HOLMAN
BIBLE
DICTIONARY

HOLMAN BIBLE DICTIONARY

With summary definitions and explanatory articles on
every Bible subject; introductions and teaching outlines for
each Bible book; in-depth theological articles;
plus internal maps, charts, illustrations,
scale reconstruction drawings, archaeological photos,
and atlas.

GENERAL EDITOR
TRENT C. BUTLER, PH.D.

CONTRIBUTING EDITORS
MARSHA A. ELLIS SMITH, PH.D.
FORREST W. JACKSON, D. MIN.
PHIL LOGAN, PH.D.
CHRIS CHURCH, PH.D.

HOLMAN BIBLE PUBLISHERS   NASHVILLE, TENNESSEE

EDITORIAL FOREWORD

The Bible is God's authoritative Word for the Christian church. Christian beliefs and practice—doctrine and lifestyle—are based on the Bible and no other book. A Bible dictionary is an essential tool for effective Bible study. It gives background information, definitions, outlines, and theological information. Bible times and characters come to life. This enables you to understand the meaning of God's Word and starts you on the path to applying the Word to your life. Such understanding gives depth and consistency to Bible interpretation, enabling the student of God's Word to believe and follow its teaching with confidence and intelligence.

Six years of work by hundreds of people have produced this *Holman Bible Dictionary* for a generation of Bible students anticipating the third Christian millennium. The editorial team presents the dictionary to the Christian world hoping that it will indeed provide the guidance and information for which every Bible student searches. You, the reader, will make our work worthwhile as you prepare sermons, draw up teaching plans, search for personal knowledge and inspiration, and wrestle with problems of interpretation and of life with the help of this dictionary. We look forward to hearing your testimonies on how God uses the dictionary to help the Bible become an even greater guide to your life. We pray that the Holy Spirit will use the information and illustrations provided here to renew His people in faith *and* practice. We also look forward to hearing questions you raise as you study the Bible with the help of this dictionary. We solicit your suggestions for making the next edition an even better tool for Bible study.

The dictionary is designed with *you* in mind. Every feature is intended to make it easier for you to find what you need to know as quickly as possible. As you begin to use this Bible study tool, turn first to pages vi–viii to see all the features available; then read through pages ix–xi to see how to use these features most effectively.

May God bless you and reveal His word for your life as you read the inspired Word and as you use this dictionary to understand its message and meaning for you.

Trent C. Butler

TABLE OF CONTENTS

1. Editorial Foreword   v
2. How to Use This Dictionary   ix–xi
3. Production Staff   xii
4. Contributors   xiii–xx
5. Time Line   xxi–xxix
6. Bible Information from A to Z   1–1444
7. Art Credits   1445–1446
8. Map Index   1447–1450
9. NASA-generated Holman Maps   1451–1458

─────── SPECIAL INTERNAL FEATURES ───────

CHARTS

1. Time Line   xxii–xxix
2. Disciples, Apostles   364
3. The Jewish Calendar   486–487
4. The Hasmonean Dynasty   611
5. The Holy / The Personal   661
6. Parables of Jesus   784–785
7. Miracles of Jesus   786
8. Discourses of Jesus   787
9. Jewish Parties in the New Testament   792–793
10. Messianic Prophecies in the Old Testament   953–955
11. Millennial Perspectives on Revelation   1184–1187
12. Table of Weights and Measures   1404–1405

SCALE RECONSTRUCTIONS

1. Roman Archer's Machine   93
2. Ark of the Covenant   99
3. First-Century Athens   126–127
4. Pool of Bethesda   170
5. Jerusalem During the Time of David   342–343
6. Temple of Artemis at Ephesus   429
7. Eighth-Century Hebrew Home   672
8. First-Century Hebrew Home   673
9. Herod's Winter Palace at Jericho   762–763
10. New Testament Jericho   763
11. Jerusalem in Jesus' Time   766–767
12. Caesarea Maritima   1080
13. Cutaway view of Solomon's Temple   1289
14. Solomon's Temple   1290
15. First-Century Synagogue   1312
16. Tabernacle of Israelites   1317
17. Herod's Temple Floor Plan   1326–1327
18. Herod's Temple   1329
19. Roman Siege Tower   1401
20. Roman Battering Ram   1402
21. First-Century Winepress   1411
22. Ziggurat   1441

INTERNAL MAPS

1. The Journeys of the Apostles 365
2. Culture and Commerce in the Ancient Near East 390–391
3. The Coming of the Israelites 452–453
4. The World of the Greeks 580–581
5. The Ancient Near East in the Second Millennium B.C. 652–653
6. The Near East in the First Millennium B.C. 656–657
7. Palestine in Graeco-Roman Times 708–709
8. The Kingdom of David and Solomon 724–725
9. The Kingdoms of Judah and Israel 728–729
10. Jesus in His Land 778–779
11. Jesus in Galilee 782
12. The Growth of Christianity 978–979
13. Palestine in the Time of the New Testament 1021
14. Palestine in the Time of the Old Testament 1047
15. The Holy Land Today 1065
16. The Land of Canaan 1066–1067
17. The Spread of the Early Church 1082–1083
18. The Roman Empire 1210–1211

——————————— MAJOR ARTICLES ———————————

BIBLE BACKGROUNDS AND CULTURE

Altar 37–40
Animals 52–58
Apocrypha 69–71
Apocrypha, New Testament 71–74
Apostolic Fathers 76–77
Archaeology and Biblical Study 83–93
Architecture in the Bibical Period 94–96
Ark of the Covenant 98–100
Arms and Armor 101–104
Art and Aesthetics 105–107
Asia Minor, Cities of 114–116
Assyria, History and Religion of 120–124
Babylon, History and Religion of 141–144
Birds 191–193
Calendars 221–222
Canaan, History and Religion of 226–230
Chronology of the Biblical Period 255–259
Cities and Urban Life 264–266
Cloth, Clothing 270–272
Coins 274–275
Commerce 280–281
Containers and Vessels 290–292
Cooking and Heating 295–298
Corinth 298–301
Court Systems 306–308
Crimes and Punishments 316–319
Damascus 330–332
Disciples, Apostles 362–366
Diseases 367–370
Ebla 387–388

Economic Life 389–394
Edom 395–397
Education in Bible Times 397–398
Egypt 399–403
Ephesus 424–428
False Worship 474–475
Festivals 484–490
Food 503–504
Gestures 545–547
Gnosticism 558–559
Gods, Pagan 562–565
Government 570–572
Greece 578–583
Hammurabi 599–601
Hellenism 632–634
High Priest 645–648
Hittites and Hivites 654–659
House 671–673
Insects 699–703
Intertestamental History and Literature 707–713
Israel, History of 722–731
Jericho 759–764
Jerusalem 765–773
Jewels, Jewelry 788–791
Jewish Parties in the New Testament 791–794
King, Kingship 842–843
Land, Ground 860–861
Library 879–881
Macedonia 907–908
Mari 917–918
Minerals and Metals 968–970
Mines and Mining 970–972
Mishnah 975–976
Moab and the Moabite Stone 982–983
Monotheism, Polytheism 985–986
Music, Instruments, Dancing 993–996

Mystery, Mystery Religions 997–998
Number Systems and Number Symbolism 1029–1031
Occupations and Professions in the Bible 1037–1040
Oracles 1051–1054
Palestine 1063–1069
Pentateuch 1088–1091
Persia 1097–1098
Philistines 1108–1109
Plants in the Bible 1116–1120
Pottery in Bible Times 1126–1129
Prophecy, Prophets 1141–1143
Rivers and Waterways in the Bible 1196–1199
Roman Law 1200–1202
Rome and the Roman Empire 1207–1212
Sacrifice and Offering 1218–1220
Samaria, Samaritans 1224–1225
Ships, Sailors, and Navigation 1269–1273
Spices 1297–1298
Synagogue 1311–1313
Syria 1313–1314
Temple of Jerusalem 1325–1332
Tools 1356–1357
Transjordan 1362–1363
Transportation and Travel 1363–1366
Tribes of Israel 1368–1371
Ugarit 1380–1382
Vessels and Utensils 1390–1392
Weights and Measures 1403–1407
Writing 1423–1426

DOCTRINES AND ETHICS

Angel   51–52
Anthropology   60–62
Atonement   128–131
Baptism   149–151
Bible, Formation and Canon
   of   177–178
Bible, Hermeneutics   178–181
Bible, History of
   Interpretation   181–183
Bible, Texts and Versions   183–
   185
Bible, Theology of   185–188
Bible, Translations   188–190
Black People and Biblical
   Perspective   196–197
Blessing and Cursing   198–199
Blood   200–201
Body   202–203
Capital Punishment   232–233
Christ, Christology   250–252
Church   259–261
Clean, Cleanness   268–270
Compassion   282–283
Confessions and Credos   286–
   287
Conversion   293–294
Covenant   308–312
Creation   313–315
Cross, Crucifixion   319–321
Deacon, Deaconess   344–345
Death   347–349
Devil, Satan, Evil,
   Demonic   358–359
Dispensation   370–371
Election   407–409
Eschatology   432–436
Eternal Life   440–441
Ethics   441–444
Expiation, Propitiation   458–
   460
Faith   469–470
Fall   471–472
Family   475–477
Fear   480–481
Flesh   497–498
Freedom   514–515
Future Hope   519–520
God   560–562
Gospel   567–570
Grace   573–575
Heaven   620–622
Hell   631–632
History   650–654
Holy   660–662
Humanity   675–676
Incarnation   693–694
Jesus Christ   775–777
Justification   829–830

Kingdom of God   843–845
Life   881–883
Lord   889–891
Love   896–898
Mercy, Merciful   947–949
Messiah   952–956
Mission   976–980
Names of God   1004–1006
Offices in the New
   Testament   1041–1042
Ordinances   1054–1057
Parables   1071–1073
Peace, Spiritual   1086
People of God   1091–1092
Prayer   1130–1132
Predestination   1133–1135
Promise   1140–1141
Providence   1147–1148
Purity, Purification   1154–1155
Reconciliation   1168–1169
Redeem, Redemption,
   Redeemer   1170–1171
Resurrection of Jesus
   Christ   1179–1180
Revelation of God   1180–1183
Righteousness   1194–1195
Salvation   1222–1224
Servant of the Lord   1248–1249
Sex, Biblical Teaching
   on   1251–1252
Sin   1281–1283
Son of Man   1291–1292
Spirit   1299–1300
Time, Meaning of   1347–1349
Trial of Jesus   1367–1368
Trinity   1372–1374
Worship   1421–1422

PEOPLE

Jacob   738–740
Jesus, Life and Ministry   777–
   788
John   803–805
Patriarchs   1077–1079
Paul   1079–1085

HOW TO USE THIS DICTIONARY

A Bible dictionary should be a friend; it can become a frustration!

It becomes a friend when you learn how to use it. It remains a frustration when you know it has information you want but you do not know how to find or use the information. Holman Bible Publishers wants to introduce a new friend to you—the *Holman Bible Dictionary.* We intend this to be the most user-friendly Bible study tool available.

• NOTE ITS FRIENDLY FEATURES •
Finding an Entry

You can find any entry easily. The dictionary is organized as one single unit. Every person, place, and topic stands in one section in simple alphabetical order. The different colored side tabs lead you immediately to the letter you seek.

You will find the topic you want. Every person and place in the Bible is included. Every major theological or doctrinal subject is included. Articles about the Bible and its background are included. If a related topic appears, the dictionary tells you to "See" the topic. You do not have to remember that a special kind of type means you should look to another reference.

You can use the Bible translation you favor. Topics and spellings from *King James Version, Revised Standard Version, New American Standard Bible, New International Version, Today's English Version, Revised English Bible,* and *New Revised Standard Version* are included. Spellings are generally those of King James, as are Scripture quotations, unless otherwise noted. Spellings of other translations will have a separate entry with a "See" pointing you to the article under an alternate spelling.

Making Bible Study Live

You can see the Bible come alive. Over six hundred color illustrations, internal maps, informative charts, and Bill Latta's tinted scale reconstructions of biblical sites, worship places, tools, and artifacts join the acclaimed Holman maps to help you place yourself in the sandals of your favorite Bible personalities.

You can know the Bible in depth. We have included as much information as possible in a single volume, especially about the nature, background, and teachings of the Bible. The list of major articles in the Table of Contents will direct you to extended reading sessions on the Bible, its background and culture, its doctrine and ethics, and its people.

You can understand every word of the dictionary. The editors have fashioned it for you to read, not for scholars to be impressed. Technical language and mysterious abbreviations of Latin words do not appear. Words you know and use daily explain, affirm, and describe the background of God's inspired Word.

Learning the Dictionary's Features

Now, let us introduce your new friend. You may want to have a pad of paper handy to write down notes reminding you of the new friend's characteristics.

1. Turn to the Table of Contents. Read through the list of major articles. Select the first three you want to read, and note them on your paper.
2. Turn to page xxi. Examine the Time Line. See the information it offers as you seek to relate Bible history to world history.

3. Use the Table of Contents to find the Artistic Scale Reconstructions. Explore two or three that interest you such as the Ark of the Covenant or a First-Century Hebrew Home. Look at the charts, perhaps the ones of Jewish Parties, Messianic Prophecies, and Millennial Perspectives on Revelation. Note how each of these features can help you understand the Bible better.

4. Look next at the maps. You will discover two sets of maps—a feature unique to the *Holman Bible Dictionary*. The "Internal Maps" are spread throughout the text. They even include a map of the Holy Land as it is today—another unique feature of this dictionary. The special Holman maps and an index to them are at the back of the dictionary. They were drawn using NASA photographs. With them you view physical features as seen from space. They will help you locate Bible places at the point in history you are studying. Use the index to find how many times a favorite place, such as Bethlehem, occurs. Find it on each map.

5. To see just how helpful the *Holman Bible Dictionary* can be for you, think of a question you want answered, perhaps one that arose recently at a church Bible study. Suppose you want to understand the background and meaning of Luke 15, the well-loved chapter with its three parables of the lost sheep, the lost coin, and the lost son. Begin by reading the article on "Luke, Gospel of." Note the bold subheads which direct you to a place of interest in the article. You will probably choose "Purpose and Readership" and "Special Emphases and Characteristics." Scan through the "Outline" to see how Luke 15 fits into Luke's overall purpose.

What is a parable? Find the article on "Parables." Notice that the beginning sentence provides a brief definition of the subject. Many times this will be all the information you want. Run your finger through the article to find specific references to Luke 15. See how many Bible references are used, assuring you the article is based on Scripture and intended to show the meaning of Scripture.

Now ask questions about Luke 15, such as: Who were the tax collectors? Why were they grouped with sinners? Look up "Tax Collector," where you will find, "See *Publican.*" Turn to "Publican." See how many of your questions are answered in the brief article. Further information is available under "Taxes." Who were

the Pharisees and scribes opposing Jesus? Brief articles on "Pharisees" and "Scribes" will refer you to "Jewish Parties" for an overview article accompanied by a chart. What difference did Jesus' mealtime associates make? "Food" and "Banquet" will help you understand. How important were sheep? What images and feelings did the mention of sheep raise? "Sheep" and "Shepherd" will begin your search leading you to "Agriculture," "Cattle," "Economic Life," "Occupations and Professions in the Bible." Read as far as you want.

"Architecture in the Biblical Period" and "House" with the accompanying art work will help you understand the type house the woman had to sweep in search of her coin. "Coins" will help you identify the coin. "Family" will provide background on the lost son as will "Inheritance." Of course, all three parables point to Jesus and the kingdom of God. Articles on "Christ, Christology," "Jesus Christ," and "Kingdom of God" will help you.

Do not stop with our suggestions. Read through Luke 15. Underline or note words that call for deeper study. See how many words you can list for further dictionary study. If you lead a Bible study, each of these words makes a good assignment for class members. That way you can work together to study and learn God's Word. Every member will feel a part of the exciting joy of studying and following God's Word.

6. Relations with your new friend may appear to have become quite complex. Often, the relationship is much simpler. You need to pronounce a name in your Bible study class. After each entry of a proper name and after many other entries where pronunciation may be a question, the *Holman Bible Dictionary* shows you how to pronounce the name. Just use the following pronunciation guide adapted from W. Murray Severance, *Pronouncing Bible Names*, Revised Edition (Nashville: Holman Bible Publishers, 1983, 1985).

7. Finally, you may find your new dictionary friend is really a reunion with old friends. Let your eyes wander through the list of contributors. You may find several names you know from other reading. You may have heard them speak in your church. You know you can trust the work they and their colleagues have done. The *Holman Bible Dictionary* is now your

friend. Be faithful to it. Use it daily as you study God's Word. Introduce it to other friends in Sunday School or other Bible study groups. Let them become the dictionary's friend too.

May this be the beginning of a long and fruitful friendship. May it lead you to a closer and deeper relationship with God's Word. Most of all, may it lead you to a closer walk with the best Friend you can ever have: Jesus, the Christ.

KEY TO PRONUNCIATION

MARK	EXAMPLE	SOUND	MARK	EXAMPLE	SOUND
ā	dāy, lāy	ay	ô	ôr, fôr	aw
ă	hăy, căt	a	ph	(unmarked) alpha	f
ä	äre, fär	ah	ş	hiş, muşe	z
â	câre, fâre	e, eh	s	(unmarked) kiss	ss
à	àbout, àbet	u, uh	ū	tūne, mūte	yoo, ew
a	(unmarked) call	aw	ŭ	ŭp, tŭb	uh
å	åfraid	u, uh	û	hûrl, fûrl	u, uh
āē	dāēmon, dēmon	ee	ü	trüth	oo, ew
ah	(unmarked) Elijah	uh	th	(unmarked) thin	th
âi	âisle	ī	th	thyme	t
ai	mail, hail	ay	ti, ci, si	attraction	sh
am	(unmarked) adam's apple	uhm	y	city	i, ih
an	(unmarked) roman	uhn			
c, ch	cord, chorus	k		**Seldom Used Marks**	
ç	çity	s, ss	aȧ	Balaȧm	uh
ē	mēte, Crēte	ee	aė	archaėology	ih
ĕ	mĕt, lĕt	e, eh (uh)	ao	(unmarked) pharaoh (ant)	oh
ē	tērm	u, uh	au	(unmarked) author	aw
ė	ėlastic	i, ih	eā	seā	ee
ḡ	ḡet	g	eȧ	zeȧlous	eh
ġ	ġerm	gh, j	ēē	ḡēē	ee
ī	pīne, fīne	ī	eu, ew	brew	oo, ew
ĭ	hĭm, pĭn	ih	ia	(unmarked)	ya
î	machîne	ee	īo	legīon	uh
ī	fīrm	u, uh (uhr)	îo	savîor	yaw
ō	nōte, rōde	o, oh	ôi	bôil	oy
ŏ	nŏt, rŏt	ah	on	(unmarked) onion	uhn
o	(unmarked) amok	uh	ou	(unmarked) out	ow

PRODUCTION STAFF

———————— ADMINISTRATION ————————

President, Holman Bible Publishers, Johnnie C. Godwin
Director, Bibles and Books Tom Clark

———————— EDITORIAL ————————

General Editor Trent C. Butler
Contributing Editors Marsha A. Ellis Smith, Archaeology
Forrest W. Jackson, Bible content
Phil Logan, New Testament
Chris Church, Biblical theology

Copy Editors June Swann
Sharon Wegman

Design Editor Candace Morris McKibben

Editorial Assistant Jean Jenkins

Production Support Staff Diane Stem, Office Supervisor
Donna Easlick
Tracie Gregory
Cindy Kephart

———————— GRAPHICS ————————

Designer Ernie Couch / Consultx
Jacket Design Jim Bateman
Graphics Director W. Don Rogers
Graphics Manager Jack Jewell
Artists Emma Jane Vidrine
Gene Elliott
Bill Latta
Wayne Curtis

———————— PRODUCTION ————————

Procurement Director James Shull
Procurement Manager James Nash
Procurement Buyers Karl Huddleston
Bob Morrison
Procurement Assistants Janie Ralph
Daniel Halpin
Typesetters Huron Valley Graphics, Inc.
Printers Arcata Graphics Company,
Kingsport, TN

CONTRIBUTORS

Albright, Jimmy, Pastor, Wyatt Park Baptist Church, St. Joseph, MO 64507

Allen, Leslie C., Professor of Old Testament, Fuller Theological Seminary, Pasedena, CA 91101-1790

Anderson, Douglas, Director, Family Ministry Department, Baptist Sunday School Board, Nashville, TN 37234

Arnold, Steve, Doctoral Candidate, Golden Gate Baptist Theological Seminary, Mill Valley, CA 94941

Baldwin, Gary D., Pastor, First Baptist Church, Rolla, MO 65401

Baskin, Joe R., Professor of Religion, Shorter College, Rome, GA 30161

Baston, Jerry W., Associate Dean, Beeson Divinity School, Samford University, Birmingham, AL 35226

Bean, Albert F., Professor of Old Testament, Midwestern Baptist Theological Seminary, Kansas City, MO 64118

Beasley-Murray, George R., Senior Professor of New Testament Interpretation, The Southern Baptist Theological Seminary, Louisville, KY 40280

Beitzel, Barry J., Associate Academic Dean, Professor of Old Testament, Trinity Evangelical Divinity School, Deerfield, IL 60025

Bellinger, Jr., W. H., Associate Professor of Religion, Baylor University, Waco, TX 79798

Berry, Donald K., Assistant Professor of Religion, Mobile College, Mobile, AL 36613

Berryman, James C., Professor of Religion and Philosophy, Ouachita Baptist University, Arkadelphia, AR 71923

Bishop, Ronald E., Pastor, Plainview Baptist Church, Bogalusa, LA 70427

Blevins, James L., Professor of New Testament, The Southern Baptist Theological Seminary, Louisville, KY 40280

Bloesch, Donald G., Professor of Theology, University of Dubuque Theological Seminary, Dubuque, IA 52001

Bond, Steve, Coordinator, Marketing Planning, Baptist Sunday School Board, Nashville, TN 37234

Bonner, Gary, Pastor, First Baptist Church, Huntsville, TX 77340

Borchert, Gerald L., J. Rupert and Lucille Coleman Professor of New Testament, The Southern Baptist Theological Seminary, Louisville, KY 40280

Boyd, Timothy, Pastor, First Baptist Church, Mulvane, KS 67110

Brangenberg, III, John H., Doctoral Candidate, Golden Gate Baptist Theological Seminary, Mill Valley, CA 94941

Bridges, Linda McKinnish, Assistant Professor of New Testament, Baptist Theological Seminary, Richmond, VA

Brisco, Thomas V., Associate Professor of Biblical Backgrounds and Archaeology, Southwestern Baptist Theological Seminary, Fort Worth, TX 76122

Brooks, James A., Professor of New Testament, Bethel Theological Seminary, Saint Paul, MN 55112

Brooks, Oscar S., Professor of New Testament, Golden Gate Baptist Theological Seminary, Mill Valley, CA 94941

Browning, Jr., Daniel C., Assistant Professor of Religion, William Carey College, Hattiesburg, MS 39401

Bruce, Barbara J., Free-lance writer, Ridgecrest, NC 28770

Bruce, Larry, Free-lance writer and professional pilot, Fort Worth, TX 76123

Bugg, Charles B., Carl E. Bates Professor of Christian Preaching, The Southern Baptist Theological Seminar Louisville, KY 40280

Butler, Bradley S., Pastor, Memorial Park Baptist Church, Stone Mountain, GA 30083

Butler, Trent C., Manager, Bibles and Textbooks, Broadman, Holman Presses, Nashville, TN 37234

Byrd, Robert O., Professor of Religion, Belmont College, Nashville, TN 37212

Cate, Robert L., Distinguished Professor of Religion, Oklahoma State University, Stillwater, OK 74075

Chance, Bradley, Assistant Professor of Religion, William Jewell College, Liberty, MO 64068

Church, Chris, Copy Editor, Broadman Press, Nashville, TN 37234

Coats, George W., Professor of Old Testament, Lexington Theological Seminary, Lexington, KY 40508

Cole, Dennis, Assistant Professor of Biblical Archaeology, New Orleans Baptist Theological Seminary, New Orleans, LA 70126

Coleson, Joseph E., Professor of Hebrew Scripture, Western Evangelical Seminary, Portland, OR 97267

Collins, Alvin O., Chairman, Department of Christianity and Philosophy, Houston Baptist University, Houston, TX 77074-3298

Compton, Bob, Professor, International Seminary, San Jose, Costa Rica

Conyers, A. J., Professor of Religion, Charleston Southern University, Charleston, SC 29411

Cook, Donald E., Professor of New Testament, Southeastern Baptist Theological Seminary, Wake Forest, NC 27588-1899

Cooper, C. Kenny, Pastor, Bellevue Baptist Church, Nashville, TN 37221

Cowen, Gerald P., Professor of New Testament Greek, The Criswell College, Dallas, TX 75218

Craig, Jr., Kenneth M., Assistant Professor of Religion, Chowan College, Murfreesboro, NC 27855

Cranford, Jeff, Pastor, First Baptist Church, Lincolnton, NC 28092

Cranford, Lorin L., Associate Professor of New Testament, Southwestern Baptist Theological Seminary, Fort Worth, TX 76122

Creech, R. Robert, Pastor, University Baptist Church, Houston, TX 77059

Creed, Brad, Pastor, First Baptist Church, Nachitoches, LA 71457

Cresson, Bruce C., Professor of Archaeology, Baylor University, Waco, TX 76798

Criswell, W. A., Pastor, First Baptist Church, Dallas, TX 75201

Crook, Roger, Professor of Religion, Meredith College, Raleigh, NC 27607

Cross, Diane, Doctoral student, Golden Gate Baptist Theological Seminary, Mill Valley, CA 94941

Culpepper, R. Alan, James Buchanan Harrison Professor of New Testament Interpretation, The Southern Baptist Theological Seminary, Louisville, KY 40280

Dalglish, Edward, Professor of Old Testament, Baylor University, Waco, TX 76798

Davies, Phillip R., Senior Lecturer, Department of Biblical Studies, The University of Sheffield, Sheffield, England

Davis, Cos, Manager, Preschool Program Section, Baptist Sunday School Board, Nashville, TN 37234

Davis, Earl C., Pastor, First Baptist Church, Memphis, TN 38111

Davis, John J., Professor of Old Testament, Grace Theological Seminary, Winona Lake, IN 46590

Davis, M. Stephen, Director of Christian Life, Houston Baptist University, Houston, TX 77074-3298

Dean, Robert J., Senior Editorial and Curriculum Specialist, Baptist Sunday School Board, Nashville, TN 37234

Dehoney, Wayne, Professor of Preaching (Ret.), The Southern Baptist Theological Seminary, Louisville, KY 40280

Denison, James C., Pastor, First Baptist Church, Midland, TX 79701

DeVries, LaMoine, Campus Minister/Lecturer, Southwest Missouri State University, Springfield, MO 65804-0095

DeVries, Simon J., Professor of Old Testament Methodist Theological School in Ohio, Delaware, OH 43015

Dockery, David S., General Editor, New American Commentary, Broadman Press, Nashville, TN 37234

Dollar, Stephen E., Pastor, Superior Avenue Baptist Church, Bogalusa, LA 70427

Dominy, Bert B., Professor of Theology, Southwestern Baptist Theological Seminary, Fort Worth, TX 76122

Drakeford, John W., Distinguished Professor of Psychology and Counseling, Emeritus, Southwestern Baptist Theological Seminary, Fort Worth, TX 76122

Draughon, III, Walter D., Pastor, Arapaho Road Baptist Church, Garland, TX 75044

Drayer, John R., Vice-President for Academic Affairs, Gardner-Webb College, Boiling Springs, NC 28017

Drinkard, Jr., Joel F., Associate Professor of Old Testament, The Southern Baptist Theological Seminary, Louisville, KY 40280

Duke, David Nelson, Chairman, Department of Religion, William Jewell College, Liberty, MO 64068

Dunham, Duane A., Professor of New Testament Language and Literature, Western Conservative Baptist Seminary, Portland, OR 97215

Duvall, J. Scott, Assistant Professor of Religion, Ouachita Baptist University, Arkadelphia, AR 71923

Eakin, Jr., Frank E., Chairman, Department of Religion, University of Richmond, Richmond, VA 23173

Eakins, J. Kenneth, Professor of Archaeology and Old Testament Interpretation, Golden Gate Baptist Theological Seminary, Mill Valley, CA 94941

Easley, Kendell, Professor of New Testament and Greek, Mid America Baptist Theological Seminary, Memphis, TN

Echols, Steven, Pastor, Bethel Baptist Church, Moody, AL 35004

Eddins, Jr., John W., Professor of Theology, Southeastern Baptist Theological Seminary, Wake Forest, NC 27588-1889

Edwards, Jr., W. T., Head, Department of Religion and Philosophy, Samford University, Birmingham, AL 35229

Ellis, Bob R., Assistant Professor of Old Testament, Southwestern Baptist Theological Seminary, Fort Worth, TX 76122

Ellis, Terence B., Pastor, Mulberry Baptist Church, Houma, LA 70360

Ellis, W. Ray, Professor of Greek, Dean of the Graduate School, Hardin-Simmons University, Abilene, TX 79698

Elmore, Vernon O., Pastor, First Baptist Church, Corpus Christi, TX 78412

Fallis, W. J., Senior Editor (Ret.), Broadman Press, Nashville, TN 37234

Feinberg, Charles Lee, Dean Emeritus, Talbot Theological Seminary, LaMirada, CA 90639

Field, Taylor, Pastor, East Seventh Baptist Ministry, New York, NY 10009

Finger, Thomas, Associate Professor of Systematic Theology, Northern Baptist Theological Seminary, Lombard, IL 60148

Fink, Michael, Manager, Adult Curriculum Section, Baptist Sunday School Board, Nashville, TN 37234

Fisher, Fred L., Academic Coordinator, Southern California Center, Golden Gate Baptist Theological Seminary, Mill Valley, CA 94941

Fleming, David M., Assistant Professor of Religion, Campbell University, Buies Creek, NC 27506

Fountain, Mark, Free-lance Author, Louisville, KY 40280

Fredericks, Daniel C., Assistant Professor of Bible, Belhaven College, Jackson, MS 39202

Fricke, Robert, Professor, International Seminary, San Jose, Costa Rica.

Fuhrman, Mike, Pastor, First Missionary Baptist Church, Benton, KY 42025

Galeotti, Gary A., Professor of Old Testament, Criswell College, Dallas, TX 75246

Garrett, Jr., James Leo, Distinguished Professor of Theology, Southwestern Baptist Theological Seminary, Fort Worth, TX 76122

Gautsch, Darlene R., Instructor in Old Testament and Hebrew, Golden Gate Baptist Theological Seminary, Mill Valley, CA 94941

George, Timothy, Dean, Beeson Divinity School, Samford University, Birmingham, AL 35229

Glaze, Joseph E., Director of Christian Social Ministries, The Richmond Baptist Association, Richmond, VA 23222

Glaze, Jr., R. E., Professor Emeritus of New Testament, New Orleans Baptist Theological Seminary, New Orleans, LA 70126-4858

Gloer, W. Hulitt, Assistant Professor of New Testament Studies, Midwestern Baptist Theological Seminary, Kansas City, MO 64118

Godwin, Johnnie C., President, Broadman Press, Nashville, TN 37234

Gower, Ralph, Southport, Lancashire, England

Graham, Charles E., Professor Emeritus of Old Testament, New Orleans Baptist Theological Seminary, New Orleans, LA 70126-4858

Gray, Elmer L., Free-lance Author, Fresno, CA 93703

Greenfield, Guy, Professor of Christian Ethics, Southwestern Baptist Theological Seminary, Fort Worth, TX 76122

Grissom, Fred A., Professor of Church History, Southeastern Baptist Theological Seminary, Wake Forest, NC 27587

Haag, Joe, Christian Life Commission, Baptist General Convention of Texas, Dallas, TX 75246

Halbrook, Gary K., Pastoral Counselor, Samaritan Counseling Center, Lufkin, TX 75901

Hancock, Jr., Omer J., Assistant Professor of Applied Christianity, Hardin-Simmons University, Abilene, TX 79698

Hardin, Gary, Design Editor, *Growing Churches,* Nashville, TN 37234

Harris, R. Laird, Professor Emeritus of Old Testament, Covenant Theological Seminary, St. Louis, MO

Harrison, R. K., Professor Emeritus of Old Testament, Wycliffe College, Toronto, Canada

Harrop, Clayton K., Professor of New Testament Interpretation, Golden Gate Baptist Theological Seminary, Mill Valley, CA 94941

Hatchett, Randy, Assistant Professor of Christianity and Philosophy, Houston Baptist University, Houston, TX 77074-3291

Hatfield, Lawson G., Former Director, Sunday School Department and Pastor (Ret.), Arkansas Baptist State Convention, Little Rock, AR 72203

Hemer, Colin J., Tyndale House, Cambridge, England

Henderson, Gene, Design Editor, Adult Bible Teacher, Nashville, TN 37234

Hendricks, William L., Director of Graduate Studies, Professor of Christian Theology and, Director of the Center for Religion and the Arts, The Southern Baptist Theological Seminary, Louisville, KY 40280

Henry, Jerry M., Pastor, Elkdale Baptist Church, Selma, AL 36701

Henry, Jim, Pastor, First Baptist Church, Orlando, FL 32805

Hepper, F. Nigel, Royal Botanical Gardens, Richmond, England

Hester, J. Michael, Director of Pastoral Counseling and Growth Center, Asheville, NC 28801

Hill, C. Dale, Pastor, Central Baptist Church, Clovis, NM 88101

Hinson, E. Glenn, David T. Porter Professor of Church History, The Southern Baptist Theological Seminary, Louisville, KY 40280

Hockenhull, Brenda R., Lay minister, Palomar Community Church, Vista, CA 92083

Hoehner, Harold W., Professor of New Testament and Greek, Dallas Theological Seminary, Dallas, TX 75204

Honeycutt, Roy L., President and Professor of Old Testament, The Southern Baptist Theological Seminary, Louisville, KY 40280

Horton, Jr., Fred L., Professor of New Testament, Wake Forest University, Winston-Salem, NC 27109

Howe, Jr., Claude L., Professor of Church History, New Orleans Baptist Theological Seminary, New Orleans, LA 70126-4858

Hubbard, Kenneth, Pastor, First Baptist Church, Smyrna, TN 37167

Huckabay, Gary C., Pastor, Woodman Valley Chapel, Colorado Springs, CO 80921

Huey, Jr., F. B., Professor of Old Testament, Emeritus, Southwestern Baptist Theological Seminary, Fort Worth, TX 76122

Humphreys, Fisher, Professor of Theology, Beeson Divinity School, Birmingham, AL 35229

Humphries-Brooks, Stephenson, Assistant Professor of Religion, Hamilton College, Clinton, NY 13323

Hunt, Jr., Harry B., Associate Professor of Old Testament, Southwestern Baptist Theological Seminary, Fort Worth, TX 76122

Ireland, Jr., William J., Pastor, First Baptist Church, Luling, LA 70070

Jackson, Paul, Doctoral Candidate, Southwestern Baptist Theological Seminary, Fort Forth, TX 76122

Jackson, Thomas A., Pastor, McLean Baptist Church, McLean, VA 22101

Johnson, Ricky L., Associate Professor of Religion, Wayland Baptist University, Plainview, TX 79072

Johnson, W. Stanley, Professor of Christian Theology, Western Evangelical Seminary, Portland, OR 97267

Joiner, E. Earl, Chairman of Department of Religion, Stetson University, Deland, FL 32720

Joines, Karen R., Professor of Religion and Philosophy, Samford University, Birmingham, AL 35229

Jones, Lynn, Highland Baptist Church, Shreveport, LA 71001

Jones, Peter Rhea, Pastor, First Baptist Church, Decatur, GA 30030

Kaiser, Jr., Walter C., Academic Dean and Vice President of Education, Professor of Semitic Language and Old Testament, Trinity Evangelical School, Deerfield, IL 60015

Keathley, Naymond, Professor of New Testament, Baylor University, Waco, TX 76798

Kelm, George L., Professor of Biblical Backgrounds and Archaeology, Southwestern Baptist Theological Seminary, Fort Worth, TX 76122

Kent, Dan G., Professor of Old Testament, Southwestern Baptist Theological Seminary, Fort Worth, TX 76122

Knight, George W., Cook-Derrick Professor of New Testament and Greek, Hardin-Simmons University, Abilene, TX 79698

Koester, Helmut, John H. Morrison Professor of New Testament Studies and Winn Professor of Ecclesiastical History, Harvard University, Cambridge, MA 02138

Lain, Gil, Pastor, Coggin Avenue Baptist Church, Brownwood, TX 76801

Langston, Scott, Doctoral Candidate, Southwestern Baptist Theological Seminary, Fort Worth, TX 76122

Laughlin, John C. H., Professor of Religion, Averett College, Danville, VA 24541

Lea, Thomas D., Professor of New Testament, Southwestern Baptist Theological Seminary, Fort Worth, TX 76122

Lee, H. Page, Bost Professor of Religion, Mars Hill College, Mars Hill, NC 28754

Lee, Phillips, Associate Pastor, St. Bernard Baptist Church, New Orleans, LA 70126

Lemke, Steve W., Assistant Professor of Philosophy of Religion, Southwestern Baptist Theological Seminary, Fort Worth, TX 76122

Leonard, Bill J., William Walker Brookes Chair of American Christianity, The Southern Baptist Theological Seminary, Louisville, KY 40280

Lewis, Floyd, Pastor, First Baptist Church, Eldorado, AR 71730

Lewis, Jack P., Walton and Margaret Lipsey Professor of Biblical Studies, Harding Graduate School of Religion, Memphis, TN 38117

Lewis, Joe O., Vice President Academic Affairs, Georgetown College, Georgetown, KY 40324-1696

Livingston, George H., Professor of Old Testament, Asbury Theological Seminary, Wilmore, KY 40390

Logan, Phil, Pastor, Emmanuel Baptist Church, Huntingtown, MD 20649

Lorenzen, Thorwald, Professor of Systematic Theology and Ethics, Baptist Theological Seminary, Ruschlikon, Switzerland

Lunceford, Joe E., Associate Professor of Religion, Georgetown College, Georgetown, KY 40324

MacRae, Allen A., Chancellor and Emeritus Professor of Old Testament, Biblical Seminary, Hatfield, PA 19118

Mallau, Hans-Harold, Professor of Old Testament, Baptist Theological Seminary, Ruschlikon, Switzerland

Maltsberger, David C., Doctoral Candidate, Southwestern Baptist Theological Seminary, Fort Worth, TX 76122

Mariottini, Claude F., Associate Professor of Old Testament, Northern Baptist Theological Seminary, Lombard, IL 60148

Marsh, C. Robert, Pastor, Second-Ponce de Leon Baptist Church, Atlanta, GA 30305

Marshall-Green, Molly T., Associate Professor of Christian Theology, The Southern Baptist Theological Seminary, Louisville, KY 40280

Martin, D. C., Chairman, Department of Christian Studies, Grand Canyon College, Phoenix, AZ 85061

Martin, D. Michael, Assistant Professor of Biblical Studies, Golden Gate Baptist Theological Seminary, Mill Valley, CA 94941

Martin, Ralph P., Professor of Biblical Studies, University of Sheffield, Sheffield, England

Martin, Tony M., Associate Professor of Religion, University of Mary Hardin-Baylor, Belton, TX 76513

Massey, Ken, Pastor, First Baptist Church, Marks, MS 38646

Matheney, Jr., M. Pierce, Professor of Old Testament and Hebrew, Midwestern Baptist Theological Seminary, Kansas City, MO 64118

Matheson, Mark E., Pastor, First Baptist Church, Windermere, FL 36786

Matthews, E. LeBron, Pastor, Chase Memorial Baptist Church, Columbus, GA 31909

Matthews, Victor H., Associate Professor of Religion, Southwest Missouri State University, Springfield, MO 65804

McCall, Emmanuel L., Director of Black Church Extension Division, Home Mission Board of SBC, Atlanta, GA 30367

McCoy, Glenn, Bible Chair, Eastern New Mexico University, Portales, NM 88130

McCready, Wayne, Associate Professor of Religious Studies, University of Calgary, Calgary, Alberta, Canada

McGee, Daniel B., Professor of Christian Ethics, Baylor University, Waco, TX 76798

McGraw, Larry, Assistant Professor in Bible Hardin-Simmons University, Abilene, TX 79698

McKinney, Larry, Instructor in Biblical Studies, Midwestern Baptist Theological Seminary, Kansas City, MO 64118

McKnight, Edgar V., Professor of Religion, Furman University, Greenville, SC 29613

McNeal, T. R., Pastor, Trinity Baptist Church, Mount Pleasant, TX 75455

McRay, John M., Professor of New Testament and Archaeology, Wheaton College Graduate School, Wheaton, IL 60187

McWilliams, Warren, Auguie Henry Professor of Religion, Oklahoma Baptist University, Shawnee, OK 74801

Meier, Janice K., Th.D. Student, New Orleans Baptist Theological Seminary, New Orleans, LA 70126

Michaels, J. Ramsey, Professor of Religious Studies, Southwest Missouri State University, Springfield, MO 65804

Mickelsen, A. Berkeley,* Professor of New Testament Emeritus, Bethel Theological Seminary, Saint Paul, MN 55112

Miller, J. Maxwell, Director of Graduate Division of Religion, Emory University, Atlanta, GA 30322

Mitchell, Michael J., Editor, *Biblical Illustrator,* Nashville, TN 37234

Morgan, Barry, Associate Professor of New Testament and Greek, Hannibal-LaGrange College, Hannibal, MO 63401

Morris, Leon, Principal, Ridley College (Ret.), Canon, St. Paul's Cathedral, Melbourne, Australia

Morris, Wilda W., Assistant Professor of Christian Education, Northern Baptist Theological Seminary, Lombard, IL 60148-5698

Mott, Stephen C., Professor of Christian Social Ethics, Gordon-Conwell Theological Seminary, South Hamilton, MA 01982

Moyer, James C., Head of Department of Religious Studies, Southwest Missouri State University, Springfield, MO 65804

Murrell, Rich, Editor, *Baptist Young Adult,* Nashville, TN 37234

Music, David W., Associate Professor of Church Music, Southwestern Baptist Theological Seminary, Fort Worth, Texas 76122

Newell, James, Pastor, Coosada Baptist Church, Coosada, AL 36020

Newman, Carey C., Assistant Professor of Religion and Philosophy, Palm Beach Atlantic College, West Palm Beach, FL 33402-3353

Newport, John P., Vice-President for Academic Affairs and Provost (Ret.), and Distinguished Professor of Philosophy of Religion, Emeritus, Southwestern Baptist Theological Seminary, Fort Worth, TX 76122

Ngan, Lai Ling Elizabeth, Doctoral Candidate, Golden Gate Baptist Theological Seminary, Mill Valley, CA 94941

Omanson, Roger L., Translator, American Bible Society, New York, NY 10023

Osborne, Grant, Professor of New Testament, Trinity Evangelical Divinity School, Deerfield, IL 60015

Owens, J. J., Senior Professor of Old Testament, The Southern Baptist Theological Seminary, Louisville, KY 40280

O'Brien, J. Randall, Pastor, Calvary Baptist Church, Little Rock, AR 72207

Parkman, Joel, Doctoral Candidate, Baylor University, Waco, TX 76798

Parsons, Mikeal C., Assistant Professor of New Testament, Baylor University, Waco, TX 76798

Patterson, Paige, President of the Criswell College, Dallas, TX 75246

Pinnock, Clark H., Professor of Systematic Theology, McMaster Divinity College, Hamilton, Ontario, Canada

Polhill, John B., Professor of New Testament, The Southern Baptist Theological Seminary, Louisville, KY 40280

Popkes, Wiard, Principal and Professor of New Testament, Hamburg Baptist Seminary, Hamburg, Germany

Potts, Donald R., Chairman of Religion Department, East Texas Baptist University, Marshall, TX 75670

Poulton, Gary, President and Professor of History, Virginia Intermont College, Bristol, VA 24201

Powell, Paul W., President and Chief Executive Officer, Annuity Board, Dallas, TX 75221-2190

Price, Nelson, Pastor, Roswell Street Baptist Church, Marietta, GA 30060

*Deceased

Prince, III, Robert W., Pastor, Hot Wells Baptist Church, San Antonio, TX 78223

Queen-Sutherland, Kandy, Professor of Old Testament, Baptist Theological Seminary, Ruschlikon, Switzerland

Reddish, Mitchell, Assistant Professor of Religion, Stetson University, Delando, FL 32720

Redditt, Paul, Chairman, Department of Religion, Georgetown College, Georgetown, KY 40324-1696

Reeves, Rodney, Chairman, Department of Religion and Philosophy, Assistant Professor of Religion, Williams Baptist College, Walnut Ridge, AR 72476

Register, M. Dean, Pastor, First Baptist Church, Gulfport, MS 39502

Reiling, J., Professor of New Testament, University of Utrecht, Utrecht, The Netherlands

Reynolds, J. A., Chairperson, Religion Department, University of Mary Hardin-Baylor, Belton, TX 76513

Ridge, Donna R., Free-lance writer, Kimberly, WI 54136

Robbins, Ray F., Professor Emeritus of New Testament and Greek, New Orleans Baptist Theological Seminary, New Orleans, LA 70126-4858

Robertson, Paul E., Associate Professor of Theology, New Orleans Baptist Theological Seminary, New Orleans, LA 71026

Robinson, Darrell W., Vice President of Evangelism Section, Home Mission Board, Atlanta, GA 30367

Rogers, Max, Professor of Old Testament, Southeastern Baptist Theological Seminary, Wake Forest, NC 27587

Ruffles, John, University of Durham, Durham, England

Sandlin, Bryce, Retired Professor of Bible and Hebrew, Howard Payne University, Brownwood, TX 76801

Saul, D. Glenn, Professor of Christian Ethics, Golden Gate Baptist Theological Seminary, Mill Valley, CA 94941

Sawyer, W. Thomas, Professor of Religion, Mars Hill College, Mars Hill, NC 28754

Scalise, Pamela J., Associate Professor of Old Testament, The Southern Baptist Theological Seminary, Louisville, KY 40280

Schweer, G. William, Professor of Evangelism, Golden Gate Baptist Theological Seminary, Mill Valley, CA 94941

Self, William L., Former Pastor, Wieuca Road Baptist Church, Atlanta, GA 30326

Sexton, James H., Ila Baptist Church, Ila, GA 30647

Sheffield, Bob, Deacon Ministry Consultant, Nashville, TN 37234

Shurden, Kay, Marriage and Family Therapist, Mercer University, Macon, GA 31207

Simeon, James E. M., Pastor, Centreville Baptist Church, Centreville, MS 39631

Simmons, Billy E., Professor of New Testament and Greek, New Orleans, Baptist Theological Seminary, New Orleans, LA 70126-4858

Skinner, Craig P., Professor of Preaching, Golden Gate Baptist Theological Seminary, Mill Valley, CA 94941

Sloan, Robert B., George Truett Professor of Religion, Baylor University, Waco, TX 76798

Smalley, Stephen S., Dean of Cathedral, Chester, England

Smith, Billy K., Professor of Old Testament and Hebrew, New Orleans Baptist Theological Seminary, New Orleans, LA 70126-4858

Smith, Gary V., Professor of Old Testament, Bethel Theological Seminary, St. Paul, MN 55112

Smith, Marsha A. Ellis, Editor/Designer, Bibles and Academic Books, Holman Bible Publishers, Nashville, TN 37234

Smith, Ralph L., Professor of Old Testament, Emeritus, Southwestern Baptist Theological Seminary, Fort Worth, TX 76115-1153

Smith, T. C., Professor of New Testament, Furman University, Greenville, SC 29613

Smothers, Thomas, Professor of Old Testament, The Southern Baptist Theological Seminary, Louisville, KY 40280

Snider, P. Joel, Pastor, Crievewood Baptist Church, Nashville, TN 37220

Soards, Marion, United Theological Seminary, Dayton, OH 45406

Songer, Harold S., Vice President for Academic Affairs, Professor of New Testament Interpretation, The Southern Baptist Theological Seminary, Louisville, KY 40280

Stagg, Robert W., Professor of Religion, Ouachita Baptist University, Arkadelphia, AR 71923

Stephens, Shirley, Free-lance Writer/Editor, Nashville, TN

Strange, James F., Professor of Religious Studies, University of South Florida, Tampa, FL 33620

Street, Jr., Robert, Professor of Old Testament, Campbellsville College, Campbellsville, KY 42718

Stricker, Barry A., Assistant Professor of Theology and Christian Philosophy, Golden Gate Baptist Theological Seminary, Mill Valley, CA 94941

Stubblefield, Jerry, Professor of Christian Education, Golden Gate Baptist Theological Seminary, Mill Valley, CA 94941

Sullivan, James L., Retired President, Baptist Sunday School Board, Nashville, TN 37234

Summers, Ray, Retired Chairman of Department of Religion, Baylor University, Waco, TX 76798

Sutherland, Dixon, Professor of Patristics, Baptist Theological Seminary, Ruschlikon, Switzerland

Swanson, Phillip J., Pastor, Beacon Light Baptist Church, Vernon, NY 13476

Talbert, Charles H., Professor of Religion, Wake Forest University, Winston-Salem, NC 27109

Tang, Samuel Yau-Chi, Professor of Old Testament Interpretation, Golden Gate Baptist Theological Seminary, Mill Valley, CA 94941

Tankersley, Bruce, Professor of Religion, East Texas Baptist University, Marshall, TX 75670

Tate, Marvin E., Professor of Old Testament Interpretation, The Southern Baptist Theological Seminary, Louisville, KY 40280

Taulman, James, Design Editor, Adult Bible Book Curriculum, Nashville, TN 37234

Thompson, J. William, Senior Design Editor, Youth Curriculum, Nashville, TN 37234

Tobias, Hugh, Pastor, First Baptist Church, Opp, AL 38467

Trammell, Timothy J., Professor of New Testament, Dallas Baptist University, Dallas, TX 75211-9800

Travis, James L., Head of Bible Department, Blue Mountain College, Blue Mountain, MS 38610

Traylor, Jr., John H., Pastor, First Baptist Church, Monroe, LA 71210

Tullock, John H., Professor of Religion, Belmont College, Nashville, TN 37212

Turnham, Tim, Pastor, Seminary Baptist Church, Seminary, MS 39479

Van Leeuwen, Raymond C., Assistant Professor of Theology, Calvin Theological Seminary, Grand Rapids, MI 49506

Vermillion, William H., Professor of Biblical Literature and Counseling, Western Evangelical Seminary, Portland, OR 97267

Vestal, Daniel, Pastor, Dunwoody Baptist Church, Dunwoody, GA 30338

Wade, Charles, Pastor, First Baptist Church, Arlington, TX 76010

Walker, Larry, Professor of Old Testament and Hebrew, Mid-America Baptist Theological Seminary, Memphis, TN 38104

Ward, Wayne E., Joseph Emerson Brown Professor of Christian Theology, The Southern Baptist Theological Seminary, Louisville, KY 40280

Warren, Bruce, Pastor, Elliott Baptist Church, Hearne, TX 77859

Watts, John D. W., Donald L. Williams Professor of Old Testament Interpretation, The Southern Baptist Theological Seminary, Louisville, KY 40280

Wilson, Johnny Lee, Pastor, Immanuel Baptist Church, La Puente, CA

Winbery, Carlton L, Professor of Religion and Chairman of the Department of Religion/Philosophy, Louisiana College, Pineville, LA 71359

Wooldridge, Judith, Design Editor, Youth Curriculum, Nashville, TN 37234

Wright, Jr., G. Al, Pastor, Mount Tabor Baptist Church, Duluth, GA 30136

Wyrick, Stephen Von, Assistant Professor of Old Testament and Hebrew, California Baptist College, Riverside, CA 92504

Yamauchi, Edwin, Professor of History, Miami University, Oxford, OH 45056

Young, J. Terry, Professor of Theology, New Orleans Baptist Theological Seminary, New Orleans, LA 70126-4858

TIME LINE

────────────────────────── Pentateuch ──────────────

BIBLICAL HISTORY

◀ **CREATION, FALL, FLOOD, BABEL** | **PATRIARCHS**

Earlier
Dating
System

| 2100 | 2000 | 1900 | 1800 |

Isaac

Abraham   Jacob   Joseph

◀ **Undatable Past - Creation, Fall, Flood, Babel** | **PATRIARCHS** | **EGYPTIAN SLAVERY**

Later
Dating
System

| 2100 | 2000 | 1900 | 1800 |

────────────────── ANCIENT HISTORY ──────────────────

WORLD HISTORY

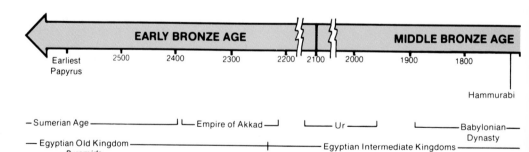

◀ **EARLY BRONZE AGE** | | **MIDDLE BRONZE AGE**

Earliest
Papyrus

| 2500 | 2400 | 2300 | 2200 | 2100 | 2000 | 1900 | 1800 |

Hammurabi

─ Sumerian Age ──────────────┘ └─ Empire of Akkad ─┘   └── Ur ──┘   └── Babylonian ──

─ Egyptian Old Kingdom ────────────────┼──── Egyptian Intermediate Kingdoms ── Dynasty

     Pyramids

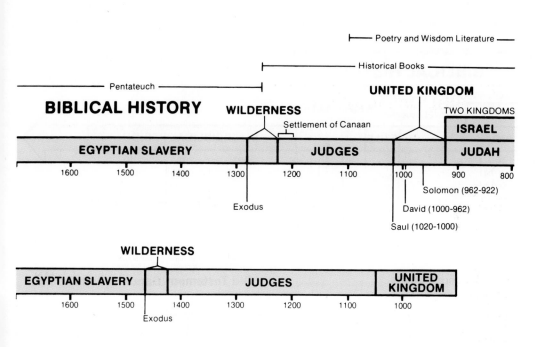

Poetry and Wisdom Literature ——

Historical Books ——

Pentateuch ——

BIBLICAL HISTORY

WILDERNESS

Settlement of Canaan

UNITED KINGDOM

TWO KINGDOMS

ISRAEL

EGYPTIAN SLAVERY

JUDGES

JUDAH

| 1600 | 1500 | 1400 | 1300 | 1200 | 1100 | 1000 | 900 | 800 |

Solomon (962-922)

Exodus

David (1000-962)

Saul (1020-1000)

WILDERNESS

| EGYPTIAN SLAVERY | | JUDGES | | UNITED KINGDOM |

| 1600 | 1500 | 1400 | 1300 | 1200 | 1100 | 1000 |

Exodus

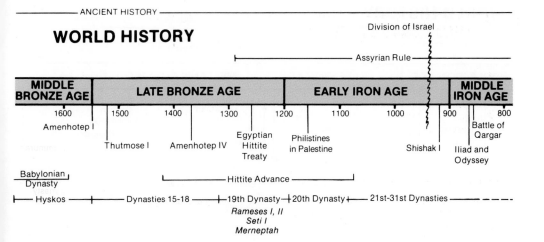

—— ANCIENT HISTORY ——

WORLD HISTORY

Division of Israel

Assyrian Rule ——

| MIDDLE BRONZE AGE | LATE BRONZE AGE | EARLY IRON AGE | MIDDLE IRON AGE |

| 1600 | 1500 | 1400 | 1300 | 1200 | 1100 | 1000 | 900 | 800 |

Amenhotep I

Thutmose I

Amenhotep IV

Egyptian Hittite Treaty

Philistines in Palestine

Shishak I

Battle of Qargar

Iliad and Odyssey

Babylonian Dynasty

—— Hyskos ——   —— Dynasties 15-18 ——   ┤19th Dynasty┤20th Dynasty┤—— 21st-31st Dynasties —— – – – –

Hittite Advance ——

Rameses I, II
Seti I
Merneptah

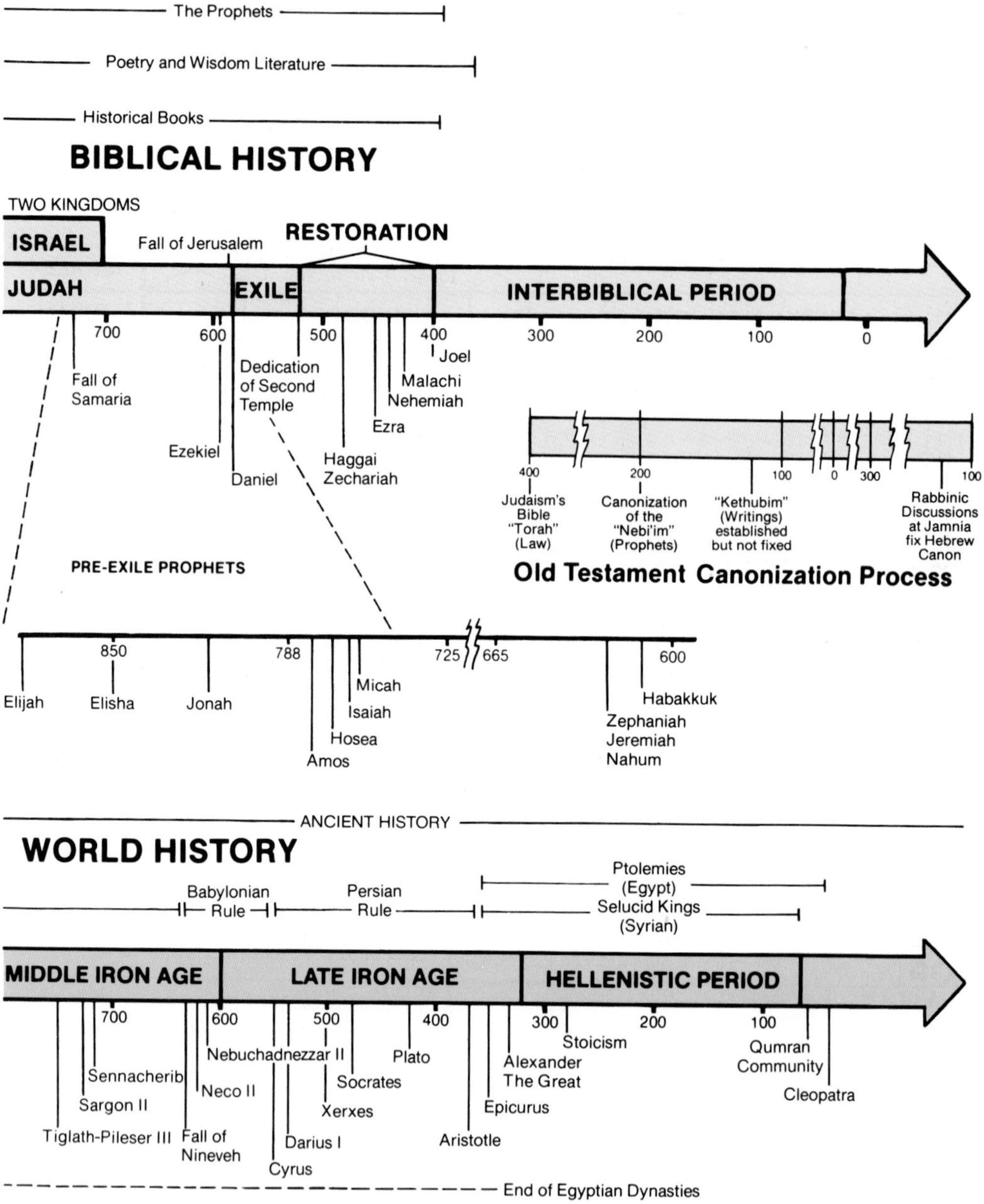

The Prophets

Poetry and Wisdom Literature

Historical Books

BIBLICAL HISTORY

TWO KINGDOMS

ISRAEL   Fall of Jerusalem   **RESTORATION**

JUDAH   **EXILE**   **INTERBIBLICAL PERIOD**

700   600   500   400   300   200   100   0

Joel

Fall of
Samaria

Dedication
of Second
Temple

Malachi
Nehemiah

Ezra

Ezekiel

Haggai
Daniel   Zechariah

Old Testament Canonization Process

400   200   100   0   300   100

Judaism's
Bible
"Torah"
(Law)

Canonization
of the
"Nebi'im"
(Prophets)

"Kethubim"
(Writings)
established
but not fixed

Rabbinic
Discussions
at Jamnia
fix Hebrew
Canon

PRE-EXILE PROPHETS

850   788   725 // 665   600

Micah

Elijah   Elisha   Jonah

Isaiah

Hosea

Amos

Habakkuk
Zephaniah
Jeremiah
Nahum

ANCIENT HISTORY

WORLD HISTORY

Babylonian
Rule

Persian
Rule

Ptolemies
(Egypt)

Selucid Kings
(Syrian)

MIDDLE IRON AGE   **LATE IRON AGE**   **HELLENISTIC PERIOD**

700   600   500   400   300   200   100

Stoicism

Qumran
Community

Sennacherib

Nebuchadnezzar II

Plato

Alexander
The Great

Sargon II   Neco II   Socrates   Epicurus

Xerxes   Cleopatra

Tiglath-Pileser III   Fall of
Nineveh

Darius I   Aristotle

Cyrus

End of Egyptian Dynasties

CHURCH HISTORY

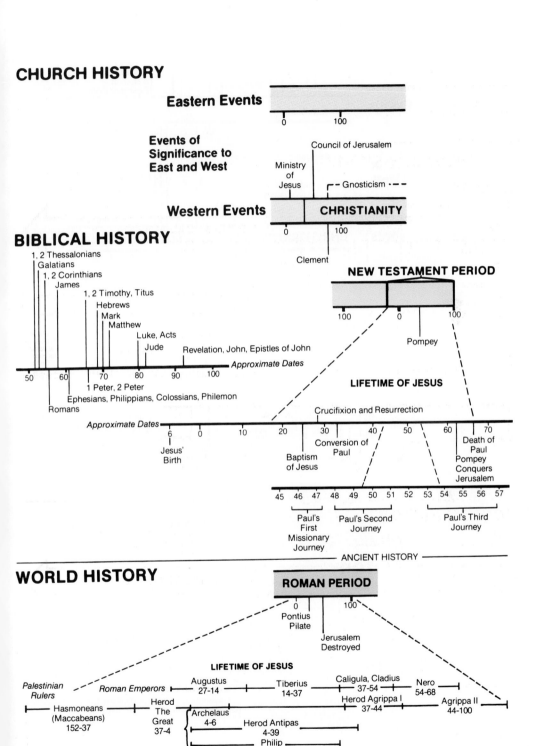

Eastern Events

0   100

**Events of
Significance to
East and West**

Council of Jerusalem

Ministry
of
Jesus

Gnosticism

Western Events   **CHRISTIANITY**

0   100

BIBLICAL HISTORY

Clement

NEW TESTAMENT PERIOD

1, 2 Thessalonians
Galatians
1, 2 Corinthians
James
1, 2 Timothy, Titus
Hebrews
Mark
Matthew
Luke, Acts
Jude   Revelation, John, Epistles of John

100   0   100

Pompey

Approximate Dates

50   60   70   80   90   100

1 Peter, 2 Peter
Ephesians, Philippians, Colossians, Philemon
Romans

LIFETIME OF JESUS

Approximate Dates

6   0   10   20   30   40   50   60   70

Jesus'
Birth

Crucifixion and Resurrection

Conversion of
Paul

Baptism
of Jesus

Death of
Paul
Pompey
Conquers
Jerusalem

45   46   47   48   49   50   51   52   53   54   55   56   57

Paul's
First
Missionary
Journey

Paul's Second
Journey

Paul's Third
Journey

ANCIENT HISTORY

WORLD HISTORY

ROMAN PERIOD

0   100

Pontius
Pilate

Jerusalem
Destroyed

LIFETIME OF JESUS

*Palestinian
Rulers*

Roman Emperors

Augustus
27-14

Tiberius
14-37

Caligula, Cladius
37-54

Nero
54-68

Herod
The
Great
37-4

Archelaus
4-6

Herod Agrippa I
37-44

Agrippa II
44-100

Hasmoneans
(Maccabeans)
152-37

Herod Antipas
4-39

Philip
4-34

CHURCH HISTORY

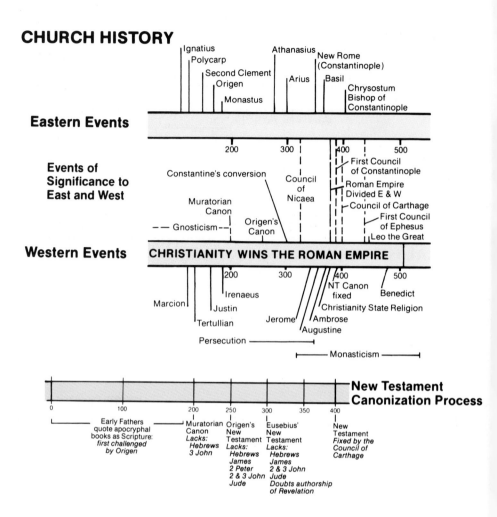

Ignatius
Polycarp
Second Clement
Origen
Monastus

Athanasius
Arius

New Rome
(Constantinople)
Basil
Chrysostum
Bishop of
Constantinople

Eastern Events

200   300   400   500

Events of Significance to East and West

Constantine's conversion

Council of Nicaea

Muratorian Canon

-- Gnosticism --
Origen's Canon

First Council of Constantinople
Roman Empire Divided E & W
Council of Carthage
First Council of Ephesus
Leo the Great

Western Events

CHRISTIANITY WINS THE ROMAN EMPIRE

200   300   400   500

Marcion
Tertullian
Justin
Irenaeus
Persecution ⟶

Jerome
Augustine

NT Canon fixed
Christianity State Religion
Ambrose
Benedict

⟵ Monasticism ⟶

New Testament Canonization Process

0   100   200   250   300   350   400

| Early Fathers quote apocryphal books as Scripture: *first challenged by Origen* | Muratorian Canon *Lacks: Hebrews 3 John* | Origen's New Testament *Lacks: Hebrews James 2 Peter 2 & 3 John Jude* | Eusebius' New Testament *Lacks: Hebrews James 2 & 3 John Jude Doubts authorship of Revelation* | New Testament *Fixed by the Council of Carthage* |

⟵ ANCIENT HISTORY ⟶ ⟵ MEDIEVAL HISTORY ⟶

WORLD HISTORY

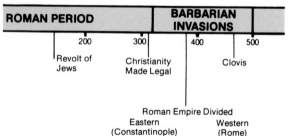

ROMAN PERIOD	BARBARIAN INVASIONS

200   300   400   500

Revolt of Jews

Christianity Made Legal

Clovis

Roman Empire Divided
Eastern (Constantinople)   Western (Rome)

CHURCH HISTORY

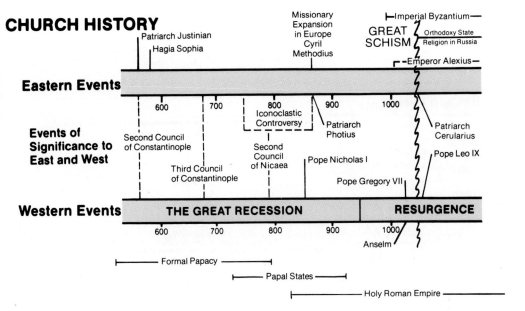

Eastern Events

Patriarch Justinian
Hagia Sophia

Missionary
Expansion
in Europe
Cyril
Methodius

Imperial Byzantium
GREAT
SCHISM
Orthodoxy State
Religion in Russia
Emperor Alexius

600   700   800   900   1000
Iconoclastic
Controversy

**Events of
Significance to
East and West**

Second Council
of Constantinople

Third Council
of Constantinople

Second
Council
of Nicaea

Patriarch
Photius

Pope Nicholas I

Pope Gregory VII

Patriarch
Cerularius

Pope Leo IX

Western Events   THE GREAT RECESSION   RESURGENCE

600   700   800   900   1000
Anselm

Formal Papacy

Papal States

Holy Roman Empire

Doctrines Addressed by the Early Church Councils

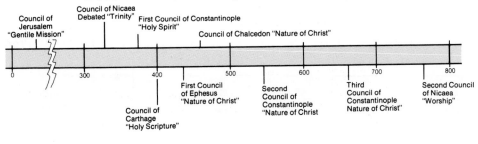

Council of
Jerusalem
"Gentile Mission"

Council of Nicaea
Debated "Trinity"

First Council of Constantinople
"Holy Spirit"

Council of Chalcedon "Nature of Christ"

0   300   400   500   600   700   800

First Council
of Ephesus
"Nature of Christ"

Second
Council of
Constantinople
"Nature of Christ"

Third
Council of
Constantinople
Nature of Christ"

Second Council
of Nicaea
"Worship"

Council of
Carthage
"Holy Scripture"

MEDIEVAL HISTORY

WORLD HISTORY

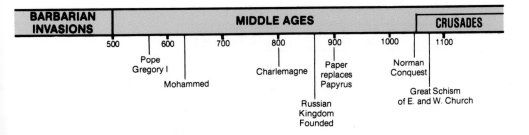

**BARBARIAN
INVASIONS**   MIDDLE AGES   **CRUSADES**

500   600   700   800   900   1000   1100

Pope
Gregory I

Mohammed

Charlemagne

Paper
replaces
Papyrus

Norman
Conquest

Great Schism
of E. and W. Church

Russian
Kingdom
Founded

CHURCH HISTORY

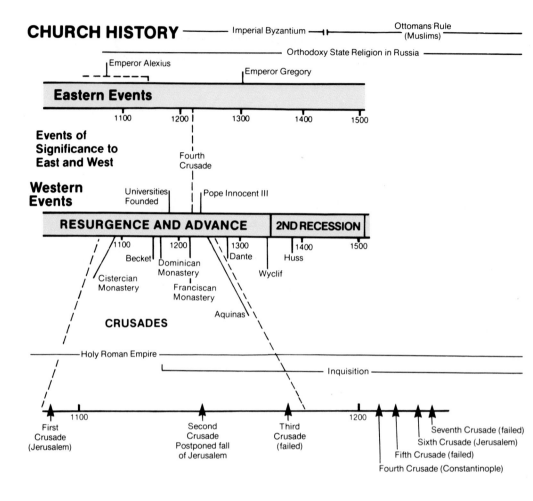

Imperial Byzantium

Ottomans Rule
(Muslims)

Orthodoxy State Religion in Russia

Emperor Alexius

Emperor Gregory

Eastern Events

1100   1200   1300   1400   1500

Events of Significance to East and West

Fourth Crusade

Western Events

Universities Founded

Pope Innocent III

RESURGENCE AND ADVANCE   2ND RECESSION

1100   1200   1300   1400   1500

Becket   Dante   Huss

Dominican Monastery

Wyclif

Cistercian Monastery

Franciscan Monastery

Aquinas

CRUSADES

Holy Roman Empire

Inquisition

1100   1200

First Crusade (Jerusalem)

Second Crusade Postponed fall of Jerusalem

Third Crusade (failed)

Seventh Crusade (failed)

Sixth Crusade (Jerusalem)

Fifth Crusade (failed)

Fourth Crusade (Constantinople)

MEDIEVAL HISTORY

WORLD HISTORY

Fall of Constantinople   Spanish Inquisition

CRUSADES   RENAISSANCE

1100   1200   1300   1400   1500

Marco Polo   Black Death   Huss burned

Discovery of New World

CHURCH HISTORY

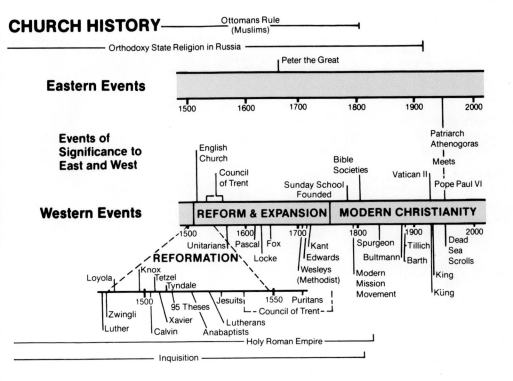

Ottomans Rule (Muslims)

Orthodoxy State Religion in Russia

Eastern Events

Peter the Great

1500   1600   1700   1800   1900   2000

Events of Significance to East and West

English Church

Council of Trent

Bible Societies

Vatican II

Patriarch Athenogoras

Meets

Sunday School Founded

Pope Paul VI

Western Events

REFORM & EXPANSION   **MODERN CHRISTIANITY**

1500   1600   1700   1800   1900   2000

Unitarians Pascal Fox   Kant   Spurgeon   Tillich   Dead
                    Locke   Edwards   Bultmann   Barth   Sea
REFORMATION   Wesleys   Modern   Scrolls
                               (Methodist) Mission   King
Loyola   Knox   Movement
            Tetzel   Küng
            Tyndale
Zwingli   95 Theses Jesuits   1550 Puritans
                                    Council of Trent
Luther   Calvin Xavier   Lutherans
                    Anabaptists

Holy Roman Empire

Inquisition

WORLD HISTORY

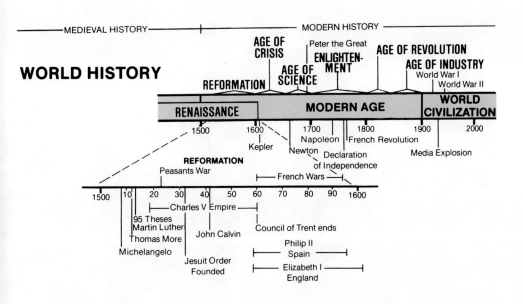

MEDIEVAL HISTORY   MODERN HISTORY

AGE OF CRISIS

Peter the Great

ENLIGHTEN-MENT

AGE OF REVOLUTION

AGE OF SCIENCE

AGE OF INDUSTRY

World War I

World War II

REFORMATION

RENAISSANCE   **MODERN AGE**   **WORLD CIVILIZATION**

1500   1600   1700   1800   1900   2000

Kepler

Newton

Napoleon French Revolution

Declaration of Independence

Media Explosion

French Wars

REFORMATION

Peasants War

1500 10 20 30 40 50 60 70 80 90 1600

Charles V Empire

95 Theses
Martin Luther

John Calvin

Council of Trent ends

Thomas More

Philip II
Spain

Michelangelo

Jesuit Order
Founded

Elizabeth I
England

The ancient Acropolis of Athens, Greece.

A

AARON (Aâr' on) Moses' brother; Israel's first high priest.

Aaron's parents Amram and Jochebed were from the tribe of Levi, Israel's tribe of priests. Miriam was his sister. See Exodus 6:16–26. With his wife Elisheba, Aaron had four sons: Nadab, Abihu, Eleazar, and Ithamar. The first two perished when they offered sacrifices with fire that God had not commanded them to make (Lev. 10:1–2; 16:1–2). Two priestly lines developed from the remaining sons: (1) Ithamar through Eli to Abiathar and (2) Eleazar to Zadok (1 Sam. 14:3; 22:20; 1 Kings 2:26–27; 1 Chron. 6:50–53).

Aaron experienced the joy of starting Israel's formal priesthood, being consecrated to the office (Ex. 28—29; Lev. 8—9), wearing the first priestly garments, and initiating the sacrificial system (Lev. 1—7). He also bore the burdens of his office as his sons were killed for their disobedience (Lev. 10:1–2), and he could not mourn for them (Lev. 10:6–7). He also bore the special rules of conduct, clothing, and ritual cleanness (Lev. 27:1—22:33).

He could not live up to such high standards perfectly. Thus he had to offer sacrifices for his own sins (Lev. 16:11). Then in his cleansed, holy office, he offered sacrifices for others. In his imperfection, Aaron still served as a symbol or type of the perfect priest as seen in Psalm 110:4, where the future king was described as eternal priest. Zechariah 6:11–15 also speaks of a priest—Joshua—in typical terms. Thus the imperfect Aaron established an office full of symbolic meaning for Israel.

Aaron's life. With all his faults, Aaron was a man chosen by God. We do not know what Aaron did during Moses' forty-year exile from Egypt, but he maintained the faith, kept contact with Israel's leaders, and did not forget his brother (Ex. 4:27–31). Ready of speech, he served nobly as Moses' spokesman before Pharaoh. More than once he stretched out Moses' staff to bring God's plagues on the land (Ex. 7:9,19). In the wilderness Aaron and Hur helped Moses hold up the staff, the symbol of God's power, so that Israel would prevail over Amalek (Ex. 17:12).

At Sinai, Aaron and his two older sons, Nadab and Abihu, were called to go up the mountain with Moses and seventy elders (Ex. 24:9). There they worshiped and ate and drank in heavenly fellowship. As Moses and Joshua went farther up, Moses left Aaron and Hur in charge (Ex. 24:14). But as Moses delayed on the mountain, the people asked Aaron for action. They cried, "Make us gods" (Ex. 32:1). Their sin was polytheism (worship of many gods) as well as idolatry. Aaron all too easily obliged and made a calf and apparently led in its worship.

On another occasion Aaron appeared in a bad light. In Numbers 12 he and Miriam spoke against Moses' marriage to the Cushite (Ethiopian) woman. (Cush was an old name for upper Egypt—approximately modern Sudan.) We are not told if this was a wife in addition to Zipporah, or if Zipporah had died, or even if Zipporah—a Midianite—had Cushite connections. Anyway, Aaron and Miriam were jealous of their younger brother. Really, their murmuring was against God's selection. Second place did not satisfy them.

Miriam was severely judged. Again, Aaron was not as harshly judged. Perhaps again he was not the instigator but the accomplice. He confessed his sin and pleaded for mercy for Miriam. When Korah, Dathan, and Abiram opposed Moses and Aaron, Aaron's intercession stopped the plague (Num. 16). Aaron's leadership was vindicated by God in the miraculous blossoming of his staff (Num. 17). When the people cried for water at Kadesh in the desert of Zin, Aaron joined in Moses' sin as they seized the power of the Lord for themselves (Num. 20:7–13). In consequence, Aaron, like Moses, was not to enter the Promised Land. Nearby on the border of Edom after forty years of his priesthood, Moses took Aaron up mount Hor, transferred his garments to his son, Eleazar, and Aaron died there at the age of 123 years (Num. 20:23–28). Israel mourned for their first high priest thirty days (Num. 20:29), as they soon would mourn for Moses (Deut. 34:8).

R. Laird Harris

AARONITES (Aâr' on īte) A term used only in the KJV to translate the name Aaron where it refers to the descendants of Aaron (1 Chron. 12:27; 27:17). Equivalent to the phrases "sons of Aaron" and "descendants of Aaron" used often in the Old Testament.

AARON'S ROD The rod Aaron used to demonstrate to the Pharaoh that the God of the Hebrews was Lord. It became a snake when cast down (Ex. 7:8–13) and brought about the first three plagues (Ex. 7:19–20; 8:5–7,16–19). This rod was also used to strike the rocks at Horeb and Kadesh to bring forth water (Ex. 17:1–7; Num. 20:7–11).

The rebellion of Korah (Num. 16:1–50) made it necessary to determine who would be eligible to come before God in the tabernacle as priests (see *Korah*). The head of each tribe was to inscribe his name on an almond rod representing his tribe, and each rod was placed in the tabernacle. The next morning, Aaron's rod had blossomed and borne almonds. This was taken as a sign from God that the house of Aaron had the right to serve Him in the tabernacle. The rod was placed inside the tabernacle (Num. 17:1–11). According to Hebrews 9:4, the rod was kept in the ark of the covenant.

AB The name for the fifth month in Jewish religious calendar corresponding to the eleventh month in the Hebrew civic calendar. It usually covered parts of July and August. The name does not appear in the Bible.

ABADDON (Å·bǎd' don; *to perish*) In the KJV Abaddon appears only in Revelation 9:11 as the Hebrew name of the angel of the bottomless pit, whose Greek name was Apollyon. Abaddon occurs six times in the Hebrew Bible (Job 26:6; 28:22; 31:12; Prov. 15:11; 27:20; Ps. 88:11). The KJV and NIV translate Abaddon as "destruction," while the NASB and RSV retain the word "Abaddon." Abaddon appears in parallel with Sheol and death. It represents the dark side of existence beyond death. See *Hell.*

ABAGTHA (Å bǎḡ' thȧ) One of seven eunuchs on the staff of Ahasuerus or Xerxes (486–465 BC), King of Persia (Esther 1:10).

ABANA (Ǎb' ȧ·nȧ) or **ABANAH** (NASB) River in Damascus in Syria. In his anger Naaman wanted to wash here rather than in the dirty Jordan (2 Kings 5:12). Many Hebrew manuscripts, the Septuagint and Targums call the river the Amana. See Song of Solomon 4:8. Its modern name is Barada, and it travels swiftly from snow-capped Mount Hermon through Damascus to end in a marsh.

The Abana River (modern Barada River) flows through the country of Syria.

ABARIM (Ābȧ·rīm) Mountain range including Mount Nebo from which Moses viewed the Promised Land (Num. 27:12; 33:47–48; Deut. 32:49). The mountain range is in Moab, east of the Dead Sea, west of Heshbon and southeast of Jericho. Jeremiah called Jerusalem to cross to Abarim and lament because her allies had been defeated (Jer. 22:20).

ABBA (Ǎb' bȧ) is the Aramaic word for "father" used by Jesus to speak of His own intimate relationship with God, a relationship that others can enter through faith.

Old Testament Although *abba* does not occur in the Old Testament, its Hebrew associate *ab* occurs frequently. *Ab* usually refers to a human father.

On occasion the Old Testament speaks of God in the role of Father to Israel (Ex. 4:22; Deut. 32:6; Isa. 45:9–11; Mal. 2:10) or to Israel's king (2 Sam. 7:14; Pss. 2:7; 89:26–27).

New Testament The idea of God's intimate relationship to humanity is a distinct feature of Jesus' teaching. God relates to believers as a father relates to his child. Some would translate *Abba* as "Daddy" to convey the close, personal meaning of the word. Even when "Father" in the New Testament translates the more formal Greek word *pater,* the idea of *abba* is certainly in the background. Jesus addressed God as *Abba* in prayer (Mark 14:36) and taught His disciples to pray in the same terms (Luke 11:1–2). Jesus' claim of intimate relationship with God offended many of His opponents because they considered *Abba* to be overly familiar in addressing God. But Jesus' usage established the pattern for the church's view of God and each believer's relationship with Him. Paul used *Abba* to describe God's adoption of believers as His children (Rom. 8:15) and the change in the believer's status with God that results (Gal. 4:6–7). *Michael Fink*

ABDA (Ǎb' dȧ) Name meaning, "servant" for two men. *1.* The father of Adoniram, whom Solomon entrusted with his labor force (1 Kings 4:6). *2.* A Levite living in Jerusalem rather than in one of the levitical cities (Neh. 11:17). He is also called Obadiah (1 Chron. 9:16).

ABDEEL (Ǎb' dė·ĕl) Name meaning, "servant of God." Abdeel's son Shelemiah was one of three attendants whom Jehoiakim (609–598 B.C.) commanded to arrest Baruch, Jeremiah's scribe, and Jeremiah (Jer. 36:26).

ABDI (Ǎb' dī) Name meaning, "my servant." *1.* A Levite whose grandson Ethan was one of the Temple musicians David appointed (1 Chron. 6:44). *2.* A Levite whose son Kish followed King Hezekiah's wishes and helped cleanse the Temple (2 Chron. 29:12). *3.* An Israelite with a foreign wife in the time of Ezra (Ezra 10:26).

ABDIEL (Ǎb' dī·ĕl) Name meaning, "servant of God." His son Ahi was a leader in the tribe of Gad (1 Chron. 5:15).

ABDON (Ǎb' dŏn) Geographical and personal name meaning "service" or "servile." *1.* A city from the tribe of Asher given the Levites (Josh. 21:30; 1 Chron. 6:74). Its modern name is Khirbet Abdeh. It lies about three miles from the Mediterranean coast between Tyre and Acco. *2.* A judge of Israel from the town of Pirathon in the tribe of Ephraim. He had a large family and personal wealth (Judg. 12:13–15). *3.* Two men of the tribe of Benjamin (1 Chron. 8:23, 30; 9:36). The second of these was an ancestor of King Saul. *4.* A member of the team named by King Josiah to seek God's guidance as to the meaning of the book Hilkiah, the priest, found in the Temple (2 Chron. 34:20). Known in 2 Kings 22:12 as Achbor or Acbor (NIV).

ABEDNEGO (Ȧ·bĕd′ nė·ḡō) In Daniel 1:7, the Babylonian name given to one of the three Hebrew youths who were conscripted along with Daniel to serve in the king's court. God delivered them from the fiery furnace (Dan. 2:48—3:30). His Hebrew name was Azariah. The precise meaning of the Babylonian name Abednego is disputed. Abed means "servant." *Nego* may include the name of a Babylonian god. See *Daniel, Book of; Azariah.*

ABEL (Ā′ bĕl) Name meaning, "breath, vapor, meadow." Abel's name is associated with the shortness of life. The second son of Adam and Eve may have been a twin because Genesis 4:2 literally reads, "And she continued to bear his brother Abel." His claim to fame is that "by faith Abel offered unto God a more excellent sacrifice than Cain" (Heb. 11:4). Some have thought that it was the better sacrifice because it was the sacrifice of an animal. However, the emphasis on "faith" in Hebrews and the idea of a "proper offering" in the Septuagint translation of Genesis 4:7 suggest that Abel's offering was made with a correct attitude and in the proper manner. Because of jealousy, Cain killed Abel. Hebrews 12:24 compares Abel's blood with Christ's blood. Abel's blood calls for vengeance, but Christ's blood carries with it the idea of forgiveness (Matt. 23:35; Luke 11:51; 1 John 1:7). Nevertheless, Abel is outstanding because he was the first person to worship God correctly, to demonstrate faith accurately, and to please God fully. Abel was the first shepherd and influenced the early Hebrews to place a priority on the pastoral life.   *Donald R. Potts*

ABEL (Ā′ bĕl) A place name used alone and as the first part of other place names as seen below. The Hebrew ʼ*Abel* is a distinct word with a different spelling from the personal name Abel (Hebrew, *hebel*). The precise meaning of the place name is uncertain. It may mean, "brook." Standing alone, Abel appears in 2 Samuel 20:14–18, probably being the same place as Abel-beth-maachah.

ABEL-BETH-MAACHAH or **ABEL-BETH-MAACAH** (NAS, NIV, RSV). (Ā′ bĕl-bĕth-mā′ ȧ·cah) See *Abel.* A city with a strong Israelite tradition, known for its wise people. Joab besieged the city when Sheba fled there after seeking to lead a rebellion against David. A wise woman delivered the city by getting the citizens to execute Sheba (2 Sam. 20:1–22). Ben-hadad, king of Syria, answered the call for help of Asa,

king of Judah (913–873), and conquered Abel-beth-Maachah from Baasha, king of Israel (1 Kings 15:20). Tiglath-pileser, king of Assyria, captured the city from Pekah, king of Israel (2 Kings 15:29). Abel-beth-maachah is identified with the modern Abil el-Oamh, twelve miles north of Lake Huleh near Dan. Its name indicates it was once part of the city state of Maachah controlled by Arameans (2 Sam. 10:6).

ABEL-CHERAMIM or **ABEL-KERAMIM** (NAS, NIV, RSV, TEV) (Ā′ bĕl-chĕr′ ȧ·mĭm) Place name meaning, "brook of the vineyards." Jephthah, the judge, extended his victory over the Ammonites as far as Abel-cheramim (Judg. 11:33), whose location east of the Jordan is not known precisely.

ABEL-MAIM (Ā′ bĕl-mȧ′ ĭm) Place name meaning, "brook of the waters." Used in 2 Chronicles 16:4 for place called Abel-beth-maachah in 1 Kings 15:20. If Abel-maim is a different city, its precise location east of the Jordan is not known.

ABEL-MEHOLAH (Ā′ bĕl-mė-hō′ lăh) Place name meaning, "brook of the round dancing." A border town or towns whose location(s) is uncertain. Gideon fought the Midianites in the territory of Issachar west of the Jordan (Judg. 7:22). Solomon places Abel-meholah in a district including Taanach, Megiddo, and Beth-shean (1 Kings 4:12). This was Elisha's home (1 Kings 19:16).

ABEL-MIZRAIM (Ā′ bĕl-mĭz′ rā′ ĭm) Place name meaning either "brook of Egypt," or if derived from a different Hebrew word with similar spelling, "mourning of the Egyptians." Jacob's children mourned him there east of the Jordan (Gen. 50:11). In giving the name the Canaanites identified Jacob's sons as Egyptians.

ABEL-SHITTIM (Ā′ bĕl-shĭt′ tĭm) Place name meaning, "brook of the acacias." The last stop of Israel before crossing the Jordan (Num. 33:49). See *Shittim.*

ABEZ or **EBEZ** (NAS, NIV, RSV, TEV) (Ā′ bĕz) Place name with unknown meaning. Town allotted to Issachar (Josh. 19:20).

ABI or **ABIJAH** (NIV) (Ā′ bī) Personal name meaning, "my father." Mother of King Hezekiah (2 Kings 18:2).

ABIA (Ȧ·bī′ ȧ) KJV for Abijah in 1 Chronicles 3:10; Matt. 1:7; Luke 1:5. See *Abijah.*

ABIAH (Ȧ·bī′ ȧh). KJV for Abijah in 1 Samuel 8:2; 1 Chronicles 2:24; 6:28; 7:8. See *Abijah.*

ABI-ALBON (Ā′ bī-ăl′ bŏn) Personal name meaning, "my father is overpowering." One of David's

30 heroes (2 Sam. 23:31). Called Abiel in 1 Chronicles 11:32. Original name in 2 Samuel may have been Abi-baal, whose letters were then transposed to a new name to avoid the idolatrous name. See *Abiel.*

ABIASAPH (Á·bī′ á·săph) Personal name meaning, "my father has gathered" or "harvested." A levitical priest in the line of Korah (Ex. 6:24). See *Ebiasaph.*

ABIATHAR (Á·bī′ á·thär) Personal name meaning, "father of abundance." The son of Ahimelech and the eleventh high priest in succession from Aaron through the line of Eli. He survived the slaughter of the priests at Nob and fled to David, hiding in the cave of Adullam from King Saul (1 Sam. 22). Having escaped with the ephod, Abiathar became the high priest and chief counselor for David (1 Sam. 23:6). Repeatedly, he inquired of the Lord for David (1 Sam. 23:9; 30:7; 2 Sam. 2:1; 5:19). Abiathar shared with Zadok the responsibility of taking the ark to Jerusalem (1 Chron. 15:11,12; 2 Samuel 15:24). While Abiathar remained faithful to David during Absalom's rebellion (2 Sam. 15), he later supported Adonijah as successor of King David instead of Solomon (1 Kings 1:7). Solomon deposed him from the priesthood and banished him to Anathoth, his home town, fulfilling the prophecy to Eli (1 Sam. 2:31–35). Only because of his faithful service to Solomon's father, King David, was he spared the death penalty (1 Kings 2:26,27).

Mark 2:26 records Jesus' statement that David took the showbread from the place of worship when Abiathar was high priest at Nob. 1 Samuel 21:1 reports that this happened when Ahimelech, the father of Abiathar, was still the high priest. However, a few days after this incident Abiathar did become high priest (1 Sam. 22:19–20). Some New Testament Greek manuscripts omit "when Abiathar was high priest." It may be that Abiathar was co-priest with his father. Or a copyist of the Gospel of Mark may have copied the text wrong. See *Priesthood; Levites; Chief Priest.*

Donald R. Potts

ABIB (Á′ bib) The month of the Exodus deliverance from Egypt (Ex. 13:4) and thus of the Passover festival (Ex. 23:15; 34:18; Deut. 16:1). A harvest month covering parts of March and April, Abib means, "ears of grain." Later the month was called Nisan (Esther 3:7). See *Calendar.*

ABIDA or **ABIDAH** (Á·bī′ dá) Personal name meaning, "my father knows." A grandson of Abraham and ancestor of the Midianites (Gen. 25:4; 1 Chron. 1:33).

ABIDAN (Ăb′ ĭ·dăn) Personal name meaning, "my father judged." Representative of the tribe of Benjamin in helping Moses and Aaron number the people in the wilderness (Num. 1:11) and captain of the tribe in the wilderness marches (Num. 2:22; 7:60,65; 10:24).

ABIEL (Á·bī′ ĕl) Personal name meaning, "my Father is God." See *Abi-albon.* Grandfather of King Saul (1 Sam. 9:1) or at least closely related to him (1 Chron. 9:36,39; 1 Sam. 14:50–51), the meaning of the texts not being absolutely clear. See *Jehiel.*

ABIEZER (Ā′ bī-ē′ zēr) Personal and place name meaning, "my Father is help." *1.* Son of Manasseh and grandson of Joseph (Josh. 17:2; 1 Chron. 7:18). *2.* Territory belonging to clan of Abiezer of tribe of Manasseh located in southwest part of Manasseh's territory and including towns of Elmattan, Ophrah, and Tetel. The territory was famous for grape production (Judg. 8:2; Samaritan, Ostraca) and was home of the judge Gideon (Judg. 6:11, 24, 34; 8:32). *3.* Member of David's 30 heroes (2 Sam. 23:27; 1 Chron. 11:28) and an administrator of David's forces in the ninth month (1 Chron. 27:12). See *Jeezer.*

ABIEZRITE (Ā′ bī-ĕz′ rīte) Descendants of Abiezer (Judg. 6:11,24; 8:32). See *Abiezer 1.* and *2.*

ABIGAIL (Ăb′ ĭ gāil) Personal name meaning, "my father rejoiced." *1.* Wife of David after being wife of Nabal. She was praised for wisdom in contrast to Nabal, her arrogant and overbearing husband, who was a large landowner and successful shepherd. Nabal held a feast for his sheep shearers while David was hiding from Saul in the wilderness of Paran. David and his six hundred men were camped near the town of Maon. He heard about Nabal's feast and requested some food. Nabal, in a drunken state, refused the request and insulted David's ten messengers. In anger, David determined to kill all of Nabal's household. Abigail anticipated David's reaction and loaded a convoy of donkeys with food to feed all of David's men. As soon as she met David, she impressed him with her beauty, humility, praise, and advice (1 Sam. 25:32–33). After Nabal became sober and heard about David's plans to kill him, he had a heart attack. Following Nabal's death, David married Abigail, the second of his eight wives. They lived first at Gath and then at Hebron, where Abigail gave birth to Chileab, who is also called Daniel. Later, Abigail was taken captive by the Amalekites when they captured Ziklag, but David rescued her (1 Samuel 30:1–18). *2.* Sister of David and the mother of Amasa (1 Chron. 2:16–17), married to Jether, an Ishmaelite (also called Ithra). Amasa, her son, was at one time the commander of David's army (2 Sam. 17:25). Abigail was the daughter of Nahash who, because of textual uncertainties has been described as (1) another name for Jesse; (2) the wife of Jesse; and (3) the father of Abigail and Zeruiah, who died and whose widow became a wife of Jesse. See *David.*   *Donald R. Potts*

ABIHAIL (Ăb′ ĭ·hāïl) Personal name meaning, "my father is a terror." *1.* Woman in family list of Judah (1 Chron. 2:29). *2.* Wife of King Rehoboam (2 Chron. 11:18). Personal name from different Hebrew spelling meaning, "my father is powerful." *3.* Father of Zuriel, a leading Levite under Moses (Num. 3:35). *4.* Father of Esther and uncle of Mordecai (Esther 2:15). *5.* A member of the tribe of God (1 Chron. 5:14).

ABIHU (Å·bī′ hū) Personal name meaning, "my father is he." The second son of Aaron; one of Israel's first priests (Ex. 6:23; 28:1). He saw God with Moses, Aaron, his brother, and 70 elders (Ex. 24). He and his brother Nadab offered "strange fire" before God (Lev. 10:1–22). The exact nature of their sin is not known. They simply did what God had not commanded. Perhaps they offered sacrifice at the wrong time or with coals or materials not properly sanctified. Compare Lev. 16:12. The result is clear. God's fire consumed them. See *Priests.*

ABIHUD (Å·bī′ hŭd) Personal name meaning, "my father is glorious." Grandson of Benjamin (1 Chron. 8:3).

ABIJAH or **ABIJAM** (Å·bī′ jäh) Personal name meaning, "my Father is Yahweh." *1.* Second son of Samuel whose crooked acts as judge led Israel to demand a king (1 Sam. 8:2–5). *2.* Son of Jeroboam, first king of the Northern Kingdom Israel. Abijah died according to prophecy of Ahijah (1 Kings 14:1–18). *3.* Son of Rehoboam and second king of divided Southern Kingdom of Judah (915–913), called Abijam in 1 Kings 15, a name meaning, "my father is Yam" (or sea), possibly a reference to Canaanite god. Abijah was his father's favorite son (2 Chron. 11:22). Abijah followed the sins of Rehoboam (1 Kings 15:3) but still maintained proper worship in Jerusalem (2 Chron. 13:10), and God gave him victory over Jeroboam of Israel (2 Chron. 13:15–20). Abijah was remembered for his large family (2 Chron. 13:21). He is listed in the ancestors of Jesus (Matt. 1:7). *4.* Wife of Hezron connected with genealogy of Caleb in a text whose meaning is not clear (1 Chron. 2:24). *5.* A grandson of Benjamin (1 Chron. 7:8). *6.* A priestly descendant of Aaron (1 Chron. 24:10). *7.* A priest under Nehemiah who signed a covenant to obey God's law (Neh. 10:7). *8.* A leading priest in the days of the return from Exile (Neh. 12:4), and then a priestly house (Neh. 12:17) to which Zechariah, father of John the Baptist, belonged (Luke 1:5). *9.* Mother of King Hezekiah (2 Chron. 29:1) and thus a power-

ful political influence. See *Abia, Abiah.*

ABIJAM See *Abijah.*

ABILENE (Ăb·ĭ·lē′ nē) Small mountainous region ruled by the tetrarch Lysanias at the time John the Baptist began his public ministry (Luke 3:7). Abilene was located about eighteen miles northwest of Damascus in the Anti-Lebanon mountain range. Its capital was Abila. In A.D. 37 Abilene came under the administrative control of Herod Agrippa I. Later it was part of the kingdom of his son, Agrippa II.

ABIMAEL (Å·bīm′ ā·ěl) Personal name meaning, "El (god) is my father." Ancestor of the Israelites as a descendant of Shem and Eber (Gen. 10:28).

ABIMELECH (Å·bīm′ ĕ·lěch) Personal name meaning, "My father is king." *1.* King of Gerar, who took Sarah for himself, thinking she was Abraham's sister rather than his wife (Gen. 20). He restored her to Abraham after a nighttime dream of God. *2.* Probably the same as *1,* a king who disputed the ownership of a well at Beersheba with Abraham and then made a covenant of peace with him (Gen. 21:22–34). *3.* King of Philistines at Gerar related to or identical with *1.* Isaac lived under his protection and fearfully passed Rebekah, his wife, off as his sister. Abimelech scolded Isaac and warned his people not to touch Rebekah. A dispute over water wells led to Isaac's leaving but finally to a treaty of peace (Gen. 26) at Beersheba. *4.* Son of Gideon, the judge of Israel (Judg. 8:31). Abimelech seized power after his father's death by murdering his brothers and having himself named king by his relatives at Shechem. This provoked Jotham's famous fable (Judg. 9:7–21). God provoked Shechem against Abimelech, who defeated an army under Gaal and then recaptured Shechem. When he tried to repeat his tactics against Thebez, a woman threw a stone down on his head and killed him (Judg. 9:23–57). Abimelech's fate served as an illustration Joab used to protect himself from David (2 Sam. 11:21). *5.* Priest under David with Zadok (1 Chron. 18:16), but correct reading of text here is probably Ahimelech as in 2 Sam. 8:17. *6.* Person mentioned in title of Psalm 34, which apparently refers to 1 Sam. 21:10–15, where Achish is David's opponent. Abimelech may have been an official title for Philistine kings.

ABINADAB (Å·bīn′ à·dăb) Personal name meaning, "my father is generous." *1.* Resident of Kirjath-jearim whose house was resting place of ark of the covenant for 20 years after the Philistines returned it. His son Eleazar served as priest (1 Sam. 7:1–2; 2 Sam. 6:3–4). *2.* Son of Jesse passed over when David was selected as king (1 Sam. 16:8; 17:13). *3.* Son of King Saul killed by Philistines in battle of Mount Gilboa (1 Sam. 31:2). *4.* Solomon's official and son-in-law over Dor, the Mediterranean seaport below Mount Carmel, was the Son of Abinadab or Ben-abinadab (1 Kings 4:11).

ABINOAM (Á·bĭn' ō·ăm) Personal name meaning, "my father is gracious." Father of Barak, army commander with Deborah (Judg. 4—5).

ABIRAM (Á·bī' răm) Personal name meaning, "my father is exalted." *1.* Leader of rebellion against Moses and Aaron seeking priestly authority. He died when God caused earth to open and swallow the rebels (Num. 16; 26:9–11). *2.* Son of Hiel sacrificed in foundation of rebuilt Jericho, fulfilling Joshua's warning (1 Kings 16:34).

ABISHAG (Ăb' ĭ·shăg) Personal name meaning, "my father strayed" or "is a wanderer." A young virgin or "maiden" (RSV) brought to David's bed in his last days to keep him warm (1 Kings 1:1–4). They had no sexual relations, but Solomon considered her David's wife when his brother Adonijah asked to marry her after David's death (1 Kings 2:17). Solomon interpreted the request as a step toward becoming king and had Adonijah executed (1 Kings 2:23–25). Abishag was from Shunem, a city guarding the Jezreel Valley.

ABISHAI (Ăb' ĭ·shā·ī) Personal name meaning, "father exists." Son of David's sister Zeruiah and brother of Joab, David's general (1 Chron. 2:15–16). He was with David when he spared Abner (1 Sam. 26:7) and with Joab pursuing Abner (2 Sam. 2:24) and killing Abner (2 Sam. 3:30). He commanded troops against Ammon (2 Sam. 10). He sought to kill Shimei for cursing David, but the king restrained him (2 Sam. 16; 19:21). He led a third of David's troops against David's son Absalom (2 Sam. 18). He commanded forces against Sheba, who led a northern rebellion against David (2 Sam. 20). He killed Isbi-benob, the Philistine giant who threatened David (2 Sam. 21:15–17). A mighty captain, he was still not among David's elite three (2 Sam. 23:8–19). He was famed for killing 18,000 Edomites (1 Chron. 18:12).

ABISHALOM (Ăb' ĭ·shá·lōm) Personal name meaning, "my father is peace." Another spelling for Absalom (1 Kings 15:2,10). See *Absalom.*

ABISHUA (Á·bĭsh' ū·á) Personal name meaning, "my father is salvation." *1.* A Levite, the great-grandson of Aaron (1 Chron. 6:4). *2.* A Benjaminite (1 Chron. 8:4). Compare 1 Chronicles 7:7.

ABISHUR (Á·bī' shûr) Personal name meaning, "my father is a wall." A descendant of Jerahmeel (1 Chron. 2:28–29).

ABITAL (Á·bī' tăl) Personal name meaning, "my

father is dew." Wife of David (2 Sam. 3:4).

ABITUB (Ā·bī' tŭb) Personal name meaning, "my father is good." A Benjaminite from Moab (1 Chron. 8:11).

ABIUD (Á·bī' ŭd) Greek spelling of Abihud for ancestor of Jesus (Matt. 1:13). See *Abihud.*

ABLUTIONS are ceremonial washings with water to make oneself pure before worship. The practice of ablutions is one background for New Testament baptism.

The Hebrew term *rachatz* is the everyday word for washing with water, rinsing, or bathing (Gen. 18:4; Ex. 2:5; Ruth 3:3). The Greek word *louein* is similar (Acts 9:37; 16:33; 2 Pet. 2:22).

Old Testament Ablutions were performed for cleansing from the impurity of an inferior or undesirable condition to prepare the person for initiation into a higher, more desirable condition. Aaron and his sons were washed before they were clothed with the priestly robes and anointed with oil (Ex. 29:4; 30:19–21; Lev. 8:6). Such washings prepared people to participate in special acts of religious service.

When a person became unclean (Lev. 11—15), becoming clean involved ablution practices. Washing could symbolize a person's claim to be pure, innocent of sin in a particular case (Deut. 21:1–9).

At times ablutions involved a general washing or bathing as when the Hebrews bathed their bodies and washed their clothes (Lev. 14:8; 15:5; Num. 19:7–8). Such washing occurred in various places—running water (Lev. 15:13), a fountain (John 9:7), in a river (2 Kings 5:10), or in a courtyard of a home (2 Sam. 11:2,4).

In some parts of the Hebrew tradition, the ritual importance of washing became a central part of religious practice with minute descriptions of how a person was supposed to wash before various activities. Some of the stricter groups would not enter a house without ablutions. They said one hand had to be washed first so it could be purified and could wash the second hand.

Old Testament teachings do not give such importance and detail to ablutions. Rather, inward, spiritual purity is the goal. Outward washing is only a symbol (Ps. 24:4; 51:7; 73:13; Prov. 30:12; Isa. 1:16; 4:4; Jer. 2:22; 4:14; Ezek. 16:4–9; 36:25–27; Zech. 13:1).

New Testament In Hebrews 6:2 the writer bid Christians to progress beyond discussion of basic matters, among which he lists "instruction about washings" (NAS). He may be describing discussions about the differences between Christian baptism and other ablutions. Hebrews 9:10 refers to "various washings" (NAS) practiced by the Hebrews under the law but no longer necessary because Christ "was once offered to bear the sins of many" (9:28).

Mark 7:4 mentions that among the traditions observed by the Pharisees was the "washing of cups and pots." They "wash their hands oft" (v. 3) before meals. They did this to hold "the tradition of the elders." Jesus called this the "tradition of men" which meant "laying aside the commandment of God" (v. 8). He cited Isaiah to call for purity of heart rather than strictness of rules (v. 6).

Examples of Jewish practice in Jesus' day have been illustrated by archaeologists in their excavations at Qumran, the Dead Sea Scroll community of the Essenes, a strict Jewish sect. Excavations revealed a vast network of ritual basins and baths used in ablutions.

For the New Testament the only washing commanded was that of baptism (Acts 22:16; 1 Cor. 6:11). Ephesians 5:26 shows that the washing of baptism is not effective as a ritual in itself but only as it shows the working of God's Word in the life of the one baptized. Inward cleansing must accompany the outward washing (Heb. 10:22).

Jimmy Albright

ABNER (Ăb' nēr) Personal name meaning, "father is a lamp." The chief military officer for King Saul and Saul's uncle (1 Sam. 14:50). At Saul's death, he supported Ish-bosheth, Saul's son (2 Sam. 2:8) until Ish-bosheth accused him of treason for taking one of Saul's concubines (2 Sam. 3:7-8). Abner transferred loyalty to David. Joab, David's general, went into a jealous rage when David welcomed Abner. Joab then killed Abner, who was buried in Hebron (2 Sam. 3). See 1 Sam. 17:55-58; 20:25; 26:5, 14-15.

ABODE OF THE DEAD See *Death; Grave; Hades; Hell; Pit; Sheol.*

ABOMINATION, ABOMINATION OF DESOLATION refers to that which is detestable to God and is particularly related to idolatry.

Abomination translates four Hebrew and one Greek word. *Ba'ash,* "stink," refers to that which becomes odious, despised, or hated as water polluted by dead fish (Ex. 7:18). Israel became a stinking abomination to the Philistines (1 Sam. 13:4). *Shiqquts,* "a detested thing," and *shaqats,* "to be filthy" refer to that which cannot be accepted in worship or eaten (Lev. 11). It often refers to idols (Deut. 29:17). *Piggul,* "stinking, rotten" refers to meat unfit for sacrifice (Lev. 7:18). *To'ebah,* "offensive, detestable," the most common word for abominable, occurring 117 times to refer to worship, cultural and moral practices which offend such as homosexuality (Lev. 18:22), Egyptians' eating with foreigners (Gen. 43:22), and particularly foreign gods (Ezek. 6:11). *Bdelugma,* "that which stinks, is disgusting," things people value are an abomination to God (Luke 16:15). See Revelation 21:27.

"Abomination of desolation" is a special term in Daniel 9:27; 11:31; 12:11; Matthew 24:15; Mark 13:14; Luke 16:15; Revelation 17:4,5; 21:27.

Daniel 9:27; 11:31; and 12:11 give evidence of a heathen idol or altar. "Abomination" (*shiqquts*) is used to describe an idol which would desecrate the holy Temple and/or altar in Jerusalem.

The term "desolation" (*shomem*) permeates the book of Daniel (8:13; 9:2,17-18,26-27; 11:31; and 12:11). The word has two root meanings: "to be desolated, ravaged" or "to be appalled, astounded." In these verses, the meaning of desolation is primary to the context.

The three occasions where the two words "abomination" and "desolation" are used together present interpreters with baffling grammatical and syntactical problems. Translators have had an impossible task in making accurate representations of the texts. Compare various translations.

In Daniel, the historical situation was apparently the building of an altar of Zeus by Antiochus Epiphanes in Jerusalem in his attempt at complete hellenization of Israel in the second century B.C. Antiochus fancied himself to be a god who greatly resembled Zeus Olympios. Zeus was known as "ba'al shamem" (lord of heaven). Hebrews did not want to write or pronounce the pagan term "ba'al" and so substituted "abomination" (shiqquts). "Shamem" in a typical "play on words" was written "desolating one" (shomem). Thus, the Zeus (lord of heaven) is loosely referred to as "abominations . . . one who makes desolate."

Antiochus selected for himself the title "Epiphanes" (God manifest). However, the people who were forced to endure his persecutions dubbed him "Epimanes" (madman). "Shamem" (desolate) could also mean "to be mad" and thus identified a more direct reference to Antiochus.

The idea of "idol worship" being conquered by The Righteous One and righteousness reaches its full and climactic expression when the Kingdom of God was inaugurated by Jesus the Messiah. The passages in Matthew, Mark, Luke, and Revelation clearly show this, pointing ahead at least to the destruction of Jerusalem by Rome in A.D. 70 and possibly beyond to the end of time.

Later literature picks up this same type of violation of proper worship in Jerusalem when Caligula (A.D. 40) sought to erect his own statue in the Jerusalem Temple. Josephus even identified the abomination of the desolator in the destruction of Jerusalem by the Roman Titus in A.D. 69-70.

Bible students give differing interpretations about the eschatological meaning of the abomination of desolation. Such interpretations often depend on the interpreter's view of the millennium. Some would interpret the "eschaton" or end time in the Book of Daniel to be the end of Antiochus

Herodian structure built over the Caves of Machpelah, Abraham's burial place for Sarah.

Epiphanes. Others see the end of any and all efforts of heathenism in the spiritual victory by Jesus over Satan. Others point to the destruction of Jerusalem by Titus. Others put off the final fulfillment to the end of all time. Some see this activity occurring repeatedly in history. Others see the fulfillment only in the final end when evil is put down finally and completely. The original passage in Daniel serves as the textual and historical presaging for later applications. One must be sensitive to the immediate interpretation of a passage as differentiated from successive applications of that same principle. *G. Beasley-Murray*

ABRAHAM (Åb ră hăm) Personal name meaning, "father of a multitude." The first Hebrew patriarch, he became known as the prime example of faith. He was the son of Terah, a descendant of Noah's son, Shem. (Gen. 11:27). His childhood was spent in Ur of the Chaldees, a prominent Sumerian city. He was known at the beginning as Abram ("father is exalted"), but this was changed subsequently to Abraham ("father of a multitude") (Gen. 17:5).

Well at modern Beersheba thought by some to be Abraham's well.

Terah, his father, moved to Haran with the family (Gen. 11:31) and after some years died there. God called Abram to migrate to Canaan, assuring him that he would father a vast nation. At different times he lived in Shechem, Bethel, Hebron, and Beer-sheba. His wife Sarai's beauty attracted the pharaoh when they moved to Egypt during a famine (Gen. 12:10), but God intervened to save her. The trouble arose partly because Abram had claimed her as his sister rather than his wife, and in fact she was his half-sister (Gen. 20:12). After returning to Palestine, Abram received further covenantal assurances from God (Gen. 15). He decided he could produce offspring by taking Sarai's handmaid Hagar as a concubine. Though the union produced a son, Ishmael, he was not destined to become Abram's promised heir. Even after another covenantal assurance (Gen. 17:1–21) in which the rite of circumcision

was made a covenantal sign, Abram and Sarai still questioned God's promise of an heir.

Then Sarai, whose name had been changed to Sarah ("princess"), had her long-promised son, Isaac ("laughter"), when Abraham was 100 years old. Ishmael's presence caused trouble in the family, and he was expelled with his mother Hagar to the wilderness of Paran. Abraham's faith and obedience were tested by God in Moriah when he was commanded to sacrifice Isaac. God provided an alternative sacrifice, however, saving the boy's life. As a reward for Abraham's faithfulness, God renewed the covenant promises of great blessing and the growth of a mighty nation to father and son.

Subsequently, Sarah died and was buried in the cave of Machpelah (Gen. 23:19), after which Abraham sought a bride for Isaac. A woman named Rebekah was obtained from Abraham's relatives in Mesopotamia, and Isaac married her gladly (Gen. 24:67). In old age Abraham remarried and had further children, finally dying aged 175 years. Abraham recognized God as the almighty Lord of all and the Author of a covenant by which the Hebrews would become a mighty nation. God Himself was known subsequently as the God of Abraham (Ex. 3:6). Through him God had revealed His plan for human salvation (Ex. 2:24). The promises to Abraham became assurance for future generations (Ex. 32:13; 33:1). Abraham became known as "God's friend forever" (2 Chron. 20:7).

John showed that descent from Abraham did not guarantee salvation (Matt. 3:9). See Romans 9. Indeed, foreigners would join him in the kingdom (Matt. 8:11). Compare Luke 16:23–30. Lost sons of Abraham, Jesus invited to salvation (Luke 19:9). True children of Abraham do the works of Abraham (John 8:39).

For Paul Abraham was the great example of faith (Rom. 4; Gal. 3). In Hebrews Abraham provided the model for tithing (Heb. 7) and played a prominent role in the roll call of faith (Heb. 11). James used Abraham to show that justification by faith is proved in works (Jas. 3:21–24).
R. K. Harrison

ABRAHAM'S BOSOM was the place to which the poor man Lazarus was carried by the angels when he died. The Roman custom of reclining at meals was common among the Jews. Such positioning placed one in the bosom of the neighboring person. To be next to the host, that is to recline in the bosom of the host, was considered the highest honor. Thus, to be in Abraham's bosom was to be in a position of honor. In Luke 16:22–23, Abraham's bosom is pictured as a place of blessedness and honor. The poor man was comforted after death by being given the place of closest fellowship with the father of the whole Hebrew nation. See *Heaven.*

ABRAM (Ā' bram) Personal name meaning, "father is exalted." The name of Abraham ("father of a multitude") in Genesis 11:26–17:4. See *Abraham.*

ABRONAH (Ă·brō' nah) Place name meaning, "pass or passage." Wilderness camp (Num. 33:34). Its location is not known, but it is apparently close to Ezion-geber at the northern tip of the Gulf of Aqaba. KJV spelling is Ebronah.

ABSALOM (Ăb' sȧ·lom) Personal name meaning, "father of peace." See *Abishalom.* Third son of King David, who rebelled against his father and was murdered by Joab, David's commander (2 Sam. 3:3; 13—19). Absalom apparently resented being ignored by his father and resented

So-called Tomb of Absalom in the Kidron Valley in Jerusalem.

his brother Ammon going unpunished for raping Tamar, Absalom's full sister. Being overindulged and ambitious, Absalom became the spokesman for the people (2 Sam. 15:1–6). They, in turn, gladly proclaimed him king in Hebron (15:10), where David was first crowned (2:4). Battle ensued. David left Jerusalem and sent his army to find Absalom but not to hurt him (15:5), but Joab murdered him (15:14). David's lament over Absalom shows the depth of a father's love over the loss of a son as well as regret for personal failures which led to family and national tragedies.

Robert Fricke

ABSHAI NAS spelling for Abishai. See *Abishai.*

ABSTINENCE is the voluntary refraining from some action, such as eating certain kinds of foods or drinking alcoholic beverages.
Old Testament The most prominent examples of abstinence in the Old Testament relate to the Sabbath (Ex. 20:8–11), food laws (Lev. 11; 19:23–25; Deut. 14), the Nazarite vow (Num. 6), and fasting. While not unique to the Israelites, observance of the Sabbath and food laws became distinguishing characteristics of Israelites in foreign cultures.

The Nazarite vow involved abstinence from fermented products and all produce of the grape vine. On occasion the vow became a lifelong commitment (Judg. 13:5–7). Fasting was practiced as an act of humbling oneself before the Lord. It involved abstinence from food and drink or on occasion only from food or drink. The Day of Atonement was the most prominent fast in Israel.
New Testament Old Testament forms of abstinence continued in the New Testament period, but the forms themselves frequently were points of controversy between Jesus and the religious leaders (Mark 2:18—3:6). Jesus refocused the prohibitive aspects of the practices by emphasizing internal motive over external observance (Matt. 6:16–18). Paul established the principle of abstaining from any activity that might offend or cause another to stumble (Rom. 14; 1 Cor. 8). This principle often guides the contemporary practice. *Michael Fink*

ABYSS (A·byss') Transliteration of Greek word *abussos* literally meaning "without bottom." KJV translates, "the deep," or bottomless pit. NAS, NIV, RSV use abyss to refer to the dark abode of the dead (Rom. 10:7). Abaddon rules the Abyss (Rev. 9:11), from which will come the beast of the end time of Revelation (11:7). The beast of the Abyss faces ultimate destruction (Rev. 17:8). Satan will be bound there during the millennium (Rev. 20:1–3). See *Hades; Hell; Sheol.*

ACACIA See *Shittim.*

Acacia tree growing in the Sinai desert.

ACBOR NIV spelling for Achbor.

ACCAD (Ăc' căd) or **AKKAD** (NIV). Place name of famous city in Mesopotamia ruled by Sargon I about 2350 B.C. (Gen. 10:10). Its exact location is not known. It gave its name to Akkadian language used by Babylon and Assyria.

ACCENT, GALILEAN The peculiarity of Peter's speech that showed he was from Galilee. The peculiarity of speech made the servant girl suspect that Peter was a follower of Jesus from Nazareth in

Galilee (Matt. 26:73; compare Judg. 12:5–6, where a person's speech betrayed his place of origin; see *Shibboleth*).

ACCEPTANCE means being received with approval or pleasure. In the Bible, things or persons are often said to be acceptable to men or to God. Human acceptance (or rejection) of other humans is affected by many things such as race, class, clan, sex, actions of the individual, prejudice, etc. On a human level Jesus shows us that all human beings are to be accepted, to be loved for their own sake, simply because they are persons created in the image of the loving Father (Gen. 1:26–27; 5:43–48).

Above all, sin keeps a person from being acceptable to God (Gen. 4:7; Isa. 59:2). From earliest days sacrifices were offered to God in an attempt to make the worshiper acceptable to Him. Later, the law revealed more clearly what one needed to do to be acceptable to God. This included ethical actions (Ten Commandments) as well as sacrifices (Leviticus). Israel succumbed to the temptation of separating sacrifice from ethical action, so the great prophets again and again hammered home the truth that no sacrifice is acceptable if it is divorced from just treatment of others (Isa. 1:10–17), Amos 5:21–24). Micah summed up the terms of acceptance in 6:6–8, "What doth the LORD require of thee, but to do justly, and to love mercy, and to walk humbly with thy God?" The proper attitude of humility is as important as right action (Ps. 51:16–17; 1 Pet. 5:5–6).

Jesus summarized the law and the prophets in the two great commandments (Matt. 22:37–40) and held them up as the requirements for eternal life (Luke 10:25–28). Paul saw that the law serves two purposes. (1) It makes known God's requirements, thus revealing human sinfulness (Rom. 3:20). (2) The moral law as a true expression of God's will remains a goal or guide, even though one no longer thinks God's acceptance is won by the law. The New Testament proclaims that Jesus has done what is necessary to make one acceptable to God. At the beginning of His ministry Jesus announced that His mission included proclaiming the acceptable year of the Lord, the time of salvation (Luke 4:19). Jesus revealed the will of God clearer than ever before (Heb. 1:1–2); He destroyed the works of the devil (1 John 3:8); but above all He put away sin "by the sacrifice of Himself" (Heb. 9:26). Paul wrote of acceptance before God mainly as justification. People are made acceptable to God because the just requirements of the law have been met by the sacrifice of Jesus (Rom. 3:21–26, 8:3–5). The Book of Hebrews presents Jesus as the true High Priest who offers the perfect sacrifice that effectively cleanses or covers sin so that it is no longer a barrier to acceptance by God (Heb. 9:11–14,26). Both Paul and Hebrews taught that for acceptance by God to be effective, one must believe—accept the offer of

The modern Mediterranean port city of Haifa a few miles south of the ancient port city of Acco in Israel.

acceptance from God in Christ and commit one-self to following the way of Jesus, confessing Him as Lord. See *Justification; Atonement; Love.*

Joe Baskin

ACCESS Permission and ability to enter into a secured area or into the presence of an important person or God. In the human realm access usually applied to persons who were permitted to see the king face to face (Esther 1:14). Thus they had a place to stand in the king's presence (Zech. 3:7). Each royal court had its own rules. The Persian court which Esther faced set the death penalty for anyone who sought access to the king without royal permission (Esther 4:11). The New Testament teaches that every person can now have access to God because Jesus' death on the cross has opened the way. Such access is actually experienced by those who express personal trust in Jesus and rely on divine grace. This brings peace and eternal hope (Rom. 5:1–2), but it is always dependent upon the heavenly King's royal favor, not upon entrance requirements established by or met by humans. Both Gentiles and Jews have an open door to the Father through Christ's death on the cross and through the work of the Holy Spirit present in the believer's life (Eph. 2:10–18). Access to God through faith in Christ was God's eternal purpose and gives the believer confidence and boldness to approach God (Eph. 3:12). Old Testament religious practices allowed only the high priest to enter the holy of holies and that only once a year (Lev. 16:2,34). Through Christ believers have constant access to the holiest place, where God is (Heb. 10:19–22).

ACCO (Ăc′ cō) KJV reads **ACCHO.** Place name for famous Mediterranean seaport north of Mount Carmel. Territory was assigned to tribe of Asher, but they could not conquer it (Judg. 1:31). The Greeks renamed Acco, Ptolemais. On his third missionary voyage, Paul spent one day in Ptolemais (Acts 21:7). The city has a long history documented by Near Eastern records reaching back to about 2000 B.C., but it plays a small role in the biblical narrative.

ACCOUNTABILITY, AGE OF The age of accountability is a concept not directly mentioned in the Bible. What the Bible teaches about personal responsibility for sin and the nature of salvation compels us to define this concept. Basically, the age of accountability is that time in the development of a person when he or she can and invariably does sin against God and thus stands in the need of personal redemption through Jesus Christ. Even under the Old Testament, the Jews recognized that children could not be held personally accountable to the law of Moses. They set the arbitrary age of twelve as the year when a child assumed adult status in religious matters.

Historically, some groups of Christians have believed that an infant is born with an immediate responsibility for sin. This view suggests that children inherit the guilt of the sins of those who have lived before them. Infant baptism has been the usual prescription for this innate sin. This position, however, misinterprets both the biblical doctrine of sin and the ordinance of baptism.

The Bible teaches clearly that persons are responsible for their own actions, not for those of their ancestors. Sin is a willful act of rebellion against God on the part of an individual (Rom. 3:9–18). Clearly, an infant or young child is not capable of such a willful act. At this point, one must be careful not to confuse bad behavior or early signs of willful actions on the part of children with sin. Such behavior does not necessarily indicate that a child has knowingly sinned.

Similarly, the Bible indicates that salvation is a deliberate act of faith on the part of individuals. To exercise this choice, persons must be able to make certain distinctions. They must be aware they are sinners before God and be able to repent of that rebellious life-style. They must be capable of transferring trust to Jesus as personal Savior and Lord. They must be able to understand that their life-styles should be patterned after the example of Christ (Rom. 10:9–14). Obviously, an infant or young child cannot make these distinctions and cannot be responsible for making such a decision.

There comes a time in the life of each child when that boundary of responsibility to God is crossed. A child invariably sins (Rom. 3:23) and stands in need of Christ. However, it is impossible to set a particular age when this will occur. Indeed, each child will vary in reaching that time.

It would seem wise to recall that Christ commanded the children be brought to Him (Matt. 18:10; 19:13–14). Yet, care must be taken that children "come to Christ" with a responsible understanding. *Timothy Boyd*

ACCURSED A translation of Hebrew *cherem,* a technical term in warfare for items captured from the enemy and devoted to God. See *Anathema; Ban; Blessing and Cursing; Devoted Thing.* TEV demonstrates the difficulty of translating the Hebrew into English, using at various times: "unconditionally dedicate" (Num. 21:2); "put everyone to death" (Deut. 2:34); "completely destroy" (Deut. 20:17); "killed" (Josh. 6:21; 8:26); "become the Lord's permanent property" (Lev. 27:21); "put a curse on . . . destroyed" (Judg. 1:17). REB uses "dedicated" (Lev. 27:21); "devoted" (Lev. 27:28–29); "utterly destroy" (Num. 21:2); "put to death under solemn ban" (Deut. 2:34); "exterminate" (Deut. 7:2); "destroyed" (Josh. 2:10); "put to death" (Judg. 21:11). NRSV consistently uses "devoted" and "utterly destroyed" to translate *cherem,* while NAS uses "set apart" and "utterly destroy." NIV uses "devoted," "totally destroyed," "completely destroyed." Devoting battle spoils to a god was practiced by Israel's neighbors also, as 2 Kings 19:11 shows. "Accursed" appears in KJV for *cherem* only in Joshua and in 1 Chronicles 2:7. In Deuteronomy 21:23 and Isaiah 65:20 KJV uses "accursed" to translate another Hebrew root, *qalal,* "to make light of, curse."

Paul used a technical Greek term, *anathema,* to call for persons to be put under a holy ban or be accursed (Rom. 9:3; 1 Cor. 12:3; Gal. 1:8–9; compare 1 Cor. 16:22). Paul used the term in the sense of the Hebrew *cherem.* See *Anathema.*

ACCUSER A legal term describing a person who claims another is guilty of a crime or a moral offense. The Hebrew word for accuser is "*Satan*" (compare Ps. 109:6 in various translations). See *Satan.* False accusation called for serious punishment (Deut. 19:15–21). The psalmist prayed for judgment against his accusers (Ps. 109:4,20,29 NAS, NIV, NRSV). False accusers led to Christ's conviction and death (Matt. 27:12). Jewish accusers (Acts 22:30) finally led Paul to appeal to Rome (Acts 25:11).

ACELDAMA (À·cĕl' dà·mà) KJV spelling for Akeldama. The field Judas Iscariot purchased, where he killed himself (Acts 1:19). The name is Aramaic and means "field of blood." Evidently it was purchased with the money that had been paid to Judas for betraying Jesus. According to Matthew 27:7, the field purchased with this money was used for the burial of strangers. See *Judas.*

ACHAIA (À·chā' ià) The Roman province in which Gallio was deputy, or proconsul, in the time of Paul the apostle (Acts 18:12). It consisted roughly of the southern half of ancient Greece, including the Peloponnesus. Major cities in Achaia included Sparta, Athens, and Corinth, which was the administrative center. Paul preached successfully in the province (Acts 18:27–28).

ACHAICUS (À chā' ĭ cŭs) Personal name of messenger who came to Paul from Corinth before he wrote 1 Corinthians (1 Cor. 16:17). His presence with Stephanas and Fortunatus encouraged Paul. The three brought news and perhaps a letter (1 Cor. 7:1) to Paul from the church at Corinth. They may have carried 1 Corinthians back to Corinth.

ACHAN (Ā' chàn) or **ACHAR** (1 Chron. 2:7). In Joshua 7:1, a Judahite whose theft of a portion of the spoil from Jericho brought divine displeasure and military defeat on the Israelite army. After the battle of Ai, the Lord told Joshua the reason for Israel's defeat was that the ban concerning the spoil of Jericho had been violated (Josh. 7:11). Achan was discovered to be the guilty party, and

he and his family were stoned to death (Josh. 7:25). See *Ai; Joshua.*

ACHAR See Achan.

ACHAZ KJV spelling of **AHAZ** (Matt. 1:9). See *Ahaz.*

ACHBOR (Ăch' bôr) Personal name meaning, "mouse." *1.* Father of king in Edom (Gen. 36:38). *2.* Man King Josiah commissioned to ask God the meaning of the Book of the Law found in the Temple. He and others commissioned obtained God's word from Huldah, the prophetess (2 Kings 22:12–14). *3.* Father of Elnathan, whom Jehoiakim sent to bring back prophet Uriah from Egypt to execute him (Jer. 26:22). Compare Jeremiah 36:12.

ACHIM (Ā' chīm) Personal name. Ancestor of Jesus of whom nothing but his name is known (Matt. 1:14).

ACHISH (Ā' chish) Philistine personal name. *1.* King of Gath, a Philistine city, to whom David fled in fear of Saul (1 Sam. 21:10). David played the madman to escape from Achish (21:13). Later David became a soldier for Achish, but cunningly expanded his own influence around Ziklag (1 Sam. 27). David joined Achish to fight Saul (28:1–2), but the Philistine leaders forced him to leave without fighting (29:1–11). Saul and his sons, including Jonathan, died in the battle (31:1–6). *2.* King of Gath to whom Shimei went to retrieve his servants but in so doing violated his agreement with Solomon and lost his life (1 Kings 2:36–46).

ACHMETHA (Ăch' mē·thà); or **ECBATANA** (NAS, NIV, RSV, TEV) The capital of the ancient Median empire, located in the Zagros Mountains in western Iran, on two major roads that lead from the south and west to the city of Tehran. Only one reference to the city is found in the canonical books of the Bible (Ezra 6:2), but it is known as Ecbatana in the apocryphal books and is referred to frequently, especially in the books of Judith, Tobit, and 2 Maccabees.

No archeological work has been undertaken at Achmetha for the simple reason that it is now occupied by the modern city of Hamadan. Surface finds, two of which are a gold dagger and a gold tablet written in cuneiform, have been made.

Bryce Sandlin

ACHOR (A' chôr) Place name meaning "trouble, affliction," or "taboo." The valley in which Achan and his household were stoned to death (Josh. 7:24–26). Later, it formed part of the border of Judah. It is the subject of prophetic promises in Isaiah 65:10 and Hosea 2:15. See *Joshua.*

ACHSA (Ach' sà) or **ACHSAH** (NAS, RSV, TEV) or **ACSAH** (NIV). Personal name meaning, "bangle, ankle ornament." Daughter of Caleb offered as wife to man who conquered Kirjath-sepher (Josh. 15:16). Othniel took the city and the woman. See Judges 1:12–13.

ACHSHAPH (Äch' shǎph) or **ACSAPH** (NIV) Place name meaning, "place of sorcery." City state which joined Jabin, King of Hazor, in opposing Joshua as he invaded northern Israel (Josh. 11:1). Achshaph was a border city for Asher (Josh. 19:25). It was probably located near Acco.

ACHZIB (Äch' zĭb) or **ACZIB** (NIV) Place name meaning, "deceitful." *1.* Town in southern Judah, perhaps modern Tel el-Beida near Lachish (Josh. 15:44). Micah 1:14 makes a wordplay using Achzib, literally the houses of deceitfulness will be deceitful. *2.* A border town of Asher (Josh. 19:29) which the Israelite tribe could not conquer (Judg. 1:31). It may be modern Tel Akhziv, near Acco.

ACRE Translation of Hebrew *tsemed,* literally a "team" of oxen. As a measure of land, it refers to the land a team can plow in one day (1 Sam. 14:14; Isa. 5:10).

ACROSTIC Literary device by which each section of a literary work begins with the succeeding letter of the alphabet. Thus in Psalm 119 the first eight verses begin with *aleph,* the first letter of the Hebrew alphabet; the next eight with *beth,* the second letter of the Hebrew alphabet, and the pattern is continued through verses 169–176, which each begin with *taw,* the last letter of the Hebrew alphabet. Other examples in the Bible include Psalms 9—10; 25; 34; 37; 111; 112; 145; Proverbs 31:10–31; Lamentations 1; 2; 3; 4. The acrostic style helped people memorize the poem and expressed completeness of subject matter from A to Z.

ACSAH NIV spelling of Achsa. See *Achsa.*

ACTS Fifth book of the New Testament tracing growth of early church.

The most significant help in discovering the author of Acts is simply recognizing this book's relationship to the Gospel of Luke: 1) Both books begin with a greeting to a man named Theophilus ("friend of God"); 2) Acts' greeting to Theophilus refers to a previous writing; 3) The end of Luke intentionally overlaps with the beginning of Acts to provide continuity between the two volumes; 4) the author's writing style, vocabulary, and attention to specific themes remain constant throughout both books.

Consequently, the reader must assume Acts was written by the same author as the gospel of Luke. In fact, many Bible readers believe Luke-

Acts is a single work which was divided into two parts as the books of the New Testament were gathered together. The size of Luke and Acts combined makes the author of these two books the chief contributor to the New Testament, having written twenty-five percent of all Scripture from the Christian era. Taken as a whole, Luke and Acts are a larger work than the combined letters of Paul.

Once readers assume Luke and Acts come from the same pen, they can begin to look for evidence within these books which points toward the author's identity.

The first piece of evidence comes in Luke 1:2. There, the writer states he was *not* an eyewitness to the ministry of Jesus. This fact eliminates any of the eleven disciples as candidates for authorship. Next, the "we" passages in Acts also offer a major, internal clue to the identity of the book's author. During the account of Paul's missionary journeys, the author occasionally changes his style from that of a third person observer to a first person participant. In Acts 16:10–17; 20:5–16; 21:1–18; and 27:1—28:16, the author speaks of "we" and "us" in relationship to Paul's travels. The language implies the author himself traveled with Paul. These "we" sections include the time when Paul was imprisoned at Rome. Scholars have determined Paul wrote Philemon, Colossians, and the Pastoral Epistles during his house arrest in that city. By searching those letters for references to Paul's fellow workers, they compiled a list of companions who could have written Luke and Acts. In 2 Timothy 4:11, Paul says, "Only Luke is with me," making him the most likely person to have written Luke-Acts.

Students of the first century church confirm the likelihood of Luke's authorship with what they call the "negative" argument. This negative argument recognizes the early church's tendency to attribute the authorship of New Testament works to recognized apostles and eyewitnesses of the ministry of the Master. We have no reason to assume early Christians would have given credit for the authorship of Luke-Acts to such an insignificant figure as Luke unless they possessed firm evidence the doctor, traveling companion of Paul, did indeed write this important document.

The Purpose of Acts Why did Luke write Acts? What purpose was the Spirit leading him to fulfill? The years have produced several different answers to those questions.

The opening verses of Luke and Acts mention Theophilus as the recipient of Luke's writings. As mentioned earlier, the name means "friend of God" and was common among Jews and Greeks in the first century. Many Bible students think Theophilus was a Roman dignitary sympathetic to the Christian cause. Perhaps Luke was writing a defense of Christianity for this official during a time of persecution to show him there was nothing subversive or sinister about the followers of Jesus. The geographical framework of Acts, the spread of the gospel from Jerusalem to Rome, lends credibility to this idea.

In addition to Luke's possible purpose as an interpreter of Christianity to the Roman world, Paul's traveling companion seems to have perceived himself specifically as a recorder of God's saving work. In 1:3 of his Gospel, Luke clearly states he is trying to make "an orderly account" of the events surrounding Jesus' ministry.

The only question which remains is Luke's reason for dividing his record of those events into Luke and Acts as he did. The obvious solution to this question would be that Luke focuses on Jesus Himself while Acts focuses on the followers of Jesus who continued their Master's work. This solution misses one important verse, Acts 1:1, where Luke says to Theophilus: "In my former book . . . I wrote about all Jesus *began* to do and teach . . ." Luke implied that Jesus continued to do and teach more, and that *His* story was incomplete where the Gospel ended. In fact, a careful reading of Acts makes it clear that Jesus remained the active, living, focus of Luke's story. In 9:4 (NIV), Jesus spoke directly to Saul and asked, "Why do you persecute *me?*" Later, in the same chapter, Peter could say directly to Aeneas, "Jesus Christ heals you" (9:34 NIV). In chapter ten, Christ made His will known to Peter concerning a ministry to the Gentiles. These are but three examples of Jesus' vital involvement in the spread of the gospel in Acts.

Therefore, despite the fact Acts begins with the ascension of Jesus, there is no evidence anyone in the early church perceived Him as "gone" from their midst. He healed, spoke, and directed the work of His disciples. Even when they preached, the disciples thought of Jesus as literally present in their preaching. They asked the listeners of those first sermons, not merely to believe facts about Jesus, but to encounter through their words the One who died, rose again, and lives forever. The ascension marked not Christ's departure, but a change in the way Christ performs His ministry of salvation and grace. Consequently, Acts is the continuing story of Jesus' work. It simply begins once He is no longer bound by the limitations of time and space. Acts tells what happened following the ascension when Jesus started to work through His new body, which is the church.

Themes of Luke Continued in Acts Because the story begun in Luke (the saving work of God) continues in Acts with the same central character (Jesus), one must expect the central themes of Luke to continue in Acts as well. What are the themes which express Luke's personal understanding of the gospel and give his record of Jesus' story his unique touch?

1. An emphasis on the work of the Holy Spirit. Luke began his Gospel with stories about individuals upon whom the Spirit descended. He described Zechariah, Mary, Simeon, and Anna as full of the Spirit and, consequently, instruments of God's efforts to save His people. Acts begins in a similar way: at Pentecost the Holy Spirit engulfed the entire community of believers who become the vehicles through which the good news of Jesus was proclaimed in "Jerusalem, and in all Judea, and in Samaria, and unto the uttermost part of the earth" (1:8).

2. A concern for outcasts and sinners. Both in the Gospel which bears his name and in Acts, Luke showed special sympathy toward persons who fell outside the traditional Jewish boundaries of acceptability. The shepherds who attended the birth of Christ would not have been admitted to the Temple or synagogue for worship because keeping sheep made them "unclean." Yet, the Spirit led Luke to record the angels' invitation to these men to gather around the manger. In Acts, Luke fully developed this theme which he began in the first volume of his work. The Ethiopian eunuch (8:26–40), Cornelius (ch. 10), and the Philippian jailer (16:22–34) all represent persons rejected by Judaism but accepted and redeemed by Christ.

3. An emphasis on women. Women constituted a special group of persons cut off from the center of Jewish worship. They were not permitted beyond their own court in the Temple, and in the synagogues they were forced to stand behind a partition while men read from the Scriptures. A prescribed morning prayer which was popular during the first century was, "Blessed be God that He did not make me a Gentile, a slave, or a woman." Luke, however, carefully recorded the importance of the role of women in the spread of the gospel. He told about the birth of Jesus from Mary's viewpoint (as opposed to Matthew's version from Joseph's experience). Luke is also the only Gospel which mentions the prophetess Anna (Luke 2:36–38), the widow at Nain (Luke 7:11–17), and the Galilean women who supported Jesus' ministry (Luke 8:2). In Acts, Luke specifically drew attention to the conversions and consequent roles of Lydia (16:11–15,40) and Priscilla (18:18–28). He also mentioned regularly the conversion of nameless women at various stops on the missionary journeys of Paul (see 17:4 as one example). Judaism allowed no room for women leaders, and Jews would not have considered female converts worth mentioning.

4. The piety of Jesus and His followers. All the principal characters of Luke's story demonstrated great personal devotion to God and tremendous personal discipline in their spiritual lives. In the Gospel, Mary and Joseph performed all of Judaism's prescribed rituals associated with childbirth and the dedication of a new infant. Jesus worshiped in the synagogue "as was his custom" (Luke 4:16), and prayed regularly. In Acts, the disciples showed the same qualities. The first few chapters constantly describe the apostles in the Temple praying. Paul's ministry was punctuated by the same type of spirituality.

Outline

I. God Prepared for Jesus' Mission to Continue (1:1—7:69).
   A. Jesus' resurrection and ascension prepared for the Spirit's coming with power (1:1–11).
   B. The waiting church organized for mission (1:12–26).
   C. The Spirit empowered God's people for mission (2:1–4).
   D. The gospel overcomes ridicule to unify the church (2:5–47).
   E. The gospel overcomes imprisonment to add to the church (3:1—3:4).
   F. The gospel overcomes tradition and threats, increasing the church's power, unity, and generosity (4:5–37).
   G. The Spirit overcomes Satan's temptations of greed and pride (5:1–16).
   H. God overcomes human jealously and fear (5:17–42).
   I. Spirit-filled leaders help the church overcome disputes and continue to grow (6:1–7).
   J. False accusers and persecution cannot halt the church's mission (7:1–60).
II. God Overcomes Human Barriers to Continue Jesus' Mission (8:1—13:52).
   A. God overcomes cultural barriers (8:1–40).
   B. God overcomes organized opposition (9:1–31).
   C. God overcomes physical barriers (9:32–43).
   D. God overcomes racial barriers (10:1—11:30).
   E. God overcomes political persecution (12:1–25).
   F. God overcomes sorcery (13:1–12).
   G. God expands the mission to "pagan peoples" (13:13–52).
III. God Expands Jesus' Mission through Geographical Boundaries (14:1—20:12).
   A. Persecution helps spread missionary work (14:1–7).
   B. Missions honors God, not missionaries, and maintains strong ties with the sending church (14:8–28).
   C. Missions is based on salvation by grace through faith without ritual burdens (15:1–35).
   D. Missionaries can disagree and spread the gospel (15:36–41).
   E. God leads missionaries in new paths (16:1–40).
   F. God can use the jealousy of religious people and the power of intellectual argument to spread His gospel (17:1–34).
   G. Missionaries preach fearlessly and follow God's will (18:1–23).
   H. Missionaries need accurate understanding as well as zeal and fervor (18:24–28).
   I. Missionaries lead people to baptism in Jesus' name and to receive God's Spirit (19:1–8).
   J. God disciplines those who seek personal gain through false use of Jesus' name (19:9–41).
   K. Missionaries visit new churches to strengthen the converts (20:1–12).
IV. Human Limits Cannot Hinder Jesus' Mission (20:13—28:31).
   A. Missionaries testify of Christ, even in the face of danger (20:13–24).
   B. Missionaries train leaders to carry on their work (20:25–38).
   C. Missionaries must be willing to die for their faith (21:1–14).
   D. Missionaries use every opportunity to share their personal testimonies (21:15—22:21).
   E. Missionaries use political rights to gain further opportunities to witness (22:22—23:11).
   F. God protects His missionaries against religious enemies (23:12–35).
   G. Enemies cannot prove their case against God's missionaries (24:1—25:27).
   H. Imprisonment lets missionaries preach forgiveness (26:1–32).
   I. God can protect His missionaries against danger (27:1—28:10).
   J. God uses fellow Christians to encourage enchained missionaries (28:11–16).
   K. Even foreign prisons cannot keep God's missionaries from preaching the gospel (28:17–31).   *Joel Snider*

ADADAH (Ăd′ ȧ·dah) Place name of city in southeastern Judah (Josh. 15:22).

ADAH (Ā′ dăh) Personal name meaning "adornment, ornament." *1.* Wife of Lamech and mother of Jabal and Jubal (Gen. 4:19–23). *2.* Wife of Esau and mother of Edomite officials (Gen. 36:2–16).

ADAIAH (Ȧ·daî′ ah) Personal name meaning, "Yahweh has adorned." *1.* Grandfather of King Josiah (2 Kings 22:1). *2.* A Levite, one of the family of Temple singers (1 Chron. 6:41). *3.* A Benjaminite (1 Chron. 8:21). *4.* A priest who returned to Jerusalem from Babylon after the Exile (1 Chron. 9:12). *5.* The father of Maaseiah, who helped make young Joash king instead of Athaliah, the queen mother (2 Chron. 23:1). *6.* Two men with foreign wives in time of Ezra (Ezra 10:29, 39). *7.* A member of the tribe of Judah in Jerusalem after the Exile (Neh. 11:5). *8.* A priest in the

Temple after the Exile (Neh. 11:12), probably the same as *4.*

ADALIA (Ăd·à·lī′ à) Personal name of Persian origin. One of ten sons of Haman, villain of Book of Esther, who was slain by Jews (Esther 9:8).

ADAM (Ăd′ am)   Place name of city near Jordan River, where waters of Jordan heaped up so Israel could cross over to conquer the land (Josh. 3:16). Its location is probably Tel ed-Damieh near the Jabbok River.

ADAM AND EVE (Ăd′ am and Ēve) The first man and woman created by God from whom all other people are descended. They introduced sin into human experience.

Old Testament The Hebrew word for Eve means "life," while the Hebrew word for Adam simply means "man." The Hebrew word *'adam* is used in at least three different ways in the Old Testament. In its most common occurence, the word *'adam* refers to mankind in general. It has this use in Genesis 1:26–27, where it includes both male and female, those who were created in the image of God. It is also used in referring to a specific man where it occurs with the Hebrew definite article (Gen. 2:24; 4:1). A third use of Adam is in reference to the city beside Zaretan (Josh. 3:16) on the Jordan. The Hebrew word for Eve is used only as reference to Adam's wife.

New Testament In the New Testament, Adam is used as a proper name, clearly referring to our ancestral parents. Jesus' genealogy is traced back to Adam (Luke 3:38). However, the most important New Testament usage treats Jesus as a second Adam (1 Cor. 15:45), where the word is used as a symbol. Furthermore, Paul in a similar manner treats Adam as a type of Christ (Rom. 5:14). As the first Adam brought death into the world, the "second Adam" brought life and righteousness (Rom. 5:15–19).

Eve is referenced two times in the New Testament. In 2 Corinthians 11:3, Eve's gullibility before the serpent is presented as undesirable. In 1 Tim. 2:11–15, women are urged to be silent and subjected to man because Adam was created before Eve and because Eve was deceived into sinning.

Theological Concerns Adam and Eve are the ancestors of humanity. They are described as being the first persons. They also produced the first offspring (Gen. 4:1–2,25). The Genesis narrative shows the development of humanity from these first parents. The interrelatedness of all humanity is stressed in Genesis.

Further the biblical writers use the story of Adam and Eve as symbolic of the universal history of all mankind. All persons reenact in their own lives the tragic story of our ancestral parents. Thus Adam and Eve are real but also symbolic.

Adam and Eve introduced sin into human experience. The first record of sinful rebellion in the Bible is found in the narrative of the first persons (Gen. 3:1–13). They fell victim to the serpent's lie (Gen. 3:4). They made the choice to disbelieve and to disobey. They were not forced to disobey God but freely chose to do so.

The consequences of Adam and Eve's sin fell not merely upon them but upon the earth as well (Gen. 3:14–19). The consequences of sin had lasting influence far beyond the two individuals. Further, following their sin, Adam and Eve hid from God; God did not hide from them (Gen. 3:8–9). Their ultimate punishment was being driven from the garden (Gen. 3:22–24). However, this was also an act of God's mercy, for it kept humanity from living forever in a sinful state. Thus an opportunity was offered for the possibility of future redemption. See *Jesus; Sin; Judgment; Wrath; Mercy.*   *Robert Cate*

ADAMAH (Ăd′ à·mah) Place name and common noun meaning, "soil, farmland." *1.* The earth or cultivated ground from whose dust God formed mankind, forming the wordplay Adam from dust of *'adamah.* (Gen. 2:7). Compare 2:19. Pottery was also made from the soil (Isa. 45:9), as were altars (Ex. 20:24). The dead return to the earth (Ps. 146:4), but the soil also produces harvests (Deut. 7:13; 11:7). *2.* A city in Naphtali's territory (Josh. 19:36) near where the Jordan River joins the sea of Tiberias, perhaps modern Hagar ed-Damm.

ADAMANT See *Minerals and Metals.*

ADAMI (Ăd′ à·mī) or **ADAMI-NEKEB** (NAS, NIV, RSV, TEV). Place name meaning, "red earth" or "red earth pass." Town in Naphtali's territory (Josh. 19:33), perhaps Khirbet Damiyeh north of Mount Tabor.

ADAR (Ā′ där) Twelfth month of Jewish calendar after the Exile, including parts of February and March. Time of Festival of Purim established in Esther (9:21).

ADBEEL (Ăd′ bĕ·ĕl) Personal name meaning, "God invites." Son of Ishmael and grandson of Abraham (Gen. 25:13).

ADDAN (Ăd′ dän) Personal name of person who returned from Exile but could not prove he was of Israelite parents. Also called Addon (Ezra 2:59; Neh. 7:61).

ADDAR (Ăd′ där) Place name and personal name meaning, "threshing floor." *1.* City on southwest border of Judah (Josh. 15:3). Also called Hazar-addar (Num. 34:4). *2.* Benjamin's grandson (1 Chron. 8:3). Also called Ard (Gen. 46:21; Num. 26:40).

ADDER (Ăd·der) See *Animals*

ADDI (Ăd′ dī) Personal name meaning, "adornment." Hebrew equivalent is Iddo. Ancestor of Jesus (Luke 3:28).

ADDON See *Addar.*

ADER (Ā′ dēr) KJV spelling of *Eder.*

ADIEL (Ăd′ ĭ·ĕl) Personal name meaning, "an ornament is god." *1.* An important leader of tribe of Simeon (1 Chron. 4:36), a shepherd people. *2.* Father of a priestly family in Jerusalem after the Exile (1 Chron. 9:12). *3.* Father of David's treasurer (1 Chron. 27:25).

ADIN (Ā′ dīn) Personal name meaning, "delightful, blissful, luxuriant." *1.* Ancestor of Jews who returned from Exile with Zerubbabel and Joshua (Ezra 2:15; Neh. 7:20). *2.* Ancestor of exiles who returned with Ezra (Ezra 8:6). *3.* Signer of the covenant of Nehemiah to obey God's Law (Neh. 10:16).

ADINA (Ăd′ ĭ·nà) Personal name meaning, "delightful, luxuriant." A captain of thirty men in David's army from tribe of Reuben (1 Chron. 11:42).

ADINO (Ȧ·dī′ nō) Personal name meaning, "loving luxury." Chief of David's captains who slew 800 men at one time (2 Sam. 23:8). Name does not appear in Septuagint, earliest Greek translation of this passage, nor in the Hebrew text of the parallel passage in 1 Chronicles 11:11. Some modern translators omit it from 2 Samuel 23:8 (NIV, RSV, TEV).

ADITHAIM (Ăd·ĭ·thā′ ĭm) Place name meaning, "elevated place." City Joshua allotted to Judah (Josh. 15:36). Its location is not known.

ADLAI (Ăd′ la·ī) Personal name of father of one of David's chief shepherds (1 Chron. 27:29).

ADMAH (Ăd′ mäh) Place name meaning, "red soil." City connected with Sodom and Gomorrah as border of Canaanite territory (Gen. 10:19). Its king was defeated along with kings of Sodom and Gomorrah by coalition of four eastern kings (Gen. 14). God destroyed Admah, one of "the cities of the plains" (Gen. 19:29), along with Sodom and Gomorrah (Deut. 29:23). God could not stand to treat Israel, the people He loved, like He had treated Admah, even though Israel's behavior resembled Admah's (Hos. 11:8). Admah may have been located under what is now the southern part of the Dead Sea.

ADMATHA (Ăd·mā′ thà) Personal name in Persian meaning, "unconquered." One of the leading advisors to King Ahasuerus (Xerxes) of Persia (Esther 1:14).

ADMIN (Ăd′ mĭn) Personal name in best Greek texts of Luke 3:33 in the ancestry of Jesus but not in Greek texts available to King James translators. Thus Admin appears in NAS, RSV, TEV but not in KJV or NIV. See NIV text note.

ADMINISTRATION *1.* A spiritual gift God gives to some members to build up the church (1 Cor. 12:28 NAS, NIV, RSV), called "governments" in KJV. The the Greek word *kubernesis* occurs only here in the Greek New Testament. It describes the ability to lead or hold a position of leadership. *2.* NAS translates Hebrew idiom "to do justice" as "administer justice" (2 Sam. 8:15; 1 Kings 3:28; 1 Chron. 18:14). Similarly, NAS translates the idiom "to judge justice" as "administer justice" (Jer. 21:12). NIV goes further with other Hebrew and Aramaic idioms translated as "administer." The person called in Hebrew "who is over the house" NIV calls the "palace administrator" (2 Kings 10:5). The Old Testament seeks to lead people in authority to establish a society in which God's law brings fairness and justice to all people without favoritism and prejudice. *3.* KJV speaks of differences of administrations (1 Cor. 12:5), translating the Greek, *diakoiōn,* "services" (NIV, RSV) or "ministries" (NAS). Leading a church involves ministering to or serving the needs of its members.

ADNA (Ăd′ nà) Personal name meaning, "joy of living." Aramaic name of *1.* A post-exile Israelite with a foreign wife (Ezra 10:30). *2.* A post-exilic priest (Neh. 12:15).

ADNAH (Ăd′ näh) Personal name meaning, "joy of living." *1.* A military leader from the tribe of Manasseh who joined David at Ziklag (1 Chron. 12:20). *2.* A military leader of Judah stationed in Jerusalem under Jehoshaphat (2 Chron. 17:14).

ADONI-BEZEK (Ăd′ ·ō·nī·bĕ′ zek) Personal name meaning, "lord of Bezek," Bezek being a place name meaning, "lightning" or "fragments." Canaanite king of Bezek. Tribe of Judah defeated him and cut off his thumbs and big toes, a sign of humiliation, before taking him to Jerusalem. There he died (Judg. 1:5–7). See *Bezek.*

ADONIJAH (Ăd·nī′ jäh) Personal name meaning, "Yah is Lord." *1.* The fourth son of David. His mother's name was Haggith (2 Sam. 3:4). In David's old age, Adonijah maneuvered to succeed his father on the throne of Israel, but his effort failed (1 Kings 1:5–50). After Solomon's accession to the throne, Adonijah gave renewed expression to his regal aspirations by asking for Abishag, David's nurse, as a wife. Solomon's response to this request was to have Adonijah put to death. (1 Kings 2:13–28). See *David*. Adonijah sought to establish hereditary kingship for Israel in which the eldest son automatically became king. Nathan, the prophet, worked with David and Bathsheba to establish a kingship in which the wishes of the dying monarch and the election by God determined the new king. *2.* A Levite Jehoshaphat sent to teach the people of Judah the book of the law (2 Chron. 8). *3.* A leader of the Jews after the Exile who signed Nehemiah's covenant to obey God's law (Neh. 10:16).

ADONIKAM (Ăd·ō·ni′ kam) Personal name meaning, "the Lord has arisen." Family head of 666 persons who returned to Jerusalem with Zerubbabel from Babylon about 537 B.C. (Ezra 2:13). Some members of the family returned with Ezra under Xerxes (Ezra 8:13). Compare Ezra 7:18. Some Bible students think Adonikam is the same person as Adonijah in Nehemiah 10:16.

ADONIRAM (Ăd·ō·nī′ ram) Personal name meaning, "the Lord is exalted." Officer in charge of the work gangs Solomon conscripted from Israel (1 Kings 4:6; 5:14). The king forced Israel's citizens to work for the state to secure materials to build the Temple and the other projects of Solomon. Apparently the same person continued administering the work force for Rehoboam, though his name is abbreviated to Adoram in 1 Kings 12:18. At that time, Isreal rebelled against making free citizens work. They stoned Adoniram to death. The name is spelled Hadoram in 2 Chronicles 10:18. Recently archaeologists uncovered a seal which probably dates to the seventh century, long after Adoniram. The seal talks of a person over the labor force.

ADONIS (Ă dō′ nĭs) God of vegetation and fertility with Syrian name meaning, "lord." Worshiped in Greece and Syria. Rites seem to include the planting of seeds which quickly produced plants and that just as quickly wilted in the sun. These were used to symbolize the dying and rising of the god and to bring blessing upon crops. Similar rites were celebrated for Osiris in Egypt and possibly for Tammuz in Babylon. REB translates Isaiah 17:10 as "your gardens in honour of Adonis." The Hebrew term appears only here in the Bible, being related to the personal name Naaman and to the Hebrew word meaning, "lovely, pleasant, agreeable." Other translations read, "finest plants" (NIV), "pleasant plants" (KJV), "delightful plants" (NAS), "sacred gardens" (TEV), "pleasant plants" (NRSV).

ADONI-ZEDEK (Ăd′ ō·nī-zē·dĕk) Personal name meaning, "the Lord is righteous" or "the god Zedek is righteous." King of Jerusalem who gathered coalition of Canaanite kings to fight Gibeon

after Joshua made a peace treaty with Gibeon (Josh. 10). Joshua marched to Gibeon's aid and defeated the coalition. Joshua made a public example of the kings before executing them (10:22–26). He exposed their bodies on trees, a further sign of humiliation, since it postponed burial.

ADOPTION *1.* The legal process whereby a person assumed parental responsibilities for another person's child as Mordecai did for Esther, his uncle's daughter (Esther 2:15). Near Eastern literature, such as the Code of Hammurabi, illustrates adoption laws, but the Bible contains no law showing the process, rights, or responsibilities involved in adoption.

Old Testament References to adoption are rather rare in the Old Testament. Other practices related to ensuring descendants were more common, and the desire to maintain the family line of the natural parents was strong.

The Old Testament examples of Moses (Ex. 2:10) and Esther (Esther 2:7,15) took place in foreign cultures and may reflect those settings more than the Hebrew practice. Some Old Testament traditions approach the idea that Israel's relationship with God was that of an adopted child (Ex. 4:22; Deut. 14:2; Hos. 11:1), though the idea is never stated explicitly (compare Rom. 9:4).

New Testament The New Testament frequently speaks of believers as God's children (Luke 20:36; Rom. 9:26; Gal. 3:26). Thus, believers are affirmed in a special and intimate relationship with God.

At the same time, the New Testament emphasizes Jesus' unique relationship to God as the "only begotten Son" (John 1:18; 3:16). He called God His "Abba" (Mark 14:36). In light of this truth, the relationship of believers to God is clearly derivative and secondary. Thus, adoption provided a means of describing the believers' relationship with God while maintaining the uniqueness of Jesus as *the* Son.

Paul is the only New Testament writer to employ the word *adoption*. He used the term to describe the status persons receive from God when they have been redeemed by Jesus Christ (Gal. 4:3–7). In belonging to Christ believers become Abraham's offspring and heirs with him of God's promise. Believers are chosen in Christ and predestined to this adoption by God's gracious will (Eph. 1:3–6).

Adoption symbolized for Paul God's love and grace in accepting believers as His children, intimate members of His family. Adoption occurs through the work of God's Spirit, giving believers power to overcome fleshly temptations and live the life in the Spirit (Rom. 8:14–15). This drives out the fear sinners experience in the presence of the holy God and provides power to pray trustingly to God as our "Abba," or "Daddy." See *Abba*. The Spirit living in the believer gives confident assurance that one is accepted fully as a child into God's family (8:15–16). This means the believer has all rights of inheritance and will join Jesus, "the only begotten Son" (John 3:16) in inheriting the glory of eternal life with God, but it does not mean the believer can escape the suffering and persecution the world dishes out to God's people (Rom. 8:17–18). The adoption process will be finalized when God restores all creation, giving His children resurrection bodies (8:23). Adoption has always been God's way of operating with His people (Hos. 11:1), for only spiritual birth, not natural birth, has determined who belonged to the covenant people (Rom. 9). Even Jews under God's law had to be redeemed by God's Son to be adopted sons (Gal. 4:4–6). *Michael Fink*

ADORAIM (Ăd·ō·rā′ ĭm) Place name meaning, "double strength." City located at modern Durah, six miles southwest of Hebron. Rehoboam fortified the city and placed troops and supplies there as part of a massive defense building program (2 Chron. 11:9). See *Rehoboam*.

ADORAM (Å·dō′ răm). See *Adoniram*.

ADRAMMELECH (Å·drăm′ mē·lĕch) Divine and personal name meaning, "Adra is king." Probably based on earlier form Hadadmelech, "Hadad is king," using name of Canaanite god. *1.* A god of the city of Sepharvaim. The Assyrian king Sargon spread the people of Israel all over his empire and replaced them with settlers from other cities he conquered (2 Kings 17:24). These new settlers tried to worship Yahweh, Israel's God, as the god of the land along with the gods they brought with them. One of these gods was from the city of Sephervaim, possibly in Assyria. His worshipers sacrificed their own children to this Semitic god (17:31–33). *2.* Murderer of Sennacherib, king of Assyria, during the king's worship in the temple of Nisroch (2 Kings 19:37). One reading of the Hebrew manuscripts describes this Adrammelech as Sennacherib's son (KJV, NIV, RSV). Other manuscripts do not have "his sons" (NAS).

ADRAMYTTIUM (Ăd·rå·myt′ tĭ·ŭm) or **ADRAMYTIAN** (NAS) Place name of a seaport on the northwest coast of modern Turkey in Roman province of Asia. Paul used a ship whose home port was Adramyttium to sail from Caesarea to Italy to appeal his case to Caesar (Acts 27:2). The ancient site is near modern day Edremit.

ADRIA (Ā′ dri·á) or **ADRIATIC SEA** (NAS, NIV) The sea separating Italy and Greece in which Paul's ship drifted for fourteen days as he sailed toward Rome to appeal his case to Caesar (Acts 27:27). Apparently Paul drifted nearly 500 miles from Clauda (27:16) to Malta (28:1).

ADRIEL (Ā′ drĭ·el) Personal name meaning, "God is my help." Saul's daughter Merab was promised as David's wife but then given to Adriel from Meholah, on the northern River Jordan (1 Sam. 18:19). His five sons David gave to the Gibeonites, who hanged them in revenge for unexplained actions Saul had taken against Gibeon (2 Sam. 21:1–9).

ADULLAM (Å·dŭl′ lam) Place name meaning, "sealed off place." City five miles south of Bethshemesh in Judah, probably modern Tell esh-Sheikh Madkur. Joshua conquered it (Josh. 12:15), though no story of its conquest appears in the Bible. Hirah, a friend of Judah, son of Jacob, was from Adullam (Gen. 38:1, 12). He took the sheep Judah had pledged to Tamar and discovered Tamar did not live where they first encountered her (38:20–22). David escaped to the cave at Adullam when he feared Achish, king of Gath (1 Sam. 22:1). There David collected an army from the lower class and outcasts of society. There he assembled an army against the Philistines (2 Sam. 23:13). Micah, the prophet, used David's experience almost 300 years later to warn his people that again their glorious king would have to flee to the caves of Adullam to escape an enemy who would take possession of the country because of Judah's sin (Mic. 1:15). In his build up of Judah's defenses King Rehoboam, Solomon's son, rebuilt Adullam's defenses, stationed soldiers, and stored supplies at Adullam (2 Chron. 11:7). After returning from the Exile, some members of the tribe of Judah lived at Adullam (Neh. 11:30).

ADULTERY is the act of unfaithfulness in marriage that occurs when one of the marriage partners voluntarily engages in sexual intercourse with a person of the opposite sex other than the marriage partner.

Old Testament Israel's covenant law prohibited adultery (Ex. 20:14) and thereby made faithfulness to the marriage relationship central in the divine will for human relationships. Many Old Testament regulations deal with adultery as the adulterous man's offense against the husband of the adulterous wife. Yet both the adulterous man and woman were viewed as guilty, and the punishment of death was prescribed for both (Lev. 20:10). The severity of the punishment indicates the serious consequences adultery has for the divine-human relationship (Ps. 51:4) as well as for marriage, family, and community relationships.

Several Old Testament prophets used adultery as a metaphor to describe unfaithfulness to God. Idolatry (Ezek. 23:27) and other pagan religious practices (Jer. 3:6–10) were viewed as adulterous unfaithfulness to the exclusive covenant that God established with His people. To engage in such was to play the harlot (Hos. 4:11–14).

New Testament Jesus' teachings expanded the

Old Testament law to address matters of the heart. Adultery has its origins within (Matt. 15:19), and lust is as much a violation of the law's intent as is illicit sexual intercourse (Matt. 5:27–28). Adultery is one of the "works of the flesh" (Gal. 5:19). It creates enmity with God (Jas. 4:4), and adulterers will not inherit the kingdom of God (1 Cor. 6:9).

Adulterers can be forgiven (John 8:3–11); and once sanctified through repentance, faith, and God's grace, they are included among God's people (1 Cor. 6:9–11). See *Divorce, Marriage*.

Michael Fink

ADUMMIM (Ả·dum′ mĭm) Place name meaning, "red ones." A rocky pass on the road descending from Jerusalem to Jericho located at modern Tal′at ed-damm. It formed the border of Judah and Benjamin in the tribal allotments Joshua made (Josh. 15:7; 18:17). Today the Inn of the Good Samaritan is there because late traditions locate the Good Samaritan narrative there (Luke 10:30–37).

ADVENT designates the coming or second coming of Christ. See *Parousia* for related biblical references. The English term *advent* comes from a Latin word meaning "coming" and is used primarily to designate a period before Christmas during which Christians prepare for the Christmas season and reflect on the meaning of the coming of Christ. Churches in many areas began to observe this period of preparation as early as the fifth century, soon after the origin of the celebration of Christmas. Lasting up to six weeks, the period was one of both penitence and joyous anticipation. By the Middle Ages, four Sundays had become the standard length of the Advent season. Since then, Advent has been considered to be the beginning of the church year. See *Church Year*.

Advent may also refer to the second coming or second advent of Christ. See *Parousia; Second Coming*.

Fred A. Grissom

ADVENTURESS RSV translation of *nokriya*, which is also translated as strange woman (KJV), adulterous woman (Prov. 23:27) (NAS), wayward wife (NIV), adulteress (NRSV), and immoral women (TEV) in Proverbs 2:16; 5:20; 6:24; 7:5; 23:27). Some see an adventuress as a woman who lives in part by her wits, but largely based upon sex. Others describe her as a woman who seeks social advancement or wealth by seduction or other immoral means. Solomon's wives were called *nokriyoth*—that is, foreign wives (1 Kings 11:1,8), so the term may refer to women cut off or ostracized from Israelite society and normal social relationships. They are feared as ones who break up marriages.

ADVERSARY An enemy either human or satanic. Psalmists often prayed for deliverance from adversaries (Pss. 38:20; 69:19; 71:13; 81:14; 109:29).

The devil is the greatest adversary and must be resisted (1 Pet. 5:8–9).

ADVOCATE is one who intercedes in behalf of another.

Old Testament While the word *advocate* is not found in the Old Testament, the concept of advocacy is found. Abraham intercedes with God in behalf of Sodom (Gen. 18:23–33); Moses intercedes with God in behalf of the Israelites (Ex. 32:11–14); Samuel intercedes with God in behalf of the children of Israel (1 Sam. 7:8–9). Other examples may be found in Jeremiah 14:7–9,13,19–22 and Amos 7:2,5–6. Modern translators often use "advocate" to refer to Job's desire for a heavenly attorney to plead his case even though he die (Job 16:19).

New Testament "Advocate" is the translation often given to the Greek *parakletos* in 1 John 2:1, a word found elsewhere only in John's Gospel as a title referring to the Holy Spirit, and there translated "Helper," "Comforter," "Counselor," or "Advocate" (John 14:16,26; 15:26; 16:7). Ancient Greeks used the term for one called in to assist or speak for another, frequently in a court setting. Rabbis transliterated the word into Hebrew, using it to denote an advocate before God. 1 John portrayed a courtroom scene in which Jesus Christ, the righteous One, intercedes with the Father on behalf of sinners. Such a portrayal stands in line with Old Testament ideas of advocacy, but supercedes it. In contrast to Old Testament advocates, Jesus is both the one righteous Advocate and the "atoning sacrifice" (NIV) for the world's sins (1 John 2:2). 1 John 2:1 parallels other New Testament descriptions of Jesus' intercessory role (Rom. 8:34; Heb. 7:25). See *Helper; Paraclete; Intercession; Jesus Christ, High Priest*.

R. Robert Creech

AENEAS (Ā·e·nē′ ȧs) Personal name of a paralyzed man Peter healed at Lydda (Acts 9:33–34).

AENON (Ā·e′ nŏn) Place name meaning, "double spring." The location where John the Baptist was baptizing during the time that Jesus was baptizing in Judea (John 3:23). The biblical text indicates that Aenon was a place richly endowed with water near Salim, which precise location is unknown. The most likely location of Aenon was in a broad open valley called Wadi-Farah, west of the Jordan and northeast of Nablus.

AFFLICTION describes the state of being pained or distressed by oppressors. In the Hebrew language as many as eleven words can be translated "affliction."

Old Testament The two primary Hebrew words used for affliction mean "to lower, humble, or deny" (*'anah*) (Lev. 16:29,31; 23:27,32; Isa. 58:3,5) and "depressed" (*'oni*) (Gen. 16:11;

Deut. 16:3; Job 30:15, 29). Both came from the same Hebrew root word.

In the Old Testament, the source of affliction is (1) God's retribution upon disobedience (Lam. 3:32–33; Isa. 30:20; Jer. 30:15); (2) the natural conditions of life (Gen. 16:11; 29:32; Psa. 25:18); (3) personal sin (Psa. 107:17); (4) forces of opposition (Isa. 51:21–23); and (5) evil spirits and/or Satan (1 Sam. 16:14; Job 1:6–12).

New Testament Three Greek words may be used for "affliction," including words meaning oppression, mistreatment, and misfortune. Suffering is sometimes used interchangably for the word "affliction," particularly in the KJV.

In the New Testament the source of affliction is (1) the natural conditions of humanity (Jas. 1:27); (2) persecution because of faithfulness to Christ (2 Cor. 6:4; 1 Thess. 1:6); (3) discipline for the purpose of maturing the Christian faith; and (4) the result of personal sin (Gal. 6:7).

Practical Concerns Affliction can be an individual matter (Phil. 4:14) or a corporate condition (Ex. 3:7; 2 Cor. 8:1–2). We can experience affliction directly (Deut. 16:3) or indirectly (Jas. 1:27). Affliction is sometimes described as overflowing all of life (Pss. 42:7; 69:1; 88:7; 124:4; Isa. 30:20; Jonah 2:5). Thus, affliction is one of the inevitable facts of our human existence. We find comfort in our afflication by remembering the promises of God and by taking specific personal actions. The promises that God has given to help mankind cope with situations of affliction are: (1) God sees and knows our affliction (Gen. 29:32; 31:42; Ex. 3:7; 2 Kings 14:26; Acts 7:34); (2) Afflication is only temporary (2 Cor. 4:17); and (3) God can deliver from any afflication (Ex. 3:17).

To endure during times of affliction, Christians should: (1) pray to the Lord (Ps. 25:18; Lam. 1:9; Jas. 5:13); (2) comfort others (Jas. 1:27; Phil. 4:14); (3) remain faithful through the patient endurance of suffering (2 Cor. 6:4; 1 Tim. 4:5; Jas. 1:2,12; 1 Pet. 4:13); (4) cultivate an attitude of joy (Jas. 1:2); and (5) follow the example of Jesus Christ (1 Pet. 2:19–23).   *Bob Sheffield*

AFTERBIRTH The placenta and fetal membranes that are expelled after delivery. Disobedience to God will result in defeat in war which in turn will result in such a lack of food that women will seek nourishment from the most disgusting sources (Deut. 28:57; compare 2 Kings 6:24–31; Lam. 2:20; 4:10).

AGABUS (Ăg′ á·bŭs) Personal name meaning, "locust." Prophet in the Jerusalem church who went to visit the church at Antioch and predicted a universal famine. His prophecy was fulfilled about ten years later in the reign of Claudius Caesar (Acts 11:27–29). His prediction led the church at Antioch to begin a famine relief ministry for the church in Jerusalem. Later, Agabus went to Caesarea and predicted that Paul would be arrested by the Jews in Jerusalem (Acts 21:10–11). Still, his friends could not persuade Paul out of going to Jerusalem.

AGAG (Ā′ găg) Agag, whose name means "fiery one," was king of the Amalekites, a tribal people living in the Negev and in the Sinai peninsula. The Amalekites had attacked the Israelites in the wilderness and were therefore cursed (Ex. 17:14). In 1 Samuel 15:8, Saul destroyed all the Amalekites but King Agag. Since the Lord had ordered the complete destruction of the Amalekites, Samuel, Saul's priest, rebuked Saul for his disobedience and reported God's rejection of Saul as king. Then Samuel himself executed Agag.

In Numbers 24:7, Agag is used to refer to the Amalekite people. Agag was a common name among Amalekite kings much as Pharaoh among Egyptian rulers.

AGAGITE (Ā′ găg-īte) Apparently, the term means a descendant of Agag. Only Haman, the arch villain in the Book of Esther, is called an Agagite (Esther 3:1). Agagite is probably a synonym for Amalekite. See *Agag.*

AGAPE See *Love; Lord's Supper.*

AGAR KJV spelling of Hagar in the New Testament. See *Hagar.*

AGATE (Ăg′ áte) A translucent quartz with concentric bands, generally white and brown. Agate translates three words in the Bible: a stone in the breastpiece of judgment (Ex. 28:19; 39:12), the material in the pinnacles of Jerusalem (Isa. 54:12; see Ezek. 27:16), and the third jewel in the foundation wall of the new Jerusalem (Rev. 21:19). See *Jewelry, Jewels, Precious Stones.*

AGEE (Ā′ gēē) Personal name perhaps meaning, "camel thorn." Father of one of David's three chief commanders (2 Sam. 23:11).

AGING describes the natural process of human beings growing older and, according to the Bible, gaining respect.

Old Testament References to aging persons in the Old Testament stress the physiological changes of aging (1 Kings 14:4; 2 Sam. 19:35; Eccl. 12:1–5; Zech. 8:4), the wisdom of the aging (Deut. 32:7; Job 12:12), the honor due the aging (Ex. 20:12; Lev. 19:32), and the continuing service of the aging (Gen. 12—50, the patriarchs; Jos. 13:1; 14:10; Ps. 92:14; Joel 2:28). Aging is presented as a normal part of the biblical view of the life cycle (Ps. 90:10; Isa. 46:4). See *Elder.*

New Testament References to aging persons in the New Testament focus on the responsibility of children or the family of faith to care for dependent or disabled aging persons (Mark 7:1–13; Matt. 15:1–6; 1 Tim. 5:4, 8; Jas. 1:27). The young are urged to honor the aging (1 Tim. 5:1–2), and the aging are encouraged to be worthy examples (Titus 2:2–3). Christians are expected to care for widows (Acts 6:1–7), and the aging are expected to serve God as did Zechariah, Elizabeth, Simeon, and Anna in Luke 1—2. Such service by the aging can bring blessings to their families, as did Timothy's grandmother and mother (2 Tim. 1:5).

Practical Concerns The biblical view of aging is unequivocally positive, though allowing for foolish elderly (Eccl. 4:13). Generally older persons have a reservoir of wisdom and understanding based on past experience (Deut. 32:7). They can experience new family joys, even after many previous sad experiences (Ruth 4:13–17). Both youth and age have their unique worth; they are not in competition (Prov. 20:29). While advancing age results in diminishing strength (Eccl. 12:1–8), God's grace and help are ever the same (Isa. 46:4). *Douglas Anderson*

AGRAPHA, "unwritten things," has been used since about 1700 to denote words of Jesus not written in the four canonical gospels. Some examples within the Bible are Acts 20:35 and 1 Corinthians 11:24–25. More are found in Apocryphal writings, Gnostic gospels, the Talmud, the Islamic sources, Oxyrhynchus Papyri, and the church fa-

Arab farmer plowing a rocky field along the Jerusalem-Jericho road in Israel.

thers. Some scholars suggest that the canonical gospels may rely in part on these sayings. Most sayings are regarded by scholars as expansions of the gospel tradition or creations by subsequent followers of Jesus, though a few of them may be authentic.
Joe Baskin

AGRICULTURE is the art of cultivating the land to grow food.

The people of biblical times, both of the Old and New Testament periods, were essentially rural. Even those who lived in towns were close to the country and usually owned gardens or farms. With the seasons as a background to their daily life, the religious calendar was partly based on the agricultural year with several festivals coinciding with significant events: e.g. Feast of Weeks or first fruits (of cereals, Ex. 32:11), Feast of Tabernacles or ingathering (of grapes, Lev. 23:34). The primary crops of the Bible include grain, grapes, and olives (Gen. 27:28; Deut. 7:13; Joel 1:10).

How were cereals cultivated? Grain crops were the staple food of rich and poor alike, although the poor may have had to consume barley bread rather than the more palatable wheat. Both were sown by scattering the grains into prepared land usually ploughed by draft animals. The parable of the sower (Matt. 13:3–23; Luke 8:5–15) provides an interesting account of grain sowing and the subsequent fate of the seed. Peasant agriculture, unlike modern farming practices, was unsophisticated with primitive implements often used in harsh conditions where rocky ground and vigor-

ous weeds militated against a good yield. Hence it would be normal for some of the scattered seed to fall on a path of compacted soil where it would not be covered and lie vulnerable to birds. Similarly, some seeds would fall at the margins of the fields where thorny thickets and rapidly growing thistles easily suffocated the germinating wheat. Shallow soil and lack of moisture during the hot dry summer encouraged the withering of the seeds that did sprout into young plants on the field's outer borders. Those seeds that fell on moist, deep soil grew and matured their ears ready for harvest.

The Book of Ruth provides a vivid picture of the harvesting scene that was carried out by whole families and extra hired men, followed by poor women gleaners picking leftovers. Barley was harvested first during April and May, followed by wheat a month later. A sickle was used to cut off the ears which were held with one hand, and then bundled together in small sheaves to be carted off to the threshing floor (1 Chron. 21:22)—a cleared area of stamped earth or stone. Animals, usually cattle, were driven over the spread-out stalks to trample out the grains. Often a cartwheel or a heavy sledge with small stones inserted in the bottom was drawn round and round the floor to hasten the threshing. The grains were swept together and separated from the useless chaff by winnowing—a process involving the throwing up of the grain in breezy weather so that the light scaly chaff is blown away, leaving a pile of clean grain ready for grinding into flour (Matt. 3:12). A proportion of the crop was always kept aside and carefully stored in dry conditions for sowing the following year (Gen. 47:24).

How did the agriculture of Egypt differ from that of Canaan? The essential difference between Egyptian and Canaanite agriculture was that Canaan depended on rainfall (Deut. 11:11), while Egypt depended on the River Nile and its annual flood (Amos 8:8). In other words, Canaan was a rain-fed agriculture, while Egypt used irrigation agriculture. In July the Nile rose following rainfall in Ethiopia and flooded the land on both sides. (Now the modern Aswan Dam impounds the water and releases it evenly throughout the year). The flood carried silt that enriched the farmland; and the water level fell later in the year, leaving behind pools of water that could be used for irrigation in channels small enough to be opened and closed by a farmer's foot (Deut. 11:10). Egypt was renowned for its rich harvests of wheat and vegetables which were missed by the Israelites fleeing the country via the desert of Sinai. There the Israelites longed for the succulent melons, cucumbers, garlic, leeks, and onions they left behind (Num. 11:5).

Were vineyards for growing grapevines? The Bible presents two accounts of vineyards that describe them in some detail. In Isaiah 5:1–7 and Mark 12:1–9 we read how the hillside was fenced and terraced to provide deep stone-free soil where the rainfall could water the vines' roots in winter. Dung and compost nourished the plants which needed to be trained over rocks or fences. Constant attention had to be given to the trailing branches of carefully chosen varieties in order to yield sweet green or black grapes. As harvest time approached, the owners of the vineyards and their families camped near the vineyards in shelters (booths) or in stone-built towers (Isa. 1:8) to protect the grapes from animals, such as jackals (foxes) and wild pigs (boar) (Ps. 80:13) and human thieves. When ripe, the grapes were picked for eating fresh (Isa. 65:21), drying in the sun as raisins (1 Sam. 30:12), or crushed for wine. Most vineyards had a winepress where the grapes were trodden under human foot (Neh. 13:15; Rev. 19:15), the juice collected in flagons or skins and fermented (Matt. 9:17). Fermentation was caused by naturally occurring yeast (*Saccharomyses*) breaking down the sugars into alcohol and carbon dioxide gas. During the winter, the long shoots of the previous year's growth had to be pruned away from the vines to leave a few buds for the next season (John 15:2).

How long do olive trees live? The huge trees in the Garden of Gethsemane (Matt. 26:36) on the Mount of Olives in Jerusalem are hundreds of years old and could potentially stretch back to New Testament times. During the siege of Jerusalem in A.D. 70 the Roman forces under Titus felled all the trees, presumably including the olives which *could* have sprouted again (Ps. 123:3) to yield the aged hollow trees still growing around Jerusalem.

Olive trees are not raised from seeds because the seedlings invariably produce very inferior ones similar to the wild stock. Selected cuttings are rooted or more often grafted on to the wild plant which has a better root system. Olive roots spread widely to gain nourishment on rocky hillsides, hence the trees are often well spaced. Although flowering begins when the trees are less than ten years old, full yield of fruit is not reached until they are 40 or 50 years old, after which branches are pruned to encourage new fruitful growth. Olives require a Mediterranean type of climate of moist cool winters and hot dry summers to be economically productive.

Olive groves usually had an oil press nearby where the heavy stone wheel crushed the fruit and its hard kernel. The pulp was placed in a press which extracted the precious yellow oil. This was used for cooking purposes as an essential part of diet (Deut. 7:13, 2 Kings 4:5, 2 Chron. 2:10). Olive oil was rubbed over skin and hair (Ps. 2:6; 23:5) and used for anointing guests (Luke 7:46 and 1 Kings 1:34). Christ was God's "anointed" one (Ps. 2:2; John 1:41; Acts 4:27), anointing being symbolic of the Holy Spirit (Isa. 61:1; Acts

10:38). Medicinally, olive oil mixed with antiseptic wine healed wounds (Luke 7:34, Jas. 5:14). Taken internally, olive oil soothed gastric disorders and acted as a laxative. Olive oil was used as fuel for lamps with a wick made of flax, producing a bright flame when lit (Ex. 25:6; Matt. 25:34). **What animals were used in agriculture?** Mainly cows (oxen) were used to pull carts (1 Sam. 6:7) and simple wooden plows (Job 1:14; 1 Sam. 14:14) tipped with iron, if the farmer could afford it (Isa. 2:4). Oxen and donkeys (asses) were driven over the harvested grain to thresh it. The use of horses and camels in agriculture appears to have been limited, presumably because they were more valuable animals, well adapted for carrying heavy loads and for use in time of war. When pairs of animals were used, they were coupled with a wooden yoke across their shoulders (Jer. 28:13; Luke 14:19). *F. Nigel Hepper*

AGRIPPA See *Herod.*

AGUE KJV translation of Hebrew word meaning "burning with fever." The Hebrew term appears in Leviticus 26:16 and Deuteronomy 28:22, KJV translating "fever" in the second passage.

AGUR (Ā′ gûr) Personal name meaning, "hired hand." Author of at least part of Proverbs 30.

AHAB (Ā′ hăb) Personal name meaning, "father's brother." *1.* The seventh king of Israel's Northern Kingdom, married a foreigner, Jezebel, and incited God's anger more than any of Israel's previous kings. Ahab, was the son and successor of Omri. His 22-year reign (874–853 B.C.), while enjoying some political and military success, was marred by spiritual compromise and failure (1 Kings 16:30).

Ruins of Ahab's palace excavated at the site of the ancient city of Samaria.

Ahab's marriage to a Phoenician princess had both commercial and political benefits. Commercially, it brought desired goods to Samaria and opened the way for expanded sea trade. Politically, it removed any military threat from Phoenicia.

During Ahab's days, Israel enjoyed peace with Judah, largely as a result of a marriage he arranged between princess Athaliah and Joram, the crown prince of Judah. The resulting alliance produced cooperative efforts in sea trade (1 Kings 22:48; 2 Chron. 20:35–37) and a joint military campaign to recapture Ramoth-gilead, which had fallen under Aramean control (1 Kings 22:2–40).

During his reign, effective control was maintained over Moab, producing revenue extracted by tribute, a tax the Moabite king paid to maintain his position (2 Kings 3:4). The oppression of Moab under Ahab and his father Omri finds expression in the famous Moabite Stone.

Ahab was successful in two major campaigns against the Syrian king, Ben-hadad, but was mortally wounded in the third. His participation in the great battle of Qarqar (853 B.C.), though not mentioned in the Bible, is recorded on an inscription of Shalmanezer III of Assyria. According to Shalmanezer, Ahab committed 2,000 chariots and 10,000 men to the battle.

The days of Ahab in Samaria were days of growing wealth and spiritual apostasy. According to 1 Kings 22:39, he built an "ivory house" for Jezebel, the remains of which were discovered in the Harvard excavations at the site. Rooms and furniture were decorated with ivory inlay which in many cases featured Egyptian deities. His surrender to the influences of idolatry is illustrated by the construction of a temple for Baal (1 Kings 16:32), the massacre of the Lord's prophets (1 Kings 18:4,19), and seizure of an Israelite's property (1 Kings 21).

Ahab appears to have been a worshiper of Yahweh, God of Israel, but probably along with other deities. He frequently consulted with Yahweh's prophets (1 Kings 20:13–14,22,28; 22:8,16), used the divine name in naming his children (Ahaziah, Jehoram, and Athaliah) and did not interfere with the execution of the priests of Baal after the contest on Mt. Carmel (1 Kings 18:40). The influence of Jezebel in his life, however, overshadowed any significant influence the prophets of the Lord had in his life. He became a prime example of evil (Mic. 6:16).

2. A false prophet living in Babylon who prophesied lies and faced Jeremiah's condemnation (Jer. 29:20–23). *John J. Davis*

AHARAH (Å·hâr′ ah) Spelling in 1 Chronicles 8:1 for Ahiram (Num. 26:38). See *Ahiram.*

AHARHEL (Å·här′ hĕl) Personal name with unknown meaning. Descendant of Judah (1 Chron. 4:8).

AHASAI (Å·hăs′ aî) KJV spelling of Ahzai.

AHASBAI (Å·hăs′ baî) Father of a leader in David's army (2 Sam. 23:34). See 1 Chron. 11:35.

He apparently came from Maacah.

AHASUERUS (Å·hăs·ū·ē′ rŭs) Hebrew spelling for Xerxes (NIV, TEV). See *Xerxes; Persia.*

AHAVA (Å·hā′ và) River in Babylon and town located beside the river where Ezra assembled Jews to return to Jerusalem from Exile (Ezra 8:15,21,31). Ahava was probably located near the city of Babylon, but the exact site is not known.

AHAZ (Ā′ hăz) *1.* The evil king of Judah (735–715). Ahaz, whose name means "he has grasped," was the son and successor of Jotham as king of Judah and the father of Hezekiah. The Bible characterizes Ahaz as an evil man who participated in the most monstrous of idolatrous practices (2 Kings 16:3). His sixteen-year reign was contemporary with the prophets Isaiah and Micah. Isaiah gave counsel to Ahaz during the Syro-Ephraimitic crisis, when Rezin, king of Syria, and Pekah, king of Israel, joined forces to attack Jerusalem. The prophet Oded rescued some captives from Israel (2 Chron. 28). Ahaz refused the prophet's advice and appealed for help to Tiglathpileser III of Assyria (Isa. 7). That appeal and the resulting entanglement had unfortunate results religiously and politically in that Ahaz surrendered to Assyrian domination. He even placed an altar made from a Syrian model in the Temple (2 Kings 16:11). Ahaz suffered the final humiliation of not being buried in the royal tombs (2 Chron. 28:15). See *Israel; Chronology of Biblical Period. 2.* A Benjaminite descended from Saul (1 Chron. 8:35–36; 9:42).

AHAZIAH (Ā·hà·zī′ ah) names two Old Testament kings, the king of Israel (850–840 B.C.) and the king of Judah (ca. 842). The name means, "Yahweh has grasped."
1. The son and successor of Ahab as king of Israel (1 Kings 22:40). He reigned two years and died after suffering a fall in his palace at Samaria (2 Kings 1:2–17). The prophet Elijah announced Ahaziah would die because he sent for help from Baal-zebub, the god of Ekron, instead of from Yahweh. *2.* The son and successor of Jehoram as king of Judah (2 Kings 8:25). He reigned for one year and died after being wounded as he fled from Jehu while visiting King Joram of Israel (2 Kings 9:27). These two kings were related to one another. Athaliah, the mother of Ahaziah of Judah, was the sister of Ahaziah of Israel.

AHBAN (Äh′ băn) Personal name meaning, "the brother is wise" or "the brother is creator." A member of the clan of Jerahmeel (1 Chron. 2:29).

AHER (Ā′ hĕr) Personal name meaning, "another." A member of tribe of Benjamin (1 Chron.

7:12); may be another spelling for Ahiram (Num. 26:38).

AHI (Ā′ hī) Personal name meaning, "my brother." 1. Member of tribe of Gad (1 Chron. 5:15), who lived in Gilead. 2. Member of tribe of Asher (1 Chron. 7:34).

AHIAH (Å·hī′ ah) Personal name meaning, "Yahweh is my brother." Variant spelling of Ahijah but not used consistently by English translations to reflect Hebrew spellings: 1. ʾachiyah—1 Sam. 14:3,18; 2 Sam. 23:34; 1 Kings 4:3; 11:29–30; 12:15; 14:2,4; 15:27–33; 1 Chron. 2:25; 8:7; 11:36; 26:20; 2 Chron. 9:29; Neh. 10:27. 2. ʾachiyahu—1 Kings 14:4–6,18; 2 Chron. 10:15. 3. ʾachyo—2 Sam. 6:3,4; 1 Chron. 8:14, 31; 9:37; 13:7. See *Ahijah.*

AHIAM (Å·hī′ ăm) Personal name whose meaning is not certain. One of David's thirty heroic soldiers (2 Sam. 23:33).

AHIAN (Å·hī′ ăn) Personal name meaning, "little brother." A member of tribe of Manasseh (1 Chron. 7:19).

AHIEZER (Ā·hī·ē′ zēr) Personal name meaning "my brother is help." *1.* An aide to Moses in the wilderness from the tribe of Dan (Num. 1:12; 2:25). He brought the tribe's offerings (7:66–71) and led the tribe on the march (10:25). *2.* The chief warrior who joined David at Ziklag. He was skilled with both hands and represented Benjamin, the tribe of King Saul, who threatened David (1 Chron. 12:1–3).

AHIHUD (Å·hī′ hŭd) *1.* Personal name meaning, "my brother is splendid or majestic" (Hebrew ʾachihud). A leader of the tribe of Asher who helped divide the Promised Land among the tribes (Num. 34:27). *2.* Meaning "my brother is a riddle" (Hebrew ʾachichud). A member of tribe of Benjamin (1 Chron. 8:7).

AHIJAH (Å·hī′ jah) See *Ahiah.* Personal name rendered several ways in Hebrew and English meaning "my brother is Yahweh." *1.* A priest of the family of Eli in Shiloh (1 Sam. 14:3–4). He brought the ark of God to Saul (1 Sam. 4:18). *2.* A scribe of Solomon (1 Kings 4:3). *3.* A prophet from Shiloh who tore his clothes in twelve pieces and gave ten to Jeroboam to signal God's decision to divide the kingdom after Solomon's death (1 Kings 11:29–39). Later when Jeroboam's son fell sick, the blind prophet recognized Jeroboam's wife through God's word. He announced the end of Jeroboam's reign and of his dynasty (1 Kings 14:1–18; 15:29). 2 Chronicles 9:29 refers to a prophecy of Ahijah in written form. *4.* Father of King Baasha of Israel from tribe of Issachar

(1 Kings 15:27). *5.* Son of Jerahmeel (1 Chron. 2:25). *6.* Son of Ehud in tribe of Benjamin, an official in Geba (1 Chron. 8:7). *7.* One of David's 30 military heroes whose home was Pelon (1 Chron. 11:36). The corresponding list in 2 Samuel 23:34 has Eliam the son of Ahithophel the Gilonite. *8.* Signer of Nehemiah's covenant to obey God's law (Neh. 10:26). *9.* The Hebrew text of 1 Chronicles 26:20 says Ahijah, a Levite, had charge of Temple treasuries under David (KJV, RSV). The Septuagint or oldest Greek translation suggests reading ʾachehem, "their brothers or relatives" (NAS, NIV, TEV).

AHIKAM (Aʹhīʹ kăm) Personal name meaning, "my brother stood up." Son of Josiah's scribe Shaphan. He took the book of the law found in the Temple to Huldah the prophetess to determine God's will (2 Kings 22:8–20). His son Gedaliah headed the Jews left in Judah after Nebuchadnezzar destroyed Jerusalem (586 B.C.) briefly before rebels killed him (2 Kings 25:22–25). Ahikam protected Jeremiah when King Jehoiakim wanted to kill the prophet (Jer. 26:24). Later, his son also protected Jeremiah (Jer. 39:14).

AHILUD (Aʹhīʹ lŭd) Personal name meaning, "a brother is born." The father of Jehoshaphat, David's court recorder (2 Sam. 8:16), who retained the position under Solomon (1 Kings 4:3). Probably the same Ahilud was father of Baana, Solomon's official to get court provisions from the province around Taanach, Megiddo, and Bethshean (1 Kings 4:12).

AHIMAAZ (A·hĭmʹ á·ăz) Personal name with uncertain meaning, "brother of anger" and "my brother is counselor," being suggestions. *1.* Saul's father-in-law (1 Sam. 14:50). *2.* Son of Zadok, one of David's priests (2 Sam. 15:27). He served as one of David's secret messengers from the court when Absalom rebelled and drove his father from Jerusalem (2 Sam. 15:36; 7:17). Once he had to hide in a well to keep from being found out (17:18–21). He was a swift runner, overtaking Cushi to bring tidings to David (18:19–29), but he did not report Absalom's death. He maintained a reputation as a "good man" (18:27). *3.* One of 12 officers over Solomon's provinces, he had charge of Naphtali. He married Solomon's daughter Basmath. He may be the same as *2.* Zadok's son (1 Kings 4:15).

AHIMAN (A·hīʹ man) Personal name with uncertain meaning. *1.* One of the giants of Anak (Num. 13:22). See *Anak.* Caleb drove him and his two brothers out of Hebron. Compare Judges 1:10, where the tribe of Judah killed the three brothers. *2.* A Levite and Temple gatekeeper (1 Chron. 9:17).

AHIMELECH (A·hĭmʹ ĕ·lĕch) Personal name meaning, "My brother is king." See *High Priest.*

AHIMOTH (A·hīʹ mŏth) Personal name meaning literally, "My brother is death" or "my brother is Mot (god of death). A Levite (1 Chron. 6:25).

AHINADAB (A·hĭnʹ á·dăb) Personal name meaning, "my brother has devoted himself" or "my brother is noble." One of Solomon's 12 province officials, he provided supplies for the royal court from Mahanaim (1 Kings 4:14).

AHINOAM (A·hĭnʹ ō·ăm) Personal name meaning, "my brother is gracious." *1.* King Saul's wife (1 Sam. 14:50). *2.* Wife of David from Jezreel (1 Sam. 25:43) who lived with him under the Philistines at Gath (27:3). When she and Abigail, David's other wife, were captured by the Amalekites, the people threatened to stone David. David followed God's word, defeated the Amalekites, and recovered his wives and the other captives (30:1–20). Ahinoam then moved to Hebron with David, where the people crowned him king (2 Sam. 2:2–4). She gave David his first son, Amnon (3:2).

AHIO (A·hīʹ ō) Personal name meaning, "my brother is Yahweh." See *Ahiah, Ahijah.* *1.* Son of Abinadab at whose house the ark of the covenant was stationed (2 Sam. 6:3). He and his brother Uzzah drove an ox and cart carrying the ark. *2.* A member of the tribe of Benjamin (1 Chron. 8:14), but the Septuagint or earliest Greek translation of the Old Testament reads "their brothers" or kinfolk. *3.* A member of Benjamin with connections to Gibeon (1 Chron. 8:31; 9:37).

AHIRA (A·hīʹ rá) Personal name meaning, "my brother is a friend." Leader of tribe of Naphtali under Moses (Num. 1:15), who presented the tribe's offerings at the dedication of the altar (7:78–83) and led them in the wilderness marches.

AHIRAM (A·hīʹ ram) Personal name meaning, "my brother is exalted." Son of Benjamin who gave his name to a clan in that tribe (Num. 26:38).

AHIRAMITE (A hīʹ rám īte) Clan established by Ahiram. See *Ahiram.*

AHISAMACH (A·hĭşʹ á·măch) Personal name meaning, "my brother has supported." Father of Oholiab, the artisan who helped Bezaleel create the artwork of the wilderness tabernacle (Ex. 31:6; 35:34; 38:23).

AHISHAHAR (A·hīʹ shā·här) Personal name meaning, "brother of the dawn." A member of tribe of Benjamin (1 Chron. 7:10) but not listed in the genealogy of 1 Chronicles 8.

AHISHAR (Å·hī′ shär) Personal name meaning, "my brother sang." Head of Solomon's palace staff (1 Kings 4:6).

AHITHOPHEL (Å·hĭth′ ō·phĕl) Personal name meaning, "brother of folly" if it is not a scribal attempt to hide an original name including a Canaanite god such as Ahibaal. See *Jerubbaal.* David's counselor who joined Absalom's revolt against King David (2 Sam. 15:12). David prayed that his counsel might be turned to foolishness (15:31) and commissioned the faithful Hushai to help Zadok and Abiathar, the priests, counteract the counsel of Ahithophel. Ahithophel led Absalom to show his rebellion was for real by taking over his father's concubines (16:15–23). Ahithophel's counsel was famous as being equal to the word of God (16:23). Hushai, however, persuaded Absalom not to follow Ahithophel's military advice (ch. 17), this being God's work (17:14). Disgraced, Ahithophel returned home to Giloh, put his house in order, and hanged himself (17:23). He may have been the grandfather of Bathsheba, David's partner in sin and wife (2 Sam. 11:3; 23:34).

AHITUB (Å·hī′ tŭb) Personal name meaning, "my brother is good." *1.* Priest, son of Phinehas and grandson of Eli ministering in Shiloh (1 Sam. 14:3). He was Ahimelech's father (22:9). *2.* Father of Zadok, the high priest under David and Solomon (2 Sam. 8:17). The name occurs twice in the Chronicler's list of priests (1 Chron. 6:7–8, 11–12, 52). Compare 9:11. Ezra descended from Ahitub's line (Ezra 7:2).

AHLAB (Âh′ lăb) Place name meaning, "mountain forest" or "fertile." Probably located at Khirbet el-Maçhalib on the Mediterranean coast four miles above Tyre. The tribe of Asher could not conquer it (Judg. 1:31).

AHLAI (Äh′ lā·ī) Personal name meaning, "a brother to me," perhaps an abbreviated form of Ahliya, "the brother is my god." Others interpret as interjection meaning, "O would that." *1.* A member of clan of Jerahmeel (1 Chron. 2:31). Ahlai's father was Sheshan. 1 Chronicles 2:34 says Sheshan had no sons, only daughters. This makes Ahlai either a daughter of Sheshan or part of a Hebrew text that is incomplete due to copying errors. Some would identify Ahlai with Sheshan's grandson Attai (1 Chronicles 2:35). Others think Sheshan changed his servant's Jarha's name to Ahlai when he made Jarha his son-in-law (v. 35). No certain answer to Ahlai's identity has been offered. *2.* Father of a valiant soldier of David (1 Chron. 11:41).

AHOAH (Å·hō′ ah) Personal name of uncertain meaning. Grandson of Benjamin (1 Chron. 8:4), but lists in 7:7; 8:7; and evidence of early translations may point to Ahijah as the original name.

AHOHITE (Å·hō′ hīte) Clan name. In time of David and Solomon military figures of this clan or place became military leaders. See 2 Samuel 23:9, 28; 1 Chronicles 11:12,29; 27:4.

AHOLAH (Å·hō′ lah) KJV spelling for Oholah. See *Oholah.*

AHOLIAB (Å·hō′ lĭ·ăb) KJV spelling for Oholiab. See *Oholiab.*

AHOLIBAH (Å·hō′ lĭ·bah) KJV for Oholibah. See *Oholibah.*

AHOLIBAMAH (Å·hō·lĭ·bā′ mah) KJV spelling of Oholibamah. See *Oholibamah.*

AHUMAI (Å·hū′ maî) Personal name meaning, "a brother is it" or "brother of water." Member of clan of Zorathites of tribe of Judah (1 Chron. 4:2).

AHUZAM (Å·hū′ zăm) or **AHUZZAM** (NAS, NIV, RSV, TEV) Personal name meaning, "their grasping" or "their property." A member of the tribe of Judah (1 Chron. 4:6).

AHUZZATH (Å·hŭz′ zàth) Personal name meaning, "that grasped" or "property." Official who accompanied Abimelech, king of Philistines, to make covenant of peace with Isaac (Gen. 26:26). Called literally "the friend of the king," he probably held an office as the closest advisor of the king. Compare KJV, NAS, NIV.

AHZAI (Äh′ zaî) or **AHASAI** (KJV) Personal name meaning, "property" or abbreviated form of Ahzaiah, "Yahweh has grasped." A priest after the return from Exile (Neh. 11:13). Sometimes said to be same as Jahzerah (1 Chron. 9:12).

AI (Ā′ ī) a city located two miles from Bethel, was the site where Abram built an altar, and Joshua and Achan suffered ruin. Ai is also spelled Aija, Aiath, and Hai. Ai means "ruin" (or possibly "heap") in the Hebrew language. The city was almost the ruin of Joshua's leadership (Josh. 7:1–9); it was the ruin of Achan and his family (Josh. 7:16–26); and it suffered complete ruin (Josh. 8:1–29). Several hundred years before Joshua, Abram built an altar on a hill just west of Ai which was also near Bethel (Gen. 12:8). He then returned to the location after visiting Egypt (Gen. 13:3). The prophets later referred to Ai as a symbol of the power of God who provided victory for his obedient people. Isaiah noted the Assyrian army marching by Ai on his way to Jerusalem, but promised God would stop their progress (Isa.

10:28). Jeremiah used the ruin of Ai as a warning to the Ammonites, who had occupied Israel's territory (Jer. 49:3). Residents of Bethel and Ai returned from Exile with Zerubbabel (Ezra 2:28).

Although the existence of Ai is well documented, its exact location is debated. The general location of the city is known to be about 10–12 miles north of Jerusalem in the central hills of Palestine. This would be about the same distance from Jericho. William F. Albright identified Beitin as the city of Bethel and then concluded that et-Tell (a site one mile southeast of Beitin) was biblical Ai. Excavations conducted in the 1920s (John Garstang), 1930s (Judith Marquet-Krause and Samuel Yeivin), and 1960s and 1970s (Joseph Callaway), however, produced some disturbing evidence in light of Albright's 1939 proposal. It seems that et-Tell was first occupied as early as the fourth millennium (3200–3000 B.C.) and continued to thrive until the end of the third millennium (2200 B.C.). The problem is that the site has no evidence of being inhabited during the next 1000 years which includes the time of the Israelite invasion. Callaway found a small village without defense walls lasting from 1220 to 1050 B.C. This has resulted in some speculations concerning Albright's theory and the Bible story.

The suggestions for solving this problem are basically three: (1) the Bible contains an inaccurate or legendary story built on the earlier fame of the city; (2) the Israelites actually destroyed Bethel (not Ai), but the twin cities (see Ezra 2:28; and Neh. 7:32) were considered to be the same, or (3) further archaeological evidence will reveal a different site for Ai. Because of the Bible's historical accuracy, many scholars today dismiss the first idea. The second and third proposals, however, will require further archaeological evidence before this dilemma is solved.

Ai's meaning goes far beyond its mysterious location. At Ai, Israel learned they could not take a city known as the ruin if they disobeyed God. Victory did not lie in military strength or wise leadership. It lay in God's presence. Israel also learned they had hope after defeat. Confession of sin and punishment of offenders helped restore God's favor. The victory at Ai (Josh. 8) frightened the other Canaanites (9:3; 10:2) and helped Israel to further victories. Israel learned to live with a punishing as well as a promising God.

Gary C. Huckaby

AIAH (Ā·ī′ ah) Personal name imitating the cry of a hawk, then meaning, "hawk." *1.* A son of Zibeon among the clans of Edom descended from Esau (Gen. 36:24). *2.* The father of Rizpah, Saul's concubine (2 Sam. 3:7) and grandfather of Miphibosheth (2 Sam. 21:8).

AIATH (Ā·ī′ ath) Alternate spelling of Ai (Isa. 10:28). See *Ai.*

AIJA (Ā·ī′ jà) Alternate spelling of Ai (Neh. 11:31). See *Ai.*

AIJALON (Ăi′ jà·lŏn) Also spelled Ajalon. Place name meaning, "place of the deer." *1.* Town and nearby valley where moon stood still at Joshua's command (Josh. 10:12). Near the Philistine border, south of Beth-horon, Aijalon belonged to Dan, according to tribal allotments (Josh. 19:42); but Dan did not conquer the territory and moved to the north (Judg. 18:1). It was one city in Dan given the Levites (Josh. 21:24). Amorites gained temporary control, but the Joseph tribes subjected them to pay tribute (Judg. 1:34–35). Saul and Jonathan won a battle between Michmash and Aijalon (1 Sam. 14:31). In post-exilic times, the Chronicler knew Aijalon as a city of the tribe of Benjamin which defeated Gath (1 Chron. 8:13). Rehoboam, Solomon's son, had fortified Aijalon (2 Chron. 11:10). King Ahaz (735–715 B.C.) asked for Assyrian help because the Philistines had taken Aijalon and other cities. Thus it was an important military location on Judah's western border. Aijalon is located at modern Yalo about fourteen miles from Jerusalem. *2.* Elon, a judge of the tribe of Zebulon was buried in a northern Aijalon (Judg. 12:12), whose location may be at Tell et-Butmeh.

AIJELETH SHAHAR (Ăi′ jĕ·lĕth shā′ här) Musical direction in title of Psalm 22, literally, "doe of the dawn." May be name of musical tune.

AIN (Ā′ ĭn) Place meaning, "eye" or "water spring." Often used as first part of a place name indicating the presence of a water source. English often uses "En" as first part of such names. See *Endor,* for example. *1.* Place on eastern border of Canaan (Num. 34:11). Location is uncertain. *2.* City of southern Judah (Josh. 15:32) belonging to Simeon (Josh. 19:7) but assigned as homestead for the Levites, who had no land allotted (Josh. 21:16), if this is not read Ashan as in some manuscripts of Joshua and in 1 Chronicles 6:59.

AIR Space beneath the sky according to the human sense description of the universe Bible writers used. English versions translate Hebrew *ruach,* "wind, breath, spirit," as "air" in Job 41:16 to describe empty space between objects on earth. Compare Jeremiah 14:6 (NAS, RSV). The birds fly in the air (Matt. 6:26). Mourners throw dust into the air (Acts 23:23). Inept boxers hit the air instead of opponents (1 Cor. 9:26). Speaking in tongues without an interpreter is vainly speaking in the air with no one understanding (1 Cor. 14:9). More theologically and symbolically, Ephesians 2:2 mentions the "prince of the power of the air," showing Satan's power to tempt and rule people here below but his lack of power in heaven. At the second coming those still alive will be caught up with those being resurrected to meet the Lord Jesus in the air (1 Thess. 4:17). The fifth angel of Revelation opens the bottomless pit, which is so dominated by fire that its smoke thus released darkened the sun and the air (Rev. 9:2). The seventh angel poured destruction into the air, thus on earth, from his vial (Rev. 16:17).

AJAH (Ā′ jah) KJV spelling of Aiah (Gen. 36:24). See *Aiah.*

AJALON Variant spelling of Aijalon. See *Aijalon.*

AKAN (Ā′ kan) Personal name of uncertain meaning. An official of Edom of Horite ancestors (Gen. 36:27). Spelled Jakan in 1 Chronicles 1:42.

AKELDAMA NIV, RSV, TEV spelling of Aceldama. See *Aceldama.*

AKHENATON (Äkh′ ĕn·ä′ tŏn) Egyptian Pharaoh (1370–1353 B.C.) Originally named Amenhotep IV, he made a radical religious switch from worshiping Amon to serving Aton, the sun disc. Often referred to as the first monotheist, he probably did not go so far as denying the existence of all other gods. Later Egyptian writers called him blasphemer and criminal. He married the famous Nefertiti, known for her beauty, and was succeeded by his son-in-law Tutankhaten, known to-

Statue of Pharaoh Akhenaton.

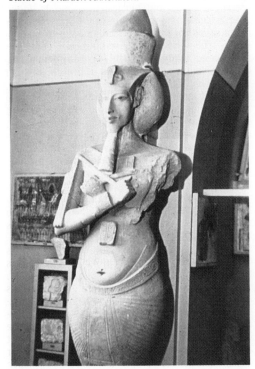

day as King Tut. He moved his capital northwards from Thebes to Akhentaton at Tell El-Amarna. During his reign he received the reports and requests from city-state rulers in Palestine that archaeologists call the Amarna letters. These show the lack of unity and harmony in Palestine which Joshua found when he entered to conquer Palestine.   *Gary C. Huckabay*

Painted floor of Pharaoh Akhenaton's summer palace.

AKIM NIV spelling of Achim.

AKKAD NIV spelling of Accad.

AKKADIAN describes the first known Semitic invaders of Mesopotamia and the language they spoke. Also spelled Accadians.

The Akkadians, under Sargon the Great, conquered Mesopotamia and established the first true empire in world history (2360–2180 BC). Their ancient capital Akkad, (Agade), is mentioned in Genesis 10:10 as one of the cities of Shinar (Mesopotamia).

Akkadian is also the ancient name of the Semitic language used in the cuneiform inscriptions and documents modern archaeologists have discovered. The earliest inscriptions in Old Akkadian date from about 2400–2000 B.C. Two main dialects evolved, Babylonian and Assyrian. These dialects are conveniently outlined in three phases: Old Babylonian and Old Assyrian, about 2000–1500 B.C., Middle Babylonian and Middle Assyrian, about 1500–1000 B.C., and Neo-Babylonian, about 1000–100 B.C., and Neo-Assyrian, about 1000–600 B.C. After about 600 B.C. Akkadian was increasingly replaced by Aramaic.

Akkadian is commonly classified as East Semitic to distinguish it from Northwest Semitic (Amorite, Ugaritic, Hebrew, etc.) and Southwest Semitic (Arabic, Ethiopic). Akkadian was the international language of diplomacy and commerce in the Near East before 1000 B.C. Consequently, collections of documents written in Akkadian originated among several non-Akkadian speaking national

The Treaty of Kadesh, between the Hittites and Egypt, is inscribed on this tablet in Akkadian.

and ethnic groups. Examples include the Amarna Tablets of Palestinian rulers addressed to Egypt, Akkadian documents from Ugarit in Syria, and the Nuzi Tablets from a Hurrian people.

Akkadian studies have had a profound effect on Old Testament studies in at least four areas. First, the meanings of many Hebrew words have been determined or clarified by Akkadian cognates. Second, the literary (poetic) texts and legal texts have provided a rich source for comparative study of Old Testament poetry and law texts. Third, historical annals and international treaties provide the wider framework for understanding biblical events and sometimes mention events and persons known also from the Bible. Fourth, the Akkadian mythico-religious texts have included accounts of creation and flood, as well as prophetic oracles, curses and blessings, and prayers, which provide a basis for understanding both the common Semitic heritage and the uniqueness of Israel's faith. See also *Cuneiform.*
Thomas Smothers

AKKUB (Ăk' kŭb) Personal name possibly meaning, "protector," or "protected one." *1.* Descendant of Solomon in post-exilic Judah about 420 B.C. (1 Chron 3:24). *2.* Gatekeeper of the Temple after the return from Exile (1 Chron. 9:17; Ezra 2:42; Neh. 7:45; 11:19). They were Levites (Neh. 12:25). Since "the children of Akkub" are

mentioned (Neh. 7:45), the family apparently served for several generations, with more than one person in the family line named Akkub. *3.* A Levite who helped Ezra teach the Law to God's returned people (Neh. 8:7). He may have been related to *2. 4.* The head of another family of Temple staff personnel (Ezra 2:45).

AKRABBIM (Ăk-rab' bĭm) Place name meaning, "scorpions." The "ascent of Akrabbim" lies southwest of the Dead Sea forming the southern border of Canaan (Num. 34:4; Josh. 15:3; Judg. 1:36). It is a mountain pass on the road southeast of Beersheba, today called Neqb es-Safa. Recent study has found the Scorpion Pass mentioned in other Near Eastern literature.

ALABASTER See *Metals and Minerals.*

ALAMETH (Ălȧ-mĕth) KJV spelling of Alemeth (1 Chron. 7:8). See *Alemeth.*

ALAMMELECH (Ȧ-lăm' mĕ-lĕch) KJV spelling of Allammelech. See *Allammelech.*

ALAMOTH (Ăl' ȧ-môth) Musical notation meaning literally "upon or according to young woman." This apparently signifies a tune for a high voice, a song for a soprano (1 Chron. 15:20; Ps. 46 title).

ALARM A signal given by shouting or playing an instrument. The Hebrew term (*teru'ah*) means literally a shout, but musical instruments were used as the trumpets of Numbers 10:1–10. The alarm called the wilderness community to march (Num. 10:5–6). The alarm was a special, unspecified, sound of the trumpets, for they could be blown without sounding the alarm to march (10:7). The alarm called later Israel to battle (10:9) and reminded them of God's presence with their armies. Compare 31:6. The alarm is sounded against the enemy of God's people (2 Chron. 13:12). Joshua 6 describes a different alarm system. The priests march with horns, instruments distinct from trumpets, and the people shout a great shout or alarm (*teru'ah*) before God's miraculous act. The trumpet could also sound the alarm on a great religious day (Lev. 25:9), and Israel could raise a shout of joy (1 Sam. 4:5). The alarm did not always bring joy. The alarm announcing the enemy coming in war brought shock, sadness, and fear (Jer. 4:19; Hos. 5:8). The greatest fear should come, however, when God sounds the alarm for His day (Joel 2:1).

ALEMETH (Ăl' ȧ-meth) Place and personal name meaning, "concealed" or "dark." *1.* A city set aside for the Levites from Benjamin's allotment (1 Chron. 6:60). Known as Almon in Joshua 21:18. *2.* Grandson of Benjamin (1 Chron. 7:8). *3.* Descendant of Saul and Jonathan in tribe of

Benjamin (1 Chron. 8:36).

ALEXANDER THE GREAT (Ăl·ĕx·ăn′ dĕr) succeeded his father as king of Macedonia and quickly conquered the Persian empire.

Alexander the Great (356–323 B.C.) was one of the greatest military leaders in history. His father was Phillip of Macedon, king of a region of Greece known as Macedonia.

When Alexander was twenty years old (336 B.C.), his father was killed, and Alexander became king. This ambitious young king immediately began to make plans to conquer Persia. Persia had extended its empire to Asia Minor (modern-day Turkey). In 334 B.C., Alexander led his troops into Asia Minor where they won a series of victories over the Persians.

Alexander the Great continued his victorious military march into Syria and Egypt. From victories there, he led his troops into Persia, Media, and as far east as northern India. He returned to Babylon, where he died in 323 B.C. at the age of thirty-three.

Alexander's most lasting legacy was his spread of Greek culture. Everywhere he went, he tried to instill that culture. While Alexander is never directly named in the Bible, the culture which he brought to Palestine greatly affected the biblical world, especially during the time between the writing of the Old and New Testaments. His empire is one element of the historical background of

Alexander the Great depicted in the famous "Battle of Issus" mosaic from Roman times.

Daniel. See *Greece, Religion and Society of* and *Alexandria.*   *Lynn Jones*

ALEXANDER (Ăl·ĕx·ăn′ dĕr) names five New Testament men including the son of Simon of Cyrene (Mark 15:21), a relative of Annas (Acts 4:6), a Jew of Ephesus (Acts 19:33), a false teacher (1 Tim. 1:19–20), and a coppersmith (2 Tim. 4:14).

ALEXANDRIA (Ăl·ĕx·ăn′ drĭ·à) The capital of Egypt from 330 B.C., founded by Alexander the Great as an outstanding Greek cultural and academic center.

Alexandria was designed to act as the principal port of Egypt located on the western edge of the Nile delta. Built on a peninsula, it separated the Mediterranean Sea and Lake Mareotis. A causeway (Heptastadion, or "seven stadia") connected the peninsula with Pharos Island and divided the harbor. The Pharos lighthouse was visible for miles at a height of over 400 feet and is remembered today as one of the seven wonders of the world.

The city was divided into sections with a substantial Jewish quarter, the Royal area, the Neapolis, and a necropolis to the far west. The city was known for its cultural and academic pursuits. The finest library in the ancient world with over 500,000 volumes attracted many scholars. The Mouseion (Museum) complimented the library as the center of worship for the Muses, goddesses of "music," dancing, and letters. It became the most important center of Judaism outside of Jerusalem.

Carved wall inside the catacombs of Alexandria, Egypt.

Jewish rabbis gathered in Alexandria to produce the Septuagint (LXX), the Greek translation of the Old Testament. Greek philosophers and mathematicians such as Euclid, Aristarchus, and Eratosthenes worked here. Octavian incorporated it into the Roman empire about 30 B.C. It quickly became second in importance to Rome. Its importance declined about 100 A.D.

The educated Jews of Alexandria contended with Stephen (Acts 6:9). Apollos, the great Christian orator, came from Alexandria (Acts 18:24), and Paul rode the ships of that port (Acts 27:6; 28:11). Although the Christians suffered persecution there, they produced a school with such

Alexandria, Egypt. The ruins of the famous ancient library can be seen in the background.

notables as Clement and Origen in leadership. The school was noted for its allegorical approach to Scripture. *Gary C. Huckabay*

ALGUM A rare wood Solomon imported from Lebanon for the Temple (2 Chron. 2:8). The exact type of wood is not known. 1 Kings 10:11–12 refers to almug wood imported from Ophir (compare 2 Chron. 9:10–11). The rare wood was used for gateways and for musical instruments.

ALIAH (Ă·lī′ ăh) Personal name meaning, "height." A leader of Edom (1 Chron. 1:51), known in Genesis 36:40 as Alvah.

ALIAN (Ă·lī′ an) Personal name meaning, "high one." A descendant of Esau and thus an Edomite (1 Chron. 1:40). Known in Genesis 36:23 as Alvan.

ALIEN A foreigner living in a community without relatives. People fleeing famine became aliens among the people where they settled. Thus Elijah was an alien in the home of the widow of Zarephath (1 Kings 17:20; "to sojourn" is to be an alien). Isaac was an alien with Abimelech, the Philistine king (Gen. 26:3). War leaves refugees who become aliens (Isa. 16:4). Compare 2 Samuel 4:3. Levites, priests not given inheritance, are aliens (Deut. 18:6). Accidents or crime could cause a person to leave home and become an alien. An alien stood between a person born in the community and a foreigner without any ties to the

community. The alien could become a soldier, as did the Amalekite who killed Saul (2 Sam. 1:13). David gathered aliens to build God's house (1 Chron. 22:2). As an alien in Sodom, Lot owned a house (Gen. 19:9). The patriarchs (Abraham, Isaac, Jacob) were aliens in Canaan, but owned large material resources (Gen. 20:1; 26:3; 32:5). The alien could worship God and was supposed to keep the sabbath (Ex. 23:12; Deut. 31:12). Israel had a special place for aliens, because Israel began history in Egypt as aliens (Ex. 23:9). Special laws provided food and clothing for aliens (Deut. 24:19–20; 26:12). Aliens had rights in the courtroom (Deut. 24:17; 27:19). The ritual expectations of the alien are not always clear (Deut. 14:21; Lev. 17:15). God loves aliens (Deut. 10:19). They may observe Passover just as any Israelite (Num. 9:14) and offer sacrifices (Lev. 17:8). They should obey sexual laws (Lev. 18:26). Unexpectedly, the prophets have little to say about aliens. See Jeremiah 7:6; 22:3; Ezekiel 22:7,29. Jeremiah does lament that God appears to be an alien (Jer. 14:8). The psalmist saw all people as aliens on earth (39:13; 119:19). God owns the land (Lev. 25:23). See *Stranger.*

ALLAMMELECH (Ăl·lăm′ mĕ·lĕch) Place name meaning, "king's oak," or "royal holy tree." Border town of Asher (Josh. 19:26) whose specific location is not known.

ALLEGORY is a means of presenting or interpreting a story by focusing on hidden or symbolic meanings rather than the literal meaning.
Background Allegory arose from the Cynic and Stoic philosophies of the Hellenistic period (fourth to second centuries B.C.). As a general phenomenon, allegorical interpretation is adopted when sacred traditions are challenged by advances in knowledge and thought. When no longer able to interpret the traditions historically, and being unwilling to discard the traditions themselves, followers of the traditions probe for deeper, symbolic meanings. In the Greek world allegory was used primarily to interpret the Homeric myths and to preserve some moral and philosophical truths from them.
Old Testament Allegory Scholars generally agree that none of the Old Testament was written allegorically. Portions of it have been interpreted allegorically by later generations. For example, interpreting the Song of Solomon as an allegory of God's love for Israel rather than as a collection of romantic love songs may have played a role in the acceptance of that book into the Old Testament canon.

Allegorical interpretation of the Old Testament arose among Hellenistic Jews in Alexandria during the second century B.C. Philo, who died about A.D. 50, was its most prolific proponent. Philo sought to preserve Old Testament traditions against Greek perspectives in science and philosophy. He applied allegory to many portions of the Old Testament where the biblical views seemed to contradict contemporary secular understandings. Jewish proponents of allegory, however, never abandoned the historical meaning of their traditions to the extent that Greek proponents did.

Jewish interpreters in Palestine were less influenced by allegorical approaches. Their allegories were less complex and remained closer to the literal meaning. The rabbis placed more emphasis on extracting legal prescriptions from the traditions, while other interpreters were more attracted to viewing the Old Testament in terms of prophecies to be fulfilled.
New Testament New Testament writers have more in common with the approaches of Palestinian Jewish interpreters of the Old Testament than with Hellenistic interpreters like Philo. Allegory is not widely used in the New Testament; and when it is employed, it does not depart far from the literal meaning. A strong prophetic-fulfillment interpretation of the Old Testament also is evident.

While Jesus never made allegorical interpretations of the Old Testament, some of His parables were interpreted as allegories. The parable of the soils (Mark 4:1–20) and the parable of the tares (Matt. 13:24–30,36–43) are prime examples. Other parables draw on obvious Old Testament images (such as the vineyard representing Israel). In general, however, parables are to be distinguished from allegories because of their simplicity, sharp focus, and direct imagery. Contemporary scholarship generally prefers the plain and obvious point of the parable over the veiled and obscure meanings that often characterize allegories.

Paul employed allegorical interpretations on four occasions (1 Cor. 5:6–8; 9:8–10; 10:1–11; Gal. 4:21–31), once employing the word *allegory* itself (Gal. 4:24). Paul's allegories generally are restrained and focus on contemporary application. First Corinthians 5:6–8 is not so much an interpretation of the Old Testament as it is the use of an Old Testament image that finds fulfillment in the sacrifice of Christ, our Passover. 1 Corinthians 10:1–11 draws heavily on the fulfillment that "followed" the Old Testament people in the person of Christ. These approaches are not far from Matthew's citations of Old Testament testimonies about Christ. They bear more resemblance to prophetic fulfillment than to allegory.

On the other hand, 1 Cor. 9:8–10 departs completely from the literal meaning of the law as it applied to muzzling oxen; and Gal. 4:21–31 is a thorough allegorization of the Old Testament. The writer of Hebrews followed in that same spirit in dealing with Old Testament themes like Melchizedek, the Old Testament priesthood, and the tabernacle.   *Michael Fink*

ALLELUIA KJV spelling of Hallelujah in New Testament. See *Hallelujah.*

ALLEMETH (Ăl′ lĕ·mĕth) Variant spelling of Alemeth in some English translations (1 Chron. 6:60). See *Alemeth.*

ALLIANCE See *Covenant.*

ALLON (Ăl′ lŏn) Personal name meaning, "oak." Leader of tribe of Simeon (1 Chron. 4:37).

ALLONBACHUTH (Ăl′ lŏn-băch′ ŭth) or **ALLONBACUTH** Place name meaning, "oak of weeping." Burial place near Bethel of Rebekah's nurse (Gen. 35:8).

ALLOTMENT describes the Old Testament concept of land allocation either by God or by lot.

The allotment of the land of Canaan to the tribes of Israel is recorded in Numbers 32 and Joshua 13–19. God directed the process through the lot of the priest (Josh. 14:1–2). See *Lots.* The tribes of Reuben and Gad, along with half the tribe of Manasseh, requested land east of the Jordan (Num. 32:33).

Ezekiel 48 also contains a version of the allotment of the land for the Jews after the Exile, revised so that each tribe received an equal share.
Ronald E. Bishop

ALMIGHTY Title of God, translating Hebrew *El Shaddai.* The early Greek translation introduced Almighty as one of several translations. Recent study has tended to see "The Mountain One" as the most likely original meaning. The name was particularly related to Abraham and the patriarchs (Gen. 17:1; 28:3; 35:11; 49:25). God gave Moses the name Yahweh, which to an extent replaced El Shaddai (Ex. 6:3). Job is the only book to use El Shaddai extensively, 31 times in all. Paul used Almighty once at the end of a series of Old Testament quotations to imitate Old Testament style and to underline divine power to bring His word to fulfillment. Revelation refers to God nine times as "Almighty," again giving a feeling of power to the vision of Revelation.

ALMODAD (Ăl·mō′ dăd) Personal name meaning, "God is a friend." Grandson of Eber and ancestor of Arabian tribes (Gen. 10:25–26).

ALMON (Ăl′ mŏn) Place name meaning, "darkness" or "hidden," or "small road sign." City given to Levites from tribe of Benjamin, called Alemeth in 1 Chronicles 6:60. The site is probably modern khirbet Almit.

ALMOND A large, nut-bearing tree and the nuts it bears. Noted as the first tree to bloom (January) and for its pretty white or pink blossoms. Jacob used the almond (KJV, "hazel") as a breeding device to increase his herds (Gen. 30:37). Jacob sent almonds as one of the best fruits of the land to satisfy the Egyptian ruler (Gen. 43:11). The bowls for the tabernacle had almond-shaped decorations (Ex. 25:33–34). Aaron's rod miraculously produced ripe almonds, showing he and his tribe were the only chosen priests (Num. 17:8). The early-appearing white bloom of the almond apparently serves as a picture of the early-graying of a person's hair, pointing the writer of Ecclesiastes to the certainty of death (Eccl. 12:5). The early blossom meant for Jeremiah that the almond watched for spring and gave the prophet a word-play on the almond (Hebrew, *shaqed*) and his task to watch (Hebrew, *shoqed*) (Jer. 1:11).

ALMON-DIBLATHAIM (Ăl′ mŏn-dĭb·lȧ·thā′ ĭm) Place name meaning, "road sign of the two figs." A stopping place near the end of the wilderness wandering near Mount Nebo (Num. 33:46–47). It may be the same as Beth-Diblathaim in Jeremiah 48:22. Location may be modern Deleilat el-Gharbiyeh which looks over three roadways.

ALMS Gifts for the poor.
Old Testament Although the Hebrew language apparently had no technical term to refer to "alms" or "almsgiving," the practice of charitable giving, especially to the poor, became a very important belief and practice within Judaism. The Old Testament taught the practice of benevolent concern for those in need. Israel's ideal was a time when no one was poor (Deut. 15:4). Every three years, for example, the tithe of the produce of the year was to be brought to the towns and made available to the Levites, the aliens in the land, the orphans, and the widows (Deut. 14:28–29). Every seventh year all debts were to be cancelled among the Israelites (Deut. 15:1–3), and the fields were to lie fallow so that the needy of the people might eat (Ex.. 23:10–11). In addition, the law instructed Israel to give generously to the needs of their Hebrew neighbors (Deut. 15:7–11). Such charitable giving was not a grudging chore nor a loan for repayment. Failure to comply would be sin (Deut. 15:9–10). Israel showed concern for the needy by not harvesting the corners of fields and by leaving the gleanings so the needy and the stranger might gather what remained (Lev. 19:9–10; 23:22; Deut. 24:19–22).
New Testament The New Testament regards alms as an expression of a righteous life. The technical term for alms (Greek, *eleēmosunē*) occurs thirteen times in the New Testament. This does not include Matthew 6:1, where the preferred reading is "righteousness" (NAS, NIV) instead of "alms" (KJV). By the first century A.D. righteousness and alms were synonymous in Judaism. Although Jesus criticized acts of charity done for the notice of men (Matt. 6:2–3), He expected

His disciples to perform such deeds (Matt. 6:4) and even commanded them (Luke 11:41; 12:33). Alms could refer to a gift donated to the needy (Acts 3:2–3,10) or to acts of charity in general (Acts 9:36; 10:2,4,31; 24:17).

The principle of deeds of mercy performed in behalf of the needy receives emphatic significance in the New Testament, since such actions are ultimately performed in behalf of the Lord (Matt. 25:34–45). Early Christians voluntarily sold their possessions and shared all things in common to alleviate suffering and need within the church (Acts 2:44–46; 4:32–35). Much of Paul's later ministry involved the supervision and collection of a contribution for the needy Christians in Jerusalem (Rom. 15:25–28; 1 Cor. 16:1–4; 2 Cor. 8—9). According to James 1:27, pure and undefiled religion consists, at least partially, in assisting orphans and widows in their distress. John also presented charitable giving as evidence of one's relationship to God (1 John 3:17–18). See *Aliens; Mercy; Hospitality;* and *Stewardship.*

Barry Morgan

ALMUG See *Algum.*

ALOE A large tree grown in India and China, producing resin and oil used in making perfumes. Balaam used the beauty of the aloe tree to describe the beauty of Israel's camp as he blessed them (Num. 24:6). The aloe perfume gave aroma to the king's garment as he was married (Ps. 45:8). Aloe also perfumed the harlot's bed (Prov. 7:17). The beloved's garden includes aloe (Song of Sol. 4:14). Nicodemus brought aloe with myrrh to perfume Jesus' body for burial (John 19:39).

ALOTH (Ā′ lŏth) Place name meaning, "the height" if not read Bealoth (NAS, RSV), "feminine baals." Center of activity for Baanah, one of Solomon's twelve district supervisors (1 Kings 4:16).

ALPHA AND OMEGA are the first and last letters of the Greek alphabet and are used in Revelation to describe God or Christ (Rev. 1:8,17; 21:6; 22:13.) "Alpha and omega" refers to God's sovereignty and eternal nature. God and Christ are "the beginning and the end, the first and last." (Rev. 22:13). Thus they control all history and all humans of all generations.

ALPHAEUS (Ăl·phāe′ ŭs) or **ALPHEUS** Personal name. *1.* Father of apostle called James the Less to distinguish him from James, the son of Zebedee and brother of John (Matt. 10:3; Mark 3:18; Luke 6:15; Acts 1:13). Mark 15:40 says James' mother, Mary, was with Jesus' mother at the cross. John 19:25 says Mary the wife of Cleophas was at the cross. This would seem to indicate that Cleophas and Alphaeus are two names for the same person. Many Bible students accept this. Others think the

language problems between Greek and Hebrew make the equation impossible so that two different Marys are meant. Some want to equate Alphaeus, Cleophas, and the Cleopas of Luke 24:18. *2.* The father of the apostle Levi (Mark 2:14). Comparison of Matthew 9:9 and Luke 5:27 would indicate Levi was also called Matthew.

ALTAR is a structure used in worship as the place for presenting sacrifices to God or gods.

Old Testament The Hebrew word for altar that is used most frequently in the Old Testament is formed from the verb for slaughter and means literally, "slaughter place." Altars were used primarily as places of sacrifice, especially animal sacrifice.

While animals were a common sacrifice in the Old Testament, altars were also used to sacrifice grain, fruit, wine, and incense. The grain and fruit sacrifices were offered as a tithe of the harvest or as representative first fruits of the harvest. They were presented in baskets to the priest who set the basket before the altar (Deut. 26:2–4). Wine was offered along with animal and bread sacrifices. Incense was burned on altars to purify after slaughterings and to please God with sweet fragrance.

Canaanite altar at Hazor in the Galilee area of northern Israel.

"Altar" is distinct from "temple." Whereas temple implies a building or roofed structure, altar implies an open structure. Altar and temple were often adjacent, though not all altars had a temple adjacent. The reference to Abraham's sacrifice of Isaac (Gen. 22) may indicate that the animal to be sacrificed was placed on the altar alive, but bound, and slaughtered on the altar. Such may have been the earliest practice. By the time of the Levitical laws, the animal was slaughtered in front of the altar, dismembered, and only the fatty portions to be burned were placed on the altar (for example, Lev. 1:2–9).

In the Old Testament, altars are distinguished by the material used in their construction. The simplest altars, and perhaps oldest, were the *earthen* altars (Ex. 20:24). This type altar was made of either mud-brick or a raised roughly shaped mound of dirt. Mud-brick was a common building material in Mesopotamia, so mud-brick altars would have appeared most likely in Mesopotamia. An earthen altar would not have been very practical for permanently settled people, for the rainy season each year would damage or destroy the altar. This type altar might be more indicative of a nomadic people who move regularly and are less concerned with the need for a permanent altar. It might also reflect the Mesopotamian ancestry of the Hebrews, since the mud-brick was the typical building material there.

The *stone* altar is the most commonly mentioned altar in biblical records and the most frequently found in excavations from Palestine. A single large stone could serve as an altar (Judg. 6:19–23; 13:19–20; 1 Sam. 14:31–35). Similarly, unhewn stones could be carefully stacked to form an altar (Ex. 20:25, 1 Kings 18:30–35). Such stone altars were probably the most common form of altar prior to the building of the Solomonic Temple. A number of examples of stone altars have been excavated in Palestine. The sanctuary at Arad, belonging to the period of the Divided Monarchy (900 B.C. to 600 B.C.) had such a stone altar. The Hebrew stone altars were not to have steps (Ex. 20:25–26), probably in part to distinguish them from Canaanite altars which did have steps. A striking circular Canaanite altar dating from 2500 B.C. to 1800 B.C. was excavated at

The summit of Mount Carmel where Elijah's altar to God and the altar of the priests of Baal were built.

Megiddo. It was 25 feet in diameter and 4½ feet high. Four steps led up to the top of the altar. Apparently in later times, the requirement forbidding steps on Hebrew altars was not enforced, for in Ezekiel's vision of the restored Temple, the altar has three levels and many steps.

Other stone altars have been excavated in Palestine. One from Beersheba, belonging also to the period of the Divided Monarchy, was of large hewn stones and had, when reassembled, horns on the four corners (Ex. 27:2; 1 Kings 1:50). Apparently the Exodus restrictions concerning unhewn stones, like those concerning steps, were not consistently followed throughout the Old Testament period.

The third type altar mentioned in the Old Testament is the *bronze* altar. The central altar in the court of Solomon's temple was a bronze altar. Its dimensions are given as 20 cubits by 20 cubits by 10 cubits high (about 30 feet square and 15 feet high) [2 Chron. 4:1]. Yet is is unclear whether the entire altar was made of bronze, or if it had a bronze overlay on a stone altar. It is also possible that the bronze portion was a grate set on top of the otherwise stone altar (Ex. 27:4). This altar is regularly known as the *altar of burnt offering*. The earlier tabernacle had a similar altar made of acacia (or shittim, KJV) wood overlaid with bronze (Ex. 27:1–2). The tabernacle altar was smaller, only 5 cubits square and 3 cubits high. The location of the altar of burnt offering of the tabernacle and Solomon's Temple is not given specifically. It is located "at" or "before" the door of the Tent of

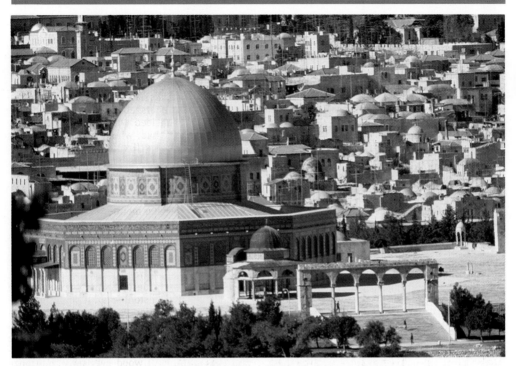

The Moslem Dome of the Rock built over the rock said to be the altar of Abraham's near sacrifice of Isaac and also built upon the site of Solomon's Temple.

Meeting, which is also the place sacrificial animals are slaughtered. Generally reconstructions of the tabernacle and Temple locate the altar in the center of the courtyard, but the text seems to favor a location near the entrance of the tabernacle/Temple structure. The rationale was probably to locate the altar as close as possible to the focal point of God's presence, near the ark itself.

Ezekiel's vision of the restored Temple had the altar of burnt offering located in the center of the courtyard. Although the dimensions are not fully given in the text, it seems that this altar was approximately 18 cubits square and 12 cubits high (Ezek. 43:13–17). Ezekiel's altar had three superimposed levels, each slightly smaller than the preceding, and had steps from the east leading up to the top.

Both the altar of the tabernacle and that of Ezekiel are described as having horns. It is likely that the altar of burnt offering in Solomon's Temple also had horns. The stone altar found at Beersheba has such horns preserved. Apparently grasping the horns of the altar was a way of seeking sanctuary or protection when one was charged with a serious offense (1 Kings 1:50–51; 2:28–34; compare Ex. 21:12–14). More importantly, the horns of the altar were the place where blood from a sacrificial animal was applied for atonement from sin (for example, Ex. 29:12; Lev. 4:7).

Jeremiah graphically described the people's sin as being so severe that they were engraved on the horns of the altar (Jer. 17:1). During certain festivals a sacred procession led into the Temple and up to the horns of the altar (Ps. 118:27). Probably this procession carried the chosen animal sacrifice to atone for the people's sin and ended at the place of sacrifice.

During the reign of Ahaz, the bronze altar or altar of burnt offering in Solomon's Temple was displaced by an altar that Ahaz had built on a Syrian model (2 Kings 16:10–16). This altar was apparently larger than the bronze altar of Solomon and was placed in the central position in the courtyard to be the main altar of sacrifice.

No biblical description exists for the altar of burnt offering from the Second Temple. However, such an altar was constructed even before the Temple was rebuilt (Ezra 3:2). Josephus described the altar in the rebuilt Temple of Herod. He wrote that the altar was fifty cubits square and fifteen cubits high with a ramp leading to the top. This altar would have been much larger than the earlier ones.

A fourth type of altar mentioned in the Bible is the *gold altar* or *altar of incense*. It was located in the inner room of the sanctuary, just outside the holy of holies (1 Kings 7:48–50). The incense altar is described in Exodus as constructed of acacia wood, overlaid with gold, with dimensions one cubit square and two cubits high (Ex. 30:1–6). Like the altar of burnt offering, the altar of incense had horns on the four corners. As its name implies, incense was burned on this altar. The incense served as a means of purification after slaughtering animals, a costly sacrifice, and also as a sweet smelling offering that would be pleasing to God.

Another Hebrew word for altar that is used infrequently in the Old Testament means literally, "high place" (Hebrew, *bamah*). Such "high places" were probably raised platforms at which sacrifices and other rites took place. The "high place" may have been itself a kind of altar, though this is not certain. The circular Canaanite altar mentioned above may be an example of a "high place," an elevated place of sacrifice and worship.

New Testament The Greek word used for altar literally translates "place of sacrifice." New Testament references to altars concern proper worship (Matt 5:23–24) and hypocrisy in worship (Matt. 23:18–20). The altar of incense described in the Old Testament (Ex. 30:1–6) is mentioned in Luke (Luke 1:11). Several New Testament references to altars refer back to Old Testament altar events (Rom. 11:3; Jas. 2:21). In Revelation, John described a golden altar (Rev. 9:13) that, like the Old Testament bronze altar, had horns.

While direct references to altar and the sacrifice of Jesus Christ are few in the New Testament (Rom. 13:10), the message that Jesus Christ is the ultimate sacrifice who puts us right with God is the theme of the New Testament.

Fragments of what was probably an altar base unearthed at the high place at Lachish in Israel.

Theological Significance Altars in the Bible were places of sacrifice. Beyond that function, altars also were places of God's presence. The patriarchal narratives regularly record the building of an altar at the site of a theophany, a place where God had appeared to an individual (Gen. 12:7; 26:24–25). It was quite natural to build an altar and commemorate the appearance of God with a sacrifice. If God had once appeared at a site, that would be a good location for Him to appear again. Thus sacrifices would be offered there with the feeling that God was present and would accept the offering. With the building of the Solomonic Temple, the presence of God was associated especially with the ark of the covenant. The altar of burnt offering then came to signify more of a sense of reconciliation or mediation. The worshiper brought a sacrifice to the altar where it was burned and thereby given to God. The acceptance of the offerings by the priest symbolized God's acceptance, manifest in blessings (Ex. 20:24) and covenant renewal.   *Joel F. Drinkard, Jr.*

ALTASHHETH (Ăl·tăsh′ hĕth) (NAS) or **ALTASCHITH** (KJV). Word in Psalm title (Pss. 57; 58; 59; 75) transliterated letter for letter from Hebrew to English by NAS and KJV but translated, "Do not destroy" by NIV and RSV. This may indicate the tune to which the people sang the Psalm.

ALUSH (Ā′ lŭsh) Wilderness camping place not far from Red Sea (Num. 33:13–14).

ALVAH (Ăl′ văh) Personal name of leader of Edom. Spelled Aliah in 1 Chronicles 1:51.

ALVAN (Ăl′ văn) Personal name meaning, "high" or "tall." A descendant of Seir (Gen. 36:23), spelled Alian in 1 Chronicles 1:40.

AMAD (Ā′ măd) Place name of unknown meaning. City allotted to tribe of Asher (Josh. 19:26).

AMAL (Ā′ măl) Personal name meaning "worker" or "trouble." Leader of tribe of Asher (1 Chron. 7:35).

AMALEKITE (Ăm′ ā·lĕk·ite) A nomadic tribe of formidable people that first attacked the Israelites after the Exodus at Rephidim. Descendants of Amalek, the grandson of Esau (Gen. 36:12), they inhabited the desolate wasteland of the northeast Sinai peninsula and the Negeb. They were the first to attack Israel after the Exodus (Num. 24:20). Israel won the initial battle (Ex. 17:8–16), but later was driven back into the Sinai wilderness by a coalition of Amalekites and Canaanites (Num. 14:39–45). Thereafter the Amalekites waged a barbaric guerrilla war against Israel (Deut. 25:17–19). Fighting continued after

Israel settled in Canaan. Because of their atrocities, God commanded Saul to exterminate the Amalekites (1 Sam. 15:2–3). Saul disobeyed, and the Amalekites were not defeated completely until late in the eighth century B.C. (1 Chron. 4:43). No archaeological data concerning the Amalekites has been discovered to date. See also *Exodus* and *Negeb.* *LeBron Matthews*

AMAM (Ā' măm) Place name in southern Judah (Josh. 15:26).

AMANA (Á·mā' nà) Place name meaning, "trusted." Mountain peak in Anti-lebanon mountains where lovers meet and then descend (Song of Sol. 4:8).

AMARIAH (Ăm·à·rī' äh) Personal name meaning "Yahweh has spoken." Popular name, especially among priests, after the Exile. Brief biblical comments make it difficult to distinguish the number of separate individuals. The following division is one attempt to separate them. *1.* A priest in line of Aaron (1 Chron. 6:7,52; Ezra 7:3. *2.* A priest in the high priestly line after Solomon's day (1 Chron. 6:11). *3.* A priestly son of Hebron in Moses' line (1 Chron. 23:19; 24:23. *4.* The chief priest and highest judge of matters involving religious law under King Jehoshaphat (2 Chron. 19:11). *5.* Priest under Hezekiah responsible for distributing resources from Jerusalem Temple to priests in priestly cities outside Jerusalem (2 Chron. 31:15). *6.* Man with foreign wife under Ezra (Ezra 10:42). *7.* Priest who sealed Nehemiah's covenant to obey the law (Neh. 10:3). *8.* Ancestor of a member of tribe of Judah living in Jerusalem during Nehemiah's time (Neh. 11:4). *9.* A priest who returned to Jerusalem from Exile in Babylon with Zerubbabel (Neh. 12:2). *10.* Head of a course of priests in Judah after the Exile (Neh. 12:13). *11.* An ancestor of Zephaniah, the prophet (Zeph. 1:1).

AMARNA, TELL EL is a site approximately two hundred miles south of Cairo, Egypt, where, in 1888, clay tablets were found describing the period of history when the Israelites were in bondage in Egypt. Amarna is not mentioned by name in the Bible. Tell el-Amarna lies on the east bank of the Nile River.

Tell el-Amarna is the present location of the ancient Egyptian city Akhenaton. That city was constructed as the new capital of a young Pharaoh, Amenhotep (or Amenophis) IV, who was in power during the mid-fourteenth century B.C.

The letters were primarily diplomatic communications between Egypt and Egyptian-controlled territories, including Syria and Palestine. Rulers of small Palestinian city-states including Shechem, Jerusalem, and Megiddo complain of mistreatment by other rulers and ask for Egyptian aid.

These letters evidence the political unrest, disunity, and instability of the period prior to the Hebrew conquest. *Hugh Tobias*

AMASA (Á·mā' sà) Personal name meaning, "burden" or "bear a burden." *1.* Captain of Judah's army replacing Joab during Absalom's rebellion against his father David (2 Sam. 17:25). He is related to David, but the texts leave some question as to the exact relationship. Abigail was Amasa's mother. His father was either Ithra an Israelite (2 Sam. 17:25) or Jether the Ishmaelite (1 Chron. 2:17). She was sister of Zeruiah, Joab's mother (2 Sam. 17:25) or sister to David and to Zeruiah, Joab's mother (1 Chron. 2:16). When he defeated the rebel forces and Joab murdered Absalom (2 Sam. 18:14), David made peaceful overtures to Judah by inviting Amasa as his relative to assume command of his army (2 Sam. 19:13). When called to battle, Amasa appeared too late (2 Sam. 20:4–5). Joab marched among David's army and cunningly killed Amasa (2 Sam. 20:10). This served as reason for David to advise Solomon to do away with Joab (1 Kings 2:5) and thus reason for Solomon to kill Joab (1 Kings 2:28–34). *2.* Leader in tribe of Ephraim who prevented Israel's soldiers from keeping captives of the army of King Ahaz of Judah, knowing this was a sin (2 Chron. 28:12–14).

AMASAI (Á·mā' saî) Personal name meaning, "burden bearer." *1.* A Levite in line of Kohath (1 Chron. 6:25). *2.* A Levite in the line of Kohath and of Heman the singer (1 Chron. 6:35), often identified with *1.* *3.* The chief of David's captains, who received prophetic inspiration from the Spirit (1 Chron. 12:18). Note that he does not appear in 2 Samuel 23. *4.* A priest and musician who blew trumpets before the ark of God in David's time (1 Chron. 15:24). *5.* Levite, father of Mahath, who helped purify the Temple under Hezekiah (2 Chron. 29:12).

AMASHAI (Á·măsh' aî) or **AMASHSAI** (NAS, TEV). Personal name of priest after the Exile (Neh. 11:13).

AMASIAH (Ăm à sī' ah) Personal name meaning "Yahweh has borne." One of the captains of Jehoshaphat (2 Chron. 17:16).

AMAW (Ăm' aw) Place name meaning, "his people." Translated "land of children of his people" (KJV) or "his native land" (NIV) or "land of the sons of his people" (NAS) in Numbers 22:5, but translated as place name in RSV, TEV. Place name also appears in Idrim Inscription about 1450 B.C. and in an Egyptian tomb inscription. It was located west of Euphrates River south of Carchemish and included Pethor, the home town of Balaam, the prophet.

AMAZIAH (Ăm·à·zī' ăh) Personal name meaning, "Yahweh is mighty." *1.* A Simeonite (1 Chron. 4:34). *2.* A Levite and a descendant of Merari (1 Chron. 6:45). *3.* A priest at Bethel who sent Amos the prophet home, saying he did not have the right to prophesy against King Jeroboam II of Israel (789–746 B.C.) in the king's place of worship (Amos 7:10–17).

4. Ninth king of Judah, the son of Joash and father of Uzziah (797–767 B.C.). He was 25 years old when he ascended the throne. He speedily avenged the murder of his father, who had been killed by court servants. Amaziah was uncommonly merciful in his avenging, as he only murdered the guilty servants, not the servants' children (2 Kings 14:5–6).

Among Amaziah's accomplishments, he conscripted an army for Judah, composed of all men age 20 and above. He also hired mercenaries from Israel, but declined to use them at the advice of a "man of God" (1 Chron. 25:7). Amaziah led his army to Seir, where he easily defeated the Edomites, making them again subject to Judah. Yet, he took Edomite idols back to Jerusalem and worshiped them. He then refused to listen to the rebuke and the forecast of doom brought by God's prophet (2 Chron. 25:11–16).

Encouraged by his victory in Edom, Amaziah challenged Joash, king of Israel, to battle. Though Joash tried to avoid a conflict, Amaziah persisted and was defeated at the hands of Israel. The Temple and royal palace were plundered, the wall of Jerusalem was pierced, and Amaziah was taken prisoner. Amaziah survived Joash by fifteen years. Because of a conspiracy against him he fled to Lachish but was murdered there. See: *Judah, Kings of; Joash; Uzziah; Jehoaddin (his mother).*
Ronald E. Bishop

AMBASSADOR ·Representative of one royal court to another. According to the KJV, NAS, and NIV reading of Joshua 9:4, the Gibeonites pretended to be official ambassadors from a foreign government as they approached Joshua. Compare NRSV. The king of Babylon sent official ambassadors to learn of Hezekiah's power (2 Chron. 32:31). Pharaoh Necho sent ambassadors to prevent King Josiah of Judah (640–609) from joining in the battle at Megiddo, but Josiah persisted and died (2 Chron. 35:21). Faithful ambassadors bring health to a nation (Prov. 13:17). Isaiah condemned Israel for sending ambassadors to Egypt seeking military aid rather than seeking God's aid (Isa. 30:4). While they suffered before God's announced salvation, the people lamented before God. This included ambassadors who had unsuccessfully worked for peace (Isa. 33:7). Israel consistently relied on ambassadors to foreign lands rather than on Yahweh and His plan (Isa. 57:9). Jeremiah announced that God had prompted an ambassador to call the nations to punish Edom (Jer. 49:14; compare Obad.

1). Ezekiel condemned King Zedekiah (597–586 B.C.) for sending ambassadors to Egypt seeking help in rebelling against Babylon (Ezek. 17:15).

Paul saw himself even in prison as an ambassador sent by the divine King to proclaim salvation through Christ to the world (Eph. 6:20; compare 2 Cor. 5:20).

AMBER (Ăm' bĕr) A yellowish or brownish translucent resin that takes a good polish. Also translated as gleaming bronze (RSV, but amber in NRSV), glowing metal (NAS, NIV), bronze (TEV, Ezek. 1:4,27; 8:2). Some think that the Greek (Septuagint) and Latin (Vulgate) translations of the Old Testament suggest the substance known as electrum—an amalgam of silver and gold. See *Jewelry, Jewels, Precious Stones.*

AMBUSH A military tactic of hiding a unit of troops for surprise attack while carrying on normal battle with the remainder of the troops. Joshua used the tactic against Ai (Josh. 8). The people of Shechem waited in hiding to attack and rob people who crossed the mountain (Judg. 9:25; compare Hos. 6:9). Abimelech used ambush to defeat Shechem (Judg. 9:43–45). Israel used ambush to attack Gibeah and the rebellious tribe of Benjamin (Judg. 20:29–43). Saul apparently used similar tactics against the Amalekites (1 Sam. 15:5). Jeroboam, king of Israel (926–909 B.C.) tried unsuccessfully to ambush Judah (2 Chron. 13:13). God set ambushes against Moab, Ammon, and Edom to defeat them for King Jehoshaphat (873–848 B.C.). God delivered Ezra from ambush attempts (Ezra 8:31).

The psalmists asked for God's help against wicked persons who sought to ambush them (Ps. 10:8; 59:3; 64:4; compare Prov. 1:11,18). Jeremiah accused his people of spiritual ambush against one another (Jer. 9:8). He also called for ambushes to defeat Babylon (Jer. 51:12). The people of Jerusalem lamented that the enemy had used ambushes to defeat and destroy the city and nation (Lam. 4:19). Paul's nephew saved him from Jewish plans to ambush him as the Roman authorities transferred him from Jerusalem to Caesarea (Acts 23:12–33; compare 25:3).

AMEN is a transliteration of a Hebrew word signifying something as certain, sure and valid, truthful and faithful. It is sometimes translated, "so be it." In the Old Testament it is used to show the acceptance of the validity of a curse or an oath (Num. 5:22; Deut. 27:15–26; Jer. 11:5), to indicate acceptance of a good message (Jer. 28:6), and to join in a doxology in a worship setting to affirm what has been said or prayed (1 Chron. 16:36; Neh. 8:6; Ps. 106:48). "Amen" may confirm what already is, or it may indicate a hope for something desired. In Jewish prayer, "amen" comes at the end as an affirmative response to a statement or wish made by others, and is so used in the New Testament epistles (Rom. 1:25; 11:36; 15:33; 1 Cor. 16:24; Gal. 1:5; Eph. 3:21; Phil. 4:20). Paul ended some of his letters with "amen" (1 Thess. 5:28; 2 Thess. 3:18).

In the gospels, Jesus used "amen" to affirm the truth of His own statements. English translations often use "verily," "truly," "I tell you the truth" to translate Jesus' amen. He never said it at the end of a statement, but always at the beginning: "Amen, I say to you" (Matt. 5:18; 16:28; Mark 8:12; 11:23; Luke 4:24; 21:32; John 1:51; 5:19). In John's Gospel, Jesus said "Amen, amen." That Jesus prefaced His own words with "amen" is especially important, for He affirmed that the kingdom of God is bound up with His own person and emphasized the authority of what He said.

Jesus is called "The Amen" in Revelation 3:14, meaning that He Himself is the reliable and true witness of God. Perhaps the writer had in mind Isaiah 65:16 where the Hebrew says "God of Amen."   *Roger L. Omanson*

AMETHYST (Ăm′ ė thyst) A deep purple variety of stone of the aluminum oxide family. Used in the breastplate of the high priest (Ex. 28:19; 39:12) and the twelfth stone in the foundation wall of the new Jerusalem (Rev. 21:20). See *Jewelry, Jewels, Precious Stones.*

AMI (Ā′ mī) Personal name, meaning uncertain. A servant in the Temple after the Exile belonging to a group called "children of Solomon's servants" (Ezra 2:55–57). Ami is apparently called Amon in Nehemiah 7:59.

AMINADAB (À·mĭn′ å·dăb) KJV spelling in New Testament of Amminadab. See *Amminadab.*

AMITTAI (À·mĭt′ taî) Personal name meaning, "loyal," "true." Father of the prophet Jonah who lived in Gath-hepher (2 Kings 14:25).

AMIZZABAD. TEV spelling of Ammizabad. See *Ammizabad.*

AMMAH (Ăm′ mah) Hill near Giah in the territory of Gibeon between Jerusalem and Bethel. There Joab and Abishai pursued Abner after he killed Asahel, their brother (2 Sam. 2:24).

AMMI (Ăm′ mī), meaning "my people," was a name given to Israel by Hosea in contrast to the name Lo-ammi (Hos. 1:9) meaning "not my people." The name Lo-ammi was given to the third child of Gomer, the wife of Hosea the prophet, to pronounce God's rejection of Israel. The name Ammi was the new name to be given the restored Israel in the day of redemption.

AMMIEL (Ăm′ mĭ·ĕl) Personal name meaning,

"people of God" or "God is of my people," that is God is my relative. *1.* The spy representing the tribe of Dan whom Moses sent to spy out the Promised Land. He was one of ten who brought bad report and led people to refuse to enter the land (Num. 13:12). *2.* Father of Machir, in whose house Mephibosheth, son of Jonathan and grandson of Saul, lived after the death of his father and grandfather. The family lived in Lo-debar (2 Sam. 9:4). See 17:27. *3.* The father of Bathshua, David's wife (1 Chron. 3:5). 2 Samuel 11:3 speaks of Bathsheba, daughter of Eliam. Many Bible students think these verses are talking about the same person, whose names have been slightly altered in the process of copying the manuscripts. *4.* Gatekeeper of Temple whom David appointed (1 Chron. 26:5).

AMMIHUD (Ăm·mī′ hŭd) Personal name meaning, "my people is splendid." *1.* Father of Elishama, who represented the tribe of Ephraim to help Moses during the wilderness wandering (Num. 1:10). He presented the tribe's offerings at the dedication of the altar (7:48) and led them in marching (10:22). He was Joshua's grandfather (1 Chron. 7:26). *2.* Father of Shemuel of the tribe of Simeon, who helped Moses, Eleazar, and Joshua allot the land to the tribes (Num. 34:20). *3.* Father of Pedahel of tribe of Naphtali, who helped allot the land (34:28). *4.* Father of King of Geshur to whom Absalom fled after he killed his brother Amnon (2 Sam. 13:37). *5.* Member of tribe of Judah who returned from Exile (1 Chron. 9:4).

AMMINADAB (Ăm·mĭn′ å·dăb) Personal name meaning, "my people give freely." *1.* Aaron's father-in-law (Ex. 6:23). Father of Nahshon, who led tribe of Judah in the wilderness (Num. 1:7). Ancestor of David (Ruth 4:19) and Jesus (Matt. 1:4; Luke 3:33). *2.* Son of Kohath in genealogy of Levites (1 Chron. 6:22), but this may be copyist's change for Izhar (Ex. 6:18,21). *3.* Head of a family of Levites (1 Chron. 15:10). He helped carry the ark of the covenant to Jerusalem (1 Chron. 15:11–29).

AMMI-NADIB (Ăm′ mĭ-nå′ dĭb) The KJV takes these words as a personal name in Song of Solomon 6:12. Most modern versions express uncertainty about the translation of this verse. Some modern translations translate *ammi-nadib* as "my noble people" (NAS) or "my people" (NIV), while others translate "my prince" (NRSV) or "chariot driver" (TEV). Some versions (NIV, REB, TEV) take the verse as spoken by the young man. The NRSV takes the words in verse 12 as coming from the maiden who spoke about her fancy (perhaps her imagination) setting her in a chariot beside her prince. Because of the confusion, James Moffatt did not even attempt a translation.

AMMISHADDAI (Ăm′ mĭ·shăd′ daî) The father of Ahiezer, the leader of the tribe of Dan in the wilderness. (Num. 1:12) The name Ammishaddai means "people of the Almighty."

AMMIZABAD (Ăm′ mĭz′ à·băd) Personal name meaning, "my people give." Son of Benaiah, one of captains of David's army (1 Chron. 27:6).

AMMONITES Semitic people living northeast of the Dead Sea in the area surrounding Rabbah who often battled with the Israelites for possession of the fertile Gilead. Ammon, the kingdom of the Ammonites, was hardly more than a city-state, consisting of the capital city itself, Rabbah or Rabbath-Ammon ("chief city," or "chief city of the Ammonites") and its immediately surrounding territory. Rabbah was located at the headwaters of the Jabbok river, where the southeastern corner of Gilead gives way to the desert. The agricultural productivity of Gilead, the waters of the Jabbok itself and of associated springs, as well as Rabbah's naturally defendable position, destined Rabbah to be a city of medium importance in ancient times. The proximity of the Ammonites to Gilead likewise destined them to be constant enemies of the Israelites, who made claims to Gilead and actually controlled it during the reigns of certain strong kings such as David, Omri, Ahab, and Jeroboam II.

Most of our information about the Ammonites comes from the Old Testament, although Ammonite kings are mentioned occasionally in the Assyrian records. We know from the latter, for example, that an Ammonite king named Ba'sha, along with Ahab of Israel and other kings of the region, defended Syria-Palestine against Shalmaneser III in 853 B.C. An Ammonite inscription, the so-called Siran Bottle Inscription and several seals/seal impressions have provided additional information about the Ammonites.

Archaeologists have excavated only a small portion of the site of ancient Rabbah (the so-called "Citadel" in the heart of the modern city of Amman). The surrounding area remains largely unexplored. In addition to the inscription and seals mentioned above, the bust of an Ammonite warrior (or god) and the remains of round stone towers thought to be Ammonite are significant archaeological discoveries shedding light on the Ammonites.

Conflict broke out between the Ammonites and Israelites as early as the time of the Judges. The Ammonites made war on the Israelites of Gilead, leading the Israelites to appeal to Jephthah, chief of a local band of renegade raiders, to organize and lead their resistance. Jephthah accepted the challenge, but only after extracting a promise from the elders of Gilead that, if he indeed succeeded in defeating the Ammonites, they would recognize him as ruler of Gilead. At the same time he vowed to Yahweh that "If thou wilt give the Ammonites into my hand, then whoever comes forth from the doors of my house to meet me, when I return victorious from the Ammonites, shall be the LORD's, and I will offer him up for a burnt offering" (Judg. 11:30b–31). Jephthah was victorious, and the Gileadites submitted to his rule; but then his little daughter greeted him upon his return (Judg. 10:6—11:40).

On another occasion when the Ammonites were attacking the city of Jabesh in Gilead and the Jabeshites attempted to negotiate terms for surrender, the Ammonites demanded nothing less than to put out the right eye of each man in the city. In desperation, the Jabeshites sent messengers to Saul at Gibeah for help. Saul organized an army, hurried to Jabesh, and lifted the siege. Consequently, the Jabeshites were strong supporters of Saul in later years (1 Sam. 11; 31:11–13). The Ammonite king Saul defeated at Jabesh was Nahash. Presumably this was the same Nahash with whom David had good dealings but whose son, Hanun, renewed hostilities (2 Sam. 10—12). The ensuing wars between Israel and Ammon involved warfare between David's troops and those of Hadadezer of Zobah (2 Sam. 10:6–19) and provided the occasion of David's affair with Bathsheba. Uriah, Bathsheba's husband, was killed while storming the walls of Rabbah (2 Sam. 11—12).

No war with the Ammonites is reported during Solomon's reign. On the contrary, Solomon took one or more Ammonite wives and allowed the worship of Milcom, the Ammonite god, in Jerusalem (1 Kings 11:1–8). Presumably the worship of Milcom continued in Jerusalem until it was stamped out by Josiah many years later (2 Kings 23:13). We know little of relations between the Ammonites and either Israel or Judah during the first half century of the separate kingdoms, probably because neither of the Hebrew kingdoms attempted to exercise influence in the Transjordan. The coalition of Syro-Palestinian kings, which included Ba'sha of Ammon and Ahab of Israel, halted the Assyrian king, Shalmaneser's march in 853 B.C. But success was only temporary. Later Shalmaneser penetrated the very heart of Syria-Palestine, exacting tribute from the Israelites and, although it is not recorded, probably also from the Ammonites. Eventually, all the petty kingdoms of the region fell to the Assyrians and either were incorporated into the Assyrian province system or controlled as satellites. Ammonite kings paid tribute to Tiglath-pileser III, Sennacherib, and Esarhaddon.

The Israelites recognized the Ammonites as relatives, although somewhat more distant than the Edomites. This relationship was expressed genealogically. Specifically, the Ammonites were said to have descended from an ancestor named Ben Ammi, one of two sons which Lot bore to his two daughters. The Moabites were said to have descended from the other son (Gen. 19:30–38). The Ammonites also are mentioned from time to time in Israel's poetical literature. See for example Amos' oracle agains the Ammonites in Amos 1:13–15.

Rabbah apparently had dwindled to an insignificant settlement by the third century B.C. when Ptolemy II Philadelphus (285–246) rebuilt the city and renamed it "Philadelphia" after himself. Philadelphia came to be regarded as one of the Decapolis cities, a federation of ten Greek cities in Palestine (Matt. 4:25), and was annexed with the whole Decapolis region to the Roman empire in A.D. 90.   *Maxwell Miller*

AMNON (Ăm′ nŏn) Personal name meaning, "trustworthy, faithful." *1.* The firstborn son of King David (2 Sam. 3:2). He raped his half-sister Tamar. Tamar's brother Absalom avenged this outrage by killing Amnon (2 Sam. 13:1–20). This incident marked the beginning of the decline of David's family following his adulterous relationship with Bathsheba and the murder of Uriah. See *David. 2.* A member of tribe of Judah (1 Chron. 4:20).

AMOK (Ā′ mŏk) Personal name meaning, "deep." A priestly family after the return from Exile (Neh. 12:7,20).

AMON (Ā′ mŏn) Personal name meaning, "faithful." *1.* Governor of Samaria when Jehoshaphat was king of Judah, who followed orders from the king of Israel and put the prophet Micaiah in prison (1 Kings 22:26). *2.* King of Judah (642 B.C.) following his father Manasseh. He followed the infamous idolatry of his father and was killed in a palace revolt (2 Kings 21:19–23). The people of Judah, in turn, killed the rebels. Good King Josiah, Amon's son, succeeded to his throne. See Matt. 1:10. *3.* An ancestor of Temple staff members after the Exile (Neh. 7:59), called Ami in Ezra 2:57. *4.* Egyptian god whose worship center at Thebes Jeremiah threated with divine destruction (Jer. 46:25). KJV translates "the multitude of No."

AMORITES A people who occupied part of the Promised Land and often fought Israel. Their history goes back before 2000 B.C. They took control of the administration of Babylonia for approximately 400 years (2000–1595), their most influential king being Hammurabi (1792–1750). Their descent to Canaan may be traced back to 2100–1800 when their settlement in the hill country helped to set the stage for the revelation of God through Israel.

Abraham assisted Mamre the Amorite in recovering his land from four powerful kings (Gen. 14), but later the Amorites were a formidable obstacle to the Israelites' conquest and settlement of Ca-

naan. They preferred living in the hills and valleys that flank both sides of the Jordan River. Sihon and Og, two Amorite kings, resisted the Israelites' march to Canaan as they approached east of the Jordan (Nu. 21:21–35); but after the Israelite victory here, Gad, Reuben and half of Manasseh settled in the conquered area. These two early victories over the Amorites foreshadowed continued success against other Amorites to the west and were often remembered in both history (e.g., Deut. 3:8; Josh. 12:2; Judg. 11:19) and poetry (Num. 21:27–30; Ps. 135:10–12; 136:17–22). West of the Jordan, the Amorites lived in the hills along with the Hivites, Hittites, and Jebusites (Num. 13:29; Josh. 11:3); but specific identification of Amorite cities cannot be certain since the term "Amorite" is used often as a very general name for all the inhabitants of Canaan, as is "Canaanite" (e.g. Gen. 15:16; Josh. 24:15; Judg. 6:10; 1 Kings 21:26). Five city-states in south Canaan formed an alliance instigated by the king of Jerusalem (Jebus, Jebusites) and intimidated an ally of Joshua, i.e. Gibeon. These "Amorites," as they are called in the general sense, were defeated by Joshua's army and the Lord's "stones from heaven" (Josh. 10:1–27). Amorites also were among those in the north who unsuccessfully united to repel the Israelites (Josh. 11:1–15). Later, two other Amorite cities, Aijalon and Shaalbim, hindered the settlement of Dan near the Philistine border (Judg. 1:34–36).

Amorite culture laid at the root of Jerusalem's decadence, according to Ezekiel (Ezek. 16:3,45); and Amorite idolatry tainted the religion of the Northern and Southern Kingdoms (1 Kings 21:26; 2 Kings 21:11). Despite the Amorite resistance and poor influence, they were subjugated as slaves (Judg. 1:35; 1 Kings 9:20,21; 2 Chron. 8:7,8). Their past hindrance is a subject of derision for the prophet Amos (Amos 2:9,10). See also *Canaanites; Jebusites; Babylon; Syria; Sihon.*

        Daniel C. Fredericks

AMOS (Ā′ mŏs) Personal name meaning, "a load." *1.* A prophet from Judah who ministered in Israel about 750 B.C. One might graphically describe the prophet Amos as a "burden bearer." He carried a heavy burden for his people. Or, from another perspective, his people were a burden he carried.

Amos was a layperson who disclaimed professional status as a prophet: "I am no prophet, nor a prophet's son, but I am a herdsman, and a dresser of sycamore trees, and the Lord took me from following the flock, and the Lord said to me, 'Go, prophesy to my people Israel' " (7:14–15 RSV). Because of God's call, Amos assumed his prophetic responsibilities as a lonely voice prophesying from both the desert and the villages. He indicted both Judah and Israel, challenging the superficial qualities of religious institutions. For

Amos, his call and his continuing ministry rested in God's initiative and in His sustaining power: "The lion has roared; who will not fear? The Lord God has spoken; who can but prophesy?' " (3:8 RSV).

Amos lived in a time of relative peace on the international political scene. Both Egypt and Assyria were in a period of decline, although Assyria was beginning to expand its power. Syria had become ineffective, but the reduction of this buffer state between Israel and Assyria was to have serious repercussions in the generation following Amos.

Internally, the political structures of both Israel and Judah were stable. Beginning his prophetic activity during the reign of Jeroboam II in the Northern Kingdom of Israel, Amos lived during an era that rivaled Solomon's generation in its stability and economic prosperity (2 Kings 14:23–27). Yet, it was precisely the social, moral, and religious problems attending that prosperity that became the focus for Amos' voice of judgment. In the Southern Kingdom of Judah, the noble king Uzziah reigned (Amos 1:1). Amos probably began his ministry with God's call in 765 B.C., "two years before the earthquake" (1:1).

Morally, Israel and Judah were suffering under the corruption generated as a by-product of Canaanite and Tyrian Baalism, as well as infidelity to the Lord's covenant. Israelite society had experi-

Chasm at Tekoa, Israel, the hometown of Amos the Prophet.

enced the inevitable decay which characterizes misdirected prosperity. It may appear strange that the corruption of Israelite society could be traced to its contemporary religious structures and to the material prosperity which Israelites so often interpreted as a sign of divine favor. Despite the contradictory nature of those circumstances, the debauched moral condition of the land was the product of both corrupt religion and perverted material prosperity. Rampant luxury and self-indulgence were clearly manifest (1:6ff; 4:1ff; 5:10ff; 6:1ff; 8:4ff).

Exploitation of the poor occurred throughout the land (2:6; 3:10; 4:1; 5:11; 8:4–6). Justice was distorted. The dynamism of personal religious experience gave way to the superficiality of institutional religion as demonstrated in the conflict

Ruins of small building, probably dating from postbiblical times, at Tekoa, Israel, Amos's hometown.

between Amos and Amaziah, the priest of Bethel (7:10ff). Amos' opposition to those moral and religious evils led him to emphasize the primary theme of the book: "let justice roll down like waters, and righteousness like an everlasting stream" (5:24 RSV).

One may divide the book of Amos into three sections. Chapters one and two are a basic section, divided into subsections which begin with a common literary introduction (1:3,6,9,11,13; 2:1,4,6). The second section of the book consists of judgment oracles directed against Israel (3:1—6:14). The third section contains the visions of Amos (7—9), which may have been the earliest revelations through the prophet. The visions were central to his call experience. Aware of the awesome reality of human sin and divine judgment, these visions shaped his prophetic messages (7:1–3,4–6,7–9; 8:1–3; 9:1–4).

The words of Amos address various issues, but the central theme stresses sin and judgment. Whether in addressing other nations, Israel, or Judah, the prophet condemned those who sin against a universal conscience (1:1—2:3), the revealed law (2:4–5), or God's redeeming love (2:6–16). Amos challenged people to live by covenant standards and condemned them for their failure to reflect the covenant in daily life. He was concerned about people who "do not know how to do right" (3:10 RSV). His word of judgment was severe for the "first ladies of Samaria" who encouraged the injustice and violence of their husbands "who oppress the poor, who crush the needy, who say to their husbands, 'Bring, that we may drink!' " (4:1 RSV). Because of such injustice and the failure to bind authentic religious experience with a social conscience, Amos claimed that the nation was already dead. One could sing Israel's funeral lament: "Fallen, no more to rise, is the virgin Israel" (5:1 RSV). For individuals who were superficially and confidently "at ease in Zion, and to those who feel secure on the mountain of Samaria" (6:1 RSV), their only hope rested in the renewal of authentic religious experience leading to a life of justice and righteousness which overflow the land (5:24). For those who rejected that way, only judgment remained: "prepare to meet your God, O Israel!" (4:12).

Outline

I. The Sermons: God Confronts His People's Sin (1:1—6:14).
  A. God's Word is revealed in human words (1:1–2).
  B. God identifies and condemns all human sin (1:3—2:16).
    1. Acts against common human decency are sinful (1:3—2:3).
    2. The rejection of God's law by substituting one's own wisdom is sin (2:4–5).

  3. Rejecting God's love is sin (2:6–16).
  C. God condemns empty religion (3:1–15).
    1. The privilege of being loved by God brings responsibility (3:1–2).
    2. God reveals His purposes to His people (3:3–8).
    3. God uses historical agents in His judgment (3:9–12).
    4. Centers of empty religion and ill-gotten prosperity will all fall (3:13–15).
  D. God's love confronts His disobedient people in judgment (4:1–13).
    1. Insatiable desire leads to sin (4:1–3).
    2. Empty and meaningless worship is sin (4:4–5).
    3. Temporal judgment is intended to lead God's people to repentance (4:6–11).
    4. God's rebellious people face an ultimate confrontation with Him (4:12–13).
  E. God calls His people to practice justice and righteousness (5:1–27).
    1. God sees the end of His sinful people (5:1–3).
    2. God's rebellious people are invited to seek Him (5:4–9,14–15).
    3. God's inescapable judgment is on His people (5:10–13,16–20).
    4. Practical righteousness is God's ultimate demand of His people (5:21–27).
  F. False security in national strength leads to ultimate downfall (6:1–14).
II. The Visions: Seeing God Properly Reveals Both His Judgment and His Mercy (7:1—9:15).
  A. God extends mercy in response to serious intercession (7:1–6).
  B. Ultimate confrontation with God can never be escaped (7:7–9).
  C. A proper view of God brings everything else into perspective (7:10–17).
    1. A false view of the nature of God's message leads to wrong decisions (7:10–13).
    2. A person transformed by a vision of God sees people and things as they really are (7:14–17).
  D. The final consequences of sin offers judgment without hope (8:1—9:4).
    1. An overripe, rotten religion is worthless (8:1–3).
    2. The empty observance of meaningless ritual leaves our morality unaffected (8:4–6).
    3. God's final judgment is a horrible sight (8:7—9:4).
  E. God's mercy can be seen beyond His judgment (9:5–15).

1. God is Sovereign over all the universe (9:5–6).
2. God's mercy still offers hope beyond temporal judgment (9:7–10).
3. God's ultimate purpose of good for His people will be fulfilled (9:11–15).

2. An ancestor of Jesus (Luke 3:25).

Roy L. Honeycutt

AMOZ (Ā′ mȧz) whose name means "strong," was the father of the prophet Isaiah (2 Kings 19:2).

AMPHIPOLIS (Ăm·phĭp′ o·lĭs) City near the Aegean Gulf between Thessalonica and Philippi. Paul and Silas passed through it on their way to Thessalonica on Paul's second missionary journey (Acts 17:1) as they travelled the famous Egnatian Way.

AMPLIAS (Ăm′ plĭ·ȧs) A Christian convert in Rome to whom Paul sent greetings (Rom. 16:8). Amplias was a common name often given to slaves. Paul referred to this individual as "my beloved in the Lord," which may suggest a particularly warm and affectionate relationship between Amplias and the apostle. Modern translations spell the name Ampliatus.

AMPLIATUS (Ăm·plĭ·ā′ tus) See *Amplias.*

AMRAM (Ăm′ răm) Personal name meaning "exalted people." *1.* Father of Moses, Aaron, and Miriam and grandson of Levi (Ex. 6:18–20). Moses' father, Amram, was the father of the Levitical family, the Amramites (Num. 3:27; 1 Chron. 26:23), who served in the wilderness sanctuary and may have served in the Temple treasuries in later years. *2.* One of the twelve sons of Bani who was guilty of marrying foreign women (Ezra 10:34). *3.* One of four sons of Dishon in 1 Chronicles 1:41. In Genesis 36:26, the four sons of Dishon are also listed, however Amram is listed as Hemdan. Translations other than the KJV list this son of Dishon as Hemdan in Chronicles as well as Genesis.

AMRAPHEL (Ăm′ rȧ·phĕl) Personal name, probably originally Akkadian, meaning, "the God Amurru paid back" or "the mouth of God has spoken." King of Shinar or Babylon who joined a coalition to defeat Sodom and Gomorrah, then other kings in Canaan and the Dead Sea area. The kings captured Lot. Hearing the news, Abraham assembled an army, defeated the coalition, and rescued Lot (Gen. 14:1–9). Amraphel cannot be equated with any other king of whom records are available from the Ancient Near East.

AMULETS (Ăm′ ū lĕts) NAS, RSV translation of rare Hebrew word for charms, oaths used to describe an ornament women wore (Isa. 3:20). NIV translates charms; KJV, earrings.

AMZI (Ăm′ zī) Personal name meaning, "my strong one," or an abbreviation for Amaziah. *1.* Member of Temple singer family (1 Chron. 6:46). *2.* Ancestor of Adaiah, who helped build the second Temple (Neh. 11:12).

ANAB (Ā′ năb) Place name meaning, "grape." Joshua eliminated the Anakim from southern Judah including Hebron, Debir, and Anab (Josh. 11:21). Joshua allotted the mountain city to Judah (Josh. 15:50). Located at modern Khirbet Anab about fifteen miles southwest of Hebron.

ANAH (Ā′ năh) Personal name meaning, "answer." *1.* Mother of Oholibamah, a wife of Esau (Gen. 36:2), and grandmother of Jeush, Jalam, and Korah (36:14). RSV reads "daughter" as "son." This would allow this Anah to be related to or identified with Anah 2 below. In Genesis 36:24 Anah is noted for having found "mules in the wilderness" (KJV) or "hot springs in the desert" (NIV; compare NAS; RSV). Here Zibeon is still Anah's father as in 36:2, but this Anah is masculine. In 36:29 Anah is a Horite chief living in Seir. *2.* A son of Seir and brother of Zibeon (Gen. 36:20).

ANAHARATH (Ȧ·nā′ hȧ·răth) Place name meaning, "gorge." City on border of Issachar (Josh. 19:19) located possibly at modern Tell el-Mukharkhash between Mount Tabor and the Jordan.

ANAIAH (Ȧ·naî′ ăh) Personal name meaning, "Yahweh answered." Ezra's assistant when Ezra read the law to the post-exilic community (Neh. 8:4). He or another man of the same name signed Nehemiah's covenant to obey God's law (Neh. 10:22).

ANAK, ANAKIM (Ā′ năk, Ăn′ ȧ·kĭm) Personal and clan name meaning, "long-necked" or "strong-necked." The ancestor named Anak had three children: Ahiman, Sheshai, Talmai (Num. 13:22). They lived in Hebron and the hill country (Josh. 11:21) before being destroyed by Joshua. Their remnants then lived among the Philistines (Josh. 11:22). These tall giants were part of the Nephilim (Gen. 6:4; Num. 13:33). Arba was a hero of the Anakim (Judg. 14:15). The spelling Anakims puts the English plural "s" on to the Hebrew plural "im."

ANAKITES NIV translation of Anakim. See *Anakim.*

ANAM (Ā′ năm) NAS reading of 1 Chronicles 1:11, interpreting Anam as an individual rather than as a tribe or nation. See *Anamim.*

ANAM MELECH (Ă·năm′ mĕ·lĕch) Personal name meaning, "Anu is king." A god of the Sepharvites, who occupied part of Israel after the Northern Kingdom was exiled in 721 B.C. Worshipers sacrificed children to this god (2 Kings 17:31).

ANAMIM (Ăn′ à·mĭm) A tribe or nation called "son of Egypt" in Genesis 10:13. No further information is known about these people. See *Anam.*

ANAMITES (Ăn′ à·mītes) NIV translation of Anamim. See *Anamim.*

ANAN (Ā′ năn) Personal name meaning, "cloud." Signer of Nehemiah's covenant to obey God (Neh. 10:26).

ANANI (Ă·nā′ nī) Personal name meaning, "cloudy" or "he heard me." Descendant of David's royal line living after the return from Exile (1 Chron. 3:24).

ANANIAH (Ăn·à·nī′ ah) Personal name meaning, "Yahweh heard me." *1.* Grandfather of Azariah, who helped Nehemiah repair Jerusalem (Neh. 3:23). *2.* Village where tribe of Benjamin dwelt in time of Nehemiah (Neh. 11:32). It may be located at Bethany, east of Jerusalem.

ANANIAS (Ăn à nī′ às) Greek form of the Hebrew name Hananiah, which means "Yahweh has dealt graciously." *1.* Husband of Sapphira (Acts 5:1–6). They sold private property, the proceeds of which they were to give to the common fund of the early Jerusalem church (Acts 4:32–34). They did not give all the proceeds from the sale, as they claimed, and both were struck dead for having lied to the Holy Spirit (Acts 5:3,10). *2.* A disciple who lived in the city of Damascus (Acts 9:10–19). In response to a vision he received from the Lord, this Ananias visited Saul (Paul) three days after Saul had his Damascus road experience. Ananias laid his hands on Saul, after which Saul received both the Holy Spirit and his sight. Acts 9:18 may imply that Ananias was the one who baptized Saul. *3.* The Jewish high priest Ananias from A.D. 47 to 58 (Acts 23:2; 24:1). As high priest, he was president of the Jewish court known as the Sanhedrin which tried Paul in Jerusalem (Acts 23). As was typical of high priests who belonged to the aristocratic Jewish group known as the Sadducees, he was quite concerned to appease Roman authorities and representatives. This desire may have prompted Ananias to take such a personal interest in the case of Paul (Acts 24:1–2), since some Roman authorities suspected the apostle of sedition against Rome (Acts 21:38). Because of Ananias' pro-Roman sentiments, he was assassinated by anti-Roman Jewish revolutionaries at the outbreak of the first great Jewish revolt against Rome in the year A.D. 66. See *Sadducees; Sanhedrin.*

ANATH (Ā′ năth) Personal name either meaning, "answer" or was the name of a Canaanite god. Father of Shamgar, a judge of Israel (Judg. 3:31).

ANATHEMA (Ă·nà′ thĕ·mà) Someone or something sacrificed to God for destruction in fulfillment of a vow. Greek translation of Hebrew *cherem,* the holy war ban imposing destruction of war booty (Lev. 27:28; Deut. 20:10–18). See *Ban.* Paul invoked the curse of the ban on anyone who did not love the Lord (1 Cor. 16:22). This may have been a technical term in the early church meaning to exclude from church membership. Paul echoed similar sentiments in Romans 9:3, saying he would be cut off from Christ if that were the means to save his Jewish people. Spiritual gifts, especially ecstatic prophecy, do not cause people to say "Jesus is anathema" (1 Cor. 12:3; NAS note). A person preaching any gospel except the gospel of grace promising justification through faith alone should be under the curse, that is anathema (Gal. 1:8–9).

ANATHOTH (Ăn′ à·thôth) Personal and place name. *1.* A city assigned to the tribe of Benjamin, located about three miles northeast of Jerusalem (Josh. 21:18). King Solomon sent Abiathar the priest there after removing him as high priest (1 Kings 2:26–27). It was also the home of Jeremiah the prophet, who may have been a priest in the rejected line of Abiathar (Jer. 1:1). Though Jeremiah was opposed and threatened by the citizens of Anathoth (Jer. 11:21–23) he purchased a field there from his cousin Hanameel in obedience to the word of the Lord to symbolize ultimate hope after Exile (Jer. 32:6–15). Anathoth was overrun by the Babylonians, but resettled following the Exile (Neh. 7:27; 11:32). *2.* The eighth of nine sons of Becher, the son of Benjamin (1 Chron. 7:8). *3.* A chief that is a family or clan leader, who along with 84 other priests, Levites, and leaders signed a covenant that the Israelites would obey the law of God given through Moses (Neh. 10:19).

ANCESTORS are those from whom a person is descended and in biblical history were honored. **Old Testament** While the word, *ancestor,* is only found in one Old Testament verse (Lev. 26:45), the number of genealogies tracing family lines in the Old and New Testament indicates that ancestors were significant to the Israelites. Israel honored her ancestors. Leaders and prophets implored the Israelites to remember their heritage and the God of their forefathers.

The Old Testament includes thirteen principal genealogical lists. (See *Genealogies.*) Scholars believe there are a number of purposes for these genealogies including identification, establishment of rights, and verification of racial purity. One of the more obvious reasons was to establish the legitimacy of an individual in office or to provide an individual with added importance. Such genealogies are generally lists of male ancestors, although women are included when of historical significance (Gen. 11:29; 22:23; Num. 26:33; 27:1–11).

A remarkable feature of the biblical account of Israel's ancestors is the fact that they are not idealized but portrayed as fallible mortals. What made them great was not their moral excellence nor heroic deeds but that God had chosen them for a purpose.

New Testament As in the Old Testament, ancestors are honored in the New Testament. Paul was encouraged by remembering the faith of Timothy's grandmother and mother (2 Tim. 1:5). In Hebrews, the preacher encouraged the Jewish converts to remember the faithful believers who have gone before them (Heb. 11).

The New Testament includes two genealogies both of which trace the lineage of Jesus Christ. Matthew traces Jesus' lineage to Abraham (Matt. 1:1–17) while Luke traces the lineage to Adam, the son of God (Luke 3:23–38).

Ancestor Worship Ancestor worship is the adoration or payment of homage to a deceased parent or ancestor. Such worship was usually reserved for deities. Among ancient Israel's neighbors, there are several instances of deification of ancestors (Mesopotamian mythology and Egyptian kings). There may be one instance of ancestor worship recorded in the Bible. Ezekiel 43:7–9 may suggest that the bodies of Israel's dead kings were being worshiped. This practice of ancestor worship was condemned and forbidden.

Cult of The Dead Much like ancestor worship, the cult of the dead involves adoration of the deceased. The cult of the dead goes a step beyond adoration, however, seeking to maintain or manage a relationship with the dead. The cult of the dead involves the beliefs that certain departed spirits must be fed or honored and that they can be channels of information with the spiritual world.

While ancestor worship was not common among Israel or her neighbors, the cult of the dead was widely practiced. The belief in an afterlife was apparently universal in the Ancient Near East. The provision of food, drink, and artifacts within tombs is an indication of the belief that the departed spirit would have need of such things.

Though Israel was forbidden to practice the cult of the dead, she often departed from God's injunctions and engaged in the worship of pagan deities. Wayward Israelites were also guilty of practicing the cult of the dead (1 Sam. 28). Israel was specifically warned not to offer to the dead (Deut. 26:14). God warned them through the prophets not to consult the dead in an effort to learn the future (Isa. 8:19; 65:4). Such acts were considered by the prophets to be dangerously at odds with God's will (1 Sam. 28:7). See *Burial; Divination and Magic; Genealogies; Necromancy.*

Larry Bruce

ANCHOR A weight held on the end of a cable that when submerged in water holds a ship in place. Anchors were made of stone, iron, and lead during biblical times. The ship on which Paul sailed to Rome let down four anchors as it approached Malta (Acts 27:29–30,40). "Anchor" is used in a figurative sense in Hebrews 6:19 where the hope of the gospel is compared to "an anchor of the soul, both sure and steadfast"—that is, a spiritual support in times of trial.

ANCIENT OF DAYS is a phrase used in Daniel 7 to describe the everlasting God. Ancient of days literally means "one advanced in (of) days" and may possibly mean "one who forwards time or rules over it."

Several biblical passages are related in terms and ideas with Daniel 7 (Gen. 24:1; Job 36:26; Ps. 50:1–6; 55:19; 1 Kings 22:19–20; Isa. 26:1—27:1; 44:6; Ezek. 1; Joel 3:2). It is impossible to determine the origin or original meaning of this term. However, in ancient Ugaritic literature, the god *El* is designated as "the father of years."

Coupled with the figures of speech in the context of Daniel 7, Ancient of days suggests age, antiquity, dignity, endurance, judgment, and wisdom. It clearly describes Yahweh, the God of Israel. *J. J. Owens*

ANDREW (Ăn′ drēw) A disciple of John the Baptist who became one of Jesus' first disciples and led his brother Simon to Jesus. Because of John the Baptist's witness concerning Jesus, Andrew followed Jesus to His overnight lodging and became one of His first disciples. Subsequently Andrew brought his brother Simon to Jesus (John 1:40–41). He was a fisherman by trade (Matt. 4:18). He questioned Jesus about His prophesy concerning the Temple (Mark 13:3). Andrew brought the lad with his lunch to Jesus, leading to the feeding of the five thousand (John 6:8). He and Philip brought some Greeks to see Jesus (John 12:22). In the Bible, he is mentioned for the last time in Acts 1:13. He figures prominently in several early extra-biblical church traditions. He is believed to have been killed on an x-shaped cross. See *Apostles; Disciples.*

ANDRONICUS (Ăn·drŏ·nī′ cŭs) An apostle and thus probably an eyewitness of the risen Christ. Paul greeted this Jewish Christian as one honored by the church, one who had suffered in prison for his faith, and one who had been a Christian longer than Paul (Rom. 16:7). Evidently he lived in Rome when Paul wrote Romans. See *Apostle.*

ANEM (Ā′ něm) Place name meaning, "fountains." A city given the Levites from the territory of Issachar (1 Chron. 6:73). Joshua 21:29 lists the city as En-gannim.

ANER (Ā′ nēr) Personal and place name. *1.* An ally of Abraham in the battle against the coalition of kings in Genesis 14. *2.* A city from tribe of Manasseh given to Levites (1 Chron. 6:70). In Joshua 21:25 the Levites' city is called Taanach. See *Taanach.*

ANETHOTHITE KJV reading for Anathothite in 2 Samuel 23:27. See *Anathoth.*

ANGEL is a heavenly messenger who either delivers a message to humans, carries out God's will, praises God, or guards God's throne.
Bible Terms The term "angel" is derived from the Greek word *angelos* which means "messenger." *Angelos* and the Hebrew equivalent, *malak* (which also means "messenger"), are the two most common terms used to describe this class of beings in the Bible. In general, in texts where an angel appears, his task is to convey the message or do the will of the God who sent him. Since the focus of the text is on the message, the messenger is rarely described in detail.

Another set of terms used to describe angels focuses not on angels as mediators between God and persons, but on God's heavenly entourage. Terms such as "sons of God," "holy ones," and "heavenly host" seem to focus on angels as celestial beings. As such, these variously worship God, attend God's throne, or comprise God's army. These terms are used typically in contexts emphasizing the grandeur, power, and/or acts of God.

A third category of heavenly beings is that of winged angels. Cherubim and seraphim make their most memorable appearances in the visions of Ezekiel (1:4–28; 10:3–22) and Isaiah (6:2–6). Cherubim function primarily as guards or attendants to the divine throne. Seraphim appear only in Isaiah's vision and there attend God's throne and voice praises. All three categories present us with heavenly beings in service to God.
Angelic Hierarchy Some scholars suggest that a heavenly "host" (i.e. "army") must have order and that references to archangels (1 Thess. 4:16; Jude 9) and a special class of angels which has intimate fellowship with God such as the seraphim of Isaiah 6:2–6, indicate that angels are organized in a rigidly fixed rank system. Some authors even attempt to list their ranks and duties.
Angelic Appearance The appearance of angels varies. Only cherubim and seraphim are represented with wings. Often in the Old Testament angels appear as ordinary men. Sometimes, however, their uniqueness is evident as they do things or appear in a fashion clearly non-human (Gen. 16:7–11; Ex. 3:2; Num. 22:23; Judg. 6:21;

13:20; John 20:12). The brilliant white appearance common to the New Testament angel is not a feature of the Old Testament image.
Creation of Angels Angels are created beings. Only God is eternal. But when God created angels the Bible never reveals. If the "us" in Genesis 1:26 is a reference to God's angelic court, then the angels are simply present at the creation; their origin is not explained.
Guardian Angels Jesus' comment in Matthew 18:10 and some passages which assign protective roles to angels (for example, Michael, angelic prince over Israel, Dan. 12:1; angels of specific churches in Daniel 10:13; Acts 12:15; Revelation 1:20; 2—3) imply that a heavenly counterpart represents each person in heaven. This evidence is commonly used to assert that each individual has a "guardian" angel assigned to him or her by God. The term, "guardian angel," however, is not biblical, and the idea is at best only implied in these passages.
Old Testament Each of the various types of literature in the Old Testament has its own concerns, and angels appear in the texts in ways appropriate to each. Those books which narrate the great acts of God (Gen., Ex., Num., Judg., 1 and 2 Sam. and 1 and 2 Kings) contain numerous references to angels. In these books, especially at key points, God reveals Himself and acts on behalf of His people. Sometimes He does this directly, sometimes in the person of an angel. Often the distinction between God's action and the angel's is blurred to the point that they seem synonymous (Gen. 19:13,24; Ex. 3:2,4).

The angel's function as messenger or agent of God is acted out in terms of proclamation: revealing the will of God and/or announcing key events (Gen. 19:1–22; Ex. 3:2–6; Judg. 2:1–5; 13:2–23); protection: ensuring the well-being or survival of God's people (Ex. 14:19,20; 1 Kings 19:1–8); and punishment: enforcing the wrath of God on the wicked among the Jews and the Gentiles (Gen. 19:12–13; 2 Sam. 24:17; 2 Kings 19:35). In addition, some passages reflect popular ideas about angels (2 Sam. 14:17,20) which the text records but does not necessarily affirm.

In the books of the prophets, angels rarely are mentioned. The most prominent exceptions are the heavenly visions of Isaiah and Zechariah.
New Testament Much of the pattern observed in the Old Testament is repeated in the New. The majority of references to angelic activity are in the narrative books (the Gospels and Acts). The epistles include only some brief references to angels; several books do not mention them specifically at all. Hebrews with its lengthy contrast between Jesus and the angels is exceptional (Heb. 1:3—2:16). The Apocalypse of John in its visionary nature, apocalyptic style, and reference to angels is comparable to parts of Daniel, Zechariah, and Isaiah.

The basic tasks of proclamation, protection, and punishment are again the focus (Matt. 1:20–24; 4:11; Acts 12:7–11) while references to the nature of angels are very brief.

What is perhaps most remarkable is what the New Testament texts do not say about angels. The interbiblical period, under Persian and Greek influences, had seen an explosion of speculation about angels. Angels (or comparable spiritual beings) in detailed hierarchies came to be understood by many as necessary mediators between God and humanity. Knowing the names, ranks, and how to manipulate these lesser spiritual beings enabled one to gain blessings in this life and attain the level of the divine in the next.

The New Testament texts contain no developed angelic hierarchy and do not present angels as semi-independent lesser gods. Angels are not used to explain the existence of evil, nor are they needed as intermediaries or as agents of revelation. See *Cherubim; Demons; Seraphim.*

Mike Martin

ANGER See *Wrath.*

ANGLE, THE, THE ANGLE OF THE WALL See *Turning of the Wall.*

ANIAM (Å·nī′ ăm) Personal name meaning, "I am a people," "I am an uncle," or "mourning of the people." A member of tribe of Manasseh (1 Chron. 7:19).

ANIM (Ā′ nĭm) Place name meaning, "springs." City given tribe of Judah (Josh. 15:50). Located at modern Khirbet Ghuwein at-Tahta, eleven miles south of Hebron.

ANIMALS Animals populate the biblical world, giving life and interest to many biblical episodes. We do not always have the specific information we would like about these characters of the Bible. **Mammals** A mammal is defined as any class of higher vertebrates including humans and all other animals that nourish their young with milk secreted by mammary glands and have their skin more or less covered with hair." Numerous kinds of animals that fall into this category are mentioned in the Bible. Those mentioned in the New Testament, as a general rule, can be identified with a high degree of certainty. Those in the Old Testament are not as easy to identify. **Domestic** The people of Scripture tamed many animals for use in food production, military endeavors, and transportation.

1. ASS The ass or donkey was a common beast of burden in biblical times and was similar to donkeys of today but larger. This animal appears more than 120 times in Bible.

Centuries before the age of the patriarchs, the ass had been domesticated in Western Asia. They appear in Mesopotamia (onager) and Egypt three thousand years before Christ. The Nubian wild ass of Egypt has been identified as the ass of Palestine and the Bible. A larger animal than the European ass of today, this animal was used for riding (Num. 22:21; Judg. 5:10), as a beast of burden (1 Sam. 16:20), and for agricultural work (Deut. 22:10). When the Israelites returned to Palestine from the Babylonian captivity, they brought with them 6,720 asses (Ezra 2:67), about six times the number of horses and camels they possessed. While some people used the ass for food, this animal was considered unclean by the Israelites and thus considered unacceptable to eat. The ass was covered by the sabbath rest regulations, and the firstborn was redeemed (Ex. 13:13). While the horse was the primary mount for the warrior, the ass was used by those who traveled in peace. Jesus' choice of an ass as His riding animal for His triumphal entry into Jerusalem symbolized His role as the Prince of Peace (Zech. 9:9; Matt. 21:1–5). Before the twentieth century, ass caravans crossed the Sahara Desert, traveling between Morocco and the Red Sea.

2. CAMEL A camel is a large, hump-backed ruminant (chews cud) of Asia and Africa. It was used to transport burdens or passengers.

The camel has been called the "ship of the desert," being a primary mode of transportation

The horse, originally brought into Palestine from Persia, is still useful to Israeli shepherds.

The camel, particularly adapted to travel in hot, dry climates, is thus a valuable commodity in Israel.

for taking goods and people across dry, hot terrain. Recent discoveries show it was domesticated before 2000 B.C. When camels were introduced into Palestine is a matter of ongoing debate. Since this animal has the capacity to store several days' supply of water in its stomach, it is ideally suited for such work. In addition, the storage of fat in its hump makes it possible for the camel to subsist on little food when taking a desert journey. They were counted among the riches of Job (Job 1:3). Camel hair was used for tents and for clothes (Mark 1:6).

3. CATTLE Cattle are domesticated quadrupeds used as livestock. In the Bible, the term commonly refers to all domesticated animals.

Ox, bull, calf, and cow are among the names for cattle in the Bible. Sheep, goats, and other domesticated animals are also included under the designation of cattle (Gen. 1:24; John 4:12). The land of Goshen, where the Hebrews settled during the time of Joseph, was rich in cattle. From bones found at Megiddo, one archaeologist has identified cattle in ancient Israel as the present small Beiruti race, while another has identified five types of cattle of Gezer. Cattle were valued for sacrifices, for food and as work animals (Deut. 25:4; Luke 14:19). They were divided into clean and unclean classifications (Lev. 5:2) and were covered by the law of firstlings and sabbath rest (Ex. 13:12; 20:12). Bullocks and calves were used for sacrifices. Possession of considerable live-stock was a sign of wealth (Gen. 13:2; 1 Sam. 25:2).

4. COW Cow designates domestic bovine animals, especially the female.

Cows are mentioned in relation to giving birth and nurturing calves (Lev. 22:27–28; 1 Sam. 6:7). They were among the cattle gift that Jacob offered to Esau (Gen. 32:15). Amos called the wealthy, selfish women of Samaria "cows of Bashan" (Amos 4:1), referring to the area that was well known for raising cows (Deut. 32:14). See *Cattle* above.

5. DOG The dog was a scavenger animal that often ran wild. They were sometimes kept as house pets. In Mark 7:27, Jesus probably was referring to the small dogs that people kept as pets. Some dogs evidently were used to herd sheep (Job 30:1). See below *Wild Dogs.*

6. DONKEY See *Ass* above.

7. GOAT A goat was a hollow-horned ruminant with long, floppy ears, usually covered with long, black hair. Sometimes, they were speckled.

One type of goat mentioned in the Bible has been identified as the Syrian or Mamber goat. Domesticated long before the biblical era, the goat in biblical times probably had long ears and backward-curving horns. Both male and female had horns. The most common color was black. It was a prominent source of food; the male also was used for sacrifices (Lev. 22:27). A goat (called a scapegoat) was selected at random once a year on the Day of Atonement to bear symbolically the sins of the nation of Israel (Lev. 16:10–22). The skin of the goat was used to make garments, musical instruments, and water bottles; goat hair was woven into fabrics (Ex. 26:7). Goats are extremely destructive to vegetation and thereby contribute to erosion, as they tear plants out of the soil. Some of the earliest drawings available depict goats eating on trees. Sheep and goats grazed in the same pasture, but it was necessary to separate the herds because the male goat was often hostile toward the sheep (Matt. 25:32). Today, goats are found in colors of black, grey, brown, white, and a variety of patterns and mixtures. See *Ibex* below.

8. HORSE A horse was a solid-hoofed animal that was used for riding, as a war animal, and for transporting goods.

Evidence indicates that the horse was introduced into the Middle East two thousand years before Christ. These animals evidently were brought to the area from Persia by the Hyksos warriors who invaded Egypt. It is believed that the horse originally came from Central Asia. The horse is mentioned more than 150 times in the Bible, with the earliest reference being found in Genesis 47:17. However, there is no indication that the horse was in common use in Israel until the time of David and Solomon. The number of horses owned by Solomon was as many as twelve thousand. They were used to draw chariots (1 Kings 4:26; 10:26). Since the Mosaic law forbad the breeding of horses, Solomon imported horses from Egypt (Deut. 17:16; 2 Chron. 1:16). Likely, because of the superiority of the horse for warfare, this law was later ignored. The ruins of Solomon's well-known horse stables at ancient Megiddo are today marked as an historical and archeological site.

9. MULE A mule was the result of cross-breeding of a female horse and a male ass.

Since the Mosaic law forbade cross-breeding (Lev. 19:19), the Israelites imported mules (Eze. 27:14). They were used as war animals, for riding, and for carrying burdens (2 Kings 5:17). They were especially good for moving heavy burdens in mountainous areas, being better than the horse, ass, or camel. During David's reign, mules, along with horses, were a popular riding animal for royalty (1 Kings 1:33).

10. OX An ox is a large domesticated bovine. In the Old Testament it was extremely valuable as a work animal.

An important animal in the economy of Israel, oxen were essential for farm work. They were often yoked in pairs to do farm work and were used to transport burdens. Permitted as food, they were also offered as sacrifices (Deut. 14:4–6; Lev. 17:3–4). See *Cattle* above; *Wild Ox* below.

11. SHEEP A sheep is a stocky animal, larger than a goat, but has no beard.

A prominent animal in the sacrificial system of Israel, sheep are first mentioned in the Bible in Genesis 4:2 where Abel is identified as a keeper of sheep. They were the primary wealth of pastoral people. The sheep found in the Bible usually are the broad-tailed variety. The tail, weighing as much as fifteen pounds, was sometimes offered as a sacrifice (Ex. 29:22; Lev. 3:9). Of this species only the male had horns; females of other species did have horns. Rams' horns were used as trumpets (Josh. 6:44) and as oil containers (1 Sam. 16:1). Sheep were also a source for food and clothing. The Bible contains hundreds of references to sheep. Often, they are referred to as small cattle.

12. SWINE Swine are stout-bodied animals that have a large snout and thick skin.

The swine of the Bible, in most instances, probably were the wild pig, still common in Palestine. While Canaanite pagans kept herds of swine, the Mosaic law classified this animal as "unclean" and thus forbade the eating of its flesh (Lev. 11:7; Deut. 14:8). Isaiah condemned the eating of swine, dogs, and mice (65:4; 66:3,17). One who tended swine was barred from the Temple. A scavenger in ancient times, this animal became a symbol for baseness and paganism (Matt. 7:6). The fact that the prodigal son resorted to tending swine points to the extreme humiliation he experienced. Interestingly, Hezir, a proper Jewish name, is the same word as that translated swine (1 Chron. 24:15; Neh. 10:20).

Wild Wild animals provided food and sport, and were feared by biblical people.

1. ANTELOPE A fleet-footed animal with horns and about the size of a donkey, the antelope has a mane on the underside of its neck that makes it look like a large goat.

The pygarg (KJV), found in a list of animals in Deuteronomy 14:5, has not been identified with certainty but is considered by a number of scholars to be an antelope. Pygarg literally means "white rump" and is the Greek name for a kind of antelope. This animal has been connected with one that is native to North Africa. It has greyish-white hinder parts with a white patch on the forehead and twisted and ringed horns that point upward and backward. It also has been identified with the Arabian Oryx, an antelope of Iraq that has long horns stretching backward.

2. APE An ape is a large, semi-erect primate.

Apes are mentioned only twice in the Old Testament and are not described. The ape was not native to the Holy Land, but the Israelites were familiar with it. Some types were kept as pets. They were among the gifts that the navy of Hiram brought to Solomon (1 Kings 10:22; 2 Chron. 9:21).

3. BADGER The badger is a burrowing mammal, largest of the weasel family.

Disagreement exists about the translation of badger's skin in Exodus 25:5; 26:14 (badger, KJV; goat, RSV; sea cows, NIV; porpoise, NAS; fine leather, TEV, NRSV). This animal has also been

An Arab shepherd tends his herd in the Judean hills.

identified as the rock hyrax or coney. See *Coney* below.

4. BAT A bat is a quadruped with wings that nurses its offspring.

The Hebrew word translated *bat* is the generic name for many species of this mammal found in Palestine. Although the bat is listed among unclean birds in the Bible (Lev. 11:19), it belongs to the mammals, because it nurses its young. They live in caves. Modern zoologists have cited at least twenty different species in the area of Palestine.

5. BEAR The bear is a large, heavy mammal with long, thick, shaggy hair. It eats insects, fruit, and flesh.

The bear of the Bible has been identified with a high degree of certainty as the Syrian bear. They may grow as high as six feet and weigh as much as five hundred pounds. In biblical times the bear was a threat to vineyards and to herds of sheep and goats (1 Sam. 17:34–35). The two largest and strongest beasts of prey—the bear and the lion— are often listed together in the Bible (1 Sam. 17:37). A narrative about Elisha recorded in the Bible pictures the ferocity of the bear (2 Kings 2:23–24). Within the last century the Syrian bear has disappeared from the Holy Land, with the last bear being killed in Galilee just before World War II. It still survives in Syria, Persia, and Turkey.

6. BEHEMOTH A large beast.

Described in detail in Job 40:15–24, this animal has been variously identified as an elephant, hippopotamus, and the water buffalo, with the hippopotamus the more likely. Identification as a hippopotamus is based on the description in Job 40 of its size and strength, where it lived, and its manner of eating. The modern Hebrew word for the animal means *beast* or *cattle*. In Leviticus 11:2 the word translated *beasts* (KJV) is translated *animals* in the NIV.

7. BOAR A boar is a male swine (wild pig).

The boar was considered unclean by the Israelites. A menace to crops, it is mentioned only once in the Bible (Ps. 80:13). See *Swine* above.

8. CONEY The coney resembles a rabbit in size and color. The badger of Exodus 25:5; 26:14 has been identified by some scholars as the Syrian coney. See *Badger* above. It lives in rocky areas from the Dead Sea Valley to Mt. Hermon. The design of its feet helps the coney keep footing on slippery rocks.

9. DEER The deer is an antlered animal (all male and some female have antlers) with two large and two small hooves. It is believed that three species of deer lived in Palestine in Bible times: red, fallow, and roe. The red deer seems to be the one most easily identified and probably was the specie in the list of daily provisions for Solomon's table (1 Kings 4:23). The hart is the male red deer (Ps. 42:1), and the hind, the female (Job 39:1). The fallow deer, a small specie with especially large horns, is native to the Middle East and still survives in northern parts of that area. The tribe of Naphtali is described as "a doe set free that bears beautiful fawns" (Gen. 49:21). Certain characteristics of deer are noted in the Bible in the form of similes (Prov. 5:19; Isa. 35:6; Hab. 3:19).

10. DOG The dog was a scavenger animal that ran wild and was sometimes kept as a house pet. The dog in Bible times was considered an unclean animal. No specific breed has been identified. Dogs ran wild in village streets, often in packs (Ps. 22:16–21; 59:6). The term "dog" was a designation for the wicked (Isa. 56:10–11). Jews contemptuously called Gentiles, "dogs."

11. DUGONG The dugong is an aquatic mammal; the male has tusk-like teeth. The skin of the dugong is mentioned as a covering for the tabernacle (Ex. 25:5; KJV has badger's skins NAS, porpoise; NIV, sea cows; RSV, goat; NRSV, fine leather).

12. ELEPHANT While elephants are not specifically referred to in the Bible, ivory is mentioned in connection with King Solomon. Ivory was among the riches he imported (1 Kings 10:22).

13. GAZELLE The gazelle is a fleet-footed animal noted for its attractive eyes. See *Antelope* above. Native to the Middle East, this animal resembles an antelope but is smaller. They were considered clean by the Israelites and thus were permitted as food (Deut. 12:15,22).

14. HARE The hare is a long-eared animal that is a close relative of the rabbit. The hare was classed as unclean (Lev. 11:6; Deut. 14:7) and

Goats and a ram graze on a mountainside in Turkey. These animals were often chosen as offerings in ceremonies of sacrifice in biblical times.

were forbidden for Israelites to eat.

15. HIPPOPOTAMUS See *Behemoth* above.

16. HYENA The hyena is a striped scavenger that looks like a fox. The Hebrew word for hyena is found in the Bible as a geographical name (1 Sam. 13:18, Valley of Hyenas) and as the name of a town (Zeboim, Neh. 11:34). Once numerous in Palestine, the hyena appears only at night. Because of its scavenger activity of digging up graves, the hyena was a repulsive animal in the ancient world. They were easily tamed, and the Egyptians kept them as pets.

17. IBEX The ibex resembles a goat. The ibex has been identified as the wild goat of the Bible (1 Sam. 24:2; Ps. 104:18). The Nubian Ibex is found today in the area of Ein Gedi, an oasis near the Dead Sea.

18. JACKAL The jackal is a flesh-eating animal that resembles a fox. The same Hebrew word is translated both "jackal" and "fox." (In Judg. 15:4, NEB has jackals; NIV has foxes.) In Micah 1:8 and Isaiah 34:13 another Hebrew word is translated as "jackals" (KJV, dragon; NEB, wolf). The animals look similar, with the jackal having a broader head and shorter nose and ears than the fox. In temperament they are quite different. A noisy animal, the jackal is characterized by a nightly wailing. The jackal is a scavenger, while the fox is not. In contrast to the solitary character of the fox, the jackal is gregarious, but a place they haunt, humans have deserted (Isa. 13:22; Jer. 10:22). Luke 13:32 refers to the cunning and crafty nature of the fox.

19. LEOPARD The leopard is a large cat with yellow fur with black spots that form patterns. This animal was one of the most dangerous both to animals and human beings. Known for its gracefulness and speed, it was common in Palestine in Old Testament times, especially in the forests of Lebanon, but is seldom found there now. Five were killed around Jerusalem just before World War II, and one was killed in Southern Palestine near Beersheba soon after the war. The leopard still survives in Israel and is protected by the government. Two locations suggest habitats of leopards—Beth-nimrah ("leopards' house," Num. 32:36) and "waters of Nimrim" ("waters of leopards," Isa. 15:6; Jer. 48:34). In Hosea 13:7, the lurking, noiseless movement of the leopard symbolizes God's wrath. Isaiah illustrated the serene peace of God's kingdom as creating the seemingly impossible occurrence of a leopard lying down with the goat (Isa. 11:6). Some translate Habakkuk 1:8 as cheetah.

20. LION The lion is a large, swift-moving cat. The male has a heavy mane. Mentioned approximately 135 times in the Old Testament, the lion is the proverbial symbol for strength (Judg. 14:18). In Palestine, lions seemed to prefer the vegetation of the Jordan valley (Jer. 49:19). The Bible describes the lion as powerful and daring (Prov. 30:30) and distinguished by a terrifying roar (Isa. 5:29). It was a sign of the tribe of Judah (Gen. 49:9; Rev. 5:5). David defended his father's flock against lions and bears (1 Sam. 17:34–35). One of the most well-known stories in the Bible is about a young man being cast into a den of lions (Dan. 6:16–23). Since untamed lions were put in pits, it is possible that Daniel was cast into such a pit. Lions were kept as pets by pharaohs. The Hebrews seemed to make closer distinctions than does English in the lion family, since five unrelated Hebrew words are translated, "lion." They have disappeared from Palestine, with the last one killed near Megiddo in the thirteenth century.

21. MOLE The mole is a large rodent, grey in color. In Leviticus 11:30 some translate the Hebrew word as *chameleon* (NIV, NAS, RSV). Others translate, "mole" in Leviticus 11:29 (NAS, NEB), or in Isaiah 2:20 (NAS, RSV, KJV) See *Rodent* below.

22. MOUSE A mouse is a rodent with a pointed snout. As such it is unclean (Lev. 11:29). Mice were apparently feared as carriers of the plague (1 Sam. 6:4). See *Rodent* below.

23. OX The wild ox was a large beast that is believed to be the ancestor of domestic cattle. It symbolized ferocious strength. The Hebrew word translated *unicorn* in Numbers 23:22 (KJV) has been identified as the word for wild ox (NAS, NIV, RSV). Compare Psalm 22:21; 92:10. See *Ox* above.

24. PORCUPINE The porcupine or hedgehog is a large rodent that has stiff, sharp bristles mixed with its hair. Disagreement exists about the translation of the Hebrew word. Some feel porcupine is the correct translation. Others have various translations (NIV, owl; KJV, bittern; NEB, bustard).

25. PYGARG See *Antelope* above.

26. RAT A large rodent listed among the unclean animals (Lev. 11:29) but were eaten by a disobedient people (Isa. 66:17). See *Rodents* below.

27. RODENTS All small rodents are designated by the Hebrew *akhbar,* a generic word including both mice and rats. The Mosaic prohibition against eating rodents (Lev. 11:29) reveals their presence in the Holy Land. As a guilt offering for stealing the ark of the covenant, the Philistines were advised to send "five golden mice" to the Israelites when they returned the ark to them (1 Sam. 6:4, KJV; "rats," NIV). More than twenty varieties of small rodents have been identified in the Holy Land today.

28. WEASEL The weasel is a small mammal that is related to the mink. The weasel was common in the Holy Land, although mentioned only once in the Bible (Lev. 11:29; compare NAS, mole).

29. WHALE The whale is a large aquatic mammal that resembles a large fish (Ezek. 32:2; Jon. 1:17; Matt. 12:40).

The Greek word translated, "whale" in Matthew 12:40 (KJV) is also called "a great fish" (Jonah 1:17, NIV), "great creature" (Gen. 1:21; Ps. 148:7, NIV), "monster" (Job 7;12; Ezek. 32:2, NIV). The exact identification of the animal is impossible with present knowledge.

30. WOLF The wolf is a large wild canine that is thought to be the primary ancestor of the domestic dog. Common in Palestine in biblical times, the wolf constantly threatened sheep and shepherds and earned a reputation for viciousness (Gen. 49:27; Matt. 7:15; Luke 20:3). The wolf stalked prey at night (Jer. 5:6; Zeph. 3:3). Its method of attack is described in John 10:12. Its name is used symbolically to describe deceitful and greedy people (Ezek. 22:27; Acts 20:29).

Reptiles A reptile has been defined as "an animal that crawls or moves on its belly or on small short legs." This category of animals includes alligators, crocodiles, lizards, snakes, and turtles. It is generally agreed that, in many instances, the reptiles in the Bible cannot be specifically determined. Many times the same Hebrew word is translated in different ways. Leviticus 11:30 is a case in point. The same Hebrew word translated *lizard* in a number of translations is translated *crocodile* in the RSV. There does, however, seem to be a grouping of reptiles in this verse, even though the specific names may be difficult to determine.

1. ADDER The adder is a venomous snake. See *Serpent* below.

2. ASP The asp is a venomous snake. Modern

translations often use "cobra." See Isaiah 11:8 in various translations. See *Serpent* below.

3. CHAMELEON The chameleon is a kind of lizard that changes color according to its surroundings. See *Mole* above. The unique design of its eyes characterizes the chameleon. Each eyeball moves independently; thus it can look two ways at the same time. Feeding mostly on insects, the chameleon is harmless. In Palestine it lives in trees and bushes and hangs onto branches with its long tail.

4. COBRA The cobra is a deadly poisonous snake with loose skin on its neck that forms a hood when the cobra is excited. See *Asp.*

5. COCKATRICE Cockatrice designates a venomous snake. Cockatrice is the name for a legendary serpent. As used in the KJV, however, it is a venomous snake. Later versions translate the Hebrew word "adder" (RSV) and "viper" or "venomous snake" (NIV).

6. CROCODILE The crocodile is a large, thick-skinned, aquatic reptile. See *Lizard* below.

7. FROG The frog is a web-footed, amphibious animal. Frogs are mentioned prominently in connection with the ten plagues in Egypt, where frogs were quite common. The psalmist reminded the Israelites of plague devastation in Psalms 78; 105.

8. GECKO The gecko is a wall lizard. The gecko is a common type of lizard in the Holy Land. Sucking-disc toes enable it to run over walls and ceilings. Early versions translated the Hebrew word "ferret," while later scholars believe gecko is the correct translation (NAS, RSV, NIV). It is a harmless but repulsive-looking reptile.

9. LIZARD The lizard is a long-bodied reptile that is distinguished from the snake by two sets of short legs. Several kinds of lizards are mentioned in Leviticus 11:30: gecko, monitor lizard, wall lizard, skink, and chameleon (NIV). One traveler identified as many as forty-four different species in Palestine.

10. SERPENT Serpent seems to be a general name for long-bodied reptiles, specifically snakes such as the adder and viper. The serpent is mentioned numerous times in the Bible. At least thirty-three different species may be found in Palestine. Translators use various terms to translate the eight Hebrew terms. The serpent—usual name for snake—has been a continuing symbol of evil and of the evil one. See *Adder; Asp; Cockatrice; Cobra;* above and *Viper* below.

11. SKINK The skink is a small lizard listed among the unclean animals (Lev. 11:30 NIV). Other translations render, "sand reptile" (NAS), "snail" (KJV), "sand lizard" (NRSV).

12. SNAKE See *Serpent* above.

13. TORTOISE The tortoise is a land turtle listed among the unclean animals (Lev. 11:29 KJV). Other versions have "great lizard" (RSV; NAS; NIV) instead of tortoise.

14. VIPER The viper is a venomous snake. See *Serpent* above.

See *Birds; Insects.* *Shirley Stephens*

ANISE (Ăn' īse) The KJV translation of the Greek term more properly translated as dill in Matthew 23:23. The KJV translates the corresponding Hebrew word as fitches in Isaiah 28:25,27 (but see *Fitches*). Dill is a leafy plant, resembling parsley. Dill was grown for its seeds, which were aromatic and used in cooking as a seasoning. See *Spice, Spices.*

ANKLET Ornamental rings worn above the ankles. The KJV has "tinkling ornaments about their feet" (Isa. 3:18; compare 3:16). Anklets were luxury items worn by the women of Jerusalem during the days of Isaiah. Archaeologists have recovered anklets that date to the biblical period. They are made of bronze, from $2\frac{1}{2}$ to $4\frac{1}{2}$ inches in diameter and from about $\frac{2}{10}$ to $\frac{4}{10}$ of an inch wide.

ANNA (Ăn' nà) An aged prophetess who recognized the Messiah when He was brought to the Temple for dedication (Luke 2:36). Anna, whose name means "grace," was the daughter of Phanuel of the tribe of Asher. After seven years of marriage, she was widowed and became an attendant of the Temple. She was eighty-four when she recognized the Messiah, thanked God for Him, and proclaimed to all hope for the redemption of Jerusalem.

ANNAS (Ăn' nàs), son of Seth, was a priest at the time John the Baptist began his public preaching (Luke 3:2). Evidently, Annas, whose name means "merciful," was appointed to the high priesthood about A.D. 6 by Quirinius, governor of Syria. Though he was deposed in A.D. 15 by Gratus, he continued to exercise considerable influence. When Jesus was arrested, He was taken before Annas (John 18:13). After Pentecost, Annas led other priests in questioning Peter and the other church leaders (Acts 4:6).

ANNUNCIATION Act of announcing or of being announced. The name is given the announcement to Mary by the angel Gabriel that she would give birth to a son who was to be named Jesus (Luke 1:26–38). This followed the account of Gabriel's announcement to Zacharias that he and his wife Elizabeth were to become the parents of John the Baptist. While the announcement to Mary about the Incarnation has become associated with the annunciation, the announcements to Samson (Judg. 13:2–5), Joseph (Matt. 1:20–25), and Zechariah (Luke 1:11–20) follow a similar pattern.

The Feast of the Annuniciation is celebrated on March 25 (Lady Day) by Roman Catholics, Anglicans, and Orthodox Christians. The first references to the feast, besides the Gelasian and Gregorian sacramentaries, are in acts of the Council of Toledo (656) and of the Trullan Council (692).

ANOINT describes the procedure of rubbing or smearing a person or thing, usually with oil, for the purpose of healing, setting apart, or embalming. A person can anoint himself, be anointed, or anoint another person or thing. While olive oil is the most common element mentioned in the Bible for use in anointing, oils produced from castor, bay, almond, myrtle, cyprus, cedar, walnut, and fish were also used. In Esther 2:12, for example, the oil of myrrh is used as a cosmetic.

The Hebrew verb *mashach* (noun, *messiah*) and the Greek verb *chrio* (noun, *christos*) are translated "to anoint." From ancient times the priests and kings were ceremonially anointed as a sign of official appointment to office, and as a symbol of God's power upon them. The act was imbued with an element of awe. David would not harm King Saul because of the anointing the king had received (1 Sam. 24:6). Likewise, Israel (Ps. 89:38), and even Cyrus (Isa. 45:1) are called God's anointed because of God's working through them. Israel came to see each succeeding king as God's anointed one, the *messiah* who would deliver them from their enemies and establish the nation as God's presence on the earth.

In the New Testament anoint is used to speak of daily grooming for hair (Matt. 6:17), for treating injury or illness (Luke 10:34), and for preparing a

Church of the Annunciation in Nazareth commemorating Gabriel's unprecedented announcement to Mary.

body for burial (Mark 16:1).

Christians see Jesus as God's Anointed One, the Savior (Acts 10:38). The same symbolism as in the Old Testament is employed in this usage: God's presence and power are resident in the anointing. Likewise, the Christian is anointed by God (2 Cor. 1:21; 1 John 2:27) for the tasks of ministry.   *Mike Mitchell*

ANON (Ă nŏn′) Archaic word meaning "immediately."

ANT See *Insects.*

ANTEDILUVIANS meaning, "before the Deluge," refers to those who lived before the Flood described in Genesis 6–8. The early chapters of Genesis affirm that the God of Israel is the God who created the world and who guides all of human history. Those chapters connect the history of all humankind to that of God's covenant people, and thus to salvation history.

The genealogy in Genesis 4 is framed by two accounts of violence—1) the murder of Abel by Cain and God's promise of seven-fold vengeance on anyone who harmed Cain (Gen. 4:8–16), and 2) the war song of Lamech, threatening seventy-seven fold vengeance for any injury (Gen. 4:23–24). In between we are told of the cultural achievements of the antediluvians. Cain is credited with building the first city. The three sons of Lamech are attributed with the origins of cattle raising (Jabal), music (Jubal), and metallurgy

(Tubal-cain). Since cultural achievements were often attributed to the gods in the Ancient Near East, the Scripture wants to emphasize that they are achievements of human beings created by the one God. The text is aware of parallel developments—beside the achievements of civilization stood the perennial violence which threatened it and used its technology for destructive purposes. This perpetual struggle to maintain order and to insure the proper use of cultural advances is a part of the human condition.

The longevity attributed to the antediluvians in Genesis 5 is the subject of study and debate. The ages of the antediluvians are reported somewhat differently in the Hebrew Bible (Masoretic Text), the Samaritan Pentateuch, and the Greek Old Testament (Septuagint). One traditional view is that these people lived longer because they were closer to the state in which God created human beings. Others say that their more simple life and vegetarianism (Gen. 2:16–17; 3:18b; and Gen. 9:3) allowed for longer life spans. Some consider the numbers symbolic.

The discovery of lists of Sumerian kings who reigned before the Flood has thrown light on the theological significance of the text. The Sumerian kings, who were considered gods, were said to have lived for tens of thousands of years. In contrast, the biblical antediluvians were clearly human. Genesis emphasizes the oneness of God and the distinction between the Creator and human beings who were created. See *Flood.*

Wilda W. Morris

ANTELOPE A grass-eating deerlike animal which does not appear in the KJV but does in NAS, NIV, NRSV, TEV, translating Hebrew *te'o,* a word translated in different ways by the earliest translations. The references may be to a large white antelope or oryx (*oryx leucoryx*) with striking long horns, black markings, and a tuft of black hair under its neck. It had a divided hoof and chewed the cud and so qualified as a clean animal to be eaten (Deut. 14:5). They were hunted and caught with nets (Isa. 51:20).

The Rhorr gazelle found in the biblical region is one species in the biblical family of antelopes.

ANTHOTHIJAH (Ăn·thō·thī′ jăh) A descendant of Benjamin (1 Chron. 8:24). The name may represent connection with city of Anathoth.

ANTHROPOLOGY The study of human beings; in biblical understanding involves who humans are in light of God's revelation in holy Scripture. **Old Testament** The Old Testament accounts of history, the poetry of Wisdom Literature, and the pronouncements of the prophets work together to provide the Old Testament picture of humans.

Stated in its most pointed form, the anthropological question asks, "What is man that thou art mindful of him, and the son of man that thou dost care for him?" (Ps. 8:4 RSV). The psalmist's intense wondering has no simple solution. Indeed, the biblical portrait of humans is complex and often paradoxical. On one hand, humans are depicted as the crowning center of God's creative activity, fearfully and wonderfully made (Gen. 1:26–31; 2:4–7; Ps. 8:6–8). On the other hand, humans are "like a breath," physically frail, spiritually weak, and unable to stand before the holiness and righteousness of God (Pss. 90:5–6; 103:13–16; 144:3–4; 146:3–4). In traditional theological studies, the doctrines of humanity and sin have often been examined as one. Indeed, they are different sides of the same coin.

The scriptural picture of persons is constantly confirmed by human experience. The biblical awareness and understanding of humanity is both personal and profound because God knows human beings even better than they know themselves. Psalm 139 is a poignant and frightening expression of this kind of knowledge. The conclusion of the psalmist in praise to God is "Thou knowest me right well" (Ps. 139:14b RSV). God's deep knowledge of humanity points out both humanity's significance and insignificance, worth and unworthiness, capabilities and inadequacies. Wherever humanity is found, the condition and situation of humanity is tempered by the intimate and passionate knowledge of God. Because of that knowledge, humans need never be alone. Because of that knowledge, humans are unable to hide from God (Ps. 139:7–12). Indeed, it is *only* God who knows humanity (Jer. 17:9–10).

God's profound knowledge of humanity is rooted in His initial act of creation. Simply stated, the Creator knows the created. Although the Genesis account of creation intentionally and purposefully tells much about God, the account also speaks volumes about humans. Genesis 1—2, for example, boldly affirms God as Creator and Lord of all. At the same time, though, the passage declares just as boldly that God's creation is good, indeed humanity is very good (Gen. 1:31). The passage explicitly portrays humans as the highest of God's created beings, the center of God's marvelous creation (Gen. 1:26–30). Much more than a proclamation of honor or favored position, this pronouncement should be regarded as a serious statement of responsibility. (See Luke 12:48.)

Two anthropological truths become recurring themes throughout the biblical record. First, a human being is a totality of being, not a combination of various parts and impulses. According to the Old Testament understanding, a person is not a body which happens to possess a soul. Instead, a person is a living soul. Genesis 2:7 relates God forming man "of dust from the ground" and breathing into his nostrils "the breath of life." (See Jer. 18:6.) The man became human when God breathed the breath of life. Because of God's activity, humanity became a special and unique part of creation. Because of God's breath of life, the man became "a living being" (Gen. 2:7). A person, thus, is a complete totality, made up of human flesh, spirit (best understood as "the life-force"), and *nephesh* (best understood as "the total self" but often translated as "soul"). Human flesh cannot exist alone. Neither can spirit or *nephesh* exist alone. Together, however, they comprise a complete person.

A second major anthropological truth originally proclaimed in the Genesis account of creation and echoed by later biblical writers affirms that a person is created in the image and likeness of God. The idea is explicitly stated in Genesis 1:26–31; 5:1–3; and 9:1–7. The idea is more implicit, but still present in Psalm 8. Specific New Testament references to the concept include 1 Corinthians 11:7; Colossians 3:1; and James 3:9. The created bears some kind of resemblance to the Creator. "Image" and "likeness" simply intensify the same truth. The two words do not signify different or unique aspects of the human person.

A better understanding of the image of God stresses the truth that all human beings are equally included. The image of God is expressed by two parallel ideas. First, the image of God refers to the human *capability* to respond to God and to enter into relationship with God. Second, the image of God refers to the human *responsibility* to respond to God and to enter into relationship with God. Obviously, this understanding of the image of God is unrelated to any kind of physical similarity. At the same time, it claims that the image and likeness include the total self, not only reasoning ability or traits of personality. Seeing the image of God in this light leads to the conclusion that people occupy a high place in God's creation. In fact, people are God's representative on earth, the possessor of God-given power and dominion over creation, and the only part of creation reflecting God in this way.

New Testament The place of people in God's activity of creation is parallelled by their place in God's activity of redemption. The New Testament insists that people have failed to accept the responsibility given in Genesis 1:29–30. It is equally insistent that God's high regard for humans has

not diminished. New Testament writers stress human sin throughout (Rom. 3:9–20; 6:23); still, the broader theme of God's love for all humanity is echoed at every turn. John 3:16 speaks of an intense and passionate love of a mighty God for all creation. The New Testament teachings about humanity, God, and salvation are clear: *despite* humanity's unworthiness, God loves with an everlasting love. In fact, the worth or value claimed by Scripture for humans is *because* of God's initial act of creation or God's great sacrifice through Jesus Christ. Human worth and dignity, whatever that may entail, is unavoidably tied to God. As a result, a proper theological conclusion would be "God loves people; *therefore* a person has value and worth." Human worth is based upon relationship with God.

The Old Testament truth that people exist as a totality remained firm in New Testament writings. In the New Testament scheme, four dimensions of life are designated in place of the Hebraic flesh, spirit, and *nephesh.* The body (Greek, *sōma*) is simply the shape or form of a person (1 Pet. 2:24; although Rom. 12:1 can best be translated "selves"). The soul (Greek, *psuche,* related to the Old Testament *nephesh*) points to the "total self." John 10:11 tells of Jesus "laying down his life for his sheep." The Greek word normally translated "life" in John 10:11 is *psuche,* the word for "soul." Jesus sacrificed *His total self* or *His whole being* for His sheep. Life in the spiritual dimension is called spirit (Greek, *pneuma*). Like its Old Testament counterpart, the New Testament root meaning of spirit refers to "wind," "breath," or "force." Spirit, therefore, is the energizing life-force, the innermost part of human beings (1 Cor. 2:10–11). While spirit seems to be the dimension whereby humans can cooperate with and respond to God, flesh is that dimension that represents human finitude and weakness. Similar to its Old Testament counterpart, flesh (Greek, *sarx*) in the New Testament suggests physical failing and the inability to transcend the physical dimension. It would be unwise, however, to conclude that, in itself, flesh is evil. (See John 1:14.) Jesus, the Word made flesh, was certainly not evil.

The New Testament illustrates four specific and distinct dimensions of human existence, but the writers of the New Testament affirm with the Old Testament writers that a human being is a totality, a complete whole. Quoting Deuteronomy 6:4, Jesus taught that "you shall love the Lord your God with all your heart, and with all your soul, and with all your mind, and with all your strength" (Mark 12:30). The message is clear: true love of God is love with the total person— heart, soul, mind, and strength. In the same light, "no one can serve two masters" (Matt. 6:24). Because a human being is a complete whole, a divided allegiance is impossible. This biblical idea of humans carries with it profound ethical and social implications. To understand the truth that a person is a total being is to see that ministry must focus upon every dimension of existence. True ministry is, therefore, concerned with the spiritual, the social, the physical, and the psychological.

While the Old Testament seems to affirm the survival of the image of God in people even after the Fall, it is also true that the original relationship between the Creator and the created has been altered. New Testament writers, in general, note the existence of the image even in "natural man" but, more significantly, see the proper restoration of the image of God in people through redemption in Jesus Christ (Rom. 8:29; 1 Cor. 11:7; Jas. 3:9). Proper relationship with God through Jesus Christ allows for the renewal of the true image of God. Unique to the New Testament view is the idea that ultimately the true image of God can be seen in Christ (John 12:45; 14:9; Col. 1:15; Heb. 1:3). With this in mind, Paul developed the theologically potent distinction between "the first man Adam" and "the last Adam" (1 Cor. 15:45–47).

From the standpoint of the complete biblical record, the doctrine of humanity includes at least two additional ideas. First, the doctrine of humanity is primarily based upon a concept of relationship. At its ultimate level, this relationship is portrayed as the encounter of a loving, seeking, powerful God with a weak, finite, sinful human being. Granting purpose and life to men and women, this relationship necessarily leads to relationships between human beings. The relationship of God and humanity in the Old Testament vision points directly to the relationships of human beings within Christ's church, a community of human beings called out to minister to all of God's creation.

A second idea is closely related to this. For the biblical writers, humans are at once individuals standing alone before God *and* members of a corporate community standing before God. The individual nature of humanity can be seen in God's call of Abraham, the psalmist's description of God's intimate knowledge, the ministry of Jesus with specific individuals in need, and Paul's understanding of humans as individual sinners. The corporate nature of humanity can be seen in the Old Testament concepts of family, tribe, nation, and kingdom, Jesus' calling out of a redemptive community of followers, and the establishment of the church as the corporate body of God's people on earth.

Theological Affirmations Despite the diversity and complexity of the biblical doctrine of humanity, several significant theological conclusions may be affirmed.

1. *Human beings have worth.* The biblical record explicitly and implicitly affirms the value and worth of humanity. This positive statement is grounded in God's creative activity, the ultimate plan of redemption that has been revealed in Jesus

Christ, and the ongoing care that God provides for all creation. The worth of humanity is not based on anything inherent in people but is the result of God choosing to grant worth and dignity to people. As such, the value of humanity is a God-given value.

2. *Human beings are frail and sinful.* The Bible affirms both explicity and implicity the weaknesses and shortcomings of human beings. Manifest as both physical weakness and spiritual failing, this frailty is seen properly in contrast to the holiness and righteousness of God. The condition of humanity leads to the conclusion that all individuals are dependent upon God and that salvation truly is a matter of God's grace, not human effort or striving.

3. *Human beings exist as individuals before God.* God confronts, convicts, and calls out human beings as individuals. God's knowledge of people is intimate, personal, and profound. God's love is offered to human beings individually. The relationship between humanity and God is the most significant and vital part of human existence.

4. *Human beings exist in community.* God also confronts, convicts, and calls out communities of people. The relationship of an individual with God is necessarily tied to relationships with others. This profound theological truth leads to serious questions of group identity, corporate responsibility, and ethical consciousness. Related to this affirmation is the biblical truth that humans exist primarily for relationship. This seems to be a central focus of creation, salvation, and corporate Christian identity.

5. *Human beings exist as complete, total beings.* Although the biblical picture of humanity acknowledges several distinct dimensions of existence, the dimensions form one whole. In biblical terms, the physical dimension, the spiritual dimension, and the social dimension are absolutely and inseparably tied together. God created humans to be total persons. As a result, the church is called to minister and to proclaim the message of Jesus Christ to the total person. See *Salvation; Sin; Ethics; Death; Eternal Life; Creation.*

Barry Stricker

ANTHROPOMORPHISM (Ăn·thrō·pō·mŏr-phĭs·m) is the process of applying human characteristics to a god, an animal, or an inanimate object. The English word is derived from combining two Greek words—*anthropos,* which means "man" or "mankind," and *morphe,* which means "form" or "shape." Thus, anthropomorphism is giving human form to something not inherently human. In biblical studies the term focuses on those human characteristics applied to God.

The Biblical Tension Biblical faith emerged in a world where deities often were portrayed in human and/or animal form and were worshiped as physical images. Persons in primitive religions first sought spiritual reality in their daily experiences. Rocks, trees, the sun, the earth, or other natural objects were the focus for their sense of mystery and awe. Later religious thought centered in human experience, and mankind began to personify its gods in graven or molten images.

Despite its prohibitions against idolatry, Israel's faith did not flee from every attempt to personify God. Unlike some philosophical religions, biblical faith does not reduce God to mere abstractions. Instead, God is affirmed as active in daily life. Though eternal and transcendent, He also is personal and present. He reveals Himself through historical actions and relationships with His people.

Actions and Relationships Anthropomorphism grows naturally in a faith that views God as active and relational. Israel received God's revelation and expressed its faith in this personal God who had chosen them. Its religious expressions also were drawn from life (and especially from personal relationships); but the form of God was preserved in mystery, and His character was revealed rather than conceived.

Thus anthropomorphic imagery thrives in the Bible. In the typically concrete fashion of the Hebrew mind, the inspired writers of the Old Testament speak of God's eyes, ears, hands, and feet; but they meticulously avoid letting the descriptions become too tangible and concrete. God's movement among humanity is described as walking; His acceptance of sacrifice is through smell; His awareness of human plight is through sight; His feelings are represented in terms of human emotion. He rules as king, tends as shepherd, loves as father. This picturesque language is metaphor, but it is more. It is faith affirming the reality, uniqueness, and sovereignty of God.

The Image of God Behind the anthropomorphisms of the Old Testament lies another foundational concept. Genesis speaks of mankind—both male and female—being created in God's "image" and "likeness" (Gen. 1:26–27; 5:1–2; 9:6). Here is the reverse of anthropomorphism. Rather than creating an image of God out of personal experience or imagination, mankind *is* an image of God.

In some ways, then, anthropomorphic presentations of God and theomorphic (in the form or image of *theos,* "God") presentations of mankind are reciprocal. What we are intended to be is most fully reflected in what He is (see 1 John 3:2). What He is can be understood more fully in the familiar and concrete images of daily life and experience. Jesus' teachings certainly underscore this mutual relationship. His parables especially speak of God in anthropomorphic terms.

The Incarnation While the Old Testament concept of the image of God is reflected in the New Testament (see 1 Cor. 11:7; Jas. 3:9), the idea is transformed in light of the incarnation. In a sense, the ultimate anthropomorphism is seen in the eternal Word of God becoming flesh and dwelling among us (John 1:14). The uniqueness of God's revelation in Christ so overshadows the earlier concept that some New Testament writers present the image of God in terms of the perfect image revealed in Christ (2 Cor. 4:4; Col. 1:15; Heb. 1:3; compare John 1:14; 12:45; 14:9). The image of God in mankind is so eclipsed by the revelation in Christ that one must "put on the new man, which is renewed in knowledge after the image of him that created him" (Col. 3:10; see Eph. 4:24).

Michael Fink

ANTICHRIST describes a particular individual or a group of people who oppose God and His purpose.

Old Testament The Old Testament described the antichrist in various ways. Especially in Daniel, there arose the expectation of one who would oppose the Lord and His people Israel. This evil leader was referred to as the king of the north (11:40) who would come with a mighty army to crush the nations, to persecute the righteous (7:25), to bring death (8:10), and to set up his throne in the Temple (8:13). This latter event the Jews term the "abomination of desolation." Many Jews viewed the arrival of Antiochus Epiphanes IV as the embodiment of these verses. Yet in the mind of many Jews, the rule of Antiochus did not meet the full expectations of these Scriptures. There evolved a permanent expectation of an antichrist figure in Judaism. In later Jewish history such Roman figures as Pompey and Caligula were identified with the antichrist.

In Daniel one also finds a collective antichrist. In 7:7–28 the Fourth Empire was viewed as a collective antichrist. In later Judaism, the Fourth Kingdom or the collective antichrist was viewed as the Roman Empire (2 Baruch 26–40; 4 Ezra 5:3–4).

New Testament In the New Testament, the only use of the term "antichrist," is in the Johannine epistles. 1 John 2:18 speaks of the antichrist who is the great enemy of God and, in particular, antichrists who precede that great enemy. These antichrists were human teachers who had left the church. Such antichrists deny the incarnation (1 John 4:3) and Christ's deity (1 John 2:2). In 2 John 7, the antichrists are identified as deceivers who teach that Jesus Christ did not come in the flesh. The concept of the antichrist appears in the term "false Christ" (pseudo christos) (Matt. 24:24; Mark 13:22). Mark and Matthew apparently expected a Roman ruler to once again enter the Temple as did Antiochus and Pompey. In Revelation 13:3, the beast from the sea is often viewed as an antichrist figure. There John may have looked for a return of the emperor Nero.

In 2 Thessalonians 2:1–12, the antichrist figure is armed with satanic power and is fused with Beliar, a satanic being. In this passage the Roman government is viewed as restraining its power. In Revelation, the Roman caesar is the evil force.

Contemporary Concerns Christians today have differing views of the antichrist figure. Dispensationalists look for a future Roman ruler who will appear during the tribulation and will rule over the earth. Those in the amillennialist school interpret the term symbolically.   *James L. Blevins*

ANTIMONY (An' tĭ mō ny) A silvery-white, brittle, metalic chemical element of crystalline structure, found only in combination. It is used in alloys with other metals to harden them and increase their resistance to chemical actions. Compounds of antimony are used in medicines, pigments, matches, and fireproofing. In the NRSV and the NAS antimony is used as a translation of the Hebrew terms *'abne-puk* to describe the materials used to build the Temple (1 Chron. 29:2; see Isa. 54:11; NIV has turquoise; REB and TEV stones for mosaic work; KJV, glistering stones and stones with fair colors, respectively). It is likely that *'abne-puk* refers to some sort of cement or mortar used in the creation of mosaics, which it is suggested, would make precious stones appear larger and more colorful. In two other passages (2 Kings 9:30; Jer. 4:30), *puk* is consistently translated as eye paint. One of Job's daughters was named Keren-hapuk—that is, "horn of eye paint" (Job 42:14).

A great Roman aqueduct at Antioch of Pisidia brought water to the city from the mountains to the north.

ANTINOMIANISM (Ăn tĭ nō' mĭ ăn ĭsm) The false teaching that since faith alone is necessary for salvation, one is free from the moral obligations of the law. The word *antinomianism* is not used in the Bible, but the idea is spoken of. Paul appears to have been accused of being an antinomian (see Rom. 3:8; 6:1,15). While it is true that obedience to the law will never earn salvation for anyone (Eph. 2:8–9), it is equally true that those who are saved are expected to live a life full of good works (see, for example, Matt. 7:16–20; Eph. 2:10; Col. 1:10; Jas. 2:14–26). Since we have been freed from the dominion of sin through faith in Jesus, we have also been freed to practice the righteousness demanded by God (Rom. 6:12–22).

ANTIOCH (Ăn' tĭ-ŏch) names two New Testament cities one of which was home to many Diaspora Jews (Jews living outside of Palestine and maintaining their religious faith among the Gentiles) and the place where believers, many of whom were Gentiles, were first called Christians.

1. The largest city of the Roman empire after Rome in Italy and Alexandria in Egypt. Because so many ancient cities were called by this name, it is often called Antioch on the Orontes (River) or Antioch of Syria. Antioch was founded around 300 B.C. by Seleucus Nicator. From the beginning it was a bustling maritime city with its own seaport. It lay about 20 miles inland from the Mediterranean in ancient Syria on the Orontes River nearly three hundred miles north of Jerusalem.

Many Jews of the Diaspora lived in Antioch and engaged in commerce, enjoying the rights of citizenship in a free city. Many of Antioch's Gentiles were attracted to Judaism. As was the case with many of the Roman cities of the east, Antioch's patron deity was the pagan goddess Tyche or "Fortune."

In the New Testament only Jerusalem is more closely related to the spread of early Christianity. Luke mentioned Nicholas of Antioch in Acts 6:5 among the Greek-speaking leaders of the church in Jerusalem. The persecution that arose over Ste-

Pisidian Antioch in the mountains of Asia Minor (modern Turkey) north of the Mediterranean Sea.

phen resulted in Jewish believers scattering to Cyprus, Cyrene, and Antioch (Acts 11:19). In Antioch the believers were first called Christians (11:26), and it was to Antioch that Barnabas fetched Saul (Paul) from Tarsus so that they could teach this mixed congregation of Jewish and Gentile followers of the Lord. At Antioch the Christian prophet Agabus foretold the famine that would shortly overtake the Roman world (11:28). The disciples responded with the work of famine relief for the church in Jerusalem, directed and carried out from Antioch. The church at Antioch felt the leading of the Holy Spirit to set aside Barnabas and Saul for what was the first organized mission work (13:1–3). Barnabas and Saul left for Seleucia (also known as Pieria, Antioch's Mediterranean sea-

A small first-century marble statue of a sleeping traveler reminiscent of Paul from Antioch of Syria.

port) to begin their preaching. The church at Antioch heard the reports of Paul and Barnabas on return from their first missionary journey (14:27) and likely their second missionary journey (18:22). This was a missionary effort to both Jews and Gentiles, about which Paul says in Galatians 2:11 that he had to oppose Peter to his face at Antioch.

Archaeological excavations at Antioch have been very fruitful, revealing a magnificent, walled Roman city of theatres, forums, a circus, and other public buildings. The language of the city was Greek, as inscriptions and public records show, but the language of the peasantry around this mighty city was Syriac, a dialect of Aramaic.

2. A city in Pisidia, Asia Minor, west of Iconium. Like the Syrian Antioch, this Antioch was founded by Seleucus Nicator. Under Roman rule, this city was called Caesarea. Paul preached in a

The Cilician Gates through the Taurus Mountains north of Antioch of Syria through which Paul passed.

synagogue there on his first missionary journey (Acts 13:14) and was warmly received (13:42–44). Jewish jealously led to a separate ministry to Gentiles (13:46). Finally, Jews drove Paul and Barnabas from the city. These Jews from Antioch followed Paul to Lystra and stirred up trouble there (14:19). Despite this, Paul returned to Antioch to strengthen the church (14:21). Paul used the experience to teach Timothy (2 Tim. 3:11).

James F. Strange

ANTIOCHUS (Ăn·tī′ ŏ·chŭs) Name of thirteen rulers of Syria Palestine headquartered in Antioch. They were part of the Seleucid dynasty which inherited part of Alexander the Great's kingdom. No Antiochus is specifically mentioned in Scripture. Many Bible students think the Book of Daniel originally had its attention focused on the Seleucid kings, particularly Antiochus IV (175 to 164 B.C.). The Maccabean revolt and Jewish intertestamental history occurred during the reigns of the Antiochus kings. See *Daniel; Intertestamental History; Maccabees.*

ANTIPAS (Ăn′ tĭ·pàs) names a martyr in Revelation and the son of Herod the Great. *1.* The tetrarch of Galilee at the time John the Baptist and Jesus began their public ministries (Luke 3:1). Antipas, whose name is an abbreviation of Antipater, ordered John the Baptist beheaded (Matt. 14:3). Pilate sent Jesus to Antipas prior to the crucifixion. On that occasion, he treated Jesus with scornful contempt (Luke 23:11). This won the friendship of Pilate. See *Herod.*
2. According to tradition, the martyr of the church of Pergamum in Revelation 2:13 was roasted in a brazen bowl at Domitian's request.

ANTIPATRIS (Ăn·tĭ·pät′ rĭs) Place name meaning, "in place of father." City Herod the Great built to honor his father Antipater in 9 B.C. It was 40 miles from Jerusalem and 25 miles from Caesarea on the famous Via Maris, "way of the sea," international highway. Roman soldiers taking Paul from Jerusalem to Caesarea spent the night at Antipatris (Acts 23:31). It is located on the site of Old Testament Aphek. See *Aphek.*

ANTONIA, TOWER OF names a fortress near the Temple built around A.D. 6 that served as a palace residence for King Herod, barracks for the Roman troops, a safe deposit for the robe of the high priest, and a central courtyard for public speaking. The tower of Antonia is not mentioned directly in the Bible. It served various functions between A.D. 6 and A.D. 66, the time of its destruction by Titus. Herod the Great built the tower at the northwest corner of the Temple court to replace the Maccabean fort. The tower was 75 feet high and was named for Herod's friend, Mark Anthony. Although the name "Antonia" is not used in the Bible, several references from the first century Jewish historian, Josephus, describe the appearance and function of the tower of Antonia.
Josephus describes the splendor of the tower with spacious apartments, elaborate baths, and beautiful courtyards. The tower served as an official residence for the Roman procurators. Capable of accomodating at least a Roman cohort (500–600 men), the tower housed portions of the Roman army used to guard the Jews inside the Temple court. Herod required that the vestments of the high priest be kept in the tower to maintain control over the worship festivals of the Jews.
The pavement beneath the modern convent of Notre Dame de Sion has been thought to be the place of the tower's courtyard, traditionally consid-

Antonia Fortress (Tower of Antonia) in the model of first-century Jerusalem (Holyland Hotel, Jerusalem).

ered the site of Jesus' trial before Pilate (John 19:13). Recent archeological evidence, however, has shown that the pavement dates from the second century and not the time of Jesus.

Linda McKinnish Bridges

ANTOTHIJAH (Ăn·tō·thī' jah) KJV spelling of Anthothijah. See *Anthothijah.*

ANTOTHITE (Ăn' tō·thīte) Person from Anathoth in KJV spelling. See *Anathoth.*

ANXIETY The state of mind wherein one is concerned about something or someone. This state of mind may range from genuine concern (see Phil. 2:20,28; 2 Cor. 11:28) to obsessions that originate from a distorted perspective of life (Matt. 6:25–34; Mark 4:19; Luke 12:22–31). Jesus did not prohibit genuine concern about food or shelter, but He did teach that we should keep things in their proper perspective. We should make God's kingdom our first priority; everything else will fall in line after we do that (Matt. 6:33).

ANUB (Ā' nŭb) Personal name meaning, "grape," or "with a mustache." A member of tribe of Judah (1 Chron. 4:8).

APE Solomon imported animals in international shipping (1 Kings 10:22). The Hebrew term *qoph* may refer to apes (*papio hamadrias arabicus*), using a loanword from Egyptian, but the exact animal referred to by this term is far from certain, the animal apparently being an imported novelty for the people of Solomon's day.

APELLES (Å·pĕl' lĕs) A Christian in Rome whom Paul saluted as "approved in Christ" (Rom. 16:10), which may mean he had been tested by persecution and proved faithful.

APHARSACHITES (Å·phär' săch·ītes) or **APHAR-SATHCHITES** KJV transliteration of Aramaic terms in Ezra 4:9; 5:6; 6:6. Modern translations translate the term to indicate government officials: governors (RSV); officials (NIV; NAS). The term in 4:9 may represent officials representing the Persian king in the provinces of his kingdom. The term in 5:6 and 6:6 may refer to government investigators or inspectors.

APHARSITES (Å·phär' sītes) KJV transliteration of Aramaic term in Ezra 4:9 variously translated and interpreted by modern translators and Bible students: men from Persia (NIV); Persians (RSV); secretaries (NAS). The verse is difficult to read in the original language, and no satisfactory interpretation has been offered.

APHEK (Ā' phĕk) Place name meaning "bed of brook or river" or "fortress." *1.* City whose king

Joshua defeated (Josh. 12:18), where Philistine armies formed to face Israel in days of Samuel (1 Sam. 4:1) resulting in Philistine victory and capture of Israel's ark of the covenant. Philistine armies including David and his men gathered in Aphek to fight Saul. The Philistine commanders forced Achish to send David back from battle (1 Sam. 29). Eventually the Philistines defeated Israel, bringing death to Saul and Jonathan.

Aphek is located at modern Tell Ras el' Ain near the source of the Yarkon River in the Sharon plain northeast of Joppa. Egyptian execration texts from about 1900 B.C. apparently refer to Aphek. Aphek became known as Antipatris in the New Testament era. See *Antipatris. 2.* Northern border city which Joshua did not conquer (Josh. 13:4).

Late Bronze Age palace excavated at Aphek-Antipatris.

This may be modern Afqa, fifteen miles east of ancient Byblos and 23 miles north of Beirut, Lebanon. *3.* City assigned to Asher (Josh. 19:30) but not conquered (Judg. 1:31). This may be modern Tell Kerdanah three miles from Haifa and six miles southeast of Acco. *4.* City east of Jordan near the Sea of Galilee where Benhadad led Syria against Israel about 860 but met defeat as a prophet predicted for Israel (1 Kings 20:26–30). A wall of Aphek fell on 27,000 Syrians (1 Kings 20:30). Also Elisha promised Joash victory over the Syrians in Aphek (2 Kings 13:17).

APHEKAH (Å·phē' kăh) City Joshua assigned to tribe of Judah (Josh. 15:53). Its location is unknown.

APHIAH (Ā·phī' ah) Personal name meaning "forehead." An ancestor of King Saul from the tribe of Benjamin (1 Sam. 9:1).

APHIK (Ā·phĭk) Variant Hebrew spelling of Aphek (Judg 1:31). See *Aphek, 3.*

APHRAH (Ăph' rah) KJV interpretation of place name in Micah 1:10, also called Beth Ophrah (NIV) or Beth·le·aph' rah (RSV; NAS); or Beth Leaphrah (TEV). The longer name used in modern translations means "house of dust" and is used to make a wordplay by Micah, the meaning of the name being more important than the actual city. The city has not been located. It may be modern tel et-Taijibe near Hebron.

APHSES (Ăph′ sēs) KJV spelling of Happizzez. See *Happizzez.*

APIS (Ā′ pĭs) Sacred bull worshiped in Memphis, Egypt. RSV and TEV divide the words in Jeremiah 46:15 differently than does printed Hebrew text. They thus translate, "Why has Apis fled?" (RSV) or "Why has your mighty God Apis fallen?" (TEV). Other translations retain the present Hebrew text and read, "Why are thy valiant men swept away?" (KJV)

APOCALYPTIC describes: (1) writings from God that employ symbolic language to tell of a divine intervention soon to take place; (2) the doctrinal system explicit in these writings; and (3) the movement(s) that produced the writings and doctrines.

Old Testament While portions of Joel, Amos, Zechariah, and Isaiah have apocalyptic features, Daniel is the only Old Testament book which is wholly apocalyptic.

New Testament "Apocalyptic" is derived from the Greek verb *apokalupto,* "to uncover," and so figuratively "to disclose, reveal." Its use, however, is due to the opening word of the Book of Revelation, *apokalupsis,* which means an "uncovering," "a disclosure, a revelation." This term has passed into English as "apocalypse." When writers refer to "*the* Apocalypse," they mean the Book of Revelation; when they speak of an apocalypse, or apocalypses, or apocalyptic writings, they mean works written in a similar style to the Book of Revelation. The first sentence of the Book of Revelation is noteworthy in this connection: "The *Revelation of Jesus Christ,* which *God gave to him,* to shew unto his servants *things which must shortly come to pass;* and he *sent* and *signified it by his angel unto his servant John:* who bare record. . .of *all things that he saw."* The italicized expressions illustrate the fundamental features of the genre of apocalyptic: these writings claim to originate from *God;* they most frequently tell of a divine intervention *soon* to take place; their authors often use *sign* language—i.e. they "sign-ify," employing pictorial language which is also parabolic; an *angelic intermediary* commonly explains to the prophet the meaning of the message conveyed to him; and the prophet makes known to others his *visions* ("all that he saw"). John's "apocalypse" is specifically stated to be a Christian revelation: it is "the revelation *of Jesus Christ,"* received from God; accordingly it is described as "the Word of God and the testimony of Jesus Christ." It is thereby declared to be an authentic apocalypse. John the prophet would have been aware that there were many other works which possessed similar literary characteristics as his own, the most notable being the Book of Daniel.

Extra-biblical Sources The other apocalyptic writings are outside the Bible and mainly belong to the period 200 B.C.–A.D. 100. The best known of the extra-biblical apocalyptic books are 1 Enoch (often called "Ethiopic Enoch," since it survives in that language), 2 Enoch, 4 Ezra, and 2 Baruch. With these Jubilees, Psalms of Solomon, Testaments of the Twelve Patriarchs, and the Sibylline Oracles are generally classed, although their form differs from that of "classic apocalyptic." It is not clear, however, that we should postulate a standard structure of apocalyptic writing; the use of symbolism, whether of animals or of mythical monsters, of visions and of messianic woes varies greatly.

Apocalyptic Movement The so-called "apocalyptic movement" which gave birth to the apocalyptic literature had its roots in Israel's history. The creation myths of the Semitic world supplied quarries for the picture language employed by the prophets and apocalyptists. The leading literary features and apocalyptic message were conditioned above all by Israel's history and experience of God. Historical alienation created the conditions wherein apocalypticism flourished. Estrangement resulted from the disintegration of society, caused by oppression or the ravages of war. The isolation of a group within its society also caused alienation. While the Jewish literature that concerns us was the offspring of Old Testament prophecy, the apocalyptic movement had parallels in the contemporary world of the Middle East. Other nations resisted Greek rule and created hopes of a renewal of a native kingship. They divided history into four successive kingdoms and expected a god to intervene to restore order and bring victory. This shows the links between the religious thought of nations of the ancient world, of their response to aggressive oppression, and of their hope in deliverance from God.

Characteristics of Apocalyptic Writing The characterics of Jewish apocalyptic writings are widely discussed, sometimes without due regard for the diversity in these writings. It is commonly agreed that three major features characterize apocalyptic thinking: dualism, determinism, and pessimism. Dualism is the dominant characteristic and is expressed in two ways: (1) in a dual *spacial* order—powers of heaven and powers of hell, hence angels and demons in abundance, spirits of good and spirits of evil, a holy Spirit and an evil prince of this world; (2) in a *historical* dualism—the present age is ruled by the evil powers and is wholly wicked, but it will be succeeded by the age to come, which will be ruled by God and therefore will be good. The ordering of the ages for the accomplishment of God's purpose in the coming age often entails a determinism, which can be applied to the last detail of history. This means God has already planned each historical event regardless of human choices and acts. This in turn can lead to pessimism, such as that in 4 Ezra. Examples of dualism or determinism in some literature does not mean every writer of apocalytic works believed in a world dominated by dualism and determinism. Persian religion had the ultimate dualism. The powers of good and evil were co-equal. This was impossible in Jewish thought, whose main belief was one God without equal. The idea that the devil is *lord* of the present age was not shared by all apocalyptists; for example, in Daniel 4:25, Nebuchadnezzar was told that he would be humbled until he learned that "the most High ruleth in the kingdom of men, and giveth it to whomsoever he will," (compare Rev. 13:5–10). Positively, we should view these insights as subsumed under the heading of the sovereignty of God. He is Lord of the universe, and so of all powers; the good are His ministers, the evil have to contribute to His will. The two ages are a clarification of the prophetic view of history leading to the day of the Lord, the coming of God, and the fulfillment of His purpose in the victorious kingdom of God. The determinism of which these writings speak is an attempt to set forth God's will as done on earth as in heaven. Such a faith is not rightly described as pessimism. It certainly postulates the inability of humanity to save itself and thus looks to God to complete history in the kingdom of glory. The end therefore is *good!*

Most apocalyptic works are ascribed to an ancient saint, as their names imply (for example, the books of *Enoch,* the Apocalypse of *Abraham,* of *Noah,* of *Ezra,* of *Baruch*). The reason for this form is still uncertain; it obviously includes the desire for a book to gain a hearing, but it also expresses the conviction that the revelations have come down from ancient times, somewhat as the Pharisees believed that their tradition went back to Moses. Pseudonymity, however, was not a necessary adjunct of apocalyptic work; the literature of Qumran is without it, and the supreme example of apocalyptic writing, the Book of Revelation, was issued in the name of its author.

Significance The chief importance of the apocalyptic literature was its enabling the prophetic faith in God and hope for His kingdom to burn brightly in oppressive times. At its best it was more than maintenance of dogma. It encouraged people to be ready for and participate in God's final victory in history. Thus it encouraged an alienated, estranged, defeated people to live for God and to hope in His promised coming. Apocalyptic writing found its correction and true fulfillment in the message of Jesus, and in His living, dying, rising, and the hope of His appearance.

George Beasley-Murray

APOCRYPHA Jews did not stop writing for centuries between the Old Testament and the New. The Intertestamental Period was a time of much literary production. We designate these writings as Apocrypha and Pseudepigrapha. See *Pseudepigrapha.* They did not attain canonical status, but some of them were cited by early Christians almost on a level with the Old Testament writings, and a few were copied in biblical manuscripts. Some New Testament authors were familiar with various non-canonical works, and the Epistle of Jude made specific reference to at least one of these books. They were ultimately preserved by the Christians rather than by the Jews.

Meaning "things that are hidden," apocrypha is applied to a collection of fifteen books written between about 200 B.C. and A.D. 100. These are not a part of the Old Testament but are valued by some for private study. The word "apocrypha" is not found in the Bible. Although never part of the Hebrew Scriptures, all fifteen apocryphal books except 2 Esdras appear in the Greek translation of the Old Testament, the Septuagint. They were made a part of the official Latin Bible, the Vulgate. All except 1 and 2 Esdras and the Prayer of Mannasseh are considered canonical (in the Bible) and authoritative by the Roman Catholic Church. From the time of the Reformation, the apocryphal books have been omitted from the canon of the Protestant churches. The Apocrypha represent various types of literature: historical, historical romance, wisdom, devotional, and apocalyptic.

First Esdras is a historical book from the early first century A.D. Parallelling material in the last chapters of 2 Chronicles, Ezra, and Nehemiah, it covers the period from Josiah to the reading of the law by Ezra. In a number of places, it differs from the Old Testament account. It is believed that this writing drew from some of the same sources used by the writers of the canonical Old Testament books. The Three Guardsmen Story, 3:1—5:3, is the one significant passage in 1 Esdras that does not occur in the Old Testament. It tells how Zerubbabel was allowed to lead the exiles back to Palestine.

The most important historical writing in the Apocrypha is **1 Maccabees.** It is the primary source for writing the history of the period it covers, 180 to 134 B.C. The emphasis is that God worked through Mattathias and his sons to bring deliverance. He did not intervene in divine, supernatural ways. He worked through people to accomplish His purposes. The writer was a staunch patriot. For him nationalism and religious zeal were one and the same. After introductory verses dealing with Alexander the Great, the book gives the causes for the revolt against the Seleucids. Much detail is given about the careers of Judas and Jonathan. Less attention is given to Simon, although emphasis is placed upon his being acclaimed leader and high priest forever. Brief reference to John Hyrcanus at the close suggests that the book was written either late in his life or after his death, probably shortly after 100 B.C.

Second Maccabees also gives the history of the early part of the revolt against the Seleucids, covering the period from 180 to 161 B.C. It is based upon five volumes written by Jason of Cyrene, about which volumes nothing is known. Second Maccabees, written shortly after 100 B.C., is not considered as accurate historically as 1 Maccabees. In places the two books disagree. This book begins with two letters written to Jews in Egypt urging them to celebrate the cleansing of the Temple by Judas. In the remainder of the writing, the author insisted that the Jews' trouble came as the result of their sinfulness. He emphasized God's miraculous intervention to protect the Temple and His people. Great honor was bestowed upon those who were martyred for their faith. The book includes the story of seven brothers and their mother who were put to death. The book clearly teaches a resurrection of the body, at least for the righteous.

Tobit is a historical romance written about 200 B.C. It is more concerned to teach lessons than to record history. The story is of a family carried into exile in Assyria when Israel was destroyed. The couple, Tobit and Anna, had a son named Tobias. Tobit had left a large sum of money with a man in Media. When he became blind, he sent his son to collect the money. A man was found to accompany the son Tobias. In reality he was the angel Raphael. Parallel to this is the account of a relative named Sarah. She had married seven husbands, but a demon had slain each of them on the wedding night. Raphael told Tobias that he was eligible to marry Sarah. They had caught a fish and had preserved the heart, liver, and gall. When burned, the heart and liver would drive away a demon. The gall would cure blindness. Thus Tobias was able to marry Sarah without harm. Raphael collected the money that was left in Media, and the blindness of Tobit was cured by means of the fish's gall. The book stresses Temple attendance, paying of tithes, giving alms, marrying only within the people of Israel, and the importance of prayer. Obedience to the law is central along with separation of Jews from Gentiles. It introduces the concept of a guardian angel.

The book of **Judith**, from 250 to 150 B.C. shows the importance of obedience to the law. In this book Nebuchadnezzar, the king of the Assyrians, reigned at the time the Jews returned from Exile. This shows it is not historically accurate, for Cyrus of Persia was king when the Jews returned from Exile (538 B.C.). The story may be based upon some event where a woman played an heroic role in the life of her people. In the story Nebuchadnezzar sent one of his generals, Holofernes, to subjugate the nations in the western part of his empire. The Jews resisted. Holofernes laid siege to the city of Bethulia (unknown except for this reference). Because of a shortage of water, the city decided to surrender in five days if God did not intervene. Judith had been a widow for three years and had been careful to obey all the law. She stated that God was going to act through her to save His people. She went with her maid to the camp of Holofernes, claiming that God was going to destroy the people because of their sin. She promised to show the general how he could capture the city without loss of a life. At a banquet a few days later, when Holofernes had drunk himself into a coma, she cut off his head and took it back to the city. The result was a great victory for the Jews over their enemies. This book places emphasis upon prayer and fasting. Idolatry is denounced, and the God of Israel is glorified. The book shows a strong hatred of pagans. Its moral content is low, for it teaches that the end justifies the means.

The Apocrypha contains **additions to the book of Esther.** The Hebrew text of Esther contains 163 verses, but the Greek contains 270. These additions are in six different places in the Greek text. However, in the Latin Vulgate they are all placed at the end. These sections contain such matters as the dream of Mordecai, the interpretation of that dream, the texts of the letters referred to in the canonical book, (Esther 1:22; 3:13; 8:5,10; 9:20,25–30) and the prayers of Esther and Mordecai. The additions give a more obviously religious basis for the book. In the Old Testament book of Esther, God is never named. This omission is remedied by the additions which were probably made between 125 and 75 B.C.

The Song of the Three Young Men is one of three additions to the book of Daniel. It follows Daniel 3:23 in the Greek text. It satisfies curiosity about what went on in the furnace into which the three men were thrown. The final section is a hymn of praise to God. It emphasizes that God acts to deliver His people in response to prayer. This writing, along with the other two additions to Daniel, probably comes from near 100 B.C.

The story of **Susanna** is added at the close of the Book of Daniel in the Septuagint. It tells of two judges who were overpowerd by the beauty of Susanna and sought to become intimate with her. When she refused, they claimed they had seen her being intimate with a young man. Authorities believed their charges and condemned the young lady to death. Daniel then stated that the judges were lying, and he would prove it. He asked them, separately, under what tree they saw Susanna and the young man. When they identified different kinds of trees, their perjury became apparent. They were condemned to death, and Susanna was vindicated.

The third addition to Daniel is **Bel and the Dragon,** placed before Susanna in the Septuagint. Bel was an idol worshiped in Babylon. Large quantities of food were placed in Bel's temple each night and consumed before the next morning. King Cyrus asked Daniel why he did not worship Bel, and Daniel replied that Bel was only a man-made image. He would prove to the king that Bel was not alive. Daniel had ashes sprinkled on the floor of the temple and food placed on Bel's altar before sealing the temple door. The next morning the seals on the doors were intact, but when the doors were opened the food was gone. However, the ashes sprinkled on the floor revealed foot-prints of the priests and their families. They had a secret entrance and came at night and ate the food brought to the idol. The second part of the story of Bel and the Dragon concerned a dragon wor-shiped in Babylon. Daniel killed the dragon by feeding it cakes of pitch, fat, and hair. The people were outraged, and Daniel was thrown into the lions' den for seven days. However, the lions did not harm him. These stories ridicule paganism and the worship of idols.

The next four apocryphal books are examples of Wisdom literature. The **Wisdom of Solomon** which was not written by Solomon, was probably written about 100 B.C. in Egypt. The first section of the book gave comfort to oppressed Jews and condemned those who had turned from their faith in God. It shows the advantages of wisdom over wickedness. The second section is a hymn of praise to wisdom. Wisdom is identified as a per-son present with God, although it is not given as much prominence as in some other writings. The final section shows wisdom as helpful to Israel throughout its history. This writing presents the Greek concept of immortality rather than the bibli-cal teaching of resurrection.

The **Wisdom of Jesus the Son of Sirach** is also known as **Ecclesiasticus**. It emphasizes the impor-tance of the law and obedience to it. Written in Hebrew about 180 B.C., it was translated into Greek by the author's grandson shortly after 132 B.C. The book has two main divisions, 1—23 and 24—51, each beginning with a description of wisdom. The writer was a devout Jew, highly educated, with the opportunity to travel outside Palestine. Thus he included in his writing not only traditional Jewish wisdom but material that he found of value from the Greek world. He pictured the ideal scribe as one who had time to devote himself to the study of the law. Chapters 44—50 are a praise of the great fathers of Israel, some-what similar to Hebrews 11. Wisdom is highly exalted. She is a person made by God. She goes into the earth to seek a dwelling place. After she is rejected by other people, she is established in Zion. Wisdom is identified with the law.

The Book of **Baruch** is also in the wisdom category. It is a combination of two or three differ-ent writings. The first section is in prose and claims to give a history of the period of Jeremiah and Baruch. However, it differs from the Old Testament account. The second section is poetry and a praise of wisdom. The final section is also poetic and gives a word of hope for the people. As in Sirach, wisdom and law are equated. It was written shortly before 100 B.C.

The **Letter of Jeremiah** is often added to Ba-ruch as chapter 6. As the basis for his work, the author evidently used Jeremiah 29:1–23, in which Jeremiah did write a letter to the exiles. However, this letter comes from before 100 B.C. It is a strongly worded condemnation of idolatry.

The **Prayer of Manasseh** is a devotional writ-ing. It claims to be the prayer of the repentant king whom the Old Testament pictured as very wicked (2 Kings 21:10–17). Second Kings makes no suggestion that Manasseh repented. However, 2 Chronicles 33:11–13,18–19 states that he did repent and that God accepted him. This writing from before 100 B.C. is what such a prayer of repentance might have been.

The final book of the Apocrypha is **2 Esdras,** written too late to be included in the Septuagint. Chapters 1—2 and 15—16 are Christian writ-ings. Chapters 3—14, the significant part of the work, are from about 20 B.C. This writing is an apocalypse, a type of writing popular among the Jews in the Intertestamental Period and which became popular among Christians. See *Apocalyp-tic.* Second Esdras contains seven sections or visions. In the first three, Ezra seeks answers from an angel about human sin and the situation of Israel. The answer he receives is that the situation will change only in the new age that God is about to inaugurate. The third section pictures the Mes-siah. He will remain four hundred years and then die. The next three visions stress God's coming intervention and salvation of His people through the pre-existent Messiah. The final section states that the end will be soon and reports that Ezra was inspired to write ninety-four books. Twenty-four are a rewrite of the canonical Old Testament while the other seventy are to be given to the wise. The last two chapters of 2 Esdras contain material common to the New Tesament. See *Pseu-depigrapha.*   *Clayton Harrop*

APOCRYPHA, NEW TESTAMENT is a collec-tive term referring to a large body of religious writings dating back to the early Christian centu-ries that are similar in form to the New Testament (Gospels, acts, epistles, and apocalypses) but were never included as a part of the canon of Scripture. **Meaning of the Term "Apocrypha"** When the term *apokryphos* occurs in the New Testament, it simply means "hidden things." This original sense does not include the later meanings associated with it. In the formation of the Christian canon of Scripture, "apocrypha" came to mean works that were not divinely inspired and authoritative. The term was also used by certain groups (for example, Gnostics) to describe their writings as secretive.

They believed their writings were written much earlier but kept hidden until the latter days. Such writings were even then only available to the properly initiated. Since the church recognized works that were read openly in services of public worship, the term "apocrypha" came to mean "false" and began to be used to describe heretical material. In contrast to portions of the Old Testament Apocrypha which have been accepted by some branches of the Christian Church, none of the New Testament Apocrypha (with the possible exception of the *Apocalypse of Peter* and the *Acts of Paul*) has ever been accepted as Scripture. Though some scholars allow the term to describe writings that are neither a part of the New Testament nor strictly apocryphal (e.g., apostolic fathers), it seems best to restrict the term to material that was not received into the canon of Scripture, yet, by form and content, claimed for itself a status and authority equal to Scripture.

Purpose of the Apocrypha Three general reasons explain the existence of the New Testament Apocrypha. First, some groups accepted apocryphal writings because they built on the universal desire to preserve the memories of the lives and deaths of important New Testament figures. Regardless of whether the transmitted traditions were true or false, the desire of later generations to know more detail made the apocryphal writings attractive. The second purpose is closely related to the first. Apocryphal works were intended to supplement the information given in the New Testament about Jesus or the apostles. This may be the motivation behind the *Third Epistle to the Corinthians* (to provide some of the missing correspondence between Paul and the Corinthian church) and the *Epistle to the Laodiceans* (to supply the letter referred to in Col. 4:16). For the same reason, the apocryphal acts made certain to record the events surrounding the death of the apostles, a matter on which the New Testament is usually silent. Third, heretical groups produced apocryphal writings in an attempt to gain authority for their own particular views.

1. The apocryphal gospels. This large group of writings can be further classified into infancy gospels, passion gospels, Jewish-Christian gospels, and gospels originating from heretical groups.

Infancy Gospels is the name given to apocryphal works that in some way deal with the birth or childhood of Jesus or both. Though Matthew and Luke stressed the same basic story line, they emphasized different aspects of the events surrounding the birth of Jesus, primarily because of their audience and their own particular purpose in writing. The writers of these apocryphal infancy gospels attempted to correct what they viewed as deficiencies in the canonical accounts and to fill in the gaps they believed existed. Most of the material is concerned with the silent years of Jesus'

childhood. The two earliest infancy gospels, from which most of the later literature developed, are the *Protoevangelium of James* and the *Infancy Gospel of Thomas*. The *Protoevangelium of James* seems to have been written to glorify Mary. It includes the miraculous birth of Mary, her presentation in the Temple, her espousal to Joseph (an old man with children), and the miraculous birth of Jesus. This second-century work was extremely popular and undoubtedly had an influence on later views of Mary, the mother of Jesus. The *Infancy Gospel of Thomas* depicts Jesus in a crude manner as a wonder boy, using his miraculous powers as a matter of personal convenience. This work attempts to fill in the silent years of Jesus' childhood, but does so in a rather repulsive and exaggerated manner.

As legend continued to expand, many later infancy gospels developed including the *Arabic Gospel of the Infancy,* the *Armenian Gospel of the Infancy,* the *Gospel of Pseudo-Matthew,* the *Latin Infancy Gospel,* the *Life of John According to Serapion,* the *Gospel of the Birth of Mary,* the *Assumption of the Virgin,* and the *History of Joseph the Carpenter.*

Passion Gospels, another class of apocryphal gospel, are concerned with supplementing the canonical accounts by describing events surrounding the crucifixion and resurrection of Jesus. The two most important works in this category are the *Gospel of Peter* and the *Gospel of Nicodemus* (sometimes called the *Acts of Pilate*). The *Gospel of Peter* is a second-century work which downplays Jesus' humanity, heightens the miraculous, and reduces Pilate's guilt, among other things. The *Gospel of Nicodemus* (*Acts of Pilate*) is another example of an apocryphal passion gospel. The trial and death of Jesus is expanded as Nicodemus, the chief narrator, tells of one witness after another coming forward to testify on Jesus' behalf. Pilate gives in to popular demand and hands Jesus over to be crucified. The *Gospel of Nicodemus* also includes a vivid account of Jesus' "Descent into Hell," much like that of a Greek hero invading the underworld to defy its authorities or rescue its prisoners. Another apocryphal work that might be classified as a passion gospel is the *Book of the Resurrection of Christ by Bartholomew the Apostle.*

Jewish-Christian Gospels are works that originated among Jewish-Christian groups. They include the *Gospel of the Ebionites,* the *Gospel of Hebrews,* and the *Gospel of the Nazarenes.* Although some scholars equate the *Gospel of Hebrews* and the *Gospel of the Nazarenes,* the evidence is inconclusive. The *Gospel of the Hebrews,* perhaps the most prominent, appears to have been in some ways a paraphrase of the canonical Gospel of Matthew and places a special emphasis on James, the brother of the Lord.

Heretical Gospels cover a wide variety of apocryphal gospels, most of which are considered Gnostic gospels. Gnosticism developed in the second century as a widespread and diverse religious movement with roots in Greek philosophy and folk religion. The *Gospel of Truth* contains no references to the words or actions of Jesus. Some heretical gospels are attributed to all or one of the twelve apostles. These include the *Gospel of the Twelve Apostles* and the gospels of Philip, Thomas, Matthias, Judas, and Bartholomew. Written before A.D. 400, the *Gospel of Thomas* (of no relation to the *Infancy Gospel of Thomas*) is a collection of 114 secret sayings "which Jesus the living one spoke and Didymus Judas Thomas wrote down." This document is one of almost fifty discovered in 1945 near Nag Hammadi in Upper Egypt as a part of what many scholars believe was the library of a Gnostic community. The heretical emphases of the *Gospel of Thomas* are countered in advance by the canonical Epistle of 1 John, which emphasizes the gospel of Jesus Christ as the message of life, available for every person to experience. Other gospels in this class include those under the names of Holy Women (for example, the *Questions of Mary* and the *Gospel According to Mary*), and those attributed to a chief heretic such as Cerinthus, Basilides, and Marcion.

2. The apocryphal acts. A large number of legendary accounts of the journeys and heroics of New Testament apostles sought to parallel and supplement the Book of Acts. The five major apocryphal acts are second and third-century stories named after a "Leucius Charinus" and therefore known as the *Leucian Acts.* Even though they show a high regard for the apostles and include some historical fact, much of what they offer is the product of a wild imagination, closely akin to a romantic novel (with talking animals and obedient bugs).

The *Acts of John* is the earliest of the group (A.D. 150–160). It contains miracles and sermons by John of Asia Minor and has a distinct Gnostic orientation. It tells the story of John's journey from Jerusalem to Rome and his imprisonment on the isle of Patmos. After many other travels, John finally dies in Ephesus.

The *Acts of Andrew,* written shortly before A.D. 300, is, like the *Acts of John,* distinctly Gnostic.

The *Acts of Paul* was written before A.D. 200 by an Asian presbyter "out of love for Paul." He was later defrocked for publishing the writing. It is divided into three sections: (1) the Acts of Paul and Thecla, a girl from Iconian who assisted Paul on his missionary travels, (2) correspondence with the Corinthian church, and (3) the martyrdom of Paul.

The *Acts of Peter* is a late second-century writing that tells of Peter defending the Church from a heretic named Simon Magus by public preaching.

Peter, who is forced to flee, later returns to be crucified upside down. Like the other acts, it is ascetic, that is, it promotes a life-style of self-denial and withdrawal from society as a means of combating vice and developing virtue.

The *Acts of Thomas* is a third-century work, thought by most scholars to have originated in Syriac Christianity. It tells how Judas Thomas, "Twin of the Messiah," was given India when the apostles divided the world by casting lots. Thomas, though he went as a slave, was responsible for the conversion of many well-known Indians. The ascetic element is again present in Thomas' emphasis on virginity. In the end he was imprisoned and martyred.

Other later apocryphal acts include: the *Apostolic History of Abdias,* the *Fragmentary Story of Andrew,* the *Ascents of James,* the *Martyrdom of Matthew;* the *Preaching of Peter, Slavonic Acts of Peter,* the *Passion of Paul, Passion of Peter, Passion of Peter and Paul;* the *Acts of Andrew* and *Matthias, Andrew and Paul, Paul and Thecla, Barnabas, James the Great, Peter and Andrew, Peter and Paul, Philip,* and *Thaddaeus.*

3. The apocryphal epistles. We know of a small group of apocryphal epistles or letters many of which are ascribed to the Apostle Paul. The *Epistle of the Apostles* is a second-century collection of visions communicating post-resurrection teachings of Christ. The *Third Epistle to the Corinthians* was purported to be Paul's reply to a letter from Corinth. Though it circulated independently, it is also a part of the *Acts of Paul.* The *Latin Epistle to the Laodiceans* is a gathering of Pauline phrases probably motivated by Col. 4:16.

Other important apocryphal epistles include the *Correspondence of Christ and Abgar,* the *Epistle to the Alexandrians,* the *Epistle of Titus,* of *Peter to James,* of *Peter to Philip,* and of *Mary to Ignatius.*

4. The apocryphal apocalypses. The Book of Revelation is the only apocalyptic book in the New Testament, though there are apocalyptic elements in other books (such as Mark 13 and parallels; 2 Thess. 2:1–12). The term "apocalypse" or "apocalyptic" means "to uncover" and is used to describe a category of writings that seek to unveil the plan of God for the world using symbol and visions. See *Apocalyptic.* While the New Testament apocalyptic material emphasizes the return of Christ, the later apocryphal apocalypses focus more on heaven and hell. The most popular of these, the *Apocalypse of Peter,* seems to have enjoyed a degree of canonical status for a time. It presents visions of the resurrected Lord and images of the terror suffered by those in hell. The *Apocalypse of Paul* is probably motivated by Paul's reference in 2 Corinthians 12:2 of a man in Christ being caught up to the third heaven. The author is thoroughly convinced this was Paul's personal experience and proceeds to give all the details.

A

Other apocalypses include the *Apocalypse of James, of Stephen, of Thomas, of the Virgin Mary,* and several works discovered at Nag Hammadi.

5. Other apocryphal works. These include the *Agrapha* (a collection of sayings attributed to Jesus), the *Preachings of Peter,* the *Clementine Homilies* and *Recognitions,* the *Apocryphon of John,* the *Apocryphon of James,* and certain Gnostic writings such as the *Pistis Sophia,* the *Wisdom of Jesus,* and the *Books of Jeu.*

Relevance of the New Testament Apocrypha
The New Testament Apocrypha is significant for those who study church history. Even though these writings were not included in the canon, they are not worthless. They give a sample of the ideas, convictions, and imaginations of a portion of Christian history. The New Testament Apocrypha also serves as a point of comparison with the writings contained in the canon of the New Testament. By way of contrast the apocryphal writings demonstrate how the New Testament places a priority on historical fact rather than human fantasy. While the New Testament Apocrypha is often interesting and informative, it is usually unreliable historically and always unauthoritative for matters of faith and practice.

J. Scott Duvall

APOLLONIA (Ăp·ol·lō′ nĭ·à). Place name meaning, "belonging to Apollo." Paul visited Apollonia on his second missionary journey, though the Bible reports no activity there (Acts 17:1). The city is in northern Greece or Macedonia on the international highway called Via Egnatia, 30 miles from Amphipolis and 38 miles from Thessalonica.

APOLLOS (Ă·pŏl′ lŏs), meaning "destroyer," names an Alexandrian Jew who came to Ephesus following Paul's first visit and was taught Christian doctrine by Priscilla and Aquila. An educated man, Apollos handled the Old Testament Scriptures with forcefulness. However, he was lacking in a full understanding of the way of God, so Priscilla and Aquila took him aside and instructed him (Acts 18:26). Apollos became even more successful in his ministry. He went from Ephesus to Greece with the encouragement of the Asian believers and a letter of introduction (Acts 18:27). He greatly strengthened the believers by using the Scriptures to demonstrate that Jesus was the Christ (Acts 18:28).

Apollos is last mentioned in the Book of Acts as being in Corinth (19:1). Paul referred to Apollos frequently, particularly in 1 Corinthians. Here the majority of the references (1 Cor. 1:12; 3:4–6,22) have to do with the schisms in the Corinthian church centering on personalities. Paul noted that some believers championed Paul; some, Apollos; and some, Cephas. What is important is that believers belong to Christ, not to individual leaders. Such references show that

Apollos must have been a dynamic figure to be compared with Paul or Peter. In 1 Corinthians 4:6 Paul placed Apollos on the same level as himself. They both sought to defeat the arrogance and superiority which comes from being self-centered rather than Christ-centered.

Paul referred to Apollos in 1 Corinthians 16:12 as "our brother," showing how much Paul considered him as one of the team. This is also demonstrated in Titus 3:13 where Paul asked Titus to help Apollos on his way. A learned and gifted preacher, Apollos was willing to receive more instruction and be part of the team.

Because of Apollos' knowledge of the Old Testament, Luther suggested that Apollos might well be the writer of the Book of Hebrews. See *Priscilla and Aquila; Ephesus; Corinth; Corinthians, 1 and 2.*

William Vermillian

APOLLYON (Ă·pŏll′ yon) Greek name for Abaddon (Rev. 9:11). See *Abaddon.*

APOSTASY (ă·pŏs′ tà·sȳ) is the act of rebelling against, forsaking, abandoning, or falling away from what one has believed.

Old Testament The Old Testament speaks of "falling away" in terms of a person's deserting to a foreign king (2 Kings 25:11; Jer. 37:13–14; 39:9; 52:15). Associated ideas, however, include the concept of religious unfaithfulness: "rebellion" (Josh. 22:22); "cast away" (2 Chron. 29:19); "trespass" (2 Chron. 33:19); and "backslidings" (Jer. 2:19; 8:5). NAS uses "apostasy" in Jeremiah 8:5 and Hosea 14:4 with the plural in Jeremiah 2:19; 5:6; 14:7.

The prophets picture Israel's history as the history of turning from God to other gods, from His law to injustice and lawlessness, from His anointed king to foreign kings, and from His word to the word of foreign kings. This is defined simply as forsaking God, not fearing Him (Jer. 2:19). Such action was sin, for which the people had to ask forgiveness (Jer. 14:7–9) and repent (Jer. 8:4–7). The basic narrative of Judges, Samuel, Kings is that Israel fell away from God, choosing selfish ways rather than His ways. Exile resulted. Still God's fallen people had hope. In freedom God could choose to turn away His anger and heal their "backsliding" (Hos. 14:4).

New Testament The English word "apostasy" is derived from a Greek word (*apostasia*) that means, "to stand away from." The Greek noun occurs twice in the New Testament (Acts 21:21; 2 Thess. 2:3), though it is not translated as "apostasy" in the King James Version. A related noun is used for a divorce (Matt. 5:31; 19:7; Mark 10:4). The corresponding Greek verb occurs nine times.

Acts 21:21 states an accusation made against Paul that he was leading Jews outside Palestine to abandon the law of Moses. Such apostasy was defined as failing to circumcise Jewish children and to observe distinctive Jewish customs.

In 2 Thessalonians 2:3 Paul addressed those who had been deceived into believing that the day of the Lord had already come. He taught that an apostasy would precede the day of the Lord. The Spirit had explicitly revealed this falling away from the faith (1 Tim. 4:1). Such apostasy in the latter times will involve doctrinal deception, moral insensitivity, and ethical departures from God's truth.

Associated New Testament concepts include the parable of the soils, in which Jesus spoke of those who believe for a while but "fall away" in time of temptation (Luke 8:13). At the judgment, those who work iniquity will be told to "depart" (Luke 13:27). Paul "withdrew" from the synagogue in Ephesus (Acts 19:9) because of the opposition he found there, and he counseled Timothy to "withdraw" from those who advocate a different doctrine (1 Tim. 6:3–5). Hebrews speaks of falling away from the living God because of "an evil heart of unbelief" (3:12). Those who fall away cannot be renewed again to repentance (Heb. 6:6). Yet God is able to keep the believer from falling (Jude 24).

Implications Apostasy certainly is a biblical concept, but the implications of the teaching have been hotly debated. The debate has centered on the issue of apostasy and salvation. Based on the concept of God's sovereign grace, some hold that, though true believers may stray, they will never totally fall away. Others affirm that any who fall away were never really saved. Though they may have "believed" for a while, they never experienced regeneration. Still others argue that the

St. John's Monastery (Patmos)—traditional site where John the Apostle received the Book of Revelation.

biblical warnings against apostasy are real and that believers maintain the freedom, at least potentially, to reject God's salvation.

Persons worried about apostasy should recognize that conviction of sin in itself is evidence that one has not fallen away. Desire for salvation shows one does not have "an evil heart of unbelief."

Michael Fink

APOSTLES Persons sent to accomplish a mission, especially the twelve apostles Jesus commissioned to follow Him. An apostle represents the

The traditional site, in St. John's Monastery, Patmos, where the apostle John may have laid his head.

one sending and has authority to represent the sender in business, political, or educational situations. See *Disciples, Apostles.*

APOSTOLIC COUNCIL The meeting in Jerusalem at which the apostles and elders of Jerusalem defended the right of Paul and Barnabas to preach the gospel to the Gentiles without forcing con-

verts to obey the Jewish law (Acts 15). A "decree" from the council did ask Gentile converts not to eat food that had been sacrificed to idols, not to eat meat with blood in it, not to eat animals which had been strangled, and not to commit sexual immorality (Acts 15:28–29). These requirements may all be taken from Leviticus 17–18, which set up requirements not only on the "house of Israel" but also on "the strangers which sojourn among you" (Lev. 17:8).

In Galatians 2 Paul described the work of the council from his perspective, though some Bible students have long tried to distinguish between the events of Acts 15 and Galatians 2. Paul used the council experience to show that his gospel without circumcision was accepted by the leaders in Jerusalem to the point Titus could be with him in Jerusalem and not be circumcised.

The council showed the working of the early church with strong leadership yet involving the voice of the congregation (Acts 15:12,22), the messengers sent from Jerusalem to Antioch not being part of the twelve apostles.

APOSTOLIC FATHERS Early Christian authors believed to have known the apostles. The Apostolic Fathers are not mentioned in the Bible. Five Apostolic Fathers appear in the original seventeenth century list: Barnabas, Clement, Ignatius, Polycarp, and Hermas. Today the list usually includes nine items, adding *The Didache, The Epistle to Diognetus, Papias,* and *Apology of Quadratus.* Although scholars dispute whether any of the writers knew the apostles, all but possibly two of the writings, *The Epistle to Diognetus* and the *Apology of Quadratus,* originated before A.D. 156.

The Didache or **Teaching of the Twelve Apostles** was not rediscovered until 1883 despite the fact that it had considerable usage in early centuries. An early church manual, it may be the earliest of the Apostolic Fathers, in its current form no later than A.D. 100 but possibly much earlier. Part one (chs. 1–6) contains the Jewish catechetical material known as "The Two Ways" adapted to Christian usage by insertion of teachings of Jesus. Part two gives directions concerning baptism (7), fasting and prayers (8), the eucharist (9–10), travellers who seek hospitality (11–13), worship on the Lord's day (14), and bishops and deacons (15). An exhortation to watchfulness concludes *The Didache.* Several allusions indicate Syria (perhaps Antioch) as the place of origin.

The Apostolic Fathers include two writings under the name of Clement, a Roman presbyter-bishop at the end of the first century, but only his letter to the Corinthians, the **Epistle of 1 Clement** can be considered authentic. What is entitled **The Second Letter of Clement to the Corinthians** is actually an early sermon which dates from around A.D. 140.

Clement, whom early lists named as the third bishop of Rome (after Linus and Anacletus), composed his letter, reliably dated A.D. 96, in response to a disturbance in the church at Corinth. A group of younger members had revolted against the presbyter-bishops and driven them out. In part one (1–36) Clement appealed on behalf of the Church of Rome for unity, using numerous biblical examples. In part two (37–61) he discussed the divisions at Corinth and called for the restoration of order by submission to persons appointed presbyters by the apostles and their successors. Interestingly he drew his organizational pattern from the military structure used at Qumran. In his conclusion (62–65) he expressed hope that the letter bearer would return with news of reconciliation.

The so-called **Second Letter of Clement** urges hearers to repent for too great attachment to the "world." The author cited authoritative writings that are now definitely identified as Gnostic in the library discovered at Nag Hammadi in Egypt.

En route to Rome, where he suffered martyrdom during the reign of Trajan (98–117), Ignatius, Bishop of Antioch, wrote seven letters called the **Epistles of Ignatius.** At Smyrna he composed letters thanking the churches of Ephesus, Magnesia, and Tralles for sending messengers to greet him. From there he also sent a letter to the church at Rome begging them not to intercede on his behalf with the Emperor since he desired to be "ground by the teeth of wild beasts" so as to become "pure bread of Christ." (Rom. 4:1). At Troas he learned that persecution had ceased at Antioch and wrote to the churches of Philadelphia and Smyrna as well as to Polycarp, Bishop of Smyrna, entreating them to send messengers to Antioch to congratulate the faithful on the restoration of peace. In his letters Ignatius mentioned tensions within the communities to which he wrote and urged, as a solution, acceptance of episcopal authority. His special pleading would suggest that the churches of Asia Minor had not yet accepted rule by a single bishop with presbyters and deacons subordinate to him.

Papias was a bishop of Hierapolis in Asia Minor who, according to Irenaeus his pupil, was a hearer of John, the disciple and a friend of Polycarp. He wrote a five-volume work called **Interpretation of the Lord's Oracles** of which only fragments remain in the writings of others. The date of his writing is disputed either being around 110 or 120.

Polycarp's **Epistle of Polycarp** is a cover letter sent with "as many as he had" of the letters of Ignatius at the request of the church of Philippi. Because in its present form the letter is a virtual mosaic of quotations from the collected letters of Paul, P. N. Harrison proposed a two-letter hypothesis. According to this proposal, chapter 13 would be the cover letter written at the time of Ignatius's martyrdom, chapters 1–12 a later composition dated around 135. The letter is primarily an exhortation to true faith and virtue.

Included in the Apostolic Fathers is **The Martyrdom of Polycarp,** the oldest account of a martyr's death recorded soon after it happened in 156. Written to strengthen faith in time of persecution, the account is somewhat embellished by miraculous happenings, for example, so much blood spurting from a wound in Polycarp's side that it extinguished the fire consuming him. **The Martyrdom** is notable as the first Christian writing to use the word "catholic" in reference to the church.

The so-called **Epistle of Barnabas** is neither a letter nor the work of Barnabas, Paul's companion and fellow missionary. An allusion to the destruction of the temple in A.D. 70 (16:3–4) as an event of the distant past precludes such an early date. The main part of this sermon or treatise (chs. 1–17) attempts to prove that the Jews misunderstood the Scriptures from the beginning because they interpreted them literally. Had they interpreted properly, they would have recognized Jesus as the fulfillment of the law. The author himself engaged in some rather fanciful allegorical exposition. To the apology is appended a Jewish document known as "The Two Ways" (of life and death).

Identified by the *Muratorian Canon* as the brother of Pius, Bishop of Rome around 140–150, Hermas indicates that he had been brought to Rome after being taken captive and was purchased by a woman named Rhoda. Using the form of an apocalypse or revelation, the **Shepherd of Hermas** deals with the heatedly debated question of repentance for serious post-baptismal sins such as apostasy, adultery, or murder. Some in Rome, evidently following Hebrews, took an inflexible stance: those who committed such serious offenses should suffer permanent exclusion. Hermas proposed one repentance following baptism, a view widely accepted in the early churches.

The Epistle to Diognetus, is misnamed and misplaced. An attractive apology or defense of Christianity, it is of uncertain but considerably later date than the Apostolic Fathers, perhaps as late as the third century. The author contrasts the unsatisfying faith of other religions with Christian teachings concerning love and good citizenship.

Like the **Epistle to Diognetus,** the **Apology of Quadratus** is believed to be dated considerably later than the Apostolic Fathers. The writing which is a fragment from a defense of Christianity addressed to the Emperor Hadrian, is preserved by Eusebius. Some scholars believe the **Epistle to Diognetus** and the **Apology of Quadratus** are the same.

While the writings designated Apostolic Fathers differ in the precision of their dating and authorship, as writings that predate the formation of the New Testament canon, they are invaluable resources for understanding post-apostolic Christianity.   *E. Glenn Hinson*

APOTHECARY (Å pŏth' ĕ câr y) KJV translation of a word translated as perfumer in modern versions (Ex. 30:25,35; 37:29; 2 Chron. 16:14; Neh. 3:8; Eccl. 10:1). See *Perfume, Perfumer.*

APPAIM (Ăp' pā·ĭm) Personal name meaning, "nostrils." Member of clan of Jerahmeel of tribe of Judah (1 Chron. 2:30–31).

APPEAL TO CAESAR When Paul was brought before Festus for trial on charges made against him by Jews from Jerusalem, Festus asked him if he wanted to return to Jerusalem for trial. Paul, fearing the Jews would kill him, asked that his case be heard by the emperor as he had done nothing deserving of death (Acts 25:1–12). By all appearances, Paul's Roman citizenship gave him the right to have his case heard by the emperor. There are cases, however, where Roman citizens in Africa were refused the right of appeal and were crucified by Galba, the governor of the province. Paul was granted his appeal, though it was later determined that he need not have appealed his case as he had done nothing wrong (Acts 26:32). We do not know the results of Paul's appeal since Acts ends with Paul still in prison awaiting trial. It is probable that Paul's case was dismissed after two years and he was released from prison.

APPENDAGE OF THE LIVER See *Caul.*

APPHIA (Ăp' phĭ·å) Christian lady Paul greeted as "beloved" while writing Philemon (v.2). Early Christian tradition identified her as Philemon's wife, a claim that can be neither proved nor disproved.

APPI FORUM (Ăp' pĭ fō' rŭm) KJV translation of Acts 28:15 reference to Forum of Appius or Market of Appius. See *Forum of Appius.*

APPIUS (Ăp' pĭ·ŭs) See *Forum of Appius.*

APPLE OF THE EYE An English expression that refers to the pupil of the eye and therefore to something very precious. Three different Hebrew words or phrases are rendered as the apple of the eye: (1) the word in Deuteronomy 32:10 and Proverbs 7:2 literally means "little man" and evidently refers to the reflection of a person in the eye of another; (2) the word in Psalm 17:8 and Lamentations 2:18 (KJV) literally means "the daughter of the eye" with possibly the same significance as (1); and (3) the word in Zechariah 2:8 literally means "gate." The reference in Lamentations 2:18 is to the pupil of the eye as the source of tears; the other references are metaphorical of something that is precious.

APPLE TREE A tree known in the Old Testament for its fruit, shade, beauty, and fragrance (Joel 1:12; Prov. 25:11; Song of Sol. 2:3,5; 7:8; 8:5). Some scholars doubt that the Hebrew text is referring to the apple tree. They think the common apple tree was only recently introduced to Palestine, and that the wild variety hardly matches the description given to the tree and its fruit in the Bible. The citron, quince, and apricot have been proposed as the tree spoken of in the Bible. Of the three, the apricot seems to have the best support. Having been introduced from China prior to the time of Abraham, the apricot is widespread in Palestine. When conditions for it are right, the apricot tree can grow to a height of about thirty feet with spreading branches, which make it a good shade tree. Hebrew *tappuach* "apple" does appear as a place name in the Bible and may indicate apple trees were known as unusual occurrences in some Palestinian sites.

APRON Translation of a Hebrew word in the Old Testament otherwise translated as girdle (1 Sam. 18:4; 2 Sam. 18:11; 20:8; 1 Kings 2:5; Isa. 3:24). In Genesis 3:7, the fig leaves sown together by Adam and Eve are called aprons to hide their nakedness. In the Old Testament the girdle was an inner garment wrapped around the waist. In the New Testament the girdle was wrapped around the waist of the outer garment. In Acts 19:12 the aprons and handkerchiefs of Paul had healing powers.

AQABA, GULF OF TEV translation in 1 Kings 19:26 to show that the part of the Red Sea meant is the eastern arm below the Dead Sea. Its northern port city is Eloth (or Elath, NIV). See *Eloth; Ezion-geber.*

AQUEDUCTS were troughs cut out of rock or soil or pipes made of stone, leather, or bronze that were used from very early times in the Middle East to transport water from distant places into towns and cities.

Old Testament The simplest aqueducts were troughs cut out of rock or soil and sometimes lined with mortar. These troughs carried water from hillsides to the valleys below. Jerusalem was served by a system of aqueducts which brought mountain spring water first to collecting reservoirs outside the city, and then into the city itself. Hezekiah's tunnel, the Siloam tunnel, was a twisting underground aqueduct that diverted water from the Gihon Spring to the Pool of Siloam (2 Kings 20:20).

Roman Aqueducts The Romans excelled in building aqueducts, and the remains of these systems are impressive. Ancient aqueducts, the non-pressure type, carried water downhill by means of gravity. Although most conduits were beneath the ground, lowlands were crossed on high, arched structures, each containing a built-in slope so that water flow was not impeded. Sometimes these elevated sections, while also carrying several chan-

Island of Pharaoh, in the Gulf of Aqaba.

nels of water, served as footbridges. The Romans built many aqueducts, the longest of which covered fifty-seven miles. Pipes were made of various materials such as stone, leather, or bronze.

Diane Cross

Roman aqueduct at Caesarea Maritima which transported water to the city from the Carmel Mountains.

AQUILA and PRISCILLA were a married couple who came from Italy to Corinth after the emperor Claudius ordered Jews expelled from Rome, became Christians, and assisted Paul in his ministry. They were tentmakers by trade (2 Tim. 4:19). They came into contact with Paul, who was a tentmaker, in Corinth (Acts 18:2). It is not clear whether they became Christians before or after meeting Paul; but, they became workers in the gospel, and accompanied Paul to Ephesus (Acts 18:19). There they instructed Apollos in the Christian faith (18:25). A church met in their home, and they joined Paul in writing to the Corinthian church (1 Cor. 16:19).

Aquila and Priscilla were apparently influential among the "churches of the Gentiles" (Rom. 16:3). This reference in Romans probably indicates that Priscilla and Aquila moved back to Rome. Some scholars think the church at Ephesus received a copy of the last chapter of Romans. The reference to the couple in 2 Timothy 4:19 may indicate the couple was in Ephesus.

Paul thanked Aquila and Priscilla for risking their own lives for him (Rom. 16:4). The circumstances of this incident are unknown, although it may have occurred during Paul's trouble with Demetrius the silversmith (Acts 20:23–41).

Taylor Field

AR (Är) Place name meaning, "city." Town or northern border of Moab on southern bank of Arnon River (Num. 21:15, 28). Israel celebrated its defeat with a proverbial taunt song (Num. 21:28). God refused to let Israel occupy Ar, having designated it for Lot's descendants, the Moabites (Deut. 2:9). Israel could only pass through Ar (Deut. 2:18), evidently the region controlled by the city-state. Ar provided provisions for the Israelites as they passed through on the last legs of the

wilderness wandering (Deut. 2:29). Isaiah used a threatening situation in Ar to announce a time when Moab would seek protection from Judah (Isa. 15:1). The exact location of the city is not known.

ARA (Ā' rà) Leader in tribe of Asher (1 Chron. 7:38).

ARAB (Ă' răb) Place name meaning "ambush." A city in the hill country of Judah near Hebron (Josh. 15:52). Usually identified with modern er-Rabiyeh. See *Arbite; Paarai.*

Reconstruction of the stone altar at Arad.

The Citadel, first temple of the Hebrew kings, was built by King David on the highest point in Arad.

ARABAH (Ăr' à·bāh) Place name meaning, "dry, infertile area" and common Hebrew noun meaning desert with hot climate and sparse rainfall. *1.* Modern usage refers specifically to the rift area below the Dead Sea to the Gulf of Elath or Aqaba, a distance of 110 miles. This was a copper-mining region and was guarded by military fortresses. Control of the Arabah along with control of the Red Sea port on its southern end meant control of valuable trade routes and sea routes connecting to southern Arabia and eastern Africa. See Deut. 2:8; 1 Kings 9:26–27. *2.* The wilderness of Judah encompassing the eastern slopes of the mountains of Judah with little rain, deep canyons, and steep cliffs where David hid from Saul (1 Sam. 23:24–25). *3.* The entire Jordan Valley running 70 miles from the Sea of Galilee to the Dead Sea, or more precisely the desert areas above the actual Zor or lushly fertile areas on the immediate shore of the Jordan. See Deut. 3:17 (RSV; NIV); Josh. 8:14 (TEV; NIV); 11:2, 16; 12:8 (NAS; NIV); 2 Sam. 2:29 (NAS; NIV); Jer. 39:4 (NAS; NIV); Ezek. 47:8 (NAS; NIV); Zech. 14:10 (NIV).

4. Sea of the Arabah is the Dead Sea. See NAS, NIV, RSV of Deut. 3:17; 4:49; Josh. 3:16; 2 Kings 14:25. *5.* The Araboth of Moab or plains of Moab includes the eastern shore of the Dead Sea south of the wadi Nimrim. Notice NEB translation as "lowlands of Moab." See Num. 22:1; 31:12; 36:13; Deut. 34:1; Josh. 13:32. *6.* The desert area or the eastern border of the Jordan River from the Sea of Galilee to the Dead Sea. See Joshua 12:1 (NAS, NIV, RSV). *7.* The Araboth of Jericho or plains of Jericho represent the area near the Jordan once dominated by the city state of Jericho. (Josh. 4:13; 5:10; 2 Kings 25:5; Jer. 39:5). *8.* The brook of the Arabah represents the southern border of Israel (Amos 6:14), possibly the River Zered, the wadi el-Qelt, or the wadi Hefren.

ARABIA (Á·rā′ bī·á) names an Asian penisula lying between the Red Sea on the west and the Persian Gulf on the east incorporating over 1,200,000 square miles of territory.

Old Testament The Arabian peninsula, together with the adjoining lands which were home to the biblical Arabs, includes all of present-day Saudi Arabia, the two Yemens (San'a' and Aden), Oman, the United Arab Emirates, Qatar, and Kuwait, as well as parts of Iraq, Syria, Jordan, and the Sinai Peninsula. The vast Arabian peninsula was divided into two distinct economic and social regions. Most biblical references to Arab peoples or territory are to the northern and western parts of this whole, but sometimes includes both the northern and southern portions.

In the northern portion of Arabia the mountains of the Anti-Lebanon, the Transjordanian Highlands, and the mountains of Edom flank the desert on the west. The mountains continue all the way down the western edge of the Arabian Peninsula bordering the Red Sea and are actually much higher and more rugged in the south. The central and northern portions of the peninsula, and extending north into Syria and Iraq, are vast expanses of sandy and rocky desert, including some of the driest climate in the world.

The name Arab comes from a Semitic root which in Hebrew is 'arab, probably meaning "nomad" or bedouin. This refers to the people of the northwestern parts of the Arabian territory, whom the Old Testament writers knew as nomadic herders of sheep and goats, and later, of camels. Sometimes 'arab simply refers to the economic status of nomads without geographical or ethical reference. Proper understanding of Scripture includes determining the specific meaning of Arab in each context.

The Arabs are also called in the Bible "the sons (or childen) of the east." Furthermore, many of the names of the Old Testament refer to people or tribes who were ethnically and linguistically Arab. These include the Midianites, the Ishmaelites, the people of Kedar, the Amalekites, the Dedanites, the Temanites, and others. The Israelites recognized their blood relationship with the Arabs. Most of these groups are linked with Abraham through his son Ishmael or through his second wife Keturah (Gen. 25).

The inhabitants of southern Arabia, in the mountains fringing the Red Sea and the Indian Ocean, were town-dwellers with a sophisticated system of irrigation. They possessed considerable wealth from incenses and spices which they grew, from gold, silver, and precious stones, which they mined in their own territory, and from these and other products which they transported and traded to the Mediterranean world and Mesopotamia from as far away as East Africa, India, and China.

New Testament The New Testament references to Arabia are fewer and less complex. The territory of the Nabatean Arabs is probably intended in each instance. The Nabateans controlled what is today southern Jordan and the Negeb of Israel; for a time they controlled as far north as Damascus. Arabs heard the gospel at Pentecost (Acts 2:11). Paul went to Arabia after his conversion (Gal. 1:17).

Joseph Coleson

ARABIM (Är′ à·bĭm) NAS transliteration of name of waterway mentioned in Isaiah 15:7. Other translations include: "brook of the willows" (KJV); "Ravine of the Poplars" (NIV); Valley of Willows (TEV); "Wadi of the Willows (NRSV). The water source indicated may be the wadi el-Chesa at the southern end of the Dead Sea in Moab.

ARAD (Ā′ rad) names two towns of significance to the Old Testament and two Old Testament men.

1. One town is referred to in the Bible during the time of Moses, and another was inhabited during the period of the monarchy. Both are located in the dry, semi-desert region known as the Negeb in the southern extreme of Judah's territory.

The Arad of Numbers 21:1–3 (probably Tel Malhata) was a Canaanite city about eleven miles west southwest of Beersheba. Its king attacked the Israelites as they were moving on to Canaan after the wilderness wandering. He was successful temporarily, taking captives; but after vowing to God that they would destroy the city, Israel struck back effectively and renamed the devastated city Hormah. Victory over this king is recorded in Joshua 12:14. Subsequently the Kenites settled in Arad near the tribe of Judah (Judg. 1:16–17).

Another Arad location about seventeen miles west northwest of Beersheba is not mentioned in the Bible, but was an important fortress for Judah from Solomon's time to Josiah, over three hundred years. A temple has been found there with architecture much like the biblical tabernacle and Temple, having similar chambers including a holy of holies. Even the names of priestly families of Israel have been found here, Pashhur (Ezra 2:38; 10:22) and Meremoth (Ezra 8:33; Neh. 10:5). The Temple may well have been destroyed during Josiah's reforms which tolerated only the one Temple in Jerusalem.

2. One of six sons of Beriah the Benjamite (1 Chron. 8:15,16) who was one of the major inhabitants of Aijalon. (See *Aijalon.*) Another Old Testament Arad was a Canaanite king who attacked the Israelites near Mount Hor and was defeated (Num. 21:1).   *Daniel C. Fredericks*

ARAH (Ā' răh) Personal name meaning, "ox" or "traveller." *1.* Clan of 775 people who returned to Jerusalem with Zerubbabel from Babylonian Exile about 537 B.C. (Ezra 2:5). Nehemiah 7:10 gives the number as 652. *2.* Father of Schechaniah, father-in-law of Tobiah, who led opposition to Nehemiah (Neh. 6:18). May be identical with clan head of *1* above. *3.* Member of tribe of Asher (1 Chron. 7:39).

ARAM (Ā' răm) Personal, ethnic, and geographical name. *1.* Arameans. See *Aramean.* *2.* Original ancestor of Arameans, the son of Shem and grandson of Noah (Gen. 10:22–23). *3.* Grandson of Nahor, Abraham's brother (Gen. 22:21). *4.* Member of tribe of Asher (1 Chron. 7:34). See various compound names with Aram below and *Beth Rehob; Padan-Aram; Geshur; Maacah; Tob;* Zobah.

ARAMAIC (Ăr·à·mā' ĭc) A North Semitic language similar to Phoenician and Hebrew was the language of the Arameans whose presence in northwestern Mesopotamia is known from about 2000 B.C.

A funerary inscription of the second burial of King Uzziah written in Aramaic during Herod's time.

Old Testament Although the Arameans never founded a great national state or empire, by the eleventh century they had established several small states in Syria, and their language came to be known from Egypt to Persia.

The oldest inscriptions in Old Aramaic are from Syria around 800 B.C. In the ninth century official or Royal Aramaic appeared. This was a dialect known from documents from Assyria and known best from documents from the Persian empire, for which Aramaic had become the official court language. Before 700 B.C. Aramaic had begun to supplant Akkadian as the language of commerce and diplomacy (2 Kings 18:26). Important for biblical history are the fifth century papyri from Elephantine, the site of a Jewish colony in Egypt. Official Aramaic continued to be used widely throughout the Hellenistic period.

Parts of the Old Testament were written in Aramaic: Ezra 4:8—6:18; 7:12–26; Daniel 2:4*b*—7:28; Jeremiah 10:11. Two words in Genesis 31:47, *Jegar-sahadutha* (heap of witness) are in Aramaic. A number of Aramaic words came into common Hebrew usage, and several passages in the Hebrew Bible show Aramaic influence.

New Testament The wide diffusion of Aramaic, along with its flexibility and adaptability, resulted in the emergence of various dialects. In Syria-Palestine the western group includes Jewish Palestinian Aramaic, Samaritan, Palmyrene, and Nabataean. Jewish Palestinian Aramaic words and phrases occur in the New Testament, such as *Abba* (father) (Mark 14:36), *talitha, qumi* (maiden, arise) (Mark 5:41), *lama sabachthani* (why hast thou forsaken me?) (Mark 15:34). The Palestinian Talmud and the Targums (translations of Old Testament books into Aramaic) also were written in Palestinian Jewish Aramaic. The eastern (Mesopotamian) group includes Babylonian Jewish Aramaic, Mandaean, and Syriac.

                              Tom Smothers

ARAMEAN (Ăr·à·mē' ăn) consisted of the loose confederation of towns and settlements spread over what is now called Syria as well as in some parts of Babylon from which Jacob and Abraham came (Deut. 26:5). The Arameans were rarely gathered into a cohesive political group; rather they lived as independent towns and tribes settled by nomads prior to 1000 B.C. Although the Arameans were quick to form alliances with each other or with other countries if threatened, once the crisis was ended they disbanded and often fought among themselves and against their former allies.

The Old Testament records interactions between Israel and the Arameans on a number of occasions. Deuteronomy 26:5 contains what has become an important confession for Jews—"A wandering Aramean was my father . . ." (RSV)—which claims Aramean lineage for Jacob and by extension for Abraham. The first mention of Arameans outside of the Bible dates from the reign of Tiglath-pileser I of Assyria (1116–1076 B.C.). Thus roughly at the start of Israel's monarchy, the Arameans became a potent political force. They were able to seize large portions of Assyrian lands, defeating Tiglath-pileser I and II and Ashur-rabi II. At the same time they suffered losses to David on the western front (2 Sam. 8:9–10). He demanded tribute from Hadadezer, king of Zobah, and married Maacah the daughter of Talmui, king of Geshur. It was Maacah who bore Absalom (2 Sam. 3:3). Both Zobah and Geshur were Aramean states.

The most important city of the Arameans was Damascus. Although the political influence of the Arameans was relatively unimportant, they made a lasting contribution with their language. See *Assyria; Damascus; Aramaic.*

Tim Turnham

ARAMITESS (Är′ à·mīt·ĕss) KJV translation in 1 Chronicles 7:14 for an unnamed concubine from Aram, thus an Aramean or Syrian. She was mother of Machir, son of Manasseh.

ARAM-MAACAH (Ā′ răm-Mā′ à·căh) Territory in Syria (1 Chron. 19:6), also called Syria-Maachah, Maacah, Maachah. See *Maacah.* In 2 Samuel 10:6 only Aram-Zobah is named.

This mountain (in modern Turkey) may be Mt. Ararat where Noah's ark came to rest after the flood.

ARAM-NAHARAIM (Ā′ răm-Nā·hȧ·rā′ īm) Country name meaning, "Aram of the two rivers." Appears in title of Psalm 60 in KJV. Transliterated from Hebrew also in Genesis 24:10; Deuteronomy 23:4; Judges 3:8; and 1 Chronicles 19:6 by NIV. It refers to the land between the Tigris and Euphrates River. Nahor, Abraham's brother, lived there; and Rebekah, Isaac's wife, came from there. Balaam, the prophet Balak hired to curse Israel as they entered Moab from the wilderness, came from Aram-Naharaim. So did Cushan-Rishathaim, who oppressed Israel before Othniel delivered them. The Ammonites bought military help from Aram-Naharaim to fight David.

ARAM-ZOBAH (Ā′ răm-Zō′ bah) Alternate name for the Aramean town and kingdom of Zobah found in the superscription of Psalm 60. See *Zobah.*

ARAN (Ā′ răn) Personal name perhaps meaning, "ibex." A Horite descended from Seir (Gen. 36:28).

ARARAT (Âr′ à·răt) A mountainous region in western Asia mentioned on four occasions in the Bible: (1) the place where the ark came to rest after the flood (Gen. 8:4); (2) the region where Sennacherib's sons, Adrammelech and Sharezer, fled for refuge after murdering their father (2 Kings 19:37); (3) Isaiah's version of 2 Kings 19:37 (Isa. 37:38); (4) Jeremiah's prophetic call for a war league as judgment against Babylon (Jer. 51:27). The references in Kings and Isaiah are rendered

'Armenia' in KJV, following the Septuagint tradition.

Geography The Ararat of the Old Testament is known as the land of Urartu in sources outside the Bible, especially Assyrian sources. The people of the region identified themselves as "children of Haldi" (the national god) and their land as *Biainae.* The country was southeast of the Black Sea and southwest of the Caspian, where the head waters of the Tigris and Euphrates Rivers were found. Near the center of the land was Lake Van; Lake Sevan lay on its northern border; and Lake Urmia was found in its southeast corner. Modern Turkey, Iran, and Soviet Armenia occupy parts of the ancient land area of Urartu. Mt. Ararat is located to the northeast of Lake Van.

Ararat rises from the lowlands of the Aras River to a height of 17,000 feet. Considering the high elevation, the region is remarkably fertile and pasturable. Archaeologists believe that Ararat received more rainfall in biblical times than it does today, an observation which suggests that the area would have been even more productive as farmland in ancient times.

History of Ararat The height of Urartian political prominence was between 900 and 700 B.C. Culturally the Urartians were akin to the earlier Hurrians and to the Assyrians whose empire stretched to the south. From after 1100 until after 800 B.C., Urartu remained independent of Assyria, and in many ways was a political rival. The rise of Tiglath-pileser III (745–727 B.C.) in Assyria, followed by Sargon II (721–705 B.C.), crushed any political ambitions Urartu might have had in the region.

See *Noah; Ark;* and *Flood.*   *A. J. Conyers*

ARARITE (Âr′ ā·rīte) NAS spelling of Hararite (2 Sam. 23:23) reflecting distinctive Hebrew spelling of written text, which has already been marked for change by early Hebrew scribes. See *Hararite.*

ARAUNAH (Å·raū′ näh) Personal name of unknown meaning. A Jebusite whose threshing floor David purchased as a site for sacrifice, following the prophetic command of God, holding back a divine plague after David disobeyed by taking a census (2 Sam. 24:15–25). 2 Chronicles 3:1 and 1 Chronicles 21:15–30 refer to Araunah as Ornan.

ARBA (Är′ bà) Personal name meaning, "four." Father of Anak for whom Kiriath-arba was named (Josh. 14:15; 15:13). The city became known as Hebron. Arba was the outstanding warrior among the Anakim. See *Anakim.*

ARBATHITE (Är′ bằth·īte) Resident of Beth-Arabah (2 Sam. 23:31). See *Beth-Arabah.*

ARBITE (Är′ bīte) Native of Arab, a village in

Judah near Hebron (Josh. 15:52), identified as modern er-Rabiyeh. See *Paarai.*

ARCH KJV rendering of a Hebrew word in Ezekiel 40:16–36. The KJV translates the word as porch elsewhere (for example, 1 Kings 6:3; 7:12,19,21). Other versions translate the word as porch (NAS), portico and galleries (NIV), vestibule and walls (RSV), and entrance room and galleries (TEV). Aside from 1 Kings 7:6 (where the word describes a covered porch whose roof is supported by columns; see *Hall of Pillars*), the word refers to the entrance room to the main building of the

Graeco-Roman arches in the ruins of Gerasa (modern Jerash, Jordan), a city in the Decapolis.

Temple just outside the holy place. The entrance was about thirty by fifteen feet and forty-five feet high (1 Kings 6:2–3; but compare 2 Chron. 3:4). In Ezekiel's vision of the Temple, each gate leading into the court of the Gentiles also had a vestibule (40:7–26) as did the gates to the court of the Israelites (40:29–37).

ARCHAEOLOGY AND BIBLICAL STUDY Archaeology is a study of the past based upon the recovery, examination, and explanation of the material remains of human life, thought, and activity, coordinated with available information concerning the ancient environment.

Biblical archaeology, a discipline largely developing since 1800, searches for what can be learned about biblical events, characters, and teachings from sources outside the Bible. Dealing with what ancient civilizations left behind, its goal is to give a better understanding of the Bible itself.

Students of the Bible are particularly interested in the archaeology of ancient Canaan and its adjacent regions. Today, this is the land forming the countries of Israel, Lebanon, Syria, and Jordan. In addition, the biblical world included other regions such as Egypt, Greece, Italy, Cyprus, the Arabian Peninsula, and the large areas occupied by present-day Turkey, Iraq, and Iran.

Objective The Bible lands have as yet been only partly investigated. Few mounds have been completely excavated. The significance of the objects

Step trench cut into the tel of Old Testament Jericho by archaeologists to uncover levels of destruction.

found is subject to diverse interpretation, and conclusions once held are often abandoned in favor of new hypotheses. In using archaeological data, biblical students need to take precautions to be current. They also need to be conscious of what archaeology can and cannot do. The basic affirmations of the Bible—that God is, that He is active in history, and that Jesus is His Son raised from the dead—are not subject to archaeological verification. One can demonstrate from archaeological materials that Sennacherib invaded Judah in the time of Hezekiah, but that he was a tool in the hand of the Lord can only be known from biblical assertion. That claim is not open to archaeological verification.

The goal of excavation now is to reconstruct, in as far as possible, the total ancient environment of the site, making materials previously ignored to be important. Epigraphers, anthropologists, botanists, bone, pottery, and architectural specialists are all essential to the effort.

A brief history of archaeology The work of archaeologists in the biblical world in general, and in ancient Canaan in particular, can be divided into three over-lapping periods.

1. Stage One In the earliest period, prior to about A.D. 1900, the practice of archaeology was primarily a "treasure hunt" with no organized, systematic way of going about the work. Individuals set forth to find spectacular items from the past. No clearly determined methodology was followed. Pits and trenches dug into ancient cities often destroyed more than they revealed. Since the area occupied by ancient Israel was relatively poor in "treasure," much of this work was carried out in Egypt and in Mesopotamia, the ancient homeland of the Assyrians and Babylonians (the present site of the country of Iraq).

Before 1800 little was known of the biblical world except from often inaccurate data transmitted by classical writers. The secrets of Egypt opened following the discovery in 1799 of the Rosetta stone and its decipherment by Champollion. The secrets of Mesopotamia began to unfold following the copying and decipherment of the Behistun inscription by Rawlinson begun in 1835, and by the later discovery in 1852 of Ashurbanipal's library by Rassam. Architecture, art, and written sources recovered from numerous ancient sites began to cast rays of light on the Bible, particularly on the Old Testament. About the middle of the nineteenth century, English archaeologists excavated portions of the city of Nineveh, capital of the ancient Assyrian Empire at the height of its power.

Among the discoveries at Nineveh were two great palaces. The huge palace of the Assyrian king, Sennacherib (704–681 B.C.), contained hundreds of feet of wall space lined with sculptured reliefs depicting the exploits of the king. Included is a striking picture of the siege of the important biblical fortress-city of Lachish which was captured by the Assyrians in 701 B.C. Also among the discoveries was the Taylor Prism which contains a written Assyrian version of their invasion of the kingdom of Judah in 701 B.C. The biblical account of the siege of Jerusalem at this time is found in 2 King 18:13—19:37. It is interesting to compare the two records. Although Sennacherib does not claim to have captured Jerusalem, he makes no mention of the calamity suffered by his troops as described in the biblical account.

The palace of King Asshurbanipal (668–633 B.C.) was also uncovered. The most significant find here was a great library of written documents which the king had collected from many portions of the empire. These have provided the student of the Bible with much primary source material from this portion of the ancient world. Of particular interest are mythological stories relating traditions of creation and of a great flood as understood by the people of ancient Mesopotamia.

2. Stage Two Near the beginning of the twentieth century, significant developments in the discipline of archaeology began to occur. In 1890, Sir Flinders Petrie, an English archaeologist who had done important works in Egypt, began excavations at Tell el-Hesi in southwestern Palestine. This work was continued in 1891–92 by an American, F. J. Bliss.

The word "tell" refers to an ancient mound built

up over a long period of time by the occupational debris of persons living at the site. People chose to live at a site for certain reasons. The presence of a water supply was crucial. The site might need to be defended from enemies and, therefore, high ground was usually chosen. Fertile soil, the presence of minerals or other natural resources, and accessibility to trade routes were also important factors.

In time, a site was often abandoned, either briefly or for a long duration. The reason might be destruction by an enemy or by a natural catastrophe, such as an earthquake. A town might be deserted because of an epidemic of disease. Another important and probably common reason for people leaving a site was a weather change such as drought. Regardless of why people left, the reasons for settling there in the first place often drew them back. The debris of the earlier occupation was made smooth by leveling off and filling in, and a new village was built on top of the ruins. This process, along with the ordinary accumulation of debris and rebuilding that occurs in any area of human occupation, gradually over the centuries and millennia resulted in the site becoming higher and higher—a "tell" was formed, containing many strata (layers). A large number of these artificially formed mounds dot the biblical landscape.

The work of Petrie and Bliss referred to above was highly significant in two interrelated ways. First, they tried very carefully to excavate Tell el-Hesi layer by layer. Second, they made careful notes of the style of pottery found in each layer. Since the way pottery was made changed through the years, the type found in any one layer permitted the archaeologist to assign an approximate date to that level. Almost a century of study of pottery now enables archaeologists to give almost an absolute date for each strata excavated. Petrie and Bliss's work marks the beginning of a scientific, disciplined approach to archaeology in Palestine. The principles of stratagraphic excavation (isolating each layer) and of pottery analysis are still basic to sound methodology, although many improvements have occurred since the beginning of the twentieth century.

Archaeologists attempt to determine when they are leaving one layer and entering another on the basis of such items as changes in the color, consistency, and content of the soil, or, in some cases, the presence of ashes between strata. A stratum may be very thin or quite thick depending on the nature of the occupation and how long it lasted.

During the first half of the twentieth century, many archaeological expeditions from numerous countries were sent to the biblical world. Stratigraphic excavation and pottery analysis became more precise and exact. Careful records (written reports, drawings, photographs) were kept.

Much was learned. Space permits only one illustration at this point. Samaria was the capital of the Northern Kingdom of ancient Israel. The city was built by the Hebrew Kings Omri and his son Ahab in the first half of the ninth century B.C. During the first third of the twentieth century, excavations sponsored by Harvard University, with the help of several other institutions, partially recovered this old capital city of the Northern Kingdom.

Among the many interesting discoveries at Samaria was a group of over sixty ostraca, probably from the time of King Jeroboam II (782–743 B.C.). An ostracon (plural, ostraca) is a piece of broken pottery that has been written upon. Ancient peoples often employed pieces of pottery as a writing surface and used these for records, lists, and letters. The ostraca from Samaria contain the records of supplies, including grain, oil, and wine, which had been sent in for the support of the royal palace by persons living in various towns. From these, some information can be deduced about the economy and the political organization of the land. In addition, the presence of names of several persons containing Baal as a component (eg. Abibaal, Meribaal) reveal the continued influence of Baalism in the land.

A comparison of these ostraca with Amos 6:1–7 also suggests that the "tax" levied on the common people was being used to support a life-style of luxury and debauchery on the part of the high officials in the government. The passage in Amos also mentions "beds of ivory" (v. 4; see 3:15; 1 Kings 22:39). Several hundred pieces of ivory were found in the excavations of Samaria. Many of these had been used as inlays in furniture.

Overview of the excavations at tel Arad in Israel, showing the Citadel built by David (right background).

In addition to Samaria, excavations began or were continued at a large number of sites in the biblical world during the first six or seven decades of the twentieth century. The list includes such important places as Babylon and Ur in ancient Mesopotamia and Ai, Bethel, Hazor, Jericho, Jerusalem, Lachish, Megiddo, Shechem, and many other sites in ancient Israel.

3. Stage Three Beginning about 1960, a new stage in the history of archaeology in the Ancient

Near East began to emerge. It was prompted in part by a new question that people began to ask: "What does it all mean?" Archaeologists and others began to realize that it was not enough to make discoveries and to describe those discoveries. They needed synthesis of information and the explanation of data.

During the second stage of archaeology, primary attention had been paid to art, architecture, pottery and written sources, with little or no thought given to the investigation of other possible windows of information to the past. As the third stage began to unfold, it became clear that to determine the meaning of the evidence being recovered and to understand more fully the people and civilizations of the past required additional information.

This stage of archaeology, sometimes called the "New Archaeology," is characterized by a multidisciplinary team approach to the archaeological task. The approach also emphasizes the use of volunteer help and a strong educational program. In the previous stage much of the labor of digging had been done by persons living in the region who were paid for their services. The third stage of archaeology also is characterized by a growing tendency to think in terms of a regional approach rather than concentrating exclusively on one site. Interest is growing in the investigation of small villages as opposed to an almost total concentration in the past on large, "important" cities.

In Israel, the modern approach was pioneered at Tell Gezer in the 1960's and early 1970's and was continued at numerous sites, such as Tell el-Hesi and Tell Halif in the 1970's and 1980's. The professional staff of an archaeology team in the new stage includes not only field archaeologists, but also botanists, geologists, zoologists, and anthropologists with various areas of expertise and interest. The plant and animal life of an ancient site can now be determined. This allows one to reconstruct the diet of the people and may shed significant information about weather patterns in the past. Examination of human skeletons and burial customs provides important clues about the health of the people and about some of their religious beliefs. Careful analysis of stone tools sheds light on the kinds of industry common in the community. Examination of the constituents in the clay used for pottery often permits one to determine where the vessel was made and may provide helpful information about commerce and trade routes.

All of this permits a much more complete picture than is available from buildings, pottery forms, and even from many written sources. Now there seems to be a real possibility that information about the everyday life of ordinary men and women during the biblical period can be gained.

Contributions of Archaeology to Biblical Study
The purpose of archaeology is not to "prove the Bible." This lies outside the scope of archaeology and, in any case, the Bible does not need to be "proved." Archaeology can, however, make considerable contribution to one's understanding of the Bible. It can help clarify and illuminate the Bible in many important ways.

1. Archaeology and the Biblical Text The oldest complete copy of the Old Testament in Hebrew, the Leningrad Manuscript, has a date of A.D. 1008. The major Greek manuscripts from which the New Testament is translated came from the fourth century A.D. The Bible, particulary the Old Testament, was copied by hand many times before reaching the form found in the manuscripts just mentioned. During that process some mistakes were inevitably made by the human scribes. Also, some words in the Bible, particularly in the Old Testament, are obscure—their meaning is not certain. This can be a particularly difficult problem when a word is used only once or twice in the Bible.

Archaeology, through the recovery of ancient Hebrew and Greek copies of the Scripture, plus the discovery of other old literature written in related languages has helped scholars to determine a more exact text of the Bible than was available previously. It has also demonstrated that the scribes were very careful in their work.

At the end of the last century in a rubbish room (now known as the Cairo Geniza) of an old synagogue in Cairo, Egypt, an invaluable find of Hebrew materials was made. In 1947 archaeologists began to see the Dead Sea Scrolls found in eleven caves. This moved knowledge of Hebrew manuscripts back from the Middle Ages to the period 250 B.C. to A.D. 70.

A new Old Testament critical text is being prepared by the Hebrew University in Jerusalem from an old codex from the synagogue at Aleppo, Syria, with comparisons with the new materials.

The Dead Sea Scrolls are from Qumran, an old community located near the northwest shore of the Dead Sea. At least a fragment of every Old Testament book except Esther was found in the Qumran caves. A complete copy of the Book of Isaiah was written about 100 B.C. The text of this manuscript is very close to that found eleven hundred years later in the Leningrad Manuscript. During all those years, the scribes did their job very well. In a handful of cases, however, minor problems which had crept into the text of Isaiah could be corrected by use of the older scroll. Modern translations of the Old Testament usually include these improvements.

Knowledge of *writing* has greatly increased. The earliest documents now known from Syria-Palestine would be the Ebla texts (the first of which were found in 1975) dating about 2400 B.C., followed by the Ugaritic texts (found 1929–1937) on the coast of Syria and dating about 1400 B.C. Examples of eight different writing scripts in Palestine which antedate the time of Moses have solved the question debated in the last century of whether or not Moses could have known writing. Examples of decipherable Hebrew found by archaeologists begin at about the time of Solomon with the Gezer calendar.

In 1929 French archaeologists began to excavate the ancient city of Ugarit near the coast of Syria. Many clay tablets containing ancient writing were unearthed. Most of these were written in a previously unknown language, soon called Ugaritic. Ugaritic is a Northwest Semitic language. Hebrew belongs to this same family of languages. Ugaritic is the earliest example of a language written in an alphabetical script. A study of Ugaritic has helped Old Testament scholars better understand the nature and development of the Hebrew language, and it has been of particular value in the clarification of some of the ancient Hebrew poetry contained in the Bible.

Earlier scholars defined Old Testament words by comparison with Arabic and by meanings derived from rabbinic tradition. Discovery and decipherment of previously unknown ancient Middle Eastern languages like Sumerian, Akkadian, Hittite, Ugaritic, Aramaic, and Eblite give a wider base for definition of words, making (by the study called Comparative Semitics) for a substantial reorientation of Old Testament vocabulary.

In 1 Samuel 13:21 there is a Hebrew word, *pim,* which occurs nowhere else in the Bible. The meaning of this word was not known to early readers and translators of the Bible. Although the translators of the *King James Version* of 1611 chose the word *file* to translate *pim,* there was no firm basis for the choice. Since that time archaeologists have found several small weights from ancient Israel bearing the word *pim*. A *pim* appears to have weighed a little less than a shekel. Now it is clear that the word *pim* refers to the charge made by the Philistines for working on the Hebrew's iron tools. Recent translations of the Bible reflect this new understanding.

With reference to the New Testament, during the last one to two centuries, numerous old papyrus manuscripts have been found, mainly in Egypt, which contain portions of the biblical text. At least a small portion of every book in the New Testament, except 1 and 2 Timothy, has been found in these ancient Greek papyri. The oldest of these is known as the Rylands Papyrus dated about A.D. 125. It contains John 18:31–33,37–38. These papyri are useful to scholars involved in the task of determining the best textual base of the New Testament. The number of Greek manuscripts and fragments known has increased from about 1,500 in 1885 to 5,373 in 1986. Included are ninety-three papyrus items which carry knowledge of the text behind the fourth century codices previously depended upon to the second century for the parts of the text covered. New Greek

critical texts are being prepared to make all the material available to students, and already English translations are reflecting the new finds.

The non-biblical papyrus find made in Egypt at the end of the last century furnished new insights into everyday Greek usage and vocabulary which have now become the substance of New Testament language study.

Related to the matter of text is the question of canon. Why were some books included in the Bible and others omitted? How and when did this selection take place? The Dead Sea Scrolls from Qumran throw some limited light on these questions. For example, some parts of the canon were still not finalized during the time of this Jewish community (ca. 150 B.C. to A.D. 68). Scrolls containing the Book of Psalms have been found in cave eleven which differ in several ways from the Book of Psalms as it was finalized by the Jews about A.D. 100. The Qumran material contains some psalms that eventually were left out of the Bible and omit some that were finally included.

Also, the Qumran group had two different old Hebrew copies of the Book of Jeremiah. One, a longer version, was eventually accepted as the standard by the Jewish people and is the one now translated in the Christian's Old Testament. The shorter version can be found in the Septuagint, the ancient translation of the Old Testament into Greek.

2. Archaeology and Biblical Geography As late as A.D. 1800, the location of many of the places mentioned in the Bible was unknown. In 1838, an American explorer by the name of Edward Robinson, and his assistant, Eli Smith, made a trip through Palestine on horseback. On the basis of their study of geography and the analysis of place names, they were able to identify over one hundred biblical sites. Robinson returned for further exploration in 1852.

Since the time of Robinson, archaeologists have been able to identify a great many of the sites mentioned in the Bible, including the places visited by the apostle Paul on his travels. Not only have villages and cities been identified, but entire kingdoms have been located. For example, excavations beginning in 1906 by German archaeologists in what is now Turkey recovered the lost empire of the Hittites.

The location of places like Jerusalem and Bethlehem were never forgotten. Other places were destroyed and their location lost. Edward Robinson developed a technique by which literary information and travelers' reports, coupled with local historical memory, could give probable identities. Excavation of the ruins in the areas has helped. Twenty-eight jar handles found in the cistern at El Jib made certain the location of ancient Gibeon; six stone carvings with the name "Gezer" identify that place, and "Arad" seven times scratched on a potsherd confirms its location.

A

3. Archaeology and Biblical History The Bible makes no attempt to give a complete history of the people of God, much less of the entire biblical world. The material included in the Bible was carefully selected under the guidance of God, and the history contained therein is theologically interpreted. Today's reader, far removed from the ancient event, often wishes for a more complete understanding of the historical context. Archaeology has helped a great deal in this regard by recovering many ancient historical records, including documents from Assyria, Babylonian, and Egypt. This

information fills in some of the blank spaces, illuminating the biblical narrative and making the sacred accounts more understandable and interesting.

Egyptian reports like "The Tale of Sinuhe" show how Palestine appeared to Egyptians about the time of Abraham. The Tell Amarna tablets found by a peasant woman in Egypt are letters from Palestinian rulers to the reigning pharaohs; but they show the unstable conditions in Palestine prior to the Israelite conquest which enabled Israel to conquer the enemy one by one.

The Egyptian Pharaoh Merneptah (1213–1204 B.C.) invaded Syro-Palestine during his brief reign. A monument found in his mortuary chamber at Thebes contains a record of this venture and includes the oldest reference to Israel outside of the Bible. Israel is called a people, rather than a nation. Merneptah claimed to have utterly destroyed them. Here is clear evidence that Israelites were in the land of Canaan by no later than the thirteenth century B.C., and it supports the biblical picture that the people were not organized as a nation by this date.

The discovery of the law code of Hammurabi in 1901 at Susa with its preamble and 282 laws opened the way for interesting comparisons with Israel's laws. Archaeologists now have five cuneiform law codes which were written before the time of Moses: those of Ur-Nammu, Eshnunna, Lipit-Ishtar, Hammurabi, and the Hittites. Slightly later are the Middle Assyrian laws. Interesting comparisons in the "eye for an eye" law, the case of rape on the mountain as contrasted with in the city, possession of the goring ox, kidnapping, killing a thief in the house, and matters of deposited property can be made between these laws and those of Moses. Contrasts include the number of acts for which the accused is subjected to the ordeal (Num. 5) and the punishments of mutilation (Deut. 25:12). While these codes have both similarities and differences from the laws of Moses, the claim of borrowing cannot be established. The varieties of bodily mutilation prescribed by Hammurabi are absent in Israel's laws as are also the unlimited floggings.

Though searched for in the Jericho area, the location of Gilgal, the Israelites' camping place, remains elusive. Despite what now seems to have been unfounded claims earlier made for Jericho by John Garstang, archaeological evidence for the conquest of Jericho, Ai, and Gibeon, after excavation of the sites, remains debated. K. Kenyon demonstrated that Garstang misdated the walls which he assumed were those Joshua took. Debate continues over whether archaeological evidence shows a cultural change which could be identified with Israel's conquest of the land. Cities on the Palestinian hill

Continuing archaeological excavations along the southern border of the Temple Mount in Jerusalem.

country like Shiloh, Bethel, Gibeah, Bethzur, Debir, and Hazor underwent destruction in the late Bronze Age, and poorer cities rose on their mounds; but the destroyer and rebuilder remain unidentified.

The Philistines, a part of the "Sea Peoples" who came into the land following their being blocked in Egypt by Rameses III, and who left their name on the land, offered major opposition to the Israelites. Rameses III depicted his battle with them on sea and land on the walls of the temple at Medinet Habu. Philistine levels have been identified on numerous Palestine sites.

Interesting sidelights on the general period of the Judges and Kings include the Egyptian custom of counting the victims of a campaign from stacks of severed hands (compare Judg. 8:6), the putting out of an eye (1 Sam. 11:1–11), or both eyes (2 Kings 25:7), and depiction of circumcised men on a Megiddo ivory [as well as on an Egyptian papyrus] where the subject described his ordeal.

Tell el-Balatah (ancient Shechem) had foundations of a temple from the late Bronze Age conjectured to be those of Baal-Berith (Judg. 9). The Danites migrated north to Laish (Judg. 18:1–31), the site known as Tel Dan. Later Dan became a shrine city, and excavation has yielded an inscription from about A.D. 200 in Greek and Aramaic, "To the god who is in Dan." Dagon to whose temple the ark was taken while in Philistine territory (1 Sam. 5:2) is now known from occurrences of his name all over the Middle East to have been a grain god rather than a combined man-fish as he was hypothetically depicted in old dictionaries. In Ugaritic texts, Baal is the "son of Dagon."

Remains of similar city gates, conjecturally identified as Solomonic, have been found at Hazor, Megiddo, and Gezer. Remains of pagan temples of the Solomonic period, coupled with biblical data, enable scholars to do reconstruction of what Solomon's Temple must have been like. A potsherd from Tel Qasile is inscribed "Gold of Ophir to Bethhoron." Assyrian occurrences of the term "Que" make clear that it is a place in what is now southern Turkey from which Solomon got his horses rather than the "linen yarn" of the KJV (1 Kings 10:28). Claims of having found remains of Solomon's stables, as well as of finding his mines and smelter, have been abandoned.

The law (Ex. 22:26–27) forbids keeping overnight a man's garment in pledge. Amos 2:8 faults those who have used pledged garments at worship shrines. An ostracon found at Mesad Hashaviahu has the seventh century complaint of a man whose garment had been taken but who sought redress from the governor.

Inscriptions with the name of Yahweh, Israel's God, begin with the Mesha stone in the ninth century and stretch to the fifth century Elephantine papyri. They come from a wide geographical area, including Arad, Jerusalem, and Kuntillet ᶜAjrud. Numerous ostraca have names that are compounds of Yahweh.

After the death of Solomon (ca. 922 B.C.), the Hebrew kingdom divided into two portions, the Northern Kingdom (Israel) and the Southern Kingdom (Judah). One powerful nation thereby became two weak nations, and the Egyptian ruler Shishak took advantage of the situation by invading the land about 918 B.C. (1 Kings 14:25–28). The biblical account is very brief and only tells of an attack on Jerusalem. Shishak, however, recorded his exploits on a wall in the temple of the god Amun in Karnak, Egypt. He claims to have captured over 150 towns in Palestine, including places in the Northern Kingdom. The probability that this invasion was a greater blow to the Hebrew kingdoms than is obvious from the brief account in 1 Kings is suggested not only by the Egyptian record, which may have been inflated to some degree, but also by the archaeological evidence that several of the cities named were indeed destroyed at about this time. Here is an example of archaeology helping to provide a larger historical context which enriches the study of Scripture.

Mesha, king of Moab, on the Moabite stone gave his account of his servitude to the Israelite kings and his effort to free himself which seems parallel to the record in 2 Kings 3. The name of Omri, of Mesha, of the Lord, of Chemosh, and of numerous Palestinian cities are listed on this stone. The policy of *cherem* by which a place is totally devoted to the deity as Jericho earlier was (Josh. 6:21) is illustrated. Other records enlarge our knowledge of biblical characters. Such are the records of Ahab's participation in the battle of Qarqar in 853 B.C. on a monument set up by Shalmaneser III, and of Jehu's tribute to Shalmaneser III recorded on the black obelisk now in the British Museum. Neither episode is mentioned in the Bible.

Omri was king of the Northern Kingdom about 876–869 B.C. During his short reign he moved the capital from Tirzah to the newly built city of Samaria. He was an evil king, and the Bible devotes little space to him (1 Kings 16:15–28). The surrounding nations, however, perceived Omri as a very strong and able ruler. He made such an impression on the Assyrians that for over a hundred years their records continue to refer to Israel as "the House of Omri," even after his dynasty no longer ruled. This reminds one that, from a biblical perspective, faithfulness to God is considered to be much more important than ability in warfare and government.

Assyrian records furnish information on Tiglath-pileser, Sargon, Sennacherib, and Ashurbanipal who are significant in the Old Testament. They also mention the kings of Israel and Judah, chronicling the exchange of the last kings of Israel and the

exiling of Samaria. Until the excavation of Sargon's palace by Emil Botta, Sargon was known only from the Bible. Sargon's invasion of Ashdod (Isa. 20) was recorded by Sargon, and a fragment of a stele set up in Ashdod was found there. Sennacherib depicted his siege of Lachish in his palace and told on a cylinder of his bringing Hezekiah to his knees. A water tunnel in Jerusalem is conjectured to be that which Hezekiah built at this time. Its inscription tells of the excavation required to build the tunnel. A record tells of Sennacherib's murder by his son. The Babylonians told of the downfall of Nineveh, of the battle of Carchemish, and of the capture of Jerusalem in a record which establishes March 15/16, 597 B.C. as its date.

The prophetic movement is one of the most distinctive features of Old Testament life. Search for antecedents has looked at Ebla, where an occurrence of the equivalent of the Hebrew word is reported. More than twenty texts from Mari on the Euphrates report prophetic-like figures with visions and spoken messages given to the heads of state. The eleventh century tale of Wen-Amon's mission to Byblos continues to be the classic example of ecstatic behavior. The eighth century Zakir inscription from Afis, Syria, has the deity Baᶜal-sheman speak through his seers (*chozim*). The excavation of Tell Deir ᶜAlla yielded Balaam texts in Aramaic from the sixth century, the first prophetic text of any scope outside the Old Testament (compare Num. 22—24). Even at that date this "seer of the God" was still being revered at some places. None of these areas have a prophetic literature comparable to that of the writing prophets.

Nahum's description of the fall of Nineveh can be better understood by a study of the depiction of ancient warfare on the Assyrian monuments. These picture attacks of cities, war chariot charges, and the exiling of people. Nahum 3:8 compared the date of Nineveh to that of Thebes. The Assyrian records also depict the siege of an Egyptian city plus a description of the capture of Thebes.

The poignant statement in Jeremiah 34:6–7 that the Bablyonian army had captured all the fortified cities in Judah except Jerusalem, Lachish, and Azekah is highlighted by a group of twenty-one ostraca found by archaeologists at Lachish. These ostraca are rough, draft copies of a letter the Hebrew commander at the doomed city of Lachish was preparing to send to a high official in Jerusalem. Among other things, he wrote that signals were no longer being received from Azekah. Apparently he was writing shortly after the time of Jeremiah 34. Now only two major cities were still resisting the Babylonian onslaught—Azekah had fallen.

The fate of Israelite people in Exile is illustrated in a list of rations found in excavations at the Ishtar Gate of Babylon which are for Yaukin (Jehoiachin) and his sons. Banking records found at Nippur show that people of Jewish names were doing business there while in Exile. Although there is as yet no known text which specifically calls Belshazzar a king, this figure once known only from the Bible is abundantly known in texts.

The return from Exile was accomplished by means of a decree of Cyrus. Cyrus's cylinder, now in the British Museum, though not mentioning the Jews or their Temple, makes clear that such a project was in keeping with Cyrus's general policy. Papyri found at Elephantine Island in Egypt dating about the time of Nehemiah show the condition of Jews in that area, but also permit a dating of Nehemiah's work. Sons of Sanballat are mentioned; and these documents together with Samaritan papyri found in a cave northwest of Jericho make clear that a series of figures bore this name.

Archaeology and Ancient Culture A vast gulf separates the cultures of today, especially those found in the western hemisphere, from those of the biblical period. One of the greatest contributions of archaeology lies in its ability to break down barriers of time and culture and to move the reader of the Bible back into its ancient context, providing fresh insight and increased understanding of the Scripture.

The list of biblical objects which has been found in excavations, allowing us to know exactly what a word means, is large. Examples of weights and measures, plow points, weapons, tools, jewelry, clay jars, seals, and coins are all included. Ancient art depicts clothing styles, weapons, modes of transportation, methods of warfare, and styles of life. Excavated tombs show burial customs which in themselves reflect beliefs about life and death. The Beni Hasan tomb in Egypt from around 1900

Archaeological field worker in background is drawing a scaled sketch of the area just excavated.

B.C. shows how Semites coming to Egypt would have been dressed. It is our nearest approach to what a patriarch might have looked like, and it moves students away from the Bedouin analogy previously made.

Archaeology furnishes much knowledge of the cultures of Israel's neighbors—the Canaanites, Egyptians, Hittites, Philistines, Moabites, Assyrians, Arameans, Babylonians, and Persians. Finds reveal the gods they worshiped, their trade, wars, and treaties.

The tables found at Ugarit provide much primary source information about Canaanite faith and practice. They present a fairly clear picture of what life was like in the land where the Israelites settled down. See *Canaan.*

The Ugaritic texts reveal the Canaanite pantheon with the worship practices of the Canaanite people against which the Hebrew prophets like Elijah, Elisha, and Hosea struggled. The Samaritan ostraca (broken pottery with ink writing) from after 700 B.C. containing numerous names about half of which are compounds of the name Baal, and the Kuntillet ʿAjrud inscription which speaks of "Yahweh and his Asherah" (female counterpart) reveal the syncretism into which Israel was drawn.

Archaeological studies have aided with *chronology.* The Hebrews dated from the beginning of years of the reign of the kings but did not develop a consecutive dating system with one beginning point. They simply began anew with each king. By cross comparisons of biblical with Egyptian, Assyrian, and Babylonian data, scholars can assign reasonably accurate dates in modern terms to many Old Testament events.

Claims of discovery of parallels to patriarchal customs once made are now being reevaluated because of a methodological flaw in the arguments made. In some cases scholars were not careful to note specifically what the Bible said; in others they felt free when finding a custom to make a slight modification in Scripture statement and then to claim a parallel to the modification. An example is the claim that Rachel wanted the teraphim to get a special position for her husband. While such a benefit may be in the Nuzi texts, Scripture nowhere suggests this aim was Rachel's motive.

Genesis 15:1–6 indicates that Abraham and Sarah had made Eliezer, a member of their household staff, their official heir. They may have adopted him to do so, apparently in response to the long delay in the birth of a promised child. A bit later, as recorded in Genesis 16:1–16, Sarah took the further step of having a child by proxy. At her urging, Abraham fathered a son, Ishmael, by the Egyptian maid, Hagar. What was the stimulus for these actions? Clay tablets have been found at the ancient northeastern Mesopotamian city of Nuzi which cast some light on this question. The tablets came from a time a few centuries after

A

Abraham, but contain a record of customs practiced over a long period of time. These tablets reveal that both the adoption of a son and the birth of a son by proxy were common practices for a barren couple. Careful laws were enacted to safeguard the rights of all parties. Abraham's roots were in Mesopotamia (Gen. 11:27–32), and he must have known of these customs. Abraham and Sarah appear to have followed the generally accepted cultural norms of their day.

Genesis 15:7–21 greatly puzzles the modern reader. The passage is difficult to understand. What is actually happening? At least partial light has been shed on this passage by the recovery of numerous clay tablets from the northern Mesopotamian city of Mari. The tablets are from the eighteenth century B.C., a time not too distant from the probable date of Abraham. The tablets indicate that the ceremony used at that time for sealing an agreement or covenant included the cutting of a donkey into half. The persons involved in the contract would then walk between the severed pieces of the animal. One sees that God gave Abraham instructions regarding the ceremony that would have been familiar to the patriarch. God met Abraham in his own cultural context. It is of interest that when people in later Old Testament times made a covenant, they are said, in the Hebrew language, to have "cut a covenant."

The value of archaeology to history and to textual study merges in an interesting passage in 2 Kings 23:29–30. The 1611 *King James Version* indicates that the Egyptian Pharaoh, Neco, went up *against* the Assyrian king. When the Hebrew king, Josiah, sought to interfere, he was killed by the Egyptians in a battle at Megiddo (622 B.C.). Recovered Babylonian documents indicate, however, that the Pharaoh was going up to the aid of the Assyrians. The problem revolves around the translation of the Hebrew preposition which can mean *against,* but can also mean *to,* or *unto.* There is no reason to doubt the accuracy of the Babylonian record at this point. Therefore, recent translations of the Old Testament indicate that Neco was going *to* the Assyrians (to their aid) rather than against them.

New Testament The contribution of archaeology to New Testament study is as exciting as that to the study of the Old Testament. The Dead Sea Scroll discoveries show that Judaism was more complicated than previously suspected. The Nag Hammadi documents from Egypt show how the Gnostics misinterpreted Jesus.

Tombs with rolling stones in place, and the bones of a crucified man with the nails in his heel bones have been found. Remains of first century synagogues at Masada, the Herodium, and Ostia have been identified; and the Theodotos inscription from Jerusalem tells of the building of a synagogue. Coins of the Herods and the Procurators have been found. At Caesarea an inscription mentioning a structure by Pontius Pilate in honor of Tiberius Caesar was found in the theater.

The New Testament rightfully presents Herod the Great as a ruthless and wicked king (Matt. 2:1–23). Very few details of his life are given. A more complete picture of this complex man is now available through the writings of the first century A.D. Jewish historian, Josephus, and through the work of archaeologists. Herod was one of the greatest builders of the ancient world. A visitor to the Holy Land can now see numerous remains from Herod's building program. These include the Temple platform in Jerusalem, the harbor city of Caesarea, the strong fortress of Masada, the striking ruins of Samaria, and the Herodium, the fortress palace where Herod was buried. These, and numerous other sites excavated by archaeologists, remind one that the world in which Jesus lived continued to be dominated to a large degree by Herod—not only through the rule of his sons, but also by the monuments of stone that he left behind. In Jerusalem the thirty-five acre platform on which Herod built his Temple still stands, and parts of the tower of David at the Citadel are Herodian. Inscription stones warning the Gentiles not to proceed into the court of Israel have been found.

Alleged relics of New Testament figures can never be demonstrated to be genuine. Claims for having located the house of Peter at Capernaum and for having located his tomb in Rome are based on pious asssumptions. Pilgrims have been going to Palestine since the second century when Melito of Sardis went "to see the places." Many have left records of what they were shown; but sites like the place of Jesus' birth, baptism, and burial have only long veneration to establish their claim.

Most Pauline cities and those of the Book of Revelation have been located, and many excavated. Corinth has supplied its inscription "synagogue of the Hebrews," and that of Erastus who laid the pavement at his own expense (compare Rom. 16:23). Papyrus documents from Egypt contain invitations to pagan dinners which are good illustrations of the Corinthian problem of being invited to a dinner where food has been offered to idols.

These examples are only a beginning of the materials relevant to New Testament study which archaeology has brought to light. See William H. Stephens, *The New Testament World in Pictures* (Nashville: Broadman Press, 1987).

Archaeology has supplied *older manuscripts* of Bible texts than those previously depended on, examples of objects spoken of in the Bible, numerous items that illuminate the cultural background, and at times offers information which enlarges knowledge of a specific biblical character or event. The idea that archaeology proves the Bible is very much frowned upon in archaeological circles. Its main task is illumination rather than proving. The gulf in time, language, and culture between our own day and the time depicted in the Bible makes knowledge of the archaeological contribution essential for biblical study.

J. Kenneth Eakins and Jack P. Lewis

ARCHANGEL The English term archangel is based on a Greek term *archangelos* which means "chief, or first angel."

In religious texts dating from the post-exilic period, there appears to be substantial change in perception of angels. Hierarchies emerge in the literature that stressed particular groupings headed by archangels [that is, chief angels] who were counted among number designations such as seven (Tobit 12:15; 4 Ezra 5:20), four (Enoch 4; 87:2−3; 88:1), three (Enoch 90:31). The archangels Michael (Dan. 10:13; 12:1; Enoch 9:1; 10:11), Gabriel (Dan. 8:16; Enoch 9:1; 20:7; 40:9), Raphael (Tobit 3:17; 12:15; Enoch 10:4; 40:9) and Uriel (Enoch 9:1; 19:1; 20:2) gain particular hero status. These special archangels function as mediators between God and humans, and frequently there is a perceptible character that stands in contrast (but not necessarily in opposition) to the messenger function. The archangels are interpreters of the message. Although angels generally represented a "guardian role," common to the ancient near eastern world, archangels seem to be of a superior category. In particular, Michael (Dan. 10:13,21; 12:1; Jude 9; Assumption of Moses 12:7−9), Gabriel (*gabriel*, "hero of God"; Dan. 8:16; 9:21; Lk 1:19,26), and Raphael (*rapa,el* "God has healed"; a chief figure in the book of Tobit, see 3:16−17) were cast as important interpreters, advocates, and intercessors.

The New Testament continues the idea of angels as messengers of God. Among the numerous references, an angel advises Joseph of Jesus' birth (Matt. 1:20), and warns of the advisability of the flight into Egypt (Matt. 2:13,19). The archangel, Gabriel, is the messenger who speaks of the birth of John in Luke 1:11, 19, and tells Mary of the birth of Jesus (Luke 1:26). The Book of Revelation appears to reflect tradition of archangels found in Enoch (although the term *archangelos* is found only in 1 Thess. 4:16 and Jude 9) that have holy creatures waiting on the throne of God, presiding over the corners of the earth, and are part of the cosmic reordering at the end of time (Rev. 1:4; 4:5; 7:1; 12:7; Enoch 9:1; 10:1; 40:2; 90:21). See *Angel*.   *Wayne McCready*

ARCHELAUS (Är·chḕ·lā′ ŭs) Son and principal successor of Herod the Great (Matt. 2:22). When Herod died in 4 B.C., his sons Herod Antipas and Philip were named tetrarchs; but his son Archelaus was the principal successor. Aware of the hostility of the Jews toward his family, Archelaus did not attempt to ascend the throne immediately. First, he tried to win the Jews over. His efforts were not successful; as the Jews revolted, and Archelaus ordered his army to retaliate.

Archelaus encountered opposition to his reign from his brothers, in particular Herod Antipas, who felt entitled to the throne. The brothers presented their case to the emperor Augustus, who gave Archelaus one half of his father Herod's land and split the remainder between Antipas and Philip. Archelaus was given the title Tetrarch, but was promised the title of King if he reigned virtuously.

Archelaus interfered in the high priesthood, married against Jewish law, and oppressed the Samaritans and Jews through brutal treatment. In revolt, the people sent deputations to Caesar to have Archelaus denounced. His rule was ended in A.D. 6 when the Roman government banished him to Gaul and added his territory to Syria.

Joseph was warned in a dream to avoid Judea because of Archelaus' rule. He decided to take Mary and the child Jesus to Galilee when they returned from Egypt rather than go to Judea (Matt. 2:22).

ARCHER One who shoots an arrow from a bow. Archery was used in ancient times for the hunting of both small and large game and in warfare. An archer trained from childhood until he could pull a 100-pound bow that would shoot an arrow a distance of 300-400 yards. Several Old Testament passages mention archery in warfare (Gen. 49:23−24; 2 Sam. 11:24). See *Arms and Armor*.

Reconstruction of an ingenious Roman archer's machine of the first-century A.D.

ARCHEVITES (Är′ chė·vītes) Group who joined Rehum the commander in writing a letter to King Artaxerxes of Persia protesting the rebuilding of Jerusalem under Zerubbabel's leadership about 537 B.C. NAS, NIV, NRSV translate Archevites as people or men of Erech. See *Erech*.

ARCHI (Är′ chī), **ARCHITE** An unknown group of people who gave their name to a border point of the tribes of Ephraim and Benjamin (Josh. 16:2). They may have been a clan of Benjamin, or more likely remnants of the ancient "Canaanite" inhabitants. Their only representative in the Bible was David's Counselor Hushai. See *Hushai*.

ARCHIPPUS (Är·chĭp pŭs) Personal name meaning, "First among horsemen." A Christian Paul greeted in Colossians 4:17 and Philemon 2, entreating him to fulfill the ministry God gave him. Some have suggested he was the son of Philemon and Appia, but this can be neither proved or disproved. The nature of his ministry has also been widely discussed without firm conclusions. Paul's use of "fellow soldier" to describe him seems to indicate a strong participation in church leadership. Evidently, he preached in the church at Colossae.

ARCHITECTURE IN THE BIBLICAL PERIOD reflects the construction, the techniques, and the materials used in building the structures of the Ancient Near East.

Atrium of the Roman villa of the Poet Menander in Pompeii (destroyed in A.D. 79).

Old Testament The people of the Ancient Near East used many types of building materials. Utilizing natural resources, they most often exploited stone, wood, reeds, and mud. Used naturally, mud served as mortar. It also was formed into bricks and then sun dried. Religious or large public buildings used the more expensive lumber that came from cedar, cypress, sandalwood, and olive trees. The sycamore tree served as a less costly lumber. Limestone and basalt were common stones used in construction.

    1. Public Structures. As a basic element of city architecture, walls served three general purposes. Protective walls encircled the city to keep out enemy forces. These city walls usually did not support any load. Retaining walls had the purpose of keeping in place any weight that was behind them. In agricultural terracing, they prevented erosion and created a level place for farming on the sides of hills. This type of wall also was placed below city walls to stop any erosion of the soil which ultimately might weaken the city walls. Lastly, buildings and houses used walls to bear loads or keep out the weather.

    Walls were made of several layers or courses of stones placed one on top of the other with mud bricks often set on the stone courses. Composed of large field stones, the first few layers served as the foundation of the wall. The placing of the large stones into trenches gave the wall a more stable foundation. In houses and public buildings, the stone courses above the ground may have been given smooth surfaces so as to produce a uniform look, but this was not always done. Large public building projects commonly made use of a technique called headers and stretchers. The builders alternated laying the stones lengthwise and breadthwise to form the wall.

    During the time of Solomon, a common type of city wall was the casemate wall. This was composed of two parallel walls with perpendicular walls placed at intervals in between the parallel ones. The empty spaces formed between the walls, called casemates, commonly were filled with stones, earth, or debris. Sometimes the people used the spaces for living quarters, guardrooms, or storehouses. The outer parallel wall averaged about 5 1/2 feet in width, while the inner parallel wall averaged about 4 feet. This type of wall had an advantage over a solid wall due to its greater strength and its saving of material and labor. Excavations at Gezer, Megiddo, and Hazor uncovered the remains of casemate walls.

    The inset-offset wall came into use as a city wall after the time of Solomon. Its name came from the technique used to build it. After erecting one stretch of the wall, the next stretch was slightly recessed by about 1/2 yard. The following section then was built slightly forward with the next section placed slightly behind it. Each stretch of the wall was placed alternately either slightly ahead or slightly behind the previous section. This "insetting" and "offsetting" of the city wall allowed the city's defenders to fire at any attackers from three angles: head on and to the right and left of the attackers. As a solid structure composed of stone or mud bricks placed on a stone foundation, this type of wall contrasts with the casemate wall. The remains of an inset-offset wall, eleven feet in thickness, were excavated at Megiddo.

    The city gate was an important part of public architecture because it was the weakest part of the city's defenses. It also served as a meeting

The Pantheon in Rome, built in the first century A.D., was the first large dome ever built.

place for the various city activities. Remains of Solomonic gates at Megiddo, Gezer, and Hazor show that two square towers flanked the entrance into the gate. The gate complex was composed of three successive chambers or rooms on each side (six chambers in all). A gate separated each pair of chambers, and the six rooms probably served as guardhouses. At Dan, a later gate had the two towers, but only four chambers instead of six. This gate complex measured 58 x 97 feet. The approach to the gate from outside the city usually was placed at an angle. This forced any attackers to expose their flanks to the defenders on the city walls. Should the attackers be able to get inside the gate area, the angle caused the attackers to move at a slower pace.

As a prominent public structure, the temple acted as the house of the god. Two types of temple structures were common in Palestine during the biblical period. The broadroom temple was a rectangular structure with its entrance in the middle of one of the long sides. The plan of the temple, therefore, was oriented around a room that was broader than it was long. The longroom temple likewise was a rectangular structure, but its entrance was in the middle of one of the short sides. This caused the building to be longer than it was broad.

As a longroom temple, Solomon's sanctuary in Jerusalem consisted of three main sections. A courtyard with an altar preceded the building. The Temple proper actually was one building divided into two parts, the holy place and the holy of holies. The main room, or the holy place, was entered from the courtyard. A partition separated the holy place from the holy of holies.

Another Israelite temple dating from after 1000 B.C. was uncovered at Arad. It was a broadroom temple entered from the east. The holy of holies was a niche protruding out of the western wall opposite the entrance.

2. Private Structures. Houses in the period of the Old Testament usually were built around a central courtyard and entered from the street. They often were two stories high with access to the upper story coming from a staircase or a ladder. The walls of the house consisted of stone foundations with mud bricks placed on the stone layers or courses. They subsequently were plastered. Floors either were paved with small stones or plaster, or they were formed from beaten earth. Large wooden beams laid across the walls composed the supporting structure of the roof. Smaller pieces of wood or reeds were placed in between the beams and then covered with a layer of mud. Rows of columns placed in the house served as supports to the ceiling. Since the roof was flat, people slept on it in the hot seasons and also used it for storage. Sometimes clay or stone pipes that led from the roof to cisterns down below were used to catch rainwater.

The most common type of house was the so-called "four-room" house. This house consisted of a broadroom at the rear of the house with three parallel rooms coming out from one side of the broadroom. The back room ran the width of the building. Rows of pillars separated the middle parallel room from the other two rooms. This middle room actually was a small, unroofed courtyard and served as the entrance to the house. The courtyard usually contained household items such as silos, cisterns, ovens, and grinding stones and was the place where the cooking was done. The animals could have been kept under a covered section in the courtyard. The other rooms were used for living and storage.

Ovens were constructed with mud bricks and then plastered on the outside. One side of the oven had an air hole. A new oven was created whenever the old one filled up with ashes. By breaking off the top of the old oven and then raising the sides, a new oven was made.

Storage structures were common in the biblical period. Private and public grain silos were round and dug several feet into the ground. The builders usually erected circular mud brick or stone walls around the silo, but sometimes they did nothing to the pit or simply plastered it with mud. Rooms with clay vessels also served as storage space.

While the "four room" house was the most common plan in Palestine, other arrangements existed. Some homes had a simple plan of a courtyard with one room placed to the side. Other houses had only two or three rooms; still others may have had more than four. The arrangement of the rooms around the open courtyard also varied. The broadroom at the rear of the house seems to be common to all plans.

New Testament In this time period, architecture in Israel was greatly influenced by Greek and Roman ideas. Some of the primary cities in Israel show this influence in their public buildings.

1. Public Structures. Over twenty Roman theaters were built in Palestine and Jordan. At Caesarea, the theater contained two main parts, the auditorium and stage, and the stage building. These two parts formed one building complex. Six vaulted passageways served as entrances. The auditorium was semicircular with upper and lower sections used for seating. The lower tier had six sections of seats, and the upper tier had seven for a total capacity of 4,500 people. A central box was reserved for dignitaries and important guests. The wall of the stage was as high as the auditorium. Other similar theaters were located at Scythopolis (Beth-Shan), Pella, Gerasa, Petra, Dor, Hippos, and Gadara.

Arenas for chariot racing, called hippodromes, were long, narrow, and straight with curved ends. Gerasa, Caesarea, Scythopolis, Gadara, and Jerusalem had hippodromes. Erected in the second century A.D., the one at Caesarea was 1/4 of a mile long and 330 feet wide with a seating capacity of 30,000.

The Temple in Jerusalem was destroyed in 586 B.C. and rebuilt in 515 B.C. Herod the Great refurbished it during the first century B.C. As a result, the Temple became widely known for its beauty. It retained the same plan as its predecessor, but the area around it was doubled. Retaining walls that marked the boundaries of the Temple complex were built, and marble porticos were added all around the Temple mount. The stones of the Temple mount's retaining walls were about four or five feet high and weighed three to five tons.

2. Private Structures. Houses usually followed a plan that arranged the rooms around a courtyard. A stairway on the outside of the house led to the upper stories. A stone or timber projected out from the wall at intervals and supported the staircase. This architectural technique is known as corbelling. The walls and ceiling were plastered, and arches sometimes supported the roof. Houses at Avdat and Shivta used arches that came out from the walls to form the roof. After placing thin slabs of limestone over the arches, the builders plastered the entire roof. In the lower city of Jerusalem, houses constructed with small stones were crowded closely together. Yet, they still maintained small courtyards.

Houses of the rich often had columns placed around a central court that had rooms radiating out from it. Kitchens, cellars, cisterns, and bathing pools may have been located underneath the ground. In Jerusalem, one house covered about 650 square feet, a large house by first century standards. In the courtyard, four ovens were sunk into the ground, and a cistern stored the house's water supply. Inside the house on one of the walls, three niches raised about five feet off the ground served as cabinets for storing the household vessels. *Scott Langston*

ARCHIVES See *House of the Rolls.*

ARCTURUS (Ärc·tū′ rŭs) A constellation of stars God created (Job 9:9; 38:32) of which exact identification was not clear to the earliest Bible translators and continues to be debated. Modern translations generally use "Bear" (NAS, NIV, NRSV). TEV uses "the Dipper." Some scholars prefer, "the lion." Whatever the identification, the star points to the sovereign greatness of God beyond human understanding.

ARD (Ärd), **ARDITE** Personal name meaning, "hunchbacked." *1.* A son of Benjamin and grandson of Jacob (Gen. 46:21). *2.* A grandson and clan father of Benjamin (Num. 26:40). Apparently listed as Addar in 1 Chron. 8:3.

ARDON (Är′ dŏn) Son of Caleb (1 Chron. 2:18).

ARELI (Ȧ·rē′ lī) **ARELITES** Son of Gad (Gen. 46:16) and original ancestor of clan of Arelites (Num. 26:17).

AREOPAGITE (Âr·ė·ŏp′ ȧ·gīte) A member of the highly respected Greek council which met on the Areopagus in Athens. See *Areopagus; Athens; Dionysius.*

AREOPAGUS (Âr·ė·ŏp′ ȧ·gŭs) The site of Paul's speech to the Epicurean and Stoic philosophers of Athens (Acts 17:19). It was a rocky hill about 370 feet high, not far from the Acropolis and the Agora (marketplace) in Athens, Greece. The word also was used to refer to the council that originally met on this hill. The name probably was derived from Ares, the Greek name for the god of war known to the Romans as Mars.

ARETAS (Âr′ ė·tȧs) Personal name meaning, "moral excellence, power." The ruler of Damascus in New Testament times. He sought to arrest Paul after his conversion (2 Cor. 11:32). The name Aretas was born by several Arabian kings centered in Petra and Damascus. Aretas IV ruled from Petra (9 B.C.–A.D. 40) as a subject of Rome. Herod Antipas married, then divorced his daughter to marry Herodias (Mark 6:17–18). Aretus joined with a Roman officer to defeat Herod's army in A.D. 36.

ARGOB (Är′ gŏb) Personal and geographical name meaning, "mound of earth." *1.* Man who joined Pekah (2 Kings 15:25) in murdering Pekahiah, king of Israel (742–740 B.C.). The Hebrew text is difficult to read at this point. Some scholars omit Argob as a copyists' error duplicating part of verse 29 here (TEV). NIV translation can be interpreted to mean Pekah also killed Argob. *2.* A territory in Bashan in the hill country east of the Jordan River. Argob was probably in the center of the fertile tableland and was famous for its strong cities (Deut. 3:4). Moses gave this land of giants to Manasseh (Deut. 3:13). Manasseh's son Jair conquered Argob (Deut. 3:14) and changed the name to Bashan-havoth-jair.

ARIDAI (Ȧ·rĭd′ ā·ī) Persian personal name, perhaps meaning, "delight of Hari" (a god). Son of Haman, Esther, and the Jews' archenemy. He died as the Jews reversed Haman's scheme and gained revenge (Esther 9:9).

ARIDATHA (Är·ĭ·dā′ thȧ) Persian personal name perhaps meaning, "given by Hari" (a god). Brother of Aridai, who shared his fate. See *Arida.*

ARIEH (Ȧ·rī′ ĕh) Personal name meaning, "lion." Paired with Argob in 2 Kings 15:25 with same text problems involved. See *Argob.* Compare KJV, NAS, NIV, NRSV.

ARIEL (Â′ rĭ·ĕl) Personal name meaning, "God's lion." *1.* Jewish leader in captivity who acted as Ezra's messenger to the Levites to send people

with Ezra to Jerusalem about 458 B.C. (Ezra 8:16). *2.* Code name for Jerusalem in Isaiah 29. Ariel apparently referred to the top of the altar on which the priests burned sacrifices. Jerusalem under Assyrian attack was like the altar. It did not burn but caused everything around it to burn. The sins of Jerusalem had led to the devastation of the rest of Judah in 701 B.C.

ARIMATHEA (Är·ĭ·mȧ·thē′ ȧ) City of Joseph, the disciple who claimed the body of Jesus following the crucifixion, and in whose own new tomb the body was placed (Matt. 27:57). The location of Arimathea is not certainly known. In Luke 23:51, Arimathea is described as a Jewish city. See *Joseph of Arimathea.*

ARIOCH (Âr′ ĭ·ŏch) Personal, probably Hurrian, name meaning, "servant of the moon god." *1.* King of Ellasar, who joined alliance against Sodom and Gomorrah (Gen. 14) but was eventually defeated by Abraham. See *Amraphel, Ellasar.* Parallel names have been found in early Akkadian documents and at Mari and Nuzi, but no other reference to the biblical Arioch can be shown. *2.* Commander of bodyguard of King Nebuchadnezzar (Dan. 2:14–25). He confided in Daniel, who was able to interpret the king's forgotten dream and prevent the death of the wise counselors of Babylon.

ARISAI (Ȧ·rīs′ ā·ī) Persian personal name. Son of Haman (Esther 9:9) who suffered his brothers' fate. See *Aridai.*

ARISTARCHUS (Âr·ĭs·tär′ chŭs) Personal name perhaps meaning, "best ruler." Paul's companion caught by the followers of Artemis in Ephesus (Acts 19:29). Apparently the same person was the Thessalonian who accompanied Paul from Greece to Jerusalem as he returned from his third missionary journey (Acts 20:4). Aristarchus also accompanied Paul when he sailed for Rome (Acts 27:2). Paul sent greetings from Aristarchus, a fellow prisoner and worker, in his letters to the Colossians (4:10) and Philemon (24). Later church tradition said Nero put Aristarchus to death in Rome.

ARISTOBULUS (Ȧ·rīs·tō·bū′ lŭs) Head of a Christian household in Rome whom Paul greeted (Rom. 16:10).

ARK Boat or water vessel and in particular one built by Noah under God's direction to save Noah, his family, and representatives of all animal life from the flood.
Old Testament God warned Noah of His intentions to destroy the earth because of the wickedness of humanity. Noah was commanded to build an ark to God's specifications to save his family

and representatives of all animals from the flood (Gen. 6:18–19). As such, the ark became both a symbol of a faith on the part of Noah and a symbol of grace on the part of God (Gen. 6:8,22).

The shape of the ark was unusual. Although the Bible does not give enough detail to enable a full model to be made, the ark was apparently not shaped like a boat, either ancient or modern. The shape more closely approximates a giant block. The length was 300 cubits (about 450 feet), the width was 50 cubits (about 75 feet), and the height was 30 cubits (about 45 feet), overall dimensions that resemble the dimensions of a giant house (Gen. 6:15). The ark had three floors filled with rooms (Gen. 6:14,16) and one window and one door (Gen. 6:16).

The ark was built of gopher wood (Gen. 6:14) which may have been a variety of cypress. It has also been suggested that gopher wood referred to a particular shape or type of plank or beam, rather than a type of wood. Our limited knowledge makes it impossible to make a final conclusion.

The ark was a testimony of Noah's faith because no large body of water stood nearby on which Noah could have floated such a large boat. Hence people could see no obvious or visible need for such a vessel.

The ark was also a symbol of God's grace. Obviously, the ark was intended by God as an instrument of deliverance to preserve both human and animal life upon the earth (Gen. 6:17–18). As such, it came to be understood as a symbol of His grace and mercy (Heb. 11:7a).

New Testament The gospel references to the ark are in connection with Jesus' teachings regarding the second coming. The expectancy of some at the second coming is likened to those who were destroyed by the flood. In the Book of Hebrews, the preacher lists Noah as a man of faith who prepared an ark even though the danger was at that point unseen. The last New Testament reference to the ark points to the evil of humanity and God's patient salvation (1 Pet. 3:20).

Extra-biblical Sources The Babylonian flood story, called the Gilgamesh epic, also tells of a large boat by which its hero survived the flood. There, however, the ark was not a symbol of the grace of the gods but of their folly and faulty planning.

Searches for the ark have proven fruitless. Numerous newspaper articles and paperback books record attempts to discover the ruins of Noah's ark. While the ark has not yet been recovered, the discovery of such remains are unnecessary to demonstrate the authenticity of the story. Faith which requires proof is not faith at all. See *Flood; Noah.*

Robert Cate

ARK OF BULRUSHES KJV translation of a Hebrew word in Exodus 2:3–5 usually translated basket.

ARK OF THE COVENANT names the original container for the Ten Commandments and the central symbol of God's presence with the people of Israel.

Old Testament The ark of ancient Israel is mysterious in its origins, in its meanings, and its ultimate fate. Its many names convey the holy sense of God's presence. The Hebrew word for ark means simply "box, chest, coffin," as is indicated by its use for the coffin of Joseph (Gen. 50:26) and for the Temple collection box of King Joash (2 Kings 12:9–10).

The names used for the ark define its meaning by the words which modify it. The word "covenant" in the name defines the ark from its original purpose as a container for the stone tablets upon which the Ten Commandments (sometimes called the "testimony") were inscribed. Sometimes it is identified rather with the name of diety, "the ark of God," or "the ark of the Lord" (Yahweh), or most ornately "the ark of the covenant of the Lord of hosts (Yahweh Sabaoth) who is enthroned on the cherubim" (1 Sam. 4:4).

Stone carving of what is thought to be the ark of the covenant in the synagogue ruins at Capernaum.

The origin of the ark goes back to Moses at Sinai. The mysterious origin of the ark is seen by contrasting the two accounts of how it was made in the Pentateuch. The more elaborate account of the manufacture and ornamentation of the ark by the craftsman Bezalel appears in Exodus 25:10–22; 31:2,7; 35:30–35; 37:1–9. It was planned during Moses' first sojourn on Sinai and built after all the tabernacle specifications had been communicated and completed. The other account is found in Deuteronomy 10:1–5. After the sin of the golden calf and the breaking of the original decalogue tablets, Moses made a plain box of acacia wood as a container to receive the new tables of the law.

A very ancient poem, the "Song of the Ark" in Numbers 10:35–36, sheds some light on the function of the ark in the wanderings in the wilderness. The ark was the symbol of God's presence to guide the pilgrims and lead them in battle (Num. 10:33,35–36). If they acted in faithlessness, failing to follow this guidance, the consequences could be drastic (Num. 14:39–45). Some passages suggest the ark was also regarded as the throne of the invisible deity, or his footstool (Jer. 3:16–17; Ps. 132:7–8). These various meanings of the ark should be interpreted as complementary rather than contradictory.

The ark was designed for mobility. Its size (about four feet long, two and a half feet wide, and two and a half feet deep) and rectangular shape were appropriate to this feature. Permanent poles were used to carry the ark, since no one was allowed to touch it, and only priestly (Levitical) personnel were allowed to carry it. The ark was the most important object within the tabernacle of the desert period, though its relationship to the tabernacle was discontinued sometime after the conquest of Canaan.

The ark played a prominent role in the "holy war" narratives of the crossing of the Jordan and the conquest, of Jericho (Josh. 3—6). After the conquest, it was variously located at Gilgal, Shechem (Josh. 8:30–35; see Deut. 11:26–32; 27:1–26) or Bethel (Judg. 20:26), wherever the tribal confederacy was gathered for worship. Finally, it was permanently located at Shiloh, where a temple was built to house it (1 Sam. 1:9; 3:3).

Because of the faithless superstition of the wicked sons of Eli, the Hebrew tribes were defeated in the battle of Ebenezer, and the ark was

Shiloh in Israel where the ark of the covenant was brought after the conquest and rested for 400 years.

captured by the Philistines (1 Sam. 4). The adventures of the ark in the cities of Ashdod, Gath, and Ekron are told to magnify the strength and glory of the Lord of the ark. The Lord vanquished Dagon and spread bubonic plagues among the enemy until they propitiated the God of Israel by symbolic guilt offerings and a ritually correct sending away of the dread object (1 Sam. 5:1—6:12). The men of Bethshemesh welcomed the return of the ark, until they unwisely violated its holiness by looking into it (1 Sam. 6:13–15,19–20). Then it was carried to Kiriath-Jearim, where it remained in comparative neglect until David recovered the symbolism it had for the ancient tribal confederacy and moved it to his new capital and sanctuary in Jerusalem (1 Sam. 6:21—7:2; 2 Sam. 6). Abinadab and his sons (2 Sam. 6:3) seemed to have served the Lord of the

Reconstruction of the Ark of the Covenant drawn in the Egyptian style, reflecting 400 years of captive influence in Egyptian bondage.

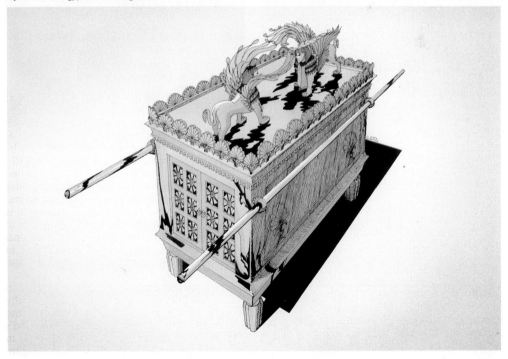

ark faithfully until one son, Uzzah, was smitten for his rash touching of the holy object during David's first attempt to transport the ark from its "hill" at Kiriath-Jearim to his own city. In fear, David left the ark with Obed-edom the Gittite, whose household was blessed by its presence. More cautiously and with great religious fervor, David succeeded the second time in taking the ark into his capital city (2 Sam. 6:12–19).

Recent scholarship has suggested that on coronation occasions or annually at a festival of enthronement this ark ceremony was reenacted. Such an occasion would re-emphasize the promise to the Davidic dynasty, as well as the glory of the Lord of Hosts (Ps. 24:7–10;132). Finally, Solomon built the Temple, planned by David, to house the ark, which he then transported into the holy of holies with elaborate festival cermonies (1 Kings 8; 2 Chron. 5).

The precise time of the theft or destruction of the ark is unknown. Some have suggested Shishak of Egypt plundered the Temple of this most holy object (1 Kings 14:25–28), but it seems more likely, from Jeremiah 3:16–17, that the Babylonians captured or destroyed the ark in 587 B.C. with the fall of Jerusalem and the burning of the Temple. As Jeremiah predicted, the ark was never rebuilt for the second Temple, the holy of holies remaining empty.

Other mysteries of the ark are its relation to the cherubim, its ornate lid called the "mercy seat," and its precise ritual usage during the time of the monarchy. Because the ark of the covenant was the central symbol of God's presence with His people Israel, its mysteries remain appropriately veiled within the inner sanctuary of the living God. See *Holy of Holies; Mercy Seat; Tabernacle; Temple.*
New Testament Hebrews 9:1–10 shows the ark was a part of the old order with external regulations waiting for the new day of Christ to come with a perfect Sacrifice able to cleanse the human conscience. Revelation 11:19 shows the ark of the covenant will be part of the heavenly temple when it is revealed. *M. Pierce Matheney, Jr.*

ARKITE (Är' kīte) Canaanite clan listed in the table of nations (Gen. 10:17). They apparently centered around Arqa, modern Tell Arqa in Syria 80 miles north of Sidon. Thutmose III of Egypt conquered it. It appears in the Amarna letters. Tiglath-pileser III of Assyria conquered it in 738 B.C. Romans called it Caesarea Libani and noted its Astarte worship.

ARM The upper limb of the human body used to symbolize power and strength. Such power can oppress people (Job 35:9), but such arms will be broken (Job 38:15). No human arm or power is comparable to God's (Job 40:9). In prayer the faithful can ask God to break the arm of the wicked (Ps. 10:15). Human arms cannot save (Ps.

44:3). God's outstretched arm does (Ex. 6:6; 15:16; Deut. 5:15). People can trust in God's arm (Isa. 51:5). On seeing Mary as she waited for the birth of Jesus, Elizabeth confessed that in bringing Jesus, God showed "strength with his arm" (Luke 1:51).

ARMAGEDDON (Är·má·gĕd' dŏn) A Middle East site of the final battle between the forces of good and evil (Rev. 16:16). The word "Armageddon" appears once in Scripture and is not found in Hebrew literature. Translators transliterate the term from Greek into English in several ways: Armageddon (KJV); Har Magedon (NAS); and Harmageddon (Moffatt). The Greek is a transliteration of the Hebrew *har megiddo,* literally, "mountain of Megiddo." Revelation promises that in the face of defeat of God's saints by military forces from the east, south, and the north, the Lord Jesus Christ will return to defeat His enemies and deliver His people. See *Megiddo.* *Ken Hubbard*

ARMENIA (Är·mē′ ni·à) KJV translation for land of Ararat (2 Kings 19:37). See *Ararat.*

ARMLET A band or ring worn around the upper arm that should be distinguished from a bracelet worn around the wrist. The Hebrew word is translated as chain (Num. 31:50) and bracelet (2 Sam. 1:10). A related word is rendered as ornaments of the legs (Isa. 3:20) in the KJV.

Gold Persian armlet from the treasury of the Oxus.

ARMONI (Âr·mō′ nī) Personal name meaning, "born in Armon." Son of Rizpah and Saul, whom David gave to the Gibeonites in revenge for Saul's earlier killing of Gibeonites (2 Sam. 21:7–9). See *Rizpah.*

ARMOR BEARER See *Arms and Armor.*

ARMOR OF GOD See *Arms and Armor.*

ARMS and ARMOR include instruments and body coverings for defense and or protection.
Old Testament The offensive arms of the Old

Testament include long, medium, and close range arms, and the defensive items include shields and armor.

Long Range Arms The bow and arrow were effective arms from long-range (300–400 yards) and were used widely by the nations of the Bible. Israel had expert archers in men from Benjamin (1 Chron. 8:40; 2 Chron. 17:17) and the eastern tribes of Reuben, Gad, and Manasseh (1 Chron. 5:18). Jonathan and Jehu were individual marksmen. At least four Israelite kings were severely or fatally wounded by enemy arrows: Saul (1 Sam. 31:3), Ahab (1 Kings 22:34), Joram (2 Kings 9:24), and Josiah (2 Chron. 35:23). Bows were constructed with single pieces of wood, or more effectively with glued layers of wood, horn, and sinew, and possibly even with added bronze (2 Sam. 22:35; Job 20:24). The size varied from approximately three to six feet in length. Arrows were made of wood shafts or reeds, tipped with metal heads which were forged differently to meet the diverse defenses of the enemy. The arrow was guided by feathers, especially from the eagle, vulture, or kite. A leather quiver strapped to the back or hung over the shoulder carried between 20 and 30 of these arrows, or if strapped to a chariot, perhaps as many as 50. Frequently a leather arm guard was also used on the bow arm to protect it from the gut string that propelled the arrow.

One might be most familiar with the slingshot through reading about David's encounter with Goliath (1 Sam. 17:40–50), without realizing that it was a conventional artillery weapon for deadly long-range use by armies throughout the Middle East. Because of the long-range capabilities, expert slingers were stationed by the hundreds near the archers. It was especially valuable to have those who could sling from the left hand as well as from the right (Judg. 20:16; 1 Chron. 12:2). A patch of cloth or leather with two braided leather cords on either end would hold a smooth stone. The slinger then twirled the pocketed missile above his head. Release of one of the cords would eject the stone towards its victim. The blow would disarm, destabilize, knock out, or even kill the enemy. King Uzziah of Judah developed large catapults that projected arrows and stones long-range to defend Jerusalem (2 Chron. 26:15).

Medium Range Arms A javelin is a spear thrown obviously a shorter distance than the archers could arch their arrows or slingers could sling their sling stones. However, as a hurled weapon, its medium range is to be differentiated from the close range thrusting spear of the phalanxed foot-soldier. David faced the javelin while successfully challenging Goliath (1 Sam. 17:6) and while peacefully attempting to soothe Saul's spirit. Twice the disturbed Saul hurled his javelin at David (1 Sam. 18:10,11; 19:9,10) and even once at his own son Jonathan (1 Sam. 20:33). Usually made of wood or reed, some javelins had one or both of two features that aided its flight: some had a leather cord wrapped around its shaft that caused the released weapon to spin when the cord was retained in the hand, and a counter-weight was sometimes fixed on the butt of the shaft. The latter could be even sharp enough to be stuck in the ground to stand the javelin (1 Sam. 26:7) or even used to kill (2 Sam. 2:23). A quiver was used often to aid the soldier in carrying more than one javelin at a time.

Close Range Arms Hand-to-hand combat brought different weapons to the fore: some sharp, some dull, some long, some short. The thrusting spear was longer and heavier than the javelin and could have been thrown if needed. The soldiers from the tribes of Judah and Naphtali carried spears as a tribal weapon (1 Chron. 12:24,34). Guards protected the Temple with these arms (2 Chron. 23:9). Front battle lines often featured foot soldiers equipped with rectangular shields carrying spears jutting out beyond the walls of shields and pressing forward at the expense of the enemy front line.

Two types of swords were used in the biblical times, the single edge and the two-edged sword (Ps. 149:6, Prov. 5:4). The single edge was used most effectively by swinging it and hitting the enemy to lacerate the flesh. The blade could be straight or curved to a great degree. In the latter case the sharp edge of the sword was on the outside of the curve. The double-edged sword was used primarily for piercing rather than lacerating, though it could obviously be used either way if necessary. The sword was carried in a sheath attached to the belt. The varieties of the overall width and length of swords in proportion to the hilts were numerous. The difference between a straight sword and the dagger is simply the length. The earliest blades were more daggers than swords. They were lengthened gradually through the ages. Ehud probably used a long dagger in assassinating King Eglon of Moab, since it measured about 18 inches (one cubit, Judg. 3:16–26).

The mace and battle ax are seldom mentioned in the Bible (Prov. 25:18; Jer. 51:20; Ezek. 9:2); yet they played a significant role in hand-to-hand combat in the biblical lands. The mace was a war club that was used to crush the head of the enemy. The heavy metal or stone head of the weapon would be of various shapes such as round, oval, or pear-shaped. Its wooden handle would fasten by going through the head like a modern hammer or axe. The handle was formed with some flaring at the bottom to keep the weapon from sliding out of the hand. With the pervasive introduction of armor, especially the helmet, the mace gave way in popularity to the piercing edge of the battle ax. These axes with narrow heads could penetrate more easily a helmet or other armor with their elongated shape. Other blades were designed with wider edges to cut and open the flesh where

less or no armor was worn.

Armor bearers accompanied the military leaders to bring along extra weapons and defensive equipment that would be expended during a battle (arrows, javelins, shields). They sometimes aided the soldier as well by positioning their shields for them, as in the case of Goliath, and at times killing those enemy soldiers who were left helplessly wounded by preceding combatants.

Battering rams, as modelled by Ezekiel in his object lesson for the Israelites (Ezek. 4:2), were actually rolled on wheels and had metal ends attached to wooden shafts to withstand the collision force with city gates or stone walls.

Defensive Arms Defense against all these arms consisted of the shield which was carried or armor which was worn. Shields were made of wicker, or of leather stretched over wooden frames with handles on the inside. These were much more maneuverable than heavier metal, but obviously less protective. A cross between metal and leather was achieved by attaching metal disks or plates to the leather over a portion of the surface. Two different sizes are referred to in the Bible and in many ancient illustrations (2 Chron. 23:9). One was a round shield used with lighter weapons and covered half the body at most. The tribe of Benjamin preferred these along with the bow and arrow (2 Chron. 14:8). So did Nehemiah when he equipped his men for protection while rebuilding the city walls of Jerusalem (Neh. 4:16). The gold and brass shields made by Solomon and Rehoboam respectively were ceremonial and decorative in function (1 Kings 14:25–28) and were of this size. A larger shield was more rectangular and covered nearly, if not all, the body and was so large at times that a special shieldbearer was employed to carry it in front of the weapon bearer. Both Goliath and one of these assistants faced David (1 Sam. 17:41). The tribes of Judah (2 Chron. 14:8), Gad (1 Chron. 12:8), and Naphtali (1 Chron. 12:34) used this type of shield with the long thrusting spear or lance as the offensive weapon in the other hand. Bowmen also stood behind standing shields while they flung their arrows.

Armor is essentially a shield that is worn directly on the body. Since the body is most fatally vulnerable in the head and chest regions, it was especially there where armor was clad. Saul and Goliath wore helmets (1 Sam. 17:5,38), as did the entire army of Judah, at least in the time of Uzziah (2 Chron. 26:14). The helmet was usually made of leather or metal and was designed with various shapes depending on the army and even on the unit within an army so that the commander could distinguish one unit from another from a higher vantage point. The differently decorated and constructed helmets helped the soldier tell whether he was near an enemy or comrade in the confusion of tight hand-to-hand combat.

With the rise in popularity of the arrow and with its speed of flight and imperceptible approach on its victim, the mail came to be more and more necessary to cover the torso. Fishscale-like construction of small metal plates sewn to cloth or leather was the breastplate for the ancient soldier. These scales could number as high as 700–1000 per "coat." Each coat obviously could be quite heavy and expensive to produce in volume. The distant enemy units of archers who might find themselves firing on each other would wear mail especially, as well as those archers riding in chariots. While in a chariot, Ahab was hit and killed by an arrow exactly where the mail was least protective—at the seam where the sleeve and breast of the coat met (1 Kings 22:34).

Leg armor, like the bronze leglets of Goliath (1 Sam. 17:6), was not regularly used in the Old Testament times.

New Testament Arms and armor surface on only a few occasions in the New Testament. Of course, the New Testament times found Roman imperial soldiers equipped with metal helmets, protective leather and metal vests, leg armor, shields, swords and spears. Christ accepted a legal, defensive use of the sword (Luke 22:36–38), but he rebuked Peter's illegal and more offensive strike against Malchus at a time of arrest (John 18:10–11). Often the New Testament uses arms and armor symbolically as in the Old Testament poets and prophetic books. The Word of the Lord and its piercing, penetrating effect is referred to as a sword (Eph. 6:17; Heb. 4:12; Rev. 1:16; 2:16; 19:15,21). Paul used both arms and armor of a soldier to express the virtues necessary to defend the believer against Satan (Eph. 6:10–17; compare Isa. 59:16–17).

Metaphorical Use In the Old Testament, the devastating effect of a vicious tongue is compared with the destructive purpose of the sword and arrow (Ps. 57:4; 64:3; Prov. 12:18). However, when weapons are used metaphorically in the Old Testament, it is usually to help convey the supreme sovereignty of God. For instance, one's primary dependence on military arms is considered foolish, since they are not the ultimate source of deliverance, whether it be by the bow or sword (Josh. 24:12; Ps. 44:6; Hos. 1:7). This is because God overpowers and shatters the bow and arrow, spear, sword, and shield (Ps. 46:9; 76:3). In other places, God's judgment is spoken of as a bow or sword (Ps. 7:12–13; Isa. 66:16; Jer 12:12). He also uses the literal weapons of conquering nations to judge Israel (Isa. 3:25). Finally, that God is the faithful protector of His people is often expressed by referring to Him as "a shield unto them that put their trust in Him" (Prov. 30:5), just as He Himself encouraged Abraham,

Roman Emperor Trajan in armor (cuirass, kilt, and boots).

"Fear not, Abram: I am thy shield" (Gen. 15:1).

Dan Fredericks

ARMY A nation's military personnel organized for battle. Thus in Egypt, Israel could be referred to as having "armies" even when they did not have a political organization (Ex. 6:26; 7:4; 12:17). Goliath learned that to defy God's people was to defy the "armies of the living God" (1 Sam. 17:26,36), for God was the "God of the armies of Israel" (1 Sam. 17:45). In face of God, humans can only confess, "Is there any number of his armies?" (Job 25:3). Israel recognized God's anger when God did not go out with their armies (Ps. 44:9). To announce salvation, the prophet proclaimed the fury of God upon all armies (Isa. 34:2).

In the New Testament the writer of Hebrews looked back on the heroes of faith and proclaimed that through faith they "turned to flight the armies of the aliens" (Heb. 11:34). John's vision of the end time included the armies of heaven following the King of kings to victory over the beast and the false prophet (Rev. 19:11–21).

A sarcophagus relief depicting a battle scene between Greeks and Galatians.

Armies were organized in different ways during Israel's history. The patriarchs called upon servants and other members of the household (Gen. 14). In the wilderness Joshua led men he had chosen to defend against the Amalekites (Ex. 17:9–10). In the conquest Joshua led the tribes of Israel into battle after being commissioned by the "captain of the host of the Lord" (Josh. 5:14). At times tribes joined together to take territory (Judg. 1:3; 4:6).

Deborah summoned many of the tribes to battle, but some did not answer (Judg. 5). Other judges summoned clans (6:34) and tribes (6:35; 7:29). Saul first established a standing, professional army in Israel (1 Sam. 13:2), at first leading it himself with his son but then appointing a professional commander (1 Sam. 17:55). David apparently hired foreign troops loyal to him personally (2 Sam. 9:18; 15:18). Solomon enhanced the foot soldiers with a chariot corps and calvary (1 Kings 10:26). The army was organized into various units with officers over each, but the precise chain of command cannot be determined (2 Chron. 25:5). Humanitarian laws determined who was excused from military service and how war was conducted (Deut. 20).

ARNAN (Är′ năn) Personal name meaning, "quick." Person in messianic line of King David after the return from Exile (1 Chron. 3:21).

ARNI (Är′ nī) Ancestor of Jesus in difficult text of Luke 3:33. NAS, NIV read Ram, correlating with list in 1 Chronicles 2:10.

ARNON (Är′ nŏn) Place name meaning, "rushing river" or "river flooded with berries." River forming border of Moab and Amorites (Num. 21:13). Sihon, the Amorite king, ruled from the Arnon to the Jabbok (Num. 21:24), land which Israel took under Moses. The Arnon then served as the southern limit of territory Israel took east of the Jordan River (Deut. 3:8). It became the southern border of the tribe of Reuben (Josh. 13:16). The king of the Ammonites tried to retake the Arnon in Jephthah's day, but God's Spirit led Jephthah to victory (Judg. 11:12–33). Hazael, king of Damascus, retook the territory from Jehu of Israel (841–814 B.C.). Isaiah pictured Moab as scattered baby birds trying to cross the Arnon (16:2). Jeremiah called for a messenger to announce Moab's defeat by the Arnon (48:20). Near the Dead Sea, the Arnon is large and deep, one of Palestine's impressive sights. The wide river valley rises 1700 feet to the top of the cliffs above. The modern name is wadi-el-Mojib.

AROD (Ā′ rŏd) or **ARODI** Personal name meaning, "humpbacked." Arodi (Gen. 46:16) or Arod (Num. 26:17) was son of Gad and grandson of Jacob. He was the original ancestor of the Arodite clan.

AROER (Á·rō′ er) Place name meaning "juniper." *1.* City on north rim of Arnon Gorge east of Dead Sea on southern boundary of territory Israel claimed east of the Jordan River (Josh. 13:9). It figured in territorial claims of Reuben (Josh. 13:16), though the tribe of Gad originally built it (Num. 32:34). Compare Deuteronomy 3:12. Sihon, king of the Amorites, ruled it prior to Israel's conquest (Deut. 4:48; Josh. 12:2). Israel claimed a three hundred year history in the area (Judg. 11:26). Jehu's sins brought God's punishment on Israel, including the loss of Aroer to Hazael of Damascus (about 840 B.C.) (2 Kings 10:33). Compare Isaiah 17:2. Jeremiah asked Aroer to witness God's coming judgment on Moab (Jer. 48:19). The Moabites had gained control of Aroer under King Mesha, as his inscription on the Moabite Stone witnesses (about 850 B.C.). Spanish excavations show Aroer to have been more a border fortress than a major city. It is located at khirbet Arair two and one-half miles east of the highway along the Arnon River.

2. A city of the tribe of Gad (Josh. 13:25) near Rabbah, capital of the Ammonites. This may be the Aroer where Jephthah defeated the Ammonites (Judg. 11:33).

3. Town in southern Judah about twelve miles southeast of Beersheba with whose leaders David divided the spoil of battle (1 Sam. 30:28). This is located at modern Khirbet Arara. The text of Joshua 15:22 may have originally read Aroer. Two of David's captains hailed from Aroer (1 Chron. 11:44).

ARPACHSHAD (Är·păch′ shăd) or **ARPHAXAD** (New Testament spelling) Third son of Shem, son of Noah, and ancestor of the Hebrew people (Gen. 10:22). He was born two years after the flood and was the grandfather of Eber. In the New Testament the name Arphaxad appears in Luke's genealogy of Jesus (Luke 3:36). Luke seems to identify Arphaxad as the great-grandfather, rather than the grandfather, of Eber. This suggests the possibility that the genealogy in Genesis 10 was not intended to be exhaustively complete.

ARPAD (Är′ pad) or **ARPHAD** A city-state in northern Syria closely identified with Hamath. The Rab-shakeh, representing Sennacherib, Assyria's king, taunted the people of Judah in 701 B.C. (2 Kings 10:34; 19:13). He reminded the people walled up in Jerusalem that the gods of Arpad did not save it from Sennacherib. Isaiah mimicked such statements, saying Assyria was only a rod of Yahweh's anger and would soon face punishment for its pride (Isa. 10:5–19). Jeremiah noted Arpad's confusion as he pronounced doom on Damascus (Jer. 49:23). Arpad is modern tell Erfad about 25 miles north of Aleppo. Assyrian kings Adadnirari (806 B.C.), Ashurninari (754 B.C.), Tiglath-pileser (740 B.C.), and Sargon (720 B.C.) all mention victories over Arpad.

ART AND AESTHETICS are the making and recognition of objects of beauty produced by the use of skill and understanding. Though neither word appears in the Bible as such, the concepts which they represent certainly do.

The Old Testament Era Though no one knows for sure when or where artistic endeavors began, they may go back to the beauty of the creating events themselves (Gen. 1—2). However, human beings sinned and marred the relationship which they had both with the world in which they lived and the God who gave it to them (Gen. 3). Despite this, God still loved them and gave them not only the ability to provide a living, but also to design objects of beauty and grace to make their lives more enjoyable (Gen. 4:21–22). Thus, in time, many groups achieved a very high level of artistic accomplishment.

Unfortunately, the ancient Canaanites were not so lucky, for they were usually subservient to some foreign power. Apparently the Israelites were no better off, for though they did gain their

Mosaic design (which originated in Ur in 2500 B.C.) is seen in this famous mosaic map of Palestine.

A

freedom from Egypt, the struggle to claim the Promised Land was a long and difficult one. Moreover, when peace did come, it did not last long. Therefore, since they had little time for aesthetic pursuits, they simply borrowed such artifacts from their neighbors (particularly from the Egyptians and the Mesopotamians).

Not all of the Israelites' lack of artistic ability was the result of their political difficulties, for their religious teachings concerning the making and worshiping of idols (Ex. 20:4–6) also cast a shadow upon artistic endeavors. Yet, the warning was not so much against the art objects themselves as it was against their misuse. After all, God had commanded the Israelites not only to accept the Egyptian artifacts when they left Egypt (Ex. 12:35), but also to use them to build the tabernacle (Ex. 25—27; 35:20–29) with its fancy ark (Ex. 37:7–9, 1 Sam. 4:4), elaborate veils (Ex. 36:35–37), and other furnishings (Ex. 36:9—38:20). In all likelihood, most of it was done either by outsiders or at least by those trained elsewhere.

Apparently, this trend continued until the time of the monarchy when Israel developed an expanding and refining of artistic talents. By the time of David, music and dance had become a popularly accepted media for artistic presentation (1 Sam. 18:6; 2 Sam. 6:14). With the building of the magnificent Temple (1 Kings 5—6; 7:13–51) and the other royal edifices (1 Kings 7:1–12) during Solomon's reign, Israel had come into its own in

More carved stone pillars from the excavated synagogue at Capernaum.

the field of artistic endeavors. Even then, most of the intricate wood work on the walls and doors (such as the fancy carvings, applique palmettes, and guilloched borders—1 Kings 6:14–36) as well as the fancy metal work (1 Kings 7:23–50) was done by foreigners (1 Kings 5:18; 7:13–14). The Israelites were slowly developing their own craftsmen (1 Kings 5:18).

Intricate stone carving on top of pillar in the ruins of Capernaum.

Before long, they not only built fancy public edifices, but also enhanced the beauty of their own homes (1 Kings 22:39; Jer. 22:14; Ezek. 23:14). Unfortunately, this led to their placing more emphasis upon themselves than upon God and His work. As a result, prophets delivered God's strong condemnation (Ps. 45:8; Isa. 30:20; Hos. 13:2; Amos. 3:15; Hag. 1:4). All was not

lost. After the purging of their sin, God promised to restore them unto Him and provide for them a new and better place to live (Ezek. 40—48; Amos 9:9–15). Quite naturally, the main structure in that new place would be a new and more elaborately decorated temple (Ezek. 41).

The Intertestamental Era The days which followed the Babylonian Exile proved difficult for the Jewish remnant. Before they could get on their feet, Alexander the Great conquered their world. Though he soon died, he left behind a strong Greek influence. Much of this influence is still visible in the remains of the ornate columns, fancy gables, and beautiful paintings and mosaics. Though some of these do depict mythological motifs (such as the zodiac, the chariot of the sun god, etc.), most of them are of more traditional Jewish themes (such as the candlestick, the Star of David, etc.).

The New Testament Era Though the New Testament has little to say directly about art and aesthetics, artistic endeavors such as singing (Matt. 26:30; Luke 15:25) and dancing (Matt. 14:6; Mark 6:22) were apparently quite common. Certainly, Paul was not a bit intimidated by the Aeropagus in Athens, but rather used its theological significance to preach the gospel (Acts 17:22–29). As a result, those who were involved in the making and worshiping of idols became very angry and tried to kill him (Acts 19:23–31). God did not disapprove of their skills, but just the way they used them. When God began to reveal the nature of the new kingdom, He did so not only with the accompaniment of music (Rev. 5:9), but also with great strokes of artistic beauty (Rev. 21:9–21).

Since most of the early Christians came out of a Jewish background which warned against idolatry, they were careful to make a clear distinction between the work of art and the object which it represented. They were aware of the teaching value which art might have. Even though the political situation did not let them openly display

Decorative mosaic floor in Herod the Great's fortress palace atop the large hill in Israel called Masada.

their works, they did manage to paint religious symbols and scenes on the walls of the catacombs (or burial chambers). As Christianity gradually became more accepted, the practice of meeting in private homes was replaced by meeting in buildings which were especially designed for worship. Such buildings were usually elaborately decorated with paintings of biblical stories (such as those of Moses, David, Jonah, Daniel, Christ, and the disciples).   *Harry Hunt*

ARTAXERXES (Är·tȧ·xẽr′ xēs) Persian royal name meaning, "kingdom of righteousness," belonging to four Persian rulers and forming a major piece of evidence in dating Ezra and Nehemiah. See *Ezra; Nehemiah. 1.* Son of Xerxes I, Artaxerxes I ruled Persia from 465 to 424 B.C. He was called Longimanus or "long-handed." Most scholars place Ezra's trip to Jerusalem in the seventh year of his reign or 458 B.C. (Ezra 7:7). He had already received complaints from the inhabitants of Palestine who wanted to stop the returned exiles from rebuilding and had stopped the Jewish builders (Ezra 4:7–24). The Temple had been completed under Darius II (522–486) and thus before Artaxerxes (Ezra 6:15). Artaxerxes supported Ezra's work (Ezra 7:6–26). Nehemiah served as cupbearer to Artaxerxes (Neh. 2:1), and the king proved sensitive to Nehemiah's mood (Neh. 2:2). He granted Nehemiah's request to go to Judah (Neh. 2:5–6), making him governor of Judah (Neh. 5:14). *2.* Artaxerxes II ruled Persia 404 to 359 B.C. Some Bible students identify him as ruler under whom Ezra worked. *3.* Artaxerxes III ruled 358–337 B.C. *4.* Ruled Persia 337–336 B.C. See *Persia.*

ARTEMAS (Är′ tė·màs) Personal name probably shortened from Artemidoros, meaning, "gift of Artemis." If this is the case, then the parents worshiped the Greek goddess Artemis. Paul promised to send Artemas or Tychicus to Titus, so Titus could join Paul in Nicopolis (Titus 3:12). Artemas would apparently take over Titus' pastoral duties in Crete. Tradition says Artemas became bishop of Lystra.

ARTEMIS (Är′ tė·mĭs) names the Greek goddess of the moon, the daughter of Zeus and Leto, whose worship was threatened by Paul's preaching of the gospel. Artemis was the goddess who watched over nature for both humans and animals. She was the patron deity of wild animals, protecting them from ruthless treatment and at the same time regulating the rules of hunting activities for humans. She was considered the great mother image and gave fertility to humankind. In the Greek homeland she was usually portrayed by the statues as a young, attractive virgin, wearing a short tunic and having her hair pulled back on her head. In Ephesus and western Asia Minor she was portrayed as a more mature woman. Her robe is draped in such a way as to expose her bosom which is covered with multiple breasts, depicting her gift of fertility and nurture. Often standing beside her is a fawn or stag on each side representing her relation to the animal world. The official local statue was carefully housed in a temple honoring Artemis.

The most famous statue was located in the city of Ephesus, the official "temple keeper" for Artemis. Artemis was the chief deity of Ephesus, and her temple was one of the seven wonders of the ancient world. See *Ephesus.* The temple ceremonies were carried out by priests who were eunuchs and priestesses who were virgins. They conducted the daily ceremonies caring for the deity and for the gifts brought by worshipers, as well as an annual festival on May 25, when numerous statues of the goddess were carried in procession to the amphitheater in Ephesus for a celebration of music, dancing, and drama. This could be the background of the outcry in Acts 19:28: "Great is Artemis of the Ephesians."

The statues of the goddess, often miniature models of the temple with an image of the goddess within, were sold widely. In Acts, a silversmith named Demetrius rallied support against Paul's preaching of the gospel for fear that it might damage his business selling statues.

Diana was a Roman diety somewhat similar to the more popular Artemis. As the Italic and Greek

Artemis (Diana), patron goddess of Ephesus, covered with eggs (or breasts) as symbols of fertility.

divinities met, she was quickly identified with Artemis.

ARUBBOTH (Á·rŭb′ bŏth) City name meaning, "smoke hole" or "chimney." One of Solomon's provincial officials made headquarters there and administered over Sochoh and the land of Hepher (1 Kings 4:10). This would be territory belonging to the clan of Hepher of the tribe of Mannasseh in the northern part of the Plain of Sharon, southwest of Megiddo and southeast of Dor. Arubboth is modern Arabbah nine miles north of Samaria.

ARUMAH (Á·rū′ măh) Place name meaning, "exalted" or "height." Abimelech, the judge, lived there while he fought to control Shechem (Judg. 9:41). It may be modern khirbet el-Ormah south of Shechem.

ARVAD (Är′ văd) **ARVADITE** Place name of unknown meaning. It provided sailors and soldiers for Tyre (Ezek. 27:8,11). It was probably the rocky island called Rouad today, off the coast of Syria. It is related to Canaan in the family of nations (Gen. 10:18).

ARZA (Är′ zà) Personal name meaning, "wood worm" or "earthiness." Steward of the house of King Baasha (908–886 B.C.) in Tirzah. The king was drunk in Arza's house when Zimri killed Baasha (1 Kings 16:8–10).

ASA (Ă′ sà) Personal name meaning, "doctor" or "healing." *1.* Son and successor of Abijam as king of Judah (1 Kings 15:8). He reigned for forty-one years (913–873 B.C.). A pious man, he instituted several reforms to remove foreign gods and foreign religious practices from the land, even removing his mother from political power (1 Kings 15:13). After his death, apparently from natural causes, he was succeeded by his son Jehoshaphat or Josaphat (KJV). Asa was rebuked by the prophet Hanani (2 Chron. 16:7) for relying on the king of Syria rather than on the Lord (1 Kings 15:17–20). The chronicler further reported that when Asa developed a disease in his feet, he relied on physicians rather than on the Lord (2 Chron. 16:12). Matthew 1:7–8 lists Asa among Jesus' ancestors. See *Israel; Chronology of Biblical Period.*

2. A Levite who returned from the Exile to Jerusalem. He was the head of a family in the villages of the Netophathites near Jerusalem (1 Chron. 9:16).

ASAHEL (Ăs′ à·hĕl) Personal name meaning "God acted" or "God made." *1.* Brother of Joab and Abishai, David's nephew (2 Sam. 2:18). He was a commander in David's army (2 Sam. 23:24). He was a fleet-footed individual who pursued Abner as the latter fled following his defeat at Gibeon. Unable to dissuade Asahel from pursuing him, Abner slew him. That act led at last to the murder of Abner by Asahel's brother Joab (2 Sam. 3:27–30). *2.* A Levite during the reign of Jehoshaphat, Asa's son. Asahel was sent out along with several princes, other Levites, and priests to teach the people of Judah the book of the law of God (2 Chron. 17:8). *3.* A Levite under Hezekiah, the king of Judah following Ahaz. Asahel, along with ten others, assisted the chief officers in charge of contributions, tithes, and dedicated objects. Asahel's title was that of overseer. *4.* The father of Jonathan who along with Jahaziah opposed Ezra's direction for the men of Judah to separate themselves from the foreign wives they had married. Ezra indicated they had sinned in marrying foreign women (Ezra 10:15).

ASAHIAH (Ăs·à·hī′ ah) See *Asaiah.*

ASAIAH (Å·sai′ ăh) Personal name meaning, "Yahweh made." *1.* Servant of King Josiah sent with others to Huldah, the prophet, to determine meaning of book of law found in the Temple about 624 B.C. *2.* A leader of tribe of Simeon who helped drive out people of Ham from pastures of Gedor when Hezekiah was king of Judah (715–686 B.C.). See *Gedor. 3.* A musical Levite in line of Merari (1 Chron. 6:30). He is apparently the same as the chief of the sons of Merari, who led 220 of his clan in helping bring the ark of the covenant from the house of Obed-edom to Jerusalem (1 Chron. 15). *4.* Leader of clans from Shilo who returned from Babylonian Exile about 537 B.C. (1 Chron. 9:5).

ASAPH (Ā′ săph) Personal name meaning, "he collected." *1.* Father of court official under King Hezekiah (715–686 B.C.), who in sadness reported the threats of Assyria to the king (2 Kings 18). *2.* Levite musician David appointed to serve in the tabernacle until the Temple was completed (1 Chron. 6:39). Asaph was the father of the clan of Temple musicians who served through the history of the Temple. A member of the clan was among the first to return from Exile in 537 B.C. (1 Chron. 9:15). Part of the musical responsibility included sounding the cymbal (1 Chron. 15:19). David established the tradition of delivering psalms to Asaph for the Temple singers to sing (1 Chron. 16:7). Asaph and the singers ministered daily (1 Chron. 16:37). Their musical service could be called "prophesying" (1 Chron. 25:1–7). Descendants of Asaph delivered prophetic messages under God's Spirit (2 Chron. 20:14–19). Later generations sang the songs of Asaph "the seer" (2 Chron. 29:30). Psalms 50, 73–83 are titled "Psalms of Asaph" or similar titles. This may refer to authorship, the singers who used the Psalms in worship, or to a special collection of Psalms. See *Psalms.*

ASAREL (Å·sā′ rĕl) or KJV **ASAREEL** Personal name meaning, "God has sworn" or "God rejoiced." A member of tribe of Judah (1 Chron. 4:16).

ASARELAH (Ăs·à·rē′ lăh) KJV, NIV, NRSV spelling of Asharelah (NAS, RSV, TEV) in 1 Chronicles 25:2. This appears to be a variant of Jesharelah or Jesarelah in 1 Chronicles 25:14. The person is a descendant or son of Asaph among the Temple singers.

ASCENSION Act of going to heaven in bodily form from earthly life. Experienced by Enoch (Gen. 5:24) and Elijah (2 Kings 2:1–2) but supremely by Jesus Christ (Acts 1:9). Jewish literature outside the canon of the Bible developed long stories and explanations of the ascension of many religious heroes. See, for example, the Assumption of Moses. The Bible gives only brief notices. Still, the ascension of Jesus provides important theological foundations. It concluded the earthly ministry of Jesus, allowing eyewitnesses to see both the risen Christ on earth and the victorious, eternal Christ returning to heaven to minister at the right hand of the Father. The ascension expanded Christ's ministry from its geographically limited earthly dimensions to its universal heavenly dimensions. The ascension (1) allowed Jesus to prepare a heavenly place for His followers (John 14:2), (2) return to the Father (John 16:5), (3) send the Holy Spirit to the disciples (John 16:7) to bring conviction of sin, open the way to righteousness through faith, and condemn the devil, (4) comfort those suffering for Him through visions of the Ascended One (Acts 7:54–60), (5) call persons to fulfill His missionary task (Acts 9:1–18), (6) open doors of ministry for His people (2 Cor. 2:12–14), (7) demonstrate God's power and His rule over all who would exercise power and authority on earth or in heaven (Eph. 1:20–23), (8) give gifts for ministry to His people (Eph. 4:7–12), (9) give hope to troubled followers showing they would join Him in glory (Col. 3:1–4), (10) rescue His servants from persecution so they can preach His gospel (2 Tim. 4:16–18), (11) demonstrate that glory, not death, is God's final word for the Son and for disciples (Heb. 2:9), (12) exercise a heavenly priesthood (Heb. 4:14), (13) make revelation of future trials and final victory possible (Rev. 1:1), (14) discipline His church so He may have fellowship with it and provide final full fellowship in ruling with Christ (Rev. 3:19–22).

Most of all the ascension combined with the resurrection exalted Christ (Phil. 2:9). Contrasted to Christ's act of humbling Himself to move from heaven to earth and especially to the cross (Phil. 2:5–8) is God's act of exalting Jesus to the highest position in the universe, in charge of everything that exists and all that happens. Thus in ascension Jesus showed He had defeated death for good and made eternal life possible. The ascension thus calls on all people to bow in worship and obedience to the Ascended One (Phil. 2:10).

ASCENTS, SONG OF See *Degrees, Song of.*

ASENATH (Ăs′ ĕ·năth) Egyptian name meaning, "Belonging to Neith" (a goddess). Wife of Joseph and daughter of a priest in Egyptian temple at On or Heliopolis. Asenath was Pharaoh's present to Joseph (Gen. 41:45). She was mother of Ephraim and Manasseh (Gen. 41:50−51).

ASER New Testament spelling of Asher in KJV (Luke 2:36; Rev. 7:6).

ASH KJV translation in Isaiah 44:14. Some manuscripts of the Hebrew text have the word for cedas, which is very similar to the word found in the text translated by the KJV. Modern versions differ. The word is translated fir (NAS), pine (NIV), cedar (NRSV, REB), and laurel tree (TEV).

ASHAN (Ā′ shăn) Place name meaning, "smoke." City in western hills of tribe of Judah (Josh. 15:42) given to tribe of Simeon (Josh. 19:7). The Aaronic priests claimed Ashan as one of their cities (1 Chron. 6:59; called Ain in Josh. 21:16). See *Bor-asan.* Ashan was located at modern Khirbet Asan just northwest of Beersheba.

ASHARELAH (Ăsh·à·rē′ lăh) See *Asarelah.*

ASHBEA (Ăsh·bē′ à) KJV, TEV translation. NIV, NAS, NRSV read Beth Ashbea. See *Beth Ashbea.*

ASHBEL (Ăsh′ bĕl) **ASHBELITES** Personal name meaning, "having a long upper lip." Son of Benjamin, grandson of Jacob, and original ancestor of Ashbelite clan (Gen. 46:21).

ASHCHENAZ (Ăsh′ chĕ·năz) **ASHKENAZ** Personal and national name given two spellings in KJV but spelled Ashkenaz in modern translations. A son of Gomer (Gen. 10:3) and original ancestor of people called kingdom of Ashkenaz (Jer. 51:27). Usually identified with Scythians. See *Scythians.*

ASHDOD (Ăsh′ dŏd) One of five principal cities of the Philistines, where the Philistines defeated Israel and captured the ark of the covenant.

Asdod was ten miles north of Ashkelon and two and a half miles east of the Mediterranean Sea on the Philistine plain. It was the northernmost city of the Philistine pentapolis recorded in Joshua 13:3. Ashdod occurs in written history first in the Late Bronze period where it is mentioned in the trade documents of the Ras Shamra tablets discovered at Ugarit (ancient trade center near the Mediterranean coast in northern Syria). Ashdod is described as a manufacturer and exporter of textiles, specifically purple wool. The city name also occurs in the Egyptian list of names, *Onomasticon of Amanope* (263).

Old Testament In the Old Testament Ashdod was a place where some of the Anakim remained during the time of Joshua (Josh. 11:22). See *Anakim.* As one of the five chief cities of the Philistines it stood yet to be possessed by Joshua (Josh. 13:3), who allocated it to the tribe of Judah (Jos. 15:46−7). David subdued the Philistines, implicitly including Ashdod (2 Sam. 5:25; 8:1), but it was not described as under Israel's control until Uzziah (783−742 B.C.) captured it (2 Chron. 26:8). Perhaps the most infamous contact between Ashdod and Israel is reported in 1 Sam. 4−6 when the Philistines defeated the army of Israel in battle, killed the two sons of Eli, Hophni and Phinehas, and captured the ark of the covenant.

Although the city was captured by Uzziah, it did not remain long under Judah's control and regained enough strength to revolt from Sargon II in 711 B.C. The Assyrians were able quickly to subdue the Philistines, and they remained under Assyrian control until captured by the Egyptian Pharaoh Psammetichus I (664−610) after a 29-year seige as reported by Herodotus. Under Nebuchadnezzar (604−562 B.C.), Babylon soon captured this territory and took the king of Ashdod prisoner.

The prophets of Israel spoke about the city of Ashdod in various military, political and moral contexts (Neh. 13:23−24; Isa. 20:1−6; Jer. 25:20; Amos 1:8; Zech. 9:6). Throughout the Persian period the city remained a threat to Israel.

Extra-biblical Sources In the Greek period Ashdod was known as Azotus and was a flourishing city until being captured by Israel during the Maccabean period. Judas Maccabeus destroyed altars and images in Ashdod (1 Maccabees 5:68), and Jonathan later burned the temple of Dagon, those who took refuge there, and ultimately the city itself (1 Maccabees 10:84−87).

Josephus reported that Pompey separated Ashdod from Israel after his victory (63 B.C.), Gabinius rebuilt the city, and it was joined to the province of Syria. Augustus granted it to Herod the Great. Herod left it to his sister Salome, who in turn willed it to Julia, the wife of Augustus. Its greatness as a city ended with the Roman destruction of A.D. 67, although it was occupied at least through the sixth century.

Archaeological Evidence The major archaeological work on Ashdod was done from 1962−72 under the direction of D. N. Freedman and others. Some evidence remains from Chalcolithic and Early Bronze times, but the major remains date from Middle Bronze and later including a walled city dating around 1625 B.C. A major destruction of the city was indicated by a three foot layer of ash and debris dating about 1250 B.C. Two extensive Philistine occupation levels date from the twelfth and eleventh centuries B.C. The Iron Age showed a flourishing community, and an Iron II temple yielded many cultic artifacts.   *George W. Knight*

ASHDOTH-PISGAH (Ăsh′ dŏth-Pĭs′ gah) KJV for "slopes of Pisgah." See *Pisgah.*

ASHER (Ăsh′ ēr) or **Aser** (New Testament Greek spelling) Personal, tribal, and place name meaning, "fortune," "happiness." *1.* Eighth son of Jacob, born of Zilpah, the concubine (Gen. 30:13). His four sons and one daughter began the tribe of Asher (Gen. 46:17). Jacob's blessing said Asher would have rich food that he would give a king (Gen. 49:20), perhaps suggesting a period when the tribe would serve a foreign king. *2.* The tribe of Asher numbered 53,400 in the wilderness (Num. 26:46), having grown from 41,500 (Num. 1:41). They formed part of the rear guard in the wilderness marches (Num. 10:25−28). Asher's territorial allotment was in Phoenicia in the far northwest reaching to Tyre and Sidon on the Mediterranean coast (Josh. 19:24−31). They could not drive out the Canaanites and had to live among them (Judg. 1:31−32). When Deborah summoned the tribes to action, Asher did not respond but "continued on the seashore" (Judg. 5:17). Apparently, Asher was working for the Canaanites in the ports of the Mediterranean. Moses' blessing gives another view of Asher, calling the tribe "most blessed," "favored by his brothers," and strong (Deut. 33:24−25). Asher produced no judge in the Book of Judges; nor did it have a tribal leader in the chronicler's list (1 Chron. 27:16−22). Asher did provide troops for Gideon (Judg. 6:35; 7:23) and 40,000 for David at Hebron (1 Chron. 12:36). Some people from Asher made the pilgrimage to Jerusalem to keep Hezekiah's Passover (2 Chron. 30:11). Perhaps Asher's greatest hero was Anna, the prophetess who bore witness to the baby Jesus (Luke 2:36−38). Twelve thousand from Asher are among the 144,000 sealed out of great tribulation to be fed by the Lamb (Rev. 7).
3. Apparently a border town in Manasseh (Josh. 17:7) but possibly a reference to the border joining the tribal territories of Manasseh and Asher. See *Tribes of Israel.*

ASHERAH (À·shē′ răh) A fertility goddess, the mother of Baal, whose worship was concentrated in Syria and Canaan and the wooden object that represented her. The King James Version translated Asherah "grove" and the proper noun "Ashtaroth."
The writers of the Old Testament did not provide an actual description of an "asherah" or the origin of the worship of Asherah. Other religious writings from the Ancient Near East indicate that "Asherah" was the Hebrew name for an Amorite or Canaanite goddess who was worshiped in various parts of the Ancient Near East. The biblical

writers sometimes did not make a clear distinction between references to Asherah as a goddess and as object of worship. According to ancient mythology, Asherah, the mother goddess, was the wife of El and mother of seventy gods, of whom Baal was the most famous. Asherah was the fertility goddess of the Phoenicians and Canaanites. She was called "Lady Asherah of the Sea." See *Canaan.*
Scholars who have studied art work from the Ancient Near East have suggested that some figures in drawings could be representations of the fertility goddess Asherah. Drawings of plain and carved poles, staffs, a cross, a double axe, a tree, a tree stump, a headdress for a priest, and several wooden images could be illustrations of an Asherah. Passages such as 2 Kings 13:6; 17:16; 18:4; 21:3; and 23:6,15 have been interpreted as a definition of an asherah as a wooden object constructed or destroyed by man. The object stood upright and was used in the worship of a goddess of the same name.
The Asherah existed in both the Southern and Northern Kingdoms of Israel. Jezebel of Tyre apparently installed Asherah worship in the north when she married King Ahab (1 Kings 18:18−19). The principle cities in which the objects were located were Samaria, Bethel, and Jerusalem. According to 1 Kings 14:23, the people "built for themselves high places, and pillars, and Asherim (plural) on every hill and under every green tree."
See *Baal; Idolatry.*   *James Newell*

ASHERIM Plural of Asherah. See *Asherah.*

ASHERITES Members of tribe of Asher. See *Asher.*

ASHEROTH Plural of Asherah. See *Asherah.*

ASHES often were associated with sacrifices, mourning, and fasting. Grief, humiliation, and repentance were expressed by placing ashes on the head or by sitting in ashes. Dirt, sackcloth, fasting, the tearing of clothing, and ashes visibly demonstrated the person's emotions. At times the ashes that remained from a sacrifice were kept and used for ritual purification. They also symbolized the results of divine destruction. The use of ashes to express grief and repentance continued into the New Testament period. Their use in purification rites are contrasted with the cleansing brought by Christ's blood. They also represent the devastating effect of God's wrath on Sodom and Gomorrah (2 Pet. 2:6).   *Scott Langston*

ASHHUR (Ăsh′ hŭr) Modern translation spelling of Ashur (KJV, TEV). Personal name meaning, "to be black," or "belonging to Ishara." Son of Hazron, born after his father's death (1 Chron.

2:24). He had two wives, each of whom bore him children (1 Chron. 4:5–7). His title, "Father of Tekoa," may indicate he founded the city later famous for native son Amos, the prophet. See *Tekoa*. Some Bible students understand Caleb to be Ashhur's father in 1 Chronicles 2:24 (TEV, RSV, but not NRSV).

ASHIMA (Å·shī' mà) Syrian god made and worshiped in Hamath (2 Kings 17:30). The Hebrew word *'asham* means, "guilt." Hebrew writers may have deliberately written a word associated with guilt instead of the name of the god or goddess. Hamath's goddess may have been Asherah. See *Asherah*. Amos 8:14 says Israel swore by or made oaths by the "sin" (KJV) "guilt" (NAS) or "shame" of Samaria. NRSV and NIV footnote propose "Ashimah of Samaria." Samaria worshiped falsely. They may have incorporated the god of Hamath into their worship. See *Hamath.* The exilic Elephantine papyri from a Jewish community in Egypt mention an "Ashim-bethel" who may have been worshiped by Egyptian Jews as a counterpart to Yahweh.

ASHKELON (Ăsh' kė·lŏn) One of five principal cities of the Philistines (pentapolis), located on the Mediterranean coast on the trade route, Via Maris, and designated for Judah in the conquest. Ashkelon was a Mediterranean coastal city twelve miles north of Gaza and ten miles south of Ashdod. It is the only Philistine city directly on the seacoast. Its history extends into the Neolithic Period. The economic importance came from both its port and its location on the trade route, the Via Maris.

The location in southern Palestine put Ashkelon under considerable Egyptian influence throughout much of its history. The first mention of the city was in the nineteenth century B.C. Execration Texts, where a curse on the ruler and his supporters was written on pottery, then smashed, symbolizing breaking his power. A fifteenth century B.C. papyrus speaks of Ashkelon's loyalty to Egypt, and the fourteenth century Amarna Letters confirm that relationship with the ruler Widia claiming submission to the Pharaoh, although the ruler of Jerusalem claimed that Ashkelon had given supplies to the 'Apiru. In this period the goddess Astarte was worshiped here by the Canaanites. The city revolted from Egypt and was subsequently sacked by Ramses II (1282 B.C.). Later that same century Pharaoh Merneptah captured the city.

The Old Testament record concerns the city after it had come under Philistine control. It was ruled by a ruler or *seren* supported by a military aristocracy. Joshua had not taken Ashkelon in the conquest of the land (Josh. 13:3), but it was included in the territory designated for Judah. It appears that Judah did take the city (Judg. 1:18), but it belonged to the Philistines in the Samson account (Judg. 14:19) and under Saul and David (1 Sam. 6:17; 2 Sam. 1:20). Ashkelon subsequently was independent or under the control of Assyria, Egypt, Babylon, and Tyre. Amos 1:8 and Jeremiah 47:5, 7 refer to Ashkelon and her evils. With the coming of the Greeks, Ashkelon became a Hellenistic center of culture and learning. During the Maccabean Period the city flourished and apparently did not have hostilities with the Jews (1 Maccabees 10:36; 11:60). In fact, many Jews lived there. Rome granted the status "free allied city" in 104 B.C. A tradition was known in Christian circles that Herod the Great was born in Ashkelon, the son of a temple slave of Apollo. Herod did have family and friends there and gave the city some beautiful buildings, built a palace there, and left the city to his sister, Salome, at his death. The city was attacked by the Jews in the first Roman Revolt (66 A.D.) but survived and was faithful to Rome.   *George W. Knight*

ASHKENAZ See *Ashchenaz.*

ASHNAH (Ăsh' năh) Place name. *1.* A city in the valley of the tribe of Judah (Josh. 15:33), possibly modern Aslin. *2.* A second city in the valley or shephelah of Judah (Josh. 15:43), possibly modern Idna, about eight miles northwest of Hebron.

ASHPENAZ (Ăsh' pĕ·năz) Chief eunuch guarding the family of Nebuchadnezzar, king of Babylon (605–562 B.C.) (Dan. 1:3). He administered the diet and life-style of Daniel and his three friends, giving them new Babylonian names (Dan. 1:7). Daniel developed a close, loving relationship with him.

ASHRIEL (Ăsh' rĭ·ĕl) KJV spelling for Asriel. See *Asriel.*

ASHTAROTH (Ăsh' tȧrŏth) is the plural form of Ashtoreth, a Canaanite goddess of fertility, love, and war and the daughter of the god El and the goddess Asherah. *1.* The Old Testament uses the plural form, Ashtaroth, more than the singular form, Ashtoreth. The only references to Ashtoreth come in 1 Kings 11:5,33; 2 Kings 23:13. The Hebrew scribes replaced the vowels of the name Ashtart or Ashteret with the vowels from the Hebrew word for shame, *boshet,* to bring dishonor to the memory of the goddess. This exchanging of vowels formed the word Ashtoreth. The Greek form of the name is Astarte.

In Canaanite mythology, she appears to be the sister of the goddess Anath and the spouse of the god Baal. Anath also was the spouse of Baal, as well as the goddess of love and war. Some confusion, therefore, exists with regards to Ashtaroth's relationship to Anath. Anath and Ashtaroth may have referred to the same goddess, or they may have been two separate deities. Among the people of Palestine, Ashtaroth may have taken over

Anath's role. The Egyptians gave the title "Lady of Heaven" to Astarte, Anath, and another goddess, Qudshu. In Moab, Astarte was the spouse of the major god, Chemosh. The Babylonians and Assyrians called her Ashtar and worshiped her as goddess of fertility and love. The people of the Ancient Near East during the Hellenistic and Roman periods referred to her as Aphrodite-Venus.

Apparently, the word "ashtaroth" at one time meant "womb" or "that which comes from the womb." This word, "ashtaroth," appears in Deuteronomy 7:13 and 28:4,18,51 to describe the young of the flock. This use may demonstrate the link between the goddess Ashtaroth and fertility.

The biblical writers often coupled Baal with Ashtaroth as a designation of pagan worship (Judg. 2:13; 10:6; 1 Sam. 7:3–4; 12:10). In addition to her worship by the Canaanites, the Old Testament mentions the people of Sidon (1 Kings 11:5) and the Philistines (1 Sam. 31:10) as reverencing her. At Beth-Shan, the Philistines erected a temple to Ashtaroth (1 Sam. 31:10). The reference to the Queen of Heaven (Jer. 7:18) may have Ashtaroth in mind, but this is uncertain. The Israelites worshiped her, and the biblical writers specifically refer to Solomon's leadership in promoting the worship of Ashtaroth (1 Kings 11:5). She was only one of many foreign deities revered by the Israelites. Josiah destroyed the shrines built to her (2 Kings 23:13).

2. Egyptian documents dating from the eighteenth century B.C. onward refer to a city called Ashtartu or Ashtarot in the region of Bashan. Joshua 21:27 mentions a city with the name Be-eshterah in Bashan, while a man named Uzzia is called an Ashterathite (1 Chron. 11:44). Og, king of Bashan, reigned in the city of Ashtaroth (Deut. 1:4; Josh. 9:10; 12:4, 13:12, 31; 1 Chron. 6:17). The sons of Machir received it as a part of their inheritance in the land (Josh. 13:31).

Once the city is called Ashteroth-karnaim (Gen. 14:5) or "Ashtaroth of the two horns." A seventeenth century B.C. stone mould for making bronze figurines of Astarte was uncovered at Nahariyah. She was represented as a woman with two horns on her head. Many other clay figurines of Astarte have been found at sites throughout Palestine. The city's name, Ashtaroth, may reflect that she was worshiped by the citizens of this settlement.

The city is located at modern Tel Ashtarah about 20 miles east of the Sea of Galilee. It was located on a major branch of the Via Maris, or Way of the Sea and in the King's Highway, the major highway for traffic east of the Jordan.

Scott Langston

ASHTEROTH KARNAIM (Ăsh′ tė·rŏth Kär′ - na·ĭm) See *Ashtaroth.*

ASHTORETH (Ăsh′ tō·rĕth) See *Ashtaroth.*

ASHUR KJV spelling for Ashhur. See *Ashhur.*

ASHURBANIPAL (Ă′ shŭr·băn′ ĭ·păl) Assyria's

Ashurbanipal (668–629 B.C.) was ruler of Assyria during its last years of decline. This relief from Nimrud depicts an earlier period of great power—the reign of Ashurnasirpal II (883–859 B.C.).

last great king who is identified in Ezra 4:10 as the king of Assyria who captured Susa, Elam, and other nations and settled their citizens in Samaria.

The son of the King Esarhaddon was the heir apparent from about 673 B.C. He actually ruled from 668 to 629 B.C. Ashurbanipal's legacy is his famous library which contained more than 20,000 clay tablets. The library was located in the Assyrian capital of Nineveh and was discovered in 1853. Ashurbanipal's copyists not only transcribed Assyrian books but also preserved Sumerian and Akkadian literature. Most of what we know about the Assyrian Empire is derived from his library.

A wall relief (dating ca. 650 B.C.) in alabaster from Nineveh depicting Asshurbanipal on a lion hunt.

Ashurbanipal was also known by the name Osnappar and appears in the KJV as Asnapper. His name appears only once in the Bible (Ezra 4:10), the only report of such a settlement in Samaria. The Greeks called him Sardanapalus. His reign was contemporary with the reigns of Manasseh, Amon, and Josiah, Kings of Judah. See *Assyria.*

M. Stephen Davis

ASHURITE (Ăsh' ŭr·īte) or **ASHURI** (NIV) Apparently a tribe or clan over which Ish-bosheth, Saul's son, ruled (2 Sam. 2:9). The textual tradition among the earliest translations is not clear here with some evidence that the tribe of Asher or the city-state of Geshur is meant. In KJV of Ezekiel 27:6 Ashurites made "benches of ivory" for Tyre. Most modern translations use a different division of words in the Hebrew text and see a type of wood used: boxwood (NAS), cypress (NIV), pine (TEV, RSV), cedar (Jerusalem). If people from Ashur are meant in either of the original texts, we know nothing else about them.

ASHVATH (Ăsh' văth) Personal name meaning, "that which has been worked" (as iron). Descendant of Asher (1 Chron. 7:33).

ASIA (Āsià) in the New Testament refers to a Roman province on the west of Asia Minor whose capital was Ephesus.

The Roman province of Asia comprised generally the southwest portion of Anatolia. Its first capital was Pergamum, but the capital was later changed to Ephesus. Asia residents were in Jerusalem at Pentecost (Acts 2:9). Paul the apostle traveled and preached extensively in Asia (Acts 19:10,22) especially in the neighborhood of Ephesus; but God forbad him to preach there prior to his Macedonian call (Acts 16:6). Men of Asia led to Paul's arrest in Jerusalem (Acts 21:27). 1 Peter was addressed to Christians in Asia. Asia was the location of the seven churches to whom the Book of Revelation was addressed. Asia was known for its worship of Artemis (Acts 19:27). See *Rome; Roman Empire.*

ASIA MINOR, CITIES OF (Ā' sià Mī' nŏr) The cities located on the Anatolian peninsula (modern-day Turkey). Cities of Asia Minor important to the New Testament accounts included Alexandria Troas, Assos, Ephesus, Miletus, Patara, Smyrna, Pergamum, Sardis, Thyatira, Philadelphia, Laodicea, Colossae, Attalia, Antioch, Iconium, Lystra, Derbe, and Tarsus. The cities figured prominently in the apostle Paul's missionary journeys, several of the churches receiving epistles. Among the list are the "Seven Cities" of the Revelation.

Geography and History The geography of Asia Minor greatly influenced the development of settlements in the area. The region can be described as the point where "East meets West," linking the continent of Europe with the Near East. The peninsula is a high plateau surrounded by steep mountain ranges. The mountains isolate Asia Minor from much of the outside world. Narrow passes through the mountains connect the interior with the Near East. Deep ravines cut by numerous and often navigable rivers linked the cities of the plateau with the western coastline. Cities developed in locales vital to trade and commerce, such as near the mouths of rivers and mountain passes.

The history of Asia Minor reflects the region's unstable position between the east and west. The Hittite Empire thrived in the eastern portion of the peninsula during the second millennium B.C. (before 1000). Exposed on the west to the Aegean Sea, the coastal area became the home to numerous Greek colonies beginning after 1200 B.C. Centered in Sardis, the Lydian Empire began to expand about 600 B.C., but the Persians soon conquered the area. Control passed to Alexander the Great during the fourth century, and upon his death Asia Minor fell under the rule of the Seluccids. Beginning about 200 B.C. Roman control of the peninsula increased until all of Anatolia was absorbed into the Roman provincial system. At this time, "Asia" designated the provinces of only western Anatolia. Galatia, Cappadocia, and Cilicia comprised the eastern provinces, while Bithynia and Pontus bordered the Black Sea to the north. The Anatolian peninsula was probably first termed "Asia Minor" during the fifth century A.D.

Coastal Cities The name *Troas* described both the northwest region of Asia Minor as well as the port city. Located 10 miles south of the site of ancient Troy, Alexandria Troas was founded as a Roman colony during the period of Augustus and served as a primary port for trade passing between Asia Minor and Macedonia. Remains of the ruined city wall and a bath complex of the second century A.D. are still visible. As with many ancient ports, the once busy harbor silted up and became unusable. Paul set sail from Troas to Greece in response to his vision of the "Macedonian man" (Acts 16:8). On his third journey, Paul's companions embarked on a ship sailing toward the port of *Assos,* 20 miles south (Acts 20:13–14). A bustling port city surrounded by a wall dating to the fourth century B.C., Assos' temple of Athena sat high on the acropolis overlooking the harbor. At Assos, Paul joined the ship carrying Luke and several others after journeying on foot from Troas.

Ephesus served as the primary trading center of all Asia Minor. The large port facility provided ample anchorage for ships carrying goods east from Greece and Italy, as well as for those which took to Rome the wares brought overland from Asia and the Far East. A well-laid road linked the port facilities at Ephesus with *Tarsus* to the east. The road approached the city from the southeast, entering a monumental gateway near the public baths. Remains of the city's immense theater, capable of seating 24,000 spectators, stand today as a reminder of the great crowd which, in protest to Paul, filled the seats and for several hours shouted, "Great is Diana of the Ephesians!" (Acts 19:34). The city's temple honoring Diana was one of the Seven Wonders of the world. Known as the Artemision to the Greeks, the temple possessed 127 pillars, each 60 feet high, which held up the roof of the largest all-marble structure in the Hellenistic world. The city's harbor, built around the outlet of the Cayster River, gradually filled with silt; and the site now lies some six miles away from the sea. As the chief port and city of Asia, Paul's choice of Ephesus as a center of ministry provided the perfect base from which the gospel could be spread throughout the Roman world.

During the early period of Greek colonization, *Miletus* exercised extensive control over southwestern Anatolia. As a major sea power, the city remained independent throughout the time of Lydian rule in the region. The city was able to withstand attempted incursions by the Persians until 494 B.C. Once a wealthy port for the wool industry, Miletus was a city of little significance during the New Testament era (Acts 20:15).

Acts 21 recounts how Paul sailed for *Tyre* from Patara. The city served as a popular port for ships traveling eastward during the early autumn months when favorable winds made travel to Egypt and the Phoenician coast easier. The harbor sat near the outlet of the Xanthus River and was the main shipping facility of provincial Lydia.

Smyrna surrounded a well protected harbor on the Aegean coast at the outlet of the Hermus River. Extensive trade into and out of Asia passed through the city. During the first century A.D. Smyrna reigned as one of the grandest cities of all Asia. A large temple dedicated to the Emperor Tiberius boasted the close alliance of the city with the Empire. Numerous other temples dedicated to a wide range of Roman deities as well as scores of beautifully adorned public buildings decorated the city.

Cities of the Interior Located 15 miles inland overlooking the Caicus River, *Pergamum* contained the first temple in Asia dedicated to a Roman Emperor, Augustus, in 29 B.C. The city possessed a commanding position on a hill high above the valley. Located on the Upper Acropolis were a large theater, library, agora, palace, barracks, and altar of Zeus. The larger altar area may be that referred to by John as the "throne of Satan" (Rev. 2:13). The city was well-known as a center of worship for the gods Asklepios, Zeus, Demeter and Persephone, Serapis, Isis, as well as the cult of the emperor.

The greatest city in Lydia, *Sardis* is remembered as the first municipality to mint coins of silver and gold. Set in the fertile Hermus valley, Sardis served as the capital of the Lydian king Croesus, a name synonymous with wealth. The city fell to the Persian armies of Cyrus in 549 B.C. and to the Romans in 188 B.C. A tremendous earthquake in A.D. 17 struck Sardis, a blow from which it was never fully able to recover.

Following the Hermus River inland from Sardis one reached *Philadelphia,* the name commemorating the brotherly love between Attalus Philadelphus and Eumenes. Founded during the second century B.C., the city was set amidst vast vineyards and led in the worship of Dionysius. The terrible earthquake of A.D. 17 was followed by dangerous tremors for the next twenty years, each one debilitating the city further. The apostle John's reference to the giving of a "new name" (Rev. 3:12) may be a wordplay on the proposed dedication of the city as "Neocaesarea" in honor of aid Tiberius sent.

Journeying inland from Miletus, a traveller followed the course of the Meander River until it joined the Lycus. In the center of the valley sat *Laodicea.* Situated along the major east-west trade route, the city prospered greatly. As the chief city of the wealthy province of Phrygia, Laodicea boasted of a large number of banks. In 51 B.C. Cicero recounted how he stopped to cash drafts at one of the city's banks. The great wealth of Laodicea allowed it to finance its own rebuilding after a destructive earthquake in A.D. 60, refusing help from the Senate of Rome. The city was also known

A

for clothes and carpets woven from the rich, glossy black wool raised in the valley. Laodicea served as home to a medical school renowned for production of collyrium, an eye salve. Revelation makes mention of the riches of the city, admonishing believers to seek instead spiritual gold of eternal worth, and to anoint their eyes with a spiritual salve. John's description of "white garments" to cover their nakedness contrasts the Laodicean preference for "home-grown" black wool, a symbol of worldly prosperity (Rev. 3:14–18).

Eleven miles south of Laodicea lay *Colossae.* The city was well-known as early as the fifth century B.C. as a commercial center, famous for red-dyed wool. The establishment of Laodicea, however, led to the decline of Colossae's prosperity. Several remains are still visible, including a small theater on the city's southeast side. The apostle Paul never personally evangelized the city. Instead, the church was established by Epaphras during Paul's third missionary journey (Col. 1:7,12,13). Paul wrote to the church during his Roman imprisonment, complementing the work of Philemon and his servant Onesimus (Col. 4:9).

Cities of Eastern Asia Minor Much of Paul's Asian ministry centered around the provinces of Galatia and Lycaonia. On his first journey, Paul and Barnabas most likely arrived by sea at *Attalia,* a relatively small and unimportant harbor. Moving northward from the port and crossing Pamphylia, the group arrived at Antioch in the province of Galatia. Luke's *"Antioch of Pisidia"* carried the title of *Colonia Caesarea Antiocheia,* a colony established in 25 B.C. upon a much earlier Hellenistic city. Antioch had been renovated by Rome to provide for the defense of Galatia. A temple to Augustus dominated the central plaza, and the official inscription telling of his victories and achievements was displayed in the city. Wagons bearing Anatolian marble passed through Antioch on their way to ships at Ephesus to be used in the decoration of the Empire.

Moving southeast from Antioch, Paul and his companions traveled to *Iconium.* Located in a fertile, well-watered plain, Iconium supplied large amounts of fruit and grain for the surrounding provinces. Several years after Paul's visit, the Emperor Claudius allowed the town to be renamed Claudiconium in his honor, a reminder of the strong ties it shared with Rome.

Lystra lay twenty miles to the south of Iconium along the *Via Sebaste.* About 6 B.C. Augustus conferred the title of *Julia Felix Gemina Lustra* upon this Roman colony. Connected by a fine road with Antioch to the west, the city honored Zeus and Hermes as patron gods. A statue dedicated to the two was discovered in the 1800's, reminiscent of the city's identification of Paul and Barnabas with the gods (Acts 14). Timothy was a native of Lystra (Acts 16:1). The ruins of the city are today near the small Turkish town of Katyn Serai.

Derbe was situated sixty miles from Lystra at the present-day site of Kerti Huyuk. Although a large city of Lycaonia, Derbe was relatively unimportant. Paul's decision to visit the city implies a large Jewish population in the region. It is possible that some believers had already advanced the gospel to Derbe, having been earlier expelled from Iconium.

The boyhood home of the apostle Paul, *Tarsus* of Cilicia lay on the eastern end of the east-west trade route beginning at Ephesus. At Tarsus, merchants had the option of going south into Syria and Palestine, or continuing across the mountains on to Zeugma and the East. The Cydnus River provided Tarsus with an outlet to the Mediterranean Sea, ten miles away. Lumber and linen were the main industries of Tarsus, but the related manufacture of goat's-hair cloth was practiced by many, including Paul. This skill served as his main source of income wherever he traveled. Tarsus also housed a university and school of philosophy, an academic atmosphere which formed the basis of Paul's latter rabbinic career.

David C. Maltsberger

ASIARCHS (Ā′ sī·àrchs) A somewhat general term for public patrons and leaders named by cities in the Roman province of Asia. They used their wealth for the public good, especially for supporting worship of the emperor and of Rome. They underwrote expenses of games sponsored in connection with religious festivals. Having served in the position, a person seemed able to continue to use the title. Paul won friends among this elite class (Acts 19:31), and they helped protect him from a religious riot in Ephesus. Note that some versions transliterate Asiarchs from Greek while others translate it to chiefs or officials.

ASIEL (Ăs′ ĭ·ĕl) Personal name meaning, "God has made." A descendant of Simeon and clan leader who settled in Gedar in rich pasture lands (1 Chron. 4:35–40).

ASKELON Alternate KJV spelling of Ashkelon. See *Ashkelon.*

ASNAH (Ăs′ năh) Proper name possibly with Egyptian origins relating to the god Nah. One of the Nethanims or Temple servants who returned to Jerusalem with Zerubbabel from Exile about 537 B.C. (Ezra 2:50).

ASNAPPER (Ăs·năpēr) KJV reading in Ezra 4:10. Modern translations read Osnappar (NAS, RSV) Ashurbanipal (TEV, NIV). See *Osnappar.*

ASP KJV translation for a dangerous, poisonous snake (Deut. 32:33; Job 20:14,16; Isa. 11:8; Rom. 3:13). Other translations use serpent, viper, or cobra at some or all of these places. The Hebrew term *pethen* occurs also in Psalm 58:4, where KJV translates, "adder." Recent work points to the cobra *naja chaje,* but this identification is not certain. Whatever the specific identification, they serve as symbols of dangerous poison (Deut. 32:33). They can be described as deaf (Ps. 58:4) either as a natural characteristic or as an unusual case. The deafness makes them immune to the snake charmer and thus even more dangerous with their poison. Riches that become the center of life turn out to be as poisonous as asps (Job 20:14,16). The prophetic vision is God's restoration of the world order so that small children can play around the holes of poisonous snakes without fear (Isa. 11:8). Until that day sin continues to dominate humanity, turning speech into poisonous lies (Rom. 3:13).

ASPATHA (Ăs·pā′ thà) Persian personal name. Son of Haman killed by Jews (Esther 9:10).

ASRIEL (Ăs′ rĭ·ĕl) Personal name meaning, "God has made happy." A son of Gilead and clan, As-rielites, in the tribe of Manasseh (Num. 26:31). They received a land allotment (Josh. 17:2). In 1 Chronicles 7:14 KJV spells Ashriel.

ASS Beast of burden and wild animal to KJV but translated, "donkey" in most modern translations. Six different Hebrew words and two Greek words lie behind the English translations. *1. 'athon* is a female animal used for riding (Gen. 49:11; Num. 22:21–33; Judg. 5:10; 2 Kings 4:22) and as a beast of burden (Gen. 45:23). Saul's father lost his female asses (1 Sam. 9:3). This indicated loss of pride and prestige, for asses were apparently the riding animals for leaders and for the nobility (compare Judg. 10:4; 12:14; see below on *'ayir*). Warriors rode female asses (Judg. 5:10). Wealthy persons owned numbers of asses (Gen. 12:16; 32:15; 1 Chron. 27:30; Job 1:3). They grazed the grasslands for food (Job 1:14). God used a talking ass to teach a prophet a lesson in obedience (Num. 22). Zechariah pictured the Messiah as riding on "a colt the foal of an ass" (*'athon*), thus emphasizing the animal was a purebred ass and not a crossbred mule (Zech. 9:9).

2. Chamor is the male ass, probably a reddish color according to the basic meaning of the Hebrew term. The original homeland of the ass (*equus asinus*) was probably Africa. It was both a riding animal (Gen. 22:3) and a beast of burden (Gen. 42:26), which could be used for plowing (Deut. 22:10, which forbids yoking an ass with an ox). For his hard work Issachar was pictured as a donkey (Gen. 49:14). An ass was valuable enough that the first born ass had to be ritually redeemed through sacrifice of a lamb (Ex. 13:13; 34:20) or by killing the newborn ass. In extreme famine conditions people would go so far as to pay astronomical prices for the head of an ass which they could eat (2 Kings 6:25). The ass was used to illustrate rampant sexual lust (Ezek. 23:20). A donkey's burial was an unceremonious dumping on the garbage heap for the vultures and scavengers to eat up (Jer. 22:19). The rich possessed herds of donkeys (Gen. 24:35; 30:43) though the Egyptian farmers suffering under the famine also had asses to bring to Joseph in exchange for food (Gen. 47:17; compare Ex. 9:3; 20:17). The Messiah would ride on a donkey (Zech. 9:9), the animal of the nobility in days when Israel did not have a king. The animal constrasted to the horse used in the kings' military exploits after Solomon's time (1 Kings 10:26) in violation of Deuteronomy 17:16. The picture in Zechariah 9 thus joins the humble suffering servant and the royal Messiah.

3. 'Ayir refers to the stallion or young, vigorous male ass. These were apparently riding animals reserved for nobility (Judg. 10:4; 12:14; Zech. 9:9). Isaiah described an unusual caravan on the way to Egypt including young donkeys and camels. The older donkeys would have been the more usual caravan members (Isa. 30:6). Nomads in the desert often led caravans of donkeys and camels loaded with wares to sell. The day of God's salvation would include luxurious food for the donkeys who pulled the plows (Isa. 30:24). The young wild ass can also be called *'yir* (Job 11:12).

4. 'Arad and *'arod* refers to the wild ass (*asinus hemippus*) that God created for freedom in the wilderness rather than to do slave labor for humans (Job 39:5). Such animals explore mountain pastures for food (Job 39:8).

5. Pere' is a wild donkey or onager which some Bible students identify with the zebra, but no evidence exists for zebras in Palestine. The Hebrew in Genesis 16:12 calls Ishmael "a wild ass of a man" (NRSV; see NIV; TEV; NAS), because he would live in opposition to all other people. The wild donkey was known for its braying and for eating grass (Job 6:5). Such a wild animal can never be human (Job 11:12; compare various translations). It lives in the wilderness searching for food and helpless before the cold and rain (Job 24:5–8; compare 39:5). Without pastures, it breathes its last dying gasp (Jer. 14:6). They ventured into cities only when the cities were forsaken ruins (Isa. 32:14). God had created them to be accustomed to life in the Judean wilderness (Jer. 2:24), where they freely pursued natural instincts and lusts. (Compare Hos. 8:9).

6. Onarion refers to a small donkey and appears only in John 12:14 to show the promise of Zechariah 9:9 was being fulfilled.

7. Onos can refer either to a male or female donkey. John 12:15 sees the ass as the parent of the colt on which Jesus rode, while Matthew 21:2 sees both an ass and a colt involved. These animals were kept in stalls and watered as a natural part of peasant life (Luke 13:15). They could easily get loose and fall into a pit (Luke 14:5). Jesus

The donkey, or ass, is still used as a beast of burden and mode of transportation in the Middle East.

showed care for the animals which stricter Jews were prone to let lie in pits in order to obey religious rules.

8. Hupozugion literally means, "one under a yoke." This is Matthew's term for the parent of the "foal of an ass" predicted in Zechariah 9:9 (Matt. 21:5). Peter used the term to refer to the animal which spoke to Balaam (2 Pet. 2:16).

The precise difference in meaning of the various words for "ass" is not always evident to modern Bible students, though the differences were surely clear to the original writers and readers.

ASSASSINS Organized Jewish group who attempted to win freedom from the Romans. The word in Greek is derived from the Latin term *Sicarii,* and literally means "dagger men." Josephus described them as hiding small daggers in their clothing, which they used in crowded situations to kill their victims. "Sicarii" was used by the Romans to refer to those Jews who engaged in the organized killing of political figures. Perhaps this group should be associated with the Zealots of the New Testament (see *Zealots*). The Sicarii were often called robbers, and it is likely that the thieves crucified with Jesus were suspected of

Ruins of the ancient seaport city of Assos on the Gulf of Adramyttium.

belonging to this group. In Acts 21:38, Paul was mistaken as a leader of four thousand Sicarii. KJV calls them murderers; REB and TEV, terrorists.

ASSAYER One who tests ore for its silver and gold content. According to modern versions of Jeremiah 6:27, the calling of Jeremiah was to be an assayer of the people. He did not find them to be a precious metal. The KJV takes the word from the Hebrew root for tower, which is spelled the same as the root word for assayer. Modern versions, however, seem to make the best sense of the Hebrew text (see the entire context; 6:27–30). See *Bellows.*

ASSEMBLY The official gathering of the people of Israel and of the church. See *Congregation.*

ASSHUR (Ăs′ shŭr) **ASSHURIM, ASSHURITES** (NIV) Personal and national name. *1.* Son of Shem and thus a Semite, as were the Hebrew people (Gen. 10:22). *2.* An otherwise unknown Arabian tribe (Gen. 25:3). This tribe may also be meant in Balaam's oracle (Num. 24:22–24), but a reference to Assyria is more likely. *3.* The nation Assyria and its inhabitants are generally meant by the Hebrew term *Asshur.* This is the likely meaning in Genesis 10:11; Ezekiel 27:23; 32:22; Hosea 14:3. See *Assyria.*

ASSIR (Ăs′ sĭr) Personal name meaning, "prisoner." *1.* A son of Korah (Ex. 6:24), the leader of

the rebellion against Moses (Num. 16:1–35). *2.* Great grandson of *1* above (1 Chron. 6:23) or grandson of *1* above with Elkanah and Ebiasaph being brothers. Compare 1 Chronicles 6:37. *3.* A son of King Jeconiah (or Jehoiachin) in KJV of 1 Chronicles 3:17, but this should probably be interpreted as a common noun, "captive," referring to Jehoiachin (NIV, NAS, NRSV).

ASSOS (Ăs' sŏs) Seaport city on the Gulf of Adramyttium, an offshoot of the east coast of the Aegean Sea. Paul visited there briefly and met Luke and others there as he sailed to Jerusalem from his third missionary journey (Acts 20:13–14).

ASSUR (Ăs' sŭr) KJV spelling in Ezra 4:2; Psalm 83:8 for Assyria. See *Assyria.*

ASSURANCE See *Security of the Believer.*

ASSURBANIPAL See *Ashurbanipal.*

ASSYRIA, HISTORY AND RELIGION OF Assyria (Ăs·sўr' ĭ·à) was a nation in northern Mesopotamia in Old Testament times that became a large empire during the period of the Israelite kings. Assyrian expansion into the region of Palestine (about 855–625 B.C.) had enormous impact on the Hebrew kingdoms of Israel and Judah.

Relief of King Sargon of Assyria and his visier.

History Assyria lay north of the region of Babylonia along the banks of the Tigris River (Gen. 2:14) in northern Mesopotamia. The name Assyria (in Hebrew, *Ashshur*) is from Asshur, its first capital, founded about 2000 B.C. The foundation of other Assyrian cities, notably Calah and Nineveh, appears in Genesis 10:11–12.

The history of Assyria is well documented in royal Assyrian annals, building inscriptions, king lists, correspondence, and other archaeological evidence. By 1900 B.C. these cities were vigorously trading as far away as Cappadocia in eastern Asia Minor. An expanded Assyria warred with the famous King Hammurabi of Babylon shortly before breaking up into smaller city states about 1700 B.C.

Beginning about 1300 B.C., a reunited Assyria made rapid territorial advances and soon became an international power. Expanding westward, Tiglath-pileser I (1115–1077 B.C.) became the first Assyrian monarch to march his army to the shores of the Mediterranean. With his murder, however, Assyria entered a 166-year period of decline.

Assyria awoke from its dark ages under Adad-nirari II (911–891 B.C.), who reestablished the nation as a power to be reckoned with in Mesopotamia. His grandson, Ashurnasirpal II (883–859 B.C.) moved Assyria toward the status of an empire. Ashurnasirpal II used a well-deserved reputation for cruelty to extort tribute and taxes from states within the reach of his army in predatory campaigns. He also rebuilt the city of Calah as the new military and administrative capital. Carved stone panels in Ashurnasirpal's palace there show violent scenes of the king's vicious campaigns against unsubmissive enemies.

Ashurnasirpal's son Shalmaneser III (858–824 B.C.) continued a policy of Assyrian expansion through his annual campaigns in all directions. These were no longer mere predatory raids. Rather they demonstrated a systematic economic exploitation of subject states. As always, failure to submit to Assyria brought vicious military action. The results, however, were not always a complete victory for Assyria. In such a context Assyria first encountered the Hebrew kingdoms of the Bible. In 853 B.C., at Qarqar in north Syria, Shalmaneser fought a coalition of twelve kings including Hadad-ezer (Ben-Hadad, 1 Kings 20:26,34) of Aram-Damascus and Ahab of Israel. This confrontation is not mentioned in the Bible, but it may have taken place during a three-year period of peace between Israel and Aram-Damascus (1 Kings 22:1). In his official inscriptions Shalmaneser claims victory, but the battle was inconclusive. In 841 B.C., he finally defeated Hazael of Damascus and on Mt. Carmel received tribute from Tyre, Sidon, and King Jehu of Israel. A scene carved in relief on the Black Obelisk of Shalmaneser, unearthed at Calah, shows Jehu groveling before Shalmaneser, the only known depiction of an Israelite king.

With the death of Shalmaneser, Assyria entered another period of decline during which she was occupied with the nearby kingdom of Urartu. For the next century only one Assyrian king seriously affected affairs in Palestine. Adad-nirari III (810–783 B.C.) entered Damascus, taking extensive tribute from Ben-hadad III. He is probably the "savior" of 2 Kings 13:5, who allowed Israel to escape domination by Aram-Damascus. Nevertheless, Adad-nirari also collected tribute from Jehoash of Israel.

Assyrian preoccupation with Urartu ended with the reign of Tiglath-pileser III (744–727 B.C.). The true founder of the Assyrian Empire, he made changes in the administration of conquered territories. Nations close to the Assyrian homeland were incorporated as provinces. Others were left with native rule, but subject to an Assyrian overseer. Tiglath-pileser also instituted a policy of mass deportations to reduce local nationalistic feelings. He took conquered people into exile to live in lands vacated by other conquered exiles. Compare 2 Kings 17:24.

As Tiglath-pileser, also called Pul, arrived on the coast of Phoenicia, Menahem of Israel (2 Kings 15:19) and Rezin of Aram-Damascus brought tribute and became vassals of Assyria. An anti-Assyrian alliance quickly formed. Israel and Aram-Damascus attacked Jerusalem about 735 B.C. in an attempt to replace King Ahaz of Judah with a man loyal to the anti-Assyrian alliance (2 Kings 16:2–6; Isa. 7:1–6) and thus force Judah's participation. Against the protests of Isaiah (Isa. 7:4,16–17; 8:4–8), Ahaz appealed to Tiglath-pileser for assistance (2 Kings 16:7–9). Tiglath-pileser, in response, campaigned against Philistia (734 B.C.), reduced Israel to the area immediately around Samaria (2 Kings 15:29; 733 B.C.), and annexed Aram-Damascus (732 B.C.), deporting the population. Ahaz, for his part, became an Assyrian vassal (2 Kings 16:10; 2 Chron. 28:16,20–22).

Little is known of the reign of Tiglath-pileser's successor, Shalmaneser V (726–722 B.C.), except that he besieged Samaria for three years in response to Hoshea's failure to pay tribute (2 Kings 17:3–5). The city finally fell to Shalmaneser (2 Kings 17:6; 18:9–12), who apparently died in the same year. His successor, Sargon II (722–705 B.C.), took credit in Assyrian royal inscriptions for deporting 27,290 inhabitants of Samaria.

Sargon campaigned in the region to counter rebellions in Gaza in 720 B.C. and Ashdod in 712 (Isa. 20:1). Hezekiah of Judah was tempted to join in the Ashdod rebellion, but Isaiah warned against such action (Isa. 18). Meanwhile, unrest smoldered in other parts of the empire. A rebellious king of Babylon, Merodach-baladan, found support from Elam, Assyria's enemy to the east. Though forced to flee Babylon in 710 B.C.,

These human-faced monumental bulls from Assyria date from the time of Ashurnasirpal II (ninth century B.C.)

Merodach-baladan returned some years later to reclaim the throne. He sent emissaries to Hezekiah in Jerusalem (2 Kings 20:12–19; Isa. 39), apparently as part of preparations for a concerted anti-Assyrian revolt.

News of Sargon's death in battle served as a signal to anti-Assyrian forces. Sennacherib (704–681 B.C.) ascended the throne in the midst of widespread revolt. Merodach-baladan of Babylon, supported by the Elamites, had inspired the rebellion of all southern Mesopotamia. A number of states in Phoenicia and Palestine were also in rebellion, led by Hezekiah of Judah. After subduing Babylon, Sennacherib turned his attentions westward. In 701 B.C., he reasserted control over the city-states of Phoenicia, sacked Joppa and Ashkelon, and invaded Judah where Hezekiah had made considerable military preparations (2 Kings 20:20; 2 Chron. 32:1–8,30; Isa. 22:8*b*–11). Sennacherib's own account of the invasion provides a remarkable supplement to the biblical version (2 Kings 18:13—19:36). He claims to have destroyed 46 walled cities (see 2 Kings 18:13) and to have taken 200,150 captives. Sennacherib's conquest of Lachish is shown in graphic detail in carved panels from his palace at Nineveh. During the siege of Lachish, an Assyrian army was sent

A colossal stylized bull with human face from the time of Sargon II of Assyria.

against Jerusalem where Hezekiah was "made a prisoner . . . like a bird in a cage." Three of Sennacherib's dignitaries attempted to negotiate the surrender of Jerusalem (2 Kings 18:17–37), but Hezekiah continued to hold out with the encouragement of Isaiah (2 Kings 19:1–7,20–35). In the end, the Assyrian army withdrew, and Hezekiah paid an enormous tribute (2 Kings 18:14–16). The Assyrian account claims a victory over the Egyptian army and mentions Hezekiah's tribute but is rather vague about the end of the campaign. The Bible mentions the approach of the Egyptian army (2 Kings 19:9) and tells of a miraculous defeat of the Assyrians by the angel of the Lord (2 Kings 19:35–36). The fifth century B.C. Greek historian Herodotus relates that the Assyrians suffered defeat because a plague of field mice destroyed their equipment. It is not certain whether these accounts can be combined to infer an outbreak of the plague. Certainly, Sennacherib suffered a major setback, for Hezekiah was the only ruler of the revolt to keep his throne.

On a more peaceful front, Sennacherib conducted some major building projects in Assyria. The ancient city of Nineveh was rebuilt as the new royal residence and Assyrian capital. War continued, however, with Elam, which also influenced Babylon to rebel again. An enraged Sennacherib razed the sacred city in 689 B.C. His murder, at the hands of his own sons (2 Kings 19:37) in 681 B.C., was interpreted by Babylonians as divine judgment for destroying their city.

Esarhaddon (681–669 B.C.) emerged as the new king and immediately began the rebuilding of Babylon, an act which won the allegiance of the local populace. He warred with nomadic tribes to the north and quelled a rebellion in Phoenicia, while Manasseh of Judah remained a loyal vassal. His greatest military adventure, however, was an invasion of Egypt conducted in 671 B.C. The Pharaoh Taharqa fled south as Memphis fell to the Assyrians, but returned and fomented rebellion two years later. Esarhaddon died in 669 B.C. on his way back to subjugate Egypt.

After conducting a brief expedition against eastern tribes, Esarhaddon's son, Ashurbanipal (668–627 B.C.), set out to reconquer Egypt. Assisted by 22 subject kings, including Manasseh of Judah, he invaded in 667 B.C. He defeated Pharaoh Taharqa and took the ancient capital of Thebes. Some 1,300 miles from home, Ashurbanipal had no choice but to reinstall the local rulers his father had appointed in Egypt and hope for the best. Plans for revolt began immediately; but Assyrian officers got wind of the plot, captured the rebels, and sent them to Nineveh. Egypt rebelled again in 665 B.C. This time Ashurbanipal destroyed Thebes, also called No-Amon (Nah. 3:8, NAS). Phoenician attempts at revolt were also crushed. Ashurbanipal ruled at Assyria's zenith but also saw the beginning of her swift collapse. Ten years after the destruction of Thebes, Egypt rebelled yet again. Assyria could do nothing because of a war with Elam. In 651 B.C., Ashurbanipal's brother, the king of Babylon, organized a widespread revolt. After three years of continual battles Babylon was subdued, but remained filled with seeds of hatred for Assyria. Action against Arab tribes followed, and the war with Elam continued until a final Assyrian victory in 639 B.C. That same year the official annals of Ashurbanipal came to an abrupt end. With Ashurbanipal's death in 627 B.C., unrest escalated. By 626, Babylon had fallen into the hands of the Chaldean Nabopolassar. Outlying states, such as Judah under Josiah, were free to rebel without fear. War continued between Assyria and Babylon until, in 614 B.C., the old Assyrian capital Asshur was sacked by the Medes. Then, in 612 B.C., Calah was destroyed. The combined armies of the Babylonians and the Medes laid siege to Nineveh. After two months, the city fell.

An Assyrian general claimed the throne and rallied what was left of the Assyrian army in Haran. An alliance with Egypt brought a few troops to Assyria's aid; but in 610 B.C. the Babylonians approached, and Haran was abandoned. Assyria was no more.

Religion Assyrian religion, like that of most Near Eastern nations, was polytheistic. Essentially the same as Babylonian religion, official Assyrian religion recognized thousands of gods; but only about twenty were important in actual practice.

Younger gods were usually associated with a newer city or none at all. Adad, the Canaanite Hadad, was the god of storms and thus both beneficial and destructive. Ninurta, the god of war and hunting, became a fitting patron for the Assyrian capital Calah. Most important, however, is the unique figure of Asshur. As patron god and namesake of the original Assyrian capital Asshur and the state itself, Asshur rose in importance to be lord of the universe and the supreme god. Since the god Asshur stood above all others, the Assyrian king was duty-bound to show his corresponding dominance on earth. Most Assyrian military campaigns were initiated "at the command of Asshur." See *Babylon, History and Religion of.*

Daniel C. Browning, Jr.

ASTAROTH See *Ashtaroth.*

ASTARTE See *Ashtoreth.*

ASTROLOGER Person who "divided the heavens" (literal translation of Hebrew phrase of Isa. 47:13) to determine the future. Particularly the Babylonians developed sophisticated methods of reading the stars to determine proper times for action. The prophet mocked Babylon's tireless and tiring efforts in astrology. Daniel shows repeatedly that Babylon's well-educated, professional magicians could not match Daniel and his friends. Daniel apparently has magicians and masters of incantations and spells rather than astrologers. The "Chaldeans" of Daniel 2:2; 4:7; 5:7,11 may be the nearest reference to astrologers in the book. The Bible does not seek to describe the skills, tactics, or methods of foreign personnel engaged in various practices to determine the opportune time. Rather the Bible mocks such practices and shows that God's word to the prophets and the wise of Israel far surpasses any foreign skills.

ASUPPIM (Ă·sŭp′ pĭm) KJV interpretation in 1 Chronicles 26:15,17. Modern translations read, "storehouse."

ASWAN (Ă′ swän) NIV, TEV reading in Ezekiel 29:10; 30:6 for Syene. See *Syene.*

ASYLUM See *Avenger.*

ASYNCRITUS (Ă·sў̆r′ crĭ·tŭs) Personal name meaning, "incomparable." Roman Christian whom Paul greeted (Rom. 16:14).

ATAD (Ā′ tăd) Personal name meaning, "thorn." Owner of threshing floor east of the Jordan River where Joseph stopped to mourn the death of his father before carrying Jacob's embalmed body across the Jordan to Machpelah for burial. The place was named Abel-mizraim (Gen. 50:10–11). See *Abel-mizraim.*

ATARAH (Ăt′ ȧ·răh) Personal name meaning "crown" or "wreath." Second wife of Jerahmeel and mother of Onam (1 Chron. 2:26).

ATAROTH (Ăt′ ȧ·rŏth) Place name meaning, "crowns." *1.* Town desired and built up by tribe of Gad (Num. 32:3,34). Mesha, king of Moab, about 830 B.C. claims he captured Ataroth but admits it belonged to Gad "from of old" and had been built by an Israelite king. It is located at modern Khirbet Attarus, eight miles northwest of Dibon and eight miles east of the Dead Sea. *2.* Village on border of Benjamin and Ephraim (Josh. 16:2,7) It may be modern Khirbet el-Oga in the Jordan Valley.

ATAROTH-ADDAR (Ăt′ ȧ·rŏth-Ăd′ där) Place name meaning, "crowns of glory." A border town in Ephraim (Josh. 16:5), bordering Benjamin (Josh. 18:13), probably modern Khirbet Attara at the foot of tell en-Nasbeh or possibly identical with tell en-Nasbeh and thus with biblical Mispah.

ATER (Ā′ tēr) Personal name meaning either, "crippled" or "left-handed." Clan of which 98 returned from Babylonian Exile with Zerubbabel about 537 B.C. (Ezra 2:16). They were Temple gatekeepers (Ezra 2:42). The head of the clan signed Nehemiah's covenant to keep God's Law (Neh. 10:17).

ATHACH (Ā′ thăch) Place name meaning, "attack." Town in southern Judah to which David sent spoils of victory while he fled Saul among the Philistines (1 Sam. 30:30). May be the same as Ether (Josh. 15:42), a small copying change causing the difference. See *Ether.*

ATHAIAH (Ȧ′ ·thaî′ ah) Leader of tribe of Judah who lived in Jerusalem in time of Nehemiah (Neh. 11:4).

ATHALIAH (Ăth·ȧ·lī′ ăh) Personal name meaning, "Yahweh has announced His exalted nature," or "Yahweh is righteous." *1.* Wife of Jehoram, king of Judah, and mother of Ahaziah, king of Judah. She was either the daughter of Ahab and Jezebel of Israel (2 Kings 8:18) or of Omri, king of Israel (2 Kings 8:26); according to a literal reading of text as in KJV; an interpretation of text extends Hebrew word for daughter to mean female descendant and thus "granddaughter as in NAS; NIV; RSV). Some have suggested Omri was her father, but her brother Ahab raised her at court and thus functioned as her father. She brought the northern court's devotion to Baal to the court of Judah. She exercised great political influence during her son's reign of one year (1 Kings 8:27–28). At her son's death from battle wounds, she tried to gain power for herself by having all male heirs killed. She managed to rule Judah for six years (2 Kings 11:1–4), being the only woman to do so. Finally, Jehoiada, the priest, led a revolt, crowning the child Josiah as king and bringing about Athaliah's death (2 Kings 11:5–20).
  2. Son of Jeroham in tribe of Benjamin (1 Chron. 8:26). *3.* Father of Jeshaiah, who led 70 men back to Jerusalem from Exile with Ezra (Ezra 8:7).

ATHARIM (Ăth′ ȧ·rĭm) Hebrew word of uncertain meaning. It names a roadway the king of Arad took to attack Israel under Moses. After an initial setback, Israel prayed and found victory under God (Num. 1:1–3). KJV translates "spies" following the Septuagint, the earliest Greek translation. Modern translations simply transliterate the Hebrew. The site may be Tamar a few miles south of the Dead Sea.

First-century Athens, Greece, as it appeared during the time of Paul. The view is from the northwest of the Agora (market, business, and civic center) of the lower city, which is in the foreground. The Acropolis (upper city) with the famous Parthenon, dedicated to the goddess Athena is in the background. The Aeropagus (Mars Hill) where Paul addressed the citizens of Athens is at right.

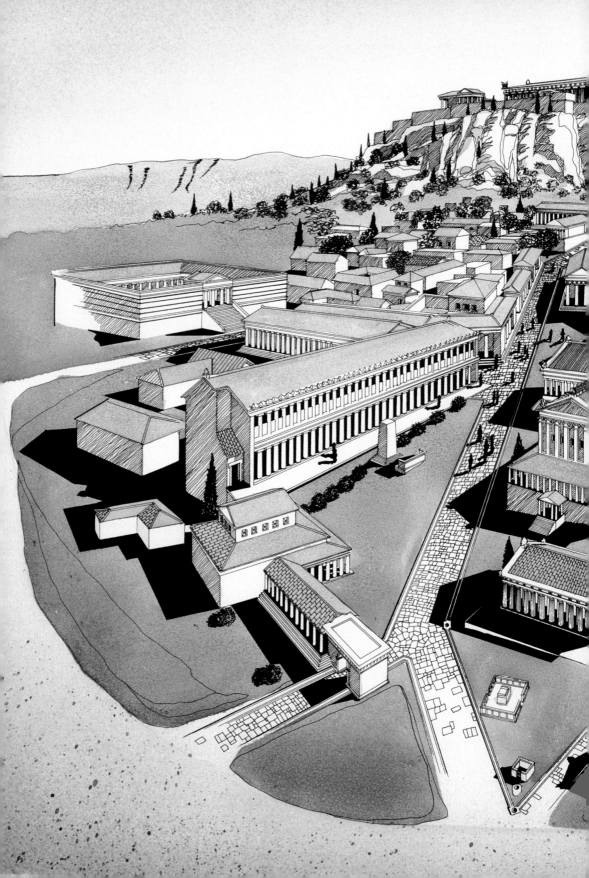

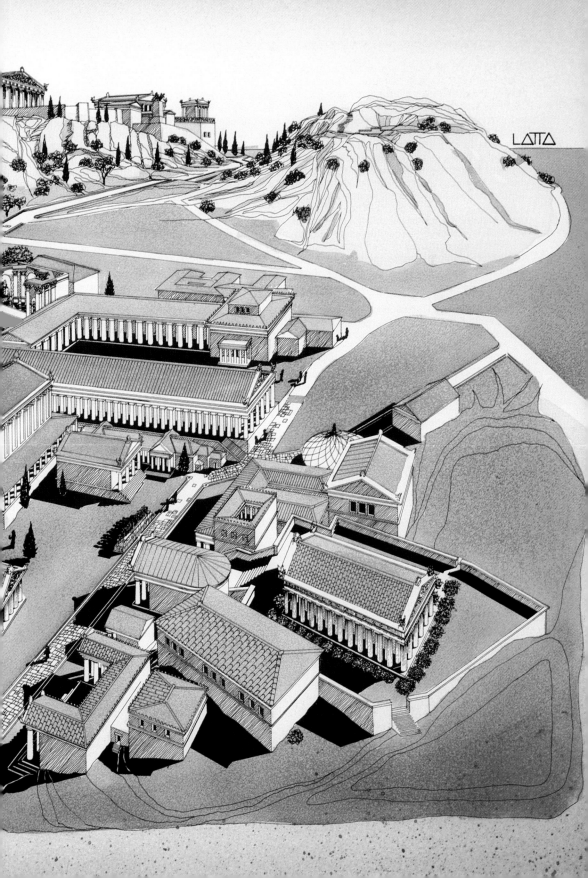

LATTA

ATHENS (Ăth′ ĕns) Capital of Attica, an ancient district of east central Greece, where Paul preached to the Greek philosophers (Acts 17:15–34). Paul saw the Athenians were very religious and even had an altar to an unknown God. He based his sermon on this. Though some converts were won to faith in Christ, no biblical record exists of a viable church being established. The city, which probably was named for the wisdom goddess Athene, was already an ancient place by the time Paul visited it. Indeed, human occupation of the area seems to date before 3000 B.C. In the sixth century B.C. Athens became the scene of the world's first great experiment with democratic government. It was destroyed by the Persians early in the fifth century B.C., but during the administration of Pericles the city was rebuilt into an architectural wonder.

ATHLAI (Ăth′ laî) Personal name meaning, "Yahweh is exalted." A man who agreed under Ezra's leadership to divorce his foreign wife and return to faithfulness to Yahweh.

ATONEMENT (Ȧ·tōne′ mĕnt), meaning reconciliation, was associated with sacrifical offerings to remove the effects of sin and in the New Testament, refers specifically to the reconciliation between God and humanity effected by the death, burial, and resurrection of Christ.

Old Testament Primarily in the Old Testament,

The Parthenon, dedicated to Athena (goddess of wisdom), on the Acropolis at Athens.

The Doric columns of the Parthenon at Athens.

atonement refers to the process God established whereby humans could make an offering to God to restore fellowship with God. Such offerings, including both live and dead animals, incense, and money, were required to remove the bad effects of human sin.

The only fast day stipulated in the Mosaic law was the annual day of Atonement (Yom Kippur), observed on the tenth day of Tishri (September–October) at the conclusion of ten days of penitence. The day of Atonement was the only day of the year that the priest entered the holy of holies to make sin offerings for himself, his family, and the "assembly of Israel." After making these offerings, the nation's sins were symbolically laid on the scapegoat "Azazel" that was released into the wilderness to die.

While atonement in the Old Testament most frequently refers to humans offering sacrifices to God for their wrongdoing, several references are made to God making atonement. In Psalm 78:38, the Hebrew for "atoned for" is used where the KJV translates "forgave" as is also true in Deuteronomy 21:8. Because God "atones for" or "covers" human sin, atonement is best understood as expiation, that is removing the barrier that sin creates rather than propitiation or appeasing an angry God, though both views of atonement continue to be taught by Bible students.

New Testament The New Testament rarely uses a word for atonement. The basic Greek word is

katallassō, usually translated "to reconcile," and the corresponding noun, *katallagē,* meaning "reconciliation." The basic meaning is to establish friendship. This is used in human relationships in 1 Corinthians 7:11, referring to the restoration of relationship between an estranged husband and wife. Paul used the term in reference to Christ's work of salvation in Romans 5:10–11; 11:15; 2 Corinthians 5:18–20. The Greek term *hilaskomai,* "to forgive" or "show mercy" along with the nouns *hilasmos,* "means of forgiveness," and *hilastērion,* "means or place of forgiveness" are the important words in the discussion of expiation and propitiation. They occur in Luke 18:13; Romans 3:25; Hebrews 2:17; 9:5; 1 John 2:2; 4:10.

Atonement and the Cross The focal point of God's atoning work is Christ's death on the cross. Paul wrote that "when we were enemies, we were reconciled to God by the death of his Son" (Rom. 5:10). These words not only define the meaning of atonement, they reveal the heart of the gospel as well.

The primacy of the cross is emphasized throughout the New Testament. At the beginning of His ministry, Jesus was identified as "the Lamb of God which taketh away the sin of the world" (John 1:29). The purpose of His coming was "to give his life a ransom for many" (Mark 10:45). He explained His death in terms of the "blood of the new testament, which is shed for many" (Mark 14:24).

The relation of the cross to forgiveness of sins was implicit in the earliest Christian preaching (Acts 2:21; 3:6,19; 4:13; 5:31; 8:35; 10:43). Paul proclaimed that "Christ died for our sins"(1 Cor. 15:3), that He was a "propitiation" (Rom. 3:25 KJV; "sacrifice of atonement," NRSV, NIV; "expiation," RSV), that He became "a curse for us" (Gal. 3:13), and that those "who sometimes were far off are made nigh by the blood of Christ" (Eph. 2:13). Furthermore, "Christ was once offered to bear the sins of many" (Heb. 9:28) and has become "a new and living way" (Heb. 10:20) into God's presence. He is the one who "bare our sins in his own body on the tree" (1 Pet. 2:24).

Though atonement is focused in the cross, the New Testament makes clear that Christ's death is the climax of His perfect obedience. He "became obedient unto death, even the death of the cross" (Phil. 2:8). "Though he were a Son, yet learned he obedience by the things which He suffered" (Heb. 5:8). Romans 5:12–19 contrasts Christ's obedience with Adam's disobedience. His sinless obedience qualified Him to be the perfect Sacrifice for sin (Heb. 6:8–10).

Furthermore, the New Testament interprets the cross in light of the resurrection. "At-one-ment" is the achievement of Christ crucified *and risen.* So important is this emphasis that Paul affirms, "And if Christ be not raised, your faith is vain; ye are yet in your sins" (1 Cor. 15:17).

The Necessity of Atonement The necessity for Christ's atoning work is occasioned by the breach in the relationship between the Creator and the creature. This breach is the result of humanity's sinful rebellion. "But your iniquities have separated between you and your God, and your sins have hid *his* face from you, that he will not hear" (Isa. 59:2). Thus, in their unreconciled state people are God's "enemies" (Rom. 5:10), have "enmity against God" (Rom. 8:7), and have "no hope" (Eph. 2:12). There is no difference between Jew and Gentile in this respect, "for all have sinned and come short of the glory of God" (Rom. 3:23).

The Origin of Atonement The atonement for sin provided by Christ's death had its origin in divine love. No other reason can explain why "God reconciled us to himself by Jesus Christ" (2 Cor. 5:18). The anthem that continuously peals from the the Bible is that "God so loved the world, that he gave his only begotten Son" (John 3:16; see 1 John 4:9–10). This does not mean that God loves us because Christ died for us. Rather, Christ died for us because God loves us. Thus, "God commendeth his love toward us, in that, while we were yet sinners, Christ died for us" (Rom. 5:8). Because atonement issues from love, it is always seen as a divine gift, never as human achievement.

Yet, divine love is not sentimental or merely emotional. It is a righteous love which blazes out against all that opposes God's will. The New Testament affirms that "God is love" (1 John 4:8); it also affirms that "our God *is* a consuming fire" (Heb. 12:29). Thus, the cross is simultaneously a manifestation of God's will to save and of His wrath against sin.

Atonement: Representation and Substitution In His atoning work Christ is both representative and substitute. As representative, Christ acted on behalf of His race. An example of representation is Paul's contrast between Adam and Christ (Rom. 5:12–21; 1 Cor. 15:45–49). Adam and Christ represent two heads of two races of people. Adam is the head of the race of fallen persons. Sin and death came into the world through him. Because of our fallenness, all people belong to Adam's race, the old humanity.

Christ, the last Adam, represents a new race of people. These are the people who have been saved from sin. Where Adam failed, Christ succeeded. Those who belong to Christ through faith belong to the new humanity He created (2 Cor. 5:17; Eph. 2:14–22).

As substitute, Christ acted *in our place.* Whereas representation emphasizes Christ's relation to the race, substitution stresses His relation to the individual. He experienced as substitute the suffering and death each person deserved. Substitution is implied in such references as 2 Corinthians 5:21; Galations 3:13; 1 Peter 2:24.

In thinking of Christ as substitute, however, His oneness with the Father must be emphasized. Christ is not a third party who comes between God and humanity to absorb all the punishment God can inflict. Substitution means that in Christ, God Himself bears the consequences of human sin. God reconciles people at great cost to Himself, not at cost to a third party.

Images of Atonement To describe the meaning of atonement New Testament writers used images drawn from different areas of experience. Each image says something important about the cross. No one image, however, is adequate by itself. Each image needs the others to produce the whole picture.

1. Atonement and ransom. Ransom is an image drawn from ancient economic life. The picture is a slave market or prison. People are in bondage and cannot free themselves. Someone comes and pays the price (provides the ransom) to redeem those in captivity.

The New Testament emphasizes both the fact of deliverance and the ransom price. Jesus said that He came "to give his life a ransom for many" (Mark 10:45). Paul wrote, "ye are not your own; For ye are bought with a price" (1 Cor. 6:19–20; compare 7:23). Peter declared that "ye were not redeemed with corruptible things, as silver and gold, . . . But with the precious blood of Christ" (1 Peter 1:18–19*a*). The main idea in this imagery is rescue from bondage through the costly self-giving of Jesus.

2. Atonement and victory. In this imagery, Satan, the head of evil forces and archenemy of God, has humanity in his power. Christ is the Warrior of God who enters the battle, defeats the devil, and rescues humanity.

This conflict motif pervades the gospels (Matt. 4:1–11; 12:28; Mark 3:27; John 12:31). The warfare between Jesus and Satan was real. Yet, divine victory was so certain that Jesus could say in anticipation, "I beheld Satan as lightning fall from heaven" (Luke 10:18).

Victory imagery is also prominent in the epistles. "For this purpose the Son of God was manifested, that he might destroy the works of the devil" (1 John 3:8). Christ came so "that through death he might destroy him that had the power of death, that is, the devil; And deliver them who through fear of death were all their lifetime subject to bondage" (Heb. 2:14–15). That Christ triumphed is clear: "And having spoiled principalities and powers, he made a shew of them openly, triumphing over them in it" (Col. 2:15).

3. Atonement and sacrifice. Not surprisingly, the atoning power of Christ's death is often expressed in terms drawn from Old Testament sacrificial practices. Thus, Christ's death is called a "sacrifice for sins" (Heb. 10:12) and a "sacrifice to God" (Eph. 5:2). Christ is variously identified

with the Passover lamb (1 Cor. 5:7), the sacrifice which initiates the new covenant (Luke 22:20), and the sin offering (Heb. 9:14,25–28).

Sacrificial imagery is another way of expressing the costliness of Christ's atoning work. It is a continual reminder that divine love has assumed the shape of the cross (Gal. 2:20). Furthermore, sacrifice witnesses to the effectiveness of Christ's death. Through it, sin is forgiven (Eph. 1:7), and the conscience is cleansed (Heb. 9:14).

4. Atonement and glory. In much of the New Testament the glorification of Jesus is associated with His resurrection and ascension. John's Gospel shifts perspective. The whole life and work of Jesus is a revelation of divine glory. This glorification climaxes in Jesus' death on the cross (John 12:23–24; 13:31–32).

Consistent with this theme is the emphasis on the cross as "lifting up." This verb has the double meaning of "to lift up on a cross" and "to exalt." The meanings are combined in John's Gospel. " 'And I, if I be lifted up from the earth, will draw all *men* unto me.' This he said, signifiying what death he should die." (John 12:32–33; compare 3:14; 8:28). The meaning is not that Jesus was glorified as a reward for His death. Rather it means that divine glory was revealed in the death He died for sins. See *Propitiation; Expiation; Redeem.*   *Bert Dominy*

ATROTH (KJV) or **ATROTH-BETH-JOAB** (Ăt' rŏth-bĕth-Jō' ab) Place name meaning "crowns of the house of Joab." A "descendant" of Caleb and Hur (1 Chron. 2:54), the name apparently refers to a village near Bethlehem.

ATROTH-SHOPHAN (Ăt' rŏth-shō' phăn) Town built by tribe of Gad of unknown location (Num. 32:35). Earliest translations spelled name various ways: Shophar, Shaphim, Shopham, Etroth Shophan.

ATTAI (Ăt' tā-ī) Personal name meaning, "timely." *1.* Member of clan of Jerahmeel in tribe of Judah (1 Chron. 2:35–36). *2.* Warrior of tribe of Gad who served David in the wilderness as he fled from Saul (1 Chron. 12:11). *3.* Son of Maachah (1 Chron. 11:20), the favorite and beloved wife of King Rehoboam of Judah (931–913 B.C.).

ATTALIA (Ăt-tȧ-lī' ȧ) Seaport city on northern Mediterranean cost in Asia Minor where Paul stopped briefly on first missionary journey (Acts 14:25). Modern Antalya continues as a small seaport with some ancient ruins.

AUGUSTAN COHORT A unit of the Roman army stationed in Syria from about A.D. 6. The cohort's place among the rest of the Roman army is indicated by the fact that it was named after the emperor. This special unit was given charge of

Paul on his way to Rome (Acts 27:1). In Luke's eyes, this demonstrated the importance of Paul, and more importantly, the gospel that Paul preached.

AUGUSTUS (Aū·gŭs′ tŭs) A title meaning, "reverend" the Roman Senate gave to Emperor Octavian (31 B.C.–A.D. 14) in 27 B.C. He ruled the Roman Empire, including Palestine, when Jesus was born and ordered the taxation that brought Joseph and Mary to Bethlehem (Luke 2:1). He was the adopted son of Julius Caesar. Born in 63 B.C. he first gained power with Antony and Lepidus at Julius Caesar's death in 44 B.C. He gained sole control at the Battle

Cameo of Augustus Caesar.

of Actium in 31 B.C., where he defeated Antony and Cleopatra, who both committed suicide. This brought Egypt into the system of Roman provinces. He thus founded the Roman Empire and ruled with popular acclaim. At his death the Senate declared him a god. Herod the Great ruled as appointed by Augustus, even though Herod originally supported Antony. Herod built temples to Augustus as a god in Caesaria and Samaria. The title Augustus passed on to Octavian's successors as emperors of Rome. Thus it is applied to Nero in Acts 25:21,25, when Paul appealed to Caesar. Note the various translations: the Emperor (NIV, NAS), his Imperial Majesty (NRSV).

AUTHOR, AUTHOR OF LIFE See *Prince of Life.*

AUTHORITY in biblical usage, describes the absolute power and freedom of God, and claims that He is the source of all other authorization or power.

The word "authority" is used rarely in the Old Testament. In the English New Testament it translates the Greek *exousia,* a word for which there is no exact correspondence in Hebrew or Aramaic. The Greek "exousia" expresses both freedom and legal rights, and is used in the Bible in numerous ways.

Old Testament Two Hebrew words are translated "authority," but occurrences are not common. Examples include Proverbs 29:2, describing the rejoicing of the people when the righteous are "in authority;" Esther 9:29, speaking of "full written authority" (RSV) Esther and Mordecai exercised; Daniel 4:17, declaring that "the most High rules the kingdom of men" (RSV); and Daniel 7:13–14, prophesying that eternal authority will be given to the "Son of Man." God gave authority to humans over nature (Gen. 1:28), to husband over wife (Gen. 3:16), and to parents over their children (Lev. 19:3).

New Testament "Exousia" is found in the New Testament in a variety of usages, although always consistent with the belief that "there is no authority except from God" (Rom. 13:1 RSV; see John 19:11). "Exousia" describes first the freedom of God to act (Luke 15:5; Acts 1:7). Second, it signifies the divinely given power and authority of Jesus Christ as deriving from the Father (Matt. 28:18; John 10:18; 17:2), enabling Him to forgive sin (Mark 2:10), and signifying His power to heal and to expel demons, which He gave His disciples (Mark 3:15). Third, it describes the freedom God gives His people for salvation (John 1:12) and from legalism (1 Cor. 6:12). Fourth, it denotes the authority God imparted to the leaders to build up the church (2 Cor. 10:8; 13:10). Fifth, "exousia" signifies the power God displayed through agents of destruction in the last days (Rev. 6:8; 9:3,10,19; 14:18; 16:9; 18:1). Sixth, the word denotes the dominion God allows Satan to exercise (Acts 26:18; Eph. 2:2). Seventh, it describes the "authorities" created by God, both heavenly (Col. 1:16) and secular (Rom. 13:1; Titus 3:1).

As "exousia" denotes an authority manifested in power, translators sometimes render the word "power" (KJV, Matt. 9:6,8; 10:1; 28:18). "Exousia" sometimes denotes as well the sphere in which authority is exercised (Luke 23:7).

Historical Survey of Religious Authority The scriptural views of authority have undergone major shifts in interpretation in church history. The early leaders of the church were virtually unanimous in viewing the Bible as the primary source of revelation and authority. The church soon began ascribing authority to its tradition as well as to the Scriptures. By the fourth century church tradition was viewed as of equal authority with the Bible. The medieval church especially emphasized the church as the sole interpreter of Scripture, through its tradition and creeds, councils, and pope.

The Reformation rejected this duality of authority in Bible and church, claiming "sola scriptura" ("only the Bible"). The Reformers argued that all authority, even that of the church, is derived from the Bible itself, and valuable only as it is consistent with Scripture. The Anabaptists and early Baptists made this view of biblical authority the foundation for their theological beliefs, maintaining that all church doctrine and practice must be entirely consistent with the Bible itself.

The Catholic church responded to the Reformation with an increased emphasis on the authority of the church and its tradition, culminating in its assertion of papal infallibility in all areas of faith and practice in 1870. Vatican II, held in 1962–65, modified this position by balancing papal authority with that of the bishops and interpreting both authorities in a ministerial context.

The nineteenth century movement of "Liberal Protestantism" defined religious authority in yet another way, locating authority in man's reason and experience. The Bible was seen as normative only insofar as it is consistent with reason and personal experience, and people are to interpret it subjectively. The movement called "Pietism" alternately located religious authority in man's evangelical experience.

Conclusions It is the uniform witness of the Bible that all authority is located in God. People possess authority only as the Lord gives it (Rom. 13:1). Religious authority derives from the authority of the Father, as that authority is revealed in the Son, manifested by the Holy Spirit, and given in and through the Bible to the church and the world. While each of the approaches to authority described in the above historical survey is still practiced and taught today, Scripture says all legitimate authority comes directly or indirectly from God.

Such a position will have obvious implications for contemporary Christian faith and practice. The church and its ministry possess genuine religious authority only as they serve the mission of Jesus in faithfulness to the Bible and in building up the church (Matt. 28:18–20). The Christian accepts the truth of Scripture as authoritative by faith, and the command of Scripture as authoritative in obedience, and so demonstrates love for the Lord (John 14:15).   *James C. Denison*

AVA (Ā′ và) or **AVVA** A people the Assyrians conquered and settled in Israel to replace the people they took into Exile (2 Kings 17:24). Their gods did not help them against the Assyrians and could be used as an example to call Jerusalem to surrender (2 Kings 18:34, where Ivvah refers to the same people). Compare 2 Kings 19:13. Avva was apparently in Syria, but their homeland is unknown. Some would suggest tell Kafr Ayah on the Orontes River. The Avites who made the god Nibhaz (2 Kings 17:31) may refer to these people.

AVEN (Ā′ vĕn) Hebrew noun meaning, "wickedness," used in place names to indicate Israel's understanding of the place as site of idol worship. *1.* Referred to On or Heliopolis in Egypt (Ezek. 30:17). *2.* Referred to major worship centers of Israel such as Bethel and Dan (Hos. 10:8). *3.* Referred to a valley, perhaps one in place of popularly-known names such as Beth-aven for Beth-el (Josh. 7:2; 18:12). See *Beth-aven.*

AVENGER is the person with the legal responsibility to protect the rights of an endangered relative. Avenger translates Hebrew *go'el,* which in its verbal form means to redeem. Redemption applies to repossessing things consecrated to God (Lev. 27:13–31) or to God's actions for His people (Ex. 6:6; Job 19:25; Ps. 103:4; Isa. 43:1). Ultimately God is the *go'el* (Isa. 41:14).

The human avenger is tied closely to the institutions of cities of refuge, land ownership, and levirate marriage. Cities of refuge offered people who killed without intention or hatred a place of escape from the avenger of blood (Ex. 21:12–14; Num. 35:6–34; Deut. 4:41–43; 19:1–13; Josh. 20:1–9). The human *go'el* may be a brother, an uncle, a cousin, or another blood relative from the family (Lev. 25:48–49). An established order among these determined the one legally responsible to act as *go'el* (Ruth 3:12–13). The avenger or *go'el* is responsible to take the life of one who killed a family member (Num. 35:12), to receive restitution for crimes against a deceased relative (Num. 5:7–8), buy back property lost to the family (Lev. 25:25), redeem a relative who sold himself into slavery (Lev. 25:48–49), or marry the widow of a relative without sons and perpetuate the family (Deut. 25:5–10). Avenging the death of a relative is placed under strict limits. The murderer must have intentionally waited to kill the relative (Ex. 21:13) or willfully attacked the relative (Ex. 21:14). Vengeance could be exercised only before the murderer reached the city of refuge or after the court either at the victim's hometown or at the murder site judged the case (Num. 35:12). The avenger was free to act if an iron object was used to commit the murder (Num. 35:16), or if a stone or wood object was used (Num. 35:17–18). Pushing a person to death because of hatred made one liable to the avenger (Num. 35:20–21). Unintentional acts could not be punished (Num. 35:22–24).

A killer judged to have committed the crime without hatred or intentional planning was sent to the city of refuge until the death of the high priest. The avenger could not touch the killer in the city of refuge, but if the killer left the city of refuge for any reason, the avenger could reap vengeance even against the unintentional killer (Num. 35:22–28). This shows that even unintentional murder involved sin for which a penalty had to be paid. The law of the avenger thus prevented the shedding of innocent blood while also purging the guilt of murdering the innocent (Deut. 19:11–13). The law maintained the reverence for human life created in the image of God (Gen. 9:5–7).

The New Testament sets up government to avenge evil doing (Rom. 13:4), while noting God's role in avenging wrong against a brother (1 Thess. 4:6).

AVIM (Ā′ vĭm) AVIMS, AVITES, AVVIM, AVVITE 1. A people of whom nothing is known outside biblical sources. They lived on the Philistine coast before the Philistines invaded about 1200 (Deut. 2:23). 2. A city in the tribal territory of Benjamin (Josh. 18:23) about which nothing is known.

AVITH (Ā′ vĭth) City name meaning, "ruin." Capital city of Hadad, king of Edom, before Israel had a king. Its location is unknown.

AWE appears in different passages in different English translations as the translation of different Hebrew and Greek words. Of ten occurrences in the NAS, it translates eight distinct Hebrew and Greek words. It appears only three times in KJV translating three different Hebrew words. NIV uses "awe" sixteen times, repeating only six of the NAS usages. The term refers to an emotion combining honor, fear, and respect before someone of superior office or actions. It most appropriately applies to God.

AWL An instrument or tool made of flint, bone, stone, or metal to bore holes. Biblical references refer to using the awl to pierce a servant's ear (Ex. 21:6; Deut. 15:17). Perhaps a ring or identification tag was placed in the hole. This marked the slave as a permanent slave for life. Excavators in Palestine unearth many such boring tools.

AWNING The usage in Ezekiel 27:7 suggests a deck covering to protect the ship's passengers from the sun. It may be similar to the covering of Noah's ark (Gen. 8:13) and the tabernacle (Ex. 26:14).

AX, AX HEAD The English translation of several Hebrew terms indicating cutting instruments used in normal small industry and in war. 1. *Barzel* is the Hebrew term for iron and is used for the iron portion of an ax (Isa. 10:34; 2 Kings 6:5). The ax was used to fell trees. Elisha was able through miraculous power to make the ax head float. 2. *Garzen* is a hatchet or a tool for cutting stone (Deut. 19:5; 20:19; 1 Kings 6:7; Isa. 10:15). It was made of iron and could be used to cut trees. The iron head was attached to a wooden handle. It was not to be used to destroy a city's trees in war. 3. *Chereb* is a

weapon or tool used to destroy enemies' towers in battle (Ezek. 26:9). The term also is used for flint knives Joshua used in circumcision (John 5:2), for two-sided daggers (Judg. 3:16), a tool to shape stone (Ex. 20:25), and of battle swords (Judg. 7:20). 4. *Magzerah* was a tool used in brick work. David apparently forced the Ammonites to tear down their own city walls and then to produce bricks for Israel (2 Sam. 12:31). 5. *Ma atsad* is the craftsman's tool (Jer. 10:3; NIV, "chisel") produced by the blacksmith working with iron (Isa. 44:12 NAS; NRSV). It was apparently used to trim or prune trees or lumber. 6. *Qardom* was an iron tool which has to be sharpened (1 Sam. 13:20) and was used for cutting trees (Judg. 9:48). Skillful use of this tool made a person famous (Ps. 74:5). 7. *Keylaph* appears only in Psalm 74:6 and is variously translated: hammer (KJV, NAS, NRSV), hatchet (NIV), sledge hammer (TEV), or crowbar (some lexicons). 8. *Kashshil* appears only in Psalm 74:6 in combination with 7. above. It is variously translated as ax (KJV, NIV, TEV) or hatchet (NAS, NRSV). Whatever the precise nature of these tools, they could be used for destruction as well as construction. 9. *Axine* was used to chop down trees (Matt. 3:10).

AYYAH (Ăy′ yah) Place name meaning, "ruin." In the unclear Hebrew text of 1 Chronicles 7:20, modern translations read Ayyah as a city on the border of Ephraim. Some identify this with Ai. See *Ai*. Others follow a Greek text tradition which apparently read Gaza.

AZAL (Ā′ zăl) KJV spelling of Azel. See *Azel*.

AZALIAH (Ăz·à·lī′ ăh) Personal name meaning, "Yahweh has reserved." Father of Shaphan, Josiah's scribe (2 Kings 22:3). See *Shaphan*.

AZANIAH (Ăz·à·nī′ ăh) Personal name meaning, "Yahweh listened." Father of Levite who signed Nehemiah's covenant to obey God's law (Neh. 10:9).

AZARAEL (Ăz·à·rā′ ĕl) KJV spelling of Azarel (Neh. 13:36). See *Azarel*.

AZAREEL (Ăz′ à·reêl) KJV spelling for Azarel. See *Azarel*.

AZAREL (Ăz′ à·rĕl) Personal name meaning, "God helped." 1. David's soldier at Ziklag, skilled with bow and arrow and able to sling stones with either hand (1 Chron. 12:6). 2. Leader of a course of priests selected by lot under David (1 Chron. 25:18). 3. Leader of tribe of Dan under David (1 Chron. 27:22). 4. Priest who had married a foreign wife under Ezra (Ezra 10:41). 5. Father of Amashai, head of a priestly family who lived in Jerusalem under Nehemiah (Neh. 11:13). 6. Priest who played a musical instrument in time of Nehemiah (Neh. 12:36), probably the same as *5.* above.

AZARIAH (Ăz·a·rī′ ăh) Personal name meaning, "Yahweh has helped." *1.* Son and successor of Amaziah as king of Judah (792–740 B.C.). Also called Uzziah. See *Uzziah. 2.* High priest under Solomon (1 Kings 4:2) listed as son of Zadok (1 Kings 4:2) or of Ahimaaz (1 Chron. 6:9), the son of Zadok (2 Sam. 15:27). If the latter is accurate, then son in 1 Kings 4:2 means descendant. *3.* Son of Nathan in charge of the system of obtaining provisions for the court from the twelve government provinces (1 Kings 4:5). He would have supervised the persons listed in 1 Kings 4:7–19. *4.* Great grandson of Judah (1 Chron. 2:8). *5.* A member of the clan of Jerahmeel in the tribe of Judah (1 Chron. 2:38–39). *6.* High priest, son of Johanan (1 Chron. 6:10). *7.* High priest, son of Hilkiah (1 Chron. 6:13–14) and father of Seraiah, who is listed as Ezra's father (Ezra 7:1). The list in Ezra is not complete. Apparently some generations have been omitted. *8.* Member of family of Kohath, the Temple singers (1 Chron. 6:36). Apparently called Uzziah in 6:24. *9.* A priest, son of Hilkiah (1 Chron. 9:11) may be same as *7.* above. *10.* Prophet, son of Oded, whose message gave King Asa (910–869 B.C.) courage to restore proper worship in Judah (2 Chron. 15:1–8). *11.* Two sons of Jehoshaphat, king of Judah (873–848 B.C.) according to 2 Chron. 21:2. Perhaps the boys had different mothers, each of whom gave the son the common name Azariah. *12.* Son of Jehoram, king of Judah (852–841) according to 2 Chronicles 22:6, but the correct name is probably Ahaziah as in 2 Kings 8:29. Azariah represents a copyist's error in Chronicles. *13.* Two military commanders of 100 men who helped Jehoiada, the high priest, depose and murder Athaliah as queen of Judah and install Joash as king (835–796). *14.* High priest who led 80 priests to oppose King Uzziah of Judah (792–740) when he tried to burn incense in the Temple rather than let the priests. God struck Uzziah with a dreaded skin disease (2 Chron. 26:16–21). *15.* A leader of the tribe of Ephraim under Pekah, king of Israel (752–732 B.C.), who rescued captives Pekah had taken from Judah, cared for their physical needs, and returned them to Jericho (2 Chron. 28:5–15). *16.* A Levite whose son Joel helped cleanse the Temple under Hezekiah, king of Judah (715–686) (2 Chron. 29:12–19). *17.* A Levite who helped cleanse the Temple (2 Chron. 29:12–19). See *16.* above. *18.* Chief priest under King Hezekiah who rejoiced with the king over the generous tithes and offerings of the people (2 Chron. 31:10–13). *19.* Son of Meraioth in the list of high priests and father of Amariah (Ezra 7:3) Since list in Ezra is incomplete, this Azariah may be same as *6.* above. *20.* Helper of Nehemiah in rebuilding wall of Jerusalem (Neh. 3:23). *21.* Man who returned from Exile with

Zerubbabel (Neh. 7:7) about 537 B.C. He is called Seraiah in Ezra 2:2. *22.* Man who helped Ezra interpret the law to the people in Jerusalem (Neh. 8:7). *23.* Man who put his seal on Nehemiah's covenant to obey God's law (Neh. 10:2). *24.* A leader of Judah, possibly a priest, who marched with Nehemiah and others on the walls of Jerusalem to celebrate the completion of rebuilding the city defense walls (Neh. 12:33). He may be identical with any one or all of *20.–23.* above. *25.* Friend of Daniel renamed Abednego by Persian officials. God delivered him from the fiery furnace (Dan. 1:7; 4:1–30). See *Abednego; Daniel. 26.* Son of Hoshaiah and leader of Jewish people who tried to get Jeremiah to give them a word from God directing them to go to Egypt after the Babylonians destroyed Jerusalem. When Jeremiah said not to go, they accused him of lying (Jer. 42:1—43:7). Hebrew text reads Jezaniah in 42:1.

AZARIAHU (Ăz·a·rī′ a·hü) Long form of Azariah used by NAS, NIV in 2 Chronicles 21:2 to differentiate two men named Azariah. See *Azariah.*

AZAZ (Ā′ zăz) Personal name meaning, "he is strong." A descendant of tribe of Reuben (1 Chron. 5:8).

AZAZEL (Å·zā·zĕl) See *Scapegoat; Atonement.*

AZAZIAH (Ăz·a·zī′ ăh) Personal name meaning, "Yahweh is strong." *1.* Levite David appointed to play the harp for the Temple worship (1 Chron. 5:21). *2.* Father of leader of tribe of Ephraim under David (1 Chron. 27:20). *3.* Overseer among the priests under Hezekiah (715–686 B.C.) (2 Chron. 31:13).

AZBUK (Ăz′ bŭk) Father of a Nehemiah who repaired Jerusalem under the leadership of Nehemiah, son of Hachaliah (Neh. 3:16).

AZEKAH (Å·zē′ kăh) Place name meaning, "cultivated ground." *1.* City where Joshua defeated southern coalition of kings led by Adonizedek of Jerusalem (Josh. 10:10), as God cast hailstones from heaven on the fleeing armies. In the battle Joshua commanded the sun and moon to stand still (Josh. 10:12). Joshua allotted it to Judah (Josh. 15:35). Near it, the Philistines lined up their forces for battle against Saul (1 Sam. 17:1), resulting in the David and Goliath confrontation. Rehoboam, king of Judah, (931–913 B.C.), built up its fortifications (2 Chron. 11:9). The tribe of Judah occupied it in Nehemiah's day (Neh. 11:30), after it had been one of the last cities to fall to Nebuchadnezzar of Babylon in 588 B.C. (Jer. 34:7). One of the letters found at Lachish tells of searching for signal lights from Azekah but not being able to see them. This can be dated to 588 B.C. An earlier Assyrian inscription, perhaps from 712

B.C. speaks of Azekah's location on a mountain ridge, being inaccessible like an eagle's nest, too strong for seige ramps and battering rams.

Later tradition connected Azekah with the tomb of the prophet Zechariah and then with Zechariah the father of John the Baptist, to whom a large church was dedicated. Thus the Madeba map from about 550 A.D. calls Azekah, "Beth Zechariah," or "house of Zechariah" and pictures a large church there.

Azekah is located at tell Zakariya five and one half miles northeast of Beth Govrin above the Valley of Elah. Excavations show the site was occupied before 3000 B.C. and had a strong fortress in the period of the judges.

AZEL (Ā′ zĕl) Personal and place name meaning, "noble." *1.* Descendant of Saul in tribe of Benjamin and father of six sons (1 Chron. 8:37–38). *2.* Unclear word in Hebrew text of Zechariah 14:5 which may be a place name, perhaps near Jerusalem, or a preposition meaning "near to," "beside," or a noun meaning, "the side." Translations vary: "Azal" (KJV, NRSV), "the other side" (TEV), "Azel" (NAS, NIV), "the side of it" (RSV).

AZEM (Ā′ zĕm) KJV spelling of Ezem. See *Ezem*.

AZGAD (Ăz′ găd) Personal name meaning, "Gad is strong." *1.* Clan of which 1222 (Neh. 7:17 says 2,322) returned from Exile in Babylon with Zerubbabel to Jerusalem in 537 B.C. (Ezra 2:12). One hundred eleven more returned with Ezra about 458 B.C. (Ezra 8:12). *2.* A Levite who signed the covenant Nehemiah made to keep God's law (Neh. 10:15).

AZIEL (Ā-zī′ ĕl) Short form of Jaaziel in 1 Chronicles 15:20. See *Jaaziel*.

AZIZA (Ȧ-zī′ zȧ) Personal name meaning, "strong one." Israelite who agreed under Ezra's leadership to divorce his foreign wife to help Israel remain true to God (Ezra 10:27).

AZMAVETH (Ăz·mā′ veth) Personal and place name meaning, "strong as death" or "death is strong." *1.* Member of David's elite 30 military heroes (2 Sam. 23:31). He lived in Barhum or perhaps Baharum (NRSV). See *Baharum*. *2.* Descendant of Saul in tribe of Benjamin (1 Chron. 8:36). *3.* Father of two of David's military leaders (1 Chron. 12:3), probably identical with *1.* above. *4.* The treasurer of David's kingdom (1 Chron. 27:25). He, too, may be identical with *1.* above. *5.* A city probably the same as Bethazmaveth. See *Beth-azmaveth*. Forty-two men of the city returned to Jerusalem from Exile in Babylon with Zerubbabel in 537 B.C. (Ezra 2:24). Levites on the Temple staff as singers lived there. It apparently is near Jerusalem, perhaps modern

Hizmeh, five miles northeast of Jerusalem (Neh. 12:29).

AZMON (Ăz′ mŏn) Place name meaning, "bones." Place on southern border of Promised Land (Num. 34:4). Joshua assigned it to Judah (Josh. 15:4). It is located near Ain el-Quseimeh, about 60 miles south of Gaza. Some would identify it with Ezem.

AZNOTH-TABOR (Ăz′ nŏth-Tā′ bôr) Place name meaning, "ears of Tabor." A border town of the tribe of Naphtali (Josh. 19:34). It may be modern Umm Jebeil near Mount Tabor.

AZOR (Ā′ zôr) Personal name of an ancestor of Jesus (Matt. 1:13–14).

AZOTUS (Ȧ·zō′ tŭs) See *Ashdod; Philistines.*

AZRIEL (Ăz′ rĭ·ĕl) Personal name meaning, "God is my help." *1.* Head of a family of eastern part of tribe of Manasseh (1 Chron. 5:24). *2.* Head of tribe of Naphtali under David (1 Chron. 27:19). *3.* Father of royal officer commanded to arrest Baruch, Jeremiah's scribe (Jer. 36:26).

AZRIKAM (Ăz·rī′ kăm) Personal name meaning, "my help stood up." *1.* Descendant of David after the Exile (1 Chron. 3:23). *2.* Descendant of Saul of tribe of Benjamin (1 Chron. 8:38). *3.* Father of a Levite who led in resettling Jerusalem after the Exile (1 Chron. 9:14). *4.* Officer in charge of palace for Ahaz, king of Judah. Zicri, a soldier in Israel's army, killed him when Israel attacked Judah about 741 B.C. (2 Chron. 28:7).

AZUBAH (Ȧ·zū′ bah) Personal name meaning, "forsaken." *1.* Queen mother of Jehoshaphat (1 Kings 22:42), king of Judah (873–848 B.C.). *2.* First wife of Caleb, son of Hezron (1 Chron. 2:18–19).

AZUR (Ā′ zûr) KJV spelling (Jer. 28:1; Ezek. 11:1) for Azzur. See *Azzur.*

AZZAH KJV translation or spelling of Gaza (Deut. 2:23; 1 Kings 4:24; Jer. 25:20). See *Gaza.*

AZZAN (Ăz′ zăn) Personal name meaning, "he has proved to be strong." Father of representative of tribe of Issachar in assigning territorial lots to the tribes after God gave Israel the Promised Land (Num. 34:26).

AZZUR (Ăz′ zur) Personal name meaning, "one who has been helped." *1.* Jewish leader who sealed Nehemiah's covenant to obey God's law (Neh. 10:17). *2.* Father of Hananiah, the prophet, in Jeremiah's days (Jer. 28:1). *3.* Father of Jaazaniah, Jewish leader in Jerusalem who plotted evil in Ezekiel's day (Ezek. 11:1).

B

An Arab baker in old Jerusalem delivers a fresh batch of bread.

BAAL (Bā′ ȧl) Lord of Canaanite religion and seen in the thunderstorms, Baal was worshiped as the god who provided fertility. He proved a great temptation for Israel. "Baal" occurs in the Old Testament as a noun meaning, "lord, owner, possessor, or husband," and as a proper noun referring to the supreme god of the Canaanites, and often to the name of a man. According to 1 Chronicles 5:5, Baal was a descendant of Reuben, Jacob's firstborn son, and the father of Beerah. Baal was sent into exile by Tiglath-pileser, king of Assyria. The genealogical accounts of Saul's family listed in 1 Chronicles 9:35−36 indicates that the fourth son of Jehiel was named Baal.

The noun comes from a verb that means to marry or rule over. The verb form occurs in the Hebrew text 29 times, whereas the noun occurs 166 times. The noun appears in a number of compound forms which are proper names for locations where Canaanite deities were worshiped, such as Baal-peor (Num. 25:5; Deut. 4:3; Ps. 106:28; Hos. 9:10), Baal-hermon (Judg. 3:3; 1 Chron. 5:23), and Baal-gad (Josh. 11:17; 12:7; 13:5). See *Canaan*.   *James Newell*

BAALAH (Bā′ ȧ·lăh) Place name meaning, "wife, lady," or "residence of Baal." *1.* City on northern border of tribe of Judah equated with Kirjath-jearim (Josh. 15:9−11). David kept the ark there before moving it to Jerusalem (1 Chron. 13:6). It is located at modern Deir el-Azar, eight miles west of Jerusalem. It is called Baale of Judah (2 Sam. 6:2) and may be the same as Kirjath-baal (Josh. 15:60). See *Kirjath-jearim*. *2.* Town on southern border of Judah (Josh. 15:29) that may be same as Balah (Josh. 19:3) and as Bilhah (1 Chron. 4:29). Tribe of Simeon occupied it. Its location is unknown. *3.* A mountain on Judah's northern border between Jabneel and Ekron. It may be the same as Mount Jearim.

BAALATH (Bā′ ȧ·lăth) Place name meaning, "feminine Baal." City in original inheritance of tribe of Dan (Josh. 19:44). Same or different town which Solomon rebuilt (1 Kings 9:18). It may have been near Gezer on the road to Beth-horon and Jerusalem. Some would identify Solomon's town with Simeon's Balah, with Kirjath-jearim, or with Baalath-beer.

BAALATH-BEER (Bā′ ȧ·lăth-bē′ ēr) Place name meaning, "the baal of the well" or the "lady of the well." A city in the tribal allotment of Simeon (Josh. 19:8), identified with Ramath of the south (KJV) or Ramah of the Negev (NAS, NIV, NRSV). It may be identical with Baal (1 Chron. 4:33) and/or with Bealoth (Josh. 15:24).

Statuette of Baal, the Canaanite weather god, from Minet-el-Beida (15th−14th century B.C.).

BAALBEK See *Heliopolis.*

BAAL-BERITH (Bā′ al-bē·rĭth) In Judges 8:33, a Canaanite deity whom the Israelites began to worship following the death of Gideon. The name means "lord of covenant," and the god's temple was located at Shechem. The precise identity of this deity cannot be determined. The designation, "lord of covenant," may mean that a covenant between the Israelites and the Shechemites was agreed to and annually renewed in his shrine. See *Shechem.*

BAALE (KJV), **BAALE-JUDAH** (NAS, NRSV) (Bā′ á·lē·jū′ dăh) Place name meaning, "Baals of Judah" or "lords of Judah." 2 Samuel 6:2 may be read as "from the lords of Judah" or as went from Baale Judah. If the latter reading is correct, then Baale Judah is a place name where the ark of the covenant was before David took it to Jerusalem. 1 Chronicles 13:6 calls the place Baalah of Judah and identifies it with Kirjath-jearim. See *Kirjath-jearim.*

BAAL-GAD (Bā′ ál-găd) Place name meaning, "Baal of Gad" or "lord of Gad." Town representing northern limit of Joshua's conquests (Josh. 11:17) in Valley of Lebanon at foot of Mount Hermon. It has been variously located at modern Hasbeya and at Baalbek, over 50 miles east of Beirut where imposing ruins of Greek and Roman worship remain.

BAAL-HAMON (Bā′ ál-hā′ mōn) Place name meaning, "lord of abundance." Location of Solomon's vineyard according to Song of Solomon 8:11.

BAAL-HANAN (Bā′ ál-hā′ năn) Personal name meaning, "Baal was gracious." *1.* King of Edom prior to any king ruling in Israel (Gen. 36:38). *2.* Official under David in charge of olive and sycamore trees growing in Judean plain or Shephalah (1 Chron. 27:28).

BAAL-HAZOR (Bā′ ál-hā′ zôr) Place name meaning "Baal of Hazor." Village where David's son Absalom held celebration of sheepshearing (2 Sam. 13:23). During festivities, Absalom had his employees kill his brother Amnon, who had violated his sister Tamar. The village is modern Jebel Asur, five miles northeast of Bethel.

BAAL-HERMON (Bā′ ál-hĕr·mŏn) Place name meaning, "Baal of Hermon" or "lord of Hermon." A mountain and village Israel could not take from the Hivites, whom God left to test Israel (Judg. 3:3). It marked the Hivites' southern border and Manasseh's northern border (1 Chron. 5:23). Its location is unknown. Some would equate it with Baal-gad. Others, modern Baneas or Caesarea Philippi.

BAALI (Bā′ ál·ī) Form of address meaning, "my lord," or "my Baal." Hosea used a play on words to look to a day when Israel would no longer worship Baal (Hos. 2:16). He said Israel, the bride, would refer to Yahweh, her God and husband, as "my man" (Hebrew, ′ishi) but not as "my lord" (Hebrew, baali). Even though baal was a common word for lord or husband, Israel could not use it because it reminded them too easily of Baal, the Canaanite god. See *Baal; Canaan.*

BAALIM (Bā′ á·līm) Hebrew plural of Baal. See *Baal; Canaan.*

BAALIS (Bā′ á·lĭs) Personal name of king of Ammon who sent Ishmael to kill Geduliah, governor of Judah immediately after Babylon captured Jerusalem and sent most of Judah's citizens into the Exile (Jer. 40:14).

BAAL-MEON (Bā′ ál-mē′ on) Place name meaning, "lord of the residence" or "Baal of the residence." City tribe of Reuben built east of Jordan (Num. 32:36), probably on the tribe's northern border. Mesha, king of Moab about 830 B.C., claims to have rebuilt Baal-meon, meaning he had captured it from Israel at that date. Ezekiel 25:9 pronounces judgment on Baal-meon as a city of Moab about the time of the Exile in 587. Baal-meon is located at modern Main, ten miles southwest of Heshbon and ten miles east of the Dead Sea.

BAAL-PEOR (Bā′ ál-pē′ ôr) In Numbers 25:3, a Moabite deity that the Israelites worshiped when they had illicit sexual relations with Moabite women. The guilty Israelites were severely punished for this transgression, and the incident became a paradigm of sin and divine judgment for later generations of Israelites (Deut. 4:3; Ps. 106:28; Hos. 9:10). See *Moab; Peor.*

BAAL-PERAZIM (Bā′ ál-pĕr′ á·zīm) Place name meaning, "Lord of the breakthroughs" or "Baal of the breaches." Place of David's initial victory over the Philistines after he became king of all Israel at Hebron, then captured and moved to Jerusalem (2 Sam. 5:20). The location is not known. It is probably identical with Mount Perazim (Isa. 28:21).

BAAL-SHALISHAH (Bā′ ál-shăl′ ĭ′ shăh) Place name meaning, "Baal of Shalishah" or "lord of Shalishah." Home of unnamed man who brought firstfruits to Elisha, who used them to feed a hundred men (2 Kings 4:42–44). The "land of Shalishah" was evidently in the tribal territory of Ephraim (1 Sam. 9:4). Baal-shalishah may be modern Kefr Thilth, twenty miles southwest of Shechem. See *Shalishah.*

BAAL-TAMAR (Bā′ ál-tā′ mär) Place name meaning, "Baal of the palm tree" or "lord of the palm tree." Place where Israelites attacked and defeated tribe of Benjamin for killing concubine of traveling Levite (Judg. 20:33). It must have been near Gibeah. It may be ras et-Tawil north of Jerusalem.

BAAL-ZEBUB (Bā′ ȧl-zē′ bŭb) Deity's name meaning, "lord of the flies." In 2 Kings 1:2, a Philistine deity from which the Israelite King Ahaziah sought help after injuring himself in a fall. Though the Philistines themselves may have used this name, it is more probable that it is intentionally used to distort the god's actual name. The problem of identification is further complicated by references in the New Testament. Jesus is reported to have used the name Beel-zebub in reference to the prince of demons (Matt. 10:25). Beel-zebub is clearly a variation of Baal-zebub. However, the Greek text of the New Testament has Beelzebul. The meaning of Beelzebul is disputed. One suggestion is "lord of the dwelling." A second, and more likely possibility is "lord of dung." Regardless of the exact meaning of the name, Jesus clearly used it in reference to Satan. See *Baal; Philistines; Satan.*

BAAL-ZEPHON (Bā′ ȧl-zē′ phôn) Place name meaning, "lord of the north" or "Baal of the north." Place in Egypt near which Israel camped before miracle of crossing the sea (Ex. 14:2,9). The exact location is not known. Some suggest tell Defenneh known in Egypt as Tahpanhes in the eastern Nile delta. See *Exodus.*

BAANA (Bā′ ȧ·nȧ) or **BAANAH** Personal name of uncertain meaning. Some have suggested, "son of grief" or "son of Anat." English spelling variations reflect similar Hebrew spelling variations. *1.* One of Solomon's district supervisors to provide food one month a year for the court. His territory encompassed the great central plain with the famous cities of Beth-shean, Taanach, and Megiddo (1 Kings 4:12). *2.* Another district supervisor over Asher, the western slopes of Galilee in the north. His father Hushai may have been "David's friend" (2 Sam. 15:37). *3.* Father of Zadok, who repaired walls of Jerusalem under Nehemiah (Neh. 3:4). *4.* A captain of Ishbosheth's army after Saul died and Abner deserted to David and was killed by Joab. Baanah and his brother killed Ishbosheth and reported it to David, who had them killed (2 Sam. 4). *5.* Father of Heleb, one of David's thirty heroes (2 Sam. 23:29). *6.* Man who returned with Zerubbabel from Babylonian captivity about 537 B.C. (Ezra 2:2). *7.* One who signed Nehemiah's covenant to obey God's law (Neh. 10:27).

BAARA (Bā′ ȧ·rȧ) Personal name meaning, "burning" or a name intentionally changed from one honoring Baal. Wife of Shaharaim in tribe of Benjamin (1 Chron. 8:8).

BAASEIAH (Bā·ȧ·seî′ ah) Personal name of unknown meaning. A Levite ancestor of Asaph (1 Chron. 6:40).

BAASHA (Bā′ ȧshȧ) The king of Israel who was at war against Asa, king of Judah (1 Kings 15:16). Baasha gained the throne of Israel by violence. He conspired against and killed his immediate predecessor Nadab, the son of Jeroboam I (1 Kings 15:27). Furthermore, he exterminated the entire line of Jeroboam (15:29). Baasha reigned over Israel for twenty-four years (908–886 B.C.). His capital was at Tirzah. He died, apparently from natural causes, and was succeeded by his son Elah. See *Israel; Chronology; Tirzah.*

BABBLER A derogatory term the Epicureans and Stoics used against Paul in Athens (Acts 17:18). The Greek word literally means "seed picker" and was used of birds (especially crows) who lived by picking up seeds. It was applied to people who lived parasitically by picking up pieces of food off the merchants' carts. In the field of literature and philosophy the term was applied to those who plagiarize without the ability to understand or properly use what they had taken. The philosophers referred to Paul as a babbler because they considered Paul an ignorant plagiarist.

Another Greek word *bebēlos* refers to something outside the religious sphere. It appears in 1 Timothy 4:7; 6:20; 2 Timothy 2:16; Hebrews 12:16, usually in reference to chatter or babbling talk about worldly things, an activity Christians should avoid. In Hebrews it refers to a godless person.

BABEL (Bā′ bĕl) Babel is a Hebrew word meaning "confusion," derived from a root which means "to mix." It was the name given to the city which the disobedient descendants of Noah built so they would not be scattered over all the earth (Gen. 11:4,9). Babel is also the Hebrew word for Babylon.

The tower and the city which were built were intended to be a monument of human pride, for they sought to "make a name" for themselves (Gen. 11:4). It was also a monument to mankind's continued disobedience. They had been commanded to fill up the earth but were seeking to avoid being scattered abroad (Gen. 9:1; 11:4). Further, it was a monument to human engineering skills, for the techniques of its building described the use of fired clay bricks as a substitute for stone. Bitumen, found in relative abundance in the Mesopotamian Valley, was used to bind the bricks together.

Ruins of numerous temple-towers, called ziggurats, have been found in the region of Babylon. It is possible that ruins of the great temple-tower to Marduk found in the center of ancient Babylon is the focus of this narrative.

To bring the people's monumental task to an end, God confused their language. The inspired writer apparently considered this to be the basis for the origin of the different human languages. When the builders were no longer able to communicate with each other, they then fled from one another in fear. The city of Babylon became to the Old Testament writers the symbol of utter rebellion against God and remained so even into the New Testament (Rev. 17:1–5). See *Babylon.*

Bob Cate

BABOON The NIV translation of *thukkiyim* (1 Kings 10:22; 2 Chron. 9:21). The TEV and REB translate the same word as "monkeys." The KJV, NAS, and NRSV give the translation "peacocks" (but see NRSV margin). There is a strong similarity between *thukkiyim* and the Egyptian word for monkey which leads many to accept baboon or monkey as the correct translation.

BABYLON, HISTORY AND RELIGION OF Babylon was a city-state in southern Mesopotamia during Old Testament times, which eventually became a large empire that absorbed the nation of Judah and destroyed Jerusalem.

History The city of Babylon was founded in unknown antiquity on the river Euphrates, about 50 miles south of modern Baghdad. The English names Babylon and Babel (Gen. 10:10; 11:9) are

The site of the ancient city of Babylon in modern Iraq—a general overview of the ruins.

translated from the same Hebrew word (*babel*). See *Babel.* Babylon may have been an important cultural center during the period of the early Sumerian city-states (before 2000 B.C.), but the corresponding archaeological levels of the site are below the present water table and remain unexplored.

Babylon emerged from anonymity shortly after 2000 B.C., a period roughly contemporary with the Hebrew patriarchs. At that time, an independent kingdom was established in the city under a dynasty of Semitic westerners, or Amorites. Hammurabi (1792–1750 B.C.), the sixth king of this First Dynasty of Babylon, built a sizable empire through treaties, vassalage, and conquest. From his time forward, Babylon was considered the political seat of southern Mesopotamia, the region called Babylonia. See *Hammurabi.*

The Amorite dynasty of Babylon reached its apex under Hammurabi. Subsequent rulers, however, saw their realm diminished, and in 1595 B.C. the Hittites sacked Babylon. After their withdrawal, members of the Kassite tribe seized the throne. The Kassite Dynasty ruled for over four centuries, a period of relative peace but also stagnation. Little is known up to about 1350 B.C., when Babylonian kings corresponded with Egypt and struggled with the growing power of Assyria to the north. After a brief resurgence, the Kassite dynasty was ended by the Elamite invasion in 1160 B.C.

When the Elamites withdrew to their Iranian homeland, princes native to the Babylonian city of Isin founded the Fourth Dynasty of Babylon. After

a brief period of glory in which Nebuchadnezzar I (about 1124–1103 B.C.) invaded Elam, Babylon entered a dark age for most of the next two centuries. Floods, famine, widespread settlement of nomadic Aramean tribes, and the arrival of Chaldeans in the south plagued Babylon during this time of confusion.

During the period of the Assyrian Empire, Babylon was dominated by this warlike neighbor to the north. A dynastic dispute in Babylon in 851 B.C. brought the intervention of the Assyrian king Shalmaneser III. Babylon kings remained independent, but nominally subject to Assyrian "protection."

A series of coups in Babylon prompted the Assyrian Tiglath-pileser III to enter Babylon in 728 B.C. and proclaim himself king under the throne name Pulu (Pul of 2 Kings 15:19; 1 Chron. 5:26). He died the next year. By 721 B.C., the Chaldean Marduk-apal-iddina, Merodach-baladan of the Old Testament, ruled Babylon. With Elamite support he resisted the advances of the Assyrian Sargon II in 720 B.C. Babylon gained momentary independence, but in 710 B.C. Sargon attacked again. Merodach-baladan was forced to flee to Elam. Sargon, like Tiglath-pileser before him, took the throne of Babylon. As soon as Sargon died in 705 B.C., Babylon and other nations, including Judah under King Hezekiah, rebelled from Assyrian domination. Merodach-baladan had returned from Elam to Babylon. It is probably in this context that he sent emissaries to Hezekiah (2 Kings 20:12–19; Isa. 39). In 703 B.C., the new Assyrian king, Sennacherib, attacked Babylon. He defeated Merodach-baladan, who again fled. He ultimately died in exile. After considerable intrigue in Babylon, another Elamite-sponsored revolt broke out against Assyria. In 689 B.C., Sennacherib destroyed the sacred city of Babylon in retaliation. His murder, by his own sons (2 Kings 19:37) in 681 B.C., was interpreted by Babylonians as divine judgment for this unthinkable act.

Esarhaddon, Sennacherib's son, immediately began the rebuilding of Babylon to win the allegiance of the populace. At his death, the crown prince Ashurbanipal ruled over Assyria, while another son ascended the throne of Babylon. All was well until 651 B.C. when the Babylonian king rebelled against his brother. Ashurbanipal finally prevailed and was crowned king of a resentful Babylon.

Assyrian domination died with Ashurbanipal in 627 B.C. In 626 B.C., Babylon fell into the hands of a Chaldean chief, Nabopolassar, first king of the Neo-Babylonian Empire. In 612, with the help of the Medes, the Babylonians sacked the Assyrian capital Nineveh. The remnants of the Assyrian army rallied at Haran in north Syria, which was abandoned at the approach of the Babylonians in 610 B.C. Egypt, however, challenged Babylon for the right to inherit Assyria's empire. Pharaoh Necho II, with the last of the Assyrians (2 Kings 23:29–30), failed in 609 to retake Haran. In 605 B.C., Babylonian forces under the crown prince Nebuchadnezzar routed the Egyptians at the decisive Battle of Carchemish (Jer. 46:2–12). The Babylonian advance, however, was delayed by Nabopolassar's death which obliged Nebuchadnezzar to return to Babylon and assume power.

In 604 and 603 B.C., Nebuchadnezzar II (605–562 B.C.), king of Babylon, campaigned along the Palestinian coast. At this time Jehoiakim, king of Judah, became an unwilling vassal of Babylon. A Babylonian defeat at the border of Egypt in 601 probably encouraged Jehoiakim to rebel. For two years Judah was harassed by Babylonian vassals (2 Kings 24:1–2). Then, in December of 598 B.C., Nebuchadnezzar marched on Jerusalem. Jehoiakim died that same month, and his son Jehoiachin surrendered the city to the Babylonians on March 16, 597 B.C. Many Judeans, including the royal family, were deported to Babylon (2 Kings 24:6–12). Ultimately released from prison, Jehoiachin was treated as a king in exile (2 Kings 25:27–30; Jer. 52:31–34). Texts excavated in Babylon show that rations were allotted to him and five sons.

Nebuchadnezzar appointed Zedekiah over Judah. Against the protests of Jeremiah, but with promises of Egyptian aid, Zedekiah revolted against Babylon in 589 B.C. In the resultant Babylonian campaign, Judah was ravaged and Jerusalem besieged. An abortive campaign by the Pharaoh Hophra gave Jerusalem a short respite, but the attack was renewed (Jer. 37:4–10). The city fell in August of 587 B.C. Zedekiah was captured, Jerusalem burned, and the Temple destroyed (Jer. 52:12–14). Many more Judeans were taken to their Exile in Babylonia (2 Kings 25:1–21; Jer. 52:1–30).

Apart from his military conquests, Nebuchadnezzar is noteworthy for a massive rebuilding program in Babylon itself. The city spanned the Euphrates and was surrounded by an eleven-mile long outer wall which enclosed suburbs and Nebuchadnezzar's summer palace. The inner wall was wide enough to accommodate two chariots abreast. It could be entered through eight gates, the most famous of which was the northern Ishtar Gate, used in the annual New Year Festival and decorated with reliefs of dragons and bulls in enameled brick. The road to this gate was bordered by high walls decorated by lions in glazed brick behind which were defensive citadels. Inside the gate was the main palace built by Nebuchadnezzar with its huge throne room. A cellar with shafts in part of the palace may have served as the substructure to the famous "Hanging Gardens of Babylon," described by classical authors as one of the wonders of the ancient world. Babylon contained many temples, the most important of which was Esagila, the temple of the city's patron god, Marduk. Rebuilt by Nebuchadnezzar, the temple was lavishly decorated with gold. Just north of Esagila lay the huge stepped tower of Babylon, a ziggurat called Etemenanki and its sacred enclosure. Its seven stories perhaps towered some 300 feet above the city. No doubt Babylon greatly impressed the Jews taken there in captivity and provided them with substantial economic opportunities.

Nebuchadnezzar was the greatest king of the Neo-Babylonian Period and the last truly great ruler of Babylon. His successors were insignificant by comparison. He was followed by his son Awel-marduk (561–560 B.C.), the Evil-Merodach of the Old Testament (2 Kings 25:27–30), Neriglis-sar (560–558 B.C.), and Labashi-Marduk (557 B.C.), murdered as a mere child. The last king of Babylon, Nabonidus (556–539 B.C.) was an enigmatic figure who seems to have favored the moon god, Sin, over the national god, Marduk. He moved his residence to Tema in the Syro-Arabian Desert for ten years, leaving his son Belshazzar (Dan. 5:1) as regent in Babylon. Nabonidus returned to a divided capital amid a threat from the united Medes and Persians. In 539 B.C., the Persian Cyrus II (the Great) entered Babylon without a fight. Thus ended Babylon's dominant role in Near Eastern politics.

Babylon remained an important economic center and provincial capital during the period of Persian rule. The Greek historian Herodotus, who visited the city in 460 B.C., could still remark that

Painted relief of a bull from the famous Ishtar Gate of Babylon.

"it surpasses in splendor any city of the known world." Alexander the Great, conqueror of the Persian Empire, embarked on a program of rebuilding in Babylon which was interrupted by his death in 323 B.C. After Alexander the city declined economically, but remained an important religious center until New Testament times. The site was deserted by A.D. 200.

The ruins of the Hanging Gardens of Babylon (modern Iraq), one of the seven wonders of the ancient world.

In Judeo-Christian thought, Babylon the metropolis, like the Tower of Babel, became symbolic of man's decadence and God's judgment. "Babylon" in Revelation 14:8; 16:19; 17:5; 18:2 and probably in 1 Peter 5:13 refers to Rome, the city which personified this idea for early Christians.

Religion. Babylonian religion is the best known variant of a complex and highly polytheistic sys-

tem of belief common throughout Mesopotamia. Of the thousands of recognized gods, only about twenty were important in actual practice. The most important are reviewed here.

Anu, Enlil, and Ea, were patron deities of the oldest Sumerian cities and were each given a share of the Universe as their dominion. Anu, god of the heavens and patron god of Uruk (biblical Erech; Gen. 10:10) did not play a very active role. Enlil of Nippur was god of the earth. The god of Eridu, Ea, was lord of the subterranean waters and the god of craftsmen.

After the political rise of Babylon, Marduk was also considered one of the rulers of the cosmos. The son of Ea and patron god of Babylon, Marduk began to attain the position of prominence in Babylonian religion in the time of Hammurabi. In subsequent periods, Marduk (Merodach in Jer. 50:2) was considered the leading god and was given the epithet *Bel* (equivalent to the Canaanite term Baal), meaning "lord" (Isa. 46:1; Jer. 50:2; 51:44). Marduk's son Nabu (the Nebo in Isa. 46:1), god of the nearby city of Borsippa, was considered the god of writing and scribes and became especially exalted in the Neo-Babylonian Period.

Astral deities—gods associated with heavenly bodies—included the sun-god Shamash, the moon-god Sin, and Ishtar, goddess of the morning and evening star (the Greek Aphrodite and Roman

Relief of King Nabonidus standing before emblems of the moon-god, sun-god, and war/love goddess.

Venus). Sin was the patron god of Ur and Haran, both associated with Abraham's origins (Gen. 11:31). Ishtar, the Canaanite Astarte/Ashtaroth (Judg. 10:6; 1 Sam. 7:3–4; 1 Kings 11:5), had a major temple in Babylon and was very popular as the "Queen of Heaven" (Jer. 7:18; 44:17–19).

Other gods were associated with a newer city or none at all. Adad, the Canaanite Hadad, was the god of storms and thus both beneficial and destructive. Ninurta, god of war and hunting, was patron for the Assyrian capital Calah.

A number of myths concerning Babylonian gods are known, the most important of which is the *Enuma elish,* or Creation Epic. This myth originated in Babylon, where one of its goals was to show how Marduk became the leading god. It tells of a cosmic struggle in which, while other gods were powerless, Marduk slew Tiamat (the sea goddess, representative of chaos). From the blood of another slain god, Ea created mankind. Finally, Marduk was exalted and installed in his temple, Esagila, in Babylon.

The *Enuma elish* was recited and reenacted as part of the twelve-day New Year Festival in Babylon. During the festival, statues of other gods arrived from their cities to "visit" Marduk in Esagila. Also, the king did penance before Marduk, and "took the hand of Bel" in a ceremonial processing out of the city through the Ishtar Gate.

The gods were thought of as residing in cosmic localities, but also as present in their image, or idol, and living in the temple as a king in his palace. The gilded wooden images were in human form, clothed in a variety of ritual garments, and given three meals a day. On occasion the images were carried in ceremonial processions or to visit one another in different sanctuaries. It is very difficult to know what meaning the images and temples of the various gods had for the average person, and even more difficult to ascertain what comfort or help he might expect through worship of them. It seems clear, however, that beyond the expectations of health and success in his earthly life, he was without eternal hope. *Dan Browning*

BACA (Bā′ cà) Place name meaning, "Balsam tree" or "weeping." A valley in Psalm 84:6 which reflects a poetic play on words describing a person forced to go through a time of weeping who found God turned tears into a well, providing water.

BACHRITE (Băch′ rīte) KJV spelling of Becherites (NAS, NRSV) or Bekerite (NIV). See *Becher.*

BACKSLIDING Term used by the prophets to describe Israel's faithlessness to God (Isa. 57:17 RSV; Jer. 3:14,22; 8:5; 31:22; 49:4; Hos. 11:7; 14:4). In these passages it is clear that Israel had broken faith with God by serving other gods and by living immoral lives. See *Apostasy.*

BADGER See *Animals.*

BADGER SKINS KJV translation of the skin used to cover the tabernacle (Ex. 26:14; 36:19; 39:34), the ark, and other sacred objects (Num. 4:6–14). The leather was also used for shoes (Ezek. 16:10). Bible students do not agree on the kind of skin intended. The KJV translation of "badger skin" seems doubtful as the word used is not the normal word for badger. In addition, the badger was considered an unclean animal making it very doubtful that the skin of the badger would have been used as a covering for sacred objects. In addition, it is doubtful that the badger was plentiful enough to provide the necessary hides. The translation of "goatskin" (RSV) also fails on the grounds that the word used is not a normal word for goat. Thus NRSV reads "fine leather" with a note that the meaning of the Hebrew is uncertain. Some have proposed the simple translation, "leather," noting the similarity of the Hebrew and Egyptian words for leather (TEV). Others have proposed dolphin or "porpoise skins," noting the similarities between the Hebrew and Arabic words for dolphin or porpoise (NAS). Still others have proposed "hides of sea cows" (that is, dugongs, REB)—sea creatures that have been found in the Red Sea (NIV). Would either the dolphin or dugong have been considered "clean" for the purpose of covering sacred objects; and, further, would the hides of these animals have been readily available to the small inland Israelite community? It is doubtful. There seems to be no clear answer to the question: What kind of hides were used as a covering for the tabernacle, ark, and other sacred objects?   *Phil Logan*

BAG Flexible container that may be closed for holding, storing, or carrying something. Several kinds are mentioned in the Bible: *1.* Large bags in which large amounts of money could be carried (2 Kings 5:23; Isa. 3:22, KJV has "crisping pins"). *2.* A small bag (purse) used to carry a merchant's weights (Deut. 25:13; Prov. 16:11; Mic. 6:11) or smaller sums of money (Prov. 1:14; Isa. 46:6). This may be the same as the purse mentioned in the New Testament (Luke 10:4; 12:33; 22:35–36). *3.* A cloth tied up in a bundle is translated as bag (Job 14:17; Prov. 7:20; Hag. 1:6) or bundle (Gen. 42:35; 1 Sam. 25:29; Song of Sol. 1:13). The size of the bundle would depend on its use. This type of bag was used to hold money (Gen. 42:35; Prov. 7:20; Hag. 1:6; see 2 Kings 12:10 where the verb form, "to tie up in bags," is used) or something loose such as myrrh (Song of Sol. 1:13). This term for bag is used figuratively to speak of one's sins being bundled up (and perhaps sealed; "bag of transgressions," Job 14:17) and one's life being bundled up and protected by God ("bundle of the living," 1 Sam. 25:29). *4.* The shepherd's bag (KJV "scrip" or "vessel").

Used by shepherds and travelers to carry one or more days' supplies, it was made of animal skins and slung across the shoulder. Joseph's brothers carried grain in such a bag (Gen. 42:25). Saul's bag was empty of bread when he went to meet Samuel (1 Sam. 9:7), and David collected stones in his shepherd's bag when confronting Goliath (1 Sam. 17:40,49). An Israelite traveler whose bag of provisions was empty could eat from a fellow Israelite's vineyard, but was not permitted to fill his bag for the rest of the journey (Deut. 23:24). Jesus commanded His disciples not to carry a bag when He sent them out to preach (Matt. 10:10; Mark 6:8; Luke 9:3; 10:4). They were to be totally dependent on God and the hospitality and support of God's people (compare Num. 18:31; 1 Cor. 9:3–14). The disciples learned from this experience that they would be cared for; but because of the critical nature of what they were about to face, Jesus later instructed His disciples to begin carrying a purse, bag, and—very curiously—a sword (Luke 22:35–36). The Hebrew word for shepherd's bag is also translated as "carriage." See *Carriage.*

5. A large sack used to carry grain (Gen. 42:25,27,35; Josh. 9:4; see Lev. 11:32). The same Hebrew word is translated as sackcloth worn during times of mourning or humiliation. See *Sackcloth.*

6. KJV translates *glossokomon* as bag in John 12:6; 13:29. The *glossokomon* was actually a money box. See *Money Box.*   *Phil Logan*

BAGGAGE See *Carriage.*

BAGPIPE Modern translation of a musical instrument translated as "dulcimer" by the KJV (Dan. 3:5,10,15). See *Musical Instruments.*

BAHARUM (Bá·hā′ rŭm) NRSV reading of Baharumite (KJV, NAS, NIV). A person from Bahurim. See *Bahurim.*

BAHURIM (Bá·hū′ rĭm) Place name meaning, "young men." Village on road from Jerusalem to Jericho in tribal territory of Benjamin. David demanded Ishbosheth, Saul's son, send back Michal, Saul's daughter and David's wife. Ishbosheth took her from her husband Phaltiel, who followed her weeping to Bahurim until Abner, the general, forced him to return home (2 Sam. 3:16). When David fled from his son Absalom, a kinsman of Saul named Shimei met him at Bahurim, cursed him, and threw stones at his party. David prevented immediate punishment (2 Sam. 16:5; 19:16). Two messengers taking secret messages about Absalom from the priests hid from Absalom's servants at Bahurim (2 Sam. 17:18). Solomon followed David's orders and had Shimei of Bahurim killed (1 Kings 2:8–9,36–46). Azmaveth, one of David's valiant soldiers, was from Bahurim (1 Chron. 11:33). 2 Samuel 23:31 lists the city as Barhum, due to a copyist's mistake. Bahurim was probably located at modern Ras et-Tmim, east of Mount Scopus near Jerusalem.

BAJITH (Bā′ jĭth) KJV reading in Isaiah 15:2. Modern translations read, "temple." KJV interprets as name of Moabite worship place.

BAKBAKKAR (Băk·băk′ kär) A Levite living in Judah after the Exile (1 Chron. 9:15).

BAKBUK (Băk′ bŭk) Personal name meaning, "bottle." Levite who was a Temple servant after returning from Babylonian Exile with Zerubbabel about 537 B.C. (Ezra 2:51; Neh. 7:53).

BAKBUKIAH (Băk·bū·kī′ ăh) Personal name meaning, "Yahweh's bottle." Leader among the Levites in Jerusalem after the Exile (Neh. 11:17; 12:9,25).

BAKEMEATS Old English term for any food prepared by a baker.

BAKER'S STREET Street in Jerusalem known as "baker's street" where most, if not all, the bakeries of the city were located. It was common in ancient cities for trades and crafts to locate near others of the same kind. In all likelihood, the baker's residence was part of the bakery. Zedekiah promised Jeremiah, whom he had imprisoned,

The village baker prepares dough for baking in his stone oven (on the left).

that he would have food for as long as bread was available on baker's street (Jer. 37:21).

BAKING The Old Testament speaks most often of the baking of bread and cakes, which were the main part of the meal for Hebrews and Canaanites alike (Gen. 19:3; Ex. 12:39; Lev. 26:26; 1 Kings 17:12–13; Isa. 44:15). The bread of the presence (Lev. 24:5) and other offerings (Lev. 2:4–6) were also baked. See *Bread; Bread of the Presence; Cooking and Heating; Food and Meals in the Bible; Kneading, Kneading Bowl.*

BALAAM (Bā′ lȧȧm) A non-Israelite prophet whom Balak, king of Moab, urged to curse the invading Israelites for a fee.

Old Testament Balaam was one of many prophets of eastern religions who worshiped all the gods of the land. Many of these false teachers had great power and influence. When they pronounced a blessing or a curse, it was considered as true prophecy. When Moses led his people across the wilderness, God commanded him not to attack Edom or Moab (Deut. 2:4–9). He did not. When Edom attacked, "Israel turned away from him" (Num. 20:21). As the great nation journeyed north on the east side of Jordan, King Balak of Moab faced the invasion of Israel. Balak sought a strategy other than battle to stop Moses. He decided to use a prophet to curse Israel. Balaam was chosen. Balak sent his messengers with fees to secure Balaam's services. Balaam asked God's permission to curse Israel. Permission was refused,

but Balaam journeyed to confer further with Balak. On this journey, Balaam's donkey talked with him as he traveled a narrow trail (Num. 22:21–30; 2 Pet. 2:16). Here Balaam clearly understood that an angel's drawn sword enforced his obedience to speak only God's message to Balak. Later in four vivid messages Balaam insisted that God would bless Israel (Num. 23—24). God used Balaam to preach truth. He even spoke of a future star and scepter (Num. 24:17) a prophecy ultimately fulfilled in the coming of Jesus as the Messiah. Balak's actions brought God's anger upon Moab (Deut. 23:3–6). In a battle against the Midianites, Balaam died (Num. 31:8; Josh. 13:22). Balaam could not curse Israel, but he taught the Moabites to bring the men of Israel into Baal worship with its immorality. For this God would punish Israel. What Balaam could not accomplish with a curse he did so through seductive means.

New Testament Peter warned against false teachers and described their destruction. He referred to the fallen angels, the watery destruction of the unbelievers in Noah's time, and the fiery judgment on lawless Sodom and Gomorrah in Lot's day. Peter described his generation of false leaders as those with eyes full of adultery, who never stop sinning by seducing the unstable. He further said that they bore a curse as experts in greed. Peter wrote that they left the straight way and followed the way of Balaam (2 Pet. 2:15). In Revelation 2:14, the church at Pergamos was complimented for faithfulness under persecution, but also warned that some followed after Balaam in offering meat to idols and in immorality.

Lawson Hatfield

BALAC (Bā' lăc) KJV spelling of Balak. See *Balak.*

BALADAN (Băl' á·dăn) Akkadian personal name meaning, "God gave a son." Father of Merodach Baladan, king of Babylon (722–711; 705–703 B.C.). See *Merodach–Baladan.*

BALAH (Bā' lăh) Place name meaning, "used, worn out." City in tribal territory of Simeon (Josh. 19:3), apparently the same as Baalah (Josh. 15:29) and Bilhah (1 Chron. 4:29). Location in southwest Judah is unknown.

BALAK (Bā' lăk) In Numbers 22:2, the king of Moab who sent for Balaam the prophet to pronounce a curse on the Israelites. Balaam, however, spoke no curse; and Balak was denied a military victory over Israel. See *Moab; Balaam.*

BALANCES were used to measure weights early in the development of civilization. Balances were well known to the Hebrews and in common use in the Old Testament (Lev. 19:36; Job 6:2; Hos. 12:7). They consisted of two pans hung on cords

attached to a balancing beam. The beam was suspended by a cord in its center. Sometimes the beam was suspended by a ring or hook. Sometimes balances were held in the hand. The Hebrews probably used the common balances of Egypt, which are shown in Egyptian tomb reliefs and papyri writings.

Balances were the basis of economic life. Money came in weighted units of gold and silver. These had to be weighed in the balance for every business transaction or purchase (Jer. 32:9–10). Balances could be easily manipulated, especially by having weights which did not measure up to the proper amount or by having two sets of weights, one for buying and one for selling. God called on Israel for economic justice that began with proper weights and balances. (See Proverbs 11:1; 16:11; 20:23; Ezek. 45:9–12; Hos. 12:7; Amos 8:5; Mic. 6:10–11.) In a figurative sense the balance was employed in the Bible to ask for a fair trial or judgment for the persecuted (Job 31:6; Ps. 62:9).

Balances help teach about God. Only He can weigh the mountains in a balance (Isa. 40:12–13). Just balances show a person belongs to Him (Prov. 16:11), while foolish people weigh out lavish amounts of gold to make idols to worship (Isa. 46:6).

Jimmy Albright

BALD LOCUST See *Insects; Locust.*

BALDNESS Natural baldness was apparently rare in Israel. It is mentioned only in the Levitical laws on leprosy (Lev. 13:40–43), where the bald man is declared "clean" unless the bald area has evidence of redness or swelling. Archaeology has uncovered no depictions of bald men from Israel. Elisha was ridiculed for being bald, but he may have shaved his head to mourn Elijah's departure (2 Kings 2:23). Shaving the head for appearance or in grieving for the dead was prohibited by law (Lev. 21:5; Deut. 14:1), and especially for priests (Ezek. 44:20). However, Isaiah told of God calling the people to acknowledge their sin with baldness and the wearing of sackcloth (Isa. 22:12). A shorn head is frequently mentioned in conjunction with shaving the beard and wearing sackcloth to signify loss of loved ones or loss of hope (Isa. 3:24; 15:2–3; Jer. 48:37). Deuteronomy 21:11 may refer to a practice of making captives bald, to baldness in mourning, or to a symbol of a change in life-style. Ezekiel described men made to work so hard "every head was made bald, and every shoulder was peeled" (Ezek. 29:18), but there is no evidence that slaves were forced to shave their heads.

See *Mourning; Leprosy; Hair.*   *Tim Turnham*

BALLAD SINGERS Refers to the makers and repeaters of proverbs (Num. 21:27). KJV "they that speak in proverbs" gives the sense.

B

BALM Aromatic resin or gum widely used in the ancient Near East for cosmetic and medical purposes. Egyptians used them for embalming. Despite the widespread usage, balm is difficult to identify. Ancient writers refer to balm by a variety of names, which adds to the difficulty of identification. Most ancient references seem to be to the resin from *Balsamodendron opobalsamum* or balm of Gilead. At times the reference seems to be to *Balanites aegyptiaca* Delile—a small shrub that still grows in North Africa and exudes a sticky resin used for medicinal purposes (Gen. 37:25; Jer. 8:22; 46:11; 51:8). In another place the mastic tree (*Pistacia lentiscus*) seems to be referred to (Gen. 43:11). A yellow aromatic resin was extracted from the mastic tree by cutting the branches.

BALM OF GILEAD A substance known in the ancient world for its medical properties. Exported from Gilead to Egypt and Phoenicia (Gen. 37:25; Ezek. 27:17). For the identification of this substance, see *Balm.*

BALSAM Translation of two Hebrew words. *Baka'* is translated as balsam trees in the modern versions (2 Sam. 5:23–24; 1 Chron. 14:14–15; NAS, NIV, NRSV, and TEV). The KJV reads "mulberry trees," while REB has "aspens." Neither the balsam nor mulberry tree has been known to grow around Jerusalem, making the identification of the tree uncertain. Poplar and mastic tree have also been suggested as translations. Balsam is also a translation of *basam* in the NAS, where other versions have "spice" and "spices" (Song of Sol. 5:1,13; 6:2).

BAMAH (Bā′ măh) Hebrew noun meaning, "back, high place." Word is used frequently to describe places of worship, usually false worship of Yahweh containing Canaanite elements. See *High Place.* In Ezekiel 20:29 a particular place is named Bamah in a wordplay ridiculing high places. If a location was intended for Bamah, it can no longer be found.

BAMOTH (Bā′ mŏth) Place name and common noun meaning, "high places." A place in Moab where Israel stayed during the wilderness wanderings (Num. 21:19–20). Some would equate it with Bamoth-baal.

BAMOTH-BAAL (Bā′ mŏth-bā′ ăl) Place name meaning, "high places of Baal." Mesha, king of Moab about 830 B.C., mentioned it in the Moabite stone. Numbers 22:41 speaks of Bamoth or high places of Baal near the Arnon River. There Balak and Balaam could see all Israel. Joshua 13:17 lists it as a city Moses gave the tribe of Reuben. It may be modern gebel Atarus.

BAND KJV translation in Matthew 27:27; Mark 15:16. Modern translations have battalion. See *Battalion.*

BAND, MAGIC See *Magic Bands.*

BANI (Bā′ nī) Personal name meaning, "built." *1.* Man from tribe of Gad in David's special thirty warriors (2 Sam. 23:6). *2.* Levite descended from Merari (1 Chron. 6:46). *3.* Ancestor of Uthai of tribe of Judah who was among first Israelites to return to Palestine from Babylonian Exile about 537 B.C. (1 Chron. 9:4). *4.* Original ancestor of clan of whom 642 returned from Babylonian Exile with Zerubbabel about 537 B.C. (Ezra 2:10). Nehemiah 7:15 spells the name Binnui and says 648 returned. Same clan apparently had members who had married foreign wives and agreed to divorce them to avoid bringing religious temptation to the covenant community (Ezra 10:29,34,38). *5.* Father of Rehum, a Levite who helped Nehemiah repair the wall of Jerusalem (Neh. 3:17). May be same man who helped Ezra interpret the law to the people (Neh. 8:7), led the worship service of repentance leading to Nehemiah's covenant to obey God's law (Neh. 9:4–5; a second Bani was also involved here), sealed Nehemiah's covenant along with the second Bani (Neh. 10:13–14). His son Uzzi was overseer of the Levites (Neh. 12:22).

BANKING Ancient Israel had no lending institutions or banks in the modern sense. Commercial transactions and the lending of credit were entirely in the hands of private individuals, landowners, and merchants. Contemporary cultures in Mesopotamia lent money or produced at interest (in some cases as much as $33\frac{1}{3}$ percent per annum). The temptation among the Israelites to do this was suppressed by laws forbidding the charging of interest on loans (Ex. 22:25; Lev. 25:36–37; Ezek. 18:8). According to these statutes, only foreigners could be charged interest on a debt (Deut. 23:20).

Pledges were sometimes required to guarantee a loan (Gen. 38:17), but essential items, like a cloak, could not be kept past nightfall (Deut. 24:12; Amos 2:8). A strict protocol of debt collection was also to be followed with the lender forbidden to enter the home of the debtor to "fetch his pledge" (Deut. 24:10–11). In periods of famine or high taxation a man might mortgage his home and fields, pledging his labor as a debt-slave or the labor of his family to satisfy the loan (Neh. 5:1–5; Ps. 119:11). Abuse of this system occurred often enough that the prophets condemned it (Neh. 5:6–13; Ezek. 22:12), Proverbs called it folly (17:18; 22:26).

The widespread introduction of coined money after 500 B.C. and the expansion of travel and commerce in the Roman empire aided the establishment of banking institutions in the New Testament period. Money lending (Gk. *trapezítēs,* from the table *trápeza* where business was conducted) was a common and acceptable activity in the cities. Jesus' parables of the talents (Matt. 25:14–30) and the pounds (Luke 19:11–27) lend credence to the practice of giving sums to the bankers to invest or to draw interest. The older custom of burying one's money for safe keeping (Josh. 7:21) Jesus condemned as "wicked and slothful" (Matt. 25:25–27).

Some who were involved in finance, however, took advantage of the large number of currencies in circulation in Palestine. Farmers and merchants came to them to weigh coinage and exchange it for the Tyrian drachma favored in the city. The regulations regarding the Temple tax in Jerusalem also worked in the financiers' favor. The "moneychangers," known as *kollybistēs,* charged a fee of 12 grains of silver (a *kóllybos*) and set up their tables in the Court of the Gentiles. They exchanged foreign currency for the silver didrachma required by the law (Matt. 17:24). Jesus' cleansing of the Temple may have been in part a response to the unfair practices of these money-changers (Matt. 21:12–13; Mark 11:15–17; John 2:14–16).

With sums coming into the Temple from Jews throughout the empire, the Temple itself became a bank, lending money to finance business, construction, and other programs. Pilate raised a storm of protest when he tapped one of the Temple funds (*Qorban*), which was to be used exclusively for religious purposes, to build an aqueduct. After the destruction of the Temple in A.D. 70, the Roman emperor Vespasian ordered the continued payment of the tax and its deposit in the Temple of Jupiter.

Victor H. Matthews

BANNER was a sign carried to give a group a rallying point. Hebrew terms translated with the English word *banner* are "*degel*" and "*nes.*" A third term, "*oth* ("sign")," seems related to these, as "*degel*" and "*oth*" appear in the same verse (Num. 2:2), "Every man of the children of Israel shall pitch by his own standard ("degel"), with the ensign ("oth") of their father's house . . .". The terms may describe two different banners, or the terms may be in parallel, expressing the same thing in different words.

A banner was usually a flag or a carved figure of an animal, bird, or reptile. It may have been molded from bronze, as was the serpent in Numbers 21:8–9. Each tribe of Israel may have had some such animal figures as their standard, or banner. The banner was used as a rallying point for groups with a common interest, such as a call for an army to assemble, or as a signal that a battle was to begin. When the Israelites left Sinai for the land of Canaan, they marched under the banner of four major tribes: Judah, Reuben, Ephraim, and

Dan (Num. 10). The prophet Isaiah used the term in reference to a signal God would raise against Babylon as a warning of impending destruction (Isa. 13:2). In Isaiah 49:22 God's upraised hand is a signal ("*nes*") for the nations to bring the sons of the exiles home to the land of Canaan. The practice of using banners, or standards, was widespread in ancient times in many cultures and lands. Israel probably borrowed the custom from her neighbors.   *Bryce Sandlin*

BANQUET An elaborate meal, sometimes called a feast. In the Old Testament and New Testament, banquets and feasts are prominent in sealing friendships, celebrating victories, and for other joyous occasions (Dan. 5:1; Luke 15:22–24). The idea of hospitality ran deep in the thought of those in the Near East (Gen. 18:1–8; Luke 11:5–8).

Most banquets were held in the evening after the day's work. Usually only men were invited. The women served the food when no servant was present. Hosts sent invitations (Matt. 22:3–4) and sometimes made elaborate preparations for the guests. Those who dined reclined on bed-like seats and lay at right angles to the table. Even though our English translations usually speak of "sitting down" at a meal, the Greek actually means "recline" (Mark 6:39; Luke 12:37).

Typical foods served at banquets were fish, bread, olives, various kinds of vegetables, cheeses, honey, dates, and figs. Beef or lamb was used only by the rich or on special occasions (Mark 14:12; Luke 15:23). Wine was also an important part of the feasts, so that they were sometimes called "a house of drinking" in the Hebrew (KJV, "banqueting house," Song of Sol. 2:4) or "drinkings" in the Greek (KJV, "banquetings," 1 Pet. 4:3).

Some "seats" at the banquet table were preferred over others (Mark 10:37; Luke 14:7–11; John 13:23). In Luke 14:8–10, Jesus referred to these "lowest" and "highest" places. He often used banquets and feasts to present His message to various people (Matt. 9:9–10; Mark 14:1–9; Luke 7:36–50; 19:1–6; John 2:1–11; 12:1–8).

The image of the feast as an occasion of celebrating victory is seen in Jesus' reference to the messianic banquet (Matt. 8:11; Luke 13:29). Also in the Book of Revelation, the final victory day is described in terms of a "marriage supper of the Lamb" of God (Rev. 19:9).   *W. Thomas Sawyer*

BAPTISM The immersion or dipping of a believer in water symbolizing the complete renewal and change in the believer's life and testifying to the death, burial, and resurrection of Jesus Christ as the way of salvation.
Jewish Background As with most Christian practices and beliefs, the background of baptism lies in practices of the Jewish community. The Greek word *baptízo,* "immerse, dip, submerge" is used

metaphorically in Isaiah 21:4 to mean, "go down, perish" and in 2 Kings 5:14 for Naaman's dipping in the Jordan River seven times for cleansing from his skin disease. The radical Qumran sect which produced the Dead Sea Scrolls attempted to cleanse Judaism. The sect laid great emphasis on purity and purifying rites. These rites normally involved immersion, though the term *baptízo* does not seem to appear in their writings. It is quite possible that such a rite was used to initiate members into the community. Along with the rite, the Essenes at Qumran emphasized repentance and submission to God's will.

At some point close to the time of Jesus, Judaism began a heavy emphasis on ritual washings to cleanse from impurity. This goes back to priestly baths prior to offering sacrifices (Lev. 16:4,24). Probably shortly prior to the time of Jesus or contemporary with Him, Jews began baptizing Gentile converts, though circumcision still remained the primary entrance rite into Judaism.

John's Baptism John the Baptist immersed repen-

tant sinners: those who had a change of mind and heart (John 1:6,11). John's baptism—for Jews and Gentiles—involved the same elements later interpreted in Christian baptism: repentance, confession, evidence of changed lives, coming judgment, and the coming of the kingdom of God through the Messiah, who would baptize with the Spirit and with fire (Matt. 3:11). John thus formed a purified community waiting for God's great salvation.

Jesus' Baptism John also baptized Jesus, who never sinned (Matt. 3:13–17; John 1:13–16). Jesus said that His own baptism was to fulfill all righteousness (Matt. 3:15). Thus Jesus acknowledged that the standard of life John demanded was correct for Himself and for His followers. In this way He was able to identify with sinful mankind and to be a model for others to follow. In this way Jesus affirmed John and his message. The coming of the Spirit and the voice from heaven showed that Jesus represented another point in God's revelation of Himself and formed the connection between baptism and Christ's act of redemption.

Christian Baptism John's baptism prepared repentant sinners to receive Jesus' baptism of the Holy Spirit and of fire. (Note that Jesus did not do the

Ancient Byzantine baptistry at Avdat, Israel, showing the importance given baptism by the early church.

water baptizing; His disciples did—John 4:1–2.) Jesus' baptism and the baptizing by His disciples thus connected baptism closely with the Holy Spirit. When Jesus comes into a life, the Holy Spirit comes with His saturating presence and purifies. He empowers and cleanses the believer in a spiritual baptism. The main differences between John's baptism and Jesus' baptism lie in the personal commitment to Christ and the coming of the Holy Spirit in Jesus' baptism (John 1:33).

A thorough study of the Holy Spirit is helpful to understand what "baptism with the Holy Spirit" means (John 1:33). The sequence of baptism and the coming of the Spirit into individual lives will show some differences (Acts 8:12–17). The usual sequence of events is: the Spirit comes into a person's life at conversion, and then the believer is baptized. The Holy Spirit is the gift who comes with salvation (Acts 2:38) and is its seal (Eph. 4:30). The Holy Spirit saturates the new Christian's life. Or we might say that Jesus baptizes the new Christian by plunging the person into the Holy Spirit's presence and power (John 14:16–17; Acts 11:15–16).

To be baptized is to clothe oneself with Christ (Gal. 3:27 NRSV, NIV). Baptism refers to the suffering and death of Christ (Mark 10:38–39; Luke 12:50). Christian baptism is in a sense a sharing of this death and resurrection and all that brought Christ to those events (Rom. 6:1–7; Col. 2:12). Baptism shows that a person has died to the old way of life and has been raised to a new kind of life—eternal life in Christ (Matt. 28:19–20; Col. 3:1; 2 Tim. 2:11). The resurrection from the water points to the Christian's resurrection also (Rom. 6:1–6).

Believers' Baptism In the New Testament baptism is for believers (Acts 2:38; 8:12–13,36–38; Eph. 4:5). Water apart from personal commitment to Christ makes no difference in the life of anyone. In the New Testament baptism occurs when a person trusts Christ as Lord and Savior and obeys the command to be submerged in water and raised from it as a picture of the salvation experience that has occurred. Baptism comes after conviction of sin, repentance of sin, confession of Christ as Lord and Savior. To be baptized is to preach a personal testimony through the symbol of baptism. Baptism testifies that "ye are washed . . . ye are sanctified . . . ye are justified in the name of the Lord Jesus, and by the Spirit of our God" (1 Cor. 6:11).

Church Practice The church has attempted to build its practice upon that of the New Testament but has not found agreement always as to what the practice was. Several church groups practice the baptism of infants. This necessarily moves away from immersion to sprinkling as the mode. See *Infant Baptism.*

The setting of baptism is often restricted to a church setting with an ordained person. In the

New Testament baptism takes place in varied settings wherever there is another person to do the baptizing (Acts 8:36–39; 9:18; 10:47–48). Both Jesus and Paul let others do the baptizing, so that the restriction of baptism to a leading professional minister does not seem to be the New Testament practice.

Rebaptism Scriptural baptism (baptism because of belief in Christ) occurs once. Sometimes people are baptized again because they feel they were not saved when they were first baptized. If that was the case, the first baptism simply wasn't scriptural baptism. Others are baptized because something changes in their beliefs—other than their salvation experience—and they either want to be or are urged by someone else to be rebaptized. The purpose of baptism was never to affirm each change in beliefs. For example, Apollos got his understanding corrected, but no mention is made of his rebaptism (Acts 18:24–28). The disciples grew spiritually and changed in understandings, but no mention is made of their rebaptism. Christians are to become learners along with their baptism, but no mention is made of any need to rebaptize them if they were scripturally baptized the first time. Rebaptism in the New Testament seemingly occurred only when a group of people never had received the Holy Spirit, who is the seal of salvation (Eph. 4:30; see also Acts 1:4–5; 2:38,41; 8:12–13,36–39). Although the dozen people focused on in Acts 19:1–7 had John's baptism, they were then properly scripturally baptized as they trusted in Jesus and received the promised Holy Spirit.

Baptism and Salvation Baptism is not a requirement of salvation, but it is a requirement of obedience. Baptism is a first step of discipleship. Although all meanings of baptism are significant, the one that most often comes to mind is water baptism as a picture of having come to know Christ as Lord and Savior. Baptism is never the event but, rather, the picture of the event. So the pattern of obedience is to come to Christ in trust and then to picture that through the symbol of baptism.

Johnnie Godwin

BAPTISM FOR THE DEAD Some Christians at Corinth denied the resurrection of the dead (1 Cor. 15:12). Paul saw that as a serious error. If there is no resurrection from the dead, then Christ was not raised, there can be no salvation, and Paul's preaching and the Corinthians' faith would all be in vain. Thus Paul argued in 1 Corinthians 15 for the reality of the resurrection of the dead. As part of his argument he mentioned a practice of some of the people at Corinth—that is, the practice of baptizing "for the dead" (1 Cor. 15:29). Two things are important to note here. First, we are not sure exactly what is entailed in the practice of baptizing for the dead. Chrysostom (an early church father) explained the practice of an early Christian group of hiding a living person under the bier of a dead person. The corpse would be approached and asked if he would like to be baptized. The person hiding underneath would answer in behalf of the corpse that he desired baptism. The living person would then be baptized for the dead one. It is possible that something along this line was being practiced in Corinth.

Second, Paul was not advocating the practice of baptizing for the dead. Paul was pointing to the inconsistency in the thought of the Corinthians in trying to convince them of the reality of the resurrection of the dead. The argument seems to be: "If, as some of you Corinthians claim, there is no resurrection from the dead, then why do you go to the trouble of baptizing for the dead? Only those who hope for life after death would attempt to influence the eternal fate of those who have died. Your thinking on the subject is contradictory. You claim there is no resurrection, but your actions betray that you really believe there is something beyond this life."

Other Bible students think the Corinthians believed life in the Spirit made the body unnecessary. Baptism for the dead in this view ensured the dead would enjoy the same spiritual life as would the living but without a body.

Phil Logan

BAPTISM OF FIRE The phrase, "He shall baptize you with the Holy Ghost, and with fire," occurs twice in the New Testament (Matt. 3:11; Luke 3:16). To be baptized with fire is certainly not to be taken literally (as some in the history of the church have taken it).

Fire is one of the physical manifestations of God's presence. This is illustrated several times in the Bible: the making of the covenant with Abraham (Gen. 15:17), the appearance in the burning bush (Ex. 3:2), God leading the Israelites by a pillar of fire by night (Ex. 13:21–22; 14:24; Num. 9:15–16; 14:14; etc.), His appearance on Mount Sinai (Ex. 19:18; 24:17; Deut. 4:11–36; 5:4–26; etc.), and others (1 Kings 18:24,38; 1 Chron. 21:26; 2 Chron. 7:1,3).

Fire was used symbolically in Israel's worship to represent God's constant presence with Israel (Lev. 6:12–13). God's presence as fire represented both judgment and purification (the words purify and purge come from the Greek word for fire). To be in God's presence is to be in the presence of absolute holiness where no sin or unrighteousness can stand. To be in the presence of God is to have the overwhelming sense of one's uncleanness and the overwhelming desire to be clean (see Isa. 6:1–6). God is able to judge and destroy the sin and purify the repentant sinner.

The Holy Spirit is the gift Jesus gave His disciples (John 20:22) and is the presence of God at work in the life of the believer and in the world.

Because the Holy Spirit is God's presence in the life of the believer and in the world, the believer and "the world" are made aware of sin and God's judgment on sin and of the necessity of being righteous in God's presence (John 16:8). The presence of God's Spirit brings the overwhelming sense of one's uncleanness and the overwhelming desire to be clean.

The statement "He shall baptize you with the Holy Ghost, and with fire," means that Jesus had and has the ability to immerse (baptize) people in the presence of God so that they are aware of their sin and the need they have to be cleansed of that sin. To be baptized with the Holy Spirit and fire is to be convicted concerning sin and righteousness and judgment (John 16:8).

To be baptized with the Holy Spirit has a wider application than this; but when the Holy Spirit is coupled with fire (as in the phrase in Matt. 3:11; Luke 3:16), the particular aspect of the Holy Spirit's work as described here is in view. See *Baptism of the Holy Spirit; Holy Spirit* for a more complete view of the work of the Holy Spirit.

Phil Logan

BAPTISM OF THE HOLY SPIRIT Ever since the days of Joel, God's people have looked for the pouring out of God's Spirit (Joel 2:28–32). The Gospels and Acts speak of a baptism of the Holy Spirit (Mark 1:8; John 1:33; 7:37–39; Acts 1:5; see Matt. 3:11; Luke 3:16. See *Baptism of Fire* for one specific aspect of being baptized with the Spirit). The Book of Acts shows the fulfillment of this promise (Acts 2:3–4,16–21; compare 10:44 with 11:16). But what does it mean to be "baptized with the Holy Spirit"?

Being baptized in the Holy Spirit means being immersed (baptized) in the presence and being of God. One immersed in the presence of God is made aware of his or her sinfulness and desires cleansing and purification (John 16:8; see *Baptism of Fire*). The result of this cleansing is life in the true sense of the word (see *Eternal Life; Life*).

One baptized with the Holy Spirit is also empowered to do works of ministry (Luke 24:49; Acts 1:8). The ministry for which empowerment comes included witnessing (Acts 1:8; see John 15:26–27) and working miracles (John 14:12; Acts 3:4–10; 5:12). As part of the empowerment for ministry, believers are given the necessary spiritual gifts (Rom. 12:4–8; 1 Cor. 12:1—14:40; Eph. 4:1–16; 1 Tim. 4:16; 1 Pet. 4:10–11) and knowledge and guidance (John 14:26; 16:13).

Phil Logan

BAPTIST See *John the Baptist.*

BAR Aramaic translation of the Hebrew word, "ben." Both words mean "son of." Bar is often used in the New Testament as a prefix for names of men telling whose son they were: Barabbas

(Matt. 27:16–26), Bar-Jesus (Acts 13:6), Bar-Jona (Matt. 16:17), Barnabas (Acts 4:36; 9:27; etc.), Barsabas (Acts 1:23; 15:22), Bartholomew (Matt. 10:3; Acts 1:13), and Bartimaeus (Mark 10:46). See *Ben.*

BARABBAS (Bà·ràb′ bàs) A murderer and insurrectionist held in custody at the time of the trial of Jesus (Mark 15:17). All four Gospels record that when Pilate offered to release Jesus, the assembled crowd demanded the release of Barabbas instead. Pilate gave in to the demand, ordered Jesus crucified, and set Barabbas free. Nothing is known of his subsequent history.

According to Origen, supported by a relatively small number of late manuscripts at Matthew 27:16, Barabbas was named "Jesus Barabbas." Though not well attested, the reading is possible. If it is correct, Pilate's question to the crowd in Matthew 27:17 would have added poignancy. See *Christ; Cross; Crucifixion.*

BARACHEL (Bär′ à·chĕl) Personal name meaning, "God blessed." Father of Job's friend Elihu (Job 32:2).

BARACHIAH (Bär′ à·chī′ äh) NRSV spelling of Berechiah in New Testament. See *Berechiah.*

BARACHIAS (Bĭ·à·chi′ ăs) KJV spelling of Berechiah in New Testament. See *Berechiah.*

BARAK (Bā′ răk) The son of Abinoam whom the prophetess Deborah summoned to assume military leadership of the Israelites in a campaign against Canaanite forces under the command of Sisera (Judges 4:6). Barak mustered Zebulunite and Naphtalite troops and set out to engage the Canaanites in battle near Mt. Tabor. Though the Canaanites were routed, Sisera escaped. He was subsequently killed by Jael, the wife of Heber the Kenite. In 1 Samuel 12:11, where he is called Bedan, Barak is mentioned as one who delivered the Israelites from their enemies. See *Judges.*

BARAKEL (Bär′ à·kĕl) NIV, TEV spelling of *Barachel.* See *Barachel.*

BARBARIAN The term originally referred to stammering, stuttering, or any form of unintelligible sounds. Even the repeated syllable "bar-bar" mimics this. The term "barbarian" came to be synonymous with "foreigner," one who did not speak Greek, or one who was not a Greek. The Septuagint or earliest Greek translation translated Psalm 114:1 using barbarian for "a people of strange language." In the New Testament, barbarian occurs six times. Paul uses the term twice in 1 Corinthians 14:11 where he deals with the problem of unintelligible speech in the church. The more common use of "barbarian" seems related to

those who spoke a foreign language, especially other than Greek. Paul's description of the islanders of Melita (Acts 28:2,4) as barbarians meant only that they did not speak Greek. With the rise of the Greek empire there was the tendency to include all who were not privy to this language and culture as barbarians. Thus, Paul makes the distinction between Greek and non-Greek in Romans 1:14. Also in Colossians 3:11, "Barbarians" are distinguished from the Greeks. As the Romans came to power and absorbed the Greek culture, they removed themselves from barbarian classification. The term came to be a reproach during the Persian wars and in time was associated with those who were crude and contemptible. See *Gentile; Greeks; Hellenist.*   *C. Kenny Cooper*

BARHUMITE (Bär·hū′ mīte) Variant Hebrew spelling for Baharumite. See *Bahurim.*

BAR-JESUS (Bär·jē′ sŭs) A Jewish magician and false prophet at Paphos (Acts 13:6). Paul the apostle denounced him, and he was struck blind. In Acts 13:8, he is called Elymas.

BAR-JONA (Bär·jō′ nà) The surname of Simon Peter (Matt. 16:17). The meaning is "son of John."

BAR-KOCHBA (Bär·Kōchbà) Bar-Kochba means "son of the star" and was the title given by Jewish rebels to Simeon bar Kosevah, the leader of their revolt in A.D. 132–135. The title designated him as the Messiah (Num. 24:17). The revolt erupted because the Roman Emperor Hadrian had begun to rebuild Jerusalem as a pagan city with plans to replace the ruined Jewish Temple with one dedicated to Jupiter. Circumcision was also forbidden. At first, the Jews prepared for war secretly. When Hadrian left Syria, they openly revolted. By using guerrilla tactics, they were able to overpower the Roman forces and liberate Jerusalem in A.D. 132. Bar-Kochba was the civil leader of the people, and Eleazar was the high priest. Their initial success led to such widespread rebellion that even some Gentiles and Samaritans joined them. Hadrian had to recall Severus from Britain to suppress them. It was a long and costly war for the Romans. Severus avoided direct confrontation, weakening the rebels instead by capturing them in small groups, cutting supply lines, besieging fortresses, and starving them. Bar-Kochba made his last stand at Betar, where most of the remaining insurgents died in 135. Some retreated to caves in the Judean desert and had to be starved to death.

Ricky L. Johnson

BARKOS (Bär′ kŏs) Aramaic name possibly meaning, "son of Kos (a god)." The original ancestor of a clan of Nethinim or Temple employees who returned to Jerusalem from Exile in Babylon with Zerubbabel about 537 B.C. (Ezra 2:53).

BARLEY A grain for which Palestine was known (Deut. 8:8). The failure of the barley crop was a disaster (Joel 1:11). Barley was the food of the poor (Lev. 23:22; Ruth 3:15,17; 2 Sam. 17:28; 2 Kings 4:42; 7:1,6,18; 2 Chron. 2:10,15; 27:5; Jer. 41:8). Barley flour was used to make bread (Judg. 7:13; Ezek. 4:12) and was the kind of bread Jesus used to feed the multitude (John 6:9,13). Barley was also used as feed for horses, mules, and donkeys (1 Kings 4:28). There was a spring variety (*Hordeum vulgare*) and a winter variety (*Hordeum hexastichon*).

BARLEY HARVEST The barley harvest (Ruth 2:23) began in late April or early May and preceded the wheat harvest by about two weeks (Ex. 9:31–32). At the beginning of the barley harvest, the first fruits were offered as a consecration of the harvest (Lev. 23:10).

BARN In the Bible, a barn is a storage place for seed (Hag. 2:19) or grain (Matt. 13:30). A full barn is a sign of prosperity (Deut. 28:8; Prov. 3:10; Luke 12:18) while empty barns are signs of calamity of some kind (either drought, war, etc; Joel 1:17). Equivalent to modern granaries or silos.

BARNABAS (Bär′ na·bas) The name Barnabas appears 23 times in Acts and 5 times in Paul's letters and probably means "son of prophecy" or one who prophesies or preaches ("son of exhortation," Acts 4:36).
Barnabas in Acts Barnabas was a Levite and native of the island of Cyprus, named Joseph (Joses), before the disciples called him Barnabas. He sold his property and gave the proceeds to the Jerusalem church (Acts 4:36–37). He introduced Saul of Tarsus to the Jerusalem church (9:26–27). The church chose Barnabas to go to Syrian Antioch to investigate the unrestricted preaching to the Gentiles there. He became the leader to the work and secured Saul as his assistant. They took famine relief to the Jerusalem church (11:19–30). On Paul's "first missionary journey," Barnabas at first seems to have been the leader (chs. 13—14). Paul and Barnabas were sent to Jerusalem to try to settle the questions of how Gentiles could be saved and how Jewish Christians could have fellowship with them (15:1–21). They agreed to go on another missionary journey but separated over whether to take John Mark with them again (15:36–41).
Barnabas in Paul's Letters In Galatians 2:1–10, Paul recalled how he went with Barnabas to Jerusalem and how the apostles approved of their Gentile mission (probably the same event as Acts 15). In Galatians 2:13, however, Paul indicated that on one occasion Barnabas wavered on the issue of full acceptance of Gentile Christians. In 1 Corinthians 9:6, Paul commended Barnabas for following his (Paul's) practice of supporting himself

rather than depending upon the churches. Colossians 4:10 simply states that Mark was Barnabas' cousin.
Barnabas in Later Legend In the third century Clement of Alexandria identified Barnabas as one of the seventy of Luke 10:1; Tertullian referred to him as the author of Hebrews; and the Clementine Recognitions stated he was the Matthias of Acts 1:23,26. All of these are most unlikely. In the second century an epistle bearing Barnabas' name appeared, became quite popular, and even received some consideration for a place in the New Testament. Later an apocryphal Acts of Barnabas and perhaps even a Gospel of Barnabas were circulated. Barnabas had nothing to do with the writing of any of these.   *James A. Brooks*

BARREL KJV translation found in 1 Kings 17:12–16; 18:33. Modern versions translate the same word as "jar." Jars were used for carrying water and storing flour. See *Pottery.*

BARREN, BARRENNESS Term used to describe a woman who is unable to give birth to children: Sarai (Gen. 11:30), Rebekah (Gen. 25:21), Rachel (Gen. 29:31), Manoah's wife (Judg. 13:2), Hannah (1 Sam. 1:5), and Elizabeth (Luke 1:7,36). Also described as "solitary" (Job 3:7), "desolate" (2 Sam. 13:20; Isa. 49:21; 54:1), or "dead, deadness" (Rom. 4:19). Barrenness was considered a curse from God (Gen. 16:2; 20:18; 1 Sam. 1:5), which explains Elizabeth's statement that God had taken away her "reproach among men"—that she was a sinner and cursed by God as evidenced by her barrenness (Luke 1:25). The barrenness of Sarai, Rebekah, and Rachel (the mothers of the Israelite nation) is significant in that their ability to finally bare children is a sign of the grace and favor of God toward His elect people.

BARSABAS (Bär′ sa·bas) (KJV) or **BARSABBAS** Personal name meaning, "son of the Sabbath." *1.* Name given Joseph Justus, candidate not elected when church chose replacement for Judas, the traitor (Acts 1:23). *2.* Last name of Judas, who Jerusalem church chose to go with Paul and Silas to Antioch after the Jerusalem council (Acts 15:22). See *Apostle; Judas; Joseph; Justus.*

BARTHOLOMEW (Bär·thŏl′ ō·mēw) One of the twelve apostles (Mark 3:18). The name Bartholomew means "son of Talmai," and may have been a patronymic, a name derived from that of the father or a paternal ancestor. It occurs in all four lists of the apostles in the New Testament (Matt. 10:2–4; Mark 3:16–19; Luke 6:14–16; Acts 1:13); in each of the Gospels it immediately follows the name of Philip. The name does not occur at all in John's Gospel. In the first chapter of John, however, the account of Philip's call to discipleship is closely related to the call of a person named Nathanael (vv. 43−51). This circumstance has led to the traditional identification of Bartholomew with Nathanael. See *Nathaniel; Apostles; Disciples.*

BARTIMAEUS (Bär·tĭ·maē′ ŭs) or **BARTIMEUS** (KJV) Blind beggar on highway near Jericho who asked Jesus for mercy despite crowd's efforts to silence him. Jesus said his faith had made him whole. Able to see, Bartimaeus followed Jesus (Mark 10:46−52).

BARUCH (Bā′ rŭch) The son of Neriah who served as Jeremiah's scribe and friend. He helped Jeremiah purchase a field from the prophet's cousin Hanameel and used the purchase as a symbol of hope (Jer. 32:12). Baruch, whose name means "blessed," served Jeremiah as an amanuensis or scribe. He appears, moreover, to have had a close personal association with the prophet and to have exercised a significant influence in the ministry of Jeremiah. He wrote down Jeremiah's preaching and read it to the king's counselors who took it to the king. Jehoiakim burned it, but Jeremiah dictated it again (Jer. 36). Jeremiah was even accused of being a mere instrument of Baruch's enmity (Jer. 43:3). The prophet counseled Baruch to place his confidence wholly in the Lord and not to seek great things for himself (Jer. 45). A wide range of later literature was attributed to Baruch in Jewish tradition. See *Jeremiah.*

BARZILLAI (Bär·zĭl′ lā·ī) Personal name meaning, "made of iron." *1.* Man from Gilead east of the Jordan who met David at Mahanaim as he fled from Absalom. Barzillai and others gave needed supplies for David's company (1 Sam. 17:27−29). When David returned to Jerusalem, the eighty-year-old Barzillai accompanied him across the Jordan but refused to go to Jerusalem (1 Sam. 19:31−39). Barzillai may have served as David's host while he stayed east of the Jordan. His sons went to Jerusalem, and the dying David ensured their welfare (1 Kings 2:7). *2.* Father of Adriel whose sons David delivered to the Gibeonites for execution in payment for Saul's inhumane slaying of Gibeonites (1 Sam. 21:8). This Barzillai could be the same as *1.* above. *3.* A priestly clan whose ancestor had married the daughter of *1.* above and taken his name. Some of these priests returned from Exile in Babylon with Zerubbabel about 537 B.C. (Ezra 2:61).

BASEMATH (Băs′ ĕ·măth) Personal name meaning, "balsam." *1.* A Hittite woman whom Esau married, grieving his parents, Isaac and Rebekah (Gen. 26: 34−35; 27:46). Some differences in her name and ancestors appear. In Genesis 28:9, Esau married Mahalath, daughter of Ishmael and sister of Nebajoth. In Genesis 36:3, Basemath is Ishmael's daughter and Nebajoth's sister. Apparently, all three passages refer to the same woman.

How one explains the complexity of names, relationships, and backgrounds is not certain. Some talk of literary sources; others of new names given women at marriage; others of copyists' changes of the text. Reuel, Basemath's son, became father of four clans in Edom (Gen. 36:10,13,17). *2.* Daughter of Solomon who married Ahimaaz, district supervisor providing supplies for the royal court from Naphtali (1 Kings 4:15).

BASHAN (Bā′ shăn) The northernmost region of Palestine east of the Jordan River. Though its precise extent cannot be determined with certainty, it was generally east of the Sea of Galilee. In the time of Moses it was ruled over by a king named Og, whom the Israelite army defeated (Num. 21:33−35). It was assigned to the tribal area of Manasseh (Deut. 3:13; Josh. 13:29−31). Probably on account of its frontier location, it changed hands several times during the course of Israelite history. It was known as a particularly fertile area (Deut. 32:14; Ezek. 39:18). See *Geography of Palestine.*

BASHAN-HAVOTH-JAIR (Bá′ shăn-hā′ vŏth-jáĭr) KJV translation of Havoth-jair. See *Havoth-jair.*

BASHEMATH (Băsh′ ĕ·măth) KJV spelling of Basemath. See *Basemath.*

BASIN (KJV: Bason)—"Basin" and "bowl" are used interchangeably in the Bible to refer to various sizes of wide hollow bowls, cups, and dishes used for domestic or more formal purposes (John 13:5). In Bible times the most common material used to make such instruments was pottery. However, basins were also made of brass (Ex. 27:3), silver (Num. 7:13), and gold (2 Chron. 4:8). The largest basins were usually banquet bowls or mixing bowls for wine, although one of the largest was used in the sacrificial ritual at the great altar of the Temple (Zech. 9:15). Generally, the largest basins were also used as lids for other vessels. The basin used by Jesus to wash the disciples' feet (John 13:5) was of a special sort. The Greek word is found nowhere else in Scripture, but from the context is understood to mean a vessel specifically suited for washing a particular part of the body, such as the hands or the feet, and is therefore used with a definite article, "the basin." See *Sacrifice; Offerings; Laver.*   C. Dale Hill

BASKET Five kinds of baskets are mentioned in the Old Testament. The precise distinctions of size and shape are not clear. Some had handles, others lids, some both, others neither. The most common term always refers to a container for carrying food (Gen. 40:16−18). Another term is used to signify a cage or "bird net" (Amos 8:1−2). A third type basket is the common household utensil used in harvesting grain (Deut. 26:2;

B

28:5). A fourth term refers to a larger basket used for heavy burdens such as clay for bricks or even the heads of the seventy sons of Ahab delivered to Jehu (2 Kings 10:7). The final term was used to describe both the basket (ark) in which Moses was placed as an infant (Ex. 2:3,5) and the ark which Noah built (Gen. 6:14–16). The New Testament uses two words for basket. The smaller basket is referred to in the story of the feeding of the 5000 (Matt. 14:20). The larger basket is mentioned in the feeding of the 4000 (Matt. 15:37). The apostle Paul also used the larger basket as a means of escape over the wall of Damascas (Acts 9:25). It might logically be considered a hamper. See *Ark*.   *C. Dale Hill*

BASMATH (Băs' măth) KJV spelling for Basemath in 1 Kings 4:15. See *Basemath*.

BASON KJV form of basin. See *Basin*.

BASTARD An illegitimate child, but not necessarily a child born out of wedlock. The term could refer to offspring of an incestuous union or of a marriage that was prohibited (Lev. 18:6–20; 20:11–20). Illegitimate children were not permitted to enter the assembly of the Lord (Deut. 23:2). According to Hebrews, those who do not have the discipline of the Lord are illegitimate children (12:8). Also translated as "a mongrel people" (Zech. 9:6 NRSV).

BATH A liquid measure roughly equivalent to five and one half gallons (U.S.). It was used to measure the molten sea in the Temple (1 Kings 7:26,38) as well as oil and wine (2 Chron. 2:10; Ezra 7:22; Isa. 5:10; Ezek. 45:14). The bath was one-tenth of a homer (Ezek. 45:11,14). See *Weights and Measures*.

BATHING The biblical languages make no distinction between washing and bathing primarily because the dry climate of the Middle East prohibited bathing except on special occasions or where there was an available source of water (John 9:7). Therefore, where "bathe" occurs in the biblical

Bathing room in the baths at Roman Herculaneum (modern Italy), showing mosaics and shelves.

The second century Roman baths in the upper Agora at Ephesus.

text, partial bathing is usually intended. However, two notable exceptions are: (1) that of Pharaoh's daughter in the Nile River, (Ex. 2:5), (2) that of Bathsheba on her rooftop, (2 Sam. 11:2). The public baths of the Greek culture were unknown in Palestine before the second century. The chief use of the word has to do with ritual acts of purification (Ex. 30:19–21). It is probably safe to say that the masses of people in both the Old Testament and New Testament had neither the privacy nor the desire for bathing as we know it today. Priests washed clothes, hands, feet, or bodies before approaching the altar for sacrifice. Ceremonial defilement was removed by bathing the body and washing the clothes (Lev. 14:8). During a time of mourning or fasting, the face and clothes were left unwashed (2 Sam. 12:20), a practice forbidden by Jesus (Matt. 6:17). Lambs were washed at shearing time (Song of Sol. 4:2), babies after birth (Ezek. 16:4), and bodies in preparation for burial (Acts 9:37). Sometimes other elements such as wine and milk were used to symbolize washing in a metaphorical sense. According to Josephus, the Essene community practiced daily bathing for ceremonial reasons, a practice which excavations at Qumran appear to confirm. See *Clean; Unclean*.   *C. Dale Hill*

BATH-RABBIM (Băth-răb' bĭm) Place name meaning, "daughter of many." A gate of Heshbon near which were pools of fish. Song of Solomon 7:4 uses its beauty as comparison for the beauty of the beloved lady's eyes. See *Heshbon*.

BATHSHEBA (Băth-shē' bà) The daughter of Eliam and the wife of Uriah the Hittite (2 Sam. 11:3). She was a beautiful woman with whom David the king had an adulterous relationship (2 Sam. 11:4). When David learned that she had become pregnant as a result of the intrigue, he embarked on a course of duplicity that led finally to the violent death of Uriah. David then took Bathsheba as his wife. She became the mother of Solomon and played an important role in ensuring he became king (1 Kings 1:11—2:19). See *David*.

BATHSHUA (Băth′ shū·à) Personal name meaning, "daughter of nobility." *1.* Canaanite wife of Judah and mother of Er, Onan, and Shelah (1 Chron. 2:3 NAS, TEV, NRSV). KJV, NIV read, "daughter of Shua." Genesis 38:2 says her name was Shuah, while Genesis 38:12 calls her daughter of Shuah or Bath-shua. See *Shuah. 2.* Name for Bathsheba in 1 Chronicles 3:5. See *Bathsheba.*

BATS Any of an order (*Chrioptera*) of nocturnal placental flying mammals with forelimbs modified to form wings. Listed among the unclean birds (Lev. 11:19; Deut. 14:18). According to Isaiah 2:20, they are creatures found in dark caves where idols were to be thrown.

BATTALION RSV translation of one-tenth of a Roman legion—about six hundred men. KJV translates "band." When Pilate handed Jesus over to be crucified, the whole battalion assembled together before Jesus (Matt. 27:27; Mark 15:16). This battalion would have been the Second Italian Cohort. See *Cohort.*

BATTERING RAM See *Arms and Armor.*

BATTLE See *Peace and War.*

BATTLE-AX See *Arms and Armor.*

BAVAI (Bā′ vā·ī) (KJV), **BAVVAI** (NAS, TEV, RSV) Government official in Keilah who helped Nehe-

Modern Middle Eastern market on the island of Crete reminiscent of an ancient bazaar.

miah rebuild wall of Jerusalem (1 Chron. 3:18). See *Keilah.* NRSV, NIV read Binnui on basis of 1 Chron. 3:24 and other textual evidence. See *Binnui.*

BAY KJV translation of a term referring to horses in Zechariah 6:3,7. The KJV took the term as referring to the color of the horses. The earliest translators had trouble with the word as do modern versions. Recent interpreters take the Hebrew word as referring to the strength of the horses (NIV, NAS), though NRSV reads "gray" in verse 3 and "steeds" in verse 7, while REB omits the word in verse 3 and emends the text in verse 7.

BAY TREE KJV translation in Psalm 37:35. The Hebrew word (*'ezrah*) means "native" or "indigenous." While the bay tree is native to Palestine, Psalm 37:35 gives no indication of referring to that tree. The NRSV and TEV hardly come closer to a correct translation with cedar tree. NAS, NIV, and REB come closer to the meaning of the Hebrew text when they speak of a tree in its native soil.

BAZAAR A section of a street given over to merchants. Benhadad of Damascus gave Ahab permission to set up bazaars in Damascus as Benhadad's father had done in Samaria (1 Kings 20:34).

BAZLITH (Băz′ lĭth) Personal name meaning, "in the shadow" or "onions." Original ancestor of

clan of Temple employees who returned from Exile in Babylon with Zerubbabel in 537 B.C. (Neh. 7:54). Name is spelled Bazluth in Ezra 2:52, which NIV reads in Nehemiah 7:54.

BAZLUTH (Băz' lŭth) See *Bazlith.*

BDELLIUM Translation of *bedolah,* a word of uncertain meaning. It has been identified as a gum or resin, pearl, or stone. Genesis 2:12 mentions bdellium, gold, and onyx as products of Havilah. Numbers 11:7 likens manna to bdellium in appearance. Terms in other languages using words very similar to *bedolah* favor the identification with a resinous gum. In droplet form, the gum may have the appearance of a pearl or stone.

BEADS RSV translation of a term for articles of gold jewelry (Num. 31:50). The exact identification of these objects is uncertain. They are variously identified as tablets (KJV), armlets, pendants (REB, NRSV), necklaces (TEV, NIV, NAS), and breastplates.

BEALIAH (Bē·à·lī' ah) Personal name meaning, "Yahweh is Lord." Literally, "Yahweh is baal." Soldier who joined David at Ziklag while he fled from Saul and served the Philistines (1 Chron. 12:5).

BEALOTH (Bē' ā·lŏth) Place name meaning, "female Baals" or "ladies." *1.* Town on southern border of tribal territory of Judah (Josh. 15:24). This may be the same as Baalath-beer (19:8). *2.* Region with Asher making up a district to supply food for Solomon's court (1 Kings 4:16). KJV, NIV read, "in Aloth." This could be a common noun meaning, "in the heights." If a town is meant, its location is unknown.

BEANS A leguminous plant (*Faba vulgaris,*) grown in the ancient world as food. The beans mentioned in the Bible (2 Sam. 17:28; Ezek. 4:9) were the horse or broad bean. These beans were sown in the autumn and harvested sometime in mid-April just before the barley and wheat. They were cooked green in the pods or were cooked after being dried. Dried beans were threshed and winnowed like other grains.

BEAR See *Animals.* For the constellation, see *Arcturus.*

BEARD Hair growing on a man's face often excluding the mustache. Ancient Hebrews are often depicted in ancient Near Eastern art with full rounded beards. This is in contrast to Romans and Egyptians who preferred clean shaven faces and to otner desert nomads and others living in Palestine who often clipped or cut their beards (on the latter see Jer. 9:26; 25:23; 49:32). Israelites were forbidden to mar the edges of their beards by cutting them (Lev. 19:27), and priests were forbidden to cut the corners of their beards (Lev. 21:5). To have one's beard shaved was an insult (2 Sam. 10:4–5; Isa. 50:6) or used as a sign by the prophets of coming destruction (Isa. 7:20; 15:2; Jer. 41:5; 48:37; Ezek. 5:1). The regular Hebrew word for "beard" (*zaqan*) also means "old" and was applied to men (Judg. 19:16), slaves (Gen. 24:2), women (Zech. 8:4), and elders (Ex. 19:7). The word translated as "beard" in 2 Sam. 19:24 (*sapam*) probably means "mustache." The same word is also translated "lip" (Lev. 13:45; Ezek. 24:17,22; Mic. 3:7, KJV, NRSV), "[lower part of the] face" (NIV, TEV), "mouth" (Mic. 3:7, NAS, REB), "mustache" (Lev. 13:45; Ezek. 24:17,22, NAS), "upper lip" (Lev. 13:45, REB), and "beard" (Ezek. 24:17,22, REB).

BEAST Several Hebrew and Greek words and phrases are translated as "beast." "Beast" may refer to any animal in distinction from people (Eccl. 3:18–21), reptiles (Gen. 1:24), and sometimes cattle (Gen. 1:30). Beasts were divided into categories of clean and unclean (Lev. 11:1–8), and wild and domesticated (Gen. 1:24; 2:20; Ex. 19:13; 22:10; Num. 3:13; etc.). See *Animals.*

Apocalyptic literature such as Daniel and Revelation utilize beasts of various sorts in their symbolism (see *Apocalyptic*). The Old Testament used "beast" as a symbol for an enemy, and the writers of Daniel and Revelation may have built on that (Ps. 74:19; Jer. 12:9). Daniel saw four great beasts who represented four great kings arise out of the sea (Dan. 7:2–14). These four beasts would threaten God's kingdom, but God's people would prevail over them (Dan. 7:18).

The Book of Revelation speaks of two beasts. The first beast arises out of the sea (Rev. 13:1), is seven headed, and derives its authority from the dragon (Rev. 12:3; 13:4). This beast has several of the characteristics of the four beasts of Daniel 7. The second beast arises out of the earth (Rev. 13:11). It serves the first beast by seeking devotees for it and is referred to as the "false prophet" (Rev. 16:13; 19:20; 20:10). Both the beast and the false prophet persecute the church but are finally judged by Christ (Rev. 19:20; see 2 Thess. 2:6–12). See *Behemoth; Leviathan.*

BEATEN GOLD Thin sheets of gold produced by hammering and used to overlay objects of lesser value. Several objects were overlayed with gold in this manner: the golden shields of Solomon (1 Kings 10:16–17), the lampstands of the tabernacle (Ex. 25:18,31,36; 37:7,22; Num. 8:4), and idols (Isa. 40:19).

BEATEN OIL The highest grade of olive oil produced by crushing ripe olives in a mortar. The second grade of oil was produced by pressing the olives. The third grade of oil was produced by further crushing and pressing the pulp. Beaten oil was used in the lamps of the sanctuary (Ex. 27:20; Lev. 24:2) and with the daily sacrifices (Ex. 29:40; Num. 28:5). Solomon also used beaten oil in his trade with Hiram (1 Kings 5:11).

BEATEN SILVER Thin sheets of silver produced by hammering and used to overlay objects of lesser value such as the wooden core of an idol (Jer. 10:6–10).

BEATING See *Scourging.*

BEATITUDES are the opening sentences of Jesus in the Sermon on the Mount which describe the quality of life of a citizen of the kingdom of God.

The word "Beatitude" comes from a Latin word meaning "happy" or "blessed." Various forms of the word "bless" are used many times in both the Old and New Testaments, but this passage alone is known as the Beatitudes. The Sermon on the Mount (Matt. 5—7) sets forth the spiritual principles of the kingdom of God. They define the character of a child of the King. The Beatitudes are not to be seen as separate blessings for different believers. All the Beatitudes are to be applied and developed in all disciples both now and in the future. The eight Beatitudes have continuity. 1. "The poor in spirit" denotes the fact of sin

Mount of Beatitudes as viewed from the Sea of Galilee. Church of the Beatitudes is in center of photo.

(5:3). 2. "They that mourn" means to repent of sin (5:4). 3. "The meek" describes not the weak, but rather strength that is surrendered to God in a new birth experience (5:5). 4. To "hunger and thirst after righteousness" signifies the strong desire to become more Christ-like (5:6). 5. "The merciful" show an attitude of forgiveness (5:7). 6. "The pure in heart" strive daily for clean living

Church of the Beatitudes on the traditional site of the Sermon on the Mount by the Sea of Galilee.

(5:8). 7. "The peacemakers" exert a calming influence in the storms of life (5:9). 8. "They which are persecuted" denotes faithfulness under stress (5:10–12). Each Beatitude carries with it a strong promise of ultimate good for those who develop the blessed life.   *Lawson Hatfield*

BEAUTIFUL GATE The scene of the healing of a lame man by Peter and John (Acts 3:2,10). Nei-

ther the Old Testament nor other Jewish sources mention a "Beautiful Gate." Christian tradition has identified the gate with the Susa (or Shushan) or Golden Gate on the east side of the Temple leading from outside into the Court of the Gentiles. Modern scholars, however, identify the gate as the one on the east side of the Court of Women leading from the Court of the Gentiles. Others place it east of the Court of the Men. Josephus, a Jewish historian in the first century, described a gate of "Corinthian bronze" outside the sanctuary. Jewish sources refer to this gate as Nicanor's Gate. See *Jerusalem; Temple.*

BEBAI (Bē′ bā-ī) Babylonian personal name meaning, "child." *1.* Original ancestor of clan of whom 623 (Neh. 7:16, 628) returned with Zerubbabel from Exile in Babylon about 537 B.C. (Ezra 2:11). His son, or at least a member of the clan, led 28 men from Babylon to Jerusalem with Ezra (Ezra 8:11). Members of the clan had married foreign wives (Ezra 10:28). *2.* Signer of Nehemiah's covenant to obey God's law (Neh. 10:15).

BECHER (Bē′ chēr) or **BEKER** (NIV) *1.* Personal name meaning, "firstborn" or "young male camel." Son of Benjamin and grandson of Jacob (Gen. 46:21). He had nine sons (1 Chron. 7:8). *2.* Original ancestor of clan in tribe of Ephraim (Num. 26:35). 1 Chronicles 7:20 spells the name Bered.

Bedroom in Herculaneum showing the Roman-style bed and walls originally decorated with frescoes.

BECHERITE (Bē′ chēr-īte) Member of clan of Becher. See *Becher.*

BECHORATH (Bē-chō′ răth) KJV spelling of Becorath. See *Becorath.*

BECORATH (Bē-cō′ răth) Personal name meaning, "firstborn." An ancestor of King Saul (1 Sam. 9:1).

BED, BEDROOM A bed is a place to sleep or rest and may be a simple straw mat or an elaborate frame of wood, metal, stone, or ivory. A bedroom is a designated room designed for sleep or rest.

A bed for the very poor was a mere thin straw mat or cloth pad rolled out on the ground with no more than a stone for a pillow (Gen. 28:10–11; John 5:9) and an outer garment for cover. For the more fortunate poor, a multi-purpose, one room, mud house served as protection from the elements, and as a kitchen, work space, and sleeping quarters. For the very few affluent, households and palaces contained many rooms including kitchens, living rooms, libraries, and bedrooms with elaborately decorated beds (Esther 1:6; Prov. 7:16–17; Amos 6:4). A bed of iron attracted attention (Deut. 3:11). Sometimes the bed was a symbol of both the highest and the lowest moral codes of mankind. The bed is a symbol that there is no secret place secure from deception (2 Kings 6:12). In Isaiah 28:20, the bed that is too short and the cover too narrow is a symbol that there is no escape from judgment. The Scripture teaches

that marriage is honorable among all people, that the marriage bed should be kept undefiled, and that God will judge the adulterer and the sexually immoral (Heb. 13:4; Rev. 2:22).

Lawson Hatfield

BEDAD (Bē′ dăd) Personal name meaning, "scatter," or "be alone." Father of Hadad, king of Edom (Gen. 36:35).

BEDAN (Bē′ dăn) Personal name of uncertain meaning. *1.* Listed as a judge in 1 Samuel 12:11. This is usually seen as work of copyist, but the original reading is uncertain. The closest name of the judges would be Barak (Judg. 4—5). Bedan is a son of Gilead in 1 Chron. 7:17 and could be another name for Jephthah, a son of Gilead (Judg. 11:1). Early Jewish rabbis read *ben-Dan,* "son of Dan" and thought Samson was intended (Judg. 13:2, 24). Others read Abdon (Judg. 12:13–15). NIV, TEV, NRSV read Barak for Bedan. *2.* A descendant of Machir and Manasseh (1 Chron. 7:17).

BEDEIAH (Bē-dē′ iàh) Personal name meaning, "Yahweh alone" or "branch of Yahweh." Man with foreign wife who divorced her under Ezra's leadership to prevent tempting Israel with foreign gods (Ezra 10:35).

BEE See *Insects.*

BEELIADA (Beê-lī′ à-dà) Personal name meaning, "Baal knows" or "the Lord knows." Son of David born in Jerusalem (1 Chron. 14:7). In 2 Samuel 5:16 the Baal part of the name is replaced with "El," a Hebrew word for God, becoming, "Eliada."

BEELZEBUB (Bē-ēl′ zē-bŭb) (KJV, NIV) or **BEEL-ZEBUL** (NAS, TEV, NRSV) Name for Satan in New Testament spelled differently in Greek manuscripts. The term is based on Hebrew Baal-zebub, "lord of the flies." See *Baal-zebub.*

BEER (Bē′ ĕr) Place name meaning, "well." It frequently occurs in compound constructions of place names. For example, Beer-sheba means "well of seven." The generally arid climate of much of Palestine made wells particularly significant locations. *1.* One of the camps of the Israelites during the wilderness wandering (Num. 21:16). *2.* Jotham fled to Beer when he feared his brother Abimelech would kill him (Judg. 9:21). This may be modern Bireh.

BEERA (Bē-ē′ rà) Personal name meaning, "a well." A descendant of the tribe of Asher (1 Chron. 7:37).

BEERAH (Bē-ē′ răh) Personal name meaning, "a well." A leader of the tribe of Reuben taken captive by Tiglath-pileser, king of Assyria, about 732 B.C. (1 Chron. 5:6).

BEER-ELIM (Bē′ ĕr-ē′ lĭm) Place name meaning, "well of the rams, the heroes, the terebinths, or the mighty trees." Place involved in mourning according to Isaiah's lament over Moab (Isa. 15:8). It is probably the same as Beer (Num. 21:16), where Israel sang the song of the well. The location may be in the wadi et-Temed, northeast of Dibon.

BEERI (Bē-ē′ rī) Personal name meaning, "well." *1.* Hittite father of girl Esau married, grieving his parents Isaac and Rebekah (Gen. 26:34–35; 27:46). *2.* Father of Hosea, the prophet (Hos. 1:1).

BEER-LAHAIROI (Bē′ ĕr-là-haî′ roî) Place name meaning, "well of the Living One who sees me." Interpretation of the name and location of the place are difficult. After Sarai had Abraham put Hagar out of the house, an angel appeared to her announcing the birth of a son. Hagar interpreted this as a vision of the living God and named the well where she was, Beer-lahairoi (Gen. 16:14). Isaac passed there as he went to meet and wed Rebekah (Gen. 24:62). Isaac lived there after his father Abraham died (Gen. 25:11).

BEEROTH (Bē-ē′ rŏth) Place name meaning, "wells." *1.* The wells of the sons of Jaakan, where Israel camped in the wilderness (Num. 33:31; Deut. 10:6). *2.* A city of the Gibeonites to which Joshua and his army came to defend the Gibeonites after making a covenant with them (Josh. 9:17). The city was allotted the tribe of Benjamin (Josh. 18:25). Ishbosheth's army captains came from Beeroth (2 Sam. 4:2), whose citizens had fled to Gittaim when Israel, possibly under Saul, conquered Beeroth (2 Sam. 4:3). Compare 2 Samuel 21:1–9 for Saul's dealing with the Gibeonites. Joab's armorbearer, one of David's 30 heroes, came from Beeroth (2 Sam. 23:37). Citizens of Beeroth returned with Zerubbabel from Exile in Babylon about 537 B.C. (Ezra 2:25).

The city had to be close to Gibeon, but its exact location is debated. Among suggestions are: el-Bireh, tell en-Nasbeh, Nebi Samwil, Khirbet el-Burj, Biddu, Khirbet Raddana, ras et-Tahune.

BEEROTH-BENE-JAAKAN (Bē-ē′ rŏth-bē′ nē-jā′ à-kăn) NAS, NRSV translation in Deuteronomy 10:6. See *Beeroth.*

BEER-SHEBA (Bē′ ĕr-shē′ ba) Beer-sheba and its surrounding area factors significantly in the Old Testament from the earliest sojurns of the patriarchs (Gen. 21; 22; 26) to the return of the Hebrew exiles with Nehemiah (Neh. 11:27,30). Since it was an important crossroad to Egypt in the geographic center of the dry, semi-desert region known as the Negeb, Beersheba also served as the administrative center of the region. Settlement of the Beersheba area began before 3000 B.C.

Abraham and a nearby king, Abimelech, swore to protect Abraham's right to the water of this region (Gen. 21:22–33). Abraham then named the place "Beer-sheba," meaning "well of the oath" or preferably "well of the seven," referring to seven lambs involved in the agreement. Here he called on the Lord (Gen. 21:33) and lived for some time (Gen. 22:19). The Lord confirmed His promises with Isaac at Beer-sheba (Gen. 26:23–25), where Isaac renamed his father's well "Shibah." A well is found today outside the ruins of biblical Beer-sheba (Tell es-Saba'), however, it cannot be the patriarchal well since it is dated much later, around the twelfth century. Isaac also lived in the area of Beer-sheba, and his son Jacob left there for Haran to seek a wife (Gen. 28:10). A crossroad to Egypt, Beer-sheba was a stopping place for Jacob many years later when he was encouraged by the Lord to continue on to Egypt where Joseph was awaiting him (Gen. 46:1–5). Because of these patriarchal events at Beer-sheba, it is thought that the city eventually and unfortunately became a pilgrimage destination for idolatry later during the monarchy (Amos 5:5; 8:14).

Joshua gave Beer-sheba to the tribe of Judah (Josh. 15:28), and then to the tribe of Simeon whose territory lay within Judah's boundaries

Excavated storerooms at the site of ancient Beersheba in the Negeb.

(Josh. 19:1,2,9). Samuel's sons Joel and Abiah were unfair judges in Beer-sheba right before the monarchy began with Saul (1 Sam. 8:1–3).

Beer-sheba is mentioned idiomatically twelve times to indicate the northern and southern extremes of Israel, "Dan to Beersheba" (2 Sam. 24:2, 1 Kings 4:25). This type of phrase served to

A well found at Beersheba which may date as early as 13th–14th centuries B.C.

speak of Israel in its entirety and its unity; for instance, in its resolve to punish the tribe of Benjamin (Judg. 20:1) and its recognition of Samuel as a true prophet (1 Sam. 3:20). This idiom also served to show the extent of the reforms of three southern kings: Jehoshaphat (2 Chron. 19:4, "Beer-sheba to mount Ephraim"), Hezekiah (2 Chron. 30:5, "Beer-sheba even to Dan"), and Josiah (2 Kings 23:8, "from Geba to Beer-sheba").

Archaeology has shown Beer-sheba to be the administrative center of the Negeb by uncovering its large commercial storerooms and fortifications which were superior to the lesser cities in the area. The fortifications were inadequate, however, against the Assyrians who sacked the city and left in ruins until the Persian period. After the punitive Exile of Judah, the people returned to Beer-sheba and its surrounding satellite towns with Nehemiah in the fifth century (Neh. 11:27,30).

Various millstones and stone mortars from the area around Beersheba.

As the "gateway to the desert," Beer-sheba was in a precarious place climatically, which is the backdrop of two person's prayers concerning death. Hagar pleads at a distance not to see her son die (Gen. 21:14–16), and Elijah prays for death in the desert rather than at the order of Queen Jezebel (1 Kings 19:3,4).

Daniel C. Fredericks

BEESHTERAH (Bē·ĕsh'tė·räh) Place name meaning, "in Ashtaroth" or representing a contraction of "Beth Ashtaroth," which means, "house of Ashtaroth." Place east of the Jordan from territory of tribe of Manasseh set aside for the Levites (Josh. 21:27). 1 Chronicles 6:71 spells name "Ashtaroth." See *Ashtaroth.*

BEGINNING AND END See *Alpha and Omega.*

BEHEADING See *Crimes and Punishments.*

BEHEMOTH (Bē'hė·mŏth) Animal God created known for enormous strength and toughness. See *Animals; Leviathan.*

BEKA One-half a shekel. The amount contributed

by each Israelite male for the use of the Temple (Ex. 38:26). See *Weights and Measures.*

BEKAH See *Beka.*

BEKER NIV spelling of Becher. See *Becher.*

BEL (Bĕl) Name of Babylonian god, originally as city patron of Nippur, but then as a second name for the high god Marduk of Babylon. Isaiah mocked Babylon by describing their gods burdening down donkeys in procession out of the city into captivity. People did not bow before them. The idols bowed down to get out of the city gates (Isa. 46:1). Similarly, Jeremiah prophesied shame coming on Bel (Jer. 50:2). Bel would have to spit out the nations he had swallowed up (Jer. 51:44). An apocryphal book is called Bel and the Dragon.

BELA (Bē'là) or **BELAH** Personal and place name meaning, "he swallowed." *1.* Name for Zoar. See *Zoar.* Its king joined coalition to fight off attacks from eastern kings (Gen. 14:2). *2.* King of Edom who ruled in city of Dinhabah before Israel had a king (Gen. 36:32). *3.* A son of Benjamin and grandson of Jacob (Gen. 46:21). He became original ancestor of clan of Belaites (Num. 26:38; 1 Chron. 7:7). *4.* A descendant of Reuben (1 Chron. 5:8).

BELAITES Descendants of Bela (Num. 26:38). See *Bela.*

BELIAL (Bē'lĭ·ȧl) The transliteration of a Hebrew common noun meaning, "useless" or "worthless." KJV interprets it as a proper name sixteen times, but modern translations translate it as a common noun, "worthless" or "wicked." It is a term of derision (Deut. 13:13). In Nahum 1:15, where the King James Version translates it as "the wicked," Belial appears to be the name of some specific malevolent power.

In the New Testament the word occurs one time (2 Cor. 6:15). There Paul the apostle declared the mutual irreconcilability of Christ and Belial, who thus appears to be equated with Satan. See *Satan; Antichrist.*

BELIEVE, BELIEF See *Faith.*

BELL A golden object fastened to the garments of the high priest which served as a signal or warning of the high priest's movements (Ex. 28:33–35; 39:25–26).

BELLOWS Instrument that blows air on a fire making it burn hotter. The term is used only in Jeremiah 6:29. God appointed Jeremiah as the assayer of His people to test their purity. God's people remained like impure metal despite the fact that the bellows had blown fiercely on the fire making it hot enough to consume lead. The refining process was in vain; the wicked remained; the people were like refuse silver. The idea of a bellows is alluded to elsewhere in the Bible (See Job 20:26; 41:21; Isa. 54:16; Ezek. 22:20–21). See *Assayer.*

BELOVED DISCIPLE Term used only in John's Gospel to refer to a disciple for whom Jesus had deep feelings. He has been variously identified as Lazarus, an anonymous source or author of the Gospel, an idealized disciple, or John's reference to himself without using his own name. Church tradition and interpretation of biblical evidence appear to point to John. Modestly he declined to put his name on his literary works. For this reason the onetime "son of thunder" referred to himself as the other disciple whom Jesus loved. See *John.*

Lawson Hatfield

BELSHAZZAR (Bĕl·shăz′ zàr; *Bel's prince*) The Babylonian king whose drunken feast was interrupted by the mysterious appearance of the fingers of a human hand that wrote a cryptic message on the palace wall (Dan. 5:1). When the Babylonian seers were unable to interpret the writing, Daniel the Hebrew was called. He interpreted the message for the king, explaining that it meant the kingdom would be taken from Belshazzar and given to the Medes and Persians (Dan. 5:28). According to Daniel 5:30, Belshazzar was slain on the very night of this incident. See *Babylon.*

BELTESHAZZAR (Bĕl·tĕ·shăz′ zàr) Babylonian name meaning, "protect the king's life." Name prince of eunuchs under Nebuchadnezzar, king of Babylon, gave to Daniel (Dan. 1:7). See *Daniel.*

BEN (Bĕn) Hebrew noun meaning, "son of." A Levite who became head of a clan of Temple porters under David (1 Chron. 15:18 NAS, KJV). Other translations follow the Septuagint or earliest Greek translation and some Hebrew manuscripts that omit Ben.

BEN-ABINADAB (Bĕn-á-bĭn′ á-dăb) Personal name meaning, "son of Abinadab." The district supervisor over Dor in charge of provisions for Solomon's court one month a year. He married Solomon's daughter, Taphath (1 Kings 4:11). KJV reads, "son of Abinadab."

BENAIAH (Bē·naî′ ah) Personal name meaning, "Yahweh has built." *1.* Captain of David's professional soldiers (2 Sam. 8:18; 20:23), known for heroic feats such as disarming an Egyptian and killing him with his own sword as well as killing a lion in the snow (2 Sam. 23:20–23). Still he was not among the top three military advisors of David (2 Sam. 20:23). His unquestioned loyalty to David led Adonijah not to include him as he attempted to replace David as king instead of Solomon (1 Kings

1:8–26). He followed David's orders and helped annoint Solomon as king (1 Kings 1:32–47). He became Solomon's executioner (1 Kings 2:25–46) and army commander (1 Kings 4:4). *2.* A. Pirathonite who is listed among the elite warriors of David known as the "thirty" (2 Sam. 23:30). *3.* In 1 Chronicles 4:36, a Simeonite prince who was involved in a defeat of the Amalekites. *4.* In 1 Chronicles 15:18, a Levitical musician involved in the processional when the ark of the covenant was brought to Jerusalem. *5.* In 1 Chronicles 15:24, a priest who sounded a trumpet when the ark was brought to Jerusalem. *6.* In 2 Chronicles 20:14, an Asaphite, the grandfather of Jahaziel. *7.* In 2 Chronicles 31:13, one of the overseers who assisted in the collection of contributions in the house of the Lord during the reign of Hezekiah. *8.* In Ezekiel 11:1, the father of Pelatiah. *9.* In Ezra 10, the name of four Israelite men who put away their foreign wives.

BEN-AMMI (Bĕn-ăm′ mī) Personal name meaning, "son of my people." Son of Lot and his younger daughter after his two daughters despaired of marriage and tricked their father after getting him drunk (Gen. 19:38). Ben-ammi was the original ancestor of the Ammonites. See *Ammon.*

BENCHES KJV translation for the planks of a ship's deck (Ezek. 27:6). Modern translations give the wood of the deck variously: boxwood (NAS); pine (NRSV, TEV), or cypress (NIV, REB). These translations understand the deck to be inlaid with ivory rather than made of ivory as the KJV suggests.

BEN-DEKER (Bĕn-dē′ kēr) Personal name meaning, "son of Deker" or "son of bored through." Solomon's district supervisor in charge of supplying the royal court one month a year. His district bordered the Philistine territory on the west, reached to Aphek in the north, and to Bethshemesh in the south (1 Kings 4:9).

BENE-BERAK (Bĕn′ ė-bē′ răk) Place name meaning, "sons of Barak" or "sons of lightning." City of tribe of Dan (Josh. 19:45). It is located at modern Ibn Ibraq, four miles southeast of Joppa. Sennacherib, king of Assyria, in 701 B.C. claims he conquered Bene-berak.

BENEDICTION A prayer for God's blessing or an affirmation that God's blessing is at hand. The most famous is the priestly benediction (or Aaronic blessing) in Numbers 6:24–25. Most New Testament epistles close with benedictions as well (Rom. 15:13; 16:25–27; 1 Cor. 16:23; 2 Cor. 13:14; Gal. 6:18; Eph. 3:20–21; 6:23–24; Phil. 4:23; 1 Thess. 5:28; 2 Thess. 3:18; 1 Tim. 4:20*b;* 2 Tim. 4:22; Titus 3:15*b;* Philemon 25; Hebrews 13:20–21,25; 1 Pet. 5:14*b;* 2 Pet. 3:18; 3 John 15*a;* Jude 24–25). See *Blessing and Cursing.*

BENEDICTUS Latin word meaning "blessed." The first word in Latin of Zacharias' psalm of praise in Luke 1:68–79 and thus the title of the psalm. See *Magnificat; Nunc Dimittis.*

BENEFACTORS An honorary title bestowed on kings or other prominent people for some meritorious achievement or public service. The title in Greek is *Euergetes* and was held by some of the Hellenistic kings of Egypt. One would not earn the title "benefactor" from service rendered in the kingdom of God. In contrast to the conspicuous work needed to earn the title "benefactor," the members of the kingdom are to devote themselves to humble, obscure, and perhaps menial service (Luke 22:24–27).

BENEJAAKAN (Bĕn´ė·jā´ à·kan) Place name meaning, "sons of Jaakan." Same as Beeroth-bene-jaakan. See *Beeroth-bene-jaakan.*

BEN-GEBER (Bĕn-gē´ bēr) Personal name meaning, "son of Geber" or "son of a hero." Solomon's district supervisor in the towns northeast of the Jordan River around Ramoth-gilead (1 Kings 4:13). He provided supplies for the royal court one month a year. KJV reads, "son of Geber."

BEN-HADAD (Bĕn-hā´ dăd) Personal name or royal title meaning, "son of (the god) Hadad." Biblical references to Israel's interaction with Damascus and other city-states in Syria show the power of the kings of Damascus. The kings either bore a title, "ben-hadad," son of the god, much like Israel's kings seem to have been called "son of God" at their coronation (Ps. 2:7) and as emperors of Rome were called caesars, or Ben-hadad was the personal name of several kings. See *Damascus; Syria.*

BEN-HAIL (Bĕn-hā´ ĭl) Personal name meaning, "son of strength." Official under King Jehoshaphat of Judah (873–848), who sent him to help teach God's law in the cities of Judah (2 Chron. 17:7).

BEN-HANAN (Bĕn-hā´ năn) Personal name meaning, "son of the gracious one." Son of Shimon in lineage of Judah (1 Chron. 4:20).

BEN-HESED (Bĕn-hē´ sĕd) Personal name meaning, "son of mercy." Solomon's district supervisor over the Mediterranean coastal region between Aphek on the south and Hepher. He supplied the royal court one month a year (1 Kings 4:10).

BEN-HINNOM (Bĕn-hĭn´ nŏm) Place name meaning, "son of Hinnom." A valley south of Jerusalem serving as northern border of tribe of Judah (Josh. 15:8) and southern boundary of tribe of Benjamin (Josh. 18:16). Pagan child sacrifices occurred here, some kings of Judah included (Ahaz, 2 Chron. 28:3; Manasseh, 2 Chron. 33:6). Jeremiah announced God's judgment on the valley because of such practices (Jer. 19:1–15). The valley would be renamed, "valley of slaughter" (Jer. 19:6). The sin of the valley gave God reason to bring the Babylonians to destroy Jerusalem (Jer. 32:35). King Josiah defiled and did away with the altars there (2 Kings 23:10). The valley served as the northern boundary of the Judean villages where the returning exiles settled (Neh. 11:30).

BEN-HUR (Bĕn-hûr´) Personal name meaning, "son of a camel" or "son of Horus." Solomon's district supervisor over Mount Ephraim in charge of supplying the royal court one month a year (1 Kings 4:8).

BENINU (Bē-nī´ nū) Personal name meaning, "our son." A Levite who sealed the covenant Nehemiah made to obey God's law (Neh. 10:13).

BENJAMIN (Bĕn´ jà mĭn) Personal name meaning, "son of the right hand" or "son of the south." The second son Rachel bore to Jacob. He became the forefather of the tribe of Benjamin. His birth was difficult, and his mother named him Benoni, which means "son of my sorrow." She died giving him birth. His father Jacob, however, did not let that name stand. He gave the child the name Benjamin.

The tribe of Benjamin occupied the smallest territory of all the tribes. Yet, it played a significant role in Israelite history. Saul, Israel's first king, was a Benjamite. Furthermore, the city of Jerusalem was near the border between the territories of Benjamin and Judah and may have been in Benjamin originally (Josh. 18:16; Judg. 1:21). Benjamin's appetite for territory may be seen in Jacob's blessing (Gen. 49:27). Moses' blessing highlights Benjamin's special place in God's care (Deut. 33:12). Late in the period of the judges, Benjamin almost disappeared from history when they mistreated a Levite and his concubine (Judg. 19—21).

In the New Testament, the apostle Paul proudly proclaimed his heritage in the tribe of Benjamin (Rom. 11:1; Phil. 3:5). See *Tribes of Israel; Patriarchs.*

BENJAMIN GATE A gate of Jerusalem (Jer. 37:13; 38:7). Identified by some with Nehemiah's Sheep Gate or with the Muster Gate, it could indicate gate which led to tribal territory of Benjamin. See *Jerusalem.*

BENO (Bē´ nō) Proper name meaning, "his son." A Levite under David (1 Chron. 24:26–27).

BENONI (Bĕn ō´ nī) Personal name meaning, "son of my sorrow." See *Benjamin.*

BEN-ZOHETH (Bĕn-zō' hĕth) Personal name meaning, "son of Zoheth." Son of Ishi in the tribe of Judah (1 Chron. 4:20).

BEON (Bē' ŏn) Place name of uncertain meaning. Probably a copyist's change from original Meon (Num. 32:3), a short form of Beth-meon or Beth-baal-meon. See *Beth-baal-meon.*

BEOR (Bē' ôr) Proper name meaning, "burning." *1.* Father of Bela, king of Edom centered in Dinhabah, before Israel had a king (Gen. 36:32). *2.* Father of prophet Balaam (Num. 22:5). See *Balaam.*

BERA (Bē' rà) Personal name perhaps meaning, "with evil" or "victory." King of Sodom in days of Abraham and Lot (Gen. 14:2). He joined coalition of local kings against group of invading eastern kings.

BERACAH (Bĕr' à·căh) Personal name meaning, "blessing." *1.* Skilled soldier able to use right or left hand with slingshot and with bow and arrows. He joined David's band in Ziklag, when David fled from Saul and joined the Philistines (1 Chron. 12:3). *2.* Valley where King Jehoshaphat of Judah (873–848 B.C.) and his people blessed God after He provided miraculous victory over Ammon, Moab, and Edom (2 Chron. 20:26). A valley near Tekoa and a modern village retain the name: wadi Berekut and khirbet Berekut.

BERACHAH (Bĕr' à·chäh) KJV spelling of Bĕracah. See *Beracah.*

BERACHIAH (Bĕr·à·chī' äh) KJV spelling for Berechiah in 1 Chronicles 6:39. See *Berechiah.*

BERAIAH (Bĕ·raî' äh) Personal name meaning, "Yahweh created." A descendant of the tribe of Benjamin (1 Chron. 8:21).

BERAKIAH (Bĕr·à·kī' ah) NIV New Testament spelling of Berechiah in Matthew 23:35. See *Berechiah.*

BEREA (Bĕ·rē' à) Place name meaning, "place of many waters." City in Macedonia to which Paul escaped after the Jews of Thessalonica rioted (Acts 17:10). See *Macedonia.*

BERECHIAH (Bĕr·ē·chī' äh) Personal name meaning, "Yahweh blessed." *1.* A descendant of David in period after Jews returned from Exile in Babylon (1 Chron. 3:20). *2.* Father of Asaph (1 Chron. 6:39). See *Asaph.* *3.* A leader of the Levites after the return from Exile who lived around the city of Netophah (1 Chron. 9:16). *4.* A Levite in charge of the ark when David moved it to Jerusalem (1 Chron. 15:23). He could be identical with *2.* above. *5.* A leader of the tribe of Ephraim who

rescued prisoners of war Pekah, king of Israel (752–732), had taken from Ahaz, king of Judah (735–715) (2 Chron. 28:12). *6.* Father of Meshullam, who repaired the wall with Nehemiah (Neh. 3:4). His family was tied in marriage to Tobiah, Nehemiah's enemy (Neh. 6:17–19). *7.* Father of the prophet Zechariah (Zech. 1:1; Matt. 23:35).

BERED (Be' rĕd) Personal name meaning, "cool." *1.* Place used by Bible to locate Beer-lahai-roi (Gen. 16:14), but a place that cannot be located today. *2.* A son of Ephraim (1 Chron. 7:20). Numbers 26:35 spells the name Becher.

BERI (Bē' rī) Personal name of unknown meaning. A descendant of Asher (1 Chron. 7:36). Many Bible students think a copyist has changed original text which may have read, *bene* (sons of).

BERIAH (Bĕ·rī' äh) Personal name meaning, "Yahweh created." *1.* Son of Asher and grandson of Jacob (Gen. 46:17). He thus became original ancestor of clan of Beriites (Num. 26:44). *2.* Son of Ephraim born after his sons Ezer and Elead died in battle against Gath. Beraiah's name is explained here not as a compound of *bara'* + *Yah* (*Yahweh created*) but as a compound of *b* + *ra'ah* (*with evil*). His daughters built the two cities named Beth-horon (1 Chron. 7:20–25). *3.* A clan leader of the tribe of Benjamin in the area of Ajalon. He helped drive out the inhabitants of Gath (1 Chron. 8:13). 4. A Levite under King David (1 Chron. 23:10).

BERIITE (Bĕ·rī' īte) Member of clan descended from Beriah. See *Beriah.*

BERITE (Bē' rīte) Word of unknown meaning (2 Sam. 20:14). Some Bible students think original text read Bichrites, referring to clan to which Sheba, son of Bichri belonged (2 Sam. 20:13). See TEV, NRSV. Some would identify the Berites as residents of a town called Biria in northern Palestine.

BERITH (Bē' rīth) Hebrew word meaning, "covenant." See *Baal-berith; Covenant.*

BERNICE (Bĕr nī' cĕ; *gift*) The companion of Herod Agrippa II (Acts 25:13). She was the daughter of Herod Agrippa I, born probably about A.D. 28. Prior to her appearance in Acts, she had been married first to a person named Marcus, then to her own uncle Herod. Two sons were born as a result of the latter union before Bernice was widowed in A.D. 48. In the following years, an incestuous relationship is suggested between Agrippa II and her. Later she was married again, to Polemo, the king of Cilicia. According to the Roman historian Tacitus, she was also the mistress of the Roman emperor Titus. See *Herod.*

BERODACH BALADAN (Bê·rō′ dăch Băl′ á·dăn) King of Babylon who wrote Hezekiah, king of Judah (2 Kings 20:12). Parallel passage in Isaiah 39:1 reads Merodoch Baladan, so most Bible students think Berodach resulted from a copyist's change in the text. Compare NIV, TEV, NRSV. See *Merodach Baladan.*

BEROEA (Bê·rōe′ á) NRSV spelling of Berea. See *Berea.*

BEROTHAH (Bê·rō′ thăh) Place name meaning, "wells." Northern border town in Ezekiel's vision of restored Promised Land (Ezek. 47:16). It may be located east of the Jordan River about seven miles south of Baalbeck at Bereiten. See *Berothai.*

BEROTHAI (Bē·rō′ thaî) Place name meaning, "wells." City in Syria from which David took brass as tribute after he defeated King Hadadezer (2 Sam. 8:8). The parallel passage (1 Chron. 18:8) reads Chun or Cun and says Solomon used the brass for Temple vessels. The exact relationship of Berothah, Berothai, and Cun cannot be determined. The three are usually identified as the same place, but some Bible students dispute this. At the date when Chronicles was written, Cun may have been better known than nearby Berothai. See *Cun.*

BEROTHITE (Bē′ rŏth·īte) Person from Beeroth (1 Chron. 11:39). See *Beeroth.*

BERYL (Bē′ rўl) A light green precious stone closely related to emeralds and aquamarines. See *Minerals and Metals.*

BESAI (Bē′ saî) Personal name of unknown meaning. A clan of Temple employees who returned from Exile in Babylon with Zerubbabel about 537 B.C. (Ezra 2:49).

BESODEIAH (Bĕs·ō·deî′ ah) Personal name meaning, "in Yahweh's counsel." Father of Meshullam, who helped Nehemiah repair the gate of Jerusalem (Neh. 3:6).

BESOM Broom made of twigs (Isa. 14:23 KJV).

BESOR (Bē′ sôr) Place name perhaps meaning, "wadi of the good news." Brook where David left 200 weary soldiers while he and the remaining 400 pursued the Amalekites after they had burned Ziklag and captured David's wives (1 Sam. 30:9–10). David rewarded those who stayed as well as those who fought (1 Sam. 30:21–24). The Besor is probably wadi Ghazzeh about fifteen miles south of Ziklag.

BESTIALITY Sexual intercourse between a human and an animal, punishable by death in Old Testament legal codes. (Ex. 22:19; Lev. 20:15–16; see Lev. 18:23; Deut. 27:21). Israel's neighbors practiced bestiality in fertility worship and worship of animal gods.

BETAH (Bē′ tăh) Place name meaning, "security." City from which King David took brass after defeating King Hadadezer (2 Sam. 8:8). See *Berothai.* 1 Chronicles 18:8 lists Betah as Tibhath. See *Tibhath.* Thus NIV reads Tebah in 2 Samuel 8:8.

BETEN (Bē′ tēn) Place name meaning, "womb." Border town of tribe of Asher (Josh 19:25). It may be located at khirbet Abtun eleven miles south of Acco.

BETH-ABARA (Bĕth-ăb′ á·rà) Place name meaning, "house of crossing." KJV reading for Bethany in John 1:28 following some Greek manuscripts. See *Bethany.*

BETH-ANATH (Bĕth-ā′ năth) Place name meaning, "house of Anath." A fortified city in the territory of the tribe of Naphtali (Josh. 19:38). The tribe could not drive out the Canaanites from the city (Judg. 1:33). Beth-anath was apparently a worship center for the Canaanite goddess Anath. It may have been located at modern Safed el-Battik, fifteen miles east of Tyre.

BETH-ANOTH (Bĕth-ā′ nŏth) Place name meaning, "house of Anath" or "house of being heard." A city of Judah (Josh. 15:59). A temple to the Canaanite goddess Anath may have been here. The modern location may be khirbet beit Ainur, one and a half miles southeast of Halhul.

BETHANY (Bĕth′ á nў) Known primarily in the Gospels as the home of Mary, Martha, and Lazarus, ancient Bethany occupied an important place in the life of Jesus. Jesus often found Himself staying in Bethany at the home of his closest friends as He ministered in Jerusalem.
Background of the City Located on the Mt. of

View of the ancient city of Bethany, the hometown of Mary, Martha, and Lazarus.

Olives' eastern slope, Bethany sat "about two miles" (John 11:18, NIV) southeast of Jerusalem. Bethany became the final stop before Jerusalem just off the main east-west road coming from Jericho. Being at the foot of the mountain, the people could not see Jerusalem, thus giving Bethany a sense of seclusion and quietness. The road between Bethany and Jerusalem provided a ready avenue for travel across Olivet with the journey taking about fifty-five minutes to walk.

Role of the City in the Bible The primary event in the New Testament taking place in Bethany involved the raising of Lazarus from the dead (John 11–12). This magnificent miracle by Jesus demonstrated His authority, prepared for His resurrection, and was even magnified through the name of His friend, Lazarus (an abbreviation of Eleazar, "God has helped").

Another significant event in Jesus' life occurred in Bethany at the home of Simon the Leper (Matt. 26:6; Mark 14:3). Late on the Tuesday night of Jesus' last week, a woman (recognized as Mary in John 12:3) gave Jesus His "burial anointment." Coming to Jesus in the sight of all, she brought a costly alabaster vial of perfume and emptied its contents upon Jesus' head ("feet" in John 12:3).

Besides a number of smaller references to Bethany, one final event took place there. Bethany provided the location for Jesus' final blessing to His disciples and His subsequent parting. This encounter made up the final scene of ascension in Luke's Gospel (24:50–53).   *Larry McGraw*

BETH-ARABAH (Bĕth-är' a·bäh) Place name meaning, "house of the desert." A border town of tribe of Judah (Josh. 15:6, 61) also claimed as a city of Benjamin (Josh. 18:22). It may be modern Ain el-Gharbah southeast of Jericho.

BETH-ARAM KJV spelling of Beth-haram. See *Beth-haram.*

BETH-ARBEL (Bĕth-är' bĕl) Place name meaning, "house of Arbel." Sight of infamous battle Hosea could use as example of what would happen to Israel (Hos. 10:14). The battle is unknown to us. The site may be Irbid in Gilead, four miles northwest of Tiberius. See *Shalman.*

BETH-ASHBEA (Bĕth-ăsh' bē·a) Place of unknown location in Judah known for clans of linen workers, thus giving evidence of craft guilds in Israel (1 Chron. 4:21).

BETH-AVEN (Bĕth-ā' vĕn) Place name meaning, "house of deception" or "of idolatry." *1.* A city near Ai east of Bethel (Josh. 7:2). It formed a border of Benjamin (Josh. 18:12) and was west of Michmash (1 Sam. 13:5). Saul defeated the Philistines here after God used his son Jonathan to start the victory (1 Sam. 14:23). The exact location is

not known. Suggestions include Burqa, south of Bethel; tell Maryam; and Ai. *2.* Hosea used the term as a description of Beth-el. Instead of a house of God, Beth-el had become a house of deception and idolatry. Thus he commanded worshipers to refuse to go there (Hos. 4:15), to prepare for battle against an army marching from the south against Benjamin (5:8), and to be afraid of the golden calves in the worship place of Beth-el, not because they represented the fearful presence of God but because they brought disaster on the nation (10:5). All the worship places were Aven, deception and idolatry (10:8).

BETH-AZMAVETH (Bĕth-ăz·mā' vĕth) Place name meaning, "house of the strength of death." Home town of 42 people who returned to Palestine with Zerubbabel from Exile in Babylon about 537 B.C. (Neh. 7:28). Ezra 2:24 calls the town Azmaveth. It may be modern Hizmeh about two miles north of Anathoth.

BETH-BAAL-MEON (Bĕth-bā' ăl-mē' ŏn) Place name meaning, "house of Baal's residence." City allotted tribe of Reuben (Josh. 13:17). Same as Baal-meon. See *Baal-meon.*

BETH-BARAH (Bĕth-bâr·ah) Place name meaning, "house of God." A ford over the Jordan River and/or the village there if text of Judges 7:24 is correct. Many Bible scholars think copyists have changed the original text, introducing a place name not in the text.

BETH-BIREI (Bĕth-bir' ē·ī) KJV spelling of Beth-biri. See *Beth-biri.*

BETH-BIRI (Bĕth-bir' ī) Place name meaning, "house of my creation." Town allotted tribe of Simeon (1 Chron. 4:31). It is apparently the same as Lebaoth (Josh. 15:22) and Beth-lebaoth (Josh. 19:6). The location is uncertain.

BETHCAR (Bĕth' cär) Place name meaning, "house of sheep." Final site of battle where God thundered from heaven to defeat the Philistines for Samuel (1 Sam. 7:11). The location is not known unless copyists changed an original Beth Horon as some Bible students think.

BETH-DAGON (Beth-da' gŏn) Place name meaning, "house of Dagon." Apparently the name indicates a worship place of Philistine god Dagon. *1.* Town in tribal territory of Judah (Josh. 15:41). It is probably modern khirbet Dajun on the road connecting Ramalleh and Joppa. *2.* Town in Asher (Josh. 19:27) without certain present location.

BETH-DIBLATHAIM (Bĕth-dīb·la·thā' īm) Place name meaning, "house of the two fig cakes."

Town in Moab on which Jeremiah prophesied judgment (Jer. 48:22). About 830 B.C., Mesha, king of Moab, bragged that he built the city, as recorded on the Moabite Stone. It may be present-day khirbet et-Tem. See *Almon-diblathaim.*

BETH-EDEN (Běth-ē′ děn) Place name meaning, "house of bliss." Amos announced God's threat to take the royal house out of Beth-eden or the "house of Eden" (KJV) (Amos 1:5). He was obviously referring to a place in Syria. Assyrian records refer to Bit-adini, a city-state between the Euphrates and Balik rivers, somewhat north of Syria proper. Ashurbanipal II conquered it in 856 B.C. An Assyrian representative bragged about conquering Beth-Eden, urging Hezekiah to surrender about 701 B.C. (2 Kings 19:12). Ezekiel included Eden as one of the states who had traded with Tyre (Ezek. 27:23).

BETH-EKED (Běth-ē′ kěd) Place name meaning, "house of shearing" (KJV, "shearing house"). Place where Jehu, after slaughtering all members of King Ahab's house in Jezreel, met representatives from King Ahaziah of Judah and killed them (2 Kings 10:12–14). It is traditionally located at beit Qad, four miles northeast of Jenin, but recent studies question this location. Whatever its location, it must have been a meeting place and perhaps a marketplace for shepherds.

BETHEL (Běth′ ēl; *house of God*) *1.* Bethel was important in the Old Testament for both geographic and religious reasons. Because of its abundant springs, the area was fertile and attractive to settlements as early as 3200 B.C., and first supported a city around the time of Abraham. Today the village of Beitin rests on much of the ruins of Bethel. Located at the intersection of the main north-south road through the hill country and the main road from Jericho to the coastal plain, Bethel saw much domestic and international travel. Bethel became a prominent border town between tribes and the two kingdoms later. Religiously, Bethel served as a sanctuary during the times of the patriarchs, judges, and the divided kingdom, hence was second only to Jerusalem as a religious center.

Entering Canaan, Abraham built an altar at Bethel, calling "upon the name of the LORD" (Gen. 12:8), and returned here after his time in Egypt (Gen. 13:3). His grandson, Jacob, spent the night here on his way to Syria to find a wife. In a dream the Lord confirmed the Abrahamic covenant, and Jacob responded by renaming this locale which was previously called Luz, "Bethel" ("house of God"; Gen. 28:10–22). Probably the name "Bethel" is referred to but out of chronological sequence in the earlier Abraham passages. When he returned with his large family, Jacob came to Bethel again to hear the Lord's confirmation of the covenant and his name was changed to "Israel." Here again Jacob set up a stone monument (Gen. 35:1–16; Hos. 12:4,5). Extensive fortification of Bethel came after this patriarchal period.

At the time of the conquest, Bethel and Ai were taken together (Josh. 7:2; 8:3–17; 12:9,16), but the definitive defeat of Bethel is recounted later in Judges 1:22–26. It was a Benjamite border town initially (Josh. 16:1,2; 18:13,22). Later it was a part of the Northern Kingdom (1 Chron. 7:28), only briefly annexed to Judah by Abijah (2 Chron. 13:19).

The ark of the covenant was kept in Bethel during a period of the judges (Judg. 20:27), so the tribes converged there upon Benjamin to avenge the moral atrocity at Gibeah (Judg. 20:18–28), offering sacrifices and seeking the Lord's direction (Judg. 21:1–4). Bethel also was a place where both Deborah (Judg. 4:5) and Samuel (1 Sam. 7:16) judged the civil and religious affairs of the Israelites in the area. Bethel was evidently vulnerable at the time of the judges, since archaeology shows it to have been destroyed several times in this period.

David considered the city significant enough to send it gifts during his flight as a fugitive from Saul, hoping to establish a friendship of diplomatic value in the future (1 Sam. 30:27). When he eventually named Jerusalem his capital, Bethel grew and prospered.

Whereas Bethel had been a place of orthodox worship from Abraham to the judges, Jeroboam I made it a religious center of his innovative, apostate religion of the Northern Kingdom. He erected a golden calf both here and in Dan with non-Levitic priests and an illegitimate feast to compete with the celebrations and religion of Jerusalem, ten and a half miles to the south in Judah (1 Kings 12:29–33). Bethel was the prominent site over Dan. There an anonymous prophet from Judah found and rebuked Jeroboam I and brought destruction to the king's altar (1 Kings 13:1–10). Another anonymous prophet from Bethel entrapped the first prophet into disobedience. Because of his disobedience, the Lord caused a lion to kill the first prophet (1 Kings 13:11–25).

Other true prophets seem to have been attached to Bethel even during the time of northern apostasy, since Elijah encountered a group of them there as he traveled (2 Kings 2:2–3). Amos was sent to Bethel to rebuke the kingdom of Jeroboam II in the eighth century (Amos 7:10–13) since it was the center of northern idolatry and a royal residence. He met the resistance of Amaziah, the priest, who vainly ordered him to leave the city. In addition to Amos' prophetic charges against those who sacrificed there (Amos 4:4), he predicted the destruction of Bethel and its false altars (Amos 3:14, 5:5,6), as did Hosea (Hos. 10:14,15). Hosea seems to have played with the name of Bethel ("city of God"), by referring to it as "Beth-aven" ("city of a false [god]," Hos. 5:8,9; 10:5).

The religious significance of Bethel is confirmed also by Assyria's appointment of a priest to this city to teach the new residents of the north who displaced the Israelites (2 Kings 17:28). Later, Josiah desecrated another false altar of Bethel during his reforms (2 Kings 23:4–19) and perhaps annexed the city to his Southern Kingdom.

Bethel was destroyed in the sixth century during the Exile; however, some returned there when released by the Persians (Ezra 2:28; Neh. 7:32; 11:31).

Since it was a late first century Roman garrison town, it was probably a city of importance at the time of Christ. *2.* Another city variously spelled Bethul (Josh. 19:4), Bethuel (1 Chron. 4:30), and Bethel (1 Sam. 30:27). This may be modern khirbet el Qaryatein north of Arad.

2. Bethel was apparently the name of a West Semitic god. Many scholars find reference to this deity in Jeremiah 48:13. Others would find the mention of the deity in other passages (especially Gen. 31:13; Amos 5:5). *Daniel C. Fredericks*

BETHELITE (Bĕth'el·īte) Resident of Bethel (1 Kings 16:34). See *Bethel.*

BETH-EMEK (Bĕth-ē' mĕk) Place name meaning, "house of the valley." A border town in the tribal territory of Asher (Josh. 19:27). Located at modern tel Mimas, six and a half miles northeast of Acco.

The Pool of Bethesda at Jerusalem. A spring-fed pool near the Sheep Gate at Jerusalem, used by the sick for healing. Jesus healed a man there who had been stricken with an unidentified infirmity for thirty-eight years.

BETHER (Bē' thēr) Place name meaning, "division." A mountain range used as an emotional image in Song of Solomon 2:17. NIV reads, "rugged hills."

BETHESDA (Bē thĕs' dà) The name of a pool in Jerusalem where Jesus healed a man who had been sick for thirty-eight years (John 5:2). The name, appropriately, means "house of mercy." Most ancient manuscripts identify Bethesda as the place of the pool. Some ancient manuscripts name it Bethzatha or Bethsaida. The third edition of the United Bible Societies Greek New Testament places Bethzatha in the text and the other readings in footnotes. The waters of the pool were popularly believed to possess curative powers. Truly, the man who was healed after thirty-eight years experienced the outpouring of God's mercy on the sabbath. The references to the pool being stirred by angels (John 5:3*b*–4) are not found in either the oldest or the majority of manuscripts. However, regardless of the disagreement among manuscripts on the name of the pool or the angel passage, the pool did exist. Today this pool is identified with the series of pools found near the church of St. Anne. See *Healing.*

BETH-EZEL (Bĕth-ē' zĕl) Proper name meaning, "house of the leader" or "house at the side." City Micah used in a wordplay to announce judgment on Judah about 701 B.C. All support would be taken away from the house of the leader or the house beside (Mic. 1:11). The location may be deir el-Asal two miles east of tell beit Mirsim.

BETH-GADER (Bĕth-gā' der) City founded by or controlled by descendants of Hareph, a descendant of Caleb (1 Chron. 2:51). It is probably the same as Geder (Josh. 12:13), if that is the proper reading. Some students of Joshua suggest the original text read Gezer or Gerar.

BETH-GAMUL (Bĕth-gā' mŭl) Place name meaning, "house of retaliation." City in Moab on which Jeremiah announced judgment (Jer. 48:23). Its location was modern khirbet el-Jemeil about seven miles east of Dibon.

BETH-GILGAL (Bĕth-gĭl' găl) Place name meaning, "house of the wheel or circle." A village of Levitical singers near Jerusalem whose occupants participated in the dedication of the newly built city wall under Nehemiah (Neh. 12:29). It is probably the same as Gilgal. See *Gilgal.*

BETH-HACCEREM (Bĕth-hăc' ce·rĕm) or **BETH-HACCHEREM** Place name meaning, "house of the vineyard." City used to signal that enemies approached from the north (Jer. 6:1). Its leading official helped Nehemiah repair the dung gate (Neh. 3:14). It is probably modern Ramat Rahel halfway between Jerusalem and Bethlehem. Archaeological excavations show it was founded about 800 B.C. It sits high on a hill surveying the surrounding countryside. One of the later kings of Judah built a grand palace there. Apparently Jehoiakim (609–597) built the palace, which fits the description of Jeremiah 22:13–19. After the return from Exile, it served as an administrative center.

BETH-HAGGAN (Bĕth-hăg′ găn) Place name (NIV, TEV, NRSV) or common noun (KJV, NAS) meaning, "house of the garden." King Ahaziah of Judah (841 B.C.) fled there from Jehu, but Jehu finally caught up and killed him (2 Kings 9:27). It is probably modern Jenin, southeast of Tanaach.

BETH-HANAN (Bĕth-hā′ năn) Place name meaning, "house of grace." A city in Solomon's second district (1 Kings 4:9 TEV). See *Elon-beth-hanan.*

BETH-HARAM (Bĕth-hā′ răm) Place name meaning, "house of the exalted one," or "house of height." (KJV, Beth-aram). A city Moses allotted the tribe of Gad (Josh. 13:27). It is probably tell er-Rameh though others suggest tell Iktanu. It is probably the same as Beth-haran. See *Beth-haran.*

BETH-HARAN (Bĕth-hā′ răn) Place name meaning, "house of height." Town east of the Jordan the tribe of Gad strengthened after Moses gave it to them (Num. 32:36). It is probably the same as Beth-haram. See *Beth-haram.*

BETH-HOGLAH (Beth-hŏg′ lăh) Place name meaning, "house of the partridge." Border city between tribes of Judah and Benjamin (Josh. 15:6; 18:19,21). It is probably modern Ain Hajlah four miles southeast of Jericho.

BETH-HORON (Bĕth-hō′ rŏn) Place name of uncertain meaning. Suggestions include, "house of caves," "house of anger," "house of the hollow," "house of (the god) Hauron." Twin cities, one higher than the other, and so called Upper and Lower Beth Horon. An important road here dominates the path to the Shephelah, the plain between the Judean hills and the Mediterranean coast. Joshua used the road to chase the coalition of southern kings led by the king of Jerusalem (Josh. 10:10). Here God cast hail stones on the enemies. The border between the tribes of Ephraim and Benjamin was at Beth-horon (Josh. 16:3,5; 18:13–14). The city belonged to Ephraim but was set aside for the Levites (Josh. 21:22). The Philistines sent one unit of their army the way of Beth-horon to attack Saul and Jonathan (1 Sam. 13:18). Solomon rebuilt the lower city as a stone city and as a defense outpost (1 Kings 9:17). The chronicler preserved an even earlier tradition of a descendant of Ephraim, a woman named Sherah,

building the two cities (1 Chron. 7:22–24). When King Amaziah of Judah (796–767 B.C.) followed a prophet's advice and sent home mercenary soldiers he had hired from Israel, those soldiers fought the cities of Judah, including Bethhoron (2 Chron. 25:13). Upper Beth Horon is modern beit Ur el-Foqa, five miles northwest of Gibeon and ten miles northwest of Jerusalem. It is 1750 feet above sea level. Lower Beth Horon is two miles to the east and only 1050 feet above sea level. It is modern beit Ur et-Tahta.

BETH-JESHIMOTH (Bĕth-jĕsh′ ĭ-mŏth) or **BETH-JESIMOTH** (KJV spelling at Num. 33:49). Place name meaning, "house of deserts." A town in Moab where Israel camped just before Moses died and Joshua led them across the Jordan (Num. 33:49). Joshua 12:3 lists it as land Israel took from Sihon, king of the Amorites. Moses gave it to the tribe of Reuben (Josh. 13:20). Ezekiel described it as one of three frontier cities of Moab, these being "the glory of the country" (Ezek. 25:9), but one facing God's judgment. It is usually located at modern tell el-Azeme, twelve miles southeast of Jericho.

BETH-LE-APHRAH (Bĕth-lĕ-aph′ răh) Place name meaning, "place of dust." Town Micah used in a wordplay to announce judgment on Judah. The house of dust would roll in dust, a ritual expressing grief and mourning (Mic. 1:10). The location is uncertain, perhaps et-Taijibe between beit Gibrin and Hebron. KJV reads, "house of Aphrah"; NIV, "Beth Ophrah."

BETH-LEBAOTH (Bĕth-lĕb′ ā-ŏth) Place name meaning, "house of lionesses." City in territorial allotment of tribe of Simeon (Josh. 19:6). It is apparently the same as Lebaoth in Judah's inheritance (Josh. 15:32). This is called Beth-birei in the parallel passage (1 Chron. 4:31). Its location is not certain.

BETHLEHEM (Bĕth′ lĕ hĕm) Place name meaning, "house of bread," "fighting," or "Lahamu" [god]. *1.* Approximately five miles southwest of

Overview of the city of Bethlehem in Israel.

Jerusalem just off the major road from Jerusalem to the Negeb lies the modern Arabic village Bethlehem. The popular understanding is that the name, beth lehem, means "house of bread." Perhaps the first mention of the village occurred before 1300 B.C. in the Amarna letters (No. 290) where the ruler of Jerusalem complained to the Egyptian pharaoh that the people of *Bit–Lahmi* had gone over to the side of the "Apiru," apparently a people without local citizenship who caused disturbances in Canaanite society.

Small entrance to the Church of the Nativity in Bethlehem. Archway was filled to keep out horsemen.

In the Old Testament the parenthetical reference to Bethlehem in Genesis 35:19 is perhaps derived from a traditional burial site for Rachel near the village. Bethlehem appears in Judges 17:7–13 as the home of the Levite who became priest to Micah. The concubine of the Levite of Ephraim was from the village of Bethlehem (Judg. 19). The Book of Ruth takes place in the region of Bethlehem (Ruth 1:1–2,19,22; 2:4; 4:11). This story leads to the events that gave major importance to the village as the home and place of anointing of David (1 Sam. 16:1–13; 17:12,15).

Other Old Testament references to the village include the mention of a Philistine garrison being there during David's early kingship (2 Sam.

Traditional site of the manger of the infant Jesus, inside the Church of the Nativity in Bethlehem.

23:14), Elhanan's home (2 Sam. 23:24), the burial place of Asahel (2 Sam. 2:32), and a fort of Rehoboam (2 Chron. 11:6). Bethlehem is also

Stained glass window depicting the nativity scene at the Church of the Nativity in Bethlehem.

mentioned with reference to the Babylonian Exile (Jer. 41:17; Ezra 2:21).

It is the relationship of Bethlehem to Christ that has insured its place in Christian history. Micah 5:2 was understood to indicate that the Messiah, like David, would be born in Bethlehem not Jerusalem. Matthew (2:1–12), Luke (2:4–20), and John (7:42) report that Jesus was born in that humble village. It appears that early Christians believed that some caves east of the village were the holy site of the birth.

A field southeast of town has been identified as the place where the shepherds had the vision of the angels. *2.* A town in the territory of Zebulun, about seven miles northwest of Nazareth (Josh. 19:15), which was the burial site of Ibzan (Judg. 12:10), in modern beit Lahm. *3.* A personal name as in 1 Chronicles 2:51, 54. *George W. Knight*

BETHLEHEM-EPHRATAH (KJV) or **BETHLEHEM-EPHRATHAH** (NAS, NIV, NRSV) Place name used by Micah 5:2 to designate birthplace of new David who would come from Bethlehem, David's birthplace, and of the clan of Ephratah, that of Jesse, David's father (1 Sam. 17:12). See *Bethlehem.*

BETHLEHEMITE Citizen of Bethlehem. See *Bethlehem.*

BETH-MAACAH (Bĕth-mā′ ȧ·cäh) (NAS, NRSV) or **BETH-MAACHAH** (KJV) Place name meaning, "house of Maacah" or "house of pressure." Usually appears as Abel Beth-Maacah (always so in NIV). See *Abel-Beth-Maacah.* Form Beth-Maacah apparently appears as final stop on Sheba's trip through Israel to gain support against David (2 Sam. 20:14).

BETH-MARCABOTH (Bĕth-mär′ cȧ·bŏth) Place name meaning, "house of chariots." City allotted to tribe of Simeon (Josh. 19:5). Its location is uncertain.

BETH-MEON (Bĕth-mē′ ŏn) Place name meaning, "house of residence." City in Moab on which

Jeremiah pronounced judgment (Jer. 48:23). Apparently the same as Beth-baal-meon and Baal-meon. See *Beth-baal-meon; Baal-meon.*

BETH-MILLO (Bĕth-mîl′ lō) Place name meaning, "house of fulness." *1.* A part of Shechem or a fortress guarding Shechem, where the citizens of Shechem proclaimed Abimelech king. Jotham, Jerubaal's (or Gideon's) son asked citizens to overthrow Abimelech at Beth Millo (Judg. 9:6,20). See *Millo, Shechem. 2.* A fortification in Jerusalem where two of his servants killed King Joash (835-796 B.C.—1 Kings 12:19). It is also called, "Millo." See *Jerusalem; Millo.*

BETH-NIMRAH (Beth-nĭm′ răh) Place name meaning, "house of the panther." City east of the Jordan that tribe of Gad rebuilt after Moses allotted it to them (Num. 32:36). It provided good grazing land (Num. 32:3). It is located at either tell Nimrin or nearby at tell el-Bleibil, about ten miles northeast of the mouth of the Jordan.

BETH-OPHRAH (Bĕth-ōph′ răh) NIV spelling of Beth-le-Aphrah. See *Beth-le-Aphrah.*

BETH-PALET (Bĕth-pā′ lĕt) KJV spelling in Joshua 15:27 of Beth-pelet. See *Beth-pelet.*

BETH-PAZZEZ (Bĕth-păz′ zĕz) Place name meaning, "house of scattering." Town in tribal allotment of Issachar (Josh. 19:22). It may be modern kerm el-Hadetheh.

BETH-PELET (Bĕth-pē′ lĕt) Place name meaning, "house of deliverance." Southern town in tribal allotment of Judah (Josh. 15:27). After the return from Exile in Babylon, the Jews lived there (Neh. 11:26). KJV spellings are Beth-palet, Beth-phelet. The location is not known.

BETH-PEOR (Bĕth-pē′ ôr) Place name meaning, "house of Peor." A temple for the god Peor or Baal Peor probably stood there. See *Baal Peor.* Town in whose valley Israel camped as Moses delivered the sermons of the Book of Deuteronomy (Deut. 3:29). It had belonged to Sihon, king of the Amorites (Deut. 4:46). Moses died and was buried near there (Deut. 34:6). It belonged to tribe of Reuben (Josh. 13:20). It was located at modern khirbet Uyun Musa, twenty miles east of the north end of the Dead Sea. Numbers does not use the place name, but evidently at least part of the shameful worship of Baal Peor (Num. 25:1–5) occurred at Beth-peor. Hosea described the actions of Peor as a turning point in Israel's blissful honeymoon with God (Hos. 9:10). See *Peor.*

BETHPHAGE (Bĕth′ phȧġē) Place name meaning, "house of unripe figs." A small village located on the Mount of Olives near Bethany on or near the road between Jerusalem and Jericho. Reference is made to the village in each of the Synoptic Gospels (Matt. 21:1; Mark 11:1; Luke 19:29). In each account Bethphage was where Jesus gave instruction to two disciples to find the colt on which he would ride into Jerusalem for His triumphal entry. This may also be the place where the fig tree was cursed (Matt. 21:18–22; Mark 11:12–14, 20–26). Today one may still find rolling stone tombs in Bethphage, such as our Lord was buried in. See *Mt. of Olives; Triumphal Entry.*   *William Vermillion*

BETH-PHELET (Bĕth-phē′ lĕt) See *Beth-pelet.*

BETH-RAPHA ((Bĕth-rā′ phà) Place name meaning, "house of a giant." 1 Chronicles 4:12 says the otherwise unknown Eshton "became the father of Beth-rapha" (NAS). This apparently describes the beginning of a clan who lived at the town whose name is not known. The name could have distant relationships to the Rephaim (Deut. 3:11), though the Bible nowhere makes such relationships.

BETH-REHOB (Bĕth-rē′ hŏb) Place name meaning, "house of the market." Town near where tribe of Dan rebuilt Laish and renamed it Dan (Judg. 18:28). Rehob was the father of Hadadezer, the Syrian king of Zobah (2 Sam. 8:3). Beth-rehob may have been their hometown. When the Ammonites made David angry by humiliating his officials, Ammon sent to Beth-rehob for Syrian soldiers, evidently indicating that Syria controlled the city. The town lay at the southern foot of Mount Hermon. See *Rehob.*

BETHSAIDA (Bĕth sā′ ĭ dà) Place name meaning, "house of fish." The home of Andrew, Peter, and Philip (John 1:44; 12:21), located on the northeast side of the Sea of Galilee. This town was rebuilt under Philip the tetrarch, one of Herod the Great's sons, who named it Julius in honor of the Emperor Augustus' daughter. Near here Jesus fed the 5,000 (Luke 9:10) and healed a blind man (Mark 8:22). Jesus pronounced judgment upon Bethsaida for its lack of response to His message and miracles (Matt. 11:21; Luke 10:13). The site of Bethsaida has yet to be identified archaeologically. Some scholars do propose two sites named Bethsaida: The one northeast of the Sea of Galilee, as already discussed; and another, west of the Sea of Galilee, close to Capernaum. This postulation is based on Mark 6:45, where following the feeding of the 5,000 outside Bethsaida, Jesus tells His disciples to sail to Bethsaida. However, there is no contemporary mention of two Bethsaidas, and the Mark 6 text can just as easily refer to a short trip to the known city of Bethsaida-Julias as to an unknown town.   *William Vermillion*

BETH-SHAN or **BETHSHAN** (Bĕth-Shän) See *Beth-Shean.*

The Graeco-Roman theater at Beth-shean (tel el-Husn) in Israel.

BETH-SHEAN (Bĕth-shē′ an) Place name meaning, "house of quiet." Beth-shean stood at the crossroad of the Jezreel and Jordan Valleys, commanding the routes north-south along the Jordan and east-west from Gilead to the Mediterranean Sea. Tell el-Husn, site of ancient Beth-shean, stands above the perennial stream of Harod, the city's primary water supply, giving the city a commanding view of the two valleys.

Excavation of tell el-Husn and its surroundings were carried on by the University of Pennsylvania in several campaigns from 1921 to 1933. Settlements at Beth-shean were found to date back to the Neolithic and Chalcolithic periods. The city

Excavations showing entrances to the Graeco-Roman theater at Beth-shean (tel el-Husn) in Israel.

became an important Canaanite site in the Early and Middle Bronze Ages (3300−1500 B.C.), but came under the domination of Egypt's 18th dynasty in the Late Bronze Age. The name Beth-shean (or -*shan*) is mentioned in the Egyptian texts of Thutmose III (1468 B.C.), the Amarna letters (1350 B.C.), Seti I (1300 B.C.), Ramses II (1280 B.C.) and Shishak (925 B.C.). Excavations have confirmed the Egyptian role in the life of Beth-shean in these periods (for example, through the discovery of scarabs and a cartouche bearing the name Thutmose III).

Biblical references to Beth-shean relate to the period from Joshua until the United Monarchy. The city is listed among the allocations of the tribe of Manasseh, though the city was within the territory of Issachar (Josh. 17:6). Yet Manasseh was unable to control Beth-shean until the Canaanites were subdued in the reign of David (Josh. 17:16; Judg. 1:27). After the defeat of Saul and the Israelite army by the Philistines (ca. 1006 B.C.), the bodies of Saul and his sons were hung on the walls of Beth-shean, where a temple to the Ashtaroth was located. Some valiant men from Jabesh-gilead rescued the bodies from this sacrilege and disposed of them in Jabesh (1 Sam. 31). Later the bodies were brought by David's men in Benjamin (2 Sam. 21:12−14). The city is listed among those under the administration of Baana (fifth district) during Solomon's reign (1 Kings 4:12). Though the city is not specifically mentioned in the 1 Kings 14:25−28 account of the invasion of Shishak from Egypt, Beth-shean is listed among the

Excavations at Beth-shemesh showing what appears to be a portion of the massive city walls.

cities plundered. Afterward, the city played little role in Israelite history, though the city was occupied by Israelites of the Northern Kingdom from 815–721 B.C.

The city remained abandoned for the most part until the Hellenistic period (third century B.C.), when it was rebuilt and renamed Scythopolis ("city of Scythians"). This city formed the foundation of a significant Hellenistic and Roman occupation that included temples, theater, amphitheater, colonnaded street, hippodrome, tombs, and many public buildings, which had spread to the northern, eastern, and southern quadrants around the earlier "tell." Scythopolis was the largest city of the Decapolis (Matt. 4:25; Mark 5:20), and the only city of the league west of the Jordan River. The city continued to flourish in the Byzantine period until it was destroyed by Arabs in A.D. 636. The modern village of Beisan preserves the ancient name of the city.   *Dennis Cole*

BETH-SHEMESH (Bĕth-shē′ mĕsh) Place name meaning, "house of the sun." Beth-shemesh is a name applied to four different cities in the Old Testament. The name probably derives from a place where the Semitic god Shemesh (Shamash) was worshiped. *1.* Beth-shemesh of Issachar was situated on the tribal border with Naphtali between Mt. Tabor and the Jordan River (Josh. 19:22). Present scholarship identifies the city with either el-ʿAbeidiyeh, two miles south of Gali-

lee, or khirbet Shemsin, east of Tabor. *2.* Beth-shemesh of Naphtali was probably located in central upper Galilee because of its association with Beth-anath (Josh. 19:38; Judg. 1:33). This Canaanite town remained independent and unconquered until the time of David. The site khirbet er-Ruweisi has been suggested as a possible location. *3.* Beth-shemesh of Egypt is to be identified with Heliopolis (five miles northeast of Cairo) according to the Septuagint or early Greek translation (Jer. 43:13). Jeremiah told of the Lord's judgment upon the gods of Egypt by depicting the destruction of the worship centers. *4.* Beth-shemesh of Dan is located on the south tribal border with Judah (Josh. 15:10; 19:41) overlooking the Sorek Valley about 24 miles west of Jerusalem. The ancient name was preserved in the Arab village of Ain Shems, and the "tell" is identified with tell er-Rumeilah. Beth-shemesh guarded the lush farmlands of the Sorek Valley at the point at which the Shephelah (foothills) borders the Judean hill country. It was also situated in the strategic "buffer zone" between the Philistines and the Israelites during the judges period.

The Danite tribe was unable to control the lands of its inheritance because of the Amorites (Judg. 1:34–35) and/or the Philistines. Some were forced into the hills near Zorah and Eshtaol (as was Samson's family, Judg. 13:1–2). Beth-shemesh was apparently controlled by Israel (ca. 1050 B.C.) when the ark of the covenant passed through the city upon returning from the Philistines (1 Sam. 6:13). Around 795 B.C., the city was the scene of a battle in which Jehoash of Israel was victorious over Amaziah of Judah, resulting in the pillaging of the Temple (2 Kings 14:11–14; 2 Chron. 25:21–24). Beth-shemesh is last mentioned in Scripture during the decadent reign of Ahaz. The Philistines captured Beth-shemesh from Judah (ca. 734), seen as judgment from God (2 Chron. 28:18–19).

Beth-shemesh was excavated by D. Mackenzie in 1911–1912 and Haverford College in 1928–31,1933. The city was first settled about 2200 B.C. by a relatively small group. The city achieved importance after being conquered and rebuilt by the Hyksos about 1720 B.C. A huge city wall, three defensive towers, and several tombs were uncovered. The Hyksos city was captured by the Egyptians of the Eighteenth Dynasty about 1550 B.C. Beth-shemesh flourished in the Late Bronze Age under Egyptian and Canaanite rule, evidenced by imported wares from Mycenae and Egypt, as well as quality Canaanite finds, including inscriptions. Iron Age I (Judges) finds show that Beth-shemesh was heavily influenced by the Philistines, but the city was in general decline. After David defeated the Philistines, the city was rebuilt. Excavations indicate the Israelite city had olive oil, wine, copper, fabric dyeing, and wheat production industries. After Beth-shemesh was destroyed by the Babylonians (588–587 B.C.) under Nebuchadrezzar, the city was largely unoccupied, except for remnants of the Roman/Byzantine city at Ain Shems (monastery on the corner of the tell). *Dennis Cole*

BETH-SHEMITE (Bĕth-shē' mite) A resident of Beth-shemesh. See *Beth-shemesh.*

BETH-SHITTAH (Bĕth-shĭt' tăh) Place name meaning, "house of Accacia." Battle scene when Gideon and his 300 men defeated the Midianites (Judg. 7:22). It may be modern tell es-Saidiya or tell umm Hamad. It may be east of the Jordan River.

BETH-TAPPUAH (Bĕth-tăp' pū-ăh) Place name meaning, "house of apples." Town assigned tribe of Judah in Judean hills (Josh. 15:53). It is modern Taffah, about four miles west of Hebron.

BETH-TOGARMAH (Beth-tō-gär' măh) Place name meaning, "house of Togarmah." Listed in table of nations (Gen. 10:3) as son of Gomer and great grandson of Noah, Togarmah is a city mentioned in Assyrian and Hittite texts. It was north of Carchemish on an Assyrian trade route. It may be related to modern Gurun between the Halys and Euphrates Rivers. Ezekiel notes Togarmah's

trading relations in horses and mules with Tyre (Ezek. 27:14) and warned it of judgment along with Gog (Ezek. 38:6).

BETHUEL (Bĕ-thū' ĕl) Place name and personal name meaning, "house of God." *1.* Nephew of Abraham and son of Nahor (Gen. 22:22). His daughter Rebekah married Isaac (Gen. 24:15,67). He was an Aramean or Syrian from Padan-aram (Gen. 25:20). His relationship to Rebekah's brother Laban (Gen. 24:29) is not clear, since Laban takes the chief role protecting Rebekah (Gen. 24:55; 27:43), and Nahor is Laban's father (Gen. 29:5). Genesis 28:5 says Laban was the son of Bethuel. Nahor was actually Bethuel's father (Gen. 22:22–23). *2.* A town where the children of Shimei lived (1 Chron. 4:30). Joshua 19:4 apparently reads the same town as Bethul. It may be modern khirbet el-Qarjeten, three miles north of tell Arad.

BETHUL (Bē' thul). See *Bethuel.*

BETHZATHA (Bĕth-zā' tha) TEV, NSRV reading of place name in John 5:2 based on different Greek manuscripts than those followed by other translators. See *Bethesda.*

BETH-ZUR (Bĕth' zûr) Place name meaning, "house of the rock." *1.* A city allotted to tribe of Judah (Josh. 15:58). Rehoboam, Solomon's son and successor as king of Judah (931–913 B.C.), built it up as a defense city (2 Chron. 11:7) in view of the threat of Shishak of Egypt (2 Chron. 12:2). A city official of Beth-zur helped Nehemiah repair Jerusalem and its wall (Neh. 3:16). It played a significant role in the wars of the Maccabeans in the period between the Testaments. It is located at khirbet et-Tubeiqeh, eighteen miles southwest of Jerusalem and four miles north of Hebron on a major highway intersection. This is one of the highest sites above sea level in Palestine.

2. Son of Maon in line of Caleb (1 Chron. 2:45), apparently indicating the clan that settled the city.

BETONIM (Bĕt' ō-nĭm) Place name meaning, "pistachios." A border town in tribal allotment of Gad (Josh. 13:26). It is located at khirbet el-Batne, two and a half miles southeast of es Salt on Mount Gilead.

BETROTHAL was the act of engagement for marriage in Bible times and was as binding as marriage.

Old Testament The biblical terms, betrothal and espousal, are almost synonymous with marriage, and as binding. Betrothal and marriage comprised a moral and spiritual principle for the home and society. The penalty under the law of Moses for disrupting this principle by adultery, rape, fornication, or incest was death by stoning (Deut. 22:23–30). Later under some circumstances the

Jewish legal system allowed divorce. The forgiving love and grace of God for his adulterous people is demonstrated by Hosea buying back his adulterous wife and restoring her to his home and protection (Hos. 2:19–20). This means that forgiveness takes precedence over stoning or divorce.

New Testament Mary and Joseph were betrothed but did not live together until their wedding. When Mary came to be with child during betrothal, Joseph decided to quietly divorce her. In a dream from God, the apparent unfaithfulness of Mary was explained to Joseph as a miracle of the Holy Spirit. This miracle gave emphasis to the unique human and divine nature of Jesus Christ. Paul used the betrothal concept to explain the ideal relationship that exists between the church as a chaste virgin being presented to Christ (2 Cor. 11:2).   *Lawson Hatfield*

BEULAH (Beû' lah) A symbolic name meaning, "married," used in reference to Jerusalem (Isa. 62:4). The other name, Hephzibah, means "my delight in her." Both names connote good fortune. The name symbolizes the closeness of Zion and her sons, and that Zion is restored to her God. The name suggests fertilty in the Messianic Age based on righteousness, with the Lord as husband (Isa. 62:1–2).

BEVELED WORK NRSV translation describing scrollwork on the bronze stands of the laver in Solomon's Temple (1 Kings 7:29; KJV "thin work"; NAS, "hanging work"; REB, NIV, "hammered work"). It was wreathlike in appearance and may have been gold plating.

BEWITCH KJV translation of two Greek words. In Galatians 3:1, Paul criticized the Galatians for being "captivated by the falsehood" (*baskaino*) of the Judaizers to the point of straying from the Gospel. The Greek word used here has a history in magical evil and the casting of spells. "Bewitch" is also used as a translation of another word (*existemi*) that modern versions translate as "amazed," "astonish," or "astound" (Acts 8:9,11).

BEYOND THE JORDAN Often used to describe the territory on the east side of the Jordan river (also referred to as the Transjordan). Five times the phrase describes the territory on the west side of the Jordan (Gen. 50:10–11; Deut. 3:20,25; 11:30).

BEYOND THE RIVER A phrase that refers to the Euphrates River in Mesopotamia. From the perspective of those living in Palestine, "beyond the river" meant on the east side of the Euphrates River. The expression is often used when speaking of the ancestral home of the patriarchs (Josh. 24:3,14–15; KJV has "on the other side of the flood"). From the perspective of those living in

Persia, "beyond the river" meant on the west side of the Euphrates River. Darius I, the great organizer of the Persian empire, named his fifth satraphy "Beyond the River" (Ebir-nari). This satrapy included Syria and Palestine. The official Persian usage is reflected in the Books of Ezra (4:10–20; 5:3,6; 6:6,8,13; 7:21,25; 8:36) and Nehemiah (2:7,9; 3:7).

BEZAI (Bē' zā·ī) A contraction of Bezalel. See *Bezalel*. *1.* A clan of 323 (Ezra 2:17) who returned from Babylonian Exile with Zerubbabel about 537 B.C. *2.* A man who signed Nehemiah's covenant to obey God's law (Neh. 10:18).

BEZALEEL (Bĕz' à leêl) Personal name meaning, "in the shadow of God." *1.* The son of Uri, a member of the tribe of Judah (Ex. 31:2) and great grandson of Caleb (1 Chron. 2:20). He and another man, the Danite Aholiab, were skilled craftsmen who were responsible for making the tabernacle, its furnishings, and trappings. His skill derived from his being filled with the Spirit of God. Most modern translations of the Bible render the names of these men Bezalel and Oholiab. *2.* Man who followed Ezra's leadership and divorced his foreign wife (Ezra 10:30).

BEZALEL (Bĕz' à·lel) See *Bezaleel*.

BEZEK (Bē' zĕk) Place name meaning, "lightning." Place where Judah and Simeon defeated Canaanites who were led by Adoni-bezek (literally, "lord of Bezek") (Judg. 1:4). In Bezek Saul numbered the Israelites to rally an army against Nahash the Ammonite and deliver Jabesh-gilead (1 Sam. 11:8). Bezek was located at khirbet Ibziq, twelve miles northeast of Shechem and thirteen miles from Jabesh-Gilead, six miles north of Tirzah, though the Judges' site may be a distinctive city. If so, it would be at tell Bezqah near Gezer.

BEZER (Bē' zēr) Place name meaning, "inaccessible." *1.* A city of refuge in tribal territory of Reuben (Deut. 4:43; Josh. 20:8), set aside as a city for the Levites (Josh. 21:36). It may be Umm el-Amad, eight miles northeast of Medeba. Mesha, king of Moab about 830 B.C., claimed to have rebuilt Bezer as a Moabite city.

BIBLE, FORMATION AND CANON OF The word "Bible" was formed from a Greek term meaning books in the plural. Our Bible is, in fact, the collection of books written by various authors that possesses final authority in Christian communities. It has no rival in its pervasive influence upon Western culture, and increasingly over world culture.

Why does the Bible exist? The answer has to do with the transmission of the gospel down through the generations. Once God had revealed Himself and His plan of salvation to Israel and to the believers surrounding Jesus, the question arose how this truth would be passed along to posterity without its suffering distortion from later interpreters. The only obvious answer to this question was written documentation. It would be necessary to secure the revelation in a fixed, written, and authentic form so that the truth would not be lost in the transmission.

Does the Bible itself give this answer? You can see that it does when you consider, first, the fact that leading figures in the Bible, such as Moses, Jeremiah, Luke, and Paul, are described as writing things down precisely for people who are unable to talk with them directly. Second, you find that Jesus and the apostles in the New Testament had a very high view of the divine authority of the Hebrew Scriptures which they believed God gave by inspiration (2 Tim. 3:16). The idea of the Bible was not a late afterthought in the history of salvation but was in the process of being formed almost from the first.

How did the Bible take shape? A general acquaintance with the book goes a long way toward answering this question. In the case of the Old Testament, people must have told and retold the stories of God's interaction with Israel before they were collected into the books we now possess. They carefully preserved the law of God given through Moses and accepted it as binding on them. The inspired prophecies could not be allowed to be forgotten even when they were painful. Of course, the wisdom of the sages and the hymns of the people had to be preserved. The process of formation can thus be viewed both from the point of view of God's purpose and with an eye on the natural historical dynamics. In the case of the New Testament, it is clear that four writers undertook the task of presenting the life of Jesus, each of them with some special emphases and with a particular audience in view. The apostle Paul, as well as some others, had the practice of writing letters to groups of people to communicate with them when visiting was difficult. Writing was a way of instructing them in the things of God from a distance. One can see how the Bible must have been formed just by looking at it. Each of its parts was created and preserved because it met a need in the covenant community and qualified to be treasured for transmission to posterity.

How was the canon of Scripture decided on? The word *canon* comes from a Sumerian term meaning "reed," and it came to designate the list of books which were normative and sacred. The simplest answer to this question is a practical one: the books which ended up on the canonical lists in the end were those which proved themselves in a variety of ways to be God's Word to His people as they used them over the years. The historical answer is a little less clear. We just do not know as much about the process of canonization as we would like. The best clues are in the Bible itself. The law of Moses was written down and became the core of the later Old Testament. This is the assumption of all the later documents. There is much less said about the composition and preservation of the other writings. Certainly the divine authority claimed by the great prophets of Israel attached to the books which preserved their preaching. It is possible that the Old Testament canon as we know it took shape under the influence of the scribe Ezra who rounded off the task long in process. This would explain the tenacity of the Jews ever since to preserve their Hebrew canon. As for the New Testament, the books involved are many fewer and were composed over a mere half century. The respect for the words and deeds of Jesus is obvious and would explain both the preparation and the respect accorded the four Gospels. Paul's apostolic authority guaranteed respect for his epistles from the beginning. Respect grew later when the original witnesses began to die off and the epistles circulated among the churches. The authority of a prophecy like the Revelation of John, if deemed authentic, would be automatic. An extraneous factor which speeded the process toward developing a canon was the work of second century reformer Marcion, who proposed dropping the Old Testament and much of the New Testament as well, forcing orthodox Christians to make up their minds on the question of the canonical list. The die was already cast in the Muratorian Canon of 170 A.D. where one finds the essential New Testament as we know it today.

Is there an interplay then of subjective and objective factors in the determination of the canon of Scripture? Yes, we need to view it in terms of God's providence guiding and directing His people in this matter. God sent His messengers and the Scriptures in their wake. God's Word to the people had to make its own impact upon human minds. There is the historical solidity of God's revelation in history, but there is also the need for God's sheep to hear the voice of their Shepherd. God has given us His written Word and allowed it quietly and unhurriedly to make its impact upon us. It did not require a big council when the decision would come down from the leaders of the churches. All that was needed was that God's people be satisfied in the matter of the historical authenticity and then of the practical efficacy of the books in question. The fact that substantially the whole church came to recognize the same books as canonical is remarkable when we remember the agreement was not at all contrived.

Clark Pinnock

BIBLE, HERMENEUTICS The science of interpreting the Bible (or any piece of literature) is

Contemporary Jews show respect for the Scripture as they carry the Torah to the Wailing Wall in Jerusalem.

called hermeneutics. The word comes from a Greek word, *hermeneuo,* which means to interpret or to explain. Interpreting the Bible is not a simple process of reading what has been written. **Questions to Ask** The meaning of a piece of writing is seldom clearly self-evident to anyone who happens to read it. Especially is this true if the writing is a very old document, written for someone who lived in a very different cultural-historical setting. If we want to interpret a piece of literature, we must ask at least five questions: 1) Who was the writer and to whom was he writing? 2) What was the cultural-historical setting of the writer? 3) What was the meaning of the words in the writer's day? 4) What was the intended meaning of the author and why was he saying it? 5) What should this mean to me in my situation today? These basic questions lead into other questions that must be explored in a serious attempt to understand the message of the Bible. The reader today must somehow try to enter the world of the biblical writer and seek to understand what the writer was saying. Then he must bring that ancient message into today's world where the reader lives.

There are some basic principles that should be observed by the interpreter of the Scriptures. 1) The Bible is a divinely inspired book (2 Tim. 3:16) and should be reverently approached. Perhaps the reader should hear what was said to Moses as he stood before the burning bush: "Put off your shoes from your feet, for the place on which you are standing is holy ground" (Ex. 3:5). We must be careful to reverence the divine character of Scripture. 2) The Bible has a genuinely human element, also, since God used ordinary people to write the Scriptures. Recognition should be given to the human elements utilized by the Holy Spirit in giving us God's Word. To miss the human element is as much a mistake as to miss the divine element. 3) The primary aim of the interpreter is to discover the original meaning of the author who wrote the passage under consideration. 4) Preference should be given to the interpretation which is clearest and simplest, the most obvious. 5) Only one meaning should be given to any passage of Scripture, unless a later passage of Scripture assigns it a second meaning. Only an inspired writer of Scripture can be allowed to give a passage more than one meaning. 6) Careful attention must be given to the literary form of a passage in determining its meaning. 7) Careful attention must be given to the historical situation of a portion of Scripture.

Historical Task Interpretation begins with a historical task. The interpreter needs to know as much as possible about the writer and his cultural-historical setting. If we know nothing concerning who wrote a passage, when it was written, or under what conditions it was written, we are almost left to guess what its meaning might

be. Knowing what an author has experienced and what the thought forms of his day were aids us in understanding his writing. It is important to know the approximate date when a passage was written. For instance, words about God's Spirit written before the coming of the Holy Spirit at Pentecost might be given one meaning while they would be given a different meaning after Pentecost. The reader also needs to know who the intended recipients of a passage were. Words addressed to unbelievers would be interpreted very differently from words addressed to believers. The meaning of a passage might depend upon knowing whether the original audience was Jewish or Gentile. The interpreter also needs to know what occasioned the writing, or why the writer wrote his message and what his purpose was.

Literary Task A literary task follows the historical task of the interpreter. The literary task begins with the task of translation of the Scripture from the ancient Hebrew and Greek into the language best understood by the interpreter. Translation is itself a stage of interpretation. For translation is more than simply substituting English words for the Greek and Hebrew words. If you cannot do a good job of translating Greek and Hebrew into English (or whatever your language is), then you must rely upon good translations of the Bible. You really should utilize several good translations to help you understand what the ancient writer was trying to say to you.

Lexical study is the next phase of your literary study of the Bible. You must consult a lexicon or dictionary to find the meaning key words had when the original writer used them. His words may have a different meaning today, and you must know what they meant when originally used.

The next stage of the literary task of the interpreter is the grammatical or syntactical phase. Here, you must examine the form of the writer's grammar: what is signified by the grammatical constructions, the verb forms used, what is given emphasis in a sentence, the relationships of the words to each other, etc. The tense, voice, mode, case, etc. of the words used is very important in understanding what the writer was trying to say to you, the reader. These matters are acutely important in the work of translation, but they also must not be overlooked in the process of interpretation. You should consult good critical commentaries that analyze these grammatical matters for you, even if you do your own translation.

Rhetorical analysis is another important phase of the literary task of interpretation. Here, the interpreter seeks to determine what kind of rhetoric, or language, the ancient writer was using. It is extremely important to recognize the various literary forms that are used by the different writers of the Bible. Major portions of the Bible are written in ordinary prose, plain descriptive narrative. Other portions are pure poetry. Sometimes vivid figures of speech are incorporated in narrative portions. Such figures of speech must be interpreted in their symbolic sense rather than as literal, descriptive language. Portions of the Bible are written in apocalyptic language, a well-known literary style often used in the ancient world, but hardly known to us today. Apocalyptic literature employs vivid symbols and fanciful images to convey some message or mystery or prophecy in a veiled, highly imaginative way. The Book of Revelation and certain portions of Daniel and Ezekiel are examples of apocalyptic literature in the Bible.

Consideration must be given to the context of a passage of Scripture. No portion of Scripture ought to be interpreted without regard to its content. The context is the setting in which the particular passage is located. Generally, the paragraph in which a statement appears is the minimum context. However, the context of a passage may be the whole chapter in which a verse occurs; it could even be the entirety of a book, in the case of the shorter books of the Bible. Meaning that is given to a verse, without regard to its context, is very likely to be the wrong meaning.

The literary task of the interpreter must include comparing the meaning given to a passage to what is taught elsewhere in the Scriptures. This does not mean that we should arbitrarily force one viewpoint upon all of the Scriptures. But it does mean that we should be careful not to interpret Scriptures in such a way that we introduce contradictions into our interpretation of the Bible. There is an overall unity to the Bible; it teaches one theme, one message. But within that unity, there is also diversity. There is diversity due to the vast amount of time spanned in the writing of the Bible. There is diversity due to the many different authors employed by the Holy Spirit. There is diversity due to the progressive nature of revelation. God gradually revealed more and more of Himself and of His will for humans as the message of the Bible proceeded from Genesis to Revelation. While there is progression, there is not contradiction in the Scriptures. The careful interpreter will always want to compare an interpretation of a passage with what the Bible teaches elsewhere to see if the interpretation "fits" with what the Bible says in other places.

Spiritual Task There is a personal, spiritual task of the interpreter. One who would be a good interpreter must be devoted to diligent, careful study of the Scriptures (2 Tim. 2:15), prayerfully seeking the leadership of the Holy Spirit continually while interpreting the Scriptures (John 16:12–15; 2 Pet. 1:19–21). Only illumination or divine guidance can lead to correct interpretation. On the one hand, the Bible is a piece of literature that is to be interpreted just like any other piece of literature. On the other hand, the Bible is unique in that it is inspired by God through the Holy Spirit; one who reads the Bible should therefore seek the guidance of God in understanding what is written there.

One additional task remains for the interpreter. Seek to apply the teaching of the Bible to your present situation. It is important to know what the Bible said to its original readers, the people to whom it was originally addressed. But it is equally important to apply the ancient message to us today in our life situation which may be very different from that of the ancient world of Moses or Jesus or Paul. If the Bible is a living revelation of God to us, as we say it is, then we must do more than decipher its ancient history. We must apply the principles discerned in that ancient history to our life situation today.   *J. Terry Young*

BIBLE, HISTORY OF INTERPRETATION

Biblical interpretation, or hermeneutics, has had a long and checkered history. The way in which almost all Christians today read and interpret the Bible only gradually developed. It was not until the era of the Renaissance and Reformation that the science of biblical interpretation was clarified. Today we follow what is generally known as the literary historical method of interpretation.

Origen (who died in 254 A.D.) was the first major biblical interpreter and Christian theologian. In addition to the obvious, simple, literal meaning of a passage, which Origen believed was only for the simple believer, Origen found a hidden or deeper meaning embedded in the words of Scripture. This hidden meaning was the pure word of God to the mature Christian, and much to be preferred over the simple, literal meaning. Origen made extensive use of allegorical interpretation to derive this deeper, preferred meaning of Scripture. This allowed Origen to import his underlying philosophical position into the Scriptures, as though this was the message of God to us.

The School of Antioch was the bright spot in the ancient world, so far as biblical interpretation was concerned. The biblical interpreters associated with this school insisted that the Bible be interpreted in the light of the literary form and historical situation of a particular passage. They carefully avoided reading philosophical and speculative preconceptions into the text in the fashion of Origen and his followers. Today, this would seem to be the obvious way that Scripture should be interpreted, but that was not the general opinion in the ancient world. Not until the time of the Reformation (1517) did this kind of biblical interpretation become the dominant approach to the Scripture.

In the Middle Ages (500–1500), Origen's allegorical approach to the interpretation of Scripture was the accepted pattern. Indeed, Middle Ages interpreters expanded on Origen's two meanings and found anywhere from four to seven different levels or types of meanings. A fourfold meaning was usually sought in Scripture: the literal-historical, for the simple believer; the allegorical, which supplies a deeper meaning for faith; the moral, which guides conduct; and the anagogical, a mystical interpretation which points towards the ultimate goal of the Christian in his pilgrimage. Various terms were used to denote these four different levels of meaning.

With biblical interpretation so complicated, it is no wonder that the Roman Catholic Church took the Bible out of the hands of the lay people and left biblical interpretation to the clergy. The ordinary person could not possibly know how to derive from four to seven different levels of meaning out of a given passage.

Biblical interpretation as we know it today began in the period of the Renaissance and Reformation. In the age of the Renaissance, people began to realize the true literary character of the Bible. Luther learned anew the important place of the Bible and made a determined effort to put the Bible back in the hands of the people. One of Luther's cardinal principles was "sola scriptura," only by Scripture, or Scripture alone. Luther and other Reformers insisted on the perspicuity of Scripture—Scripture is clear enough that the ordinary believer can read and understand it by observing the grammatical and historical elements of the text. Calvin insisted (in the preface to his commentary on Romans) "It is the first business of an interpreter say what he [the Scripture writer] does, instead of attributing to him what we think he ought to say."

Following the time of the Reformation, great emphasis was placed on letting the Bible speak for itself. The science of textual criticism was developed. This was the analysis of all of the available biblical manuscripts, comparing the variant readings, and making an informed judgment as to what the original text of the Scriptures really was.

In the earnest search for accurate, faithful interpretation of the Bible, the historical-critical method of interpretation was developed. The word "critical" comes from a Greek word which means to judge or to make a decision in the light of evidence. With this type of interpretation, more attention is given to historical considerations than merely clarifying the historical context in which a passage of Scripture is set. Some developers of this method saw history as a closed system. They thought everything must be explained on the basis of forces and causes that are resident within the normal historical experience of humans. Thus, by definition, miracles could not be explained on the basis of an act of God who reaches into history; some natural explanation had to be found for what appears in the Scripture record as a miracle.

What is at fault here is not the method of interpretation as such, but the presupposition that miracles are impossible. This hermeneutical approach is often confused with the literary-historical interpretation practiced by more conservative interpreters. The two are very similar, differing primarily in the presupposition of the interpreter rather than in method as such.

Many varieties of so-called "scientific exegesis" have been developed as refinements of the historical-critical method. They employ very sophisticated and technical methods to analyze the factors that lie behind the text as we have it: who the author was, what the motive was in writing, identification of various sources of material used by the writer, the writer's position among God's people, the relationship to other biblical writers, how and why each idea was developed, the meaning the writer was trying to convey.

Another approach to biblical interpretation is in the form of the history of religions hermeneutic. In this type of biblical interpretation, parallels are sought between what is found in Scripture and what is found in the development of other systems of religion. This shows what biblical writers shared with their culture, what they adopted and adapted from the culture, and what they had in unique distinction from their culture. An extreme position here can expect biblical teaching to be little different from what is found in other religions. A more conservative position recognizes that God used the culture to teach His people but also that He pointed the way to be a holy people distinct from the culture.

As a reaction to the radical insistence on history being closed to outside influences, another approach to biblical interpretation has developed. It is called the new hermeneutic and is often based upon the philosophy of existentialism. According to this approach, the message of the Bible is not to tell me what happened hundreds or thousands of years ago. It is to create in me new spiritual experiences, or encounters with God; or, at least, it is to show me the possibilities that are open to me when I place my faith in Christ.

The dominant type of biblical interpretation used by conservative Christians today is the literary-historical method. See *Bible, Hermeneutics*.   *J. Terry Young*

BIBLE, METHODS OF STUDY Conscious, organized approaches that help one arrive at the meaning of God's Word without pre-determined conclusions.

Certainly we cannot and must not try to limit or master God's sovereign self-revelation by human methods. The living activity of the Holy Spirit is above and beyond all systems of communication. Methodology is appropriate and necessary, however, insofar as the Bible was written and is read by human beings. Methods serve to clarify and prepare the understanding of the Bible; their character is auxiliary. They help to remove obstacles hindering or falsifying the process of listening to the message. Adequate methodology reflects the manifold dimensions of life. The Biblical message originated in life and aims at being experienced anew in life. This process comprises various cultures, ages, circumstances, societies, people, languages, traditions, emotions. Methods follow certain presuppositions, concerning what people can know and communicate. Methodology, therefore, touches our understanding of reality, experience, and reason. Methods must be open to general testing, not self-contradictory, and evident. Not everyone has the same experiences which others have; and we must be aware of so far unknown aspects of reality. This requires from methodology that it does not narrow down experiences to be communicated, but rather leaves room for all the dimensions of life.

The methods need not be mutually exclusive but should assist each other. In addition, every method must be aware of the wide range of reality. Every event and document can and must be considered from the various perspectives of human knowledge, such as social and political sciences, humanities, economy, psychology of religion, value systems, etc.

Practical Suggestions No set of methods can claim to be the most perfect one. We should avoid any schematism, too. There are, however, certain steps in the interpretation of Biblical texts, following a rather natural sequence, gained from experience.

1. After the first reading of the text the interpreter's own relation to it needs some clarification. Is the text new or familiar—perhaps too familiar? Does it remind you of previous events (sermons, situations)? What are your feelings about the text: do you like it, or is it alien or rather abstract? The interpreter thus reflects on a personal attitude to the text. Furthermore, you try to formulate a preliminary description of what the text speaks about.

2. The interpreter continues considering the text as a whole to define its character more clearly. Is the passage a more or less independent unit? Where does it begin and end? What are its relations to the context? After that, the structure of the text may be analysed. Are there indications of subsections with logical or other links? Does it lead to a climax? What is of central importance? In the same way the key persons and/or terms should be located. Does the text contain essential points of activity, qualification, description, judgment, etc.? In the course of these observations the nature of the text receives further clarification. Is it a narrative, a hymn, a psalm, an admonition, an argumentation, etc.? What can be normally expected in such portions? What is surprising?

3. It is advisable to ask at this point the so-called journalist's questions: Who wrote, when, where, to whom, why, what for? These questions cannot be answered with the same accuracy for all parts of the Bible, since we lack information some-

times. The available information is collected in handbooks, introductions, and commentaries to the Bible. It helps to reconstruct the original situation of the text, to understand the needs and expectations of the people involved, to see the manifold aspects of reality touched, and to avoid wrong applications if important aspects have changed today. The interpreter should ask the question, what is really helpful to understand the message, in order not to do too little or too much.

4. The background of the text is further analysed along the lines of "this reminds of . . ." or "this seems to be taken from . . .". Every author uses traditions, often in smaller, sometimes even in larger units. Are there any quotations or allusions? Bible concordances and dictionaries are the best help at this point, not to forget a sound Bible knowledge. It is important to locate the specific message of a text in the longer course of God's history with His people.

5. A detailed analysis of the passage can now be made. It is helpful to compare different translations; occasionally they may even reflect variant readings of the original. Helpful, too, is the method of translators to cut a text into its smallest components of meaning, i.e. into short and simple sentences. (Even a single adjective e.g. might be transformed into a small sentence). The translation and analysis thus becomes a paraphrase, i.e. a reformulation in our own words, usually somewhat longer than the original.

6. What is the contribution of the text, first in the original situation, then also in the history of the early church, the entire history of salvation? Contribution comprises both effect and message, activity and doctrine. What could have happened if these words had not been given to Jeremiah's or James' generation? What would be lacking if that message had not been preserved by Luke? Which details would cause us to suffer clarity or completeness in our knowledge about Jesus Christ, the church, or ethics? In so asking the interpreter will get a better glance of the specific value of the text.

7. As an interpreter, you must not think you are the first and only recipient of the text. Others in the history of the church have read it before; their experiences and reactions are worth a comparison (so-called "history of reception," found in good commentaries). This may also help avoiding a one-sided interpretation by pointing to a more balanced picture of the Biblical revelation. Equally, the Biblical message was and is not given just to individuals but rather to the people of God. The essential life-setting, therefore, is the church and its service. The final test to an adequate interpretation of the Bible is whether it leads to gratitude and praise, to service and mission.

Wiard Popkes

BIBLE, TEXTS AND VERSIONS The preservation and transmission of the Bible from the time that it was written until the present involves two areas of study. The study of the process by which the documents (66 in all) were written, used, collected into groups, and elevated to the authoritative place that they occupy today is called the study of the canon. The other is the process of preserving in writing and translations the text of the documents. This is the study of text and versions.

There are two periods in the history of the text of the Bible. The first is from the time the documents were written until the time of printing (A.D. 1453). The second is from that date until the present. The invention of printing was very important for the transmission of the text of the Bible. Before that date, the only way that a person could have a copy of any written work was to make a copy (or have it made) by hand, letter by letter. This was slow and often expensive. Some have calculated that the cost of one complete Bible made by a professional scribe in the fourth century would equal the salary of a member of the Roman legion for forty years. Certainly not every church, let alone every Christian, could afford to have a copy of the Scriptures.

The Period of the Handwritten Text The story of the Bible is really the story of two Testaments, the Old and the New. The story came together for Christians in the second century A.D., when the Christian writings began to be equated with the Hebrew Scriptures and thus published side by side as the Christian Scriptures. Even then, however, the history of the text used by Christians differed some from the text used and preserved by Jews.

1. Old Testament Text and Versions. The difficulty of tracing the history of the Old Testament text is the scarcity of manuscripts that go back beyond the ninth and tenth century. One reason for this scarcity is the practice by Jewish scribes of burying old manuscripts in a storehouse called a *genizah* and then destroying these manuscripts. The text from that period is called the Masoretic Text because it derives from the work of a group of Hebrew scribes known as Masoretes, whose work spans the time from A.D. 500 to 1000. The manuscripts used most frequently in editing the Old Testament today are of this variety.

Textual scholars use several tools to trace the text behind the Masoretic Text. One is the *Samaritan Pentateuch.* This refers to the text of the first five books of the Old Testament as it was preserved among the Samaritans after their separation from Judah about 400 B.C. until the present. This text is preserved in Israel today by a few hundred Samaritans who still live at Nablus (near Mt. Gerazim where their ancient temple stood, John 4:20) and just south of Tel Aviv. The importance of this text is that it was preserved independently of the Masoretic text even though the oldest copies in existence were not made until the eleventh century. Only in a few instances do scholars think that the Samaritan Pentateuch preserves readings superior to the Masoretic text.

Another tool to trace the history behind the Masoretic text is the Aramaic paraphrases of the Old Testament known as the *Targums.* They originated because the Jews in the synagogues in the Middle East could not understand the Hebrew Scripture. Someone stood alongside the reader of the text (read in Hebrew) and recited Aramaic paraphrases, which in time became stereotyped. The earliest of these to be written down came before the time of Christ (a fragment of a Targum on Job was discovered among the Dead Sea Scrolls in the eleventh cave from Qumran). Most of the manuscripts of the Targums originated 500 to 1000 A.D. Because they are paraphrases and not strict translations, the Targums are more of interest for determining Jewish doctrine in the time of their origin than for determining the early stages of the text of the Old Testament.

A much more important source for textual history is the *Septuagint.* This is a Greek translation of the Old Testament made from about 250 to 100 B.C. or shortly thereafter. It was made in Alexandria, Egypt, to meet the needs of Jews and others who wanted to read the Old Testament but lacked the facility to read Hebrew. The Septuagint represents an official translation which likely replaced a variety of earlier unofficial translations. Basic problems in using a translation to seek to study the earlier wording of the Hebrew text are: the difficulty of determining the exact readings of Hebrew text(s) used by the original translators because of the innate differences in all languages, the difficulties in establishing the original readings of the Greek translation by studying the many manuscripts of it, and uncertainty concerning the quality of the translation itself. Nevertheless, the Septuagint does preserve some readings (especially in Exodus, Samuel, and Jeremiah) that appear to be superior to the Masoretic text. Some of them are supported by copies of the Hebrew texts found at Qumran. There are other Greek translations of the Old Testament made by Jews to replace the Septuagint. The two most famous were made in the second century A.D. by Aquila and Theodotion.

The most important source for textual information beyond the Masoretic Text is the *Dead Sea Scrolls.* Most of these were discovered in the caves by the wadi Qumran on the shores of the Dead Sea beginning in 1947. Others were found further south in the wilderness of Judea and at Masada. The oldest copies of Old Testament Scriptures found in these discoveries are manuscripts written in the second century before Christ. They are over a thousand years older than the basic manuscripts of the Masoretic texts. They represent the remains of a library of a group of separatist Jews who lived in the caves in the area and worked in a type of monastery. Along with Old Testament manuscripts, the caves preserved documents written by the participants in the community and their founders. Biblical manuscripts have been found containing fragments or complete copies from every book of the Old Testament except Esther. The scrolls from Qumran do differ from the Masoretic text in some places (1375 places in Isaiah), but most are insignificant.

Other versions of the Old Testament such as the Syriac, Old Latin, the Latin Vulgate, etc. can be used, but none of these yield many significant variants from the Masoretic texts. The copies of the Hebrew Bible available today are the work of very careful Hebrew scribes. Though there are variations, the text of the Hebrew Bible is essentially as it existed in the time before Christ. The early Christians had access to either the Hebrew text or to the Septuagint. When the Septuagint was no longer used by the Jews (about A.D. 90), it was preserved by the Christians and used by them. About half of the Old Testament quotes in Paul are from the Septuagint as are almost all of the quotes in 1 Peter, James, and Hebrews. The famous Latin Vulgate of Jerome contained the books in the Septuagint not found in the Hebrew Bible plus 2 Esdras. These are called the Apocrypha.

2. New Testament Text and Versions. From near the middle of the second century on most Christians equated many Christian writings with the Scriptures of the Jews. The term "Old Testament," implying a "New Testament," was first used by Christians in A.D. 187. These writings were preserved at first mostly on papyrus, a form of paper made from the papyrus plant which grew in the Nile Delta. It was perishable, and very few copies survived. In 1976, only 88 separate fragments of papyrus New Testament manuscripts were known. Few of them contain in their present state more than a part of a single page of text. The original papyrus manuscripts contained only portions of the New Testament, such as the Gospels and Acts or Paul's letters or the Revelation or some or all of the General Epistles. The earliest of these date from the second and third centuries. During that period the New Testament did not circulate as a single volume. Apparently all New Testament manuscripts so far discovered were made in the leaf form of books, not on rolls.

The New Testament circulated as a single volume in the time of the great parchment manuscripts. Parchment was made from the skins of animals. The earliest of these to contain the New Testament also contain the Old Testament (in the form of the Septuagint with the outside books) and other Christian writings such as 1 and 2 Clement or The Shepherd of Hermas and the Letter of Barnabas. The earliest of these were written in the middle of the fourth century.

Not only manuscripts written in Greek, the language of the New Testament, but also Christian writings which quote from the Greek New Testament furnish evidence for the text of the New Testament. However, some of the Christian "fathers" were very loose in their quotes or quoted from faulty memories. Another factor is that not all the writings were preserved carefully.

Another major source of information about the text of the New Testament is the versions. From the very beginning of the Christian story, translation has been an essential part of the process. We have less than a dozen words of Jesus preserved in Aramaic, the language which He spoke. Hence, almost all that he said was translated into Greek before it was written down. The accusation written over the cross was written in the three languages used in Palestine: Latin, Hebrew (probably Aramaic), and Greek. When the Christians, fleeing from the persecution in which Stephen died, arrived in Antioch, they needed to use Syriac to evangelize the surrounding areas. By the middle of the second century, extensive efforts had been made to translate all the Scriptures into the Old Latin and Syriac. From the third century on followed translations into the various dialects of the Egyptian languages, the languages of Armenia, Georgia, Ethiopia, Arabia, Nubia, and the areas of Europe.

In the West, Latin became the major language of the church. The Latin Vulgate, produced about 400 A.D. by Jerome, became the Bible of the Latin Church. Among the Eastern Orthodox, Greek remained the official language of the Scriptures. Thus during the long period from 400 to 1500, most New Testament Greek manuscripts used the official text of the Orthodox Church. Hence, today most Greek New Testament manuscripts are of the type designated as Byzantine, Ecclesiastical, *Koine,* Standard, or Eastern. The earlier and (for most scholars) the most reliable ones are of the Alexandrian (also called Neutral, Egyptian, and African) type. When the printers in the fifteenth and sixteenth centuries looked for manuscripts from which to edit the earliest printed Greek New Testaments, all that they could find were those of the Byzantine type. Since then, the process of discovery and editing of manuscripts has brought to light over 5,300 handwritten copies of all or part of the New Testament. The process of editing and utilizing all of this material in producing the earliest possible text for readers today is the task of textual criticism. It is a painstaking job done mostly by scholars in the universities, colleges, seminaries, and Bible societies. As always, a major impetus for this work is missionary. Without textual criticism no modern Bibles in any language would be possible.   *Carlton L. Winbery*

BIBLE, THEOLOGY OF Biblical theology is one of four primary types of theology and needs to be carefully distinguished from the other three. *1.* In common usage, the single word "theology" usually denotes the study of doctrine in a *systematic* or orderly, organized form. It draws insight both from the Bible and from history and numerous other fields of study to give the widest possible application of the biblical principles. Systematic theology may be done in a denominational context. For instance, Baptist theology or Methodist theology is the Christian doctrines presented as Baptists or Methodists understand them. Such a doctrinal statement of belief may be strongly influenced by biblical teaching, but insight is also drawn from the history of Baptists (or Methodists, etc.). No denomination's theology is a presentation of "pure" biblical thought; its theology draws insight from its own history, and seeks to apply biblical principles to its current life setting. Systematic theology seeks to give a comprehensive statement of belief, describing all of the major points of belief in their contemporary significance.

2. Historical theology is a study of the doctrinal teachings in various ages, usually tracing the development from ancient times to the present, bringing out the distinctive and changing emphases from age to age. This discipline is closely related to church history, but it is historical study narrowly focused on theology or doctrine.

3. *Philosophical* theology is a statement of Christian belief which seeks to take the basic elements of the teachings of the Bible and translate them into philosophical concepts. It may also seek to use the creative powers of human reason to create a system of belief. Such a statement may be fairly closely related to biblical thought. On the other hand, such a system of belief may be entirely speculative, going far afield from biblical teachings.

4. *Biblical* theology is a narrowly focused field of study, as compared to these other types of theology. Usually, biblical theology does not even seek to give the doctrinal or theological teachings of the Bible as a whole. It seeks to isolate and express the theological teachings of a specific portion of Scripture, such as the theology of the Pentateuch (first five books of the Old Testament), or the theology of the prophets, or the theology of the Synoptic Gospels (Matthew, Mark, Luke), or the theology of John, or the theology of the Pauline writings, etc. Such study seeks to show the development of thought from early times to the close of the New Testament. As some people do biblical theology, such a study only emphasizes the diversity found in the Bible. Others find an overall unity of theological thought, but trace considerable diversity within that unity. Some will interpret the theology of the Bible in such a way that there is only unity, allowing for no development of thought, or diversity, from Genesis to Revelation. Some who seek to develop biblical theology will finally synthesize the teachings of the Bible as a whole as the end product of their study of the theology of the Bible. They choose not to leave biblical theology as a series of statements of differing beliefs found in various periods of the Bible. Such a statement should not be taken to mean that the Bible teaches exactly that point of view at every point in the Scriptures. Rather, this is a statement of the biblical teaching in its completed form, allowing for development of the various themes from the beginning to the end of the Bible.

Many credit J. P. Gabler, German biblical scholar, with beginning the field of biblical theology. In his inaugural address in a professorship in 1787, Gabler called for a sharp distinction between dogmatic (systematic or doctrinal) theology and biblical theology. For Gabler, biblical theology must be strictly a historical study of what was believed in the various periods of biblical history, independent of any modern denominational, doctrinal, philosophical, or cultural considerations.

In general, the principles that Gabler called for were right, and he influenced the development of biblical theology for many years to come. However, it should be noted, that there is no such thing as "a study of the Bible alone with complete objectivity." Every interpreter brings certain presuppositions to the task. These have considerable influence upon the process of interpreting the Scriptures. As a result, the field of biblical theology is a checkered field with every imaginable variation in what is held to be the theology taught by the Bible.

Biblical theology is utterly dependent upon the hermeneutics of the theologian (See *Bible, Hermeneutics; Bible, History of Interpretation*). The methods employed in interpreting Scriptures are crucially important to doing biblical theology. One's biblical theology can be no better than his methods used to interpret Scriptures.

Content. What, then, is the theology of the Bible as a traditional conservative theologian views it? Biblical theology today needs to give due consideration to the real history recorded in the Bible and seek to interpret the Scriptures in the light of historical considerations, with due regard for their literary form and construction. Such theology recognizes an overall unity of the Bible. The Bible is much more than a book of miscellaneous, disconnected religious ideas that emerged over a period of nearly two thousand years. These theologians recognize a development of teaching, a progressive revelation, as God has worked with His people leading them from a point of beginning to the climax of New Testament Christianity. Many New Testament teachings are not found, or even hinted at, in the Old Testament. These New Testament advances are the completion or fulfillment of what was started in the Old Testament, not a contradiction. Later revelation does not contradict earlier revelation; the later expands, fulfills, or interprets the earlier. With the development, historical diversity, and progression, God has led to a unity of teaching. A distinct difference separates the Old Testament and the New Testament, but a fundamental unity joins the two Testaments. The Old Testament is the preparation for the New. The New Testament is the fulfillment of the Old. Theological themes begun in the Old Testament are often carried to completion in the New Testament. For instance, the practice of sacrifice which began as early as Genesis 4:4 (apparently without any divine command) and became an officially commanded practice of the Old Testament under the law given through Moses, was carried through to the climactic once-for-all sacrifice of Jesus Christ as the Lamb of God slain from the foundation of the world.

Central Theme. One central theme runs through the Bible from first to last. God is the central character in the Bible. His work to bring redemption to humans is the central theme. The Bible is a religious book, focused narrowly upon redemption and its implications for our lives.

The Bible begins with the religious teaching that God created humans and the world in which they live. Human responsibility to God is grounded in the religious truth that humans come from God's creative hand. The first man and woman sinned in deliberate rebellion against God, breaking their fellowship with God. Their sin spread from them to all of their descendants, making sinful alienation from God the number one problem of all of us as human beings. The spread of this sin is not an automatic process but one which involves the personal, willful act of each of us so that we are all accountable for our sins. The Bible then proceeds to develop the theme of God's redemptive grace, tracing various stages of God's revelation of Himself: the call of Abraham; the establishment of the covenant with the Israelite community as His chosen people; the institution of the sacrificial system, teaching the people the proper way to approach God for forgiveness; the life, death, and resurrection of Jesus as the provision of forgiveness and regeneration for those dead in sin; the church as the new covenant community, the redeemed people of God on mission for Him in the world; finally, the life to come, in heaven for the redeemed, and in hell for the unregenerate.

The theme of the two covenants is crucially important to the unity of the Bible. God's plan of redemption, bringing people into a right relationship to Himself, begins with the call of Abraham and the establishment of a covenant with him. Subsequently, this covenant was reaffirmed with his son Isaac; with Isaac's son Jacob, whose name was changed to Israel; and finally the covenant was reaffirmed with the whole nation of Israel. It was an unconditional covenant on God's part but a conditional covenant from the human side: God's people must live up to the covenant respon-

sibilities. The major portion of the Old Testament is the story of repeated failure to live up to the covenant responsibilities. The prophet Jeremiah looked forward to a new day when God would write His covenant on the hearts of the people so that it could not be broken (Jer. 31:31–34), a prophecy of the new birth referred to by Jesus in John 3:1–8. Jesus termed His death on the cross as the sacrifice instituting the new covenant referred to by Jeremiah (Luke 22:20). This shows the remarkable unity of the Old and New Testaments as anticipation and fulfillment.

God. The doctrine of God begins in the Old Testament with the work of God in creation. The Old Testament has four major emphases concerning God. *1.* First, and most basic, is the *unity of God:* one and only one God exists and rules this world. The theme was hard to establish in the minds of the people who repeatedly fell into worship of idols and pagan deities. *2. The holiness of God* teaches the wholly otherness of God. God's holiness is the qualitative difference between God and all else. It is supremely important for humans to learn that God is holy and must be treated with reverence. *3. God's sovereignty* is often expressed as His lordship. Since God is sovereign, He must be obeyed at all costs; all persons must give account to Him. *4. God's faithfulness.* God is not fickle and changeable like the gods of the pagans. He is faithful and unchanging. The New Testament completes the doctrine of God by sharpening the focus on God as Father and the primacy of God's love.

A person is a creature of God but a very special creature. A person is made in the image of God. This means that God has created a spiritual being, made primarily to live in fellowship with God and act responsibly in maintaining God's creation. In an act of selfish rebellion the first people sinned against God. Sin corrupted human nature, leaving all people highly susceptible to sin. Except for Jesus Christ, each person who has lived since Adam and Eve has followed in their footsteps, sinning against God.

A person's need for redemption has at least five aspects: 1. guilt must be forgiven and removed; 2. people must learn responsible obedience; 3. they must learn reverence and respect for God; 4. they must learn to live by faith; 5. they must learn to live for God's purposes, not selfish whims. The whole Bible is the unfolding story of how God has met each of these needs through the salvation that unfolded finally in its completed form through the life, death, and resurrection of Jesus Christ.

Jesus Christ. Jesus Christ is the eternal Son of God who took on human life, living as one Person who was both God and human in a single human life on this earth. His coming was prophesied in the Old Testament as the coming of a Messiah, a Suffering Servant who would redeem His people. In the New Testament, His life unfolded as a revelation from God of what God Himself is like. He spoke the ultimate message from God, in clearer, more forceful ways than God had ever spoken by prophet or priest in other times. He died on the cross and was raised the third day as the ultimate fulfillment of the ancient sacrificial system. New Testament writers saw His death variously, not only as the ultimate sacrifice, but also the ultimate expression of God's forgiving love. They saw Jesus' death and resurrection as the way in which God conquered sin and death, and opened regeneration to mankind as God shares the power of Jesus' resurrection with those who come to Him by faith.

Following Jesus' personal ministry on the earth, He ascended to the Father in heaven to resume His rightful place at the right hand of God. In His place, the Holy Spirit of God came as the very presence of Jesus with the disciples of Jesus, dwelling in each believer. The Holy Spirit is the agent of regeneration and supplies both nurture and guidance to the Christian, equipping each believer for an effective life of service to God in the church and in the world.

Salvation. Salvation comes to the individual person upon a response of faith in receiving the free gift of God's grace. Salvation includes both the forgiveness of sin and the regeneration of the sinful human nature. Salvation issues in a new style of living under the leadership of God, with the Christian living for the purposes of God in this world. Salvation, properly understood, should include a life of spiritual growth, ever moving towards the goal of Christlike living.

The church is seen as the new covenant community, the fulfillment of the old covenant community in the Old Testament. It is not a radical break with the old covenant community but is the logical outgrowth of the people of God in the Old Testament era. It is described as the body of Christ, with Christ as the head of the body, His life flowing out into all parts of the body, as He gives direction to it and works through it in the world just as once He worked through His own physical body in the world.

The Bible points to a time of ultimate fulfillment when God shall complete what He has been doing in this world from the beginning of creation. Jesus will return to this earth, the kingdom of God will be consummated, the dead will be resurrected, and all persons will have continued existence, with the unregenerate spending eternity in hell and believers in Christ spending eternity with God in heaven.

J. Terry Young

BIBLE, TRANSLATIONS The Old Testament was written in Hebrew and Aramaic and the New Testament in Greek, the languages both of the writers and of those who were expected to read the books in the first instance. The complete Bible has been translated into 293 languages and dialects, the New Testament into 618 additional ones, and individual books into 918 more languages. The process of translation is ongoing in the effort to make God's Word available to all in languages which everyone can understand.

Early Translations The Samaritan Pentateuch used by the Samaritan community is a form of Hebrew written in a different script (Samaritan characters) from that which the Jewish community later came to use. The Aramaic translations called Targums have their beginning in the pre-Christian period and are represented in the Qumran finds; but the major Targums came later.

The Old Testament was translated into Greek about 250 B.C. for the royal library of Alexandria. Named from the seventy translators who are said to have made it, the Septuagint, though made by Jews, has come down to us through Christian channels. Later Greek translations were made in the early period by Aquila, Symmachus, and Theodotion.

The evangelistic thrust of the early church gave impetus for many translations to impart the gospel to peoples in diverse language areas of the Roman empire. Before the 400 A.D., the Bible had been made available in Latin, Syriac, Coptic, Ethiopic, Armenian, and Georgian. The succeeding centuries brought still other translations.

In the West, the church primarily used Latin after the end of the second century, and unofficial translations were made. In the fourth century Pope Damascus invited Jerome to revise current Latin translations based on Hebrew and Greek manuscripts. Jerome completed the new translation after eighteen years of work at Bethlehem. Jerome's translation came to be the accepted Bible, and by 1200 A.D. was called the Vulgate, the official version for the Roman Catholic Church.

Reformation Translations The invention of printing in 1443 and the onset of the Protestant Reformation in 1517 stimulated great interest in Bible translation. Most of the modern languages of Europe had printed translations made at that time: German, 1466; Italian, 1471; Spanish, 1478; and French, 1487. Each of these areas has a long history of manuscript translation prior to printing.

English Translations Efforts to render Scripture into English began with Caedmon's paraphrases into Anglo-Saxon (A.D. 670). Bede (A.D. 735) is said to have translated the Gospel of John, completing it on the last day of his life. It was, however, John Wyclif and his associates (A.D. 1382) who are given credit for having first given the English the complete Bible in their own language.

Erasmus printed the Greek New Testament for the first time in 1516. Luther made his German translation in 1522–1524; and William Tyndale in 1525 brought out his English New Testament—the first printed one to circulate in England. Making use of Tyndale's material where available, Miles Coverdale brought out his complete Bible in 1535.

From this point the history of the English Reformation and the history of the English Bible go hand in glove with each other. Coverdale's Bible was followed by Matthew's Bible in 1537. Then in 1539, Coverdale with the king's approval brought out the Great Bible, named for its large size.

With the coming of Mary Tudor to the throne in 1553, the printing of Bibles was temporarily interrupted; but the exiles in Geneva, led by William Whittingham, produced the Geneva Bible in 1560. This proved to be particularly popular, especially with the later Puritans. Matthew Parker, Archbishop of Canterbury, then had the Bishops' Bible prepared, primarily by bishops of the Church of England, which went through twenty editions. Roman Catholics brought out their Rheims New Testament in 1582 and then the Old Testament in 1610. The period of Elizabeth was the time of England's greatest literary figures.

With Elizabeth's death and the coming of King James I to the throne at the Hampton Court Conference in January 1604, the king accepted the proposal that a new translation be made. The outcome was the King James Version of 1611. It is number nine in the sequence of printed English Bibles and is a revision of the Bishops' Bible. The KJV was heavily criticized in its early days; but in time, with official pressure, it won the field and became "the Bible" for English-reading people—a position it has held for almost four hundred years. The KJV has undergone numerous modifications so that the currently circulating book differs from that of 1611 in many ways, though the basic text is essentially the same.

By 1850, large numbers of people felt the time had come for a revision. A motion made by Bishop Wilberforce in the Convocation of Canterbury carried, setting in operation the making of the Revised Version whose New Testament appeared in 1881 and its complete Bible in 1885. The best British scholars of the day participated in the revision, and American scholars were also invited for a limited role. Though launched with great publicity, the revision eventually provoked harsh criticism. In time it became obvious that people still preferred the KJV. The revised edition was more accurate; however, the style was awkward.

The Americans waited out the fifteen years which they had promised before they would bring out a rival revision. The American Standard Revised Version was issued in 1901 with the American preferences in the text and the British in an appendix. It was more accurate than the KJV; but the revisers made the mistake of using an English style not native to English at any time. Wishing a literal translation, they produced one which is really English in Greek and Hebrew grammar and word order.

English Bible Translations in the Twentieth Century At the turn of the century Adolf Deissmann, using study of the papyri from Egypt, persuaded scholars that the New Testament was in the common language (the Koine) of the first century, giving impetus to an effort to present the Bible in the language of the twentieth century. Accompanying this development was the rise of archaeological discovery which gave new manuscripts of both the Old and New Testaments. The Cairo Genizah collection of Hebrew manuscripts was found at the end of the last century, and the Dead Sea Scrolls in 1947. Perhaps twenty-five Greek manuscripts of the New Testament could have been used in 1611. Now 5357 are known. The papyri which now total ninety-three items and are older than the great codices were found. Wider knowledge of the nature of the biblical and related languages has been gained, making for more accurate definitions. New scholarly grammars, dictionaries, and anthologies of texts grew out of these developments. Besides these matters is the simple fact that the English language continually changes so that what is understandable at one period becomes less so at a later one.

The first half of the twentieth century saw a spate of translations which abandoned the effort to revise the KJV and attempted to reflect new trends, each from its own viewpoint. They had a limited vogue in some circles while being criticized in others. Some were works of groups; others were prepared by one person; none seriously threatened the dominance of the KJV.

The Revised Standard Version, with its New Testament ready in 1946 and the complete Bible in 1952 bore the brunt of criticism of modern translations because it was the first serious challenge after 1901 to the long dominance of the KJV. It retained the Old English forms in liturgical and poetic passages, as well as using Old English pronouns when deity is addressed. Eventually an edition was issued with modifications to make it acceptable for use by Greek Orthodox and Roman Catholics which is called the "Common Bible." After forty years the RSV is rapidly becoming archaic. The New Revised Standard Version appeared in 1990.

The British have prepared the New English Bible (1970) which represents certain trends in British biblical scholarship. The American reader will see differences between British English and American English.

Roman Catholics issued the Jerusalem Bible, which with its notes is used both in and out of Catholic circles. Of more widespread influence is the New American Bible (1970) which was used in preparing the English version of the liturgy of the Roman church. While making some concessions, its notes support Catholic doctrine.

The Jewish community has produced the New Jewish Publication Society translation (1962–1982).

The paraphrase found a champion in Kenneth Taylor with his Living Bible Paraphrased (1971), which has more recently been issued under the name The Book. Taylor attempts to restate the biblical message in different words from those used by the writers, hoping to make it more understandable. Taylor, not a Hebrew or Greek scholar, paraphrased the American Standard Version. The accuracy of his work has been heavily criticized by Greek and Hebrew scholars. A revision was being prepared as this article was written.

Those who prefer literal translation found their representatives in the New American Standard Bible (NAS) prepared by the Lockman Foundation (1963). An attempt to give the ASV new life, this effort removes many archaisms from the ASV; it reflects different judgments on textual questions from the ASV, and its generous use of items which have been supplied by the translators in italics invites reinterpretation of passages.

An effort to preserve as much of the old as possible is the New King James Bible (1982). This is a "halfway house" for those who know that something needs to replace the KJV but who are not willing to have a translation which represents the current state of knowledge and which uses current language.

An effort to meet the needs of those who have English as a second language or those who have a limited knowledge of English is Today's English Version (TEV), also known as the Good News Bible (1976). Recasting of language, consolidation of statements, and paraphrasing have all been employed in the effort to make the message simple enough to be grasped by the reader.

The New International Version was issued in 1978 by the International Bible Society from a cooperative project in which more than 110 scholars representing thirty-four religious groups participated. Abandoning any effort to revise the KJV line of Bibles, the NIV is a new translation aiming at accuracy, clarity, and dignity. It attempts to steer a middle course between literalness and paraphrase while attaining a contemporary style for the English reader.

The translation effort in all its forms is a sincere effort on the part of many people of many different religious persuasions to make the Bible accessible and understandable to people to whom it might otherwise be a closed book. A diligent study of any of the efforts will increase one's understanding of the Bible. The ultimate translation is one that influences the behaviors in readers' lives and brings them hope. The task of translation is not finished. New discoveries and new students of God's Word will bring still more translations of the Bible to serve the church and its mission in generations to come.   *Jack P. Lewis*

BICHRI (Bĭch′ rī) Personal name meaning, "firstborn" or clan name, "of the clan of Becher." Father of Sheba, who led revolt against David after Absalom's revolt (2 Sam. 20:1).

BICHRITE (Bĭch′ rīte) RSV reading of Berites. See *Berites.*

BICRI (Bĭc′ rī) NIV spelling of Bichri. See *Bichri.*

BIDKAR (Bĭd′ kär) Officer of Jehu who took body of Joram, king of Israel (852–841 B.C.), and threw it on Naboth's land after Jehu murdered the king (2 Kings 9:25). Bidkar and Jehu had originally served as chariot officers for Ahab, Joram's father.

BIER Litter or bed upon which a body was placed before burial. They were portable (2 Sam. 3:31; Luke 7:14). Biers in biblical times have been compared to the wooden boards used in Muslim funerals to carry bodies today. Asa's bier was of a more elaborate type of burial couch that was probably placed in the tomb. The Hebrew word for bier (*mitta*) is the normal word for bed and is translated bier only when referring to burials.

BIGTHA (Bĭg′ thà) Persian personal name possibly meaning, "gift of God." A eunuch who served King Ahasuerus of Persia and took command to Queen Vashti to come to party (Esther 1:10). Bigthan (Esther 2:21) may be same person. See Bigthan.

BIGTHAN (Bĭg′ thăn) May be identical with Bigtha. See *Bigtha.* He plotted with Teresh, another of the king's eunuchs, to assassinate King Ahasuerus of Persia (Esther 2:21). Mordecai foiled the plot, thus setting up the king's need to honor Mordecai at Haman's expense (Esther 6:1−12).

BIGTHANA (Bĭg·thā′ nà) Alternate spelling in Hebrew of Bigthan (Esther 6:2). See *Bigthan.*

BIGVAI (Bĭg′ và-ī) Persian name meaning, "god" or "fortune." 1. Leader with Zerubbabel of exiles who returned from Babylon about 537 B.C. (Ezra 2:2). Either he or another person of same name was original clan ancestor of 2,056 people who returned (Ezra 2:14). When Ezra returned about 458 B.C., 72 members of the clan returned (Ezra 8:14). 2. One who sealed Nehemiah's covenant to obey God's law (Neh. 10:16).

BIKRI (Bĭk′ rī) TEV spelling of Bichri. See *Bichri.*

BILDAD (Bĭl′ dăd) Proper name meaning, "the Lord loved." One of the three friends of Job (Job 2:11). He is identified as a Shuhite, perhaps a member of a group of nomadic Arameans. His speeches reveal him as a defender of traditionalist theological views. He argues that a just God does not punish the innocent (ch. 8). Job should admit he was suffering the just fate of the wicked (ch. 18), and no person can be righteous before the awesome God (ch. 25). See *Job.*

BILEAM (Bil' ē·ăm) City given to Levites from tribal territory of western Manasseh. It is often identified with Ibleam. See *Ibleam.* Joshua 21:25, a parallel passage reads, "Gath-rimmon."

BILGAH (Bil' găh) Personal name meaning "brightness." *1.* Original ancestor of one of divisions of priesthood (1 Chron. 24:14). *2.* Priest who returned from Exile with Zerubbabel about 537 B.C. (Neh. 12:5).

BILGAI (Bil' ga·ī) Priest who sealed Nehemiah's covenant to obey God's law (Neh. 10:8).

BILHAH (Bil' häh) Personal name meaning, "unworried." The handmaid of Rachel (Gen. 29:29). When Rachel failed to bear children to her husband Jacob, Bilhah became his concubine at Rachel's instigation. Bilhah became the mother of Dan and Naphtali (Gen. 29:29; 30:4–7). See *Patriarchs; Tribes of Israel.*

BILHAN (Bil' hăn) Personal name perhaps meaning, "afraid" or "foolish." *1.* Descendant of Seir or Edom (Gen. 36:27). *2.* A descendant of Benjamin (1 Chron. 7:10).

BILL OF DIVORCEMENT See *Divorce.*

BILSHAN (Bil' shăn) Akkadian personal name meaning, "their lord." Leader of returning exiles with Zerubbabel from Babylon about 537 B.C. (Ezra 2:2).

BIMHAL (Bim' hăl) Descendant of tribe of Asher (1 Chron. 7:33).

BINDING AND LOOSING describe the concept that the church has the power and means to announce that sin was condemned or forgiven.

The keys to the kingdom given to Peter was a symbol in locking or unlocking sins and illustrate his authority in binding or loosing (Matt. 16:19). Later (Matt. 18:18) the same power was given to the apostles and the church as a whole. It is not an exclusive gift to any one person or church. The question of how sins are forgiven is raised in the meaning of binding and loosing. Whatever the church declared to be wrong or right would have been anticipated and ratified in heaven by divine sanction. This means that whatsoever shall have been forgiven on earth shall have been forgiven in heaven. Heaven sets the standard, earth follows heaven's lead. It is the responsibility of believers to have a forgiving spirit and to teach the conditions of forgiveness (Matt. 6:12). In John 20:23

Jesus said "Whose soever sins ye remit, they are remitted unto them; and whose soever sins ye retain, they are retained." This means that the church is to proclaim the way of salvation and those who accept Him are forgiven, but those who reject Him are condemned. Binding and loosing is determined by the hearer's response. Sins have been washed (loosed) by the blood of Jesus (Rev. 1:5)   *Lawson Hatfield*

BINEA (Bin' ē·à) A descendant of the tribe of Benjamin (1 Chron. 8:37) and of King Saul (1 Chron. 10:43).

BINNUI (Bin' nū·ī) Personal name meaning, "built." *1.* A Levite who assured the Temple treasures Ezra brought back from Exile were correctly inventoried (Ezra 8:33). *2.* Two men who divorced foreign wives when Ezra sought to remove temptation to idolatry and purify the community (Ezra 10:30,38). *3.* Man who helped Nehemiah repair the wall of Jerusalem (Neh. 3:24). *4.* Clan leader of 648 members who returned with Zerubbabel from Babylon about 537 B.C. (Neh. 7:15; Ezra 2:10—spells it "Bani" with 642 people). *5.* Levite who sealed Nehemiah's covenant to obey God's law (Neh. 10:9). Could be same as any of the above. He came up with Zerubbabel from Babylonian Exile (Neh. 12:8).

BIRDS The Bible contains approximately three hundred references to birds, scattered from Genesis to Revelation. The Hebrew people's keen awareness of bird life is reflected in the numerous different Hebrew and Greek names used for birds in general or for specific birds. Although bird names are difficult to translate, many birds of the Bible can be identified from the descriptions of them given in the Scriptures.

General Terminology Several general terms for birds occur in the Bible. In the Old Testament the Hebrew term *'oph,* the most general term for birds, is used collectively to refer to flying creatures or fowl, as well as to winged insects. The term *'oph* occurs repeatedly in the creation narrative of Genesis 1 and 2 (Gen. 1:20, 21, 22, 26, 28, 30; 2:19, 20). Genesis 6:20 notes the division of birds into species. Leviticus 20:25 categorizes them as clean or unclean. Leviticus 11:13–19 and Deuteronomy 14:12–18 list the specific birds which the Hebrews regarded as unclean and therefore not to be eaten. All birds of prey, including eagles, vultures, hawks, and falcons, were classified as unclean.

A second general term used for birds in the Old Testament is *tsippor.* Like *'oph, tsippor* may refer to birds of every kind (Gen. 7:14; Deut. 4:17), but it usually denotes game birds (Ps. 124:7; Prov. 6:5) or the perching birds (passerines, Ps. 102:7; Dan. 4:12). From the term *tsippor* the name of Moses' wife (Zipporah) is derived.

In the New Testament the Greek term *peteinon* is used for birds in general (Matt. 6:26; 8:20; 13:4; Luke 9:58; 12:24; Acts 10:12; 11:6; Rom. 1:23). The term *orneon* is used in Revelation to describe the completeness of Babylon's destruction (18:2) and to refer to flesh-eating fowl (19:17, 21).

Specific Birds Named in the Bible Apart from the general terminology, the Bible mentions a great number of birds by name. Translators use different English equivalents to refer to the various birds. Among the birds specifically named in the RSV translation of the Bible are:

Cock The crowing of the cock is probably the most well-known bird sound in the Bible. All of the New Testament references to the cock (except the mention of "cockcrow" in Mark 13:35) relate to Peter's denial of Christ. Jesus warned Peter that before the cock crowed twice, Peter would deny Him three times (Mark 14:30). Roosters first crowed about midnight and a second time around three o'clock in the morning. Their crowing occurred so punctually that the Romans relied on this bird sound to signal the time to change the guard.

Dove/Turtledove The term "dove" is applied rather loosely to many of the smaller species of pigeon. The first mention of the dove in the Bible occurs in Genesis 8:8–12. Noah released a dove from the ark to determine if the flood waters had subsided from the earth.

The moaning of the dove sometimes functions metaphorically (Isa. 38:14; 59:11; Ezek. 7:16). Psalm 55:6 notes the dove's powers of flight; Jeremiah 48:28 describes its nesting habits; Psalm 68:13 indicates its rich colors. Because of the gentleness of the dove and because of its faithfulness to its mate, this bird is used as a descriptive title of one's beloved in the Song of Solomon (2:14; 5:2; 6:9). In Matthew 10:16 the dove symbolizes innocence.

All four Gospels describe the Spirit of God descending like a dove upon Jesus after His baptism (Matt. 3:16; Mark 1:10; Luke 3:22; John 1:32).

The term "turtledove" also is applied to any of the smaller varieties of pigeon. The turtledove played a significant sacrificial role in the Bible (Gen. 15:9; Lev. 1:14; 5:7,11; 12:6; 14:22, 30; 15:14; Luke 2:24). For those who could not afford a lamb, the law prescribed that two turtledoves or pigeons be offered for the sacrifice of purification after childbearing. Mary brought such an offering after the birth of Christ (Lev. 12:8; Luke 2:24). The turtledove also signified the arrival of spring (Song of Sol. 2:12; Jer. 8:7).

Eagle The term "eagle" refers to several large birds of prey active in the daytime rather than at night. The Hebrew term translated "eagle" (*nesher*) also sometimes is translated "vulture." The eagle, the largest flying bird of Palestine, may reach a wingspread of eight feet or more. The Palestinian eagle builds great nests of sticks on rocky crags in the mountains (Job 39:27–28; Jer. 49:16). As one of the most majestic birds, it occupies a prominent role in the Bible. The eagle appears in the lists of unclean birds (Lev. 11:13; Deut. 14:12). Old Testament writers noted the eagle's swift movement (Deut. 28:49; 2 Sam. 1:23; Jer. 4:13), the sweep and power of its flight (Prov. 23:5; Isa. 40:31), and the eagle's concern for its young (Ex. 19:4; Deut. 32:11).

In the ancient world the eagle or vulture often was associated with deity. The prophets and apocalyptists chose this bird to play a figurative or symbolic role in their writings (Ezek. 1:10; 10:14; Dan. 7:4; Rev. 4:7; 8:13).

In Exodus 19:4 and Deuteronomy 32:11 the eagle is used figuratively of God's protection and care. In these passages God is pictured as a loving parent who redeems and protects His people even as the parent eagle cares for its young.

Hen The Greek word translated "hen" can refer to the female of any bird, not just the domesticated fowl. Only two references to the hen occur in the Scriptures (Matt. 23:37; Luke 13:34). In both instances the term is used figuratively of God's care for His people. The hen stands as a figure of the self-sacrifice and tender motherliness of God revealed in Christ.

Ostrich The ostrich, the largest of birds, is a swift, flightless fowl. One passage in Job (39:13–18) describes some of the characteristic habits of the ostrich. The female lays her eggs in the sand. The male does most of the incubating, mainly at night. Unhatched eggs serve as food for the young. Although the parent bird leaves the nest when it senses danger, this diversionary tactic actually is a protective measure. However, such habits may have created the impression that the ostrich was indifferent to its young (Lam. 4:3). The ostrich is listed as unclean (Lev. 11:16; Deut. 14:15), probably because of its eating habits.

Pigeon "Pigeon" is a general term referring to any of a widely distributed subfamily of fowl (*Columbinae*). The term "pigeon" basically is employed when referring to the use of these birds for sacrificial offerings. In Leviticus pigeons serve as burnt offerings and as sin offerings (Lev. 1:14; 5:7,11). They also play a role in the rituals for purification following childbirth (Lev. 12:6,8) and for the cleansing of a healed leper (Lev. 14:22,30). Along with turtledoves, pigeons are the least expensive animal offerings. Mary offered a pigeon and two turtledoves after Jesus' birth (Luke 2:24).

Quail The Hebrew term translated "quail" in the Old Testament is found only in connection with God's provision of food for Israel in the wilderness (Ex. 16:13; Num. 11:31–32; Ps. 105:40). Probably the quails which visited the Hebrew camp were a migrating flock. Enormous numbers of quails migrate north during the spring after wintering in Africa. When the fatigued birds stop to rest, they can be caught easily. In God's timing the birds came to provide for the needs of His people.

The quails mentioned in the Old Testament differ from the North American bobwhite quails. Besides being migratory, the quails of the Bible are mottled brown in color and are smaller than the bobwhite quails. The quails mentioned in the Old Testament have short wings and weak powers of flight.

Raven The raven, conspicuous because of its black color (Song of Sol. 5:11), is a member of the crow family. The raven acts as a scavenger and is listed among the unclean birds (Lev. 11;15; Deut. 14:14). Biblical writers cite the raven as an example of God's care for His creation (Job 38:41; Ps. 147:9; Luke 12:24).

The raven was the first bird Noah sent forth from the ark following the flood (Gen. 8:7). He may have selected the raven for several reasons. It can fly without rest for long spans of time. Also the raven makes its home in the rocky crags, and thus it would scout out mountain peaks emerging from the flooded earth. Finally, the raven is a resourceful bird with a remarkable memory.

God sent ravens to sustain Elijah by the brook Cherith (1 Kings 17:4–6). Ravens often store surplus food beneath leaves or in rocky crevices. Although ravens often have been viewed as birds of evil omen, in the Elijah story they serve as symbols of God's love for His servant and of His mighty sovereignty over nature.

Sparrow The sparrow belongs to the finch family. In the Old Testament the Hebrew term translated "sparrow" (*tsippor*) also carries the general meaning "bird." The translation "sparrow" occurs in the Revised Standard Version text in Psalm 84:3 and in Proverbs 26:2. The King James Version also translates *tsippor* "sparrow" in Psalm 102:7.

In Psalm 102:7, the translation "sparrow" may be inappropriate because the verse refers to a bird "alone upon the house top," and the most common sparrows always appeared in flocks. On the other hand, the psalmist may have intended this contradiction to emphasize the depth of loneliness and utter desolation which he was experiencing.

Two passages in the New Testament refer to the sparrow (Matt. 10:29–31; Luke 12:6–7). In these parallel passages Jesus taught His disciples to have confidence in God's love. The God who cares for all of His creation, even the insignificant sparrow, certainly cares for people.

Vulture Both carrion vulture and vulture are listed separately in the unclean bird lists (Lev. 11:13–19; Deut. 14:12–18 RSV). The term "vulture" refers to several different birds of prey. The English word "vulture" is used to translate several different Hebrew terms.

The Bible does not permit a positive identification of the types of vultures known during the biblical period. In contrast to eagles and hawks, which usually kill living prey, vultures feed on dead animals.

The Hebrew term *nesher,* sometimes translated "eagle," is translated "vulture" in Hosea's threat to Israel (8:1). Lack of a proper burial was viewed as a great horror in biblical times. The common belief was that as long as a body remained unburied, the person could not be gathered to the fathers and experience rest in Sheol. Goliath and David threatened one another with this fate (1 Sam. 17:44,46). The curses in Deuteronomy warned the disobedient of this horrible consequence (Deut. 28:26). Ultimately the author of Revelation used the image of the birds of prey to picture the defeat of evil before the reign of Christ (Rev. 19:17–21; compare Ezek. 29:5; 32:4; 39:4, 17–20).   *Janice Meier*

BIRDS OF ABOMINATION List of twenty birds not to be consumed by Israelites (Lev. 11:13–19). The reason for the exclusion of these birds is unclear. Some have suggested that the birds were prohibited because they were associated with the worship of idols. Others have suggested that they were excluded because they ate flesh which contained blood or because they had contact with corpses—both of which would make one ritually unclean (see Lev. 7:26; 17:13–14; 21:1–4,11; 22:4; Num. 5:2–3; 6:6–11). See *Birds.*

BIRSHA (Bĭr' shå) Personal name with uncertain meaning, traditionally, "ugly." King of Gomorrah who joined coalition of Dead Sea area kings against eastern group of invading kings (Gen. 14:2).

BIRTH The act or process of bringing forth young from the womb. The biblical writers, like other ancient people, did not fully understand the process of conception. Having no knowledge of the woman's ovum, they thought that only the male's semen (his "seed") produced the child. The woman provided her womb as a receptacle for the protection and growth of the child.

Midwives were often used in the birthing process (Gen. 35:17; 38:28; Ex. 1:15). Birthstools were also used (Ex. 1:16; see *Birthstool*). The infant's navel cord was cut immediately after birth; the child was cleaned, rubbed with salt, and wrapped in cloths (Ezek. 16:4). Often the child was named at birth (Gen. 21:3; 29:32,35; 30:6–8). The woman was considered ritually unclean for a period of from 40 to 80 days following birth (Lev. 12:1–8; see Luke 2:22).

When a son was born, he was placed immediately on his father's knees (Gen. 50:23; Job 3:12). The psalmist's words, "Upon thee was I cast from my birth," reflects the father's receiving of his new son and signifies God's care from the moment of birth (Ps. 22:10; 71:6). Rachel, by receiv-

B

ing Bilhah's child upon her knees at birth, was adopting him as her own (Gen. 30:3–8).

Birth could be premature because of the shock of bad news (1 Sam. 4:19). The untimely birth—here, stillborn (see *Untimely Birth*)—enters the dark, finds rest, and does not know the agony of life (Eccl. 6:4–5; Job 3:11–13). A miscarriage was caused by accident or violence (Ex. 21:22–25), or may have been considered as divine judgment (Ps. 58:8; Hos. 9:14).

The birth of a child was a time of rejoicing, especially the birth of a son (Ruth 4:13–14; Jer. 20:15; Luke 1:14,57–58; 2:13–14; John 16:21). One's birthday was an occasion for celebration (Gen. 40:20; Matt. 14:6). If life became unbearable, one might be moved to curse the day of birth (Job 3:3; Jer. 20:14).

The birthing process was used in a figurative way in describing the relationship of God to His people. In Deuteronomy 32:18, God gave birth to Israel as a mother would give birth to a child. Therefore, when the Israelites said to the tree, "You are my father," and to the stone, "You gave me birth," they turned away from their true parent (the tree and stone pillar were symbols in the worship of idols). According to Jesus, it is just as necessary to be born of the Spirit as it is to be born of a woman (John 3:1–7). The birthing process is also used as an image to describe God's creative activity (Job 38:29). God is even pictured as a midwife (Isa. 66:7–9).

Many biblical writers used the pain of childbirth in a metaphorical way. Kings before God tremble like a woman giving birth (Ps. 48:6). The coming of the day of the Lord will cause anguish similar to childbirth. There will be pangs, agony, cries, gasping, and panting (Isa. 13:8; 42:14; Jer. 6:24; 13:21; 22:23; 30:6; 48:41; 49:24; 50:43; John 16:21; Rev. 12:2). *Phil Logan*

BIRTHRIGHT Esau forfeited his birthright to his brother Jacob for the sake of a meal of lentil stew and bread (Gen. 25:29–34). The birthright consisted of the special privileges that belonged to the firstborn male child in a family. Prominent among those privileges was a double portion of the estate as an inheritance. If a man had two sons, his estate would be divided into three portions, and the older son would receive two. If there were three sons, the estate would be divided into four portions, and the oldest son would receive two. The oldest son also normally received the father's major blessing. Indeed, the Hebrew word for blessing (*berakah*) is virtually an anagram of the word that means both birthright and firstborn (*bekorah*). Legal continuation of the family line may also have been included among the privileges of the firstborn son. Deuteronomy 21:15–17 prohibited a father from playing favorites among his sons by trying to give the birthright to other than the firstborn.

BIRTHSTOOL An object upon which a woman sat during labor (Ex. 1:16). The birthstool may have been of Egyptian origin. The same Hebrew word (*obnayim*) is also translated as "potter's wheel" (Jer. 18:3).

BIRZAITH (Bĭr-zā' ĭth) Descendant of Asher (1 Chron. 7:31).

BIRZAVITH (Bĭr-zā' vĭth) KJV spelling of Birzaith. See *Birzaith.*

BISHLAM (Bĭsh' lăm) Personal name or common name meaning, "in peace." Apparently representative of Persian government in Palestine who complained about building activities of the returned Jews to Artaxerxes, king of Persia (464–423 B.C.).

BISHOP The English word "bishop" is the normal translation of the Green noun *episkopos,* which occurs five times in the New Testament (Acts 20:28; Philem. 1:1; 1 Tim. 3:2; Titus 1:7; 1 Pet. 2:25).

Prior to the advent of Christianity *episkopos* meant "inspector," "watchman," or "overseer." It was used of the finance officers of Greek guilds and of the officers Athens sent to its subject-states. Finance officers administered revenues for Greek temples.

One of the five usages of *episkopos* in the New Testament was as a title applied to Jesus: "the Shepherd and Bishop of your souls" (1 Pet. 2:25). The other four uniformly referred to one who had a role or office in an early Gentile Christian congregation. In addressing the elders of the church of Ephesus the Apostle Paul stated, "the Holy Ghost hath made you overseers (*episcopous*), to feed the church of God" (Acts 20:28). In the salutation to his Epistle to the Philippians he greeted "the bishops and deacons" of the church at Philippi (1:1). In 1 Timothy 3:1–7 qualifications were given for a "bishop": reputation, marital status, character traits, hospitality, teaching ability, non-drunkenness, attitude toward money, responsible parenthood, and length of time as a Christian. A similar list of qualifications for a "bishop" appears in Titus 1:6–9.

The noun *episkopē,* meaning "overseership," "bishopric," or "office," appears in Acts 1:20 (a quotation from Ps. 109:8*b*) and in 1 Timothy 3:1. The verb *episkopeō,* meaning "to exercise oversight," appears in some Greek New Testament manuscripts and hence some English translations (KJV, ASV) in 1 Peter 5:2.

Paul, addressing the Ephesian "elders," reminded them that the Holy Spirit made them "overseers" (*episkopous*) "to feed (verb which is cognate to the noun "pastor") the church of the Lord." From this many conclude that in Paul's time "elder," "bishop," and "pastor" were terms used to describe three different functions of the same Christian leader, not three distinct ministerial offices. Moreover, according to Philippians 1:1 the church at Philippi had more than one bishop.

During the second century A.D. churches came to have a single bishop, and then that bishop came to exercise oversight over nearby rural churches as well as the city church so that his ecclesiastical territory became known as a "diocese" or "see" ("eparchy" in the East). Bishops of churches that had been founded by apostles were said to be in succession to the apostles, and hence their teaching was held to be authentic and their authority collegial. By 400 A.D. in the West, the bishop of Rome began to assume extraordinary authority above other bishops.

Today the Roman Catholic Church, the Eastern Orthodox churches, the Old Catholic Church, the Anglican communion, and the (Lutheran) Church of Sweden teach the doctrine of apostolic (or episcopal) succession. Other Lutheran bodies, the United Methodist Church (USA), and the Moravian Church have bishops who serve as superintendents.   *James Leo Garrett, Jr.*

BIT The metal bar fastened to the muzzle end of the horse's bridle. The bit is inserted in the horse's mouth between the teeth and is used to control the horse. The bit had loops on either end for attaching the reins. Some bits from the biblical period have spikes which would have stuck in the side of the horse's mouth when the reins were applied; the pain made the horse more responsive to the rider's commands. The bit and bridle were used figuratively in the Bible to refer to different forms of control (James 1:26; 3:2; see 2 Kings 19:28; Isa. 37:29).

BITHIA (Bĭ' thĭ' à) NAS spelling of Bithiah. See *Bithiah.*

BITHIAH (Bĭth' ĭ-äh) Personal name meaning, "daughter of Yahweh" or Egyptian common noun meaning, "queen." Daughter of an Egyptian pharaoh whom Mered, a descendant of tribe of Judah, married (1 Chron. 4:17 NAS, RSV; 4:18 KJV; NIV). The verse stands in verse 18 in Hebrew but relates to the content of verse 17. Bithiah was the mother of Miriam, Shammai, and Ishbah. Throughout its history, Israel incorporated foreigners into its tribes.

BITHRON (Bĭth' rŏn) Place name meaning, "ravine" or common noun meaning, "morning." As David ruled Judah in Hebron and Ishbosheth ruled Israel in Mahanaim, their armies clashed under generals Joab and Abner. Abner retreated. Joab and his brothers pursued. Abner killed Asahel. Finally Joab quit pursuing. Abner crossed the Jordan and marched through "Bithron," either a ravine or mountain pass (KJV, NIV, TEV) or the forenoon (RSV, NAS).

BITHYNIA (Bĭthўn' ĭà) A district in northern Asia Minor that Paul's missionary company desired to enter with the gospel (Acts 16:7). The Holy Spirit prevented them from doing so and directed them instead to Macedonia. Though no record exists of how the Christian faith took root in Bithynia, believers lived there during the first century. Those to whom 1 Peter was addressed included persons in Bithynia (1 Pet. 1:1).

BITTER HERBS Herbs eaten with the Passover meal (Ex. 12:8; Num. 9:11). They were interpreted as symbolizing the bitter experiences of the Israelites' slavery in Egypt. Some have suggested that the bitter herbs comprised a salad including lettuce, endive, chicory, and dandelion. The word translated "bitterness" in Lamentations 3:15 is the same word translated "bitter herbs."

BITTER WATER The water drunk by a woman suspected of adultery (Num. 5:11–31). If a man suspected his wife had been unfaithful to him but was not a witness to the act and could not produce witnesses to the act, the woman was taken to the priest who arranged an ordeal to determine the woman's innocence or guilt. When the man brought the woman to the priest, he brought an offering of jealousy or remembrance (a cereal offering of barley). The priest seated the woman before the sanctuary facing the altar. The woman's hair was unbound as a sign of her shame. The woman held the offering, and the priest held the vessel containing the bitter water. The bitter water was a combination of holy water and dust from the sanctuary floor. At this point the woman took an oath: if she was innocent, the water would not harm her; if she was guilty, then her "thigh would rot" and her "body swell." The woman affirmed the oath with a double, "amen." The priest wrote the curse (Num. 5:21–22) on a parchment and washed the ink off the page into the water. The priest then took the offering and burned it upon the altar, after which the woman drank the bitter water. If she was innocent, she would not be harmed and would conceive children as a blessing. If she was guilty, the curse would take effect. The man bore no guilt if his suspicions proved false—that is, he had not willingly broken the ninth commandment against bearing false witness. The woman, on the other hand, bore the consequences of her guilt (Num. 5:31).

BITTERN KJV translation for an animal of desolation mentioned three times in the Bible (Isa. 14:23; 34:11; Zeph. 2:14). The name "bittern" is applied to any number of small or medium sized herons (*Botaurus* and related genera) with a characteristic booming cry. Bittern and heron are marsh and water birds and do not seem to be the animal referred to by the biblical writers. A number of alternatives have been suggested: bustard (REB), (screech) owl (NIV, TEV), porcupine, hedgehog (NAS, NRSV), and lizard. Of these suggestions, hedgehog and porcupine have the widest support. The animal represents the wild and mysterious world humans do not control. See *Animals.*

BITUMEN A mineral pitch or asphalt (KJV has "slime';' NAS, NIV, "tar pits") found in solid black lumps in the cretaceous limestone on the west bank of the Dead Sea (see Gen. 14:10). Other forms are found in Asia Minor. Bitumen was used as a mortar in setting bricks in the buildings and ziggurats in Mesopotamia (see Gen. 11:3) and as a caulking for rafts and basket boats on the Euphrates (see Ex. 2:3; compare Gen. 6:14). See *Pitch.*

BIZIOTHIAH (Bĭz' ĭ-ō-thī' ăh) Place name meaning, "scorns of Yahweh." Southern town in tribal allotment of Judah (Josh. 15:28). The parallel list in Nehemiah 11:27 reads, *benotheyha* ("her villages"), which the Joshua text of the Septuagint or early Greek translation also read. If that is not the correct reading in Joshua 15:27, then the location of Biziothiah is not known.

BIZJOTHJAH (Bĭz·jŏth' jah) KJV spelling of Biziothiah. See *Biziothiah.*

BIZTHA (Biz' thà) Persian personal name of uncertain meaning. One of seven eunuchs who served King Ahasuerus in matters relating to his wives (Esther 1:10).

BLACK Often used to denote the color of physical objects: hair (Lev. 13:31,37; Song of Sol. 5:11), skin (Job 30:30; Song of Sol. 1:5–6; Lam. 4:8), the sky as a sign of rain (1 Kings 18:45), and animals (Gen. 30:32–43; Zech. 6:2,6; Rev. 6:5). "Black" is also used figuratively to describe mourning (Job 30:28; Jer. 4:28; 8:21; 14:2), a visionless day (Micah 3:6), the abode of the dead (Job 3:5; Jude 13), and the treachery of Job's friends (Job 6:16). See *Colors.*

BLACK PEOPLE AND BIBLICAL PERSPECTIVES Black people in America have a deep affinity for the Bible. This affinity has evolved despite the negative ways in which the Bible was used from 1620 to 1865. Then, the Bible was used to reinforce attitudes of subservience and servility. It became a weapon for enforcing certain moralisms designed to keep the slaves under control.

Black people found positive reasons for turning to the Bible. During the protracted revival meetings called the "Great Awakenings" (1740's and 1798—1820) they heard the Bible used to proclaim the good news of salvation. The new life in

Christ surpassed anything they had ever known, and it was proclaimed under the authority of the Bible.

Some slaves felt the divine call to preach. For those given permission to preach, the Bible became the textbook from which they learned to read. Some were forbidden the opportunity of learning to read, but legends tell of secret instructions by beneficent persons. Often the Bible was the textbook.

Black people also developed love for the Bible because of the stories of deliverance and hope that it contains. These were memorized, embellished, and became their daily spiritual substance. Black people identified with the Israelites moving from Egyptian servitude to the Promised Land. They took courage in God's provisions during the wilderness wanderings. The miraculous battles of Joshua, Gideon, Samson, and David were inspiring to them. Black sermonic themes from those days until the 1950's emphasized God's deliverance as illustrated in Daniel and "the Hebrew Boys"; Ezekiel and the Valley of Dry Bones; the messianic passages of the prophets; the miracles of Jesus; His death, burial, and power over death. Some sermon themes became attention-getters sure to draw crowds (The Valley of Dry Bones, The Eagle Stirreth Her Nest, The Lions Den, The Firey Furnace).

These stories were told over again by God-called men who were denied formal training; but who, having heard others read from the Bible, committed those verses to memory and could retell Bible stories in ways that made them come to life. Black preachers became masters at "telling the story." They practiced narrative theology long before it was suddenly "discovered" by some seminaries in the 1970's. Even though the congregations had heard these Bible stories, they were anxious to hear them again. Not only did the repetition reinforce the story, but each man gave the stories new vitality through his interpretation.

Black people also "sang the story." Bible stories became the substance of spirituals and jubilee songs: "Didn't My Lord Deliver Daniel, Then Why Not Every Man," "Go Down Moses," "Joshua Fit the Battle of Jericho," "Little David, Play On Your Harp," "O Mary, Don't You Weep." Music not only reinforced the telling of the story but put it in a medium to be easily remembered. Memorization through music is an experience common to humanity. Black people have maximized music as a communicative medium.

The 1960's and '70's birthed another interest of Black people in relation to the Bible. The quest for Black history and Black pride led to in-depth studies of Bible personalities believed to be Black or with African identification. This has resulted in some deeper affinities for the Bible since Black people now know they are positively represented. Pride is expressed in the rescue of the prophet

Jeremiah by Ebedmelech, an Ethiopian (Jer. 38:7–13; 39:15–18). Simon of Cyrene, identified as an African, was considered heroic for helping Jesus carry the cross (Mark 15:21). Black people felt included in the embryonic spread of Christianity when seeing that representatives from African countries were among those upon whom the Holy Spirit fell at Pentecost (Acts 2:5–11,39). Historical notions were rethought when it was discovered that Christianity did not originally come to Africa through Western missionaries, but more likely from the dispersion after Pentecost, the influence of the powerful government official whom Philip baptized (Acts 8:26–37), and from the early church fathers. Recent research has determined that nine of the eighteen church fathers were African (Clement, Origen, Tertullian, Cyprian, Dionysius, Athanasius, Didymus, Augustine, and Cyril). These were men who guided the formation, crystallization, and propagation of Christian thought during the first to the third centuries A.D.

The only Bible passages some Black people have difficulty with are the Pauline passages which seem to ignore the problem of slavery as an evil. These are 1 Corinthians 7:20–24; Ephesians 6:5–9; Colossians 3:22–25; Titus 2:9–10; Philemon. One other passage, though not Pauline, is in this category, 1 Peter 2:18–25.

These passages have become less objectionable when viewed with the "interim ethic" idea. Paul expected the return of Christ to be so immediate that he gave little place for social change. Some Black theologians now think that had Paul known Jesus would have been this long in returning he would have tackled this social evil straight forwardly.

The Bible continues to be loved and reverenced by Black people. Some non-Christians regard it as sacred even though refusing to commit their lives to the Christ of the Bible. Most people, however, regard the Bible as God's Word. They believe it literally, may apply some passages allegorically, and will contemporize it for practical application.

In more recent years the Bible is used less for its story content as for a practical guide in dealing with issues from a Black perspective. These issues include salvation, moral guidance, ethical behavior, and spiritual nurture. The preacher who only "tells the story" is in less demand. The person who applies the truths of the stories to contemporary situations is taken more seriously. As more Black people move into decision-making roles, they will become more dependent upon biblical and spiritual resources to guide that mobility. Many Black people are definite about the place of the Bible in their pilgrimage. It remains in the forefront. *Emmanuel McCall*

BLAINS KJV word for sores in Exodus 9:9–10. See *Boils*.

BLASPHEMY is a transliteration of a Greek word meaning literally "to speak harm." In the biblical context, blasphemy is an attitude of disrespect that finds expression in an act directed against the character of God.

Old Testament Blasphemy draws its Christian definition through the background of the Old Testament. It is significant that blasphemy reflects improper action with regard to the use of God's name. God revealed His character and invited personal relationship through the revelation of His name. Therefore, the use of God's name gave the Israelites the opportunity of personal participation with the very nature of God.

Leviticus 24:14–16 guides the Hebrew definition of blasphemy. The offense is designated as a capital crime, and the offender is to be stoned by the community. Blasphemy involves the actual pronunciation of the name of God along with an attitude of disrespect. Under the influence of this interpretation, the personal name of God (Yahweh) was withdrawn from ordinary speech and the title of Adonai (Lord) was used in its place.

Israel, at various times, was guilty of blasphemy. Specifically mentioned were the instances of the golden calf (Neh. 9:18) and the harsh treatment of the prophets (Neh. 9:26). David was accused by Nathan of making a mockery of God's commands and giving an occasion for the enemies of Israel to blaspheme—to misunderstand the true nature of God (2 Sam. 12:14).

The enemies of Israel blasphemed God through acts against the people of God. The Assyrians claimed that God was powerless when compared to their mighty army (2 Kings 19:6,22; Isa. 37:6,23). A contempt of God was shown by the Babylonians during the Exile, as they continually ridiculed God (Isa. 52:5). Edom was guilty of blasphemy when it rejoiced over the fall of Jerusalem (Ezek. 35:12). God responded with judgment (2 Kings 19:35–37) or promised judgment (Isa. 52:6; Ezek. 35:12–15) to defend the dignity of His name.

New Testament The New Testament broadens the concept of blasphemy to include actions against Christ and the church as the body of Christ. Jesus was regarded by the Jewish leaders as a blasphemer Himself (Mark 2:7). When tried by the Sanhedrin, Jesus not only claimed messianic dignity, but further claimed the supreme exalted status (Luke 22:69). Such a claim, according to the Sanhedrin, fit the charge of blasphemy and, therefore, deserved death (Matt. 26:65; Mark 14:64). However, according to the New Testament perspective, the real blasphemers were those who denied the messianic claims of Jesus and rejected His unity with the Father (Mark 15:29; Luke 22:65; 23:39).

The unity of Christ and the church is recognized in the fact that persecutions against Christians are labeled as blasphemous acts (1 Tim.

1:13; 1 Pet. 4:4; Rev. 2:9). It is also important that Christians avoid conduct that might give an occasion for blasphemy, especially in the area of attitude and speech (Eph. 4:31; Col. 3:8; 1 Tim. 6:4; Titus 3:2).

The sin of blasphemy is a sin that can be forgiven. However, there is a sin of blasphemy *against the Holy Spirit* that cannot be forgiven (Matt. 12:32; Mark 3:29; Luke 12:10). This is a state of hardness in which one consciously and willfully resists God's saving power and grace. It is a desperate condition that is beyond the situation of forgiveness because one is not able to recognize and repent of sin. Thus one wanting to repent of blasphemy against the Spirit cannot have committed the sin.   *Jerry M. Henry*

BLASTING Reference to the hot east winds which blow across Palestine for days at a time (Deut. 28:22 KJV and RSV; other versions read "blight"). This blasting wind dries up vegetation and ruins crops (Isa. 37:27; see Ps. 90:5–6; 102:3–4; Isa. 40:6–8). This wind represents one of the great natural calamities (1 Kings 8:37; 2 Chron. 6:28) and one of the judgments of God upon the disobedient (Deut. 28:22; Amos 4:9; Hag. 2:17).

BLASTUS (Blăs' tŭs) Personal name meaning, "sprout." Official under Herod Agrippa I (A.D. 37–44). Won over by citizens of Tyre and Sidon, he tried to help them make peace with Herod. Herod's ensuing speech let him assume the role of God over the people, resulting in God striking him dead (Acts 12:20–23).

BLEACH See *Fuller.*

BLEMISH A condition that disqualifies an animal as a sacrifice (Lev. 22:17–25) or a man from priestly service (Lev. 21:17–24). In the New Testament, Christ is the perfect sacrifice (without blemish, Heb. 9:14; 1 Pet. 1:19) intended to sanctify the church and remove all its blemishes (Eph. 5:27). The children of God are commanded to live lives without blemishes (Phil. 2:15; 2 Pet. 3:14).

BLESSEDNESS See *Blessing and Cursing.*

BLESSING AND CURSING are primary biblical emphases, as reflected in the 516 uses of words such as bless (132), blessed (285), blesses (10), blessing (70), and blessings (19); and the 199 occurrences of such words as curse (97), cursed (74), curses (19), and cursing (9).

The English word "bless" is often used to translate *barak.* The word means "to kneel" (2 Chron. 6:13; Ps. 95:6) and thus "to bless" (Gen. 27:33; Ex. 18:10; Deut. 28:4). Old Testament individuals might bless God (Gen. 9:26; Ez. 18:10; Ruth

4:14; Ps. 68:19). God also blesses men and women (Gen. 12:23; Num. 23:20; Ps. 109:28; Isa. 61:9). Persons might also bless one another (Gen. 27:33; Deut. 7:14; 1 Sam. 25:33), or they might bless things (Deut. 28:4; 1 Sam. 25:33; Prov. 5:18). Normally, however, when used as a verb, the word is in the passive voice ("be blessed"), as though to suggest that persons do not have in themselves the power to bless.

Words of blessing also are used as a salutation or greeting, with an invocation of blessing as a stronger greeting than "peace" (*shalom,* Gen. 48:20). As such it may be used in meeting (Gen. 47:7), departing (Gen. 24:60), by messengers (1 Sam. 25:14), in gratitude (Job 31:20), as a morning salutation (Prov. 27:14), congratulations for prosperity (Gen. 12:3), in homage (2 Sam. 14:22), and in friendliness (2 Sam. 21:3).

In the New Testament, the word "bless" often translates *makarios,* meaning "blessed, fortunate, happy." The special characteristic of New Testament uses of "bless" and related words is close relationship to the religious joy people experience from being certain of salvation and thus of membership in the kingdom of God. "Bless" occurs in the New Testament only ten times, in contrast to 122 Old Testament occurrences. The New Testament never uses "blesses" and uses "blessing" only 17 times. It is reasonable to conclude that the primary use of the blessing concept in the New Testament is that of "blessed" as opposed to the verbal emphasis on "bless."

"Blessed" appears frequently in the New Testament (88). Especially is "blessed" well known for Jesus' references to the word in the Beatitudes of the Sermon on the Mount (Matt. 5:3–11) and His congratulations to those who respond positively to the kingdom of God (Matt. 23:39; 24:46; Mark 11:9; Luke 10:23; 14:15). In contrast to frequent usage in the first three Gospels (52 occurrences) the Gospel of John uses the word "blessed" in only three places (John 12:13; 13:17; 20:29).

Elsewhere, Pauline literature uses the word: "Blessed are they whose iniquities are forgiven, and whose sins are covered" (Rom. 4:7); "Blessed be God, even the Father of our Lord Jesus Christ, the Father of mercies, and the God of all comfort" (2 Cor. 1:3). John often used the word in Revelation: "Blessed is he that readeth, and they that hear the words of this prophecy, and keep those things which are written therein for the time is at hand" (Rev. 1:3); "Blessed are the dead which die in the Lord" (Rev. 14:13; cf. 16:15; 19:9; 20:6; 22:7,14).

"Cursing" is less frequently used in the Bible (199) than is "blessing" (516). The concept is almost exclusively Old Testament, which speaks of "curse" (89), "cursed" (65), "curses" (18), and "cursing" (8). The New Testament uses "curse" only 8 times, "cursed" in 9 places, "curses" in a single verse, and "cursing" in one reference. Of the 199 biblical uses of the words, 180 are in the Old Testament and only 19 in the New Testament.

An early word for "curse" in the Old Testament is 'arar and is used primarily in poetic and legal sections of the Old Testament. The word appears in the call of Abraham, "and curse him that curseth thee" (Gen. 12:3). An extended curse formula appears in Deuteronomy, where blessing and cursing are contrasted (Deut. 27:15–26; cf. 28:16–19). Later the same word refers to cursing the priests: "If ye will not hear, and if ye will not lay it to heart, to give glory unto my name, saith the Lord of hosts, I will even send a curse upon you, and I will curse your blessings: yea, I have cursed them already, because ye do not lay it to heart" (Mal. 2:2).

Another word used for "curse" in the Old Testament (qalal) has less severe implications, although it probably came to be used as a synonym for the harsher term ('arar). The basic meaning of the word is light, insignificant, or trifling. It described persons lightly esteemed (2 Sam. 6:22) and also meant "to make contemptible"; hence, to curse persons (Gen. 12:3; Ex. 21:17). The word also means to treat with contempt (2 Sam. 19:44; Isa. 23:9) or to dishonor (Isa. 8:21).

The unique concept of the spoken word, especially in the context of worship or other formal settings, is important for understanding the significance of both cursing and blessing. According to Old Testament thought patterns, the formally spoken word had both an independent existence and the power of its own fulfillment. The word once spoken assumed a history of its own, almost a personality of itself. The word also had the power of its own fulfillment. Both of these concepts are fundamental to understanding Isaiah's emphasis on God's Word: "For as the rain cometh down, and the snow from heaven, and returneth not thither, but watereth the earth, and maketh it bring forth and bud, that it may give seed to the sower, and bread to the eater: so shall my word be that goeth forth out of my mouth: it shall not return unto me void, but it shall accomplish that which I please, and it shall prosper in the thing whereto I send it" (Isa. 55:10–11; cf. Jer. 1:12). The Word of God exists as a reality and has within itself the power of its own fulfillment. Formal words of blessing or cursing also had the same power of self-fulfillment. When Isaac mistakenly blessed Jacob rather than Esau, he could not recall the blessing, for it existed in history (Gen. 27:18–41); it had acquired an identity of its own. Blessing and cursing released suprahuman powers which could bring to pass the content of the curse or the blessing.

Both blessing and cursing assumed unique power in Israel's life as they were taken into the context of worship. The Lord was the source of all blessing, and people sought to express gratitude for that blessing; indeed, to pray for the continua-tion of such blessing: "Bless the Lord, O my soul: and all that is within me, bless his holy name. Bless the Lord, O my soul, and forget not all his benefits" (Ps. 103:1–2). Central to the covenant renewal ceremony was the blessing (Deut. 28:3–6). Aaron's benediction both proclaims and petitions the Lord's blessing: "The Lord bless thee, and keep thee: The Lord make his face shine upon thee, and be gracious unto thee: The Lord lift up his countenance upon thee, and give thee peace" (Num. 6:24–26).   *Roy L. Honeycutt*

BLIGHT See *Blasting*.

BLINDNESS Physical blindness in the biblical period was very common. The suffering of the blind person was made worse by the common belief that the affliction was due to sin (John 9:1–3).

Because of their severe handicap, blind persons had little opportunity to earn a living. A blind man was even ineligible to become a priest (Lev. 21:18). Frequently, the blind became beggars (Mark 10:46).

The possibility of a blind person being mistreated was recognized and forbidden by God. The law prohibited the giving of misleading directions (Deut. 27:18) or doing anything to cause the blind to stumble (Lev. 19:14).

Physical Cause Many things caused blindness in ancient times. One could be born blind (John 9:1) due to some developmental defect or as a result of infection prior to birth. Usually, however, blindness began later. The most common cause was infection. Trachoma, a painful infection of the eye, is a common cause of blindness today and was probably prevalent in ancient times. Leprosy can also cause blindness. In old age, vision may be severely impaired in some persons (Gen. 27:1). Some develop cataracts. Some have a gradual atrophy of portions of the eye.

Ancient people used salves of various types to treat disorders of the eye. Simple surgical procedures such as the lancing of boils near the eye and the extraction of inverted eyelashes were also employed.

In reality, almost no effective treatment was available to those who suffered from diseases of the eye and blindness. There were no antibiotics, no effective surgical procedures for most problems, and no eyeglasses. Miraculous healing was often sought (John 5:2–3).

Jesus frequently healed blind persons (Matt. 9:27–31; 12:22; 20:30–34; Mark 10:46–52; John 9:1–7). Perhaps there is no greater evidence of His compassion and power than that seen in His willingness and ability to heal those who lived in darkness and hopelessness.

Spiritual blindness The Bible addresses spiritual blindness as the great human problem. Israel was supposed to be God's servant (Isa. 42:19) but was blind to the role God wanted them to fill. Called to be watchmen protecting the nation, they instead blindly preyed on the people (Isa. 56:10). As the Pharisees gained leadership, they became blind leaders of the blind (Matt. 15:14; 23:16–26). Jesus came to reverse the situation, making it clear who had spiritual sight and who was spiritually blind (John 9:39–41). Peter listed the qualities a person must have to have spiritual sight. Without these, a person is blind (2 Pet. 1:5–9). The problem is that the spiritually blind do not know they are blind (Rev. 3:17). They are blinded by the "god of this world" (2 Cor. 4:4). They walk in darkness, eventually being blinded by the moral darkness of hatred (1 John 2:11).

BLOOD has great significance in the Bible. Its meanings involve profound aspects of human life and God's desire to transform human existence. Blood is intimately associated with physical life. Blood and "life" or "living being" are closely associated. The Hebrews of Old Testament times were prohibited from eating blood. "Only be sure that thou eat not the blood: for the blood is the life; and thou mayest not eat the life with the flesh. Thou shalt not eat it; thou shalt pour it upon the earth as water" (Deut. 12:23–24). For agricultural people, this command stressed the value of life. Though death was ever-present, life was sacred. Life was not to be regarded cheaply.

Even when the Old Testament speaks of animal sacrifice and atonement, the sacredness of life is emphasized. "For the life of the flesh *is* in the blood: and I have given it to you upon the altar to make an atonement for your souls for it is the blood that maketh an atonement for the soul" (Lev. 17:11). Perhaps because an animal life was given up (and animals were a vital part of a person's property), this action taken before God indicated how each person is estranged from God. In giving what was of great value, the person offering the sacrifice showed that reconciliation with God involved life—the basic element of human existence. How giving up an animal life brought about redemption and reconciliation is not clear. What is clear is that atonement was costly. Only the New Testament could show how costly it was.

Flesh and Blood This phrase designates a *human being.* When Peter confessed that Jesus was the Messiah, Jesus told Peter, "Flesh and blood hath not revealed *it* unto thee, but my Father which is in heaven" (Matt. 16;17). No human agent informed Peter; the Father Himself disclosed this truth. When "flesh and blood" is used of Jesus, it designates His whole person: "He that eateth my flesh, and drinketh my blood, dwelleth in me and I in him" (John 6:56). The next verse shows that eating "blood and flesh" is powerful metaphorical language for sharing in the life that Jesus bestows—"so he that eateth me, even he shall live by me" (John 6:57).

When Paul used the phrase "flesh and blood" in 1 Corinthians 15:50, he referred to sinful human existence: "flesh and blood cannot inherit the kingdom of God." The sinfulness of human beings disqualifies them as inheritors of God's kingdom. In Galatians 1:16, Paul used "flesh and blood" as a synonym for human beings with whom he did not consult after his conversion. Paul said his gospel came directly from God.

In Ephesians 6:12, Paul portrayed Christians in conflict—their wrestling is "not against flesh and blood" but with higher, demonic powers, "against principalities, against powers, against the rulers of the darkness of this world, against spiritual wickedness in high places." Of course, Christians do meet opposition to Christ and the gospel from other human beings, but behind all human opposition is a demonic-Satanic opposition. Human beings choose to identify with moral evil. We wrestle with the demonic leaders of moral revolt.

Finally, the phrase "flesh and blood" sometimes designates human nature apart from moral evil. Jesus, like other children of His people, was a partaker "of flesh and blood" (Heb. 2:14). Because He did so, He could die a unique, atoning death. He was fully human, yet more than human; He was both God and man.

After the flood, God renewed the original command that Noah and his sons be fruitful and multiply (Gen. 9:1). They were not to eat the flesh with its life, that means the blood (Gen. 9:4). Then murder is forbidden (Gen. 9:5,6). The reason is explained thus: "Whoso sheddeth man's blood, by man shall his blood be shed; for in the image of God made he man." (Gen. 9:6). Since a murderer destroys one made in God's image, murder is an attack upon God.

In Deuteronomy 21:1–9, we read of an elaborate ceremony by elders concerning a person murdered in the fields near their city. They were to pray for the Lord's forgiveness by atonement: "Be merciful, O Lord, unto thy people Israel, whom thou hast redeemed, and lay not innocent blood unto thy people of Israel's charge. And the blood shall be forgiven them" (Deut. 21:8; see v. 9). The victim is assumed to be innocent, and the community is held responsible. A person who killed another accidentally had six cities to which he could flee and there establish his innocence (Josh. 20:1–9). He had to flee because the avenger of blood (the nearest of kin to the person murdered) was obligated to kill the individual who had murdered his relative (Num. 35).

When Pilate saw that justice was being distorted at the trial of Jesus, he washed his hands symbolically and declared his own innocence: "I am innocent of the blood of this just person: see ye to it [i.e., that's your affair]" (Matt. 27:24). The people replied naively, "His blood be on us, and on our children" (Matt. 27:25).

Blood of sacrifices, blood of the covenant The

great historic event of the Old Testament was the Exodus from Egypt. Central to that event was the offering of a lamb from the sheep or from the goats (Ex. 12:5). The blood of that lamb was put on the top and the two sides of the door frame (Ex. 12:7,22–23). When the angel passed through, destroying the firstborn in Egypt, he would pass by the houses in Israel's part of Egypt that were marked in this fashion. In terms of its redemptive effects, none of the daily sacrifices made throughout the Old Testament (see Leviticus) were as dramatic as the Passover sacrifice.

Almost as dramatic as the Passover was the ceremony at the dedication of the covenant treaty at Sinai between Yahweh and His covenant people, the Israelites (Ex. 24:1–8). Moses took the blood of oxen and placed it in two bowls. Half of it he dashed upon the altar and half he dashed upon the people (Ex. 24:6–8). Moses declared "Behold the blood of the covenant which the LORD hath made (literally, cut) with you concerning [or in agreement with] all these words." The people solemnly promised to act in agreement with this covenant (Ex. 24:3,7).

When Jesus inaugurated the New Covenant after His last Passover with the disciples, He declared: "This is my blood of the new testament which is shed for many for the remission of sins" (Matt. 26:28). Luke reads: "This cup is the new testament in my blood, which is shed for you" (Luke 22:20). Testament means covenant here. Jesus, the God-man, gave up His life and experienced the reality of death so that those who identify themselves with Jesus might experience His life and never taste death as He did. He died as a sin-bearer that we might live for righteousness and become healed (1 Pet. 2:24).

Blood of Christ—meaning and effects The term "blood of Christ" designates in the New Testament the atoning death of Christ. Atonement refers to the basis and process by which estranged people become at one with God (atonement = at-one-ment). When we identify with Jesus, we are no longer at odds with God. The meaning of Christ's death is a great mystery. The New Testament seeks to express this meaning in two ways: (1) in the language of sacrifice, and (2) in language pertaining to the sphere of law. This sacrificial language and legal language provide helpful analogies. However, the meaning of Christ's death is far more than an enlargement of animal sacrifices or a spiritualization of legal transactions. Sometimes, both legal and sacrificial language are found together.

In the language of sacrifice we have "expiation" (removal of sins, Romans 3:25); "sprinkling of the blood of Jesus" (1 Pet. 1:1–2); "redeemed by precious blood as of a lamb without spot and without blemish" (1 Pet. 1:19); "blood of His Son cleanses us from all sin" (1 John 1:7); "blood that cleanses the conscience" (Heb. 9:14); and "blood of an eternal covenant" (Heb. 13:20). In legal language we have "justification" (Rom. 5:9); "redemption" (Eph. 1:7); been redeemed to God by His blood (Rev. 5:9). Such metaphors show that only God could provide atonement; Jesus, the God-man was both Priest and Offering, both Redeemer and the One intimately involved with the redeemed.   *A. Berkeley Mickelsen*

BLOOD, AVENGER OF See *Avenger; Bloodguilt; Cities of Refuge.*

BLOOD, FIELD OF See *Akeldama.*

A monastery on Mount Zion marks the traditional site of Judas's suicide overlooking the Field of Blood.

BLOODGUILT Guilt usually incurred through bloodshed. Bloodguilt made a person ritually unclean (Num. 35:33–34) and was incurred by killing a person who did not deserve to die (Deut. 19:10; Jer. 26:15; Jonah 1:14). Killing in self-defense and execution of criminals are exempted from bloodguilt (Ex. 22:2; Lev. 20:9). Bloodguilt was incurred (1) by intentional killing (Judg. 9:24; 1 Sam. 25:26,33; 2 Kings 9:26; Jer. 26:15); (2) by unintentional killing (See Num. 35:22–28 where one who accidentally kills another may be killed by the avenger of blood implying that the accidental murderer had bloodguilt. See *Avenger*.); (3) by being an indirect cause of death (Gen. 42:22; Deut. 19:10*b*; 22:8; Josh. 2:19); (4) a person was under bloodguilt if those for whom he was responsible committed murder (1 Kings 2:5,31–33); and (5) the killing of a sacrifice at an unauthorized altar imputed bloodguilt (Lev. 17:4). The avenger of blood could take action in the first two instances but not in the latter three.

When the murderer was known in instance (1) above, the community shared the guilt of the murderer until the guilty party had paid the penalty of death. No other penalty or sacrifice could substitute for the death of the guilty party, nor was there any need for sacrifice once the murderer had been killed (Num. 35:33; Deut. 21:8–9). The one who unintentionally killed another [(2) above] might flee to a city of refuge and be safe. If, however, the accidental killer left the boundaries of the city of refuge, the avenger of blood could kill in revenge without incurring bloodguilt (Num. 35:31–32; Deut. 19:13). The community was held to be bloodguilty if it failed to provide asylum for the accidental killer (Deut. 19:10).

In cases where the blood of an innocent victim was unavenged, the blood of the innocent cried out to God (Gen. 4:10; Isa. 26:21; Ezek. 24:7–9; compare Job 16:18), and God became the avenger for that person (Gen. 9:5; 2 Sam. 4:11; 2 Kings 9:7; Ps. 9:12; Hos. 1:4). Even the descendants of the bloodguilty person might suffer the consequences of God's judgment (2 Sam. 3:28–29; 21:1; 1 Kings 21:29). Manasseh's bloodguilt and Judah's failure to do anything about it was the cause of Judah's downfall over 50 years after Manasseh's reign (2 Kings 24:4).

Judas incurred bloodguilt by betraying Jesus ("innocent blood," Matt. 27:4). Those who called for the crucifixion accepted the burden of bloodguilt for themselves and their children (Matt. 27:25). Pilate accepted no responsibility for the shedding of innocent blood (Matt. 27:24).

Phil Logan

BLUE The Hebrew word translated "blue" (*tekeleth*) is also translated as "purple" (Ezek. 23:6) and "violet" (Jer. 10:9). The color was obtained from Mediterranean mollusks (class of Gastropoda) and used for dyeing. Blue was considered inferior to royal purple but was still a very popular color. Blue was used in the tabernacle (Ex. 25:4; 26:1,4; Num. 4:6–7,9; 15:38), in the Temple (2 Chron. 2:7,14; 3:14), and in the clothing of the priests (Ex. 28:5–6,8,15; 39:1). See *Purple; Violet; Colors.*

BOANERGES (Bō·a·nēr′ ḡēs; *sons of thunder*) A name given by Jesus to James and John, the sons of Zebedee (Mark 3:17). The Gospel writer gave the meaning of the name as "sons of thunder," but did not explain why it was appropriate. The name may be indicative of the thunderous temperament these brothers apparently possessed. See *Apostles; Disciples.*

BOAR See *Animals.*

BOAT See *Ships, Sailors, and Navigation.*

BOAZ (Bō′ ăz) Personal name perhaps meaning, "lively." *1.* Hero of Book of Ruth, a wealthy relative of Naomi's husband. See *Ruth.* Ruth gleaned grain in his field; and he graciously invited her to remain there and enjoy the hospitality of his servants, pronouncing a blessing on her for her goodness to Naomi. As he spent the night on the threshing floor to protect his harvest from thieves, Ruth lay down at his feet. Boaz agreed to marry her, according to the custom of levirate marriage by which the nearest male relative married a man's widow. Boaz bargained with the nearest relative, who gave up his right to marry Ruth. Boaz married her and became Obed's father, David's grandfather, and an ancestor of Christ (Matt. 1:5; Luke 3:32).

2. The left or north pillar Solomon set up in the Temple (1 Kings 7:21). The function of the pillars is not known. See *Jachin.*

BOCHERU (Bŏch′ ė·rū) Personal name meaning, "firstborn." Descendant of King Saul in the tribe of Benjamin (1 Chron. 8:38).

BOCHIM (Bō′ chĭm) Place name meaning, "weepers." Place where angel of God announced judgment on Israel at beginning of the period of Judges because they had not destroyed pagan altars but had made covenant treaties with the native inhabitants. Thus the people cried and named the place Bochim (Judg. 2:1–5). It may have been between Bethel and Gilgal. An oak of weeping near Bethel was the burial place of Deborah, Rebekah's nurse (Gen. 35:8). See *Allonbachuth.*

BODY The Greek-Hellenistic culture often downplayed the value of the body. Humans were seen as having two or three parts—body and soul or body, soul, and spirit. Greek culture placed small value on the body, the mortal house of the immortal soul. Modern research, on the other hand, shows that body and soul cannot be observed separate from one another. Body and soul do not form two separate substances. Instead, they comprise the one individual human in an inseparable union. The body is one aspect of the whole individual existence. The Bible says the same thing.

Old Testament The Old Testament differs from the New in that Old Testament Hebrew does not express the idea of body. Of the thirteen words which refer to the animal or human body, the most frequent is *basar,* "flesh." It can designate the body as a whole, but the form or shape of the body or of its parts is not what is important. The focus is on the function or dynamics. See *Flesh.*

Also in the New Testament body and soul are two inseparable aspects of the one human being (Matt. 6:25).

Bible Teachings The Bible then makes basic claims about physical human existence. *1.* The body is our realm of personal evaluation. The body is created by God—mortal, with physical needs, weak and subject to temptation. The body is not, however, without significance. In the body the person lives out the "I" of human existence, relating to God and to fellow humans. The body is the place of proper worship (Rom. 12:1), the Temple of the Holy Spirit (1 Cor. 6:19–20), and thus is to be disciplined (1 Cor. 9:27). In Corinth the people emphasized spiritual life. Paul followed Jesus in opposing them by showing that the inner and outer life belong together. The inner spiritual life is not to be played off against the outer, physical life (Matt. 6:22; 1 Cor. 6:12–20; 2 Cor. 4:7,10). That means the war in the name of the spirit is not against the body but against sin. The goal is not liberation of a "divine" soul from the body but the placing of the body in service for God. Every action must be accounted for before God one day (2 Cor. 5:10).

2. The body and sexuality. Physical love is a gift of the Creator (Gen. 2:23–24). An entire book of the Bible rejoices over this reality—the Song of Solomon. Humans express love with their entire person not only with their sexual organs. This means that sexuality differs from eating and drinking, which satisfy only the requirements of the stomach. Sexual sin rules the body, that is, the entire person. Because the body of the Christian belongs to the Creator, Redeemer, and Holy Spirit, sexual sin is forbidden for the Christian (1 Cor. 6:12–20).

3. The redemption and resurrection of the body. The earthly human stands under the power of sin and of death. No persons can distance themselves from this power, but all long for redemption (Rom. 7:24; 8:23). Redemption is not guaranteed by a bodiless soul which continues to live after death. Such redemption is guaranteed only by God, who continues to care for the body and soul of humans even after death (Matt. 10:28). Death is not the redeemer; God is. He makes the gift of eternal life (Rom. 6:23) in that Jesus Christ became an earthly Human and offered Himself for us (John 1:14; Rom. 7:4). Those who follow Him in faith and baptism experience the reality that the body does not have to remain a slave of sin (Rom. 6:6,12). A person will not be redeemed from the body; rather the body will be redeemed through the resurrection of the dead (Rom. 6:5; 8:11). The existence of the resurrected is a bodily existence. The earthly body of lowliness will be renewed like the glorious body of the resurrected Jesus, becoming an unearthly body or building or house (1 Cor. 15:35–49; 2 Cor. 5:1–10; Phil. 3:21).

Resurrection of the body does not mean that the personality dissolves into an idea, into posterity, or into the society. It means, instead, the total transformation of "flesh and blood" into a "spiritual body," that is a personality created and formed anew by God's Spirit. The resurrection body is that communion with the Lord and with people that begins before death and finds an unimaginable completion through the resurrection.

4. The body of Christ. Jesus Christ had a physical, earthly body which was crucified in front of the gates of Jerusalem (Mark 15:20–47; Col. 1:22; Heb. 13:11–12). The body of Christ also designates the body of the Crucified One "given for you," with which the church is united together in the celebration of the Lord's Supper (Mark 14:24; 1 Cor. 10:16; 11:24). The continuing power of the sacrifice of Golgotha leads humans to join together in a church community, which in a real sense is joined together with the exalted Lord. Bodily is not, however, physical. The joining with the body of Christ does not occur magically through bread, but historically through the realization of the presence of the suffering and death of Jesus.

5. The church as the body of Christ. The image of the body calls the differing individual members into a unity (1 Cor. 12:12–27); however, the church is not just similar; it is one body, and, indeed, one body in Christ (Rom. 12:5; 1 Cor. 10:17). In Christ the body of the church community is incorporated. The community of Christians does not produce the body; the body is a previously given fact (1 Cor. 12:13). In the body of Christ the body of the church community lives, because Christ is greater than the church. He is the Head of the entire creation (Eph. 1:22–23; Col. 2:10) and as Head does not only belong to the church community but rather also stands over against the church. While the world stands in a relationship of subjection to Christ (Eph. 1:20–23; Phil. 2:9–11), only the church is His body (Col. 1:18,24; Eph. 4:4,12; 5:23,30), which He loves (Eph. 5:25). The church is joined to Him in organic growth (Col. 2:19; Eph. 4:15–16). The church grows by serving a future which through Christ has already begun to be incarnate (Col. 2:9,16). The growth of the body occurs as the church marches out in service to the world (Eph. 4:12), even to the demonic world (Eph. 3:10). The individual Christian is joined to Christ only as a member of the body. The Bible knows nothing of a direct, mythical union of the individual with the Lord. The Bible knows of a union with Christ only as faith embodied in the realm of the church community and with the church in the realm of the world.   *Christian Wolf*

BODYGUARD A person or group of persons whose duty it is to protect another from physical harm. In the Old Testament, soldiers were included among the king's bodyguard because of acts of bravery. Members of a king's bodyguard mentioned in the Bible include: David (1 Sam. 22:14; 28:2), Benaiah ben Jehoiada (2 Sam. 23:23), Potiphar (Gen. 37:36), Nebuzaradan (2 Kings 25:8; Jer. 39:9–13; 52:12–16), and Arioch (Dan. 2:14).

BOHAN (Bō' hăn) Place name and personal name meaning, "thumb" or "big toe." A place on the northern border of the tribal allotment of Judah called the "stone of Bohan," "the son of Reuben" (Josh. 15:6). This was the southern border of the tribe of Benjamin (Josh. 18:17). Some Bible students see this as evidence that some part of the tribe of Reuben once lived west of the Jordan. Others see an otherwise unknown heroic deed of Bohan honored with a memorial boundary stone.

BOIL A general term used in the Bible to describe inflamed swellings of the skin. Boils are mentioned in connection with blains (KJV; an inflamatory swelling or sore) in the sixth plague on Egypt (Ex. 9:9–10). Since this plague affected both animals and men, many have suggested the malignant pustule of cutaneous anthrax as the sore or boil mentioned. Hezekiah's boil (2 Kings 20:7; Isa. 38:21) is identified as a furuncle—a localized swelling and inflamation of the skin caused by the infection of a hair follicle that discharges pus and has a central core of dead tissue. The boils suffered by Job (Job 2:7) have been identified with smallpox or with treponematosis (a parasitic infection).

BOKERU (Bō′ kĕ·rü) NIV spelling of Bocheru. See *Bocheru.*

BOKIM (Bō′ kĭm) NIV spelling of Bochim. See *Bochim.*

BOLDNESS Translation of four Greek words in the New Testament. Boldness denotes two things in the New Testament. First, boldness describes the courageous manner of those who preach the Gospel (Acts 2:29; 4:13,31; 9:27–29; 13:46; 14:3; 18:26; 19:8; 26:26; 28:31; see 1 Thess. 2:2; Phil. 1:20). The word translated as "boldness" in these texts (*parresia*) was used of the free citizen of a city-state who could say anything in the public assembly. In the New Testament it denotes the moral freedom to speak the truth publicly. Second, boldness describes the confidence with which Christians can now approach God because of the redeeming work of Christ (2 Cor. 3:4–6,12; Heb. 10:19; 1 John 2:28; 4:17).

BOLLED KJV translation (Ex. 9:31) of a term that means "having bolls"—that is, having seed pods. Some see the flax in this verse as being either in bud or in blossom.

BOLSTER KJV translation that means "the place where the head is while sleeping" (1 Sam. 19:13,16; 26:7,11,12,16). REB, NRSV translate "at his head" (compare NIV, NAS).

BOND Translation of several Hebrew and Greek words with the meanings of "obligation," "dependence," or "restraint." Used literally to speak of the bonds of prisoners or slaves (Judg. 15:14; 1 Kings 14:10; Ps. 107:14; 116:16; Luke 8:29; Philem. 13). Used figuratively to speak of the bonds of wickedness or sin (Isa. 58:6; Luke 13:16; Acts 8:23), of affliction and judgment (Isa.

28:22; 52:2; Jer. 30:8; Nah. 1:13), the authority of kings (Job 12:18; Ps. 2:3), the obligation to keep the covenant (Jer. 2:20; 5:5; see Col. 2:14), the bonds of peace and love (Eph. 4:3; Col. 3:14), and the bonds of an evil woman (Eccl. 7:26).

BONDAGE, BONDMAN, BONDMAID, BONDSERVANT See *Slavery.*

BONES While often referring to the skeletal remains of humans (Gen. 50:25; Ex. 13:19; 1 Sam. 31:13), "bones" were also referred to metaphorically. "Rottenness of bones" signified one whose wife caused shame and confusion (Prov. 12:4; 14:30) or could refer to dejectedness and anticipation of approaching evil (Hab. 3:16). The "shaking of bones" denoted fear (Job 4:14) or sadness (Jer. 23:9). The "burning of the bones" indicated grief and depression (Ps. 102:3; Lam. 1:13) and the feeling of Jeremiah when he tried to refrain from proclaiming God's message (Jer. 20:9). "Dryness of bones" meant poor health (Prov. 17:22). Various other expressions using "bones" referred to mental distress (Job 30:17; Pss. 6:2; 22:14; 31:10; 38:3; 51:8; Lam. 3:4). "Bone of my bones" may mean having the same nature or being the nearest relation (Gen. 2:23; 2 Sam. 5:1).

BONNET KJV translation of two words. A conical-shaped cap placed on the head of the priest at the time of investiture. Made of fine white linen (Ex. 28:40; 29:9; 39:28; Lev. 8:13). See *Cloth, Clothing.*

BOOK OF LIFE The book of life is the heavenly record (Luke 10:20; Heb. 12:23) written by God before the foundation of the world (Rev. 13:8; 17:8) containing the names of those who are destined because of God's grace and their faithfulness to participate in God's heavenly kingdom. Those whose names are in the book have been born into God's family through Jesus Christ (Heb. 12:23; Rev. 13:8); remain faithful in worship of God (Rev. 13:8; 17:8); are untouched by the practice of abomination and falsehood (Rev. 21:27); are faithful through tribulation (Rev. 3:5); and are fellow workers in the work of Jesus Christ (Phil. 4:3). The book of life will be used along with the books of judgment at the final judgment to separate the righteous and the wicked for their respective eternal destinies (Rev. 20:12,15; 21:27).

Christ Himself determines whether the names that are recorded in the book of life remain in that record and are supported by His confession that they belong to Him at the day of judgment or are blotted out (Rev. 3:5).

The Old Testament refers to a record kept by God of those who are a part of His people (Ex. 32:32; Isa. 4:3; Dan. 12:1; Mal. 3:16). As in

Revelation, God can blot out the names of those in the book (Ex. 32:32; Ps. 69:28). In the Old Testament this may simply mean people not in the book die, leaving the list of the living. Those whose names are written in the book are destined for life in a restored Jerusalem (Isa. 4:3) and deliverance through future judgment (Dan. 12:1). See *Apocalyptic; Book; Eschatology; Judgment, Books of.*   *Jeff Cranford*

BOOK(S) Term which often refers to a scroll. A document written on parchment or papyrus and then rolled up. The "book" may be a letter (1 Kings 21:8) or a longer literary effort (Dan. 9:2). See *Writing; Letter; Library.* Several books are mentioned in the Bible:

The Book of the Covenant Moses read from this book during the making of the covenant between God and Israel on Mount Sinai (Ex. 24:7). The "Book of the Covenant" included at least the material now found in Exodus 20:23—23:33. The "Book of the Covenant" is referred to at a later time (2 Kings 23:2,21; 2 Chron. 34:30). It probably included the Exodus passage in addition to other material.

The Book of the Law During the reign of Josiah, Hilkiah, the high priest, found a copy of the "Book of the Law" in the Temple (2 Kings 22:8). Josiah based his reforms of the religion of Israel on the laws found in this book (2 Kings 23). The book is not explicitly identified in 2 Kings, but by comparing the measures undertaken by Josiah and the laws of Deuteronomy it is very likely that the "Book of the Law" was a copy of Deuteronomy.

The Book of the Wars of the Lord This book is quoted in Numbers 21:14—15 (Num. 21:17—18,27—30 may also represent quotations from this book). The part of the book quoted describes the territory conquered by God in behalf of the Israelites. The book was probably a collection of poems which relate the conquest of the land during the time of Moses and Joshua. As the title of the book suggests, the Lord (acting as commander-in-chief) was responsible for the success of the conquest.

The Books of Joshua Joshua wrote one book detailing the allotment of Canaan to the Israelite tribes (Josh. 18:9) and a book similar to the "Book of the Covenant" listed above (Josh. 24:25—26).

The Book of Jashar (or Upright) A book quoted twice in the Old Testament: Joshua's poetic address to the sun and the moon (Josh. 10:12—13) and David's lament for Saul and Jonathan (2 Sam. 1:17—27). Others would include Solomon's words of dedication of the Temple (1 Kings 8:12—13), which the earliest Greek translation attributes to the book of song (Hebrew *shir*), a transposition of letters of Hebrew *jshr* or *ishr* for Jashar. Deborah's song (Judg. 5), and Miriam's song (Ex. 15:20—21) are sometimes seen as part of Jashar. The "Book of Jashar" probably consisted of poems

on important events in Israel's history collected during the time of David or Solomon. The "Book of Jashar" is often compared to or identified with the "Book of the Wars of the Lord" discussed above.

The Book of the Acts of Solomon Probably a biographical document that included such stories as Solomon's judgment between the two harlots (1 Kings 3:16—28), Solomon's administrative arrangements (1 Kings 4:1—19), and the visit of the Queen of Sheba (1 Kings 10:1—13).

Book of the Chronicles of the Kings of Israel Perhaps a continuous journal compiled by scribes from various sources but not to be confused with 1 and 2 Chronicles in the Bible. The writer of 1 and 2 Kings mentions this book eighteen times as containing more complete information on the reigns of the kings of Israel (1 Kings 14:19; 15:31; 16:5,14,20,27; 22:39; 2 Kings 1:18; 10:34; 13:8,12; 14:15,28; 15:11,15,21,26,31).

Book of the Chronicles of the Kings of Judah Source similar to the book of the chronicles of the kings of Israel, not to be confused with 1 and 2 Chronicles in the Bible. The writer of 1 and 2 Kings mentions this book 15 times as containing more complete information on the reigns of the kings of Judah (1 Kings 14:29; 15:7,23; 22:45; 2 Kings 8:23; 12:19; 14:18; 15:6,36; 16:19; 20:20; 21:17,25; 23:28; 24:5).

Books Mentioned in 1 and 2 Chronicles The "Book of the Kings of Israel" (1 Chron. 9:1; 2 Chron. 20:34), the "Book of the Kings of Israel and Judah" (2 Chron. 27:7; 35:27; 36:8), the "Book of the Kings of Judah and Israel" (2 Chron. 16:11; 25:26; 28:26; 32:32), the "Acts of the Kings of Israel" (2 Chron. 33:18), and the "Commentary on the Book of the Kings" (2 Chron. 24:27). Many think these titles are references to the same work and refer to it as the "Midrash of the Kings." This work may contain the books of the chronicles of the kings of Israel and Judah listed above or at least be very similar in content to them.

Also mentioned in 1 and 2 Chronicles are books of various prophets: the "Book of Samuel the Seer" (1 Chron. 29:29), the "Book of Nathan the Prophet" (1 Chron. 29:29; 2 Chron. 9:29), the "Book of Gad the Seer" (1 Chron. 29:29), the "Prophecy of Ahijah the Shilonite" (2 Chron. 9:29), the "Visions of Iddo the Seer against Jeroboam the Son of Nebat" (2 Chron. 9:29), the "Book of Shemaiah the Prophet and Iddo the Seer" (2 Chron. 12:15), the "Story of the Prophet Iddo" (2 Chron. 13:22), the "Book of Jehu the Son of Hanani" (2 Chron. 20:34), the "Acts of Uzziah" (2 Chron. 26:22; written by Isaiah), the "Vision of Isaiah the Prophet" (2 Chron. 32:32), and the "Saying of the Seers" (2 Chron. 33:19). All of these, except for the last, may have been part of the "Midrash of the Kings."

Various other works are also mentioned in 1

and 2 Chronicles: genealogies of the tribe of Gad (1 Chron. 5:17), the "Chronicles of King David" (1 Chron. 27:24), an untitled work containing the plan for the Temple (1 Chron. 28:19), works on the organization of the Levites written by David and Solomon (2 Chron. 35:4), and lamentations for the death of Josiah by Jeremiah and others (2 Chron. 35:25).

Book of the Chronicles A work which contained genealogies and possibly other historical material (Neh. 7:5; 12:23) but was distinct from 1 and 2 Chronicles.

Books by the Prophets Isaiah (Isa. 30:8 compare 8:16) and Jeremiah (Jer. 25:13; 30:2; 36; 45:1; 51:60,63) are said to have written books. These may have represented the first stages of the collections of their prophecies we now have.

Book (of Records) of the Chronicles or **Book of Memorable Deeds** The royal archives of Persia which contained, among other things, the way in which Mordecai saved the life of King Ahasuerus (Esther 2:20–23; 6:1; 10:2; compare Ezra 4:15).

Book of Remembrance Book mentioned in Malachi 3:16. Probably the same as the Book of Life (see *Book of Life*).

Scripture (Book) of Truth Book mentioned in Daniel 10:21. Probably the same as the Book of Life (see *Book of Life*). *Phil Logan*

BOOT The figure mentioned in Isaiah 9:5 of the booted Assyrian warrior (KJV translates the rare Hebrew word for boot as "battle"). Assyrian reliefs from the period of Sennacherib depict soldiers wearing leather boots laced up to the knee which is in contrast to the sandals worn by the Israelite soldier of the period. God's Messiah promised full victory even over the more-impressively dressed army.

BOOTH A temporary shelter constructed for cattle (Gen. 33:17) and people (Jonah 4:5), especially for soldiers on the battlefield (2 Sam. 11:11; 1 Kings 20:12,16). Israel after an invasion is compared to a deserted booth in a vineyard (Isa. 1:8). The booth is also used as a symbol of that which is flimsy and impermanent (Job 27:18). The booths used at the Feast of Booths were made of twigs woven together (Lev. 23:40–43; Neh. 8:15).

BOOTHS, FEAST OF See *Festivals*.

BOOTY Spoils taken by individuals in battle. Includes anything that might be of value or use to the captor including persons (Num. 31:53; Jer. 15:13; Ezek. 25:7). Booty is distinguished from spoil in the sense that booty was that taken by individual soldiers whereas spoil was plunder taken by the victor nation as a right of conquest.

BOOZ (Bō' ŏz) KJV New Testament spelling of Boaz. See *Boaz*.

BOR-ASHAN (Bôr-ā' shăn) Place name meaning, "well of smoke" or "pit of smoke." Place in most manuscripts of 1 Samuel 30:30; others read Chor-ashan (KJV). A town of the tribe of Judah to whom David gave part of his spoils of victory. It is usually equated with Asham, the town of Judah in which Simeon lived (Josh. 15:42; 19:7).

BORROW In Hebrew culture borrowing indicated economic hardship, not a strategy for expanding business or household. (See Lev. 25:35–37, which assumes that borrowers are poor.) In Deuteronomy God's blessings of prosperity was understood to exclude the need to borrow (15:6; 26:12). Thus poverty was not considered to be a desirable situation for anyone in the covenant community. The dire straits requiring borrowing are illustrated in Nehemiah 5:1–5. With typical shifts in fortune borrowing was common practice in Hebrew society, and rules were needed so that the poor were not victimized by creditors. Laws for restitution were also established for borrowed property that was damaged (Ex. 22:14–15).

In Matthew 5:42, Jesus cites generosity "from him that would borrow of thee" as one example of an unexpected, loving response (instead of the typical self-protective response) to others' demands and abuses. In each example (5:38–42) the disciple's primary concern is the other person, not protecting one's own vested interests. The second person singular in verse 42 makes clear the personal nature of this response to the would-be borrower. This passage is part of Jesus' consistent emphasis on absolute loyalty to the way of God's kingdom, which necessitates a carefree regard for one's possessions (Matt. 6:24–34) and personal security (Matt. 5:43–48) as one unselfishly loves the neighbor. *David Nelson Duke*

BOSCATH (Bŏs' căth) KJV spelling of Bozkath (2 Kings 22:1). See *Bozkath*.

BOSOR (Bō' sôr) KJV New Testament spelling of Beor (2 Pet. 2:15). See *Beor*.

BOSSED, BOSSES Bosses were knobs on the flat surfaces of shields. When shields were made of leather and wood, the bosses served to strengthen the shield. When shields were made of metal, the bosses were ornamental. Job 15:26 says that the wicked oppose God with thick-bossed shield—that is, a reinforced shield. Thus some modern translations express the meaning rather than using literal translation: "strong shield" (NIV); "massive shield" (NAS).

BOTCH An old English term used in the KJV that means boil (Deut. 28:27,35).

BOTTLE Word used often in the KJV to translate several Hebrew and Greek words. Modern ver-

Painted relief of Persian soldier with lance, bow, and quiver of arrows on left shoulder.

B

Tiny Roman glass bottle.

sions often translate these words as "skin" or "wineskin." Although glass and glass bottles were known in ancient times, ancient "bottles" were almost always made of animal skins since they were easier to carry than earthenware vessels. In Psalm 33:7 many modern scholars and translators emend the Hebrew text by adding an unpronounced Hebrew letter (*aleph*) to read "bottle" or "jars" (NIV, NRSV), but the traditional reading "heap" following the Hebrew text finds support in the parallel statement of Exodus 15:8.

BOTTOMLESS PIT Literal translation of the Greek in Revelation 9:1–2,11; 11:7; 17:8; 20:1,3. It represented the home of evil, death, and destruction stored up until the sovereign God allowed them temporary power on earth. See *Abyss; Hades; Hell; Sheol.*

BOW AND ARROW See *Arms and Armor.*

BOWELS Translation used in modern versions to refer to intestines and other entrails (Acts 1:18). In the KJV, "bowels" is also used to refer to the sexual reproductive system (2 Sam. 16:11; Ps. 71:6) and, figuratively, to strong emotions (Job 30:27), especially love (Song of Sol. 5:4) and compassion (Col. 3:12). Both Hebrew and Greek picture the entrails as the center of human emotions and excitement.

B

Phrygian cut-glass bowl.

BOWL See *Basin.*

BOX KJV translation for jar or flask, a container of oil used for anointing (2 Kings 9:1; Mark 14:3).

BOX TREE KJV, REB and NAS translation in Isaiah 41:19; 60:13. The box tree grows in Asia Minor and Persia but does not occur in Palestine. The tree has been identified as the pine (NRSV) or cypress (TEV, NIV). "Box tree"is based on early Greek and Latin translations. The Hebrew word means, "to be straight" and apparently refers to the tall, majestic cypress trees. Such wonders of nature reflect the greatness of the Creator (Isa. 41:20).

BOZEZ (Bō′ zĕz) Place name perhaps meaning, "white." A sharp rock marking a passage in the wadi Suwenit near Michmash through which Jonathan and his armor-bearer went to fight the Philistines (1 Sam. 14:4).

BOZKATH (Bŏz′ kăth) Place name meaning, "swelling." Town near Lachish and Eglon in tribal allotment of Judah (Josh. 15:39). It was the home town of Adaiah, King Josiah's maternal grandmother (1 Kings 22:1). Its precise location is not known.

BOZRAH (Bŏz′ răh) Place name meaning, "inaccessible." *1.* Ancestral home of Jobab, a king in Edom before Israel had a king (Gen. 36:33). Isaiah announced a great judgment on Bozrah in which God would sacrifice His enemies (Isa. 34:6). A center of shepherds, it was known for woolen garments. God is pictured as returning from Bozrah with dyed garments as His spoil of victory (Isa. 63:1). Thus He demonstrated His righteousness and power to save from enemies. Jeremiah proclaimed doom on Bozrah (Jer. 49:13,22), as did Amos (1:12). A major city which at times served as capital of Edom, Bozrah lay about 25 miles southeast of the southern end of the Dead Sea at modern Buseirah. See *Edom.* *2.* City of Moab Jeremiah condemned (Jer. 48:24). It may be

equated with Bezer. See *Bezer.*

BRACELET An ornamental band of metal or glass worn around the wrist (as distinct from an armlet worn around the upper arm). Bracelets were common in the Ancient Near East and were worn by both women and men. They were made mostly of bronze, though examples of iron, silver, glass, and, rarely, gold bracelets have been found. The bracelets mentioned in the Bible were usually of gold (Gen. 24:22,30,47; Num. 31:50; Isa. 3:19; Ezek. 16:11; 23:42). KJV, TEV and NAS translation for armlet in 2 Samuel 1:10. See *Armlet.*

BRAIDED, BRAIDING Fixing the hair in knots or weaving a wreath into the hair. Christian women were instructed that good works and spiritual grace were more important than outward appearances (1 Tim. 2:9; 1 Pet. 3:3).

BRAMBLE Shrub (Lycium Europaeum) with sharb spines and runners usually forming a tangled mass of vegetation (see Judg. 9:8–15; Luke 6:44). It had beautiful, attractive flowers, but its thorns gave flocks trouble. Today, we know that it prevents erosion on mountain slopes.

BRANCH Translation of many Hebrew and Greek words in the Bible. Often refers to the branches of trees or vines or to the branches of the lampstands of the tabernacle and Temple. There are, however, many metaphorical usages of "branch." The palm branch may stand for nobility, while the reed is symbolic for the common people (Isa. 9:14; 19:15). One's "being a branch" denotes membership in the people of God (John 15:1–8; Rom. 11:16–21). Spreading branches can symbolize fruitfulness and prosperity (Gen. 49:22; Job 8:16; Ps. 80:11), while withered, burnt, or cut branches symbolize destruction (Job 8:16; Isa. 9:14; Jer. 11:16; Ezek. 15:2). "Branch" or "shoot" is often used as a symbol for a present or coming king of Israel (Isa. 11:1; Jer. 23:5; 33:15; Zech. 3:8; 6:12). See *Messiah.*

BRASEN SEA See *Molten Sea.*

BRASEN SERPENT See *Bronze Serpent.*

BRASS Any copper alloy was called brass by the KJV translators. Brass is the alloy of copper and zinc, a combination unknown in the ancient Near East. A common alloy was copper and tin—that is, bronze—and this is what is indicated by the Hebrew of the biblical text. Some modern translations retain brass where hardness or persistence in sin is in view (Lev. 26:19; Deut. 28:23; Isa. 48:4), but they use "bronze" as a translation elsewhere. See *Bronze.*

BRAZEN SEA See *Molten Sea.*

BRAZEN SERPENT See *Bronze Serpent.*

BRAZIER A portable fire-pot (NIV) or firepan used for heating a room during cold weather (Jer. 36:22–23; KJV has "hearth").

BREAD The word bread appears 239 times in the NAS Old Testament and 79 times in the NAS New Testament; but the seven Hebrew words which refer to bread, but are not always so translated, appear 384 times in the Old Testament and three Greek words 108 times in the New. Frequency of mention is just one indication that bread (not vegetables and certainly not meat) was the basic food of most people (except nomads and the wealthy) in Bible times. Indeed, several of the words alluded to above are often translated food. **Ingredients** A course meal was ground from wheat (Gen. 30:14) or barley (John 6:9,13). American corn was unknown. (The use of the word in the KJV is a "Britishism" meaning grain in general.) Barley bread was less appetizing but also less expensive and therefore common among the poor. Grinding was done by a mortar and pestle or with millstones turned by an animal or human being (Num. 11:8; Matt. 24:41). For special occasions and for offerings a fine flour was ground (Gen. 18:6; Lev. 2:7). The meal or flour was mixed with water, salt, sometimes leaven or yeast, sometimes olive oil, and rarely with other cereals and vegetables (Ezek. 4:9) and then was kneaded (Ex. 12:34).
Baking Baking was usually the work of wives (Gen. 18:6) or daughters (2 Sam. 13:8), although in wealthy households it was done by slaves. Large cities or the royal court had professional bakers (Gen. 40:2; Jer. 37:21). There were three means of baking: on heated rocks with the dough being covered with ashes (1 Kings 19:6); on a clay or iron griddle or pan (Lev. 2:5); and in a clay or iron oven (Lev. 2:4). Most bread that was so baked had the appearance of a disk (Judg. 7:13) about one-half inch thick and twelve inches in

Bread for sale in old Jerusalem.

diameter. Some was perforated. Some had a hole in the middle for storing or carrying on a pole. Some was heart-shaped (the word for cakes in 2 Sam. 13:6,8,10 literally means heart-shaped). Some took the shape of a small modern loaf (suggested by the arrangement of the Bread of Presence). Bread was broken or torn, not cut.
Use In addition to being used as a staple food, bread was used as an offering to God (Lev. 2:4–10). It was used in the tabernacle and Temple to symbolize the presence of God (Ex. 25:23–30; Lev. 24:5–9). Bread was also used in the Old Testament to symbolize such things as an enemy to be consumed (Num. 14:9, KJV, RSV), the unity of a group (1 Kings 18:19), hospitality (Gen. 19:3), and wisdom (Prov. 9:5). It is prefixed to such things as idleness (Prov. 31:27), wickedness (Prov. 4:17), and adversity (Isa. 30:20). In the New Testament it symbolizes Jesus Christ Himself (John 6:35), His body (1 Cor. 11:23–24), His kingdom (Luke 14:15), and the unity of His church (1 Cor. 10:17).

BREAD OF THE PRESENCE (*bread of the faces*) In Exodus 25:30, the Lord's instructions concerning the paraphernalia of worship include a provision that bread be kept always on a table set before the Holy of Holies. This bread was called the bread of presence, or shewbread. The literal meaning of the Hebrew expression is "bread of the face." It consisted of twelve loaves of presumably unleavened bread, and it was replaced each sabbath. See *Temple; Tabernacle.* Jesus took the staple diet of festival worship—unleavened Bread—and gave it to His followers to symbolize the presence of His body broken to bring salvation and the hope of His return (1 Cor. 11:17–32).
James A. Brooks

BREAKFAST See *Food and Meals in the Bible.*

BREASTPIECE OF THE HIGH PRIEST See *Breastplate 1.*

BREASTPLATE *1.* A piece of elaborate embroidery about nine inches square worn by the high priest upon his breast. It was set with twelve stones with the name of one of the 12 tribes of Israel engraved on each stone; The breastplate was a special item worn by the high priest as he ministered in the tabernacle or Temple. Made like a purse, the breastplate was constructed of gold metal, blue, purple, and scarlet yarn, and of fine linen. It was securely tied to the ephod. See *Ephod.* Inside the breastplate were placed two unknown stones, the Urim and Thummim, worn over the heart (Lev. 8:8). The breastplate was called breastplate of judgment (Ex. 28:15) because these stones were the means of making decisions (Ex. 28:28–29). See *Urim and Thummim.* The purpose of the breastplate was: (1) to show the glory and beauty of the Lord (Ex. 28:2); (2) to be a means of making decisions (Ex. 28:30); and (3) to be a continuing memorial before the Lord (Ex. 28:29). *2.* A piece of defensive armor. See *Arms and Armor.*

Paul used the military breastplate as an illustration of Christian virtues. Ephesians 6:14 reflects Isaiah 59:17 symbolizing the breastplate as righteousness. Faith and love are symbolized in 1 Thessalonians 5:8. Breastplates were also strong symbols of evil (Rev. 9:9,17).   *Lawson Hatfield*

BREATH Air coming out of or into the body of a living being. Two Hebrew terms are translated, "breath." Generally *neshamah* is used in a milder manner to refer to the fact of breath in all forms of life. It is concerned with the physiological concept of breath with a primary emphasis on breath as a principle of life. By contrast, *ruach* refers more to the force of breath in the extreme experiences of life, judgment, and death. At times it is intensified by the idea of a blast of breath. It thus contains the expanded meanings, wind and spirit. *Ruach* refers more to the psychological idea of breath by relating it to one's own will or purpose.

The term *neshamah* is often used with reference to God's breath. It identifies God as the source of life (Gen. 2:7; Job 27:3; 33:4; Dan. 5:23).

God is also the sovereign of life. He gave breath to humans initially in creation (Gen. 2:7), but He also takes breath away eventually at death (Gen. 7:22; Job 34:14). God has the power to restore life to the dead if He wishes to do so (Ezek. 37:9). He controls nature and the weather by His breath (Job 37:9,10). More important is the impact of God's breath on national life, for He can breathe anger and judgment on threatening enemies bringing festive joy to God's people (Isa. 30:33; compare Job 41:21).

Neshamah is used several times to refer to human breath. It identifies breath as fragile during the times of God's wrath and in natural calamities (Isa. 2:21,22). Breath can become weak (Dan. 10:17); it is limited (Gen. 7:22; I Kings 17:17). Breath may be taken from a person, thus the experience of death (Josh. 11:11).

Breath (*neshamah*) refers to all living creatures. Those who breathe are expected to be responsive to God by offering Him praise (Psalm 150:6). Ultimately, they are responsible to God because He has the right to demand that they be put to death (Deut. 20:16; Josh. 10:40).

The New Testament contains a few references to breath as the life principle which God gives (Acts 17:25) and as the mighty wind at Pentecost (Acts 2:2). Acts 9:1 uses breath to express Saul's anger as a breathing of threats against the early Christians. In John 20:22 Jesus breathed the Holy Spirit upon His disciples. While the word *pneuma* parallels *ruach* in the Old Testament in its multiple meanings, it is translated primarily as spirit or Holy Spirit. In Revelation 13:15 it refers to the power to breathe life into the image of the beast. See *Spirit; Life.*   *Donald R. Potts*

BREATH OF LIFE The translation of several Hebrew words and phrases. The phrase denotes the capacity for life. In the Bible, God is the source of the breath of life (Gen. 1:30; 2:7; 7:15; Isa. 57:16). Just as God gave the breath of life, so can He take it away (Gen. 6:17; 7:22; Isa. 57:16). See *Life; Immortality.*

BREECHES Priestly garments made of linen covering the thighs for reasons of modesty. They were worn by the high priest on the Day of Atonement and by other priests on other ceremonial occasions (Ex. 28:42; 39:28; Lev. 6:10; 16:4; Ezek. 44:18). The garment ensured that priests fulfilled the commandment in Exodus 20:26.

BRIBERY Giving anything of value with intention of influencing one in the discharge of his or her duties. The danger of bribery is the opportunity it presents for the perversion of justice (see 1 Sam. 8:3; Prov. 17:23; Isa. 1:23; Micah 3:11; 7:3). The poor, because they had no bribe to offer, were either discriminated against when the judgment was handed down or had difficulty getting a trial at all (see Job 6:22 where a bribe is necessary to get justice done). Bribery, because it perverted justice, is prohibited in the Bible (Ex. 23:8; Deut. 16:19).

BRICK is a building material of clay, molded into rectangular shaped blocks while moist and hardened by the sun or fire, used to construct walls or pavement.

The task of brick making was hard labor. It involved digging and moving heavy clay. Clay required softening with water which was done by treading clay pits. After molding the bricks of approximately 2 by 4 by 8 inches, they were dried

Mud-clay bricks in the ruins of the city of Ur.

in the sun or in kilns, (ovens) for fire-hardened bricks. The tower of Babel (Gen. 11:3), made of bricks, had mortar of slime, a tar-like substance. Later, because of famine, Joseph moved his family to Egypt (Gen. 46:6). The twelve families multiplied greatly in 430 years. A new Pharaoh who "knew not Joseph" (Ex. 1:6–8) enslaved the Jews. They built storehouse cities of brick in Pithom and Ramses. Egyptian bricks were sometimes mixed with straw. When Moses confronted Pharaoh for Israel's freedom, the angered Pharaoh increased his demands of the slaves. They must produce their same brick quotas and gather their own straw. Both straw-made bricks and bricks of pure clay have been found at Pithom and Ramses. When David conquered the Ammorites, he required they make bricks (2 Sam. 12:31). Isaiah (65:3) condemned Israel for their pagan-like practice of offering incense on altars of brick.

Lawson Hatfield

BRICKKILN An oven, furnace, or heated enclosure used for processing bricks by burning, firing, or drying. Some Bible students believe that sun-dried bricks were used in Palestine; they would translate the word as "brick-mold" (see Nah. 3:14 NRSV, NAS, TEV). Others give the neutral translation "brickwork" (NIV, REB). Just as the Egyptians used the Israelites to make bricks, so David put the Ammonites to making bricks (2 Sam. 12:31).

BRIDE Biblical writers have little to say about weddings or brides. They occasionally mention means by which brides were obtained (Gen. 24:4; 29:15–19). Ezekiel 16:8–14 describes bride, her attire, and the wedding ceremony. The Song of Solomon is a collection of love poems in which the bride describes her love for her bridegroom.

The imagery of the bride is used widely in the Bible as a description of the people of God. In the Old Testament, the prophets presented Israel as a bride who had committed repeated adulteries (Jer. 3; Ezek. 16; Hos. 3). The prophets also proclaimed that God was faithful to His unfaithful bride and would restore her (Jer. 33:10–11; Isa. 61:10,62:5). In the New Testament, the bride imagery is used often of the church and her relationship to Christ. The bride belongs to Christ, who is the Bridegroom (John 3:29). In Revelation, the church, as the bride of the Lamb, has prepared herself for marriage by performing righteous deeds (19:7–8). In Revelation 21, the great wedding is portrayed with the church prepared for her bridegroom (21:2,9). Finally, the bride and the Spirit issue an invitation "to come" (22:17). Paul used the metaphor of the bride to indicate his feelings toward the churches he had founded. In 2 Corinthians 11:2, Paul wrote that he had betrothed the Corinthian church to Christ. He wanted to present the church as a pure bride to Christ. The Corinthians were in danger of committing "adultery." The imagery of the bride is used by various biblcal writers, but they appear to have a single biblical purpose. The bridal imagery is used to indicate the great love which God has for His people. For these writers, no image could express better this love than the ideal love between a bridegroom and bride.   *Terence B. Ellis*

BRIDE OF CHRIST See *Bride.*

BRIDLE See *Bit.*

BRIER Translation of various Hebrew words referring to thorny plants. Used metaphorically of the enemies of Israel (Ezek. 28:24) and of land which is worthless (Isa. 5:6; 7:23–25; 55:13; compare Micah 7:4).

BRIGANDINE KJV translation at Jeremiah 46:4; 51:3. Rendered elsewhere as "coat of mail" or "armor." See *Arms and Armor.*

BRIMSTONE Combustible form of sulphur. Used as a means of divine retribution (Gen. 19:24; Deut. 29:23; Job 18:15; Ps. 11:6; Isa. 30:33; 34:9; Ezek. 38:22; Luke 17:29; Rev. 14:10; 19:20; 20:10; 21:8). It lies on the shore of the Dead Sea and can burst into flame when earthquakes release hot gases from the earth's interior.

BROAD PLACE To be set in a broad place (Job 36:16) is to be delivered from danger, anxiety, want, or distress. The phrase is also translated as "large place" (2 Sam. 22:20; Pss. 18:19; 118:5; Hos. 4:16) and "large room" (Ps. 31:8). Related is the phrase applied to Canaan, "large land" which would appear to denote Canaan—the Promised Land—as a place of deliverance (Judg. 18:10; but see Isa. 22:18).

BROAD WALL A stretch of the wall of Jerusalem on the northwest corner near the Gate of Ephraim. This section of the wall was restored by Nehemiah (Neh. 3:8; 12:38).

BROIDERED See *Embroider, Embroiderer.*

BRONZE See *Minerals and Metals.*

BRONZE SEA See *Molten Sea.*

BRONZE SERPENT Moses made a bronze serpent and set it on a pole in the middle of the Israelite camp (Num. 21). God had told Moses to do this so the Israelites bitten by serpents could express their faith by looking at it and be healed. The need for the serpent came in one of the times Israel murmured against God and Moses. The people were in the wilderness after their refusal to obey God by entering the land of Canaan.

Although God had provided food and water for them after their disobedience, they complained because of the monotony of the good provided. God sent serpents among them, therefore, to punish the people. The serpents' bites were deadly, but God relented and chose to provide a way for rescue if those bitten would accept it. The bronze serpent was God's way. It was a call to faith in God and to the way of healing He established.

Nothing more is known of the bronze serpent until it is mentioned again in 2 Kings 18:4. There, in the account of King Hezekiah's purging of the Temple, the Bible tells of the destruction of this symbol. Hezekiah wanted to purify Temple worship. Apparently, the bronze serpent had become an object of worship as the Israelites burned incense to it.

Archaeological evidence from Mesopotamian and, more importantly, Canaanite sites reveals that the crawling serpent was a symbol of the fertility of the soil. The serpent was often represented associated with the fertility goddesses, the bull, the dove (life of the heavens), and water.

Jesus made the final mention of this symbol in John 3:14. There, in His conversation with Nicodemus, Jesus compared His own purpose with that of the bronze serpent. The serpent, lifted up in the wilderness, had been God's chosen way to provide physical healing. Jesus, lifted up on the cross, is God's chosen way to provide spiritual healing for all afflicted by sin. As the serpent gave life in the wilderness, Jesus gives spiritual life. Faith was necessary to look at the serpent and be healed; faith is necessary to receive the healing (salvation) Jesus gives.

See *Moses; Wilderness; Atonement; Hezekiah.*

Albert F. Bean and Karen Joines

BROOCH Class of jewelry brought by both men and women as offerings (Ex. 35:22). The Hebrew term denotes a golden pin (the KJV has bracelets here; REB, "clasp"; TEV, "decorative pins"). At a later time brooches were bow shaped and made of bronze or iron. Some recent interpreters think "nose rings" were meant.

BROOK OF EGYPT The southwestern limit of Canaanite territory given to Israel as a possession (Num. 34:5 NAS). It is usually identified with the Wadi el-'Arish, which flows from the middle of the Sinai Peninsula to the Mediterranean Sea. It empties into the Mediterranean about midway between the sites of Gaza and Pelusium. See *Rivers and Waterways in the Bible.*

BROOK OF THE ARABAH Literally, "brook of the wilderness." A stream bed that is dry most of the year and marked the southern border of Israel, the northern kingdom (2 Kings 14:25; Amos 6:14). It has sometimes been located at the Brook of Zered which joins the Dead Sea at its southeast-

ern corner from the east. More likely, it is either the wadi el-Qelt, flowing from Jericho to the west, or the wadi el-Kefren from the northern end of the Dead Sea flowing to the east.

BROOKS OF THE WILLOWS A name appearing only in Isaiah 15:7 as one of the borders of Moab. The Hebrew name can be read as a plural form of the Brook of the Arabah, but two separate waterways are meant. Probably the same as the Brook of Zered, modern wadi el-Hesa. See *Brook of Zered.*

BROOK OF ZERED Also called "valley of Zered." The Israelites crossed this book marking an end to their wilderness wandering and entrance into the Promised Land (Num. 21:12; Deut. 2:13–14). It is usually identified with modern wadi el-Hesa which flows into the southeast end of the Dead Sea. The wadi is about 35 miles long and forms the boundary between Moab and Edom. The Brook of Zered is the same as the Brook of the Willows (Isa. 15:7), the dry stream bed of 2 Kings 3:16 (see 3:22), and perhaps the same as the Brook of the Arabah (Amos 6:14), though see *Brook of the Arabah.*

BROOM TREE A bush that often grows large enough to provide shade (1 Kings 19:4–5). Its foliage and roots were often used as fuel (Job 30:4; Ps. 120:4). Its white flowers with maroon center beautify the Dead Sea area. Bees buzz

Broom tree in southern Israel.

among its blooms. The name Rithmah—a place along the route of the Exodus (Num. 33:18–19)—was named for this shrub (*rothem*). Although KJV, NAS identify the bush as the juniper, modern scholars agree that the bush intended by the Hebrew writer was the broom tree—*Retama raetam* (NIV, REB, NRSV).

BROTHERLY LOVE A concept which appears

throughout the Bible, but the specific word for this type love appears only in the New Testament.

The word which is usually rendered "brotherly love" in the New Testament is the Greek *philadelphia* and is used only five times (Rom. 12:10; 1 Thess. 4:9; Heb. 13:1; 1 Pet. 1:22; 2 Pet. 1:7). A similar word, *philadelphos,* appears in 1 Peter 3:8, and means "loving one's brother." However, the idea of brotherly love is much more extensive than these few occurrences.

Old Testament Two words in the Old Testament cover the full range of ideas associated with "love," the Hebrew '*ahab* and *hesed,* though the latter is often associated with covenant love. Israelites were called upon to love other people in many relationships: as friend to friend (Ps. 38:11; Prov. 10:12); between slave and master (Ex. 21:5; Deut. 15:16); with the neighbor (Lev. 19:18); with the poor and unfortunate (Prov. 14:21,31); and especially significant is the command to love the stranger and foreigner (Lev. 19:34; Deut. 10:19). Often the love relationship between people is in the context of covenant, as with David and Jonathan (1 Sam. 18:1-3).

New Testament Brotherly love in the ancient Christian literature means to treat others as if they were a part of one's family. This kind of love means "to like" another person and to want what is best for that individual. The basic word used for the brotherly type of love, *phileo,* sometimes means "to kiss," which was to show close friendship (Mark 14:44). This kind of love is never used for the love of God nor for erotic love.

Jesus constantly taught His followers the principle of "brotherly love," even though the New Testament never records Him using this very word. He declared that the second great commandment is, "Thou shalt love thy neighbor as thyself" (Mark 12:31), and in the parable of the Good Samaritan He explained who that neighbor is (Luke 10:25-37). He also encouraged forgiveness of a brother (Matt. 18:23-35) and offered the Golden Rule as a guide in relating to one's brother (Matt. 7:12; Luke 6:31).

Paul spoke of "brotherly love" in the context of the community of believers, the church. Twice he used the term *philadelphia:* first in 1 Thessalonians 4:9, then in Romans 12:10. In both cases he encouraged Christians to live peaceably with one another in the church. He underlined the idea of love for the brethren in Galatians 5:14, "For all the law is fulfilled in one word,. . . Thou shalt love thy neighbor as thyself." Also in Romans 13:8-10, he declared, "Owe no man any thing, but to love one another," and in 1 Corinthians 8:13, on causing a weaker brother to stumble, he wrote, "If meat make my brother to offend, I will eat no flesh. . . . "

In the Johannine writings, brotherly love is a dominant theme. Jesus gave a new commandment "that ye love one another" (John 13:34). The idea is repeated in John 17:26, "that the love wherewith thou hast loved me may be in them." A series of emphatic statements on brotherly love in 1 and 2 John are designed to show that this is truly the central command of Jesus (1 John 2:9; 3:10,18,23; 4:8,20; 2 John 6).

In the Epistles the specific word, *philadelphia* (brotherly love) appears in Hebrews and in 1 and 2 Peter. Hebrews 13:1-2 connects it with "hospitality to strangers," 1 Peter 1:22 with being pure, and 2 Peter 1:7 has it in a checklist of virtues which Christians should possess. See *Love; Hospitality; Ethics.* *W. Thomas Sawyer*

BROTHERS In the Old Testament, the word *brother* usually refers to the blood relationship of siblings (Ex. 4:14; Judg. 9:5). In fact, the book of Genesis addresses the difficulties of sibling rivalry, or the "brother problem": Cain and Abel (Gen. 4); Jacob and Esau (Gen. 25—28); Joseph and his brothers (Gen. 37—50). In each instance, the younger brother is the one favored by God. (See also David among Jesse's sons, 2 Sam. 1:26.)

The New Testament also reflects the use of the word *brother* to designate a physical relationship. Luke mentions that Herod and Philip are brothers (Luke 3:1). Among the disciples, Simon and Andrew are siblings (Mark 1:16); so also are James and John (Mark 1:19). The four brothers of Jesus are mentioned in Mark 3:31 and named in Mark 6:3. Other examples of physical brothers are found in the Parable of the Rich Man and Lazarus (Luke 16:28), the story of the disputed inheritance (Luke 12:13), and the Parable of the Prodigal Son (Luke 15).

The term *brother* is also used in the Old Testament to signify kinsmen, allies, fellow countrymen. The word is used in Genesis 13:8 to describe the relationship of Abram and his nephew, Lot ("we be brethren"). Solomon and Hiram of Tyre are called brothers after they entered into political alliance with one another (1 Kings 9:13). Often, the term *brothers* is found in apposition to the phrase "the children of Israel" (Lev. 25:46; Deut. 3:18; 24:7; Judg. 20:13; cf. Num. 25:6). Basic to this idea is the notion that the tribes and nation of Israel descended from a common father.

This shift of focus from blood to spiritual kinship is found in the teachings of Jesus when He designated as brothers those "which hear the word of God, and do it" (Luke 8:20). The fledgling Christian community continued this emphasis on *brother* as expressing a spiritual relationship. Paul regularly addressed the Christian community as brothers (1 Cor. 1:10; 1 Thess. 1:4). In fact, in most of the New Testament passages where *brethren* is used to designate the entire Christian community (male and female), the word may be better translated as "fellow Christians" (Phil. 4:1-9). The dual function of the term *brother* as describing both a physical and spiritual relationship bears eloquent testimony to the importance in the Christian community of both the family of flesh and the family of faith. See *Sister; Early Church; Paul.*

Mikeal C. Parsons

BROTHERS, JESUS Jesus grew up in a normal family with parents and brothers. Jesus' Nazareth critics listed them in Mark 6:3 as James, Joses, Juda, and Simon. Their names appear again in the parallel passage of Matthew 13:55, except Joseph is used as the alternate spelling of Joses (see NAS). His brothers may have been among the friends in Mark 3:21 who thought Jesus was "beside himself"; ten verses later 3:31 "his brethren and his mother" tried to get His attention while He was teaching in a house. Furthermore, John 7:5 reports that "neither did his brethren believe in him." After the resurrection, however, they changed their minds and joined the disciples in times of prayer (Acts 1:14). The risen Christ appeared to one of them, James, and he became the leader of the church in Jerusalem (Acts 12:17; 1 Cor. 15:7). Nevertheless, some writings in the early centuries raised questions about the brothers to protect their developing doctrine of Mary's perpetual virginity. One of them, often called the Gospel of James, tells the life story of Mary, using much fanciful material. It claims that Jesus' brothers were the sons of Joseph by an earlier marriage. This is the view of the Greek Orthodox Church. Later a famous scholar, Jerome, argued that Jesus' brothers were really his cousins because their mother was Mary of Cleophas and the sister of Mary the mother of Jesus (see John 19:25). This is the view of the Roman Catholic Church, but Protestant scholars prefer the traditional view of the Gospels. Jesus was born of the virgin Mary. Mary and Joseph then had four sons in the way all humans normally do. *W. J. Fallis*

BROWN KJV translation of a Hebrew word rendered as "black" (NAS, NRSV, TEV, REB) or "dark-colored" (NIV) by modern translations (Gen. 30:32,33,35,40). See *Colors; Black.*

BUBASTIS (Bū′ băs·tĭs) TEV, NIV translation of Pi-beseth. See *Pi-beseth.*

BUCKET The reference is to waterskin held open at the top by a stick in the shape of a cross (Num. 24:7; Isa. 40:15). The main purpose was for drawing water from a well and is still used in Palestine today.

BUCKLER A small rounded shield which was carried in the hand or worn on the arm. Larger shields were also used which covered the entire body. See *Arms and Armor.*

BUGLE NRSV, NAS, TEV translation of a Greek word in 1 Corinthians 14:8 which is elsewhere translated as "trumpet." See *Music; Instruments; Dancing.*

BUKKI (Bŭk′ kī) Personal name shortened from Bukkiah, meaning, "Yahweh proved" or "Yahweh has emptied." *1.* Representative of tribe of Dan on commission to distribute the Promised Land among the tribes (Num. 34:22). *2.* High priestly descendant of Aaron (1 Chron. 6:5,51) and ancestor of Ezra (Ezra 7:4).

BUKKIAH (Bŭk·kī′ ăh) See *Bukki.* Son of Herman among Temple musicians David appointed (1 Chron. 25:4). He or a person of same name headed the sixth course of musicians (1 Chron. 25:13).

BUL (Bŭl) Name of eighth month or parts of October and November meaning, "harvest month." Solomon finished building the Temple in this month (1 Kings 6:38).

BULL The term is a translation of several Hebrew words: "*abbir,*" "*par,*" and "*shor.*" The difference between "abbir" and "par" is not obvious but may be of some consequence. "Abbir" is used as an adjective most frequently to mean might or valiant one, either man, angels, or animals. "Par" seems to be used in reference to the male of the bovine species.

The bull was the symbol of great productivity in the ancient world and was a sign of great strength. Moses portrayed the future strength of Joseph with the term "*shor*" (Deut. 33:17). The king of Assyria boasted of his great strength with the term "*abbir*" (Isa. 10:13). The most frequent use of the bull in the Old Testament was as a sacrificial animal. Leviticus specifies that no castrated animal could be so used and that the animal must be at least eight days old (22:17–28). The bull is specified as the sacrificial animal for a peace offering (Ex. 24:5), a burnt offering (Judg. 6:26), and as a sin offering (Ezek. 43:19). On the other hand, the sacrificial animal is not so restricted in other passages (Lev. 22:23; Num. 23:14). The bull was used most frequently in connection with the inau-

Relief of festooned bull's head from Roman Ephesus.

A colossal Persian column capital from Susa decorated with the neck and head of two stylized bulls.

guration of the sacrificial system or with sacrifices on special days. It was used in connection with the consecration of the priests (Ex. 29:1–37); at the dedication of the altar of the tabernacle (Num. 7); for the purification of the Levites (Num. 8:5–22); at the beginning of the month (New Moon [Num. 28:11–15]); the Feast of Weeks (Num. 28:26–31). The Feast of Booths had the distinction of requiring the largest numbers of bulls (seventy-one [Num. 29:12–40]).

The bull may have been introduced into the cultic system of Israel from the practice of her neighbors. It was a widespread practice in the region in which Israel resided. In the Canaanite religion, the chief of the assembly was called "father bull El." The bull was closely associated with Baal and may have influenced Jeroboam to set up the golden bulls at Bethel and Dan (1 Kings 12:28). The bronze sea in the courtyard of the temple in Jerusalem was resting on the back of twelve bronze bulls.   *Bryce Sandlin*

BULRUSH In Exodus 2:3, the material that was used to make the ark in which the infant Moses was placed to protect him from the edict of Pharaoh requiring that every male Hebrew child be drowned. It was a kind of reed plant. See *Plants of the Bible.*

BULWARK A solid wall-like structure raised for

defense, possibly a system of two walls with space between. God's salvation is a bulwark for His people (Isa. 26:1; see Ps. 8:2; 1 Tim. 3:15).

BUNAH (Bū' năh) Personal name meaning, "understanding." Member of clan of Jerahmeel in tribe of Judah (1 Chron. 2:25).

BUNDLE See *Bag 3.*

BUNNI (Bŭn' nī) Personal name meaning, "built." Levite leader of worship service confessing Israel's sin in days of Ezra (Neh. 9:4). A man of same name, probably same man, signed Nehemiah's covenant to obey God's Law (Neh. 10:15). His son Hasabiah was one of the Levites living in Jerusalem in time of Nehemiah (Neh. 11:15).

BURGLARY See *Crimes and Punishments.*

BURIAL Partly because of the warm climate of Palestine and partly because the corpse was considered ritually impure, the Hebrews buried their dead as soon as possible and usually within twenty-four hours of death (Deut. 21:23). To allow a body to decay or be desecrated above the ground was highly dishonorable (1 Kings 14:10–14; 2 Kings 9:34–37), and any corpse found by the wayside was required to be buried (2 Sam. 21:10–14).

Though the Bible nowhere systematically describes Hebrew mortuary practice, several features can be gleaned from individual passages. Joseph closed his father's eyelids soon after Jacob's death (Gen. 46:4). Jesus' body was prepared for burial by anointing with aromatic oils and spices and wrapping in a linen cloth (Mark 16:1; Luke 24:1; John 19:39). The arms and legs of Lazarus' body were bound with cloth, and the face covered by a napkin (John 11:44). The body of Tabitha was washed in preparation for burial (Acts 9:37).

The dead were buried in caves, rock-cut tombs, or in the ground. It was desirable to be buried in the family tomb, so Sarah (Gen. 23:19), Abraham (Gen. 25:9), Isaac, Rebekah, Leah (Gen. 49:31)

Bulrushes at the so-called "Moses' Well" in the Sinai desert.

and Jacob (Gen. 50:13) were all buried in the cave of Machpelah, east of Hebron. Burial sites were marked by trees (Gen. 35:8), pillars (Gen. 35:19–20), and piles of stones (Josh. 7:26). The burials of the wealthy or politically powerful were sometimes accompanied by lavish accessories, including robes, jewelry, furniture, weapons, and pottery (1 Sam. 28:14; Isa. 14:11; Ezek. 32:27).

In contrast to its wide usage among the Greeks and Romans, cremation is not described as normal practice in the Bible. Bodies were cremated only in exceptional cases such as decay following mutilation (1 Sam. 31:12) or the threat of plague. Even in these instances, cremation was partial so that the bones remained. Embalming is mentioned only in the burial accounts of Jacob and Joseph (Gen. 50:2–3, 26) and there only because of the Egyptian setting and plans to move the bodies. Apparently, embalming was an Egyptian practice.

When preparations for burial were completed, the body was usually placed on a bier and carried to the burial site in a procession of relatives, friends, and servants (Amos 6:10). The proces-

Burial caves carved out of bedrock along the south slope of the Hinnom Valley in Jerusalem.

sion carried out the mourning ritual, which could include (1) baldness and cutting of beard, (2) rending garments and wearing sackcloth, (3) loud and agonized weeping, and (4) putting dust on the head and sitting in ashes (2 Sam. 1:11–12; 13:31; 14:2; Isa. 3:24, 22:12; Jer. 7:29; Ezek. 7:18; Joel 1:8). The Canaanite practices of laceration and mutilation are forbidden in the Torah (Lev. 19:27–28; 21:5; Deut. 14:1).

The period of mourning varied in response to circumstances. Mourning for Jacob lasted seventy days (Gen. 50:3), while for Aaron and Moses it lasted thirty days (Num. 20:29; Deut. 34:5–8). Women captured in war were allowed to mourn the deaths of their parents one month before having to marry their captors (Deut. 21:11–13).

The deaths of the famous prompted poetic laments. David mourned for the deaths of Saul and Jonathan (2 Sam. 1:17–27), and Jeremiah lamented the death of Josiah (2 Chron. 35:25).

Professional mourners are referred to in Jeremiah 9:17–18 and Amos 5:16 as "such as are skilled in lamentation," and in Matthew 9:23 as "minstrels." In the latter account Jesus seemed to dismiss them as He healed the ruler's daughter. It is interesting to note that Jesus' own response to Lazarus' death was comparatively simple; He wept quietly at the tomb (John 11:35–36).

Israel's mourning rites reflect in part the belief that death is something evil. All contact with death—whether it happened by touching a corpse, the bones of a corpse, a grave, or a house which contained a dead body—made the Israelite unclean and in need of purification. In addition to personal sorrow, the mourning rites reflected at least to a degree the mourner's humiliation because of his necessarily close contact with the body of the deceased. *Joe Haag*

BURNING BUSH In Exodus 3:2, Moses' attention was arrested by the sight of a bush that burned without being consumed by the fire. When he turned aside to investigate, the Lord spoke to him from the bush, instructing him to return to Egypt to deliver the Hebrew people from slavery. Some attempts have been made to explain the phenomenon by claiming that the bush had foliage of a brilliant fiery color, or that its leaves reflected the sunlight in an unusual manner. It is best, however, to regard the burning of the bush as a unique act of God. It appears to have had significance primarily, perhaps solely, as a means of attracting Moses' interest and so enabling him to hear the divine word. See *Moses; Exodus.*

BURNT OFFERINGS See *Sacrifice and Offering.*

BUSHEL See *Weights and Measures.*

BUTLER Translation of a Hebrew word that literally means "one who gives drink." The butler was an officer of the royal court who had charge of wines and other beverages. The butler was a trusted member of the royal court as this person helped prevent the poisoning of the king. The term that is translated "butler" (Gen. 40:1–23; 41:9) is also translated "cupbearer" (1 Kings 10:5; 2 Chron. 9:4; Neh. 1:11).

BUZ (Bŭz) Place and personal name meaning, "scorn." *1.* Son of Nahor, brother of Abraham (Gen. 22:21). *2.* A member of tribe of Gad (1 Chron. 5:14). *3.* A land in eastern Arabia (Jer. 25:23) which Jeremiah condemned.

BUZI (Bū′ zī) Personal noun meaning, "scorn." Priest and father of Ezekiel, the prophet and priest (Ezek. 1:3).

BUZITE (Bŭz′ īte) Citizen of Buz. See *Buz.*

BYWORD An object of derision among other peoples. Used in the Bible to speak of the fate of faithless Israel (Deut. 28:37; 1 Kings 9:7; 2 Chron. 7:20; Job 17:6; 30:9; Ps 44:14).

C

The ruins of Corinth with the Acrocorinth in the distance.

CAB See *Kab; Weights and Measures.*

CABBON (Căb' bŏn) Place name of uncertain meaning. Town in tribal allotment of Judah (Josh. 15:40). Its location is uncertain.

CABIN KJV translation of Hebrew word appearing only in Jeremiah 37:16 and meaning vault, cellar, or prison cell.

CABUL (Cā' bûl) Place name meaning, "fettered" or "braided." *1.* Town on northeast border of Asher (Josh. 19:27). May be located at modern Kabul nine miles southeast of Acco. *2.* Region of cities in Galilee Solomon gave Hiram, king of Tyre, as payment for materials and services in building the Temple and the palace. Hiram did not like them and called them Cabul, a Hebrew word play meaning, "as nothing." Apparently, the "gift" expected a gift in return, according to Near Eastern etiquette, for Hiram gave Solomon 120 talents of gold (1 Kings 9:10–14).

CAESAR (Cāe' sàr) Family name of Julius Caesar assumed by following emperors as a title. Some Pharisees and Herodians asked Jesus about the propriety of paying taxes to Caesar. In reply, the Lord said that those things pertaining to Caesar should be rendered to Caesar and those things pertaining to God should be rendered to Him (Matt. 22:15–21). In this passage, the name Caesar is virtually a symbol for civil authority. Originally, Caesar was the family name of the founder of the Roman Empire. Julius Caesar was assassinated on March 15, 44 B.C. His successors kept Caesar's memory alive, and eventually his name

Bust of Caligula, the Roman Caesar from A.D. 37–41.

came to be used as a title. Caesars mentioned or referred to in the New Testament include Augustus, Tiberius, Claudius, and probably Nero. See *Rome; Roman Empire.*

CAESAREA (Caĕs à rē' à) Located on the Mediterranean Sea 23 miles south of Mt. Carmel is the city of Caesarea, known also as Caesarea-on-the-Sea (Maritima), Caesarea Sebaste, Caesarea of Palestine, and Caesarea of Judea.

Byzantine street at Caesarea Maritima with two colossal statues, one possibly of the Emperor Hadrian.

The turbulent waters of the Mediterranean Sea as seen from Caesarea Maritima.

Because of the lack of natural harbor between Sidon and Egypt, a Sidonian king, Abdashtart established an anchorage in the 4th century B.C. It became known as Strato's Tower, using the king's Greek name. A fortified town developed on this site. The first literary record is from the archive of the Egyptian Zenon who put in there for supplies in 259 B.C. The Hasmonean ruler Alexander Jannaeus brought it under Jewish control in 96 B.C., but Pompey returned it to Gentile rule in 63 B.C. The Jewish community apparently continued to thrive. Mark Anthony gave it to Cleopatra, but Octavian or Augustus defeated Antony at Actuim and placed Caesarea under Herod in 30 B.C.

Herod determined to build a fine port facility and support it by a new city. The harbor, which he named Sebastos (Latin, Augustus), was a magnificently engineered project. The southern breakwa-

The Mediterranean Sea as seen through the arches of the Herodian aqueduct at Caesarea Maritima.

Performances are once again held at the restored Herodian theater at Caesarea Maritima.

Water was provided for Caesarea Maritima by an extensive system based upon this Herodian aqueduct.

ter was built of huge mortared stones placed in a semicircle about 2000 feet long, and the northern one is of similar construction almost 900 feet long. Great statues of Augustus and Roma were erected at the entrance. An inner harbor appears to have been dug into the land where mooring berths and vaulted warehouses were constructed. Josephus described the construction of the harbor and accompanying city in grandiose detail. The city was Hellenistic in design and style and named

Caesarea for Caesar. In addition to the many buildings a platform was raised near the harbor upon which a temple was built for Caesar with a Colossus of Caesar.

After Archelaus was removed in 6 A.D., Caesarea became the capital of the province of Judea and served as the official home of the procurators. Hostilities between the Jewish and Gentile population apparently had been a way of life in this city. One of the public outbreaks resulted in the desecration of the synagogue Knestha d'Meredtha in 66 A.D. which precipitated the Jewish-Roman War. Vespasian gave it the status of Colony.

The city appears in the book of Acts as a place of witness, travel, and the seat of government. Philip, having witnessed to the Ethiopian eunuch, is mentioned as arriving at Caesarea after a preaching mission. Peter led a centurion, Cornelius, who was stationed there to become a Christian (Acts 10). Paul had several reported contacts with the city as a port (Acts 9:30; 18:22; and perhaps 21:8) and a place of imprisonment and trial (Acts 23:23, 25:1–7). Herod Agrippa I had a residence there and died there (Acts 12:19–23).

George W. Knight

CAESAREA PHILIPPI (Caĕs á rē′ á Phĭl′ ĭp pī) About 1,150 feet above sea level, Caesarea Philippi is located on a triangular plain in the upper Jordan Valley along the southwestern slopes of Mt. Hermon. Behind it rise bluffs and rugged mountain peaks. The area is one of the most lush and beautiful in Palestine, with groves of trees and grassy fields abounding. Water is in abundance, for the city is near the spot where the spring Nahr Baniyas, one of the sources of the Jordan, gushes from a cave in the bluffs. The city is also in a strategic location, guarding the plains in the area. The extent of its ruins indicate that it was a city of considerable size. The modern town, which has dwindled drastically, is known as Banyas.

History Caesarea Philippi seems to have been a religious center from its earliest days. The Canaanite god Baal-gad, the god of good fortune, was worshiped here in Old Testament times. Later, in the Greek period, a shrine in the cave was dedicated to the god Pan. In addition, many niches in the cave held statues of the Nymphs. When Herod the Great was king of the Jews, he built a temple out of white marble near the same spot and dedicated it to Emperor Augustus.

The city also has an important place in the history of the area. Paneas, as it was called before its name was changed, was the site of a famous battle (198 B.C.) in which Antiochus the Great defeated the Egyptians and thereby took control of Palestine for the Seleucids. In 20 B.C., the Romans under Augustus, who then controlled the area, gave the territory to Herod the Great. After Herod's death, it passed to his son Philip who ruled there from 4 B.C. until his death in A.D. 34. Philip rebuilt the city into a beautiful place and renamed it Caesarea Philippi in honor of Tiberias Caesar and himself.

Ruins of a Christian chapel on Mount Hermon near Caesarea Philippi, the site of Peter's confession.

Stone niche at Caesarea Philippi (Banias), in which the statue of a pagan god was placed.

When Herod Agrippa II (grandson of Herod the Great) inherited the city, he renamed it Neronias in honor of the emperor Nero. But, after Nero's death the name was dropped. During the Jewish-Roman War of A.D. 66–70, the Roman general Vespasian rested his army here. After the war, Titus, who succeeded his father as general of the Roman armies, held gladiatorial shows here during which a number of Jewish prisoners were put to death. After subduing the Jews, the Romans changed its name back to Paneas.

New Testament Near here Jesus asked His disciples the famous question about His identity. When He asked them who men said He was, they answered that people were identifying Him with Elijah, John the Baptist, or one of the prophets (Mark 8:27–33; Matt. 16:13–23). Jesus then asked them, "But whom say ye that I am?" (Matt. 16:15). Peter, acting as the group's spokesman, replied with his famous statement that Jesus is the Christ.

The transfiguration, which occurred about a week after the confession at Caesarea Philippi, was probably also in the area. Caesarea Philippi, which had been the center for pagan worship, thus became an important site for Christians because of Jesus' association with it.

See *Agrippa II; Augustus; Baal; Herod the Great; Herod Philip; Nero.*　　*W.T. Edwards*

CAESAR'S HOUSEHOLD In Philippians 4:22, Paul the apostle sent greetings to the Philippian Christians from certain believers who were of Caesar's household. The phrase was used to refer to all persons, both slave and free, who were in the service of the emperor. In Philippians 1:13 Paul had indicated that the fact he was imprisoned for the cause of Christ had become well known throughout the praetorian guard. Quite possibly, some members of the praetorian guard were included among the believers of Caesar's household. See *Caesar; Rome.*

CAIAPHAS (Caí a phàs) Personal name meaning "rock" or "depression." The high priest at the time of Jesus' crucifixion (Matt. 26:3). He was the son-in-law of Annas and a leader in the plot to have Jesus arrested and executed. Little is known about Caiaphas beyond what can be learned from the New Testament. Evidently he was appointed high priest about A.D. 18 and removed from office about A.D. 36 or 37. See *Priests and Levites; Cross; Crucifixion.*

CAIN (Cāin) Personal name meaning, "*acquisition.*" The firstborn son of Adam and Eve (Gen. 4:1). Although the meaning of the name is disputed, Eve's rationale for giving it suggests a relationship with a Hebrew root that means "to acquire." Cain was a farmer, and his brother Abel was a shepherd. When the two men each brought an offering to the Lord, Abel's was accepted; but Cain's was not. Subsequently, Cain murdered Abel his brother. In punishment, God took from him the ability to till the ground productively and made him to be a wandering vagabond. God marked him off to protect him from anyone seeking to avenge Abel's murder.

CAINAN (Cā-ī′ nan) Personal name of unknown meaning. *1.* Ancestor of Noah (Gen. 5:10–14), sometimes seen as a variant spelling of Cain (Gen. 4:17). He is included in Christ's ancestry (Luke 3:37). In 1 Chronicles 1:2 the name is spelled Kenan, a spelling used in other places by many modern translators. *2.* Descendant of Noah listed in the Septuagint of Genesis 11:12 but not of Hebrew. Luke used this early Greek translation of the Old Testament and included Cainan in Christ's ancestors (Luke 3:36).

CAKE A term referring more to the shape of a loaf of bread (flat and round) than to the type of batter or dough used to make the loaf. See *Bread.*

CALAH (Cā′ läh) Assyrian place name. City Nimrod built along with Nineveh and Rehoboth (Gen. 10:8–12). It is modern tell Nimrud on the east bank of Tigris River where it joins Upper Zab River twenty miles south of Nineveh. Ashurnasirpal II (883–859 B.C.) made it the capital of Assyria. Major Assyrian archaeological discoveries including the six-acre palace of Ashurnasirpal have been dug up. See *Assyria.*

CALAMUS (Căl′ à·mŭs) An ingredient of holy anointing oil (Ezek. 30:23). It was a good-smelling spice made from an imported reed. It is also translated "fragrant cane" (NIV, NAS) or aromatic cane (NRSV).

CALCOL (Căl′ cŏl) Personal name of uncertain meaning. Wise man who served as comparison for Solomon's unsurpassed wisdom (1 Kings 4:30). 1 Chronicles 2:6 makes him a grandson of Judah, the son of Jacob.

CALDRON A cooking pot made of various materials used by different English translations for various Hebrew words. Use both in the home and in the Temple (1 Sam. 2:14; 2 Chron. 35:13; Job 41:20; Ezek. 11:3,7,11; Jer. 52:18,19; Micah 3:3). See *Pottery.*

CALEB (Cā′ lēb) **CALEBITE** Personal and clan name meaning, "dog." Caleb the son of Jephunneh, was one of the twelve spies sent by Moses to reconnoiter the territory of Canaan (Num. 13:6). He was one of only two who brought back a positive report (Num. 13:30). Because of his steadfast loyalty to the Lord, God rewarded him by letting him survive the years of wilderness wandering and giving him the region of Hebron as his portion in the Promised Land. At the age of eighty-five Caleb conquered Hebron (Josh. 14).

The ethnological identity of the Calebites is uncertain. In Numbers 13:6, Caleb is identified with the tribe of Judah. However, according to Numbers 32:12, his father Jephunneh was a Kenezite. The Kenezites apparently were of Edomite origin (Gen. 36:9–11). Perhaps Caleb represented a Kenezite clan that had joined the Israel-

ites and become incorporated into the tribe of Judah.

CALEB EPHRATAH (KJV) or **CALEB-EPHRATHAH** (modern translations) (Cā′ leb Eph-′ ră·täh) Place where Hezron, Caleb's father died (1 Chron. 2:24). The RSV (not NRSV) follows a slight change of Hebrew text to make Ephrathah the wife of Hezron whom Caleb took after his father's death. Ephrathah was another name for Bethlehem. See *Bethlehem; Ephrathah.* Otherwise, Caleb-ephrathah is unknown.

CALENDARS The Old Testament mentions days, months, and years, the basic elements of a calendar; but it has no prescription for regulating one. It was in the rabbinical period that the written treatise on Jewish traditions, *Rosh Hashanah,* a part of the Mishna, organized the biblical data into the detailed calendrical system that the Jews observe today. We can assume that what the rabbis codified was in general practice among the Jews of the first century, the time of Christ and the apostles, but the New Testament offers little direct calendrical data. Periods into which certain important events are dated mention not the day and month, but the name of one or another of the ancient Jewish festivals: the Passover (usually in the passion pericopes, Matthew 26, Mark 14, Luke 22, John 18–19; otherwise at Luke 2:41 and at seven passages in John preceding the passion); the day of Pentecost (the Jewish feast of Weeks), Acts 2:1, 20:16, 1 Corinthians 16:8; and the feast of dedication (Jewish Hanakkah), John 10:22–23. The New Testament offers no evidence that the Jews inside or outside Palestine observed the Roman calendar commencing on January 1, but the apocryphal book 1 Maccabees and the Jewish historian Josephus do substitute Greek (Macedonian) month names for Jewish month names. We may assume that in business dealings Greek-speaking Jews made free use of them. This was little more than a linguistic convention, however, since the Greek months corresponded with the Jewish months, making little difference in the basis of calendrical reckoning.

The year Anthropological evidence from many regions show that it was possible in the most ancient times to chart the course of the sun in its annual orbit, which occurs in approximately 365¼ days. The vernal and autumnal equinoxes (the day in the spring and fall, respectively, when days and nights are of equal lengths) were commonly designated as the beginning of a new year. From biblical data and from Near Eastern writings we know that all the peoples from the Mesopotamian area, as well as the Arabians, the Greeks, and the Romans, chose the first, unquestionably because spring is when new life sprouts forth. In Phoenicia, Canaan, and Israel, however, the fall date was chosen, probably for the reason that harvesting marked the end of one agricultural cycle and prepared for the next. In the exilic and postexilic periods, the Jews shifted to the spring new year, but since rabbinic times the fall new year has been observed.

From biblical and archaeological evidence we are able to describe three different ways for reckoning the years and dividing up the months from one new year to the next. Each of them reflects a different social system and religious ideology.

First, a basically agricultural society is reflected in the "Gezer Calendar" discovered by R.A.S. Macalister. This is actually a schoolboy exercise in which primitive Hebrew letters are scratched on a clay tablet. It reads:

His two months are (olive) harvest,
His two months are planting (grain),
His two months are late planting;
His month is hoeing up of flax,
His month is harvest of barley,
His month is harvest and feasting;
His two months are vine-tending,
His month is summer fruit.

(trans. by W.F. Albright, *Ancient Near Eastern Texts*)

Two things are important to observe: (1) the list commences in the fall and ends with the following summer; (2) because it alternates between two-month and one-month periods and does not name or number the months, we can see that the succession of agricultural activities determines the order of items, and that the year is conceived on the succession of agricultural events rather than on astronomical observation.

Second, the entire Old Testament moves on to a lunar-solar calendar that is based on observation of the heavenly bodies and regulates a more sophisticated order of economic and religious activity. This type of calendar had wide currency among the more advanced societies. It is called "lunar-solar" because it allowed the sun's orbit to mark the years' beginning, but based the beginning of months on observation of the phases of the moon. The first appearance of the new moon would mark the new month. According to the Talmud, the priests would watch for this and proclaim it by sending messengers and blowing trumpets. The problem is, first, that the moon's circuit is about 29½ days, forcing a vacillation between a 30-day and a 29-day month; and second, that twelve of these moon/months equal 354¼ days, about eleven days short of the solar year. From the Babylonians the Hebrews learned to add an extra month every two or three years. In rabbinical times this "intercalary" month was inserted seven times in nineteen years.

Third, a sect known as the Essenes created a purely solar calendar that combined mathematical calculation with a special ideology. Discarding observation of the new moon, the Essenes gave each month thirty days but added a special day at the end of each three-month period, giving a year of 364 days. We have reason to believe that when this party tried to put this calendar into practice, the Temple authorities drove them into exile. It would have disrupted the official religious festival cycle based on the lunar-solar year. We know about this erratic calendar only from sectarian books like the scrolls of Qumran.

The month In addition to knowing that the length of months varied and that a new-year date in the spring or fall determined which of them was first, we are able to observe through Israel's history an interesting development in the naming of the months. These names reflected the presence of one or another dominating cultural influence, first that of the Canaanites, then that of Mesopotamia.

The earliest practice was to use the Canaanite month-names, of which four survive in the Bible: Abib (March–April); Ziv (April–May); Ethanim (September–October); and Bul (October–November) (Ex. 13:4; 23:15; 34:18; 1 Kings 6:1,37–38; 8:3). The other Canaanite months are known from Phoenician inscriptions. These are all agricultural names and reflect a seasonal pattern of reckoning, as in the Gezer calendar.

The usual practice in the Old Testament is to simply number the months from first to twelfth. Some of these numbered months are found in the passages mentioned above, hence the practice must be at least as early as the time of the Israelite monarchy. Because the first month is always in the spring, we must trace this practice back to the patriarchs, who would have learned it in Mesopotamia (Gen. 11:31).

When the Jews returned from Babylonian Exile, they brought with them the names of the Babylonian calendar, at the same time counting the new year from the spring. Although the rabbis returned to an autumnal new year, Judaism retains these Babylonian names as its own: Nisan (March–April); Iyyar (April–May); Sivan (May–June); Tammuz (June–July); Ab (July–August); Elul (August–September); Tishri (September–October); Marcheshvan (October–November); Chislev (November–December); Tebeth (December–January); Shebat (January–February); Adar (February–March). The intercalated year is called *WeAdar,* "and-Adar."   Simon J. De Vries

CALF The young of the cow or other closely related animals. Calves were fattened in stalls to provide veal on special occasions (Gen. 18:7–8; 1 Sam. 28:24; Luke 15:23,27,30). Calves were also used in sacrificial settings (Lev. 9:2–3; Jer. 34:18; compare Gen. 15:9–10). A calf symbolized the bullish Gentile armies (Ps. 68:30) and Egyptian mercenary soldiers (Jer. 46:21). The feet of one of the cherubim described by Ezekiel looked like those of a calf (Ezek. 1:7). One of the four creatures around the throne resembled a calf (Rev. 4:7 KJV; modern translations read, "ox"). For other religious uses of the calf, see *Golden Calf.*

CALIGULA Roman emperor, A.D. 37–41. See *Rome, Roman Empire.*

CALKERS, CALKING Those who place some substance like bitumen into the seams of a ship's planking to make it watertight (Ezek. 27:9,27). See *Bitumen.*

CALL, CALLING Invitation, summons, commission, or naming.
Old Testament Five main uses of call appear in the Old Testament. First, "to call" means "to invite or summon." For example, God called to Adam (Gen. 3:9); Moses called the elders together (Ex. 19:7); and Joel gave a command to call a solemn assembly (Joel 1:14).

Second, the verb can have the sense of "calling on God," hence, to pray. We first meet this expression in Genesis 4:26: "Then began men to call upon the name of the Lord." (See also Ps. 79:6; 105:1; Isa. 64:7; Jer. 10:25; Zeph. 3:9).

Third, "to call" is used very often in the sense of naming, whether of things (Gen. 1:5–30; day, night, heaven, earth; Gen. 2:19, the animals), or of persons (Gen. 25:26, Jacob; 30:6–24, Jacob's sons), of a city (2 Sam. 5:9, the city of David), or of qualities (in Isa. 35:8 a way and in Ex. 12:16 a day are called holy).

Fourth, God calls by name with a view to service. The call of Moses (Ex. 3:4–22) and the call of Samuel (1 Sam. 3) are good examples.

Fifth, "to call" may be used in the sense of "to call one's own," to claim for one's own possession and to appoint for a particular destiny. Especially noticeable is Isaiah 43:1, when the Lord addressed Israel: "I have called thee by thy name; thou art mine." This calling of Israel stands closely related to its election (Isa. 45:4). It thus points to the covenant relation in which Israel is called to salvation, is given its name, and has the function of God's witness.
New Testament All the senses found in the Old Testament appear again in the New Testament. The meaning "invite/summon" is encountered principally in the parables of the great banquet (Luke 14:16–25) and the marriage feast (Matt. 22:2–10). Calling in the sense of naming has special importance in the infancy narratives (Matt. 1:21; Luke 1:60; 2:21). Calling on the name of the Lord is found in a quotation from Joel in both Acts 2:21 and Romans 10:13. The choosing of the apostles can be expressed in terms of calling (Mark 1:20). Finally, Christ's people are those whom He has called and who are rightly called by His name (Rom. 8:28; Gal. 1:6; 1 Thess. 2:12; 1 Pet. 1:15).

The New Testament refers to the Christian life as a calling (Eph. 1:18; 4:1; 2 Tim. 1:9; Heb. 3:1; 2 Pet. 1:10). The basic call is to Christ as Lord and Savior; thus, all Christians are "called ones." It is employed in a comprehensive way to depict what has happened to those who through the Father's love are now called children of God (1 John 3:1). However, there are further callings to special ministries (Acts 13:2).

The noun "calling" takes on great significance in the New Testament, especially in the writings of Paul. First, there is the goal of calling. We are called to salvation, holiness, and faith (2 Thess. 2:13–15), to the kingdom and glory of God (1 Thess. 2:12), to an eternal inheritance (Heb. 9:15), to fellowship (1 Cor. 1:9), and to service (Gal. 1).

The means of calling is clearly stated as being through grace (Gal. 1:6) and through the hearing of the gospel (2 Thess. 2:14).

The ground of calling is specifically established in 2 Timothy 1:9. The starting point for the divine calling is not works but the purpose and grace of God in Christ Jesus.

The nature of God's calling is described as an upward (Phil. 3:14), heavenly (Heb. 3:1), holy (2 Tim. 1:9) calling. It is filled with hope (Eph. 1:18; 4:4). Christians are urged to lead lives that are worthy of their calling (Eph. 4:1; 2 Thess. 1:11). Also, they are urged to make their calling and election sure (2 Pet. 1:10). Finally, the "called, and chosen, and faithful" are with the Lamb (Rev. 17:14) indicating that those whom God called (saved) He glorified (Rom. 8:30). The stress is on the initiative of God. The one who experiences God's calling can only break forth in praise with Paul: "O the depth of the riches both of the wisdom and knowledge of God! how unsearchable are his judgments, and his ways past finding out!" (Rom. 11:33). See *Election; Predestination.*

J.A. Reynolds

CALNEH (Căl′ nĕh) Place name of uncertain meaning. *1.* A part of kingdom of Nimrod in Babylonia (Gen. 10:10). The location or identity with any other recorded city is not known. *2.* City in Syria under Israel's control in the days of Amos and Isaiah (around 740 B.C.). Amos invited Israel to view Calneh's fate as a conquered city and see if Israel was really better in any way (Amos 6:2). Similarly, Isaiah warned Jerusalem that Calno (another spelling of Calneh) was as good as Jerusalem and yet had suffered conquest by Tiglath-Pileser of Assyria in 738. This Calneh may be modern Kullan Koy in northern Syria, six miles from Arpad.

CALNO (Căl′ nō) Variant spelling in Hebrew of Calneh in Isaiah 10:9. See *Calneh.*

CALVARY (Căl′ vå rў) Place name meaning, "a bare skull." The place where Jesus was crucified. Our English word "Calvary" comes from the Latin *calvaria.* This word is a translation of the Greek *kranion,* meaning "skull." The Greek is a translation of the Aramaic *golgotha,* also meaning "skull." The word is used twice in the Greek translation of the Old Testament (Judg. 9:53; 2 Kings 9:35) to designate the skulls of Abimelech and Jezebel.

"Calvary" appears in the New Testament, only in the story of the crucifixion (Matt. 27:33; Mark 15:22; John 19:17). The gospel writers name it as the place where Christ was led to be executed.

Exactly why the place was called this is not known. The logical explanation would be because the skull symbolized death. A place of execution would see its share of skulls.

Archeologists are uncertain where Calvary was located. John 19:20 and Hebrews 13:12 say that Jesus was taken *outside* the city to be crucified. Mark 15:29 suggests that a road may have been nearby.

Two sites are held today as Calvary. The older, more traditional Church of the Holy Sepulchre is a complex of religious shrines venerated as the place of Christ's cross and tomb.

In the 4th century A.D., Queen Helena, mother of Constantine, had the site revealed to her in a vision. A pagan temple on the site was razed and a shrine built in its place. Several destructions and rebuildings have taken place over the centuries.

Since 1842, a rocky hill outside the Damascus Gate has vied for veneration as Calvary. Discovered by Otto Thenius, the site gained fame when Charles Gordon wrote in 1885 that this was in-

Gordon's Calvary is one of two sites considered to be the possible location of Jesus' crucifixion.

deed Calvary. A garden tomb nearby, discovered in 1849, had drawn little attention until Gordon made his assertion.

Executions during the first century *were* conducted outside the city walls. This might tend to make Gordon's Calvary the logical site. However, at the time of Jesus' crucifixion the outer wall of Jerusalem was much closer to the center of the city. This would make the traditional site more plausible.

Perhaps the most telling fact between these places is the *type* of tombs they represent. Jewish tombs appear to have had small niches carved out of the walls in which bodies were placed. Later Byzantine tombs used trough-like slabs. This places the weight of authenticity with the Church of the Holy Sepulchre.   *Mike Mitchell*

CALVES, GOLDEN Representation, of young bulls used to symbolize the god's presence in the worship place. The bull was used to represent many gods in the Ancient Near East, particularly Amon-Re in Egypt and El and Baal in Canaan. As Moses was on Mount Sinai, Aaron formed a golden calf to use in a "feast to Yahweh" (Ex. 32:4–5). Similarly, Jeroboam placed calves in Dan and Bethel for the Northern Kingdom to use in its worship of Yahweh (1 Kings 12:28) so the people would not have to go to Jerusalem, the southern capital, to worship. In both instances the calves represent the gods who brought Israel up from Egypt. Thus the sin of the calves is not worshiping the wrong god but worshiping the true God in the

wrong way, through images. See Psalm 106:19–20. Israel tried to make pedestals on which the invisible God could ride. The only such pedestal Old Testament teaching allows was the ark of the covenant. (See 1 Samuel 4:4.) See *Bull*.

CALVES OF THE LIPS KJV translation of a very difficult Hebrew phrase in Hosea 14:2. If this is the correct translation, the meaning is very obscure, possibly referring to vows to sacrifice cattle (REB). Modern translations supply different vowels to the consonants of the Hebrew text and read "fruit of the lips," which means giving praise to God.

CAMEL Large hump-backed mammal of Asia and Africa used for desert travel to bear burdens or passengers.
Old Testament The camel is adapted for desert travel with padded feet, a muscular body, and a hump of fat to sustain life on long journeys. A young camel can walk one hundred miles in a day. Wealth was measured by many things including camels (Gen. 24:35). The Jews were forbidden to eat the ceremonially unclean camel, which chews the cud, but does not have a split hoof (Lev. 11:4).

Camels are still used by Bedouins and others as a mode of travel in the Middle East.

An ill-tempered camel in an unhampered rampage could quickly trample down the tents of a family or clan. Jeremiah thus described the sins of Israel saying they were as a swift she-camel, running wild (Jer. 2:23). The wise men who worshiped Jesus are traditionally pictured as riding camels (Matt. 1:1). This may be a prophecy of Isaiah 60:6 which describes camel riders from Sheba coming to bring gold, incense, and praises of the Lord.
New Testament John the Baptist, a desert preacher, wore the rough and plain clothes of camel's hair. His clothing and diet were revolutionary and consistent with his role as a forerunner of Jesus. A proverb picturing things impossible to accomplish was quoted by Jesus when he said it is easier for a camel to pass through the eye of a needle than for a rich man to enter heaven. A traditional but non-biblical illustration describes an unburdened camel kneeling to creep under a low gate in a Jerusalem wall. This means that if a rich man will rid himself of pride and humble himself (kneel) he can get into heaven. Jesus describes hypocrites as persons who are very careful to strain out a gnat from a cup of drink, but swallow a camel without notice. They tithe the leaves of a small household herb, but omit judgment, mercy, and faith. *Lawson Hatfield*

CAMEL'S HAIR A very coarse material was woven from the hair of a camel's back and hump. A finer material was woven from the hair taken from underneath the animal. John the Baptist wore coarse camel's hair (Mark 1:6). Jesus contrasted John's cloak to the "soft raiment" of the members of the court (Matt. 11:8). Wearing a hairy mantle was the mark of a prophet (Zech. 13:4; compare 2 Kings 1:8).

CAMON (Cā′ mŏn) KJV spelling of Kamon. See *Kamon*.

CAMP, ENCAMPMENT A temporary settlement for nomadic and military people. In the Old Testament English translators usually use "camp" or "encampment" to translate Hebrew *machaneh*. A *machaneh* is a temporary settlement of travelers or warriors. Before the settlement in the Promised Land, Israel was a group of tribes on the move. Hence the frequent reference to "the camp" or "the camp of Israel" (Ex. 14:19; 16:13). Leviticus and Deuteronomy contain laws regulating life "in the camp."

Each tribe also had its own camp: Numbers 2:3 speaks of "the camp of Judah"; Numbers 2:25 of "the camp of Dan." After each tribe had secured a permanent place of residence in the Promised Land, the term "camp" designated a military settlement, whether of Israel (1 Sam. 4:3; 14:21) or of an enemy (2 Kings 7:10). The Hebrew word *machaneh* is often rendered "company" (Gen. 32:8,21), "host" (Ex. 14:24), and "army" (1 Sam. 17:1). The context in these instances calls for a word which designates the people of the camp rather than the settlement as such.

In the Greek translation of the Old Testament *machaneh* is rendered *parembolē*, literally "a putting alongside." See *Castle*. *Thomas A. Jackson*

CAMPHIRE Variant spelling of camphor. KJV translation in Song of Solomon 1:14; 4:13. Most modern versions read "henna." See *Henna*.

CANA (Cā′ nà) Place name meaning, "the nest." In John 2:1, the town that was the scene of a wedding during which Jesus changed water into wine. Its exact location is uncertain, though it was in Galilee. In Cana an unnamed nobleman sought out Jesus to ask Him to heal his son in Capernaum (John 4:46). Cana was also the home of Nathanael, one of the apostles (John 21:2).

CANAAN, HISTORY AND RELIGION OF The territory between the Mediterranean Sea and the Jordan River reaching from the brook of Egypt to the area around Ugarit in Syria or to the Euphrates. This represents descriptions in Near Eastern documents and in the Old Testament. Apparently, Canaan meant different things at different times. Numbers 13:29 limits Canaanites to those who "dwell by the sea and by the coast of Jordan." Compare Joshua 11:3. Israel was aware of the larger "Promised Land" of Canaan (Gen. 15:18; Ex. 23:21; Num. 13:21; Deut. 1:7; 1 Kings 4:21; etc.) Israel's basic land reached only from "Dan to Beersheba" (2 Sam. 24:2–8,15; 2 Kings 4:25). At times Israel included land east of Jordan (2 Sam. 24:5–6). At times the land of Gilead was contrasted to the land of Canaan (Josh. 22:9). After the conquest, Israel knew "there remaineth yet very much land to be possessed" (Josh. 13:1). Canaan thus extended beyond the normal borders of Israel, yet did not include land east of the Jordan. At times land of Canaanites and land of Amorites are identical. Whatever the land was called, it exercised extraordinary influence as the land bridge between Mesopotamia and Egypt and between the Mediterranean and the Red Sea.

History The word *Canaan* is not a Semitic name, although its appearance about 2300 B.C. in the Ebla texts attests to its antiquity. Because of the final "n," it has been conjectured to be a Hurrian form. Quite probably the name was derived from a merchant designation; certainly Canaanite was ultimately equated in the biblical text with "trader" or "merchant" (Zech. 14:21). Isaiah 23:8 uses *Canaanites* as a common noun meaning "merchants" or traders as the aristocracy to Tyre in the prophet's day. Similar association may be found in passages such as Hosea 12:7–8; Ezekiel 17:4; Zephaniah 1:11. Canaan's identity as merchants probably goes back to a time when Canaan was limited to the area of Phoenicia, the rather small and narrow country along the seacoast of Canaan. Phoenicia was particularly known for a special purple dye produced from crushed mollusks. This product was shipped throughout the

Mediterranean world. The word Canaan may be related to the special colored dye.

The biblical genealogical references are not particularly helpful in clarifying our understanding of Canaan. According to Genesis 9:18 and 10:6, Canaan was a son of Ham, one of the three sons of Noah. Genesis 10:15–20 clarifies the implications of this Hamitic descent in the sons of Canaan: Sidon, Heth, the Jebusites, the Amorites, the Girgasites, the Hivites, the Arkites, the Sinites, the Arvadites, and Zemarites, and the Hamathites. All of these peoples are characizerized by being generally within the Egyptian sphere of influence.

Settlement within the land of Canaan is attested from Paleolithic times. Further, a Semitic presence in the area is evidenced at least by 3000 B.C. Some of the best examples of cities indicating Semitic influences are Jericho, Megiddo, Byblos, and Ugarit.

The best attested period in Canaanite history is the Bronze Age (ca. 3200–1200 B.C.). During the Old Kingdom (ca. 2600–2200 B.C.), Egypt's power extended as far northward as Ugarit. From recoveries at several sites including Byblos and Ugarit, it is clear that Egypt controlled the area during the period of the Twelfth Dynasty (1990–1790 B.C.). From this general time period come the Egyptian Execration Texts which list peoples and princes of the area who owe their allegiance to Egypt. Egyptian control over Canaan waned, being withdrawn about 1800.

Canaan had to contend with other aggressors besides Egypt. Approximately 2000 B.C., the Amorites invaded the area, having migrated via the Fertile Crescent from the southern Mesopotamian Valley. In addition, the Canaanites were beset by the Hyksos, who controlled Egypt from 1720 until 1570. Hurrians and Hittites also sought control of Canaan. The mingling of so many cultural influences still resulted in a rather unified culture.

When the Egyptians were able to expel the Hyksos in the sixteenth century, the Egyptians were able to extend their power over Canaan. Again, however, Egyptian power weakened. By 1400, a number of small, established nations in the area struggled with each other. From the fourteenth century are the Amarna Letters are derived. These are approximately 350 letters written in cuneiform Akkadian. They represent correspondence between the Egyptian court at Tell el-Amarna and numerous Canaanite cities, including Jerusalem, Megiddo, and Shechem. These letters indicate the unrest characteristic of these Canaanite principalities socially and politically.

Prior to Israel's entrance into Canaan, the country seems to have been organized around major cities creating rather small principalities. There was apparently no attempt to organize centrally for defense, thus making possible the success the

A Canaanite altar located at Megiddo in Israel.

These twin basalt column bases are a part of one of four Canaanite altars excavated at Beth-shean.

Israelites enjoyed in the thirteenth century and the parallel success of the Philistines in the twelfth century. The biblical evidence is scant for any type of concerted Canaanite aggression against the Israelites. Stories in the book of Joshua (9:1–2; 10:1–5) indicate that in emergency situations the independent city-state kings formed defense coalitions, but no one had power to unite all Canaan against Israel. In the Book of Judges only one Judge, namely Deborah (Judges 4—5), is depicted as having fought against the Canaanites. Rather than struggling with each other after the conquest, the Canaanites and Israelites gradually melded together, a phenomenon essentially completed by the end of David's rule.

The most significant finds have been the cuneiform tablets discovered in the royal library and/or temple in Ugarit. These tablets date from ca. 1400 B.C., near the final fall of Ugarit in ca. 1200 B.C. Their portrayal of the deities and religious perspectives represent Canaanite thought between 2000 and 1500 B.C.

The Pantheon A pantheon of deities was worshiped at Ugarit. On the one hand, each deity had a clear duty assignment, while on the other hand considerable fluidity flowed in deity perception. The role(s) of any given deity might be assumed by another.

El was acknowledged as the titular head of the pantheon. As king of the gods, he was both the creator god and a fertility god. He had earlier been more strongly associated with fertility than was

true in the fourteenth century, although he was still depicted in the form of a bull. El lived at some distance from Ugarit upon a mountain (Mt. Saphon) located to the north.

El was joined by *Athirat,* apparently his wife, who is represented in the Old Testament as *Asherah,* with both feminine (*Asheroth*) and masculine (*Asherim*) plurals. Athirat was acknowledged as the mother of the deities, having given birth to some seventy gods and goddesses. Thus, she was predominately a fertility goddess and designated "creatress of the gods."

Baal was the chief god in the popular worship of the people. Baal means "master" or "lord" and could refer to any one of the numerous Baalim (Baals) who had authority in various locations. The Ugaritic Baal, however, referred to the ultimate Baal!

Whereas El was located at some distance from the people, Baal was easily accessible. Baal statues have been recovered. These depict Baal wearing a conical hat with horns that conveys the strength and fertility associated with bull imagery. In his right hand Baal holds a club that represents his military strength as well as thunder. In his left hand he grasps a stylized lightening bolt which symbolizes his role as a storm god. He is sometimes portrayed as seated on a throne, indicating his authority as king of gods.

Baal was joined in his task by *Anat,* represented in the Bible as *Anath.* She was portrayed as both sister and consort of Baal. In her role she was both goddess of love, the perpetual virgin, and the goddess of warfare, whose exploits in Baal's behalf were sometimes remarkably cruel.

As Baal gradually supplanted El, many of the prerogatives earlier associated with El were naturally transferred to Baal. The biblical text derives from the period when this symbolic struggle between the deities had in essence been accomplished. Thus in the Bible Baal is often depicted with Asherah (i.e., Athirat) rather than Anath (i.e., Anat), as in Judges 3:7 (NIV).

Two additional gods fulfilled important roles in the popular mythology. Mot was the god of death and sterility. (In the Hebrew language the word for death is also *mot*.) Mot was associated with death, whether that refers to the seasonal cycle of vegetation, the sabbatical understanding of a seventh year of agricultural rest, or in some fashion to the individual's death. Mot was clearly understood as a power capable of rendering impotent Baal's regenerative powers.

Yam was called both "Prince River" and "Judge River." (Again, the Hebrew word for sea is *Yam*.) In the Ugaritic texts Yam was the chaotic god of the sea, capable of turning cosmos into chaos. The people of Ugarit, like their Mesopotamian counterparts (and unlike the Egyptians), apparently recognized both their dependency upon as well as the dangers associated with water. Cultically, the fear of chaos overcoming cosmos was represented in Baal's struggle with Yam.

This sampling of some of the more important members of the pantheon indicates that the Ugaritic schema, and thus that of the Canaanites in general, offered abundant options for worship. The mode of worship was tied especially to procreative sympathetic magic. The sexual union of god and goddess assured the fertility of mankind, the animals, and the larger world of nature. Crucial for this mode of worship was the worshiper's possibility to assist the process via sympathetic magic. In the temple a male priest or devotee fulfilled the god role, and the female priestess or devotee fulfilled the goddess role. These two individuals became for the moment as god and goddess. In sympathetic magic, humans ordain when and how the god and goddess act. This mode of human arrogance undergirded the tower of Babel story in Genesis 11. Practically all ancient worship structures operated from such a fertility-sympathetic magic orientation. The Israelites encountered this thought pattern when they entered Canaan. It took many centuries (note King Josiah's removal from the Jerusalem Temple about 621 B.C. of the vessels made for Baal and Asherah as well as the houses of the male cult prostitutes—2 Kings 23) for Israel in daily practice of popular religion to resist Canaanite practices. The teachings of inspired leaders and the actual practice of religion often stood in stark contrast.

Canaanite Mythology The seven tablets upon which the Ugaritic mythological material was found is often mutilated, frequently making diffi-

cult an assured rendering of the material.

The mythology apparently centered around three primary exploits of Baal. Through these events he established himself as the god of supreme power within the pantheon, built the palace or temple which he merited by virtue of his victory over Yam, and in the third scenario struggled with, succumbed to, and ultimately escaped from the clutches of Mot.

El is portrayed as having been unashamedly afraid of Yam, this chaotic god of the sea. In fact, El was so frightened that he hid beneath his throne, fearful himself to encounter Yam but encouraging anyone to come forward who would confront this agent of chaos. Eventually, following some negotiations having to do with his role if successful against Yam, Baal stepped forward and proceeded to engage Yam. Baal was successful, bringing Yam under control by dividing him and thus making helpful an otherwise destructive, chaotic force. By this act Baal demonstrated himself worthy of exaltation.

The second mythological sequence emphasized that Baal was now worthy of his own palace or temple. Given the cyclic view of reality and the recurring danger posed by Yam, it is understandable that Baal did not want any windows in his palace. After all, the threat of chaotic flooding would surely occur again, for such recurrence is characteristic of mythological thought. Eventually Baal was convinced otherwise. Anat secured El's permission to build the palace, and the master craftsmen erected the structure. Baal opened the completed palace to all the pantheon for a type of sacred meal. During the meal, Baal opened one of the windows and bellowed out the window, surely understood as an indication of thunder's origin, given Baal's association as god of the storm.

All should be well, but Baal had one more enemy to confront, Mot. According to the mythology, the two met in battle. Baal was defeated, being consigned thereby to the nether world. When Baal was separated from Anat, sterility reigned on earth. The wadis dried up, and Anat anxiously searched for Baal. While she could not find Baal, one day she chanced upon Mot. She had with her a blade with which she cut Mot into many pieces, which pieces she then sifted, with the remains being scattered across the ground, probably an allusion to some type of grain festival. Regardless, this action by Anat enabled Baal to escape from his confinement. Rapidly thereafter, fertility returned! Thus the full cycle has been traversed, whether the intent be the annual cycle experienced in the world of nature, the seven-year sabbatical cycle, or perhaps the human birth-to-death cycle. What is transparent is the cyclic nature of the highly sensual, sympathetic magic worship. The Israelites were forced to contend with this mythology upon their entrance to Canaan. They faced a worship structure which had proved itself successful in the view of the Canaanites. Apparently, the Israelites had to offer in exchange a non-agrarian wilderness God who had no record of success in agriculture!

Old Testament Relationships The Israelites settling into Canaan were not impervious to their surroundings. In the Ancient Near East people assumed that as a people migrated from one area to another they would take over the gods and religion of the new area in which they settled. At the least, they would incorporate the new religion into their own old religious structure. After all, these gods and goddesses had demonstrated their capability in meeting the inhabitants' needs. For the Israelites the most natural thing would have been to embrace Baalism, although perhaps not to the exclusion of Yahwism.

Strong argument can be made that a type of Yahwism—Baalism synthesis gradually established itself, particularly in the Northern Kingdom. During the period of Joshua and the Judges, a cultural struggle was waged which had to do more with the conflict between wilderness (Israelite) and agrarian (Canaanite) cultural motifs than between Yahweh and Baal. As earlier indicated, in the Book of Judges only one Judge, Deborah, is depicted as fighting directly against the Canaanites. Another judge could be called Jerabaal (Judg. 6:32), having a father with an altar to Baal (Judg. 6:25). Without leadership Israel worshipped Baal-berith ("Baal of the covenant") mixing Baalism with the covenant of Yahweh (Judg. 8:33).

The early monarchical period demonstrates the same type of syncretistic behavior. Saul assuredly did not struggle to eliminate Baalism, and he even named a son Eshbaal ("man of Baal," 1 Chron. 8:33). Jonathan had a son, Merib-baal (1 Chron. 8:34). In like manner David named a son Beeliada ("Baal knows," 1 Chron. 14:7). Solomon was even more of a syncretist. Solomon's crowning glory, the Temple, was designed and built by Canaanite architects. In such an atmosphere lines of demarcation were loosely drawn. Solomon's politically-motivated marriages brought many other gods and their worship into Jerusalem (2 Kings 11:1–8).

Following Solomon's death and the disruption of the United Monarchy, the identity crisis continued in both north and south, but not as much in the south as in the north. Judah was the base for worship of Yahweh and the site of the Jerusalem Temple. In addition, Judah was geographically isolated from the northern Canaanite area where Baalism was more regularly practiced.

In Israel, however, the initial king, Jeroboam I (922–901 B.C.), erected rival shrines to the Jerusalem Temple at Dan and Bethel. These shrines, in the shape of bulls, are viewed by most scholars as being associated in some fashion with Baalism (recall that both El and Baal could be represented in the form of a bull). Regardless, the adherence to Jeroboam's shrines was for the biblical writers the mark of apostasy for Israel's kings.

During the Omrid Dynasty, Ahab (869–850 B.C.) married Jezebel, a princess from Tyre, as a sign of the diplomatic relationship between Israel and Tyre. Jezebel brought the clearest infusion of Baalism into Israel. Amidst the building of a Baal temple in the capital city of Samaria and the persecution of Yahweh's prophets, the prophet Elijah emerged on the scene. In a classical story of cultural confrontation, Elijah encouraged a contest atop Mount Carmel (1 Kings 18–19). On the one hand, the contest was an attempt to determine which deity could give the life-giving rain. On the other hand, it had a much greater significance. It clarified that a person must worship *either* Yahweh *or* Baal. It was not possible to worship both, for Yahweh demanded exclusive allegiance.

The struggle Elijah initiated with this either-Yahweh-or-Baal imperative, King Jehu (842–815) carried forward politically. Religiously, in the Northern Kingdom, Hosea gave voice to the anti-Baalistic message.

In the South, two kings led the anti-Baalistic struggle. Hezekiah (715–687 B.C.) is remembered as a reforming king (2 Chron. 29–31), Josiah (640–609 B.C.) was the reformer *par excellence.*

Judah also had its vocal prophetic spokesmen against Baalism. Isaiah about 740–700 addressed the issue. Jeremiah from 615 B.C. onwards issued the strongest denunciation of Baalism.

The Baalistic Canaanites influenced Israel in many ways: Temple construction, sacrificial rituals, the high places, a rejection of any sexual motif as a worship instrument (Deut. 23:17–18), and a lessening of the purely mythical with a concomitant emphasis upon the historical happening as with Yahweh's splitting of the sea (*Yam Suph*) rather than a struggle with a mythological Yam—(Ex. 14–15).

It is too easy for the biblical interpreter to focus on the numerous ways that Israel found the Canaanite religion to be offensive. In some cases, such as the use of sex in worship, the level of antipathy witnessed in the Old Testament may not always have characterized Israel's actual practice, as prophetic denouncements like Hosea's show. The marked hostility (Deut. 20:16–18) which clamored for the wholesale destruction of the Canaanites came from inspired religious leaders who did not represent the majority of Israel's population. A priest could call a prophet to leave the king's place of worship (Amos 7:12–13). The prophet could command people not to go to traditional worship places (Amos 5:5).

In summary the Israelites did not settle into a cultural vacuum upon entering Canaan. They encountered a people with a proud history and a thriving religion. Historically speaking, that encounter could potentially have led to the elimination of Yahwism. It did not. Rather, a long historical process led to the eventual elimination of baalism and other elements of Canaanite religion. Israel's battle with Canaanite religion gave new dimensions and depth to Israel's faith. The biblical record affirms that Yahweh, the Lord of history, has used the reality of historical encounter as a means to bring biblical religion to its mature development as revealed in the full canon of Scripture. See *Amorites; Anath; Asherah; Baal; El; Elijah; Israel; Phoenicia; Ugarit.*   *Frank E. Eakin, Jr.*

CANALS Translation of a Hebrew word that refers to the branches of the Nile river (Ex. 7:19; 8:5; Isa. 19:6). The KJV uses "rivers."

CANANAEAN (Cā nǎn′ an) One of the twelve apostles is identified (Mark 3:18 RSV) as Simon the Cananaean (KJV renders "Simon the Canaanite"). In some other New Testament references this individual is called Simon the Zealot. Cananaean is probably the Aramaic equivalent of Greek zealot. See *Apostles; Disciples; Zealot.*

CANDACE (Căn′ dȧ cē) In Acts 8:27, the queen of Ethiopia whose servant became a believer in Christ and was baptized by Philip. It is generally agreed that Candace was a title rather than a proper name, though its meaning is uncertain. The title was used by several queens of Ethiopia.

CANDLE, CANDLESTICK KJV translation. Candles as we know them were in use in biblical times. The reference is to 'lamp" or 'lampstand." See *Lamps, Lighting, Lampstand.*

CANE See *Calamus.*

CANKER KJV translation in 2 Timothy 2:17 and James 5:3. In general, canker may refer to any source of corruption or debasement. In 2 Timothy 2:17 the reference is to gangrene which is the local death of soft tissues due to loss of blood supply—a condition that can spread from infected to uninfected tissue. In James 5:3 the reference is to rust. See *Rust.*

CANKERWORM KJV translation in Joel 1:4; 2:25; Nahum 3;15–16. The Hebrew refers to a type of locust. See *Insects; Locust.*

CANNEH (Căn′ něh) Northern Syrian city which traded with Tyre and gained Ezekiel's mention in condemning Tyre (Ezek. 27:23). It may be variant spelling of Calneh or a city called Kannu in Assyrian documents.

CANTICLES See *Song of Solomon.*

CAP See *Bonnet.*

CAPERBERRY A fruit—*capparis spinosa*—thought to increase sexual powers and used by Ecclesiastes to symbolize the dying physical desire of the aging (Eccl. 12:5 NAS). Most modern translations omit the symbolism of the Hebrew and translate, "desire."

CAPERNAUM (Cȧ pēr′ nā um; *village of Nahum*) On the northwest shore of the Sea of Galilee

A house at Capernaum venerated by early local Christians as the home of the apostle Simon Peter.

C

Some of the intricately carved column pieces discovered in the excavations at Capernaum.

about 2½ miles west of the entrance of the Jordan is located the New Testament town of Capernaum.

Capernaum appears in the biblical record only in the Gospels where it is mentioned 16 times. As an economic center in Galilee it was more significant than tradition has often allowed. The designation "city" distinguishes it from the "fishing village" category. Perhaps the proximity to a major east-west trade route explains the need for a cus-toms station there. The importance of the city is further demonstrated by the location of a military installation there under the command of a centurion. Fishing and farming were important to the economy and archaeological evidence suggests that there were other light industries contributing to the local prosperity.

In the New Testament Capernaum was chosen as the base of operations by Jesus when He began His ministry. Teaching in the synagogue (Mark 1:21) and private homes (Mark 2:1) was basic to His work there, but the miracles performed there

An overview of the third-century synagogue at Capernaum.

The foundational material of this third-century synagogue may possibly date from the first century.

appear to have precipitated the controversy and opposition. The religious leadership challenged the direction of Jesus' ministry (Mark 2:24, 7:5) and the popular following attempted to take over and force Him into a political position (John 6:15). Mark (2:1) referred to Capernaum as *Jesus' home* and Matthew (9:1) described it as "his own city." It appears that several of the disciples also lived in that town including Peter, Andrew, Matthew, and perhaps John and James. The populace apparently did not accept His messianic role because they fell under the same condemnation as Chorazin and Bethsaida for failing to repent (Matt. 11:20–24). *George W. Knight*

CAPHTOR (Căph' tôr) The original home of the Philistines (Amos 9:7). In Jeremiah 47:4 and in Deuteronomy 2:23, its inhabitants are called Caphtorim (compare Gen. 10:14). Though several places have at times been proposed for its location, current scholarship is generally agreed that Caphtor is the island of Crete. See *Philistines; Crete.*

CAPHTORIM or **CAPHTORITES** (NIV) (Căph'-tō·rĭm) Citizens of Caphtor or Crete. See *Caphtor.*

CAPITAL PUNISHMENT The death penalty legally sanctioned by a society or government for extremely serious offenses. Capital punishment was legislated in ancient Israel and appears to be divinely ordered. Whether this divine sanction was for all time and places is a matter of biblical interpretation for today.

Offenses Calling for Capital Punishment: *1.* Intentional homicide (Ex. 21:12; Lev. 24:17; Num. 35:16–21,29–34); *2.* False witnessing in capital cases (Deut. 19:16–21); *3.* Idolatry (Lev. 20:1–5; Deut. 13:2–19; 17:2–7); *4.* Abducting persons for slavery (Ex. 21:16; Deut. 24:7); *5.* Sexual acts of incest, homosexuality, and bestiality (Ex. 22:19; Lev. 20:11–17); *6.* Rape (Deut. 22:23–27) including the girl if she did not cry for help; *7.* Adultery (Lev. 20:10–12; Deut. 22:22); *8.* Sex relations outside of marriage: (a) before marriage, but discovered afterward (Deut. 22:20–21), the woman alone to be executed; (b) relations with another's betrothed (Deut. 22:23–24), both to be executed; (c) the harlotry of a priest's daughter (Lev. 21:9); *9.* Witchcraft and false claim to prophecy (Ex. 22:18; Lev. 20:27; Deut. 13:1–5; 18:20; 1 Sam. 28:3,9); *10.* Profaning the Sabbath (Ex. 31:14–17; 35:2; Num. 15:32–36); *11.* Blasphemy (Lev. 24:14–16,23; 1 Kings 21:13; Matt. 26:65–66); *12.* Cursing or striking one's parents (Ex. 21:15,17).

Forms of Capital Punishment Stipulated or Mentioned: *1.* Stoning was the usual method in Israel (Ex. 19:13; Lev. 20:27; Deut. 22:24; Josh. 7:25; compare Luke 20:3–6; Acts 7:58). At least two witnesses were needed to verify a charge, and they had to throw the first stones (Deut. 17:6–17; compare John 8:7). *2.* Burning was the penalty for incest (Lev. 20:14); harlotry (Gen. 38:24), particularly by a priest's daughter (Lev. 21:9). *3.* Sword (Ex. 32:27; Deut. 13:15), spear (Num. 25:7ff.), and shooting by arrow (Ex. 19:13). *4.* Beheading was reserved especially for those who cursed or insulted royalty (2 Sam. 16:9; 2 Kings 6:31–32). *5.* Crucifixion was carried out in New Testament times only by Roman decree and by Roman soldiers (Matt. 27:22–26,33–50; Luke 23:13–33; John 18:28—19:30) for those convicted of political insurrection against Rome. Jewish authorities under Roman rule were not normally permitted to execute anyone (John 18:31), although rare exceptions are recorded (Acts 5:27–33; 7:57–60; 26:10); whether these were approved by Rome is difficult to say.

Does Scripture Require Capital Punishment? How do we reconcile Exodus 20:13 ("Thou shalt not kill") with Genesis 9:6 ("Whoso sheddeth man's blood, by man shall his blood be shed")? If an individual kills another, it is murder; if the state kills, it is not murder, some would say. Is Genesis 9:6 the mandate for capital punishment? Its rationale appears to be the unique value of persons, "for in the image of God made he man" (9:6). Yet what about other commands in Genesis 9? What about the prohibition against eating meat with blood in it (9:4), or the execution of animals who kill humans (9:5; compare Ex. 21:28–36). Has the Lord spoken forever against eating rare meat and for executing killer animals? Is it sound biblical interpretation if we interpret "by man shall his blood be shed" as a divine command for capital punishment yet consistently ignore the other commands in the context in which it is found?

How do we explain the Lord's protection of Cain in Genesis 4:15 where a "mark" was placed on him to fend off self-appointed executioners? God's grace spared the original first-degree murderer.

Maybe Genesis 9:6 is more descriptive than prescriptive much like Jesus' words, "for all they that take the sword shall perish with the sword" (Matt. 26:52). Genesis 9:6 seems too broad to be a divine order requiring all societies in all ages to kill their killers.

What about Paul's instruction regarding the role of the state in preserving order? The political ruler is a "minister of God to thee for good"; the ruler "beareth not the sword in vain: for he is . . . a revenger to execute wrath upon him that doeth evil" (Rom. 13:4). It seems that the authority of the state is divinely established to protect the good and punish the evil. Is authority to punish a mandate to kill? If the sword is to be taken literally and the state's hold on the sword is a mandate to kill, then capital punishment should be the primary punishment the state has available to use, and it should always be by a literal sword. Literalism presents serious problems. However, if the sword is symbolic, then various forms of punishment and deterrence are available to the state.

Scripture does not present capital punishment as always mandatory. The early Christians apparently did not believe so. All Scripture should be filtered through the perspective of the apostolic tradition and especially through the mind of Jesus Christ who himself was a victim of capital punishment on the cross.

Does Scripture Permit Capital Punishment? If Scripture does not require the state to execute killers, does it allow such action by way of excep-

tion? A generally accepted principle of killing not subject to punishment is self-defense, whereby killing is forced on us as the only way to prevent someone from killing us. In this sense capital punishment may be a form of self-defense on the part of the state. Killing in a just war is a similar response. Does the state have a right to defend its people by executing killers? The Scripture certainly does not prohibit the state from exercising this right.

Arguments For and Against Capital Punishment
1. Deterrence: capital punishment will discourage murdering. Yet the only one who is knowingly deterred from killing again is the executed offender. No scientific evidence is available to prove that the death penalty lowers homicide rates. Since most murders are among friends and relatives, these "crimes of passion" are the least likely to be repeated of all offenses by the same people. *2.* Protection: Capital punishment protects other prisoners and guards from killers sentenced to life in prison. If released these may kill again. Capital punishment protects the other citizens. Yet the available statistics do not support this argument. *3.* Economics: It is cheaper to execute than to imprison. Again, statistics do not support this. *4.* The Complexities and Inequalities of the Criminal Justice System: The system favors the rich over the poor. It is so often inefficient, inept, and sometimes wrong in its judgments. Some innocent people have been executed. The guilty are often set free over legal technicalities. *5.* Punishment: This is the only argument that has any Scriptural support. Yet, are there more humane ways of punishment than execution? Many see that life in prison without possibility of parole is a greater punishment than death. A sense of justice requires that a murderer be punished, yet nonlethal punishment preserves the life-valuing role of the state. Is this more in line with a biblical sense of justice which also values life? To be effective, punishment should be certain, swift, and impartial. Yet with capital cases in many courts, this is rare.

In summary, the Bible prescribed capital punishment for certain cases in its society. It also set up love for human beings in being like Christ as the highest ethical norm. The modern student of Scripture must ask if cases in our society really find parallels in biblical society. Which methods of biblical interpretation allow us to determine where capital punishment should apply? How do biblical forms of capital punishment relate to modern society? Does Scripture absolutely require capital punishment? In what situation(s) does a government have the right and/or responsibility to carry out capital punishment? Are there scriptural answers to the arguments for and against capital punishment? *Guy Greenfield*

CAPPADOCIA (Cắp-pả-dō′ cǐ-ả) A Roman province in Asia Minor mentioned twice in the New Testament: Acts 2:9; 1 Peter 1:1.

Although the extent of Cappadocia varied through the centuries depending on the currently dominant empire, it lay south of Pontus and stretched about 300 miles from Galatia eastward toward Armenia, with Cilicia and the Taurus Mountains to the south. Although mountainous country, its mostly rural population raised good crops, cattle, and horses. While in New Testament times its mines were still producing some minerals, a large number of tablets written in cuneiform script discovered in 1907 at Tanish, now known as Kultepe, revealed that Assyrians were mining and exporting silver ore from Cappadocia about 1900 B.C.

From Acts 2:9 we know that Jews from Cappadocia were in Jerusalem when Peter preached at Pentecost. Those converted to Christianity that day must have given a good witness when they returned home because in 1 Peter 1:1 believers there are mentioned along with others in Pontus.

Today the region of Cappadocia is in central Turkey, which is ninety-eight percent Muslim.

A region of Cappadocia where Christians hid from invading Moslems in cities carved in the mountains.

CAPTAIN English translation of several Hebrew words usually referring to an officer or leader of some kind. As the term is applied to Christ, see *Prince of Life.*

CAPTAIN OF THE TEMPLE The officer second in authority only to the high priest. Pashhur ("chief governor in the house of the Lord," Jer. 20:1) and Seraiah ("ruler of the house of God," Neh. 11:11) held this office in the Old Testament times. In Acts it appears that one of the main functions of this officer was to keep order in the Temple (Acts 4:1; 5:24,26). The plural (Luke 22:4,52) may refer to officers under the command of the captain of the Temple.

CAPTIVITY Term used for Israel's Exile in Babylon between 597 B.C. and 538 B.C. See *Exile.*

CARAVAN A company of travelers (usually merchants) on a journey through desert or hostile regions with a train of pack animals (see Gen. 37:25; Judg. 5:6; 1 Kings 10:2; Job 6:18–19; Isa. 21:13). Palestine lay along the main travel route between Egypt, Arabia, and Mesopotamia and had many caravans passing through it.

CARBUNCLE (Cär' bŭn cle) A precious stone used in the priest's breastpiece (Ex. 28:17) and part of the king of Tyre's apparel in the Garden of Eden according to Ezekiel's ironic description (Ezek. 28:13). Equation with a stone used today is difficult if not impossible. NAS and NRSV read, "emerald"; NIV, "beryl." KJV translates a different Hebrew term, "carbuncle," in Isaiah 54:12. There NAS reads, "crystal"; NRSV, "jewels"; and NIV, "sparkling jewels." In English, carbuncle is an obsolete term referring to various red jewels. See *Jewelry, Jewels.*

CARCAS (Cär' càs) Persian name meaning, "hawk." Eunuch under King Ahasuerus of Persia commanded to bring Queen Vashti to the king's party. (Esther 1:10). See *Abagtha; Esther.*

CARCHEMISH (Cär' chĕm ĭsh; *fort of Chemosh*) (modern Jerablus) was an important city on the great bend of the Euphrates River. It was on the west bank of the river, at an important river crossing point on the international trade route. Carchemish lies mostly on the Turkish side of the modern Turkish-Syrian border.

Carchemish is mentioned about 1800 B.C. as the capital of a kingdom in alliance with the Assyrian king Shamshi-adad I against Yahdun-lim, king of Mari.

After the Mari period, there is a short break in the known history of the city. When sources again become available, Carchemish was first under Hurrian influence, then was included within the Hittite sphere. Carchemish was a vassal and ally of the Hittite King Muwatallis against the Egyptian Pharaoh Ramses II at the important battle of Kadesh in 1286 B.C.

Following the destruction of the New Hittite Kingdom at the hands of the Sea Peoples shortly after 1200 B.C., Carchemish became the most important heir of the Hittite culture. The land of Hatti and the Hittites mentioned in the Bible are probably these successors to the Anatolian Hittites centered on Carchemish. Carchemish again became the head of an independent kingdom and successfully resisted capture by the Assyrian Empire during the whole of its first period of expansion. Only under Sargon II were the Assyrians able to capture and destroy Carchemish in 717 B.C. Sargon helped to rebuild the city, and it became the capital of a western Assyrian province. Assyria's ultimate capture of the city was noteworthy enough that Isaiah used it as a rhetorical example in one of his oracles (Isa. 10:9).

The most important battle at Carchemish, however, was not fought over possession of the city. At the very end of the Assyrian period, when Nebuchadrezzar was incorporating all former Assyrian territory within the new Babylonian Empire, Pharaoh Neco II of Egypt came to Carchemish to try to save the remnants of the Assyrian army. He hoped to preserve a weak Assyria as a buffer between him and a strong and aggressive Babylon. He arrived too late to save the Assyrians, perhaps held up by Josiah's unsuccessful challenge at Megiddo (2 Chron. 35:20–24). Nebuchadrezzar defeated Neco at Carchemish. This victory gave Babylon authority over all of western Asia within the next few years; for this reason it ranks as one of the most decisive battles of all time. Jeremiah and the Chronicler both took note of it; Jeremiah composed a poetic dirge commemorating the Egyptian defeat (Jer. 46:2–12). The city of Carchemish appears to have declined after the Babylonian period of power, for references to it cease.

Carchemish and its ruins were visited by western travelers repeatedly during the eighteenth and nineteenth centuries. Excavations were carried out on the site from 1878–1881, and again from 1911–1914 and in 1920. A cuneiform inscription found during the excavations confirms the site as Carchemish.   *Joseph Coleson*

CAREAH (Cà·rē' äh) KJV spelling for Kareah (2 Kings 25:23). See *Kareah.*

CARITES (Cär' ī·tēs) A term of uncertain meaning in 2 Kings 11:4,19 and in Hebrew text of 2 Sam. 20:23, where Cherethites is usually read. The Carites were either mercenary soldiers recruited from Cilicia by Judah and other countries such as Egypt, or the meaning of the term can no longer be determined. They were military personnel who helped Jehoiada, the priest, install Joash as king and assassinate the queen mother Athaliah.

CARKAS (Cär' kàs) NAS, NRSV, TEV spelling of Carcas. See *Carcas.*

CARMEL (Car' mel) Place name meaning, "park, fruitful field." *1.* A village in the tribal territory assigned Judah (Josh. 15:55). King Saul set up a monument after he defeated the Amalekites there (1 Sam. 15:12). There Nabal treated David and his men with disrespect and disregard, an action eventually resulting in Nabal's death and David's marriage to his widow Abigail (1 Sam. 25:2–40). The village is modern khirbet el-Kirmil, seven miles south of Hebron. *2.* The towering mountain (1 Kings 18:19) where Elijah confronted the prophets of Baal. The mountain is near the Mediterranean coast of Palestine between the Plain of Acco to the north and the Plain of Sharon to the south. It reaches a maximum elevation of about 1,750 feet. The Bible frequently mentions Carmel as a place of great beauty and fertility.

CARMEL, MOUNT (Cär' mĕl) In 1 Kings 18:19, the scene of the confrontation between the prophet Elijah and the prophets of Baal. The mountain is near the Mediterranean coast of Pales-

The western summit of Mount Carmel overlooking the modern Israeli port city of Haifa.

tine between the Plain of Acco to the north and the Plain of Sharon to the south. It is frequently mentioned in the Bible as a place of great beauty and fertility.

CARMELITE (Cär′ mēl īte) A citizen of Carmel. See *Carmel.*

CARMELITESS (Cär′ mēl ī tĕss) A woman who resided in or was a citizen of the town of Carmel. See *Carmel.*

CARMI (Cär′ mī) Personal name meaning, "my vineyard." *1.* A son of Reuben (Gen. 46:9) and thus original ancestor of a clan in the tribe of Reuben (Num. 26:6). *2.* Father of Achan (Josh. 7:1). *3.* A son of Judah (1 Chron. 4:1).

CARMITE (Cär′ mīte) Member of clan of Carmi (Num. 26:6). See *Carmi.*

CARNAL Anything related to the fleshly or worldly appetites and desires rather than to the godly and spiritual desires. Basic human nature is carnal, sold out to sin and thus living in the realm of death, unable to observe God's spiritual law (Rom. 7:14). People walk either in the flesh or in the Spirit, leading to death or to life. The carnal person is hostile to God, unable to please God (Rom. 8:1–11). Jesus Christ in human flesh over-

came the condemnation of the fleshly way to offer the free life of the Spirit's way. Paul said that Gentiles had received the spiritual gospel through the Jews and should thus minister to the fleshly or material needs of the Jews (Rom. 15:27). Compare 1 Corinthians 9:11.

Even church members can be carnal, being only babes in Christ, as Paul indicated in writing the Corinthians (1 Cor. 3:1–4). Such Christians are jealous of one another and quarrel with one another. Christians should solve their problems with different "weapons" (2 Cor. 10:4). Such weapons serve God's purposes, destroy human arguments and human divisions, and bring glory to Christ.

Hebrews teaches that Christ had a distinct kind of priesthood from that of Jewish priests. Priests had always served on the basis of commandments written to meet fleshly needs. Christ served on the basis of His indestructible, eternal life (Heb. 7:16). In 9:10 the writer of Hebrews made clear the fleshly nature of the law. It consisted of commandments for the old order dealing with external matters until Christ came to deal with the spiritual matters of eternal redemption, sanctification, cleansing, and eternal life.

Using the same Greek word (*sarkikos),* Peter issued a battle cry against "fleshly lusts" so that glory would go to God and people would be attracted to His way of life (1 Pet. 2:11).

CARNELIAN (Car ne′ li an) Hard, red precious stone, a variety of chalcedony. It was used to decorate the king of Tyre (Ezek. 28:13 NRSV) and could be used to describe the one sitting on the heavenly throne (Rev. 4:3 NIV, NRSV) and formed part of the wall of the New Jerusalem (Rev. 21:20 NIV, NRSV).

CARPENTER The trade lifted to a high position of honor by Jesus (Mark 6:3). See *Occupations*.

CARPUS (Cär' pŭs) Personal name meaning, "fruit." A Christian friend with whom Paul left his cloak in Troas. He asked Timothy to retrieve it for him (2 Tim. 4:13).

CARRIAGE KJV translation of several general Hebrew and Greek terms referring to utensils, baggage, supplies, or anything which can be carried. The term has nothing to do with transportation vehicles, as a more modern use of carriage would imply. Compare various translations of Judges 18:21; 1 Samuel 17:22; Isaiah 10:28; 46:1; Acts 21:15.

CARRION VULTURE NAS, NRSV translation of bird of prey (Lev. 11:18; Deut. 14:17). See *Birds*.

CARSHENA (Cär shē' nà) Wise counselor of King Ahasuerus of Persia to whom the king turned for advice on how to deal with his disobedient wife Vashti (Esther 1:14).

CASEMENT A window with lattice work. The wisdom teacher looked through a latticed window to observe a foreign woman dealing with a naive youth (Prov. 7:6). Sisera's mother looked through a similar window as she impatiently waited for her son to return from the battle which he had lost to Deborah and Barak and after which he was killed by Jael (Judg. 5:28). Archaeologists have found such lattice windows in royal palaces. The queen or a goddess looking out the royal window seems to have been a popular motif in the Ancient Near East.

CASIPHIA (Cà sīph' ĭ à) Place name meaning, "silversmith." Place in Babylon where Levites settled in Exile (Ezra 8:17) and from which Ezra summoned Levites to return with him to Jerusalem. The place is unknown outside this passage.

CASLUH (Căs' lŭh), **CASLUHIM** (Căs' lū hĭm), **CASLUHITES** (Căs' lū hītes) Clan name of "sons of Mizraim (or Egypt)" and "father" of the Philistines in the Table of Nations (Gen. 10:14). Their origin is not known.

CASSIA Bark of an oriental tree (*Cinnamomum cassia* Blume) related to cinnamon. One of the ingredients used to make anointing oil (Ex. 30:24), it was acquired through trade with Tyre (Ezek. 27:19) and was desired for its aromatic qualities (Ps. 45:8). One of Job's daughters was

named Kezia(h) (Job 42:14), a name that means "cassia."

CASTANETS See *Musical Instruments*.

CASTAWAY KJV translation of Greek *adokimos*, referring to battle-testing of soldiers, qualifications for office, or testing of metals to make sure they are genuine. Paul used his own example of personal discipline to ensure that his preaching proved true in life as a call to others to do the same (1 Cor. 9:27). He did not want to be cast away as impure metal or disqualified as an unworthy soldier or candidate. Paul played on the words *dokimos*, "qualified," and *adokimos*, "disqualified," in 2 Corinthians 13:5–7. The Corinthians demanded a test or proof that Christ spoke through him (v. 3). Paul turned the argument on them, saying they needed to prove themselves that they had not failed the test of Christ and become reprobates. He hoped the Corinthians would recognize in Paul's life that he had not failed the test and was thus not a reprobate. He prayed the Corinthians would not do wrong, not to prove himself qualified but so that the Corinthians would do what was right even if Paul proved to be unqualified.

Paul warned Timothy of evil persons in evil times with people resisting the truth, having corrupt minds, and being unqualified in the faith (2 Tim. 3:8). Similarly, he wrote Titus of persons professing to know God but unqualified in good works (Titus 1:16). With similar purpose, Hebrews compares people to ground which bears thorns and briers and is thus unqualified and fails to pass the test (Heb. 6:8).

CASTLE KJV translation for six Hebrew and one Greek word. NAS uses "castle" only for one Hebrew term in 2 Kings 15:25 and Proverbs 18:19. RSV uses castle in Proverbs 18:19 and for a different Hebrew term in Nehemiah 7:2. NIV does not use "castle." See *Fortified Cities*.

'Armon refers to the large, fortified home of the king, often translated palace or citadel (1 Kings 16:18). The term apparently referred to the massive masonry structures connected with the defense of the palace and possibly of the homes of other leading citizens (Amos 6:8; compare 1:4). Apparently they served as storehouses for royal treasures and goods taken in battle (Amos 3:10). Israel prayed for peace in her fortress, but no fortress gave security from God's anger (Isa. 25:2; 34:13; Hos. 8:14). God promised to rebuild the fortified palaces of His people (Jer. 30:18). The palaces should witness to God's strength (Ps. 48:3,13–14). The wisdom teacher knew a more stubborn defense system than castles—that of humans (Prov. 18:19).

Birah is a late loan word from Accadian and refers to the fortified acropolis, usually built at the highest and most easily defensible part of a city (Neh. 1:1; Esther 1:2). It referred to the fortress near the Temple in the rebuilt Jerusalem (Neh. 2:8). A military commander ruled the fortress (Neh. 7:2). The Chronicler used the term for Solomon's Temple (1 Chron. 29:1,19) and used the term in the plural to describe Jehoshaphat's and Jotham's building (2 Chron. 17:12; 27:4).

Tirah refers to a stone wall used for protection around a camp of tents (Gen. 25:16; Num. 31:10; Ps. 69:25; Ezek. 25:4). Compare 1 Chronicles 6:54; Ezekiel 46:23*b*.

Migdal is a defense tower which may stand alone in the countryside as a watchtower (1 Chron. 27:25). They were also used to protect vineyards and other crops (Isa. 5:2). A famous *migdal* crowned one area of Shechem or served as a military outpost for Shechem (Judg. 9:46–49). See *Shechem.* Uzziah fortified the Jerusalem gates with such towers on top of which he placed modern weaponry (2 Chron. 26:9–10,15). Battle axes were used to break down such towers (Ezek. 26:9).

Matsad and *metsudah* are closely connected to the Canaanite or Jebusite city of Jerusalem that David conquered (2 Sam. 5:7,9; 1 Chron. 11:5,7). The *metsudah* of Zion was probably a military citadel protecting the southeastern hill of Jerusalem, that part Israel called, "city of David." See *David, City of.* In general, the word described any place of hiding or refuge (Judg. 6:2; 1 Sam. 23:14).

The basic biblical lesson is that Yahweh is our stronghold, refuge, and fortress (Ps. 18:2; 31:3).

Parembole is the Greek term for a fortified camp and designated the Roman army barracks or headquarters in Jerusalem (Acts 21:34; 22:24; 23:10). Hebrews refers to Old Testament offerings burned outside the camp, comparing this to the place of Jesus' suffering and inviting Christians to be willing to suffer outside the camp, accepting disgrace as did Jesus (Heb. 13:11–13). Compare Revelation 20:9.

Trent C. Butler

CASTOR (Căs' tôr); **POLLUX** (Pŏl' lŭx *sons of Jupiter)* In Acts 28:11, the sign or figurehead of the ship which carried Paul from Malta toward Rome. Castor and Pollux were Greek deities, the twin sons of Zeus, who were supposed particularly to watch over sailors.

CATERPILLAR The wormlike larvae of butterflies and moths. The term appears in different English versions to translate various Hebrew words, NIV not referring to caterpillars at all.

Chasil refers to a particular stage of the grasshopper or locust. Apparently in this stage wings have begun to develop but are not folded together. They could cause famine in a land, eating all the crops (1 Kings 8:37; Joel 1:14). They symbolized gathering booty or spoil of battle (Isa. 33:4). They made their mark on Israelite history in the plagues in Egypt (Ps. 46).

Yeleq is the first stage after emerging from the egg. The flying apparatus has begun to develop but is invisible. The word could be used to describe the plague on Egypt (Ps. 105:34). They were noted for covering or filling up an area (Jer. 51:14). They swarmed over a land as an army in formation marched into a country (Jer 51:27; Joel 2:25). They multiplied quickly and ate up all in front of them before flying away to attack another land (Nah. 3:15–16). Obviously such language is not fully appropriate for the first stage of the animal, showing that the various terms became synonyms and could be used interchangeably to describe typical activities of the grasshopper or locust.

Gazam is traditionally defined as the just matured grasshopper ready for flight. Other scholars would identify it as the true caterpillar. Its name comes from a Hebrew root word meaning, "to cut off," thus describing the animal's destructive ability to bite through weeds, grain, fig leaves, grapes, olive trees, fruit, and even small twigs and branches. Compare Amos 4:9; Joel 1:4; 2:25. This stage is variously translated as "palmerworm" (KJV), "gnawing locust" or "caterpillar" (NAS), "locust" (NIV), "cutting locust" (NRSV).

'Arbeh is the mature, swarming locust—*schistocera gregaria*—which grows to six centimeters in length. The Exodus plague narrative features them (Ex. 10:14–19). They were classified as hopping animals (Job 39:20) with jointed legs and so were clean for Israel to eat (Lev. 11:20–23). Their devouring habits made them a part of God's threatened curses on a disobedient people (Deut. 28:38). Their wandering and swarming resembled that of an army (Judg. 6:5; 7:12; Prov. 30:27; Jer. 46:23; Nah. 3:17). They were harmless to the human body, since people could easily shake them off (Ps. 109:23).

CATHOLIC EPISTLES The New Testament letters not attributed to Paul and written to a more general or unidentifiable audience: James; 1 and 2 Peters; 1, 2, and 3 John; Jude. The title is from tradition and cannot be defined by modern standards.

CATTLE See *Animals.* English translations use "cattle" for at least thirteen different Hebrew words and six Greek words.

'Eleph or *'aluph* refers to tame animals living in a herd. It is variously translated as "herd," "cattle," "oxen," "kine." It includes animals used in plowing (Isa. 30:24).

Behemah is a general term for animals (Ex. 9:9; Isa. 30:6), for four-footed animals (1 Kings 4:33), wild animals (Deut. 28:26; 1 Sam. 17:44), as well as for domestic cattle including both herds of cattle and flocks of sheep and goats (Lev. 1:2) and oxen and donkeys (Deut. 5:14). Compare Genesis 47:17–18 . It includes all animals belonging to a household (Gen. 34:23). They were used as riding animals (Neh. 2:12–14).

Be'ir is a general term including beasts of burden (Gen. 45:17) who graze in a field (Ex. 22:5). They are the property of an individual or community (Num. 20:4,8).

Baqar were important members of an Israelite household (Gen. 47:1), even being included in prayer and fasting by people of Nineveh (Jonah 3:7). They are the most important work animals, pulling the plow (1 Sam. 11:5; 1 Kings 19:19; Job 1:14) and the wagon (1 Chron. 13:9). These oxen, especially the young, provided meat for special occasions (Gen. 18:7; 1 Kings 1:9). The royal palace ate such food daily (1 Kings 4:22). The cattle produced milk from which yogurt was made (Deut. 32:14) and also cheese (2 Sam. 17:29 NAS). Such cattle could be fattened in the pasture (1 Kings 4:23) or in stalls (Hab. 3:17). The high value placed on oxen can be seen in the penalty for stealing one (Ex. 22:1).

Mala'kah is a basic Hebrew word for business or work which came to designate the wares or things connected with work and thus is used to refer to cattle in Genesis 33:14.

Meri' is based on the root meaning, "fat." It refers to calves fattened for people to eat. David sacrificed these before the ark (2 Sam. 6:13; compare 1 Kings 1:9). Isaiah reminded Israel that such sacrifices were not God's first priority for His people (Isa. 1:11; compare Amos 5:22). Some have suggested the animal meant here is a buffalo—*bubalus buffalus.*

Miqneh is the Hebrew word for "possessions" and most frequently refers to herds and flocks (Gen. 26:14) and possibly to a longer list of animals (Gen. 47:17–18; Ex. 9:3; Job 1:3).

'Egel and *'eglah* are young steers and cows. The golden calves of the wilderness were formed like an *'egel* (Ex. 32:4) as were the calves King Jeroboam placed in Bethel and Dan (1 Kings 12:28). An *'egel* was the son of a *baqar* (Lev. 9:2).

Par or *parah* represents a bull or cow which has matured enough to be capable of reproduction (Job 21:10). They are older than an *'egel* or *'eglah* and belong to the collective term *baqar.*

Shor is a collective term for either bull or cow and most often refers to a single animal. See *Bull.*

Threma refers to a domesticated animal, usually a sheep or a goat (John 4:12).

Ktēnos refers to domesticated animals, often ones used for riding or for pack animals. Revelation 18:13 apparently refers to cattle. The same word may refer to a donkey in Luke 10:34. Compare Acts 23:24.

KJV refers to cattle in Luke 17:7, but the Greek term *poimaino* refers to the activity of a herdsman leading sheep or goats to pasture. Compare 1 Corinthians 9:7.

Tauros is a bull or ox used in sacrifices and for banquets. It is the Greek translation of Hebrew *shor.* See Matthew 22:4; Acts 14:13; Hebrews 9:13; 10:4.

Bous is an ox or cow. Kept in stalls, they had to be led to water even on the sabbath (Luke 13:15). Compare Luke 14:5. They were yoked for plowing (Luke 14:19). Jesus found people selling them in the Temple for sacrifices (John 2:14). It can also translate Hebrew *shor* (1 Cor. 9:9).

Moschos is a young bull or heifer, basically equivalent to Hebrew *par* or *parah.* See Luke 15:23; Hebrews 9:12,19; Revelation 4:7.

Damalis is the Greek equivalent for Hebrew *'eglah* and is used in the New Testament to refer to the red heifer of Numbers 9:2–9. See Hebrews 9:13. *Trent C. Butler*

CAUDA (Cāū' dà) or **CLAUDA** A small island whose name is variously spelled in the Greek manuscripts. Paul sailed by the island on his way to Malta and ultimately to Rome (Acts 27:16). The island is modern Gavdos, southwest of Crete.

CAUL The part of the liver which appears to be left over or form an appendage to the liver, according to KJV. Other translations refer to the "lobe" (NAS), "covering" (NIV), or "appendage" (NRSV) of the liver. See Exodus 29:13. In Hosea 13:8 KJV speaks of the "caul of their hearts," which modern translations render more freely. The Hebrew apparently refers to the chest cavity in which the heart is located. KJV also uses "caul" to translate a rare Hebrew word in Isaiah 3:18 taken by modern linguists to mean, "headbands."

CAULKERS, CAULKING See *Calkers, Calking.*

CAVALRY The mounted soldiers of an army. Israel faced cavalry and chariots in the Exodus (Ex. 14:9,18,28) and during the period of the judges (Judg. 4). God would not allow Israel to rely on the wealth and security represented by military horses (Deut. 17:16). David captured horses and chariots from Syria (2 Sam. 8:4). Solomon then developed a military force featuring horses (1 Kings 4:26; 9:17; 10:26). These references to horsemen may all refer to personnel connected with chariots rather than to individual riders or cavalry units. The Hebrew term *parash* refers to both with the context the only guide to interpretation. Evidence outside Israel points to Assyria using cavalry troops shortly after 900 B.C. The cavalry provided a line of defense, served as scouts, and chased a defeated army. God warned Israel not to depend upon horses for security (Isa. 31:1).

CAVES Numerous caves pit the cliffs and mountains of Palestine. Such caves provided housing

The east face of the mount of transfiguration showing caves used for shelter by the people of the area.

and burial sites for prehistoric people. Although occupation was not continuous, evidence for human habitation in some of the caves exists up until the Roman period. At this time, they became places of refuge for Jews fleeing Roman persecution.

In the Bible, caves were often used as burial places. Abraham brought the cave of Machpelah as a tomb for Sarah (Gen. 23:11–16,19). Lazarus was buried in a cave (John 11:38). David used the cave of Adullam for refuge (1 Sam. 22:1), as did five Canaanite kings at Makkedah (Josh. 10:16).

Diane Cross

CEDAR A tree grown especially in Lebanon and valued as building material (probably *Cedrus libani).* Cedar played a still-unknown role in the purification rites of Israel (Lev. 14:4; Num. 19:6). Kings used cedar for royal buildings (2 Sam. 5:11; 1 Kings 5:6; 6:9—7:12). Cedar signified royal power and wealth (1 Kings 10:27). Thus the cedar symbolized growth and strength (Ps. 92:12; compare Ezek. 17). Still, the majestic cedars could not stand before God's powerful presence (Ps. 29:5). The cedars owed their existence to God, who had planted them (Ps. 104:16). See *Plants in the Bible.*

CEDRON (Cē′ drŏn) KJV spelling for Kidron in John 18:1. See *Kidron.*

CELESTIAL BODIES Paul contrasted celestial bodies (sun, moon, and stars) with terrestrial bodies in explaining the difference between the present human body (physical) and the resurrection body (spiritual body, 1 Cor. 15:35–50). The two types of bodies are of an entirely different nature; one weak and perishing, the other glorious and eternal.

CELIBACY Abstention by vow from marriage. The practice of abstaining from marriage may be alluded to twice in the New Testament. Jesus said that some have made themselves eunuchs for the sake of the kingdom and that those who were able to do likewise should do so (Matt. 19:12). This statement has traditionally been understood as a reference to celibacy (See *Eunuch*). Paul counseled the single to remain so (1 Cor. 7:8). Both Jesus (Mark 10:2–12) and Paul (1 Cor. 7:9, 28, 36–39; 9:5), however, affirmed the goodness of the married state. One New Testament passage goes so far as to characterize the prohibition of marriage as demonic (1 Tim. 4:1–3).

CENCHREA (Cĕn′ chrē à) or **CENCHREAE** The eastern port city of Corinth. Phoebe served in the church there (Rom. 16:1), and Paul had his head shaved there when he took a vow (Acts 18:18).

CENSER In Leviticus 10:1, a vessel used for offering incense before the Lord. Nadab and Abihu used it improperly to bring God's destruction. It probably was also used for carrying live

One of the "cedars of Lebanon."

The ruins of Cenchrea with the waters of its bay seen in the background of the photo.

coals employed in connection with worship in the tabernacle or the Temple, each priest having one (compare Num. 16:17–18). Use of the censer in Temple worship was restricted to members of the Aaronic priesthood, as King Uzziah discovered in shocking fashion (2 Chron. 26:16–21). The heavenly worship also involved censers and incense, according to John's vision (Rev. 8:3–5). See *Containers and Vessels; Tabernacle; Temple.*

CENSUS The enumeration of a population for the purpose of taxation or for the determination of manpower of war.

Moses took a census of Israel at Mount Sinai and assessed a half-shekel tax to each male over twenty to support the tabernacle (Ex. 30:13–16). Another census counted Israel's manpower available for war. This census excluded the Levites, separating them for service in the tabernacle (Num. 1). Another census was taken in Moab at the end of the wilderness wanderings, again excluding the Levites. The Hebrew may indicate the units used in the count reflect tribal units and not thousands, thus accounting for the large totals. David also counted Israel's warriors. Second Samuel 24 says that the Lord incited David to carry out the census, and 1 Chronicles 21 says that Satan moved David to do so. In both accounts a pestilence was sent upon Israel because of the census. Ezekiel 2 accounts for those who came out of Exile with Zerubbabel and Nehemiah.

The first census referred to in the New Testament concerns the decree by Caesar Augustus "that all the world should be taxed." This "first census" was taken by Cyrenius, the governor of Syria (Luke 2:1–5). Luke used this benchmark both as a general time reference and, more importantly, to set the birth of Jesus in Bethlehem, the ancestral city of David. This passage has presented problems in that: one, there is no specific record of such a census outside the Lukan account and two, the date of Cyrenius's governorship (A.D. 6–9) appears to be inconsistent with the previous statement that Jesus' birth was in the reign of Herod the Great (Luke 1:5), who died in A.D. 4. However, Luke's account is consistent with Roman practices, and such a census could well have been ordered by Cyrenius functioning as a military governor alongside the political governor Sentius Saturnius around 6 B.C., when most scholars date the birth of Jesus. The other reference is that of Gamaliel's remark about Judas of Galilee, who rose up "in the days of the census" only to later perish (Acts 5:37 NIV).   *Joel Parkman*

CENTURION An officer in the Roman army, nominally in command of one hundred soldiers. In Matthew 8:5, a centurion who lived at Capernaum approached Jesus on behalf of his ailing servant. In Mark 15:39, a centurion who witnessed the crucifixion identified Jesus as the Son of God. In Acts 10, the conversion of the centurion Cornelius marked the beginning of the church's outreach to the Gentile world. In Acts 27:3, the centurion Julius treated the apostle Paul with courtesy. These passages illustrate the generally favorable impression made by the centurions who appear in the New Testament. They were usually career soldiers, and they formed the real backbone of the Roman military force.

CEPHAS (Cē' phàs) See *Peter.*

CEREAL OFFERINGS See *Sacrifices and Offerings.*

CEREMONIAL LAW Laws which pertained to the festivals and cultic activities of the Israelites. See *Festivals; Laws; Priests and Levites; Sacrifices and Offerings; Worship.*

CERTIFICATE OF DIVORCE See *Family; Divorce.*

CHAFF The husk and other materials separated from the kernel of grain during the threshing or winnowing process. It blew away in the wind (Hos. 13:3) or was burned up as worthless (Isa. 5:24; Luke 3:17).

CHAINS The English translation of at least eight different Hebrew terms for materials interlaced together into ornamental or restraining objects. *1.* An ornament worn around the neck either signifying investiture in office with political award (Gen. 41:42; Dan. 5:7) or for personal jewelry (Num. 31:50). Animals such as camels might also wear ornamental chains (Judg. 8:26). *2.* Decorations of gold worn on the high priest's breastplate (Ex. 28:14). *3.* A series of chains formed a partition in Solomon's Temple (1 Kings 6:21). *4.* Architectural ornaments on the Temple walls (2 Chron. 3:5,16). *5.* Restraining chains preventing prisoners from escaping (Jer. 39:7; Acts. 28:20). God could loose His minister from chains (Acts 12:7).

CHALCEDONY Transliteration of Greek name of precious stone in Revelation 21:19. See *Jewels.*

CHALCOL (Chăl' cŏl) KJV spelling for Calcol in 1 Kings 4:31. See *Calcol.*

CHALDEA (Chăl·dē' ·à) refers either to a geographical locality (Chaldea) or to the people who lived there (Chaldeans). Chaldea was situated in central and southeastern Mesopotamia, i.e., the land between the lower stretches of the Tigris and Euphrates Rivers. Today Chaldea lies in the country of Iraq, very close to its border with Iran, and touching upon the head of the Persian Gulf.
The Chaldeans In Old Testament times different peoples occupied southeastern Mesopotamia at various times. One such group was the Chaldeans, whose name derives from the ancient term *Kaldai,* which refers to several Aramean tribes who moved into lower Mesopotamia between 1000 and 900 B.C. Their new homeland was a flat, alluvial plain of few natural resources, many marshes, spring flooding, and very hot summers.
Relation to Babylonia At first the Chaldeans lived in tribal settlements, rejecting the urban society of the Babylonians to the northwest

As time passed, the Chaldeans gradually acquired domination in Babylonia. In the process they also took on the title "Babylonians," or more exactly, "Neo-Babylonians." As a result, the terms *Chaldea(ns)* and *(Neo-)Babylonia(ns)* may be used interchangeably (Ezek. 1:3, RSV, NIV; 12:13, NIV). See *Babylon, History and Religion of.*

In the eighth century B.C., the Chaldeans emerged as the champions of resistance against Assyria, a dangerous, aggressive imperial force in upper Mesopotamia. At this time the Chaldeans begin to appear in the Old Testament, first, as possible allies with Judah against Assyria, but later, as a direct threat to Judah and Jerusalem.

Tony M. Martin

CHALDEES (Chăl' dēēs) Another expression for Chaldeans. See *Chaldea.*

CHALKSTONE Soft stone easily crushed used for comparison to destruction of altar (Isa. 27:9).

CHAMBER English translation of at least seven Hebrew words referring to a portion of a house or building. Included are sleeping quarters (2 Kings 6:12); bathroom (Judg. 3:24); private inner room reserved for a bride (Judg. 15:1; Joel 2:16); private, personal cubicle in the Temple furnished with benches (1 Sam. 9:22; 2 Kings 23:11); storage rooms (Neh. 12:44); a cool upper room built on the roof (Judg. 3:20) or over the city gate (2 Sam. 18:33); and the ribs or beams forming side rooms in the Temple (1 Kings 7:3). The New Testament speaks of inner rooms of a house (Matt. 6:6; 24:26; Luke 12:3) or of a storeroom (Luke 12:24). See *Architecture.*

CHAMBERING KJV translation of a Greek word in Romans 13:13 rendered as "debauchery" or "sexual promiscuity" in modern versions.

CHAMBERLAIN High military or political official whose title is related to Hebrew term meaning, "castrated" or "eunuch" but may be actually derived from Accadian term for royal official. That all officials bearing the Hebrew title, *saris,* were actually eunuchs is doubtful. The Rab-saris of 2 Kings 18:17 is literally, "chief of eunuchs" but more likely signifies the office held by a high military and administrative official. Compare Jeremiah 39:3; Daniel 1:3. Potiphar is described as Pharaoh's *saris* but had a wife (Gen. 37:36; 40:7). The Persian officials in Esther 1:10 may have been eunuchs, since they apparently protected the king's wives and harem. Compare 2 Kings 9:32. Hebrew officials also carried the title: 1 Samuel 8:15; 1 Kings 22:9; 2 Kings 8:6; 23:11; 24:12,15; 25:19. See *Eunuch.*

CHAMBERS OF IMAGERY Phrase of uncertain meaning (Ezek. 8:12). It could refer to secret rooms containing idols or pictures on the walls (see Ezek. 8:10; 23:14) probably related to pagan religions. Whatever "chambers of imagery" refers to, that which was taking place in the Temple during the days of Ezekiel was displeasing to God.

CHAMBERS OF THE SOUTH Reference to some unknown phenomenon in the skies. Since "chambers of the south" is mentioned along with other stellar constellations (Job 9:9), the phenomenon is usually taken to mean some sort of constellation or group of constellations. Some have taken "chambers of the south" to be a reference to the bright portion of the sky from Argus to Centauri. Others have taken the term as a reference to the zodiac or perhaps to the southern portion of the zodiac. Compare Job 37:9; 38:22. See *Astrology; Astronomy; Heavens.*

CHAMELEON An unclean animal that moves on the ground (Lev. 11:30), usually identified as the *Chamaeleo chamaeleo.* A Hebrew word with the same spelling but perhaps with different historical derivation occurs in Leviticus 11:18 and Deuteronomy 14:16, where it is apparently the barn owl, *Tyto alba.*

CHAMOIS A small antelope (*rupicapra*) that stands about two feet high and is found in mountainous regions. Translated as "mountain-sheep" in modern versions (Deut. 14:5). See *Animals.*

CHAMPAIGN Open, unenclosed land or plain (Deut. 11:30 KJV). Hebrew has preposition meaning in front of or opposite Gilgal and Arabah. See *Arabah.*

CHAMPION The Hebrew phrase in 1 Samuel 17:4,23 is literally "the man of the space between"—that is the man (like Goliath) who fights a single opponent in the space between two armies. The Hebrew word translated "champion" in 1 Samuel 17:51 is a different word meaning "mighty one, warrior."

CHANAAN (Chā′ nản) KJV form of Canaan in Acts 7:11; 13:19.

CHANCELLOR Title of a royal official of the Persian government living in Samaria and helping administer the Persian province after Persia gained control of Palestine. English translations vary in the way they render the title, but it apparently refers to political administration rather than to military command and represents a high official but not the highest provincial office, that of governor. See Ezra 4:8–9,17.

CHANT See *Music, Instruments, Dancing.*

CHAOS The transliteration of the Greek word "*chaos.*" In the Old Testament, several Hebrew words convey the idea meaning emptiness, waste, desolation, and void. Hebrew verbs denote sinking into obscurity, becoming nothingness, or falling prey to weakness. In Isaiah 24:10, God announced judgment on the whole earth. This included breaking down the city of chaos so that no one could enter. Through God's power, the line of desolation and the plumbline of emptiness are stretched over Edom (Isa. 34:11). In Jeremiah 4:23–26, the land is described as desolate, formless, void, and without light, a wilderness unfit for habitation. En route to Canaan, God cared for Israel in a howling wilderness waste (Deut. 32:10). God's power caused mighty leaders and princes to wander in the pathless wastes (Job 12:24, Ps. 107:40). Job compared his friends to waterless riverbeds that had lost themselves in nothingness (Job 6:18). Later Job longed for a place of deep shadow, of utter gloom without order (Job 10:21–22).

In Hebrew thought, however, the most prominent concept of chaos is that of the primeval disorder that preceded God's creative activity. When "darkness was upon the face of the deep," God through His word destroyed the forces of confusion (Gen. 1:2).

Throughout the Scriptures, chaos is personified as the principal opponent of God. In ancient Semitic legends, a terrible chaos-monster was called Rahab (the proud one), or Leviathan (the twisting dragon-creature), or Yam (the roaring sea). While vehemently denouncing idolatry and unmistakably proclaiming the matchless power of the One Almighty God, biblical writers did not hesitate to draw upon these prevalent pagan images to add vividness and color to their messages, trusting that their Israelite hearers would understand the truths presented.

God demonstrated His power in creation graphically in the crushing defeat of chaos. He quieted the sea, shattering Rahab, making the heavens fair, and piercing the fleeing serpent (Job 26:12–13). His victory over Leviathan is well-known (Job 41:1–8; Isa. 27:1); Leviathan and the sea are at His command (Ps. 104:26). In creation He curbed the unruly sea and locked it into its boundaries (Job 38:1–11). He stretched out the heavens and trampled the back of Yam, the sea (Job 9:8).

A second use of the chaos-monster figure involved God's victories at the time of the Exodus, using the term Rahab as a nickname for Egypt. Through His power God divided the sea and crushed Leviathan (Ps. 74:13–14). He calmed the swelling sea and smashed Rahab like a carcass (Ps. 89:9–10). By slaying the monster Rahab, God allowed the people to pass through the barrier-sea (Isa. 51:9–10). Mockingly, Isaiah called Egypt a helpless, vain Rahab whom God exterminated (Isa. 30:7). The psalmist anticipated the day when Rahab and Babylon would be forced to recognize God's rule (Ps. 87:4). In Ezekiel 29:3; 32:2, the Pharaoh of Egypt is called the river-monster that will be defeated at God's will.

Thirdly, the chaos theme is implied, if not used, in the New Testament depicting God's victory in Christ. In the Gospels Christ confidently demonstrated mastery over the sea (Mark 4:35–41, 6:45–52; John 6:16–21). In Revelation, when the ancient serpent, personified as the satanic dragon, rises out of the sea challenging His kingdom, Christ utterly defeats the adversary forever.

So, beginning with Genesis 1:2, when God conquered the formless waste, and continuing through all the Scriptures, God's mighty power over chaos is shown repeatedly. Finally, the triumphal note is sounded in Revelation 21:1, "there was no more sea." A new heaven and new earth are proof once again that chaos is conquered!

Alvin O. Collins

CHAPITER KJV translation of Hebrew architectural term meaning a capital made to stand on top of a pillar (1 Kings 7:16) or the base on which the actual capital is placed. In Exodus 36:38; 38:17,19,28 KJV translates the Hebrew word for "head" as chapiter, while a different Hebrew term is so translated in 2 Chronicles 3:15. See *Architecture.*

CHAPMAN Old English word for trader (2 Chron. 9:14 KJV).

CHARASHIM (Chär′ à shǐm) KJV spelling of Geharashim. See *Ge-harashim.*

CHARCHEMISH Variant spelling of Carchemish. See *Carchemish.*

CHARGER(S) *1.* A large flat serving dish (Num. 7:13–85; Matt. 14:8,11 KJV). *2.* Horses used in battle to charge or attack (Nah. 2:3 NRSV; compare TEV, REB based on early Greek translations; compare Isa. 31:1,3; Jer. 8:6; Rev. 6:2).

CHARIOTS Two-wheeled land vehicles, made of wood and strips of leather, and usually drawn by horses. They were used widely in Mesopotamia before 3000 B.C. and were introduced into Canaan and Egypt by the Hyksos about 1800–1600 B.C. Their primary function was as mobile firing platforms in battles. They were also used for hunt-

ing, for transportation of dignitaries, and in state and religious ceremonies.

Old Testament Egyptian chariots were the first to be mentioned in the Bible (Gen. 41:43; 46:29; 50:9). The iron chariots of the Philistines were fortified with plates of metal which made them militarily stronger than those of the Israelites (Judg. 1:19; 4:3, 13–17; 1 Sam. 13:5–7).

Chariots became an important part of Solomon's army and his commercial affairs (1 Kings 4:26; 9:15–19; 10:28–29). The military strength of Israel under Ahab was noteworthy because of the number of chariots available for use. According to Assyrian records, Ahab brought 2,000 chariots into the Battle of Qarqar in 853 B.C. Chariots were also seen in prophetic visions (Zech. 6:1–8) and applied figuratively to Elijah's and Elisha's power (2 Kings 2:12; 13:14).

New Testament Chariots were used in prophetic imagery (Rev. 9:9; 18:13) and for transportation of the Ethiopian eunuch (Acts 8:26–38).

See *Arms and Armor.*

Lai Ling Elizabeth Ngan

CHARIOTS OF THE SUN RSV translation in 2 Kings 23:11 for a sculpture that Josiah removed from the Jerusalem Temple. Other translations speak of horses the kings of Judah had dedicated to the sun. The Assyrians called the sun god, "chariot rider," so this could represent statuary introduced when Judah began to pay tribute to the Assyrian kings. Deuteronomy 17:3 records God's injunction to Israel not to worship the sun, but Ezekiel attested to persons in the Temple worshiping the sun (Ezek. 8:16).

CHARITY KJV translation of Greek *agape.* See *Love.* NAS uses "charity" to translate Greek *ekdidomai,* "to give out" in relation to helping the poor (Luke 11:41; 12:33; Acts 9:36).

CHARM Human grace and attractiveness; magic objects intended to ward off evil; and a method used to prevent poisonous snakes from biting. *1.* Human charm can be deceitful (Prov. 31:30), yet the Hebrew term used—*chen*—is a characteristic of God's gift of the Spirit (Zech. 12:10). God gave Joseph the ability to be charming or gain favor with the Egyptian jailer (Gen. 39:21). God also gives such grace to the afflicted (Prov. 3:34). Generally the term means to find favor or acceptance from another person (Gen. 6:8; 32:8), but English translations use grace or favor rather than charm as the translation at these points. Charm is used in cases like the harlot of Nahum 3:4. *2.* Magic charms sewn as wristbands (Ezek. 13:18 NIV) to ward off evil spirits and diseases receive prophetic condemnation. Compare Isaiah 3:20. *3.* Snake charmers exercised power in the community because they knew "magic words" or "magic acts" to prevent poisonous snakes from harming people. The psalmist compared the wicked to deaf snakes who were immune to such charmers (Ps. 58:4–5). The "enchanters" (NAS, NIV, NRSV) are listed among community leaders the prophet condemned (Isa. 3:3). Jeremiah warned God would send snakes whom no one could charm to punish His disobedient people (Jer. 8:17). The writer of Ecclesiastes reminded his audience that the price of unsuccessful charmers was great (Eccl. 10:11).

CHARRAN Greek and KJV spelling of Haran (Acts 7:2,4) See *Haran.*

CHASTE Holy purity demanded of God's people with special reference to the sexual purity of women. The Greek word *hagnos* originally referred to the holy purity of deities. Paul used the term to urge the Corinthians to remain pure so he could present them to Christ in the last days as a pure, virginal bride (2 Cor. 11:2–3). Titus was to teach young women to be pure in sincere worship, in general moral behavior, and in sexual matters (Titus 2:5; compare 1 Pet. 3:2). Similarly, church leaders must be pure (1 Tim. 5:22). Purity is an essential element of Christian ethics (Phil. 4:8; Jas. 3:17). Even preaching the gospel can be done from impure motives (Phil. 1:17). To be pure can also appear in a legal context, meaning to be declared innocent of a charge as Paul did in reference to the Corinthians (2 Cor. 7:11). Ultimately, Jesus is the pure One (1 John 3:3).

CHASTEN, CHASTISEMENT refers to an act of punishment intended to instruct and change behavior. Two basic Hebrew words express the idea—*yakach,* "to settle a dispute, reprove"; *yasar*—"to instruct, a discipline." People fear the experience of God's angry chastisement (Ps. 6:1; 38:1). Still, the Father must correct His children (2 Sam. 7:14; compare Deut. 8:5; 21:18; Prov. 13:24; 19:18). God's people should not despise God's chastening, for it leads to healing (Job 5:17–18; compare Prov. 3:11; Heb. 12:5). Such chastisement is God's choice, not that of humans (Hos. 10:10; compare 7:12). The purpose of chastising is to lead to repentance (Jer. 31:18–19) and bring blessing (Ps. 94:12), not to kill (Ps. 118:18). It shows God's greatness and power (Deut. 11:2). The climactic Old Testament word on chastisement is that the Suffering Servant has borne our chastisement, so that we do not have to suffer it (Isa. 53:5). Ultimately, chastisement shows God's love for the one chastised (Rev. 3:19). He seeks to lead us away from eternal chastisement (1 Cor. 11:32; compare Heb. 12:10).

CHEBAR (Chē′ bär) River in Babylon where Ezekiel had visions (Ezek. 1:1; 3:15; 10:15; 43:3). This is probably to be identified with the nar Kabari, a channel of the Euphrates River southeast of Babylon. It may be the modern Satt-en-nil.

CHECKER WORK Part of the decoration of the pillars of the Temple (1 Kings 7:17). The Hebrew word also denotes a lattice (2 Kings 1:2) or net (Job 18:8). With reference to the pillars of the Temple, it thus denotes a criss-crossed design.

CHEDOR-LAOMER (Chĕd ôr-lā′ ō mēr) King of Elam who joined coalition of kings against kings of Sodom and Gomorrah, leading to Abraham's involvement and victory (Gen. 14:1). His Elamite name means, "son of La'gamal," (a god). He apparently led the eastern coalition. He does not appear in the fragmentary Elamite records known today, so nothing else is known except what Genesis 14 records. See *Elam.*

CHEESE A dairy product forming a basic part of the diet. The three occurrences of cheese in English translations reflect three different Hebrew expressions. Job 10:10 refers to cheese; 1 Samuel 17:18 speaks literally of a "slice of milk," and 2 Samuel 17:29 uses a word usually interpreted as meaning, "curds of the herd."

CHELAL (Chē′ lăl) Personal name of a man with foreign wife in the post-exilic community (Ezra 10:30).

CHELLUH (Chĕl′ lŭl) Personal name of a man with a foreign wife in post-exilic community (Ezra 10:35).

CHELUB (Chē′ lŭb) *1.* A descendant of the tribe of Judah (1 Chron. 4:10), probably to be identified with Caleb, the hero of the spy narrative of Numbers 13—14. See *Caleb. 2.* Father of Ezri, overseer of workers on David's farms (1 Chron. 27:26).

CHELUBAI (Chĕ lū′ baî) Hebrew variant of Caleb, the hero of the spy narratives (Num. 13—14). See *Caleb.*

CHELUHI (Chĕl′ ūh ĭ) TEV, NRSV, NAS spelling of Chelluh. See *Chelluh.*

CHEMARIM (Chĕm′ à rĭm) KJV transliteration of Hebrew word meaning, "priests of foreign or false gods" in Zephaniah 1:4. The Hebrew term also appears in 2 Kings 23:5; Hosea 10:5.

CHEMOSH (Chē′ mŏsh) Divine name meaning, "subdue." The deity the Moabites worshiped (Num. 21:29). He was expected to provide land for Moab (Judg. 11:24). Solomon erected a sanctuary for Chemosh on a mountain east of Jerusalem (1 Kings 11:7). Josiah subsequently defiled the sanctuary (2 Kings 23:13). Jeremiah pronounced doom on Chemosh and his people (Jer. 48:7, 13,46).

CHENAANAH (Chẻ nā´ å năh) *1.* Personal name meaning, "tradeswoman." Father of the false prophet Zedekiah (1 Kings 22:11). See *Zedekiah*. *2.* A member of tribe of Benjamin (1 Chron. 7:10).

CHENANI (Chẻ nā´ nī) Personal name meaning, "one born in month of Kanunu." A Levite who led Israel in a prayer of renewal and praise (Neh. 9:4).

CHENANIAH (Chĕn å nī´ ăh) Personal name meaning, "Yahweh empowers." *1.* Chief of the Levites under David who instructed people in singing and played a leading role in bringing the ark back to Jerusalem (1 Chron. 15:22, 27). *2.* A Levite whose family had charge of business outside the Temple, including work as officials and judges (1 Chron. 26:29).

CHEPHAR-AMMONI (Chẻ´ phär-ăm´ mō nī) Place name meaning, "open village of the Ammonites." A village in the tribal territory of Benjamin (Josh. 18:24). Its location is not known.

CHEPHAR HA-AMMONAI KJV spelling, including the Hebrew definite article, "ha," for Chephar-ammoni. See *Chephar-ammoni.*

CHEPHIRAH (Chẻ phī´ răh) Place name meaning, "queen of the lions." It is located at khirbet Kefire about four miles west of Gibeon. One of the four cities of the Gibeonites which Joshua delivered from the coalition led by the king of Jerusalem (Josh. 9:17). Joshua assigned it to the tribe of Benjamin (Josh. 18:26). Some of its exiled inhabitants returned to the post-exilic village with Zerubbabel (Ezra 2:25).

CHEPHIRIM (Chĕph´ ĭ rĭm) Hebrew term for villages that NAS transliterates as place name in Nehemiah 6:2.

CHERAN (Chē´ răn) Descendant of Seir (or Edom) listed in Genesis 36:26.

CHERETHITES, CHERETHIM A people who lived south of or with the Philistines (1 Sam. 30:14). They were probably related to or paid soldiers for the Philistines. Crete may have been their original home. David used some of these soldiers as a personal bodyguard (2 Sam. 8:18). Ezekiel pronounced judgment on them (Ezek. 25:16), as did Zephaniah (Zeph. 2:5).

CHERITH (Chē´ rĭth) Place name meaning, "cutting" or "ditch." A wadi or brook east of the Jordan River, the modern wadi Qilt south of Jericho. Elijah pronounced God's judgment in the form of a two-year drought and then found God's protection at the Cherith, where he had water to drink (1 Kings 17:3). When Cherith finally went dry, he found refuge with the widow of Zarephath.

CHERUB (Chĕr´ rŭb) Man who left Tel-melah in Babylonian Exile to go to Jerusalem with Zerubbabel about 537 B.C. He could not provide a family list to prove he was an Israelite (Ezra 2:59).

CHERUB, CHERUBIM (Chĕr´ ŭ-bĭm) Class of winged angels. The Hebrew *cherub* (plural, *cherubim),* is of uncertain derivation. In the Old Testament it is the name of a class of winged angels who functioned primarily as guards (Gen. 3:24) or attendants (Ezek. 10:3–22). The only New Testament reference to cherubim is in a description of the furnishings of the holy of holies (Heb. 9:5).

Texts descriptive of the appearance and activities of cherubim reflect two contexts. One is in the visions of the presence of God attended by living creatures (cherubim and seraphim, Isa. 6:2–6; Ezek. 1:4–28; 10:3–22). The other is Temple worship and the representations of cherubim which were a part of its furnishings (Ex. 25:18–22; 1 Kings 6:23–35; 2 Chron. 3:7–14).

The most impressive of the Temple cherubim were the large sculptures (probably winged quadrupeds) in the holy of holies. If these were arranged as was common in the ancient Near East, the two cherubim would together form a throne. Their legs would be the legs of the throne, their backs the arm rests, and their wings the back of the throne. Consistent with the idea of a cherub throne are the texts which envision God dwelling between, enthroned upon, or riding upon the cherubim (1 Sam. 4:4; 2 Sam. 6:2; 22:11; 2 Kings 19:15; 1 Chron. 13:6; 28:18; Ps. 18:10; 80:1; 99:1; Isa. 37:16). Even Ezekiel's vision depicts the glory of God resting upon or between the cherubim as something of a living throne. See *Angels.*   *Michael Martin*

CHESALON (Chĕs´ å lŏn) Place name meaning, "on the hip." Village on eastern border of territory of tribe of Judah (Josh. 15:10). It is equated with Mount Jearim and is modern Kesla, about ten miles west of Jerusalem. See *Jearim.*

CHESED (Chē´ sĕd) Personal name meaning, "one of the Chaldeans." Son of Nahor, the brother of Abraham (Gen. 22:22). His name may indicate he was the original ancestor of the Chaldeans. See *Chaldea.*

CHESIL (Chē´ sĭl) Place name meaning, "foolish." A city of the tribe of Judah (Josh. 15:30). A similar list giving the boundary of Simeon in Joshua 19:4 spells the name Bethul, a reading supported for Joshua 15:30 by the Septuagint, the earliest Greek translation. First Chronicles 4:30 also reads Bethuel. Chesil is thus identical with Bethuel.

CHESTNUT KJV translation for plane tree in

Genesis 30:37. It apparently refers to the smooth-barked *Platanus orientalis.*

CHESULLOTH (Chḗ sŭl' lŏth) Place name meaning, "on the hips." A border town of the tribe of Issachar (Josh. 19:18), probably the same as the border town of Zebulon called Chisloth-tabor in Joshua 19:12. It is the modern Iksal, four miles south of Nazareth.

CHEZIB (Chē' zĭb) Place name meaning, "deceiving." Birthplace of Shelah, son of Judah and Shuah, a Canaanite (Gen. 38:5). Chezib is probably the same as Achzib. See *Achzib.*

CHICKEN A nesting, brooding bird. Both tame and wild chickens were known in Bible times, but they play an insignificant role in the Bible, appearing only in Jesus' comparison of His care for Jerusalem to the care of a mother hen for her nestlings. The Greek terms are general terms for birds and nestlings (Matt. 23:37; Luke 13:34).

CHIDON (Chī' dŏn) Personal name meaning, "crescent sword." 1 Chronicles 13:9 reads Chidon for Nacon in 2 Samuel 6:6. See *Nacon.* Chidon could be a place name in the text.

CHIEF The English translation of at least thirteen different Hebrew words designating a leader in political, military, religious, or economic affairs. *'Abir* means the powerful one and is used of the chief of Saul's shepherds (1 Sam. 21:7). *'Ayil* is one who holds official power (Ex. 15:15; 2 Kings 24:15; Ezek. 17:13; 32:21). *'Aluph* is the leader of a clan or tribe (Gen. 36:15–43; Zech. 12:5–6). *Gibbor* is the manly one or hero (1 Chron. 9:26). *Gadol* is the great one or the big one (Lev. 21:10). *Ba'al* is the lord or master (Lev. 21:4). *Kohen* is literally a priest and then a leader (2 Sam. 8:18). *Nagid* is a leader (1 Chron. 23:22; 2 Chron. 11:11; Isa. 55:4; Jer. 20:1; Ezek. 28:2). *Nitstsab* is the one in charge, the overseer or foreman (1 Kings 9:23). *Menatstseach* is the eminent one or supervisor and is used in the titles of many Psalms (Ps. 4:1), apparently referring to the choir director. *Nasi'* is a sheikh or tribal chief (Num. 25:18; Josh. 22:14). *Pinnah* is the corner or cornerstone (Judg. 20:2; 1 Sam. 14:38; Zech. 10:4). *'Attud* is a ram or he-goat and is used metaphorically for a chief or leader (Isa. 14:9; Zech. 10:3). *Qatsin* is the last one, the one who has to decide and thus the leader (Josh. 10:24; Judg. 11:6; Prov. 6:7; Isa. 1:10; Mic. 3:1). *Ro'sh* is the head (Num. 25:4; 2 Sam. 23:8; 2 Sam. 25:18; Job 29:25 and often in Chronicles, Ezra, Nehemiah). *Ri'shon* is number one, the first (Dan. 10:13). *Re'shith* is the first or beginning one (Dan. 11:41). *Sar* is one with dominion or rule, thus an official or ruler (Gen. 40:2; 1 Sam. 17:18; 1 Kings 4:2; 5:16; 1 Chron. 24:5; Dan 10:20). *Rab*

means numerous or great and is used in several compound words to represent the chief or greatest one (2 Kings 18:17; Jer. 39:13; Dan. 5:11).

In the New Testament the Greek word *arche* means beginning or chief and is used in several compound words to represent the chief priest or ruler (Matt. 2:4; 16:21; Luke 11:15; 19:2; John 12:42; Acts 18:8; 19:31; 1 Pet. 5:4). *Hegeomai* means to lead to command with official authority (Luke 22:26; Acts 14:12). *Protos* means first or foremost (Matt. 20:27; Luke 19:47; Acts 13:50; 16:12; 25:2; 28:7). *Chiliarchos* is the commander of a military unit supposed to have 1,000 members (Acts 21:31; 25:23; Rev. 6:15).

CHIEF PRIEST See *Aaron; Priests; Levites.*

CHILD See *Family.*

CHILDREN (SONS) OF GOD Although the phrase refers at times to heavenly beings (Gen. 6:1–4; Job 1:6; 2:1; 38:7; Ps. 29:1; 89:6), it usually denotes those people who acknowledge God as the source and goal of their life and who enter into a relationship of trust and love with God. All people are the creation of God, and as such all people bear the image of God and should therefore be treated with the greatest respect and dignity; but not all people can be called the children of God in the sense in which the phrase is used in the Bible. All people are, however, potential children of God.

Jesus was, is, and always shall be the preeminent Child of God. The parent/child relationship with God was completely realized only by Jesus (Matt. 11:27; John 3:35; 13:3). Jesus had an unbroken knowledge of and communion with God (John 17:20–26; see Matt. 3:17; 17:5). For Jesus, being God's Son meant knowing what God willed and doing what God willed (John 5:19,30; 8:29; 15:10; 17:4; Phil. 2:8; Heb. 5:8). The parent/child relationship (with the obedience implied in that relationship) so dominated the life and thought of Jesus that being God's Son was the defining characteristic of Jesus' being. Jesus was God's *only* begotten or unique Son (John 1:14,18; 3:16,18; 1 John 4:9).

Of course, God intended for all people to be His children. God wanted all people to have an unbroken knowledge of and communion with Him. God wanted all people to know and do His will. God wanted the parent/child relationship to be the dominating characteristic of every life. But people in every place and in every time have rejected God as the source and goal of their lives and have refused to enter into a relationship of complete trust and love with God (Rom. 3:23). People who continue to live in this state of rebellion against God or sin have lost the actuality of being God's children.

All people ("whosoever," John 3:15) retain the

potentiality of becoming children of God. This is so because God, out of His great love, gave His only Son for the salvation of the world (John 3:16). Jesus, in turn, gave to all who would receive Him the power to become children of God (John 1:12).   *Phil Logan*

CHILDREN OF THE EAST See *Kadmonites.*

CHILEAB (Chĭl' ė ăb) Personal name meaning, "everything of the Father." David's second son (2 Sam. 3:3) born to Abigail. The name appears as Daniel in 1 Chronicles 3:1. Whatever his exact name, David's second son disappeared from history here and did not figure in the later disputes over who would succeed David as king. His name could be associated with the clan of Caleb.

CHILION (Chĭl' ĭ-ŏn) Personal name meaning, "sickly." One of the two sons of Elimelech and Naomi (Ruth 1:2). With his parents, he emigrated to Moab, where he married a Moabite woman named Orpah. Afterwards, he died in Moab. See *Ruth.*

CHILMAD (Chĭl' măd) Place name meaning, "marketplace." A trading partner of Tyre according to Hebrew text of Ezekiel 27:23, but many Bible students think copyists inadvertently changed the text from "all of media" or a similar reading. Otherwise, Chilmad is identical with Kulmadara, a city in the Syrian Kingdom of Unqi. Its location may be modern tell Jindaris.

CHIMHAM (Chĭm' hăm) Personal name meaning, "paleface." *1.* Apparently the son of Barzillai, the patron of David when he fled to Mahanaim east of the Jordan before Absalom (2 Sam. 19:37). Chimham returned with David to Jerusalem when Barzillai refused to leave his home. *2.* A village near Bethlehem. Johanan gathered his people there after the assassination of Gedaliah. From there they escaped to Egypt (Jer. 41:17).

CHINNERETH (Chĭn' nė rěth) Place name meaning, "harp-shaped." *1.* The sea or lake otherwise called the Sea of Galilee, Lake of Gennesaret, or Sea of Tiberias. It formed the eastern border of Canaan, the Promised Land (Num. 34:11), marking the western boundary of the tribe of Gad (Josh. 13:27). *2.* A city on the western edge of the Sea of Chinnereth, also called Chinneroth (Josh. 11:2), though this could be a reference to the Sea. The city belonged to the tribe of Naphtali (Josh. 19:35). The city apparently gave its name to the Sea and to the surrounding region with its several bays, thus explaining the plural form in 1 Kings 15:20, which tells of Ben-hadad of Syria defeating the area in answer to the request of King Asa of Judah. Thothmes III of Egypt also claimed to have conquered the city about 1475 B.C. The city is the modern tell al-Oreimeh.

CHINNEROTH (Chĭn' nė rōth) Hebrew plural form of Chinnereth. See *Chinnereth.*

CHIOS (Chī' ŏs) Island with city of same name. Paul stopped here while returning from third missionary journey (Acts 20:15). The Greek poet Homer supposedly came from Chios. It lies in the Aegean Sea five miles off the coast of Asia Minor. It is now called Scio.

CHISEL The English term NIV uses to translate several Hebrew expressions for working with wood and stone. The verb *pasal* means to hew out or dress stone (Ex. 34:1; Deut. 10:1; 1 Kings 5:18; Hab. 2:18). *Garzen* is an ax used in the stone quarries or forests (Deut. 19:5; 1 Kings 6:7). *Hoqqi* is a verbal noun meaning cutting out or engraving (Isa. 22:16; 30:8). Isaiah employs a word used nowhere else and meaning a carpenter's tool for forming an idol. KJV, NAS, NRSV read "planes." *Ma'atsad* is apparently a small, curved cutting tool, perhaps an adze (Isa. 44:12; Jer. 10:3). KJV reads "tongs" in Isaiah 44:12.

CHISLEU (Chĭs' lēū) or **CHISLEV** The name of the ninth month of the Jewish calendar after the Exile, apparently borrowed from the Babylonian name Kisliwu. See Nehemiah 1:1; Zechariah 7:1.

CHISLON (Chĭs' lŏn) Personal name meaning, "clumsy." Father of Elidad, who represented the tribe of Benjamin on the commission that divided the land for Israel (Num. 34:21).

CHISLOTH-TABOR (Chĭs' lōth-tā' bôr) See *Chesulloth.*

CHITLISH (Chĭt' lĭsh) Place name of foreign origin. It was a city of the tribe of Judah near Lachish (Josh. 15:40). KJV reads Kithlish; NIV, Kitlish.

CHITTIM See *Kittim.*

CHIUN (Chī' ŭn) KJV spelling of divine name meaning, "the constant, unchanging one" (Amos 5:26). NRSV reads "Kaiwan;" NAS, "Kiyyun;" NIV, "pedestal." The Hebrew word *kiyun* appears to represent an intentional change by the Hebrew scribes, inserting the vowels of *siqquts,* "abomination," for an original reading, *Kaiwan,* the name of a Babylonian God of the stars equivalent to the Greek god Saturn. Amos condemned the people of Israel for priding in their sophisticated worship of foreign gods. He called them back to the simple worship of the wilderness. See *Sikkuth.*

CHLOE (Chlō' ē) Personal name meaning, "verdant." A woman whose household members informed Paul of dissension within the church at Corinth (1 Cor. 1:11). Where she lived and how her people learned of the situation in Corinth are not known.

CHOINIX is a dry measure used to measure grain and was equivalent to about a quart, or a daily ration for one person (Rev. 6:6). See *Weights and Measures.*

CHORASHAN (Chôr ăsh′ ăn) See *Bor-ashan.*

CHORAZIN (Chō·rā′ zĭn) One of the cities Jesus censured because of the unbelief of its inhabitants (Matt. 11:21). It was located in Galilee. It has been identified with modern khirbet Kerazeh,

Excavations at the site of Chorazin showing the synagogue area.

ruins located about two miles north of the site of Capernaum. Chorazin is mentioned in the Talmud as a place famous for its wheat. In the time of Jesus it must have been an important place, but by the second half of the third century A.D. it had ceased to be inhabited.

CHOSEN PEOPLE Israel as the elect of God. See *Election.*

CHOZEBA (Chō zē′ bà) KJV spelling of Cozeba. See *Cozeba.*

CHRIST, CHRISTOLOGY "Christ" is the English rendering of the Greek *Christos,* meaning "anointed." See *Messiah* which translates the corresponding Hebrew term *mashiach,* the anointed one.

Old Testament and Jewish Background See *Messiah.*

Jesus as the Christ in the Gospels The first three Gospels give less prominence to the title "Christ" (the Messiah) than we might have expected. Jesus never openly paraded His Messiahship, nor did He overtly claim to be the Messiah in the sense of announcing an aspiration to be Israel's warrior king. Yet He did claim to be the One in whom the kingdom of God was present (Mark 1:14,15; Luke 11:20). His parables enunciated both the arrival

of the kingdom and its character, setting a pattern for living for those who would enter God's realm as His children (Matt. 13; Mark 4). His mighty acts in healing the sick and casting out demons were demonstrations of the power and presence of God at work in His ministry (Luke 5:17). His teaching on prayer was based on the awareness He had of God as His Father in an intimate sense, calling him "Abba," my dear Father, which is a nursery word used of an earthly parent by Jewish children (Mark 14:36; Luke 10:21–22; 11:2). See *Abba.* His entire mission was seen as heralding the coming of the divine kingdom which, He believed, was closely tied in with His final journey to Jerusalem (Luke 9:51; 13:32–35) and His sacrifice there on the cross (Mark 8:31–32; 9:31; 10:32–34). Only in this way, Jesus knew, could God's kingdom come and God's will be done by His anointed Servant and Son (Luke 4:16–19).

For this reason—that God's redemption of Israel would take place only by the suffering of the Messiah—Jesus took a reserved and critical attitude to the title "Christ." When Peter confessed "Thou art the Christ" (Mark 8:29), Jesus' response was guarded: not denying it, but distancing Himself from the political and social connotations which a nationalist Judaism had accepted as commonplace in the expected Deliverer. (See Mark 10:35–45; Luke 24:19–21; Acts 1:6 for the evidence that even the disciples entertained such a hope.) At the trial Jesus was interrogated on this point. The balance of the evidence points in the direction that He still maintained a reserve (Matt. 26:63,64; Luke 22:67,68), with the same reluctance to be identified with a worldly messiah-king evident, too, in the interview with Pilate (Mark 15:2: "Art thou the King of the Jews?" asked Pilate. "Thou sayest it," Jesus replied; but the answer is probably noncommittal meaning, "It is your word, not mine"). At all events, Jesus was sentenced to death on the trumped-up charge of being a messianic claimant and a rival to the emperor in Rome (Mark 15:26,32). The Gospels make it clear that there was no direct and supportable evidence that Jesus so claimed to be such a figure. Instead, He consistently viewed His life and mission as fulfilling the role of the "Son of man" (a title drawn from Dan. 7:13,14 where it stands for God's Representative on earth who suffers out of loyalty to the truth and is at length rewarded by being promoted to share the throne of God) and God's chosen Servant, a pattern for ministry which Jesus evidently found in Isaiah's servant songs (Isa. 42:1–4; 49:5–7; 52:13—53:12). If this is the correct background to Jesus' self-awareness, both of His relationship to God and to His mission, it helps to explain how He looked confidently beyond defeat and death to His vindication by God in the resurrection. Whatever destiny of suffering and rejection by His people awaited Him, He saw, like Isaiah's servant, that God would bring Him out of death to newness of life. Also, the significance Jesus attached to His death as an atoning sacrifice in such sayings as Mark 10:45; 14:24 requires some such background as the vicarious sacrifice of the Suffering Servant in Isaiah 53:5,10 to give it coherent meaning.

In the apostolic church this understanding of Jesus' life and ministry was given clearer definition (Acts 2:22–36; 8:26–40), and in the hands of the New Testament theologians such as Paul (Rom. 3:24–26) and the author of Hebrews (ch. 8—10) the conviction regarding the person, work, and glory of Jesus Christ is clearly articulated. At this point we have entered the realm of Christology, the teaching about the person of Jesus Christ.

Christology: Methods Any approach to Christology (that is, the teaching on Christ's person as both a figure of history and the object of the church's worship) must face the issue of methodology. Specifically, this means that a choice has to be considered whether the interpreter will begin with creedal formulations that confess that Jesus Christ is "true God" and "true man," and then work backward to the way this teaching arose in the early church and the New Testament. This method is called seeking Christology "from above." The alternative approach, called by modern scholars a Christology "from below," begins with the factual data of the historical and theological records of the New Testament Scriptures, and from there it proceeds to trace the way the church's understanding of the Lord developed until the creeds were framed. Another way of putting this choice—which we shall stress is not so momentous as it appears, since both methods add up to the same conclusion—is to ask whether New Testament Christology is ontological (that is, concerned with Christ's transcendent role in relation to God, the world, and the church) or primarily functional. The latter term means that the New Testament writers were concerned mainly to relate the person of Jesus Christ to His achievement as Savior and Lord and to set this in the context of His earthly ministry.

The two methods do seem to proceed from different starting points. The first one asks, "Who is Christ and how is He related to God?" The second raises the questions, "What did Jesus do in His human life, and how did it come about that the church accorded Him titles of divinity?" At a practical level we can see that the choice is one which can be put in personal terms. Is Jesus rightly called the Son of God because He saves me? This is the standpoint of functional Christology. Or is it true that He saves me because He is the Son of God? That is the language of ontological Christology. Yet the two approaches reach the same goal in the end, we believe. As methods, they are different. In what follows we adopt the approach of "Christology from below" on the

ground that this method more adequately respects the way the New Testament teaching has come to us and so can be seen in the pages of the New Testament. We do not deny that there are ontological overtones, in such places as John 1:1–18; Philippians 2:6–11; and Hebrews 1:1–4. They are implicit rather than explicit. One of the exciting discoveries in recent scholarship has been to see how even the indirect evidence of the Gospels and Epistles witnesses to the truth enshrined in the creeds, and provides the "raw materials" out of which the later church built its confession, "Thou art the King of glory, O Christ. Thou art the everlasting Son of the Father" (The *Te Deum* of the fifth century liturgy).

The Course of New Testament Christology

The early believers in Jerusalem were Jews who had come to faith in Jesus as Messiah and risen Lord (Acts 2:32–36). Their appreciation of who Jesus was took its point of departure from the conviction that, with His resurrection and exaltation, the new age of God's triumph, described in the Old Testament and the intertestamental writings, had indeed dawned, and the Old Testament Scriptures (notably Ps. 110:1) had been fulfilled. The cross had also to be explained, since Jesus' death at the hands of the of the Roman political powers stood in direct and obvious contradiction to all that pious Jews believed about the Messiah, God's expected Deliverer of His people and a glorious Figure. The crux is seen in Deuteronomy 21:23 which prescribed that anyone hanging on a tree died under God's curse (the verse is quoted in Gal. 3:13) A rationale was found in two ways: it came by asserting (1) that Jesus' rejection was already foreseen in the Old Testament, notably Psalm 118:22; Isaiah 53, and that His implicit claims to be the Messenger and embodiment of God's kingdom revealed only human unbelief; and (2) that at the resurrection God had reversed this verdict, vindicated His Son, and installed Him in the place of honor and power. The first Christological statement therefore was based on the fact of two stages in Jesus' existence: He was the Son of David in His human descent, and since the resurrection He is known as the Son of God with power and alive in the Spirit (Rom. 1:3,4). The implicit messianic claims of His earthly life were made overt since His exaltation, and the hiddenness of His true being was revealed in glory. The proof of the new age He inaugurated was seen in the coming of the Holy Spirit (Acts 2:16–21, quoting Joel 2:28).

At a practical level this way of seeing Jesus' life and resurrection gave these believers a personal relationship with Jesus as a present reality. He did not appear as a simple figure of the past, however recent. Hence the first Christian prayer of which we have any record is "Maranatha" (meaning "our Lord, come") addressed to the risen Lord and placing Him on a par with Yahweh, Israel's covenant God (1 Cor. 16:22; Rom. 10:9–13; compare Acts 7:55, 56,59) as worthy of worship.

Further meditation on Old Testament Scripture gave a clue to Jesus' secret identity and explained His use of the mysterious title "Son of man." Drawn from Daniel 7:13–18, the Son of man title is one of authority and dignity, two ideas that the resurrection of Jesus confirmed (Acts 7:56). The church preserved this teaching on the Son of man from Jesus' lips and set it in the framework of His earthly life to accomplish several objectives: (1) to show how Jesus was misunderstood and rejected as a messianic pretender, since "Son of man" spoke of God's kingdom and made Him a sharer of the divine throne; (2) to indicate how Jesus brought in a new age in which God's revelation was not tied to the law of Moses but was universalized for all people. The "Son of man" in Daniel 7:22, 27 is the head of a worldwide kingdom, far outstripping the narrow confines of Jewish hopes; and (3) to find a missionary impulse which led these believers, notably under the leadership of Stephen and his followers, to reach out to non-Jews (Acts 7:59—8:1; 11:19–21; 13:1–3).

Such a mission brought the church into the world of Greek religion in the setting of Greco-Roman society. The most relevant title in this religious milieu was "Lord," a title used of gods and goddesses in the mystery religions which were partly oriental, partly Greco-Roman. More significantly, "Lord" was an appellation of honor and divinity that came to be associated with emperor worship and applied to the Roman Caesar. Both areas proved fertile ground for the application to Jesus of the commonest New Testament Christological title, Lord. It was already in use as the name of Yahweh in the Greek Bible of the Old Testament, and it now was applied to the exalted Christ. It became useful as establishing a meeting point between Christians and pagans who were familiar with the deities of their religious world (1 Cor. 8:5,6). Later, the term "Lord" became the touchstone for marking off Christian allegiance to Jesus when the Roman authorities required that homage should be paid to the emperor as divine as in the setting of the Book of Revelation in the 90's A.D., when the Emperor Domitian proclaimed himself "lord and god." (See Rev. 17:14.)

The final step in New Testament Christology was taken in the churches whose life we see reflected in the Letter to the Hebrews and the Johannine writings. The author of Hebrews sets out to prove the finality of Christ's revelation as Son of God (1:1–4) and great "high priest" (5:5; 7:1—9:28). John's writings are clearest in their ascription to Jesus of the names Logos (Word) and (only) God. (See John 1:1,14,18; 20:28, along with the claims of Jesus registered in the affirmations of "I AM," recalling Exodus 3:14; Isaiah 45:5; 46:9; compare John 8:24; 10:30,33.) John's indebtedness is evidently to the Old Testa-

ment and intertestamental or early Jewish wisdom teaching where "wisdom" and "word" (often linked with the Mosaic law) are treated as mediators in God's act of creating the world (Prov. 8) and as a preexistent revelation of God (in the early Jewish book The Wisdom of Solomon, written in the second century B.C.). John boldly claimed both roles for Jesus of Nazareth (John 1:3,18; 14:6,9). He set the earthly life of Jesus against the backdrop of His eternal Being as one with the Father and the visible glory of the unseen God, thus superseding the law of Moses (John 1:17; compare 5:46,47) and the claims of the Roman emperor (John 20:28: "My Lord and my God").

Yet even these most explicit statements, along with other teachings in Paul (Phil. 2:6; Col. 1:15; Titus 2:13; possibly Rom. 9:5) and Hebrews (Heb. 1:1–4) never compromised the belief in the unity of God, an inheritance the Christians took from their Jewish ancestry as a cardinal element of Old Testament monotheism (belief in one God in a world of many gods). Nor did they lend countenance to the view that Jesus was a rival deity in competition with His Father (John 14:28; 1 Cor. 11:3; Phil. 2:9–11). God the Father is always regarded as the Fount of deity; Jesus is His Son in a unique way, but He is never confounded with Him. The worship of the church is properly directed to God who has revealed Himself once-for-all and uniquely in the Son whom He loves (Col. 1:13), and who mirrors the perfect expression of the divine nature (2 Cor. 4:4–6). How to relate the two sides to Jesus' person—the human and the divine—is not explained in the New Testament; and the writers there bequeath a rich legacy to the later church which formed the substance of the Christological debates leading to the Council of Chalcedon in A.D. 451. There it was decreed and expressed that Christ's two natures are united in one Person, and this belief has remained the centralist position of the church ever since. See Messiah; Son of God; Lord.

Ralph P. Martin

CHRISTIAN (Chrĭs′ tian) The Greek *Christianos* originally applied to the slaves belonging to a great household. It came to denote the adherents of an individual or party. A Christian is an adherent of Christ; one committed to Christ; a follower of Christ. The word is used three times in the New Testament. *1.* Believers "were called Christians first in Antioch" because their behavior, activity, and speech were like Christ (Acts 11:26). *2.* Agrippa responded to Paul's witness, "Almost thou persuade me to be a Christian" (Acts 26:28). He spoke of becoming an adherent of Christ. *3.* Peter stated that believers who "suffer as a Christian" are to do so for the glory of God (1 Pet. 4:16). A Christian is one who becomes an adherent of Christ, whose daily life and behavior facing adversity is like Christ. *Darrell W. Robinson*

CHRISTIAN FESTIVALS See *Church Year.*

CHRISTMAS Of the major Christian festivals, Christmas is the most recent in origin. The name, a contraction of the term "Christ's mass," did not come into use until the Middle Ages. In the early centuries, Christians were much more likely to celebrate the day of a person's death than the person's birthday. Very early in its history the church had an annual observance of the death of Christ and also honored many of the early martyrs on the day of their death. Before the fourth century, churches in the East—Egypt, Asia Minor, and Antioch—observed Epiphany, the manifestation of God to the world, celebrating Christ's baptism, His birth, and the visit of the Magi.

In the early part of the fourth century, Christians in Rome began to celebrate the birth of Christ. The practice spread widely and rapidly, so that most parts of the Christian world observed the new festival by the end of the century. In the fourth century, the controversy over the nature of Christ, whether He was truly God or a created being, led to an increased emphasis on the doctrine of the incarnation, the affirmation that "the Word was made flesh" (John 1:14). It is likely that the urgency to proclaim the incarnation was an important factor in the spread of the celebration of Christmas.

No evidence remains about the exact date of the birth of Christ. The December 25 date was chosen as much for practical reasons as for theological ones. Throughout the Roman Empire, various festivals were held in conjunction with the winter solstice. In Rome, the Feast of the Unconquerable Sun celebrated the beginning of the return of the sun. When Christianity became the religion of the Empire, the church either had to suppress the festivals or transform them. The winter solstice seemed an appropriate time to celebrate Christ's birth. Thus, the festival of the sun became a festival of the Son, the Light of the world. See *Church Year.*   *Fred A. Grissom*

CHRONICLES, BOOKS OF (Chrŏ′ nĭ clēs)
Nature and Focus of Chronicles 1 and 2 Chronicles are the first and second books of a four-book series that includes Ezra and Nehemiah. These four books provide a scribal (priestly) history of Israel from the time of Adam (1 Chron. 1:1) to the rebuilding of the house of God and the walls of Jerusalem and the restoration of the people in the worship of God according to the law of Moses (Neh. 13:31).

The special focus of these books is on the fortunes of God's house in Jerusalem upon which God has set His name forever (2 Chron. 7:16). David found Israel to be like scattered sheep. As God's chosen shepherd and line through whom God would build His house, David sought to order the life of Israel around the worship of God. Under God

he made the city of Jerusalem his capital (1 Chron. 11:4–9), transferred the ark of God to the city (1 Chron. 16:1), and began to prepare for the building of the Temple (1 Chron. 22:1–2). Solomon, his son, built the Temple (2 Chron. 2:1), and Zerubbabel, his son of succeeding generations, rebuilt the Temple (Ezra 3:8). The intervening sons of David, who served as kings of Judah, were judged by whether or not they were faithful to God and to His house. Compare, for example, the reign of wicked King Ahaz with that of good King Hezekiah (2 Chron. 28:1–4, 29:1–11).

Significance of the Title The two books now called 1 and 2 Chronicles were originally one book. The division into two books was first made after 300 B.C. by the Jewish elders who translated the Hebrew Old Testament into Greek, producing the Septuagint. The reason for their making Chronicles into two books is quite simple. The Hebrew manuscript, which usually contained no vowels, could be written on one large roll. The Greek translation with its vowels, however, required nearly twice as much space. The division seems quite appropriate with 1 Chronicles concluding the reign of David, and 2 Chronicles beginning the reign of Solomon.

The English title "Chronicles" is derived from the Latin *Chronicon,* which was applied to these writings by Jerome. He described these materials as "a chronicle of the whole of sacred history." The Septuagint (Greek) title is *Paraleipomena,* meaning "omitted things." That title reflects their understanding of Chronicles to be a supplement to the materials found in Samuel and Kings.

Closest to the heart is the Hebrew title. It means "the acts or deeds of the day or times." However, the books do more than recount the various acts of the people of that day. Chronicles focuses on the most important deeds of that time or indeed of any time—building the house of God. God's house was, of course, the Temple in Jerusalem. But God's house transcends that building. David's dwelling "in the house of the Lord for ever" (Ps. 23:6) means dwelling forever with God and His people in the abode of God. In the ultimate sense we would equate God's house with His kingdom. Accordingly, the writer(s) of Chronicles reminds us that the most important of all deeds are those by which God's kingdom is built in the hearts of people.

Significance of Chronicles' Place in the Canon Chronicles, Ezra, and Nehemiah stand among the *Hagiographa,* meaning "holy writings," which is the third division of the Old Testament. The order of English versions with Chronicles, Ezra, and Nehemiah after Samuels and Kings goes back to the Septuagint.

The Hebrew Bible places Chronicles as the last book in the Old Testament after even Ezra and Nehemiah. Chronicles doubtless occupied this position in the time of Christ, since he cited Zechariah as the last named prophet who suffered a violent death (2 Chron. 24:20–22; Matt. 23:35; Luke 11:51).

Three explanations are given as to why the Hebrews concluded the Old Testament with Chronicles. One is the view that Chronicles was the last book to be accepted in the Old Testament canon. The second is that the author(s) first wrote Ezra-Nehemiah and then Chronicles. The third and most likely is to have the Old Testament conclude with God's providential control of history to build (rebuild) His house in Jerusalem. The final admonition of the Hebrew Old Testament then is for God's people to go up to Jerusalem to build God's house (2 Chron. 36:23). Moreover, God's final promise is to bless with His presence those who indeed go up to build (2 Chron. 36:23).

Authorship, Date, and Sources We do not know for sure who wrote Chronicles. As has been noted, tradition names Ezra the "ready scribe," a priest descended from Zadok and Phinehas (Ezra 7:1–6), as author of Chronicles, Ezra, and Nehemiah. This tradition cannot be proved, but there is no valid objection to it. If he did not, we do not know who did. The position of these books in the *Hagiographa* indicates that the author was not a prophet. Moreover, the emphasis upon the priests and Levites suggests the author to be someone like Ezra who was one of them. Also, in the seventh year of his reign, Artaxerxes Longimanus, the Persian king from 465 to 425 B.C., sent Ezra to Jerusalem to order the civil and religious life of the Jews according to the law of Moses (Ezra 7:8,14). Accordingly, Ezra was the leader of the spiritual restoration effort these books were written to accomplish. An editor(s) could account for any material extending beyond the time of Ezra.

The use of sources by the author(s) is obvious. Much of the material came from the biblical Books of Samuel and Kings. However, other sources are evident such as official chronicles (1 Chron. 27:24), the writings of the prophets (1 Chron. 29:29), and commentaries on the events of that day (2 Chron. 24:27). The genealogies reflect the carefully kept records of the Levites. Sources for the Temple materials include "the works of Asaph and David" (2 Chron. 29:30) and the God-given "pattern" (1 Chron. 28:19).

Purposes and Enduring Value The principal purpose of 1 and 2 Chronicles is to show God's control of history to fulfill His desire to dwell among His people in a perfect relationship of holiness in which God is God and the redeemed are His people. God first shared His desire with Moses (Ex. 25:8). The tabernacle and the Temple symbolize that desire. God is fulfilling His desire through the Lord Jesus Christ—the Son of David. When Christ shall have completed His redemptive work, "the tabernacle of God" will be "with men, and he will dwell with them, and they shall

be his people, and God himself shall be with them, and be their God" (Rev. 21:3). Chronicles shows how God worked from the time of Adam but particularly in the times of David through Ezra and Nehemiah to accomplish His desire to dwell in holiness with His people.

A second purpose is to show God's choice of a person and a people to build His house. The person is the Son of David—the Messiah. Solomon built the temple in Jerusalem, but the Son who is building and shall build to completion God's true house and the Son whose reign God will establish forever is the Lord Jesus Christ (1 Chron. 17:12; Luke 1:31–33; Acts 15:14–16). The people are those of faith whose lineage goes back to Adam through Seth to Shem to Abraham (1 Chron. 1:1,17,28) to whom God made the promise of the seed (the Christ) through whom He would bless all nations (Gen. 12:1–4; 15:4–6; 17:7; 22:16–18; Gal. 3:16). His people are those of Israel and indeed of all nations who will put their trust in Him.

A third purpose is to show that God who dwells in holiness must be approached according to the law that God gave to Moses. David, in seeking to unite his people around the presence of God, learned that God must be sought in the proper way (1 Chron. 15:13). Basic is the necessity to come to God by way of the altar of sacrifice as ministered by the Levitical priesthood. God in His merciful forgiveness of David revealed the place of the altar of sacrifice to be in Jerusalem at the threshingfloor of Ornan (1 Chron. 21:18—22:1. There David erected the altar and built the Temple according to God's directions. But most importantly, there the Son of God, our great High Priest, sacrificed Himself on the cross in our stead to bring His people into the glorious presence of God (Heb. 2:17; 5:1–10).

A fourth purpose of Chronicles is to encourage God's people to work together with God and one another to build God's house. That is the reason the author(s) shared with his people the challenge of God through King Cyrus to go up to Jerusalem to build God's house. That is the reason he shared with them God's promise to be with them to bless as they obediently went up to build. (See 2 Chron. 36:23.) That is the reason he shared with them the history of the fortunes of God's house and God's people. He demonstrated thereby God's blessing upon those who built and otherwise honored God's house, but God's judgment upon those who neglected, thwarted the building of, or desecrated the house of God. As such, 1 and 2 Chronicles stands as a challenge to God's people of every generation to devote themselves with all their heart to building God's house. Accordingly, "who is there among you of all his [God's] people? The Lord his God, be with him, and let him go up" (2 Chron. 36:23).

1 and 2 Chronicles: Blessings for Building

God's House
I. Israel's People of Faith (1:1—9:44)
  A. Godly line of Adam (1:1–4)
  B. Sons of Noah focusing on Shem (1:5–27)
  C. Sons of Abraham focusing on Isaac (1:28–34a)
  D. Sons of Isaac focusing on Israel (1:34b–54)
  E. Sons of Israel focusing on Judah and Levi (2:1–9:44)
II. David's Learning Obedience (10:1—22:1)
  A. God's replacing rebellious Saul with David (10:1–14)
  B. God's bringing David to power (11:1–12:40)
  C. David's seeking to build around God's presence: David's son to build God's house (13:1—17:27)
  D. David's marring his victories by his sin (18:1—21:17)
  E. God's revelation in mercy of the site of the Temple and the place of the altar of sacrifice (21:18—22:1)
III. David's Preparing to Build God's House (22:2—29:30)
  A. Preparing workmen and materials (22:2–5)
  B. Preparing Solomon to build (22:6–16)
  C. Charging the princes to help Solomon (22:17–19)
  D. Making Solomon king (23:1)
  E. Ordering the priests and Levites and princes for service (23:2—27:34)
  F. Charging Solomon and the people (28:1–21)
  G. Inspiring gifts to build (29:1–9)
  H. Worshiping God and enthroning Solomon (29:10–25)
  I. Summarizing David's reign (29:26–30)
IV. Solomon's Building God's House (2 Chron. 1:1—9:31)
  A. God's blessing of Solomon to build (1:1—17)
  B. Construction and consecration (2:1—7:22)
  C. Solomon's other achievements (8:1–18)
  D. Solomon's wisdom and wealth and fame (9:1–28)
  E. Concluding Solomon's reign (9:29–31)
V. God's Judging Judah's Kings by Their Faithfulness to His House (10:1—36:21)
  A. The wicked reign of Rehoboam (10:1–12:16)
  B. The wicked reign of Abijah (13:1–22)
  C. The sin-marred reign of good King Asa (14:1—16:14)
  D. The godly reign of Jehoshaphat (17:1–21:1)
  E. The wicked reign of Jehoram (21:2–20)
  F. The wicked reign of Ahaziah (22:1–9)
  G. The wicked reign of Athaliah (22:10–23:21)
  H. The good reign of Joash (24:1–27)
  I. Imperfect devotion of Amaziah (25:1–28)
  J. Uzziah's violation of the priestly office (26:1–23)
  K. Good but imperfect reign of Jotham (27:1–9)
  L. Wicked reign of Ahaz (28:1–27)
  M. Unqualified good reign of Hezekiah (29:1—32:33)
  N. Conversion of wicked King Manasseh (33:1–20)
  O. Wicked reign of Amon (33:21–25)
  P. Unqualified good reign of Josiah (34:1—35:27)
  Q. Wicked reigns of Jehoahaz and Jehoiakim: beginning of Exile (36:1–8)
  R. Wicked reigns of Jehoiachin and Zedekiah: final stage of Exile (36:9–21)
VI. Providential Decree to Rebuild God's House (36:22–23)
  A. Date and origin of decree (v. 22a)
  B. Purpose of decree (v. 22b)
  C. Motivating force of decree (v. 23)
  D. Substance of decree (v. 23)

John H. Traylor Jr.

CHRONICLES OF KINGS OF ISRAEL AND OF JUDAH Sources of information to which the writer of 1 and 2 Kings referred readers for more data concerning the various kings about whom he wrote. (See 1 Kings 14:19.) These are not the biblical books 1 and 2 Chronicles. They probably were official court records compiled for the use of each of the kings. Such records apparently were available to the author of Kings writing after the destruction of Jerusalem, but they are not available today. See *Kings.*

CHRONOLOGY OF THE BIBLICAL PERIOD When speaking of chronology, one must differentiate between relative and absolute chronology. Absolute chronology is tied to fixed dates—events which are known to have occurred on a specific date (i.e. John F. Kennedy was assassinated on November 22, 1963). Relative chronology places events in their chronological order but without a fixed date (i.e., Jesus was baptized, then tempted, then began His public ministry). Most of the biblical events are dated relatively rather than absolutely. For this reason many chronological charts have differences in specific dates B.C. or A.D., but generally agree on the relative order of most events.

The Old Testament Period The Patriarchal period is usually dated in the Middle Bronze Age between about 1800 and 1600 B.C. Recent finds at Ebla have indicated a high degree of civilization in Syria-Palestine at least 500 years earlier. It is generally assumed that the Hebrews migrated to

Egypt during the Hyksos period about (1700 to 1500 B.C.) when Semitic people ruled Egypt. The Exodus is usually associated with the reign of Ramsees II shortly after 1290 B.C. Following the wilderness-wandering period of forty years, the conquest of Canaan began about 1250 B.C. Pharaoh Merneptah (1224–1214 B.C.) mounted a campaign against Canaan in the fifth year of his reign (about 1220). In his record of that campaign, he records that, among others, Israel was utterly destroyed. Thus by that date, the people Israel were a recognized group in Canaan.

The period of the Judges lasted from shortly after the conquest until ca. 1025 B.C., when Saul was made king. The length of his reign is uncertain, 1 Samuel 13:1 reads, "Son of a year was Saul in his ruling, and two years he ruled over Israel." Acts 13:21 says he ruled 40 years. Compare several translations. It is often put at about 20 years. The forty-year reigns of David and Solomon would then have lasted to about 924 B.C. One major event during the reign of Solomon was the building of the Temple in Jerusalem, beginning in the fourth year in his reign (1 Kings 6:1) and completed in the eleventh year of his reign (1 Kings 6:38). The divided monarchy of Israel and Judah began with the ascension of Rehoboam following Solomon's death, and lasted until the fall of Samaria in 722 B.C. The destruction of Jerusalem in 586 B.C. ended Judah's existence as a monarchy. This period of the monarchy is also the period of the pre-exilic prophets (such as Amos, Hosea, Isaiah, Jeremiah). 1 and 2 Kings gives many synchronisms between the kings of Judah and Israel, following this pattern; "In the ——— year of ——— —, son of ———, king of Judah, ——— began to reign over Israel in Samaria." (See 1 Kings 22:51; 2 Kings 3:1.) Even with these synchronisms, some difficulty remains in establishing dates and precise parallels because the kings of Judah and Israel figured their reigns differently during a portion of this time. The kings of Judah figured their reign from their first full year as king. A part of a year would be designated as the former king's last year of rule. In Israel, a part year was designated as the previous king's last year and the new king's first year. Therefore, the length of reign for a king of Israel was counted as one year longer than a similar reign for a king of Judah.

The last days of the kingdom of Judah involve the kings of Babylon, thus giving an outside source to date Judah's history. These external synchronisms can be used to fix the date of the fall of Jerusalem at ca. 586 B.C.

The period of Exile began with the capture of Jerusalem, the destruction of the Temple, and the second deportation of leading citizens in 586 B.C. (An earlier deportation in 597 B.C. had taken King Jehoiachin and his family and many top officials to Babylon.) Ezekiel is a leading prophet among the exiles during this time. Exile ended in 538 B.C. after the capture of Babylon by the Persians under Cyrus in 539 B.C. and Cyrus' edict permitting displaced persons to return to their homelands. The rebuilding of the Temple is dated between 520 and 515 B.C. according to dates from Haggai 1:1; Zechariah 1:1; and Ezra 4:24, 6:15.

Much more difficult is the date of Ezra and Nehemiah. Ezra returned from Exile in the seventh year of Artaxerxes (Ezra 7:1,6–7). Nehemiah returned to Judah in the twentieth year of Artaxerxes (Neh. 1:1). What is difficult is whether these two came during the reign of Artaxerxes I (464–423 B.C.) or Artaxerxes II (404–358 B.C.), or even if both returned during the reign of the same king.

The Intertestamental Period During the In-

SIGNIFICANT DATES IN OLD TESTAMENT BIBLE HISTORY

Periods of History		Critical		Traditional
Patriarchs		1700–1500		2000
(Abraham, Issac, Jacob)				
Exodus		1290		1450
Conquest		1250		1400
Judges		1200–1025		1360–1025
Kings				
Kings of United Israel				
Saul		1025–1005		1020–1004
David		1005–965		1004–965
Solomon		965–925		965–931
Kings of the Divided Kingdom				
Judah	**Israel**			
Rehoboam			924–907	931–913
	Jeroboam	924–903	926–909	
Abijam (Abijah)			907–906	913–910
Asa			905–874	910–869
	Nadab	903–902	909–908	

King				
Baasha	902–886		908–886	
Elah	886–885		886–885	
Zimri	885		885	
(Tibni, 1 Kings 116:21)	885–881		885–880	
Omri	885–873		885–874	
Jehoshaphat		874–850		873–848
Ahab	873–851		874–853	
Ahaziah	851–849		853–852	
Jehoram (Joram)		850–843		853–841
Jehoram	849–843		852–841	
Ahaziah		843		841
Athaliah		843–837		841–835
Jehu	843–816		841–814	
Joash (Jehoash)		837–796		835–796
Jehoahaz	816–800		814–798	
Amaziah		798–767		796–767
Joash (Jehoash)	800–785		798–782	
Uzziah (Azariah)		791–740		792–740
Jeroboam II	785–745		793–753	
Jotham		750–742		750–732
Zechariah	745		753–752	
Shallum	745		752	
Menahem	745–736		752–742	
Jehoahaz I (Ahaz)		742–727		735–715
Pekahiah	736–735		742–740	
Pekah	735–732		752–732	
Hoshea	732–723		732–723	
Hezekiah		727–698		715–686
Fall of Samaria	722		723/722	
Manasseh		697–642		696–642
Amon		642–640		642–640
Josiah		639–606		640–609
Jehoahaz II		609		609
Jehoiakim		608–598		609–597
Jehoiachin		598–597		597
Zedekiah		597–586		597–586
Fall of Jerusalem		586		586

BABYLONIAN EXILE AND RESTORATION UNDER PERSIAN RULE

Jehoiachin and leaders exiled to Babylon including Ezekiel	597
Jerusalem destroyed, remaining leaders exiled to Babylon	586
Gedaliah set over Judea	586
Gedaliah assassinated	581 (?)
Jeremiah taken with other Judeans to Egypt	581 (?)
Judeans deported to Babylon	581
Cyrus, king of Persia	559–530
Babylon captured	539
Edict allowing Jews to return to Jerusalem under Zerubbabel	538
Temple restoration begun but quickly halted	538
Cambysses, king of Persia	530–522
Darius, king of Persia	522–486
Haggai and Zechariah lead rebuilding of Temple	520–515
Temple completed and rededicated	515
Xerxes, king of Persia	486–465
Artaxerxes I, king of Persia	465–424
Ezra returns to Jerusalem and teaches the law	458
Nehemiah returns to Jerusalem and rebuilds the walls	445

NOTE: Overlapping dates of kings such as between Uzziah and Jotham result from coregencies, that is, a father installing his son as king during the father's lifetime and allowing the son to exercise royal power. Critical dates are adapted from a system proposed by J. Maxwell Miller and John H. Hayes. Traditional dates are adapted from a system proposed by E. R. Thiele.

tertestamental Period, Palestine was first under the control of the Persians. Persian rule ended with the conquest of Palestine by Alexander the Great in 333–332 B.C. After the death of Alexander, Palestine fell first under Ptolemaic rule (323–198 B.C.) and then under Seleucid rule (198–164 B.C.). During the period of Ptolemaic rule the Septuagint (Greek translation of the Old Testament) was made in Egypt. Seleucid rule brought a strong move to bring Hellenistic culture to Palestine, ending with the desecration of the Temple in Jerusalem and the persecution of Jews by Antiochus IV (Epiphanes) in 167 B.C. The following Jewish revolt led by Judas Maccabeus resulted in the defeat of the Seleucids and the Second Jewish Commonwealth (164 B.C.-63 B.C.). The Temple was reconsecrated in 164 B.C. These events are recorded in the Apocrypha in 1 Maccabees 1—4. The successors to the Maccabees are usually called the Hasmonean rulers. Hasmonean rule ended in 63 B.C. when Pompey occupied Jerusalem and Judea was again under foreign domination.

The New Testament Period One might expect that the chronology of the New Testament would be much more certain than that of the Old Testament. In some respects that is the case, but not entirely so. Granted we have Greek and Roman histories and annals, but most of the biblical events still cannot be placed precisely in an absolute chronology. The complicating factors are at least twofold. In the first place, the events of the New Testament were not reported by the Greek and Roman historians, nor were many precise events from Greek and Roman history included in the New Testament. Secondly, the Romans and Jews used different calendars. The Romans had a solar calendar with the year beginning in January, but reckoned most events from the accession date of the emperor. Thus they had internal differences in their own calendar. The Jewish calendar only confused the matter more. Basically, the Jews used a lunar calendar of 354 days. Periodically, they added an additional month to keep their calendar in line with the seasons. Because of several calendar changes, the Jews in their history had two New Year's days, one in the fall and the other in the spring. The spring New Year marked the beginning of the cultic calendar and the beginning of the next year's reign of the Jewish king. The fall New Year marked the beginning of the civil year. The reign of foreign rulers was noted from this fall New Year. With such differences, it is no wonder that absolute chronology for New Testament events is very difficult.

The Life and Ministry of Jesus The births of both Jesus (Matt. 2:1) and John the Baptist (Luke 1:5) are set in the reign of Herod the Great. From Josephus we learn that Herod died in the thirty-seventh year after the Roman Senate decree naming him king (40 B.C). This would place his death

in 4 B.C. The further evidence Luke gives of a census while Cyrenius was governor of Syria presents some difficulty (Luke 2:2). Cyrenius conducted a census while serving as governor in 6–7 A.D., but there is no corroborating historical reference to a census during Herod's reign, nor to Cyrenius serving as governor at that time. This simply means that we cannot verify Luke's statement from presently available evidence. Luke may have referred to the census of 6–7 A.D. in Acts 5:37. With Herod's death placed in 4 B.C., Jesus' birth should probably be dated about 7 or 6 B.C.

The beginning of John the Baptist's ministry is set in the fifteenth year of Tiberius (Luke 3:1–2). This would be A.D. 28 or 29, if Tiberius' reign is set following the death of Augustus. If, however, the years of Tiberius' co-rule with Augustus are included, his fifteenth year would be A.D. 26 or 27. This latter date would fit better with Luke's statement that Jesus was about thirty when He began His ministry (Luke 3:23). Jesus' ministry would thus have began about A.D. 27 or 28. The length of Jesus' ministry is also much debated. None of the four Gospels gives enough details to determine the precise length of the ministry. Lengths of one, two, and three years are most often proposed. John's Gospel mentions three Passover feasts (2:13; 6:4; 11:55). If these are distinct Passovers, then they would seem to indicate at least a ministry extending slightly more than two years.

Even the information concerning the date of Jesus' crucifixion is uncertain. All the Gospel accounts agree that Jesus died on Friday of Passover week. The Synoptics indicate that the Last Supper was a Passover meal (Matt. 26:17–20; Mark 14:12; Luke 22:7–8). Passover was eaten on the evening of Nisan 15. John, on the other hand, indicates that Passover was eaten after Jesus was crucified (18:28; 19:14). Then by John's account, Jesus was crucified on Nisan 14. Nisan 14 and 15 fell on a Friday four times within this time frame: A.D. 27, 29, 30, and 33. The most likely date for the crucifixion is Nisan 14 or 15, A.D. 30.

The Apostles Dating the events and activities of the apostles is as vexing as dating the events of Jesus' life. There are very few fixed dates. The death of Herod Agrippa I, mentioned in Acts 12:23, occurred in A.D. 44 according to Josephus. Likewise, the edict of Claudius expelling Jews from Rome (Acts 18:2), is usually dated to A.D. 49, and Gallio's term as deputy (Acts 18:12) belongs to A.D. 51–52.

Other events in Acts must be dated relatively, and problems remain. In particular, there is great difficulty in matching the chronology of Acts with the information in the Pauline epistles. However, in general, we can sketch with approximate dates the ministry of Paul as follows:

Conversion A.D. 33

First visit to Jerusalem, A.D. 36

Second visit to Jerusalem, during famine, A.D.
46
First missionary journey, A.D. 47–48
Conference in Jerusalem, A.D. 49
Second and third missionary journeys, A.D.
50–56
Final visit to Jerusalem, A.D. 57
Reaches Rome, A.D. 60
The datable events in the New Testament all
occurred before the fall of Jerusalem and destruc-
tion of the Temple in A.D. 70.

Joel F. Drinkard, Jr.

CHRYSOLITE See *Minerals and Metals.*

CHRYSOPRASE See *Minerals and Metals.*

CHUB (Chŭb) KJV transliteration of Hebrew
name of a people in Ezekiel 30:5. Other translations follow an interpretation of the Septuagint,
the earliest Greek translation, to find meaning in
the text, reading "Lud" for "Chub," and translating "Libya." If "Libya" is not the original reading,
"Chub" remains a people about whom nothing is
known except that Ezekiel announced judgment
on them as a partner of Egypt. See *Libya.*

CHUN (Chŭn) KJV spelling of Cun. See *Cun.*

CHURCH Church is the term used in the New
Testament most frequently to describe a group of
persons professing trust in Jesus Christ, meeting
together to worship Him, and seeking to enlist
others to become His followers.
The meaning of the term "church" Church is
the English translation of the Greek word
ekklesia. The use of the Greek term prior to the
emergence of the Christian church is important as
two streams of meaning flow from the history of
its usage into the New Testament understanding
of church. First, the Greek term which basically
means "called out" was commonly used to indicate an assembly of citizens of a Greek city and is
so used in Acts 19:32, 39. The citizens who were
quite conscious of their privileged status over
against slaves and noncitizens were called to the
assembly by a herald and dealt in their meetings
democratically with matters of common concern.
When the early Christians understood themselves
as constituting a church, no doubt exists that they
perceived themselves as called out by God in Jesus
Christ for a special purpose and that their status
was a privileged one in Jesus Christ (Eph. 2:19).
Second, the Greek term was used more than
one hundred times in the Greek translation of the
Old Testament in common use in the time of
Jesus. The Hebrew term (*qahal)* meant simply
"assembly" and could be used in a variety of ways,
referring for example to an assembling of prophets
(1 Sam. 19:20), soldiers (Num. 22:4), or the
people of God (Deut. 9:10). The use of the term in

the Old Testament in referring to the people of
God is important for understanding the term
"church" in the New Testament. The first Christians were Jews who used the Greek translation of
the Old Testament. For them to use a self-
designation that was common in the Old Testament for the people of God reveals their understanding of the continuity that links the Old and
New Testaments. The early Christians understood
themselves as the people of the God who had
revealed Himself in the Old Testament (Heb. 1:1–
2), as the true children of Israel (Rom. 2:28–29)
with Abraham as their father (Rom. 4:1–25), and
as the people of the New Covenant prophesied in
the Old Testament (Heb. 8:1–13). As a consequence of this broad background of meaning in
the Greek and Old Testament worlds, the term
"church" is used in the New Testament of a local
congregation of called-out Christians, such as the
"church of God which is at Corinth"(1 Cor. 1:2),
and also of the entire people of God, such as in the
affirmation that Christ is "the head over all things
to the church, Which is his body" (Eph. 1:22–
23).
What church means in the New Testament is
further defined by a host of over one hundred
other descriptive expressions occurring in relationship to passages where the church is being
addressed. Three basic perspectives embrace
most of these other descriptions. First, the church
is seen as the body of Christ; and a cluster of
images exists in this context as emphasis falls on
the head (Eph. 4:15–16), the members (1 Cor.
6:12–20), the body (1 Cor. 12:12–27), or the
bride (Eph. 5:22–31). The church is also seen as
God's new creation (2 Cor. 5:17), the new persons (Eph. 2:14–15), fighters against Satan (Eph.
6:10–20), or bearers of light (Eph. 5:7–9).
Thirdly, the church is quite often described as a
fellowship of faith with its members described as
the saints (1 Cor. 1:2), the faithful (Col. 1:2), the
witnesses (John 15:26–27), or the household of
God (1 Pet. 4:17).
Major characteristics of the life of the church
The preeminent characteristic of the church in
the New Testament is devotion to Jesus Christ as
Lord. He established the church under His authority (Matt. 16:13–20) and created the foundation
for its existence in His redeeming death and demonstration of God's power in His resurrection.
Christ's position as the Lord evoked, sustained,
and governed the major characteristics of the life
of the church in the way members were admitted,
treated one another, witnessed to His power, worshiped, and lived in hope of His return.
Persons were admitted to the local congregation only upon their placing their trust in Christ as
Savior (Acts 3:37–42), openly confessing this
(Rom. 10:9–13), and being baptized (Acts
10:44–48). Baptism or immersion in water was
performed because Christ had commanded it

(Matt. 28:18–20) and was itself a dramatic symbolic picturing of the burial and resurrection of Christ (Rom. 6:3–4). Joining the church made one a fully participating member in it, unlike many of the religious groups in the first century in which there was a substantial period of probation before full acceptance. When Christ accepted the person, the congregation did also, even though the members might be aware of weaknesses (Rom. 14:1–4).

The way in which members of the church were called on to treat one another was modeled by what God had done in Christ for the church. They were to forgive one another (Col. 3:12–14) and to love one another (Eph. 5:1–2; 1 John 3:16) because God had done this for all of them in Christ.

Members of the church were called on to demonstrate the power of Christ's redemption in their own lives by exemplary conduct, embracing every area of life (Rom. 12:1—13:7; Col. 3:12—4:1). The overcoming of sins in the lives of Christians was a witness to the redeeming power of Christ in action in the community (Gal. 5:22–26), and the sins to which the communities were prone were clearly identified and challenged (Gal. 5:19–21).

The worship of the early church demonstrated the lordship of Christ, not only in the fact that He was extolled and praised but also in the fact that worship demonstrated the obligation of Christians to love and to nurture one another (1 Cor. 11:17–22; 14:1–5). In distinction from worship as it was practiced in the pagan cults of Greece and Rome, Christian worship not only stressed the relation of a person to the Diety but went beyond this to stress that worship should edify and strengthen the Christians present (1 Cor. 14:26) and should challenge pagans to accept Christ (1 Cor. 14:20–25). Christian worship was often enthusiastic and usually involved all Christians present as participants (1 Cor. 14:26). This openness both inspired creativity and opened the way for excesses which were curbed by specific suggestions (1 Cor. 14:26–33a; 1 Tim. 2:1–10) and by the rule that what was done should be appropriate to those committed to a God of peace (1 Cor. 14:33a).

All of these characteristics of the life of the church existed in the context of an urgency created by the awareness that Christ was going to return (1 Thess. 1:9–10). Christ's return would bring judgment to the unbelievers (1 Thess. 5:1–10) and thus made witnessing to them an urgent concern. How central this belief was to the early church is illustrated by the fact that the Lord's Supper, which they observed at His command was seen as proclaiming "the Lord's death till he come (1 Cor. 11:26). The return of Christ was to result in glorious joy and the transformation of the Christians—a hope that sustained them in difficult times (2 Thess. 1:5–12).

Organization of the New Testament churches A striking feature of the organization of the early churches is that every member of the church was seen as having a gift for service which was to be used cooperatively for the benefit of all (Rom. 12:1–8; 1 Pet. 4:10). Paul used the imagery of the human body to illustrate this unique feature of the church's life, stressing that every Christian has a necessary function and a responsibility to function with an awareness of his or her share in the body of Christ (1 Cor. 12:12–31).

In the context of this strong belief that every member has a ministry, certain persons were designated to fulfill specific tasks in relation to the functioning of the church such as apostles, bishops, elders, and deacons. As these offices are examined, it is important to remember that the organization of the early churches was not necessarily the same in every locality. A large church would need more organizational structure than a small one, and the presence of an apostle or his designated representative would cause the other leaders in a given church to be seen in a different light. In addition to these variables, the church was in a period of rapid growth; and as it responded to the needs of ministry, roles or offices, such as the appointment of the seven in Acts 6:1–7, were created to enable the church to fulfill its ministry in Christ. See *Offices.*

The organization of the early churches was not governed by a rigid plan that each church had to follow. The guiding principle was that the church was the body of Christ with a mission to accomplish, and the church felt free to respond to the leading of the Holy Spirit in developing a structure that would contribute to its fulfilling its responsibilities (Rom. 12:1–8; 1 Cor. 12:4–11; Eph. 4:11–16).

The growth and expansion of the early church Jesus taught His disciples that by following Him they were to be involved in a movement that would continue (Matt. 16:13–20; John 14:12–14), but it was after the resurrection of Jesus that the mission of the church really began (Matt. 28:16–20; John 20:19–23; Acts 1:6–11). The earliest Christians were Palestinian Jewish followers of Jesus and found it difficult to witness to non-Jews (Acts 10:1–48). The bridge to the Gentiles was the Hellenistic Jewish Christianity, which sprang into existence with the conversion of Jews from the dispersion who were visiting in Jerusalem and converted at Pentecost (Acts 2:5–47). These Jews whose residence had been in the cities of the Roman Empire were called Hellenistic because they were generally more open to the Greco-Roman culture than their Palestinian colleagues. They spoke and wrote Greek as their primary language, gave their children Greek names (such as Stephen which means "crown"in Greek), and were more willing to relate to Gentiles. It was this group of the early Christians that was the major channel in spreading the gospel to the Gentiles (Acts 19:11–26).

Paul was a Hellenistic Jew (Acts 21:39); and when he became a Christian, he was called to and accepted a ministry to the Gentiles (Acts 22:21; Eph. 3:1–13). Significantly, he inaugurated his ministry of founding new churches from the base of a church composed of both Gentiles and Hellenistic Jewish Christians (Acts 11:19–26; 13:1–3). Paul's strategy was to visit synagogues in the cities of the Roman Empire and to proclaim Jesus as the Christ (Acts 18:5). The usual result was that some Jews and some Gentiles who were interested in Judaism (called God-fearers, Acts 18:7) believed in Christ, were expelled from the synagogue, and formed the nucleus for a growing church (Acts 18:5–11; 19:8–10).

The Acts of the Apostles gives only a glimpse of the early Christian heroes and heroines with a focus on Peter, Paul, and a few others (Acts 18:1–4, 24–28). There were, however, many heroic Christian witnesses unknown to us who first carried the gospel to Rome (Acts 28:14–15) and to the limits of the Empire in India, Egypt, and the outlying areas of Europe. See *Apostle; Bishop; Deacon; Elders; Missions.*   Harold S. Songer

CHURCH YEAR Although the dates of observance and specific practices of the Christian festivals developed over the centuries, the major festivals all center on the life of Christ. As the church grew and the need for ordered worship increased, the need for focusing on the central affirmations at the heart of the Christian message also increased. By the fifth century, the basic elements of the church calendar were firmly established, although modifications continued to be made throughout the Middle Ages and the Reformation. Even today, the symbols and rituals of the festivals vary according to denomination, culture, and personal preference.

The original Christian festival and the basic building block for all the church year is the Lord's day, Sunday. The earliest Christians set aside Sunday, the day of the resurrection, as a time of special remembrance of Christ. By the second century, most Christians were observing a special celebration of the resurrection at Easter. In most areas, the season before Easter, later called Lent, was a time of penitence and the training of new Christians. Similarly, the fifty-day period after Easter was one of triumph during which fasting and kneeling to pray were forbidden. This period culminated in Pentecost, which means "fiftieth day," the celebration of the descent of the Holy Spirit. By the next century, at least in the East, many churches held a special observance of Christ's birth and baptism at Epiphany. In the fourth century, most Christians began to celebrate Christ's birth at Christmas and to observe Advent as a period of preparation.

As the dates and practices for these celebrations became more standard throughout the Christian world, the dimensions of the church year were established. Advent came to be regarded as the beginning of the church year and the half-year between Advent and Pentecost, the period during which all the major festivals occurred, came to be regarded as a time for Christians to concentrate on the life and work of Christ. The rest of the year, from Pentecost to Advent, became a time for concentrating on the teachings of Jesus and the application of those teachings in the lives of Christians. The development of the church calendar helped to assure that Christian worship would deal with the entire breadth and depth of the Christian gospel.

See *Advent; Christmas; Easter; Epiphany; Holy Week; Lent; Lord's Day.*   Fred A. Grissom

CHUSHAN-RISHATHAIM (Chū' shăn-rĭsh·à· thā·ĭm) KJV spelling of Cushan-rishathaim. Mesopotamian king who oppressed Israel until he was defeated by Othniel the son of Kenaz (Judg. 3:8). The name of this Mesopotamian ruler means Chushan of double iniquity. It probably was a derogatory epithet rather than his actual name. See *Judges.*

CHUZA (Chū' zà) Personal name meaning, "seer." The steward of Herod Antipas (Luke 8:3). He was the husband of Joanna, one of the women who provided material support for Jesus. See *Joanna.*

CILICIA (Cĭ lĭc' ĭ à) A geographical area and/or Roman province in southeastern Asia Minor. The region was home to some of the people who opposed Stephen (Acts 6:9). It was located on the coast of the Mediterranean Sea in the southeast part of Asia Minor. One of its important cities was Tarsus, the birthplace of Paul the apostle (Acts 21:39; 22:3). By the time of the Council of Jerusalem (Acts 15), Christianity had already penetrated Cilicia. Paul passed through the region during the course of his missionary travels (Acts 15:41; 27:5; Gal. 1:21).

The western portion of the geographical area was about 130 miles long east to west and 50 to 60 miles wide, consisted almost entirely of the westernmost extension of the Taurus Mountains, was called "mountainous" Cilicia, and was sparsely populated and important primarily for timber. The eastern portion was about 100 miles long east to west and 30 to 50 miles wide, consisted of a fertile coastal plain, and was called "level" Cilicia. Through the Cilician Gates (pass) in the Taurus Mountains to the north, through "level" Cilicia itself, and through the Syrian Gates in the Ammanus Mountains to the east ran the great international highway between central Asia Minor and Syria, Mesopotamia, and Egypt.

The famous Cilician Gates, a mountain pass thirty miles north of Tarsus, through the Taurus mountains.

The area was conquered by the Romans between 102 and 67 B.C. Until A.D. 72 the western portion had the status of a client kingdom or was part of another such kingdom. In 38 B.C. the eastern portion was joined to the Province of Syria, the name of which then became Syria and Cilicia. In A.D. 72 the parts were united in a separate province.

In the Old Testament the same region is called Kue (1 Kings 10:28; 2 Chron. 1:16, RSV, NAS, NIV). See *Kue; Paul; Tarsus.*   *James A. Brooks*

CINNAMON A spice used in making fragrant oils. Such oil was used to anoint the wilderness tent of meeting (Ex. 30:23). It was part of the lucrative international spice trade (Rev. 18:13). Compare Prov. 7:17; Song of Solomon 4:14. Cinnamon comes from the bark of a large tree belonging to the laurel family. Both the English and Greek words are derived from the Hebrew *qinnamon.* See *Spices.*

CINNEROTH (Cĭn' nē rōth) KJV spelling of Chinneroth in 1 Kings 15:20. See *Chinnereth; Chinneroth.*

CIRCUIT A circular route that a person, a geographical feature, or a natural object follows. Underlying the English word are at least four Hebrew words indicating round, surround, around, or turning. Samuel went around a circuit of cities to judge Israel (1 Sam. 7:16). The human eye views heaven as a circular vault or dome, where God takes His daily walk (Job 22:14). Similarly, the sun passes along the circuit of the heavens (Ps. 19:6). The wind appears to run a meaningless circular course going nowhere (Eccl. 1:6). Jerusalem within its walls represented a circle or circuit, which David repaired (1 Chron. 11:8 NRSV). The villages around Jerusalem formed a circuit (Neh. 12:28 NRSV). Compare 2 Kings 3:9 NAS.

CIRCUMCISION Circumcision is the act of removing the foreskin of the male genital. In ancient Israel this act was ritually performed on the eighth day after birth upon children of natives, servants, and aliens (Lev. 9:3). Circumcision was carried out by the father initially, utilizing a flint knife (compare Josh. 5:3). Later specialists were employed among the Jewish people.

Origin Several theories seek to explain and describe the nature and origin of circumcision: (1) initiatory rite—before marriage (as the Shechemites in Gen. 34:14–24) or at puberty; (2) physical hygiene—to prevent the attraction or transmission of diseases; (3) tribal mark of distinction; (4) rite of entry into the community of faith. In the Old Testament the origin of Israelite practice was founded upon the circumcision of Abraham as a sign of the covenant between God and the patriarch (Gen. 17:10).

Ancient Near Eastern background Several Semitic and non-Semitic peoples practiced circumcision according to biblical and other sources. Jeremiah depicts Egyptians, Edomites, Ammonites, Moabites, and the desert-dwelling Arabians as circumcised peoples (Jer. 9:25–26; compare Ezek. 32:17–32). On the other hand Philistines, Assyrians, and Babylonians are counted among the uncircumcised. That the Canaanites are not mentioned in either regard is noteworthy. Evidence of their perspective of circumcision is lacking.

Ethical implications of circumcision can be observed in the metaphorical usage of the term. The uncircumcised are those who are insensitive to God's leadership. Circumcision of the heart implies total devotion to God (Deut. 10:16; Jer. 4:4); however, the uncircumcised ear cannot hear so as to respond to the Lord (Jer. 6:10); and the uncircumcised of lips cannot speak (Ex. 6:12). Circumcision was therefore an external sign of an internal singularity of devotion of Yahweh.

Circumcision and Christianity Controversy arose in the early church (Acts 10—15) as to whether Gentile converts need be circumcised. First century A.D. Jews disdained the uncircumcised. The leadership of the apostle Paul in the Jerusalem Council was crucial in the settlement of the dispute: circumcision was not essential to Christian faith and fellowship. Circumcision of the heart via repentance and faith were the only requirements (Rom. 4:9–12; Gal. 2:15–21).   *R. Dennis Cole*

CIS (Cĭs) KJV transliteration of Greek for Kish in Acts 13:21. See *Kish.*

CISTERN The translation of a Hebrew term that means "hole," "pit," or more often "well." The difference between *cistern* and *well* often is not apparent. The innumerable cisterns, wells, and pools that exist in Palestine are evidence of the efforts of ancient people to supplement the natural water supply. The cistern of Palestine was usually a bottle or pear-shaped reservoir into which water could drain from a roof, tunnel, or courtyard. The porous limestone out of which the

A cistern with a stone mortar in the foreground probably used for grinding grain at Beersheba.

cisterns were dug allowed much of the water put into the cistern to escape. After 1300 B.C. cisterns began to be plastered, which resulted in a more efficient system of water storage. The mouth of a cistern was sometimes finished and covered with a stone. Some cisterns have been found with a crude filter to trap debris.

The water system at Gibeon was based on this large rock-cut pool connected by tunnel to another cistern.

The biblical writers revealed that cisterns were used for purposes other than holding water. Joseph was placed in a "broken" cistern by his brothers (Gen. 37:20–29). The prophet Jeremiah was imprisoned in the cistern of Malchijah, King Zedekiah's son, (Jer. 38:6 NAS). In Jeremiah 14,

Large, extensive water cistern at Masada, Herod's mountain fortress.

The circular opening to a cistern at the site of Lachish in Israel.

the pagan gods were symbolized as broken cisterns that could not hold water. Cisterns also served as convenient dumping places for corpses (Jer. 41:7,9).

See *Waterworks; Wells.*   *James Newell*

CITADEL NRSV, NAS, NIV translation of Hebrew *'armon.* See *Castle.*

CITIES AND URBAN LIFE Cities form a major indicator of civilization. Indeed, the emergence of cities often marks the move to civilization. The oldest city excavated to date is found in Palestine; it is tell es-Sultan, Old Testament Jericho. This site was already a bustling city between 8000 and 7000 B.C. Even before its citizens used pottery, the city had a massive defense wall and a high circular watch tower inside the wall.

The terms "city" and "urban life" had quite a different meaning in the biblical period, especially in the earlier times. Modern usage has given us at least five terms to describe a range of population. In increasing size of population we speak of open country, village, town, city, metropolis. The Old Testament uses two words for "city" (*'eer* and *kiriah*) and one for "village" (*chatsair*). The Old Testament differentiation seems to be based not on size primarily, but on the presence or absence of a defense wall. Cities had walls, while villages were unwalled.

Size of cities Ancient cities tended to be much smaller in both size and population than our typical understanding of a city. The oldest walled city at Jericho mentioned above covered less than ten acres. Even during the Old Testament period, Jericho was no more than ten acres in area. Some of the great cities of Mesopotamia were much more like the size we consider for a city. At the height of the Assyrian empire in the eighth century B.C., Nineveh covered approximately 1720 acres or over two and a half square miles. The mound of Calah (ancient Nimrud) covered over 875 acres or one and a quarter square miles. None of the cities in Palestine from the Old Testament period come close to the size of the great cities of

Mesopotamia. Jerusalem at the time of Solomon covered only 33 acres; even at the time of Jesus it covered less than 200 acres. This is not to say that Palestine had no larger cities. Hazor, in northern Israel, was over 175 acres in area. However, most of the well-known biblical sites were smaller rather than larger.

Closely related to the area of a town is its population. Recent population projections based on the density of cities from cultures similar to those of biblical times along with a count of the number of house units found in excavations suggest that most cities could support 160–200 persons per acre. Thus Shechem might have had a population of 2,000 to 2,500 during the Old Testament period; Jerusalem in Solomon's time could have supported 5,000 to 6,500. Even when Jerusalem expanded in Josiah's time, it would have had no more than 25,000 inhabitants. An inscription found at Ebla in northern Syria and dated to about 2400–2250 B.C. states that Ebla had a population of 250,000. However, it is unclear whether this figure referred to the city, or the entire kingdom controlled by Ebla, or was an exaggeration to impress others of the size of Ebla. By A.D. 300, the city of Rome may have had nearly a million inhabitants.

Cities and the Surrounding Region At least two types of phrases are used to describe the region surrounding a city. One phrase described the chief city of a region in relation to the smaller villages around it. Thus in a literal translation the Old Testament speaks of a city "with its villages" (Josh. 19:16; Neh. 11:30) or "with its daughters" (Num. 21:25; 2 Chron. 13:19). These two phrases indicate that the city was the most important center of activity for the region. Outlying villages were closely related to the central city for their existence. Most of the commercial activity for the region was carried out in the city. Usually, the city was located on the main highway or intersection of highways and trade route through the area. The major sanctuary or worship place would be most frequently located in the city, making it a center of religious pilgrimages and celebrations. Whenever war or invasion threatened, the people of the surrounding villages would flee to the walled city for protection.

Why was a city built at a particular location? Among the chief concerns would be the presence of food and water nearby, along with the raw materials for shelter, tools, and industry. Furthermore, a site that was easy to defend would be most likely to be chosen.

A number of common features may be found in the typical city of the Ancient Near East. Each of these features will be discussed briefly.

1. Walls City walls in the Ancient Near East were formed of courses of stone or mudbrick, at times quite thick. The rampart at Hazor in northern Israel about 1700 B.C. is almost 50 feet high at places and up to 290 feet thick! Furthermore, the perimeter of this enclosed area was over two miles. See *Architecture.*

2. Gate The most important and most vulnerable part of the wall structure was the gate. Massive guard towers usually flanked the gate. The entrance itself was narrow, usually twelve to fifteen feet wide. Two heavy wooden doors could be shut and braced with metal bars at night or in case of attack. The gate complex itself had two or three separate sets of doors through which one had to pass to gain entry to the city. See *Architecture.*

3. Water supply Adequate water supply was another necessity for a city. During peaceful times, the water supply could be outside the wall and within a reasonable distance from the city. A protected water supply accessible from within the city was necessary to endure a siege during wartime. Most cities were located near springs, streams, or wells. Many homes had cisterns, especially in the more arid regions. The springs were usually at the foot of the tell outside the city wall. Hazor, Megiddo, and Gibeon provide examples of water systems the Israelites constructed during the monarchy. Extensive water tunnel and pool systems were built by cutting through the bedrock of the tell to reach the level of the springs. At Hazor, the tunnel system had to cut through 70 feet of soil and rock to reach the water level. Hezekiah's tunnel in Jerusalem is another example of the water tunnel system. Second Kings 20:20 mentions the construction of this system about 700 B.C. The Romans often constructed great aqueducts to bring water from long distances to a city. Portions of two such aqueducts still remain at Caesarea-by-the-Sea which brought the water from over five miles away. One of the Hellenistic-Roman aqueducts at Jerusalem covers nearly 25 miles.

4. Agricultural land Earliest towns were surely self-sufficient and must have had fertile farming land nearby. The Old Testament speaks of the fields of a city or village (Lev. 25:34; Josh. 21:12; Neh. 11:25,30), and indicates that some of the land was held in common and some was owned by a family or clan. Large cities would not have had enough land surounding to meet its food needs, so they would depend on the trade of the surplus produce from the smaller villages. The villages in turn would depend on the cities for the manufactured goods and items of trade from distant areas. Agricultural land was not supposed to be sold out of the family or clan (Lev. 25:25–28). Isaiah strongly denounced those wealthy who would add "field to field, until there be no place" (Isa. 5:8).

5. Acropolis The highest elevation of many cities often formed an acropolis or inner citadel. In addition to serving as a stronghold, the acropolis also served as residence for the aristocracy or royalty. As one might expect, the houses located here would be the largest and best constructed of the city. Not only would the security be strongest in the acropolis, but the higher elevation would catch any breeze and cool the house in the summer. In addition, the major shrines or temples were often located on the acropolis.

6. *Street plan* Ancient Near Eastern cities usually had a regular street plan. In Babylon, major streets led from the gates into the city center. In the period of the monarchy, Israelite cities regularly had an open court just inside the gate. A circular street led from the court around the perimeter of the city. This circular street gave easy access to all sections of the city, as well as providing the military with quick access to any part of the city wall. Other streets branched off this circular street and led into the center of the city. In the Roman cities, the major road was usually the cardo, a wide, flagstone paved highway which ran north-south. The major east-west road was the decumanus. A section of the cardo of Jerusalem has been excavated recently in the Jewish Quarter. Although the portion excavated belongs to the Byzantine period, it may well reflect what the Roman cardo there was like. The street was colonnaded, and was 39 feet wide. It had covered sidewalks, each an additional 17 feet wide. The street even had a covered drainage system.

7. *House plans* Along with street plan, one can note something of a development in house plans in Israel. The earliest houses had one main room and courtyard. By the period of the monarchy, the typical Israelite house was a four room house.

Dramatic changes took place in the Hellenistic and Roman periods. The successors to Alexander the Great built many Greek cities in Palestine. Greek culture was the pattern in the Decapolis and other Hellenistic cities. See *Architecture.*

Joel F. Drinkard, Jr.

CITIES OF REFUGE A safe place to flee for a person who had accidentally killed another. The city provided asylum to the fugitive by sheltering and protecting him until a trial could be held to determine his guilt or innocence. If, in the judgment of the city elders, the death had occurred accidentally and without intent, the man was allowed to stay there without fear of harm or revenge by the dead man's relatives (Josh. 20:2–6).

Four major passages in the Old Testament describe the right of asylum and the sanctuary provided by a city of refuge (Ex. 21:12–14; Num. 35:1–34; Deut. 19:1–13; Josh. 20:1–9). A literal translation of the Hebrew phrase means "a city of intaking." This right of asylum was offered before the settlement of the Promised Land, but was available only to one charged with accidental manslaughter. Exodus 21:12 records that "He that smiteth a man, so that he die, shall be surely put to death." The passage continues, however, to promise that "if a man did lie not in wait," a place would be designated to which he could flee (v.

13). Prior to the establishment of these cities, temporary safety could be gained by fleeing to a sanctuary and grasping the horns of the altar there. 1 Kings 1:50 and 2:28 record two examples of men seeking safety by clinging to the altar in Jerusalem. Neither Adonijah nor Joab were innocent, though, and later were executed.

Moses was commanded to establish six cities of refuge from the total of 48 given to the Levites (Num. 35:6–7). Three were located on each side of the Jordan. In the east were Bezer in the territory of the Reubenites, Ramoth in Gilead, and Golan in the area of Bashan (Deut. 4:43). On the west side of the Jordan were Kedesh in Galilee, Shechem in Ephraim, and Kirjath-arba or Hebron in the hill country of Judah (Josh. 20:7–8). Sanctuary was not limited to the people of Israel but was extended to the stranger and sojourner among them (Num. 35:15).

The Old Testament reveals the importance and sacredness of human life by its laws regarding the taking of life. See *Blood Guilt; Avenger.*

The reason for distributing the cities of refuge throughout Israel on both sides of the Jordan was so that a city was easily accessible to a person responsible for an accidental homicide. He needed to find asylum immediately because he would be pursued by a member of the dead man's family. The avenger of blood sought to kill the slayer of his kin for the harm done to the family or clan. In the early period of Israel's history before the development of the cities of refuge, this action could result in a blood feud that terminated only with the extinction of one family. The establishment of the cities of refuge served a humanitarian purpose by transforming a case of homicide from a private feud between two families to a judicial matter settled by a group of elders.

Numbers 35 lists several requirements to be met prior to seeking sanctuary in a city of refuge. The primary requisite was that the death must have occurred by accident, without premeditation or intent. Case studies are presented in Numbers 35:16–18, 20–21, 22–23 to provide examples of those incidents which prevented or allowed a slayer to seek refuge in such a place.

A second major requirement for asylum in a city of refuge was that the slayer, once being admitted to the city, could not leave until the death of the high priest (Num. 35:25; Josh. 20:6). If he chose to the leave the city before that time, he could be killed by the avenger of blood (Num. 35:26–28). In contrast to the temporary sanctuary offered by grasping the horns of an altar, the city of refuge provided a permanent place of asylum for the manslayer. In a punitive way, the city also served as a place of detention. The manslayer was not guiltless. He could not leave under penalty of death by the avenger of blood, nor could he buy his way out by offering a ransom to the relatives of the deceased. A similar example of this punishment may be found in Solomon's confinement of Shimei to Jerusalem under a death threat if he left the city (1 Kings 2:36–46).

The taking of a life imposed a guilt that could not be paid for by any means short of death. The death of the high priest, even as a result of natural causes, served to pay the price of the required penalty. One man died in place of another. During his life, one of the functions of a high priest was to bear the sins of the people (Ex. 28:38). In accordance with this regulation, all the cities of refuge were Levitical cities, given to that tribe during the division of the Promised Land among the Israelites. These locations probably contained local sanctuaries in which a priest served. After the death of the high priest, the one guilty of manslaughter was free to leave the city and return to his home without fear of the avenger of blood.

Brenda R. Hockenhull

CITIES OF THE PLAIN The cities of the plain (RSV, "cities of the valley") are the five cities—Sodom, Gomorrah, Admah, Zeboiim, and Zoar—thought to be located near the southern end of the Dead Sea. The narrative of Genesis 14 associates these five cities and locates them in the Valley of Siddim, the Dead Sea. All these cities except Zoar were destroyed for the wickedness of Sodom and Gomorrah (Gen. 19:24–29).

Most recent scholarship has located the five cities in the shallow water of the southern end of the Dead Sea, south of the Lisan, the tongue of land along the southeastern shore that protrudes into the sea. However, no conclusive evidence has been found to support this proposal. Excavations along the eastern shore of the Dead Sea in recent years have convinced some scholars that the cities of the plain might be located in that region, especially at Bab-ed-Dhra and Numeira near the Lisan.

The particular phrase, "cities of the plain," occurs only in Genesis 13:12 as the place Lot chose to dwell, and in Genesis 19:29 concerning the destruction. The Hebrew word translated "plain" more nearly means "round." Thus it seems better to think of these cities as being ones "around" the Dead Sea or "around" the Jordan Valley. This interpretation may indicate simply that these cities were allies that lay in the Jordan Valley near the Dead Sea. As such, these cities may have been on a trade route and themselves involved in the trade of bitumin, salt, and sulphur.

Joel F. Drinkard, Jr.

CITIZEN, CITIZENSHIP Officially recognized status in a political state bringing certain rights and responsibilities as defined by the state. Paul raised the issue of citizenship in the Bible by appealing to his right as a Roman citizen (Acts 16:37; 22:26–28). Roman citizenship rights were first formulated in the Valerian Law at the founding of the Roman Republic in 509 B.C., but

citizenship rights changed as Roman governments changed. In New Testament times the definition came in the Julian Law passed near 23 B.C.
Becoming a Citizen Roman citizenship could be gained in several ways: birth to Roman parents, including birth to a Roman woman without regards to identity of the father; retirement from the army; being freed from slavery by a Roman master; buying freedom from slavery; being given citizenship by a Roman general or emperor as an individual or as part of a political unit; purchase of citizenship. Paul was born a citizen, but how his family gained citizenship we do not know.
Citizenship Rights and Responsibilities A citizen became liable for Roman property taxes and municipal taxes. A citizen had the right to vote in Rome, though different social classes had different rights at this point. A citizen became a member of a Roman tribe. A citizen was promised a fair trial without certain forms of harsh punishment. A citizen could not be executed without a trial and would not be crucified except by order of the emperor. A citizen could appeal to Caesar and had to be taken to Rome for trial.

Paul made use of these rights as he faced opposition and persecution (Acts 16:37; 25:11).

CITRON NAS, NIV translation of Greek *thuinos,* a scented wood that formed part of the rich international trade (Rev. 18:12). KJV translates, "thyine," while NRSV has "scented."

CITY OF CONFUSION (CHAOS) A name applied to Jerusalem in Isaiah 24:10.

CITY OF DAVID In the Old Testament, the phrase "the city of David" refers to Jerusalem. The name was given to the fortified city of the Jebusites after it was captured by David (2 Sam. 5:6–10). Its original reference may have been only to the southeastern hill and the Jebusites' military fortress there. In Luke 2:4,11 the reference is to Bethlehem, the birth place of David (see John 7:42). See *Jerusalem; Zion.*

CITY OF DESTRUCTION See *Heliopolis.*

CITY OF MOAB City where Balak went to meet Balaam (Num. 22:36). Some identify the city as Ar. See *Ar.*

CITY OF PALM TREES Probably to be identified with a site near Jericho where the Kenites lived (Judg. 1:16; see Deut. 34:3; Judg. 3:13; 2 Chron. 28:15). Jericho itself lay in ruins from the time of the conquest until the time of Ahab. See *Jericho.* Some identify the region with Zoar on the south side of the Dead Sea or with Tamar about twenty miles south of the Dead Sea.

CITY OF SALT A city allotted to the tribe of Judah "in the desert" (Josh. 15:62). Its precise location is not known. Archaeological finds do not support an identification with Qumran that some have tried to make.

CITY OF THE SUN Usually taken as a reference to Heliopolis (Isa. 19:18). See *Heliopolis.*

CITY OF WATERS A city in Ammon, probably to be identified with a part of or all of Rabbah, the capital. Joab captured it for David (2 Sam. 12:27).

CLAN Term used to distinguish a kin group more extensive than a family. The boundaries of such a group are not always clearly delineated. Each clan was governed by the heads of the families (elders). Several clans formed a tribe, and twelve tribes formed Israel. The clan is sometimes referred to as "division," "kindred," "family," "thousand," or even "tribe."

CLAUDA (Clāū´ dȧ) KJV, NAS spelling of Cauda in Acts 27:16 for island where Paul landed on his way to Rome. See *Cauda.*

CLAUDIA (Clāū´ dĭ ȧ) Woman who sent greetings to Timothy (2 Tim. 4:21).

CLAUDIUS (Clāū´ dĭ ŭs) *1.* Roman emperor from A.D. 41 to 54. He made Judea a Roman province in A.D. 44. He expelled Jews from Rome

Marble bust of Claudius from the island of Malta, dating from the first century.

in about A.D. 49 (Acts 18:2), probably due to conflict between Jews and Christians in Rome. Apparently his fourth wife Agrippina poisoned him in A.D. 54 and took charge of the empire for her son Nero. The prophet Agabus announced a coming famine during Claudius' reign (Acts 11:28). See *Caesar.*

2. Roman army captain who protected Paul from Jews who wanted to assassinate him (Acts 23:26).

CLAY A basic building and artistic material for people in biblical times. Clay consisted of various types of dirt or sand combined with water to form a material which could be molded into bricks for building, sculptures, pottery, toys, or writing tablets. A piece of clay marked by a signet ring gave proof of ownership or approval. The type of dirt— sand, quartz, flint, limestone—along with coloring patterns gives archaeologists a key for dating deposits uncovered from ancient sites.

CLEAN, CLEANNESS The idea of cleanness includes a surprisingly wide range of human behavior. On the purely physical side a person is considered clean when obvious indications of dirt or similar defilement have been removed. A clean person is also one who habitually maintains a pattern of personal cleanliness and hygiene, while at the same time taking care to ensure that his or her environment is in a clean condition so as to forestall possible accidents, infection, and disease.

Because the mind is an integral aspect of the human personality, cleanness must also be applied to attitudes and motives that govern particular forms of behavior. Impure thoughts as the expression of the mind can result in shameful activities (Mark 7:15) unless they are checked firmly, and bring disgrace to the individual concerned as well as harm to others.

Cleanness, however, is a relative term when the human condition is being considered. Mankind's fall from divine grace as a result of defying God's commands and yielding to temptation has made sin a genetic issue (Gen. 3:1–19). This means that the *tendency* to sin is inborn, with the inevitable result that, as the ancient psalmist said, there is none righteous (Ps. 14:3; Rom. 3:10). Paul stated the situation with equal emphasis by proclaiming that all have sinned and come short of God's glory (Rom. 3:23). Human sin places a barrier between sinners and a just, holy God. Sinners are unclean in God's eyes.

The religious rituals of Leviticus had much to say about the way in which the sinner could be cleansed from iniquity and be reconciled to God. This was a matter of great importance to the Israelites, because God required them to be a kingdom of priests and a holy nation (Ex. 19:6). In the Ancient Near Eastern religions the idea of holiness was applied to a person in a state of consecration to the service of a deity, whose cultic worship could, and frequently did, involve acts of a gross sexual nature. For the Hebrews, holiness demanded that they should reflect in their living and thinking the exalted moral and spiritual qualities of God as revealed in His laws.

Cleanness was thus fundamental to the establishing and preservation of holiness in the Israelite community. As distinct from all other nations, the Hebrews were provided with specific instructions concerning cleanness and how to recover it when it had been lost through carelessness or disobedience. The principles of cleanness touched upon all aspects of individual and community life. They were ultimately capable of a moral interpretation, since in the holy nation secular and spiritual matters were closely connected.

God established for the Israelites a special group of laws dealing with clean and unclean animals (Lev. 11:1–47; Deut. 14:1–21) to provide guidance for dietary and other circumstances. While the nations of the Ancient Near East maintained a general distinction between clean and unclean species, the principles of differentiation were in no sense as explicit as those provided for the Hebrews. Clean animals were allowed to be eaten, but unclean ones were prohibited strictly. The terms "clean" and "unclean" were defined by illustration, and clear principles were enunciated to enable anyone to make the distinction correctly.

Very simply, whatever animal had a cleft hoof and chewed the cud was clean, and therefore suitable for food. Any animal that did not meet these specifications was unclean, and consequently was not to be eaten. If an animal such as a camel possessed only one of the two stated requirements, it was still regarded as unclean. Because birds formed part of the Israelites' diet, a list of those species suitable for food excluded the ones that might carry communicable diseases.

There has been much discussion about the purpose of these regulations. Some writers claimed that they were designed so as to avoid pagan idolatrous practices. Others have focused upon preserving the separated nature of the Israelites in matters of food as well as in ethical and religious considerations. Yet another view emphasized the hygienic aspects of the laws as a means of preventing the spread of infectious ailments. Most probably, all three concerns underlay the legislation, and therefore each should be given due weight. Animals associated with pagan cults were prohibited, as were unfamiliar or repulsive creatures, and those species that fed upon carrion. If the rules for food were followed, the Hebrews could expect to enjoy good physical health. Clearly the overall objective of the dietary laws was the prevention of uncleanness and the promoting of holiness in the community (Lev. 11:43–44).

Uncleanness also applied to certain objects and situations in life which conveyed impurity to those involved. Thus contact with a dead person (Lev. 5:2; 21:1), a creeping insect or animal (Lev. 22:4–5), the carcass of an animal (Lev. 11:28; Deut. 14:8), or a woman in labor (Lev. 12:4–5) brought about uncleanness, which required ritual purification to remove it. Leprosy was particularly dangerous as a source of uncleanness, and required special cleansing rituals (Lev. 14:13) when the sufferer was pronounced cured. Unclean persons transmitted their condition to whatever they touched, so that others who handled such things became unclean also. Even God's sanctuary needed to be cleansed periodically (Lev. 4:6; 16:15–20).

As noted previously, cleanness had a specific moral dimension. Because God's priests were to be clothed with righteousness (Ps. 132:9), the entire nation was involved in manifesting the priesthood of all who believed sincerely in the covenant relationship with God that had been forged on Mount Sinai. Thus to be clean meant not merely the negative aspects of being free from disease or defilement, but the positive demonstration in daily life of God's high moral and ethical qualities of absolute purity, mercy, justice, and grace.

Cleanness was a part of the moral stipulations of the Law. Thus murder was both a pollution of the land and a violation of the Decalogue's express commands. The killing of the innocent called for a response in justice from the entire Israelite community, based upon a principle of blood retribution (Num. 35:33; Deut. 19:10). Grave moral offenses that violated God's law and polluted the nation included adultery (Lev. 18:20)—a capital offense (Lev. 20:10)—and perverted sexual activity which included bestiality, with death as the prescribed punishment (Lev. 20:13).

Ceremonial holiness thus involved distinguishing between clean and unclean. Moral holiness required the Israelites to behave as a nation separated from the pollutions of contemporary society, and to live upright and righteous lives in obedience to God's laws (Lev. 21:25–26). For the penitent transgressor a complex system of purificatory rites cleansed from both physical and moral defilement. These involved various kinds of washing by water, as a natural cleansing process (Lev 6:28; 8:6; 14:8–9; Num. 8:7; 19:9); the use of ashes (Num. 19:17) and hyssop (Num. 19:18) for ritual and accidental contamination; and sacrificial blood, which made atonement for sin and reconciled the worshiper to God. The Law established the principle that blood made atonement for human life (Lev. 17:11), and thus a blood sacrifice involved the highest form of purification (Lev. 14:6, 19–20) or dedication to God (Lev. 8:23–24). Yet even this form of sacrifice was powerless against sins deliberately committed against the spirituality of the covenant (Num. 15:30).

In the New Testament, cleansing was associated only with the ritual customs of contemporary Judaism. Thus the infant Jesus was presented in the Temple for the traditional purification ritual (Lev. 12:2–8; Luke 2:22). Cleansing (*katharismos*) was a matter of contention between the Pharisees and the disciples of John the Baptist (John 3:25), but Christ obeyed the Law in sending healed lepers to the priest for cleansing (Lev. 14:2–32; Matt. 8:4). On other occasions He asserted His superiority to the ordinances that He would subsequently enrich and fulfill (Matt. 12:8; Mark 2:28; Luke 6:5).

In His teaching Christ made the Old Testament cultic regulations concerning cleanness even more rigorous by stressing a person's motivation rather than the external or mechanical observance of rules and regulations. He taught that adultery had been committed just as fully by a man's lusting after a woman (Matt. 5:27–28) as if the physical act had occurred. In John 15:2, the word that Christ had proclaimed made them clean by regenerating their characters and inculcating holiness of life.

Jesus was not only a moral Teacher. He came to earth to give His life as a ransom for humanity's sin (Mark 10:45). In this way He became the Lamb of God, taking away the sin of the world (John 1:29). His atoning death as our great High Priest transcended all the Law's cleansing rituals could ever be expected to do in the single offering of Himself for us on Calvary (Heb. 7:27). There He instituted a New Covenant of divine grace in His blood (Heb. 8:6), achieving human redemption and making possible eternal life for the penitent individual who has faith in His atoning work.

One of the most gracious assurances of His New Covenant is that the blood of Jesus cleanses us from all sin (1 John 1:7). Sacrifices and offerings are now unnecessary, for what Jesus demands is a penitent spirit that confesses the merits of His atonement. For the Christian the cultic provisions of the Old Testament are nullified. All meats have been declared clean (Mark 7:19; Acts 10:9–16), and the only sacrifices that God requires are those that emerge from a humble and contrite heart (Ps. 51:17).   *R. K. Harrison*

CLEMENT (Clĕm′ ĕnt) A fellow worker in the gospel with Paul (Phil. 4:3). He was apparently a member of the church at Philippi. Otherwise, no more information about him is available.

CLEOPAS (Clē′ ō·pȧs) A follower of Jesus, who with a companion was traveling toward the village of Emmaus on the day of Christ's resurrection (Luke 24:13–25). They were joined by a person whom they did not recognize. Later, they discovered that the stranger was Jesus Himself.

CLEOPHAS (Clē′ ō·phȧs) KJV spelling of Clopas (John 19:25).

CLOAK An outer garment. See *Clothing.*

CLOPAS (Clō′ pȧs) Relative of one of the Marys who were near the cross during the crucifixion (John 19:25). The Greek text describes him literally as "the of the Clopas." The most natural interpretation is that Clopas was husband of Mary. For the identification of this Mary and wider implications of Clopas' relationships, see *Mary.*

CLOSET A private room in a dwelling where Jesus encouraged people to pray (Matt. 6:6). He also noted that not even words said in the inner room privacy could be kept secret (Luke 12:3), indicating the Pharisees' hypocrisy could not be hidden. A biblical closet is an actual room, not a storage place. See *Architecture; Chamber.*

CLOTH, CLOTHING Biblical and archaeological sources concur that the earliest clothing resources were the hides of wild animals (Gen. 3:21). The Bible contains little information, however, about the process of manufacturing clothes from vegetable fibers. Technological developments predate biblical history.

Natural resources Cloth production in the ancient Near East dates to the Neolithic period when natural flax fibers were spun and woven into linen fabric. Nomadic cultures continued to prefer the hides of animals, some of which were left with small amounts of fur. The growing sedentary urban cultures preferred fabrics made from vegetable fibers such as flax and cotton and from animal fibers such as wool, goats' hair, silk, and the limited use of other wild animals.

Wild flax originated in the regions of Palestine and the Caucasus. Domesticated plants were

Modern Arab man wearing typical head cloth (called kaffiyeh) worn by Middle Easterners for millennia.

brought to Egypt early where it grew abundantly and was used to produce fine linen (Gen. 41:42) for soft garments and sails (Ezek. 27:7). Linen from Syrian flax was deemed finer than Egyptian. The importance of flax production in Palestine is reflected in the Gezer calendar. Quality fabrics were made from plants grown in Galilee and the Jordan valley. Flax stalks were also used in making sturdy baskets.

Cotton, which seems to have originated in the Indus Valley region, was grown on small trees. In the Iron Age the cotton tree was introduced into Assyria, but the climate of southern Mesopotamia was more suitable to crop cultivation. Cotton needs a warm humid climate for quality growth and processing and thus was produced less widely in Palestine. Still, it was highly prized by leaders from Egypt to Babylon for its bright color and its soft, yet durable, qualities. During the Hellenistic period, production and usage increased dramatically.

Wool was the most commonly-used raw material among the Semitic peoples for felt and other fabrics. By patriarchal times wool spinning was advanced sufficiently to warrant no description in the Bible. Natural wool tones ranged from white to yellow to gray. These gave rise to a multitude of color possibilities in conjunction with natural dyes. The development of metallic shears in the Iron Age greatly facilitated removal of wool and hair. Wool was at first plucked by hand and later by a toothed-comb. Wool fabrics were quite fashionable among the Sumerians, who spoke extensively of all aspects of wool production.

Other resources included silk, hemp, camel hair, and goat hair. Silk was imported from China and spread to Mesopotamia and eventually to the Mediterranean islands, where the moths were cultivated. Silk was generally reserved for royalty and the wealthy. Hemp and hair produced coarse garments when used alone, but when used with wool produced rugged quality garments.

The fuller would take the newly shorn wool or flax, and sometimes woven linen, and prepare the products for use in garments. Oil, dirt, or other residues were removed by first washing the material in an alkaline-based liquid made from ashes, lime, etc., and then repeatedly rinsed with clean water. Sometimes it would be tread upon and beaten against rocks in the rinse stage. Finally, the material would be left in the sun to dry, bleach, and shrink before final usage (Isa. 7:3). God's justice is compared to the fuller's wash soap (Mal. 3:2). In Jesus' transfiguration (Mark 9:3), His garments are said to have been whiter that the best fuller's work.

Weaving Biblical sources indicate that the raw materials were spun and woven into fabric sections about six feet in width and as long as necessary (Ex. 26:1–2,7–8). Egyptian murals indicate that their looms were large and technologically advanced. Three kinds of looms were employed during Bible times: the Egyptian vertical, the Greek vertical, and the horizontal. Models of the horizontal loom have been found in Egyptian tombs. The Greek vertical primarily was used in wool production. Primitive warp-weighted vertical looms, using hand-molded clay weights, were prominent even in the Iron II period in Israel. Examples of the baseball-sized loom weights have been excavated in numerous Old Testament sites. These looms consisted of two uprights, a horizontal beam, and a warp stretched between the beam and a series of loom weights. Greek vase-paintings also show many excellent examples of this type.

In the construction of the tabernacle, skilled women spun wool with their hands, and even interwove gold threads into the fabric (Ex. 35:25; 39:3). Spinning wheels were better developed in Egypt and Mesopotamia. The Book of Proverbs depicts a woman who spends much time spinning and weaving fabric (Prov. 31:13–24).

Dyes and colors Predynastic Egyptians (about 3000 B.C.) had begun to master the art of dyeing fabrics. Reds, purples, and blues (indigo) were the known natural dyes of the Mediterranean and African regions, having been derived from marine life, plants, and insects. Natural tones from different breeds of animals gave some variety to fabric colors (brown and black goats' hair; white, gray, and yellow wool). Available natural dyes and variable natural tones offered a wide spectrum of color possibilities. Mixing of dyes and fabrics could result in colors such as green, orange, brown, yellow, black, and pink, each with varied shades. Natural Tyrian purple was considered the most beautiful color of all throughout ancient history.

Those who could afford them preferred more colorful garments. Biblical descriptions indicate that dyed textiles were generally reserved for special garments and occasions. In Exodus 26:1 indigo, purple, and scarlet are listed as hues of tabernacle raiments. Jealousy over favoritism in the gift of a brightly colored coat is reflected in the Joseph conflict with his brothers (Gen. 37:3–4).

Clothing styles The Bible gives only general descriptions of the types of garments worn in biblical times. Egyptian, Assyrian, Roman, and Hittite monuments provide extensive pictorial evidence of dress in the ancient world. The need for clothing derives its origin from the shame of nakedness experienced by Adam and Eve in the garden (Gen. 3:7–8). God's provision for His people is reflected in the animal skin garments given in response to human need.

Men and women wore tunics made of linen or wool hanging from the neck to the knees or ankles. The Beni Hasan Tableau from the tomb of Khnum-hotep in Egypt depicts tunics worn by Semitic peoples as having diverse patterns and colors.

Loin cloths or waistcloths of linen (Jer. 13:1) or leather (2 Kings 1:8) were worn by men and used to gird up the tunic for travel. For comfort it could be loosened at night or when resting. Priests were to have their hips and thighs covered (Ex. 28:42) so as not to be exposed when in service in Yahweh.

The cloak was an outer garment used for a night covering, and thus was not to be loaned (Deut. 24:13). This article is often referred to as a mantle, which was worn by sojourners (Deut. 10:18; Ruth 3:3). In John 19:2, Jesus' outer cloak was draped over him during the beatings inflicted by the Roman soldiers. Jesus' tunic was probably the garment for which the Roman soldiers cast lots at His death (John 19:23). Long sleeveless external robes of blue or purple fabric were worn by royalty, prophets, and the wealthy (1 Sam. 18:4; Ezra 9:3; Luke 15:22). Mantles of various types were worn by kings, prophets, and other distinctive persons. In times of sorrow or distress, this garment might be torn (Job 1:20). Another kind of outer garment was the ephod, usually a special white robe (1 Sam. 2:19).

Women likewise wore inner and outer garments, but the differences in appearance must have been noticeable since wearing of clothes of the opposite sex was strictly forbidden (Deut. 22:5). The undergarments were loose fitting or baggy apparel (Prov. 31:24), and the outer robes were more flowing. The woman also wore a headcloth of brightly colored or patterned material which could be used as a wrapped support for carrying loads (Isa. 3:22), a veil (Gen. 24:65; Song of Sol. 5:7) or a hanging protective garment against the hot sun. A long train or veil adorned women of high social stature (Isa. 47:2).

Festive clothing for both men and women was generally made of costly white material, adorned with colorful outer wrappings and headclothes. Gold, silver, or jewels further decorated one's festive attire (2 Sam. 1:24). Priestly dress (Ex. 39:1–31) likewise consisted of only the best of fine linen, which was dyed scarlet, indigo, and purple, and of gold ornamentation. See *Weaving; Dress; Wool; Garments.*

R. Dennis Cole

CLOUD, PILLAR OF The means by which God led Israel through the wilderness with His presence and still hid Himself so they could not see His face. By day Israel saw a pillar of cloud, while by night they saw a pillar of fire (Ex. 13:21–22). The night before the Exodus, the cloud gave light to Israel but darkness to the Egyptians so they could not come near one another (Ex. 14:19–20). God came down to speak to Israel in the cloud during crisis times (Num. 11:25; 12:5). Coming to the tabernacle in the cloud, God spoke to Moses face to face (Ex. 33:11; Num. 14:14). Paul used the protection of the cloud theme to warn

Christians that living under God's presence calls for holy living (1 Cor. 10:1–14).

CLOUDS The Old Testament uses eight different Hebrew words in 167 passages to refer to clouds of rain, dust, smoke, storm, and fog. Both meteorological (1 Kings 18:44–45) and metaphorical meanings appear. The latter can be both positive (beneficial to life, Prov. 16:15; Isa. 25:5) and negative (hindrance to life, Eccl. 12:1–2). Clouds symbolize fluidity and transitoriness (Job 30:15; Isa. 44:22; Hos. 6:4), massive expansion and height (Ps. 36:5; Ezek. 38:9,16). More important are the statements in contexts speaking of God. **Old Testament** *1.* Clouds demonstrate the power of God as Creator. Particularly Job 36—38 witness to the sovereignty of the Creator, who directs and controls the clouds.

2. The clouds accompany God's revelation. God dwells in the dark clouds (1 Kings 8:12; Ps. 18:12). When He comes forth from His unapproachable holy being for judgment or for salvation, rain, lightning, and thunder break out from the clouds (Judg. 5:4; Ps. 68:33–35; 77:14–18; 97:2). When Yahweh appears as a Warrior, the clouds are His battle chariots in which He travels (Ps. 68:34; 104:3; Isa. 19:1) and from which He shoots down the lightning as arrows (Ps. 18:14; 77:17; Zech. 9:14). Dark clouds overshadow the judgment day of Yahweh, which the prophets announced (Ezek. 30:3,18; Joel 2:2; Zeph. 1:15).

3. Clouds conceal and reveal the secrets of God at the same time. In the tent of revelation during the wilderness period (Ex. 40:34–38), in the Jerusalem Temple (1 Kings 8:10–11), on Mount Sinai (Ex. 34:5), and in His direction and protection by means of the clouds and the pillar of fire, Israel experienced that God came to them (Ex. 33:7–11) but still remained wholly other (Lev. 16:2,13) even when he came as the Son of Man (Dan. 7:13).

New Testament *1.* The strictly meterological meaning appears only in Luke 12:54. A metaphorical meaning occurs in Jude 12; 2 Peter 2:17, Hebrew 12:1 (using a distinct Greek word). Clouds are not used in the New Testament to point to the power of God as Creator except for indirect references (Matt. 5:45; Acts 14:17). All other references to clouds in the New Testament have a relationship to God.

2. The clouds accompany the revelation of God in Jesus Christ. As God on Sinai was glorified and concealed in the clouds, so was Jesus on the mountain of transfiguration and in His ascension to heaven (Mark 9:7; Acts 1:9). The clouds into which Jesus entered with Moses and Elijah as Moses had once entered on Mount Sinai (Ex. 24:18), are "light" but at the same time concealing. The voice out of the clouds no longer referred to the Torah of Moses but to the teaching of the Son. No longer must a tent be set up to experience the presence of God, for the clouds have set God's presence free to appear in Jesus alone. As the resurrected One was exalted to the Father, the clouds veiled Him.

3. The clouds mark the conclusive and final revelation of the lordship of Christ. Mark 13:26; 14:62; and Revelation 1:7 combined the motif of the Son of Man from Daniel 7 with the word of judgment from Zechariah 12:10 and referred them to the parousia or coming of Christ. Clouds thus became only signs of the revealing of the lordship amd majesty of the Lord; they no longer concealed anything. In Revelation 14:14–16 the returning Christ sits on "white" (light, shining, majestic) clouds. In this transparent purity both the living and the deceased believers are joined with their Lord (1 Thess. 4:17).

In 1 Corinthians 10:1–2 the clouds and the sea of the Exodus of Israel form a type of the baptism of Christians which had been falsely understood by the Corinthians.   *Christian Wolf*

CLOUT KJV translation in Jeremiah 38:11–12 for Hebrew word meaning, "tattered clothes, rags."

CLUB A weapon of war used in close combat to strike an enemy. See *Arms and Armor.*

CNIDUS (Cnī′ dŭs) Place name of city in southwest Turkey. Paul's ship passed by here on the way to Rome (Acts 27:7).

COAL Charred wood used for fuel. See *Cooking.* The altar of sacrifice burned coals (Lev. 16:12), as did the blacksmith's fire (Isa. 44:12) and the baker's (Isa. 44:19). Coals provided heat for refining metal (Ezek. 24:11). Burning coals became a symbol of divine judgment, apparently representing God coming to earth and causing volcanos to erupt and throw burning coals on His enemies (Ps. 18:13).

COAST The land bordering a major body of water and used by KJV in obsolete sense of territories, borders, frontiers.

COAT See *Clothing.*

COAT OF MAIL See *Arms and Armor.*

COBRA A poisonous snake. See *Animals; Adder.*

COCK See *Birds; Chicken.* The strutting, crowing bird, *Zarzir motnayim* (Prov. 30:31).

COCKATRICE See *Animals.* KJV translation of legendary serpent and poisonous snakes (Isa. 11:8; 14:29; 59:5; Jer. 8:17). It is probably the *Vipera xanthina.*

A cobra pictured in the famous Nile Mosaic.

COCKCROWING The third watch of the night in the Roman system (Mark 13:35), thus midnight until 3 a.m. The Jewish system had only three watches. The Roman had four.

COCKLE Plant whose name derives from Hebrew word for "stink." It appears in Scripture only at Job 31:40, and is identified as *Lolium temulentum.* Modern translations refer to brier or thorns.

CODEX (Cō′ dĕx)describes a collection of manuscript pages, especially of the Bible or sections of it, bound together in book form.

The word comes directly from the Latin meaning "tree trunk," possibly describing a stack of wooden tablets, each coated with wax on one side for writing and held together by leather thongs inserted in holes bored along one side. For centuries papyrus and parchment made from animal skins were popular writing materials because they could be shaped into long strips and rolled into a scroll. Using the scroll required both hands, however, and someone decided to cut a scroll into equal-sized sheets, stack them in order, and stitch them together along one edge. So, the scroll became a codex.

Biblical manuscripts produced in the codex form were all handcopied in Greek capital letters on parchment from older manuscripts. Nearly 250 of these manuscripts in codex form are now preserved in various libraries and museums. They have been dated from the fourth to the eleventh centuries. The oldest and most complete is Codex Sinaiticus now in the British Museum. It contains about 350 sheets that measure 15 by 13 1/2 inches with four columns of lettering per page. It was discovered accidentally in 1844 by a Russian scholar in a monastery at the foot of Mount Sinai. It contains all the New Testament and most of the Old. Another important codex from the fourth century is in the Vatican Library in Rome. A fifth-century manuscript of the four Gospels is known as Codex Washingtonianus and is housed in the Freer Gallery of Art in Washington, D. C.

William J. Fallis

COFFER Old English word for box in 1 Samuel 6:8,11,15 (KJV).

COHORT A Roman military unit with capacity of 1000 men; ten cohorts formed a legion. Cornelius (Acts 10:1) apparently belonged to a cohort of archers named the *Cohors II Miliaria Italica Civium Romanorum Voluntariorum* that had 1,000 members, Cornelius commanding 100 of them. Originally, the unit had been formed in Rome of freed slaves who received citizenship. It was transferred to Syria at least by 69 A.D. The Bible narrative places the cohort in Caesarea before 41 A.D. An infantry cohort was stationed in Jerusalem and protected Paul from zealous Jews (Acts 21:31). They were stationed in the citadel Antonia on the northwest corner of the Temple. A centurion attached to the cohort Augusta had command of Paul and other prisoners, transporting them from Caesarea to Rome (Acts 27:1). KJV translates "cohort" as "band."

COINS are stamped metal disks issued by a government for trade and valuation.

Before money was invented, a man might trade or swap with a neighbor something he owned for something he wanted. Because of their intrinsic value and mobility, cattle were very popular in the barter system. Such trading took place also on a grand scale. When Hiram of Tyre agreed to furnish building materials for the Temple, Solomon pledged large annual payments in wheat and olive oil (1 Kings 5:11). Eventually the discovery and use of metals for ornaments, implements, and weapons led to their dominating the primitive exchanges. Silver, gold, and copper in various forms, such as bars, bracelets, and the like represented wealth in addition to land, cattle, and slaves. The silver shekel, weighing about four

A coin from Pamphylia (190–36 B.C.).

tenths of an ounce, became the standard measure. When Abraham bought the cave of Machpelah, he "weighed out . . . four hundred shekels of silver" (Gen. 23:16). At that time the shekel was a weight rather than a coin.

The talent was another weight frequently associated in the Old Testament with gold and silver. The crown that David took from the king of the Ammonites weighed one talent (2 Sam. 12:30). After Judah's defeat at Megiddo, the victorious pharaoh appointed a puppet king and required the Jews to pay Egypt a heavy tribute in silver and gold (2 Kings 23:33). Although its weight varied slightly from one country to another, the talent was approximately 75 pounds.

Determining the weight and purity of any metal was a tedious business and sometimes subject to dishonesty. To establish some standards, the first coins were minted about the same time around 650 B.C. both in Greece and in Lydia of Asia Minor. Excavations in Shechem have uncovered a Greek silver coin dating after 600 B.C., about the time the Jews were returning from Babylon to Judah. The first mention of money in the Bible appears in Ezra 2:69, describing funds collected for rebuilding the Temple. The King James Version lists among other resources 61,000 "drams of gold," but the RSV has "darics of gold," (NAS, NIV, "*drachmas*") referring to a Persian gold coin. Years later, about 326 B.C., after Alexander overran the Persian Empire, Greek coinage was circulated widely in Palestine, according to archaeological research.

The Maccabean Revolt began in 167 B.C. Twenty-four years later (123 B.C.), Judea became an independent state, and about 110 B.C. the reigning high priest minted in bronze the first real Jewish coins. Only dominant political entities could produce silver coins. In accord with the Second Commandment, Jewish coins did not bear the image of any ruler, but they used symbols such as a wreath, a cornucopia, or the seven-branched lampstand of the Temple. Such symbols continued to be used by Herod and other appointed Jewish rulers after Palestine submitted to Roman domination. Many small copper coins from this early New Testament period have been discovered.

The coin most often mentioned in the Greek New Testament is the *denarion,* translated "penny" in the KJV and "denarius" in the RSV, NAS, NIV. It was a silver coin usually minted in Rome. It carried on one side the image of the emperor (Matt. 22:21), and on the reverse might be some propaganda symbol. Of course, the "penny" translation was an attempt to equate the value of an ancient coin with a familiar one of the King James era. Its value in New Testament times can be more accurately assessed by knowing the labor that the ancient coin could buy. The denarius was the daily pay for Roman soldiers and the wage of a day laborer in Palestine (Matt. 20:21).

Roman coins in a bowl of the same period at Caesarea Maritima on the coast of Israel.

C

Another reference to silver money occurs in Matthew 26:15 in the agreement between the high priest and Judas for betraying Jesus. Although the original text mentions only "silver" with no specific coin, scholars feel that the figure "thirty" recalls the compensation required by law for killing a slave by accident (Ex. 21:32). So, Judas' pay could have been thirty silver shekels. By this time the shekel had developed from only a measure of weight to a specific coin weighing a little less than half an ounce. It is possible also that the "large money" (KJV) paid to the soldiers guarding Jesus' tomb (Matt. 28:12) referred to large silver coins or shekels.

A third coin mentioned in the New Testament was the one the poor widow put into the Temple treasury as Jesus watched (Mark 12:42). The KJV translates the original words as "two mites, which make a farthing" while the RSV reads "two copper coins, which made a penny" (NIV: "two very small copper coins, worth only a fraction of a penny." The first noun describes the smallest *Greek* copper coin, (*lepta*)*,* and the second noun translates the Greek (*quadrans)* for the smallest *Roman* copper coin. In either case, they were the smallest coins available, but Jesus said they were greater in proportion than the other donations.

From two parables told by Jesus we get the impression that the word "talent" had come in New Testament times to represent a large sum of money, instead of just a measure of weight. In Matthew 18:24, He told of a man who owed a certain king "ten thousand talents." A few chapters later He described a wealthy man assigning different responsibilities to three servants. At the reckoning time he rebuked the one who had merely hidden his talent by saying that at least he could have deposited the money to let it earn interest (Matt. 25:27). Such a talent had been estimated to have a current value of about one thousand dollars.   *William J. Fallis*

A gold coin of Lysimachos from Thrace (323–281 B.C.).

COLHOZEH (Cŏl hō′ zĕh) Personal name meaning, "he sees everything" or "everyone a seer." Father whose son Shallun was ruler of part of Mizpah and who helped Nehemiah repair Jerusalem's gates (Neh. 3:15). Apparently he had a grandson living in Jerusalem in Nehemiah's day (Neh. 11:5). The name Colhozeh may indicate a family of prophets.

COLLAR This word is used to translate various Hebrew words and may describe (1) the opening for the head in a garment (Ex. 28:32 NIV; Job 30:18; Ps. 133:2 NIV), (2) a decorative ornament around the necks of the Midianite Kings (NRSV) or their camels (Judg. 8:26; see Prov. 1:9; Song of Sol. 4:9), (3) stocks or a pillory used to restrain a person (Jer. 29:26 NRSV, NAS), and (4) a shackle of iron placed around the neck of a prisoner (Ps. 105:18 NRSV, REB, TEV).

COLLECTION FOR THE POOR SAINTS Near the end of Paul's ministry he took up a collection for the poor of the Jerusalem church. Why the Jerusalem church had so much poverty is not clear. The Jews in Jerusalem may have isolated Christian Jews from the economic system. Paul and Barnabas promised to help (Gal. 2:1–10). This money was collected by Paul from the Gentile churches which he administered. These included churches in Philippi, Thessalonica, Corinth, and Galatia. He mentioned this offering on three occasions in his letters. In 1 Corinthians 16:1–4, Paul indicated that he wanted the church to put something aside on the first day of each week. In 2 Corinthians 8—9, Paul wrote that the churches of Macedonia had given liberally and Titus would oversee the completion of the offering in Corinth. Finally, in Romans 15:25, Paul stated that at the present time he was going to Jerusalem to deliver the gift. A sense of spiritual indebtedness to the founding church in Jerusalem prompted the offering. Luke never mentioned the offering specifically in Acts. There is a list of men in Acts 20:4 who accompanied Paul to Jerusalem. (This trip corresponds to the plans of Rom. 15:25.) The importance of this offering for Paul was twofold. First, the offering met an economic need in Jerusalem. Political instability and general economic depression were problems in Palestine. There were dependent widows (Acts 6:1), and the sharing of property offered only temporary relief (Acts 4:32–37). For this reason Paul was anxious to "remember the poor" (Gal. 2:10). Second, the offering had a theological importance for Paul. The fact that the Gentiles were willing to aid the Jews in this manner validated Paul's Gentile mission. The offering was evidence that in the Christian family there was neither "Jew nor Greek" (Gal. 3:28). *Terence B. Ellis; Lynn Jones*

COLLEGE KJV translation (2 Kings 22:14) of Hebrew word meaning, "repetition, copy, second," referring to the second district or division of Jerusalem. Compare Zephaniah 1:10.

COLONY Only Philippi is described as a colony of Rome (Acts 16:12), though many cities mentioned in the New Testament were considered as such. Roman colonization as practiced under Julius Caesar provided land for healthy individuals on the relief rolls of Rome and veteran soldiers. The cities of Corinth and Philippi were Roman colonies during the time of Caesar. Augustus founded colonies in Antioch (Psidian), Lystra, Troas, and Syracuse (all mentioned in Acts). Other Roman colonies included Ptolemais (Acco) and Iconium. Colonies had autonomous local governments and in some cases were exempt from poll and land taxes. The functioning of the local governments of Roman colonies is seen in Acts 16:12–40.

COLORS

Color Awareness in Biblical Literature The writers of biblical literature reflected little or nothing of an abstract sense of color. Nevertheless, they made frequent references to a select group of colors when their purposes in writing so demanded it.

References to Colors in the Bible Moving beyond color in the abstract sense, one does find in the Bible frequent references to certain objects which have color designations. When reference is made to a particular color or colors, it is likely made for one of two basic reasons. First, a writer may wish to use color in a descriptive sense to help identify an object or clarify some aspect about that object.

A second reason for color designations in the Bible involves a more specialized usage. At times a writer may use color in a symbolic sense to convey theological truth about the subject of his writing. Color designations have general symbolic significance. For instance, white may be symbolic of purity or joy; black may symbolize judgment or decay; red may symbolize sin or life-blood; and purple may be symbolic of luxury and elegance. Color symbolism became for the writers of apocalyptic literature (Daniel, Revelation) an appropriate tool for expressing various truths in hidden language. In their writings one may find white representative of conquest or victory, black representative of famine or pestilence, red representative of wartime bloodshed, paleness (literally "greenish-gray") representative of death, and purple representative of royalty.

Color Designations of Frequent Use The color designations which appear in the Bible offer relatively little in the way of variety. The matter is further complicated by the fact that of those colors which appear a precise translation of the underlying Hebrew and Greek terms is difficult.

The colors mentioned most frequently in the Bible are those which refer to the dyed products manufactured by the peoples of Israel and her neighbors. Particularly common are the varying shades in the red-purple range. Purple was the most valued of the ancient dyes and was used in the coloring of woven materials. The peoples of Crete, Phoenicia, and Canaan produced the dye from mollusks taken from the Mediterranean Sea. Purple is noted to be the color of some of the tabernacle furnishings and priests' garments in the Old Testament (Ex. 26:1; 28:4–6). In the New Testament the robe put on Christ and Lydia's occupation are associated with the color purple as well (Mark 15:17; Acts 16:14). By varying the dye-making process, other shades of blue became possible and are noted in Scripture (Ex. 28:5–6; Ezek. 23:6; Rev. 9:17).

Shades of red dye were produced from the bodies of insects, vegetables, and reddish-colored minerals. These were, likewise, used to color garments. In addition, natural objects are sometimes designated red, scarlet, or crimson, including such items as pottage, wine, the sky, and horses (Gen. 25:30; Prov. 23:31; Matt. 16:2–3; Rev. 6:4). Isaiah used the color red as a symbol of the nature of sin (Isa. 1:18).

The neutrals, white and black, are mentioned on occasion in the Bible. Natural objects such as milk, leprous skin, and snow are designated white (Gen. 49:12; Lev. 13:3–4; Isa. 1:18). White is used in the New Testament of the garments of Jesus and angels to indicate the glory of the wearer (Matt. 17:2; 28:3; Acts 1:10). Natural objects designated black in the Bible include such items as hair, skin, the sky, and even the sun itself (Lev. 13:31; Job 30:30; 1 Kings 18:45; Rev. 6:12).

Other color designations used less frequently but not any less significantly in the Bible are green, yellow, vermillion, and gray. *James Sexton*

COLOSSIANS (Cō·lŏs' sĭans) A letter from Paul to the Church at Colosse. It is one of the Prison Epistles (along with Ephesians, Philemon, and Philippians). The traditional date and place of writing is A.D. 61 or 62 from Rome. The letter itself does not name the place where Paul was imprisoned, and Caesarea and Ephesus have been suggested as alternatives to Rome. If written from Ephesus, the time of writing would be in the mid-50's; if from Caesarea the late 50's. The primary purpose of Colossians was to correct false teachings which were troubling the church.

Authorship of Colossians The authenticity of Colossians has been debated, as has also the exact nature of the relationship between Ephesians and Colossians. In favor of Pauline authorship it may be noted that the letter was accepted as genuinely Pauline by the early church. While it is true that the style and vocabulary differ somewhat from Paul's other letters, this occurs primarily in the section which attacks the Colossian heresy (1:3—2:23). The unusual terminology in this section is at least partly the result of addressing an unusual problem.

Some would rule out Pauline authorship by identifying the heresy attacked in Colossians as second century gnosticism. Such arguments are not convincing, however, because (1) the heresy cannot be identified with certainty, and (2) gnostic thought was already encroaching on the church by the middle of the first century.

One should note also the relationship between Philemon and Colossians. They mention many of the same people and were apparently carried by the same messenger (Col. 4:7–18; Philem. 1,2,10,23,24). The undoubted authenticity of Philemon argues in favor of the Pauline authorship of Colossians as well.

The City of Colosse Colosse was located in the southwest corner of Asia Minor in what was then the Roman province of Asia. Hierapolis and Laodicea were situated only a few miles away. All three were in the Lycus River valley. A main road from Ephesus to the east ran through the region. See *Asia Minor*.

Colosse was prominent during the Greek period. By Paul's day it had lost much of its importance, perhaps due to the growth of the neighboring cities. Extremely detrimental to all of the cities of the region were the earthquakes which occasionally did severe damage. Shortly after Paul wrote Colossians, the entire Lycus Valley was devastated by an earthquake (about A.D. 61) which probably ended occupation of the city.

The region included a mixture of people native to the area, Greeks, Romans, and transplanted Jews. The church probably reflected the same diversity. As far as we know, Paul never visited Colosse. His influence was felt, however, during his ministry in Ephesus. (Acts 19:10 records that all Asia heard the gospel.) The letters to Philemon and to the Colossians indicate that many of Paul's fellow workers (if not Paul himself) had worked among the churches of the Lycus Valley. As a result, the relationship between the apostle to the Gentiles and the Colossian church was close enough that when trouble arose some of the church turned to Paul for instruction.

Content Colossians may be divided into two main parts. The first (1:3—2:23) is a polemic against false teachings. The second (3:1—4:17) is made up of exhortations to proper Christian living. The introduction (1:1–2) is in the form of a Hellenistic, personal letter. The senders (Paul and Timothy) and the recipients (the Colossian church) are identified, and a greeting is expressed (the usual Pauline "grace and peace" replaced the usual secular "greeting").

Typical of Paul, a lengthy thanksgiving (1:3–8) and prayer (1:9–14) lead into the body of the letter. Paul thanked God for the faith, hope, and love (1:4–5) which the Colossians had by virtue of their positive response to the gospel. He prayed that they might have a full knowledge and understanding of God's will and lead a life worthy of redeemed saints, citizens of the kingdom of Christ (1:9–14).

The doctrinal section which follows begins with a description of the grandeur of the preeminent Christ (1:15–20). Though the precise meaning of some words and phrases is uncertain, there is no doubt as to Paul's intent. He meant to present Jesus as fully God incarnate (1:15,19), as supreme Lord over all creation (1:15–17), as supreme Lord of the church (1:18), and as the only Source of reconciliation (1:20).

The origin of this grand statement on the nature and work of Christ is debated. The structure, tone, and vocabulary of the passage have led many to speculate that 1:15–20 is a doctrinal statement (hymn) that was in use in the church of Paul's day. This passage and Philippians 2:6–11 are thought by the majority of scholars to be the most obvious examples of pre-Pauline tradition in the letters of Paul. However, difficulty in recreating a balanced hymnic structure has convinced most that Paul rewrote portions of the hymn, if indeed he was not the author of the entire confession. Author or not, the apostolic stamp of approval is on these words which Paul used to state unambiguously that Christ is Lord and Savior of all.

The Lycus River Valley (which was devastated ca. A.D. 61 by an earthquake) as seen from Colosse.

A view of the tell of Colosse.

The purpose of the first two chapters was to correct the false teaching which had infiltrated the church. The heresy is not identified, but several characteristics of the heresy are discernible: (1) An inferior view of Christ is combated in 1:15–20. This Christological passage implies that the heretics did not consider Jesus to be fully divine or perhaps did not accept Him as the sole Source of redemption. (2) The Colossians were warned to beware of plausible sounding "philosophies" which were antichrist (2:8). (3) The heresy apparently involved the legalistic observance of "traditions," circumcision, and various dietary and festival laws (2:8,11,16,21; 3:11). (4) The worship of angels and lesser spirits was encouraged by the false teachers (2:8,18). (5)Asceticism, the deprivation or harsh treatment of one's "evil"

fleshly body, was promoted (2:20−23). Finally, (6) the false teachers claimed to possess special insight (perhaps special revelations) which made them (rather than the apostles or the Scriptures) the ultimate source of truth (2:18,19).

Scholars cannot agree on who these false teachers were. Some of the characteristics cited above seem to be Jewish; others sound like gnostic teachings. Some see the teachings of a mystery religion here. Dozens of alternatives have been proposed by very capable authors. It is even argued that Paul was not attacking one specific heresy (or if he was, he did not have a clear understanding of it himself), but rather was warning the Colossians about a variety of false teachings which had troubled the church, or which might trouble it in the future. While the passage does not clearly identify the heretics, it does clearly state that Christ (not angels, philosophies, rituals, traditions, asceticism, nor anything else) is the Source of redemption.

Colossians 3:1−4 provides the link connecting the theology of chapters 1 and 2 with the exhortations to live a Christian life in chapters 3 and 4. The command to "put to death" (3:5 NIV) and to "rid yourselves of all such things" which will reap the wrath of God (3:5−11) is balanced by the command to "clothe yourselves with" (3:12 NIV) those things characteristic of God's chosen people (3:12−17). The changes are far from superficial, however. They stem from the Christian's new nature and submission to the rule of Christ in every area of one's life (3:9,10,15−17).

Rules for the household appear in 3:18—4:1. The typical first century household is assumed, thus the passage addresses wives and husbands, fathers and children, masters and slaves. Paul made no comment about the rightness or wrongness of the social structures; he accepted them as givens. Paul's concern was that the structures as they existed be governed by Christian principles. Submission to the Lord (3:18,20,22; 4:1), Christian love (3:19), and the prospect of divine judgment (3:24—4:1) must determine the way people treat one another regardless of their social station. It is this Christian motivation which distinguishes these house rules from those that can be found in Jewish and pagan sources.

A final group of exhortations (4:2−6) and an exchange of greetings (4:7−17) bring the letter to a close. Notable in this final section are (1) the mention of Onesimus (4:9), which links this letter with Philemon, (2) the mention of a letter at Laodicea (4:16), which may have been Ephesians, and (3) Paul's concluding signature which indicates that the letter was prepared by an amanuensis (secretary) (4:18).

Outline

I. Warnings Against Heresy (1:1−2:23)
  A. Greeting, thanksgiving, and prayer (1:1−14)
  B. Christ and no other is supreme in the universe (1:15−17).
  C. Christ, having reconciled all creation to God and embodying the fullness of God, is supreme in the church (1:18−20).
  D. Believers experience Christ's supremacy in the saving power of the gospel (1:21−23).
  E. The supreme Christ fulfills God's eternal saving purpose (1:24−29).
  F. Christians should have full confidence in Christ's supremacy and forget heretical teachings (2:1−5).
  G. Elemental human traditions must not lead away from faith in Christ (2:6−10).
  H. Legal practices cannot supplement Christ's work of salvation on the cross (2:11−23).
II. The Supreme Rule of Christ Leads to Rules for Life with Christ (3:1−4:18).
  A. Believers seek the fullness of the new life in Christ (3:1−4).
  B. Life in Christ cleanses believers of old practices (3:5−11).
  C. The life in Christ gives power for unity, mutual love, and forgiveness (3:12−14).
  D. Church life includes mutual encouragement and worship (3:15−17).
  E. Life in Christ brings faithfulness and compassion in family relationships (3:18−4:1).
  F. Closing greetings and blessings for those in Christ (4:2−18)

Michael Martin

COLT The young of various riding animals. *1.* Young camels (Gen. 32:15), noted by the Hebrew term for "sons." *2.* Young donkeys (Gen. 49:11), also "son" in Hebrew. Compare Judges 10:4; 12:14, where Hebrew is "donkeys." The New Testament uses the reference in Zechariah 9:9 as a prediction of Jesus' triumphal entry into Jerusalem (Matt. 21; Mark 11; Luke 19; John 12:15). Zechariah apparently used parallelism, the basic structure of Hebrew poetry, to describe a rider on one young donkey. Mark, Luke, and John told the story of Jesus' entry with reference to one animal. Matthew mentioned two animals, including both the ass and the colt from Zechariah as separate animals.

COMFORTER KJV translation of the special word for the Holy Spirit in John 14—16 (in Greek *parakletos.* NAS translates, "Helper"; NIV, "Counselor"; NRSV, "Advocate." The background of the Greek term lies in the law court where the Paraklete helped someone. The Holy Spirit is another "Helper" alongside Jesus for the believer. As Jesus helped disciples during His earthly ministry, so the Spirit helps them after the ascension as they face a hostile world. Meanwhile, Jesus is the

Paraklete in the heavenly court (1 John 2:1). See *Advocate; Holy Spirit.*

COMMANDMENTS, TEN See *Ten Commandments.*

COMMERCE Commercial activity in the ancient Near East took many forms. The economy centered around agriculture, but some manufactured goods were produced and natural resources mined. Farm goods, products, and resources had to be transported to market centers and other countries. Barter and the buying and selling of goods and services held a prominent place in the life of villages and towns. This is demonstrated by the large number of economic texts uncovered in excavations and the importance placed on transactional dialogue and the use of commercial scenes to highlight major events in the biblical text.

Products The irrigated fields of Mesopotamia and Egypt and the terraced hillsides of Palestine produced a variety of agricultural products. Barley and wheat were crushed, winnowed, sieved, and distributed on the threshingfloor (*gōren)* for local consumption (Deut. 15:14; Ruth 3:15). Surpluses were transported to regional marketplaces and major cities. Whole grain, meal, flax, nuts, dates, olive oil, fish in the Galilee area, and a variety of animal by-products found their way into every home and paid the taxes imposed by the government. The kings like Uzziah (2 Chron. 26:10) also had large holdings of land and vast herds that contributed to the overall economy.

Village craftsmen produced pottery, metal and wooden implements, weapons, and cloth. Evidence of their commercial self-sufficiency is seen in the recovery of loom weights in excavations of private homes throughout Israel. These balls of clay provide evidence of how widespread the local weaving and cloth-making industries were in ancient times. Manufactured products were distributed among the inhabitants of the village. The finer items were traded to traveling merchants or transported overland to Jerusalem or some other commercial center.

Manufactured goods most commonly introduced into national or international commerce included fine pottery, weapons, glassware, jewelry, cosmetics, and dyed cloth. Distinctive styles or fine workmanship created markets for these products and thus made it worth the costs and hazards of sea and overland transport. Evidence of how widespread trade was in the ancient world can be traced by the different styles and decoration of pottery. Seal markings showing place of origin are also found on many jugs and storage jars used to transport wine, oil, grain, and spices.

Another indication of the diversity of trading products that circulated throughout the ancient Near East is found in Ezekiel's "lamentation over Tyre," one of the principal Phoenician seaports (Ezek. 27:12–24). Their ships and those of Tarshish carried iron, tin, and lead, exchanging them for slaves, horses, mules, ivory, and ebony at various ports of call. Aram or Edom (NIV with footnote) traded "emeralds, purple, embroidered work, fine linen, coral, and rubies" (27:16 NAS), and Judah sent honey, oil, and balm along with wheat as trade goods to Tyre (Ezek. 27:17). The Phoenicians also supplied their trading partners with wool and cloth dyed purple with a glandular secretion from the murex mollusk.

Merchant quarters were established in many trading centers like that at Ugarit, a seaport in northern Syria (1600–1200 B.C.). The Phoenician seaports of Tyre and Sidon also had their resident alien communities, adding to the cosmopolitan nature of these cities and facilitating transmission of culture and ideas. The economic and political importance of these trading communities is seen in Solomon's construction of storehouse cities in Hamath (2 Chron. 8:4 and in Ahab's negotiations with Ben-Hadad of Syria for the establishment of "market areas in Damascus" (1 Kings 20:34 NIV).

Places of Business Metropolitan centers, like Babylon and Thebes, had open areas or market squares where commerce took place. This was also the case in the Hellenistic cities of the Near East which had one or more *agoras.* The narrow confines of the villages and towns in Palestine, however, restricted commercial activity to shops or booths built into the side of private homes or to the open area around the city gate.

For most Palestinian villages and towns, the gate was a vital place where commercial, judicial, and social activities of all sorts took place. Lot sat in the gate, demonstrating his status as a privileged resident alien (Gen. 19:1). The gate of Samaria served as a market center where the people purchased measures of barley and fine meal (2 Kings 7:18). In Proverbs 31:23, one sign of a prosperous man with a well-ordered house was his ability to sit with the elders in the gate.

Large urban centers, like Jerusalem, had several gates and commercial districts, thus allowing for diversification of commercial activity throughout the city. Jeremiah 18:2 speaks of the Potsherd Gate (author's translation; known as the Dung Gate in Neh. 2:13) where Jeremiah enacted a prophecy of doom by smashing a pot. He also mentions the bakers' street as the principal area of production and supply of bread in Jerusalem (Jer. 37:21). In the Roman period, Josephus lists several commercial activities in the city: wool shops, smithies, and the clothes market.

Weights and Measures Inscribed stone, clay, or metal weights were used throughout the Near East and have been found in large quantities by archaeologists. They range from the talent (2 Sam. 12:30; 2 Kings 18:14) to the mina (Ezra 2:69 NAS), the shekel (2 Sam. 14:26; Ezek. 4:10), and various smaller weights. Until the establishment of the monarchy, commercial transactions were governed in each Israelite town by a local standard of exchange. Evidence has been found (markings on the weights) of the use of both the Egyptian standard of weights as well as Babylonian measures. Even these standards were apparently negotiable, however, and sometimes subject to abuse. Thus, Abraham was forced before witnesses in the gate of Hebron to pay an exorbitant rate (400 shekels of silver) for the cave of Machpelah (Gen. 23:16), and Amos condemned those merchants who were "making the ephah small, and the shekel great, and falsifying the balances by deceit" (8:5).

Until coinage was introduced after 600 B.C., foodstuffs and other goods were obtained through barter in the marketplace or purchased with weights of previous metals (Gen. 33:19; Job 42:11). When minted coinage came into general use during the Hellenistic period (after 200 B.C.), it created a revolution in commerce. See *Coins*. Transactions in accepted coinage, known to bear a definite weight, added to the confidence of the public and eliminated some of the abuses of the marketplace. Coins also facilitated the payment of taxes (Mark 12:15–17) and wages (Matt. 20:2). **Business Law** Hammurabi's law code (about 1750 B.C.) contains a model of business law in the Ancient Near East. Many facets or trade are governed by this code. They are sometimes echoed in the biblical codes as well. For instance, Hammurabi's law protected a man who consigned a portion of his grain to storage from losses due to natural events and the corrupt practices of the owner of the storage room. (Compare Ex. 22:7–9). Lending at interest to fellow Israelites was forbidden in Exodus 22:25 and Deuteronomy 23:19. This injunction, however, does not seem to apply to the practice of investment of surplus capital found in Matthew 25:14–30 and Luke 19:12–25.

The parables of the pounds and the talents suggest the existence of a sophisticated banking and investment community, which lent out sums for commercial enterprises and garnered profits for those who left their money with them. A portion of the vast sums that came into the Temple treasury in Jerusalem as taxes each year (Matt. 17:24) were probably lent out as investment capital. Several of Hammurabi's laws speak of similar practices requiring that those who engage in commercial transactions obtain receipts to show proof of their investments and sales.

Trade and Trade Routes From earliest times caravans of traders carried goods throughout the Near East. Obsidian, brought by Neolithic traders from Anatolia, has been discovered at sites hundreds of miles from its place of origin. Palestine, situated on a land bridge between Mesopotamia and Africa, naturally became a center of commercial travel. Groups of Semitic traders, like the Ishmael-

ites and Midianites (Gen. 37:27–28), are recorded in Egyptian texts and on the walls of tombs, such as the Beni-hasen tomb paintings (about 1900 B.C.), which depict whole families with their donkeys transporting "ox-hide" ingots of metal. They used hilltop pathways as well as the Via Maris coastal highway and the King's Highway in Transjordan to move between Mesopotamia and Egypt. Eventually, the introduction of the camel and the establishment of caravansaries (inns where caravans can rest at night) as storage and rest centers, made it possible for merchants to take a more direct route across the deserts of northern Syria and Arabia. These lucrative trade routes were controlled in the Roman period by the city of Tadmor, the capital of the Palmyran kingdom, and by the Nabateans.

During the monarchy period, Israel's trade horizon expanded. Solomon imported vast quantities of luxury and exotic goods (ivory, apes, peacocks—1 Kings 10:22*b)* from all over the Near East. He also purchased horses and chariots for his fortress garrisons like those at Gezer, Hazor, and Megiddo (1 Kings 10:26). The nation had no deep water ports on its coastline, so the Gulf of Aqaba became the prime point of entry for goods coming from Africa (spices, precious stones, gold from Ophir, algum wood). The Aqaba port of Elath (Ezion-geber) served the needs of the court of Solomon and subsequent kings as well. The shipping trade of Israel, as well as many other nations, joined with or was carried by Phoenician merchantmen (1 Kings 10:22). These more experienced sailors could avoid the storms and other hazards that sank many ships in the Mediterranean (2 Chron. 20:37 NIV).

Even in New Testament times, shipping was restricted to particular routes and seasons (Acts 27:12). Travel seems to have been more common in this period as seen by the movements of Paul, the other apostles, and those associated with the establishment of the early church, such as Aquila and Priscilla (Rom. 16:3). Passengers and cargo might be transported on one leg of a journey on one ship and then transferred to a number of others to complete their journey (Acts 27:1–8). Underwater excavations off Cyprus and the Herodian port of Caesarea Maritima demonstrate, however, that many of these ships never made it to port (Acts 27:39–44).

For those who chose to take the overland routes, instead, the Romans constructed paved roads that facilitated the movement of their armies, as well as people and wagons loaded with goods for sale. Mile markers set up along these roads show how often they were repaired and which emperors took a special interest in the outlying districts of his domain. See *Agriculture; Banking; Economic Life; Marketplace; Transportation and Travel; Weights and Measures.*

Victor H. Matthews

COMMON In the Old Testament, that which was common (alternately profane) was contrasted with that which was holy. Thus common bread was contrasted with the bread of the Presence (1 Sam. 21:4); the common journey was contrasted with the military campaign for which David and his men would need to be consecrated (1 Sam. 21:5). The common people (*am ha arets,* "people of the land") were contrasted with rulers or people of standing in the community (Lev. 4:22,27) and were buried in cemeteries for the common people (2 Kings 23:6; Jer. 26:23). By New Testament times, the concept of "common" also carried with it the connotation of "unclean." Thus Peter declares that he has never eaten anything "common or unclean." The response to Peter was: "What God hath cleansed, that call not thou common" (Acts 10:14–15).

COMMON LIFE See *Community of Goods.*

COMMONWEALTH A group of people united by common interests. Before the coming of Christ the Gentiles were separated from the commonwealth of Israel (Eph. 2:12). Paul reminded the Philippians that more important than their citizenship in a Roman colony was their citizenship in heaven (Phil. 3:20). See *Citizen, Citizenship.*

COMMUNION Paul's term describing the nature of the Lord's Supper and thus the term used by many church groups to refer to their celebration of Jesus' final, memorial supper with His disciples. Paul used the Greek term *koinonia* to express the basic meaning of the Christian faith, a sharing in the life and death of Christ which radically creates a relationship of Christ and the believer and of the believers with one another in a partnership or unity. See *Fellowship; Lord's Supper.*

COMMUNITY OF GOODS The Jerusalem church's practice of holding "all things in common" (Acts 2:41–47; 4:32–37) had contemporary parallels: the Greek utopian ideal of common property among friends; the compulsory communalism of the Jewish sect at Qumran; and even the precedent of Jesus and the twelve (Luke 8:3; John 13:29). The immediate context of both references in Acts (2:1–40; 4:31) indicates that the community of goods was not an ideal to which the church aspired, but was itself evidence of the community's nature: that the entire range of their life together was shaped and directed by the Holy Spirit.

"Common" (*koina*) in 2:44 and 4:32 has the same root as *koinonia* ("fellowship" in 2:42); thus the issue was not economic theory but the common life together ("daily" in 2:46) with no separation between physical and spiritual needs. (See 6:1ff. which depicts the investment in care for the needy.) The parallel between Acts 4:34 and Deuteronomy 15:4 indicates that the early church fulfilled God's intention for Israel to be generous.

The Jerusalem church chose to practice the selfless generosity in a form which closely resembled the life-style of Jesus and the twelve. Other early churches practiced sacrificial generosity in different forms (Acts 11:27–30; 1 Cor. 16:1–4; Rom. 12:13; 1 John 3:17), for Jesus' call to set aside possessions took more than one form. Compare Matthew 19:16–22 with Luke 19:1–10. What these incidents have in common is an emphasis on sacrificial giving (Luke 21:1–4), requiring a complete change of heart so that God, not possessions, is served (Matt. 6:24) with a clear recognition of riches' dangers (Mark 10:23–31; Luke 6:24; 12:13–31).

This danger of riches manifested itself in the context of the community of goods (Acts 4:36—5:11). In contrast to Barnabas who sold some land and gave the proceeds to the apostles, Ananias and Sapphira held back some of the proceeds from their sale. Their subsequent deaths testified to the severity of abandoning the common life for selfish interest. Possessiveness led to lying to the Spirit (5:3,9) and therefore rejecting the bond ("one heart and of one soul" in 4:32) created by the Spirit. The voluntary nature of this community of goods was therefore not a matter of individuals independently choosing when and if to give, but the ongoing spontaneous generosity of a community unified and directed by the Spirit. (See TEV translation of Acts 2:45 and 4:34*b* ("*would* sell") which identifies the *ongoing* nature of the generosity. See *Holy Spirit; Jerusalem Church; Koinonia; Fellowship; Qumran; Essenes; Riches; Gifts; Possessions; Borrow; Generosity; Mammon; Ananias and Sapphira; Teachings of Jesus.*

David Nelson Duke

COMPASSION To feel passion with someone, to enter sympathetically into their sorrow and pain. Compassion in English translations represents at least five Hebrew and eight Greek terms. *Chamal* means "to regret," "be sorry for," "grieve over," or "spare someone." Thus the rich man "refrained" (NIV) from taking his own sheep and took the poor man's (2 Sam. 12:4). Pharaoh's daughter "had pity" on the baby Moses (Ex. 2:6). David spared Mephibosheth for Jonathan's sake (2 Sam. 21:7). Often it expresses God's anger and decision no longer to show mercy and pity (Zech. 11:6). Beyond this the Bible points to God's plans to again have compassion for His people (Joel 2:18; compare Mal. 3:17; Gen. 19:16; 2 Chron. 36:15; Isa. 63:9).

Chen represents what is aesthetically beautiful. It means then to possess grace and charm and to be gracious. God looked to pour out a spirit of grace or "compassion" (Zech. 12:10 NRSV) on His people so they would mourn for the one they pierced. Bildad told Job to "implore the compassion of the Almighty" (Job 8:5 NAS).

Chus is an emotional expression of crying and feeling with someone who is hurting. With the emotion goes the intent to help. God could forbid Israel to have such pity (Deut. 7:16). God refuses to have pity on a disobedient people (Ezek. 5:11). God's history had been a history of compassion in which He did not destroy His people (Ezek. 20:17). God's people should pray for Him to "spare" them (Joel 2:17). Jonah had "compassion" (Jonah 4:10 NAS) on a plant but did not want God to have compassion on a city (Jonah 4:11). Nehemiah asked for "compassion" (Neh. 13:22). *Chus* most often appears in Hebrew in a formula which may be translated, "Do not let your eye cry over, or have regrets over" something.

Nichum or nocham means to "be sorry for," "regret," "comfort," "console." It is more than emotion. It includes a will to change the situation. Thus God "was sorry" He made people (Gen. 6:6 NAS). Still God acted to preserve human life (Gen. 8:21), for He identifies with human weakness. In His basic nature He does not "change His mind" (1 Sam. 15:29 NAS), translating Hebrew *nicham*. Still Scripture describes times when Yahweh "repented" (Ex. 32:14; 2 Sam. 24:16; Jonah 3:10 as examples). In His freedom God can announce one set of plans, see the response and weakness of the people affected, and decide not to carry out the plans. Thus Hosea 11:8 concludes, "my repentings are kindled together" (KJV) or "all my compassion is aroused" (NAS). At another time God can say, "I will have no compassion" (Hos. 13:14 NAS).

Racham is related to the Hebrew word for "womb" and expresses a mother's (Isa. 49:15) or father's (Ps. 103:13) love and compassion, a feeling of pity and devotion to a helpless child. It is a deep emotional feeling seeking a concrete expression of love (Gen. 43:14; Deut. 13:17). This word always expresses the feeling of the superior or more powerful for the inferior or less powerful and thus never expresses human feeling for God. The word seeks to bring security to the life of the one for whom compassion is felt. The majority of Bible uses of *racham* have God as subject. Compare Hosea 2:4,23; Zechariah 1:16; 10:6. God "has compassion on all he had made" (Ps. 145:9).

The New Testament builds on the Old Testament understanding of God's compassion. The central New Testament words are *eleeo* and *splagxnizomai*. The first—*eleeo*—is used in the Greek Old Testament to translate most of the Hebrew words listed above. It represents the emotion aroused by another person's undeserved suffering or pain. It is something an orator tries to kindle in an audience or a lawyer seeks to elicit from a judge. Jesus commanded the Pharisees to learn God's desire for compassion (Matt. 9:13; 12:7). Jesus said even slaves should practice compassion as He taught Peter about forgiveness (Matt. 18:33). God showed compassion in healing the demoniac (Mark 5:19). Christians need to show compassion to those who waver or doubt (Jude 22). God's commands for compassion from disciples finds its roots in the nature of God, who is full of compassion (Eph. 2:4; 1 Pet. 1:3). See *Mercy.*

Splagxnizomai is related to the Greek noun for inward parts much as Hebrew *rachemim.* Here is located the center of personal feelings and emotions. Before Christ's appearance the Greeks apparently did not use this word to speak of compassion and mercy, it being more closely related to courage. It is not clear when the shift in meaning to compassion occurred. Some of the apocryphal Jewish writings before Christ do use the term to mean mercy. In the parable of the unforgiving servant, the master had compassion and forgave the servant's debt (Matt. 18:27). The prodigal son's father had compassion on him (Luke 15:20). The Good Samaritan had compassion for the injured traveler (Luke 10:33). Jesus had compassion on the crowds (Mark 6:34). People needing help asked Jesus for compassion (Mark 9:22; compare Matt. 9:36; 20:34). Paul saw compassion as a quality expected of believers (Phil. 2:1; Col. 3:12). Paul said he related to his readers in the compassion of Christ (Phil. 1:8), that is, the quality is not an achievement by the believer but a result of being in Christ. The love of God dwells only in those who are compassionate to a person in need (1 John 3:17; compare Eph. 4:32; 1 Pet. 3:8). Compassion finds its source in God's compassion (Jas. 5:11). In compassion He has provided salvation and forgiveness (Luke 1:78).

Oiktiro is related to lamentation and grief for the dead and came to mean sympathetic participation in grief. Such sympathy or compassion stands ready to help the one who has suffered loss. In the Greek Old Testament translation *oiktiro* translates words related to *chen* and *racham.* Paul taught that God is the Father and source of compassion (2 Cor. 1:3; compare Jas. 5:11). He has total freedom in exercising compassion (Rom. 9:15). Humans can sacrifice themselves for God's causes only because God has sacrificed Himself in mercy (Rom. 12:1; compare Luke 6:36; Phil. 2:1; Col. 3:12).

Sumpatheo means to suffer what someone else suffers. It came to mean to suffer with, alongside, to sympathize. Peter listed it among the basic Christian virtues (1 Pet. 3:8). Having come to earth and endured all kinds of human temptations, Jesus exercises sympathy for our weaknesses (Heb. 4:15). The writer of Hebrews could recall his readers' experience of having sympathy for and thus helping others imprisoned for their faith (Heb. 10:33–34).

Metriopatheo refers to the ability to be moderate in emotions or passions. An Old Testament or human minister realizes personal weaknesses and thus moderates personal anger at another's weaknesses (Heb. 5:2).

CONANIAH (Cŏn å nī′ åh) Personal name meaning, "Yahweh has established." *1.* Levite in charge of collecting Temple offerings under King Hezekiah (2 Chron. 31:12). *2.* He and other Levites contributed 5,000 sheep and goats and 500 bulls for Josiah's Passover offering (2 Chron. 35:9). He may have been a grandson of *1.* above.

CONCISION Archaic English noun meaning, "a cutting off." KJV uses "concision" in Philippians 3:2 to describe Paul's opponents who insisted on circumcision as necessary for right relationship with God (Phil. 3:2). See *Circumcision; Paul.*

CONCOURSE KJV translation of Hebrew "noisy places" in Proverbs 1:21 referring to a place of community gathering and meeting.

CONCUBINE A secondary wife. The taking of concubines dates back at least to the patriarchal period. Both Abraham and Nahor had concubines (Gen. 22:24; 25:6; 1 Chron. 1:32). Concubines were generally taken by tribal chiefs, kings, and other wealthy men. Gideon had a concubine (Judg. 8:31). Saul had at least one concubine, named Rizpah (2 Sam. 3:7; 21:11). David had many (2 Sam. 5:13), but Solomon took the practice to its extreme, having 300 concubines, in addition to his 700 royal wives (1 Kings 11:3). Deuteronomy 17:17 forbid kings to take so many wives.

The concubines (and wives) of chiefs and kings were symbols of their virility and power. Having intercourse with the concubine of the ruler was an act of rebellion. When Absalom revolted against his father, David, he "went in unto his father's concubines in the sight of all Israel" (2 Sam. 16:22) on the palace roof. When David returned to the palace, the ten concubines involved were sent away to live the rest of their lives in isolation (2 Sam. 20:3).

A concubine, whether purchased (Ex. 21:7–11; Lev. 25:44–46) or won in battle (Num. 31:18), was entitled to some legal protection (Ex. 21:7–12; Deut. 21:10–14), but was her husband's property. A barren woman might offer her maid to her husband hoping she would conceive (Gen. 16:1ff.; 30:1ff.).

Although the taking of concubines was not totally prohibited, monogamous marriage was more common and seems to be the biblical ideal (Gen. 2:24; Mark 10:6–9).

See *Marriage; Polygamy; Slavery.*

Wilda W. Morris

CONCUPISCENCE KJV translation of Greek *epithumia,* "desire, lust." The Greeks used the term to mean excitement about something in a neutral sense and then in an evil sense of wrongly valuing earthly things. The New Testament knows desire can be good (Matt. 13:17; Luke 22:15; Phil. 1:23; 1 Thess. 2:17). In fact, the New Testament uses the verb form more often in a good sense than in a bad.

The bad sense of *epithumia* is desire controlled by sin and worldly instincts rather than by the Spirit (Gal. 5:16). Everyone has been controlled by such desires before their commitment to Christ (Eph. 2:3; Titus 3:3). Such desire is part of the old life without Christ and is deceitful (Eph. 4:22). Such desire can be for sex (Matt. 5:28), material goods (Mark 4:19), riches (1 Tim. 6:9), and drunkenness (1 Pet. 4:3). The Christian life then is a war between desires of the old life and desire to follow the Spirit (Gal. 5:15–24; 1 Pet. 2:11), the Spirit-led life crucifying worldly desires (Gal. 5:24). (Note the list of fleshly desires in (Gal. 5:19–21.) As the new life comes through the Spirit, so old desires come through Satan (John 8:44) and the world of which he is prince (1 John 2:16). Such desires can make slaves of people (2 Pet. 2:18–20). Desire brings temptation, leading to sin, resulting in death (Jas. 1:14–15). People cannot blame God, for He allows them freedom to choose and gives them over to what they choose (Rom. 1:24). God did give the law which defined wrong desires as concupiscence or sin. The power of sin then changed the good commandment into an instrument to arouse human desires to experience new arenas of life. Thus they sin and die rather than trust God's guidance through the law that such arenas are outside God's plan for life and thus should not be experienced (Rom. 7:7–8). Either sin brings death, or believers in Christ murder evil lusts (Col. 3:5).

In a very limited sphere of life, Paul called on believers to rise above the normal activities caused by lust in society. He called on faithfulness in marriage rather than on the immoral practices of the Greek and Roman world of his day (1 Thess. 4:4–5).

CONDEMN is the act of pronouncing someone guilty after weighing the evidence.
Old Testament The word appears first in the context of a court of law (Ex. 22:9) where a judge hears a charge against a thief and condemns the culprit. Another juridical instance appears in Deuteronomy 25:1 where judges are instructed to hear cases, decide on the issue, and "condemn the wicked." In Psalm 94:20–21 the writer accuses corrupt judges who "condemn the innocent," and in Psalm 109:31 he thanks God for saving the poor man "from those who condemn him to death" (TEV).

"Condemn" is also used in making everyday personal judgments as in the Book of Job. Feeling helpless before God's power and righteousness,

Job knew that no matter how he tried to defend himself, his own mouth would condemn him (9:20). He begged God not to condemn him but to explain why He was making him suffer (10:2). After Job's advisors had had their say, Elihu saw that all three "had condemned Job" (32:3). Other instances of the word being used in everyday judgments appear in Isaiah 50:9; 54:17.

The more significant use of "condemn" is in connection with God's judgment. In dedicating the new Temple, Solomon prayed that God would judge His people, "condemning the wicked . . . and justifying the righteous" (1 Kings 8:32). The writer of Proverbs expected the Lord to condemn "those who plan evil" (12:2 TEV). The psalmist was sure God would not forsake a good man or allow him "to be condemned when he is on trial" (37:33 TEV). On the other hand, the Lord asked Job whether he wanted to condemn Him just to prove his own righteousness (40:8).

New Testament Several Greek words are translated "condemn" and "condemnation" with a progression of meaning from just making a distinction to making an unfavorable judgment. The three-way usage of the word in the Old Testament continued into the New. The law court context is seen in Jesus' prediction of His coming trial in Jerusalem (Matt. 20:18), in a remark of one of the men crucified with Jesus (Luke 23:40), and in the final vote of the Sanhedrin (Mark 14:64).

"Condemn" was also used in Jesus' day in making personal judgments of others. For instance, Jesus said the men of Nineveh would condemn His own unrepentant generation (Matt. 12:41); James warned the brethren that teachers were subject to greater criticism (Jas. 3:1); and Paul urged Titus to use healthful speech in his teaching to avoid criticism (Titus 2:8). As in the Old Testament, God is also the source of condemnation in the New. He was responsible for the destruction of Sodom and Gomorrah (2 Pet. 2:6), and He condemned sin in human nature by sending His own Son (Rom. 8:3).

New Testament usage of "condemn" is unique in its reference to the final judgment, expecially in John 3:17-19. A similar teaching appears in John 5:24. Paul felt that avoiding that final condemnation was a reason for accepting the Lord's chastening in this life (1 Cor. 11:32).   *William J. Fallis*

CONDUIT A water channel or aqueduct in or near Jerusalem channeling water into the city (2 Kings 18:17; 20:20; Isa. 7:3). The same Hebrew word refers to a trench built up to conduct water flow (1 Kings 18:32-38; Job 38:25; Ezek. 31:4). The location of the Jerusalem conduit is a matter of debate with different scholars favoring the Pool of Siloam, the Gihon Spring, or outside the wall to the northwest of the city beside the major north-south highway leading to Samaria. The latter location may be the most likely. Aque-

ducts had been built for Jerusalem before David conquered it with a tunnel providing water for the city (2 Sam. 5:8). Israel's kings evidently supplemented this. In a marvelous engineering feat, Hezekiah had workmen start at both ends and meet in the middle to construct a water tunnel connecting Gihon Spring and the Pool of Siloam (2 Kings 20:20; 2 Chron. 32:2-4,30). The tunnel was discovered in 1880.

CONEY A wild hare—*Procavia syriaca* also called *Hyrax syriacus.* See *Animals.* It was unclean because it did not have a divided hoof (Lev. 11:5; Deut. 14:7). They established their home in the rocky cliffs (Ps. 104:18; Prov. 30:26).

CONFECTIONER One who mixes ointments or perfumes. KJV translation. Modern translations read, "perfumer" (Ex. 30:25,35; 1 Sam. 8:13; Neh. 3:8). See *Perfumers.*

CONFESSION Confession, an admission, declaration, or acknowledgment, is a significant element in the worship of God in both Old and New Testaments. The majority of the occurrences of the term can be divided into two primary responses to God: the confession of sin and the confession of faith.

Confession of Sin Numerous Old Testament passages stress the importance of the confession of sin within the experience of worship. Leviticus speaks of ritual acts involving such admission of sin: the sin (or guilt) offering (5:5—6:7) and the scapegoat that represents the removal of sin (16:20-22). Furthermore, confession can be the act of an individual in behalf of the people as a whole (Neh. 1:6; Dan. 9:20) or the collective response of the worshiping congregation (Ezra 10:1; Neh. 9:2-3). Frequently, it is presented as the individual acknowledgment of sin by the penitent sinner (Ps. 32:5; Prov. 28:13; see also Pss. 40 and 51 which are individual confessions although the word "confession" is not used).

Likewise, in the New Testament confession of sin is an aspect of both individual and corporate worship. At the Jordan, John's followers were baptized, confessing their sins (Matt. 3:6; Mark 1:6). Similar confessions were made by Paul's converts in Ephesus (Acts 19:18). Christians are reminded that God faithfully forgives the sins of those who confess them (1 John 1:9). James admonished his readers not only to pray for one another but also to confess their sins to one another (5:16), probably within the context of congregational worship. By the end of the first century, routine worship included confession as the prelude to the observance of the Lord's Supper as seen in *Didache* 14:1. See *Apostolic Fathers.*

Confession of Faith Closely related to the confession of sin in the Old Testament is the confession of faith, that is, the acknowledgment of and commitment to God. In 1 Kings 8:33,35 (as well as

2 Chron. 6:24,26) acknowledgment of the name of God results in forgiveness of sins. Such acknowledgment came to be standardized in the confessional formula known as the Shema (Deut. 6:4–5).

Such declaration of commitment to God, or particularly to Christ, is also found in the New Testament. One's public acknowledgment of Jesus is the basis for Jesus' own acknowledgment of that believer to God (Matt. 10:32; Luke 12:8; compare Rev. 3:5). Furthermore, as Paul described the process by which one is saved, he explicitly drew a parallel between what one believes in the heart and what one confesses with the lips (Rom. 10:9–10). Belief and confession are two sides of the same coin! Probably the earliest confession of faith was the simple acknowledgment of the lordship of Christ (Rom. 10:9; 1 Cor. 12:3; Phil. 2:11), but the rise of heresy seems to have caused the addition of specific data *about* Christ to the confession—for example, that He is Son of God (1 John 4:3,15) or that He has come in the flesh (1 John 4:2). A firmly set outline of Christian beliefs then appears to be what is meant by confession in later New Testament writings (Heb. 5:14).

See *Faith; Scapegoat; Sin; Repentance.*

Naymond Keathley

CONFESSIONS AND CREDOS Confessions and credos are the articulate and corporate expressions of the faith in response to the revelatory and saving acts of God. They are articulate because they do not express human emotions but recite the acts of God; they are corporate because they do not belong to individuals but to the people of God (Old Testament) or to the church (New Testament). The difference in meaning between the two terms as far as the Bible is concerned is hard to describe. For the sake of clarity we understand confession to have its primary place in worship and preaching, and credo to belong to the teaching ministry and to refer in the first place to doctrine. Confession implies a note of allegiance and commitment, credo, a note of authority.

Old Testament A fine example of a confession in action is found in Joshua 24. The setting was the meeting of Joshua with the elders, the heads, the judges, and the officers. Joshua spoke to them as a prophet: "Thus saith the Lord God of Israel (vv. 2). God spoke through the mouth of Joshua and recapitulated His mighty acts for Israel (vv. 2–13). Then follows an injunction by Joshua in his own name to serve the Lord and to put away the strange gods of their fathers (vv. 14–15). The people responded by confessing the Lord as their God (vv. 16–17); this confession was followed immediately by a recitation of the acts of God to Israel and a renewed confession (vv. 17–18). Here we find side by side the two types of confessions of the Bible, the nominal type (the Lord is our God) and the verbal type which relates the acts of God.

Two examples of the verbal type appear in Deuteronomy 6: 21–25 and 26: 5–9. Both recite the redeeming acts of God to Israel in Egypt and in the Promised Land in similar though not identical words, but each has a very different setting. The first serves as an explanation and justification of the commandments of the Lord; the second is said at the offering of the firstfruit to God and relates the offering to the saving acts of God.

The nominal confession "The Lord is our God" has its origin in the revelatory introduction to the Ten Commandments: "Thou shalt have no other gods before me" (Ex. 20: 3; see also Deuteronomy 5:6). Confessions of this type are found throughout the Old Testament, often embedded in hymns and psalms of praise or invocation (Pss. 3:8; 7:2,4; 10:12; 100:3). Elaborate recitals of the acts of God are found in Psalm 105:8–45 (preceded by an appeal to give thanks and praise to God, vv. 1–6, and the nominal confession of His lordship, v. 7), in Psalm 135, and in Psalm 136. These examples confirm the place of the confession of the acts of God in the framework of worship.

New Testament Jesus and the early church shared the faith in God of their fellow Jews. The Old Testament confessions of that faith were also theirs. The new element was the revelatory acts of God in Jesus, the Christ. His person and ministry called forth new confessions and credos giving expression to the believers' relationship with Him. In the development of these confessions three stages can be distinguished:

(a) The first stage is the life and ministry of Jesus on earth. Our Lord referred to Himself as the Son of Man, thereby presenting Himself as the fulfilment of the prophecy of Daniel 7:13. This, however, did not lead to a confession of Jesus as the Son of Man in the church. Jesus did not rebuke Peter for confessing Him to be the Messiah but ordered His disciples not to divulge this secret (Mark 8:29–30). During His presence on earth, confessing Jesus meant to express personal allegiance and commitment to Him and to His cause (Matt. 10:32; Luke 12:8).

(b) The second stage began after Jesus' resurrection and exaltation. Already on the day of Pentecost Peter proclaimed that God had made Jesus both Lord and Christ (Acts 2:36). The first title expressed His authority, having been exalted to the right hand of God; the second identified the crucified Jesus as the fulfilment of the messianic prophecies of the Old Testament. Here and throughout this stage, confessing was the corollary of preaching the gospel. At this stage confession began to be formulated to express in one sentence the church's faith in Christ. The same distinction between nominal and verbal confessions applies here as well. Nominal confessions consist of a subject (Jesus or Christ or Jesus Christ) and a predicate. The most common confession of this type is: Jesus is Lord (Rom. 10:9; 1 Cor. 12:3; Phil. 2:11; each time in a different context). Here also belongs the confession Jesus is the Son of God (Acts 8:37, not in all manuscripts and hence in most modern translations only in a footnote). Conceivably these confessions were baptismal confessions. Confessions of Jesus as the Messiah or Christ are found only rarely (John 20:31), since this title did not carry a religious or a theological meaning with the non-Jews. It gradually developed into a part of the name of our Lord. Verbal confessions tell the story of Christ in a pointed and condensed form. Impressive confessions of this type are Philippians 2:5–11 reaching its climax in the proclamation of Jesus Christ as Lord (see above); Colossians 1:15–20; 1 Timothy 3:16; 1 Peter 3:18–22. Hebrews 1:1–3 belongs here, too. Paul's wording of the Gospel, preached by him and the other apostles, has also a clear note of confession (1 Cor. 15:3–5) and shows how closely associated witness to the gospel and confessing Jesus are to one another.

(c) The third stage began when the gospel had to be safeguarded from false interpretation. Here the function of confessions is primarily doctrinal and credal and no longer a part of proclamation as in the second stage. This stage presupposes the presence of false teachers and false doctrine. This is the case in the Pastoral letters, 2 Peter and Jude though the confessions or credos which give the right expression to the gospel are usually not quoted specifically but referred to or woven into the text of the letters. In the letters of John, however, the specific wording of the doctrinal credo is quoted explicitly: Jesus Christ has come in the flesh (1 John 4:2; 2 John 7); Jesus is the Christ (1 John 5:1) or the Son of God (1 John 5:5). The former credo emphasized the full humanity of the divine Son of God; the latter, the divinity of the earthly Jesus. Understood together they form the doctrine of Christ (2 John 9).

See *Faith; Gospel; Preaching; Doctrine.*

J. Reiling

CONFIRM To establish an agreement and to show that a word is true and reliable. English translations use confirm for general Hebrew terms meaning, "to prove reliable, trustworthy," "to be strong," "to fill, fulfill," "to stand," "to rise." The Greek terms mean, "to be reliable" and "to set up." The terms are regularly used to speak of humans establishing God's words, covenant, or law by practicing them (Deut. 27:26) and more often of God confirming His message or His covenant by setting it up with His people and bringing to pass the promises He made (Lev. 26:9; 2 Sam. 7:25; 1 Chron. 16:17; Isa. 44:26; Rom. 15:8). At times human agreements or promises are confirmed (Ruth 4:7; 1 Kings 1:14; Esther 9:29; Jer. 44:25; Heb. 6:16). One could also establish themselves in a position or institution (2 Kings 15:19;

1 Chron. 17:14). Believers seek to confirm the gospel message through a Christian life (1 Cor. 1:6; Phil. 1:7). In so doing one also confirms the individual's calling and election (2 Pet. 1:10).

CONFISCATION Appropriation of private property for public or governmental use. Confiscation was not practiced in Israel until the rise of the monarchy and was not permitted by God. This practice was foretold by Samuel before Israel elected its first king (1 Sam. 8:14) as an inherent danger of Kings following Near Eastern patterns. Ahab exercised this royal right when he confiscated the property of a person (Naboth) executed by the state (1 Kings 21:15–16), but he had to bear God's punishment for his act (1 Kings 21:18–19). Ezekiel reacted strongly against the abuses of this royal prerogative (Ezek. 45:7–8; 46:16–18).

CONGREGATION The assembled people of God. Congregation translates the Hebrew words *'edah* and *qahal* primarily. These terms may apply to any individual or class collectively such as "the wicked," "the hypocrites," etc. While *'edah* is once used to refer to a herd of bulls (Ps. 68:30) and once to a hive of bees (Judg. 14:8), both words primarily describe the Israelite people as a holy people, bound together by religious devotion to Yahweh rather than by political bonds. There is no apparent distinction in meaning between the two. Every circumcised Israelite was a member of the congregation. The congregation was subdivided into the tribe and then the most basic unit, the family. The congregation of Israel functioned in military, legal, and punishment matters.

In the Greek Old Testament *'edah* was usually translated by *sunagōgē, qahal* by *ekklēsia.* In late Judaism *sunagōgē* depicted the actual Israelite people and *ekklēsia* the ideal elect of God called to salvation. Hence *ekklēsia* became the term for the Christian congregation, the church. *Sunagōgē* in the New Testament is almost entirely restricted to the Jewish place of worship. (An exception is Jas. 2:2, which may refer to a Christian assembly.) The English word "synagogue" is merely a transliteration of *sunagōgē. Ekklēsia* means "called out," and in classical Greek referred to the body of free citizens called out by a herald. In the New Testament the "called out ones" are the church, the assembly of God's people. There is a direct spiritual continuity between the congregation of the Old Testament and the New Testament church. Significantly the Christian community chose the Old Testament term for the ideal people of God called to salvation (*ekklēsia),* rather than the term which described all Israelites collectively (*sunagōgē). Joe E. Lunceford*

CONGREGATION, MOUNT OF The mountain considered by Israel's neighbors to stand in the far north and serve as a meeting place of the gods. Babylon's king was so proud he thought he could storm the meeting (Isa. 14:13).

CONIAH (Cō·nī′ ăh) See *Jehoiachin.*

CONQUEST OF CANAAN The Book of Joshua and the first chapter of the book of Judges describe the conquest of Canaan, which resulted in Israel's settlement in the land of promise.

Historical Setting The Israelite conquest came at a time when Egyptian control of Canaan was weakened. Historians have not been able to pinpoint the time when the conquest of Canaan occurred. The difficulty lies in the fact that the date of the Exodus is uncertain. Scholars have proposed quite a number of dates for this important event. The most commonly accepted period for the Exodus is around 1280 B.C. Such a date would place the conquest at about 1240–1190 B.C. Other scholars prefer to date the Exodus around 1445 B.C., which would suggest that the conquest occurred about 1400–1350 B.C.

While it is not possible to be definitive about the date of the conquest, it is possible to draw some general conclusions regarding the situation of Canaan in the approximate time frame of the conquest. Shortly after 1500 B.C., Egypt subdued Canaan. Canaanite society operated according to a feudal system whereby the kings of city states paid tribute to their Egyptian overlords. The city states were numerous in the heavily-populated Palestinian coastal plain; the mountainous regions were lightly populated. From about 1400 B.C. onward, Egyptian control of Canaan weakened, opening the land up for possible invasion by an outside force.

Joshua's Strategy Joshua led a three-campaign invasion of Canaan. At the close of the wilderness wanderings the Israelites arrived on the plains of Moab in the Transjordan ("beyond the Jordan"). There they subdued two local kings, Sihon and Og (Num. 21:21–35). Some of the Israelite tribes—Reuben, Gad, and half of the tribe of Manasseh—chose to settle in this newly conquered territory (Num. 32).

After Moses died, Joshua became the new leader of the Israelites. As God instructed him, Joshua led the people across the Jordan River into Canaan. The crossing was made possible by a supernatural separation of the water of the Jordan (Josh. 3—4). After crossing the river the Israelites camped at Gilgal. From there Joshua led the first military campaign against the Canaanites in the sparsely-populated central highlands, northwest of the Dead Sea. The initial object of the attack was the ancient stronghold of Jericho. The Israelite force marched around the city once a day for six days. On the seventh day they marched around it seven times, then blasted trumpets and shouted. In response the walls of Jericho col-

lapsed, allowing the invaders to destroy the city (Josh. 6).

The Israelites then attempted to conquer the nearby city of Ai, where they met with their first defeat. The reason for the failure was that Achan, one of the Israelite soldiers, had kept some booty from the invasion of Jericho—an action which violated God's orders to destroy everything in the city. After Achan was executed, the Israelites were able to destroy Ai (Josh. 7—8).

Not all of the Canaanites tried to resist Israel's invasion. One group, the Gibeonites, avoided destruction by deceiving the Israelites into making a covenant of peace with them (Josh. 9). Alarmed by the defection of the Gibeonites to Israel, a group of southern Canaanite kings, led by Adonizedek of Jerusalem, formed a coalition against the invading force. The kings threatened to attack the Gibeonites, causing Joshua to come to the defense of his new allies. Because of supernatural intervention, the Israelites were able to defeat the coalition. Joshua then launched a southern campaign which resulted in the capture of numerous Canaanite cities (Josh. 10).

Joshua's third and last military campaign was in northern Canaan. In that region King Jabin of Hazor formed a coalition of neighboring kings to battle with the Israelites. Joshua made a surprise attack upon them at the waters of Merom, utterly defeating his foe (Josh. 11:1–15).

The invasion of Canaan met with phenomenal success; large portions of the land fell to the Israelites (Josh. 11:16—12:24). However, some areas still remained outside their control, such as the heavily-populated land along the coast and several major Canaanite cities like Jerusalem (Josh. 13:1–5; 15:63; Judg. 1). The Israelites struggled for centuries to control these areas.

Israelite Settlement The Israelite tribes slowly settled Canaan without completely removing the native population. Even though some sections of the land remained to be conquered, God instructed Joshua to apportion Canaan to the tribes which had not yet received territory (Josh. 13:7). Following the land allotments, Israel began to occupy its

Ruins of a temple at Hazor destroyed by Joshua in the conquest of Canaan.

territory. Judges 1 describes the settlement as a slow process whereby individual tribes struggled to remove the Canaanites. In the final analysis the tribes had limited success in driving out the native population (Judg. 1). As a result, Israel was plagued for centuries by the infiltration of Canaanite elements into its religion (Judg. 2:1–5).

Conquest Reconstructions Scholars have proposed varying models for understanding the conquest of Canaan. The previous description of the nature of the conquest and settlement presents a traditional, harmonizing approach to the interpretation of the biblical material. Some scholars have proposed other interpretive models. One is the immigration model, which assumes that there was no real conquest of Canaan but that peoples of diverse origins gradually immigrated into the area after 1300 B.C. They eventually took control of the city states and became the nation of Israel. The difficulty with this model is that it ignores the general biblical picture of God constituting the nation of Israel in the desert and leading them to invade the Promised Land.

Other scholars have put forth a revolt model for understanding the nature of the conquest. This approach suggests that there was no major invasion of Canaan from an outside force but simply the immigration of a small group of people who inspired a revolt of the Canaanite peasants. The result was the overthrow of the feudal city-state kings and the emergence of what became the Israelite nation. This interpretation of the conquest diverges from the biblical record in its claim that the bulk of the population of Israel was made up of former Canaanite peasants. It also reveals a tendency to read back into Israelite history modern Marxist theory about the struggle between classes. The best approach to understanding the conquest of Canaan is one which is rooted in the biblical materials.

See *Achan; Ai; Exodus; Gilgal; Jericho; Joshua.*
Bob R. Ellis

CONSCIENCE refers in general to that human moral awareness that judges an action right or wrong.

Although the word "conscience" does appear in the Old Testament, the Hebrew word usually translated "heart" does refer to conscience in a number of passages, for example, "Afterward. . . David's heart smote him" (1 Sam. 24:5). Compare 2 Samuel 24:10; Job 27:6. The New Testament also uses this Hebraic reference to conscience: "if our heart condemn us" (1 John 3:20–21.) The word for "reins" or "kidneys" sometimes refers to conscience. In Psalm 16:7 the psalmist thanked God for giving him counsel and because his reins or kidneys admonished him, meaning his conscience reproved him. (See Ps. 73:21 for "heart" and "reins" in the same verse.)

"Conscience" in the New Testament is the translation of a Greek word derived from a verb that means "to know with." This suggests a moral consciousness which compares an action with a standard. Paul, it seems, took a word from popular Greek usage in Corinth and used it to reply to some of the Corinthian Christians. For Paul, God is the Creator and Sustainer of all things. God judges persons by His standards as revealed in Jesus Christ. These standards are reflected in His creation and especially in persons who are morally responsible because of their capacity of choice. To Paul the "conscience" is a person's painful reaction to a past act which does not meet the standard. A person can react wrongly because of wrong information, wrong environment, and wrong habit. Yet Paul would have said that, in spite of these liabilities, a person's conscience must be obeyed. Paul, however, would not have said that a person has no other guide. If past actions have not been such as to produce painful reactions, the person is said to have a "pure conscience" (1 Tim. 3:9; 2 Tim. 1:3). When sensitive and active in judging past acts, the conscience is said to be "good" (Acts 23:1; 1 Tim. 1:5,19; 1 Pet. 3:16,21; Heb. 13:18) or "void of offence toward God" (Acts 24:16). If the conscience is not active in judging past acts, it is said to be "weak" (1 Cor. 8:7,10,12) and may be wounded (1 Cor. 8:12). When the conscience is insensitive, it is "seared" (1 Tim. 4:2). The sinful conscience is "defiled" (Titus 1:15) or "evil" (Heb. 10:22).

In 1 Corinthians 4:4, Paul used the verb from which the word for "conscience" is derived. He wrote: "For I know nothing by myself." This phrase means "my conscience does not accuse me." Paul completed the sentence by saying: "yet am I not hereby justified: but he that judgeth me is the Lord." Paul, in short, taught that a pure conscience is valuable, but that Christ is the final standard by which a person is judged.
H. Page Lee

CONSECRATION refers to persons or things being separated to or belonging to God. They are holy or sacred. They are set apart for the service of God. The Hebrew *kadosh* and Greek *hagiazo* are translated by several different English words: holy, consecrate, hallow, sanctify, dedicate.

Old Testament God is said to be *kadosh* or "holy." When persons or things were "consecrated," they were separated to or belonged to God. "Ye shall be holy: for I the Lord your God am holy" (Lev. 19:2). "Ye shall be unto me a kingdom of priests, and an holy nation" (Ex. 19:6). When persons were "consecrated," they were set apart to live according to God's demands and in His service.

In the Old Testament the ordination of persons to the service of God is indicated by the phrase "to fill the hand." This phrase is usually translated "consecrate" or "ordain."

Numbers 6:1–21 sets forth the vow of the Nazirite. *Nazar* from which Nazirite is derived, means "to separate" and is translated "consecrate" in Numbers 6:7, 9, 12.

New Testament This ethical understanding of God's holiness is found throughout the New Testament. In Matthew 23:16–24 Jesus criticized the scribes and Pharisees on the basis of their neglect of justice, mercy, and faith. He said it is "the altar that sanctifieth the gift" (Matt. 23:19). The cause to which persons give themselves determines the nature of the sacrifice. When the cause is God's, the gift is consecrated. Jesus' mission was to sanctify persons. Paul said that Christians are called to be "saints," and their sanctification comes through Christ.   *H. Page Lee*

CONSOLATION Comfort which eases grief and pain. The Hebrew terms are closely related to the words for compassion—*nichum, nocham.* See *Compassion.* Job's integrity with God's instructions gave him consolation despite his grief and pain (Job 6:10). David sent servants to console Hanun, king of Ammon, after his father died (2 Sam. 10:1–2). People brought food and drink to console the grieving (Jer. 16:7; compare John 11:19). God's response to prayer brings consolation to the worried soul (Ps. 94:19). Even as God destroyed Jerusalem, He provided consolation in the person of faithful survivors (Ezek. 14:22–23).

Israel's ultimate hope was the consolation only the Messiah could bring. The faithful waited expectantly for this (Luke 2:25; compare Isa. 40:1–2). Those who trust in riches rather than in the coming of the Son of Man have all the consolation they will receive (Luke 6:24). Believers receive consolation through the ministry of proclamation (1 Cor. 14:3).

CONSTELLATIONS See *Astrology, Astronomy, Heavens.*

CONSUMMATION The end of history and the fulfillment of God's kingdom promises. The term comes from Daniel 9:27 speaking of the complete destruction God had decreed on the prince who threatened His sanctuary. See *Eschatology.*

CONSUMPTION A wasting or emaciating disease that would be inflicted upon those who disobeyed the law (Lev. 26:16; Deut. 28:22). The disease has been identified as pulmonary tuberculosis (phthisis) or as the side effects of wasting and emaciation from prolonged bouts of malarial fever. Some have even suggested cancer. The KJV uses consumption in Isaiah 10:22; 28:22 where modern versions translate "destruction."

CONTAINERS AND VESSELS were hollow receptacles used to hold dry or liquid substances. The Bible mentions numerous containers and vessels. They range from pottery dishes, bowls, urns, and jugs to baskets, metalware, cloth and leather bags and on to wooden boxes and bowls and glassware of all shapes and sizes. By far the most common vessel was made of clay.

Stoneware was the first to be produced. Archaeologists have found crude stone vessels from the oldest periods of mankind's history, dating them from the Paleolithic (Old Stone) and Epipaleolithic (Middle Stone) Ages (700,000 to 8300 B.C.). The Neolithic (New Stone) and Chalcolithic Ages (8300 to 3100 B.C.) saw advances in the production of stoneware as humans became producers of food rather than merely gatherers and hunters. Larger and deeper vessels were needed. In the Ancient Near East the Egyptians excelled at the craft of making stoneware.

As mankind progressed through the Neolithic Age, the most marked change in containers was the ability to form them by mixing clay, water, and fire. The first pottery vessels were simple, unglazed bowls and jars.

Early clay vessels were "fired" simply by letting them stay out in the sun. Unfortunately, they could not be used to hold liquids; for they returned to their muddy stage if they came in contact with a fluid. Firing progressed to the next stage probably by accident when a house burned and the mud-clay pottery inside hardened beyond anything yet produced. This led to a more advanced firing by simply holding the molded vessels over an open flame.

The Chalcolithic era brought about another monumental change in pottery making. A slow potter's wheel was introduced. This made production faster and more uniform. The Egyptians claim responsibility for this development.

Incense bowls and jars are other large categories of vessels produced during the Chalcolithic period. The bowls usually were broad and half-rounded. The jars ranged from small hole-mouthed and high-necked containers decorated with red bands to the large storage vessels deco-

A large copper (or bronze) caldron of the Phrygian period from Gordion in Asia Minor.

This imported Mycenean pottery and local ware (14th century B.C.) from Hazor indicates trade with Greeks.

rated with bands that resemble ropes set in relief.

Bronze Age (3100–1200 B.C.) pottery containers marked a distinct individuality based on different regions. Typical of the vessels from northern Palestine are jars of the grain-wash or band-slip techniques. Potters painted the containers with criss-crossing bands in vivid colors (dark and light brown, red, and yellow). Also indicative of this region are burnished vessels, those polished to a luster.

In southern Palestine a different type of pottery emerged during the Bronze Age. Red painted wares have been found in abundance in the south. Vessels of all shapes and sizes, including jugs, juglets, jars, and even "teapots" with long spouts and loop handles exhibit the same decorative characteristics.

During the Middle Bronze Age (2200–1550 B.C.) several new features were introduced to the vessels and containers of Palestine. Carinated (ridged rims) bowls and goblets, deep kraters, and storage jars with rounded shoulders marked a further advance in the potter's skill. Primary to all these advances was the ability to produce the entire vessel on the wheel. This enabled a potter to make the more intricate shapes.

The Late Bronze Age (1550–1200 B.C.) saw the introduction of bowls with tapering or rounded sides. Black and red bands painted on the inside were the normal form of decoration. Imports from Cyprus and Mycenae abounded, espe-cially large, rounded bowls with wishbone handles. These came to be known as "milk bowls." Highly distinctive decorations were used by the Mycenaeans. They painted their ware with bands, spirals, scales, and even leaves.

Major changes marked the transition from the Bronze Age to the Iron Age (1200–586 B.C.). Instead of the rounded shapes, containers became more angular. Burnishing replaced painted decorations. Many potters began putting multiple handles on their ware, often as many as four. Chalices were very popular. With the rise of the monarchy came jar handles stamped with the royal seals.

Philistine ware made its debut during this period. Some of the liquid containers had strainers in the spouts to prevent the dregs (pulp and debris that usually settled to the bottom) from coming

Chalice and bowl in situ at the excavations at biblical Timnah.

out with the liquid. Philistine ware is an amalgamation of Mycenaean types with clear influences from Egypt and Canaan. Red and black decorations, especially people and animals, are typical of this type pottery.

Alexander the Great brought to the Middle East the Hellenistic culture and its large variety of ceramic ware. Large, heavy vessels mark this period. They show a uniformity of style owing to the Greek dominance of all major production centers.

By the time Rome conquered Palestine in 63 B.C., a new type of cylindrical jar with angular to rounded shoulders appeared. It had a ring base and a rim made to receive a lid. This type vessel made an excellent storage jar for solids, especially scrolls. The famous Dead Sea Scrolls were kept in these finely-crafted containers for almost two thousand years.

Metalware has been found in abundance in the lands of the Bible. Although palaces and temples often had vessels made of gold or silver, by far the most common material for metalware was an alloy

Storage jars (dating from the Minoan Age) at the palace of Minos at Knossos on the island of Crete.

of copper and tin called bronze. Pure copper rarely was used.

Wood was used to produce storage boxes and bowls. Boxes were made by nailing together planks, whereas bowls usually were hollowed from single pieces of wood. More wooden containers have been found in Egypt partly because the climate is more conducive to their preservation than other parts of the Middle East.

Glass has a long history in the Middle East. Obsidian (volcanic glass) was brought into Palestine from Anatolia as early as 5000 B.C. Manufactured glass began to appear after 2500 B.C., but vessels made of glass did not appear until about 1500 B.C.

Glass containers were made by molding the molten material around a solid core of the desired shape. Highly-skilled artisans created pieces that imitated precious stones such as lapis lazuli and turquoise.

Again, only royalty and temples owned glassware. Practically all found so far in Palestine was

imported from Egypt. The glass industry reached its zenith there between 1400 and 1300 B.C. One of the few artifacts not from Egypt is a conical beaker from Mesopotamia, found at Megiddo.

Glass drinking bowls became popular in Palestine by 200 B.C. Most of that found in Palestine originated in Phoenicia. The method used still was molding the glass over an object. About 50 B.C. came the revolutionary invention of glass blowing. This method was quicker and less expensive than creating molds for each desired type of vessel. Discovered probably in Phoenicia, blown glass became the vessels of choice in Palestine during the Roman period. Palestinian artists became famous for their brown glass. Many even began signing their creations—the first known designer products in history.　　*Mike Mitchell*

CONTENTMENT An internal satisfaction which does not demand changes in external circumstances. The New Testament expresses this with the Greek word *arkew* and its derivatives. Hebrews 13:15 summarizes the teaching in advising believers to be free of the love of money and to depend on God's promise not to forsake His people. Food and lodging should be enough for the godly (1 Tim. 6:6–10; compare Matt. 6:34; contrast Luke 12:19). The believer can be content no matter what the outward circumstances (Phil. 4:11–13). Believers are content to know the Father (John 14:8–9) and depend on His grace (2 Cor. 12:9–10; compare 2 Cor. 9:8–11).

CONTRIBUTION FOR THE SAINTS An offering for the church at Jerusalem that Paul raised among the churches outside of Jerusalem. When Paul and Barnabas visited the church in Jerusalem, they made a commitment to the leaders there to remember the poor in Jerusalem (Gal. 2:1–10).

Exactly why the church in Jerusalem had so many poor people is not clear. These Christians may have been economically isolated by the other Jews in Jerusalem.

Paul was true to his promise to help the poor in Jerusalem. He organized an offering among the churches he visited and established on his second and third missionary journeys.

Paul urged the church at Corinth to give to this offering (1 Cor. 16:1–4). He evidently promoted the offering in the churches of Galatia (1 Cor. 16:1) and in the churches of Macedonia (2 Cor. 8:1). When the offering lagged in Corinth, he encouraged the church to give generously (2 Cor. 8—9).

He mentioned the offering to the Romans (Rom. 15:25–28). He pointed out that the offering was prompted by the sense of spiritual indebtedness that all of the other churches had toward the church in Jerusalem. Paul probably also promoted the offering as a way of building unity between Jewish and Gentile Christians.

When the offering was completed among the churches, the money was sent to Jerusalem. Paul accompanied some members of those churches to Jerusalem to deliver the offering (1 Cor. 16:3, Acts 24:17). See *Jerusalem; Stewardship; Paul; Corinth.* *Lynn Jones*

CONTRITE To be humble and repentant before God, crushed by the sense of guilt and sinfulness. This Old Testament concept is expressed by the Hebrew word *daka'* and its derivatives. The basic meaning is to be crushed or beaten to pieces. This meaning appears in the crushing of the golden calf (Ex. 32:20) or the crushing of grain during threshing (Isa. 28:28). Crushing enemies is a frequent theme (Ps. 89:11). God taught Israel not to crush the poor (Prov. 22:22). Indeed, the king is to crush the oppressor who harms the poor (Ps. 72:4). In Psalm 9:9, the poor are referred to as the crushed (literal translation) and assured God is their "refuge." Compare Ps. 143:3. They can thus come to God in prayer, knowing what God wants is a broken spirit and a contrite heart (Ps. 51:17). God will revive the spirit of such a one (Isa. 57:15; compare 66:2; Ps. 34:18).

God's plan of salvation rests on God being pleased to crush His Suffering Servant (Isa. 53:10 NAS). This One will finally be exalted (Isa. 52:13).

CONVERSATION Communication between two or more people (Jer. 38:27 in modern translations) or personal conduct or behavior in KJV's now obsolete use of the term (Ps. 37:14; Gal. 1:13; Jas. 3:3).

CONVERSION A person's turning to God. Conversion is the experience of an individual who encounters God's reality or purpose and responds to that encounter in personal faith and commitment.

The Old Testament frequently uses the term both in a noun and verb form. The psalmist said that, "The law of the Lord is perfect, converting the soul" (19:7). He affirmed that "sinners shall be converted unto thee" (51:13). God declared to Isaiah that "Zion shall be redeemed with judgment, and her converts with righteousness" (Isa. 1:27). Isaiah was told that Israel's heart would be hardened lest the people would "understand with their heart, and convert, and be healed" (6:10).

The New Testament uses the noun form only once in referring to "the conversion of the Gentiles" (Acts 15:3) but uses the term repeatedly in other forms. Three of the Gospels make reference to Isaiah 6:10 (Matt. 13:15; Mark 4:12, John 12:40). Jesus admonished His disciples, "Except ye be converted, and become as little children, ye shall not enter into the kingdom of heaven" (Matt. 18:3). He told Simon Peter, "When thou art converted, strengthen thy brethren" (Luke 22:32). The Book of Acts refers repeatedly to the importance of conversion, beginning with Peter's words, "Repent ye therefore, and be converted" (3:19). Acts uses the term most frequently in describing a person turning to God (Acts 15:19, 26:20) or turning "from darkness to light" (26:18), or from "these vanities unto the living God" (14:15). Other New Testament references speak of turning from idols to serve the living God (1 Thess. 1:9) and turning so that "the veil shall be taken away" (2 Cor. 3:16). James encourages us with the words "that he which converteth the sinner from the error of his way shall save a soul from death" (Jas. 5:20).

Biblical Examples of Conversion The Old Testament records experiences of several men who in the most basic sense turned to God (they were converted). Of course, they did not have the benefit of later revelation or the understanding that comes from the gospel; but they were confronted by God in a way that made them conscious of sin. As a result, they turned to God in self-surrender. Jacob's experience with God at Bethel was a kind of conversion (Gen. 32). Moses, at the burning bush, was surely given a call to mission, and some would call it a conversion (Ex. 3). Isaiah had an experience with God that undoubtedly changed his life (Isa. 6). One of the most notable conversions in the Old Testament would have to be that of the Babylonian king Nebuchadnezzar, who through a series of unusual circumstances turned to "the King of heaven, all whose works are truth, and his ways judgment: and those that walk in pride he is able to abase" (Dan. 4:37).

In the New Testament the list of conversions is much more lengthy. In a very real sense all of the apostles were converted to the messiahship of Jesus and forsook everything to follow Him. The Gospels recount numerous encounters that Jesus had with individuals that resulted in their acknowledging Him as the Christ. They then experienced a radical change in their lives: Zacchaeus (Luke 19), the woman at the well at Sychar (John 4), the sinful woman in the house of Simon (Luke 7), and Nicodemus (John 3). The Book of Acts records a number of individual conversions, the most notable of which are the Ethiopian eunuch (Acts 8), Saul of Tarsus (Acts 9), and Cornelius (Acts 10). In addition, several references to large numbers of conversions appear (Acts 2:41; 9:35; 11:21).

The biblical evidence, both within the Old and New Testaments, emphasizes the importance of conversion. Persons need to be converted. They are commanded to be converted and can be converted. Conversion is necessary because of sin. Conversion is made possible by the goodness and grace of God.

The Character of Conversion Christian conversion is the experience of an individual in which one turns from sin and trusts in Jesus Christ for salvation. It is personal and inward in nature, but is results in a public and outward change. Each individual's conversion is unique; yet the requirements of conversion are the same for everyone. An individual's conversion will be influenced by temperament, knowledge, and people; but each conversion is the result of the same gospel and the same Spirit.

The characteristics of conversion are summarized in 2 Corinthians 5:17, "If any man be in Christ, he is a new creature: old things are passed away; behold, all things are become new." A change of the mind, emotions, and will is the result of conversion. The mind is changed in that it seeks to know the truth and accept the truth, whereas before conversion the mind resisted the truth. The emotions are changed in that evil is hated and righteousness is loved, whereas before conversion evil was loved and righteousness was hated. In conversion the will is changed so that it turns away from sin in humble submission to the will of God.

Conversion does not result in Christian maturity, but it does begin the process that leads to maturity. Conversion does not cause perfection, but it radically redirects the personality.

The Causes of Conversion The cause of conversion is the sovereign grace and mercy of God. "God commendeth his love toward us, in that, while we were yet sinners, Christ died for us" (Rom. 5:8). The finished work of Christ on the cross is the basis and foundation of individual conversion. That finished work is the result of God's grace. Whatever means and methods God uses to influence individuals—the preaching and teaching of truth, the prayers of the church, the circumstances of life—are the result of God's grace. In conversion God takes the initiative; God causes understanding; God creates desire; God enables response.

The cause of conversion is a confrontation and encounter with God. In genuine conversion one is confronted with the living Christ and faced with decision. It is a personal event, concentrated and focused. Surely every person's conversion will not be as dramatic as someone else's may be, but every person must personally come face to face with Jesus Christ to claim a conversion. Confrontation is not just acceptance of ideas or intellectual assent to plan of salvation. It is not just agreeing to some facts. It involves acceptance of a Person and acknowledging that acceptance to Him. Confrontation is saying to Jesus Christ, "I accept You as my Lord. I trust You for my salvation."

The cause of conversion is conviction that is the result of the Holy Spirit's witness to the Word of God (John 16:7–11). Christian conversion must be preceded by a basic understanding of the gospel story, some cognitive grasp of truth, a minimal acquaintance with God's redemptive work in Christ. "Faith cometh by hearing, and hearing by the word of God" (Rom. 10:17). The truth of the gospel causes concern and leads people to ask the question asked of Simon Peter after his Pentecost sermon, "Men and brethren, what shall we do?" (Acts 2:37). The clear presentation of God's requirements, man's failures, and God's provision for sinful man in Jesus Christ creates the opportunity for conversion as well as the opportunity for rejection.

The Conditions of Conversion If conversion is the result of grace on God's part, it is the result of repentance and faith on a person's part. Repentance is turning from sin and self-centeredness to God and His will. It is a redirection of life, a change of mind, a radical break with the past.

Faith is essentially trust. Faith is trust in Christ and His redemptive sacrifice. It is believing in Him alone for salvation. Faith is receiving the grace God revealed through the Person and work of His Son. The numerous admonitions of Scripture are to believe on the Lord Jesus Christ for salvation (John 3:16; Acts 16:31; 1 John 5:13). Belief is more than acceptance of the historical Jesus. It is a personal trust in the living Christ who lived, died, and rose again. It is trust to the point of commitment and surrender to the will of Christ.

See *Regeneration; Repentance.*   *Daniel Vestal*

CONVICTION A sense of guilt and shame leading to repentance. The words "convict" and "conviction" do not appear in the King James Version. The word "convince" (KJV) comes closest to expressing the meaning of "conviction."

The Hebrew word *yakah* expresses the idea of conviction. It means "to argue with," "to prove," "to correct." God may be the subject and persons the object (Job 22:4) or a person may be the subject who convicts another person (Ezek. 3:26).

The Greek term meaning "convict" is *elegxo*. It means "to convict" "to refute," "to confute," usually with the suggestion of shame of the person convicted. Young ministers like Timothy and Titus had the responsibility of "convicting" (rebuking, refuting) those under their charge (1 Tim. 5:20; 2 Tim. 4:2; Titus 1:13; 2:15). John the Baptist "convicted" Herod Antipas because of his illicit marriage to Herodias, his brother's wife (Luke 3:19). No one could convict Jesus of sin (John 8:46).

John 16:8–11 is a classic passage on conviction. The Holy Spirit is the One who convicts, and the (inhabited) world is the object of conviction. A study of this passage yields the following results. First, conviction for sin is the result of the Holy Spirit awakening humanity to a sense of guilt and condemnation because of sin and unbelief. Second, more than mental conviction is intended. The total person is involved. This can lead to action based on a sense of conviction. Third, the conviction results in hope, not despair. Once individuals are made aware of their estranged relationship with God, they are challenged and encouraged to mend that relationship. The conviction not only implies the exposure of sin (despair) but also a call to repentance (hope).

See *Sin; Forgiveness; Repentance.*

Glenn McCoy

CONVOCATION, HOLY See *Festivals.*

COOKING AND HEATING Only in recent times have cooking and heating become separated, so that central heating, for example, works independently of the microwave. In Bible times, the means of heating was the means of cooking. Heating was by open fire, and cooking was done at the same time.

The basic focus for cooking and heating was the open fire. The bedouin encampment could be recognized by the fires at night outside and in front of the tents. The fire was laid in a hollow scooped out of the ground or on flat stones. The fire was ignited by friction or by firing tinder with sparks (Isa. 50:7,11). Many of the stories of the Bible were preserved, originally as folk memories, remembered word for word around the camp fires lit for warmth on cool evenings in the arid climate or in the high terrain. The people of the Bible were fortunate because the white broom plant was useful in making fires. Its embers stayed hot for a long time and could be fanned into a blaze even when they looked dead. Less useful, but equally combustible materials were thorns (Isa. 10:17), dried grass (Matt. 6:30), charcoal (John 18:18), sticks, and dried animal dung (Ezek. 4:15).

When people of the Bible moved from tents and settled in houses, fires for cooking were still generally lit out-of-doors. If the house had a courtyard, the fire was made somewhere in the corner as the farthest place away from the smoke. Very few houses had a chimney; and even though the fire

Middle Eastern woman sifting grain with a type of sifting frame.

Arab woman using an ancient hand mill to grind grain.

was put into an earthenware box or was contained in a metal brazier, there was no exit for the smoke. Life must have been quite miserable during the damp and cold winters of the Holy Land. A fire was necessary to keep warm, but the only window needed rough curtaining with a blanket. The smoke had little space to exit, so it blackened the rough ceiling and made the householders choke and splutter. Later better homes were provided with a chimney, and the houses of royalty actually had a form of central heating in which the heat of underfloor fires was ducted underneath paved rooms.

In patriarchal times food consisted basically of bread, milk products, meat, and honey. Wine was the most common drink. Cooking, therefore, consisted of the preparation of such foods. Grain (spelt, barley, or wheat—preferred in that order) had first to be cleaned and selected. It was necessary to remove any poisonous seeds such as darnel (tares Matt. 13:25). Then it was ground either in a pestle and mortar or in a hand mill. The hand mill was made of two disks of stone about twelve inches in diameter. The lower stone had an upright wooden peg at its center, and the upper stone had a hole through the center which fitted over the peg. A handle fixed to the upper stone allowed it to be rotated about the peg. Grain was fed through the central hole. As the upper stone was rotated the grain was crushed, coming out as flour between the two stones and falling onto a cloth placed below. Any woman could manage a hand mill, but it was much easier if two women shared in the task, sitting with the mill between them and alternately turning the handle (Matt. 24:41). It was a chore and was therefore given to the slaves when this was possible (Lam. 5:13), but it was a chore which made a sound always associated with home. (See Jer. 25:10.) The flour was mixed with water and formed into dough cakes in a trough called a kneading trough. Salt was added, and most days of the year, leaven was added too. Leaven was fermented dough from the previous day's baking. It took longer to penetrate the dough than if fresh yeast was used, but that was reserved for the time following the festival of Unleavened Bread, and the normal method was just as certain. Some of the grain was finely ground and was given a special name. It was the finely ground flour which was used in sacrificial offerings (Ex. 29:40).

Cooking consisted of the application of (relatively) clean heat. In some cases large flat stones were put in the hot fire. When the flames had died down, the dough was placed on the hot stones. In other cases, where the fire was placed in a hole in the ground, the dough was actually placed on the hot sides of the depression. Another common method was to invert a shallow pottery bowl over the fire, and place the dough cakes on the bowl's convex surface. It was many years before the pottery "oven" was invented. It consisted of a truncated cone which was placed over the fire. The cakes of bread were then placed on the inside of the cone at the top, away from the flames. Not until Roman times were pottery ovens in use where the firebox was separated from the cooking area by a clay dividing piece. This method was maintained for centuries. The cooking resulted in different shapes of bread. Some loaves were paper-thin and were most suitable for scooping food from a common pot (Matt. 26:23). Other loaves (John 6:9) were heavier, like biscuits, and a still heavier loaf is described in Judges 7:13 where it knocked down a tent.

As communities grew larger, the baker developed his trade and provided facilities for the whole village. His oven was tunnel-shaped. Shelves lined the sides for the dough, and fires were lit on the floor. It was possible for the housewife to take her own dough to be cooked in the communal oven, and possible for the children to collect hot embers at the end of the day for kindling fires in their own homes. (See Hos. 7:4–7.) Jeremiah received a bread ration from the local bakery while he was in prison (Jer. 37:21).

Not all of the grain was ground. A metal baking sheet was sometimes placed over the hot fire and grain put on the metal surface. The grain "popped" and provided what the Bible calls parched corn (1 Sam. 25:18), which was used as an occasional snack.

The basic food to go with the bread was vegetable soup prepared from beans, green vegetables, and herbs. A large cooking pot was put directly on the fire and was used for this purpose. The pottage which Jacob gave to Esau was a lentil soup (Gen. 25:30). It was eaten by forming a scoop with a piece of bread, and dipping it in the central pot. When soups were made, the cook had to remember that ritual law forbad the mixing of seeds for this purpose (based on Lev. 19:19). When a special occasion was called for, as at the arrival of a guest, meat would be added to the stock. Most meat was boiled or stewed in this way and was taken either from the herd or in the hunt. Boiling was the easiest way to deal with meat because ritual law required that the blood should be drained from the animal (Lev. 17:10–11). It

Bread is being cooked here in an outdoor truncated cone-shaped "pottery oven."

Bread being cooked on an inverted shallow skillet over an open flame.

was therefore easiest to cut up the carcass before putting it in a stew. Meat was normally roasted only at festivals and very special days such as Passover (Ex. 12:8–9). It was sometimes roasted on a spit which was speared through the animal and supported over the fire. Since the main altar at Temple and tabernacle was a kind of barbecue in which the carcass was laid on a grill above a fire, it would be unusual if similar arrangements were not sometimes used domestically. Meat was always available from the sheep and goats of the flock, but the hunting of wild animals which came up from the jungle in the Jordan Valley was popular. Veal was served to Abraham's guests in Genesis 18:7, while Gideon's guests ate goat meat (Judg. 6:19). Milk, too, was used as a basic cookery material; but it was forbidden to stew a kid in its mother's milk (Ex. 23:19). The reason for this is not clear. Guesses have been made that the commandment was given for "humanitarian" reasons, or that the practice was somehow associated with magic in contemporary religious life.

By the time the Jewish people had settled in the Promised Land, additions had been made to their diet. While they were in Egypt, they had gotten used to some of the food which was popular in that country—cucumber, garlic, leeks, onions, and melons (Num. 11:5). Some of these plants were uncooked and were used to eat with bread or as a salad. Others were cooked to give additional flavor to the cooking pot. The leek was a salad leek, and the cucumber the "snake cucumber" which was common in Egypt. With the growth of trade under the Israelite monarchy, these items became fairly common in the diet. In addition to onions and garlic, herbs were used in cooking to add to the flavor. Salt was collected during the hot season from the shores of the Dead Sea after evaporation had left it behind. Salt was used for preservation as well as for seasoning. Liberal use was made of dill, cummin (Isa. 28:25–27) and coriander and sugar. Spicy chutneys were also prepared to give added flavor to the food. The charoseth used at the Passover was a chutney made of dates, figs, raisins, and vinegar.

The big difference when the settlement took place was that the Jews began to use fruit from the trees. They built plantations and orchards. Most significant in this respect was the olive. After the olives had been beaten from the trees and crushed in the olive press, the olive oil was used both for binding the flour instead of water, and for frying. A whole new era of cookery was opened. The woman from Zarephath who cared for Elijah needed only some flour (meal) and some olive oil to be able to survive through the time of famine (1 Kings 17:12). Other trees provided basic food which was eaten either raw or stewed—figs, sycamore figs, pomegranates, and nuts.

Milk has already been mentioned as a liquid for stewing meat and vegetables. It was also drunk for itself and used in the preparation of other foods. Some milk was fermented to produce yogurt. It is in fact still called "milk" in some versions of the

Bible (Judg. 4:19). Milk was used to make cheese (1 Sam. 17:18) and when placed in a skin bag to be shaken and squeezed by turn, butter was produced. Buttermilk was presumably used as well, but there is no mention of this in the Bible.

By New Testament times, fish was a common addition to the diet. Much of the fish was imported from the Phoenicians, who caught fish in the Mediterranean. Fishing industry also thrived on the Sea of Galilee. Fish was most commonly grilled over a fire (John 21:9) or was salted and eaten later. Magdala, the home of Mary Magdalene, was a well-known center for the salting of fish.

Wine was always available, even among the nomadic people. When entry to the Promised Land took place, it was possible for the people of the Bible to go into viticulture in a big way, and the preparation of the grapes was an important aspect of cooking. Some grapes were dried in the hot sun to become raisins—a substantial snack when they were needed. Most of the grapes however were crushed to obtain their juice. This was a long "cooking" operation. Picked between July and September, the grapes were placed in a winepress—a stone "tank" cut out of the ground with an exit hole in the bottom where the juice ran out and could be collected outside. The juice stood in the collecting vessels for about six weeks to allow natural fermentation to take place. It was then carefully poured off to leave any sludge undisturbed in the bottom and was placed in another jar, sealed except for a small hole to allow gases to escape until the fermentation process was complete. The wine was the natural and safest drink because water supplies were often suspect. Not all of the wine was used for drinking. The housewife sometimes boiled up the juice to make a simple grape jelly or jam, which was spread on the bread. This was so plentiful that it may well be the "honey" which is referred to in the phrase referring to the "land flowing with milk and honey" (Ex. 3:8, 17). *Ralph Gower*

COOS (Cō′ ŏs) KJV spelling for Cos. See *Cos.*

COPING Traditional translation of a Hebrew architectural term in 1 King 7:9. The meaning of the Hebrew word is unknown. NIV, TEV reads "eaves." Recent scholars see it as the "framework" meaning a row of stone or wood headers and stretchers above the various levels of the foundation on which bricks were laid. The Hebrew word also occurs in Exodus 25:25; 37:12; Isaiah 48:13.

COPPER See *Minerals and Metals.*

COPPERSMITH A term applied in ancient times to metal-workers or blacksmiths in general. The

Miniature copper tools for shawabtis (small god symbols) from Egypt, New Kingdom.

name Kenite means "smith" (see *Kenite*). A certain Alexander was a coppersmith who caused trouble in the early church (2 Tim. 4:14).

COR A large liquid and dry measure of unknown quantity. See *Weights and Measures.*

CORAL Calcareous or horny skeletal deposit produced by anthozoan polyps. The red or precious coral found exclusively in the Mediterranean and Adriatic seas (*Corallium rubrum*) is the type known to the biblical writers. The value of wisdom surpasses the value of gold, silver, a variety of precious stones, crystal, or coral (Job 28:12–18). Coral was among the goods of trade between Israel and Edom (Ezek. 27:16).

CORBAN (Côr′ băn) A gift particularly designated for the Lord, and so forbidden for any other use (Mark 7:11). Jesus referred to some persons who mistakenly and deliberately avoided giving needed care to their parents by declaring as "corban" any money or goods that could otherwise be used to provide such care. Thus what began as a religious act of offering eventually functioned as a curse, denying benefit to one's own parents. See *Sacrifice; Offering.* *Gene Henderson*

CORE (Cō′ rė) KJV transliteration of Greek spelling of Korah in Jude 11. See *Korah.*

CORIANDER SEED A herb (*Coriandrum sativum*) of the carrot family with aromatic fruits used much as poppy, caraway, or sesame seeds are today. The manna of the wilderness period was like coriander seed either in appearance (Ex. 16:31) or taste (Num. 11:7).

CORINTH One of four prominent centers in the New Testament account of the early church, the other three being Jerusalem, Antioch of Syria, and Ephesus. Paul's first extended ministry in one city was at Corinth. On his first visit to Corinth, he remained for at least eighteen months (Acts

The columns of the temple of Apollo at Corinth.

18:1–18). Paul's three longest letters are associated with Corinth. First and Second Corinthians were written to Corinth, and Romans, from Corinth. Prominent Christian leaders associated with Corinth include Aquila, Priscilla, Silas, Timothy, Apollos, and Titus.

History of Corinth Corinth was located on the southwest end of the isthmus that joined the southern part of the Greek peninsula with the mainland to the north. The city was located on an elevated plain at the foot of Acrocorinth, a rugged hill reaching 1,886 feet above sea level. Corinth was a maritime city located between two important seaports: the port of Lechaion on the Gulf of Corinth about two miles to the north and the port of Cenchreae on the Saronic Gulf about six miles east of Corinth.

Corinth was an important city long before becoming a Roman colony in 44 B.C. In addition to the extant works of early writers, modern archaeology has contributed to knowledge of ancient Corinth.

The discovery of stone implements and pottery indicates that the area was populated in the Late Stone Age. Metal tools have been found that reveal occupation during the Early Bronze Age (between 3000 B.C. and 2000 B.C.). The rising importance of Corinth during the classical period began with the Dorian invasion about 1000 B.C.

Located at the foot of Acrocorinth and at the southwest end of the isthmus, Corinth was relatively easy to defend. The Corinthians controlled the east-west trade across the isthmus as well as trade between Peloponnesus and the area of Greece to the north. The city experienced rapid growth and prosperity, even colonizing Siracuse on Sicily and the Island of Corcyra on the eastern shore of the Adriatic. Pottery and bronze were exported throughout the Mediterranean world.

For a century (about 350 to 250 B.C.) Corinth was the largest and most prosperous city of mainland Greece. Later, as a member of the Achaean League, Corinth clashed with Rome. Finally, the city was destroyed in 146 B.C. L. Mummius, the Roman consul, burned the city, killed the men, and sold the women and children into slavery. For a hundred years the city was desolate.

Julius Caesar rebuilt the city in 44 B.C., and it quickly became an important city in the Roman Empire. An overland shiproad across the isthmus connected the ports of Lechaion and Cenchreae. Cargo from large ships was unloaded, transported across the isthmus, and reloaded on other ships. Small ships were moved across on a system of rollers. Ships were able, therefore, to avoid 200 miles of stormy travel around the southern part of the Greek peninsula.

Description of Corinth in Paul's Day When Paul visited Corinth, the rebuilt city was little more than a century old. It had become, however, an important metropolitan center. Except where the city was protected by Acrocorinth, a wall about six miles in circumference surrounded it. The Lechaion road entered the city from the north, connecting it with the port on the Gulf of Corinth. As the road entered the city, it widened to more

A first century A.D. street at Corinth. The Acrocorinth (mountain) is in the background.

than twenty feet with walks on either side. From the southern part of the city a road ran southeast to Cenchreae.

Approaching the city from the north, the Lechaion road passed through the Propylaea, the beautiful gate marking the entrance into the agora (market). The agora was rectangular and contained many shops. A line of shops divided the agora into a northern and a southern section. Near the center of this dividing line the Bema was located. The Bema consisted of a large elevated speaker's platform and benches on the back and sides. Here is probably the place Paul was brought

The "bema," or judgment seat, at Corinth.

before Gallio (Acts 18:12–17).

Religions of Corinth Although the restored city of Paul's day was a Roman city, the inhabitants continued to worship Greek gods. West of the Lechaion road and north of the agora stood the old temple of Apollo. Probably partially destroyed by Mummius in 146 B.C., seven of the original thirty-eight columns still stand. On the east side of the road was the shrine to Apollo. In the city were shrines also to Hermes, Heracles, Athena, and Poseidon.

Corinth had a famous temple dedicated to Asclepius, the god of healing, and his daughter Hygieia. Several buildings were constructed around the temple for the sick who came for healing. The patients left at the temple terra cotta replicas of the parts of their bodies that had been healed. Some of these replicas have been found in the ruins.

The most significant pagan cult in Corinth was the cult of Aphrodite. The worship of Aphrodite had flourished in old Corinth before its destruction in 146 B.C. and was revived in Roman Corinth. A temple for the worship of Aphrodite was located on the top of the Acropolis.

Summary The city of Corinth as Paul found it was a cosmopolitan city composed of people from varying cultural backgrounds. Being near the site of the Isthmian games held every two years, the Corinthians enjoyed both the pleasures of these games and the wealth that the visitors brought to the city. While their ships were being carried across the isthmus, sailors came to the city to spend their money on the pleasures of Corinth. Even in an age of sexual immorality, Corinth was known for its licentious life-style.   *R.E. Glaze*

1 CORINTHIANS First Corinthians is a practical letter. Paul dealt with problems concerning the church as a whole and also with personal problems.

Paul's First Ministry in Corinth A brief survey of Paul's contacts with Corinth will aid in understanding his correspondence with Corinth. In a vision at Troas on his second missionary journey, Paul heard the call, "Come over into Macedonia, and help us" (Acts 16:9). Paul and his party went to Philippi and established work there. Following their release from prison, Paul and Silas went to Thessalonica. Although a work was established there, persecution arose due to the jealousy of the Jews. Paul and Silas moved on Berea, where they were well received. However, Jews from Thessalonica came and stirred up the crowds.

The decision was made for Paul to minister alone in Athens. A comparison of Acts 17:13–15 with 1 Thessalonians 3:6 indicates that Timothy returned to Thessalonica. Silas probably remained at Berea. Paul's ministry was brief in Athens. Some converts were made, but a church was not established. Paul left Athens alone and probably discouraged.

Paul went from Athens to Corinth, where later Silas and Timothy joined him (Acts 18:5). Paul

The excavations at Corinth showing the shops in the Agora.

ministered in Corinth at least eighteen months (Acts 18:1–18). He began working with Aquila and Priscilla in tentmaking. Probably, they already were Christians.

Paul left Corinth accompanied by Aquila and Priscilla (Acts 18:18). He left them at Ephesus and promised the Ephesians that he would return. In the meantime, Aquila and Priscilla instructed Apollos; and he left for Corinth, where he preached for some time (Acts 18:24–28). After visiting Jerusalem and Antioch of Syria, Paul returned to Ephesus for a ministry of more than two years (Acts 19:8–10).

Paul's Contacts with Corinth During His Ephesian Ministry During Paul's Ephesian ministry a series of disturbing events took place relative to Corinth: (1) A party spirit arose in Corinth (1 Cor. 1:12–13; 3:3–4). (2) A series of reports came to Paul, some by those of Chloe (1 Cor. 1:11). These reports included attacks upon Paul (1 Cor. 2:1–10) and problems of immorality (1 Cor. 5:1). (3) Paul wrote a letter warning against fellowship with sexually immoral people (1 Cor. 5:9). This letter is lost unless a portion of it remains in 2 Cor. 6:14—7:1. (4) The Corinthians wrote to Paul (1 Cor. 7:1), asking about certain problems concerning marriage, fornication, and disorders in public worship. (5) A delegation came from Corinth (Stephanas, Fortunatus, and Achaicus) with news from Corinth (1 Cor. 16:17). (6) Apollos quit his work in Corinth and returned to Ephesus. Even under Paul's urging, he refused to go back to Corinth (1 Cor. 16:12). (7) Paul sent Timothy to Corinth (1 Cor. 4:17) in an effort to heal the

problems. Timothy probably went by way of Macedonia (Acts 19:22; 1 Cor. 16). (8) Paul wrote 1 Corinthians from Ephesus (1 Cor. 16:8), expecting them to receive the letter before the arrival of Timothy (1 Cor. 16:10).

Purpose for Writing First Corinthians Paul wrote 1 Corinthians to give instruction and admonition that would lead to the solving of the many problems in the congregation. Some of these problems may have arisen out of a "super spiritualist" group that had been influenced by incipient gnostic teachings. All of the problems in chapters 1—14 were grounded in egocentric or self-centered attitudes in contrast to self-denying, Christ-centered attitudes. Chapter 15 concerning the resurrection may reflect sincere misconceptions on the part of the Corinthians.

Theme of 1 Corinthians The egocentric life is contrasted with the Christocentric life, or, the mature Christian is characterized by *giving*, not *getting.*

Outline

Introduction (1:1–9)

I. Divisions Revealing Carnality and Immaturity Rather than Growth under the Lordship of Christ (1:10—4:21).
   A. Fragmentized by a party spirit (1:10–17)
   B. Christ crucified: a stumbling block to the world in its wisdom, yet the power and wisdom of God (1:18–31)
   C. Paul's preaching by the power of God, not by the wisdom of the world (2:1–5)
   D. God's wisdom revealed to those having the mind of Christ (2:6–16)
   E. The inability of the Corinthians to receive the full message of the gospel (3:1–9)
   F. Responsibility and judgment (3:10–23)
   G. The role of the apostles—"ministers of Christ and stewards of the mysteries of God" (4:1–13)
   H. The intent of Paul's rebuke—not to shame but to admonish (4:14–21)

II. Problems of Sexual Immorality (5:1—6:20)
   A. A case of incest (5:1–8)
   B. The right attitude and relationship of the church to fornicators (5:9–13 and 6:9–11)
   C. The error of antinomianism in relation to sex (6:12–20)
   D. Litigation in pagan courts (6:1–8)

III. Marriage and Celibacy (7:1–40)
   A. The sexual relation in marriage (7:1–7)
   B. Advice to the unmarried in view of the sex drive (7:8–9)
   C. Admonition to Christian partners to remain married (7:10–11)
   D. The Christian's responsibility when the marriage partner is not a Christian (7:12–24)
   E. Circumstances under which Paul ad-

vised the unmarried to remain as they were (7:25–35)
   F. The responsibility of a father for his virgin daughter (7:36–38)
   G. Advice to widows (7:39–40)

IV. Meat Offered to Idols and Christian Liberty (8:1—11:1)
   A. Liberty and responsibility in relation to meat offered to idols (8:1–13)
   B. Paul's own surrender of apostolic privileges (9:1–23)
   C. The necessity for self-discipline (9:24–27)
   D. Admonition from Israel's wilderness history (10:1–13)
   E. The impossibility of partaking both of the table of the Lord and the table of demons (10:14–22)
   F. A summary of guiding principles (10:23—11:1)

V. Problems in Public Worship (11:2—14:40)
   A. The veiling of women (11:2–16)
   B. Disorders connected with the Lord's Supper (11:17–34)
   C. Spiritual gifts and the supremacy of love (12:1—14:40)

VI. The Resurrection (15:1–58)
   A. The resurrection of Jesus (15:1–29)
   B. The relevance of the hope of the resurrection for the struggles of this life (15:30–34)
   C. The resurrection of the body (15:35–58)

VII. Practical and Personal Matters (16:1–24)

R.E. Glaze

2 CORINTHIANS After writing 1 Corinthians, Paul continued his ministry at Ephesus. This ministry was so successful that "they which dwell in Asia heard the word of the Lord Jesus, both Jews and Greeks" (Acts 19:10). Not so successful, however, was his attempt to solve the problems at Corinth. Even after the writing of 1 Corinthians, trouble continued to grow worse, especially the Corinthians' harsh attacks upon Paul. Divisions within the church and their attacks upon Paul denied the very essence of the gospel that "God was in Christ, reconciling the world unto himself . . . and hath committed unto us the word of reconciliation" (2 Cor. 5:19).

Contacts between Paul and the Corinthians continued. Reports from Corinth indicated increasing hostility toward Paul. Timothy, whom Paul had sent with the hope that he could resolve the problems, returned to Ephesus and was with Paul when he wrote 2 Corinthians (2 Cor. 1:1).

Paul made a painful visit to Corinth that is not recorded in Acts. Second Corinthians contains three references to this visit. After making this visit, Paul wrote, "But I determined this with myself, that I would not come again to you in heaviness" (2 Cor. 2:1). The first visit of Acts

18:1–18 was not a painful visit; therefore, the painful visit was a second visit. Also, 2 Corinthians 12:14 and 13:1 indicate that Paul's forthcoming visit would be his third visit.

Paul also wrote a letter of strong rebuke that he regretted after sending it (2 Cor. 7:8). Later, he rejoiced because the letter provoked them to repentance. Titus probably was the bearer of this letter (2 Cor. 8:7, 16–17). This letter was not preserved unless it is chapters 10—13 of 2 Corinthians.

After Titus departed for Corinth, Paul left Ephesus. His heart was heavy because of Corinth. He expected Titus to meet him at Troas with news of reconciliation. Titus did not meet him. Even though Paul found an open door at Troas, his heart was so heavy that he could not minister (2 Cor. 2:12–13). He went on to Macedonia, where Titus finally met him (2 Cor. 7:6–7) and reported improved conditions at Corinth. In response, Paul wrote 2 Corinthians, promising an early visit to them.

Questions have been raised concerning the unity of 2 Corinthians. These questions concern 6:14—7:1 and chapters 10—13. Some see 6:14—7:1 as a part of the previous letter mentioned in 1 Corinthians 5:9. Two arguments favor this view: (1) The verses interrupt the thematic connection between 6:13 and 7:2. (2) Their content fits the description of the letter in 1 Corinthians 5:9. Two arguments oppose this view: (1) There is no manuscript evidence for these verses ever existing outside of 2 Corinthians. (2) It was characteristic of Paul to insert other matters into his main argument.

The suggestion has been made that chapters 10—13 refer to the letter written "out of much affliction and anguish of heart" (2 Cor. 2:4). Two arguments favor this: (1) The tone changes between chapters 9 and 10. Chapters 1—9 reflect restored relations and the absence of hostility. Chapters 10—13 are filled with rebuke and Paul's defense of his apostleship and conduct. (2) Chapters 1—9 reflect Paul's joy and optimism. This is hard to account for if even a minority remained stubborn. Two arguments are given against chapters 10—13 being the harsh letter: (1) There is no manuscript evidence for such a division. (2) Chapters 1—9 could be addressed to the repenting majority and chapters 10—13 to an unrepenting minority.

We can be sure that all was written by Paul and is God's message given to Paul through divine inspiration. Paul wrote 2 Corinthians to deal with problems within the church and to defend apostolic ministry in general and his apostleship in particular. In so doing, Paul revealed much about himself, his apostleship, and his apostolic ministry. This epistle is essential for anyone who would know as much as possible about Paul.

Second Corinthians is relevant for today in its teachings concerning ministers and their ministries. Among these teachings are the following: (1) God was in Christ reconciling the world to Himself and has given to us a ministry of reconciliation. (2) True ministry in Christ's name involves both suffering and victory. (3) Serving Christ means ministering in His name to the total needs of persons. (4) Leaders in ministry need support and trust from those to whom they minister.

Outline
Salutation (1:1–3)
I. The Nature of Apostolic Ministry (1:3—7:16)
   A. Defined in terms of Paul's relations with the Corinthians (1:3—2:17)
   B. Defined in light of its glory and shame (3:1—7:16)
II. The Expression of Apostolic Ministry Through the Collection for Jerusalem (8:1—9:15)
   A. Examples of sacrificial giving (8:1–15)
   B. Care in handling the collection (8:16–24)
   C. An appeal for a generous response (9:1–15)
III. Paul's Defense of His Apostolic Ministry (10:1—12:13)
   A. Defended by answering allegations (10:1–18)
   B. Defended by resorting to the foolishness of boasting (11:1—12:13)
IV. Paul's Future Plans (12:14—13:10)
   A. Anticipation of a third visit to Corinth (12:14–21)
   B. Paul's warning that he will deal forthrightly when he comes (13:1–10)
Farewell (13:11–14)   *R.E. Glaze*

CORMORANT Large seafowl (*Phalacrocorax carbo carbo*) listed among the unclean birds (Lev. 11:17; Deut. 14:17). Other translators call it a Fisher-owl (REB). See *Birds.*

CORN A general term used by the translators of the KJV for any grain.

CORNELIUS (Côr nē′ lĭ ŭs) A centurion in the Roman army who lived at Caesarea (Acts 10:1). Although he was a Gentile, he was a worshiper of the one true God. He also treated the Jewish people with kindness and generosity. After an angel appeared to this pious soldier, he sent to Joppa for Simon Peter, who came to him with the message of forgiveness of sins through faith in the crucified and risen Christ. Cornelius became a Christian as a result of this incident. His conversion marked the beginning of the church's missionary activity among Gentiles. It also helped to set the stage for an important early controversy in the church, for it raised the question of the possibility of salvation for those who were not Jews. See *Peter; Acts.*

CORNER BUTTRESS, THE NAS translation in 2 Chronicles 26:9. See *Turning of the Wall.*

CORNER GATE A gate of Jerusalem in the northwest corner of the city not far from the Ephraim Gate (2 Kings 14:13; 2 Chron. 25:23). It is not mentioned in Nehemiah's restoration of Jerusalem.

CORNERSTONE The stone laid at the corner to bind two walls together and to strengthen them. Used symbolically as a symbol of strength and prominence in the Bible. The figure is often applied to rulers or leaders (Ps. 118:22; 144:12; Isa. 19:13 NIV, REB, NAS; Zech. 10:4). God promised through Isaiah that Zion would be restored, resting on the cornerstone of the renewed faith of Israel (Isa. 28:16). Jeremiah declared that Babylon would be so utterly devastated that nothing useful would remain, not even a stone for use in a foundation (Jer. 51:26).

In the New Testament Psalm 118:22 and Isaiah 28:16 are quoted (or alluded to) and applied to Christ. The symbolism is clear: Jesus Christ is the only sure foundation of faith. The Synoptic gospels quote Psalm 118:22 after the parable of the wicked tenants to show the rejection and ultimate triumph of Christ (Matt. 21:42; Mark 12:10; Luke 20:17; compare Acts 4:11; Eph. 2:20–22).

In 1 Peter 2:4–8, the two cornerstone passages are quoted in addition to Isaiah 8:14. Here the appeal to the reader is to come to the living stone (Jesus) the people rejected but precious in God's sight. This is substantiated by a quote from Isaiah 28:16. There then comes a warning: those who believe consider the stone to be something precious; but those who do not believe are warned that the stone which they have rejected has become the head of the corner (Ps. 118:22) and, further, this stone will make them stumble and fall (Isa. 8:14; compare Rom. 9:33). Believers are encouraged to become themselves living stones like *the* Living Stone and be built into a spiritual house (1 Pet. 2:5). See *Rocks and Stones.*

Phil Logan

CORNET KJV translation for several different kinds of musical instruments. See *Music, Instruments, Dancing.*

CORNFLOOR KJV translation for threshing floor in Hosea 9:1.

CORRUPTION Used especially in the KJV to denote the transient nature of the material world—that is, the world's bent toward change and decay (see especially Rom. 8:21; 1 Cor. 15:42–57; 1 Pet. 1:4). The world's corruption stands in contrast to the permanent, eternal nature of the resurrection hope.

CORRUPTION, MOUNT OF Hill east of Jerusalem near the Mount of Olives where Solomon built altars to the gods of his foreign wives (1 Kings 11:7). These places of worship were destroyed by Josiah (2 Kings 23:13). The name is probably a word play by the biblical writer on Mount of Oil, an early name of the Mount of Olives and a word spelled much like Mount of Corruption or Destruction.

COS (Cŏs) Island and its chief city between Miletus and Rhodes where Paul landed briefly on his return voyage after his third missionary journey (Acts 21:1). It was a center for education, trade, wine, purple dye, and ointment. Hippocrates founded a school of medicine there. It is modern Kos.

COSAM (Cō′ săm) Personal name meaning, "diviner." Ancestor of Jesus (Luke 3:28).

COSMETICS Materials used for personal care and beautification. In the Ancient Near East, cosmetics were used by both men and women. Men primarily made use of oil, rubbing it into the hair of the head and the beard (Ps. 133:2; Eccl. 9:8). Women used cosmetic preparations which included eye paint, powders, rouge, ointments for the body, and perfumes. There are only limited references made to cosmetics in the Bible.

Utensils, Colors, and Manufacture of Cosmetics Cosmetic utensils of glass, wood, and bone have been found in archeological excavations in Palestine, Egypt, and Mesopotamia. In Ur, utensils have been discovered dated as early as 2500 B.C. In Egypt, a scene on a sarcophagus dated about 2000 B.C. depicts a woman holding a mirror. In Palestine, most frequently uncovered are limestone bowls or palettes. These are ordinarily in the form of small bowls, about four inches in diameter, with flat bases and a small shallow hole in the center. The wide rim was usually decorated with incised geometric designs. They were used to prepare colors for making up the face. Mixing was done by means of bone spatulas or small pestles. Possibly imported from Syria, the palettes were common in the northern part of Palestine from about 1000 B.C. on.

Other paraphernalia uncovered include small glass vials and small pottery juglets used as perfume containers, alabaster jars used for ointments, ivory flasks, cosmetic burners, and perfume boxes such as that mentioned in Isaiah 3:20. Ivory combs, bronze mirrors, hairpins, kohl sticks, unguent spoons, and tweezers also were used by women in biblical times. In the excavations at Lachish, an object was discovered which appears to be a curling iron and is dated about 1400 B.C. In the Cave of Letters, one of the hiding places of some rebels of the Bar Kochba War (A.D. 132–135), a woman's possessions found included a mirror and cosmetic utensils of glass, wood, and bone.

The colors for cosmetic preparations came from various minerals. Red ocher was used for lip color. White was obtained from lead carbonate. Green eyelid coloring was derived from turquoise or malachite, and black was often made from lead sulphate. Kohl or manganese was used for outlining of the eyes. Colors were also produced from ivories, bitumen, and burned woods.

Expert craftsmen made the cosmetics. They imported many of the raw ingredients, especially from India and Arabia. Oils for the skin creams were extracted from olives, almonds, gourds, other trees and plants, and animal and fish fats. Fragrances came from seeds, plant leaves, fruits, and flowers, especially roses, jasmines, mints, balsams, and cinnamon.

Eye Paint Women used paint to enhance their eyes and make the eyes appear larger (Jer. 4:30 NAS). There may also have been some medicinal value by preventing dryness of the skin of the eyelid or discouraging disease-carrying flies. However, biblical references often seem to associate the practice of painting the eyes with women of questionable reputation (2 Kings 9:30; Ezek. 23:40).

Dry powders for eye-coloring were stored in pouches, reeds, reed-like tubes of stone, or small jars. The reference to Job's daughter, "Kerenhappuch" (horn of antimony or eye-paint, Job 42:14), indicates the powders were also carried in horns. The powders were mixed with water or gum and applied to the eyelids with small rods made of ivory, wood, or metal. Egyptian women favored the colors of black and green, painting the upper eyelid black and the lower one green. Mesopotamian women preferred yellows and reds. Heavy black lines were traced around the eyes to make them appear more almond-shaped.

Ointments and Perfumes Creams, ointments, and perfumes were especially important in the hot Near Eastern climate. Creams protected the skin against the heat of the sun and counteracted body odors. Ointments were applied to the head (Matt. 6:17) or to the whole body (Ruth 3:3) as part of hygienic cleansing. They were considered part of the beautification process (Esther 2:12). Anointing one's head with oil was a sign of gladness (Ps. 45:7). In worship services, anointing was a special part of consecration (Ex. 30:30–32). The formula was given by God and was a priestly secret (Ex. 30:22–38). Ointments were used by prophets in anointing new kings. Elijah anointed Jehu (2 Kings 9:3), and Jehoiada anointed Joash (2 Kings 11:12). In New Testament times a good host displayed hospitality by anointing guests with ointments (Luke 7:37–50). Ointment was sometimes used to anoint the sick (Jas. 5:14). Perfumed ointments were part of the preparation for burial (Mark 14:8; Luke 23:56).

The use of perfume is an ancient practice. The first recorded mention is on the fifteenth century B.C. tomb of Queen Hatshepsut who had sent an expedition to the land of Punt to fetch frankincense. Herodotus (450 B.C.) mentioned Arabia's aromatics. To the Magi who bore gifts to the Christ child, the offering of frankincense symbolized divinity.

Perfumes mentioned in the Bible include aloes (Num. 24:6); balm (Ezek. 27:17); cinnamon (Prov. 7:17); frankincense (Isa. 43:23; Matt. 2:11); myrrh (Song of Sol. 5:5; Matt. 2:11); and spikenard (John 12:3). The perfumes were derived from the sap or gum of the tree (frankincense, myrrh), the root (spikenard), or the bark (cinnamon). They were often quite expensive and imported from Arabia (frankincense, myrrh), India (aloes, spikenard, and Ceylon (cinnamon).

The perfumes could be produced as a dry powder and kept in perfume boxes (Isa. 3:20), or as an ointment and kept in alabaster jars, such as the spikenard with which Mary anointed Jesus (John 12:3). They could also be obtained in the natural form as gum or pellets of resin. In this form, they were placed in cosmetic burners and the resin burned. In close or confined quarters, the resulting incense-smoke would act as a fumigation for both the body and the clothes, such as that which seems to be described in the beautification process noted in Esther 2:12.

See *Perfumes; Anointing; Eye-paint; Trade Routes.* *Darlene R. Gautsch*

COULTER KJV word for both mattock and plowshare.

COUNCIL, HEAVENLY A meeting of God and His heavenly hosts. The concept of a heavenly council arose as a corollary to Israel's thoughts about the transcendence of God. They conceived of God as exalted above the world. God's dwelling place was in the heavens, not on the earth (Eccl. 5:2). One prophet asserted that God sits "upon the circle of the earth" (Isa. 40:22). There Yahweh presided over His heavenly council like some earthly king presiding over an assembly of his subjects.

God's heavenly council was made up of angelic servants often called "sons of God" (Job 1:6; 2:1). Micaiah saw the Lord sitting on His throne with "all the host of heaven" standing by to serve Him (1 Kings 22:19). God sent these servants from the council from time to time to do His bidding (Job 1—2). Satan, the adversary, was among these "sons of God" in the prologue to Job. In his vision Isaiah entered the council and received a commission to preach to his people (Isa. 6). The psalmist gave this insight into God's exalted being: "For who in the skies is comparable to the Lord? Who among the sons of the mighty is like the Lord, a God greatly feared in the council of the holy ones . . . ?" (Ps. 89:6–7 NAS). Eliphaz questioned Job's status with God: "Have you listened in the council of God?" (Job 15:8*a*). For Jeremiah the sign of false prophets was that they had not "stood in the counsel of the Lord" (Jer. 23:18). Had they done so they would have proclaimed God's word to God's people (Jer. 23:22). The servants of the Lord in good standing are those who obey their Sovereign's will (Pss. 103:21; 148:1–6).

Billy K. Smith

COUNCIL OF JERUSALEM The name given to the meeting described in Acts 15:6–22. The purpose of the council was to determine the terms on which Gentile converts to Christianity would be received into the church. The occasion of the meeting was a significant turning of Gentiles to Christ as a result of missionary activity by Barnabas and Paul. Some maintained that all Gentile converts must submit to circumcision and observe the whole of the Mosaic law. Paul and Barnabas, however, contended that imposing such requirements on Gentiles was unreasonable. The solution proposed by the Jerusalem council was that Gentile believers would not be required first to become Jewish proselytes, but that they would be asked to refrain from idolatry, from sexual misconduct, and from eating blood. See *Acts; Paul*.

COUNSELOR One who analyzes a situation and gives advice to one who has responsibility for making a decision. Israelite kings seem to have employed counselors on a regular basis (see 2 Sam. 16:23; 1 Kings 12:6–14; 1 Chron. 26:14; 27:32,34; 2 Chron. 25:16; Isa. 1:26; 3:3; Mic. 4:9). God is often regarded as a counselor (Ps. 16:7; 32:8; 33:11; 73:24) as is His Messiah (Isa. 9:6; 11:2) and the Holy Spirit (John 14:16,26; 15:26; 16:7). See *Advocate*.

COUNTENANCE The face as an indication of mood, emotion, or character (see Gen. 4:5–6; Deut. 28:50; Job 9:27; Ps. 10:4; Prov. 15:13; Eccl. 7:3; Mark 10:22). To speak of God lifting up His countenance upon one is a way of speaking about being in God's presence (Ps. 21:6). Being in God's presence—having God's countenance lifted toward one—may bring peace (Num. 6:25–26), blessing (Pss. 4:6; 90:15), or victory (Ps. 44:3). It may also bring destruction (Ps. 80:16) or judgment for sin (Ps. 90:8).

COUNTERVAIL Old English word meaning to equal, be commensurate with, compensate for in Esther 7:4.

COURIERS Members of the royal guard who carried messages throughout the kingdom (2 Chron. 30:6,10; Esther 3:13,15; 8:10,14). Roman couriers were empowered to confiscate transportation or the help of citizens of the empire in

the fulfillment of their duties (Matt. 5:41; Mark 15:21).

COURT OF THE GUARD See *Court of the Prison*.

COURT OF THE PRISON An open court in the Jerusalem palace reserved for the detention of prisoners during the day of Jeremiah (Jer. 32:8,12; 33:1; 37:21; 38:6,13,28; 39:14–15). Translated in the modern versions as "court of the guard."

COURTS OF THE GENTILES, WOMEN, ISRAELITES, PRIESTS See *Temple*.

COURT SYSTEMS The court systems of ancient Israel are not fully described in the Old Testament or in any extra-biblical source. Laws governing the conduct of judges and witnesses, reports about leaders who were consulted for legal decisions, and narratives of judicial proceedings supplement the accounts of Moses' appointment of assistant judges (Ex. 18) and Jehoshaphat's judicial reform (2 Chron. 19). Archaeological investigation has not yet discovered court documents from ancient Israel.

Legal disputes could be settled at the level of society in which they arose. The head of a family had authority to decide cases within his household without bringing the matter before a professional judge (Gen. 31; 38). The law codes limit his authority in some cases (Num. 5:11–31; Deut. 21:18–21; 22:13–21). When persons from more than one family were involved, the case was taken before the elders of the town, who were the heads of the extended families living together in that place and represented the community as a whole. The elders would serve as witnesses to a transaction (Deut. 25:5–10; Ruth 4:1–12), decide guilt or innocence (Deut. 19; 22:13–21; Josh. 20:1–6), or execute the punishment due the guilty party (Deut. 22:13–21; 25:1–3). The elders helped to preserve the community by seeing that disputes were settled in a manner that everyone would recognize as just.

Disputes between tribes were more difficult to resolve. When a Judahite woman who was the concubine of a Levite living in the territory of Ephraim was raped and murdered in Gibeah of Benjamin, several tribes were involved (Judg. 19—21). The Levite, therefore, appealed to all the tribes of Israel for justice. The initial attempts at negotiation were rebuffed when the men of Benjamin refused to hand over the guilty persons for punishment. Israel then went to war against the whole tribe of Benjamin, defeated them, and vowed not to let them intermarry with the rest of the tribes. The biblical historian comments regretfully that this sort of thing happened when there was no king to execute the law (Judg. 21:25).

During the period of Israelite history covered by the book of Judges, special judicial authority was possessed by several individuals appointed by God. The so-called "minor judges" (Judg. 10:1–5; 12:8–15) are not credited with delivering Israel from oppression by military means, so their function may have been purely judicial or political. Some scholars have identified their office as "judge of all Israel" in the tribal league, but others have argued that their jurisdiction was over a smaller area. Deborah, and later Samuel, also decided cases. Their judicial activities took place in a limited area (Judg. 4:4–5; 1 Sam. 7:15–17). We do not know whether they only heard cases on appeal. The Bible does not say how any of these individuals came to possess their authority as judges. Both Deborah and Samuel were prophets. The other deliverer judges were called by God and possessed by God's Spirit, so judicial authority was probably also a divine gift.

A hierarchical system of courts and judges could exist when political authority was centralized. In Exodus 18:13–26 Moses appointed assistant judges to decide the smaller cases so that his own energy could be preserved for the difficult ones. A system in which local courts referred complex cases to the supreme judges is described in Deuteronomy 17:2–13; 19:16–19. This was not an appeals court to which dissatisfied parties could bring their cases for reconsideration; it was a court of experts who could pass judgment in cases too complicated for the local judges to decide themselves. The court system instituted by Jehoshaphat also followed this pattern (2 Chron. 19:4–11). Although appointed by the king, the judges were responsible directly to God (2 Chron. 19:6). It is not clear whether the residents of Jerusalem went directly to the central court. We only know that Jeremiah was tried in Jerusalem by "the princes of Judah" after being charged by the priests and prophets with a crime worthy of death. The system described in Deuteronomy 17; 19; 2 Chronicles 19 has both priests and secular officials as judges in the central court in Jerusalem.

The king possessed limited judicial authority. Despite his supreme political power, he was not personally above the law. Saul's death sentences on Jonathan (1 Sam. 14:39) and the priests at Nob (1 Sam. 22:6–23) were not accepted by the people. Jonathan was not punished, and the priests were finally killed by a non-Israelite. David was led to convict himself of his crimes against Uriah and his mistreatment of Absalom (2 Sam. 12:1–6; 14:1–24). Unlike Saul, David and Solomon were able to exercise authority to execute or spare persons who represented a threat to their reigns (2 Sam. 1:1–16; 4:1–12; 19:16–23; 21:1–14; 1 Kings 2:19–46). Jezebel used the existing town court to dispose of Naboth and confiscate his vineyard. She and Ahab, however, were punished by God for having Naboth executed on trumped-up charges even though Ahab was king (1 Kings 21—22). Deuteronomy 17:18–20 places the king at the same level as his subjects with respect to the requirements of God's law. In Israel the king did not have the authority to enact new laws or to make arbitrary legal rulings contrary to the prevailing understanding of justice.

The ideal of the just king who oversees the dispensing of justice for all his subjects was known in Israel. In this role the king himself was the leading example of a just and honest judge and was personally involved in hearing cases as well as appointing other judges. Absalom was able to take advantage of David's failure to live up to this ideal (2 Sam. 15:1–6). Solomon is the supreme example of the just king, having been granted discernment and wisdom by God (1 Kings 3).

The relationship of the king's court to the rest of the judicial system is uncertain. The wise woman from Tekoah appealed to David, a decision which had been made within her extended family (2 Sam. 14). The Shunammite widow successfully appealed to the king of Israel for the restoration of her house and land, which she had abandoned during a time of famine (2 Kings 8:1–6). The famous case of the two prostitutes and their infant sons was brought directly to Solomon without any previous judgment (1 Kings 3:16–28). All of these cases seem to be exceptional. Powerful third parties were involved in the first two cases; Joab set up the audience with David, and the Shunammite had an advocate present in the person of Gehazi, Elisha's servant. The two prostitutes had no families to settle their dispute. We are not certain, therefore, what these accounts can tell us about how cases usually came to be heard by the king. There are no Old Testament laws which define the process of judicial appeal to the king.

Priests also possessed judicial authority. The passages about the high court in Jerusalem mention priests alongside the secular judge (Deut. 17:9; 19:17; 2 Chron. 19:8,11). Some scholars believe that this division between religious and civil courts reflects the post-exilic period, in which the secular authority was that of the Persian king and Jewish priests administered the law of God (Ezra 7:25–26). Israelite priests, however, possessed a body of knowledge from which they ruled on matters pertaining to the worship of God and the purity of the community. The cult and the judicial system were both concerned with removing blood-guilt from the community (Deut. 21:1–9). We cannot determine how the priestly judges were related to the other court systems or how cases were assigned to the various judges.

Actual court procedures may be partially reconstructed as follows. There were no prosecutors or defense attorneys; accuser and accused argued their own cases. The burden of proof lay with the defendant. Physical evidence was presented when necessary (Deut. 22:13–21), but proving one's case depended primarily on testimony and persuasive argument. The word of at least two witnesses was required to convict (Deut. 19:15). The system depended on the honesty of witnesses and the integrity of judges (Ex. 18:21; 20:16; 23:1–3,6–9; Lev. 19:15–19; Deut. 16:19–20; 19:16–21; 2 Chron. 19:6–7). The prophets condemned corrupt judges (Isa. 1:21–26; Amos 5:12,15; Mic. 7:3) and those who supported them (Amos 5:10). Cases brought by a malicious witness giving false testimony were referred to the central court (Deut. 19:16–21). In some circumstances the accused could submit to an ordeal or an oath to prove his or her innocence (Ex. 22:6–10; Num. 5:11–31; Deut. 21:1–8). If guilty, he or she would be punished directly by God. Casting lots to discover the guilty party was another extraordinary procedure. In both cases reported in the Bible the person identified also confessed his guilt (Josh. 7; 1 Sam. 14:24–46). The judges were responsible to administer punishment, often with the whole community participating (Deut. 21:21). The court systems could only function well when the community agreed with their decisions and cooperated to enforce them. By judging justly, the courts taught God's law and the principles of divine justice. The courts worked together with the people to restore the community to peace and wholeness under God whenever they recognized the one in the right and imposed an appropriate penalty on the guilty one.

Pamela J. Scalise

COUSIN At times the KJV uses cousin when a distant relative is referred to (Luke 1:36; see also Mark 6:4; Luke 1:58; 2:44; 14:12). The same Greek word in all these passages means relatives, kin, or countryman.

COVENANT A pact, treaty, alliance, or agreement between two parties of equal or of unequal authority. The convenant or testament is a central, unifying theme in Scripture, God's covenants with individuals and the nation Israel finding final fulfillment in the new covenant in Christ Jesus. God's covenants can be understood by humans because they are modelled on human covenants or treaties.

Near Eastern Covenants Biblical covenants do not represent something brand new in their world. They are built on normal patterns used in economics and politics of the day. Studies of political and economic agreements in the Ancient Near East have revealed the basic structure of a treaty, agreement, or covenant. Two types of treaties are available for study: those from the Hittite empire about 1400–1200 B.C. and those from the Assyrian Empire about 850–650 B.C. We have several Hittite examples but few Assyrian ones for study.

Neither fits a rigid, unchangeable pattern, but the Hittite treaties between a king and vassal kings or between two kings of equal authority can be described with the following structure:

1. Royal Titles naming and identifying the Hittite king making the treaty:

2. Historical prologue reviewing in personal terms the past relationships between the two parties to the treaties, emphasizing the gracious acts of the Hittite king;

3. Treaty stipulations or agreements, often stating first the primary agreement or obligation agreed to by the two parties and then detailing the specific demands or agreements in a longer list;

4. A clause describing the way the treaty is to be stored and to be read regularly to the citizens affected by it; this does not always appear;

5. List of witnesses to the treaty including the gods and natural phenomena such as mountains, heaven, seas, the earth, etc;

6. List of curses and blessings brought on by violating or observing the treaty demands.

The Assyrian treaties often do not have the historical prologue or the blessings.

The Book of Deuteronomy, Joshua 24, and other Old Testament texts show that Israel was familiar with these treaty forms and used them in their literature. They may also show that Israel used these forms in their worship, renewing regularly the covenant relationship with God. No Old Testament text precisely follows the treaty forms without change, and no text states explicitly that covenant renewal ceremonies formed the center of Israel's worship.

Covenants among Humans In biblical language, people "cut" a covenant with another person or group of people. Abraham and Abimelech cut such a covenant as equal partners, agreeing that the well at Beersheba belonged to Abraham (Gen. 21:22–34). Sacrifices acompanied the covenant making. Apparently, Abraham gained the right to live among Abimelech's people, the Philistines (v. 34). Jonathan and David cut a covenant of friendship in which Jonathan acknowledged David's right to the throne (1 Sam. 18:3; 23:18). Such an agreement was a "covenant of the Lord" (1 Sam 20 8), that is the Lord was its witness and guarantee. At the time Jonathan possessed greater authority than David, but in the covenant he acknowledged David's coming authority over him. Abner led the tribes of northern Israel to cut a covenant with David, making David king over the north as well as over southern Judah (2 Sam.3; Compare 5:3; 1 Chron. 11:3). David, who occupied the position of power and authority in the agreement, demanded that Abner also produce Saul's daughter who David had married earlier. Solomon and Hiram made a covenant of peace which apparently included certain trade agreements (1 Kings 5:12).

King Zedekiah made a covenant with the people of Jerusalem, releasing the Hebrews from slavery (Jer. 34:8).

Ezra reformed the restored Jewish community by leading them to make a covenant together in God's presence. They would agree to divorce foreign wives and separate themselves from the children so strongly influenced by the foreign mothers (Ezra 10:3).

Hosea denounced the northern kingdom's covenant or vassal treaty with Assyria (Hos. 12:1; compare 7:8–14; 8:9; 10:4; 2 Kings 17:3–4). Such treaties sought to gain military protection from foreign countries rather than relying upon Yahweh, the covenant God. (See Ex. 23:32; 34:12,15; Deut. 7:2).

When Athaliah tried to usurp the throne and kill off the royal family, the priest Jehoiada made a covenant agreement with the army (2 Chron. 23:1) and with all the people (v. 3) to support the king Joash against Athaliah (compare 2 Kings 11).

Israel had a long history of making covenant agreements with foreigners, despite God's warnings not to do so. The Gibeonites deceived Israel under Joshua into making a vassal treaty. Israel easily occupied the position of authority in the treaty and subjected the Gibeonites to temple service, but still this violated God's commandments (Josh. 9; compare Judg. 2:2). The Israelites in Jabesh Gilead begged for a treaty from Nahash, the Ammonite, but he demanded severe conditions. Saul delivered them, leading to affirmation of Saul's kingship (1 Sam. 11).

Ben-Hadad, king of Damascus in Syria, promised to return captured cities to Israel and to provide Israel with markets for its products in Damascus if the king of Israel would make a peace treaty or political alliance with him (1 Kings 20:31–35). Earlier, Asa, king of Judah, had used the Temple treasury to pay tribute to Ben-Hadad of Damascus to entice Ben-Hadad to break his vassal treaty with Baasha, king of Israel, and enter into a similar treaty with Judah (1 Kings 15:19; 2 Chron. 16:3). This is the typical example of a political covenant. One party desires privileges from the other party and pays for the privileges. Such payment may be enforced by a victorious king or may be offered by a weak king needing help against enemies. Members of such a covenant alliance were called "*baals* of the covenant" or lords, owners of the covenant (Gen. 14:13), a technical term for allies. They could also be called "men of the covenant" (Obad. 7). Covenant treaties carried exprectations of humane and moral treatment of other members of the covenant, the covenant being literally a covenant of brothers (Amos 1:9; compare 1 Kings 20:32–33).

Each covenant had special conditions effecting the power in authority and the one becoming a vassal or imposing demands on each partner of a covenant between equals. Breaking covenant conditions meant treason and extreme punishment (Ezek. 17:12–18; compare Amos 1:9).

Marriage involved covenant obligations with God as the witness (Mal. 2:14). This could be used to describe the covenant relationship between God and His people (Ezek. 16:8; Hos. 2:19–20).

Isaiah spoke menacingly of a covenant of death political leaders had made (Isa. 28:15). They thought they had bought protection from their enemies. The prophet reminded them nothing made them secure against God's judgment. The action behind the covenant of death can be variously interpreted: a ritual with a foreign god of the underworld or of death, a mutual alliance to fight to the death, a treaty with a foreign power that brought God's judgment and thus death.

God's Covenants with His People God's grace in relating to His people by initiating covenants with them is a major theme of the Bible.

Noah received God's first covenant (Gen. 9:9–17). This was a divine oath or promise not to repeat the flood. This covenant extended beyond Noah to all the animals who had experienced the massive destruction and death associated with the flood. The rainbow stands eternally as a sign of God's promise. This covenant called for no human response. It was solely a promise and oath from God. God's covenant with Noah was not a divine afterthought to the flood, a way of making up to His creation for all the destruction. God established the covenant relationship prior to the flood (Gen. 6:18). The Hebrew verb here means literally, "to cause to stand." Some interpreters take this to mean that even in Genesis 6 God was confirming a covenant already established, though most see this as a formula for the establishment of the covenant. All agree that the formula underlines the lasting guarantee behind the covenant. The covenant is established and will stand. God's first covenant protected life—both human and animal—in the face of massive destruction. That priority on and protection of life remains the foundation of God's relationship with His creation. Neither "natural" catastrophe nor human sin (compare 6:5; 8:21) can prevent God from maintaining His priority on life.

God made His second covenant with Abraham (Gen. 15:18; 17:2). As the covenant with Noah involved a righteous man (Gen. 6:8–9), so the covenant with Abraham involved a man of faith (Gen. 15:6). God initiated His covenant with this type of person, but this does not mean that the person earned God's covenant with good works. Rather, this type of person was open to God's actions and could be directed by God for His purposes. The covenant with Abraham, like that with Noah, involved divine promises, not human obedience. God promised to give the land of Canaan to Abraham's descendants after a long sojourn to a foreign land. He symbolized this promise through an ancient covenant ceremony (compare Jer. 34), known from other cultures also, in which animals are cut and covenant participants pass through. Normally, the human covenant partners swear that they will abide by covenant conditions or will face the fate of the animals. For Abraham, the rite became a sacrifice to God and a sign of his devotion to the rite even when attacking birds threatened to spoil it. Abraham did not walk through the divided animals. Symbols of God's presence did. God made the oath to keep His promise. Genesis 17 shows the initiation of circumcision as the sign of the covenant. God's covenant promise was extended to include international-relations, many descendants, and to be God of the people descended from Abraham forever.

Redemption from Egyptian slavery found its climax in God's covenant with Israel. This covenant differed from those with Noah and Abraham. The situation was not an affirmation of human faithfulness or righteousness, but the confession of God's salvation (Ex. 19:4). The oath or promise came not from God but from the people. They were to "obey my voice indeed, and keep my covenant." Then they would be "a peculiar treasure unto me above all people . . . a kingdom of priests . . . an holy nation" (Ex. 6:5–6). Covenant law was then revealed to God's people. They had responsibilities within the covenant relationship. The people accepted this responsibility in a solemn ceremony in which covenant law was read from the "book of the covenant" and "the blood of the covenant" was sprinkled on the altar and on the people (Ex. 24:3–8). The covenant with Yahweh meant Israel could make covenants with no other gods (Ex. 23:32). Within the covenant agreement, God included the sabbath covenant, Israel's perpetual promise to observe the seventh day as a day of rest, reflecting God's practice in creation (Ex. 31:16).

Israel refused to take covenant commitment seriously almost from the start. While Moses climbed the mountain and stayed in God's presence to receive the Ten Commandments, the people worshiped golden calves (Ex. 32). God renewed the covenant with His people, making explicit His covenant promise to conquer miraculously the land of Canaan promised to Abraham (Ex. 34; note verse 10). Again, covenant with Israel involved Israel's pledge to make no other covenants (34:12,15; Deut. 7:2) and God's commandments as His expectations of a covenant people (Ex. 34:27–28; Deut. 4:13). See *Ten Commandments.*

Israel's sacrificial worship included reminders of the covenant relationship. Salt added to offerings was the "salt of the covenant" (Lev. 2:13). Salt symbolized covenant relationships among Arabs and Greeks and probably other peoples of Israel's day. The symbolic meaning is not precisely known. It may have reflected on understanding of salt as something eternal and thus as a sign of the

everlasting effect of the agreements reached in a covenant relationship (compare Num. 18:19; 2 Chron. 13:5). The bread of the altar also symbolized Israel's everlasting covenant (Lev. 24:8).

Israel apparently celebrated its covenant with ceremonies helping the people identify themselves as the covenant people as they heard, "The Lord our God made a covenant with us in Horeb. The Lord made not this covenant with our fathers, but with us, even us, who are all of us here alive this day" (Deut. 5:2–3; compare 29:1,12,14–15; Josh 8:30–35; 24:1–28). Israel's ceremonies had some of the same components that Near Eastern covenants or treaties had, particularly blessings for covenant obedience and cursings for disobedience (Ex. 23:25–30; Lev. 26:1–46; Deut. 27:11–26; 28:1–68). A major element of blessing is that God will make His covenant stand for His people (Lev. 26:9). Curses come when God's people break the covenant (Lev. 26:15; Deut. 29:25; 31:16; Josh. 7:11,15,23:16; Judg. 2:20). Curse is not the final word for covenant breaking, however. After covenant curse or punishment takes effect, God expects the people to confess sin and return to Him (Lev. 26:40; Deut. 4:30–31; 30:1–3). God, on the other side, does not "break my covenant with them: for I am the Lord their God" (Lev. 26:44; compare Deut. 7:9, 12: Judg. 2:1; Zech. 11:10). For the sake of His promises to the ancestors and because of His nature as Yahweh, the God of Israel, God "will for their sakes remember the covenant of their ancestors" (Lev. 26:45). God's eternal devotion to His covenant does not nullify the effect of the curses. They are real and enforced, for "the Lord thy God is a consuming fire, even a jealous God" (Deut. 4:24).

God's covenant is not simply the selfish demands of a victorious, powerful overlord placing unreasonable demands on His subjects. God works for His covenant people. He protected them in the wilderness, gave them the land, and gave "power to get wealth" (Deut. 8:18; 29:9). The blessings of the covenant are more than part of a ceremony. They become reality in the life of His people. Why? Not so the people can become conceited and self-confident (Deut. 8:17) but that God can have a powerful people with whom to establish His covenant and thus to accomplish His purposes for His creation (Deut. 8:18). This did not mean that all God's people would be rich or that only the rich could enter the covenant. God invited persons from every economic level of Israelite society to join His covenant (Deut. 29:10–12). Even those not physically present at the covenant ceremony were covenant members (Deut. 29:15).

God's covenant with Abraham and with Israel found its special climax in God's covenant with David (2 Sam. 23:5; compare 7:12–16; 2 Chron. 13:5; Ps. 89:3–34; 132:12). God would establish the house of David to rule His people forever.

Perennial disobedience led to Judah's exile and complaint, "thou hast made void the covenant of thy servant" (Ps. 89:39).

Making covenants with His people characterized God and distinguished Him from the other gods of the nations. Israel's God was the one "who keepest covenant and mercy with thy servants that walk before thee with all their heart" (1 Kings 8:23; 2 Chron. 6:14; Neh. 1:5; 9:32; Ps. 105:8, 10; compare Isa. 54:10).

Sadly, God's people did not mirror Him in faithfulness to covenant. David's son King Solomon blazed the trail of covenant-breaking, worshiping other gods and setting a model Israel consistently followed through their history (1 Kings 11:11). Israel chose to listen to Dame Folly's strange wooings and forget the covenant with God (Prov. 2:17). God had to punish. Even in punishment, He remained faithful, preserving two tribes for the family of David (1 Kings 11:12–13) and protecting the people from enemies (2 Kings 13:23; 2 Chron. 21:7). Israel's covenant breaking, on the other hand, became so extreme that a lonely, persecuted prophet could claim, "I, even I only, am left; and they seek my life" (1 Kings 19:10). Occasionally, faithful people gained control and led the people to renew the covenant with God (2 Kings 17:35; 23:3; 2 Chron. 15:12; 29:10; 34:31–32). Eventually, covenant-breaking led God to send the northern kingdom into eternal exile (2 Kings 17:15–18; 18:11–12). Punishment was not God's final word. He heard His people's cry and "remembered for them his covenant" (Ps. 106:45).

The covenant relationship became so characteristic for Israel and their God that the Psalmists in worship and in wisdom teaching called Israel to remember God and His covenants. Covenant keeping led to mercy and truth (Ps. 25:10; 103:18) and to participation in the intimate covenant relationship (25:14). In times of trouble the worshiper could call on God, claiming "neither have we dealt falsely in thy covenant" (44:17). In worship the covenant people gathered to hear God's judgment (50:5; compare 78:10, 37: Jer. 11:2–3). A strong word of judgment rebuked those who entered God's covenant with false intentions and results (50:16). In worship they also claimed God's covenant promises, asking deliverance from trouble by calling on God to "have respect unto the covenant" (74:20). They praised God for covenant faithfulness (111:5,9).

God also made a covenant with the priests, acknowledging their obedient and even heroic acts by promising them the office of the priest forever (Num. 25:12–13; Ex. 40:15; compare Deut. 33:8–11). Even the priests proved unfaithful and drew God's anger (Neh. 13:29; Mal. 2:1–9).

God's covenant has a future. It was not limited to a brief period of human history. God's covenant with Israel was a covenant pointed to all the earth, to the Gentiles (Isa. 42:6; compare 49:8). If Israel would not be God's servant to fulfill the Gentile mission, God would raise up a servant who would be a "light to the Gentiles." This passage has led to several interpretations, making Cyrus of Persia the servant and seeing the command to impose God's obligations on the nations rather than to bring salvation to people. Such interpretations appear to miss the larger biblical context and message as well as imposing an unnecessary limitation on Israel's theological horizons.

God extended His covenant with David for the sake of the nations. The entire nation of Israel would fulfill David's role and would bring the nations streaming to Jerusalem to find God's glory (Isa. 55:1–5). God extended His covenant to the outsiders among His own people—eunuchs otherwise forbidden to worship (Isa. 56:3–5; compare Deut. 23:1) and foreigners (Isa. 56:6; compare Deut. 23:2–9).

The emphasis on a covenant with the nations did not diminish God's covenant care for His people. He continued His promise to come and redeem them from the power of the capturing nations (Isa. 59:21; 61:8).

Hosea condemned Israel for transgressing the covenant (Hos. 6:7; 8:1). This involved making an international alliance or covenant with Assyria, seeking protection from enemies and freedom from Assyrian attack (Hos. 12:1). Egypt was also involved in such international treaty making with Israel. Still, Hosea pointed forward to a day of hope when God would renew the covenant with Israel (2:18).

Jeremiah based his preaching on the covenant (11:6,8), claiming Israel of his day had broken the covenant just like those in Moses' day (11:10). He could also use God's covenant faithfulness as the theological basis of his prayer for deliverance and restoration (14:21). He could explain Israel's disaster as resulting from breaking the covenant (22:9). Jeremiah's strongest contribution to covenant theology was his portrait of God's promise of a new covenant, a covenant whose stipulations would not stand on tables of stone as did the old one but whose obligations would be deeply nested in the hearts of the people so they would have will and power to obey (33:31–34; compare 32:40–44; 50:5). Forgiveness would characterize God's relationship to the new covenant people. Jeremiah's new covenant preaching extended to the covenant with David (33:19–26).

Ezekiel related the history of Israel as God's covenant of mercy, broken by a people who despised it but renewed in an eternal covenant (16:8,59–63; compare 20:37). The new covenant would bring a new David and a new era of peace not only with human enemies but with the beasts of the natural world (34:22–31; compare 37:24–28). Ezekiel judged Israel for having broken the law of Numbers 18:4 by bringing "unclean" foreigners into the Temple (Ezek. 44:7). He also interpreted King Zedekiah's breaking of his vassal covenant with Babylon as a breaking of Israel's covenant with God (17:19).

Zechariah promised that exiles would return to Jerusalem because God would be true to the covenant of blood He made with Moses (Zech. 9:11; compare Ex. 24). The prophetic vision of Zechariah 11 has produced many interpretations: "And I took my staff, even Beauty, and cut it asunder, that I might break my covenant which I had made with all the people." The prophet denounced the wicked leaders of God's people and claimed the leadership role for himself in the vision. He could not get cooperation and turned against the people, breaking his covenant and breaking the union of Israel and Judah (v. 14). The broken covenant could be between king and people, between king and allied nations, between God and His people, or between God and the nations. Whichever interpretation is correct, it shows that a covenant agreement could be brought to an end.

Malachi joined the chorus condemning Israel for ignoring God's covenant expectations by treating each other "treacherously" (2:10).

Old Testament covenant language ends in Malachi 3:1 with God's announcement that the "messenger of the covenant" will come representing God, proving the covenant relationship is not a thing of the past. He will show God continues to punish those who ignore or reject His covenant. **Covenant in the New Testament** The New Testament by use of the Greek *diatheke* transformed covenant into testament, *diatheke* referring to a binding will a person made to ensure proper disposal of goods upon the death of the person making the will (see Gal. 3:15; Heb. 9:17). Still, the New Testament followed the Septuagint, the earliest Greek translation, in using *diatheke* to translate the Hebrew *berith* or covenant. New Testament language is thus Greek with a strong Hebrew flavoring.

Jesus used the last supper as opportunity to interpret His ministry, and particularly His death, as fulfillment of Jeremiah's new covenant prophecy. His death represented the shedding of the blood of the new covenant. People who repeated the rites of the last supper drank the blood of the new covenant, remembering His death as the sacrifice for sins (Matt. 26:28; Mark 14:24; Luke 22:20; 1 Cor. 11:25).

Zechariah, father of John the Baptist, interpreted the announcement of John's birth as evidence that God had remembered His holy covenant (Luke 1:72). Peter told skeptical Jews that they were children of the covenant with Abraham and that Christ had come first to them to fulfill the promise of blessing to Abraham by turning them away from their sinful ways (Acts 3:25). Stephen reminded those who would murder him that the covenant of circumcision with Abraham contin-

ued as part of God's history of salvation leading to Jesus (Acts 7:8). Paul confirmed that just as a human last will and testament could not be changed by another person, so God's covenant with Abraham could not be changed or annulled (Gal. 3:15–17). Paul asserted that with the coming of Christ and Israel's rejection of Him, God still had a covenant to save Israel (Rom. 11:27). Paul interpreted Christ as the one who had made the meaning of the Old Testament plain, removing the veil that caused the Jews to continue looking only to Moses rather than to look to Christ as God's final revelation (2 Cor. 3:14). Paul was a minister of the new covenant, not of the old (2 Cor. 3:6), a ministry of the Spirit and of life, not of dead literalism.

In the New Testament only Hebrews makes covenant a central theological theme. The emphasis is on Jesus, the perfect High Priest, providing a new, better, superior covenant (Heb. 7:22; 8:6). Jesus represented the fulfillment of Jeremiah's new covenant promise (Heb. 8:8,10; 10:16). Jesus was the perfect covenant Mediator (Heb. 9:15), providing an eternal inheritance in a way the old covenant could not (compare 12:24). Jesus' death on the cross satisfied the requirement that all covenants be established by blood (Heb. 9:18,20) just as was the first covenant (Ex. 24:8). Christ's blood established an everlasting covenant (Heb. 13:20). If Israel suffered for breaking the Sinai covenant (Heb. 8:9–10), how much more should people expect to suffer if they have "counted the blood of the covenant, wherewith he was sanctified, an unholy thing" (Heb. 10:29).

The Greek word testament eventually gave its name to the two parts of our Bible—the Old and the New Testaments. In many ways the name is appropriate to show that the two parts of Scripture rest on God's gracious action in redeeming His people and making a covenant with them.

Trent C. Butler

COVENANT BOX TEV name for the ark of the covenant. See *Ark of the Covenant.*

COVENANT OF SALT Salt was often utilized in covenant making probably as symbolic of that which preserves and prevents decay. The hope was that the covenant thus enacted would endure (Num. 18:19; 2 Chron. 13:5). Salt was an essential element of the cereal offerings made to God (Lev. 2:13).

COVERING OF THE LIVER See *Caul.*

COVERING THE HEAD In 1 Corinthians 11:1–16, Paul dealt with the matter of covering the head in worship services. This extended treatment shows that this must have been a subject of considerable interest in Corinth.

The Jewish custom was for all women to cover

their heads with a veil when they went outside their homes. To appear in public without a veil was a sign of immodesty and lack of virtue. To appear in a worship service without a veil was unthinkable.

Some of the Corinthian Christian women had evidently appeared in worship without a veil on their heads. Perhaps they had understood Paul's emphasis on Christian freedom to mean that they no longer had to observe any of the old Jewish customs—including that of wearing a veil.

The effects of such a change in dress style had been disruptive to the worship services and Christian witness in Corinth. This led Paul to state that a woman should cover her head during the worship service. At the same time, he encouraged the men to follow the Jewish custom of worshiping with uncovered heads.

Paul cited various reasons in 1 Corinthians 11:1–16 for his position. He referred to: (1) the order in creation (v. 3), (2) social customs of the time (vv. 4–6), (3) the presence of angels (v. 10), (4) nature itself (vv. 13–15), and (5) the common practice in the churches (v. 16).

The principle here is that Christians must be sensitive to the cultures in which they live. They should not needlessly flout local customs unless there is some moral reason to do so. To be insensitive to the culture in which one lives causes one to offend many of the people whom the church is trying to win to Jesus Christ. It diverts attention away from the most important thing and focuses it on peripheral matters.

See *Corinth; Worship; Women.* *Lynn Jones*

COVET, COVETOUS The inordinate desire to possess what belongs to another, usually tangible things.

While the Hebrew word for "covet" can also be translated "to desire," in the Tenth Commandment it means an ungoverned and selfish desire that threatens the basic rights of others. Coveting was sinful because it focused greedily on the property of a neighbor that was his share in the land God had promised His people. After Israel's defeat at Ai, Achan confessed that his selfish desire for treasure was so great that he disobeyed God's specific commandment (Josh. 7:21). In defense of Judah's poor, Micah declared the Lord's judgment against the land-grabbers for coveting small farms and actually seizing them from their powerless owners (Mic. 2:2). Although the commandment against coveting seems concerned only with motivation, some passages indicate that coveting in the heart was expected to end with taking what was desired.

In the New Testament the same Greek word is translated "covet" in the King James Version and "earnestly desire" in the Revised Standard Version (1 Cor. 12:39). So, covet could be used in good sense. Another Greek word describes the ruthless self-assertion that the Tenth Commandment forbids (Luke 12:15; Eph. 5:5). In the Luke passage Jesus said that the covetous man will not be "rich toward God." In the Ephesian passage Paul classed the covetous man with the idolater. So, the greedy person—one who covets—denies his faith in God and scorns His values.

William J. Fallis

COZ (Cŏz) KJV, TEV spelling of Koz. See *Koz.*

COZBI (Cŏz' bī) Personal name meaning, "my falsehood." A Midianite woman who was slain by Phinehas after being brought into the tent of an Israelite man named Zimri (Num. 25:15). When both she and Zimri were executed, a plague that was sweeping through the Israelite camp was stopped.

COZEBA (Cō zē' bȧ) Place name meaning, "deceptive." Home of descendants of Judah (1 Chron. 4:22). Its location is uncertain.

CRACKNEL Old English word for a hard brittle biscuit (1 Kings 14:3 KJV).

CRAFT Occupation or trade requiring manual dexterity or artistic skill. Several crafts were practiced in biblical times: carpentry, boatbuilding, carving (wood, ivory, ebony, and alabaster), metalworking (gold, silver, bronze, and iron), weaving and spinning, tanning, tentmaking, basket weavers, potter's trade, fuller's trade, dyeing, sculpting, jeweler's trade, glassworking, perfumery, embroidering, masonry, plastering, etc. See *Occupations, Professions in the Bible.*

CRANE KJV translation of the Hebrew word in Isaiah 38:14; Jeremiah 8:7. Modern translations read, "swift" (NIV, NAS, REB) or dove (Isa. 38:14 REB). See *Birds.*

CRAWLING THINGS NRSV translation of Hebrew term in Micah 7:17. The Hebrew word also appears in Deuteronomy 32:34, where it refers to poisonous snakes. See *Creeping Things, Snakes.*

CREATION From ancient times persons have had a keen interest in the origin of the universe. Stories or fragments of stories about creation have survived in the literature of several ancient nations. Biblical writers may reflect an awareness of these extra-biblical accounts, but their consistent testimony is that Israel's God was the Creator. His creative activities proceeded in orderly and methodical fashion toward the fulfillment of His purpose to create "good heavens" and "a good earth."

Biblical References to Creation Probably the best known reference to creation in the Bible is Genesis 1:1—2:4a. That certainly is not the only place in Scripture where the subject is treated. Psalmists mentioned creation or the Creator frequently

(Pss. 8:3, 4; 74:17; 95:5; 100:3; 104:24,30; 118:24; 40:5; 51:10; 64:9; 24:1—2; 102:25; 145:10). The second half of Isaiah (chs. 40—66) has four direct references to creation (Isa. 40:28; 43:7, 15; 45:7; 65:17). Job alluded to creation in two speeches (Job 10:8; 26:7), and God's answer to Job contains one reference to the subject (Job 38:4).

The New Testament reveals that Jesus "made" all things (John 1:3) and that "all things were created by him, and for him" (Col. 1:16). Paul's assertion recorded in Ephesians 3:9 is that God "created all things." The writer of Hebrews notes that Jesus was the agent God used to create the world (Heb. 1:2). Because God created all things, He is worthy of "glory and honor and power" (Rev. 4:11). Luke testified that the living God "made heaven, and earth, and the sea, and all things that are therein" (Acts 14:15). The consistent report of the Bible is that God is the Source of the whole created order.

The Function of Biblical Creation References
Genesis is a book about beginnings. The centerpiece of the book is God's redemptive activity following the fall of man. God began by calling Abram out of Ur, by entering into a covenant with him, and by making promises to bless him and to bless all the families of the earth through him.

Genesis 1—11 is prologue to the patriarchal stories (Gen. 12—50). It sets a world stage on which God acted in choosing one man in order to bless all men. Genesis 1—2 contain two accounts of creation, the order of man's creation coming at the end in the first and at the beginning in the second. God's creation, "good" as it was (Gen. 1:4,10,12,21,25,31), soon became bad through human rebellion against God. The accounts of creation in Genesis 1—2 prepare the reader for the record of the first people being placed in the Garden of Eden, temptation by the serpent, rebellion against God, expulsion from the garden, and the degenerating effect of sin in society.

God's judgment on sin in the form of a flood did not put an end to sin (Gen. 6—9). Noah himself carried sin into the society that survived the flood. Even destroying the tower of Babel, confusing the people's language, and scattering them over the face of the earth did not stop the spread of sin (Gen. 11). Genesis 11 ends by introducing Terah, the father of Abram, through whom God would bless the world in spite of its rebellion against Him. The link between creation and redemption is clear.

Isaiah reminded weary exiles that the God he proclaimed as their Redeemer and Sustainer was "the everlasting God, the Lord, the Creator of the ends of the earth" (Isa. 40:28). The prophet linked God's redemptive activity with His creative activity (Isa. 43:7,15). He went on to declare God's plan to "create new heavens and a new earth" as well as a new people (Isa. 65:17—18).

Job lamented that God's hands "made and fashioned" him but for some unexplained reason turned about to "destroy" him (Job 10:8). In a later speech Job expressed the effortless manner in which God created the universe (Job 26:7—11) and defeated Rahab and the serpent (26:12—13). The Lord's speech in response to Job (Job 38—39) makes clear that God is the Creator and that man had no part in creation.

The psalmists' concerns with God as Creator were related to people's place in creation (Ps. 8:3,4), to God's redemptive activity (Pss. 74:17; 95:5), and to praise for the Creator (Pss. 100:3; 104; 24:1,2). One psalmist referred to the creation to contrast its perishable nature with the imperishable nature of the Creator (Ps. 102:25—27).

The three doxologies in Amos (4:13; 5:8—9; 9:5—6) magnify God the Creator and Controller of creation. Malachi's reference to God as Creator stresses the fact that one God created all people (Mal. 2:10). This fact forms the basis of the prophet's appeal for faithfulness among covenant members.

John based God's worthiness to receive "glory and honor and power" on His creative activity (Rev. 4:11). By God's will "all things" existed and were created. John's testimony is that "the Word" made all things (John 1:3) and that Jesus is the Word (John 1:14).

Paul's perspective was that Christians represent God's workmanship "created in Christ Jesus for good works" (Eph. 2:10). The gospel that God called Paul to preach had been hidden in God who "created all things" (Eph. 3:9). He agreed with John that Jesus the Savior, the firstborn of all creation, was Himself the Source of all creation (Col. 1:16—17).

The author of Hebrews wrote of God's revelation through prophets of old, but "in these last days" God spoke through a Son (Heb. 1:1—2). The Son created the world. Like many Old Testament passages, this passage in Hebrews links God's creative activity with His redemptive activity.

The people of Lystra took Barnabas and Paul to be gods (Acts 14:11). Paul and Barnabas set the record straight as they pointed to "the living God which made heaven, and earth, and the sea, and all things that are therein" (Acts 14:15).

Relationship of Biblical and Extra-biblical References to Creation The Enuma Elish ("When on High") is probably the best known extra-biblical reference to creation. This Mesopotamian account reflects a striking correspondence in various details and in order of events when it is compared with the biblical references to creation. What is the explanation for these similarities?

Based on the dating of Babylonian and biblical materials, apparently biblical writers were aware of Babylonian prototypes. Though the two accounts are similar in some ways, they are poles apart in other ways. Conflict between rival deities dominates the Babylonian story of creation. The biblical accounts feature one God creating a good, orderly, and harmonious universe. Their cosmogony (theory of the origin of the universe) is similar; their religion is radically different. Biblical writers seem to be conscious of Babylonian sources, but they take a critical position toward them.

Human Place in Creation Both detailed stories of creation in the Bible feature people at center stage, even though the creation of persons is last in the order of creative acts in Genesis 1:1—2:4*a* but first in Genesis 2:4*b*–24. The author of Psalm 8 seems surprised at the attention the Creator gives to mortal humans formed from the dust (Ps. 8:4). Yet God gave humans a place of prominence and set them over the rest of creation (Ps. 8:5–8). "For thou hast made him a little lower than the angels" (Ps. 8:5*a)* may be a commentary on the Genesis statement that God "created man in his own image" (Gen. 1:27).

New Creation and Physical Creation The Old Testament is consistent in its use of the verb "create" (*bara'*). Only God serves as subject of the verb. Creation is the work of God. People may "make" (*'asah)* and "form" (*yatsar).* God alone creates (*bara').*

Psalm 51:10 may reflect a transition in usage of "create" (*bara')* to designate a purely physical work. A clean heart is the object of the verb "create" in this Psalm. Isaiah employed "create" in reference to "new heavens and a new earth" as well as "Jerusalem" and "her people" (Isa. 65:17–18). Paul wrote to the Corinthians about being "in Christ" and thereby being "a new creation" (2 Cor. 5:17). "Created in Christ Jesus" is Paul's terminology for spiritual salvation in Ephesians 2:10. The point in all of these references is that God alone is the Author of spiritual redemption.

God is the Creator of all things. All things belong to God. God gave humans dominion over creation, a stewardship assignment. Therefore, people are accountable directly to God for their use or abuse of creation. God created "good" heavens and a "good" earth. The entrance of human sin has had an adverse effect on creation (Hos. 4:1–3). Paul pictured that the whole of creation "groaneth and travaileth" under the burden of human sin (Rom. 8:22). He also wrote of a time when "the creation itself also will be set free from its slavery to corruption into the freedom of the glory of the children of God" (Rom. 8:21 NAS). Paul anticipated a day when God would restore the whole of creation to its original goodness. *Billy K. Smith*

CREATURE A being with life. The phrase used in the Hebrew Bible *nephesh chayah* is translated by "creature," "living [thing, soul]," and "beast." In Genesis 2:7 it is used of mankind and translated

"living soul." In all of the other references the phrase applies solely to animals. Because the same term is used of mankind and the other creatures, interpreters believe that it applies to the similar physical makeup (same matter) rather than the higher relationship with God that is special to humans. *Mike Mitchell*

CREDIT, CREDITOR See *Loans.*

CREEPING THINGS English translation sometimes used for a general Hebrew term designating small animals that appear to creep or crawl along the ground. English translators sometimes use "moving things" or other equivalents for the Hebrew word. The term was applied to all land animals in general (Gen. 1:24–26,28; 7:23; 9:3), fish (Pss. 69:34; 104:25; Hab. 1:14), forest animals (Ps. 104:20), and swarming creatures (that is, weasels, mice, lizards, snails, moles, and perhaps even crocodiles, NRSV, NAS; Lev. 11:29–30,44,46).

CRESCENS (Crĕs' cĕns) Personal name meaning, "growing." Christian worker with Paul who had gone to Galatia when 2 Timothy was written (2 Tim. 4:10).

CRESCENTS Translation used in some modern versions for the ornamental jewelry in the shape of the crescent moon worn on necklaces. It probably had magical connotations. Midianites (Judg. 8:21,26) and unfaithful Israelites (Isa. 3:18) wore them.

CRETANS (Crē' tăns), **CRETES, CRETIANS** Citizens of Crete. See *Crete.*

CRETE (Crēte) A long, narrow, mountainous island south of mainland Greece, running 170 miles east-west but never more than about 35 miles wide. Crete was the center of the Minoan maritime empire named after the legendary King Minos, and associated especially with the famous palaces of Cnossos and Phaestos, which flourished from 2000 to 1500 B.C. This artistically brilliant civilization fell suddenly, perhaps by earthquake followed by conquest, about 1400 B.C., leaving written tablets in the oldest known scripts of Europe, including the undeciphered "Linear A" and the apparently later proto-Greek "Linear B," found also on the mainland. The Minoans of Crete were known to the Egyptians as "Keftiu," which may be the same as biblical "Caphtor," though the biblical term may include a wider reference to coastlands and islands of the Aegean area. The Philistines came to Palestine from Caphtor (Jer. 47:4; Amos 9:7) and may have been part of the widespread migrant "Sea Peoples" rather than Cretans proper.

In classical Greek times Crete had many city-states, but they played relatively little part in mainstream Greek history. It had become a center of piracy before the Roman occupation in 67 B.C. Under the Romans it became part of a double province Crete with Cyrene, under a governor with the title "proconsul," who ruled the island and the opposite coast of North Africa from the Roman capital Gortyna. This had already been among the cities to whom the Romans had appealed a century before for fair treatment of their Jewish minorities (1 Macc. 15:23). Cretans were among those listed as present in Jerusalem on the day of Pentecost (Acts 2:11), and the gospel may first have reached the island through them.

Paul made his voyage to Rome as a prisoner on a Roman grain ship. The voyage followed the route south of Crete, which gave partial shelter from the northwest winds and avoided the peril of the lee shore on the north coast, while still involving the need to beat up against largely adverse winds. The journey had already been very slow, and it was getting dangerously late in the summer sailing season. The ship doubled Salmone, the eastern cape of Crete, and with difficulty reached Fair Havens, a small anchorage near the city of Lasea (Acts 27:8). There the emergency council called by the centurion and shipmaster overruled Paul's advice, and a risky attempt was made to reach Phoenix, a regular port for servicing the grain ships, some 40 miles further west along the coast. The gentle south wind gave way to a violent northeaster (Euroclydon, Acts 27:14) when they came out of the shelter of Cape Matala (Loukinos) into an open bay, and the ship was driven helplessly, managing only some emergency action in the lee of the offshore island of Cauda, and thence to shipwreck on Malta.

The only other references to Crete in the New Testament are in the epistle to Titus. Paul had left Titus in Crete to exercise pastoral supervision over the churches there (Titus 1:5). The character of the people is described in a quotation from a prophet of their own: "Cretians are always liars, evil beasts, slow bellies" (Titus 1:12), words attributed to the Cretan seer Epimenides, who was also credited with having advised the Athenians to set up altars to unknown gods (compare Acts 17:23).

It is a problem to know when Paul (or Titus) visited Crete, apart from Paul's voyage as a prisoner. It is difficult to fit the occasions of the Pastoral Epistles (to Timothy and Titus) into Paul's life as recorded in Acts. The most satisfactory answer to this difficulty still seems to be that which argues that Paul was released from his two years' imprisonment in Rome (Acts 28:30), and undertook further travels in the East which can only be traced in these epistles. At this last period of his life he may have focused his work on establishing and strengthening the churches throughout the Greek East.   *Colin J. Hemer*

CRIB Feeding trough for the ox (Prov. 14;4 KJV) or the ass (Isa. 1:3; compare Job 39:9) and proba-

bly for any number of other domesticated animals.

CRICKET The Hebrew term translated "cricket" (Lev. 11:22 NIV, NAS, NRSV, TEV) is difficult to identify, probably a locust or grasshopper. See *Insects.*

CRIMES AND PUNISHMENTS Israel, like most peoples in the Ancient Near East, considered their law to be the direct revelation from God. Since the law came from God, any transgression of the law was a transgression of God's revealed will.

The responsibility for the fulfillment and enforcement of the law lay with the entire community. The transgression of the law by one person or group within Israel involved the whole community in the guilt of the act. This is especially true in cases of homicide, idolatry, and sexual offenses (see, for example, Deut. 19:10; 21:1–9; 2 King 24:1–7). When Israel failed to purge the offender and rebellion against God's Law from their midst, God punished Israel (Lev. 18:26–28; 26:3–45; Deut. 28).

Israelite Law with respect to crime and punishment was distinct from the laws of other cultures in several ways. First, Israel, in contrast to many of its neighbors, did not consider crimes against property to be capital crimes. Israel observed a system of corporal punishment and/or fines for lesser crimes. Second, Israel restricted the law of retaliation (eye for an eye; *lex talionis*) to the person of the offender. Other cultures permitted the family to be punished for the crimes of the offender. Third, Israel did not observe class differences in the enforcement of the Law to the extent that their neighbors did. Nobility and commoner, priest and lay people were treated equally in theory. However, slaves and sojourners (foreigners) did not have an equal standing with free Israelites—though their treatment in Israel was often better than in surrounding nations; and women did not have equal standing with the men in Israelite culture—especially in regard to marriage and divorce laws and laws pertaining to sexual offenses. Finally, Israelites (in contrast to the people of surrounding nations) could not substitute sacrifices for intentional breaches of the law; sin and guilt offerings were allowed only in the cases of unwitting sins (Lev. 4—5).

Crimes and Capital Punishment in the Old Testament Israelite law considered some crimes serious enough to warrant capital punishment. See *Capital Punishment.*

Being "Cut Off" from Israel Often in the Old Testament the punishment for a particular crime is termed being "cut off" from Israel. The meaning of the phrase is somewhat ambiguous. Some interpret the phrase to mean excommunication or exile from Israel or the community of faith while

The palace of Minos at Knossos on the island of Crete dates from the end of the Minoan Age.

others interpret it as the pronouncement of the death penalty. The latter position is accepted in this article. Often the phrase "cut off" is used in parallel with words or phrases or in contexts which clearly indicate death (Ex. 31:14; Deut. 12:29; 19:1; 2 Sam. 7:9; 1 Kings 11:16; Jer. 7:28; 11:19; Ezek. 14:13,17,19,21; 17:17; 25:7; 29:8; Amos 1:5,8; 2:3; Obad. 9–10; Nah. 3:15; Zech. 13:8). See *Excommunication*.

The offenses that make one liable to being "cut off" are: the men of Israel who are uncircumcised (Gen. 17:14; compare Ex. 4:24; Josh. 5:2–9), eating leavened bread during the feast of unleavened bread (Es. 12:15,19), trying to copy or using the holy anointing oil on outsiders (30:33), profaning the sabbath (Ex. 31:14), partaking of sacrifices in an unclean state (Lev. 7:20–21,25; 19:8; compare 1 Sam. 2:33), eating blood (Lev. 7:27; 17:10,14), offering sacrifices in a place other than the tabernacle (Lev. 17:3–4,8–9), certain sexual offenses (18:29; 20:17–18), child sacrifices to Molech (Lev. 20,3,5), consulting wizards or mediums (Lev. 20:6; Mic. 5:12), approaching holy things in an unclean state (Lev. 22:3; Num. 19:13,20), improperly observing the Day of Atonement (Lev. 23:29), not observing the Passover (Num. 9:13), committing a high handed sin (sinning intentionally or defiantly; Num. 15:30–31), idolatry (1 Kings 9:6–7; 14:9–10,14; 21:21; Ezek. 14:7–8; Mic. 5:13; Zeph. 1:4; Zech. 13:2), and those God curses (Ps. 37:22). The idea of being "cut off" is also mentioned in the New Testament (Rom. 9:3; 11:22; compare 1 Cor. 16:22; Gal. 1:6: 5:12).

Crimes and Corporal Punishment in the Old Testament Crimes of a lesser nature (usually those involving premeditated bodily injury) were punished with some sort of corporal punishment. The law of retaliation (eye for an eye; *lex talionis*) was the operative principle in most cases involving corporal punishment (Ex. 21:23–25; Lev. 24:19–22; Deut. 19:21).

The law of retaliation may seem to some to be rather harsh and even crude. In our own modern world, we would sue a person responsible for putting out an eye before we would put that person's eye out. In the ancient world, however, the law of retaliation served to restrict the vengeance taken on one who inflicted bodily injury. For example, it prevented the killing of a person who had put out the eye of another. The law of retaliation helped make the punishment fit the crime.

Besides the law of retaliation, corporal punishments also included scourging (Deut. 25:1–3), blinding (Gen. 19:11; 2 Kings 6:18; compare Judg. 16:21; 2 Kings 25:7), plucking out hair (Neh. 13:25; Is. 50:6), and the sale of a thief into slavery who could not pay the monetary penalties (Ex. 22:1–3; compare Lev. 25:39; 2 Kings 4:1; Neh. 5:5). In one instance, mutilation is prescribed (Deut. 25:11–12).

Crimes and Fines in the Old Testament Fines were always paid to the injured party. Fines were prescibed for causing a miscarriage (Ex. 21:22), deflowering a virgin (Ex. 22:16–17; compare Deut. 22:29), sexually violating a slave woman promised to another man in marriage (Lev. 19:20), and in some cases where an ox gored a person causing death (Ex. 21:28–32). A thief (one who steals by stealth) may be fined double, four-fold, or five-fold the value of the stolen goods, depending on what was stolen (Ex. 22:1–4,9). A robber (one who steals by force or intimidation) must return the stolen property plus one-fifth of its value plus make a guilt offering (Lev. 6:1–7). The difference between the penalties for thievery and robbery is difficult to explain. Should a man falsely accuse his bride of being unchaste, the man is fined double the marriage present (100 shekels of silver; Deut. 22:19). One who inflicted unpremeditated bodily injury must compensate the victim for the loss of income plus pay the costs of recovery (Ex. 21:18–19). If a person should cause the loss of eye or tooth of his slave, the slave was freed (Ex. 21:26–27).

Crimes and Punishments in the New Testament There is no body of legal material in the New Testament comparable to that found in the Old Testament. Jesus did comment in the Sermon on the Mount on some of the matters discussed above. He expanded the prohibition of killing to include anger (Matt. 5:21–26) and the prohibition against adultery to include lust (Matt. 5:27–30). In contrast to the Old Testament, Jesus forbade divorce except on the grounds of unchastity (Matt. 5:31–32). With regard to the law of retaliation, Jesus desired that his disciples waive their rights to reparations (Matt. 5:38–42).

During the period of the New Testament, the Jews seem to have had relative autonomy in the matters of their religious law and customs. Even Jewish communities outside Palestine were under the authority of the high priest (Acts 9:1–2) and were allowed some measure of autonomy in religious matters (Acts. 18:12–17).

Whether or not the Jews had the authority under the Roman government to impose the death penalty is a debated question. When Jesus was brought to trial, the Jews' reason for bringing him to Pilate was that they did not have the power to execute criminals (John 18:31). One ancient rabbinic tradition in the Babylonian Talmud (Abodah Zarah 8b) holds that the Jews lost the power to execute criminals for about 40 years. However, incidents in the New Testament seem to indicate otherwise: statements made at Peter's trial (Acts 5:27–42), the stoning of Stephen (Acts 7:57–60), attempted lynchings (Acts 9:23–24; 14:19; 23:12–15), the authority to kill foreigners caught trespassing in certain areas of the temple (Acts 21:28–31, a practice reported by Josephus, an ancient Jewish historian), and a statement made by Paul (Acts 26:10). Other ancient Jewish records of stonings and burnings indicates that the Jews may have had the authority to impose the death penalty.

The Jews during the period of the New Testament had the power to impose corporal punishment. This consisted primarily of scourgings (Matt. 10:17; Acts 5:40; 22:19; 2 Cor. 11:24) and excommunication (Luke 6:22; John 9:22; 12:42; 16:2).

The procurator was Rome's legal representative in the provinces of the Roman empire. He intervened in local affairs when the public peace and order were threatened—especially by sedition, riot, or brigandage (compare Acts 5:36–37). The charge against Jesus was a claim to be "King of the Jews" (Matt 27:37). Roman punishments included crucifixion (usually reserved only for slaves and the lower classes), beheading (see Matt. 14:10; Rev. 20:4), lifetime sentences to work in the mines (that is, kept in bonds; Acts 23:29; 26:31), scourging (Acts 16:22; 22:24), and imprisonment (Acts 16:23–24). See *Appeal to Caesar.*

Phil Logan

CRIMSON A red color taken from the bodies of dead kermes (*Coccus ilicis,* wich attached itself to the kermes oak—*Quercus coccifera*) or cochineal insects (*Coccus cacti*). The same Hebrew words translated as crimson are also translated "scarlet" ("red" comes from a root word from which the Hebrew word "blood" comes and designates a different color.) Crimson or scarlet thread (Gen. 38:28,30), cord (Josh. 2:18,21), and cloth (Lev. 14:4; Num. 4:8; 2 Sam. 1:24; 2 Chron. 2:7,14; 3:14; Prov. 31:21; Jer. 4:30; Nah. 2:3) are mentioned in the Bible. Crimson or scarlet along with purple were considered royal colors (Matt. 27:28; Rev. 17:3–4; 18:11–12,16). Isaiah used scarlet as the imagery to describe sins (Isa. 1:18). See *Colors.*

CRISPING PIN KJV translation in Isaiah 3:22. A crisping pin was used for curling the hair. Modern versions translate the word "handbag," or "flounced skirt" (REB). See *Bag 1.*

CRISPUS (Crĭs′ pŭs) Personal name meaning, "curly." Leader of synagogue in Corinth (Acts 18:8) and one of few whom Paul personally baptized (1 Cor. 1:14). Church tradition says he became bishop of Aegina.

CROCUS See *Flowers.*

CROSS, CRUCIFIXION The method the Romans used to execute Jesus Christ. The most painful and degrading form of capital punishment in the ancient world, the cross became also the means by which Jesus became the atoning sacrifice for the sins of all mankind. It also became a symbol for the sacrifice of self in discipleship (Rom. 12:1) and for the death of self to the world (Mark 8:34).

Historical Development Originally a cross was a wooden pointed stake used to build a wall or to erect fortifications around a town. Beginning with the Assyrians and Persians, it began to be used to display the heads of captured foes or of particularly heinous criminals on the palisades above the gateway into a city. Later crucifixion developed into a form of capital punishment, as enemies of the state were impaled on the stake itself. The Greeks and Romans at first reserved the punishment only for slaves, saying it was too barbaric for freeborn or citizens. By the first century, however, it was used for any enemy of the state, though citizens could only be crucified by direct edict of Caesar. As time went on, the Romans began to use crucifixion more and more as a deterrent to criminal activity, so that by Jesus' time it was a common sight.

The eastern form of crucifixion was practiced in the Old Testament. Saul was decapitated and his body displayed on a wall by the Philistines (1 Sam. 31:9–10), and the "hanging" of Esther 2:23; 5:14 may mean impalement (compare Ezra 6:11). According to Jewish law (Deut. 21:22–23) the offenders were "hung on a tree," which meant they were "accursed of God" and outside the covenant people. Such criminals were to be removed from the cross before nightfall lest they "defile the land." During the intertestamental period the western form was borrowed when Alexander Janneus crucified 800 Pharisees (76 B.C.), but on the whole the Jews condemned and seldom used the method. Even Herod the Great refused to crucify his enemies. The practice was abolished after the "conversion" of the emperor of Constantine to Christianity.

A person crucified in Jesus' day was first of all scourged (beaten with a whip consisting of thongs with pieces of metal or bone attached to the end) or at least flogged until the blood flowed. This was not just done out of cruelty but was designed to hasten death and lessen the terrible ordeal. After the beating, the victim was forced to bear the crossbeam to the execution site in order to signify that life was already over and to break the will to live. A tablet detailing the crime(s) was often placed around the criminal's neck and then fastened to the cross. At the site the prisoner was often tied (the normal method) or nailed (if a quicker death was desired) to the crossbeam. The nail would be driven through the wrist rather than the palm, since the smaller bones of the hand could not support the weight of the body. The beam with the body was then lifted and tied to the already affixed upright pole. Pins or a small wooden block were placed halfway up to provide a seat for the body lest the nails tear open the wounds or the ropes force the arms from their sockets. Finally the feet were tied or nailed to the post. Death was caused by the loss of blood circulation and coronary failure. Especially if the victims were tied, it could take days of hideous pain as the extremities turned slowly gangrenous; so often the soldiers would break the victims legs with a club, causing massive shock and a quick death. Such deaths were usually done in public places, and the body was left to rot for days, with carrion birds allowed to degrade the corpse further.

Four types of crosses were used: 1) The Latin cross has the crossbeam about two-thirds of the way up the upright pole; 2) St. Anthony's cross (probably due to its similarity to his famous crutch) had the beam at the top of the upright pole like a T. 3) St. Andrew's cross (supposedly the form used to crucify Andrew) had the shape of the letter X; 4) the Greek cross has both beams equal in the shape of a plus sign.

The Crucifixion of Jesus Jesus predicted His coming crucifixion many times. The Synoptic Gospels list at least three (Mark 8:31; 9:31; 10:33–34 and parallels), while John records three others (3:14; 8:28; 12:32–33). Several aspects of Jesus' passion are predicted; 1) it occurred by divine necessity ("must" in Mark 8:31); 2) both Jews ("delivered") and Romans ("killed") were guilty (Mark 9:31); 3) Jesus would be vindicated by being raised from the dead; 4) the death itself entailed glory (seen in the "lifted up" sayings which imply exaltation in John 3:14; 8:28; 12:32–33).

The narration of Jesus' crucifixion in the Gospels emphasized Jewish guilt, but all four carefully separated the leaders from the common people, who supported Jesus all along and were led astray by the leaders at the last. Yet Roman guilt is also obvious. The Sanhedrin was no longer allowed to initiate capital punishment; only the Romans could do so. Furthermore, only Roman soldiers could carry it out. Roman customs were followed in the scourging, mock enthronement, bearing the crossbeam, and the crucifixion itself. The site on a hill and the size of the cross (the use of the hyssop reed shows it was seven to nine feet high) showed their desire for a public display of a "criminal." The Jewish elements in the crucifixion of Jesus were the wine mixed with myrrh (Mark 15:23), the hyssop reed with vinegar (Mark 15:36), and the removal of Jesus' body from the cross before sunset (John 19:31).

The four Gospels look at Jesus' crucifixion from four different vantage points and highlight diverse aspects of the significance of His death. Mark and Matthew centered upon the horror of putting the Son of God Himself to death. Mark emphasized the messianic meaning, using the taunts of the crowds to "save yourself" (15:30–31) as an unconscious prophecy pointing to the resurrection. Matthew took Mark even further, pointing to Jesus as the royal Messiah who faced His destiny in complete control of the situation. Jesus' vindication was found not only in the rending of the veil and the centurion's testimony (Matt. 27:51,54 paralleling Mark) but in the remarkable raising of the Old Testament saints (vv. 52–53) which links the cross and the open tomb. For Matthew the cross inaugurated the last days when the power of death is broken, and salvation is poured out upon all people.

Luke has perhaps the most unique portrayal, with two emphases: Jesus as the archetypal righteous Martyr who forgave His enemies and the crucifixion as an awesome scene of reverence and worship. Luke omitted the negative aspects of the crucifixion (earthquakes, wine with myrrh, cry of dereliction) and overturned the taunts when the crowd "returned home beating their breasts" (23:48 RSV). Luke included three sayings of Jesus which relate to prayer (found only in Luke): "Father, forgive them" (v. 34, contrasted with the mockery); "today you will be with me in paradise" (v. 43, in response to the criminal's prayer); and "Father into thy hands I commend my spirit" (v. 46). A wondrous sense of stillness and worship color Luke's portrayal.

John's narration is perhaps the most dramatic. Even moreso than Luke, all the negative elements disappear (the darkness and taunts as well as those missing also in Luke), and an atmosphere of calm characterizes the scene. At the core is Jesus' sovereign control of the whole scene. The cross becomes His throne. John noted that the inscription on the cross ("JESUS OF NAZARETH, THE KING OF THE JEWS") was written in Aramaic, Latin, and Greek (19:19–20), thereby changing it into a universal proclamation of Jesus' royal status. Throughout the account to the final cry, "It is finished" (v. 30), Jesus was in complete control.

One cannot understand Jesus' crucifixion until all four Gospels are taken into account. All the emphases—the messianic thrust, Jesus as Son of God and as the righteous Martyr, the sacrificial nature of His death, the cross as His throne—are necessary emphases of the total picture of the significance of His crucifixion.

Theological Meaning While a theology of the cross is found primarily in Paul, it clearly predates him, as can be demonstrated in the "creeds" (statements of belief/teaching) Paul quoted. For instance, 1 Corinthians 15:3–5 says Paul had "received" and then "delivered" to the Corinthians the truth that Jesus "died for our sins according to the Scriptures." Three major themes are interwoven in this and other creeds (Rom 4:25; 6:1–8; 8:32; Col. 2:11–12; 1 Tim. 3:16; Heb. 1:3–4; 1 Pet. 1:21; 3:18–22): Jesus death as our substitute (from Isa. 53:5; compare Mark 10:45; 14:24); Jesus' death and resurrection as fulfilling Scripture; and Jesus' vindication and exaltation by God.

For Paul the "word of the cross" (1 Cor. 1:18

NAS) is the heart of the gospel, and the preaching of the cross is the soul of the church's mission. "Christ crucified" (1 Cor. 1:23; compare 2:2; Gal. 3:1) is more than the basis of our salvation; the cross was the central event in history, the one moment which demonstrated God's control of and involvement in human history. In 1 Corinthians 1:17—2:16 Paul contrasted the "foolishness" of the "preaching of the cross" with human "wisdom" (1:17–18), for only in the cross can salvation be found and only in the foolish "preaching of the cross" and "weakness" can the "power of God" be seen (1:21,25). Jesus as the lowly One achieved His glory by virtue of His suffering—only the crucified One could become the risen One (1:26–30). Such a message certainly was viewed as foolish in the first century; Roman historians like Tacitus and Suetonius looked upon the idea of a "crucified God" with contempt.

The cross is the basis of our salvation in Paul's epistles (Rom. 3:24–25; Eph. 2:16; Col. 1:20; 2:14), while the resurrection is stressed as the core in the Book of Acts (2:33–36; 3:19–21; 5:31). Romans 4:25 makes both emphases. The reason for the distinct emphases is most likely seen in the fact that Acts chronicles the preaching of the early church (with the resurrection as the apologetic basis of our salvation) and the epistles the teaching of the early church (with the crucifixion the theological basis of our salvation). The three major terms are: "redemption," stressing the "ransom payment" made by Jesus' blood in delivering us from sin (Titus 2:14; 1 Pet. 1:18); "propitiation," which refers to Jesus' death as "satisfying" God's righteous wrath (Rom. 3:25; Heb. 2:17); and "justification," picturing the results of the cross, the "acquittal" ("declaring righteous") of our guilt (Rom. 3:24; 4:25; Gal. 2:16–21; 3:24).

The cross did even more than procure salvation. It forged a new unity between Jew and Gentile by breaking down "the dividing wall of hostility" and "made the two one" (Eph. 2:14–15 NIV), thereby producing "peace" by creating a new access to the Father (v. 18). In addition the cross "disarmed" the demonic "powers" and forged the final triumph over Satan and his hordes, forcing those spiritual forces to follow his train in a victory procession (Col. 2:15 NIV). The cross was Satan's great error. When Satan entered Judas in betraying Jesus, he undoubtedly did not realize that the cross would prove his greatest defeat. He could only respond with frustrated rage, knowing that "his time is short" (Rev. 12:12 NIV). Satan participated in his own undoing!

The Symbolic Meaning Jesus Himself established the primary figurative interpretation of the cross as a call to complete surrender to God. He used it five times as a symbol of true discipleship in terms of self-denial, taking up one's cross, and following Jesus (Mark 8:34; 10:38; Matt. 16:24; Luke

9:23; 14:27). Building upon the Roman practice of bearing the crossbeam to the place of execution, Jesus intended this in two directions: the death of self, involving the sacrifice of one's individuality for the purpose of following Jesus completely; and a willingness to imitate Jesus completely, even to the extent of martyrdom.

Closely connected to this is Paul's symbol of the crucified life. Conversion means the *ego* "no longer live(s)" but is replaced by Christ and faith in Him (Gal. 2:20). Self-centered desires are nailed to the cross (Gal. 5:24), and worldly interests are dead (Gal. 6:14). In Romans 6:1–8 we are "buried with him" (using the imagery of baptism) with the result that we are raised to "newness of life" (v. 4). This is taken further in 2 Corinthians 5:14–17. The believer relives the death and resurrection by putting to death the old self and putting on the new. In one sense this is a past act, experienced at conversion. Yet according to Ephesians 4:22,24 this is also a present act, experienced in the corporate life of the church. In other words, both at conversion and in spiritual growth, the believer must relive the cross before experiencing the resurrection life. The Christian paradox is that death is the path to life! See *Atonement; Christology; Justification; Passion; Propitiation; Redemption.*   Grant Osborne

CROWN A special headdress worn by royalty and other persons of high merit and honor.

The crown probably evolved from the cloth headband or turban worn by a tribal leader; the headband eventually became a metal diadem, with or without ornamentation. Some years ago archaeologists discovered in a Jericho tomb a copper headband or crown dating from about 2000 B.C.

Both the king and the high priest of Israel wore crowns, but we have been told more about the latter than the former (Ex. 28:36–37; 29:6, Lev. 8:9). David's golden crown was a prize of battle (2 Sam. 12:30). As a symbol of his authority, the crown was worn when the king was on his throne and when leading his forces in combat (2 Sam. 1:10). The word "crown" was also used figuratively referring to the old man's gray head (Prov. 16:31), a man's virtuous wife (Prov. 12:4), and God's blessings on mankind (Ps. 8:5). Occasionally the word referred to a festive wreath of leaves or flowers (Song of Sol. 3:11).

While most references to "crown" in the Old Testament point to the actual headdress, in the New Testament it usually has a figurative significance. Paul envisioned "a crown of righteousness" for himself and others (2 Tim. 4:8), and James anticipated "the crown of life" (Jas. 1:12). While the winning runner of that day received a garland of myrtle leaves, Paul looked forward to a crown that would not decay (1 Cor. 9:25). Not even the victorious athlete would receive his reward unless he obeyed the rules (2 Tim. 2:5). Conversely, the word evokes revulsion when we read of Roman soldiers weaving briers into a crown of Jesus' head (Matt. 27:29).

In the Book of Revelation crowns are both realistic and figurative. The twenty-four elders seated around God's throne were wearing "crowns of gold" (4:4), and as they worshiped, they "cast their crowns before the throne" (4:10). Later, a seven-headed dragon appeared wearing a crown on each head (12:3), but opposing all the evil forces was the "Son of man" wearing "a golden crown" (14:14). In each case the crown symbolized power, either good or evil. *William J. Fallis*

CROWN OF THORNS The crown made by the Roman soldiers to mock Jesus, the "King of the Jews" (Matt. 27:29; Mark 15:18; John 19:3; not mentioned in Luke). The identification of the plant used to plait this crown is unknown. Jesus used the imagery of "thorns" in his teaching in a negative sense (Matt. 7:16; Mark 4:7,18; see Heb. 6:8). See *Plants of the Bible.*

CRUCIBLE A melting pot or "fining pot" (KJV), probably made of pottery, used in the refining of silver. The crucible is used in the Bible as a figure for testing of people (Prov. 17:3; 27:21).

CRUSE An elongated pottery vessel about six inches tall used for holding liquids such as oil (1 Kings 17:12,14,16) or water (1 Kings 19:6). Modern readers would understand the vessels to serve the purpose of a modern canteen (1 Sam. 26:11–16). The bowl (2 Kings 2:20 NIV) reflects a different Hebrew term but a similar type vessel.

CRYSTAL A nearly transparent quartz which may be colorless or slightly tinged. "Crystal" is the modern translation of several Hebrew and Greek words used to describe something valuable (Job 28:18), a clear sky (Ezek. 1:22), a calm sea or river (Rev. 4:6; 22:1), or the radiance of the new Jerusalem (Rev. 21:11). Translators differ in their usage in the various passages.

CUB See *Chub.*

CUBIT A unit of measure. It was reckoned as the distance from a person's elbow to the tip of the middle finger, approximately eighteen inches. See *Weights and Measures.*

CUCKOW KJV translation for an unclean bird (Lev. 11:16; Deut. 14:15); also spelled cuckoo. Since the bird in question is grouped with carrion-eating or predatory birds, the cuckoo would seem to be eliminated since it only eats insects. Modern versions read "sea gull."

CUMMIN An herb of the carrot family (*Cuminum*

Fragment of a slate measuring rod divided into fractions of the cubit, from Egypt, Akhenaton's reign.

cyminum L.) mentioned with dill. Used in Bible times to season foods. Isaiah portrayed the planting and threshing of cummin (Isa. 28:25,27). Jesus faulted the Pharisees for giving attention to small things like tithing mint, dill, and cummin while ignoring the weightier matters of the law (Matt. 23:23; see Luke 11:42).

CUN (Cūn) Place name of city in Syria belonging to Hadadezer, king of Zobah. David took bronze from the city as tribute, and Solomon used the materials in furnishing the Temple (1 Chron. 18:8). The parallel passage in 2 Samuel 8:8 reads, "Berothai." The two are apparently separate cities, Cun being northeast of Byblos and Berothai southeast of Byblos. Apparently, Cun was more familiar to the Chronicler's readers than Berothai. See *Berothai.*

CUNEIFORM (Cū·nē′ ĭ·fŏrm) The most widely-used system of writing in the Ancient Near East until it was supplanted by alphabetic scripts like Aramaic. The word cuneiform is derived from the Latin *cuneus,* wedge, and is used to refer to characters composed of wedges. The system of writing was originated apparently by the Sumerians before 3000 B.C. The earliest documents are commercial tablets consisting of pictographs (of sheep, grain, etc.) and numbers. Because the documents

Cuneiform tablet and its envelope dealing with the sale of some land.

were written on tablets of moist clay, the scribes soon found it more convenient to indicate objects with stylized pictures composed of wedges made by a stylus. The earliest cuneiform signs were ideographs (a sign standing for a word); but as literary needs increased, the signs were given phonetic values.

The cuneiform system of writing was adapted and developed to suit the requirements of several other languages, including Akkadian, Hurrian, Hittite, Elamite, and Eblaite. The people at Ugarit and the Persians used wedges to form their alphabetic scripts.

The decipherment of the cuneiform scripts of Mesopotamia was aided by the existence of trilingual inscriptions, such as the Behistun Rock inscriptions written in Persian, Babylonian, and Elamite cuneiform. The decipherment of the Persian written in an alphabetic cuneiform opened the way for the decipherment of the more difficult syllabic Babylonian and Elamite scripts. Due to the pioneering efforts of H. Rawlinson, E. Hincks, and J. Oppert and others, by the end of the nineteenth century it was possible to read with confidence the cuneiform inscriptions known up to that time.

The decipherment of the Ugaritic alphabetic cuneiform script was accomplished simultaneously but independently by H. Bauer, E. Dhorme, and Ch. Virolleaud in 1930–31. Unlike any other cuneiform writing, Ugaritic consists of thirty-one signs or characters used to record documents in a language similar to Phoenician and Hebrew. The Ugaritic inscriptions and documents date from the fourteenth century and are of crucial importance for the study of the Bible.

See *Akkadian; Assyrian; Babylonian; Sumerian; Writing.*   *Thomas Smothers*

CUP The cup was a drinking vessel made of pottery or various metals such as gold, silver, or bronze. During biblical times cups came in two different forms. Some resembled their modern

Gold cup decorated with gazelles, late second millennium B.C., from southwest Caspian area.

counterparts. However most ancient cups were shallow bowls which were produced in a multitude of sizes. They also could be used in divination (Gen. 44:5). In addition, the term cup was used to designate the receptacles for holding lamps on the lampstand of the tabernacle (Ex. 25:31–35 NAS).

In the Bible the word "cup" frequently is used in a figurative sense. The contents of the cup are accentuated, since symbolically God serves the drink. Thus the cup might represent blessings or prosperity for a righteous person (Ps. 16:5; 23:5; 116:13). Likewise, it portrayed the totality of divine judgment on the wicked (Ps. 11:6; 75:8; Isa. 51:17,22; Jer. 25:15; 49:12; 51:7; Ezek. 23:31–34; Rev. 14:10; 16:19; 17:4; 18:6). Jesus voluntarily drank the cup of suffering (Matt. 20:22; 26:39,42; Mark 10:38; 14:36; Luke 22:42; John 18:11). For Jesus that cup was His death and everything that it involved.

The cup had a prominent place in the liturgy of the Jewish Passover meal, and so, subsequently, in the Lord's Supper. In the Christian ordinance the cup is a symbolic reminder of the atoning death of Jesus (Matt. 26:27–28; Mark 14:23–24; Luke 22:20; 1 Cor. 11:25–26).

See *Divination; Lampstand; Lord's Supper; Passover; Pottery.*   *LeBron Matthews*

CUPBEARER A high ranking official in the courts of Ancient Near Eastern kings. The cupbearer was responsible for serving wine at the king's table and protecting the king from poisoning. The cupbearer was often taken into the king's confidence and had no small amount of influence on the king's decisions. The "chief butler" of the Joseph story (Gen. 40:2) was a cupbearer who was overseer of a staff of his own. Nehemiah was the highly esteemed cupbearer for Artaxerxes (Neh. 1:11; see also 1 Kings 10:5; 2 Chron. 9:4). The Rabshakeh may have been the title given to cupbearers in the Assyrian court (2 Kings 18:17–37; Isa. 36:2).

CURDS Fermented milk product equivalent to the modern leban (translated as "butter" in the KJV). Curds are prepared by churning fresh milk with a small amount of curds from a previous batch in a goatskin. They are frequently served with honey and wine and are considered a delicacy among the nomads in the ancient Near East (see Gen. 18:8; Deut. 32:14; Judg. 5:25; 2 Sam. 17:29; Job 20:17; Isa. 7:15,22).

CURSE See *Blessing and Cursing.*

CURTAIN A piece of cloth or other material, sometimes arranged so that it can be drawn up or sideways, hung either for decoration or to cover, conceal, or shut off something. "Curtain" is often used synonymously with "tent" (Song of Sol. 1:5;

Isa. 54:2; Jer. 4:20; 10:20; 49:29; Hab. 3:7). The tabernacle which was constructed to carry the ark of the covenant was made of ten curtains (Ex. 26:2). At a later time in Israelite history, two curtain were used to close off the holy place and the holy of holies in the Temple. The curtain separating the holy of holies and the holy place was torn from top to bottom at the time of Jesus' death signifying the access that all people had to God from that time forward (Matt. 27:51). The writer of Hebrews speaks of the curtain in the heavenly sanctuary (Heb. 6:19; 9:3). Jesus also opened this curtain to his followers by his death (Heb. 10:20).

CUSH (Cŭsh) *1.* A member of the tribe of Benjamin about whom the psalmist sang (Ps. 7:1). Nothing else is known of him. *2.* Son of Ham and grandson of Noah (Gen. 10:8). Thus in this Table of Nations he is seen as the original ancestor of inhabitants of Cush, the land.

3. A nation situated south of Egypt with differing boundaries and perhaps including differing dark-skinned tribes (Jer. 13:23) at different periods of history. The Hebrew word *Cush* has been traditionally translated Ethiopia, following the Septuagint, or earliest Greek translation, but Cush was not identical with Ethiopia as presently known. Moses' wife came from Cush (Num. 12:1), probably a woman distinct from Zipporah (Ex. 2:21). Cush was an enemy of Egypt for centuries, being controlled by strong pharaohs but gaining independence under weak pharaohs. Zerah, a general from Cush, fought against Asa, king of Judah (910–869) (2 Chron. 14:9). Finally, Piankhi of Cush conquered Egypt and established the twenty-fifth dynasty of Egyptian rulers (716–656) with their capital at Napata above the fourth cataract. Isaiah 18 may describe some of the political activity involved in Cush's establishing their power in Egypt. Tirhakah (2 Kings 19:9) was one of the last of the pharaohs from Cush. Isaiah promised that people who fled from Judah and were exiled in Cush would see God's deliverance (Isa. 11:11; compare Zeph. 3:10). Isaiah acted out judgment against Cush, probably as the rulers of Egypt (Isa. 20:3–5; compare 43:3; 45:14; Ps. 68:31; Jer. 46:9; Ezek. 30:4–5,9). In Ezekiel's day Cush represented the southern limit of Egyptian territory (Ezek. 29:10). Cush's strength could not help Thebes escape from Ashurbanipal, king of Assyria, in 663 B.C. Nahum used this historical example to pronounce doom on Nineveh, the capital of Assyria (Nah. 3:9). Ezekiel listed Cush as one of the allies of Gog and Magog in the great climatic battle (Ezek. 38:5). The psalmist proclaimed that God's reputation had reached even unto Cush (Ps. 87:4). Job saw Cush as a rich source of minerals, especially topaz (Job 28:19).

By the time of Esther, Cush represented the southwestern limits of Persian power (Esther

1:1). Cambyses (530–522) conquered Cush for Persia.

Cush is mentioned in Genesis 2:13 as surrounded by the Gihon River. The Gihon is usually associated with Jerusalem as a spring (1 Kings 1:33). Some Bible students identify Cush here with the Kassites, the successors to the old Babylonian empire, who controlled Babylon between about 1530 and 1151 B.C. Such students connect this with Genesis 10:8, where Cush is associated with Nimrod, whose kingdom centered in Babylon (Gen. 10:10). Other Bible students would see Gihon here as another name for the Nile River and Cush as referring to the land south of Egypt. A clear solution to this problem has not been found.

CUSHAN (Cū' shăn) A tent-dwelling people Habakkuk saw as experiencing God's wrath (Hab. 3:7). The parallel with Midian makes people think of an Arabian tribe, possibly nomads. Some identify Cushan with Cush, either as a territory controlled by Cush or as an otherwise unknown kingdom of Cush on the northeast shore of the Gulf of Aqabah near Midian. This would account for Cushites near Arabs (2 Chron. 21:16).

CUSHAN-RISHATHAIM (Cū' shăn- rĭsh ȧ thā' ĭm) Personal name meaning, "dark one of double evil." King of Aram Naharaim to whom Yahweh gave Israel in the early period of the Judges (Judg. 3:8). Othniel finally defeated him. We have no other information about him. Some have tried to see Aram as an unintentional copying error for an original Edom, but no evidence exists for this conjecture. See *Aram Naharaim.*

CUSHI (Cū' shī) Personal name meaning, "Cushite." *1.* Father of the prophet Zephaniah (Zeph. 1:1). *2.* Ancestor of a royal official under King Jehoiakim (Jer. 36:14).

CUSHITE (Cū' shīte) Citizen or inhabitant of Cush. See *Cush.* The Hebrew word is the same as the proper name, "Cushi." God has concern for and control over them just as He does for His own people (Amos 9:7). An unnamed Cushite served as Joab's messenger to bring the news of Absalom's death to David (2 Sam. 18:21–32). A eunuch under King Zedekiah who helped Jeremiah escape from a cistern into which the king had had him thrown (Jer. 38:6–12; 39:16). See *Ebedmelech.*

CUSTODIAN Wealthy Greek and Roman families often had a slave who attended boys under the age of about 16. The major responsibilities of the custodian was to escort the boys to and from school and to attend to their behavior. The pedagogue or custodian had responsibility to discipline or punish the boy. Once the boys reached manhood, they no longer needed the services of the custodian. Often the young man rewarded the custodian by granting him freedom. Paul spoke of the law as the custodian of God's people until Christ came (Gal. 3:23–26). The law could not save; but it could bring us to the point where we could have faith in Christ by showing us our unrighteousness (Gal. 3:19; compare Rom. 7:7–12). Of course, the law was not nullified by Christ's death nor by becoming Christians. We are still expected to live according to the moral principles found in the law (Rom. 7:12,16; compare Matt. 5:17–20,21–48).

CUTH (Cŭth), **CUTHAH** Place names with two spellings in Hebrew and English. Cuthah was the center of worship of Nergal, god of death in Mesopotamia. See *Nergal*. Residents of the city were exiled by the Assyrians to live in Israel (2 Kings 17:24). Once settled, they made an idol to worship Nergal (2 Kings 17:30), thus aggravating the tendency to worship Yahweh of Israel along with other gods. Cuth was located at tell Ibrahim, about 18 miles northeast of Babylon.

CUZA (Cü' zà) NIV spelling of Chuza. See *Chuza.*

CYMBAL See *Music, Instruments, Dancing.*

CYPRIAN (Cy̆' prĭ an) Citizen or resident of Cyprus. See *Cyprus.*

Limassol, a modern city on the southern coast of Cyprus.

CYPRUS (Cy̆' prŭs) A large island in the eastern Mediterranean Sea mentioned most prominently in Acts. In the Old Testament scattered references refer to the island as Kittim (Chittim, Isa. 23:1; Jer. 2:10), although in some passages the term has a wider scope and includes lands other than Cyprus lying west of Palestine (Dan. 11:30). The island is 138 miles long east to west and 60 miles wide from north to south; it is eclipsed in size only by Sicily and Sardinia. Much of Cyprus is mountainous; the Troodos Mountains (5900 feet) dominate the western and central sections, while the Kyrenia Mountains (3100 feet) extend along the northern coast.

Historically Cyprus was important as a source for timber used in shipbuilding and copper, both vital commodities in the ancient world. The strategic position of Cyprus just off the coasts of Asia Minor and Syria coupled with the presence of favorable currents and reliable summer winds encouraged wide-ranging trade contacts. Evidence of trade with Cyprus between 2000 and 1000 B.C. has been found in Asia Minor, Egypt, Palestine, and Syria; contacts also were maintained with Crete, the Aegean Islands, and Greece. After 1500 B.C., Cyprus was influenced heavily by the Mycenean culture of mainland Greece which left an indelible stamp.

After 1000 B.C., several city-states, each ruled by a king, were the basis of the political structure on Cyprus. Among the most important cities were Salamis and Kition. The Phoenicians, a Semitic people who established a trading empire through-

A portion of the agora area at the site of ancient Salamis on the island of Cyprus.

out the Mediterranean, colonized Kition about 850 B.C. Tyre and Sidon were the center of Phoenician trade, and the Old Testament underscores the connection between these cities and Cyprus in several passages (Isa. 23:1–2, 12; Ezek. 27:4–9).

From the time the kings of Cyprus submitted to Sargon II of Assyria in 707 B.C., the political fortunes of the island were determined by successive empires which dominated the Near East. Egyptian and Persian kings controlled Cyprus prior to the coming of Alexander the Great in 333 B.C. After his death, Cyprus became a part of the Ptolemaic Empire (294–258 B.C.). During this period many Jews settled on the island, forming an important part of the population. In 58 B.C., Rome annexed Cyprus; with the establishment of the Roman Empire under Augustus, the island became a Senatorial Province in 22 B.C. governed by a proconsul from Paphos.

Cyprus is first mentioned in the New Testament as the birthplace of Joseph surnamed Barnabas, a Hellenistic Jewish convert who later accompanied Paul (Acts 4:36–37). As a result of the persecu-

tion associated with the martyrdom of Stephen in Jerusalem, Jewish Christians journeyed to Cyprus and preached the gospel to the Jewish community on the island (Acts 11:19–20). In A.D. 46 or 47, Paul undertook his first missionary journey accompanied by Barnabas and John Mark (Acts 13). Arriving at Salamis on the eastern side of Cyprus, the group crossed the island to Paphos preaching the new faith. The reference to Paphos is to Neapaphos, "New Paphos," founded in the fourth century B.C. and the center of Roman government on Cyprus. The conversion of the deputy, Sergius Paulus, was brought about in part by the blinding of the magician Bar-jesus. Whether Paul visited Paleapahos, "Old Paphos," is unclear; Paleapaphos was an ancient city associated with the worship of the Greek goddess Aphrodite, who reputedly emerged from the foam of the sea nearby.

John Mark and Barnabas returned to Cyprus a second time after parting company with Paul (Acts 15:39). Later, Paul twice passed by the island on voyages, once on a return to Jerusalem (Acts 21:3)

The excavations at Paphos on Cyprus showing the traditional site of Paul's whipping.

and finally while traveling to Rome (Acts 27:4). See *Kittim; Phoenicians.*   *Tommy Brisco*

CYRENE (Cȳ rē′ nē) The home of a certain Simon who was compelled to carry Jesus' cross to the place of crucifixion (Matt. 27:32). Located in northern Africa, it was the capital city of the Roman district of Cyrenaica during the New Testament era. Cyrenaica and Crete formed one province. Simon of Cyrene may have belonged to the rather large population of Greek-speaking Jews who resided in the city during the first part of the first century A.D. See *Simon of Cyrene.*

CYRENIAN (Cȳ rē′ nĭ ăn) Citizen and/or resident of Cyrene. See *Cyrene.*

CYRENIUS (Cȳ rē′ nĭ ŭs) The Roman official mentioned in Luke 2:2 as the governor of Syria when the birth of Jesus took place. Some translations of the New Testament use the name Cyrenius, an Anglicized form of his Greek name, while others use the Latin form Quirinius. His full name is Publius Sulpicius Quirinius. Throughout his varied career, Quirinius served as consul of Rome, military leader, tutor to Gaius Caesar, and legate (governor). He died in A.D. 21.

Luke's reference to Quirinius as governor during the nativity has caused some scholars to question Lucan historical accuracy. It is established that Quirinius was legate in Syria from A.D. 6–9, but this date is far too late for Jesus' birth, which occurred prior to the death of Herod the Great who died in 4 B.C. Luke's historical reference seems in direct conflict with non-biblical sources establishing that either Saturninus (9–7 B.C.) or Varus (6–4 B.C.) was legate of Syria during Christ's birth.

The discovery of an ancient inscription has shown that a legate fitting the description of Quirinius served two different times in Syria. Apparently the nativity occurred during Quirinius' first tenure in Syria as legate with primary responsibilities for military affairs, while Varus was the legate handling civil matters. Quirinius served a second term in A.D. 6–9.

This solution affirms Lucan accuracy without overlooking other known historical sources.
          Stephen Dollar

CYRUS (Cȳ′ rŭs) The third king of Anshan, Cyrus (the Great) assumed the throne about 550 B.C. According to the best histories Cyrus was reared by a shepherd after his grandfather, Astyages, king of Media, ordered that he be killed. Apparently, Astyages had dreamed that Cyrus would one day succeed him as king before the reigning monarch's death. The officer charged with the execution instead carried the boy into the hills to the shepherds.

As an adult, Cyrus organized the Persians into an army and revolted against his grandfather and father (Cambyses I). He defeated them and claimed their throne.

One of his first acts as king of Medio-Persia was to launch an attack against Lydia, capital of Sardis and storehouse for the riches of its king, Croesus. Turning eastward, Cyrus continued his campaign until he had carved out a vast empire, stretching from the Aegean Sea to India.

The Babylonian Empire next stood in his path, an obstacle which appeared to be insurmountable. Engaging the Babylonian army at Opis, Cyrus' troops routed them and moved on Babylon. The

The Cyrus Cylinder, inscribed with the famous Edict of Cyrus the Great (538? B.C.).

people in the capital welcomed Cyrus with open arms, seeing him as a liberator rather than a conqueror. All that remained was Egypt, which he left for his son, Cambyses II. Cyrus truly was the ruler of the world.

Cyrus' military exploits have become legendary. However, he is best remembered for his policies of peace. His famous decree in 538? B.C. (2 Chron. 36:22–23; Ezra 1: 1–4) set free the captives Babylon had taken during its harsh rule. Among these prisoners were the Jews taken from Jerusalem in 586 B.C. They were allowed to return to rebuild the Temple and city. Along with this freedom Cyrus restored the valuable treasures of the Temple taken during the Exile. Since the Jews had done well in Babylon financially, many of them did not want to return to the wastes of Judah. From these people Cyrus exacted a tax to help pay for the trip for those who did wish to rebuild Jerusalem.

An astute politician, Cyrus made it a practice to publicly worship the gods of each kingdom he conquered. In so doing, he won the hearts of his subjects and kept down revolt. He is referred to as Yahweh's shepherd and anointed (Isa. 44:28–45:6) because of his kindness to the Jews and worship of Yahweh.

His last years are obscure. Cyrus was killed while fighting a frontier war with the nomadic Massagetae people. His tomb is in Pasargadae (modern Murghab).   *Mike Mitchell*

D

Storehouses along the southeastern rim of Masada with a beautiful view of the Dead Sea in the distance.

DABAREH (Dăb′ å rĕh) KJV spelling of Daberath (Josh. 21:28). See *Daberath.*

DABBASHETH (Dăb′ bå shĕth), **DABBESHETH** Place name meaning, "hump." A border town of the tribe of Zebulun (Josh. 19:11). It is modern tell esh-Shammam northwest of Jokneam.

DABERATH (Dăb′ ĕ răth) Place name meaning, "pasture." Border city of Zebulun near Mount Tabor (Josh. 19:12). In Joshua 21:28 it is a city given the Levites from the territory of Issachar. It is modern Daburiyeh at the northwest foot of Mount Tabor.

DAGGER KJV translation for the short, double-edged weapon of Ehud, the judge (Jdg. 3:16–22). Other translations use sword. Ehud's weapon was one cubit in length (18-22 inches), enabling him to conceal it under his cloak.

DAGON (Dā′ gŏn) Name of god meaning, "little fish," or "dear." Dagon is a god associated with the Philistines. However, his origins were in Mesopotamia during the third millennium B.C. By 2000 B.C. a major temple was erected for him in the maritime city of Ugarit. Ugaritic commerce carried his cult into Canaan when Canaan was still a part of the Egyptian empire. When the Philistines conquered the coastal region of Canaan, they adopted Dagon as their chief deity.

According to a popular etymology of Dagon, the name came from the Hebrew word for fish, and so it was postulated that he was a sea god. However, archaelogical evidence does not support this view. The name probably was derived originally from the word for grain, or possibly from a word for clouds. Thus Dagon was a grain god or a storm god, much like Baal. According to Ugaritic documents from the fourteenth century B.C., Dagon was the father of Baal. Little else is known about his mythology or cult.

After the Philistines subdued Samson, they credited the victory to Dagon (Judg. 16:23). However, when Samson collapsed Dagon's temple upon himself and the Philistines, he proved the superiority of Israel's God. Likewise the overthrow of the idol of Dagon before the ark of the covenant demonstrated God's predominance (1 Sam. 5:1–7). Nevertheless the Philistines, later, displayed the head of Saul as a trophy in the temple of Dagon (1 Chron. 10:10).

See *Philistines.*   *LeBron Matthews*

DALAIAH (Då laî′ ăh) KJV spelling of Delaiah. See *Delaiah.*

DALMANUTHA (Dăl må nū′ thå) Place to which Jesus and His disciples came following the feeding of the four thousand (Mark 8:10). Its location is not known. The parallel reference in Matthew 15:39 suggests it was in the area of Magdala. See *Magdala.*

DALMATIA (Dăl mā′ tĭ å) Place name referring to the southern part of Illyricum north of Greece and across the Adriatic Sea from Italy. At the writing of 2 Timothy, Titus had left Paul to go to Dalmatia (2 Tim. 4:10). Paul had preached in Illyricum (Rom. 15:19). Illyricum included most of modern Yugoslavia and Albania.

DALPHON (Dăl′ phŏn) Personal name apparently derived from Persian word perhaps meaning, "sleepless." One of ten sons of Haman, chief enemy of Mordecai and Esther. The sons were killed when the Jews protected themselves against the Persian attack (Esther 9:7).

DAMARIS (Dăm′ å rĭs) Personal name meaning, "heifer." An Athenian woman who became a Christian following Paul's sermon at Mars' Hill, the highest court in Athens (Acts 17:34).

DAMASCENE (Dăm′ å scēne) Resident and/or citizen of Damascus. See *Damascus.*

DAMASCUS (Då măs′ cŭs) Capital of important city-state in Syria with close historical ties to Israel. Apparently Damascus has been occupied continuously for a longer period of time than any other city in the world and can claim to be the world's oldest city.

Setting Its geographical location enabled Damascus to become a dominant trading and transportation center. Standing 2300 feet above sea level, it lay northeast of Mount Hermon and about 60 miles east of Sidon, the Mediterranean port city. Both major international highways ran through Damascus—the *Via Maris* from Mesopotamia in the east through Damascus and the Jezreel Valley to the Plain of Sharon and the Mediterranean coast, then south to Egypt; and *the King's Highway* from Damascus south through Ashtaroth, Rabbath-ammon, and Bozrah to Elath on the Red

Wall of the New Testament period in Damascus from which Paul escaped to begin his ministry.

Sea and to Arabia. By the same token, Damascus saw armies march along the highways, often using Damascus as the staging area.

History Archaeology cannot contribute much to the study of Damascus, since the continued existence of the city makes excavation difficult, if not impossible. Explorations do indicate settlement from before 3000 B.C. Tablets from the Syrian center of Ebla mention Damascus about 2300 B.C. Thutmose III of Egypt claimed to have conquered Damascus about 1475 B.C. The Hittites battled Egypt for control of Damascus until the Hittites were defeated by the Sea Peoples about 1200 B.C. At this time Arameans from the nearby desert came in and took control of an independent Damascus, gradually establishing a political power base.

In the Bible Abraham chased invading kings north of Damascus to recover Lot, whom they had taken captive (Gen. 14:15). Abraham's servant Eliezer apparently came from Damascus (Gen. 15:2).

Soldiers of Damascus attempted to help Hadadezer, king of Zobah—another Syrian city-state—against David. David won and occupied Damascus (2 Sam. 8:5–6). The weakness of Zobah encouraged Rezon to organize a renegade band, much as David had in opposing Saul (1 Sam. 22:2). Rezon became the leader of Syria headquartered in Damascus (1 Kings 11:23–25). God used him to harass Solomon.

The new Syrian city-state faced a strong opponent from the east as Assyria rose to power. Benhadad strengthened Damascus to the point that Asa, king of Judah (910–869), paid him tribute to attack Baasha, king of Israel, and relieve pressure on Judah (1 Kings 15:16–23). This gave Damascus reason to interfere repeatedly in politics in Palestine.

1 Kings 20 also features Ben-hadad of Damascus, giving reason to believe that Ben-hadad (literally, "son of Hadad) was a royal title in Syria, identifying the king of Damascus as a worshiper of the god Hadad, another name for Baal. See *Baal; Ben-hadad.* The Syrian king attacked Samaria under King Ahab (874–853). A prophet revealed the way to victory for Ahab over a drunken Benhadad. The Syrian king decided Israel's God controlled the hills but not the plains, so he attacked at Aphek (1 Kings 20:26). Again a prophet pointed the way to Israel's victory. Ahab agreed to a covenant treaty with the defeated Syrian king, for which he met a prophet's strong judgment (1 Kings 20:35–43).

Naaman, a Syrian officer, sought Elisha's help in curing his skin disease but decided Abana and Pharphar, the great rivers of Damascus, offered greater help than did the Jordan (2 Kings 5:12). These rivers made Damascus an oasis in the midst of the desert. Elisha helped deliver Samaria when Ben-hadad besieged it (2 Kings 6–7). Elisha also

The city wall of biblical Damascus.

prophesied a change of dynasty in Damascus, naming Hazael its king (2 Kings 8:7–15). Shalmaneser III of Assyria (858–824) claimed to have defeated both Ben-hadad and Hazael. The first important battle came at Qarqar in 853 B.C. Ahaziah, king of Judah (841), joined Joram, king of Israel (852–841), in battle against Hazael with Joram being wounded. Jehu took advantage of the wounded king and killed him (2 Kings 8:25—9:26).

Having fought against Damascus in campaigns in 853, 849, 848, and 845, Shalmaneser III of Assyria severely weakened Damascus, besieging it in 841 and then receiving tribute again in 838. After this, Hazael of Damascus exercised strong influence, gaining influence in Israel, Judah, and Philistia (2 Kings 10:32–33). His son Ben-hadad maintained Damascus' strength (2 Kings 13:3–25). Finally, Jehoash, king of Israel (798–782), regained some cities from Damascus (2 Kings 13:25). Jeroboam II, king of Israel (793–753), expanded Israelite influence and gained control of Damascus (2 Kings 14:28). This was possible because Assyria threatened Syria again, as Adadnirari III, king of Assyria (810–783), invaded Syria from 805 to 802 and again in 796. About 760 B.C. Amos the prophet condemned Damascus and its kings Hazael and Ben-hadad (Amos 1:3–5).

Tiglath-pileser III, king of Assyria (744–727), threatened Damascus anew. King Rezin of Damascus joined with Pekah, king of Israel, about 734 B.C. in an effort to stop the Assyrians. They marched on Jerusalem, trying to force Ahaz of Judah to join them in fighting Assyria (2 Kings 16:5). The prophet Isaiah warned Ahaz not to participate with Syria and Israel (Isa. 7). He also said that Assyria would destroy Damascus (Isa. 8:4; compare ch. 17). Rezin of Damascus had some military success (2 Kings 16:6), but he could not get Ahaz of Judah to cooperate. Neither could Isaiah. Instead, Ahaz sent money to Tiglath-pileser, asking him to rescue Judah from Israel and Damascus. The Assyrians responded readily and captured Damascus in 732 B.C., exiling its leading people (2 Kings 16:7–9). Damascus had one last influence on Judah; for when Ahaz went to Damascus to pay tribute to Tiglath-pileser, he

The window of the city wall of Damascus which may be the site of Paul's escape in a basket from the city.

liked the altar he saw there and had a copy made for the Jerusalem Temple (2 Kings 16:10–16). Damascus sought to gain independence from Assyria in 727 and 720 but without success. Thus Damascus became a captive state of first the Assyrians, then the Babylonians, Persians, Greeks, Ptolemies, and Seleuccids. Finally, Rome gained control under Pompey in 64 B.C. Jews began to migrate to Damascus and establish synagogues there. Thus Saul went to Damascus to determine if any Christian believers were attached to the synagogues there so that he might persecute them (Acts 9). Thus the Damascus Road became the sight of Saul's conversion experience and Damas-

The traditional "Street called Straight" in Damascus, Syria.

cus the sight of his introduction to the church. He had to escape from Damascus in a basket to begin his ministry (2 Cor. 11:32). Damascus gained importance, eventually becoming a Roman colony. See *Hadad; Syria.*   *Trent C. Butler*

DAN (Dăn) Personal name meaning, "judge." *1.* First son born to Jacob by Rachel's maid Bilhah (Gen. 30:6). He was the original ancestor of the tribe of Dan. When the Israelites entered Canaan, the tribe of Dan received land on the western coast. They could not fully gain control of the territory, especially after the Philistines settled in the area. The last chapters of Judges show Samson of the tribe of Dan fighting the Philistines. Eventually, Dan migrated to the north and was able to take a city called Laish. They renamed the city Dan and settled in the area around it. Dan was always a small tribe, and it never exercised significant influence in Israel. The most prominent Danites mentioned in the Bible are Oholiab and Samson. See *Tribes of Israel; Patriarchs.*

2. The biblical city of Dan is often mentioned in the description of the land of Israel, namely "from Dan even to Beersheba" (Judg. 20:1). It has been identified with modern tell el-Qadi (or tell Dan). The tel, which covers about 50 acres, is situated at the northern end of the richly fertile Huleh Plain at the base of Mt. Hermon. The abundant springs of the site provide one of the three main sources of the Jordan River.

Base for a canopy at Dan, probably from the time of Ahab.

The city was formerly named Laish (Judg. 18:7 or Leshem in Josh. 19:47) when occupied by the Canaanites. This city is mentioned in the Egyptian execration texts and Mari tablets from the eighteenth century B.C. Later Thutmose III listed Laish among the cities conquered in his 1468 B.C. campaign.

Excavation of tell Dan has been led by A. Biran of Hebrew University in Jerusalem since 1966. Laish was founded at the end of the Early Bronze II Age (about 2700 B.C.) near the springs and flourished until about 2300 B.C. Significant pottery remains of this era were uncovered along with remains of floors and walls. The city probably remained unoccupied until the Middle Bronze II period (about 2000 B.C.), when a large, well-fortified city was constructed. A massive earthen rampart similar to that of Hazor was built for defensive purposes, and set into the rampart (about 1750 B.C.) was a well-preserved, mudbrick "triple-arched gate." The fifteen meter square gate system stood twelve meters above the surrounding plain and contained the earliest arched entryways known in the world.

The Late Bronze Age is represented by a richly-

Excavations at Dan showing the stone steps leading to the mud brick gate in the background.

supplied tomb containing Mycenaean and Cypriote imported wares; ivory inlaid cosmetic boxes; gold, silver, and bronze objects; and forty-five skeletons of men, women, and children.

Iron Age Laish was rebuilt by local inhabitants in the late thirteenth century B.C. but destroyed about 1100 B.C. by the migrating tribe of Dan. Scripture describes the conquest of the city as if the local people were unsuspecting of the coming invasion. Danites utilized the earlier rampart for defense and built their homes on the ruins of the previous city. The first Danite city, which contained some Philistine pottery remnants, was destroyed a century after its founding. The city was soon rebuilt and became a prominent Israelite city of the Iron Age.

Following the establishment of the Israelite

View of the mud brick arched gateway just after its discovery and before it was completely uncovered.

kingdom under David and Solomon, Jeroboam led the Northern tribes in revolt against Rehoboam (about 925 B.C.). As an alternative to worship in Jerusalem, Dan and Bethel were fortified as border fortress/sanctuaries (1 Kings 12:29) with temples containing golden calf representations of Yahweh. This may have represented a combination of Baal worship with worship of Yahweh. The extent to which the Baal cult influenced Northern Israel is seen in the reign of Jehu, who did not destroy the altars at Dan and Bethel, despite eradicating the Baal priests from the land (2 Kings 10:32). Excavations at Dan have uncovered the "high place" of Jeroboam along with a small horned altar, the city gate (with royal throne) and walls (12 feet thick), hundreds of pottery vessels, buildings, and inscribed objects. This city was soon taken by Ben-hadad of Aram and then recaptured by Jeroboam II in the eighth century B.C. (2 Kings

Canopied structure at Dan, possibly a throne from Ahab's reign.

14:25). The Israelite city of Dan fell to the Assyrians under Tiglath-pileser III (Pul of Old Testament) about 743 B.C. (2 Kings 15:29). He annexed the city into an Assyrian district. Many Danites were deported to Assyria, Babylon, and Media following the fall of Samaria in 722 or 721 B.C. (2 Kings 17:6) to Sargon II. Foreigners were brought in from Babylon, Aram, and other lands to settle Israel's territory. The writer of Kings ascribed the fall of the kingdom to the worship of gods other than Yahweh (2 Kings 17:7–20), and Dan was one of the key centers of this idolatry.

As Josiah came to the throne of Judah in 639 B.C., Assyria was on the decline. Josiah incorporated the former Northern Kingdom territories into a united country, restoring the classical borders of Israel to "from Dan to Beersheba." An upper gate to the city was built during this period, and the inscription found at this level, "belonging to Ba'alpelet," demonstrates that Baal worship continued to influence this area after the Assyrian destruction. The partially rebuilt city survived until the onslaught of the Babylonian army of Nebuchadnezzar (about 589 B.C.; compare Jer. 4:14–18).

Dan again was occupied in the Hellenistic, Roman, and Byzantine periods. In the area of the high place, statues and figurines of Greco-Roman and Egyptian gods such as Osiris, Bes, and Aphrodite have been excavated. The Greek and Aramaic inscription, "To the god who is in Dan, Zoilos made a vow," further evidences the religious significance of the city. *Dennis Cole*

DANCING Dancing was an essential part of Jewish life in Bible times. According to Ecclesiastes 3:4, there is "a time to mourn, and a time to dance." Dances were performed on both sacred and secular occasions, though the Hebrew mind would not likely have thought in these terms.

The Old Testament employs eleven terms to describe the act of dance. This suggests something about the Hebrew interest in the subject. The basic Hebrew term translated "dance" means to twist or to whirl about in circular motions. Other terms for dance mean "to spring about," "to jump," "to leap," "to skip." One term seems to have been used of processional marches or dances at feasts and holidays.

The Greek terms for dance mean "row" or "ring." The two terms are used five times in the New Testament (Matt. 11:17; 14:6; Mark 6:22; Luke 7:32; 15:25). Dances were performed for different purposes. The mood behind the dance was one of celebration and praise.

Jewish men dancing during a private ceremony in the Court of the Men at the Wailing Wall in Jerusalem.

Dances celebrated military victories. Women sang and danced, accompanied by musical instruments. Miriam and other Israelite women sang and danced in celebration of the victory at the Red Sea (Ex. 15:20–21). Jephthah's daughter danced before her victorious father (Judg. 11:34) as did the Israelite women when David returned from having defeated the Philistines (1 Sam. 18:6). Men also danced to celebrate military victory (1 Sam. 30:16).

Dances were customary at weddings. On some occasions young ladies, dressed in their best clothing, danced in a bride-choosing ceremony (Judg. 21). Marriage processions involved dancing with timbrels and other musical instruments (Ps. 45:14–15). Dances were performed in honor of the bride (Song of Sol. 6:13).

Some dances were performed for the sheer entertainment of guests. Salome danced before the princes and politicans gathered to celebrate her father's birthday (Matt. 14:6; Mark 6:22). Children played games of "dance" (Job 21:11), often with the accompaniment of a musical instrument (Matt. 11:17; Luke 7:32). The return of a long lost son was cause for celebration and dancing (Luke 15:25).

Religious celebration was most often the occasion for dancing. David danced before the ark as it was brought into Jerusalem (2 Sam. 6:14,16; 1 Chron. 15:29). The psalmist exhorted others to praise God with music and dancing (Ps. 149:3; 150:4). Also pagans used the dance as a means of honoring their gods (1 Kings 18:26).

In summary, the dance of the Jewish people was similar to what we today call the folk dance. It was performed by both males and females, though apparently not in mixed groups. Both group and individual dances were performed. *Glenn McCoy*

DANIEL (Dăn' iĕl) Personal name meaning, "God is judge" or "God's judge." *1.* A son of David and Abigail, the Carmelitess (1 Chron. 3:1), who is also called Chileab in 2 Samuel 3:3. *2.* A priest of the Ithamar lineage (Ezra 8:2; Neh 10:6) who returned with Ezra from the Babylonian captivity.

3. Daniel of Ezekiel 14:14,20; 28:3 is spelled differently in Hebrew from all the other forms in the Old Testament. This Daniel was a storied figure of antiquity mentioned with Noah and Job. He was famous for wisdom and righteousness. Due to the similarity in the spelling of the name and the common attributes of wisdom and righteousness, some interpreters identify this Daniel with the Daniel of the canonical book of Daniel.

Most interpreters, however, take note of the differences in the spelling and also the fact of antiquity. Some identify the "Daniel" of Ezekiel with "Danel" of ancient Ugaritic literature.

4. The most common usage of "Daniel" refers to the hero of the Book of Daniel. This young man of nobility was taken captive by Nebuchadnezzar, king of Babylon, and elevated to high rank in the Babylonian and Persian kingdoms.

The Babylonians sought to remove all vestiges of Daniel's nationality and religion. For this reason, they sought to change the name of Daniel to Belteshazzar (Dan. 1:7; 2:26; 4:8,9,18,19; 5:12; 10:1).

Daniel was transported from Judah to Babylon in his early youth at the battle of Carchemish, 605 B.C. The text does not indicate his precise age. He was trained in the arts, letters, and wisdom in the Babylonian capital. Eventually, he rose to high rank among the Babylonian men of wisdom.

He was active throughout the long reign of Nebuchadnezzar (604–562 B.C.). No mention is made in Daniel of the times of Evil-Merodach (561–560 B.C.), Neriglissar (559–555 B.C.), or Labashi-Marduk (555 B.C.). However, much information is provided concerning Daniel's involvement during the reign of Nabonidus (555–539 B.C.). While Nabonidus was absent from his country for extended periods of time, he put his son Belshazzar in charge of the affairs of government.

Daniel was in Babylon when the forces of Cyrus, the Persian, captured Babylon. Successively, Daniel was a high governmental official during the reigns of Cyrus (539–529 B.C.) and Cambyses (529–522 B.C.). He served also during his old age into the reign of Darius I, the son of Hystaspes (522–486 B.C.). Daniel would probably have celebrated his one hundredth birthday during the reign of Darius.

He had outstanding physical attraction. He demonstrated at an early age propensities of knowledge, wisdom, and leadership. In addition to his wisdom, he was skilled in dream interpretation.

Throughout his entire life he demonstrated an unshakable faith in his God. It took courage to resist the temptations and threats which confronted him repeatedly. He recognized that God was continuously judging him. He remained faithful.   *J. J. Owens*

DANIEL, BOOK OF High hopes and great expectations highlight the Book of Daniel. It provides the highest example of Old Testament ethics and the climax of Old Testament teaching about the future of God's people. It also provides Bible students some of the most perplexing questions they ever seek to answer.

Literary Features Daniel combines characteristics of prophecy, wisdom, and apocalyptic writing into a unique type of literature. Matthew identified Daniel as a prophet (Matt. 24:15). The book addresses a current situation with a call for moral uprightness, as did the prophets. It also points to hope for the future rising out of God's words and promises. It focuses on the nations as well as Israel, as did the other prophets. It does not, however, use the literary forms of the prophets, particularly the standard formulas such as, "Thus says the Lord"; nor does it represent a collection of prophetic sermons.

As did the wisdom writers, Daniel served in a royal court counseling a ruler. He was highly-educated. The book seeks to instill moral wisdom in young persons. Yet it does not string proverbs or wisdom poetry together nor delve into the problems Job or Ecclesiastes tackled. It is wisdom literature and more.

Apocalyptic literature best describes Daniel for most Bible students. Apocalyptic writings originate from times of national, communal, or personal tribulations. See *Apocalyptic.*

The visions and angelic figures of Daniel along with its strongly figurative, symbolic language tie it closely to the apocalyptic. Its opening stories serve as the tie to times of persecution and call for moral living. The letters to the churches serve a similar function in Revelation.

Daniel uses two languages—Aramaic (2:4*b*–7:28) and Hebrew (1:2–2:4*a*; 8:1—12:13)—plus loan words from Persian and Greek to write the complex work of prophecy, wisdom, and apocalyptic writing. This is apparently a combination of the language of worship (Hebrew) and the language of daily life (Aramaic). The two languages combine to form two distinctly separate sections of the book (1—6; 7—12), the first told in narrative form about Daniel and his friends with a historical conclusion (6:28) and the second told in form of Daniel's visions.

Canon and Authority The basic twelve chapters of Daniel appear in the Hebrew Bible between Esther and Ezra in the last section called the Writings rather than in the Law or the Prophets. The Greek translation called the Septuagint introduced Daniel into the prophets and also introduced additional materials: the prayer of Azariah, the song of the three children, story of Susanna, Bel and the Dragon. See *Apocrypha.* The Christian church has followed the Septuagint in placing Daniel among the prophets, but Protestant Christianity has not accepted the additions, whereas the Catholic tradition has. All agree the basic Book of Daniel is God's authoritative Word for His people. Questions rise in interpretation not in the book's authority.

Unity Many things appear to separate Daniel into unrelated parts. The position of the person Daniel differs in various portions of the book. He is more central in chapters 1—2 and 4—7 than in the rest of the book. In chapters 1—6 Daniel is spoken of in the third person in the form of a biography. In chapters 7—12, however, Daniel speaks in the first person in the form of autobiography (except 10:1).

In chapters 1—6 the dreams or phenomena come to heathen kings, but in chapters 7—12 Daniel has the visions. In chapters 1—6 Daniel is the one who interprets the dreams, but in 7—12 "someone" else interprets the dreams and visions to Daniel. Chapters 1—6 have simplicity, whereas chapters 7—12 are complex.

The Book of Daniel acts as a unit despite these differences in languages used and types of literature employed. Each of the twelve chapters contributes to this unity. The unifying theme is that God expects His followers to maintain fidelity in face of threats, wars, legal pronouncements, or changing customs.

Outline

I. The Faithful Young Men in a Foreign Court (1:1—6:28)
A. Loyalty to God leads Daniel and his friends to high political positions (1:1—21).
B. Interpretation of the king's dream leads to the king's confession of God and to important positions for the friends (2:1—49).
C. Loyalty to God brings deliverance from the fiery furnace, royal decree protecting the right to worship God, and further promotion for the friends (3:1—30).
D. Interpretation and fulfillment of the king's dream leads the king to praise God (4:1—37).
E. Loyalty to God and His rewards allows interpretation of the handwriting on the wall, brings promotion in the kingdom, and spells doom for Babylon (5:1—31).
F. Faithfulness in prayer despite secular laws overcomes conspiracy, brings deliverance from the lions' den, leads the king to command fear of the true God, and brings political prosperity (6:1—28).

II. Daniel's Visions Point the Way Through Persecution to Hope (7:1—12:13).
A. Vision of four beasts shows four kingdoms to be overcome by Son of man and saints of the Most High, who will reign forever (7:1—28).
B. Vision of ram, he goat, and four horns points to passing of Persians, Medes, and of proud Greeks, one of whom will interrupt daily sacrifices of Temple for a while (8:1—27).
C. Daniel confesses the nation's sins, seeks forgiveness, and learns meaning of Jeremiah's 70 weeks as pointing to Messiah and to desolation of Jerusalem (9:1—27).
D. A heaven-sent vision shows that Scripture points to battles between north and south until the northern king proudly triumphs and persecutes the people of God's covenant, taking away their sacrificial system and desecrating the Temple, but facing disaster in the end (10:1—11:45).
E. Heavenly intervention will bring the time of the end and the resurrection of God's faithful people (12:1—13).

Meaning Daniel encouraged the reader to remain faithful to God, God's law, and to the scriptural traditions of God's people. War, danger, threat, heathen kings, temptation, greedy desire for luxury, prosperity, and position lead away from God's way. Daniel encouraged the faithful to stand firm in faithfulness to the heritage of Israel.

Daniel 1:8—6:28 shows how in history Israelite heroes stood firm in their resolve to stay true to God and their heritage. In six different situations an Israelite hero faced extreme pressure to forsake God and tradition for personal safety and gain. In each case the hero resisted threats or danger of loss of life with no assurance of victory other than his faith.

Daniel 7:1—12:13 brought these truths to bear upon an extremely tense situation. Throughout the book the author focused upon the "fourth kingdom," that of a tyrannical despot. As the ancient heroes remained faithful, so people facing the despot could double their resolve and experience victorious faith. They faced the choice: believe a ruthless foreign conqueror, or stay true to the faith of the fathers and the God of their history.

Interpretation The literary features, authority, outline, and meaning of the book are rather clear. The historical setting and details of interpretation bring varying opinions. The basic issue is the nature of inspired prophecy and Daniel's relationship to prophecy. All agree that prophecy is both exhortation of a present generation to faithfulness and painting of a future hope. The point at issue among interpreters is the fidelity to detail that prophecy must contain and whether Daniel with its wisdom and apocalyptic overtones must have the same type of historical setting and perspective as do the classic prophets of Israel.

To simplify the picture, two major stances on Daniel can be summarized. The first sees Daniel standing in the precise line of previous prophets, so that every detail of his visions points to the future and not the past. This assumes that Daniel in the sixth century B.C. wrote the book and described the history of contemporary Babylonian, Median, and Persian history and future Greek, Ptolemaic, Seleuccid, Maccabean, and Roman history, as well as the events of end time. Those interpreters who use a dispensational system (see *Dispensations)* to interpret Daniel see antichrist, tribulation, and the final kingdom pictured in Daniel.

A second stance emphasizes Daniel's relationship to other apocalyptic literature in which writers often use the names of ancient heroes to describe history long past to bring a message to a present generation facing extreme persecution. Writing in the name of the ancient hero gives authority to the writing and protection in the situation of extreme danger. This stance views Daniel as the hero but not the author of the book. The author is an unknown inspired writer who lived in the time of Antiochus Ephiphanes shortly before 164 B.C. The author used contemporary methods of interpreting the prophecies of Ezekiel, Jeremiah, and others to give hope to his generation when many Jews were seeking favor with the Syrian government of Antiochus by adopting a Hellenistic life-style and ignoring Jewish traditions. He used biblical traditions and other knowledge of his day to review the history of Babylon, the Medes, Persia, Greece, the Ptolemies of Egypt, and the Seleuccids of Syria. He then pointed to an immediate future when God would judge Antiochus and his followers who enforced the present persecution of God's people. This interpretation may then take another step and say that the book lends itself to valid new interpretations in light of Jesus Christ and the Christian hope, but that these were not necessarily the main points of the original author.

Whichever stance one takes in interpreting the details of Daniel, the inspired book continues to give hope, strength, and courage to God's people, especially in times of persecution, and to call for ultimate faithfulness no matter the temptations faced. *J. J. Owens and Trent C. Butler*

DANITE (Dăn′ īte) Resident and/or citizen of city of Dan or member of tribe of Dan. See *Dan*.

DAN-JAAN (Dăn-jā′ ȧn) Place name of uncertain meaning in 2 Samuel 24:6. Many Bible students think the scribes have not preserved the correct Hebrew text at this point and read only "Dan" (NRSV) or "Dan and Ijon" (NEB). If the present Hebrew text is correct, the location of the town is not known except that it is apparently in ′the territory of the tribe of Dan.

DANNAH (Dăn′ năh) Place name meaning, "fortress." Town assigned tribe of Judah in the hill country (Josh. 15:49). Its location is uncertain.

DAPPLED The variegated grey color of the horses in the vision in Zech. 6:3,6. KJV translates the rare Hebrew term as "bay." Modern translators follow the earliest Greek translation in reading "dappled." The Hebrew term also appears in Genesis 31:10,12 and in a few manuscripts of Nehemiah 5:18. KJV reads "grisled," while modern translations have, "spotted," "speckled," or "mottled."

DARA (Dâr′ ȧ) Hebrew reading in 1 Chronicles 2:6 for Darda of 1 Kings 4:31. See *Darda*.

DARDA (Där′ dȧ) Personal name possibly meaning, "pearl of knowledge." Famous wise man whose father is listed as Mahol in 1 Kings 4:31 but as Zerah in what appears to be a parallel list in 1 Chronicles 2:6. Mahol may mean, "dancer," "musician," or "chorister," representing an occupation or guild rather than the father's name.

DARIC A Persian gold coin equivalent to four days' wages, probably introduced by Darius I (522–486 B.C.), and possibly the earliest coined money used by the Jews who became acquainted with it during the Exile. Offerings for the reconstruction of the Temple were made in darics (Ezra 2:69; Neh. 7:70,72). Some interpreters understand the 20 gold basins in Ezra 8:27 to be worth 1,000 darics each. Others take this as a weight of about 19 pounds or 8.5 kilograms.

DARIUS (Dȧ rī′ ŭs) King of Persia (522–486 B.C.) Successor to Cambyses II in the Persian Empire, Darius spent his early years as king putting down revolts in Media, Persia, and Egypt. After solidifying his power in the Middle East, he set out to reconquer the Scythians and Greeks who had rebelled under his predecessor. He was successful in this venture until the Battle of Marathon in 490 B.C. From that time the kingdom began a gradual regression until finally conquered by Alexander the Great in 331 B.C.

Relief of Darius I giving an audience.

Darius brought a new sense of unity to his empire. He enlarged on the policies of Cyrus the Great in making restoration to those disenfranchised by the Assyrian and Babylonian dominations. The Jews received additional financial aid for finishing the Temple in Jerusalem (Ezra 6:8–9).

Unlike Cyrus, Darius organized a tightly-knit centralized state and vested himself with absolute power. Twenty satrapies (provinces) were established. Each had a system of checks and balances, with each official watching the actions of his colleagues.

A common code of laws was established in the empire, administered by royal judges. A system of weights and measures were standardized throughout the kingdom to help stimulate the economy and make transactions easier. Several major roads were built, making travel quicker and safer. What may have been the first gold currency was issued by Darius. Aramaic was decreed as the official language of the empire. The people were infused

Remains of the throne of Darius the Great.

with a new sense of pride as the king made these many improvements. Unfortunately, Darius' successors were unable to maintain his policies after his death.   *Mike Mitchell*

DARKNESS The absence of light is used in both physical and figurative senses in both the Old and New Testaments. The darkness which covered the deep before God's creation of light symbolizes chaos in opposition to God's orderly creation (Gen. 1:2,3). Elsewhere darkness, as well as light, is recognized as the creation of God (Isa. 45:7). Darkness is a place for evil doers to hide (Job. 34:22); however, darkness does not hide one from God (Ps. 139:11–12; Dan. 2:22).

Darkness was thought of as a curse. Thus the Old Testament speaks of death as a land of darkness (Job 10:21–22; 17:13; Ps. 88:6). Darkness is frequently associated with supernatural events involving the judgment of God, such as the plagues of Egypt (Ex. 10:21), the coming of the Lord (Isa. 13:9–10; Joel 2:31; Matt. 24:29), and Christ's crucifixion (Matt. 27:45). The day of God's judgment is often described as a day of darkness (Joel 2:2; Amos 5:18–20). Elsewhere darkness forms part of God's punishment on the disobedient (Deut. 28:29; 1 Sam. 2:9; Job 5:14; 15:30; 20:26; Ps. 107:10; Isa. 47:5; Jer. 13:16; Ezek. 32:8).

In the New Testament, the place of punishment for humans and sinful angels is designated "the outer darkness" (Matt. 8:12; 22:13; 25:30; compare 2 Pet. 2:4; Jude 6,13). Darkness often has an ethical sense. Scripture speaks of ways of darkness (Prov. 2:13; 4:19), walking in darkness (John 8:12; 1 John 1:6; compare 2 Cor. 6:14; Eph. 5:8), and works of darkness (Rom. 13:12; Eph. 5:11). In this ethical sense God has no darkness in Himself (1 John 1:5). Powers hostile to God can be termed darkness. People thus face a choice of whether to yield allegiance to God or to darkness (Luke 22:53; John 1:5; 3:19; Col. 1:13; 1 Thess. 5:5). Darkness also symbolizes ignorance, especially of God and of God's ways (Isa. 8:22; 9:2; John 12:46; Acts 26:18; 1 Thess. 5:4; 1 John

2:9). God's deliverance (either from ignorance or hostile powers) is described as lighting the darkness (Isa. 9:2; 29:18; 42:7–16; Mic. 7:8; 1 Pet. 2:9). See *Light*.   *Chris Church*

DARKON (Där' kŏn) Personal name perhaps meaning, "hard." A servant of Solomon whose descendants returned from Exile with Zerubbabel about 537 B.C. (Ezra 2:56).

DART A thrusting or throwing weapon used for medium range combat either similar to a spear or javelin (2 Sam. 18:14) or else an arrow (Prov. 7:23; Eph. 6:16). The use of flaming arrows (Ps. 7:13; 120:4) becomes in Eph. 6:16 a picture of the assault of the evil one on believers. KJV uses darts to translate two different Hebrew words, the first meaning "stick" or "staff" and the second, "arrows."

DATES The fruit of the date palm (*Phoenix dactylifera*), highly valued by desert travelers who consume dates fresh, dry them, or form them into cakes for a portable and easily-storable food. As part of the celebration of bringing the ark to Jerusalem, David gave gifts of food to each Israelite gathered in Jerusalem (2 Sam. 6:19; 1 Chron. 16:3). The meaning of the Hebrew term is uncertain. NAS and NIV use "cake of dates" at 2 Samuel 6:19 (also TEV margin). Other modern translations follow the KJV, understanding the food as a piece of meat. The NIV, but not the NAS, uses "cake of dates" in the parallel account in 1 Chronicles.

Dates growing on a date palm tree.

The NAS of Song of Solomon 5:11 describes the hair of the king as "like a cluster of dates," perhaps a reference to a full head of hair. The REB translates the same term as "like palm-fronds". Other translations speak of bushy hair (KJV), curly hair (KJV margin), or wavey hair (NIV, NRSV, TEV). See *Palms*.

DATHAN (Dā' thăn) Personal name meaning, "fountain" or "warring." The son of Eliab and brother from the tribe of a Reuben, Dathan and

An Arab date vendor.

his brother Abiram were leaders of a revolt challenging Moses' authority over the Israelites. The attempted coup failed, and Dathan and Abiram, along with their families, were swallowed up by the earth (Num. 16). See *Numbers; Abiram.*

DAUGHTER-IN-LAW The wife of one's son. Famous daughters-in-law include Sarah, daughter-in-law of Terah (Gen. 11:31); Tamar, daughter-in-law of Judah (Gen. 38:11,16; 1 Chron. 2:4); and Ruth, daughter-in-law of Naomi (Ruth 2:20,22; 4:15). Daughters-in-law might be addressed simply as daughter (Ruth 2:2,8,22). Marriage made them an integral member of the family. Ruth was hailed as more to Naomi than seven sons (Ruth 4:15). The breakdown of the relationship between mother-in-laws and daughters-in-law illustrated the collapse of moral society (Mic. 7:6). In the New Testament, differing responses to the gospel created the same breakdown of relationship (Matt. 10:35; Luke 12:53). Jewish law prohibited incest between a man and his daughter-in-law (Lev. 18:15). This crime was punishable by death (Lev. 20:12). In Ezekiel 22:11 this crime illustrates the moral decline of the nation. See *Family.*

DAVID (Dā′ vĭd) Personal name probably meaning, "favorite" or "beloved." The first king to unite Israel and Judah and the first to receive the promise of a royal messiah in his line. David was pictured as the ideal king of God's people. He ruled from about 1005 to 965 B.C.

Selection as King When Saul failed to meet God's standards for kingship (1 Sam. 15:23,35; 16:1), God sent Samuel to annoint a replacement from among the sons of Jesse, who lived in Bethlehem (1 Sam. 16:1). God showed Samuel He had chosen the youngest who still tended sheep for his father (16:11–12). David's good looks were noteworthy.

In Saul's Court David's musical talent, combined with his reputation as a fighter, led one of Saul's servants to recommend David as the person to play the harp for Saul when the evil spirit from God troubled him (16:18). Saul grew to love David and made him armorbearer for the king (16:21–22).

At a later date the Philistines with the giant Goliath threatened Israel (1 Sam. 17). David returned home to tend his father's sheep (17:15). Jesse sent David to the battlefield with food for his warrior brothers. At least one brother did not think too highly of him (17:28). Saul tried to persuade David, the youth, from challenging Goliath; but David insisted God would bring victory, which He did.

Saul's son Jonathan became David's closest friend (1 Sam. 18:1). David became a permanent part of Saul's court, not returning home (18:2). Saul gave David a military commission, which he fulfilled beyond expectations, defeating the Philistines and winning the hearts of the people. This stirred Saul's jealousy (18:8). Moved by the evil spirit from God, Saul tried to kill David with his spear; but God's presence protected David (18:10–12). David eventually earned the right to marry Michal, Saul's daughter, without being killed by the Philistines as Saul had hoped (18:17–27). With the help of Michal and Jonathan, David escaped from Saul and made contact with Samuel, the prophet (19:18). Jonathan and David made a vow of eternal friendship, and Jonathan risked his own life to protect David (1 Samuel 20).

Independent Warrior David gathered a band of impoverished and discontented people around him. He established relationships with Moab and other groups and gained favor with the people by defeating the Philistines (1 Sam. 22—23), but all Saul's efforts to capture him failed. God protected David, and David refused to injure Saul, instead promising not to cut off Saul's family (24:21–22).

Abigail of Maon intervened with David to prevent him from punishing her foolish husband Nabal. God brought Nabal's death, and David married Abigail. He also married Ahinoam of Jezreel, but Saul gave Michal, David's first wife, to another man (1 Sam. 25).

After again refusing to kill Saul, the Lord's anointed, David attached himself to Achish, the Philistine king of Gath. Saul finally quit chasing him. Achish gave Ziklag to David, who established a headquarters there and began destroying Israel's southern neighbors (1 Sam. 27). Despite the wishes of Achish, the other Philistine leaders would not let David join them in battle against Saul (1 Sam. 29). Returning home, David found the Amalekites had destroyed Ziklag and captured his wives. David followed God's leading and defeated the celebrating Amalekites, recovering all the spoils of war. These he distributed among his followers and among the peoples of Judah (1 Sam. 30).

King of Judah Hearing of the deaths of Saul and Jonathan, David avenged the murderer of Saul and sang a lament over the fallen (2 Sam. 1). He moved to Hebron, where the citizens of Judah crowned him king (2 Sam. 2). This led to war with Israel under Saul's son Ishbosheth. After much intrigue, Ishbosheth's commanders assassinated him. David did the same to them (2 Sam. 4).

King of Israel The northern tribes then crowned David king at Hebron, uniting all Israel under him. He led the capture of Jerusalem and made it his capital. After defeating the Philistines, David sought to move the ark of the covenant to Jerusalem, succeeding on his second attempt (2 Sam. 6). He then began plans to build a temple but learned from Nathan, the prophet, that he would instead build a dynasty with eternal dimensions (2 Sam. 7). His son would build the Temple.

David then organized his administration and subdued other nations who opposed him, finally gaining control of the land God had originally promised the forefathers. He also remembered his promise to Jonathan and cared for his lame son Mephibosheth (2 Sam. 9).

A Sinner David was a giant among godly leaders, but he remained human as his sin with Bathsheba and Uriah showed. He spied Bathsheba bathing, desired her, and engineered the death of her faithful warrior husband, after committing adultery with her (2 Sam. 11). Nathan, the prophet, confronted David with his sin, and David confessed his wrongdoing. The newborn child of David and Bathsheba died. David acknowledged his helplessness in the situation, confessing faith that he would go to be with the child one day. Bathsheba conceived again, bearing Solomon (2 Sam. 12:1–25).

Family Intrigue Able to rule the people but not his family, David saw intrigue, sexual sins, and murder rock his own household, resulting in his isolation from and eventual retreat before Absalom. Still, David grieved long and deep when his army killed Absalom (2 Sam. 18:19–33). David's kingdom was restored, but the hints of division between Judah and Israel remained (2 Sam. 19:40–43). David had to put down a northern revolt (2 Sam. 20). The last act the Books of Samuel report about David is his census of the people, bringing God's anger but also preparing a place for the Temple to be built (2 Sam. 24). The last chapters of 1 Chronicles describe extensive preparations David made for the building and the worship services of the Temple. David's final days involved renewed intrigue among his family, as Adonijah sought to inherit his father's throne, but Nathan and Bathsheba worked to insure Solomon became the next king (1 Kings 1:1—2:12).

Prophetic Hope David thus passed from the historical scene but left a legacy never to be forgotten. He was the role model for Israelite kings (1 Kings 3:14; 9:14; 11:4,6,33,38; 14:8; 15:3,11; 2 Kings 14:3; 16:2; 22:2). David was the "man of God" (2 Chron. 8:14), and God was "the God of David thy father" (2 Kings 20:5). God's covenant with David was the deciding factor as God wrestled with David's disobedient successors on the throne (2 Chron. 21:7). Even as Israel rebuilt the Temple, they followed "the ordinance of David king of Israel" (Ezra 3:10).

God's prophets pointed to a future David who would restore Israel's fortunes. "Of the increase of his government and peace there shall be no end, upon the throne of David, and upon his kingdom, to order it, and to establish it with judgment and with justice from henceforth even forever" (Isa. 9:7). Jeremiah summed up the surety of the hope in David: "If ye can break my covenant of the day, and my covenant of the night, and that there should not be day and night in their season; Then may also my covenant be broken with David my servant, that he should not have a son to reign upon his throne. . . . As the host of heaven cannot be numbered, neither the sand of the sea measured: so will I multiply the seed of David my servant" (Jer. 33:20–22). For further references, compare Jeremiah 33:15, 17, 25–26; Ezekiel 34:23–24; 37:24–25; Hosea 3:5; Amos 9:11; Zechariah 12:6–10.

In the New Testament The New Testament tells the story of Jesus as the story of the Son of God but also as the story of the Son of David from His birth (Matt. 1:1) until His final coming (Rev. 22:16). At least twelve times the Gospels refer to Him as "Son of David." David was cited as an example of similar behavior by Jesus (Matt. 12:3); and David called Him, "Lord" (Luke 20:42–44). David thus took his place in the roll call of faith (Heb. 11:32). This was "David the son of Jesse, a man after mine own heart, which shall fulfill all my will" (Acts 13:22).

DAVID, CITY OF *1.* The most ancient part of Jerusalem on its southeast corner representing the city occupied by the Jebusites and conquered by David (2 Sam. 5:7). The Kidron Valley bordered it on the east, and the Tyropoeon Valley on the west. The entire area occupied no more than ten acres. It is also called Zion. See *Jerusalem; Zion.*

A view of the excavations led by Kathleen Kenyon of the City of David.

This part of Jerusalem dates back at least to about 2500 B.C., when it is mentioned in the Ebla documents. See *Ebla.* Its strong defense walls on which the Jebusites prided themselves originated about 1750 B.C.

DAWN The first appearance of light in the morning as the sun rises. Job 3:9 indicates that the stars are still visible at dawn. Dawn is used in the literal sense of the beginning of the day (Josh. 6:15; Judg. 19:26; Matt. 28:1; Acts 27:33). Matthew 4:16 uses the picture of the dawn in Isa. 9:2–3 as a figure for the new age of hope and promise which Jesus brought.

DAY OF ATONEMENT The tenth day of the seventh month of the Jewish calender (Sept.— Oct.) on which the high priest entered the inner

sanctuary of the Temple to make reconciling sacrifices for the sins of the entire nation (Lev. 16:16–28). The high priest was prohibited from entering this most holy place at any other time on pain of death (Lev. 16:2). Nor was any other priest permitted to perform duties within the Temple proper during the ritual for the Day of Atonement (Lev. 16:17). The days' ritual required the high priest to bathe and be dressed in pure linen garments as a symbol of purity (Lev. 16:4). The ceremony began with the sacrifice of a young bull as a sin offering for the priest and his family (Lev. 16:3,6). After burning incense before the mercy seat in the inner santuary, the high priest sprinkled the blood from the bull on and in front of the mercy seat (16:14). The priest cast lots over two goats. One was offered as a sin offering. The other was presented alive as a scapegoat (16:5,7–10,20–22). The blood of the goat used as the sin offering was sprinkled like that of the bull to make atonement for the sanctuary (16:15). The mixed blood of the bull and goat were applied to the horns of the altar to make atonement for it (16:18). The high priest confessed all of the people's sins over the head of the live goat which was lead away and then released in the wilderness (16:21–22). Following the ceremony, the priest again bathed and put on his usual garments (16:23–24). The priest then offered a burnt offering for the priest and the people (16:24). The bodies of the bull and goat used in the days' ritual were burnt outside the camp (16:27–28). The Day of Atonement was a solemn day, requiring the only fast designated by the Mosaic law. All work was also prohibited (16:29; 23:27–28).

The writer of Hebrews developed images from the Day of Atonement to stress the superiority of Christ's priesthood (8:6; 9:7,11–26). Hebrews 13:11–12 uses the picture of the bull and goat burned outside the camp as an illustration of Christ's suffering outside Jerusalem's city walls. According to one interpretation Paul alluded to the day's ritual by speaking of Christ as a sin offering (2 Cor. 5:21). See *Atonement.*

Chris Church

DAY OF CHRIST See *Day of the Lord, Judgment Day.*

DAY OF THE LORD The time when God reveals His sovereignty over human powers and human existence. The day of the Lord rests on the He-

View of Jerusalem from the southwest during the time of David (1000–962 B.C.), showing the Tabernacle pitched atop the threshing floor of Araunah (or Ornan) the Jebusite (upper right). David's palace (center, right) overlooked the Tabernacle. The Citadel fortress (center), and City of David (left, center) can also be seen. The Tyropoeon Valley (top, center) and the Kidron Valley (lower right) flanked each side of the city perched high on the escarpment of Zion.

D

brew term, *yom,* "day," the fifth most frequent noun used in the Old Testament and one used with a variety of meanings: time of daylight from sunrise to sunset (Gen. 1:14; 3:8; 8:22; Amos 5:8); 24-hour period (Gen. 1:5; Num. 7:12,18; Hag. 1:15); a general expression for "time" without specific limits (Gen. 2:4; Ps. 102:3; Isa. 7:17); the period of a specific event (Isa. 9:3; Jer. 32:31; Ezek. 1:28). The "day of the Lord" then does not give a precise time period. It may mean either the daylight hours, the 24-hour day, or a general time period, perhaps characterized by a special event. Zechariah 14:7 even points to a time when all time is daylight, night with its darkness having vanished.

"Day of the Lord" does not in itself designate the time perspective of the event, whether it is past, present, or future. Lamentations 2:2 can speak of the "day of the Lord's anger" in past tense, describing the fall of Jerusalem. Joel 1:15 could describe a present disaster as the "day of the Lord."

The Old Testament prophets used a term familiar to their audience, a term by which the audience expected light and salvation (Amos 5:18), but the prophets painted it as a day of darkness and judgment (Isa. 2:10–22; 13:6,9; Joel 1:15; 2:1–11,31; 3:14–15; Amos 5:20; Zeph. 1:7–8,14–18; Mal. 4:5). The Old Testament language of the day of the Lord is thus aimed at warning sinners among God's people of the danger of trust in traditional religion without commitment to God and to His way of life. It is language that could be aimed at judging Israel or that could be used to promise deliverance from evil enemies (Isa. 13:6,9; Ezek. 30:3; Obad. 15). The day of the Lord is thus a point in time in which God displays His sovereign initiative to reveal His control of history, of time, of His people, and of all people.

New Testament writers took up the Old Testament expression to point to Christ's final victory and the final judgment of sinners. In so doing, they used several different expressions: "day of Jesus Christ" (Phil. 1:6,10), "day of our Lord Jesus" (1 Cor. 1:8; 5:5); "day of the Lord" (1 Thess. 5:2); "day of Christ" (Phil. 2:16); "day of judgment" (1 John 4:17); "the day" (1 Thess. 5:4); "that day" (2 Tim. 1:12); "day of wrath" (Rom. 2:5).

People who take a dispensational perspective on Scripture often seek to interpret each of the terms differently, so that the "day of Christ" is a day of blessing equated with the rapture, whereas the day of God is an inclusive term for all the events of end time (2 Pet. 3:12). See *Dispensations.* In this view the day of the Lord includes the great tribulation, the following judgment on the nations, and the time of worldwide blessing under the rule of the Messiah.

Many Bible students who do not take a dispensational viewpoint interpret the several expressions in the New Testament to refer to one major event: the end time when Christ returns for the final judgment and establishes His eternal kingdom.

Whichever interpretation one makes of specific details, the day of the Lord points to the promise that God's eternal sovereignty over all creation and all nations will one day become crystal clear to all creatures.

DAY'S JOURNEY The customary though inexact measure of distance traveled in a day. The distance varied with the terrain and with the circumstances of the traveler. The typical day's journey of the Jews was between 20 and 30 miles, though groups generally travelled only 10 miles per day. (See Gen. 30:36; 31:23; Ex. 3:18; 8:27; Deut. 1:2; Luke 2:44).

DAYSMAN The KJV term for a mediator, arbitrator, or umpire (Job. 9:33). In the Near East such mediators placed their hands on the heads of the parties in a dispute. The mediator may have attempted to bring both parties together in reconciliation or may have had authority to impose a settlement on both parties. Job's point is that no human is capable of standing in judgment of God. The New Testament points to "the man Christ Jesus" as the "one mediator between God and men" (1 Tim. 2:5).

DAY STAR NRSV translation of Hebrew term called "Lucifer" by KJV and morning star or star of the morning by other translations. The planet Venus appears as a morning "star" at dawn. Isaiah 14:12 compares the splendor of the Babylonian king to the Day Star. Second Peter 1:19 describes Christ as the morning star which outshines the light of the earlier prophetic witness. The Hebrew term appears only in Isaiah 14:12. The translation "Lucifer" comes from the Latin translation called the Vulgate. See *Lucifer.*

DEACON, DEACONESS The term "deacon" is derived from the Greek word *diakonos,* which is usually translated "servant" or "minister." Only a few times in the New Testament (Phil. 1:1; 1 Tim. 3:8,12, and, in some translations, Rom. 16:1) is it translated "deacon" and used to denote one holding a church office. The noun form comes from a verb which means "to serve," probably originally in the sense of waiting on tables. It came to be used to signify a broad range of types of service. In the New Testament, the noun is used to refer to ministers of the gospel (Col. 1:23), ministers of Christ (1 Tim. 4:6), servants of God (2 Cor. 6:4), those who follow Jesus (John 12:26), and in many other similar ways.

Although Philippians 1:1 and 1 Timothy 3 clearly indicate that the office of deacon existed in New Testament times, no explicit Bible reference describes the duties of deacons or refers to the origin of the office. In Philippians 1:1 and in numerous references in early Christian literature outside the New Testament, bishops and/or elders and deacons are mentioned together, with deacons mentioned last. Because of this order, and because of the natural connotations of the word *diakonos,* most interpreters believe that deacons, from the beginning, served as assistants of the church leaders. Certainly, that was clearly the role of deacons by the second century. Deacons continued to fill an important role in the ministry of the early church, serving the needs of the poor, assisting in baptism and the Lord's Supper, and performing other practical ministerial tasks.

The nature of the qualifications of deacons outlined in 1 Timothy 3: 8–13 perhaps indicates the function of deacons in the New Testament period. In most respects, the qualifications of deacons mirror those of the "bishops," the leaders of the churches. The high standards of morality and character expected of both demonstrates the church's serious regard for the offices and the importance of their functions. The requirements that deacons must have a clear understanding of the faith (1 Tim. 3:9) and that their faithfulness already be proven (1 Tim. 3:10) indicate that their duties consisted of more than menial chores. The exclusion of those who are "doubletongued" (v. 8) may be evidence that the work of the deacons brought them into close contact with the everyday lives of the church members, as would occur in visiting the sick and ministering to the other physical needs of fellow Christians. Such service would both give them greater knowledge of items for gossip and allow them greater opportunity to spread such gossip, thus making it crucial that they should not be prone to talebearing. The requirement that deacons not be greedy may indicate that they were responsible for collecting and distributing church funds.

Whether the deacons' functions extended to leading in worship is not clear. Gifts for teaching, a requirement for "bishops," are not mentioned in the qualifications for deacons. The connotations of table service in the word *diakonos* and the centrality of the Lord's Supper in the worship of the early church strongly imply that distributing the elements and, in the early years, serving the *agape* meal were important functions of deacons.

Many interpreters believe that the account of the choosing of the seven in Acts 6 describes the selection of the first deacons, although the term *diakonos* is not used in the passage and the term *diakonia* ("service" or "ministry") is used only for the work of the twelve. The tasks that the seven performed, however, later seem to be principal functions of deacons. On the other hand, two of the seven, Stephen and Philip, are known to us as prominent preachers and evangelists, roles which may not have been common for deacons. The seven were set apart for their task in a ceremony in which the apostles "laid their hands on them" (Acts 6:6). This ceremony may reflect the origin of later ordination practice. Other than this passage, which may or may not represent usual practice, the New Testament does not mention ordination of deacons.

The list of qualifications in 1 Timothy 3:11 requires that "women" *must* "likewise" (NAS) be similar in character to the men. Although this remark may refer to the wives of male deacons (KJV, NIV) it probably should be interpreted as a parenthetical reference to female deacons, or deaconesses (NIV footnote; NAS footnote; NRSV footnote). Romans 16:1 refers to Phebe as a *diakonos* of the church at Cenchrea. Williams New Testament translates this as deaconess. The NRSV uses "deacon." Other translations use "servant." In this verse, Phebe's role as "helper" and Paul's obvious regard for her work seem to support the conclusion that she functioned as a deacon in her church. Deaconesses are mentioned prominently in Christian writings of the first several centuries. They cared for needy fellow believers, visited the sick, and were especially charged with assisting in the baptism of women converts. *Fred A. Grissom*

DEAD SEA Inland lake at the end of the Jordan Valley on the southeastern border of Canaan with no outlets for water it receives; known in the

The Dead Sea's high salt content makes it virtually impossible for a person to sink in its waters.

Bible as Salt Sea, Sea of the Plain, and Eastern Sea. Its current English name was applied to it through writings after A.D. 100. It is about fifty miles long and ten miles wide at its widest point. The surface of the sea is 1292 feet below the level of the Mediterranean Sea. At its deepest point the lake is 1300 deep. At its most shallow it is only ten to fifteen feet deep.

The main source of water for the sea is the Jordan River, but other smaller rivers empty into the sea also. The Jordan River empties an average of six million tons of water every twenty-four hours into the sea. Despite this and the fact that the sea has no outlet, the surface does not rise more than ten to fifteen feet. The reason for this lies in the rapid evaporation of the water because of the heat and acidness of its location below sea level.

This plus other geographical factors gives it a salt content which is approximately five times the concentration of the ocean. This makes it one of the world's saltiest. It also causes a condition where no form of marine life can live even though some fish have reportedly been found in adjacent less salty pools. The surrounding land area can support vegetation and life, however. These features of the Dead Sea plus its location in an hot and arid area inspired the biblical writers to use it as an example of a life apart from the law of God.

Bob Sheffield

Dead Sea Scroll fragment.

Aerial photo of central Israel showing the topography of the Dead Sea area. Courtesy of NASA.

DEAD SEA SCROLLS The Dead Sea Scrolls were discovered between 1947 and 1960 in a cave on the western Dead Sea shore near a ruin called *khirbet Qumran.* Eleven caves from the Qumran area have since yielded manuscripts, mostly in small fragments. About sixty percent of the scrolls have so far been published. These were composed or copied between 200 B.C. and A.D. 70, mostly around the lifetime of Jesus, by a small community living at Qumran.

Contents They comprise three main kinds of literature: (1) copies of Old Testament books, the oldest we now possess; (2) some non-biblical Jewish books known from elsewhere (such as 1 Enoch and Jubilees), probably written by the Essenes; (3) the community's own compositions, including: biblical commentaries (for example, on Habakkuk and Nahum), which interpret biblical prophecies as applying to the community and its times; rules of community conduct; and liturgical writings such as prayers and hymns.

The Essenes The Qumran community belonged to the Essenes, one of four major Jewish religious movements described by the first century A.D. historian Josephus, but, strangely, unmentioned in the New Testament. The origins of the Essenes are uncertain: one major view is that they descended from the "Pious," who had fought for religious independence with the Maccabees; on another view they originated in Exile in Babylonia, returning to Palestine sometime in the third or second century B.C. They opposed the cultic laws operating at the Temple, rejecting its priesthood, and following a different calendar. They lived apart from other Jews in strictly-disciplined groups. One such rather special group lived at Qumran. Unlike many Essene groups, they were celibates, and they traced their origin to a "Teacher of Righteousness," a messianic figure of whom little is known except that he was a priest, possibly a high priest. The Qumran biblical commentaries speak of his confrontation with a "Wicked Priest," possibly a Maccabean high priest of about 150 B.C.

The Shrine of the Book (Museum for the Dead Sea Scrolls) in Jerusalem, Israel.

Caves of the Qumran area in which the Dead Sea Scrolls were discovered.

Beliefs and Practices The Scrolls show a surprising variety of beliefs, accounted for by two hundred years of community history, beginning with a belief In an eminent "end of days" which faded as the fulfilment did not materialize. Like other Essenes, they believed that by observing their own interpretation of the Jewish law and by frequent ritual bathing they preserved a faithful remnant. Thus they were ready for the restoration of the land by God, who would punish the wicked through two messiahs—one priestly, one lay. They had an interest in angels, astrology, and prophetic prediction. Peculiar to Qumran was a dualistic view of the world in which God had appointed an angel of light (one of his names

being Melchizedek; see Gen. 14; Heb. 7) and an angel of darkness to govern the world, all persons being assigned to the realm of one or the other. They also avoided the Temple and developed distinctive liturgical beliefs and practices based on a communion between earthly and angelic worship.

Philip R. Davies

DEAFNESS The inability to hear. According to the Old Testament God makes persons deaf or hearing (Ex. 4:11). The deaf were protected by the Mosaic law (Lev. 19:14). The inability to hear is used as an image for waiting on God rather than resisting attackers (Ps. 38:13–14). Deafness is also symbolic of inattentiveness to and rebellion against God (Isa. 42:18–20; 43:8). Part of the future hope of the prophets is that the deaf will hear (Isa. 42:18–20; 43:8). The enemies of Israel would experience deafness in response to God's restoration of Israel (Mic. 7:16).

The New Testament interprets Jesus' healing of the deaf as evidence of Jesus's Messiahship (Matt. 11:5; Luke 7:22). Strangely, only Mark narrated the healing of a deaf person (Mark 7:33–35; compare 9:14–29). Mark 9:25 attributes deafness to an evil spirit. The parallel narratives (Matt. 17:14–19; Luke 9:37–42) emphasize epilectic-like fits rather than deafness.

DEATH Unlike the Greeks, who largely understood a person as a soul entrapped in a body, the ancient Hebrews depicted the person as a psychosomatic (body-soul) unity. When this body-soul union failed in death, the Hebrews did not visualize the escape of the soul from the body, but the actual death of the self.

The Old Testament does not, however, teach that persons were annihilated at death. Rather, the dead in some sense remained in Sheol, the place of the dead located deep beneath the earth. This belief is expressed in the Genesis 25:8 report of Abraham's death. Abraham survived after a fashion with and in the vicinity of his ancestors because he was buried in the family grave (Gen. 15:15; 35:29; Judg. 8:32). Existence in Sheol was a "shade" existence, symbolized by the bones which remained and survived in the grave.

To the Israelite, death and Sheol were both acceptable and unacceptable. Especially when life was long and blessed (Abraham, Gen. 25:8; David, 1 Chron. 29:28), the Israelites accepted death with some degree of grace. They found consolation in long life, many children, remembrance of the family name, and burial in the family grave (Gen. 15:15).

When death occurred in the prime of life or without children or without proper burial, it was strictly understood as a curse. In fact, because of the Hebrews' love of life and conviction that Yahweh was the Author of life, death and Sheol always represented either a potential or actual threat. The Old Testament calls Sheol "the pit" (Isa. 38:17–18; Ezek. 26:19–21; Jonah 2:1–6), personifies it as "the king of terrors" (Job 18:13–14), and describes it as a house or city with bars (Job 17:16) where gloomy darkness prevails (Ps. 88:12).

Furthermore, because of the Hebrews' emphasis on group identity, death could be accepted in that the *group* survived. Injustice could be accepted in individual lives (for example, prosperity among the wicked, misfortune among the righteous) because it was assumed that justice eventually prevailed in the *group*. By the time of the Babylonian Exile, this pattern of passive acceptance began to change. Job and Ecclesiastes questioned the idea that justice is always served in this life. Ezekiel and Jeremiah affirmed that God's justice could not be satisfied simply by reference to the group, but had to apply to the individual (Jer. 31:29–30,33–34; Ezek. 18:19–20). Finally, the Book of Daniel teaches that to serve justice in individual lives, the dead had to be raised by God, "some to everlasting life, and some to shame and everlasting contempt" (Dan. 12:2). Some Bible students see resurrection hope suggested or even clearly taught in other Old Testament passages. See *Resurrection.*

The Old Testament recognized the theological meaning of death as well as its physical meaning. The account of Adam and Eve in the Garden of Eden (Gen. 2—3) clearly points to sin as the reason humans must experience death (2:17; 3:3). Other passages echo the same teaching (Num. 18:22; Prov. 6:12–19; Jer. 31:29–30; Ezek. 18:1–32).

Death in the Synoptic Gospels and Acts Several passages in the Synoptic Gospels (Matthew, Mark, and Luke) and Acts imply a positive, or at least neutral, attitude toward death. In Luke's birth narrative, for example, Simeon asked God to let him "depart in peace" because he had seen God's salvation (2:29). Similar to the Old Testament accounts of some of the partriarchs, Simeon's death would be the peaceful resignation of a life dedicated to God. In a Sermon on the Mount

saying (Matt. 6:27; Luke 12:25), Jesus counseled His hearers with a rhetorical question, "and which of you by being anxious can add a single cubit to his life's span?" (NAS). If this translation is correct (some interpreters prefer "stature" to "span of life"), the teaching implies that mortality is a fact which must be accepted by Jesus' followers and entrusted to God.

In other passages death is seen as ominous and threatening. In the account of the stilling of the storm (Matt. 8:23–27; Mark 4:35–41; Luke 8:22–25), the disciples cried out desperately against the raging water. In Acts 5:1–11 Ananias and Sapphira died because they committed perjury against the Holy Spirit. Luke 1:79 and Matthew 4:16 use the phrase "shadow of death" as a negative image. In Luke 7:22–23, Jesus vindicated His ministry in the face of John the Baptist's question by revealing His power against the realm of death: the dead are raised, the demons are cast out, the lame walk, the deaf hear, the blind see.

The most striking feature of the Synoptic Gospels' understanding of death is the central place given to Jesus' death. In His death the positive and negative aspects just discussed come together: Jesus overturned death in the community and ran toward His own death; He agonized over His fate in Jerusalem and wished it were already accomplished; He announced with word and deed the Resurrection Age, but He could not completely welcome His own accursed death which resurrection would vindicate. Above all else, death in the Synoptic Gospels is interpreted by the paradoxical death of the Servant who found life through the means of death.

Death in the Letters of Paul Paul's understanding of Jesus' death and resurrection determined his depiction of death as a quality of human existence. The most fundamental facet of this understanding is that death has been defeated (1 Cor. 15:26; 2 Tim. 1:8–10). Paul's conviction was confirmed: (1) through his assurances to the Thessalonians that their dead were not disadvantaged (1 Thess. 4:13–18); (2) through his concept of the firstfruits (Rom. 8:23; 1 Cor. 5:20); (3) through his doctrine of the eventual transformation of the resurrection body (1 Cor. 15:35–58), and (4) through his conviction that the proper Christian response to death and all of its signs is an indomitable hope (Rom. 8:31–38; 1 Cor. 15:58; 1 Thess. 4:18). Simply put, Paul pictures the Christian's death as nonfinal and nonthreatening.

Death is nonetheless an enemy. It is intimately connected with sin (Rom. 3:23; 5:12–21). Paul used death imagery to characterize sinful existence (Rom. 6:13, 7:7–25, 8:6–8; Eph. 2:1, 5; Col. 2:13). If the "old" existence should be thought of as death, conversion to Christ is nothing less than rebirth (Rom. 6:5–11; Gal. 2:20). Paul's image of rebirth is realistic to the extent that he acknowledged the incompleteness of our death and resurrection with Christ. In the same paragraph that he announced our union with Christ, he felt compelled to remind Christians that they should consider themselves dead to sin but alive to God in Christ (Rom. 6:11).

Death in the Writings of John As much or more than Paul, John redefined death (and life) in relationship to Jesus. In the fourth Gospel especially, how the hearers respond to Jesus is a matter of life and death: "Verily, verily, I say unto you, He that heareth my word, and believeth on him that sent me, hath everlasting life, and shall not come into condemnation; but is passed from death unto life" (John 5:24). The account of Lazarus' resuscitation in John 11 makes this point more dramatically. Jesus waited until Lazarus had been dead four days and declared to Martha, "I am the resurrection, and the life: he that believeth in me, though he were dead, yet shall he live: And whosoever liveth and believeth in me shall never die" (John 11:25–26). Jesus went on to call Lazarus from the tomb; but in doing so, he ironically sealed His own death in the plans of the Jewish authorities (John 11:45–53).

Conclusions The New Testament assumed the Old Testament concept of body-soul unity and the late Old Testament and intertestamental concept of resurrection. Unlike Greek philosophers who downplayed the significance of death by emphasizing the immortality of the soul, the biblical writers affirmed that death is real. Because the Bible also affirms the value of life as a gift from God, death is sometimes depicted as threatening and never entirely desirable. The doctrine of resurrection is an affirmation that even the realm of the dead belongs to God and that death is overcome only at His gracious command.

The distinctive contribution of the New Testament is that it relentlessly defines human life, death, and resurrection in light of Jesus' life, death, and resurrection. Thus death is removed from its normal context at the end of life and placed in the very middle of life; in *Christ* we die and are raised as we commit our lives to Him.

Joe Haag

DEATH OF CHRIST See *Cross, Crucifixion; Christ; Jesus.*

DEATH, SECOND Final separation from God; spiritual death following physical death. Revelation describes the second death with the images of the lake of fire (20:14) and a lake burning with fire and sulphur (21:8). The second death has no power over those who remain faithful in persecution (2:11), who are martyred (20:6), or for those whose names are written in the book of life (20:15). Some stress everlasting punishment in literal fire. Others stress the spiritual state of separation from God. Still others interpret the second death in terms of anihilation on the basis

of comparison with Matthew 10:28. The alternative is eternal life with God.

DEBIR (Dē′ bĭr) Personal and place name meaning, "back, behind." As a common noun, the Hebrew term refers to the back room of the Temple, the holy of holies. *1.* King of Eglon who joined in Jerusalem-led coalition against Joshua and lost (Josh. 10:3). Nothing else about him is known. See *Eglon.*

2. Important city in hill country of tribe of Judah whose exact location is debated by archaeologists and geographers. Joshua annihilated its residents (Josh. 10:38; compare 11:21; 12:13). Joshua 15:15 describes Caleb's challenge to Othniel to capture Debir, formerly called Kiriath Sepher. Compare Judges 1:11. Joshua 15:49 gives yet another name, Kiriath Sannah, to Debir. It became a levitical city for the priests (Josh. 21:15). Different scholars locate Debir at tell beit Mirsim, thirteen miles southwest of Hebron; khirbet Tarrameh, five miles southwest of Hebron; and khirbet Rabud, seven and a half miles west of Hebron. It may have been the most important town south of Hebron.

3. A town on the northern border of Judah (Josh. 15:7). This may be located at thoghret ed Debr, the "pass of Debir," ten miles east of Jerusalem.

4. A town in Gad east of the Jordan given various spellings in the Hebrew Bible: *Lidebor* (Josh. 13:26); *Lwo Debar* (2 Sam. 9:4–5); *Lo' Debar* (2 Sam. 17:27); *Lo' Dabar* (Amos 6:13). The city may be modern Umm el-Dabar, twelve miles north of Pella. It apparently was near Mahanaim, where first Ish-bosheth and then David while fleeing Absalom, made their headquarters. Some Bible students have suggested a location at tell el-Chamme or khirbet Chamid.

DEBORAH (Dĕb′ ô räh) Personal name meaning, "bee." Deborah is the name of two women in the Bible, Rebekah's nurse (Gen. 35:8; 24:59) and a leader of pre-monarchic Israel (Judg. 4—5).

1. Deborah, Rebekah's nurse, died and was buried near Bethel. She had been part of the household of Jacob, Rebekah's son.

2. Deborah, the leader of Israel, is identified as a prophetess, a judge, and the wife of Lapidoth (Judg. 4:4). She probably lived about 1200 B.C. or slightly later during a period of Canaanite oppression. Deborah is described in Judg. 5:7 as "a mother in Israel" because of her role in delivering God's people. After Moses, only Samuel filled the same combination of offices: prophet, judge, and military leader.

Deborah served regularly as a judge, hearing and deciding cases brought to her by the people of Israel. She held court at "the palm tree of Deborah," in the southern part of the territory of Ephraim, between Ramah and Bethel (Judg. 4:4–5).

Nothing is said about the procedures at her court or about the extent of her jurisdiction.

As a prophet, Deborah summoned Barak and delivered an oracle giving him God's instructions for a battle in the Jezreel Valley against the Canaanite army commanded by Sisera (Judg. 4:6–9; compare Samuel in 1 Sam. 15:2–3 and the unnamed prophet in 1 Kings 20:13–15). Barak obeyed, and the Israelites won the battle. Some scholars believe that Deborah as prophet also composed the victory poem she and Barak sang in Judges 5. Deborah's authority under God was evidenced by Barak's desire to have her present with him in the army camp (Judg. 4:8,14) and by the testimony to her leadership in the song (Judg. 5:7,12,15). *Pamela J. Scalise*

DEBT, DEBTOR See *loan.*

DECALOGUE See *Ten Commandments.*

DECAPOLIS (Dė căp′ ō lĭs) Place name meaning, "ten cities." A group of Greek cities referred to in Matthew 4:25; Mark 5:20; 7:31, originally ten in number but including more cities at a later time. The second century A.D. writer Pliny named the ten cities as Damascus, Philadelphia (modern Amman), Canatha, Scythopolis, Pella, Hippos, Gadara, Dion, Raphana, and Gerasa (modern Jerash). Ptolemy, another second century writer, names eighteen cities in the Decapolis, omitting Raphana but adding nine others. A later source mentioned fourteen cities in the group. Thus the number varied from time to time. They were established after the time of Alexander the Great and were predominantly Greek in culture and influence. These cities were scattered south and east of the Sea of Galilee. Only Scythopolis was west of the Jordan River. Josephus named it as the greatest of the group.

The "Decapolis" is mentioned only in Matthew and Mark in the Bible. In Mark 5:20, Jesus healed a demoniac after which the man "began to publish in Decapolis how great things Jesus had done for him." Mark 7:31 states that after Jesus went to

Colonnade along the main road through the ruins of the ancient Decapolis city of Gerasa (modern Jerash).

the region of Tyre and Sidon he went "through the midst of the coasts of Decapolis." Matthew 4:25 adds no more to our knowledge of these cities.

Traditionally the Decapolis is assumed to be a league of cities which preserved the stronghold of

Graeco-Roman theater in Amman, Jordan (the ancient Decapolis city of Philadelphia).

Greek thought and life in Palestine and resisted the Semitic influences of the Jews. According to Pliny, however, it was not a very solid political alliance. A recent view is that it was not even a league, but a geographical region. These cities do seem to have much in common; they were centers for the spread of Greco-Roman culture and had no great love for the Jews. They were associated with one another closely enough that in some ways they were considered as a group, if not as a league. See *Palestine.* *W. Thomas Sawyer*

DECISION, VALLEY OF See *Jehoshapat, Valley of.*

DECREE A royal order. Decrees were proclaimed publically by criers (Jonah 3:5–7) designated "heralds" (Dan. 3:4) often throughout the territory of the monarch (1 Sam. 11:7; Ezra 1:1). Decrees were written and stored in archives for later reference (Ezra 6:1–2). Scripture attributes just decrees to divine wisdom (Prov. 8:15). Scripture also recognizes unjust decrees (Isa. 10:1). Some important decrees include: Cyrus' decree on rebuilding the Temple (Ezra 6:3–5); Esther's decree on the celebration of Purim (Esther 9:32); and the decree of Caesar Augustus which set the scene for the birth of Christ (Luke 2:1).

As King of the earth, God issues decrees regulating the world of nature (the sea, Prov. 8:29; rain, Job 28:26) and of humanity (Dan. 4:24). God also decrees the reign of the Messianic King (Ps. 2:7).

The KJV uses "decree" to describe the decision of the Apostolic Council (Acts 16:4) and of a human inward decision not to marry (1 Cor. 7:37). NIV refers to God's righteous decree of death for sinners (Rom. 1:32). NAS uses "decree" for God's law which led to disobedience and death

(Col. 2:14,20). NRSV uses "decree" to speak of God's eternal wisdom and plan for creation. Any translator using "decree" is interpreting the meaning of a more general Hebrew or Greek term, resulting in each translation using "decree" for several different words of the original language.

DEDAN (Dē´ dăn) Personal and place name of unknown meaning. *1.* The original ancestor of an Arabian tribe listed in the table of nations as a son of Cush (Gen. 10:27). See *Cush. 2.* A grandson of Abraham (Gen. 25:3). Here as in 10:27, Dedan's brother is Sheba. Three otherwise unknown Arabian tribes descended from Dedan, according to Genesis 25:3. *3.* The Arabian tribe centered at al-Alula, 70 miles southwest of Tema and 400 miles from Jerusalem. It was a station on the caravan road between Tema and Medina. Jeremiah pronounced judgment against the Arabian tribes (Jer. 25:23), perhaps looking to Nebuchadnezzar's raid in Arabia in 599–598 B.C. Nabonidus, king of Babylon (556–539), left control of his kingdom to his son Belshazzar and worked in Arabia for a period, controlling Dedan among other cities. Dedan was a caravan center for incense trade (Isa. 21:13). Isaiah warned the traders from Dedan to avoid the regular caravan stations and spend the night in the wilderness. Neighbors from Tema would have to meet their food needs. Jeremiah warned merchants from Dedan working or staying in Edom to flee the country because God was bringing judgment on it (Jer. 49:8). Ezekiel warned Edom that their soldiers fleeing even to Dedan would be struck down (Ezek. 25:13). In judging Tyre, Ezekiel noted they, too, traded with Dedan (Ezek. 27:15,20). Compare Ezekiel 38:13.

DEDANIM (Dĕd´ å nĭm) or **DEDANITE** (Dĕd´ ån īte) A resident or citizen of the tribe of Dedan. See *Dedan.*

DEDICATE, DEDICATION A general term used in the Bible to describe an act of setting apart or consecrating persons or things to God (or gods), persons, sacred work, or ends. The act is usually accompanied by an announcement of what is being done or intended and by prayer asking for divine approval and blessing. In the Old Testament the people who were set apart included all Israel (Ex. 19:5,6; Deut. 7:6; 14:2) and the priests (Ex. 29:1–37). The things that were set apart included the altar in the tabernacle (Num. 7:10–88), images of pagan deities (Dan. 3:2,3), silver and gold (2 Sam. 8:11), Temple (1 Kings 8:63; Ezra 6:16–18), walls of Jerusalem (Neh. 12:27), and private dwellings (Deut. 20:5). The idea of dedication is embodied in the New Testament word "saints." The whole church is set apart to God (Eph. 5:26). The individual believer is one of a dedicated, sanctified, consecrated, priestly people; set apart "to offer up spiritual sacrifices,

acceptable to God by Jesus Christ" (1 Pet. 2:5).
Ray Robbins

DEDICATION, FEAST OF The term for Hanukkah in John 10:22. See *Festivals; Hanukkah.*

DEEP, THE English translation of the Hebrew term *tehom.* The deep constitutes the primeval waters of creation in Genesis 1:2. This concept is echoed dramatically in Psalm 104:5–7, where God is pictured as rebuking the waters of the deep, separating the waters from the mountains and valleys, and setting the boundaries for each. Creation includes the concept of bringing order by separating or dividing what is made, and keeping each in its proper place (Prov. 8:22–31). This thought is expressed in an interesting metaphor in Psalm 33:7, where God is said to have gathered the waters into a bottle (NRSV) and put the deeps into a storehouse.

In the account of the Exodus from Egypt, God's action in parting the waters for the Israelites to pass is expressed poetically as a dividing of the waters of the deep (Ex. 15:8). God held the waters in place as the Israelites crossed the sea, and released the waters when they reached the other side, shielding them from the Egyptians (Ps. 77:16–20). This was, theologically speaking, an act of creation—creating a people for the Lord, by freeing them from slavery in Egypt.

The waters of the deep can be destructive or constructive, curse or blessing. When the waters of the deep burst their bounds, the result is a flood (Gen. 7:11). At the extreme described in Genesis 7, it is a reversal of creation which can only be checked when God again sends the wind or spirit (*ruah*) which began creation (Gen. 1:2) and closes the fountains of the deep (Gen. 8:1–3). Storms at sea are also associated with the deep (Ps. 107:23–26; compare Jonah 2:6). In the poetry of the Psalms, the deep is a metaphor for the trials of life which seem overwhelming (Ps. 69:14–15). It could even represent the abode of the dead (Ps. 71:20).

On the other hand, the waters of the deep are a blessing, without which life could not continue. Deuteronomy 8:7 describes the Promised Land as a land of brooks, fountains, and deeps, which irrigate the land so that grain and fruit can be grown (Ezek. 31:4). When Jacob blessed his son Joseph with "blessings of the deep that lieth under," he was attempting to bestow fertility on Joseph and his offspring and on their land (Gen. 49:25; compare Deut. 33:13–17). As blessing and as curse, the deep reflects as power which only the creator God can control (Ps. 95:4).

The Greek Bible or Septuagint translated *tehom* as "abyss," bringing it into relationship with the pit, the abode of the dead (Rom. 10:7) and place of evil spirits (Luke 8:31), including the beast of the apocalypse (Rev. 17:8).   *Wilda W. Morris*

D

DEER See *Animals in the Bible.*

DEFILE To make ritually unclean. See *Clean, Cleanness.*

DEGREES, SONG OF The KJV phrase used in the titles of 15 Psalms (Pss. 120—134). Modern speech translations render the phrase, "Song of Ascents". Though the origin of the phrase is obscure, the generally accepted view is that the Hebrew term *ma‘aloth* (goings up) is a reference to pilgrims' going up to Jerusalem for the 3 required festivals. (Pss. 42:4; 122:4). Jerusalem was surrounded by mountains (Pss. 121:1; 125:2; 133:3), thus such trips involved a literal going up. It is conjectured that these psalms were sung on such occassions (Isa. 30:29; Ps. 132:7). Others have suggested that "ascents" is a reference to the rising melody of the psalms, the step-like poetic form of some of the psalms, or to the steps upon which the Levites performed music in the Temple. Jewish tradition relates the title to the fifteen steps leading from the court of the women to the court of Israel in the Temple.

DEHAVITE (Dė hā′ vīte) KJV transliteration of Aramaic text in Ezra 4:9. Modern translators read the text as two Aramaic words—*di-hu′*—meaning, "that is."

DEKAR (Dē′ kär) KJV reads "son of Dekar" in 1 Kings 4:9, where modern translations transliterate the Hebrew text to read, "Ben-deker." See *Ben-deker.*

DELILAH (Dė lī′ läh) Personal name meaning, "with long hair hanging down." A woman from the valley of Sorek who was loved by Samson (Judg. 16:4). She was probably a Philistine. She enticed Samson into revealing to her that the secret of his great strength lay in his hair, which had never been cut. Then, she betrayed him to the Philistines. While he slept, she had his head shaved, and he was captured, blinded, and bound by the Philistines. See *Samson; Judges.*

DELIVERANCE, DELIVERER Rescue from danger. In Scripture God gives deliverance (Pss. 18:50; 32:7; 44:4), often through a human agent. In the Old Testament deliverance most often refers to victory in battle (Judg. 15:18; 2 Kings 5:1; 13:17; 1 Chron. 11:14; 2 Chron. 12:7). Joseph was God's agent to deliver His people from famine (Gen. 45:7). The Old Testament consistently stresses God as the giver of deliverance rather than the human agent. Thus Mordecai warned Esther that is she failed to act out her role as deliverer God would provide another way (Esther 4:14). KJV also uses "deliverance" to describe the remanant that survives a battle or exile (Ezra 9:13). In KJV both New Testament uses of deliver-

ance refers to release of prisoners (Luke 4:18; Heb. 11:35). Modern translations use "deliverance" to refer to rescue from danger in Acts 7:25; Philippians 1:19.

A deliverer is one who rescues from danger. Two of the judges, Othniel and Ehud (Judg. 3:9,15), are called deliverers in the sense of military heroes. More often God is spoken of as the Deliverer of His people (2 Sam. 22:2; Ps. 18:2; 40:17; 144:2). The picture of God as deliverer is paralled with the images of a rock, fortress, helper, and strong tower. Acts 7:35 refers to Moses as a deliverer. Romans 11:26–27 refers to the Messianic King as the Deliverer who will take away Israel's sins.

The verb "deliver" is used in a wide range of contexts. According to Job 5:19–26 God delivers in 7 ways; from famine, war, the scourge of the tongue, the wild animals, to safety, abundant offspring, and long life. Scripture also speaks to deliverance from sin (Ps. 39:8; 79:9); the way of evil (Prov. 2:12); the power of evil (Matt. 6:13; Gal. 1:4; Col. 1:13); the body of death (Rom. 7:24); the law (Rom. 7:6); and the coming wrath of God (1 Thess. 1:10). God is the agent of deliverance in Colossians 1:13 and Romans 7:24–25. Christ is the agent in 1 Thessalonians 1:10 and Galatians 1:4, where Christ brings deliverance by giving Himself for sins.

DELUGE See *Flood.*

DEMAS (Dē′ màs) A companion and co-worker of Paul the apostle (Col. 4:14). Though in Philemon 24 Paul identified Demas as a "fellowlabourer," 2 Timothy 4:10 indicates that this man later deserted Paul, "having loved this present world."

DEMETRIUS (Dė mē′ trĭ ŭs) Personal name meaning, "belonging to Demeter, the Greek goddess of crops." *1.* A silversmith in Ephesus. He incited a riot directed against Paul because he feared that the apostle's preaching would threaten the sale of silver shrines of Diana, the patron goddess of Ephesus (Acts 19:24–41). Demetrius may have been a guild master in charge of producing small silver copies of Diana's temple with a figure of the goddess inside. *2.* Apparently a convert from the worship of Demeter, the god worshiped in the mystery religion at Eleusis near Athens. John commended him, saying, he "hath good report of all men, and of the truth itself" (3 John 12). He may have carried 3 John from John to its original readers.

DEMON POSSESSION The control of an individual's personality so that actions are influenced by an evil demonic spirit. Most of those described as demon-possessed in the New Testament are adult men, but certain women were also delivered from the influence of evil spirits (Luke 8:2; 13:11,16). The signs of demon possession in the New Testament include: speechlessness (Matt. 9:33); deafness (Mark 9:25); blindness (Matt. 12:22); fierceness (Matt. 8:28); unusual strength (Mark 5:4); convulsions (Mark 1:26); and foaming at the mouth (Luke 9:39). Most of the New Testament references to demon possession appear in the Gospels and represent the outburst of satanic opposition to God's work in Christ.

The Scripture writers are careful to distinguish between demon possession and disease. In Matthew 4:24 demon possession is listed with a variety of symptoms of other diseases including pain, epilepsy, and paralysis. The Gospel writers could distinguish between demon possession and these other diseases.

The features demonstrated by those who are demon possessed are incompatible with a theory of mere bodily or mental illness. The healing of the Gadarene demoniac in Mark 5 had fatal effects upon a nearby herd of swine (Mark 5:11–13). The same demoniac made an assertion of Christ's deity when the disciples of Jesus had not as yet shown any recognition of this fact (Mark 4:41; 5:7). Epilepsy and insanity would not cause such effects as these.

Descriptions of the experience of demon possession do not separate the actions of the possessed person from the actions of the demon (Mark 1:23; Luke 8:28). The power of the demon dominates the personality of the possessed person. Such bizarre behavior as masochism (Mark 5:5) and an unnatural voice (Mark 5:7) stems from the demon's control of the individual's self-expression.

Jesus treated the cases of demon possession as realities. He was neither putting on a performance nor pretending to agree with superstitious attitudes of the Jews. In His discussions with the Jews He assumed the reality of demon possession when He affirmed that His casting out of devils showed that the kingdom of God had come to His hearers (Matt. 12:23–27). The Jews of Jesus' time superstitiously believed that demons were lurking at every corner. They thought they could find them in rivers, seas, and on mountaintops. Demons were blamed for toothaches, headaches, broken bones, and outbursts of jealousy and anger. By way of contrast to this practice, the response of Jesus and the New Testament writers is very restrained.

The cure for demon possession in the New Testament is always faith in the power of Christ. The New Testament never shows Jesus or the apostles using magical rites to deliver the afflicted from demon possession. Whenever Christ spoke the word, the demons were forced to obey Him (Mark 1:27; Luke 4:41). Jesus entrusted this same power of exorcism to His disciples as they went out on mission for Him (Matt. 10:8).

Missionaries and Christian workers in foreign countries have encountered the biblical type of demon possession in some of their work. Those individuals who have experienced a release from demon possession by spiritual means have been able to lead normal healthy lives. Psychiatrists would describe demon possession in terms quite different from the Bible. The most useful solution to the problem will assume that the evil of human nature renders the mind especially susceptible to the influence of personal agents of evil.

Thomas D. Lea

DENARIUS (De năr′ ĭ ŭs) A coin representing a typical day's wage for an ordinary laborer (Matt. 20:2). The King James Version translates it "penny." This unit of Roman currency is the most frequently mentioned coin in the New Testament. See *Coins; Economic Life.*

A Roman denarius.

DEN OF LIONS A place where lions live, at times a thicket (Jer. 50:44) or cave (Nah. 2:12). See *Animals.*

DENY To disown or disassociate oneself from someone or to dispute that an assertion (Mark 14:70) or event (Acts 4:16) is true. The Old Testament speaks of disassociating oneself from God (Josh. 24:27; Prov. 30:9). Peter's denial of Jesus (Matt. 26:34,69–75; Mark 14:30,66–72; Luke 22:34,56–62) should be understood in this sense, since Peter three times disassociated himself from Jesus, claiming not to be one of His group. Fear of death or persecution leads some to deny, that is, disassociate themselves from Jesus (Matt. 10:33; Mark 8:38; Luke 12:9; 2 Tim. 2:12), resulting in Jesus' disassociation from them at the judgment. It is possible that 2 Peter. 2:1 and Jude 4 should be understood in this sense as well. To deny oneself is a special case in which a person disassociates oneself from self interest to serve a higher cause. Here the idea of denial is paralleled by the picture of taking up Jesus' cross and following Him (Matt. 16:24; Mark 8:34; Luke 9:23).

John the Baptist denied or disputed the assertion that he was the Christ (John 1:19–20). The "antichrists" of 1 John 2:22 disputed the teaching that Jesus is the Christ. Possibly 2 Peter 2:1 and Jude 4 are to be understood in this sense.

DEPOSIT Something given as a downpayment (See *Pledge*); money invested with a banker for the purpose of drawing interest (Matt. 25:27); something given to another for safekeeping (Ex. 22:7). Ex. 22:7–13 gives guidelines for cases in which property left for safekeeping is stolen or a deposited animal is injured or dies. Lev. 6:2–7 gives guidelines for one wishing to confess mishandling a deposit.

DEPTHS The deep places of the sea (Ex. 15:5,8; Pss. 68:22; 77:16; 78:15), an underground spring (Deut. 8:7; Prov. 8:24), the earth's interior (Ps. 95:4; Isa. 44:23), and by extension Sheol, the subterranean abode of the dead (Pss. 63:9; 71:20). "The depths" is used figuratively for the unsearchable (Prov. 25:3), for the womb (Ps. 139:15), and perhaps for tragedy (Ps. 130:1). See *Deep*.

DEPUTY An official of secondary rank (1 Kings 22:47); KJV term for a Roman proconsul (Acts 13:7; 18:12; 19:38). See *Proconsul*.

DERBE (Dêr' bè) Important city in region of Lycaonia in province of Galatia in Asia minor. It is apparently near modern Kerti Huyuk. The residents of Derbe and Lystra spoke a different language from the people to the north in Iconium. Paul visited Derbe on his first missionary journey (Acts 14:6), fleeing from Iconium. Persecution in Lystra led to a successful preaching mission in Derbe (14:20–21). On the second journey, Paul returned to Derbe (Acts 16:1). He apparently visited again on the third journey (18:23). Paul's fellow minister Gaius was from Derbe (20:4).

DESCENT The path down a mountain (Luke 19:37); a geneology, line of ancestors (Heb. 7:3,6).

DESCENT TO HADES A phrase taken from the Apostles' Creed describing the work of the resurrected Christ. The idea of descent to Hades was a theme of many ancient religions to describe the work of a religious hero. First Peter 3:19 says Christ "went and preached unto the spirits in prison." Many interpretations have been given for this. The time may be seen as the days of Noah (v. 20) and thus describe the work of the preexistent Christ or the work of Christ's spirit through Noah. It may be seen as immediately following Christ's resurrection. The content of His preaching may have been judgment; it may have been affirmation of His victory over "angels, authorities, and powers" (v. 22); it may have been release from Sheol

or Hades for saints who preceded Him. The spirits may have been the "sons of God" of Genesis 6:2, the people of Noah's day, the Old Testament sinners, Old Testament people who were true to God, fallen angels, the evil spirits or demonic powers whom Jesus contested in His earthly ministry. The prison may have been Sheol or Hades according to Old Testament thinking, a special place of captivity for sinners, a place of punishment for fallen angels, a place of security for such angels where they thought they could escape Christ's power, or a place on the way to heaven where the faithful of old waited to hear the message of Christ's final atoning victory. Whatever the detailed explanation of each of the phrases, the ultimate purpose is to glorify Christ for His completed work of salvation through His death, resurrection, and ascension, showing He has control of all places and powers.

DESERT Areas with little rainfall to the east and south of Palestine and inhabited by nomads with flocks and herds. Three major deserts figure in biblical events: the plateau east of the mountains to the east of Jordan River; the area south of Edom, and the triangle bordered by Gaza, the Dead Sea, and the Red Sea. The Bible pictures raiders from the desert—Amalekites, Midianites, Ishmaelites—threatening Palestine farmers. Saul relieved some of this pressure (1 Sam. 14:48).

Palestine's desert areas received brief if hard rains in March and April. At times they blossomed briefly, but long dry spells returned its normal desert characteristics. The Hebrew language distinguishes with several words what English describes as desert or wilderness.

Midbar is the most prominent and inclusive term but is used in several different contexts with differing meaning. It can describe the southern boundary of the Promised Land (Ex. 23:31; Deut. 11:24). This southern wilderness can be divided into various parts: Shur (Ex. 15:22); Sin (Ex. 16:1); Paran (Num. 12:16); Zin (Num. 13:21). This entire southern desert region can be called the wilderness of Sinai (Ex. 19:1) above which rises Mount Sinai. North of this is the wilderness of Judah (Judg. 1:16), lying east of the road connecting Jerusalem and Hebron. Here deep, narrow gorges lead down from the Judean hills to the Dead Sea. *Midbar* also describes the area surrounding a settlement where herds are pastured (1 Sam. 23:24; 24:1; 2 Chron. 20:20; compare Josh. 8:24). Settlements in the desert arose particularly during times of political stability and served as military stations against bedouin invasions and as protection for commerce on the desert trade routes.

'Arabah often appears as a synonym for *midbar*. This is the basic term for the long rift reaching from the Sea of Galilee to the Dead Sea and on down to the Red Sea. It describes ground domi-

nated by salt with little water or plants. *'Arabah* is never used to describe pasturelands. It serves as the eastern boundary of the Promised Land and is often translated, "plain," if it is not transliterated as "Arabah" (Deut. 3:17; Josh. 12:1).

Yeshimon designates the wasteland which is unproductive. The word appears either in parallel with *midbar* or as part of a territorial designation such as in 1 Samuel 23:24. See *Jeshimon.* God holds out hope for restoration of the wild lands (Isa. 43:19–20).

Chorbah describes hot, dry land or land with destroyed settlements. It can designate dry land opposed to water-covered land (Gen. 7:22; Ex. 14:21). It describes the desert in Psalms 102:7; 106:9; Isaiah 25:5; 50:2; 51:3; 64:10; Jeremiah 25:9.

Tsiyyah points to a dry region (Job 30:3; Ps. 78:17; 105:41; Isa. 35:1; Jer. 50:12; Zeph. 2:13).

Shamamah is a desolate and terrifying land and often indicates God's destruction of a place (Ex. 23:29; Lev. 26:33, Jer. 4:27; Ezek. 6:14; 23:33).

Negeb refers to the dry land and is a technical name for the southern desert whose northern border lies north of Beersheba. Annual rainfall ranges from 100 to 300 millimeters a year. Rainfall varies drastically year to year. Negeb came to mean "south" in Hebrew and could be translated the "south country" (Gen. 24:62).

Wasteland of the northern Negeb (Negev) in southern Israel.

The dry, mostly uninhabited desert held fear and awe for Israel. It could be described like the original chaos prior to creation (Deut. 32:10; Jer. 4:23–26). Israel was able to go through the desert because God led them (Deut. 1:19). Its animal inhabitants caused even more fear—snakes and scorpions (Deut. 8:15); wild donkeys (Jer. 2:24). The desert lay waste without humans or rain (Job 38:26; Jer. 2:6). The desert was a "terrifying land" (Isa. 21:1 NAS). The only expectation for a person in the wilderness was death by starvation (Ex. 16:3).

God's judgment could turn a city into desert (Jer. 4:26), but His grace could turn the wilderness into a garden (Isa. 41:17–20).

In the New Testament the desert was the place of John the Baptist's ministry (Luke 1:80; 3:4) and where demon-possession drove a man (Luke 8:29). The crowds forced Jesus into the unpopulated desert to preach (Mark 1:45). Jesus took His disciples there to rest (Mark 6:31). See *Wilderness.*   *Trent C. Butler*

DESIGN Modern translations' reading for an artistic pattern (Ex. 31:4; 39:3; 2 Chr. 2:14; KJV, "cunning works"); RSV translation for plans, generally in the negative sense of schemes or wiles (Job 10:3; 2 Cor. 2:11). KJV has "Counsel" and "devices."

DESIRE OF ALL NATIONS Phrase Haggai used in his prophecy of a renewed Temple (Hag. 2:7). Some translations (KJV, NIV) interpret the underlying Hebrew as a prophecy of the coming Messiah. Other translations render the phrase "treasure" (TEV, NRSV, REB) or "wealth" (NAS) of all nations in parallel to the gold and silver of 2:8. The messianic interpretation first appears in the Latin Vulgate translation, while the treasures would show Yahweh's power to restore the glory of His house despite the people's poverty.

DESOLATION, ABOMINATION OF See *Abomination of Desolation.*

DESTINY Word used in modern translations for God's act in electing or predestinating people and nations. See *Election; Fate; Predestination.*

DESTROYER An invading army (Isa. 49:17; Jer. 22:7) or a supernatural agent of God's judgment (Ex. 12:23; Heb. 11:28), often termed an angel (2 Sam. 24:15–16; 2 Kings 19:35; Ps. 78:49). All stand under God's sovereign control as he directs human affairs.

DESTROYING LOCUSTS See *Insects.*

DETAINED BEFORE THE LORD To remain in the presence of the Lord at the Tabernacle or Temple (1 Sam. 21:7). The reason for Doeg's remaining at the Tabernacle is not given. Perhaps he was there to fulfill a vow, receive an oracle, perform an act of penance, or to celebrate a holiday. 1 Sam. 21:6 suggests that it was the Sabbath. (See Mark 2:25–26).

DEUEL (Dēū′ ĕl) Personal name meaning, "God knows." In Numbers 1:14, the father of Eliasaph, the leader in the wilderness of the tribe of Gad. Numbers 2:14 identifies Eliasaph's father as Reuel. Deuel and Reuel may be alternative forms of the same name, probably representing a copyist's misreading of Hebrew "d" and "r," which are quite similar.

DEUTERONOMY, THE BOOK OF English name of fifth book of Old Testament taken from Greek translation meaning, "second law." Deuteronomy is the last of five books of Law and should not be read in isolation from the other four books (Genesis, Exodus, Leviticus, Numbers). Pentateuch (five books) is the familiar title associated with these five books of Law, the first and most important division of the Hebrew Bible. By longstanding tradition these books have been associated with Moses, the human instrument of God's deliverance of Israel from bondage in Egypt and the negotiator of the covenant between God and Israel.

Title The probable origin of the title "Deuteronomy" is the translation in the Septuagint (Greek translation of the Hebrew Old Testament) of Deuteronomy 17:18–19. These two verses contain instructions to the king about making "a copy of this law" to be read regularly and obeyed faithfully. The Septuagint translators rendered the above phrase "this second law" instead of "a copy of this law." The Septuagint translation implies a body of legislation different from that contained in the previous books of Law. That does not seem to be the point of the instruction in Deuteronomy 17:18–19. This apparent Greek mistranslation is the likely source of the title "Deuteronomy."

The title used in the Hebrew Bible, "these (are) the words" (two words in Hebrew), follows an

The hands of a Jewish man with the long strips of his phylactery intertwined with his fingers as he prays.

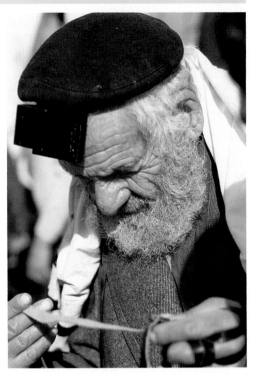

Jewish man in prayer at the Wailing Wall wearing his phylactery (containing Scripture from Deuteronomy).

ancient custom of using words from the first line of the text to designate a book. Sometimes the title in the Hebrew Bible was shortened to "words." This title more accurately defines the contents of the book than our familiar English title, Deuteronomy. In the main the book consists of the words by which Moses addressed Israel prior to their entry into the Promised Land. The style is sermonic, that of a preacher addressing his congregation with words designed to move them to obedience and commitment.

Background Deuteronomy is not primarily a law book or a book of history. It claims to be the words of Moses addressed to Israel on the eve of their entry into Canaan. Their wanderings in the wilderness were at an end. Their early efforts at conquest of the Promised Land east of the Jordan had met with success.

Israel's Exodus from Egypt and the covenant at Sinai were the stages of Israel's birth as a nation. As yet they were a nation without a homeland. God's covenant with Israel at Sinai was in part a renewal of earlier covenants made with the patriarchs. Included in those covenants were the following promises: (1) that Israel would be God's special nation, (2) that Yahweh God would be their God, (3) that they would be obedient to God, and (4) that God would give them a homeland and innumerable descendants.

Now Israel was poised on the borders of Canaan

ready to enter and to possess the Land of Promise. Moses, knowing that Israel's future hung on their obedience and commitment to God, led the people in a covenant renewal ceremony. Moses' approaching death and resulting transfer of human leadership to Joshua, plus Israel's approaching battles in conquest of the land, formed the basis for renewal of the covenant.

Contents Deuteronomy contains not one, but three (or more) addresses from Moses to Israel. Most interpreters agree that the structure of the book is patterned after Near Eastern vassal treaties.

Deuteronomy 1:1–5 is an introduction, giving the time and place of the addresses. The time is "the fortieth year" (Deut. 1:3) of wilderness wandering, "in the eleventh month, on the first day of the month." The place is "on this side Jordan in the wilderness" (Deut. 1:1) and, more particularly, "in the land of Moab" (Deut. 1:5).

Deuteronomy 1:6—4:40 is Moses' first address in which he recounted Israel's journey from Horeb to Moab and urged Israel to be faithful to Yahweh. Moses used Israel's immediate past history to teach the present generation of Israelites the importance of trusting God. Israel's obedience was imperative if they were to expect to possess

A Jewish rabbi opening a Torah (Genesis through Deuteronomy) case for a ceremony at the Western, or Wailing, Wall in Jerusalem. Jewish people consider the wall sacred but were forbidden to worship at it during Turkish, British, and Jordanian rule.

the land of Canaan. Moses set up cities of refuge on the east bank of the Jordan (Deut. 4:41–43).

Deuteronomy 4:44—28:68 contains Moses' second address to Israel. The address is introduced in Deuteronomy 4:44–49. Then Moses proceeded to teach Israel lessons from the law. These are not laws to be used in the courts to decide legal cases, but instructions for life in the land of Canaan.

Moses' third address is found in Deuteronomy 29:1—30:20. The focus is upon covenant renewal. Repentance and commitment would assure life and the blessings of God. Rebellion would result in their death as a nation. The choice was theirs.

Deuteronomy 31:1–29 is Moses' farewell address. The song of Moses is given in Deuteronomy 31:30—32:52. Moses' blessing is reported in chapter 33, and his death is recounted in chapter 34.

Date and Authorship The date when Deuteronomy was put in its final form was relatively late. Internal evidence seems to favor a time after the Mosaic era. The author makes third person references to Moses instead of first person statements about himself as one would expect Moses to do. "Beyond the Jordan," a common phrase used for the territory east of that river, gives the perspective of a writer within the land of Canaan.

The Near Eastern vassal treaty form of Deuteronomy has been used by scholars to argue for a date for the book in the Mosaic period or shortly thereafter. Other scholars use the same information to argue for a date closer to 600 B.C. Differences in form between early Hittite treaties and later Assyrian treaties when compared to Deuteronomy are the bases for deciding in favor of an early or a later date for Deuteronomy. Such comparisons of the structure of Deuteronomy with the structure of Near Eastern vassal treaties do not provide firm evidence for dating Deuteronomy either early or late.

The "book of the law" found during the repair of the Temple in the eighteenth year of Josiah's reign (621 B.C.) has been identified as Deuteronomy since the early church fathers shortly after 300 A.D. That identity cannot be proved, but the nature of the reforms of Josiah and the contents of Deuteronomy show an interesting similarity. For example, the call for centralization of worship (Deut. 12) is matched by Josiah's destruction of all altars except the one in the Temple in Jerusalem (2 Kings 23:4–20).

All the basic material in Deuteronomy seems to be quite ancient, but the book seems to have been edited after the death of Moses. No doubt Moses gave such addresses to Israel as the book reflects when it became known to him that God would not permit him to lead Israel into the Promised Land.

Purpose The sermonic style of Deuteronomy suits

it well to serve just as most interpreters agree that it served originally. Deuteronomy is a call to repentance, a plea for God's disobedient people to mend their ways and renew the covenant God made with them at Sinai. Moses had led Israel to the borders of Canaan nearly forty years before, but in rebellion and unbelief the people turned back into the wilderness. Now the new generation of Israelites stood on the borders of the Promised Land. Would they turn back in rebellion and unbelief?

The approaching death of Moses put urgency into his appeal for covenant renewal. He called for obedience through love to Yahweh, the loving God, who had established the covenant with Israel. Moses was convinced that only through a renewed relationship with God could the new generation of Israelites hope to succeed under Joshua's leadership in possessing the land. No doubt Joshua used the materials of Deuteronomy when he led Israel in a covenant renewal ceremony at Shechem (Josh. 8:30—35). Later, covenant renewal became a regular feature of Israel's cult. Deuteronomy must have been used in these ceremonies.

Teaching Deuteronomy continues to exercise strong influence on God's people. In many ways it remains a guide to life under God. It reminds of the great things God has done and wants to do for His people. It calls to faith and action in response to God's acts. It holds high the belief in the uniqueness of God as the only God without rivals. Thus it points to worship of any other god as vain, without meaning or hope. It shows the Ten Commandments as the center of the covenant relationship for believers. It holds up love of God as the basic relationship God wants with His people. It calls for total separation from pagan practices and godless life-styles. It seeks to establish a community at rest, free from internal strife and external war. It focuses on the needs of the least privileged members of society, calling on God's people to meet their needs. It teaches that the commitment of people finds reflection in action. It pronounces curses on evildoers who forsake God's covenant and blessings on those faithful to the covenant. From first to last, it calls for repentance and renewal of faith.

Outline

I. Introduction: Historical Setting (1:1–5)
II. Moses' First Sermon: Learn from God's Saving Acts (1:6—4:43)
    A. Historical memories call for present faith action (1:6—3:29)
    B. God's Word is the foundation for His people's life (4:1–43)
III. Second Sermon: God's Law Guides and Gives Unique Identity to God's People (4:44—28:68)
    A. Covenant faith demands total allegiance and unchanging love for God (4:44—11:32)
    B. God expresses His demands in worship, leadership, daily life, business life, legal practices, family life, and care for others (12:1—28:68).
IV. Third Sermon: God Seeks to Renew Covenant Relationships (29:1—30:20).
V. Conclusion: God Seeks Continuity in Leadership for His People (31:1—34:12).

Billy K. Smith

DEVIL, SATAN, EVIL, DEMONIC The personal dimension of that which opposes God's purposes in His world. For some people, belief in a personal Satan is part of mankind's nursery furniture. The concept of a personal Satan, however, has remained a part of evangelical thought. The present-day Christian who accepts the biblical teaching concerning Satan is not committed to all of the crude imagery that has sprung up around belief in Satan. In the light of medieval and modern distortions, a careful consideration of the biblical teaching concerning Satan is especially needed.

Old Testament Teaching A fully defined doctrine of Satan is not fund in the Bible until New Testament times. A number of reasons have been suggested for the relatively limited material on Satan in the Old Testament.

God began His self-revelation in the ancient world of polytheism (belief in many gods). God wanted to lead His people to a dynamic practical monotheism (the belief in and worship of one God). In the Old Testament a primary emphasis is placed on the supremacy of and the power of the God of Abraham, Isaac, and Jacob, who delivered the Hebrews from the slavery of Egypt.

Satan, the chief of the fallen angels, is mentioned in a number of places in the Old Testament. It is clear that from the very moment of the creation of this world that Satan and fallen angels were on the scene, rebels against God. Satan was evidently perfect in his original state. Pride seems to have been the cause of his fall. Disguised as a serpent, he was the agent of temptation for the first man and woman (Gen. 3:10; Rev. 12:9; 20:2). When Satan does appear in the Old Testament he is always the adversary of God's people. He seeks to lead God's people into presumption (1 Chron. 21:1) or slanders them to God's face (Zech. 3:1).

The most extensive Old Testament discussion of Satan is in Job. Here he is seen as God's agent and minister, who tested human fidelity. He makes a wager with God using Job as the stake. He acts, however, with the express permission of God and keeps within the limits which God has fixed for him (Job 1:12; 2:6).

New Testament Teaching By the time the New Testament books were written, God had led their authors to a clear-cut doctrine of Satan. This doctrine located an origin of evil in Satan. This recognizes the reality of evil outside and beyond the scope of human will. The New Testament avoids identifying evil with the direct will of God and keeps it always and finally subordinate to God.

Matthew, Mark, and Luke clearly accept and teach a doctrine of a personal Satan and his agents called fallen angels or demons (Mark 3:22). Matthew 4:1 tells of Jesus being tempted by the devil in the wilderness. In Matthew 25:41 even hell is described as being prepared for the devil and his angels. Satan and demons are seen as able to inflict disease (Matt. 17:5–18; Luke 13:16). Satan possessed Judas (Luke 22:3). John saw Satan as the prince of this world (John 12:31; 14:30; 16:11) with the whole world in his power (1 John 5:19).

The apostle Paul's world view teaches that Satan is the god of this age. The cosmos or unredeemed world is at present under Satan's power. Satan is now the "commander of the spiritual powers of the air" (Eph. 2:2 REB) and leads "the superhuman forces of evil in the heavenly realms" (Eph. 6:12 REB).

The general New Testament Epistles describe Satan's activities graphically. Second Peter 2:4 speaks of the "angels that sinned" and Jude 6 of the "angels which kept not their first estate." The constant use of violence and deceit by Satan requires that believers manifest courage and extreme vigilance (Jas. 4:7; 1 Pet. 5:8–9).

The book of Revelation sees Satan's activities as involving not only individuals but communities. Political forces can become servants of the devil (Rev. 12; 13). Revelation 2:13 even speaks of a throne of Satan.

It should be remembered that the New Testament teaches that Satan and his demonic allies are not coequal with God. He is a created being who has rebelled and can tempt—but not force. The main concern of the Bible is not with the devil but with God and the gospel of His grace. Satan and the demonic forces have been overcome by the life, death, and resurrection of Jesus Christ. The New Testament never allows complete pessimism. In the end Satan and his angels will be completely overcome. In fact, Jesus came into the world to "destroy the works of the devil" (1 John 3:8). The cross was a decisive victory over Satan and Satan's host (Col. 2:15). This victory insured that countless numbers would be delivered from the dominion of darkness and transferred to the kingdom of Christ (Col. 1:13).

Limitations of Satan Today, people continue to concretize their fears. They want a scapegoat to deliver them from responsibility. Satan is a created, rebellious and tempting evil power active in the universe, but his powerful existence does not exclude a person from responsibility. Satan and the demonic forces cannot dominate or possess us except by our own consent. Believers will not be tempted beyond our power of resistance (1 Cor.

10:13). The power of Satan is limited. He acts within the limits set by divine sovereignty. The believer has God's armor—the biblical gospel, integrity, peace through Christ, faith in Christ, prayer—as spiritual security (Eph. 6:11–18).

The recent fascination with Satan and demons is in reaction to an earlier disbelief. Christians should beware of excessive gullibility as well as extreme oversimplification. Knowledge about Satan and evil angels alerts Christians to the danger and subtlety of satanic temptation. We should not become too absorbed in satanic forces. Satan and demonic forces are active, but they are limited. We must remember that the main thrust of Christianity is on the availability of God's power and love in Jesus Christ and the Spirit.

John P. Newport

DEVOTED, DEVOTED TO DESTRUCTION See *Anathema; Ban.*

DEVOUT Careful in fulfilling religious duties, pious; used only in Luke and Acts. Simeon is described as righteous and devout person who welcomed the coming of the Messiah and on whom the Holy Spirit rested (Luke 2:25). Cornelius is described as a devout person who reverenced God, gave alms, and prayed continuously (Acts 10:2). Ananias is described as a devout person according to the standard of the Jewish law. He was well-spoken of by all (Acts 22:12).

DEW Dew is the moisture which forms into drops of water upon the earth during a cool night. Moist air drawing from the sea is largely responsible for the dewfall in western Palestine. Downward dew occurs in the summer when the soil is loose, thus providing good cooling conditions. Upward dew results from the condensation of water vapor from damp soil and is, therefore, more frequent in the winter season.

Dew is used in the Bible as a symbol of refreshment (Deut. 32:2; Ps. 133:3); a symbol of the loving power of God which revives and invigorates (Prov. 19:12); a symbol of the sudden onset of an enemy (2 Sam. 17:12); a symbol of brotherly love and harmony (Ps. 133:3); a symbol of God's revelation (Judg. 6:36–40); and a symbol of God's blessing (Gen. 27:28). *Gary Bonner*

DIADEM English translation of three Hebrew terms designating a head covering symbolizing authority and honor. *Mitsnepheth* is the turban of the high priest (Ex. 28:4,39) or king (Ezek. 21:26). The priest's was made of fine linen (Ex. 28:39) with a golden plate (KJV, NAS, NIV) or a flower rosette of pure gold (NRSV) on its front. The plate or rosette is apparently called a *nezer* (literally, "sign of dedication") in Exodus 29:6 ("crown" NAS, KJV; "diadem" NIV, NRSV). Compare Exodus 39:30.

The turban was worn by both religious and royal persons. Aaron the High Priest wore one (Ex. 28:37; 29:6; Lev. 16:4; Zech. 3:5) as did Queens Vashti (Esther 1:11) and Esther (Esther 2:17).

Tsaniph or *tseniphah* is the turban worn by a man (Job 29:14) or woman (Isa. 3:23) or by the king (Isa. 62:3) or high priest (Zech. 3:5). *Tsephirah* is a braided crown, garland, or wreath signifying God's glorious power and authority to come (Isa. 28:5).

The word "diadem" was used in a metaphorical sense of the prudent person (Prov. 14:18), of justice (Job 29:14), of God (Isa. 28:5), of God's presence (Ezek. 21:26), and of Jerusalem (Isa. 62:3).

Just before the New Testament era, diadem was applied by Greeks to the symbol of royalty worn by the Persians. Since all levels of people wore the turban, the king's diadem was distinguished by its color and perhaps by jewels worn on it. To the Greeks and Romans the diadem was the distinctive badge of royalty and was usually white. Later, a wreath was used as a crown for Greek kings.

The diadem should be distinguished from the wreath given for victory in athletic games (1 Cor. 9:25), for civil accomplishments, for military bravery, and for weddings.

In Revelation 12:3; 13:1; 19:12 the diadem conveys the idea of power and authority.

Glenn McCoy

DIAL See *Sundial.*

DIAMOND Precious stone used in jewelry and engraving. It is the hardest mineral known, formed of pure carbon crystals. Two Hebrew words stand behind English, "diamond." *Yahelom* is a stone on the high priest's breastplate (Ex. 28:18; NIV, "emerald"; NRSV, "moonstone") and among the jewels of the king of Tyre (Ezek. 28:13). *Shamir* is the stone used on the point of an engraving tool to cut into stone surfaces (Jer. 17:1; NIV, "flint"; others suggest "emery"). The term also appears in Ezekiel 3:9; Zechariah 7:12 as the hardest stone known.

Apparently Alexander the Great around 330 B.C. first discovered diamonds for the western world in India. This would indicate "diamonds" are not meant in the Old Testament references. Emery stones or adamant stones were widely used for engraving. Emery was a variety of corundum and was composed of aluminum oxide.

DIANA (Dī ăn′ ȧ) Roman goddess with similar characteristics to the Greek Artemis. KJV reads "Diana" in Acts, where Greek and most modern translations read "Artemis." See *Artemis.*

DIASPORA The scattering of the Jews from the land of Palestine into other parts of the world and the Jews thus scattered. The term "dispersion" is also often used to describe this process.

The diaspora took place over several centuries. While its exact beginnings are difficult to date, two major events greatly contributed to it. In 722 B. C. the Assyrians captured the Northern Kingdom (Israel). Following this victory, the Assyrians resettled large numbers of the Israelites in Assyria (2 Kings 17:6). In 586 B. C. the Babylonians captured the Southern Kingdom (Judah) and followed the same policy of resettlement. Many of the residents of Judah were transported to Babylon (2 Kings 25:8–12). While some of these persons later returned to Judah, many of them remained permanently in Babylon. Later, other wars fought by the Greeks and Romans in Palestine helped scatter more of the Jewish people.

The result of the diaspora was that by New Testament times as many Jews lived outside of Palestine as lived within the land. In almost every city which Paul visited on his missionary journeys, he found a Jewish synagogue (Acts 14:1; 17:1,10; 18:4). The diaspora thus helped pave the way for the spread of the gospel. See *Assyria; Babylonia; Exile; Synagogue.*

Lynn Jones

DIBLAH (Dĭb′ lăh) or **DIBLATH** (Dĭb′ lăth) Place name with variant manuscript spellings and English transliterations in Ezekiel 6:14. The Hebrew term many mean, "cake of figs." Ezekiel used the term to describe the northern border of Israel as joined with the southern wilderness to describe all the territory of Israel which faced judgment—"from the desert to Diblah" (NIV). With slight manuscript support from the Latin Vulgate, many Bible students read "Riblah" supposing that in the earliest history of the text tradition a copyist made the simple mistake of changing a Hebrew "r" to a Hebrew "d," the two letters being easily confused. See *Riblah.*

DIBLAIM (Dĭb lā′ ĭm) Personal or place name meaning, "two fig cakes." Hosea 1:3 lists Diblaim as a parent of Gomer, Hosea's harlot wife. Some Bible students see Hosea's father-in-law so named; others, his mother-in-law. The latter case is combined with an understanding that she was also a harlot whose price was two fig cakes. Others would equate Diblaim with the place name Beth-diblathaim. See *Beth-diblathaim.* The most direct explanation seems to be that Diblaim is Gomer's father, of whom nothing more is known.

DIBON (Dī′ bŏn) or **DIBON-GAD** (Dī′ bŏn-găd) Place name possibly meaning, "pining away" or "fence of tubes." *1.* Capital city of Moab captured by Moses (Num. 21:21–31). Gad and Reuben asked for it as their tribal territory (Num. 32:3). Gad took control and fortified Dibon (Num. 32:34). It thus became known as Dibon-gad and was one of Israel's camping spots east of the Jordan (Num. 33:45–46). Joshua reported that Moses gave Dibon to the tribe of Reuben (Josh.

13:9,17). In pronouncing judgment on Moab, Isaiah described the religious mourning at the worship place in Dibon (Isa. 15:2), showing that Moab had gained control of Dibon by about 730 B.C. The Moabite stone of King Mesha, discovered in Dibon, shows that Moab controlled Dibon about 850 B.C. About 700 B.C. Jeremiah again announced destruction for Moab and Dibon (Jer. 48:18–22).

Dibon stood on the northern hill across the valley from modern Dhiban. It is about 40 miles south of Amman, Jordan, and three miles north of the Arnon River. Occupation of the site apparently goes back to about 2500 B.C., but the main occupation period began after 1200 B.C., climaxing about 850 with Mesha. Nebuchadnezzar destroyed the city in 582 B.C.

Nabateans built a temple there during Jesus' childhood. It was apparently abandoned about A.D. 100.

2. In Nehemiah's day (about 445 B.C.) Jews lived in a Dibon in Judah. This may be the same as Dimonah. See *Dimonah.*

DIBRI (Dĭb′ rī) Personal name meaning, "talkative" or "gossip." Israelite woman who had a son with an Egyptian father. The son cursed God's name and was stoned to death (Lev. 24:10–23).

DIDACHE See *Apostolic Fathers.*

DIDRACHMA A Greek coin worth two drachmas or a Jewish half shekel, the amount of the Temple tax paid by every male Jew above age 19 (Matt. 17:24). After the Temple's destruction in A.D. 70, the Roman government apparently continued to collect the Temple tax, possibly to support a Roman temple. The first readers of Matthew's Gospel would have understood the Temple tax in the Roman context.

DIDYMUS (Dĭd′ ў mŭs) Personal name meaning, "twin." An alternative name for the apostle Thomas (John 11:16). It appears only in John's Gospel. See *Thomas.*

DIGNITIES KJV translation of Greek *doxas* (literally, "glorious ones") in 2 Peter 2:10. The people 2 Peter condemned willingly blasphemed the dignities, who are evil good angels or evil angels. Compare Jude 8.

DIKLAH (Dĭk′ läh) Personal name apparently meaning, "date palm." Grandson of Eber (Gen. 10:27). He was apparently the original ancestor of a tribe in Arabia which settled in an oasis where dates were grown, but nothing more is known of him.

DILEAN (Dī′ lė ăn) Place name meaning, "protrusion" or "ledge." Village in tribal territory of Judah (Josh. 15:38). Tell en-Najileh southwest of tell el-Hesi has been suggested as a possible modern site.

DILL Spice cultivated in Israel (Isa. 28:25–27). KJV translates, "fitches"; NIV, "caraway." It was probably black cummin, *Nigella satina.* Jesus accused the scribes and Pharisees of tithing their dill but neglecting justice, mercy, and faith (Matt. 23:23). See *Plants.*

DIMNAH (Dĭm′ năh) Place name meaning, "manure." Town in tribal territory of Zebulun given to Levites (Josh. 21:35). First Chronicles 6:77 appears to refer to the same city as Rimmon. Compare Joshua 19:13. A scribe copying the text could easily confuse the two names. See *Rimmon.*

DIMON (Dī′ môn) Place name perhaps meaning, "blood." City in Moab on which Isaiah announced judgment (Isa. 15:9). Dead Sea Scrolls text and Latin Vulgate read "Dibon" here. This may be the original reading, but that would go against the normal type of copying mistakes scribes make in that it would substitute an unknown place for a famous place. It may be that transcription of a Moabite name into the Hebrew language or the development of the language resulted in a change of pronunciation, so that the two names represent one place. If Dimon is a separate town, it was probably located at modern khirbet Dimme, about seven miles north of Kerak. Jeremiah 48:2 calls a Moabite town, "Madmen." The Hebrew word, *madmen,* may involve a play on words referring to Dimon. See *Dibon.*

DIMONAH (Dī mō′ năh) Place name related to Hebrew word for blood. A town on southeast border of tribal allotment of Judah (Josh. 15:22). Some have suggested its location at tell ed-Dheib near Aroer. It may be the same as Dibon mentioned in Nehemiah 11:25.

DINAH (Dī′ năh) Personal name meaning, "justice" or "artistically formed." The daughter of Jacob and Leah (Gen. 30:21). According to Genesis 34, she was sexually assaulted by a man named Shechem, who wished to marry her. Simeon and Levi, her brothers, took revenge by killing the male residents of the city of Shechem. See *Jacob; Leah; Shechem; Patriarchs.*

DINAITE (Dī′ nȧ īte) KJV transliterations of Aramaic word in Ezra 4:9. Modern translations translate the word as "judges."

DINHABAH (Dĭn′ hȧ băh) City name of unknown meaning. Residence of one of earliest kings of Edom in period prior to Saul in Israel (Gen. 36:32). Nothing else is known of the city.

DIONYSIUS (Dī ō nўs′ ĭ ŭs) An Athenian aristocrat who was converted to Christianity through the preaching of Paul the apostle (Acts 17:34). He was a member of the Areopagus, an elite and influential group of officials. See *Areopagus.*

DIOTREPHES (Dī ŏt′ rė phēs) Personal name meaning, "nurtured by Jove." An individual whose self-serving ambition is cited unfavorably (3 John 9). The writer of the letter declared that Diotrephes rejected his (the writer's) authority. See *3 John.*

DIPHATH (Dī′ phăth) NRSV, NAS reading of great grandson of Noah in 1 Chronicles 1:6. KJV, NIV follow other Hebrew manuscripts and versions and Genesis 10:3 in reading Riphath. See *Riphath.*

DIRECTIONS (GEOGRAPHICAL) How did the people of the Bible orient themselves within the "four corners of the earth" (Isa. 11:12)? The word "orient" gives the key, pointing us eastward. To orient oneself, the biblical person faced eastward toward the sunrise. Thus in front is east and behind is west, where the sun sets. On the left hand is north and to the right hand is south. In this Israel differed from the Egyptians, who oriented themselves to the south, the source of the Nile River.

Israel combined its sunrise-based system with a geographical viewpoint. Thus west could be referred to as the Sea with reference to the Mediterranean Sea. East could be referred to as the wilderness, and south could be called the Negeb, the dry south country (Gen 24:62). The north was designated as the mountains.

Israel lay in the central position between the nations, at the connecting point of three continents via land and water. Israel saw Jerusalem with its Mount Zion as the center of the world (Isa. 2:2; Ezek. 5:5). As expressed later in the Jewish midrash, "just as the navel is in the center of a person, so is the land of Israel in the middle of the world." Christians in the first centuries after Christ took over this type of geographical description and made Golgotha, considered the grave of Adam and of Christ, the middle point of the world.

East and West The most important words for east and west are rising and setting, with reference to the sun. Joined together, the two expressions signified the expanse of the world between its most widely-separated points (Ps. 50:1; Isa. 45:6). At times a Babylonian/Assyrian viewpoint describes Palestine as the land of the Amorites, that is the wild west, or the land beyond the river with reference to the Euphrates. From an Israelite perspective, however, the land beyond the river refers to the east, across the Jordan (Josh. 24:2–3). The great sea of the sun's setting (Josh. 1:4) or more simply the sea is the west. West can also be

called the back side in contrast to the front side (Isa. 9:12), where inhabitants of Transjordan, that is the sons of the front side, the east people originated (Gen. 29:1; Judg. 6:3,33).

North and South "From Dan to Beersheba" (2 Sam. 3:10) describes the stretch of land the tribes of Israel claimed after their entrance into the land. The description ranges from north to south. For the Hebrew language north is the left and south is the right. Benjamin means literally, "son of the right" or "son of the south." Genesis 35:18 calls them the sons of good fortune since the right was seen as the lucky side.

Teman or the south is a place in Edom. The Negeb, a designation for the southern dry country south of the Judean hills, also stands for the south. Zaphon, the mountain on the northern Syrian Mediterranean Coast, stands for the north. For the Canaanites, Zaphon represented the dwelling place of Baal, while in the Old Testament it is an attribute of the throne of Yahweh (Isa. 14:13; Ps. 48:2–3).

Some prophets spoke of the enemy from the north, which was called the punishing tool of God on Israel. This was recognized in the appearance of the Babylonians from the north. Compare especially Jeremiah 4—6. *Christian Wolf*

DIRGE Modern translation term for lamentation. See *Music; Psalms.*

DISCERNING OF SPIRITS One of the gifts of the Spirit (1 Cor. 12:10). It apparently refers to the God-given ability to tell whether a prophetic speech came from God's Spirit or from another source opposed to God.

DISCHARGE Modern translation term for bodily excretion which rendered one ceremonially unclean (Lev. 15:2–25: Num. 5:2; KJV, issue.) The nature of the discharge of males (Lev. 15:2–25) is unclear. Suggestions include hemorrhoids, spermatorrhea, that is, the involuntary release of sperm due to a weakening of the sexual organs, or a discharge related to an inflamation of the urinary tract. In the case of women, the discharge is the monthly period (15:19) or bleeding outside this period (15:25). A discharge rendered unclean the person and anything or anyone coming into contact with the source of uncleanness.

DISCIPLES; APOSTLES Followers of Jesus Christ, especially the commissioned twelve who followed Jesus during His earthly ministry.

Background of Apostle The English word "apostle" comes from the Greek term *apostolos,* which means a messenger, envoy, or ambassador. Related to the verb, "to send," it refers to one who is "sent" on behalf of another. The conceptual background of the New Testament term *apostolos* has been variously represented. Many scholars believe that the rabbinic office of the *shaliach*—attested by 150 A.D.—constitutes the proper background for understanding the New Testament term "apostle." The *shaliach* was established as a legal institution in rabbinic Judaism to insure that an appointed "messenger" was given due regard as the legal representative of his sender. The *shaliach* functioned with the full authority of the one who commissioned him. According to Jewish tradition, "A man's agent (*shaliach)* is like to himself" (Mishnah Berakoth 5:5; Rosh ha-Shanah 4:9; compare 1 Sam. 25:40–41; 2 Sam. 10:1–19). It is not certain that the legal rabbinic notion of a *shaliach* was established before the time of Christ. Moreover, even if it were in use by that time, the differences between the rabbinic of *shaliach* and that of the New Testament term *apostolos* are significant enough to urge caution in relating the two terms too closely. The *shaliach,* for example, had a function that was more legal than religious (to serve documents, collect money, carry information), was applied generally to human representation (whether individuals or groups), and lasted for only a limited period. The New Testament apostle, on the other hand, emerges as a divinely appointed, lifetime witness to the saving acts of God, specifically, the death and resurrection of Jesus.

The Old Testament notion of a *shaliach* also differs from the rabbinic conceptions of that term and appears to be of more significance for understanding the New Testament term "apostle." The "sending" and commissioning of the great prophetic figures Moses and Isaiah (Ex. 3:10; Isa. 6:8 where the Hebrew verb for sending, *shalach,* is translated by *apostello* in the *Septuagint,* the Greek Old Testament, as divine spokesmen surely influenced the New Testament word, "apostle." We may also note that the same "sending" terminology is applied to other noteworthy characters such as Elijah (2 Kings 2:2,4,6), Jeremiah (Jer. 1:7), and Ezekiel (Ezek. 2:3,4). As a reference to a divine spokesman, Old Testament ideas of a "sent one" are certainly in line with the New Testament term "apostle." Compare Jeremiah 7:25.

Apostle in the New Testament The term "apostle" in the New Testament is used primarily to designate that group of leaders within the early church(es) who were historical witnesses of the resurrected Lord and proclaimers of God's saving mercies enacted through the death and resurrection of Jesus. Jesus originally gave the title to His closest circle of friends, the twelve (Luke 6:13). He especially indicated their status as emissaries He had set apart to announce (as He had done) the good news of the kingdom (Matt. 10:1–23; Luke 8:1; 9:1–6). After the first Easter, the term was expanded by the early church to refer not only to the twelve, but to a wider circle of authoritative preachers and witnesses of the resurrected Lord

(Acts 14:4,14; Rom. 16:7; 1 Cor. 4:9; 15:5–9; 2 Cor. 11:13; Gal. 1:19; 2:7–9).

The early church's expansion of the term was certainly justified given both the self-understanding of Jesus as One sent from God (Matt. 5:17; 10:34; Mark 2:17; 10:45; Luke 4:18; 9:48; John 5:19–47; 6:29–57; 8:14–42; compare Heb. 3:1) and His designation of His followers as those who, as His representatives, carried on His work (Matt. 28:16–20; Luke 24:44–49; John 20:21; Acts 1:6). Those facts coupled with the early church's actual sense of continuity with the person and mission of the historical Jesus made rather natural their extended application of the term "apostle" to more than the original twelve, though not, as we shall see, to all Christian witnesses. Thus, the choice, meaning, and ongoing use by the early church of the term "apostle" as a reference to a unique class of witnesses is in large measure derived from its actual use by Jesus.

The term "apostle" did not, however, have limitless application in the New Testament period. It extended to gospel witnesses other than the twelve but not to all proclaimers of the gospel. It was never so broad in New Testament use as to be an ancient equivalent to the modern term "missionary." The term "apostle," most immediately brought to mind its central function: to preach the gospel; but all those who preached the gospel were not designated "apostles." There is, for example, a striking absence of the term with reference to Timothy (2 Cor. 1:1; Phil. 1:1; Col. 1:1; 1 Thess. 1:1; 2 Thess. 1:1), Sosthenes (1 Cor. 1:1), and Silas (1 Thess. 1:1, 2 Thess. 1:1), who were certainly not only Paul's fellow workers but also preachers of the gospel (compare 2 Cor. 1:19). Thus, others in the Pauline missionary party were called, for example, "brother," "fellow worker," or "bond servant" (Rom. 16:3; Phil. 2:25; Col. 4:7–14; 1 Thess. 3:1); but the term "apostle" had a more exclusive, and thus more restricted, meaning.

The decisive criterion for the term's application seems to have been the eyewitness status of some with respect to the resurrected Lord. Though the criteria employed for replacing Judas among the twelve (Acts 1:12–22) included being an eyewitness not only of the resurrected Jesus but also of the ministry of Jesus from the days of His baptism by John, there developed in the early church a slightly broader application of the term "apostle" which did not demand an eyewitness knowledge of Jesus' ministry. James the brother of Jesus (Matt. 13:55) was certainly no follower of his Brother during His ministry (Mark 3:21,31–35; John 7:3–5). He still became an "apostle" and leader of the Jerusalem church (Acts 15:1–21; Gal. 1:18,19) following his encounter with the resurrected Lord (1 Cor. 15:7). In a similar way, Paul's vision of, and calling by, the resurrected

Lord won for him the designation "apostle" (1 Cor. 9:1; 15:8–11; Gal. 1:11—2:10); though this distinction was apparently not conceded by all (2 Cor. 3:1; 12:11–13). We may presume that Barnabas (Acts 14:4,14), Apollos (1 Cor. 4:6–13), and also Andronicus and Junias (Rom. 16:7) were likewise witnesses of the resurrected Lord.

To be sure, Paul did speak of certain others as "apostles" who likely were not eyewitnesses of the risen Lord (2 Cor. 8:23 NAS and RSV notes; Phil. 2:25); but such passages are only apparent exceptions, for the helpers in question are called "apostles" (normally translated "representatives" or "messengers") *of the churches,* clearly suggesting a status different from that of the "apostle *of Jesus Christ."* Therefore, because it referred to a specific set of historical witnesses, the New Testament office of apostle, by definition, died with its first representatives. The New Testament certainly speaks of a succession of witnesses to the apostolic *tradition* (1 Tim. 6:20; 2 Tim. 1:14), so that the gospel they preached—the apostolic *theology*—has been handed on (the New Testament itself being the inspired, literary remains of that theology). No true personal or ecclesiastical succession of apostles continues in any New Testament sense of that term.

Background of Disciple The term "disciple" comes to us in English from a Latin root. Its basic meaning is "learner" or "pupil." The term is virtually absent from the Old Testament, though there are two related references (1 Chron. 25:8; Isa. 8:16).

In the Greek world the word "disciple" normally referred to an adherent of a particular teacher or religious/philosophical school. It was the task of the disciple to learn, study, and pass along the sayings and teachings of the master. In rabbinic Judaism the term "disciple" referred to one who was committed to the interpretations of Scripture and religious tradition given him by the master or rabbi. Through a process of learning which would include a set meeting time and such pedagogical methods as question and answer, instruction, repetition, and memorization, the disciple would become increasingly devoted to the master and the master's teachings. In time, the disciple would, likewise, pass on the traditions to others.

Jesus' Disciples In the New Testament 233 of the 261 instances of the word "disciple" occur in the Gospels, the other 28 being in Acts. Usually the word refers to disciples of Jesus, but there are also references to disciples of the Pharisees (Matt. 22:16; Mark 2:18), disciples of John the Baptist (Mark 2:18; Luke 11:1; John 1:35), and even disciples of Moses (John 9:28).

The Gospels often refer to Jesus as "Rabbi" (Matt. 26:25,49; Mark 9:5; 10:51; 11:21; John 1:38,49; 3:2,26; 6:25; 20:16 NIV). One can assume that Jesus used traditional rabbinic teaching techniques (question and answer, discussion, memorization) to instruct His disciples. In many respects Jesus differed from the rabbis. He called His disciples to "Follow me" (Luke 5:27). Disciples of the rabbis could select their teachers. Jesus oftentimes demanded extreme levels of personal renunciation (loss of family, property, etc.; Matt. 4:18–22; 10:24–42; Luke 5:27–28; 14:25–27; 18:28–30). He asked for lifelong allegiance (Luke 9:57–62) as the essential means of doing the will of God (Matt. 12:49–50; John 7:16–18). He taught more as a bearer of divine revelation than a link in the chain of Jewish tradition (Matt. 5:21–48; 7:28–29; Mark 4:10–11. In so doing Jesus announced the end of the age and the long-awaited reign of God (Matt. 4:17; Luke 4:14–21,42–44).

The Twelve As the messianic Proclaimer of the reign of God, Jesus gathered about Himself a special circle of twelve disciples, clearly a symbolic representation of the twelve tribes (Matt. 19:28). He was reestablishing Jewish social identity based upon discipleship to Jesus. The twelve represented a unique band, making the word "disciple" (as a reference to the twelve) an exact equivalent

Matthew 10:2–4	Mark 3:16–19	Luke 6:13–16	Acts 1:13–14
Simon Peter	Simon Peter	Simon Peter	Peter
Andrew	James, son of Zebedee	Andrew	James
James, son of Zebedee	John	James	John
John	Andrew	John	Andrew
Philip	Philip	Philip	Philip
Bartholomew	Bartholomew	Bartholomew	Thomas
Thomas	Matthew	Matthew	Bartholomew
Matthew the publican	Thomas	Thomas	Matthew
James, son of Alphaeus	James the son of Alphaeus	James, son of Alphaeus	James, son of Alphaeus
(Lebbeus) Thaddeus	Thaddaeus	Simon Zelotes	Simon Zealotes
Simon the Canaanite	Simon the Zealot	Judas, brother of James (compare John 14:22)	Judas brother of James
Judas Iscariot	Judas Iscariot	Judas Iscariot	(Judas Iscariot) Matthias (v. 26)

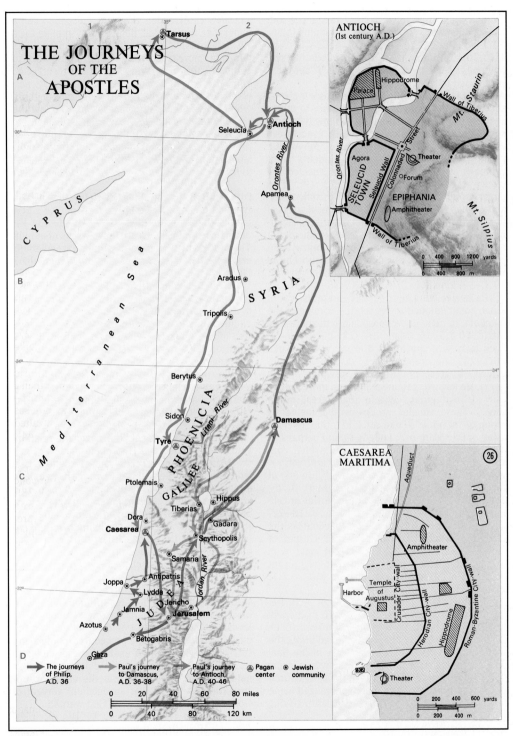

THE JOURNEYS OF THE APOSTLES

ANTIOCH
(1st century A.D.)

Hippodrome
Palace
Wall of Staurin
Mt. Tiberius
Orontes River
Colonnaded Street
Agora
Theater
Forum
SELEUCID TOWN
Seleucid Wall
EPIPHANIA
Amphitheater
Mt. Silpius
Wall of Tiberius

0   400   800   1200   yards
0   400   800   m

Tarsus

Seleucia   Antioch

Orontes River

Apamea

C Y P R U S

Aradus

S Y R I A

M e d i t e r r a n e a n   S e a

Tripolis

Berytus

Sidon

Damascus

Tyre

Litani River

P H O E N I C I A

G A L I L E E

Ptolemais

Hippus

Tiberias

Dora

Gadara

Caesarea

Scythopolis

Samaria

Jordan River

Joppa   Antipatris

Lydda

Jericho

Jamnia

J U D E A

Jerusalem

Azotus

Betogabris

Gaza

CAESAREA MARITIMA

26

Aqueduct

Amphitheater

Temple of Augustus

Harbor

Crusader City-wall

Herodian City-wall

Hippodrome

Roman-Byzantine City-wall

Theater

0   200   400   600   yards
0   200   400   m

➤ The journeys of Philip, A.D. 36

➤ Paul's journey to Damascus, A.D. 36-38

➤ Paul's journey to Antioch, A.D. 40-46

⊛ Pagan center

⊛ Jewish community

0   20   40   60   80 miles
0   40   80   120 km

© carta

to "apostle" in those contexts where the latter word was also restricted to the twelve. The four lists of the twelve in the New Testament (Matt. 10:1–4; Mark 3:16–19; Luke 6:12–16; Acts 1:13,26) also imply from their contexts the synonymous use of the terms "disciples"/"apostles" when used to refer to the twelve.

A Larger Group of Followers The Gospels clearly show that the word "disciple" can refer to others besides the twelve. The verb "follow" became something of a technical term Jesus used to call His disciples, who were then called "followers " (Mark 4:10). These "followers" included a larger company of people from whom He selected the twelve (Mark 3:7–19; Luke 6:13–17). This larger group of disciples/followers included men and women (Luke 8:1–3; 23:49) from all walks of life. (Even the twelve included a variety: fishermen, a tax collector, a Zealot.) Jesus was no doubt especially popular among the socially outcast and religiously despised, but people of wealth and of theological training also followed (Luke 8:1–3; 19:1–10; John 3:1–3; 12:42; 19:38–39).

The twelve were sent out as representatives of Jesus, commissioned to preach the coming of the kingdom, to cast out demons, and to heal diseases (Matt. 10:1,5–15; Mark 6:7–13; Luke 9:1–6). Such tasks were not limited to the twelve (Luke 10:1–24). Apparently Jesus' disciples first included "a great multitude of disciples" (Luke 6:17). He formed certain smaller and more specifically defined groups within that "great multitude." These smaller groups would include a group of "seventy" (Luke 10:1,17), the "twelve" (Matt. 11:1; Mark 6:7; Luke 9:1), and perhaps an even smaller, inner group within the twelve, consisting especially of Peter, James, and John— whose names (with Andrew) always figure first in the lists of the twelve (Matt. 10:2; Mark 3:16–17; Luke 6:14; Acts 1:13), whose stories of calling are especially highlighted (Matt. 4:18–22; John 1:35–42 and the tradition that John is the "Other"/"Beloved Disciple" of the Gospel of John—13:23; 19:26; 20:2; 21:20), and who alone accompanied Jesus on certain significant occasions of healing and revelation (Matt. 17:1; Mark 13:3; Luke 8:51).

All Followers of Jesus The Book of Acts frequently uses the term "disciple" to refer generally to all those who believe in the risen Lord (6:1–2,7; 9:1,10,19,26,38; 11:26,29). In addition, the verb form "to disciple" as it appears in the final commissioning scene of Matthew's Gospel (28:19–20) also suggests a use in the early church of the term "disciple" as a more generalized name for all those who come to Jesus in faith, having heard and believed the gospel.

Conclusion We have seen that, as references to the twelve, the words "apostle" and "disciple" could be synonymous. However, just as the term "disciple" could mean other followers of Jesus

than the twelve in the time of His ministry, so also after His resurrection the term "disciple" had a wider meaning as well, being clearly applied to all His followers. Whereas the term "apostle" retained a more specific meaning, being tied to certain historical eyewitnesses of the resurrected Lord, the word "disciple" tended to lose its narrower associations with the twelve, and/or those who followed the historical Jesus, or who saw the risen Lord, and became a virtual equivalent to "Christian" (Acts 11:26). In every case, however, the common bond of meaning for the various applications of the word "disciple" was allegiance to Jesus. *Robert Sloan*

DISCIPLINE In the Bible, discipline has a positive and essential place in the lives of God's people. God had prescribed a way of life for His people. They had to learn how to be obedient. The process by which God's people learned obedience was the "discipline of the Lord" (Deut. 11:2 NIV).

Discipline comes from a Latin word *"disco"* which means to learn or get to know, a direct kind of acquaintance with something or someone. Discipline refers to the process by which one learns a way of life. A disciple was like an apprentice who was learning a trade or craft from a master. Such learning required a relationship between the master who knew the way of life (discipline) and a learner (a disciple). Within this relationship, the master led a learner through a process (the discipline) until the learner could imitate or live like the master.

In the Old Testament, the covenant relationship between God and His people made Yahweh the Master. Through praise and correction, God led His people. The goal was to bring His people to a kind of maturity where obedience was the rule rather than the exception. Parents, judges, kings, prophets, and wisemen worked with God in teaching His people. Successful discipline resulted in a life pleasing to God. The earliest setting for discipline was the family (Deut. 6:20–25).

The prophets established "schools of the prophet." Elijah became a master to Elisha (1 Kings 19:19–21). Isaiah chose some Judeans who would learn his message through living with him (Isa. 8:16). This pattern was followed by Jewish rabbis. The rabbi would discipline his disciples (*talmidim)* through a procedure of praise and correction. This process enabled the disciples to learn the law. Correction was seldom physical in nature. Reproof or rebuke was the usual form of correction. The goal was an obedient servant of God, who knew and did what God wanted.

Jesus called twelve men to be His disciples. Through His call, He established a master-learner relation with them. As they lived and worked with Him, Jesus disciplined them in His understanding of what God wanted.

The Great Commission places the responsibility for discipling disciples in the hands of the church. The believers are to teach them "to observe all things whatsoever I have commanded you" (Matt. 28:20). "To observe" is much more than simple knowledge. Observance is to live in obedience to the commands of Jesus. Learning and doing what Jesus wants requires a process, a discipline. Becoming like Christ is the result of the discipline of the Lord Jesus Christ, exercised in and through His church. Hence, churches throughout their history have sought to teach their members the way of the Lord through "church discipline."

Apart from the Gospels, the concept of discipline appears most prominently in the ethical teachings of Paul and the Letter to the Hebrews. Paul admonished the Ephesians to bring their children up "in the discipline and instruction of the Lord" (Eph. 6:4*b* NAS). Such an education was to avoid the heavy-handed, physical brutality practiced by their pagan neighbors. Discipline was not to evoke anger from the children (Eph. 6:4*a)*. The writer of Hebrews pictures God treating the faithful as sons (Heb. 12:7). As a loving Father, God disciplines the believing community. Such discipline is evidence of His love because the end result of such action is blessing (Heb. 12:10).

Discipline, biblically understood, results in blessing. God's people learn how to serve Him. Through praise and correction, their lives are shaped into a pattern of consistent obedience and love. Within "the discipline of the Lord," expressed in and through the Lord Jesus Christ, one can live the kind of life which is pleasing to God and of benefit to others.   *James Berryman*

DISEASES Physical and/or mental malfunctions that limit human functions and lessen the quality of life. Successful treatment of disease depends primarily on prompt, correct diagnosis and the use of effective therapeutic agents. Unfortunately, people living in biblical times had limited means to diagnose and treat illness. The best-educated people in biblical times had a meager understanding of human anatomy and physiology and even less knowledge about the nature of disease and its effect on the body. No one knew about bacteria and viruses. This fact hampered diagnosis. Illness was often attributed to sin or to a curse by an enemy. The main diagnostic tools were observation and superficial physical examination. The physician had few aids to use in his work.

Providers of Medical Care Ancient Near Eastern literature contains numerous references to physicians and medical practice. A Sumerian physician, Lulu, lived in Mesopotamia about 2700 B.C. A few decades later, a famous Egyptian named Imhotep established a reputation as a physician and priest. He also became noted as a great architect. He designed the Step Pyramid at Saqqara.

The Code of Hammurabi, from about 1750 B.C., contains several laws regulating the practice of medicine and surgery by physicians in the Old Babylonian Kingdom. Although the profession of medicine was in its infancy, the many practitioners slowly improved their skills.

The Egyptians made more rapid progress in medical knowledge and its application to patients than did the Babylonians. Their physicians tended to specialize. Each would limit his practice to one part of the body, such as the eye, the teeth, or the stomach. Egyptian doctors, like others, often used herbs in their medications. These were collected from many areas of the world and were often grown in gardens connected with the temples of Egypt. Egyptian physicians became respected throughout the ancient world. Their skill was even admired in a later period by the Greeks, who eventually became the foremost physicians.

The Old Testament has only a few references to physicians. These persons most likely had been trained in Egypt. Physicians were called upon to embalm the body of Jacob (Gen. 50:2). King Asa sought medical care from physicians for his diseased feet (2 Chron. 16:12). Some non-medical references are made to physicians (Jer. 8:22; Job 13:4). It is unlikely that many trained physicians lived among the ancient Hebrews.

The great Greek physician, Hippocrates, born about 460 B.C., is often referred to as the Father of Medicine. Hippocrates believed that disease had natural causes. He relied mainly on diet and various herbs to treat his patients. Around 300 B.C. the Greeks established an important medical school in Alexandria, Egypt, which flourished for several centuries and trained many physicians. The school was noted for its large library and laboratory facilities. Dissection of the human body was permitted, and some limited advances were made in the knowledge of anatomy.

By the time of Jesus, the city of Rome had become an important medical center. Many physicians practiced there. Originally they were in the slave class, but their profession gradually became esteemed. Julius Caesar granted Roman citizenship to Greek physicians practicing in Rome. The Romans made significant contributions in the area of public health, including the provision of a relatively pure water supply, an effective sewage disposal system, and the establishment of a food inspection program. The Romans also established a network of hospitals, initially founded to care for the needs of the army.

Outlying regions of the empire, such as Palestine, apparently had few well-trained doctors, although little information is available concerning professional medical care outside the large cities. The majority of people probably were born and died without ever being treated by a trained physician.

The New Testament mentions physicians only a few times. Jesus noted the purpose of a physician is to treat the ill (Matt. 9:12; Mark 2:17; Luke 5:31), and he referred to a common proverb, "Physician, heal thyself" (Luke 4:23). Mark and Luke related the story of a woman who had sought the help of physicians but had not been healed (Mark 5:25–34; Luke 8:43–48). Paul, in Colossians 4:14, remarks that his colleague, Luke, was a physician. Luke was a Gentile, but his hometown is unknown. The source of his medical training is also unknown, but it is possible that he went to medical school in Tarsus, Paul's hometown.

In many lands, priests were assigned medical duties. This was true among the ancient Hebrews, where priests were major providers of medical services. They were especially responsible for the diagnosis of diseases which might pose a threat to the community (Lev. 13). Priests in Israel apparently played little role in the actual treatment of ill persons.

During the time of the New Testament, the Roman god of healing, Aesculapius (known by the Greeks at an earlier time by the name of Asklepios), was popular. Many of his temples, staffed by his priests, were scattered throughout the Mediterranean world. Persons seeking healing thronged these temples. They often brought small replicas of the portion of the body that was afflicted by disease to these temples and left them with the priests. Other sites, for one reason or another, became renowned as places of healing. A good biblical example of this is the Pool of Bethesda (John 5:1–15). The pool of Siloam also is connected with Jesus' ministry of healing (John 9:7).

Most of the medicine practiced in ancient Palestine and in other outlying parts of the Roman Empire was probably unprofessional. This was certainly true in Old Testament times. Women, trained by apprenticeship and experience served as midwives. Some persons became adept at setting broken bones. Families were left to apply their own folk remedies in most cases of illness, perhaps in consultation with someone in the community who had become known for his or her success in the treatment of various ailments. Fortunately, the human body has considerable ability to heal itself. Despite obvious medical limitations, many of the patients recovered; and many of the remedies used were "successful."

Methods of Treating Disease The Bible contains little information about the treatment of disease, except through miraculous means. Much of the data concerning this subject has to be obtained from other ancient literature. Most of these records come from the ancient Babylonians, Egyptians, Greeks, and Romans. Some are even older. For example, a clay tablet containing fifteen prescriptions from a Sumerian source has been found. This dates to about 2200 B.C.

An examination of these old records, often frag-

mentary and obscure, reveals that most medicines were derived from three sources. The majority came from various parts of many different plants. Early physicians also used substances obtained from animals, such as blood, urine, milk, hair, and ground-up shell and bone. In addition, certain mineral products were commonly used, including salt and bitumen. The use of these medicines was often accompanied by magical rites, incantations, and prayers. In the earliest periods, in particular, lines were not clearly drawn between religion, superstition, and science.

Modern doctors and Bible students have an almost impossible task as they try to diagnose accurately ailments mentioned in the Bible. Various infectious diseases undoubtedly accounted for a large number of the cases of serious illness and death. Nutritional deficiencies, birth defects, and injuries were common. The symptoms produced by these and other types of physical afflictions were treated by a variety of means.

Prevention is always the best form of treatment. Since the cause of most illness was unknown in the biblical period, relatively little could be done, however, to prevent disease. Ancient people did realize a contagious nature to some illnesses. In these cases, attempts were made to quarantine the afflicted person and prevent close contact with healthy individuals (Lev. 13).

The Hebrew word translated, "leprosy," in Leviticus 13 is a general term used to describe a number of different skin eruptions. Although true leprosy occurred in ancient times and often caused changes in the skin, many of the persons brought to the priests undoubtedly suffered from more common bacterial and fungal infections of the skin. The priests had the duty of determining, on the basis of repeated examination, which of these eruptions posed a threat to others. They had the authority to isolate persons with suspected dangerous diseases from the community.

Isaiah 38 relates the story of the very serious illness of King Hezekiah. The cause of his illness was a "boil" (v. 21). The Hebrew word translated, "boil," is translated, "sore boils," in Job 2:7. It is also the word used to describe the eruption occurring on men and beasts mentioned in Exodus 9:8–11 (compare Lev. 13:18–20; Deut. 28:27).

The illness of Hezekiah was treated by applying a poultice of figs (Isa. 38:21). Hezekiah almost certainly had some type of acute bacterial infection of the skin. Prior to the discovery of antibiotics, these dangerous infections could cause death. Although it is unlikely that the figs had any medicinal value, they were probably applied in the form of a hot compress. Heat is an effective treatment for infections of the skin.

The use of hot and cold compresses and baths was widely employed in the ancient world to treat illness, although the Bible itself has little to say about this.

Medical care in biblical times frequently employed the use of different kinds of salves and ointments. Olive oil was used widely, either alone or as an ingredient in ointments. The use of oil for the treatment of wounds is mentioned in Isaiah 1:6 and Luke 10:34. Oil also became a symbol of medicine, and its use was coupled with prayer for the ill (Mark 6:13; James 5:14).

Herbs and various products obtained from many different plants were among the most popular of ancient medicines. These were applied to the body as a poultice, or, in many cases, taken by mouth. Frankincense and myrrh—gum resins obtained from trees—were commonly used to treat a variety of diseases, although their main use was in perfumes and incense.

Wine was commonly thought to have medicinal value. One of its uses was to alleviate pain and discomfort. Wine, mixed with gall and myrrh, was offered to Jesus prior to His crucifixion, but He refused to drink it (Matt. 27:34; Mark 15:23). Wine also was used to sooth stomach and intestinal disorders (1 Tim. 5:23) and to treat a variety of other physical problems. Beer was also widely used as an ingredient in several medicines, especially by the Babylonians.

Mental illness and epilepsy were not uncommon in the ancient world, and the victims suffered greatly. Their sickness was usually associated with demonic powers. The afflicted person was often isolated, and even abused in some cases. King Saul became mentally unstable, and it is of interest that he gained some help from music (1 Sam. 16:23), a form of therapy that has proved to be beneficial in some cases of mental illness. Perhaps the most dramatic example of mental illness related in the Bible concerns the Babylonian king, Nebuchadnezzar (Dan. 4). No treatment is described, but the king's sanity was restored when he acknowledged the true God.

Sterility was a great burden in biblical times. A childless couple was pitied by all. When Leah suffered a temporary period of sterility, she sent her son, Reuben, to the field to obtain mandrakes. Her barren sister, Rachel, also asked for some of the mandrakes (Gen. 30: 9–24). The root of the mandrake was widely used in the ancient world to promote conception, although there is no reason to believe it was truly effective. It was also used as a narcotic.

Most babies were born without the benefit of a physician. Midwives were frequently sought to give help, especially in the case of difficult deliveries (Gen. 35:16–21; 1 Sam. 4:19–22). Babies were often born with mothers seated on a special stool (Ex. 1:16). Many mothers and babies died during childbirth, or in the first few days and weeks after delivery. The high death rate was due to infection, blood loss, poor nutrition, and the absence of good medical care before, during, and after childbirth. The custom of breast-feeding for-

tunately did help prevent some illness.

Several examples of sickness are mentioned in the Bible where no description of the treatment given is described. King Asa had a disease of the feet (2 Chron. 16:12). The nature of the treatment provided by his physicians is not given, but it was unsuccessful, and he died after two years. He may have been afflicted with gout, but this is uncertain.

King Jehoram died with a painful intestinal disorder (2 Chron. 21:18–20). King Uzziah died of leprosy (2 Chron. 26:19–23). King Herod Agrippa I died of some kind of parasitic disease (Acts 12:21–23). Several kings died of injuries received in battle. Ahaziah died following a fall from the upper portion of his home in Samaria (2 Kings 1:2–17). When illness or accident occurred in the ancient world, it mattered little whether one was a royal person or a commoner—in either case, only limited medical help was available.

Several illnesses accompanied by fever are mentioned in the Bible (Matt. 8:14–15; John 4:46–52; Acts 28:8). In the last cited reference, the ill man also had dysentery. Dysentery has several causes, but a very common and serious type in the biblical world was caused by amoeba, an intestinal parasite. Most fevers were due to infectious diseases, including malaria. There was no effective treatment for any of these infections, and death was all too often the outcome. Infections of the eye often resulted in blindness.

Small children were particularly vulnerable to illness, and the death rate could be high. The Bible tells of many children who suffered illness and sometimes death (2 Sam. 12:15–18; 1 Kings 17:17–24; 2 Kings 4:18–37; Luke 7:11–15; 8:40–56; John 4:46–52).

Since there was relatively little good medical care available and since illness so often led to disastrous results, it is not unexpected that sick persons in biblical times frequently asked for divine help. The Hebrew people were no exception to this practice. They often sought the help of God directly through prayer or through some person who was believed to possess special God-granted power to heal. A large number of the miracles described in the Bible are miracles of healing.

Surgery The only surgical procedure mentioned in the Bible is circumcision. This was done for religious rather than medical reasons and was not ordinarily performed by a doctor. In many ways, however, advances in surgery occurred more rapidly than progress in other branches of medicine in many countries. Descriptions of operations have been found in ancient literature, and some old surgical tools have been found in the ruins of ancient cities. Skeletons and mummies sometimes bear the traces of ancient surgical procedures.

Boils were lanced; broken bones were set; arms and legs were amputated. Holes were drilled into skulls to relieve pressure, and stones were removed from the urinary bladder. Teeth were also extracted. Ancient mummies have been found with gold fillings in their teeth. In addition, false teeth, using human or animal teeth, were being prepared by at least 500 B.C. Other kinds of daring operations were performed. Surgery called for boldness both on the part of the doctor and the patient.

Jesus and the Treatment of Disease One of the major ministries of Jesus was the healing of ill persons. They flocked to Him in large numbers, often after having tried all the remedies available in their day. They were desperate for help.

Jesus did not believe that all illness was the direct result of sin (John 9:1–3). He had the power, however, both to forgive sin and to heal (Matt. 9:1–8; compare Mark 2:1–12; Luke 5:17–26). Ordinarily, He did not use any kind of secondary means to treat the afflicted, although on several occasions He used spittle (Mark 7:32–35; 8:22–25; John 9:6–7). Some of the illnesses treated by Jesus probably had a psychosomatic basis; but many others undoubtedly had organic causes, including birth defects, accidental injuries, and infections.

Regardless of the cause of their distress, people found that Jesus could truly help. There can be no doubt that the ability of Jesus to perform miracles is seen most vividly in His healing ministry. The blind, the deaf, the lame, and sufferers of all varieties found in Him the help that was often not available through regular medical channels.

Kenneth Eakins

DISH A utensil for holding or serving food. The Old Testament uses three terms for dish: a large, shallow metal dish (Judg. 5:25; 6:38), a platter (2 Kgs 21:13), and a deep dish or bowl (Ex. 25:29; 37:16; Nm. 4:7; 7:13). Dishes were generally made of earthenware. Those made of wood were more highly prized (Lev. 15:12). Dishes made of precious metal were used by the rich and in the Temple. In the Ancient Near East those gathered at a meal usually ate out of one central dish (Matt. 26:23; Mark 14:20). To offer a person a choice piece of food from the common dish was a special sign of hospitality.

DISHAN (Dī′ shăn) Personal name meaning, "bison" or "antelope." This may be a variant spelling/pronunciation of Dishon. See *Dishon.*

A Horite chief and son of Seir (Gen. 36:21,28,30). Apparently, these Horites controlled the land of Edom before the Edomites entered the land. See *Edom; Horites; Seir.*

DISHON (Dī′ shŏn) See *Dishan.* Name of Horite chief of Edom (Gen. 36:21,25,26,30). The name may be the same as Dishan with the variant spelling used to identify the separate individuals.

DISHONOR See *Shame and Honor.*

DISPENSATION An administration, ministry, or stewardship for which a person has responsibility in God's administration of salvation. In certain interpretations of Scripture, a period of time during which people are tested in respect to their obedience to a specific revelation of God's will. "Dispensation" appears four times in the King James Version (1 Cor. 9:17; Eph. 1:10; 3:2; Col. 1:25). Each time it translates the Greek *oikonomia,* which normally refers to an office and the management functions related to the office. See Luke 16:2–4. In Ephesians 3:9 KJV translates the term, "fellowship," and in 1 Timothy 1:4, "edifying." Modern translations differ in translating *oikonomia* in the four basic passages.

The New American Standard translates *oikonomia* as "stewardship" in all but the Ephesians 1:10 passage which translates it "administration." New Revised Standard Version translates it "commission" except for Ephesians 1:10 for which the translation is "plan." The New International Version translates *oikonomia* differently in each passage: 1 Corinthians 9:17, "trust"; Ephesians 1:10, "put in effect"; Ephesians 3:2, "administration"; Colossians 1:25, "commission."

The New Testament thus uses *oikonomia* to refer either to Paul's ministry in his apostolic office or God's administration of the world and of His plan of salvation for it. Paul thus had a part in working out God's eternal plan of salvation.

Modern Technical Usage The word "dispensation" became prominent in biblical studies in a recent eschatological movement which dates back to 1830 in Scotland. This movement called "dispensationalism" can be traced back to the visions of Margaret McDonald, a member of the Plymouth Brethren Church. She believed that the return of Christ would be in two distinct stages. The believer would be caught up to the Lord in the air before the days of the antichrist. Then there would be a final revelation of Christ at the end of the age.

The Role of J.N. Darby This two-stage return of the Lord, unheard of before 1830, became the platform for a movement called "dispensationalism." Miss McDonald's pastor J. N. Darby (1800–1882) picked up on her idea and began to make use of it in his sermons. Darby was responsible for developing the two-stage coming of Christ into a fully developed eschatology or theology. He had been an Anglican clergyman until 1827 when he left the church to join the Plymouth Brethren.

Darby set forth the idea that God has set up seven time periods called dispensations for His work among human beings. The seventh or last dispensation will be the millennial reign of Christ (Rev. 20). In each dispensation, people are tested in reference to the obedience of God's will according to a specific revelation of that will.

The Role of C. I. Scofield Darby visited the United States on several occasions and won many advocates to his theology. However, C. I. Scofield popularized the dispensational system in his study Bible of 1909. He set forth seven dispensations in God's dealing with human beings.

1. Innocency (Gen. 1:28) This is the period of time in the Garden of Eden.

2. Conscience (Gen. 3:23) This is the awakening of human conscience and the expulsion from the garden.

3. Human Government (Gen. 8:20) This is the new covenant made with Noah, bringing about human government.

4. Promise (Gen. 12:1) This is the new covenant made with Abraham.

5. Law (Ex. 19:8) This is the period of acceptance of the Jewish law.

6. Grace (John 1:17) This dispensation begins with the death and resurrection of Jesus.

7. Kingdom (Eph. 1:10) This constitutes the final rule of Christ.

Program of Eschatology Beyond the seven dispensations, the Darby movement had a definite program of eschatology in five steps.

1. A two-stage coming of Christ—rapture and parousia.

2. Seven years of tribulation on earth for those not raptured. The last three and a half years will be the time of the antichrist. One hundred forty-four thousand Jews will accept Christ and become evangelists.

3. Christ will return with the church, conclude the battle of Armageddon, and rule for a thousand years.

4. Belief in an unconditional covenant with Israel. Thus God is working through Israel and the church. In the millennium, national Israel will be restored.

5. All Old Testament prophecy will be fulfilled literally.

Some of the more popular advocates of dispensationalism have been C. H. MacKintosh, W. E. Blackstone, H. A. Ironside, A. C. Gaebelein. More recently Hal Lindsey has made the system a best seller in *The Late Great Planet Earth.* The Book of Revelation has become a key book in the dispensational approach. Dispensationalists see the rapture taking place in Revelation 4:1 and the rest of the book (chs. 4—18) dealing with the seven years of tribulation. Thus the book has very little significance for Christians who will not be on earth during that time. See *Millennium; Revelation.*   *James L. Blevins*

DISPERSION See *Diaspora.*

DISSIPATION Deceptive desires leading to a lifestyle without discipline resulting in the dizzy hangovers of drunkenness. The Greek word *apatē* means, "deception" caused by riches (Matt.

13:22) and sin (Heb. 3:13). This is founded in the deceptive lusts of the unredeemed human heart (Eph. 4:22). People following such a way of life will suffer "the penalty for doing wrong" as they continue "reveling in their dissipation" (2 Pet. 2:13 NRSV). *Asotia* means to be hopelessly sick and refers to a life-style by which one destroys oneself. It is the prodigal son's "wild living" (Luke 15:13 NIV). It is the life of "dissipation" resulting from drinking wine (Eph. 5:18 NAS). Compare Titus 1:6; 1 Peter 4:3–4. The Bible speaks against a disorderly life, whereas the Greeks used the term to mean a wasteful or luxurious life. The Bible teaches believers to avoid both life-styles.

DISTAFF A part of the spindle used in spinning wool (Prov. 31:19). The obscure Hebrew word may refer to a small disk at the bottom of the spindle used to make the wheel spin faster.

DISTRICT Translates several different Hebrew and Greek words referring to a region, territory, or land. In the Old Testament district often connotes a part of a larger whole, either the provinces of an empire (1 Kings 20:14–19), regions within a country (2 Chron. 11:23), or sections of a city (Neh. 3:9–18). In the New Testament district often refers to the area around a city (Matt. 15:21; 16:13; Mark 8:10). At Acts 16:21 the reference is to an administrative area (perhaps Matt. 2:22 also). At times district means no more than the general area (Matt. 9:26,31).

DIVES (Dī' vēs) The name sometimes given to the rich man of whom Jesus spoke in Luke 16:19–31. *Dives* actually is the Latin word for "rich" used in Luke 16:19 in the Vulgate translation. The idea that this was the name of the man emerged in medieval times. See *Lazarus.*

DIVIDED KINGDOM The two political states of Judah and Israel that came into existence shortly after the death of Solomon and survived together until the fall of Israel in 722 B.C. The Northern Kingdom, known as Israel, and the Southern Kingdom, known as Judah, were operated as separate countries from approximately 924 B.C. until 722 B.C. At times, the two countries were at war with one another. At other times, they cooperated in a friendly alliance. The Northern Kingdom came to an end in 722 B.C., when the Assyrians destroyed the capital city, Samaria. The Southern Kingdom fell to the Babylonians in 587 B.C.

James Newell

DIVINATION AND MAGIC An attempt to contact supernatural powers to determine answers to questions hidden to humans and usually involving the future. The practice was widely known in the ancient Middle East, especially among the Babylonians who developed it into a highly respected discipline. Ezekiel 21:21 records, "For the king of Babylon stood at the parting of the way, at the head of the two ways, to use divination: he made his arrows bright, he consulted with images, he looked in the liver."

The ancient Babylonians and Assyrians employed several methods. The Babylonians commonly used hepatoscopy, divination by the liver. The liver of a sacrifical animal by virtue of being considered the seat of life could be observed carefully by specially trained priests to determine the future activities of the gods.

Other methods included augury (foretelling the future by natural signs, especially the flight of birds), hydromancy (divination by mixing liquids; see Gen. 44:5), casting lots (Jonah 1:7-8), astrology (2 Kings 21:5), necromancy (1 Sam. 28:7-25), observing the Urim and Thummim (1 Sam. 28:6), and by consulting the liver (Ezek. 21:21).

The use of magic is seen often in the literature of the ancient Middle East, employed both by the gods and by human beings. As superhumans, the gods themselves were subject to the higher power of magic. In *Enuma Elish,* the Babylonian Creation Story, the god of wisdom, Ea, killed his father Apsu, god of the fresh river waters, after reciting a spell. In the same epic, Marduk, the leader of the pantheon, went into battle against Tiamat, goddess of the chaotic sea, with a talisman of red paste in his mouth. Likewise, Tiamat relied on the recitation of a charm to cast a spell. To demonstrate his supreme position in the godhead, Marduk through the magical power of his word caused a piece of cloth to vanish and to reappear. To assure her reappearance on the earth, Ishtar, the goddess of love and fertility, donned charms before descending to the underworld.

Similar beliefs in magic are evident from ancient Canaanite myths. The supreme Canaanite deity El acted to heal the ill king Keret by working magic. The goddess Anath through magical means restored the dead Baal to the earth. Paghat, the daughter of the legendary king Daniel, observed the movements of water and of the stars.

The Old Testament often attests to the practice of magic by the Hebrews themselves, reflecting how entrenched it was. Saul, the first Hebrew king, is said to have "put away those that had familiar spirits, and the wizards, out of the land" (1 Sam. 28:3), but even he later sought out a necromancer (1 Sam. 28:7). Jehu responded to the question of Joram, king of Israel, as to whether he came in peace, "What peace, so long as the whoredoms of thy mother Jezebel and her witchcrafts are so many?" (2 Kings 9:22). Isaiah 2:6 accuses the house of Jacob of being "full of diviners from the east and of soothsayers like the Philistines" (NRSV). Isaiah 3:2-3 reflects that the society attaches the same importance to "the diviner," "the skillful magician," and "the expert in

charms" as to "the mighty man, and the soldier, the judge, and the prophet" (RSV). Consequently, King Manasseh could make public use of such services (2 Chron. 33:6). The people acted in a similar fashion. Jeremiah 27:9 admonishes the people not to heed "your [false] prophets, . . . your diviners, . . . your dreamers, . . . your enchanters, or your sorcerers." (Compare 29:8).

Although varying kinds of divination and magic are reported to have been practiced widely in ancient Israel and among her neighbors (Deut. 18:9-14; 1 Sam. 6:2; Isa. 19:3; Ezek. 21:21; Dan. 2:2), Israel herself was clearly and firmly admonished to have no part in such activities. "You shall not practice augury or witchcraft" (Lev. 19:26 RSV). "Do not turn to mediums or wizards; do not seek them out to be defiled by them" (Lev. 19:3 RSV). *Karen Joines*

DIVINER'S OAK A place visable from the gate of Shechem (Judg. 9:35,37). Some translations understand the underlying Hebrew to refer to a plain (KJV, plain of Meonenim; NRSV, Elon-meonenim). Others translate as the diviner's oak (NAS), Soothsayers' terebinth (REB), soothsayers' tree (NIV) or "oak tree of the fortune tellers" (TEV). In this case the tree formed part of a sanctuary. The terebinth was designated the diviner's or soothsayer's tree since persons would go to the sanctuary seeking an oracle. The tree is perhaps that associated with Abraham (Gen. 12:6), Jacob (Gen. 35:4), and Joshua (Josh. 24:26). Compare Deuteronomy 11:30, Judges 9:6. It may well have played an important role in Canaanite worship at Shechem before Israel took over the ancient worship place. It was apparently located near the east gate of the city.

DIVINE FREEDOM Absolute freedom is one of the chief attributes of God. God is self determining. He acts according to His own choosing to accomplish His plans and purposes. In so doing He pleases the requirements of His nature (Ps. 115:3; Ps. 135:6; Isa. 42:21; Eph. 1:11). No person or entity puts God under necessity. He is in all ways and at all times free to choose and act as He pleases. The only necessity that God has upon Him derives from His nature (Job 34:13; Ps. 135:5; Isa. 45:7; Jer. 18:6; Lam. 3:37-38; Matt. 20:15; Rom. 11:33-36). God does not at any time act contrary to His nature (Heb. 1:12). God's freedom does not mean, therefore, that He authors those things which are imperfect or calculated to bring harm to the person or purposes of His creation (Jas. 1:17).

God's nature is the source of His freedom. Several aspects of His nature clarify God being able to act freely at all times. One of these is God's supremacy. God is a unique Being. He is not one of many gods but reigns as supreme over all (1 Chron. 29:11; Neh. 9:6; Ps. 24:1; Isa. 44:6).

He is self-existent and independent within Himself (Ex. 3:14; Deut. 32:40; Jer. 10:10; John 5:26). As absolutely supreme, He is free to act as He wishes.

God's power gives Him absolute freedom (1 Chron. 29:12). This enables Him to accomplish anything consistent with His nature (Luke 1:37). God is also Spirit (John 4:24). He is thus totally free of the space or time limitations of this universe (Ps. 139:7–12). God is free to be anyplace at anytime with anybody.

Since God is free, He always wills and acts voluntarily and without compulsory outside influence. This does not mean that there is no influence to which God responds. The influence exerted upon God comes from God's nature. Some of the characteristics of God's nature that influence His actions toward His creation are grace (2 Cor. 8:9), justice (Zeph. 3:5), love (John 3:16), and mercy (Mic. 7:18; Titus 3:5).

The implications of divine freedom for mankind are vast. God's creation was established with the qualities of God inherent in it. History involves free interaction between people and God. A fatalistic view of creation or of mankind in particular is not in keeping with the way God exercises His freedom. God's freedom gives humans confidence that God cares for His creatures and works for their good (Rom. 8:28). God is interested in people and takes an active, positive role in the affairs of His creation. *Bob Sheffield*

DIVINE RETRIBUTION Process of God's meting out merited requital—punishment for evil or reward for good. Retribution involves the act of paying someone back according to their behavior. Thus, many (incorrectly) think that "divine retribution" means only an expression of God's wrath. "Divine retribution," however, involves both reward and punishment, blessing and curse. The notion of divine retribution involves questions concerning time (when will one be judged?) and method (on what basis will judgment occur?). These questions, in turn, call to mind other issues such as suffering, evil, and God's justness.

Though the exact phrase "divine retribution" does not occur in the Old Testament, the idea is quite prevalent: people will be repaid in this life for what they do—blessing for good, punishment for evil. Both sides of divine retribution can be detected in the history of ancient Israel. Abraham's obedient response to God's call resulted in his being blessed and becoming the mediator of blessing to all the world (Gen. 12:1–3). Israel, if they heard and obeyed God's word, would be blessed (Deut. 6:1–9). However, banishment from Eden, the flood, and multiplication of languages followed on the heels of sin. Pharaoh and all Egypt incurred God's judgment for not yielding to God's will. Even Israel, because of her failure to place her trust in God, experienced the judgment

of Exile. The Psalms affirm that the same process occurs on an individual level that occurs on the corporate. The book of Job, however, issues a proviso to such a mechanical view of God and suffering in this life. It is dangerous to interpret all suffering as punishment. Humans cannot determine the causes of suffering and should never overlook God's patience, forgiveness, and mercy.

The New Testament also affirms that humans are rewarded and punished by God in this life (Gal. 6:7–8). In fact, the wage earner is a profound image for the life of Jesus' disciple. Blessing and reward come to those who live life in accordance with the reality of the Kingdom of God (Matt. 5—7; Mark 10:41; Luke 10:7; John 9:36). The remarkable development in the New Testament is that reward/punishment in this life is a foretaste of that which will be experienced at the end of time. As in the Old Testament, the standard for reward and punishment is still God's character, His faithfulness. The standard has been revealed to all creation in the events surrounding the life, death, and resurrection of Jesus Christ. The Gospel is the standard by which God will reward and punish (Rom. 2:16). Furthermore, since it is a revelation both of God's faithfulness and of His wrath, Gospel preaching enacts the process of end-time judgment. Divine retribution, both as reward and punishment, is found in the gospel preaching and is a foretaste of the final reckoning that is to occur on that great and glorious day. See *Eschatology; Eternal Life; Everlasting Punishment; Future Hope.* *Carey C. Newman*

DIVINITY OF CHRIST See *Christ, Christology; Incarnation; Jesus; Pleroma.*

DIVORCE The legal ending of a marriage. From early time provision was made for divorce among the Israelites (Deut. 24:1–4). Presumably prior to this decree, a wife could be put out of the home at the pleasure of the husband. Now he was required to write out "a bill of divorce" and give it to his wife as proof that he was divorcing her. This gave some dignity and protection to the divorced woman.

Divorce was common enough among the Jews in New Testament times to cause division among the rabbis as to the valid basis for divorce. The passage in Deuteronomy did not give clear guidelines. "Because he hath found some uncleanness in her" (Deut. 24:1) left room for interpretation. One group of rabbis insisted that divorce could be granted only if the wife was immoral. Another group argued that divorce could be secured by the husband if the wife displeased him in any way. Among the Jews, only the husband had the right to secure a divorce. The wife might leave her husband, but she could not divorce him. The situation was different in the Roman world. There the wife had equal rights with the husband in the matter of divorce.

The teachings of Jesus are the clearest to be found in the Bible concerning divorce. He refused to be drawn into the rabbinical controversy over the possible valid basis for divorce. When such an attempt was made (Matt. 19:3–9; Mark 10:2–12), Jesus referred His questioners to the Old Testament law. They cited the permission granted in Deuteronomy 24. Jesus pointed out that this was not God's original intent. Divorce was permitted only because of "the hardness of your heart" (Mark 10:5). Then Jesus went back to God's original intent which was permanent monogamy, one man and one woman together for life. He supported this by referring back to Genesis 1:27 and 2:24. God intended marriage to be permanent.

On another occasion as Jesus taught about divorce (Matt. 5:31–32), He referred to the passage in Deuteronomy 24 as common knowledge among His hearers. He did not give His approval to the practice of divorce. Rather, He showed the consequences of divorce in the lives of people. If a man divorced his wife, he made her an adulteress unless the basis of the divorce was her own immorality. This statement has been understood in various ways. One idea is that Jesus was giving here a justifiable ground for divorce. If the wife violated her marriage vows, the husband had the right to divorce her. However, another suggestion is that Jesus was not making a law. Instead, he was saying that the husband would make the wife become an adulteress unless she had already become one by her own action. A divorced woman in Palestine of that day had few choices. To survive she could remarry or become a prostitute. In either case she was guilty of adultery. In a few instances, the divorced wife might have been able to return to live with her parents. Whichever interpretation of Jesus' statement is considered best, He indicated that God's intention was permanent marriage.

On only one occasion did Paul deal with the matter of divorce in his writings. The church at Corinth asked him questions concerning marriage. In his response to their questions, he had to give advice in matters relating to the marriage of a Christian with another Christian and that of a Christian with a nonbeliever (1 Cor. 7:10–13). With regard to the marriage of two Christians, he cited the teaching of Jesus. The Christian man should not divorce his wife, and the Christian woman should not separate from her husband. In the matter of a Christian married to a nonbeliever, Paul did not have a specific teaching from Jesus. But he gave his advice under the guidance of God's Spirit (1 Cor. 7:40). He stated that a Christian was not to take the initiative to divorce the nonbeliever. So long as the nonbeliever was willing to live in a proper marriage relationship, the Christian was to maintain that relationship.

Clayton Harrop

DIZAHAB (Dĭz' á hăb) Place name meaning, "place of gold." Place east of Jordan River used in Deuteronomy 1:1 to locate where Moses spoke to Israel. Nothing else is known of it. It may be located in Moab in modern ed-Dhebe.

DOCTOR See *Physician.*

DOCTRINE The basic body of Christian teaching or understanding (2 Tim. 3:16). Christian doctrine is composed of teachings which are to be handed on through instruction and proclamation. The teacher attempts to offer a clear and connected interpretation, for doctrine must be a coherent explication of what the Christian believes. **The Heart of Doctrine** The basic question for human beings is: "can we know the transcendent," that is, God? Religious doctrine deals with the ultimate and most comprehensive questions.

We speak as persons addressed; God has spoken to us (Heb. 1:1). With all the limitations of human language, we still attempt to reflect upon what we have heard through God's Word of revelation in history, Scripture, and the Christ. **The Flexibility of Doctrine** God and His Word remain consistent and unchanging. Human teaching about God has to be stated anew for each generation in the language that generation speaks. Without abandoning crucial affirmations, the church must address itself to the issues of each new day. It goes without saying that most Christian doctrines reflect something of the culture in which they were brought to speech and Scripture. **The Shaping of Christian Doctrine** Three factors guide a believer in the formulation of Christian doctrines: Scripture, experience, and intellect.

1. Scripture The Bible witnesses to the revelatory activity of God. The Bible functions both as witness to and bearer of revelation. Its authority lies in the events to which it points and the One to whom it testifies.

Scripture may, however, become bound to tradition. The church may become a servant to and rely only on inherited interpretations of Scripture. The church may adopt definitions having no other basis than earlier church statements and teachings. The result is traditionalism. This leads a church to become deaf to the Word of God and to fail to penetrate to the core of scriptural teaching. Doctrine may be perceived, then, as static and unchanging, or worse, irrelevant and meaningless.

Priority of apostolic tradition collected as Scripture over church tradition was the decision of the church. This was also the basic thrust and tenet of the Reformation. It is still a basic presupposition of Protestant Christianity: Scripture over tradition. Each generation must listen to the Word rather than simply depending on the church.

2. Experience A person has doctrine before being able to read and interpret Scripture. This comes through experience as an individual and as a part of a church community. Experience is not the most important factor in shaping or guaranteeing the truth of doctrine. Several aspects of one's experience do contribute to the shaping of Christian doctrine. These include personal, church, and cultural experience.

Personal experience includes one's moral struggle, intellectual quest, and mystical awareness of God, whether dramatic/emotional or quiet/contemplative. These are all integral to doctrinal understanding, providing evidence and understanding. Personal experience ensures doctrine is related to life and valid. It can also make doctrine idiosyncratic, untested by and unrelated to the experiences of history, of others, and to the truths of Scripture.

A church with its own tradition introduces us to faith. Christian nurture shapes our attitudes toward the Bible, our social consciousness, and our attitudes toward the goodness of life. The doctrine of our denomination takes root in us. Such shaping gives us doctrine roots and strength. It may also make us provincial, out of touch with the rest of God's people and ignorant of the world and its questions.

Culture shapes the way we think, the values we hold, the choices we make, and the way we relate to others. Peer pressure from our culture and our socioeconomic status affect our doctrine. Culture enriches and gives depth to life. It may so shape our expectations that it blinds us to truth.

There must be scope for the free activity of Christian feeling rooted in experience. When feeling, however, comes to be considered an immediate fountain of knowledge, the intellect is deprived of its rights, and the Bible sinks below its proper level. We must always guard against absolutizing our experience (or that of anyone else) as normative.

3. Intellect The church has framed the canon, creeds, and confessions as a means of giving coherent interpretation to the witness of the earliest church. Of course, the key question is: did these distort or accurately develop the tradition of the New Testament?

There must be as much scope for the free activity of the intellect in framing Christian doctrine as for Christian feeling. The exaggeration of the intellectual factor can also pervert doctrine. Mystery is difficult to explain logically. We must learn from the church's history and thus use confessions, creeds, and abstracts, to formulate Christian teaching for the present generation. At the same time we should retain a suspicion of any claim to have arrived at a comprehensive, exhaustive, definitive, or infallible statement of doctrine. The human intellect tests experience of personal life, church, and culture by the truth of Scripture to describe the church's beliefs in current language. Such descriptions remain open to correction and revising.

In the final analysis, every heresy is the inappropriate use of any one of the factors used to form doctrine. Scripture must be interpreted in language appropriate to present experience and in categories shaped by human intellect. Thus, the church must continue to clarify the focus of its teaching.   *Molly Marshall-Green*

DODAI (Dō' daî) Personal name related to Hebrew word meaning, "favorite" or "beloved." 1 Chronicles 27:1–15 describes David's army as being divided into twelve monthly divisions with an officer over each. Dodai was in charge for the second month. See *Ahohite*. Second Samuel 23:9 and 1 Chronicles 11:12 refer to Dodo the Ahohite, which is probably a variant spelling referring to the same person as Dodai. See *Dodo*.

DODANIM (Dō' dä nĭm) Great grandson of Noah and son of Javan in the table of nations (Gen. 10:4). In 1 Chronicles 1:7 the name is Rodanim. Early copyists made the easy confusion between Hebrew "r" and "d." If Rodanim is correct, the reference may be to inhabitants of Rhodes. If Dodanim is original, the identification of the people is not simple. It could refer to a land of Danuna known from the Amarna letters. This was apparently north of Tyre. A people with a similar name were among the Sea People who fought with Rameses III. Homer says Danaeans besieged Troy. Sargon II describes Yadanana who lived on Cyprus. Despite specific information, they were apparently from the Greek area and may have been Greek-speaking.

DODAVAH (Dŏd' å väh) or **DODAVAHU** (Dō dä vȧ' hū) Personal name meaning, "beloved of Yahweh." Father of Eliezer the prophet (2 Chron. 20:37).

DODO (Dō' dō) Personal name meaning, "his beloved." *1.* Grandfather of Tola, the judge (Judg. 10:1). *2.* Father of Eleazar, one of David's three mighty men (2 Sam. 23:9). In 1 Chronicles 27:4 he is called Dodai. *3.* Citizen of Bethlehem and father of Elhanan, one of David's warriors (2 Sam. 23:24).

DOE Modern translation where KJV has "hind" or "roe." The Hebrew has two words. *Ya'aalah* refers to the female ibex or mountain goat (Prov. 5:19), the mate of the ibex, *Capra nubiana* or *Capra sinaitica* (Ps. 104:18). *'Ayalah* is the female fallow deer (Gen. 49:21; 2 Sam. 22:34; Job 39:1; Pss. 18:33; 29:9; Jer. 14:5; Hab. 3:19; Song of Sol. 2:7; 3:5). The male, *Cervus captrolus,* is the hart or deer of Deuteronomy 12:15,22; 14:5; 15:22; 1 Kings 4:23; Isaiah 35:6; Psalm 42:2; Song of Solomon 2:9,17; Lamentations 1:6. See *Animals.*

DOEG (Dō' ĕg) Personal name meaning, "full of fear." An Edomite in the service of King Saul (1 Sam. 21:7). He was present at Nob at the time David arrived there during the course of his flight from Saul. Doeg subsequently reported to Saul that the priest Ahimelech had given assistance to David. After confronting Ahimelech, Saul ordered his guards to slay the priests of Nob. When the guards refused to obey, Saul told Doeg to kill the priests. In a grisly show of obedience, Doeg took the lives of eighty-five people. The title of Psalm 52 refers to this incident. See *Saul*.

DOG See *Animals*. Dogs served as watchdogs for herds (Isa. 56:10; Job 30:1) and for the dwelling (Ex. 11:7). Some were trained for hunting (Ps. 22:17, 21), but some ran stray in the streets (Ex. 22:30; 1 Kings 14:11). Metaphorically, "dog" was a term of contempt (1 Sam. 17:43) and self-abasement (1 Sam. 24:15). "Dog" may refer to a male cult prostitute (Deut. 23:19), though the exact meaning of "dog's wages" is disputed. The prophet insulted the priests by saying their sacrifices were no better than breaking a dog's neck and sacrificing the dog (Isa. 66:3). This means sacrifices is not needed in the new age and that the priests had neglected their first task, that of determining God's will.

Jesus used dogs to teach people to be discriminating in whom they chose to teach (Matt. 7:6). Paul insulted his Judaizing opponents, calling them dogs (Phil. 3:2; compare 2 Pet. 2:22; Rev. 22:15).

DOMINION Either political authority (Num. 24:19; Dan. 7:6,12,14) or the realm in which such authority is exercised (1 Kings 4:24; 9:19). Dominion may have a positive connotation as when humankind is given dominion over creation (Gen. 1:26,28; Ps. 8:6) or a negative connotation that approximates the idea of domination (Gen. 37:8; Judg. 14:4; Neh. 9:28). Though humans exercise dominion in the political sphere and over creation, ultimate dominion belongs to God (Ps. 72:8; Dan. 4:3,34). Dominion is used figuratively for the authority of the law (Rom. 7:1) and for the domination of sin (Ps. 119:113; Rom. 6:14) and death (Rom. 6:9). The dominion of Col. 1:16 are angelic powers which are subordinated to Christ.

DOMITIAN See *Rome, Roman Empire*.

DONKEY See *Ass*.

DOOR An opening for entering or leaving a house, tent, or room. At least five Hebrew words and one Greek term are translated "door" in the English Bible. The two most common Hebrew words have distinct usages, though they may be interchanged. *Petha* refers to the doorway, to the actual opening itself. *Deleth* alludes to the door

proper, usually made of wood sheeted with metal, though a slab of stone could be used. The Greek term *thura* is used for both of these Hebrew words.

"Door" is often used in a figurative sense in the Bible. In the Old Testament, "sin lieth at the door" (Gen. 4:7) means that sin is very near. The valley of Achor, a place of trouble (Josh. 7:26), is later promised as "a door of hope" (Hos. 2:15). It will become a reason for God's people to trust Him again.

In the New Testament Jesus calls Himself "the door" (John 10:7,9). Faith in Him is the only way to enter the kingdom of God. God gave to the Gentiles "the door of faith," or an opportunity to know Him as Lord (Acts 14:27). Paul constantly sought a "door of service," an occasion for ministry in the name of Christ (1 Cor. 16:9). Jesus stands at the door and knocks (Rev. 3:20). He calls all people to Himself, but will not enter without permission. *Bradley S. Butler*

DOORKEEPER A person guarding access to an important or restricted place. Temple doorkeeper was an important office in biblical times. The doorkeepers collected money from the people (2 Kings 22:4). Some Levites were designated doorkeepers (or "gatekeepers") for the ark (1 Chron. 15:23–24). The Persian kings used eunuchs for doorkeepers (Esther 2:21). Women also served this function (John 18:16–17; Acts 12:13).

The Hebrew word underlying the translation "doorkeeper" in Ps. 84:10 (KJV, RSV, NIV) appears only once in the Old Testament. The root idea is threshold. Thus some translations (NASV, REB, TEV) render the word by "at the threshold" or some similar expression. The reference is those waiting outside the Temple either to beg alms or to seek admission. The thought of the verse is that it is better to be standing outside the Temple than to be inside the tents of the wicked.

DOPHKAH (Dŏph' kăh) Place name perhaps meaning, "(animal) drive." Station in the wilderness between wilderness of Sin and Rephidim where Israel camped (Num. 33:12). It has been located at modern Serabit el-Chadim, but this is uncertain.

DOR (Dôr) Place name meaning, "dwelling." Canaanite city located at modern khirbet el-Burj, twelve miles south of Mount Carmel. Its early history shows connections with Egypt under Rameses II and with the Sea Peoples, who are closely related to the Philistines. Apparently the Tjeker, one of the Sea Peoples, destroyed the city shortly after 1300 B.C. Its king joined the northern coalition against Joshua (Josh. 11:2; 12:23) but met defeat. The Hebrew expression here, "*Naphoth Dor,*" or heights of Dor is unexpected,

View of the ancient harbor at Dor in Israel.

since Dor lies on the seacoast. The reference must be to Mount Carmel. Dor lay in the territory assigned Asher, but the tribe of Manasseh claimed it (Josh. 17:11). The Canaanites maintained political control (Josh. 17:12; Judg. 1:27). Dor served as a district headquarters under Solomon, governed by Solomon's son-in-law Ben-abinadab (1 Kings 4:11).

DORCAS (Dôr′ càs) Personal name meaning, "gazelle." A Christian woman of Joppa who was known for her charitable works (Acts 9:36). She was also called Tabitha, an Aramaic name. When she became sick and died, friends sent for the apostle Peter. He came to Joppa. Through him Dorcas was restored to life. This was the first such miracle performed through any of the apostles, and it resulted in many new believers.

DOT REB translation of Greek term "little horn" (Matt. 5:18; compare Luke 16:17), rendered in various ways in English translations (e.g. tittle, KJV; stroke of a letter or pen, NASV, NRSV, NIV). The dot is generally held to be a mark distinguishing similarly shaped letters, either the raised dot distinguishing *sin* from *shin* or else the hooks used to distinguish others (e.g., *beth* and *kaph*). Others suggest the letter *waw* is intended. *Iota,* translated "jot" or "smallest letter" is the smallest Greek vowel and is generally taken to represent the smallest Hebrew letter, *yodh.* Jesus thus contended that is was easier for heaven and earth to pass away than for the smallest detail of the law to be set aside. Matthew's qualification "until all is accomplished" is perhaps a reference to the saving work of Christ as the fulfillment of all Scripture.

DOTHAN (Dō′ thăn) Place name of uncertain meaning, also known as Dothaim. A city of the tribe of Manasseh, west of the Jordan, northeast of Samaria, southeast of Megiddo, and now identified as Tell Dotha. It was located in an area less productive for agriculture and was traversed by roads used for commerce. Dothan is the area to which Joseph traveled to find his brothers (Gen.

37:17). From there, Joseph was sold to a caravan of Ishmaelites and carried to Egypt, following an ancient trade route over the Plain of Dothan to Egypt. Dothan was the place Elisha stayed (2 Kings 6:13). The king of Syria sought to capture Elisha by laying siege to the city. Elisha then

Excavations of the ruins at Dothan in Israel.

led the Syrian army away from Dothan to Samaria and defeat. Dothan is 5 miles southwest of Genin, 11 miles northeast of Samaria, and 13 miles north of Shechem.   *David M. Fleming*

DOUBLE-MINDED An expression James used (1:7–8; 4:8) to express the opposite of purity of heart. Ps. 12:1–2 forms the Old Testament background of the term. There the faithful are contrasted with liars who speak from a double heart, that is, from divided loyalties. Jesus' teaching on the impossibility of serving two masters (Matt. 6:24; Luke 16:13) forms the New Testament background. This teaching is expressed in James 4:4 as the impossibility of maintaining friendship with the world and friendship with God.

James urged those who pray to do so without doubting. This doubting is not so much intellectual doubt (Does God exist?), but doubt about commitment (Am I committed to this God to whom I pray? Will I make use of this wisdom for which I pray?). Such doubt is described as double-mindedness. The double-minded are unstable in all their ways, that is, they vacillate between following God's way and their own way (1:7–8). The solution to double-mindedness is to draw near to God who can purify the heart (4:8).

DOUBLE-TONGUED One of the qualifications of deacons is that they not be double-tongued, that is, inconsistent in speech (1 Tim. 3:8). James 3:9–10 warns of the inconsistency of those who bless God while cursing those made in the image of God. 1 John 3:18 encourages consistency of loving words with loving actions. Inconsistency of speech might be taken as thinking one thing and saying another or as saying one thing to one, another thing to another.

DOUGH Flour or meal mixed with liquid, usually water but sometimes olive oil as well, which is baked as bread. Dough was normally leavened, given time to rise, and then kneaded before baking (Jer. 7:18; Hos. 7:4). The necessity for haste at the Hebrews' departure from Egypt caused them to carry their dough before it was leavened (Ex. 12:34). See *Bread.*

DOVE See *Birds.*

DOVE ON FAR OFF TEREBINTHS Part of the superscription of Psalm 56 (NRSV; compare REB, NIV) probably a reference to the secular tune to which the psalm was to be sung. "Hind of the Dawn" (Ps. 22 REB) and "Lilies" (Ps. 45 NIV) are possibly other hymn tunes. An alternative explanation relates to the association of doves with the ritual of atonement. In this case the title indicates an atonement psalm. See *Terebinths.* KJV transliterates the Hebrew, Jonath-elem-rechokim.

DOVE'S DUNG An item sold as food for an incredible price (2 Kings 6:25) during the seige of Samaria. Some interpret dove's dung as bird droppings. 2 Kings 18:27 indicates that in time of seige persons could be reduced to eating their own excrement and drinking their own urine. Others have suggested that the dung was to be used as fuel or as a salt substitute. Others have suggested that Dove's Dung refers to a bulbous plant similar to a wild onion which was edible after boiling or roasting. Still others emend the text to read some type of bean pods (REB, NIV).

DOWRY A marriage present that ensured the new wife's financial security against the possibility her husband might forsake her or might die. The husband-to-be or his father paid the dowry or bride price to the bride's father to be kept for the bride. The bride could protest if her father used the dowry for other purposes (Gen. 31:15). In addition the bride received wedding gifts from her father and husband (Gen. 24:53; 34:12; Judg. 1:15). The amount of the dowry depended on customs of the specific tribes or clans and upon the economic and social class of the parties involved (1 Sam. 18:23–27, a passage also showing that service could be substituted for money; compare Gen. 29:15–30; Josh. 15:16–17). Besides guaranteeing future financial security, the dowry also compensated the bride and her family for the economic loss represented to her family by her leaving to join her husband's family. Deuteronomy 22:29 apparently puts the price at fifty shekels of silver, a much larger price than paid for a slave—thirty shekels (Ex. 21:32; compare Lev. 27:1–8). Payment of the dowry made the marriage a legal fact even before the official wedding ceremonies or consumation of the marriage. Ancient Near Eastern texts from different cultures show similar practices. Often the bride receives the dowry directly or indirectly through her father. See *Marriage; Family.*

DOXOLOGY A brief formula for expressing praise or glory to God. Doxologies generally contain two elements, an ascription of praise to God (usually referred to in third person) and an expression of His infinite nature. The term "doxology" ("word of glory") itself is not found in the Bible, but both the Old and New Testaments contain many doxological passages using this formula.

Biblical doxologies are found in many contexts, but one of their chief functions seems to have been as a conclusion to songs (Ex. 15:18), psalms (Ps. 146:10), and prayers (Matt. 6:13), where they possibly served as group responses to solo singing or recitation. Doxologies conclude four of the five divisions of the Psalter (Ps. 41:13; 72:19; 89:52; 106:48), with Psalm 150 serving as a sort of doxology to the entire collection. Doxologies also occur at or near the end of several New Testament books (Rom. 16:27; Phil. 4:20; 1 Tim. 6:16; 2 Tim. 4:18; Heb. 13:21; 1 Pet. 5:11; 2 Pet. 3:18; Jude 25) and figure prominently in the Revelation (1:6; 4:8; 5:13; 7:12).

David W. Music

DRACHMA (Drăch' mă) See *Coins.*

DRAGNET A large fishing net equipped with a weighted bottom edge for touching ("dragging") the river or lake bottom and a top with wooden floats allowing the net to be spread across the water (Isa. 19:8). Such nets were normally let down from a boat and then drawn to shore by a crew positioned on the beach. In the case of a large catch the net was hauled to shore by boat (John 21:6–8).

Habakkuk 1:14–17 pictures the residents of Judah as helpless fish before the Babylonian army, pictured as the fishermen. Here the fishing nets and hooks symbolize the Babylonian military machinery. The text is not evidence that ancient fishermen sacrificed to their nets or that the Babylonian sacrificed to their weapons of war. Rather the text points to the worship of military might.

Jesus compared the kingdom of God to a dragnet, containing both good and bad fish until the time of separation and judgment (Matt. 13:47).

DRAGON The term used by the KJV to translate two closely related Hebrew words (*tannim* and *tannin*). At times the terms appear to be interchangeable. Context indicates that the first term refers to a mammal inhabiting the desert (Isa. 13:22; 35:7; 43:20; Lam. 4:3). Most modern speech translations equate the animal with the jackal, though perhaps the wolf (REB) is intended. The second term has four possible uses: (1) "great sea monster" (KJV, "great whales") in the sense of a large sea creature (Gen. 1:21; Ps. 148:7), possibly a whale; this sense of *tannin* as created being may serve as a correction of sense 4; (2) a snake (Ex. 7:9–10,12; Deut. 32:33; Ps. 91:13); (3) a crocodile (Jer. 51:34; Ezek. 29:3; 32:3); here the beast is used as a symbol of Nebuchadnezzar of Babylon or the Egyptian Pharaoh; (4) a mythological sea monster symbolic of the forces of chaos and evil in opposition to God's creative and redemptive work (Ps. 74:12–14; Job 7:12; 26:12–13; Isa. 27:1; 51:9–10). Leviathan and Rehab are used as parallel terms.

In the New Testament Revelation develops sense 4, describing the dragon as a great, red monster with seven heads and ten horns. This dragon is clearly identified with Satan (the Devil) and is termed the deceiver and the accuser of the saints. As in the Old Testament texts, the dragon is put under guard (Rev. 20:1–3; see (Job 7:12) and later released for final destruction (Rev. 20:7–10; see Isa. 27:1).

DRAGON WELL A Jerusalem landmark in the time of Nehemiah which can no longer be identified with certainty (Neh. 2:13). The water source is described as a well (KJV, NAS, NIV), a spring (REB, NRSV), or a fountain (TEV). The NIV takes the underlying Hebrew word as Jackal rather than dragon. The Dragon Well has been identified with the Gihon spring, the main water source during the time of Hezekiah, the Siloam pool which was fed by the Gihon, the En-rogel spring located 210 meters south of the confluence of the Hinnom and Kidron valleys, or with a spring along the east side of the Tyropoeon Valley which has since dried up.

DRAWERS OF WATER Water carriers. See *Occupations, Professions in the Bible.*

DREAMS In the Ancient Near Eastern world dreams were real. They were not an extension of one's conscious or unconscious mind. Dreams were the world of the divine and the demonic. Dreams had meaning, too. They often revealed the future. They could show the dreamer the right decision to make. People even went to temples or holy places to sleep in order to have a dream which would show them the decision to make.

The dreams of common people were important to them, but the dreams of kings and of holy men or women were important on a national or international scale. One of the results was that many of the nations surrounding Israel had religious figures skilled in the interpretation of dreams. These figures could be consulted at the highest level of government for important decisions. In such nations as Egypt and Assyria, these interpreters even developed "dream books" by which they could give interpretations according to the symbols of a dream.

Dreams were important in the Old Testament,

too. Israel was forbidden to use many of the divining practices of her neighbors, but over a dozen times God revealed something through a dream. When we recognize that night visions and dreams were not strictly distinguished, we can find many more times in the Old and New Testaments that God used this method to communicate. In fact, prophecy and the dreaming of dreams were to be tested in the same way according to Deuteronomy 13.

What Dreams Were Interpreted? Not every dream was thought to be from God. Not every dream was a significant. Some could be wishful thinking (Ps. 126:1; Isa. 29:7,8). In times of need and especially when a person sought a word from God, dreams could be significant.

Not every dream needed to be interpreted. To note this we can distinguish three types of dreams. A simple "message dream" apparently did not need interpretation. For instance, Joseph, in Matthew 1 and 2, understood the dreams concerning Mary and Herod even though no mention is made of interpretation. A second type, the "simple symbolic dream," used symbols, but the symbolism was clear enough that the dreamer and others could understand it. The Old Testament Joseph had this kind of dream in Genesis 37. Complex symbolic dreams, though, needed the interpretive skill of someone with experience or an unusual ability in interpretation. The dreams of Nebuchadnezzar described in Daniel 2 and 4 are good examples of this kind of dream. Even Daniel himself had dreams in which the symbolism was so complex that he had to seek divine interpretation (Dan. 8).

Were Dreams Ever Wrong or Wrongly Interpreted? Dreams were neither foolproof nor infallible. Both Jeremiah and Zechariah spoke against relying on dreams to express the revelation of God. Dreams could come without being God's word (Jer. 23:28). Jeremiah lumped dreamers together with soothsayers, sorcerers, and false prophets (Jer. 27:9). He cautioned exiles in Babylon not to listen to dreamers and false prophets who told them that the Exile would not be long (Jer. 29:8). Zechariah pointed people toward the Lord, apparently because they were relying on dreamers and others to give them the truth (Zech. 10:1–2). Thus, while dreams were often used by God to reveal His will, there is a warning, too, not to rely on this method to know the will of God.
See *Inspiration; Oracles; Prophets; Revelation.*
Albert Bean

DRESS See *Clothing.*

DRESSER OF SYCAMORE TREES One of the occupations of the prophet Amos (Amos 7:14). The tending involved slitting the top of each piece of fruit to hasten its ripening and to produce a sweeter, more edible fruit. Fruit infested with insects might be discarded at this time as well. The significance of Amos' trade is twofold: (1) He was a prophet solely because of the call of God, not because of training in a prophetic school; and (2) contrary to the accusation of the priest Amaziah (7:12), Amos did not earn his living by prophesying.

DRIED GRAPES Raisins. Grapes were dried in clusters for a food that was easily stored and transported (1 Sam. 25:18; 30:12; 2 Sam. 16:1; 1 Chron. 12:40). Nazarites were prohibited from eating dried grapes (Num. 6:3).

DRINK Beverages. Water was the primary drink. It was drawn from cisterns (2 Sam. 17:18; Jer. 38:6) or from wells (Gen. 29:2; John 4:11). In times of draught it was necessary to buy water (Deut. 2:28; Lam. 5:4). Milk was also a common beverage though it was considered a food rather than a drink. Several types of wine were consumed. "New" or "sweet" wine was likely wine from the first drippings of juice before the grapes had been trodden. Some interpreters argue that new wine was unfermented. Some texts in which it is mentioned, however, allude to its intoxicating effects (Hos. 4:11; Acts 2:13). In a hot climate before the invention of refrigeration, it was not possible to keep wine many months past the harvest before fermentation began. Sour wine, perhaps vinegar mixed with oil, was a common drink of day laborers (Ruth 2:14; Luke 23:36). Wine was considered a luxury item which could both gladden the heart (Ps. 104:15) or cloud the mind (Isa. 28:7; Hos. 4:11). See *Milk; Water; Wine.*

DRINK OFFERING See *Sacrifice and Offering.*

DROMEDARY A species of camel. See *Animals.*

DROPSY Edema, a disease with fluid retention and swelling. Dropsy is a symptom of disease of the heart, liver, kidneys, or brain. The condition involves the accumulation of water fluid in the body cavities or in the limbs. Thus the TEV speaks of a man whose arms and legs were swollen (Luke 14:2).

DROSS Either the refuse from impure metal which is separated by a process of smelting (Prov. 25:4; 26:23) or else the base (impure) metal before the smelting process. Litharge (lead monoxide) from which silver was to be extracted is perhaps meant at Isaiah 1:22,25. The same sense is required if the reading dross is preferred over the emendation glaze (REB, NRSV, NIV) at Proverbs 26:23. Dross is a symbol of impurity. The wicked are pictured as dross (Prov. 25:4; Ps. 119:119) that renders the whole of society impure. Both Isaiah 1:22,25 and Ezekiel 22:18–19

speak of silver turned to dross as a picture of Israel's lost righteousness.

DRUNKENNESS A state of dizziness, headaches, and vomiting resulting from drinking alcoholic beverages. From Genesis 9:21 on, the Bible describes the shameful state of the drunken person and the shameful actions resulting from the state. Too much partying led to drunkenness and failure of communication between husband and wife (1 Sam. 25:36). It left a person defenseless against enemies (1 Kings 16:9–10; 20:16). They sang loud songs ridiculing other people (Ps. 69:12) and could not walk straight (Job 12:25; Ps. 107:27). They vomited (Jer. 25:27) and were in a daze, unaware of events around them (Joel 1:5). They ruined their future (Prov. 23:20–21). They could not protect themselves against unnecessary injuries such as avoiding a thornbush (Prov. 26:9). Drunken leaders ruin a nation (Isa. 28:1–9). Being drunk became a figure of speech for having to drink the disaster God was sending (Isa. 49:26; 51:21–22; Jer. 25:27–29; Ezek. 39:17–20).

The Jewish leaders tried to discredit Jesus, saying He was a drunkard (Matt. 11:19). Jesus warned that the cares of life may lead to anxiety and drunkenness (Luke 21:34). Paul repeatedly warned against the dangers of drunkenness (Rom. 13:13; 1 Cor. 5:11; Gal. 5:21; 1 Thess. 5:7). Timothy 3:3 and Titus 1:7 warn church leaders they must not be drunkards. Drunkenness is a pagan custom, not a Christian one (1 Pet. 4:3). Drunkards are among these who will not "inherit the kingdom of God" (1 Cor. 6:10).

DRUSILLA (Drū sĭl′ là) Wife of Felix, the Roman governor of Judea who heard Paul's case. Drusilla was a Jew and listened to Paul's arguments with her husband (Acts 24:24). She was the youngest daughter of Herod Agrippa I. She had been engaged to Antiochus Ephiphanes of Commagene, but he refused to become a Jew. King Aziz of Emesa did agree to be circumcised, and they were married. Atomos, a magician from Cyprus, helped Felix win Drusilla away from her husband. Apparently, her son Agrippa died when Mount Vesuvius erupted in A.D. 79. She may have also died in this disaster. See *Herod.*

DUKE KJV translation of Hebrew word for "chief." See *Chief.*

DULCIMER Apparently a Greek word used to name a musical instrument in Daniel 3:10. Many think the bagpipes are meant here (NAS). NRSV translates, "drum."

DUMAH (Dū′ măh) Place name meaning, "silence" or "permanent settlement." *1.* A son of Ishmael and the original ancestor of the Arabian tribe (Gen. 25:14) centered in the oases of Dumah, probably modern el-Gof, also called Dumat el-Gandel, meaning Dumah of the Rocks. Rulers in Dumah apparently led coalitions supported by Damascus and later by Babylon against Assyria between 740 and 700 B.C. Thus Assyria punished Dumah in 689 when they also defeated Babylon. Sennacherib conquered Dumah. The remainder of Assyrian history is filled with troubled relationships with Arabian vassals, particularly those around Dumah. Isaiah proclaimed an oracle against Dumah (Isa. 21:11). *2.* A city of the tribe of Judah (Josh. 15:52). It is probably modern khirbet ed-Dome about nine miles southwest of Hebron. It may be mentioned in the Amarna letters.

DUMBNESS See *Muteness.*

DUNG The excrement of man or beast. "Dung" translates several different Hebrew and Greek words. An ash heap or rubbish heap was used to convey the haunt of the destitute (1 Sam. 2:8; Luke 14:35).

The first mention of dung in the Bible was in connection with the sacrificial rites. The sacred law required that the dung, along with other parts of the animal, should not be burned on the altar but should be burned outside the camp (Ex. 29:14; Lev. 4:11–12).

A major disgrace for a Jew was to have one's carcass treated as dung (2 Kings 9:37). Dung has been used as fertilizer for centuries. It is recorded in Luke 13:8 and Isaiah 25:10 that the people of Palestine used it for that purpose. Dry dung was and is often used as fuel (Ezek. 4:12–15). Animal dung was used as fuel when it was mixed with straw and dried to a suitable state for heating the simple bread ovens.

The dung gate, one of the eleven gates of Jerusalem during Nehemiah's time (Neh. 3:14), was located in the southwest corner of the wall and was used for the disposal of rubbish, garbage, and dung. It led out to the Valley of Hinnom.

Paul used a powerful metaphor with the word dung when he made a comparison between his personal knowledge of Christ and those who did not know Christ (Phil. 3:8). The word is used also in Scripture to indicate symbolically the degradation to which a person or a nation might fall (2 Kings 9:37; Jeremiah 8:2).   *Gary Bonner*

DUNG GATE A Jerusalem landmark in the time of Nehemiah (Neh. 2:13; 3:13–14; 12:31). Located at the southwest corner of the wall, the gate was used for the disposal of garbage which was dumped into the Hinnom Valley below. Referred to as the Refuse Gate by KJV, NAS and Rubbish Gate by TEV.

DUNGEON See *Prison, Prisoners.*

DURA (Dū' ră) Accadian place name meaning, "circuit wall." Plain in Babylonia where King Nebuchadnezzar set up a mammoth golden image of a god or of himself (Dan. 3:1). The common place name does not lend itself to an exact location.

DUST Loose earth, used both literally and figuratively. Dust is used in figures of speech for a multitude (Gen. 13:16; Num. 23:10; Isa. 29:5) or for an abundance (of flesh, Ps. 78:27; of silver, Job 27:16; of blood, Zeph. 1:17). Dust is used as a metaphor for death, the grave, or Sheol (Job 10:9; Eccl. 12:7; Dan. 12:2). Dust on a balance is a picture of something insignificant (Isa. 40:15). Human lowliness in relationship with God as well as humanity's close relationship with the rest of creation is expressed in the making of persons from dust (Gen. 2:7; Job 4:19; Ps. 104:29). To return to dust is to die (Gen. 3:19; Job 10:9; 17:16). To place dust on one's head was a sign of mourning (Lam. 2:10; Ezek. 27:30; Rev. 18:19). This act was sometimes accomplished by rolling in dust (Mic. 1:10). Dust on the head may have been a sign of defeat and shame as well as mourning in Joshua 7:6. To throw dust was a sign of contempt (2 Sam. 16:13), though to throw it in the air may have been a demand for justice (Acts 22:23).

The Dung Gate in old Jerusalem.

D

To defile a crown in dust (Ps. 89:39) was to dishonor the office of king. To eat or lick dust (Gen. 3:14; Ps. 72:9; Isa. 65:25; Lam. 3:29; Mic. 7:17) was to suffer humiliation and powerlessness before an enemy. To lay one's horn (glory) in the dust was to experience humiliation and loss of standing (Job 16:15). To lay a soul in the dust (Ps. 7:5; 22:15) is to kill. To make something dust (Deut. 9:21; 2 Kings 13:7) is to completely destroy it. To raise from the dust (1 Sam. 2:8) is to rescue or exalt. To sit in the dust (Isa. 47:1) is to suffer humiliation.

For Jews to shake dust off their feet was a sign that Gentile territory was unclean. In the New Testament this action indicates that those who have rejected the gospel have made themselves as Gentiles and must face the judgment of God (Matt. 10:14–15; Acts 13:51).   *Chris Church*

DWARF A person of abnormally small size, especially one with abnormal body proportions. The Hebrew word translated as dwarf by most English translations of Lev. 21:20 is used in Gen. 41:3,23 to describe the emaciated cows and shrivelled heads of grain. Some thus understand the word to mean lean or emaciated. The early Greek and Latin versions understood the word to mean a type of eye disorder (compare REB). Though denied the privilege of making the offering to God, priests with such a blemish were permitted to eat the holy food with other priests and Levites.

DWELLING A place where someone lives, in biblical times either a tent (Gen. 25:27), house (2 Sam. 7:2), or the territory in which one lives (Gen. 36:40,43). The Old Testament repeatedly promises that those who keep the covenant will dwell in safety (Lev. 25:18–19; Zech. 2:10–11).

References to the dwelling place of God highlight both the imminence and transcendence of God. References which focus on God's drawing near to speak, listen, and fellowship include the following references to God's dwelling place: in the bush at Sinai (Deut. 33:16); in the tabernacle (Ex. 25:8; 29:45–46; 2 Sam. 7:2); at Shiloh (Ps. 78:60); in the land of Israel (Num. 35:34); in the Temple (Pss. 26:8; 43:3; 135:2; Matt. 23:21); on Mount Zion (Pss. 9:11; 20:3; 132:14) ; and in Jerusalem (Pss. 76:2; 135:21; Ezra 7:15). The Old Testament idea of God's dwelling with His people (Ezek. 37:27) is developed in a variety of ways in the New Testament.

The Word become flesh dwelt among humankind (John 1:14). The church is the dwelling place of God (Eph. 2:22). Christ dwells in believers' hearts (Eph. 3:17). Believers are the temple of God (1 Cor. 3:16) and their bodies the temple of His Holy Spirit (6:19). The New Testament closes with an echo of Ezekiel's hope of God's dwelling with His people in Revelation 21:3.

References focusing on the transcendency of God include those in which God is said to dwell in clouds and thick darkness (1 Kings 8:12), in a high and holy place (Isa. 57:15), or in light (1 Tim, 6:16). Though heaven is spoken of as God's dwelling (1 Kgs 8:30,39,43,49) even heaven cannot contain God (1 Kings 8:27).

Dwelling is used figuratively for the body. To dwell in a house of clay (Job 4:19) is to possess a mortal body. The heavenly dwelling of 2 Corinthians 5:2 is the resurrection body.   *Chris Church*

DYEING The process of coloring materials. The dying process is not mentioned in Scripture, though dyed material is. Blue, purple, and scarlet thread was used in the making of the tabernacle curtains (Ex. 25:4; 36:8,35,37). Dyed material was an important part of the spoils of war (Judg. 5:30). The work of the guild of linen workers (1 Chron. 4:21) may have included dyeing thread. Solomon requested the King Hiram of Tyre send him someone skilled in dyeing purple, blue, and crimson for the Temple curtains (2 Chron. 2:7; 3:14). Job 38:14 as emended by some modern translators (NRSV) speaks of the dawn's "dyeing" the sky. In the New Testament, Lydia was a seller of purple dyed goods (Acts 16:14).

The dyeing process involved soaking the material to be dyed in vats of dye then drying it. This process was repeated until the dyed stuff was the desired color. The process was concluded by soaking in a fixing agent which rendered the cloth colorfast. Blue dye was made from the rind of pomegranates, crimson from grubs or worms that fed on oaks, and purple from the shell of the murex shellfish. Since this shellfish was found only in the vicinity of Acre on the Phoenician coast and since only a small amount of a dye material could be extracted from each shell, this dye was especially valued. Archeological evidence suggests that in Palestine of Biblical times thread was dyed rather than whole cloth.

DYSENTERY A disease characterized by diarrhea, painful bowel spasms, and ulceration and infection of the bowels resulting in blood and pus in the excreta. Modern speech translations of Acts 28:8 render the "bloody flux" of the KJV as dysentery. Many interpreters also understand the chronic bowel disease which afflicted King Jehoram (2 Chron. 21:15,18–19) as dysentery. The non-technical language of the account does not permit a precise diagnosis excluding other diseases of the bowels such as chronic diarrhea or colitis. There is some disagreement on the nature of the symptoms given in 2 Chronicles 21:15. The REB together with many commentators understand the phrase usually rendered his bowels came out as a reference to a prolapsed bowel, that is, his bowel slipped from its normal position. Others understand the text to refer to excretion of the bowel itself.

E

View of the Eastern or Golden Gate of the temple area.

EAGLE See *Birds.*

EAR The physical organ of hearing. In the Old Testament the ears are involved in several rites. The right ear of priests were consecrated with blood (Ex. 29:20; Lev. 8:24). The right ears of lepers were also sprinkled with blood and oil as part of their cleansing (Lev. 14:14,17). If a slave volunteered to serve a master for life, the slave's ear was pierced with an awl into the master's doorpost (Ex. 21:6; Deut. 15:17).

The ears appear in a variety of expressions in both Testaments. To speak to someone's ears was to speak to them or speak in their hearing (Gen. 44:18; 50:4). To incline the ear was to listen (2 Kings 19:16) or even to obey (Jer. 11:8). To give ear was to pay careful attention (Job 32:11). To turn the ears toward wisdom (Prov. 2:2) was to desire understanding. Dull, heavy, closed, or uncircumcised ears expressed inattentiveness and disobedience (Isa. 6:10; Jer. 6:10; Acts 7:51). To stop the ears was to refuse to listen (Acts 7:57). Open ears were obedient, hearing ears. Open ears are a gift of God (Ps. 40:6) who sometimes uses adversity to open deaf ears (Job 36:15). To awake the ears was to make someone teachable (Isa. 50:4). To uncover or open the ear was to reveal something (Isa. 50:5). To let words sink into ones ears was to thoroughly understand (Luke 9:44). Sometimes the functions of the mind were attributed to the ear. Thus the ear exercised judgment (Job 12:11) and understanding (13:1).

EARLY RAIN See *Rain.*

EARNEST Sincerity and intensity of purpose or a deposit paid to secure a purchase. *1.* Earnest does not relate directly to any Hebrew or Greek word, but represents the attempts of translators to relay the sense of several grammatical constructions and words. For instance, KJV uses "earnest" or "earnestly" 24 different times as the translation of 13 different words, phrases, or constructions in the original languages. Some expressions have important theological significance. The fallen creation waits earnestly for redemption (Rom. 8:19). The Corinthians' earnest desire for Paul's welfare comforted him (2 Cor. 7:7). Believers should give earnest heed to Christian teachings (Heb. 2:1). In the agony of the cross Christ prayed earnestly (Luke 22:44). Paul urged the Corinthians to "covet earnestly the best (spiritual) gifts" (1 Cor. 12:31). Christians earnestly wait the new resurrection body (2 Cor. 5:2). Meanwhile, they earnestly contend for the faith (Jude 3).

2. The Greek *arrabon* is a first payment on a purchase which obligates the purchaser to make further payments. A payment made in advance, it secures legal claim to an article or validates a sales contract before the full price is paid. The concept is a Semitic one with the word being adopted into

Greek. The related Hebrew term appears in Genesis 38:17, where Judah promised to send Tamar a young goat and she asked for a pledge to hold until she received the promised animal. God has given believers the Holy Spirit in their hearts as an earnest or pledge of the salvation to come (2 Cor. 1:22; 5:5; Eph. 1:14). Daily relationship with the Spirit brings total confidence that God will complete His plan and the believer will share His gift of eternal life.

EARRING See *Jewelry, Jewels; Precious stones.*

EARS OF GRAIN The fruit-bearing spike of a cereal such as maize which included both seed and protective structures. American corn was unknown in the Ancient Near East. It is more proper to speak of the common grains of that area, namely, wheat and barley, as having heads. The law permitted passersby to handpick heads of grain from a neighbor's field (Deut. 23:25).

EARTH, LAND Earth and land are the principle meanings of the Hebrew word *'erets.* Earth and land differ in the degree of space involved: "earth" encompasses the whole planet; "land" designates a limited area.

'Erets **as Entire Created Sphere or Material Realm** In Genesis 1:1,2 the earth (*'erets*) is created with the heavens. However, the sentence structure stresses the earth more than the heavens. Creation brought to the earth both form and content. Light made the earth's form and content visible. The waters were separated and put in appropriate places. An earth that was exceedingly good came from God's creation (Gen. 1:31).

Other parts of the Bible also speak of God creating the earth (Isa. 40:28; 45:12). The Bible stresses God's personal involvement: "Mine hand also hath laid the foundation of the earth" (Isa. 48:13*a*). Compare Job 26:7; Isa. 42:5; 45:18.

'Erets **as Specific Territory or Land** Interpreters and translators must decide whether *'erets* means the whole earth or a specific land. The literary context (that which comes before and after the word) helps determine the precise meaning.

Naaman, the commander of the army of Syria, came to Elisha to be healed of leprosy. The maid of Naaman's wife told her mistress that Elisha could cure Naaman of leprosy. She was called "the maid that is of the land (*'erets*) of Israel" (2 Kings 5:4). Naaman, however, said of Elisha's God, "I know that there is no God in all the earth (*'erets*), but in Israel" (2 Kings 5:15). The context indicates that the same word in one verse means "land" and in another verse means the more comprehensive "earth."

'Erets **as Ground that Produces** The prophet Haggai condemned his people for being concerned with their own houses while the house of the Lord lay in ruins. The Lord had judged them.

A literal translation would be, "There has been no dew from the heavens, and the land [or ground] has withheld its produce" (Hag. 1:10).

'Erets as What Is Beneath the Earth or Land—the Underworld The prophet Ezekiel wrote literally of "the *land* of lowest places" (Ezek. 26:20). People of Tyre were going there (Ezek. 26:15,20). The people of Egypt were going there (Ezek. 31:2,14,16,18; 32:18,24). The RSV translates *'erets* in this case as "the nether world." The NIV uses "the earth below." Sheol was another name for the place of the departed dead (Ezek. 31:15–17 NAS).

In the Old Testament, the heavenly realm, the earthly realm, and the sub-earthly realm all described the place of God and angels, the place of people now alive, and the place of those who have died. The New Testament reveals more. Believers go to be with Christ (Phil. 1:21–24). In both the Old and New Testaments, earthly decisions and actions influenced future destiny.

Theological Questions Regarding 'Erets To whom did the land of Canaan belong? Who was to own and use the land?

According to Joel 2:18,19, the land of Canaan belonged to Yahweh. God was jealous "for his land." He would judge the nations because they had "parted my land" (Joel 3:2). God promised Abraham that He would establish His covenant with Abraham and with his descendants as an everlasting covenant; all the "land of Canaan" was to be for an everlasting possession (Gen. 17:8–9).

Do these verses tell us *who* is to own and use the land? No, because Israel broke that covenant. Paul spoke of an old covenant and a new covenant (2 Cor. 3:6, 14). Jeremiah spoke about both covenants. The new covenant was not like the old "which my covenant brake, although I was an husband unto them, saith the Lord" (Jer. 31:32). The Holy Spirit testifies to Christians about the new covenant (Heb. 10:15–18). The land belongs to the Lord, and He may apportion it to whomever He pleases.

Use and Ownership of Land ('erets) Those who joined land to land, house to house, field to field (in land monopolies) were condemned (Isa. 5:8–10). Woe was pronounced on selfish wealthy people—those at ease in Zion, those who lay on beds of ivory (Amos 6:1,4). Micah pronounced woes upon those who "covet fields, and take them by violence, and houses, and take them away" (Mic. 2:2). To prevent consolidation of land in the hands of a few, Leviticus proposed a fifty-year jubilee to return property to families (Lev. 25). "The land shall not be sold for ever: for the land is mine; for ye are strangers and sojourners with me" (Lev. 25:23). People were to permit redemption of the land to prevent its being controlled by only a few. The Lord of heaven and earth is also the Lord of individual lands. All of the earth as well as specific parts should be used to promote a good life for the inhabitants. People are to give thanks to the One who provided them with the means to achieve such a life.

A. Berkeley Mickelsen

EARTHQUAKE A shaking or trembling of the earth due to volcanic activity or, more often, the shifting of the earth's crust. Severe earthquakes produce such side effects as loud rumblings (Ezek. 3:12–13), openings in the earth's crust (Num. 16:32) and fires (Rev. 8:5). Palestine has two to three major quakes a century and two to six minor shocks a year. The major quake centers in Palestine are Upper Galilee,—near the biblical town of Shechem (Nablus)—and near Lydda on the western edge of the Judean mountains. Secondary quake centers are located in the Jordan Valley at Jericho and Tiberias.

The Bible mentions an earthquake during the reign of Uzziah (Amos 1:1; Zech. 14:5). The oracles of Amos are dated two years before this earthquake. The precise year of this quake has not been settled to everyone's satisfaction. Most would view the period between 767 and 742 B.C. as the likely dates for the earthquake.

Earthquakes are used symbolically in the Bible. Many times God's judgment or visitation is described using the imagery of an earthquake (Ps. 18:7; Isa. 29:6; Nah. 1:5; Rev. 6:12; 8:5; 11:13; 16:18) and is often seen as a sign of the end of time (Matt.24:7,29). Many times an earthquake is a sign of God's presence or of God's revelation of Himself (1 Kings 19:11–12; Ps. 29:8; Ezek. 38:19–20; Joel 2:10; 3:16; Acts 4:31; Rev. 11:19). At times the whole universe is described as being shaken by God (Isa. 13:13; 24:17–20; Joel 3:16; Hag. 2:6–7; Matt. 24:29; Heb. 12:26–27; Rev. 6:12; 8:5).

Even though earthquakes were usually seen in the Bible as things to escape (Isa. 2:19,21; possibly Amos 2:13–16; 9:1–4), they could be used by God for good purposes (Acts 16:26). The earth quaked in revulsion at the death of Jesus (Matt. 27:51–54) and the earth quaked to move the stone from Jesus' tomb (Matt. 28:2). Those who love God and are faithful to Him have no need to fear the trembling of the earth (Ps. 46:2–3).

Phil Logan

EAST See *Directions, Geographic.*

EAST COUNTRY A designation for territories lying in the direction of the rising sun. At Genesis 25:6 the reference signifies desert lands more than direction. At 1 Kings 4:30 the wisdom of the East, either of Mesopotamia or of the desert dwelling Arabs, together with the wisdom of Egypt signifies all wisdom. The East Country of Ezekiel 47:8 lies in the direction of the Dead Sea. The East Country and West Country of Zechariah 8:7 refer to the whole world.

EAST GATE This designation refers to three different gates. (1) KJV refers to the East Gate of Jerusalem as leading to the Hinnom Valley (Jer. 19:2). This valley lies to the south of the city rather than the east. Modern speech translations render this phrase Potsherd Gate. This gate may be identified with the Valley Gate (2 Chron. 26:9; Neh. 2:13,15; 3:13) or perhaps to the Refuse or Dung Gate (Neh. 2:13; 3:13–14; 12:31) located 1,000 cubits away. (2) The East Gate of the outer court of the Temple. Since the Temple faced east, this gate was the main entrance to the Temple complex (Ezek. 47:1). Levites in charge of the East Gate of Solomon's Temple had responsibility

The Golden Gate, sometimes called the East Gate, with the Kidron Valley in the foreground.

for the free-will offerings (2 Chron. 31:14). In a vision, Ezekiel saw the glory of the Lord depart through the East Gate before the destruction of the city (10:19). His vision of the new Temple included the return of God's glory through the same gate (43:1–2). God's use of this gate rendered it holy. It was to remain closed. Only the prince (messianic king) was allowed to enter it (44:1–3). (3) The East Gate of the inner court of the Temple. This gate was closed on the six working days but open on the sabbath (Ezek. 46:1).

EAST SEA Ezekiel's expression for the Dead Sea (Ezek. 47:18). See *Dead Sea.*

EAST WIND See *Wind.*

EASTER The special celebration of the resurrection at Easter is the oldest Christian festival, except for the weekly Sunday celebration. Although the exact date was in dispute and the specific observances of the festival developed over the centuries, it is clear that Easter had special significance to the early generations of Christians. Since Christ's passion and resurrection occurred at the time of the Jewish Passover, the first Jewish Christians probably transformed their Passover observance into a celebration of the central events of their new faith. In the early centuries, the annual observance was called the "pascha," the Greek

word for Passover, and focused on Christ as the paschal Lamb.

Although the New Testament does not give any account of a special observance of Easter and evidence from before A.D. 200 is scarce, the celebrations were probably well-established in most churches by A.D. 100. The earliest observance probably consisted of a vigil beginning on Saturday evening and ending on Sunday morning and included remembrance of Christ's crucifixion as well as the resurrection. Evidence from shortly after A.D. 200 shows that the climax of the vigil was the baptism of new Christians and the celebration of the Lord's Supper. By about A.D. 300 most churches divided the original observance, devoting Good Friday to the crucifixion and Easter Sunday to the resurrection. See *Church Year.*

Fred A. Grissom

EATING See *Cooking; Food.*

EBAL (Ē' bȧl) Personal and place name possibly meaning, "bare." *1.* Grandson of Seir and son of clan leader Shobal among the Horite descendants living in Edom (Gen. 36:23). *2.* Son of Joktan in line of Shem (1 Chron. 1:22). He is called Obal in Genesis 10:28 through a scribal copying change.

3. Mountain near Shechem on which Moses set up the curse for the covenant ceremony (Deut. 11:29; 27:13). An altar was also on Ebal (Deut. 27:4–5). Ebal rises 3100 feet with its stark rock, bare of vegetation, giving the appearance of curse. On the north of Shechem, it stands opposed to the fruitful Mount Gerazim, the mount of blessing to the south. Joshua carried out the covenant ceremony on Ebal and Gerazim (Josh. 8:30–35; compare 24:1–27), building an altar on Ebal. Later the Samaritans built their temple on Mount Ebal (compare John 4:20). See *Gerazim and Ebal.*

EBED (E' bĕd) Personal name meaning, "servant." *1.* Father of Gaal, who led revolt in Shechem against Abimelech (Judg. 9:26–40). See *Abimelech; Gaal.*

2. Clan leader who returned from Exile under Ezra (Ezra 8:6).

EBED-MELECH (Ē' bĕd mē' lĕch) Personal name meaning, "servant of the king." An Ethiopian eunuch in the service of King Zedekiah of Judah (Jer. 38:7). When Jeremiah was imprisoned in a cistern used as a dungeon, Ebed-melech was responsible for the prophet's rescue. As a result of his faith in the Lord, he received the promise recorded in Jeremiah 39:15–18.

EBENEZER (Ĕb' ĕn ē' zēr) Personal name meaning, "stone of help." The name of a site near Aphek where the Israelites camped before they fought in battle against the Philistines (1 Sam. 4:1). During the second of two engagements in the area, the Philistines captured the ark of the covenant. Later, after the recovery of the ark and a decisive Israelite victory over the Philistines, Samuel erected a monument to which he gave the name Eben-ezer.

EBER (Ē′ bēr) Personal name meaning, "the opposite side." *1.* The ancestor of Abraham and the Hebrew people, and a descendant of Shem (Gen. 10:21–25; 11:14–17). Numbers 24:24 apparently refers to him as the original ancestor of a people associated with the Assyrians and threatened by Balaam with destruction by Kittim. Precisely who was meant at this point is not known. *2.* A member of the tribe of Gad, called Heber by KJV (1 Chron. 5:13). The name entered Israel's record about 750 B.C. (v. 17). *3.* Clan leader in tribe of Benjamin (1 Chron. 8:12). *4.* Another clan leader of Benjamin (1 Chron. 8:22). *5.* Head of priestly family of Amok (Neh. 12:20) in days of Jehoiakim (609-597 B.C.).

EBEZ (Ē′ bĕz) Spelling of Abez in modern translations. See *Abez.*

EBIASAPH (Ė bī′ ȧ săph) Personal name meaning, "my father has collected or taken in." See *Abiasaph,* which has same Hebrew spelling. A Levite descended from Kohath (1 Chron. 6:23). The same person may be mentioned in verse 37, but the precise relationship of these family lists is uncertain with one or both possibly incomplete. He and his family kept the gate of the tabernacle (1 Chron. 9:19). The Abiasaph of Exodus 6:24 is apparently the same person.

EBLA (Ěb′ la) A major ancient site located in Syria about 40 miles south of Aleppo. Covering about 140 acres, the mound is known today as Tell Mardikh. Excavations have been conducted since 1964 by an Italian team headed by P. Matthiae. The discovery of over 17,000 clay tablets in the mid-1970's revealed a major Syrian civilization in the mid-third millennium and brought the site worldwide prominence by the late 1970's.

Excavations have revealed fourteen occupation levels at Ebla dating from 3500 B.C. to 600 A.D. Only four levels, dating from 2000–1600 B.C., cover the whole site and indicate the greatest power and prosperity of Ebla.

Level IIB1 (2600–2250 B.C.): This is the best known but also the most controversial period. Matthiae dates this period about 2400–2250 B.C. while the original epigrapher, G. Pettinato, dates it about 2600–2400 B.C. In any event, it is during this period that Ebla became a major city. It was the largest in northern Syria and the capital of a major kingdom with a population estimated as high as 260,000. Though the boundaries of the kingdom are uncertain, it probably extended

Near the ancient city of Shechem lies Mount Ebal.

across all of northern Syria into Mesopotamia. There Elba was challenged by Sargon and Naram-Sin of Akkad; the latter eventually destroyed Ebla about 2250 B.C.

Level IIB2 (2250–1900 B.C.): Though little excavation has been done on this level, Ebla was rebuilt and had some prosperity judging from references to it in contemporary Mesopotamian sources.

Level IIIA (1900–1800 B.C.): Ebla was again rebuilt with extensive fortifications. Some evidence indicates a new culture imposed by the Amorites which is also attested in Mesopotamia, Syria, and Palestine.

Level IIIB (1800–1600 B.C.): During this period Ebla was absorbed by the kingdom of Yamhad, a major kingdom to the north. Though not destroyed at the outset, Ebla's prosperity suffered. This period ended around 1600 B.C. when the Hittites under Hattusili I or Mursili I destroyed Ebla. Ebla never really rose to prominence again though limited occupation continued down to the Byzantine period around 600 A.D.

The 17,000 clay tablets have attracted the most interest at Ebla. Though few are published yet, they appear to date from about 2500 B.C. Most were discovered in the two rooms of Palace G in fallen debris, but in a way that allowed for reconstructing the original shelving. They are written in a cuneiform script similar to that used in Mesopotamia. Sumerian was used on a limited scale as well as a new language that has come to be called Eblaite. The later language was correctly assumed to be Semitic so that decipherment was almost immediate. Nevertheless, the complexity of reading the cuneiform signs has created significantly different readings, with attending controversies. At least four categories of texts are known: (1) administrative texts relating to the palace make up the majority (about 80%), (2) lexical texts for the scribes, (3) literary and religious texts, including accounts of creation and a flood, and (4) letters and decress.

Many early attempts to draw connections between Ebla and the Bible have not proven to be convincing. The term Ebla never occurs in the Bible, and no Biblical personalities or events have yet been identified in the Ebla tablets. Some Biblical personal names such as Ishmael have been attested at Ebla; but since they can be attested elsewhere in the Ancient Near East, this has no special significance. Claims that the Ebla tablets mention Biblical cities such as Sodom, Gomorrah, Jerusalem, and Hazor have not been substantiated. Efforts to identify the Israelite God Yahweh with the -ya elements of Eblaite personal names have not been compelling because these -ya elements can frequently occur in both Semitic and non-Semitic languages.

On the other hand, valuable general information can be gleaned from Ebla for the study of the Bible. Ebla was a major religious center, and over 500 gods are mentioned in the texts. The chief god was Dagon, a vegetation deity associated in the Bible with the Philistines (1 Sam. 5:2). Other gods include Baal, the Canaanite god of fertility, and Kamish (the Biblical Chemosh), god of the Moabites (Judg. 11:24). In addition, there is reference to "the god of my father" (compare Gen. 43:23). Some similarities between prophets at Ebla and Mari can be drawn with Israelite prophets, especially their call by the deity and their role as messengers of the deity to the people

Actually, contacts between Ebla and the Bible are by necessity limited for three reasons:

1. The illumination of the Bible using other Ancient Near Eastern civilizations is usually general cultural background rather than specific and direct connection.

2. A more specific limitation in this case is that the Elba tablets are generally too early to have specific bearing on the Old Testament.

3. Finally, the study of Ebla is in its infancy with very few texts already published. As more texts are published, we can expect additional information to illuminate not only the Bible but the rest of the Ancient Near East as well.   *James C. Moyer*

EBONY See *Plants, foreign trees.*

EBRON (Ē′ brŏn) City in territory of Asher (Josh. 19:28), spelled Hebron in KJV. Several manuscripts in Joshua 19:28 plus the lists in Joshua 21:30; 1 Chronicles 6:39 have Abdon. See *Abdon.*

EBRONAH (Ē brō′ năh) KJV spelling for Abronah. See *Abronah.*

ECBATANA (Ĕc′ bă tả nả) Modern translation spelling of Achmetha. See *Achmetha.*

ECCLESIASTES, BOOK OF Ecclesiastes is the English title of this wisdom book derived from the Greek Septuagint's translation of the original Hebrew, "Qoheleth." The word Qoheleth (1:1;

7:27; 12:8) suggests one who has a function as teacher or preacher in the assembly.

Date and Author An almost universal agreement, even among conservative scholars, thinks that Ecclesiastes was not written by Solomon. Solomon's name is never mentioned in the book. Qoheleth refers to gaining more wisdom than "all they that have been before me in Jerusalem" (1:16), which does not fit Solomon who had only David as his royal predecessor. Elsewhere, the writer speaks as if he were a subject rather than a ruler (4:13; 8:2; 9:14–16; 10:16–17,20) in a time of oppression (4:14), injustice (5:8), and social confusion (10:6–7). Moreover, the language of the book is clearly late, being the closest to postbiblical Mishnaic Hebrew of any book in the Bible. From these and other clues, scholars conclude that a later writer used a literary device, the "didactic autobiography" to present his teaching, probably between 300 and 200 B.C. Some scholars continue to argue for Solomon as author, thinking this is the only way 1:1 can be interpreted.

Literary Character After the title (1:1) and the introductory poem on the vanity of all things (1:2–11), the book takes the form of a "didactic autobiography" which recounts Qoheleth's project "to study and explore by wisdom all that is done under heaven" (1:13 NIV). Qoheleth undertook great building projects, enjoyed the best of life's pleasures, and in every regard achieved the pinnacle of human success. Still, he concluded that all this, including work and play, is merely "vanity." Qoheleth loosely maintained the form of the autobiography (2:9,24; 3:10,16; 4:7; 7:15; 9:13) as a device to weave together a great many wisdom forms and reflections on life, elaborating the theme of vanity. He concluded with an allegory on death. The autobiography is framed by the observation which began the book: "Vanity of vanities . . . all is vanity (1:2; 12:8). The book ends with a short third person epilogue, probably by an editor, which puts Qoheleth and his difficult book in theological perspective (12:9–14).

Content Ecclesiastes is a book which focuses upon the limits of life to teach wisdom. The point of view is that of the Solomon-like Qoheleth whose wealth, wisdom, and glory placed him at the upper limit of human success. From his royal pinnacle Qoheleth surveyed life and judged it to be vanity because of the inescapable limits God and sin place on even the most successful human being. Thus the book cannot be dismissed as the disillusioned pessimism of one whom life had cheated. Human limits are various: humans cannot make straight what is crooked (1:15); what is lacking cannot be numbered (7:13); nor can humans remove injustice (3:16) and oppression (4:1–2; 5:8) from the earth. Sometimes good folk receive evil while the wicked prosper (7:15; 8:14; compare Ps. 73). Thus, humans are unable to achieve their dreams and ambitions because of sin and because of their limited knowledge, power, and goodness. In his focus on limits Qoheleth, like Job, attacked those who selectively misuse traditional wisdom to promote a false gospel of unlimited success for the "righteous." Even if humans do seem to succeed, like Qoheleth himself, had even this is vanity, because their knowledge is limited and imperfect: "no man (*adam*) can find out the work that God maketh from the beginning to the end" (3:11). Moreover, even the best, richest, and wisest life is ended by death. Thus even the greatest goods and achievements, indeed, "everything under the sun" must be labeled as "vanity."

The Hebrew word translated as "vanity" is *hevel* whose literal meaning is "breath" or breeze. The author used this word metaphorically, often with the added phrase "striving after wind," to express the transience, weakness, and nothingness of human life. All things pass away.

Since life is vanity, what then is good? Qoheleth's answer has two points which are repeated several times in the book (though many commentators overlook this aspect of the book's teaching). The first point is summarized by the editor at the end of the book: "Fear God, and keep his commandments: for this is the whole duty of man" (12:13). God's sovereign actions are beyond human ability to change (7:13); God has done this "that men should fear before him" (3:14). It is God who has set the limits on human life and knowledge (7:14). Thus Qoheleth's world is "vain," but only in the sense noted above. It is not a world without God. Apart from God, "who can eat and who can have enjoyment?" (2:25 NAS). Even if a person experiences injustice (3:16; 5:8; 7:15; 8:14), God is still a just Judge (3:17–18) who acts in His own time (8:6; 11:9). For Qoheleth, worship of God and vows made to Him are matters of utmost seriousness (5:1–2,4). Since God judges sin (5:6), people should avoid foolish talk and "fear God" (5:7). "Although a sinner does evil a hundred times and may lengthen his life, still I know that it will be well for those who fear God, who fear Him openly. But it will not be well for the evil man and he will not lengthen his days, like a shadow, because he does not fear God" (8:12–13 NAS; compare 7:18).

Qoheleth's second point is: humans do not have sovereign control over life, being limited by vanity in all its forms, especially death. Because of this, they should enjoy life and its ordinary pleasures of work and play, food and drink, love and family, all as gifts from God (2:24–26; 3:12–13; 5:18–20; 9:7–10). If there is resignation in Qoheleth, it is that of one who has left the riddles and painful mysteries of life in God's hands, while accepting its limited joys with sober thanks.

Outline
I. Life is vanity because nothing new ever occurs (1:1–11).
II. Wisdom produces only vanity (1:12–18).
III. Pleasure and possessions are all vanity (2:1–11).
IV. Wisdom is no better than folly (2:12–17).
V. Labor brings only vanity (2:18–26).
VI. God plans the world but hides the plan (3:1–11).
VII. The wise conclusion: seek to enjoy life (3:12–22).
VIII. Illustrations show life is vanity (4:1–16).
IX. The wise conclusion: fear God (5:1–7).
X. Wealth brings no advantage (5:8—6:12).
XI. Proverbs illustrate the way of wisdom (7:1–14).
XII. Righteousness results in vanity (7:15–25).
XIII. Warnings are needed against the wiles and devices of women (7:26–29).
XIV. Wise conclusion: obey the King (8:1–9).
XV. Righteousness goes unrewarded (8:10–17).
XVI. All people share the same ultimate fate (9:1–12).
XVII. Wisdom does not provide the ultimate answer (9:13—10:20).
XVIII. Wise conclusion: act in the face of vanity (11:1–8).
XIX. Youth has the advantage (11:9—12:7).
XX. Wise conclusion: everything is vanity (12:8).
XXI. Parting advice: Learn from the teacher and obey God (12:9–14).

Raymond C. Van Leeuwen

ECONOMIC LIFE Economic life in ancient Palestine involved the simple desire to improve the condition of life and to expand contact with other peoples. The people's success in doing this was determined to a large extent by the environmental conditions in which they lived. Adequate rainfall or water sources, arable farm and grazing lands, and the availability of natural resources were the most important of these ecological factors. Once the nation was formed and the monarchy established, the demands of the local and international markets, government stability, and the effects of international politics also came into play. Throughout their history, however, the economic life of the people of Israel was at least in part governed by the laws of God which concerned the treatment of fellow Israelites in matters of business and charity.

Like most of the rest of the Near East, the economy of ancient Palestine was primarily agricultural. However, unlike the major civilizations of Mesopotamia and Egypt, Israel's economy was not as completely dominated by the concerns of palace or temple as they were in other nations. For instance, there was no state monopoly on the ownership of arable land. Private ownership of

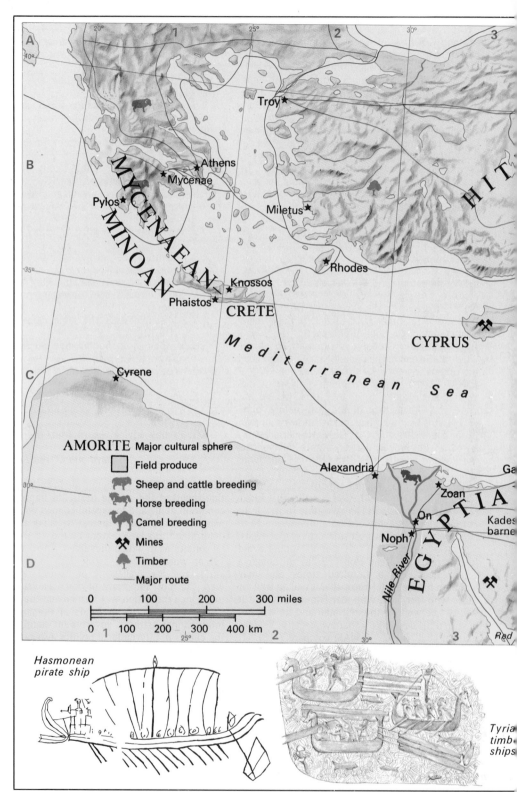

A
1   25°   2   30°   3
40°

Troy ★

B   H I T

Athens ★
Mycenae ★
MYCENAEAN-

Pylos ★   Miletus ★
MINOAN

Rhodes ★

35°

Knossos ★
Phaistos ★   CRETE

Mediterranean Sea   CYPRUS

C   Cyrene ★

AMORITE Major cultural sphere
         ☐   Field produce
         🐂   Sheep and cattle breeding
         🐎   Horse breeding   Alexandria ★   Ga
         🐪   Camel breeding
                                                           Zoan ★
         ⚒   Mines   On ★   E G Y P T I A   Kades
30°   barne
         🌳   Timber   Noph ★
D   N i l e   R i v e r
         ──   Major route

         0   100   200   300 miles

         0   100   200   300   400 km
                        25°   2   30°   3   Red

Hasmonean
pirate ship

Tyria
timb
ships

© carta

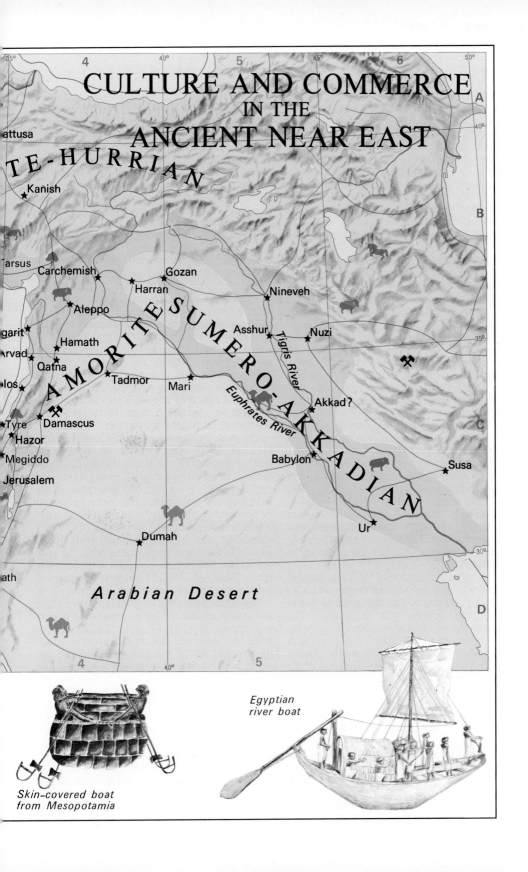

CULTURE AND COMMERCE
IN THE
ANCIENT NEAR EAST

TE-HURRIAN

Kanish

AMORITE

SUMERO-AKKADIAN

Hattusa

Tarsus

Carchemish   Gozan

Harran   Nineveh

Aleppo

Ugarit   Hamath   Asshur   Nuzi

Arvad   Qatna

Ios   Tadmor   Mari

Tyre   Damascus   Akkad?

Hazor

Megiddo   Babylon   Susa

Jerusalem

Dumah   Ur

ath

Arabian Desert

Tigris River

Euphrates River

*Egyptian
river boat*

*Skin-covered boat
from Mesopotamia*

land and private enterprise were the rule during the early history of the tribes of Israel. This changed somewhat after the establishment of the monarchy when large estates were formed (2 Sam. 9:10) to support the kings and the nobility. Attempts were also made by the royal bureaucracy to control as much of the country's land and economic activity as possible (1 Kings 4:1–19).

Further changes took place after the conquest of the nation by Assyria and Babylon. From that point on, the economic efforts (farm production, industry, and trade) of the nation were largely controlled by the tribute demands of the dominant empires (2 Kings 18:14–16) and the maintenance of international trade routes. This pattern continued into the New Testament period when Roman roads speeded trade, but also held the populace in submission. The economy, while relatively stable, was burdened with heavy taxes (Matt. 22:17–21) to support the occupation army and government.

Environmental Conditions Many aspects of the economic life of the people were determined by the environmental conditions in which they lived. Palestine has a remarkably varied geographic pattern and huge shifts in climate. Within its environs are steppe and desert to the south and east in the Negev and the corresponding areas of the Transjordan. In these areas only dry or irrigation farming is possible, and much of the land is given over to pastoralists guiding their flocks and herds. A desolate wilderness region lies near the Dead Sea, while well-watered farm lands are found in the Shephelah plateau (between the coastal plain and the hill country) and in the Galilee area of northern Palestine. Rolling hill country dominates the center of the country where agriculture must be practiced on terraced hillsides and where water conservation and irrigation are necessary to grow crops.

The semi-tropical climate of Palestine includes a hot, dry summer and autumn during which no rains fall for six months. The drought is broken in September or October with rains continuing throughout the winter and into March and April. Yearly amounts of rainfall, which may all come in torrents within a few days, average 40 inches a year in the north and in the western areas of the hill country and Shephelah. Under the influence of the desert winds and the barrier of the hill country, these amounts decrease to the south and east, with less than eight inches a year in the desert regions of the Judean wilderness and the Negev. Average temperatures also vary widely, again with the highlands and northern coastal strip remaining cooler while the desert regions and low lying areas see temperatures well into the 90 degree range.

Uncertain climatic conditions often determined the economic activity of the local village, the region, and the nation. The fact that Abram's first experience in Palestine was a famine (Gen. 12:10) is not surprising. Drought, which destroyed crops (1 Kings 17:1; Jer. 14:1–6), had a ripple effect on the rest of the economy. Some people left the country for the more predictable climate of Egypt (Gen. 46:1–7) or went to areas in Transjordan unaffected by a famine (Ruth 1:1). Economic hardship brought on by climatic extremes also hurt the business of the local potter, tanner, blacksmith, and weaver.

Local Village Economy Agriculture in ancient Palestine took three basic forms: grain production (barley and wheat), cultivation of vines and fruit trees, and the care of oleaginous plants (olive, date, sesame) from which oil was extracted for cooking, lighting, and personal care uses. Most of the energies of the village population were taken up with plowing fields (1 Kings 19:19) and the construction and maintenance of the hillside terraces where vineyards (Isa. 5:1–6; Mark 12:1) and grain were planted. In the hill country, water sources were usually in the valleys, and thus it would have been too much work to carry water up to the hillside terraces. As a result, irrigation channels were dug to insure that the terraces were evenly watered by rain and dew. Roof catch basins and plastered cisterns were constructed to augment water supplies from the village's wells and springs during the dry summer months.

The ideal situation for every rural Israelite was to spend his days "under his vine and under his fig tree" (1 Kings 4:25). To insure this possibility for his sons, a man's ownership of land was considered part of a family trust from one generation to the next. Each plot of land was a grant to the household by Yahweh and as such had to be cared for so that it would remain productive (Deut. 14:28–29). Its abundance was the result of hard work (Prov. 24:30–34) and was to be shared with the poor (Deut. 24:19–21). Yahweh's grant of the land was repaid (Num. 18:21–32) through the payment of tithes to the Levites and through sacrifices.

The family's holdings were duly marked off. It was strictly against the law to remove the boundary stones (Deut. 19:14; Prov. 22:28). Inheritance laws were well defined with every eventuality provided for in the statutes. Normally, the oldest son inherited the largest portion of the lands of his father (Deut. 21:17; Luke 15:31). Sometimes this was all a man had to pass on to his children. It thus became traditional that land not be permanently sold outside the family or clan (Lev. 25:8–17). The tradition was so strong that Naboth could refuse King Ahab's request to purchase his vineyard saying he could not give him "the inheritance of my fathers" (1 Kings 21:3). In later periods, however, the prophets spoke of rich men who add "house to house, that lay field to field" (Isa. 5:8), taking advantage of the poor farmer whose land has been devastated by invading armies (Mic. 2:2) or drought.

If a man died without a male heir, his daughters would receive charge of the land (Num. 27:7–8), but they were required to marry within the tribe to insure it remained a part of the tribal legacy (Num. 36:6–9). A childless man's property passed to his nearest male relative (Num. 27:9–11). The tragedy of childlessness was sometimes resolved through the levirate obligation. In these cases the nearest male relative married the dead man's widow to provide an heir for the deceased (Gen. 38). The duty of the redeemer, or *go'el,* as the relative was called, also included the purchase of family lands which had been abandoned (Jer. 32:6–9).

Since life was uncertain and disease and war often took many of the village's inhabitants, laws were provided to insure that the widow, the orphan, and the stranger would not go hungry. Each field owner was required to leave a portion of the grain unharvested and some grapes on the vine (Lev. 19:9–10). This belonged to the poor and the needy who had the right to glean in these fields (Ruth 2:2–9). The land was also protected from exhaustion by the law of the sabbatical year which required that it be left fallow every seventh year (Lev. 25:3–7).

Despite the back-breaking work of harvesting fields with flint-edged sickles (Joel 3:13), the grain and the fruits meant the survival of the village and was cause for celebration (Judg. 21:19). Following the harvest, the threshingfloor became the center of the economic activity of the village and countryside (Joel 2:24). The sheaves of grain from the harvested fields of the district were brought here (Amos 2:13) to be trampled by oxen (Deut. 25:4) and threshing sledges (2 Sam. 24:22; Isa. 41:15). The grain was further separated from the chaff with winnowing forks (Ruth 3:2; Isa. 41:16; Jer. 15:7), and finally with sieves (Amos 9:9; Luke 22:31). Once this process was complete, the grain was guarded (Ruth 3:2–7) until it could be distributed to the people. The village may have had a communal granary, but most kept their grain in home storage pits or private granaries (Matt. 3:12).

Because of the importance this distribution held for the well-being of the people, the threshingfloor gradually became associated with the administration of justice for the community. This is seen in the Ugaritic epic of Aqhat (dated to about 1400 B.C.) where the hero's father Daniel is said to be judging the cases of widows and orphans at the threshingfloor. Similarly, Ruth's coming to Boaz as he lay on the threshingfloor after the winnowing (Ruth 3:8–14) may have been an attempt to obtain justice regarding the ownership of her dead husband's estate. In another instance from the monarchy period, it can be seen how the threshingfloor evolved into a symbolic place of judgment used by kings to augment their authority. First Kings 22:10 (NAS, NIV) portrays Kings Ahab and Jehoshaphat sitting enthroned before the gates of Samaria on a threshingfloor as they judge the statements of the prophet Micaiah.

Village economies also included the maintenance of small herds of sheep and goats. Nomadic pastoralism, like that described in the patriarchal narratives, was not a part of village life. The flocks were moved to new pastures in the hill country with the coming of the dry summer season (1 Sam. 25:7–8), but this would have required only a few herdsmen (1 Sam. 16:11). Only the shearing of the sheep would have involved large numbers of the community (Gen. 31:19; 1 Sam. 25:4; 2 Sam. 13:23–24).

What little industry existed in Israelite villages was designed to complement agricultural production and provide both necessities and some trade goods. This activity included the making of bricks and split timbers for house construction, and the weaving of material for clothing. Some households (usually consisting of a group of related families—Judg. 18:22) had the skill to shape cooking utensils and farm tolls from clay, stone, and metal. Few, however, had the ability to shape their own weapons, relying in many cases on clubs and ox goads (Judg. 3:31) for protection.

In exceptional cases village craftsmen may have set up stalls or business where they provided some of the more specialized items, especially fine pottery, bronze weapons, and gold and silver jewelry. Anything additional could either be done without or obtained in trade with other villages or nations who might possess a particularly fine artisan (1 Sam. 13:20). It is also possible that during a yearly visit to the city (Luke 2:41) to attend a religious festival the villager could visit the stalls of traders from all over the Near East and buy their wares.

Urban Economic Life Local trade expanded beyond the sale of surplus commodities and handcrafted items as the villages and towns grew in size. Population growth, sparked by the establishment of the monarchy and social stability, also increased the needs and appetites for metals (gold, tin, copper, iron), luxury items, and manufactured goods. A network of roads gradually developed to accommodate this economic activity and to tie together the villages and towns throughout the nation. More sophisticated road construction, designed to allow heavy vehicular traffic, was introduced by the kings who marshalled large numbers of corvée workers (persons who worked in lieu of paying taxes) to construct public works projects (1 Kings 9:15–22). Ezion-geber, a port on the Red Sea, was acquired from the Edomites and serviced a fleet of ships bringing gold from Ophir and rare woods and other luxury items to the royal court (1 Kings 9:26; 10:11–12). Another fleet joined that of Hiram of Tyre in the Mediterranean trade (1 Kings 10:22).

Within the walled cities and towns, most commercial activity occurred within the gate complex or its environs. This would have been the site of the heaviest traffic in any town and the most likely spot, other than private homes (Jer. 18:2–3), for stalls and shops to be set up for business. Since legal matters were also handled here (Deut. 21:18–19), business contracts could be witnessed (Gen. 23:15–16), and disputes settled (Ruth 4:1–6). Shops may have also been established within the walls of those cities which had hollow-wall (casemate) construction.

Since this was an economy without coined money until about 550 B.C., barter and specified weights (shekel, mina, talent) of precious metals were used as rates of exchange. Prices, as always, were determined by the law of supply and demand (2 Kings 6:25; Rev. 6:6), with an extra markup to cover the costs of transport, and, where applicable, manufacturing. For instance, luxury items such as spices and perfumes from Arabia and ivory and rare animals commanded high prices. They were portable enough to make the venture worthwhile.

Weights and measures also fitted into the sale of commodities in the town marketplace. These weights varied from one district and time period to the next (2 Sam. 14:26; Ezek. 45:10). However, the law required that Israelites provide a fair measure to their customers (Lev. 19:35–36). The fact that the law did not prevent fraud in every case is seen in the prophets' cries against deceitful weights (Mic. 6:11) and false balances (Amos 8:5). Archaeological evidence shows some attempt by the royal administration to standardize shekel weights. Hieratic symbols on these markers demonstrate a reliance on the Egyptian system of weights and measures.

Slave labor was also an outgrowth of the urbanization of Israel and the constant military campaigns of the kings. The large number of military prisoners joined the levies of forced labor gangs (1 Kings 5:13; 9:20–22) building roads and repairing the walls of the fortresses which guarded the kingdom. Royal estates were managed by stewards (1 Chron. 27:25–31) and worked by large bands of state-owned slaves and a levy of free men (1 Sam. 8:12).

It is unlikely that private individuals held as many slaves as the monarchy or the social elite. Since the laws regarding slaves were quite stringent (Ex. 21:1–11,20,26; Lev. 25:39–46), it is more likely that day laborers were hired by most landowners (Matt. 20:1–5). The leasing of land to tenant-farmers was another alternative to the labor problem, but this was not common in Israel until the New Testament period (Matt. 21:33–41; Mark 12:9).

Israelites could sell their families or themselves into slavery to resolve a debt (Ex. 21:7–11; Lev. 25:39; Matt. 18:25). This was regulated by the law so that the normal term of slavery or inden-

ture was no more than six years. Then the slave was to be released and given a portion of the flock and the harvest with which to make a new start (Deut. 15:12–14). Perpetual slavery was only to occur if the Israelite himself chose to remain a slave. This choice might be made because he did not want to be separated from a wife and children acquired during his term of enslavement (Ex. 21:1–6) or because he did not feel he would have a better life on his own (Deut. 15:16).

Urbanization and the imposed demands of foreign conquerors brought greater complexity to the economic life of the people of Palestine. Travel and trade increased, and the variety of goods and services was magnified by the increased demands of consumers and the influx of new ideas and technologies from outside the country. Agriculture remained the staple of the economy, but it was augmented by the public works projects of the kings and foreign rulers. The increase in commercial and private traffic was facilitated by better highways and means of transport. Slave labor also became more common, but the majority of slaves came from a pool of military prisoners acquired in the wars that solidified and protected the nation's borders. See *Agriculture; Commerce; Transportation and Travel; Slavery; Weights and Measures.*

Victor H. Matthews

ECSTASY The state of being in a trance, especially a mystic or prophetic trance. The derivation of our word "ecstasy" (from the Greek *ek,* out plus *stasis,* state) suggests an out of body state (2 Cor. 12:2–3) or the state of being out of control. In the Old Testament ecstasy was associated with bands or schools of prophets (1 Sam. 10:5,9; 19:20; 2 Kings 9:1). The ecstatic state was often accompanied by music (1 Sam. 10:5; 2 Kings 3:15–16) and rhythmic dance, though the "prophetic frenzy" was brought on by the onrush of the Spirit of God (1 Sam. 10:6,10; 19:20,23) or hand of the Lord (2 Kings 3:15). Prophetic ecstasy could be accompanied by irrational behavior (1 Sam. 19:24; perhaps 21:15) leading prophets to be identified with madmen (2 Kings 9:11; Jer. 29:26; Hos. 9:7). Efforts to control such prophetic expression (Jer. 29:26) were regarded as ill-founded (29:31).

In the New Testament Paul's experience of being caught up into the third heaven or paradise (2 Cor. 12:2–4) is an example of an ecstatic experience. Paul twice pleaded ignorance of whether this experience was "in or out of the body." Paul preferred to boast in his weakness than in such spiritual experiences (12:5). The gift of speaking in tongues is thought by some to involve an ecstatic state. See *Prophecy, Prophets; Tongues, Gift of.*

ED (Ĕd) Place name meaning, "witness." Altar that the tribes assigned territory east of the Jordan built as a witness that Yahweh is God of both the eastern and western tribes. The building resulted in a dispute between the two groups of tribes, but Phinehas, the priest, helped settle the dispute, ensuring the altar was a symbol and would not be used for burnt offering (Josh. 22:34). NAS, NIV, NRSV read, "witness."

EDAR (Ē′ där) KJV spelling of Eder in Genesis 35:21. See *Eder.*

EDEN (Ē′ dĕn) Garden of God. "Eden" is probably derived from the Sumerian-Akkadian *edinu,* meaning "flatland" or "wilderness." The similarity to the Hebrew verb *'adan,* meaning "delight" or "pleasure," resulted in the Septuagint's translation of the expression "garden of Eden" as "garden of delight," hence paradise.

"Eden" appears twenty times in the Old Testament but never in the New Testament. Two usages refer to men (2 Chron. 29:12; 31:15). Twice the name is used to designate a city or region in the Assyrian province of Thelassar (Isa. 37:12; 2 Kings 19:12). Ezekiel 27:23 mentions a region named Eden located on the Euphrates. Amos 1:5 refers to the ruler of Damascus as holding the scepter of the house of Eden.

The fourteen remaining appearances relate to the idyllic place of creation. In Genesis (2:8,10,15; 3:23,24; 4:16) the reference is to the region in which a garden was placed. Though details seem precise, identification of the rivers which flow from the river issuing forth from Eden cannot be accomplished with certainty. The Euphrates and the Tigris can be identified, but there is no agreement on the location of the Pishon and the Gihon.

Joel 2:3 compares Judah's condition before its destruction with Eden. In Isaiah 51:3 and Ezekiel 36:35, Eden is used as an illustration of the great prosperity God would bestow on Judah. These exilic prophets promised that the nation God restored after the Exile would be like Eden's garden. Ezekiel also refers to the trees of Eden (31:9,16,18) and calls Eden the garden of God (28:13). See *Paradise.*   *Robert Anderson Street*

EDER (Ē′ dĕr) Place and personal name meaning, "water puddle" or "herd." *1.* Tower near Bethlehem (Gen. 35:21; compare verse 19). The exact location is not known. Micah referred to Jerusalem as the "tower of the flock," the same Hebrew expression as in Genesis (Mic. 4:8). *2.* A town in the southern limits of the tribal territory of Judah near Edom (Josh. 15:21). Its location is not known. *3.* A Levite of the clan of Merari (1 Chron. 23:23; 24:30). *4.* A leader of the tribe of Benjamin (1 Chron. 8:15); KJV spelling is Ader.

EDICT See *Decree.*

EDIFICATION Literally "building up," it approximates encouragement and consolation (1 Cor. 14:3; 1 Thess. 5:11), though with edification focus falls on the goal, defined as being established in faith (Col. 2:7) or attaining unity of faith and knowledge, maturity, and the full measure of Christ (Eph. 4:13). Edification is the special responsibility of the various church leaders (Eph. 4:11–12) and is the legitimate context for the exercise of their authority (2 Cor. 10:8; 13:10). The work of building up is, however, the work of all Christians (1 Thess. 5:11). Spiritual gifts are given for the edification of the Church. Of these gifts, those which involve speaking are especially important (Acts 20:32; 1 Cor. 14; Eph. 4:29). All elements of Christian worship should contribute to edification (1 Cor. 14:26). Prophecy and instruction are especially important (1 Cor. 14:3, 18–19). Edification is not all talk, however, but involves demonstrating love (1 Cor. 8:1) and consideration for those weak in faith (Rom. 15:1–2).

EDOM (Ē′ dom) The area southeast and southwest of the Dead Sea, on opposite sides of the Arabah, was known as Edom in biblical times and was the home of the Edomites. The name "Edom" derives from a Semitic root which means "red" or "ruddy" and characterizes the red sandstone terrain of much of the area in question. Moreover, the Edomite area was largely "wilderness"—semi-desert, not very conducive to agriculture—and many of the inhabitants were semi-nomads. Thus the boundaries of Edom would have been rather ill-defined. Yet not all of Edom was wilderness; the vicinity of present-day Tafileh and Buseireh, east of the Arabah, is fairly well watered, cultivable land, and would have boasted numerous villages during Old Testament times. This would have been the center of Edomite population. Buseireh is situated on the ruins of ancient Bozrah, the capital of Edom. Note that the modern name, "Buseireh," preserves memory of the ancient one, "Bozrah."

Most of the biblical passages pertaining to Edom refer to this Edomite center east of the Arabah. Isaiah 63:1, for example, speaks of one that " . . . cometh from Edom, with dyed garments from Bozrah, . . . glorious in his apparel, travelling in the greatness of his strength." (See also Jer. 49:22; Amos 1:11–12). Yet there are other passages which presuppose that the territory west of the Arabah, south of the Judean hill country and separating Judah from the Gulf of Aqaba, was also part of Edom. See especially the description of Judah's boundary in Numbers 34:3–4 and Joshua 15:1–3, where Judah's south side is described as extending "even to the border of Edom the wilderness of Zin." Certain of the tribal groups which ranged this wilderness area south of Judah are listed in the Edomite genealogy of Genesis 36. In New Testament times, even the southern end of the Judean hill country (south of approximately Hebron) was known officially as Idumea (Edom).

The "land of Seir" seems to be synonymous with Edom in some passages (Gen. 32:3; 36:8; Judg. 5:4). Egyptian texts from about 1300 to 1100 B.C. know of *Shasu* (apparently semi-nomadic tribes) from Seir and Edom. "Teman" also is used in apposition to Edom in at least one biblical passage (Amos 1:12), but normally refers to a specific district of Edom and possibly to a town by that name. One of Job's visitors was Eliphaz the Temanite (Job 2:11; compare Ezek. 25:13).

The Israelites regarded the Edomites as close relatives, even more closely related to them than the Ammonites or Moabites. Specifically, they identified the Ammonites and Moabites as descendants of Lot, Abraham's nephew, but the Edomites as descendants of Esau, Jacob's brother (Gen. 19:30–36; 36). Thus Edom occasionally is referred to as a "brother" to Israel (Amos 1:11–12). Edomites seem not to have been barred from worship in the Jerusalem Temple with the same strictness as the Ammonites and Moabites (Deut. 23:3–8). Yet, as is often the case with personal relations, the closest relative can be a bitter enemy. According to the biblical writers, enmity between Israel and Edom began already with Jacob and Esau (when the former stole the latter's birthright) and was exacerbated at the time of the

Israelite Exodus from Egypt (when the Edomites refused the Israelites passage through their land). Be that as it may, much of the conflict also had to do with the fact that Edom was a constant threat to Judah's frontier, and moreover blocked Judean access to the Gulf of Aqaba.

Both Saul and David conducted warfare with the Edomites—probably frontier wars fought in the "wilderness" area southwest of the Dead Sea (1 Sam. 14:47–48; 2 Sam. 8:13–14). David achieved a decisive victory in the valley of salt, probably just southwest of Beersheba where the ancient name still is preserved in modern Arabic wadi el-Milk. Apparently this secured Davidic control of the Edomite area west of the Arabah as well as access to the Gulf of Aqaba. Thus we read that Solomon built a fleet of ships at Ezion-geber and sent them to distant places for exotic goods. Later Hadad of the royal Edomite line returned from Egypt and became an active adversary to Solomon. This would have involved Edomite attacks on Solomon's caravans which passed through traditionally Edomite territory from Ezion-geber to Jerusalem (1 Kings 11:14–22).

Apparently Judah gained the upper hand against Edom again during the reign of Jehoshaphat. Once again we read of a Judean attempt (unsuccessful this time) to undertake a shipping venture from Ezion-geber (1 Kings 22:47–50). Edom regained independence from Judah under Joram, who succeeded Jehoshaphat to the throne (2 Kings 8:20–22). A later Judean king, Amaziah, is reported to have defeated the Edomites again in

The mountainous landscape of the land of Edom.

The hills of Edom between Petra and Bozrah toward the Wadi Arabah.

the valley of salt and then to have pursued ten thousand survivors to "the top of the rock" from which they were thrown down and dashed to pieces (2 Chron. 25:11–12).

Conflict between Judah and Edom and efforts on the part of Judean kings to exploit the commercial possibilities of the Gulf of Aqaba continued (2 Kings 14:22; 16:6; 2 Chron. 26:1–2; 28:17) until eventually the Edomites, like the other peoples and petty kingdoms of Syria-Palestine, fell under the shadow of the major eastern empires — the Assyrians, then the Babylonians, finally the Persians and the Greeks. Some scholars hold that the Edomites aided the Babylonians in their attacks on Jerusalem in 597 and 586 B.C. and then took advantage of the Judeans in their helpless situation. This would explain, for example, the bitter verbal attacks on Edom in passages such as Jeremiah 49:7–22 and the Book of Obadiah. Yet there is no clear evidence to support this view.

By New Testament times a people of Arabic origin known as the Nabateans had established a commercial empire with its center in the formerly Edomite territory east of the Arabah. Their chief city was Petra, and the whole region southeast of the Dead Sea had come to be known as Nabatea. Only the formerly Edomite territory west of the Arabah was still known as Idumea (Edom). Herod the Great was of Idumean ancestry. See *Transjordan; Esau; Bozrah; Nabateans; Petra; Sela.*

EDOMITES See *Edom.*

EDREI (Ĕd′ rĕ ī) Place name of unknown meaning. 1. Royal city of Og, king of Bashan (Josh. 12:4). Invading Israel defeated Og there (Num. 21:33–35). It is also known from Egyptian records. Its location is modern Dera halfway between Damascus and Amman. The clan of Machir in the tribe of Manasseh laid claim to the city (Josh. 13:31). *2.* A fortified city in the tribal territory of Naphtali (Josh. 19:37).

EDUCATION IN BIBLE TIMES While the word "school" occurs in the Bible only once (Acts 19:9), there are numerous references to teachers and teaching in both Testaments. There are many references in the Old Testament to the importance of religious training but there is no Mosaic legislation requiring the establishment of schools for formal religious instruction.

Education in Old Testament Times The primary purpose of education among the Jews was the learning of and obedience to the law of God, the Torah.

The secondary purpose in education was to teach about the practical aspects of everyday life: a trade for the boy and the care of the house, application of dietary laws and how to be a good wife for the girl.

The home was considered the first and most effective agency in the education process, and parents were considered the first and most effective teachers of their children. This responsibility is expressed in Genesis 18:19 where God states his expectation that Abraham will train his children and his household to walk in the ways of the Lord. Proverbs 22:6 is another familiar exhortation for parents to teach their children according to the way of the Lord.

Deuteronomy 6:7 gives an interesting insight into how parents were to teach their children about God: "And thou shalt teach them diligently unto thy children, and shalt talk of them when thou sittest in thine house, and when thou walkest by the way, and when thou liest down, and when thou risest up." The parent was to use the various ordinary activities of life as avenues to teach about God. All of life was permeated by religious meaning and teaching about God should flow naturally from its activities.

Training in the Torah began very early. The father had an obligation to teach his children the Law by words and example. A child could observe his father binding the phylacteries on his arm and head. The natural question, "What are you doing?", could be used to teach the child that it was everyone's duty to "Love the Lord your God with all your heart, and with all your soul, and with all your might" (Deuteronomy 6:5).

When the son reached the age of twelve, the Jews believed his education in the Torah was complete enough to help him know the Law and keep it. He was then known as a "son of the Law." As a symbol of this attainment, the father would fasten the phylacteries upon the arm and forehead of his son. The box placed on the forehead indicated that the laws must be memorized. The other box was placed on the left arm so that it would press against the heart when the arms were folded or the hands were clasped in prayer. The box pressed against the heart would symbolize that the laws were to be loved and obeyed.

Girls received their education at home. A girl's mother taught her what she needed to know to be a good wife and mother.

A girl learned how to make the home ready for special holidays and Sabbath. In such preparation she learned the maning of the customs and history behind the events. This heritage she would be able to pass on to her own children in their very early years.

The girl would learn a variety of skills such as weaving, spinning, and treating illnesses. She might also learn to sing and dance and play a musical instrument such as a flute or harp.

The Jewish people had opportunity to receive religious education from priests and Levites (Lev. 10:10–11). The priests and Levites were to be supported by the offerings of the people and were to be the religious teachers of the nation. Apparently the educational function of their work was not well maintained. During the revival under King Jehoshaphat, the teaching function of Priests and Levites was resumed and the people were taught the ordinances of the Law. (2 Chron. 17:7–9).

The ineffective work of the priests was supplemented by the teaching of the prophets. The first of these prophets, Samuel, attempted to make his reform permanent by instituting a school of the prophets in Ramah (1 Sam. 19:19–20). Later other schools of the prophets were begun at other places. The main study at these centers was the Law and its interpretation. Not all of the students of these schools had predictive gifts nor were all the prophets students in such schools. Amos is a notable example of a prophet who was not educated in one of these schools (Amos 7:14–15).

Education in New Testament Times. The synagogue apparently came into existence during the Babylonian captivity when the Jews were deprived of the services of the Temple. During captivity they began meeting in small groups for prayer and Scripture reading. When they returned to Israel the synagogue spread rapidly and developed into an important educational institution. Synagogue services made an important educational contribution to the religious life of the community. The elementary school system among the Jews developed in connection with the synagogue. Even before the days of Jesus, schools for the young were located in practically every important Jewish community.

The teacher was generally the synagogue "attendant." An assistant was provided if there were more than twenty-five students. The primary aim of education at the synagogue school was religious. The Old Testament was the subject matter for this instruction. Reading, writing and arithmetic were also taught. Memorization, drill and review were used as approaches to teaching.

Boys usually began formal schooling at the "house of the book" at age five. He would spend at least a half day, six days a week for about five years, studying at the synagogue. Parents brought their son at daybreak and came for him at midday.

While not at school the boy was usually learning a trade, such as farming or carpentry.

If a boy wanted training beyond that given in a synagogue, he would go to a scholarly scribe. Saul of Tarsus received such advanced theological training "at the feet of Gamaliel" in Jerusalem (Acts 22:3).

No formal educational approach is described in the New Testament. However, Jesus is pictured as teaching large crowds (Mark 4:1–2). While Jesus was much more than a teacher, he was recognized as a teacher by his contemporaries. He was a God-sent teacher who taught with an authority and challenge which held his audiences captive.

As risen Lord, Jesus commissioned his followers to carry their evangelism and teaching ministry into all the world (Matt. 28:19–20). As seen in Acts 2:42, 4:1–2; 5:21,28, teaching became an important work in the early church in Jerusalem.

The New Testament places importance on the teaching function of the church. Teaching is regarded as a primary function of the pastor (1 Tim. 3:2). Volunteer teachers are also important to the work of the church (James 3:1).   *Cos Davis*

EGLAH (Ĕg′ lăh) Personal name meaning, "heifer, young cow." David's wife and mother of his son Ithream (2 Sam. 3:5).

EGLAIM (Ĕg′ lā ĭm) Place name meaning, "two cisterns." Place in Moab used by Isaiah to describe far limits of Moab's distress. It is modern *rugm el-Gilimeh,* southeast of *el-Kerak.* It is distinct in location and Hebrew spelling from En-eglaim (Ezek. 47:10).

EGLATH-SHELISHIYAH (Ĕg′ lăth-shĕ lĭsh′ ĭ yăh) Place name meaning, "the third heifer." Place apparently in Moab where Moab fugitives fled in Isaiah's description of disaster (Isa. 15:5). The name has given translators and interpreters many problems. The location is not known. The words do not apparently fit the poetic structure and are unexpected in the syntax and context, there being no adverb or preposition between Zoar and Eglath-Shelishiyah in the Hebrew. King James makes the phrase an identifying statement with Zoar—"an heifer of three years old." The same problems arise in the closely related Jeremiah 48:34.

EGLON (Ĕg′ lŏn) *1.* A Moabite king who oppressed the Israelites (Judg. 3:12). Aided by the Amalekites and Ammonites, Eglon dominated Israel for eighteen years. He was finally slain by the Benjamite judge Ehud, who ran the obese monarch through with a short sword.

2. A Canaanite city whose king entered an alliance with four other Canaanite rulers against Gibeon (Josh. 10:3). The Gibeonites had made a treaty with Israel (Josh 9). Subsequently, Eglon was captured by the Israelite army under Joshua. It became a part of the territory of the tribe of Judah. Most scholars long held that the modern site of tell el-Hesi was the location of ancient Eglon. More recently, however, some have contended for tell Eton. Both places are to the southwest of Lachish. See *Joshua; Judges; Ehud.*

EGYPT A land in northeastern Africa, home to one of the earliest civilizations, and an important cultural and political influence on ancient Israel. **Geography** Egypt lies at the northeastern corner of Africa, separated from Palestine by the Sinai Wilderness. In contrast to the modern nation, ancient Egypt was confined to the Nile River valley, a long, narrow ribbon of fertile land (the "black land") surrounded by uninhabitable desert (the "red land"). Egypt proper, from the first cataract of the Nile to the Mediterranean, is some 750 miles long.

Classical historians remarked that Egypt was a gift of the Nile. The river's three tributaries converge in the Sudan. The White Nile, with its source in Lake Victoria, provides a fairly constant water flow. The seasonal flow of the Blue Nile and Atbara caused an annual innundation beginning in June and cresting in September. Not only did the innundation provide for irrigation, but it replenished the soil with a new layer of fertile, black silt each year. The Nile also provided a vital communication link for the nation. While the river's flow carried boats northward, prevailing northerly winds allowed easy sailing upstream.

Despite the unifying nature of the Nile, the "Two Lands" of Egypt were quite distinct. Upper Egypt is the arable Nile Valley from the First Cataract to just south of Memphis in the north. Lower Egypt refers to the broad Delta of the Nile in the north, formed from alluvial deposits. Egypt was relatively isolated by a series of six Nile cataracts on the south and protected on the east and west by the desert. The Delta was the entryway to Egypt for travelers coming from the Fertile Crescent across the Sinai.

History The numerous Egyptian pharaohs were

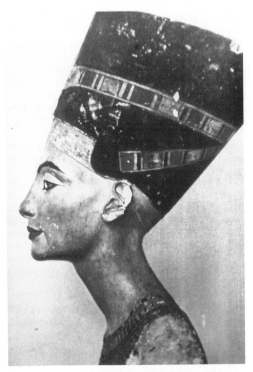

Bust of the Egyptian queen Nefertiti, wife of Pharaoh Akhenaton.

divided by the ancient historian Manetho into thirty dynasties. Despite certain difficulties, Manetho's scheme is still used and provides a framework for a review of Egyptian history.

The unification of originally separate kingdoms of Upper and Lower Egypt about 3100 B.C. began the Archaic Period (First and Second Dynasties). Egypt's first period of glory, the Third through Sixth Dynasties of the Old Kingdom (2700–2200 B.C.) produced the famous pyramids.

Low Nile innundations, the resultant bad harvests, and incursions of Asiatics in the Delta region brought the political chaos of the Seventh through Tenth Dynasties, called the First Intermediate Period (2200–2040 B.C.). Following a civil war, the Eleventh Dynasty reunited Egypt and began the Middle Kingdom (2040–1786 B.C.). Under the able pharaohs of the Twelfth Dynasty, Egypt prospered and conducted extensive trade. From the Middle Kingdom onward, Egyptian history is contemporary with biblical events. Abraham's brief sojourn in Egypt (Gen. 12:10–20) during this period may be understood in light of a tomb painting at Beni Hasan showing visiting Asiatics in Egypt about 1900 B.C.

Under the weak Thirteenth Dynasty, Egypt entered another period of division. Asiatics, mostly Semites like the Hebrews, migrated into the Delta region of Egypt and began to establish independent enclaves, eventually consolidating rule over

Funerary statuettes from the tomb of King Tut (Pharaoh Tutankhamun).

Lower Egypt. These pharaohs, being Asiatics rather than native Egyptians, were remembered as Hyksos, or "rulers of foreign lands." This period, in which Egypt was divided between Hyksos (Fifteenth and Sixteenth) and native Egyptian (Thirteenth and Seventeenth) dynasties, is known as the Second Intermediate or Hyksos Period (1786–1550 B.C.). Joseph's rise to power (Gen. 41:39–45) may have taken place under a Hyksos pharaoh. See *Hyksos.*

The Hyksos were expelled and Egypt reunited about 1550 B.C. by Ahmose I, who established the Eighteenth Dynasty and inaugurated the Egyptian New Kingdom. Successive Eighteenth Dynasty pharaohs made military campaigns into Canaan and against the Mitannian kingdom of Mesopotamia, creating an empire which reached the Euphrates River. Foremost among the pharaohs was Thutmose III (1479–1425 B.C.), who won a major victory at Megiddo in Palestine. Amenhotep III (1391–1353 B.C.) ruled over a magnificent empire in peace—thanks to a treaty with Mitanni—and devoted his energies to building projects in Egypt itself. The great successes of the Empire led to internal power struggles, especially between the powerful priesthood of Amen-Re and the throne.

Amenhotep III's son, Amenhotep IV (1353–1335 B.C.), changed his name to Akhenaton and embarked on a revolutionary reform which promoted worship of the sun disc Aton above all other gods. As Thebes was dominated by the powerful priesthood of Amen-Re, Akhenaton moved the capital over two hundred miles north to Akhetaton, modern tell el-Amarna. The Amarna Age, as this period is known, brought innovations in art and literature; but Akhenaton paid little attention to foreign affairs, and the Empire suffered. Documents from Akhetaton, the Amarna Letters, represent diplomatic correspondence between local rulers in Egypt's sphere of influence and pharaoh's court. They especially illuminate the turbulent situation in Canaan, a century prior to the Israelite invasion.

The reforms of Akhenaton failed. His second successor made clear his loyalties to Amen-Re by changing his name from Tutankhaton to Tutankhamen and abandoning the new capital in favor of Thebes. He died young, and his comparatively insignificant tomb was forgotten until its rediscovery in 1921. The Eighteenth Dynasty would not recover. The General Horemheb seized the throne and worked vigorously to restore order and erase all trace of the Amarna heresy. Horemheb had no heir and left the throne to his vizier, Ramses I, first king of the Nineteenth Dynasty.

Seti I (1302–1290 B.C.) reestablished Egyptian control in Canaan and campaigned against the Hittites, who had taken Egyptian territory in North Syria during the Amarna Age. See *Hittites.*

Construction of a new capital was begun by Seti I in the eastern Delta, near the biblical Land of Goshen. Thebes would remain the national religious and traditional capital.

Ramses II (1290–1224 B.C.) was the most vigorous and successful of the Nineteenth Dynasty pharaohs. In his fifth year, he fought the Hittites at Kadesh-on-the-Orontes in north Syria. Although ambushed and nearly defeated, the pharaoh rallied and claimed a great victory. Nevertheless, the battle was inconclusive. In 1270 B.C. Ramses II concluded a peace treaty with the Hittites recognizing the status quo. At home he embarked on the most massive building program of any Egyptian ruler. Impressive additions were made to sanctuaries in Thebes and Memphis, a gigantic temple of Ramses II was built at Abu Simbel in Nubia, and his mortuary temple and tomb were prepared in Western Thebes. In the eastern Delta, the new capital was completed and called Pi-Ramesse ("domain of Ramses;" compare Gen. 47:11), the biblical Ramses (Ex. 1:11). Indeed, Ramses II may have been the unnamed pharaoh of the Exodus.

Ramses II was succeeded, after a long reign, by his son, Merneptah (1224–1214 B.C.). A stele of 1220 B.C. commemorates Merneptah's victory over a Libyan invasion and concludes with a poetic account of a campaign in Canaan. It includes the first extra-biblical mention of Israel and the only one in known Egyptian literature. After Merneptah, the Nineteenth Dynasty is a period of confusion.

Egypt had a brief period of renewed glory under Ramses III (1195–1164 B.C.) of the Twentieth Dynasty. He defeated an invasion of the Sea Peoples, among whom were the Philistines. The remainder of Twentieth Dynasty rulers, all named Ramses, saw increasingly severe economic and civil difficulties. The New Kingdom and the Empire petered out with the last of them in 1070 B.C. The Iron Age had taken dominance of the Near East elsewhere.

The Late Period (1070–332 B.C.) saw Egypt divided and invaded, but with occasional moments of greatness. While the high priesthood of Amen-Re controlled Thebes, the Twenty-first Dynasty ruled from the east Delta city of Tanis, biblical Zoan (Num. 13:22; Ps. 78:12; Ezek. 30:14; Isa. 19:11; 30:4). It was likely a pharaoh of this dynasty, perhaps Siamun, who took Gezer in Palestine and gave it to Solomon as his daughter's dowry (1 Kings 3:1; 9:16). The Twenty-second Dynasty was founded by Shoshenq I (945–924 B.C.), the Shishak of the Bible, who briefly united Egypt and made a successful campaign against the newly-divided nations Judah and Israel (1 Kings 14:25; 2 Chron. 12). Thereafter, Egypt

Sailboat on the Nile River near Luxor.

E

was divided between the Twenty-second through Twenty-fifth Dynasties. The "So king of Egypt" (2 Kings 17:4) who encouraged the treachery of Hoshea, certainly belongs to this confused period, but he cannot be identified with certainty. Egypt was reunited in 715 B.C., when the Ethiopian Twenty-fifth Dynasty succeeded in establishing control over all of Egypt. The most important of these pharaohs was Taharqa, the biblical Tirhakah who rendered aid to Hezekiah (2 Kings 19:9; Isa. 37:9).

Assyria invaded Egypt in 671 B.C., driving the Ethiopians southward and eventually sacking Thebes (biblical No-Amon; Nah. 3:8) in 664 B.C. Under loose Assyrian sponsorship, the Twenty-sixth Dynasty controlled all of Egypt from Sais in the western Delta. With Assyria's decline, Neco II (610–595 B.C.) opposed the advance of Babylon and exercised brief control over Judah (2 Kings 23:29–35). After a severe defeat at the Battle of Carchemish (605 B.C.), Neco II lost Judah as a vassal (2 Kings 24:1) and was forced to defend her border against Babylon. The Pharaoh Hophra (Greek Apries; 589–570 B.C.) supported Judah's rebellion against Babylon, but was unable to provide the promised support (Jer. 37:5–10; 44:30). Despite these setbacks, the Twenty-sixth Dynasty was a period of Egyptian renaissance until the Persian conquest in 525 B.C. Persian rule (Twenty-seventh Dynasty) was interrupted by a period of Egyptian independence under the

View of Giza, Egypt, showing two of the three pyramids located here and the famous sphinx.

Twenty-eighth through Thirtieth Dynasties (404–343 B.C.). With Persian reconquest in 343 B.C., pharaonic Egypt had come to an end.

Alexander the Great took Egypt from the Persians in 332 B.C. and founded the great city of Alexandria on the Mediterranean coast. After his death in 323 B.C., Egypt was home to the Hellenistic Ptolemaic Empire until the time of Cleopatra, when it fell to the Romans (30 B.C.). During the New Testament period, Egypt, under direct rule of the Roman emperors, was the breadbasket of Rome.

Religion Egyptian religion is extremely complex and not totally understood. Many of the great number of gods were personifications of the enduring natural forces in Egypt, such as the sun, Nile, air, earth, and so on. Other gods, like Maat ("truth," "justice"), personified abstract concepts. Still others ruled over states of mankind, like Osiris, god of the underworld. Some of the gods were worshiped in animal form, such as the Apis bull which represented the god Ptah of Memphis.

Many of the principal deities were associated with particular cities or regions, and their position was often a factor of the political situation. This is reflected by the gods' names which dominate pharaohs' names in various dynasties. Thus the god Amen, later called Amen-Re, became the chief god of the Empire because of the position of Thebes. The confusion of local beliefs and political circumstances led to the assimilation of different gods to certain dominant figures. Theological systems developed around local gods at Hermopolis,

The temple of Luxor, Egypt.

Memphis, and Heliopolis. At Memphis, Ptah was seen as the supreme deity which created the other gods by his own word, but this notion was too intellectual to be popular. Dominance was achieved by the system of Heliopolis, home of the sun god Atum, later identified with Ra. Similar to the Hermopolis cycle, it involved a primordial chaos from which appeared Atum who gave birth to the other gods.

Popular with common people was the Osiris myth. Osiris, the good king, was murdered and dismembered by his brother Seth. Osiris' wife, Isis, gathered his body to be mummified by the jackal-headed embalming god Anubis. Magically restored, Osiris was buried by his son, Horus, and reigned as king of the underworld. Horus, meanwhile, overcame the evil Seth to rule on earth. This cycle became the principle of divine kingship. In death, the pharaoh was worshiped as Osiris. As the legitimate heir Horus buried the dead Osiris, the new pharaoh became the living Horus by burying his dead predecessor.

The consistent provision of the Nile gave Egyptians, in contrast to Mesopotamians, a generally optimistic outlook on life. This is reflected in their preoccupation with the afterlife, which was viewed as an ideal continuation of life on earth. In the Old Kingdom it was the prerogative only of the king, as a god, to enjoy immortality. The common appeal of the Osiris cult was great, however, and in later years any dead person was referred to as "the Osiris so and so."

To assist the dead in the afterlife, magical texts were included in the tomb. In the Old Kingdom they were for royalty only, but by the Middle Kingdom variations were written inside coffin lids of any who could afford them. In the New Kingdom and later, magical texts known as *The Book of the Dead* were written on papyrus and placed in the coffin. Pictorial vignettes show, among other things, the deceased at a sort of judgment in which his heart was weighted against truth. This indicates some concept of sin, but the afterlife for the Egyptian was not an offer from a gracious god, but merely an optimistic hope based on observation of his surroundings.

The Bible mentions no Egyptian gods, and Egyptian religion did not significantly influence the Hebrews. There are some interesting parallels between biblical texts and Egyptian literature. An Amarna Age hymn to the Aton has similarities to Psalm 104, but direct borrowing seems unlikely. More striking parallels are found in wisdom literature, as between Proverbs 22 and the Egyptian *Instruction of Amen-em-ope.*

Daniel C. Browning, Jr.

EGYPTIAN, THE The leader of an unsuccessful attempt to capture Jerusalem in about A.D. 54. In Acts 21:38 the tribune commanding the Antonia fortress mistook Paul for this revolutionary who led 4,000 "Assassins" into the wilderness. Josephus mentioned two incidents involving the same, or similar, character. In the first, an Egyptian false prophet led a group into the desert. The procurator Felix dispersed this revolutionary band with calvary and foot soldiers. Later the Egyptian gathered 30,000 in the wilderness, leading the multitude to the Mount of Olives from which, so he promised, they would see the walls of Jerusalem fall at his command. Felix again responded with force, killing 400 and taking 200 captive. The Egyptian ringleader escaped.

Such a sizeable following suggests that either an Egyptian Jew or a proselyte to Judaism was the leader of the revolt rather than a pagan Egyptian. The tribune presumed that the Egyptian was a barbarian (unable to speak Greek). This presumption together with Paul's response that he was a Jew of Tarsus, an important city of Cilicia, suggests a rural origin for the Egyptian rebel.

EHI (Ē′ hī) Personal name meaning, "my brother." A son of Benjamin (Gen. 46:21). He does not appear in the lists of Benjamin's sons in Numbers 26:38–40; 1 Chronicles 8:1–2.

EHUD (Ē′ hŭd) Personal name meaning, "unity, powerful." *1.* A lefthanded Benjamite whom the Lord raised up to deliver the Israelites from Moabite oppression (Judg. 3:15). By a ruse, he gained access to the Moabite King Eglon and assassinated him. *2.* Great grandson of Benjamin and clan leader in that tribe (1 Chron. 7:10). *3.* Clan leader in tribe of Benjamin who originally lived in Geba but were deported by someone unknown to Manahath (1 Chron. 8:6). The name Ehud appears unexpectedly in the text, so that scholars search for other names in the lists of Numbers 26 and 1 Chronicles 8:1–5 who might be the same person without sure results.

EKER (Ē′ kēr) Personal name meaning, "root" or "offspring." Son of Jerahmeel and grandson of Hezron in the tribe of Judah (1 Chron. 2:27).

EKRON (Ĕk′ rŏn) Ekron is the northernmost of the five major Philistine cities known as the pentapolis. The site of ancient Ekron has been much debated, but now is generally agreed to be modern tell Miqne, about 14 miles inland from the Mediterranean Sea and 10 miles from Ashdod. The site is one of the largest in Palestine, covering some 50 acres. Ekron lies on the road leading from Ashdod into the Judean hill country and up to Jerusalem through the Sorek Valley.

Ekron was assigned to both Judah (Josh. 15:11,45–46) and Dan (Josh. 19:43) in the tribal allotments. It probably lay on the border between the tribes. Judges 1:18 reports that Judah captured Ekron along with other parts of the Philistine coast, but Ekron was certainly in Philistine hands at the time the ark was captured (1 Sam. 5:10). It was also the place to which the Philis-

tines retreated after David slew Goliath (1 Sam. 17:52). Ahaziah, the son of King Ahab of Israel, called on the god of Ekron, Baal-zebub, when he was sick (2 Kings 1:2–16).

Excavations at tell Miqne have discovered much pottery that is typically Philistine. From the last period before tell Miqne was destroyed by the Babylonians, the excavators found an important industrial complex near the city gate. A hoard of iron agricultural tools was found. Hundreds of whole pottery vessels were present. Perhaps most importantly, a well-preserved olive press was discovered. This press is the largest and best preserved known in Israel. A horned altar was also found during the excavations. *Joel F. Drinkard, Jr.*

EL (Ĕl) One of several words for God found in biblical Hebrew and the name of the high god among the Canaanites. The word is common to Hebrew, Aramaic, and Arabic, yet the origin and root from which the word was derived is obscure. "El" is a general term that expresses majesty or power.

Biblical Usage "El" occurs 238 times in the Old Testament, most frequently in Psalms and Job. The normal biblical usage is as a simple noun for deity. "El" is a synonym for the more frequent noun for God: Elohim. "El" refers to the God of Israel and in other passages to one of the pagan gods. In some instances, qualifying words are associated with "El" in order to distinguish which god is being addressed. Exodus 34:14 is an example of the expression "other god"; Psalm 44:20 and Psalm 81:9 are translated "strange god."

"El" was frequently combined with nouns or adjectives to express the name for God with reference to particular attributes or characteristics of His being. El Shaddai, "God Almighty," appears in Genesis 17:1. El-elohe-Israel, in Genesis 33:20, was used to distinguish the God of Israel from all others. El Elyon, in Genesis 14:18 and Psalm 78:35, was written to suggest the exalted nature of God. El Gibbor (Isa. 9:6; Jer. 32:18) has been interpreted as a portrayal of God as a mighty warrior. El Roi, the God who sees, is found only in Genesis 16:13. See *Canaan.*   *James Newell*

ELA (Ē′ là) Personal name of unknown meaning, perhaps related either to *'el,* Hebrew word for God, or to Elah, a slightly different Hebrew spelling not noted in KJV. See *Elah.* Father of one of Solomon's district superintendents (1 Kings 4:18).

ELADAH (Ĕl′ à dăh) KJV spelling of Eleadah. See *Eleadah.*

ELAH (Ē′ lăh) Personal and place name meaning, "oak," "mighty tree," or "terebinth." See *Terebinth. 1.* Clan chief descended from Esau (Gen. 36:41) and thus an Edomite. See *Edom;*

Esau. 2. A valley where Saul and his army set up battle lines against the Philistines (1 Sam. 17:2). The valley runs east and west just north of Socoh. There David defeated Goliath (1 Sam. 21:9). 3. King of Israel (886-885 B.C.), killed while he was drunk during rebellion Zimri, his general, led successfully (1 Kings 16:6–14). 4. Father of Hoshea, who led a revolt and became king of Israel (886-885 B.C.) (2 Kings 15:30). 5. Son of Caleb and father of Kenaz among clans of Judah (1 Chron. 4:15). 6. Head of a clan from Benjamin who settled in Jerusalem after the Exile (1 Chron. 9:8).

ELAM (Ē′ lăm) A personal name and a place name 1. Elam was a son of Shem, one of the sons of Noah (Gen. 10:22; 1 Chron. 1:17). He may have given his name to the region known as Elam. 2. The region of Elam is on the western edge of ancient Persia, modern Iran. The Zagros Mountains lie east and north while the Persian Gulf is to the south and the Tigris River is on the west. The ancient capital of the area is Susa. The region has been inhabited since before 3000 B.C., but only a few of the periods are of importance for biblical history.

Elam appeared in history when Sargon of Akkad subdued it about 2300 B.C. Soon, though, Elamites reversed the role, sacked Ur, and set up an Elamite king in Eshnunna. The Elamite presence continued in Babylon until the time of Hammurabi about 1700 B.C.

After Hammurabi, Kassites invaded Elam. Their rule lasted until about 1200 B.C. The next century was the high point of Elam's power. All of western Iran was theirs. Again the Babylonians brought Elamite power to an end. The Assyrian Ashurbanipal brought an end to the periods of strength and weakness. He swept through the region in a series of campaigns and captured Susa in 641 B.C. He may have moved some Elamites to Samaria at that time (Ezra 4:9). Earlier, Elam had incorporated Anshan, later home of Cyrus the Great, into the kingdom. As Assyria weakened, Elam and Anshan became part of the kingdom of the Medes. Thus, they participated, with the Babylonians, in the defeat of the Assyrian empire. Elam had little subsequent independent history, but it continued to be part of the Medes' and the Persians' empires. In Scripture Elam's importance may have been due to its role as a vassal of the great empires, supplying troops for them.

Elam is mentioned in Scripture in narratives and oracles. Abraham fought Chedorlaomer, king of Elam, to secure the return of Lot and others (Gen. 14). Although this king cannot be identified from other records, the events may have occurred during Elam's time of strength prior to Hammurabi. Prophets mentioned Elam in oracles.

Other biblical references mention Elam as a personal name or homeland. Perhaps most interesting is the presence of men from Elam on the day of Pentecost. These may have been Jews from the region of Elam or converts to Judaism (Acts 2:9). God was still gathering His people from there. See *Persia; Cyrus; Assyria.*

3. A clan head of tribe of Benjamin living in Jerusalem (1 Chron. 8:24). 4. A priestly gatekeeper under David (1 Chron. 26:3). 5. Two clan leaders among the exiles who returned to Jerusalem with Zerubbabel in 537 B.C. (Ezra 2:7,31). Compare Ezra 8:7; 10:2, 26. 6. A post-exilic leader who signed Nehemiah's covenant to obey God (Neh. 10:14). 7. A priest who helped Nehemiah lead the people in celebrating the completion of the Jerusalem wall (Neh. 12:42).

Albert F. Bean

ELASAH (Ĕl ā′ săh) Personal name meaning, "God has made." 1. Son of Shaphan, the royal scribe. He took Jeremiah's message to the exiled community in Babylon while on a mission for King Zedekiah (Jer. 29:3). 2. Descendant of Jerahmeel in tribe of Judah (1 Chron. 2:39–40); spelled Eleasah in English translations. 3. Descendant of Saul and Jonathan in tribe of Benjamin (1 Chron. 8:37); spelled Eleasah in English translations. Compare 9:43. 4. Priest with a foreign wife who agreed to divorce her to avoid temptation of foreign gods in time of Ezra (Ezra 10:22).

ELATH (Ē′ lăth) or **ELOTH** (Ē′ lōth) Place name meaning, "ram," "mighty trees," or "terebinth." See *Terebinth.* Port city on northern end of Red Sea. Israel passed through it on way through Edom in wilderness (Deut. 2:8). It was significant enough to serve as a point of reference to identify Ezion-geber, where King Solomon made his naval vessels (1 Kings 9:26; compare 2 Chron. 8:17–18). Later King Uzziah (792-740) rebuilt the seaport and controlled it for Judah (2 Kings 14:22). Archaeologists have usually identified Elath as another name for Ezion-geber and located it at *tell el-Kheleifeh.* More recent archaeological work has attempted to show that Ezion-geber was the port

Aqaba, Jordan, at the mouth of the Gulf of Aqaba. In the distance is Elath.

city on the island of Jezirat Faraun. Elath would then be the mainland base to which goods were transferred for loading onto pack animals for the long caravan travels northward to Judah, Israel, Syria, or Phoenicia or for travels eastward to Assyria or Babylonia or westward to Egypt. See *Ezion-geber.*

EL-BERITH (El-běr′ ĭth) Name of god meaning, "god of the covenant." A god worshiped in a temple at Shechem. It had a stronghold or citadel guarding it. There the citizens of Shechem sought protection when Abimelech attacked them, but Abimelech set the citadel on fire (Judg. 9:46–49). KJV translates "god Berith." See *Baal-berith; Shechem.*

EL-BETHEL (Ĕl-běth′ ēl) Place name meaning, "god of the house of El (god)." Either Bethel or place in or near Bethel, where Jacob built an altar to God as memorial to his previous visit to Bethel, when he had seen a vision of God (Gen. 35:7; compare 28:10–19). Apparently the name used for God was used as a place name. See *God of the Fathers.*

ELDAAH (Ĕl dā′ ăh) Personal name meaning, "God has called," "God has sought," or "God of wisdom." Son of Midian and grandson of Abraham thus original ancestor of clan of Midianites (Gen. 25:4).

ELDAD (Ĕl′ dăd) Personal name meaning, "God loved." Along with Medad, he was one of seventy elders of Israel God selected to help Moses, but the two did not meet at the tabernacle with the others. Still the Spirit came upon Eldad and Medad in the camp, and they prophesied. Joshua attempted to stop them, but Moses prayed that all God's people might have the Spirit (Num. 11:16–29). See *Prophet; Spirit; Medad*

ELDER Prominent member of both Jewish and early Christian communities. In the Old Testament, "elder" usually translates the Hebrew word *zaqen* from a root which means "beard" or "chin." In the New Testament, the Greek word is *presbuteros,* which is transliterated in English as "presbyter" and from which the word "priest" was derived.

Elders in the Old Testament From the beginning of Israelite history, the elders were the leaders of the various clans and tribes. When the tribes came together to form the nation of Israel, the elders of the tribes naturally assumed important roles in governing the affairs of the nation. Moses was commanded to inform the "elders of Israel" of the Lord's intention to deliver Israel from Egypt and to take the elders with him to confront the pharaoh (Ex. 3:16,18). Similarly, seventy of the elders participated with Moses at the covenant meal at Sinai (Ex. 24:9–11). As the task of governing Israel grew in complexity, part of the burden was transferred from Moses to a council of seventy elders (Num. 11:16–17).

During the period of the Judges and the monarchy, the elders were prominent in the political and judicial life of Israel. They demanded that Samuel appoint a king (1 Sam. 8:4–5); they played crucial roles in David's getting and retaining the throne (2 Sam. 3:17; 5:3; 17:15; 19:11–12); and they represented the people at the consecration of the Temple of Solomon (1 Kings 8:1,3). In the legal codes of Deuteronomy the elders are responsible for administering justice, sitting as judges in the city gate (Deut. 22:15), deciding cases affecting family life (Deut. 21:18–21, 22:13–21), and executing decisions (Deut. 19:11–13; 21:1–9).

Although elders were less prominent in the post-exilic period and the term was apparently not much used in Jewish communities outside Palestine, the "council of elders" was an integral part of the Sanhedrin at Jerusalem. In the New Testament, frequent reference is made to the elders of the Jews, usually in conjunction with the chief priests or scribes (for example, Matt. 21:23; Mark 14:43). In this context the elders, apparently members of leading families, had some authority but were not the principal leaders in either religious or political affairs.

Elders in the New Testament In the earliest Jewish Christian churches, at least the church in Jerusalem, the position of "elder" was almost certainly modeled after the synagogue pattern. Although there are few specific details about the function of elders in the Jerusalem church, they apparently served as a decision-making council. They are often mentioned in conjunction with the apostles, and some passages give the impression that the apostles and elders of Jerusalem considered themselves to be a decision-making council for the whole church (Acts 15; 21:17–26).

Other churches also had elders. Acts 14:23 reports that Paul and Barnabas appointed elders in churches on their missionary journey. These elders do not seem to fit the Jewish pattern, however. In the address to the Ephesian elders Paul referred to them as overseeing the church and serving as shepherds of the church (Acts 20:28). Paul did not use the term "elders" often usually referring to the functions of ministry rather than titles of offices. For example, in Romans 12:6–9, Paul referred to those with gifts for prophecy, serving, teaching, and several other aspects of ministry (compare 1 Cor. 12). Although those exercising such gifts in churches are not expressly called elders, it is likely that at least some of them were elders. Thus, elders in the Pauline churches were probably spiritual leaders and ministers, not simply a governing council.

One of the most debated questions concerning

the pattern of early Christian ministry is the relationship between bishops and elders. Some scholars believe the two terms are interchangeable; others argue that they refer to distinct offices. Nowhere in the letters of Paul is there any explicit reference to the duties of either, nor is there any listing of the qualifications of elders. Titus 1: 5–9 is the only passage which mentions both terms. The passage begins with a direction that elders be appointed in every town and continues with a description of the qualifications for a bishop. The context leads to the conclusion that the directions and the qualifications refer to the same persons, thus implying that the terms are interchangeable.

The qualifications in Titus 1:6–9 and in 1 Timothy 3:1–7 apparently apply to elders. It becomes apparent that the elders were the spiritual leaders of the churches. Taken as a whole, the qualifications describe one who is a mature Christian of good repute, with gifts for teaching, management, and pastoral ministry. The only specific reference to the ministry of elders is the description (Jas. 5:14–15) of elders praying for and anointing a sick person. Although "bishop" usually occurs in the singular form, none of these passages indicate that there was only one elder in each congregation. The nature of the relationship between the various elders is nowhere described.

Fred A. Grissom

ELEAD (Ĕl′ ė ăd) Personal name meaning, "God is a witness." Member of tribe of Ephraim killed by men of Gath for stealing their cattle (1 Chron. 7:21). See *Ezer.*

ELEADAH (Ĕl′ ė ā dăh) Personal name meaning, "God adorned Himself." Modern translation spelling for KJV Eladah, a descendant of Ephraim (1 Chron. 7:20).

ELEALEH (Ĕl ė ā′ lĕh) Moabite place name meaning, "God went up" or "high ground." Town that tribe of Reuben requested from Moses and strengthened (Num. 32:3,37). Isaiah announced judgment on the town (Isa. 15:4; 16:9; compare Jer. 48:34). It is modern el-ʿAl, a mile north of Heshbon in a fertile plain.

ELEASAH (Ĕl ė ā′ săh) Personal name meaning, "God acted," or "God made," using same Hebrew spelling as Elasah. *1.* A member of clan of Jerahmeel in tribe of Judah (1 Chron. 2:39–40). *2.* A descendant of Saul and Jonathan in tribe of Benjamin (1 Chron. 8:37; 9:43).

ELEAZAR (Ĕl ė ā ′ ză r) Personal name meaning, "God helps." *1.* The third son of Aaron (Ex. 6:23) and high priest of Israel (Num. 20:28). After Aaron's death, Eleazar took his place as Moses' helper. It was in the presence of Eleazar that Moses commissioned Joshua (Num. 27:22). According to Joshua 14:1, Eleazar and Joshua were the key figures in the distribution of Canaanite territories among the Israelite tribes. When he died, Eleazar was buried on a hill belonging to his son Phinehas (Josh. 24:33). He was an ancestor of Ezra the scribe (Ezra 7:5). See *Aaron; Priests and Levites.*

2. The son of Abinadab who was sanctified by the men of Kirjath-jearim to have responsibility for the ark of the Lord (1 Sam. 7:1).

3. One of David's renowned warriors, the son of Dodo (2 Sam. 23:9).

4. A son of Mahli who died having had no sons, but only daughters (1 Chron. 23:21–22).

5. The son of Phinehas who assisted in weighing out the silver and gold utensils in the house of God (Ezra 8:33).

6. One of the sons of Parosh in a list of persons who had married foreign wives. He later put away his wife because of Ezra's reform banning foreign marriage (Ezra 10:25).

7. A musician involved in the dedication of the wall of Jerusalem (Neh. 12:42).

8. The son of Eliud and father of Matthan. He was an ancestor of Joseph the husband of Mary (Matt. 1:15).

ELECT LADY The recipient of John's second letter (2 John 1) sometimes understood to be an individual but the phrase probably is a way of referring to a local church congregation. The members of the church would then be the "children" who are mentioned in the same verse. The "elect sister" of verse 13 would be another congregation whose members were sending greeting.

ELECTION God's plan to bring salvation to His people and His world. The doctrine of election is at once one of the most central and one of the most misunderstood teachings of the Bible. At its most basic level, election refers to the purpose or plan of God whereby He has determined to effect His will. Thus election encompasses the entire range of divine activity from creation, God's decision to bring the world into being out of nothing, to the end time, the making anew of heaven and earth. The word "election" itself is derived from the Greek word, *eklegomai,* which means, literally, "to choose something for oneself." This in turn corresponds to the Hebrew word, *bachar.* The objects of divine selection are the elect ones, a term found with increasing frequency in the later writings of the Old Testament and at many places in the New (Matt. 22:14; Luke 18:7; Col. 3:12; Rev. 17:14). The Bible also uses other words such as "choose," "predestinate," "foreordain," "determine," and "call" to indicate that God has entered into a special relationship with certain individuals and groups through whom He has decided to fulfill His purpose within the history of salvation.

Israel as the Object of God's Election The doctrine of election is rooted in the particularity of the Judeo-Christian tradition, that is, the conviction that out of all the peoples on earth God has chosen to reveal Himself in a special, unique way to one particular people. This conviction resonates through every layer of Old Testament literature from the early awareness of Israel as "the people of Yahweh" through the Psalms (147:19–20a, "He sheweth his word unto Jacob, his statutes and his judgments unto Israel. He hath not dealt so with any nation"; compare Isa. 14:1; Ezek. 20:5). Five major motifs in the Old Testament portray God's election of Israel.

(1) Election is the result of the sovereign initiative of God. At the very beginning of Israel's role in salvation history is the call of Abraham to leave his homeland for a new one which would be shown unto him (Gen. 12:1–7). This directive came to Abraham from God who also promised to bless his descendants and all peoples on earth through them. While Abraham responded to this call in obedience and faith, his election was not the result of his own efforts, but solely of God's decision. (2) The central word in Israel's vocabulary for describing their special relationship with God was *covenant*. This covenant was not a contract between equal partners, but a bond established by God's unmerited favor and love. The gracious character of the covenant is a major theme in Deuteronomy. "For thou art an holy people unto the Lord thy God: the Lord thy God hath chosen thee to be a special people unto himself, above all people that are upon the face of the earth. The Lord did not set his love upon you, nor choose you, because ye were more in number than any people; for ye were the fewest of all people" (Deut. 7:6–7). (3) Within the covenanted community God selected certain individuals to fulfill specific functions. The following persons are said to be elected in this sense: Abraham (Neh. 9:7), Moses (Ps. 106:23), Aaron (Num. 16:1–17:13), David (Ps. 78:70), Solomon (1 Chron. 28:10), and Zerubbabel (Hag. 2:23). Kings, priests, and prophets are all chosen by God, though in different ways and for various purposes. Jeremiah believed that he had been elected and set apart as a prophet even before he was born (Jer. 1:4–5). (4) Israel's election was never intended to be a pretext for pride, but rather an opportunity for service. "I the Lord have called thee in righteousness, . . . for a light of the Gentiles" (Isa. 42:6). From time to time the children of Israel were tempted to presume upon God's gracious favor, to assume, for example, that because the Lord had placed His temple at Jerusalem, they were exempt from judgment. Again and again the prophets tried to disabuse them of this false notion of security by pointing out the true meaning of the covenant and their mission among the nations (Jer. 7:1–14; Amos 3:2; Jonah). (5) In the later Old Testament writings, and especially during the intertestamental period, there is a tendency to identify the "elect ones" with the true, faithful "remnant" among the people of God. The birth of the Messiah is seen to mark the dawn of the age of salvation for the remnant (Ezek. 34:12–13, 23–31; Mic. 5:1–2). The community of Essenes at Qumran saw themselves as an elect remnant whose purity and faithfulness presaged the Messianic Age.

Election and the New Covenant The early Christians saw themselves as heirs of Israel's election, "a chosen generation, a holy nation, a peculiar people" (1 Pet. 2:9). Paul treats this theme most extensively, but we should not overlook its central importance for the entire New Testament. Again, certain individuals are singled out as chosen by God: the twelve apostles (Luke 6:13), Peter (Acts 15:7), Paul (Acts 9:15), and Jesus Himself (Luke 9:35; 23:35). In the Synoptic Gospels the term "elect ones" is always set in an eschatological context, that is, the days of tribulation will be shortened "for the elect's sake, whom he hath chosen" (Mark 13:20). Many of the parables of Jesus, such as that of the marriage feast (Matt. 22:1–14) and that of the laborers in the vineyard (Matt. 20:1–16), illustrate the sovereignty of God in salvation. In John, Jesus is the unmistakable Mediator of election: "Ye have not chosen me, but I have chosen you," He reminded the disciples (John 15:16a). Again, His followers are those who have been given to Him by the Father "before the world was" and "none of them is lost" (John 17:5,12). Also in John the shadow side of election is posed in the person of Judas, "the son of perdition." Though his status as one of the elect is called into question by his betrayal of Christ, not even this act was able to thwart the fulfillment of God's plan of salvation.

There are three passages where Paul deals at length with different aspects of the doctrine of election. In the first (Rom. 8:28–39) divine election is presented as the ground and assurance of the Christian's hope. Since those whom God has predestinated are also called, justified, and glorified, nothing can separate them from the love of God in Christ Jesus. The second passage (Rom. 9–11) is preoccupied with the fact of Israel's rejection of Christ which, in the purpose of God, has become the occasion for the entrance of Gentile believers into the covenant. In the third passage (Eph. 1:1–12) Paul pointed to the Christocentric character of election: God has chosen us *in Christ* before the foundation of the world. We can refer to this statement as the evangelical center of the doctrine of election. Our election is strictly and solely in Christ. As the eternal Son, He is along with the Father and the Holy Spirit, the electing God; as the incarnate Mediator between God and humankind, He is the elected One. We should never speak of predestination apart from this central truth.

Election and the Christian Life Paul admonished the Thessalonians to give thanks because of their election (2 Thess. 2:13), while Peter said that we should make our "calling and election sure" (2 Pet. 1:10). However, in the history of Christian thought few teachings have been more distorted or more misused. The following questions reveal common misperceptions. (1) Is not election the same thing as fatalism? Predestination does not negate the necessity for human repentance and faith; rather it establishes the possibility of both. God does not relate to human beings as sticks and stones but as free creatures made in His own image. (2) If salvation is based on election, then why preach the gospel? Because God has chosen preaching as the means to awaken faith in the elect (1 Cor. 1:21). We should proclaim the gospel to everyone without exception, knowing that it is only the Holy Spirit who can convict, regenerate, and justify. (3) Does the Bible teach "double predestination," that God has selected some for damnation as well as some for salvation? There are passages (Rom. 9:11–22; 2 Cor. 2:15–16) which portray God as a potter who has molded both vessels of mercy and vessels of destruction. Yet the Bible also teaches that God does not wish any one to perish but for all to be saved (John 3:16; 2 Pet. 3:9). We are not able to understand how everything the Bible says about election fits into a neat logical system. Our business is not to pry into the secret counsel of God but to share the message of salvation with everyone and to be grateful that we have been delivered from darkness into light. (4) Does not belief in election result in moral laxity and pride? Paul says that God chose us "to salvation through sanctification of the Spirit" (2 Thess. 2:13). We are to work out our salvation with fear and trembling, even though to be sure, it is God who is at work within us both to will and do His good pleasure (Phil. 2:12–13). The proper response to election is not pride but gratitude for God's amazing grace which saves eternally. Election, then, is neither a steeple from which we look in judgment on others, nor a pillow to sleep on. It is rather a stronghold in time of trial and a confession of praise to God's grace and to His glory. *Timothy George*

EL-ELOHE-ISRAEL (Ĕl-ė1 ō′ hĕ-Ĭs′ rā ĕl) Divine name meaning, "God, the God of Israel." The name Jacob gave altar he set up in land he bought near Shechem (Gen. 33:20). See *Patriarchs.*

EL-ELYON See *El; God.*

ELEMENTS, ELEMENTAL SPIRITS (Greek *stoicheia*) The basic idea of *stoichei* is a member in a series. At Hebrews 5:12 the term means basic or fundamental principles of Christian belief. The meaning of the term in other New Testament

contexts is disputed. In the Pauline uses (Ga. 4:3,9; Col. 2:8,20) English translations are divided between rudiments, that is, basic principles, (KJV, NAS, NIV) and elementary spirits (NRSV, REB, TEV). At 2 Peter 3:10,12 most English translation render *stoicheia* as elements, that is, component parts. TEV takes the term with the preceding phrase, thus rendering it heavenly bodies.

ELEPH (Ė′ lĕph) KJV spelling of Haeleph. See *Haeleph.*

EL-HANAN (Ĕl hā′ năn) Personal name meaning, "God is gracious." The Bethlehemite who slew the brother of Goliath (2 Sam. 21:19). The Hebrew text, however, does not contain the words "the brother of." It states that El-hanan killed Goliath. First Chronicles 20:5 *does* indicate that El-hanan killed Lahmi, the brother of Goliath. A further variation in the texts from 2 Samuel and 1 Chronicles lies in the name of El-hanan's father: in 2 Samuel 21:19 it is Jaare-oregim; in 1 Chronicles 20:5, Jair. The proper reconciliation of these two passages, along with their relationship to 1 Samuel 17 (according to which Goliath was slain by David), constitutes one of the Old Testament's more baffling puzzles. See *David.*

ELI (Ē′ lī) Personal name meaning, "high." The priest at Shiloh who became the custodian of the child Samuel (1 Sam. 1:3). He was the father of Hophni and Phinehas. After Samuel's birth Hannah, his mother, brought him to the sanctuary at Shiloh in fulfillment of a vow she had made to the Lord. Eli thereby became the human agent largely responsible for the religious and spiritual training of the boy. When Samuel mistook the voice of God for the voice of Eli, Eli instructed him to ask the Lord to speak the next time he heard the voice (1 Sam. 3). Eli's death was precipitated by the news of the death of his sons and the capture of the ark of God by the Philistines (1 Sam. 4:18).

ELI, ELI, LAMA SABACHTHANI This cry of Jesus on the cross, traditionally known as the "fourth word from the cross" means, "My God, my God, why hast thou forsaken me?" (Matt. 27:46; Mark 15:34). It is a quotation from Psalm 22:1. The Markan form, *Eloi,* is closer to Aramaic than Matthew's more Hebraic *Eli.*

This saying of Jesus from the cross strikes a dissonant chord for some Christians, because it seems to indicate that Jesus felt forsaken by the Father. There are several ways to consider the meaning of this passage in reverent faith. It is possible to interpret these words as a beautiful testimony to Jesus' love of His Bible, the Old Testament, and His quoting of it in this hour of darkest crisis. In this case, such verses in Psalm 22 as 5, 7, 8, 12, 14, and 18 indicate that Jesus sees Himself and His fate in this Psalm. However, since the Gospels record only the first verse of the Psalm and we do not know whether Jesus quoted the entire Psalm, this view may run the risk of not taking the phrase at face value.

Another view sees this cry as indicating a genuine forsaking of Jesus by the Father, a forsaking which was necessary for our redemption. This view leads some to questions about the nature of the godhead and theories of atonement which we cannot address in this brief discussion. Perhaps the most serious difficulty of this view is that it raises the question of whether the idea of God the Father turning His back on the obedient Son is consistent with the general biblical teaching of the steadfastness and faithfulness of God. Would He desert a trusting child in such an hour?

A view which takes into consideration the full humanity—as well as full divinity—of Jesus seems most helpful. Obviously Jesus *felt* deserted as He bore the burden of human sin and suffered the agony of crucifixion. This feeling of His death as a "ransom for many" may, indeed, have obscured for a time His feeling of closeness with the Father, so that even in dying He was tempted as we are. Rather than forsaking the Father in that moment, He cried out to Him in prayer.   *Earl Dans*

ELIAB (Ē lī′ ăb) Personal name meaning, "God is father." *1.* Leader of tribe of Zebulun under Moses (Num. 1:9). He brought the tribe's offering at the dedication of the altar (Num. 7:24). *2.* Member of tribe of Reuben and father of Dathan and Abiram. See *Abiram; Dathan. 3.* First son of Jesse to pass by and be rejected when Samuel searched for king to replace Saul (1 Sam. 16:6). He fought in Saul's army (1 Sam. 17:13) and became angry at David's interest in fighting Goliath (1 Sam. 17:28). His daughter married King Rehoboam (2 Chron. 11:18). He is apparently called Elihu in 1 Chronicles 27:18. *4.* A Levite in the line of Kohath and ancestor of Samuel (1 Chron. 6:27). The same person is apparently called Elihu in 1 Samuel 1:1 and Eliel (1 Chron. 6:34). *5.* A Levite appointed as a Temple musician under David (1 Chron. 15:18,20; 16:5). *6.* A military leader from the tribe of Gad under David (1 Chron. 12:9).

ELIADA (Ē lī′ ă dà) Personal name meaning, "God has known." *1.* Son born to David after he established his rule in Jerusalem (2 Sam. 5:16). In 1 Chronicles 14:7 he is listed as Beeliada ("Baal has known" or "the lord has known"). *2.* Father of Rezon, who established himself as king of Damascus after David conquered Zobah (1 Kings 11:23). *3.* A military commander of the tribe of Benjamin (2 Chron. 17:17) under King Jehoshaphat (873-848 B.C.).

ELIADAH (Ē lī′ ă däh) KJV spelling of Eliada in 1 Kings 11:23. See *Eliada.*

ELIAH (Ē lī′ äh) KJV spelling of Elijah in 1 Chronicles 8:27; Ezra 10:26. See *Elijah.*

ELIAHBA (Ē lī′ äh bá) Personal name meaning, "God hides in safety" or "my god is Chiba." A leading soldier in David's army (2 Sam. 23:32).

ELIAKIM (Ē lī′ ă kĭm) Personal name meaning, "God will raise up." The son of Hilkiah who was in charge of the household of King Hezekiah of Judah (2 Kings 18:18). That responsibility had previously belonged to Shebna; Isaiah 22:15–25 deals with the displacing of Shebna by Eliakim.
2. The son of Josiah who was placed on the throne of Judah by Pharaoh Neco of Egypt (2 Kings 23:34). The Pharaoh changed the name of Eliakim to Jehoiakim. The latter name is the one by which this individual is more familiarly known. See *Jehoiakim. 3.* A priest who was involved in the dedication of the wall of Jerusalem (Neh. 12:41). *4.* An ancestor of Joseph the husband of Mary (Matt. 1:13). *5.* The son of Melea, mentioned in Luke's genealogy of Jesus (Luke 3:30).

ELIAM (Ē lī′ ăm) Personal name meaning, "God is an uncle or relative" or "God of the people." *1.* Father of Bathsheba (2 Sam. 11:3). The two parts of his name are reversed in 1 Chronicles 3:5, becoming Ammiel. *2.* A leading warrior under David (2 Sam. 23:34). The related list in 1 Chronicles 11 does not have Eliam but in a similar position has Ahijah ("my brother is Yahweh").

ELIAS (Ē lī′ às) KJV New Testament spelling of Elijah, transliterating the Greek spelling. See *Elijah.*

ELIASAPH (Ē lī′ ă săph) Personal name meaning, "God has added." *1.* The leader of the tribe of Gad under Moses (Num. 1:14). He presented the tribe's offerings at the dedication of the altar (Num. 7:42). *2.* A Levite of the family of Gershon (Num. 3:24).

ELIASHIB (Ē lī′ ă shĭb) Personal name meaning, "God repays or leads back." *1.* A descendant of David in Judah after the return from Exile in Babylon (1 Chron. 3:24). *2.* A leading priest under David (1 Chron. 24:12). *3.* High priest in time of Nehemiah who led in rebuilding the sheep gate in the Jerusalem wall, a gate through which sheep were led to the nearby Temple for sacrifice (Neh. 3:1). His house was built into the city wall (Neh. 3:20). He was the son of Joiakim and the father of Joiada (Neh. 12:10). His grandson married the daughter of Sanballat, who strongly opposed Nehemiah's efforts (Neh. 13:28), possibly indicating some tension between Nehemiah and the priestly leaders. He may be the Eliashib whose son had a room in the Temple (Ezra 10:6). *4.* A priest in the time of Nehemiah who administered the Temple storerooms and provided a place for Tobiah, Nehemiah's strong opponent (Neh. 13:4–9). This may be the Eliashib of Ezra 10:6. *5.* A Levite and Temple singer in Ezra's day who agreed to divorce his foreign wife to avoid tempting Israel to worship other gods (Ezra 10:24). *6.* Two Israelites who agreed to divorce his foreign wife under Ezra's leadership (Ezra 10:27,36).

ELIATHAH (E lī' a thäh) Personal name meaning, "my God has come." A Temple musician appointed under David to play and prophesy (1 Chron. 25:4). He headed a division of Temple workers (1 Chron. 25:27, where the Hebrew spelling of the name varies slightly). Many scholars of the Hebrew language think the names of the last nine sons of Heman in verse *4b* originally formed a verse of a Hebrew psalm in which Eliathah would have meant, "My God are you."

ELIDAD (E lī' dăd) A personal name meaning, "God loved" or "My God is uncle or friend." The name in Hebrew is a variant spelling of Eldad. See *Eldad.* Representative of tribe of Benjamin on commission God chose to help Joshua and Eleazar divide the land of Canaan among the tribes (Num. 34:21).

ELIEHOENAI (Ĕl' ĭ ē hō ē' nāi) Personal name meaning, "to Yaho are my eyes." Compare Psalm 123:2. *1.* One of the Temple porters or gatekeepers under David (1 Chron. 26:3). *2.* One of the twelve clan heads who returned to Jerusalem from Babylon with Ezra (Ezra 8:4). See *Elihoenai.*

ELIEL (E lī' ĕl) Personal name meaning, "my God is God" or "my God is El." *1.* A clan leader in the tribe of Manasseh east of the Jordan River (1 Chron. 5:23). *2.* A Levite and ancestor of the singer Heman (1 Chron. 6:34). *3.* A member of the tribe of Benjamin (1 Chron. 8:20). *4.* Another Benjaminite (1 Chron. 8:22). *5.* Military leader under David (1 Chron. 11:46), not listed in 1 Samuel 23. *6.* Another military leader under David not listed in 1 Samuel 23 (1 Chron. 11:47). *7.* A warrior from the tribe of Gad who served under David in the wilderness (1 Chron. 12:11). *8.* A chief Levite in the time of David (1 Chron. 15:9, 11) *9.* An overseer of Temple offerings among the Levites (2 Chron. 31:13) under King Hezekiah (715-686 B.C.).

ELIENAI (Ĕl ĭ ē' nāi) An abbreviated form of the Hebrew personal name Eliehoenai. See *Eliehoenai.* The abbreviated form's literal meaning is "my God my eyes." A member of the tribe of Benjamin (1 Chron. 8:20).

ELIEZER (Ĕl ĭ ē' zēr) Personal name meaning,

"God helps." *1.* The servant of Abram who would have been the patriarch's heir if Abram had remained childless (Gen. 15:2). *2.* The second son of Moses and Zipporah (Ex. 18:4). *3.* One of the sons of Becher the Benjamite (1 Chron. 7:8).

4. One of the priests who blew the trumpets when the ark of the covenant was brought to Jerusalem (1 Chron. 15:24). *5.* A ruler of the Reubenites (1 Chron. 27:6). *6.* The son of Dodavah, who prophesied against Jehoshaphat (2 Chron. 20:37).

7. One of the leaders whom Ezra sent for (Ezra 8:16). *8.* A priest who put away his foreign wife (Ezra 10:18). *9.* A Levite who put away his foreign wife (Ezra 10:23). *10.* A member of the clan of Harim who put away his foreign wife (Ezra 10:31). *11.* The son of Jorim mentioned in the genealogy of Jesus (Luke 3:29).

ELIHOENAI (Ĕl ĭ hō ē' nāi) KJV spelling of Eliehoenai in Ezra 8:4. See *Eliehoenai.*

ELIHOREPH (Ĕl' ĭ hō' rĕph) Personal name meaning, "my God repays," or "my God is the giver of the autumn harvest," or borrowed from Egyptian, "Apis is my God." One of Solomon's two royal scribes with his brother Ahijah (1 Kings 4:3). Their father may have been Egyptian. The name could indicate that Solomon's father-in-law (1 Kings 3:1) had helped him organize and staff his administration. Shisha, the name of Elihorep's father, is the Egyptian word for scribe. REB takes Elihoreph as a title: "adjutant-general."

ELIHU (E lī' hū) Personal name meaning, "he is God." *1.* The son of Barachel the Buzite who addressed Job after the latter's first three friends had ended their speeches (Job 32:2). Elihu's words fill Job 32—37. Interpreters differ with regard to the significance of Elihu's speeches. His words seem to be somewhat more insightful than those of the other three friends, yet they still prove finally unsatisfactory as an explanation of Job's suffering. See *Job.*

2. Samuel's great grandfather (1 Sam. 1:1). *3.* A member of tribe of Manasseh who defected to David (1 Chron. 12:20). *4.* Mighty military hero under David (1 Chron. 26:7). *5.* David's brother in charge of the tribe of Judah (1 Chron. 27:18).

ELIJAH (E lī' jäh) Personal name meaning, "my God is Yah." The prophet from the ninth century B.C. from Tishbe of Gilead in the Northern Kingdom has been called the grandest and the most romantic character that Israel ever produced. See 1 Kings 17:1—2 Kings 2:18.

He was a complex man of the desert who counseled kings. His life is best understood when considered from four historical perspectives which at times are interrelated: his miracles, his struggle against Baalism, his prophetic role, and his eschatological relationship to Messiah.

Miracles His first miracle was associated with his prophecy before King Ahab (1 Kings 17:1) in which he said there would be no rain or dew apart from his declaration. Immediately after the prophecy, he retreated to the brook Cherith where he was fed by ravens.

His next refuge was Zarephath where he performed the miracle of raising the widow's dead son (1 Kings 17:17–24). Here he was first called "a man of God."

On Mount Carmel his greatest public miracle involved his encounter with the 450 prophets of Baal and the 400 prophets of Asherah (1 Kings 18:19–40). The contest was to determine the true God. The false prophets called on their gods, and Elijah called on His God to see which would rain fire from heaven. After the false prophets

The Chapel of Elijah on Mt. Sinai, commemorating the traditional site to which Elijah fled.

failed to hear from their gods, Elijah wet the wood on his altar to the true God by pouring four jars of water over it three times. In response of Elijah's prayer, Yahweh rained fire from heaven to consume the wet wood. As a result of their deception, Elijah ordered the false prophets killed.

Elijah next prophesied that the drought was soon to end (1 Kings 18:41) after three rainless years. From Carmel, Elijah prayed. He sent his servant seven times to see if rain was coming. The seventh time a cloud the size of a hand appeared on the horizon. Ahab was told to flee before the storm. Elijah outran his chariot and the storm to arrive at Jezreel.

Baalism Interwoven in the life of Elijah is his struggle with Baalism. Jezebel, daughter of Ethbaal, king of Sidon and Tyre (1 Kings 16:31), was Ahab's wife and Israel's queen. She brought the worship of her god Baal into Ahab's kingdom. Even "Ahab served Baal a little" (2 Kings 10:18). The contest on Carmel showed a contrast between the contesting dieties. Yahweh's power and Baal's impotence was further revealed through the drought. A later involvement with Naboth showed the moral superiority of Elijah's faith (2 Kings 9:25–37).

Jezebel planned revenge toward Elijah for ordering the false prophets slain, so Elijah retreated to Judah and finally Mount Horeb. There he observed the power of the wind, earthquake, and fire; but the Lord was not seen in these forces. In a small voice the Lord commanded him to go anoint Hazael king of Syria, Jehu king of Israel, and Elisha as his own successor (1 Kings 19:1–17).

Prophet His prophetic role constantly placed Elijah in opposition to the majority of the people of his nation. His prophetic confrontations involved King Ahab and later his son Ahaziah. Their toleration of polytheism was the ongoing reason for Elijah's prophetic denunciations.

When Ahaziah fell and injured himself, he sent messengers to ask Baal-zebub (lord of flies) about his fate. Elijah intercepted them and sent word back to Ahaziah that he was soon to die (2 Kings 1). Ahaziah sent three different detachments of fifty soldiers each to arrest Elijah. The first two units were destroyed by fire from heaven. The captain of the third group pleaded for his life. He safely escorted Elijah to the king where he delivered the prophecy of his pending death personally.

Relationship to Messiah Elijah and Elisha were involved in the schools of the prophets when Elijah struck the waters of the Jordan and they parted to allow their crossing (2 Kings 2:1–12).

Malachi promised God would send Elijah the prophet before the coming "day of the Lord" (Mal. 4:5). John the Baptist was spoken of as the one who would go before Messiah "in the spirit and power" of Elijah (Luke 1:17). John personally denied that he was literally Elijah reincarnate (John 1:21,25). Some considered Jesus to be Elijah (Matt. 16:14; Mark 6:15).

Entrance to Elijah's cave near Tyre.

Elijah appeared along with Moses on the Mount of Transfiguration with Jesus to discuss His "departure." Here Peter suggested that three tabernacles be built for Jesus, Moses, and Elijah (Matt. 17:4; Mark 9:5; Luke 9:33).

The two witnesses referred to in Revelation 11:6 are not identified by name, but their capacity "to shut heaven, that it rain not . . . " leads many to conclude they are Moses and Elijah.

Nelson Price

ELIKA (Ē lī′ ká) Personal name meaning, "my God has arisen" or "my God has vomited." One of David's military heroes from the village of Harod (2 Sam. 23:25). He does not appear in the parallel list in 1 Chronicles 11.

ELIM (Ē′ līm) Place name meaning, "trees." One of the encampments of the Israelites after the Exodus from Egypt (Ex. 15:27). It was the first place where they found water. It had twelve wells of water and seventy palm trees (Num. 33:9). Its exact location is unknown.

ELIMELECH (Ē līm′ ē lĕch) Personal name meaning, "my God is king." The husband of Naomi, who led his family from Bethlehem to Moab to escape famine and then died in Moab. This prepared the scene for the Book of Ruth (Ruth 1:2–3; compare 4:3).

ELIOENAI (Ēl ĭ ō ē′ nâi) Personal name meaning, "to Yo are my eyes," a Hebrew spelling variant of Eliehoenai. See *Eliehoenai.* *1.* A post-exilic descendant of David, maintaining Israel's royal line (1 Chron. 3:23–24). *2.* Clan leader of the tribe of Simeon (1 Chron. 4:36). *3.* A grandson of Benjamin and thus great grandson of Jacob (1 Chron. 7:8). *4.* A priest who agreed under Ezra's leadership to divorce his foreign wife to protect the community from false worship (Ezra 10:22). *5.* An Israelite who agreed to divorce his foreign wife (Ezra 10:27). *6.* A priest who led in the service of dedication and thanksgiving for the completion of repairs of the wall around Jerusalem (Neh. 12:41).

ELIPHAL (Ē lī′ phăl) Personal name meaning, "God has judged." Military hero under David (1 Chron. 11:35). In 2 Samuel 23:34 the name appears as Eliphelet.

ELIPHALET (Ē līph′ á lĕt) KJV spelling of Eliphelet (2 Sam. 5:16; 1 Chron. 14:7). See *Eliphelet.*

ELIPHAZ (Ĕl′ ĭ phăz) Personal name meaning, "my god is gold." *1.* A son of Esau by his wife Adah the daughter of Elon the Hittite (Gen. 36:4). Eliphaz became the ancestor of the chieftains of several Edomite clans (Gen. 36:15–16).

2. One of three men who visited Job and engaged the sufferer in dialogue (Job 2:11). He is identified as a Temanite, meaning he was from Teman in Edom. His recorded speeches to Job are marked by a simplistic theological traditionalism and a tone of moral superiority. He may have been a descendant of Eliphaz the son of Esau. See *Job.*

ELIPHELEH (Ē līph′ ē lĕh) KJV spelling of Eliphelehu (1 Chron. 15:18,21) based on early Greek transliteration of the Hebrew. See *Eliphelehu.*

ELIPHELEHU (Ē līph′ ē lē hū) Personal name meaning, "God treated him with distinction." Levite and musician in Temple under David (1 Chron. 15:18,21).

ELIPHELET (Ē līph′ ē lĕt) Personal name meaning, "God is deliverance." *1.* David's son born in Jerusalem (2 Sam. 5:16). He is apparently listed twice in both 1 Chronicles 3:6,8 and 14:5,7, with an abbreviated Hebrew spelling in 14:5. See *Elpalet.* *2.* A descendant of Saul and Jonathan in the tribe of Benjamin (1 Chron. 8:39). *3.* A clan leader who accompanied Ezra on his return from Exile in Babylon (Ezra 8:13). *4.* A man who divorced his foreign wife under Ezra's leadership to avoid false worship among God's people (Ezra 10:33). *5.* A famous warrior under David (2 Sam. 23:34).

ELISABETH (E′ līs ′ á bĕth) Personal name meaning, "my God is good fortune" or "my God has sworn an oath." A woman descended from Aaron who was the wife of Zacharias the priest (Luke 1:5). Both she and her husband are described in Luke 1:6 as being noteworthy examples of piety and devotion to the Lord. However, she was barren in her old age. God removed from her the stigma of childlessness, and she became the mother of John the Baptist, forerunner of Christ. She also was kin to Mary the mother of Jesus; but the Bible does not indicate the exact degree of relationship between the two women. See *John the Baptist; Annunciation.*

ELISEUS (Ĕl ĭ sē′ ŭs) KJV spelling of Elisha, following the Greek transliteration of the Hebrew, in Luke 4:27. See *Elisha.*

ELISHA (E lī′ shà) Personal name meaning, "my God is salvation." A ninth century B.C. Israelite prophet, son of Shaphat of Abel-meholah (1 Kings 19:16).

His Name and Call Experience Elisha was plowing one day when "Elijah passed by him, and cast his mantle upon him." (1 Kings 19:19). This action symbolically manifested God's plan to bestow the prophetic powers of Elijah upon Elisha. The chosen one understood the call of God for, "he left the oxen, and ran after Elijah. . . . " (1 Kings 19:20). That Elisha felt the call of prophetic succession is again clear following Elijah's dramatic ascent into heaven. There Elisha "took up also the mantle of Elijah that fell from him. . . . " (2 Kings 2:13).

The beginning of Elisha's ministry should be dated to the last years of King Ahab's rule (1 Kings 19) or approximately 850 B.C. The prophet then served faithfully during the reigns of Ahaziah (about 853 B.C.), Jehoram or Joram (852 B.C.), Jehu (c. 841 B.C.), Jehoahaz (c. 814 B.C.), and Jehoash or Joash (798 B.C.).

His Miracles After Elijah insisted to his chosen successor that he, "Ask what I shall do for you, before I am taken from you," Elisha answered, "Let me inherit a double portion of spirit" (2 Kings 2:9 NIV). Taking up the mantle of the departed prophet, he parted the Jordan River. Following this miracle the prophetic order or "sons of the prophets" declared, "The spirit of Elijah is resting on Elisha" (2 Kings 2:15).

Soon thereafter, Elisha made bad water wholesome (2 Kings 2:19–22). His reputation soon assumed so sacred an aura that harassment of the prophet merited severe punishment. For mocking the bald prophet, 42 boys were attacked by two she-bears (2 Kings 2:23–24).

The prophet used his power to provide a widow with an abundance of valuable oil to save her children from slavery (2 Kings 4:1–7). He made a poisonous pottage edible (2 Kings 4:38–41), fed a hundred men by multiplying limited resources (2 Kings 4:42–44), and miraculously provided water for thirsting armies (2 Kings 3:13–22). Once he made an iron ax head float (2 Kings 6:5–7).

Some of the miracles of Elisha are quite well known and loved. Who has not been moved by the story of the Shunammite woman and her son? This barren woman and her husband who had

Elisha's spring at Jericho which is the source for Elisha's well (located in the covered area).

graciously opened their home to the prophet had in turn been given a son by the Lord. One day while the boy worked in the field with his father, he suffered an apparent heartstroke and died. The compassion and tenacious hope of the mother met its reward when she sought and found the man of God and pleaded for help. God's power through Elisha raised the boy from the dead (2 Kings 4:8–37).

Yet another well-known story is the healing of Naaman the leper and the subsequent affliction of Gehazi the dishonest servant of Elisha (2 Kings 5:1–27). The miraculous powers of the prophet were prominently displayed still further in the war between Syria and Israel. The Syrian soldiers were blinded, then made to see. Then, at last, divine intervention totally foiled the Syrian seige of Samaria (2 Kings 6:8–7:20).

Elisha's power did not end at death. For when a dead man was thrown into Elisha's grave and touched his bones, "he revived, and stood up on his feet" (2 Kings 13:21).

In carrying out the second and third commands of the "still small voice" to Elijah (1 Kings 19:11–16), Elisha enhanced his legacy beyond the realm of miracle worker. He played a major role in Hazael becoming king of Syria (2 Kings 8:7–15) and also in the anointing of Jehu as king of Israel (2 Kings 9:1–13).

Powerful enough to perform miracles and appoint kings, yet sensitive enough to weep over the fate of Israel (2 Kings 8:11,12), Elisha, disciple and successor to Elijah, proved to be both prophet and statesman.   *J. Randall O'Brien*

ELISHAH (Ē lī′ shăh) Place name of unknown meaning. Elishah, or Alashiya as it appears in Hittite, Akkadian, and Ugaritic texts, is a name for all or part of the island of Cyprus, which exported copper and purple cloth. Others would locate it as the present Haghio Kyrko in Crete. Among the Amarna letters from Egypt are letters from the king of Elishah to the pharaoh mentioning copper exports. The Greeks established a colony on Cyprus by about 1500 B.C. This would explain the relationship of Elishah as a son of Javan or the Greeks in the Table of Nations (Gen. 10:4). Compare 1 Chronicles 1:7. Ezekiel noted in his lament over Tyre that Tyre had imported from Elishah the purple fabric for which Tyre was famous (Ezek. 27:7).

ELISHAMA (Ē lĭsh′ à má) Personal name meaning, "God heard." *1.* Leader of the tribe of Ephraim under Moses in the wilderness (Num. 1:10). He presented the tribe's offerings at the dedication of the altar (Num. 7:48–53). Compare 1 Chronicles 7:26. *2.* David's son born after he captured and moved to Jerusalem (2 Sam. 5:16). He is apparently listed twice in 1 Chronicles 3:6,8, though 1 Chronicles 14:5 reads the first

Elishama as Elishua, as in 2 Samuel 5:15. *3.* A royal scribe under King Jehoiakim (609-597 B.C.). Baruch's scroll of Jeremiah's preaching was stored in Elishama's room before it was taken to be read to the king (Jer. 36:12–21). *4.* An ancestor with royal bloodlines of Ishmael, the person who murdered Gedaliah and took over political control of Judah immediately after Babylon had destroyed Jerusalem (2 Kings 25:25). *5.* A descendant of the clan of Jerahmeel in the tribe of Judah (1 Chron. 2:41). *6.* Priest under King Jehoshaphat (873-848 B.C.). He taught the book of the law to the people of Judah at the king's request (2 Chron. 17:7–9).

ELISHAPHAT (E lĭsh′ ȧ phăt) Personal name meaning, "God had judged." Military captain who helped Jehoiada, the priest, overthrow Queen Athaliah and establish Joash (835-796 B.C.) as king of Judah (2 Chron. 23:1).

ELISHEBA (E lĭsh′ ē bä) Personal name meaning, "God is good fortune." Wife of Aaron, the high priest (Ex. 6:23).

ELISHUA (Ĕl′ ĭ shū ȧ) Personal name meaning, "God is salvation." David's son born after he captured and moved to Jerusalem (2 Sam. 5:15). See *Elishama, 2.*

ELIUD (E lī′ ŭd) Personal name meaning, "God is high and mighty." Great, great grandfather of Joseph, the earthly father of Jesus (Matt. 1:14–15).

ELIZABETH (E lĭz′ ȧ bĕth) Americanized spelling used in modern translations of KJV Elisabeth. See *Elisabeth.*

ELIZAPHAN (Ĕl′ ĭ zā phăn) Personal name meaning, "God has hidden or treasured up." *1.* A clan leader among the sons of Kohath among the Levites in the wilderness with Moses (Num. 3:30). Compare 1 Chronicles 15:8; 2 Chronicles 29:13. *2.* Representative of tribe of Zebulun on the council to help Joshua and Eleazar divide the land among the tribes (Num. 34:25).

ELIZUR (E lī′ zûr) Personal name meaning, "God is a rock." Leader of tribe of Reuben under Moses in the wilderness (Num. 1:5). He presented the tribe's offerings at the dedication of the altar (Num. 7:30–35).

ELKANAH (Ĕl kā′ nah) Personal name meaning, "God created." *1.* One of the sons of Korah, the priest (Ex. 6:24).
2. The son of Jeroham. He became the father of Samuel (1 Sam. 1:1). *3.* A person named in a list of Levites (1 Chron. 6:23–26). *4.* The father of Asa who is mentioned in a list of Levites (1 Chron. 9:16). *5.* A Benjaminite warrior who deserted

Saul and joined David (1 Chron. 12:6).
6. One of two gatekeepers for the ark of the covenant (1 Chron. 15:23).
7. An official in the service of King Ahaz of Judah who was assassinated by Zichri the Ephraimite (2 Chron. 28:7). See *Samuel.*

ELKOSH (Ĕl′ kŏsh) Place name of unknown meaning. The home of Nahum the prophet (Nah. 1:1). Although several traditions exist that identify various places as the site of Elkosh, its location remains unknown. That it was in Judea is fairly likely.

ELLASAR (Ĕl lā′ sär) Babylonian place name of unknown meaning. The capital city of King Arioch, who joined the eastern coalition against Sodom and Gomorrah, resulting in Abraham's involvement in war (Gen. 14:1). Identification with Larsa in Babylon was based on a false identification of Arioch. The Mari texts mention Ilanzura between Carchemish and Harran. Other scholars suggest Ellasar is an abbreviation for Til-Asurri on the Euphrates River. Others suggest it is located on the southern coast of the Black Sea near Pontus in Asia Minor. Thus the question of exact identification still remains open.

ELM See *Plants in the Bible; Terebinth.*

ELMADAM (Ĕl mā′ dám) Personal name of unknown meaning. An ancestor of Jesus Christ (Luke 3:28).

ELMODAM (Ĕl mō′ dăm) KJV spelling of Elmadam. See *Elmadam.*

ELNAAM (Ĕl nā′ ăm) Personal name meaning, "God is a delight." Father of military leaders under David (1 Chron. 11:46). He is not listed in 2 Samuel 23.

ELNATHAN (Ĕl nā′ thàn) Personal name meaning, "God has given." *1.* Father of King Jehoiachin's mother (2 Kings 24:8). *2.* Possibly to be identified with *1.* He was the member of King Jehoiakim's advisory staff who brought the prophet Uriah back to the king from Egypt for punishment (Jer. 26:22–23). He tried to prevent the king from burning Baruch's scroll of Jeremiah's preaching (Jer. 36:12–26). *2.* Three men of the same name plus a "Nathan" are listed in Ezra 8:16 as part of the delegation Ezra sent to search for Levites to return from Babylon to Jerusalem with him. Many Bible students feel that copying of the manuscripts has introduced extra names into the list.

ELOI (E lō′ ī) Greek transliteration of Aramaic *'elohi,* "my God." See *Eli Eli Lama Sabachthani.*

ELON (Ē′ lŏn) Personal and place name meaning, "great tree" or "tree of god." Compare Genesis 12:6; Judges 9:6,37. See *Terebinth*. *1*. A son of Zebulun and grandson of Jacob (Gen. 46:14). A clan in Zebulun was thus named for him (Num. 26:26). *2*. A judge from the tribe of Zebulun (Judg. 12:11–12). City in tribal territory of Naphtali (Josh. 19:33), often transliterated into English as Allon. See *Allon*. The reference may simply be to a large tree which served as a boundary marker. *4*. The site where Deborah, Rebekah's nurse, was buried, called, "Allon-bachuth" or "the oak of weeping" (Gen. 35:8). See *Allonbachuth*. The same point may be referred to as the "oak of Tabor" (1 Sam. 10:3) or the "palm tree of Deborah" (Judg. 4:5). See *Bochim*. *5*. A leader in the tribe of Simeon (1 Chron. 4:37).

A different Hebrew spelling underlies other examples of Elon in English translations. *1*. The Hittite father of Esau's wife Bashemath (Gen. 26:34). *2*. The Hittite father of Adah, Esau's wife (Gen. 36:2), Bashemath being listed as Ishmael's daughter (36:3). See *Basemath*. *3*. City in tribal territory of Dan (Josh. 19:43). It may be located at khirbet wadi Alin. It is probably the same place as Elon-beth-hanan (1 Kings 4:9), though some read Ajalon and Bethhanan or "Elon, and Beth-hanan" (REB).

ELON-BETH-HANAN (Ē′ lŏn-bĕth-hā′ năn) See *Elon*.

ELONITE (Ē′ lŏn īte) Citizen of Elon. See *Elon*.

ELOTH (Ē′ lŏth) Variant spelling of Elath. See *Elath*.

ELPAAL (Ĕl pā′ ăl) Personal name meaning, "God has made." A clan name in the tribe of Benjamin, mentioned twice in 1 Chronicles 8 (vv. 11-12,18). Bible students debate whether the references refer to the same clan ancestor or to two individuals. It is also uncertain whether he or his sons receive credit for building Ono and Lod (v. 12).

ELPALET (Ĕl pā′ lĕt) KJV spelling of Elpelet. See *Elpelet*.

ELPARAN (Ĕl pā′ rán) Place name meaning, "tree of Paran." The place where the eastern coalition of kings extended its victory over the Horites (Gen. 14:6). It is apparently a place in or near Elath. See *Elath; Paran*.

ELPELET (Ĕl pĕl′ ĕt) David's son born after he captured and moved to Jerusalem (1 Chron. 14:5). This is apparently an abbreviated spelling of Eliphelet. See *Eliphelet*.

EL-SHADDAI See *El; God*.

ELTEKE or **ELTEKEH** (Ĕl tĕ kĕ) Place name meaning, "place of meeting," "place of hearing," or "plea for rain." A city in Dan (Josh. 19:44) assigned to the Levites (Josh. 21:23). Egyptian pharaohs claim to have conquered an Altaku, which may be the same. Sennacherib of Assyria met an Egyptian army there about 701 B.C. It has been variously located at khirbet el-Muqenna′ on the eastern edge of the coastal plain, at tell esh-Shalaf, and at tell el-Melat, northwest of Gezer.

ELTEKON (Ĕl tĕ′ kŏn) Place name meaning, "securing advice." Village in tribal territory of Judah in southern hill country (Josh. 15:59). Its location is unknown, though some have suggested khirbet ed-Deir west of Bethlehem.

ELTOLAD (Ĕl tō′ lăd) Place name meaning, "plea for a child." Village in tribal territory of Judah (Josh 15:30), given to tribe of Simeon (Josh. 19:4). First Chronicles 4:29 apparently abbreviates it as Tolad. Its location is not known.

ELUL (Ē′ lūl) Sixth month of Hebrew year, name taken over from Accadian. It included parts of August and September. See Nehemiah 6:15.

ELUZAI (Ē lū′ zā ī) Personal name meaning, "God is my strength." A member of King Saul's tribe Benjamin, who became a military leader for David, while he lived as a fugitive in Ziklag (1 Chron. 12:5).

ELYMAS (Ĕl′ y̆ măs) Personal name possibly meaning, "wise." A magician and false prophet also known as Bar-jesus (Acts 13:6–11). At Paphos on the island of Cyprus, Elymas tried to dissuade the deputy Sergius Paulus from listening to the words of Barnabas and Paul. He was denounced by Paul and stricken temporarily blind. See *Sergius Paulus*.

ELYON See *El; God*.

ELZABAD (Ĕl zā′ băd) Personal name meaning, "God made a gift." *1*. Soldier who fought for David while he was a fugitive in Ziklag (1 Chron. 12:12). *2*. A Levite and grandson of Obed-Edom, identified as a valiant man (1 Chron. 26:7). He was a porter or gatekeeper in the Temple.

ELZAPHAN (Ĕl zā′ phăn) Personal name meaning, "God has hidden or treasured up." An abbreviated form of Elizaphan. A son of Uzziel, Aaron's uncle (Ex. 6:22). He helped carry the dead bodies of Nadab and Abihu out of the wilderness camp after God punished them (Lev. 10:4–5).

EMBALMING The process of preserving bodies from decay. Embalming originated in Egypt and was seldom used by the Hebrews. The practice is rarely mentioned in the Bible, and the human remains unearthed in Palestinian tombs generally show no signs of having been embalmed. In Genesis 50:2–3, it is recorded that Joseph ordered the embalming of Jacob's body and that "physicians" required forty days to perform the process. Verse 26 says Joseph was embalmed and laid to rest in Egypt. The embalming of these two patriarchs testifies both to their importance in the community and to plans to remove their bodies for burial in Canaan (Gen. 50:13; Ex. 13:19).

Related passages include 2 Chronicles 16:14 which describes the burial of Asa and the John 19:39–40 account of Jesus' burial. The use of spices mentioned in both of these passages did not constitute embalming but ceremonial purification.

The Egyptian art of mummification was an elaborate version of embalming which required seventy days for completion.   *Joe Haag*

EMEK-KEZIZ (Ē′ mĕk-kē′ zĭz) Place name meaning, "the cut off valley" or "the valley of gravel." It is listed as one of the cities assigned the tribe of Benjamin (Josh. 18:21). Its location is not known.

EMERALD See *Minerals and Metals.*

EMERODS An archaic form of the word hemorrhoids used by the KJV for the disease(s) in Deuteronomy 28:27 and 1 Samual 5—6. It is impossible to identify the disease with certainty. Whatever its precise nature, the disease was regarded as incurable and fatal. Modern speech translations are agreed that the malady is likely not hemorrhoids. The underlying Hebrew term is rendered tumors except for the passage in Deuternomy where NRSV and TEV opt for ulcers or sores. The presence of tumors associated with an infestation of mice has suggested bubonic plague to some interpreters. On the basis of the earliest Greek Old Testament reading, the NIV includes the margin reading "tumors of the groin."

EMIM (Ē′ mĭm) National name meaning, "frightening ones." They lost a war to the eastern coalition of kings (Gen. 14:6) and are identified with a place in northern Moab, Shaveh Kiriathaim. They were ancient giants or Rephaim (Deut. 2:10–11). See *Rephaim.*

EMITES (Ē′ mītes) NIV translation of Emim. See *Emim.*

EMMANUEL (Em măn′ ū ĕl) See *Immanuel.*

EMMAUS (Ĕm mā′ ŭs) Place name meaning, "hot baths." A village that was the destination of two of Jesus' disciples on the day of His resurrection (Luke 24:13). As they traveled, they were joined by a person whom they later realized was the risen Christ. Emmaus was about 60 furlongs (approximately seven miles) from Jerusalem. That statement is the only clue to its location. As many as four sites have been proposed as the location of Emmaus, but certainty is not possible. See *Resurrection.*

EMMOR (Ĕm′ môr) KJV spelling of Hamor in Acts 7:16. See *Hamor.*

EMPEROR WORSHIP The practice of assigning the status of deity to rulers and high ranking officials so honored by the ruler.

Old Testament Kings who conquered a nation would displace the local gods in favor of their own as a way of establishing authority. Frequently this included worshiping the king himself (or queen). The assumption was that only a god could rise to such a high position on earth. Entire religions were built around the worship of the ruler, including ceremonies, sacrifices, statues, and images.

In the Book of Esther, Haman was made part of the imperial cult by King Ahasuerus; all the people were required to bow to him and hail him (Esther 3:1–5). The most obvious example of emperor worship in the Old Testament is the well-known story of Shadrach, Meshach, and Abednego (Dan. 3). King Nebuchadnezzar made an image of gold, presumably of himself, and commanded everyone to fall down and worship the image or be killed (3:5–6). Shadrach, Meshach, and Abednego refused to commit idolatry by worshiping the image (3:16–18). They were thrown into a furnace, but were not burned (3:27). Thereafter, Nebuchadnezzar permitted them to worship their God unhindered (3:29).

New Testament Emperor worship was firmly in place in the Roman Empire in the early days of Christianity. During the reigns of Nero, Domitian, and other Roman emperors, persecution of Christians was severe because of gross misconceptions regarding the practice of the Christian faith. Christians were considered undesirable and were vigorously rooted out. Standing trial if they worshiped the pagan gods, that is, the emperor and the

Forum and Temple of Augustus in Rome—the major center of emperor worship.

imperial cult, they would be freed. If not, they would suffer all manner of punishments and death. All the suspected Christian had to do was sprinkle a few sacrificial grains of incense into the eternal flame burning in front of the statue of the emperor. Since the punishments were so horrible and the means of escape so easy, many Christians gave in. Many did not and were burned alive, killed by lions in the arena, or crucified.

A specific New Testament example of emperor worship is the worship of the beast in the Book of Revelation. Revelation 13 speaks of a beast that is given ruling authority. An image is made of the beast, and all are commanded to worship it (13:4,12, 14–15). *Donna R. Ridge*

ENAIM (Ě nā′ ĭm) Place name meaning, "two eyes or springs." A village near Timnah, where Tamar seduced Judah (Gen. 38:14). It is probably the same as Enam in the tribal territory of Judah (Josh. 15:34). The exact location is not known. See *Timnah.*

ENAM (Ē′ năm) See *Enaim.*

ENAN (Ē′ năn) Personal name meaning, "eyes or springs." Father of Ahira, the leader of the tribe of Naphtali under Moses (Num. 1:15). See *Ahira.*

ENCHANTER See *Magic; Sorcery; Divination.*

ENDOR (Ěn′ dôr) Place name meaning, "spring of Dor, that is, "spring of settlement." *1.* Home of witch who brought up Samuel from the grave (1 Sam. 28:7). Psalm 83:10 says Jabin died there. Compare Judges 4—5. It is modern khirbet Safsafe, three miles south of Mount Tabor. *2.* City tribe of Manasseh claimed but could not conquer (Josh. 17:11; compare Judg. 1:27).

ENEAS (Ě nē′ ȧs) Variant spelling of Aeneas. See *Aeneas.*

EN-EGLAIM (Ěn-ěg′ lā ĭm) Place name meaning, "spring of the two calves." A spring near the Dead Sea, where Ezekiel predicted a miracle, the salt waters being made fresh and becoming a paradise for fishing (Ezek. 47:10). It is apparently Ain Feshcha on the western coast of the Dead Sea.

ENEMY An adversary, foe, or hater. An enemy is one who dislikes or hates another and seeks to harm the person. It can refer to an individual opponent or to a hostile force, either a nation or an army.

The natural inclination of all people is to hate their enemies. Some have even misconstrued God's law to teach hatred. Jesus taught rather to love one's enemies and to seek their good (Matt. 5:43–47). This is also the teaching of the Old Testament (Prov. 24:17; 25:21).

In the Bible, a person who disobeys divine commands is declared to be God's enemy. Paul referred to sinners as the enemies of God (Rom. 5:10). Job felt that God had become his enemy, too (Job 13:24). Because of this severed relationship, God has made provision for our forgiveness in the life, death, and resurrection of Jesus Christ.

Satan is also called "the enemy" (1 Tim. 5:14–15). He has revealed himself as such throughout history by seeking to hurt men and women, leading them away from God.

The greatest and final enemy is death itself (1 Cor. 15:24). It is feared by all because of its finality and unknown nature. But the Bible teaches that Jesus has "abolished" death once for all (2 Tim. 1:10). Death need not be feared by those who have trusted Christ for the salvation He freely gives. *Bradley S. Butler*

EN-GANNIM (Ěn-găn′ nĭm) Place name meaning, "the spring of gardens." *1.* A town in the tribal territory of Judah located in the Shephalah (Josh. 15:34). It has been located at modern Beit Jemal, about two miles south of Beth-shemesh or at 'umm Giina one mile southwest of Beth-shemesh. *2.* Town in tribal territory of Issachar designated as city for Levites (Josh. 19:21; 21:29). Anem (1 Chron. 6:73) is apparently an alternate spelling. The same place may be meant in 2 Kings 9:27 by Beth Haggan (NIV, REB, NRSV) or the "garden house" (KJV, NAS). It is located at modern Jenin west of Beth-shean and about 65 miles north of Jerusalem.

ENGEDI (Ěn′ gĕ dī) Place name meaning, "place of the young goat." A major oasis along the western side of the Dead Sea about 35 miles southeast of Jerusalem. The springs of Engedi are full, and the vegetation is semitropical. Both biblical and extra-biblical sources describe Engedi as a source of fine dates, aromatic plants used in perfumes, and medicinal plants (Song of Sol. 1:14). It was a chief source of balsam, an important plant used for perfumes, and a major source of income for the area. Engedi apparently lay on a caravan route that led from the east shore of the Dead Sea around to its south, then up the west side to Engedi. From there the road went up to Tekoa and then to Jerusalem.

Engedi, also called Hazazon-tamar (2 Chron. 20:2), was inhabited by Amorites in the time of Abraham and was subjugated by Chedorlaomer (Gen. 14:7). In the tribal allotments, it was given to Judah and was in the district of Judah known as the wilderness district (Josh. 15:62). When David was fleeing from Saul, he hid in the area of Engedi (1 Sam. 23:29). Saul was in a cave near Engedi when David cut off a piece of his robe but spared

The only natural waterfall in Israel is located at Engedi on the west side of the Dead Sea.

E

his life (1 Sam. 24). During the reign of Jehoshaphat, Moabites, Ammonites, and others gathered at Engedi to attack Judah (2 Chron. 20:1–2).

Recent excavations at Engedi have uncovered a fortress belonging to the period of the monarchy, a workshop used in producing perfumes, and a sanctuary belonging to the Chalcolithic or Early Bronze Age. *Joel F. Drinkard, Jr.*

ENGINE A catapult or battering ram. See *Arms and Armor.*

ENGRAVE To impress deeply, to carve. Many materials were engraved including clay writing tablets (Isa. 8:1), metal, precious gems, stone (Zech. 3:9), and wood. Engraving was frequently done with an iron pen, a stylus, sometimes with a diamond point (Job 19:24; Jer. 17:1). Signet rings engraved with the sign or symbol of the owner were quite common throughout the ancient world (Gen. 38:18; Esther 3:12; Jer. 22:24). In fact, "like the engravings of a signet" ring or cylinder is a set phrase used to describe the various engraved gems of the high priest's vestments (Ex. 28:11, 21,36; 39:6,14). The Hebrew words translated engrave are used both for carving wood and working with precious stones in the construction of the tabernacle and Temple (Ex. 31:5; 35:33; 1 Kgs. 6:18,35; 2 Chron. 2:7). A graven image (Ex. 20:4) is a carved idol (as opposed to one cast in a mold).

EN-HADDAH (Ĕn-hăd′ dàh) City in tribal lot of Issachar (Josh. 19:21). It is apparently el-Hadetheh about six miles east of Mount Tabor.

EN-HAKKORE (Ĕn-hăk′ kōr rè) Place name meaning, "spring of the partridge" or "spring of the caller." Place where God gave Samson water from the jawbone he had used to kill a thousand Philistines (Judg. 15:18–19). It is near Lehi, or literally translated, "Jawbone," which is probably near Beth-shemesh.

EN-HAZOR (Ĕn-hā′ zôr) Place name meaning, "spring of the enclosed village." A fortified city in the tribal territory of Naphtali (Josh. 19:37). It may be located at khirbet Hazireh, west of Kadesh. Others would locate it southwest of Kedesh on the border joining Naphtali and Asher.

EN-MISHPAT (Ĕn-mĭsh′ pàt) Place name meaning, "spring of judgment." Another name for Kadesh, where the eastern coalition of kings defeated the Amalekites and Amorites. The location is usually called Kadesh-Barnea and identified with the oasis now called ain Hudeirat. See *Kadesh-Barnea.*

ENOCH (Ē′ nôch) Personal name meaning, "dedicated." *1.* The son of Jared taken up to God

without dying (Gen. 5:18). He became the father of Methuselah. Enoch lived in such close fellowship with God that he was translated into the presence of God without dying. Hebrews 11:5 attributes his translation to faith. According to Jude 14, he prophesied. The name of Enoch is associated with a large body of ancient extra-biblical literature. See *Genesis; Resurrection; Apocalyptic; Apocrypha; Pseudepigrapha.*

2. Son of Cain for whom Cain built a city and named it (Gen. 4:17–18).

ENON CITY (Ē′ nŏn Cĭ′ tỷ) TEV translation of Hazar-enan (Ezek. 47:17). See *Hazar-enan.*

ENOS (Ē′ nōs) or **ENOSH** (Ē′ nōsh) Personal name meaning, "humanity"or "a man." The son of Seth and therefore the grandson of Adam (Gen. 4:26). The period following his birth is identified as the time when people began to worship Yahweh. See Genesis 5:6–11.

EN-RIMMON (Ĕn-rĭm′ mŏn) Place name meaning, "spring of the pomegranate." A town in Judah (Neh. 11:29) where people lived in Nehemiah's day (about 445 B.C.). Ain and Rimmon or Remmon appear as separate cities in the tribal territory of Judah (Josh. 15:32), settled by the tribe of Simeon (Josh. 19:7). These two are often read as one city (19:7, RSV but not NRSV), but this makes the numbers of the cities in the lists inaccurate. It is located at khirbet er-Ramamin, about two miles south of Lahav.

EN-ROGEL (Ĕn-rō′ gĕl) Place name meaning, "spring of the fuller" or "spring of the foot." A border town between the tribal territory of Judah (Josh. 15:7) and that of Benjamin (Josh. 18:16). Jonathan and Ahimaaz, the priests' sons, stayed at En-rogel as messengers to relay to David what the priests might learn from Absalom when he took over Jerusalem from his father (2 Sam 17:17). Adonijah staged a party there to proclaim himself as David's successor as king of Judah (1 Kings 1:9). En-rogel lay near Jerusalem where the Kidron and Hinnom valleys met at modern Bir Ayyub.

ENROLLMENT Term used by the KJV of Luke 2:1–5 for the census or registration. See *Census.*

EN-SHEMESH (Ĕn-shē′ mĕsh) Place name meaning, "spring of the sun." Town on border between tribal territories of Judah (Josh. 15:7) and Benjamin (Josh. 18:17). It is located at ain el-Hod, "the spring of the apostles," about two miles east of Jerusalem on the eastern edge of Bethany.

EN-TAPPUAH (Ĕn-tăp pū′ ăh) Place name meaning, "spring of apple." A spring near the town of Tappuah which marked the border of the tribe of

Manasseh and Ephraim (Josh. 17:7). See *Tappuah.*

ENTRANCE ROOM See *Arch.*

ENVY A painful or resentful awareness of another's advantage joined with the desire to possess the same advantage. The advantage may concern material goods (Gen. 26:14) or social status (30:1). Old Testament wisdom frequently warns against envying the arrogant (Ps. 73:3), the violent (Pr. 3:31), or the wicked (Ps. 37:1; Pr. 24:1,19). In the New Testament envy is a common member of vice lists as that which comes out of the person and defiles (Mark 7:22), as a characteristic of humanity in rebellion to God (Rom. 1:29), as a fruit of the flesh (Gal. 5:21), as a characteristic of unregenerate life (Tit. 3:3) and as a trait of false teachers (1 Tim. 6:4). Envy (sometimes translated jealousy by modern translations) was the motive leading to the arrest of Jesus (Matt. 27:18; Mark 15:10) and to opposition to the gospel in Acts (Acts 5:17, 13:45; 17:5). Christians are called to avoid envy (Ga. 5:26; 1 Peter 2:1).

Envy is sometimes a motive for doing good. The Preacher was disillusioned that hard work and skill were the result of envying another (Eccl. 4:4). Paul was, however, able to rejoice that the gospel was preached even if the motive were envy (Phil. 1:15).

En-Rogel with the traditional site of Jacob's Well located under the dome in the center of the photo.

The KJV rightly understood the difficult text in Jas. 4:5, recognizing that it is a characteristic of the human spirit that it "lusteth to envy". Contrary to modern translations, the Greek word used for envy here (*phthonos*) is always used in a negative sense, never in the positive sense of God's jealousy (Greek *zealos*). God's response to the sinful longings of the human heart is to give more grace (4:6). See *Jealousy.*

EPAENETUS (E pāe̅' nĕ tŭs) Personal name meaning, "praise." The first Christian convert in Achaia and thus a friend with special meaning for Paul (Rom. 16:5). See *Achaia.*

EPAPHRAS (Ĕp' à phrăs) Personal name meaning, "lovely." A Christian preacher from whom Paul learned of the situation of the church in Colosse (Col. 1:7). He was a native of Colosse whose ministry especially involved Colosse, Laodicea, and Hierapolis. Later he was a companion of Paul during the latter's imprisonment. Though Epaphras is mentioned in the New Testament only in the letters to the Colossians and to Philemon, Paul evidently held this man in high regard.

EPAPHRODITUS (E păph' rō dī' tŭs) Personal name meaning, "favored by Aphrodite or Venus." A friend and fellow worker of Paul and the apostle (Phil. 2:25). He had delivered to Paul a gift from the church at Philippi while the apostle was in prison. While he was with Paul, Epaphroditus became seriously ill. After his recovery, Paul sent him back to Philippi, urging the church there to receive him "with all gladness" (Phil 2:29). The name Epaphroditus was common in the first century Greek-speaking world.

EPENETUS (E pē' nė tŭs) Variant spelling of Epaenetus. See *Epaenetus.*

EPHAH (Ē' pháh) Personal name meaning, "darkness." *1.* Son of Midian and grandson of Abraham (Gen. 25:4). The line came through Abraham's wife Keturah rather than Sarah and did not inherit as did Isaac. Ephah was thus the original ancestor of a clan of Midianites, and the clan name could be used in poetry in parallel with Midian to talk about the Midianites (Isa. 60:6). *2.* Concubine of Caleb and mother of his children (1 Chron. 2:46). *3.* Son of Jahdai and apparently a descendant of Caleb (1 Chron. 2:47).

An entirely different Hebrew word with a different first letter lies behind the English "ephah" as a dry measure of grain. It is one-tenth of a homer and equal to one bath of liquid (Ezek. 45:11). It is also equal to 10 omers (Ex. 16:36). Thus it is about 40 liters, though we do not have enough information to make precise estimates. Estimates place it about half a bushel. The vision of Zechariah 5:7 of a woman sitting in an ephah basket contains the imaginative images of visions, for any ephah would be far too small for a woman to sit in. Israel was constantly warned not to have two ephah measures, one to buy by and one to sell with (Deut. 25:14; Prov. 20:10). Compare Leviticus 19:36; Ezekiel 45:10; Amos 8:5.

EPHAI (Ē′ phăī) Personal name meaning, "bird." Father of men who joined Ishmael in revolt against and murder of Gedaliah, the governor of Judah after Babylon captured and destroyed Jerusalem in 586 B.C. (Jer. 40:8). Ephai was from Netophah near Bethlehem.

EPHER (Ē′ phēr) Personal name meaning, "young deer." *1.* Son of Midian, grandson of Abraham through his wife Keturah, and clan father among the Midianites (Gen. 25:4). *2.* A descendant of Caleb in the tribe of Judah (1 Chron. 4:17). *3.* Original ancestor of clan in tribe of Manasseh (1 Chron. 5:24).

EPHES-DAMMIN (Ē′ phĕs-dăm′ mĭn) Place name meaning, "end of bloodshed." Town between Shocoh and Azekah where Philistines gathered to fight Saul (1 Sam. 17:1) preceding David's killing of Goliath. It is apparently the same as Pasdammim (1 Chron. 11:13). It is modern Damun, four miles northeast of Shocoh.

The entrance to the Basilica of St. John at the ancient port of Ephesus in western Asia Minor.

EPHESIANS, BOOK OF (E′ phē′ sians) While it is not the longest of the Pauline Epistles, Ephesians is the one which best sets out the basic concepts of the Christian faith.

Paul and the Ephesians Precise information on the introduction of Christianity to Ephesus is not available. From Acts 13:1—14:28 we know Christianity was introduced to the Asian peninsula early. Paul and Barnabas, during the first missionary journey about A.D. 45–48, established Christianity in Cilicia, Pamphylia, and Phrygia. The newly-established religion moved inevitably westward to the coast and to the flourishing city of Ephesus, a city of multiple religions, gods, and goddesses.

At the close of his second missionary journey about A.D. 49–52, Paul left Achaia (Greece) taking Aquila and Priscilla with him. They stopped at Ephesus and surveyed the situation in that city where religions flourished. The Ephesians urged Paul to stay there, but he declined. Leaving Aquila and Priscilla and perhaps Timothy there to carry on the Christian witness (Acts 18:18–21), Paul sailed to Antioch. He returned to Ephesus during a third missionary journey and experienced the triumph over the challenge of Jewish religious leaders as well as that of the Greco-Roman religions represented in the worship of the Greek goddess Artemis (Roman name—Diana; Acts 19:24).

His ministry in Ephesus lasted three years (Acts 20:31). From there he journeyed to Jerusalem where he was arrested by the Jews and turned over to the Romans. He was imprisoned in Caesarea for two years (Acts 21:15—26:32). He was sent to Rome where he was imprisoned for another two years (Acts 27:1—28:31).

Interpreters are divided in opinion as to the time and place of the writing of Ephesians. These two imprisonments of Paul are the only ones which might bear on the question of where and when the Imprisonment Epistles were written. In all four of these epistles, Paul mentioned his imprisonment.

A related and much debated question is the year of Paul's writing each epistle and the place. To our knowledge only two places appear to be viable options—Caesarea and Rome. Majority opinion through Christian history has favored Rome. A much smaller minority of interpreters have argued for Caesarea. The case for Caesarea has been posited on speculative questions such as: (1) Would it be easier for Paul to get letters to the three places involved (Ephesus, Colosse, and Philippi) from Caesarea or from Rome? (2) Would it be easier for the runaway slave, Onesimus, to meet Paul in a prison in faraway Rome or the much closer Caesarea?

A third opinion has grown out of Colossians 4:16 in which Paul urged the church at Colosse to exchange letters with the church at neighboring

Laodicea so both might get the benefit of both letters. This opinion, which was never widely held, took the position that Paul was writing from an imprisonment in Ephesus and that the "Laodicean" letter was what we have as "Ephesians."

Careful review of this very extensive and complex issue leaves the subjective opinion that all four Prison Epistles were written by Paul during his imprisonment in Rome about A.D. 61–62. Also subjective is the opinion that they were written in this order: Ephesians A.D. 61; Colossians A.D. 61; Philemon A.D. 61; Philippians A.D. 62. **Introduction to the Epistle** Paul's experiences in Ephesus combined with the work of his associates qualified him for writing to that church the Queen of the Epistles. Granting the inspiration of the Holy Spirit as the compelling reason for his writing this epistle as well as the related epistle to the Colossians, from the life-situation in the Mediterranean world of the first century A.D., what was the apostle's motive for writing? His motive was the challenge which Christianity faced in confrontation with other religions and philosophies of the day. Paul was convinced that the religion he proclaimed was the *only* way of redemption from sin and sonship to God.

The challenge was the struggle for human minds as they sought the "good life." Even in Judaism, the cradle in which it was born, Christianity faced that aggressive encounter.

Paul opposed a Judaism he considered to have become a religion of human attainment, doing the works of the law as a means of being right with God. He offered instead Christianity as a religion of divine provision, salvation by faith in God's providing what humans could never attain.

That distinction was also what brought Christianity into conflict with Greek philosophy and with the Greco-Roman nature religions. The Christian view is that the "good life" comes by faith, not by intellectual processes, speculations, and rules of conduct in the integration of personality. **Analysis of the Epistle: Theology and Ethics** Following the pattern of all of his epistles, Paul introduced himself as an apostle of Christ Jesus by the will of God—not by human will, not even by his own will, but God's will. That was the driving force in his life.

The expression "at Ephesus" is not in the oldest manuscripts of Ephesians, but it is in many of the best ones. Its absence has led to speculation that in writing the epistle Paul left a blank space, that he meant the epistle to be a circular one to go to several churches. As the epistle was read in the churches, the public reader would insert the name of that church; such as, at Laodicea, at· Hierapolis, at Colosse, etc. Indeed one manuscript of about the middle of the second century had "at Laodicea" in that place.

"Grace be to you, and peace, from God our Father, and from the Lord Jesus Christ" (Eph.1:2)

is in all of Paul's epistles. It is always in that order, grace and peace. Grace is the work of the Father by which salvation from sin comes. Peace is the condition of the believer's heart after grace has done its work. They are in that order because there can be no peace in the heart until grace has done its work.

Following a frequently used pattern in Paul's epistles, two basic themes are developed. First there is a major section on some theological theme. Second there follows a major section in ethics growing out of the theological theme. In the New Testament, theology and ethics are bound together; they are never to be separated.

In his theological part (1:13—3:21) Paul centered attention on the plan and propagation of redemption. He began with a literary pattern of a poem or song to praise God for what He has done in providing salvation for sinful humanity. The provision of redemption is presented as the work of the Trinity: Father, Son, and Holy Spirit. A refrain "to the praise of the glory of His grace" repeats itself after each section, each with a slight variation.

Paul turned to thanksgiving to show the blessings of redemption (1:15—2:10). He wanted his readers to know Christ better, the Christ who enables believers to have the incomparable power that resurrected Christ and that now rules in this age and the one to come. This power can come to persons who were dead in sin but are saved by grace, being raised up with Christ to participate in His rule but also to live out of grace in the good works God has planned for His people to do.

Paul turned to the language of imperative to explain the propagation of redemption (2:11—3:21). A people without hope, separated from the people of the covenant have been brought to salvation through the blood of Christ. Thus unity of all races is accomplished through Him. In the cross He brought peace and provided access to God through the one Holy Spirit. All are joined together in Christ's church built on the foundation of the apostles and serving as the residence of God the Spirit. This good news is a mystery, a mystery God calls people to share with other people through His grace and a mystery which allows all people to approach God in confidence and freedom.

Paul turned to prayer to conclude this section and reveal the goal of redemption (3:14–21). His prayer was that Christ may dwell in the believers who will be rooted in love and can grasp the marvelous greatness of that love.

In his ethical part (4:1—6:24) Paul looked at the application of redemption to the church, to personal life, and to domestic life. Ethical imperatives dominate the section. He sought unity in the Spirit—one body, one Spirit, one hope, one Lord, one faith, one baptism, one God and Father. Within the unity he celebrated the diversity of the individuals within the church, a diversity stemming from the differing gifts Christ gives. The use of the gifts within the church leads to maturity for the church and its members. Maturity involves growing in Christ, in His love, each doing the work Christ gives and not seeking to do the work assigned another.

This has consequences for personal life, calling for a complete transformation from the life-styles of unbelievers. Without faith the individual is devoted to selfish lust and earthly dissipation. The believer becomes like God in holiness, purity, and righteousness. A central element of this is human speech, speaking the truth and saying that which helps build up others. Anger and malice must turn to love, compassion, and forgiveness. Walking in the light means pleasing God and showing the sinfulness of evil deeds. This is the wise path avoiding spirits that make one drunk but turning to the one Spirit which leads to praise and worship. This changes one's role at home. Submission to one another becomes the key, a submission motivated by loyalty to Christ and love to the marital partner. That love follows the example of Christ's love for His church. Parents expect honor from children while training children in the Lord's way of love. Similarly, masters and servants respect and help one another.

To complete his letter, Paul called his readers to put on God's armor to avoid Satan's temptations. This will lead to a life of prayer for self and for other servants of God. This will lead to concern for and encouragement from other Christians. As usual, Paul concluded his letter with a benediction, praying for peace, love, faith, and grace for his beloved readers.

Outline

I. Salutation: The apostle greets the church (1:1–2).

II. Theology: The plan of redemption leads to the propagation of redemption (1:3—3:21)
   A. The plan of redemption (1:3—1:14)
      1. The work of the Father: He has blessed and chosen us in Christ, predestining us for sonship in Him (1:3–6).
      2. The work of the Son: He brings redemption and forgiveness from sin through His blood (1:7–12).
      3. The work of the Spirit: He seals us as God's cherished possession (1:13–14).
   B. The blessings of redemption (1:15–2:10)
      1. A clear insight into the nature of redemption (1:15–19)
      2. A full insight into the nature of Christ (1:20–23)
      3. A transition from spiritual death to spiritual life (2:1–9)
      4. A life of good works wrought out in Christ (2:10)

   C. The propagation of redemption (2:11—3:21)
      1. Redemption is for all without regard to race (2:11–13).
      2. Redemption makes all people one in Christ (2:14–22).
      3. Redemption is to be revealed to people through other people (3:1–13).
      4. Redemption has a goal: revelation of the nature of God's love through Christ (3:14–21).

III. Ethics: Redemption is applied in church life, personal life, and domestic life (4:1—6:24).
   A. The application of redemption in church life (4:1–16)
      1. The Holy Spirit produces unity (4:1–6).
      2. Christ provides a diversity of gifts (4:7–11).
      3. The Spirit's unity and Christ's gifts result in maturity (4:12–16).
   B. The application of redemption in personal life (4:17—5:21)
      1. Desires and practices of old life are ended (4:17–32).
      2. In the new way of life the redeemed learn to walk in love (5:1–5).
      3. In the new way of life the redeemed learn to walk in light (5:6–14).
      4. In the new way of life the redeemed learn to walk in wisdom (5:15–21).
   C. The application of redemption in domestic life (5:22—6:9)
      1. Mutual duties of husbands and wives to each other (5:22–33)
      2. Mutual duties of parents and children to each other (6:1–4)
      3. Mutual duties of masters and servants to each other (6:5–9)

IV. Conclusion: Prepare for the spiritual conflict of life (6:10–24).
   A. Know God is your Ally and Satan your enemy (6:10–12).
   B. Put on the armor God supplies (6:13–17).
   C. Pray for boldness for Christian leaders (6:18–20).
   D. Communicate with and encourage one another (6:21–22).
   E. Live under God's benediction of peace, love, faith, and grace (6:23–24).

Ray Summers

EPHESUS (Ĕph' ē sŭs) One of the largest and most impressive cities in the ancient world, a political, religious, and commercial center in Asia Minor. Associated with the ministries of Paul, Timothy, and the apostle John, the city played a significant role in the spread of early Christianity. Ephesus and its inhabitants are mentioned more than twenty times in the New Testament.

Location The ancient city of Ephesus, located in western Asia Minor at the mouth of the Cayster River, was an important seaport. Situated between the Maeander River to the south and the Hermus River to the north, Ephesus had excellent access to both river valleys which allowed it to flourish as a commercial center. Due to the accumulation of silt deposited by the river, the present site of the city is approximately five to six miles inland.

Historical Background The earliest inhabitants of Ephesus were a group of peoples called Leleges and Carians who were driven out around 1000 B.C. by Ionian Greek settlers led by Androclus of Athens. The new inhabitants of Ephesus assimilated the native religion of the area, the worship of a goddess of fertility whom they identified with the Greek goddess Artemis, the virgin huntress. (Later the Romans identified Artemis with their goddess Diana.)

Around 560 B.C. Croesus of Lydia conquered Ephesus and most of western Asia Minor. Under Croesus' rule, the city was moved farther south and a magnificent temple, the Artemision, was constructed for the worship of Artemis. In 547 B.C., following the defeat of Croesus by Cyrus of Persia, Ephesus came under Persian control. Disaster struck the city in 356 when fire destroyed the Artemision.

Alexander the Great, who was reportedly born

A part of the Roman Harbor Baths and Gymnasium complex excavated at ancient Ephesus.

The Great Theater of Ephesus with the Arcadian Way in the background leading to the ancient harbor.

on the same day as the Artemision fire, took over the area in 334 B.C. His offer to finance the ongoing reconstruction of the temple was diplomatically declined. The rebuilt temple, completed about 250 B.C., became known as one of the Seven Wonders of the World.

Lysimachus, one of Alexander's generals, ruled over Ephesus from about 301 to 281 B.C., when he was killed by Seleucus I. Under Lysimachus the city was moved again, this time to higher ground

A baptismal pool from the Roman period located in the Double Church of Mary at ancient Ephesus.

to escape the danger of flooding. City walls were built; a new harbor was constructed; and new streets were laid out. After the death of Lysimachus, Ephesus fell under the control of the Seleucids until their defeat by the Romans in 189 B.C. Rome gave the city to the king of Pergamum as a reward for his military assistance. In 133 B.C., at the death of the last Pergamum ruler, the city came under direct Roman control.

Under the Romans, Ephesus thrived, reaching the pinnacle of its greatness during the first and second centuries of the Christian era. At the time of Paul, Ephesus was probably the fourth largest city in the world, with a population estimated at 250,000. During the reign of the emperor Ha-

The Great Theater of ancient Ephesus as viewed from the Arcadian Way on the way to the harbor.

E

Curetes Street in ancient Ephesus with the Library of Celsus in the background.

drian, Ephesus was designated the capital of the Roman province of Asia. The grandeur of the ancient city is evident in the remains uncovered by archaeologists, including the ruins of the Artemision, the civic agora, the temple of Domitian, gymnasiums, public baths, a theater with seating for 24,000, a library, and the commercial agora, as well as several streets and private residences. Also discovered were the head and forearm of a colossal statue of the emperor Domitian. Today the Turkish town of Seljuk occupies the site of ancient Ephesus.

See *Asia Minor; Ephesians; Revelation, Book of; Timothy.*   Mitchell G. Reddish

A carved paving stone in ancient Ephesus which is probably an advertisement for a brothel.

EPHLAL (Ĕph′ lăl) Personal name meaning, "notched" or "cracked." Descendant of Jerahmeel in tribe of Judah (1 Chron. 2:37).

EPHOD (Ē′ phŏd) A priestly garment connected with seeking a word from God and used in a wrong way as an idol. The exact meaning and derivation of the term "ephod" are not clear.

In early Old Testament history, there are references to the ephod as a rather simple, linen garment, possibly a short skirt, apron, or loin cloth. It is identified as a priestly garment (1 Sam. 14:3; 22:18). It was worn by Samuel (1 Sam. 2:18) and by David when he danced before God on the occasion of the transfer of the ark of the covenant to David's capital city of Jerusalem (2 Sam. 6:14). From its earliest forms and uses, it appears that the ephod was associated with the presence of God or those who had a special relationship with

The re-erected marble facade of the Library of Celsus at ancient Ephesus.

God. It is portrayed as a source of divine guidance, as when David wanted to know if he should trust the people of Keilah (1 Sam. 23:9–12) or when he wanted to know if he should pursue the Amalekites (1 Sam. 30:7–8).

There are references to a special ephod associated with the high priest. It appears to have been an apron-like garment worn over the priest's robe and under his breastplate. It is described in detail in Exodus 28—35. Woven of gold, blue, purple, and scarlet materials, it was very elaborate and ornate. On top of each of the shoulders the ephod was fastened by two onyx clasps on which were engraved the names of six of the twelve tribes. Twelve gem stones on the breastplate contained the names of the twelve tribes. Some scholars believe that this breastplate also contained a pouch where the sacred lots, Urim and Thummim, were kept (Ex. 28:30). The ephod was fastened around the waist by a beautiful and intricately woven girdle. The robe worn with the ephod was equally elaborate. It was blue in color, with a fringe at the bottom comprised of golden bells and blue, purple, and scarlet pomegranates (Ex. 28:31–34). Apparently, the ephod of the

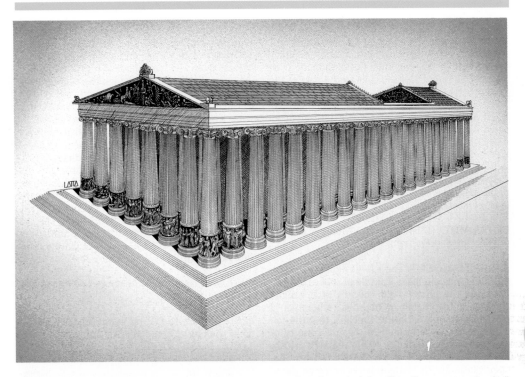

Reconstruction of the Artemesion, the great Temple of Artemis (Roman Diana) at Ephesus in ancient Asia Minor (modern Turkey) which was begun in 360 B.C. to honor the ancient many-breasted mother goddess of the Anatolian region. The cult was adopted by the conquering Alexander the Great of Greece and renamed Artemis (Roman Diana). The temple was completed by the Greeks and was recorded as one of the seven wonders of the ancient world—four times larger than the Parthenon at Athens.

high priest was not only worn by the high priest, but also prominently displayed in the tabernacle. It may have been placed upon a divine image and used as an object of worship at some times in Israel's history. This usage, plus the importance of the ephod, may have led to idolatrous use in worship during the time of the judges (Judg. 8:27; 17:5–6).

The importance of the ephod in Hebrew worship is seen in the fact that, even after the division of the nation into the Northern and Southern Kingdoms, there is mention of the ephod in worship in the Northern Kingdom (Hos. 3:4).

See *Priests; Tabernacle; Ark of the Covenant; Teraphim.* *Daniel B. McGee*

EPHPHATHA (Ĕph′ phȧ thȧ) The Aramaic expression that Jesus spoke when He healed a person who was deaf and had a speech impediment. It is translated, "be opened." When Jesus had said it, the individual was healed.

EPHRAIM (Ē phrȧ ĭm) Personal and tribal name meaning, "two fruit land" or "two pasture lands." The younger son of Joseph by the Egyptian Asenath, daughter of the priest of On (Gen. 41:52). He was adopted by his grandfather Jacob and given precedence over his brother Manasseh (Gen. 48:14). He was the progenitor of the tribe of Ephraim, which occupied a region slightly to the northwest of the Dead Sea (Josh. 16) and was the leading tribe of the Northern Kingdom, ever ready to assert its rights (Josh. 17:15; Judg. 3:27; 4:5; 7:24—8:3; 12:1).

Ephraim played an important role in Israelite history. Joshua was an Ephraimite (Josh. 19:50). Samuel was an Ephraimite (1 Sam. 1:1). Jeroboam I was an Ephraimite (1 Kings 12:25). The important sanctuary at Shiloh was located in the territory of Ephraim. From the eighth century B.C., Ephraim was often used as a designation for Israel (Isa. 11:13; Jer. 7:15; Hos. 5:13). See *Tribes of Israel; Patriarchs.*

EPHRAIM, CITY OF Another name for Ephron. See *Ephron.*

EPHRAIM, FOREST OF The densely wooded site of the battle between the forces of King David and the rebel army of Absalom (2 Sam. 18:6,8). The location of the forest presents difficulties. The account in 2 Samuel suggests a site on the east side of the Jordan near enough to the city of Mahanaim in the Jabbok valley to allow David to send reinforcements. The difficulty arises since the tribal allotment for Ephraim was west of the

E

Jordan. Joshua 17:14–18 predicts Ephraim's expansion north into the wooded Jezreel valley and the vicinity of Beth Shan, both within Issachar's territory. It is possible that this dominant tribe also settled in the wooded hills to the east of the Jordan.

EPHRAIM GATE An entrance to Jerusalem located 400 cubits (about 200 yards) from the Corner Gate (2 Kings 14:13). The section of wall between these two gates was destroyed by King Jehoash of Israel in eighth century. In Nehemiah's time the city square at the Ephraim Gate was one of the sites where booths for the celebration of the feast of tabernacles were set up (Neh. 8:16).

EPHRAIMITE (Ē′ phră ĭm īte) Member of tribe of Ephraim. See *Ephraim.*

EPHRAIM, MOUNT The KJV designation for the hill country belonging to Ephraim. Modern translations use the phrase "hill country of Ephraim" since an entire region is intended rather than a particular mount. Scripture specifies that the following cities were located in the hill country of Ephraim: Bethel (Judg. 4:5); Gibeah (Josh. 24:33); Ramah (Judg. 4:5); Shamir (10:1); Shechem (Josh. 20:7); Timnath-heres or -serah (Josh. 19:50; Judg. 2:9).

EPHRAIN (Ē′ phră în) KJV reading of city in 2 Chronicles 13:19 following the earliest Hebrew scribal note. Hebrew text reads, "Ephron," as do most modern translations. See *Ephron.*

EPHRATAH (Ĕph′ rà tăh) Place and personal name meaning, "fruitful." Modern translations spell Ephrathah. *1.* Town near which Jacob buried his wife Rachel (Gen. 35:16–19; usually translated in English as Ephrath). Genesis 36:16 seems to indicate that Ephrath(ah) must have been near Bethel. This is supported by 1 Samuel 10:2; Jeremiah 31:15 which place Rachel's tomb near Ramah on the border between the tribal territories of Ephraim and Benjamin. Genesis 35:19, however, identifies Ephrath(ah) with Bethlehem. Compare Genesis 48:7. It is part of Judah's tribal territory according to the earliest Greek translation of the Old Testament, words omitted in current Hebrew manuscripts (Josh. 15:59 REB). Micah 5:2 also appears to equate Bethlehem and Ephrath(ah) as the home of the coming Messiah. This, in turn, was based on Bethlehem (1 Sam. 16:1) and Ephrath(ah) (1 Sam. 17:12) as the home of David's father Jesse and thus of David. In sending Messiah, God chose to start over at David's birthplace. Naomi's husband Elimelech was an Ephrathite from Bethlehem (Ruth 1:2). In Ruth 4:11 Bethlehem and Ephrathah are apparently identified in poetic parallelism. It may be that Ephrathah was a clan name of a family in Bethle-

hem whose importance made the clan name a synonym for the city. The parallelism in Psalm 132:6 seems to equate Ephrathah with "the field of Jaar" (NAS and most modern translations). This would be Kiriath-jearim, though two different resting points of the ark—Bethlehem and Kiriath-jearim—may be intended here. The identification with Kiriath-jearim could be supported by the genealogy in 1 Chronicles 2 which lists both personal and place names. Shobal, the founder of Kiriath-jearim, was the son of Ephrathah, Caleb's wife (1 Chron. 2:19,50). In 1 Chronicles 4:4 Ephrathah's son Hur was the father of Bethlehem. Ephrathah may have been a clan name associated with several different geographical localities, the most famous of which was Bethlehem. The textual and geographical connections are not always easy to figure out. *2.* Caleb's wife (1 Chron. 2:50; spelled Ephrath in 2:19; compare 4:4).

EPHRATH (Ē′ phrăth) Alternate spelling of Ephratah. See *Ephratah.*

EPHRATHAH (Ĕph′ rà thăh) Modern translations' spelling of Ephratah. See *Ephratah.*

The entrance to the Church of the Nativity in Bethlehem, or Ephratah.

EPHRATHITE (Ĕph′ rà thīte) Citizen or clan member of Ephratah. See *Ephratah.*

EPHRON (Ē′ phrŏn) Personal and place name meaning, "dusty." *1.* A Hittite who sold the cave of Machpelah to Abraham (Gen. 23:8–20). The narrative follows the normal manner of concluding a purchase agreement among Near Eastern people. Abraham was also buried in the cave with Sarah (Gen. 25:9–10). It became the patriarchs' burying place (Gen. 49:30–33; 50:13). *2.* A mountain marking the tribal border of Judah with Benjamin (Josh. 15:9). It is located northwest of Jerusalem near Mozah at el-Qastel. *3.* A city King Abijah of Judah (913-910 B.C.) took from King Jeroboam of Israel (926-909 B.C.), according to spelling of Hebrew text (2 Chron. 13:19). The earliest Hebrew scribes suggested that Ephrain was the correct spelling (KJV). It is apparently identical with Ophrah in Benjamin (Josh. 18:23; 1 Sam. 13:17), located at et-Taiyibeh about four miles north of Bethel. The city of Ephraim (2 Sam. 13:23; John 11:54) is probably the same city. If et-Taiyibeh is the correct location, it is a high city, 300 feet higher than Jerusalem and could be quite cold. Some would locate the city of Ephraim in the lower valley at ain Samieh, on the edge of the desert.

EPICUREANISM (Ĕp ĭ cū rē′ ăn ĭsm) A school of philosophy which emerged in Athens about 300 B.C.

The school of thought was founded by Epicurus who was born in 341 B.C. on the Greek island of Samos. Epicurus founded his school (The Garden) in Athens. Around him he gathered his students and refined his philosophy. Epicurean thought had a significant impact on the Hellenistic world and later, Rome. Paul met Epicureans as he preached about Jesus and the resurrection in Athens (Acts 17:18).

Epicurean philosophy centered on the search for happiness. Pleasure is the beginning and fulfillment of a happy life. Often today, Epicurus' ideas are distorted. Many think he proposed a life of sensual pleasure and gluttony. This concept is far from his philosophy and his own life-style. To Epicurus happiness could only be achieved through tranquillity and a life of contemplation. The goal of Epicureanism was to acquire a trouble-free state of mind, to avoid the pains of the body, and especially mental anguish. Epicureans sought seclusion from worldly temptations. Epicurus taught that a man should not become involved in politics or affairs of the state. These activities simply served to distract one from the life of contemplation.

He believed in gods, but he thought that they were totally unconcerned with the lives or troubles of mortals. *Gary Poulton*

EPILEPSY A disorder marked by erratic electrical discharges of the central nervous system resulting in convulsions. In ancient times epilepsy was thought to be triggered by the moon. The term at Matt. 4:24 translated as epilepsy by most modern translations is literally "moonstruck". The KJV term "lunatic" from the Latin *luna* (moon) assumes the same cause for the disorder. Many interpreters understand the symptoms of the boy in Mark 9:17–29 (inability to speak, salivation, grinding teeth, rigid body, convulsions) as expressions of epilepsy.

EPIPHANY The term "epiphany" comes from a Greek word which means "appearance" or "manifestation." In Western Christianity the festival of Epiphany, observed on the sixth of January, celebrates the manifestation of Christ to the Gentiles, the coming of the Magi to see the child Jesus

(Matt. 2:1–12). The twelve days between Christmas and Epiphany have often been called the "Twelve Days of Christmas."

In much of Eastern Christianity, Epiphany is a celebration of the baptism of Jesus, a recognition of His manifestation to humanity as the Son of God (Mark 1:9–11). In the early centuries, before the observance of Christmas, Epiphany celebrated both the birth of Jesus and His baptism. See *Church Year.* *Fred A. Grissom*

EPISTLE See *Letters.*

ER (Er) Personal name meaning, "protector" or "watchful." *1.* Oldest son of Judah and grandson of Jacob (Gen. 38:3). He married Tamar but was so wicked that God killed him (Gen. 38:6–7). *2.* A grandson of Judah (1 Chron. 4:21).

ERAN (Ē′ răn) Personal name meaning, "of the city," or "watchful." Some of the earliest translations and the Samaritan Pentateuch read "Eden" rather than Eran. Eran was grandson of Ephraim and a clan leader in the tribe of Ephraim (Num. 26:36).

ERANITE (Ē′ răn īte) Member of clan of Eran (Num. 26:36).

ERASTUS (Ē răs′ tŭs) Personal name meaning, "beloved." *1.* Disciple Paul sent with Timothy from Ephesus to Macedonia to strengthen the churches during his third missionary journey (Acts 19:22). *2.* City financial officer of Corinth who joined Paul in greeting the church at Rome (Rom. 16:23). He may have been a slave or a freed slave working for the city government; he may well have been a high-ranking and influential government leader—city treasurer. If so, he would have political power, prestige, and probably some wealth. *3.* A disciple who remained at Corinth and was not with Paul when he wrote Timothy (2 Tim. 4:20). He may have been identical with either of the other men named Erastus or may be a separate individual.

ERECH (Ē′ rĕch) Hebrew transliteration of Akkadian place name: Uruk, one of the oldest Sumerian cities founded before 3100 B.C. Genesis' Table of Nations reports that Nimrod, the mighty hunter, included Erech in his kingdom (Gen. 10:10). Ashurbanipal, king of Assyria (668-629 B.C.), exiled "men of Erech" (NAS) to Samaria about 640 B.C. (Ezra 4:9). Sumerian literature lists Erech as one of the first cities after the flood. Gilgamesh, the hero of Akkadian flood stories, appears as king of Erech. Excavations at Erech provide early evidence of pictographic writing and numerical notation on clay tablets and reveal an astronomical observatory and a scribal school. It is modern Warka, about 120 miles southeast of Babylon and 40 miles northwest of Ur.

E

ERI (Ē' rī) Personal name meaning, "of the city of" or "watchful." A son of Gad and grandson of Jacob (Gen. 46:16). Original ancestor of clan of Erites (Num. 26:16).

ERITE (Ē' rīte) Member of clan of Eri. See *Eri.*

ESAIAS (Ė sâi' ás) KJV transliteration of Greek spelling of Isaiah in New Testament. See *Isaiah.*

ESARHADDON (Ē' sär hăd' dŏn) Assyrian royal name meaning, "Ashur (the god) has given a brother." King of Assyria (681–669 B.C.). He was the favorite son of Sennacherib, who he succeeded as king.

There are many references to Esarhaddon in the Bible (2 Kings 19:36–37; Ezra 4:2; Isa. 19:4; 37:37–38). In Isaiah 19:4 he is probably the "cruel lord" and "fierce king" who conquered Egypt. In Ezra 4:2 he is recognized as the king who colonized Samaria. See *Assyria.*

M. Stephen Davis

ESAU (Ē' sāū) Personal name whose meaning is not known. Son of Isaac and Rebekah; elder twin brother of Jacob (Gen. 25:24–26; 27:1,32,42; 1 Chron. 1:34); father of the Edomite nation (Gen. 26; Deut. 2:4–29; Mal. 1:2–3). At birth his body was hairy and red "and they called his name Esau" (Gen. 25:25,30; 27:11,21–23). The second born twin, Jacob, father of the nation Israel, held Esau's heel at birth (Gen. 25:22–26); thus depicting the struggle between the descendants of the two which ended when David lead Israel in the conquest of Edom (2 Sam. 8:12–14; 1 Chron. 18:13; compare Num. 24:18).

From the first Jacob sought to gain advantage over Esau (Hos. 12:3). Esau, the extrovert, was a favorite of his father and as a hunter provided him with his favorite meats. Jacob was the favorite of his mother Rebekah.

As a famished returning hunter, Esau, lacking self-control, sold his birthright to Jacob for food (Gen. 25:30–34). Birthright involved the right as head of the family (Gen. 27:29) and a double

A well which marks the traditional site where Jacob met Esau.

share of the inheritance (Deut. 21:15–17). This stripped Esau of the headship of the people through which Messiah would come. Thus, the lineage became Abraham, Isaac, and Jacob.

Having lost his birthright, he was still eligible to receive from Isaac the blessing of the eldest son. Rebekah devised a deception whereby Jacob received this blessing (Gen. 27:1–30).

Years later the two brothers were reconciled when Jacob returned from Mesopotamia. Esau had lived in the land of Seir. As Jacob neared Palestine, he made plans for confronting his wronged brother and allaying his anger. Esau, with an army of 400, surprised Jacob, his guilty brother, and received him without bitterness (Gen. 33:4–16).

The two reconciled brothers met again for the final time at the death of their father (Gen. 35:29). Though their hostility was personally resolved, their descendants continue to this day to struggle against one another. *Nelson Price*

ESCHATOLOGY The teaching concerning the last things in world history. The Greek word *eschatos* means "last" or "final." Accordingly, eschatology is the study of the things expected to occur at the end of history. There are two basic ways of approaching eschatology. The first, which has been most common over the centuries, focuses on those final events or situations which have not yet occurred. These are, chiefly, Jesus' return, the millennium, the last judgment, the final resurrection, and heaven and hell. Over the last century, however, scholars have generally agreed that the New Testament was written in an atmosphere pervaded by eschatology. Early Christianity was rooted in the paradoxical conviction that the last things had "already" occurred, even though they were "not yet" fully completed. (Jesus' resurrection, for instance, was understood as the beginning of the final resurrection of the dead [1 Cor. 15:20]). This conviction lay at the heart of the early church's joy and hope. It shaped its understanding of Jesus, salvation, mission, and all else. Accordingly, when scholars speak of eschatology today, they are often referring not simply to events which have "not yet" occurred, but chiefly to the way in which the last things are "already" present, and to the attitudes and expectations which this arouses.

The Millennium For the last century or so, different overall eschatological perspectives have usually been classified according to their viewpoint regarding the millennium. The "millennium" (from the Latin *mille,* meaning "a thousand") refers to the 1,000 year reign of Christ and His saints described in Revelation 20:4–6. Not all proponents of the various millennial views, however, insist that this period must last exactly 1,000 years. There have been three basic millennial perspectives. Each has existed in a more general and a more specific form, although these have not been entirely consistent with each other.

1. Premillennialism Premillennialists hold that Jesus will return before ("pre-") He establishes a millennial kingdom on this earth. This return will be necessary because forces hostile to God will be governing the world, and Christ must conquer them before He can rule. Towards the end of the millennium evil will again arise, and it will have to be defeated once more before God's cosmic rule is perfected. Until the fourth century, the early church was generally premillennial. This perspective, which placed the church in sharp conflict with the Roman Empire, declined rapidly after Constantine made Christianity the Empire's favored religion. In subsequent centuries premillennialism was often held by radical groups at odds with state-supported religion. Those who hold the general expectation that Jesus will return before establishing an earthly millennium are called "historic premillennialists."

Premillennialism's more specific form is qualified by the adjective "dispensational." Dispensational premillennialism acquired its specific shape during the ministry of John Nelson Darby (1800–1882), founder of the Plymouth Brethren. It has remained popular among many American fundamentalists and conservative evangelicals. Dispensationalism contrasts God's way of working in at least two historical "dispensations": those of Israel and of the church. See *Dispensation.*

2. Postmillennialism Whereas premillennialists hold that Jesus will return before the millennium, postmillennialists maintain that He will return after ("post-") an earthly kingdom is established. This means, however, that the millennium will be simultaneous with an era of ordinary human history. This viewpoint was first comprehensively articulated by Augustine (354–430), who regarded the establishment of the church since about Constantine's time as the rule of Christ with His saints. Postmillennialism has often been the general perspective of Roman Catholic, Reformed, and other socially established churches. It became popular during the eighteenth and nineteenth century evangelical revivals, which emphasized social transformation. Today some socially-minded evangelicals are reviving it.

In a general sense, postmillennialism serves as a label for any eschatology which expects religious and social activity to play a large role in establishing God's kingdom. All such movements acknowledge that this kingdom is not yet fully established, for much evil still exists. They also grant that evil may sometimes gain the upper hand. Nevertheless, they hold that history and society in general have been and will be brought increasingly under Christ's rule and that the kingdom's advance is closely related to that of certain social and religious forces.

3. Amillennialism By adding the prefix "a-" (meaning "not"), amillennialists express their conviction that no historical period called the millennium does or will exist. In general sense, amillennialism can refer to everyone who interprets all language about a final, earthly realm of peace in a spiritual manner.

Paradoxically, it was during late antiquity, as many church leaders were adopting a postmillennial perspective, that much popular piety ceased hoping for any historical millennium and, focusing entirely on the afterlife, became amillennial. In this general sense, amillennialism tends to be individualistic, concentrating on the heavenly destiny of each person rather than on the future of this earth. It includes much medieval mysticism. Even modern existentialist theologians, such as Rudolf Bultmann, who regard futurist eschatology as mythological and emphasize encounter with God in the present, can be included under this general label.

During the nineteenth century, however, "amillennialism" was applied increasingly to a more specific eschatology. Like postmillennialists, these amillennialists believed that Christ was already reigning with His saints. They argued that He was doing so, however, in heaven with departed Christians, and not through specific ecclesiastical or social movements. Like premillennialists, these amillennialists expected Jesus to return, to conquer His enemies and to rule over a transformed earth. His perfected rule, however, would be established immediately, and not preceeded by an interim called the millennium. This specific form of amillennialism, then, is far less individualistic than the general one, and views history before Jesus' return much as does the more general, or "historic," premillennialism.

People claim the Bible describes five major final events: Jesus' return, defeat of evil, resurrection, judgment, and renewal of the cosmos. Postmillennialists and amillennialists expect them to occur more or less together and to be preceeded by a troubled time called the Great Tribulation (Mark 13:19) during which the antichrist will rule. They also anticipate a large-scale conversion of Jews before the end.

Historic premillennialists also expect Israelite conversion and the Great Tribulation to occur before Christ's return. However, they divide each of the other four final events into two phases. (1) At Jesus' return: antichrist will be defeated, and Satan will be bound (though not wholly destroyed); then "the just" alone shall rise from their graves; they will be judged and rewarded for their good works; and the millennial kingdom will be established. (2) Then, after the millennium: Satan and all evil will be destroyed; then the "unjust" will rise; they will be judged for their evil works; and the new heavens and new earth will descend (compare Rev. 21).

Dispensational premillennialists further subdivide this scheme. They distinguish two phases in Jesus' return. In the first, He will rapture the church. The Tribulation and Israel's conversion will follow (although in some versions, the rapture will occur in the middle of or even after the Tribulation). Then Jesus will return to defeat antichrist, bind Satan, and establish a Judeo-centric millennial kingdom. From then on, events will proceed much like those of historic premillennialism. The resurrection, however, must now occur in three phases: at the rapture, all who have died in Christ to that time will be raised; at Jesus' second return, those martyred during the Tribulation will rise; finally, after the millennium, the "unjust" will be resurrected. Judgment, too, will proceed somewhat differently: "the just" who join the rapture will be rewarded then, while those raised at Jesus' second return will be rewarded only after the millennium, when "the unjust" are raised and judged.

The Last Judgment While traditional eschatological discussion has been preoccupied with millennial issues for over a century, several other doctrines have received attention through much longer periods of history. Many ordinary Christians and theologians have been concerned not with exactly when the last judgment will occur, but with how many will be judged favorably, and with how the condemned will be punished.

1. Universalism Over the centuries, most Christians have believed that some people will finally be saved while others will be lost. They often assumed that the latter would outnumber the former. By the early third century, however, Origen (185—254) was teaching "universalism": the doctrine that everyone would finally be saved. (Origen even included the devil in that number, although this particular addition brought the church's official condemnation.) While universalism was revived from time to time, it was never widely accepted until the nineteenth century, when liberal Protestantism emphasized the goodness of human nature and often extolled God's love to the exclusion of final judgment. In this century, although talk of divine judgment has become more acceptable, even some fairly conservative theologians, such as Karl Barth, have apparently been universalists.

Numerically speaking, opponents of universalism have more biblical texts on their side. The Old Testament abounds with annihilating judgments (Ex. 14:23–28; Josh. 7:24–26; Jer. 51:39–40). Jesus proclaimed negative judgments in parables (Matt. 13) and many other sayings (Matt 5:29–30; 11:21–24; 23:33). Paul often spoke of future condemnation (Rom. 2:5–9; 2 Cor. 5:10; 1 Thess. 1:10) as do other New Testament writings (2 Peter 3:7; Jude 14,15; Rev. 20:11–15).

Universalists, however, can cite passages emphasizing God's desire that everyone be saved (1 Tim. 2:4; 2 Peter 3:9). They also argue that the scope of salvation becomes continally wider as biblical history advances (Rom. 5:15). Finally, certain texts seem to directly teach universalism: "For as in Adam all die, even so in Christ shall all be made alive" (1 Cor. 15:22; "[Jesus'] act of righteousness leads to acquittal and life for all" (Rom. 5:18 RSV; compare Eph. 1:10; Col. 1:20; 1 Tim. 4:10; 1 John 2:2).

Positions on universalism, however, are not influenced by specific biblical texts alone. One's views on the character of God and of humanity and of salvation play important roles—sometimes in emotional ways. Universalists find negative judgment incompatible with God's overwhelming love and the dignity of the human person. Opponents of universalism feel that it seriously undercuts the urgency of the call to repentance and the firmness of God's justice and ignores too many biblical texts.

2. The Nature of Hell Negative judgment results in consignment to hell. Most Christians have supposed that this will involve eternal conscious torment. This seems to be taught by texts which speak of hell as enduring forever (Isa. 66:24; Mark 9:48; Rev. 14:9–11). Others, however, have argued that such texts should be taken figuratively since for them such a penalty is incompatible with God's mercy and also is disproportionate to all sins that a finite being could commit. Moreover, some find the eternal existence of hell inconsistent with the perfected rule of God over the cosmos. Accordingly, some have proposed that hell consists simply in the annihilation of "the unjust," involving their immediate loss of consciousness. Others have suggested that a gradual annihilation or deterioration of the wicked may be involved. Most evangelical Christians continue to expect a literal hell of torment. See *Hell.*

The Final Resurrection While the hope of resurrection has frequently been expressed in liturgy, hymns, and playful speculation, it has received far less theological discussion than have hell and judgment. Perhaps this is because most have regarded the affirmation of resurrection as far less problematic. In recent decades, however, some have questioned whether resurrection is compatible with another notion widely held since the first Christian centuries: the immortality of the soul.

Belief that the soul is inherently immortal implies, first, that every person passes immediately and automatically into God's presence at death. Yet this seems contrary to the biblical depiction of Death as an enemy barring the way to God and overcome only by Jesus' painful dying struggle and His resurrection. Second, since only the soul is immortal, this view implies only one part of the person comes directly into God's presence. This seems to contradict the biblical emphasis on resurrection of the body. Finally, if the soul passes immediately into God's full presence, eschatological hope would focus on the individual's death rather than on the return of Christ and the renewal of the cosmos. In other words, belief in inherent immortality of the soul tends to make one's eschatology spiritualistic and individualistic; belief in resurrection emphasizes eschatology's physical, historical, and corporate dimensions.

If a future resurrection be our ultimate hope, though, many will wonder: where are our departed loved ones, if they are not yet fully enjoying God's presence? Some, such as the Adventists, have long responded that souls simply sleep until the resurrection. Some talk of a distinction in eternity and historical time. Others think it best to simply affirm that the dead are somehow "in Christ." While the uncertainty involved may unsettle some who are bereaved, this approach can also help people deal realistically with the tragedy that is still involved in death.

Event and Meaning As judgment and resurrection have been discussed, it has become increasingly clear that eschatological discussions arise not merely from speculation about future events, but also from the hopes, fears, and perplexities which anticipation of these events arouses. Upon closer examination, this also proves to be true of millennial questions. For when people ask about the relationship between the millennium and the present, they often are seeking to determine what kind of actions and attitudes are appropriate in the present. For instance, postmillennialists will usually conclude that because the millennium is already here, vigorous involvement in certain social movements is imperative. Premillennialists may conclude that because the millennium is not yet here, social involvement is not appropriate; or perhaps that radical, counter-cultural criticism and involvement are called for.

In any case, the more one penetrates into the questions which underlie traditional eschatological discussions, the more one recognizes that eschatology has to do not only with the future, but also with the present. The last things, at least insofar as they arouse hope, fear, and perplexity, are already alive in the present.

New Testament Eschatology What features were essential to the eschatological atmosphere that pervaded the New Testament era—and therefore to a full understanding of eschatology in general? Jesus' contemporaries felt that they were living at the end of an "old Age" dominated by forces which opposed God. Pagan gods and pagan political rulers seemed to hold all things in their grip. They afflicted Yahweh's righteous remnant with suffering and death. Pious Israelites cried out for deliverance. They expected Yahweh to intervene radically in world affairs. More specifically, they expected God, first, to judge and defeat His enemies; second, to rescue His people and raise the righteous dead; and third, to inaugurate the "new Age" of life and peace through the Spirit.

The gospel story tells how God did these very things—though in an unforeseen and surprising way. Instead of coming as a warrior Messiah to destroy the pagan nations and their gods, God came as a humble Servant who was put to death, but then was unexpectedly resurrected. Yet as the early Christian community pondered these things, they began to acknowledge that they had rejected Jesus and had therefore participated, whether actively or passively, in putting Him to death. However, this meant that not only pagans, but they, too, were God's enemies (Rom. 5:10). By crucifying Jesus, they, too, had come under God's judgment. In fact, the last, decisive judgment of the world had "already" occurred.

The early church also discovered that the anticipated resurrection of the righteous dead had "already" occurred—although again in a surprising form. For instead of all the righteous being raised, Jesus alone had been, as the "firstfruits" of final harvest (1 Cor. 15:20, 23). His resurrection had two astounding consequences. On one hand, since Jesus was again alive and continuing to offer love and forgiveness, no one who had rejected Him need remain under God's judgment. Those who repented of their sin could receive new life in fellowship with Him. On the other hand, by overcoming death, Jesus had conquered the strongest of those evil forces which oppose God (1 Cor. 15:26,54–57). Since this power had been defeated, no other power in heaven and earth could separate those who participated in Jesus' resurrection from God (Rom. 8:37–39; Eph. 1:18–23; 1 Pet. 3:21–22).

Third, the early Christian community discovered that the "new Age" of life and peace had "already" begun among them through the outpouring of God's Spirit. They began to understand that the Spirit, like Jesus, was the "firstfruits" of a new creation (Rom. 8:23), while those who turned to Christ became the firstfruits of a new humanity (Rom. 16:5; Jas. 1:18; Rev. 14:4). Yet the "new Age," too, was present in an unexpected way. For although the powers which dominated the old Age had already been defeated, they were "not yet" wholly destroyed. Indeed, even as the Spirit impelled the early Christians to spread the good news among all nations, they experienced opposition much like that which Jesus had suffered.

The early church, then, continued to live in an atmosphere charged with eschatology. Like Jesus' contemporaries, they continued to struggle with forces which opposed God and to long eagerly for God's final triumph and deliverance. Yet they did so with a difference. For their conviction that the new Age had broken in imbued them with certainty of victory. Convinced that new ways of living were possible through the Spirit, they began to serve each other, to share their wealth, to bring people from all social groups into their fellowship.

General Implications for Eschatology Traditionally, the study of eschatology has suffered from two attitudes: neglect and overemphasis. Since eschatology has focused on events which have not yet occurred, many Christians have ignored it; and many theologians have treated it as an appendix at the end of their systems. Other Christians and theologians, however, have become so obsessed with these events that they have dealt with little else. Both attitudes have been encouraged by the separation of eschatology from the rest of Christian life and doctrine. If the "last things" have been occurring since Jesus' time, they must be far more relevant to the main themes of Christian activity and thought.

When the last judgment is regarded solely as a future event, it often arouses perplexity as to who will be rewarded or condemned and fear as to whether I might be condemned. It is more in line with biblical thinking to affirm that the last judgment, in the most decisive sense, has already occurred in Jesus' death and resurrection. Final judgment is not determined primarily by how many good or evil deeds one will do, but by how one responds to the judgment which these events already make upon oneself and the world. This emphasis, indeed, may not relieve all discomfort. It speaks about judgment in relation to concrete historical events and not solely in reference to an unknown future. It speaks, moreover, of events through which God's love, forgiveness, and triumph as well as condemnation are revealed. If eschatology can deal with the last judgment in this light, it might appear more clearly not only as an exercise of God's wrath, but also as the manifestation of His love and the consummation of His triumph.

When resurrection is regarded as wholly future, it often seems to stand in sharp contrast to one's present life. Earthly existence appears as a struggle which we must endure, largely on our own, until we are suddenly translated into a totally different realm. If resurrection, in the most decisive sense has already occurred in Jesus' triumph, then the strength which it unleashes is available to us now. Further, if all resurrection is rooted in Jesus' resurrection and if one's own resurrection is not totally a distant, isolated event, then the resurrection life already brings one into fellowship with Jesus and with all others who participate in it. If eschatology can deal with future resurrection in this light, it might appear more clearly as the joyous manifestation, perfection, and culmination of the life which all Christians now share in Him.

Finally, a deeper understanding of the "already-not yet" life on the new Age might help Christians relate more effectively to society at large. Postmillennialists, emphasizing that God's kingdom is already present, have usually been active in society, but have sometimes been unduly optimistic about possibilities for positive social change. Premillennialists, on the other hand, regarding God's kingdom as partially or wholly future, have often recognized the massive scope of evil in the world; but they have sometimes been unduly pessimistic about the value of social involvement. Perhaps a recognition that the new Age is both present and future and that neither side of this paradox dare be ignored could help the church maximize the strengths of different millennial perspectives without being overcome by the weaknesses of any.

See *Christology; Kingdom of God; Millennium; Revelation, Book of.*   *Thomas Finger*

ESDRAELON (Ĕs drā´ ē lŏn) Greek translation of the word Jezreel, indicating the low-lying area separating the mountains of Galilee from the mountains of Samaria.

Old Testament Esdraelon, also called the Great Plain of Esdraelon or the Plain of Jezreel, is the area assigned to Zebulun and Issachar (Josh. 19:10–23). It extends from the Mediterranean Sea to the Jordan River at Beth-Shean. Included are the Valley or Plain of Megiddo in the east and the Valley of Jezreel in the west.

Sources disagree on the actual naming of the area. Some scholars say that the Valley of Jezreel is the name for the entire region; Esdraelon being the western portion, comprised of the Plain of Accho and the Valley of Megiddo. Whatever the entire region is called, it is assumed that references to Jezreel indicate both the town of Jezreel and the valley in which it is located; and references to Megiddo indicate both the town and the plain on which it is located.

The historical and biblical significance of Esdraelon in the Old Testament is its association with war and bloodshed. As a battleground, it was a strategically-favored place. It was occupied by Canaanites who were less than willing to relocate when the tribes of Israel tried to settle there (Judg. 1:27). The Song of Deborah in Judges 5 celebrates the battle "at Tanaach by the waters of Megiddo" (Judg. 5:19) where Barak finally routed the Canaanites.

Other important battles were fought in Esdraelon. Frequently the question of Israel's leadership was settled there. Josiah died in battle against Pharaoh Neco at Megiddo (2 Chron. 35:20–24). Saul and Jonathan died at the hands of the Philistines in the Valley of Jezreel (1 Sam. 29:1,11; 31:1–7). Jehu killed his rivals Joram and Ahaziah at Jezreel (2 Kings 9). He later slaughtered all the men of Ahab and Azariah and all the prophets of Baal there (2 Kings 10).

Brutal slaughter for other than political reasons took place in Esdraelon. Naboth owned a vineyard in Jezreel. Jezebel and Ahab wanted to buy the vineyard, but Naboth refused because it had been handed down to him from his ancestors (1 Kings

The Valley of Armageddon, or Plain of Esdraelon, as seen from the site of ancient Megiddo.

21:3). Jezebel arranged Naboth's murder so Ahab could take possession of the vineyard (1 Kings 21:5–16).

The tragedies at Esdraelon did not go unnoticed by God. For her part, Jezebel was later murdered at Jezreel as prophesied by Elijah (1 Kings 21:23; 2 Kings 9:36). Hosea prophesied vengeance on the house of Jehu for his role in the slaughter at Jezreel (Hos. 1:4–5).

New Testament Esdraelon is mentioned in the New Testament as Armageddon or har-Megiddon, meaning hill or city of Megiddo. Revelation 16:16 echoes the Old Testament portrayal of Esdraelon as a place of war and tragedy. The final battle of the Lord will be waged there (Rev. 16:14–16; 19:19).   *Donna R. Ridge*

ESEK (Ē′ sĕk) Place name meaning, "strife." A well Isaac's servants dug in the valley near Gerar to find water for their herds. The shepherds of Gerar disputed Isaac's claim to the watering place. Isaac apparently gave in to the claim without warfare, thus receiving God's assurance of blessing (Gen. 26:18–22).

ESHAN (Ē′ shăn) Place name meaning, "I lean on." Town in the hill country of Judah assigned to tribe of Judah (Josh. 15:52). KJV spells Eshean. A text tradition in the earliest Greek translation reads, "Soma," instead of Eshan, possibly pointing to a location at modern khirbet hallat Sama. Otherwise, the location is not known.

ESH-BAAL (Ĕsh-bā′ ál) Personal name meaning, "man of Baal." Son of Saul, the first king of Israel (1 Chron. 8:33; 9:39). In 2 Samuel 2:8 the name is Ish-bosheth, "man of shame," apparently an intentional corruption in the Hebrew tradition to avoid the name of the Canaanite god and to characterize the person with such a name. First Samuel 14:49 lists Ishui or Ishvi as Saul's son, possibly another way of respelling the name to avoid Baal. In Saul's day "baal" may have been a title applied to Yahweh indicating, "He is Lord or Master." In this case Esh-baal would mean, "the man of the

Lord." Otherwise, Saul's name for his son would seem to indicate some devotion to the Canaanite god Baal at the period in his life when he named the son. Saul's son Jonathan named his son Merib-baal. See *Ish-bosheth; Ishvi; Merib-baal; Jonathan.*

ESHBAN (Ĕsh′ băn) Personal name of unknown meaning. An Edomite listed as a descendant of Seir the Horite (Gen. 36:26).

ESHCOL (Ĕsh′ cŏl) Place name meaning, "valley of grapes," or "cluster." *1.* A valley in Canaan that was explored by the twelve Israelites sent to spy out the land (Num. 13:23). From the valley of Eshcol they brought back an exceptionally large cluster of grapes. Apparently the valley was given the name on account of grape clusters such as the one found by the Israelite spies. *2.* Brother of Mamre and Aner (Gen. 14:13). He and his brothers were Amorites who were allies of Abram in the defeat of Chedorlaomer.

ESHEAN (Ĕsh′ ė ăn) KJV spelling of Eshan. See *Eshan.*

ESHEK (Ē′ shĕk) Personal name meaning, "oppression" or "strong." A member of the tribe of Benjamin descended from King Saul (1 Chron. 8:39).

ESHKALONITE (Ĕsh′ kȧ lŏn īte) Citizen of Ashkelon. See *Ashkelon.*

ESHTAOL (Ĕsh′ tā ŏl) Place name meaning, "asking (for an oracle)." Town in lowlands of Shephelah of Judah allotted to the tribe of Judah (Josh. 15:33) but also to the tribe of Dan (Josh. 19:41). Near there, God's Spirit stirred Samson of the tribe of Dan (Judg. 13:25). Samson was buried near Eshtaol (Judg. 16:31). The tribe of Dan sent men from Eshtaol to seek a new homeland (Judg. 18:2–11). Its citizens were kin to the clan of Caleb and to residents of Kiriath-jearim (1 Chron. 2:53). It may be located at modern Irtuf, a mile south of Ishwa.

ESHTAOLITE (Ĕsh′ tȧ ō līte) Citizen of Eshtaol. See *Eshtaol.*

ESHTARAH (Ĕsh′ tȧ răh) NIV spelling of Beeshterah. REB reads "Be-ashtaroth. See *Beeshterah.*

ESHTAULITE (Ĕsh′ tȧ ū līte) KJV spelling of Eshtaolite. See *Eshtaolite.*

ESHTEMOA (Ĕsh tė mō′ á) Place and personal name meaning, "being heard." The name may indicate an ancient tradition of going to Eshtemoa to obtain an oracle or word of God from a prophet or priest. *1.* City in tribal allotment of Judah (Judg.

15:50, with variant Hebrew spelling; see *Eshtemoh).* God set it aside for the Levites (Josh. 21:14). While living in exile in Ziklag, David sent some of the plunder from his victories to Eshtemoa (1 Sam. 30:28). *2.* A member of clan of Caleb in tribe of Judah (1 Chron. 4:17), probably listed as the clan father of those who settled in Eshtemoa. The relation between the two Eshtemoas in 1 Chronicles 4:17,19 is not clear. The city is the modern es-Samu about eight and a half miles south-southwest of Hebron and fourteen miles northeast of Beersheba.

ESHTEMOH (Ĕsh' tė mōh) Variant Hebrew spelling of Eshtemoa (Josh. 15:50). See *Eshtemoa.*

ESHTON (Ĕsh' tŏn) Personal name of uncertain meaning. A member of tribe of Judah (1 Chron. 4:11–12).

ESLI (Ĕs' lī) Personal name of unknown meaning. Ancestor of Jesus (Luke 3:25), spelled Hesli in NAS. Some scholars equate him with Elioenai (1 Chron. 3:23). See *Elioenai.*

ESPOUSAL See *Betrothal.*

ESROM (Ĕs' rŏm) KJV New Testament spelling of Hezron. See *Hezron.*

ESSENES Members of a Jewish sect that existed in Palestine during the time of Christ. They are not mentioned in the New Testament. They were ascetics who practiced community of goods, generally shunned marriage, refrained from attending

The ruins of ancient Qumran probably inhabited by Essenes from 130 B.C. until A.D. 70.

worship in the Temple, and attached great importance to the study of the Scriptures. Many scholars associate the Dead Sea Scrolls discovered in 1947 with an Essene community. See *Dead Sea Scrolls; Qumran.*

ESTHER (Ĕs' thĕr) Persian personal name meaning, "Ishtar." Heroine of biblical Book of Esther whose Jewish name was Hadassah. Esther is the

The traditional site of the tombs of Esther and Mordecai in the modern country of Iran.

story of a Jewish orphan girl raised by her uncle, Mordecai, in Persia. She became queen when Queen Vashti refused to appear at a banquet hosted by her husband, King Ahasuerus. Esther did not reveal that she was Jewish.

Mordecai heard about a plot against the king's life which he reported through Esther. Haman was made prime minister and began to plot against Mordecai and the Jews because they would not pay homage to him. The king issued a decree that all who would not bow down would be killed. Esther learned of the plot and sent for Mordecai. He challenged her with the idea, "Who knoweth whether those art come to the kingdom for such a time as this?" (Esther 4: 14). She asked Mordecai and the Jews to fast with her while she decided. She entered the king's presence unsummoned which could have meant her death. The king granted her request.

Haman was tricked into honoring Mordecai, his enemy. At a banquet, Esther revealed Haman's plot to destroy her and her people, the Jews. Haman was hanged on the gallows prepared for Mordecai. Mordecai was promoted, and Esther got the king to revoke Haman's decree to destroy the Jews. The Jews killed and destroyed their enemies. The book closes with the institution of the festival of Purim.

The Book of Esther The Book of Esther has been placed among the writings in the Old Testament. It, along with four others small books—Song of Solomon, Ruth, Ecclesiastes, and Lamentations, was placed on one scroll called the "Meghilloth" and was used for festival readings. Many scholars feel that the Book of Esther is a short historical novel or short story sprinkled with historical data and names to make its message more urgent and important. Thus it would be comparable to Jesus' parables. Others think it is an attempt to write history with free interspersion of speeches and conversation following the conventions of history writing of its day. Others insist on the historicity of every detail, pointing to Esther 10:2.

The Purpose of the Book The purpose is not clear from a reading of the book. It considers the question of destruction or survival of the Jews under persecution. Though the book deals with religious issues, the name of God is never mentioned in the book. The writer deliberately avoids the name of God. When Esther prepares herself to present herself unrequested into the presence of the king, prayer does not accompany fasting. Also vengeance is more prominent than devotion. An important function of the book is to explain the observance of the festival of Purim. The Purim festival was a Jewish commemoration of deliverance—deliverance of the Jews from the hands of the Babylonians.

If this is the purpose of the book, then that explains the absence of the name of God. The book was intended to be read at the Purim festival—a festival of merrymaking, noise, and conviviality. Thus the major theme of the book, persecution returning on the head of those who initiate it, leads through all the details of the story to the final victory which Purim celebrates.

Theological Teachings Many feel that the religious concepts taught in the book are sub-Christian. Probably the persons who can understand and appreciate the attitudes of Esther are those who have lived through persecution and occupation by others. In times of peace it is incomprehensible and unforgivable that hard suffering creates such rigidity and callousness. Though the book does not mention the name of God, it has a definite theology. Throughout, the book points to justice and indicates that faithfulness to the covenant people is a duty whether it pays or not. Mordecai's insistence that Esther must intervene to save her people is based on the idea that a good Jew must worship and be loyal to the covenant God and to Him alone. To be faithful to Him means to be faithful to His people.

The book teaches the axiom that "the Lord helps those who help themselves." During the days of oppressive persecution the very survival of the people depended upon the Jews doing something. The book shows the sovereignty of God working in a foreign land to preserve His people. It shows God working through people of unpretentious backgrounds as they prove faithful to Him. It shows ultimate punishment for those who oppose God's people. It calls for celebration of God's deliverance.

Outline

I. Humble faithfulness can lead to large responsibilities (1:1—2:18).
   A. Political power of ungodly rulers may be far-reaching (1:1–8).
   B. Protection of personal rights may result in loss of position and rights (1:9–15).
   C. Family relationships and respect cannot be enforced by political means (1:16–22).
   D. Self-giving love and loyalty to family, nation, and God may require hiding one's identity to gain opportunity to serve (2:1–11).
   E. Humble obedience can lead to opportunities to serve (2:2–18).
II. Faithfulness to one's people can be expressed through service to a foreign ruler (2:19—3:15).
   A. Loyalty to one's people does not require participation in conspiracy against foreign rulers (2:19–23).
   B. Loyalty to the foreign ruler does not mean participating in immoral government practices (3:1–2).
   C. Loyalty to God and godly traditions over loyalty to foreign rulers may cause personal and even national persecution (3:3–15).
III. Positions of influence bring responsibility to act for God's people (4:1–17).
   A. Mourning rites are appropriate responses to national danger (4:1–4).
   B. God's people must act and pray in times of danger (4:5–17).
IV. Responsible actions for God are honored by God's actions for His people (5:1—8:17).
   A. Self-giving action is rewarded in unexpected ways (5:1–8).
   B. Human pride leads to rash actions (5:9–14).
   C. Honor comes to God's faithful at the opportune moment (6:1–3).
   D. Human pride often leads to humiliation (6:4–12).
   E. God's people will experience vindication eventually (6:13–14).
   F. Brave action for God's people brings deliverance (7:1–10).
   G. God's providence brings reward for faithfulness and joy to God's people (8:1–17).
V. Celebration through the ages helps God's people remember His salvation and the lessons of history (9:1–32).
VI. Work for God's people can bring new opportunities for service and honor (10:1–3).

Jerry Stubblefield

ETAM (Ē′ tăm) Place name meaning, "place of birds of prey." *1.* A rocky crag where Samson camped during his battles with the Philistines (Judg. 15:8–13), conferring there with men of Judah who wanted to bind him and hand him over to the Philistines. The exact location is not known. It must be near Lehi. See *Lehi. 2.* A town in territorial allotment of tribe of Judah according to earliest Greek translation of the Old Testament but omitted from present Hebrew manuscripts (Josh. 15:59 REB). Rehoboam, king of Judah (931-913 B.C.), fortified the city (2 Chron. 11:6), which seems to indicate that Etam stood between Bethlehem and Tekoa. Rehoboam probably feared attack from Egypt, which had sheltered Jeroboam, king of Israel (2 Chron. 10:2). Pharaoh Shishak did, indeed, attack (2 Chron. 12:2–4). Some scholars think Rehoboam's fortification program came after Shishak's attack. A road ran along the ridge through or near Hebron, Beth-zur, and Bethlehem to Jerusalem. Etam protected the approach to this road from the east. Etam is located at khirbet el-Khokh, southwest of Bethlehem. 3. Member of tribe of Judah and apparently clan father of town of same name associated with Jezreel (1 Chron. 4:3). 4. A village assigned to Simeon (1 Chron. 4:32), though it is not listed in Simeon's tribal territory in Joshua 19:7. It may be modern Aitun, about eleven miles southwest of Hebron.

ETERNAL LIFE The quality of life including the promise of resurrection which God gives to those who believe in Christ. This important term in the New Testament is emphasized in the Gospel of John, but also appears in the other Gospels and in Paul's writings. Eternal life in the New Testament eliminates the boundary line of death. Death is still a foe, but the one who has eternal life already experiences the kind of existence that will never end.

Yet in this expression, the emphasis is on the *quality* of life rather than on the unending duration of life. Probably some aspects of both quality and duration appear in every context, but some refer primarily to *quality of life* and others point to *unending life* or a *life to be entered into* in the future.

"Quality of life" involves (1) life imparted by God; (2) transformation and renewal of life; (3) life fully opened to God and centered in Him; (4) a constant overcoming of sin and moral evil; and (5) the complete removal of moral evil from the person and from the environment of that person.
Eternal Life As Experience in the Present This term in John has important implications. The one trusting in the Son has eternal life; the one disobeying the Son has the wrath of God abiding on him (John 3:36). Trusting and obeying go together; they leave no room for neutrality. The one who hears Christ's message and believes or trusts in the Father who sent Him has eternal life. This person does not come into condemnation but has passed out of death into life (John 5:24). The perfect tense—one who has passed and remained in the state of having passed from death into life—emphasizes eternal life as a permanent, present reality. But no presumption is possible here. Eternal life is a present reality for the one hearing and trusting (John 5:24).

The bold metaphors of *eating* and *drinking* point to active involvement with Christ. "The one eating my flesh and drinking my blood, has eternal life" (John 6:54*a*). (Translations in this article are the author's.) Verse 57 explains: "The one eating

me will live because of *me*." Since Christ is our life, we must make that life part of us by "sharing in Christ," by actively coming to Him and drawing life-giving strength from Him.

Eternal life is defined in Jesus' high priestly prayer: "Eternal life is this: that people be constantly knowing you, the only genuine God and Jesus Christ whom You sent" (John 17:3). The present tense of the verb "to know" indicates that this knowledge is by experience—not from intellectual facts. Genuine knowledge of God by experience brings eternal life. Such experience transforms life.
Eternal Life as Experienced in the Present and Future John compared the lifting up of the serpent in the wilderness to the lifting up of the Son of Man on the cross and His exaltation to heaven. People who respond to Christ by constant trust have eternal life (John 3:15). They have healing from something more deadly than snakebite—the destructive effects of sin. Here eternal life involves a present healing, a present reality. But John 3:16 refers both to the present and the future.

Christ defined His true sheep as those who hear or listen to His voice and follow Him (John 10:27). To such disciples, He gives eternal life, and they will not perish (John 10:28). Again, no presumption is possible. Those are secure who persistently listen, hearken, and follow. For such people eternal life is both a present and a future reality.
Eternal Life as a Future Experience "What shall I do that I may inherit eternal life?" the rich young ruler asked. (Mark 10:17; compare Matt 19:16; Luke 18:18). He saw eternal life as a final inheritance. His earnestness moved Jesus, and Jesus loved this young man (Mark 10:21). But he had to make a decision: Would he follow Jesus without his possessions? (Mark 10:22). He answered, "No." He could not part with his possessions first and then follow Jesus.

In Matthew 19:27 Peter asked Jesus, "What then shall be to us?" The disciples had left their dear ones and their possessions to follow Jesus. Jesus promised them loved ones and lands (possessions) with persecutions. Then He added: "And in the coming age, *eternal life*" (Mark 10:30). Eternal life here refers to an unending future reality.

John 12:20–26 tells of some Greeks who wanted to see Jesus. We do not know how Jesus interacted with these Greeks. We do know He spoke about His death and what it meant to be a disciple: "The one loving his life [or soul] will lose it; but the one hating his life [or soul] in this world will guard the soul unto eternal life" (John 12:25). Jesus here contrasted eternal life with the present life. Believers are to guard their persons or souls by serving Christ and following Him (John 12:26). Such servants will be where Christ is, and the Father will honor them (John 12:26). To be where Christ is means to come into eternal life—a life freed from sin or moral evil.

Paul declared that "the one sowing to the Spirit will reap eternal life from the Spirit" (Gal. 6:8). Eternal life is given by Jesus and the Holy Spirit. This future reality, already experienced to some limited degree in the present, involves the Father, Son, and Spirit. Fellowship in life eternal means fellowship with the Triune God.

A. Berkeley Mickelsen

ETHAM (Ē′ thăm) Place name meaning, "fort." The second station in Israel's wilderness wandering out of Egypt (Ex. 13:20; Num. 33:6–8). The nearby wilderness was called the wilderness of Etham (Num. 33:8). Its precise location is not certain.

ETHAN (Ē′ thăn) Personal name meaning, "long-lived." *1.* A man so famous for his wisdom that Solomon's outstanding wisdom could be described as exceeding Ethan's (1 Kings 4:31). Ezrahite may indicate Ethan was at home in Canaan before Israel entered, though this is uncertain. See *Ezralite.* A list similar to 1 Kings 4:31 appears among the descendants of Judah in 1 Chronicles 2:6,8. *2.* A Levite and Temple singer (1 Chron. 6:42,44; 15:17) and instrumentalist (1 Chron. 15:19). He is associated with Psalms 88 and 89 in their titles.

ETHANIM (Ĕth′ à nĭm) Canaanite name of the seventh month taken over by Israel (1 Kings 8:2), who also called the month Tishri. This was the first month of the civil year. Ethanim means, "always flowing with water" and refers to the flooding streams fed by heavy fall rains.

ETH-BAAL (Ĕth-bā′ ăl) Personal name meaning, "with him is Baal." King of Sidon and father of Jezebel (1 Kings 16:31), who married Jeroboam II, king of Israel (793-753 B.C.). Through her influence Baal worship pervaded the Northern Kingdom. See *Jezebel.*

ETHER (Ē′ thēr) Place name meaning, "smoke of incense." *1.* Town in tribal territory of Judah (Josh. 15:42). *2.* A town occupied by tribe of Simeon (Josh. 19:7). Some Bible students identify this with the town in Judah, since Simeon's territory was within Judah's boundaries. Other scholars warn us not to identify the two places. Ether in Judah is modern khirbet Attir, south of Lahav and a mile northwest of Beth Gibrin.

ETHICS The study of good behavior, motivation, and attitude in light of Jesus Christ and biblical revelation. The discipline of ethics deals with such questions as: "What ought I do?" "How should I act so as to do what is good and right?" "What is meant by good?" "Who is the good person?"

Biblical ethics likewise addresses some of the identical questions. While neither Testament has an abstract, comprehensive term or definition which parallels the modern term "ethics," both the Old Testament and the New Testament are concerned about the manner of life that the Scripture prescribes and approves. The closest Hebrew term in the Old Testament for "ethics," "virtue" or "ideals" is the word *mûsār,* "discipline" or "teaching" (Prov. 1:8) or even *derek,* "way or path" of the good and the right. The closest parallel Greek term in the New Testament is *anastrophē,* "way of life, life-style" (occurring nine times in a good sense with 2 Pet. 3:11 being the most significant usage). Of course the Greek terms *ethos* or *ēthos* appear twelve times in the New Testament (Luke 1:9; 2:42; 22:39; John 19:40; Acts 6:14; 15:1; 16:21; 21:21; 25:16; 26:3; 28:17 and Heb. 10:25). The plural form appears once in 1 Corinthians 15:33. It is usually translated "conduct," "custom," "manner of life," or "practice."

The Biblical Definition of Ethics is Connected With Doctrine The problem with trying to speak about the ethics of the Bible is that ethical contents are not offered in isolation from the doctrine and teaching of the Bible. Therefore, what God is in His character, what He wills in His revelation, defines what is right, good, and ethical. In this sense then, the Bible had a decisive influence in molding ethics in western culture.

Some have seriously questioned whether there is a single ethic throughout the Bible. Their feeling is that there is too much diversity to be found in the wide variety of books and types of literature in the Bible to decide that there is harmony and a basic ethical stance and norm against which all ethical and moral decisions ought to be made. Nevertheless, when following the *claims* made by the books of the Bible, some conceive their message to be a contribution to the ongoing and continuous story about the character and will of God. This narrative about the character and will of God is the proper basis for answering the questions: "What kind of a person ought I to be?" "How then shall we live so as to do what is right, just, and good?"

As some have pointed out, the search for diversity and pluralism in ethical standards is as much the result of a prior methodological decision as is the search for unity and harmony of standards. One may not say the search for diversity is more scientific and objective than the search for harmony. This fact must be decided on the basis of an internal examination of the biblical materials; not as an external decision foisted over the text.

Three Basic Assumptions Can ethical or moral decisions rest on the Bible, or is this idea absurd and incoherent? Three assumptions illustrate how a contemporary ethicist or moral-living individual may be able to rest his or her decision on the ethical content of the biblical text from a past age. The three are: (1) the Bible's moral statements were meant to be applied to a universal class of peoples, times, and conditions, (2) Scripture's teaching has a consistency about it so that it presents a common front to the same questions in all its parts and to all cultures past and present; (3) the Bible purports to direct our action or behavior when it makes a claim or a demand. In short the Bible can be applied to all people. The Bible is consistent. The Bible seeks to command certain moral behavior.

To take Scripture's universalizability first: every biblical command, whether it appeared in a biblical law code, narrative text, wisdom text, prophetic text, gospel, or epistle was originally addressed to someone, in some place, in some particular situation. Such particulars were not meant to prejudice their usage in other times, places, or persons. Lurking behind each of these specific injunctions can be found a universal principle. From the general principle a person in a different setting can use the Bible to gain direction in a specific decision.

Are our problems, our culture, and our societal patterns so different that even though we can universalize the specific injunctions from Scripture, they have no relevance to our day? Can we assume consistency between cultures and times for this ethic? All that is required here is that the same biblical writer supplied us elsewhere with a whole pattern of ethical thought that has led up to this contextualized and particular injunction. If we may assume that the writer would not change his mind from one moment to the next, we may assume that he would stand by his principle for all such similar situations regardless of times or culture.

Finally, the Bible claims to command mortals made in the image of God. Whether the ethical materials are in the imperative or indicative moods makes little difference. The writers of Scripture intended to do more than offer information; they purported to direct behavior.

Five Basic Characteristics of Biblical Ethics In contrast to philosophical ethics, which tends to be more abstract and human—centered, biblical morality was directly connected with religious faith. Hence immoral men and women were by the same token irreligious men and women, and irreligious persons were also immoral persons (Ps. 14:1).

Biblical ethics are, first of all, *personal.* The ground of the ethical is the person, character, and declaration of an absolutely holy God. Consequently, individuals are urged, "Ye shall be holy: for I the Lord your God am holy" (Lev. 19:2).

In the second place, the ethics of the Bible are emphatically *theistic.* They focus on God. To know God was to know how to practice righteousness and justice.

Most significantly, biblical ethics are deeply concerned with the *internal* response to morality rather than mere outward acts. "The Lord looketh on the heart" (1 Sam. 16:7) was the cry repeatedly announced by the prophets (Isa. 1:11–18; Jer. 7:21–23; Hos. 6:6; Mic. 6:6–8).

Scripture's ethical motivation was found in a *future orientation.* The belief in a future resurrection of the body (Job 19:26–27; Ps. 49:13–15; Isa. 26:19; Dan. 12:2–3) was reason enough to pause before concluding that each act was limited to the situation in which it occurred and bore no consequences for the future.

The fifth characteristic of biblical ethics is that they are *universal.* They embrace the same standard of righteousness for every nation and person on earth.

The Organizing Principle: God's Character That which gives wholeness, harmony, and consistency to the morality of the Bible is the character of God. Thus the ethical directions and morality of the Bible were grounded, first of all, in the character and nature of God. What God required was what He Himself was and is. The heart of every moral command was the theme that appeared in Leviticus 18:5,6,30; 19:2,3,4,10,12,14,18,25, 31,32,34,36,37, "I am the Lord" or "Ye shall be holy: for I the Lord your God am holy." Likewise, Philippians 2:5–8 agreed: "Let this mind be in you, which was also in Christ Jesus: Who, being in the form of God, . . . yet he humbled himself, and became obedient unto death—even the death of the cross."

The character and nature of the holy God found ethical expression in the will and word of God. These words could be divided into *moral law* and *positive law.* Moral law expressed His character. The major example is the Ten Commandments (Ex. 20:1–17; Deut. 5:6–21). Another is the holiness code (Lev. 18—20). Positive law bound men and women for a limited time period because of the authority of the One who spoke them. Positive law claimed the peoples' allegiances only for as long and only in as many situations as God's authority determined when He originally gave that law. Thus the divine word in the Garden of Eden, "you must not eat from the tree of the knowledge of good and evil" (Gen. 2:17 NIV) or our Lord's, "Untie [the colt]" (Luke 19:30) were intended only for the couple in the garden of Eden or the disciples. They were not intended to be permanent commandments. They do not apply to our times. A study of biblical ethics helps us distinguish between the always valid moral law and the temporary command of positive law.

The moral law is permanent, universal, and equally binding on all men and women in all times. This law is best found in the Decalogue of Moses. Its profundity can be easily grasped in its comprehensiveness of issues and simplicity of expression. A few observations may help in interpreting these Ten Commandments. They are:

[1] The law has as a prologue. This established the grace of God as seen in the Exodus as the basis for any requirement made of individuals. Ethics is a response to grace in love not a response to demand in fear.

[2] All moral law is doublesided, leading to a positive act and away from a negative one. It makes no difference whether a law is stated negatively or positively, for every moral act is at one and the same time a refraining from a contrary action when a positive act is adopted.

[3] Merely omitting or refraining from doing a forbidden thing is not a moral act. Otherwise, sheer inactivity could count as fulfilling a command, but in the moral realm this is just another name for death. Biblical ethics call for positive participation in life.

[4] When an evil is forbidden in a moral command, its opposite good must be practiced before one can be considered obedient. We must not just refuse to murder, but we must do all in our power to aid the life of our neighbor.

The essence of the Decalogue can be found in three areas: [1] right relations with God (first command, internal worship of God; second, external worship of God; third, verbal worship of God); [2] right relations with time (fourth command), and [3] right relations with society (fifth command, sanctity of the family; sixth, sanctity of life; seventh, sanctity of marriage and sex; eighth, sanctity of property; ninth, sanctity of truth; and tenth, sanctity of motives).

The Content of Biblical Ethics Biblical ethics is based on the complete revelation of the Bible. The Decalogue and its expansions in the three other basic law codes join the Sermon on the Mount in Matthew 5—7 and the Sermon on the Plain in Luke 6:17–49 as the foundational texts of the Bible's teaching in the ethical and moral realm. All other biblical texts—the narratives of wrongdoing, the collection of Proverbs, the personal requests of letters—all contribute to our knowledge of biblical ethics. The Bible does not offer a list from which we pick and choose. It hammers home a life-style and calls us to follow.

Several examples of the content of biblical ethics may help to better understand how the character of God, especially of His holiness, sets the norm for all moral decision-making.

Honor or respect for one's parents was one of the first applications of what holiness entailed according to Leviticus 19:1–3. This should come as no surprise, for one of the first ordinances God gave in Genesis 2:23–24 set forth the monogamous relationship as the foundation and cornerstone of the family.

Husband and wife were to be equals before God. The wife was not a mere possession, chattel, or solely a childbearer. She was not only "from the Lord" (Prov. 19:14) and her husband's "crown"

(Prov. 12:4), but she also was "a power equal to" him (the word "helper" Gen. 2:18 NIV is better translated "strength, power"). The admonition to honor parents was to be no excuse to claim no responsibility to help the poor, the orphan, and the widow (Lev. 25:35; Deut. 15:7–11; Job 29:12–16; 31:16–22; Isa. 58; Amos 4:1–2; 5:12). The oppressed were to find relief from the people of God and those in authority.

Similarly, human life was to be regarded as so sacred that premeditated murder carried with it the penalty of capital punishment in order to show respect for the smitten victim's being made in the image of God (Gen. 9:5–6). Thus the life of all persons, whether still unborn and in the womb (Ex. 21:22–25; Ps. 139:13–6) or those who were citizens of a conquered country (Isa. 10; Hab. 3), were of infinite value to God.

Human sexuality was a gift from God. It was not a curse, nor an invention of the devil. It was made for the marriage relationship and meant for enjoyment (Prov. 5:15–21), not just procreation. Fornication was forbidden (1 Thess. 4:1–8). Sexual abberrations, such as homosexuality (Lev. 18:22; 20:13; Deut. 23:17) or bestiality (Ex. 22:19; Lev. 18:23–30; 20: 15–16; Deut. 27:21) were repulsive to the holiness of God and thus condemned.

Finally, commands about property, wealth, possessions, and concern for the truth set new norms. These norms went against the universal human propensity for greed, for ranking things above persons, and for preferring the lie as an alternative to the truth. No matter how many new issues were faced in ethical discourse, the bottom line remained where the last commandment had laid it: the motives and intentions of the heart. This is why holiness in the ethical realm began with the "fear of the Lord" (Prov. 1:7; 9:10; 15:33).

The greatest summary of ethical instruction was given by our Lord in Matthew 22:37–39: it was to love God and to love one's neighbor. There also was the Golden Rule of Matthew 7:12. The best manifestation of this love was a willingness to forgive others (Matt. 6:12–15; 18:21–35; Luke 12:13–34).

The New Testament, like the Old, included social ethics and one's duty to the state as part of its teaching. Since God's kingdom was at work in the world, it was necessary that salt and light also be present as well in holy living.

While both Testaments shared the same stance on issues such as marriage and divorce, the New often explicitly adopted different sanctions. Thus, church discipline was recommended in the case of incest in 1 Corinthians 5 rather than stoning.

The main difference between the two Testaments is that the New Testament sets forth Jesus as the new Example of uncompromising obedience to the will and law of God. He came not to abolish the Old, but to fulfill it. The New Testa-

E

ment is replete with exhortations to live by the words and to walk in the way set forth by Jesus of Nazareth, the Messiah (1 Cor. 11:1; 1 Thess. 1:6; 1 Pet. 2:21–25).

Some of the motivators to live ethical and moral lives carry over from the previous Testament, but to these are added: the nearness of God's kingdom (Mark 1:15); gratitude for God's grace in Christ (Rom. 5:8); and the accomplished redemption, atonement, and resurrection of Jesus Christ (1 Cor. 15:20–21). Like the Old Testament, love is a strong motivator; however, love does not take the place of law. Love is not itself the law; it is a "how" word, but it will never tell us "what" we are to do. Love is a fulfillment of the law (Rom. 13:9) because it constrains us to comply with what the law teaches. Thus, love creates an affinity with and an affection for the object of its love. It gives willing and cheerful obedience rather than coerced and forced compliance.

Finally, the content of biblical ethics is not only personal, but it is wide-ranging. The letters of Paul and Peter list a wide range of ethical duties; toward one's neighbors, respect for the civil government, and its tasks, the spiritual significance to work, the stewardship of possessions and wealth, and much else.

The ethic which Scripture demands and approves has the holiness of the Godhead as its standard and fountainhead, love to God as its impelling motivation, the law of God as found in the Decalogue and Sermon on the Mount as its directing principle, and the glory of God as its governing aim. *Walter C. Kaiser, Jr.*

ETHIOPIA (Ē thī ō′ pī á) The region of Nubia just south of Egypt, from the first cataract of the Nile into the Sudan. Confusion has arisen between the names Ethiopia and Cush. The Old Testament Hebrew (and Egyptian) name for the region was Cush. The ancient Greek translation of the Old Testament, the Septuagint, rendered Cush by the Greek word Ethiopia, except where it could be taken as a personal name. English translations have generally followed the Septuagint in designating the land as Ethiopia and its inhabitants as Ethiopians. In some passages such as Genesis 2:13 and Isaiah 11:11, various English versions alternate between Cush and Ethiopia. See *Cush.*

The biblical Ethiopia should not be confused with the modern nation of the same name somewhat further to the southeast. In biblical times, Ethiopia was equivalent to Nubia, the region beyond the first cataract of the Nile south, or upstream, of Egypt. This region, with an abundance of natural resources, was known to the Egyptians as Cush and was occupied by them during periods of Egyptian strength. During the New Kingdom (1550–1070 B.C.), Ethiopia was totally incorporated into the Egyptian Empire and ruled through

an official called the "viceroy of Cush."

When Egyptian power waned, Nubia became independent under a line of rulers who imitated Egyptian culture. When Egypt fell into a period of chaos about 725 B.C., Nubian kings extended their influence northward. In 715 B.C., they succeeded in establishing control over all of Egypt and ruled as pharaohs of the Twenty-fifth Dynasty. The most influential of these Ethiopian pharaohs was Taharqa (biblical Tirhakah), who rendered aid to Hezekiah of Judah during the Assyrian invasion of Sennacherib in 701 B.C. (2 Kings 19:9; Isa. 37:9).

The Assyrian Empire invaded Egypt in 671 B.C., driving the Ethiopian pharaohs southward and eventually sacking the Egyptian capital Thebes (biblical No-Amon; Nah. 3:8) in 664 B.C. Thereafter, the realm of Ethiopian kings was confined to Nubia, which they ruled from Napata. Ethiopia continued to be an important political force and center of trade (Isa. 45:14). Some time after 300 B.C., Napata was abandoned and the capital moved further south to Meroe, where the kingdom continued for another six hundred years. Excavations in Nubia have revealed numerous pyramid tombs at Napata and Meroe as well as several temples to the Egyptian god Amun.

In New Testament times, several queens of the kingdom of Meroe bore the title Candace. The Ethiopian eunuch to whom Philip explained the gospel was a minister of "the Candace, queen of the Ethiopians" (Acts 8:27 RSV). Candace should be understood as a title rather than a personal name. *Daniel C. Browning, Jr.*

ETHIOPIAN EUNUCH (Ē thī ō′ pī ăn) An unnamed person who was returning to his homeland after having been to Jerusalem to worship (Acts 8:27). He was an official in the court of the queen of Ethiopia. As he traveled, he met Philip the evangelist. Philip had come to the desert area in response to God's call. Philip declared the gospel to the eunuch, and the eunuch received Christian baptism at Philip's hands. His conversion illustrates the Christian faith transcending national boundaries and embracing one whose physical mutilation would have excluded him from full participation in Judaism.

ETHKAZIN (Ĕth kā′ zĭn) Place name perhaps meaning, "time of the chieftain." Town in tribal territory of Zebulun (Josh. 19:13). Its location is not known.

ETHNAN (Ĕth′ năn) Personal name meaning, "gift." Member of tribe of Judah (1 Chron. 4:7).

ETHNI (Ĕth′ nī) Personal name meaning, "I will give." Levite, ancestor of Asaph (1 Chron. 6:41).

EUBULUS (Ēu bū′ lŭs) Personal name meaning,

"good counsel." Companion of Paul who sent greetings to Timothy (2 Tim. 4:21).

EUNICE (Ēu′ nĭce) Personal name meaning, "victorious." The mother of Timothy (2 Tim. 1:5). Both she and her mother Lois were commended by Paul for their faith. She was a Jewish woman whose husband was a Gentile. No details are known about her conversion to Christianity. See *Timothy.*

EUNUCH A male deprived of the testes or external genitals. Such were excluded from serving as priests (Lev. 21:20) and from membership in the congregation of Israel (Deut. 23:1). Eunuchs were regarded as especially trustworthy in the Ancient Near East and thus were frequently employed in royal service. By extension, the Hebrew word translated eunuch could be used of any court official (At Gen. 37:36 and 39:1 the reference is to a married man). The Greek term translated eunuch is literally one in charge of a bed, a reference to the practice of using eunuchs as keepers of harems (Esth. 2:3,6,15). Part of Isaiah's vision of the messianic era was a picture of the eunuch no longer complaining of being "a dry tree," one without hope of descendants, because God would reward the faithful eunuch with a lasting monument and name in the Temple which would be far better than sons or daughters (Isa. 56:4–5). Ethiopian eunuch of Acts 8:27 was reading from Isaiah's scroll.

A "eunuch for the sake of the kingdom of heaven" (Matt. 19:12) is likely a metaphor for one choosing single life in order to be more useful in kingdom work. Compare 1 Cor. 7:32–34.

EUODIA A female leader in the church at Philippi whose disagreement with Syntyche concerned Paul (Phil. 4:2–3). The name Euodia means either prosperous journey or pleasant fragrance. Euodia and Syntyche were perhaps deacons or else hostesses of house churches that met in their respective homes. Paul commended these women as two who struggled by his side for the spread of the gospel in a way comparable to Clement and other church leaders.

EUODIAS (Ēu ō′ dĭ ås) Personal name meaning, "good journey." A member of the church at Philippi (Phil. 4:2). The correct form of the name is generally recognized to be Euodia rather than Euodias. She and another church member, Syntyche, were quarreling with one another, and Paul urged them to resolve their differences. See *Philippians.*

EUPHRATES AND TIGRIS RIVERS (Ēu phrā′ tēs and Tī′ grĭs) Two of the greatest rivers of Western Asia. They originate in the Armenian mountains and unite about ninety miles from the Persian Gulf to form what is now called the Shatt-al-Arab which flows into the gulf. In ancient times the Tigris flowed through its own mouth into the

Boats on the Euphrates River in modern Iraq (ancient Mesopotamia).

gulf. The Euphrates and Tigris were included among the four rivers of Paradise (Gen. 2:14).

The Euphrates was known as "the great river" (Gen. 15:18; Josh. 1:4) or "the river" (Num. 22:5) to the Hebrews. It formed the northern boundary of the land promised by Yahweh to Israel (Gen. 15:18; Deut. 1:7). The Euphrates is mentioned in the Book of Revelation as the place where angels were bound (9:14) and where the sixth vial was poured out (16:12).

A young Iraqi man gazing across the Euphrates River which flows through Iraq and into the Persian Gulf.

The Euphrates is the longest, largest, and most important river in Western Asia. Many significant cities were located on the Euphrates, Babylon being the most important. Others located on its banks were Mari and Carchemish, the latter being the site of a famous battle between Babylon and Egypt in 605 B.C. (Jer. 46:2).

The Tigris is not as prominent in the Bible as is the Euphrates, but it is the site of the major vision of the prophet Daniel (Dan. 10:4). Like the Euphrates, some significant cities were located on its banks. Nineveh, the ancient capital of the Assyrian Empire, was located on its east bank. Farther south was the site of Asshur, religious center and original capital of Assyria.

See *Babylon; Nineveh.*   *M. Stephen Davis*

EURAQUILO (Ēu rǎ′ quǐ lō) NAS transliteration of Greek name for northeast wind in Acts 27:14. See *Euroclydon.*

EUROCLYDON (Ēu rŏc′ lў dŏn) Noun meaning, "southeast wind raising mighty waves." KJV reading of traditional Greek text in Acts 27:14, but most modern translations follow other Greek texts which read *Eurakulon,* the northeast wind. Whichever reading is correct, the wind created a mighty storm which shipwrecked the ship taking Paul to Rome.

EUTYCHUS (Ēu′ tў chǔs) Personal name meaning, "good fortune." A young man who listened to Paul the apostle preach in Troas (Acts 20:9–10). Overcome with sleep, Eutychus fell from a third

floor window sill and was picked up dead. Paul, however, embraced the youth, and Eutychus was restored to life.

EVANGELISM The active calling of people to respond to the message of grace and commit oneself to God in Jesus Christ. While many think of evangelism as a New Testament phenomena, profound concern for all people is also obvious in the Old Testament (1 Kings 8:41–45; Ps. 22:27–28; Isa. 2:2–4). God's care for the first couple after they had sinned, His plan to "bless" all people through the Israelite nation, and His continuing attempts through the prophets and through discipline to forge His people into a usable nation all speak of His concern.

While Israel's influence was primarily national and magnetic in nature, there were instances of individual and external witness (Dan. 3—6; 2 Kings 5:15–18; Jonah 3:1–10). Though Israel was largely a failure in carrying out her mission, the large number of God-fearers at the beginning of the Christian era show that her magnetic attraction and proselyting efforts were not entirely unfruitful.

It is, however, the New Testament which manifests the dynamic thrust of evangelism. While the word "evangelism" does not occur in the Bible, it is woven into the very fabric of Scripture.

Despite its obvious importance, a wide range of opinion seeks to define what it means and what it should include. Definitions range from the extremely narrow to the exceedingly broad.

Evangelism is derived from the Greek word *euaggélion,* meaning "gospel" or "good news." The verbal forms of *euaggelízesthai,* meaning "to bring" or "to announce good news" occur some fifty-five times (Acts 8:4, 25, 35; 11:20) and are normally translated with the appropriate form of the word "preach." Evangelism has to do with the proclamation of the message of good news.

In the light of the wide range of definitions and the continuing debate, it is well to consider two kinds of definitions. First, many insist on defining evangelism only in the strictest sense of the above New Testament words. It is preaching the gospel, communicating God's message of mercy to sinners. Such a definition places strict limits to arrive at a precise definition of evangelism. It refuses to speak in terms of recipients, results, or methods, laying all its emphasis on *the message.*

This type of definition is certainly correct, as far as it goes. It would represent the view of many evangelicals concerning evangelism. Many others, however, believe that such definitions are inadequate for the present day and that they are partly responsible for a truncated sort of evangelism too often practiced in the past.

Many would, therefore, prefer what might be described as a "holistic" definition, or one that takes into account the "good news of the kingdom." This might be stated: evangelism is the Spirit-led communication of the gospel of the kingdom in such a way or ways that the recipients have a valid opportunity to accept Jesus Christ as Lord and Savior and become responsible members of His church. Such a definition takes into account the essential work of the Holy Spirit, the various ways of conveying the good news, holistic concern for the persons involved, the need for actual communication and understanding of the message, and the necessity of productive church membership on the part of the convert.

Luke 8:2–56 shows how Jesus brought the good news. He not only preached; He demonstrated His power over the forces of nature in saving His fearful disciples. He exorcised a demon, healed a poor woman that had hemorrhaged for twelve years, and raised Jairus' daughter from the dead. Clearly he brought the good news by word and deed, and not by word only.

Paul, in similar fashion, described how he had been used to "win obedience from the Gentiles, by word and deed, by the power of signs and wonders, by the power of the Spirit of God so that . . . I have fully proclaimed the good news of Christ" (Rom. 15:18–19 NRSV).

Some warn that such definitions are dangerous, opening the door to an overemphasis on the social dimension of the gospel to the exclusion of the spoken message. Indeed they can be. A complete evangelism will include the verbalized gospel. Balance is a necessity, although different situations may sometimes call for more emphasis on one aspect or the other. The biblical mandate remains "to become all things to all men, that I may by all means save some" (1 Cor. 9:22 NAS).

G. William Schweer

EVE (Ēve) Personal name meaning, "life." The first woman created and thus original ancestor of all people (Gen. 3:20; compare 4:1–2,25). She also faced the serpent's temptation first (3:1; 2 Cor. 11:3; 1 Tim. 2:13–14). Her fall illustrates the ease with which all persons fall into sin (2 Cor. 11:3). See *Adam and Eve.*

EVERLASTING PUNISHMENT Protracted, continual and eternal judgment.

"Everlasting" immediately calls to mind end-of-time realities. "Punishment" introduces the ideas of wrongdoing and evil. Thus, to wrestle with the idea of "everlasting punishment" is to grapple with notions of time, justice, evil, and the end of time. The Old Testament seldom directly addresses the issue of "everlasting punishment." It emphasizes that God, His attributes, His word, His covenant, His dwelling place, and His possessions are everlasting (for example, Gen. 21:33; Deut. 33:27; Ps. 41:13; Isa. 33:27). "Punishment" in the Old Testament is normally executed within history (plagues, wars, famine, sickness,

exile). Though one can find expressions of individual guilt, punishment, and forgiveness in the Psalms, and though one can find the language of universal judgment in the prophets that unfaithful Israel and all the nations of the world will be historically punished—it is not until after the Old Testament that the notions of "eternal punishment" or "everlasting judgment" are fully developed (see 1 Enoch 104:5; Testament of Abraham 11:11; 4 Macc. 9:9; 10:15; 12:12; 13:15; 15:3). Still, the Old Testament builds a foundation with its glimpses, warning of judgment on God's enemies, judgment that can occasionally be described as everlasting (compare Isa. 33:14. Jer. 20:11; 23:40). Daniel 12:2 placed eternal punishment on an individual level.

Part of the early church's teaching (Heb. 6:2), the eternal fate of creation and human beings is bound up with gospel preaching and thus with the end-of-time events of Jesus' death, resurrection and promised return. The opposite of "eternal life," "everlasting punishment" is thought of as an "eternal fire," a "second death," or an "eternal destruction." The language paints a picture of endless suffering, loss, doom, and separation from the presence of God. Such end-of-time trauma befalls the evil, angelic powers which oppose God (Matt. 25:41; Jude 6; Rev. 19:3) and those human beings who willfully continue in "sin"—a decision which demonstrates solidarity with the evil powers (Matt. 25:46; Mark 3:29; Jude 13; Rev. 14:11). The remarkable New Testament teaching is that "everlasting punishment" in some ways has already begun in the revelation of the gospel. The gospel is a present, historical revelation of end-of-time righteousness and wrath (Rom. 1:16–17). To some, the gospel brings eternal life—for others, eternal death (2 Cor. 2:15–16). This eternal judgment which begins with the preaching of the Gospel will be culminated and concluded at the end of time. At the time of Jesus' mighty, majestic, and powerful appearance, all evil will be destroyed; all humans who continued in opposition to God will receive their eternal sentencing (2 Thess. 1:9). *Carey C. Newman*

EVI (Ē′ vī) Personal name of uncertain meaning, perhaps "desire." King of Midian killed in battle by Israelites during wilderness wanderings (Num. 31:8). He apparently ruled as a vassal of Sihon (Josh. 13:21).

EVIL That which is opposed to God and His purposes or that which, defined from human perspectives, is harmful and non-productive.
The Problem of Evil Evil is a major theoretical and practical problem for a Christian. Evil is of two types. First, there is natural evil. There are destructive forces in nature, ranging from earthquakes and tidal waves to cancer. Second, there is moral evil which has its source in the choice and

action of humans. This type of evil includes war, crime, cruelty, and slavery.

If God is all-powerful and good, as the Bible affirms, why does He allow evil?

Natural Evil Concerning natural evil, several emphases should be noted. First, moral evil accounts for much of natural evil. In Genesis, evil and suffering appeared only after the Fall (Gen. 3:16–19). By contrast, the original creation is very good (Gen. 1:31). The new heavens and and new earth will have no more suffering (Rev. 21:4). This means that evil and suffering are not eternally inevitable. Rather they are bound up with the actions of sinful humans. Physical suffering and pain and finally death have been introduced as a consequence of the Fall (Gen. 3:16–19).

Second, God disciplines His people collectively and individually, even through natural evil and pain, to bring them closer to His purposes (Prov. 3:11–12; Jer. 18:1–10). This emphasis is also found in the New Testament (Heb. 2:10; 5:8–9; 12:5–11).

Third, personal life cannot develop except in a stable environment. God limited Himself by the establishment of regularity and law. This regularity of nature is an important factor in developing human personality. The earthquake, volcano, and storm, which cause human suffering, all belong to nature's regularity. Some so-called natural evil, therefore, can be attributed to the necessary operation of natural uniformities.

Fourth, natural evils may be used for judgment upon sin. It is deeply ingrained in the Bible that physical evils have been used by God for the punishment of individual and national wickedness. Noah's flood, the destruction of Sodom and Gomorrah, and the fall of Jerusalem are examples. This does not mean that all physical evils are the punishment of physical sins.

Moral Evil There are also some biblical teachings which help us to understand moral evil from the Christian perspective.

First, God limited Himself in giving people and angels freedom. To be truly human, a person must have the power of choice.

Second, humans used freedom in such a way as to bring in evil. The Bible tells us that with the Fall, humanity's first sin, a radical change took place in the universe. Death came upon mankind (Gen. 2:17; 3:2–3, 19). God pronounced a curse upon mankind which is represented by certain specifics: anguish in childbearing (3:16), male domination over the wife (v. 16), toilsome labor (v. 17), and thorns and thistles (v. 18). These are probably only a sample of the actual effects upon the creation. Paul in Romans 8:22 said that the whole creation has been affected by human sin and is now in bondage to decay.

Third, back of human revolt stood Satan. In Genesis 3 we read that the serpent tempted Eve. Thus, an evil force was present within the cre-

ation. It was Satan's appeal which stirred within Adam and Eve the desire which led them to sin. Compare Revelation 12:9.

It is clear, then, that God did not create evil and sin. He merely provided the options necessary for human freedom. People sinned, and before that, the fallen angels, not God.

Fourth, even though evil is because of human revolt and failure, God continues to be active in redeeming people from their self-imposed evil.

Fifth, God deals with evil through judgment and wrath. This judgment can be seen in the Old Testament (Deut. 28:20,21; Isa. 3:11). The wrath of God is not divine vindictiveness, but is dynamic, persistent opposition to sin (Rom. 1:18). Thus, a principle of judgment upon, and annulment of, evil can be discerned at work in history and even in individual lives.

Sixth, God deals with evil through the incarnation, the cross, and the resurrection. The Bible teaches that God Himself in Jesus Christ became the victim of evil so that there might be victory over evil. It is also indicated in such passages as Colossians 1:24; Philippians 3:10; and 2 Corinthians 12:7 that the Christian can bear suffering for others and assist in God's redemptive purpose.

After all the solutions are considered, we still realize that the problem of evil is not completely solved on an intellectual level from our limited human perspective. However, on the practical and experiential level we can say with the apostle Paul that "in all these things we are more than conquerors through him that loved us" (Rom. 8:37).

John P. Newport

EVIL-MERODACH (Ē′ vĭl-mē rō′ dăch) Babylonian royal name meaning, "worshiper of Marduk." Babylonian king (562–560 B.C.) who treated Jehoiachin, king of Judah, with kindness (2 Kings 25:27). The Babylonian form of the name is Amel-Marduk. He was the son of Nebuchadrezzar. See *Babylon.*

EXACTOR The KJV term for a taskmaster or a tax collector used only at Isaiah 60:17. Most often the KJV translated the underlying Hebrew word as oppressor (Job. 3:18; Isa. 3:12; 9:3; 14:2,4; Zech. 9:8; 10:4). Elsewhere the term is translated taskmaster, one who "exacts" labor (Ex. 3:7) or as raiser of taxes (Dan. 11:20). The image is of one who drives people like a mule driver drives his beast (Job 39:7). Isaiah's picture is striking. In the future God is preparing the only "rule" known will be peace, the only "oppression" known will be righteousness (60:17).

EXCOMMUNICATION The practice of temporarily or permanently excluding someone from the church as punishment for sin or apostasy.
Old Testament In the Old Testament, excommunication came as a curse from God as punishment

for sin (Deut. 27:26; 28:15; Ps. 119:21; Mal. 2:2–9; 4:6). The Jewish community assumed authority to curse on God's behalf (Num. 23:8; Isa. 66:5). Old Testament terms for excommunication include: *Karath,* to be excluded or cut off (Ex. 12:15, 19; Lev. 17:4, 9); *cherem,* banish, devote, or put to destruction (Ex. 22:19; Lev. 27:28–29; Josh. 6:17); and *qelalah,* desolation or thing of horror (2 Kings 22:19; Jer. 25:18). The covenant community protected itself from curse and temptation by distancing covenant-breakers from the community even to the point of executing them. **New Testament** Expulsion from the synagogue was one form of New Testament excommunication. Christians were frequently subject to expulsion, which was punishment for blasphemy or for straying from the tradition of Moses (Luke 6:22; John 9:22; 12:42; 16:2). Many early Christians thus endured excommunication from the worship place of their fathers to be Christians. The apostles practiced excommunication based on the binding and loosing authority Jesus gave to them (John 20:23; Matt. 18:18). See *Binding and Loosing.* They excommunicated church members for heresy (Gal. 1:8) for gross, deliberate sin (1 Cor. 5; 2 John 7) and perhaps for falling away from church belief and practice (Heb. 6:4–8). The purpose was to purify the church and to encourage offenders to repent (1 Cor. 5:5–6; 2 Cor. 2:6–10; 2 Thess. 3:15). Punishment ranged in scope from limited ostracism to permanent exclusion and may even have included some form of physical punishment if the church continued synagogue practice (Luke 4:28–30; John 8:2–11; Acts 5:1–5; 7:58). New Testament terms for excommunication include: being delivered to Satan (1 Cor. 5:5; 1 Tim. 1:20); anathema or cursed and cut off from God (Rom. 9:3; 1 Cor. 16:22; Gal. 1:8). The New Testament churches apparently used excommunication as a means of redemptive discipline. See *Apostasy.*

In Church History During the Middle Ages, when church and state became intertwined, excommunication was often used as a political tool. In 1054, the Catholic church was divided into east and west. Each claimed primacy as the true church. They "resolved" the issue by excommunicating each other.

Contemporary In its broadest sense, excommunication now means denial of sacraments, congregational worship, or social contact of any kind. Excommunication is practiced in this manner by both Protestant and Catholic churches. However, the term itself is used mainly in the Catholic church and usually indicates the permanent ban. Lesser punishments are called censures.

Donna R. Ridge

EXECRATION The act of cursing; an object of cursing. The term appears in the KJV twice (Jer. 42:18,44:12), both times in reference to the fate of the remnant who disobeyed God's word and sought safety in Egypt. The text may be understood in at least two ways. First, their name would become an object of cursing (NIV), that is, others would curse the remnant. Alternately, their name might be used as a curse (TEV) in the form "May you be like the remnant whom God destroyed." See *Blessing and Cursing.*

EXECUTIONER One who puts another to death, especially as a legal penalty. The KJV uses the term only once (Mark 6:27 for the one beheading John the Baptist). Some modern translations prefer a more generic term such as "soldier of the guard" (NRSV, REB) or simply "guard" (TEV). The Old Testament law does not know the role of the representative executioner who acts on behalf of the society. Where "official" executioners are mentioned, they are portrayed as the agents of despotic rulers (Dan. 2:14,24; Mark 6:27). The execution of Jesus is the chief example of such an abuse of power. See *Capital Punishment.*

EXHORTATION Argument (Acts 2:40) or advice intended to incite hearers to action. The ability to exhort or encourage to action is a spiritual gift (Rom. 12:8) sometimes associated with prophets/preachers (Acts 15:32; 1 Cor. 14:3). Elsewhere mutual exhortation is the responsibility of all Christians (Rom. 1:12; 1 Thess. 5:11,14; Heb. 3:13, 10:24–25). The Hebrew Scriptures provided New Testament preachers with a source of exhortation (Rom. 15:14; Heb. 12:5–6). The synagogue sermon was described as a "word of exhortation" (Acts 13:15). As such it called for applying the truths of the scriptural text to life. Indeed, exhortation is the goal of orderly worship (1 Cor. 14:31). Letters of exhortation were common in the ancient world. Messengers often supplied additional encouragement to supplement the written message (2 Sam. 11:25; Eph. 6:22; Col. 4:8). Two New Testament documents describe themselves as exhortations (1 Pet. 5:12; Heb. 13:22). The effect of the letter of the Apostolic Council was similarly described as exhortation (Acts 15:21). Though it does not designate itself as such, the Epistle of James is an exhortation.

EXILE (Ex' īle) The events in which the northern tribes of Israel were taken into captivity by the Assyrians and the events in which the southern tribes of Judah were taken into captivity by the Babylonians. Sometimes the terms "captivity," and "carried into captivity" refer to the exiles of Israel and Judah.

In Old Testament times the Assyrians and Babylonians introduced the practice of deporting captives into foreign lands. Deportation was generally considered the harsher measure only when other means had failed. Rather than impose deportation,

Assyria demanded tribute from nations it threatened to capture. As early as 842 B.C., Jehu, king of Israel, was paying tribute to Shalmaneser, king of Assyria. Not until the reign of Tiglath-pileser (745–727 B.C.) did the Assyrians began deporting people from the various tribes of Israel.

In 734 B.C., Tiglath-pileser captured the cities of Naphtali (2 Kings 15:29) and carried away as captives the inhabitants of the tribes of Naphtali, Reuben, Gad, and the half-tribe of Manasseh (1 Chron. 5:26). In 732, Tiglath-pileser took control of Damascus, the capital city of Syria. At that time he appointed Israel (the Northern Kingdom) her last king—Hoshea (732–723 B.C.). Hoshea rebelled about 724 B.C. and was taken captive by the Assyrians (2 Kings 17:1–6).

Samaria, the capital city of Israel, held out until early 721 B.C. Shalmaneser V (727–722 B.C.) laid seige to the city. The eventual fall of Samaria occurred at the hands of Sargon II (722–705 B.C.). These events marked the end of the ten northern tribes (2 Kings 17:18).

The Assyrians exiled the Israelites into Halah, Gozan, and Media (2 Kings 17:6; 18:11; Obad. 20). The Assyrians brought into Samaria people from Babylon, Cuthah, Ava, Hamath, and Sepharvaim (2 Kings 17:24; Ezra 4:10). Sargon II recorded that 27,290 Israelites were deported.

The prophets Hosea and Amos had prophesied the fall of Israel. These two prophets proclaimed that Israel's fall was due to moral and spiritual degeneration rather than to the superior military might of the Assyrian nation. Assyria was only the "rod of mine anger"' (Isa. 10:5).

History of the Exile of Judah More than a hundred years before the Babylon Exile, Isaiah, the prophet, had predicted Judah's fall (Isa. 6:11, 12; 8:14; 10:11). In addition, the prophets Micah, Zephaniah, Jeremiah, Habakkuk, and Ezekiel agreed that Judah would fall.

There were three deportations of Jews to Babylon. The first occurred in 598 B.C. (2 Kings 24:12–16). The second deportation took place in 587 B.C. (2 Kings 25:8–21; Jer. 39:8–10; 40:7; 52:12–34). After the second deporation, Gedeliah was appointed governor of Judah by the Babylonians but was assassinated (2 Kings 24:25). A third deportation, a punishment for Gedaliah's assassination, occurred in 582 B.C. (Jer. 52:30).

Life in the Exile meant life in five different geographical areas: Israel, Judah, Assyria, Babylon, and Egypt. We possess little information about events in any of these areas between 587 B.C. and 538 B.C.

1. Israel Assyria took the educated, leading people from the Northern Kingdom and replaced them with populations from other countries they had conquered (2 Kings 17:24). They had to send some priests back to the area to teach the people the religious traditions of the God of the land (2 Kings 17:27–28). Such priests probably served a

population which contained poor Jewish farmers dominated by foreign leaders. When Babylon took over the area, they established a provincial capital in Samaria. Leaders there joined with other provincial leaders to stop Zerubbabel and his people from rebuilding the Temple (Ezra 4:1–24). Gradually, a mixed population emerged (Ezra 10). Still, a faithful remnant attempted to maintain worship of Yahweh near Shechem, producing eventually the Samaritan community. See *Samaritans.*

2. Assyria Exiles from the Northern Kingdom were scattered through the Assyrian holdings (2 Kings 17:6). Apparently, their small communities, isolated from other Jews, did not allow them to maintain much national identity. We do not know what happened to these poeple, thus the popular title—the lost tribes of Israel. Some may have eventually returned to their original homeland. Others may have established the basis of Jewish communities which appear in later historical records.

3. Judah The Babylonians did not completely demolish Judah. They left farmers, in particular, to care for the land (Jer. 52:16). Some citizens who had fled the country. before the Babylonian invasion returned to the land after Jerusalem was destroyed (Jer. 40:12). The Babylonians set up a government which may or may not have been dependent on the provincial government in Samaria. Jews loyal to the Davidic tradition assassinated Gedaliah, the governor (2 Kings 25:25). Then many of the people fled to Egypt (2 Kings 25:26; Jer. 43). People remaining in the land continued to worship in the Temple ruins and seek God's word of hope (Lamentations). Many were probably not overjoyed to see Jews return from Babylon claiming land and leadership.

4. Babylon The center of Jewish life shifted to Babylon under such leaders as Ezekiel. Babylon even recognized the royal family of Judah as seen in 2 Kings 25:27 and in recovered Babylonian records. Exiled Jews based their calendar on the exile of King Jehoichin in 597 (Ezek. 1:2; 33:21; 40:1). Jehoiachin's grandson, Zerubbabel, led the first exiles back from Babylon in 538 (Ezra 2:2; Hag. 1:1). Most of the exiles in Babylon probably followed normal Near Eastern practice and became farmers on land owned by the government. Babylonian documents show that eventually some Jews became successful merchants in Babylon. Apparently religious leaders like Ezekiel were able to lead religious meetings (Ezek. 8:1; compare Ezra 8:15–23). Correspondence continued between those in Judah and those in Exile (Jer. 29), and Jewish elders gave leadership to the exiles (Jer. 29:1; Ezek. 8:1; 14:1; 20:1). First Chronicles 1—9, Ezra, and Nehemiah show that genealogies and family records became very important points of identity for the exiles. People were economically self-sufficient, some even owning slaves (Ezra 2:65) and having resources to fund the return to Jerusalem (Ezra 1:6; 2:69).

Still, many longed for Jerusalem and would not sing the Lord's song in Babylon (Ps. 137). They joined prophets like Ezekiel in looking for a rebuilt Temple and a restored Jewish people. They laughed at Babylonian gods as sticks of wood left over from the fire (Isa. 44:9–17; 45:9–10; 46:1–2,6–7; Jer. 1:16; Ezek. 20:29–32). A Babylonian Jewish community was thus established and would exercise strong influence long after Cyrus of Persia permitted Jews to return to Judah. These Jews established their own worship, collected Scriptures, and began interpreting them in the Aramaic paraphrase and explanations which eventually became the Babylonian Talmud, but continued to support Jews in Jerusalem.

5. *Egypt* Jews fled Jerusalem for Egypt (2 Kings 25:26) despite God's directions not to (Jer. 42:13—44:30). Many Jews apparently became part of the Egyptian army stationed in northern border fortresses to protect against Babylonian invasion. As such, they may have joined Jews who had come to Egypt earlier. Archaeologists have discovered inscriptions at Elephantine in southern Egypt showing a large Jewish army contingent there also. They apparently built a temple there and worshiped Yahweh along with other gods. These military communities eventually disappeared, but Jewish influence in Egypt remained. Finally, a large community in Alexandria established itself and produced the Septuagint, the earliest translation of the Hebrew Bible into Greek.

The Edict of Cyrus in 538 B.C. (2 Chron. 36:22–23; Ezra 1:1–4) released the Jews in Babylon to return to their homeland. Though conditions in the homeland were dismal, many Jews did return. The preaching of Haggai and Zechariah (520–519 B.C.) urged these returning captives to rebuild their Temple in Jerusalem. The Temple was completed in 515 B.C., the date which traditionally marks the end of the Babylonian Exile.

Gary Hardin

EXODUS Israel's escape from slavery in Egypt and journey towards the Promised Land under Moses. The most important event in the Old Testament historically and theologically is Israel's Exodus from Egypt. More than a hundred times in all parts of the Old Testament except the Wisdom Literature, Yahweh is proclaimed as "the one who brought you up from the land of Egypt, out of the house of bondage." Israel remembered the Exodus as God's mighty redemptive act. She celebrated it in her creeds (Deut. 26:5–9; 1 Sam. 12:6–8). She sang of it in worship (Ps. 78; 105; 106; 114; 135; 136). The prophets constantly reminded Israel that election and covenant were closely related to the Exodus (Isa. 11:16; Jer. 2:6; 7:22–25; Ezek. 20:6,10; Hos. 2:15; 11:1; Amos 2:10; 3:1; Mic. 6:4; Hag. 2:5). (The English word "Exodus" does not occur in the King James Version). The Exodus in the Old Testament was to Israel what the death and resurrection of Christ was to Christians in the New Testament. Just as Israel commemorated her deliverance from Egyptian bondage in the feast of Passover, Christians celebrate their redemption from sin in the observance of the Lord's Supper (Luke 22:1–20; 1 Cor. 11:23–26).

Historicity The only explicit account of the Exodus we have is the biblical account (Ex. 1—15). No extra-biblical witnesses directly speak of the sojourn of Israel's ancestors in the land of the Nile. However, Egyptian sources do confirm the general situation that we find in the end of Genesis and the beginning of the Book of Exodus. There are many reports in Egyptian sources of nomadic people called *Habiru* coming into Egypt from the east fleeing from famine. Extra-biblical evidence from Egypt indicates that Egypt used slave labor in building projects (Ex. 1:11). At one time the land in Egypt was owned by many landholders; but after the reign of the Hyksos kings the Pharaoh owned most of the land, and the people were serfs of the king (Gen. 47:20). Old Testament scholars accept the essential historicity of the Exodus.

The Nature of the Event Some scholars see the Exodus as the miraculous deliverance of the people of God from the grip of Pharaoh's army at the Red Sea. Others see it as an escape across a sprawling wilderness and sweltering desert of a small mixed band of border slaves. Some argue that the military language in the account indicates that the event was a military skirmish. Such language may be the language of holy war.

The Bible stresses that the Exodus was the work of God. God brought the plagues on Egypt (Ex. 7:1–5). The miracle at the sea was never treated merely as a natural event or as Israel's victory alone. In the earliest recorded response to the event Miriam sang, "Sing to the Lord, for he has triumphed gloriously; the horse and his rider he has thrown into the sea" (Ex. 15:21 RSV).

Elements of the wonderful and the ordinary contributed to the greatest Old Testament events. The natural and supernatural combined to produce God's deliverance. The Exodus was both miraculous and historical. An air of mystery surrounds this event as all miraculous events. We are not told when the Exodus occurred. We do not know precisely where it happened since the Hebrew term may have meant the Red Sea as we know it, one of its tributaries, or a "sea of reeds" whose location is unknown. We do not know who or how many may have been involved. The record makes it clear that God delivered Israel from bondage because of His covenant with the patriarchs and because He desired to redeem His people (Ex. 6:2–8).

The Date of the Exodus The Bible does not give an incontrovertible date for the Exodus. First

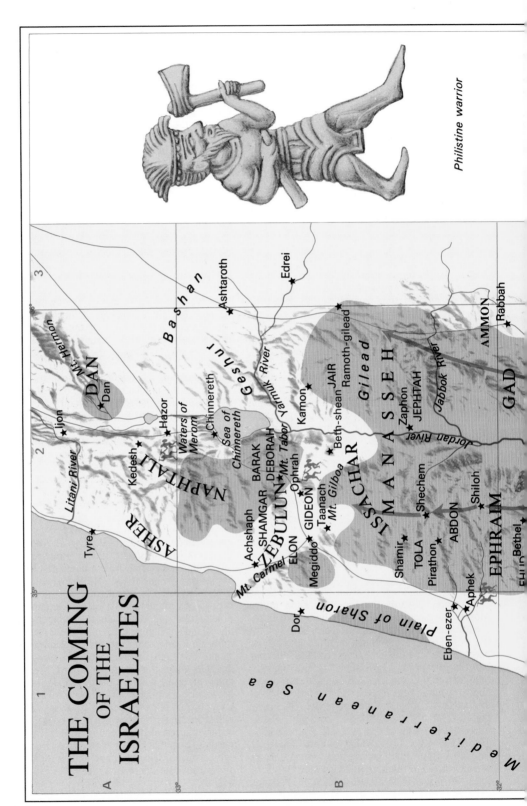

THE COMING
OF THE
ISRAELITES

Philistine warrior

Mediterranean Sea

Plain of Sharon

Tyre

Dor

Megiddo

Mt. Carmel

Achshaph

Kedesh

Litani River

Ijon

Mt. Hermon

DAN

Dan

Hazor

Waters of Merom

Chinnereth

Sea of Chinnereth

NAPHTALI

ASHER

SHAMGAR

BARAK DEBORAH

ZEBULUN

ELON

GIDEON

Ophrah

Mt. Tabor

Taanach

Mt. Gilboa

Bashan

Geshur

Yarmuk River

Kamon

Beth-shean

JAIR

Ramoth-gilead

Gilead

MANASSEH

Zaphon

JEPHTAH

Jabbok River

Jordan River

Shechem

Shiloh

ISSACHAR

Shamir

TOLA

Pirathon

ABDON

EPHRAIM

Ehud Bethel

Aphek

Eben-ezer

GAD

AMMON

Rabbah

Ashtaroth

Edrei

© carta

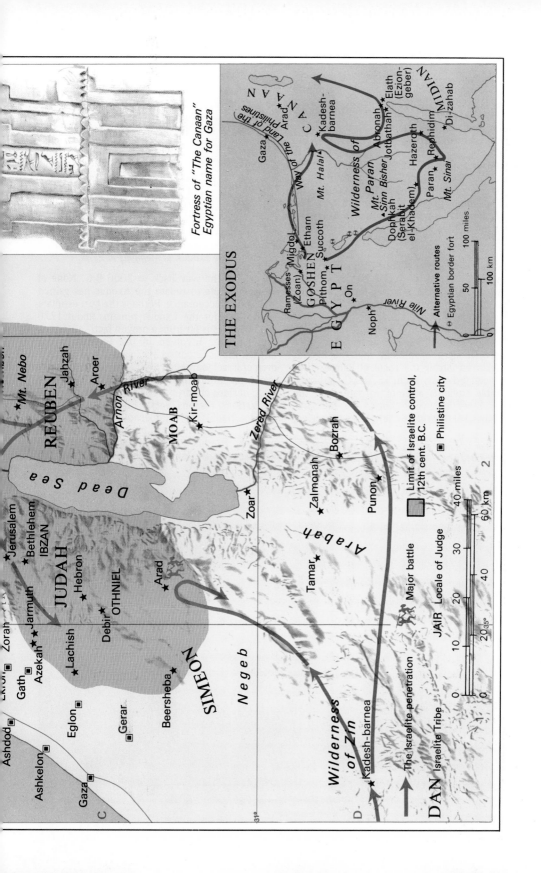

Fortress of "The Canaan"
Egyptian name for Gaza

THE EXODUS

CANAAN

Way of the Land of the Philistines

Gaza
Arad
Kadesh-barnea

Ramesses (Zoan)
Migdol
Etham
GOSHEN
Pithom
Succoth
On
Noph

E G Y P T

Mt. Halal

Wilderness of Paran

Mt. Sinai Bisher Jotbathah
Dophkah (Serabit el-Khadem)
Paran Rephidim
Hazeroth
Abronah
Elath (Ezion-geber)

M I D I A N

Di-zahab

Nile River

Alternative routes
⊕ Egyptian border fort

0   50   100 km
0   100 miles

Mt. Nebo
REUBEN
Jahzah
Aroer

Arnon River

Dead Sea

MOAB
Kir-moab

Zered River

Zoar

Jerusalem
Bethlehem
IBZAN
JUDAH
Hebron
Arad
OTHNIEL
Debir

Gath
Azekah
Jarmuth
Lachish
Zorah

Ashdod
Ashkelon
Gaza
Eglon
Gerar
Beersheba

SIMEON

Negeb

Zalmonah
Bozrah

Arabah

Punon

Tamar

Wilderness of Zin

Kadesh-barnea

The Israelite penetration

DAN Israelite Tribe
JAIR Locale of Judge

⚔ Major battle

Limit of Israelite control, 12th cent. B.C.

■ Philistine city

0   10   20   30   40 miles
0   20   40   60 km
35°

C

D

Kings 6:1 says, "In the four hundred and eightieth year after the children of Israel were come out of the land of Egypt, in the fourth year of Solomon's reign over Israel, in the month of Zif, which is the second month, that he began to build the house of the Lord." But this verse refers primarily to the beginning of the building of Solomon's Temple and only in a general way to the time of the Exodus. We do not know the precise dates of Solomon's reign. If we use 961 B.C. as the beginning of Solomon's reign, his fourth year would be 957 B.C. If we take the 480 years of 1 Kings 6:1 literally, the Exodus would be dated in 1437 B.C. Exodus 1:11 says, however, that the Israelites in Egypt built the store cities of Pithom and Raamses for Pharaoh. Evidently the name Raamses was not used in Egypt before 1300 B.C. If one of the store cities was named for a king by that name, the Exodus could not have happened before 1300 B.C. Thus some scholars believe the Exodus must have taken place after 1300 B.C.

It has been the opinion of most scholars since the rise of modern Egyptology that the Exodus likely occurred during the reign of Ramses II in the nineteenth dynasty about 1270 B.C., although many Bible students attempt to date it in the earlier eighteenth dynasty about 1447 B.C. Several variations of these dates have been suggested,

The monumental statue of Ramses II, probably the pharaoh of the Exodus, at Memphis in Egypt.

ranging all the way back to 2000 B.C. None of these attempts to redate the Exodus has gained widespread acceptance. Perhaps the best estimate of the date for the Exodus remains about 1270 B.C., but this is far from a proven fact.

The Number Involved in the Exodus In our English Bibles Exodus 12:37 says, "And the children of Israel journeyed from Rameses to Succoth, about six hundred thousand on foot, that were men, besides children." For a very long time and for various reasons some Bible scholars have asked: Should the number 600,000 be understood literally? It seems to be an excessively large number. Exodus 23:29–30 and Deuteronomy 7:22 suggest the number was so small that the

Lake Timsah, possibly the place where the Hebrews crossed the Red Sea.

The lower half of a broken monumental statue of Ramses II at Tanis, the possible start of the Exodus.

people would be endangered by wild beasts. Many scholars believe the Hebrew word *'eleph,* usually translated "thousand," can also be translated "clan" or "fighting unit." Perhaps this is the meaning in Exodus 12:17. Assuming this, conservative scholars have estimated the number at between 6,000 and 72,000. We may not know the exact date, route, or number of people in the Exodus. But the significant thing is we know and believe that such an event happened and that we interpret it as a saving act of God.

The Exodus was the work of God. It was also a historical event involving a superpower nation and an oppressed people. God acted redemptively in power, freedom, and love. When the kingdom of God did not come, the later prophets began to look for a second Exodus. That expectation was fulfilled spiritually in Christ's redemptive act.

Ralph L. Smith

EXODUS, BOOK OF The central book of the Old Testament, reporting God's basic saving act for Israel in the Exodus from Egypt and His making of His covenant with the nation destined to be His kingdom of priests.
Literary Setting The Book of Exodus is the second book of the Old Testament and of the Pentateuch. See *Pentateuch* for discussion of date and authorship. Exodus builds on the narrative of creation, human sin, divine punishment and renewal, the call of Abraham to bless the world, and the struggles of Isaac and then Jacob to carry out God's call. This ends with Joseph taking his father's family into Egypt to avoid the harsh sufferings of famine. Exodus takes up the story of the children of Jacob in Egypt, now under a new pharaoh and seen as feared foreigners instead of welcomed deliverers from famine. Israel thus became slave laborers in Egypt (ch. 1). God delivered the baby Moses from danger, and he grew up in pharaoh's court as son of pharaoh's daughter. Still he cared for the Israelites. Trying to protect one of his own people, he killed an Egyptian. Thus Moses had to flee to the wilderness of Midian, where he helped seven endangered shepherd girls. He settled among them and married one of the girls. There, God called him at the burning bush of Mount Horeb/Sinai and sent him back to rescue Israel from Egypt (chs. 2—4). With his brother Aaron, he faced a stubborn pharaoh, who refused to release the Israelites. When pharaoh made life harder for Israel, the Israelites griped about Moses. God took this as opportunity to reveal Himself to Israel, to pharaoh, and to the Egyptians. God brought the plagues upon Egypt. Pharaoh stubbornly refused to let Israel go until his firstborn son and the eldest sons of all Egypt died in the final plague. This tenth plague became the setting for Israel's central religious celebration, that of Passover and Unleavened Bread in which Israel reenacted the Exodus from Egypt and rejoiced at God's supreme act of salvation for His people (chs. 5—13). As Israel fled Egypt, the pharaoh again resisted and led his army after them. The miracle of the Red Sea (or perhaps more literally, the Sea of Reeds) became the greatest moment in Israel's history, the moment God created a nation for Himself by delivering them from the strongest military power on earth as He led them through the divided waters of the sea and then flooded the sea again as the Egyptians tried to follow (ch. 14).

After celebrating the deliverance in song and dance (15:1—21), Israel followed God's leadership into the wilderness, but soon the difficult wilderness life proved too hard. The Israelites cried for the good old days of Egypt, even after God supplied their food and drink needs and after He defeated the Amalekites (15:22—17:15). Moses' father-in-law Jethro brought Moses' wife and children back to him in the wilderness and praised God for all that He had done for Moses and the people. Jethro also advised Moses how to organize a more efficient judicial system, relieving Moses of stress (ch. 18). Then Israel came to Sinai, where God called them to become His covenant people, a holy nation to carry out Abraham's mission of blessing the nations. God gave the Ten Commandments and other laws central to the covenant (chs. 19—23), and then confirmed the covenant in a mysterious ceremony (ch. 24). Moses went to the top of the mountain to receive the

E

remainder of God's instructions, especially instructions for building the sacred place of worship, the tabernacle (chs. 24–31). Impatient Israel got Aaron to build an object of worship they could see, so he made the golden calf. The people began worshiping. This angered God, who sent Moses back down to the people. Moses prayed for the people despite their sin, but then saw the people's sinful actions and threw the tablets with the law to the ground, breaking them. Moses again went up and prayed for the people. God punished them but did not destroy them as He had threatened. God showed His continued presence in the Tent of Meeting and in letting His glory pass by Moses (chs. 32–33). God then gave Moses the law on two new tablets of stone and renewed the covenant with the people, providing further basic laws for them. Such intense communication with God brought radiance to Moses' face (ch. 34). Moses then led Israel to celebrate the sabbath and to build the tabernacle (chs. 35—39). Moses set up the tabernacle and established worship in it. God blessed the action with His holy, glorious presence (ch. 40). This provided the sign for Israel's future journeys, following God's cloud and fire.

Theological Teaching In Exodus Israel learned the basic nature of God and His salvation. They also learned the nature of sin, the characteristics of God's leader, the components of worship, and the meaning of salvation. In Exodus Israel learned the identity of the people of God.

God is Ruler of the world, able to act for His people even on the home territory of the world's most powerful political and military force. God chooses to act for the people He elects. God knows the situation of His people even when another nation has forced them into slavery. God saved His people through calling out a leader to communicate God's will and to face their enemies. God empowered the leader at a time of the leader's personal weakness rather than at a time of strength. He worked in the forces of nature to show His unequalled power and to demonstrate His concern for His own people.

Salvation, power, and concern was not all God revealed of Himself. He also showed a holy nature in that special preparations were made to enter His presence. He revealed His great glory, so majestic even the leader could not view it. Most of all, He revealed His will to be present among His people and lead them through their daily activities.

In so doing, He showed the way He expected His people to live, a way of holiness, a way of priesthood among the nations. This way centered on life guided by the Ten Commandments. Such a life reflected the nature of God Himself, who could be identified as "The Lord God, merciful and gracious, longsuffering, and abundant in goodness and truth, Keeping mercy for thousands, forgiving iniquity and transgression and sin, and that will by no

means clear the guilty" (Ex. 34:6–7).

God expected His people to live the way of holiness, the way of the Ten Commandments. Failure to do so is sin. Sin centers particularly in giving another god credit for what God has done and in worshiping what human hands have made rather than the true God who allows no images of Himself. To avoid sin, God's people had to follow God's chosen leader, even when the path led through the wilderness and demanded a life-style lacking in some of the food and luxuries they had learned to take for granted. The leader followed God's will and not the people's. In so doing, the leader interceded with God for a sinful people, willing to give up his own place with God in exchange for the people's salvation. Only a leader who communed face to face with God could develop such an attitude. Thus Moses became the leader without parallel for Israel.

The leader's lasting role included the establishment of a worship place and worship practices. God's people gained their identity in worship. The leader showed them when, where, and how to worship.

The people offered worship because They had experienced God's salvation. For them salvation meant physical deliverance in military action against a powerful world enemy. It involved following God's instructions and waiting for God's miraculous help. Salvation set up a relationship between God and the people, a relationship based on God's initiative in delivering the people and on God's initiative in inviting the people into covenant relationship. See *Covenant.* This meant the people could trust God to lead them through their personal and national history. It also meant that God expected a trusting people to obey Him as He set out the way of life they should follow. Salvation was not just receiving God's salvation. It was following in faith the life-style God described for them.

Outline

I. God Saves His People (1:1—4:17).
    A. God's people face oppression in fear (1:1–22).
    B. God raises up a deliverer for His oppressed people (2:1—4:17).
II. God Sends His Leader on a Difficult Mission (4:18—7:2).
    A. God uses all means to accomplish His will against an ungodly ruler (4:18–26).
    B. God fulfills His angry promise to provide a helper for His leader (4:27–31).
    C. God's leader delivers God's message to pagan leaders (5:1–23).
    D. God promises deliverance to a deaf people (6:1–9).
    E. God reaffirms His insecure leaders (6:10—7:2).
III. God Reveals Himself in Punishing His Enemy (7:3—12:30).

A. God is sovereign over enemy powers (7:3–13).

B. Miracles do not bring belief (7:14–25).

C. Enemy powers seek compromise not conversion (8:1–15).

D. God's power convinces enemy religious leaders (8:16–19).

E. Political deceit cannot defeat God's purposes (8:20–32).

F. God's power is superior to pagan religious symbols (9:1–7).

G. God's power affects people as well as animals (9:8–12).

H. Terror and admission of sin are not adequate responses to the actions of the only God (9:13–35).

I. God's saving acts are to be taught to coming generations (10:1–20).

J. God's will must be followed completely (10:21–29).

K. God distinguishes between His people and His enemies when He punishes (11:1–10).

L. God judges other gods but preserves an obedient people (12:1–13).

M. God's people are to remember and celebrate His deliverance (12:14–28).

N. God punishes His proud, stubborn enemies (12:29–30).

IV. God Reveals Himself by Delivering His People from Bondage (12:31—15:21).

A. God delivers and blesses His people and those who join them (12:31–51).

B. God instructs His people to remember, celebrate, and teach His mighty salvation (13:1–16).

C. God leads and protects His obedient people (13:17–22).

D. God gains glory and evokes faith by saving His troubled people (14:1–31).

E. God's people praise Him for their deliverance (15:1–21).

V. God Provides for His Doubting, Complaining People (15:22—18:27).

A. God promises healing to an obedient people (15:22–27).

B. God reveals His glory and tests His people's faith while meeting their needs (16:1–36).

C. Doubting people test God's presence (17:1–7).

D. God delivers His people and permanently curses their enemy (17:8–16).

E. Foreign relatives testify to God's superiority over all gods (18:1–12).

F. God's people must have effective teaching and administrative leadership (18:13–27).

VI. God Covenants with His People (19:1—20:21).

A. God's covenant is based upon His act of deliverance and upon the people's obedience as a kingdom of priests (19:1–8).

B. God prepares His people for His coming down to make a covenant (19:9–15).

C. God's awesome presence confirms His covenant (19:16–25).

D. The Ten Commandments are God's covenant ground rules for life with Him (20:1–17).

E. Awestruck people need a human mediator with the holy God (20:18–21).

VII. God Gives Civil, Ceremonial, and Criminal Laws to Help His People (20:22—23:33).

A. Instructions for acceptable worship (20:22–26)

B. Treatment of Hebrew slaves (21:1–11)

C. Dealing with a person who injures or kills another person (21:12–32)

D. Justice for damage done to another's property (21:33—22:15)

E. Justice when a virgin is seduced (22:16–17)

F. Punishment for sorcery, bestiality, and idolatry (22:18–20)

G. Care for the stranger, widow, orphan, and poor (22:21–27)

H. Respect for God and human rulers, dedication of children, and being holy (22:28–31)

I. Practice honesty; do not hurt the righteous or innocent (23:1–9).

J. Keep the sabbatic year, the sabbath day, sacred occasions (23:10–19).

K. God will provide spiritual guidance (23:20–33).

VIII. God and His People Must Ratify the Covenant (24:1–18).

A. The people commit themselves to do God's will (24:1–11).

B. God ratifies the covenant with His holy presence (24:12–18).

IX. God Plans to Be Present with His People (25:1—31:17).

A. As their hearts move them, people are to give for God's worship place (25:1–7).

B. God will dwell among His peple in His place of holy worship (25:8—27:21).

C. God's minister mediates His holy presence for a holy people (28:1—29:37).

D. People respond to the holy Presence with sacrificial giving (29:38—30:38).

E. Craftsmen respond to the holy Presence by dedicating God-given skills (31:1–11).

F. People respond to the holy Presence with sabbath worship (31:12–17).

X. God Restores a Sinful People (31:18—34:35).

A. God provides guidelines for life in His presence (31:18).

B. An impatient people break the covenant by making and worshiping other gods (32:1–6).

C. God reacts against a disobedient people in wrath (32:7–10).

D. Intercessory prayer brings divine repentance (32:11–14).

E. Judgment comes to a disobedient people through God's chosen leaders (32:15–29).

F. A mediator's majestic intercession is not sufficient (32:30–35).

G. God withdraws His immediate presence from a sinful people (33:1–4).

H. Mourning and repentance, even by a disobedient people, catch God's attention (33:5–6).

I. Worship at God's chosen place is an essential element in restoring the covenant (33:7–11).

J. The unseeable presence of God reaffirms the covenant relationship (33:12–23).

K. God renews His covenant with His people (34:1–35).

XI. God Honors the Obedience of His People with His Holy Presence (35:1—40:38).

A. God gives His people specific requirements (35:1–19).

B. Obedient people provide resources and skills needed for God's work (35:20—36:7).

C. Obedient people use their resources to build God's dwelling place (36:8—39:43).

D. The leader of God's people prepares for worship (40:1–33).

E. God's presence fills the worship place continually for His obedient people (40:34–38). *Trent C. Butler*

EXORCISM The practice of expelling demons by means of some ritual act. Although the Hebrew Bible does make reference to demonic beings (Lev. 17:7; Deut. 32:17; Isa. 13:21; 34:14; 2 Chron. 11:15; Ps. 106:37 NRSV), there is no account of demons being cast out of a person or a place. The office of the exorcist, long known in the religious practice of Mesopotamia, is totally absent from the Hebrew Bible. The demons that are mentioned there are usually dreadful earthly beings, sometimes resembling goats or satyrs who live in dry regions. Twice a loan-word, *shĕdîm* (Akkadian: *shêdû*, "protecting spirit"), is used to describe the foreign gods (Deut. 32:17; Ps. 106:37) and is usually translated "demons" in English.

In the New Testament the demons were earthly powers or spirits allied with Satan. Jesus' power to exorcise is demonstration in the Synoptic Gospels

of His power over Satan (Matthew 15:21–28; Mark 1:23–38; 5:1–20; 7:24–30; 9:14–29). Exorcism is included in the list of wonders Jesus performed at Capernaum and in the Galilee (Mark 1:34,39). Mark 3:11 reports that Jesus had to silence the unclean spirits because they recognized Him and proclaimed Him Son of God.

Jesus gave His disciples authority over unclean spirits (Mark 3:14–15; 6:7) which they generally exercised with success (Mark 6:13), but not always (Mark 9:18). Mark 9:38–41 makes reference to someone who did exorcisms in the name of Jesus even though he was not a follower of Jesus. Jesus told the disciples not to forbid him. In another vein, Acts 19:13–16 tells of wandering Jewish exorcists in Ephesus who attempted to exorcise demons in the name of the Jesus preached by Paul but without success.

John says nothing of Jesus exorcising demons, but the issue of demons is not lacking in that Gospel, for His opponents often accused Jesus of being possessed (John 7:20; 8:48–49,52; 10:20). Similarly, in the Synoptics, the scribes accused Him of casting out demons by the power of the prince of demons (Mark 3:22).

The usual technique of exorcism, as shown by contemporary magical papyri, was to adjure the demon (by name, if possible) through the power of one or more gods to depart the one possessed. This was often accompanied by preparations of herbs and the imposition of amulets. Magical words of extended, repeated syllables were also part of almost all exorcistic formulas. By contrast, the exorcisms of Jesus in the Synoptics involved His command without reference to other divine beings (Mark 1:25; 9:25) and with only a single reference to anything like technique in saying about the boy the disciples could not exorcise that the demon involved could only be cast out by prayer (Mark 9:29). Something close to the usual technique of exorcism was demonstrated by the Gerasene demoniac who tried unsuccessfully to exorcise Jesus, calling Him by title and adjuring Him in the name of the Most High God to leave him alone (Mark 5:7). Jesus relied on His own unique power to demonstrate demons had no place or power in His Kingdom. See *Miracles; Magic; Healing; Demon.* *Fred L. Horton, Jr.*

EXPIATION, PROPITIATION (Ĕx pĭ ā´ tion; Prō pĭ tĭ ā´ tion) Terms used by Christian theologians in attempts to define and explain the meaning of Christ's death on the cross as it relates to God and to believers. Expiation emphasizes the removal of guilt through a payment of the penalty, while propitiation emphasizes the appeasement or averting of God's wrath and justice. Both words are related to reconciliation, since it is through Christ's death on the cross for our sins that we are reconciled to a God of holy love (Rom. 5:9–11;

2 Cor. 5:18–21; Col. 1:19–23).

Biblical Vocabulary The point of difference in interpretation for theologians has centered on the Greek word *hilasmos* in 1 John 2:2; 4:10. A look at various translations show the distinctions here: "propitiation" (KJV, NAS); "expiation" (RSV); "atoning sacrifice for our sins" (NIV, NRSV, compare REB); "means by which our sins are forgiven" (TEV). Related Greek words occur in Matthew 16:22; Luke 18:13; Romans 3:25; Hebrews 2:17; 8:12; 9:5. KJV uses various translations of these words: "be merciful," "make reconciliation," "*to be* a propitiation," "the mercy-seat," "be it far from thee," "I will be merciful."

In Greek writings *hilasmos* refers to soothing the anger of the gods. In the Septuagint, the earliest Greek translation of the Old Testament, *hilasmos* appears in Leviticus 25:9 in the expression, "day of atonement"; in Psalm 130:4 to confess that there is "forgiveness" with God; in Numbers 5:8 in the expression the "ram of the atonement"; and in Ezekiel 44:27 as a "sin-offering." Daniel 9:9 uses the plural form to speak of "forgivenesses" which are a character trait of God.

Some scholars interpret these Old Testament references to mean that God has acted as the subject to cover and forgive sins. He has removed the uncleanness or defilement of sin. Other scholars see God as the object receiving the offering for sin which then in some sense pacifies His anger and meets His holy need for justice. In the New Testament setting, this would mean that on the cross Jesus either dealt with the evil nature of human sin and covered it so that God forgives it, or it means that Jesus satisfied God's holy anger and justice so that forgiven sinners could freely enter the presence of the holy God. Some scholars would see both ideas present in the word *hilasmos,* so that God in grace initiated the sacrifice of Jesus to provide covering and forgiveness for human sin but that He also received the sacrifice which satisfied His anger and justice.

The background of the idea is the Old Testament sacrificial system. The whole system sought to procure God's favor through obediently following ways He commanded. God promised to show His mercy after His faithful people followed certain ritual requirements. These included the burnt offering (Lev. 1:3–17), the peace offering (3:1–17), the sin offering (4:1—5:13), and the guilt offering (5:15—6:6). None of these dealt with "defiant sins" (Num. 15:20–31), only with "sin through ignorance" (Lev. 4:2). The high point of the sacrificial cult was the annual day of atonement when the sins of the people were laid on a scapegoat by the high priest and the sin-laden animal was then driven into the wilderness to perish (Lev. 16:1–34).

In the Old Testament, the note of grace is clearly present. God did not simply wait for His people to bring before Him the appropriate sacrifices. He took the initiative in specifying which sacrifices would be needed. When Abraham showed willingness to sacrifice Isaac, God Himself supplied the adequate substitute offering (Gen. 22:1–19). The Old Testament repeats its promise that God remains gracious even in our sinning, that He stands ready to forgive even before we are ready to repent (Pss. 78:21–28; 89:28–34; Isa. 65:1–2; Jer. 31:1–3, 31–34; Hos. 6:1–2). God expects people both to repent of sin and to commit themselves to obey His covenant.

The New Testament shows how Jesus fulfilled the Old Testament system of sacrifices and thus replaced it with His own work on the cross. The Old Testament system could not purify the consciences of those who offered them (Heb. 8:7, 13; 10:1–4). In their stead, God provided a perfect Sacrifice, that of His own Son. This sacrifice is eternal, not provisional; it is sufficient to cover or expiate all human sin, not just specific sins (Heb. 7:26–28; 9:25–26). The sacrifice of Jesus Christ on Calvary restored the broken relationship between God and His people and did not need to be repeated. He made reconciliation available to all people in all times. Such reconciliation involves a change both in God's attitude toward us and in our attitude toward God. The cross of Calvary was God's eternal plan to deal with human sin so that John could describe Jesus as the "Lamb slain from the foundation of the world" (Rev. 13:8). God chose to forgive us before the sacrifice was enacted in history, but His forgiveness could not reach us until this sacrifice took place.

To understand the need for propitiation and for expiation, we have to remind ourselves that the God of the Bible is both holy and loving. His holiness means that sin cannot be condoned. His love signifies that the sinner can be accepted if the claims of divine holiness are recognized. The atoning sacrifice of Christ both satisfies the demands of His holy law and demonstrates His boundless love, the love that goes beyond the law. God was not waiting to be appeased (as in the pagan, Greek conception). Rather, God condescended to meet us on our level to remedy the situation. He provided the sacrificial offering that expiates human sin and makes reconciliation possible. Both Old and the New Testaments proclaim that only God's grace opens the door to salvation. All ritual requirements for sacrifice in the Old Testament are replaced by the sacrifice of the cross, which wipes away the record of our debts to God (Col. 2:14; Heb. 10:14–18). The only sacrifices now required of the Christian are those of praise and thanksgiving, which take the form of worship in spirit and in truth and the obedience of discipleship (Rom. 12:1; Heb. 13:15–16; 1 Pet. 2:5). God calls us to demonstrate our gratefulness for His self-sacrifice by leading lives of holiness,

E

lives that give the world a sign and witness of God's great love for us shown in Jesus Christ.

In conclusion, the doctrine of the atonement includes both the dimensions of propitiation—averting the wrath of God—and expiation—taking away or covering over human guilt. By the expiation of human guilt, the wrath of God is turned away, the holiness of God is satisfied. Yet it is God who in the person of His Son performs the sacrifice of expiation. It is God who in the person of His Son swallows up evil within Himself through vicarious identification with the sin of His people. A sacrifice was necessary to satisfy the demands of His law, but God Himself provided the Sacrifice out of His incomparable love. What human ritual offerings could not do, God has done once for all by giving up His Son for the sins of the whole human race.

See *Atonement; Blood; Christology; Salvation.*
Donald G. Bloesch

EYE The organ of sight. Literal uses. The eyes were especially valued organs. If a master stuck a slave, blinding him in an eye, the slave was to go free as compensation for the eye (Ex. 21:26). The Old Testament law of retribution limited vengeance of personal loss to "an eye for an eye" (Lev. 24:20). Jesus replaced this concept of justice with His requirement of love for enemies (Matt. 5:38). An eye defect disqualified one for priestly service (Lev. 21:20). An exceptionally cruel punishment was to gouge out the eyes of a enemy (Judg. 16:21; 2 Kings 25:7). This act was interpreted as bringing disgrace on the land of the blinded ones (1 Sam. 11:2). The description of Leah's eyes (Gen. 29:17) is of uncertain meaning. The KJV rendering tender can be understood either positively (lovely, NRSV) or negatively (weak, NAS).
Extended uses The Old Testament often speaks of the eye where we would speak of the person, reflecting the Hebrew concept of bodily parts as semi-independent entities. The eye can thus approve actions (Job 29:11). The eyes can be full of adultery (2 Peter 2:14) and can desire (Ps. 54:7) or lust (Num. 15:39; 1 John 2:16). The eyes despise (Esther 1:17), are dissatisfied (Prov. 27:20; Eccl. 4:8), and can dwell on past provocation (Job 17:2). Job even spoke of entering a covenant with his eyes as if they were a second party (31:1). Eyes can be evil, that is, greedy or stingy. Such an evil eye refuses to loan when the sabbatical year is near (Deut. 15:9) and begrudges a brother food (28:54). The evil eye of Matthew 6:23 is often interpreted as an unhealthy eye in contrast to the single (whole, healthy) eye of 6:22. The Matthean context of teaching on treasure in heaven (6:19) and serving mammon or riches (6:24) as well as the usage in Matthew 20:15 suggest that the familiar Old Testament idea of the evil eye as the stingy eye is in mind here also. The eyes can be generous to the poor

(Prov. 22:9). The eyes can scorn and mock (Prov. 30:17), spare an enemy (1 Sam. 24:10; Isa. 13:18), or wait for a time to sin (Job 24:15). The eyes can offend (Matt. 5:19), that is, cause someone to sin. Jesus' call to pluck out the offending eye is an exaggerated call to let nothing cause one to sin.
Expressions The "apple of the eye" is a description of the pupil. Proverbs 7:2 called for making God's law the apple of one's eye, that is, something of value to be guarded (kept) carefully. To "make any baldness between your eyes" (Deut. 14:1 KJV) means to shave one's forelocks (NRSV, REB). Bribes blind the eyes of judges causing them to ignore justice (Deut. 16:19; 1 Sam. 12:3). The difficult expression "covering the eyes" (Gen. 20:16 KJV), denotes either compensation for injury (REB), covering the offense (NIV), or else exoneration or some similar term (NRSV, NAS, TEV). In some way Sarah was vindicated; Abimelech and his company could see nothing to criticize in her behavior; and her marriage was saved.

The difficult expression, "daughter of the eye" (Lam. 2:18 NAS margin), rendered "apple of the eye" by the KJV is generally understood as a poetic equivalent for the eye. To see "eye to eye" (Isa. 52:8) is either to see in plain sight (NRSV) or to see with one's own eyes.

Eyes which have been enlightened or brightened (1 Sam. 14:27) are likely an image for being

Sunrise ("eyelids of the morning" in Job 3:9) over the Mediterranean coast of Israel.

refreshed (REB, TEV). Compare Psalm 13:3. Light of the eyes can parallel strength (Ps. 38:10; compare Prov. 15:30). The Lord's commands could enlighten the eyes (Ps. 19:8) in this sense of giving strength or in the sense of giving understanding.

To fasten one's eyes (Acts 11:6) is to look closely. Heavy eyes (Mark 14:40) are drowsy eyes. To have one's eyes opened (Gen. 3:5; 21:19) is to be made aware or to recognize. The image of "tearing out ones eyes" (Gal. 4:15) pictures willingness to do anything. Winking one's eyes (Ps. 35:19; Prov. 6:13; 10:10; compare 16:30) is associated with hate, treachery, and trouble-making.

God's eye(s) God's eye or eyes is a frequent picture of God's providential care. God guides with His eye (Ps. 32:8), that is, gives counsel while offering His watchcare. Deliverance from death and famine result from God's watchful eye (Ps. 33:18–19). The image of God's eye(s) ranging throughout the earth (2 Chron. 16:9; Prov. 15:3; Jer. 16:17) symbolizes God's knowledge of all human activity and His control over it. Apocalyptic pictures involving numerous eyes (Ezek. 1:18; 10:12; Rev. 4:6), likewise, reassure of God's awareness of His people's plight wherever they might be.

Other uses The Hebrew term for eye is used in a variety of expressions not related to sight or seeing. The word can be translated spring (Gen. 16:7; Num. 33:9). The term can refer to the (sur)face of the land (Ex. 10:5,15; Num. 22:5,11) or to facets (faces) of a stone (Zech. 3:9). The term is used for the sparkling of wine (Prov. 23:31) perhaps in reference to bubbles that resemble eyes. The word translated "color" in Numbers 11:17 is also a word for eye.   *Chris Church*

EYELIDS OF THE MORNING A phrase meaning "the glow of dawn" used to describe the eyes of Leviathan (Job 41:18). See *Leviathan.*

EYE PAINT See *Cosmetics.*

EZAR (Ē′ zăr) KJV spelling of Ezer in 1 Chronicles 1:38. See *Ezer.*

EZBAI (Ĕz′ bā ī) Personal name of unknown meaning. Father of one of David's military leaders (1 Chron. 11:37). The parallel list (1 Sam. 23:35) contains a word of similar appearance—"the Arbite." The Samuel reading may be the original with the Chronicles reading the result of early copying, but no certain decision can be made.

EZBON (Ĕz′ bŏn) Personal name perhaps meaning, "bare." *1.* Son of Gad and grandson of Jacob (Gen. 46:16). Numbers 26:16 has a similar sounding Hebrew name, "Ozni." The Samaritan Pentateuch has a longer Hebrew name of similar sound, so that the precise spelling and pronunciation of

the name are not known. Whatever the name, he was one of the Hebrews who entered Egypt with Joseph.

EZEKIAS (Ĕz ĕ kī′ ás) KJV spelling of Ezekiel in the New Testament following the Greek spelling there. See *Ezekiel.*

EZEKIEL (E zē′ kĭ ĕl) Personal name meaning, "God will strengthen." A sixth-century B.C. prophet during the Babylonian Exile, son of Buzi (1:3), and priest as well as prophet. He was taken captive to Babylon in 597 B.C. by King Nebuchadnezzar along with King Jehoiachin and 10,000 others, including political and military leaders and skilled craftsmen (2 Kings 24:14–16). He lived in his own house at Tel-Abib near the river Chebar, an irrigation canal that channeled the waters of the Euphrates River into the surrounding arid region.

Ezekiel's call came in 593 B.C., the "thirtieth year" (1:1), probably Ezekiel's age (though it has been interpreted as 30 years since the discovery of the law book in 622, 30 years since Jehoiachin's imprisonment, or a system of Babylonian chronology).

Scholars have long debated whether Ezekiel was in Babylon or Jerusalem during his ministry. The book bearing his name points unmistakably to a Babylonian locale (1:1–3; 3:15; 8:1–3; 33:21). However, it has been argued that since most of the messages were addressed to the people of Jerusalem (16:2; 21:2; 22:2), it would have been meaningless to deliver them to the exiles. Also, some believe his intimate knowledge of events in Jerusalem (for example, his description of worship practices in the Temple, 8:1–18; Pelatiah's death, 11:13) would require that he was in Jerusalem. To resolve the difficulties, some have suggested that he was in Babylon part of the time and in Jerusalem at other times.

All objections to the Babylonian locale can be answered satisfactorily, however. Prophets frequently delivered messages for audiences not present (for example, the messages against foreign nations as in chapters 25—32). Furthermore, the genuine visionary experience (through which Ezekiel claimed to receive his knowledge) cannot be dismissed arbitrarily. Of course, visitors from Jerusalem could have kept him informed about events at home and carried his messages back when they returned. Therefore, there is no need to reject Babylon as the location of Ezekiel's entire ministry.

Ezekiel was married, but little else is known about his family life. His wife died suddenly during the siege of Jerusalem (24:18). Ezekiel continued to preach until at least 571 B.C. (29:17). His ministry can be divided into two phases: (1) 593–587, characterized by warnings of coming judgment on Judah and Jerusalem, and (2) 587–571, a period characterized by messages of encouragement and hope for the future.

Much has been written about Ezekiel's personality. He has been labeled neurotic, paranoid, psychotic, or schizophrenic because of his unusual behavior (for example, lying on one side for 390 days and on the other for 40 days, 4:4–6; shaving off his hair, 5:1–4; and his many visions). A better explanation for his strange behavior is that anyone who conscientiously obeys God will be considered "strange" by some people. Nothing God asked Ezekiel to do seemed too difficult. Only once was he reluctant to obey a command that would have made him ceremonially unclean (4:14). His objection reflected his priestly training.

Historical Background Ezekiel lived in a time of international crisis and conflict.

In 605, a showdown between Egypt and Babylonia at Carchemish established Babylonia as the dominant world power. Judah was able to maintain her independence by transferring her allegiance to Babylonia. During the last century of her existence, Judah was governed by a succession of wicked kings, with one exception. Josiah (640–609 B.C.) was deeply committed to God and instituted sweeping religious reforms during his reign (2 Kings 23:1–25). His son Jehoahaz was deposed by the Egyptians after a three-months' rule and was succeeded by another son, Jehoiakim (609–598 B.C.), who rebelled against his Babylonian overlords. Nebuchadnezzar led an army to quell the insurrection. During the crisis that followed, Jehoiakim died or perhaps was killed by those in his own court. His son Jehoiachin (598–597 B.C.) was taken as prisoner to Babylon after a three-months' rule, along with Ezekiel and others. The last of Judah's kings, Zedekiah (597–587 B.C.), did not heed the warnings of Ezekiel and Jeremiah. He also rebelled, and Nebuchadnezzar led an army that besieged Jerusalem for eighteen months before the city fell.

Difficulties with Understanding the Book The messages of Ezekiel are not easy to understand because of their frequent use of symbolic imagery. The modern reader is not alone in struggling to understand Ezekiel. There is evidence of opposition to the book for liturgical purposes and public reading that continued into the first century A.D., although it had been recognized as part of the canon for several centuries. At one time those under age 30 were not allowed to read the first chapter and chapters 40—48. Rabbi ben Hezekiah burned 300 jars of "midnight oil" in an attempt to harmonize the text. He concluded that he had solved all its problems.

Influence of Ezekiel on the New Testament Allusions to Ezekiel in the New Testament are found most prominently in the Gospel of John and the Book of Revelation. Jesus' presentation of Himself as the Good Shepherd in John 10 surely was intended as a contrast to the wicked shepherd in

Ezekiel 34. His comparison of Himself to the vine in John 15 may have had in mind the parable of the vine of Ezekiel 15.

Allusions to Ezekiel are found more frequently in the Book of Revelation than any other New Testament book. The living creatures of Ezekiel 1 reappear in Revelation 4:6–9. The throne of God (Ezek. 1:26–28) is described similarly in Revelation 4:2–3. "Gog, the land of Magog" (Ezek. 38:2) becomes "Gog and Magog" in Revelation 20:8. The Temple vision of Ezekiel 40—48 has several parallels in Revelation 21—22, with its focus on the Holy City Jerusalem and the river flowing from the throne of God.

Jesus' frequent reference to Himself as the Son of man is generally considered to have its origin in Daniel 7:13, but he may have appropriated it from the 93 times God addressed Ezekiel as "son of man."

Stylistic Characteristics of Ezekiel The Book of Ezekiel has been described by scholars as an artistic masterpiece. It contains a number of distinctive stylistic characteristics. Less than 10 percent of the messages are in a poetic format as compared to the frequent use of poetry in Isaiah and Jeremiah.

Few other books in the Old Testament contain such a rich blend of symbolic actions, visions, figurative speech, and allegories to communicate God's messages. There are at least 11 symbolic acts performed by Ezekiel (3:26–27; 4:1–3,4–8,9–17; 5:1–4; 12:1–16,17–20; 21:6,18–23; 24:15–24; 37:15–23). Visions form the content of 17 of the 48 chapters (1–3; 8–11; 37:1–14; 40–48). The imaginative use of figurative language was characteristic of Ezekiel (the watchman, 3:17–21; 33:1–9; a refining furnace, 22:17–22; Tyre as a merchant ship, 27:1–36; Pharaoh as a crocodile, 29:2–5). Ezekiel proclaimed many messages by means of allegory (15:1–8; 16:1–63; 17:1–24; 23:1–49; 24:3–14).

God first appeared to Ezekiel in a storm cloud seated on a throne surrounded by cherubim (1:1–28; 10:15). He commissioned Ezekiel to go to an "impudent children and stiffhearted" (2:4) and gave him a scroll to eat (3:1–3), symbolizing his complete identification with God's Word.

After Ezekiel returned to the exiles in Tel-Abib, God spoke to him again, addressing him as "watchman" (3:17) as a reminder of his responsibility to His people. God imposed silence on him for the next seven and one half years so that he could not speak unless he had a message from God (3:26–27; 33:21–22).

Ezekiel's ministry began with the performance of a series of symbolic acts, all designed to communicate God's warnings of the coming siege of Jerusalem and the scattering of its people (4:1—5:17). Chapters 8—11 contain an extended vision that took Ezekiel to Jerusalem where he saw abominable worship practices in the Temple (8:1–18).

Ezekiel pronounced woes on the false prophets and prophetesses who were leading the people astray (13:1–23). However, he did not exempt each individual from his or her responsibility before God (18:1–32). God told Ezekiel not to weep when his wife died during the siege of Jerusalem to communicate to the people that God's sympathy for His disobedient people was exhausted (24:16–17, 22–24).

Along with all the prophets except Hosea, Ezekiel did not limit his messages to the covenant people. Chapters 25—32 contain a series of messages against the surrounding nations. Though seemingly unrelated to the prophet's task of warning his own people, these messages served as solemn warnings that the covenant people could not expect to escape punishment if God would also punish nations which did not acknowledge Him.

After Jerusalem fell, Ezekiel changed the emphasis of his messages. There was no longer need for warning of impending punishment. Instead, the devastated nation needed encouragement that there was hope for the future. Therefore, the rest of the book, beginning with chapter 33, contains mainly messages of hope. The vision of the valley of dry bones dramatically proclaimed the future resurrection of the nation (37:1–14). The prophecies concerning Gog of the land of Magog gave assurance that God would protect His people from their enemies (38:1—39:29).

The closing vision of the restored community announced hope for God's people in the future (40:1—48:35). These chapters are interpreted by some to be a literal description of the Temple to be rebuilt after the Exile, by some as an allegorical picture of the church, by others as a literal temple to be rebuilt as part of the fulfillment of the dispensational premillennial interpretation of Daniel's seventieth week (Dan. 9:2–27), and by others as an example of apocalyptic language to describe God's coming kingdom in understandable terms of the destruction of wickedness and the establishment of a sanctified people in whose midst God would dwell.

Major Themes Prominent themes of the book include God's presence (1:26–28; 48:35), the sovereign authority of God over all nations (Israel as well as pagan nations), individual responsibility (18:1–32), righteousness (18:5–9), submission to God as the key to blessing (9:4; 16:60–63; 18:30–32; 36:22–38), and hope for the future of the people of God (37—48).

Outline

I. Introduction: Yahweh's Glory Watches Over the Captives in Babylon (1:1–28).

II. The Glory Brings Divine Judgment on Israel. (2:1—24:27)
   A. By calling Ezekiel to be a prophet (2:1—3:27)
   B. By predicting the fall of Jerusalem (4:1—5:17)
   C. By condemning Jerusalem's idolatry and sins (6:1—7:27)
   D. By describing and explaining why the Glory departed from the city (8:1—11:25)
   E. By showing the futility of the nation's leadership (12:1—15:8)
   F. As a means of providing reconciliation (16:1—18:32)
   G. Resulting in the nation's destruction (19:1—23:49)
   H. As seen in two events of unparalleled sadness (24:1–27)
      1. In the siege and destruction of Jerusalem (24:1–14)
      2. In the death of Ezekiel's wife (24:15–27)

III. The Glory Brings Divine Judgment to the Nations. (25:1—32:32)
   A. Against Ammon because of her joy over Israel's distress (25:1–7)
   B. Against Moab because of her failure to recognize Israel's revelatory status (25:8–11)
   C. Against Edom because of her lust for vengeance (25:12–14)
   D. Against Philistia because of her perpetual hostility (25:15–17)
   E. Against Tyre because of her greed for self-gain at Israel's expense (26:1—28:19)
   F. Against Sidon because of her constant threat to Israel's welfare (28:20–26)
   G. Against Egypt because of her pride and deceit (29:1—32:32)

IV. The Glory Brings Restoration to Israel. (33:1—48:35)
   A. Through Ezekiel's faithful role as a watchman (33:1–33)
   B. By means of the messianic leader, "my servant David" (34:1–31)
   C. For the entire land (35:1—36:38)
      1. By the total destruction of Edom (35:1–15)
      2. In the deliverance of Israel (36:1–21)
      3. In the implementation of the new covenant (36:22–38)
   D. To revive the hopeless state of the people who felt they had perished (37:1–28)
   E. By defeating the ungodly forces of the nations under Gog of Magog (38:1—39:29)
   F. Resulting in the pure worship of the restored people (40:1—48:35)
      1. With the throne of Yahweh's glory replacing the ark (40:1—43:12)
      2. With the presence of Yahweh's glory providing far-reaching blessings (44:1—47:12)

E

3. With a firm inheritance in the land (47:13—48:35)   *F. B. Huey, Jr.*

EZEL (Ē′ zĕl) Place name of uncertain meaning, perhaps, "disappearance." Rock where David hid from Saul and watched for Jonathan's signal (1 Sam. 20:19). He had hidden there previously, an apparent reference to David's escape in 1 Samuel 19:2. In 1 Samuel 20:41 the Hebrew text apparently refers to the same place as the "south side" (NAS), using a word for side which sounds much like Ezel. Early translations and modern translators have sought a different text to read at this point. Thus "the pile of stones there" (TEV; compare NRSV) or "the mound there" (REB). The name and location of the site is uncertain. The point of the narrative is clear: David used a natural hiding place to escape Saul and to gain vital information from his friend, the king's son.

EZEM (Ē′ zĕm) Place name meaning, "mighty" or "bone." Town in Judah's tribal territory but settled by tribe of Simeon (Josh. 15:29; 19:3; 1 Chron. 4:29). KJV spells Azem in Joshua. Ezem is modern Umm el-Azam about fifteen miles south of Beersheba and southwest of Aroer. Archaeologists at tell esh-Sharia about thirteen miles northwest of Beersheba have found a broken piece of pottery with the name Ezem on it.

EZER (Ē′ zĕr) English spelling of two Hebrew names with different spellings and meanings. The first Hebrew meaning is "gathering" or "pile." Ezer was a leader in Edom and a descendant of Esau (Gen. 36:21,27,30). He was a Horite and lived in Seir or Edom.

The second Hebrew meaning is "help" or "hero." *1.* A descendant of Judah (1 Chron. 4:4) in the clan of Caleb. *2.* Son of Ephraim and grandson of Jacob. With his brother Elead, he was killed as he tried to take cattle from the inhabitants of Gath (1 Chron. 7:21). Ephraim was born and lived in Egypt with his family (Gen. 46:20). When any of his immediate family would have had opportunity to visit Gath and steal cattle is a difficult question. It may be history of clans of Ephraim and refer to a moment of mourning in the history of families descended from Ephraim. The place in the middle of the list of descendants of Ephraim and ancestors of Joshua points to a time after that of Ephraim himself. Otherwise, a different Ephraim from the son of Jacob is meant, or Ephraim, the son of Jacob, entered Palestine, but the Bible did not preserve a story of his travels. *3.* Member of tribe of Gad who joined David's wilderness army before he became king (1 Chron. 12:9). *4.* Person who helped Nehemiah repair the Jerusalem wall. His father had political authority over Mizpah (Neh. 3:19). *5.* Temple musician who helped Nehemiah dedicate the completion of the Jerusalem wall (Neh. 12:42, with a slightly different Hebrew spelling). See *Ebenezer.*

EZION-GABER KJV variant spelling of Ezion-Geber (Num. 33:35—36; Deut. 2:8; 2 Chron. 20:36). See *Ezion-Geber.*

EZION-GEBER (Ē′ zĭ ŏn-gē′ bĕr) A port city of Edom located on the northern shore of the Gulf of Aqabah. It is first mentioned in the Bible among the cities on the route of the Exodus (Num. 33:35–36; Deut. 2:8). Solomon utilized this city for ship-building purposes. During this time it was a port from which ships manned by Phoenician sailors sailed to Ophir for gold and other riches (1 Kings 9:26–28; 10:11, 22; 2 Chron. 8:17).

Nelson Glueck led excavations of the site of the ancient city and discovered the remains of four towns, the first dating to the time of Solomon. Interestingly, this first city shows evidence of being a carefully laid out complex built at one time according to a plan, rather than gradually. A notable feature of this first town was a series of structures with flues and air ducts in the floors and walls. Glueck concluded that this city was a refinery for the copper and iron which were mined in the area. However, in 1962 Rothenburg challenged this view and persuaded Glueck that the remains indicate that the city was a large storehouse for grain and supplies.

After the division of the kingdom, the city fell to the kingdom of Judah. It was destroyed probably during the invasion of Palestine by Shishak (925 B.C.). The city was rebuilt by Jehoshaphat, king of Judah who attempted a similar enterprise as Solomon, but with disastrous results (1 Kings 22:48; 2 Chron. 20:35–37). The city was again destroyed in the reign of Jehoram when the Edomites revolted (2 Kings 8:20–22). Azariah rebuilt the city, and according to many scholars it was renamed Elath (2 Kings 14:22; 2 Chron. 26:2), though recent study sees Elath as a separate city. During the reign of Uzziah, the Edomites regained possession of the city. From that time on the city remained under the control of the Edomites. It was abandoned sometime between the eighth and fourth centuries B.C. and was never rebuilt.

Recent archaeological study has questioned the identification of Ezion-geber with tell el-Kheleifeh. Its lack of a good harbor and of the proper pottery finds has led to exploration of the island of Jezirat Faraun, where a natural harbor exists. Also known as Pharaoh's Island and Coral Island, it is seven miles south of modern Eilat and 900 feet offshore from the Sinai Peninsula. The island is 1,000 feet from north to south and 200 feet from east to west. It may have served as the harbor and port, while tell el-Kheleifeh was Elath. See *Commerce; Elath.*   *Paul E. Robertson*

EZNITE A word of uncertain meaning describing the family or tribal relationship of Adino (2 Sam. 23:8), but most modern translations take a clue from the parallel text in 1 Chronicles 11:11 and from the earliest Greek translation, omitting Adino the Eznite from the text. Compare modern translations. See *Adino.*

EZRA, BOOK OF (Ĕz′ rà) The name Ezra means "Yahweh helps." Several had the name: a family head in Judah (1 Chron. 4:17), a priest in the return with Zerubbabel (Neh. 12:1,13), and a prince at the dedication of Jerusalem's walls built by Nehemiah (Neh. 12:32–33). The most famous is the chief character in the Book of Ezra.

The Book of Ezra is intimately connected with Chronicles and Nehemiah. The connection is so obvious that possibly one person wrote and compiled all three. This unknown person is referred to as the Chronicler.

Ezra and Nehemiah were actually one book in the ancient Hebrew and Greek Old Testament. Each book contains materials found in the other (e.g., the list in Ezra 2 is also in Neh. 7). Each book completes the other; Ezra's story is continued in Nehemiah (chs. 8—10). Both are necessary to the history of Israel. A whole century would be unknown (538–432 B.C.), historically, apart from Ezra and Nehemiah. They are the next chapter of the history recorded in Chronicles.

Ezra lived during the reign of Artaxerxes (7:1), king of Persia, but which one? Artaxerxes I (Longimanus), 465–425 B.C., or Artaxerxes II (Mnemon) 404–359 B.C.? If it is Longimanus, then "the seventh year of Artaxerxes the king" (7:7) was 458 B.C.; but if Mnemon, it was 398 B.C. Scripture possibly intimates that Nehemiah preceded Ezra to Jerusalem. For example, Ezra prayed as though walls were already in place in Jerusalem (9:9), yet they were built by Nehemiah. Also Nehemiah's reforms (Neh. 13) seem to have preceded Ezra's teaching the law and his reforms. There are real problems either way, but it seems logical to stay with the biblical order and date Ezra's journey to Jerusalem in 458 B.C.

Ezra was a priest and a scribe. He descended from Aaron through Phinehas and later Zadok (Ezra 7:1–5; 1 Chron. 6:4–14).

Ezra's purpose for going to Jerusalem was "to study the law of the Lord, and to do it, and to teach the statutes and ordinances in Israel" (7:10 NRSV). He was well equipped for this task as a priest and scribe. Jerusalem needed the law of God. The permanence of the Jews was threatened by opposition from non-Jews and by the Jews' careless disregard for the things of God. Ezra's teaching was needed to give solidity and strength to the Jewish community struggling against pressures to surrender its ethnic and theological identity.

Ezra was written from this kind of perspective. A variety of sources was used, either by Ezra or by another who gave the book its present form. Jewish tradition is strong that Ezra was the actual author of the entire book, as well as Chronicles and Nehemiah. Vivid details and the use of the first person pronoun permit scholars to speak of the Ezra Memoirs (7:27—9:15).

The book has two major stories, that of Zerubbabel and the group of returnees who rebuilt the Temple (chs. 1—6), and that of Ezra (chs. 7—10, completed in Neh. 8—10). Peculiarities in the book include the naming of Sheshbazzar (ch. 1) as the leader of the first group to return and not Zerubbabel. Two approaches are possible. One is that Sheshbazzar was a real historical person who actually led a small group of anxious Jews to Jerusalem. The other is that Sheshbazzar might have been another name for Zerubbabel. But it seems unlikely that a Jew would have two Babylonian names.

Another peculiarity, found in both Ezra and Nehemiah, is the use of lists. The list in Ezra 2 of those who returned with Zerubbabel is in Nehemiah 7. Other lists include those who returned with Ezra (Ezra 8:1–14); "the sons of the priests there were found who had taken strange wives" (Ezra 10:18–43).

Another peculiarity is the Aramaic in Ezra. This was a widely used language of Ezra's era, related to Hebrew, used by Jews and Gentiles alike. Most of the book is written in Hebrew, but there are two large sections of Aramaic (Ezra 4:7—6:18; 7:12–26). The Aramaic generally deals with official correspondence between Palestine and Persia.

The lists and the Aramaic show that the author was determined to use official documents where possible. Establishing the legitimacy of the Jews was an important objective, and these helped do that.

Ezra begins with the story of Sheshbazzar and Zerubbabel and the first Jews to return to Jerusalem from captivity in 538 B.C. Their main objective was to rebuild the Temple. Its foundation was laid in 536 B.C. Then there was a long delay. Haggai and Zechariah (Ezra 5:1) in 520 B.C. had encouraged the people to finish the project, which they did in 515 B.C. (6:14–15), and they "celebrated the dedication of this house of God with joy" (6:16 NRSV).

Almost sixty years passed before Ezra went to Jerusalem (458 B.C.), six decades of silence. He left Persia with "the letter that the king Artaxerxes gave unto Ezra the priest, the scribe" (7:11), giving him unusual power and authority (7:12–26). As he "viewed the people, and the priests, and [he] found there none of the sons of Levi" (8:15). These were essential for his teaching program to implement the law of God in Jerusalem. During a three-day delay more than 200 "ministers for the house of our God" (8:17) were enlisted. Four months later the group, probably less than 2,000, arrived in the Holy City.

Soon Ezra was informed of the most glaring sin of the Jews, intermarriage with non-Jews, those

E

not in covenant relation with Yahweh (9:2). Ezra was greatly upset (9:3–4). He prayed (9:6–15). In assembly people reached what must have been a heartrending decision: "Let us make a covenant with our God to put away all the wives, and such as are born of them" (10:3). The book concludes with the carrying out of this decision (ch. 10).

Ezra's story reaches its climax in Nehemiah (Neh. 8—10). There he read from "the book of the law of Moses, which the Lord had commanded to Israel" (Neh. 8:1). A great revival resulted. Ezra is not heard of again.

Ezra's greatest contribution was his teaching, establishing, and implementing "the book of the law of the Lord" (Neh. 9:3) among the Jews.

Ezra evidenced strong theology. He believed in the sovereignty of God, who could use a Cyrus, an Artaxerxes, and a Darius to accomplish His purposes. He believed in the faithfulness of God, who brought home as many exiles as He could. He believed in the sacredness and practicality of the Scriptures; he read them to his people and insisted that their teachings be carried out. He was a person of prayer; note his long confessional prayers (Ezra 9:5–15; Neh. 9:6–37). He was a preacher: he used a pulpit (Neh. 8:4); he publicly read the Scriptures; and he helped to interpret them to his congregation (8:8).

The value of the contributions of Ezra to the Jews is immeasurable. What he did probably saved them from disintegration. His efforts helped guarantee the ethnic and theological continuance of descendants of Abraham. He might not have been the father of Judaism, but he contributed greatly to saving the Jews' identity as a people of God.

Outline

I. God's Worship Must Be Restored (1:1—6:22)
   A. God can use a pagan "to fulfill the word of the Lord." (1:1–4)
   B. God's people respond to God's ways. (1:5–6)
   C. God will recover and reclaim His possessions. (1:7–11)
   D. God's people, by name and as individuals, are important. (2:1–67)
   E. God's people are generous givers for a good cause. (2:68–70)
   F. God's people worship, regardless of the circumstances. (3:1–6)
   G. God's people will give and organize to get a job done. (3:7–9)
   H. God's people praise Him in success or in disappointment. (3:10–13)
   I. God's people must reject some offers of help. (4:1–3)
   J. God's work can be opposed and stopped. (4:4–24)
   K. God's work and workers must be encouraged. (5:1–2)
   L. God's work and workers are in His watchcare. (5:3–5)

   M. God's work may get pagan authorization and support. (5:6—6:12)
   N. God's work must ultimately be completed. (6:13–15)
   O. God's work must be dedicated publicly with joyful celebration. (6:16–22)
II. God's Word Must Be Followed. (7:1—10:44)
   A. God's Word needs skilled teachers and helpers. (7:1–7)
   B. God's Word elicits commitment. (7:8–10)
   C. God's work accepts all the help it can get from many different sources. (7:11–26)
   D. God blesses His workers and expects to be praised. (7:27–28)
   E. God's work warrants good records. (8:1–14)
   F. God's work must enlist trained workers. (8:15–20)
   G. God's work calls for faith, prayer, and humility. (8:21–23)
   H. God's work warrants division of responsibility. (8:24–30)
   I. God's work necessitates good stewardship and generous sacrifice. (8:31–36)
   J. Gross violations of God's Word must be acknowledged. (9:1–5)
   K. Acknowledged sin leads to prayer and confession with deep theological insights. (9:6–15)
   L. God's grace and human confession call for active commitment. (10:1–4)
   M. God's people must act unitedly. (10:5–9)
   N. God's call for the separated life must be made clear by God's leaders to God's people. (10:10–11)
   O. God's way utilizes practical solutions for difficult problems. (10:12–17)
   P. God's way expects "fruit in keeping with repentance" (Matt. 3:8) from all who are guilty. (10:18–44)   *D. C. Martin*

EZRAH (Ĕz′ răh) Modern translation spelling of Ezra in 1 Chronicles 4:17 to reflect different final letter in Hebrew spelling. This Ezra is a descendant of Judah of which nothing else is known. The spelling of his name may be a Hebrew form, whereas the more common spelling is Aramaic. See *Ezra*.

EZRAHITE (Ĕz′ rȧ hīte) A term used to describe the family relationships of Ethan, a famous wise man (1 Kings 4:31). The precise meaning of the Hebrew word is debated. It may mean one born in the land with full citizenship rights and point to a Canaanite origin for Ethan. A related word appears in Exodus 12:19,49; Leviticus 17:15; Joshua 8:33, and other places. See *Ethan*.

EZRI (Ĕz′ rī) Personal name meaning, "my help." Supervisor of royal farm labor under David (1 Chron. 27:26).

F

A variety of orchid—one of the many flowers found in the Middle East.

FABLE A short, fictitious story that uses animals or inanimate objects as characters to teach ethical or practical lessons. Typically, the characters are portrayed as having human personality traits that are good or evil. The practical or moral lesson is obvious in the story when these character traits lead to either failure or success. Fables are rarely found in the Bible. There are two clear examples in the Old Testament. The fable of the trees of the forest selecting a king (Judg. 9:8–15) is designed to warn Israel of the dangers in selecting a weak and ruthless king. In 2 Kings 14:8–10 (2 Chron. 25:17–19), there is a fable addressed to Amaziah, king of Judah, about the folly of arrogance. In this story a thistle thinks that it is equal to the giant cedars of Lebanon and gets trampled by a wild beast of the forest. *Daniel B. McGee*

FACE The front of a person's head. In the Bible several words are translated as "face." In the Old Testament, *panim* is the most common and has the actual meaning of face. ʾAph (nose) and ʿayin (eyes, aspect) are also at times translated as face. In the New Testament the words used are *opsis* and *prosōpon.*

The word "face" has a variety of meanings. It is used literally to refer to the face of man or animals (Gen. 30:40), seraphim (Isa. 6:2), and the face of Christ (Matt. 17:2). Figuratively, it is used in reference to the face of the earth (Gen. 1:29), waters (Gen. 1:2), sky (Matt. 16:3), and moon (Job 26:9). Also, the word "face" is used theologically with regard to the "presence of God" (Gen. 30:17–23). Face may be the physical "face" or the surface seen. Being "face to face" (literally, "eye to eye") is being squared off with each other, front to front, and fully visible (Num. 14:14). The face (eye) of the earth is the visible surface of the earth (Ex. 10:5, 15), and the face of the waters is that surface which is seen (Gen. 1:2).

The word "face" may stand for the entire countenance. It is in the face that the emotions are expressed. The face of the sky expresses the weather, stormy and red, or fair (Matt. 16:2–3). Bowing one's face (nose or face) expresses reverence or awe (Num. 22:31; Luke 5:12). Bowing one's face (nose) toward the ground also includes the involvement of the entire person (1 Sam. 20:41; Matt. 26:39), indicating complete submission. When angry or sad, one's countenance (face) will fall (Gen. 4:5). "A merry heart maketh a cheerful countenance (face)" (Prov. 15:13). To express displeasure or disgust, the face is averted or "hid" (Ezek. 39:23; Ps. 102:2); to "seek his face" is to desire an audience (Ps. 105:4). To "set my face against" is to express hostility (Jer. 21:10), while turning away the face shows rejection (Ps. 132:10). To "set their faces to" indicates determination (Jer. 42:17; Luke 9:51). The wicked man "hardeneth his face"(Prov. 21:29), and "covered his face with his fatness" (Job

15:27). When in mourning, the face is covered (2 Sam. 19:4).

Because the face reflects the personality and character of person, the word is frequently translated as "person" (Deut. 28:50; 2 Sam. 17:11; 2 Cor. 2:10), or "presence" (Ex. 10:11). Sometimes it is translated merely as the indefinite pronoun "many" (2 Cor. 1:11). Frequently, the word "face" is translated with the phrase "respect persons," (KJV), or "being partial" (RSV), (Deut. 1:17; Prov. 24:23; Matt. 22:16; Gal. 2:6).

Many idioms and phrases also apply to "the face of God." His face shines (Ps. 4:6), indicating good will and blessing. He sets His face against sinners (Lev. 17:10), and hides His face (Ps. 13:1). Frequently, the word "face" is used in a theological sense with regard to the person or presence of God. Sometimes "face" is translated as "presence" (Gen. 4:16; Ex. 33:14; 2 Thess. 1:9). In the tabernacle, the "shewbread" (KJV) or "Bread of the Presence" (RSV), was a local manifestation of the presence of God. The literal Hebrew reads "bread of the faces." At other times, other words are substituted although the direct meaning is the "face of God." Moses asked to see God's "glory" (Ex. 33:18), but God answered that "thou canst not see my face" (Ex. 33:20). The correlation indicates that in seeing God's face, one would experience His actual presence, and thereby be exposed to God's nature and character. Sinful and non-holy beings cannot survive being in God's holy presence without God's grace or merciful intervention (Ex. 33:17–23). Thus Moses (Ex. 3:6), Elijah (1 Kings 19:13), and the seraphim (Isa. 6:2) hide their faces in God's presence.

See *Glory; Shewbread; Presence; Eye.*

Darlene R. Gautsch

FACETS NRSV, TEV translation of the Hebrew *ayinim,* meaning small plane surfaces, especially those on a cut gem (Zech. 3:9). The basic idea of the Hebrew *ayin,* as reflected in most English versions, is eye. By extension the root can designate a face or surface, hence the translation facet. Some commentators understand the Hebrew root to mean springs of water (compare Gen. 16:7). The translation "eyes" points ahead to "the seven eyes of God which roam throughout the world" (4:10), a symbol of the omniscience or omnipresence of God. The translation "springs" fits well with the idea of the removal of iniquity (3:9b). The eschatological spring or stream is well-known in visions of the Temple (Joel 3:18; Ezek. 47; Zech. 13:1; 14:8). Zechariah 3:9, however, uses the masculine plural form rather than the feminine form used in other references to springs. Perhaps the masuline form is an Aramaism. Some scholars believe the stone was a stone slab occupying the place held by the ark of the covenant in the first Temple. In this case the seven eyes represent the full presence of God in a way corresponding to the ark of the covenant.

FAIR HAVENS (Fair Hā′ vẻns) An open bay on the southern coast of Crete near the city of Lasea. Protected only by small islands, it did not appear to be a safe harbor for winter, so the sailors of the ship carrying Paul to Rome decided to try to reach Phenice. They refused to listen to Paul's warnings and were caught in a ferocious storm (Acts 27:8–20).

FAITH Trusting commitment of one person to another, particularly of a person to God. Faith is the central concept of Christianity. One may be called a Christian only if one has faith.

Our English word "faith" comes from the Latin *fides,* as developed through the Old French words *fei* and *feid.* In Middle English (1150–1475) "faith" replaced a word that eventually evolved into "belief." "Faith" came to mean "loyalty to a person to whom one is bound by promise or duty." Faith was fidelity. "Belief" came to be distinguished from faith as an intellectual process having to do with the acceptance of a proposition. The verb form of "faith" dropped out of English usage toward the end of the sixteenth century.

Old Testament Expressions The word "faith" occurs in the Old Testament only twice in the KJV, eighteen times in the RSV, and sixteen times in the NIV. This discrepancy becomes even more interesting when we note that the RSV and the NIV agree on only five of these verses of Scripture (Deut. 32:51; Judg. 9:16,19; Isa. 26:2; Hab. 2:4), and the KJV concurs with them only on the translation of Habakkuk 2:4. These differences revolve around problems with the translation of two Hebrew roots, *ma̓ al* and *̓aman.*

The first of these roots, *ma̓ al,* is a negative term that means "to be deceitful, treacherous, or unfaithful." The RSV, NAS, and the NIV translate this word with the phrase "broke faith" (Deut. 32:51; Josh. 22:16) or with "acted unfaithfully" (Deut. 32:51; Josh. 7:1). The KJV translates this root in those same verses with the word "trespass."

The second root, *̓aman,* is more difficult to translate because its meaning changes as it passes through the various Hebrew verb forms. There are seven such forms, but this root occurs in only three of them. In the first and most basic verb form the root means to support or nourish and is used of a parent's care for a child. In the second verb-form one encounters a range of meanings having to do with being secure.

Only the third verb form was rendered with the Greek word for faith in the New Testament and in the Septuagint, an early Greek version of the Old Testament originating in Alexandria. *̓Aman* expresses the idea of stability and steadfastness in this form and is translated as standing firm (Job 39:24, RSV; Isa. 7:9*b* NIV), or "to trust" (a per-

son) or "to believe" (a statement). One stands firm in one's convictions. In relationships, one trusts persons and believes their testimony or promises. Thus, we find no Hebrew noun for "faith" in the Old Testament, only verbs that have been translated with "faith" because of New Testament influence.

If we do not find the noun "faith" in the Old Testament, we surely find the concept named with other words. In the Old Testament faith is described as the "fear of God" (Gen. 20:11; Ps. 111:10; Eccl. 12:13; Mal. 4:2), and in terms of trust (2 Chron. 20:20; Ps. 4:5, Isa. 26:4), and obedience (Ex. 19:5; 1 Sam. 15:22, Jer. 7:23). Faith is a New Testament concept that encompasses and enriches these Old Testament concepts.

Because the Old Testament does not have a word equivalent to the English noun, "faith," does not mean the idea of faith is unimportant for the Old Testament. Habakkuk 2:4 was properly taken by Paul as the center of Old Testament religion. God prepared the way for His people in mercy and grace, then called them to obedience. To accept the responsibilities of God's covenant was to trust His word that He alone was God and to commit one's life to His promises for the present and future. That is faith.

New Testament Expressions The Greek noun, *pistis* (faith), is related to the verb *pisteuo* (I have faith, trust, believe). The noun and verb are found virtually everywhere in the New Testament, with the notable exception that the noun is absent altogether from John's Gospel and occurs only once in 1 John. The verb form does not occur in Philemon, 2 Peter, 2 and 3 John, or Revelation.

In the New Testament "faith" is used in a number of ways, but primarily with the meaning "trust" or "confidence" in God. This basic meaning is particularly evident in the Synoptic Gospels. Mark 1:15 introduces and summarizes the Gospel with Jesus' charge to his hearers to "repent ye, and believe the gospel." (The word usually translated "believe" in this verse is the verb form of "faith" for which there is no English equivalent. The call is repeated as "Have faith in God," using the noun form, in Mark 11:22.) Thus, Jesus called His hearers to place their confidence in God. It is common in the Synoptics for Jesus to say after healing someone, "thy faith hath made thee whole" (Matt. 9:22; Mark 5:34; Luke 7:50; 8:48.) One's confidence in or allegiance to God makes one whole. John expressed a similar understanding of faith in 6:29 and 14:1 where people are called to have faith in the Christ.

Outside the Gospels faith is related to the keynote *concepts* of the Christian message: the state of salvation (Eph. 2:8–9), sanctification (Acts 26:18), purification (Acts 15:9), justification or imputed righteousness (Rom. 4:5; 5:1; Gal. 3:24), adoption as children of God (Gal. 3:26).

F

Each of these comes by faith. As in the Gospels, faith is an attitude toward and relationship with God mediated by Christ Jesus. It is surrender to God's gift of righteousness in Christ rather than seeking to achieve righteousness alone.

Faith is also called a fruit of the Holy Spirit (Gal. 5:22)—something God creates in a person. In another place "faith" is used quite differently as a gift of the Holy Spirit that is given to some but not to others (1 Cor. 12:8–9). Apparently such special gifts of faith refer to the ability to do great acts for God, what Jesus called moving mountains (Matt. 17:20; 1 Cor. 13:2).

The New Testament sometimes uses "faith" to designate Christianity itself or that which Christians believe (Acts 6:7; Eph. 4:5; Col. 1:23; 1 Tim. 1:19; Jude 3). In this usage it is clear that an element of what we call belief is essential to the personal relationship we are calling "faith." Here it would be well to note Hebrews 11:6 also—"But without faith it is impossible to please him: for he that cometh to God must believe that he is. . . . " In this verse also the word translated "believe" is the Greek verb form of "faith." Context here dictates that we understand it in the sense of intellectual acceptance of a proposition, "belief." To have a right relation with God, it is necessary to "believe" that God is, that God has revealed Himself in Christ, and to accept God accepts you.

If faith is the religion itself, it is so in more than an intellectual way. Faith is also the living out of the religion; it is Christianity in action. This is the meaning of "We walk by faith, not by sight" (2 Cor. 5:7). "Walking" represents the totality of one's way of life. Paul wrote that "faith," both in the sense of Christian piety and of the trust and confidence one puts in God, determines action in life. Faith changes the standards and priorities of life. Similarly, using the imagery of a soldier's armor, Paul said that faith is a shield against sin and evil in our lives (Eph. 6:16; 1 Thess. 5:8).

If Christianity itself may be called "the faith," then it is a small step to the New Testament usage of the participle of the verb form of faith to designate Christians. This form is often translated "believers" (it occurs most often in the plural) or "those who believe" (Acts 4:32; Rom. 1:16).

The nearest the New Testament comes to presenting a definition of "faith" *per se,* is in Hebrews 11:1. Here faith is called "the assurance of things hoped for, the conviction of things not seen" (RSV). Thus, Hebrews very closely ties faith to Christian hope. The personal conviction of faith encourages the Christian to continue hoping for the fulfillment of the promises of God, but it is not the substance (as in the KJV) of these "things hoped for" in any normal sense of "substance." The "things hoped for" have a reality greater than anyone's hoping for them. Faith is then meant as a sort of foretaste of the hoped for things.

Faith as the Way to Salvation The concept of faith is primarily that of a personal relationship with God that determines the priorities of one's life. This relationship is one of love that is built on trust and dependence. We receive it by trusting the saving work of Jesus. Faith is the basic Christian experience, the decision for Christ Jesus. It is the acceptance of Christ's lordship (i.e., His God-given, absolute authority). In this sense faith is doubly a break from the past: it is one's removal from sin, and it is one's removal from all other religious allegiances (1 Thess. 1:9). As a break from the past, faith is the beginning of relation to God and not an end. It is, especially in Paul's letters, the inauguration of incorporation "in Christ," in which one continues to grow and develop.

If faith is primarily a relationship into which one enters through acceptance of Jesus' authority, it also includes a certain amount of "belief." As a derived use, then, "faith" may also denote the content of what is believed. In this sense faith is the conviction that God acted in the history of Israel and "that God was in Christ, reconciling the world unto himself" (2 Cor. 5:19). In theological usage "the faith" may refer to many more doctrines and dogmas that have been developed since New Testament times, but in the New Testament "that which must be believed" was more limited as Romans 10:9–10 may demonstrate.

Conclusion Faith is what we believe, it is Christianity itself, but primarily it is the relationship we have with God through what Jesus accomplished in His death and resurrection.   *William L. Self*

FAITHFUL Steadfast, dedicated, dependable, and worthy of trust. It is derived from the Hebrew root having the basic meaning "to trust (a person)," or "to believe (a statement)." This is the same root that gives us the word "amen." The derived meaning is that the one so described is trustworthy, dependable, trusting, or loyal. Moses was faithful in all God's household (Num. 12:7). "Faithful" is used to describe the relation of God and Israel (Deut. 7:9). The faithful God keeps His covenant, and the faithful people keep His commandments.

In the New Testament the adjective "faithful" is a derivative of the Greek noun meaning "faith." Here we get the translation "faithful" as a natural derivative of faith. Once again the fundamental meaning is that the one so described is trustworthy and loyal. The root idea is that one has fidelity toward another person or toward God. For example, in 1 Corinthians 7:25 Paul commended himself to the Corinthians as one who is "faithful" (KJV) or "trustworthy" (NAS). In Revelation 2:10 the church in Smyrna and subsequent readers are commanded "be thou faithful unto death." And, in Ephesians 1:1 Paul addressed the letter "to the faithful in Christ Jesus." In other cases, however, "faithful" describes God's mode of relation toward persons or toward God's creation.

Many of these passages speak of God as faithful in order to comfort and encourage Christians. "If we confess our sins, he is faithful and just to forgive us our sins, and to cleanse us from all unrighteousness" (1 John 1:9). "God is faithful, who will not suffer you to be tempted above that ye are able" (1 Cor. 10:13). "Faithful is he that calleth you, who also will do it" (1 Thess. 5:24).

The faithful person is steadfast, unchanging, and thoroughly grounded in relation to the other. This sort of fidelity, or faithfulness, is used in both the Old Testament and the New Testament to describe God's relation to the world and to describe the quality of relationship that Israel and Christians are called upon to have with God and with one another.

See *Faith; Trust; Trustworthy.*   *William L. Self*

FALCON See *Birds.*

FALL The traditional name for the first sin of Adam and Eve which brought judgment upon both nature and mankind.

In Genesis people are the dominion-havers created in the image of God (Gen. 1:26-28). Man and woman are placed on earth with a commandment to obey (Gen. 1:28). The biblical understanding of dominion suggests a serving stewardship rather than mere power (Matt. 20:25-28). **Sin in the Garden** Genesis pictures humans as the special creation of God (2:7) placed in the special garden created by God (2:8-15). Three features are crucial for understanding the human role in the garden: (1) Adam was put in the garden to "dress it and to keep it" (2:15). God provided this vocation for man's fulfillment. (2) The first people were granted great freedom and discretion in the garden. This freedom permitted them to take from the goodness of God's creation (2:16). (3) Yet their freedom and discretion were limited. God prohibited the taking of the fruit from the tree of knowledge of good and evil (2:17). Scholars have pointed out that these three features belong uniquely to humans. Each person faces (1) vocation, (2) freedom, and yet (3) prohibition. Full humanity is experienced only when all three of these are maintained.

The "knowledge of good and evil" would make humans godlike in some way (Gen. 3:5,22). Some Bible students understand the tree to hold (1) all knowledge—that is the complete range of experience. Others claim the tree provides (2) knowledge of a moral nature. Some claim the acquired knowledge was simply (3) sexual experience.

The tree's purpose within the narrative provides a clue toward a more satisfactory explanation. The tree was the object and symbol of God's authority. The tree reminded Adam and Eve that their freedom was not absolute but had to be exercised in dependence upon God. In prideful rebellion the couple grasped for the capacity to be completely self-legislating—establishing an absolute self-directing independence. Such absolute dominion belongs only to God. Their ambition affected every dimension of human experience; for example, they claimed the right to decide what is good and evil.

The Serpent The serpent made a sudden intrusion into the story. The serpent is identified in Genesis only as a creature. Theological reflection has identified him as an instrument of Satan and, thus, legitimately cursed and pictured as the enemy of woman's seed (Gen. 3:14-15). Later Scripture also declares that Satan is the ultimate tempter (1 John 3:8; Rev. 12:9). His presence, however, does not diminish mankind's responsibility. Scripture stipulates that man cannot blame his sin on demonic temptation (Jas. 1:12-15).

The serpent began the conversation with a question that obviously distorted or at least extended God's order not to eat of the tree (Gen. 3:1). The questioner invited the woman to enter into a conversation about God and to treat Him and His word as objects to be considered and evaluated. Moreover, the serpent painted God as one who sadistically and arbitrarily placed a prohibition before the couple to stifle their enjoyment of the garden.

The woman apparently felt inclined to defend God's instruction. In her response to the serpent she included a citation of God's command. The text does not tell us how she or the snake came to know God's command. Adam may have passed on this information that he initially received prior to woman's creation (Gen. 2:17-18). She may thus represent all who receive the word of God through "human" instrumentality but who are nevertheless called to believe (compare John 20:29). She responded with a restatement of God's permission to eat freely of the garden provision (Gen. 3:2). She then told of God's prohibition of that one tree in the middle of the garden. Perhaps anxiety over doubting God's character moved her then to add to God's own words; she extended the instruction to include touching the tree, thereby making her own law. It is interesting that the first challenge to God's word did not involve deletion, but addition by both the serpent and the woman. Mankind's first surrender to temptation began with doubting God's instruction and His loving character.

The woman's willingness to judge and her addition to God's instruction, though seemingly harmless, permitted the serpent boldly to continue with a direct attack on God's character. He declared that the couple would not really die. Instead, he argued that God's motive was to keep the couple from being like God. The serpent claimed that the phrases "your eyes shall be opened, and ye shall be as gods, knowing good and evil" (Gen. 3:5) are God's reasons for giving the prohibitive command; in reality, these phrases express the human reasons for breaking the command. The couple was unhappy with their freedom as long as they thought more could be had. They sought unrestricted freedom—to be responsible to no one, not even God. The serpent seemed sure that eating would produce equality not death.

The woman stood before the tree. Crudely, she saw the fruit was good for food. In a more refined manner she judged it to be pleasant to the eye. More appealing to her vanity still was the newfound faith that it would bring knowledge (Gen. 3:6; compare 1 John 2:16). She ate of the fruit and gave it to Adam who ate as well.

Results of Sin Sin had immediate results in the couple's relationship; the self-first and self-only attitude displayed toward God affected the way they looked at one another. The mutual trust and intimacy of the one-flesh bond (Gen. 2:24) was ravaged by distrust. This does not suggest that the knowledge of good and evil was sexual awareness. Intercourse was the command and blessing of God prior to the fall (Gen. 1:28). In the absence of mutual trust, complete intimacy implies complete vulnerability (Gen. 3:7).

The couple also felt compelled to hide from God when they heard Him walking in the garden. When loving trust characterized the couple's attitude, they were apparently comfortable in God's presence. After their sin, shame appropriately marked their relationships—both human and divine (Gen. 3:8). The sinners could not remain hidden. God pursued, asking, "where art thou" (Gen. 3:9). This may be a normal question, but some see it as God's sorrowful anticipation of what follows. Sinners finally must speak to God. Adam admitted that God's presence now provoked fear, and human shame provoked hiding (Gen. 3:10).

God's next question drew the man's attention away from his plight to his sin (Gen. 3:11). The couple had to face their maker. The man admitted his sin, but only after emphatically reminding God that the woman was instrumental in his partaking. Woman shared equally in the deed, but she quickly blamed the deceiving serpent (Gen. 3:12–13). Along with shame, blame comes quite naturally to humankind.

God moved immediately to punish. The serpent was not interviewed because he was not an image-bearer in whom God sought a representation and relationship. The snake's behavior foreshadowed the reversal of created order and mankind's dominion. Once appealing and crafty, the cursed snake became lower than other animals. The judgment included the strife between snakes and humans. Some believe a fuller meaning of the verse promises Christ's ultimate victory over Satan (Gen. 3:14–15).

The woman's punishment was linked to her distinctive role in the fulfillment of God's command (Gen. 1:28). Her privilege to share in God's creative work was frustrated by intense pain. Despite this pain she would nevertheless desire intimacy with her husband, but her desire would be frustrated by sin. Their mutuality and oneness were displaced by male domination (Gen. 3:16).

Adam's punishment also involved the frustration of his service. He was guilty of following the woman's sinful advice and eating of the forbidden tree (Gen. 3:17). The fruitful efficiency known prior to the Fall was lost. Now even his extreme toil would be frustrated by the cursed earth. The earth was apparently cursed because it was within Adam's domain. This corporate mentality is strange to us, but biblical writers recognize nature's need for redemption (Isa. 24; Rom. 8:19–23; Col. 1:15–20).

Results—Epilogue Man's prerogative to name woman (Gen. 3:20) was a sign of the fallen order, but hope persists. Mankind can carry on because the woman has the capacity to bear children. Hope ultimately emerged from divine determination to preserve His creation. Some may expect God to retreat and leave the sinful people alone to taste the misery that would follow, but grace-giving Yahweh provided clothing for fallen mankind (Gen. 3:20–21).

Yahweh acknowledged the partial truth of the serpent's claim: Adam's and Eve's autonomy had made them like the divine (Gen. 3:5,22). In these circumstances, access to the tree of life is inappropriate. Numerous questions regarding the conditional nature of the tree of life are left unanswered here (Ezek. 47:12; Rev. 2:7; 22:2,14,19). As a tragic judgment, the sinful pair was driven out of the garden, intended by God as His dwelling place. Guardian cherubim protected the garden and the tree (Gen 3:22–24) and, thus, graciously protected people from entering into an infinite period of struggle. The serpent's lie concerning death (Gen. 3:4) became visible. Human sin brought death (Gen. 3:19,22). Some readers question why death did not come "on that day" as God had apparently promised (Gen. 2:17), but the Hebrew expression may mean simply "when" (NIV; compare REB). One should also be reminded of God's grace to allow life to continue and the Hebrew understanding that death involves separation from God as much as physical death (Job 7:21; Ps. 88:5,10–12; Isa. 38:18–19).

New Testament The New Testament writers assumed the fallen state of both humans and nature. Both groan for redemption (Rom. 8:19–23). When comparing Adam and Christ, Paul declared that sin and death gained entrance into the world through Adam and that sin and death are now common to all people (Rom. 5:12; 6:23). Adam may be pictured as a representative of mankind, all of whom share in his penalty (Rom. 5:19).

Randy Hatchett

FALLOW DEER See *Animals*.

FALLOW GROUND Virgin soil or else soil which has not recently been planted (Jer. 4:3; Hos. 10:12). The central thrust of the prophetic message is clear: the nation Israel, "Jacob", is to return to Yahweh by "cultivating" the covenant values of righteousness and steadfast love. The precise significance of the fallow ground is unclear. Perhaps the unplowed earth represents Israel's failure to do what was needed to keep the covenant. Or perhaps the virgin soil represents a new relationship with God. Here the call is for Israel to abandon the worn out fields of unrighteousness (symbolized by thorns) and to move on to the new, fertile (Prov. 13:23) ground of covenant living.

FALSE APOSTLES A designation for Paul's opponents in 2 Corinthians 11:13, also designated deceitful workers (11:13) and ministers of Satan (11:15). Such "apostles" were characterized as preaching a "rival Jesus" (likely a lordly, miracle-working "success story"), possessing a different spirit (a self-seeking motivation evidenced by a different lifestyle than Paul's), and a different gospel which disregarded the cross (and its corollary of suffering for those who follow Christ). The false apostles appear to have been Jewish Christians (11:22), well-trained in speech (11:6), who perhaps claimed "visions and revelations of the Lord" (12:1) as authenticating marks of apostleship (Compare the role of Paul's Damascus Road experience, Acts 9:15; 22:14–15; 26:16–19). Though they cut in on Paul's missionary territory, the "false apostles" are characterized as boasting (2 Cor. 10:13–16) according to human standards. Their leadership style was oppressive (11:20). In contrast to Paul, these false apostles relied on the Corinthian Christians for financial support (11:7–11,20; 12:14). They perhaps accused Paul of being "paid what he was worth." Paul countered that suffering for Christ was the mark of true apostleship (11:23). Weakness, not dominating power, reveals God's power (11:30; 12:5,9). If the "super-apostles" (11:5; 12:11 NRSV, REB, NIV) are identified with the leaders of the Jerusalem church, they should be distinguished from the false apostles at Corinth. The latter may have claimed the authority of the former.

The false apostles of Revelation 2:2 are characterized as evil men and liars. They should perhaps be identified with the Nicolaitans active at Ephesus (2:6) and Pergamos (2:15), and with the followers of the "false prophetess" at Thyatira (2:20).

FALSE CHRISTS Imposters claiming to be the Messiah (Christ in Greek). Jesus associated the appearance of messianic pretenders with the fall of Jerusalem (Matt. 24:23–26; Mark 13:21–22).

Jesus warned His followers to be skeptical of those who point to signs and omens to authenticate their false messianic claims. Jesus also urged disbelief of those claiming the Messiah was waiting in the wilderness or was in "the inner rooms" (perhaps a reference to the inner chambers of the Temple complex). Josephus mentioned several historical figures who might be regarded as false christs: (1) Theudas, who appeared when Fadus was procurator (A.D. 44–46) and summoned the people to the Jordan River wilderness with the promise that he would divide the Jordan like Joshua and begin a new conquest of the land; (2) various "imposters" during the term of Felix (A.D. 52–59) who led crowds into the wilderness with promises of signs and wonders; (3) an "imposter" during the term of Festus (A.D. 60–62) who promised deliverance and freedom from the miseries of Roman rule for those who would follow him into the wilderness; (4) Manahem ben Judah (alias "the Galilean") during the term of Florus (A.D. 64–66) who came to Jerusalem "like a king" and laid seige to the city. These messianic imposters and the barely distinguishable false prophets repeatedly urged the Jewish people to take up armed resistance to Rome or to stay in Jerusalem to fight. In contrast, Jesus urged His disciples to attempt to save themselves by fleeing the city. The Christian inhabitants of Jerusalem remembered this advice when the war with Rome broke out (A.D. 66) and fled to safety in Pella in Trans-Jordan. Some interpreters expect false christs to arise before the future coming of Christ.

FALSE PROPHET A person who spreads false messages and teachings, claiming to speak God's words.

Old Testament While the term "false prophet" does not occur in the Old Testament, references to false prophets are clear. The pages of the Old Testament are filled with men and women who fit the description of a false prophet given in Jer. 14:14 (NAS): "The prophets are prophesying falsehood in My name. I have neither sent them nor commanded them nor spoken to them; they are prophesying to you a false vision, divination, futility and the deception of their own minds." Other examples are in Jeremiah 23:21–33 and Zechariah 10:2. Punishment for prophesying falsely was severe. False prophets were cast away from God's presence and permanently humiliated. They suffered the destruction of their cities (Jer. 7:14–16; 23:39).

A false prophet was also one who prophesied on behalf of another God. A familiar example is the story of Elijah and the prophets of Baal (1 Kings 18:20–39). In a test against Elijah and the true God, the prophets of Baal suffered humiliating defeat.

Israel could not always distinguish between the true and the false prophet as seen in 1 Kings 22;

Jeremiah 28. The prophet could only say, wait and see whose prophecy proves true in history (Deut. 18:22; 1 Kings 22:28; Jer. 29:9). Compare 1 Kings 13.

New Testament Jesus and the apostles spoke many times about false prophets. In the Sermon on the Mount, Jesus taught about the marks of a false prophet and the consequences of being one (Matt. 7:15–23). He also cautioned His followers to beware of false prophets who would arise during times of tribulation and in the end times (Matt. 24:11,24; Mark 13:22). He said to be careful when the world loves a prophet's words, because a prophet who is false is apt to be popular (Luke 6:26).

The apostles instructed believers to be diligent in faith and understanding of Christian teachings, in order to discern false prophets when they arise (2 Pet. 1:10; 1:19–2:1; 1 John 4:1). The tests of a prophet are: 1) Do their predictions come true (Jer. 28:9)? 2) Does the prophet have a divine commission (Jer. 29:9)? 3) Are the prophecies consistent with Scripture (2 Pet. 1:20–21; Rev. 22:18–19)? 4) Do the people benefit spiritually from the prophet's ministry (Jer. 23:13,14,32; 1 Pet. 4:11)?

Punishments for false prophets were just as severe in the New Testament as they were in the Old. Paul caused a false prophet to be stricken with blindness (Acts 13:6–12), but most other punishments were more permanent in nature. Jesus said the false prophets would be cut down and burned like a bad tree (Matt. 7:19). Second Peter 2:4 describes being cast into pits of darkness. The ultimate punishment appears in Revelation 19:20; 20:10—the false prophet, the beast, and the devil will be thrown into a lake of fire and brimstone and be tormented forever.

See *Prophets.* *Donna R. Ridge*

FALSE WORSHIP A broad category *of acts and attitudes* which includes the worship, reverence, or religious honoring of any object, person, or entity other than the one true God. It also includes impure, improper, or other inappropriate acts directed toward the worship of the true God.

Worship offered to a false object is the most obvious and easily recognized form of false worship. The worship of idols is but a part of false worship in the biblical world. Many times other gods were worshiped, not because of the appeal of the idols or images but out of a false sense of the power of the "god." The most consistent problem with false worship seen in the Old Testament is with the nature or fertility deities—Baals and Ashtaroth, Anath, Astarte—the male and female representations of reproduction and growth. Understanding of the basic form and nature of this kind of false worship has been clarified by discoveries made at Ugarit and the subsequent interpretation and study of these. Baal was commonly believed to have control over growth of all crops and reproduction of all flocks. Many of the forms of this false worship involved sexual acts—activities abhorred in the Old Testament laws. Yet the appeal and practice of these rituals continued, probably because of Baal's reputed power in those areas so intwined with life and livelihood of the ancient Hebrews. During the time of great Assyrian power in the ancient world, even the Hebrews seem to have thought that the Assyrian gods were more powerful than their Yahweh; so they began to worship them. The prophet Zephaniah, who lived and prophesied in this time, condemned those who "worship the host of heaven upon the house tops" (Zeph. 1:5). Associated with this type of worship was the fairly prevalent view in the Old Testament world that a god had his own territory and that he was relatively powerless outside that place. Perhaps the most direct statement of this is in the story of Naaman (2 Kings 5, especially v. 17). After the Syrian commander was cured of his leprosy, he requested a "two mules' burden" of dirt from Israel to take with him to Syria so that he could worship the true God.

The many references to false gods with obviously false worship in the Old Testament coupled with the almost total absence of such in the New Testament might suggest that there was little problem with other gods in the New Testament world. Such is far from true. The world of the first century was filled with religions other than Judaism and Christianity. The presence of falseness in worship because it was directed to false gods continued to be a religious problem. Native national gods and fertility deities similar to Baal and Ashtaroth of the Old Testament period still abounded. A new force was present in the mystery religions—Hellenistic religions which focused on the hope for life beyond death. The Orphic and Eleusinian mysteries were perhaps the most common of these. Emperor worship was a serious challenge in the days of the early church. Probably most Romans saw the emperor cult as merely an expression of patriotism and loyalty to the state. However, the Christian standard was to "render therefore unto Caesar the things which be Caesar's, and unto God the things which be God's" (Luke 20:25). Often the Christian was faced with imperial orders to participate in this kind of false worship. Refusal could bring serious penalties, often execution. In late New Testament times and the years following, Mithraism became the primary competitor with Christianity. This pagan worship of Mithra, represented by *sol invictus* (the invincible sun) was a powerful challenge to Christianity. Exclusively a male religion, emphasizing power and strength, Mithraism was especially popular in the Roman army.

False worship does not necessarily center in practice of pagan or idolatrous cults. It is often a problem for those who proclaim worship of the one true God. False worship of this sort usually centers in some form of deliberate or unintentional disobedience. Its presence in the Bible extends from the self-exalting disobedience in the Garden of Eden to compromising accommodation with the emperor cult and other pagan religions seen in the Book of Revelation.

The primary forms of false worship are addressed in the Decalogue (Ex. 20): "Thou shalt have no other gods before [in addition to] me" (v. 3)—a command for exclusive loyalty to and worship of Yahweh; "Thou shalt not make unto thee any graven image" (v. 4a) —a clear requirement of imageless, that is, spiritual worship; and "Thou shalt not take the name of the Lord thy God in vain" (v. 7a) —a command to honor in all of life the God whose name the Hebrews claimed and bore.

The Hebrews were guilty of syncretistic or artificially mixed religious practices. The temples built by Jeroboam, son of Nebat, the first king of Israel (the Northern Kingdom) after its break from the Jerusalem-centered Kingdom of Judah, were probably dedicated to such worship. When these temples were established in Bethel and Dan, Jeroboam the King "made two calves of gold, and said unto them, It is too much for you to go up to Jerusalem: behold thy gods, O Israel, which brought thee up out of the land of Egypt" (1 Kings 12:28). This mixing of the gold calf—a symbol of Baal—with the worship of the God who delivered the Hebrews from their Egyptian bondage was false worship.

A very similar practice was prevalent in the time of Elijah. In his confrontation with the Baal prophets on Mt. Carmel in the time of Ahab and Jezebel (1 Kings 18:20–46), the prophet of the Lord addressed the assembled people. "How long halt ye between two opinions? if the Lord be God, follow him: but if Baal, then follow him" (1 Kings 18:21).

False worship includes trusting in military power (Isa. 31:1), trusting in the "works of your hands" (Jer. 25:7), serving God in order to receive physical and material blessings (as Job's friends), offering unacceptable, tainted or maimed sacrifices to God instead of the best (Mal. 1:6–8). False worship also occurs when one prays, fasts, or gives alms "before men to be seen of them" instead of in sincere devotion to God (Matt. 6:1–18).

The subjects of false and true worship are best presented in Micah 6:8, "What doth the Lord require of thee, but to do justly, and to love mercy, and to walk humbly with thy God" and in the words of Jesus to the Samaritan woman in John 4:23–24: "true worshippers shall worship the Father in spirit and in truth: for the Father seeketh such to worship him. God is a Spirit: and they that worship him must worship him in spirit and in truth."

See *Canaan, Religion and History of; Worship.*

Bruce C. Cresson

FAMILIAR SPIRIT See *Medium.*

FAMILY The basic household unit which provides a person's central relationships, nurture, and support. The basic composition of a family changes from the Old Testament to the New Testament. Therefore, the search for the traditional biblical family is difficult.

Old Testament The span of the Old Testament allowed for much transition in the family. Their understanding of the nature of God as well as of their culture influenced much of the Hebrew family life.

Structure The Old Testament family represents a larger body that the English word suggests. There are two Hebrew words which are used to refer to the family. One word (*mishpachah*) was used to describe the larger patriarchal clan which included those persons related by blood, marriage, slaveship, and even animals (as found in the fourth commandment, Ex. 20:10). Occasionally even strangers or sojourners could be included in the larger household.

The second word (*bayith*) was used to suggest the place of residence or household. It had multiple meanings. It represented a clan of descendents

A modern Jewish family (grandfather, daughter, and grandchildren) on an afternoon outing in Tel Aviv.

(Gen. 18:19), or property and persons of a particular place or residence on which and on whom one depended (Job 8:15).

Central to this household was the oldest male relative who was viewed as the "father," master, and ultimate authority, thus signifying the family as the father's house. All who belonged to him and claimed their allegiance to him were considered part of the household and were similar in beliefs and values. In Genesis 7:1 Noah and his household were directed to enter the ark. Beyond the household was the larger clan, the tribe, and the nation which were descendants of Abraham, the origin of the people of Israel.

Relationships With the oldest male as center of

F

the household, he was expected to marry and often have more than one wife (Gen. 38:8–10; Deut. 25:5–10). Polygamy was common, though monogamy was widely practiced in Israel. Abraham, Jacob, and David were all husbands of more than one wife, and they also had concubines which were recognized as a lower status than a wife. See *Concubine.* Jacob's family numbered sixty-six persons in all, not including his sons' wives (Gen. 46:26). The creation story (Gen. 1–2) modeled the monogamous relationship of one male and one female, as does much of the Bible.

The authority of the father was quite significant, even though he may actually have been the grandfather or great-grandfather. His responsibilities included begatting, instructing, disciplining, and nurturing. Abraham had the power to sacrifice his son (Gen. 22). The father could even destroy family members if they enticed him from his loyalty to God (Deut. 13:6–10). However, the father was also to be loving, and the divine mercy of the New Testament was based on the compassionate Old Testament father (Ps. 103).

In the marriage, the male had power over the female or females (Gen. 3:16). They were often considered property of the male. He could have relationships with other women as long as he did not destroy property rights. Therefore, divorce was a male option only. He could divorce for almost any reason. As an example, he might "lose favor" (Deut. 24:1). He simply had to write a note and place her out. Both persons were free to marry again.

The Hebrew "mother" often saw her primary function as having children. The account of creation, however, described the female as being created equal with the male. After the Fall, women were relegated to the child-bearing role. The mother exercised significant authority over family life and often gave directions. Her primary role was to provide love and care for the members. The prophet Isaiah used the image of the mother to describe the compassion of God (Isa. 66:13). The mother was the object of love and honor and is praised in Proverbs 31 for her good works.

Children were very important to the family and were considered proof of God's love (Ps. 127:3–5). They were under absolute authority and control of the father. Sons were especially important and were considered second to the father in significance. Descent was through the male which also determined the perpetuation of the family name and the personality. Therefore, sons were trained in the traditions of the community and in the meaning of wisdom (Prov. 3:12; 13:24; 19:18). Daughters were often considered of secondary importance. The fathers were responsible for arranging marriages for the sons (Gen. 24:4) and writing contracts for the daughters.

Commitment The Old Testament family was close-knit, and family loyalty was very strong. The family was held together around the central dominant figure of the father. Family honor and respect was high. The covenant was central to understanding Old Testament family relationships as well as relationships with God. A covenant had both an interior bonding and an exterior binding quality. Steadfast love (*hesed)* was the basis of the covenant which created a sense of loyalty, justice, and high regard. Covenants were personal and caring and were greater than contracts for directing the family. Hebrew marriages were covenant marriages (Mal. 2:14). Hosea especially revealed the importance of steadfast love (Hos. 2:19–20).

Functions The family of the Old Testament had the purposes of reproduction, instruction, care giving, maintaining traditions, and conveying wisdom. The primary function, however, was the teaching of religion, thus providing guidelines and instruction which were central to Hebrew family well-being. They carefully guarded the family from outside influences. When the family moved from a rural to an urbanized culture, their traditions and values were threatened. Consequently, ancient customs were reaffirmed, and faith was used to undergird them.

New Testament The New Testament introduced major changes in understanding the family, and it provided new and creative ways to appreciate the nature of family and the nature of faith.

Structure As in the Old Testament the Greek words used to describe family did not refer exclusively to our understanding of the nuclear family. One word (*patria)* was used to identify lineage and descent from a specific ancestor (Luke 2:4; Acts 3:25; Eph. 3:15). Another term (*oikos)* meant a house or a building but could also refer to a lineage or clan much like the Old Testament word for household (1 Cor. 1:16). A similar term (*oikia)* also referred to a building (Matt. 7:24) but was used to describe a household including husband, wife, children, and others.

The New Testament household or family, especially the Christian family, probably had one husband and one wife, children, relatives, slaves, servants, and others who lived there for various reasons. The household codes of the New Testament outlined duties for the members including husband/wife, father/child, and master/slave (Eph. 5:21—6:4; Col. 3:18—4:1).

The importance of lineage in the New Testament shifted from a focus on the lineage from an ancestor to lineage from God. In Matthew, Jesus said, "call no man your father upon the earth: for one is your Father, which is in heaven" (23:9). The focus of family structure and family lineage changed from the "earthly father" and was replaced by a lineage from "God the Father," accessible to anyone through Jesus Christ. Therefore, all who believed on Jesus became part of a broader family of God.

Relationships Jesus used the relationships of His own family as well as natural families to define the nature of God's relationships with His people (Matt. 7:9–10; 11:16–17; 21:28–32; Luke 11:7; 14:11–32). Jesus even gave greater importance to relationships within the family of God than to the natural family. He said, "whosoever shall do the will of my Father which is in heaven, the same is my brother, and sister, and mother" (Matt. 12:50). Following Jesus often meant leaving one's family (Mark 1:16–20; Luke 9:59–60).

The primary relational dynamic Jesus and the New Testament taught was love (*agape).* This New Testament love expanded the Old Testament understanding of steadfast love (*hesed)* by developing an unconditional, accepting love known initially in the love of God (John 3:16; 1 Cor. 13). This love permeated and transformed the relationships of families and all persons.

Marriage in the New Testament was founded on a love bond experienced by both male and female in contrast to the arranged marriage of the Old Testament. Women were not to be considered property by men but rather were to be loved and nurtured (Eph. 5:25).

The roles of men and women were transformed by the love of Christ. The father was no longer the central figure of the family but was replaced by God the Father and faith in Jesus Christ. The authority of the male became like the sacrificial, servant authority of Jesus Christ (Eph. 5:25–33).

The role and status of a woman were not linked intrinsically to her function as a wife and mother. Her identity and personhood were discovered in her faith commitment to Jesus Christ and in doing the will of the Father. Therefore, women did not have to be married or have children to be important in the family of God (Gal. 3:28).

The marriage relationship was important in the New Testament. There was to be marriage between one man and one woman (Mark 10:6–8; Eph. 5:31). The relationship was to be permanent. Jesus addressed the issue of divorce because it was so commonly and easily exercised (for the man). Jesus believed that the love bond made the marriage vows sacred, and they were not to be broken (Mark 10:11–12; Luke 16:18). Jesus affirmed the value of marriage but did not view it as more important than the family of God.

The nature of the Christian marriage relationship, guided by Christlike love, called for both man and woman to give themselves voluntarily and sacrificially to each other (Eph. 5:21). This mutual love commitment was a radical departure from the Old Testament marriage model. The New Testament marriage union was based on an equal and mutual sharing guided by love (1 Cor. 7:4).

Children were given a place of high honor by Jesus (Mark 10:13–16). Having a child created an opportunity for parents to become co-creators with God in helping earthly children to become children of God (Rom. 9:8). Therefore, the focus of the parent/child relationship was on love, honor, and respect as well as discipline and instruction (Eph. 6:1–4).

Commitment The Old Testament concept of covenant became the foundation for the new covenant in Jesus Christ. Steadfast love was enhanced by Christlike love. Covenants and commitments, in family relationships and faith relationships, were deepened by the new covenant of love which was infused with grace and forgiveness. All relationships were guided by grace and the sacrificial love of Jesus Christ (1 John 3:16). Christian family relationships called for a commitment which was based on openness and compassion, forgiveness and understanding.

This image of family commitment was so significant that it was used by the early church to describe the relationship of Christ and the church (Eph. 5).

Function The function of the family in the New Testament was secondary to the primary purpose of the family of God. Obedience to Christ and doing God's will was the calling for everyone. This faith commitment, then, shaped the purpose and function of the family. The family was guided by Christlike love, and the purpose of the family was to give witness to the love of God and bring people to a saving relationship with God through Jesus Christ, thus creating the larger family of God.

See *Father; Mother; Marriage; Sex; Woman; Children; Divorce.*   *J. Michael Hester*

FAMINE AND DROUGHT A famine is an extreme shortage of food, and a drought is an excessive dryness of land. The Bible reports or predicts the occurrence of several famines and droughts. **Causes of Famine** Drought was the most common cause of famines mentioned in the Bible. Drought caused famines in the time of Abraham (Gen. 12:10), Isaac (Gen. 26:1), Joseph (Gen. 41:27), and the judges (Ruth 1:1). Drought and famine also plagued the Israelites in the days of David (2 Sam. 21:1), Elijah (1 Kings 18:2), Elisha (2 Kings 4:38), Haggai (Hag. 1:11), and Nehemiah (Neh. 5:3). At times the coming of droughts and famines was predicted by prophets (2 Kings 8:1; Isa. 3:1; Jer. 14:12; Acts 11:28). Other natural forces also caused famines: locusts, wind, hail, and mildew (Joel 1:4; Amos 4:9; Hag. 2:17). The Israelites also experienced famines caused by enemies. Occasionally oppressors destroyed or confiscated food (Deut. 28:33,51; Isa. 1:7). The siege of cities also resulted in famine, such as the siege of Samaria by Ben-hadad (2 Kings 6:24–25) and the siege of Jerusalem by Nebuchadnezzar (2 Kings 25:2–3).

The famines which Israel experienced were often severe, some lasting for years (Gen. 12:10;

F

41:27; Jer. 14:1–6). During famines, starving people resorted to eating such things as wild vines, heads of animals, garbage, dung, and even human flesh (2 Kings 4:39; 6:25,28; Lam. 4:4–10).

Famine and Drought as the Judgment of God God created the world as a good environment which would normally provide ample water and food for mankind (Gen. 1). However, the productiveness of the earth is related to people's obedience to God. For example, the sins of Adam, Eve, and Cain resulted in unfruitfulness of the earth (Gen. 3:17–18; 4:12). Israel's relationship with God also directly affected the fertility of the Promised Land. When the people obeyed God, the land was productive (Deut. 11:11–14). However, when they disobeyed, judgment came on the land by drought and famine (Lev. 26:23–26; Deut. 11:16–17; 1 Kings 8:35). Furthermore, the New Testament reports that famine will be a part of God's coming judgment of the earth in the last days (Matt. 24:7; Rev. 6:8).

While the Bible states that some famines and droughts are the judgment of God (2 Sam. 21:1; 1 Kings 17:1; 2 Kings 8:1; Jer 14:12; Ezek. 5:12; Amos 4:6), not all such disasters are connected to divine punishment (Gen. 12:10; 26:1; Ruth 1:1; Acts 11:28). When God did send drought and famine on His people, it was for the purpose of bringing them to repentance (1 Kings 8:35–36; Hos. 2:8–23; Amos 4:6–8). Moreover, the Old Testament contains promises that God will protect His faithful ones in times of famine (Job. 5:20,22; Pss. 33:18–19; 37:18–19; Prov. 10:3). *See Benhadad; Jerusalem; Nebuchadnezzar; Samaria; Water.* *Bob R. Ellis*

FAN KJV term for a long wooden fork used to toss grain into the air so that the chaff is blown away. Shovels were also used for this purpose (Isa. 30:24). Modern translations render the underlying Hebrew and Greek terms shovel, winnowing fork, or winnowing shovel.

FARM, FARMING See Agriculture

Ox turning an ancient type of water pump used for irrigation in the Goshen area of Egypt.

A relief of a plowing scene from the Roman period.

FARMER See *Occupations and Professions in the Bible; Agriculture.*

FARTHING See *Coins.*

FASTING Refraining from eating food. The Bible describes three main forms of fasting: 1) The Normal Fast, involving the total abstinence of

Young Israeli farmer plowing furrows behind his donkey-drawn wooden plow.

Arab farmer plowing his field with a simple double-yoked plow and team of two donkeys.

food. Luke 4:2 reveals that Jesus "did eat nothing." Afterwards "He was hungered." Jesus abstained from food but not from water. 2) In Acts 9:9 we read of an Absolute Fast where for three days He "neither did eat nor drink." The abstinence from both food and water seems to have lasted no more than three days (Ezra 10:6; Esther 4:16). 3) The Partial Fast—in Daniel 10:3 the emphasis is upon the restriction of diet rather than complete abstinence. The context implies that there were physical benefits resulting from this partial fast. However, this verse indicates that there was a revelation given to Daniel as a result of this time of fasting.

Fasting is the laying aside of food for a period of time when the believer is seeking to know God in a deeper experience. It is to be done as an act before God in the privacy of one's own pursuit of God (Ex. 34:28; 1 Sam. 7:6; 1 Kings 19:8; Matt. 6:17).

Fasting is to be done with the object of seeking to know God in a deeper experience (Isa. 58; Zech. 7:5). Fasting relates to a time of confession (Ps. 69:10). Fasting can be a time of seeking a deeper prayer experience and drawing near to God in prevailing prayer (Ezra 8:23; Joel 2:12). The early church often fasted in seeking God's will for leadership in the local church (Acts 13:2). When the early church wanted to know the mind of God, there was a time of prayer and fasting.

C. Robert Marsh

FATE That which must necessarily happen. The Old Testament speaks of death as the common fate of humankind (Pss. 49:12; 81:15; Eccl. 2:14; 3:19; 9:2,3). The Old Testament similarly speaks of violent death as the destiny of the wicked (Job 15:22; Isa. 65:12; Hos. 9:13). See *Election* and *Predestination.*

FATHER See *Family; God.*

FATHERLESS A person without a male parent, often rendered orphan by modern translations. Orphans are often mentioned with widows as representatives of the most helpless members of society (Ex. 22:22; Deut. 10:18; Ps. 146:9). In societies where the basic social unit was the clan headed by a father (the eldest male relative, perhaps a grandfather or uncle), those without a father or husband were social misfits without one to provide for their material needs and represent their interests in the court (Job 31:21). Life for the fatherless was harsh. Orphans were often forced to beg for food (Ps. 109:9–10). They suffered loss of their homes (Ps. 109:10), land rights (Prov. 23:10), and livestock (Job 24:3). The fatherless were subject to acts of violence (Job 22:9), were treated as property to be gambled for (6:27 TEV, NRSV, NAS, NIV), and were even murdered (Ps. 94:6).

God, however, has a special concern for orphans and widows (Deut. 10:18; Pss. 10:14–18; 146:9; Hos. 14:3) evidenced in the title "a father of the fatherless" (Ps. 68:5). Old Testament law provided for the material needs of orphans and widows who were to be fed from the third year's tithe (Deut. 14:28–29; 26:12–13), from sheaves left forgotten in the fields (24:19), and from fruit God commanded to be left on the trees and vines (24:20–21). Orphans and widows were to be included in the celebrations of the worshiping community (Deut. 16:11,14). God's people were repeatedly warned not to take advantage of orphans and widows (Ex. 22:22; Deut. 24:17; 27:19; Ps. 82:3; Isa. 1:17). In the New Testament, James defined worship acceptable to God as meeting the needs of orphans and widows (1:27).

God's exiled people were described as orphans without home or inheritance (Lam. 5:2–3). The Old Testament image of the orphan without a helper at the court perhaps forms the background for Jesus' promise that His disciples would not be left orphans (John 14:18, NAS, NIV, NRSV; "comfortless", KJV; "bereft", REB). They would not be defenseless since the Holy Spirit would act as their advocate (14:16). Paul described his painful separation from the Thessalonian Christians as being orphaned (1 Thess. 2:17, NRSV).

Chris Church

FATHER'S HOUSE A name given to extended family units in the Ancient Near East reflecting a social organization in which a dominant male headed the family. These units might be large (Jacob's house included 66 descendants when he entered Egypt, Gen. 46:26). A father's house could designate the clans within a tribe (Ex. 6:14–25) or even an entire tribe (Josh. 22:14). The common designations "house of Jacob" (Ex. 19:3; Amos 3:13), "house of Israel" (Ex. 40:38) and the unusual designation "house of Isaac" (Amos 7:16) all refer to the nation Israel in terms of a father's house.

During patriarchal times a marriage was expected to be within the house of one's father (Gen. 11:29; 20:12; 24:4,15,38,40; 29:10; Ex. 6:20; Num. 36:8–10). Some of these marriages within the clan were later prohibited (Lev. 18:9,12; 20:17,19). In patriarchal times married women were regarded as remaining part of their father's house (Gen. 31:14; compare 46:26 where the enumeration of Jacob's house does not include his sons' wives). In later times married women were regarded to have left their father's houses (Num. 30:3,16). Widows were expected to return to their fathers' houses (Gen. 38:11). Genesis 31:14 suggests that in patriarchal times married women might normally expect to share in their father's inheritance. Later law limited this right to cases in which there were no sons to inherit (Num. 27:8).

In John 2:16 "My father's house" is a designation for the Temple which was then equated with Christ's body (2:21). The reference to "My Father's house" with its many dwelling places (14:2) can be explained in two ways. House can be understood as a place or as a set of relationships, a household. Already in the Psalms the Temple is the house of God where the righteous hope to dwell (23:6; 27:4). It is a short step to the idea of heaven as God's dwelling where there is ample room for the disciples. If house is understood as household, the focus is on fellowship with God. In contrast to servants, a son abides in his father's house (John 8:35). As Son of God, Jesus enjoys unique fellowship with God. By believing in Christ, we are empowered to become children of God (1:12), members of God's household, and share in fellowship with the Father. The two meanings do not exclude each other. Both may be included in Jesus' promise in John 14:2.

Chris Church

FATHOM Measure of depth equalling six feet (Acts 27:28). See *Weights and Measures.*

FATLINGS, FATTED Generally a young animal put up to be fed for slaughter. Sometimes a general reference to the strongest or choice among a flock or herd is intended. In Pharoah's dream fat cows (Gen. 41:2,18) symbolized years of prosperity. Saul was tempted to spare the choice animals of the Amalekites (1 Sam. 15:9). In Ezekiel 34:3,16,20 the fat sheep symbolize the prosperous leaders of Israel. As choice specimens, fattened animals made an appropriate offering to God (2 Sam. 6:13; Ps. 66:15; Amos 5:22). Fattened animals are often associated with banquets.

Fattened cattle formed part of the menu for the wedding banquet of the king's son in the parable in Matthew 22:4. In the parable of the loving father a son is welcomed home with a banquet of a fatted calf (Luke 15:23,27,30). Fattened animals were used as a symbol for slaughter. In the New Testament, James pictured the oppressive rich as fattening their hearts for a day of slaughter, perhaps a reference to God's judgment on them (5:5).

FAWN Young deer; term used in modern translations for KJV "hind" and "roe." See *Animals.*

FEAR A broad range of emotions that embrace both the secular and the religious worlds. Secular fear is the natural feeling of alarm caused by the expectation of imminent danger, pain, or disaster. Religious fear appears as the result of awe and reverence toward a supreme power.
Terminology The English word "fear" is used to translate several Hebrew and Greek words. In the Old Testament, the most common word used to express fear is *yirʾah,* which means "fear, "terror" (Isa. 7:25; Jonah 1:10,16). In the New Testament, the word used most often to express fear is *phobos* which means "fear," "dread," "terror"

(Matt. 28:4; Luke 21:26).

Secular Fear arises in the normal activities and relationships of life.

Human Fear Animals fear humans (Gen. 9:2), and humans fear the animals (Amos 3:8); individuals fear individuals (Gen. 26:7), and nations fear nations (2 Sam. 10:19). People are afraid of wars (Ex. 14:10), of their enemies (Deut. 2:4), and of subjugation (Deut. 7:18; 28:10). People are afraid of death (Gen. 32:11), of disaster (Zeph. 3:15–16), of sudden panic (Prov. 3:25), of being overtaken by adversity (Job 6:21), and of the unknown (Gen. 19:30). Fear can reflect the limitations of life (Eccl. 12:5) as well as the unforeseen consequences of actions (1 Sam. 3:15). Fear can be the regard the young owes to the aged (Job 32:6), the honor a child demonstrates toward parents (Lev. 19:3), the reverential respect of individuals toward their masters (1 Pet. 2:18), and to persons in positions of responsibilities (Rom. 13:7). Fear also can be the sense of concern for individuals (2 Cor. 11:3) as well as the respect for one's husband (1 Pet. 3:2).

Fear as consequence of sin Fear may come from a strong realization of sin and disobedience. Man and woman were afraid after their act of disobedience (Gen. 3:10). Abimelech was afraid when he realized that he had committed an offensive act by taking the wife of Abraham to be his wife (Gen. 20:8–9). This sense of estrangement and guilt that comes as consequence of sin produces in the heart of individuals the fear of the day of the Lord because they will appear before the judgment of God (Joel 2:1).

Freedom from fear Freedom from fear comes as individuals trust in the God who protects (Ps. 23:4) and helps them (Isa. 54:14). The New Testament teaches that perfect love casts out fear (1 John 4:18). Christians are no longer slaves of fear, for Christ has given them not a spirit of timidity or cowardice, but a spirit of power, of love, and of self-control (2 Tim. 1:7).

Religious Fear is the human response to the presence of God.

Fear of God A prominent element in Old Testament religion is the concept of the fear of God. Most often the sense of fear comes as individuals encounter the divine in the context of revelation. When God appears to a person, the person experiences the reality of God's holiness. This self-disclosure of God points to the vast distinction between humans and God, to the mysterious characteristic of God that at the same time attracts and repels. There is a mystery in divine holiness that causes individuals to become overwhelmed with a sense of awe and fear. They respond by falling down or kneeling in reverence and worship, confessing sin, and seeking God's will (Isa. 6).

God as a fearful God The God of Israel is an awe-producing God because of His majesty, His power, His works, His transcendence, and His holiness. Yahweh is a "great and terrible God" (Neh. 1:15); He is "fearful in praises, doing wonders" (Ex. 15:11); His name is "fearful" (Deut. 28:58) and "terrible" (Ps. 99:3). The fear of God comes as people experience God in a visible manifestation (Ex. 20:18), in dreams (Gen. 28:17), in visible form (Ex. 3:6), and in His work of salvation (Isa. 41:5). God's work, His power, majesty, and holiness evoke fear and demand acknowledgment. The fear of God is not to be understood as the dread that comes out of fear of punishment, but as the reverential regard and the awe that comes out of recognition and submission to the divine. It is the revelation of God's will to which the believer submits in obedience.

The basis for God's relationship with Israel was the covenant. The personal relationship that came out of the covenant transformed the relationship from a sense of terror to one of respect and reverence in which trust predominated. This fear which produces awe can be seen in the worship of Israel. The Israelites were exhorted to "serve the Lord with fear" (Ps. 2:11). Fear protected Israel from taking God for granted or from presuming on His grace. Fear called to covenant obedience.

Fear as obedience Deuteronomy sets out a relationship between the fear of God and the observance of the demands of the covenant. To fear the Lord is one of the ways by which Israel expresses its obedience and loyalty to Yahweh and to His divine requirements: "And now, Israel, what doth the Lord thy God require of thee, but to fear the Lord thy God, to walk in all his ways, and to love him, and to serve the Lord thy God with all thy heart and with all thy soul, to keep the commandments of the Lord and his statutes, which I command thee this day for thy good?" (Deut. 10:12–13; compare 6:24–25; 10:20; 13:4). Fear becomes a demand that can be learned (Deut. 17:19). Fear of God was part of the religious life of every Israelite, where the acknowledgment of it required a specific behavior from each individual. Fear of God was a requirement demanded from every judge (Ex. 18:21). The kings of Israel should rule in the fear of the Lord (2 Sam. 23:3); even the messianic King would live in the fear of the Lord (Isa. 11:2). To fear God was the beginning of wisdom and thus of the pathway to true life (Prov. 1:7; 9:10; 15:33).

"Fear not" The expression "fear not" (also translated "do not fear" or "do not be afraid") is an invitation to confidence and trust. When used without religious connotation (15 times), "fear not" is an expression of comfort. These words come from an individual to another providing reassurance and encouragement (Gen. 50:21; Ruth 3:11; Ps. 49:16). When "fear not" is used in a religious context (60 times), the words are an invitation to trust in God. These words appear in the context of the fear and terror that follows divine revelation. God invites His people not to be

F

afraid of Him (Gen. 15:1; 26:24); the angel of the Lord seeks to calm an individual before a divine message is communicated (Dan. 10:12,19; Luke 1:13,30); a person acting as a mediator of God invites the people to trust in God (Moses, Deut. 31:6; Joshua, Josh. 10:25).

The "God-fearers" The "God-fearers" were those who were faithful to God and obeyed His commandments (Job 1:1; Pss. 25:14; 33:18). Those who fear God are blessed (Ps. 112:1); they enjoy God's goodness (Ps. 34:9) and God's provision (Ps. 111:5). In the New Testament "God-fearers" became a technical term for uncircumcised Gentiles who worshiped in the Jewish synagogue.

Fear in the New Testament Some Christians tend to de-emphasize the fear of God in the New Testament by placing the love of God above the fear of God. There is indeed a greater emphasis on the love of God in the New Testament. However, the element of fear was part of the proclamation of the early church.

Paul admonished believers to work out their salvation "with fear and trembling" (Phil. 2:12). The early church grew in number as they lived "in the fear of the Lord" (Acts 9:31). The fear of God is related to the love of God. The revelation of God to people in the New Testament contains the element of God's mysterious otherness calling for reverent obedience. The New Testament church stands in awe and fear in the presence of a holy God, for fear is "the whole duty of man" (Eccl. 12:13). *Claude F. Mariottini*

FEAR OF ISAAC Name or title that Jacob used in referring to God (Gen 31:42; compare 31:53; 46:1). Evidently the patriarchs used various names to refer to God until He revealed His personal name to Moses (Ex 6:3). Some scholars translate the Hebrew expression "Kinsman of Isaac" or "Refuge of Isaac." See *Patriarchs; God of the Fathers.*

FEASTS See *Festivals.*

FELIX (Fē' lix) The procurator of Judea at the time Paul the apostle visited Jerusalem for the last time and was arrested there (Acts 23:24). Antonius Felix became procurator of Judea in A.D. 52, succeeding Cumanus. He remained in office until A.D. 60, when the emperor Nero recalled him. He is depicted in Acts as a man who listened with interest to Paul's defense but failed to make any decision with regard to the case or with regard to the personal implications of Paul's message. Rather he hoped Paul would pay him a bribe (Acts 24:26). Contemporary historians Tacitus and Josephus paint Felix as a brutal, incompetent politician who was finally replaced. Compare Acts 24:27. See *Paul; Roman Empire.*

FELLOES Term used by KJV, REB for the rim of a wheel (1 Kings 7:33).

FELLOWSHIP The bond of common purpose and devotion that binds Christians together and to Christ. "Fellowship" is the English translation of words from the Hebrew stem *hbr* and the Greek stem *koin-*. The Hebrew *hbr* was used to express ideas such as common or shared house (Prov. 21:9), "binding" or "joining" (Ex. 26:6; Eccl. 9:4), companion (Eccl. 4:10), and even a wife as a companion (Mal. 2:14). *Haber* was used for a member of a Pharisaic society. Pharisees tended to form very close associations with one another in social, religious, and even business affairs. A most important dimension in the life of these *heberim* was a sharing together in the study of Scripture and law, and table fellowship.

The Gospels record no sayings of Jesus in which He used the *koin-* stem to describe "fellowship" among disciples, though certainly the close association shared by Jesus and His followers laid the foundation for the church's post-Easter understanding of fellowship.

Koinonia was Paul's favorite word to describe a believer's relationship with the risen Lord and the benefits of salvation which come through Him. On the basis of faith believers have fellowship with the Son (1 Cor. 1:9). We share fellowship in the gospel (1 Cor. 9:23; Phil. 1:5). Paul probably meant that all believers participate together in the saving power and message of the good news. Believers also share together a fellowship with the Holy Spirit (2 Cor. 13:14), which the apostle understood as a most important bond for unity in the life of the church (Phil. 2:1–4).

The tendency of many Christians to refer to the Lord's Supper as "communion" is rooted in Paul's use of the term *koinonia* in the context of his descriptions of the Lord's Supper. He described the cup as "communion of the blood of Christ," and the bread as "communion" of the body of Christ (1 Cor. 10:16). Paul did not explain precisely how such "communion" takes place through the Supper. He emphatically believed the Supper tied participants closer to one another and to Christ. Such "communion" could not be shared with Christ and with other gods or supernatural beings. Thus Paul forbad his readers from partaking in pagan religious meals, which would result in sharing "fellowship" with evil, supernatural forces or demons (1 Cor. 10:19–21).

Immediately after Paul spoke of "fellowship" with Christ through participation in the Lord's Supper (1 Cor. 10:16), he said, "since there is one bread, we who are many are one body" (1 Cor. 10:17 NAS). This illustrates clearly Paul's belief that fellowship with Christ was to issue into fellowship between believers. Once we grasp this, it is easy to understand why Paul was so angry over the mockery that the Corinthians were making of the Lord's Supper. While claiming to partake of this sacred meal, many Corinthian Christians ignored the needs of their brothers and sisters and actually created factions and divisions (1 Cor. 11:17–18), "for when the time comes to eat, each of you goes ahead with your own supper, and one goes hungry and another becomes drunk" (1 Cor. 11:21 NRSV). Because the "fellowship" among the Corinthians themselves was so perverted, Paul could go so far as to say "when you come together, it is not really to eat the Lord's supper" (1 Cor. 11:20 NRSV).

Koinonia with the Lord results not only in sharing His benefits (the gospel and the Holy Spirit), but also sharing His sufferings (Phil. 3:10; Col. 1:24). These texts express clearly just how intimate was Paul's perception of the close relationship between the believer and the Lord. The pattern of self-sacrifice and humility, demonstrated most profoundly through Jesus' suffering on the cross (Phil. 2:5–8), is to mark the current life of the disciple. Just as Jesus gave so completely of Himself for the sake of His people, so, too, are believers to give completely of themselves for the sake of the people of God (2 Cor. 4:7–12; Col. 1:24). The pattern of following Christ in suffering continues for the believer, in that just as Christ entered into glory following His suffering (Phil. 2:9–11), so, too, will the believer in the future share in the glory of Christ "if so be that we suffer with him" (Rom. 8:17; compare Phil. 3:10–11).

Paul believed that Christians were to share with one another what they had to offer to assist fellow believers. Paul used the *koin-* stem to refer to such sharing. One who has received the word ought to "share" it with others (Gal. 6:6). Though it is not translated "fellowship" in English versions, Paul actually used the term *koinonia* to denote the financial contribution which he was collecting from Gentile believers to take to Jerusalem for the relief of the saints who lived there (Rom. 15:26; 2 Cor. 8:4; 9:13). The reason he could refer to a financial gift as *koinonia* is explained by Romans 15:27: "If the Gentiles have come to share in their [the Jewish Christians'] spiritual blessings, they ought also to be of service to them in material things" (NRSV). In this case, each offered what they were able to offer to benefit others: Jewish Christians their spiritual blessings, Gentile Christians their material blessings. Such mutual sharing of one's blessings is a clear and profound expression of Christian fellowship.

Finally, for Paul, *koinonia* was a most appropriate term to describe the unity and bonding that exists between Christians by virtue of the fact that they share together in the grace of the gospel. When Paul wished to express the essential oneness of the apostolic leadership of the church he said concerning James, the Lord's brother, Peter, and John, that they "gave to me . . . the right hands of fellowship" (Gal. 2:9). When we realize

that this expression of *koinonia* came on the heels of one of the most hotly debated issues in the early church, namely the status of Gentiles in the people of God (Gal. 2:1–10; Acts 15), we can see how powerful and all encompassing Paul's notion of Christian fellowship actually was.

Like Paul, John also affirmed that *koinonia* was an important aspect of the Christian pilgrimage. He affirmed emphatically that fellowship with God and the Son was to issue in fellowship with the other believers (1 John 1:3, 6–7).

See *Lord's Supper; Holy Spirit.*

Bradley Chance

FENCED CITY KJV term for a fortified or walled city. See *Cities and Urban Life; Fortified Cities.*

View from the inside of the outer defensive wall of the ancient city of Arad in Israel.

FERRET White European polecat mentioned by KJV in Leviticus 11:30. Other translations read, "gecko." See *Animals in the Bible*

FERTILE CRESCENT refers to the crescent-shaped arc of alluvial land in the Near East stretching from the tip of the Persian Gulf to the southeastern corner of the Mediterranean Sea. The term was coined by James Henry Breasted in 1916 and does not occur in the Bible.

Conditions in the Fertile Crescent in antiquity were favorable for settled life, and the rise of civilization occurred along its river valleys. This band of land between the desert and the mountains was suitable for farming and was somewhat isolated by geographical barriers on all sides. The northeast is bordered by the Zagros Mountains, the north by the Taurus and Amanus ranges. On the west lies the Mediterranean Sea, and the concave southern limit is determined by the vast Syro-Arabian Desert. The Fertile Crescent is composed of Mesopotamia in the east and the Levant, or Palestine and Syria in the west. See *Mesopotamia, Palestine.*

Egypt was separated from Palestine by the Sinai, and thus is not a part of the Fertile Crescent. The Nile River, however, provided an ideal situation for the rise of early civilization parallel to that of Mesopotamia.   *Daniel C. Browning, Jr.*

FERTILITY CULT A general term for religions marked by rites which reenact a myth accounting for the orderly change of the seasons and the earth's fruitfulness. Such myths often involve a great mother-goddess as a symbol of fertility and a male deity, usually her consort but sometimes a son, who like vegetation dies and returns to life again. In Mesopotamia the divine couple was Ishtar and Tammuz (who is mourned in Ezek. 8:14), in Egypt Isis and her son Osiris, in Asia Minor Cybele and Attis. In Syria the Ugaritic myths of the second millenium B.C. pictured Baal-Hadad, the storm god, as the dying and rising god. (A local manifestation of this god is mourned in Zech. 12:11; Syrian kings derived their names from this deity, 1 Kings 15:18; 2 Kings 6:24; 13:24). His wife was the goddess Anath. In the earliest Ugaritic myth Asherah, the great mother-goddess, was the consort of El, the chief god in the pantheon. As Baal replaced El as the major deity, he became associated with Asherah (Judg. 6:25–30; 1 Kings 18:19). Ashtoroth, the daughter of Asherah, is used as the Hebrew word for womb or the fruit of the womb (Deut. 7:13; 28:4,18,51).

Fertility cults attribute the fertility of the cropland and herds to the sexual relations of the divine couple. Sacral sexual intercourse by priests and priestesses or by cult prostitutes was an act of worship intended to emulate the gods and share in their powers of procreation or else an act of imitative magic by which the gods were compelled to preserve the earth's fertility (1 Kings 14:23; 15:12; Hos. 4:14). Transvestism (prohibited in Deut. 22:5) may have been part of a fertility rite like that practiced by the Hittites. Sacrifices of produce, livestock, and even children (2 Kings 17:31; 23:10) represented giving the god what was most precious in life in an attempt to restore order to the cosmos and ensure fertility.

Elijah's struggle with the priests of Baal and Asherah at Mount Carmel is the best known conflict between worship of Yahweh and a fertility cult (1 Kings 18:17–40). Under Ahab, Baalism had become the state religion (1 Kings 16:31). The account of the priests of Baal lacerating themselves (1 Kings 18:28) is illuminated by the Ugaritic myths where El gashes his arms, chest, and back at the news of Baal's death. The priests of Baal customarily reenacted this scene from the myth at plowing time. Both skin and earth were cut as a sign of mourning (prohibited by Deut. 14:1). Baal's resurrection came with the return of the rains. The Biblical narrative is clear that Yahweh, not Baal, is the Lord who withholds and gives rain (1 Kings 17:1; 18:20–45).

The Israelites' sacred calender celebrated the same seasons as their neighbors (barley harvest = feast of unleavened bread; wheat harvest = Pentecost; fruit harvest = booths). The Israelites interpreted these seasons in light of God's redemptive acts in their history. Israel recognized the one God as the one responsible for rain (1 Kings 18), grain, wine, oil, wool, and flax (Hos. 2:8–9). Israel conceived of the earth's fruitfulness in a way quite unlike that of her neighbors. Yahweh had no consort; thus fertility was not tied to Yahweh's return to life and sexual functioning. Rather, the ability of plants and animals to reproduce their own kind was rooted in creation (Gen. 1:11–12,22,28). The orderly progression of the seasons was not traced to a primordial battle but was rooted in God's promise to Noah (Gen. 8:22). The fertility of the land was ensured not by ritual reenactment of the sacred marriage but by obedience to the demands of the covenant (Deut. 28:1,3–4,11–12).

In the New Testament, Diana or Artemis of the Ephesians (Acts 19:35) was a many-breasted fertility goddess. Aphrodite was also associated with fertility. Her temple at Corinth was the home of cult prostitutes responsible for the city's reputation for immorality. (Compare 1 Cor. 6:15–20.) Many of the mystery religions which competed with Christianity in the early centuries of the church developed the myths of the older fertility cults. See *Asherah; Ashtoroth; Baal; Canaan, History and Religion of; Dagon; Diana; Gods, Pagan; High Place; Prostitution; Tammuz; Ugarit.*

Chris Church

FESTAL GARMENTS, FESTAL ROBES Translations used by modern translations for two Hebrew expressions. The Hebrew expressions underlying "festal garments" mean a change of clothing (Gen. 45:22; Judg. 14:12–13,19; 2 King 5:5,22–23); the term underlying "festal robes" means clean, pure, or white clothing (Isa. 3:22; Zech. 3:4). Modern translations are not consistent in translating the terms, translation depending on the context. In the Ancient Near East possession of sets of clothing was regarded as a sign of wealth. Common people would own few clothes. Thus a change of clothes might suggest clothes reserved for a special occasion as reflected in some translations (Judg. 14:12–13,19 NRSV, TEV; 2 King 5:5,22–23 TEV). The white garments of Isaiah 3:22 are likely fine linen robes. The reference in Zechariah 3:4 is either to the high priest's robes (perhaps the special robes reserved for the Day of Atonement, Zech. 3:9) which represent the restoration of the priesthood or a simple reference to clean robes as a symbol of Joshua's innocence of any charges (symbolized by the filthy rags).

FESTIVALS Regular religious celebrations remembering God's great acts of salvation in the history of His people. Traditionally called "feasts" in the English Bibles, these can conveniently be categorized according to frequency of celebration. Many of them were timed according to cycles of seven. The cycle of the week with its climax on the seventh day, provided the cyclical basis for much of Israel's worship: as the seventh day was observed, so was the seventh month (which contained four of the national festivals), and the seventh year, and the fiftieth year (the year of Jubilee), which followed seven cycles each of seven years. Not only were the festivals as a whole arranged with reference to the cycle of the week (Sabbath), two of them (the feast of unleavened bread and the feast of tabernacles) lasted for seven days each. Each began on the fifteenth of the month—at the end of two cycles of weeks and when the moon was full. Pentecost also was celebrated on the fifteenth of the month and began fifty days after the presentation of the firstfruits— the day following seven times seven weeks.

The Sabbath See *Sabbath*. The seventh day of each week was listed among the festivals (Lev. 23:1–3). It functioned as a reminder of the Lord's rest at the end of the creation week (Gen. 2:3) and also of the deliverance from slavery in Egypt (Deut. 5:12–25). The sabbath day was observed by strict rest from work from sunset until sunset (Ex. 20:8–11; Neh. 13:15–22). Each person was to remain in place and not engage in travel (Ex. 16:29; Lev. 23:3). Despite such restrictions even as kindling a fire (Ex. 35:3) or any work (Ex. 31:14; 35:2), the sabbath was a joyful time (Isa. 58:13–14).

The New Moon This festival was a monthly cele-

A Jewish mother and child celebrate the Jewish tradition of the lighting of the candles at Hanukkah.

A young modern Jewish boy receives his first phylactery during his Bar Mitzvah celebration.

bration characterized by special offerings, great in quantity and quality (Num. 28:11–15), and blowing of trumpets (Num. 10:10; Ps. 81:3). According to Amos 8:5, business ceased. The festivals of the new moon and sabbath are often mentioned together in the Old Testament (Isa. 1:13; 66:23; Ezek. 45:17; 46:1,3). This festival provided the occasion for King Saul to stage a state banquet and for the family of David to offer a special annual sacrifice (1 Sam. 20:5,6,24,29). David's arrangements for the Levites included service on the new moon (1 Chron. 23:31), and the ministry of the prophets was sometimes connected with this occasion (2 Kings 4:23; Isa. 1:13; Ezek. 46:1; Hag. 1:1). Ezekiel mentioned four times receiving a vision on the first day of the month (Ezek. 26:1; 29:17; 31:1; 32:1). This day (along with others) is included in prophetic denunciations of abuses of religious observances (Isa. 1:13, 14). The new moon of the seventh month apparently received special attention (Lev. 23:24; Num. 29:1–6; Ezra 3:6; Neh. 8:2). Although the Exile brought a temporary cessation (Hos. 2:11), the festival was resumed later (Neh. 10:33; Ezra 3:1–6). It was on the first day of the seventh month that Ezra read the law before the public assembly (Neh. 7:73b—8:2). For Paul, new moon festivals were viewed as only a shadow of better things to come (Col. 2:16–17; compare Isa. 66:23).

Annual Festivals required the appearance of all males at the sanctuary (Ex. 34:23; Deut. 16:16). These occasions—called "feasts to the Lord," (Ex. 12:14; Lev. 23:39,41)—were times when freewill offerings were made (Deut. 16:16,17).

Passover The first of the three annual festivals was the Passover. It commemorated the final plague on Egypt when the firstborn of the Egyptians died and the Israelites were spared because of the blood smeared on their doorposts (Ex. 12:11,21,27,43,48). Passover took place on the fourteenth day (at evening) of the first month (Lev. 23:5). The animal (lamb or kid) to be slain was selected on the tenth day of the month (Ex. 12:3) and slaughtered on the fourteenth day and then eaten (Deut. 16:7). None of the animal was

F

The Jewish Calendar

Year	Sacred	1	2	3	4	5	6
	Civil	7	8	9	10	11	12
Month		Nison/Abib 30 days	Iyyar/Ziv 29 days	Sivan 30 days	Tammuz 29 days	Ab 30 days	Elul 29 days
English Months (nearly)		April	May	June	July	August	September
Festivals		1 New Moon 14 The Passover 15-21 Unleavened bread	1 New Moon 14 Second Passover (for those unable to keep first)	1 New Moon 6 Pentecost	1 New Moon 17 Fast. Taking of Jerusalem	1 New Moon 9 Fast. Destruction of temple	1 New Moon

Seasons and Productions		Spring rains (Deut. 11:14) Floods (Josh. 3:15) Barley ripe of Jericho	**Harvest** Barley Harvest (Ruth 1:22) Wheat Harvest Summer begins No rain from April to Sept. (1 Sam. 12:17)	**Hot Season** Heat increases	The streams dry up Heat intense Vintage (Lev. 26:5)	Heat intense (2 Kings 4:19) Grape harvest (Num. 13:23)

Note 1

The Jewish year is strictly lunar, being 12 lunations with an average of 29-1/2 days making 354 days in the year.

The Jewish sacred year begins with that new moon of spring which comes between our March 22 and April 25 in cycles of 19 years.

We can understand it best if we imagine our New Year's Day, which now comes on Jan. 1, without regard to the moon, varying each year with Easter, the time of the Passover, of the time of the full moon which, as a new moon had introduced the New Year two weeks before.

7 1	8 2	9 3	10 4	11 5	12 6	13 Leap year
Tishri/Ethanim 30 days	Marchesran/ Bul 29 days	Chislev 30 days	Tebeth 29 days	Shebat 30 days	Adar 29 days	Veadar/Adar Sheni
October	November	December	January	February	March	March/April
1 New Year Day of Blowing of Trumpet Day of Judgment and Memorial (Num. 29:1) 10 Day of Atonement (Lev. 16) 15 Booths 21 (Lev. 23:24) 22 Solemn Assembly	1 New Moon	1 New Moon 25 Dedication (John 10:22, 29)	1 New Moon 10 Fast. Siege of Jerusalem	1 New Moon	1 New Moon 13 Fast. of Esther 14-15 Purim	1 New Moon 13 Fast. of Esther 14-15 Purim
Seed time Former or early rains begin (Joel 2:23) Plowing and sowing begin	Rain continues Wheat and barley sown	Winter Winter begins Snow on mountains	Coldest month Hail and snow (Josh. 10:11)	Weather gradually warmer	Thunder and hail frequent Almond tree blossoms	Intercalary Month

Note 2	Hence the Jewish calendar contains a 13th month, Veadar or Adar Sheni, introduced 7 times in every 19 years, to render the average length of the year nearly correct, and to keep the seasons in the proper months.
Note 3	The Jewish day begins at sunset of the previous day.

to be left over on the following morning (Ex. 34:25). The uncircumcised and the hired servant were not permitted to eat the sacrifice (Ex. 12:45–49).

The Passover was also called the feast of unleavened bread (Ex. 23:15; Deut. 16:16) because only unleavened bread was eaten during the seven days immediately following Passover (Ex. 12:15–20; 13:6–8; Deut. 16:3–8). Unleavened bread reflected the fact that the people had no time to put leaven in their bread before their hasty departure from Egypt. It was also apparently connected to the barley harvest (Lev. 23:4–14).

During New Testament times large crowds gathered in Jerusalem to observe this annual celebration. Jesus was crucified during the Passover event. He and His disciples ate a Passover meal together on the eve of His death. During this meal Jesus said, "This is my body," and "this cup is the new testament in my blood" (Luke 22:7, 19–20). The New Testament identifies Christ with the Passover sacrifice: "For even Christ our Passover is sacrificed for us" (1 Cor. 5:7). See *Passover.*

Feast of Weeks The second of the three annual festivals was Pentecost, also called the feast of weeks (Ex. 34:22; Deut. 16:10,16; 2 Chron. 8:13), the feast of harvest (Ex. 23:16), and the day of firstfruits (Num. 28:26; compare Ex. 23:16; 34:22; Lev. 23:17). It was celebrated seven complete weeks, or fifty days, after Passover (Lev. 23:15,16; Deut. 16:9); therefore, it was given the name Pentecost.

Essentially a harvest celebration, the term "weeks" was used of the period of grain harvest from the barley harvest to the wheat harvest, a period of about seven weeks. At this time, the Lord was credited as the source of rain and fertility (Jer. 5:24). It was called "day of firstfruits" (Num. 28:26) because it marked the beginning of the time in which people were to bring offerings of firstfruits. It was celebrated as a sabbath with rest from ordinary labors and the calling of a holy convocation (Lev. 23:21; Num. 28:26). It was a feast of joy and thanksgiving for the completion of the harvest season. The able-bodied men were to be present at the sanctuary, and a special sacrifice was offered (Lev. 23:15–22; Num. 28:26–31). According to Leviticus 23:10–11,16,17, two large loaves were waved before the Lord by the anointed priests. These were made of fine flour from the new wheat and baked with leaven. They were a "wave offering" for the people. They could not be eaten until after this ceremony (Lev. 23:14; Josh. 5:10–11), and none of this bread was placed on the altar because of the leaven content. Also two lambs were offered. The feast was concluded by the eating of communal meals to which the poor, the stranger, and the Levites were invited.

Later tradition associated the feast of weeks with the giving of the law at Sinai. It had been concluded by some that Exodus 19:1 indicated the law was delivered on the fiftieth day after the Exodus. Some thought that Deuteronomy 16:12 may have connected the Sinai event and the festival, but Scripture does not indicate any definite link between Sinai and Pentecost. In the New Testament the Holy Spirit came upon the disciples at Pentecost (Acts 2:1–4), at the festive time when Jews from different countries were in Jerusalem to celebrate this annual feast. See *Pentecost.*

The Day of Atonement The third annual festival came on the tenth day of the seventh month (Tishri-Sept./Oct.) and the fifth day before the feast of tabernacles (Lev. 16:1–34; Num. 29:7–11). According to Leviticus 23:27–28, four main elements comprise this most significant feast. First, it was to be a "holy convocation," drawing the focus of the people to the altar of divine mercy. The holy One of Israel called the people of Israel to gather in His presence and give their undivided attention to Him. Secondly, they were to "humble their souls" ("afflict your souls," Lev. 23:27 KJV). This was explained by later tradition to indicate fasting and repentance. Israel understood that this was a day for mourning over their sins. The seriousness of this requirement is reiterated in Leviticus 23:29, "If there is any person who will not humble himself on this same day, he shall be cut off from his people" (Lev. 23:29 NAS). Thirdly, offerings are central to the day of atonement. The Bible devotes an entire chapter (Lev. 16) to them; they are also listed in Numbers 29:7–11. In addition to these, when the day fell on a sabbath, the regular sabbath offerings were offered. The fourth and final element of the day involved the prohibition of labor. The day of atonement was a "sabbath of rest" (Lev. 23:32), and the Israelites were forbidden to do any work at all. If they disobeyed, they were liable to capital punishment (Lev. 23:30).

The center point of this feast involved the high priest entering the holy of holies. Before entering, the high priest first bathed his entire body, going beyond the mere washing of hands and feet as required for other occasions. This washing symbolized his desire for purification. Rather than donning his usual robe and colorful garments (described in Ex. 28 and Lev. 8), he was commanded to wear special garments of linen. Also, the high priest sacrificed a bullock as a sin offering for himself and for his house (Lev. 16:6). After filling his censer with live coals from the altar, he entered the holy of holies where he placed incense on the coals. Then he took some of the blood from the slain bullock and sprinkled it on the mercy seat ("atonement cover," Lev. 16:13 NIV) and also on the ground in front of the ark, providing atonement for the priesthood (Lev. 16:14–15). Next he sacrificed a male goat as a sin offering for the people. Some of this blood was then also taken into the holy of holies and sprinkled there on behalf of the people (Lev. 16:11–15). Then he took another goat, called the "scapegoat" (for "escape goat"), laid his hands on its head, confessed over it the sins of Israel, and then released it into the desert where it symbolically carried away the sins of the people (Lev. 16:8,10). The remains of the sacrificial bullock and male goat were taken outside the city and burned, and the day was concluded with additional sacrifices.

According to Hebrews 9—10, this ritual is a symbol of the atoning work of Christ, our great high Priest, who did not need to make any sacrifice for Himself but shed His own blood for our sins. As the high priest of the Old Testament entered the holy of holies with the blood of sacrificial animals, Jesus entered heaven itself to appear on our behalf in front of the Father (Heb. 9:11,12). Each year the high priest repeated his sin offerings for his own sin and the sins of the people, giving an annual reminder that perfect and permanent atonement had not yet been made; but Jesus, through His own blood, accomplished eternal redemption for His people (Heb. 9:12). Just as the sacrifice of the day of atonement was burned outside the camp of Israel, Jesus suffered outside the gate of Jerusalem so that He might redeem His people from sin (Heb. 13:11,12).

Feast of Tabernacles The fourth annual festival was the feast of tabernacles (2 Chron. 8:13; Ezra 3:4; Zech. 14:16), also called the feast of ingathering (Ex. 23:16; 34:22), the feast to the Lord (Lev. 23:39; Judg. 21:19). Sometimes it was simply called "the feast" (1 Kings 8:2; 2 Chron. 5:3; 7:8; Neh. 8:14; Isa. 30:29; Ezek. 45:23,25) because it was so well known. Its observance combined the ingathering of the labor of the field (Ex. 23:16), the fruit of the earth (Lev. 23:39), the ingathering of the threshingfloor and winepress (Deut. 16:13), and the dwelling in booths (or "tabernacles"), which were to be joyful reminders to Israel (Lev. 23:41; Deut. 16:14). The "booth" in Scripture is not an image of privation and misery, but of protection, preservation, and shelter from heat and storm (Pss. 27:5; 31:20; Isa. 4:6). The rejoicing community included family, servants, widows, orphans, Levites, and sojourners (Deut. 16:13–15).

The feast began on the fifteenth day of Tishri (the seventh month), which was five days after the day of atonement. It lasted for seven days (Lev. 23:36; Deut. 16:13; Ezek. 45:25). On the first day, booths were constructed of fresh branches of trees. Each participant had to collect twigs of myrtle, willow, and palm in the area of Jerusalem for construction of the booths (Neh. 8:13–18). Every Israelite was to live for seven days in these during the festival, in commemoration of when their fathers lived in such booths after their Exodus from Egypt (Lev. 23:40; Neh. 8:15). The dedication of Solomon's Temple took place at the feast (1 Kings 8:2).

After the return from Exile, Ezra read the law and led the people in acts of penitence during this feast (Neh. 8:13–18). Later, Josephus referred to it as the holiest and greatest of the Hebrew feasts. Later additions to the ritual included a libation of water drawn from the pool of Siloam (the probable background for Jesus' comments on "living water," John 7:37–39) and the lighting of huge Menorahs (candelabra) at the Court of the Women (the probable background for Jesus' statement, "I am the light of the world," John 8:12). The water and the "pillar of light" provided during the wilderness wandering (when the people dwelt in tabernacles) was temporary and in contrast to the continuing water and light claimed by Jesus during this feast which commemorated that wandering period.

Feast of Trumpets Modern *Rosh Hashanah* is traced back to the so-called "Feast of Trumpets," the sounding of the trumpets on the first day of the seventh month (Tishri) of the religious calendar year (Lev. 23:24; Num. 29:1). The trumpet referred to here was the *shofar,* a ram's horn. It was distinctive from the silver trumpets blown on the other new moons.

This day evolved into the second most holy day on the modern Jewish religious calendar. It begins the "ten days of awe" before the day of atonement. According to Lev. 23:24–27 the celebration consisted of the blowing of trumpets, a time of rest, and "an offering made by fire." The text itself says nothing specifically about a New Year's Day, and the term itself (*rosh hashanah)* is found only one time in Scripture (Ezek. 40:1) where it refers to the tenth day. The postexilic assembly on the first day of the seventh month, when Ezra read the law, was not referred to as a feast day (Neh. 8:2–3). The fact that the Old Testament contains two calendars—a civil and a religious one—further complicates our understanding of the origins of this holiday. Until modern times this day did not appear to be a major feast day. See *New Year Festival.*

Two feasts of postexilic origin are noted in Scripture—Purim and Hanukkah.

Purim Purim commemorating the deliverance of the Jews from genocide through the efforts of Esther (Esther 9:16–32) derives its name from the "lot" (pur) which Haman planned to cast in order to decide when he should carry into effect the decree issued by the king for the extermination of the Jews (Esther 9:24). In the apocryphal book of 2 Maccabees (15:36) it is called the day of Mordecai. It was celebrated on the fourteenth day of Adar (March) by those in villages and unwalled towns and on the fifteenth day by those in fortified cities (Esther 9:18,19). No mention of any religious observance is connected with the day; in later periods, the Book of Esther was read in the synagogue on this day. It became a time for rejoicing and distribution of food and presents.

Hanukkah The other postexilic holiday was *Hanukkah,* a festival which began on the twenty-fifth day of Kislev (Dec.) and lasted eight days. Josephus referred to it as the Feast of Lights because a candle was lighted each successive day until a total of eight was reached. The festival commemorates the victories of Judas Maccabeus in 167 B.C. At that time, when Temple worship was reinstituted, after an interruption of three years, a celebration of eight days took place. The modern celebration does not greatly affect the routine duties of everyday life. This feast is referred to in John 10:22, where it is called the feast of dedication.

Two festivals occurred less often than once a year; the sabbath year and the year of jubilee.

Sabbatic year Each seventh year Israel celebrated a sabbath year for its fields. This involved a rest for the land from all cultivation (Ex. 23:10,11; Lev. 25:2–7; Deut. 15:1–11; 31:10–13). Other names for this festival were sabbath of rest (Lev. 25:4), year of rest (Lev. 25:5), year of release (Deut. 15:9), and the seventh year (Deut. 15:9). The sabbatic year, like the year of jubilee, began on the first day of the month Tishri. This observance is attested by 1 Maccabees 6:49, 53 and Josephus. Laws governing this year of rest included the following: 1) the soil, vineyards, and olive orchards were to enjoy complete rest (Ex. 23:10,11: Lev. 25:4–5); 2) The spontaneous growth of the fields or trees (Isa. 37:30) was for the free use of the hireling, stranger, servants, and cattle (Ex. 23:10,11; Lev. 25:6–7). A fruitful harvest was promised for the sixth year (Lev. 25:20–22). 3) Debts were released for all persons, with the exception of foreigners (Deut. 15:1–4). Probably this law did not forbid voluntary payment of debts. Also no one was to oppress a poor man. 4) Finally, at the feast of tabernacles during this year, the law was to be read to the people in solemn assembly (Deut. 31:10–13).

Jewish tradition interpreted 2 Chronicles 36:21 to mean that the seventy years' captivity was intended to make up for not observing sabbatic years.

Year of Jubilee This was also called the year of liberty (Ezek. 46:17). Its relation to the sabbatic year and the general directions for its observance are found in Leviticus 25:8–16,23–55. Its bearing on lands dedicated to the Lord is given in Leviticus 27:16–25.

After the span of seven sabbaths of years, or seven times seven years (49 years), the trumpet was to sound throughout the land; and the year of jubilee was to be announced (Lev. 25:8–9).

The law states three respects in which the jubilee year was to be observed: 1) rest for the soil—no sowing, reaping, or gathering from the vine (Lev. 25:11); 2) reversion of landed property (Lev. 25:10–34; 27:16–24)—all property in fields and houses located in villages or unwalled towns, which the owner had been forced to sell through poverty and which had not been redeemed, was to revert without payment to its original owner or his lawful heirs. (Exceptions to this are noted in Lev. 25:29,30; 27:17–21.) 3) redemption of slaves—every Israelite, who through poverty had sold himself to another Israelite or to a foreigner settled in the land, if he had not been able to redeem himself or had not been redeemed by a kinsman, was to go free with his children (Lev. 25:39–41).

It appears that the year of jubilee was a time of such complete remission of all debts that it became a season of celebration of freedom and grace. In this year oppression was to cease, and every member of the covenant family was to find joy and satisfaction in the Lord of the covenant. God had redeemed His people from bondage in Egypt (Lev. 25:42), and none of them was again to be reduced to the status of a perennial slave. God's child was not to be oppressed (Lev. 25:43,46); and poverty could not, even at its worst, reduce an Israelite to a status less than that of a hired servant, a wage earner, and then only until the year of jubilee (Lev. 25:40).

After the institution of the year of jubilee laws (Lev. 25:8–34), the year is mentioned again in Numbers 36:4. No reference to the celebration of this festival is found in Scripture apart from the idealistic anticipation of Ezekiel 46:17, but the influence of such laws illuminate such passages as the conduct of Naboth and Ahab in 1 Kings 21:3–29; and the prophetic rebukes found in Isaiah 5:8 and Micah 2:2.   *Larry Walker*

FESTUS (Fĕs' tŭs) The successor of Felix as procurator of Judea (Acts 24:27), He assumed this office at Nero's appointment in A.D. 60. He held it until his death in A.D. 62. Paul the apostle appealed to Porcius Festus for the opportunity of being tried before Caesar, and Festus granted that request. See *Paul; Herod; Roman Empire.*

FETTER Translation of several Hebrew and Greek terms refering to something that constrains, especially a shackle for the foot. Fetters were made of wood, bronze (Judg. 16:21; 2 Chron. 33:11), or iron (Ps. 149:8). Fetters worn on the feet were often joined by a rope or chain to hobble the prisoner (Mark 5:4). Fetters were painful to the feet (Ps. 105:18). Paul claimed that though he wore fetters, the word of God was not fettered (2 Tim. 2:9 REB, RSV).

FEVER An elevated body temperature or a disease accompanied by such symptoms. The "burning ague" (Lev. 26:16) is an acute fever marked by regular periods of fever, sweating, and then chills. Fever accompanying "consumption" or "wasting disease" (Deut. 28:22 REB) could refer to any number of diseases: malaria, typhoid, typhus, dysentery, chronic diahhrea, or cholera. The "extreme burning" of Deuteronomy 28:22 is understood by most modern translations as a reference to the weather ("fiery heat" RSV, NAS; "scorching wind" TEV) rather than to a fever. Jesus healed two persons afflicted with fevers—Peter's mother-in-law (Matt. 8:14; Mark 1:30; Luke 4:38) and an official's son (John 4:52). In Luke the healing was portrayed as an exorcism. In Acts 28:8 Paul healed Publius of a fever and dysentery ("bloody flux" KJV). See *Diseases, Treatment of.*

FIELD Unenclosed land. In the Hebrew definition of field, both the use of land (pasture, Gen. 29:2; 31:4; cropland, Gen. 37:7; 47:24; hunting ground, Gen. 27:3,5) and the terrain [mountaintops, Num. 21:20 (literal translation, "field of Moabi"); Judg. 9:32,36;] were insignificant. The crucial distinction is between what is enclosed and what is open. A field may be contrasted with a tent (Num. 19:14,16), a camp (Lev. 14:3,7), vineyards which were customarily enclosed (Ex. 22:5; Lev. 25:3–4), or with a walled city (Lev. 14:53; Deut. 28:3,16). Villages without walls were regarded as fields (Lev. 25:31). Fields were likewise distinguished from barren wasteland (Ezek. 33:27). Fields were marked with landmarks (Deut. 19:14).

The NRSV translated the Hebrew term *shedemah,* one of the words generally translated field, as vineyard at Deuteronomy 32:32. The REB rendered the term differently each place it was used (terraces, Deut. 32:32; slope, 2 Kings 23:4; vineyard, Isa. 16:8; field, Jer. 31:40; orchards, Hab. 3:17).

FIELD OF BLOOD See *Akeldama.*

FIERY SERPENT God used snakes of fiery appearance or burning bite to teach His people. The Hebrew word for burning or fiery is the same as for seraphim in Isaiah 6 but refers to different kinds of creatures. To punish the Israelites for complaining about their lot in the wilderness, God sent fiery serpents among them. As a result, many died. The serpents were natural residents of the wilderness (Deut. 8:15). Subsequently, God directed Moses to make a representation of a fiery serpent and place it on a pole. The brass serpent made by Moses became the means of healing for those who had been bitten by the fiery serpents but had not died. Jesus used this to point to His own fate of being lifted up on a cross (John 3:14). Compare John 12:32. See *Numbers; Moses.*

Isaiah used the fear of snakes to warn complacent Philistines that God would raise up a more fearful enemy who could be compared only to a serpent (*saraph)* which flew or darted (Isa. 14:29 NIV). Compare Isaiah 30:6.

FIG, FIGTREE See *Plants in the Bible.*

FIGURED STONE An idol of carved stone (NIV) in contrast to one of molten metal, associated with Canaanite worship (Lev. 26:1; Num. 33:52), according to modern translations. KJV reads, "image of stone" and "pictures." The same Hebrew term is used in Ezekiel 8:12 for idolatrous shrines decorated with base reliefs of gods in the form of animals (8:10; prohibited in Deut. 4:17–18). Various identifications of the animals have been suggested, beasts similar to the lions and serpent-dragons of the "Ishtar Gate" in Babylon, animals similar to those serving as mounts for the gods in stone carvings at Maltaya, Egyptian mortuary deities, and totem animals.

FIGUREHEAD An emblem on the prow of a ship (Acts 28:11 NIV, NRSV, NAS). The figure ("sign" KJV) in Acts is the Twin Brothers Castor and Pollow, sons of Zeus and Leda, identified with the constellation Gemini. Sight of the constellation was a good omen in bad weather. Thus the figurehead was something of a good luck charm.

FILIGREE Modern translation of ornamental work, especially of fine metal wire. KJV reads, "ouches"; REB, "rossettes." Gold filigree was used in the settings of precious stones (Ex. 28:11,20; 39:6,13) and as clasps (Ex. 28:13,25; 39:16,18) for clothing or jewelry. The design in Exodus was likely a rosette or simple floral pattern.

FILLETS Either metal bands binding the tops of pillars used in construction of the Tabernacle (Ex. 36:38; 38:10–12,17,19) or else rods connecting the pillars to one another (TEV). Jeremiah 52:21 uses a different Hebrew word to refer to a measuring line used to measure the circumference of a pillar.

FINERY Modern translation of Hebrew term for the luxuriousness of the jewelry and clothing worn by the society women of Jerusalem (Isa. 3:18). KJV reads "bravery"; NAS, "beauty." The Hebrew word describes the beauty or glory of Aaron's priestly clothes (Ex. 28:2), the glory of God's house (Isa. 60:7), battle field honor (Judg. 4:9), and the pompous (NAS) pride (NIV) of the Assyrian King (Isa. 10:12). Thus finery in itself is not bad, but prideful human attitudes concerning it soon became sinful.

FINGER OF GOD A picturesque expression of God at work. The finger of God writing the Ten Commandments illustrated God's giving the law without any mediation (Ex. 31:18; Deut. 9:10). Elsewhere the finger of God suggests God's power to bring plagues on Egypt (Ex. 8:19) and in making the heavens (Ps. 8:3). Jesus' statement "If I with the finger of God cast out devils, no doubt the kingdom of God is come upon you" (Luke

11:20) means that since Jesus cast out demons by the power of God, God's rule had become a reality among His hearers.

FINING POT KJV term for a crucible (NRSV, NIV) or smelting pot (REB), a vessel used to heat metal to a high temperature as part of the refining process (Prov. 17:3; 27:21).

FIR TREE KJV term for a tree most often identified with the aleppo pine (NIV, REB, TEV). Others have identified the tree with the juniper (NAS at Isa. 41:19 and 60:13 only) or cypress (NRSV, NAS elsewhere). See *Plants in the Bible.*

FIRE The product of burning which produces heat, light, and flame. One of the earliest human discoveries, probably first seen as a result of lightning. Humans soon discovered ways to use it and found it to be not only a very useful servant, but also a dreaded master. The invention of fire antedates history, but no nation has yet been discovered which did not know the use of fire. According to Greek mythology, Prometheus stole fire from Olympus, when Zeus denied it to immortal beings, and gave it to humans. For this crime he was punished by being chained to a rock in the wilderness of Scythia. The Bible does not explain the invention of fire. In the account of the Abrahamic covenant (Gen. 15:17), one reads of a smoking furnace and a flaming torch. Fire has been from early times the object of man's worship. This worship among the Canaanites is frequently mentioned in Scripture with the adjoining prohibition for God's people to refrain from the abominable practice (Lev. 18:21; Deut. 12:31; 2 Chron. 28:3).

Fire is a consistent element in the relationship of God with His people, often being used as an instrument of His power, either in the way of approval or destruction. The Abrahamic covenant (Gen. 15:17), the appearance of the burning bush (Ex. 3:2), the pillar of fire by night to lead the children of Israel into the Promised Land (Ex. 13:21–22), and God's appearance in fire on Mt. Sinai (Ex. 19:18; 24:17), are well known illustrations of such. The appearance of Christ in John's vision (Rev. 1:14; 2:18), was with eyes "as a flame of fire," and the descent of the Holy Spirit on the day of Pentecost (Acts 2:3), was accompanied by "tongues like as of fire." Fire is used often as a symbol of holiness and often equates the idea of God's presence with God's holiness. God Himself is compared to fire not only to illustrate His holiness, but also to illustrate His anger against sin (Isa. 10:17; Heb. 12:29).

Our English word "purify" is a cognate of the main Greek word used in the New Testament for fire. As such, it denotes one of the main metaphors of the use of fire, namely as purification. God uses the fire of experience to test us (Job

23:10). Ultimately all of our works done on earth in our lifetime will be tested "as by fire" (1 Cor. 3:12–15).

In the context of biblical religion, fire was used to consume the burnt offerings and incense offerings. Fire was to be continually burning upon the altar as a visible sign of the continuous worship of God. If for some reason the fire was extinguished, according to the Talmud, it was to be rekindled only by friction. If fire was used for sacred purposes and obtained other than from the altar, it was called "strange fire" (Lev. 10:1,2), for which use Nadab and Abihu, two sons of Aaron, were punished immediately by divine execution.

The law prohibited any fire to be kindled on the sabbath, even for cooking purposes (Ex. 35:3). Anyone kindling a fire that caused damage to crops was compelled by law to make restitution (Ex. 22:6). Capital punishment was occasionally made even more shameful by burning the body of the criminal after death (Lev. 20:14; 21:9; 2 Kings 23:16).

Fire is also used to symbolize: God's people victorious over all enemies (Obad. 18); the word of God (Jer. 5:14); the Holy Spirit (Isa. 4:4; Acts 2:3); the zeal of the saints (Pss. 39:3; 119:139); of angels (Heb. 1:7); of lust (Prov. 6:27,28); of wickedness (Isa. 9:18); of the tongue (Jas. 3:6); and of judgment (Jer. 48:45).

The final destiny of all the enemies of God is the "lake of fire" (Rev. 19:20; 20:10). The earth will be consumed by fire (2 Pet. 3:7–12).

See *Baptism of Fire; Molech; Lake of Fire.*

C. Dale Hill

FIREPAN A utensil made of bronze (Ex. 27:3) or gold (1 Kings 7:50, KJV, "censers") used to carry live coals from the altar of burnt offering (Ex. 27:3; 38:3), as censers for burning incense (Num. 16:6,17), and as trays for collecting the burnt wicks from the tabernacle lamps (Ex. 25:38; 37:23; the "snuffdishes" of the KJV).

FIRKIN A unit of liquid measure (John 2:6). Firkin is an archaic English word that was used to translate a Greek term referring to a measure of approximately ten gallons. See *Weights and Measures.*

FIRMAMENT The great vault or expanse of sky that separates the upper and lower waters. The firmament was created by God on the second day to separate the "waters from the waters" (Gen. 1:6–7). One use of "heaven" in the Bible is to refer to the ceiling or canopy of the earth. Heaven in this sense is also referred to as the firmament or sky (Gen. 1:8). Into this expanse, God set the sun, moon, and stars (Gen. 1:14–18).

In Genesis 1:6 the firmament separates the mass of waters and divides them into layers. The firmament is mentioned nine times in Genesis, the Psalms, Ezekiel, and Daniel. It is described as bright, transparent like crystal, revealing the handiwork of God, and signifying His seat of power (Pss. 19:1; 150:1; Ezek. 1:22; Dan. 12:3).

Some scholars argue that the Hebrews had a primitive cosmology where the firmament was visualized as a rigid, solid dome—a celestial dam (Gen. 7:11; 2 Sam. 22:8; Job. 26:8; 37:18; Prov. 8:28; Mal. 3:10). Above the firmament flowed the heavenly waters. The firmament was punctuated by grilles or sluices, "windows of heaven" through which rain was released. Others argue that such interpretations are unsound, in that they confuse poetic and figurative language with literal prose. Others say Israel's inspired writers used language of experience and appearance rather than language of precise scientific description.

See *Heavens*.   *Paul Robertson*

FIRST AND LAST See *Alpha and Omega*.

FIRSTBORN First son born to a couple and required to be specially dedicated to God. The firstborn son of newly married people was believed to represent the prime of human vigor (Gen. 49:3; Ps. 78:51). In memory of the death of Egypt's firstborn and the preservation of the firstborn of Israel, all the firstborn of Israel, both of man and beast, belonged to Yahweh (Ex. 13:2,15; compare 12:12−16). This meant that the people of Israel attached unusual value to the eldest son and assigned special privileges and responsibilities to him. He was presented to the Lord when he was a month old. Since he belonged to the Lord, it was necessary for the father to buy back the child from the priest at a redemption price not to exceed five shekels (Num. 18:16). The husband of several wives would have to redeem the firstborn of each.

The birthright of a firstborn included a double portion of the estate and leadership of the family. As head of the house after his father's death, the eldest son customarily cared for his mother until her death, and he also provided for his sisters until their marriage. The firstborn might sell his rights as Esau did (Gen. 25:29−34) or forfeit them for misconduct as Reuben did because of incest (Gen. 35:22; 49:3,4).

The firstborn of a clean animal was brought into the sanctuary on the eighth day after birth (Ex. 22:30). If it were without blemish, it was sacrificed (Deut. 15:19; Num. 18:17). If it had a blemish, the priest to whom it was given could eat it as common food outside Jerusalem (Deut. 15:21−23), or it could be eaten at home by its owner. Apparently the firstborn of clean animals were not to be used for any work since they belonged to the Lord (Deut. 15:19).

The firstborn of an unclean animal had to be redeemed by an estimation of the priest, with the addition of one-fifth (Lev. 27:27; Num. 18:15).

According to Exodus 13:13; 34:20, the firstborn of an ass was either ransomed by a sheep or lamb, or its neck had to be broken.

Figuratively, Israel was God's "firstborn" (Ex. 4:22; Jer. 31:9) and enjoyed priority status. God compared His relationship to Israel with the relationship of a father and his firstborn son. Within Israel, the tribe of Levi represented the firstborn of the nation in its worship ceremony (Num. 3:40−41; 8:18).

Christ is the "firstborn" of the Father (Heb. 1:6 NIV) by having preeminent position over others in relation to Him. He is also described as "firstborn among many brethren" (Rom. 8:29) and "firstborn of all creation" (Col. 1:15 NAS). Paul (Col. 1:18) and John (Rev. 1:5) refer to Christ as "firstborn from the dead"—the first to rise bodily from the grave and not die again.

Hebrews 12:23 refers to the "church of the firstborn, which are written in heaven." Christian believers, united with and as joint heirs with Christ, enjoy the status of "firstborn" in God's household.   *Larry Walker*

FIRSTFRUITS The choice examples of a crop harvested first and dedicated to God. In accordance with Mosaic law, individual Israelites brought to the house of the Lord "the first (that is, "the best") of the firstfruits of thy land" (Ex. 23:19; 34:26), including grain, wine, and oil, which were used—except for the grain (Lev. 2:14−16)—for the support of the priests (Num. 18:12; Deut. 18:4). According to Deuteronomy 26:1−11, the offering was brought in a basket to the sanctuary for presentation. The Book of Proverbs promises prosperity to those who honor the Lord with the firstfruits (Prov. 3:9).

According to Leviticus 23:9−14, the first sheaf of the new crop of barley was presented as a wave offering before the Lord. This took place on the day after the Passover sabbath and was a public acknowledgment that all came from God and belonged to Him (Num. 28:26; compare Ex. 23:16; 34:22). Not only were the Israelites to be mindful that the land of Canaan was the Lord's possession and that they had only the rights of tenants (Lev. 25:23), but they were also to be aware that the fertility of Canaan's soil was not due to one of the Baals but rather to the Lord's gift of grace.

Israel was described as God's "firstfruits" (Jer. 2:3). Christ in His resurrection is described as the "firstfruits" of them that slept (1 Cor. 15:20,23). The Holy Spirit is spoken of as a "firstfruits" (Rom. 8:23), and believers are also spoken of as "a kind of firstfruits" (Jas. 1:18). The saved remnant within Israel is described as "firstfruits" (Rom. 11:16), as are the 144,000 of the tribulation period (Rev. 14:4). The first converts of an area

Fishing boats on the Nile River in Egypt.

were designated "firstfruits" (Rom. 16:5; 1 Cor. 16:15). In each case the emphasis was on special dedication and blessing.   *Larry Walker*

FIRST RAIN KJV term at Deuteronomy 11:14 for the early rain. See *Rain*.

FISH, FISHING Animals living in water and breathing through gills; the profession and/or practice of catching fish to supply a family or society's need for food. Fish abounded in the inland waters of Palestine, was well as in the Mediterranean.

Old Testament Fish are mentioned often in the Bible but not by the different kinds. Fish were a favorite food and a chief source of protein (Num. 11:5; Neh. 13:16). The law regarded all fish with fins and scales as clean. Water animals that did not have fins and scales were unclean (Lev. 11:9–12).

Methods of catching fish included angling with a hook (Job 41:1), harpoons and spears (Job 41:7), use of dragnets (John 21:8), and thrown hand nets (Matt. 4:18). Fish caught in the Mediterranean were brought to ports such as Tyre and Sidon. The Sea of Chinnereth or Galilee was also a fishing center. The fish were preserved in salt and brought to Jerusalem where they were sold at a specially named "Fish Gate" in the city. The strong currents of the Jordan River carried many fish to the Dead Sea where they died (Ezek. 47:7–11).

References to fishing as an occupation are rare in the Old Testament because, for the most part, in Old Testament times the Mediterranean coast was controlled by the Philistines and Phoenicians. The Israelites depended largely on foreign trade for their fish (Neh. 13:16). Two Old Testament texts (Song of Sol. 7:4; Isa. 19:10) speak of fishpools and fish ponds, possibly an indication of commercially raised fish or of fish farming.

The most famous Old Testament fish was the great fish of the Book of Jonah (Jonah 1:17), one God prepared especially for the occasion and one whose species the Old Testament does not indicate.

New Testament During New Testament times

A building stone from Ephesus carved with the figure of a fish.

commercial fishing businesses were conducted on the Sea of Galilee by fishermen organized in guilds (Luke 5:7,11). Fishermen were hard workers, crude in manner, rough in speech and in their treatment of others (John 18:10). Fishermen owned their ships, took hirelings into their service, and sometimes joined to form companies (Mark 1:20; Luke 5:7).

Fish provided food for the common people (Matt. 14:17; 15:34). The risen Lord ate fish with the disciples in Jerusalem (Luke 24:42) and by the Sea of Galilee (John 21:13). The primary method of preparing fish was broiling (John 21:9). The most famous New Testament fish was the one used to pay the Temple tax for Jesus and Peter (Matt. 17:27).

Theological The Bible contains numerous figurative uses of fish and fishing. Human helplessness is compared to fish taken in a net (Eccl. 9:12; Hab. 1:14). Fish caught in a net symbolized God's judgment (Ps. 66:11; Ezek. 32:3). Jesus mentioned fishing when He called disciples to be witnesses (Matt. 4:18–19). Jesus compared the kingdom of heaven to a net thrown into the sea and loaded with fish of many varieties (Matt. 13:47).

In early Christian churches, the Greek word for fish (*ichthus*) came to be interpreted as a cipher for Jesus. The first letter of each of the Greek words for "Jesus Christ, Son of God, Saviour" spell *ichthus*. We do not know when this cipher was first used; but once the identification was made, the fish became a standard Christian symbol.   *Gary Hardin*

FISH GATE A north gate of the second quarter of Jerusalem (Zeph. 1:10) mentioned in connection with fortifications built by Manasseh (2 Chron. 33:14). The gate was rebuilt during the time of Nehemiah (Neh. 3:3; 12:39). The name is perhaps derived from the proximity of the gate to the fish market. (Compare Neh. 13:16–22.)

FISHHOOK A curved or bent device of bone or iron in biblical times used for catching or holding fish (Job 41:1–2; Isa. 19:8—KJV, "angle"; Matt. 17:27). Habakkuk described God's people as helpless fish who would be captured by hooks (1:15) and nets. Amos 4:2 refers to the practice of ancient conquerors of leading captives with hooks through their lips. Such was the fate of Manasseh according to one interpretation (2 Chron. 33:11, NAS, NIV, TEV).

FITCHES KJV term for two different plants. The first is black cummin (Isa. 28:25,27). Ezekiel 4:9 refers to either spelt, an inferior type of wheat (NAS, NIV, TEV), or else vetches (REB), a plant of the bean family. See *Plants in the Bible*.

FLAG KJV term for a water plant generally translated as reed (Ex. 2:3,5; Job 8:11) or rush (Isa. 19:6) by modern translations. See *Plants in the Bible*.

FLAGON A large, two handled jar for storing wine (Isa. 22:24 KJV; Ex. 25:29; 37:16; REB, NRSV). The Hebrew term *ashishah* translated as flagon by the KJV (2 Sam. 6:19; 1 Chron. 16:3; Song of Sol. 2:5; Hos. 3:1) refers to a cake of raisins, often used as offerings to idols.

Statue of an aged woman holding in her lap a flagon of wine.

FLAGSTAFF A pole on which a standard is displayed (Isa. 30:17). The same Hebrew term is translated mast elsewhere (Isa. 33:23; Ezek. 27:5). The REB used the translation mast at Isaiah 30:17 as well. The NAS preferred the translation flag for this text though the margin note, pole, can account for all occurrences of the term.

FLASK A general term translators use to describe vessels. It does not appear in KJV. The term refers to a small container of perfumed oil in 2 Kings 9:1–3. The same Hebrew word appears in 1 Sam. 10:1. At Jeremiah 19:1 (RSV) refers to an earthenware water jar or jug. The vessel perhaps had a narrow neck making it impossible to mend (19:10). This Hebrew word recurs in 1 Kings 14:3. At Matthew 25:4 small containers for lamp oil are meant. The Greek term appears only here in the New Testament. Luke 7:37 refers to a small alabaster container such as had been used for expensive perfumes for thousands of years.

FLAX The plant (*Linum usitatissimum*) used to make linen. The fibers of the flax stem are the most

ancient of textile fibers. Flax was cultivated by the Egyptians before the Exodus (Ex. 9:31) and by the Canaanites before the Conquest (Josh. 2:6). The making of linen was a common household chore in Biblical times. Proverbs 31:13 described the virtuous wife as one who sought wool and flax. The linen making process involved pulling and drying flax stalks (often on rooftops, Josh. 2:6). The stalks were deseeded, soaked until the fibers were loosened (retted), and redried. A hackle, a comb or board with long teeth, was used to separate the outer fibers from the inner core. Further combing (carding) cleansed and ordered the fibers so that they might be spun into thread for weaving (Isa. 19:9). The remaining short, tangled fibers (the tow) were used to weave a course fabric or make twine (Judg. 16:9; Isa. 1:31).

Flax fibers were also used to make torches and lamp wicks. Isaiah 43:17 pictures armies as a wick which the Lord would extinguish. In Isaiah 42:3 the Servant of the Lord is one who will not quench a dimly burning wick. The picture suggests one who will help and comfort the powerless rather than bring harsh judgment. Matthew understood Jesus' ministry as the fulfillment of this Scripture (Matt. 12:20).

FLEA See *Insects*.

FLEET A group of ships. Solomon built a fleet of ships at Ezion-Geber with the help of Hiram of Tyre (1 Kings 9:26–27; 10:11,22). The KJV translated fleet as navy or navy of ships. Solomon's fleet was used for commercial rather than military purposes. See *Ezion-Geber; Ships, Sailors, and Navigation*.

FLESH The skin and/or meat of animals and humans used to represent human dedication to physical desires rather than to obedience to God. **Literal use** It often refers to the muscular part of the body, both of humans (Gen. 2:21; Job 10:11) and animals (Deut. 14:8; 1 Cor. 15:39). Even dead, a person is still called flesh (1 Sam. 17:44) until the body returns as dust to the earth (Eccl. 12:7).
Food and Sacrifice The flesh of animals is used for food by humans (Gen. 9:3–4; 1 Sam. 2:13,15), while human flesh may be eaten by animals (Gen. 40:19; Rev. 19:17–18). The flesh of animals is used for sacrifice (Ex. 29:31).
Body The term "flesh" can denote the human body in its entirety—the part referring to the whole (Judg. 8:7; 1 Kings 21:27; Eph. 5:29; Heb. 9:13). It can also denote the opposite where the whole refers to the part, especially when referring to the sexual organs such as the circumcision of the flesh (Gen. 17:14; Gal. 6:13; Eph. 2:11; Phil. 3:3; Col. 2:13; compare Lev. 15:2, 3, 7, 19). It may signify a comprehensive sense whereby "all flesh" refers to all of humanity (Joel 2:28; Matt. 24:22) or including both the human and animal

F

creation (Gen. 6:13, 17; 7:16; Lev. 17:14).

Relationship Adam said of Eve's creation that she is the "bone of my bones, and flesh of my flesh" (Gen. 2:23; compare 29:14) denoting a kinship between the two, thus Adam and Eve were regarded as one flesh (Gen. 2:24; Matt. 19:5; 1 Cor. 6:16; Eph. 5:31). Jesus was related to David with reference to the flesh (Rom. 1:3).

Whole Person The term may denote the entire person and not just the physical aspects. It can refer to the outward expression of a person paralleling the inward action of the person as seen in Psalm 63:1 where the "soul thirsts" and the "flesh faints" NRSV and in Psalm 84:2 where the "heart and flesh sing for joy" (NRSV). Peter, quoting from Psalm 16, paralleled the flesh with the heart and soul (Acts 2:26–27). Paul spoke of his sufferings for Christ as his flesh suffering (Col. 1:24). Hence, the biblical view asserts a dualism of man but not in the Greek sense. Greek philosophers saw the soul, heart, or mind distinguished from and superior to the flesh. The biblical view sees the inward and outward aspects of man very closely tied together. Hence, the psalmist (Ps. 73:26) referring to his "flesh and heart" sees the person in its entirety. Paul's reference to the flesh denotes all of humanity when he stated that no flesh is justified by the works of the law (Rom. 3:20; Gal. 2:16).

Theological Significance Biblically, the flesh is viewed as the created and natural humanity. It is not automatically sinful, but it is weak, limited, and temporal. Such qualities make it vulnerable to sin. Adam and Eve were created as fleshly human beings. They succumbed to the temptations of Satan, who promised them that they would be like God, knowing good and evil (Gen. 3:5). Because of the limited perspective and the weakness of the flesh, Adam and Eve accepted Satan's lie. The weakness of the flesh is seen in the Garden of Gethsemane where Jesus found the disciples sleeping. He enjoined them to watch and pray lest they enter into temptation for "the spirit indeed is willing, but the flesh is weak" (Matt. 26:41; Mark 14:38). Here, the flesh was not sinful, but rather limited and weak due to fatigue, and easy to succumb to sleep.

In its weakness and limitation, the flesh tends to yield to the temptation of what seems good naturally. Since sin promises pleasure and fulfillment, the natural propensity is for the flesh to yield to sin's promises. Thus, doing what comes naturally is yielding to sin's will. This is contrary to God's will and commands. Those who follow the impulses of the flesh are governed by the flesh and are characterized as those who live "after the flesh" (Rom. 8:5). They are those who yield to sinful passions and produce works contrary to God and His law (Gal. 5:16–17, 19–21,23–24; compare 1 John 2:16; 1 Pet. 4:2; 2 Pet. 2:10). Being enslaved to the desires of the flesh (Eph. 2:3),

they have the mindset of the flesh (Rom. 8:5–7). Hence, the natural person controlled by the flesh does not and cannot submit to God's will or please God (Rom. 8:7–8; 1 Cor. 2:14; compare Gen. 6:13). The limitation of the flesh appears clearly in the human inability to discern God's revelation of Himself (Matt. 16:17; Gal. 1:13–24). Only death succeeds in convincing those who live according to the flesh of the fleeting, temporal nature of the flesh (Rom. 6:23; 8:6,13). Flesh-driven people are the children of wrath (Eph. 2:3). They cannot inherit the kingdom of God (1 Cor. 6:9–10; Gal. 5:19–21; Eph. 2:11–12; 5:5).

Flesh is weak but not naturally sinful. Christ came in the "likeness" of sinful flesh (John 1:14; Rom. 8:3; Heb. 4:15) to redeem those who are in sinful flesh. That is, Christ became a flesh and blood person but did not give in to the desires of the flesh. Instead, perfect in life and death, He died to provide salvation for all other persons, since they do give in to fleshly desires. Those who trust in God's provision in Christ remain physically "in" the flesh but do not live "according to" the flesh (Gal. 2:20; Phil. 1:22–24). They are characterized as those who are not in the flesh but in the Spirit (Rom. 8:9) because they are governed not by the flesh but by the Spirit (Rom. 8:6, 11–17). They are those who are led by the Spirit to put to death the deeds of the flesh, not the flesh itself (Rom. 8:13; Gal. 5:24). Believers must be careful not to be tricked into thinking that they have any obligation to the flesh and its sinful, selfish desires (Rom. 8:12–13; Gal. 3:3). The flesh serves as a base of operation for sin (Rom. 7:8, 11) and thus enslaves a person to sin (Rom. 6:15–23; 7:25). This does not imply that flesh is automatically sinful, but its history in Adam shows the weakness of flesh and its strong tendency to yield to the commands of sin.

In conclusion, the term "flesh" can be a neutral term referring to created humans and animals who are limited and weak, or it can refer to humans controlled by sin and its passions. See *Anthropology; Body.*   *Harold W. Hoehner*

FLESH AND SPIRIT Two important terms often contrasted with one another in referring to human existence. Bible readers often suppose that any mention of the word "flesh" is automatically in contrast with the concept of "spirit" and is, therefore, intrinsically evil. However, the early appearances of the word "flesh" in the Bible contrast with spirit only in the sense that the flesh is material substance, while the spirit is immaterial substance. The first mention of flesh occurs in Genesis 2:21, the account of the creation of woman from the side of man. The Bible simply records that God closed up Adam's flesh. Adam's own judgment in Genesis 2:23 was that this is now "bone of my bones, and flesh of my flesh."

Thus Adam recognized that whatever he was, Eve was the same. Genesis 2:24 suggests that the man and his wife would become "one flesh," apparently indicating the sexual as well as the psychological union. All that God created in Genesis is called "very good." Therefore, it may be safely concluded that the concept of "flesh" as such is not an evil concept but a part of the artistry and design of God.

Nevertheless, it remains true that the Bible frequently contrasts flesh with spirit. Once our first parents had sinned, all subsequent offspring were born with a tendency toward evil that manifests itself particularly in the flesh. Hence, we are told in Mark 14:38 (NAS) that "the spirit is willing but the flesh is weak." Thus, we are introduced to the fact that many of the temptations to which the human family is subject are those that relate to the flesh. We are, therefore, instructed not to fulfill "the lust of the flesh" (1 John 2:16). We are warned, in fact, that "the flesh lusteth against the Spirit" (Gal. 5:17). Perhaps the fifth chapter of Galatians, verses 16 and 17, focuses on the problem more decisively than any other verses. Paul wrote,

> "Walk in the Spirit, and ye shall not fulfil the lust of the flesh. For the flesh lusteth against the Spirit, and the Spirit against the flesh: and these are contrary the one to the other: so that ye cannot do the things that ye would."

The walk of obedience to the Holy Spirit, who is enshrined in the human spirit of twiceborn men, is the only way to avoid allowing the flesh to rule. Essentially, the emphasis that Paul provides is not intended to suggest that the Spirit is good and the flesh is evil, but rather that the flesh should never rule the spiritual life of a man. Instead, the flesh must be subjugated and made useful to the spiritual purposes and goals of humanity.

Sometimes the Bible speaks of carnality. The word translated carnal, for example, in Romans 8:7, in which we are told that the "carnal mind" is enmity against God is a derivative of the Greek word for "flesh." Some Christians are carnal Christians (1 Cor. 3:1) meaning that, while they have been saved, they nevertheless are ruled more by their fleshly desires than by the Spirit.

See *Anthropology; Flesh; Spirit.* W. A. Criswell

FLESH HOOK A large fork used for handling large pieces of meat, especially at the sacrificial altar. Those in the tabernacle were of brass (Ex. 27:3; 38:3), those in the Temple of bronze (2 Chron. 4:16) or gold (1 Chron. 28:17).

FLESH POT A kettle used for cooking meat. The murmuring of the Israelites against Moses (Ex. 16:3) included the exaggerated claim that they customarily relaxed by the flesh pots in Egypt and had more than enough bread. In the Ancient Near East meat was not part of the common people's regular diet.

FLINT Flint translates three Hebrew terms which are applied loosely to any hard, compact rock or specifically to nearly opaque, cryptocrystaline varieties of quartz. Flint may be flaked to give a very sharp, hard edge. Flint tools, including scrapers, axheads, knives (Ex. 4:25; Josh. 5:2–3 REB, NIV, NAS, NRSV, TEV), arrow heads, sickle blades, and other tools were used from the earliest prehistoric times.

The hardness of flint is proverbial. God's miraculous provision for the Israelites in the wilderness is pictured as water (Deut. 8:15; Ps. 114:8) or oil (Deut. 32:13) flowing from flinty rock. God protected the prophet Ezekiel by making his forehead harder than flint (Ezek. 3:9). A face set like flint pictured the determination of the Servant of the Lord (Isa. 50:7; compare Luke 9:51). Zechariah 7:12 pictures the people's unwillingness to repent as hearts of flint.

FLOAT KJV translation of two Hebrew terms (1 Kings 5:9; 2 Chron. 2:16) rendered raft by modern speech translations. The pine and cedar logs for construction of the Temple were lashed together to form rafts which were floated down the coast.

FLOCK Sheep and goats under the care of a shepherd (Gen. 30:31–32). God' people are sometimes described as sheep without a shepherd (Num. 27:17; Ezek. 34:5,8; Matt. 9:36; Mark 6:34), that is, in need of leaders who would rule

Flock of sheep in central Israel.

them justly and nurture them spiritually. God's people can be described as a flock shepherded by God (Ps. 100:3; Jer. 23:3; Ezek. 34:31) or by Christ, the "great Shepherd of the sheep" (Heb. 13:20; compare John 10:11; 1 Peter 5:4).

The unity of all Christians is pictured by the image of one flock composed of many folds (John 10:16). Flocks can refer to individual congregations under the care of a pastor (1 Peter 5:2–3).

Judgment is sometimes pictured as the sorting of a flock. In Ezekiel 34 the fat, strong sheep (the oppressive leaders of Israel) are separated from the weak sheep that they victimized (34:16–17,20–21). In Matthew 25:32–46 sheep are separated from goats on the basis of concrete acts of love shown to the needy.

FLOGGING Punishment by repeated lashes or blows of a whip or rod(s). The Old Testament recognized flogging as a form of punishment (Deut. 25:1–3) though limiting it to 40 blows so that the neighbor who was punished would not be degraded. Children were disciplined with rods (Prov. 23:13–14). Floggings were sometimes inflicted unjustly (Prov. 17:26; Isa. 53:5).

Jesus warned His disciples that they would face flogging (Matt. 10:17; beatings, Mark 13:9) in the synagogue. Paul had believers flogged in his days as a persecutor of the church (Acts 22:19–20). The apostles were flogged by order of the Sanhedrin (Acts 5:40). Paul received the "forty lashes less one" at the hands of the synagogue five times (2 Cor. 11:24). Paul was also beaten with rods three times (11:25), perhaps at the hands of Gentile officials as at Philippi (Acts 16:22–23).

FLOOD A miraculous deluge of water God used to discipline His world made evil through human sin. **Its Structural Background** The literary theme of a flood was a natural motif for the Sumerian and Akkadian peoples who resided between the Tigris and Euphrates Rivers in a plain prone to flood. The oft-repeated flood experience found literary expression in a Sumerian flood story and in two or more Akkadian ones: the Atrahasis Epic and the Epic of Gilgamesh. The Akkadian and Hebrew stories parallel each other in the following ways: the naming of the hero (Utnapishtim/Noah), the divine announcement of a flood, instructions to build a ship, the inclusion of animals in the ship, the dispatch of birds, the sacrifice the hero offered after the waters subsided, and other related details.

It must be admitted that the identification of a flood that gave rise to the Sumero-Akkadian and Hebrew Flood accounts has proved illusive. In every geological or archaeological endeavor to use sedimentary deposits to develop a time frame for such a catastrophic deluge and all efforts to recover an ark have failed. Such scientific efforts have not proven the Flood narrative.

The drama of Israel's Flood story is the drama of God reacting to the habitual sin of His creatures. Scene after scene exhibits a disclosure of God, the moral nature of His acts, His self-consistent righteousness, His ever abiding love, His determined will to extricate humanity from its self-inflicted ruin, His determination never to see wrong as ultimately victorious, but to see the fulfilment of His purposes finally and fully.

To an ancient story form known widely in the Ancient Near East, the inspired Hebrew writer joined Israel's theological affirmation to form an educational means to teach the community of Israel the ways of Yahweh (Gen. 18:19).

Theological Proclamation of the Flood God took account of earth's wickedness, the persistent human bent toward evil, the corruption that filled the earth with injustice. Still, God did not overlook Noah. Self-consistency demanded justice equal to the wickedness and prompted a determination to blot out mankind. This was a matter of deep regret and sorrow, but the purpose invested in human creation was not to be thwarted. God announced His intentions to Noah and instructed him to build an enormous ark for himself, his family, and the lower orders—even for unclean, creeping things! The expansiveness of the ark was expressive of the greatness of God's love; the extension of safety to "every" type of fauna elaborates the wideness of His concern. The destruction of all people existing before the Flood indicated the abhorrence of evil. The rescue of the family of Noah shows God's yearning love to save. When Noah offered a sacrifice to Yahweh after the Flood, the act prompted God to exercise His concern for the new race. Accordingly, He vowed never to doom the world again despite the enormous, continuing evil of the human creatures, an evil inconsistent with all God made and intended. Rather than destroy, God affirmed the continuity of seasons without respite. Moreover, the narrative pictured the equal rights and opportunities for all members of the new race based on each person representing the image of God. Most notable of all was the covenant of continued earthly security for mankind and the rainbow as the symbol of that everlasting covenant.

If God saw the evil in the earth, He saw also the righteous Noah—blameless in his generation, one who walked with God. Noah had found grace in the eyes of God. Informed, instructed, provided for, covenanted with to become the head of a new race and blessed to be productive and to increase on earth, Noah was made the mediator of a world-encompassing covenant where the image of God would guarantee equality in society. Here the Flood account highlights a person's potential: to walk with God, to be blameless and righteous in a wicked world, to be a mediator of divine grace possible for all people, and to know that the future was safe and sure by the oath God had sworn.

FLOUR Fine-crushed and sifted grain used in making bread (Ex. 29:2; 1 Sam. 28:24), often translated as fine or choice flour. Typically meal, which was ground course from the whole kernels of grain together with the bran, was used to make bread (Lev. 2:16; 1 King 17:12). The first fruits cereal offering was of course grain since it repre-sented the common table fare. Most often cereal offerings were of fine flour (Lev. 2:1,2,4,5,7), ground from the inner kernels of wheat only, the best part of the grain (Deut. 32:14). Fine flour was a luxury item (2 Kings 7:1; Ezek. 16:13; Rev. 18:13) such as might be baked as bread for an honored guest (Gen. 18:6; 1 Sam. 28:24).

An ancient flour mill in Capernaum.

Another type of ancient flour mill from the Roman period. The flour falls into the wooden box.

FLOWERS Colorful blooms containing a plant's reproductive organs. Flowers grew abundantly during springtime in Palestine. Flowers grew mostly in open fields, since flower gardens as we now know them were not cultivated. See *Garden*. Flowers grew in crop fields and in groves of trees around houses. Numerous kinds of wild flowers could be found in the plains and mountains of Palestine. The words "flower" or "flowers" refer to (1) colorful blossoms, (2) towering plants, (3) open flowers, and (4) flourishing flowers. In Palestine the warm spring temperatures joined with the winter rains to produce beautiful, blooming plants and flowers.

(1) *Almond blossoms* (Gen. 43:11; Ex. 25:33–34; 37:19–20; Num. 17:8; Eccl. 12:5). This tree, a member of the rose family, had beautiful pink blossoms that the Israelites used as models for engravers to adorn the cups of the golden lampstand.

(2) *Bulrush* (Ex. 2:3; Job 8:11; Isa. 18:2; 35:7), sometimes is referred to as "flag," "papyrus" (NIV), "reed" (NAS), or "rush" (NEB). This tall, slender reedlike plant grew along the banks of the Nile River and provided the earliest known mate-rial for making paper and covering the frames of boats (Isa. 18:2).

(3) *Calamus leaves* (Ex. 30:23; Song of Sol. 4:14; Isa. 43:24; Jer. 6:20; Ezek. 27:19). The leaves from this plant were a sweet-smelling cane or ginger grass. The leaves, when crushed, gave a much relished ginger smell. It was apparently imported from India for use in worship (Jer. 6:20). Several Hebrew expressions lie behind "calamus." The basic Hebrew term *qaneh* means, "cane." It is modified in Exodus 30:23 by the word for balsam, apparently referring to sweet cane or *Cymbopogon.* A similar plant may be meant by *qaneh tob* in Jeremiah 6:20, *tob* meaning either "good" or "perfumed." Elsewhere, *qaneh* occurs without modification and may refer to different types of cane. For example, in 1 Kings 14:15 the giant reed *Arundo donax* may be meant. Compare Job 40:21; Isaiah 19:6; 35:7.

(4) *Camphire flowers* (sometimes referred to as Henna) (Song of Sol. 1:14; 4:13; 7:11—see REB). The camphire was a small plant or shrub that bore beautiful cream-colored flowers that hung in clusters like grapes and were highly scented. It was used for orange dye.

(5) *Caperberry flowers* (Eccl. 12:5). The caperberry was a prickly shrub which produced lovely flowers and small, edible berries as it grew in rocks and walls. It was supposed to stimulate sexual desires and powers. KJV, NRSV, NIV, TEV translate the Hebrew term as "desire" in Ecclesiastes 12:5, but REB and NAS follow recent Hebrew

Cyclamen, pictured here, is one of the flowers of Israel.

The blossoms and fruit of a pomegranate tree growing in Israel.

dictionaries in translating, "caperberry."

(6) *Cockle flowers* (Job 31:40) were the purplish red flowers of a noxious weed called the "cockle" or "darnel" (*Lolium tenulentum*). This plant grew abundantly in Palestinian grain fields. Its Hebrew name is spelled like the Hebrew word for "stink" and thus is translated "stinkweed" by NAS.

(7) *Crocus* (Song of Sol. 2:1; Isa. 35:1) was a spring flowering herb with a long yellow floral tube tinged with purple specks or stripes. It is sometimes translated as rose. Technically, it was probably the asphodel (REB).

(8) *Fitch* (Isa. 28:25—27) KJV calls this flower the "fitch," but the better designation is probably the nutmeg flower. This flower was a member of the buttercup family and grew wildly in most Mediterranean lands. The plant was about two feet high and had bright blue flowers. The pods of the plant were used like pepper. Technically the plant is probably dill (NRSV, NAS, REB) or more precisely black cummin (*Nigella sativa*). NIV translates, "caraway."

(9) *Leek* (Num. 11:5), a member of the lily family, was a bulbous biennial plant with broad leaves. The bases of the leaves were eaten as food. The bulbs of this plant were used as seasoning. Israel relished the memory of leeks (*Allium porrum*) from Egypt.

(10) *Lily* (1 Kings 7:19,22,26; 2 Chron. 4:5; Songs of Sol. 2:1,2,16; 5:13; 6:2,3; 7:2; Hos. 14:5). The term "lily" covered a wide range of flowers. The most common was *Lilius candidum.* The lily mentioned in Song of Solomon 5:13 refers to a rare variety of lily that had a bloom similar to a glowing flame. The "lily of the valley" (Song 2:1,2,16) is known as the Easter lily. The lily mentioned in Hosea 14:5 is more akin to an iris. The beautiful water lily or lotus was a favorite flower in Egypt and was used to decorate Solomon's Temple (1 Kings 7:19,22,26; 2 Chron. 4:5). The "lilies of the field" (Matt. 6:28; Luke 12:27) were probably numerous kinds of colorful spring flowers such as the crown anemone.

(11) *Mandrake* (Gen. 30:14–16; Song of

Sol.7:13). The mandrake, a herb of the night-shade family, had a rosette of large leaves and mauve flowers during winter and fragrant and round yellow fruit during spring. The mandrake grew in fields and rough ground. It was considered to give sexual powers and probably can be identified as *Atropa Mandragora,* often used for medicine in ancient times.

(12) *Mint* (Matt. 23:23; Luke 11:42) was an aromatic plant with hairy leaves and dense white or pink flowers, probably *jucande olens.* Mint was used to flavor food. The Jews scattered it on the floors of houses and synagogues for its sweet smell.

(13) *Myrtle branches* (Neh. 8:15; Isa. 41:19; 55:13; Zech. 1:8–11). Myrtle bushes (*Myrtus communis*), which grew on Palestinian hillsides, had fragrant evergreen leaves and scented white flowers. The flowers on the myrtle branches were used as perfumes.

(14) *Pomegranate blossoms* (Ex 28:33, Num. 13:23; 1 Sam. 14:2; 1 Kings 7:18) from the pomegranate tree (*Punica granatum*) had dark green leaves with large orange-red blossoms. Decorators carved pomegranates on public buildings. The fruit symbolized fertility and was used to tan leather and for medicine.

(15) *Rose* (Song of Sol. 2:1; Isa. 35:1). Several varieties of roses could be found in Palestine. The rose was a member of the crocus family. Tradition-

Israel's Star of Bethlehem flower.

ally, what is considered a rose is not the flower mentioned in Scripture. The "rose" is more generally considered an asphodel. See *Crocus* above.

(16) *Saffron* (Song of Sol. 4:14). Saffron (*Curcuma longa* or *Crocus sativas*) is a species of crocus. In ancient times the petals of the saffron flower were used to perfume banquet halls. The type meant in Song of Solomon 4:14 may be an exotic plant imported from India.

Other Though not specifically mentioned by kind in the Bible, other varieties of flowers grew in Palestine. Appearing as early as January were the pink, white, and lilac blossoms of the cyclamen. Dominating many landscapes were the various shades of reds and pinks of the crown anemones, poppies, and mountain tulips. Some short-lived summer flowers were the yellow and white daisylike chrysanthemums.

Figurative Uses of "Flowers" The striking manner in which flowers burst into bloom for a few short weeks in spring and then faded into withered leaves was viewed as an illustration of the transient nature of human life (Job 14:2; Ps. 103:15; Isa. 40:6; 1 Pet. 1:24). The flowers of spring (Song of Sol. 2:12) signify renewal. The "fading flower" of Isaiah 28:1 represented the downfall of God's disobedient people. The "lilies of the field" (Matt. 6:28) grew unassumingly and without any outward signs of anxiety. If God takes care of the lilies, so God will take care of His children who need not worry uselessly. The phrase "flower of her age" (1 Cor. 7:36) described a girl reaching womanhood. The rich pass away just as quickly as the period of time for blooming flowers passes away (Jas. 1:10–11).   *Gary Hardin*

FLUTE See *Music, Instruments, Dancing.*

FLUX, BLOODY KJV term for dysentery (Acts 28:8). See *Dysentery.*

FODDER Feed for domestic animals. The Hebrew suggests a mixed feed, either of several grains (though barley was the common grain for livestock, Judg. 19:19; 1 Kings 4:28) or a mix of finely cut straw, barley, and beans formed into balls. Silage refers to fodder which has been moistened and allowed to ferment slightly (Isa. 30:24 NRSV). Fodder was salted to satisfy the animals' need for salt and to give a tastier feed.

FOOD When Jesus was Himself a guest at a meal, He referred to the two main meals of the day: "When thou makest a dinner or a supper, call not thy friends. But when thou makest a feast, call the poor, the maimed, the lame, the blind" (Luke 14:12–13). There were only two main meals for the Jewish family. Breakfast was taken informally soon after getting up and normally consisted of a flat bread cake and a piece of cheese, dried fruit, or olives. Sometimes the bread was wrapped

F

round the appetizer, and sometimes the bread was split open to make a bag where the morsels might be placed. To eat bread for a meal in such a way was so natural and normal that "eating bread" came to have the same meaning as "having a meal." "Give us this day our daily bread" is a request that God will meet our need for daily food (Matt. 6:11). It was quite usual for the men and boys to leave the house for their work, eating their breakfast as they went, while mother, daughters and the younger children were kept at home. There was no midday meal as such, although a rest may have been taken for a drink and a piece of fruit. When Ruth stopped with the reapers she ate parched corn moistened with wine (Ruth 2:14 NRSV).

While the men in the family were at work, the women and children would, among their daily activities, prepare for the evening meal. Water for cooking was collected by the older girls who drew it from the well or spring at the beginning of the day before it began to get hot, and the goats were milked too. Water collection was quite a serious business as well-water could be polluted by animal usage, and house run-off from mud roofs was not normally safe to drink. Water collected, the girls then went to the market to purchase food for the meal. Fresh vegetables were bought from traders who sat with their produce around them on the ground of the market place, and if needed, olive oil and seasoning. Some families collected bread from the village baker who owned a communal oven, returning the bread which each family had left as dough the night before (see Hosea 7:4–6). Other families got on with baking their own bread on their return home. The house had in the meantime been cleaned (Luke 11:25) and the washing done. Grain had been crushed in the handmill and the fire fanned so that it was hot enough for baking bread. After the midday rest, the evening meal was prepared on the fire; a vegetable or lentil stew was made in the large cooking pot, herbs and salt being used to add to the flavor. Only on special occasions such as a sacrifice or festival day was any meat added to the stew, and only on very rare occasions was the meat roasted or game or fish eaten. When the time came for the meal, the pot was placed on a rug on the floor (Gen. 18:8), the whole family sitting round. A blessing or thanksgiving was made and each membeer of the family used a piece of bread as a scoop to take up some of the contents of the pot because there was no cutlery. (Communal dipping into the pot made it essential that hands were washed before the meal). Later in history a table and benches sometimes replaced the rug on the ground (1 Kings 13:20), but the communal pot was still at the center. At the close of the meal, fruit would be eaten and everything washed down with wine.

Formal meals were always preceded by an invitation (which was politely refused as a matter of course). The host then insisted that people came until the invitations were accepted (Luke 14:16–24). When the guests arrived, their feet were washed by the most humble slaves, and their sandals were removed (John 13:3–11). This was to protect the carpeted floors from dirt as well as to make it more confortable to sit on one's heels. Their heads were anointed with olive oil scented with spices. The oil was rubbed into the hair (Luke 7:36–50). Drinking water was then provided. In large houses the special guest moved to the "top table" in a room with a raised floor and would sit on the right-hand side of the host. The second guest would sit on the host's left-hand side (see Luke 14:7–11; 20:46).

One did not so much "sit" at table as recline at table. Couches were drawn up to the tables, head towards the table and cushions provided so that guests could rest on their left arm and use the right to serve themselves from the table. Using this arrangement it was possible for the servants to continue to wash the feet (Luke 7:46), but to make conversation persons had to turn almost on their backs and literally be "on the bosom" of the person to the left (John 13:23–25). In the time of Jesus, the triclinium or couch arranged around three sides of a table, was the height of fashion. The open side was used by servants so that they had access to the tables to bring in or to take away dishes of food.

The meal started with a drink of wine diluted with honey. The main dinner which followed was of three courses, beautifully arranged on trays. There were no forks, so guests ate with their fingers except when soup, eggs, or shellfish were served. Then spoons were used. Finally there was a dessert of pastry and fruit. During the meal the host provided entertainment of music, dancing (individual, expressive dances), and readings from poetry and other literature. Such an occasion was an important local event, and people of humbler means were able to look in from the darkness outside (Luke 7:37). When the meal was completed, there was a long period devoted to talking. Stories were related, and gossip was shared. Such festivities were always the envy of poorer people who tried to copy them in their own way. Martha was probably trying to do something of this sort at Bethany when Jesus reminds her "but one thing is needful " (Luke 10:42).

Whether such meals were formal or informal, abundant or scant, there were always food laws which had to be observed. Only animals which chewed the cud and had divided hoofs, fish which had fins and scales, and birds which did not eat carrion could be eaten (Lev. 11:1–22), and the practice grew that soups should not be made with a mixture of vegetables (Deut. 9:9) and meat and milk dishes were not to be taken together (see Ex. 23:19).

Ralph Gower

FOOD OFFERED TO IDOLS A cause of controversy in the early church centering on what Christians were permitted to eat.

"Food offered to idols" is a translation of a single Greek word which has also been rendered "things offered unto idols" (KJV) and "meat sacrificed to idols" (NIV). The identification of the object of the offering by the term "idol" suggests that it was a name which originated outside first-century paganism. It reflects the perspective and conclusion of someone who spoke as a Jew or Christian.

Pagan sacrifices could be thought of as typically consisting of three portions. One small part would be used in the sacrificial ritual. A larger portion would be reserved for the use of the priests or other temple personnel. The largest part would be retained by the worshiper to be used in one of two ways. The one who offered the sacrifice sometimes used the remaining portion as the main course in a meal which might be served at or near the pagan temple. It is this type of religio-social event that stands behind the question raised by the letter (1 Cor. 7:1; 8:1) from the church at Corinth to Paul and consequently as the background for Paul's response in 1 Corinthians 8. The second method of disposing of the worshiper's portion would be to offer it for sale at the local marketplace. Meat that was sold in this fashion would be bought and then served as a part of a regular family meal. This situation is reflected in Paul's comments in 1 Cor. 10:23—11:1.

Robert Byrd

FOOL, FOOLISHNESS, AND FOLLY Translations of several uncomplimentary words which appear approximately 360 times throughout the Old and New Testaments to describe unwise and ungodly people. The words are especially predominant in the Wisdom Literature of the Old Testament. Persons who do not possess wisdom are called "fools"; their behavior is described as "folly." The picture which emerges from the biblical material is quite simple: folly is the opposite of wisdom, and a fool is the opposite of a wise person. Both wisdom and folly are depicted as philosophies or perspectives on life. The religious person chooses wisdom, whereas the nonreligious person opts for folly. Wisdom leads to victory; folly to defeat. Wisdom belongs to those who fear God, and the "fear" of the Lord is the beginning of wisdom (Prov. 1:7). Wisdom is the essence of life. The foolish person is the one who is thoughtless, self-centered, and obviously indifferent to God.

Old Testament Usage Seven different Hebrew words are usually translated by the single English word, "folly." Some of the shades of meaning suggested by these various words include: a) deliberate sinfulness; b) simplemindedness; c) malicious simple-mindedness; and d) brutal or subhuman activity.

The fool may be the one who is aloof. He "foldeth his hands" (Eccl. 4:5 a). This aloofness is also described in terms of the farmers who "follow worthless pursuits" instead of tending to the farm (Prov. 12:11 b NRSV).

In other passages the fool is described as the one who denies that God exists: "The fool hath said in his heart, There is no God" (Ps. 14:1). Foolish behavior is also characterized by an inability to recognize the true character of God. Job chastised his wife for behaving as the foolish do when she denied the steadfast love of God (Job 2:10).

The simple-minded fool is encouraged to change in Proverbs 9:4–6. But the fool may be the one who is intentionally perverse. Nabal and Saul represent this kind of intentional and malicious folly toward David (1 Sam. 25:25; 26:21).

New Testament Usage The contrasting elements of wisdom and folly evident in the Old Testament were clearly in the mind of Paul when he asked, "hath not God made foolish the wisdom of this world?" (1 Cor. 1:20 b). However, in the New Testament, this polarity between wisdom and folly is not always stressed. In fact, it is possible that a certain kind of wisdom can actually be folly. In Matthew 7:26; 25:2,3; Romans 2:20 "folly" is used synonymously with "experiental wisdom." Wisdom based only on human intellect and experiences without considering God is folly.

In Matthew 23:17, folly is equated with blindness. The characteristics of folly include thoughtlessness, the pursuit of unbridled aspirations, and a life-style characterized by envy, greed, and pride.

Foolishness is also described in paradoxical terms in the New Testament. In 1 Corinthians 1—3, the incarnation is portrayed as "foolishness," but it is precisely this kind of perceived "foolishness" which is better than worldly wisdom. Our understanding of this paradoxical relationship affects the manner in which Christ is proclaimed (1 Cor. 1:18—2:5). We must rely on God's gift and power of proclamation not on human powers and wisdom. The writer of Matthew records Jesus stating that "whosoever shall say, Thou fool, shall be in danger of hell fire" (5:22 b).

See *Wisdom*. *Kenneth Craig*

FOOT A part of the human and animal body used for walking. In Scripture "foot" refers mainly to the human foot (Ex. 12:11; Acts 14:8). It may also be used of the feet of animals (Ezek. 1:7) or, anthropomorphically, of God's feet (Isa. 60:13). The "foot" as a measure of length does not appear in Hebrew or Greek, but some English versions give the equivalent in feet (Gen. 6:15, NIV; KJV "cubits").

In the ancient world with unpaved roads, feet easily became dirty and had to be washed often.

From earliest times, hosts offered to wash their guests' feet (Gen. 18:4), usually done by the lowest servant (John 13:3–14). High honor was paid by anointing another's feet (Deut. 33:24; Luke 7:46; John 12:3).

Because it was so easy to soil one's feet, to remove the shoes was a sign of getting rid of dirt and so indicated holiness in worship (Ex. 3:5). To shake the dust off one's feet meant total rejection of that place (Acts 13:51). For both the Israelites and the Romans, punishment might include binding the feet in stocks (Job 13:27; Acts 16:24). Often "feet" symbolize the whole person, since it is hard to act without using the feet ("refrained my feet from every evil way" means "kept *myself* from evil," Ps. 119:101; compare Luke 1:79; Acts 5:9; Rom. 3:15).

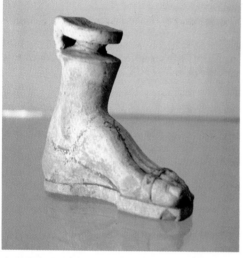

A perfume bottle in the shape of a sandaled foot from ca. 550 B.C. in Sicily.

Several biblical expressions contain "feet." "Put your feet upon the necks of these" suggested total victory over someone (Josh. 10:24). This was also implied by the phrase to put someone "under your feet" (Rom. 16:20; 1 Cor. 15:25). "To fall at someone's feet" showed humble submission, often when one had a request (1 Sam. 25:24; Luke 17:16). "To cover one's feet" was a euphemism for relieving oneself (1 Sam. 24:3). For one's foot "to slip" or "to be taken in a snare" meant calamity (Pss. 9:15; 66:9). "The feet of him that bringeth good tidings" meant their coming (Isa. 52:7). To sit "at the feet" meant to be a listener or disciple of someone (Acts 22:3) "Laid them down" at someone's feet suggested that the thing was a gift (Acts 4:35).   *Kendell Easley*

FOOTMAN KJV translation of two unrelated Hebrew terms. The first refers to foot soldiers as distinguished from cavalry (2 Sam. 8:4), to sol-

diers in general (1 Sam. 4:10; 15:4), or to men of military age (Ex. 12:37). The second term refers to a runner who served in the honor guard which ran ahead of the king's chariot (1 Sam. 8:11; 2 Sam. 15:1), to the king's guards in general (1 Kings 14:27–28; 2 Kings 10:25), or to royal couriers (Esther 3:13,15).

Bronze statuette from the Roman period of two soldiers carrying a wounded comrade.

FOOTSTOOL A piece of furniture for resting the feet, especially for one seated on a throne (2 Chron. 9:18; Jas. 2:3). The footstool of Tutankhamin of Egypt was carved with pictures of his enemies. Other Pharaohs were portrayed with their feet on their enemies' heads. The footstool thus became a symbol for dominion. God is pictured as a king enthroned in heaven with the earth as His footstool (Isa. 66:1; Matt. 5:35). In Psalm 99:5 and Lamentations 2:1 it is difficult to determine with certainty whether God's footstool is the ark, the Temple, or Zion. (Compare Isa. 60:13; Ezek. 43:7.) Only 1 Chronicles 28:2 is an unambiguous reference to the ark as a resting place for God's feet.

In Psalm 110:1 God makes the Messianic King triumph over His enemies, who are then made his footstool. This text is quoted six times in the New Testament. It served as the basis for Jesus' riddle about David's son who is also his lord (Matt. 22:44; Mark 12:36; Luke 20:43). Elsewhere, the Scripture was applied to the ascension of Christ (Acts 2:34–35), the exaltation of Christ (Heb. 1:13), and the future victory of Christ (Heb. 10:13).

FOOTWASHING An act necessary for comfort and cleanliness for any who have traveled dusty Palestinian roads with feet shod in sandals. Customarily, a host provided guests with water for washing their own feet (Judg. 19:21; Luke 7:44, where the complaint was that Simon had not provided water). Footwashing was regarded as so lowly a task that it could not be required of a Hebrew slave. In this context the statement of John the Baptist that he was unworthy to untie the sandal (to wash the feet) of the One coming after him (Mark 1:7) indicates great humility. As a sign of exceptional love, a disciple might wash a master's feet (contrast John 13:13–14) or a wife volunteer to wash her husband's (Joseph and Asenath 20:1–5). The initiative of the woman who was a "sinner" in washing Jesus' feet (Luke 7:37–50) was more than expected hospitality. Hers was an act of great love which evidenced the forgiveness of her sins (7:47).

Jesus' washing of the disciples' feet (John 13:4–5) has both an ethical and symbolic sense. The ethical sense is emphasized in John 13:14–15 where Jesus presented Himself as the example of humble, loving service. (Compare Luke 22:27.) The command to do for each other what Christ had done for them ought not to be confined simply to washing feet. What Jesus did for the disciples was to lay down His life for them (John 15:13). Thus the ethical imperative calls for giving our lives in extravagant acts of selfless service. Footwashing is one expression of this. The footwashing in John occupies the place taken by the institution of the Lord's Supper in Matthew, Mark, and Luke. Like the Supper, the footwashing is an enacted sermon on the death of Christ. This symbolic sense is highlighted in the picture of Jesus' laying aside his garments and then taking them up (a picture of Christ's laying down and taking up his life, John 10:17–18), the note that the footwashing is necessary for the disciples to receive their inheritance ("part" 13:8), and the statement that it affects cleansing (13:10). Some interpreters see a connection with baptism (and the Eucharist) as sacraments of cleansing. Instead, the footwashing, like baptism and the Supper, bears witness to the same salvific event, the selfless giving of Christ in the humilitating death of the cross.

Washing the feet of other Christians was a qualification for service as a "widow" in the early church (1 Tim. 5:10). Footwashing is here representative of humble acts of service (TEV).

The ceremonial washing of feet is first attested by Augustine in connection with Easter baptism. The association of the rite with Maundy Thursday was fixed by the council of Toledo (694). The developed Catholic practice involves a priest washing the feet of twelve poor men. Martin Luther criticized ecclesiastical authorities who washed feet as an act of humility and then demanded greater humility in return. The Anabaptists practiced footwashing as a symbol of washing in the blood of Christ and to impress the example of Christ's deep humiliation. Footwashing was commonly practiced by Baptists in early America. Today the regular practice is confined to smaller Baptist bodies, Mennonites, and some others.

Chris Church

FORBEARANCE Specifically, a refraining from the enforcement of a punishment; generally, a synonymn for patience. Forbearance makes it possible to influence a ruler (Prov. 25:15 NAS; patience NIV, NRSV; patient persuasion TEV). Jeremiah prayed that God not take him way in His forbearance (15:15 NRSV), that is, that God not be so patient with Jeremiah's enemies as to allow them to destroy him. In Romans 2:4; 3:25 forbearance refers to God's patience expressed in God's willingness to hold back judgment for a time. God's forbearance does not mean that God condones sin, but that God gives opportunity for repentance. God is able to maintain God's reputation as a righteous judge in spite of God's overlooking the past sins of Israel and the present sins of those who place faith in Christ (3:26), because the cross was an effective sacrifice of atonement. God's forbearance is an opportunity for salvation (2 Pet. 3:15).

FORD A shallow place in a stream or river that permits crossing by foot. The Romans were the first to build bridges in Palestine. Before their time river crossings were generally limited to fords. Fords are mentioned in connection with three rivers in Palestine: the Arnon (literally "rushing torrent" Isa. 16:2), the Jabbok (Gen. 32:22), the Jordan. All three rivers have swift currents and offer few fording places. Fords were thus strategic points. To secure the fords meant success in battle (Judg. 3:28; 12:5,6); their loss meant defeat (Jer. 51:32).

FOREHEAD Part of the face above the eyes. Because it is so prominent, the appearance of the forehead often determines our opinion of the person.

The Emblem of Holiness was placed on Aaron's forehead (Ex. 28:38). This symbolized acceptance before the Lord. A mark was put upon the foreheads of those in Jerusalem who mourned for the wickedness of Jerusalem. They were spared in a time of terrible judgment (Ezek. 9:4).

The Bible indicates that a person's character can be determined by observing the forehead. A set forehead indicates opposition, defiance, and rebellion (Jer. 3:3). Hardness of the forehead indicates determination to persevere (Isa. 48:4; Ezekiel 3:8–9). It has been used as a representation of Satan (Rev. 13:16–17). The forehead is used as a very dishonorable word when read of the harlot's forehead (Jer. 3:3), indicating utter shamelessness. At the same time, it stands for courage as when God told Ezekiel that He had made the prophet's forehead harder than flint against the foreheads of the people (Ezek. 3:9).

In the apocalyptic literature of the New Testament the foreheads of the righteous were marked (Rev. 7:3; 9:4; 14:1; 22:4). The apocalyptic woman dressed in purple and scarlet had her name written on her forehead (Rev. 17:5).

See *Face.* *Gary Bonner*

F

FOREIGNER See *Stranger.*

FOREKNOWLEDGE Awareness and anticipation of events before they occur. The words "foreknowledge" and "foreknow" are rarely used in the Bible, but the concept of God's foreknowledge is found throughout Scriptures. Other terms such as "election" and "predestination" are closely related to foreknowledge.

In the Bible, God alone has foreknowledge. Nothing is outside of His knowledge—past, present, or future. Nothing is hidden from Him, and only fools think they can hide their deeds from God (Pss. 10:11; 11:4–5; Prov. 15:11; Isa. 29:15–16). God knows completely the thoughts and doings of human beings (Ps. 139). Jesus taught that God has complete knowledge of human beings (Matt. 10:29–31), and the author of Hebrews wrote that "nothing in all creation is hidden from God's sight" (Heb. 4:13*a* NIV).

Foreknowledge of the Future God's foreknowledge encompasses future events. The perspective of faith can say that all that happens has been previously planned by God. Events of history are perceived in faith as the unfolding of God's eternal plans (Gen. 45:4–8; Isa. 14:24–27; 42:9; Jer. 50:45). The New Testament writers perceived in the life, death, and resurrection of Jesus the outworking of God's eternal plans to save sinful humanity. Thus Paul proclaimed the gospel which God had promised beforehand through His prophets in the holy Scriptures (Rom. 1:2). The gospels similarly declare that those things which the prophets had said were now fulfilled in the life and death of Jesus (Matt. 1:22–23; 2:5–6:15; John 19:24). Acts 2:23 and 1 Peter 1:20 declare that the crucifixion of Christ was not a chance happening of history. It was according to the foreknowledge of God, according to His eternal plan.

Foreknowledge and God's Will In the Bible, God's foreknowledge of people is not primarily a reference to His intellect, but to His kind will by which He sets people apart to Himself. So Jeremiah heard God's word to him saying, "Before I formed you in the womb I knew you, before you were born I set you apart; I appointed you as a prophet to the nations" (Jer. 1:5 NIV). Similarly, the apostle Paul perceived that God had "separated me from my mother's womb . . . that I might preach him among the heathen" (Gal. 1:15–16). God's foreknowledge must be understood in terms of personal relationship of God to His creation. To affirm God's foreknowledge is a statement of faith—that God's purpose existed before mankind's response to God (Ps. 139:16). The initiative lies with God.

In Romans Paul wrote that those whom God foreknows, He predestines to be conformed to the image of His Son; and those whom God predestines, He calls; and those whom He calls, He justifies; and those whom He justifies, He glorifies

(8:29–30). In the same letter, Paul declared that God had not rejected the Jewish people whom He foreknew (Rom. 11:2).

Foreknowledge and Human Freedom Such statements raise the difficult theological question of human freedom. If God already knows in advance who will be saved or elected, does that not eliminate free human will? Does God predestine some people to salvation and others to damnation?

One major attempt to answer this question is associated with James Arminius (1560-1609) who argued, as did the pre-Augustinian church fathers, that God's foreknowledge is a prescient knowledge, that is, God knows in advance what a person's response will be, so He elects to salvation in advance those whom He knows will freely accept Christ. This Arminian view is called *conditional predestination,* since the predestination is conditioned on God's foreknowledge of the individual's acceptance or rejection of Christ.

Another major Christian tradition is the Augustine-Luther-Calvin tradition. This view claims that God's foreknowledge is not simply God's foreknowledge of faith. Rather, for God to foreknow means that His knowledge determines events. He predestines some to be saved, but not on the foreknowledge of how they will respond; rather in His foreknowledge He foreordains apart from any human response.

Both views are supported by texts from Scripture. While Romans 8:29–30 are key verses in any discussion of God's foreknowledge, it is perhaps more correct to interpret these verses in terms of the doctrine of assurance rather than of predestination. Paul's point in Romans 8:29–30 is not to discuss who is foreknown and predestined to be saved and who is not. This passage may naturally give rise to that question, but it does not lead to any one answer. The doctrine of predestination was developed in the reformed tradition in an attempt to solve problems raised by Paul's writings and by other biblical texts. Paul's concern in this passage was rather to assure the Christian readers that their security is based upon God's eternal purpose and not upon the Christian's initiative. Nothing, therefore, can separate them from God's love!

First Peter 1:20 also declares that the Christian readers in Asia Minor were chosen by God according to His foreknowledge. Directed to Christians experiencing persecution because of their faith in Jesus, 1 Peter's reference to the foreknowledge of God was intended to bring assurance that their existence is part of God's will and plan and that they have a sure and certain hope that is not tied to changing circumstances or events. Other such affirmations in the New Testament (Eph. 1:4,11–12; 2 Thess. 2:13; Rev. 17:8) should be read from the same faith perspective. The writers were not attempting to answer the question of whom God saves and whom He rejects, nor were they intending to limit free human choice. They were rather expressing the conviction and assurance of faith that the individual's salvation lies entirely and securely in God's hand and in God's eternal purpose.

See *Knowledge; Election; Predestination.*

Roger L. Omanson

FORERUNNER The Greek term *prodromos* (one who runs ahead) occurs only once in the New Testament (Heb. 6:20) where it serves as a designation for Christ. In secular Greek the term was frequent as a military term for advanced scouts or cavalry that prepared for a full assault. This sense is seen in the Septuagint or earliest Greek translation of the Old Testament once (Wisdom of Solomon 12:8) where wasps were the forerunners of the armies of Israel. (Compare Ex. 23:28; Deut. 7:20; but also Joshua 24:12 where the hornets completed driving out the Amorite kings so that no Israelite assault was necessary.) Elsewhere in the Septuagint *prodromos* is used metaphorically for the first ripe fruit (Num. 13:20; Isa. 28:4). This usage suggests that the Christian hope of entering God's presence is guaranteed by the forerunner's already reaching this goal. (Compare the idea of Christ as first fruits of the dead, 1 Cor. 15:20,23.) A similar idea is expressed in the image of Christ as the pioneer of salvation (Heb. 2:10), the first of many children that God brings to glory through suffering. Significantly, Christ is forerunner *for* us. Having run ahead on the road of suffering, Christ became the source of salvation which makes our following possible (Heb. 5:8-10).

In English forerunner indicates one who precedes and indicates the approach of another. In this sense John the Baptist is termed the forerunner of Jesus, though the New Testament does not use this term of John. The Old Testament used the common image of advance agents sent ahead of a king to make arrangements for his travel to picture the mission of a prophetic messenger preparing the way for God's coming (Isa. 40:3; Ma. 3:1). The application of these texts to John by the New Testament writers (Matt. 11:10; Mark 1:2; Luke 1:76; 7:27) affirm that the coming of Jesus is the coming of God.

FORESAIL A small sail used to steer a vessel in strong wind (Acts 27:40). KJV refers to the "mainsail." Paul's ship likely had a large central mast with a long yard arm supporting the large, square mainsail and a smaller foremast, slopping forward like a bowsprit, which carried the foresail.

FORESKIN The loose fold of skin covering the glans of the penis which is removed in circumcision. Removal of the foreskin was a bodily reminder of God's covenant with Abraham (Gen. 17:11,14,23-25). In Deuteronomy 10:16 the "foreskin of the heart" is associated with stubborn-

ness in disobedience. The difficult text in Habakkuk 2:16 is likely a scribal corruption of the word "stagger" involving the inversion of two letters. NRSV, TEV, and REB thus translate "stagger" together with the Dead Sea Scrolls and several ancient versions. The reading in the Masoretic text, "to show oneself to be uncircumcised," does not mean simple exposure (NIV, NAS), but to be recognized as one cut off from the covenant. See *Covenant; Circumcision.*

FOREST Large, naturally-wooded areas, characteristic of the central hill country, the Galilee, and the Bashan.

Large expanses of forest covered the majority of the hills in Palestine during the Old Testament period. Because of their locations on hilly, rocky soil, forests were considered unfarmable in early periods. After the Exodus, the inability of the Israelite tribes to conquer much of their inheritance forced them to develop new settlements and camps in the wooded hill country. Unable to rescue their portion from the hands of the Canaanites, the clans of Ephraim and Manasseh cleared the forests among the hills in their territory to provide room for settlement (Josh. 17:15-18). Forests also provided excellent staging areas for warfare, such as the rebellion of Absalom against David which ended with a battle in the forests of Ephraim (2 Sam. 18:6-8). The valuable cedars of Lebanon were imported from Tyre by Solomon for his extensive building projects in Jerusalem (1 Kings 5:8-10). Solomon's palace, "The house of the forest of Lebanon," was so named for its extensive use of these cedars (1 Kings 7:2). As the population expanded, forested areas were cut down, and terraced orchards took their place. Large portions of the forests around Jerusalem were destroyed during the Roman seige of the city in A.D. 70.   *David Maltsberger*

FOREST OF LEBANON, HOUSE OF See *House of the Forest of Lebanon.*

FORGE See *Furnace.*

FORGETFULNESS, LAND OF A name for Sheol, the abode of the dead, in Psalm 88:12. See *Sheol.*

FORGIVENESS An act of God's grace to forget forever and not hold people of faith accountable for sins they confess; to a lesser degree the gracious human act of not holding wrong acts against a person. Forgiveness has both divine and human dimensions. In the divine relationship, it is, first of all, the gracious act of God by which believers are put into a right relationship to God and transferred from spiritual death to spiritual life through the sacrifice of Jesus. It is also, in this divine dimension, the ongoing gift of God without which our lives as Christians would be "out of joint" and

F

full of guilt. In terms of a human dimension, forgiveness is that act and attitude toward those who have wronged us which restores relationships and fellowship.

Everyone Needs Forgiveness The basic facts of the Bible are God's creative power and holiness, human rebellion, and the efforts of our merciful God to bring us back to an intended relationship of sonship and fellowship. The need of forgiveness is first seen in the third chapter of Genesis, as Adam and Eve willfully disobeyed God, choosing rather to satisfy their own self-will. The result was guilt (Gen. 3:8,10), separation from God, loss of fellowship (Gen. 3:8,23–24), and a life of hardship, anxiety, and death (Gen. 3:16–24) lived under the wrath of God. David expressed this terrible condition of the unforgiven sinner graphically in Psalm 51. He spoke of being unclean (v. 2,7,10), of being sinful by his very nature (v. 5), of his grief and sorrow at being separated from God (v. 8,11,12), and of his guilt (v. 14). Sinners cannot live rightly without God, and yet as a sinner a person is cut off from the holy God. Only through the mercy of God can one find peace and forgiveness.

Forgiveness in the Old Testament The primary means of obtaining forgiveness in the Old Testament is through the sacrificial system of the covenant relationship, which God established when He brought His people out of Egypt. The sacrificial system expressed the dynamics of the sinful human condition. The bringing of the sacrifice showed the sense of need; the laying of the hands on the living sacrifice symbolized identification of the person with the sacrifice, as did the releasing of the life of the animal through the sacrificial slaughter. Emphasis on an unblemished sacrifice stressed the holiness of God contrasted with human sinfulness. The forgiveness of God, channeled through the sacrificial offering, was an act of mercy freely bestowed by God, not purchased by the one bringing the offering.

An emphasis upon God's demand for a repentant heart as the basis for forgiveness, while not totally absent earlier (see Ps. 51), gained its full expression in the prophets (Isa. 1:10–18; Jer. 7:21–26; Hos. 6:6; Amos 5:21–27). This element does not negate but rather deepens the understanding of the sacrifice. The Old Testament sacrificial system could never give once-for-all forgiveness. It had to be repeated over and over (Heb. 10:1–4).

Forgiveness in the New Testament Jesus is the perfect and final Sacrifice through which God's forgiveness is mediated to every person (Rom. 3:25; Heb. 10:11–12). The connection of Jesus with forgiveness is seen in His own self-understanding. According to the Old Testament, only God could forgive sins; yet Jesus declared that He could do so, and He did (Mark 2:1–12; John 8:2–11). He saw His own death as the fulfillment of the Old Testament sacrificial system. At the Last Supper He spoke of His death as "my blood of the new testament [covenant]" (Mark 14:24). Jesus Himself is the unblemished Sacrifice (Isa. 53:3–7), offered once for all (Heb. 9:28) not by a human being, but by God Himself in Christ Jesus for the sins of mankind (Heb. 9:14; Rom. 3:25; Acts 13:38). Forgiveness through the sacrifice of Christ is available for everyone who truly repents (Luke 23:39–43; John 8:2–11).

The Sin Which is Unforgivable It is true that Jesus spoke of an unforgivable sin (Matt. 12:22–32; Mark 3:22–30; Luke 12:10). It is not a question of God's ability or desire to forgive, but rather a matter of human willingness to meet the conditions for forgiveness. The background of the saying was the controversy between Jesus and the religious leaders of His time. The Pharisees refused to see the merciful hand of God in the work of Jesus, and rather attributed His miracles to the power of Satan. For such who deliberately closed their minds to the work and invitation of God in Christ to draw near, repent, and receive forgiveness, there is no hope. But the fault lies with them, rather than with God.

Human Forgiveness in the New Testament As a part of His teaching about human need for forgiveness and the means of receiving it, Jesus spoke of the human dimension of forgiveness. A firm condition for the receiving of God's forgiveness is the willingness to forgive others. In the Lord's Prayer (Matt. 6:12; Luke 11:4) and the parable of the Unforgiving Servant (Matt. 18:12–35) Jesus clearly indicated such is the case: "But if ye forgive not men their trespasses, neither will your Father forgive your trespasses" (Matt. 6:15). The forgiven life is the forgiving life.

Human forgiveness reflects our experience and understanding of divine forgiveness. Love, not wooden rules, governs forgiveness (Matt. 18:21–22). Jesus powerfully demonstrated this teaching on the cross, as He asked for forgiveness for His executioners (Luke 23:34).

See *Cross; Mercy; Redemption; Sin.*

Earl C. Davis

FORK A pronged implement. Two types of forks are mentioned in Scripture, an implement used in the sacrificial cult (See *Fleshhook*) and a farm tool used to winnow grain (See *Fan*).

FORMER RAIN KJV term at Joel 2:23 for the early rain. See *Rain.*

FORNICATION (Fōr nĭ cā' tion) Various acts of sexual immorality, especially being a harlot or whore.

Old Testament Normally women are the subject of the Hebrew verb *zanah,* but in Numbers 25:1 men "began to commit whoredom." The clearest example is that of Tamar sitting on the roadway to entice Judah (Gen. 38:12–34). Such action was subject to criminal prosecution bringing the death penalty (Gen. 38:24; compare Lev. 21:9; Deut. 22:21). Fornication meant being unfaithful to a marriage commitment (Judg. 19:2).

Israel's neighbors practiced a fertility religion in which prostitution was part of the worship. This led naturally to describing worship of other gods as prostitution (Ex. 34:15–16; Judg. 8:27,33; Hos. 4:13). This concept is central for Hosea's preaching based on his experience with his unfaithful wife Gomer. Ezekiel also used this concept (Ezek. 16; 23) and extended it to include political treaties with foreign enemies (Ezek. 16:26, 28; 23:5).

New Testament The New Testament also condemns prostitution. Here again prostitution played a central role in worship in places like Corinth and Athens. Greek philosophers could even distinguish the roles of prostitutes for pleasure, slave mistresses to give daily care to the master's body, and wives to produce legitimate children. Some Stoic philosophers reacted against such practices and condemned sex outside marriage. Many women used the situation to take slave lovers for themselves or become lesbians.

Jesus went against Jewish tradition and forgave prostitutes and opened the way for them to enter God's kingdom through faith (Matt. 21:31–32; compare Heb. 11:31; Jas. 2:25), though He still regarded fornication as evil (Mark 7:21).

Paul extended the use of the Greek term for fornication to cover all sinful sexual activity. He dealt with the problem particularly in writing the Corinthians who faced a society permeated with sexual religion and the sexual sins of a seaport. A believer must decide to be part of Christ's body or a prostitute's body (1 Cor. 6:12–20). The believer must flee sexual immorality and cleave to Christ, honoring Him with the physical body. Fornication is thus a result of sinful human nature (Gal. 5:19) and unsuitable for God's holy people (Eph. 5:3; 1 Thess. 4:3).

The Book of Revelation also says much about fornication, condemning those guilty to eternal punishment (Rev. 2:21–22). Revelation, as well as the prophets, extends the meaning of fornication to include political and religious unfaithfulness (Rev. 14:8; 17:2,4; 18:3; 19:2).

As a whole, the New Testament uses *porneia*, most often translated fornication, in at least four ways:

1. Voluntary sexual intercourse of an unmarried person with someone of the opposite sex (1 Cor. 7:2; 1 Thess. 4:3).

2. A synonym for adultery (Matt. 5:32; 19:9). See *Adultery; Divorce.*

3. Harlotry and prostitution (Rev. 2:14,20).

4. Various forms of unchastity (John 8:41; Acts 15:20; 1 Cor. 5:1).   *Gary Hardin*

FORT, FORTIFICATION Walled structures built defense against enemy armies. Cities of the ancient world were fortified for defensive purposes as far back as archaeological records exist. The oldest fortifications in Israel are at Jericho, where a Neolithic stone tower and part of a wall have been dated to 7,000 B.C. No other examples exist until 3,000 B.C., the Chalcolithic Period (about 4,000-3,000 B.C.) being one of open villages without fortification. Beginning in the Early Bronze Age mudbrick walls, towers, and gates were built on stone foundations at Ai, Arad, Beth Yerah, Gezer, Jericho, Megiddo, and elsewhere. From this time until the Roman Period (the time of Christ), cities were almost always surrounded by walls. The stone foundations and those portions of wall above the ground which utilized stone construction were made of uncut field stone. In the

Masada, the site of a palace built by Herod the Great, provides its own natural fortification.

time of Solomon, however, well-dressed ashlars (carefully trimmed limestone blocks) began to be used in the construction of unique fortification systems. These included casemate walls (that is, two parallel stone walls with dividing partitions connecting them) and huge six-chambered gates allowing easy entrance and exit for his chariots (a gate plan introduced much earlier by the Hyksos invaders, around 1700 B.C., who also used chariots). Similar, but smaller four-chambered gates were used later in the time of Ahab and Jeroboam II, attached to offsets-insets solid walls. A glacis was sometimes built against the outside wall for added protection against the battering ram. A glacis was a sloping embankment of beaten earth, clay, gravel and stones, sometimes covered with plaster. Examples of huge, dressed stone walls and gate towers of the Hellenistic/Roman Periods may be seen today at Samaria, Caesarea Maritima, and Tiberias. Citadels were often built on the acropolis of the enclosed city.   *John McRay*

FORTIFIED CITIES The term "fortified city" (often "fenced city" or "defenced city" in the KJV) refers to a town with strong defenses, usually a massive wall structure and inner citadels or strongholds. In general the fortified city was a major military or administrative center for a region. Size was not so much the factor, though many of the fortified cities were large cities. Location was much more critical.

The Bible contains two lists of fortified cities, one for Naphtali (Josh. 19:35–38), and a list of cities Rehoboam fortified for Judah (2 Chron. 11:5–12). These two lists seem to include most of the walled cities within the tribal area.

Fortified cities served a strategic function. They could guard a major highway (as did Lachish and Hazor). They could protect mountain passes (Megiddo and Taanach). They could serve as border fortresses (Arad and Hazor). Surely troops would be garrisoned in a fortified city. At times of imminent danger, much of the populace from the surrounding area might find protection in a fortified city (Jer. 4:5; 8:14).

Other closely related terms used in the Bible include chariot cities and store cities (1 Kings 9:19). Chariot cities were major military centers where the chariot troops were garrisoned. Store cities probably served as central supply bases for the military. *Joel F. Drinkard, Jr.*

FORTUNATUS A Corinthian Christian who together with Stephanus and Achaicus ministered to Paul at Ephesus (1 Cor. 16:17). The three perhaps brought Paul a letter from Chloe's household in Corinth. In view of their anticipated return to Corinth, they perhaps delivered First Corinthians as indicated in the superscription of the Textus Receptus.

FORTUNE See *Destiny.*

FORUM The open place of a market town or the town itself. The Appii Forum (Acts 28:15) or market town of Appius was located 43 miles to the southeast of Rome on the Appian Way.

FORUM OF APPIUS A station along the Appian Way where Paul and his companions were met by a group of believers from Rome (Acts 28:15). It

A panoramic view of the ruins of the forum of ancient Rome.

was some 43 miles southeast of Rome. Paul was on the way to Rome to be tried before Caesar.

FOUNDATION That on which a building is built; the first layer of a structure that provides a stable base for the superstructure. Bedrock was the preferred foundation (Matt. 7:24). The best alternative was a solid platform of close-fitting cut stone (1 Kings 5:17). Modest homes had foundations of rough stone. Generally, building sites were leveled by filling in the foundation trenches with gravel or small stones. Often, the foundation is all that remains of ancient structures. The prohibition of laying a foundation for Jericho (Josh. 6:26) was a prohibition of rebuilding the city as a fortified site rather than of inhabiting the place. The splendor of the new Jerusalem is pictured in its foundation of precious stones (Isa. 54:11; Rev. 21:19).

The Old Testament pictured the earth (dry land) as resting on foundations (2 Sam. 22:16; Ps. 18:15; 82:5). God is pictured as a builder who marked out the foundations (Prov. 8:29) and set the stone (Ps. 104:5). The mountains (Deut. 32:22; Ps. 18:7) and the vault of the heavens (2 Sam. 22:8; Job 26:11) are also pictured as resting on foundations. God's great power is expressed in the images of the earth's foundations trembling (Isa. 24:18) or being exposed (2 Sam. 22:16) before the Almighty. "From the foundations of the earth" means from the time of creation (Isa. 40:21; Matt. 13:35; John 17:24).

Christ's teaching is compared to a rock solid foundation (Matt. 7:24; Luke 6:48). Foundation serves as a metaphor for the initial preaching of the Gospel (Rom. 15:20; Heb. 6:1–2 which outlines the foundational topics), for the apostles and prophets as the first generation of preachers (Eph. 2:20; compare Rev. 21:14,19); and for Christ as the content of preaching (1 Cor. 3:10–11).

The foundations of Psalms 11:3 are the foundations of life, security, community, justice, and religion. To lay a good foundation for the future (1 Tim. 6:19) is to be generous and ready to share. The foundation of 2 Timothy 2:19 is an enigma. The context suggests that God's foundation is the core of true believers known only to God. Other suggestions include Christ, God's work, the church, Christ's teaching, and God's eternal law. *Chris Church*

FOUNTAIN A spring of water flowing from a hole in the earth. The limestone rock of Palestine is especially suited for the formation of springs. In semi-arid country springs are highly prized as water sources and often determine the location of settlements. Thus the frequency of the Hebrew root *En,* meaning spring, in place names: En-dor (Josh. 17:11); En-eglaim (Ezek. 47:10); En-gannim (Josh. 15:34); En-gedi (15:62); En-haddah (19:21); En-hakkore (Judg. 15:19); En-

During the Roman period manmade fountains such as this one at Pompeii (first century A.D.) supplemented natural spring-fed fountains.

hazor (Josh. 19:37); En-rimmon; (Neh 11:29); En-rogel and En-shemesh (Josh. 15:7); and En-tappuah (17:7). Enaim (Enam, Josh. 15:34) means "two springs." The goodness of Canaan was seen in its abundant water supply, "a land with flowing streams, with springs and underground waters welling up in valleys and hills" (Deut. 8:7 NRSV).

The Old Testament portrays the earth's dry land resting on foundations over the fountains of the deep (Gen. 7:11). The unleashing of these waters amounted to a return to the chaos before the creation (Gen. 1:1,9).

Provisions of spring water is an expression of God's providential care (Ps. 104:10). God's spe-

Another manmade public fountain area at Hierapolis.

cial concern for the poor and needy is pictured in terms of providing fountains and springs (Isa. 41:17–18). The blessedness of the endtime includes pictures of fountains flowing from the Temple (Ezek. 47:1–12; Joel 3:18), Jerusalem (Zech. 14:8), or the throne of God (Rev. 22:1–2) with amazing life-giving powers.

The metaphorical use of fountain for source is common. The teaching of the wise is a fountain (source) of life (Prov. 13:14; contrast 25:26).

Chris Church

FOUNTAIN GATE A city gate at the southeast corner of the walls of ancient Jerusalem (Neh. 2:14; 3:15; 12:37), probably so named because people brought water from the En-rogel or Gihon springs into the city through this gate. The gate is possibly identical with the "gate between the two walls" (2 Kings 25:4; Jer. 39:4; 52:7).

FOWL See *Birds.*

FOWLER One who traps birds. All Biblical references are figurative. A variety of means are mentioned in Scripture: snares (Ps. 91:3; 124:7); traps (Ps. 141:9; Jer. 5:26–27); ropes (Job 18:10 KJV, "snare"); and nets (Hos. 7:12). God is praised as One who delivers from the fowler's snare (Ps. 91:3; 124:7), an image of the power of the wicked. Opposition to the prophet Hosea is pictured as a fowler's snare set in the Temple (Hos. 9:8). Hosea 7:12 pictures Israel as a dumb bird which God will catch with a net so the nation can be disciplined. Proverbs 6:1–2,5 pictures indebtedness as a snare to be avoided. Jesus warned that the day of God's coming judgment would be as unexpected as the closing of a trap (Luke 21:35).

FOX See *Animals.*

FRACTURE The breaking of a bone (Lev. 24:20, KJV "breach"). The law of retribution limited retaliation to "fracture for fracture."

FRAME Term used by modern translations to render a number of Hebrew terms. Frame refers to the "carrying frame" (NRSV) for the lamps and Tabernacle utensils (Num. 4:10,12; KJV, NAS "bars"; REB "poles"); to the rim that served as a brace for the legs of the table of the presence (Ex. 25:25,27; KJV "border"); to the frames for the side panels of the stands used to transport the Temple lavers (1 Kings 7:28–36; 2 Kings 16:17; KJV "ledge"); to the skeletal structure over which the Tabernacle curtains were spread (Ex. 26:15–29; 35:11; KJV, NAS "boards"); and to the casing of windows and doors (1 Kings 7:4–5). Frame is also used in reference to the human form (Job 41:12; Ps. 103:14; 139:15). Frame can be interpreted either as "how we are formed" (NIV) or "what we are made of" (TEV). Frame is also used as a verb. The tongue's "framing words" is a picturesque expression for speech (Ps. 50:19). Most often frame means to plan or devise (Ps. 94:20) or to act on plans (Jer. 18:11).

FRANKINCENSE An ingredient used in making the perfume for the most holy place in the tabernacle (Ex. 30:34). It is a resinous substance derived from certain trees in the balsam family. Frankincense was one of the gifts presented to the child Jesus by the Magi (Matt. 2:11).

FREE WILL OFFERING A gift given at the impulse of the giver (Ex. 35:21–29; 36:3–7; Lev. 7:16). The distinctive mark of the free will offering was the "stirred hearts" and "willing spirits" of the givers. The Tabernacle was constructed using materials given as free will offerings (Ex. 35:29). The people's desire to give was so great that Moses was compelled to ask that no more gifts be given (Ex. 36:3–7). Free will offerings were traditionally given at Pentecost (Deut. 16:10). See *Sacrifice and Offerings.*

FREEDMEN, SYNAGOGUE OF THE A Greek-speaking synagogue in Jerusalem involved in instigating the dispute with Stephen (Acts 6:9; KJV "Synagogue of the Libertines"). The Greek syntax suggests two groups of disputants. The first consisted of the Synagogue of the Freedmen, composed of Cyrenians and Alexandrians (so NAS, TEV). It is possible that this first group has three parties, the freedmen (freed slaves), the Cyrenians, and Alexandrians. Some early versions have Libyans in place of "libertines," giving three groups of North African Jews. The second party in the dispute was composed of Greek-speaking Jews of Asia and Cilicia. These may have belonged to the Synagogue of the Freedmen as well (REB). Some have identified the freedmen as the descendants of Pompey's prisoners of war (63 B.C.).

FREEDOM The ability of a person or group to be and do what they want instead of being controlled by another. It is popular today to believe that the individual is or should be in full control of him or her self. Such an understanding is alien to the Bible, which never depicts the individual as having total command or freedom over self. In one sense the Scripture does affirm that we are in control of ourselves. We are able to choose our actions and attitudes, our responses to others and to God. In another sense, we cannot be and do what we want because we are not independent of others or God. We do not have the power to do what we want to, whether that be to fulfill the law, love others, or save ourselves. The Bible constantly affirms that the kind of freedom all persons have is the kind of freedom that slaves have.

Old Testament Teaching In the Old Testament, "freedom" is used to describe what God desires and grants to Hebrew slaves. According to the law, no person is to have complete mastery of another. Consequently, the Law stipulates that a person can only be used as a slave for six years. Even so, if they are mistreated during that time, they are to be released. Also, every fifty years, all slaves are to be freed, regardless of how many years of their slavery they have served (Ex. 21:2–11,26,27; Lev. 25:10; Deut. 15:12–18). In the example of the Exodus and the preaching of the prophets, whoever is oppressed is viewed as a slave, and God desires that the oppression stop.

Throughout the Old Testament, freedom is predominantly used to express control over the physical circumstances of life. By the time of the New Testament, it was widely recognized that no persons are free to such an extent that they have control of their physical circumstances. Even the rich are subject to war, drought, and other calamities. Nevertheless, an influential group called Stoics believed that anyone could still attain true freedom, because no person or force of nature can control the inner life. Thus, the individual is ultimately in control of self, though not of the environment.

New Testament Teaching In contrast to the Stoics, the New Testament recognizes that no one has such absolute control. Everyone is considered to be a slave in some sense. But being a slave in the first century world did not mean being without freedom.

Slaves during the New Testament era had much freedom of choice in daily affairs, and their decisions were not just trivial. They served in every position in society, including being the emperor's advisors and filling other government positions. They were allowed to conduct their own personal affairs, earn and save money for themselves, own property, and even own their own slaves. Just as Roman slaves usually had much control over their daily affairs, every time the New Testament commands us to do something, it implicitly affirms that we have control over our daily decisions.

Most slaves of the first century were slaves from birth. They were children of slaves, and they served their parents' owners. But few remained slaves for life. They were usually freed when their owners died, or after ten to twenty years of adult service to their owner. They also had the opportunity to buy their freedom if they could save or borrow the money their owner charged for freeing them. In fact, before the New Testament era was over, a large percentage of the free population of the Roman Empire had either been slaves at one time or had parents who were slaves. The New Testament depicts all persons as being in slavery—the slavery of sin (John 8:34; Rom. 3:9–12; 2 Pet. 2:19). Just as Roman slaves usually had the opportunity to gain their freedom, so all people have the opportunity to obtain release from bondage to sin by choosing to follow Christ (Rom. 6:12–14; 10:9–12). Though slaves, our free will is intact, and our decisions are real and meaningful.

The New Testament also affirms that we are not our own rulers. We do not have ultimate control of our lives. Just as we are not in control of our physical circumstances because nature or some other person is more powerful than ourselves, so we are not in full control of even our inner selves because the powers of sin and grace are stronger than ourselves (Rom. 7:15–25). Just as the slave's master determines the service that the slave is to perform, since the master is more powerful than the slave, so it is our master, not ourselves, who determines the general direction of our life (Rom. 6:16).

When we yield to sin as our master, sin uses the law to deceive us into thinking that we are so in control of ourselves that by our own works we can save ourselves by obeying the law. In reality, on our own we do not have the power, the freedom, to live righteously. Indeed, "I can will what is right, but I cannot do it." (Rom. 7:18 NRSV). So our attempts to fulfill the law by ourselves simply increase our pride, thus strengthening the control of sin over us. As we continue to live under the rule of sin, the daily choices we make become more and more consistently obedient to sinful purposes and lead to death.

If, however, we yield to grace, given through Jesus Christ, the Spirit has the power to lead us into life and truth (Rom. 6:19; Eph. 1:11–14). As we continue to live in Christ, He uses His power to mold us more and more into His image (2 Cor. 3:18; Phil. 1:6).

Since Jesus established His church, some people have always thought that we are no longer bound by the law but are "free" in Christ to act however we like. The Scriptures constantly remind us that following our every desire is not what freedom is. We are free from our former master, sin; but we are still servants. As servants of Christ, though we have the freedom to disobey our master, it is our responsibility to direct our actions to fulfill the purposes of Christ (Rom. 6:1,2,15,18,22; 1 Pet. 2:16).

Do we have freedom? Yes. Are we free? No. The Bible affirms that our choices are not determined; we make them ourselves. But it also demonstrates that we are not in total control of ourselves. We live under the ultimate control and direction of a power greater than ourselves. The comforting thing about this is that "in everything, . . . he (God) cooperates for good with those who love God" (Rom. 8:28 REB).

See *Election, Slavery.*   *Steve Arnold*

FRIEND, FRIENDSHIP A close trusting relationship between two people. Nowhere does the Bible present a concise definition of "friend" or "friendship." Instead, both the Old and New Testaments present friendship in its different facets.

Two Hebrew root words, r'h and ahv, are used to describe friendship. *R'h* denotes an associate or companion, while *ahv* connotes the object of one's affection or devotion—a friend. Consequently, friendship may be simple association (Gen. 38:12; 2 Sam. 15:37) or loving companionship, the most recognizable example being that between David and Saul's son, Jonathan (1 Sam. 18:1,3; 20:17; 2 Sam. 1:26).

Friendship, however, was not limited to earthly associates. The Old Testament also affirms friendship between God and human persons. The relationship between God and Moses (Ex. 33:11) is likened to friendship because they conversed face to face. Both 2 Chronicles 20:7 and Isaiah 41:8 characterize Abraham as the friend of God. Friendship between God and His people is alluded to in Isaiah 5:1–7, the song of the vineyard. Proverbs features the most references to friendship, nearly all of them cautioning against dubious friendships or extolling the virtues of a true friend (14:20; 17:17–18; 18:24; 19:4,6; 22:11,24; 27:6,10,14).

In the New Testament, the predominant word for friend is *philos.* A derivative, *philia,* is often used for friendship. Jesus is described as the "friend of sinners" (Matt. 11:19). He called His disciples "friends" (Luke 12:4; John 15:13–15). The New Testament highlights the connection between friends and joy (Luke 15:6,9,29), as well as warning of the possibility of friends proving false (Luke 21:16). Echoing the Old Testament, James pointed to Abraham, the friend of God, as one whose example of active faith is to be followed (Jas. 2:23). James also warned against friendship with the world (Jas. 4:4).

Only in 3 John 14 is "friend" a self-designation for Christians. As a means of describing the relations between church members, friendship was overshadowed by the model of family relations, brotherhood and sisterhood (1 Tim. 5:1–3; 1 Pet. 1:22; 2:17).

See *Body of Christ; David; Love; Neighbor; Jonathan.*   *William J. Ireland, Jr.*

FRIEND OF THE KING The title of a court official (1 Kings 4:5). The King's Friend was counselor and companion to the monarch. He functioned somewhat as a Secretary of State. Hushai evidently held this office in David's court; Zabud held it in Solomon's.

FRINGE Tassels of twisted cords fastened to the four corners of the outer garment, worn by observant Jews as a reminder of covenant obligations (Num. 15:38,39; Deut. 22:12; compare Zech. 8:23). The woman suffering from chronic hemorrhage touched the tassel of Jesus' cloak (Matt.

9:20, Luke 8:44). The English translations (with the exception of the NRSV) obscure this point by using different terms to translate the Greek *kraspedon* when it refers to Jesus' outer cloak (hem, KJV; fringe, NAS; edge; NIV, TEV; simply garment, RSV) and to the outer garment of the Pharisees (borders, KJV; tassels, NAS, NIV, TEV; fringe, RSV). Such translation contributes to a picture of a Jesus who was not really a Jew. Though Jesus observed the Old Testament requirement, He criticized those who wore excessively long tassels to call attention to their piety (Matt. 23:5).

FROG See *Animals.*

FRONTLETS Objects containing Scripture passages worn on the forehand and between the eyes, primarily at prayer times. Jews followed scriptural commands, literally, writing Exodus 13:1–10,11–16; Deuteronomy 6:4–9; 11:13–21 on small scrolls, placing these in leather containers and placing these on their forehead and left arm. See Exodus 13:9,16; Deuteronomy 6:8; 11:18.

By New Testament times, the frontlets were known as *phylacteries* (Matt. 23:5). Jewish men wore phylacteries during prayer times, except on the sabbath and feast days.

Phylacteries were bound with thongs to the forehead, though some phylacteries were worn on the upper arm so that when a person crossed his arms the Scriptures contained in the phylactery would be close to the heart.

Jesus condemned individuals who called attention to themselves by wearing larger than usual phylacteries (Matt. 23:5).   *Gary Hardin*

FRUIT The edible pulp surrounding the seed(s) of many plants.

Literal uses Various types of fruit are mentioned frequently in Scripture. Among the most common are grapes, figs, olives, pomegranates, and apples (perhaps to be identified with apricots or quince). Israel, in contrast to her neighbors, recognized the process by which trees reproduce by means of seeds carried in fruit to be a part of God's good plan at creation (Gen. 1:12,29). The continuing fruitfulness of Israel's trees was dependent on faithfulness to the covenant (Deut. 28:4,11,18). The first fruit to ripen was offered to God (Ex. 23:16; Neh. 10:35).

Figurative uses The fruit of the womb is a common expression for descendants (Gen. 30:2; Deut. 7:13; Ps. 127:3; Isa. 13:18). Fruit often indicates a thought close to our word results. The fruit of the Spirit is the results of the Spirit's workings in the lives of believers (Gal. 5:22–23). Similar is the use of fruit where we would speak of manifestations or expressions. The fruits of righteousness (Phil. 1:11; Jas. 3:18), of repentance

A modern orthodox Jewish man praying at the Wailing Wall in Jerusalem wearing his frontlet.

(Matt. 3:8), of light (Eph. 5:9) are expressions of righteousness, repentance, and moral purity. Jesus cautioned that false prophets could be identified by the fruit they produced (Matt. 7:15–20), that is, by the qualities manifested in their lives. Jesus similarly warned of the necessity of bearing fruit that was compatible with citizenship in the kingdom of God (Matt. 21:43). Fruit sometimes has the sense of reward (Isa. 3:10; John 4:36; Phil. 4:17). Fruit is also used as a picture for Christian converts (Rom. 1:13; 1 Cor. 16:15).

FRYING PAN KJV term for the vessel used for cooking the cereal offering (Lev. 2:7; 7:9), simply pan in modern translations. A kettle for deep fat frying is perhaps intended.

FUEL Materials used to start and maintain a fire. Numerous types of fuel are mentioned in Scripture: wood (Isa. 44:14–16); charcoal (Jer. 36:22; John 18:18); shrubs (Ps. 120:4); thorn bushes (Eccl. 7:6; Nah. 1:10); grass (Matt. 6:30); weeds (Matt. 13:40); vines (Ezek. 15:4,6); branch trimmings (John 15:6); animal or even human dung (Ezek. 4:12); and the blood-stained clothing of fallen warriors (Isa. 9:5). Oil was used as a fuel for lamps (Matt. 25:3). Coal was not known to the Hebrews.

Fuel is frequently used figuratively as a symbol of total destruction. Disobedient Israel is portrayed as "fuel for the fire" (Isa. 9:19; Ezek. 15:6; 21:32). For Jesus, God's extravagant love evidenced in clothing grass destined to be burned as fuel with beautiful flowers illustrated even greater care for human beings (Matt. 6:30).

FULFILL The verb fulfill is used in three senses that merit special attention: an ethical sense of observing or meeting requirements; a prophetic sense of corresponding to what was promised, predicted, or foreshadowed; and a temporal sense related to the arrival of times ordained by God. The ethical sense of fulfill appears in the Old Testament only in connection with meeting the requirements of a vow (Lev. 22:21; Num. 15:3), never in connection with the law. In the New Testament Jesus submitted to John's baptism, identifying Himself with sinful people, in order "to fulfill all righteous" (Matt. 3:15), that is, to meet God's expectation for His life. Jesus described His mission not as coming "to abolish the law or the prophets" but "to fulfill" (Matt. 5:17). The New Testament repeatedly speaks of love as the fulfilling of the law (Rom. 13:8–10; Gal. 5:14; Jas. 2:8).

Fulfill is most common in Scripture in the prophetic sense of corresponding to what was promised, predicted, or foreshadowed. The fulfillment of prophecy in the life of Jesus is a major theme in Matthew's Gospel. Isaiah's prophecy (7:4) found fulfillment not only in Christ's virgin birth but also in His nature as "God with us" (Matt. 1:22–23; compare 28:20). Jesus' ministry in both word (Matt. 4:14–17) and deed (8:16–17) fulfilled Scripture (Isa. 9:1–2; 53:4). Jesus' command of secrecy (Matt. 12:16) and His habit of teaching in parables (13:35) likewise fulfilled Scripture (Isa. 42:1–3; Ps. 78:2), as did His humble entry into Jerusalem (Matt. 21:4–5; Zech. 9:9) and His arrest as a bandit (Matt. 26:56). At several points Jesus' life story gave new meaning to the history of Israel. Like Israel, Jesus was God's Son called out of Egypt (Matt. 2:15; Hos. 11:1). The suffering of Israel's mothers (Jer. 31:15) was echoed by the mothers of Bethlehem (Matt. 2:17–18). Both foreshadowed the fate of the Christ child who was spared only to die at a later time.

Luke and Acts are especially interested in Christ's suffering and later glorification as the fulfillment of the expectations of all the Old Testament, the law, prophets, and writings (Luke 24:25–26,44–47; Acts 3:18; 13:27–41) Jesus interpreted His journey to Jerusalem as a second "exodus" (Luke 9:31), an event that would result in freedom for God's people.

In John the failure of the people to recognize God at work in Jesus' signs or to accept Jesus' testimony was explained as fulfillment of Scripture (12:37–41; compare Mark 4:11–12). John also viewed details of the passion story as the fulfillment of Scripture (John 19:24,28; Pss.

22:18; 69:21). Typological fulfillment in which Jesus corresponded to Old Testament institutions is more common than correspondence to predictive prophecy. Jesus was "the lamb of God who takes away the sin of the world" (1:29), likely a reference to the Passover lamb (John 19:14). Like Bethel (Gen. 28:12) Jesus offered access between heaven and earth (1:51). At Cana Jesus' gift of wine corresponded to the blessings of God's future (John 2:1–11; Isa. 25:6; Joel 3:18; Amos 9:13; Zech. 9:17). Jesus' body which was to be destroyed and raised was identified with the Temple (John 2:19,21). In His being lifted up on the cross (John 3:14), Christ corresponded to the serpent Moses raised in the wilderness (Num. 21:9). In the same way, Christ in giving His life corresponded to the life-giving manna from heaven (John 6:31–32; Ex. 16:15). Often, time references in the Gospel of John suggest that Jesus gave new meaning to the celebrations of Israel (Passover, 2:13; 6:4; 11:55; Booths, 7:10; Dedication, 10:22).

Paul spoke of Christ as the One in whom "every one of God's promises is a 'yes' " (2 Cor. 1:20 NRSV). Like John, Paul made frequent use of typology. Christ was foreshadowed by Adam (Rom. 5:12–21; 1 Cor. 15:22,45–49), by the rock in the wilderness (1 Cor. 10:4), and by the Passover lamb (1 Cor. 5:7).

Temporal phrases such as "the time is fulfilled" point to times ordained by God, for example, the time of Christ's ministry (Mark 1:15; Gal. 4:4; Eph. 1:10), the time of Gentile domination of Israel (Luke 21:24), or the time of the appearance of the lawless one (2 Thess. 2:6).

Chris Church

FULLER One who thickens and shrinks newly-shorn wool or newly-woven cloth; also one who washes or bleaches clothing. The Hebrew term comes from the root "to tread" and refers to the common method of cleansing clothing by treading them by foot. Cleansing was also done by beating clothing with sticks. The ancient Hebrews were not acquainted with bar soap. Clothing was cleansed in a solution of alkali obtained by burning wood to ash. Putrid urine was sometimes used in the process. Due to the foul smell, fullers worked outside the city gates. All the biblical references are metaphorical (Ps. 51:7; Jer. 2:22; 4:14; Mal. 3:2) and refer to cleansing from sin.

FULLER'S FIELD A site outside Jerusalem's walls, located near the conduit between the Gihon Spring and the upper pool (2 Kings 18:17; Isa. 7:3; 36:2). The road to the Fuller's Field was the scene of an encounter between Rabshakeh, agent of the king of Assyria, who stopped within hearing distance of those on the city walls, and the leaders of Jerusalem. See *Rabshakeh.*

FULLNESS Completeness or totality. "The earth is the Lord's, and the fulness thereof" (Ps. 24:1). Scripture sees that nothing is really complete until it serves the purpose for which God has created it. Thus Ephesians 1:23 (NRSV) speaks of God as "him who fills all in all." He is the one who gives everything its ultimate significance and richness. This fullness is most clearly expressed in Jesus Christ (Col. 1:19; 2:9) from whom all true believers receive the divine life of fullness (John 1:16; 10:10). It is a life full of joy (John 15:11) and peace despite the fact of tribulations in this world (John 16:33).

See *Eternal Life* ; *Pleroma*.

Joe Baskin

FULLNESS OF TIME The traditional rendering of two similar Greek expressions in Galatians 4:4 and Ephesians 1:10. The first refers to a past event, the sending of Christ to redeem those born under the law. While the sending of God's Son encompasses the whole of Christ's incarnate ministry, the New Testament specifically relates the sending to Christ's death as a saving event (John 3:17; Rom. 8:3; 1 John 4:9–10). The sending of Christ in the fullness of time refers not so much to world conditions in the sense that the prevalence of Greek as a common spoken language, Roman roads, and the Roman enforced peace made the rapid spread of the gospel possible. Rather the emphasis is on God whose sending of Christ is not a "last ditch effort" but part of God's gracious plan from the beginning.

The reference to the fullness of time in Ephesians is more difficult. Some translations understand the time when all things are gathered together in Christ to lie in the future (NIV, TEV); others, in the past (REB). A major theme of Ephesians is that Christ has already broken down the dividing wall of hostility between Jew and Gentile (2:11–22, especially 2:14,21). Therefore, it seems likely that the crucial shift in time between the past with its hopelessness and hostility and the present age of reconciliation has already occurred.

Chris Church

FURNACE A device, generally of brick or stone, used to heat materials to high temperatures. In Biblical times furnaces were not used for central heating. Rather furnaces were used to smelt ore, melt metal for casting, heat metal for forging, fire pottery or bricks, and to make lime. The furnace of Daniel 3 was probably a large furnace used for smelting ore or for firing bricks. Biblical references to furnaces are mostly figurative for experiences of testing (of the Egyptian bondage, Deut. 4:20; 1 Kings 8:51; Jer. 11:4; of adversity, Isa. 48:10). God's stubbornly rebellious people are pictured as "rejected silver" (Jer. 6:30) and as dross, the waste product of the smelting process (Ezek. 22:17–22). Such pictures may form the background of the furnace of fire which symbolizes divine punishment (Matt. 13:42,50).

FURNACES, TOWER OF KJV and NAS designation (Neh. 3:11) for a tower designated "Tower of the Ovens" in other modern translations. The tower was adjacent to the "corner gate" located at the northwest angle in the second or middle wall of Jerusalem. The "Baker's Street" (Jer. 37:21) may have passed by this tower.

FURNITURE Equipment in a home used for rest, beautification, storage, and work space.

Sacred Furniture Biblical interest in furniture focuses on the sacred furnishings of the tabernacle and the Temple. We have in Exodus 25—27; 30; 37—38 a full description of the tabernacle with all its objects of furniture. Lovingly detailed accounts of the ark of the covenant, the altar of incense, and other furnishings are so clear that we can easily visualize and reconstruct them in the form of models. Likewise, 1 Kings 6–7 provides similar data about the Temple of Solomon. See *Tabernacle; Temple.*

Common Furniture But this is not the case regarding the furniture of the common people living out their daily lives in their tents and houses. The Bible occasionally refers to basic furniture items such as beds, chairs, etc. But we have virtually nothing about manufacturers, building materials, designs, or appearances.

Biblical terminology illustrates the problem. Old Testament Hebrew has no word equivalent to the English terms "furniture" or "furnishings." The Hebrew word *keli* is so translated in passages such as Exodus 31:7, but in this very same context the very same word (*keli*) is also rendered as "utensils," "articles," or "accessories." In fact, the word *keli* is so fluid that it may refer to any humanly manufactured material object.

Similarly, the New Testament carries us no further, for it uses no word which could be translated as "furniture" in the English versions.

Sources of Data The Bible remains a source of data, however, at least to the degree that it refers to such items as beds and chairs. Beyond the Bible itself we must resort to artifacts recovered by archaeology. Palestine, however, does not enjoy the climate which would have saved wooden furnishings for study today. Only a few such objects have survived, and even these have greatly disintegrated over time. This being the case, we must resort to secondary artifacts such as written records, seals, sculpture, ivories, and tombs.

Individual Objects of Furniture Domestically, Israelite furniture reflected the simplicity of the ordinary household dwelling. Some Israelites preferred to live in tents (Jer. 35), preserving the traditions of nomadic and wilderness days. The furnishings of such a living place would have to be readily portable and as light as possible. Chests of some sort would be used when the family or clan was settled then double as carriage crates when on the move. A few simple rugs covered the ground floor. The tent itself and all its paraphernalia—pegs, ropes, interior curtains for separating the "rooms" inside—along with a few sleeping mats, might be all the "furniture" such a family owned. The same would apply to those living in small shelters.

A more permanent home would be furnished according to the family's relative wealth or poverty. Like the tent-dwellers mentioned above, a poorer family would own, at the minimum, simple bedding and kitchen equipment. Reed mats would be rolled out on the floor for resting and sleeping. In some cases these mats would have to serve as tables and chairs, as well, since real ones were probably beyond the means of poorer families. All homes needed interior lighting, of course, so even the poor would own, in all probability, several lamps, i.e., saucer-shaped bowls with a pinch in the rim for a wick fueled by a pool of olive oil; such a lamp often sat on a supporting stand. Wide-mouth jars for food and water were essential, as were also some sort of stone and clay oven, and a grinding mill for preparing grain. A few of these houses might also have stone or wooden benches, some covered with cloth or carpet material around the inner walls; but this was likely the exception among the poor rather than the rule. Since most homes of biblical days had few windows, they would also have had few—if any—curtains.

Even the homes of the comfortable and the wealthy would also seem all but bare in contrast to the homes of any socioeconomic class in a developed nation of the West today. Consider the home of the "wealthy woman" of Shunem (in lower northern Palestine about five miles east of Megiddo), found in 2 Kings 4:8–37. Because of her special concern for the prophet Elisha, she and her husband built "a small room on the roof" (4:10 NIV) of their house for him to use when he was passing through their vicinity. They furnished it with "a bed and a table, a chair and a lamp" (4:10 NIV), for which he was sincerely grateful.

Only a century later Amos (760-750 B.C.) condemned the decadent prosperity of the wealthy class in his day. He spoke of the mansions of Samaria (Amos 3:15; 5:11; 6:11) and their opulent beds and couches encrusted with ivory (3:12, 15; 6:4). By then the gap between the relatively poor and the relatively rich had grown to scandalous proportions, as evidenced by the quality of their furniture (compare Esther 1:6). It seems most likely that apart from the highly ornamented furniture mentioned in Amos, the household furniture of the vast majority of Israelites was merely functional, rather than aesthetic.

Furniture and Artifacts Archaeology has shed some (but not much) light on ancient Palestinian furniture. The excavation of ancient Jericho in the 1950s discovered a series of tombs containing both the skeletal remains of the dead and practical provisions to serve their needs in the afterlife. The pertinent finds date to about 1600 B.C. Furniture styles were slow to change, and the artifacts found at Jericho were probably like those used by the Israelites long after.

One body had been laid on a wooden bed consisting of a rectangular frame enclosing wooden crosspieces tenoned to the rails. The crosspieces and rails enclosed five panels of woven rush. The bed probably supported a mattress about six inches above the floor.

Beside the bed was a table measuring about fifty-eight inches by sixteen inches, supported by only three legs about ten inches above the floor. Each leg tenoned into a rounded corner extension below the underside of the table. Survivors left a wooden platter of mutton on the table.

Two cylinder seals from Tell es-Sa'idiyeh on the Jordan River and dated to about 750 B.C. show simple chairs in their impressions. One has a tall straight back and, apparently, a seat of woven rush. Further details are unclear. The other chair has a curved, ladder-back design with four cross-slats.   *Tony M. Martin*

FURROW A narrow trench cut in the earth by a plow (1 Sam. 14:14; Job. 31:38; 39:10; Ps. 65:10; 129:3; Hos. 10:4; 12:11). The KJV rendered two Hebrew terms as furrow which are best translated otherwise. At Ezekiel 17:7,10 modern translations opt for bed (NAS, RSV), plot (NIV), or garden (TEV). At Hosea 10:10 modern translations understand a reference to two sins (iniquity, NRSV; guilt, NAS; sin, NIV, TEV; shameful deed, REB).

FUTURE HOPE The expectation of individuals after their death and of the world when God brings present world affairs to an end.

Future hope focuses upon the expectancy of the consummation of the individual's salvation at the close of the age. With the ushering in of the eternal order at the return of Christ, the believer's hope becomes experienced reality rather than anticipation of future experience (Rom. 8:24–25). This eschatological orientation of New Testament future hope grows out of the Old Testament prophetic anticipation of God's future deliverance (Ps. 40; 42:11; 62:5–6; Isa. 25:9; 40:31; 42:4; 51:5; Jer. 29:4–15; 31:17, 31–34; Ezek. 36—37; Mic. 7:7). See especially Paul's use of Isaiah 11:10 in Romans 15:12.

Old Testament Terms for Future Hope In the Hebrew Old Testament several terms are used to convey the idea of hope: *qawah* (to be stretched out towards, to long after, wait for [with God as object 26 times]), *yahal* (to wait, long [for God, 27 times]), *hakah* (to wait [for God, 7 times]) *sabar* (to wait, hope [for God, 4 times]). The corresponding nouns are not commonly used; only nine times in reference to hope in God. Of the 146 uses of these verbs or nouns, only half have the thrust to spiritual reality rather than a nonreligious meaning. In these 73 religious uses the concept of hope is closely related to trust. God is the ground and frequent object of hope; "to hope in Yahweh," "to wait for Yahweh" are common expressions. Implicit to hoping in God is submission to His sovereign rule. Consequently, hope and fear of God are often expressed together (Pss. 33:18–20; 147:11; Prov. 23:17–18). To hope in God is to stand in awe of Him and His power with the confidence that God will faithfully perform His word. Thus hope becomes trust in the righteous character of Yahweh.

Between the Testaments In the interbiblical period the eschatological thrust of hope became prominent but also confusing with its differing expectations. This future hope was often directed toward the expectation of the Messiah and the restoration of the kingdom of Israel. With the emergence of numerous individuals making messianic claims, arousing the expectations of the people, but then collapsing into defeat and destruction, the future hope of Israel took on a pessimistic tone especially in rabbinical thought. Not before Israel achieved complete obedience to the law could God's kingdom be established.

This national uncertainty tended to create a personal uncertainty about what constitutes the required obedience for pleasing God, thus insuring the resurrection of the body and inclusion in that coming messianic kingdom. In contrast to this pessimistic view, one finds in Qumran a confident eschatological hope. However, this hope was only possible for the select few who were the elect of God. In Hellenistic Judaism, future hope was submerged into the Greek concept of the immortality of the soul, as Philo's writings illustrate.

Hope in the New Testament The writers in the New Testament express the concept of future hope primarily by the Greek word *elpis* and its cognates.

The use of hope in reference to the return of Christ is seen in Matthew 24:50 (also Luke 12:46) and in 2 Peter 3:12–14. In Jesus' teaching on watchfulness, failure to be expecting the return of the Son of man can cause disaster. In 2 Peter this expectation of the day of the Lord stands as the incentive to holy living. In both passages the element of uncertainty often associated with the Greek word has disappeared and is replaced with the sense of confidence based upon the promise of the Lord to come again.

Content of Future Hope The objects of the various Greek words relating to future hope provide insight into what constitutes this hope. Most basic is the expectancy of the return of Christ, described as the revelation of our Lord Jesus Christ (1 Cor. 1:7) and as the coming of the day of God (*parousian;* 2 Pet. 3:12), or just simply as hope in our Lord Jesus Christ (1 Thess. 1:3; compare Luke 12:36; Phil. 3:20; Heb. 9:28). This expectancy constitutes a blessed hope and is defined as the manifestation of the glory of our great God and our Savior Jesus Christ (Tit. 2:13; compare Rom. 5:2; Col. 1:27). Accompanying this manifestation of Christ is the expectancy of a new heaven and a new earth (2 Pet. 3:13; Rev. 21:1); the resurrection of the righteous and the wicked (Acts 24:15); the revelation of the sons of God (Rom. 8:19); our adoption as sons which is defined as the redemption of our bodies (Rom. 8:23); the mercy of our Lord Jesus Christ for life eternal (Jude 21); God's grace (1 Pet. 1:13). As Abraham awaited the Holy City, so the believer looks forward to it (Heb. 11:10). The hope of Israel in the promise of God is realized in the Christian hope of resurrection (Acts 26:6–8). These constitute the hope of life eternal long promised beforehand (Titus 1:2; 3:7), of salvation (1 Thess. 5:8) and of righteousness (Gal. 5:5).

The basis of this hope lies in God. In Him who is the Savior of all mankind one puts hope (1 Tim. 4:10; 5:5; Rom. 15:12; 1 Pet. 1:21), rather than in uncertain riches (1 Tim. 6:17); in His name is hope placed (Matt. 12:21), or in Christ (1 Cor. 15:19). This hope is linked closely to the gospel (Col. 1:23), to our calling into God's grace (Eph. 1:18; 4:4) and to faith and the presence of the Holy Spirit (Gal. 5:5). It is a dynamically living hope (1 Pet. 1:3) which motivates one to holy and righteous living (2 Pet. 3:14). As such it stands as member of the Christian triad of faith, hope, and love (1 Cor. 13:13; 1 Thess. 1:3; Col. 1:4–5).

See *Hope; Day of the Lord; Return of Christ; Eternal Life; Salvation; Eschatology; Resurrection; Faith.* *Lorin L. Cranford*

G

The green farmland and citrus groves of central Israel.

GAAL (Gā' ál) Personal name meaning, "abhorrence," "neglect," or perhaps "dung-beetle." Man who usurped Abimelech's leadership in Shechem but met sudden defeat from Abimelech and left the city (Judg. 9:26–41). The early translations spell his name and that of his father in several different ways, showing perhaps that Israelites intentionally distorted his name to shame his reputation.

GAASH (Gā' ăsh) Personal name meaning, "rising and falling noisily." A height in the hill country of Ephraim which cannot be located any more precisely. Joshua was buried there (Josh. 24:30). Hiddai, one of David's thirty military heroes, came from the brooks of Gaash (2 Sam. 23:30).

GABA (Gā' bà) KJV spelling of Geba. See *Geba.*

GABBAI (Găb' bā ī) Personal name traditionally interpreted as meaning, "tax collector." Member of tribe of Benjamin who settled in Jerusalem in time of Nehemiah (Neh. 11:8). Many modern commentators think copying errors have introduced the name into the text from an original Hebrew text meaning, "heroic men," though no existing Hebrew text has this reading.

GABBATHA (Găb' bà thà) English transliteration of Greek transliteration of Aramaic place

Entrance to the Church of St. Gabriel in Nazareth.

name meaning, "elevation." A platform in front of the praetorium or governor's palace in Jerusalem, where Pilate sat in judgment over Jesus (John 19:13), pronouncing the sentence to crucify Jesus. Before announcing the decision, however, Pilate introduced Jesus as King of the Jews, giving the Jewish leaders one last chance to confess their Messiah. The Greek name for the place was *lithostrotos,* or "stone pavement." The location is either the fortress Antonia or Herod's palace. Tourists see the Antonia site at the present Convent of the Sisters of Zion, but archaeologists have dated the pavement there later than Jesus' time.

GABRIEL (Gā' brǐ ēl) Personal name meaning, "strong man of God." The heavenly messenger who interpreted to Daniel the meaning of the vision of the ram and the goat. He appears four times in the Bible, each time bringing to human beings a message from the Lord. Twice he appeared to Daniel (8:15–27; 9:20–27). In the New Testament he appeared to announce the births of John the Baptist (Luke 1:8–20) and Jesus (Luke 1:26–38). See *Angels.*

GAD (Găd) Personal name meaning, "good fortune." *1.* The seventh son of Jacob and the progenitor of the tribe of Gad (Gen. 30:9–11). His mother was Leah's maid Zilpah. At the conclusion of the period of wilderness wandering, when the Israelites were preparing to occupy Canaan, the tribe of Gad requested permission, along with the tribe of Reuben and half the tribe of Manasseh, to settle east of the Jordan. Their reason was that they owned large numbers of livestock and the territory east of the Jordan was particularly suitable for raising livestock (Num. 32). This territory became known as Gad (Jer. 49:1). Though the exact limits of Gad's tribal territory are difficult to determine, the Gadites generally occupied land to the northeast of the Dead Sea (Josh. 13:24–28). See *Tribes of Israel. 2.* Syrian god known from inscriptions from Phoenicia and Palmyra and used in biblical names such as Baal-gad (Josh. 11:17) and Migdal-gad (Josh. 15:37). It also apparently is meant in Isaiah 65:11 where the prophet condemned the people for setting "a table for Fortune" (NAS; Hebrew, *Gad*). 3. Prophet who advised David as he fled from Saul (1 Sam. 22:5) and who brought God's options for punishment after David took a census of Israel (2 Sam. 24:11–14). Gad also brought David God's orders to build an altar, apparently on the site of the future Temple (2 Sam. 24:18–19). The Chronicler pointed his readers to records of David's reign by Gad (1 Chron. 29:29) and of Gad's assistance in showing David God's plan for Temple worship (2 Chron. 29:25).

GADARA (Găd' à rà) Place name for home of Gadarenes used in TEV (Matt. 8:28). See *Gadarenes.*

G

GADARENE (Găd′ å rēne) A resident of Gadara, one of the cities of Decapolis (Mark 5:1). In the New Testament, it is mentioned only in the Gospel accounts of the healing of the Gadarene man who was afflicted by demons (Matt. 8:28–34; Mark 5:1–17; Luke 8:26–37). The textual tradition in the Greek manuscripts of each of these passages shows confusion among Gadarenes, Gerasenes, and Gergesenes. Textual evidence appears to favor Gadarenes in Matthew, Gerasenes in Mark and Luke. Origen, an early church father, apparently introduced Gergesenes into the tradition. Gadarene, in the context, would have to refer to the larger area, not just the city of Gadara. Gergasenes points to the modern city of Kersa on the lake's edge. Gerasene comes from the city of Gerasa about 30 miles southeast of the lake. Early tradition may have confused the Hebrew or Aramaic spelling of Gedara and Gerasa or may have seen Gerasa as the dominant town in the area. Whatever the original name, Gentiles and their pigs dominated the area. It has been identified with modern Um Keis, approximately five miles southeast of the Sea of Galilee. The designation "country of the Gadarenes" evidently applied to an area that extended as far as the shore of Galilee.

GADDI (Găd′ dī) Personal name meaning, "my good fortune." Spy from the tribe of Manasseh sent by Moses to examine the land of Canaan prior to Israel's conquest (Num. 13:11).

GADDIEL (Găd′ dī ēl) Personal name meaning, "God is my good fortune." Spy from tribe of Zebulun Moses sent to examine Canaan, the land to be conquered (Num. 13:10).

GADFLY A stinging insect (stinging fly, TEV), either a horsefly (*Tabanidae, NAS*) or a botfly (Oestridae). See *Insects.*

GADI (Gă′ dī) Personal name meaning, "my good fortune." A variant Hebrew spelling of Gaddi using same word as Gadite. Father of Menahem, king of Israel (752-742 B.C.) (2 Kings 15:14, 17).

GADITE (Găd′ īte) Member of tribe of Gad. See *Gad.*

GAHAM (Gă′ hăm) Personal name meaning, "flame." Son of Nahor, Abraham's brother, by his concubine Reumah (Gen. 22:24).

GAHAR (Gă′ här) Personal name meaning, "drought" or "small in spirit" or "red-faced." Clan head of family of Temple servants who returned from Babylonian captivity with Zerubbabel about 537 B.C. (Ezra 2:47).

GAIUS (Gă′ iŭs) Greek form of Latin name Caius meaning, "I am glad, rejoice." *1.* A Macedonian Christian who was one of Paul's traveling companions (Acts 19:29). Along with Aristarchus, he was seized during the riot in Ephesus incited by Demetrius the silversmith. *2.* A Christian from Derbe who accompanied Paul the apostle into Asia (Acts 20:4). *3.* Paul the apostle's host in Corinth (Rom. 16:23). According to 1 Corinthians 1:14, he was one of the individuals in Corinth whom Paul personally had baptized. *4.* The Christian John loved and to whom he addressed 3 John (3 John 1).

GALAL (Gā′ lăl) Personal name meaning, "roll" or "turtle." *1.* A Levite in among those who settled in Jerusalem after the Exile (1 Chron. 9:15). *2.* Grandfather of Adda, a Levite who led in Nehemiah's thanksgiving (Neh. 11:17). He came up and settled in Jerusalem after the Exile (1 Chron. 9:16).

GALATIA (Gå lā′ tiå) Geographical name derived from Gaul because its inhabitants were Celts or Galli (Gauls). The original settlement was in central Asia Minor. See *Asia Minor.* King Nicomedes of Bithynia invited the Celtic warriors across the Bosporus River to help him fight his brother in 278 B.C. The invaders fought on their own capturing cities until stopped by Antiochus I in 275 B.C. They then occupied the northern part of Asia Minor, bounded on the north by Pontus and Bithynia, on the east by Tavium and Pessinus in the west. For the most part, true Galatians lived in open areas, leaving city occupation to their predecessors, the Phrygians. The true Galatians constantly switched sides in ongoing battles in the area. Finally, in 25 B.C. Rome made Galatia a province of the empire and extended its borders, adding Lycaonia, Isauria, and Pisidia with Ancyra serving as the governmental center. Various Roman rulers added and subtracted territory from the province, so its precise boundaries are difficult to draw. Paul visited Galatia (Acts 16:6; 18:23), though his precise route is not clear. Did he visit Phrygian-dominated cities or the true Galatians in the countryside? Was his letter addressed to the original territory in the north or to the Roman province with its southern additions? See *Galatians.* Compare 1 Corinthians 16:1; 2 Timothy 4:10, where some manuscripts have Gaul, and 1 Peter 1:1.

GALATIAN (Gå lā′ tian) Specifically, a member of the Celtic or Galli tribes which invaded and settled Galatia, but more generally any resident of the territory or province of Galatia. See *Galatia.*

GALATIANS, LETTER TO THE (Gå lā′ tians) Paul's letter to the church at Galatia defending his interpretation of the gospel of Christ. Paul's heated defense of justification by faith and freedom in the Spirit has endeared this epistle to all

G

who hold such to be the living core of the Christian faith. From the time of Jesus the sufficiency of faith alone for salvation has been a major issue among Christians. The issue initially came to the forefront in Paul's day when Gentiles believed in Jesus Christ. Must the Gentiles become a part of the Jewish faith to be fully Christian? Certain Jewish Christians, called Judaizers, said that the Gentiles must also obey the law of Moses and be circumcized to be saved. Paul declared that the Gentiles' faith in Jesus, apart from the Jewish faith, was sufficient for salvation.

The churches of Galatia, to whom Paul wrote, were churches he himself founded (Gal. 1:8,9; 4:19). He preached the gospel to them the first time because of a physical problem (4:13). The nature of this ailment is not certain, but it did not hinder the Galatians from hearing Paul's preaching (4:14). In 4:13, the term "at first" normally meant "the former of two times," meaning Paul visited Galatia twice before he wrote the epistle, a factor important for determining the dating of the epistle and its destination. The readers were Gentiles converted from paganism (4:8; 5:2; 6:12), although there may have been Jewish Christians and proselytes in the church as well.

Paul did not specifically locate these churches, (4:2), with a resulting confusion. The place name "Galatia" belonged to a large province of the Roman Empire. The name was used earlier to designate the northern territory of the province inhabited by a particular people know as "Galatians." In Acts 13:14—14:24 (first missionary journey) Paul founded churches at Antioch of Pisidia, Iconium, Lystra, and Derbe, cities in the southern part of the Roman province. Paul visited Lystra and Derbe again in Acts 16:1–6 (second missionary journey). In 16:6 Paul then went through the "region of Phrygia and Galatia," as he did also in 18:23 (third missionary journey). Does "Galatia" in Acts 16:6 and 18:23 refer to the southern portion of the Roman province, or does it indicate that Paul went north and founded churches in the territory of Galatia? Paul probably addressed his epistle to the churches in the southern part of the Roman province, for two reasons: *1)* When describing churches founded by him, Paul normally used the titles of the Roman provinces in which the churches were located as in 2 Corinthians 9:2; *2)* Acts specifically mentioned that Paul founded churches in the southern region, but was silent concerning churches in the north.

Determining the date Paul wrote the epistle involves reconciling Gal. 1:11— 2:14 with Acts. Paul mentioned two visits to Jerusalem (Gal. 1:18; 2:1), but Acts recorded five visits (Acts 9:26; 11:27 and 12:25; 15:4; 18:21; 21:17). Probably Galatians 1:18 and Acts 9:26 record Paul's first visit to Jerusalem after his conversion. Paul did not mention the Acts 11:30; 12:25 visit because he was concerned to relate only his contact with the twelve apostles. This second visit was with the elders, not the twelve. Acts 15:1–29 and Galatians 2:1–10 are both probably accounts of the Jerusalem Council. Though there are differences in the accounts (Paul made no reference in the epistle to the decree of Acts 15:23–29), the principal characters (Paul, Barnabas, Peter, James), and the main issue (whether faith in Jesus is sufficient for salvation or circumcision and obedience to the law of Moses were also necessary) in each account are the same. The council is usually dated A.D. 49 or 50. After the Council, Paul made his second visit to Galatia (Acts 16:1–6), matching the two visits he indicated in the epistle (Gal. 4:13). Then he moved on to Corinth (A.D. 51–52). It was perhaps from Corinth that he wrote the epistle.

Sometime after Paul's last visit (Acts 16:1–6), heretical teachers, who "distort the gospel" (Gal. 1:17 NAS) and trouble the churches (1:7; 5:10, 12), came among the Galatians. They were on the verge of leading the Galatians away from the truth of the gospel. These Judaizers were Jews who unquestionably claimed to be Christians and to faithfully preach the gospel. They taught that circumcision was necessary for salvation (5:2; 6:12–16), as was obedience to the law of Moses, even the observation of days, months, seasons, and years (4:10). They were acting out of false and selfish motives, those of personal ambition (4:17; 6:13) and offense at the cross of Christ (6:12). To lead the Galatians away from Paul's gospel, they sought to discredit him personally.

Paul gave such a fiery response to this disturbance because of the very real threat of a large-scale abandonment by the Galatians of the gospel. In 1:1–5 Paul gave greetings to the churches, but he omitted the statement of praise or thanksgiving which normally followed. Paul was too disturbed to give thanks or praise. Instead, in 1:6–9 Paul expressed distress at their fickle faith. The Galatians had received the one and true gospel but were turning away from it. Paul pronounced a curse on those who preached something different from the gospel he had preached to them.

The major portion of the epistle (1:10—6:10) can be divided into three parts. *1)* 1:10—2:21 In this section Paul defended his qualifications as an apostle against the attacks of the Judaizers. He was called to be an apostle by God, and the gospel of grace he preached came from God, independent of the Jerusalem apostles (they even approved of it). Paul closed this section with the main theme of the epistle, a choice between faith in Christ and obedience to the law. Justification (a sinful person coming into a right relationship with God) came not by living bound to the law but by faith in Christ. Faith alone was sufficient for salvation. To be in Christ meant being free from the legal requirements of the law.

2) 3:1—5:12 This section is the major argument of the epistle, where the differences between Paul's gospel and the Judaizer's heresy came to full light. Paul supported his thesis of faith alone on three principles: the gift of the Spirit, the promise and faith of Abraham, and the curse of the law. The gift of the Spirit came to them through faith, not the law. Abraham received the promise and righteousness by faith 430 years before the law was given. People of faith were true children of Abraham and heirs of the promise. Because people did not keep the law when it came, they fell under its curse. The law could only condemn sinners. Christ removed the curse of the law. The law was given as an interim provision until Christ came. Now He has come, and the believer is free. To turn back to the law was to return to slavery. With the coming of Christ, faith and law had become mutually exclusive as ways to approach God.

3) 5:13—6:10 In this final section, Paul guarded against abuse of this freedom from the law. Christian freedom required the believer to walk by the Spirit, which was contrary to the desires and works of the flesh. Christian freedom must be tempered by Christian love.

Paul closed (6:11—18) again urging them not to yield to circumcision and all it represented.

Outline

I. The Players (1:1–5)
   A. Paul's credentials came not from humans but from the risen Christ (1:1).
   B. The churches of Galatia receive grace and peace (1:2).
   C. Christ gave Himself for our sins (1:3–5).

II. The Problem: The Nature of the Gospel (1:6–10)
   A. People who follow a different gospel desert God (1:6).
   B. People who advocate another gospel confuse the church (1:7).
   C. People who preach another gospel are condemned eternally (1:8–9).
   D. The minister of the true gospel pleases God, not people (1:10).

III. The Answer, Part I: Believers Are Justified Simply by Faith in Christ (1:11—5:12).
   A. Personal example proves faith is the only requirement to be right with God (1:11—2:21).
      1. The gospel comes from Christ, not people (1:11–24).
      2. The gospel of grace has apostolic endorsement (2:1–10).
      3. Whoever adds to the gospel of grace is a hypocrite (2:11–14).
      4. Faith in Christ saves, but legalism cannot save (2:15–21).
   B. To return to legalism is to accept slavery instead of sonship (3:1—5:12).
      1. Faith in the crucified Christ, not legalism, brings the indwelling Spirit

(3:1–5).
      2. Abraham's inheritance comes through faith to both Jews and non-Jews (3:6–9).
      3. Christ has provided redemption for all who believe (3:10–14).
      4. Christ is the true heir of Abraham (3:15–16).
      5. The law cannot annul the justification by faith promised to Abraham (3:17–22).
      6. The law was used as a tutor to bring believers to Christ (3:23–25).
      7. Faith in and baptism into Christ make us one in Christ (3:26–29).
      8. The law acted as guardian until believers became full sons of God through Christ's redemption (4:1–7).
      9. Return to legalism from faith is a son's return to slavery (4:8–11).
      10. Zeal must be directed to the source of your joy—Christ (4:12–19).
      11. Interpretation of Scripture shows legalism leads to slavery, while Christ leads to the promised freedom of sons (4:20—5:1).
      12. Return to legalism is to fall away from the grace of Christ, which expresses itself in love (5:2–12).

IV. The Answer, Part 2: Believers Are Justified Simply by Faith in Christ to Serve Freely in the Spirit through Love (5:13—6:10).
   A. Scripture shows love fulfills the whole law (5:13–15).
   B. Life in the Spirit overcomes the weakness of the law (5:16–24).
   C. Believers should live and walk by the Spirit (5:25—6:10).

V. Conclusion: Boast Only that You Are New Creations in Christ (6:11–18).
   A. Summary (6:11–17)
      1. Legalism is not true to its own claims (6:11–13).
      2. Christ recreates us to meet God's claims (6:14–17).
   B. Farewell: May Christ's grace be with the Christian family (6:18).   *Bruce Warren*

GALBANUM See *Plants in the Bible.*

GALEED (Găl′ ė ĕd) Place name meaning, "pile for witness." Place where Jacob and his father-in-law Laban made a formal agreement or covenant determining the boundary line between their peoples and agreeing not to harm one another (Gen. 31:43–52). The place was also called Sahadutah and Mizpah. The heap of stones marking Galeed was in Gilead, north of the Jabbok River. See *Mizpah.*

G

GALILEAN (Găl ĭ lē' ăn) Person who lived in Galilee. Their speech distinguished them from Jews in Jerusalem and Judah, particularly their difficulty in distinguishing the sounds of the gutturals which are important in Hebrew and Aramaic. Peter's Galilean speech set him apart from the courtyard crowd during Jesus' trial (Mark 14:70; compare Acts 2:7). Jesus was identified as being from Galilee (Matt. 26:69). Pilate used this as an excuse to get Herod to hear Jesus' case (Luke 23:6–7). Galileans had a reputation for rebellion and disregard of Jewish law (Acts 5:37), so they could be regarded as sinners (Luke 13:2). Apparently, Pilate had killed some Galileans while they offered the Passover sacrifices in Jerusalem (Luke 13:1). On His return to Galilee from Judea and Samaria, Jesus received a warm welcome from the Galileans. This surprising statement is modified by the following story showing the welcome apparently depended on an expectation of miracles not on appreciation for who Jesus was or from faith in Him (John 4:43–54).

GALILEE (Găl' ĭ lēē) Place name meaning, "circle" or "region." The northern part of Palestine above the hill country of Ephraim and the hill country of Judah (Josh. 20:7). The Septuagint or early Greek translation referred to a king of the nations of Galilee in Joshua 12:23, though the Hebrew reads, "Gilgal." Many scholars see the Greek as original (NRSV, REB). This would indicate a leader of a coalition of city-states whom Joshua defeated. Kedesh in Galilee was a city of refuge (Josh. 20:7) and a city for the Levites (Josh. 21:32). Solomon paid Hiram of Tyre twenty cities of Galilee for the building materials Hiram supplied for the Temple and royal palace (1 Kings 9:11), but the cities did not please Hiram, who called them Cabul, meaning, "like nothing" (1 Kings 9:12–13). Apparently, Galilee and Tyre bordered on each other. The cities may have been border villages whose ownership the two kings disputed. The Assyrians took the north under Tiglath-pileser in 733 (2 Kings 15:29) and divided it into three districts—the western coast or "the

Looking eastward over the Sea of Galilee.

way of the sea" with capital at Dor, Galilee with capital at Megiddo, and beyond Jordan or Gilead (Isa. 9:1).

The term "Galilee" apparently was used prior to Israel's conquest, being mentioned in Egyptian records. It was used in Israel but not as a political designation. The tribes of Naphtali, Asher, Issachar, Zebulun, and Dan occupied the territory which covered approximately the forty-five-mile stretch between the Litani River in Lebanon and the Valley of Jezreel in Israel north to south and from the Mediterranean Sea to the Jordan River west to east.

In the time of Jesus' Galilee, Herod Antipas governed Galilee and Perea. Jesus devoted most of His earthly ministry to Galilee, being known as the Galilean (Matt. 26:69). After the fall of Jerusalem in A.D. 70, Galilee became the major center of Judaism, the Mishnah and Talmud being collected and written there.

GALILEE, SEA OF (Găl' ĭ lēē) Place name meaning, "circle." A freshwater lake nestled in the hills of northern Palestine. Its surface is nearly 700 feet below the level of the Mediterranean, some thirty miles to the west. The nearby hills of Galilee reach an altitude of 1,500 feet above sea level. To the east are the mountains of Gilead with peaks of more than 3,300 feet. To the north are the snow-covered Lebanon mountains. Fed chiefly by the

Sea of Galilee with the boat landing at Capernaum in view.

Jordan River, which originates in the foothills of the Lebanon Mountains, the sea of Galilee is thirteen miles long north and south and eight miles wide at its greatest east-west distance. Because of its location, it is subject to sudden and violent storms which are usually of short duration.

In the Old Testament this sea is called Chinnereth. See *Chinnereth*. It is named only rarely, however, and all references to it relate to the Hebrew conquest of Palestine under Joshua. In New Testament times it was also called the "lake of Gennesaret." Luke referred to it by that name once (5:1); the Jewish historian Josephus always called it by that name, and so did the author of

The Sea of Galilee as viewed from the northwest.

First Maccabees. Once John called it the "sea of Tiberias" (6:1).

In the first century the sea of Galilee was of major commercial significance. Most Galilean roads passed by it, and much travel to and from the east crossed the Jordan rift there. Fish was a major food in the area, and the fishing industry flourished because there was no other significant freshwater lake in the region. Capernaum, which played a major role in the ministry of Jesus, was a center of that industry. The other lake towns of importance were Bethsaida, which means "the fishing place", and Tiberias, a Gentile city constructed by Herod Antipas when Jesus was a young man.   *Roger Crook*

GALL (herb) A bitter, poisonous herb (perhaps *Citrullus colocynthis*), the juice of which is thought to be the "hemlock" poison Socrates drank. Gall was frequently linked with wormwood (Deut. 29:18; Jer. 9:15; 23:15; Lam. 3:19; Amos 6:12) to denote bitterness and tragedy. Wormwood and gall were often associated with unfaithfulness to God, either as a picture of the unfaithful (Deut. 29:18) or as their punishment. Modern speech translations generally translate the Hebrew word for gall in light of the context of the passage (poisonous growth, Deut. 29:18 NRSV; poisonous water, Jer. 8:14; 9:5; 23:15 NRSV; poison, Amos 6:12 NRSV). Gall is still used at Lamentations 3:19. On the cross, Jesus was offered sour wine drugged with gall, perhaps opium, which He refused (Matt. 27:34; compare Ps. 69:21). Simon the magician was described as full of the gall of bitterness (Acts 8:23) because he wanted to prostitute the gift of the Holy Spirit.

GALL (of livers) Gall expressed by two different Hebrew words is used in three senses in connection with the liver: *1.* as an organ, either the liver or the gallbladder, through which a sword might pass when one was run through (Job 20:25); *2.* as bile, a sticky, yellow-greenish, alkaline fluid secreted by the liver, which might be poured out on the ground when one was disemboweled (Job 16:13); *3.* in a figurative sense (Job 13:26) for bitterness (bitter things, NAS, NIV, NRSV; bitter charges, REB, TEV).

GALLERY An architectural feature of the Temple annex (Ezek. 41:15–16) and two buildings near the Temple (42:3,5). The English "gallery" is an ambiguous term referring to a number of features: a corridor (REB); a roofed walkway or colonade; an outdoor balcony or terrace. The meaning of the underlying Hebrew word is contested. Some suggest the meaning was passage way on the basis of similarities with Akkadian. Others suggest the term means slope or embankment. In this case the Temple measurements in 41:15–16 would refer to the base of the elevated inner court. English translators understand either a reference to interior corridors of the Temple annex or columned porches (contrast 42:6). The two buildings in chapter 42 were apparently constructed "stairstep" style with each floor smaller than the one beneath it. Here the gallery is perhaps the terrace formed by the flat roof of the floor below. Others have suggested the Hebrew refers to underlying rock formations that protruded into the structure.

GALLEY A long, narrow ship propelled mainly by oars. The galleys were used as warships (Isa. 33:21). Such vessels were designed to sail near the shore or on rivers. The image in Isaiah is of a Jerusalem free from the threat of invasion.

GALLIM (Găl′ lĭm) Place name meaning, "piles." Village near Anathoth in tribal territory of Benjamin. Saul gave his daughter Michal as wife to a citizen of Gallim after taking her away from David (1 Sam. 25:44; compare 2 Sam. 3:14–15). See *Michal.* Gallim lay on the road conquerors took from Bethel down to Jerusalem (Isa. 10:30). It may be modern khirbet Kakul, northwest of Anathoth or even further to the northwest just south of Ramah at khirbet Ercha.

GALLIO (Găl′ lĭ ō) Personal name of unknown meaning. The deputy or proconsul of Achaia headquartered in Corinth, where his judgment seat has been discovered. Certain Jews brought Paul before Gallio seeking to get Roman punishment of him. They charged that Paul advocated an unlawful religion (Acts 18:12–17). Gallio refused to involve himself in Jewish religious affairs, even ignoring the crowd's beating of Sosthenes, the ruler of the synagogue.

Gallio was the son of Marcus Annaeus Seneca, a Spanish orator and financier, and the elder brother of Seneca, the philosopher and tutor of Nero. Lucius Junius Gallio, a rich Roman, adopted Gallio, naming him Lucius Junius Gallio Annaeus. Gallio's name appears on an inscription at Delphi that refers to the 26th acclamation of Claudius as emperor. This places Gallio in office in Corinth between A.D. 51 and 53. He was apparently proconsul from May 1, 51, to May 1, 52, though dates a year later are possible. The date gives evidence from outside the Bible for the time Paul was in Corinth and founded the church there.

Finding the climate at Corinth unhealthy, Gallio apparently welcomed the opportunity to return to Rome, where he counselled Nero until he and Seneca joined a conspiracy against the emperor. First Seneca died; then Nero forced Gallio to commit suicide about A.D. 65. See *Achaia; Corinth; 1 and 2 Corinthians; Paul; Roman Empire.*

GALLON See *Weights and Measures.* Word used by modern translations to transfer Greek *metretes* into modern terminology. A *metretes* contained about nine gallons. Compare John 2:6. KJV reads firkins.

GALLOWS In English "gallows" refers to the platform on which a person was hanged. The Hebrew term translated "gallows" in Esther (2:23; 7:9–10; 9:25) is the word for tree. It is frequently suggested that tree should be understood as "stake" and that those executed by the Persians were impaled rather than hung. The earliest Greek translation understood the passage in this sense.

GAMAD (Gā′ măd) (NRSV, TEV) or **GAMMAD** (NIV, REB) Place name of uncertain meaning in Ezekiel 27:11. The early translations apparently read slightly a different Hebrew text with letters easily confused with those of Gamad and meaning, "watchers." Others interpreted it as "dwarf" or "pygmies." Others have pointed to a people called Kumudi from northern Syria listed in early Egyptian sources. They were apparently allies of Tyre in its fight against Babylon. See *Gammadim(s).*

GAMALIEL (Gȧ mā′ lĭ ĕl) Personal name meaning, "God rewards with good." *1.* The son of Pedahzur; a leader of the tribe of Manasseh, who helped Moses take the census in the wilderness (Num. 1:10). Compare Numbers 7:54–59. *2.* A highly regarded Pharisee who was a member of the Sanhedrin (Acts 5:34). He squelched a plan by the Sanhedrin to kill the apostles by reminding the members that interference with what the apos-

The interior of the traditional site of the tomb of Gamaliel.

tles were doing might prove to be opposition to God. If the work of the apostles were a purely human work, Gamaliel said, it would come to nothing anyway. According to Acts 22:3, this Gamaliel had been Paul's teacher. He was the grandson of the great Rabbi Hillel. He died about A.D. 52. *3.* A leading Jewish rabbi in the late first and early second centuries A.D. He was the grandson of the Gamaliel mentioned in the Book of Acts. He is credited with many of the adaptations in Judaism necessitated by the destruction of the Temple in A.D. 70.

GAMES Although the Bible contains references

Mosaic of gladiators from the Roman period with the victor standing triumphantly over the fallen one.

to sports (2 Sam. 2:14–16) along with allusions to children's entertainment (Isa. 11:8; Zech. 8:5), it is silent as to the nature of these games. Archaeology provides the most valuable information on games and athletics in the ancient world. Drawings and paintings on tomb and palace walls, sculptures and reliefs, as well as numerous artifacts illustrate recreational activities.

Board Games Over 4000 years old, board games were common throughout the Middle East. Game pieces moved from one square to another according to certain rules which are still unknown. A throw of dice, knucklebones, or even heelbones (lots) determined play. In the Old Testament, lots decided things such as slave allotments

A training track for footracing at Olympia.

(Nah. 3:10), apportionment of land (Josh. 18:6), and care of the Temple (Neh. 10:34; 1 Chron. 24:5). Their use of dice or "lots" gradually extended to gambling, then to simple table games. Soldiers cast lots for Jesus' garment at the crucifixion (John 19:24).

The oldest surviving game board was discovered in Egypt. Made of clay and divided into squares, it has eleven cone-shaped playing pieces, all dated before 4000 B.C. Another game commonly referred to as "hounds and jackals" was played throughout the Fertile Crescent (Tigris-Euphrates and Nile valleys with intervening land).

Playing pieces of varying designs as well as game boards of ivory and stone have been discovered at Samaria, Gezer, Megiddo, and other sites in Palestine. Excavations at Debir (tell beit Mirsim) in Southern Palestine unearthed a limestone board with ten glazed playing pieces and an ivory "die." Boards for a game called "fifty-eight holes" have been found at Megiddo and in Egypt and Mesopotamia as well.

Public Games The four Greek Panhellenic Games were the largest public sports contests in the Near East. Some believe that Paul was a spectator at the Isthmian Games (near Corinth), one of these international spectacles. It is evident that the apostle was familiar with athletics (Gal. 2:2; Phil. 3:13–14; 2 Tim. 2:5; 1 Cor. 9:25–27). Among the events were the pentathlon (long-jump, javelin and discus throws, running, and wrestling) and chariot races. All races were run on a long track or *stadion* with pylons at each end. Runners or char-

Children in present-day Jerusalem playing a game in the street on the Via Dolorosa.

ioteers rounded the pylons, racing back and forth instead of circling an oval track.

Athletes were rubbed with oil and participated without clothing. Competitive spirit was vigorous, and contests were governed by few rules. Prizes for winners of the Panhellenic Games were simple wreaths of olive, wild celery, laurel, and pine. At Rome, one could see basically these same events until wild beasts were introduced into the arena. Sometimes as many as ten thousand gladiators fought at the Roman games which might last for several weeks. Herod the Great built many amphitheaters in Palestine, including one near Jerusalem where men condemned to death fought with wild animals.

A Roman courtyard and garden in the Villa of Menander at Pompeii.

The process of hellenization (the forcing of Greek culture on the Jews) brought amphitheaters and gymnasia to Palestine. Orthodox Jews were repelled by nude athletes and games dedicated to Caesar. Trophies of ornamented wood were considered images and thus forbidden. Add to this the cruelty of the games, and it is understandable why devout Jews hated the games.   *Diane Cross*

GAMMADIM(S) (Găm′ mȧ dĭm) Citizens of Gamad. See *Gamad.*

GAMUL (Gā′ mŭl) Personal name meaning, "receiver of good deeds." Head of one of the priestly divisions in the Temple under David and Solomon (1 Chron. 24:17).

GANGRENE The Greek *gangraina* (2 Tim. 2:17) can refer either to gangrene, a death of soft tissue resulting from problems with blood flow (NAS, NRSV, REB) or to an ulcer (canker, KJV; open sore, TEV). In 2 Timothy *gangraina* is used figuratively for false teachings which destroy people who accept them.

GARDEN In biblical times, an enclosed plot of ground on which flowers, vegetables, herbs, and fruit and nut trees were cultivated (Gen. 2:8; 1 Kings 21:2; Esther 1:5; Isa. 51:3; John 18:1–2). **Characteristics** The primary Old Testament words for "garden" (*gan* and *gannah*) derive from a root meaning "to surround." Gardens were plots of ground enclosed or surrounded by walls or hedges. Some were large (Esther 1:5), the most prominent gardens being royal ones (2 Kings 25:4; Neh. 3:15; Jer. 39:4). Most gardens were situated close to the owner's residence (1 Kings 21:2). Occasionally a house might be located in the garden (2 Kings 9:27). An abundant supply of water was especially important (Gen. 13:10; Num. 24:6; Isa. 1:30; 58:11; Jer. 31:12). Gardeners were employed to tend the more substantial gardens, sowing seed and watering (Deut. 11:10; John 20:15). Orchards or small vineyards were sometimes called gardens.

The Garden of Gethsemane looking west toward the city wall of old Jerusalem.

Uses Obviously a garden provided food for its owner (Jer. 29:5,28; Amos 9:14), but it also served other aesthetic and utilitarian purposes. It was a place of beauty where plants were pleasing to the sight (Gen. 2:9). As a guarded and protected place (Song of Sol. 4:12), persons could retreat there for prayer (Matt. 26:36–46), for quiet or solitude (Esther 7:7), or even for bathing (Susanna 1:15). It provided a cool escape from the heat of the day (Gen. 3:8; Susanna 1:7). Friends could meet in gardens (John 18:1–2), or banquets could be served there (Esther 1:5). It thus was often associated with joy and gladness (Isa. 51:3). On the other hand, pagan sacrifices were sometimes offered in gardens (Isa. 65:3; 66:17); and gardens were used as burial sites (2 Kings 21:18,26; John 19:41–42).

Important Gardens The garden of Eden (Gen. 2:8; 3:23–24) was planted by God (2:8) and entrusted to Adam for cultivating and keeping (2:15). Following their sin, Adam and Eve were banished from the garden; but "Eden the garden of God" (Ezek. 28:13) continued as a symbol of blessing and bounty (Ezek. 36:35; Joel 2:3). The "king's garden" in Jerusalem was located near a gate to the city that provided unobserved exit or escape (2 Kings 25:4; Neh. 3:15; Jer. 39:4; 52:7). The "garden" (John 18:1) called Gethsemane (Matt. 26:36; Mark 14:32) was a place where Jesus often met with His disciples (John 18:2) and where He was betrayed and arrested.

Michael Fink

GAREB (Gā′ rĕb) Personal and place name meaning, "scabby." A member of David's personal army (2 Sam. 23:38). *2.* Hill in Jerusalem marking point of city wall which Jeremiah promised would be rebuilt (Jer. 31:39).

GARLAND Garland translates in modern translations two Hebrew and one Greek term, all referring to wreaths worn on the head. Garlands symbolized instruction or the benefit of wisdom (Prov. 1:9; 4:9). In Isaiah 61:3,10 garlands form part of the bridegroom's wedding apparel. Israel's days of Exile, pictured as mourning, would give way to the celebration of God's salvation, pictured as a wedding. At Acts 14:13 the priest of Zeus brought Paul and Barnabas garlands. In Greek mythology

A sculpture of a garland around the altar of the pagan god Aesculapius at Pergamum.

the gods were frequently portrayed wearing garlands. Mistaking the apostles for Zeus and Hermes, the priest deemed garlands a suitable gift.

GARLIC See *Plants in the Bible.*

GARMITE (Gär′ mīte) A title or designation meaning, "my bone" used for Keilah in the line of the tribe of Judah (1 Chron. 4:19). The Hebrew text and the exact meaning of Garmite are obscure.

GARNER KJV term for a barn, storehouse, or granary (Ps. 144:13; Joel 1:17; Matt, 3:12; Luke 3:17). To garner (Isa. 62:9, NAS, NRSV) means to gather (a crop) for storage. See *Granary.*

GARRISON A body of troops stationed for defense, often in the sense of occupying forces. In the tenth century B.C. the Philistines had garrisons deep in Jewish territory at Gibeath-elohim (1

Sam. 10:5), Geba (1 Sam. 13:3), and Bethlehem (2 Sam. 23:14). David, in turn, placed garrisons in Damascus (2 Sam. 8:6) and in Edom (2 Sam. 8:14) with the result that the natives became his servants, that is, they were subjugated and forced to pay tribute.

The KJV has garrisons at Ezekiel 26:11 where modern translations have a reference to pillars in honor of the gods of Tyre. The KJV of 2 Corinthians 11:32 mentions that the city of Damascus was guarded with a garrison. Modern versions simply note the city was guarded. The parallel in Acts 9:24 only mentions guards at the gate.

GASH In modern translations to cut the skin as a sign of mourning (Jer. 41:5; 47:5; 48:37) or in the worship of pagan dieties (1 Kings 18:28). See *Fertility Cults.*

GASHMU (Găsh′ mū) Aramaic form of Geshem used in Nehemiah 6:6. See *Geshem.*

GATAM (Gā′ tăm) Personal name of uncertain meaning. Son of Eliphaz and grandson of Esau (Gen. 36:11). He headed a clan of Edomites (Gen. 36:16).

GATE BETWEEN THE TWO WALLS A city gate on the southeast side of Jerusalem, perhaps identical with the Fountain Gate. Zedekiah and his sons were captured by the Babylonians after escaping through this gate (2 Kings 25:4; Jer. 39:4; 52:7).

GATEKEEPER One who guards access to a place, either a city (2 Sam. 18:26; 2 Kings 7:10–11), a residence (John 18:17), the sacred precincts of the ark (1 Chron. 15:23–24), or the Temple (1 Chron. 23:5). KJV uses porter. Temple gatekeepers were charged with preventing anyone

The Joppa (modern Jaffa) Gate at Jerusalem.

unclean from entering the Temple (2 Chron. 23:19) and with guarding the Temple treasuries and storehouses (1 Chron. 9:26; 26:20–22; Neh. 12:25).

The Dung Gate at Jerusalem was the entry to Jerusalem from the area of the Tyropoeon Valley.

GATES OF JERUSALEM AND THE TEMPLE Jerusalem's many gates have varied in number and location with the changing size and orientation of its walls throughout its long history. Persons could enter through an important city gate on the west from Jaffa (Tel Aviv) Road, as they do today. On the east, entrance from the Kidron Valley was signed principally through the Sheep Gate (modern Stephen or Lion Gate) in New Testament times and by a recently found gate (Spring, 1986) south of the modern city walls in Old Testament times. This latter gate may date to the reign of Solomon, being similar to Solomonic gates found at Megiddo, Gezer, and Hazor. Entrance to the Temple itself was on its eastern side through the Beautiful gate (Acts 3:10), near the Golden Gate recently found beneath the city eastern wall. On the north, the principal gateway (Damascus Gate) opened onto the Damascus Road. Seven gates now allow entrance to the old city of Jerusalem. *John McRay*

GATH (Găth) Gath was one of the five cities that comprised the Philistine city-state system (1 Sam. 6:17). See *Philistines.* The inhabitants of Gath

Stephen's (or Lion's) Gate at Jerusalem.

The Damascus Gate at Jerusalem as seen from outside the old city walls.

were referred to as the Gittites (1 Sam. 17:4; 2 Sam. 6:10–11). Because the Hebrew term *gath/gat* meant "winepress" and since vineyards and winepresses were widespread in the land, a number of towns in Palestine were named Gath. Usually the name was used with another name which helped distinguish one site from another, such as, Gath-Hepher, Gath-Rimmon and Moresheth-Gath.

By far the most frequently mentioned Gath in the Old Testament is Gath of the Philistines. In addition to Gath, the other towns of the Philistine city-state system were Ekron, Ashdod, Ashkelon and Gaza (1 Sam. 6:17). We may reasonably assume that Gath was the principal city among the five and served as the hub of the pentapolis.

Gath was strategically located for Philistine purposes. While we do not know the exact location, we do know the general area in which Gath was located. Based on information from the biblical accounts, Gath was located inland as opposed to the other Philistine towns which were on or near the coast. It was located in the Shephelah, that is, the band of foothills which lay between the

Panoramic view of the tel of ancient Gath.

coastal plain on the west and the central hill country on the east. Since the Israelites, at least during the period of the settlement, occupied the central hill country, Gath was in a position to protect Philistine territory from raids by the Israelites. At the same time it was convenient for the Philistines to initiate raids on Israelite communities from the city of Gath. Since a number of sites have been eliminated in recent years based on archaeological excavations, one of the most likely candidates for Philistine Gath is tell es-Safi, twelve miles east of Ashdod.

A number of the highlights of Gath's history are reflected in the Old Testament. Prior to the coming of the Israelites, Gath was a Canaanite city occupied by the Anakim, a group known for their large stature (Josh. 11:21–22). During the conquest of Canaan, Joshua and the Israelites apparently did not take the sites of Gaza, Gath, and Ashdod (Josh. 11:22). We may assume that these towns were taken by the Philistines at this point.

G

Gath was one of the locations to which the Philistines took the ark (1 Sam. 5:8–9) and was the hometown of Goliath (1 Sam. 17:4) and Obed-edom (1 Chron. 13:13). One of the most interesting bits of information is that at one point while Saul was in pursuit of David, David found sanctuary with Achish, the king of Gath, and perhaps became a vassal of the Philistines (1 Sam. 27:1–7). Eventually David defeated the Philistines and made Gath an Israelite town (1 Chron. 18:1). Apparently Achish continued to be the king of Gath, perhaps as a vassal king, even during the reign of Solomon (1 Kings 2:39). During the period of the divided monarchy, Gath's history went through a series of changes. Rehoboam, the king for Judah (931-913 B.C.) fortified Gath and made it a fortress city of Judah (2 Chron. 11:5–12). Hazael, king of Syria (about 843-797 B.C.), beseiged the city and captured it (2 Kings 12:17). Shortly thereafter, the inhabitants of Gath apparently rebelled against Hazael and established to some degree their independence. Finally, Uzziah, king of Judah (792-740 B.C.), partially destroyed Gath and made it once again a part of the territory of Judah (2 Chron. 26:6). Around 711 B.C., Sargon II, the king of Assyria, conquered and perhaps destroyed the city. Apparently, at this point, Gath's history came to an end. This conclusion is reinforced by the fact that Gath is obviously omitted in the lists of Philistine sites mentioned by the prophets (Jer. 25:20; Amos 1:6–8; Zeph. 2:4; Zech. 9:5–6).   *LaMoine DeVries*

A mythical figure wearing a gauze-thin garment of Roman style.

GATH-HEPHER (Gath-hē′ phēr) Place name meaning, "winepress on the watering hole." A city on the eastern border of Zebulun's tribal allotment (Josh. 19:13). The prophet Jonah came from Gath-hepher (2 Kings 14:25). It is located at modern el-Meshed or nearby khirbet ez-Zurra, three miles northeast of Nazareth.

GATH-RIMMON (Găth-rĭm′ mon) Place name meaning, "winepress on the pomegranate tree." Town in tribal territory of Dan (Josh. 19:45) and set aside for Levites (Josh. 21:24). It is usually located at tell Jerisheh on the Yarkon River in modern Tel Aviv, but some scholars locate it two miles to the northeast at tell Abu Zeitun. 1 Chronicles 6:69 lists Gath-rimmon in the tribe of Ephraim, but this is usually understood as a copyist's omission of a sentence at the beginning of verse 69. Gath-rimmon also appears in the Hebrew text of Joshua 21:25 though not in the earliest Greek translation or in the parallel in 1 Chronicles 6:70. Most scholars recognize that a copyist repeated Gath-rimmon from verse 24, the original reading probably being Ibleam. See *Ibleam.*

GAUZE, GARMENTS OF One of the fine items associated with Jerusalem socialites (Isa. 3:23, NRSV). The meaning of the underlying Hebrew is

debated. The sense is either a gauze garment (NRSV; interpreted as a revealing garment, TEV; scarves of gauze, REB) or a mirror (hand mirror, NAS). The KJV has glasses in the sense of looking glasses. At this time a mirror would be a piece of polished metal. At Isaiah 8:1 the Hebrew word translated as gauze garment (or mirror) is translated as (writing) tablet.

GAZA (Gā′ zà) Place name meaning, "strong." Philistine city on the coastal plain about three miles inland from the Mediterranean Sea. It was the southernmost town of the Philistine city-state system which also included Ashkelon, Ashdod, Ekron, and Gath (1 Sam. 6:17).

While the site is especially associated with the Philistines, many other groups have inhabited it throughout history. That history extends from a period prior to the arrival of the Philistines, a period when the Avvim occupied the village (Deut. 2:23), on down to the present. The inhabitants of Gaza at times were referred to as the Gazites or Gazathites (Judg. 16:2).

Gaza's important role in ancient history was due to its strategic location on the major coastal plain highway which connected Egypt with the rest of the Ancient Near East. Because of its strategic location, Gaza witnessed the passage of numerous caravans and armies and often got caught in the middle of the political struggles of the Ancient

Near East. This is reflected in a brief review of the highlights of Gaza's history. According to the records of Thutmose III, Thutmose captured Gaza on his first campaign to Palestine and made it a major Egyptian center. The Amarna Letters identify Gaza as the district headquarters for Egyptian holdings in southern Palestine. For Solomon, Gaza was the major center on the southern border of his kingdom which ran "from Tiphsah even to Azzah (Gaza)" (1 Kings 4:24).

Gaza was often affected by the political struggles and turnovers that took place during the Assyrian and Babylonian periods. Tiglath-pileser III collected tribute from Gaza during his military campaign against Israel and Syria about 734 B.C. Hezekiah "smote the Philistines, even unto Gaza" as he tried to re-establish Judah's independence (2 Kings 18:8) about 705-704 B.C. Sennacherib reinforced his control of Gaza as a vassal state as he invaded Judah in 701 B.C. Pharaoh Neco conquered Gaza about 609 B.C. and made it an Egyptian holding,

Gold cup decorated with the raised figure of a gazelle from the Treasure of the Oxus.

Bedouin woman from the area of Gaza.

but it remained in Egyptian hands for only a few years. Sometime after 605 B.C. the Babylonian King Nebuchadnezzar conquered Gaza and made it a part of his empire.   *LaMoine DeVries*

GAZATHITE (Gā′ zȧth īte) KJV spelling of Gazite in Joshua 13:3. See *Gazite.*

GAZELLE See *Animals.*

GAZER (Gā′ zēr) KJV spelling of Gezer based on Hebrew accented form (2 Sam. 5:25; 1 Chron. 14:16). See *Gezer.*

GAZEZ (Gā′ zĕz) Personal name meaning, "sheepshearing." Name both of Caleb's son and grandson (1 Chron. 2:46). As other names in the list represent cities in southern Judah occupied by the clan of Caleb, Gazez may also be a city, though nothing else is known about it.

GAZITE (Gā′ zīte) Citizen of Gaza. See *Gaza.*

GAZZAM (Găz′ zam) Personal name meaning, "caterpillar" or "bird of prey." Leader of a clan of Temple servants who returned from Babylonian captivity with Zerubbabel (Ezra 2:48).

GEAR The context of Acts 27:17 indicates that the Greek term underlying gear (RSV) refers to some type of nautical equipment or apparatus. The two interpretations most often given are "lowered the sail" (KJV, TEV) and "let out the (sea) anchor" (NAS, NIV, NRSV, REB). Some commentators suggest that the passage means that all the ship's gear (ropes, sails, yards, pulleys) was secured or stored below deck.

GEBA (Gē′ bà) Place name meaning, "hill," and variant Hebrew spelling of Gibeah, with which it is sometimes confused though the two represent different towns in the territory of Benjamin. Geba was given Benjamin (Josh. 18:24) but set aside for the Levites (Josh. 21:17). This is evidently the base camp for Saul and Jonathan in their fight with the Philistines (1 Sam. 13:16—14:18), though the Hebrew texts and modern translations confuse Geba and Gibeah here. King Asa of Judah

The southern site of Geba, modern Jeba, a few miles north of Jerusalem.

(910-869 B.C.) strengthened the city (1 Kings 15:22). In the days of King Josiah (640-609 B.C.) Geba apparently represented the northern border of Judah as opposed to the southern border in Beersheba (2 Kings 23:8). Isaiah described the ominous march of the Assyrian army coming through Geba on its way to Jerusalem (Isa. 10:29). For Zechariah (Zech. 14:10), Geba represented the northern border of a Judah to be flattened out into a plain dominated by God ruling on Mount Zion in Jerusalem. At some period Geba's inhabitants were forced to move to Manahath (1 Chron. 8:6), perhaps when the tribe of Benjamin first settled there or during the Exile. Exiles returned to Geba under Zerubbabel (Ezra 2:26). Some citizens of Geba lived in Michmash and other cities in Nehemiah's day, unless the Hebrew text is read differently (REB) to mean they lived in Geba as well as the other towns (Neh. 11:31). Levite singers lived there (Neh. 12:29).

Geba is variously located, some scholars going so far as to locate a southern Geba of Benjamin at Jeba across the wadi Suweinit from Michmash, about five and a half miles north of Jerusalem, and a northern Geba (Josh. 18:24) at khirbet et-Tell, seven miles north of Bethel. At neither of these places has archaeology yet shown evidence to correlate with the biblical materials.

GEBAL (Gē′ bàl) Place name meaning, "mountain." *1.* Seaport known to Greeks as Byblos whose help for Tyre Ezekiel described (Ezek. 27:9). Mentioned in Egyptian texts before 2,000 B.C. and in many Egyptian and Assyrian texts through the centuries, Gebal was located at modern Dschebel about 25 miles north of Beirut. It was the most famous of the Syrian ports. It belonged to land that remained for Joshua to conquer (Josh. 13:5). Stone masons from Gebal cut stones for Solomon's Temple (1 Kings 5:18). Archaeologists have discovered settlements here as early as 8,000 B.C. The fine sarcophagus of King Ahiram found there contained the earliest evidence we have of the Phoenician alphabet. About 900 B.C. Tyre replaced Gebal as the strongest city of Phoenicia. Still its fame for building ships and trading throughout the world continued.

2. A member of a coalition against Israel which the psalmist lamented (Ps. 83:7). It is the northern part of Arabia near Petra in the mountainous country south of the Dead Sea. The Genesis Apocryphon from the Dead Sea Scrolls also mentions it.

The ruins of the ancient seaport city of Byblos (Gebal), located in the modern country of Lebanon.

GEBALITE (Gē′ bà īte) Citizens of Gebal. See *Gebal.*

GEBER (Gē′ bēr) Personal name meaning, "young man" or "hero." Solomon's district governor for Gilead beyond the Jordan (1 Kings 4:19) was the son of Uri. He collected provisions to supply the royal court. The district governor over Ramoth-gilead was Ben-geber or the son of Geber. See *Ben-geber.*

GEBIM (Gē′ bīm) Place name meaning, "water ditch." It lay on the line of march conquerors took against Jerusalem (Isa. 10:31). The exact site is not known, but it lay between tell el-Ful and Mount Scopus near Jerusalem.

GECKO See *Animals, Reptiles.*

GEDALIAH (Gĕd à lī′ ah) Personal name meaning, "Yahweh has done great things." *1.* The son of Ahikam who was appointed ruler of Judah by Nebuchadnezzar of Babylon in 587 B.C. (2 Kings 25:22). Jerusalem had fallen to the Babylonians, and many of the residents of Judah had been deported. Ahikam, the father of Gedaliah, was an ally of the prophet Jeremiah (Jer. 26:24; 39:14), and Gedaliah may have been in sympathy with Jeremiah's political views. That could explain why Nebuchadnezzar selected Gedaliah to be governor. Gedaliah's time in office was brief. After only two months he was murdered by a group of fanatically zealous nationalists under the leadership of Ishmael (Jer. 40:1—41:18). *2.* A royal official under King Zedekiah (597-586 B.C.) who was with the group that got the king's permission to imprison Jeremiah in a cistern (Jer. 38). *3.* Temple singer and prophet who played the harp with his father Jeduthan and five brothers (1 Chron. 25:3). He headed one of the twenty-four divisions of Temple servants (1 Chron. 25:9).

An abbreviated form of the Hebrew name is given a priest with a foreign wife under Ezra (Ezra 10:18) and the grandfather of the prophet Zephaniah (Zeph. 1:1).

GEDEON (Gĕd′ ė on) KJV transliteration of Greek for Gideon in Hebrews 11:32. See *Gideon.*

GEDER (Gē′ dẽr) Place name meaning, "stone wall." City whose king Joshua killed (Josh. 12:13). The site is unknown and could be easily confused with several places called Beth-geder, Gederah, Gederoth, or Gederothaim. Some scholars believe a copyist confused this text with the preceding Gezer or miscopied a similar-appearing Gerar. First Chronicles 27:28 mentions an official from Geder, but the relationship of this Geder to that of Joshua 12 to the other cities mentioned above cannot be determined.

GEDERAH (Gė dē′ rah) Place name meaning, "sheepfold" or "stone wall." A village in the Shephalah or valley of Judah (Josh. 15:36). It is located at modern tell el-Judeireh north of Maraeshah and ten miles southeast of Lod. Villagers were noted for skill in making pottery, much of which was made for the king (1 Chron. 4:23). The home of one of David's soldiers (1 Chron. 12:4) apparently belongs in Benjamin (1 Chron. 12:2), but he may have been living in Judah before joining David at Ziklag. Otherwise, this is a different Gederah located at Jedireh near Gibeon. See *Geder.*

GEDERATHITE (Gė dē′ rȧ thīte) See *Gederah.*

GEDERITE (Gė′ dẽr′ īte) Citizen of Geder. See *Geder.*

GEDEROTH (Gė dē′ rŏth) Place name meaning, "walls." City in tribal allotment of Judah in the Shephelah or valley (Josh. 15:41). It may be an alternate spelling of Gederah or Qatra near Lachish. When the Philistines took Gederoth with other cities, King Ahaz (735-715 B.C.) sent to Assyria for help (2 Chron. 28:18). See *Geder; Gederah.*

GEDEROTHAIM (Gĕd′ ė rō thā′ ĭm) Place name meaning, "two walls" or common noun referring to sheepfolds (compare REB translation, namely both parts of Gederah). A town in the valley or Shephelah of Judah allotted to Judah (Josh. 15:36). The list contains fourteen cities without Gederothaim, causing several commentators to identify Gederothaim as a part of Gederah

or as a copyist's duplication. See *Gederah.*

GEDOR (Gē′ dôr) Place name meaning, "wall." *1.* Town in hill country of Judah allotted to tribe of Judah (Josh. 15:58). It is located at khirbet Judur three miles north of Hebron and Beth-zur and west of Tekoa. The genealogy of Judah in 1 Chronicles 4 includes city names among the list of "sons." In verse 4, Penuel is the father or perhaps founder of the city. *2.* In 1 Chronicles 4:18 Jered is the father of Gedor. Its location is disputed. See *Socho; Zanoah.* The Gedor in 1 Chronicles 4:39 probably represents an early copyist's change from Gerar, which is quite similar in appearance in Hebrew and appears in the earliest Greek translation. If Gedor is the original reading, its location in the tribal allotment of Simeon (1 Chron. 4:24) is not known. A Benjaminite from Gedor had two sons in David's wilderness army (1 Chron. 12:7). This could be a city in Benjamin of unknown location or one of other Gedors discussed above. A member of the tribe of Benjamin was named Gedor (1 Chron. 8:31). See *Geder; Gederoth.*

GEHARASHIM (Gē hä rä′ shĭm) Place name meaning "valley of the handcrafts workers." A member of the genealogy of Judah and Caleb in 1 Chronicles 4:14, a list which often includes place names. It is listed as a place where members of the tribe of Benjamin lived in the time of Nehemiah (Neh. 11:35). This might indicate that descendants of Judah and Caleb had once occupied territory in Benjamin. It is apparently near Lod in Benjamin's allotment about 30 miles northwest of Jerusalem. See *Charashim.*

GEHAZI (Gė hā′ zī) Personal name meaning, "valley of vision" or "goggle-eyed." Servant of the prophet Elisha (2 Kings 4:12). The Bible portrays him as a man of questionable character. On one occasion he tried to force a grieving woman away from the prophet (2 Kings 4:27). Despite the prophet's commission, he could not restore a child to life (2 Kings 4:31). Later he tried to secure for himself the reward Elisha had refused from Naaman the Syrian and then lied to Elisha (2 Kings 5:20–25). For his duplicity with regard to Naaman, Gehazi was stricken with the disease of which Naaman had been cured. Gehazi did testify to the king of Elisha's good deeds and helped the widow get her lands restored (2 Kings 8:1–6). See *Elisha.*

GEHENNA (Gė hĕn′ nă) English transliteration of the Greek word that is a transliteration of the Hebrew place name meaning, "valley of whining" or "valley of lamentation" and came to be used in New Testament times as a word for hell. See *Hinnom.* The valley south of Jerusalem called the Valley of the son of Hinnom (Josh. 15:8; 18:16; 2 Chron. 33:6; Jer. 32:35) became the place of

View of the Valley of Gehenna (Hinnom Valley) looking northeast toward the new city of Jerusalem.

child sacrifice to foreign gods. In the period between the Old and New Testaments Jewish writing used the term to describe the hell of fire in the final judgment. In some writings but not in the Bible Gehenna was also seen as the place of temporary judgment for those waiting the final judgment.

The New Testament uses Gehenna to speak of the place of final judgment. Jesus warned that those who called another, "Thou fool," faced the danger of the fire of Gehenna (Matt. 5:22). He taught it is better to destroy a part of one's body than to have one's whole body thrown into Gehenna (Matt. 5:29; 18:9; Mark 9:43,45,47). In Gehenna worms are constantly at work in a fiery environment that burns forever (Mark 9:48). Only God can commit people to Gehenna and so is the only One worthy of human fear (Matt. 10:28; Luke 12:5). Jesus condemned the Pharisees for making converts but then turning them into sons of Gehenna, that is, people destined for hell (Matt. 23:15). He scolded the Pharisees, warning they had no chance to escape Gehenna through their present practices (Matt. 23:33). For many people James warned that they could not control their tongues that Gehenna had set on fire (Jas. 3:6). See *Hell.*

GELILOTH (Gĕl′ ĭ lŏth) Place name meaning, "circles" or "regions." A border point north of Jerusalem in tribal allotment of Benjamin (Josh. 18:17). It appears to correspond to Gilgal in the description of Judah 15:7. See *Gilgal.*

GEM See *Jewelry, Jewels, and Precious Stones; Minerals and Metals of the Bible.*

GEMALLI (Gė măl′ lī) Personal name meaning, "my camel" or "camel driver." Spy who represented tribe of Dan in searching out the land of Canaan (Num. 13:12).

GEMARA A portion of the Talmud containing commentary on the Mishnah. See *Mishnah.* The word Gemara (Aramaic, "to learn") refers specifically to the discussions on the Mishna conducted in the rabbinic academies of ancient Palestine and Babylon. The Mishna and Gemara combined comprise the Talmud. Most of the Gemara is written in Aramaic. Two Gemaras exist, the Palestinian and the Babylonian.

GEMARIAH (Gĕm ȧ rī′ ah) Personal name meaning, "Yahweh has completed or carried out." *1.* Messenger King Zedekiah (597-586 B.C.) sent to Babylon. He carried a letter from Jeremiah to the exiles (Jer. 29:3). *2.* Son of Shaphan, the court scribe, who had a room in the Temple, where Baruch read from Jeremiah's sermons to the congregation (Jer. 36:10). Later, Gemariah sought to keep the king from burning Jeremiah's scroll (v. 25). See *Shaphan.*

GENEALOGIES (Gē nē ăl′ ō gĭes) Records of family lineage that trace the descent of a person, family, or group from an ancestor.

Old Testament Genealogies are recorded in the Old Testament as early as Genesis 4. Various enrollments by family lineage are referenced at significant junctures in Old Testament history (Num. 1:19–49; Ezra 8). The writer of Chronicles offered abundant genealogical records (1 Chron. 1—9).

Genealogies occur in several different forms. A linear genealogy lists one person in each generation, usually father, son, grandson, etc. A segmented genealogy lists several people of at least the first generation and often of following generations, usually the sons of a father, the children of each son, the children in the next generation, etc. Descending genealogies begin with a parent and list the following generations. Ascending genealogies begin with the last member named and trace ancestry back through parent, grandparent, great grandparent, etc. to the original ancestor of the family, clan or nation. The linear genealogy seeks to show that the final person listed has a legitimate right to the position or honor the person occupies or claims. Such legitimation comes from the first ancestor listed or from the established family position. A segmented genealogy shows the relationship between the various individuals or groups named. Genealogies may serve family, political, or religious purposes. In their purposes of legitimation, genealogies describe not only kinship relationships but also geographical, social, economic, religious, and political relationships.

At least nine functions of genealogies may be described: *1.* Demonstrate the relationships and the differences between Israel and other nations (Gen. 10); *2.* Demonstrate the unity and coherence of Israel (Ex. 1:1–5) or of all nations (Gen. 10); *3.* Build a historical bridge connecting Israel through periods of history for which few narratives are available (1 Chron. 1–9); *4.* Reveal a pattern of cycles in world history (Matt. 1:1–17); *5.* Describe military functions (Num. 1:5–16); *6.* Show a person or group's right to an office or function (1 Chron. 6; 24–26); *7.* Preserve the purity of the nation (see Ezra 10); *8.* Assure a sense of national continuity and unity in a period of national despair (1 Chron. 5); *9.* Show the movement of history toward God's goal (Gen. 4; 5; 11:10–32; 1 Chron. 1—9).

New Testament Matthew began his Gospel with a genealogy tracing Jesus' lineage from Abraham through David. Luke also included a genealogy reaching back to Adam and God (3:23–38). The relationship between these two records is not clear, though a respective focus on messiahship and salvation offered to all mankind is apparent.

Genealogies later came under question. Hebrews 7:3,6 assigns value to the fact that Melchizedek was a priest without genealogy—a fact that set him apart from the Jewish priesthood. Paul condemned a distorted use of genealogies in his later writings (1 Tim. 1:4; Titus 3:9), though the exact role such genealogies played is not certain. They perhaps were the source of disputes about authority and leadership in some churches.

Michael Fink

GENERAL With reference to Sisera (Judg. 4:7) and Joab (1 Chron. 27:34), a general (NRSV) is the highest ranking officer in command of an army. General, commander, and (chief) captain are used interchangeably for such an officer in English translations. KJV consistently translates "captain" or "chief captain."

GENERATION A period of time and its significant events comprising the lifespan of a person but also used to talk of a more indefinite timespan. Two Hebrew words are at times translated, "generation." The more significant of these is *toledoth,* derived from the Hebrew verb, "to bear children." *Toledoth* gives structure to the Book of Genesis (2:4; 5:1; 6:9; 10:1,32; 11:10,27; 25:12,13,19; 36:1,9; 37:2). Thus creation, Adam, Noah, Noah's sons, Shem, Terah, Ishmael, the sons of Ishmael, Isaac, Esau, and Jacob each provide a generation and a structural unit in the Genesis narrative. In writing a narrative this way, Israel followed a pattern long used by Near Eastern neighbors, that of describing creation as a series of births. Israel, as so often under divine inspiration, radically changed the pattern. Israel's neighbors spoke of the birth of gods, such births representing at the same time a part of the universe, since the sun, the moon, the stars were all looked upon as gods. Israel simply spoke of the birth of creation by God's words and actions. This started a process by which human generations would endure as long as the creation generation endured. Each human generation lasts from the death of the father through the death of the son. This was the time when the son functioned as head of the larger Hebrew extended family. Often the aged patriarch presided over the active leadership of his sons as seen particularly in the cases of Isaac and Jacob. Human history in its simplest form of family history is then the way God tells His story of working with human beings to bless them and to accomplish His purposes for them. He works not only in miraculous, unique events; He works also in the continuing series of human births and deaths. Elsewhere *toledoth* appears in genealogical lists such as Exodus 6, Numbers 1, 1 Chronicles 1—9.

The Hebrew term *dor* is related to the word for circle and refers to the life circle of an individual, either from birth to death or from birth to the birth of the first child. It can have extended uses in metaphorical language. *Dor* occurs over 160 times in the Old Testament. A generation was a general term for those persons living at a particular time. A generation did not necessarily have a specific number of years. Genesis 15:13–16 apparently equates 400 years with four generations, thus 100 years per generation. Numbers 32:11–13 may reckon a generation as 60 years, it including people twenty and above and giving them forty more years to die. Or one may interpret this to mean a generation is the forty years of adulthood between ages 20 and 60. God promised Jehu his sons would rule to the fourth generation, apparently meaning four sons (2 Kings 10:30; 15:12). Jehu began ruling about 841 B.C., his first son Jehoahaz about 814 B.C. and the fourth generation Zechariah died about 752 B.C. The five generations ruled less than 90 years, while the four sons' generations ruled about 60 years. This is reducing a generation to a quite small number. After his tragedies Job lived 140 years and saw four generations (Job 42:16). This would make a generation about 35 years. Basically, generation is not a specific number of years but a more or less specific period of time. (Compare Job 8:8; Isa. 51:9.) The literal Hebrew expression "generation and generation" thus means through all generations or forever (Ps. 49:11). Similarly, "to your (his, their) generations" means forever (Num. 10:8).

The generations come and go (Eccl. 1:4). This should establish wisdom on which a present generation can draw (Deut. 32:7). A generation also represents those who can gather for worship, so that the gathered worship community forms a generation (Pss. 14:5; 24:6; 73:15). The generations of people change, but God has given His name Yahweh to be remembered through all generations (Ex. 3:15). He is the refuge for all generations (Ps. 90:1). The danger is that a generation will arise that does not know Yahweh (Judg. 2:10; compare Ps. 12). Thus one generation must tell God's acts and write them down for the next generation (Pss. 22:30–31; 102:18 NRSV; compare Ps. 79:13).

God's people must be taught faithfulness. God is faithful to a thousand generations by His very nature (Deut. 7:9). His salvation is available through the generations; that is forever (Isa. 51:8).

In the New Testament "generation" refers to a specific contemporary audience. Jesus often used the term to describe the evil nature of the people He addressed (Matt. 11:16; 12:39; Luke 17:25). The message of the New Testament can be summarized: "To him be glory in the church and in Christ Jesus to all generations, forever and ever" (Eph. 3:21 NRSV). *Trent C. Butler*

GENESIS First book of the Bible, providing a universal setting for God's revelation and introducing basic biblical teachings. Genesis moves in two parts: (1) universal creation, rebellion, punishment, and restoration; (2) God's choice of a particular family through whom He promises to bless the nations.

Contents The first eleven chapters of Genesis provide the universal setting for Israel's story. Taking up themes and motifs prominent in the literature of their neighbors, the inspired writer showed how only one God participated in creation of the whole world and in directing the fortunes of all its nations. The focus narrows from creation of the universe to creation of the first family (1:1—2:25). Trust in a wily serpent rather than in God brings sin into the world and shows God's judgment on sin. Thus human life is lived out in the suffering, pain, and frustration of the world we know (ch. 3). In that world God continues to condemn sin, bless faithfulness, and yet show grace to sinners (4:1–15). From the human perspective, great cultural achievements appear, but so does overwhelming human pride (4:16–24). Thus humans multiply their race as God commanded; they also look for a better life than that of pain and toil (4:25–5:32). Help comes, but only after further punishment. Through the flood, God eliminates all humanity except the family of Noah, then makes a covenant with that family never again to bring such punishment (6:1—9:17), but human sin continues on the individual and the societal levels, bringing necessary divine punishment of the nations at the tower of Babel (9:18–11:9). God thus establishes a plan to redeem and bless the humanity that persists in sin. He calls one man of faith—Abraham—and leads him to a new beginning in a new land. He gives His promises of land, nation, fame, and a mission of blessing for the nations. This works itself out in blessing nations that help Abraham and punishing those who do not. It climaxes in God's covenant with Abraham in which Abraham shows faithfulness in the sign of circumcision.

New generations led by Isaac and Jacob find God continuing to lead them, to call them to be His people, and to renew His promises to them. Human trickery and deception personified in Jacob do not alter God's determination to carry out His redemptive plan.

Thus is established the heritage of God's people in the triad of patriarchal fathers—Abraham, Isaac, and Jacob. God's promises and revelation to them became the foundation of Israel's religious experience and hope. See *Creation; Flood; Sin; Humanity; Anthropology; Earth; Image of God; Abraham; Isaac; Jacob; Joseph; Adam and Eve; Noah; Names of God; God of the Fathers.*

Critical Problems Critical scholars have raised many questions as they have sought reverently to study and understand the Book of Genesis. Comparison with other creation and flood stories, especially those coming from Sumeria, Babylon, and Assyria, have shown striking similarities to the biblical narrative. Why does the biblical account follow the same basic outline of other creation and flood narratives? Has one copied the other? Does God inspire a writer to react to other literature and write the authentic version? What role does oral tradition play in one nation learning of the literature of another nation? The least that can be said is that Israel's creation and flood narratives present a consistent picture of a sovereign God concerned with and in control of all nations. It shows a realistic picture of humanity in their great strengths and weaknesses. It has proven itself true through the centuries and millennia, whereas the other stories have become relics of a past civilization, recovered only by the accident of the archaeologists' spadework. See *Creation; Flood.*

Genesis has given rise to theories of the origin and compilation of the book and of the Pentateuch or first five books of the Bible. Do use of later names such as land of the Philistines (Gen. 21:32), closely resembling, almost duplicate stories (12:10–20; 20:1–18; 26:1–11), the use of different names for God (Yahweh in ch. 15; Elohim in ch. 17), the use of different facts (man made with woman in 1:27 but man made, then the animals, then woman in ch. 2) point to different authors of parts of the book, sources used by an author, or literary and theological techniques used to deliver the divine message?

In the 1960s many scholars thought they had reached agreement on the answers. The 1980s opened the questions anew with widely differing theories. The theories each try to explain how God produced and provided this book. The constant fact is that Genesis is both a classic piece of literature and the word of God inspired to teach His people about Him, His plan of redemption, and the nature of the world and people He created. See *Pentateuch.*

Teachings A brief article can merely list a few of the important teachings of Genesis. Human reflection upon the book from the point of its origin onward has not completely understood its theological richness and its call to covenant faithfulness and hope. God is Creator and Redeemer. He provided the best of all possible worlds for the best of all possible creatures, humanity created in His image. Human sin, inspired by a tempting part of the creation, brought divine judgment, resulting in the world of pain, labor, and frustration we now experience.

God is Judge and Savior. He takes human sin seriously but works constantly to form permanent relationships with people of faith. He calls people to follow and serve Him, promising them blessings suited for their needs and His purposes. God's judgment is limited by His covenant promises. God's salvation is limited only by human refusal to trust and believe. People of faith are not perfect. They deceive and connive, but they leave themselves open to God's leadership and become instruments of His plan.

God is universal sovereign and individual God. He created and directs the nations, blessing and cursing according to His purposes. He reveals Himself to, calls, enters into covenant with, and promises to bless individual people. Such work with individuals is part of His plan to bless nations.

Outline

I. The Nature of Human Life (1:1—11:9)
 A. Humans are made in His image and are the climax of His creation (1:1–2:4).
 B. Human nature has needs and limits (2:2–25).
 C. Human sin brings alienation and punishment (3:1–24).
 D. God punishes human pride and irresponsibility, yet His grace protects the sinner (4:1–15).
 E. Human nature produces astonishing cultural achievements and deadly pride (4:16–24).
 F. Humans respond to God, develop into a large society, but seek relief from their burdens (4:25–5:32).
 G. God punishes sinful society but preserves a faithful remnant (6:1—8:22).
 H. God renews His commission to the creature made in His image and makes a covenant not to repeat the disastrous punishment of the flood (9:1–17).
 I. Sin and disrespect set the pattern for international relations (9:18—10:32).
 J. Pride and failure to trust God and other people bring separation and loss of communication (11:1—9).

II. The Mission and Nature of God's Family (11:10—50:26)
 A. The Lord has a redemptive plan for His world (11:10—25:18).
  1. God's family originated in a foreign land (11:10–32).
  2. The Lord calls people to Himself (12:1–9).
  3. God plagues the nations which misuse God's people (12:10–20).
  4. God renews His promises and blessings when His family blesses the nations (13:1—15:21).
  5. The promises depend on God's grace, not human cunning (16:1—17:27).
  6. God's faithful servant intercedes with God for the wicked nations (18:1—19:38).
  7. Even deception by God's servant can result in blessing to God-fearing nations (20:1–18).
  8. God fulfills His promises both to His family and to the nations (21:1–21).
  9. God's obedient servant wins recognition from the nations (21:22–34).
  10. God tests His servant and renews His promises to the faithful servant (22:1–24).
  11. God's people begin to own the land (23:1–20).

G

12. God proves His faithfulness for the next generation (24:1–67).
13. God cares for the Arabian tribes (25:1–18).
B. God works through human conflicts to protect His people and His land (25:19—36:43).
   1. God works His purpose even in family conflicts (25:19–34).
   2. God renews His promises because of obedience of the old generations (26:1–5).
   3. God works through international conflict to preserve His people (26:6–35).
   4. God directs and blesses His people and the nations despite their family disputes (27:1—33:20).
   5. Human revenge and trickery accomplish nothing (34:1–31; compare 49:5–7).
   6. Recommitment to God brings renewal of His covenant promises (35:1–15).
   7. Death and sin do not mean the end of God's covenant people (35:16–29).
   8. God's leadership is evident even in the history of neighboring nations (36:1–43).
C. God brings reconciliation even in exile in an enemy land (37:1—50:26).
   1. Human jealousy brings hatred, separation, and grief (37:1–36).
   2. God works out His purposes despite human sin, injustice, and conniving (38:1–30).
   3. God's presence is the only blessing His servant needs (39:1–23).
   4. God leads through hardship to blessing and responsibility (40:1—41:52).
   5. God brings reconciliation through trial, confession, acceptance of responsibility, and forgiveness (41:53—45:28).
   6. God leads and rules even in a foreign kingdom (46:1—47:31).
   7. The patriarchal blessings belong to the tribes of Israel (48:1—49:33).
   8. Israel must responsibly fulfill the charges of the patriarchs (50:1–14).
   9. God renews His promises to a forgiving, faithful people (50:15–26).

Trent C. Butler

GENNESARET (Gĕn nĕs′ å rĕt) See *Galilee, Sea of.*

GENTILES (Gĕn′ tīles) People who are not part of God's chosen family at birth and thus can be considered "pagans." Though not synonymous in English "Gentiles," "nations," "pagans," "hea-thens" are variants chosen by translators to render *goyim* in Hebrew and *ethnoi* in Greek. "Gentile" and "nation" suggest race or territory, while "pagans" and "heathen" suggest religion.

The doctrine of election in which Israel became a holy nation (Ex. 19:16; Lev. 19:2) among the nations by the covenant at Sinai draws attention to the fact that no other nation has such a God or such laws. The writer of Deuteronomy forbad communion with the nations (Deut. 7:3,6,16). The Old Testament noted the filthy ways (Ezra 6:21) and worship abominations (2 Kings 16:3) of the nations.

Affliction by other nations increased tension between Israel and the nations which gave rise to invoking curses on the nations in the Psalms (Pss. 9; 59; 137). The ultimate punishment of Israel for disobedience was being scattered among the nations.

According to the prophets, the nations were under God's control and were unconsciously being used (Isa. 10:5–7); but in turn would be punished (Isa. 10:12–16). Joel depicted the judgment of the nations who had abused Israel in the valley of Jehoshaphat (Joel 3:12–16).

Solomon's prayer of dedication made clear that the door was never closed to the foreigner who wished to serve the Lord (1 Kings 8:41–43), and prophetic words and some Psalms depict the nations gathering to worship the God of Jacob (Pss. 86:9; 102:15–17; Isa. 2:2–4; Zeph. 3:9–10). The Lord is the sole God of all peoples (Isa. 45:22–24). Israel's mission was to bring justice (Isa. 42:1) and light to the nations (Isa. 49:6).

Jesus' ministry is interpreted in the Gospels in terms of Old Testament expectations for the Gentiles. He was a light to the Gentiles (Matt. 4:16–17; Luke 2:32). Though Jesus directed His work to Jews (Matt. 15:24) and at first limited His disciples to them (Matt. 10:5), He threatened that the kingdom would be taken from the Jews and given to a nation bringing its fruits (Matt. 21:43). Though Jesus was crucified by Gentiles (Matt. 20:19), equal blame is placed on both Gentiles and Jews (Acts 4:27).

Following the resurrection of Jesus, the commission included "all nations" (Matt. 28:19). The judgment scene in Jesus' parable envisioned "all nations" gathered before the glorious throne (Matt. 25:31,32). The promises included all those afar off (Acts 2:39). At the house of Cornelius, the Spirit was poured out on the Gentiles (Acts 10:45; 11:1,18; 15:7). The apostolic gathering in Jerusalem, by the apostolic letter, freed Gentiles from obedience to the law (Acts 15:19; compare 21:19,21,25).

In the apostolic preaching the promise to Abraham (Gen. 12:3; 18:18) found fulfillment (Gal. 3:8). Though in times past the Gentiles had been without God (Eph. 2:12–22), God in Christ broke through all boundries. Paul, sent to preach among the Gentiles (Acts 9:15; 22:21; 26:17; Gal. 1:16; 2:9) was in perils (2 Cor. 11:26). When rejected in the synagogues, he turned to the Gentiles (Acts 13:46; 18:6; 28:28), understanding his work in the light of Old Testament predictions (Acts 13:47,48; Rom. 15:9–12). As the apostle to the Gentiles (Gal. 2:8,9), claiming that in Christ racial distinctions were obliterated (Gal. 3:28), Paul proclaimed an equal opportunity of salvation (Rom. 1:16; 9:24; Col. 3:11; compare Acts 26:20,23). Gentiles were the wild branches in the allegory grafted into the olive tree (Rom. 11:16–25).

Paul experienced great resentment among the Jews because of the opportunity he was offering the Gentiles (2:15–16). Nevertheless, in New Testament thought, the church made up of Jew and Gentile was the holy nation, God's own people (1 Pet. 2:9).

The apocalypse with its shifting views, depicts a redeemed multitude of all nations (Rev. 5:9; 7:9), and the One who overcomes has power over the nations (Rev. 2:26), Babylon (Rev. 14:8; 18:2,23), the beast (Rev. 13:4), and the harlot (Rev. 17:15) are the deceivers of the nations. The devil is bound to deceive them no more (Rev. 20:3). All nations come to worship (Rev. 15:4) One born to rule with a rod of iron (Rev. 12:5). In the closing scenes of the book the nations walk in the light of the lamp of the Lamb; the glory of the nations is brought into the city (Rev. 21:23–24,26); the leaves of the tree of life are for the healing of the nations (Rev. 22:2).   *Jack P. Lewis*

GENUBATH (Gė nū′ băth) Personal name meaning, "theft" or "foreign guest." Son of Hadad, king of Edom, and the sister of Tahpenes, the wife of Egypt's pharaoh (1 Kings 11:19–20). The name of the Egyptian pharaoh is not known. See *Hadad.*

GERA (Gē′ rȧ) Personal name meaning, "stranger," "alien," or "sojourner." *1.* A son of Benjamin and grandson of Jacob (Gen. 46:21). *2.* Grandson of Benjamin (1 Chron. 8:3,5). Son of Ehud and clan head in Geba who was exiled to Manahath (1 Chron. 8:6–7). *3.* The Father of Ehud (Judg. 3:15, see *1.* above). *4.* Father of Shimei, who cursed David (2 Sam. 16:5). See *Shimei.*

GERAH (Gē′ rah) The smallest biblical measure of weight equaling one-twentieth of a shekel. See *Shekel; Weights and Measures.* Archaeological discoveries show a gerah weighed about half a gram.

GERAR (Gē′ rär) Place name possibly meaning, "drag away." City located between Gaza and Beersheba. Abraham and Isaac made treaties with the king of Gerar (Gen. 20; 26). Gerar was on the border of Canaanite territory (Gen. 10;19). TEV reads Gerar with the earliest Greek translation of 1 Chronicles 4:39–40. Other translations follow the

Hebrew reading Gedor. Gerar was the limit of Asa's pursuit of the defeated Ethiopians (2 Chron. 14:13–14). The site is possibly that of tell Abu Hureirah on the northwest side of Wadi Esh-Sheriah. Numerous potsherds from the Middle Bronze period (1800–1600 B.C.) indicate that the city flourished during the time of the patriarchs.

GERASA (Gĕr′ ȧ sȧ) Two places bear this name. One of them is referred to in the Bible; the other is not. See *Gadarene.*

The ruins of ancient Gerasa located in the modern country of Jordan.

The other Gerasa was located some twenty-six miles north of present-day Amman in Jordan. Its ruins are among the most excellently preserved in the Middle East. See *Arabia.*

G

The forum and colonnaded road of Gerasa (modern Jerash) as seen from the temple of Zeus.

GERASENES (Gĕr′ ȧ sēnes) Citizens of Gerasa. See *Gerasa.*

GERGESENES (Gēr′ gē sēnes) KJV reading in Matthew 8:28. Modern translations read, "Gadarenes." See *Gadarenes.*

GERIZIM AND EBAL (Gēr′ ĭ zĭm and Ē′ bȧl) Closely related place names meaning, "cut off ones" and "stripped one" or "baldy." Two mountains which form the sides of an important east-west pass in central Israel known as the valley of Shechem. Ancient Shechem lies at the east entrance of this valley, and modern Nablus stands in the narrow valley between the two mountains.

Gerizim (modern Jebel et-Tor) stands 2,849 feet above the Mediterranean and 700 feet above the valley. Ebal (modern Jebel Eslamiyeh) was located directly opposite Gerizim and is 2,950 feet above sea level. Both of the mountains are steep and rocky and perhaps gave reason to the probable meaning of Shechem: "shoulder(s)." The mountains, standing like two sentinels, could be fortified and assure control of this important valley.

When the Israelites conquered central Israel, Joshua carried out the directive given by Moses, and placed half of the tribes on Mount Gerizim to pronounce the blessing (Deut. 27:12) and the other half on Mount Ebal to pronounce the curses (Deut. 11:29; Josh. 8:30–35). Joshua built an altar on Ebal (Josh. 8:30).

Jotham proclaimed his famous kingship fable to the citizens of Shechem from Mount Gerizim (Judg. 9:7), thus using its sacred tradition to reinforce the authority of his message. After the Assyrians captured the Northern Kingdom, the mixed race of people began mixing pagan worship and worship of Yahweh (2 Kings 17:33).

Gerizim disappears from biblical history until after the Babylonian Exile and the Persian restoration. The Jewish historian Josephus reported that Alexander the Great gave permission to the Samaritans to build a temple on Mount Gerizim. Archaeologists think they have found remains of this temple, 66 x 66 feet and 30 feet high, built of uncut rocks without cement. Josephus also reported that John Hyrcanus destroyed the temple in 128 B.C. Archaeologists have also found remains of the temple to Zeus Hypsistos which Hadrian, the Roman emperor, built after A.D. 100. Over 1500 marble steps led to the pagan temple. The small Samaritan community continues to worship on Gerizim today, just as they did in Jesus' lifetime when He met the Samaritan woman drawing water from Jacob's well. She pointed to traditional worship on the mountain (John 4:20). See *Samaritans.*   *Jimmy Albright*

GERSHOM (Gēr′ shŏm) Personal name meaning, "sojourner there," "expelled one," or "protected of the god Shom." *1.* Firstborn son of Moses and Zipporah (Ex. 2:22). The inspired writer interpreted his name to mean "stranger" or "sojourner" from the Hebrew word *ger,* "sojourner." His birth became a further sign for Moses that he had done right in escaping Egypt, the birth occurring in Midian. Apparently Gershom was the son circumcised in the unusual ritual of Exodus 4:24–26 in which Zipporah delivered Moses when God sought to kill him. Thus Gershom represented protection for Moses. *2.* A son of Levi and head of a clan of Levitic priests (1 Chron. 6:16–20,43,62,71; 15:7). First Chronicles 23:14 shows that Moses' sons had been incorporated into the line of Levites. Compare 1 Chronicles 26:24. *3.* A man who accompanied Ezra on the return from Babylon to Jerusalem (Ezra 8:2). See *Gershon; Levites; Moses.*

GERSHOMITES (Gēr′ sho mītes) NRSV term for "sons of Gershom." See *Gershom.*

GERSHON (Gēr′ shŏn) Personal name meaning, "expelled" or "bell." Eldest son of Levi (Gen. 46:11). He was the progenitor of the Gershonites, who had specifically assigned responsibilities regarding the transporting of the tabernacle during the years of Israel's nomadic existence in the wilderness. Compare Exodus 6:16–17; Numbers 3:17–25; 4:22–41; 7:7; 10:17; 26:57; Joshua 21:6,27. First Chronicles often spells the name Gershom. See *Gershom; Levi; Priests and Levites.*

GERSHONITE (Gĕr' shŏn īte) Descendant of Gershon. See *Gershon.*

GERUTH (Gē' rüth) Part of a place name meaning, "hospitality" (Jer. 41:17) translated differently—KJV: "habitation of Chimham"; NAS, NRSV: "Geruth Chimham"; REB: "Kimham's holding." Fugitives stopped there near Bethlehem on their way to Egypt fleeing from Ishmael, who had killed Gedaliah, whom Babylon had appointed governor of Judah after the fall of Jerusalem in 586 B.C. It apparently designated an inn or lodging place near Bethlehem. It may have represented the first stop across the border from Judah into Egyptian-controlled territory.

GESHAM (Gĕsh' ăm) Personal name with variant spellings perhaps meaning, "rain." Son of Jahdai (1 Chron. 2:47). Earliest translations give varying spellings, followed by modern translators. Thus NAS, NIV, NRSV, REB read, Geshan, which is the actual Hebrew spelling. The early Greek traditions read Gershom and Sogar. Many of the names in the list are towns associated with Caleb, so that Gesham (Geshan) may also be a town.

GESHAN (Gĕsh' ăn) Personal name of uncertain meaning. See *Gesham.*

GESHEM (Gĕsh' ĕm) Personal name meaning, "rain." Arabian ruler of Kedar who joined Sanballat and Tobiah in opposing Nehemiah's efforts to rebuild the wall of Jerusalem (Neh. 2:19; 6:1–19). His name appears on a silver vessel dedicated by his son Qainu to the goddess Han-Ilat at tell el-Maskhuta in Lower Egypt. An inscription found in Dedan also appears to describe extensive territories Geshem controlled. He was in name a vassal of Persia but apparently wielded great personal power with tribes in the Syrian desert, southern Palestine, the delta of Egypt, and northern Arabia. He may have hoped to gain further control in Palestine and certainly did not want a local power to threaten him there. In 6:6 a variant spelling of his name—Gashmu—appears.

GESHUR (Gē' shûr) Place name perhaps meaning, "bridge." Small Aramean city-state between Bashan and Hermon. It served as a buffer between Israel and Aram. David married Maacah, daughter of the king of Geshur, who became mother of Absalom (1 Sam. 3:3), which caused the two lands to be on friendly terms. Absalom later retreated to his mother's homeland (2 Sam. 13:37–38). Nowhere do David's battle reports mention Geshur (2 Sam. 8; 10). Many scholars think Joshua 13:2 and 1 Sam 27:8 refer to a group of southern Philistine cities about which nothing else is known.

GESHURI (Gĕ shū' rī) KJV spelling for Geshurites. See *Geshur.*

GESHURITE (Gĕsh' ū rīte) Citizen of Geshur. See *Geshur.*

GESTURES Movements of either a part or part of the body to communicate one's thoughts and feelings. Gestures often may involve external objects such as the tearing of one's clothing (Joel 2:13) or the casting down of one's crown before God (Rev. 4:10). A gesture does not have to accompany verbal speech. Just a piercing look (Luke 22:61) is sufficient to communicate persuasively. In a certain sense all gestures are visual symbols.

Cultural-Corporal Gestures These are the most common to the everyday life and customs of the Ancient Near East.

Whole Body Gestures 1. Standing to pray indicates respect to God (1 Sam. 1:26; 1 Kings 8:22; Mark 11:25). *2.* Sitting may communicate several things. David's sitting before the Lord indicated reverence, humility, and submission (2 Sam. 7:18), while the sitting down of Jesus at the right hand of God indicates finality and completion as well as power and authority. (Heb. 10:12). *3.* Kneeling and bowing express honor, devotion, and submission in worship (1 Kings 19:18; Isa. 45:23; Rev. 4:10; 5:8) and reverence in prayer (1 Kings 8:54; 1 Kings 18:42; Dan. 6:10; Luke 22:41). *4.* Weeping is not only a sign of sorrow (Job 16:16; Jer. 9:10; Luke 22:62; John 11:35), but also of happiness (Gen. 46:29). *5.* Dancing shows joy (Ex. 15:20; Judg. 11:34) and celebration in praise (2 Sam. 6:16; Ps. 149:3). *6.* Tearing of one's clothes and heaping of ashes upon one's head signify deep grief (2 Sam. 1:11; 13:19), shocking horror (Num. 14:6; Josh. 7:6), and sudden alarm (Matt. 26:65; Acts 14:14).

Head Gestures 1. Shaking one's head communicates scorn and reproach (Ps. 22:7; Lam. 2:15; Matt. 27:39; Mark 15:29). *2.* Lifting one's head can indicate exaltation (Ps. 27:6), contempt (Ps. 83:2), and freedom (2 Kings 25:27). *3.* Bowing of one's head shows reverence in worship and prayer (Gen. 24:26; Neh. 8:6).

Face Gestures 1. Eye gestures are numerous and quite expressive. Winking the eye may show mischief and deceit (Prov. 6:13), which also can lead to sorrow (Prov. 10:10). Wanton eyes are sensual eyes that deserve condemnation (Isa. 3:16). Jesus' looking at Peter at the point of his denial is an example of eyes showing both hurt and condemnation (Luke 22:61). The lifting up of one's eyelids expresses haughtiness and pride (Prov. 30:13). One's eyes can show anger (Mark 3:5). The eyes, when uplifted in prayer, signify not only respectful acknowledgment of God, but also devotion to Him (Mark 6:41; Luke 9:16). To fail to lift one's eyes up to God while praying indicates one's sense of unworthiness (Luke 18:13). Jesus' lifting up of His eyes upon the disciples shows His personal regard for them

G

(Luke 6:20). *2.* Mouth gestures also are plentiful in the Scriptures. To smile and laugh can mean more than just happiness and joy; it also can show goodwill (Job 29:24), scorn (Ps. 22:7; Mark 5:40; Luke 8:53) or even rebuke (Ps. 2:4). The shooting out of the lip communicates the idea of contempt (Ps. 22:7). Kissing is an act that expresses the warmth of a friendly greeting (Rom. 16:16; 1 Cor. 16:20), the affection of one for another (Song of Sol. 8:1), the sorrow of one who dearly cares for another (Ruth 1:14; Acts 20:37), the deceit of one who hides true intentions (Prov. 27:6; Matt. 26:48), the submission of the weak to the strong (Ps. 2:12), and the seduction of a foolish man by a loose woman (Prov. 7:5–23). Spitting is an emphatic way of showing contempt in order to shame another (Deut. 25:9; Isa. 50:6; Matt. 26:67; 27:30). *3.* To incline one's ear is to give attention to another (Ps. 45:10; Jer. 7:26). *4.* An obscure gesture is the putting of the branch to the nose. This pagan gesture is an offense to God and possibly has obscene connotations (Ezek. 8:17). *5.* A hardened neck indicates stubbornness (Neh. 9:16; Prov. 29:1; Jer. 7:26), while an outstretched neck reveals haughtiness (Isa. 3:16).

Hand Gestures 1. The raising of hands in prayer is a gesture signifying one's request is unto God (Ps. 141:2; 1 Tim. 2:8). The raising of one's hands can also be a symbol of blessing (Lev. 9:22; Neh. 8:6; Luke 24:50), or it can be an act that gives emphasis to an oath (Deut. 32:40; Ezek. 20:5,15,23,28). *2.* The covering of one's mouth with the hand signifies silence (Job 29:9). *3.* The lifting up of one's hand or the shaking of one's fist means defiance (2 Sam. 18:28; Isa. 10:32; Zeph. 2:15). *4.* The laying of a hand or hands on someone can mean violence (Gen. 37:22), or it can mean favor and blessing as on a son (Gen. 48:14) or in healing (Luke 4:40; Acts 28:8). The placing of hands on someone's head shows favor and blessing as in the acknowledgment of an office (Acts 6:6) or in the coming of the Holy Spirit (Acts 8:17). The striking or shaking of hands indicates a guarantee or confirmation (Prov. 6:1; 17:18; 22:26), while the giving of one's hand to another is a sign of fellowship (2 Kings 10:15; Prov. 11:21). *5.* To clap one's hands can mean either contempt (Job 27:23; Lam. 2:15; Nah. 3:19) or joy and celebration (2 Kings 11:12; Pss. 47:1; 98:8; Isa. 55:12). *6.* The waving of one's hand can mean to beckon (Luke 5:7; John 13:24), to call for silence in order to speak (Acts 12:17; 13:16; 19:33), or to call on God for healing (2 Kings 5:11). *7.* The dropping of hands shows weakness and despair (Isa. 35:3; Heb. 12:12). *8.* A hand on one's head communicates grief (2 Sam. 13:19; Esther 6:12; Jer. 2:37). *9.* The washing of one's hands in public declares one's innocence (Deut. 21:6–7; Matt. 27:24). *10.* The pointing of a finger can show ill favor (Prov. 6:13) or accusation (Isa. 58:9). *11.* The hand or arm outstretched is a sign of power and authority (Ex. 6:6). *12.* To hug or embrace is to show warmth in greeting another (Gen. 33:4).

Feet Gestures 1. The placing of a foot upon one's enemy is a twofold gesture: it shows victory and dominance for the one standing and defeat and submission for the one downfallen and vanquished (Josh. 10:24; Ps. 110:1; 1 Cor. 15:25). *2.* To shake the dust off of one's feet is a sign of contempt and separation (Matt. 10:14; Acts 13:51). *3.* To wash the feet of another is to humble oneself as a servant (John 13:5–12). *4.* The lifting of one's heel against another shows opposition (Ps. 41:9; John 13:18). *5.* To cover one's feet is to relieve oneself with some degree of privacy (Judg. 3:24; 1 Sam. 24:3). *6.* To uncover one's feet or to walk barefooted indicates grief or repentance (2 Sam. 15:30; Isa. 20:2). *7.* The act of uncovering one's feet as in the case of Ruth with Boaz (Ruth 3:4) was an established practice indicating not only one's willingness to marry, but also the protection of the husband over his wife.

Religious-Ceremonial Gestures These are a more specialized category of gestures in which prescribed body movements take on a more clearly religious meaning than that found in the previous category.

Old Testament Sacrificial Gestures Two examples are sufficient to represent this limited category of gestures. *1.* Within the instructions given by Moses concerning the Passover are the following words: "And thus shall ye eat it; with your loins girded, your shoes on your feet, and your staff in your hand; and ye shall eat it in haste: it is the Lord's passover" (Ex. 12:11). All of these actions symbolize urgency and readiness. This whole body gesture is one of the profound ways that God chose to emphasize the abruptness and costliness of their freedom from bondage.

2. Another whole body gesture with special emphasis upon the hands is the act of offering a burnt offering unto God. If the offering came from the herd it was to be a male without blemish, and it was to be offered at the door of the tabernacle of the congregation as a free will offering. "And he shall put his hand upon the head of the burnt offering. . . . And he shall kill the bullock before the Lord . . . " (Lev. 1:4–5). The offering of this sacrifice emphasized God's holiness (a male without blemish) and human sinfulness and separation (only as far as the altar could a sinful person enter into the court of the tabernacle). The act expressed the need for substitution and death (the killing of the animal) and mediation (the ministry of the priests). In an ideal sense the act of coming to the entrance of the tabernacle was a public testimony of confession and commitment. The offering of a sacrifice was the language of covenant acted out in prayerful imagery. The act of putting one's hand upon the head of the animal and killing it served as the focal point of the offering for the sinner.

New Testament Sacrificial Gestures The two ordinances of the church continue the sacrificial theme. Both ordinances testify to the sacrificial death of Jesus Christ. *1.* The ordinance of baptism is a whole body gesture that expresses one's identification with Christ's atoning work: His death, burial, and resurrection. To be baptized (Matt. 28:19) is to testify publicly of one's total commitment to Jesus Christ as Savior and Lord. *2.* The Lord's Supper (Matt. 26:26–30; 1 Cor. 11:23–29) also emphasizes one's identification with the sacrificial death of Christ. It is through the observance of the Lord's Supper that one testifies to a willingness to deny oneself, and take up the cross (Matt. 16:24) to follow Christ.

Prophetic-Symbolical Gestures Prophets dramatized their message with symbolic gestures. Here examples are limited to the prophets Isaiah, Jeremiah, and Ezekiel. The use of symbolical gestures by the prophets could range from the simple and obvious, such as Ezekiel's mock attack against a clay model of Jerusalem to symbolize God's impending judgment on the city (Ezek. 4:1–3) to the complex and theological, such as Jeremiah's purchase of a field (Jer. 32:1–44) to symbolize God's future restoration of the Southern Kingdom as its Kinsman (*go' el)* Redeemer.

In Isaiah 20:3, Isaiah "walked naked and barefoot three years" as a symbol of the humiliation that Egypt and Ethiopia were to know when As-

syria conquered them. In Jeremiah 27:1–7, Jeremiah wore a yoke of wood around his neck as a symbol of the future domination of the Babylonians over Judah and her neighbors; therefore, Jeremiah's message was one of submission to Babylonian rule. Ezekiel more than any other was known for his use of prophetic-symbolic acts. His laying on his side for many days (Ezek. 4:4–8) indicated a year for each day of their iniquity and of their impending siege. His eating of scant rations (Ezek. 4:9–17), the cutting of his hair and its various consequences (Ezek. 5:1–17), and the setting of his face toward the mountains of Israel (Ezek. 6:1–7) were all symbolic gestures which showed the judgment of God that soon was to come upon his people. (See also Ezek. 12:1–28 for additional examples.) See *Festivals; Ordinances; Prophets; Sacrifice and Offering; Symbol.*   *Gary A. Galeotti*

GETHER (Gē' thēr) Aramean tribal name of uncertain meaning. They are Semites, their original ancestor being the grandson of Shem and great grandson of Noah (Gen. 10:23). Nothing else is known of them.

GETHSEMANE (Gĕth sĕm' å nē) Place name meaning, "olive press." Place where Jesus went after the Last Supper, a garden outside the city, across the Kidron on the Mount of Olives (Matt. 26:36–56; Mark 14:32–52; Luke 22:39–53; John 18:1–14). Here Jesus charged the disciples to "watch" as He prayed. Judas led the enemies of

Looking toward the Garden of Gethsemane with the Church of All Nations in the center of the photo.

G

Jesus to Gethsemane where Jesus was arrested and taken away for trial. Here Jesus, the Son, showed He had learned obedience to the Father even in suffering (Heb. 5:7–9).

Gethsemane was probably a remote walled garden (Jesus "entered" and "went out") where Jesus went often for prayer, rest, and fellowship with His disciples.

See *Mount of Olives; Kidron; Judas.*

Wayne Dehoney

Inside the Garden of Gethsemane the olive trees and foliage provide a beautiful and tranquil scene.

GEUEL (Gē ū′ ēl) Personal name meaning, "pride of God." Spy from tribe of Gad Moses sent to inspect the land before conquering it (Num. 13:15).

GEZER (Gē′ zẽr) Place name meaning, "isolated area." Major Canaanite city nineteen miles northwest of Jerusalem at tell Gezer on the edge of the foothills of Judah near the Shephelah, seven miles southeast of Ramleh. It provides a military post for the highway junction of the Via Maris and the road leading to the valley of Ajalon to Jerusalem, Jericho, and over the Jordan. A site of 30 acres, it was one of the largest and most important cities in Palestine from 1800 B.C. onwards, though occupation reaches back to 3500 B.C. Archaeologists have found important inscriptions here such as the Gezer calendar, one of, if not the, earliest

Tel Gezer.

(before 900 B.C.) examples of Hebrew writing known. Even earlier is an inscribed piece of broken pottery in the "Proto-Sinaitic" script. The largest stone structure in Palestine, a fifty-foot wide wall from about 1600 B.C. was found here. A high place or sanctuary with ten stone stele or masseboth demonstrates Canaanite worship practices about 1600 B.C. Some of these tower over nine feet high. Egyptian sources mention Gezer about 1410 B.C., as do the Amarna letters of 100 years later. Three different kings of Gezer wrote the Egyptian pharaoh. Merneptah's stele from about 1200 B.C. claims the pharaoh captured Gezer. Tiglath-pileser III of Assyria pictured the capture of Gezer about 734 B.C. in his palace at Nimrud.

Joshua defeated the king of Gezer when he tried to aid the king of Lachish (Josh. 10:33). Gezer formed the boundary for Ephraim's tribal allotment (Josh. 16:3), but Israel did not control the city (Josh. 16:10; Judg. 1:29). Still, it was assigned as a city for the Levites (Josh. 21:21). David finally wrested control of it from the Philistines (2 Sam. 5:25; 1 Chron. 20:4). A few years later, Egypt's pharaoh captured the city from the Canaanites and gave it to Solomon as a wedding gift for Solomon's marriage with the pharaoh's daughter. Solomon rebuilt its walls (1 Kings 9:15–17). Between the Testaments, Gezer became known as Gazara.

GEZRITE (Gĕz′ rīte) KJV spelling of name of people in 1 Samuel 27:8, where the Hebrew text tradition shows both Girzites (NIV, NAS, NRSV, TEV) and Gezrite. REB reads Gizrite. Gezrite or Gizrite would refer to inhabitants of Gezer, but Gezer is too far north for the Samuel context. We know nothing else of the Girzites. First Samuel 27:8 says they had lived in the southwestern edge of Palestine from time immemorial and that David raided them from his base at Ziklag.

GHOST The KJV uses ghost in two senses, for the human life force and for God's Holy Spirit. The KJV never uses ghost for the disembodied spirits of the dead. All eleven Old Testament references involve the phrase "give up the ghost" (for example, Gen. 25:8; 35:29) which means to cease breathing or simply to die. This phrase occurs eight times in the New Testament (Matt. 27:50; Acts 5:5; 12:23). The predominant New Testament use is for the Holy Spirit.

Modern translations use ghost (rather than spirit as the KJV) for the disembodied spirits of the dead. Jesus' disciples mistook Him for a ghost when He walked on water (Matt. 14:26; Mark 6:49) and when He appeared after the resurrection (Luke 24:37,39).

GIAH (Gī′ ah) Place name meaning, "bubbling." Place where David's general Joab confronted Abner, Saul's general, after Abner killed Joab's brother Asahel (2 Sam. 2:24). The earliest translations saw Giah as a common noun meaning, "valley." Its location near Gibeon is not known.

GIANTS Persons of unusual stature who often are reputed to possess great strength and power. **Old Testament** The earliest biblical reference to giants is to the *nephilim* born to the "daughters of men" and the "sons of God" (Gen. 6:1–4). Interpreters differ on the origin of these giants. Some understand the "sons of God" to be angelic beings who intermarried with human women (see Jude 6). Others view them as descendants of Seth who intermarried with the ungodly. Later descendants of the *nephilim* were called "the sons of Anak" (Num. 13:33) or *Anakim* (Deut. 2:11; 9:2). They inhabited the land of Canaan prior to Israel's conquest. Egyptian records testify to their presence as early as 2000 B.C. Similar races of giants had also inhabited Moab (Deut. 2:9–10) and Ammon (Deut. 2:19–20).

A second class of giants who inhabited pre-Israelite Palestine was the *rephaim*. Their last survivor was Og, king of Bashan (Deut. 3:11,13). A valley near Jerusalem (Josh. 15:8; 18:16) and part of the wooded country in the tribal territory of Ephraim (Josh. 17:15) retained their name.

The Old Testament also records cases of individual giants. The well-known Goliath (1 Sam. 17) was a Philistine champion. A family of giants from Gath were among the Philistine enemies slain by David and his followers (2 Sam. 21:16–22; 1 Chron. 20:4–8).   *Michael Fink*

GIBBAR (Gĭb' bär) Personal name meaning, "young, powerful man." A man, ninety-five of whose descendants returned from Babylonian captivity with Zerubbabel in 537 B.C. (Ezra 2:20). The corresponding list in Nehemiah 7:25 has Gibeon.

GIBBETHON (Gĭb' bĕ thŏn) Place name meaning, "arched," "hill," or "mound." City in the tribal territory of Dan (Josh. 19:44) but assigned to the Levites (Josh. 21:23). During the monarchy the Philistines controlled Gibbethon. Nadab of Israel (909-908 B.C.) besieged it. During the siege Baasha murdered Nadab and assumed the kingship (1 Kings 15:25–28). The Israelite army was encamped against Philistine Gibbethon when Zimri assumed rule by assassinating Elah, the son of Baasha (1 Kings 16:15–17). Gibbethon has been variously identified as tell el-Melat north of Ekron, and with Agir, two and a half miles west of tell el-Melat.

GIBEA (Gĭb' ĕ à) Personal name meaning, "hill." Son of Caleb by his concubine Maacah (1 Chron. 2:49). See *Gibeah.*

GIBEAH (Gĭb' ĕ àh) Place name meaning, "a hill," closely related to names of Geba and Gib-

eon. Gibeah or Gibeath was the name of four different places in the Old Testament. *1.* City in hill country of Judah allotted to tribe of Judah (Josh. 15:57). This may be the home of King Abijah's wife Maacah (2 Chron. 13:2) and could be same as the place name presupposed in the list of Caleb's descendants (1 Chron. 2:49), a list including city names rather than personal names, perhaps indicating the clans who originally inhabited the cities. This Gibeah has usually been located at el-Jeba, seven and a half miles southwest of Bethlehem, but this is too far north to be connected with clans of Caleb. Otherwise, the location is not known.

2. A city closely connected with Phinehas, the high priest and grandson of Aaron. Phinehas buried his father Eleazar there (Josh. 24:33). Some try to locate this on a hill near Shechem or Bethel. Others would identify it with the levitical city of Geba in Joshua 21:17 in the territory of Benjamin. The Bible simply uses the general term "hill country of Ephraim." It could even be near Shiloh.

3. The ark was lodged on a hill (Hebrew, Gibeah) during the period between its return by the Philistines and David's initial effort to move it to Jerusalem (2 Sam. 6:4 KJV). The Hebrew word is probably not a proper noun (Hebrew writing not distinguishing proper names with capital letters as does English). The best translation may be "hill" (NAS, NIV, NRSV, REB; compare 1 Sam. 7:1–2). The hill here is apparently near Kiriath-jearim or Baalah. See *Baalah;* compare Joshua 15:9–11.

4. The most significant Gibeah was the city in the tribal territory of Benjamin (Josh. 18:28). A bloody civil war between Benjamin and the other Israelite tribes broke out when the men of Gibeah raped a traveling Levite's concubine (Judg. 19:1—21:25). Saul had close family connections to the city (1 Chron. 8:29–33 also connects them with the nearby and similar-sounding Gibeon; see *Gibeon)* and made it his capital after he became king (1 Sam. 10:5,26; 15:34; 23:19). If the "hill of God" (1 Sam. 10:5 KJV, NAS, REB) or "Gibeath-elohim" (NRSV) should be translated "Gibeah of God" (NIV) and equated with Gibeah of Saul, then the Philistines controlled the city prior to Saul gaining control. Apparently the Philistines built a fortress there which Saul took over, or Saul constructed his own royal complex, since archaeologists have uncovered a fortress from this period. After Saul's death, the city declined. Hosea and Isaiah referred to it during the eighth century B.C. (Isa. 10:29; Hos. 5:8; 9:9; 10:9). Isaiah shows it was on the natural path of march for an enemy army such as the Assyrians attacking Jerusalem from the north. Archaeologists have shown the city flourished once more after the destruction of Jerusalem and again in the Maccabean age.

Gibeah is located at tell el-Ful on a high ridge three and a half miles north of Jerusalem. See *Benjamin; Geba; Saul.*   *LeBron Matthews*

G

GIBEATH (Gĭb′ ė äth) Alternative Hebrew spelling for Gibeah (Josh. 18:28) preserved in KJV spelling. See *Gibeah.*

GIBEATH-ELOHIM (Gĭb′ ē äth-ĕ lō′ hĭm) Place name meaning, "hill of God." See *Geba; Gibeah.*

GIBEATH-HAARALOTH (Gĭb′ ė äth-hä är′ ȧ lōth) Place name meaning, "hill of foreskins." KJV translates the place name in Joshua 5:3, while modern translations transliterate it. Joshua used traditional flint stone knives rather than more modern metal ones to circumcise the Israelite generation about to conquer Canaan.

GIBEATHITE (Gĭb ė′ ȧ thīte) Citizen of Gibeah (1 Chron. 12:3). See *Gibeah.*

GIBEON (Ḡĭb′ ė ŏn) Place name meaning, "hill place." This "great city" (Josh. 10:2) played a significant role in Old Testament history—especially during the conquest of Canaan. Archaeology has demonstrated that the city was a thriving industrial area which made it a primary community in Canaan.

Background of the City Little was known of Gibeon's exact location until the twentieth century. Originally, the city was assigned to the tribe of Benjamin following Israel's victory in Canaan (Josh. 18:25) and made a city for Levites (Josh. 21:17). Beginning in 1956, excavations led by James B. Pritchard gave proof that the modern city of el-Jib was the site of ancient Gibeon. Lying eight miles northwest of Jerusalem, Gibeon was in an area of moderate climate, ample rainfall, with a wine-led economy. With an elevation of about 2400 feet Gibeon towered above most other cities, making it easily defended. Dating to about 3000 B.C., Gibeon served as the fortress city at the head of the valley of Ajalon which provided the principal access from the coastal plain into the hill country. Gibeon's power was strong as archaeology has found no sign of the city's destruction.

Role of the City in the Bible Forty-five Old Testa-

The pool at ancient Gibeon with a spiral staircase leading down to the water level.

ment references are made to Gibeon. Its first major appearance in Israel's history involved the conquest of Canaan. The people of Gibeon concocted a deceptive strategy to protect themselves from the Israelites (Josh. 9). Pretending to be foreigners also, the Gibeonites made a treaty with Joshua. When Joshua later discovered the truth, he forced the Gibeonites to become water carriers and woodcutters for the Israelites. Honoring this covenant, Joshua led Israel against the armies of five kings who had attacked Gibeon. During these victories the Lord caused the sun and moon to stand still (Josh. 10; compare Isa. 28:21).

By the time of David, Gibeon had become part of Israel's United Monarchy. Saul's family seems to have had some connections to Gibeon (1 Chron. 8:29–33; 9:35–39). See *Gibeah.* Following Saul's death a crucial meeting occurred in Gibeon involving Abner and Joab, the respective generals of Saul and David (2 Sam. 2:12–17). A "sporting" battle (v. 14) by the pool of Gibeon ensued in which the men of Joab proved to be victorious. Archaeologists have discovered a spiraling shaft and tunnel with circular stairway leading to water and providing the city a way to get water inside the city walls during enemy attacks. Gibeon also played host to part of Sheba's rebellion against David (2 Sam. 20:8–13). Joab pursued Amasa, a leader of the revolt, to the great stone in Gibeon where Joab left him "wallowing in his blood in the middle of the highway" (v. 12 NAS). Discovering that Saul had broken the covenant by killing some of the Gibeonites, David gave seven of Saul's male descendants to the people of Gibeon who then put the seven to death (2 Sam. 21:1–9). During one of the sacrifices Solomon made in Gibeon, the Lord appeared and granted the new king's request for wisdom (1 Kings 3:3–14; compare 9:2). Apparently Gibeon was Israel's major place of worship before Solomon built the Temple.

The next references to Gibeon took place about 600 B.C. Jeremiah spoke of the coming destruction of Jerusalem, contradicting Hananiah of Gibeon who predicted Nebuchadnezzar's doom (Jer. 28). Fleeing from justice, Ishmael, the murderer of the Babylonian-appointed "governor" Gedaliah, was overtaken at Gibeon (Jer. 41).

Final references to Gibeon highlighted the city's role in post-exilic Israel. The Gibeonites assisted in rebuilding Jerusalem's walls (Neh. 3:7). Nehemiah's list of the returning exiles also included an entry concerning the number of "the children of Gibeon" (7:25).

See *Canaan; David; Joshua.* *Larry McGraw*

GIBEONITE (Gĭb′ ė on īte) Citizen of Gibeon. See *Gibeon.*

GIBLITE (Gĭb′ līte) KJV spelling of Gibalites. See *Gebal.*

GIDDALTI (Gĭd dăl′ tī) Personal name meaning, "I brought from there" or "I made great, praised." Son of Heman to whom David gave the task of prophesying through playing musical instruments (1 Chron. 25:4). He became a leader of a clan of Temple musicians (1 Chron. 25:29).

GIDDEL (Gĭd′ dĕl) Personal name meaning, "he made great, praised." *1.* The clan leader of a group of Temple servants who returned from the Babylonian captivity with Zerubbabel about 537 B.C. (Ezra 2:47). *2.* Original clan father of a group of royal servants who returned from the Babylonian Exile with Zerubbabel about 537 B.C. (Ezra 2:56).

GIDEON (Gĭd ė on) Personal name meaning, "one who cuts to pieces." The fifth major judge of twelfth century Israel. He was also called Jerubbaal and was the son of Joash of the tribe of Manasseh. He judged for forty years (Judg. 6:11— 8:35). See *Jerubaal.*

Gideon was given the task of delivering the Israelites from the Midianites and Amalekites, desert nomads who repeatedly raided the country. Their use of the camel allowed them to ride in, destroy crops, take plunder, and then escape back into the desert with such speed the Israelites could not catch them. Gideon was not a willing volunteer. Although he knew the will of God, twice he laid out the fleece in what seems an effort to avoid the will of God by imposing impossible conditions. God met his conditions both times and then set out the strategy that would guarantee victory for Israel.

To reduce their number, two tests were given to the 32,000 men in Gideon's army. This was done that Israel could not claim victory by any other means than continued dependence upon God. Those who were afraid and those who knelt down to get a drink of water were sent home. The remaining 300 were given pitchers, torches, and trumpets, and placed around the Midianite encampment. The strategy was one of terror: at Gideon's signal the pitchers were broken, the torches then became visible, and the trumpets sounded, giving the enemy the impression they were surrounded. They took flight, their leaders were killed, and the Midianite oppression was brought to an end.

The hero of faith (Hebrews 11:32) ended life on a sad note. He angrily punished Succoth and Penuel for not helping in his war against the Midianite kings (Judg. 8:1–17). He refused the people's offer to crown him king, testifying that only God was King (Judg. 8:22–23), but he ordered the people to give him their golden earrings, taken as war spoil from the Ishmaelites. He made a worship symbol, an ephod, out of it and led his people astray with it (Judg. 8:24–27). His family did not follow his God (Judg. 8:33).

See *Camel; Judge; Midianites.*

Darlene R. Gautsch

GIDEONI (Gĭd ė ō′ nī) Personal name meaning, "one who cuts down or cuts to pieces." Father of Abidan, a leader of the tribe of Benjamin during the encampment in the wilderness (Num. 1:11; 2:22; 7:60; 10:24).

GIDOM (Gī′ dŏm) Place name meaning, "cleared land." Place where tribes of Israel punished tribe of Benjamin by killing 2,000 of Benjamin's soldiers (Judg. 20:45) for grossly mistreating a traveling Levite and his concubine. REB follows some scholars in omitting Gidom. No one knows its exact location between Gibeah and Bethel.

GIFT, GIVING A favor or item bestowed on someone. Gifts were given on numerous occasions for a variety of purposes: as dowry for a wife (Gen. 34:12); as tribute to a military conqueror (2 Sam. 8:2); as bribes (Ex. 23:8; Prov. 17:8; Isa. 1:23); as rewards for faithful service and to insure future loyalty (Dan. 2:48); and as relief for the poor (Esth. 9:22). Since gifts might be required by custom, law, or force, modifiers are sometimes used to specify gifts given voluntarily: "willing" or freewill offerings or gifts (Ex. 35:29); free gift or "gift by grace" (Rom. 5:15–17; 6:23); bountiful gift not motivated by covetousness (2 Cor. 9:5).

Both Testaments witness to God as the giver of every good gift (1 Chron. 29:14; Jas. 1:17). Human life is God's gift (Job 1:21), as are all things necessary for physical life: the sun for light (Jer. 31:25); plants (Gen. 1:29) and animals for food (Gen. 9:3); water (Num. 21:16); clothing (Gen. 28:20); grass for herds (Deut. 11:15); seasonal rains for crops (Lev. 26:4); companionship of male and female (Gen. 2:18–24; compare 3:12); the ability to have children (Gen. 17:16); and sleep (Ps. 127:2). Various human abilities are likewise given by God: the ability to work (Deut. 8:18); artistic abilities (Ex. 31:6); the ability to acquire learning and master communication skills (Dan. 1:17). These gifts demonstrate God's general providence.

Scripture also witnesses to God's gifts as evidence of a special providence. In the Old Testament such gifts include: the Promised Land (Gen. 12:7)—including its successful conquest (Deut. 2:36), possessing its cities (Deut. 6:10), and its spoils (Deut. 20:14); the sabbath (Ex. 16:29); the promises (1 Kings 8:56); the covenants (2 Kings 17:15); the law (Ex. 24:12); and peace (Lev. 26:6). In the New Testament God's special providence is especially evident in the gift of God's Son (John 3:16) and of God's Holy Spirit (Luke 11:13).

G

The springs of Harod where Gideon divided his men for battle against the Midianites.

God makes relationship with Himself possible by giving His people wisdom (1 Kings 4:29), understanding (1 Kings 3:9), a new heart (1 Sam. 10:9), and a good Spirit to teach them (Neh. 9:20). The New Testament expresses these gifts as the power to become children of God (John 1:12), justification from sin (Rom. 3:24; 5:15–17); and eternal life (John 10:28; Rom. 6:23).

Both Testaments witness to God's gift of leadership to God's people as: priests (Num. 8:19; Zech. 3:7); Davidic kings (2 Chron. 13:5); deliverers (2 Kings 13:5); shepherds with Godlike hearts (Jer. 3:15); apostles, prophets, evangelists, and pastor-teachers (Eph. 4:11–12). Paul spoke of God's giving the ministry of reconciliation (2 Cor. 5:18), authority for building up the church (2 Cor. 10:8), and grace for sharing the gospel with the Gentiles (Eph. 3:8). The New Testament also stresses God's gift of spiritual abilities to every believer (Rom. 12:6; 1 Cor. 12:4; 1 Pet. 4:10).

God's gifts should prompt the proper response from the recipients. This response includes not boasting (1 Cor. 4:7; Eph. 2:8); amazement at God's inexpressible goodness (2 Cor. 9:15); the using of gifts for the furtherance of Christ's kingdom (1 Tim. 4:14; 2 Tim. 1:6–11); and a life of good works (Eph. 2:10).   *Chris Church*

GIFTS, SPIRITUAL See *Spiritual Gifts.*

GIHON (Gī' hon) Place name meaning, "gushing fountain." The primary water supply for Jerusalem and one of the four rivers into which the river of Eden divided (Gen. 2:13). The river cannot be identified with any contemporary river.

During the Old Testament period the spring of Gihon was the primary water supply for the city of Jerusalem. The name comes from a Hebrew word meaning, "a bursting forth," and is descriptive of the spring which is located in the Kidron Valley. It does not produce a steady flow, but gushes out at irregular intervals, twice a day in the dry season to four or five times in the rainy season. Water issues from a crack sixteen feet long in the rock. At some point in the ancient past a wall was built at the eastern end of the crack, diverting water into a cave at the other end. In the Jebusite period before David a shaft went from the spring to a pool under the city. Water jugs were let down into the pool through another vertical shaft. This probably was the way Joab entered into the city and captured it for David (2 Sam. 5:8; 1 Chron. 11:6). During the early Israelite occupation, water was collected outside the city walls in an open basin called the "upper pool" (Isa. 7:3). An open aqueduct carried water from there to the "old pool" at the southern end of the city (Isa. 22:11; cf. Isa. 8:6). Along this conduit Isaiah confronted Ahaz (Isa. 7:3), and later Sennacherib's army demanded the city's surrender (2 Kings 18:17). Before Sennacherib's arrival, Hezekiah plugged the aqueduct and dug his famous water tunnel (2 Kings 20:20; 2 Chron. 32:30).

See *Eden; Hezekiah; Jerusalem; Kidron Valley; Siloam; Water.*   *LeBron Matthews*

GILALAI (Gĭl' á laî) Personal name perhaps meaning, "rolled away." Temple musician who helped Nehemiah lead the thanksgiving service for the completion of the Jerusalem wall (Neh. 12:36).

GILBOA (Gĭl bō' á) Place name of uncertain meaning, perhaps, "hill country" or "bubbling fountain." Location of an Israelite encampment (1 Sam. 28:4). The Israelites under Saul were preparing to do battle against the Philistines. At

Mount Gilboa in the distance.

Mount Gilboa Saul and his three sons were slain (1 Sam. 31:8). David sang a lament over the Gilboa tragedy (2 Sam. 1:17–27). Mount Gilboa has been identified with modern Jebel Fuqu'ah, on the eastern side of the Plain of Esdraelon. See *Palestine; Saul.*

GILEAD (Gĭl' ė ád) Place and personal name meaning, "raw" or "rugged." *1.* The north-central section of the transjordanian highlands. The name may originally have applied to a very small area. The usage of the name then grew and could be applied in different contexts depending on present political situations. Compare Judg. 10:17; Hos. 6:8. It occupies the mountain slopes and tableland east of the Jordan, northeast of the Dead Sea. Gilead is bisected by the Jabbok River; in Old Testament times the kingdom of Ammon occupied its eastern fringe. It was often contested by other nations (Amos 1:3). Gilead extends about 50 miles from southern Heshbon not quite to the Yarmuk River in the north. Its east-west extent is about twenty miles.

Physically, Gilead is a rugged country; the Hebrew name *Gil'ad* may be translated "rugged." Some of its peaks reach over 3500 feet. It also has plains with grassland suitable for cattle, and in antiquity the northern half of the region particu-

The rugged hill country of Gilead.

larly was heavily forested. The King Highway, an important international trade route, passed through Gilead. Gilead was an agriculturally significant region as well. It was famous especially for its flocks and herds, and also for the balm of Gilead, an aromatic and medicinal preparation, probably derived from the resin of a small balsam tree.

Many famous persons and events are associated with Gilead. The judges Jair and Jephthah (Judg. 11:1), Israel's King Jehu, and the prophet Elijah were all Gileadites. Jacob and Laban met at its northeastern border (Gen. 31:22–23). Jacob encountered the angel of God at Peniel in Gilead (Gen. 32:30). Saul's son Ish-bosheth (2 Sam. 2:8), David (2 Sam. 17:24), and Jesus all retreated to Gilead for a time. Old Testament cities of importance were Heshbon in the south, Rabboth-ammon on the eastern desert fringe, Jabesh-gilead, and Ramoth-gilead. Rabboth-ammon is the New Testament Philadelphia; Pella and Jerash (Gerasa) are other important New Testament cities.

2. Great grandson of Joseph and original clan leader in tribe of Manasseh (Num. 26:28–32; 36:1). The clan was so strong it could be listed with Israel's tribes in Deborah's song (Judg. 5:17). They fought for recognition among other tribes (Judg. 12:4–7).   *Joseph Coleson*

GILEADITE (Gĭl′ ė ȧd īte) Citizen of Gilead. See *Gilead.*

GILGAL (Gĭl′ gȧl) Place name meaning, "circle," and probably referring to a circle of stones or a circular altar. Such a circle of stones could be found almost anywhere in Palestine and led easily to naming towns "Gilgal." The many references to Gilgal in the Old Testament cannot thus be definitely connected to the same town, since several different Gilgals may well have existed.

1. Gilgal is most closely associated with Joshua, but the number of Gilgals involved continues an unsolved question. After crossing the Jordan, Joshua established the first camp at Gilgal (Josh. 4:19). There Joshua took twelve stones from the bed of the river to set up a memorial for the miraculous crossing. Gilgal, the first foothold on Palestinian soil, became Israel's first worship place, where they were circumcised and observed the Passover. There God appeared to Joshua and affirmed his mission (Josh. 5). This Gilgal apparently became Israel's military base of operations (Josh. 9:6; 10:6; 14:6), though some scholars would identify this with a Gilgal farther north near Shechem. Joshua set up Gilgal as the border between Judah and Benjamin (Josh. 15:7; compare 18:17), though many Bible students think the border town must be south of the original camp. Ehud, the judge, passed Gilgal in his mission to slay the king of Moab (Judg. 3:19,26). David passed through Gilgal as he fled from Absalom (2 Sam. 19:15,40). This Gilgal is often located at modern khirbet Mefjir, a little more than a mile east of Jericho. Others would locate it at khirbet en-Nitleh, two miles southeast of Jericho.

Still others remain baffled at finding a location. The boundary town is often seen as khan el-Ahmar or 'Araq ed-Deir. The military camp is at times located at tell Jiljulieh east of Shechem but without archaeological support. This could be the same Gilgal of Deuteronomy 11:30, if Joshua's original town is not meant. Gilgal was also one of the three places where Samuel annually held circuit court (1 Sam. 7:16). This could be near tell Jiljulieh or at Joshua's first landing place near the Jordan. Saul was both crowned and rejected as king at Gilgal (1 Sam. 11:14–15; 13:14–15). Gilgal established itself as a major place of worship for Israel with ancient traditions. However, it also permitted worship associated with other gods and became the object of prophetic judgment (Hos. 4:15; Amos 4:4; 5:5).

2. Elijah and Elisha were associated closely with Gilgal. At one time Elisha made his headquarters there (2 Kings 4:38), where Elijah was taken up into heaven (2 Kings 2:1). This was apparently tell Jiljulieh about three miles southeast of Shiloh, though it could still be Joshua's original Gilgal.

3. Gilgal of the nations is mentioned as a royal city near Dor (Josh. 12:23). The earliest Greek translation reads this as "kings of the nations in Galilee," which many scholars think is the original reading, a copyist of the Hebrew text using the word "Gilgal" since it had become familiar in the earlier chapters of Joshua. If the Hebrew Gilgal is original, its location is not known.

See *Beth-gilgal; Elisha; Joshua; Samuel; Saul.*
Kenneth Craig

GILO (Gī' lō) RSV, TEV spelling of Giloh to refer to Gilonite (2 Sam. 23:34). See *Giloh.*

GILOH (Gī' lōh) Place name meaning, "uncovered" or "revealed." Town in tribal allotment of Judah in Judean hills (Josh. 15:51). David's counselor Ahithophel came from Giloh (2 Sam. 15:12). Some scholars locate it at khirbet Jala in the suburbs of Jerusalem, but most think Giloh was actually further south.

GILONITE (Gī' lō nīte) Citizen of Giloh. See *Giloh.*

GIMZO (Gĭm' zō) Place name of uncertain meaning. Town in the Shephelah or valley of Judah which the Philistines captured from King Ahaz of Judah (735-715 B.C.), leading him to ask Assyria for help and pay tribute to them (2 Chron. 28:18). It is located at Gimzu, about four miles east of Ramleh and three miles southeast of Lod.

GIN KJV term for a trap or snare. With the exception of Amos 3:5, all scriptural uses are figurative, either of the fate of the wicked (Job 18:9; Isa. 8:14) or of the schemes of the wicked (Pss. 140:5; 141:9). See *Fowler.*

GINATH (Gī' năth) Place name or personal name meaning, "wall" or "enclosure." Father of Tibni, the favorite of half of Israel for kingship when Omri became king about 885 B.C. (1 Kings 16:21). See *Tibni.*

GINNETHO (Gĭn' nė thō) KJV spelling in Nehemiah 12:4 of Levite who returned from Babylonian captivity with Zerubbabel about 537 B.C. Hebrew texts have various spellings followed by modern translations: Ginnethon (NIV; REB); Ginnethoi (NAS, TEV, NRSV). This is apparently the same person listed as head of a clan of priests in 12:16. Probably the person who signed Nehemiah's covenant (10:6) belonged to the same family.

GINNETHOI (Gĭn' nė thôi) See *Ginnetho.*

GINNETHON (Gĭn' nė thŏn) See *Ginnetho.*

GIRDLE Several items of clothing in KJV: (1) an ornate sash worn by the officiating priests (Ex. 28:4,40) and by the wealthy of Jerusalem (Isa. 3:24); (2) a decorated band (NRSV), woven belt (TEV, NAS), or waistband (NIV, REB) for the high priest's ephod (Ex. 28:8,27,28); (3) a belt on which a sword or bow might be carried (1 Sam. 18:4; 2 Sam. 20:8; perhaps Isa. 5:27); a leather belt forming part of the proverbial garb of the prophets (2 Kings 1:8; Matt. 3:4); (4) an undergarment (Job 12:18; Jer. 13:1–11), often rendered waistcloth or loincloth.

To gird up one's loins means literally to tuck the loose ends of one's outer garment into one's belt. Loins were girded in preparation for running (1 Kings 18:46), for battle (Isa. 5:27), or for service for a master (Luke 12:35). The call to "gird up the loins of your minds" (1 Peter 1:13) means to be spiritually alert and prepared. See *Cloth, Clothing.*

GIRGASHITE (Gĭr' ġȧ shīte) Tribal name possibly meaning, "sojourner with a deity." One of the list of original tribal groups inhabiting Canaan, traced back to Canaan, son of Ham and grandson of Noah (Gen. 10:16). The Ugaritic texts from Ras Shamra also apparently mention them.

GIRGASITE (Gĭr' ġȧ sīte) KJV spelling for Girgashite in Genesis 10:16. See *Girgashite.*

GIRZITE (Gĭr' zīte) See *Gezrite.*

GISHPA (Gĭsh' pȧ) Personal name of uncertain meaning. Supervisor of Temple servants in days of Nehemiah (Neh. 11:21). It does not appear in the lists in Chronicles and Ezra, so some Bible students think the name is a copyist's change from Hasupha, which the Jews would pronounce similarly (Ezra 2:43; Neh. 7:46).

GISPA (Gĭs' pà) KJV spelling of Gishpa. See *Gishpa.*

GITTAH-HEPHER (Gĭt' tăh-hē' phĕr) KJV spelling for Gath-hepher (Josh. 19:13) based on a variant Hebrew spelling in the text. See *Gath-hepher.*

GITTAIM (Gĭt' tā ĭm) Place name meaning, "two winepresses." City to which people of Beeroth fled after Israel entered Canaan. The Bible does not tell the precise time (2 Sam. 4:3). After the Exile, part of the tribe of Benjamin settled there (Neh. 11:33). This could be the same as the Gath of 1 Chronicles 7:21; 8:13, but that is not certain. The location is not certain, probably near Lydda and thus in Philistine territory at Rash Abu Hamid.

GITTITE (Gĭt' tīte) A citizen of Gath.

GITTITH (Gĭt' tĭth) A word of uncertain meaning used in the titles of Psalms 8; 81; 84. It may represent a musical instrument resembling a Spanish guitar, a musical tune, or a rite or ceremony as part of a festival.

GIZONITE (Gī' zō nīte) Citizen of Gizah or Gizon, a place not otherwise mentioned. It may be modern beth-Giz southwest of Latrun. David had military leaders from there (1 Chron. 11:34), though Gizonite does not appear in the parallel in 2 Samuel 23:34. Some Greek manuscript evidence points to Guni as the original reading. See *Guni.* Some Bible students suggest the original reading was Gimzoni from Gimzo. See *Gimzo.*

GIZRITE (Gĭz' rīte) Citizen of Gezer. REB reading in 1 Samuel 27:8 for Girzite. See *Girzite.*

GLAD TIDINGS KJV phrase for good news (Luke 1:19), a synonym for gospel as the news Jesus brought of God's kingdom (Luke 8:1; Acts 13:32; Rom. 10:15). See *Gospel.*

GLASS An amorphous substance, usually transparent or translucent. Glass is formed by a fusion of silicates (sometimes oxides of boron or phosphorus) with a flux and a stabilizer into a mass that cools to a rigid condition without crystallization.

Glass was known in the ancient world from about 2600 B.C. in Egypt. In Egypt and Phoenicia glass was opaque and was used chiefly to make ornamental objects—especially beads, jewelry, and small bottles. The value of glass in ancient times may be indicated in Job where the value of glass is equated with that of gold and is used in parallel with jewels (Job 28:17). The Egyptians and Phoenicians made small bottles for perfume by welding sticks of glass round a core of sand and clay built around a bar of metal. The core and bar

were removed after the glass cooled.

Transparent glass was not made until New Testament times as a luxury item. During this period, Alexandria, Egypt, became world famous as a center for the production of glassware. Such items as beakers, bowls, flasks, goblets, and bottles were made from the transparent glass. Corinth became known for the production of glass after the time of Paul.

John probably had the transparent variety of glass in mind when he wrote Revelation. He described the walls and streets of the new Jerusalem being made of pure gold. The gold of the walls and streets was so pure, it was as clear as glass (Rev. 21:18,21).

Glass vase in the shape of a fish from Tel el-Amarna in Egypt.

John also described the sea as being like glass (Rev. 4:6; 15:2). Here the reference is probably not so much to transparency as to calmness. It has often been stated that the Israelites had a fear of the sea which always seemed to be in a state of chaos and tumult. The sea that John saw around the throne of God was not in a constant uproar; this sea was as smooth as glass.

The KJV uses glass in five other passages where a polished metal mirror is probably being referred to (Job 37:18; Isa. 3:23; 1 Cor. 13:12; 2 Cor. 3:18; Jas. 1:23). Glass was not used to make mirrors in biblical times.   *Phil Logan*

GLAZE An oxide mixture (usually of silica and aluminum) applied to ceramic surfaces that renders them impervious to moisture and gives them a glossy appearance. Some modern translations (NIV, REB, NRSV, TEV) divide the consonants of the Hebrew text of Proverbs 26:23 differently than the KJV and find a reference to a glaze rather than to silver dross. The TEV gives the sense of the passage: "Insincere talk that hides what you are really thinking is like a fine glaze on a cheap clay pot." See *Pottery.*

GLEANING The process of gathering grain or produce left in a field by reapers or on a vine or tree by pickers. Mosaic law required leaving this portion so that the poor and aliens might have a means of earning a living (Lev. 19:9–10; 23:22; Deut. 24:19–21; compare Ruth 2). Isaiah compared the few grapes or olives left for gleaners to the small remnant of Israel God would leave when He judged them (Isa. 17:5–9). One day, however, God would again gather or glean His remnant one by one and return them to worship in Jerusalem (Isa. 27:12).

GLEDE KJV term for an unclean bird of prey (Deut. 14:13). The identity of the bird (Hebrew *raah*) is impossible to determine. The following suggestions have been offered: buzzard (NRSV); kite (REB); red kite (NIV, NAS). The Hebrew root suggests a bird with keen eyesight, for example a member of the hawk family. An easily-confused Hebrew word (*daah*) occurs in Leviticus 11:14 and in some manuscripts and early translations of Deuteronomy 14:13. The bird in question may be the red kite (*Milvus milvus*). See *Birds.*

GLISTERING STONES See *Antimony.*

GLORY The weighty importance and shining majesty which accompany God's presence. The basic meaning of the Hebrew word *kabod* is heavy in weight. (Compare 1 Sam. 4:18; Prov. 27:3.) Thus it can refer to a heavy burden (Ex. 18:18; Ps. 38:4; compare more idiomatic uses in Gen. 12:10; 47:4; Ex. 4:10; 7:14). On the other side, it can describe extreme good fortune or mass numbers, a use with many different English translations (compare Gen. 13:2; Ex. 12:38; Num. 20:20; 1 Kings 10:2).

The verb thus often comes to mean, "give weight to, honor" (Ex. 20:12; 1 Sam. 15:30; Ps. 15:4; Prov. 4:8; Isa. 3:5). Such honor which people give to one another is a recognition of the place of the honored person in the human community. A nation can have such honor or glory (Isa. 16:14; 17:3). This is not so much something someone bestows on another as a quality of importance which a person, group, or nation has and which another recognizes.

"To give glory" is to praise, to recognize the importance of another, the weight the other carries in the community. In the Psalms people give such glory to God, that is they recognize the essential nature of His Godness that gives Him importance and weight in relationship to the human worshiping community. (Compare Pss. 22:23; 86:12; Isa. 24:15.) Human praise to God can be false, not truly recognizing His importance (Isa. 29:13; compare 1 Sam. 2:30). At times God creates glory for Himself (Ex. 14:4, 17; Ezek. 28:22). As one confesses guilt and accepts rightful punishment, one is called upon to recognize the righteousness and justice of God and give Him glory (Josh. 7:19; 1 Sam. 6:5). God thus reveals His glory in His just dealings with humans. He

also reveals it in the storms and events of nature (Ps. 29; compare Isa. 6). Glory is thus that side of God which humans recognize and to which humans respond in confession, worship, and praise. (Compare Isa. 58:8; 60:1.) Still, for the Old Testament, the greatest revelation of divine glory came on Sinai (Deut. 5:24). Yet such experiences are awesome and fearful (Deut. 5:25). Such revelation does not, however, reveal all of God, for no person can see the entirety of the divine glory, not even Moses (Ex. 33:17–23).

The New Testament uses *doxa* to express glory and limits the meaning to God's glory. In classical Greek *doxa* means opinion, conjecture, expectation, and then praise. New Testament carries forward the Old Testament meaning of divine power and majesty (Acts 7:2; Eph. 1:17; 2 Pet. 1:17). The New Testament extends this to Christ as having divine glory (Luke 9:32; John 1:14; 1 Cor. 2:8; 2 Thess. 2:14).

Divine glory means that humans do not seek glory for themselves (Matt. 6:2; John 5:44; 1 Thess. 2:6). They only look to receive praise and honor from Christ (Rom. 2:7; 5:2; 1 Thess. 2:19; Phil. 2:16).

GLOSSOLALIA Technical term for speaking in tongues (Greek *glossa*, tongue). See *Tongues, Gift of.*

GLUTTON One habitually given to greedy and voracious eating. Gluttony was associated with stubbornness, rebellion, disobedience, drunkenness, and wastefulness (Deut. 21:20). A more general meaning for the Hebrew term as a "good-for-nothing" (Prov. 28:7 TEV) is reflected in some translations: wastrel (Deut. 21:20 REB); profligate (Deut. 21:20 NIV; Prov. 28:7 REB); riotous (Prov. 28:7 KJV). When Jesus was accused of being a "glutton and wine-drinker" (Matt. 11:19; Luke 7:34), it was in this expanded sense of being one given to loose and excessive living. The Bible knows gluttony makes one sleepy and leads to not working and poverty (Prov. 23:21).

GNASHING OF TEETH Grating one's teeth together. In the Old Testament, gnashing of teeth was an expression of anger reserved for the wicked and for one's enemies (Job 16:9; Pss. 35:16; 37:12; Lam. 2:16). In the New Testament, gnashing of teeth is associated with the place of future punishment (for example, Matt. 8:12; 13:42,50). There the gnashing of teeth is perhaps an expression of the futility of the wicked before God's judgment or else a demonstration of their continuing refusal to repent and acknowledge the justness of God's judgment. (Compare Rev. 16:9, 11.) See *Hell; Punishment, Everlasting.*

GNAT See *Insects.*

GNOSTICISM (Gnŏs' tĭ cĭsm) Modern designation for certain religious and philosophical perspectives that existed prior to the establishment of Christianity and for the specific systems of belief, characterized by these ideas, which emerged in the second century and later. The term "gnosticism" is derived from the Greek word *gnosis* (knowledge) because secret knowledge was so crucial a doctrine in gnosticism.

Importance of Gnosticism The significance of gnosticism for students of Christianity has two dimensions: the first is its prominence in the history of the church, and the second is its importance for interpreting certain features of the New Testament. Gnosticism emerged in schools of thought within the church in the early second century and soon established itself as a way of understanding Christianity in all of the church's principal centers. The church was torn by the heated debates over the issues posed by gnosticism. By the end of the second century many of the Gnostics belonged to separate, alternative churches or belief systems viewed by the church as heretical. Gnosticism was thus a major threat to the early church; and the early church leaders, such as Irenaeus (died about 200), Tertullian (died about 220), and Hippolytus (died about 236), wrote voluminously against it. Many of the features of gnosticism were incorporated into the sect of the Manichees in the third century, and Manichaeism endured as an heretical threat to the church into the fourth century.

Gnosticism is also important for interpreting certain features of the New Testament. Irenaeus reported that one of the reasons John wrote his Gospel was to refute the views of Cerinthus, an early Gnostic. Over against the gnostic assertion that the true God would not enter our world, John stressed in his Gospel that Jesus was God's incarnate Son.

Heretical Gnostic Sects The Gnostics who broke away or were expelled from the church claimed to be the true Christians, and the early Christian writers who set themselves to refute their claims are the major source for descriptions of the heretical gnostic sects. Although wide variations existed among the many gnostic sects in the details of systems, certain major features were common to most of them—the separation of the god of creation from the god of redemption; the division of Christians into categories with one group being superior; the stress on secret teachings which only divine persons could comprehend; and the exaltation of knowledge over faith. The church rejected such teachings as heretical, but many people have continued to find attraction in varieties of these ideas.

Gnostics generally distinguished between an inferior god whom they felt was responsible for the creation and the superior god revealed in Jesus as the Redeemer. This was a logical belief for them because they opposed matter to thought in a radical way. Matter was seen as inferior, sin-causing, and always deteriorating; thought or knowledge distinguished persons from matter and animals and was imperishable, capable of revealing god, and the only channel of redemption. The gnostic Marcion thus rejected the Old Testament, pointing out that the lesser or subordinate god revealed in it dealt with matter, insisted on law rather than grace, and was responsible for our decaying, tragedy-filled world. The god who revealed himself in Jesus and through the additional secret teachings was, on the other hand, the absolute god, and was not incarnate in human flesh because the absolute god would not enter evil matter—Christ only seemed or appeared to be a person, but He was not.

Gnostics divided Christians into groups, usually the spiritual and the carnal. The spiritual Christians were in a special or higher class than the ordinary Christians because they had received, as the elect of the good deity, a divine spark or spiritual seed in their beings which allowed them to be redeemed. The spiritual Christians were the true Christians who belonged to the heavenly world which was the true one. This belief that the spiritual Christians did not really belong to this world resulted in some Gnostics seeking to withdraw from the world in asceticism. Other gnostic systems took an opposite turn into antinomianism (belief that moral law is not valid for a person or group). They claimed that the spiritual Christians were not responsible for what they did and could not really sin. Thus they could act in any way they pleased without fear of discipline.

Gnostics placed great stress on secret teachings or traditions. This secret knowledge was not a product of intellectual effort but was given by Jesus, the Redeemer from the true deity, either in a special revelation or through His apostles. The followers of the gnostic Valentinus claimed, for example, that Theodus, a friend of Paul's, had been the means of transmission of the secret data. The secret knowledge was superior to the revelation recorded in the New Testament and was an essential supplement to it because only this secret knowledge could awaken or bring to life the divine spark or seed within the elect. When one received the *gnosis* or true knowledge, one became aware of one's true identity with a divine inner self, was set free (saved) from the dominion of the inferior creator god, and was enabled to live as a true child of the absolute and superior deity. To be able to attain to one's true destiny as the true deity's child, one had to engage in specific secret rituals and in some instances to memorize the secret data which enabled one to pass through the network of powers of the inferior deity who sought to keep persons imprisoned. Salvation was thus seen by the gnostics in a cosmic rather than a moral context—to be saved was to be enabled to return to the one true deity beyond this world.

The Gnostics thought faith was inferior to knowledge. The true sons of the absolute deity were saved through knowledge rather than faith. This was the feature of the various systems that gave the movements its designation: they were the Gnostics, the knowers. Yet what this precise knowledge was is quite vague. It was more a perception of one's own existence that solved life's mysteries for the Gnostic than it was a body of doctrine. The knowledge through which salvation came could be enhanced by participation in rituals or through instruction, but ultimately it was a self-discovery each Gnostic had to experience.

Origins of the Gnostic Concepts Gnosticism would not have been a threat to the early church if it had not been quite persuasive in the first centuries of the Christian era, and the question of where such ideas came from and what human needs they met must be addressed.

The classic answer to the question of why gnosticism arose is that it represents the "radical Hellenizing of Christianity." In this view, gnosticism resulted from the attempt of early Christian thinkers to make Christianity understandable, acceptable, and respectable in a world almost totally permeated by Greek assumptions about the reality of the World.

This classic view of the heretical gnostic sects as distortions of Christianity by Hellenistic thought has much strength because it is easily demonstrated how the Gnostics could use New Testament texts, bending them to their purposes. In 1 Corinthians 3:1–4, for example, Paul chides the Corinthian Christians for being "people of the flesh" (NRSV) or carnal when they should be spiritual. This text could with ease be used as the foundation for supporting the Hellenistic idea of the superiority of certain persons in the Christian community.

The classic explanation does leave some problems unsolved, however. Little doubt exists that there are ideas, attitudes, and practices incorporated into many of the gnostic heresies that are found outside of Hellenistic thought and much earlier than the second century of the Christian era. In particular, the ultimate goal of the Gnostics—to return to the absolute deity beyond matter and to be in some sense absorbed into the deity—belongs to near eastern pre-Christian mystical thought and not primarily to the Hellenistic world.

Although the radical conclusions of some scholars regarding a highly developed pre-Christian gnosticism have been discounted, it does seem clear that there were many ideas, assumptions, and perceptions about deity, reality, and the relationships of persons to gods and the world that were incorporated into the gnostic sects from outside Hellenistic sources. Two literary discoveries have both inspired and tended to support this line of research—the Dead Sea Scrolls at Qumran in 1946 and the Nag Hammadi library in 1945 with many gnostic documents.

The value of the study of gnosticism for interpreting the New Testament is greatest from the point of view that there was a pre-Christian gnosticism which was not an organized religion but was more a general attitude among thoughtful persons that although ignorance abounded, one could through knowledge come to understand one's true identity and find union or relationship with the absolute deity. This way of conceiving of a pre-Christian gnosticism supplements the classic view by providing an explanation for the rapid and widespread development of so many diverse gnostic heretical sects so quickly. This view also offers an explanation of why the New Testament could so easily be exploited by gnostic sects. The early Christian preachers and writers, seeking to speak and write to be understood, used terms current in the first century world in the vague context of gnostic religious longings and gave them new meaning in the context of the incarnation, death, and resurrection of Jesus.

Harold S. Songer

GOAD A rod, generally about eight feet long, with a pointed end used to control oxen. During the time of the judges, the Israelites hired Philistine blacksmiths to "sharpen the goads" (1 Sam. 13:21), either by fashioning metal points for the pointed ends or making metal casings for the blunt end which might be used to knock dirt clods from the plow. Goads might be used as a weapon (Judg. 3:31). The sayings of the wise are "goads" that "prod" thought (Eccl. 12:11). God warned Paul not to "kick against the goads" (KJV pricks) by refusing to submit to the heavenly vision (Acts 26:14).

GOAH (Gō′ äh) Place name meaning, "low" (as a cow) or "bellow." A place, apparently on the west side of Jerusalem, where Jeremiah promised the walls would be restored after the Babylonian destruction (Jer. 31:39).

GOAT See *Animals.*

GOATH (Gō′ äth) KJV and REB transliteration of Hebrew in Jeremiah 31:39 for Goah. See *Goah.*

GOATSKIN Hide of goats desert dwellers used for clothing (Heb. 11:37) and for containers for water (Gen. 21:14) and wine (Josh. 9:4). In Genesis 27:16 Rachel placed goatskin on Jacob's neck and arms as part of the plan to deceive Isaac into giving his blessing. See *Animals in the Bible.*

GOB (Gŏb) Place name meaning, "back" or "mountain crest." Site where David and his men fought two battles with the Philistines, killing Philistine giants (2 Sam. 21:18–19). The parallel passage (1 Chron. 20:4) names Gezer as the place. Some Hebrew manuscripts read Benob or "in Nob" as in verse 16. The Greek manuscripts presuppose either in Gath or in Gezer. The location of Gob is not known, though it appears to be a Philistine city.

GOBLET KJV term for a bowl-shaped drinking vessel without handles (Song of Sol. 7:2). In contemporary English a goblet is a drinking vessel with a foot and stem. Modern translations are divided over the reference in Song of Solomon: bowl (RSV, TEV), goblet (NAS, NIV, REB). The underlying Hebrew term is translated basin (Ex. 24:6) and bowls (Isa. 22:24) elsewhere.

GOD The personal Creator worthy of human worship because of His holy nature and His perfect love revealed in creating the universe, electing and redeeming His people, and providing eternal salvation through His Son Jesus Christ.

God is *unique* in nature. No person, object, or idea can be compared to God. Anything said about God must be based on His revelation of Himself to us. Anything said about God must be said in human terms, the only terms we have and understand. The reality of God is always much greater than human minds can understand or express.

God as the Bible's Primary Subject The Bible and history begin with God (Gen. 1:1). The last chapter of the Bible describes God as the "Alpha and Omega, the first and the last, the beginning and the end" (Rev. 22:13 NRSV). All the way through Scripture God is primary. For Christians the primacy of God is reassuring, liberating, and instructive. It reassures us that God controls all existence. It liberates us to know the loving, redeeming God seeks to set us free. It instructs us to be able to look for signs of God throughout His universe.

God as Present with Us God is present in His world in a unique manner. He is never separated from any part of His creation. As spirit, God has the perfect capability of being present everywhere in the world at once.

The Bible speaks of God's presence in two major ways: in space and in relationships. Theologians used the term *omnipresence,* derived from Latin, to speak of God's presence everywhere in all the world's space. Moses experienced that presence on a wilderness mountain (Ex. 3); Isaiah, in the Jerusalem Temple (Isa. 6); and Paul, on an international highway (Acts 9). Most often the Bible speaks in terms of God being present in relationships. He called Israel to be His people (Ex. 19:3–6). He appeared to Elijah in a "still, small voice" (1 Kings 19:12). Most of all God appeared Person to person in the human flesh of His Son Jesus.

God as Mystery Revealed in Christ The personal presence of God in Jesus Christ is the central and normative source of knowledge about God. Christ is known today through the witness of inspired Scripture and through the personal witness of the Holy Spirit. Still, what is revealed is the mystery of Christ. Even as it is revealed, God's revelation in Jesus Christ remains mysterious (Rom. 16:25–26; Eph. 3:1–10; Col. 1:24–27; 4:2–4). Faith believes that what remains hidden in mystery is totally consistent with what is revealed in Christ.

Revelation of Christ in the form of Bible narrative allows us to describe God but not to define Him. Perhaps the closest we can come to a definition is that God is the holy Being who is love in servant form. This rises out of Bible statements: "the Lord our God is holy" (Ps. 99:9); "God is love" (1 John 4:8,16). These contain partial descriptions, not definitions. The norm for a definition comes in Jesus, who said, "but I am among you as one who serves" (Luke 22:27 NRSV). Thus Christian preaching echoes Paul: "we do not proclaim ourselves; we proclaim Jesus Christ as Lord; and ourselves as your slaves for Jesus' sake" (2 Cor. 4:5 NRSV).

God's Unique Nature God is the only God. He is not simply the greatest of many gods—He is the only true God. God is the *living* God. This separates Him from all other gods and idols, which are merely forms humans have created in the image of things God created (Isa. 41:22–24; 44:9–20; 46:1–2,6–7). "The Lord is the true God, he is the living God, and an everlasting king" (Jer. 10:10; compare 1 Thess. 1:9). Christians see this in Jesus, joining Peter in confessing, "Thou art the Christ, the Son of the living God" (Matt. 16:16).

The living God is also Lord and Master. In English translations He is Lord in two ways. Lord spelled with small caps represents the Hebrew *Yahweh,* the personal name of God, by which He introduced Himself to Moses (Ex. 3:15; 6:3). See *Names of God; Yahweh.* Lord with lowercase letters represents the Hebrew *'adonai* and the Greek *kurios.* See *Lord.* This refers to the master, the boss, the owner, the person with authority over another. As Lord, God is sovereign Ruler over all the earth; He is the Creator and Judge of all persons. Thus the Hebrew identifies God as "the Lord God (Yahweh), the God of Israel" (Ex. 34:23). He is "Lord of lords" (Deut. 10:17). The New Testament proclaims, "let all Israel be assured of this: God has made this Jesus, whom you crucified, both Lord and Christ" (Acts 2:36 NIV). Thus Jesus receives the same titles as the Father, leading to a doctrine of the Trinity.

God is *holy.* The most basic word we have to describe God is holy. This is the unique quality of God's existence that marks Him off as separate and distinct from all else. Holiness includes the ideas of righteousness and purity, but it is more. Holiness belongs to God alone. It sets Him above us in majesty, power, authority, righteousness, and love. Persons or objects can be said to be holy only by virture of being drawn into relationship with God. (Compare Isa. 5:16; 6:3; 1 Pet. 1:15–16.)

God is *eternal.* He has no beginning and no ending. All else begins and ends as an expression of the will of God, but God has always existed and will always continue to exist.

God is *spirit.* He is not material or physical as we are. As spirit, He does not have the limitations of material form. Spirit is the highest form of existence. It enables God to be with His people everywhere simultaneously. As spirit, God chose to humble Himself and take on the form of human flesh (Phil. 2:6–11).

God is *love.* "God is love itself" is the nearest humans can get to making a non-symbolic statement about God (1 John 4:8,16). His love is coordinated perfectly with His righteousness. God's love is always righteous, and His righteousness is always marked by love. Love is the primary motivation behind revelation (John 3:16). God's love is expressed as His mercy in forgiving sinners and in rescuing or blessing those who do not deserve His attention.

God is *Father.* The love of God finds supreme expression as Father. God is known in Scripture as Father in three separate senses that must not be confused: *(1)* He is Father of Jesus Christ in a unique sense—by incarnation (Matt. 11:25–27; Mark 14:36; Rom. 8:15; Gal. 4:6; 2 Pet. 1:17); *(2)* He is Father of believers—by adoption or redemption (Matt. 5:43–48; Luke 11:2, 13; Gal. 3:26); *(3)* He is Father of all persons—by creation (Ps. 68:5; Isa. 64:8; Mal. 2:10; Matt. 5:45; 1 Pet. 1:17).

God is *intimate.* He is not an impersonal force like gravity, exerting influence in some mechanical, automatic way. He has personal characteristics, just as we do. God is living, working in His world, and relating to His people. He is aware of what is going on, makes plans, and carries them out. He forms relationships and has purpose and will. He is a *jealous* God, taking himself seriously and insisting that others take Him seriously (Ex. 34:14; Nah. 1:2; 1 Cor. 10:22). He wants more than divided loyalty or indifference from His people.

Attributes of God God has distinctive qualities that summarize what He is like.

God's *glory* refers to the weight or influence He carries in the universe and to the overwhelming brilliance when He appears to people (Ex. 16:7–10; Isa. 6:3; Eph. 1:12–17; Heb. 1:3). It is His presence in all His sovereign power, righteousness, and love. Sometimes the Bible describes the glory of God as a physical manifestation. Sometimes it is a spiritual perception as in a sense of tremendous awe before God.

God's *wisdom* is His perfect awareness of what is happening in all of His creation in any given moment. This includes His knowledge of the final outcome of His creation and of how He will work from beginning to ending of human history (Job 11:4–12; 28:1–28; Ps. 139; Rom. 11). It also includes His ability to know what is best for each and every one of His creatures. Sometimes this is called His omniscience.

God's *power* is His ability to accomplish His purposes and carry out His will in the world. He can do what needs to be done in any circumstance (Job 36:22–33; Isa. 40:10–31; Dan. 3:1–30; Matt. 19:16–26; 1 Cor. 1:18–25). This is sometimes called His omnipotence.

God's *righteousness* expresses itself in many ways (Ex. 2:23–25; Josh. 23:1–16; Ps. 71:14–21; Isa. 51:5–8; Acts 10:34–35; Rom. 3:5–26). He is the ultimate standard of right and wrong. He is faithful, constant, and unchanging in His character. He works for the right, seeking to extend righteousness and justice throughout the world. He defends the defenseless, helpless, victimized, and oppressed. He opposes evil through personal expressions of His wrath, anger, judgment, punishment, and jealousy. He sits in present and eternal judgment on those who do evil.

His attributes show that God is able to accomplish His will. Nothing can limit Him except limits He places on Himself.

God at Work in His World God is not an inert being far removed from the world. God is the personal God who cares about and works in the world He created. Creation was His first work but certainly not His last.

God works as *Redeemer* to save the sinful, rebellious human creatures and to renew His fallen creation. He makes salvation possible. His love makes Him a saving kind of God. He redeemed Israel in the Exodus from Egypt (Ex. 1—15); through the prophets He promised a Messiah who would save His people, and in Jesus Christ provided that salvation (John 3:16). Redemption in Christ completes creation, carrying out the purposes of God and making final, complete salvation possible.

God works *in history.* The sovereign God exercises His lordship or ownership of the world by continuing to work in His world and through His people. God allows people the freedom to be themselves and make their own free choices but works within those choices to accomplish His eternal purposes. This is called God's providence. God has not predetermined all the events of human history; yet He continues to work in that history in ways we do not necessarily see or understand.

God works toward and in the *end time* to fulfill His eternal purposes. God will one day bring His purposes to fulfillment, bringing history to a close and ushering in eternity. The sovereign, absolute Lord will accomplish His will in His world.

G

God as Trinity Finally, God has revealed Himself as Father and Creator, as Son and Savior, and as Holy Spirit and Comforter. This has led the church to formulate the uniquely Christian doctrine of the Trinity. New Testament passages make statements about the work and person of each member of the Trinity to show that each is God; yet the Bible strongly affirms that God is one, not three (Matt. 28:19; John 16:5–11; Rom. 1:1–4; 1 Cor. 12:4–6; 2 Cor. 13:14; Eph. 4:4–6). The doctrine of the Trinity is a human attempt to explain this biblical evidence and revelation. It is an explicit formulation of the doctrine of God in harmony with the early Christian message that "God was in Christ, reconciling the world unto himself" (2 Cor. 5:19). It expresses the diversity of God the Father, God the Son, and God the Holy Spirit in the midst of the unity of God's being. See *Christ; Holy Spirit; Trinity.*

John W. Eddins, Jr. and *J. Terry Young*

GOD OF THE FATHERS A technical phrase used as a general designation of the God of the patriarchs. Some references to the formula within the biblical narratives speak of the "God of my [your, thy, his, their] father" (Gen. 31:5, 29; 43:23; 49:25; 50:17), without mention of a particular father. Other references include the name of a particular patriarch, as "the God of Abraham" (Gen. 31:53; 26:24; 28:13; 32:9), "the God of Isaac" (Gen. 28:13; 32:9; 46:1), or "the God of Nahor" (Gen. 31:53). Given the polytheistic environment of the time, originally the formula could refer to tribal or clan gods (Josh. 24:2, 14–15). Each of the patriarchs apparently had a special name for God: "Fear of Isaac" (Gen. 31:42), "Mighty One of Jacob" (Gen. 49:24).

The "burning bush" story (Ex. 3) identified the "God of the Fathers" with Yahweh.

The biblical witness consistently uses the formula to emphasize continuity between the God who is revealed to Moses and the God who guided the patriarchs, even by a different name. Likewise, in the Old Testament, "God of thy fathers" or "God of our fathers" functions to link the author's generation to the God of earlier generations, especially with reference to the promises to the patriarchs (Deut. 1:11, 21; 4:1; 6:3; 12:1; 26:7; 27:3). In contrast, abandonment of this historic connection is also emphasized (1 Chron. 12:17; 2 Chron. 20:33; 24:24; 29:5; 30:7; 36:15; Ezra 7:27). In the New Testament the formula is transformed to mark the continuity between historic Israel and Christianity. The God revealed in Jesus Christ is the same as the God revealed to the patriarchs (Matt. 22:32; Mark 12:26; Acts 3:13; 5:30; 7:32; 22:14).

See *Names of God; Patriarchs; Yahweh.*

Dixon Sutherland

GODHEAD A word used witn reference to God

when one speaks of God's divine nature or essence or of the three persons of the Trinity. See *Trinity.*

GODLESSNESS An attitude and style of life which excludes God from thought and ignores or deliberately violates God's laws. Romans 1:20–32 is a classic characterization of godlessness: the godless refuse to acknowledge God in spite of the evidence of creation (1:22), engage in willful idolatry (1:25), and practice a life-style unconstrained by divine limits (1:26–31). The godless not only have no fear of God's judgment but seek to involve others in their wickedness (1:32). "Godless myths and old wives' tales" (NIV) refers to speech that encourages an attitude and life-style of godlessness (1 Tim. 4:7; compare 6:20; 2 Tim. 2:16).

GODLINESS An attitude and style of life that acknowledges God's claims on human life and seeks to live in accordance with God's will. In pagan Greek sources *eusebeia* (godliness, piety) refers to worship of the gods and to respect for the representatives of institutions regarded as divinely ordained (parents, judges, the emperor). *Eusebeia* was sometimes distinguished from *dikaiosyne* (righteousness) as concerning one's relationship with the gods rather than with other persons.

Acts 3:12 contrasts "piety" with faith in the name of Jesus, the real source of healing. Acts uses the adjective godly to describe religiously observant Gentiles (10:2,7; 17:23).

Only 1, 2 Timothy, Titus, and 2 Peter use words with the *euseb-* root for Christian piety. Individuals can be trained in godliness (1 Tim. 4:7). Godly teaching (1 Tim. 6:3) is that which results in godly lives (Tit. 1:1). False teachers sought to make their godliness a source of financial gain (1 Tim. 6:5). When "godliness" appears in lists with other virtues, it perhaps retains its earlier sense of respect for God and divinely ordained institutions (1 Tim. 6:11; Titus 2:12; 2 Peter 1:3–7). The form of godliness lacking the power of godliness (2 Tim. 3:5) likely refers to professed godliness that failed to shape moral lives since the profession was not accompanied by a vital relationship with God.

GODS, PAGAN One of the great distinctives of Judeo-Christian religion is monotheism—the recognition and reverence of only one God. By contrast, pagan religions of the biblical world were polytheistic, worshiping many gods.

Old Testament Many pagan gods had their origin as gods of certain places such as cities or regions. In Old Testament times, such gods or a combination of gods became nationalistic symbols as their cities or regions struggled for political dominance. The names of Near Eastern kings thus frequently contained a national god's name. The kings of Israel and Judah, for example, often bore names which contained a shortened form of the Hebrew name of Yahweh: Jo-, Jeho-, or -iah. A by-product of the connection between gods and certain locales was the belief that a god's power was limited to certain regions. Thus, officials of the Syrian king advised a battle with Israel on the plains observing, "their gods are gods of the hills" (1 Kings 20:23). Israel, against the background of this common belief, struggled with the concept that God was the Lord over all aspects of creation.

Egyptian Gods Egyptian religion included a great number of gods. Many were personifications of the enduring natural forces in Egypt, such as the Sun (Re or Atum), sky (Nut), earth (Geb), and so on. Certain gods were associated with a particular place, such as Ptah of Memphis. Other gods, like Maat (truth and justice), Sekhmet (war and disease), and Bes (god of childbirth) ruled over aspects of life. Still others combined these categories so that Thoth was god of Hermopolis, the moon, and wisdom, while Hathor was goddess of Denderah, the sky, and love. Some of the gods were worshiped in animal form, such as the Apis bull which represented the god Ptah of Memphis.

The Osiris myth was popular with the common people and became the principle of divine kingship. See *Egypt*.

The position of certain deities was a factor of the political situation. The gods' names which dominate pharaohs' names in a dynasty show both the dominant city and its dominant god. Thus the god Amen, later called Amen-Re, became the chief god of the empire because of the position of Thebes. Under Amenhotep III, the successes of the empire led to internal power struggles between the powerful priesthood of Amen-Re and the throne. Amenhotep IV changed his name to Akhenaton and embarked on a revolutionary reform which promoted worship of the sun disc Aton above all other gods. The reforms of Akhenaton failed. His second successor made clear his loyalties to Amen-Re by changing his name from Tutankhaton to Tutankhamen and abandoning the new capital in favor of Thebes. The following dynasty, while promoting Amen-Re seems to have favored gods of the north. The names of the gods Seth of Avaris, Ra of Heliopolis, and Ptah of Memphis are evident in the Nineteenth Dynasty names Seti, Ramses, and Merneptah.

No Egyptian gods are mentioned in the Bible, and the complex Egyptian religion did not significantly influence the Hebrews. Some have tried to posit a relationship between the reforms of Akhenaton and the monotheism of Moses, but the differences between Atonism and the Mosaic view of God are far greater than the similarities.

Mesopotamian Gods The complex system of belief common throughout Mesopotamia included thousands of gods. The most important are reviewed here.

The patron deities of the oldest Sumerian cities became the high gods of the Mesopotamian pantheon. Anu, god of the heavens and patron of Uruk (biblical Erech; Gen. 10:10), did not play a very active role. Enlil of Nippur ruled over the earth. The god of Eridu, Ea, was lord of the underground waters and the god of craftsmen. The feared Nergal of Cutha was the god of plague and the underworld. Gods of other cities became prominent through political circumstance. Thus, the god and namesake of the original Assyrian capital, Ashur, rose in importance with the rise of that empire. Ninurta, god of war and hunting, was patron for the Assyrian capital Calah. After the political rise of Babylon, Marduk was considered the chief god and was given the epithet *Bel* (equivalent to the Canaanite term Baal), meaning "lord" (Isa. 46:1; Jer. 50:2; 51:44). The *Enuma elish,* or Babylonian Creation Epic, tells of a cosmic struggle in which, while other gods were powerless, Marduk slew Tiamat (the sea goddess, representative of chaos). From the blood of another slain god, Ea created mankind. Marduk's son Nabu (Nebo in Isa. 46:1), the god of nearby Borsippa and of scribes, became especially exalted in the neo-Babylonian period as seen in the name Nebuchadnezzar.

Several important gods were associated with heavenly bodies. Shamash was god of the sun and played a prominent role. The moon god Sin was revered in the cities of Ur and Haran, both associated with Abraham's origins (Gen. 11:31). Ishtar (the Canaanite Astarte/Ashtaroth) was goddess of the morning and evening star. In addition to her astral associations, Ishtar fulfilled a dual role as the goddess of war and the goddess of love and fertility. Temple prostitution was an important part of her cult and gave Uruk, the city of her older Sumerian equivalent, Inanna, a sordid reputation. Among the masses Ishtar was very popular and referred to as the "queen of heaven" (Jer. 7:18; 44:17–19). Closely connected with Ishtar was her consort, the spring vegetation god Tammuz. A myth tells of Tammuz' betrayal by Ishtar, his subsequent death, and descent into the underworld. This event was commemorated by an annual mourning for the god in the fourth month which fell during summer. Ezekiel lamented this pagan practice by certain women of Jerusalem (Ezek. 8:14). The death of Tammuz reflected and coincided with the annual wilting of spring vegetation in the Near East. Also associated with fertility was the storm god Adad, the Canaanite Hadad.

In addition to their cosmic nature, the gods were thought of as present in their image, or idol, and living in the temple as a king in his palace. The gilded wooden images were in human form, clothed in a variety of ritual garments, and provided with meals. On occasion the images were carried in ceremonial processions or to "visit" one another in different sanctuaries.

Canaanite Gods The gods of the Canaanites

made the greatest impact on the Israelites. While many of these are related to Mesopotamian gods, Canaanite religion was not well understood until the discovery of religious texts in the 1920s at the Syrian city of Ugarit. See *Canaan.*

The chief god of the Canaanite pantheon was called El, the generic Semitic word for "god." El, however, was viewed as a grandfatherly, retiring god and did not play an active role. By far the most prominent role must be assigned to Baal around whom the Ugaritic myths revolve. These myths represent Baal as the storm god with power over rain, wind, and clouds, and thus over the fertility of the land. The cycle of the seasons is represented in the myths by Baal's struggle with Mot (literally, "death"), who represented drought and brought forth dry barren fields. During the dry season (summer) Baal was forced temporarily into the underworld by Mot, but his recurring return brought forth the rainy season (winter) and restored fertility to the land. In another myth, Baal defeated Yamm (literally "sea"), the god of chaos, in much the way that the Babylonian Marduk defeated Yam (literally, "sea"), the god of chaos.

In the Ugaritic myths, Baal's sister/consort Anat, goddess of war and love, assisted in his victories. Closely associated with Anat and more important in Palestine was another goddess of war/love, Astarte, the Mesopotamian Ishtar. Astarte (a Greek form of the name) appears in the Old Testament in the singular as "Ashtoreth, the goddess of the Zidonians" (1 Kings 11:5,33; 2 Kings 23:13) as well as in the plural form, Ashtaroth (Judge. 10:6, 1 Sam. 7:4; 12:10), representing local manifestations of the godess. As the female counterpart of Baal, Astarte/Ashtoreth seems to have been worshiped through sacred prostitution designed to promote fertility. Another goddess of fertility was Asherah, in the Ugaritic texts the wife of El. Worship of Asherah was apparently quite pronounced throughout Palestine (1 Kings 14:23 NIV). See *Asherah.*

The fertility aspects of the Canaanite gods was an inviting snare to the Israelites. New to farming and having just settled in Canaan after a generation of nomadic life in the desert, the Israelites were particularly tempted to serve the gods said to control the fertility of that land. A great deal of syncretism must have occurred, mixing elements of Baalism with worship of God. Indeed, Jeroboam's golden calves at Dan and Bethel may have been an attempt to identify Yahweh of Israel with the Baal of the Canaanite elements of the kingdom and to combine their traditions. Archaeological evidence of such syncretism can be seen in the recent discovery in the Sinai of a jar inscribed with prayer to "Yahweh of Samaria and his Asherah."

Various other deities of Palestine impacted the Old Testament story. The Arameans of Damascus (Syria) worshiped the generic Semitic storm god Hadad, frequently referred to by the epithet Rimmon (2 Ki. 5:18), meaning "thunder." Sometimes the names Hadad and Rimmon were coupled (Zech. 12:11). The god Dagon of the Philistines (Judg. 16:23) was apparently a Semitic god of grain mentioned in the Ugaritic texts as Dagan, the father of Baal. The Philistines worshiped Dagon in temples at Ashdod (1 Sam. 5:1–5) and Beth Shean (1 Chron. 10:10).

The national god of the Ammonites was called Molech (1 Kings 11:7). There are no vowels in Hebrew, so in ancient times Molech was written with the same consonants (MLK) as the Hebrew/ Semitic word for king, *melek.* Thus, Molech may have served as a title ("the king"; compare Amos 1:15) for the Ammonite god much as Baal served as a title for the storm god. The pronunciation Molech comes from the substitution for the original vowels with those from the Hebrew word *bosheth,* "shame," and is an intentional insulting misvocalization. The alternate name Milcom (1 Kings 11:5; Jer. 49:1,3 TEV) is a corruption of a variant form meaning "their king." Worship of Molech involved human sacrifice, especially making one's children "pass through the fire" (Lev. 18:21; 20:2–5; 2 Kings 23:10; Jer. 32:35). In Judah, this practice was conducted at Tophet in the Valley of Hinnom on the southwest side of Jerusalem (2 Chron. 28:3). Jephthah's reply to the Ammonites (Judg. 11:24) refers to Chemosh as their god. Chemosh, the national god of the Moabites (Num. 21:29; Jer. 48:46), thus may be identical to Molech although they are listed separately as abominations brought to Jerusalem by Solomon (1 Kings 11:7). Chemosh is mentioned prominently in the famous Moabite Stone. Mesha, king of Moab, probably offered up his son Chemosh (2 Kings 3:27). The Canaanite god Horon was evidently worshiped in the two cities of Bethhoron ("house of Horon"). Resheph (Hebrew for "flame" or "pestilence" Hab. 3:5) was a god of plague, equivalent to the Nergal of Mesopotamia. **New Testament** The pagan gods of the New Testament world were the deities of the Greco-Roman pantheon and certain eastern gods whose myths gave rise to the mystery religions. The conquests of Alexander the Great of Macedon took the Greek culture throughout the Near East.

A few of the Greco-Roman gods are mentioned in the New Testament. At the head of the Greek pantheon was Zeus, the Roman Jupiter, god of the sky, originally the weather or storm god. With the syncretism of the Hellenistic period following Alexander the Great's conquests, Zeus was equated with the Semitic storm god Hadad. As the supreme Greek deity, however, Zeus was readily identified with the chief god of any region. Thus, when Antiochus IV attempted to force Hellenism on the Jews in 167 B.C., he transformed the Jewish Temple into a temple to Zeus. A huge altar to Zeus at Pergamum is probably the "Satan's throne" of Revelation 2:13. The messenger of the Greek gods was Hermes (Roman, Mercury). When the people of Lystra assumed Barnabas and Paul to be gods (Acts 14:8—18), they called Paul Hermes because he was the spokesman; and they identified Barnabas with Zeus or Jupiter. The oxen and garlands they brought forward were appropriate offerings for Zeus. Hermes was also the god of merchants and travelers. Artemis was the Greek goddess of the wildwood, of childbirth, and, consequently, of fertility. The great mother goddess of Asia Minor worshiped at Ephesus was identified with Artemis, the Roman Diana. Her temple at Ephesus was one of the seven wonders of the aancient world and an object of pilgrimages. Artemis of the Ephesians was depicted in statues at Ephesus with many breasts, perhaps inspired by a sacred stone (a meteorite?; Acts 19:35) kept in the temple. Paul's work in Ephesus resulted in an uproar incited by the silversmiths who sold souvenirs to the pilgrims (Acts 19:23—41).

Other Greco-Roman gods are not mentioned in the New Testament but formed an important part of Hellenistic culture. The most popular of the gods was Apollo, pictured in Greek art as the epitome of youthful, manly beauty. He served as the god of medicine, law, and shepherds. Aphrodite was the Greek goddess of sexual love and beauty. She was identified with the Semitic godddess Ishtar/Astarte and with the Roman Venus. Although not mentioned in the New Testament, a temple to Aphrodite at Corinth was said to employ a thousand cultic prostitutes and contributed to the city's reputation for immorality. Athena, namesake and patron of the city of Athens, was a virgin goddess connected with arts and crafts, fertility, and war. She was identified with the Roman Minerva. Hera, whose Roman equivalent was Juno, was the wife of Zeus and goddess of marriage, women, and motherhood. Also not mentioned is the important Poseidon, Neptune to the Romans, god of the sea, earthquakes, and—oddly—horses. The war god of Greece was Ares, equated with the Roman god Mars. Hephaistos, the Roman Vulcan, was god of fire and the patron of smiths. Hades, called by the Romans Pluto, was the Greek god of the underworld. His name became the Greek word used in the New Testament for the abode of the dead (Matt. 11:23; 16:18; Luke 10:15; 16:23; Acts 2:27,31; Rev. 1:18; 20:13—14).

Certain Greek gods became the centers of cults which were quite influential in New Testament times. Foremost among these is the cult of Demeter or the Eleusinian mysteries. Demeter was the Greek goddess of grain who, according to the myth, ceased to function when her daughter Persephone was abducted into the underworld by Hades. Persephone was eventually released to her mother but forced to spend a third of each year in the underworld, a cycle which reflected the annual growth cycle of grain. Secret rites of initiation into the cult took place annually at Eleusis. The Greek god of wine, intoxication, and fertility was Dionysus, the Roman Bacchus. His cult involved orgiastic feasts in which wild animals were torn apart alive and eaten raw, originally only by groups of women. Sick persons appealed to the popular god of healing, Asclepius, by visiting special sanctuaries in certain cities. See *Fertility Cult; Mystery/Mystery Religions. Daniel C. Browning Jr.*

GOG AND MAGOG (Ḡŏḡ and Mā′ ḡŏḡ) *1.* In Ezekiel 38—39, Gog of the land of Magog is the leader of the forces of evil in an apocalyptic conflict against Yahweh. In Revelation 20:8, Gog and Magog appear together in parallel construction as forces fighting for Satan after his 1,000 year bondage. The identity of Gog and Magog has been the subject of an extraordinary amount of speculation. In general, however, attempts to relate these figures to modern individuals or states have been unconvincing.

Ezekiel's prophecy is apparently built on Jeremiah's sermons against a foe from the north (Jer. 4—6). Ezekiel's historical reference may have been Gyges, king of Lydia, who asked Ashurbanipal, king of Assyria, for help in 676 B.C. but then joined an Egyptian-led rebellion against Assyria about 665 B.C. His name became a symbol for the powerful, feared king of the north. Magog is apparently a Hebrew construction meaning, "place of Gog."

2. A descendant of the tribe of Reuben (1 Chron. 5:6).

GOIIM (Gôi′ ĭm) Proper name meaning, "nation," particularly a "Gentile, foreign nation." *1.* Land whose King Tidal joined the eastern coalition against a coalition from Sodom and Gomorrah. This action led to a war in which Abraham became involved (Gen. 14:1). To which nation the general term "Goiim" applies here is uncertain. Some would suggest the Hittites, since several Hittite kings between 1750 and 1200 B.C. were named Tudhaliya or Tidal. Others point to the Manda people, barbarian invaders who entered Mesopotamia about 2000 B.C. and had some association with Elamites. Goiim may mean a coalition of Hittite, Luvian, and/or other peoples. One Greek manuscript tradition points to Pamphylia, which means "rich in peoples." *2.* Joshua 12:23 lists a king of Goiim in Gilgal as one Joshua conquered. The earliest Greek translation reads "king of goiim of Galilee," a reading many Bible students adopt since the immediate context refers to areas near Galilee and the copyist would easily write Gilgal since it plays such an important role in the early narratives of Joshua. Whatever the correct reading, we do not know the precise location or peoples referred to. *3.* Isaiah 9:1 also refers to Galilee of the nations. This

may represent the Hebrew way of referring to Assyria's governmental district which the Assyrians called Megiddo. Assyria controlled this region after its wars with Israel in 733 and in 722 B.C.
4. In Judges 4:2 Sisera's residence was in Harosheth of the Gentiles (KJV) or Harosheth-ha-goiim (NRSV). See *Harosheth-hagoiim.*

GOLAN (Gō′ lăn) Place name meaning, "circle" or "enclosure." It was a city of refuge for people who unintentionally killed someone and was located in Bashan for the part of the tribe of Manasseh living east of the Jordan River (Deut. 4:43). It was also a city for the Levites (Josh. 21:27). It was located at modern Sahem el-Jolan on the eastern bank of the River el-Allan. See *Cities of Refuge; Levitical Cities.*

GOLD See *Minerals and Metals.*

GOLDEN CALF An image of a young bull, probably constructed of wood and overlaid with gold, which the Hebrews worshiped in the wilderness and in the Northern Kingdom of Israel.
Ancient Near Eastern Background and Biblical References Living bulls were important in the religion of some regions of ancient Egypt, and bull images appear in the art and religious texts of Mesopotamia, Asia Minor, Phoenicia, and Syria. The primary references to "golden calf" in the Bible are Exodus 32:1–8 and 1 Kings 12:25–33. The former passage records that the people summoned Aaron to make an image to go before them. The image was apparently intended to represent Yahweh, the Lord of Israel. The latter reference states that Jeroboam I constructed at Bethel and Dan two golden bulls, which were probably meant to represent the pedestals of God's throne. Interestingly, these passages are closely related to each other because they use the same terminology in the dedication of these images (Ex. 32:4; 1 Kings 12:28), and they both explore the sin of idolatry at crucial junctures in Israel's history.
Theological Significance These accounts demonstrate Israel's strong conviction that God cannot be lowered to the level of pictorial representation. God, as sovereign Lord, allows no physical image of Himself, and any human effort to create such an image invites His judgment.

See *Aaron; Bethel; Bull; Dan; Exodus; Jeroboam I; Moses; Yahweh.*

Robert William Prince, III

GOLDEN RULE The name usually given to the command of Jesus recorded in Matthew 7:12 and Luke 6:31—do to others as you would like them to do to you. The designation "Golden Rule" does not appear in the Bible, and its origin in English is difficult to trace. The principle of the Golden Rule can be found in many religions, but Jesus' wording of it was original and unique.

GOLDSMITH See *Occupations, Professions in the Bible.*

GOLGOTHA (Gōl′ gō thà) Place name transliterated from Aramaic and or Hebrew into Greek and then into English meaning, "skull." In Mark 15:22, the Hebrew name for the place where Jesus was crucified. The Latin equivalent is *calvaria.* Both words mean "skull." See *Crucifixion; Calvary.*

The hill of Golgotha, or Place of the Skull.

GOLIATH (Gō lī′ àth) In 1 Samuel 17:4, the huge Philistine champion who baited the Israelite army under Saul in the valley of Elah for forty

Azekah in the Valley of Elah where young David killed Goliath.

days. He was slain by the youthful David. See *Elhanan.*

GOMER (Gō′ mēr) Personal name meaning, "complete, enough," or "burning coal." *1.* Daughter of Diblaim and wife of Hosea the prophet (Hos. 1:3). She is described in Hosea 1:2 as "a wife of whoredoms." Various explanations have been offered for that designation. Some have maintained that she was a common prostitute. Others have maintained that she was a cultic prostitute in the service of Baal. Some have suggested she symbolized Israel's worship of many gods. Still others have believed she was an ordinary woman who became unfaithful after her marriage to Hosea. Her unfaithfulness to her husband became a sort of living parable of Israel's unfaithfulness to Yahweh. See *Hosea. 2.* Son of Japheth and grandson of Noah in the Table of Nations (Gen. 10:2). He is apparently seen as representing the Cimmerians, an Indo-European people from southern Russia who settled in Cappadocia in Asia Minor. Assyrian sources show they threatened Assyria after 700 B.C. He was the father of Ashkenaz or the Scythians of Jeremiah 51:27 who displaced the Cimmerians from their home in Russia. Gomer was also the father of Riphath (or Diphath in 1 Chron. 1:6) and of Togarmah.

GOMORRAH (Go môr′ rah) See *Sodom and Gomorrah.*

GONG (KJV "brass") A loud percussion instrument, perhaps like a type of cymbal used in the Temple worship (1 Cor. 13:1). The Greek is literally, "noisy brass" referring to the metal from which the instrument was made.

GOOD In contrast to the Greek view of "the good" as an ideal, the biblical concept focuses on concrete experiences of what God has done and is doing in the lives of God's people. Scripture affirms that God is and does good (1 Chron. 16:34; Ps. 119:68). The goodness of God is experienced in the goodness of God's creative work (Gen. 1:31) and in God's saving acts (liberation of Israel from Egypt, Ex. 18:9; return of a remnant from captivity, Ezra 7:9; personal deliverance, Ps. 34:8; salvation, Phil. 1:6). God's goodness is extended to God's name (Ps. 52:9), God's promises (Jos. 21:45), God's commands (Ps. 119:39; Rom. 7:12), God's gifts (Jas. 1:17), and God's providential shaping of events (Gen. 50:20; Rom. 8:28). Though God alone is truly good (Ps. 14:1,3; Mark 10:18), Scripture repeatedly speaks of good persons who seek to live their lives in accordance with God's will. Christians have been saved in order to do good (Eph. 2:10; Col. 1:10) with the Holy Spirit's help.

GOODMAN KJV term for a husband or for the head of a household. At Proverbs 7:19 goodman renders the Hebrew *ish,* the usual word for man. KJV on occasion translates the Greek term *oikodespotes* (rendered "goodman" at Matt. 20:11; 24:43; Mark 14:14; Luke 22:11) as master of the house (Matt. 10:25) or householder (Matt. 13:27). Modern translations use equivalents such as landowner or owner of the house.

GOPHER WOOD In Genesis 6:14, the material out of which Noah was instructed to construct the ark. The etymology of the Hebrew word is unknown, and there is no certainty as to the type of wood to which it refers. Even the earliest translators were uncertain. See *Ark.*

GOSHEN (Gō′ shēn) *1.* The phrase, "land of Goshen," appears in the general description of territory occupied by Joshua's forces (Josh. 10:41; 11:16). Apparently it refers to the hill country between Hebron and the Negev. Some believe the phrase refers to a country.
2. The "land of Goshen" may have been named after the city of Goshen located in the district of Debir (Josh. 15:51). Goshen may have been the chief city of the region at one time. The ancient city was either located at Tell el Dhahiriyeh, twelve miles southwest of Hebron or at a location further east.
3. Goshen is primarily recognized as an area in the northeast sector of the Nile Delta. It was occupied by the Hebrews from the time of Joseph until the Exodus.

Goshen is significant for biblical studies for four reasons. (1) The pharaoh assigned Goshen to Joseph's family when they entered Egypt (Gen. 47:6,11). The "Hebrew Sojourn" occurred there. (2) The territory lay on a route from Palestine to Egypt. (3) It may be possible to date Joseph's entrance to Egypt with the Hyksos control of the Delta. (4) Both the two cities which the Hebrews built, Rameses and Pithom, and the Hyksos capital at Zoan are key issues for settling on a date for the Exodus.

Gary D. Baldwin

GOSPEL is the English word used to translate the Greek word for "good news." Christians use the word to designate the message and story of God's saving activity through the life, ministry, death, and resurrection of God's unique Son Jesus.
Development in the Old Testament *Bisar* is the Hebrew verb which means "to proclaim good news." Unlike the English language, Hebrew is able to convey the subject of the proclamation in the verb's root; no direct object was needed with the verb *bisar* to make clear that the subject of an announcement was "good news." Originally, the word was used to describe the report of victory in battle (2 Sam. 4:10). Because the Israelites believed God was actively involved in their lives

The fertile land of Goshen in the delta country of northern Egypt.

(including battles and wars) *bisar* came to have a religious connotation. To proclaim the good news of Israel's success in battle was to proclaim God's triumph over God's enemies.

The transition from the use of *bisar* in a military setting to its use in a personal context is not difficult to envision. If Israel proclaimed good news when God delivered the nation from its enemies, individuals ought also to proclaim good news when God delivered them from personal distress (Ps. 40:10). The nation's victories in war and a person's individual salvation both called for the announcement of what God had done.

The Book of Isaiah marks the full religious development of the term within the Old Testament. By this time the word is most often used to describe the anticipated deliverance and salvation which would come from the hand of God when the long-awaited Messiah appeared to deliver Israel (Isa. 52:7). The military-political and personal connotations of the word were fully united in the hope of a Deliverer who would both triumph over the earthly enemies of God's people and usher in a new age of salvation.

Usage in the New Testament In the New Testament "gospel" has two shades of meaning: it is both the actual message on the lips of Jesus about the reign of God (Mark 1:14), and it is the story told about Jesus after His death and resurrection (Gal. 1:11–12). In each case "gospel" refers to the work which God alone initiates and com-

pletes. Inasmuch as God has chosen to bring about the world's reconciliation in this one particular way, there is only one gospel (Heb. 1:1–2). Furthermore, since God is the One working through the saving activity of Jesus, God is also the Author of the gospel (1 Thess. 2:13). The gospel is God's message to humankind (Rom. 15:16). Only God calls and commissions the messengers of this good news, and, in addition, only God gives the messengers the story they are to make known (Rom. 10:14–15; 1 John 1:5).

Therefore, the proclamation of the good news is the continuation of the work which God began in Jesus Christ. God's messengers are not merely telling about the history of salvation when they proclaim the good news; rather, they are an integral part of the work which continues through their efforts. The living Lord, Jesus Christ Himself, confronts listeners through the words of the messengers. To alter the message by adding extra requirements or by omitting crucial details is to pervert the gospel into a false message which ceases to have saving power (2 Cor. 11:3–4; Gal. 1:6–7).

The Message of the Gospel The most basic summary of Jesus' preaching appears in Mark 1:15. "The time is fulfilled," He said. "The kingdom of God is at hand: repent ye, and believe the gospel."

The need for good news assumes a bad situation. The bad situation in which humans find themselves and the reason they need good news is that sin has entered each of their lives (John 8:7;

Rom. 3:23). Sin is a power that controls them and shapes their destinies (Rom. 3:9; 6:22).

Because humans cannot overcome the power of sin by themselves, God has intervened on their behalf through Jesus. Jesus has come to seek out all persons so they may respond to God's grace (Luke 15:1–10; 19:10). God's grace, which Jesus bears within Himself (John 1:14), overcomes sin's power and offers forgiveness for individual sins (Mark 2:5; Rom. 6:14). See *Grace.*

While God offers grace freely to everyone, this grace is not effective in overcoming the power of sin in a person's life until that person accepts it (Matt. 19:20–22; John 1:12). Because Jesus bears God's grace in Himself, grace is accepted only by receiving him (John 14:9–12). The marks of having accepted Jesus are repentance (Luke 13:3) and a changed life (Matt. 3:8; 1 John 1:5–7).

The fact that forgiveness, freedom from sin, and a new life are possible is good news. Because all this is possible only through Jesus Christ, His message and His story are called the "gospel."

Development of Written Gospels Within the New Testament, the word *euanggelion* always refers to oral communication, never to a document or piece of literature. Not until the beginning of the second century and the writings of the "church fathers" do we find references to "gospels" in the plural, indicating written documents. How did this transition from a spoken message to written books take place?

Literacy was uncommon in the ancient world. Books and writing equipment were expensive and the education needed to use them was usually reserved for the rich alone. Consequently, many societies preserved and transmitted their national stories, traditions, and faith by word of mouth. These societies stressed the importance of telling and remembering their traditions from one generation to another. Such a system may seem fragile and unreliable by modern standards, but ancient societies trusted the methods and forms they developed to sustain the process.

In times of crisis (such as an invasion by a foreign nation), however, certain learned individuals would try to guarantee the preservation of their society's oral traditions by writing them down. They often wrote out of the fear of what would happen if their nation was defeated or destroyed and no one was left to transmit orally the living traditions to the next generation.

The gospels of the New Testament developed along a pattern similar to other ancient writings. For many years the stories and teachings of Jesus were communicated primarily by word of mouth. In addition to the fact of limited literacy, members of the early church believed Jesus would return soon, so they felt no urgency to write down His teachings for the future. Then, about thirty years after Jesus' ascension, three interrelated crises began to impinge upon the church. As a result of these crises, individuals responded to the leadership of God's Spirit to write down the teachings, stories, and message of Jesus into what we call the Gospels.

The first of these crises was persecution. The Emperor Nero initiated the first official persecution so he could use Christians as scapegoats for his own insane actions.

The second crisis involved the passing away of the generation of people who had actually seen Jesus in the flesh, heard His teachings, and witnessed His miracles. Some died in the persecutions and others simply aged enough to pass away from natural causes. The early church placed a high value on the experience of actually having seen and heard Jesus (Luke 1:2; 1 John 1:1). Therefore, the death of members of the original generation of Christians was viewed as a potential break in their linkage to the historical roots of their faith.

The third crises was the perceived delay in Christ's return to earth. Preaching recorded in the New Testament has a distinct sense of urgency about it. The apostles believed that Jesus would be returning any day and that it was imperative for them to give as many people as possible the opportunity to respond to Him. Their constant emphasis was to communicate the gospel today, not to preserve it for the future. As a longer and longer period of time passed after Jesus' ascension, the church became more and more concerned about preserving the message.

The Purposes of the Evangelists From approximately A.D. 60 until A.D. 90, four individuals responded to the inspiration of God by writing down the message of, and about, Jesus. As they did, these individuals surely held several goals in common. Responding to the crises around them, they wanted to preserve the gospel message in an accurate form for believers who would follow in future generations. In this sense the authors were each trying to produce a book for the Christian community. They wrote down the good news of Jesus to strengthen, to educate, and to encourage those who already accepted its message.

It is also clear that they intended to use a written form of the gospel as an additional tool for evangelism (John 20:30–31). The evangelists envisioned the written gospel as a vehicle to spread faith in Jesus Christ. In this sense, each evangelist was trying to produce a missionary book.

Understanding the missionary character of the four Gospels is an important factor in their study. The Gospel writers' primary interest was not to produce great works of literature, nor was their intention to write a biography in the modern sense of the word. Their principal objective was to convert individuals to faith in Christ. Thus, they wrote primarily to convince, not to record facts.

The primary intention of the evangelists determined the shape and content of the written Gos-

G

pels. One may wish the Gospel writers had included additional information about Jesus' home life, His adolescence, or some other area of interest; but the Gospel writers were not led to believe that kind of data was crucial for faith. The evangelists structured their works to give the message maximum impact on the readers. They included material they felt was essential for the reader to know to be able to make a decision about Jesus' identity. All other concerns regarding form and content of the Gospels was secondary to the missionary objective.

While the teaching of the New Testament affirms that there is only one, true gospel, the books contained therein stand as testimony to the fact that *the* gospel is influenced by each personality which proclaims it. The church does not possess one account of the message of and work of Jesus which stands alone as the official record of His activity. Rather, the early church recognized the inspiration of four different accounts of the gospel. Each one was written from a slightly different perspective; each one had a different audience in mind; each one was designed to highlight the elements of the gospel which the author felt most important. The four Gospels witness both the divine inspiration of God and the individual, human personalities of their authors.

Out of several gospels and other accounts of the life of Jesus (Luke 1:1–2), God led the early church to choose four which He had inspired. See *Matthew; Mark; Luke; John.*

Rejected Gospels The early church perceived God's inspiration in the four Gospels of the Bible, yet several other books which presented themselves as gospels also circulated during the church's early history. These "gospels" were either inadequate Jewish interpretations of Jesus, or works heavily influenced by Gnostic heretics. All of the known rejected gospels were written much later than the four included in the New Testament, most commonly between A.D. 120 and 150. Among these works are *The Gospel of the Ebionites, The Gospel According to the Hebrews, The Gospel According to the Egyptians, The Gospel of the Naassenes, The Gospel of Peter,* and *The Gospel of Thomas.*

God did lead the church to preserve four gospels so that it could continue to preserve and proclaim the richness of the gospel message of salvation to the diverse peoples of the world in their diverse needs. *P. Joel Snider*

GOSPEL OF THOMAS See *Apocrypha, New Testament; Gnosticism.*

GOUGING THE EYES A cruel and degrading punishment sometimes inflicted on conquered peoples in biblical times. The Philistines put out Samson's eyes (Judg. 16:21). Nahash offered to make peace with the people of Gilead on the condition that he put out the right eye of every man in the city and thus bring disgrace upon all Israel (1 Sam. 11:2). After executing King Zedekiah's sons in his sight, the Babylonians put out his eyes (2 Kings 25:7). Scripture records such events as cruelty, not as examples to follow.

GOURD A hard-rinded, inedible fruit of the genera *Lagenaria* or *Cucurbita.* Gourd motifs were used in the ornamentation of the interior of the Temple (1 Kings 6:18, KJV knobs) and of the rim of the bronze sea (1 Kings 7:24). The gourd of Jonah 4:6–10 cannot be identified precisely. The KJV followed the earliest Greek translation with its rendering gourd. The Vulgate or early Latin translation understood the plant as ivy. Many modern translations simply refer to a plant (NAS, RSV, TEV) or bush (NRSV). The NIV renders the term "vine"; REB, "climbing gourd." Many interpreters think a castor oil plant (*Ricinus Communis*) is meant.

GOVERNMENT may be defined in two general ways, either in terms of the officials or the institutions. In reference to officials, government refers to the sovereign authority over a body of people. In reference to institutions, government refers to the customs, mores, laws, and institutions of a people.

Many standard definitions of civilization include the presence of a strong centralized government as a constitutive element. The rise of the first empires at the beginning of the Early Bronze Age is related in part to the rise of centralized governments. Centralized government was necessary for the building and maintaining of canals used for irrigation in Mesopotamia. It was also necessary for the development of a standing army. Extensive international trade required more centralized governmental power over the economic institutions.

In understanding the biblical conception of government, one must remember that biblical theology presents early Israel as a theocracy, having God as king and ruler (Judg. 8:22–23; 1 Sam. 8:7–9; Pss. 93—99; Rom. 13:1–4). Ultimate authority resides in God and God alone. Human government is, therefore, always limited and always intended to be within the framework of God's will. The best ruler will be the one who best carries out God's design for just rule.

Early Hebrew Patterns of Government An understanding of biblical patterns of government must begin with the Patriarchal period. During this time, the Hebrews had no centralized government. The major unit was the extended family or, on a larger basis, the tribe. The government was family based. The first unit of authority or government was the household or the father's house.

This unit of society corresponds best to our designation of the extended family and would often involve two or more generations living together. The oldest male was usually the head of the family, the patriarch. As such, he was the chief official of family and government. The next level of social organization was the clan, often designated by the Old Testament as the family (Hebrew *mishpahah).* The clan was composed of several related extended families. One individual might be designated as chief or head of each clan. The next larger social level was the tribe (Hebrew *shevet),* composed of several clans. A tribe might have a chief or even a prince as its leader. Finally, a group of tribes could be known as a people (Hebrew ʿ*am).* The tribe was the most frequent social unit mentioned apart from the household or extended family. We should not necessarily consider the tribe to be overly large, but more as rather small and isolated groups, especially before Saul and David.

It has been argued recently that the tribal and clan structures were based not on kinship, but on grouping for common defense. Thus a clan might be formed by two or three villages banding together and a tribe by two or three of the clan units. This would be true for the period after the conquest of Canaan. Thus many scholars would argue that in the Song of Deborah (Judg. 5) the warriors are related to their tribal territories more than their tribes as a kinship group.

It is usually assumed that the patriarchal society was nomadic or semi-nomadic. Following the pattern of modern nomadic tribes with a patriarchal organization, the Hebrew society was probably democratic. Tribal decisions would be made on the basis of discussion by all the adult men. Not all men had equal authority. The elders held a major source of authority during this period and later periods as well.

The elders for a clan were probably the heads of the households that comprised the clan. For a tribe, the elders would have been all the household heads, or selected elders from each clan. Thus the elders were the leaders of the local community. They had the responsibility to decide many of the everyday matters, religious and judicial. The elders were representatives of the community as a whole in religious and military matters. They often accompanied the leader. The elders could conclude a covenant (2 Sam. 5:3) or treaty on behalf of the people. The elders regularly dispensed justice at the city gate (Deut. 21:19). The elders continued to function well into the period of the monarchy as a governing body. See *Elder.*

Beginning with the Exodus, the Old Testament presents Israel as a people composed of numerous tribes but with one leader. Moses as leader was succeeded by Joshua, who was succeeded in turn by the judges. Although the depiction indicates a central leader, there is no indication of a centralized government. Granted, the leader has great authority; but the leader was not surrounded by the structure of a centralized government. A confederation of tribes was in existence during this period. In addition to the elder, Israel also had, following the period of Moses and Joshua, the office of judge. The judge was not primarily a judicial official, but rather a charismatic military leader. Typically, the judge would rally the forces of Israel and defeat an oppressing power. From the time of Moses, the office of judge had included the element of deciding cases (Deut. 1:16; 16:18–20; 17:8–9). Much more frequently, the emphasis was upon the military prowess of the judge (Judg. 3:7–11, 12–30; etc.). The book of 1 Samuel brings a change in the emphasis of the judge. The judge became a priestly official, as in the case of Eli and Samuel. Thus the term "judge" seems to have a broader meaning than just a judicial term. Certainly the judge seems to have been the chief official of the confederacy of tribes in that period prior to the monarchy. It may be that the term was not specific as to the type of leader—priestly, military, or judicial—but simply indicated the leader. Although there were some cases where one judge attempted to have his sons succeed him (as did both Eli and Samuel), the office was not regularly hereditary. Compare the problems of Abimelech (Judg. 8:22—9:56). In this respect particularly, the office of judge differed from that of king which followed.

Although the period of judges may have led to the development of the monarchy, the two are quite different. The judge still retained a tribal character. Although several tribes might join together to fight a common enemy under the leadership of a judge, judgeship carried no sense of the permanence, hereditary character, or royal court of the monarchy. The judge was just an extension of the tribal chief or leader carried to a somewhat larger realm of a leader for several combined tribes. In actual function, the judge seldom played a strong role in maintaining the people's religious traditions until Samuel (Judg. 2:10; 17:6; 21:25). **Government during the Monarchy** With the rise of the monarchy, a totally new organizational pattern emerged. Not only did the king stand as a single ruler for all the people, as a sort of chief raised to a national level; but the king was also surrounded by a new structure. The king had his royal court to carry out his mandate. Alongside the older tribal and town leaders, the king had a new cadre of officials. His officials included military officers and a professional army alongside the old militia from the tribes. The nation was divided into administrative districts with administrators who stood alongside the old system of elders. A royal court and professional army required revenue, so a taxation system was developed with its attendant officials. Evidence for this taxation system is found in the Samaria ostraca, which record the receipt of taxes paid from various estates to the government. Similarly, the "*lamelek*" jar handles (which bear an inscription literally meaning, "for the king") indicate either taxation or produce of royal farms. Building projects required massive labor, and so the *corvee* or forced-labor contingents were organized. The old system of local government based on the city and the elder still existed, but a burgeoning bureaucracy developed parallel to the old system. The government also entered the international arena at this time, conducting warfare against international as well as local nations. It would negotiate treaties and alliances, trade and commercial agreements, and even arrange royal marriages. Surrounding the royal court were such officials as "the one who is over the house" a sort of Secretary of State or Prime Minister; the recorder who was a herald, press secretary, and chief of protocol combined; the chief scribe; counselors; priests; and prophets (1 Kings 4). In addition, many attendants would minister to the king. The king embodied the rule of the entire nation. As he and his officials were just and faithful in ruling, the nation prospered. As he and the officials were unjust, the nation suffered. Likewise, the unjust actions of lesser officials ultimately was the responsibility of the king. Thus the prophets accused the king of his actions and of the actions of those under him.

Government Under the Foreign Empires If the shift to a monarchy was the most revolutionary change in Israel's government, the collapse of the monarchy then marked the second most significant change. Self government and independence were lost. In all likelihood this change was felt more on the national level than on the local level. The elders continued to function as local leaders, but the royal officials were replaced by new imperial and military officials of the conquering power—first Assyria, then successively, Babylon, Persia, and Hellenistic and Roman states. Now the tax revenues went to the treasury of that foreign state, and a new legal system had to be obeyed alongside the Hebrew law. This is seen especially in the trial of Jesus which involved hearings before the religious court (at that time the highest Jewish court) and before the Roman authorities. The chief ruler became a local governor appointed by the foreign power as was Nehemiah, or even a foreigner as were the Roman procurators. When local kings were allowed to rule, it was only at the pleasure of the foreign power and under the watchful eye of foreign military.

Beginning with the post-exilic period, Jewish government fell more and more into priestly hands. The monarchy had ceased. The restructuring of society prevented too much power in political hands. The priesthood was strengthened and gradually assumed more and more of the judicial authority. Even the elders came to have an especially religious role as judicial officers. "Law" became virtually synonymous with the religious

covenant, so that obeying the law meant keeping God's covenant. This affected every area of life. Such a conception was not necessarily new; it relates to the idea of God as king. The manner in which power was concentrated entirely in the sacred realm, as opposed to the secular, was new to the post-exilic and later periods. Since political power was not possible for the most part, power was consolidated where it could still be exercised, in the religious area. Religion was simply expanded to cover all of life.

In the New Testament we find Judea governed by a Herodian king appointed by the Roman government. Later direct Roman rule replaced the king. Religious authority still existed. The high priest and the priesthood exercised considerable authority, though it remained in name "religious" authority. The elders belonged to a formal body, the Sanhedrin, as also did certain priests. Just as in the case of the monarchy, two structures of authority existed side by side. Civil government now belonged basically to the foreign overlord, but religious power rested in the hands of the priests and Sanhedrin.   *Joel F. Drinkard, Jr.*

GOVERNOR (Gov'er nor) Generally an appointed civil official charged with the oversight of a designated territory.

The King James Version uses *governor* to translate a variety of Hebrew, Aramaic, and Greek terms. These terms represent a wide range of meanings that encompass almost every form of leadership or oversight. For example *governor* is used of city and tribal leaders (Judg. 5:9; 1 Kings 22:26), rulers (Ps. 22:28), temple officials (Jer. 20:1), managers of households (John 2:8; Gal. 4:2), and even pilots of ships (Jas. 3:4). Recent versions of the Bible have translated the Hebrew word more specifically with words like ruler, leader, prince, commander, chief officer, master, manager, trustee, and ethnarch. This has allowed *governor* to be used to describe those officials serving under a rule who have administrative responsibility for assigned territories or projects. Generally the governor exercised both law enforcement and judicial functions as a representative of his superior.

Old Testament The most widely used term for *governor* in the Old Testament is the Accadian loanword *pechah*. This word first occurs in Ezra and Nehemiah as a title for Tattenai (KJV Tatnai), the Persian administrator of the province "beyond the River" (Ezra 5:3). Tattenai's response to Darius' decree (Ezra 6:13) is indicative of the governor's allegiance to the king and responsiveness to the king's command.

The title also is used of Sheshbazzar (Ezra 5:14) to describe his appointment as "governor of the Jews" (Ezra 6:7). Cyrus had commissioned him to rebuild the temple in Jerusalem at the end of the Babylonian exile. Nehemiah described his appointment by Artaxerxes I as "governor in the land of Judah" (Neh. 5:14). The prophet Haggai addressed his message to "Zerubbabel the son of Shealtiel, governor of Judah" (Hag. 1:1). *Pechah* is used of other leaders in the Old Testament as well (see 2 Kings 18:24; 20:24; Isa. 36:9).

New Testament The Greek word *hēgemōn* and its derivatives predominate in the New Testament occurrences of *governor*. The term often is used to describe Roman officials who exercised the tax and military authority of the emperor. Quirinius (Luke 2:2), Pontius Pilate (Luke 3:1; Matt. 27:2), Felix (Acts 23:24), and Porcius Festus (Acts 24:27) are specifically named. Joseph's rule in Egypt also is classified as that of a governor (Acts 7:10).

Because governors are sent by the king "to punish evildoers and for the praise of them that do well" (1 Pet. 2:13–14), believers are to submit to their authority. Sent out by Christ, however, Christians will be brought before governors and kings for judgment. Faithfulness in such situations will bear witness for His sake (Matt. 10:18).

Michael Fink

GOZAN (Gō′ zăn) Place name of uncertain meaning, possibly, "quarry." A Syrian city-state to which the Assyrians exiled many of the people from Israel after they defeated Israel in 732 (1 Chron. 5:26) and 722 (2 Kings 17:6; 18:11). Assyria had previously conquered Gozan (2 Kings 19:12). Gozan is probably located at modern tel Halaf in northwestern Mesopotamia on the southern bank of the River Khabur. Archaeology shows the city was built after 1000 B.C., though some Stone Age habitation is evidenced. The city included 150 acres with temples and government buildings. Excavators found documents with apparently Hebrew names, perhaps people deported by Assyria.

GRACE Undeserved acceptance and love received from another, especially the characteristic attitude of God in providing salvation for sinners. For Christians, the word "grace" is virtually synonymous with the gospel of God's gift of unmerited salvation in Jesus Christ. To express this, the New Testament writers used the Greek word *charis,* which had a long previous history in secular Greek. Related to the word for joy or pleasure, *charis* originally referred to something delightful or attractive in a person, something which brought pleasure to others. From this it came to have the idea of a favor or kindness done to another or of a gift which brought pleasure to another. Viewed from the standpoint of the recipient, it was used to refer to the thankfulness felt for a gift or favor. These meanings also appear in the biblical use of *charis,* but only in the New Testament does it come to have the familiar sense which "grace" bears for Christians.

Grace in the Old Testament No one word in the Hebrew Old Testament is equivalent to the New Testament use of *charis* for God's unmerited gift of salvation. The translators of the Greek Old Testament characteristically translated the Hebrew word *chanan/chen* as *charis,* and the King James Version likewise often translates this as "grace" or "favor" or "mercy." The Hebrew verb *chanan* occurs some 56 times in the Old Testament and refers to the kind turning of one person to another in an act of assistance, such as aid to the poor (Prov. 14:31). In the Psalms it is frequently used to call upon the gracious assistance of God in times of need (Pss. 4:1; 6:2; 25:16; 31:9; 86:3; 86:16; 123:3). In other instances God is said to make one attractive or favorable in the eyes of another (Gen. 39:21; Ex. 3:21; 11:3; 12:36). It is the latter meaning of "favor" which the noun *chen* especially conveys. Of its 70 occurrences in the Old Testament, 43 are in the stereotyped expression "to find favor/grace in the eyes/sight of another." Most commonly this expression refers to persons seeking or obtaining the favor of another (Jacob from Esau—Gen. 32:5; 33:8; Joseph from Potiphar—Gen. 39:14; Ruth from Boaz—Ruth 2:2,10; Esther from Ahasuerus—Esther 2:17). More rarely it refers to a person receiving God's special favor (Noah—Gen. 6:8; Moses—Ex. 33:12–19; Gideon—Judg. 6:17). In none of these instances, however, is there any emphasis on the recipient's lack of merit as in the New Testament concept of "grace." Closest to this idea are the few passages in the prophets which refer to God's gracious favor to Israel in delivering her from captivity and restoring the nation (Jer. 31:2; Zech. 4:7; 12:10).

Other Hebrew words convey the idea of God's grace, such as *racham/rachamim* ("mercy") and *chesed* ("steadfast covenant love"). These words are often combined with *chen* to refer to the one merciful, loving, gracious God (Ex. 34:6; Neh. 9:17; Pss. 86:15; 103:8; 145:8; Joel 2:13; Jonah 4:2). Together they convey something of the New Testament sense of God's grace, but even then they lack the sense of this being an unmerited favor of God. To be sure, the idea that Israel did not deserve God's mercy and love is found in the Old Testament (Deut. 7:7–10; 9:4–6). God promised David that He would not remove His love from David's successor, even though the successor sinned (2 Sam. 7:14–16). The entire Book of Jonah deals with God's merciful concern to save the wicked Ninevites, and Hosea powerfully conveys God's undeserved mercy and grace with the image of the prophet's love for the faithless Gomer. God's grace shines forth clearly in the Exodus, where God delivered an undeserving people before they entered into His covenant.

Grace in the New Testament We owe our distinctly Christian understanding of grace to the apostle Paul. The Pauline epistles employ the word *charis* and its related forms twice as frequently as the rest of the New Testament writings combined. Paul sometimes employed the word with its more secular meanings. He urged his readers to make their speech "gracious" or "attractive" (Col. 4:6; Eph. 4:29), and referred to his visit to Corinth as a "grace" which would bring them pleasure (2 Cor. 1:15 NAS text note). The idea of gift also appears, especially in reference to his collection for the Jerusalem saints (1 Cor. 16:3; 2 Cor. 8:1,4,6,7,19). Often he used *charis* to mean thanks, as in the thanksgiving over a meal (1 Cor. 10:30) or in songs of praise (Col. 3:16). Frequently he employed the set expression "Thanks" ("*charis* be to God" (Rom. 6:17, 7:25; 1 Cor. 15:57; 2 Cor. 2:14; 8:16; 9:15; 1 Tim. 1:12; 2 Tim. 1:3). One wonders if for Paul this common Greek idiom did not carry a deeper nuance. It was precisely his experience of God's grace that led to his profound sense of thanksgiving.

Paul's sense of God's grace owed much to his experience of being turned from the persecutor of the church to Christ's missionary to the Gentiles (1 Cor. 15:9–10; 1 Tim. 1:12–14). So convinced was he that this was all God's doing and not of his own merit that he could describe his apostolic calling as coming even before his birth (Gal. 1:15). He was an apostle solely because of God's grace (Rom. 1:5), and his entire ministry and teaching were due to that divine grace (Rom. 12:3; 15:15; 1 Cor. 3:10; 2 Cor. 1:12; Gal. 2:9; Eph. 3:2,7,8).

Paul had too profound a sense of human sin to believe that a person could ever earn God's acceptance (Rom. 3:23). As a Pharisee, he had sought to do that by fulfilling the divine law. Now he had come to see that it was not a matter of earning God's acceptance but rather of coming to accept God's acceptance of him through Jesus Christ. So, he came to see a sharp antithesis between law and grace. Law is the way of self-help, of earning one's own salvation. Grace is God's way of salvation, totally unearned (Rom. 3:24; 4:4; 11:6; Eph. 2:8). Grace is appropriated by faith in what God has done in Christ (Rom. 4:16). God's grace comes to sinners, not to those who merit God's acceptance (Rom. 5:20–21). It is through Christ's atoning work on the cross that God's grace comes to us, setting us free from the bondage of sin (Rom. 3:24–31). Christ is the Representative who breaks the reign of sin and brings life and acceptance with God through divine grace (Rom. 5:15, 17). God's grace is so bound up with Christ that Paul could speak of the "grace of our Lord Jesus Christ" (2 Cor. 8:9; 2 Tim. 2:1). It was in the beloved Son that God's grace came supremely to mankind (1 Cor. 1:4; Eph. 1:6–7; compare 2 Tim. 1:9).

For Paul, grace is practically synonymous with the gospel. Grace brings salvation (Eph. 2:5, 8).

Grace brings eternal life (Rom. 5:21; Titus 3:7). To share in the gospel is to be a partaker of grace (Phil. 1:7; Col. 1:6). In Christ Jesus, God's grace is open to all people (Titus 2:11; compare 2 Cor. 4:15); but the experience of God's grace is conditional upon human response. It can be rejected or accepted (2 Cor. 6:1; Gal. 1:6; 5:4).

From the human perspective, the divine grace is a power which undergirds the present life. God's grace abides *in* us (2 Cor. 9:14); we stand in it (Rom. 5:2). Our calling, our witness, our works are all based on the power of God's grace in our lives (2 Thess. 1:11–12). Paul sharply rejected any antinomian perversion of the gospel which failed to recognize that the true experience of God's grace changes one's life in the direction of righteousness (Rom. 6:1,14–15). Grace never gives freedom to sin. His own experience had shown him a new power of the divine grace active in his ministry in spite of his human weakness ·(2 Cor. 12:9). In fact, all who experience God's grace have gifts of that grace for ministry and service (Rom. 12:6; Eph. 4:7).

So pervasive was Paul's sense of God's grace that he always referred to it in the opening or closing of his letters. His usual salutation includes a wish for "grace" and "peace" upon his readers (Rom. 1:7; 1 Cor. 1:3). Here Paul played upon the normal word of salutation in Greek letters (*chairein*-joy). *Charis* has a similar sound, but a world of difference. For the Christian, a reminder of God's grace in their lives is the richest word of greeting and the fullest source of joy.

Surprisingly the word "grace" does not occur in Matthew or Mark. The concept is there, in Jesus' ministry to sinners and outcasts, in His healing ministry, and in such teachings as the parable of the laborers in the vineyard (Matt. 20:1–8). Luke, however, made extensive use of *charis* in both his writings. Sometimes he used it with basically secular meanings, such as "credit, benefit" (Luke 6:32–34 NAS), as "thanks" (Luke 17:9), or as attractiveness in speech (Luke 4:22). The familiar Old Testament idea of "favor" appears a number of times, sometimes referring to the favor of one human to another (Acts 2:47; 7:10; 24:27; 25:3,9; Luke 2:52), sometimes to God's favor bestowed on individuals (Luke 1:28,30; 2:40; Acts 7:46). Reminiscent of Paul are the references in Acts which refer to salvation or to the gospel as "grace" (Acts 11:23; 13:43; 18:27; 20:24,32). Particularly Pauline is the reference to salvation through the grace of the Lord Jesus in Acts 15:11. Also like Paul are those places where grace is described as an enabling power in the ministries of various Christians (Acts 4:33; 6:8 NAS; 14:26; 15:40).

Grace only occurs three times in John's Gospel, all in the prologue (ch. 1), and all in a sense reminiscent of Paul. Grace is equated with truth (1:14), its gift nature is emphasized (1:16), and it is set in antithesis to the law of Moses (1:17). In the remainder of the Johannine corpus, grace occurs only three times, all in benedictions (2 John 3; Rev. 1:4; 22:21). In the Johannine writings the idea of God's unmerited gift in Christ is very present, but conveyed by a different word—*agape* (love).

References to grace in the other New Testament writings do not extend beyond the meanings found in the Pauline epistles and Luke-Acts. Secular meanings of *charis* occur, such as "gratitude" (Heb. 12:28) and "credit" (1 Pet. 2:19–20 NAS). Grace is connected with God's mercy (Heb. 4:16) and with the atoning death of Christ (Heb. 2:9). It is virtually equated with the gospel (1 Pet. 5:10) and with salvation (1 Pet. 1:10,13). It is seen as a power which strengthens life (Heb. 13:9), undergirds those who are persecuted (1 Pet. 5:10), and grants gifts for Christian service (1 Pet. 4:10). God's grace can be spurned (Heb. 10:29; 12:14–15) or turned into a perverted gospel promising freedom from the law and thus freedom to sin without judgment (Jude 4). Above all, grace is the hallmark of the Christian experience and thus a frequent component in benedictions (Heb. 13:25; 1 Pet. 1:2; 2 Pet. 1:2).

See *Mercy; Love; Justification.*   *John Polhill*

GRAFT To unite a scion (the detached, living portion of a plant which provides the leafy portion of a graft) with a stock (the part of the graft providing the roots). Olives were frequently caused to multiply by removing shoots from the base of a cultivated tree (compare Ps. 128:3) and grafting them onto the trunks of wild olive trees. Paul's illustration (Rom. 11:17–24) portrays the incomprehensible grace of God who does what no farmer would do—break off cultivated limbs (representing descendants of Israel) to graft in wild limbs (representing Gentile believers). The illustration also serves as a warning to believing Gentiles not to be proud and despise the contribution of Israelites who made their faith possible but to stand firm in faith.

A large grain silo at ancient Megiddo with a spiral access staircase leading down into it.

GRAIN A general term for the edible seed of cultivated grasses. Common grains in the biblical world included wheat (Gen. 30:14), spelt or emmer (REB vetches) (Ex. 9:32), barley (Ex. 9:31), and millet (Ezek. 4:9). The KJV normally renders grain as corn which means not maize (as in American usage) but any grain.

Various types of grains for planting on sale at an Arab market in old Jerusalem.

GRANARY A storage facility for threshed and winnowed grain. Archeological evidence indicates that granaries varied in size and format. Granary might refer simply to jars or bags of grain (Gen. 42:25), to plastered or unplastered pits, to silos (perhaps Luke 12:18), or even to large structures with numerous rooms (Hezekiah's storehouse, 2 Chron. 32:28, or those used by Joseph to store large amounts of grain, Gen. 41:49). Empty granaries was a sign of God's displeasure (Jer. 50:26; Joel 1:17). Gathering of grain into granaries was a picture of God's gathering of the righteous (Matt. 3:12; Luke 3:17). See *Garner.*

GRAPES See *Plants in the Bible.*

GRASS Herbage suitable for consumption by grazing animals (Job 6:5). English translations use grass to translate at least five Hebrew words.

1. Deshe appears to be a comprehensive term for things that sprout and turn green (Gen. 1:11), being translated grass (KJV), vegetation (NAS,

Excavated grain storehouses (granaries) at the site of ancient Beersheba.

An Arab vineyard worker examining grapes on the vines in his field.

NRSV, NIV), all kinds of plants (TEV), or growing things (REB). With rain it forms green pastures (Ps. 23:2). See Isaiah 66:14; 2 Kings 19:26.

2. *Dethe,* the Aramaic equivalent of *deshe,* depicts the vegetation to be grazed in the field (Dan. 4:15,23).

3. *Yereq* refers to pale yellow, green, or gold plants: the green herbs animals eat (Gen. 1:30; 9:3; Num. 22:4); the green sprouts of trees (Ex. 10:15); God's judgment destroys the green things (Isa. 15:6). *Yereq* can modify *deshe* to emphasize the green color (2 Kings 19:26; Ps. 37:2; Isa. 37:2). The related term *yaraq* describes garden vegetables (Deut. 11:10; 1 Kings 21:2; Prov. 15:17).

4. *Eseb* are the annuals the early rains bring forth (Gen. 1:11,29) as contrasted with the perennials; thus they are the herbs of the field (Gen. 1:30; 2:5; 9:3). Humans depend on God to make grass grow (Ps. 104:14; Mic. 5:7; Zech. 10:1). Grass illustrates the brevity of human life (Ps. 102:4,11) but also the rich, flourishing growth (Ps. 72:16; 92:7) and the king's enriching flavor (Prov. 19:12).

5. *Chatsir* is a general term for wild grass growing on roofs (2 Kings 19:26), mountains (Ps. 147:8), and even resistantly hanging on by watering places during drought (1 Kings 18:5). Humans in their mortality can be compared to grass in contrast to God's word (Isa. 40:6–8; compare 51:12; Pss. 90:5; 103:15). The lily (Matt. 6:28) is later referred to as grass (v. 30).

GRASSHOPPER See *Insects.*

GRATE, GRATING A framework of crisscrossed bars. The grating of the tabernacle altar was made of bronze and held rings through which carrying poles could be inserted (Ex. 27:4–7; 35:16; 38:4,5,30; 39:39).

GRATITUDE See *Thanksgiving.*

GRAVE The pit or cave in which a dead body is buried. The variety of grave sites used by the Hebrews was determined by several factors: the circumstances of death, the surrounding terrain, and the time available for preparation and burial. The most usual grave was the shaft or trench. While the use of pits for collective burial sites is not mentioned in the Bible, several have been excavated in Palestine. Caves were often chosen as a convenient alternative to the cost and time involved in cutting a rock tomb. Because they offered both an abundance of caves and ideal locations for constructing rock hewn shafts, Palestinian hillsides were a common choice for grave sites.

The tomb cut out of rock was sometimes fashioned to serve as a multiple grave with separate chambers. Ledges were often constructed to hold individual family members; and when the tomb was full, the bones from previous burials were set aside to make more room. The bones were placed in jars or stone boxes called ossuaries, which resembled vessels used by the Romans to store ashes after cremation. Ossuaries sometimes held the bones of more than one person and were frequently marked with decorative or identifying designs. The entrances to tombs were secured either by hinged doorways or large flat stones which could be moved by rolling.

The most desirable grave site was the family tomb to which ample reference is made in the patriarchal narratives of Genesis. The Hebrews apparently envisioned a "shade" existence in death and preferred proximity to ancestors over solitude for the placement of their loved ones' remains.

While most graves were left unmarked, some were marked with trees (Gen. 35:8) or stone pillars. Second Samuel 18:18 anticipates the use of pillars, but this practice was never widespread in biblical times. The graves of the infamous dead were often marked with a pile of stones (Achan, Josh. 7:26; Absalom, 2 Sam. 18:17; the king of Ai and the five Canaanite kings, Josh. 8:29; 10:27). In New Testament times graves were whitewashed each spring so people could see them easily and avoid touching them to prevent ritual defilement during the Passover and Pentecost pilgrimages (Matt. 23:27; compare Luke 11:44).

Coffins were generally not used in ancient Palestine. The body was placed on a simple bier and

Roman version of graves—tombs with niches (for jars containing cremated remains) like these at Pompeii.

transported to the grave site. While Canaanites often placed containers of food and water in their tombs, the Israelites largely avoided this custom.

In Hebrew thought graves were not simply places to deposit human remains. They were in a sense extensions of Sheol, the place of the dead. Since the realm of Sheol was threatening and since each grave was an individual expression of Sheol, the Israelites avoided burial sites when possible and treated them with circumspection. They performed purification rites when contact was unavoidable.

See *Death; Eternal Life; Sheol.* Joe Haag

GRAVEL Loose, rounded fragments of rock. One image of the suffering of conquered Zion was teeth broken by gravel (Lam. 3:16), perhaps the same as licking dust before the feet of the conqueror.

GRAVEN IMAGE See *Idols.*

GRAVING TOOL A sharp implement used to finish shaping the rough form of a statue cast from a mold (Ex. 32:4) or used for engraving tablets with writing (Jer. 17:1).

GRAY See *Colors.*

GREAT A title claimed by the Samaritan magician Simon (Acts 8:9–10). The title represents a claim to divine honors though the precise meaning of the title is unclear. Justin Martyr held that the Samaritans revered Simon as the highest god of the Canaanite pantheon. Others have argued that Simon claimed to be a lesser god who represented the power of the high god, such as Baal Zebul or Athena.

GREAT LIZARD See *Animals.*

GREAT OWL See *Birds.*

GREAT SEA Mediterranean Sea (Num. 34:6,7; Josh. 15:12). See *Mediterranean Sea.*

The Mediterranean Sea along the coastline near Caesarea Maritima.

GRECIA (Grē´ cĭ à) KJV spelling of Greece in Daniel 8:21; 10:20; 11:2. See *Greece.*

GRECIAN (Grē´ cian) Proper adjective referring to things or to people with origins in Greece. In the New Testament this refers to Jews who had adopted the Greek culture and language. They formed a significant part of the early church and created problems because of prejudice within the church (Acts 6:1; 9:29).

GREECE (Grēēce) Located between the Italian Peninsula and Asia Minor, Greece itself is a peninsula with the Adriatic and Ionian Seas on the west and the Aegean Sea on the east. These seas, in turn, are a part of the larger Mediterranean Sea. Greece owes its rough terrain to the fact that it is the southern end of the central European mountain range. Another geographical feature is the numerous islands that lie in close proximity to the Greek mainland. The southernmost area, the Peloponnesus, is itself virtually an island, connected to the mainland by only a narrow neck of land known as the Isthmus of Corinth.

Its mountainous nature has played an important role in the development of the country. First of all, it has an unusually long shoreline for such a small area, resulting from the fact that there are numerous bays and inlets, giving it many natural harbors. Since its mountains were heavily forested in

Terracotta of woman with Grecian dress and hairstyle, dating from the second to first century B.C.

earlier times, shipbuilding and the sea trade developed. Secondly, the rough terrain discouraged a sense of unity among its people since communication between them was not easy. Finally, the land for agriculture, while fertile, was limited so that what was produced could not sustain a large population. Small grains, grapes, and olives were the main agricultural products while the mountains provided pastures for sheep and goats.

Historical Developments About the time of the great prophets in Israel (after 800 B.C.), city-states began to develop in Greece. The limited food supplies had forced Greeks to leave the homeland. As a result, colonies were established on the Mediterranean islands, Asia Minor, Sicily, Italy, and in the Black Sea area. Colonies provided the basis for trade; and trade, in turn, encouraged the growth of cities since the economy was not tied to agriculture.

The high-water mark for the city-states was 500-404 B.C. The dominant city-states of the period were Athens and Sparta. About 500-475 B.C. Athens beat off a threat from the Persians. There followed what is known as the Golden Age of Athens. Under its great leader—Pericles—art, architecture, and drama flourished. Peloponnesian city-states feared the power of Athens, however,

The Erechtheum with the Porch of the Maidens on the Acropolis of ancient Athens in Greece.

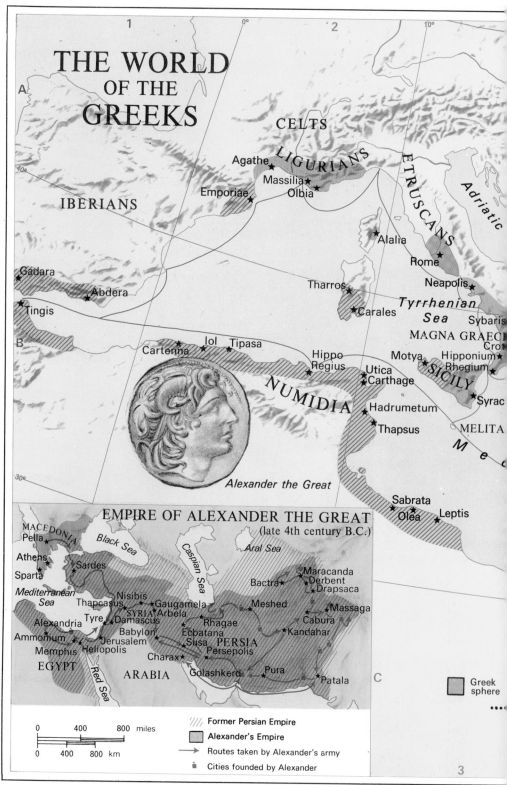

THE WORLD
OF THE
GREEKS

CELTS

LIGURIANS

Agathe
Massilia
Emporiae
Olbia

ETRUSCANS

Adriatic

IBERIANS

Alalia

Rome

Neapolis

Gadara
Abdera

Tharros

Tyrrhenian
Sea
Sybaris

Tingis

Carales

MAGNA GRAECI
Cro

Iol   Tipasa
Cartenna

Hippo
Regius

Motya   Hipponium
Utica   Rhegium
Carthage   SICILY

NUMIDIA

Hadrumetum

Syrac

Thapsus

MELITA

M

Alexander the Great

Sabrata
Olea   Leptis

EMPIRE OF ALEXANDER THE GREAT
(late 4th century B.C.)

MACEDONIA
Pella

Black Sea

Aral Sea

Caspian Sea

Maracanda
Derbent
Drapsaca

Athens
Sparta

Sardes

Bactra

Mediterranean
Sea
Thapcasus
Nisibis
Gaugamela
SYRIA Arbela
Tyre Damascus
Babylon
Jerusalem
Heliopolis

Meshed

Massaga

Alexandria
Ammonium
Memphis

Rhagae
Susa   Ecbatana
PERSIA
Persepolis

Cabura
Kandahar

EGYPT

Charax

Red Sea

ARABIA

Golashkerd

Pura

Patala

C

Greek
sphere

0 400 800 miles	
0 400 800 km	

|////| Former Persian Empire |
| Alexander's Empire |
| → | Routes taken by Alexander's army |
| | Cities founded by Alexander |

© carta

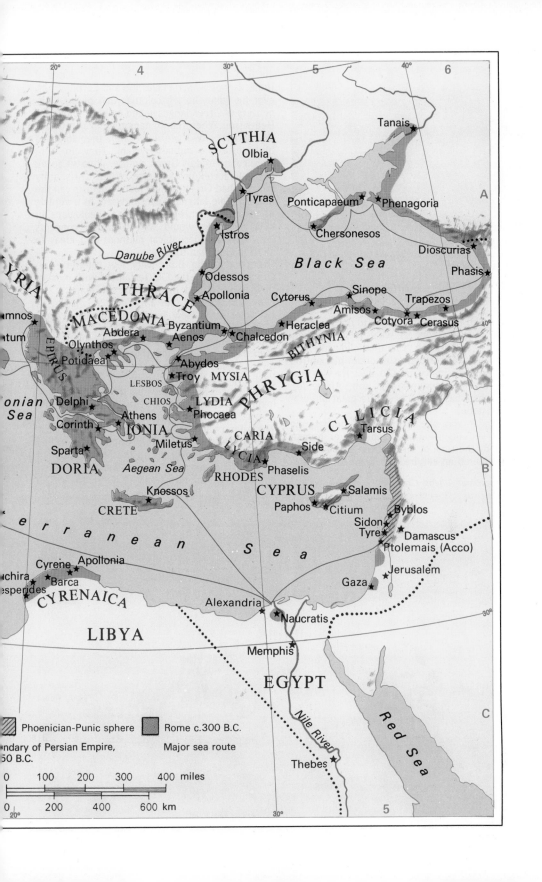

SCYTHIA

Tanais ★

Olbia ★

Tyras ★

Ponticapaeum ★ ★ Phenagoria

Istros ★

Chersonesos ★

Dioscurias ★

Danube River

Odessos ★

Black Sea

Phasis ★

THRACE

Apollonia ★

Cytorus ★

Sinope ★

Trapezos ★

YRIA

MACEDONIA

Byzantium ★

Heraclea ★

Amisos ★

Cotyora ★ Cerasus ★

EPIRUS

mnos ★

Abdera ★

Aenos ★

Chalcedon ★

BITHYNIA

tum

Olynthos ★

PHRYGIA

Potidaea ★

Abydos ★

★ Troy MYSIA

LESBOS

CILICIA

onian Sea

Delphi ★

CHIOS

LYDIA

Corinth ★

Athens ★

Phocaea ★

Tarsus ★

IONIA

CARIA

Sparta ★

Miletus ★

LYCIA

Side ★

DORIA

Aegean Sea

RHODES

Phaselis ★

Knossos ★

CYPRUS

Salamis ★

CRETE

Paphos ★

Citium ★

Byblos ★

Sidon ★

Tyre ★

Damascus ★

Mediterranean Sea

Ptolemais (Acco) ★

Cyrene ★ Apollonia ★

Jerusalem ★

chira ★

Barca ★

esperides ★

Gaza ★

CYRENAICA

Alexandria ★

LIBYA

Naucratis ★

Memphis ★

EGYPT

Nile River

Red Sea

Thebes ★

Relief of the myth of Telephus, son of Hercules, and his encounter with Achilles, a myth crucial to Greek history and culture.

and united under the leadership of Sparta to war against Athens. The defeat of Athens in 404 B.C. began a period of decline for the city-states.

About 350 B.C. Philip II came to the throne of Macedonia, a territory in what is now largely northern Greece. In the years that followed Philip brought all the Greek peninsula under his control, only to be assassinated in 336 B.C. He was succeeded by his twenty-year-old son, Alexander, whose schoolmaster had been the great philosopher, Aristotle.

Alexander was one of the most outstanding military and organizational geniuses of human history. By the time of his death in 323 B.C., he had conquered an empire that spanned the Mid-

The Acropolis at Athens, Greece.

dle East from Greece to the western reaches of India, as well as Syria-Palestine and Egypt. Wherever he went, he left colonies that became dispensers of Greek language and culture, known as Hellenism. When the Romans took over much of this territory two centuries later, they imposed their legal and military system. They, in turn, were conquered by Greek culture. Thus we speak of the Graeco-Roman culture. When Christianity arose, it had Greek, which many linguists call the most flexible language ever devised, as a vehicle to spread its concepts. Christian theologians in later centuries would wed Christian concepts with Greek philosophical methods and ideas to develop Christian theology.

Greece and the Bible Very few references to Greece appear in the Old Testament with most of them being found in the Book of Daniel (Dan. 8:21; 10:20; 11:2. See also Zech. 9:13). This is not true of the New Testament, however, especially as regards Paul's ministry. Some of his most fruitful work was done in Greek cities. Philippi, in Macedonia, was the first church founded by Paul on European soil (Acts 16). It would become Paul's special favorite among his churches and would be the recipient of his most intimate and loving letter, the Epistle to the Philippians. In the district of Thessaly, Paul founded two churches, Thessalonica and Berea (Acts 17:1–14). The Thessalonians also would be the recipients of Pauline letters, two of which are in the New Testament (1 and 2 Thessalonians). Just as Paul had problems while at Thessalonica (Acts 17:1–9), so he had

problems explaining to the church about the return of the Lord.

Bible students have long debated about Paul's success or lack of it at Athens (Acts 17:16–33). While the worship of the Greek gods had declined, Paul's experience in the marketplace at Athens shows that it was not entirely dead. It was, however, the sense of the failure of the older religions that led to the rapid acceptance of the Christian religion throughout the Roman empire. Paul, however, did not win a large number of converts at Athens, but he did win some.

No city received more attention nor provoked more correspondence from Paul than Corinth. Located on the narrow isthmus that connects the Peloponnesus to the rest of Greece, Corinth was a brawling, sinful seaport town, the crossroads of the Mediterranean (Acts 18:1–17). Here Paul met two people who would be among his most valuable helpers, Priscilla and Aquila. He would be brought to trial; he would establish one of his most troublesome and controversial churches, and later he would write at least four letters to that church. Two survived to become a part of the New Testament.

The Greek influence on the New Testament and Christianity is immeasurable. *Koine,* the Greek of the streets, is the language of the New Testament. At least five New Testament books are written to churches in Greek cities (Philippians, 1 and 2 Thessalonians, 1 and 2 Corinthians). All the other books in the New Testament are written in the Greek language. As the Christian gospel moved out into the Mediterranean world, it had to communicate its values to people who were steeped in Greek culture and religion. Both gained from the relationship with people being transformed by the gospel and Christianity gaining a vehicle for its spread.   *John H. Tullock*

GREED An excessive or reprehensible desire to acquire; covetousness. The greed of Eli's sons for the best part of the sacrifices disqualified them from the priesthood (1 Sam. 2:29). Hosea condemned priests who were greedy for the people's iniquity (4:8 NRSV), that is, greedy for the sin offerings.

Jesus warned against all types of greed (Luke 12:15; KJV covetousness). The Pauline standard for Christian ministry gave no pretext for greed (1 Thess. 2:5; 1 Tim 3:3,8). Greed marked the Gentile or pagan way of life (Eph. 4:19).

GREEK LANGUAGE The Greek language has had a long and illustrious history and continues to this day as a vital and viable language.

Like English, Greek is classified as a part of the Indo-European family of languages. It is a more highly inflected language than English. These inflections identify the uses and functions of the words in a sentence. The stems of Greek words are modified by the addition of prefixes, by the changing of the endings of words, and by the insertion of a letter or letters in the midst of words. In the hands of a skilled writer, the Greek language is able to communicate the nuances of philosophy and the deep emotional feelings of a Sophoclean tragedy.

The origins of the Greek language are buried in antiquity. Its development centered in the Greek mainland and the coastal areas around the Aegean Sea. Prior to the time of Alexander the Great, there was no central form of government which held power over all Greek-speaking people. Their territory, for the most part, was comprised of a series of independent city-states. Because these city-states were relatively isolated a variety of Greek dialects developed. The major literary dialects were Attic, Ionic, Doric, and Aeolic. In time the Attic dialect became dominant. The less influential dialects did continue to be used in many parts of the land.

The extant literature which represents the earliest form of literary Greek begins with Homer and the *Iliad* and *Odyssey.* These epic poems reflect the richness of the language from ancient times. Homer used the Greek language to portray the heroic portions of humanity. On the other hand, Hesiod, who lived about a century later, left a different type of poetic literature. In his *Works and Days,* Hesiod pictured the daily human struggle to survive.

The Golden Age of Greece differs from the other periods in two ways. It spanned a relatively brief period of time, lasting less than a century. In addition, the literary brilliance of the period was limited primarily to the Attic Greek dialect and to Athens. Its influence, however, has been far reaching. The tragic and comic playwrights left an indelible imprint on the theater of succeeding generations. Similarly Plato, Aristotle, and other writers from the Golden Age of Greece have influenced modern philosophy, logic, ethics, and even science.

The Golden Age of Greece was followed by the Hellenistic Greek period. This period lasted from about 300 B.C. to A.D. 600. It was succeeded by the Byzantine period with its political and ecclesiastical separation between East and West.

Of all of the linguistic periods in the development of the Greek language, the Hellenistic period is of particular importance. During this time Greek became the universal language of the "known" world.

Although Rome was the dominant military and political force throughout Europe and Asia Minor during the Hellenistic period, Greek rather than Latin maintained its domination as the language of the people. Latin was the language of the Roman government; Greek was the language of the Empire, the *lingua franca.* Popularly, it has been referred to as *koine* Greek. The word "*koine*" is a

G

transliteration of the Greek word which means "common." The word itself had reference to that which was everyday, that which was of ordinary people, that which was "vulgar" or common.

Biblical scholars have long known that the Greek of the New Testament is considerably different from the Greek of the Golden Age. The differences were explained by referring to the New Testament Greek as "Biblical Greek" or "Holy Ghost Greek." This implied that, although the roots of the New Testament were in the Greek language, its style and form differed sharply from the literary Attic Greek with which scholars were familiar.

Toward the close of the nineteenth century, archeologists began to find fragments of papyri, the "paper" of the ancient world. Much of this papyri was found in Egypt in the garbage heaps of some of the major cities. Adolph Deissmann, one of the important scholars of the day, realized that much of the Greek which he was finding in the papyri was similar to that found in the Greek New Testament. He published the results of his investigation in a work called *Light from the Ancient East.* This work along with that of others revolutionized biblical study. Scholars were able to demonstrate that the Greek found in the New Testament was the same as that found in other writings of the day. It was not some special dialect or Holy Ghost language. The New Testament was written in the universal language of the Empire.

The understanding of the New Testament has been enhanced by the discovery of secular texts which were written during the Hellenistic period. These texts include the papyri, pieces of broken pottery called "ostraca," inscriptions on monuments, as well as a number of formal works by such authors as Josephus, Epictetus, Philo, and Plutarch. A study of this material has revealed a wide variation in literary skills and style of the writers. They ranged from the semiliterate to the highly stylized. The latter attempted to imitate style and form of the Golden Age of Greece and were called Atticists. As should be expected, the

Greek inscription on a sarcophagus at Thyatira containing the word "Thyatira" verifying the site's identity.

literary style of the writers of the New Testament falls somewhere between these two extremes. Consequently, the average citizen who lived in Alexandria (Egypt), in Jerusalem, or in Rome could have easily understood the writings found in the Greek of the New Testament. *W. Ray Ellis*

GREEN See *Colors.*

GREETING A salutation on meeting; an expression of good wishes at the opening (or in Hellenistic times times also the close) of a letter.

Among Semitic peoples the usual greeting was and is peace: "Peace be to you, and peace be to your house, and peace be to all that you have" (1 Sam. 25:5–6 NAS; compare Luke 10:5). The usual Greek greeting on meeting is *charein,* translated "hail" or "greeting" (Luke 1:28; Matt. 28:9). A kiss was frequently a part of such greeting (Gen. 29:13; Rom. 16:16; 1 Cor. 16:20; 2 Cor. 13:12; 1 Thess. 5:26; 1 Pet. 5:14). The command not to stop to exchange greetings (2 Kings 4:29; Luke 10:4) underlines the urgency of the commission given.

The opening greetings of ancient letters typically took the form: X (sender) to Y (addressee), greeting (Acts 15:23; 23:26; Jas. 1:1). A letter addressed to a social superior took the form: To Y (addressee) from X (sender), greeting (Ezra 4:17). James is the only New Testament book to begin with the normal Greek greeting *charein.*

Paul transformed the customary greeting *charein* into an opportunity for sharing the faith, substituting "grace [*charis*] to you and peace from God our Father and the Lord Jesus Christ" (Rom. 1:7; 1 Cor. 1:3; 2 Cor. 1:2; Gal. 1:3; Eph. 1:2; Phil. 1:2; Tit. 1:4). In Paul's opening greeting these terms always occur in this order, witnessing to the truth that peace cannot be experienced apart from the prior experience of God's grace.

The greetings of Hellenistic letters typically contained a prayer for the health of the recipients. 3 John 2 provides the best New Testament example: "Beloved, I pray that all may go well with you and that you may be in good health, just as it is well with your soul" (NRSV). Paul greatly expanded his opening prayers. Most of his letters

begin with a prayer of thanksgiving, usually for the recipients. Ephesians begins with a benediction rather than a prayer of thanksgiving (also 1 Peter 1:3–5; Rev. 1:4–6). In the Pauline corpus only Galatians lacks an opening prayer.

Hellenistic letters frequently included closing greetings. Most often these are "third person" greetings of the form X sends you greetings (by me) (1 Cor. 16:19–20; Col. 4:10–14) or send my greetings to Y (who is not directly addressed; e.g., Col. 4:15). Closing greetings often included a prayer or benediction. The simplest is "Grace be with you" (Col. 4:18; 1 Tim. 6:21; Titus 3:15; Heb. 13:25). Elsewhere the benediction is expanded (Rom. 16:25–27; 1 Cor. 16:23–24; Gal. 6:16; Eph. 6:23–24; Phil. 4:23). Some of the most familiar benedictions used in Christian worship come from such closing greetings: "The grace of the Lord Jesus Christ, and the love of God, and the communion of the Holy Ghost" (2 Cor. 13:14); "Now the God of peace, that brought again from the dead our Lord Jesus, that great shepherd of the sheep . . . make you perfect in every good work to do his will . . ." (Heb. 13:20–21); "Now unto Him that is able to keep you from falling . . . to the only wise God our Savior" (Jude 24–25).   *Chris Church*

GRIEF AND MOURNING Practices and emotions associated with the experience of the death of a loved one or or of other catastrophe or tragedy. The Bible tells us of life and death. When it mentions death, the Bible frequently relates the experience of the participants. So we are told of the mourning of Abraham for Sarah (Gen. 23:2). Jacob mourned for Joseph, thinking he was dead. "And Jacob rent his clothes, and put sackcloth upon his loins, and mourned for his son many days . . . he refused to be comforted; and he said, For I will go down into the grave unto my son mourning. Thus his father wept for him" (Gen. 37:34–45). The Egyptians mourned for Jacob 70 days (Gen. 50:3). Leaders were mourned, often for 30 days: Aaron (Num. 20:29), Moses (Deut. 34:8), and Samuel (1 Sam. 25:1).

Mary and Martha wept over their brother Lazarus (John 11:31). After Jesus watched Mary and her friends weeping, we are told, "Jesus wept" (John 11:35).

Weeping was then, as now, the primary indication of grief. Tears are repeatedly mentioned, "My tears have been my meat day and night" (Ps. 42:3*a*).

The loud lamentation was also a feature of mourning. The Egyptians lifted up their voices, "There was a great cry in Egypt; for there was not a house where there was not one dead" (Ex. 12:30). Not only did the actual relatives mourn, but they hired professional mourners, "because man goeth to his long home, and the mourners go about the streets" (Eccl. 12:5*b*). "Consider ye,

and call for the mourning women" (Jer. 9:17). In this same verse they are also referred to as "cunning women," which suggests that there were certain techniques which these women practiced with unusual skill. Jesus went to Jairus's house to heal his daughter and "saw the minstrels and the people making a noise" (Matt. 9:23).

Yet another feature was personal disfigurement which was probably done to convince onlookers that the person was really grieving. Sometimes they tore their garments, "Reuben . . . rent his clothes" (Gen. 37:29). On others they wore sackcloth, "And David said . . . Rend your clothes, and gird you with sackcloth, and mourn" (2 Sam. 3:31). The women wore black or somber material, "feign thyself to be a mourner, and put on now mourning apparel, and anoint not thyself with oil, but be as a women that had a long time mourned for the dead" (2 Sam. 14:2). Mourners covered their heads, "David . . . wept . . . and had his head covered, . . . and all people that was with him covered every man his head" (2 Sam. 15:30).

Job's friends came to help him, "So they sat down with him upon the ground seven days and seven nights, and none spake a word unto him: for they saw that his grief was very great" (Job 2:13). From this and other statements we can learn ways in which we can minister to grief-stricken people:

1) Realize the gift of presence. Just calling and being there can be of value.

2) Do not overtalk the grieving person. Provide the awesome power of the listening ear.

3) Let them know it is alright for them to grieve. Even Jesus wept over the death of His friend Lazarus.

4) Be ready to minister to the griever for a long time. It sometimes takes as much as two years to work through a grief experience.

5) Tactfully remind the griever of Him who said, "I am the resurrection, and the life: he that believeth in me, though he were dead, yet shall he live" (John 11:25), and invoke His blessing.
                                                    John W. Drakeford

GREYHOUND KJV translation of an obscure Hebrew term (Prov. 30:31). Modern translations read "strutting cock" or rooster.

GRIDDLE A flat surface on which food is cooked by dry heat (Lev. 2:5; 6:21; 7:9 modern translations; KJV, pan). In earlier days this would have been of stone. Later griddles were made of iron (Ezek. 4:3 where the same Hebrew word is often rendered plate).

GRISLED KJV term for dappled (spotted) grey.

GROVE In Genesis 21:33, a tree planted in Beer-sheba by Abraham. More than likely it was a tamarisk. The King James Version of the Bible also uses the word "grove" to translate the term "Asherah." See *Asherah; Idols.*

GUARD An individual or body of troops assigned to protect a person or thing. Guard translates numerous Hebrew and Greek terms. *Tabbach* (literally butcher or slaughterer) is a Hebrew term used only for officers of foreign kings (of Pharaoh, Gen. 37:36; 39:1; of Nebuchadnezzar, 2 Kings 25:8–20; Jer. 39:9–13). Two of the terms for guards are derived from the root *shamar* (to hedge about, guard, protect). The KJV often translated these terms by "watch" (Neh. 4:9; 7:3). The most common designation for the guards of the kings of Israel and Judah was "runners" (1 Sam. 22:17; 1 Kings 1:5; 14:27–28) from the use of such guards to escort the king's chariot. Modern translation frequently use the expression "court of the guard" where the KJV used "court of the prison" (Neh. 3:25; Jer. 32:2). Two terms for guard are used only one time. The first refers to the large guard gathered to defend the boy king Joash (2 Chron. 23:10). The second refers to God as the guard of His people (Zech. 9:8).

Three Greek nouns are translated as guard. *Hypēretēs* is used for those guarding the high priest's quarters (Matt. 26:58; Mark 14:54). *Koustōdia* (Matt. 27:66; 28:11) is a Latin loan word, suggesting that this guard was indeed a Roman guard. *Philakē* is used for stations of guards in Acts 12:10.

GUARDIAN An adult responsible for the person and property of a minor (2 Kings 10:1,5). The Greek term *epitropos,* translated guardian at Galatians 4:2 (KJV tutor), is a general word for a manager. Modern translations render the term as steward, foreman, or manager when it occurs elsewhere (Matt. 20:8; Luke 8:3). The basic thrust of Paul's message is clear: Before experiencing of God's grace in Christ, the believers' lives were lives of slavery (4:3,8). The guardian appears to be an image for the "elemental things of the world," that is, of celestial or demonic powers regarded as gods by pagan Gentiles. Paul earlier pictured the Jews as under the charge of the law (Gal. 3:22–25).

GUDGODAH (Gŭd gō′ dah) Place name of uncertain meaning. A stop on the Israelites' wilderness journey (Deut. 10:7). It is apparently the same place as Hor-hagidgad (Num. 33:32). The location is uncertain with some scholars looking at the area near the wadi Chadachid.

GUEST One invited to a feast (1 Sam. 9:24; 2 Sam. 15:11). Jesus outraged those in Jericho by being a guest at the home of Zachaeus, a well-known sinner (Luke 19:7). Peter crossed racial barriers by welcoming the Gentile messengers sent by Cornelius as guests in his home (Acts 10:23).

Figurative uses of guest include Zephaniah 1:7 where consecrated guests are an image of invading armies the Lord invited to punish Judah. Jesus described His disciples as guests at a wedding feast who cannot mourn as long as He, the bridegroom, is with them (Matt. 9:15). God's salvation is pictured as a wedding hall full of guests who must have proper attire (Matt. 22:10–13).

GUEST ROOM or CHAMBER A single room where travelers could lodge. The guest room of Mark 14:14; Luke 22:11 was a room borrowed for the celebration of the Passover meal. The same Greek term is traditionally translated as inn at Luke 2:7.

GUILE Crafty or deceitful cunning; teachery; duplicity; deceit. Jacob dressed in his brother's clothes with the goatskins on his arms and neck is Scripture's best-known illustration of guile (Gen. 27:35; KJV, subtilty; modern translations, deceitfully). Jesus perhaps had this image of Jacob (Israel) in mind when pronouncing Nathanael "an Israelite indeed in whom is no guile" (John 1:47; compare John 1:51 with Gen. 28:12). First Peter 2:22 describes Christ as one without guile in His mouth. Paul encouraged Christians to be "guileless as to what is evil" (Rom. 16:19 NRSV; compare 1 Pet. 2:1), that is, innocent or naive when it comes to evil.

GUILT A sense of shame at personal wrongdoing. Guilt implies being responsible for an offense or a wrongdoing. It is a situation that exists because one has done something forbidden or failed to do something that was required. The source of the forbidden thing or omitted thing may be religious, legal, social, or personal. It may be a wrongdoing against something written or unwritten.

Guilt may be either a fact or a feeling. For example, a direct violation of law would make one guilty of violating that law. The guilt in this case would be present whether or not the person feels guilty. The condemnation may come from oneself, others, or from God. Or the condemnation might not occur at all. Nevertheless, the person is guilty because a real violation has taken place.

The Bible frequently contrasts those who are guilty with expressions that signify righteousness or just behavior. For example, Job insisted on his righteousness before the Lord (Job 27:1–6). His friends inisisted that he was wicked and therefore guilty (Job 22:5; 35:1–8). To be guilty can mean the same thing as to be wicked. In Psalm 1 it is assumed that the wicked, sinners, and scoffers are guilty of sin and that they will ultimately perish. When Pilate said that he found no guilt in Jesus, he meant that He was innocent of the charges brought against Him (Luke 23:14; John 19:4,6). There was no basis on which to charge Him.

Guilt is connected with sin in the Bible. Sin is

basically against God or against God's law. It can mean rebellion against God, or a willful transgression. Sin can also mean to miss the mark.

The Hebrew writers generally did not distinguish between the act of sin and the guilt that came from the act. The various words used for sin in the Old Testament also expressed the idea of guilt. To sin, therefore, is to become guilty.

To connect sin and guilt is a way of saying that human beings are responsible before God for their actions. Paul, in the Book of Romans went to great lengths to show that all mankind is guilty before God (Rom. 1:18–20). If all have sinned (Rom. 3:23), then all are guilty and cut off from God. Something must be done to remove the guilt.

The Old Testament describes several things that could be done to remove guilt. Sinners could confess their sins and make restitution for the wrongs they had committed (Num. 5:6–10). Various sacrifices could be brought to the priests for a guilt offering (Lev. 5:6–7:38). Restitution, sacrifice, or ritual penalty had to be made for sin and guilt.

A new idea presents itself in passages like Isaiah 53: it is the idea that a righteous one can suffer for the guilt of others. One can bear the sin of many and intercede for their transgressions (Isa. 53:12). In the New Testament, Jesus fulfilled the role of the one suffering for the sins of many . . . "Christ died for the ungodly," and we are reconciled to God (Rom. 5:6–11; compare Eph. 1:7; Col. 1:19–20).

The idea of a sacrifice or offering for sin and guilt is picked up by other New Testament writers. Jesus was made a merciful High Priest to make propitiation for the sins of the people (Heb. (2:17). Twice 1 John says that Jesus is the propitiation for our sins (1 John 2:2; 4:10). This emphasis shows how seriously the Bible takes sin and guilt. Guilt has to be dealt with in an objective way. Guilt, according to these New Testament writers, requires the sacrifice of the Son of God. See *Expiation and Propitiation.*

Guilt is both corporate and individual in the Bible. The corporate aspect can be seen in 2 Chronicles 24:18. The king and officials of the nation abandoned God, and their guilt brought wrath on the nation. Ezra lamented the guilt that had come upon the people for their sins (Ezra 9:3–6). The individual nature of guilt can be seen in passages like Psalm 32. There the psalmist acknowledged his own transgression and asked for forgiveness from guilt (v. 5). Jeremiah in speaking of the New Covenant declared that all people would be held responsible for their own sins (Jer. 31:30).

As a feeling, "guilt" refers to the emotional aspects of a person's experience. An individual may feel himself or herself to be condemned or to have sinned. The feeling may bear little or no apparent relationship to the fact with which it is

associated. In other words, one may feel guilty when there is no evidence to suggest a reason for guilt.

However, feeling is often a legitimate expression of guilt. The bitter lament Psalm 51 carries both an awareness of sin and deep feelings of remorse and repentance. Psalm 38 paints a picture of a suffering sinner weighed down with sin and guilt. Guilt is a burden (Ps. 38:4) that creates anxiety (Ps. 38:18).

Because human beings are so complex, it is often difficult to separate guilt feelings from real guilt. These guilt feelings must be taken seriously. If a person cannot resolve these guilt feelings before God, it may be wise to seek a counselor to help determine where the guilt feelings originate. Unresolved guilt can have a paralyzing effect on a person. Asking for and receiving forgiveness is one of the major ways that we can be absolved from guilt. God in His faithfulness has promised to forgive us from all iniquity (1 John 1:9)

See *Atonement; Christ; Forgiveness; Reconciliation; Sin.*   *D. Glenn Saul*

GUILT OFFERING See *Sacrifice and Offering.*

GULF Term used by the KJV and REB for the gorge or pit separating the rich man's place of torment from Lazarus' place of comfort in the presence of Abraham (Luke 16:26).

GULL See *Birds.*

GUM A yellow to yellowish-brown product formed from the excretions of certain plants. Gum was an item of the Ishmaelites' caravan trade with Egypt (Gen. 37:25; KJV, spicery) and was regarded as one of the choice products of the land (Gen. 43:11). Some English translations focus on the nature of the substance (gum, NRSV; aromatic gum, NAS). Others focus on the use of the material (spices, KJV, NIV, TEV). Ladanum spice (Gen. 37:25, NAS margin) is the soft, dark resin of rock roses used in making perfume. Gum tragacanth (REB) is a resin used in the arts and in pharmacy.

GUNI (Gū′ nī) Personal name meaning, "black-winged partridge." *1.* Son of Naphtali and grandson of Jacob (Gen. 46:24), thus head of the Gunite clan (Num. 26:48). *2.* Member of tribe of Gad (1 Chron. 5:15).

GUNITE (Gū′ nīte) Descendant of Guni and member of clan originated by Guni. See *Guni.*

GUR (Gŭr) Place name meaning, "foreign sojourner" or "young animal." An unidentified mountain road near Ibleam where Jehu's men caught up with and mortally wounded Ahaziah, king of Judah (841 B.C.) (2 Kings 9:27).

GUR-BAAL (Gŭr-bā' ȧl) Place name meaning, "foreign sojourner of Baal" or "young animal of Baal." An Arabian or bedouin city which God helped King Uzziah of Judah (792-740 B.C.) attack (2 Chron. 26:7). Greek manuscript evidence does not have Baal in the name. This would mean the city was Gur, also mentioned in the Amarna letters and situated east of Beersheba. Other scholars would identify the town with Jagur (Josh. 15:21).

GUTTER KJV translation of two Hebrew terms. That in Genesis 30:38,41 is rendered (drinking) troughs (NIV, REB, NRSV TEV) or runnels, a small stream (RSV). The term used at 2 Samuel 5:8 is rendered water shaft (NIV, NRSV) or water tunnel (NAS, TEV).

A restored gymnasium at the ancient city of Sardis.

The ruins of Ezion-Geber showing a water gutter, or water shaft.

GYMNASIUM The Greek educational center. The word comes from a Greek word (*gymnos)* which means naked. In ancient Greece, the gymnasium was the center for physical and intellectual education for aristocratic adolescent boys. The gymnasium originated in Athens where the citizens sought the ideals espoused by Pericles that men should have wisdom without the loss of manly vigor. Physical education included wrestling, swimming, running, and use of the bow and sling, all in the nude. Intellectually, the boys were trained in reading, writing, mathematics, politics, philosophy, and music. As time passed, the gymnasiums became open to all citizens and were an integral part of all Greek cities.

During the second century B.C., when the Seleucids under Antiochus Epiphanes tried to convert the Jews to Greek culture, Jason, one of the Jewish high priests, built a gymnasium in Jerusa-

lem. (See 1 Maccabees 1:14; 2 Maccabees 4:7.) Aristocratic Jewish young men began to frequent the gymnasium and to participate in Greek activities. The pious Jews were shocked at both their nudity, prohibited by Jews, and their practice of wearing the broad-brimmed Greek hats, associated with the worship of the Greek god Hermes. In addition some of the young men became ashamed of and tried to hide their circumcision. These practices were one of the causes for the Maccabean rebellion of 175 B.C.

There is no mention of the gymnasium in the New Testament, but there are references to the activities associated with it. In 1 Timothy 4:8, the expression "bodily exercise" is from the word for gymnasium. Paul also used metaphors from the gymnasium in 1 Corinthians 9:24−27; Galatians 2:2; 5:7; Philippians 1:30; 2:16. No bad connotations are associated with the word in these passages. *W. T. Edwards*

The open area (palaestra) of the gymnasium at Pompeii, with the gladiators' rooms to the left.

H

View of the ornate carving of the ruins at Baalbek (Heliopolis) in Lebanon.

HAAHASHTARI (Hā′ å hǎsh′ tå rī) Personal and national name in Persian language meaning, "kingdom." Member of tribe of Judah and clan of Caleb (1 Chron. 4:6), the form of the word indicating as in many biblical genealogies a political group as well as the ancestor. Nothing else is known of the person or nation.

HABAIAH (Hå bā′ iåh) Personal name meaning, "Yahweh hides, keeps safe." Clan leader of exiled priests who returned from Babylon to Jerusalem with Zerubbabel about 537 B.C. (Ezra 2:61).

HABAKKUK (Hå′ bǎk′ kǔk) A prophet of the late seventh century B.C., contemporary to Jeremiah. One explanation has his name based on a root meaning "to embrace." The Greek Old Testament spelling "Hambakoum" suggests a root meaning "plant" or "vegetable."

The Times Judah had just experienced the exhilaration of the glorious days of Josiah, marked by freedom, prosperity, and a great religious revival. The Assyrians, once the scourge of the Middle East, were only a shadow of their former selves. In their place, however, stood the Babylonians. In the Book of Habakkuk, they are called the Chaldeans, so named for the region from which their rulers came. The Babylonian armies were led by the energetic Nebuchadnezzar, who was soon to succeed his father Nabopolassar as king.

Nineveh, Assyria's capital, fell in 612 B.C. The powerful poetry of Nahum celebrates its fall. In 609 B.C., disaster struck. King Josiah, attempting to block the Egyptians as they moved north along the Palestinian coast to aid Assyria, was killed at Megiddo in northern Palestine. In his place the Egyptians set up Josiah's son, Jehoiakim. Unlike his father, Jehoiakim was a petty tyrant. Over the next ten or eleven years, Jehoiakim tried to play the Babylonians off against the Egyptians until he finally exhausted the patience of Nebuchadnezzar. In 598, he laid siege to Jerusalem. That same year, Jehoiakim died, leaving his son, Jehoiachin, to become Nebuchadnezzar's prisoner when Jerusalem fell in 597 B.C. People from the upper classes and skilled workmen were also among those taken to Babylon as captives.

The Man Other than his work as a prophet, nothing for certain of a personal nature is known about Habakkuk. Tradition makes him a priest of the tribe of Levi. The apocryphal work *Bel and the Dragon* (vss. 33–39) tells a story about Habakkuk being taken to Babylon by an angel to feed Daniel while he was in the lions den.

The Book The Book of Habakkuk gives us the best picture of the prophet. After a brief statement identifying the prophet (1:1), the book falls into three distinct divisions:

A. The Prophet's Questions and the Lord's Answers (1:2—2:5)

B. Five Woes against Tyrants (2:6–20)

C. A Prayer of Habakkuk (3:1–19)

Of these three parts, only one, the woes (2:6–20) fits the traditional pattern of the prophets. The great prophets of the Lord saw themselves as spokesmen for the Lord to the people. In the first section (1:2—2:5) in what has been called "the beginning of speculation in Israel," Habakkuk spoke to the Lord for the people. He asked two questions, the responses to which give Habakkuk a unique niche in the prophetic canon. The first question, Why does violence rule where there should be justice (1:2–5) expressed the prophet's sense of dismay, either about conditions within his own land caused by Jehoiakim, or by the oppression of weak countries by stronger powers. In light of what follows, internal injustice seems to have been the object of his concern.

In response, the Lord told the prophet that He was at work sending the Chaldeans as the instrument of His judgment (1:5–11).

The prophet shrank from such an idea and posed another question: Lord, how can you use someone more sinful than we are to punish us? (1:12–17). When the answer was not forthcoming immediately, he took his stand in the watchtower to wait for it. It was worth the wait: "Behold, he whose soul is not upright in him shall fail, but the righteous shall live by his faith" (2:4 RSV). The term "faith" has more of the sense of faithfulness or conviction that results in action.

The woes (2:6–20), not unlike those of the other prophets, denounce various kinds of tyranny: plunder (2:6–8); becoming rich and famous by unjust means (2:9–11); building towns with blood (2:12–14); degrading one's neighbor (2:15–17); and idol worship (2:18–19). This section ends with a ringing affirmation of the sovereignty of the Lord.

The final section (3:1–19) is, in reality, a psalm, not unlike those found in the Book of Psalms. It is a magnificent hymn, extolling the Lord's triumph over His and His people's foes.

Habakkuk in History This book was a favorite of the people of the Dead Sea Scrolls. They interpreted the first two chapters as prophecy of their triumph over the Romans who were the overlords of Palestine at that time. Unfortunately, the Romans prevailed.

More important to us, however, is the influence this book had on the apostle Paul. Habakkuk's declaration that "the just (righteous) shall live by his faith" (2:4) was taken by Paul as a central element in his theology. As he did with many Old Testament passages, he used it with a slightly different emphasis. Through Paul, this passage came alive for an Augustinian monk named Martin Luther, setting off the Protestant Reformation, one of history's greatest religious upheavals. Thus a so-called "Minor" prophet had a major influence on those who followed him.

Outline

I. A Prophet Perplexed: Why Does God Permit Injustice? (1:1–17)
  A. Prophet's first protest: A cry for deliverance from violence and iniquity (1:1–4).
  B. God's first reply: The worst is yet to be (1:5–11).
  C. Prophet's second protest: How can a holy God use such a cruel instrument as this evil people? (1:12–17)
II. A Prophet Perceiving: The Righteous Shall Live by Faithfulness (2:1–20).
  A. God's second reply (2:1–5)
    1. Revelation comes to one prepared to wait (2:1).
    2. Revelation must be easy to understand (2:2).
    3. Revelation will prove true in God's time (2:3).
    4. Persistent faith—not pride, parties, nor plunder—is the distinguishing mark of the righteous (2:4–5).
  B. God taunts His materialistic enemy (2:6–20).
    1. First taunt song: Woe because of pride and ambition (2:6–8)
    2. Second taunt song: Woe because of arrogance and greed (2:9–11)
    3. Third taunt song: Woe because of cruelty (2:12–14)
    4. Fourth taunt song: Woe because of drunkenness (2:15–17)
    5. Fifth taunt song: Woe because of idolatry (2:18–19)
    6. Conclusion: A call for universal worship of the holy God (2:20)
III. A Prophet Praying and Praising: A Psalm of Confidence Is the Proper Response to Revelation (3:1–19).
  A. Prayer asks God to repeat His acts of deliverance (3:1–2).
  B. Prayer gains confidence by recounting the holy God's redeeming acts (3:3–15).
  C. Prayer responds in awesome fear and confident joy to God's history with His people (3:16–18).
  D. Prayer claims God's strength for present crisis (3:19).   *John H. Tullock*

HABAZINIAH (Hăb′ a zĭ nī′ ah) Personal name meaning, "Yahweh inflated or caused to make merry." Grandfather of Jaazaniah, the Rechabite leader Jeremiah tested with wine (Jer. 35:3). See *Jaazaniah.*

HABAZZINIAH (Hăb ăz zĭ nī′ ah) Modern translations' spelling of Habaziniah.

HABERGEON A short coat of mail covering the neck and shoulder worn as defensive armor. The KJV uses harbergeon to translate three Hebrew words. The first (2 Chron. 26:14; Neh. 4:16) is translated coats of mail or armor, body armor, or breastplate by modern translations. Modern translations agree that the second term (Job 41:26) refers to an offensive weapon, the javelin. There is much uncertainty regarding the meaning of the third term (Ex. 28:32; 39:23). NAS, NRSV follow the KJV in retaining coat of mail. Other translations include: collar (NIV); garment (RSV); oversewn edge (REB following the earliest Greek translation). See *Arms and Armor.*

HABIRU (Hă bī′ rū) People mentioned in ancient texts written about 2000 to 1200 B.C. in Mesopotamia, Syria-Palestine, and Egypt. The word apparently means "outcast" or "renegade."
Identity of the Habiru Scholars have offered several theories attempting to identify these Habiru. Because the word sounds much like the name "Hebrew," some scholars thought it referred to ethnic Israel. Since it appears in texts written earlier than Abraham lived and since the Habiru seemed numerous during the patriarchal period, it does not appear to designate ethnic Hebrews. Most scholars treat the term as the name of a social class: outcasts or renegades. In letters written from Palestine to Amarna in Egypt, they appear as rebels attacking cities belonging to the pharaohs of the fourteenth century, and in one text they are further identified as former slaves who had revolted.
Relation to Hebrews If the Habiru are rebels and not an ethnic group, are they nevertheless somehow related to the Hebrews? Some scholars have said yes, seeing the Habiru as nomads who might have included the patriarchs to Joshua, or as peasants who revolted. The Bible, however, depicts the patriarchs, not as nomads, but as pastoralists (shepherds who settled beside other shepherds and farmers). Neither was Joshua a nomad, nor do the books of Joshua and Judges depict a revolt by peasants. About the only possible relationship is that the Hebrews might have included some Habiru from Egypt or Canaan.   *Paul Redditt*

HABITATION Dwelling place; home; KJV translation of ten different Hebrew words. Habitation is used for the dwellings of humans (Ex. 35:3; Isa. 27:10) and of birds (Ps. 104:12). Of special interest are references to the habitation of God. God's habitation is designated as heaven (Deut. 26:15; 2 Chron. 30:27), the Temple (2 Chron. 29:6), or Jerusalem (Ps. 46:4). Jeremiah 50:7 pictures the Lord as the dwelling place of justice or "their true pasture" (NIV; compare Pss. 71:3; 91:9). Ephesians 2:22 speaks of believers as the "habitation of God through the Spirit." Revelation 18:2 announces the fall of "Babylon," which "is become the habitation of devils."

HABOR (Hā′ bôr) Akkadian river name. A major

tributary of the Euphrates River. The Assyrians resettled many exiles from Israel there near Gozan when they captured the northern kingdom in 722 B.C. (2 Kings 17:6). See *Gozan.*

HACALIAH (Hăc å lī′ ah) Personal name meaning, "wait confidently on Yahweh." Father of Nehemiah. See *Nehemiah.*

HACHALIAH (Hăch å lī′ ah) KJV spelling of Hacaliah.

HACHMON (Hăch′ mon) Clan name meaning, "wisdom." Original ancestor of an Israelite clan called the Hachmonites. Most translations transliterate the Hebrew clan name as Hachmoni, including the Hebrew ending "*i*" that indicates membership in the clan or English "ite." TEV translates Hachmon (1 Chron. 11:11). Jashobeam, leader of David's army, was either a Hachmonite (1 Chron. 11:11) or a Tachmonite (2 Sam. 23:8), a copyist having either added or subtracted a "t" in transmitting the clan name. Jehiel, another of David's advisors, also belonged to the clan (1 Chron. 27:32). See *Jashobeam; Jehiel.*

HACHMONI (Hăch′ mō nī) See *Hachmon.*

HACHMONITE (Hăch′ mō nīte) See *Hachmon.*

HACMONI (Hăc′ mo nī) NIV spelling of Hachmoni.

HACMONITE (Hăc′ mo nīte) NIV spelling of Hachmonite.

HADAD (Hā′ dăd). Personal name meaning, "mighty." *1.* An Edomite king (Gen. 36:35). The name Hadad was borne by several members of the royal household of Edom. *2.* Hadad was also the name of the chief deity of the Ugaritic pantheon. This deity was identified as a storm-god. See *Canaan; Ugarit.*

HADAD-EZER (Hăd ăd-ē′ zēr) Syrian royal name meaning, "Hadad (god) helps." City-state king of Zobah in Syria whom David defeated to establish his control over Syria (2 Sam. 8:3–13). Apparently, Hadar-ezer (2 Sam. 10:16) represents a copyist's change from Hadad-ezer in transmitting the text. Ammonites saw David was too strong for them and hired Syrian troops, including those of Hadad-ezer, to help them, but Joab, David's general, defeated them (2 Sam. 10:6–19). Hadadezer regrouped the Syrians but again met defeat. Some Bible students think the narrative in chapter 8 may be a summary looking forward to the fuller account in chapter 10 of the same event. Others think two separate battles are described.

First Kings 11:23 shows the troubled situation in Syria. Rezon revolted against Hadad-ezer (possibly the son of the one in 1 Sam. 8; 10 or the same king). Rezon then established a kingdom for himself in the Syrian city of Damascus. Syria was thus a group of small city-states fighting among themselves for domination.

HADAD-RIMMON (Hā′ dăd-rĭm′ mon) Names of two Syrian gods combined into one word. Zechariah 12:11 describes the tragedy of the day of the Lord, including weeping and mourning in the Valley of Megiddo for Jerusalem. Such mourning could be compared only to the "mourning of Hadad-rimmon," apparently a reference to pagan worship ceremonies, perhaps for a dying and rising god. The exact interpretation of the passage is difficult, Hadad-rimmon being mentioned nowhere else.

HADAR (Hā′ dăr) Apparently a copyist's change of the name Hadad, a Syrian god, in Genesis 36:39 and in some manuscripts of Genesis 25:15. Translations differ on their readings, KJV reading Hadar in both cases. NIV, TEV read Hadad in both cases, while NAS, REB, NRSV retain Hadar in 36:39 but Hadad in 25:15. See *Hadad.* Parallel texts in 1 Chronicles read Hadad for both (1 Chron. 1:30, 50–51). A reverent copyist may not have wanted to introduce the name of the pagan god into Genesis.

HADAREZER (Hăd′ är-ē′ zēr) Copying change in some manuscripts for Hadad-ezer. See *Hadadezer.*

HADASHAH (Hå dăsh′ ah) Town name meaning, "new." Town in tribal territory of Judah situated in vicinity of Lachish (Josh. 15:37).

HADASSAH (Hå dăs sah) Personal name meaning, "myrtle." In Esther 2:7, another name for Esther. It was either her original Hebrew name or a title that was given to her. In the former case, it would mean "myrtle"; in the latter case, "bride." See *Esther.*

HADATTAH (Hå dăt′ tah) Place name meaning, "new." Part of name Hazor-hadattah (Josh. 15:25). The earliest Greek translations apparently read the Hebrew word for "their villages" that reappears in this section of Joshua instead of Hadattah. Some Bible students think Greek had the original reading. See *Hazor-Hadattah.*

HADES (Hā′ dēs) the abode of the dead. In the King James Version of the Bible, the Greek word is generally translated "hell." It differs, however, from the term "Gehenna," which more precisely refers to hell. Hades is the Greek equivalent of the Hebrew term "Sheol," which refers in general to the place of the dead. See *Hell.*

HADID (Hā′ dĭd) Place name meaning, "fast" or

"sharpened." Home of people returning from exile with Zerubbabel (Ezra 2:33). Town is modern el-Hadite about three miles east of Lydda. Compare Nehemiah 11:34.

HADLAI (Hăd' lā ī) Personal name meaning, "quit" or "fat sack." Leader in tribe of Ephraim and father of Amasa (2 Chron. 28:12). See *Amasa.*

HADORAM (Hȧ dō' răm) Personal and tribal name perhaps meaning, "Hadad (god) is exalted." *1.* Arabic tribe descended from Shem through Eber and thus distantly related to Hebrews according to the Table of Nations (Gen. 10:27). They lived in southern Arabia. *2.* Son of Tou, city-state ruler in Hamath of Syria. Hadoram brought tribute to David after David had defeated Hadad-ezer of Zobah (1 Chron. 18:10). See *Hadad-ezer.* *3.* "Taskmaster over the forced labor" (2 Chron. 10:18 NRSV) under Rehoboam, Solomon's son and successor as king of Judah. Rehoboam sent Hadoram to collect tribute from the Northern Kingdom immediately after they rebelled and refused to acknowledge Rehoboam as king. The children of Israel killed Hadoram. Thus they showed their contempt for Rehoboam's forced labor policies and made final the division between Israel and Judah, beginning the period of the divided monarchy.

HADRACH (Hā' drăch) City-state name of uncertain meaning. Zechariah 9:1 claims this Syrian city-state will become a part of God's territory, though the precise meaning of the verse is difficult to interpret. Assyrian inscriptions frequently mention Hatarikka or *Hzrk* as an opponent Tiglath-pileser III finally conquered and made part of his empire in 738 B.C. It was apparently the large mound tell Afis, 28 miles southwest of Aleppo, and served as capital of Luhuti, which was an ally of Hamath from 854 to 773.

HAELEPH (Hȧ ē' lĕph) Place name meaning, "the ox." KJV reads the initial "h" as the Hebrew definite article and thus has "Eleph." Some interpreters combine the preceding town name in Joshua 18:28 to read, "Zelah Haeleph" as one town, following early Greek manuscript evidence. Town in tribal territory of Benjamin (Josh. 18:28). The location is not known. See *Zelah.*

HAFT KJV term for the hilt or handle of a dagger (Judg. 3:22).

HAGAB (Hā' găb) Personal name meaning, "grasshopper" or "chamberlain." Clan of Temple servants who returned to Jerusalem from Babylonian Exile with Zerubbabel (Ezra 2:46). The name also occurs on an ostracon from Lachish.

HAGABA (Hăg' ȧ bȧ) Clan of Temple servants who returned home from Babylonian Exile with Zerubbabel about 537 B.C. (Ezra 2:45).

HAGAR (Hā' găr) Personal name meaning, "stranger." The personal servant of Sarah, who was given as a concubine to Abraham and became the mother of Ishmael (Gen. 16:1–16; 21:8–21; 25:12; Gal. 4:24–25). Genesis 16:1–7 details the events of the initial conflict of Sarah with Hagar and the flight of Hagar. Verses 8–16 detail the visit of the messenger of Yahweh bringing the promise of a son to the mother in distress, encouraging Hagar to return to Sarah. These conflicts were related to the wife's and concubine's positions in the family and community. (Compare similar conflicts in Gen. 29—30.) Genesis 21:8–21 gives the story of the expulsion of Hagar and Ishmael and their miraculous deliverance. Pauline interpretation (Galatians) relates the superiority of a son born according to the Spirit over the son born according to the "flesh." In Galatians 4 Paul used the Hagar story to stand for slavery under the old covenant in contrast to freedom of the new covenant symbolized by Isaac. *David M. Fleming*

HAGARENE (Hăg' ȧ rēne) KJV spelling in Psalm 83:6 for Hagarite. See *Hagarite.*

HAGARITE (Hăg' är īte) Name of nomadic tribe whom the tribe of Reuben defeated east of the Jordan River (1 Chron 5:10,19–20). Reuben won because they called on and trusted in God. The tribal name is apparently taken from Hagar, Sarah's maid and mother of Ishmael (Gen. 16). David's chief shepherd was a Hagarite (1 Chron. 27:31). The Psalmist asked God not to be silent when the Hagarites joined a coalition against God's people (Ps. 83:6). First Chronicles 11:38 names a Hagarite among David's military heroes, but some interpreters think that 1 Samuel 23:36 is evidence of an original Gadite, which would be written quite similar to Hagarite in Hebrew.

HAGERI (Hā' gĕr ī) REB transliteration of Hebrew for Hagarite in 1 Chronicles 11:38. See *Hagarite.*

HAGGADAH, HALAKAH In Judaism, rabbinic teaching is divided into two categories: *halakah* and *haggadah* (also spelled *aggadah*). Both of these terms refer to the oral teaching of the rabbis. Halakah refers to the legal teachings that are considered authoritative for religious life. Haggadah refers to the remaining non-legal teachings.

Halakah according to the early rabbis goes back to oral law given to Moses at Sinai along with the written law (*Torah*) embodied in the Bible primarily found in the Pentateuch. Therefore, the halakah is considered as binding as the written Torah. Modern scholars recognize that the halakah is the means by which the written Torah is interpreted

H

to each new generation. Halakah extends the Torah of Moses into every aspect of Jewish life including personal, social, national, and international relations.

Haggadah consists of a variety of amplifications of biblical texts primarily in the form of illustrative stories, parables or allegories, or, frequently, poetry. Many portions of the haggadah may go back to early Jewish synagogue preaching.

Much of early rabbinic halakah was eventually written down in the *Mishnah* (about 220 A.D.) and *Talmud* (about 360 A.D.) although it continues to be referred to as oral law even after these codifications. Likewise, haggadah was written down in various biblical commentaries as well as the Talmud.

These two types of rabbinic teaching are especially important as an aid in understanding Judaism at the time of Jesus and during the formation of the early church since some of these materials have their origin during the first century. Jesus probably referred to Pharisaic halakah (in part a precursor to rabbinic halakah) in Mark 7:1–23 and its parallel (Matt. 15:1–20). See *Mishnah; Talmud; Pharisees; Torah.*

Stephenson Humphries-Brooks

HAGGAI (Hăḡ′ ḡaî). Personal name of a sixth century prophet meaning, "festive" and of the book preserving his preaching. Compared to most of the writing prophets, we have very little information on the personal life of Haggai. Haggai has no genealogy.

The book consists of a series of addresses by Haggai together with the results of his work. The specific historical details presented makes possible exact dating of the book between the sixth and the ninth month of the year 520 B.C. The final form of the book may have been the work of someone other than the prophet who put the collection together.

When Cyrus took over Babylon in 538 B.C. and established the kingdom of Persia, the Hebrews came under a Persian governor. Permission was given for the exiles to return and restore their temples. After the death of Cyrus, and of his son Cambyses, Darius became ruler and continued the benevolent policies of Cyrus. Then Darius appointed Zerubbabel as governor with the specific responsibility of resuming work on the Temple, begun earlier by Shesh-bazzar. At first, it appears that Judah was part of the administrative district of Samaria, but the appointment of Zerubbabel may have represented a move in the direction of autonomy for Judah which became a reality in the time of Ezra and Nehemiah a few decades later.

Apparently the adjustments required of the returning exiles were so difficult that rebuilding their own homes and the Temple at the same time put a strain on their resources. They despaired of

ever restoring the Temple to its former glory. Work on the Temple ceased. Haggai, along with Zechariah, helped Zerubbabel gain the support and help he needed from the returning exiles to carry out his assigned task. Haggai may have viewed the restoration of order by Darius and the appointment of Zerubbabel as a sign of the end of Gentile rule and preparation for the messianic kingdom.

The Book of Haggai is very important for several reasons. One is that he laid the foundations of later Judaism on which Christianity was to build. Another was the stress on the linking of worship and work, a characteristic feature of Jesus' teaching and of the New Testament in general. Also, he revived hope for the future in a dejected community. Finally, the book provides important historical data on the post-exilic period where information is scanty. Some scholars think he neglected the moral element, but he really stressed a return to the basics of worship and a close relationship between worship and work. Both are important.

The book consists of five short addresses and a description of the results of Haggai's efforts to persuade his people to resume work on the Temple. The recipients of Haggai's message included Zerubbabel and Joshua, the high priest. Haggai suggested how they should respond to the excuses people were making for not resuming work on the Temple (1:2). Haggai's answer was that if it was right for them to rebuild their own houses, it was also right for them to rebuild the Temple (1:3–4). Haggai noted that in rebuilding their own houses they had done well, but they were still not happy. His diagnosis was that they had neglected their spiritual lives. He said the way to correct their neglect was to rebuild the Temple (1:3–11). In response they resumed work on the Temple.

In the second speech, Haggai assured them of the Lord's presence and approval (1:13), and the Lord stirred the spirit of both leaders and people as they worked together (1:14–15).

In the third address, given to both the leaders and the people (2:1–2), Haggai asked the older members of the community to recall the glory of the former Temple and thus to stir the new generation to new enthusiasm. He promised that God would bring treasures from other nations to make the splendor of the new Temple even greater than the former one (2:6–9).

The fourth address (2:10–19) returns to the theme of the first address in linking worship, work, and the blessings of God. The point seems to be that carelessness in observing accepted rules reflected a lack of seriousness in their purpose. The results were that they robbed themselves of the full measure of God's blessing.

The final speech, delivered the same day as the previous one (2:20–23), was addressed only to Zerubbabel. It announced the imminent overthrow of the kingdoms of the world and the role that Zerubbabel would play in the triumphant victory of God's kingdom on earth.

Outline

I. God's People Must Reconsider Materialistic Priorities in Light of God's Call (1:1–15).
   A. Materialistic pride and greed must not cause procrastination in fulfilling God's priority tasks (1:1–4).
   B. God withholds blessing and fertility from a selfish people who do not glorify Him (1:5–11).
   C. Faithful leadership and God's presence can motivate God's people to carry out His priorities (1:12–15).
II. God's People Must Reconsider Priorities in Light of God's Promises and Power (2:1–9).
   A. Comparisons with past achievements may discourage God's people from doing God's work (2:1–3).
   B. Trust in God's promises and power to provide every need encourages His people to continue His work (2:4–9).
III. God's People Must Reconsider the Priority of a Pure Life (2:10–19).
   A. Impure people produce only more impurity (2:10–14).
   B. God does not bless an impure people who do not repent (2:15–17).
   C. God will bless His attentive people in the future (2:18–19).
IV. God's People Must Reconsider God's Power to Overcome Opposition (2:20–23).
   A. God will overcome all opposition (2:20–22).
   B. God will empower His chosen servant (2:23).   *E. Earl Joiner*

HAGGEDOLIM (Hăg′ gĕ dō′ lĭm) Personal name meaning, "the great ones." Zabdiel a leading priest was the son of Haggedolim (Neh. 11:14 KJV, "the great men"; TEV, "a leading family"). Bible students have suggested that *haggedolim* is probably not a Hebrew proper name and have interpreted it as a copyists' change of an unfamiliar name for a more familiar word or title, an honorary title for a leading family, or a title for the high priest.

HAGGERI (Hăg gē′ rī) KJV transliteration of Hebrew for Hagarite in 1 Chronicles 11:38. See *Hagarite.*

HAGGI (Hăg′ gī) Personal name meaning, "my festival," indicating birth on a holy day. Son of Gad and grandson of Jacob and thus original ancestor of clan of Haggites (Gen. 46:16; Num. 26:15).

HAGGIAH (Hăg gī′ ah) Personal name meaning, "Yahweh is my festival." A Levite in the line of Merari (1 Chron. 6:30).

HAGGITE (Hăg′ gīte) Member of clan of Haggi. See *Haggi.*

HAGGITH (Hăg′ gĭth) Personal name meaning, "festival." Wife of David and mother of Adonijah, who was born at Hebron (1 Sam. 3:4).

HAGIOGRAPHA Greek term meaning "holy writings" used as a designation for the third and final major division of the Hebrew Bible. In contrast to the first two divisions (the law and the prophets), "the writings" (Hebrew, *Kethubim*) are a miscellaneous collection. The hagiographa in their Hebrew order include: Psalms, Proverbs, and Job; the "five scrolls" (*Megilloth*) read at major festivals, namely, Song of Solomon, Ruth, Lamentations, Ecclesiastes, and Esther; Daniel; and Ezra-Nehemiah and Chronicles. These books were the last portion of the Hebrew Bible to be recognized as canonical. Luke 24:44 uses "psalms" as a designation for these writings.

HAGRI (Hăg′ rī) Tribal or personal name probably referring to the Hagarites (1 Chron. 11:38) or a miscopying of "the Gaddite" from 2 Samuel 23:36. See *Hagarite.*

HAGRITE (Hăg′ rīte) Alternate spelling for Hagarite in modern translations. See *Hagarite.*

HAHIROTH (Hȧ hī′ rŏth) Reading of some manuscripts and translations for Pi-hahiroth in Numbers 33:8. See *Pi-hahiroth.*

HAI (Hā′ ī) KJV reading for Ai in Genesis 12:8; 13:3. See *Ai.*

HAIL (GREETING) See *Greeting.*

HAIL (METEROLOGICAL) Precipitation in the form of small balls consisting of layers of ice and compact snow, regarded as a plague by biblical writers. Hailstones generally have a diameter of half an inch to one inch. Large hailstones can destroy crops (Ex. 9:25,31; Ps. 78:47; Hag. 2:17; Rev. 8:7) and kill livestock and persons caught in the open (Ex. 9:19,25; Josh. 10:11; Ps. 78:48). The Bible speaks of hail to speak of divine presence, action, and punishment.

HAIR The covering of the human head and of animals. Ordinarily human hair is meant in biblical references (Num. 6:5), though animal hair (wool) may be in mind (Matt. 3:4). Beautiful hair has always been desirable for both women and men (Song of Sol. 5:11). In Old Testament times both men and women wore their hair long. Both Samson and Absalom were greatly admired for their long locks (Judg. 16:13; 2 Sam. 14:25–26). In the New Testament era, men wore their hair much shorter than women did (1 Cor. 11:14–15).

Gray or white hair was a respected sign of age (Prov. 20:29). But baldness could be considered embarrassing or even humiliating (2 Kings 2:23;

Jewish men of the orthodox tradition are prohibited from cutting off the hair above their ears.

Ezek. 7:18). In Leviticus 13, which gives extensive instruction on the diagnosis of leprosy (probably including other skin diseases), the color of the hairs in an infected area of skin indicated whether the disease was present or had been cured. A cured leper was required to shave his entire body (Lev. 14:8–9).

Hair among the Israelites required good care. Women usually wore their hair loose, but sometimes they braided it (2 Kings 9:30). New Testament writers cautioned against ostentation in women's hairstyles (1 Tim. 2:9; 1 Pet. 3:3). Hair that was anointed with oil symbolized blessing and joy (Ps. 23:5; Heb. 1:9). Some hosts provided oil to anoint honored guests (Luke 7:46). Mourn-

Silver decorative bucket with scene of a servant combing the hair of her mistress.

ing was indicated by disheveled, unkept hair (Josh. 7:6; 2 Sam. 14:2). Jesus told His followers not to follow the custom of the Pharisees, who refused to care for their hair while they were fasting (Matt. 6:17).

Israelite men trimmed their hair, but the law prohibited them from cutting off the hair above their ears (Lev. 19:27). This restriction probably originally forbade some pagan custom (Deut. 14:1–2), but orthodox Jews still wear long sidecurls. Those who took a Nazirite vow were forbidden from cutting their hair during the course of their vow, but afterward, their entire head was to be shaved (Num. 6:1–21; Acts 18:18; 21:24).

Because hairs are so many, they may symbolize the concept of being innumerable (Ps. 40:12). Because they seem so unimportant, they can stand for insignificant things (Luke 21:18).

Kendell Easley

HAKELDAMA (Hả kĕl′ dả mả) NAS, NRSV spelling for Aceldama or Akeldama (Acts 1:19). See *Aceldama.*

HAKILAH (Hả kī′ lah) NIV spelling of Hachilah. See *Hachilah.*

HAKKATAN (Hăk kả′ tăn) Personal name meaning, "the small one, the lesser." Father of the clan leader who accompanied Ezra from Babylon to Jerusalem about 458 B.C. (Ezra 8:12).

HAKKORE (Hăk′ kō rė) TEV reading of En-hakkore (Judg. 15:19), translating En as spring. See *En-hakkore.*

HAKKOZ (Hăk′ kŏz) Personal and clan name meaning, "the thorn." *1.* Clan leader in tribe of Judah (1 Chron. 4:8). See *Coz. 2.* Clan of priests (1 Chron. 24:10). Compare Nehemiah 3:4,21. In the time of Ezra and Nehemiah members of this clan could not prove their family roots, so they were not allowed to function as priests (Ezra 2:61). See *Koz.*

HAKUPHA (Hả kū′ phả) Personal name meaning, "bent." Original ancestor of clan of Temple servants (Ezra 2:51).

HALAH (Hā′ lah) City-state or region in northern Mesopotamia to which Assyrians exiled some leaders of the Northern Kingdom after capturing Samaria in 722 B.C. (2 Kings 17:6). Some Bible students think the original text of Obadiah 20 contained a promise for the captives in Halah. They read the Hebrew word for "host" as Halah. Halah may have been Hallahhu, northeast of Nineveh.

HALAK (Hā′ lăk) Place name meaning, "barren" or "naked." Mountain marking southern extent of

Joshua's conquests (Josh. 11:17; 12:7). It is identified with jebel Halak, about 40 miles southwest of the Dead Sea in Edom.

HALF TRIBE Used to designate a segment of the tribe of Manasseh which received territory on both sides of the Jordan river. The term usually refers to that part of Manasseh dwelling to the east of the Jordan along with Reuben and Gad (Num. 32:33; Deut. 3:13; Josh 1:12; 4:12; 22:1). Those living west of the Jordan are sometimes called "the rest of the tribe of Manasseh" (Josh. 17:2 NRSV) or the "other half" (22:7). See *Tribes of Israel.*

HALF-SHEKEL TAX The Temple tax required annually of every Israelite twenty years of age and upwards (Ex. 30:13,15; 38:26). Such payment brought atonement, but atonement price was equal for all (30:15). At Matthew 17:24 this tax is called the *didrachma* ("the two drachma") tax. The coin in the fish's mouth was a *stater,* a coin worth four drachmas or the Temple tax for two (17:27). See *Atonement.*

HALHUL (Hăl′ hŭl) Place name perhaps meaning, "circles." Town in hill country of Judah assigned to the tribe of Judah (Josh. 15:58). It is modern Halhul, four miles north of Hebron.

HALI (Hā′ lī) Place name meaning, "jewel." Border town assigned to tribe of Asher (Josh. 19:25). It may be khirbet Ras Ali, north of Mount Carmel.

HALL A large, usually imposing building, often used for governmental functions; the chief room in such a structure. The NIV uses hall for the main room of the Temple (1 Kings 6:3,5,17,33). Other translations have house (KJV), nave (NAS, NRSV), or sanctuary (REB). Modern translations designate several of Solomon's building projects as halls. The Hall of Pillars (KJV porch of pillars) was part of the palace complex (1 Kings 7:6). It is unclear whether this hall was a separate building or the entrance to the House of the Forest of Lebanon or even the whole palace complex. The Hall of the Throne or Hall of Judgment (1 Kings 7:7; KJV porch) was the throne room where legal decisions were rendered. The king's hall of Esther 5:1 was, likewise, the audience chamber of the Persian king. Archeological research indicates that Ahasuerus' Hall of Pillars was 193 feet square. The hall's name stemmed from the 36 massive pillars supporting the roof.

Banqueting halls are frequently mentioned. The hall of 1 Samuel 9:22 (KJV parlour) was a chamber connected with the sanctuary where sacrificial meat was eaten. Belshazzar's banqueting hall (KJV banquet house) was the scene of the famous handwriting on the wall (Dan. 5:10). This room was likely the large throne room (50 by 160 feet)

which has been excavated.

KJV used the term hall to translate the Greek term *aule* (Luke 22:55). Elsewhere KJV translated the term "palace" (for example Matt. 26:58; Mark 14:54; John 18:15). Modern translations use "courtyard." KJV also used hall for the praetorium or Roman governor's headquarters (Pilate's Matt. 27:27; Mark 15:16; John 18:28; Herod's Acts 23:35).

HALLEL A song of praise. The name derives from the Hebrew "Praise Thou." The singing of psalms of praise was a special duty of the Levites (2 Chron. 7:6; Ezra 3:11). The "Egyptian" Hallel (Pss. 113—118) was recited in homes as part of the Passover celebration (compare Ps. 114:1; Matt. 26:30). The "Great Hallel" was recited in the Temple as the Passover lambs were being slain and at Pentecost, Tabernacles, and Dedication. Scholars disagree as to the original extent of the "Great Hallel" with some limiting the Hallel to Psalm 136, some including Psalm 135, and still others including the "Songs of Ascents" (Pss. 120—134).

HALLELUJAH (Hăl lĕ lū jäh) Exclamation of praise that recurs frequently in the Book of Psalms meaning, "Praise Yahweh!" In particular, Psalms 146—150 sometimes are designated the Hallelujah Psalms. In the Psalms God is praised for His power, His wisdom, His blessings, and the liberation of His people. See *Psalms.*

HALLOHESH (Hăl lō′ hĕsh) Personal name meaning, "the exorcist." Father of Shallum, who helped Nehemiah repair the Jerusalem wall. He is called, "ruler of the half part of Jerusalem" (Neh. 3:12), apparently meaning he administered one of the outlying districts near Jerusalem. The same man or a man of the same name sealed his name to Nehemiah's covenant (Neh. 10:24).

HALLOW To make holy; to set apart for holy use; to revere. See *Dedicate, Dedication; Holy; Sanctification.*

HALT A term KJV sometimes uses as an alternate translation for lame (Matt. 18:8; Mark 9:45; Luke 14:21; John 5:3).

HAM (Hăm) Personal name meaning, "hot." Second of Noah's three sons (Gen 5:32). Following the Flood, he discovered Noah, his father, naked and drunken and reported it to Shem and Japheth (Gen. 9:20–29). When Noah learned of the incident, he pronounced a curse on Canaan the son of Ham. Ham became the original ancestor of the Cushites, the Egyptians, and the Canaanites (Gen. 10:6). See *Noah.*

HAMAN (Hā′ man) Personal name meaning,

"magnificent." The Agagite who became prime minister under the Persian king Ahasuerus (Esther 3:1). He was a fierce enemy of the Jews, and he devised a plot to exterminate them. In particular, he had a gallows erected on which he hoped to hang Mordecai because Mordecai would not bow to him. Through the intervention of Esther, however, his scheme was unmasked; and he was hanged on the gallows he had designed for Mordecai the Jew. See *Esther.*

HAMATH (Hā′ măth) Place name meaning, "fortress" or "citadel." City-state located in the valley of the Orontes River, roughly 120 miles north of Damascus. Excavation indicates this mound was occupied as early as Neolithic times. Hieroglyphic inscriptions first discovered by J. L. Burckhardt in 1810 attest early Hittite influence in Hamath. Throughout much of its existence, Hamath functioned as the capital of an independent kingdom.

The southern boundary of Hamath served as the northern boundary of Israel during the reigns of Solomon (1 Kings 8:65; 2 Chron. 8:4) and Jeroboam II (2 Kings 14:25,28). The "entrance of Hamath" was treated as the northern border of Israel (Num. 34:8; Josh. 13:5; Ezek. 47:15–17,20; 48:1) and served as an accepted geographical expression (Num. 13:21; Judg. 3:3).

Toi, king of Hamath, sent his son to congratulate David after David defeated King Hadadezer of Zobah. Toi had frequently fought with Hadadezer (2 Sam. 8:9–10; 1 Chron. 18:3,9–10). See *Toi.* In 853 B.C. King Irhuleni of Hamath joined a coalition including Ben-hadad II of Damascus and Ahab of Israel which successfully thwarted the advance of Shalmaneser II of Assyria into northern Syria. In about 802 B.C. Adad-nirari III of Assyria crushed Damascus and levied a heavy tax upon it. During the following decades, the king of Hamath, probably named Zakir, waged a successful rivalry with Damascus. Hamath reached the zenith of its power between 800 and 750 B.C.

In 738 B.C. Tiglath-pileser III of Assyria exacted tribute from Hamath together with other states including Israel. Following the fall of Samaria in 722–721 B.C., Hamath was devastated in 720 B.C. by Sargon II of Assyria (Amos 6:2). Refugees from Samaria may have been exiled to Hamath by the Assyrians, while refugees from Hamath were brought to Samaria along with their god, Ashima (2 Kings 17:24,30; Isa. 11:11). From this time, Hamath's history seems to merge with that of Damascus (Jer. 49:23).

In the Hellenistic period, Antiochus IV changed its name to Epiphania. It was known by this name in the Graeco-Roman period, though the natives continued to call it Hamath (modern Ḥamah).

Max Rogers

HAMATH-ZOBAH (Hā′ măth-zō′ bah) Place name meaning, "hot place of Zobah." City Solomon captured in Syria (2 Chron. 8:3). Both Hamath and Zobah are cities in Syria that David controlled (2 Sam. 8). See *Hamath; Zobah.* Some interpreters see the combination here as the result of a damaged text available to the Chronicler. Others think the Chronicler reflects the Babylonian and Persian administrative system of his day including the two cities in one administrative district. Other think this was simply another name for Zobah. The Chronicler in distinction from 2 Samuel 8 also combines the two cities into "Zobah-hamath" (1 Chron. 18:3 REB, reflecting the literal Hebrew text).

HAMATHITE (Hā′ măth īte) Citizen of Hamath and originally descended from Canaan, son of Ham, son of Noah (Gen. 10:18). See *Hamath.*

HAMITES (Hăm′ ītes) NIV designation for descendants of Ham (1 Chron. 4:40–41). See *Ham.*

HAMMATH (Hăm′ măth) Place name meaning, "hot spot," probably due to hot spring, and personal name meaning, "hot one." *1.* Fortified city in the tribal territory of Naphtali (Josh. 19:35); probably the same as the levitical town of Hammoth-dor (21:32). It may be located at tell Raqqat, just north of Tiberias. Others have tried to locate it at the famous hot springs of Hammam Tabiriyeh, south of Tiberias, but archaeologists have found no evidence of Iron Age occupation there. First Chronicles 6:76 reads "Hammon," apparently the same place, in listing the Levitical towns. *2.* Original ancestor of Kenites and Rechabites (1 Chron. 2:55; KJV reads, "Hamath"; TEV, REB see a verbal construction meaning, "intermarried" or "connected by marriage."). The context and grammatical construction of the verse makes certain understanding impossible. Hammath could be the founder of the city Hammath.

HAMMEDATHA (Hăm mė dā′ thà) Personal name meaning, "given by the god." Father of Haman, the villain of the Book of Esther (Esther 3:1).

HAMMELECH (Hăm′ mė lĕch) According to KJV, personal name meaning, "the king" (Jer. 36:26; 38:6). Modern translations read, "son of the king."

HAMMER A striking tool. The earliest hammers were simply smooth or shaped stones. Beginning in the Bronze Age, stones were hallowed out to give a better grip or to receive a handle. Mallets of bone and wood were used (Judg. 5:26), though these have not normally been preserved. Hammers with metal heads were rare in Palestine, possibly because metal was reserved for tools needing a cutting edge.

Hammers were used in cutting stone (1 Kings

6:7), working common and precious metals (Isa. 41:7; 44:12), and for woodworking (Jer. 10:4). A hammer-like weapon was also used in battle (Jer. 51:20 "shatterer" NAS margin; Ezek. 9:2 "shattering weapon"). See *Arms and Armor.*

The hammer was a symbol of power. God's word is pictured as a hammer (Jer. 23:29). Babylon is mocked as a hammer whose strength has failed (Jer. 50:23). See *Tools.*

HAMMOLECHETH (Hăm mŏl′ ĕ chĕth) Personal name meaning, "queen." Sister of Gilead in genealogy of Manasseh in the unparalleled list of 1 Chronicles 7:18. This spelling appears in TEV, NRSV, NAS. See *Hammoleketh.*

HAMMOLEKETH (Hăm mō′ lĕ kĕth) KJV, NIV, REB spelling of Hammolecheth.

HAMMON (Hăm′ mon) Place name meaning, "hot spot," probably from a hot spring. *1.* Town in tribal allotment of Asher (Josh. 19:28). It may be modern Umm el-awamid near the Mediterranean coast in Lebanon about five miles northeast of Rosh ha-niqra. *2.* See *Hammath.*

HAMMOTH-DOR (Hăm′ moth-dôr) See *Hammath.*

HAMMUEL (Hăm′ mū ĕl) Personal name meaning, "El is my father-in-law" or "God is hot with anger." Member of tribe of Simeon (1 Chron. 4:26).

HAMMURABI (Hăm mū rā′ bī) King of Babylon about 1700 B.C. who issued a famous code of law. His name probably means, "Hammu (the god) is great." The name Hammurabi belongs to the family of Semitic, not Akkadian, personal names and began appearing in cuneiform texts about 2000 B.C. Two kings of Yamhad, who were contemporaries of the king of Babylon, bore the name. In addition, the name was borne by the king of Kurda and by an official from the Old Babylonian period. Prior to Hammurabi, the kings of Babylon had Akkadian names.

Kingdom Hammurabi was the sixth king of the First Dynasty of Babylon. He was the son of Sin-muballit and the father of Samsu-iluna. He ruled over Babylon for 42–43 years. Although we have more and better evidence for his reign than any other king of his dynasty, the precise years he ruled cannot be determined. Four positions are held. The ultra-high chronology holds 1900 B.C. for his first year of his reign. Probably, the most widely-held view is that his first year to rule was 1792 B.C. Others hold a middle chronology with 1728 B.C. as his first year. The low chronology places 1642 B.C. as the first year.

Although most scholars present Hammurabi as one of the great kings of his era, a recent scholar

sees him as a minor king in comparison to his peers, pointing to the correspondence found at Mari as evidence. For the first ten years of Hammurabi's reign, Babylon appears to be subservient to Assyrian rule. Later, his serious rivals were Zimri-Lim of Mari, Rim-sin of Larsa, and Ibal-pi-El of Eshnunna along with his Elamite allies.

From his seventh to eleventh years he destroyed Malgum, attacked Rapiqum, warred against Emutbal, and captured both Isin and Uruk (Erech).

Despite an uneasy truce with Assyria and Eshnunna, Hammurabi spent the middle twenty years of his reign preoccupied with local affairs. Evidently, he was consolidating and organizing his kingdom. He built religious shrines, civic buildings, defensive walls, and canals during this period. The archives at Mari reveal about 140 letters sent between Babylon and Mari during this era. Four of the letters are addressed by Hammurabi to either the king or court officials at Mari.

In year 29 of his reign, he won a decisive victory over a coalition holding the east side of the Tigris River, which opened the way for him two years later to attain victory over Larsa and gain control of the southern cities. Change in the balance of power resulted. The last twelve years of his rule were uninterrupted warfare. In year 35 he dismantled Mari and Malgium. In year 38 he conquered Eshnunna. Yet these latter wars at best were an "offensive defensive" against the pressures of invading peoples. In the latter years he built walls along the Tigris and Euphrates and in year 43 fortified Sippar with an earthen wall. While the early years witnessed military and political expansion which was probably initiated by his father, Sin-muballit, the latter years saw the kingdom shrink.

Religion Scholars assign the famous staged-temple-tower or ziggurat "E-temen-an-ki" to his reign. The name means "The House of the Foundation Platform of Heaven and Earth." It was one of the seven wonders of the world. This giant structure may have influenced the biblical writer in his narrative of the Tower of Babel (Gen. 11:4–9). Hammurabi placed Marduk, a local deity, at the head of the Babylonian pantheon, where he remained for subsequent centuries.

Lawgiver In 1898 some fragments were published of cuneiform tablets from the library of Ashurbanipal, king of Assyria. These fragments were thought to be part of an old "book of Law" dating to the First Babylonian Dynasty. In December 1901 and January 1902 in the old royal city of Susa, a diorite stone measuring two and a quarter meters high and almost two meters in circumference was found. The stone was a relief of Hammurabi with 44 columns of ancient cuneiform writing. The stele proved to contain the collection of Hammurabi laws.

The stone was engraved late in Hammurabi's

H

reign. It was probably set in the great Esagil Temple of Marduk in Babylon with copies sent to other centers. In 1160 B.C., following a successful raid on Babylon, the Elamite Shutruk-nahhunte carried it to Susa.

The relief of Hammurabi shows him receiving a sceptre and a ring from Shamash, the divine lawgiver. The sceptre and ring are symbols of justice and order. The stele begins by describing the king's divine call to "make justice to shine forth in the land, to destroy the evil and the wicked, that the strong might not oppress the weak . . . to give light to the land."

The diverse elements of the expanded kingdom demanded a precise definition of individual rights. The large economic dependence upon slavery and the overwhelming personal indebtedness provided the means and reason for developing a standard of law. By setting the wages for technical and agricultural laborers and by decreeing the release from debt or slavery, the king could control much of the life of the nation. This was done by a periodical "pronouncement of righteousness." This usually occurred in a king's first year of reign. In his first year, Hammurabi decreed the standard of law which would govern the economic and religious life of all Babylonians. This compares to the "reforms" of the Hebrew kings, who by restating allegiance to the Torah in their first year as king, "did the right in the eyes of the Lord" (2 Kings 18:3).

Hammurabi's laws probably date from his first year as king, but they were not compiled and edited until the conclusion of his reign.

Two hundred eighty-two paragraphs or judgments of Hammurabi remain. These are not comparable to modern codes. The cases are grouped by subjects, but rarely are they stated in terms of general application. The laws are primarily the king's verdicts regarding specific cases. Some of the cases are similar to the law codes of Lipit-Ishtar of Isin, Eshnunna, and the Hebrew laws. The code in general does not discuss religious affairs. Punishments include immersion in the river, "lex talionis," fines, restitution by labor or in kind, and death. Penalties varied according to the class of the offender. Three classes were recognized: freedman, state-dependent, and slave. The code covers the following subjects:

(1) Various offenses and crimes (¶ 1–25). These include false witness similar to Deuteronomy 5:20; 19:16–17; witchcraft, which is forbidden in Deuteronomy 18:10; Exodus 22:18; action against evil judges similar to Exodus 23:6–9; Leviticus 19:15; Deuteronomy 16:18–21. The death penalty was imposed for robbery or receipt of stolen merchandise from a palace or a temple. Hebrew law allowed for restoration for such offenses (Ex. 22:1; Lev. 6:2). The penalty for dereliction was death or thirty- or ten-fold restitution depending on the class of the accused. Hebrew

law asked for double-restitution (Ex. 22:1–4,7). The death penalty was prescribed for kidnapping, theft of slaves, looting, and robbery.

(2) Property (¶ 26–99). Distinction was made between crown-tenants, fief holders, and tenant farmers. Much is stated about loans of either money or seeds against future crops. A farmer had four years to produce a fruit crop from trees before repaying his loan. In Hebrew law, the first-fruits of the fourth crop had to be dedicated to God.

(3) Commercial law (¶ 100–126). These laws regulated partnerships and agencies, sales, and transporting merchandise. These treat slaves and debtors more harshly than do the Hebrew laws.

(4) Marriage (¶ 127–161). These cases involve the rights of both parties, dowry settlements, bridal gifts, marriage offenses, and divorce. Adultery with a married woman, as in Hebrew law (Deut. 22:22), resulted in death for both individuals. Death was the punishment for rape as in Deuteronomy 22:25. An adulterous wife was sentenced to trial by ordeal in both codes (Num. 5:13–22). A husband captured abroad had his marriage protected. Likewise, this was the intent of Deuteronomy 24:5. The references to concubinage and the protection of the female from reduction to slavery or divorce, except for offenses against the first wife, shed light on patriarchal practices (Gen. 16:2,4; 21:8). Incest is prohibited by each.

(5) Firstborn. As in Hebrew law (Ex. 13:2; Deut. 21:15–17), the first-born had special rights.

(6) Adoption (¶ 185–194). Males could be granted sonship or disowned by oral pronouncements. Unruly, violent sons were corrected by cutting off the offending limb.

(7) Assault (¶ 195–208). Damage to persons and property were thoroughly discussed. Liabilities of builders and surgeons were especially noted. Hurting pregnant women was severely punished as in the Hebrew law (Ex. 21:22–25).

(8) Agricultural work and offenses (¶ 241–267). As in Exodus 21:28–32 the owners' responsibilities for gorings by oxen are discussed in great detail.

(9) Rates and wages (¶ 268–277). The differences between the conditions in early Israel and the urban communities of Babylon are evident in these paragraphs.

(10) Slaves (¶ 278–282). These paragraphs discuss the purchase and sale of slaves.

A particular genre of Ancient Near Eastern literature is known as the "law code." Nine separately identifiable law codes are known to have existed in the Old Testament era. Seven of them are in the form of cuneiform documents: Ur-Nammu, Lipit-Ishtar, Eshnunna, Hammurabi, Assyrian Laws, Hittite Laws, and Neo-Babylonian Laws. The other two that are comparable are found in the Bible (Ex. 21:1—22:16; Deut. 21—

25). All nine are remarkably similar in form and content. All are casuistic in style, dealing with specific cases with an if . . . then form.

What is the purpose for such law codes? Some scholars believe they are more literary than legal. In this view their purpose was never legislative. They were "royal apologia." They were to lay before the public, posterity, future kings, and the gods, evidence of the king's execution of the divinely ordained mandates. Other scholars say that the codes are "scribal exercises." This views Hammurabi more as a scribe than as a judge. Thus, his work is theoretical literature designed to illustrate his wisdom. Others understand the law codes to be from a tradition similar to compiling lists of omens, medical prognoses, and other scientific treatises. The purpose of these series was to act as reference works for the royal judges in deciding difficult cases. This probably began as an oral tradition and gradually became a systematic written corpus.

Significance The Hammurabi code resembles Hebrew law in form, style, and general content. Thus some scholars believe the Hebrews were influenced by Hammurabi's code through the Canaanites among whom they settled.

Whatever the similarities, important differences are obvious. First, the Hammurabi code presupposes an aristocratic class system that did not prevail in Israel. Second, Israel could never have viewed the state as the custodian of the law. Third, Hebrew law is characterized by a more humane spirit. Fourth, Hebrew law maintains a high ethical emphasis. Fifth, the pervading religious fervor makes the Hebrew code unique. Sixth, Hebrew law is set within a covenant relationship.

Gary D. Baldwin

HAMON-GOG (Hā´ mŏn-gŏg) Place name meaning, "horde of Gog." Place where Ezekiel predicted burial of defeated army of Gog (Ezek. 39:11,15). Its location is not known. See *Ezekiel; Gog; Hamonah.*

HAMONAH (Hà mō´ nah) Place name meaning, "horde." Town in valley of Hamon-gog where Israel would bury the defeated army of God (Ezek. 39:16). The exact meaning and location of the city are not clear except that Ezekiel was determined that Israel would keep the land ritually pure in all circumstances. TEV, REB translate Hamonah as "nearby" or "great horde" and thus do not mention the city. See *Ezekiel; Gog; Hamon-gog.*

HAMOR (Hā´ môr) Personal name meaning, "donkey" or "ass." In Genesis 33:19, the father of Shechem. From the children of Hamor, Jacob purchased a parcel of land on which he erected an altar. Later the remains of Joseph, Jacob's son, were buried on this parcel of land (Josh. 24:32). Hamor and Shechem were killed by Simeon and

Levi in an act of revenge for the outrage committed against Dinah (Gen. 34:25–26). Hamor was the original clan ancestor of the city of Shechem (Judg. 9:28).

HAMRAN (Hăm´ răn) Personal name of uncertain meaning, perhaps, "vineyard." Member of family of Esau and Seir (1 Chron. 1:41). KJV spells the name, Amram. The parallel list has Hemdan (Gen. 36:26); NIV picks up Hemdan in 1 Chronicles along with some Hebrew and Greek manuscripts. Apparently early copyists misread similar Hebrew letters. See *Hemdan.*

HAMSTRING To cripple by cutting the leg tendons. Horses captured in war were frequently hamstrung (KJV, hough) (Josh. 11:6,9; 2 Sam. 8:4; 1 Chron. 18:4). The hamstringing of oxen (Gen. 49:6 modern translations) is an example of rash anger.

HAMUEL (Hăm´ ū ĕl) KJV spelling of Hammuel.

HAMUL (Hā´ mŭl) Personal name meaning, "pitied, spared" or "El is father-in-law" or "El is hot, angry." Son of Pharez and grandson of Judah (Gen. 46:12) and thus a clan leader in Judah (Num. 26:21).

HAMULITE (Hā´ mŭl īte) Member of clan of Hamul (Num. 26:21). See *Hamul.*

HAMUTAL (Hà mū´ tăl) Personal name meaning, "father-in-law or kindred of the dew." Mother of King Jehoahaz (2 Kings 23:31) and King Zedekiah (2 Kings 24:18) of Judah. See *Jehoahaz; Zedekiah.*

HANAMEEL (Hà năm´ ė ĕl) Personal name meaning, "God is gracious." Uncle of Jeremiah from whom the prophet bought the field in Anathoth (Jer. 32:7–12). Jeremiah's act symbolized God's long-range plans to restore the people to the land after Exile.

HANAMEL (Hăn´ à mĕl) Modern translation spelling of Hanameel. See *Hanameel.*

HANAN (Hā´ năn) Personal name meaning, "gracious." Personal name probably originally connected to divine name such as El, Yahweh, or Baal. *1.* Clan or guild of prophets or priests living in the Temple. Jeremiah used their Temple chamber for his meeting with the Rechabites (Jer. 35:4). *2.* Clan of Temple servants who returned to Jerusalem from Babylonian Exile with Zerubbabel about 537 B.C. (Ezra 2:46). *3.* Man Nehemiah appointed as assistant Temple treasurer to receive and disperse tithes brought to care for the Levites (Neh. 13:13).

4. One of David's military heroes (1 Chron. 11:43). *5.* Levite who instructed the people in the

H

Lord's law while Ezra read it (Neh. 8:7). *6.* Levite who sealed Nehemiah's covenant to obey God's law (Neh. 10:10). *7.* Another signer of Nehemiah's covenant (Neh. 10:22). *8.* Another who signed Nehemiah's covenant (Neh. 10:26).

9. Member of tribe of Benjamin (1 Chron. 8:23). *10.* Descendant of Saul in tribe of Benjamin (1 Chron. 8:38).

HANANEEL (Hȧ năn' ė ĕl) KJV spelling of Hananel.

HANANEL (Hăn' ȧ nĕl) Place name meaning, "God is gracious." Tower marking northern wall of Jerusalem. Jeremiah predicted its rebuilding in the day of the Lord to come (Jer. 31:38; compare Zech. 14:10). Nehemiah led the nation to rebuild the tower along with the rest of the Jerusalem wall (Neh. 3:1; 12:39). It may well have been part of the earliest fortress protecting the Temple (Neh. 2:8; 7:2 NAS).

HANANI (Hȧ nā' nī) Personal name meaning, "my grace" or a shortened form of "Yahweh is gracious." *1.* Father of prophet Jehu (1 Kings 16:1,7; 2 Chron. 19:2). *2.* Man who agreed under Ezra's leadership to divorce his foreign wife to protect the Jews from temptation to worship idols (Ezra 10:20). *3.* Nehemiah's brother who reported the poor conditions in Jerusalem to him while Nehemiah was still in Persia (Neh. 1:2). Nehemiah placed him in charge of the military protection of the restored Jerusalem (Neh. 7:2). Some have tried to identify him with the Hunani mentioned in the Elephantine Papyri, but this is far from certain. *4.* Priest musician at dedication of Jerusalem walls (Neh. 12:36). *5.* Temple musician and descendant of Heman (1 Chron. 25:4). Some would equate him with *4.* above *6.* Original leader of one course of Temple musicians (1 Chron. 25:25). *7.* Prophetic seer who condemned King Asa of Judah (910–869 B.C.) for paying tribute to King Ben-hadad of Damascus rather than relying on God (2 Chron. 16:7). Asa imprisoned Hanani (2 Chron. 16:10).

HANANIAH (Hăn ȧ nī' ah) Personal name with two Hebrew spellings meaning, "Yah(weh) is gracious." *1.* Prophet from Gibeon who opposed Jeremiah by promising immediate deliverance from Babylon. Jeremiah could combat this false prophecy only by telling the people to wait until they saw it fulfilled in history (Jer. 28:8–9). Jeremiah could not even oppose Hannaniah when he tried to embarrass Jeremiah by breaking the symbolic yoke Jeremiah was wearing (vv. 10–11). Only later did Jeremiah receive a countering word from God to oppose Hananiah (vv. 12–17). *2.* Father of Zedekiah, a court official, in time of Jeremiah (Jer. 36:12). *3.* Grandfather of captain of guard who

arrested Jeremiah as he left Jerusalem (Jer. 37:13). *4.* Jewish name of Daniel's friend Shadrach (Dan. 1:7). See *Shadrach.* *5.* Son of Zerubbabel in the royal line of David (1 Chron. 3:19). See *Zerubbabel 6.* Clan head in tribe of Benjamin living in Jerusalem (1 Chron. 8:24). *7.* Son of Heman among the priestly musicians in the Temple (1 Chron. 25:4). He may be the same as the head of a course of priests (v. 23), though the latter's name has a slightly variant spelling in Hebrew. *8.* Military leader under King Uzziah of Judah (792–740 B.C.) (2 Chron. 26:11). *9.* Man who followed Ezra's leadership and divorced his foreign wife to protect Judah from the temptatio to worship foreign gods (Ezra 10:28). *10.* A member of the perfumers' guild who helped Nehemiah repair the Jerusalem wall (Neh. 3:8 NAS). *11.* Man who helped Nehemiah repair the Jerusalem wall (Neh. 3:30). *12.* Ruler of the Temple fortress under Nehemiah (Neh. 7:2 NAS). Nehemiah set him up as one of two administrators of Jerusalem because he was trustworthy and reverenced God more than other men. *13.* Man who signed Nehemiah's covenant to obey God's law; perhaps the same as *12.* above (Neh. 10:23). *14.* A priest immediately after the time of return from Babylonian Exile (Neh. 12:12) when Joiakim was high priest. *15.* Priest musician who helped Nehemiah celebrate the completion of the Jerusalem wall (Neh. 12:41).

HAND Part of the human body, namely the terminal part of the arm which enables a person to make and use tools and perform functions. The Greek and Hebrew words that are translated by the English word "hand" appear approximately 1800 times in the Bible. Of these occurrences to which "hand" is referred, the literal sense is intended some 500 times, and the figurative sense some 1300 times.

The references to "hand" in the Bible often encompassed the idea of parts of a hand. Thus, in Genesis 41:42, when Pharaoh took his signet ring "from his hand" and placed it "upon Joseph's hand," "hand" was used in the place of "finger." Likewise, in Ezekiel 23:42, hand was used to mean wrists: ". . . which put bracelets upon their hands." The context in which the word appears determines the meaning and usage of the word.

The largest number of figurative uses of "hand" relate to God. The "hand of God" or "in thine hand" is an idiom referring to the supreme and almighty power and authority of God (1 Chron. 29:12). In Isaiah 59:1, God's hand was described as mighty. Exodus 13:3–16 described God's deliverance of Israel from Egypt by His "strong hand." The creative work of God involved the use of His hands to make the heavens and the earth (Ps. 8:6; 95:5). God uses His hand to uphold and guide the righteous (Ps. 37:24; 139:10). Punishment and affliction come from the hand of God (Ex. 9:3;

Deut. 2:15; Judg. 2:15; 1 Sam. 7:13; 12:15; Ruth 1:13).

The hand of God can be upon someone in either a good or bad sense. In a good sense, it meant to bring aid, while the negative connotation meant to hinder or distress (Amos 1:8).

The phrase "into someone's hand" was used figuratively to convey the idea of authority involving responsibility, care, or dominion over someone or something (Gen. 9:2). Examples of this concept include: Sarah's authority over Hagar (Gen. 16:6,9), Joseph's administration of Potiphar's house (Gen. 39:3–8), and the role of Moses and Aaron as leaders of Israel (Num. 33:1). Victory and deliverance were portrayed also by the use of this phrase. "Victory over someone" was conveyed by the phrase "delivered into hand of" (Gen. 49:8; Josh. 6:2), while deliverance was understood as "out of the hand of" (Ex. 3:8).

Functions of the hand were often used by biblical writers to identify certain uses of the word. Since a person takes possession of objects with the hand, the Biblical writers adapted "hand" to mean possession. A literal translation of Genesis 39:1 would include the statement that Potiphar brought Joseph "from the hand of the Ishmaelites." In 1 Kings 11:31, Jeroboam was told that the Lord was about to tear the kingdom "from the hand" of Solomon.

"To give the hand" meant that one had pledged or submitted to another, as in 2 Kings 10:15 and Ezra 10:19. Submission to the Lord is implied in 2 Chronicles 30:8, where "yield to" is literally, "give hand to."

"To stretch the hand" was used to convey two thoughts: attacking the enemy in battle (Josh. 8:19,26) and an intense desire for communion with God (Ps. 143:6).

Work or the action in which one is involved is expressed by the words "works of thy hand" (Deut. 2:7; 30:9). In 1 Samuel 23:16 Jonathan's helping David is literally, "he strengthened his hand in God," that is increased his faith and hope in God's help.

The Hebrew phrase "high hand" indicated willful rebellion against God (Num. 15:30; see Deut. 32:27) but also military power (Ex. 14:8; Mic. 5:9). A similar image is projected by the phrase "shaking the hand" (Isa. 10:32; 11:15). The movement of the hand was interpreted as a sign of contempt and displeasure, or lack of respect. When used in reference to God, it symbolized God's warning and punishment.

Hebrew "to fill the hand" expressed the consecration of a priest (Judg. 17:5) or a congregation's dedication (2 Chron. 29:31).

The word "hand" was used in a number of specialized ways. It came to mean "side," perhaps because of the location of the hands and arms on the body. A peculiar use was that of hand for "monument" (1 Sam. 15:12). The spreading of the hands denoted a large "space" (Gen. 34:21). See *Work; Worship; Laying on of Hands.*

James Newell

HANDBAG See *Bag 1.*

HANDBREADTH An ancient measurement equal to the width of the hand at the base of the fingers (about three inches). Ezekiel's long cubit was six handbreaths, one more than the common cubit (Ezek. 40:5). In Psalm 39:5 "a few handbreadths" illustrates the shortness of life.

HANDKERCHIEF The Greek term *soudarion* is borrowed from a Latin term used for a table napkin or a handkerchief. The term derives from the Latin root for sweat, suggesting that a *soudarion* was a cloth for wiping sweat or a sweatband. Such a cloth is likely intended at Acts 19:12. The same Greek term is used for a cloth in which money was buried (Luke 19:20) and for the cloth used to cover the face of the dead (John 11:44; 20:7).

HANDLES (Literally hands) The thumb pieces or knobs of the bolt or latch of a door (Song of Sol. 5:5).

HANDMAIDEN See *Maid.*

HANDS, LAYING ON OF See *Laying on of Hands.*

HANDSTAVE A wooden staff used as a weapon by foot soldiers. KJV used handstave to translate a weapon at Ezekiel 39:9. The nature of the weapon is unclear though the weapon was made of wood (39:10). The NRSV renders the term handpike; NAS and NIV, war clubs; REB, throwing sticks. See *Arms and Armor.*

HANDWRITING See *Writing.*

HANES (Hā′ nēs) Egypt place name. City to which Israel sent ambassadors in time of Isaiah to seek military and economic help (Isa. 30:4). Isaiah condemned the government policy of seeking Egyptian help rather than trusting Yahweh. Hanes has often been located at Heracleopolis Magna in southern Egypt just north of the Nile Delta, modern Ahnas. This would be a natural parallel to northern Zoan or Tanis. See *Zoan.* A more likely identification, however, is Heracleopolis Parva, modern Hanes, almost directly east of Tanis and much more likely to be the goal of Judah's ambassador's than the distant southern Heracleopolis. Ashurbanipal of Egypt also mentions Hanes in listing Egyptian cities.

HANGING A method of ridiculing, shaming, and desecrating an enemy. Hanging was not regarded as a means of capital punishment according to biblical law, although it was practiced by the Egyptians (Gen. 40:19,22) and the Persians (Esther 7:9). The Israelites, after putting an enemy or criminal to death, might hang them on a gibbet or tree for public scorn as added degradation and warning (Gen. 40:19; Deut. 21:22; Josh. 8:29; 2 Sam. 4:12), but biblical law demanded that the corpses be taken down and buried the same day (Deut. 21:22, 23). Joshua 8:29; 10:26,27 record that the bodies of the kings of Ai and the kings of the Amorites were taken down and buried at sundown on the same day they were hanged. Contrast the undetermined length of exposure allowed by Pharaoh (Gen. 40:19), the Philistines (1 Sam. 31:10), and the Gibeonites (2 Sam. 21:8–10). A hanged man was considered an insult to God (Gal. 3:13) and therefore defiled the land.

According to the first century Jewish historian, Josephus, all executed criminals were afterward hanged. The Mishna prescribes hanging only for those put to death by stoning. Some Bible students think hanging was prescribed only for blasphemers and idolaters.

Hanging oneself is mentioned only once in the Old Testament and once in the New Testament. Ahithophel, David's counselor, joined the conspiracy of Absalom, David's son (2 Sam. 15:31). Feeling his ploy for personal power evaporate, he set his house in order and hanged himself (2 Sam. 17:23). Judas, one of the twelve disciples of our Lord, in a desperate effort to resolve guilt and atone for the misdeed of betraying Jesus for thirty pieces of silver, went out into the night and hanged himself (Matt. 27:5). Acts 1:18 says he fell headlong and burst asunder, presumably as the rope broke. *C. Dale Hill*

HANIEL (Hăn′ ĭ ĕl) KJV variant spelling of Hanniel (1 Chron. 7:39). See *Hanniel.*

HANNAH (Hăn′ nah) Personal name meaning, "grace." One of the wives of Elkanah and mother of Samuel (1 Sam. 1:2). Because she had been barren for many years, she vowed to the Lord that if she should give birth to a son, she would dedicate the child to God (1 Sam. 1:11). Subsequently, she gave birth to the child Samuel. She fulfilled her vow by bringing her son to the sanctuary at Shiloh, where he served the Lord under the direction of Eli. Later on, Hannah had other sons and daughters. See *Samuel.*

HANNATHON (Hăn nă′ thŏn) Place name meaning, "grace." Town on northern border of tribal territory of Zebulun (Josh. 19:14). The El-Amarna tablets and the annals of Tiglath-pileser III of Assyria also mention it. It is probably present-day tell el-Badawiye, about six miles north of Nazareth.

HANNIEL (Hăn′ nĭ ĕl) Personal name meaning, "God is gracious." *1.* Representative of tribe of

Manasseh on council which helped Joshua and Eleazar divide the land among the tribes (Num. 34:23). *2.* Member of tribe of Asher (1 Chron. 7:39).

HANOCH (Hā′ nŏch) Personal name with same Hebrew spelling as Enoch meaning, "dedicated" or "vassal." See *Enoch. 1.* Son of Reuben and grandson of Jacob (Gen. 46:9) and thus a clan leader in Israel (Ex. 6:14; Num. 26:5). *2.* Son of Midian and grandson of Abraham and thus one of the Midianites (Gen. 25:4). See *Midian.*

HANOCHITE (Hā′ nŏch īte) Member of clan of Hanoch. See *Hanoch.*

HANUKKAH An eight-day festival that commemorated the cleansing and rededication of the Temple following the victories of Judas Maccabeus in 167/165 B.C. See *Festivals.*

HANUN (Hā′ nŭn) Personal name meaning, "blessed" or "favored." *1.* King of Ammon whom David sought to honor and with whom he sought to renew the peace treaty. Hanun and his advisors misinterpreted David's act and treated David's messengers shamefully. David's military response brought victory over Ammon and Syria (2 Sam. 10). This set the stage for David's sinful relationship with Bathsheba. *2.* Man who repaired the valley gate of Jerusalem under Nehemiah (Neh. 3:13). See *Jerusalem. 3.* Another man who worked under Nehemiah to repair the Jerusalem wall (Neh. 3:30).

HAPHARAIM (Hăph à rā′ ĭm) Modern translations reading of KJV's Haphraim. See *Haphraim.*

HAPHRAIM (Hăph rā′ ĭm) Place name meaning, "two holes" or "two wells." Town in tribal territory of Issachar (Josh. 19:19). It is modern et-Taiyibeh, about nine miles northwest of Bethshean.

HAPPIZZEZ (Hăp pĭz′ zĕz) Personal name meaning, "the shattered one." Leader of one course of the priests (1 Chron. 24:15) and thus the original ancestor for that priestly clan. KJV, REB spell the name Aphses.

HAR-HERES (Här-hē′ rēs) NRSV reading in Judges 1:35 for Mount Heres, NRSV transliterating *har,* Hebrew word for mountain. See *Heres.*

HAR-MAGEDON (Här-Mà gĕd′ ŏn) NAS, NRSV transliteration of Greek transliteration from Hebrew in Revelation 16:16 for place name other English translations transliterate as Armageddon. See *Armageddon.*

HARA (Hā′ rà) Place name of uncertain meaning. City or region in northern Mesopotamia where,

H

according to 1 Chronicles 5:26, the Assyrians under Tiglath-pileser settled some of the exiles from east of the Jordan in the Northern Kingdom in 734 B.C. The name does not occur in the parallel passages (1 Kings 17:6; 18:11). The scribe copying Chronicles may have copied part of the Hebrew word for either Habor or for river a second time in a way later generations made into the name Hara. The accounts in 1 Kings place the exile to these cities in 722 B.C.

HARADAH (Hả rā′ dah) Place name meaning, "quaking" or "terror." Station in Israel's wilderness journey (Num. 33:24–25). It is probably modern el-Harada, over 50 miles south of Aqaba.

HARAN (Hā′ răn) Personal and place name meaning, "mountaineer" or "caravan route." Three men and an important city of northern Mesopotamia located on the Balikh River. *1.* Terah's son and Lot's father (Gen. 11:26–29,31). *2.* Son of Caleb's concubine (1 Chron. 2:46). *3.* Son of Shimei and a Levite (1 Chron. 23:9). *4.* The city became Abraham's home (Gen. 11:31–32; 12:4–5) and remained home for his relatives like Laban (Gen. 27:43). Jacob went there and married (Gen. 28:10; 29:4). In the eighth century Assyria conquered it (2 Kings 19:12; Isa. 37:12). It was a trade partner of Tyre (Ezek. 27:23). Through excavations begun in the 1950s, the city was determined to have been established by the middle of the third millenium and was occupied through the Assyro-Babylonian period until Islamic times. The city was also a major center of worship for the moon god Sin. Its name is spelled differently from that of the men in Hebrew.   *David M. Fleming*

HARAR (Hā′ rảr) Geographical name perhaps related to Hebrew word for "mountain." The word appears in slightly difficult forms in its appearances in the Hebrew Bible. Three of David's military heroes are related to Harar (2 Sam. 23:11,33; 1 Chron. 11:34–35). Harar can either be a town, a region, a tribe, or a general reference to mountain country.

HARARITE (Hā′ rả rīte) Person from Harar. See *Harar.*

HARBEL (Här′ běl) TEV reading of place name in Numbers 34:11, usually translated Riblah but spelled in Hebrew with beginning "h," which can be the Hebrew definite article. See *Riblah.*

HARBONA (Här bō′ nả) Persian personal name perhaps meaning, "barren." A eunuch on the staff of King Ahasuerus of Persia (Esther 1:10; 7:9).

HARBONAH (Här bō′ nảh) Alternate spelling of Harbona, based on Hebrew text's alteration between Hebrew and Aramaic spelling. See *Harbona.*

HARD SAYING Teaching difficult to understand or accept (John 6:60).

HARDNESS OF THE HEART A stubborn attitude that leads a person to reject God's will. The Bible speaks of the attitude both as stemming from the human heart and from God's action.

The Bible makes it clear that humans can resist God who respects the free human will. One of the most important ways of resisting God is for a person to "harden his heart." The analogy is to a rock or a millstone so that the individual has no feeling and is like a piece of stone.

When God's people were in captivity in Egypt, "Pharaoh hardened his heart" (Ex. 8:32) as he refused to let the Israelites go. One of the puzzling aspects of this hard heart is that in the next chapter in the contest between God and Pharaoh, "the Lord hardened the heart of Pharaoh, and he hearkened not unto them" (Ex. 9:12).

The explanation of saying God hardened Pharaoh's heart seems to be that this is the way of punishment which comes as the consequence of his own initial self hardening. Pharaoh hardened his own heart and then became confirmed in his obstancy. Sin has become its own punishment. This makes more relevant the warning in the Psalms, "Harden not your heart" (Ps. 95:8).

In the New Testament Jesus took up the same theme as He warned His disciples, "Have ye your heart yet hardened?" (Mark 8:17). Hardening the heart was also seen as evidence of skepticism, "They considered not the miracle of the loaves: for their heart was hardened" (Mark 6:52).

God's people can have hardened hearts and begin to complain when God's ethical standards seem too high. Discussing the permanence of marriage and the concession that Moses made to the children of Israel, Jesus said, "For the hardness of your heart he wrote you this precept. But from the beginning of the creation God made them male and female." (Mark 10:5–6). Even though the word was part of Scripture (Deut. 24:1), it was simply a concession to the hardness of the people's hearts.

Failure to hear the voice of God may come from a hardened heart (Prov. 28:14; 29:1).

Scottish people speak about falling in love as "having a soft heart," and God's people must constantly maintain a soft heart towards their Lord, ever remembering the exhortation of the writer of the Hebrews letter, "Today if ye will hear his voice, harden not your hearts" (Heb. 4:7).
                                                          John Drakeford

HARE A member of the rabbit family (Leporidae), especially those born with open eyes and fur. Hares were regarded as unclean (Lev. 11:6; Deut. 14:7). See *Animals.*

HAREPH (Hā′ rěph) Personal name meaning,

"clever" or "reproach." Descendant of Caleb and thus member of tribe of Judah (1 Chron. 2:51).

HARETH (Hā' rĕth) Place name meaning, "woodland." Forest where David went at advice of Gad, the prophet, as he hid from Saul (1 Sam. 22:5). It was in Judah, but the exact location is debated. Some students place it at khirbet Khoreisa two miles south of Ziph and about six miles southeast of Hebron. Others think it is near the village of Kharas near Keilah. For modern translations' spelling, see *Hereth.*

HARHAIAH (Här hâi ' ah) Personal name of uncertain meaning. Member of goldsmiths' guild whose son helped Nehemiah repair the wall of Jerusalem (Neh. 3:8).

HARHAS (Här' hăs) Foreign name of uncertain meaning. Grandfather of the husband of Huldah, the prophet (2 Kings 22:14). Second Chronicles 34:22 spells the name Hasrah with other manuscript evidence pointing to Hasdah or Harham. Many Bible students think Hasrah is original.

HARHUR (Här' hūr) Personal name meaning, "glow, burn," possibly describing fever of mother at birth. A Temple servant who returned from Babylonian Exile with Zerubbabel about 537 B.C. (Ezra 2:51).

HARIM (Hā' rĭm) Personal name meaning, "dedicated." *1.* Clan leader from Bethlehem whose family returned from Babylonian Exile with Zerubbabel about 537 B.C. (Ezra 2:32). *2.* Head of one course of priests appointed under David's leadership (1 Chron. 24:8; compare Ezra 2:39; Neh. 12:15). Some members of this clan agreed under Ezra's leadership to divorce their foreign wives to protect the people from the temptation of false worship (Ezra 10:21). *3.* Another Israelite clan with members having to divorce foreign wives under Ezra (Ezra 10:31). The clan name may have come from an original ancestor but more likely from the town of residence—Charim, eight miles northeast of Joppa. One of these clan members helped Nehemiah build the Jerusalem wall (Neh. 3:11). *4.* Priest who signed Nehemiah's covenant to obey God's law (Neh. 10:5). *5.* Clan leader who signed Nehemiah's covenant (Neh. 10:27).

HARIPH (Här' ĭph) Personal name meaning, "sharp" or "fresh." *1.* Israelite clan whose members accompanied Zerubbabel in returning from Babylonian Exile about 537 B.C. (Neh. 7:24). *2.* Leader of people who signed Nehemiah's covenant to obey God's law (Neh. 10:19).

HARLOT A prostitute. The most famous harlot in the Bible is Rahab of Jericho, who saved the Israelite spies sent by Joshua to scout out the Promised Land (Josh. 2). Israel spared her and her family when they conquered and destroyed Jericho. She continued to dwell with the Israelites (Josh. 6:23–25). She is listed in the genealogy of Jesus (Matt. 1:5). Her action on behalf of the Israelite spies won her a place in the roll call of the faithful (Heb. 11:31; compare Jas. 2:25).

The Bible gives few details of the ways in which harlots like Rahab practiced their trade. Evidently, harlots might solicit along the roadside (Gen. 38:14–15). Brothels, which often served as taverns and inns, were also known in the Ancient Near East. Rahab's house may have been one (Josh. 2:1). It is possible that the prostitute had a distinctive mark on her forehead (Jer. 3:3) and breasts (Hos. 2:2). She might attract attention by her clothing, jewelry and make-up (Jer. 4:30; Ezek. 23:40; Rev. 17:4). Flattering with words (Prov. 2:16) and making sweet music (Isa. 23:16) might be used to lure or soothe a client. Her payment might be in money, or it could be in jewelry (Ezek. 23:42) or other items of value (Gen. 38:15–18; compare Luke 15:30).

Although harlots were considered socially inferior, they did have legal rights, as is evident from the incident recorded in 1 Kings 3:16–22.

See *Fornication; Prostitution. Wilda W. Morris*

HARMON (Här' mon) Place name of uncertain meaning in Amos 4:3 as translated by NRSV, NAS, NIV. KJV reads, "palace," changing the first letter of the Hebrew word to a common Hebrew noun for royal fortresses. TEV does not translate the final Hebrew word, saying it is unclear. REB changes two Hebrew letters slightly to translate, "dunghill." The earliest Greek translation read, "Mount Rimmon." Some Bible students change the first letter slightly to read, "Mount Hermon." If Harmon, the unchanged Hebrew text, is read, we know nothing of the place meant. Whatever the precise reading of the original, Amos' intention was to describe the drastic fate waiting the sinful women of Samaria, a fate using terminology connected with slaughter of animals and exile.

HARMONY OF THE GOSPELS The arrangement of the gospels in parallel columns for the purpose of studying their similarities and differences. Andreas Osiander (1498–1552), a German Bible scholar of the Protestant Reformation, was the first person to use the phrase "harmony of the gospels" for a parallel organization of gospel texts which he designed. By choosing a musical term as a metaphor for his columnar arrangement, Osiander likened the total picture of Jesus supplied by all four gospels to the sound of several musical notes being played together in one chord. A harmony of the gospels may also be called a synopsis or a parallel of the gospels.

History of Harmonies While the term "harmony of the gospels" was not used until the sixteenth century, Bible scholars began efforts to compare and harmonize the four accounts of Jesus as early as the second century. At that time, Tatian, a Christian from Syria, compiled the four gospels into a single paraphrased narrative called the *Diatessaron*. All we know about Tatian's work is from references to it by other writers.

The *Diatessaron* represents one approach to harmonizing the gospels: the weaving together of material from the gospels to present one, continuous narrative of Jesus' life. Several biblical scholars in the past two hundred years have attempted similar works.

Few contemporary scholars give credence to attempts to "harmonize" either the texts or the information contained in the gospels into one, exhaustive record of Jesus. Rather, they recognize the differences and compare the variations between the gospels and use their findings as an aid for interpretation. The first great work in this second approach to harmonizing the gospels was done by Amonnius of Alexandria in the third century. Ammonius took the text of Matthew and wrote beside the text in parallel columns any passages from the other three gospels which corresponded to them. Consequently, Ammonius' work only showed the relationship between Matthew and the other three gospels. Any parallels which existed independently among the other three were ignored. In the fourth century, the church historian Eusebius developed a cross-reference system which provided a way to locate and study a passage which had parallels in any of the other gospels.

J. J. Griesbach, another German, made one of the most significant contributions to this field when he produced his *Synopse,* a parallel arrangement of the texts of the first three gospels, in 1776. Griesbach derived his title from the Greek word which means "to view at the same time," and, consequently gave Matthew, Mark, and Luke the designation "synoptic gospels" because of their similar perspective (in contrast to John) on the life of Jesus. Greisbach's work still serves as the basic model for scholars who make comparisons between the gospels in order to aid their interpretation of a given text.

Need for Comparative Study Even the most casual reading of the New Testament reveals the need and helpfulness of a comparative study of Matthew, Mark, and Luke. Note the following:

1. Some of the material contained in one gospel is repeated almost word for word in one or both of the other gospels (the story of Jesus' disciples plucking grain on the sabbath, Mark 2:23–27, Matt. 12:1–8; Luke 6:1–5).

2. Some material, part of which appears vital to the record of Jesus' teaching, is included in only one gospel (the parable of the Prodigal Son, Luke 15:11–32).

How are these facts to be explained, and what help do their answers provide for understanding the gospels? A comparative study helps answer these questions.

The Synoptic Problem As noted above, scholars have long noted the particular similarities which abound between Matthew, Mark, and Luke. In all three gospels:

1) The appearance of John the Baptist, Jesus' baptism and temptation, and the initiation of Jesus' public ministry are linked together.

2) Jesus' ministry is confined to Galilee until He attended the Passover celebration in Jerusalem where He was crucified.

3) The story ends with His crucifixion and resurrection.

In addition to the rough similarity in their plots and similar points of view, the three gospels exhibit an undeniable interrelatedness with respect to actual content: Luke contains 50 per cent of the substance of Mark's verses, while Matthew contains a full 90 per cent of Mark. Yet, for all these similarities, the three gospels also possess significant differences. How does one explain these facts? Scholars have labeled the issues surrounding this question "the synoptic problem."

1. An Early Solution One of the earliest and most influential answers to the synoptic problem was offered by Augustine (A.D. 354–430). He decided that Matthew wrote first and that Mark produced his gospel by abridging what Matthew had written. Luke was thought to be dependent on both of them. Augustine's position was the orthodox view for over 1400 years.

2. Later Solutions During the 1800's, advances were made in archaeology and the study of ancient languages. New methods were introduced to biblical studies. These changes produced several fresh solutions to the synoptic problem.

The first "modern" solution focused on the hypothesis of a single, original gospel which is now lost to us. Some scholars believed it may have been an orally transmitted gospel which had become formalized through constant repetition, while others believed it was an actual document. In either case, those who believed this hypothesis assumed Matthew, Mark, and Luke individually selected material from this gospel as they wrote their accounts.

Other solutions to the problem centered on the belief that two documents were used by the gospel writers. Reversing the established view that Matthew was written first, proponents of the two document theory concluded that Mark was actually the first gospel and that the other two synoptic gospels were dependent upon Mark. Because of the similarities between teaching passages contained in both Matthew and Luke, these scholars also theorized that Matthew and Luke both had one other source, a collection of Jesus' teachings.

3. The Four Document Hypothesis In the early part of the twentieth century, B. H. Streeter, a

H

British scholar, proposed the four document theory as a solution to the synoptic problem. Streeter agreed with the two document theory to a point, but thought it failed to go far enough in explaining the existence of material which was exclusive to either Matthew or Luke. Therefore, Streeter offered the hypothesis that the writers of the synoptic gospels used a total of four documents as sources for their works.

a. The Priority of Mark Like the proponents of the two document theory, Streeter believed Mark was written first and served as a source for both Matthew and Luke. Several facts led to this belief. First, all three gospels usually agree on the order in which they arrange their material. However, when they do disagree, Matthew and Mark frequently agree compared to Luke, or Luke and Mark will agree compared to Matthew. Matthew and Luke hardly ever agree compared to Mark. The same is true in word usage and sentence structure. Mark often agrees with Matthew or Luke against the other, but Matthew and Luke rarely agree against Mark. These two facts would indicate Mark was used by the other writers. A third piece of evidence indicating the priority of Mark is that statements in Mark which could offend or perplex readers are either omitted or presented in a less provocative form by the other two synoptics (compare Mark 4:38 with Matthew 8:25 and Luke 8:24). Streeter believed that when taken together, these three facts can only lead to the conclusion that Mark was written first and used by Matthew and Luke.

b. The Existence of "Q" Streeter also agreed with the proponents of the two document theory that Matthew and Luke used a common source other than Mark. German scholars gave this source the name "Q" from the German *Quelle,* which means "source." Its content can only be deduced by comparing passages common to Matthew and Luke but absent from Mark. Scholars agree that Q was primarily a collection of Jesus' teachings with little narrative and no mention of the crucifixion and resurrection. The most significant contribution of Q is the Sermon on the Mount (Matthew 5—7 and Luke 6:20–49).

c. The "M" Source Streeter believed Matthew had access to a body of material unknown to (or at least unused by) Mark and Luke. This source derives its name "M" from the initial for Matthew. Because Matthew's infancy story differs from Luke, it is considered part of the material contained in this source. M also contained many Old Testament proof texts related to Jesus' role as Messiah.

d. The "L" Source The fourth and final source in the four document hypothesis is believed to contain the material exclusive to Luke. This source contained at least an infancy story and many parables. The stories of the Good Samaritan and the Prodigal Son are a part of this "L" source.

The Place of Inspiration Many persons believe the discussion of "sources" used by the gospel writers impinges on the inspiration of the Scriptures. If Matthew, Mark and Luke used other documents to write their gospels, does God still have a place in their authorship? Careful thought will reveal that "sources" and inspiration are not mutually exclusive. Old Testament writers clearly show they used written sources (Josh. 10:13; 2 Sam. 1:18; 1 Kings 11:41; 2 Chron. 9:29).

Luke says, "Many have undertaken to draw up an account of the things that have been fulfilled among us, just as they were handed down to us by those who from the first were eyewitnesses and servants of the word. Therefore, since I myself have carefully investigated everything from the beginning, it seemed good also to me to write an orderly account for you . . . (Luke 1:1–3). Luke made an important admission in this statement: he indicated knowledge of other accounts of Jesus' life and message. No known theory of inspiration violates a person's humanity to the point of negating his or her memory. Therefore, the gospel authored by Luke would certainly have had something in common with the sources known to him. Additionally, no theory of inspiration states that the human authors of biblical material used information or words which, until the precise moment of writing, had been entirely unknown to the writer. To assume that inspiration cannot involve the process of helping a human being to recognize divine truth and to shape that truth into the specific message God wants communicated is to limit the abilities of God's Spirit. Inspiration of both Testaments included God's leading writers to proper sources and directing in the use of the sources.

Summary While most contemporary scholars hold to the four document theory (or a theory very similar to it), one must recognize any solution to the synoptic problem is a theory and not a proven fact. Many Bible students today are returning to the view Matthew was written first. It must be admitted that many of the answers we desire about the origins of the gospels are not available to us. Therefore, some modern questioners will find themselves extremely frustrated when they expect scientifically precise answers about documents, the original purpose of which was to be religiously reliable about the exciting good news from God through Jesus Christ. We can trust and obey the gospels without having the answer to every question about their origins and relationships.

P. Joel Snider

HARNEPHER (Här' nē phēr) Egyptian personal name meaning, "Horus (god) is good." Member of tribe of Asher (1 Chron. 7:36).

HARNESS KJV translation of a term meaning breastplate (1 Kings 22:34; 2 Chron. 18:33) or weapons (2 Chron. 9:24), where RSV translation myrrh and REB perfumes reflect a different Hebrew text, changed to weaponry in NRSV. See *Arms and Armor.*

HAROD (Hā′ rŏd) Place name meaning, "quake," "terror," or "intermittent spring." Place where God led Gideon to test his troops to reduce their numbers before fighting Midian (Judg. 7:1). It is modern ain Jalud near Gilboa, half way between Affulah and Beth Shean. It is about two miles east southeast of Jezreel. It was home for two of David's heroes (2 Sam. 23:25), though the parallel text in 1 Chronicles 11:27 reads, "Harorite," representing a copyist's confusion of two letters similar in appearance. The "fountain" of 1 Samuel 29:1 was probably Harod. Some Bible students see a reference to Judges 7:1 in Psalm 83:10 and make a slight change in the Hebrew text to read "Harod" instead of "En-dor." Compare REB.

HARODITE (hā′ rŏd īte) Citizen of Harod. See *Harod.*

HAROEH (Hå rō′ ĕh) Personal name meaning, "the seer." Descendant of Caleb in tribe of Judah (1 Chron. 2:52). The same person is apparently called Reaiah in 1 Chronicles 4:2, an easy change to make in copying Hebrew and probably the original name. As other names in the list, this may represent a place name as well as a personal name.

HARORITE (Hā′ rō rīte) Copyist's spelling of Harodite (1 Chron. 11:27). See *Harod.*

HAROSHETH (Hå rō′ shĕth) Place name meaning, "forest land." First part of compound Hebrew place name Harosheth-hagoiim, meaning Harosheth of the Gentiles (KJV, REB, TEV) or nations. Home of Sisera, captain of the army of Jabin of Hazor (Judg. 4:2). He mustered his troops there and marched them to the river Kishon to face Barak and Deborah (v. 13). Barak chased the army back to Harosheth and killed them there (v. 16). It may be the same as Muhrashti of the Amarna letters. Its location is debated, some favoring tell el-Ama at the foot of Mount Carmel about nine miles south of Haifa near the Arab village of Haritiyeh. Others would see Haroseth as a common noun meaning, "woods" and locate it in the woods or forests of Galilee, using some evidence from the earliest Greek translation. This view would read Joshua 12:23, "king of Goiim in Galilee" (TEV, NRSV) and equate the king with the ruler of the Galilean forests.

HAROSHETH HAGGOYIM (Hå rō′ shĕth Håg goy′ īm) NIV spelling for Harosheth. See *Harosheth.*

HAROSHETH-HAGOIIM (Hå rō′ shĕth-hå gôi′ īm) Full Hebrew name of Harosheth. See *Harosheth.*

HAROSHETH-HAGOYIM (Hå rō′ shĕth-hå goy′ īm) NAS spelling of Harosheth. See *Harosheth.*

HARP See *Music, Instruments, Dancing.*

HARPOON A barbed (KJV) spear or javelin used in hunting large fish or whales, mentioned as an inadequate weapon for catching the sea monster Leviathan (Job. 41:7) and thus showing God's sovereignty over human inadequacy.

HARROW To pulverize and smooth the soil by means of a harrow, a cultivating implement with spikes, spring teeth, or disks. The modern harrow was unknown in ancient Egypt. The biblical references to harrowing or breaking clods (Job. 39:10; Isa. 28:24; Hos. 10:11) distinguish this process from plowing. Perhaps the dragging of branches to smooth the soil over seed is what is intended. The NIV replaced harrow with "till" (Job 39:10) and with "break up the ground" (Hos. 10:11).

Modern translations replace the harrow of the KJV with iron picks (NIV, NRSV); iron hoes (TEV), or sharp iron instruments (NAS) at 2 Samuel 12:31; 1 Chronicles 20:3. See *Agriculture; Tools.*

HARSHA (Här′ shà) Personal name meaning, "unable to talk, silent" or "magician, sorcerer." Clan of Temple servants who returned with Zerubbabel from Babylonian Exile about 537 B.C. (Ezra 2:52). Tel-Harsha (Ezra 2:59 NAS) was one of the places where Jewish exiles lived in Babylon, so that the clan could have taken its name from the Babylonian home or given its name to the Babylonian home.

HART An adult male deer (Ps. 42:1; Isa. 35:6). See *Animals.*

HARUM (Hā′ rŭm) Personal name meaning, "the exalted." A member of the tribe of Judah (1 Chron. 4:8).

HARUMAPH (Hå rū′ măph) Personal name meaning, "split nose." Father of worker who helped Nehemiah rebuild the wall of Jerusalem (Neh. 3:10).

HARUPHITE (Hå rū′ phīte) Clan or place name meaning, "early" or "reproach." Reading of early Hebrew scribes in 1 Chronicles 12:5. Written Hebrew text has Hariphites. Haruph is otherwise unknown. It could be a clan or a town from which Shephatiah came. Hariphite would refer to citizen or descendent of Hariph. See *Hariph.*

HARUZ (Hā′ rŭz) Personal name meaning, "gold"

or "industrious." Maternal grandfather of Amon, king of Judah (642–640 B.C.). He was from Jotbah (2 Kings 21:19). The home may not be in Judah and thus represent foreign influence on the king. See *Jotbah.*

HARVEST The festive occasion for gathering the crops, usually marked by important religious festivals.

Among the more important crops grown were wheat, grapes, and olives. Other crops included barley, flax, and various vegetables and fruits. Crops that had been planted were harvested at various times. Olives were harvested between mid-September to mid-November by beating the trees with long sticks (Deut. 24:20; Isa. 17:6). Flax was gathered in the spring by cutting it off near the ground and then laying the stalks out to dry (Josh. 2:6). Barley was harvested from April to May; wheat from May to June; and summer fruits from August to September. The average harvesting period was set at a period of seven weeks (Lev. 23:15; Deut. 16:9).

All members of the family were expected to work during harvest (Prov. 10:5; 20:4). Significant events were connected with harvest times (Ex. 34:18–20; Deut. 16:13–16; Josh. 3:15; 1 Sam. 16:13). Harvest time became the occasion for joyful festivals (Ex. 34:22; Isa. 9:3). See *Festivals.*

Several laws governed the harvest. Part of the crop was not harvested (Lev. 19:9) out of concern for the poor. The firstfruits of the harvest were presented as an offering to God (Lev. 23:10).

The Old Testament provides several figurative uses of harvest. A destroyed harvest represented affliction (Job 5:5; Isa. 16:9). The "time of harvest" sometimes represented the day of destruction (Jer. 51:33; Joel 3:13). "The harvest is past" meant the appointed time was gone (Jer. 8:20).

Jesus spoke often of the harvest in connection with the harvesting of souls (Matt. 9:37; Mark 4:29; John 4:35). In the parable of the tares, Jesus related harvest to the end of the world (Matt. 13:30–39). The rhythm of harvest time (sowing and reaping) provided an illustration of a spiritual truth (Gal. 6:7–8). *Gary Hardin*

HARVEST, FEAST OF An alternate name for Pentecost or the Feast of Weeks (Ex. 23:16; 34:22). See *Festivals; Pentecost.*

HARVESTER See *Occupations and Professions in the Bible.*

HASADIAH (Hăs á dī' ah) Personal name meaning, "Yahweh is gracious." Son of Zerubbabel and descendant of David (1 Chron. 3:20). See *Zerubbabel.*

HASENUAH (Hăs é nū' ah) KJV spelling of Hassenuah in 1 Chronicles 9:7. See *Hassenuah.*

HASHABIAH (Hăsh á bī' ah) Personal name meaning, "Yahweh has reckoned or imputed," appearing in longer and shorter Hebrew spellings. *1.* Ancestor of Merari among the Levite leaders (1 Chron. 6:45). *2.* Another member of the Merari priesthood (1 Chron. 9:14; Neh. 11:15). *3.* Temple musician and Levite under David (1 Chron. 25:3) and leader of course of Levites (1 Chron. 25:19). *4.* Family of Levites from Hebron given authority to carry out God's business in the service of the king west of the Jordan (1 Chron. 26:30). This shows the close connection between Temple and palace, religious and political activity in Israel. *5.* Leader of the tribe of Levi possibly connected with taking the ill-fated census under David (1 Chron. 27:17). He may be identical with *4.* above. *6.* Levite leader under Josiah who provided animals for the Levites to celebrate Passover (2 Chron. 35:9). *7.* Levite leader Ezra conscripted to return to Jerusalem with him from Babylonian Exile about 458 B.C. (Ezra 8:19). He shared responsibility for transporting Temple treasures on the journey (vv. 24–30). Compare Nehemiah 12:24. *8.* Israelite called to divorce his foreign wife to protect the people from tempation to false worship according to Greek manuscripts of Ezra 10:25 (NRSV). *9.* Levite with administrative duties over city of Keilah who joined Nehemiah in repairing wall of Jerusalem (Neh. 3:17). He is probably the same one as the signer of Nehemiah's covenant to obey God's law (Neh. 10:11) and could be the same as both *7.* and *8.* above. *10.* Ancestor of chief Levite in Jerusalem in Nehemiah's day (Neh. 11:22). *11.* Priest one generation after the return from Exile (Neh. 12:21).

HASHABNAH (Hă shăb' nah) Personal name perhaps meaning, "reckoning." Signer of Nehemiah's covenant to obey God's law (Neh. 10:25).

HASHABNEIAH (Hăsh áb nē ī' ah) Personal name meaning, "Yahweh has imputed to me." *1.* Father of man who helped Nehemiah repair the Jerusalem wall (Neh. 3:10). *2.* Levite who led worship in Nehemiah's covenant ceremony in which people reaffirmed their commitment to obey God (Neh. 9:5).

HASHABNIAH (Hăsh áb nī' ah) KJV spelling for Hashabneiah. See *Hashabneiah.*

HASHBADANA (Hăsh bá dā' na) KJV spelling of Hashbaddanah. See *Hashbaddanah.*

HASHBADDANAH (Hăsh băd dá' nah) Personal name of uncertain meaning. A member of the community leaders who stood with Ezra as he read the law to the people (Neh. 8:4). Some early translations provide evidence for a copyist having joined two names—Hashub and Baddanah into one. The precise function of these leaders is not stated.

HASHEM (Hā' shěm) Personal name meaning, "the name." Father of some of David's heroes (1 Chron. 11:34) and said to be a Gizonite. See *Gizonite.* The parallel passage in 2 Samuel 23:32 may preserve the original spelling—Jashen. See *Jashen.*

HASHMONAH (Hăsh mō' nah) Place name of uncertain meaning. A station in Israel's wilderness journey (Num. 33:29–30). Some Bible students identify it with Azmon (Num. 34:4). See *Azmon.*

HASHUB (Hăsh ŭb) KJV spelling of Hasshub in Nehemiah 3:11,23; 10:23; 11:15. See *Hasshub.*

HASHUBAH (Hȧ shū' bah) Personal name meaning, "highly treasured." Son of Zerubbabel in the royal line of David (1 Chron. 3:20).

HASHUM (Hā' shŭm) *1.* Personal name meaning, "flat-nosed." Clan leader of group returning from Babylonian Exile with Zerubbabel about 537 B.C. Some clan members divorced their foreign wives under Ezra's leadership to rid the community of religious temptations (Ezra 10:33). *2.* Community leader who stood with Ezra while he read the law to the people (Neh. 8:4). He also signed Nehemiah's covenant to obey God (Neh. 10:18).

HASHUPHA KJV form of Hasupha.

HASIDEANS A militant, religious community active in the Maccabean revolt (begun 168 B.C.). The group's name derived from the Old Testament concept of the *Hasidim,* the "saints" or "faithful." The Pharisees and the Essenes likely derived from different streams of the Hasidean movement. See *Intertestamental History and Literature; Jewish Parties.*

HASMONEAN (Hăs mō nē' an) Name given to the dynasty that ruled ancient Judea for almost a century, from the Maccabean wars (that ended in approximately 145 B.C.) until Roman occupation of ancient Palestine, in 63 B.C. See *Intertestamental History.*

HASRAH (Hăs' rah) Personal name perhaps meaning, "lack." See *Harhas.*

HASSENAAH (Hăs sė nā' ah) Personal or place name perhaps meaning, "the hated one." Apparently the same name without *h,* the Hebrew definite article, appears as Senaah. A clan who returned with Zerubbabel from Babylonian Exile about 537 B.C. (Ezra 2:35). Members of the clan helped Nehemiah rebuild the fish gate of the Jerusalem wall (Neh. 3:3).

HASSENUAH (Hăs sė nū' ah) Personal name meaning, "the hated one." Leader in tribe of Benjamin (1 Chron. 9:7). The name without the Hebrew article *h* appears in Nehemiah 11:9 as father of a leader in post-exilic Jerusalem from the tribe of Benjamin.

THE HASMONEAN DYNASTY

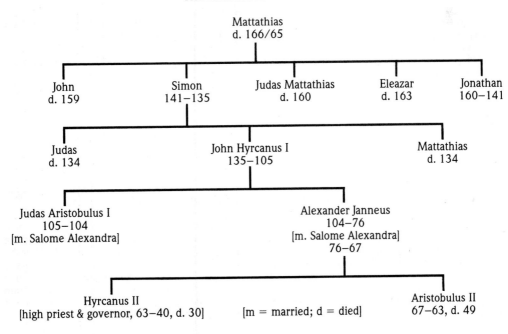

Mattathias d. 166/65				
John d. 159	Simon 141–135	Judas Mattathias d. 160	Eleazar d. 163	Jonathan 160–141

Judas d. 134 — John Hyrcanus I 135–105 — Mattathias d. 134

Judas Aristobulus I 105–104 [m. Salome Alexandra] — Alexander Janneus 104–76 [m. Salome Alexandra] 76–67

Hyrcanus II [high priest & governor, 63–40, d. 30] — [m = married; d = died] — Aristobulus II 67–63, d. 49

HASSHUB (Hăs' shŭb) Personal name meaning, "one to whom He has imputed or reckoned." *1.* Man who helped Nehemiah repair the Jerusalem wall (Neh. 3:23). He was apparently a Levite at the Temple (1 Chron. 9:14; Neh. 11:15). *2.* Man who helped repair the bakers' ovens and apparently two parts of the wall, Nehemiah 3:23 describing the "other piece" or a "second section" (REB). He may be the one who signed Nehemiah's covenant to obey God (Neh. 10:23).

HASSOPHERETH (Hăs sō' phè rĕth) Personal name meaning, "the scribe" or "scribal office." Ezra 2:55 indicates it was either a family name of persons returning from Babylonian Exile with Zerubbabel about 537 B.C. or a guild of scribes who returned. The parallel passage (Neh. 7:57) omits *h,* the Hebrew article, from the name, possibly indicating a guild is indicated.

HASUPHA (Hà sū' phà) Personal name meaning, "quick." A clan returning with Zerubbabel from Babylonian Exile about 537 B.C. (Ezra 2:43).

HAT An article of clothing for the head (Dan. 3:21). The root word is similar to the Akkadian term for a helmet or cap. The NAS rendered the term cap; NIV, turban. See *Cloth, Clothing.*

HATACH (Hā' tăch) Personal name perhaps of Persian origin meaning, "runner." A eunuch serving King Ahasuerus in the Persian court whom the king assigned as Esther's servant (Esther 4:5–6). Esther assigned him to find why Mordecai was troubled, thus initiating Esther's appearances before the king to save her people.

HATE, HATRED A strong negative reaction, a feeling toward someone considered an enemy as well as loving someone less than another.
Hatred of Other People Hatred of other people is a common response in human relations. Conflict, jealousy, and envy often result in animosity, separation, revenge, and even murder (Gen. 26:27; 27:41; Judg. 11:7; 2 Sam. 13:15,22). Some Hebrew laws explicitly deal with hatred or favoritism (Deut. 19:11–13; 21:15–17; 22:13–21).

Hatred of other people is frequently condemned, and love toward enemies is encouraged (Lev. 19:17; Matt. 5:43–44). Hatred characterizes the old age and the sinful life (Gal. 5:19–21; Titus 3:3; 1 John 2:9,11). Although Jesus cited the attitude of hating enemies (Matt. 5:43), the Old Testament does not give an explicit command like this. The Dead Sea Scrolls, however, indicate that the Essenes at Qumran cultivated hatred for enemies, but they discouraged retaliation. Jesus stressed loving our enemies and doing good to those who hate us (Luke 6:27).

Believers can experience or practice hatred in certain contexts. For example, they are to hate whatever opposes God. Not a malicious attitude, this hate reflects agreement with God's opposition to evil (Pss. 97:10; 139:19–22; Prov. 8:13; 13:5; Amos 5:15). Although some of the psalms may sound vindictive, they leave punishment of the wicked to God's prerogative.

Jesus' disciples would have to hate their families to follow him (Luke 14:26). Hate here refers not to emotional hostility but to the conscious establishment of priorities. Hate means to love family less than one loves Jesus (Matt. 10:37). Similarly, one should hate personal life to gain eternal life (John 12:26).

Disciples can expect to be hated, just as Jesus was hated by the world (John 15:18–24; 17:14; 1 John 3:13). Hatred and persecution will also occur near the end of time (Matt. 24:9). Jesus encouraged His disciples to rejoice at this opposition (Luke 6:22–23).

Hatred of God People sometimes hate God (Ps. 68:1; 81:15) and His people. They are enemies of God who stubbornly rebel at His will and will be punished.

Divine Hatred Although God is love (1 John 4:8), some texts point to divine hatred. A holy, jealous God is displeased with human sin. For example, God hates pagan idolatry (Deut. 12:31) as well as hypocritical Hebrew worship (Isa. 1:14; Amos 5:21). God hates sin (Prov. 6:16–19; 8:13; Mal. 2:16), but He desires the sinner's repentance (Ezek. 18:32). Some texts imply God's hate is directed primarily to sinful actions rather than to sinful persons (Heb. 1:9; Rev. 2:6).

God's hate is not the vindictive, emotional hate often felt by human beings but is a strong moral reaction against sin. Divine hate is often closer to the sense of loving less. God hates Esau (Mal. 1:2–5; Rom. 9:13) stresses divine freedom in election, not an emotional reaction.

See *Enemy; Love; Retaliation; Revenge; Wrath.*
Warren McWilliams

HATHACH (Hā' thăch) Modern translations' spelling of Hatach. See *Hatach.*

HATHATH (Hā' thăth) Personal name meaning, "weakling." Son of Othniel in the family line of Caleb and the tribe of Judah (1 Chron. 4:13).

HATIPHA (Hà tī' phà) Aramaic personal name meaning, "robbed." Clan who returned from Babylonian Exile with Zerubbabel about 537 B.C. (Ezra 2:54).

HATITA (Hà tī' tà) Aramaic personal name meaning, "bored a hole" or "soft" or "festival." Clan of Temple gatekeepers who returned from Babylonian Exile with Zebrubbabel about 537 B.C. (Ezra 2:42).

HATTIL (Hăt' tĭl) Personal name meaning, "talkative, babbling" or "long-eared." Clan of Temple servants who returned from Babylonian Exile with Zerubbabel about 537 B.C. (Exra 2:57).

HATTUSH (Hăt' tŭsh) Personal name of uncertain meaning. *1.* Man in David's royal line after the return from Exile (1 Chron. 3:22). He returned from Babylonian Exile with Ezra about 458 B.C. (Ezra 8:2). His high place in the list may indicate that Ezra and his followers still placed hope in a Davidic monarch. *2.* A priest who signed Nehemiah's covenant to obey God (Neh. 10:4). It is not impossible that this was the same as *1.* above. *3.* Priest who returned from Babylonian Exile with Zerubbabel about 537 B.C. (Neh. 12:2). *4.* Man who helped Nehemiah repair the Jerusalem walls (Neh. 3:10).

HAURAN (Haūr' ăn) Geographical name of uncertain meaning. One of four or five provinces through which the Assyrians and their successors administered Syria. Its northern boundary was Damascus; eastern, the Jebel Druze; western, the Golan Heights; and Southern, the Yarmuk River. It was a battle ground among Assyria, Syria, Israel, Judah, and Egypt, appearing in Egyptian and Assyrian records. Ezekiel promised it would be in the restored Promised Land (Ezek. 47:16,18). The Maccabeans did control it for a time. The region was noted for its black basalt rocks, volcanoes, and rich harvests of grain.

HAVEN A place which offers safe anchorage for ships (Gen. 49:13; Ps. 107:30; Isa. 23:10 NRSV, NIV). See *Fair Havens.*

HAVILAH (Hăv' ĭ lah) Place name meaning, "sandy stretch." Biblical name for the sand-dominated region to the south covering what we call Arabia without necessarily designating a particular geographical or political area. The river from Eden is described as flowing "around the whole land of Havilah" (Gen. 2:11 NAS), a land noted for gold and other precious stones. The Table of Nations lists Havilah as a son of Cush or Ethiopia, showing Havilah's political ties (Gen. 10:7). Some Bible students think the name is preserved in modern Haulan in southwest Arabia. Havilah is also mentioned in the Table of Nations as a son of Joktan, the grandson of Shem (Gen. 10:29). The descendants of Ishmael, Abraham's son, lived in Havilah (Gen. 25:18). Saul defeated the Amalekites from "Havilah as you go to Shur, which is east of Egypt" (1 Sam. 15:7 NAS), a description whose meaning Bible students continue to debate. Some seek to change the Hebrew text slightly. Others look for a Havilah further north and west than Havilah is usually located. Others talk of the fluid boundaries of the area. Thus Havilah refers to an area or areas in Arabia, but the precise location is not known.

HAVOTH-JAIR (Hā' vŏth-Jā' ĭr) Place name meaning, "tents of Jair." Villages in Gilead east of the Jordan which Jair, son of Manasseh, captured (Num. 32:41). Deuteronomy 3:14 says Jair took the region of Argob and named Bashan after himself—Havoth-Jair. This passage equates land of Rephaim, Argod, Bashan, and Havoth-Jair. Compare Joshua 13:30; 1 Kings 4:13. Judges 10:3−4 concern Jair the Gileadite, a judge in Israel for 22 years. He "had thirty sons that rode on thirty ass colts, and they had thirty cities, which are called Havoth-Jair unto this day, which are in the land of Gilead." First Chronicles 2:18−23 describes the genealogy of Caleb and his father Hezron. In late life Hezron married the daughter of Machir, the father of Gilead. She bore Segub, the father of Jair, who had 23 towns in Gilead. "But Geshur and Aram took from them Havvoth-Jair, Kenath and its villages, sixty towns. All these were descendants of Machir, father of Gilead" (1 Chron. 2:23 NRSV). Apparently a group of villages east of the Jordan, perhaps varying in number at different times, were called Havoth-Jair. Israel laid claim to them and connected the name to that of different Israelite heroes at various time periods.

HAVVOTH-JAIR (Hăv' vŏth-Jā' ĭr) Modern translations' spelling of Havoth-Jair, following Hebrew text more literally. See *Havoth-Jair.*

HAWK See *Birds.*

HAZAEL (Hăz' ā ĕl) Personal name meaning, "El (a god) is seeing." A powerful and ruthless king of the Syrian city-state of Damascus during the last half of the eighth century B.C. While an officer of Ben-hadad, king of Syria, Hazael was sent to Elisha the prophet to inquire about the king's health (2 Kings 8:7−15). Elisha prophesied Hazael's future kingship and his cruel treatment of Israel. Hazael returned to his master, murdered him, and became king of Syria in 841 B.C. These events had also been forecast by the prophet Elijah (1 Kings 19:15−17). Soon after becoming king of Syria, Hazael joined in combat against both Ahaziah, king of Judah, and Joram, king of Israel (2 Kings 8:28−29; 9:14−15). He eventually extended his rule into both the Northern Kingdom of Israel (2 Kings 10:32−33; 13:1−9, 22) and the Southern Kingdom of Judah (2 Kings 12:17−18; 2 Chron. 24:23−24). He was prevented from capturing the holy city of Jerusalem only by being allowed to carry off everything that was portable and of value in the city and the Temple. The memory of Syria's ruthless power under Hazael was etched in Israel's memory. Half a century later, Amos used his name as a symbol of Syria's oppression that would be judged by God (Amos 1:4).

See *Damascus; Syria.*   *Daniel B. McGee*

H

HAZAIAH (Hȧ zā́i' ah) Personal name meaning, "Yahweh sees." Member of tribe of Judah and ancestor of Jerusalem descendants in Nehemiah's day (Neh. 11:5).

HAZAR A Hebrew term meaning a court or enclosed space. *Hazar* is a common element in place names: Hazar-enan (Ezek. 47:17); Hazar-gaddah (Josh. 15:27); Hazar-shual (Josh. 15:28); Hazar-susah (Josh. 19:5). The place names perhaps recall the pitching of tents or building of homes in a circle for protection, resulting in an enclosed space. Alternately, settlements bearing the name *Hazar* were enclosed with walls or other defenses (compare Num. 13:28; Deut. 1:28). See *Cities and Urban Life.*

HAZAR-ADDAR (Hā' zär-ăd' där) Place name meaning, "threshing floor." Station on Israel's wilderness journey (Num. 34:4) near Kadesh, possibly ain Qedesh. See *Addar; Kadesh.*

HAZAR-ENAN (Hā' zär-ē' nan) Place name meaning, "encampment of springs." Site marking northeastern border of Promised Land (Num. 34:9–10; Ezek. 47:17). Its exact location is not known, but some locate it at Qaryatein about 70 miles east north east of Damascus.

HAZAR-ENON (Hā' zär-ē' nōn) Variant Hebrew spelling of Hazar-enan in Ezekiel 47:17 and reflected in NRSV. TEV calls the place Enon City. See *Hazar-enan.*

HAZAR-GADDAH (Hā' zär-găd' dah) Place name meaning, "village of good luck." Town in tribal territory of Judah of unknown location near Beersheba (Josh. 15:27).

HAZAR-HATTICON (Hā' zär-hăt' tĭ cŏn) Place name meaning, "middle village." Ezekiel named it as the border of the future Israel (47:16). Some Bible students think the original text read Hazor-enan as in 47:17; 48:1 (REB). The location is not known.

HAZAR-MAVETH (Hā' zär-mā' věth) Place name meaning, "encampment of death." Name in the Table of Nations for son of Joktan in the line of Eber and Shem (Gen. 10:26). It is the region of Hadramaut east of Yemen.

HAZAR-SHUAL (Hā' zär-shū' ȧl) Place name meaning, "encampment of the foxes." Town near Beersheba in tribal territory of Judah (Josh. 15:28) but allotted to tribe of Simeon (Josh. 19:3; 1 Chron. 4:28). Jews returning from Exile in Babylon lived there (Neh. 11:27). It may be modern khirbet el-Watan.

HAZAR-SUSAH (Hā' zär-sū' sah) Place name meaning, "encampment of a horse." Town in tribal allotment of Simeon (Josh. 19:5). As most towns of Simeon also appear in Judah's allotment (compare 19:1), many Bible students think this is another name for Sansannah in Joshua 15:31. Instead of the feminine form Susah, 1 Chronicles 4:31 has the plural form Susim. It may be located at Sabalat Abu Susein.

HAZAR-SUSIM (Hā' zär-sū' sĭm) See *Hazar-susah.*

HAZAZON-TAMAR (Hăz' ȧ zŏn-tā' mȧr) Place name meaning, "grave dump with palms." Home of Amorites who fought eastern coalition led by Chedorlaomer (Gen. 14:7). Edom (NIV; TEV; NRSV; REB following one Hebrew manuscript; most manuscripts and early translations read, "Aram," meaning Syria, as read by NAS; KSV). captured the city and then attacked Jehoshaphat of Judah (873–848 B.C.), the text noting that Hazazon-tamar was another name for Engedi (2 Chron. 20:2). See *Engedi.* Some Bible students think Hazazon-tamar was actually located six miles north of Engedi at wadi Hasasa, while others point to Tamar in southern Judah, Kasr Ejuniyeh or ain Kusb, twenty miles southwest of the Dead Sea.

HAZEL KJV translation of a term meaning almond rather than hazelnut (Gen. 30:37).

HAZELELPONI (Hăz' ě lěl pō' nī) Personal name meaning, "Overshadow my face." Daughter of Etam in the tribe of Judah (1 Chron. 4:3 NAS; NIV, TEV, REB, NRSV). KJV follows Hebrew text, which reads "these the father of Etam." Many Bible students think a copyist omitted something in Hebrew. They would restore the text to read, "these were the sons of Hareph: the father of Etam, ..." Since many of the other names in the list are names of towns (for example, Penuel, Bethlehem), Hazeleponi may also represent a town name. If so, its location is not known.

HAZER-HATTICON (Hā' zẽr-Hăt' tĭ cŏn) NAS, NIV, NRSV spelling of Hazar-hatticon.

HAZERIM (Hȧ zē' rĭm) KJV interpretation and transliteration of Hebrew word meaning, "villages" or "hamlets" in Deuteronomy 2:23. Modern translations interpret as common noun meaning villages near Gaza. See *Gaza.*

HAZEROTH (Hȧ zē' rŏth) Place name meaning, "villages" or "encampments." Wilderness station on Israel's journey from Egypt (Num. 11:35). There Aaron and Miriam challenged Moses' sole authority, using his Cushite wife as an excuse (Num. 12). God punished Miriam with a hated skin disease. Deuteronomy 1:1 uses Hazeroth as one focal point to locate Moses' speech to Israel. Some geographers would locate it at moder ain Khadra, south of Ezion-geber. Some Bible students try to locate all the sites in Deuteronomy 1:1 near Moab. If they are right, the the Hazeroth mentioned there is different from the wilderness station.

HAZEZON-TAMAR (Hăz′ ė zŏn-tā′ mȧr) KJV spelling of Hazazon-tamar.

HAZIEL (Hā′ zĭ ĕl) Personal name meaning, "God saw." A leading Levite in the time of David (1 Chron. 23:9).

HAZO (Hā′ zō) Abbreviated form of personal name Haziel meaning, "God saw." Son of Abraham's brother Nahor (Gen. 22:22). The twelve sons of Nahor apparently represented a closely-associated group of tribes. Some Bible students think Hazo represents the city of Hazu known from an Assyrian source and located at al-Hasa near the Arabian coast by Bahrein.

HAZOR (Hā′ zôr) Place name meaning, "enclosed settlement." *1.* Hazor was located in upper Galilee on the site now known as tell el-Qedah, ten miles north of the Sea of Galilee and five miles southwest of Lake Huleh.

The site of Hazor is composed of a 30-acre upper tell or mound rising 40 meters above the surrounding plain and a 175-acre lower enclosure which was well fortified. These dimensions make Hazor the largest city in ancient Canaan. Estimates set the population at its height at over 40,000.

The upper tell had twenty-one separate levels of occupation beginning between 2750 and 2500 B.C. and continuing down to the second century B.C. Canaanites occupied Hazor until Joshua destroyed it. The Israelites controlled it until 732 B.C. when the Assyrians captured the city. Hazor then served as a fortress for the various occupying powers until the time of the Maccabees.

The lower enclosure had five levels of occupation beginning about 1750 B.C. and continuing

Israelite storehouses dating from the ninth century B.C. at ancient Hazor in Israel.

until Joshua destroyed it. It was never rebuilt.

Hazor's location was strategic both economically and militarily. It overlooked the Via Maris, the major overland trade route from Egypt to the north and east, and thus became a major trading center. It is mentioned extensively in both Egyptian and Mesopotamian records in conjunction with the other major trading cities of the day. Hazor also overlooked the Huleh Valley, a critical defense point against armies invading from the north.

Joshua 11:1–15; 12:19 relate how Jabin, king of Hazor, rallied the forces of the northern cities of Canaan against Joshua. Hazor was "the head of all those kingdoms" (Josh. 11:10), that is, it was the dominant city-state of the Canaanite kingdoms. Joshua defeated the Canaanite forces, slew the leaders, including Jabin, and burned the city of Hazor. Modern archaeology lends support to this biblical account. The size and location of the city of Hazor, as well as references to it in other ancient literature, would indicate that Hazor probably controlled a vast portion of Canaan. Yadin's excavation of Hazor indicated that the city was destroyed by fire in the second third of the thirteenth century B.C.

The next mention of Hazor in the Old Testament is troublesome. In Judges 4 we again find a Jabin as king of Canaan ruling from Hazor. His troops led by Sisera of Harosheth-hagoyim were routed by Deborah and Barak. Some Bible students see a discrepancy between this story and the story in Joshua, saying Jabin was killed generations earlier and Hazor destroyed and taken into Israelite control. The traditional solution to this discrepancy stresses that Jabin is referred to in the past tense—"who reigned in Hazor." Jabin was not alive at the time of the battle with Deborah, but Sisera had previously been commander of Jabin's forces. Hazor need not exist at this time as Sisera lived at Harosheth-hagoiim (location unknown.) A different solution on the basis of archaeological excavations claims the story concerning Jabin in Joshua is accurate. The city was destroyed by Joshua and was not rebuilt as a city until the time of Solomon. The most ancient account of the defeat of Sisera by Deborah and Barak appears in the poetic account of Judges 5, which mentions neither Jabin nor Hazor (compare 1 Sam. 12:9). This approach sees Judges 4 as a later account influenced by the story in Joshua. The straight biblical narrative seems to assume Joshua destroyed but did not occupy it, though it was allotted to Naphtali: (Josh. 19:36). The Canaanite dynasty of Jabin maintained or regained control with one or more kings named Jabin. First Kings 9:15 mentions that Solomon rebuilt the walls of Hazor, Megiddo and Gezer. Excavations have discovered conclusive evidence to support this short portion of Scripture. Two layers of Israelite occupation of Hazor between the destruction of the Canaanite city by Joshua and the rebuilding of the city

H

Overview of the excavations at Tel el-Qedah (ancient Hazor) north of the Sea of Galilee.

by Solomon show merely semi-nomadic Israelite encampments, evidenced by tent or hut foundation rings, cooking pits, and storage pits. Apparently, no formal city or fortifications existed during the time of the Judges. The city was clearly rebuilt at the time of Solomon, evidenced by the characteristically Solomonic gate structures, that is, casemate walls and a six-chamber gatehouse (three on each side) with two square towers. Comparing the gates at Hazor with those at Gezer and Megiddo, Yadin found them to be identical in both design and dimension. The Solomonic city was much smaller than the Canaanite city. It only covered half of the upper tell.

Second Kings 15:29 records that Tiglath-pileser III, king of Assyria, captured Hazor and carried its people captive to Assyria. The evidence of this destruction is very great. No less than three feet of ashes and rubble cover the ruins left by this destruction. Prior to the Assyrian invasion, Hazor had been greatly enlarged and strengthened by King Ahab of Israel in anticipation of the attack. The city had grown to fill the entire upper tell. Its fortifications had been strengthened and enlarged, and a special water shaft and tunnel 40 meters deep was dug down to the water table to bring the water supply inside the city.

2. Town in tribal inheritance of Judah (Josh. 15:23), probably to be read with earliest Greek translation as Hazor-Ithnan. This may be modern el-Jebariyeh.

3. Town in southern part of tribal inheritance of Judah, probably to be read as Hazor-Hadattah (Josh. 15:25) with most modern translations. This may be modern el-Hudeira near the Dead Sea's southern end.

4. Town identified with Hezron (Josh. 15:25). See *Hezron.*

5. Town where part of tribe of Benjamin lived in time of Nehemiah (Neh. 11:33). This may be modern khirbet Hazzur four miles north northwest of Jerusalem.

6. Name of "kingdoms" that Nebuchadnezzar of Babylon threatened (Jer. 49:28–33). Apparently, small nomadic settlements of Arab tribes are meant. Such settlements would still have rich treasures the Babylonian king coveted.

John Brangenberg

HAZOR-HADDATTAH (Hā′ zôr-há dăt′ tah) Place name meaning, "new Hazor." Town in tribal territory of Judah (Josh. 15:25). Its location is not known.

HAZZEBAIM (Hăz zĕ bā′ ĭm) See *Pochereth-hazzebaim.*

HAZZELELPONI (Hăz zĕ lĕl pō′ nī) Modern translations' spelling of Hazelelponi.

HAZZOBEBAH (Hă zō bĕ′ băh) The NIV rendering of the name of the son of Coz (or Kos) and grandson of Helah (1 Chron. 4:8). Other English translations use the feminine name Zobebah.

HE The fifth letter of the Hebrew alphabet; it carries the numerical value five. In Judaism *he* is used as an abbreviation for the divine name Yahweh (tetragrammaton). In some English versions *he* appears as a superscript to verses 33–40 of Psalm 119 each of which begin with this letter. See *Hebrew Language; Writing.*

HE ASS A male donkey. See *Animals.*

HEAD Literally, the uppermost part of the body considered to be the seat of life, but not the intellect and figuratively for first, top, or chief. The Jewish notion was that the heart was the center or seat of the intellect. "Head" meant the physical head of a person (Gen. 48:18; Mark 6:24) or of animals, such as a bull's head (Lev. 1:4). It was often used to represent the whole person (Acts 18:6). Achish made David "keeper of mine head," that is his bodyguard (1 Sam. 28:2).

"Head" was used frequently to refer to inanimate objects such as the summit of a mountain (Ex. 17:9), or the top of a building (Gen. 11:4). The word "head" often has the meaning of "source" or "beginning," that of rivers (Gen. 2:10), streets (Ezek. 16:25), or of periods of time (Judg. 7:19, translated here as "beginning").

In Psalms 118:22, "head of the corner" (cornerstone) refers metaphorically to a king delivered by God when others had given him up (compare Matt. 21:42; Acts 4:11; 1 Pet. 2:7, where it is used in reference to the rejection of Christ). "Head" designated one in authority in the sense of the foremost person. It can mean leader, chief, or prince (Isa. 9:15), and it can have the idea of first in a series (1 Chron. 12:9). Israel was the "head" (translated "chief") nation, God's firstborn (Jer. 31:7). Damascus was the "head" (capital) of Syria (Isa. 7:8). A husband is the "head of the wife" (Eph. 5:23).

A distinctive theological use of the word "head" was seen in the New Testament concept of the "headship" of Christ. Christ is the "head" (*kephalē*) of His body the church; the church is His "bride" (Eph. 5:23–33). In His role as "head," Christ enables the church to grow, knits her into a unity, nourishes her by caring for each member, and gives her strength to build herself up in love (Eph. 4:15–16). Not only is Christ "head" of the church, but also He is "head" of the universe as a whole (Eph. 1:22) and of every might and power (Col. 2:10). The divine influences on the world result in a series: God is the "head" of Christ; Christ is the "head" of man; man is the "head" of the woman, and as such he is to love and care for his wife as Christ does His bride (1 Cor. 11:3). This theological use of the word may be an extension of the Old Testament use of the word "head" for the leader of the tribe or community or may be a reaction to early Gnostic tendencies. See *Gnosticism.*

Because the head was the seat of life, value was placed on it. Injury to it was a chief form of defeating an enemy (Ps. 68:21). As part of contemptuous insult, the soldiers struck Jesus' head with a reed and crowned Him with a crown of thorns (Mark 15:16–19). Decapitation was a further insult after the defeat. Herodias, through treachery and out of spite, had John the Baptist beheaded (Matt. 14:1–11). David cut off Goliath's head and brought it before Saul (1 Sam. 17:51). The Philistines cut off Saul's head (1 Sam. 31:9), and the sons of Rimmon cut off that of Ishbosheth (2 Sam. 4:7). Attested to in many inscriptions and portrayed on several monuments, it was common for the Babylonians, Assyrians, and the Egyptians to cut off the heads of their dead enemies slain in battle.

Conversely, blessing comes upon the head (Gen. 49:26); and, therefore, hands are laid on it (Gen. 48:17). Anointing the head with oil symbolized prosperity and joy (Ps. 23:5; Heb. 1:9). In the service for ordination of priests and dedication to priestly service, the head of the high priest was anointed with oil (Ex. 29:7; Lev. 16:32). Human sins were transferred to the animal of the sin offering by laying on of hands upon the head of the animal (Ex. 29:10,15,19).

The head is involved in several colloquial expressions. The Jew swore by his head (Matt. 5:36). Sadness or grief was shown by putting the

Unidentified sculpture of a head from the Roman period in Israel.

H

hand on the head or putting ashes on it (2 Sam. 13:19). In other instances, grief was shown by shaving the head (Job 1:20). To "heap coals of fire upon his head" was to make one's enemy feel ashamed by returning his evil with good (Prov. 15:21–22; Rom. 12:20). Wagging the head expressed derision (Mark 15:29), but bowing the head was a sign of humility (Isa. 58:5). Finally, "The hoary head is a crown of glory, if it be found in the way of righteousness" (Prov. 16:31).

Darlene R. Gautsch

HEAD OF THE CHURCH A title for Christ (Eph. 4:15; Col. 1:18). In Ephesians, the metaphor of Christ as head of His body, the church, is carefully developed. Headship includes the idea of Christ's authority (1:22; 5:23) and of the submission required of the church (5:24). More is in view than a statement of Christ's authority. The focus is on the character of Christ's relationship with the church. Unlike self-seeking human lords (Luke 22:25), Christ exercises His authority for the church (Eph. 1:22 NRSV, NIV), nourishing and caring for the church as one cares for one's own body (5:29). Christ's headship also points to the interrelationship of Christ and the church. The mystery of husband and wife becoming "one flesh" is applied to Christ and the church (5:31), which is "the fullness of him that filleth all in all" (1:23). In Colossians 1:18, the idea of Christ as head is again complex, including not only the idea of head as authority but of head as source (1:15–20). The church is called to follow its head and to rest secure in its relationsip with Him.

HEADBAND, HEADDRESS Headband refers to a head ornament, headdress to an ornamental head covering. Modern translations use headband to render an item of finery in Isaiah 3:18. KJV rendered the same term as caul, a loose-fitting, netted cap. KJV used headband to translate a different Hebrew term at Isaiah 3:20. Modern translations render this term sash. The same term is rendered attire (NAS, NRSV), wedding ribbons (REB), or wedding ornaments (NIV) at Jeremiah 2:32.

Modern translations use headdress for a third Hebrew term (Isa. 3:20; KJV, bonnet). Such a headdress was wound around the head like a turban (Ezek. 24:17). The same Hebrew term is used for the bridegroom's "garland" (Isa. 61:10) and for the linen turbans of the priests (Ezek. 44:18). See *Cloth, Clothing.*

HEADSTONE KJV term for a top stone (NAS) or capstone (NIV) at Zechariah 4:7. Zerubbabel's vision of a capstone quarried from the mountaintop was interpreted as an assurance that he would see the Temple completed (4:8–9). New Testament writers spoke of Christ as a stone rejected by the builders which has become the head of the corner (Acts 4:11; 1 Pet. 2:7). Here, head of the corner refers either to a capstone (coping), a keystone of an arch, or to a cornerstone. See *Cornerstone.*

HEALING, DIVINE God's work through instruments and ways He chooses to bring health to persons sick physically, emotionally, and spiritually. The Bible not only tells of people's spiritual status but is also concerned about their physical condition. This concern appears in the emphasis on healing, particularly in the ministry of Jesus and in the early church. Nearly one-fifth of the Gospels report Jesus' miracles and the discussions they occasioned. The gospels record fourteen distinct instances of physical and mental healing.

Jesus commissioned His disciples to continue His basic ministry, including healing (Matt. 10:5–10; Mark 6:7–13; Luke 9:1–6). In the Book of Acts the healing ministry continued.

Psychosomatic is a word which literally means "soul and body," referring to the close relationship of body and spirit. The soul affects the body, and the health of the soul may be an indication of the health of the body. In the Bible John wished for his friend Gaius, "above all things that thou mayest prosper and be in health, even as thy soul prospereth" (3 John 2).

Most Christians believe in healing through faith; but trying to decide what techniques are scriptural, decorous, and psychologically helpful

Headdresses and head coverings are still worn by the men and women of the Middle East.

confuses the believer. Jesus used different methods in His healing ministry. They included calling upon the faith of the person or bystanders to be healed, touching the sick person, praying, assuring forgiveness of sin, uttering commands, and using physical media. On several occasions the faith of the individual was an important factor in the healing. Speaking to the woman who was hemorrhaging Jesus said, "thy faith hath made thee whole" (Mark 5:34; compare Matt. 9:29).

The faith of other people became a factor. Jesus stated to the father of the sick boy that healing was possible if people had faith, and the man responded, "Lord, I believe; help thou mine unbelief" (Mark 9:23–24). When the centurion sought Jesus to ask for healing his servant, the Savior responded, "I have not found so great faith, no, not in Israel. . . . And his servant was healed in the selfsame hour" (Matt. 8:10,13; compare Mark 2:5).

Christians are often confused about the ministry of healing, but these biblical teachings clearly appear:

1) The Bible clearly states that Jesus believed in healing of the body.

2) Jesus spoke of doctors in a positive way as He compared those in good health who have no need of a physician with those who do, (Matt. 9:12; Mark 2:17; Luke 5:31). God has often healed by the way He has led dedicated scientists into the discovery of body function.

3) The methods of healing Jesus used included prayer, laying on of hands, anointing with oil, and assurance of forgiveness of sins. The church continued to use these methods (Jas. 5:14–16).

4) Jesus did not use healing as a means of gaining attention but tried to keep the experience private. "Bless the Lord . . . who healeth all thy diseases" (Ps. 103:2–3).   *John W. Drakeford*

HEALING, GIFT OF See *Spiritual Gifts; Divine Healing.*

HEALTH The condition of being sound in body, mind, or spirit; used especially for physical health. Neither Hebrew or Greek has a direct equivalent for our concept of health. Since a variety of terms are employed, English translations vary considerably in their use of the term health. The KJV has the most numerous references to health (17 times). Modern translations frequently replace health with other terms. The substitutions of the NRSV are typical. The most common substitution is healing for health (Prov. 3:8; 4:22; 12:18; 13:17; Isa. 58:8). Elsewhere the NRSV substituted well as a broader statement of well-being (Gen. 43:28; 2 Sam. 20:9) or help (Pss. 42:11; 43:5) and saving power (Ps. 67:2) as more specific instances of God's assistance. The NRSV substituted recovery for health at Jeremiah 33:6, though rendering the underlying Hebrew as

health elsewhere (Jer. 8:22; 30:17) as in KJV. At Acts 27:34 the NRSV has "help you survive" in place of "for your health".

The health wish of 3 John 2 is typical of Hellenistic letters (Compare 2 Macc. 1:10; 3 Macc. 3:12; 7:1). The basic Greek concept of health is what is balanced. Thus the Greeks frequently used the adjective "healthy" (*hygiēs*) to mean rational or intelligible. The adjective is frequently translated sound in the New Testament (1 Tim. 1:10; 6:3; 2 Tim. 1:13; 4:3; Titus 1:9; 2:1,8).

See *Diseases; Healing, Divine.*

HEART The center of the physical, mental, and spiritual life of humans.

First, the word heart refers to the physical organ and is considered to be the center of the physical life. Eating and drinking are spoken of as strengthening the heart (Gen. 18:5; Judg. 19:5; Acts 14:17). As the center of physical life, the heart came to stand for the person as a whole.

The heart became the focus for all the vital functions of the body; including both intellectual and spiritual life. The heart and the intellect are closely connected, the heart being the seat of intelligence: "For this people's heart is waxed gross . . . lest at any time they should . . . understand with their heart, and should be converted" (Matt. 13:15). The heart is connected with thinking: As a person "thinketh in his heart, so is he" (Prov. 23:7). To ponder something in one's heart means to consider it carefully (Luke 1:66; 2:19). "To set one's heart on" is the literal Hebrew that means to give attention to something, to worry about it (1 Sam. 9:20). To call to heart (mind) something means to remember something (Isa. 46:8). All of these are functions of the mind, but are connected with the heart in biblical language.

Closely related to the mind are acts of the will, acts resulting from a conscious or even a deliberate decision. Thus, 2 Corinthians 9:7: "Every man according as he purposeth in his heart, so let him give." Ananias contrived his deed of lying to the Holy Spirit in his heart (Acts 5:4). The conscious decision is made in the heart (Rom. 6:17). Connected to the will are human wishes and desires. Romans 1:24 describes how God gave them up "through the lusts of their own hearts, to dishonor their own bodies."

Not only is the heart associated with the activities of the mind and the will, but it is also closely connected to the feelings and affections of a person. Emotions such as joy originate in the heart (Ps. 4:7; Isa 65:14). Other emotions are ascribed to the heart, especially in the Old Testament. Nabal's fear is described by the phrase: "his heart died within him" (1 Sam. 25:37; compare Ps. 143:4). Discouragement or despair is described by the phrase "heaviness in the heart" which makes it stoop (Prov. 12:25). Again, Ecclesiastes 2:20 says, "Therefore I went about to cause my heart to despair of all the labor which I took under the sun." Another emotion connected with the heart is sorrow. John 16:6 says, "because I have said these things unto you, sorrow hath filled your heart." Proverbs 25:20, describes sorrow as having "an heavy heart." The heart is also the seat of the affection of love and its opposite, hate. In the Old Testament, for example, Israel is commanded: "You shall not hate your brother in your heart, but you shall reason with your neighbor, lest you bear sin because of him" (Lev. 19:17 RSV). A similar attitude, bitter jealousy, is described in James 3:14 as coming from the heart. On the other hand, love is based in the heart. The believer is commanded to love God "with all your heart" (Mark 12:30; compare Deut. 6:5). Paul taught that the purpose of God's command is love which comes from a "pure heart" (1 Tim. 1:5).

Finally, the heart is spoken of in Scripture as the center of the moral and spiritual life. The conscience, for instance, is associated with the heart. In fact, the Hebrew language had no word for conscience, so the word heart was often used to express this concept: "my heart shall not reproach me so long as I live" (Job 27:6). The Revised Standard Version translates the word for "heart" as "conscience" in 1 Samuel 25:31 (RSV). In the New Testament the heart is spoken of also as that which condemns us (1 John 3:19–21). All moral conditions from the highest to the lowest are said to center in the heart. Sometimes the heart is used to represent a person's true nature or character. Samson told Delilah "all his heart" (Judg. 16:17). This true nature is contrasted with the outward appearance: "man looks on the outward appearance, but the Lord looks on the heart" (1 Sam. 16:7 RSV).

On the negative side, depravity is said to issue from the heart: "The heart is deceitful above all things, and desperately wicked: who can know it?" (Jer. 17:9). Jesus said that out of the heart comes evil thoughts, murder, adultery, fornication, theft, false witness, slander (Matt. 15:19). In other words, defilement comes from within rather than from without.

Because the heart is at the root of the problem, this is the place where God does His work in the individual. For instance, the work of the law is "written in their hearts," and conscience is the proof of this (Rom. 2:15). The heart is the field where seed (the Word of God) is sown (Matt. 13:19; Luke 8:15). In addition to being the place where the natural laws of God are written, the heart is the place of renewal. Before Saul became king, God gave him a new heart (1 Sam. 10:9). God promised Israel that He would give them a new spirit within, take away their "stony heart" and give them a "heart of flesh" (Ezek. 11:19). Paul said that a person must believe in the heart to be saved, "for with the heart man believeth unto righteousness" (Rom. 10:10). (See also Mark

11:23; Heb. 3:12.)

Finally, the heart is the dwelling place of God. Two persons of the Trinity are said to reside in the heart of the believer. God has given us the "earnest of the Spirit in our hearts" (2 Cor. 1:22). Ephesians 3:17 expresses the desire that "Christ may dwell in your hearts by faith." The love of God "is shed abroad in our hearts by the Holy Ghost which is given unto us" (Rom. 5:5).

Gerald Cowen

HEARTH A depression in a floor, sometimes bricked to retain heat (Jer. 36:23), used for cooking food (Isa. 30:14). KJV used hearth to translate four Hebrew terms. Modern translations retain hearth at Isaiah 30:14. Elsewhere modern translations substituted other terms: furnace (NRSV), oven (REB), or glowing embers (NIV) at Psalm 102:3; brazier (REB, NAS, NRSV) or firepot (NIV) at Jeremiah 36:22,23; blazing pot (NRSV), brazier (REB), or firepot (NAS, NIV) at Zechariah 12:6. The altar hearth of Ezekiel 43:15–16 refers to the upper part of the altar upon which the sacrifice was burnt (compare Lev. 6:9). See *Cooking and Heating.*

HEATH A shrubby, evergreen plant of the heather family, used by the KJV (Jer. 17:6; 48:6). Various translations have been offered: juniper (NAS); bush (NIV); shrub (NRSV, 17:6). At Jeremiah 40:8, the RSV and TEV follow Aquila's Greek translation in substituting wild ass for the plant name. The REB takes the Hebrew figuratively for one destitute. Arabic evidence points to the juniper (*Juniperus oxycedrus* and *Juniperus phoenicea*). See *Plants in the Bible.*

HEATHEN See *Gentiles.*

HEAVE OFFERING In Exodus 29:27–28, the portion of an offering or sacrifice that was set apart and reserved for Yahweh and for the priests. The priests were to eat their portions of the offerings of the people in a clear place. See *Sacrifice and Offerings.*

HEAVEN The part of God's creation above the earth and the waters including "air" and "space" and serving as home for God and His heavenly creatures. The Hebrew word *shamayim* is plural in form and was easily related by the common people to the word *mayim,* "waters." Biblical writers joined their contemporaries in describing the universe as it appeared to the human eye: heavens above, earth beneath, and waters around and beneath the earth. Heaven could be described as a partition God made to separate the rain-producing heavenly waters from the rivers, seas, and oceans below (Gen. 1:6–8). The heavenly lights—sun, moon, and stars—were installed into this partition (Gen. 1:14–18). This partition has windows

H

or sluice gates with which God sends rain to irrigate or water the earth (Gen. 7:11). This heavenly partition God "stretched out" (Isa. 42:5; 44:24; Ps. 136:6; compare Ezek. 1:22–26; 10:1). The clouds serve a similar rain-producing function, so that KJV often translates the Hebrew word for "clouds" as "sky" (Deut. 33:26; Ps. 57:10; Isa. 45:8; Jer. 51:9; compare Ps. 36:6; 108:4).

Only God has the wisdom to "stretch out" the heaven (Jer. 51:15). "Heaven" thus becomes the curtain of God's tent, separating His dwelling place from that of humanity on earth (Ps. 104:2; Isa. 40:22). Like a human dwelling, heaven can be described as resting on supporting pillars (Job 26:11) or on building foundations (2 Sam. 22:8; though the parallel in Ps. 18:7 applies the foundations to mountains). Just as He built the partition, so God can "rend" it or tear it apart (Isa. 64:1). Thus it does not seal God off from His creation and His people. English translations use "firmament" (KJV), "expanse" (NAS, NIV), "dome" (TEV, NRSV), or "vault" (REB) to translate the special Hebrew word describing what God created and named "Heaven" (Gen. 1:8).

Hebrew does not employ a term for "air" or "space" between heaven and earth. This is all part of heaven. Thus the Bible speaks of "birds of the heavens," though English translations often use "air" or "sky" (Deut. 4:17; Jer. 8:7; Lam. 4:19). Even Absalom hanging by his hair from a tree limb was "between heaven and earth" (2 Sam. 18:9; compare 1 Chron. 21:16; Ezek. 8:3). The heaven is the source for rain (Deut. 11:11; Ps. 148:4), dew (Gen. 27:28), frost (Job 38:29), snow (Isa. 55:10), fiery lightning (Gen. 19:24), dust (Deut. 28:24), and hail (Josh. 10:11). This is the language of human observation and description, but it is more. It is the language of faith describing God in action in and for His world (Jer. 14:22). Heaven is God's treasure chest, storing treasures such as the rain (Deut. 28:12), wind and lightning (Jer. 10:13), and snow and hail (Job 38:22). The miraculous manna came from God's heavenly storehouses for Israel in the wilderness (Ex. 16:11–15).

Heaven and earth thus comprehend the entire universe and all its constituents (Jer. 23:24), but God fills all these and more so that no one can hide from Him (compare 1 Kings 8:27–30; Isa. 66:1). Yet this One also lives in the humble, contrite heart (Isa. 57:15).

As God's dwelling place, heaven is not a divine haven where God can isolate Himself from earth. It is the divine workplace, where He sends blessings to His people (Deut. 26:15; Isa. 63:15) and punishment on His enemies (Ps. 2:4; 11:4–7). Heaven is a channel of communication between God and humans (Gen. 28:12; 2 Sam. 22:10; Neh. 9:13; Ps. 144:5).

As God's creation, the heavens praise Him and display His glory and His creativity (Ps. 19:1; 69:34) and righteousness (Ps. 50:6). Still, heaven remains a part of the created order. Unlike neighboring nations, Israel knew that heaven and the heavenly bodies were not gods and did not deserve worship (Ex. 20:4). It belonged to God (Deut. 10:14). Heaven stands as a symbol of power and unchanging, enduring existence (Ps. 89:29), but heaven is not eternal. The days come when heaven is no more (Job 14:12; ; Isa. 51:6). As God once spread out the heavenly tent, so He will wrap up the heavens like a scroll (Isa. 34:4). A new heaven and new earth will appear (Isa. 65:17; 66:22).

The Old Testament speaks of heaven to show the sovereignty of the Creator God and yet of the divine desire to communicate with and provide for the human creature. It holds out the tantalizing examples of men who left earth and were taken up to heaven (Gen. 5:24; 2 Kings 2:11).

New Testament In the New Testament, the primary Greek word translated "heaven" describes heaven as being above the earth, although no New Testament passage gives complete instructions regarding the location or geography of heaven. Other than Paul's reference to the three heavens (2 Cor. 12:2–4), the New Testament writers spoke of only one heaven.

The New Testament affirms that God created heaven (Acts 4:24), that heaven and earth stand under God's lordship (Matt. 11:25), and that heaven is the dwelling place of God (Matt. 6:9).

Jesus preached that the kingdom of heaven/ God had dawned through His presence and ministry (Mark 1:15). By using the image of a messianic banquet, Jesus spoke of heavenly life as a time of joy, celebration, and fellowship with God (Matt. 26:29). Jesus taught that there would be no marrying or giving in marriage in heaven (Luke 20:34–36).

Christians should rejoice because their names are written in heaven (Luke 10:20). Jesus promised a heavenly home for His followers (John 14:2–3).

According to Paul, Christ is seated in heaven at the right hand of God (Eph. 1:20). Paul believed heaven is the future home of believers (2 Cor. 5:1–2). Paul referred to the hope of heaven as the hope of glory (Col. 1:27). The Holy Spirit is the pledge of the believer's participation in heaven (2 Cor. 5:5). Peter affirmed that heaven is the place where the believer's inheritance is kept with care until the revelation of the Messiah (1 Pet. 1:4).

The word "heaven" occurs more frequently in Revelation than in any other New Testament book. The Revelation addresses heaven from the standpoints of the struggle between good and evil and of God's rule from heaven. The most popular passage dealing with heaven is Revelation 21:1 to 22:5. In this passage, heaven is portrayed in three

H

different images: (1) the tabernacle (21:1–8), (2) the city (21:9–27), and (3) the garden (22:1–5). The image of the tabernacle portrays heavenly life as perfect fellowship with God. The symbolism of the city portrays heavenly life as perfect protection. The image of the garden shows heavenly life as perfect provision.

Trent C. Butler and Gary Hardin

HEAVEN OF HEAVENS KJV designation rendered "highest heaven" by most modern translations (1 Kings 8:27; 2 Chron. 2:6; 6:18). According to an ancient understanding of the universe, above the canopy of the sky was a further canopy above which God dwelt. TEV understands "heavens of heavens" as "all (the vastness) of heaven".

HEAVENLY CITY, THE The fulfillment of the hopes of God's people for final salvation. To the ancient world cities represented ordered life, security from enemies, and material prosperity. See *Cities and Urban Life.* Hebrews says the city "has foundations;" its "architect and builder is God" (11:10 NAS); God has prepared it (11:16); and it is "the city of the living God, the heavenly Jerusalem" (12:22). This city is the home to "an innumerable company of angels" (12:22), to the assembly of the firstborn (12:23; an image of believers redeemed by the death of Christ; compare Ex. 13:13–15), and to the righteous made perfect by God (12:23; perhaps the Old Testament saints). Some interpreters take these descriptions literally. The Christian goal is, however, not something that can be touched and sensed like Israel's Sinai experience (12:18). Indeed, believers have already come (12:22) to the heavenly Jerusalem, at least in part. Some interpreters thus take the Heavenly City as an image of the redeemed people of God whose "foundation" is the apostles and prophets (Eph. 2:20). The experience of the patriarchs whose hope lay beyond their earthly lives (Heb 11:13–16) points to a final fulfillment of salvation in heaven.

The Heavenly City of Revelation 21:9—22:7 has also been interpreted both literally and figuratively. One interpretation sees the Heavenly City suspended above the earth like a space platform. Others see an earthly city. Still others a city suspended in the air that later descends to earth. Others, pointing to the equation of the city as the bride of Christ (21:2,9), take the city as a symbol of the church. Whether understood as a literal city or as representing God's redeemed people experiencing their final salvation, the city is a place of fellowship with God (21:3,22), of God-ensured safety (21:4,25), and of God-given provision (22:1–2,5). *Chris Church*

HEAVENS, NEW A technical, eschatological term referring to the final perfected state of the created universe. It often is connected with the

concept of a new earth.

The promise of a re-creation of the heavens and earth arose because of human sin and God's subsequent curse (Gen. 3:17). The biblical hope for mankind is tied to the conviction that persons cannot be completely set free from the power of sin apart from the redemption of the created order—earth as well as the heavens. The idea of a renewed universe is found in many passages of the Bible (Isa. 51:16; Matt. 19:28; 24:29–31; 26:29; Mark 13:24–27,31; Acts 3:20–21; Rom. 8:19–23; 2 Cor. 5:17; Heb. 12:26–28; 2 Pet. 3:10–13). However, the phrase "new heavens" is found in only four passages (Isa. 65:17; 66:22; 2 Pet. 3:13; Rev. 21:1).

The nature of the "new heavens and earth" is variously described in the Bible. First, God is the cause of this new creation (Isa. 65:17; 66:22; Rev. 21:22). In Hebrews 12:28 the new heaven and earth are described as a "kingdom which cannot be moved." This new heaven and earth will last forever (Isa. 66:22). In 2 Peter 3:13 the new world is described as one "in which righteousness dwells" (NAS).

In Revelation, the nature of the new heaven and earth stands in marked contrast to the old heaven and earth. The Greek word translated "new" designates something which already exists, but now appears in a new way. The new world is the old world gloriously transformed. Purity (Rev. 21:27) and freedom from the wrath of God (Rev. 22:3) are marks of the new heaven and earth. Further, the new world is marked by perfect fellowship of the saints with one another and with God. God and His people dwell together in the new age (21:1,3).

Clearly, God will bring the new order into existence at the end of history. But, scholars disagree as to when this will occur within the events associated with the end times. Two main views are held. First, the new heavens and earth are created immediately after the second coming of Christ. Even among those within this camp there is disagreement. Some believe that the creation of the new heavens and earth will occur immediately after the "great white throne" judgment. Amillennialists generally hold to this theory. Some premillennialists associate the creation of the new heavens and earth with the beginning of the thousand year millennial reign of Christ. A second viewpoint commonly held by many premillennialists is that the new heaven and new earth are created at the end of the millennial reign of Christ.

See *Angel; Creation; Eschatology; Heaven; Hell; Kingdom; New Jerusalem.*

Paul E. Robertson

HEBER (Hē′ bēr) Personal name meaning, "companion." *1.* Grandson of Asher and great grandson of Jacob (Gen. 46:17). He was the original clan ancestor of the Heberites (Num. 26:45). *2.* Kenite related to family of Moses' wife (Judg. 4:11). His wife Jael killed Sisera, the Canaanite general, breaking a political alliance between Heber's clan and Jabin, Sisera's king (Judg. 4:17). This completed the great victory of Deborah and Barak over the Canaanites. *3.* A member of the tribe of Judah in a Hebrew text (1 Chron. 4:18) which apparently lists two mothers of Heber, one an Egyptian. Commentators generally change the text or consider that some words have fallen out of the text as it was copied. Heber was the father of Socho and thus apparently recognized as founding ancestor of town of Socho. See *Socho. 4.* A member of the tribe of Benjamin (1 Chron. 8:17). *5.* A different Hebrew word lies behind Eber (1 Chron. 5:13; 8:22), which KJV spells Heber. See *Eber.* The Heber in Luke 3:35 (KJV) is the Eber of Genesis 11:15.

HEBERITE (Hĕb′ ĕr īte) See *Heber.*

HEBREW (Hē′ brew) The language in which the canonical books of the Old Testament were written, except for the Aramaic sections in Ezra 4:8—6:18; 7:12–26; Daniel 2:4*b*—7:28; Jeremiah 10:11, and a few other words and phrases from Aramaic and other languages. The language is not called "Hebrew" in the Old Testament. Rather, it is known as "the language (literally, lip) of Canaan" (Isa. 19:18) or as "Judean" (NAS), that is the language of Judah (Neh. 13:24; Isa. 36:11). The word "Hebrew" for the language is first attested in the prologue to Ecclesiasticus in the Apocrypha. See *Apocrypha.* In the New Testament the references to the "Hebrew dialect" seem to be references to Aramaic.

Biblical or classical Hebrew belongs to the Northwest Semitic branch of Semitic languages which includes Ugaritic, Phoenician, Moabite, Edomite, and Ammonite. This linguistic group is referred to commonly as Canaanite, although some prefer not to call Ugaritic a Canaanite dialect.

Hebrew has an alphabet of twenty-two consonants. The texts were written right to left. The script was based on that of the Phoenicians, a circumstance which did not make it possible to represent or to distinguish clearly among all the consonantal sounds in current use in classical Hebrew.

The distinguishing characteristics of Hebrew are for the most part those shared by one or more of the other Semitic languages. Each root for verbs and nouns characteristically had three consonants, even in later periods when the use of four consonant roots was increased. Nouns are either masculine or feminine. They have singular, plural, or even dual forms, the dual being used for items normally found in pairs, such as eyes, ears, lips. While most nouns were derived from a verbal root, some were original nouns which gave rise to verbs (denominatives). The genitive relationship (usually expressed in English by "of") is expressed by the construct formation in which the word standing before the genitive is altered in form and pronunciation (if possible).

The Hebrew verb forms indicate person, number, and gender. There are seven verbal stems which serve to indicate types of action: simple action, active or passive; intensive action, active, passive, or reflexive; and causative action, active or passive. In classical Hebrew the isolated verb form did not indicate a tense, but rather complete or incomplete action. Thus verbs are often referred to as perfect or imperfect, there being no past, present, future, past perfect, present perfect, or future perfect. The tense can be determined only in context, and sometimes even that procedure produces uncertain results. Classical Hebrew is a verb oriented language rather than a noun oriented or abstract language. The usual word order of a sentence is verb, subject, modifiers, direct object. The language is quite concrete in expression. However, the relatively simple structure and syntax of classical Hebrew did not keep biblical writers from producing countless passages of unparalleled beauty and power.

While historical development took place in classical Hebrew from the eleventh century to the emergence of Mishnaic Hebrew, it does not seem possible to write the history of that development. It is generally agreed that the most archaic texts are poetic, such as Genesis 4:23–24; Exodus 15; Judges 5, although often it is difficult to decide what is archaic and what may be the result of an archaizing style. Books written toward the close of the Old Testament period, such as Ezra, Nehemiah, Chronicles, and Ecclesiastes, show the Hebrew language undergoing a number of significant changes due primarily to Aramaic influence. Most

Pottery handle from Lachish stamped with a Hebrew pottery seal containing a Hebrew inscription.

H

of the Hebrew Bible now shows a homogeneous style which was most likely due to scribes in the late pre-exilic period copying the older texts in the dialect of Jerusalem. Thus, to be able to date an extant text does not necessarily mean that one can date the material contained in the text. There is some evidence of dialectical variations in the Hebrew spoken in biblical times. For example there is the *shibboleth-sibboleth* incident in Judges 12:5–6. Some Bible students think many of the difficulties of the text of Hosea may be clarified by considering the Hebrew of that book as an example of northern or Israelite idiom.

The growing number of Hebrew inscriptions dating from the pre-exilic age provides an important supplement to the study of classical Hebrew. These inscriptions were chiseled into stone, written on ostraca (broken pieces of pottery), or cut into seals or inscribed on jar handles and weights. Some of the most important inscriptional evidence includes the Gezer calendar (tenth century), the Hazor ostraca (ninth century), the Samaria ostraca (early eighth century), the Siloam inscription (late eighth century), Yavneh-yam ostracon (late seventh century), jar handles from Gibeon (late seventh century), the Lachish ostracon (early sixth century), and the Arad ostraca (late seventh and early sixth centuries). To these may be added the Moabite Stone (Stele of Mesha, ninth century) and the Ammonite stele (ninth century) which contain inscriptions in languages very similar to classical Hebrew. Several benefits may be gained from these and other inscriptions for the study of classical Hebrew. First, we now have available an adequate view of the development of Hebrew script and orthography from the tenth century to New Testament times. Second, it now appears that literacy was earlier and more widespread in Israel than was thought previously. Third, the addition of new words and personal names and the like have enriched our knowledge of classical Hebrew. And fourth, details of the texts add new data on matters of history, material culture, and religion.

Thomas Smothers

HEBREW (Hē′ brew) A descendant of Eber. See *Eber.* It differentiates early Israelites from foreigners. After David founded the monarchy the term Hebrew seems to disappear from the Hebrew language. The designation apparently begins with Abraham (Gen. 14:13), showing that he belonged to an ethnic group distinct from the Amorites. It distinguished Joseph from the Egyptians and slaves of other ethnic identity (Gen. 39:14,17; 41:12; 43:32). Abraham's land has become the land of the Hebrews (Gen. 40:15), and his God, the God of the Hebrews (Ex. 5:3). Given the ethnic identity, special laws protected Hebrew slaves (Ex. 21:2; Deut. 15:12; compare Lev. 25:40–41; Jer. 34:8–22). After the death of Saul

(1 Sam. 29), the term "Hebrew" does not appear in the historical books, pointing possibly to a distinction between Hebrew as an ethnic term and Israel and/or Judah as a religious and political term for the people of the covenant and of God's nation. See *Habiru.*

HEBREWS (Hē′ brews) Nineteenth book of the New Testament, calling for faithfulness to Jesus, the perfect fulfillment of Old Testament institutions and hope.

Authorship Although Paul has traditionally been seen as the author of Hebrews, this is not a view commonly held by modern scholars. The style, vocabulary, form, content, and theology are unlike anything found in the letters of Paul. Besides this, the author describes himself as belonging to the second generation of Christians who were dependent on the eyewitnesses of the apostles (Heb. 2:3). Paul, who considered himself an eyewitness of the resurrection of Jesus (1 Cor. 15:8–11), would not describe himself in this way. Paul felt his experience with the risen Lord put him on a par with the other apostles.

Since the author is not named in the book itself, many have speculated as to who the author was. Luke, Clement of Rome, Priscilla, Barnabas, Apollos, or a Hellenist like Stephen have all been suggested. The early Church Father, Origen, was probably more correct when he said that only God knew who wrote Hebrews. Hebrews was not accepted as part of the New Testament canon in the Western church until after A.D. 367 when the Western church finally accepted the Eastern church's theory of Pauline authorship.

The Form of Hebrews Hebrews does not have the normal opening that the letters of Paul have. (Compare, for example, Rom. 1:1–7; 1 Cor. 1:1–3; 2 Cor. 1:1–2.) It does conclude like a normal letter (Heb. 13:20–25; see *Letters in the Bible*). Many have speculated that Hebrews was originally a sermon preached to a church in Rome (notice the reference to "hearing" and "teaching" in Heb. 5:11) and later sent to a church outside of Rome (Heb. 13:24), perhaps experiencing similar circumstances. In this case, Hebrews 1—12 would represent the original sermon, and Hebrews 13 would represent the brief note (Heb. 13:22) attached for the second congregation.

Date Many have pointed to the description of the Jewish sacrificial system in Hebrews 8—10 as evidence that Hebrews was written before the destruction of the Temple in A.D. 70. In actuality, the description of the sacrificial system describes the tabernacle—not the Temple—and comes from the pages of the Old Testament—not through observance of the Temple service.

Other evidence, however, does point to a time of writing before the destruction of the Temple. Hebrews 10:32–34 describes a time of persecution endured by the original recipients. The persecution seems to have only included the loss of property. These circumstances would fit the edict of Claudius in A.D. 49 banning Christians from the city of Rome. Many believers lost their property as a result. The author then warned of greater tests ahead, probably referring to the persecutions underway during the reign of Nero in A.D. 64. If this is true, the writing of Hebrews would be sometime during or just after A.D. 64.

Others see Hebrews 10:32–34 as a reference to the persecution of Nero and place the writing during a persecution assumed to have taken place during the reign of Domitian (A.D. 81–96). This seems less likely, as the severity of Nero's persecutions does not seem to be reflected in Hebrews. Hebrews 12:4 says that the readers had not experienced bloodshed. This confirms the experience of a milder form of persecution in the past (such as the one of Claudius in 49) but suggests the intensity of the persecution to come (such as the one of Nero in 64).

The Historical Situation Early Christians were often the objects of persecution. In the beginning Christians were persecuted by Jews as can be seen in Acts (for example, 4:17–18; 5:27–42; 7:54—8:1a). Herod Agrippa I executed James and had Peter imprisoned about A.D. 44 (Acts 12:1–5). Such persecution often resulted in the spread of the gospel (Acts 8:4–25; 11:19–26).

Revelation, 1 Peter, and possibly the Gospel of Mark were written in times of such persecution. See *Persecution.*

The recipients of Hebrews faced the possibility of persecution when the book was written. As was often true when Christians faced persecution, the temptation was to deny being Christians so as to avoid persecution. Some biblical scholars think the recipients of Hebrews had been converted to Christianity from Judaism and were tempted to return to their Jewish faith and the relative safety from persecution that being Jewish brought. Thus, the writer of Hebrews went to great length to demonstrate to the recipients that Jesus and the Christian faith were superior to the Jewish faith. Exactly what form of Judaism is in view in Hebrews is unsure. It included a reverence for angels, Moses, and the Levitical sacrificial system. Some feel that a form of Judaism similar to that found among the Essenes at Qumran is the most likely.

Others feel the recipients were Gentile Christians who were also tempted to deny their Christian faith to avoid persecution. The interest in the Old Testament cult is explained by the fact that the Septuagint (the Greek translation of the Hebrew Old Testament) was the Bible of the early Gentile church. The writer, in this case, was explaining the meaning of the sacrificial elements in the Old Testament for the new people of God. This same interest in the Old Testament elements of worship was strong in the second century Church Fathers, who were also Gentiles.

The Writer's Response Whether the recipients were Jewish or Gentile Christians, the writer saw a clear and present danger. The writer's response was to point to the superiority of Jesus.

Jesus is God's superior revelation (1:1–4); He is superior to the angels (1:5—2:18) and to Moses (3:1—4:13). Jesus is superior to the earthly high priest. He has a superior ministry that establishes a superior covenant that is able to bring to maturity those who have faith (4:14—10:31). As the author and finisher of the faith, Jesus is the superior model of faith (12:1–2).

Because of the superiority of Jesus, the writer exhorted the readers not to neglect such a great salvation (2:3). The readers should enter God's rest while it is still available (4:1–13); they should go on to maturity (6:1–8). Because Jesus' high priesthood is superior and because He has a superior ministry that establishes a superior covenant, the readers should draw near God's throne in confidence (10:19–25).

The writer of Hebrews also confronted directly the recipients' fear of suffering. He thought that God's children suffer because they are His children (12:7–8). Suffering functions as a discipline that leads God's children to maturity or perfection. Jesus was perfected in this way (2:10; 5:8) and was qualified to stand in God's presence in the heavenly sanctuary as High Priest (2:17–18; 5:9–10).

The readers could also be qualified to stand in God's presence by means of the discipline of suffering. God disciplines His children for their good, that they might share his holiness (12:10). Without holiness no one will see God—that is, stand in His presence (12:14). Suffering may seem harsh at the time, but "later it yields the peaceful fruit of righteousness" to those who have been trained by suffering (12:11 NRSV). The "peaceful fruit of righteousness" is the peace that comes from having acquired the right and privilege to stand before God in confidence (see 10:19–25). Therefore, the writer exhorted the recipients to go to Jesus "outside the camp, bearing the disgrace he bore" (13:13 NIV).

The recipients were not alone in their suffering, however. Because Jesus has suffered as they were about to suffer and was tempted as they were being tempted, Jesus was able to help them (2:18; 4:15). Jesus could "sympathize" with the weakness that the recipients experienced when facing the prospects of suffering (4:15 NAS).

Thus, just as Jesus learned what it meant to be obedient to God through suffering (5:8), the readers were exhorted to exhibit the same kind of obedience in their suffering (10:36–39). "Shrinking back" from God in the face of suffering is a sin that God detests (3:12–19; 10:26–31). Jesus was tempted (2:18; 5:7) but did not sin (4:15). Because Jesus remained faithful and did not sin during the hour of His suffering, He became the "source of eternal salvation for all who obey him" (5:9 REB).

The writer also encouraged the recipients to remain faithful in the midst of suffering by giving them examples of others who were able to remain faithful (11:1–39). The writer reminded them of their own past faithfulness in suffering (10:32–39) and of the example of their former leaders (13:7). Those who remain obedient to God in the midst of suffering are able to do so by means of their faith, because "to have faith is to be sure of the things we hope for, to be certain of the things we cannot see" (11:1 TEV).

This is not to say, however, that the writer of Hebrews, felt that persons could, on the basis of their own obedience, qualify themselves to stand before God. Entrance before the throne of grace is permitted on the basis of the obedience and offering of Christ. Jesus is the one who sanctifies those who follow Him (2:11; 10:19–20; 13:12). To gain personal access to the throne of grace a person must obey (5:9). Just as Jesus learned what it meant to be obedient in suffering and was thereby brought to maturity, so, too, His brothers and sisters must be willing to demonstrate the same obedience.

Outline

I. Jesus Is God's Ultimate Revelation (1:1—2:4).
   A. Jesus, God in person, fulfills and surpasses the prophetic word (1:1–3).
   B. Jesus is superior to angels (1:4–14).
   C. Jesus provides salvation which we dare not ignore (2:1–4).
II. Jesus Is God's Son and Our Brother (2:5–18).
   A. The world is subjected to Jesus, the crucified Lord, who dies for us (2:5–9).
   B. Jesus is our brother and the Author of our salvation (2:10–13).
   C. Jesus died to conquer Satan and free us from the fear of death (2:14–15).
   D. Jesus, our High Priest, atoned for our sins and helps us overcome temptation (2:16–18).
III. Jesus Provides a Way of Faith that Assures and Perseveres (3:1—4:13).
   A. Believers must focus on Jesus, the High Priest, who is more faithful than Moses (3:1–6).
   B. Believers must be aware of the danger of disbelief (3:7–19).
   C. Believers must claim God's promised rest in faith (4:1–11).
   D. God, through His Word, is the only Judge (4:12–13).
IV. Jesus, the Sinless High Priest, Is the Only Source of Salvation (4:14—5:10).
   A. Through the sinless High Priest we can approach God in confidence (4:14–16).
   B. The obedient High Priest met all the

qualifications and became the Source of eternal salvation (5:1–10).
V. Jesus, the Eternal High Priest, Calls His Followers to Christian Maturity (5:11—6:20).
   A. Believers need to mature in Christ (5:11—6:3).
   B. Believers must show their faith is genuine and persevere in Christ (6:4–12).
   C. God's faithful promises provide secure hope (6:13–20).
VI. Jesus, the Perfect Sacrifice, Is the Only Priest Believers Need (7:1—10:39).
   A. Jesus is the promised, permanent Priest who offers a better covenant and complete salvation (7:1–25).
   B. Jesus is the perfect Priest who meets our need (7:26–28).
   C. Jesus' ministry in the heavenly worship place is superior to all other priests (8:1–13).
   D. Jesus' sacrifice of His own blood provides eternal redemption from sin in a new covenant (9:1–22).
   E. Jesus' sacrifice was once for all and pointed to His return to bring eternal salvation (9:23–28).
   F. Jesus' sacrifice provided perfect forgiveness and made all other sacrifices unnecessary (10:1–18).
   G. Jesus' sacrifice calls for His followers to live faithfully, even under persecution (10:19–39).
VII. Jesus Inspires Us to a Life of Faith (11:1–40).
   A. Faith lays claim to the unseen realities of God and His purpose (11:1–7).
   B. Faith presses on even when some of God's promises remain unfulfilled (11:8–22).
   C. Faith risks everything for God and His purpose (11:23–31).
   D. Faith endures even when earthly deliverance does not come (11:32–40).
VIII. Jesus, the Perfect Example of Faith, Inspires Believers to Persevere (12:1–29).
   A. Jesus' example of suffering encourages perseverance in the face of difficulties (12:1–6).
   B. Suffering should be seen as the Father's discipline (12:7–13).
   C. To see Jesus, believers must live holy lives (12:14–17).
   D. Believers listen to God's warnings and worship in gratitude before the divine Judge (12:18–29).
IX. Jesus, the Unchanging Savior, Expects His Followers to Live a Life of Love (13:1–25).
   A. Christian love includes all people (13:1–3).
   B. Christian love leads to pure marriage (13:4).
   C. Christian love does not love money

H

(13:5–6).

D. Christian love imitates worthy leaders (13:7).

E. Christian love centers on the unchanging Christ (13:8).

F. Christian love does not follow strange teachings (13:9–10).

G. Christian love endures isolation and persecution (13:11–14).

H. Christian love praises God and shares with others (13:15–16).

I. Christian love obeys and prays for Christian leaders (13:17–19).

J. Christian love does God's will (13:20–21).

X. Conclusion (13:22–25)   *Phil Logan*

HEBRON (Hē′ brŏn) Place name and personal name meaning "association" or "league." A major city in the hill country of Judah about nineteen miles south of Jerusalem and fifteen miles west of the Dead Sea. The region is over 3,000 feet above sea level. The surrounding area has an abundant water supply, and its rich soil is excellent for agriculture. According to archaeological research the site has been occupied almost continuously since about 3300 B.C.

After his separation from Lot, Abraham moved to Hebron. At that time the area was known as Mamre and was associated with the Amorites (Gen. 13:18; 14:13; 23:19). Abraham apparently

The mosque of the patriarchs at Hebron built over the traditional site of the Cave of Machpelah.

remained at Mamre until after the destruction of Sodom and Gomorrah. When Sarah died, the place was called Kirjath-arba; and the population was predominantly Hittite (Gen. 23:2; Josh. 14:15; 15:54; Judg. 1:10). From them Abraham purchased a field with a burial plot inside a nearby cave. Abraham and Sarah, Isaac and Rebekah, and Jacob and Leah were buried there (Gen. 23:19; 25:9; 35:29; 49:31; 50:13).

Four centuries later, when Moses sent the twelve spies into Canaan, the tribe of Anak lived in Hebron. According to Numbers 13:22 Hebron was "built" seven years prior to Zoan, the Egyptian city of Tanis. Archaeological evidence suggests that the reference was to Tanis' establishment as the Hyksos capital around 1725 B.C. and not its beginning. Indeed both cities already were inhabited long before 2000 B.C. Therefore, the date may indicate that it was rebuilt by the Hyksos at that time, or it may specify when Hebron became a Canaanite city. After the Israelite conquest of Canaan, Hebron was given to Caleb (Josh. 14:9–13). It also became a city of refuge (Josh. 20:7). Later, Samson put the gates of Gaza on a hill outside of Hebron (Judg. 16:3).

After the death of Saul, David settled in the city (2 Sam. 2:3) and made it his capital during the seven years he ruled only Judah (1 Kings 2:11). His son, Absalom, launched an abortive revolt against David from Hebron (2 Sam. 15:10). Between 922 and 915 B.C. Rehoboam fortified the city as a part of Judah's defense network (2 Chron. 11:5–10). According to inscriptions found on pot-

tery fragments, royal pottery was made in the city between 800 and 700 B.C.

When the Babylonians destroyed Jerusalem in 587 B.C., the Edomites captured Hebron. It was not recaptured until Judas Maccabeus sacked the city in 164 B.C. Although Herod the Great erected pretentious structures there, no mention of the city is made in the New Testament. The city was raided by both Jewish revolutionaries and Roman legions in A.D. 68 during the Jewish Revolt.

Two individuals in the Old Testament also were named Hebron. The first was a Levite (Ex. 6:18; Num. 3:19; 1 Chron. 6:2,18; 23:12). The second is listed in the Calebite genealogy (1 Chron. 2:42–43).

See *City of Refuge; Machpelah; Mamre.*

LeBron Matthews

HEBRONITE (Hē' brŏn īte) Citizen of Hebron. See *Hebron.*

HEDGE A boundary formed by a dense row of usually thorny shrubs. In ancient Palestine hedges served to protect vineyards from damage by animals or intruders (Ps. 80:12–13; Isa. 5:5). To put a hedge around someone means to protect (Job 1:10). To hedge in means to hem in or obstruct (Job 3:23; Lam. 3:7; Hos. 2:6).

Stone fences on the island of Patmos with portions covered with thorny briars for added protection.

HEDGEHOG See *Animals; Bittern.*

HEDGEHOG NAS, NRSV translation of the Hebrew *quippod,* a term of uncertain meaning (Isa. 14:23; 34:11; Zeph. 2:14). The term either refers to the hedgehog (or porcupine) or else to a type of bird. The decision of the NAS and RSV translators was based on the supposed Hebrew root *qpd* (meaning to roll up, which is what hedgehogs do when frightened) and on cognate Arabic and Syriac words referring to hedgehogs and porcupines. Other English versions follow the KJV in seeing a reference to a type of bird. Context favors a reference to a bird. Various identities of the bird have been proposed: bittern, a nocturnal heron (KJV); owl, screech owl (NIV); owl (TEV); bustard, a game bird (REB).

HEEL, LIFTED HIS To lift one's heel against someone is to turn one's back and join rank with the enemies. Jesus applied the expression to Judas, who accepted Jesus' hospitality but then plotted His arrest (John 13:18).

HEGAI (Hē' gâi) Persian name of unknown meaning. Eunuch in charge of King Ahasuerus' harem who befriended Esther (Esther 2:8–9,15).

HEGE (Hē' gē) KJV spelling of Hegai in Esther 2:3 based on variant spelling in Hebrew text.

HEGLAM (Hĕg' lam) NRSV interpretation of Hebrew text in 1 Chronicles 8:7, taking as a proper name giving a second name to Gera what other translations translate as "who deported them."

HEIFER A young cow, especially one that has not yet calved. Heifers were used for plowing (Deut. 21:3; Judg. 14:18) and for threshing grain (Hos. 10:11). Heifers were valued for milk (Isa. 7:21) and were used as sacrificial animals (1 Sam. 16:2). Heifers (or cows) were used in three different rites: to ratify a covenant (Gen. 15:9); to remove the guilt associated with a murder by an unknown person (Deut. 21:1–9); and to remove the uncleanness associated with contact with a corpse (Num. 19:1–10). The Hebrew term for the red "heifer" of Numbers 19 is the common term for cow.

Samson characterized scheming with his wife as "plowing with my heifer" (Judg. 14:18). One of David's wives (2 Sam. 3:5) was named Eglah (heifer). The heifer was used as a symbol for the splendor of Egypt (Jer. 46:20) and of Babylon (50:11). Hosea 10:11 pictures obedient Ephraim as a trained heifer. In contrast, disobedient Israel is a stubborn cow.

HELAH (Hē' läh) Personal name meaning "jewelry for the neck." Wife of Ashur in the tribe of Judah (1 Chron. 4:5,7).

HELAM (Hē' lam) Place name meaning "their army." The earliest Greek translation of Ezekiel 47:16 apparently locates it between Damascus and Hamath in Syria. First Maccabees 5:26 seems to indicate a place in the northern part of the territory east of the Jordan. Helam is the region, rather than a city, where David defeated the army of Hadadezer and thus gained control of Syria (2 Sam. 10:15–19).

HELBAH (Hĕl' bah) Place name meaning "forest." City in tribal territory of Asher which Asher could not drive out (Judg. 1:31). Some have seen this as an inadvertent copying of Ahlab. Most identify Helbah with Mahalib, mentioned in Assyrian monuments. It is four miles northeast of Tyre. See *Mahalab.*

H

HELBON (Hĕl′ bŏn) Place name meaning "forest." City known for its trade in wine mentioned in Ezekiel's lament over Tyre (Ezek. 27:18). It is modern Halbun about eleven miles north of Damascus.

HELDAI (Hĕl′ dā ī) Personal name meaning, "mole." *1.* Officer in charge of David's army for the twelfth month of the year (1 Chron. 27:15). He is apparently the same as Heled, David's military hero (1 Chron. 11:30), called Haleb in 2 Samuel 23:29. *2.* Man who returned from Exile in Babylon, apparently with a gift of silver and gold, which God told Zechariah to take and have made into a crown for Joshua, the high priest (Zech. 6:10). Verse 14 calls him Helem, which probably represents a copying change. Some students think Heldai was a nickname and Helem the official name. The earliest Greek translation took the names in this verse as common nouns rather than as proper names, translating Heldai as "the rulers."

HELEB (Hē′ lĕb) Personal name meaning, "fat" or "the best." One of David's military heroes (2 Sam. 23:29), probably a copyist's change from Heled in the parallel passage (1 Chron. 11:30), Heled also appearing in many manuscripts of 2 Samuel. See *Heldai.*

HELECH (Hē′ lĕch) Transliteration of Hebrew noun in NRSV, NIV which KJV, TEV, NAS interpret as meaning "your army." REB interprets Helech with many modern Bible students and reference books to refer to Cilicia. The precise meaning in the context is not known. Ezekiel described the good days of Tyre as having its massive city walls protected by foreign soldiers, but the precise home of these soldiers is not certain (Ezek. 27:11).

HELED (Hē′ lĕd) Personal name meaning, "life." See *Heldai; Heleb; Helem.*

HELEK (Hē′ lĕk) Personal name meaning, "portion." Son of Gilead from the tribe of Manasseh and original clan ancestor of the Helekites (Num. 26:30). The clan received an allotment in the tribe's share of the Promised Land (Josh. 17:2).

HELEKITE (Hē′ lĕk īte) Member of clan of Helek. See *Helek.*

HELEM (Hē′ lĕm) Personal name meaning, "beat, strike." Member of tribe of Asher (1 Chron. 7:35), probably the same name with a copying change as Hotham (v. 32). The same English spelling is derived from a different Hebrew word meaning, "power." The name appears in Zechariah 6:14 as a variant to Heldai in 6:10. See *Heldai.*

HELEPH (Hē′ lĕph) Place name meaning, "re-

placement settlement" or "settlement of reeds." Border city of the tribal allotment of Naphtali (Josh. 19:33). It is often identified with khirbet Arbathah just northeast of Mount Tabor, but some Bible students think this location is too far south. Others think Heleph represents the southern border of Naphtali.

HELEZ (Hē′ lĕz) Personal name perhaps meaning, "ready for battle." *1.* David's military hero (2 Sam. 23:26) in charge of the army for the seventh month (1 Chron. 27:10). *2.* Member of the family of Caleb and Jerahmeel in the tribe of Judah (1 Chron. 2:39).

HELI (Hē′ lī) Hebrew personal name meaning, "high." The son of Matthat and father of Joseph, Jesus' earthly father (Luke 3:23–24). His relationship to Jesus is variously explained by Bible students in light of Matthew 1:16 which makes Joseph's father to be Jacob. He has been seen as the father of Joseph, a more remote ancestor of Joseph, or an ancestor of Mary. Either Jacob and Heli are variant names of the same person, "son of" means "descendant of" as in other genealogies, or Luke preserved the genealogy of Mary rather than of Joseph. A totally satisfactory answer to the question has not been found. The name probably represents a Greek form of the Hebrew Eli (NAS).

HELIOPOLIS (Hē lĭ ŏp′ o lĭs) 1. Greek name for Egyptian city of On, meaning "city of the sun" or Beth Shemesh in Hebrew. See *On.* 2. Ancient city

View of the magnificent architectural ruins at ancient Baalbek (Heliopolis).

located in the Beqaa Valley of Lebanon. Although its Greek designation is Heliopolis ("City of the Sun"), it is more widely known by the name Baalbek ("Lord of the Valley"). Baalbek was an important city in early times, but declined through both the Hellenistic period and the early part of the Roman era. During the days of the later

Columns of the temple of Jupiter at Baalbek in Lebanon.

Roman Empire, its influence grew as a center for the cult worship of Jupiter, Mercury, and Venus (which was based upon an older cult worship of the Semitic gods Hadad, Atargatis, and Baal). Impressive ruins have been excavated at Baalbek including a temple to Jupiter, a temple to Baachus, and one to Venus.

HELKAI (Hĕl′ kā ī) Personal name meaning, "my portion." Priest when Joiakim was high priest one generation after the return from the Exile under Zerubbabel (Neh. 12:15).

HELKATH (Hĕl′ kăth) Place name meaning, "flat place." Border town in the tribal allotment of Asher (Josh. 19:25) given to the Levites (Josh. 21:31). It is called Hukok in the parallel passage (1 Chron. 6:75). It is either modern tell Qassis on the west bank of the Kishon River or tell tel-Harbaj just south of Acco.

HELKATH-HAZZURIM (Hĕl′ kăth-hăz zū′ rĭm) Place name meaning, "field of flint stones" or "field of battle." Site of "play" (2 Sam. 2:14) battle between young warriors of Saul and those of David leading to defeat of Ish-bosheth's army (2 Sam. 2:12–17). The somewhat obscure Hebrew play on words to name the field near Gibeon has led to numerous translation attempts. REB reads, "Field of Blades."

HELL The abode of the dead especially as a place of eternal punishment for unbelievers. Hell is an Anglo-Saxon word used to translate one Hebrew word and three Greek words in the King James Version of the Old and New Testaments. The Hebrew word that "hell" translated was *Sheol*. (Compare NAS). The word *Sheol* occurs sixty-five times in the Hebrew Bible. The King James Version translates thirty-one of the occurrences as "hell"; another thirty-one occurrences as "grave"; and three occurrences as "pit" (Num. 16:30,33; Job 17:16). The Revised Standard Version never uses "hell" to translate *Sheol*. It does use "grave" one time as a translation of *Sheol* (Song of Sol. 8:6). Sixty-four times it simply transliterates the word as *Sheol*. NAS always uses Sheol, while NIV intentionally avoids Sheol, using grave.

Sheol is a Hebrew word that has taken on the properties of a proper name. The Old Testament uses the word to refer to a place in the depths of the earth. The expressions "go down" or "brought down" are used twenty times in connection with Sheol. The "depths of Sheol" are mentioned six times (Deut. 32:22; Ps. 86:13; Prov. 9:18; 15:24; Isa. 7:11; 14:15). Four times Sheol is described as the farthest point from heaven (Job 11:8; Ps. 139:8; Isa. 7:11; Amos 9:2). Often Sheol is parallel with the "pit" (Job 17:13–14; 33:18; Ps. 30:3; 88:3–4; Prov. 1:12; Isa. 14:15; 38:18; Ezek. 31:14–17). Nine times it is parallel

with death (2 Sam. 22:6; Ps. 18:4–5; 49:14; 89:48; 116:3; Prov. 5:5; Isa. 28:15,18; Hos. 13:14; Hab. 2:5). Sheol is described in terms of overwhelming floods, water, or waves (Jonah 2:2–6). Sometimes, Sheol is pictured as a hunter setting snares for its victim, binding them with cords, snatching them from the land of the living (2 Sam 22:6; Job 24:19; Ps. 116:3); Sheol is a prison with bars, a place of no return (Job 7:9; 10:21; 16:22; 21:13; Ps. 49:14; Isa. 38:10). People could go to Sheol alive (Num. 16:30,33; Ps. 55:15; Prov. 1:12). With rare exceptions, such as Elijah (2 Kings 2:1–12), all people were believed to go to Sheol when they die (Job 3:11–19; Ps. 89:48).

The three Greek words often translated "hell" are *hades, gehenna,* and *tartaroō*. *Hades* was the name of the Greek god of the underworld and the name of the underworld itself. The Septuagint—the earliest Greek translation of the Old Testament—used *hades* to translate the Hebrew word *Sheol*. Whereas in the Old Testament, the distinction in the fates of the righteous and the wicked was not always clear, in the New Testament *hades* refers to a place of torment opposed to heaven as the place of Abraham's bosom (Luke 16:23; Acts 2:27,31). In Matt. 16:18 *hades* is not simply a place of the dead but represents the power of the underworld. Jesus said the gates of *hades* would not prevail against His church.

Gehenna is the Greek form of two Hebrew words *ge hinnom* meaning "valley of Hinnom." The term originally referred to a ravine on the south side of Jerusalem where pagan deities were worshiped (2 Kings 23:10; Jer. 7:32; 2 Chron. 28:3; 33:6). It became a garbage dump and a place of abomination where fire burned continuously (2 Kings 23;10; compare Matt. 18:9; Mark 9:43,45,47; Jas. 3:6). *Gehenna* became synonymous with "a place of burning."

One time the Greek word *tartaroō* "cast into hell" appears in the New Testament (2 Pet. 2:4). The word appears in classical Greek to refer to a subterranean region, doleful and dark, regarded by the ancient Greeks as the abode of the wicked dead. It was thought of as a place of punishment. In the sole use of the word in the New Testament it refers to the place of punishment for rebellious angels.

Punishment for sin is taught in the Old Testament, but it is mainly punishment in this life. The New Testament teaches the idea of punishment for sin before and after death. The expressions "the lake of fire" and "second death" indicate the awfulness of the fate of the impenitent. Some insist that the fire spoken of must be literal fire, so to interpret the language as figurative means to do away with the reality of future punishment. One can, however, maintain this position only if they see no reality expressed by a figure of speech. Jesus spoke of a place of punishment as "outer

H

darkness" (Matt. 8:12; 22:13; 25:30). Can a place have both literal fire and literal darkness? What reason does one have for taking one expression as literal and not taking taking the other as literal? Literal fire would destroy a body cast into it.

Language about hell seeks to describe for humans the most awful punishment human language can describe to warn unbelievers before it is too late. Earthly experience would lead us to believe that the nature of punishment will fit the nature of the sin. Certainly, no one wants to suffer the punishment of hell, and through God's grace the way for all is open to avoid hell and know the blessings of eternal life through Christ. See *Gehenna; Hades; Heaven; Salvation; Sheol.*

Ralph L. Smith

HELLENISM The impact of Greek culture on the civilizations of the ancient world located in the Mediterranean basin. Aspects of Hellenism include professional contacts, mixed populations, adoption of Greek culture, religion and language, and the assimilation of Orientalized Greeks and Hellenized Orientals.

The history of contact of Greek-speaking peoples with the Eastern Mediterranean is long. Mycenaean pottery dating from before 1400 B.C. has been found on both sides of the Jordan. David employed mercenaries from Crete (2 Sam. 8:18).

Colossal statue of the Roman god Mars (Greek: Ares). Dual Graeco-Roman gods was a mark of Hellenism.

The Temple of Apollo at the international Hellenistic shrine of Delphi.

Contacts increased dramatically after Alexander the Great conquered Palestine in 332 or 331 B.C. **Koine** Beginning about 300 B.C., Jews wrote in Greek both in the diaspora and in Palestine. The writer might be a Hellenized aristocrat, diplomat, mercenary, merchant, or any Jew living in a Greek-speaking area of the diaspora. Beginning about 200 B.C., Jewish worship was conducted in Greek in Egypt. The use of the Greek term synagogue (assembly) for a Jewish congregation or place of worship is a continuing witness to Hellenization. The ready acceptance of Greek by Egyptian Jews is evidenced by the surviving synagogue inscriptions from Ptolemaic Egypt, all of which are in Greek. The Zenon correspondence (259 B.C.) demonstrates that Greek was the language of state business in Palestine under the Ptolomies.
Greek Names By 300 B.C. Egyptian Jews were using adopted names derived from names of Greek gods: Apollonius; Artimidorus; Diosdotus (gift of Zeus); Dionysius; Heracleia; and Hermaios. Before 200 B.C. the author of the "Epistle" of Aristeas assumed that the majority of the elders who came to Alexandria from Jerusalem to translate the Hebrew Bible into Greek, producing eventually the Septuagint, would have had Greek names and access to Greek education. Greek names are found even among "conservative" Palestinian Jews before 100 B.C.

The envoys Judas Maccabee sent to Rome had Greek names: Eupolemus and Jason (1 Macc. 8:17; 2 Macc. 4:11). Both the envoys Jonathan Maccabee sent to Rome and Sparta and their fathers had Greek names: Numensius, son of Antiochus, and Antipater, son of Jason (1 Macc 12:16; 14:22).
Bilingual Palestine Part of the success of Jewish diplomatic missions to Rome and Sparta before 100 B.C. stemmed from the ability to speak and write proper *koine* Greek (2 Macc. 4:5–6; 14:4–5; 1 Macc. 8; 12:1; 14:16). The high social standing of Egyptian Jews in relation to native Egyptians hinged in large part on the Jewish adoption of the Greek language. (Compare Acts

H

21:37–38 where the commander of the Jerusalem cohort mistook Paul for an Egyptian agitator *until* he learned he spoke Greek.) Jesus, like most Galileans of His day, would have understood Greek. Jesus visited the Hellenistic cities of the Decapolis (Mark 5:20; 7:31). One of these cities, Gadara, was home to the famous Cynic philosopher Menippus and the "Syrian" epigrammatist Meleager (about 60 B.C.). Damascus was home to the well-known historian and peripatetic philosopher Nicholas.

Literature In contrast to the sparse Hebrew literature which has survived from the time before A.D. 100, a remarkably large body of Jewish literature has survived in Greek. The most important representative of this literature is the Septuagint, the Greek translation of the Old Testament, which served as the Bible of the early church. Extensive works of both Philo and Josephus survive as well as numerous pseudepigrapha. Even the Qumran texts written in Hebrew witness the influence of Greek ideas.

Politics The *polis* (city-state with a Greek-type constitution) was one of the principle factors in the spread of Hellenism. The *polis* was composed of free citizens with some degree of political and economic autonomy. The *polis* made use of Greek forms of government: the *boule* (senate), the *demos* (citizens' assembly), and the *archontes* (elected rulers).

Bust of Demosthenes (384-322 B.C.), famous Greek philosopher absorbed into Graeco-Roman thought.

The Seleucid king Antiochus refounded Jerusalem as "Antioch" in Judea with the status of *polis* in 175 B.C. The Sanhedrin served as the city's *boule;* the Mosaic law, as its constitution. The Hellenized high priest Jason displaced his more conservative brother Onias III and functioned as *archon.* Jason constructed a gymnasium and introduced Greek secondary education, training the elite youths as *ephebes* or citizens in training. Jason was succeeded as high priest by the even more radical Hellenists: Menelaus, Lysimachus, and Simon. Resistance to Hellenism resulted in Antiocus' reducing Jerusalem's status to *katoikia* (garrison town), with Syrian troops stationed in the city in 169 or 168 B.C.

The Maccabean revolt was in part a class struggle of the pious poor who clung to the traditional ways and the aristocracy who embraced Hellenism as a means to get ahead. Though the Maccabees succeeded in gaining political autonomy for Palestine, they were unable to stem the tide of Hellenism. The new rulers (called Hasmoneans) grew increasingly Hellenized. Jonathan was recognized by the Seleucids as king and high priest (150 B.C.) becoming in effect a Seleucid official. The Maccabees opposed the religious syncretism of Hellenism but succumbed to the broader culture of Hellenism.

The following were founded or refounded as Hellenistic cities in Palestine by 200 B.C.: Philoteria on Gennesaret (Bet Yerah); Scythopolis (Beth Shean); Berenice (Pella); Arsinoe (Damascus); Philadelphia (Rabbat-Ammon); Heliopolis (Baalbek). Herod the Great (37–4 B.C.) established Caesarea Maritima, Hebron, and Herodium. He began rebuilding of the Jerusalem Temple in Hellenistic style. Herod Antipas (4 B.C.–A.D. 39) founded Tiberias on the sea of Galilee. John's Gospel refers to the sea as "the Sea of Tiberias" (6:1; 21:1). Herod Philip raised Beth-saida to city-state status, renaming it Julias after the wife of Emperor Tiberias.

Religion/Philosophy Perhaps the most striking characteristic of the Hellenistic religion was its syncretism. The gods of the Middle East were identified with the ancient Greek and Roman gods. Hellenistic religion was characterized by a new emphasis on the individual. Religious fraternities dedicated to the worship of eastern gods offered individuals immortality. Hellenistic religion was also characterized by the public worship of the older gods of the city states and the new ruler cults. In the case of the ruler cult, the practice spread from east to west as rulers saw the unifying possibilities of a state religion.

Synagogue worship in contrast to Temple worship was purely verbal, consisting in prayer, singing, the reading of the law, and its interpretation. Such worship gave the appearance of being a philosophy to pagan Greeks. This identification of Judaism with philosophy was likewise encouraged

H

by the strong ethical emphasis of Judaism. See *Intertestamental History and Literature.*

Chris Church

HELLENISTIC (Hěl lě nĭs′ tĭc) Word derived from Greek, *hellas,* the Greek name for Greece. It describes customs or features of the Greek culture. Hellenistic people are those speaking Greek and following Greek culture even though they are not necessarily Greek by race. In the New Testament differences arose in the early church between those Christians more closely tied to Hebrew and Jewish practices and culture and those identifying themselves more closely with Greek language and culture (Acts 6:1; 9:29).

Hellenistic tombs outside the west gate at Hierapolis.

HELLENISTS (Hěl′ lě nĭsts) See *Hellenistic.*

HELMET See *Arms and Armor.*

HELON (Hē′ lŏn) Personal name meaning, "powerful." Father of the leader of the tribe of Zebulun under Moses (Num. 1:9).

HELP, HELPS In addition to the usual sense of assistance, the KJV used helps in two technical senses: for equipment used to secure a ship in storm (Acts 27:17) and for a gift of ministry (1 Cor. 12:28). Modern translations understand the "helps" of Acts 27 in various senses: ropes (NIV, TEV); supporting cables (NAS); tackle (REB); or generally as measures to undergird the ship (NRSV). The helps of 1 Corinthians refers to the ability to offer help or assistance. In the Septuagint, God is known as the help of those who lack strength and live in poverty (Sirach 11:12). It has been suggested that Paul refers to the ministry of the deacons who care for the poor and the sick. A general reference to all those who demonstrate love in their dealings with others is possible.

HELPER NAS translation of *parakletos,* a distinctive title for the Holy Spirit in the Gospel of John (14:16,26; 15:26; 16:7). Other versions translate the term "Comforter" (KJV), "Advocate" (R EB),

or "Counselor" (RSV, NIV). Because *parakletos* is difficult to translate with any single word, some interpreters opt for making "Paraclete" an English word and allowing the relevant Johannine passages to provide its meaning.

The Helper, who could not come until Jesus departed (John 16:7), functions as the abiding presence of Jesus among His disciples (John 14:16–18). Nearly everything said of the Helper is also said of Jesus in the Gospel, and the Helper actually comes as "another *parakletos*" (John 14:16), implying that Jesus had been the first (1 John 2:1).

Jesus described the role of the Helper primarily with verbs of speaking. The Helper would be sent by the Father to "teach" the disciples and to bring to remembrance all Jesus "said" to them (John 14:26; 16:14–15). Like Jesus, the Helper was "sent" to "bear witness" (John 15:26–27). The Helper's function in relation to the world involves "reproving" it concerning sin, righteousness, and judgment (John 16:8). The Helper would also "guide" Jesus' disciples into all truth by "speaking" what He hears and "showing" what is to come (John 16:13). By so doing He would "glorify" Jesus (John 16:14). See *Advocate; Comforter; Counselor; Holy Spirit; Paraclete.*

R. Robert Creech

HELPMEET KJV term for woman as a helper precisely adapted to man (Gen. 2:18). Modern translations supply various equivalents: a helper suitable for him (NAS, NIV); a helper as his partner (NRSV); a suitable companion for him (TEV). The noun translated helper or partner does not suggest subordination. Elsewhere the term is used of God as Helper (1 Chron. 12:18; Pss. 30:10; 54:4; 121:1) or of military allies (Jer. 47:4; Nah. 3:9). The adjective "meet" (translated suitable, comparable, or corresponding) stresses that woman, unlike the animals (Gen. 2:20), can be truly one with man (2:24), that is, enjoy full fellowship and partnership in humanity's God-given task (Gen. 1:27–28).

HELVE KJV term used for the handle of an ax (Deut. 19:5).

HEM The border of a cloth article doubled back and stitched down to prevent the cloth from unraveling. Biblical references to the "hem" of a garment refer more generally to its edge or border. The border of Aaron's high priestly robe was decorated with blue, purple, and scarlet pomegranates and gold bells (Ex. 28:31–35; 39:22–26). Sometimes the woof (the verticle filling threads in woven cloth) were left long to prevent unraveling. The result of these long threads was a fringed border. The fringe on the corners of their garments was to remind the Israelites of the law of God (Num. 15:38–39). The fringed "hem" of

Jesus' garment conveyed healing power to those who in faith touched it (Matt. 9:20; 14:36; Mark 6:56; Luke 8:44).

HEMAM (Hē' măm) Personal name of uncertain meaning. Descendant of Seir (Gen. 36:22). The parallel passage spells the name Homam (1 Chron. 1:39).

HEMAN (Hē' măn) Personal name meaning, "faithful." *1.* In Genesis 36:22, one of the sons of Lotan mentioned among the descendants of Esau. KJV renders the name *Hemam. 2.* In 1 Kings 4:31, a notable sage to whose wisdom that of Solomon is compared. *3.* In 1 Chronicles 6:33, the son of Joel, a Kohathite. He was one of the Temple singers under David and Solomon. In 1 Chronicles 25:5, he is called a seer. Elsewhere in that chapter he is said to have prophesied using musical instruments. He may be the same as the Heman mentioned in 1 Kings 4:31. The psalm title attributes Psalm 88 to Heman.

HEMATH (Hē' măth) KJV spelling of Hammath and Hamath. See *Hammath; Hamath.*

HEMDAN (Hĕm' dăn) Personal name meaning, "beauty, charm." Descendant of Seir and thus an Edomite (Gen. 36:26). The parallel passage spells the name Hamran (1 Chron. 1:41 NAS).

HEMLOCK KJV translation of two Hebrew terms. Modern translations agree in translating that in Hosea 10:4 as poisonous weed(s). The term at Amos 6:12 is translated as bitterness (NAS margins, NIV); poison (REB), and wormwood (NRSV, NAS). See *Gall.*

HEMORRHAGE Heavy or uncontrollable bleeding. The KJV translates the underlying Hebrew and Greek terms as "issue of blood" (Lev. 12:7; Matt. 9:20) or "fountain of blood" (Mark 5:29). Modern translations render these terms as hemorrhage, flow, or discharge of blood. Mosaic law said any discharge of blood, whether associated with the birthing process (Lev. 12:7), with menstruation (Lev. 15:19), or continued bleeding (Lev. 15:25; Matt. 9:20), rendered a woman unclean. Those ritually unclean were separated from God (represented by the tabernacle, Lev. 15:31) and from the congregation of Israel (Num. 5:2). The woman suffering from a hemorrhage (Matt. 9:20; Mark 5:29; Luke 8:43–44) was thus a religious and social outcast who only dared approach Jesus from behind. Contrary to expectations, the woman did not give her uncleanness to Jesus. Rather Jesus' healing power made the woman clean.

HEMORRHOIDS A mass of dilated veins and swollen tissue in the vicinity of the anus. The KJV

translators understood the affliction of Deuteronomy 28:27; 1 Samuel 5:6,9,12 as hemorrhoids (or emerods). Modern versions are divided in their understanding of the term in Deuteronomy. Some take a reference to tumors (NAS, NIV, REB). Others find a reference to sores (TEV) or ulcers (NRSV). Modern versions agree that the affliction of 1 Samuel was tumors, probably associated with bubonic plague.

HEN (FOWL) See *Birds.*

HEN (PERSON) Hebrew word for "grace, favor" used as either a proper name or a title (meaning "favored one") of Josiah son of Zephaniah (Zech. 6:14; compare 6:10) if the present Hebrew text is original. The Syriac version (followed by the NRSV, REB, TEV) has the name Josiah in place of Hen in 6:14. The earliest Greek version understood the name as a title.

HENA (Hē' nà) Place name of uncertain meaning. City Sennacherib, king of Assyria, captured prior to threatening Hezekiah and Jerusalem in 701 B.C. (2 Kings 18:34). Sennacherib used the historical example to brag and to persuade Hezekiah not to rely on God for protection against Sennacherib. Hena may be the same as Ana or Anat at the middle of the course of the Euphrates River.

HENADAD (Hĕn' ȧ dăd) Personal name meaning, "grace of Hadad (the god)." Clan of Levites who supervised the rebuilding of the Temple under Zerubbabel after 537 B.C. (Ezra 3:9). Clan members also helped Nehemiah rebuild Jerusalem's walls (Neh. 3:18,24) and signed Nehemiah's covenant of obedience (Neh. 10:10).

HENNA See *Plants in the Bible.*

HENOCH (Hē' nŏch) KJV spelling for Enoch (1 Chron. 1:3,33).

HEPHER (Hē' phĕr) Personal name meaning, "well" or "shame." *1.* Original family ancestor in clan of Gilead and father of Zelophehad (Num. 26:28–37). He belonged to the tribe of Manasseh (Josh. 17:1–2). *2.* A hero in David's wilderness army (1 Chron. 11:36). *3.* Member of the tribe of Judah (1 Chron. 4:6).

HEPHERITE (Hē' phĕr īte) Descendant of family of Hepher. See *Hepher.*

HEPHZIBAH (Hĕph' zĭ băh) Personal name meaning, "my delight is in her." *1.* In 2 Kings 21:1, the mother of Manasseh, king of Judah. *2.* In Isaiah 62:4, it is used as a symbolic name for Jerusalem. When Jerusalem is restored, she will no longer be forsaken and desolate; she will be called Hephzibah, for God's delight will be in her.

HERALD An official messenger. The herald of Daniel 3:4 was responsible for publicizing the king's law and the penalty of disobedience. Noah is described as a herald of righteousness (2 Pet. 2:5), that is, one who announced God's requirements. Paul was appointed as a herald or preacher of the gospel. First Timothy 2:5–7 outlines Paul's message as the uniqueness of God, Christ's unique role as mediator between God and humanity, and Christ's death as ransom. Second Timothy 1:9–11 outlines Paul's gospel as the good news that God has given grace by sending Christ who abolished death and brought life.

HERBS See *Plants in the Bible.*

HERBS, BITTER A salad of bitter herbs was eaten as part of the Passover observance (Ex. 12:8; Num. 9:11). Such a meal could be quickly prepared and was appropriate to commemorate Israel's hasty retreat from Egypt (Ex. 12:11). Later the bitter herbs were associated with the bitterness of Egyptian slavery (compare Ex. 1:14). Bitter herbs possibly included lettuce, chicory, eryngo, horseradish, and sowthistle. See *Plants in the Bible.*

HERD A number of animals kept together under human control. In biblical usage herd generally refers to cattle in contrast to flock which refers to sheep or goats. Herds were a source of meat and dairy products, of agricultural labor (1 Chron. 12:40; Isa. 46:1), and of sacrifices (Num. 7:3; Ps. 69:31; Isa. 66:3). Herds were regarded as a sign of wealth (Gen. 13:5; 32:7; 45:10). Cattle were generally kept in open pasture. Pen-fed beef was a luxury item (Amos 6:4; Hab. 3:17). See *Cattle.*

HERDSMAN One who cares for cattle in contrast to a shepherd who cares for sheep. Amos served as a herdsman before receiving his prophetic call (Amos 7:14). Herdsmen were sometimes included among high-ranking officials of ancient kings (1 Chron. 27:29; 28:1; compare Gen. 46:34). Herdsmen were sometimes paid from the products of the herd (1 Cor. 9:7).

HERES (Hē′ rĕs) Place name meaning "sun." A mountain pass over which Gideon traveled in returning from his battle with the Midianites (Judg. 8:13). It is distinct from the more western Mount Heres in Judges 1:35, often identified with Beth-Shemesh ("house of the sun"). KJV translates 8:13 as "before the sun was up" as compared to NAS, "by the ascent of Heres." Location of Gideon's pass is not known, though some scholars now locate it as the Ascent of Horus which leads to tell Deir Alla east of the Jordan. Strong manuscript evidence reads "city of Heres" or Heli-

opolis in Isaiah 19:18 (compare REB, TEV, NRSV). See *Heliopolis.*

HERESH (Hē′ rĕsh) Personal name meaning, "unable to speak." Levite who lived near Jerusalem after the return from Exile about 537 B.C. (1 Chron. 9:15).

HERESY (Hĕr′ ĕ sў) An opinion or doctrine not in line with the accepted teaching of a church; the opposite of orthodoxy. Our English word is derived from a Greek word which has the basic idea of *choice.* In ancient classical Greek it was used predominantly to refer to the philosophical school to which one chose to belong. Later, it came to be associated with the teaching of philosophical schools.

The word had a similar usage in Jewish writings. Josephus, a Jewish historian of the first century from whom we learn much of what we know about the Judaism of New Testament times, used the word to refer to the various Jewish parties (or schools of thought) such as the Pharisees, Sadducees, and Essenes. Jewish rabbis employed the term in a bad sense applying it to groups who had separated from the main stream of Jewish teaching.

The word has several usages in the New Testament, but never has the technical sense of "heresy" as we understand it today. It may be classified as follows:

1. Most frequently, especially in Acts, it has the same meaning as Josephus. In Acts 5:17, 15:5; and 26:5, where it refers to the Pharisees and Sadducees, it simply means party or sect.

2. In Acts 24:14 and 28:22 it is used in a slightly derogatory sense, referring to Christians as they were viewed to be separatists or sectarians by the Jews. This usage conforms to that of the rabbis.

3. Paul used the term to refer to groups which threatened the harmonious relations of the church. In 1 Corinthians 11:19, where he was writing about the disgraceful way in which the Corinthians were observing the Lord's Supper, the word has to do with the outward manifestations of the factions he mentioned in verse 18. In Galatians 5:20, it is one of the works of the flesh and is in a grouping including strife, seditions, and envyings. It apparently has to do with people who choose to place their own desires above the fellowship of the church. Titus 3:10 speaks of a man who is a heretic. Since the context of the verse has to do with quarreling and dissensions, the idea in this passage seems to be that of a fractious person.

4. In 2 Peter 2:1 it comes closest to our meaning of the term. It clearly refers to false prophets who have denied the true teaching about Christ. Since the remainder of 2 Peter 2 refers to the immoral living of the false prophets, the word also refers to their decadent living. The reference to

the heretic in Titus 3:10 may belong to this category since the verse mentions disputes about genealogies, a doctrinal matter.

It is clear that in the New Testament, the concept of heresy had more to do with fellowship within the church than with doctrinal teachings. While the writers of the New Testament were certainly concerned about false teachings, they apparently were just as disturbed by improper attitudes.

In the writings of Ignatius, a leader of the church in the early second century, the word takes on the technical meaning of a heresy. Most frequently in the writings of the early church fathers, the heresy about which they were concerned was Gnosticism, a teaching which denied that Jesus was fully human.

See *Christology; Error; Gnosticism.*

W. T. Edwards, Jr.

HERETH (Hē′ rĕth) Modern translation spelling of Hareth, place name meaning "cut in to." Forest in which David hid from Saul after settling his parents with the king of Moab (1 Sam. 22:5). Some identify it with Horesh (1 Sam. 23:15) located at khirbet Khoreisa two miles south of Ziph. Others place it at the village of Kharas near Keilah. From Hereth, David attacked the Philistines at Keilah (1 Sam. 23:1–5).

HERITAGE Legacy, inheritance, birthright. The Old Testament frequently refers to the promised land as Israel's heritage from God (Ex. 6:8; Pss. 16:6; 135:12). Children are regarded as a heritage from God (Ps. 127:3). The law and God's protective care are likewise called a heritage (Ps. 119:111; Isa. 54:17). Israel is called God's heritage (Ps. 94:5; Jer. 12:7; Joel 3:2). This image is applied to the church in 1 Peter 5:3 (compare NAS margin, allotment). Revelation 21:7 speaks of the water of life as the heritage of those martyrs who conquered through their faithfulness. See *Inheritance.*

HERMAS (Hēr′ màs) Personal name and name of Greek God. Christian to whom Paul sent greetings (Rom. 16:14). His name, the variant spelling of the Greek god Hermes, may indicate he was a slave, since many slaves were named for gods. See *Apostolic Fathers.*

HERMENEUTICS See *Bible, Hermeneutics, Bible, History of Interpretation.*

HERMES (Hēr′ mēs) In Acts 14:12, the Greek deity for whom the superstitious people at Lystra took Paul. KJV uses the god's Latin name, Mercurius. Hermes was known as a messenger of the gods and was associated with eloquence. Paul's role as chief speaker made the Lystrans think of Hermes.

HERMETIC LITERATURE A body of writings composed in Greek in Egypt between 100 and 300 A.D. associated with the name "Hermes Trimegistos" (Thrice-great Hermes). The Hermetic literature is a diverse collection. Some of the texts are primarily astrological, magical, or alchemical. Others are primarily religious and philosophical texts. Some of the texts are monistic (viewing all reality as a unity) and pantheistic (seeing God present in everything that is). Others are dualistic (seeing God and the creation as separate).

The best-known Hermetic writing is the tractate titled Poimandres (perhaps from the Coptic for "knowledge of the sungod"). Poimandres offers to reveal to Hermes the secret nature of creation and God. According to the myth, God created the *nous* (mind, intelligence) which in turn created (physical) nature. God then created the *anthropos,* the original man. In the fall, this man united with nature to produce the seven androgynous persons who were the source of the human race. Thus each person consists of a body (from nature) which imprisons the soul (from God). Salvation from the body and deliverance from the oppressive fate of the stars was achieved by receiving knowledge of the nature of things. Reception of such knowledge is described as re-

Marble head of Hermes dating from the first century B.C. to the first century A.D. from Dalmatia.

H

birth. By repressing the bodily senses, the faithful Hermetic hoped to ascend past the seven astral spheres and to reunite with God.

The Hermetic doctrine has similarities with gnostic teaching. The Hermetic writings unlike gnosticism did not regard nature as itself evil nor the direct agent of creation (*demiurge*) as the enemy of God. Some scholars have seen the influence of Hermetic doctrine in the Gospel of John (creation by the *logos,* rebirth). More likely, both John and the later Hermetics developed earlier Jewish and Greek ideas independently. See *Gnosticm; John.*

HERMOGENES (Hĕr mŏg' ė nēs) Personal name meaning, "born of Hermes." Follower who deserted Paul, apparently while he was in prison in Ephesus (2 Tim. 1:15). Paul's statement indicates acute disappointment in Hermogenes but does not say he became an apostate. Nothing else is known of him.

HERMON, MOUNT (Hĕr' mon) Place name meaning, "devoted mountain." Site of sanctuary of Baal and northern boundary of Israel. The name Hermon was called Sarion (Sirion) by the Sidonians (Phoenicians) (Deut. 3:9; Ps. 29:6) and Sanir (Senir) by the Amorites (Deut. 3:9). Both appellations signify "breast plate," evidently because of the mountain's rounded snow-covered tip, that gleaned and shone in the sunlight. The latter name appears twice in the Old Testament, seemingly as the name of a peak adjacent to Hermon (1 Chron. 5:23; Song of Sol. 4:8). It is also called Sion (Deut. 4:48), probably on account of its height. Once it is called "Hermons." KJV mistakenly renders this as "the Hermonites" (Ps. 42:6). This is probably a reference to the triple summits of the mountain.

The Hermon range is the southern spur of the Anti-lebanon chain of mountains which runs parallel to the Lebanon range being separated from it by the valley of Beqaa. Hermon, being 9,100 feet above sea level, is the highest mountain in Syria. It can be seen from as far away as the Dead Sea— 120 miles. The range is approximately 28 miles in length and reaches a width of 15 miles. Its peak is covered with snow two-thirds of the year. Water from its melting snow flows into the rivers of the Hauran and provides the principal source for the Jordan River. Although Hermon receives about 60 inches of precipitation (dew, snow, rain) per year, practically no vegetation grows above the snow line, where there is an almost complete absence of soil. Below it, the mountain slopes are covered with trees and vineyards. Wolves, leopards, and Syrian bears live in its forests. The biblical record praises: the dew of Hermon (Ps. 133:3), its lions

Beautiful view of Mount Hermon from the ancient city-mound of Hazor in northern Galilee.

(Song of Sol. 4:8) and its cypresses (Ezek. 27:5).

The mount is significant for four reasons. (1) It was the northern border of the Amorite kingdom (Deut. 3:8; 4:48). (2) It marked the northern limits of Joshua's victorious campaigns (Josh. 11:17; 12:1; 13:5). (3) It has always been regarded as a sacred mountain. (4) Some scholars believe the transfiguration of Jesus occurred on Hermon. *Gary Baldwin*

HERMONITE (Hĕr' mon īte) Resident of Mount Hermon, according to KJV translation of Psalm 42:6. See *Hermon.*

HERMONITES KJV translators understood the Hebrew plural "Hermans" (Ps. 42:6) to refer to the inhabitants of the slopes of Mount Hermon. Modern translations take the plural to refer to the three "peaks of Hermon" (NAS).

HEROD (Hĕr' od) The name given to the family ruling Palestine immediately before and to some degree during the first half of the first Christian century. Their family history was complex, and what information has come down has been frequently meager, conflicting, and difficult to harmonize. The chief sources are the references in the New Testament, the Jewish historian Flavius Josephus, and a few obscure references by Roman historians, such as Dio Cassius, Plutarch, and Strabo.

Overview of the excavations of Herod's Palace at Jerusalem as viewed from the Tower of David.

H

The most prominent family member and ruler was Herod, son of Antipater who had been appointed governor of Idumea by Alexandra Salome, the Maccabean queen who ruled Palestine 78–69 B.C. With the permission of the Romans, Antipater left his son Phasael as Prefect of Jerusalem and his second son, Herod, governor of Galilee. See *Intertestamental History.*

Other Herods named in the New Testament include the following:

Agrippa I, the son of Aristobulus and grandson of Herod. He ruled with the title of king from A.D. 41–44. Agrippa I ordered James the son of Zebedee killed with the sword and imprisoned Peter (Acts 12:1–23).

Agrippa II, the son of Agrippa I, heard Paul's defense (Acts 25:13–27; compare Acts 26:32). With his death the Herodian dynasty came to an end, in title as well as in fact.

Drusilla (Acts 24:24) was the third and youngest daughter of Agrippa I. She had been married briefly at age 14 to Azizus, king of Emessa, probably in the year 52. In 53 or 54 she was married to Felix, the Roman procurator.

Bernice was the sister of Drusilla and Agrippa II, and also his wife. Paul appeared before them in Acts 25.

Herod Philip was the son of Herod the Great and Cleopatra of Jerusalem (Luke 3:1). He built Caesarea Philippi and was governor of the Northeastern districts of Iturea, Gaulinitis, Trachonitis, and Decapolis. He was married to Salome, the daughter of Herodias.

A Herod Philip is mentioned in Mark 6:17 as the first husband of Herodias. In some places he is mentioned simply as Herod, or Herod II. Most scholars do not believe that he was the same person as the governor of the northeastern districts.

Herodias (Matt. 14:3) was the daughter of Aristobulus (son of Herod and Mariamne I) and Bernice, the daughter of Herod's sister, Salome. She was the second wife of Herod Antipas and called for the head of John the Baptist (Matt. 14:3–12; Mark 6:17–29; compare Luke 3:19–20).

Salome was the daughter of Herodias. She was married to Philip. After his death in 34, she married a relative Aristobulus, prince of Chalcis and had three children (Matt. 14:6–12; Mark 6:22–29).

Herod was a paradox. He was one of the most cruel rulers of all history. His reputation has been largely one of infamy. He seemed fiercely loyal to that which he did believe in. He did not hesitate to murder members of his own family when he deemed that they posed a threat to him. Yet marital unfaithfulness and drunkenness did not seem to be among his vices. Because of his effective administration, he virtually made Palestine what it was in the first Christian century. He has gone down in history as "the Great," yet that epithet can only be applied to him as his personality and accomplishments are compared to others of his family. *Robert W. Stagg*

HEROD'S PALACE The probable scene of Herod's interrogation and mockery of Jesus (Luke 23:6–12). The palace was located along the western wall of the upper city to the west of the people's assembly hall. The palace was surrounded by a 45 foot wall surmounted by ornamental towers at fixed intervals. The palace was renowned for its circular porticoes, fine gardens, and a banquet hall seating over 100 guests. The palace was destroyed in September of 70 A.D.

HERODIAN (Hẻ rō′ dĭ an) Member of an aristocratic Jewish group who favored the policies of Herod Antipas and thus supported the Roman government. Apparently they lived in Galilee, where Antipas ruled, and joined the Jerusalem religious authorities in opposing Jesus. They tried to trap Jesus into denying responsibility for Roman taxes (Matt. 22:15–22; Mark 12:13–17). Their plots began the road to Jesus' crucifixion (Mark 3:6). See *Herod.*

This aqueduct built by Herod the Great brought fresh water to Caesarea Maritima.

HERODIAS (Hẻ rō′ dĭ ȧs) In Mark 6:17, the wife of Herod Antipas. She was the daughter of Aristobulus and Bernice. She was first married to the half brother of her father, identified in Mark 6:17 as Philip. By Philip she bore a daughter named Salome. Antipas, however, who was Philip's brother, divorced his own wife and wooed Herodias away from Philip. It was this gross marital misconduct that was denounced by John the Baptist. See *Herod; John the Baptist.*

HERODION (Hẻ rō′ dĭ on) Christian man to whom Paul the Apostle sent a greeting (Rom. 16:11). Paul referred to him as a kinsman. This probably means that he was of Jewish birth. His name suggests that he might have a member of the family of Herod. This possibility is strengthened by the fact that the name immediately preceding his is Aristobulus (Rom. 16:10). Herodion could have been one of those in the household of Aristobulus.

H

A view inside the Herodium, the magnificent fortress-palace built by Herod the Great.

HERODIUM A fortress-palace built by Herod the Great about four miles southeast of Bethlehem. Herod was buried there. The fortress, captured in A.D. 72, was one of the last strongholds of Jewish resistance in the war with Rome. The Herodium served as a supply depot in the unsuccessful revolt of A.D. 132–135.

The famous silhouette of the Herodium against the Israeli sky.

HERON Any of a family of wading birds with long necks and legs (*Areidae*), which were regarded as unclean (Lev. 11:19; Deut. 14:18). See *Birds.*

HESED (Hē′ sĕd) Personal name meaning "grace" or "covenant love." Father of one of Solomon's district governors (1 Kings 4:10 KJV). Modern translations transliterate *ben* (Hebrew "son of"). He brought provisions for the royal court one month a year from his district of Arubboth. See *Arubboth.*

HESHBON (Hĕsh′ bŏn) Place name meaning, "reckoning." City in Moab ruled by Sihon and captured by Moses (Num. 21:21–30). Ancient Heshbon, to be identified with present-day tell Hesban, was one of several ancient cities situated on the rolling and fertile plateau east of the Dead Sea and north of the Arnon River (present-day Wadi Mojib). Two of the other cities nearby, often mentioned by the biblical writers in connection with Heshbon, were Elealeh and Medeba (Medeba.) The agriculturally-productive region in which these cities were located was much disputed territory during Old Testament times. Generally it was regarded as part of Moab, as is assumed in Isaiah 15—16 and Jeremiah 48. Yet the Israelite tribes of Reuben and Gad ranged with their sheep in this region (Num. 32:3,37). The Israelites laid claim to it on the grounds that Moses had taken all of the territory as far south as the Arnon from Sihon, an Amorite king who ruled from Heshbon (Num. 21:21–31). Certain of the stronger Israelite kings (David, Omri, and Ahab) were able to control all of that area. Apparently, the Ammonites claimed the region as well, as implied by the exchange of messages between Jephthah and the Ammonite king related in Judges 11:12–28.

Heshbon was assigned to the tribe of Gad and designated as a Levitical city according to Joshua 13:27–28; 21:38–39. Song of Solomon 7:4, describing a maiden's beauty, proclaims "thine eyes like the fishpools in Heshbon." Herod the Great fortified the site, and it became a flourishing city (called Esbus) during late Roman times.

Excavations at tell Hesban, conducted between 1968 and 1978, produced occupational remains ranging from the beginning of the Iron Age (about 1200 B.C.) through medieval times. No evidence of pre-Iron Age occupation was discovered at the site. That is the period when King Sihon was supposed to have ruled from the city.

See *Gad; Moab; Reuben; Sihon.*

Maxwell Miller

HESHMON (Hĕsh′ mŏn) Place name meaning, "flat field." Town in tribal territory of Judah (Josh. 15:27). Its location is not known.

HESLI (Hĕs′ lī) NAS spelling of Esli. See *Esli.*

HETH (Hĕth) Personal name of unknown meaning. Son of Canaan, great grandson of Noah, and original ancestor of the Hittites, some of the original inhabitants of Palestine (Gen. 10:15). See *Hittites.* Abraham bought his family burial ground from "sons of" or descendants of Heth (Gen. 23).

HETHLON (Hĕth′ lŏn) Place name of unknown meaning on the northern border of Israel's Promised Land, according to Ezekiel's vision (Ezek. 47:15). Some see the word as a scribe's Hebrew abbreviation for mountain of Lebanon. Others see it as another name or a scribal change for Lebohamath (Num. 34:8). Others would identify it as modern Heitela, northeast of Tripoli, two and a half miles south of Nahr el-Kebir. Ezekiel pointed to a road near this place, perhaps the important transportation road otherwise known as Eleutheros.

HEW To cut with blows from a heavy cutting

H

instrument. The references to "hewers of wood" together with drawers of water (Josh. 9:21,23,27; Deut. 29:11) probably refer to those who gathered firewood. Such work was a despised task relegated to foreigners and slaves. The "hewers that cut timber" (2 Chron. 2:10; compare Jer. 46:22) were skilled lumberjacks. The "hewers of stone" (1 Kings 5:15) or "stonecutters" were royal servants mining rock from the mountains for royal building projects. Houses of "hewn stone" rather than rough stone were regarded as an extravagance (Amos 5:11).

HEXATEUCH A modern designation for the first six books of the Old Testament viewed as a literary unity. The term was coined by source critics impressed with the supposed similarity of sources behind Joshua and the Pentateuch as well as the need for fulfillment of the promise of land to Abraham in the conquest of Cannan. More recent scholarship has evidenced a renewed appreciation of the canonical arrangement in which Joshua begins the "former prophets" or history of Israel from its entrance into the Promised Land until its departure with the Exile. Joshua forms something of a bridge linking the promises to the Patriarchs and the story of Moses with the later history of Israel.

HEZEKI (Hĕz′ ĕ kī) KJV spelling of Hizki in descendants of Benjamin (1 Chron. 8:17).

King Hezekiah's tunnel which brought water from the Spring of Gihon to the pool of Siloam.

HEZEKIAH Son and successor of Ahaz as king of Judah (716/15—687/86 B.C.) Hezekiah began his reign when he was twenty-five years old. At this time in history, the nation of Assyria had risen to power.

Hezekiah began his reign by bringing religous reform to Judah. Hezekiah was not willing to court the favor of the Assyrian kings. The Temple in Jerusalem was reopened. The idols were removed from the Temple. Temple vessels that had been desecrated during Ahaz's reign were sanctified for use in the Temple. The sacrifices were initiated with singing and the sounds of musical instruments. The tribes in the Northern Kingdom (Israel) had been subjected to Assyrian dominance. Hezekiah invited the Israelites to join in the celebration of the Passover in Jerusalem. Places of idol worship were destroyed. Hezekiah even destroyed the bronze serpent Moses had erected in the wilderness (Num. 21:4–9) so the people would not view the bronze serpent as an object of worship. Hezekiah organized the priests and Levites for the conducting of religious services. The tithe was reinstituted. Plans were made to observe the religious feasts called for in the Law.

In 711 B.C., just a few years after Hezekiah had become king, Sargon II of Assyria captured Ashdod. Hezekiah anticipated the time when he would have to confront Assyrian armies. Hezekiah fortified the city of Jerusalem and organized an army. Knowing that a source of water was crucial, Hezekiah constructed a tunnel through solid rock

from the spring of Gihon to the Siloam pool. The city wall was extended to enclose this important source of water.

Isaiah warned Hezekiah not to become involved with Assyria (Isa. 20:1–6). The critical time for Hezekiah came in 705 B.C. when Sennacherib became king of Assyria. From Hezekiah, Sennacherib obtained a heavy tribute of silver and gold.

In 701 B.C., Hezekiah became seriously ill (Isa. 38:1–21). Isaiah warned the king to prepare for his approaching death, but Hezekiah prayed that God would intervene. God answered by promising Hezekiah fifteen more years of life and deliverance of Jerusalem from Assyria (Isa. 38:4–6).

In the meantime, Sennacherib had besieged Lachish. Aware that Hezekiah had trusted God for deliverance, Sennacherib sent messengers to the Jerusalem wall to urge the people to surrender. Sennacherib boasted of having conquered 46 walled cities and having taken 200,000 captives. Sennacherib's messengers taunted that God would not come to Judah's defense. Hezekiah, dressed in sackcloth and ashes, went to the Temple to pray. He also called for Isaiah, the prophet. Isaiah announced that Sennacherib would "hear a rumour" and return to his own land where he would die by the sword (2 Kings 19:7).

Hezekiah's faith and physical recovery brought him recognition from the surrounding nations (2 Chron. 32:33). The Babylonian leader, Merodachbaladan, even congratulated Hezekiah on his recovery. Hezekiah hosted this Babylonian leader at a reception, but Isaiah met this event with a warning that succeeding generations would be subjected to Babylonian captivity (Isa. 39:1–8).

Sennacherib destroyed the city of Babylon in 689 B.C. He then marched toward Egypt. Hoping to ward off any interference from Judah, Sennacherib sent letters to Hezekiah ordering him to surrender (Isa. 37:9–38). Hezekiah took the letters to the Temple and prayed for God's help. From Isaiah came the message that Sennacherib would not prevail. In fact, Sennacherib's army was destroyed in a miraculous way (2 Kings 19:35–37). In 681 B.C., Sennacherib was killed by two of his sons as had been predicted by Isaiah in 701 B.C. Hezekiah died in 687/86 B.C. Manasseh, his son, succeeded him, although Manasseh had become co-regent with Hezekiah about 696 B.C.

The Gospel of Matthew lists Hezekiah in the genealogy of Jesus (Matt. 1:9–10).   *Gary Hardin*

HEZION (Hē′ zĭ ŏn) Personal name meaning, "vision." Grandfather of King Ben-hadad of Damascus (1 Kings 15:18). His relationship to Rezon, founder of the Damascus dynasty, is not certain. Some think Hezion is a scribal change from Rezon in Hebrew. Others think both names have been changed from an original Hezron or Hazael.

A more probable opinion is that Hezion is a personal name, while Rezon is a Syrian royal title or throne name. See *Rezon.*

HEZIR (Hē′ zīr) Personal name meaning, "wild pig." Ugaritic texts apparently show that the name came from the profession of herding swine. *1.* Leader of one of the 24 courses of priests (1 Chron. 24:15). *2.* A Levite who signed Nehemiah's covenant to obey God's law (Neh. 10:20).

HEZRAI (Hĕz′ rā ī) Personal name meaning, "his stalk" or "stem." KJV reading of name of David's military hero (2 Sam. 23:25) following an early scribal note on the Hebrew text. The written text and modern translations read Hezro with 1 Chronicles 11:37, where many early translations read Hezrai.

HEZRO (Hĕz′ rō) See *Hezrai.*

HEZRON (Hĕz′ rŏn) Personal and place name meaning, "camping place" or "reeds." *1.* Son of Reuben, grandson of Jacob (Gen. 46:9), and original clan ancestor of Hezronites (Num. 26:6). *2.* Grandson of Judah, great grandson of Jacob (Gen. 46:12), original clan ancestor of Hezronites (Num. 26:21) through whom David was born (Ruth 4:19). He was father of Caleb (1 Chron. 2:18) and of Segub (1 Chron. 2:21). The Hebrew text of 1 Chronicles 2:24 can be interpreted and translated in different ways. KJV makes Hezron the father of Ashur (compare NAS, NRSV, NIV). Some Bible students follow the lead of the earliest translations, changing the Hebrew text somewhat so that Caleb is the father of Ashur, Ephratah being Caleb's wife (compare REB, TEV, RSV). Hezron's first son was Jerahmeel, original ancestor of the Jerahmeelites (1 Chron. 2:25).

HEZRONITE (Hĕz′ rŏn īte) Clan descended from Hezron both in tribe of Reuben and of Judah. See *Hezron.*

HIDDAI (Hĭd′ dā ī) Personal name, perhaps a short form for Hodai, meaning, "my majesty." One of David's military heroes (2 Sam. 23:30). The parallel passage in 1 Chronicles 11:32 spells the name Hurai. He was from Gaash. See *Gaash.*

HIDDEKEL (Hĭd′ dė kĕl) Hebrew name for the third river flowing from the Garden of Eden (Gen. 2:14). Most modern translations translate it as Tigris. This shows the dependence of the important areas of subsequent world history owed their fertility to God's original garden of creation. KJV also retains the transliteration for Tigris in Daniel 10:4. See *Tigris.*

HIEL (Hī′ ĕl) Personal name meaning, "God lives" or, following the Greek translation, a short form of Ahiel, "brother of God." Man from Bethel who rebuilt Jericho at the price of the life of two of his sons (1 Kings 16:34), fulfilling the divine curse Joshua issued when he destroyed Jericho (Josh. 7:26).

HIERAPOLIS (Hī ēr äp′ ō lĭs) Place name meaning, "sacred city." Site of early church where Epaphras worked (Col. 4:13). Nothing else is known of the church. The city was twelve miles northwest of Colossae and six miles north of Laodicea on the Lycus River a short way above its junction with the Meander River. It is now called Pambuck Kulasi. Its fame rested on textile and

Mineral deposits from the hot springs of Hierapolis used as a health spa during the Roman period.

The Roman west gate of Hierapolis with triple arches set between two defense towers (first century A.D.).

cloth dyeing industries. It began as a center for worship of the Phrygian mother goddess. A large Jewish community is evidenced by grave inscriptions and other literary remains.

HIEROGLYPHICS Greek term meaning "sacred carvings," referring to the pictographic symbols used in ancient Egyptian writing. Normally hieroglyphs were carved in stone, though sometimes they were written with pen on papyrus. These

Hieroglyphics on the wall of a partially restored temple at Saqqara, Egypt.

picture-symbols consisted in both ideograms (representing an entire word or phrase) and phonograms (representing a consonant). A simplified cursive script (hieratic) was developed early. This was in turn simplified into the demotic script about 700 B.C.

HIGGAION (Hĭg ḡā′ iŏn) Transliteration of Hebrew word meaning, "whispering" (Lam. 3:62 NAS) or "meditation" (Ps. 19:14) or musical sound a stringed instrument produces (Ps. 92:3). It appears as a worship notation with uncertain meaning in Psalm 9:16. It may mean to play quietly or to pause for meditation.

HIGH GATE, HIGHER GATE KJV designations for a gate of the Jerusalem Temple (2 Kings 15:35; 2 Chron. 23:20; 27:3). Most modern translations prefer the designation "Upper Gate". TEV reads "North Gate" or "Main Gate." Its location is not clear, possibly being the same as the Benjamin Gate. Parallel to 2 Chronicles 23:20, 2 Kings 11:19 uses "guard" or "herald" as the gate's name, probably reflecting a change of names through history. See *Gates of Jerusalem*.

HIGH HEAPS KJV translation of a Hebrew term

which occurs only at Jeremiah 31:21. Modern translations render the term as guideposts (NAS, NIV, NRSV) or signpost (REB).

HIGH PLACE. An elevated site, usually found on the top of a mountain or hill; most high places were Canaanite places of pagan worship.

Heathen Worship at the High Place The average high place would have an altar (2 Kings 21:3; 2 Chron. 14:3), a carved wooden pole that depicted the female goddess of fertility (Asherah), a stone pillar symbolizing the male deity (2 Kings 3:2), other idols (2 Kings 17:29; 2 Chron. 33:19), and some type of building (1 Kings 12:31; 13:32; 16:32–33). At these places of worship the people sacrificed animals (at some high places children were sacrificed according to Jer. 7:31), burned incense to their gods, prayed, ate sacrificial meals, and were involved with male or female cultic prostitutes (2 Kings 17:8–12; 21:3–7; Hos. 4:11–14). Although most high places were part of the worship of Baal, the Ammonite god Molech and the Moabite god Chemosh were also worshiped at similar high places (1 Kings 11:5–8; 2 Kings 23:10). Scripture speaks negatively about these heathen places of worship; still they played a central role in the lives of most of the people who lived in Palestine before the land was defeated by Joshua. Archaeologists have discovered the remains of high places at Megiddo, Gezer, and numerous other sites.

God's Hatred of the High Places. When the Israelites came into the land of Canaan, they were ordered to destroy the high places of the people who lived in the land (Ex. 23:24; 34:13; Num. 33:52; Deut. 7:5; 12:3) lest the Israelites be tempted to worship the Canaanite false gods and accept their immoral behavior. The Israelites were to worship God at the tabernacle at Shiloh (Josh 18:1; 1 Sam. 1:3).

An exception to this practice existed in the years between the destruction of Shiloh by the Philistines and the construction of the Temple in Jerusalem by Solomon. During this short period Samuel worshiped inside a city (possibly Ramah)

The rock-cut altars of the high place at Petra in southern Jordan.

Stone fragments of what is probably an altar base (possibly Israelite) at the high place at Lachish.

at a high place dedicated to the worship of the God of Israel (1 Sam. 9:12–25), and a group of prophets of God worshiped at the "hill of God" (1 Sam. 10:5, probably Gibeah or Gibeon). David and Solomon worshiped the God of Israel at the high place at Gibeon where the tabernacle and the altar of burnt offering were located (1 Chron. 16:1–4,37–40; 21:29; 2 Chron. 1:3–4,13).

False Worship at High Places in Judah After the Temple was constructed, the people were to worship God at this place which He had chosen (Deut. 12:1–14), but Solomon built high places for the gods of his foreign wives and even worshiped there himself (1 Kings 11:1–8). Because of the seriousness of this sin, God divided the nation by removing ten tribes from the kingdom of his son Rehoboam (1 Kings 11:9–13,29–38). Following this, each new king that ruled in the Southern Kingdom of Judah and in the Northern Kingdom of Israel was evaluated in the books of Kings and Chronicles according to what they did with high places where false gods were worshiped.

False Worship at High Places in Israel When Jeroboam created the new kingdom of Israel after the death of Solomon, he put two golden calves at high places at Dan and Bethel (1 Kings 12:28–32). An unnamed man of God came to Bethel and pronounced God's curse on this high place (1 Kings 13:1–3), but the following kings of the Northern Kingdom of Israel followed in the ways of Jeroboam and did not remove the high places where the false gods were worshiped.

The Israelite prophets also condemned the high places of Moab (Isa. 15:2; 16:12), Judah (Jer. 7:30–31; 17:1–3; 19:3–5; 32:35), and Israel (Ezek. 6:3,6; 20:29–31; Hos. 10:8, Amos 7:9) because they were places of sin where false gods were worshiped.

See *Asherah; False Gods; Golden Calves; Prostitution.*   *Gary V. Smith*

HIGH PRIEST Priest in charge of the Temple (or tabernacle) worship. A number of terms are used to refer to the high priest: *the* priest (Ex. 31:10); the anointed priest (Lev. 4:3); the priest who is

H

chief among his brethren (Lev. 21:10); chief priest (2 Chron. 26:20); and high priest (2 Kings 12:10).

Responsibilities and Privileges The high priesthood was a hereditary office based on descent from Aaron (Ex. 29:29–30; Lev. 16:32). Normally, the high priest served for life (Num. 18:7; 25:11–13; 35:25,28; Neh. 12:10–11), though as early as Solomon's reign a high priest was dismissed for political reasons (1 Kings 2:27).

A special degree of holiness was required of the high priest (Lev. 10:6,9; 21:10–15). This meant he had to avoid defilement by contact with the dead, even in the case of his own parents and was forbidden to show any outward sign of mourning. He could not leave the sanctuary precincts. Such legislation identified the high priest as one totally dedicated to the Lord, always ritually pure and ready to serve the Lord.

If the high priest sinned, he brought guilt upon the whole people (Lev. 4:3). The sin offering for the high priest (Lev. 4:3–12) was identical to that required "if the whole congregation of Israel commits a sin" (4:13–21).

The consecretation of the high priest was an elaborate seven-day ritual involving special baths, putting on special garments, and anointing with oil and with blood (Ex. 29:1–37; Lev. 6:19–22; 8:5–35). The special garments of the high priest included (1) a blue robe with an ornate hem decorated with gold bells and embroidered pomegranates, (2) an ephod of fine linen with colorful embroidered work and shoulder straps bearing stones engraved with the names of the twelve tribes, (3) a breastplate with twelve precious stones engraved with the names of the twelve tribes, and (4) a linen turban with a gold plate inscribed "Holy to Yahweh" (Ex. 28:4–39; 39:1–31; Lev. 8:7–9). The engraved plate and the stones engraved with the tribal names highlight the role of the high priest as the holy representative of all Israel before the Lord (Ex. 28:12,29). In his "breastplate of judgment," the high priest kept the sacred lots, the Urim and Thummim, which were used to inquire of the Lord (Ex. 28:29–30; Num. 27:21). See *Breastplate; Ephod; Lots; Urim and Thummim.*

The high priest shared in general priestly duties. Only the high priest, however, was allowed to enter the holy of holies and then only on the Day of Atonement (Lev. 16:1–25; for the details of the ritual, see *Day of Atonement*).

The death of the high priest marked the end of an epoch. One guilty of involuntary manslaughter was required to remain in a city of refuge until the death of the high priest (Num. 35:25, 28,32; Josh. 20:6). The expiatory death of the high priest removed blood guilt that would pollute the land (compare Num. 35:33).

History of the Office Some argue that the developed priesthood characterized by three divisions (high priest, priests, and Levites) was a late, possibly postexilic, development in the history of Israel's worship. Others take the Biblical texts at face value and accept Mosaic institution of the fully developed priesthood.

The term high priest occurs in only one brief passage in the Pentateuch (Num. 35:25,28,32), once in Joshua (Josh. 20:6 where the legislation of Num. 35 is enacted), and never in the Book of Judges. Aaron, Eliezar, and Phineas are typically called *the* priest. Neither Eli, Ahimelech, Abiathar, nor Zadok are called high or chief priest, though all four headed priestly families and are mentioned in connection with items usually associated with the high priest (the ark, the ephod, the Urim and Thummim: 1 Sam. 3:3; 4:4–11; 21:6,9; 2 Sam. 15:24–29).

Eleazar was charged with supervision of the Levites (Num. 3:32; compare 1 Chron. 9:20) and of the sanctuary apparatus (Num. 4:16). He figures in the narrative of Numbers 16 where the offering of incense is affirmed as the exclusive prerogative of the priests and in the red heifer ceremony (Num. 19). The account of Eleazar's donning Aaron's priestly robe (Num. 20:25–28; compare Deut. 10:6) provides Scripture's best report of high priestly succession. As chief priest Eleazar assisted Moses with the census (Num. 26). Eleazar served as an advisor to Moses (Num. 27:1) and to Joshua, consulting the Lord by means of the sacred lots. Such counsel formed the basis for the apportionment of the Promised Land among the tribes (Num. 34:17; Josh. 14:1; 17:4; 19:51; 21:1). One indication of the significance of Eleazar is that the Book of Joshua concludes with the death of this chief priest (24:33).

Phinehas, son of Eleazar, is best known for his zealous opposition to intermarriage with the Moabites and the concomitant idolatry (Num. 25:6–13). For his zeal Phinehas was granted a covenant of perpetual priesthood (Num. 25:13) and was reckoned as righteous (Ps. 106:30). Phinehas accompanied the sanctuary vessels in holy war (Num. 31:6). Part of his ministry before the ark involved consulting the Lord for battle counsel (Judg. 20:27–28). Phinehas served as the major figure in the resolution of the conflict over the "commemorative" altar the tribes east of the Jordan built (Josh. 22:13,31,32).

Aaron, Eleazar, and Phinehas appear in Biblical history as distinct personalities. Until Eli's appearance at end of the period of the judges, a puzzling silence surrounds the high priesthood. First Chronicles 6:1–15 offers a (partial?) list of seven high priests between Phinehas and Zadok, a contemporary of David and Solomon. Of these nothing is known except their names. Nor is Eli included among this list, though he functioned as the chief priest of the Shiloh sanctuary.

Eli is best known for his rearing of Samuel (1 Sam. 1:25–28; 3) and for his inability to control his own sons (1 Sam. 2:12–17,22–25; 3:13), which, in time, resulted in the forfeiture of the high priesthood by his line (1 Sam. 2:27–35). Following the death of Eli, the Shiloh priesthood apparently relocated to Nob. Saul suspected the priesthood of conspiracy with David and exterminated the priestly family of Ahimelech (1 Sam. 22:9–19). Only Abiathar escaped (22:20). When David moved the ark to Jerusalem, Abiathar and Zadok apparently officiated jointly as chief priests (2 Sam. 8:17; 15:24–29,35; 19:11), though Zadok already appears as the dominant figure in 2 Samuel. Solomon suspected Abiathar of conspiracy with his brother Adonijah and exiled him to his ancestral home (1 Kings 2:26–27). The high priesthood remained in the family of Zadok from the beginning of Solomon's reign (about 964 B.C.) until Menelaus bought the high priesthood (171 B.C.) in the days of Antiochus Epiphanes.

Azariah, the son of Zadok, was the first individual to be explicitly identified as the "high priest" (1 Kings 4:2). At times during the monarchy, individual high priests exercised major roles in the life of Judah. Jehoshabeath, wife of the high priest Jehoida (2 Chron. 22:11), saved the infant Joash from the murderous Athaliah. Six years later, Jehoida was the mastermind of the coup de'etat in which Joash was crowned king (2 Kings 11:4–17). A second Azariah was known for opposing King Uzziah's attempt to usurp the priests' right to offer incense (2 Chron. 26:17–18). The high priest Hilkiah discovered the "Book of the Law," perhaps the Book of Deuteronomy, which provided the incentive for King Josiah's reforms (2 Kings 22:8). Hilkiah removed all traces of Baal worship from the Jerusalem Temple (2 Kings 23:4).

In the early postexilic period, the high priest Joshua is presented as the equal of the Davidic governor Zerubbabel (Hag. 1:1,12,14; 2:2,4). Both high priest and governor shared in the rebuilding of the Temple (Ezra 3; 6:9–15; Hag. 1—2). Both are recognized as anointed leaders (Zech. 4:14; 6:9–15). A further indication of the heightened importance of the high priesthood in the postexilic period is the interest in succession lists of high priests (1 Chron. 6:1–15,50–53; 9:11; Ezra 7:1–5; Neh. 12:10–11), a new development in biblical literature.

In the period before the Maccabean revolt the high priesthood became increasingly political. Jason, a Hellenistic sympathizer, ousted his more conservative brother Onias III (2 Macc. 4:7–10,18–20). Jason was, in turn, ousted by the more radically Hellenistic Menelaus who offered the Seleucid rulers an even larger bribe to secure the office (2 Macc. 4:23–26). With Menelaus the high priesthood passed out of the legitimate Zadokite line.

The Maccabees combined the office of high priest with that of military commander or political leader. Alexander Balas, a contender for the Seleucid throne, appointed Jonathan Maccabee "high priest" and "king's friend" (1 Macc. 10:20). Simon Maccabee was, likewise, confirmed in his high priesthood and made a "friend" of the Seleucid King Demetrius II (1 Macc. 14:38). Temple and state were combined in the person of Simon who was both high priest and *ethnarch* (1 Macc. 15:1–2).

The Romans continued the practice of rewarding the high priesthood to political favorites. During the Roman period, Annas (high priest A.D. 6 to 15) was clearly the most powerful priestly figure. Even when deposed by the Romans, Annas succeeded in having five of his sons and a son-in-law, Joseph Caiaphas (high priest A.D. 18 to 36/37) appointed high priests. Some confusion has resulted from New Testament references to the joint high priesthood of Annas and Caiaphas (Luke 3:2). The passage is perhaps best understood as an acknowledgment of Annas as the power behind his immediate successors. Another possibility is that Annas retained the title of respect on the grounds that the high priesthood was for life. Ananias, one of Annas' sons, was the high priest to whom Paul was brought in Acts 23:2; 24:1.

High Priest and Chief Priests The ordination rite for the high priest included the consecration of his sons as well (Ex. 29:8–9,20–21). A number of terms refer to leading priests other than the high priest: anointed priests (2 Macc. 1:10); chief priests (Ezra 8:29; 10:5; Neh. 12:7); senior priests (2 Kings 19:2; Isa. 37:2; Jer. 19:1). More specific titles are also found. Zephaniah was described as the "second priest" (2 Kings 25:18; Jer. 52:24). Pashur was the "chief officer in the house of the Lord" (Jer. 20:1).

Table of High Priests
Aaron (Ex. 28–29)
Eleazer (Num. 2:25–28; Deut. 10:6)
Phinehas (Josh. 22:13–32; Judg. 20:28)
Eli (1 Sam. 1:9; 2:11)
Ahimelech (1 Sam. 21:1–2; 22:11)
Abiathar (2 Sam. 20:25; 1 Kings 2:26–27)
Zadok (1 Kings 2:35; 1 Chron. 29:22)
Azariah (1 Kings 4:2)
Amariah (2 Chron. 19:11)
Jehoiada (2 Kings 11:9–10,15; 12:7,9,10)
Azariah (2 Chron. 26:20)
Urijah (2 Kings 16:10–16)
Hilkiah (2 Kings 22:10,12,14; 22:4,8; 23:4)
Seraiah (2 Kings 25:18)
Joshua (Hag. 1:1,12,14; 2:2,4; Ezra 3; Zech. 3:6–7; 4:14; 6:9–15)
Eliashib (Neh. 3:1,20)
Simon the Just (Sirach 50:1–21)
Onias III (1 Macc. 12:7; 2 Macc. 3:1)
Jason (2 Macc. 4:7–10,18–20; 4 Macc. 4:16)
Menelaus (2 Macc. 4:23–26)
Alcimus (1 Macc. 7:9)
Jonathan Maccabee (1 Macc. 10:20; 14:30)

H

Simon Maccabee (1 Macc. 14:20,23)
John Hyrcanus (1 Macc. 16:23–24)
Annas (Luke 3:2; John 18:14; Acts 4:6)
(Joseph) Caiaphas (Matt. 26:57; John 18:13)
Ananias (Acts 23:2; 24:1)   *Chris Church*

HIGHEST A KJV designation for God (Luke 1:32,35,76; 6:35). Modern translations prefer "Most High" (NAS, NIV, NRSV) or "Most High God" (TEV). In the Old Testament, Most High often occurs as a designation for the God of Israel when Gentiles are in view (Gen. 14:18–22; Num. 24:16; and frequently in Daniel). In the intertestamental period, the Highest or Most High became the most common designation for the Jewish God, occurring about 120 times in the Apocrypha.

HIGHEST HEAVEN See *Heaven of heavens.*

HIGHWAY A road, especially an elevated road (Isa. 62:10). In addition to literal uses, there are figurative uses, especially in Isaiah. In Proverbs 15:19 the highway of the righteous is an image for their way of conduct. The highway of Isaiah 11:16 and 35:10 is an assurance that the exiles will have safe and speedy passage home. Isaiah 40:3 speaks of preparing a highway for the Lord. See *Transportation and Travel; Palestine.*

HILEN (Hī' lĕn) Place name perhaps meaning, "power." City in tribal territory of Judah given to Levites (1 Chron. 6:58). The parallel passage (Josh. 21:15; compare 15:51) reads Holon. The Hebrew text in Chronicles actually reads "Hilez." Copying changes affected the various manuscript readings of this little-known town. See *Holon, Levitical Cities.*

HILKIAH (Hĭl kī' ăh) Personal name meaning, "Yah's portion." *1.* Father of Amaziah (1 Chron. 6:45). He was a Levite who lived before the time of David the king. *2.* Levite and Temple servant who lived during the time of David (1 Chron. 26:11). *3.* Father of Eliakim, who was in charge of the household of King Hezekiah (2 Kings 18:18). *4.* Father of Jeremiah the prophet (Jer. 1:1).
    5. Father of Gemariah, who was an emissary from Zedekiah to Nebuchadnezzar, king of Babylon (Jer. 29:3). *6.* High priest who aided in Josiah's reform movement (2 Kings 22:4). *7.* Person who stood with Ezra the scribe at the reading of the law (Neh. 8:4). *8.* Priest who was among the exiles that returned (Neh. 12:7).

HILL OF GOD (Hebrew *Gibeath-elohim*) Site of a Philistine garrison and of a place of worship. Here Saul met a band of ecstatic prophets and joined them in their frenzy (1 Sam. 10:5).

HILL OF THE FORESKINS (Hebrew *Gibeath-*

haaraloth) Place near Gilgal where Joshua circumcised the Israelites born during the wilderness wandering (Josh. 5:3).

HILL, HILL COUNTRY Elevated land, usually distinguished as lower than a mountain or with a less distinct peak. Hills separating the Mediterranean coastal plain from the Jordan valley run the length of Palestine. The area to the east of the Jordan and the Dead Sea is likewise hill country. The common Hebrew terms for hill and hill country (*Gibeah* and *Har*) lack precise English equivalents, so a detailed knowledge of geography is required for proper translation. The RSV translated *Gibeah* as hill or hills 65 times. The RSV translated *Har,* the usual term for mountain, as hill 40 times and as hill country 92 times. The KJV and REB understood the Hebew *Ophel* as a fortress or citadel (2 Kings 5:24; Isa. 32:14; Mic. 4:8). Many English translations like NAS translated the term as hill. KJV uses tower, fort, and stronghold in the three passages.

HILLEL (Hĭl' lĕl) Personal name meaning, "praise." *1.* Father of the judge Abdon (Judg. 12:13). *2.* An influential rabbi and Talmudic scholar who flourished just prior to the time of the ministry of Jesus. He and his colleague Shammai presided over the two most important rabbinic schools of their time. Hillel was the more liberal of the two, and his emphases have largely determined the direction taken by Judaism since his era.

HILT The handle of a sword or dagger (Judg. 3:22 NRSV and REB). Other translations prefer haft (KJV) or handle (NAS, NIV, TEV).

HIN (hĭn) Unit of liquid measure reckoned as one sixth of a bath (Ex. 29:40). It would have been approximately equivalent to a gallon. See *Weights and Measures.*

HIND A female deer; doe (Prov. 5:19). To make my feet like hinds' feet is a common expression (2 Sam. 22:34; Ps. 18:33; Hab. 3:19) of God's care in dangerous situations. See *Animals.*

HINGE A flexible device on which a door turns. Proverbs 26:14 compares a lazy person turning in bed to a door turning on its hinges. The meaning of the term translated hinges at 1 Kings 7:50 (KJV, NAS, TEV) is disputed. NIV, NRSV prefer the translation sockets on the grounds that ancient doors swung on doorpins set in sockets rather than on jointed hinges. REB translates, panels.

HINNOM, VALLEY OF (Hĭn' nŏm) Place name of uncertain meaning; also called the valley of the son(s) of Hinnom. The valley lies in close proximity to Jerusalem (2 Kings 23:10), just south of the

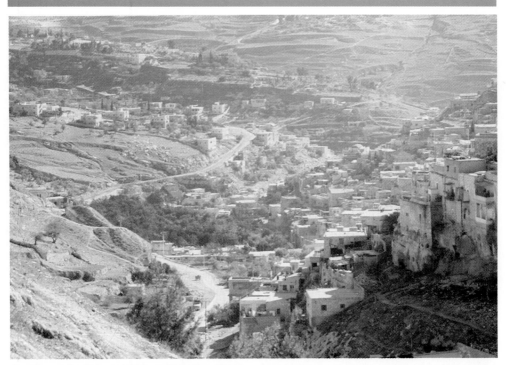

The Hinnom (or Gehenna) Valley in Jerusalem, just south of the ancient city.

ancient city (Josh. 15:8). The valley had a somewhat unglamorous history during the Old Testament period. The worshipers of the pagan deities, Baal and Molech, practiced child sacrifice in the valley of Hinnom (2 Kings 23:10). The first specific mention of human sacrifice in Israel is in 2 Kings 16:3 and in Judah is in 2 Kings 17:17. The parallel passage in 2 Chronicles 28:3 indicates that the scene of the abomination was the valley of Hinnom.

See *Baal; Gehenna; Hell; Jerusalem; Molech.*

Hugh Tobias

HIP The part of the body where the thigh and torso connect. Jacob's hip came out of socket when he wrestled with God at the Jabbok (Gen. 32:25). The Israelites commemorated this encounter by not eating the thigh muscle on the hip socket (Gen. 32:32). To strike an enemy "hip and thigh" (Judg. 15:8) is to attack him fiercely (TEV) or viciously (NIV). Belshazzar's fear at the handwriting on the wall (Dan. 5:6 NAS) was evidenced by his hip joint going slack.

HIPPOPOTAMUS A large, thick-skinned, amphibious, cud-chewing mammal of the family *Hippopotamidae*. The Hebrew *behemoth* (Job. 40:15–24) is sometimes understood as the hippopotamus (NAS, TEV margins). Others prefer to identify *behemoth* with the crocodile (REB), elephant (KJV margin), or with a mythical creature

(TEV margin). Hippopotamus remains dating between 1200 and 300 B.C. have been found along the coastal plain near Tel Aviv. It is possible that the hippopotamus was also found in the Jordan River at this time, though archeological confirmation is lacking. See *Behemoth.*

HIRAH (Hī′ răh) Personal name of unknown meaning. A friend of Judah, the son of Jacob, whom Judah was visiting when he met Shuah, who bore three of his sons (Gen. 38:1–12). Hirah was from the Canaanite city of Adullam, about nine miles northwest of Hebron.

HIRAM (Hī′ răm) Personal name apparently meaning, "brother of the lofty one." *1.* King of Tyre, associated with David and Solomon in building the Temple. He is called Hiram (Samuel and Kings) and Huram (Chronicles), but both names refer to the same individual. Other information about him comes from the ancient Jewish historian, Josephus.

Hiram was the son of Abibaal ("my father is Baal") and was nineteen years old when he succeeded his father as king of Tyre on the Phoenician coast, just north of Israel. He reigned some thirty-four years and is said to have died at age fifty-four, although the biblical references to him seem to necessitate a longer reign.

When he became king, he began to improve and to expand his kingdom. He raised banks at the eastern part of Tyre which enlarged the city, and he built a causeway to connect the city with the

H

island temple of Jupiter Olympius in the harbor, after which he modernized the temple.

When David became king of Israel, Hiram sent congratulatory gifts to him, including men and materials to build a palace (2 Sam. 5:11). The friendship between the men grew and was evidenced by the commerce which developed between their two nations. The close relationship continued into Solomon's reign, and the two men made an agreement which resulted in the construction of the Temple in Jerusalem (1 Kings 5:1–12).

This relationship between Israel and Tyre was mutually beneficial. Jerusalem was inland and had the advantages of the overland trade routes. Tyre, as a major seaport, offered the advantages of sea trade. Hiram controlled the maritime trade during this time and was himself a respected world trader. His friendship with David and Solomon undoubtedly explains, at least in part, the prosperity and success of their reigns.

See *David; Phoenicia; Solomon; Tyre.*

2. Craftsman who did artistic metal work for Solomon's Temple (1 Kings 7:13–45). He lived in Tyre, his father's home town but had a widowed Jewish mother from the tribe of Naphtali.

Hugh Tobias

HIRELING A worker paid wages; a laborer; a hired hand. The work of hired laborers was generally difficult (Job 7:1–2). Mosaic law required paying workers at the close of the day so that they might provide for their families (Deut. 24:14–15). Workers were frequently exploited (Mal. 3:5; Jas. 5:4). John 10:12–13 contrasts the cowardice of a hired shepherd with an owner's self-sacrificing concern for his sheep.

HISS A sound made by forcing breath between the tongue and teeth in mockery or to ward off demons. In the Old Testament an army or nation hissed at their enemy's city or land that suffered defeat or disaster (Jer. 19:8). Most often the reference is to astonishment at the fate of Israel, Jerusalem, or the Temple lying in ruins (1 Kings 9:8; Jer. 18:16, 19:8; Lam. 2:15–16). Other nations and cities were also the objects of hissing: Edom (Jer. 49:17); Babylon (Jer. 50:13); Tyre (Ezek. 27:36); and Nineveh (Zeph. 2:15). Hissing was sometimes accommpanied by wagging the head, clapping hands, gnashing teeth (Lam. 2:15–16), and shaking the fist (Zeph. 2:15).

HISTORY The events which have already occurred and filled time for individuals and for political entities and provided meaning for life. The central importance the Bible places on history distinguishes it from other religions and philosophies of life. History in the Bible is the stage on which God related to people and in which God revealed His nature and purposes to people. It is through studying and understanding history's meaning and direction that Bible truths can be applied today.

Views of History Most human societies have pondered the meaning of events and the goal or direction of history. This has produced widely-differing viewpoints:

1. The chaotic view claims the human story has no purpose, pattern, or significance. No one controls history, and no one knows when, if, or how it will end.

2. The circular or cyclical view focuses on history repeating its patterns in cycles of various lengths or in a spherical pattern with some movement but as basically repetitious. Observation of natural seasons and life cycles advances such a theory, as seen in the Baal religion that tempted Israel. The Greeks described history as a "wheel of unending recurrences," thus a periodic repetition that saw growth and decay again and again. Not surprisingly, the cyclical view provided little ground for the hope that life has ultimate meaning.

3. The Bible's linear view of history gives history a beginning and an end as well as a purpose or direction. The Bible is uniquely tied to history. Christianity links Christian experience with God to certain historical occurrences. Scripture notes God's blessing for the ordering of the seasons (Gen. 8:20–22) and recognizes that apart from God the cycle may lead to a hopeless understanding of life (Eccl. 1:4). Old Testament saints recited their confession by recounting what God had done (Deut. 26:5–9). New Testament saints tell the good news of God's actions through Jesus: that Christ died, that He was buried, and that He rose.

4. A mechanistic view of history attempts to tell mankind's story while seeing humans as a product of nature and completely subject to outside influences. According to this view, the environment determines our history, making our freedom no more than an illusion.

5. A progressive or developmental view of history consists of many varieties with a common belief that to understand the past one must trace the "history" of institutions and movements from their emergence at a simple stage to the culminating, complex stage. Understanding a topic "historically" is often explicitly identified with imposing a developmental scheme.

History in the Biblical Story The biblical narrative reveals the major characteristics of a biblical approach to history. The Bible tells history as a series of God's acts in which He interacts with people to reveal Himself and His saving will for them.

1. Creation and Fall Asserting that God is the Creator of the earth suggests that He is ultimately responsible for all of history and nature. God's power to speak the world into existence implies that the world is not divine or eternal.

Creation also implies that God is free. He does not need creation but desired it and loves His creation. Because of the loving nature of God, His people have confidence that a future awaits mankind. In God's sovereign freedom He grants humans restricted freedom. This reality is crucial because the biblical narrative suggests that people mysteriously have a role in shaping history. Neither the Creator nor the environment has so determined history that human decisions and human actions make no difference. Rather, God remains in sovereign control of history even as He lets free human actions determine the course of individuals and nations. The Bible does not try to solve this mysterious interworking of God's sovereignty and human freedom.

The Fall is the story of humans' first prideful misuse of freedom (Gen. 1—3). Human freedom and sin are crucial to history's telling, for the Fall means that human freedom will often be used in ways which oppose the Creator's will. History thus becomes not only the story of human events but the story of response and interaction between God and sinful humans.

2. Covenant with Israel The spread of sin despite God's punishment and grace explains why God chose one people—Abraham's family. God diligently worked with this stubborn family. His selection was not out of favoritism. He intended and still intends to bless the whole world through His chosen people (Gen. 12:3; Acts 3:25–26). Thus the reader of biblical history comes to accept that the universal and eternal significance of God's work emerges from His work with an individual people or person. Biblical history focuses tightly upon this particular people, giving a selective view of their history. Israel's story is set in universal history, with all the features of general history such as economics and politics, but it is told from a theological point of view. The Bible concentrates on the relationship of God and people. This relationship takes the form of a series of covenants—with Noah (Gen. 9:9–17), Abraham (Gen. 15; 17), and all Israel through Moses (Ex. 19—24; renewed in 34). History thus becomes the unfolding of God's covenant promises and the covenant faithulness or unfaithfulness of the people. See *Covenant*.

3. The Exodus Redemption The covenant with Israel that Moses mediated was founded on God's act in history in which He miraculously saved a slave people from the tyranny of the world's most powerful nation by leading them in the Exodus across the sea and into the wilderness out of Egypt (Ex. 1:1—15:21). This set the pattern for the Bible's understanding of history. History centered on the relationship between people and God, a relationship begun by God's acts of grace—in creation and in redemption. God's acts of redemption show He wants the best for His human creatures and is willing to act on their behalf. History

can be seen to have purpose and meaning because God has shown His intention to provide that meaning and purpose. God's acts of salvation thus pattern human moral action as response to the expectations of a saving, caring God.

The story of Israel derives from God's activity. History is the medium through which God chooses to reveal Himself. This distinctive historical dimension of Christianity needs to be stressed, especially when addressing more skeptical hearers. God reveals Himself by what He says as well as what He does. God's work is not left to mere human discernment but is entrusted to inspired prophetic interpretation. The inspired oral or written interpretation of history ensures the revelatory quality of God's enacted history.

4. The Incarnation also represents God's dramatic, invasive activity in history. His supreme Revelation (Heb. 1:1–4) became a historical Man (John 1:14; Gal. 4:4; Heb. 2:18, 4:15). God's becoming human affirmed His commitment to history as the place for His revelation. Jesus stands at the center of biblical history. His ministry inaugurates God's kingdom; His return will signal its consummation. Jesus' miracles and exorcisms are the delivering works of God which show that history is the place of spiritual warfare. The kingdom of God is breaking in through the person of Jesus (Matt. 12:28). The cross shows God's determination regarding history; the love displayed when Jesus bears our sins must be played out on the field of history. Mysteriously, God can sovereignly work His redemption even by using sinful men, such as those who crucified Jesus. Jesus' victory over sin, death, and evil on the cross, and the confirming resurrection, reveal that history will end, and it will end well.

5. The resurrection (assuming the life and death of Jesus) is the crucial point of defense of the historical validity of Christianity (1 Cor. 15:14). Evidence for the resurrection is significant: the empty tomb, the appearances (1 Cor. 15:5–8), the prophecy of the Scriptures and Jesus (Luke 24:25–27,44), and the ongoing witness of the church. The empty tomb provides an illustration of the relationship between historical evidence and faith. All four Gospel writers confess that the discovery of the empty tomb did not produce faith in a living Jesus. (John 20:8 presents the only partial exception.) These disciples were made full disciples only by a confrontation with the risen Jesus. The role of evidence is limited: an empty tomb does not a resurrection make. Evidence is important, however, because an occupied tomb would disprove the resurrection. So it is with most biblical evidence, accepting God's Word involves more than being convinced by the facts. The testimony of these eyewitnesses calls one to believe beyond mere evidence; they did not, however, ask one to believe *against* the evidence. The nature and historical reality of the resurrection is

H

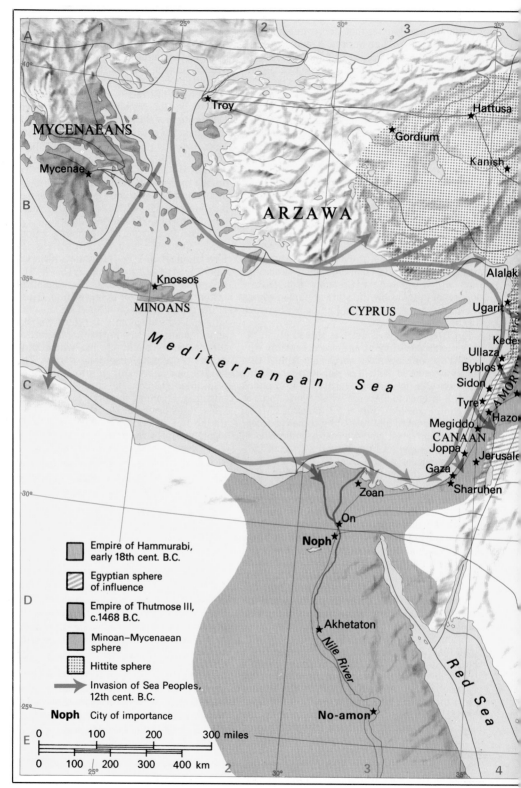

MYCENAEANS

Mycenae ★

★ Troy

ARZAWA

★ Hattusa

★ Gordium

Kanish ★

Alalak

★ Knossos

MINOANS

CYPRUS

Ugarit ★

Kede

Ullaza ★

Byblos ★

Sidon ★

A M O R I

Tyre ★

Hazo

Megiddo ★

CANAAN

Joppa ★

Jerusale

Gaza ★

Sharuhen ★

M e d i t e r r a n e a n   S e a

★ Zoan

★ On

Noph ★

Empire of Hammurabi,
early 18th cent. B.C.

Egyptian sphere
of influence

Empire of Thutmose III,
c.1468 B.C.

Minoan–Mycenaean
sphere

Hittite sphere

Invasion of Sea Peoples,
12th cent. B.C.

Noph   City of importance

★ Akhetaton

Nile River

No-amon ★

Red Sea

0   100   200   300 miles

0   100   200   300   400 km

© carta

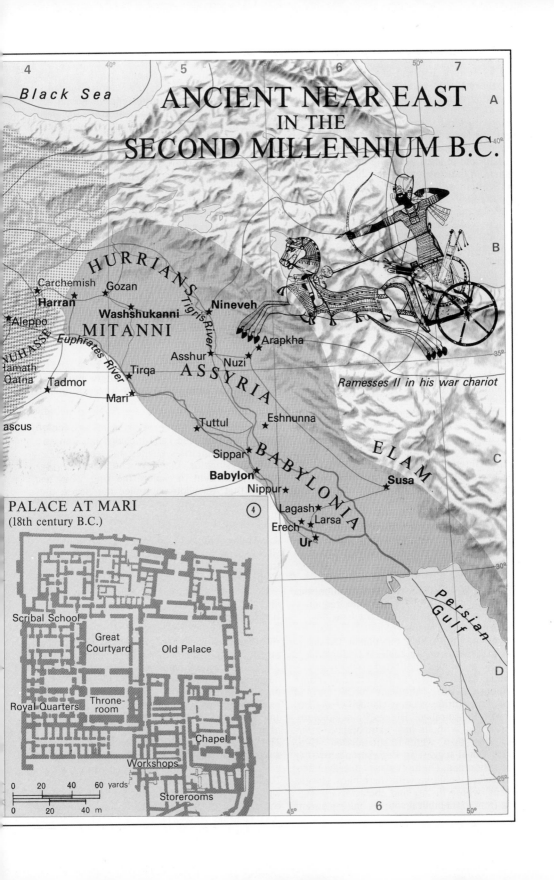

4 · 40° · 5 · 6 · 50° · 7

Black Sea

ANCIENT NEAR EAST
IN THE
SECOND MILLENNIUM B.C.

A

B

HURRIANS

Carchemish · Gozan

Harran · **Washshukanni** · **Nineveh**

Aleppo

NUHASSE

MITANNI

Euphrates River · Tigris River

Hamath · Asshur · Nuzi

Qatna · Tirqa · ASSYRIA

Tadmor

Mari

Ramesses II in his war chariot

ascus

Tuttul · Eshnunna

ELAM · C

Sippar · BABYLONIA

Babylon · Susa

Nippur

Lagash · Larsa

Erech

Ur

Persian Gulf

D

PALACE AT MARI
(18th century B.C.)

Scribal School

Great Courtyard · Old Palace

Royal Quarters · Throne-room

Chapel

Workshops

0 20 40 60 yards
0 20 40 m

Storerooms

6

crucial for history. Because of Christ's resurrection, believers may anticipate a historical and transforming resurrection for themselves (1 Cor. 15:42–44).

History for Jesus' followers will be marked by tension. Believers live between two decisive acts of God; they live between the partial realization of God's kingdom in Jesus' first coming and the final fulfillment of the kingdom when Christ will come again. Believers will suffer because they bear witness to the King the world does not acknowledge; they live by the principles of the kingdom (Matt. 5—7) the world does not acknowledge. Despite the inevitable suffering the church is sustained by the Holy Spirit. The church's history is the story of the Spirit's transforming, empowering, and equipping for mission.

6. Christ's return will signal the end of world history and the full revelation of its meaning. The prophetic vision of God's final kingdom will be realized fully. History will close as the one family of faith is inducted to a qualitatively greater future and fellowship with God.

Hints for Historical Interpretation (1) Language, historical language included, is multi-purposeful. For example, biblical language often intends to report (about history) but it also seeks to evoke faith (John 20:21). Thus the biblical documents are valuable as historical reports, but their full comprehension demands faithful response. (2) Historians must acknowledge the Bible's openness to God's miraculous intervention. An experience of Christ's saving power in the present provides a point of comparison for an understanding of God's past and future saving acts. (3) The interpreter must discern the context within Israel's history to insure that he or she does not advocate a divine concession but God's full intention (Matt. 19:4–9). God's greatest revelation, Jesus, is the guide to interpretation.

Randy Hatchett

HITTITES AND HIVITES Non-Semitic minorities within the population of Canaan who frequently became involved in the affairs of the Israelites.

Hittite and Hivite peoples of Indo-European origin, identified within the population of Canaan (as "sons" of Canaan) in the Table of Nations (Gen. 10:15,17), seemingly infiltrated from their cultural and political centers in the north and settled throughout Palestine. Although the history and culture of the Hittites is being clarified, a problem exists with the so-called "Hivites," a name of unknown origin without any extra-biblical references. That they were uncircumcised (Gen. 34:2,14) would suggest an Indo-European rather than Semitic origin. The more acceptable identification therefore would be with the biblical Horites (Hurrians) whose history and character are well-known from extra-biblical sources and consistent with role attributed to them in the biblical text. The Septuagint reading "Choraios" (Horite) for the

Massoretic "Hivite" in Gen.34:2 and Josh. 9:7 suggests this identification (see *Horites; Hurrians*). **Hittites in the Bible** Hittites appear among the ethnic groups living in urban enclaves or as individuals in Canaan interacting with the Israelites from patriarchal times to the end of the monarchy (Gen. 15:20; Deut. 7:1; Judg. 3:5). As a significant segment of the Canaan's population, these "children of Heth" permanently became identified as "sons" of Canaan (Gen. 10:15). In patriarchal times, the reference to King Tidal (in Hittite Tudhaliya II) in Gen. 14:1 is a possible link to early imperial Hatti. In Canaan, the Hittites established a claim on the southern hill country, especially the Hebron area. As a result, Abraham lived among this native population as a "stranger and a sojourner" (Gen. 23:4). He was forced to purchase the Cave of Machpelah from Ephron the Hittite as a family tomb, specifically for the immediate burial of Sarah (Gen. 23). Esau's marriage to two Hittite women ("daughters of Heth . . . daughters of the land") greatly grieved and displeased his parents (Gen. 26:34,35; 27:46).

The geographical reference to "all the land of the Hittites" (Josh.1:4) on the northern frontier of the Promised Land may indicate a recognition of the Hittite/Egyptian border treaty established by Rameses II and the Hittites under King Hattusilis III of about 1270 B.C. Moses' listing of the inhabitants of the Promised Land included the Canaanites, Hittites, Amorites, Hivites, and Jebusites (Ex. 13:5), a situation that was confirmed by the twelve spies sent to explore the land. They reported that Amalekites occupied the Negev, the Hittites, the Jebusites, and Amorites lived in the hill country, and the Canaanites were concentrated along the Mediterranean coast and the Jordan Valley (Num. 13:29; Josh. 11:3); thus the Hittites were doomed to displacement by the infiltrating and invading Hebrews (Ex. 3:8,17; 23:23; 33:2; etc.).

Devastation and pressures from the west by the Phrygians and the Sea Peoples brought another Hittite population to Canaan about 1200 B.C. Ezekiel recalled that Jerusalem had Amorite and Hittite origins (Ezek. 16:3,45). David purchased a threshing floor from Araunah the Jebusite (2 Sam. 24:16–25) whose name may suggest a Hittite noble status ("*arawanis*" in Hittite meaning "freeman, noble"). Later, the account of David's illicit love affair with Bathsheba indicates that Uriah and possibly other Hittites were serving as mercenaries in David's army (2 Sam. 11:3,6; 23:39). The Hittite woman among Solomon's foreign wives was probably the result of a foreign alliance with a neo-Hittite king of north Syria (1 Kings 10:29—11:2; 2 Chron. 1:17). Hittites together with other foreign elements appear to have been conscripted to forced labor during Solomon's reign (1 Kings 9:20–21).

Languages of the Hittite World Records of the

Ruins of the great temple at Boghaskoy, Turkey, the site of the ancient Hittite capital.

Assyrian trade colonies in the "Land of Hatti" suggest an earlier sub-stratum of linguistic and cultural development in the vicinity of Kanesh. This non-Indo-European language also found in texts from the Boghazkoy archives has been called "Hattic." It appears to have been at least one of the languages spoken in central Anatolia before the coming of the Hittite-Luwian branch of Indo-Europeans.

Speakers of an Indo-European language appear to have arrived in Anatolia from the north shortly before 4000 B.C. and gradually spread southward. These northwestern Anatolian settlers between 4000 and 3000 B.C. spoke an early form of Greek. The impression in Central Anatolia is of a generally peaceful spread of influence and language from the south and to a lesser extent from the west of Indo-Europeans whose ancestors recently had arrived from southeastern Europe. As a result from 3000 to 2000 B.C. much of Anatolia was occupied by various Indo-European elements who spoke closely related languages that included Hittite and Luwian (the Arzawans). However, soon after 1800 B.C., the kings of Kussara on the eastern frontier of Indo-European Anatolia assumed control. They conquered Kanesh and other central cities and established their capital at Hattusas.

Hittite Old Kingdom The growing pressure of the Hurrians about 1780 B.C. forced a Hittite consolidation and the eventual establishment of their fortress capital at Hattusas within the crescent of the Halys River. There, Hattusilis I quickly consolidated and expanded what is referred to as the Old Hittite Kingdom.

Hittite Empire The vitality of the Hurrian kingdom of Mitanni and the Egyptian military incursions into Syria under Thutmose III about 1450 B.C. stifled Hittite development until the death of the Egyptian pharaoh about 1436 B.C. Tudhaliyas I, the new Hittite king, relieved of Egyptian trib-

Hittite ornament portraying two stags standing on what may be an altar and encircled by a wreath.

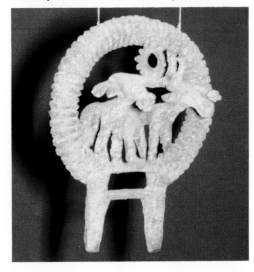

H

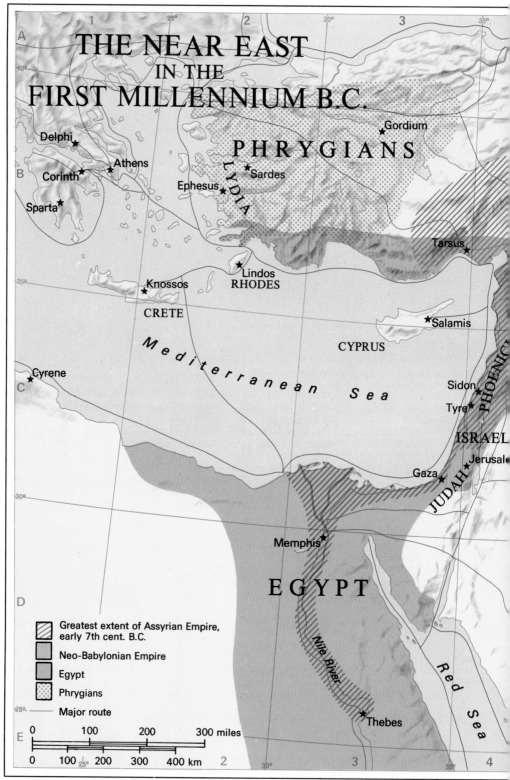

THE NEAR EAST
IN THE
FIRST MILLENNIUM B.C.

PHRYGIANS

Gordium

Delphi

Athens

Sardes

Corinth

LYDIA

Ephesus

Sparta

Tarsus

Lindos
RHODES

Knossos

CRETE

Salamis

CYPRUS

Mediterranean Sea

Cyrene

Sidon

Tyre

PHOENIC

ISRAEL

Jerusal

Gaza

JUDAH

Memphis

EGYPT

Nile River

Red Sea

Thebes

Greatest extent of Assyrian Empire,
early 7th cent. B.C.

Neo-Babylonian Empire

Egypt

Phrygians

Major route

0	100	200	300 miles

0	100	200	300	400 km

© carta

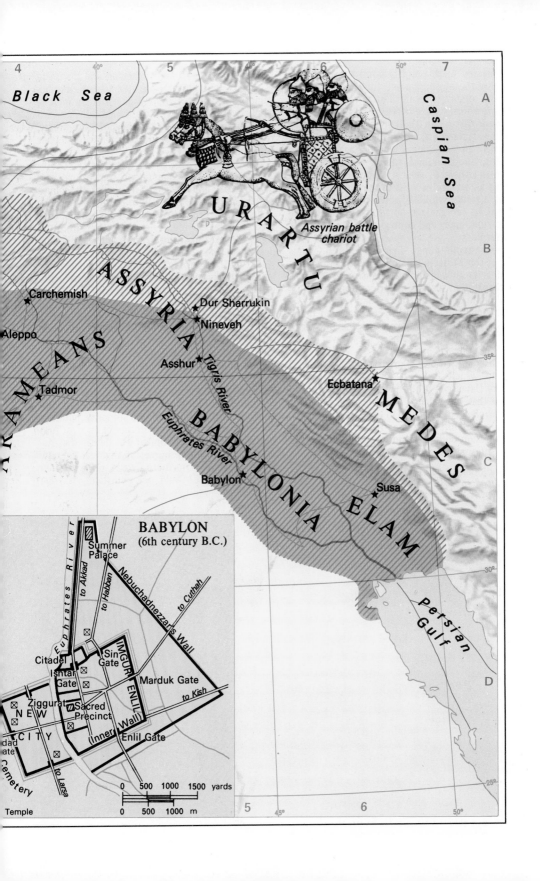

Black Sea

Caspian Sea

U R A R T U

Assyrian battle chariot

A S S Y R I A

Carchemish

Aleppo

Dur Sharrukin

Nineveh

A R A M E A N S

Asshur

Tigris River

Tadmor

Ecbatana

M E D E S

B A B Y L O N I A

Euphrates River

E L A M

Babylon

Susa

Persian Gulf

BABYLON
(6th century B.C.)

Euphrates River

to Akkad

Summer Palace

to Habban

Nebuchadnezzar's Wall

to Cuthah

Citadel

Sin Gate

Ishtar Gate

IMGUR ENLIL

Marduk Gate

to Kish

Ziggurat

Sacred Precinct

NEW

(Inner Wall)

CITY

Enlil Gate

dad ate

to Larsa

Cemetery

Temple

| 0 | 500 | 1000 | 1500 | yards |

| 0 | 500 | 1000 | m |

ute, defeated Aleppo and Mitanni and reclaimed control of the Mesopotamian trade route. During his reign other significant battles were won, but Hittite territories were besieged on all sides with the result that when Tudhaliyas died, the Hittite kingdom suffered a disastrous decline. About 1380 B.C. after a series of victories against Hittite enemies, Suppiluliumas gained the throne and moved southward against Mitanni. He soon claimed all territories west of the Euphrates. Following a treaty with Babylon and domination of Mitanni, he reorganized northern Syria to ensure Hittite supremacy and control of the trade routes of the region.

When Suppiluliumas died in 1334 B.C., his younger son Mursilis II followed with a very successful reign that included expansion in the west and preparation for the major confrontation that would come during his successor's reign. Muwatillis (about 1308–1285 B.C.) concentrated all the forces of the Hittite Empire in northern Syria to meet the challenge of Ramses II of Egypt at Kadesh. Although the battle in 1286 was indecisive, the subsequent treaty sixteen years later (1270 B.C.) in which Egypt conceded all territories north of Damascus to the Hittites would seem to suggest that the balance of power, for a time at least, favored the Hittites. On the eastern frontier, however, Mitanni became an Assyrian vassal.

Dangers on both east and west were magnified by an internal power struggle between Mursilis

The King's Gate at the Hittite city of Hattusas in Asia Minor (modern Turkey).

III, Muwatallis' son and successor, and his uncle Hattusilis, who ultimately exiled Mursilis and became king (about 1278). Western lands in Asia Minor were lost. Assyria continued its westward move and, in spite of the Egypt-Hittite treaty, reached the Euphrates and cut off Hittite copper supplies.

During the early reign of Tudhaliyas IV (1250–1220), the Hittites maintained control over the Syrian coast and invaded Cyprus for its copper mines. The Hittite treaty with Amurru, along the Syrian coast, prohibited trade with Assyria. The greater threat existed in new migrations from the west. Hittite lands were overrun and their capital destroyed by the hordes identified as "Sea Peoples," who, dislodged from their traditional homelands in the Greek-Aegean world, swept into Anatolia and the Levant (about 1200 B.C.). The Hittite empire was destroyed, and its capital was burned to the ground. For 250 years it had been a leading power by maintaining control over the vital trade routes and the distribution of mineral and agricultural wealth of the ancient Near East.

Neo-Hittite Period Following the end of the Hittite empire, a large number of Hittite principalities were established in northern Syria, Cilicia, and the regions of the Taurus and Anti-Taurus. They maintained a distinct identity as a minority within a predominantly Semitic environment for over four hundred years. When Urartu was defeated as Assyria's rival for the resources of Anatolia, the neo-Hittite states of northern Syria, now without Urartian support, could not withstand Assyrian

Hittite relief showing the king Tudhaliya IV being protected by the god Sharruma (in the king's hand).

pressure. By the end of 700 B.C. the Hittites had been absorbed into the Assyrian empire.

George L. Kelm

HIVITES A name that occurs twenty-five times in the Bible though not in texts outside the Bible. Hivites are found in Gibeon (Josh 9:7; 11:19), Shechem (Gen. 34:2), below Hermon in the land of Mizpah (Josh. 11:3), and in the Lebanon mountains (Judg. 3:3). Most frequently the name appears in the list of nations God would drive out of the land during the Israelite conquest (for example, Deut. 7:1).

Zibeon is identified as a Hivite (Gen. 36:2), but is listed among the Horites in Genesis 36:20,29. In addition, the Septuagint or earliest Greek translation reads "Horite" for "Hivite" in some texts (Gen. 34:2; Josh. 9:7). This may indicate an early linguistic confusion of "Horite" and "Hivite." It is unlikely that the two are identical, although the exact relationship is unclear. See *Horites.*

James C. Moyer

HIZKI (Hĭz′ kī) Personal name meaning, "my strength" or a shortened form of "Yah is my strength." Modern translation spelling of Hezeki, a Benjaminite (1 Chron. 8:17).

HIZKIAH (Hĭz kī′ ah) Personal name meaning, "Yah is my strength." *1.* Abbreviated form in

Hebrew for Hezekiah and used as alternate spelling of the king's name (2 Kings 18; Prov. 25:1). The ancestor of Zephaniah, the prophet, may have been the same king (Zeph. 1:1). See *Hezekiah; Zephaniah. 2.* Apparently the Hebrew name of a clan which returned from Babylonian exile with Zerubbabel about 537 B.C., the Babylonian name being Ater (Neh. 7:21; parallel passage Ezra 2:16 in Hebrew has another variant spelling—Jehizkiah). Both Ater and Hizkijah appear, however, in the list of those who signed Nehemiah's covenant to obey God's law (Neh. 10:17). This would apparently represent men of the next generation. *3.* A descendant of David living after the return from Exile (1 Chron. 3:23).

HIZKIJAH (Hĭz kī′ jah) KJV spelling of Hizkiah in Nehemiah 10:17. Modern translations usually use Hezekiah. See *Hizkiah.*

HOARFROST, HOAR FROST KJV terms for frost from "hoar" (white) and "frost" (Ex. 16:14; Job 38:29; Ps. 147:16).

HOBAB (Hō′ băb) Personal name meaning, "beloved" or "cunning." Father-in-law of Moses (Num. 10:29; Judg. 4:11). Some uncertainty exists concerning the identity of Moses' father-in-law. Jethro (Ex. 3:1; 18:2) and Reuel (Ex. 2:16) are also given as names for the father-in-law of the great lawgiver. Several explanations have been offered. Some say different groups within Israel handed down the story of Moses in oral tradition with different names for his father-in-law. Others say Reuel and Jethro were different names for the same person, while Hobab was the son of Reuel or Raguel (Num. 10:29) and thus the brother-in-law of Moses. Others say that the Hebrew term for father-in-law really has the more general meaning of "related by marriage." Moses urged Hobab to accompany the Israelites through the wilderness as a guide. See *Moses; Jethro; Reuel.*

HOBAH (Hō′ bah) Place name probably meaning "guilt" in Hebrew but "land of reeds" in Akkadian. Town in Syria to which Abraham pursued the coalition of eastern kings, who kidnapped Lot (Gen. 14:15). Attempts to identify Hobah with Apum or Upe in the Amarna letters from Egypt have recently been questioned. The town or region must lie somewhere north of Damascus, but its precise location is not known. It symbolizes Abraham's ability to drive his enemies completely out of the land of promise.

HOBAIAH (Hō bā′ iah) Personal name meaning, "Yah hides." Clan of priests in time of Zerubbabel who did not have family records to prove their descent from pure priestly lines and were excluded from the priesthood (Ezra 2:61; Neh. 7:63). Some translations use Habaiah in one or both texts.

H

HOD (Hŏd) Personal name meaning, "majesty." Member of tribe of Asher (1 Chron. 7:37).

HODAIAH (Hō dā′ iah) KJV, REB spelling of Hodaviah (1 Chron. 3:24) based on Hebrew text in which copyist has obviously transposed two letters and early scribes have noted proper reading in margin of text. See *Hodaviah.*

HODAVIAH (Hō dȧ vī′ ah) Personal name meaning, "praise Yah." The longer form Hodaviahu appears in the scribal marginal note correcting the Hebrew text of 1 Chronicles 3:24. See *Hodaiah.* *1.* The final generation of the sons of David which the Chronicler listed (1 Chron. 3:24). He appears to have been born about 420 B.C. The listing of seven brothers may be a cryptic note of hope in the Davidic dynasty for the Jewish community after the Exile. *2.* Original ancestor of clan in half-tribe of Manasseh living east of the Jordan (1 Chron. 5:24). The list leads to an explanation of Israel's loss of land east of the Jordan because of sin and idolatry. *3.* A member of tribe of Benjamin (1 Chron. 9:7). *4.* A clan of Levites who returned to Judah under Zerubbabel about 537 B.C. (Ezra 2:40). He was kin to the leading priest Joshua or to a Levite with the same name (compare Ezra 2:2,36). Ezra 3:9 reads Judah instead of Hodaviah, probably a copyists' change from the less familiar to the more familiar word. Similarly, in Hebrew Nehemiah 7:43 has Hodevah, a copyist omitting one letter.

HODESH (Hō′ dĕsh) Personal name meaning, "new moon." Wife of Shaharaim of tribe of Benjamin who bore children in Moab (1 Chron. 8:9).

HODEVAH (Hō′ dė văh) Transliteration of Hebrew text in Nehemiah 7:43 for original Hodaviah. See *Hodaviah.*

HODIAH (Hō dī′ ah) Personal name meaning, "Yah is majestic." *1.* Member of tribe of Judah (1 Chron. 4:19), though Hebrew text had led translators to interpret Hodiah as a wife (REB, KJV), the husband of Naham's sister (TEV), or the father (NAS, NIV, NRSV). Other scholars would assume copyists have changed the text from an original "sons of his wife the Jewess." *2.* A Levite who helped Ezra explain the meaning of the Law to the people (Neh. 8:7; note KJV spelling, Hodijah) and had a leading part in Israel's confession of sin and worship (Neh. 9:5). He signed Nehemiah's covenant to obey God's law (Neh. 10:10). Another Levite and a leader of the people with the same name also signed the covenant (Neh. 10:13,18).

HODIJAH (Hō dī′ jah) KJV spelling of Hodiah. See *Hodiah.*

HOE A tool for loosening the soil and cutting out weeds around cultivated plants (Isa. 7:25; KJV, mattock). See *Tools.*

HOGLAH (Hŏg′ lah) Personal name meaning, "partridge." Daughter of Zelophehad in tribe of Manasseh (Num. 26:33). See *Zelophehad.* Her marriage to a son of her father's brothers helped ensure the family land inheritance remained within the tribe (Num. 36:11). See also *Beth-hoglah.*

HOHAM (Hō′ hăm) Personal name of uncertain meaning, perhaps related to "unlucky." King of Hebron who joined forces with the king of Jerusalem to punish Gibeon for making an alliance with Joshua (Josh. 10:3). He was one of five kings shut in cave, used to show Israel's superiority over the kings by the symbol of Israel's captains putting their feet on the kings' necks, and then killed and hung on a tree (Josh. 10:15–26). Thus Joshua gained control of the south, destroying Hebron (10:36–37).

HOLD KJV term for a (fortified) place of refuge. Modern translations generally render the underlying Hebrew as stronghold (for example, Judg. 9:46,49; 1 Sam. 22:4; 2 Sam. 5:7). Occasionally other terms are used in place of hold: fortress (2 Sam. 24:7 NIV, NRSV); hill (Mic. 4:8 NRSV, perhaps in the sense of citadel); fortified cities (Hab. 1:10 NIV); refuge (Nah. 1:7 NIV). In Acts 4:3 to be put in the hold means to be put in custody (NRSV) or in jail (NIV). See *Fort, Fortification.*

HOLM TREE Small, holly-like, evergreen oak (*Quercus ilex*). The identity of the tree of Isaiah 44:14 is disputed: cypress (NAS, NIV); ilex (REB); holm oak or tree (NAS margin, NRSV); oak (TEV).

HOLON (Hō′ lŏn) Place name meaning, "sandy spot." *1.* Town in the hill country of Judah allotted to tribe of Judah and given as city for Levites (Josh. 15:51; 21:15). It may be modern khirbet Illin near Beth-zur. The parallel passage (1 Chron. 6:58) has Hilez or Hilen in different manuscripts. *2.* City of Moab that Jeremiah condemned (Jer. 48:21). Its location is not known.

HOLY A characteristic unique to God's nature which becomes the goal for human moral character. The idea of "holy" is important for an understanding of God, of worship, and of the people of God in the Bible. Holy has four distinct meanings. First is "to be set apart." This applies to places where God is present, like the Temple and the tabernacle, and to things and persons related to those holy places or to God Himself. Next, it means to be "perfect, transcendent, or spiritually pure, evoking adoration and reverence." This applies primarily to God, but secondarily to saints or godly people. Next, it means something or someone who evokes "veneration or awe, being frightening beyond belief." This is clearly the application to God and is the primary meaning of "holy." It is continued in the last definition, "filled with superhuman and potential fatal power." This speaks of God, but also of places or things or persons which have been set apart by God's presence. A saint is a holy person. To be sanctified is to be made holy.

God is holy. Fire is the symbol of holy power. Jealousy, wrath, remoteness, cleanliness, glory, and majesty are related to it. He is unsearchable, incomprehensible, incomparable, great, wonderful, and exalted. His name is Holy.

Holiness is in tension with relational personhood. Holiness tends toward separation and uniqueness. Personhood determines relations and close communion. Holiness inspires awe and fear. Personhood inspires love and the wish to be near. Both are in the Bible as necessary ways to think of and experience God. Both are necessary if one is to avoid shallow, one-sided thinking about God. Neither holiness nor personhood alone can do justice to the biblical portrayal of God. Both in their mutual tension help capture a more adequate doctrine and experience of God.

The biblical view combines these. Leviticus 17—25 presents all laws to be kept so that persons may be holy as God is holy. Holiness in God is seen as moral perfection in Psalm 89:35. Holiness in believing Christians was attained through the cross and is to be preserved in clean and moral living. Holiness comes to imply the fullness and completeness of God and godliness in all its facets and meanings.

Thus "holy" defines the godness of God. It also defines places where God is present. For the holy God to be present among His people special holy places were set apart where God and people could safely come together. The tabernacle and Temple filled this purpose. Special restrictions on access were established for the safety of the worshipers. Rules of sacrifice and cleanliness helped them prepare for this contact. A special place, the holy of holies, was completely cut off from common access. Only the high priest could enter there, and then only once a year after special preparation.

Holy also applied to persons who were to meet God. The priests had to undergo special rites that sanctified and purified them for service in the Temple. God wanted all His people to share His presence. They had to be instructed in the character and actions what would accomplish that. The Holiness Code (Lev. 17—25) commands the people to obey God's laws in all parts of life in order to be "holy: for I the Lord your God am holy" (19:2). Here holiness is seen to include a moral character as well as cultic purity. Sin and disobedience works the opposite and has to be cleansed or atoned by sacrifice (Lev. 1—7; 16).

An understanding of holiness is needed for New Testament study to appreciate the cross and the results of God's work through the cross. The Gospels make clear that Jesus came to save His people from their sins (Matt. 1:21; Luke 1:31–35). The crucifixion is portrayed as Christ shedding His blood and giving His body for the remission of sins (Matt. 26:26–29; Mark 14:22–25; Luke 22:19–20). Faith in Christ is portrayed as acceptance of His full atonement for sin (1 John 2:2; 3:5; Rev. 5:9).

The Holy Spirit is the agent of holiness for the church and its leaders (Acts 1:8; 2:4; 5:32; 13:2–4). He keeps the church pure (Acts 5:1–11). He promotes holiness in its members (1 Cor. 6:19; 1 Thess. 4:7).

Christians are called to holy living (1 Cor. 1:2; 3:17). They are saints who lead godly, righteous lives. Being sanctified, or made holy, is a work of the Holy Spirit on the basis of Christ's atonement that calls for obedient submission from those who have been saved. Christians are holy because of their calling in Christ, because of His atonement for their sins, and because of the continual minis-

H

The Holy	The Personal
Cannot be comprehended rationally.	Understood in terms of relationships.
Sensed and protected against. Avoided in contact and sight.	One can receive, respond, accept, and love.
Sins must be expiated and purged.	Sins can be forgiven with fellowship restored.
Beyond time—yet claims sacred times.	Redemption shows will, action, goal.
Beyond space—yet claims sacred space.	Creator—creature.
Life-threatening—yet strangely necessary to life.	Father—child.
Repels—yet fascinates and draws.	Judge—sinner, rebel.
Always awesome, mysterious, unnerving.	Savior—needy suppliant.
Here one worships and submits.	Lord—servant.
Portrayed in the sacrificial system, in tabernacle, Temple, priesthood, and in the cross.	Here one believes, loves, serves.
	Portrayed in the incarnation and in the gift of the Holy Spirit, in Israel as the people of God, and in the church.

trations of the Holy Spirit. They are holy inasmuch as they receive and submit to these saving and sanctifying agents.   *John D. W. Watts*

HOLY CITY Designation for Jerusalem (Neh. 11:1,18; Isa. 48:2; 52:1; Dan. 9:24; Matt. 4:5; 27:53; Rev. 11:2) and for the new, heavenly Jerusalem (Rev. 21:2,10; 22:19) because the holy God lived there. See *Holy.*

HOLY CONVOCATION See *Festivals.*

HOLY GHOST KJV designation for the Holy Spirit. See *Holy Spirit.*

HOLY OF HOLIES The innermost sanctuary of the Temple. Separated from the other parts of the Temple by a thick curtain, the holy of holies was specially associated with the presence of Yahweh. In the early years of the existence of the Temple the holy of holies contained the ark of the covenant. See *Temple.*

HOLY ONE OF ISRAEL In Isaiah 1:4, a designation for Yahweh. The title stresses God's nature as holy and His unique relationship to Israel. In the Old Testament, this designation is used especially in the Book of Isaiah. In the New Testament Jesus is referred to as the Holy One. See *God; Holy.*

HOLY PLACE The courts, the inner room, and the outer room of the tabernacle (Ex. 26:33). Later the expression was used in reference to the Temple and its environs. It was a holy place in the sense of being a place set apart for Yahweh. See *Temple.*

HOLY SPIRIT The mysterious third Person of the Trinity through whom God acts, reveals His will, empowers individuals, and discloses His personal presence in the Old and New Testament.
Old Testament The term "Holy Spirit" in the Old Testament is found only in Psalm 51:11; Isaiah 63:10–11. References to the spirit of God, however, are abundant. In one sense the Spirit of God is depicted as a mighty wind, Hebrew using the same word *ruach* for wind, breath, and spirit. During the time of the Exodus, God deployed this wind to part the sea thus enabling the Israelites to pass through safely and elude Pharaoh and his army (Ex. 14:21). God used this agent in two ways: as a destructive force that dries up the waters (Hos. 13:15), or as the power of God in gathering clouds to bring the refreshing rain (1 Kings 18:45). The spirit exercised control over the chaotic waters at the beginning of creation (Gen. 1:2; 8:1; Compare Ps. 33:6; Job 26:13). Of the eighty-seven times that the Spirit is described as wind, thirty-seven describe the wind as the agent of God, mostly baneful, and ever strong and intense. This property of the Spirit clearly reflects

the power of God. An additional quality of the Spirit is that of mysteriousness. Psalm 104:3 demonstrates that the Spirit as wind is able to transport God on its wings to the outer limits of the earth. No one can tell where He has been or where He is going. Power and mystery state the nature of God.

God's Spirit can be expressed as an impersonal force, or it can manifest itself in individuals. The Old Testament has numerous examples when God inspired the prophets indirectly by the Spirit. The prime revelation of the Spirit in the Old Testament, in the personal sense, is by means of prophecy. Joseph's dreams are perceived to be divinely inspired (Gen. 41:38); King David, as a mouthpiece for God, proclaimed that "the Spirit of the Lord speaks" (2 Sam. 23:2); and Zechariah announced the word of the Lord to Zerubbabel, "Not by might, nor by power, but by my Spirit,' saith the Lord of Hosts" (Zech. 4:6). Much like the power of the wind, the Spirit equipped the heroes of Israel with extraordinary strength (Judg. 14:6). The judges are described as being Spirit-possessed individuals as in the case of Othniel (Judg. 3:10). Sometimes, The Spirit came upon individuals mightily, so as to alter their normal behavior (1 Sam. 10:16; 19:23–24).

The Spirit is also the ultimate origin of all mental and spiritual gifts, as it is in the underlying inspiration of the men of wisdom (Ex. 31:1–6; Isa. 11:2; Job 4:15; 32:8). Not only did the prophets benefit from the influence of the Spirit, but also the Spirit will be shed upon the people of God (Isa. 44:3) and upon all the people (Joel 2:28). Ezekiel and Isaiah express the idea of the Spirit more than any other Old Testament source. Many of Ezekiel's allusions to the Spirit are in regard to Israel's restoration in the future. The reception of the new Spirit, prophesied in Ezekiel and Jeremiah, is dependent upon repentance (Ezek. 18:31) and is associated with the creation of a new heart (Jer. 31:31–34). This prophetic foreshadowing, in light of the individual, sporadic, and temporary manifestation of the Spirit in the Old Testament, looked forward to a time when the Spirit of God would revitalize His chosen people, empower the Messiah, and be lavishly poured out on all humankind.
New Testament When John the Baptist burst on the scene proclaiming the advent of the kingdom of God, the spirit-inspired prophetic voice returned after a 400-year absence. Zechariah and Elizabeth, John's parents, were informed that their son will "be filled with the Holy Ghost, even from his mother's womb" (Luke 1:15). Similarly, the angel Gabriel visited Mary with the news that "The Holy Ghost shall come upon thee, and the power of the Highest will overshadow thee: therefore also that holy thing which shall be born of thee will be called the Son of God" (1:35).

A watershed in biblical history occurred at the

H

event of Jesus' baptism when He was anointed by the Spirit of God (3:22). The Holy Spirit was then responsible for thrusting Jesus out into the wilderness to undergo temptation (4:1–13). Luke has many more references to the Holy Spirit than do the other synoptic accounts. This can be accounted for by Luke's theological interests which are extended in the Acts of the Apostles, which has been rightly named "The Acts of the Holy Spirit" because of the prominence given to the Spirit.

All apostolic writers witnessed to the reality of the Spirit in the church; however, the apostle Paul, who wrote more than any other author, offers the most theological reflection on the subject. The main chapters to consult are Romans 8; 1 Corinthians 2; 12—14; 2 Corinthians 3; and Galatians 5.

Johannine theology is rich in its doctrine of the Spirit. In the Gospel of John, the Spirit possesses Christ (1:32–33); is indicative of the new birth (3:1–16); will come upon Jesus' departure (16:7–11); and will endow the believer after the resurrection (20:22). The Christian community is anointed by the Spirit (1 John 2:20); and the Spirit assures the believer of the indwelling presence of Jesus (1 John 3:24). In the prophetic Book of Revelation, John, in Old Testament fashion, depicted himself as a prophet inspired by the Spirit. See *God*.   *Paul Jackson*

HOLY SPIRIT, SIN AGAINST THE Attributing the work of the Holy Spirit to the devil (Matt. 12:32; Mark 3:29; Luke 12:10). See *Unpardonable Sin*.

HOLY WEEK The week climaxing in Easter Sunday in which the church remembers the death and resurrection of Christ. As the observance of the Easter festival developed over the first few centuries, the week prior to Easter Sunday began to take on special significance for the early church. In the early centuries Easter Sunday celebrations included remembrance of both the crucifixion and the resurrection. By about 500, Good Friday came to be the focus of the remembrance of the crucifixion.

In a similar development Christians began to regard Thursday of Holy Week as a special time for participating in the Lord's Supper. The day came to be called "Maundy Thursday," a reference to Christ's giving a "new commandment" (John 13:34) to His disciples. The word "maundy" comes from the Latin word for "commandment." Usually the early Maundy Thursday observances included a ceremonial foot-washing, in imitation of Christ's washing the feet of the disciples (John 13:5–11). See *Church Year*.   *Fred A. Grissom*

HOMAGE Special honor, respect, or allegiance, such as that shown to a king; obeisance; reverence. Homage is most often paid to the king (1 Chron. 29:20 NAS, 2 Chron. 24:17 NIV) or to a high-ranking official (Gen. 43:28; Esther 3:2,5 NAS). Homage is sometimes paid to holy men (Samuel, 1 Sam. 28:14 NAS; Daniel, Dan. 2:46 NAS, NRSV). Homage is paid to God as the King of Israel (1 Chron. 29:20; Isa. 18:7 NAS). The Roman soldiers paid Christ mock homage before the crucifixion (Mark 15:19 NRSV).

HOMAN (Hō′ măm) Personal name perhaps meaning, "confusion." Hebrew text name for grandson of Seir (1 Chron. 1:39). The parallel passage reads Hemam (Gen. 36:22).

HOMER (Hō′ měr) A unit of dry measure (Lev 27:16). According to Ezekiel 45:11, it was equal to ten ephahs. In liquid measure this was ten baths. The actual volume represented by the term has been variously estimated between 3.8 and 6.6 bushels. It was the same volume as the cor (Ezek. 45:14). See *Weights and Measures*.

HOMOSEXUALITY Sexual preference for and sexual behavior between members of the same sex, considered to be an immoral life-style and behavior pattern throughout the biblical revelation. Only heterosexual preference and behavior patterns are approved in Scripture as conforming to God's plan in the creation of man and woman. Moreover, all sexual behavior is to take place in the context of marriage. Sex is considered good so long as it takes place within these parameters.

The Bible makes no distinction between what some today refer to as "homosexual orientation" and homosexual behavior. Homosexual desires or feelings are never mentioned as such in Scripture, but homosexual behavior is strongly condemned as a deviation from God's will for human beings. Therefore, it stands to reason that any homosexual inclination, feeling, or desire must be seriously dealt with as a potentially dangerous temptation much like those temptations of a heterosexual nature such as the desire to commit fornication or adultery.

Biblical references to homosexuality are relatively few. Genesis 19:1–11 tells the story of an attempted homosexual gang rape at the house of Lot by the wicked men of Sodom. Verse 5 mentions specifically the homosexual intentions of the men of Sodom ("to know" referring to having sex). Lot considers this behavior wicked (v. 7). Raping his daughters was considered the lesser of two evils (v. 8). This evil of Sodom is mentioned elsewhere (Jer. 23:14; Ezek. 16:49–50; 2 Pet. 2:6–10; Jude 7) in the strongest terms of condemnation. The term "sodomy" has its roots here. A similar story is found in Judges 19:22–30.

In the Holiness Code of Leviticus, homosexuality is considered an abomination (18:22), and such behavior was to be punished by death (20:13).

In the New Testament the early church also considered homosexuality as sinful behavior. Although Jesus never mentioned such behavior, probably because the problem never arose during His ministry among Jewish people, Paul clearly condemned homosexuality. Romans 1:26–27 considers homosexuality to be a sign of God's wrath upon blind sinfulness. Such behavior is considered a degrading passion, unnatural, an indecent act, and an error, even worthy of death (Rom. 1:32).

Some of the Corinthian Christians apparently had been homosexuals (1 Cor. 6:9–11). Having mentioned homosexuality, Paul stated that "such were some of you" (v. 11). Through faith in Christ they had been "washed," "sanctified," and "justified" (v. 11). Paul implied here that homosexual behavior is forgivable through the gospel and that any homosexual temptations should be resisted as seriously as those toward fornication or adultery (mentioned in v. 9). Paul also taught that homosexuality was contrary to "sound doctrine" (1 Tim. 1:10).

The Bible does not recognize homosexuality as biologically consitutional or hereditary (as a kind of third sex), but sees its roots in the sinful nature of man—a psychosocial, learned behavior, expressing rebellion against God and calling for redemption. Such persons are responsible for their behavior. This is a very complex psychological problem with many possible roots or causes, calling for both Christian compassion on the part of God's people as well as God's redemptive power through the gospel. The ministry of the church to homosexuals should include: conversion, counseling, education, and support-group relationships.

Guy Greenfield

HONESTY Fairness and straightforwardness of conduct. The KJV frequently used honesty or cognates where modern translations use other words: honorable/honorably (Rom. 13:13; Phil. 4:8; Heb. 13:18; 1 Pet. 2:12); noble (Luke 8:15; Rom. 12:17); dignity (1 Tim. 2:2); properly (1 Thess. 4:12). Men of "honest report" (Acts 6:3) are men of good standing (NRSV).

Someone in the right in a law case may be described as honest (Ex. 23:7 NIV). Isaiah lamented that "no one goes to law honestly" (59:4 NRSV). Honest or just balances, weights, and measures give fair and accurate measure (Lev. 19:36; Deut. 25:15; Prov. 16:11). Job 31:6 prays God's judgment to be weighed in an honest balance so God can know the person's integrity. Scripture often refers to honest or right speech (Job 6:25; Prov. 12:17; 16:13; 24:26). Those working on the Temple construction were known for their honest business dealings (2 Kings 12:15; 22:7).

Jacob claimed honesty (Gen. 30:33) but manipulated the breeding of Laban's flocks (30:37–43). Jacob's sons repeatedly assured Joseph of their honesty (Gen. 42:11,19,31,33,34), never guessing that their brother knew their deceptive natures all too well (37:31–33).

HONEY produced by bees providing a sweet food stuff for people to eat.

Old Testament During Bible times, honey appeared in three forms: (1) honey deposited from wild bees (Deut. 32:13), (2) honey from domesticated bees (one of the products "of the field" 2 Chron. 31:5), and (3) a syrup made from dates and grape juice (2 Kings 18:32). Honey served as a food stuff (Gen. 43:11) and as an item of trade (Ezek. 27:17).

Almost all references to honey in the Old Testament are to wild honey. Bees made their honeycombs and deposited their honey in holes in the ground (1 Sam. 14:25); under rocks or in crevices between rocks (Deut. 32:13); or in the carcasses of animals (Judges 14:8).

Honey was prohibited from being used in burnt offerings because it fermented easily (Lev. 2:11). Honey was rare enough to be considered a luxury item (Gen. 43:11; 1 Kings 14:3). Honey was so ample in Canaan that the land there was described as a land "flowing with milk and honey" (Ex. 3:8).

Bee keeping is not mentioned specifically in the Old Testament. In later times bee keeping was practiced by the Jews. The hives were of straw and wicker. Before removing the combs, the bee keeper stupefied the bees with fumes of charcoal and cow dung burnt in front of the hives.

The Lord's ordinances are "sweeter than honey" (Psa. 19:10). God's goodness to Jerusalem was expressed by the phrase "you ate honey" (Ezek. 16:13).

New Testament Honey is mentioned in three New Testament passages (Matt. 3:4; Mark 1:6; Rev. 10:9–10). In New Testament times, honey was viewed as a food eaten by lowly people (Matt. 3:4; Mark 1:6). *Gary Hardin*

HONOR See *Shame and Honor*

HOOD KJV term for one of the items of finery worn by the elite women of Jerusalem (Isa. 3:23). Modern translations render the underlying Hebrew as scarf (TEV), tiara (NIV), or turban (NAS, NRSV, REB). It represented a fine Oriental head covering.

HOOF A curved covering of horn protecting the front of or enclosing the digits of some mammals. According to Mosaic law, ritually clean animals are those which both chew the cud and have cloven (divided) hooves (Deut. 14:6–7).

HOOK A curved or bent device for catching, holding, or pulling. Some biblical uses, for example, hanging curtains (Ex. 26:32; 27:10) or fishing (Isa. 19:8; Job. 40:24; Hab. 1:15; Matt. 17:27), are familiar today. (KJV often uses angle.) Less familiar is the practice of ancient conquerors who led their captives by means of hooks or thongs put through their noses or jaws (2 Chron. 33:11; Ezek. 38:4; Amos 4:2).

HOOPOE Any of the Old World birds of the family *Upupidae,* having a plumed head crest and a long, slender, curved bill. The identity of the unclean bird of Leviticus 11:19 (Deut. 14:18) is disputed: lapwing (KJV); hoopoe (modern English translations); waterhen (earliest Greek); woodcock (Targum).

HOPE Trustful expectation, particularly with reference to the fulfillment of God's promises. Biblical hope is the anticipation of a favorable outcome under God's guidance. More specifically, hope is the confidence that what God has done for us in the past guarantees our participation in what God will do in the future. This contrasts to the world's definition of hope as "a feeling that what is wanted will happen."

The Ground and Object of Hope In the Old Testament, God alone is the ultimate ground and object of hope. Hope in God was generated by His might deeds in history. In fulfilling His promise to Abraham (Gen. 12:1–3), He redeemed the Israelites from bondage in Egypt. He provided for their needs in the wilderness, formed them into a covenant community at Sinai, and led them into the successful occupation of Canaan. These acts provided a firm base for their confidence in God's continuing purpose for them. Even when Israel was unfaithful, hope was not lost. Because of God's faithfulness and mercy, those who returned to Him could count on His help (Mal. 3:6–7). This help included forgiveness (2 Chron. 7:14; Ps. 86:5) as well as deliverance from enemies. Thus, Jeremiah addressed God as the "hope of Israel, the saviour thereof in time of trouble" (Jer. 14:8; compare 14:22; 17:13).

A corollary of putting one's hope in God is refusing to place one's final confidence in the created order. All created things are weak, transient, and apt to fail. For this reason it is futile to vest ultimate hope in wealth (Ps. 49:6–12; 52:7; Prov. 11:28), houses (Isa. 32:17–18), princes (Ps. 146:3), empires and armies (Isa. 31:1–3; 2 Kings 18:19–24), or even the Jerusalem Temple (Jer. 7:1–7). God, and God only, is a rock that cannot be moved (Deut. 32:4,15,18; Pss. 18:2; 62:2; Isa. 26:4) and a refuge and fortress who provides ultimate security (Pss. 14:6, 61:3; 73:28; 91:9). An accurate summary of the Old Testament emphasis is found in Psalm 119:49–50.

A significant aspect of Old Testament hope was Israel's expectation of a messiah, that is, an anointed ruler from David's line. This expectation grew out of the promise that God would establish the throne of David forever (2 Sam. 7:14). The anointed ruler (messiah) would be God's agent to restore Israel's glory and rule the nations in peace and righteousness. For the most part, however, David's successors were disappointments. The direction of the nation was away from the ideal. Thus, people looked to the future for a son of David who would fulfill the divine promise.

The New Testament continues to speak of God as the source and object of hope. Paul wrote that it was the "God who raises the dead" on whom "we have set our hope" (2 Cor. 1:9–10 NIV). Furthermore, "we have fixed our hope on the living God, who is the Savior of all men" (1 Tim. 4:10 NAS). Peter reminded his readers that "your faith and hope are in God" (1 Peter 1:21 NAS). In the New Testament, as in the Old, God is the "God of hope" (Rom. 15:13).

For the early Christians, hope is also focused in Christ. He is called "our hope" (1 Tim. 1:1), and the hope of glory is identified with "Christ in you" (Col. 1:27). Images applied to God in the Old Testament are transferred to Christ in the New. He is the Savior (Luke 2:11; Acts 13:23; Titus 1:4; 3:6), the source of life (John 6:35), the rock on which hope is built (1 Pet. 2:4–7). He is the first and last (Rev. 1:17), the day-spring dispelling darkness and leading His people into eternal day (Rev. 22:5).

New Testament writers spoke of Christ as the object and ground of hope for two reasons. 1) He is the Messiah who has brought salvation by His life, death, and resurrection (Luke 24:46). God's promises are fulfilled in Him. "For in him every one of God's promises is a 'Yes' " (2 Cor. 1:20 NRSV). 2) They are aware of the unity between Father and Son. This is a unity of nature (John 1:1; Col. 1:19) as well as a unity in the work of redemption. Because "God was in Christ, reconciling the world unto himself" (2 Cor. 5:19), hope in the Son is one with hope in the Father.

The Future of Hope While the New Testament affirms the sufficiency of Christ's redemptive work in the past, it also looks forward to His return in the future to complete God's purpose. Indeed, the major emphasis on hope in the New Testament centers on the second coming of Christ. The "blessed hope" of the Church is nothing less than "the glorious appearing of the great God and our Saviour Jesus Christ" (Titus 2:13). See *Future Hope.*

The Assurance of Hope Christians live in hope for two basic reasons. The first reason is because of what God has done in Christ. Especially important is the emphasis the New Testament places on the resurrection by which Christ has defeated the power of sin and death. "By his great mercy he has given us a new birth into a living hope through the resurrection of Jesus Christ from the dead" (1 Peter 1:3 NRSV).

The second reason is the indwelling of the Holy

Spirit. "The Spirit itself beareth witness with our spirit, that we are the children of God" (Rom. 8:16).

Given the assurance of hope, Christians live in the present with confidence and face the future with courage. They can also meet trials triumphantly because they know "that suffering produces perseverance; perseverance character; and character, hope" (Rom. 5:3–4 NIV). Such perseverance is not passive resignation; it is the confident endurance in the face of opposition. There is, therefore, a certitude in Christian hope which amounts to a qualitative difference from ordinary hope. Christian hope is the gift of God. "We have this hope as an anchor for the soul, firm and secure" (Heb. 6:19 NIV).   *Bert Dominy*

HOPHNI AND PHINEHAS (Hŏph' nī and Phin' ė hàs) Personal names meaning, "tadpole" and "dark-skinned one" in Egyptian. In 1 Samuel 1:3, sons of Eli and priests at Shiloh. They were disreputable men who were contemptuous of sacred matters. They were slain in battle against the Philistines (1 Sam. 4:4). The news of their deaths precipitated the death of their father Eli (1 Sam. 4:18). See *Eli; Samuel.*

HOPHRA (Hŏph' rà) Egyptian divine name meaning, "the heart of Re endures." Egyptian pharaoh (589–569 B.C.). At the beginning of his reign he tried to drive the Babylonian army away from its siege of Jerusalem (Jer. 37:5). Apparently at that time Jeremiah mocked the Pharaoh, making a pun on his name, calling him a loud-voiced boaster ("King Bombast, the man who missed his opportunity" Jer. 46:17 REB). Jeremiah warned that the pharaoh would be handed over to his enemies, at the same time warning Jews living in Egypt that salvation history was reversed and they would be destroyed (Jer. 44:26–30). Hophra's death would be a sign to the Jews that Jeremiah's words were true. Hophra eventually lost his power in a revolt by his general Amasis in 569 B.C. Condemnation of Hophra showed Jeremiah's consistency in opposing any opposition to Babylon, whom God had chosen to punish His disobedient people. See *Egypt.*

HOR (Hôr) Place name, perhaps an ancient variant of Hebrew common noun, *har,* "mountain." *1.* Place where Aaron, the high priest, died, fulfilling God's word that he would be punished for rebelling at the water of Meribah (Num. 20:22–29; 33:38–39). Moses installed Aaron's son Eleazar as high priest on the mountain. It was apparently a brief journey from Kadesh and lay near the coast of Edom (Num. 20:22–23). The traditional location at Jebel Harun above Petra is too far inside Edom and too far from Kadesh, though high (4800 feet) and impressive. Recently Bible students have pointed to Jebel Madurah, northeast of

Kadesh on Edom's border. Deuteronomy 10:6 places Aaron's death at Mosera, an unknown site which may be under Mount Hor. Israel journeyed from Mount Hor to go around Edom (Num. 21:4; 33:41). *2.* Mountain marking northern boundary of Promised Land (Num. 34:7–8). The location is unknown, though some would see Hor as a variant name for Mount Hermon.

HOR-HAGGIDGAD (Hôr-hăg gĭd' găd) Place name perhaps meaning, "hill of crickets." Station on Israel's wilderness journey (Num. 33:32–33). It may be in the Wadi Geraphi, though no certain location is known. It appears to be a variant spelling of Gudgodah (Deut. 10:7).

HOR-HAGIDGAD (Hôr-hà gĭd' găd) KJV spelling of Hor-Haggidgad.

HORAM (Hō' răm) Personal name perhaps meaning, "high, exalted." King of Gezer whose attempt to deliver Lachish from Joshua resulted in his death and the annihilation of his army (Josh. 10:33), though his city remained a Canaanite stronghold (Josh. 16:10; compare 1 Kings 9:16).

HOREB An alternative name for Mount Sinai (Ex. 3:1–12; 17:6–7; Deut. 1:19; 5:2; 1 Kings 19:8). See *Sinai, Mount.*

HOREM (Hō' rĕm) Place name meaning, "split rock" but sounding like the word for "war booty under the ban." City in tribal allotment of Naphtali (Josh. 19:38). Location is unknown.

HORESH (Hō' rĕsh) Place name meaning, "forest," KJV interpreting the term as a common noun. As David hid there from Saul, Jonathan, Saul's son, came out to help him and made a covenant of mutual help (1 Sam. 23:15–18). The people of Ziph revealed David's hideout, but David still escaped. If a proper name, Horesh may be modern khirbet Khoreisa, two miles south of Ziph and six miles south of Hebron.

HORI (Hō' rī) Personal name meaning "bleached," "lesser," or "Horite." *1.* An Edomite descended from Seir (Gen. 36:22). *2.* Father of the leader of tribe of Simeon under Moses in the wilderness (Num. 13:5).

HORIM (Hō' rĭm) KJV spelling for Horites. See *Horites.*

HORITES (Hō' rites) The pre-Edomite inhabitants of Mount Seir in the southern Transjordan.

The Hebrew word for Horites corresponds to the extrabiblical Hurrians, a non-Semitic people who migrated into the Fertile Crescent about 2000 B.C. The Hurrians created the Mitannian Empire in Mesopotamia about 1500 B.C. and later became an important element in the Canaanite population of Palestine. In locations where there is extrabiblical evidence for Hurrians, the Hebrew term Hivites appears (Gen. 34:2; Josh. 9:7; 11:3,19) as a designation for certain elements of the Canaanite population. The Septuagint (the ancient Greek translation of the Old Testament), however, substitutes Horites for Hivites in Genesis 34:2 and Joshua 9:7. Also, Zibeon, son of Seir the Horite (Gen. 36:20), is identified as a Hivite in Genesis 36:2. For these reasons, many scholars equate both Horites and Hivites (the names are quite similar in Hebrew) with the extrabiblical Hurrians.

Nevertheless, the Hebrew text only mentions Horites in Mt. Seir where there is no record of Hurrians. Therefore, another suggestion holds that the biblical Horites were not Hurrians, but simply the original cave-dwelling (the Hebrew *hor* means "cave") population of Edom (Mt. Seir). The Hivites, according to this theory, should be identified with the extrabiblical Hurrians.

Daniel C. Browning, Jr.

HORMAH (Hôr' măh) Place name meaning, "split rock" or "cursed for destruction." City marking the limit of the Canaanite rout of the Israelites after the failed Israelite attempt to invade Canaan that followed the report of the twelve spies (Num. 14:45). Though the exact location of Hormah is not known, it was in the territory assigned to the tribe of Simeon (Josh. 19:4). Some identify it with tell Masos about seven miles east of Beersheba. Excavations have shown settlement in about 1800 B.C. and again just before 1200 B.C. The latter settlement apparently lasted until the time of David (compare 1 Sam. 30:30). A small fortress was built some time after 700 B.C. and destroyed shortly after 600 B.C.

The site controlled the east-west road in the Beersheba Valley and the north-south road to Hebron. Israel gained brief victory there (Num. 21:3) after their earlier defeat (Num. 14:45; compare Deut. 1:44). The list of kings Joshua defeated includes Hormah (Josh. 12:14); the battle description says Judah and Simeon combined to take Hormah after Joshua's death (Judg. 1:1,17), the city earlier being called Zephath. See *Zephath.*

HORN Curved bone-like structures growing from the heads of animals such as deer or goats and vessels or instruments made from or shaped like such horns. In Scripture horn refers to trumpets, vessels, topographical features, and figurative symbols.

Old Testament The basic meaning of horns relate to animal horns (Gen. 22:13; Deut. 33:17; Dan. 8:5). Elephant tusks were also called horns (Ezek. 27:15). Horns are mentioned being used as trumpets (Josh. 6:5). Such instruments were perforated horns of the ram or the wild ox used to sound ceremonial or military signals. Priests sounded trumpets to call to worship. Trumpets later were made of silver. See *Music.* Horns also were used as vessels. Being hollow and easy to polish, horns were used to hold liquids for drinking or storage, including ceremonial anointing oil (1 Sam. 16:1). Horn-like projections were built onto the corners of the altar of burnt offerings in the Temple and in tabernacles (Ex. 27:2). The horns were smeared with the blood of the sacrifice, served as binding posts for the sacrifice, and were clung to for safety from punishment (1 Kings 2:28).

As a topographical feature, the peaks or summits of Palestinian hills were called horns (Isa. 51:1). Metaphorically, horn signified the strength and honor of people and brightness and rays. Such references are used in Scripture as emblems of power of God (Heb. 3:4) and other physical or spiritual entities. There is an apocalyptic use of the word in Dan. 7:7. Horns budding or sprouting is a figurative language indication of a sign of revival of a nation or power.

New Testament Christ is called "an horn of salvation" (Luke 1:69), which is a methaphorical use of the word signifying strength. Other figurative uses include the Lamb with seven horns mentioned in the Book of Revelation (Rev. 5:6); the beast with ten horns rising up out of the sea (Rev. 13:1); and the scarlet beast of the great prostitute also having ten horns (Rev. 17:3,7). Those references represent antichristian powers.

J. William Thompson

HORNED OWL Any species of owl having conspicuous tufts of feathers on the head. The NIV reckons the horned owl an unclean bird (Lev. 11:16; Deut. 14:15). The precise identity of the bird is unclear. Other possibilities include: desert owl (REB); owl (KJV); and ostrich (NAS, NRSV). See *Birds in the Bible.*

HORNED SNAKE A venomous viper (*Cerastes cornutus*) of the Near East having a horny protrusion above each eye. Dan is compared to a horned snake (Gen. 49:17 NAS, REB). See *Animals, Reptiles.*

HORNETS See *Insects.*

HORONAIM (Hŏr ō nā' ĭm) Place name meaning, "twin caves." Prominent town in Moab upon which Isaiah (15:5) and Jeremiah (48:3,5,34) pronounced laments, warning of coming destruction. It apparently lay in the southwestern part of Moab, but students of biblical geography debate its exact location. Suggestions include khirbet ad-Dubababout three miles west northwest of Majra; khirbet al-Maydan, west of modern Katrabba, and ed-Dayr, about two miles northwest of Rakin.

HORONITE (Hŏr' ō nīte) Citizen of Beth-horon or of Horonaim. A description of Sanballat, who led opposition to Nehemiah (Neh. 2:10). To which of the two possible places Sanballat belonged, we do not know.

HORSE See *Animals; Megiddo.*

Relief of horses harnessed to and turning a mill, first century A.D.

HORSE GATE Gate on east side of city wall of Jerusalem near the Temple. Jeremiah promised its rebuilding (Jer. 31:40), and the priests under Nehemiah rebuilt it (Neh. 3:28).

HORSELEACH KJV term for a leech (Prov. 30:15).

HORSEMAN A rider on a horse. The plural frequently refers to a cavalry (Ex. 14:9–28; Josh. 24:6; 1 Sam. 8:11). This association of horsemen with armed forces perhaps sparked the use of the four riders of Revelation 6:2–8 as symbols of military conquest, war, economic injustice, and death and Hades.

HOSAH (Hō' sah) Personal and place name perhaps meaning, "seeker of refuge." *1.* Coastal city in tribal territory of Asher (Josh. 19:29), probably modern tell Rashidiyeh near Tyre and known in ancient Egyptian and Assyrian texts as Usu. Other biblical geographers would see the fortified

city of Tyre as tell Rashidiyeh (Usu) and locate Hosah further from Tyre and the coast. *2.* Gatekeeper of the sanctuary under David (1 Chron. 16:38). He belonged to the priestly clan of Merari (1 Chron. 26:10). He was in charge of the west gate (1 Chron. 26:16).

HOSANNA (Hō săn' nà) Cry with which Jesus was greeted on the occasion of His triumphal entrance into Jerusalem (Mark 11:9). The words with which the Savior was welcomed by the multitude are drawn from Psalm 118:25–26. "Hosanna" is a Hebrew or Aramaic word that is best translated as a prayer: "Save now," or "Save, we beseech Thee." When the residents of Jerusalem, carrying palm branches, met Jesus and hailed Him as the One who comes in the name of the Lord, they included in their acclamation a plea for salvation. See *Psalms; Triumphant Entry.*

HOSEA (Hō sē' à) Personal name meaning, "salvation." Title of the first book in the section of the Hebrew Bible called the Book of the Twelve, named after its prophetic hero. The small prophetic books that make up this section frequently are designated Minor Prophets. This title is not an assessment of worth, but a description of size as compared to Isaiah, Jeremiah, and Ezekiel. In Hebrew the name is the same as that of Joshua's original name (Num. 13:16; Deut. 32:44) and of the last king of Israel (2 Kings 17:1), who lived at the same time as the prophet. One of David's officers bore the name (1 Chron. 27:20) as did a clan chief in the time of Nehemiah (Neh. 10:23). English translators have often chosen to spell the prophet's name Hosea to distinguish him from the others, whose names they spell, Hoshea.

The prophet's name "Hosea" appears in the Bible only at Hosea 1:1,2; Romans 9:25. Assyria's rise to power posed a constant threat to Israel's national existence. Hosea's name symbolized the pressing need for national deliverance. His message pointed the nation to the deliverer (Hos. 13:4).

The Book The two broad divisions of the Book of Hosea are: (1) Hosea's Marriage, Hosea 1—3; and (2) Hosea's Messages, Hosea 4—14. A pattern of judgment followed by hope recurs in each of the first three chapters. A similar pattern is discernible in the oracles of Hosea (Hos. 4—14), though the pattern is not balanced as neatly nor revealed as clearly. Certainly the book ends on a hopeful note (Hos. 14), but most of the oracles in chapters 4—13 are judgmental in nature. The dominant theme of the book is love (covenant fidelity), God's unrelenting love for His wayward people and Israel's unreliable love for God.

The Prophet Hosea is identified in the title verse (1:1) as a genuine prophet to whom "the word of the Lord" came. That phrase designates the source of his authority and describes his credentials. Not only are Hosea's oracles (Hos. 4—14) the word of the Lord to Israel, but so also are the materials dealing with his domestic problems (Hos. 1—3). Based on information gleaned from his book, Hosea was from the Northern Kingdom of Israel. His familiarity with place names, religious practices, and political conditions in Israel suggests that he was a native. In contrast, Amos, who ministered as a prophet in Israel shortly before Hosea's ministry there, was from Tekoa in Judah. Both prophets preached judgment, Amos with a lion's roar and Hosea with a broken heart.

Placement of Hosea's ministry in the days of Uzziah, Jotham, Ahaz, and Hezekiah indicates that he was a contemporary of Isaiah. The title verse of Isaiah contains the same list of Judean kings. Jeroboam II is the only Israelite king named in the title to Hosea's book, in spite of the fact that internal evidence suggests that Hosea's ministry continued from the last days of Jeroboam II to near the end of the Northern Kingdom (approximately 750–725 B.C.).

Hosea's prophetic ministry included the period of Near Eastern history when Assyria emerged as a new world empire under the capable leadership of Tiglath-pileser III (745–727 B.C.). Hosea rebuked efforts at alliance with Assyria and Egypt as the means to national security. He witnessed the political chaos in Israel following the death of Jeroboam II. Four of the last six kings to sit on Israel's throne were assassinated. Hosea had the unenviable task of presiding over the death of his beloved nation, but he held out hope of national revival based on radical repentance (Hos. 14).

The Marriage Hosea's marriage and family life dominate chapters 1—3 and surface from time to time in the remainder of the book. References to Hosea's family serve as prophetic symbolism of God and His family Israel. God ordered Hosea to take a wife of harlotry and have children of harlotry "for the land hath committed great whoredom, departing from the Lord" (Hos. 1:2). Primary interest is not in Hosea and his family, but in God and His family. How to interpret the prophet's marriage is not a settled issue. A few take the marriage to be an allegory. Some accept it as a literal marriage to a woman who became promiscuous after marriage. Most handle it as an actual marriage to a cult prostitute. Every interpreter must keep in mind the obvious intent of the material to serve as prophetic symbolism of God's relationship to Israel.

The Theology At the heart of Hosea's theology was the relationship between God and Israel. Yahweh alone was Israel's God. Israel was Yahweh's elect people. Hosea presented Yahweh as a faithful husband and Israel as an unfaithful wife. Hosea's stress is not upon righteousness and justice, as was the case with Amos, but the knowledge of God and loyal love. God's love for Israel would not permit Him to give up on them in spite of their lack of knowledge and infidelity. Hope for Israel's future lay in their repentance and God's forgiveness and love that made Him willing to restore their relationship.

Outline

I. God Loves His Unfaithful People (1:1—3:5).
   A. God's forgiveness has its limits (1:1–9).
   B. God promises a future reversal of His judgment upon His people (1:10—2:1).
   C. God works with His people to bring about reconciliation (2:2–15).
      1. God's legal actions call for His people's reform (2:2–5).
      2. God places obstacles in the path of His people to turn them back to God (2:6–8).
      3. God removes the bounty of His people to remind them that God is the Giver (2:9–13).
      4. God lures His people into the wilderness to open a door of hope (2:14–15).
   D. God initiates a new covenant with His people (2:16–23).
   E. God's love is the basis of future hope for His people (3:1–5).

II. Unfaithfulness Is the Basis of God's Controversy with His People (4:1—9:9).
   A. Unfaithful people break covenant commitments (4:1–3).
   B. Unfaithful ministers bring judgment on the people and on themselves (4:4–12a).
   C. An alien spirit dominates unfaithful people (4:12b–19).
   D. God chastises His unfaithful people (5:1–15).
      1. God disciplines unfaithful leaders (5:1–2).
      2. God disciplines because He knows His people fully (5:3).
      3. Pride prevents repentance and promotes stumbling (5:4–5).
      4. Extravagant giving is no substitute for lapses in living (5:6–7).
      5. God is the agent of punishment for His people (5:8–14).
      6. God seeks the return of His people through discipline (5:15).
   E. Surface repentance does not satisfy the sovereign God (6:1–3).
   F. Sharp judgment comes upon fleeting loyalty (6:4–5).
   G. Loyal love and personal knowledge of God meet His requirements (6:6).
   H. Covenant-breaking hinders restoration of God's people (6:7—7:2).
   I. Making leaders by power politics shuts God out of the process (7:3–7).
   J. Compromise leads to loss of strength and alienation from God (7:8–10).

H

K. Diplomatic duplicity interferes with God's redemptive activity (7:11–13).

L. Religious perversion ends in apostasy and bondage (7:14–16).

M. God's unfaithful people reap more than they sow (8:1—9:9).

   1. The unfaithful disregard divine law (8:1–2).

   2. The unfaithful reject God's goodness (8:3).

   3. The unfaithful practice idolatory (8:4–6).

   4. The unfaithful will reap foreign domination (8:7–10).

   5. The unfaithful will reap religious and moral corruption (8:11–13a).

   6. The unfaithful will reap national destruction (8:13b–14).

   7. The unfaithful will reap exile in a foreign land (9:1–4).

   8. The unfaithful will reap punishment for their sins (9:5–9).

III. God's Loyal Love Is the Only Basis for a Lasting Relationship with His People (9:10—14:9).

A. Without God's love His people perish (9:10–17).

B. Without reverence for God, His people have no future (10:1–8).

   1. Ornate altars cannot hide deceitful hearts (10:1–2).

   2. Bad leaders produce bad times (10:3–8).

C. Without righteousness God's people cannot experience God's unfailing love (10:9–15).

D. God's love for His people will not allow Him to give them up (11:1–11).

E. Covenant-making with alien powers is infidelity to God (11:12—12:1).

F. Judgment according to deeds is a universal principle (12:2–6).

G. Deception is repaid by destruction (12:7–14).

H. Rebellion against God leads to death (13:1–16).

I. Repentance results in restoration and life for God's people (14:1–9).

Billy K. Smith

HOSEN KJV term for hose or leggings (Dan. 3:21). The meaning of the underlying Aramaic term is disputed: leggings (NAS margin); robes (TEV); shirts (REB); trousers (NAS, NIV, NRSV); tunics (RSV).

HOSHAIAH (Hō shāī′ iah) Personal name meaning, "Yah saved." *1.* Father of Jewish leader who lead delegation requesting Jeremiah's prayer support (Jer. 42:1) and then rejected Jeremiah's word from God (Jer. 43:2). *2.* Leader of Jewish group in celebration upon the completion of the Jerusalem wall under Nehemiah (Neh. 12:32).

HOSHAMA (Hōsh′ à mà) Personal name, an abbreviated form of Jehoshama, "Yahweh heard." Descendant of David during the Exile (1 Chron. 3:18).

HOSHEA (Hō shē′ à) See *Hosea*.

HOSPITALITY To entertain or receive a stranger (sojourner) into one's home as an honored guest and to provide the guest with food, shelter, and protection. This was not merely an oriental custom or good manners but a sacred duty that everyone was expected to observe. Only the depraved would violate this obligation.

Hospitality probably grew out of the needs of nomadic life. Since public inns were rare, a traveler had to depend on the kindness of others and had a right to expect it. This practice was extended to every sojourner, even a runaway slave (Deut. 23:16–17) or one's arch enemy.

The Pentateuch contains specific commands for the Israelites to love the strangers as themselves (Lev. 19:33–34; Deut. 10:18–19), and to look after their welfare (Deut. 24:17–22). The reason for practicing hospitality was that the Israelites themselves were once strangers in the land of Egypt.

Some acts of hospitality were rewarded, the most notable of which was Rahab's (Josh. 6;22–25; Heb. 11:31; James 2:25). Breaches of hospitality were condemned and punished, such as those of Sodom (Gen. 19:1–11) and Gibeah (Judg. 19:10–25). The only exception was Jael who was praised for killing Sisera (Judg. 4:18–24).

Hospitality seemed to form the background of many details in the life of Jesus and the early church (Matt. 8:20; Luke 7:36; 9:2–5; 10:4–11). It was to be a characteristic of bishops and widows (1 Tim. 3:2; 5:10; Titus 1:8) and a duty of Christians (Rom. 12:13; 1 Pet. 4:9). It was a natural expression of brotherly love (Heb. 13:1–2; 1 Pet. 4:8–9) and a necessary tool of evangelism. Furthermore, one might even entertain angels or the Lord unawares (Heb. 13:2; Matt. 25:31–46). *Lai Ling Elizabeth Ngan*

HOST OF HEAVEN The army at God's command, composed of either heavenly bodies such as sun, moon, and stars or angels.

"Host" is basically a military term connected with fighting or waging a war. The most frequent use of the word is to designate a group of men organized for war. In this sense, the Hebrew word often refers to a human army (Gen. 21:22,32; Judg. 4:2,7; 9:29; 1 Sam. 12:9; 2 Sam. 3:23; Isa. 34:2; Jer. 51:3). The term can refer to an act of war, as in Numbers 1:3,20; Deuteronomy 24:5, and Joshua 22:12. An extended meaning of "hosts" is that it designates a length of time of hard service (Job 7:1; Isa. 40:2, Dan. 10:1). The term is used in the Book of Numbers to refer to the service of the Levites in the sanctuary.

The phrase "Host of Heaven" came into use because of the close connection between the realms of earth and heaven in ancient thought. The celestial bodies were thought to be organized in the same way as earthly military bodies. The sun, moon, and stars were regarded as the "host of heaven" (Gen. 2:1). The author of Psalms 33:6 stated that God created this host by His breath. God preserved the existence of the host of heaven (Isa. 40:26).

Old Testament writers warned Israel about the danger of worshiping the heavenly bodies (Deut. 4:19) and prescribed the death penalty for the crime of worshiping the sun, or the moon, or any of the "host of heaven" (Deut. 17:2–7). Unfortunately, Israel and Judah yielded to the temptation to worship the heavenly bodies from time to time, especially during the period of Assyrian and Babylonian influence (2 Kings 17:16–23; 21:3,5).

Manasseh, king of Judah (697 to 642 B.C.), built altars in Jerusalem for all the "host of heaven" (2 Kings 21:5). He attempted to merge the worship of other gods with the worship of Yahweh. Manasseh's efforts were reversed when Josiah came to the throne (2 Kings 23:7).

Another concept of the "host of heaven" is presented in passages similar to 1 Kings 22:19, in which the prophet Micaiah stated that he saw the Lord sitting on his throne ". . . and all the host of heaven standing by him. . . ." The people of Israel drew comparisons between their God and the gods of Canaan and Babylonia. Yahweh came to be understood as a king who presided over a heavenly council, composed of angelic servants, sometimes called "sons of God." This concept is reflected in the first two chapters of Job. See *Angels; Council, Heavenly; Sons of God.*   *James Newell*

HOSTAGE A person held as security against rebellion or aggression. When King Joash of Israel defeated King Amaziah of Judah, he took hostages (2 Kings 14:14; 2 Chron. 25:24).

HOSTS, LORD OF See *Lord of Hosts.*

HOTHAM (Hō′ thăm) Personal name meaning, "seal" or "lock." *1.* Member of tribe of Asher (1 Chron. 7:32). *2.* Father of two warriors in David's army (1 Chron. 11:44). Their home was Aroer.

HOTHAN (Hō′ thăn) KJV spelling of Hotham in 1 Chronicles 11:44.

HOTHIR (Hō′ thĭr) Personal name meaning, "he caused to be a remnant." Priestly musician in the clan of Heman under David (1 Chron. 25:4). He led the twenty-first course of Levites (1 Chron. 25:28).

HOUGH KJV term meaning to hamstring (Josh. 11:6,9; 2 Sam. 8:4; 1 Chron. 18:4). See *Hamstring.*

HOUND To harass continually (Job 19:28; Ps. 109:16; Ezek. 36:3 NIV).

HOUR An appointed time for meeting or for religious festival, a brief moment of time, one twelfth of the day or of the night, and in the Gospel of John the significant period of Jesus' saving mission on earth from His triumphal entry until His death and resurrection.

Biblical Hebrew has no word for hour, only an expression for an appointed meeting time (1 Sam. 9:24 RSV). The New Testament term *hora* can refer to a general time of day, a "late hour" (Matt. 14:15 NRSV), to a brief moment of time (Rev. 18:17; compare John 5:35), or to the time of an expected momentous event (Matt. 8:13; Mark 13:11). It also designates a period of time, somewhat flexible in duration, one twelfth of the daylight hours and one twelfth of the night, a day being divided into the two periods (or watches) of light and darkness beginning at sunrise, making the seventh hour (John 4:52) about one p.m.

Jesus' hour is a central theme in John's Gospel, creating an emotional uncertainty and expectancy and a theological understanding of the central importance of Jesus' death and resurrection. In John's Gospel, "hour" usually refers to the period from the triumphant entry (12:23) until the climactic death and resurrection.

The Johannine theme of Jesus' "hour" makes a significant theological contribution to the Gospel. As the reader encounters this motif repeatedly, a perspective on Jesus' death develops that is quite different from that gained in the other Gospels. Without trivializing the reality of Jesus' suffering and death, the Gospel of John presents that event as the "hour" of Jesus' "glory," the time of His "exaltation/lifting up." Jesus' death is the means by which eternal life is provided for the world (3:14–15; 6:51–53). From that hour on human distinctions no longer apply (4:21–24; 11:51–53; 12:20–23). The glory of Jesus' death is found both in what it enabled him to offer the world (6:51–53; 7:37–39) and in its being the means by which He returned to the Father (13:1). The accounts of the empty tomb and the appearances of the risen Jesus in 20:1–21:23 serve to underscore the glory of His "hour." See *Glory; John; Time.*   *R. Robert Creech*

HOUSE A place where people live, usually in extended family units which can then be called a house.

Abraham left Mesopotamia where he lived in

houses made of mud brick (compare Gen. 11:3) and became a tent dweller (Heb. 11:9). Tents were made of goat hair and were suitable to nomadic life. His descendants apparently lived in tents until the time of Joshua, when they captured Canaan and began to build houses like the Canaanites. In the lowlands of the Jordan Valley the houses were built of mud brick because stone was not readily available. This type of construction may still be seen in the refugee camps of modern Jericho. In the hill country field stones were used. Although slight differences existed in house construction over centuries of time, those which have been excavated manifest a similar style. The homes of the poor were small and modest, consisting of one to four rooms, usually, and almost always including a courtyard on the east of the house so that the prevailing westerly winds would blow the smoke away from the house. In this courtyard the family carried on most of its activity. Food was prepared here in an oven built of clay. Storage jars were kept here, and animals were often housed here. However, the house only met the essential needs of family life such as shelter, a place to prepare food, make clothing and pottery, care for animals, etc. Social life was normally conducted at the community well or spring, the city gate, the marketplace, or in the fields at work. Because of the heat in summer and the cold in the winter, houses were built with few, if any, windows. This also provided more protection from intruders, but it meant that the houses were dark and uninviting. The only escape from the dim, cramped interior of the house was the courtyard

Reconstruction of an eighth-century B.C. Israelite house, showing rooms for sleeping on straw mats and for storage. The outer courtyard was used for food preparation, cooking, and to house small animals. Construction of houses did not change much over centuries until the New Testament period. So, this was a typical pattern for the average home of the Old Testament period.

and especially the flat roof. Here, the women of the house could do many of their daily chores— the washing, weaving, drying of figs and dates, and even the cooking. It was a wonderful place to enjoy the cool breezes in the heat of the day and to sleep in the summer (Acts 10:9; compare 2 Kings 4:10). The roof was supported by beams laid across the tops of narrow rooms, which were then covered by brush and mud packed to a firm and smooth surface. The paralytic at Capernaum was let down to Jesus through a hole "dug out" of such a roof (Mark 2:4; it was covered with clay tiles—Luke 5:19). In the time of Moses, the Israelites were required to build a bannister around the roof to prevent falling off (Deut. 22:8).

Unlike the poor, wealthy families built larger houses which sometimes utilized cut stone. They furnished them with chairs, tables, and couches which could double as beds. The poor had neither the space nor money for furniture. They ate and slept on floor mats which could be rolled out for that purpose. Most floors consisted of beaten earth, although some were made of mud and lime plaster and occasionally even limestone slabs. The wealthy in the time of the New Testament were able to cover their floors with beautiful mosaics and adorn their plastered walls with lovely frescoes. By this time, many of the better homes, under Roman influence, included atria, which added to the concept of outdoor living already experienced in the courtyards and on the roofs. There is evidence that two story houses were built throughout biblical times, the upper floor being reached by outside stairs or ladders.

John McRay

HOUSE OF THE ARCHIVES See *House of the Rolls.*

HOUSE OF THE FOREST OF LEBANON A designation for a great hall Solomon constructed as part of his palace complex in Jerusalem (1 Kings 7:2–5), so called because of the extensive use of cedar for the pillars, beams, and roofing material. In this hall were stored 300 shields of gold and vessels of gold (1 Kings 10:17–21). See *Hall.*

HOUSE OF THE ROLLS The place mentioned in Ezra 6:1 where records of the king's decrees and actions were kept. The archives were kept sometimes in the royal treasury (Ezra 5:17) or perhaps in the Temple. Jeremiah's scroll (Jer. 36:20–26) and the scroll of the law (2 Kings 22:8–9) were probably kept in such an archive. The records pertaining to the reigns of the kings of Judah and Israel were probably also kept in archives of this kind. Genealogical records may have been stored in the archives (Ezra 4:15).

Cut-away reconstruction of a first-century A.D. Israelite house.

HOUSEHOLD The term "household" is descriptive of a wide variety of relationships in both the Old and New Testaments. The root word for household in the Old Testament is *byt,* which means literally, "house." Genesis 7:1 is an example of the use of the term "house" to refer simply to kinfolk, the members of one's own family. "Household" may also refer to a family's descendants as an organized body (Gen. 18:19; Deut. 25:9; 1 Kings 11:38). The Hebrew people as a nation or any of its tribes or clans may also be indicated by the term "household" (Ex. 19:3; 40:38; Isa. 8:17; Amos 3:13; 7:16). Paternal ancestry may be in view as well when a household is mentioned (Ex. 6:14; 12:3; Num. 1:2; Josh. 22:14). Finally, the term can be used to refer simply to household affairs: persons, property, belongings, etc. (Gen. 39:4; 1 Kings 4:6; 2 Kings 15:5; Isa. 22:15, 36:3).

In the New Testament, many derivatives of *oikos* (literally, "house") are used to refer to the members and affairs of a household. Consequently, the terms "house" and "household" are often used interchangeably in translation. The term may delineate an immediate family, as well as those employed in the service of that family (Matt. 13:57; 24:45; John 4:53; Acts 16:31). Descendants of a particular nation may also be described as a house or household as in Matthew 10:6 and Luke 1:27,69. "Household" or "house," moreover, may point to the property or the management of the affairs and belongings of a family or clan (Acts 7:10).

Next to the state, the household was the most important unit in the Greco-Roman world, largely because of its role as a guarantor of stability in society. If order prevailed in the household, so it would in the state. Just as the household was basic to society, so it was to Christianity. The life of the early church centered in houses or households (e.g. Acts 2:2,46; 12:12; Rom. 16:5,23; 1 Cor. 16:19). Household groups were the basic units that made up the church in any given locale.

Not only was the church composed of household groups, the household itself was often the focus of the church's evangelistic activity. Several texts mention the conversion of entire households: Acts 11:14; 16:15,31–34; 18:8. In the world in which the early church emerged, the household was organized around the head, and solidarity was expressed in a common religion. So it was that the faith of the head of the household was the faith of the entire household. Whenever the head of a household was converted and baptized, the remainder of his house usually followed suit as an expression of loyalty and religious unity. The motivation for conversion was at times social and not wholly individual, though in baptism each confessed Christ as Lord and showed forth His death and resurrection.

Household ideals also impacted the early church in significant ways. Household terms were used by the New Testament writers to express theological ideas. The church was referred to as the "household" of faith or of God (Gal. 6:10; Eph. 2:19). Household roles were appropriated by the Christian community: Christians were "servants" of God, and their leaders were "stewards" (1 Cor. 4:1; Titus 1:7; 1 Pet. 4:10). Because the household was so central to ancient society, much attention was given to delineating and clarifying the roles of the members of a household, be they family or servant. Standardized rules for behavior or domestic codes were developed in society, and these were adapted for use in the early church. Examples of lists of house rules or codes may be found in Colossians 3:18—4:1; Ephesians 5:21—6:9; 1 Peter 2:13—3:7.

See *Marriage; Servant; Slave; Steward; Temple.*
William J. Ireland, Jr.

HOWLING CREATURES The identity of the "howling creature" (NRSV) of Isaiah 13:21 is disputed. Suggestions include: the jackal (NIV); owl (NAS, KJV, TEV), porcupine (REB), and the laughing hyena. The precise identity of the creature is not so important as the complete desolation that its presence indicates.

HOZAI (Hō′ zā ī) Personal name meaning, "seer." NAS literal transliteration of Hebrew text of 1 Chronicles 33:19 making Hozai a prophet who recorded the reign of King Manasseh. Most translations follow Greek and one Hebrew manu-script in seeing one letter omitted from Hebrew, thus reading, "records of the seers" (NIV).

HUB The central portion of a wheel to which spokes are attached (1 Kings 7:33).

HUBBAH (Hŭb′ bah) NIV, NRSV reading of Jehubbah (1 Chron. 7:34) transliterating literally the Hebrew text. Most translations follow the early scribes' marginal note and the early translations in a slight change of the first Hebrew letter. See *Jehubbah.*

HUKKOK (Hŭk′ kŏk) Place name meaning, "hewn out." *1.* Town on border of tribal allotment of Naphtali between Mount Tabor and the border of Zebulun. It has traditionally been located at Yaquq northwest of the sea of Chinnereth, but that may be too far east. Recent proposals look at khirbet el-Jemeija, two miles west of Sakhmin (Josh. 19:34). *2.* The same Hebrew word names a levitical city in the tribe of Asher (1 Chron. 6:75), but the parallel passage (Josh. 21:31) reads Helkath. See *Helkath.*

HUKOK (Hū′ kŏk) Variant English spelling of Hebrew Hukkok. See *Hukkok.*

HUL (Hŭl) Personal name meaning, "ring." A son of Aram, son of Shem, and grandson of Noah in the Table of Nations (Gen. 10:23), thus the original ancestor of an Aramean or Syrian tribe. As often in genealogy lists, 1 Chronicles 1:17 omits the father Aram to emphasize the kinship with Shem.

HULDAH (Hŭl′ dah) Personal name meaning, "mole." Prophetess, the wife of Shallum (2 Kings 22:14). She was consulted after Josiah the king of Judah saw a copy of the Book of the Law found as preparations were being made to restore the Temple. She prophesied judgment for the nation but a peaceful death for Josiah the king. See *Josiah.*

HUMAN SACRIFICE The ritual slaying of one or more human beings to please a god. This was widely practiced by many cultures in antiquity. Although the frequency of the practice is difficult to determine, the fact is that such rituals were performed for various reasons. For example, both Egyptians and Sumerians before 2000 B.C. killed servants and possibly family members to bury them with deceased kings to allow those who had served or been near the official in life to accompany him to the realm of the dead. In Mesopotamia, and perhaps elsewhere, the remains of animals and humans offered as sacrifice were deposited within foundations to protect the building from evil powers, a practice possibly reflected in 1 Kings 16:34.

In the Old Testament, Jephthah sacrificed his daughter as a fulfillment of a vow, although the incident is clearly not normative (Judg. 11:30–

40). In the ninth century Mesha, king of Moab, offered his own son as a burnt offering presumably to Chemosh, national god of Moab, upon the walls of his capital while under seige by Israel and Judah (2 Kings 3:27). The event was so shocking that the seige was terminated. However, although Israelite law specifically forbade human sacrifice (Lev. 18:21; 20:2–5), persistent references to the practice occur, especially between 800 and 500 B.C. Both Ahaz and Manasseh burned their sons as an offering in times of national peril (2 Kings 16:3; 21:6). The sacrifices were made in the valley of Hinnom which protected Jerusalem from the west and south. A portion of the valley bore the name Topheth, a name derived from the word for fireplace or hearth. Apparently Topheth was an open air cultic area where Molech sacrifices were offered. The term Molech occurs frequently in connection with human sacrifice. In the Bible and elsewhere Molech apparently was used in two ways: 1) as the name or a title of a god to whom sacrifice was made (see 1 Kings 11:7) and 2) as a specific type of sacrifice which involved the total consumption of a person, usually a child, by fire. Both usages of the term may be reflected in the Old Testament. Both Jeremiah and Ezekiel condemn such offerings as an abomination to God (Jer. 7:31–32; 19:5–6; Ezek. 16:20–21; 20:31). Josiah defiled Topheth as a part of his reformation so that "no one might burn his son or his daughter as an offering to Molech" (2 Kings 23:10 RSV).

These practices, foreign to the worship of Yahweh, must have been adopted by Israel from the surrounding peoples. Direct evidence for human sacrifice during the first millennium B.C. comes from two cultures with which Israel had contact: the Phoenician colony of Carthage and the Arameans. The Carthaginians sacrificed children to Kronos during periods of calamity caused by war, famine, or disease. Pits filled with bones of animals and children have been excavated at Carthage with inscribed stones indicating these were Molech sacrifices. The Arameans of Gozan in northwest Mesopotamia sacrificed humans to the god Hadad. Interestingly, the Sepharvites, a people from an area dominated by Arameans deported to Palestine in 721 B.C. by Sargon II, burned their children as offerings to Adrammelech and Anammelech (2 Kings 17:31). Yet the abomination of human sacrifice, stated Jeremiah, never entered the mind of Yahweh (Jer. 19:5).

See *Molech*.   *Tommy Brisco*

HUMAN SOUL See *Soul*.

HUMANITY The characteristics which unite all persons despite their many individual differences and constitute them as God's "image."

Theologians have supposed that this "image" designates what is most essential to human nature. Many patristic, Catholic, and Protestant orthodox theologians have argued that the image was reason. Although Scripture depicts humans as thinking creatures, this definition was originally derived from Greek philosophy. More accurate is the suggestion that the image consists in humankind's lordship over and stewardship of creation, for this is the theme of the following verses (Gen. 1:28–31).

The best clue comes from frequent reference to Jesus as that image to which we are to be conformed (Rom. 8:29; 1 Cor. 15:49; 2 Cor. 3:18; 4:4). The most basic characteristics of Jesus' life were His dependence upon and devotion to His Father and His loving servanthood toward His fellow humans. This suggests that the essence of being human consists in a three-fold relationship: towards God as Lord, towards other humans as fellow servants, and towards creation as entrusted to our care. The second feature is confirmed by Genesis 1:27 which, as Karl Barth noticed, practically identifies being in God's image with being female and male. For in the interdependence between the sexes, the need, desire, and delight of humans for and in each other can be most vividly symbolized.

Theologians have often discussed whether individual humans are composed of just body and soul, or of body, soul, and spirit. Yet this question has been somewhat misguided. Scripture represents people not as individuals composed of parts, but as integrated, acting units intimately interrelated with others.

Investigation of the Bible's specific terminology generally substantiates its understanding of the image of God. The significance of human life is found primarily in relationships with others and with God.

Humanity under Sin Theologians often seek to determine sin's essence through careful analysis of Genesis 3. From this episode alone, sin can appear simply as the transgression of a divine command. However, the lengthy and varied narratives concerning Israel and Jesus yield fuller insight into sin. In the Old Testament, sin indeed involves breaking the commands of God's covenant. Yet this is rooted in turning away from the relationship which Yahweh initiated, and therefore from Yahweh Himself. Moreover, turning from Yahweh involves turning towards something else. This is usually the gods of the nations and the religious and social practices which they enforced.

Therefore, just as humans are not isolated individuals, so sin is not simply individual transgression. Sin is participation in attitudes, social behaviors, and religious commitments opposed to God. Just as humanity's image is manifested most fully in Jesus, so sin was revealed most clearly in the opposition to Him. Jesus was opposed by the collective power of the Roman state, Israel's religious establishment, and the demonic forces behind them. Individuals were involved by supporting, or by refusing to oppose, these collective forces.

In brief, just as God designed humans, made in His image, for positive relationships with others and with creation, rooted in dependence upon Him; so human sin is participation in distorted social and ecological relationships, rooted in commitments to other values and powers. Individual responsibility is involved, but it takes the form of turning from God towards something else.

Humanity Participating in Salvation The fullness of human potential cannot be determined from Genesis, but only from texts, primarily in the New Testament, which describe humans as moving towards final glorification.

Theologians have debated whether the will, apart from God's irresistable grace, is wholly bound to evil, or whether it can make some small movement toward God on its own. Through its many stories of people turning from God, Scripture insists that strong divine influence is needed to counteract sin; but Scripture may not provide a precise answer to the other side of the issue—humanity's ability to turn to God. The Bible does tells us the essential nature of freedom. It is not merely liberty to choose or not choose among various possibilities. Instead, true human freedom is initiated and empowered by the divine Spirit (2 Cor. 3:17; Gal. 4:6–7; 5:13,16; Rom. 8:2). It is not simply liberty to follow our own inclinations. It is the capacity to transform our drives and habits through the Spirit who raised Jesus bodily (Rom. 8:11). It is not simply liberty to attend to our interests. It is freedom to participate in and suffer with the Spirit's transforming work throughout all creation (Rom. 8:22–23). It is not freedom *from* involvement, but freedom *for* loving relationships with other people, the whole creation, and God.

Just as sin involves participation in perverted social and religious relationships, so fulfillment of human potential involves participation in healthy ones. Since our "bodies" are channels which relate us to creation, to others, and to God, so participation in Christ's body is the primary means by which health is restored. The "body of Christ" is no pale metaphor for an ecclesiastical organization. It is a living organism where each member participates in the joys and sufferings of the others (Rom. 12:4–8; 1 Cor. 12:12–26; Eph. 4:4–16). The church is not merely an organization for occasional worship, entertainment, or service. It is the primary community through which God wills that the relationships which constitute His image should be healed and through which the fullness which He desires for all humankind should be most clearly displayed.

See *Image of God; Body; Soul; Spirit; Creation; Sin; Freedom; Spirit; Church; Body of Christ.*

Thomas Finger

HUMANITY OF CHRIST See *Incarnations; Je-*

sus, Life and Ministry of; Christ, Christology.

HUMILIATION OF CHRIST See *Jesus, Death and Resurrection; Kenosis.*

HUMILITY A personal quality in which an individual shows dependence on God and respect for other persons.

Old Testament The Old Testament connects the quality of humility with Israel's lowly experience as slaves in Egypt—a poor, afflicted, and suffering people (Deut. 26:6). The Hebrew word translated as *humility* is similar to another Hebrew word meaning "to be afflicted." In Old Testament thought, humility was closely associated with individuals who were poor and afflicted (2 Sam. 22:28).

What God desires most is not outward sacrifices but a humble spirit (Psa. 51:17; Mic. 6:8). Such a humble spirit shows itself in several ways: (1) a recognition of one's sinfulness before a holy God (Isa. 6:5); (2) obedience to God (Deut. 8:2); and (3) submission to God (2 Kings 22:19; 2 Chron. 34:37).

The Old Testament promised blessings to those who were humble: (1) wisdom (Prov. 11:2); (2) good tidings (Isa. 61:1); and (3) honor (Prov. 15:33).

The experience of many kings indicated that those who humble themselves before God will be exalted (1 Kings 21:29; 2 Kings 22:19; 2 Chron. 32:26; 33:12;19). Those who do not humble themselves before God will be afflicted (2 Chron. 33:23; 36:12). The pathway to revival is the way of humility (2 Chron. 7:14).

New Testament Jesus Christ's life provides the best example of what it means to have humility (Matt. 11:29; 1 Cor. 4:21; Phil. 2:1–11). Jesus preached and taught often about the need for humility (Matt. 23:12; Mark 9:35; Luke 14:11; 18:14). He urged those who desired to live by Kingdom standards to practice humility (Matt. 18:1; 23:12).

The person with humility does not look down on others (Matt. 18:4; Luke 14:11). Humility in the New Testament is closely connected with the quality of "meekness" (Matt. 5:5). While God resists those who are proud, He provides grace for the humble (Jas. 4:6). Primary in the New Testament is the conviction that one who has humility will not be overly concerned about his or her prestige (Matt. 18:4; 23:12; Rom. 12:16; 2 Cor. 11:7).

Paul believed that quality relationships with other people, especially those who had erred spiritually, hinged on the presence of meekness or humility (1 Cor. 4:21; Gal. 6:1; 2 Tim. 2:25). The New Testament affirms, as does the Old Testament, that God will exalt those who are humble and bring low those who are proud (Luke 1:52; Jas 4:10; 1 Pet. 5:6). The Greek world abhored the quality of meekness or humility, but the Christian community believed these qualities were worthy (2 Cor. 10:18; Col. 3:12; Eph. 4:2).

Gary Hardin

HUMP The fleshy mound on the back of a camel where food is stored in the form of fat. Isaiah 30:6 refers to burdens carried on camels' humps ("bunches KJV).

HUMTAH (Hŭm' tah) Place name meaning, "lizards." Town in hill country of Judah in tribal territory of Judah (Josh. 15:54). Its exact location is not known.

HUNCHBACK One with a humped (curved or crooked) back. According to the Holiness Code, a hunchback was excluded from priestly service though allowed to eat of the priests' holy food (Lev. 21:20). REB translates the unique Hebrew term, "misshapen brows."

HUNDRED, TOWER OF (KJV "Tower of Meah") A tower located on the north wall of Jerusalem which was restored by Nehemiah (Neh. 3:1; 12:39). The name perhaps refers to the height of the tower (100 cubits?), the number of its steps, or the number of troops in its garrison. It may have been part of the Temple fortress (Neh. 2:8).

HUNDREDS A division of 100 persons. Moses appointed leaders of hundreds to assist him in rendering legal decisions (Ex. 18:21,25). In Numbers 31:14 leaders of hundreds are commanders of forces of 100 men each. The Philistine (1 Sam. 29:2) and the Romans (see *Centurion*) also made use of divisions of 100. The seating of the crowd in groups of hundreds in Mark 6:40 is perhaps meant to recall Israel's wilderness division.

HUNDREDWEIGHT A unit of weight equal to 100 pounds (Rev. 16:21 REB, RSV). The underlying Greek means "about the weight of a talent" (KJV). Most modern translations equate the talent with 100 pounds (NAS, NIV, NRSV, TEV).

HUNGER A strong need or desire for food. Scripture contains haunting pictures of hunger. Isaiah 29:8 uses the image of a hungry person dreaming of eating only to awake hungry again. In Lamentations 4:9, those who fell by the sword are reckoned better off than those pierced by hunger. Hunger frequently takes on a theological significance. Exodus 16:3 recounts Israel's complaint that Moses led them from Egypt to kill them with hunger in the desert. God used this experience of hunger to humble the rebellious people and to teach them to hunger for His word (Deut. 8:3). Hunger was one penalty of disobedience of covenant obligations (Deut. 28:48; 32:24).

The cessation of hunger is frequently associated with God's salvation. Hannah anticipated God's reversing the fortunes of the hungry (1 Sam. 2:5; Compare Luke 6:21,25). Isaiah promised that those returning from Exile would not be plagued by hunger (49:10). Ezekiel pictured God as providing for the needs of God's sheep so there would be no hunger (34:29). Part of the blessedness of the redeemed of Revelation 7:16 is the end of their hunger.

In Matthew 5:6 Jesus spoke of those who hunger and thirst for righteousness, that is, those who earnestly desire to see God's will become a reality. In John 6:35 Jesus promised that anyone who came to Him would not hunger but would be satisfied.

HUNT/HUNTER To pursue game for food or pleasure. Hunting was an important supplementary food source, especially in the seminomadic stage of civilization. Genesis mentions several hunters by name, none of whom are Israelite ancestors (Nimrod, 10:9; Ishmael, 21:20; Esau, 25:27), perhaps suggesting that hunting was more characteristic of Israel's neighbors than of Israel. Hunting was, however, regulated by Mosaic law. The blood of captured game was to be poured out on the ground (Lev. 17:13). Deuteronomy 14:3–5 outlines what game was permitted as ritually clean food.

The tools of the hunter include bows and arrows (Gen. 21:20; 27:3), nets (Job 18:8; Ezek. 12:13), snares or pitfalls (Job 18:8), if the term does not refer to part of the net (NAS, NIV, REB); traps, snares, ropes (Job 18:9–10). Terror, the pit, and the trap of Isaiah 24:17–18 (also Jer. 48:43–44) perhaps allude to the Battue method of hunting whereby a group forms a cordon and beats over the earth, driving game into a confined area, pit, or net. Ancient Egyptian carvings depict such methods of hunting.

Hunting for pleasure was a popular pastime of ancient kings. The hunt is a popular motif in the art of the Assyrians, Egyptians, and Phoniceans. The Assyrian reliefs depicting Ashurbanipal's lion hunt are particularly well known. The Old Testament does not mention hunting as a pastime of the kings of Israel or Judah. Josephus did note Herod's love of the hunt.

Most often the hunt is used figuratively. A rare positive image is Jeremiah's picture of God's hunting the scattered exiles to return them to Israel (Jer. 16:16). Saul hunted David (1 Sam. 24:11). Matthew described the Pharisees' plotting to "entrap" Jesus (22:15), Luke their "lying in wait" for Him (11:54). The Pastorals speak of the devil's snare (1 Tim. 3:7; 2 Tim. 2:26). Ezekiel 13:17–23 pictures women practicing magical arts as fowlers ensnaring the people. In Micah 7:2 the unfaithful are portrayed as hunting each other with nets. The warning of Proverbs 6:5 is to save oneself (from evil) like the gazelle or roe flees the

H

hunter. *Chris Church*

HUPHAM (Hū′ phăm) Original ancestor of clan of Benjamin in the wilderness (Num. 26:39). Hupham may be the original reading behind Huppim in Genesis 46:21 and 1 Chronicles 7:12,15. Comparison of Genesis 46:21; Numbers 26:38; 1 Chronicles 7:6; 8:1–2 shows the difficulty in restoring precisely the names of Benjamin's sons. Similarly, the sons of Bela, Benjamin's son, are difficult to restore (Num. 26:39–40; 1 Chron. 7:7; 8:3–4). Part of the explanation may lie in the use of genealogies to claim membership in an important clan rather than to precisely reproduce family structures.

HUPHAMITE (Hū′ phăm īte) Member of clan of Hupham in tribe of Benjamin.

HUPPAH (Hŭp′ pah) Personal name meaning, "shelter" or "roof" or "bridal chamber." Leader of thirteenth course of priests under David (1 Chron. 24:13).

HUPPIM (Hŭp′ pĭm) Personal name of unknown meaning. Son of Benjamin and grandson of Jacob (Gen. 46:21). See *Hupham.*

HUR (Hûr) Personal name of uncertain meaning, perhaps "white one" or "Horite" or perhaps derived from the name of the Egyptian god "Horus." *1.* Israelite leader who accompanied Moses and Aaron to the top of the mountain in the fight against the Amalekites. Hur helped Aaron hold Moses' hands up so Israel could prevail. In some way not explicitly stated, Moses' hands were the symbol of and instrument for God's power with Israel's army (Ex. 17:10–12). Hur and Aaron also represented Moses and settled any problems among the people while Moses ascended the mountain to receive God's instructions (Ex. 24:14). This same Hur was probably the grandfather of Bezaleel of the tribe of Judah, who was the artisan in charge of making the metal works for the tabernacle in the wilderness (Ex. 31:2). He was Caleb's son (1 Chron. 2:19). A genealogy of Hur appears both in 1 Chronicles 2:50 and 4:1. The text is difficult to decipher at times. Apparently, like the Table of Nations in Genesis 10, these texts show geographical and political relationships of the descendants of Caleb. *2.* King of Midian whom Israel slew as they moved toward the Promised Land (Num. 31:8). Joshua 13:21 identifies the kings of Midian as vassals of Sihon (Num. 31). *3.* District governor under Solomon over Mount Ephraim in charge of providing the royal table with provisions one month a year (1 Kings 4:8). His name may also be translated Ben-hur. *4.* Administrator over half the district of Jerusalem under Nehemiah or father of the administrator (Neh. 3:9).

HURAI (Hū′ rā ī) Variant reading in 1 Chronicles 11:32 for David's warrior Hiddai in the parallel passage (2 Sam. 23:30).

HURAM (Hū′ răm) Personal name probably shortened from Ahuram meaning, "exalted brother." *1.* Chronicler's spelling of Hiram, king of Tyre (2 Chron. 2). Also the Chronicler's form for Hiram, the artisan King Hiram sent to help with the metal work on the Temple (2 Chron. 2:13). See *Hiram. 2.* Descendant of Benjamin, often identified with Hupham of Numbers 26:39. See *Hupham.*

HURAMABI (Hū′ răm-ä′ bĭ) Personal name perhaps meaning, "my father is an exalted brother." NAS, NIV, NRSV name for Huram/Hiram, the skilled artisan Hiram, King of Tyre, sent Solomon to help build the Temple (2 Chron. 2:13). See *Huram.*

HURI (Hū′ rī) Personal name of uncertain meaning, perhaps "white one," "linen maker," "Horite," or "my Horus" (Egyptian god). A member of tribe of Gad (1 Chron. 5:14).

HURRIANS See *Horites.*

HUSBAND The male partner in a marriage. See *Family; Household; Marriage.*

HUSBANDMAN KJV term for one who tills the soil; a farmer. Husbandry refers to farming. Modern translations replace husbandman and husbandry with other terms. The substitutions of the RSV are typical; plowman (Isa. 61:5); farmer (2 Chron. 26:10; Jer. 14:4; 31:24; 51:23; Amos 5:16); tiller of the soil (Gen. 9:20; Joel 1:11). The KJV's "ye are God's husbandry" was rendered with "you are God's field." See *Farmer; Agriculture; Occupations.*

HUSHAH (Hū′ shah) Personal and place name meaning, "hurry." Member of tribe of Judah (1 Chron. 4:4) listed along with Bethlehem and thus probably original ancestor of clan who lived in town of Hushah, perhaps modern Husan near Bethlehem. Some Bible students think that in the copying process the name was changed from an original Shuah (1 Chron. 4:11) through transposition of Hebrew letters. Two of David's soldiers came from Hushah: Sibbechai (2 Sam. 21:18) and Mebunnai (2 Sam. 23:27).

HUSHAI (Hū′ shâi) Personal name meaning, "quick," "from Hushah," or "gift of brotherhood." The name could represent copying transposition from an original Shuah. See *Hushah.* This would designate his family as from Shuhu, the Syrian state in the central Euphrates region or a state in

Edom or Arabia. The clan became a part of Israel as a clan of the tribe of Benjamin living in Archi southwest of Bethel (Josh. 16:2). Hushai was "David's friend" (2 Sam. 15:37), probably referring to an official government post as in Egypt, a close personal adviser somewhat like the secretary of state. As David escaped, leaving Jerusalem to his son Absalom, Hushai joined him, mourning (2 Sam. 15:32). David sent him back to deceive Absalom (2 Sam. 15:34; 16:16–19). His counsel to Absalom bought time for David to establish new headquarters and gather forces for new strategy (2 Sam. 17).

Solomon's commissioner in charge of collecting royal provisions in Asher was the son of Hushai, perhaps the same as "David's friend" (1 Kings 4:16).

HUSHAM (Hū′ shăm) Personal name, perhaps meaning, "large-nosed" or "with haste." One of the early kings of Edom (Gen. 36:34) from Teman.

HUSHATHITE (Hū′ shăth īte) Citizen of Hushah. See *Hushah*.

HUSHIM (Hū′ shĭm) Personal name meaning, "hurried ones." *1.* Son of Dan and grandson of Jacob (Gen. 46:23). *2.* Member of tribe of Benjamin (1 Chron. 7:12), though many Bible students think copying has caused omission of tribe of Dan in the list, Hushim here being the same as in Genesis 46:23. Dan's son is named Shuham in Numbers 26:42, perhaps resulting from a copying transposition of Hebrew letters. *3.* Wife of Shaharaim of tribe of Benjamin (1 Chron. 8:8) and mother of Abitub and Elpaal (1 Chron. 8:11). Apparently, her husband sent her away either for safety or as part of family problems before he went to Moab.

HUSHITES (Hū′ shītes) NIV translation of Hushim (1 Chron. 7:12), interpreting it as the name of a population group rather than as an individual.

HUSK The outer covering of a seed or fruit, usually either dry (as the carob) or membranous (as the grape) (Num. 6:4; 2 Kings 4:42, Luke 15:16). Modern translations replace husk with skins when referring to grapes (Num. 6:4). The term translated husk at 2 Kings 4:42 is a *hapax legomena,* a term used only once in Scripture. NAS, RSV follow the Latin Vulgate in rendering the term "sack." Other modern translations follow other ancient versions in omitting the term. Modern translations give "pods" or "bean pods" for husks at Luke 15:16. The pods of the Carob tree (*Ceratonia siliqua*) are probably intended (so NAS margin). The ripe pods are full of a dark, honeylike syrup. These are ground and used as an animal feed.

HUT Modern translations' rendering for a lean-to or temporary shelter; shack (Isa. 1:8; 24:20). The image of Isaiah 1:8 stresses the isolation of Jerusalem, the sole survivor of the cities of Judah (1:7–9). Isaiah 24:20 illustrates God's power in judgment in the picture of the earth's swaying like an unstable hut before the Lord.

HUZ (Hŭz) KJV spelling for Uz (Gen. 22:21). See *Uz.*

HUZZAB (Hŭz′ zăb) KJV transliteration of Hebrew word whose meaning in the context of Nahum 2:7 is not clear. KJV takes it as a city-state. Other translators take the word as a Hebrew verb meaning "fixed" (NAS) or "decreed" (NRSV, NIV). Others see a feminine noun: "train" of captives (REB), "queen" (TEV), "its mistress" (RSV). The verbal translation is probably correct, pointing to God's established plan announced through the prophet to defeat Assyria and its capital Nineveh. Otherwise, the term is describing Nineveh in figurative language, perhaps referring to deportation of dressed-up idols defeated in war.

HYACINTH A stone regarded as precious in ancient times. The hyacinth is sometimes identified with the sapphire (Rev. 9:17 NRSV, TEV) or turquoise (Ex. 28:19; Rev. 9:17; 21:20 REB; Ex. 28:19; Rev. 21:20 TEV). Others identify the hyacinth with zircon, a brown to greyish gem, or essonite, a yellow to brown garnet.

HYENA Any of a group of stockily-built, carnivorous mammals of the genus *Hyaena,* located zoologically between the felines and canines. Hyena feed on carrion and are knwon for their cowardess, cruelty, and disagreeable cry. All the scriptural references concern judgment on foreign nations (Babylon or Edom) which are left desolate (Isa. 13:22; 34:14; Jer. 50:39). KJV translated the term for hyena as "wild beasts of the islands." The REB identifies this animal with the jackal (so NAS Jer. 50:39). NAS uses wolves in Isaiah 34:14.

The Hebrew term for hyena is used as a man's name (Zibeon, Gen. 36:20) and as the name for a town (Zeboim, Neh. 11:34) and valley (1 Sam. 13:18) in the territory of Benjamin.

HYKSOS (Hўk′ sŏs) Racial name from the Greek form of an Egyptian word meaning "rulers of foreign lands" given to kings of the Fifteenth and Sixteenth Dynasties of Egypt. The word, which does not appear in the Bible, was later misinterpreted by Josephus as meaning "shepherd kings."

With the decline of the Middle Kingdom of Egypt (about 2000–1786 B.C.) large numbers of Asiatics, mostly Semites like the Hebrew patri-

Hypostyle Hall of the Temple at Karnak, or Thebes, home of Egyptian dynasty who replaced the Hyksos.

archs, migrated into the Nile Delta of northern Egypt from Canaan. These probably came initially for reasons of economic distress, such as famine, as did Abraham (Gen. 12:10). Unlike Abraham, many groups stayed in Egypt as permanent settlers. Under the weak Thirteenth Dynasty, some Asiatics established local independent chiefdoms in the eastern Delta region. Eventually, one of these local rulers managed to consolidate the rule of northern Egypt as pharaoh, thus beginning the Fifteenth Dynasty. The Sixteenth Dynasty, perhaps contemporary with the Fifteenth, consisted of minor Asiatic kings. As these dynasties of pharaohs were not ethnic Egyptians, they were remembered by the native population as "Hyksos."

While the Hyksos pharaohs ruled northern Egypt from Avaris in the eastern Delta, the native Egyptian Seventeenth Dynasty ruled southern Egypt from Thebes. This period is known as the Second Intermediate or Hyksos Period (about 1786–1540 B.C.). The status quo was maintained until war erupted between the Hyksos and the last two pharaohs of the Seventeenth Dynasty. About 1540 B.C., Ahmose I sacked Avaris and expelled the Hyksos. As the first pharaoh of a reunited Egypt, Ahmose I established the Eighteenth Dynasty and inaugurated the Egyptian New Kingdom or Empire.

Joseph's rise to power (Gen. 41:39–45) as pharaoh's second-in-command would have been far more likely under a Hyksos king. Joseph was related ethnically to the Semitic Hyksos rulers, while the native Egyptians regarded Semites with contempt. Ahmose I is very likely the pharaoh "who did not know Joseph" (Ex. 1:8 NRSV). If Joseph served a Hyksos pharaoh, an Egyptian king would not have "known" of him in a political or historical sense, nor would he have regarded him as significant in an ethnic sense.

Daniel C. Browning, Jr.

HYMENAEUS (Hy̆' mĕ nāē' ŭs) Personal name of the Greek god of marriage. Name of a fellow worker of Paul whose faith weakened and whose life-style changed, leading Paul to deliver him to Satan (1 Tim. 1:20). That probably means Paul led the church to dismiss Hymenaeus from the membership to purify the church, remove further temptation from the church, and to lead Hymenaeus to restored faith, repentance, and renewed church membership. Along with Philetus, Hymenaeus taught that the resurrection had already occurred (2 Tim. 2:17–18). See *Gnosticism.* Compare 1 Corinthians 5.

HYMENEUS (Hy̆ mĕ nē' ŭs) KJV spelling of Hymenaeus.

HYMN The generic term given to vocal praise in the Bible.

Old Testament Ceremonial religious singing is mentioned in the Old Testament in connection with important events, such as the songs in celebration of the Hebrews' passage through the Red Sea (Ex. 15:1–21), Deborah and Barak's triumph song after the defeat of the forces of Jabin, king of Hazor (Judg. 5:1–31), and the women's song at David's victorious return from battle with the Philistines (1 Sam. 18:6–7). Moses also gave the Israelites some of his last warnings in a great song (Deut. 32:1–43). The Book of Psalms is a hymn book. The hymns in it were written by different authors over a long period of time and used by the people of Israel in their worship. The collection of 150 psalms eventually was included in Hebrew Scripture. Hymn singing in the Jerusalem Temple was led by trained choirs, sometimes using instrumental accompaniment (2 Chron. 29:25–28). The people joined the choir in singing hymns in unison, responsively, and antiphonally.

Hymn is also the technical term for a specific literary type of material in Psalms. In this sense a hymn expresses the congregation's praise of God's greatness and majesty, usually addressing members of the congregation and inviting them to praise God. A hymn usually includes a call to the congregation to join in praise (Ps. 33:1–3), a list of reasons to praise God (Ps. 33:4–19), and a concluding call to praise or statement of trust (Ps. 33:20–22).

New Testament The Bible makes it clear that the singing of spiritual songs was a part of the early Christian church. Among the songs in the New Testament are several outstanding songs that have become a part of liturgical Christian worship: Luke 1:46–55, Mary's song—"The Magnificat"; Luke 1:68–79, Zacharias' prophetic song—"The Benedictus"; and Luke 2:29–32, Simeon's blessing of the infant Jesus and farewell—"The Nunc Dimittis." Numerous doxologies (Luke 2:14; 1 Tim. 1:17; 6:15–16; Rev. 4:8, for example) doubtless were used in corporate worship. Other passages in the New Testament give evidence of being quotations of hymns or fragments of hymns (Rom. 8:31–39; 1 Cor. 13; Eph. 1:3–14; Eph. 5:14; Phil. 2:5–11; 1 Tim. 3:16; 2 Tim. 2:11–13; Tit. 3:4–7). As for references to the word itself, the New Testament states that Jesus and His disciples sang a hymn at the end of the Last Supper (Matt. 26:30; Mark 14:26). Most Bible students think they sang part of Psalms 115—118, hymns known as the Hallel, which traditionally were sung after supper on the night of Passover. The division of Christian song into psalms, hymns, and spiritual songs (Eph. 5:19; Col. 3:16) should not be taken to mean that there were three distinct types or styles of vocal music in use in those days. The reference indicates that Christian song was used in worship, to instruct in the

H

faith, and to express joy. In another New Testament reference, Acts 16:25, the mention of singing "praises" to God obviously means that Paul and Silas sang hymns in prison. The author of the Book of Hebrews stressed in 2:12 (a quotation of the messianic Ps. 22:22) that Jesus will declare His name to the church, that He will "sing praise," or hymns.   *J. William Thompson*

HYPOCRISY (Hў pŏc′ rĭ sў) Pretense to being what one really is not, especially the pretense of being a better person than one really is. The word is based on the Greek *hypokrisis,* originally meaning to give an answer. A hypocrite in classical Greek could be an interpreter of dreams, an orator, a reciter of poetry, or an actor. Originally a neutral term, "hypocrite" gained the negative connotation of pretense, duplicity, or insincerity.

In the Bible the negative meaning prevails. Often hypocrisy refers to evil or sin in general, not pretense in particular. In the Old Testament, "hypocrite" was used by the King James Version whereas later translations (e.g. RSV, NIV) often use "godless" or "ungodly" (Job 8:13; 15:34–35; 17:8; Isa. 9:17; 33:14, etc.). This "godless" person was totally opposed to God or forgetful of God. The Hebrew word often translated "hypocrite" referred to pollution or corruption. Although the Hebrews were concerned about pretense or insincerity (Isa. 29:13; Jer. 12:2), there is no one Hebrew word exactly equivalent to "hypocrisy."

Hypocrisy in the narrower sense of playing a role is highlighted in the New Testament, especially in the teaching of Jesus in the Synoptic Gospels. Jesus criticized hypocrites for being pious in public (Matt. 6:2,5,16). They were more interested in human praise when they gave alms, prayed, and fasted than in God's reward. Hypocrites were also guilty of being judgmental of others' faults and ignoring their own (Matt. 7:1–5). Jesus often called the Pharisees hypocrites because of the conflict between their external actions and internal attitudes (Matt. 15:1–9). Their true attitudes would be revealed (Luke 12:1–3). The hypocrites could interpret the weather but not the signs of the times (Luke 12:56). They were more concerned about the rules for the sabbath than a woman's physical health (Luke 13:15). Luke noted that the religious leaders pretended to be sincere when they asked Jesus about paying tribute to Caesar (Luke 20:20). Probably the most famous discussion of hypocrisy is Matthew 23. The religious leaders did not practice what they preached (Matt. 23:3). Jesus compared them to dishes that were clean on the outside and dirty on the inside and to white-

washed tombs (Matt. 23:25–28).

Hypocrisy is a concern throughout the New Testament. Although the term does not occur, it was part of the sin of Ananias and Sapphira (Acts 5:1–11). Paul accused Peter of hypocrisy for refusing to eat with Gentile Christians in Antioch (Gal. 2:12–13). Paul warned Timothy about hypocritical false teachers (1 Tim. 4:2). Peter included hypocrisy as one of the attitudes Christians should avoid (1 Pet. 2:1).

Six times New Testament writers stress that sincerity (without hypocrisy, *anupokritos*) should characterize the Christian. Christian love (Rom. 12:9; 2 Cor. 6:6; 1 Pet. 1:22), faith (1 Tim. 1:5; 2 Tim. 1:5), and wisdom (Jas. 3:17) should be sincere.

See *Lie; Pharisees; Sin; Truth.*

Warren McWilliams

HYSSOP A small (about 27 inches), bushy plant, probably *Origanum Maru L.,* the Syrian marjoram. Stalks of hyssop bear numerous, small, white flowers in bunches. Hyssop was thus well-suited for use as a "brush" to dab the lintels of Israelite homes with the blood of the Passover lambs (Ex. 12:22). The associations of hyssop with the events of the Exodus perhaps led to its use in other rites, the cleansing of lepers (Lev. 14:4,6,49,51–52) and the cleansing of those unclean from contact with a corpse (Num. 19:6,18; see *Heifer, Red*). Psalm 51:7 applies the well-known image of hyssop to spiritual cleansing from sin.

A branch of hyssop bore the sponge used to offer vinegar to Christ at His crucifixion (John 19:29; Matt. 27:48; Mark 15:36 mention a reed). Various attempts to resolve this tension have been offered. Most exegetes have attempted to harmonize the parallel accounts: (1) by suggesting that Christ was offered vinegar twice, once using a reed and once hyssop; (2) by suggesting both a reed and hyssop were simultaneously used to support the sponge; (3) by emending John's text to read "spike" which is more easily harmonized with reed; (4) by taking hyssop to refer to a plant other than marjoram which could be described as a reed, e.g., *Sorghum vulgare.* An alternative approach is concerned primarily with the question of why (theological significance) rather than the details of what. These interpreters stress that John intends to link Jesus' death with the Exodus event that marked liberation from Egyptian slavery and/or with the Old Testament cleansing rituals involving hyssop.

Hebrews 9:19 says the people were sprinkled with hyssop at the reading of the covenant. The account of Exodus 24:6–8 lacks this detail.

H

Outside close-up view of ruins of the Colosseum of ancient Rome in Italy.

I AM A shortened form of God's response to Moses' request for the name of the God of the patriarchs (Ex. 3:13–14). The fuller form of the name may be rendered "I am who I am," "I will be who I will be," or even "I cause to be what is." See *YHWH*. God's response is not a "name" that makes God an object of definition or limitation. Rather, it is an affirmation that God is always subject, always free to be and act as God wills. The earliest Greek rendering "I am the one who is" or "I am Being" has been especially significant in the development of theology.

Jesus' "I am" response in several New Testament passages suggests more than the simple identifying "I am he." The "I am" of Mark 6:50 means "I am Jesus and not a ghost," but suggests the divine "I am" who alone "tramples down the waves of the sea" (Job 9:8; Mark 6:48–49) and made the waves hush (Ps. 107:28–29; compare Mark 4:39). John 8:24 makes recognition that Jesus is the "I am" a matter of eternal life and death: "You will die in your sins unless you believe that I am." The Jews misunderstood, thinking it was a matter of identity ("Who are you?" 8:25). Recognition that Jesus is the "I am" who is one in word and action with His Father is possible only when Jesus has been lifted up on the cross/raised from the dead (8:28). That the Jews rightly understood Jesus' claim "before Abraham was, I am" (8:58) as a divine claim is evident from their picking up stones to throw at Him. The "I am" of John 18:5 again suggests more than "I am the man you are looking for." Rather, Jesus is the "I am" whose awesome presence forced the guard back and into a posture of reverence. Here Jesus was not the object of betrayal but the subject who won the release of His disciples (18:8). Though differing in form from the "I am" sayings, the references to the one "who is and who was and who is to come" (Rev. 1:4,8; 4:8; compare 11:17; 16:5) are similar in thought. In a context of intense hardship that called into question God's sovereignty, the writer of Revelation reaffirmed Israel's faith in the "I am" who is the subject of history and not its victim. *Chris Church*

IBEX A species of wild goat with large curved horns, native to high mountain areas. The ibex is included among clean game (Deut. 14:5). KJV's pygarg is a white-rumped antelope (compare "white-rumped deer" REB). The precise identity of the animal (whether goat or antelope) is uncertain.

IBHAR (Ĭb' här) Personal name meaning, "he elected." Son born to David after he moved to Jerusalem (2 Sam. 5:15).

IBLEAM (Ĭb' lĕ am) Place name meaning, "he swallowed the people." City in tribal territory of Issachar but given to tribe of Manasseh (Josh. 17:11). Many Bible students think Ibleam was the

A vase handle in the shape of a beautiful winged ibex.

original reading for the Levite city in Joshua 21:25, where the Hebrew text now reads "Gath-rimmon," also read in verse 24. A copyist may have copied the name from verse 24 into verse 25. Some Greek manuscripts read Iebatha, perhaps a corruption of Ibleam. First Chronicles 6:70 reads Bileam, pointing to Ibleam as original. Other Greek manuscripts read Beth-Shean. Manasseh could not conquer Ibleam (Judg. 1:27). Jehu, in his coupe against Jehoram, king of Israel, also mortally wounded Ahaziah, king of Judah, near Ibleam (2 Kings 9:27). Many Bible students also read Ibleam as the place of attack in 2 Kings 15:10 (REB, TEV, RSV, but not NRSV). The Hebrew text either uses an Aramaic pronoun otherwise unknown in Hebrew meaning, "before"; or it refers to a place Kabal-am otherwise unknown. Some Greek manuscripts read Ibleam. Normal text procedure would see Ibleam as the easier reading adopted in view of 2 Kings 9:27 by a copyist or translator who did not understand the Hebrew text. Ibleam is modern bir Belalmeh about a mile southwest of Jenin.

IBNEIAH (Ĭb nêi' ah) Personal name meaning, "Yah builds." Benjaminite who returned from Exile and settled in Jerusalem (1 Chron. 9:8).

IBNIJAH (Ĭb nī' jah) Personal name meaning, "Yah builds," a variant spelling of Ibneiah. Ancestor in tribe of Benjamin of one of persons returning from Exile and living in Jerusalem (1 Chron. 9:8).

IBRI (Ĭb′ rī) Personal name meaning, "Hebrew." A Levite under King David (1 Chron. 24:27). See *Habiru.*

IBSAM (Ĭb′ săm) Personal name akin to balsam, meaning, "sweet smelling," in modern translations. KJV spelling is Jibsam. Member of tribe of Issachar (1 Chron. 7:2).

IBZAN (Ĭb′ zăn) Personal name perhaps meaning, "quick, agile." Judge of Israel from Bethlehem who participated in royal practice of marrying children to foreigners (Judg. 12:8–10).

ICE Frozen water. Job's poetry has several references to ice. Ice is described as hard as stone (38:30). In picturesque language, ice is frozen by the "breath of God" (37:10). In an even bolder image, the Lord demanded to know "Out of whose womb came the ice? and the hoary frost of heaven, who hath gendered it?" (38:29). Though lacking the knowledge of a meteorologist, the biblical writer saw clearly with wondering eyes that God was the ultimate source of weather phenomena. The Hebrew term translated ice is sometimes rendered cold or frost (Gen. 31:40; Jer. 36:30).

ICHABOD (Ĭch′ á bŏd) Personal name meaning "where is the glory?" The son of Phinehas, Eli's son (1 Sam. 4:21). His birth seems to have been precipitated by the news of the death of his father and the capture of the ark of the covenant in battle against the Philistines. The mother of Ichabod died immediately after the child's birth. See *Eli.*

ICONIUM (Ī cō′ nĭ um) City of Asia Minor visited by Barnabas and Paul during the first missionary journey (Acts 13:51). Paul endured sufferings and persecution at Iconium (2 Tim. 3:11). Its location is that of the modern Turkish provincial capital Konya. Iconium was mentioned for the first time in the fourth century B.C. by the historian Xenophon. In New Testament times it was considered to be a part of the Roman province of Galatia. Evidently it has had a continuous existence since its founding. See *Asia Minor.*

IDALAH (Ĭd′ á lah) Place name of uncertain meaning, perhaps "jackal" or "memorial." Town in tribal territory of Zebulun (Josh. 19:15), probably modern khirbet el-Hawarah south of Bethlehem in Zebulun, not to be confused with the more famous Bethlehem in Judah.

IDBASH (Ĭd′ băsh) Personal name meaning, "sweet as honey." Son of Etam in the tribe of Judah (1 Chron. 4:3), according to modern translations and earliest Greek translation. KJV follows Hebrew text in reading father rather than son of Etam.

IDDO (Ĭd′ dō) English spelling of four different Hebrew personal names. *1.* Name of uncertain meaning. Person with authority in the exilic community during the Persian period to whom Ezra sent messengers to secure Levites to join him in the return to Jerusalem (Ezra 8:17). He apparently sent the needed Levites (vv. 19—20). *2.* Personal name perhaps meaning, "his praise." Leader of the eastern half of tribe of Manasseh under David (1 Chron. 27:21). The written Hebrew text uses this name in Ezra 10:43 for a man with a foreign wife, but an early scribal note followed by English translations read Jadau. *3.* Name perhaps meaning, "Yahweh adorns Himself." A prophet whose records the chronicler refers to for more information about Solomon and Jeroboam (2 Chron. 9:29), Rehoboam (2 Chron. 12:15), and Abijah (2 Chron. 13:22). The latter indicates he wrote a *midrash* (NAS, "annotations"), which may indicate a Jewish exposition of Scripture. As early as Josephus, Iddo had been identified with the nameless prophet who spoke against the altar of Bethel in 1 Kings 13. The Hebrew texts spell his name in different ways in the different occurrences. *4.* Grandfather of Zechariah, the prophet (Zech. 1:1,7 with different Hebrew spellings). Ezra 5:1; 6:14 put Zechariah as Iddo's son, using "son" to mean descendant, as often in Hebrew. He is included among the priestly families in the early postexilic community (Neh. 12:4,16). *5.* Father of Solomon's district supervisor who supplied the royal court provisions for one month a year in the area of Mahanaim (1 Kings 4:14). *6.* A Levite (1 Chron. 6:21).

IDLE Not engaged in earning a living; depending on the labor and generosity of others for support. Scripture distinguishes between those unwilling to work who should not eat (2 Thess. 3:10) and those unable to earn a living (for example, "true" widows, 1 Tim. 5:9) for whom the community of faith is responsible. Hebrew wisdom literature frequently condemned idleness as the cause of hunger (Prov. 19:15), poverty (Prov. 10:4; 14:23), and inadequate housing (Eccl. 10:18). According to Hebrew wisdom, the ideal woman "eateth not the bread of idleness" (Prov. 31:27), but is an industrious, working woman who helps provide for the financial needs of her family (Prov. 31:16,24). In the New Testament, Paul called attention to his own example as a bi-vocational minister to encourage the Thessalonian Christians to be hard workers (2 Thess. 3:7–8). Though Scripture consistently condemns "willful" idleness, it is also aware of economic realities in

I

which some who are willing workers stand idle because no one has hired them (Matt. 20:6–7). The biblical witness likewise does not trace all poverty to idleness. Some poverty results from the rich refusing to pay their poor day laborers (Lev. 19:13; Jer. 22:13; Jas. 5:4).

IDOL Physical or material image or form representing a reality or being considered divine and thus an object of worship. In the Bible various terms are used to refer to idols or idolatry: "image", either graven (carved) or cast, "statue," "abomination." Both Testaments condemn idols, but with idols the Old Testament expresses more concern than the New, probably reflecting the fact that the threat of idolatry was more pronounced for the people of the Old Testament.

The ancient Hebrews lived in a world filled with idols. Egyptians represented their deities in various human-animal forms. Similarly, the various Mesopotamian cultures used idol representations of their deities, as did the Hittites in ancient Asia Minor. More of a threat to Hebrew worship were the Canaanite Baal and Asherah fertility images, some of which are commonly found in excavations. Use of idols in worship continued to be commonplace in Greek and Roman religion.

One of the prominent distinguishing features of biblical religion is its ideal of imageless worship. Clearly expressed in the decalogue is the command: "Thou shalt not make unto thee any graven image . . . thou shalt not bow down thyself to them, nor serve them" (Ex. 20:4,5). This is usually interpreted to be a negative statement concerning idols but with positive implications toward the spiritual worship desired by God.

Idols were a problem of long standing. The first rebellion of the Hebrews centered around the golden calf made under Aaron's leadership in the wilderness (Ex. 32). The bronze serpent illustrates the Hebrews' propensity for idol worship. Moses set it up in the wilderness to allay a plague of serpents (Num. 21), but Israel retained it and made it an object of worship (2 Kings 18:4). Joshua called on the people to put away the gods

Probable Hittite idols, one of gold and the other of stone, found at Bogaskoy.

their fathers had served in Mesopotamia and in Egypt (Josh. 24:14). Perhaps a misguided King Jeroboam intended to represent Yahweh by the gold calves set up in his temples at Bethel and Dan when he led the northern tribes to secede from the kingdom inherited by Rehoboam (1 Kings 12:28-33).

Biblical writers often denounced idolatry. None is more graphic and devastating than that in Isaiah 44:9–20. The idol is made by a workman but is powerless to sustain the workman to complete his task. Further, the idol begins as a leftover piece of a tree from which a person makes a god. He then worships no more than a block of wood.

Many scholars believe that the threat of idolatry was much less in the Jewish community after the Babylonian Exile and that it continued to be diminished though still present throughout New Testament times. The most noted problem in the New Testament concerns the propriety of eating meat which has previously been offered to an idol (1 Cor. 8—10). Paul seemingly broadened the scope of idolatry for Christianity when he identified covetousness with idolatry (Col. 3:5). See *Food Offered to Idols; Gods, Pagan.*

Bruce C. Cresson

IDOLATRY See *Idol.*

IDOLOMACY The practice of consulting images of household gods (teraphim) for advice (Ezek. 21:21; Zech. 10:2). Zechariah encouraged his contemporaries to pray to God since the teraphim were "utter nonsense."

IDUMEA Ĭd ū mē′ á) In Isaiah 34:5, a nation destined for judgment. "Idumea" is the term used in the Greek version of the Old Testament and in the writings of the Jewish historian Josephus for Edom. The region was southeast of the Dead Sea. The Herods came originally from Idumea. Crowds from Idumea followed Jesus early in His ministry (Mark 3:8). See *Edom.*

IEZER (Ī ē′ zẽr) Personal name meaning, "where is help" or a short form of "my father is help." (Hebrew Abiezer, Josh. 17:2). Son of Gilead in tribe of Manasseh and original clan ancestor of Iezerites (Num. 26:30). KJV, REB spelling is Jeezer.

IEZERITES (Ī ē′ zẽr ītes) See *Iezer.*

IGAL (Ī′ g̅ăl) Personal name meaning, "he redeems." *1.* Spy representing tribe of Issachar whom Moses sent to investigate the land of Canaan (Num. 13:7). He voted with the majority that the land was too difficult for Israel to conquer. *2.* One of David's heroic warriors, apparently a foreigner from Zobah (2 Sam. 23:36), though his name is spelled Joel, and he is the brother, not son, of Nathan in 1 Chronicles 11:38. *3.* Descen-

I

dant of David in the postexilic community (about 470 B.C.) and thus bearer of the messianic line and hope (1 Chron. 3:22), though the chronicler does not describe him in messianic terms here.

IGDALIAH (Ĭg dȧ lī' ah) Personal name meaning, "Yahweh is great." Ancestor of the prophets whose chamber in the Temple Jeremiah used to test the Rechabites loyalty to their oath not to drink wine (Jer. 35:4). This is apparently evidence for professional prophets on the Temple staff. See *Jeremiah; Rechabites.*

IGEAL (Ī' gė al) KJV spelling of Igal in 1 Chronicles 3:22. See *Igal.*

IGNORANCE Lack of knowledge or comprehension. Old Testament law distinguished between sins of ignorance or sin unintentionally (Lev. 4:2,13,14; Num. 15:24–29) and premeditated sins ("sin presumptuously" or with a high hand Num. 15:30–31). Sins committed in ignorance incur guilt (Lev. 4:13,22,27); however, the sacrificial system provided atonement for such sin (Lev. 4; 5:5–6). In contrast, "high-handed" or "presumptuous" sin is an affront to the Lord punishable by exclusion from the people of God. The Law provided no ritual cleansing for such sin (Num. 15:30–31). Common images for sins of ignorance include error (Lev. 5:18), straying (Ps. 119:10), and stumbling (Job 4:4). By extension these images can be applied to any sin. Thus Proverbs 19:27 warns against willful "erring" from words of divine counsel.

The New Testament speaks of past ignorance which God excuses. Such was the ignorance of those Jews who participated in crucifying Jesus (Acts 3:17; 13:27), of Paul who persecuted Christians (1 Tim. 1:13), and of Gentiles who did not recognize the true God (Acts 17:30). Though God "winks at" such past ignorance, He requires repentance (Acts 3:19; 17:30). Obedience characterizes lives of the converted just as ignorant desires characterize those without Christ (1 Pet. 1:14). The New Testament speaks of deliberate ignorance as well as "excusable" ignorance. Most often deliberate ignorance involves the stubborn refusal to acknowledge nature's witness to the powerful existence of God (Rom. 1:18–21; Eph. 4:18; 2 Pet. 3:5).

IIM (Ī' ĭm) Place name meaning ruins. *1.* Town on southern border of tribal territory of Judah (Josh. 15:29). Its location is not known, and it does not appear in parallel lists in Joshua 19:3; 1 Chronicles 4:29. Many Bible students think a copyist copied parts of the following Ezem twice. *2.* Used in Numbers 33:45 (KJV) as abbreviation for Iye-abarim. See *Iye-abarim.*

IJEABARIM (Ī jė ȧb' ȧ rĭm) KJV spelling for Iye-abarim. See *Iye-abarim.*

IJON (Ī' jŏn) Place name meaning, "ruin." Place in northern Israel captured by King Ben-Hadad of Damascus as a result of his agreement with King Asa of Judah (910–869 B.C.) to break the treaty between Damascus and Baasha, king of Israel (1 Kings 15:20). This forced Baasha to defend himself on the northern border and quit intruding on Judah's territory, giving Asa opportunity to strengthen his defenses (1 Kings 15:21–22). Tiglath-pileser conquered the city and carried many Israelites into captivity about 734 B.C. (2 Kings 15:29). Ijon is located near modern Marj Uyun between the rivers Litani and Hesbani at tell Dibbin.

IKKESH (Ĭk' kĕsh) Personal name meaning, "perverted, false." Father of one of David's 30 heroes from Tekoa (2 Sam. 23:26).

ILAI (Ī' lā ī) Personal name of uncertain meaning. One of David's military heroes (1 Chron. 11:29), apparently the same as Zalmon (2 Sam. 23:28), the different spelling resulting from a copyist's change.

ILLUMINATED To be spiritually or intellectually enlightened. Hebrews 10:32 refers to those who are knowledgeable of the saving message of the gospel. The same Greek term is rendered "enlightened" at Hebrews 6:4.

ILLUSTRATION See *Imagery; Parables; Proverb; Wise Saying.*

ILLYRICUM (Ĭl lȳr' ĭ cŭm) Place name of uncertain meaning. A district in the Roman Empire between the Danube River and the Adriatic Sea. The Romans divided it into Dalmatia and Pannonia. It includes modern Yugoslavia and Albania. Illyricum represented the northeastern limits of Paul's missionary work as he wrote the Romans (Rom. 15:19), though the Bible nowhere mentions his work there. His work in Macedonia was only a few miles away, so he could easily have preached in or sent his associates to Illyricum. This does not mean he had covered all of Illyricum, only that he had introduced the gospel there in the dangerous limits of the empire. Paul had thus completed his missionary ministry of preaching the gospel and planting churches in the eastern end of the empire. Paul was now ready to preach in Rome and the western parts of the Roman Empire (Rom. 15:20–24).

IMAGE OF GOD A biblical description of the unique nature of human beings in their relationship to the Creator God.

"And God said, Let us make man in our image, after our likeness" (Gen. 1:26*b*). This passage contains a key to the understanding of humans and their nature. Scholars through the ages have

I

sought to unravel the mystery of that statement. The psalmist asked, "What is man?" (Ps. 8:4). Philosophers, theologians, psychologists, and anthropologists have constantly explored that topic. All have realized that the human being "is fearfully and wonderfully made" (Ps. 139:14).

A Special Creation According to the Scriptures, humans are not an evolutionary accident but a special creation. Human beings were purposefully produced by God to fulfill a preordained role in His world. They have peculiar qualities that somehow reflect the nature of God Himself and set them apart and above all other created beings.

Image and Likeness Some Bible students have tried to make a distinction in the meaning of "image" and "likeness." Image has been considered the essential nature of humans as God's special creation, and likeness as reflecting this image in such qualities as goodness, grace, and love. They maintain that humankind in the Fall retained the image but lost the likeness. The two words, however, seem to identify the same divine act. The repetition represents the Hebrew literary style of parallelism used for emphasis. The Hebrew *selem* or image refers to a hewn or carved image (1 Sam. 6:5; 2 Kings 11:18) like a statue, which bears a strong physical resemblance to the person or thing it represents. The word *likeness, demuth,* means a facsimile. Compare 2 Kings 16:10, "fashion" or "pattern" (NAS), "sketch" (NIV, REB), "exact model" (TEV). Neither of the words imply that persons are divine. They were endowed with some of the characteristics of God. There is a likeness but not a sameness.

Persons as Body-Soul Many different views seek to explain the nature of the likeness. Genesis 2:7 says, "the Lord God formed man of the dust of the ground, and breathed into his nostrils the breath of life; and man became a living soul." In creation God endowed persons with a spiritual aspect of life. This passage says that man became a soul, not that he had a soul. A person is both body and soul, or more accurately, body-soul. The Old Testament supports this holistic view of persons who are not segmented into parts known as body, soul, and spirit. Genesis 1:20 uses the Hebrew expression, *nephesh chayah,* "living soul" for "moving creature that has life," that is the animals. Compare 1:24; 9:10,16; Lev. 11:10.

Early theologians were greatly influenced by Greek philosophy in their interpretation of the image of God. The Greeks separated between the material and the spiritual. They saw an individual as a spirit being living in a physical body. This Greek dualism was the background out of which the early Christian theologians drew their understanding. The church fathers believed that the image of God resided in the soul or the spirit of each person.

Humankind as Persons Who are humans? The Bible portrays them as self-conscious, willful, innovative entities who, under God, preside over their environment. In other words, they are persons. God made each male and female a person in the likeness of His own personhood. Nothing else in all creation can be called a person. Personhood encompasses individuals in their entirety, body and spirit, as rational, loving, responsible, moral creatures.

Reflections of Personhood A man or woman is a person, as God is a Person. Such personal uniqueness is reflected in self-awareness and God-awareness. Human individuality is implied in personhood. God said "I am that I am" (Ex. 3:14). Persons also are separate entities with individual personalities, sets of values, inclinations, and responsibilities. Every human being is an original.

Humans created in God's image share His rational nature. People have the power to think, analyze, and reflect even upon abstract matters. They cannot be defined by or confined to material attributes. As God is spiritual (John 4:24), persons are spiritual. This spiritual kinship makes possible communication with God.

The Bible teaches that human beings have purpose. They have an instinctive need to be something and to do something. They have a responsible intuition and an inner call to duty. The human race has a unique sense of "oughtness." Humans are moral creatures. They can and do make moral judgments (Gen. 2:16–27). Persons have a censoring conscience which they may defy. They are choice makers; they can obey their highest instincts or follow their most morbid urges. A human is the only creature who can say no to God. Humans are autonomous persons. God endowed them with the freedom to govern their own lives.

This same autonomy makes possible fellowship with God. No person could have a meaningful relationship with a robot. Real fellowship can take place only between two authentic persons. God created "man" in His own image because He wanted a relationship with another sovereign person. See *Body; Creation; Flesh; Humanity; Soul;*

Vernon O. Elmore

IMAGE WORSHIP See *Idol.*

IMAGE, NEBUCHADNEZZAR'S *1.* The figure in Nebuchadnezzar's dream (Dan. 2:31–45); *2.* a colossal figure Nebuchadnezzar erected on the plains of Dura (Dan. 3:1–18).

The interpretation of the statue in Nebuchadnezzar's dream is debated. Nebuchadnezzar is clearly the head of gold (2:38). The identification of the other materials (silver, bronze, iron mixed with clay) with historical references is less clear. For convenience, interpreters may be classed broadly as historicists and dispensationalists.

Historicists have proposed various solutions to the enigmatic historical references. According to one interpretation, the various materials refer to the line of Neo-Babylonian kings which came to an end with the conquest of Cyrus who is identified as the divinely ordained rock (Dan. 2:45; compare Isa. 44:28; 45:1). Others see a succession of kingdoms rather than kings, for example, (1) Babylon, Media, Persia, and Greece or (2) Babylon, Medo-Persia, Alexander the Great, and Alexander's Hellenistic successors. Interpreters divide over whether to identify the kingdom that rules the world (2:39) with that of Cyrus who made this claim or with Alexander who in fact conquered much of the known world. The fourth "divided" kingdom (2:41) is frequently identified with the division of Alexander's empire by his generals. The mixing of iron and clay is possibly a reference to failed attempts to unite these kingdoms by marriage treaties (2:43). For these interpreters, the God-ordained stone is the Maccabees who secured Jewish independence and reinstituted Temple worship. Many historicists recognize that the Maccabees only partially fulfilled the hopes of the writer of Daniel and thus find the ultimate fulfillment in the kingdom established by Christ.

Dispensationalist interpreters identify the succession of kingdoms as Babylon, Medo-Persia, Greece, and Rome. Rome is the empire divided into eastern and western halves and finally represented by a ten nation federation. The Roman period extends until the time of Christ who is the God-ordained Rock which ends the power of the Gentiles (Dan. 7; Luke 21:24; Rev. 16:19).

The charge of not worshipping the gods of Nebuchadnezzar leveled against the Jews (Dan. 3:12,14) suggests a statue of Bel-merodach, the patron deity of Babylon, though the statue was possibly of Nebuchadnezzar himself. Here religion is a political tool to unite various peoples into one empire. Readers in Maccabean and Roman times no doubt understood the statue against contemporary use of the divine ruler cult.   *Chris Church*

IMAGERY Figurative language. Scripture prefers to convey truths by pictoral representations rather than through abstract language. Scripture abounds in word-pictures for God, God's people, and their experience of salvation.

The challenge of theology ("talk about God") is to express truths about God in human language. Scripture itself witnesses the difficulty of this task, "To whom will you liken me, and make me equal, and compare me that we may be like" (Isa. 46:5). The living God is not to be equated with any one manageable image. Idolatry is essentially the attempt to reduce God to an image or label. The multiplicity of Old Testament literary images for God serves as a corrective of human attempts to box God in. Some images for God are inanimate: stone (Gen. 49:24); fortress (2 Sam. 22:2); fountain of living waters (Jer. 2:13). There is little danger of confusing God with such images. Other

images of God are personal: father (Mal. 1:6); husband (Hos. 2:16); shepherd (Ps. 23:1); judge, lawgiver, and king (Isa. 33:22); teacher (Isa. 28:26); healer (Jer. 30:17); warrior (Ex. 15:1,3); farmer (Isa. 5:2–7). With such personal images, the danger of confusing "God is like" with "God is" is real. A challenging corrective is offered by the less familiar feminine images for God, for example, that of a mother bird sheltering her young (Ruth 2:12; Ps. 17:8). Also suggestive of a mother's tenderness are the images of carrying a child from birth (Isa. 46:3), teaching a child to walk (Hos. 11:3), child feeding (Hos. 11:4), and child rearing (Isa. 1:2).

In His parables, Jesus continued the Old Testament practice of using vivid images for God: a shepherd seeking one lost sheep (Luke 15:4–7); a woman seeking one lost coin (Luke 15:8–10); a father waiting patiently for the return of one son and taking the initiative to reconcile the other (Luke 15:11–32). Images are also used to teach who Jesus the Christ is: word (John 1:1); light (John 8:12); bread and wine (Matt. 26:26–29); vine (John 15:1); the way (John 14:6).

Imagery is also used to depict the people of God and their experience of salvation. The Old Testament pictures God's people as: a faithless wife (Jer. 3:20); a wild vine (Jer. 2:21); a wild donkey in heat (Jer. 2:24); God's beloved (Jer. 11:15); God's bride (Jer. 2:2); God's servant (Jer. 30:10); and God's son (Hos. 11:1). New Testament images include: light (Matt. 5:14); salt (Matt. 5:13); vine branches (John 15:5); a new creation (2 Cor. 5:17); God's temple (1 Cor. 3:16); and a royal priesthood (1 Pet. 2:9; compare Ex. 19:6). Images for salvation are drawn from all walks of life: the law courts (Rom. 7:3; Heb. 9:16–17); slave market (Titus 2:14); marketplace (1 Cor. 6:20; 7:23); and the family (Rom. 8:17,23). The multiplicity of images again witnesses the rich experience of God's people. See *Anthropomorphism; Parables.*
                                                                    Chris Church

IMAGERY, CHAMBER OF KJV phrase (Ezek. 8:12) understood as "room of his carved images" (NAS) or "shrine of his own idol" (NIV). The picture of the representatives of Israel worshiping idols within the Jerusalem Temple in Ezekiel's vision (8:3) symbolizes the people's unfaithfulness to God.

IMAGES See *Idol.*

IMAGINATION KJV term for thought as the prelude to action, frequently in the sense of plotting or devising evil; can also refer to stubbornness from the Hebrew words meaning formed or twisted. Imagination means evil plans (Prov. 6:18; Lam. 3:60–61). At Deuteronomy 31:21 and possibly Romans 1:21, imagination refers to the inclination to do evil. God opposes the imaginations of the proud (Luke 1:51; 2 Cor. 10:5). Imagination is also used in a neutral sense (1 Chron. 28:9). Most often, imagination means stubborness (Deut. 29:19; Jer. 3:17; 7:24; 9:14; 11:8; 13:10; 16:12; 18:12; 23:17). Modern translations use imagination less frequently. For example, the RSV used imagination only four times: for the inclination to do evil (Gen. 6:5; 8:21 NRSV reads, "inclination"); for the plans of the proud (Luke 1:51 NSRV reads "thoughts"); and in connection with the making of idols (Acts 17:29) where imagination may mean creativity or more likely a depraved mind. The NIV also used imagination four times: in reference to fabricating prophecy (Ezek. 13:2,17); and for evil plans (Isa. 65:2; 66:18).

IMITATE To mimic; to do what is seen to be done by another; sometimes it approximates, "be obedient." Paul's uses can be divided into three groups: (1) To call attention to a comparison even when no conscious mimicking is in mind. The Thessalonians shared suffering at the hands of their compatriots comparable to that experienced by the earliest Judean Christians (1 Thess. 2:14). First Thessalonians 1:6 perhaps belongs here. (2) To follow an example (Phil. 3:17; 2 Thess. 3:7,9 where Paul's example of self-support is in view). Obedience may also be in mind as references to tradition (2 Thess. 3:6) and command (3:10) demonstrate. (3) An equivalent to be obedient. Paul exhorted the Corinthians to follow him not primarily by following his personal example but by following his "ways in Christ" which he taught "everywhere in every church" (1 Cor. 4:16–17). The Corinthians were to follow Paul's example by heeding his counsel to do all for the glory of God without causing offense (1 Cor. 11:1; compare 10:23–33). In Ephesians 5:1 the command to be imitators is again linked with the previous series of commands, especially that of forgiveness (4:25–32). The image of children obedient to parents is common where the thought of imitation as obedience is primary (1 Cor. 4:14–16; Eph. 5:1).

Hebrews urges imitation of the faithfulness and patient endurance of those who inherited the promises (6:12) and the faithfulness of church leaders (13:7). The command of 3 John 11 is general, though specific examples of good (Demetrius) and bad (Diotrephes) are in view.

IMLA or **IMLAH** (Ĭm′ lah) Personal name meaning, "he fills," appearing in different spelling in Kings and Chronicles. Father of the prophet Micaiah (1 Kings 22:8). See *Micaiah*.

IMMANUEL (Im măn′ ū ĕl) Personal name meaning, "God with us." Name of son to be born in Isaiah's prophecy to King Ahaz (Isa. 7:14) and fulfilled in birth of Jesus (Matt. 1:22–23).

When King Ahaz refused to show his faith by asking God for a sign (Isa. 7:10–12), Isaiah gave him a sign of the birth of Immanuel, using the traditional form of a birth announcement (7:14; compare Gen. 16:11; Judg. 13:3,5). The Hebrew language apparently indicates that the prophet and king expected an immediate fulfillment. Recent study has pointed to Ahaz's wife as the woman expected to bear the child and show that God was still with the Davidic royal dynasty even in the midst of severe threat from Assyria. Such a sign would give hope to a king who trusted God but would be a constant threat to one who followed his own strategy. The double meaning of the Immanuel sign appears again in Isaiah 8:8. The Assyrian army would flood the land until Judah was up to its neck in trouble and could only cry out, "O Immanuel"; a cry confessing that God is with us in His destructive rage but at the same time a prayer, hoping for divine intervention. Isaiah followed this with a call to the nations to lose in battle because of Immanuel, God with us (8:10).

The Bible says nothing else about the effects of the Immanuel prophecy in the days of Isaiah and Ahaz. It does announce the great fulfillment in Jesus Christ (Matt. 1:22–23). Jesus' birth showed all humanity that God is faithful to fulfill His promises in ways far beyond human expectations; for Jesus was not just a sign of God with us. Jesus was God become flesh, God incarnate, God with us in Person.

IMMATERIALITY Not composed of matter. Acts 17:29 argues that "we ought not to think that the Godhead is like unto gold, or silver, or stone." Rather "God is a spirit: and they that worship him must worship him in spirit and in truth" (John 4:24).

IMMER (Ĭm′ mēr) Personal name probably meaning, "lamb." 1. Father of Pashur, the priest and Temple administrator (Jer. 20:1). 2. A priest whose son Zadok helped Nehemiah repair Jerusalem's walls (Neh. 3:29). Ancestor of priests who dwelt in Jerusalem after the return from Exile (1 Chron. 9:12). 3. Leader of priestly division under David (1 Chron. 24:14). Son of Immer in other instances could mean, "descendant of Immer" and refer to this original priestly ancestor. Compare Ezra 2:37–38; 10:20; Nehemiah 7:40; 11:13.

IMMORALITY Any illicit sexual activity outside of marriage. Both in the Old Testament and in the New Testament the word has a figurative meaning as well, referring to idolatry or unfaithfulness to God.

In the Old Testament *zanah* regularly refers to wrongful heterosexual intercourse, primarily in regard to women (Judg. 19:2; Jer. 3:1; Hos. 4:13). The noun "harlot" or "whore" is derived from the same stem (Gen. 34:31; Josh. 2:1–3; Prov. 23:27; Hos. 4:13–14). In a figurative sense, *zanah* refers to Israel's unfaithfulness to God (2 Chron. 21:11; Isa. 1:21; Jer. 3:1–5; Ezek. 16:26–28). In addition, the sinfulness of Tyre (Isa. 23:17) and Nineveh (Nah. 3:4) are portrayed in this manner.

In Paul's letters, *porneia* and/or related words refer to an incestuous relationship (1 Cor. 5:1), sexual relations with a prostitute (1 Cor. 6:12–20), and various forms of unchastity both heterosexual and homosexual (Rom. 1:29; 1 Cor. 5:9–11; 6:9–11; 7:2; 2 Cor. 12:21; Eph. 5:3; 1 Thess. 4:3). Immorality is a sin against God (1 Cor. 3:16–17; 6:15–20; 1 Thess. 4:3–8). In the Gospels, the term, on occasion, is related to adultery (Matt. 5:32; 19:9) and in Revelation may refer to harlotry or prostitution (Rev. 2:14,20). The word "harlot" or "whore" is derived from the same root (Rev. 19:2). In Acts, the Apostolic Council requires that Gentiles avoid *porneia* (Acts 15:20,29). *Porneia,* and related words also have a figurative meaning of unfaithfulness to God (Matt. 12:39; John 8:41; Rev. 2:21; 9:21; 14:8; 19:2). See *Adultery; Sex, Teaching on.* *Donald E. Cook*

IMMORTALITY The quality or state of being exempt from death. In the true sense of the word, only God is immortal (1 Tim. 6:16; see 1 Tim. 1:17; 2 Tim. 1:10), for only God is living in the true sense of the word (see *Life*). Humans may be considered immortal only insofar as immortality is the gift of God. Paul points us in this direction. In Romans 2:7, Paul says, "To those who by patiently doing good seek for glory and honor and immortality, he will give eternal life" (NRSV). Paul also explained that the perishable nature of human life will put on the imperishable and that the mortal nature of human life will put on immortality. When that happens, the saying concerning victory over death will have been fulfilled (1 Cor. 15:53–55; see Isa. 25:8; Hos 13:14). As it is, humans in their earthly life are mortal; they are subject to death.

Thus, eternal life is not ours because we have the inherent power to live forever; eternal life and immortality are ours only because God chooses to give them to us. Most of the time, we are given immortality after death. Those who did escape death—Enoch (Gen. 5:24) and Elijah (2 Kings 2:10–11)—did so only by the power of God and not by some inherent power they had to live forever. See *Eternal Life.* *Phil Logan*

IMMUTABILITY OF GOD (Ĭm mū tă bĭl' ĭ tȳ) The unchangeability of God; in biblical theology, a reference to God's unchanging commitment and faithfulness to the salvation of humanity.
Secular Philosophical Thought In secular thought, God's immutability connotes innate divine perfection and completeness. Since God is complete in

and of Himself, relation to anything other than Himself is an addition to His completeness, an addition which is a philosophical impossibility. Since relationship requires change or response on the part of the beings in relationship, God, perfectly complete and completely perfect, cannot relate to that which is outside Himself. This kind of God, who is possessed by an immutability which prohibits relationship to His creation, is not the God portrayed by the Bible.
Biblical Teaching God, as the Scriptures portray Him, responds to the needs of His creation and, therefore, changes in the sense that He relates to what is not God. The biblical idea of immutability is couched in the constancy of God's self-revelation to humanity: He is holy (Josh. 24:19), jealous (Ex. 20:5), zealous, (Isa. 9:7), beneficent (Ps. 107); and righteous (Ex. 9:27). God expresses wrath, though He is "slow to anger" (Neh. 9:17). He expresses love (Prov. 3:12) in the election of His people for service (Hos. 11:1; Matt. 28:19–20; Eph. 1:4) and by sending His one and only Son as the Savior of the world (John 3:16; Rom. 5:8; 1 John 4:9–10). The God of the Bible is the constant, unchangeable God in His revelation and response to humanity. He gives His name as "I am that I am" (lit. "I will be what I will be," Ex. 3:14). He is the God who is and will be what He has already been in the past: "the Lord God of your fathers, the God of Abraham, the God of Isaac, and the God of Jacob. . . . this is my name for ever . . ." (Ex. 3:15).

The greatest religious significance of the unchanging God is His eternal stance of salvation toward His creation. He is eternally faithful to His people. He therefore repents of judgment when persons answer His call to obedience, as did the Ninevites in Jonah 3. The unchanging God of salvation is the eternal, free God who reveals Himself in the eternal Son (John 1:1,18). As such, he is the immutable God who comes to seek and save the lost (Mark 10:45), the God who is the same "yesterday, and to day, and for ever (Heb. 13:8). *Walter D. Draughon III*

IMNA (Ĭm' nà) Personal name meaning, "he defends." A member of the tribe of Asher (1 Chron. 7:35). See *Imnah.*

IMNAH (Ĭm' nàh) Personal name meaning, "he allots for" or "on the right hand, good fortune." *1.* A son of Asher and original ancestor of the Imnites (Num. 26:44 KJV's Jimnah). *2.* A Levite in the time of King Hezekiah (2 Chron. 31:14).

IMNITE (Ĭm' nīte) See *Imnah.*

IMPEDIMENT IN SPEECH A disturbance of the vocal organs resulting in the inability to produce intelligible sounds (Mark 7:32). In Jesus' healing of a man who could "hardly talk" (NIV), the crowds recognized a fulfillment of Isaiah 35:5–6.

I

IMPERISHABLE Not subject to decay; ever-enduring. Imperishable (KJV, incorruption) describes the spiritual resurrection body which unlike the physical body is not subject to the decay associated with death (1 Cor. 15:42–54). Imperishable describes the everlasting reward of the saints (1 Cor. 9:25; 1 Pet. 1:23). One of the Greek terms translated imperishable is also rendered immortality (Rom. 2:7; 2 Tim. 1:10). The same term is used in reference to "undying" love in Ephesians 6:24 (KJV, "in sincerity").

IMPORTUNITY Troublesome urgency; excessive persistence. In Luke 11:8 importunity results in a favorable response to a midnight request for bread (KJV, RSV). Many modern translations read persistence (NAS, NIV, NRSV, REB). The literal meaning of the term is shamelessness (NEB; compare TEV: "not ashamed to keep on asking").

IMPOSITION OF HANDS See *Laying on of Hands.*

IMPOTENT Lacking power, strength, or vigor; helpless. Impotence in the KJV never refers to sexual inability. Modern translations replace impotent with other terms: cripple (Acts 4:9 NIV); disabled (John 5:3 NIV); invalid (John 5:3 NRSV); sick (John 5:3,7; Acts 4:9 NAS). Modern translations describe the man "impotent in his feet" (Acts 14:8) as one who could not use his feet (NRSV), without strength in his feet (NAS), or crippled (NIV). See *Diseases.*

IMPRECATION, IMPRECATORY PSALMS Act of invoking a curse. In the Imprecatory Psalms the author calls for God to bring misfortune and disaster upon the enemies (Pss. 5; 11; 17; 35; 55; 59; 69; 109; 137; 140). These Psalms are an embarrassment to many Christians who see them in tension with Jesus' teaching on love of enemies (Matt. 5:43–48). It is important to recall the theological principles that underlie such Psalms. These include: (1) the principle that vengeance belongs to God (Deut. 32:35; Ps. 94:1) that excludes personal retaliation and necessitates appeal to God to punish the wicked (compare Rom. 12:19); (2) the principle that God's righteousness demands judgment on the wicked (Pss. 5:6; 11:5–6); (3) the principle that God's covenant love for the people of God necessitates intervention on their part (Pss. 5:7; 59:10,16–17); and (4) the principle of prayer that believers trust God with all their thoughts and desires. See *Blessing and Cursing.*

IMPURITY See *Clean, Cleanness.*

IMPUTE, IMPUTATION Setting to someone's account or reckoning something to another person. God reckoned righteousness to believing Abraham (Gen. 15:16). This means that God credited to Abraham that which he did not have in himself (Rom. 4:3–5). This does not mean that God accepted Abraham's faith instead of righteousness as an accomplishment meriting justification. Rather, it means that God accepted Abraham because he trusted in God rather than trusting in something that he could do.

Similarly, drawing from Psalm 32:1–3, Paul stated that only God can forgive sin. Those who are forgiven are not regarded as wicked since the Lord does not impute to them their iniquity. Instead these are considered or reckoned as children of God (Rom. 4:7–8,11,23–24).

The imputation of righteousness lies at the heart of the biblical doctrine of salvation. This righteousness is seen in Christ who purchased redemption. God grants righteousness to those who have faith in Christ (Rom. 1:17; 3:21–26; 10:3; 2 Cor. 5:21; Phil. 3:9). This righteousness imputed or reckoned to believers is, strictly speaking, an alien righteousness. It is not the believer's own righteousness but God's righteousness imputed to the believer. So, as Luther said, believers are simultaneously righteous and sinful.

Not only is the imputation of God's righteousness to the believer taught in Scripture, but the Bible in some sense implies that Adam's sin was imputed to humankind (Rom. 5:12–21; 1 Cor. 15:21–22). Likewise, it is taught that the sins of humanity were imputed to Jesus Christ (2 Cor. 5:21), although the exact nature of this divine imputation remains a mystery. The matter has been intensely debated in church history since the time of Augustine (A.D. 354–440). Nevertheless, for a consistent biblical witness, it must be maintained that in Adam God judged the whole human race guilty. Yet humankind has not merely been declared guilty; each human has acted out his or her guilt. More importantly, it is impossible for sinners to be righteous in God's sight apart from the gift of righteousness graciously granted to them in Christ through faith. *David S. Dockery*

IMRAH (Ĭm′ rah) Personal name meaning, "he is obstinate." Member of tribe of Asher (1 Chron. 7:36).

IMRI (Ĭm′ rī) Short form of personal name Amariah meaning, "Yah has spoken." *1.* Ancestor of clan from tribe of Judah living in Jerusalem after the return from Exile (1 Chron. 9:4). *2.* Father of Zaccur, who helped Nehemiah rebuild Jerusalem's wall (Neh. 3:2).

INCANTATIONS Chants used by magicians to control evil spirits and thus heal the sick or afflict enemies. No Palestinian incantations survive from the biblical period. Babylonian incantations had three parts, (1) an invocation of the names of the great gods, (2) identification of the spirit causing the illness, and (3) the call for the demon to leave. Compare Acts 19:13 where Jewish exorcists invoked the superior name of Jesus. Mosaic law prohibited the casting of spells (Deut. 18:11). The complaint that the wicked are like a snake immune to the cunning enchanter perhaps refers to the futility of incantations (Ps. 58:4–5). The Babylonians hoped to gain success and terrorize their enemies by means of incantations (Isa. 47:12). Isaiah warned their incantations would be of no avail (47:9). The tongue muttering wickedness perhaps refers to incantations (Isa. 59:3). The books of magic of Acts 19:19 were likely collections of incantations. See *Blessing and Cursing; Imprecation; Magic.*

INCARNATION (in cär nā′ tion) God's becoming human; the union of divinity and humanity in Jesus of Nazareth.

Definition of Doctrine Incarnation [Lat. *incarnatio,* being or taking flesh], while a biblical idea, is not a biblical term. Its Christian use derives from the Latin version of John 1:14 and appears repeatedly in Latin Christian authors from about A.D. 300 onward.

As a biblical teaching, incarnation refers to the affirmation that God, in one of the modes of His existence as Trinity and without in any way ceasing to be the one God, has revealed Himself to humanity for its salvation by becoming human. Jesus, the Man from Nazareth, is the incarnate Word or Son of God, the focus of the God-human encounter. As the God-Man, He mediates God to humans; as the Man-God, He represents humans to God. By faith-union with Him, men and women, as adopted children of God, participate in His filial relation to God as Father.

The Humanity of Jesus The angel of the Lord, in a prophecy of Jesus' birth, plainly stated the purpose of the incarnation: "[Mary] shall bring forth a son, and thou shalt call his name Jesus: for he shall save his people from their sins" (Matt. 1:21; compare Luke 19:10; John 3:17; 1 Tim. 1:15). The liberation of humanity from everything that would prevent relationship with God as Father requires incarnation. The biblical materials related to incarnation, though not systematically arranged, portray Jesus as the One who accomplished the mission of salvation because He was the One in whom both full divinity and full humanity were present.

Jesus referred to Himself as a man (John 8:40), and the witnesses in the New Testament recognized Him as fully human. (For example, Peter, in his sermon at Pentecost, declared that Jesus is "a man approved of God among you . . . ," Acts 2:22). That the Word was made flesh is the crux of the central passage on incarnation in the New Testament (John 1:14). The respective genealogies of Jesus serve as testimonies to His natural human descent (Matt. 1:1–17; Luke 3:23–37).

In addition, Jesus attributed to Himself such normal human elements as body and soul (Matt. 26:26,28,38). He grew and developed along the lines of normal human development (Luke 2:40). During His earthly ministry, Jesus displayed common physiological needs: He experienced fatigue (John 4:6); His body required sleep (Matt. 8:24), food (Matt. 4:2; 21:18), and water (John 19:28). Human emotional characteristics accompanied the physical ones: Jesus expressed joy (John 15:11) and sorrow (Matt. 26:37); He showed compassion (Matt. 9:36) and love (John 11:5); and He was moved to righteous indignation (Mark 3:5).

A proper understanding of the events preceding and including His death requires an affirmation of His full humanity. In the garden, He prayed for emotional and physical strength to face the critical hours which lay ahead. He perspired as one under great physical strain (Luke 22:43–44). He died a real death (Mark 15:37; John 19:30). When a spear was thrust into His side, both blood and water poured from His body (John 19:34). Jesus thought of Himself as human, and those who witnessed His birth, maturation, ministry, and death experienced Him as fully human.

Although Jesus was fully human in every sense of the word, His was a perfect humanity—distinct and unique. His miraculous conception highlights distinctiveness and originality of His humanity. Jesus was supernaturally conceived, being born of a virgin (Luke 1:26–35). To be sure, the Bible records other miraculous births such as those of Isaac (Gen. 21:1–2) and John the Baptist (Luke 1:57), but none attained to the miraculous heights of a human being supernaturally conceived and born of a virgin.

The New Testament also attests to the sinless character of Jesus. He, Himself, asked the question, "Which of you convinceth me of sin?" (John 8:46). Paul declared, God "made him to be sin for us who knew no sin" (2 Cor. 5:21). The writer of Hebrews held that Christ was "without sin" (4:15). The New Testament presents Jesus as a man, fully human, and as a unique man, the ideal human.

The Deity of Jesus Paul, in a statement on the supremacy of Christ, asserted, "For it pleased the Father that in him should all fulness dwell" (Col. 1:19; compare John 20:28; Titus 2:13). Jesus, was aware of His divine status (John 10:30; 12:44–45; 14:9). With the "I am" sayings, He equated Himself with the God who appeared to Moses in the burning bush (Ex. 3:14). The assertion of the New Testament is that Jesus was God (John 6:51; 10:7,11; 11:25; 14:6; 15:1; esp. 8:58).

The Bible affirms the preexistence of Jesus: "In the beginning was the Word, and the Word was with God, and the Word was God. The same was in the beginning with God" (John 1:1–2; see also

I

John 1:15; 8:58; 17:5; Phil. 2:5–11). Jesus realized accomplishments and claimed authority ascribed only to divinity. He forgave sins (Matt. 9:6) and sent others to do His bidding, claiming all authority "in heaven and in earth" (Matt. 28:18–20). The central proclamation of the gospel is that He is the only way to eternal life, a status held by deity alone (John 3:36; 14:6; compare Acts 4:12; Rom. 10:9). The New Testament pictures Him as worthy of honor and worship due only to deity (John 5:23; Heb. 1:6; Phil. 2:10–11; Rev. 5:12). He is the Agent of creation (John 1:3) and the Mediator of providence (Col. 1:17; Heb. 1:3). He raised the dead (John 11:43–44), healed the sick (John 9:6), and vanquished demons (Mark 5:13). He will effect the final resurrection of humanity either to judgment or to life (Matt. 25:31–32; John 5:27–29).

The titles ascribed to Jesus provide conclusive evidence for the New Testament's estimate of His person as God. Jesus is "Lord" (Phil 2:11), "Lord of lords" (1 Tim. 6:15), "the Lord of glory" (1 Cor. 2:8), "the mediator" (Heb. 12:24), and "who is over all, God blessed for ever" (Rom. 9:5). In addition, the New Testament repeatedly couples the name "God" with Jesus (John 1:18; 20:28; Acts 20:28; Rom. 9:5; 2 Thess. 1:12; Titus 2:13; Heb. 1:8; 2 Pet. 1:1; 1 John 5:20).

Formulation of the Doctrine The problems of the incarnation begins with John's assertion, "the Word was made flesh" (1:14). Clear expression of the relation of the Word to the flesh, of divinity to humanity within the person of Jesus became a matter of major concern during the first five centuries of the Christian era. The unsystematized affirmations of the New Testament were refined through controversy, a process which culminated in the ecumenical councils of Nicaea (A.D. 325), Constantinople (A.D. 381), Ephesus (A.D. 431), and Chalcedon (A.D. 451).

The Council of Nicaea marked the meeting of church representatives from throughout the Christian world. Its purpose was to settle the dispute over the teachings of Arius, a presbyter in the church of Alexandria. He taught a creature christology—that is, he denied the Son's eternal divinity. Against Arius, the council asserted that the Son was of one substance with the Father. Jesus was fully divine.

The Council of Constantinople met to clarify and refute the christology of Apollinarius, Bishop of Laodicea. Apollinarius insisted that Jesus was a heavenly man dissimilar to earthly men. If a human is body, soul, and spirit, the bishop asserted that Jesus was a body, soul, and Logos [lit. "word"], a man not having a human spirit, or mind. Against this doctrine, the council affirmed the full humanity of Christ.

The Council of Ephesus considered the marriage christology of Nestorius, Bishop of Constantinople. He held that the union of the human and divine in Jesus was like the marriage of a husband and wife. As a result, the Council accused him of teaching that there were two separate persons in Christ.

The Council of Chalcedon was perhaps the most significant church council for Christianity. It met in debate over the teaching of Eutyches, a monk from Constantinople. He denied that Jesus had two natures. This reaction against the christology of Nestorius prompted the council to express the incarnation of Jesus in terms of one person with two natures—human and divine.

The mystery of the incarnation continues, and the statements of the first four councils of the Christian church preserve that mystery. Jesus, God incarnate, was one Person in two natures—fully divine and fully human. See *Christ.*

Walter D. Draughon III

INCENSE A mixture of aromatic spices prepared to be burned in connection with the offering of sacrifices (Ex. 25:6). The word is also used to refer to the smoke produced by the burning. In the King James Version of the Bible, two Hebrew words are translated "incense"; however, the two words are practically synonymous. The incense used in worship was to be prepared according to exacting specifications and was to be offered only by the high priest. According to Luke 1:8–20, Zacharias was burning incense in the Temple when he was visited by the angel Gabriel. See *Sacrifice and Offerings.*

Incense bowl from the island of Malta.

INCENSE ALTAR See *Tabernacle; Temple.*

INCEST Sexual intercourse between persons too closely related for normal marriage. The twofold theological rationale for the prohibition of incestuous unions is the divine claim "I am the LORD your God" (Lev. 18:2,4,6) and the note that such behavior characterized the Egyptians and Canaanites whom God judged (Lev. 18:3,24–25). Leviticus 18:6–16 prohibited unions between a man and his mother, stepmother, sister, half-sister,

Incense altar from the site of ancient Hazor.

daughter-in-law, granddaughter, aunt (by blood or marriage), or sister-in-law. Leviticus 18:19 prohibited a man's involvement with a woman and her daughter or granddaughter. Leviticus 18:18 prohibited taking sisters as rival wives. Penalties for various forms of incest included childlessness (Lev. 20:20–21), exclusion from the covenant people (Lev. 18:29; 20:17–18; compare 1 Cor. 5:2,5), and death (Lev. 20:11,12,14). In patriarchal times marriage to a half sister (Gen. 20:12) and marriage to rival sisters (Gen. 29:21–30) were permissible, though such marriages proved troublesome to both Abraham and Jacob. Scriptural accounts of incest include Genesis 19:31–35; 35:22; and 2 Samuel 13.

INCH A unit of measure equal to a twelfth of a foot. Eighteen inches (Gen. 6:16 NIV, TEV) is the equivalent of a cubit. See *Weights and Measures.*

INCONTINENCY, INCONTINENT KJV term for the lack of self-control (1 Cor. 7:5). Incontinent (2 Tim. 3:3) means lacking self-control (NAS), profligate (NRSV), or even violent (TEV).

INCORRUPTIBLE, INCORRUPTION KJV terms meaning imperishable and an imperishable state. See *Imperishable.*

INCREASE Multiplication or growth. In the Old Testament, increase often refers to the reproduction of livestock and to the harvest (Lev. 26:3–4; Deut. 7:12–13). The promise of increase is contingent on Israel's fulfilling its covenant commitments. Increase is used figuratively for Israel as the firstfruits of God's increase (KJV) or harvest. Isaiah 9:7 promises the increase of the government and peace of the coming Messiah. Isaiah 29:19 promises an increase in joy (KJV; fresh joy, NRSV; compare 9:3). Isaiah 40:29 promises increased strength to the powerless.

The increase of the word of God (Acts 6:7) refers to the spread of the gospel message. Increase is used both for the numerical growth of the church (Acts 16:5) and for maturation (Eph.

4:16; Col. 2:19). Christian maturity is evidenced by an increase in love (1 Thess. 3:12; 4:10) and knowledge of God (Col. 1:10). Boasting in the results of one's work for God is without a basis since God gives the increase (1 Cor. 3:6, Col. 2:19).

INDEPENDENCE OF GOD The doctrine that God does not depend on another for His existence or for the free exercise of His divine perogatives. See *Divine Freedom; I Am; Sovereignty of God.*

INDIA The eastern boundary of the Persian Empire of Ahasuerus (Xeres) (Esther 1:1; 8:9). Biblical references to India refer to the Punjab, the area of Pakistan and northwest India drained by the Indus river and its tributaries. India was possibly a port of call for Solomon's fleet (1 Kings 10:22).

INDIA (Ĭn' dĭ à) Place name given to a Persian satrapy or province. India was the easternmost limit of the Persian Empire. The name India applies to the territory near the northwestern part of the Indus River, a territory Darius of Persia (522–486 B.C.) had conquered. In the Bible, only Esther mentions it to describe the size of the Persian Empire (1:1; 8:9). Trade between India and the biblical lands began before 2000 B.C., however.

INFANT BAPTISM Christening a baby by the church. Christian groups take varying stances on the practice and meaning of infant baptism. Those who emphasize a conscious faith response in the salvation process limit baptism to believers. Those who interpret baptism as the sign of God's new covenant reserve the rite for the children of believers (compare 1 Cor. 7:14). Those viewing baptism as a means by which God's grace becomes effective for salvation welcome all children.

Those favoring infant baptism raise the following arguments: (1) household baptisms likely included some infants (Acts 16:5,33; 18:8; 1 Cor. 1:16); (2) Jesus' welcome and blessing of children is a mandate to baptize infants (Mark 10:13–16); "hinder" is a technical term associated with baptism (Acts 8:36); (3) circumcision which prefigured baptism (Col. 2:11) included children (Gen. 17:12); (4) in the Old Testament children participated in ceremonies of covenant renewel (Deut. 29:10–13; Josh. 8:35; Joel 2:16).

Baptists and other adherents of believer's baptism raise the following arguments and counter-arguments: (1) The New Testament prerequisite of baptism is faith (Acts 18:8) which is evidenced by confession (Rom. 10:9–10) and repentance (Acts 2:38); (2) infant baptism rests ultimately on the fear that infants are held accountable for organic sin; Baptists counter with a doctrine of an age of accountability at which conscious sin occurs (Gen. 8:21; Ps. 25:7; Jer. 3:25) and at which

I

a conscious response to God is possible (1 Kings 18:12; Ps. 71:5,17); (3) household baptisms need not have included children; baptism is prefigured in the salvation of Noah and his exclusively adult household in the ark (1 Pet. 3:20–21); (4) Jesus' blessing of the children demonstates Christ's love for children; children are presented as an example to disciples rather than as disciples themselves (Matt. 18:2–4); (5) circumcision is an imperfect analogy to baptism; only males participated in circumcision, whereas in baptism there is "neither male nor female" (Gal. 3:28); the witness of the New Testament is that "what is born of the flesh is flesh" and that a spiritual birth is necessary to enter God's kingdom (John 3:5–6); it is not the Israel of the flesh that inherits the promises of God but those who are spiritual Israel by a faith commitment (Rom. 6–8; Gal. 6:16); (6) the responsibility of the faith community to its children is instruction in the way of the Lord (Deut. 4:9–10; 11:19; Prov. 22:6); participation in covenant renewel is educational for children. See *Accountability, Age of, Baptism.*   *Chris Church*

INFANT SALVATION See *Accountability, Age of; Salvation.*

INFINITE Unlimited in extent of space, duration, and quantity. Though scripture does not use the term infinite to describe God, theologians have found the term a suitable summary of several attributes of God. God is not limited by space, (Ps. 139:7–8). God is not limited by time: God existed before the creation (Gen. 1:1); the ordering of time is part of God's creative activity (Gen. 1:5). Because God is spirit (John 4:24), God cannot be quantified like a material object. God is regarded as infinite in many other qualities: God's steadfast love endures forever (Ps. 100:5); God's knowledge extends to the fall of a single sparrow and the number of hairs on our heads (Matt. 10:29–30; compare Ps. 139:1–6); God is "the Almighty" (Gen. 17:1; Ex. 6:3).

INFIRMITY Disease, suffering, or sorrow. The KJV often used infirmity where modern translations have another term (e.g., weakness, diseases, sickness, menstruation, grief). Matthew saw in Jesus healings the fulfillment of the servant of the Lord who took our diseases (Matt. 8:17; Isa. 53:4). Romans 15:1 calls upon the strong (in conscience) to bear with the weaknesses (KJV infirmity) of those without strength. See *Disease, Treatment of.*

INFLAMMATION A response to cellular injury characterized by redness, infiltration of white blood cells, heat, and frequently pain. Inflammation was one of the curses upon those disobedient to the covenant (Deut. 28:22; compare Lev. 13:28).

INGATHERING, FEAST OF Alternate name for the Feast of Booths (Ex. 23:16; 34:12). See *Festivals; Booths, Feast of.*

INHERITANCE A legal transmission of property after death. The Hebrew Bible has no exclusive term for "inheritance." The words often translated "inherit" mean more generally "take possession." Only in context can they be taken to mean "inheritance." The Greek word in the New Testament does refer to the disposition of property after death, but its use in the New Testament often reflects the Old Testament background more than normal Greek useage.

In ancient Israel possessions were passed on to the living sons of a father, but the eldest son received a double portion (Deut. 21:17). Reuben lost preeminence because of incest with Bilhah (Gen. 35:22; 49:4; 1 Chron. 5:1), and Esau surrendered his birthright to Jacob (Gen. 25:29–34). These examples show that possession of this double portion was not absolute. Sons of concubines did not inherit unless adopted. Jacob's sons by the maidservants Bilhah and Zilpah (Gen. 30:3–13) inherited (Gen. 49) because those offspring were adopted by Rachel and Leah. Sarai promised to adopt the offspring of her maid Hagar when she gave Hagar to Abram (Gen. 16:2) but went back on that promise after Isaac's birth (Gen. 21:10).

Women were not to inherit from their fathers except in the absence of a son (Num. 27:1–11). Before this ruling from the Lord, if a man had no offspring, the inheritance went to his brothers, to his father's brothers, or to his next kinsman.

Because the Hebrew words did not necessarily presuppose a death, they could be used in reference to God's granting of the land to Israel (Josh. 1:15; Num. 36:2–4). Levites had no share of the land, and the Lord Himself was their "inheritance" (Num. 18:20–24; Deut. 10:9; 18:2; Josh. 13:33). Jeremiah used the concept of "inheritance" to refer to the restoration of Israel to the land from "the north" after the time of punishment (Jer. 3:18–19).

Israel is the "inheritance" of the Lord (Jer. 10:16). Psalm 79:1 speaks of Jerusalem and the Temple as God's "inheritance." In a broader sense, however, God can be said to "inherit" all nations (Ps. 82:8).

Anything given by God can be called an "inheritance." In Psalm 16:5 the pleasant conditions of the psalmist's life were his "inheritance" because he had chosen the Lord as his lot. In Psalm 119:111 God's testimonies are an "inheritance." In Job 27:13 "heritage" refers to God's punishment of the wicked. Proverbs 3:35 compares the honor the wise "inherit" with the disgrace of the fool.

In the New Testament "inheritance" can refer to property (Luke 12:13), but it most often refers to the rewards of discipleship: eternal life (Matt.

5:5; 19:29; Mark 10:29–30 and parallels; Titus 3:7), the kingdom (Matt. 25:34; Jas. 2:5; negatively 1 Cor. 6:9–10; 15:50), generally (Acts 20:32; Eph. 1:14,18; Rev. 21:7). Christ is the Heir *par excellence* (Matt. 21:38 and parallels; Heb. 1:2). Through Christ Christians can be heirs of God and "fellow heirs" with Christ (Rom. 8:17; compare Eph. 3:6). Only Hebrews makes explicit use of the idea of "inheritance" as requiring the death of the testator, Christ. A "will" requires a death to come into effect, so the death of Christ brings the new "covenant"/"will" into effect (Heb. 9:16–17). See *Covenant; Land; Promise.*

Fred L. Horton, Jr.

INIQUITY See *Sin.*

INJURY An act that hurts, damages, or causes loss; the result of such an act. Old Testament law provided two responses to injuries; retaliation in kind ("eye for eye, tooth for tooth" (Ex. 21:24) and compensation. For example, if the victim of an assault was confined to bed, the assailant was to pay the injured party for time lost from work as well as "health care" expenses to ensure recovery (Ex. 21:22). If an owner caused a slave to loose an eye or a tooth, the slave was to be freed as compensation for the loss (Ex. 21:26). Physical injuries excluded priests from service at the altar (Lev. 21:19). As part of the Hasmonean intrigue, Aristobulus had the ears of his uncle Hyrcanus II mutilated to disqualify him from priestly service (40 B.C.).

The extended use of the term is evidenced by Proverbs 8:36 where those who miss wisdom injure themselves and Romans 14:15 where Paul warned the Roman Christians not to injure other Christians for the sake of food (compare Gal. 4:12).

INK Writing fluid. Ink for writing on papyrus (a plant product) was made of soot or lampblack mixed with gum arabic (Jer. 36:18; 2 Cor. 3:3; 2 John 12; 3 John 13). Red ink was made by replacing lampblack with red iron oxide. Because such ink did not stick well to parchment (a leather product), another ink was made from nut galls mixed with iron sulphate.

INKHORN KJV term for a case in which ingredients for making ink were kept (Ezek. 9:2–3,11). A scribe customarily carried his inkhorn in his belt.

INLET A bay or recess in the shore of a sea or lake. When Deborah and Barak went to battle against Sisera, the tribe of Asher stayed at home "by his inlets" (landings NRSV, Judg. 5:17).

INN Different kinds of shelters or dwellings. In the Old Testament the Hebrew word translated "inn" or "lodging place" might refer to a camping place for an individual (Jer. 9:2), a family on a journey (Ex. 4:24), an entire caravan (Gen. 42:27; 43:21), or an army (Josh. 4:3,8). In these passages (with the possible exception of the reference in Jeremiah) the presence of a building is not implied. Often the reference is only to a convenient piece of ground near a spring. It is doubtful that inns in the sense of public inns with a building existed in Old Testament times.

By the time of Christ, the situation is quite different. Public inns existed in Greek times and throughout the Roman period. The Greek word for "inn" in the New Testament implies some type of stopping place for travelers. At times it refers to a public inn. Such an inn of the first century consisted primarily of a walled-in area with a well. A larger inn might have small rooms surrounding the court. People and animals stayed together.

Inns generally had a bad reputation. Travelers were subjected to discomfort and at times robbery or even death. The primary services that could be depended upon were water for the family and animals and a place to spread a pallet.

In addition to referring to a public inn, the same Greek word for "inn" at times refers simply to a guest room in a private home (Mark 14:14; Luke 22:11).

In Bethlehem, Joseph and Mary could find no room at the inn (Luke 2:7). This may have been a

Pen cases from ancient Egypt with containers in the tops for ink.

guest room in a home or some kind of public inn. The reference in Luke 10:34 is clearly to a public place where the wounded could be fed and cared for by the innkeeper. See *Hospitality; House.*

Paul E. Robertson

INNER MAN; INWARD MAN The component of human personality responsive to the requirements of the law. According to Paul's understanding (Rom. 7:22–23), human personality has three components: (1) the inmost self where the law dwells; Paul equated this with reason (*nous,* vs. 23); the inmost self approximates the rabbinic *yeser hatob* (inclination to good); (2) the members or the flesh that is responsive to desire; the flesh approximates the rabbinic *yeser harah* (inclination to evil); and (3) the conscious I which is aware of both reason and desire. In rabbinic thought, the law served to tip the balance in favor of the good inclination. Paul, however, rejected this optimistic view of the law. Only the Spirit dwelling in the inner self can free the individual from the power of sin (Rom. 8:2; Eph. 3:16). The Pauline division of personality is reflected in Freud's threefold division, superego, id, and ego.

INNKEEPER One who serves as the host or hostess at an inn. The innkeeper of Luke 10:35 was responsible for providing food and medical care. A targum (early Aramaic Free translation) on Joshua 2:1 identifies Rahab as an innkeeper.

INNOCENCE, INNOCENCY The condition of not offending God; freedom from sin and guilt. In the Old Testament the adjective *innocence* is more common than the noun. Two roots are commonly translated innocent. The basic idea of the first is clean or free from (Ex. 23:7; 2 Kings 24:4); that of the second, righteousness (Gen. 20:4; Deut. 25:1; Job 9:15). Though the innocent are frequently mentioned, the biblical writers were well aware that only God can create a right heart and remove sin (Ps. 51:10; Jer. 24:7; 31:33–34).

In the New Testament four terms are used for innocent. The first means unmixed or pure (Matt. 10:16; Phil. 2:15); the second, free from (Matt. 27:4,24); the third, just, righteous, or upright (Matt. 23:35; Luke 23:47); and the fourth, clean or pure (Acts 18:6; 20:26). Innocence is always relative to some standard. Paul declared his innocence with respect to the demands of the law (Phil. 3:6). Only Christ, however, is absolutely pure (Rom. 3:9–18; 2 Cor. 5:21). Christ presents believers as holy and blameless before God (Col. 1:22; Eph. 5:27; 1 Cor. 1:8; 1 Thess. 5:23).

INNOCENTS, SLAUGHTER OF THE Herod's murder of all boys under two years of age as he attempted to destroy the Baby Jesus (Matt. 2:16–18). The Magi or wise men searched for the one born king of the Jews. Herod the Great saw a claimant to his throne. When the Magi failed to report back their finding of the Christ-child, Herod ordered the slaughter of all male children in Bethlehem two years of age or less. The Gospel writer cites this as fulfillment of the prophecy of Jeremiah 31:15.

This incident is not mentioned elsewhere in the New Testament. However, it can be found in ancient nonbiblical documents, such as the *Protoevangelium of James, Infancy Gospel of Thomas,* and *Gospel of Pseudo-Matthew.* These sources no doubt relied on the biblical Gospel for the record.

Flavius Josephus, our chief ancient source on Herod, is surprisingly silent on this episode. Nonetheless, an act of such ruthlessness on Herod's part is entirely in keeping with his character as reported by Josephus. For example, when lying near death Herod ordered that all the Jewish leaders be captured and slaughtered upon his death, thus assuring grief at his passing. Fortunately, that order was not carried out. See *Apocrypha, New Testament; Herod; Josephus; Magi.*

Larry McKinney

INQUIRE OF GOD Seek divine guidance, most often before battle (1 Sam. 23:2,4; 2 Sam. 5:19,23; 2 Kings 3:11; 2 Chron. 18:4,6–7), but in other situations as well. A variety of methods were employed to seek God's counsel: dreams (1 Sam. 28:6); priests with the ephod (1 Sam. 22:10; 23:9–13); prophets (2 Kings 3:11); and direct consultation. In the early history of Israel, priests were consulted for divine counsel (Judg. 18:14,17; 1 Sam. 22:10). The priests discerned God's will by the sacred lots, the Urim and Thummim (Num. 27:21; 1 Sam. 14:36–42). Since these lots apparently were kept in a pouch in the priest's ephod (Ex. 28:30), references to inquiring of the ephod likely refer to the lots (1 Sam. 23:9–13; 30:8). See *Ephod; Lots; Urim and Thummim.* Prophets sometimes used music as an aid to achieve an ecstatic state in which God's will could be discerned (2 Kings 3:15; 1 Sam. 10:5–6). Prophets frequently took the initiative to announce God's will when no consultation was requested. With the rise of the synagogue, direct inquiring by prayer became the primary means of ascertaining the divine will.

Not all methods of inquiring of God were looked upon with favor. The Danites consulted a Levite in charge of Micah's sanctuary (Judg. 18:5–6,14). The method used by the Levite to ascertain the divine will is not clear. The sanctuary contained an ephod (with lots?), a cast idol, and teraphim (household gods), any of which might have been consulted. Such shrines were regarded as one example of the evil that resulted when there was no king and "every man did what was right in his own eyes" (Judg. 17:6). Other methods of discerning God's will rejected by the biblical writiers include: consulting mediums, wizards, and necromancers (Deut. 18:10–11; 1 Sam. 28:3,7; Isa. 8:19); consulting teraphim (Judg. 17:5; 18:13–20; Hos. 3:4; Zech. 10:2); and consulting pagan dieties (Baal-zebub, 2 Kings 1:2–3,16; Malcham or Milcom, Zeph. 1:5). See *Prophets, Prophecy; Necromancy; Teraphim; Milcom.*

Chris Church

INSANITY Mental illness. See *Diseases.*

INSCRIPTION Words or letters carved, engraved, or printed on a surface (Mark 15:26; Luke 23:38; superscription, KJV). Pilate likely intended the inscription above the cross in a derogatory sense: "See the defeated King of the Jews." According to John 19:21, the Jewish leadership found the inscription offensive. The Gospel writers saw in Pilate's mockery the truth about Jesus who in His suffering and death fulfilled His messianic role.

INSECTS Air-breathing arthropods which make up the class *Hexapoda.* Representatives are found on land and in water. They have three distinct body parts: head, thorax, and abdomen as well as three pair of legs, one pair of antennae, and usually one or two pairs of wings. Fossil studies have shown that insects are among the most ancient of the animals. Their persistence demonstrates their ability to survive under the most difficult conditions. Today insects are the most widely distributed of all the animals. Though their numbers are limited in the polar regions, insects abound in the tropics and temperate regions. Their primary food is green plants, and they are found almost everywhere that a food source is available.

Insects are characterized by their ability to move about. Stimuli such as food, temperature, humidity, and change of season may initiate movement. Not only are insects mobile, but they are also migratory. Migration is usually a seasonal phenomenon. Many insects, such as the monarch butterfly, have an annual migration similar to some birds.

Insects comprise the largest number of species in the animal kingdom, numbering in the millions. They are abundant in population, as well as in species. This is due, in part, to the fact that insects lay enormous numbers of eggs. The average number of eggs laid by an insect is from 100 to 150, though the queen termite can lay sixty eggs per second until several million are produced. The short life cycle of insects also contributes to their great numbers. Most mature within a year. Others such as the red mite, may have several generations in one season.

Some insects are characterized by specialized methods of reproducing. Polyembryony is a process by which hundreds of offspring can be produced from a single egg. Some species are able to reproduce with no mate, a function known as parthenogenesis.

Insects are among the most injurious of the

Hieroglyphic inscriptions on a temple wall at Karnak in Egypt.

I

classes of the animal kingdom. Most everything that man grows or manufactures is susceptible to the ravages of insects. Most insects feed on plants, causing much damage to agricultural products. Many attack man and other animals, as well as woodwork, wool, and clothing. Insects also transmit diseases such as malaria, the plague, and typhoid. However, some insects are beneficial, producing honey, wax, silk, pigments, and tannins. They are also a substantial food source for other animals, including man. Other insects are scavengers, helping to dispose of decaying flesh. The pollination of plants is another benefit provided by insects.

Insects occupy a prominent place among the animals named in the Bible. At least six orders are mentioned:

Hymenoptera: Ants, Bees, and Wasps These creatures generally have four wings. The female usually has a stinger as well as an ovipositor, or egg-laying organ, at the tip of the abdomen. Many of the species are social creatures.

1. Ants live in communities, sometimes as large as one-half million individuals. The nest is a maze of tunnels, showing much less planning than the nests of the wasps and bees. Young ants do not develop inside individual cells but are carried about in the nest. The workers are female, having neither wings nor the ability to reproduce. The queen and males have wings. Females are produced from fertilized eggs while males are born of unfertilized eggs. Ants are known to domesticate and enslave other insects, such as aphids and other ants. They also practice agriculture and conduct war on other ants.

The ant (Hebrew, *nemalah*) appears in the Bible only in the Book of Proverbs. Proverbs 6:6–8 praises her as the supreme example of industry. The ant's wisdom and ability to provide food though "a people not strong" is noted in Proverbs 30:25.

2. Bees have been domesticated for centuries. Herodotus, a Greek historian, wrote of how Egyptian beekeepers moved their hives according to the change of seasons. A beehive may contain 50,000 or more bees. Bees eat pollen and produce a wax which is used to build their combs and nests. A peculiar characteristic of bees and many of their relatives is their ability to determine the sex of their offspring. To do this, the queen bee stores in her body sperm received soon after she hatched. When she lays eggs, she releases one sperm cell for each egg she lays if females are needed. Males develop from eggs which have not been fertilized.

Bees (*deborah*) are mentioned several times in the Old Testament. They were noted for their antagonism, and armies were compared to swarms of bees (Deut. 1:44). The bee gained fame in the story of Samson, for he ate honey from the carcass of a lion and later tested the Philistines with a riddle concerning the incident (Judg. 14:5–18). The bee also is referred to in Psalm 118:12 and Isaiah 7:18.

3. Wasps and hornets (*tsir'ah*) are generally social creatures but to a lesser extent than bees and ants. They construct nests by scraping dead wood and making a pulp which is used to form paper. The nest, like that of the bee, is made up of individual cells in the shape of a hexagon. Hornets are found in the Old Testament. The Hebrew word may refer also to wasps and yellow jackets, but the precise Hebrew meaning is not known. "Hornet" comes from the earliest Greek translation. Some think the Hebrew word is a more general term for "terror" or "destruction." These insects are encountered in Exodus 23:28; Deuteronomy 7:20; and Joshua 24:12. They were recognized for their venomous stings and were God's instruments for driving Israel's enemies out of Canaan. The reference could be to the hornet as traditional symbol of Egypt or as a symbol of God's terrifying Israel's enemies. The emphasis is on God's powerful action to give Israel the land.

Lepidoptera: Butterflies and Moths This order is divided into two groups: moths which generally fly at night and butterflies which are day fliers. Moths usually have feathery antennae while butterflies have hairlike or "clubbed" ones. The adults feed primarily on nectar. Larvae are called caterpillars and are plant feeders. Both butterflies and moths are characterized by wings which are covered with powderlike, overlapping scales. They have a proboscis or tongue, which may be more than twice the length of the rest of the body. Some moths have mouth parts specialized for piercing fruit and even other animals. While butterfly pupae have no covering, moths spin cocoons.

Moths and their larvae (Hebrew, *'ash, sas;* Greek, *ses*) were known for their destructive ability (Job 4:19; 13:28; 27:18; Ps. 39:11; Isa. 50:9; 51:8; Hos. 5:12; Matt. 6:19,20; Luke 12:33; Jas. 5:2). For people who had few possessions and no safe places for storage, moth infestation could be devastating.

Diptera: Flies and Gnats The majority of these insects have one pair of wings. The adults feed upon plant and animal juices. Many species are considered injurious, both to animals and plants. Some of these creatures suck blood, transmitting diseases in the process. However, many species of this order are beneficial.

1. Flies are household pests, but they are primarily associated with livestock stables. Breeding in manure, the female may lay 75–150 eggs in the course of a single laying. This process is repeated several times during her 20-day productive period. A fly may lay a total of 2,000 eggs. The eggs hatch in 24 hours, producing larvae known as maggots. The maggots are active for two to three weeks, feeding on decaying matter. Then follows a resting stage in which the transformation into an adult occurs. The life cycle of the fly is relatively short. An egg becomes an adult within 12 to 14 days. Adults may live one or two months during the summer, and longer in the winter.

The Hebrew word for fly, *zebub,* includes the common housefly as well as other species. As in modern times, flies were great pests for ancient peoples. When combined with poor sanitation and inadequate medical knowledge, flies could be a serious threat to health. The only clear references to this nuisance are found in Ecclesiastes 10:1; Isaiah 7:18. The "swarms" of Exodus 8:21–31 may have been flies. The text is not clear, since a different word is used. The KJV translators added "of flies" for clarification, indicated by italics. The same is true in Psalms 78:45; 105:31. Second Kings 1 names the god of Ekron Baal-zebub. Some interpret this name to mean "lord of the flies." If this interpretation is correct, flies may have been feared to the extent that the people worshiped a "fly-god," hoping to prevent infestation by the insects.

A cattle-biting fly, perhaps the gadfly (RSV, NIV) is found in Jeremiah 46:20. Due to the uncertain translation of the word, it also has been called a mosquito, as well as "destruction."

2. Gnats are another airborne nuisance. These insects are scarcely visible to the naked eye and leave bites which sting and burn. Some species fly at night, while others fly in the day, mainly in shaded woods. Others attack in bright sunlight. Some gnats do not bite, but swarm in dense clouds numbering perhaps a million. The larvae of some species live in water and provide a source of food for aquatic life. The Old Testament writers knew the gnat as *kinnam* or *kinnim.* As well as being pests, they also were known to be fragile creatures, as appears to be reflected in Isaiah 51:6 (RSV). Jesus used the figure of the gnat (*kōnōps*) to teach the scribes and Pharisees a lesson (Matt. 23:24). The use here simply highlights the small size of the gnat. Ancient people would strain liquids in order to remove gnats which had fallen into the open container. Jesus charged the "hypocrites" with giving attention to such details as tithing their herb gardens while neglecting more important matters.

The Egyptian plague of Exodus 8:16–18 perhaps should be understood as a plague of gnats or mosquitoes rather than lice. The Hebrew word used to describe the plague is identified by many scholars as pointing to the gnat. The same is true of the usage of the word in Psalms 105:31. Despite the uncertainty of the exact identification of the insect, the worth of the verses in question remains unaffected.

Siphonaptera: Fleas Fleas are parasites which are particularly fond of birds and mammals as hosts. These insects are quite small and wingless, having a body which is tall and thin. This body shape allows the flea to pass easily between hairs and

feathers. The adult female lays eggs on the host or in its nest or bed. Adults suck blood, while the larvae live on decaying animal and vegetable material. Adults usually feed at least once per day if a source of food is nearby, though they have been known to live more than four months without food.

The flea (*par'osh*) was a plague for people and animals during the time of the early history of Israel. Fleas were recognized both for their bite and for their size. Their small and insignificant nature even led to the formulation of proverbs of jest. Two such comparisons are found in 1 Samuel 24:14; 26:20. In both instances David stressed the difference in stature between Saul and himself, avoiding a confrontation with the king. Some scholars interpret the plague which fell upon the Assyrians as one caused by fleas, similar to the Bubonic plague (Isa. 37:36–37).

Anoplura: Lice Lice are found in at least two varieties: chewing and sucking lice. The lice of the Bible are almost certainly sucking lice. Small, wingless insects, they are noted for short legs and antennae, laterally-flattened body, and specialized mouthparts. They have claws and are parasitic upon mammals. Both adults and larvae feed upon blood. They attach themselves to clothing, body hair, and bedding. Thus, they are passed easily from one person to another. Lice are also acknowledged as carriers of some serious diseases, such as typhus and trench fever.

Lice (*kinnim*) are mentioned in the KJV in two places. The Egyptian plague of Exodus 8:16–18 is one of dust becoming lice. Psalms 105:31 reminds the reader of the plagues upon Egypt. As stated above, both these occurrences of lice also could be understood as gnats or another biting insect.

Orthoptera: Grasshoppers and Locusts The flying members of this order normally have two pairs of wings. This group contains grasshoppers, locusts, katydids, crickets, roaches, and mantids. Grasshoppers are powerful fliers with narrow wings and slender bodies. They are known to fly fifteen miles per hour and have been found some 1200 miles at sea. Locusts and grasshoppers are perhaps the best-known insects of the Bible. This group was so prolific that the Bible contains approximately a dozen words which describe them. The numerous words may indicate different species or even different stages of development. Disagreement exists as to the translation of many instances of the words. Thus, the different species cannot be identified positively from the Hebrew words.

One form of the locust, indicated by the Hebrew word *'arbeh,* has been called the migratory locust, or desert locust. It is remembered as the locust of the plague (Ex. 10:4–5). This type of locust invaded agricultural areas in immense numbers, so that they were said to "cover the face of

I

the earth, that one cannot be able to see the earth" (Ex. 10:5). The Egyptians had already suffered a hailstorm, only to have an infestation of insects that would "eat every tree which groweth for you." (Ex. 10:5). The destructive nature of this locust is highlighted again in Deuteronomy 28:38; 1 Kings 8:37; 2 Chronicles 6:28; Psalms 78:46; 105:34; Joel 1:4; 2:25. Many references point to the great numbers in which the swarms would come (Judg. 6:5; 7:12; Jer. 46:23; Nah. 3:15). Though the locust was a formidable enemy, it was not mighty in strength. This truth is reflected in Job 39:20; Psalm 109:23; Nahum 3:17. The locust is praised in Proverbs 30:27 for its ability to work in orderly fashion while having no leader. Not only was the 'arbeh destructive; it was also edible. Permission is given for its consumption in Leviticus 11:22.

The *gazam* is known as the palmerworm, certainly the caterpillar stage of one of the locust species (Joel 1:4; 2:25; Amos 4:9). Each of these citations recalls the destructive nature of the insect.

The *haghabh* generally is translated "grasshopper," but is called a locust in 2 Chronicles 7:13. This locust also was edible, as can be seen in Leviticus 11:22. It is mentioned in Ecclesiastes 12:5 as being a "burden." Two Old Testament verses recall the animal's small stature (Num. 13:33; Isa. 40:22).

The *chasil* is called a caterpillar and generally is mentioned in conjunction with "the locust." It has been suggested that the *chasil* was the second stage after the hatching of the locust egg. Others propose that it is the cockroach. Its voracious appetite is the subject of its biblical occurrences (1 Kings 8:37; 2 Chron. 6:28; Ps. 78:46; Isa. 33:4; Joel 1:4; 2:25).

The *chargol* is mentioned only in Leviticus 11:22 and is called a beetle in the KJV. It also was one of the edible varieties. Most scholars propose that it be understood as some species of locust, perhaps a katydid.

The *solam* is called "the bald locust" in Leviticus 11:22 and was also allowed for food.

The *tselatsal* has been called a katydid, cricket, mole cricket, and even a cicada. The KJV translates it "locust" in Deuteronomy 28:42, where it is one of the curses for disobedience. The great numbers of an infestation of this insect may be reflected in Isaiah 18:1. In that verse the land "shadowing with wings" reflects a group of Ethiopian ambassadors arriving in Jerusalem to enlist Judah's support in an anti-Assyrian alliance.

The *yeleq* is called the cankerworm in Joel 1:4; 2:25; Nahum 3:15,16. It is called the caterpillar (Ps. 105:34; Jer. 51:14) and the rough caterpillar (Jer. 51:27). It evidently was some form of locust larvae and was known to plague crops.

Akris is the New Testament word for locust. This insect was food for John the Baptist (Matt.

3:4; Mark 1:6). The locust also is used in Revelation 9:3,7 as an instrument of judgment.

Miscellaneous insects *Worms* Three Hebrew words and one Greek word are used to describe worms familiar to the biblical writers. The terms are rather vague and do not offer much help in identifying positively the insect in question. *Tole'ah* is used to describe maggot-like worms (Ex. 16:20; Is. 14:11). However, the same word is used to describe worms which probably were moth larvae (Deut. 28:39; Jon. 4:7). A scarlet dye was obtained from the insect, or perhaps its eggs (Ex. 25:4; Lev. 14:4). Other occurrences of this word include Job 25:6; Psalms 22:6; Isaiah 41:14; 66:24. *Rimmah* describes maggots in Exodus 16:24; Job. 7:5; 17:14; 21:26; 24:20; Isaiah 14:11. It is also used in a more general sense in Job. 25:6. These two Hebrew words are used together in Exodus 16; Job 25:6; Isaiah 14:11. Such usage demonstrates that the meanings of the words overlapped. This is understandable, for the exact identification of species was not the intent of the writers of the biblical materials. *Zochel* was viewed as a worm by the KJV translators in Micah 7:17, but in Deuteronomy 32:24 is translated "serpent," a translation modern translators use in both passages. In the New Testament, only *skolex* is used to describe a worm. In Mark 9:44,46,48 reference is made to Isaiah 66:24. A derivative of *skolex* vividly describes the fate of Herod (Acts 12:23).

Scale Insects appear in the Bible only in connection with the crimson dye extracted from them or from their eggs. In addition to the scarlet dye made from the worm named above, a coloring material was manufactured from a member of the order *Rhynchota* known for its red scales. These insects, of the genus *Kermes,* are pea-sized and of various colors. They generally are found on oak trees. At death, eggs are gathered from the females for the extraction of dye. The biblical references to these insects include 2 Chronicles 2:7, 14; 3:14. Some scholars identify the manna of Exodus 16; Numbers 11 as an excretion of scale insects, miraculously provided by God.

Insects are found often in the story of God's dealings with His people. These occurrences help the reader to understand the life of an ancient people. Insects are a part of the Bible because they were a part of life. Yet, the references to these small creatures do more than give information. From them the reader can learn much about God.

God's sovereignty is reflected in His use of hornets to accomplish His divine purpose of driving Israel's enemies out of Canaan. He also could chasten the chosen people with a locust if they should disobey. The absence of advanced methods of insect control reminds us of Israel's utter dependence upon God. The Lord would inspire His servants to use the lowly ant and locust as examples for mankind to follow. The wisdom writers would use even the disgusting fly larva to remind humanity of its mortal nature. Though insects often appear in a negative light within the Bible, its truth is enriched by their presence.

Ronald E. Bishop

INSPECTION GATE A Jerusalem city gate (Neh. 3:31 NAS, NIV). The KJV refers to the gate as the Miphkad Gate. The Hebrew word is related to that of Jeremiah 52:11, so some interpreters read, "prison tower" here. Others translate it as Muster Gate (NRSV, REB) and see it as a place where people drafted or conscripted into miltary service gathered. Some identify it with the Benjamin Gate. See *Benjamin Gate.*

INSPIRATION OF SCRIPTURE The actions of God leading to the writing, preservation, and collection of His words to His people into the Bible. The English word *inspiration* comes from the Latin word *in spiro* which mean "to breath in." Inspiration, then, is the influence of the Holy Spirit upon individuals for the purpose of producing an authoritative record of persons, teaching and events.

Sometimes the inspiration is declared explicitly in biblical assertions. Jeremiah began his prophecy by writing, "The word of the Lord came" (Jer. 1:2); throughout his book the formula is used to emphasize his experience of inspiration. At other times, the inspiration is evident in the pervading mood of the scriptural record. The Bible summarizes this by saying, "All scripture is given by inspiration of God" (2 Tim. 3:16). Often the inspiration is a revelation of that which goes beyond normal human cognitive and experiential knowledge. When this is true, then it is most obvious that the information is divinely inspired. Concerning this, the Bible says, "For no prophecy was ever made by an act of human will, but men moved by the Holy Spirit spoke from God" (2 Pet. 1:21 NAS).

As indicated in the biblical explanation, inspiration is a divine-human encounter whereby God reveals truth. It is a message from God and of God, as well as through persons and for persons. The Bible is divine in its inception. It is a record of God's self-disclosure as Truth and as the source of all truth. Its special revelation is a disclosure of truth that humans could not comprehend through ordinary thought process. Also the Bible is human in its mediation. God revealed Himself to persons He chose. They declared God's attitude toward, His relations with, and His purposes for His people and His world. Inspiration came in the experiences of real men and women with real personalities and problems. A climax to that divine-human encounter is the fact that the Scripture is focused on the divine-human person of Jesus Christ.

The evidences of divine inspiration are found internally in the record of God's revelation. Some biblical writers claimed they were verbally inspired. Repeatedly, the prophets have attested of this experience. Isaiah interjected into his report, "But I am the Lord thy God.... And I have put my words into thy mouth" (Isa. 51:15–16). Likewise, Jeremiah wrote, "And the Lord said unto me, Behold, I have put my words in thy mouth" (Jer. 1:9).

In addition to the specific statements in the Scriptures, an abundance of internal evidences show divine inspiration from its content in general. Although the Bible is a collection of books written by at least 40 writers over a period of about 1400 years, it has a unity of subject, structure, and spirit. It contains a consistent system of doctrinal and moral utterances. Its unparalleled treatment of certain themes such as the holy, the true, the good, and the future, are mysterious, authoritative, and practical. This witness of its inspiration is attested by countless thousands of testimonies from individuals who have been transformed by the reading of this Book.

Likewise, many external evidences point to divine inspiration of the Bible. The fact that the Bible is the most widely translated and circulated Book in the world is a testimony of God's providence. This is an amazing record because its early translators were killed, and many of its early readers were imprisoned. Although the Bible has been in existence for almost nineteen centuries, it is still relevant today. Both its quotations and its motifs are found in our literature, oratory, art, music, politics, law, and ethics.

The expressions of human inspiration are a part of the biblical record. Repeatedly, the biblical writers felt compelled to preface their remarks by identifying God as the sole source of their information. Ezekiel informs us that God had said to him, "You must speak my words to them, whether they listen or fail to listen, for they are rebellious" (Ezekiel 2:7 NIV). Luke affirmed that his inspiration was tied to his experience of researching the facts about Christ. He explained, "Therefore, since I myself have carefully investigated everything from the beginning, it seemed good also to me to write an orderly account for you, most excellent Theopilus" (Luke 1:3 NIV). Even more surprising is the fact that Paul identified his inspiration as a strong inner impression. With honesty, he said, "Now concerning virgins, I have no command of the Lord, but I give my opinion as one who by the Lord's mercy is trustworthy" (1 Cor. 7:25 NRSV). On other occasions, the inspiration came through dreams. Matthew wrote, "He had resolved on this, when an angel of the Lord appeared to him in a dream, and said, 'Joseph, son of David, do not be afraid to take Mary home with you to be your wife' " (Matt. 1:20 REB). At times the inspiration came through visions (Gen. 15:1; Num. 12:6; 1 Sam. 3:1, Isa. 1:1; Ezek. 1:1; Dan. 2:19; Obad. 1; Nah. 1:1; Hab. 2:2). Inspiration also came through historical situations. Paul's letter to the Corinthians is an example of this: "Now for the matters you wrote about" (1 Cor. 7:1 NIV).

These many different expressions of inspiration show that God is resourceful. His unlimited power has used a variety of techniques to reveal Himself and to communicate His message. Regardless of the method God used to inspire the individual writers, the result is the same. They wrote the Word of God. This is evident both in the content of each book and also in the preservation of all the books in the canon of the Bible.

The explanations of biblical inspiration are numerous. This is partly due to the fact that the Bible has no theory of inspiration. It simply affirms that the Bible is the inspired Word of God. Actually no theory of inspiration is necessary. For the Bible, like Jesus, must be accepted by faith as the inspired Word of God. When this is done, then the choice of a theory of inspiration is incidental.

According to the natural intuition theory, inspiration is but a higher development of that natural insight into truth which all persons possess to some degree. The biblical writers were inspired as other great genuises are inspired. This view is very subjective, making all works equally inspired, in spite of the fact that they may be contradictory. It makes the Bible a human, or natural book, rather than a supernatural Book.

By contrast, the mechanical dictation theory claims that God literally dictated the words of the Bible to the biblical writers. They were used as secretaries or passive instruments. The primary objection to the view is that it is not consistent with God's way of relating to persons. Also, it implies that all of the Bible should have the same literary style.

The general Christian theory of inspiration is simply that the illumination of the Holy Spirit is experienced by all believers. This is based on the truth that all believers experience the Spirit. Its weakness is that it overlooks the problem of opposing viewpoints among believers and that it reduces biblical writers to the level of all Christian interpretation and proclamation.

According to the partial inspiration theory, inspiration is limited to certain parts of the Bible. What the writers would have known naturally is not necessarily inspired. Likewise, incidental matters are not regarded as being inspired. This contradicts the statements of Scripture that all Scripture is inspired.

The levels of inspiration theory claims that God used different levels of control at different times in the process of inspiration. Sometimes God used superintendence. At other times, God used evaluation, direction, or suggestion. This view holds that particular passages of Scripture carry various degrees of inspiration. In such a theory, the level of inspiration may be rather arbitrary, based on human judgment not divine actions.

The infallible theory states that the Bible as a whole is without any errors because it is in its entirety the Word of God. Usually those who hold to this view are careful to distinguish between the original manuscripts and the present form of the Bible. However, some claim that this also applies to the current translations because the biblical writers never intended to mislead or deceive. Each of the differences that may be found in parallel passages are harmonized by some type of explanation.

The verbal inspiration theory states that the Holy Spirit inspired the biblical writers to choose the exact words to convey the message of God. As indicated previously, there are many passages of Scripture that support the idea of verbal inspiration. Nevertheless, some have discredited this view because it does not relate to the differences in the personalities of the biblical writers.

On the other hand, the dynamic inspiration theory suggests that the Holy Spirit had control over the process of inspiration, but He allowed the individuals to express their personalities in communicating God's message. Those who criticize this view do so on the basis that the view does not guarantee inerrancy in nonreligious matters.

There are elements of truth in all of the views, and there are also weaknesses in each of the theories. Therefore, some have attempted to splice together ideas from two or more of the theories to develop an eclectic theory. Such an approach is feasible because there is only a slight difference in some of the theories. This might be indicative of the fact that the whole process of developing a theory of inspiration is quite difficult. Phrasing a theory is really secondary to the more important fact that the Bible is the authoritative Word of God and to the calling of obeying that Word. The Bible, itself, takes this position because it has no theory of inspiration. Nevertheless, it emphatically declares itself to be the authoritative record of God's revelation. See *Bible; Revelation, Doctrine of.*   *Donald R. Potts*

INSTANT Noun meaning a brief moment of time (Isa. 29:5; 30:15; Jer. 18:7–9) and adjective in KJV used in the sense of insistent, pressing, or urgent. For example, "they were instant" (Luke 23:23, KJV) means "they kept urgently demanding" (NRSV); "continuing instant in prayer" (Rom. 12:12, KJV) means "persevere in prayer" (NRSV) or "faithful in prayer" (NIV); "be instant" (2 Tim. 4:2, KJV) means "be persistent" (NRSV) or "be prepared" (NIV).

INSTRUCTION Teaching or exhortation on aspects of Christian life and thought directed to persons who have already made a faith commitment. Instruction (*didache*) is frequently distinguished from missionary preaching (*kerygma*). Matthew's Gospel says of Jesus, "He taught them as one having authority" (Matt. 7:29). The Sermon on the Mount (Matt. 5—7) in particular is the rock-solid foundational teaching for Christian life (Matt. 7:24–27). Jesus Himself admonished His disciples to make disciples, baptizing them in the name of the Father, the Son, and the Holy Spirit, "teaching them to observe all things whatsoever I have commanded" (Matt. 28:20).

The church of Jesus Christ, therefore, is a teacher, instructing men and women in Christian faith and discipleship. The faith which the church proclaims must be strengthened by the teaching of the gospel. Paul reminded the early Christians that one of the offices of the church was the pastor/teacher who worked "to equip God's people for work in his service, for the building up of the body of Christ" (Eph. 4:12 REB).

The church's teaching ministry has numerous dimensions: *The church teaches about Jesus.* The church presents the basic details of Jesus' life and ministry: His death, burial, and resurrection. It helps members understand the meaning of these events for all times. In the early church, the *catechumens* or learners were those given instruction in Christian faith prior to receiving baptism and full membership in the community of faith. Later church leaders such as Martin Luther and John Calvin wrote catechisms, books for instructing persons in faith and doctrine. The church is called to retell the story of Jesus in every generation. See *Gospel; Kerygma; Jesus, Life and Ministry of.*

The church teaches Christian spirituality. New Christians are not to remain "babes in Christ," but to increase in "grace, and in the knowledge" of the Lord Jesus Christ (1 Cor. 3:1–3; Heb. 5:13; 2 Pet. 3:18). Christian spirituality is the process of growing in faith. In its teaching ministry, the church guides Christians in the life of faith through prayer, Bible study, meditation, and spiritual reflection.

The church teaches Christian ethics. Those who follow Christ must be conformed to His image. The church instructs its members in faithfulness, morality, honesty, and integrity. Ethical instruction is not a new law but a way of life according to Christ's new commandment to love one another (John 13:34–35). Jesus is the ultimate moral teacher and example for the people of God. See *Ethics in the Bible.*

The church instructs in Christian doctrine. The church teaches the basic truths of the Christian faith. It guides Christians in understanding significant beliefs. It opens the Scriptures to determine those doctrinal ideals upon which the church is founded. It guides faithful Christians to maturity so that its members may not be "tossed to and fro, and carried about with by every wind of doctrine, by the sleight of men, and cunning craftiness" (Eph. 4:14). All doctrinal instruction leads to Christ who is the final source of the Christian's faith. See *Doctrine; Bible, Theology of.*

A Teaching Evangel. As the church teaches, it also evangelizes. The teaching ministry of the church is another way in which the people of God declare their faith that others may know Christ and grow up in him. See *Evangelism in the Bible.*
Bill J. Leonard

INSTRUMENT KJV term for a tool, utensil (1 Chron. 28:14), weapon (Gen. 49:5; 1 Chron. 12:33,37), or musical instrument (1 Chron. 15:16; 16:42; 23:5). Modern translations generally reserve the term instrument for musical instrument.

INSULT To treat with insolence, indignity, or contempt. The term does not appear in the KJV but becomes increasingly frequent in more recent translations, such as the NIV, where it replaces such terms as abuse, mock, revile, reproach, or ridicule. According to Hebrew wisdom, the wise person ignores insults (Prov. 12:16). Proverbs 14:31 warns that oppression of the poor is an insult to God. God's prophets were sometimes the objects of insults (Jer. 20:7–8; 2 Kings 2:23). As God's ultimate representative, Jesus anticipated insults as part of His passion (Luke 18:32). The Synoptic Gospels relate these insults (Matt. 26:68; 27:29,40–44; Mark 14:65; 15:16–20,29–32; Luke 22:63–65; 23:11,35–39). By suffering insult, Christ became the model for Christians who experience insult (Rom. 15:3, quoting Ps. 69:9; 1 Pet. 3:9). Jesus blessed those who suffered insult for His sake (Matt. 5:11). Paul was content with insults which are a natural consequence of mission involvement (2 Cor. 12:10). Jesus warned that one insulting a brother was in danger of standing before the Sanhedrin, the Jewish supreme court (Matt. 5:22).

INSURRECTION Rebellion against an established government. By the time of Artaxerxes (464–423 B.C.), Jerusalem had a well-established reputation for insurrection (Ezra 4:19). Barabbas was charged with insurrection (Mark 15:7; Luke 23:19,25). The tribune in charge of Temple security confused Paul with an Egyptian insurrectionist (Acts 21:38). The insurrection of Acts 18:12 (KJV) is better rendered "united attack" (NRSV).

INTEGRITY The state of being complete or undivided. Terms which occur in parallel with integrity (Hebrew *tom, tomim*) suggest its shades of meaning: righteousness (Ps. 7:8); uprightness (Ps. 25:21); without wavering (Ps. 26:1 NRSV, NAS, NIV); blameless (Ps. 101:2 NRSV, Hebrew uses *tom* twice in verse, otherwise translated integrity). Several Old Testament characters are designated persons of integrity: Noah (Gen. 6:9); Abraham (Gen. 17:1); Jacob (Gen. 25:27); Job (Job 1:1,8; 2:3); and David (1 Kings 9:4). English

I

translations frequently render the underlying Hebrew as perfect or blameless. Inclusion of Jacob is surprising since he is better known for his deceit (Gen. 27:5–27; 30:37–43; 33:13–17). English translators describe Jacob as a plain (KJV), peaceful (NAS), or quiet man (NRSV, NIV, REB).

In the New Testament, integrity occurs only at Titus 2:7 (NRSV, NIV, REB) in reference to teaching. The idea of singleness of heart or mind is frequent: Matthew 5:8; 6:22; James 1:7–8; 4:8.

INTERCESSION (Ĭn tēr cĕs' sion) The act of intervening or mediating between differing parties; particularly the act of praying to God on behalf of another person.

Old Testament The heroes of Old Testament faith are in most cases heroes of intercessory prayer. Abraham asked God not to destroy Sodom in order to save his nephew Lot. He called on the righteous character of God, asking if God would "slay the righteous with the wicked" (Gen. 18:25). In so doing, Abraham acknowledged that he was not worthy to lay such claims before the holy God (v. 27). Abraham also interceded for Abimelech, fulfilling a prophetic function and bringing healing (Gen. 20:7,17).

Moses intervened between God and Pharaoh as he tried to get permission for the people to leave Egypt (for example, Ex. 8:8). At Sinai the people asked Moses to represent them before God since they feared to approach the awesome God (Ex. 20:19). After the people built the golden calf, Moses prayed for God's mercy, calling on God to remember His reputation among the nations and His promises to the patriarchs. As a result, God "repented of the evil which he thought to do unto his people" (Ex. 32:11–14). Through intercessory prayer, Moses sought to make an atonement for sin, identifying himself so completely with the people that he asked to be blotted out of God's book if God would not forgive the people's sin (Ex. 32:30–34). Compare Deuteronomy 9:25.

In face of the people's idolatry, Samuel asked God to forgive them (1 Sam. 7:5). Even when he did not agree with the people, Samuel took their plea for a king to God (1 Sam. 8; compare ch. 12). When God rejected Saul, Samuel prayed in grief (1 Sam. 15:11). David interceded all night on behalf of his new-born baby, even knowning God had decreed the child's death because of David's sin (2 Sam. 12:14–18). After taking a census without God's direction, David asked God to punish him and not the innocent people (2 Sam. 24:17).

In dedicating the Temple, Solomon asked God to hear the prayers of the sinful people and forgive them (1 Kings 8; compare 3:3–14). Elijah accused God of bringing "evil upon the widow with whom I sojourn, by slaying her son" (1 Kings 17:20) and prayed successfully that the child would live again. Compare 2 Kings 4:32–34.

Hezekiah took Sennacherib's letter to the Temple and opened it before God, praying for deliverance from the Assyrians (Isa. 37:14–20).

Intercession formed an important part of the prophet's task. Amos prayed that God's word would not come to pass (Amos 7:5–6). Jeremiah responded to God's word of judgment on the nation with a plea for God not to be a stranger among them who could not save themselves (Jer. 14:7–9). Lamentations is filled with prayers for the nation. The priests had intercession as part of their job description (Joel 2:17). Compare 1 Samuel 2:25. The high priest's task was to make atonement for the people (Lev. 16).

The prophet looked to a day when people from all nations could come to the Temple and make intercession (Isa. 56:7). The prophetic hope centered in the Suffering Servant who would bear the sin of all people, making intercession for transgressors (Isa. 53:6,12).

Intercession was not always effective. God told Jeremiah to forsake the prophetic duty of intercession: "Pray not thou for this people, neither lift up cry nor prayer for them, neither make intercession to me: for I will not hear thee" (Jer. 7:16). Even the great heroes of intercession would not succeed in such situations (Jer. 15:1; compare Ezek. 14:14). In the final analysis, even the most righteous of people need an intercessor with God (Job 9:32–35; 19:25; 23:1–17).

New Testament The New Testament teaches that intercession is expected of all believers (1 Tim. 2:1–3). Intercession for the sick is particularly important (Jas. 5:14). Paul in his letters constantly referred to his prayers for the readers, and Jesus set forth the supreme example of intercession (Luke 22:32; 23:34; John 17).

The Bible reveals that intercession is performed by the Holy Spirit, Christ, and Christians. Romans 8:26–27 shows that the Holy Spirit works to sustain the burdened believer, to intercede to carry even inexpressible prayers to God. Romans 8:34 offers the truth that the risen Christ will maintain His intercession for the believer, being the Mediator between God and humanity. God accepts a believer's prayers and praises through Christ's intercession. His death secured removal of sin; His resurrection bestowed life on those who believe in Him; His ascension brought exaltation to power in heaven and on earth. Now He intercedes for us at God's throne of grace. Hebrews 7:25 proclaims the complete deliverance that comes through salvation accomplished through Christ and notes that He is ever present in heaven to intercede for those who come to Him. See *Prayer.*

J. William Thompson and *Trent C. Butler*

INTEREST Sum of money a borrower pays for use of loaned capital. Mosaic law prohibited the charging of interest to fellow Israelites (Ex. 22:25; Lev. 25:36–37; Deut. 23:19). Interest could be charged to foreigners (Deut. 23:20). The motive in loaning without interest to fellow Israelites was to prevent the formation of a permanent underclass in Israel. Ezekiel regarded the charging of interest as a watershed act separating the righteous from those practicing abominations (Ezek. 18:8,13,17; 22:12). Nehemiah challenged neglect of the Mosaic prohibition which had resulted in dire poverty for some of the returned exiles (Neh. 5:6–13).

The "harsh" master who expects interest and reaps what he did not sow (Matt. 25:24,26–27; Luke 19:21–23) is hardly to be taken as a model for Christian business practice. Luke's parable in particular contains reminiscences of the hated Archelaus (Luke 19:12,14; compare Matt. 2:22). See *Archelaus.* Jesus stood firmly in the Old Testament tradition when He commanded His disciples to give freely to the needy who asked (Matt. 5:42; 10:8).

Many commentators feel compelled to defend the common, contemporary practice of charging interest. Any moral decision on the matter must carefully weigh rival claims: (1) that capital loaned at interest provides an opportunity for persons to escape poverty and (2) that the inability of both individuals and nations to pay interest on borrowed capital contributes to continued poverty. See Banking; *Loan.*

INTERMEDIATE STATE Condition in which the deceased exists between death and the resurrection or final judgment. The brief comments of the Bible about this subject have led to much difference of opinion.

Views Concerning the Intermediate State Some have understood the phrase "sleep in Jesus" (1 Thess. 4:14) to suggest that the soul is unconscious during this time. Martin Luther made statements which suggest that after death the righteous sleep without an awareness of the passage of time. Jesus awakens them at the resurrection. This interpretation seems to contradict Paul's conviction that after death he anticipated conscious fellowship with Christ (Phil. 1:23).

Others have emphasized the possibility of a second opportunity for receiving the gospel message during this intermediate period. An interpretation of 1 Peter 4:6 following this system would emphasize that the dead receive an opportunity to hear and respond to the gospel. This view overlooks the fact that the "dead" in 1 Peter 4:6 might be believers who had responded to the gospel while they were living but were now dead.

Biblical Insights about the Intermediate State Although the Bible does not provide detailed teaching concerning the intermediate state, it does provide teaching from which we can draw legitimate inferences. The conditions of the righteous and the unrighteous provide a lesson in contrasts.

Believers appear in a state of rest. This rest does not refer to inactivity but to the joy of achievement and accomplishment (Heb. 4:10; Rev. 14:13).

Several passages clearly indicate that believers are alive and conscious in the presence of God (Matt. 22:32; John 11:26). Paul expressed the hope of being with Christ in Philippians 1:23 and in 2 Corinthians 5:8. In Luke 23:43 Jesus assured the repentant thief that He would be with him in paradise. The term "paradise" comes from a Persian word which means "park" and is another way of referring to the blessedness of the presence of God. See *Paradise.*

Even though the believer enjoys life, rest, and the presence of God, there is still a sense of incompleteness. Paul centered his hope on the resurrection (Phil. 3:10–11).

The unbeliever is pictured during the intermediate state as separated from God. The separation involves a removal from the blessing of fellowship with God. In this condition God keeps the wicked in a state of punishment until the time of final judgment (2 Pet. 2:9).

The wicked also are seen as alive and conscious. Although the parable of the rich man and Lazarus (Luke 16:19–31) has many symbolic features, it clearly suggests a state of conscious existence for the wicked.

The term "Hades" is a general reference to the location of the dead between the time of physical death and resurrection. The King James Version has translated this term as "hell" or "grave." Sometimes the term is a general reference to the grave and may allow for the presence of even the righteous (Acts 2:27,31; 1 Cor. 15:55). On other occasions Hades refers to the place of the wicked dead (Luke 16:23; Rev. 20:14). See *Hades; Hell; Resurrection.*   *Thomas D. Lea*

INTERPRETATION See *Bible, Interpretation of.*

INTERTESTAMENTAL HISTORY & LITERATURE Events and writings originating after the final prophet mentioned in the Old Testament (Malachi, about 450 B.C.) and the birth of Christ (about 4 B.C.).

Shortly after 600 B.C., the Babylonians captured Jerusalem, destroyed the Temple, and took away many of the people as captives. After Cyrus overcame the Babylonian Empire, the Jews who desired were allowed to return. The Temple was rebuilt. Under the leadership of Nehemiah and Ezra, the Jewish religious community established itself, and the worship and life of the people continued. Here Old Testament history ends, and the Intertestamental Period begins.

The history of the Intertestamental Period can be divided into three sections: The Greek Period, 323 B.C. to 167 B.C.; the Period of Independence, 167–63 B.C.; and the Roman Period, 63

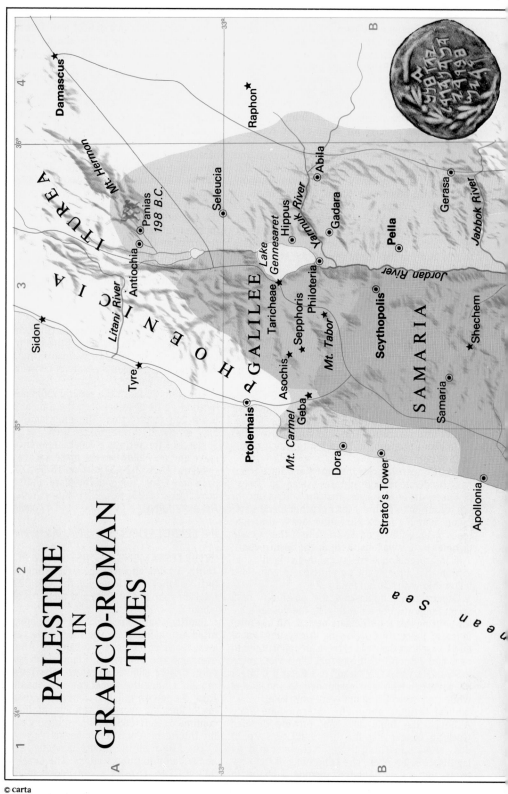

PALESTINE
IN
GRAECO-ROMAN
TIMES

Damascus

Mt. Hermon

Raphon

ITUREA

Panias
198 B.C.

Seleucia

Antiochia

Abila

PHOENICIA

Litani River

Sidon

Lake
Gennesaret

Hippus

GALILEE

Taricheae

Yarmuk River

Gadara

Tyre

Asochis

Sepphoris

Philoteria

Pella

Jordan River

Gerasa

Ptolemais

Geba

Mt. Tabor

Scythopolis

SAMARIA

Jabbok River

Mt. Carmel

Dora

Samaria

Shechem

Strato's Tower

Apollonia

nean Sea

© carta

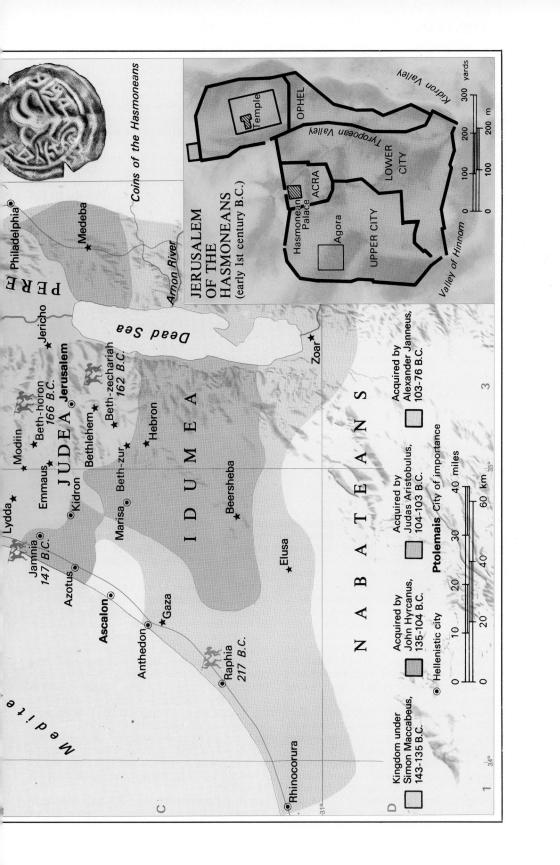

Coins of the Hasmoneans

JERUSALEM OF THE HASMONEANS
(early 1st century B.C.)

Temple

OPHEL

Kidron Valley

Tyropoean Valley

Hasmonean Palace

ACRA

LOWER CITY

Agora

UPPER CITY

Valley of Hinnom

300 yards

200 m

100

100

0

0

Philadelphia

Medeba

PEREA

Arnon River

Dead Sea

Jericho

Beth-horon
166 B.C.

Modiin

JUDEA Jerusalem

Emmaus

Bethlehem

Kidron

Beth-zechariah
162 B.C.

Hebron

Marisa   Beth-zur

IDUMEA

Beersheba

Lydda

Jamnia
147 B.C.

Azotus

Ascalon

Anthedon

Gaza

Elusa

Raphia
217 B.C.

N A B A T E A N S

Zoar

Rhinocorura

Medite

C

1

34°

310

3

35°

D

Kingdom under
Simon Maccabeus,
143-135 B.C.

Acquired by
John Hyrcanus,
135-104 B.C.

◉ Hellenistic city

Acquired by
Judas Aristobulus,
104-103 B.C.

Ptolemais City of importance

Acquired by
Alexander Janneus,
103-76 B.C.

0   10   20   30   40 miles

0   20   40   60 km

B.C. through the time of the New Testament.

The Greek Period, 323–167 B.C. Philip of Macedon sought to consolidate Greece so as to resist attack by the Persian Empire. When he was murdered in 336 B.C., his young son Alexander took up the task. He was only nineteen years of age, but he was highly gifted and educated. Within two years he set out to destroy Persia. In a series of battles over the next two years he gained control of the territory from Asia Minor to Egypt. This included Palestine and the Jews. Josephus, and Jewish historian who lived about A.D. 37–100, tells of Alexander going to Jerusalem and offering sacrifice in the Temple. Many elements of this story are undoubtedly false, but Alexander did treat the Jews well. When he founded the new city of Alexandria in Egypt, he moved many Jews from Palestine to populate one part of that city. In 331 B.C., Alexander gained full control over the Persian Empire.

Alexander's conquest had three major results. First, he sought to introduce Greek ideas and culture into the conquered territory. This is called Hellenization. He believed that the way to consolidate his empire was for the people to have a common way of life. However, he did not seek to change the religious practices of the Jews. Second, he founded Greek cities and colonies throughout the conquered territory. Third, he spread the Greek language into all of that region so that it became a universal language during the following centuries.

When Alexander died in 323 B.C., chaos resulted in his empire. Five of his prominent generals established themselves over different parts of his empire. Ptolemy chose the land of Egypt. Seleucus took control of Babylonia. Antigonus became ruler of Asia Minor and northern Syria. The other two ruled in Europe and did not have direct influence over events in Palestine.

From the beginning, Ptolemy and Antigonus struggled over the control of Palestine. The battle of Ipsus in 301 B.C. settled the matter for a century. In this battle, the other four generals fought against and killed Antigonus. Seleucus was given the territory of Antigonus, including Palestine. However, Ptolemy did not take part in the battle. Instead he took over control of Palestine. The result was that Palestine continued to be a point of contention between the Ptolemies and the Seleucids.

The Jews fared well under the Ptolemies. They had much self-rule. Their religious practices were not hampered. Greek customs gradually became more common among the people. During this period the translation of the Old Testament into Greek began during the reign of Ptolemy Philadelphus, 285–246 B.C. This translation is known as the Septuagint, often abbreviated LXX. The early Christians used the Septuagint and New Testament writers often quoted it.

Antiochus III (the Great), 223–187 B.C., attempted to take Palestine from the Ptolemies in 217 B.C. without success. At the battle of Panium, 198 B.C., however, he defeated Ptolemy IV, and he and his successors ruled Palestine until 167 B.C. The situation of the Jews changed after Antiochus was defeated by the Romans in the battle of Magnesia, 190 B.C. Antiochus had supported Hannibal of North Africa, Rome's hated enemy. As a result, Antiochus had to give up all of his territory except the province of Cilicia. He had to pay a large sum of money to the Romans for a period of years, and he had to surrender his navy and elephants. To guarantee his compliance, one of his sons was kept as hostage in Rome. So the tax burden of the Jews increased, as did pressure to Hellenize, that is, to adopt Greek practices.

Antiochus was succeeded by his son Seleucus IV, 187–175 B.C. When he was murdered, his younger brother became ruler. Antiochus IV, 175–163 B.C., was called Epiphanes ("manifest" or "splendid"), although some called him Epimenes ("mad"). He was the son who had been a hostage in Rome. During the early years of his reign, the situation of the Jews became worse. Part of it was due to their being divided. Some of their leaders, especially the priests, encouraged Hellenism.

Up to the time of Antiochus IV, the office of high priest had been hereditary and held for life. However, Jason, the brother of the high priest, offered the king a large sum of money to be appointed high priest. Antiochus needed the money and made the appointment. Jason also offered an additional sum to receive permission to build a gymnasium near the Temple. This shows the pressure toward Hellenism. Within a few years, Menelaus, a priest but not of the high priestly line, offered the king more money to be named high priest in place of Jason. He stole vessles from the Temple to pay what he had promised.

Antiochus sought to add Egypt to his territory. He was proclaimed king of Egypt; but when he returned the following year to take control of the land, the Romans confronted him, and told him to leave Egypt. Knowing the power of Rome, he returned home. When he reached Jerusalem, he found that Jason had driven Menelaus out of the city. He saw this as full revolt. He allowed his troops to kill many of the Jews and determined to put an end to the Jewish religion. He sacrificed a pig on the altar of the Temple. Parents were forbidden to circumcize their children, the sabbath was not to be observed, and all copies of the law were to be burned. It was a capital offense to be found with a copy of the law. The zeal of Antiochus to destroy Judaism was a major factor in its salvation.

Jewish Independence, 167–63 B.C. Resistance was passive at first; but when the Seleucids sent officers throughout the land to compel leading citizens to offer sacrifice to Zeus, open conflict flared. It broke out first at the village of Modein, about halfway between Jerusalem and Joppa. An aged priest named Mattathias was chosen to offer the sacrifice. He refused, but a young Jew volunteered to do it. This angered Mattathias, and he killed both the Jew and the officer. Then he fled to the hills with his five sons and others who supported his action. The revolt had begun.

Leadership fell to Judas, the third son of Mattathias. He was nicknamed Maccabeus, the hammerer. He probably received this title because of his success in battle. He was the ideal guerrilla leader. He fought successful battles against much larger forces. A group called the Hasidim made up the major part of his army. These men were devoutly committed to religious freedom. They were dedicated to obedience to the law and to the worship of God.

Antiochus IV was more concerned with affairs in the eastern part of his empire than with what was taking place in Palestine. Therefore, he did not commit many troops to the revolt at first. Judas was able to gain control of Jerusalem within three years. The Temple was cleansed and rededicated exactly three years after it had been polluted by the king, 164 B.C. (Dates through this period are uncertain and may be a year earlier than indicated.) This is still commemorated by the Jewish feast of Hannukah. The Hasidim had gained what they were seeking and left the army. Judas had larger goals in mind. He wanted political freedom. He rescued mistreated Jews from Galilee and Gilead and made a treaty of friendship and mutual support with Rome. In 160 B.C. at Elasa, with a force of eight hundred men, he fought a vastly superior Seleucid army and was killed.

Jonathan, another son of Mattathias, took the lead in the quest for independence. He was weak militarily. He was driven out of the cities and only gradually established himself in the countryside. Constant struggle engaged those seeking the Seleucid throne. The rivals offered him gifts to gain his support. In 152 B.C. he gave his support to Alexander Balas, who claimed to be the son of Antiochus IV. In return Jonathan was appointed high priest. For the first time, Jewish religious and civil rule were centered in one person. Jonathan was taken prisoner and killed in 143 B.C.

Simon, the last surviving son of Mattathias, ruled until he was murdered by his son-in-law in 134 B.C. He secured freedom from taxation for the Jews by 141 B.C. At last they had achieved political freedom. Simon was acclaimed by the people as their leader and high priest forever. The high priesthood was made hereditary with him and his descendants. The Hasmonean dynasty, named after an ancestor of Mattathias, had its beginning.

When Simon was murdered, his son John Hyrcanus became the high priest and civil ruler (134–104 B.C.). For a brief time the Seleucids exercised some power over the Jews, but Hyrcanus broke free and began to expand the territory of the Jews. In the north he destroyed the temple of the Samaritans on Mount Gerizim. He moved southeast and conquered the land of the Idumeans, the ancient kingdom of Edom. The residents were forced to emigrate or convert to Judaism. This had great significance for the Jews, for it was from this people that Herod the Great was to come.

The oldest son of Hyrcanus, Aristobulus I (104–103 B.C.), succeeded him. He had his mother and three brothers put in prison. One brother was allowed to remain free, but he was later murdered. He allowed his mother to starve to death in prison. He extended his rule to include part of the territory of Iturea, north of Galilee. He was the first to take the title of king.

Salome Alexandra was the wife of Aristobulus. When he died, she released his brothers from prison and married the oldest of them, Alexander Jannaeus. He became high priest and king (103–76 B.C.). He made many enemies by marrying the widow of his brother. The Old Testament stated that a high priest must marry a virgin (Lev. 21:14). He was an ambitious warrior and conducted campaigns by which he enlarged his kingdom to about the size of the kingdom of David. He used foreign soldiers because he could not trust Jews in his army. As high priest, he did not always follow prescribed ritual. On one occasion, the people reacted to his improper actions by throwing citrons at him. He allowed his soldiers to kill six thousand of them. At another time he had eight hundred of his enemies crucified. As they hung on the crosses, he had their wives and children brought out and slain before their eyes.

Alexandra succeeded her husband as ruler (76–67 B.C.). Of course, she could not serve as high priest, so the two functions were separated. Her oldest son, Hyrcanus II, became high priest. He was not ambitious. Her younger son, Aristobulus II, was just the opposite. He was waiting for his mother to die so he could become king and high priest.

When Salome died, civil war broke out and lasted until 63 B.C. Aristobulus easily defeated Hyrcanus, who was content to retire. This might have been the end of the story were it not for Antipater, an Idumean. He persuaded Hyrcanus to seek the help of the king of Nabatea to regain his position. Aristobulus was driven back to Jerusalem. At this point Rome arrived on the scene. Both Aristobulus and Hyrcanus appealed to Scaurus, the Roman general charged with the administration of Palestine. He sided with Aristobulus. When the Roman commander Pompey arrived later, both appealed to him. Aristobulus ended up trying to fight against the Romans. He was defeated and taken as a prisoner to Rome. The Romans took control over Palestine.

I

The Roman Period, 63 B.C.–A.D. 70 Under the Romans, the Jews paid heavy taxes; but their religious practices were not changed. Roman power was exercised through Antipater, who was named governor of Palestine. Hyrcanus was made high priest. The situation in Palestine was confused due to the efforts of Aristobulus and his sons to lead revolts against Rome. While Palestine was successively under the control of various Roman officials, Antipater was the stabilizing force. He had one son, Phasael, named governor of Judea, and a second son, Herod, made governor of Galilee. Herod sought to bring order to his area. He arrested Hezekiah, a Jewish robber or rebel, and had him executed. The Sanhedrin in Jerusalem summoned Herod to give an account of his action. He went, dressed in royal purple and with a bodyguard. The Sanhedrin could do nothing.

Antipater was murdered in 43 B.C. Antony became the Roman commander in the East in 42 B.C. In 40 B.C. the Parthians invaded Palestine and made Antigonus, the last surviving son of Aristobulus, king of Palestine. Hyrcanus was mutilated by having his ears cut or bitten off so he could not serve as high priest again. Phasael was captured and committed suicide in prison. Herod barely escaped with his family. He went to Rome to have his future brother-in-law, Aristobulus, made king, hoping to rule through him as his father had ruled through Antipater. However, the Roman Senate, at the urging of Antony and Octavian (Augustus), made Herod king (40 B.C.). It took him three years to drive the Parthians out of the country and establish his rule. He was king until his death in 4 B.C.

The years of Herod's rule were a time of turmoil for the Jewish people. He was an Idumean. Of course, his ancestors had been forced to convert to Judaism, but the people never accepted him. He was the representative of a foreign power. No matter how well he served Rome, he could never satisfy the Jews. Even his marriage to Mariamne, the granddaughter of Aristobulus II, gave no legitimacy to his rule in their sight. The most spectacular of his building achievements, the rebuilding of the Jerusalem Temple, did not win the loyalty of the Jews.

Herod had many problems which grew out of his jealousy and fears. He had Aristobulus, his brother-in-law, executed. Later Mariamne, her mother, and her two sons were killed. Just five days before his own death, Herod had his oldest son Antipater put to death. His relations with Rome were sometimes troubled due to the unsettled conditions in the empire. Herod was a strong supporter of Antony even though he could not tolerate Cleopatra with whom Antony had become enamored. When Antony was defeated by Octavian in 31 B.C., Herod went to Octavian and pledged his full support. This support was accepted. Herod proved himself an efficient administrator on behalf of Rome. He kept the peace among a people who were hard to rule. To be sure, he was a cruel and merciless man. Yet he was generous, using his own funds to feed the people during a time of famine. He never got over the execution of Mariamne, the wife he loved above all others. His grief led to mental and emotional problems.

During the reign of Herod, Jesus was born (Matt. 2:1–18; Luke 1:5). Herod was the king who ordered the execution of the male babies in Bethlehem (Matt. 2:16–18).

At his death, Herod left a will leaving his kingdom to three of his sons. Antipas was to be tetrarch ("ruler of a fourth") of Galilee and Perea (4 B.C.—A.D. 39). Philip was to be tetrarch of Gentile regions to the northeast of the Sea of Galilee (4 B.C.—A.D. 34). Archelaus was to be king of Judea and Samaria. Rome honored the will except that Archelaus was not given the title of king. He was ethnarch ("ruler of the people") of these two territories. He proved to be a poor ruler and was deposed in A.D. 6. His territories were placed under the direct rule of Roman procurators under the control of the governor of Syria.

Literature The Jews produced many writings during the Intertestamental Period. These writings can be divided into three groups. The Apocrypha are writings that were included, for the most part, in the Greek translation of the Old Testament, the Septuagint. They were translated into Latin and became a part of the Latin Vulgate, the authoritative Latin Bible. Some are historical books. First Maccabees is our chief source for the history of the period from Antiochus Epiphanes to John Hyrcanus. Other books are Wisdom Literature. Others can be classified as historical romances. One is apocalyptic, giving attention to the end of time and God's intervention in history. One writing is devotional in nature. See *Apocrypha.*

A second group of writings is the Pseudepigrapha. It is a larger collection than the Apocrypha, but there is no final agreement as to which writings should be included in it. Fifty-two writings are included in the two volumes, *The Old Testament Pseudepigrapha,* edited by James H. Charlesworth. These cover the range of Jewish throught from apocalyptic to wisdom to devotional. Their title indicates that they are attributed to noted people of ancient times, such as Adam, Abraham, Enoch, Ezra, and Baruch. For the most part they were written in the last centuries before the birth of Jesus, although some of them are from the first century A.D.

The final group of writings from this period are the Qumran scrolls, popularly known as the Dead Sea Scrolls. The first knowledge of these came with the discovery of manuscripts in a cave above the Dead Sea in 1947. During subsequent years, fragments of manuscripts have been found in at least eleven caves in the area. These writings include

Old Testament manuscripts, writings of the Qumran sect, and writings copied and used by the sect which came from other sources. These writings show us something of the life and beliefs of one group of Jews in the last two centuries before Jesus. See *Apocrypha; Pseudepigrapha; Septuagint; Seleucids; Ptolemies; Herod the Great; Herod Antipas; Herod Philip; Archelaus; Temple; Dead Sea Scrolls; Hasmoneans.*   *Clayton Harrop*

INTESTINES The tubular part of the digestive tract between the stomach and anus (2 Sam. 20:10; Acts 1:18 NIV). See *Bowels.*

IOB (Ī' ŏb) Personal name of uncertain meaning but of different Hebrew spelling than the biblical sufferer Job, a difference not made in KJV. Son of Issachar, according to Genesis 46:13; but a copyist apparently omitted one Hebrew letter, the name appearing as Jashub in Samaritan Pentateuch and some Greek manuscripts of Genesis (followed by NRSV, NIV, TEV) and in Numbers 26:24; 1 Chronicles 7:1. See *Jashub.*

IOTA See *Dot.*

IPHDEIAH or **IPHEDEIAH** (Ĭph (ė) dêi' ah) Personal name meaning, "Yah redeems." Member of tribe of Benjamin who lived in Jerusalem (1 Chron. 8:25).

IPHTAH (Ĭph' tah) Place name meaning, "he opened." Town in tribal territory of Judah in the Shephelah (Josh. 15:43). It may be located at modern Terqumiyeh, halfway between Hebron and Beit Jibrin.

IPHTAHEL (Ĭph' tah ĕl) Place name meaning, "God opens." Valley separating tribal territories of Zebulun and Asher (Josh. 19:14,27). It is modern wadi el-Melek.

IR (Ĭr) Personal name meaning, "city" or "donkey's calf." Member of tribe of Benjamin (1 Chron. 7:12). Some Bible students refer to Genesis 46:23 and think a copyist misread the name, writing Ir rather than an original Dan, which looks much like Ir in Hebrew (REB).

IRA (Ī' rȧ) Personal name meaning, "city" or "donkey's colt." *1.* Priest under David (2 Sam. 20:26). KJV and a few Bible students see "priest" here as a civil office rather than a religious one. Ira was apparently from Havoth-jair in Gilead (Num. 32:41), though some Bible students think he was from Kiriath-jearim (1 Sam. 7:1). Ira is not identified as a Levite, and his function is not related to those of Abiathar and Zadok, the official priests. Thus some have concluded that he served on David's private staff as a personal priest to the king. Similarly, David's sons served as priests (2 Sam.

8:18 NRSV, REB, TEV). *2.* Two of David's military heroes were named Ira (2 Sam. 23:26,38). Ira from Tekoa was also an officer in charge of the sixth month's "national guard" army (1 Chron. 27:9).

IRAD (Ī' răd) Personal name of uncertain meaning. Son of Enoch (Gen. 4:18).

IRAM (Ī' răm) Personal name of uncertain meaning. Tribal leader in Edom (Gen. 36:43).

IRI (Ī' rī) Personal name meaning, "my city" or "my donkey's colt." Leader in tribe of Benjamin (1 Chron. 7:7).

IRIJAH (Ī rī' jah) Personal name meaning, "Yah sees." Army captain who accused Jeremiah of treason and turned him over to the authorities for punishment (Jer. 37:13) about 586 B.C. Apparently Jeremiah was going to inspect the field he had bought in Anathoth (Jer. 32:9). Since he had been preaching about ultimate victory for Babylon over Jerusalem, Irijah thought Jeremiah was trying to escape Jerusalem and join the Babylonian army, then retreating from Jerusalem. The prophet's mission included suffering. Loyalty to God did not always mean loyalty to the government or protection from the government. Both Irijah and Jeremiah thought they were serving God. History proved Jeremiah correct.

IRNAHASH (Ĭr nā' hăsh) Place name meaning, "city of the snake" or "city of bronze." Modern deir Nahhas about five and one half miles north of Lydda or khirbet Nahash on the northern end of the Arabah. First Chronicles 4:12 lists it as a personal name in the descendants of Judah, using the device of the "Table of Nations" (Gen. 10) and other passages of listing cities by original ancestors in the form of a genealogy.

IRON Metal that was basic material for weapons and tools in biblical period. The Iron Age began in Israel about 1200 B.C., though introduction of the metal into daily life occurred slowly. The Bible mentions iron in conjunction with Moses and with the Canaanite conquest, but at this time iron was rare and used mainly for jewelry. The availability of iron was a sign of the richness of the Promised Land (Deut. 8:9), and articles of iron were indications of wealth (Deut. 3:11; Josh. 6:19). Excavations of Israelite sites dating from the eleventh and twelfth centuries have uncovered rings, bracelets, and decorative daggers made of iron.

In early forging techniques iron was not much harder than other known metals and, unlike bronze and copper, it had to be worked while hot. As improved metalworking techniques became known, however, iron gradually became the pre-

I

ferred metal for tools such as plows, axes, and picks as well as for weapons such as spears and daggers. Iron chariots were a sign of great power in warfare (Josh. 17:18; Judg. 1:19; 4:3).

Older scholars taught that the Philistines held an iron monopoly over Israel. Increased availability of iron corresponds to the period of Philistia's collapse, and 1 Samuel records that the Philistines prevented smiths from working in Israel (1 Sam. 13:19–21). However, excavations in Philistia have uncovered no more iron implements than in Israelite cities. This suggests that the prohibition of smiths in Israel may refer to workers in bronze rather than iron or that for a period of history the Philistines had an economic and perhaps technological advantage, being able to control the iron industry.

Most likely, iron became common throughout the region due to disruption of sources of other metals and to increased trading to the north and over the sea. After 1000 B.C. iron became widely used. David emphasized the importance of taking metals as spoils of war, and he later used stockpiles of iron and bronze in preparation for building the Temple (1 Chron. 22:3).

Iron is frequently used symbolically in the Bible. Related to the hardness of iron it is used as a threat of judgment (Ps. 2:9; Rev. 2:27) or as a sign of strength (Isa. 48:4; Dan. 2:40). The imagery includes other aspects of ironworking: the furnace was a symbol of oppression (1 Kings 8:51), and the cauterizing effect of hot iron was used by Paul to describe those with no conscience (1 Tim. 4:2). See *Arms and Armor; Minerals and Metals; Mining; Philistines.* *Tim Turnham*

IRON (Ī′ rŏn) Place name meaning, "fearful." Town in tribal territory of Naphtali (Josh. 19:38), sometimes spelled Yiron (RSV, TEV, NAS). It is modern Yarun in modern Lebanon a mile and a half north northwest of Baram, nine miles southwest of Lake Huleh, on the modern border between Israel and Lebanon.

IRONSMITH One who works with iron, either one who smelts ore or one who works cast pieces. Bazillai (2 Sam. 17:27–29; 19:31–39), whose name means "man of iron," perhaps served as David's ironsmith. Solomon appealed to Hiram, the king of Tyre, for a skilled ironsmith (2 Chron. 2:7). Ironsmiths were among those assisting with Jehoiada's Temple renovation (2 Chron. 24:12). The importance of smiths is highlighted by their inclusion in the classes singled out for deportation at the destruction of Jerusalem (2 Kings 24:14). Isaiah 44:12; 54:16 provide concise accounts of the ironsmith's work. See *Occupations; Iron.*

IRONY is a trope (figure of speech) in which the intended meaning is the opposite of that normally expressed by the words used. The technique is built upon the trajectories of aroused expectations and gratifications. It depends upon: (1) common vocabulary, (2) common cultural experience, and (3) common awareness of typical literary forms. Irony is normally used to express a disparity between what is actually so and what the object of the irony believes to be so. Since irony means the opposite or near opposite of what it seems to say, interpreters of the Bible need to be able to recognize it.

Uses of Irony in the Bible Irony may be the reason for individual word choice. In the Hebrew text of Job 1:5, Job offered sacrifices because he feared his children may have "blessed" (Hebrew text) God. The writer really meant "curse," as most translations render the Hebrew word, but he wrote "blessed" somewhat in the English sense of "blessed out." The euphemism seems to emphasize the extreme nature of the sin by using its exact opposite to describe it. At other times, the irony may require the entire statement. This is easily seen in Job's bitter retort in Job 12:2, "No doubt but ye are the people, and wisdom shall die with you." Job was really saying that his so-called comforters were not as important or wise as they thought they were.

In addition to the ironic use of individual words or phrases, entire narratives can be structured around an irony of situation or fate. In the first case, the outcome of events seems contradictory to what could generally be expected and results in mocking the propriety of the apparent power structure. The second case is similar, but events have unexpected consequences when the actor brings about a result contrary to the original purpose. This usually involves the introduction of an imposter (or a false message), a debate between the ironist (critic of the imposter who wins), and a conclusion which vindicates the truth (or the ironist). Balaam's desire to be made wealthy at Israel's expense in Numbers 22—24 certainly ended up backfiring upon both the soothsayer and his Moabite patron, Balak. Instead of getting rich on Moabite gold by cursing Israel, he was thwarted by God and had to bless Israel and curse Moab. This is an irony of fate. In Daniel 2, the magicians were the imposters who claimed that no one could interpret the king's dream. Daniel was the ironist who taught them where wisdom arises (v. 20) and revealed the truth (v. 30). The impossible task was accomplished; the irony of situation was complete; and the power of God emphasized! This is the usual purpose of narrative irony in the Bible.

Bible students aware of the use of irony will recognize some of the humor in the Bible which exists at the expense of God's enemies. A study of comedy, rhetoric, and satire would also be helpful. *Johnny L. Wilson*

IRPEEL (Ĭr′ pė ĕl) Place name meaning, "God

heals." Town in tribal territory of Benjamin (Josh. 18:27). Location is not known.

IRRIGATION Transportation of water by man-made means such as canals, dams, aqueducts, and cisterns.

Old Testament The dry climate of the Ancient Near East made the transportation of water, often across long distances, a necessity. Large canal systems crossed the lands of Egypt and Mesopotamia, providing the vast amounts of water necessary to support crops during the dry months of March to October. In Egypt, the second highest official, the vizier, oversaw the maintenance of canals and the allocation of water to the provinces. Joseph may have fulfilled this role during his service for Pharaoh. Water was drawn from the Nile River and offshoot irrigation canals by means of a hinged pole with a hanging bucket on the end. Egypt's canal system allowed agricultural use of the highly fertile desert lands that the annual flooding of the Nile did not cover. During the Exile of Judah in Babylon, canals as large as twenty-five yards wide and several miles long carried the waters of the Tigris and Euphrates to field and city. Commercial ships used these waterways to transport produce between outlying farms and major cities.

The irrigation of fields was not widely practiced in ancient Israel. Instead, farmers relied upon the winter rains to provide all the water necessary for crops during the coming year. Fields and gardens

At the second cataract of the Nile River a scene of primitive irrigation with the use of manpower.

close to water sources may have used small irrigation channels, and some fields may have been watered by hand in particularly dry years. Runoff from the rains was collected and diverted through conduits to both communal and private cisterns for drinking water. In larger cities such as Gezer, Megiddo, Hazor, and Jerusalem engineers and workmen produced huge underground tunnel systems to provide the citizens with ample supplies of water. These tunnels maintained the cities needs in times of siege.

New Testament During Intertestamental and New Testament times massive Roman aqueducts were built to provide fresh water for the growing cities. A two-channeled canal ran fifteen miles from its source to the coastal city of Caesarea. Water for Jerusalem was carried northward through an elaborate series of canals and pools from the Bethlehem

Ancient water wheel used to irrigate farmland with water from the nearby Nile River.

area. Along the Dead Sea, where rain seldom fell, communities with elaborate canals and catchponds thrived by capturing the runoff of rains that fell in the hill country and drained towards the Jordan Valley. Cities in the Negev developed an extensive network of dams to collect infrequent rains, allowing them to turn the desert into thriving orchards and wheat fields. *David Maltsberger*

IRSHEMESH (Ĭr shē′ mĕsh) Place name meaning, "city of the sun." Town in tribal territory of Dan (Josh. 19:41) on the border of the tribe of Judah (Josh. 15:10, called Beth-shemesh or house of the sun). See *Beth-shemesh.*

IRU (Ī′ rū) Personal name meaning, "donkey's colt" or "they protect." Son of Caleb (1 Chron. 4:15). Many Bible students think the original text read Ir, a copyist joining the final *u* to the name when it should have been the first letter of the following word, meaning, "and."

ISAAC (Ī′ ṣāac) Personal name meaning "laughter." Only son of Abraham by Sarah and a patriarch of the nation of Israel.
Old Testament Isaac was the child of a promise from God, born when Abraham was 100 years old and Sarah was 90 (Gen. 17:17; 21:5). Isaac means "he laughs" and reflects his parents' unbelieving laughter regarding the promise (Gen. 17:17–19; 18:11–15) as well as their joy in its fulfillment (Gen. 21:1–7). Sarah wanted Hagar and Ishmael banished. God directed Abraham to comply, saying that it would be through Isaac that his descendants would be reckoned (Gen. 21:8–13; compare Rom. 9:7). Abraham's test of faith was God's command to sacrifice Isaac (Gen. 22:1–19).

Isaac married Rebekah (Gen. 24), who bore him twin sons, Esau and Jacob (Gen. 25:21–28). Isaac passed her off as a sister at Gerar (as Abraham had done). He became quite prosperous, later moving to Beersheba (Gen. 26). Isaac was deceived into giving Jacob his blessing and priority over Esau (Gen. 27). Isaac died at Mamre near Hebron at the age of 180 and was buried by his sons (Gen. 35:27–29).

Though less significant than Abraham and Jacob, Isaac was revered as one of the Israelite patriarchs (Ex. 3:6; 1 Kings 18:36; Jer. 33:26). Amos used the name Isaac as a poetic expression for the nation of Israel (Amos 7:9,16).
New Testament In the New Testament Isaac appears in the genealogies of Jesus (Matt. 1:2; Luke 3:34), as one of the three great patriarchs (Matt. 8:11; Luke 13:28; Acts 3:13), and an example of faith (Heb. 11:20). Isaac's sacrifice by Abraham (Heb. 11:17–18; Jas. 2:21), in which he was obedient to the point of death, serves as a type looking forward to Christ and as an example for Christians. Paul reminded believers that "we,

brethren, as Isaac, are the children of promise" (Gal. 4:28). *Daniel C. Browning, Jr.*

ISAIAH (Ī ṣai′ ah) Personal name meaning, "Yahweh saves." Prophet active in Judah about 740 to 701 B.C.
The Historical Background Isaiah's ministry spanned the period from his call vision (about 740 B.C.) until the last years of Hezekiah (716–687) or the early years of Manasseh (687–642). The prophet lived during the reigns of the Judean kings Uzziah, Jotham, Ahaz, Hezekiah, and perhaps the first years of Manasseh. He was contemporary with the last five kings of Israel: Menahem, Pekahiah, Pekah, and Hosea. The tragic fall of Samaria to the Assyrian King Sargon II in 722 B.C. occurred during his ministry.

In northwest Mesopotamia, the energetic monarch Tiglath-pileser III (745–727) founded the mighty Assyrian Empire. A series of vigorous successors succeeded him: Shalmaneser V (726–722), Sargon II (721–705), Sennacherib (704–681), and Esarhaddon (680–669). With Asshurbanipal (668–627) the empire began to crumble and ultimately fell to the Babylonians in 612–609 under the command of Nabopolassar (625–585).

During this same period Egypt experienced a resurgence of power in the 25th Dynasty (about 716–663) and occasioned international intrigue among the Palestinian states to overthrow Assyria. The petty states of Palestine—Syria, Philistia, Moab, Edom, Ammon, Arabia, Tyre, Israel, and Judah—were ultimately conquered or made tributary to Assyria. With strong feelings of nationalism these states fomented rebellion and duplicity, a world of intrigue born of political and economic frustrations. In this era Isaiah exercised his prophetic ministry, a large part of which was politically involved with Judah and to a lesser extent Israel. He advocated policies of state in line with the religious creed of authentic prophetism.
Personal Life of Isaiah Isaiah, the son of Amoz, was born in Judah, no doubt in Jerusalem, about 760 B.C. He enjoyed a significant position in the contemporary society and had a close relationship with the reigning monarchs. His education is clearly evident in his superb writing that has gained him an eminence in Hebrew literature hardly surpassed by any other. He had a thorough grasp of political history and dared to voice unpopular minority views regarding the state and the economy. His knowledge of the religious heritage of Israel and his unique theological contributions inspire awe. He was alive to what was transpiring in the court, in the marketplace, in high society with its shallowness, and in the political frustrations of the nation.

Isaiah was called to be a prophet of Yahweh in striking visions which he experienced in the Temple about 740 B.C., the year that the aged Judean king Uzziah died (Isa. 6). The elements in that vision forecast the major themes of his preaching, particularly the transcendent nature of Yahweh, which may serve as a modern translation of Hebraic "holiness." God warned him that his ministry would meet with disappointment and meager results but also assured him that forgiveness would ever attend the penitent (Isa. 6:5–7; 1:19–20) and that the ultimate promises of God would be realized (Isa.6:13*d*).

The prophet was married and was the father of two sons whose names symbolized Isaiah's public preaching: Mahershalalhashbaz (= the spoil speeds; the prey hastes), a conviction that Assyria would invade Syria and Israel about 734 B.C., and Sherajashub (a remnant shall return), a name that publicized his belief in the survival and conversion of a faithful remnant in Israel (Isa.1:9; 7:3; 8:1,4; 10:20–23).

During the dark days when the Assyrians took over one Palestinian state after another, Isaiah firmly contended that the Judean monarchs ought to remain as neutral as possible, to refrain from rebellious acts, and to pay tribute. When the Israelites and Syrians jointly attacked Judah for refusing to join the anti-Assyrian coalition (Isa.7:1–9; 8:1–15), he deplored the dangerous policy of purchasing protection from the Assyrians. In 711 B.C. when the city of Ashdod rebelled against Assyria, Isaiah assumed the garb of a captive for three years calling on Hezekiah not to take the fatal step of joining the rebellion. No doubt he was instrumental in influencing Hezekiah to reject the seditious plot (Isa.20:1–6). That same resolute policy assured Isaiah that Jerusalem would not fall to Sennacherib in 701 B.C. despite the ominous outlook the Assyrian envoys forecast (Isa. 36—37). Isaiah soundly castigated Hezekiah for entertaining the seditious Babylonian princelet whose real purpose was to secure military aid for a rebellion in south Babylonia in an effort to overthrow Sennacherib (Isa. 39).

Literary and Theological Pronouncements Israel made no clear separation of church and state; accordingly most of the utterances of Isaiah are religious and political in character in spite of their literary diversity. Underlying his conceptual world was his inaugural vision: Yahweh was the ultimate King; His nature was infinite holiness or transcendence; His holiness manifested itself in righteousness (Isa. 5:16). Yahweh was the electing, endowing, forgiving God, possessing plans and purposes for His servant Israel by which they might secure the Abrahamic promise of world blessedness. The vision of Isaiah indicated the resistance this program would encounter but concluded with the certainty of its performance.

With this theological perspective Isaiah inveighed against the errant nation of Judah (Isa.1:2–9; 2:6–22; 3:1—4:1) even using the guise of a love song (5:1–7). He pronounced six

"woes" on the immoral nation. His wrath also attacked Israel (Isa. 9:8–21; 28:1–29). Among other travesties, Judah was rebellious, evil, iniquitous, alienated, corrupters, a sick people, unfilial in attitude, purposeless in their excessive religiosity, idolaters, proud ones whose land was filled with esoteric charlatans, brass in their defection, thankless and unappreciative, drunkards, monoplists of real estate, wise in their own eyes, morally indiscriminate. The character of true religion was absent; they needed to desist from evil, to learn to do good, to seek justice, correct oppression, defend the fatherless, plead for the widow (Isa. 1:17).

Though the indictments were severe, Isaiah still held out the hope of forgiveness to the penitent (Isa.1:18–31) and pointed to days coming when God would establish peace (Isa. 2:1–4; 4:2–6). He promised the Messiah, the son of David, who would assume the chief role in the fulfillment of the Abrahamic-Davidic covenantal promises (Isa. 9:2–7; 11:1–9).

Isaiah is remembered for his magnificent conception of God. The thrice-repeated term "holy" is equivalent to holiness to the *nth* or infinite degree (6:3). Yahweh is Lord of all, King of the universe, the Lord of history who exhibits His character in righteousness, that is, in self-consistent acts of rightness (Isa. 5:16). The prophet criticized the vanity and meaninglessness of religion's pride. He demanded social and religious righteousness practiced in humility and faith. He strongly affirmed God's plans that would not lack fulfillment, announcing that the Assyrian king was but the instrument of God and accountable to Him. He stressed, too, the Day of Yahweh, a time when the presence of God would be readily discoverable in human history. Isaiah was certain that a faithful remnant would always carry on the divine mission (Shearjashub, Isa.1:9). The messianic hope was considered the blueprint of history fulfilled, the hope of humankind toward which all creation moves.

The Disciples of Isaiah During the ministry of Isaiah when the Judeans discounted his stern warnings, he ordered that his "testimony" and "teaching" be bound and sealed—no doubt in a scroll—and committed to his disciples until history proved his words true (Isa. 8:16). Most people did not accept Isaiah's message, but he had disciples who did. They formed the backbone of a prophetic party in Judah who preserved his writings, sustained his political and religious power so that he had access to the person of the king, and arranged the final form of his preaching in written form as can be seen by constant referral to the prophet in third person rather than first.

In Isaiah's time the great military power that threatened the Palestinian states was Assyria. In much of the book that now bears the name of Isaiah, the reigning power was Babylon, which did not rise to power until after 625 B.C., over 50 years after Isaiah's death. Some Bible students think that the writings that reflect the Babylonian period may be the work of the disciples of Isaiah, who projected his thought into the new and changed situation of the Babylonian world. Others would say in the Spirit Isaiah was projected supernaturally into the future, thus able to know even the name of Cyrus, King of Persia (44:28; 45:1). **The Prophetic Critique of Foreign Affairs** Israel's prophets such as Amos, Jeremiah, Ezekiel, and Isaiah devoted considerable attention to political pronouncements regarding foreign nations. Those thus singled out included Babylon (Isa. 13—14), Moab (Is. 15—16), Damascus (Isa. 17:1–14), Ethiopia (Isa. 18), Egypt (Isa. 19—20), and Tyre (Isa. 23). The importance of these prophetic utterances are historical, though political and religious principles can be profitably drawn from them.

Every national capital hosted embassies of other friendly nations with their diplomatic staffs. Such visiting ambassadors were responsible to their home governments to report the relevant news. These prophetic speeches to the nations proved significant in that they represented a strong minority group feeling, the religious and political thought of a traditional Yahwistic block with strong backing from the right wing of the government. The speeches of Isaiah or his disciples would be relayed to the foreign capitals as a significant utterance on foreign affairs. They also informed God's people of His world plans, giving encouragement of final victory.

The "Little Apocalypse" (Isa. 24—27) Midway between prophetic prediction and apocalypticism are these four chapters. Apocalypticism is an expressive term which denotes the unveiling of the future. Portions of Ezekiel, Joel, and Daniel are written in this style marked by cosmological orientation, proximate pessimism, symbolism with few historical allusions, suprahistorical perspective—that is, the future was so bewildering and the events so vaguely perceived that the writer penned his forecast in the symbolic language of faith, pointing to a resolution of world history. In Isaiah 24—27 two opposing forces were pitted in conflict: they were presented as two cities. In the tension of history when the city of chaos triumphs, the city of God laments; when it suffers defeat, the city of God breaks forth into song. Some four hymns are in Isaiah 24—27. Ultimately, the kingdom of God is victorious with such blessing as the removal of national hatred, the overcoming of sorrow, the overcoming of death, the resurrection, in short, the resolution of history as the kingdom of God.

A Collection of Prophetic Oracles (Isa. 28—35) Since five in this series of prophecies commence with an introductory "woe," it suggests that much of this block of materials will be negative in its criticism. Thus in Isaiah 28 the inebriated aristocracy of Israel failed to discern the fading flower of

their nation; and they were supported in their dereliction by the priests and prophets. Indeed, they mimicked sarcastically Isaiah's plain speech as childish prattle, to which he retorted that if they did not understand simple Hebrew, Yahweh would speak to them in Assyrian! Yet, those that trusted in God stood on a firm foundation, a foundation laid in righteousness and justice. It alone would stand (Isa. 28:16–22).

Isaiah 29—35 are largely directed to Judah; elements of severe censure are often followed by oracles of comfort. The Judeans were reproved for their rejection of the authentic voice of prophecy, their defiant atheism, their meaningless parade of religion, their rebellious plotting with the Egyptians, and their buildup of the military. Such passages as Isaiah 28:5–6; 29:5–8,17–24; 30:18–33; 31:4–9; 32:1–5,8,15–20; 33:2–6,17–24 contrast with these passages. The conclusion of this segment includes the juxtaposition of a negative oracle against Edom, here symbolic of evil, with a paradisiacal contrast involving Israel (Isa. 34—35). Much like the theme of Isaiah 24—27, it forecasted the ultimate fulfillment of divine purposes in history.

The Historical Appendage With the exception of Isaiah 38:9–21, an original thanksgiving song of Hezekiah after a severe illness, the rest of Isaiah 36—39 duplicates 2 Kings 18:13—20:19. A similar insertion of historical materials from the Book of Kings (2 Kings 24:18—25:30) concludes the Book of Jeremiah. (Jer. 52). It provides the reader of the prophet with an historical background for the understanding of the book.

The Book of Consolation (Isa. 40—55) *Its Historical Background.* The setting of these chapters is incontestably that of the later years of the Babylonian Exile when Cyrus (Isa. 44:28; 45:1) was beginning his conquests which would ultimately overthrow the Babylonian power (550 B.C.). The city of Jerusalem and its Temple had been destroyed by the Babylonians in 587 B.C., and a considerable segment of the upper classes had been forcibly exiled to Babylon. The writer hailed Cyrus as the shepherd of Yahweh who would build Jerusalem and set the exiles free (Isa. 44:26—45:1). For some forty years the Judeans had lived as hostages in a strange land; they were discouraged by the seeming unimprovable situation. Was it their unforgivable guilt; had God forgotten them? The stunning victory of Cyrus over the mighty Babylonian power (538 B.C.) and his decree of liberation for the Jewish exiles were events too joyous to recount. But what of the long, arduous journey through the desert with its multiplied dangers? The prophetic voice assured the exiles that God would prepare a level highway for their journey, provide for their sustenance, and lead them back to their homeland (Isa. 40). The exiles were assured of divine pardon, comforted in every major problem area, and promised the restoration of Zion and its Temple.

Its Literary Structure. The prophetic voice of chapters 40—55 affirmed the purpose of God in the dark days of the Babylonian Exile. Most of the chapters articulate the various theological affirmations designed to comfort, challenge, and advise the hostage people. However, arising from the messages of comfort and dialogue are four so-called Servant Songs (Isa. 42:1–4; 49:1–6; 50:4–9; and 52:13—53:12). These songs reiterate the role of Israel as the chosen servant of God, the nation that would evangelize all nations, whose endowment by the Spirit would provide the enablement for that mission and the concomitant suffering attendant the people of God addressing a sinful society, and the ultimate success of the divine mission by his faithful servants. There can be no doubt but that the authentic Israel was the servant the prophet had in mind (Isa. 49:3). While these songs unquestionably identify the Suffering Servant as the godly in Israel, they find their ultimate fulfillment in the life, death, and resurrection of the Lord Jesus Christ, the Savior of the world. The cross-bearing Christian church (Gal. 6:14–16) carries on the Servant's mission.

The religious affirmation of Isaiah 40—55. The overwhelming majesty of these chapters have ever impressed the faithful with its sublime consolation. Against the gloom of Exile, the prophet portrayed the One Sovereign God, Creator, incomparable, unfailing, the Lord of history. What a sorry contrast was the Babylonian idolatry with its vaunted pretensions (Isa. 46—47).

The prophetic announcement disclosed the movement of God in history—the Exile was over. The Persians were about to take over the Babylonian power; they would be trustworthy and friendly to the exiles. The difficulties of the journey would be provided for by the God who programmed the Exodus and would once more duplicate that performance in the release of the exiles from Babylonian tyranny. It was Yahweh who had stirred up Cyrus, and through him His purpose would be secured. Assured of divine forgiveness and comforted in their grief, the exiles were exhorted to identify with their ancient role in the blessing of the earth's population through the dissemination of the religion through which the world would be blessed (Gen. 12:3). The Servant Songs were the blueprint for Israel's devotion and adherence—to love, to serve, to suffer, to teach the knowledge of God for the salvation of humankind.

The Concluding Prophetic Oracles (Isa. 56—66) *Its Historical Setting.* Here is a change of venue from Isaiah 40—55; no longer was Babylon the focus; Palestine was, with the Temple restored and sacrifice and worship being conducted. Many scholars place this collection sometime around 460 B.C. and attribute the diverse fields of interest, style, and religious affirmation to

prophetic voices of this period addressing themselves to major issues of their day. Others think God transported the eighth century prophet into the fifth century setting.

Its Literary Structure. The subjects handled in this section include an oracle on sabbath keeping (Isa. 56:1–8), censure of civil and religious leaders (56:9—57:12), an analysis of the meaning of fasting (ch. 58), the dilemma of the unfulfilled divine promises (ch. 59), hopeful encouragement to be anticipated (chs. 60—64), the grievous sin of Judah and the blessedness of the righteous remnant (ch. 65), and brief fragments on a number of subjects (ch. 66).

Its Theological Affirmation. This portion of inspired Scripture contains some very remarkable and advanced concepts. It places the reader in the midst of a discordant community where the righteous struggle against their powerful opponents. It censures the moral depravity of rulers, of those who succumb to pagan practices, of those who practice external rites without true identification with their meaning. A most interesting affirmation regards foreigners and eunuchs (56:3–7), they would no longer be excluded from the Temple worship. This injected grace and hope into the law of Deuteronomy 23:1. Other choice verses praise humility (Isa. 66:1–2), announce the new heaven and the new earth (Isa. 66:22); and report the anointing by the Spirit (Isa. 61:1–4). This remarkable conclusion to the Book of Isaiah discloses the struggles and aspirations of the post-exilic community. Without it we should be impoverished in our knowledge of that period.

Outline

I. God Knows His Peoples' Sins But Calls Them Back to Himself (1:1—12:6).
  A. Though your sins are many, forgiveness is possible (1:1—5:30).
  B. People need God, but God also needs people to call His people (6:1–13).
  C. National leaders may refuse God's help (7:1—8:15).
  D. Waiting for God to act is part of serving Him (8:16–22).
  E. With God the future is bright (9:1–7).
  F. Fallen nations teach lessons (9:8—10:4).
  G. Pride destroys individuals and nations (10:5–19).
  H. God can do His work with a righteous few (10:20–23).
  I. Faith in God conquers fear of all else (10:24–34).
  J. An ideal age is a human dream, but a divine accomplishment (11:1–16).
  K. Anytime is the right time for thanksgiving (12:1–6).
II. God's Sovereignty Extends to All Nations Whether Acknowledged or Not (13:1—23:18).

I

A. God's judgment is real (13:1—21:17).
B. God's judgment is impartial (22:1—23:18).
III. God's Triumph Over Evil Means Deliverance for His People (24:1—27:13).
A. God's judgment time is a time of mourning and singing (24:1–23).
B. God's judgment time is a time of thanksgiving (25:1–12).
C. God's judgment time is a time of victory (26:1–27:13).
IV. God's People Must Be Different (28:1–39:8).
A. Tragedy strikes when leaders fail (28:1—29:4).
B. The power of God overshadows the power of nations (30:1—35:10).
C. A triumphant faith is a faith that will not let go (36:1—39:8).
V. God's Word for His Confused People (40:1—55:13).
A. God comes to His people when judgment has passed (40:1–31).
B. God holds His people by the hand (41:1–29).
C. Send the light of truth to those in darkness (42:1–25).
D. God alone is Savior of His people (43:1–28).
E. Homemade gods can never save (44:1–28).
F. God may use an unbeliever (45:1–25).
G. False gods make life's load heavier (46:1–13).
H. Ruin follows wickedness as night follows day (47:1–15).
I. Let the redeemed of the Lord proclaim it (48:1—52:15).
J. Healing comes to many through the suffering of One (53:1–12).
K. God keeps His promises (54:1–17).
L. God's finest invitation: Return to Me (55:1–13).
VI. God's Word to His Imperfect People (56:1—66:24).
A. Salvation is for all people (56:1–12).
B. Idolatry is an ever present temptation (57:1–21).
C. Worship and right living are inseparable (58:1–14).
D. Repentance brings reconciliation with God (59:1–21).
E. Light from God brings life (60:1—62:12).
F. Prayer brings God's help (63:1—65:25).
G. Judgment and deliverance are rights of God alone (66:1–24).   Edward Dalglish

ISAIAH, MARTYRDOM OF A Jewish narrative elaborating the sins of Manasseh (2 Kings 21:16). The original was probably written in Hebrew or Aramaic and then translated into Greek in the pre-Christian era or perhaps in the first or early second century A.D. The narrative concerns Isaiah who makes predictions concerning the evil deeds of Manasseh. An evil priest offers Isaiah freedom if he will retract his prophecies of judgment. Empowered by God's Spirit, Isaiah resists and suffers martyrdom by being sawn in two. Hebrews 11:37 is a likely allusion to such a tradition of the faithfulness and martyrdom of Isaiah. Justin Martyr, Tertullian, and the Talmud are similarly aware of such a tradition. The familiarity of Origin (about A.D. 225) and IV Baruch (about A.D. 200) with details of the tradition suggests their dependence on the Martydom of Isaiah. See *Pseudepigrapha.*

ISCAH (Ĭs′ cah) Personal name perhaps meaning, "they look." Daughter of Haran and sister of Milcah (Nahor's wife) and Lot. Thus she was an intimate part of the ancestral family of Abraham (Gen. 11:29). Tradition has tried to make Iscah another name for Sarah or to say she was Lot's wife. No biblical information gives foundation for such late interpretations.

ISCARIOT (Ĭs câr′ ĭ ot) Personal name transliterated from Hebrew into Greek and meaning, "man of Kerioth"; or perhaps a name derived from Latin and meaning, "assassin" or "bandit." Surname of both the disciple Judas who betrayed Jesus (Mark 3:19) and of his father Simon (John 6:71). If bandit is the meaning of the name, Judas and his father may have been members of a patriotic party, the Zealots. "Man of Kerioth" is probably the meaning of the surname, referring to town of Kerioth. See *Judas; Kerioth.*

ISH-BOSHETH (Ĭsh-bō′ shĕth) Personal name meaning "man of shame." Son of Saul and his successor as king of Israel (2 Sam. 2:8). After Saul's death, Abner the commander of Saul's army proclaimed Ish-bosheth king. He reigned for two years. He was finally murdered by his own captains (2 Sam. 4:1–7). The name Ish-bosheth means "man of shame." Originally his name was Ish-baal (1 Chron. 8:33), which means "man of Baal." The repugnance with which Baal worship was regarded by the faithful in Israel frequently led to the substitution of the word for shame in the place of the name of the Canaanite deity. See *Saul.*

ISHBAH (Ĭsh′ bah) Personal name meaning, "he soothes." Member of tribe of Judah known as father of town of Eshtemoa (1 Chron. 4:17).

ISHBAK (Ĭsh′ băk) Personal name meaning, "come before, excel." Son of Abraham and Keturah (Gen. 25:2). May be the same as Yasbuq in Assyrian sources and refers to a tribal ancestor of a tribe in northern Syria.

ISHBIBENOB (Ĭsh′ bī bē nŏb) Personal name meaning, "inhabitant of Nob." See *Nob*. Philistine who tried to kill David in battle (2 Sam. 21:16–17). He is described literally as "who (was) among the children of the Raphah." Traditionally, this has been connected with the Rephaim and translated "giant" (KJV, TEV, NAS, REB, NRSV). NIV translates literally, "the descendants of Rapha." Some Bible students interpret this as being an elite group of warriors under a vow to the god Rapha. Or it may mean, "the men of the scimitar" or sword. Other Bible students use Greek manuscript evidence to replace the unusual name Ishbibenob with another—Dodo son of Joash—but this is a drastic solution. Another solution changes the text to read the name as a verb meaning, "they camped in Nob," leaving the soldier unnamed. The soldier Ishbibenob was killed by David's faithful soldier Abishai.

ISHHOD (Ĭsh′ hŏd) Personal name meaning, "man of vigor and vitality." Member of tribe of Manasseh east of the Jordan (1 Chron. 7:18).

ISHI (Ĭsh′ ī) Personal name meaning, "my deliverer or salvation." *1.* Descendant of Jerahmeel in tribe of Judah (1 Chron. 2:31). *2.* Member of tribe of Judah (1 Chron. 4:20). *3.* Father of military leaders of tribe of Simeon who successfully fought the Amalekites (1 Chron. 4:42). *4.* Clan leader in tribe of Manasseh east of the Jordan (1 Chron. 5:24). *5.* Transliteration of Hosea's wordplay between "my man" or "my husband" (Hebrew, *ishi*) and "my master" or "my lord" (Hebrew, *baali*) (Hos. 2:16 KJV, NAS). Hosea looked to the day when Israel would quit worshiping or even pronouncing the name of Baal and would be totally faithful to Yahweh as "her man" and "her master."

ISHIAH (Ĭsh ī′ ah) KJV spelling of Isshiah (I Chron. 7:3). See *Isshiah*.

ISHIJAH (Ĭsh ī′ jah) KJV, NIV spelling of Isshijah. See *Isshijah*.

ISHMA (Ĭsh′ mȧ) Short form of Ishmael meaning. "God hears." Member of tribe of Judah (1 Chron. 4:3).

ISHMAEL (Ĭsh′ mā el) Personal name meaning "God hears." Son of Abraham by the Egyptian concubine Hagar (Gen. 16:11). He became the progenitor of the Ishmaelite peoples. The description in Genesis 16:12 points to an unruly and misanthropic disposition. Ishmael and his mother were expelled from the camp of Abraham at the insistence of Sarah following the birth of Sarah's son Isaac. The boy was near death in the wilderness when the angel of God directed Hagar to a well. Genesis 21:20 explains that God was with Ishmael, and that he became an archer. See *Abraham; Patriarchs*.

ISHMAELITE (Ĭsh′ mā ĕl īte) Tribal name for descendants of Ishmael. According to Genesis 25:12–16, Ishmael was the father of twelve sons. The Ishmaelites were regarded as an ethnic group, generally referring to the nomadic tribes of northern Arabia. The Ishmaelites were not, however, exclusively associated with any geographic area. References to them in the Old Testament are relatively few. The people to whom Joseph was sold by his brothers are called Ishmaelites in Genesis 37:25. See *Ishmael; Abraham*.

ISHMAIAH (Ĭsh mâî′ ah) Long and short form of personal name meaning, "Yah(weh) hears." *1.* Military hero from Gibeon in charge of David's select "thirty" warriors (1 Chron. 12:4), though he is not listed among the "thirty" in 2 Samuel 23 or 1 Chronicles 11. He does illustrate early support for David from Saul's tribe of Benjamin. *2.* Head of tribe of Zebulun under David (1 Chron. 27:19).

ISHMERAI (Ĭsh′ mė râi) Short form of personal name meaning, "Yah protects." Member of tribe of Benjamin (1 Chron. 8:18).

ISHOD (Ī′ shŏd) KJV spelling of Ishhod. See *Ishhod*.

ISHPAH (Ĭsh′ pah) Personal name perhaps meaning, "baldhead." Member of tribe of Benjamin (1 Chron. 8:16).

ISHPAN (Ĭsh′ păn) Personal name of uncertain meaning. Member of tribe of Benjamin (1 Chron. 8:22).

ISHTAR A Mesopotamian goddess of fertility and war. In her role as goddess of fertility, Ishtar was associated with Tammuz, the god of vegetation. Ishtar was sometimes identified with the planet Venus and was designated "Mistress of Heaven" in the Amarna tablets. The goddess is perhaps the "Queen of heaven" of Jeremiah 7:18; 44:17–19,25; Ezekiel 8:14. See *Fertility Cults; Astarte; Tammuz; Babylon*.

ISHTOB (Ĭsh′ tŏb) Personal name meaning, "man of good" or "man of Tob." KJV follows early translations in interpreting this as a proper name (2 Sam. 10:6,8). The standard Hebrew manuscript apparently has two words, indicating a common noun phrase. Thus most modern translations read "men from Tob." A manuscript from the Dead Sea Scrolls has Ishtob as one word and thus as a proper name; but modern Bible students still generally follow the standard manuscript rather than the older Dead Sea Scroll. "Man of Tob" could also refer to the ruler of Tob. See *Tob*.

ISHUAH (Ĭsh′ ū ah) KJV spelling of Ishvah (Gen. 46:17). See *Ishvah*.

ISHUAI (Ĭsh′ ū âi) KJV spelling of Ishvi in 1 Chronicles 7:30. See *Ishvi.*

ISHUI (Ĭsh′ ū ī) KJV spelling of Ishvi (Gen. 46:17). See *Ishvi.*

ISHVAH (Ĭsh′ vah) Personal name meaning, "he is equal" or "he satisfies." Son of Asher (Gen. 46:17). He is not named in Numbers 26:44, leading some scholars to think that a copyist duplicated the following name Ishvi with a minor variation. KJV read the text with different vowel points than the standard Hebrew manuscript, spelling the name Ishuah.

ISHVI (Ĭsh′ vī) Personal name meaning, "he is equal," "he satisfies," or "he rules." Son of Asher (Gen. 46:17) and original clan ancestor of Ishvites (Num. 26:44).

ISHVITE (Ĭsh′ vīte) See *Ishvi.*

ISHYO REB spelling of Ishui: (1 Sam. 14:49). See *Ishui; Ishvi.*

ISLAND Tract of land surrounded by water. Modern translations sometimes replace the island or isle of the KJV with the terms coast, coastline, or coastland (compare Gen. 10:5; Esther 10:1; Ps. 97:1; Isa. 11:11; Jer. 2:10). "Islands" frequently appears in parallel to peoples/nations (Isa. 41:1; 51:5; 66:19; Jer. 31:10) and to the earth (Isa. 42:4). Often the idea of distant peoples and places is stressed by the parallelism (Isa. 41:5; 49:1). The Hebrews were not a seafaring people and so easily equated the Mediterranean islands with the ends of the earth.

Scripture mentions many islands by name: Arvad (Ezek. 27:8,11) is an island two miles offshore from northern Phoenicia. Clauda or Cauda (NRSV) is a small island off Crete (Acts 27:16). Chios (Acts 20:15) is an island off the coast of Ionia. Coos or Cos (Acts 21:1 NIV) is an island 50 miles northwest of Rhodes. Crete (the Old Testament Caphtor, Jer. 47:4; Amos 9:7) is an island 152 miles long located to the southeast of Greece (Titus 1:5, 12). Cyprus (home of the Old Testament Chittim, Jer. 2:10; Ezek. 27:6) is an island 75 miles long located toward the eastern end of the Mediterranean (Acts 4:36; 11:19–20 among others). Melita or Malta (NAS) is an island located 50 miles southwest of Sicily (Acts 27:39—28:10). Patmos is an island off the coast of Ionia west of Samos (Rev. 1:9). Rhodes is an island southwest of Asia Minor (Acts 21:1). Samos is an island located off the Ionian coast twelve miles southwest of Ephesus (Acts 20:15). Sardinia is a western Mediterranean island south of Corsica. Tyre (Ezek. 26:2) was a famous Phoenician island city.

ISMACHIAH (Ĭs mȧ chī′ ah) Personal name meaning, "Yahweh supports." Priest and administrator in the Temple under Cononiah and Shimei when Hezekiah was king of Judah (2 Chron. 31:13).

ISMAIAH (Ĭs mā′ iah) KJV spelling of Ishmaiah. See *Ishmaiah.*

ISMAKIAH (Ĭs mȧ kī′ ah) NIV spelling of Ismachiah. See *Ismachiah.*

ISPAH (Ĭs′ pah) KJV spelling of Ishpah. See *Ishpah.*

ISRAEL (Ĭṣ′ rā ĕl) Name of Northern Kingdom after Jeroboam led the northern tribes to separate from the southern tribes and form a separate kingdom (1 Kings 12).

ISRAEL (Ĭṣ′ rā ĕl) Personal name meaning, "God strives," "God rules," "God heals," or "he strives against God." Name God gave Jacob after he wrestled with the divine messenger (Gen. 32:28). Afterwards, Jacob was a changed person, limping on a damaged thigh, with new food regulations, and with a new experience of God that influenced the way he lived. His twelve sons became known as the "sons of Israel," and the resulting nation became the nation of Israel. Thus Jacob's experience at the Jabbok became the foundation for the nation of God's chosen people.

ISRAEL, HISTORY OF Chronological Outline

The Preexilic Period

The Patriarchal Period	2000–1720*
The Egyptian Period	1720–1290
The Exodus and the Wilderness Sojourn	1290–1250
The Settlement	1250–1020
The United Monarchy	1020– 922
The Divided Monarchy	922– 587
The Kingdom of Israel	922– 721
The Kingdom of Judah	922– 587
The Babylonian Exile	597/587–539/538

The Postexilic Period

The Persian Period	539– 331
The Hellenistic Period	331– 168
The Maccabean Period	168– 63
The Roman Period	63–400 A.D.

*All dates will be assumed to be B.C. unless otherwise designated. The careful interpreter cautiously suggests a dating schema given the many uncertainties. This outline is one of several academically acceptable. See *Chronology* for dating alternatives to those used in this article.

THE PREEXILIC PERIOD

1. The Patriarchal and Egyptian Periods (Genesis 12—50) Israel's roots derive from the Mesopotamian Valley. Father Abraham was associated with Ur in the southern Mesopotamian Valley. About 2000, responding to a divine command, he began a journey with his tribe which took him initially from Ur to Haran. While at Haran, Abraham's father, Terah, died, and a brother, Nahor, decided to settle at Haran. Abraham and his wife, Sarah, however, traveled onward to Canaan, where ultimately they established their home. To them was born Isaac, the son of promise, who was married to Rebekah, granddaughter of Nahor. To Isaac and Rebekah were born Jacob and Esau. Jacob, having made his way back to the region of Haran, married both Leah and Rachel, daughters of Laban, the brother of Rebekah. To Jacob and his wives were born twelve sons, who, having migrated to Egypt, became the foundation for the twelve tribes and for fulfillment of the promises originally made to Abraham. It was these tribal descendents with whom Moses was associated in the Exodus from Egypt in 1290.

2. The Exodus and the Wilderness Sojourn (Exodus 1—24; 32—34; Numbers 10—14) Israel is a product of the Sinaitic experience, begun when God called the "renegade" Moses to return to Egypt and deliver His people. Moving from Goshen in Egypt through God's leadership in the miracle at the sea to the Sinai peninsula under Moses' leadership, the Hebrews at Sinai ratified a covenant with the God Yahweh (Ex. 24), and thus Israel as a landless people came into being.

For a period of eleven months they remained at Sinai. Traditionally, it is understood that the Torah was formulated during this period, although historical criticism postulates a longer period of development. Regardless, Israel departed Sinai as a covenant people who would continually struggle with God.

The wilderness experience is set at forty years, the designation often used to indicate a generation. Through this period the generation that departed Egypt died, Yahweh's judgment upon them because they refused to believe that the God of deliverance could also lead them into Canaan.

3. The Settlement (Joshua 1—24; Judges 1—16) Eventually, however, they entered Canaan via the tranjordanian area. Under the leadership of Joshua, they crossed the Jordan River and entered the "Promised Land" at Jericho. The Book of Joshua records the settlement of the Israelites into Canaan, first in mid-country, then in the south, and finally in the north. Joshua distributed the land among the tribes and renewed the Covenant (Josh. 24).

For a period of approximately two centuries, the Israelites were centrally joined as autonomous tribes around the ark of the covenant, a loose relationship centering in common worship commitments. Over them divinely designated Judges emerged, men like Gideon and Samson, and one woman, Deborah. Gradually, any sense of unity

broke down until "every man did that which was right in his own eyes" (Judg. 21:25).

4. The United Monarchy (1 Samuel 1—3; 8—15; 2 Samuel 1—6; 9—20; 1 Kings 1—4; 6—8; 11) The period of the Judges presented problems for the Israelites, however, in that they could not assert centralized economic, political, or military strength in this disjointed condition. This situation, plus other factors such as the emergence of the Philistine threat, caused a clamoring for the establishment of kingship. Thus, about 1020, the Israelites moved politically into a monarchy.

Saul (1020–1000) was Israel's first king, although he often acted more as a Judge. Like the Judges, he understood himself designated by God to rule because of having received the Spirit of God. He fought valiantly against the Philistines, dying ultimately in the struggle. More importantly, he helped to pave the way for David, who fully lifted the nation into monarchical status.

David (1000–965) is credited with uniting the people, however tenuous that relationship (2 Sam. 5:4–5); and he lifted Israel to the full flower of monarchical establishment. Having united the north and the south, he established Jerusalem as the capital of the kingdom, contained the Philistines, expanded Israel's borders and her trade, and established a monarchical line that ruled in uninterrupted fashion, save one exception (Athaliah, 842–837), until the fall of Judah to Babylonia in 587.

David's son and successor was Solomon (965–922). Solomon inherited all that David had amassed, but he was able neither to build upon nor to maintain David's kingdom. He did temporarily intensify trade, but he is remembered primarily for building the Temple in Jerusalem. Nonetheless, when Solomon died, his legacy was a division in the kingdom, so that, henceforth, we speak of Israel in the north and Judah in the south.

5. The Divided Monarchy (1—2 Kings; Amos; Hosea; Isaiah 1—39; Micah; Jeremiah) The north was contextually tied into international politics more than was the south, in part because the primary east-west trade route traversed Israel at the Valley of Jezreel. Israel was both the larger country and the more populous area. Her involvement in the larger world of nations meant that Israel was destined to fall politically more quickly than Judah. Israel fell to Assyria in 721, while Judah was conquered by Babylonia initially in 597.

Israel emerged as a separate power under Jeroboam I (922–901 B.C.), the initial king over what became a rather turbulent nation. Nineteen kings ruled during the country's two centuries of existence, and coup attempts brought eight succession crises. Jeroboam is most remembered, however, for his establishment of rival shrines at Dan and Bethel (1 Kings 12). These shrines were in the form of bull images and were constructed as a

I

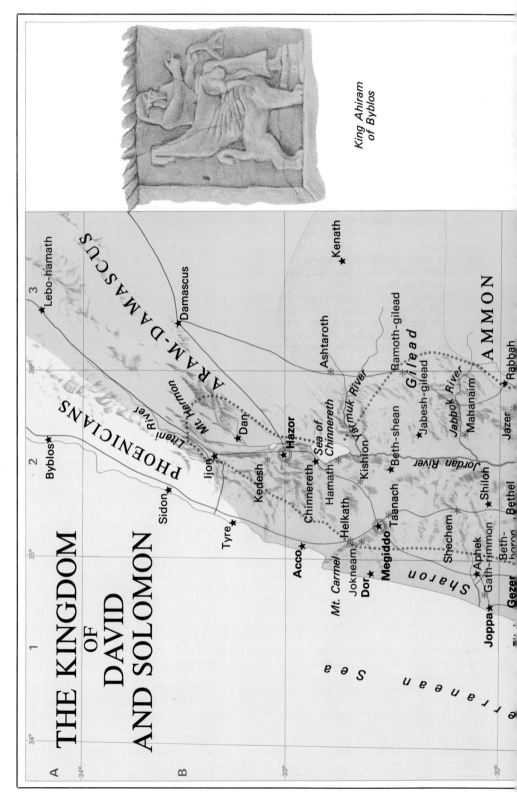

THE KINGDOM
OF
DAVID
AND SOLOMON

King Ahiram
of Byblos

Mediterranean Sea

PHOENICIANS

ARAM-DAMASCUS

Byblos

Sidon

Tyre

Lebo-hamath

Damascus

Kenath

Ijon
Dan
Kedesh
Hazor
Chinnereth
Sea of
Chinnereth
Hamath
Helkath

Mt. Hermon
Litani River
Mt. Carmel

Acco
Jokneam
Dor
Megiddo
Taanach
Kishon

Sharon

Shechem
Aphek
Gath-rimmon
Beth-
horon
Beth-
Bethel
Shiloh

Joppa
Gezer

Ashtaroth

Ramoth-gilead

Gilead

Beth-shean
Jabesh-gilead
Yarmuk River
Jordan River
Jabbok River
Mahanaim
Jazer

AMMON
Rabbah

© carta

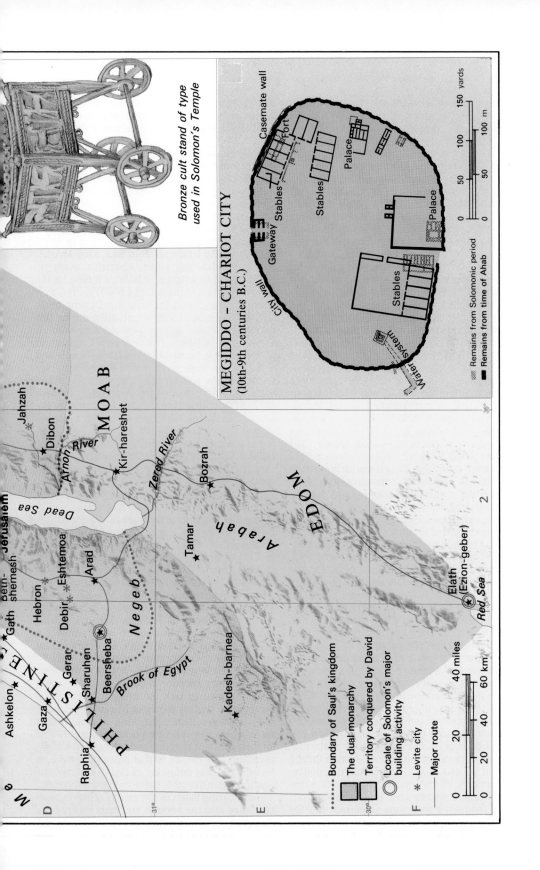

Bronze cult stand of type
used in Solomon's Temple

MEGIDDO – CHARIOT CITY
(10th–9th centuries B.C.)

Casemate wall

City wall

Gateway

Stables

Fort

Stables

Palace

Palace

Stables

Water system

Remains from Solomonic period

Remains from time of Ahab

0   50   100   150 yards

0   50   100 m

Jahzah

MOAB

Dibon

Arnon River

Kir-hareshet

Zered River

Bozrah

EDOM

Arabah

Tamar

Dead Sea

Jerusalem

Beth-
shemesh

Gath

Hebron

Debir   Eshtemoa

Arad

Gerar

Sharuhen

Beersheba

Negeb

Brook of Egypt

Kadesh-barnea

Ashkelon

Gaza

Raphia

PHILISTINES

Me

Elath
(Ezion-geber)

Red Sea

Boundary of Saul's kingdom

The dual monarchy

Territory conquered by David

Locale of Solomon's major
building activity

Levite city

Major route

0   20   40 miles

0   20   40   60 km

36°

31°

30°

2

D

E

F

conscious attempt to compete with Solomon's Temple in Jerusalem.

During the ninth century the Omride dynasty was established in Israel, beginning with Omri (876–869) and concluding with Jehoram (849–842). Perhaps the central issue during this period resulted from the emergence of overt Baalism with the clarification that Yahwism could not coexist with Baalism, the worship surrounding the indigenous Canaanite god of fertility, Baal. This issue was addressed particularly during the reign of King Ahab (869–850) and under the auspices of the prophet Elijah (1 Kings 18—19). The worshiper of Yahweh could not worship both Yahweh and Baal.

Jehu (842–815) took up the struggle against Baalism. He successfully overthrew King Jehoram (ending the Omride dynasty) and instigated a violent anti-Baalistic purge in Israel. Not only did Jehoram of Israel die; so, too, did Queen Jezebel, many of the Baal worshipers, and King Ahaziah of Judah, who just happened to visit his kin in Israel during the year of his coronation!

This struggle against Baalism was a key factor in the emergence of Israel and Judah's prophetic movement during the second half of the eighth century. During an approximate fifty-year period, two primary prophets spoke in the south—Isaiah (742–701) and Micah (724–701)—while two prophets spoke in the north—Amos (about 750) and Hosea (about 745).

Amos emphasized especially social justice (Amos 5:24). He was particularly concerned that Israel recognize her covenantal responsibility before God (Amos 3:1–2). He was convinced that judgment was inevitable for Israel. (See especially the five visions recorded in Amos 7—9).

Hosea, the only northern prophet whose message is recorded in a book bearing his name, was Israel's eighth-century proponent of ḥesed ("covenant fidelity") theology. On the analogy of his relationship with his wife Gomer (Hos. 1—3), he exhorted Israel to be faithful to Yahweh. While assuring Israel of Yahweh's love, Hosea warned her of impending judgment resulting from her abuse of the covenant relationship.

The dangers the prophets saw materialized for Israel in the first quarter of the eighth century. King Hoshea (732–721) of Israel staged an anti-Assyrian revolt in anticipation of Egypt's coming to Israel's defense. Instead, the Assyrian troops under Shalmaneser V came to Israel and took the area around Samaria quickly. A siege of Samaria lasted for three years. During the siege Shalmaneser V died. Sargon II assumed the Assyrian throne and felled Samaria in 721. As per Assyrian policy, large numbers of the people of Samaria were deported to an unknown area, while peoples from another conquered area were imported into Samaria (2 Kings 17). This policy was intended to break down nationalism and to prevent political uprisings. In Israel's case it ultimately precipitated the emergence of the hybrid people despised by the "pure" Jew. Later history designated these people as "Samaritans." The fall of Samaria in 721 marked the end of Israel as a part of the United Monarchy.

The death of Solomon in 922 marked the beginning of Judah as the separated Southern Kingdom also. Solomon left the throne in Judah to his son, Rehoboam (922–915). Rehoboam ruled over a more stable country than Israel in that a consistent line of Davidic rulers governed the country from 922 until 587, with the one exception noted. During the ninth century crisis in Israel precipitated by Jehu's revolt in 842, King Ahaziah (842) of Judah was killed. Ahaziah's death resulted in the usurpation of Judah's throne by the Queen Mother, Athaliah (842–837). Her five-year rule constituted the only non-Davidic break in the succession. More importantly, during this period a systematic attempt was made to establish Baalism also in Judah. The Southern Kingdom, in part because it housed the Jerusalem Temple and was thus the focus of Yahwism, did not embrace Baalism in the fashion of the north. Thus, when Yahwistic priests placed the young King Jehoash (837–800) on the throne, progress made by Baalism in displacing Yahwism was rapidly reversed.

As indicated above, Judah shared in the flowering of the prophetic spirit in the eighth century. Isaiah of Jerusalem, who experienced his commission (see Isa. 6) to be Yahweh's prophet at the death of King Uzziah (742), was a prophetic spokesman during three political crises. During the rule of King Ahaz (735–715), he spoke in 735 at the time of the Syro-Israelite crisis (Isa. 7). During the rule of King Hezekiah (715–687), Isaiah was a spokesman during two political crises. In 711 he warned against an Egyptian-led revolt against Assyria (Isa. 20), and in 701 he was Yahweh's spokesman when Sennacherib of Assyria laid siege to Jerusalem (Isa. 36—37; see also 2 Kings 18—19). Isaiah is primarily remembered as the proponent of faith in Yahweh, letting Yahweh struggle against those who would oppress. This God of Isaiah was One who was best described by the concept of holiness (Isa. 6:3).

Micah of Moresheth (724–701) was the other eighth-century prophet in Judah. In many ways, Micah seemed to lack the original spirit of the other eighth century prophets. Micah 6:1–8, however, is an excellent description of a courtroom scene where Yahweh's people are brought to trial for their constant rejection and transgression of the covenant. The climax to that passage, verse 8, is perhaps the best definition of eighth century prophetic religion available to the modern interpreter.

Israel having fallen in the eighth century, Judah continued into the seventh and early sixth centuries. The seventh century was both dismal and exalted. In the lengthy rule of Manasseh (687–

642), Judah jettisoned much of the concern for exclusive Yahwism. Yahwistic prophets were persecuted; Baalism was encouraged; activities associated with the Assyrian astrological rites were incorporated; and the practice of human sacrifice was revived. This was, indeed, a dark period in Judah's history.

Very soon after Manasseh, however, King Josiah (640–609) reversed the decline Manasseh had set in motion. Under Josiah, and at least as early as 621, the Deuteronomic Reformation was instituted. This reform movement had a dual focus. On the one hand, Josiah sought to take advantage of the weakened conditions of both the Mesopotamian and Egyptian powers to unite anew the Northern and Southern Kingdoms. This political aspiration was coupled with a religious fervor for combating Baalism. Even the mandate that all sacrificial worship take place in the Jerusalem Temple was partially motivated by his desire to prevent the use of Baalistic "high places" and to keep all sacrificial activity where it could be carefully monitored to prevent Baalistic assimilation. This reform had long-range repercussions on the development of Yahwism and Judaism, but the primary impetus for the reform was removed with Josiah's death in 609 as he fought against Pharaoh Necho of Egypt at Megiddo (2 Kings 23:29).

Following Josiah's death, the nation no longer had the leadership to sustain an effective reformation. Jehoiakim (609–598) waged a revolt against the nation's Babylonian overlordship. Before Nebuchadrezzar of Babylon arrived, however, Jehoiakim died, bringing his son Jehoiachin (598–597) to the throne. Thus, Jehoiachin was taken into Exile in 597 when Nebuchadrezzar conquered Jerusalem. In his place Nebuchadrezzar placed Zedekiah (597–587). His revolt against Babylon in 588 led to the ultimate fall of Jerusalem, including the razing of the Jerusalem Temple by Nebuchadrezzar in 587. Thus the kingdom of Judah was ended, and the Babylonian Exile (597/587–539/538) initiated.

The Babylonian Exile (Ezekiel, Isaiah 40—55)
The Babylonian Exile was initiated in 597 by the initial deportation of Jerusalemites to Babylon, with additional deportations in 587 and 582 (Jer. 52:15). This was a significant period in the life of the people, although relatively few persons were involved (4,600 according to Jer. 52:30). Basically, life was not completely unacceptable, because the people enjoyed a degree of social and economic freedom. Nonetheless, they were secluded from Jerusalem and the Temple and hardly desired to sing Yahweh's song in this strange land (Ps. 137).

The Babylonian Exile, in spite of its relative brevity, was the benchmark in the religious development of the people. Most importantly, during and just following the Exile the Torah was drawn essentially into its present form. This provided the basis for the emergence of what authentically is Judaism and the Jews, "the people of the book." In addition, other literary products were formulated, including most of the written record associated with the preexilic prophets, the final editorial work on the Deuteronomic History (Joshua, Judges, Samuel, and Kings), and the prophetic contributions of Ezekiel and the anonymous figure known as Deutero- or Second Isaiah.

Ezekiel was strongly nationalistic in his concerns, but nonetheless he made significant contributions. He increased the awareness that Yahweh has absolute mobility, that He was not geographically confined to Jerusalem (Ezek. 1—3). While his message is often quite cryptic, he encouraged hope in the future (Ezek. 33—39); and he suggested a type of "faith's" blueprint for a restored Jerusalem (Ezek. 40—48).

The prophecies of Isaiah 40—55 spoke to conditions near the end of the Babylonian Exile (about 540), preparing the people for a second Exodus (Isaiah 40) and impressing upon them their role as the servant people of Yahweh (Isa. 42:1–4; 49:1–6; 50:4–9; 52:13—53:12). These chapters in Isaiah provide the first undisputed literary evidence for monotheism in the Bible (Isa. 44:6; 45:5), a concept inevitably coupled with Yahweh's universality (Isa. 42:6; 45:22).

During the Exile an institution arose which was to have crucial influence on the future of Judaism, the synagogue. It was impossible to gather at the Temple in Jerusalem, so the synagogue became a social, educational, and religious center for the community. Importantly, the synagogue was never a place where sacrificial worship could be offered. Nonetheless, once Rome destroyed the rebuilt Temple in Jerusalem in A.D. 70, the synagogues preserved Judaism wherever Jews were settled.

THE POSTEXILIC PERIOD
1. The Persian Period (Ezra 1; 5—6;9—10; Nehemiah 1—6; 8—9; 13; Haggai; Zechariah; Obadiah; Malachi; Job; Ecclesiastes; Proverbs; Ruth; Jonah; Esther) Judah's postexilic era began in late 539 with the entrance of the troops of Cyrus of Persia into Babylon. In early 538 Cyrus issued a decree (Ezra 1:2–4; 6:3–5) permitting the exiles to return home. Many did return under the leadership of Zerubbabel, a descendant of King Jehoiachin. Unfortunately, Zerubbabel mysteriously disappeared, probably because the Persians recognized the inherent dangers associated with some of the Jews thinking Zerubbabel to be the anticipated messiah (Hag. 2:20–23).

Immediately following their return to Jerusalem, work was begun on rebuilding the Temple. For various reasons, they accomplished little. Eventually, primarily under the influence of the prophets Haggai and Zechariah, the Temple was rebuilt from 520 to 515; and the Temple worship reinstituted.

The city remained defenseless until Nehemiah

I

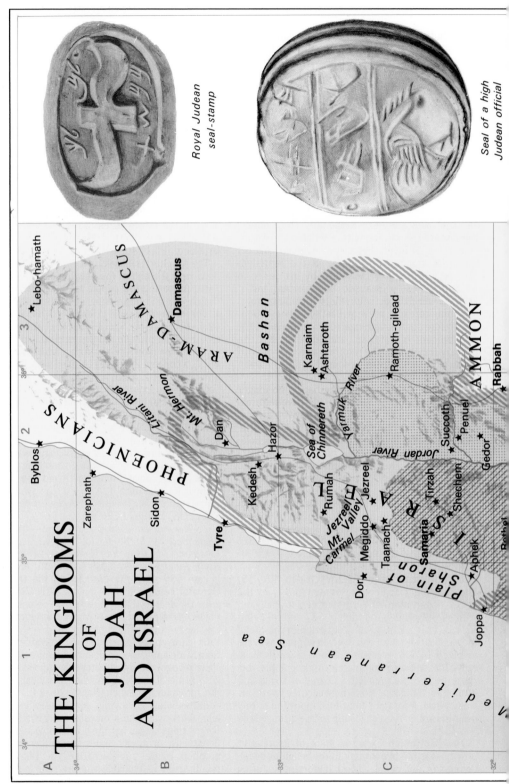

Royal Judean seal-stamp

Seal of a high Judean official

THE KINGDOMS OF JUDAH AND ISRAEL

Mediterranean Sea

PHOENICIANS

ARAM-DAMASCUS

Bashan

AMMON

ISRAEL

Plain of Sharon

Jezreel Valley

Mt. Carmel

Lebo-hamath

Byblos

Zarephath

Sidon

Tyre

Kedesh

Dan

Hazor

Damascus

Mt. Hermon

Litani River

Sea of Chinnereth

Karnaim

Ashtaroth

Yarmuk River

Ramoth-gilead

Jordan River

Succoth

Penuel

Rabbah

Gedor

Rumah

Jezreel

Jezreel

Samaria

Tirzah

Shechem

Megiddo

Taanach

Dor

Aphek

Bethel

Joppa

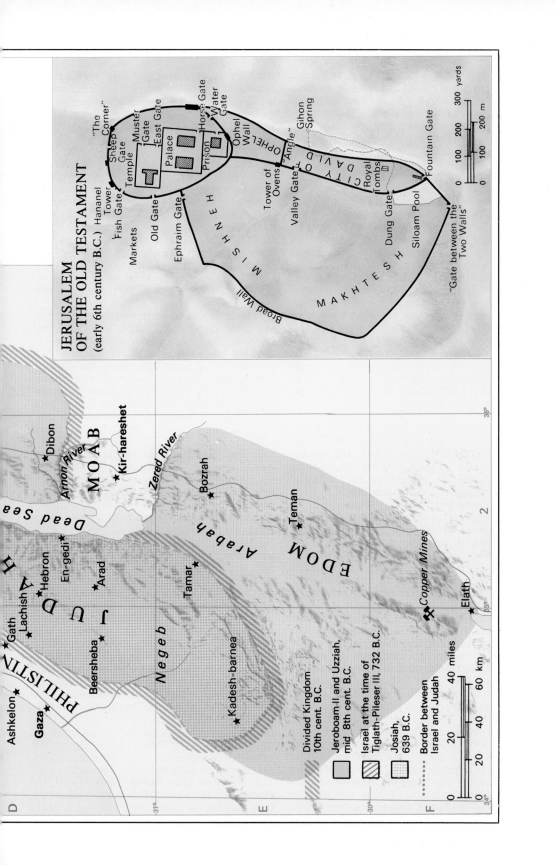

JERUSALEM OF THE OLD TESTAMENT
(early 6th century B.C.)

"The Corner"

Hananel Tower

Muster Gate

Sheep Gate

East Gate

Fish Gate

Temple

Palace

Markets

Old Gate

Prison

Ophel Wall

OPHEL

Horse Gate

Water Gate

Ephraim Gate

MISHNEH

Tower of Ovens

Valley Gate

"Angle"

Gihon Spring

CITY OF DAVID

Royal Tombs

Broad Wall

MAKHTESH

Dung Gate

Siloam Pool

Fountain Gate

"Gate between the Two Walls"

| 0 | 100 | 200 | 300 yards |

| 0 | 100 | 200 m |

PHILISTINE

Ashkelon

Gaza

Gath

Lachish

Hebron

En-gedi

Arad

Dead Sea

Arnon River

Dibon

MOAB

Kir-hareshet

Zered River

JUDAH

Beersheba

Negeb

Tamar

Bozrah

Teman

Kadesh-barnea

Arabah

EDOM

Copper Mines

Elath

Divided Kingdom, 10th cent. B.C.

Jeroboam II and Uzziah, mid 8th cent. B.C.

Israel at the time of Tiglath-Pileser III, 732 B.C.

Josiah, 639 B.C.

Border between Israel and Judah

| 0 | 20 | 40 miles |

| 0 | 20 | 40 | 60 km |

D

E

F

31°

30°

34°

35°

38°

2

(appointed twice in 445 and 432 to be Persia's governor in Judea) rebuilt and repaired the walls around the city. About the same time Ezra, (our first indication of the scribal office, lawyer of the Torah), came to Jerusalem and impressed upon the people the importance of placing Torah at the center of community life, giving birth to the modern phenomenon of Judaism.

In the interval between the completion of the Temple (515) and Nehemiah's first visit (445), several prophets spoke, each giving a sense of the period. Obadiah's brief message was a hymn of hate against the Edomites, who had assumed Judah's lands and homes when the people were taken into Exile. Joel emphasized the day of Yahweh as a day of Judah's preservation coupled with the destruction of Edom and Egypt. Malachi addressed the need for reformation in worship, condemned the activities of the priesthood, denounced the intermarriage of Jews with non-Jews, and criticized the popular piety so prevalent in his day.

One of the most important literary movements of the postexilic period was that associated with Wisdom Literature, represented in the Bible by the Books of Job, Ecclesiastes, and Proverbs, plus some of the Psalms (1; 32; 34; 37; 49; 91; 112; 119; 128). This literature borrowed heavily from Israel's neighbors, as Proverbs 22:17—23:11, directed itself predominately to the youth (note the allegory on old age in Eccl. 12:1—8), and basically sought to enhance one's ability to live a healthy and productive life, recognizing that the fear of God served as the basis for such a life.

Job recounts the difficulties experienced by Job through loss of loved ones, deprivation of material goods, and an assault upon his physical health. Throughout his ordeal he remained firm in his conviction of God's ultimate sovereignty, although his restiveness with his inability to understand (theodicy, or understanding the ways of God) certainly belies his characterization as patient. Regardless, the Book of Job does not give the reason for the suffering of innocent individuals; rather, it affirms that, if one will be submissive to God even in the midst of suffering, then one may experience a meaningful relationship with God even in the direst of circumstances. In this sense, the book was a direct attack on the idea that suffering automatically results from wrongdoing and reward from right action, as Job's friends argued.

Ecclesiastes, or Koheleth, is a very different type of book. Essentially, the author portrayed a life which can only be characterized as meaningless (Eccl. 1:2, "vanity"). The concern is whether any avenue might be successfully pursued to give meaning to life. The routes of pleasure (Eccl. 2:1–11), wisdom (Eccl. 2:12–16), wealth (most of Eccl. 4:13—6:12), and religious vows (Eccl. 5:1–6) were tried, but all to no avail. The nearest suggestion of a meaningful existence is in Ecclesi-

astes 3:1–8 which suggests that, even though persons do not understand, they might find meaning by accepting the givenness of life. Perhaps through this acceptance, they might find themselves attuned to God's purpose and hence discover meaning.

The Book of Proverbs defies any systematic analysis. It deals with a multitude of subjects and in diverse manner, usually through the short, pithy saying but at least in chapter 31 through an extended poem. The subject orientation ranges from Yahweh as the Giver of life (Prov. 1:1–7) to the importance of controlling one's tongue (Prov. 16:28). It emphasizes watchfulness in business (Prov. 6:1–5) and in friendship (Prov. 18:24). It contrasts being industrious (6:6–11) and lazy (24:30–34). While the book defies outline or categories, it is wisdom in the unique Hebraic sense.

As Judaism developed, inevitably, debate rose as regards Yahweh's availability to the non-Jew. Literarily, the Books of Ruth and Jonah encouraged the Jews to embrace all humankind within the umbrella of their faith, while the Book of Esther, which supports the highly nationalistic festival of Purim, encouraged a narrow patriotism which affirmed Yahweh to be God for the Jews protecting them from foreign enemies. This conflict was continued into New Testament times (Acts 15).

2. The Hellenistic Period Philip of Macedon was murdered in 336. This brought Alexander, his nineteen-year-old son who had earlier been tutored by Aristotle and who would later be designated Alexander the Great, to Philip's throne. After two years spent in consolidating his power, Alexander crossed the Hellespont, beginning his bid for a unified Hellenistic Empire. Alexander was not quite 33 when he died unexpectedly in 323. By the time of his death, however, an indelible Hellenistic imprint had been left on the massive area he had conquered; assuredly Canaan sensed strongly this influence.

Partly as a result of this Hellenization process, approximately 300, the chronicler's history was formulated. The chronicler's work is composed of Chronicles, Ezra, and Nehemiah. Unlike Samuel and Kings, Chronicles emphasizes the accomplishments of Judah and its Davidic kings. It ignored many events that did not suit its purpose, such as the David-Bethsheba story. The chronicler encouraged purity within the Jewish worship practices in the face of Alexander's Hellenization. Closely related, the chronicler focused upon the conflict between the supremacy of the Jerusalem cultus over that of the Samaritans. See *Chronicles.*

3. The Maccabean Period (Daniel 1—7; 12; Psalter) The apocalyptic era is usually understood to encompass the period from 200 B.C. to A.D. 200. During this period, the Jews were religiously and politically persecuted. To address this circumstance a highly symbolic, cryptic literature developed which promised the faithful community the hope of Yahweh's imminent intervention.

The emergence of the apocalyptic era coincided with events resultant to Alexander the Great's fourth-century conquest of Canaan. When Alexander died in 323, his massive kingdom was thrown into turmoil. Eventually, the control of Canaan was contested between two of his successor rulers, Seleucus and Ptolemy. Resultant to battles waged between 200 and 198, the Seleucid ruler, Antiochus III (223-187), gained control of Canaan. The significance of this transition in power became clear only with his successor, Antiochus IV (187−175), who attempted a systematic destruction of Judaism. His attempts to eradicate the faith precipitated an uprising led by a priest, Mattathias, and his four sons. One of these sons, Judas Maccabeus, was the military architect of the revolt and the individual whose name the revolt bears, the Maccabean Revolt.

The revolt was more successful than the Jews could have anticipated. On the twenty-fifth of Chislev, 165, Judas Maccabeus captured the Jerusalem Temple, purified it, and reinstituted the worship of Yahweh (the basis for the festival of Hanukkah). The Book of Daniel, clearly an apocalyptic book, focused on this era. See *Daniel.* By 142 the Jews were exempted from all Seleucid taxation, and in 129 all Seleucid soldiers were removed from the country. Once again, the Jews were totally free within the borders of their own country.

The Psalter was finally completed in this era, though many of the 150 poems are preexilic (as Psalm 29). Some are exilic (as Psalm 137); some, post-exilic (as Psalm 119). See *Psalms.* The Psalter, as the hymnbook of the second Temple, is particularly important for portraying the people as a worshiping community through her diverse historical eras and for enlightening the multitude of problems and situations she encountered.

4. The Roman Period True freedom had been achieved through the Maccabean Revolt, but unfortunately the Hasmonean rule was constantly beset by internal dissension. In addition, intermarriage of Jews with non-Jews in surrounding countries precipitated conflict. This unrest came to a climax in 63 when the constant turmoil, which now involved the governor of Idumaea and the Nabataean king, brought Pompey, the Roman general to Judea. Jerusalem fell; and the country, henceforth designated as the Roman province of Palestine, continued under Roman control until the fourth Christian century.

Jewish history beyond the Roman conquest would clearly fall within the postexilic rubric, and a rich history it is as one traces Jewish development. Nonetheless, the beginning of the Roman era is the outside limit for canonical Old Testament history and carries the thrust of this essay to its logical conclusion. See *Alexander the Great; Apocalyptic Literature; Ark of the Covenant; Assyria; Baal/Baalism; Babylon; Canaan; Covenant; Egypt; Exodus; Israel; Judah; Judge; Maccabees; Monotheism; Moses; Philistines; Prophet (see also individual prophets); Psalms; Sinai; Synagogue; Temple; Torah; Wisdom Literature; Wise Man; Yahweh.*   *Frank E. Eakin, Jr.*

ISRAEL, SPIRITUAL The church, one gathering of all believers under the lordship of Christ as the continuation of God's work with Old Testament Israel. This is in contrast to most references in the Old Testament to religious or secular assemblies or to those in the New Testament that designate a local congregation of Christians, but never in any way mean a building.

Israel is the name given to the descendants of Jacob and to the grouping of people in the twelve tribes coming from Jacob's sons. In Old Testament times they constituted the people of God, for He chose them as His own for faithful service. Scripture is clear that Christ came to earth to establish His heavenly kingdom as a substitute for the Jewish kingdom that had failed (Matt. 21:43). Throughout the New Testament the church is spoken of as the kingdom of God or the kingdom of heaven. The kingdom is presented as an actual entity ruled by God, a spiritual acceptance of the rule of God, or Jesus Christ, the One fully in submission to God and a personification of the kingdom. Paul distinguished between genealogical Israelites and the true "Israel of God," God's people, those who believe the good news and receive the peace and mercy of God (Gal. 6:16). Spiritual Israel, the Christian church, has supplanted the Jews as the elect people of God (Rom. 9:6−13; 1 Pet. 2:9). Spiritual Israel includes Jews who believe in Jesus. Christians are divided as to the fate of Israel. This centers on interpretation of passages such as Romans 11:25−36; 2 Corinthians 3:16.

Such interpretations seek to understand the mystery of divine election which began with Israel and climaxed in the life, death, and resurrection of Jesus. The history of divine election includes Israel's disobedience by depending on human achievement rather than divine mercy which led to their rejection of Jesus, and will climax in the salvation of "all Israel" (Rom. 11:26). The point at which interpretations differ is the meaning of all Israel. Is spiritual Israel the church, Israel of all generations from Abraham to the end of time, Jews at the end of the ages, or the remnant of believing Jews included in the church or brought into the church in the last days? Many interpretations have been made. What is certain is that God in His grace of election opens the door to salvation by faith to all people regardless of the race or tradition out of which they come.

J. William Thompson and Trent C. Butler

I

ISRAELITE (Ĭs′ rā ĕl īte) Citizen of nation of Israel.

ISSACHAR (Ĭs′ så chär) Personal name meaning "man for hire" or "hireling." Ninth son of Jacob, the fifth borne by Leah (Gen. 30:18). He became the progenitor of the tribe of Issachar. Almost nothing is known about his personal history. The tribe of Issachar occupied territory in the northern part of Palestine, just southwest of the Sea of Galilee (Josh. 19:17–23). The tribe was not prominent in Israel's history. Tola, one of the so-called "minor" judges, was of the tribe of Issachar (Judg. 10:1–2). So was Baasha, the successor of Nadab as king of Israel (1 Kings 15:27). The city of Jezreel, which was an Israelite royal residence, was located in the territory of Issachar. See *Tribes of Israel; Chronology of Biblical Period.*

ISSARON Transliteration of Hebrew word meaning, "a tenth." A dry measure equal to one tenth of an ephah (Ex. 29:40; Lev. 14:10, 21; 23:13;17; 24:5; Num. 15:4) or about two quarts. KJV translates a tenth deal. See *Weights and Measures; Ephah.*

ISSHIAH (Ĭs shī′ ah) Personal name meaning, "let Yahweh forget." In Hebrew the name appears in a longer form in 1 Chronicles 12:6. *1.* Leader in the tribe of Issachar (1 Chron. 7:3). *2.* Soldier from Saul's tribe of Benjamin who joined David at Ziklag while he hid from Saul (1 Chron. 12:6). *3.* Member of the Kohath branch of Levites (1 Chron. 23:20; 24:24–25). *4.* Descendant of Moses among the Levites (1 Chron. 24:21; compare 23:13–17).

ISSHIJAH (Ĭs shī′ jah) Personal name meaning, "let Yahweh forget." Same Hebrew name as Isshiah. Israelite who had married a foreign wife, threatening Israel's total allegiance to Yahweh in time of Ezra (Ezra 10:31).

ISSUE KJV term referring to offspring (Gen. 48:6; Isa. 22:24; Matt. 22:25; compare 2 Kings 20:18; Isa. 39:7) or to a bodily discharge. The KJV applied issue to male pathological discharges such as that associated with gonorrhea (Lev. 15:2–15), to normal menstruation (Lev. 15:19–24), and to female pathological discharges (Lev. 15:25–30; Matt. 9:20). Normal discharges resulted in ritual uncleanness for one day which was removed by simple washing. Pathological discharges resulted in uncleaness until seven days after the return to full health and required an atoning sacrifice. In Ezekiel 23:20 the seminal emission of stallions is one element in a graphic depiction of Judah's idolatry.

ISSUE OF BLOOD KJV phrase meaning hemorrhage (Matt. 9:20).

ISUAH (Ĭs′ ū ah) KJV spelling of Ishvah (1 Chron. 7:30). See *Ishvah.*

ISUI (Ĭs′ ū ī) KJV spelling for Ishvi in Genesis 46:17. See *Ishvi.*

ITALIAN COHORT Name of the archery unit of the Roman army to which the Gentile centurion Cornelius belonged (Acts. 10:1). KJV calls it the Italian band. Probably 1,000 men who had been mustered in Italy composed the unit. Little is known about this Italian Cohort. Extrabiblical evidence exists for the presence in Caesarea of a unit called *Cohors II Italica* after A.D. 69. That date, however, is too late for the events recorded in Acts 10. Perhaps the *Cohors II* actually was in Caesarea prior to A.D. 69. Or perhaps the Italian Cohort to which Cornelius belonged was a different unit. See *Cornelius.*

ITALY (Ĭt′ à lў) The boot-shaped peninsula between Greece and Spain which extends from the Alps on the north to the Mediterranean Sea on the south. Its long narrow shape contributed to its ethnic diversity, with so many Greeks occupying the southern part that it was called "Great

Temple of Serapis at the ancient port of Puteoli, where Paul disembarked on his journey to Rome.

Greece" by the citizens of Rome. Through the Punic Wars with Carthage (264–146 B.C.), the city of Rome extended its control over the whole country and eventually conquered the entire Mediterranean. The Roman Empire was created when Octavian became Augustus Caesar (27 B.C.) after the murder of Julius Caesar and of the demise of the Republic (44 B.C.). Italy is named in the New Testament in Acts 18:2; 27:1,6 and Hebrews 13:24. *John McRay*

ITCH A skin disorder characterized by an irritating sensation in the upper surface of the skin. The itch included among the curses on those unfaithful to the covenant (Deut. 28:27) was possibly eczema or prurigo. NIV, NRSV use itch to distinguish a minor skin disorder from leprosy (Lev. 13:30–37). The KJV termed this disorder "scall," a malady characterized by dry scales or scabs. Other translations rendered this disorder "infection" (NAS), "scale" (REB), or "sore" (TEV). It has been suggested that *alopecia areata,* which produces patches of baldness (compare Lev. 13:40–41), or ringworms are the cause of this disorder. Animals suffering from a skin disorder were unsuitable for sacrifice (Lev. 22:22). English translators divide over the nature of this disorder: eczema (NAS), itch (NRSV), scab (REB), scurvy (KJV), skin eruption (TEV). See *Diseases, Treatment of.*

ITHAI (Ī′ thā ī) Personal name perhaps meaning, "with me." A member of David's elite "Thirty" military heroes (2 Sam. 23:29).

ITHAMAR (Ĭth′ à mär) Personal name of uncertain meaning, perhaps, "island of palms," or "where is Tamar," or shortened form of "father of Tamar (palms)." Fourth son of Aaron the priest (Ex. 6:23). After the death of Nadab and Abihu, Ithamar and his surviving brother Eleazar rose to prominence. During the wilderness years Ithamar apparently was in charge of all the Levites (Ex. 38:21). Moses became angry when Ithamar and his brother did not eat part of an offering as commanded (Lev. 10:16). In addition, the house of Eli evidently was descended from Ithamar. See *Aaron; Priests and Levites.*

ITHIEL (Ĭth′ ĭ ĕl) Personal name meaning, "with me is God." *1.* Member of tribe of Benjamin in the time of Nehemiah after the return from Exile (Neh. 11:7). *2.* Person to whom Proverbs 30 is addressed, following standard Hebrew text (KJV, NAS, NIV). Many Bible students put spaces between different letters of the Hebrew text assuming an early copying change. Then the text would read, "God is not with me, God is not with me, and I am helpless" (TEV), or "I am weary, O God, I am weary, O God. How can I prevail?" (NRSV; compare REB).

ITHLAH (Ĭth′ lah) Place name perhaps meaning, "he hangs." Town in tribal territory of Dan (Josh. 19:42). Its location is not known, but some students of Bible lands geography follow some Greek manuscripts identifying Ithlah with Shithlah or Shilta, about four miles northwest of Beth-horon.

ITHMAH (Ĭth′ mah) Personal name meaning, "orphan." Moabite soldier in David's army (1 Chron. 11:46).

ITHNAN (Ĭth′ năn) Place name meaning, "flowing constantly." Town on southern border of tribal territory of Judah (Josh. 15:23). Its location is not known unless some Bible lands geographers are correct in combining Hazor-ithnan into one town, which may have been located at modern el-

Jebariyeh on the wadi Umm Ethnan.

ITHRA (Ĭth′ rà) Personal name meaning, "remnant" or "abundance." He was the father of Amasa, and the general Absalom appointed to replace David's general Joab when he revolted against his father (2 Sam. 17:25). Ithra's wife, Abigail, was Joab's aunt. Ithra is called Jether in some Greek and Old Latin manuscripts as well as in 1 Kings 2:5,32; 1 Chronicles 2:17. Some modern translations thus read Jether in 2 Samuel 17:25 (TEV, NIV). One early Greek manuscript and 1 Chronicles 2:17 identify Ithra as an Ishmaelite rather than an Israelite, as the standard Hebrew text of 2 Samuel 17:25 reads. Many Bible students think Ishmaelite was the original reading in 2 Samuel, since it would be unusual and unnecessary to identify an Israelite (REB, TEV, NRSV).

ITHRAN (Ĭth′ răn) Personal name meaning, "remnant" or "abundance." A Horite leader who lived in Edom (Gen. 36:26). *2.* Leader in the tribe of Asher (1 Chron. 7:37). He may be the same as the similarly spelled Jether (1 Chron. 7:38).

ITHREAM (Ĭth′ rḕ ăm) Personal name meaning, "remnant of the people." David's son born in Hebron to Eglah, David's wife (2 Sam. 3:5).

ITHRITE (Ĭth′ rīte) Clan name meaning, "of Jether." Descendants of Jether or Jethro (Ex. 4:18) or a clan whose home was Kiriath-jearim (1 Chron. 2:53). The latter may have been Hivites (compare Josh. 9:7,17). Two of David's valiant "Thirty" warriors were Ithrites (2 Sam. 23:38).

ITTAH-KAZIN (Ĭt′ tàh-kā′ zĭn) KJV spelling of Eth-kazin. See *Eth-kazin.*

ITTAI (Ĭt′ tā ī) Personal name meaning "with God." *1.* Gittite (from Gath) soldier who demonstrated loyalty to David by accompanying the latter in flight from Jerusalem after the outbreak of a rebellion led by David's son Absalom (2 Sam. 15:19–22). Gittite means a resident of Gath. Thus, this man was a Philistine who had cast his lot with the Israelite David. Later, Ittai shared command of David's army with Joab and Abishai (2 Sam. 18:2). See *David. 2.* One of the "Thirty" of David's army (2 Sam. 23:29) and son of Ribai of Gibeah from the tribe of Benjamin. The Hebrew text of 1 Chronicles 11:31 spells the name Ithai.

ITURAEA (Ĭt ū rāē′ à) Place name meaning, "related to Jetur." Region over which Herod Philip was governor when John the Baptist began his public ministry (Luke 3:1). It was located northeast of Galilee between the Lebanon and Anti-Lebanon mountains, though its precise boundaries are almost impossible to determine. Racially, the Ituraeans were of Ishmaelite stock; their origin probably should be traced to Jetur the son of Ishmael (Gen. 25:15). The earliest extant reference to the Ituraeans as a people dates from the second century B.C. Pompey conquered the territory for Rome about 50 B.C. Ituraea was eventually absorbed into other political districts, losing its distinct identity by the end of the first century A.D. See *Herods; Geography.*

ITUREA (Ĭt ū rē′ à) Alternate spelling for Ituraea. See *Ituraea.*

IVAH (Ī′ vah) KJV spelling for Ivvah. See *Ivvah.*

IVORY is the English translation of the Hebrew word that means "tooth." Ivory was used for decoration on thrones, beds, houses, and the decks of ships (1 Kings 10:18; 22:39; 2 Chron. 9:17; Ps. 45:8; Ezek. 27:6,15; Amos 3:15; 6:4). Archaeologists in Palestine have unearthed numerous articles made of ivory: boxes, gaming boards, figurines, spoons, and combs.

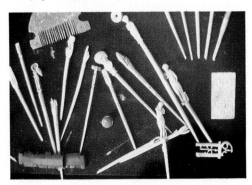

Ivory toilet articles and hair ornaments.

First Kings 10:22 is cited by scholars as a possible explanation for the source of ivory in Palestine. Apparently, Solomon's ships returned with ivory as a part of their cargo. Sources outside the Old Testament indicate that elephants existed in northern Syria during the second millennium B.C. Elephants were hunted into extinction in northern Syria by 800 B.C.

The prophet Amos mentioned ivory as a token of luxury and wealth (Amos 3:15; 6:4). Lists of booty taken by victorious armies included ivory objects. Hezekiah was credited with giving Sennacherib tribute in 701 B.C. Sennacherib's account of the tribute included couches and chairs inlaid with ivory. Ivories have been found at Samaria that are thought to be from the time of Ahab, who reigned in Israel from about 869 to 850 B.C. *James Newell*

IVVAH (Ĭv′ vah) Alternate spelling for Avva. See *Avva.*

IYE-ABARIM (Ī yē-ăb′ à rĭm) Place name meaning, "ruins of the crossings." Station in the wilderness wanderings (Num. 21:11) near Moab. It is apparently near mount Abarim. See *Abarim.* It is apparently abbreviated as Iim in Numbers 33:45 (KJV). Some Bible geographers locate it at khirbet Aii southwest of Kerak or modern Mahay, but this is far from certain.

IYIM (Ī′ yĭm) Modern translations spelling of Iim (Num. 33:45), a shortened form of Iye-abarim. See *Iye-abarim.*

IZEHAR (Ī′ zė här) KJV spelling of Izhar in Numbers 3:19. See *Izhar.*

IZEHARITE (Ĭz′ ė här īte) KJV spelling of Izharite. See *Izharite.*

IZHAR (Ĭz′ här) Personal name meaning, "olive oil" or "he sparkles." *1.* Son of Kohath and grandson of Levi, thus original ancestor of a priestly clan (Ex. 6:18). He was father of Korah (Num. 16:1). See *Korah.* Compare 1 Chronicles 23:18. *2.* The written Hebrew text of 1 Chronicles 4:7 names Izhar as a member of the tribe of Judah but uses a different letter for "h," sometimes rendered "ch" in English. The resulting name is of uncertain meaning. An early Hebrew scribal note followed by the early Syriac and Latin translations makes the name Jezoar (KJV, REB) or Zohar (NIV).

IZHARITE (Ĭz′ här īte) Clan of Levites descended from Izhar. See *Izhar.*

IZLIAH (Ĭz lī′ ah) Personal name meaning, "long-lived" or "Yahweh delivers." Leader in tribe of Benjamin living in Jerusalem after the return from Exile (1 Chron. 8:18).

IZRAHIAH (Ĭz rà hī ah) Personal name meaning, "Yahweh shines forth." Member of tribe of Issachar (1 Chron. 7:3). The same Hebrew name appears in Nehemiah 12:42 but is usually transliterated into English as Jezrahiah. See *Jezrahiah.*

IZRAHITE (Ĭz′ rà hīte) Clan name in 1 Chronicles 27:8 for which the text tradition gives several variants: Harorite (1 Chron. 11:27 KJV); Harodite (2 Sam. 23:25 KJV). Other Hebrew manuscripts read, "Zerahites." See *Harodite.*

IZRI (Ĭz′ rī) Clan leader of fourth course of Temple musicians (1 Chron. 25:11). He is probably the same as Zeri (25:3), the name change occurring in copying the text.

IZZIAH (Ĭz zī′ ah) Personal name meaning, "Yah sprinkled." Priest who repented of marrying a foreign woman and thus tempting Israel with foreign gods in time of Ezra (Ezra 10:25).

I

Beautiful inlaid tile on the wall of the Moslem Dome
of the Rock in Jerusalem.

J The sign for one of the principle sources critical scholars propose for the Pentateuch. The name derives from the personal name for God, Yahweh (German Jahveh), which characterizes this source. The source is thought to have originated in Judah earlier than the E source (about 900 B.C.). Recent research has raised radical questions about this source and theory even among critical scholars. See *Pentateuch; Bible, History of Interpretation.*

JAAKAN (Jā′ á·kăn) Personal name meaning, "to be fast." Descendant of Esau and thus tribal ancestor of Edomites (1 Chron. 1:42; compare Gen. 36:27; Num. 33:31−32; Deut. 10:6). Different translations transliterate the name differently— Akan, Jakan. The Hebrew text of Genesis 36:27 omits the first letter of the name. See *Bene-ja-jaakan.*

JAAKANITES (Jā′ á·kà·nītes) NIV translation of Bene-jaakan in Deuteronomy 10:6. See *Bene-jaakan.*

JAAKOBAH (Jā′ á·kō′ bah) Personal name meaning, "may He protect." Leader in tribe of Simeon (1 Chron. 4:36).

JAALA (Jā′ á·là) Personal name meaning, "female ibex." A member of Solomon's staff whose descendants joined Zerubbabel in returning from Babylonian Exile about 537 B.C. (Ezra 2:56; Neh. 7:58, which has an Aramaic ending rather than the Hebrew ending of the Ezra passage).

JAALAH (Jā′ á·lah) Alternate Hebrew spelling of Jaala. See *Jaala.*

JAALAM (Jā′ á·lăm) KJV, REB spelling of Jalam. See *Jalam.*

JAANAI (Jā′ á·nâi) KJV, REB spelling of Janai. See *Janai.*

JAAR (Jā′ är) Place name meaning, "forest." Modern versions' transliteration of Hebrew in Psalm 132:6 (TEV reads, Jearim, a plural form.) KJV translates, "wood." Jaar is probably a poetic abbreviation for Kiriath-jearim. See *Kiriath-jearim.* The Psalm celebrates David's returning the ark to Jerusalem from its Philistine captivity (compare 1 Sam. 7:2; 2 Sam. 6; 1 Chron. 13:5).

JAARE-OREGIM (Jā′ á·rĕ·ôr′ ĕ ḡĭm) Personal name meaning, "forests of the weavers." Father of Elhanan from Bethlehem, who killed Goliath. See *Elhanan.* Many modern Bible scholars follow early Greek translations and 1 Chronicles 20:5 and omit Oregim (REB). Others interpret Oregim as a common noun, identifying Jair as a weaver (NIV translation note). This is partly based on 2 Samuel 23:24, where an Elhanan of Bethlehem is identi-fied as the son of Dodo. Jaare may be an abbreviated form of Kiriath-jearim. See *Kiriath-jearim.*

JAARESHIAH (Jā′ á·rè·shī′ ah) Personal name meaning, "Yahweh plants." Member of tribe of Benjamin (1 Chron. 8:27).

JAASAU (Jā′ á·saū) KJV, REB spelling of Jaasu. See *Jaasu.*

JAASIEL (Jā·ăs′ ĭ·ĕl) Personal name meaning, "God makes." *1.* Leader of tribe of Benjamin under David, apparently in charge of census in his tribe when David numbered the people (1 Chron. 27:21). His father Abner may be Saul's general who became David's general. *2.* Army hero under David whose home town was Zobah (1 Chron. 11:47). See *Mesobaite.* KJV transliterates his name Jasiel.

JAASU (Jā′ á·sū) Personal name meaning, "His product," a variant spelling of Jaasiel, which the earliest Hebrew copyists noted should be pronounced differently from the printed Hebrew text. An Israelite who agreed under Ezra's leadership to divorce his foreign wife to ensure the religious purity of the nation (Ezra 11:37). See *Jaasau.*

JAAZANIAH (Jā·ăz·á·nī′ ah) Personal name meaning, "Yahweh hears." *1.* Member of party led by Ishmael who opposed Gedaliah after the Babylonians made him governor over Judah following their destruction of Jerusalem in 587 B.C. Jaazaniah may also have been in Ishmael's party that assassinated Gedaliah (2 Kings 25:23−25). His name has a slightly different spelling in Jeremiah 40:8. See *Jezaniah.* A signet seal found at tell en-Nasbeh dates from the same period and contains a depiction of a fighting cock. The seal inscription shows the seal belonged to Jaazaniah, the servant of the king. This is probably the same person and indicates he was on the king's staff, probably as an army captain. *2.* One of the elders of Israel Ezekiel found worshiping idols in the Temple (Ezek. 8:11). His father Shaphan may have been the counselor of Josiah (2 Kings 22). If so, the son did not imitate the faithful father. *3.* A government official whom Ezekiel accused with his associates of giving wicked advice. His name in Hebrew is an abbreviated form of Jaazaniah. *4.* The same abbreviated Hebrew name belonged to a Rechabite whom Jeremiah used as an example of faithful obedience to God (Jer. 35:3). See *Rechabite.*

JAAZER (Jā′ á·zēr) KJV spelling of Jazer (Num. 21:32; 32:35). See *Jazer.*

JAAZIAH (Jā·á·zī′ ah) A Levitical priest in the time of David (1 Chron. 24:26). His name means, "Yahweh nourishes."

JAAZIEL (Jā·ă′ zĭ·ĕl) Variant form of Jaaziah, meaning, "God nourishes." Levite and Temple musician (1 Chron. 15:18), apparently appearing in a variant Hebrew spelling in 15:20 as one who played the psalter (1 Chron. 15:20) or harp (NRSV, NAS, TEV) or lute (REB), or lyre (NIV). See *Aziel.*

JABAL (Jā′ băl) Personal name meaning, "stream." Son of Lamech by Adah (Gen. 4:20). A descendant of Cain, he was the first nomad, the progenitor of tent dwellers and herdsmen.

JABBOK (Jăb′ bŏk) Place name meaning, "flowing." River near which Jacob wrestled through the night with God (Gen. 32:22). Its modern name is Nahr ez-Zerqa. It is a tributary of the Jordan, joining the larger river from the east about fifteen miles north of the Dead Sea. In biblical times various sections of its approximately 50-mile course served as the western boundary of Ammon, the boundary between the kingdoms of Sihon and Og, and a division in the territory of Gilead. The existence of numerous tells points to a dense population in the Jabbok Valley in ancient times. *See Jacob.*

JABESH (Jā′ bĕsh) Place name meaning, "dry." A shortened form of Jabesh-gilead (1 Sam. 11; 1 Sam. 31; 2 Kings 15:10,13). See *Jabesh-gilead.*

Panoramic view of the Jabbok River.

JABESH-GILEAD (Jā′ bĕsh-gĭl′ ė ȧd) Place name meaning, "dry, rugged" or "dry place of Gilead." City whose residents, with the exception of four hundred virgins, were put to death by an army of Israelites (Judg. 21:8–12). The four hundred women who were spared became wives for the Benjaminites. While certainty is elusive, the area in which Jabesh-gilead probably was located is east of the Jordan River about twenty miles south of the Sea of Galilee. The story illustrates the drastic steps taken to preserve the unity of the twelve tribes of Israel.

Jabesh-gilead figured prominently in the history of Saul. His rescue of the people of Jabesh-gilead from Nahash the Ammonite marked the effective beginning of the Israelite monarchy (1 Sam. 11:1–11). Later, the men of Jabesh-gilead demonstrated the high regard in which they held Saul by retrieving the bodies of the slain king and his sons from the walls of Beth-shan (1 Sam. 31:11–13). David expressed thanks for the brave deed (2 Sam. 2:4–7), and eventually removed Saul's bones from Jabesh-gilead (2 Sam. 21:12).

JABEZ (Jā′ bĕz) Personal and place name meaning, "hollow, depression" or "he hurries." *1.* Home of scribes whose location is not known (1 Chron. 2:55). *2.* Pious Israelite who asked God for blessing and received it (1 Chron. 4:9–10). He illustrates the power of prayer.

JABIN (Jā′ bĭn) Personal name meaning, "he understands." King of Hazor (Josh. 11:1; Judg. 4; Ps. 83:10). Leader of northern coalition of kings who attacked Joshua at the water of Merom and met their death (compare Josh. 12:19–24). Jabin, king of Hazor, controlled the Israelites when they turned away from God at Ehud's death (Judg. 4:1–2). The biblical writer referred to him as "King of Canaan," a title representing his strong power in the northern part of the country, but a title kings of the other Canaanite city states probably would have strongly contested, since Canaan lacked political unity in that period. Jabin does not act in the story of Judges 4; rather Sisera, his general, represents him and is killed, leading to Jabin's loss of power. This Jabin must certainly be differentiated from the one Joshua fought, leading to the assumption by many scholars that a dynasty of kings in Hazor carried the name Jabin. Some have gone so far to identify him with Ibni-Adad, who appears in Near Eastern documents from Mari.

JABNEEL (Jăb′ nė ĕl) Place name meaning, "God builds." *1.* Town marking northwestern boundary of tribal territory of Judah in land of Philistines (Josh. 15:11); modern Yibna. Uzziah took the town, called by the shortened Hebrew form Jabneh, from the Philistines (2 Chron. 26:6). Later the city was called Jamnia and became a

J

center of scribal activity for the Jews. See *Bible, Formation and Canon of. 2.* Town in Naphtali's tribal territory (Josh. 19:33); modern tell en-Naam or khirbet Yemma, west-southwest of the Sea of Galilee and northeast of Mount Tabor.

JABNEH (Jăb' něh) See *Jabneel.*

JACAN (Jā' căn) Personal name of unknown meaning. A member of tribe of Gad (1 Chron. 5:13).

JACHAN (Jā' chăn) KJV spelling of Jacan. See *Jacan.*

JACHIN (Jā' chĭn) Personal name meaning, "Yah established." Son of Simeon and original ancestor of a clan in the tribe (Gen. 46:10; spelled Jarib in 1 Chron. 4:24). A priest who lived in Jerusalem in Nehemiah's day (Neh. 11:10; compare 1 Chron. 9:10). This represented a priestly family connected to David's organization of the priesthood (1 Chron. 24:17).

JACHIN AND BOAZ (Jā' chĭn and Bō' ăz) Proper names meaning, "he establishes" and "agile." In 1 Kings 7:21, the names of two bronze pillars that stood on either side of the entrance to Solomon's Temple. They may have been 27 feet high and 6 feet in diameter with a 10 foot capital on top. Perhaps each word was the beginning of an inscription that was engraved on the respective pillars. Analogous pillars have been found in front of temples at Khorsabad, Tyre, Paphos, and other places. Their function appears to have been primarily ornamental, though some have suggested they may have been giant incense stands. It is possible that they took on some symbolic religious significance with the passage of time. See *Temple.*

JACHINITE (Jā' chĭn-īte) Family in tribe of Simeon descended from Jachin (Num. 26:12). See *Jachin.*

JACINTH A semiprecious stone more nearly orange in color than the hyacinth. Some English translations give jacinth as a gem in the high priest's breastplate (Ex. 28:19, NAS, NIV, NRSV), the color of one of the riders' breastplates (Rev. 9:17 KJV), and the eleventh foundation stone of the new Jerusalem (Rev. 21:20, KJV, NAS, NIV, NRSV). See *Hyacinth; Minerals and Metals in the Bible.*

JACKAL Golden jackal (*Canis aureus*), a yellow-coated, carnivorous mammal resembling the wolf but considerably smaller (34–37 inches, including a tail of about one foot) with a shorter tail and ears. KJV translated the term for jackal as either dragon (Isa. 13:22; Neh. 2:13) or sea monster (Lam. 4:3). Jackals are nocturnal. They hunt ei-

ther alone, in pairs, or in packs. By hunting in packs, jackals have taken down large antelope. This reputation accounts for the horror of one abandoned to jackals (Ps. 44:19). Jackals eat small mammals, birds, fruits, vegetables, and carrion (compare Ps. 63:10). They are infamous for their distinctive. nighttime wailing (Job. 30:28–31; Mic. 1:8). Most biblical references associate jackals with desert ruins. For a city or nation to be made the haunt or lair of jackals is for it to be utterly destroyed (Isa. 13:22; 34:13; Jer. 9:11; 10:22; 49:33; 50:39; 51:37; Lam. 5:18; Mal. 1:3). See *Dragon; Foxes; Animals.*

JACKAL'S WELL Water source outside Jerusalem, accessible from the Valley Gate (Neh. 2:13, NIV, RSV). Other English translations designate this water source as the Dragon('s) fountain (TEV), spring (NRSV, REB), or well (KJV, NAS). The spring is possibly En-rogel or more likely a water source in the upper part of the Hinnom Valley. See *Jerusalem; Jackal.*

JACKDAW Black and grey bird (*Corvus monedula*) related to but smaller than the common crow (Isa. 34:11; Zeph. 2:14, NAS margin). The meaning of the Hebrew term is obscure. Other identifications include: cormorant; hawk; a species of owl; pelican; or wild bird. See *Birds.*

JACOB (Jā' cob) Personal name built on the Hebrew noun for "heel" meaning, "he grasps the heel" or "he cheats, supplants" (Gen. 25:26; 27:36). Original ancestor of the nation of Israel and father of the twelve ancestors of the twelve tribes of Israel (Gen. 25:1–Ex. 1:5). He was the son of Isaac and Rebekah, younger twin brother of Esau, and husband of Leah and Rachel (Gen. 25:21–26; 29:21–30). God changed his name to Israel (Gen. 32:28; 49:2).

Texts from Ugarit and Assyria have persons named Jacob, but these are not Israelites. Their name is often connected with one of their gods, becoming Jacob-el or Jacob-baal. In such a form, it probably means "may El protect." The Old Testament knows only one Jacob. No one else received the patriarch's name.

Between the Testaments other Jews received the name Jacob; the one New Testament example is the father of Joseph and thus the earthly grandfather of Jesus (Matt. 1:16). Jacob stands as a strong witness that the God who made all the people of the earth also worked in Israel's history, calling the patriarchs to a destiny He would fulfill even when they least deserved it.

Jacob in Genesis Jacob's story occupies half the Book of Genesis. Living up to his name, Jacob bargained for Esau's birthright. See *Birthright.* Parental partiality fostered continuing hostility between Esau, the hunter beloved of his father, and Jacob, the quiet, settled, integrated person favored

J

by his mother. The tensions between brothers seemed to threaten the fulfillment of the divine promise.

Esau's thoughtlessness lost him his birthright and allowed Jacob to have material superiority. Nevertheless, Isaac intended to bestow the blessing of the firstborn upon Esau. The oracle Rebekah received (25:23) probably encouraged her to counter Isaac's will and to gain the blessing for her favorite son by fraud. The blessing apparently conveyed the status of head of family apart from the status of heir. To his crass lies and deception, Jacob even approached blasphemy, using God's name to bolster his cause, "Because the Lord your God granted me success" (27:20 NRSV). The father's blindness deepened the pathos. The blind father pronounced the blessing he could never recall. Jacob became the bearer of God's promises and the inheritor of Canaan. Esau, too, received a blessing, but a lesser one. He must serve Jacob and live in the less fertile land of Edom, but his day would come (27:40). The split between brothers became permanent. Rebekah had to arrange for Jacob to flee to her home in Paddan-aram to escape Esau's wrath (27:46—28:1).

At age 40, Jacob fled his home to begin his life as an individual. Suddenly, a lonely night in Bethel, interrupted by a vision from God, brought reality home. Life had to include wrestling with God and assuming responsibility as the heir of God's promises to Abraham (28:10–22). Jacob made an oath, binding himself to God. Here is the center of Jacob's story; all else must be read in light of the Bethel experience.

In Aram with his mother's family, the deceiver Jacob met deception. Laban tricked him into marrying poor Leah, the elder daughter, before he got his beloved Rachel, the younger. Fourteen years he labored for his wives (29:1–30). Six more years of labor let Jacob return the deception and gain wealth at the expense of his father-in-law, who continued his deception, changing Jacob's wages ten times (31:7,41) Amid the family infighting, both men prospered financially, and Jacob's family grew. Eventually he had twelve children from four women (29:31—30:24).

Intense bargaining ensued when Jacob told Laban he wanted to follow God's call and return to the land of his birth. Supported by his wives, who claimed their father had cheated them of their dowry (31:15), Jacob departed while Laban and his sons were away in the hills shearing sheep. Starting two days later, Laban and his sons could not overtake Jacob until they reached Gilead, 400 miles from Haran.

Laban complained that he had not had an opportunity to bid farewell to his daughters with the accustomed feast. More importantly, he wanted to recover his stolen gods (31:30,32). These gods were small metal or terra-cotta figures of deities. See *Terraphim*. Without the images, his family lost the magical protection which he thought the gods provided from demons and disasters. Since no fault could be found in Jacob's conduct in Haran, all Laban could do was to suggest a covenant of friendship. Laban proposed the terms as (1) never ill-treating his daughters, (2) never marrying any other women, and (3) establishing the site of the covenant as a boundary neither would cross with evil intent. Jacob was now head of his own household. He was ready to climb to a higher plane of spiritual experience.

As Jacob approached the Promised Land, a band of angels met him at Mahanaim (32:1–2). They probably symbolized God's protection and encouragement as he headed southward to meet Esau for the first time in twenty years. Esau's seemingly hostile advance prompted a call for clear evidence of God's guarding. Shrewdly, Jacob sent an enormous gift to his brother and divided his retinue into two groups. Each group was large enough to defend itself or to escape if the other was attacked. To his scheme Jacob added prayer. He realized that it was ultimately God with whom he must deal. When all had crossed the Jabbok River, Jacob met One who wrestled with him until daybreak (ch. 32).

The two struggled without one gaining advantage, until the Opponent dislocated Jacob's hip. Jacob refused to release his Antagonist. Clinging to Him, he demanded a blessing. This would not be given until Jacob said his name. By telling it, Jacob acknowledged his defeat and admitted his character. The Opponent emphasized His superiority by renaming the patriarch. He became Israel, the one on whose behalf God strives. He named the place Peniel (face of God), because he had seen God face to face and his life had been spared (32:30).

Jacob's fear of meeting Esau proved groundless. Seemingly, Esau was content to forget the wrongs of the past and to share his life. As two contrary natures are unlikely to live long in harmony, Jacob chose the better course turning westward to the Promised Land. Esau headed to Seir to become the father of the Edomites. The twins did not meet again until their father's death (35:27–29).

From Succoth, Jacob traveled to Shechem, where he built an altar to God. The son of the city ruler raped Jacob's daughter, Dinah. Jacob's sons demanded that the Shechemites be circumcised before any intermarriages were permitted. The leading citizens followed the king in the request. They hoped to absorb the Hebrews' wealth and property into their own. While the men of Shechem were recovering from surgery and unable to defend themselves, Simeon and Levi killed them to avenge their sister. Jacob condemned their actions, but had to leave Shechem.

From Shechem, he returned to Bethel. Once again he received the patriarchal promises. Losses and grief characterized this period. The death of his mother's nurse (35:8; 24:59) was followed by the death of his beloved wife Rachel while giving birth to Benjamin at Ephrath (35:19; 48:7). About the same time Reuben forfeited the honor of being the eldest son by sexual misconduct (35:22). Finally, the death of Jacob's father, who had been robbed of companionship with both sons, brought Jacob and Esau together again at the family burial site in Hebron.

Although Chapters 37—50 revolve around Joseph, Jacob is still the central figure. The self-willed older sons come and go at his bidding.

Descent to Egypt When severe famine gripped Canaan, Jacob and his sons set out for Egypt. At Beer-sheba Jacob received further assurance of God's favor (46:1–4). Jacob dwelt in the land of Goshen until his death. Jacob bestowed the blessing not only upon his favorite son Joseph, but also upon Joseph's two oldest sons, Ephraim and Manasseh. He was finally laid to rest at Hebron in the cave Abraham had purchased (50:12–14).

Four New Testament passages recall events in his life. The woman at the well in Sychar declared to Jesus that Jacob provided the well (John 4:12). Stephen mentioned the famine and Jacob's journey to Egypt in the course of his defense before the Sanhedrin (Acts 7:8–16). Paul presented Jacob as an example of the sovereign choice of God and of the predestination of the elect (Rom. 9:10–13). The writer of Hebrews held up Jacob as one of the examples of active faith (Heb. 11:9,20–22).

Jacob's Character Throughout the narrative a persistent faith in the God of the fathers shines through. Jacob's life was a story of conflict. He always seemed to be running from someone or something—from Esau, from Laban, or from famine in Canaan. His life, like that of all Israelites, was a checkered history of rebellion and flight.

Jacob is no ideal. Jacob's better nature struggled with his sinful self. What raised Jacob above himself was his reverent, indestructible longing for the salvation of his God.

Jacob's Religion As the religion of Israel and thus the roots of Christianity claim to derive from the patriarchs, it is necessary to attempt to understand Jacob's spiritual life. See *God of the Fathers.*

Jacob's religion was consistent with the beliefs and practices of his fathers. He received instruction from Isaac concerning the history of Abraham, covenant, and the great promises. Jacob encountered God at Bethel at the moment of greatest need in his life. He was fleeing from home to distant unknown relatives. A secondhand religion would not do. Jacob's dream was his first-hand encounter with God. The threefold promise of land, descendants, and a blessing to all nations were personalized for him. Jacob saw in the vision the majesty and glory of God. At Bethel Jacob worshiped God and vowed to take Yahweh as his God.

At Peniel, Jacob wrestled face-to-face with God.

He saw how weak he was before God. It taught him the value of continued prayer from one who is helpless. Jacob emerged from Peniel willing to let his life fall into God's control. He was wounded but victorious. God gave him a crippled body but a strengthened faith. It was a new Jacob—Israel—who hobbled off to meet Esau. He had learned obedience through suffering.

Theological Significance God did not chose Jacob because of what he was but because of what he could become. His life is a long history of discipline, chastisement, and purification by affliction. Not one of his misdeeds went unpunished. He sowed deception and reaped the same, first from Laban and then from his own sons.

Jacob's story is a story of conflict. The note of conflict is even heard before his birth (Gen. 25:22–23). However, in the midst of the all-too-human quarrels over family and fortune, God was at work protecting and prospering His blessed.

With the other patriarchs God acted directly, but with Jacob God seemed to be withdrawn at times. Yet, God was no less at work. He worked through unsavory situations and unworthy persons. Even in Jacob's web of conflict and tragedy, God's hand guided, though half-hidden.

Gary D. Baldwin

JACOB'S WELL A place in Samaria where Jesus stopped to rest as He traveled from Judea to Galilee (John 4:6). There He met and conversed with a Samaritan woman on the subject of living water. The Old Testament contains no reference to it. It was located near the Samaritan city of Sychar. The well currently shown as the scene of the encounter of Jesus with the Samaritan woman certainly is an ancient well and is generally accepted to be the place referred to in the Gospel. See *Jacob; Sychar.*

JADA (Já' dà) Personal name meaning, "he knew." Grandson of Jerahmeel (1 Chron. 2:28,32).

JADAH (Jā' dah) Abbreviated form of personal name Jehoaddah meaning, "Yah adorned." NIV translation based on early Greek and Hebrew manuscripts for Jarah. See *Jarah.*

JADDAI (Jăd' dâi) Modern translations' spelling of Jadau based on textual notes by earliest Hebrew scribes. See *Jadau.*

JADDUA (Jăd' dū à) Personal name meaning, "well-known." *1.* Levite who placed his seal on Nehemiah's covenant (Neh. 10:22). *2.* A high priest, probably at the end of the Persian period when Alexander the Great approached Jerusalem about 333 B.C. (Neh. 12:11,22).

JADE See *Jewelry, Jewels; Precious Stones; Minerals and Metals.*

JADON (Jā' dŏn) Short form of personal name

Well in the city of Sychar revered by tradition as Jacob's Well.

meaning, "Yah rules" or "to be frail." Man from Meronoth near Gibeon who helped Nehemiah repair the wall of Jerusalem (Neh. 3:7).

JADUA (jă dū ȧ) KJV form of the name of a returned Exile with a foreign wife (Ezra 10:43). Modern translations render the name Jaddai.

JAEL (Jā′ ēl) Personal name meaning, "mountain goat." Wife of Heber the Kenite (Judg. 4:17). She received the Canaanite leader Sisera as he fled following his defeat by the Israelites under Deborah and Barak. Jael assassinated Sisera. Her action is celebrated in the Song of Deborah (Judg. 5:24–27). See *Deborah.*

JAGUR (Jā′ ḡûr) Place name meaning, "pile of stones." Village on southeastern border of tribal territory of Judah (Josh. 15:21). Its precise location is not known.

JAH (Jäh) Short form of divine name Yahweh in Psalm 68:4 (KJV) and in many proper names. See *God; Yahweh.*

JAHATH (Jā′ hăth) Personal name of uncertain meaning, perhaps "God will grab up." *1.* Member of clan of Zorathites in tribe of Judah (1 Chron. 4:2). *2.* Great grandson of Levi (1 Chron. 6:20; compare v. 43). *3.* A leader of the Levites in time of David (1 Chron. 23:10–11). *4.* Levite in the line of Eliezer in the clan of Izhar (1 Chron. 24:22). *5.* Levite overseer of Temple repair under King Josiah (2 Chron. 34:12).

JAHAZ (Jā′ hăz) Moabite place name perhaps meaning, "landsite." As they journeyed from the wilderness to the Promised Land, Israel defeated King Sihon there (Num. 21:23–24; Deut. 2:32–33; Judg. 11:20–21). Isaiah's oracle against Moab described the isolated city of Jahaz as hearing the mourning of Heshbon and Elealeh (Isa. 15:4). Jeremiah issued a similar warning (48:34; compare v. 21). The name also appears with the Hebrew locative *ah* ending, thus being spelled Jahaza or Jahazah. Jahzah is also a variant spelling. It became part of the tribal territory of Reuben (Josh. 13:18) and a city of the Levites (Josh. 21:36; compare 1 Chron. 6:78). On the Moabite stone, King Mesha of Moab claims an Israelite king (perhaps Jehu) built Jahaz and used it as a base in his unsuccessful fight against Mesha, Chemosh, the Moabite god driving the Israelites out. Mesha then annexed the city to Dibon. It has been variously located at Libb, six miles north of Dibon; Aleiyan; khirbet el-Medeiyineh; and khirbet Iskander, four miles north of Dibon, being the most popular suggestions.

JAHAZA (Jȧ hā′ zȧ) KJV alternate spelling for Jahaz. See *Jahaz.*

JAHAZAH An alternate KJV form of Jahaz (Josh. 21:36; Jer. 48:21). See *Jahaz.*

J

JAHAZIAH (Jā' hȧ zī' ah) Personal name meaning, "Yahweh looked." Person who opposed Ezra's plan to call for divorce in the mixed marriages (Ezra 10:15). Note the alternative interpretation of a difficult Hebrew text by KJV.

JAHAZIEL (Jȧ·hā' zī-ĕl) Personal name meaning, "Yah looks." 1. Benjaminite military hero who supported David against Saul, also of the tribe of Benjamin (1 Chron. 12:4). 2. Priest whom David appointed to blow the trumpet before the ark (1 Chron. 16:6). 3. A Levite of the clan of Hebron (1 Chron. 23:19; 24:23). 4. A Levite and a son of Asaph who received the Spirit of the Lord and prophesied, promising victory for Jehoshaphat and his people (2 Chron. 20:14–19). 5. Clan leader who led 300 men among the exiles returning to Jerusalem with Ezra (Ezra 8:5).

JAHDAI (Jăh' dā ī) Personal name meaning, "Yah leads." A descendant of Caleb (1 Chron. 2:47).

JAHDIEL (Jăh' dĭ ĕl) Personal name meaning, "God rejoices." Military hero and leader in the East Manasseh tribe (1 Chron. 5:24).

JAHDO (Jăh' dō) Personal name meaning, "his rejoicing." A member of tribe of Gad (1 Chron. 5:14).

JAHLEEL (Jăh' lē ĕl) Personal name meaning, "God shows Himself to be friendly" or "he waits for God." A son of Zebulun and grandson of Jacob (Gen. 46:14) who became a clan leader in tribe of Zebulun (Num. 26:26).

JAHLEELITE (Jăh' lē ĕl īte) Clan in tribe of Zebulun (Num. 26:26).

JAHMAI (Jăh' mā ī) Personal name meaning, "He protects me." Grandson of Issachar, great grandson of Jacob, and clan leader in tribe of Issachar (1 Chron. 7:2).

JAHWEH See *Yahweh*.

JAHZAH (Jăh' zah) Variant form of Jahaz. See *Jahaz*.

JAHZEEL (Jăh' zē ĕl) Personal name meaning, "God apportions." Son of Naphtali, grandson of Jacob, and clan leader in tribe of Naphtali (Gen. 46:24; Num. 26:48). Jahziel (1 Chron. 7:13) represents a variant spelling.

JAHZEELITE (Jăh' zē ĕl īte) Clan in tribe of Naphtali. See *Jahzeel*.

JAHZEIAH (Jăh zē' iah) Modern translation spelling of Jahaziah (Ezra 10:15). See *Jahaziah*.

JAHZERAH (Jăh' zē rah) Personal name of uncertain meaning, possibly "careful"; "crafty"; or "let him turn back." A priest (1 Chron. 9:12). A similar list in Nehemiah 11:13 lists Ahasai instead of Jahzerah.

JAHZIEL An alternate NIV form of Jahzeel (Gen. 46:24; 1 Chron. 7:13). See *Jahzeel*.

JAILER The keeper of a prison (Acts 16:23). See *Prison, Prisoners*.

JAIR (Jā' īr) Abbreviated place name meaning, "Jah shines forth." 1. Son of Manasseh who took possession of a number of villages in Gilead (Num. 32:41). See *Manasseh*. 2. A Gileadite who judged Israel for twenty-two years (Judg. 10:3–5). He was one of the so-called minor judges. His function probably was primarily judicial rather than military. He is described as having had thirty sons and thirty cities. At his death, he was buried in Camon. See *Judges*. 3. Father of Elhanan (1 Chron. 20:5), whose name comes from a different Hebrew word possibly meaning, "Jah protects." His name is Jaare-oregim in 2 Samuel 21:19, though some translators would read the text "Jair of Bethlehem" (REB). 4. A Benjamite who was the ancestor of Mordecai, Esther's guardian (Esther 2:5).

JAIRITE (Jā īr īte) Member of clan of Jair probably from Havvoth-jair, though possibly from Kiriath-jearim (1 Sam. 20:26). See *Jair*.

JAIRUS (Jāî' rŭs) Greek form of Hebrew personal name Jair meaning, "Jah will enlighten." Synagogue official who came to Jesus seeking healing for his twelve-year-old daughter (Mark 5:22). Before Jesus arrived at Jairus' house, however, the little girl died. Jesus reassured Jairus and entered the house with Peter, James, and John. Taking the girl by the hand, Jesus restored her to life, showing His power over death.

JAKAN (Jā' kan) Personal name perhaps meaning, "he was fast." Descendant of or clan inhabiting territory of Seir (1 Chron. 1:42 according to KJV and Hebrew spelling). The Chronicles list repeats that of Genesis 36:27 which reads, "Achan." Modern translations spell the name Akan or Jaakan here. (Compare Deut. 10:6; Num. 33:31–32). See *Achan; Jaakan*.

JAKEH A personal name meaning "prudent." Jakeh was the father or ancestor of Agur (Prov. 30:1).

JAKIM (Jā' kĭm) Personal name meaning, "He caused to stand." 1. Member of tribe of Benjamin living in Ajalon (1 Chron. 8:19). 2. Head of the twelfth division of priests (1 Chron. 24:12).

JAKIN (Jā′ kĭn) NIV spelling of Jachin. See *Jachin.*

JAKINITES (Jā′ kĭ nītes) NIV spelling of Jachinite. See *Jachinite.*

JALAM (Jā′ lam) Personal name meaning, "their ibex or mountain goat" or "he is hidden or dark." Son of Esau and grandson of Isaac (Gen. 36:5), a clan leader among the Edomites (Gen. 36:18). Some interpreters emend the Hebrew text of Psalm 55:19 to read, "Ishmael and Jalam, and the inhabitants of the east all together," but this is done without any textual support. KJV, REB spell the name Jaalam.

JALON (Jā′ lŏn) Personal name of uncertain meaning. Member of tribe of Judah and son of otherwise unknown Ezra (1 Chron. 4:17).

JAMBRES (Jăm′ brēs) See *Jannes.*

JAMES (Jāmes) English form of Jacob, and the name of three men of the New Testament. See *Jacob.*

1. James, the son of Zebedee and brother of John (Matt. 4:21; 10:2; Mark 1:19; 3:17; Luke 5:10). As one of the twelve disciples (Acts 1:13), he, with Peter and John, formed Jesus' innermost circle of associates. These three were present when Jesus raised Jairus' daughter (Mark 5:37; Luke 8:51), witnessed the transfiguration (Matt. 17:1; Mark 9:2; Luke 9:28), and were summoned by Christ for support during His agony in Gethsemane (Matt. 26:36–37; Mark 14:32–34).

Perhaps because of James' and John's fiery fanaticism, evidenced as they sought to call down fire from heaven on the Samaritan village refusing to receive Jesus and the disciples (Luke 9:52–54), Jesus called the brothers "Boanerges" or "sons of thunder" (Mark 3:17). James' zeal was revealed in a more selfish manner as he and John (their mother), on their behalf, in Matt. 20:20–21) sought special positions of honor for the time of Christ's glory (Mark 10:35–40). They were promised, however, only a share in His suffering.

Indeed, James was the first of the twelve to be martyred (Acts 12:2). His execution (about A.D. 44), by order of King Herod Agrippa I of Judea, was part of a larger persecution in which Peter was arrested (Acts 12:1–3).

2. James, the son of Alphaeus, one of the twelve disciples (Matt. 10:3; Mark 3:18; Luke 6:15; Acts 1:13). He is not distinguished by name in any occasion reported in the Gospels or Acts.

He may be "James the younger," whose mother, Mary, was among the women at Jesus' crucifixion and tomb (Matt. 27:56; Mark 15:40; 16:1; Luke 24:10). In John 19:25, this Mary is called the wife of Cleophas, perhaps to be identified with Alphaeus. See *Cleophas; Mary.*

3. James, the brother of Jesus. Bible students debate the precise meaning of "the Lord's brother" (Gal. 1:19). Possibilities are the literal brother or stepbrother, a cousin, or intimate friend and associate. The literal meaning is to be preferred.

During the Lord's ministry, the brothers of Jesus (Matt. 13:55; Mark 6:3; 1 Cor. 9:5) were not believers (John 7:3–5; compare Matt. 12:46–50; Mark 3:31–35; Luke 8:19–21). Paul specifically mentioned a resurrection appearance by Jesus to James (1 Cor. 15:7). After the resurrection and ascension, the brothers are said to have been with the twelve and the other believers in Jerusalem (Acts 1:14).

Paul, seeking out Peter in Jerusalem after his conversion, reported "other of the apostles saw I none, save James the Lord's brother" (Gal. 1:19). In time, James assumed the leadership of the Jerusalem church, originally held by Peter. Evidently, such was achieved not through a power struggle but by James' constancy with the church while Peter and other apostles traveled.

In a Jerusalem conference called regarding Paul's Gentile mission, James presided as spokesman for the Jerusalem church (Acts 15). See *Apostolic Council.*

James perceived his calling as to the "circumcised," that is, the Jews (Gal. 2:9), and is portrayed as loyal to Jewish tradition. He was, however, unwilling to make the law normative for all responding to God's new action in Christ.

The death of James reportedly was at the order of the high priest Ananus, and was either by stoning (according to Flavius Josephus, first century historian of the Jews) or by being cast down from the Temple tower (after Hegesippus, early Christian writer, quoted by the third-century Christian historian Eusebius). These accounts of James's death (about A.D. 66), are not confirmed in the New Testament. *Joseph E. Glaze*

JAMES, THE LETTER The Letter of James belongs to the section of the New Testament usually described as the "General Epistles." The letter is one of exhortation for practical Christianity. The author stated principles of conduct and then frequently provided poignant illustrations. The author's concerns were clearly more practical and less abstract than those of any other New Testament writer. No other New Testament book has received criticism to the extent encountered by this epistle.

Author Verse one of the letter identifies James as the "servant of God" and the author of the letter. Several possibilities for proper identification of this "James" include (1) James the brother of John and the son of Zebedee, (2) James the son of Alphaeus, one of the twelve apostles, or (3) James the half brother of Jesus, a younger son of Mary and of Joseph. Of the three, James the brother of the Lord is the most likely choice. See *James 3.*

Tradition of the early church fathers universally ascribes the letter to James, the pastor of the church in Jerusalem.

The general content of the letter is a call to holiness of life. This accords well with what is known of the life of James. Church tradition noted his exceptional piety, reporting that the knees of the saintly James were like those of a camel due to the unusual amounts of time spent on his knees before God. The author of the epistle was also steeped in the Old Testament outlook in general and in Judaism in particular.

On the other hand, James the brother of John, the son of Zebedee cannot be the author since he became an early martyr (Acts 12:1–2), his death almost certainly predating the writing of the Letter of James. Little is known of James the son of Alphaeus—too little to conjecture that he was involved in the writing of the epistle. Scholarly theories that later disciples of James gathered his teachings and published them in a Greek style too exalted for James are not necessary to explain the evidence.

Recipients Although some passages appear to address unbelievers (Jas. 5:1–6), the letter is addressed to "the twelve tribes in the Dispersion" (1:1 NRSV). Reference to the "twelve tribes" suggests that the recipients were Jews. Specifically, reference is made to the "Jews of the dispersion." This phrase recalled the scattering of the Jewish nation first in 722 B.C. when the Northern Kingdom of Israel fell to the Assyrian Empire and finally in 586 B.C. when the Southern Kingdom of Judah fell to the marauding Babylonians under Nebuchadnezzar.

However, James clearly had a still more narrow focus. Apparently, James had in mind the "Christian" Jews of dispersion. This may be conjectured from James' identification of himself (1:1) as a servant of Jesus Christ as well as from references like having "the faith of our Lord Jesus Christ" (2:1).

Date Supposing an early date of writing may account for the peculiarity of the address. James' martyrdom by A.D. 66 provides us with the latest possible date of writing. Evidences of a very early date, such as the mention of those coming into the "assembly" (Greek, *sunagogē*), point to a time very early in Christian history, perhaps prior to the Jerusalem Conference in A.D. 49–50.

Though some Bible students date James after A.D. 60, many scholars are convinced that James is the first book of the New Testament to be written, some dating it as early as A.D. 48. As such, it provides the reader with a rather remarkable insight into the developing concerns of the church in its earliest era.

Occasion The letter was evidently the product of concerns on the part of early pastoral leadership about the ethical standards of early Christians. Therefore, the subject matter includes an analysis

in chapter 1 of how to respond to temptation and trial (1:1–18). The necessity of "doing" the word as well as "hearing" the word is the focus of James 1:19–27. Treatment of the poor and the appropriate management of wealth are topics of concern in James 2:1–13 and 5:1–6. The waywardness of the tongue and the necessity of its taming are discussed in chapter 3. Conflicts and attitudes to other Christians is the subject of chapter 4. Appropriate responses to life's demands and pressures are suggested in chapter 5.

James' Contributions Some scholars have compared James to the Old Testament Book of Proverbs. In many respects the two are quite different. However, the comparison is valid from the perspective of ethical instruction. The theme of the book is that practical religion must manifest itself in works which are superior to those of the world. The essence of such works covers the areas of personal holiness and service to others, such as visiting "the fatherless and widows," and keeping onself "unspotted from the world" (1:27). These "works" further demand active resistance to the devil (4:7), submission to God (4:7), and even brokenhearted repentance for sins (4:9).

Patience in the wake of trials and temptations is the subject both of the introduction and of the conclusion of the epistle. Readers are to "count it all joy" when trials come (1:2) and expect reward for endurance of those trials (1:12). In James 5:7–11 James returns to the subject, citing both Job and the prophets as appropriate examples of patience in the midst of tribulation.

Questions and Challenges of James Two difficult and widely debated passages in James challenge Bible students. In 2:14–26, James argued that "faith if it hath not works is dead" (2:17). This *apparent* contradiction to the teaching of the apostle Paul has caused much consternation among some theologians. For example, Martin Luther referred to the book as "an epistle of straw" when compared with Paul's writings.

More careful exegesis has shown that the contradiction is apparent rather than real. James argued that a faith that is *only* a "confessing faith," such as that of the demons (2:19), is not a saving faith at all. The demons believed in God in the sense of "intellectual assent," but they were void of belief in the sense of "commitment." Orthodoxy of doctrine which does not produce a sanctified life-style is, in the final analysis, worthless.

In 5:13–18 James spoke of healing and its means. Actually, this passage only treats the subject of healing incidentally. The actual purpose of the discussion is to stress the effectiveness of the earnest prayer of a righteous man (5:15–16). This is illustrated by a reference to Elijah, whose prayers were sufficient alternately to shut up the heavens and then to open them (5:17–18).

Whatever else may be intended, clearly the prayer of faith "saves the sick." The anointing oil, whether medicinal, as some have argued, or symbolic, as others have held, is not the healing agent. God heals, when He chooses to heal (4:14), as a response to the fervent prayers of righteous men.

The Letter of James remains of lasting value and consequence to the Christian confronted by an increasingly secular world. Christ ought to make a difference in one's life. That is the theme and mandate of James.

Outline
I. Salutation (1:1)
II. True Religion Is Developed by Trials and Testing (1:2–15).
   A. Joy is the correct response to times of testing (1:2).
   B. The testing of faith can result in steadfastness which, when mature, enables us to be perfect, complete, and lacking in nothing (1:3–4).
   C. True wisdom comes from God and is available to those who ask in faith, not doubting (1:5–8).
   D. Wealth may be a test of faith, not a proof of faith (1:9–11).
   E. Perseverance under trial leads to blessing (1:12).
   F. Temptation comes from within, not from God, and is to be resisted (1:13–15).
III. True Religion Is Initiated by Faith (1:16—2:26).
   A. Salvation by faith is a gift from God, as are all good gifts (1:16–17).
   B. Salvation as an expression of God's will is related to God's Word (1:18–27).
      1. We are to receive God's Word (1:18–21).
      2. We are to do God's Word, not just hear it (1:22–25).
   C. Saving faith does not show favoritism but shows love to all (2:1–13).
   D. Saving faith issues in godly attitudes and actions (2:14–26).
IV. True Religion Is Guided by Wisdom (3:1–18).
   A. The wise person controls the tongue (3:1–12).
   B. Earthly wisdom is characterized by evil attitudes and actions (3:13–16).
   C. The wise person's life is characterized by moral behavior (3:17–18).
V. True Religion Is Demonstrated by Works (4:1—5:12).
   A. Avoid acting selfishly instead of asking God (4:1–3).
   B. Avoid being friendly with the world (4:4–5).
   C. Possess the proper attitude toward self—being humble, not proud or presumptuous (4:6–10).
   D. Avoid speaking against or judging other Christians (4:11–12).
   E. Avoid presuming on God's time (4:13–16).
   F. Do not fail to do what you know is right (4:17).
   G. Avoid depending on wealth (5:1–3).
   H. Avoid treating persons unjustly (5:4–6).
   I. Do not be impatient, for the Lord is coming (5:7–11).
   J. Do not take oaths (5:12).
VI. True Religion Is Expressed in Prayer (5:13–20).
   A. Prayer, including intercession, is a significant part of true religion (5:13–16).
      1. Prayer is a proper response to suffering and illness (5:13–14).
      2. Prayers are to be offered in faith, with right motives (5:15).
      3. Prayer includes confession of sins (5:16a).
   B. The righteousness of the person praying is related to the effectiveness of the prayer (5:16b).
   C. All humans can pray and be heard (5:17–18).
   D. Intercession for sinners is an important Christian responsibility (5:19–20).

Paige Patterson

JAMIN (Jā' mĭn) Personal name meaning, "on the right" or "good luck." *1.* Son of Simeon and grandson of Jacob, a clan leader in tribe of Simeon (Ex. 6:5; Num. 26:12). *2.* Grandson of Jerahmeel (1 Chron. 2:27). *3.* A Levite who interpreted the law for the people as Ezra read it (Neh. 8:7). *4.* A component of name Benjamin meaning "right hand."

JAMINITE (Jā' mĭn īte) Member of clan headed by Jamin. See *Jamin.*

JAMLECH (Jăm' lĕch) Personal name meaning, "May He cause to be king" known in other Near Eastern cultures. Member of tribe of Simeon (1 Chron. 4:34).

JANAI (Jā' nā ĭ) Personal name meaning, "May He answer me." Member of tribe of Gad (1 Chron. 5:12).

JANGLING, VAIN KJV expression for idle talk (1 Tim. 1:6). Translation alternatives include: foolish (TEV), fruitless (NAS), or vain (RSV) discussion; meaningless talk (NIV, NRSV); and a wilderness of words (REB).

JANIM (Jā' nĭm) Modern translation spelling of Janum following written Hebrew text (Josh. 15:53). See *Janum.*

JANNA (Jăn' nȧ) Personal name of uncertain

meaning. Ancestor of Jesus and head of final list of seven names before Jesus (Luke 3:24). Modern translations spell Jannai.

JANNAI (Jăn' nâî) Modern translations' spelling of Janna. See *Janna.*

JANNES AND JAMBRES (Jăn' nēs and Jăm' brēs) Two opposers of Moses and Aaron (2 Tim. 3:8). Though the names do not appear in the Old Testament, rabbinic tradition identified Jannes and Jambres as being among those Egyptian magicians who sought to duplicate for Pharaoh the miracles performed by Moses (Ex. 7:11). The Damascus Document from the Qumran Sect describes the two as brothers raised up by Belial, the evil one. Eusebius of Caesarea described them as sacred scribes of Egypt. The Jewish tradition makes several mentions of them, but in the end they could not match God's power displayed through Moses.

JANOAH (Jȧ nō' ah) Place name meaning, "he rests." *1.* Town in tribal territory of Ephraim (Josh. 16:6–7). It is probably modern khirbet Janun about seven miles south of Nablus. KJV transliterates the Hebrew *ah* meaning "towards" and so spells Janohah here. *2.* City in northern Israel that Tiglath-pileser, king of Assyria (744–727 B.C.), captured from Pekah, king of Israel (752–732 B.C.), about 733 B.C. Its location is uncertain, suggestions including khirbet Janun; Janua, six miles south of Megiddo, and Janoah, nine miles east of Acco. Recently, interpreters have sought to establish a military pattern in the report and locate Janoah at khirbet Niha just south of Kefar Giladi on the road south from Abel-beth-Maacah.

JANOHAH (Jȧ nō' hah) Variant spelling of Janoah. See *Janoah.*

JANUM (Jā' nŭm) Place name of uncertain meaning, perhaps "slumbering." Town in tribal territory of Judah (Josh. 15:53) near Hebron. The location is not known. KJV, NAS spelling follows vocalization by early Hebrew scribes. See *Janim.*

JAPHETH (Jā' phĕth) Personal name meaning, "may he have space." One of Noah's three sons, either the youngest or next to youngest (Gen. 5:32). Genesis 10:2 identifies Japheth's sons as Gomer, Magog, Madai, Javan, Tubal, Meshech, and Tiras. One of the titans of Greek mythology had a similar name. These names point to Japheth as having been the progenitor of the Indo-European peoples who lived to the north and west of Israel, farthest from Israel. Genesis 9:27 pronounces God's blessing on Japheth and his descendants, including living with Shem, thus getting to dwell in the land of promise, and being served by the Canaanites, thus sharing the position as God's people. Here is an early indication of non-Israelites having a share with God's people. See *Noah; Table of Nations.*

JAPHIA (Jȧ·phī' ȧ) Place and personal name meaning, "place situated high above" or "may He bring shining light." *1.* Border town of tribal territory of Zebulun (Josh. 19:3). In the Amarna Letters, the Egyptian pharaoh required the town to supply forced laborers after Labayu of Shechem destroyed Shunem. It is modern Yafa, southwest of Nazareth. *2.* King of Lachish who joined southern coalition against Joshua and met death by cave of Makkedah (Josh. 10:1–27,31–32). *3.* Son born to David in Jerusalem by unnamed wife (2 Sam. 5:15).

JAPHLET (Jăph' lĕt) Personal name meaning, "He rescues." Member of tribe of Asher (1 Chron. 7:32–33).

JAPHLETI (Jăph' lĕt ī) Place name according to KJV but name of tribal group—Japhletites—according to modern translations (Josh. 16:3). The clan's territory lay on border between Ephraim and Benjamin, though the clan apparently belonged to Asher. See *Japhlet.*

JAPHLETITE (Jăph' lē tīte) See *Japhleti.*

JAPHO (Jā' phō) KJV, TEV spelling for Joppa in Old Testament. See *Joppa.*

JAR See *Pottery in Bible Times; Vessels and Utensils.*

JARAH (Jā' rah) Personal name meaning, "goat." Descendant of King Saul (1 Chron. 9:42), apparently the same as Jehoadah in 8:36, the words being spelled the same except for one similarly written letter in Hebrew. Compare 1 Chronicles 10:6.

JAREB (Jā' rĕb) Personal name meaning, "the great one" or "he contends" (in court). Modern translations see the term as part of a Near Eastern expression "the great king" often applied to the king of Assyria, as in the Aramaic treaty inscriptions from Sefire and in the Assyrian equivalent in 2 Kings 18:19. Hosea accused Israel and Judah of turning to the "great king" of Assyria, probably Tiglath-pileser III (at least for Judah), to cure their ills rather than going to Yahweh, the great King of the universe and the Great Physician (Hos. 5:13). Hosea pronounced just punishment for Israel, their "calf-god" (REB) would be carried to Babylon as tribute to "the great king" (10:5–6).

JARED (Jā' rĕd) Personal name meaning, "slave." *1.* Father of Enoch (Gen. 5:15–20). *2.*

Member of tribe of Judah (1 Chron. 4:18; English translations usually spell the same Hebrew word Jered here rather than Jared).

JARESIAH (Jår·e·sī′ ah) KJV spelling of Jaareshiah. See *Jaareshiah.*

JARHA (Jär′ hå) Personal name of uncertain meaning. Egyptian slave used by his master Sheshan to maintain the family line in clan of Jerahmeel and tribe of Judah (1 Chron. 2:34–35).

JARIB (Jā′ rĭb) Personal name meaning, "He contends against" or "is legal opponent of" (see Ps. 35:1; Isa. 49:25). *1.* Member of tribe of Simeon (1 Chron. 4:24, but called Jachin in Num. 26:12). See *Jachin. 2.* A Levite who served as messenger for Ezra in his search for Levites to accompany him back to Jerusalem (Ezra 8:16). *3.* Priest who pledged under Ezra's leadership to divorce his foreign wife to remove the temptation to worship the foreigners' gods (Ezra 10:18).

JARMUTH (Jär′ mŭth) Place name meaning, "height" or "swelling in the ground." *1.* City whose king joined southern coalition against Joshua and Gibeon (Josh. 10). Joshua "stored" the king in the cave of Makkedah before shaming him and slaying him (compare 12:11). It lay in the western "lowlands," the "foothills" (NIV) or Shephelah (REB) of the tribe of Judah (Josh. 15:33,35). It is identified with modern tell Jarmuth three miles southwest of Beth Shemesh and fifteen miles southwest of Jerusalem. An Amarna letter from tell el-Hesi mentions it. Brief excavations have shown Early Bronze and Stone Age remains but as yet nothing from the Late Bronze or Early Iron ages. In Nehemiah's time Jewish settlers lived there (Neh. 11:29). *2.* A city of the Levites in the tribal territory of Issachar (Jos. 21:29; compare 19:21; 1 Chron. 6:58, both spelled differently and differing from *1.* above; thus spelling of Remeth, Ramoth). This city may be located at modern Kaukab el-Hawa.

JAROAH (Jå rō′ ah) Personal name meaning, "smooth, gentle" or "shown mercy." Member of tribe of Gad (1 Chron. 5:14).

JASHAR, BOOK OF (Jăsh′ år) An ancient written collection of poetry quoted by Bible authors. See *Books.*

JASHEN (Jā′ shĕn) Personal name meaning, "sleepy." Member of David's elite military corps, the "thirty" or groups of threes perhaps (2 Sam. 23:32). First Chronicles 11:34 apparently spells the same name Hashem and calls him the Gizonite. See *Gizonite.*

JASHER (Jā′ shēr) KJV spelling of Jashar. See *Jashar.*

JASHOBEAM (Jå shō′ bĕ ăm) Personal name meaning, "the uncle (or people) will return." Warrior of Saul's tribe of Benjamin who supported David at Ziklag as he fled from Saul (1 Chron. 12:6). He is listed first among the "chief of the mighty men whom David had" (1 Chron. 11:11). Some interpreters would say the text listed him as a Hachmonite, while others would see "a Hachmonite" as reference to a different individual. Second Samuel 23:8 spells the name Josheb-basshebeth (see modern translations), the last part of which represents the Hebrew word for shame, at times used by scribes instead of an original name containing the Canaanite god's name Baal, leading some interpreters to see the original name here as Yishbaal. Some Greek manuscripts actually read Ishbaal. In 2 Samuel 23:8, REB reads Ishbaal. KJV simply translates there: "that sat in the seat." Jashobeam commanded David's first course or division administering the kingdom for the first month of each year (1 Chron 27:2). Here Jashobeam is the son of Zabdiel, a descendant of Perez who belonged to the tribe of Judah. Elsewhere Jashobeam is a member of the clan of Hachmon. See *Hachmonites.*

JASHUB (Jā′ shŭb) Personal name meaning, "He turns to" or "He returns." The name is found in several Near Eastern cultures. *1.* Clan leader in tribe of Issachar (Num. 26:24). Genesis 46:13 names him Job. *2.* Man with foreign wife condemned by Ezra as bringing temptation to foreign worship into the community (Ezra 10:29). *3.* Part of name of Isaiah's son (Isa. 7:3). See *Shearjashub. 4.* Some interpreters see a town named Jashub in Joshua 17:7, a border town of the tribe of Manasseh (REB). This would be modern Jasuf, eight miles south of Shechem.

JASHUBILEHEM (Jå shū′ bī-lē′ hĕm) Personal name meaning "Jashubites of bread" or "she returns for bread." Member of tribe of Judah (1 Chron. 4:22, NAS, KJV, NIV). Hebrew text has two words which modern interpreters read in different ways: but returned to Lehem (NRSV); then settled in Bethlehem (TEV).

JASHUBITE (Jā′ shŭb īte) Member of clan founded by Jashub. See *Jashub.*

JASIEL (Jăs′ ĭ ĕl) Personal name meaning, "God makes or acts." Military leader under David (1 Chron. 11:27 KJV). Modern translations spell name Jaasiel.

JASON (Jā′ son) Personal name often used by Jews as a substitute for Hebrew Joshua or Joseph and also used by Gentiles. *1.* In Acts 17:5, Paul's host in Thessalonica. He was brought up on charges before the city officials when the angry Jewish mob were unable to find Paul (Acts 17:6–

J

7). The Jason mentioned in Romans 16:21 may have been the same person. He is identified as a Jew who joined Paul and others in greeting the Romans.

2. A Jewish high priest during the final years of Seleucid control of Palestine. His Greek name reflects the Hellenistic influence that increasingly permeated Jewish life during the period before the Maccabean revolt. See *Intertestamental History.*

JASPER Green chalcedony. Jasper commonly translates two Hebrew and one Greek term. The first term is used for the sixth stone in the headdress of the king of Tyre (Ezek. 28:13). The second term is used for a stone in the high priest's breastplate (Ex. 28:20; 39:13). This second term is rendered onyx at Ezekiel 28:13. The third term describes the face of the One seated on the throne (Rev. 4:3) and the glory of the new Jerusalem (Rev. 21:11,18,19). The NIV used jasper to translate an obscure Hebrew term at Job 28:18. Other translation options include: alabaster (REB), crystal (NAS, NRSV, TEV), and pearls (KJV). See *Minerals and Metals.*

JATHNIEL (Jăth' nĭ ĕl) Personal name meaning, "God gives." A Levite gatekeeper (1 Chron. 26:2).

JATTIR (Jăt' tīr) Place name meaning, "the remainder." Town in the hills of the tribal territory of Judah (Josh. 15:48). David gave some of war booty from victory over Amalekites to Jattir (1 Sam. 30:27). Joshua reserved it for the Levites (Josh. 20:14). It was located near modern khirbet Attir about thirteen miles south southwest of Hebron and fourteen miles northeast of Beersheba.

JAVAN (Jā' văn) Personal name meaning, "Greece." Son of Japheth (Gen. 10:2), and father of Elishah, Tarshish, Kittim, and Dodanim (Gen. 10:4), thus the original ancestor of Greek peoples. Elsewhere in the Old Testament, the name Javan is used to denote Greece. See *Greece; Table of Nations.*

JAVELIN A light spear thrown as a weapon. See *Weapons; Arms and Armor.*

JAW Either of two boney structures that border the mouth and bear the teeth. The taking of captives in war is sometimes pictured using the images of animals led with bridles in their jaws (Isa. 30:28) or fish carried away with hooks in theirs (Ezek. 29:4; 38:4). According to one understanding of Hosea 11:4, God, pictured as a farmer, "lifts the yoke from their jaws," that is, looses the yoke so that the oxen might better feed.

JAZER (Jā' zēr) Place name meaning, "May He help." Amorite city state Israel conquered while marching across the land east of the Jordan towards the Promised Land (Num. 21:32). The tribe of Gad rebuilt and settled Jazer (Num. 32:35; compare Josh. 13:25). Joshua assigned it to the Levites (Josh. 21:39). Isaiah pronounced judgment on Jazer while preaching against Moab (Isa. 16:8–9). Jeremiah echoed him (Jer. 48:32). David found outstanding leaders there (1 Chron. 26:32). It was also an important city in the period between the Testaments (1 Maccabees 5:8). Interpreters debate Jazer's exact location. German archaeologists appear to favor tell el-Areme, while Israelis point to khirbet es-Sar about eight miles west of Amman. Others point to khirbet Jazzir about two miles south of es-Salt.

JAZIZ (Jā' zĭz) Personal name meaning, "he goads." Chief shepherd under David. He was probably a foreigner. See *Hagrite.*

JEALOUSY Jealousy is used in three senses in Scripture; (1) as intolerance of rivalry or unfaithfulness; (2) as a disposition suspicious of rivalry or unfaithfulness; and (3) as hostility towards a rival or one believed to enjoy an advantage. Sense 3 approximates envy. God is jealous for His people Israel in sense 1, that is, God is intolerant of rival gods (Ex. 20:5; 34:14; Deut. 4:24; 5:9) One expression of God's jealousy for Israel is God's protection of His people from enemies. Thus

Statuette of bearded Near Eastern warrior holding a spear, or javelin, from ca. 1500 B.C.

God's jealousy includes avenging Israel (Ezek. 36:6; 39:25; Nah. 1:2; Zech. 1:14; 8:2). Phineas is described as jealous with God's jealousy (Num. 25:11,13, sometimes translated zealous for God). Elijah is similarly characterized as jealous (or zealous) for God (1 Kings 19:10,14). In the New Testament Paul speaks of his divine jealousy for the Christians at Corinth (2 Cor. 11:2).

Numbers 5:11–30 concerns the process by which a husband suspicious of his wife's unfaithfulness might test her. Most often human jealousy involves hostility towards a rival. Joseph's brothers were jealous (Gen. 37:11) and thus sold their brother into slavery (Acts 7:9). In Acts 17:5 a jealous group among the Jews incited the crowd against Paul. Jealousy, like envy, is common in vice lists (Rom. 13:13; 2 Cor. 12:20; Gal. 5:20–21). Jealousy is regarded as worse than wrath or anger (Prov. 27:4). James regarded jealousy (or bitter envy) as characteristic of earthy, demonic wisdom (3:14) and as the source of all disorder and wickedness (3:16). See *Envy.*

JEALOUSY, CEREAL OFFERING OF See *Jealousy, Ordeal of.*

JEALOUSY, IMAGE OF The term for an idol in Ezekiel 8:3,5. The meaning is either that the idol evokes God's jealousy or that the idol is identified with Asherah, the goddess of passionate love. (Compare 2 Kings 21:7; 2 Chron. 33:7.) See *Jealousy.*

JEALOUSY, ORDEAL OF A test to determine guilt or innocence of a wife suspected of adultery but who had not been caught in the act (Num. 5:11–31). The ordeal consisted of two parts: a grain offering "of memorial bringing iniquity to remembrance" (5:15) and the "bitter water that causeth the curse" (5:18). See *Bitter Water.*

JEALOUSY, WATER OF See *Bitter Water.*

JEARIM (Jē' à·rĭm) Place name meaning, "forests" or "parks." Component of several Old Testament place names including Kiriath Jearim, Mount Jearim, Fields of Jearim, and the wood of 1 Samuel 14:26. See *Kiriath Jearim; Chesalon.*

JEATERAI (Jè ăt' ĕ rāi) Personal name of uncertain meaning. A Levite (1 Chron. 6:21) perhaps to be identified with Ethni (1 Chron. 6:41).

JEATHERAI (Jē ăth' ĕ rāi) Spelling for Jeaterai in many modern translations. See *Jeaterai.*

JEBERECHIAH (Jè bĕr ė·chī' ah) Personal name meaning, "Yahweh blesses." Father of Zechariah who served as witness for Isaiah (Isa. 8:2; compare 2 Kings 18:2).

JEBEREKIAH (Jĕ bĕr ė kī' ah) NIV spelling of Jeberechiah. See *Jeberechiah.*

JEBUS (Jē' bŭs) Place name meaning, "trodden under foot." Name of tribe originally occupying Jerusalem and then of city (Judg. 19:10; compare Josh. 18:29; 1 Chron. 11:4). The name *Jebus* does not occur outside the Bible. See *Jerusalem; Jebusites.*

JEBUSI (Jĕb' ū sī) KJV reading (Josh. 18:16,28) for Jebusite. See *Jebus; Jebusite.*

JEBUSITES (Jĕb' ū sītes) Clan who originally controlled Jerusalem before David conquered the city. In the list of the descendants of Noah (Gen. 10) the Jebusites are traced through the line of Ham and Canaan and are listed alongside other clans such as the Amorites and Girgashites. In Joshua 10, the king of Jerusalem, Adonizedek, is considered one of the five Amorite kings who fought against Joshua.

In the time of the Judges, Jerusalem was attacked and burned by the men of Judah (Judg. 1:8), but the Jebusites were not expelled. Centuries later David captured the city and made it his capital. David purchased a stone threshing-floor from a Jebusite named Araunah (2 Sam. 24:16–24), and this later became the site of Solomon's Temple. The remnants of the Jebusites became bondservants during Solomon's reign (1 Kings 9:20–21). Jebusite names appear to be Hurrian rather than Semitic. See *Jerusalem.*

M. Stephen Davis

JECAMIAH (Jĕc à mī' ah) Personal name meaning, "Yah causes to stand." *1.* Member of clan of Jerahmeel in tribe of Judah (1 Chron. 2:41). *2.* Son of King Jeconiah (Jehoiachin), the Judean king exiled by Babylon (1 Chron. 3:18). English translations sometimes spell these two names differently though they are the same Hebrew name.

JECHILIAH (Jĕch ĭ lī' ah) NAS spelling in 2 Chronicles 26:3 following written Hebrew text. Other English translations follow early scribal note, versions, 2 Kings 15:2, reading Jecoliah. See *Jecoliah.*

JECHOLIAH (Jĕch ō lī' ah) KJV spelling of Jecoliah in 2 Kings 15:2. See *Jecoliah; Jechiliah.*

JECHONIAH (Jĕch ō nī' ah) NRSV spelling of Jeconiah in Matthew 1:11–12. See *Jeconiah.*

JECHONIAH (Jĕch ō nī' ah) Personal name meaning, "Jah establishes." Shortened form of Jehoiachin. See *Jehoiachin.*

JECHONIAS (Jĕch ō nī' às) KJV spelling of Jeconiah in Matthew 1:11–12. See *Jeconiah.*

JECOLIAH (Jĕc ō lī′ ah) Mother of Uzziah, king of Judah (2 Kings 15:2; 2 Chron. 26:3). See *Jechiliah; Jecholiah.*

JEDAIAH (Jè dâi′ ah) *1.* Personal name meaning, "praise Yah" or "Yah has performed a merciful deed." Man who helped Nehemiah repair the wall of Jerusalem (Neh. 3:10) and a descendant of the tribe of Simeon (1 Chron. 4:37). *2.* Personal name meaning, "Yah knows." A priest or priests heading the second course or division of priests (1 Chron. 24:7), returned from Babylonian Exile (1 Chron. 9:10; compare Ezra 2:36; Neh. 7:39; 11:10; 12:6,7,19,21). The returning Exile may be same as one from whom the prophet Zechariah received gold and silver (Zech. 6:10,14). English translations usually spell the names the same though they represent two distinct Hebrew names.

JEDIAEL (Jè dī′ ā ĕl) Personal name meaning, "the one whom God knows." *1.* Member of tribe of Benjamin (1 Chron. 7:6,10–11). *2.* Military leader under David (1 Chron. 11:45). The same or a different warrior from the tribe of Manasseh joined David when he moved to Ziklag (1 Chron. 12:20). *3.* A Levite and gatekeeper (1 Chron. 26:2).

JEDIDAH (Jè dī′ dah) Personal name meaning, "darling" or "beloved." Mother of Josiah king of Judah (2 Kings 22:1).

Valley of Jehoshaphat (or the Kidron Valley) in Jerusalem showing the Church of All Nations.

JEDIDIAH (Jĕ dĭ dī′ ah) Personal name or nickname meaning, "Yah's darling." A similar name meaning, "El's darling" appears in the Ugaritic materials. A name God told David to give to his son Solomon (2 Sam. 12:25). Despite David's sin with Bathsheba and the death of the child of their sinful relationship, God showed His love to their child Solomon, thus underlining God's forgiving nature and His continued commitment to David and his royal house.

JEDUTHUN (Jè dû′ thŭn) Personal name meaning, "praise." Prophetic musician and Levite in the service of King David (1 Chron. 25:1). The names Asaph and Heman appear along with that of Jeduthun as original ancestors of Temple musicians. In 1 Chronicles 15:17, however, Asaph and Heman are associated with Ethan, suggesting that Ethan and Jeduthun may be different names for the same person. If that is the case, Jeduthun would have been the son of Kushaiah and a member of the clan of Merari. Otherwise, nothing is known about Jeduthun's ancestry. In 1 Chronicles 25:1,3 he is said to have prophesied using musical instruments; and in 2 Chronicles 35:15 he is referred to as the king's seer, apparently working with Zadok at Gibeon (1 Chron. 16:37–42). Three of the Psalms (39; 62; 77) include his name in their titles. The exact nature of Jeduthun's relationship to these Psalms is uncertain. See *Priests and Levites; Music; Psalms.*

JEEZER (Jè ē′ zĕr) Personal name meaning, "where is help?" or a shortened form of "my

J

brother helps" or "my father helps." Original head of a clan in tribe of Gilead (Num. 26:30). Apparently, the same name is intended in Joshua 17:2 where Abiezer occurs, quite probably the original name. See *Abiezer.* Modern translations often use spelling Iezer.

JEEZERITE (Jĕ ē′ zēr·īte) Member of clan of Jeezer. See *Jeezer.*

JEGAR-SAHADUTHA (Jē′ gär·sā hȧ dū′ thȧ) Aramaic place name meaning, "stone marker." Aramaic equivalent of Galeed. See *Galeed.*

JEHALELEEL (Jĕ hȧ lē′ lĕ ĕl) Personal name meaning, "he praises God" or "God shines forth." *1.* Member of tribe of Judah (1 Chron. 4:16). *2.* Levite whose son helped King Hezekiah purify the Temple (2 Chron. 29:12). English translations are not always consistent in transliterating this Hebrew name in its two occurrences.

JEHALELEL KJV alternate form for Jehallelel at 2 Chronicles 29:12. See *Jehallelel.*

JEHALLELEL (Jĕ hăl′ lĕ lĕl) Modern translation spelling of Jehaleleel. See *Jehaleleel.*

JEHATH (Jē′ hăth) NIV spelling of Jahath (1 Chron. 6:20). See *Jahath.*

JEHAZIEL (Jĕ hăz′ ĭ ĕl) TEV spelling of Jahaziel in 1 Chronicles 23:19; 24:23. See *Jahaziel.*

JEHDEIAH (Jĕh dē′ iah) Personal name meaning, "Yahweh rejoices." *1.* A Levite listed outside the twenty-four courses of Levites (1 Chron. 24:20). *2.* Keeper of the royal donkeys under David (1 Chron. 27:30). His home was Meronoth.

JEHEZEKEL (Jĕ hĕ′ zĕ kĕl) Personal name meaning, "God strengthens." Same Hebrew spelling as prophet Ezekiel. Head of twentieth course of priests (1 Chron. 24:16).

JEHEZKEL (Jĕ hĕz′ kĕl) NAS, NIV, TEV, REB spelling of Jehezekel. See *Jehezekel.*

JEHIAH (Jĕ hī′ ah) Personal name meaning, "may he live, O Yah." Guard of the ark when David brought it up from Philistine territory (1 Chron. 15:24).

JEHIEL (Jĕ hī′ ĕl) Personal name meaning, "Let him live, O God." *1.* Apparently a variant name for Jehiah (1 Chron. 15:18; compare verse 24). See *Jehiah.* *2.* Levite musician who played the lute before the ark (1 Chron. 15:20; 16:5). *3.* A leading Levite (1 Chron. 23:8). *4.* Levite in charge of treasury for God's house under David (1 Chron. 29:8; compare 26:20–22). *5.* Guardian of the

royal sons under David (1 Chron. 27:32). *6.* Son of King Jehoshaphat slain by his brother King Jehoram when the latter ascended to the throne (2 Chron. 21:1–4). *7.* Levite who helped purify the Temple under King Hezekiah (2 Chron. 29:14) according to ancient Bible translations and scribal note; the written Hebrew text has Jehuel. Later, under Hezekiah possibly the same Jehiel served as an overseer in the Temple (2 Chron. 31:13). *8.* A leading priest under Josiah who distributed large offerings to the priests for their Passover offerings (2 Chron. 35:8). *9.* Father of man who returned with Ezra to Jerusalem from Babylon (Ezra 8:9). *10.* Father of man who proposed that men with foreign wives divorce them in order not to tempt others to worship foreign gods under Ezra (Ezra 10:1–4). *11.* Priest who agreed to divorce his foreign wife under Ezra (Ezra 10:21). *12.* Layman who agreed to divorce his foreign wife under Ezra (Ezra 10:26).

JEHIELI (Jĕ hī′ ĕ lī) Member of clan founded by Jehiel (1 Chron. 26:21–22). See *Jehiel.*

JEHIELITE (Jĕ hī′ ĕ′ līte) NAS translation of Jehieli. See *Jehieli.*

JEHIZKIAH (Jē hĭz kī′ ah) Personal name meaning, "Yahweh strengthens." *1.* Variant Hebrew spelling of Hezekiah (2 Kings 20:10; Isa. 1:1; 1 Chron. 4:41; 2 Chron. 28:27—33:3). *2.* Man of tribe of Ephraim who prevented people of Israel from bringing war prisoners from Judah into the city after Pekah of Israel defeated Ahaz of Judah about 733 B.C. (2 Chron. 28:12).

JEHOADAH (Jĕ hō′ ȧ dah) Personal name perhaps meaning, "Yahweh is ornamentation." Descendant of Saul in tribe of Benjamin (1 Chron. 8:36), the list showing a continued interest in lineage of Saul long after his death.

JEHOADDAH (Jĕ hō′ ăd dah) Modern translations' spelling of Jehoadah. See *Jehoadah.*

JEHOADDAN (Jē hō ăd′ dan) Personal name meaning, "Yahweh is bliss." Mother of king Amaziah of Judah (2 Kings 14:2).

JEHOADDIN (Jē hō ăd′ dīn) Variant spelling of Jehoaddan in written Hebrew text of 2 Kings 14:2, where early Hebrew scribal note has Jehoaddan in agreement with 2 Chronicles 25:1. See *Jehoaddan.*

JEHOAHAZ (Jĕ hō ȧ hăz) Personal name meaning, "Yahweh grasps hold." Two kings of Judah and one king of Israel bore this name. *1.* In 2 Chronicles 21:17, the son and successor of Jehoram as king of Judah (841 B.C.). He is more frequently referred to as Ahaziah. *2.* In 2 Kings

J

10:35, the son and successor of Jehu as king of Israel (814–798 B.C.). His reign is summarized in 2 Kings 13. Although 2 Kings 13:1 states that he reigned for seventeen years, a comparison of verse 1 with verse 10 seems to point to a reign of fourteen years or a coregency with his son for about three years. *3.* In 2 Kings 23:30, the son and successor of Josiah as king of Judah (609 B.C.). He is also known as Shallum.

See *Israel; Chronology of the Biblical Period.*

JEHOASH (Jẻ hō' ăsh) Personal name meaning, "Yahweh gave." Variant spelling of Joash. See *Joash.*

JEHOHANAN (Jē hō' hā năn) Personal name meaning, "Yahweh is gracious." *1.* A priest in whose Temple quarters Ezra refreshed himself and mourned for the sin of the people in taking foreign wives (Ezra 10:6). This Jehohanan is sometimes equated with the high priest of Nehemiah 12:22–23 who is considered then to be a grandson of the high priest Eliashib and also to be the high priest mentioned in the Elephantine Papyri as serving about 411 B.C. Such evidence is then used to date the ministry of Ezra to about 398 B.C. rather than being in the time of Nehemiah. See *Ezra.* The relationships between the priestly Eliashibs and Jehohanans of Scripture are too unclear to make dating decisions on them. This Jehohanan may have been related to the Eliashib of Nehemiah 13:4 who was not a high priest but was closely connected to Temple chambers. *2.* A layman with a foreign wife under Ezra (Ezra 10:28). *3.* Son of Tobiah, who opposed Nehemiah's work in Jerusalem (Neh. 6:18). Jehohanan's marriage to a prominent Jerusalem family gave Tobiah an information system concerning Jerusalem happenings. See *Meshullam; Tobiah.*
4. Head of a priestly family about 450 B.C. (Neh. 12:13). *5.* Priest who helped Nehemiah celebrate completion of Jerusalem wall (Neh. 12:42). *6.* A Levite and gatekeeper (1 Chron. 26:3). *7.* A military commander under King Jehoshaphat of Judah (2 Chron. 17:15). *8.* Father of a military commander under Jehoiada, the high priest, in the assassination of Queen Athaliah and the installation of Joash as king of Judah about 835 B.C. *9.* Father of military captain under King Pekah of Israel (2 Chron. 28:12).

JEHOIACHIN (Jẻ hoî' ȧ chin) Personal name meaning, "Yahweh establishes." In 2 Kings 24:6, the son and successor of Jehoiakim as king of Judah. He was eighteen years old when he came to the throne late in 598 B.C., and he reigned for three months in Jerusalem before being taken into captivity by Nebuchadrezzar of Babylon. The prominence in the account of his reign of his mother Nehushta suggests that she may have wielded considerable influence during the time

that her son was in office. Jehoiachin evidently was a throne name taken at the time of accession to the kingship. Jehoiachin's original name seems to have been Jeconiah or Coniah. He retained the title "king of Judah" even in Exile, but he never returned to Judah to exercise rule there. Nevertheless, he was ultimately released from prison by Evil-merodach of Babylon and accorded some honor in the land of his captivity (2 Kings 25:27–30). See *Israel; Chronology of the Biblical Period.*

JEHOIADA (Jẻ hoî' ȧ dȧ) Personal name meaning, "Yahweh knows" or "Yahweh concerns Himself for." *1.* Priest who led the coup in which Queen Athaliah, who had usurped the throne of Judah, was slain and Joash (Jehoash), the legitimate heir to the monarchy, was enthroned (2 Kings 11:4). At the time, Joash was a child of seven, and Jehoiada evidently acted as regent for a number of years. Jehoiada's role was positive and beneficial; he influenced the young king to restore the Temple. The death of Jehoiada marked a precipitous decline in the king's goodness and faithfulness to the Lord (2 Chron. 22—24). See *Joash; Athaliah; Priests and Levites.* *2.* Father of Benaiah, David's military leader (2 Sam. 8:18) apparently from Kabzeel (2 Sam. 23:20). This Jehoiada was apparently a Levite and military leader for David at Hebron (2 Chron. 12:27). *3.* Leading priest in the time of Jeremiah preceding Zephaniah (Jer. 29:25–26).

JEHOIAKIM (Jẻ hoî' ȧ kĭm) Personal name meaning, "Yahweh has caused to stand." Son of Josiah who succeeded Jehoahaz as king of Judah (609–597). Jehoiakim was a throne name given to him by Pharaoh Neco of Egypt, who deposed his brother Jehoahaz. His original name had been Eliakim (2 Kings 23:34). He and his predecessor on the throne were brothers, sons of Josiah. He reigned for eleven years. At the beginning of his reign, Judah was subject to Egypt. Probably in 605 B.C., however, Babylon defeated Egypt. Jehoiakim, who apparently had been content to be a vassal of Egypt, transferred his allegiance to Babylon, but rebelled after three years. At his death he was succeeded by his son Jehoiachin. See *Israel; Chronology of Biblical Period.*

JEHOIARIB (Jẻ hoî' ȧ rĭb) Personal name meaning, "Yahweh creates justice." *1.* Priest who was one of first settlers to return to Jerusalem from Babylonian Exile about 538 B.C. (1 Chron. 9:10; compare Neh. 12:6). *2.* Head of first course or division of priests (1 Chron. 24:7; compare Neh. 12:19). This listing follows Hebrew text. English translations are not always consistent in transliterating this name and its shortened form Joiarib. See *Joiarib.*

JEHONADAB (Jẻ hŏn' ȧ dăb) Personal name

meaning, "Yahweh incites" or "Yahweh offers Himself freely." Son of Rechab who supported Jehu in the latter's bloody purge of the house of Ahab (2 Kings 10:15). He was representative of a group of austere ultraconservatives known as the Rechabites. Jeremiah 35 relates a meeting between the prophet and Rechabites, who cited the teaching of their ancestor Jehonadab (who in Jeremiah is called Jonadab). In the context of that meeting, some of the precepts of the Rechabites are articulated. They are reminiscent of the regulations that governed the Nazirites. The Hebrew word *rechab* means "chariot," so some scholars think Jehonadab belonged to Israel's chariot forces. See *Rechabites; Jehu.*

JEHONATHAN (Jè hŏn' å than) Personal name meaning, "Yahweh gave." *1.* Longer form of Jonathan often used in Hebrew text for Jonathan as in 1 Samuel 14:6,8. *2.* Son of Abiathar, the priest (2 Sam. 15:27,36; 17:17,20). He helped King David learn Absalom's plans when Absalom drove his father from Jerusalem. *3.* King David's nephew who slew a giant from Gath (2 Sam. 21:22). *4.* Uncle of King David who served as royal counselor and scribe (1 Chron. 27:32). *5.* Military leader under David (2 Sam. 23:32). *6.* Supervisor of royal storehouses under David (1 Chron. 27:25). *7.* Scribe whose house King Zedekiah transformed into prison where he jailed Jeremiah (Jer. 37:15), a place Jeremiah did not like (v. 20; 38:26). *8.* Levite King Jehoshaphat sent to teach God's law in the cities of Judah (2 Chron. 17:8). *9.* Head of a priestly family about 450 B.C. (Neh. 12:18). *10.* Founder of priesthood at worship place in Dan (Judg. 18:30). Earliest Hebrew scribes noted that Jonathan was a descendant of Moses, but the present Hebrew text says Manasseh.

The Hebrew text is at times inconsistent in using the longer or shorter form of the name, and modern translators are as equally inconsistent. This article follows the Hebrew text. See *Jonathan.*

JEHORAM (Jè hō' ram) Personal name meaning, "Yahweh is exalted." Alternate form of Joram. See *Joram.*

JEHOSHABEATH (Jē hō shǎ' bè äth) Variant form of Jehosheba. See *Jehosheba.*

JEHOSHAPHAT (Jè hŏsh' å phăt) Personal name meaning, "Yahweh judged" or "Yahweh established the right." *1.* Son and successor of Asa as king of Judah (1 Kings 15:24). He occupied the throne for twenty-five years (873–848 B.C.). The biblical record of his reign is contained in the final chapters of 1 Kings and in 2 Chronicles 17–20. He was an able ruler and a faithful worshiper of Yahweh (1 Kings 22:43). Nevertheless, he did one thing that ultimately proved to be disastrous: he made an alliance with Ahab, king of Israel. The

immediate result was beneficial to both kingdoms. Years of conflict between them came to an end, and both kingdoms were strengthened. But, the alliance involved a marriage between Jehoshaphat's son Jehoram and Ahab's daughter Athaliah. Athaliah's influence in Judah finally proved to be horrific. See *Athaliah; Israel; Chronology of Biblical Period; Micaiah.*
2. Father of Jehu (2 Kings 9:2,14). *3.* An official at David's court (2 Sam. 8:16), called the "recorder" or "secretary of state" (REB). The Hebrew term's root meaning is "remember." Some Bible students compare the office to the Egyptian court herald who reported events to the king and made public announcements. Others think the office maintained public records, while others speak of a foreign minister. As with many Hebrew offices, certainty is not possible. Jehoshaphat retained the office under Solomon (1 Kings 4:3). *4.* Solomon's official in tribal territory of Issachar in charge of providing provisions for the royal court one month a year (1 Kings 4:17).

JEHOSHAPHAT, VALLEY OF (Jè hŏsh' å phăt) Place name meaning, "valley where Yahweh judged." Place to which the Lord summons the nations for judgment (Joel 3:2). No evidence exists that any valley actually bore this name in Joel's time. Since the fourth century A.D. the Kidron Valley has been known as the Valley of Jehoshaphat; but there is no reason for believing Joel was referring to the Kidron Valley. The reference in Joel probably is meant to be symbolic. Through Joel, God promised all nations will ultimately be called to God's place of judgment. See *Joel.*

JEHOSHEBA (Jè hŏsh' è bà) Personal name meaning, "Yahweh is fullness or fortune." Sister of King Ahaziah who, after his death, took young Joash and protected him from Queen Athaliah so Athaliah could not have him killed as she did the other royal children (2 Kings 11:2). Her name is spelled Jehoshabeath in 2 Chronicles 22:11.

JEHOSHUA (Jè hŏsh' ū à) Variant KJV spelling for Joshua in Numbers 13:16. See *Joshua.*

JEHOVAH (Jē hō' vah) English transliteration of Hebrew text's current reading of divine name Yahweh. Hebrew text, however, represents scribe's efforts to prevent people from pronouncing the divine name by combining consonants of Yahweh and vowels of Hebrew word *adonai* ("Lord") so readers would pronounce *adonai* rather than risk blasphemy by improperly pronouncing divine name. See *God; Lord; Yahweh.*

JEHOVAH-JIREH (Jĕ hō' vah-jī rĕh) Place name meaning, "Yahweh will provide" (Gen. 22:14). The name Abraham gave to the place where the Lord provided a sacrifice in place of Isaac. Modern translations translate the place name whereas KJV transliterates it. See *Jehovah.*

JEHOVAH-NISSI (Jĕ hō' vah-nĭs' sī) Transliteration of place name meaning, "Yahweh is my banner." Name Moses gave to the altar he built after defeating the Amalekites (Ex. 17:15). Modern versions translate the name instead of following KJV in transliterating it. See *Jehovah.*

JEHOVAH-SHALOM (Jĕ hō' vah-shä lom) Place name meaning, "Yahweh is peace." Name Gideon gave to the altar he built at Ophrah (Judg. 6:24). Modern versions translate the name, while KJV transliterated it. See *Jehovah.*

JEHOVAH-SHAMMA (Jĕ hō' vah Shăm' ma) Transliteration of a Hebrew name (Ezek. 48:35, margin) meaning "The Lord is there" which is better transliterated YHWH-shammah (NAS margin). See *Yahweh.* The Jerusalem of Ezekiel's vision was known by this name. Compare Isaiah 60:19–20; Rev. 21:3.

JEHOVAH-TSIDKENU (Jĕ hō' vah tsĭd kē' nū) Hebrew name meaning "The Lord [is] our righteousness" (Jer. 23:6; 33:16, margin). See *Yahweh.* The name is applied to a future Davidic king who would lead his people to do what is right and thus bring peace (23:6) and to the restored city of Jerusalem (33:16). The name is possibly a play on the name of Zedekiah ("Righteous [is] the Lord") who reigned from 597 to 587 B.C..

JEHOZABAD (Jĕ hŏz' à băd) Personal name meaning, "Yahweh bestowed." *1.* One of conspirators who killed King Joash of Judah (2 Kings 12:21). *2.* Porter or doorkeeper under King David (1 Chron. 26:4). *3.* Military commander under King Jehoshaphat of Judah about 860 B.C. (2 Chron. 17:18). See *Jozabad.*

JEHOZADAK (Jĕ hŏz' à dăk) Personal name meaning, "Yahweh deals righteously." *1.* High priest at the time Nebuchadnezzar carried Judah into Babylonian Exile about 587 B.C. (1 Chron. 6:14–15). He was the father of Joshua, the high priest who returned from Exile with Zerubbabel about 537 B.C. (Hag. 1:1; Zech. 6:11). An abbreviated Hebrew form Jozadak also appears, and English translations are inconsistent in spelling the name. See *Jozadak; Josedech.*

JEHU (Jĕ hū) Personal name meaning, "Yah is He." Son of Jehoshaphat and king of Israel (841–814 B.C.). He was a commander of the army when Elisha the prophet sent one of the sons of the prophets to Ramoth-gilead to anoint him as king (2 Kings 9:1–10). Jehu embarked on a violent and bloody course that finally led him to the throne. Along the way, he was responsible for the

deaths of Joram, king of Israel; Ahaziah, king of Judah; Jezebel, still powerful former queen of Israel, and some 70 surviving members of the household of Israel's late King Ahab. He used trickery to gather and destroy worshipers of Baal, so that Jehu destroyed Baal out of Israel (2 Kings 10:28). Jehu established a strong dynasty in Israel. He and his descendants held the throne for approximately a century. See *Israel, Chronology of Biblical Period; Elijah.*

2. A prophet who proclaimed God's judgment on King Baasha of Israel (1 Kings 16:1–12). He warned King Jehoshaphat of Judah (2 Chron. 19:2) and recorded the acts of Jehoshaphat in a record to which the Chronicler referred his readers (2 Chron. 20:34).

3. Member of David's army at Ziklag (1 Chron. 12:3). His home was Anathoth, in the tribal territory of David's opponent Saul. *4.* Leader of tribe of Simeon (1 Chron. 4:35).

JEHUBBAH (Jĕ hŭb' bah) Personal name perhaps meaning, "He has hidden." Member of tribe of Asher (1 Chron. 7:34).

JEHUCAL (Jĕ hū' căl) Personal name meaning, "Yahweh proves to be mighty." Messenger King Zedekiah sent to ask Jeremiah to pray for him as he began to rule. Apparently, Zedekiah wanted blessing on his efforts to cooperate with Egypt against Babylon about 587 B.C. (Jer. 37:3). Jucal in 38:1 is probably a shortened form of the same name. See *Jucal.*

JEHUD (Jē' hŭd) Place name meaning, "praise." Town in tribal territory of Dan (Josh. 19:45). It is located at modern Yehud about three miles south of Petah Tikvah and eight miles north of Joppa.

JEHUDI (Jĕ hū' dī) Personal name meaning, "Judean or Jewish." Messenger for Jewish leaders calling Baruch to read Jeremiah's preaching to them and then messenger of the king to get the scroll so the king could read it. Jehudi read the scroll to King Jehoiakim and then cut it up and threw it into the fire about 604 B.C. Still, God preserved His prophetic word (Jer. 36:11–32).

JEHUDIJAH (Jē' hū dī' jah) Personal name or proper adjective meaning, "Jewess or Judean woman." KJV transliteration from Hebrew which modern translations read as adjective, "Judean" or "Jewish." TEV reads, "from the tribe of Judah" (1 Chron. 4:18).

JEHUEL (Jĕ hū ĕl) Personal name meaning, "God proves Himself active and alive." Written Hebrew text of 2 Chronicles 29:14 followed by NRSV, TEV. Other translations read Jehiel, following early Hebrew scribes. Levite who helped cleanse the Temple under Hezekiah.

JEHUSH (Jē′ hŭsh) Variant spelling of Jeush. See *Jeush.*

JEIEL (Jē ī′ ĕl) Personal name possibly meaning, "God is strong" or "God heals." The early Hebrew scribes often used Hebrew vowel points in the text to indicate the name should be read as Jeiel where the written text indicated Jeuel (1 Chron. 9:35; 11:44; 2 Chron. 26:11; 29:13). The early translations point to similar early confusion at 1 Chronicles 9:5. This article will deal with both Jeiel and Jeuel, since all occurrences of Jeuel show early textual evidence of being read Jeiel. *1.* Leader in the tribe of Reuben (1 Chron. 5:7). *2.* One of early members of tribe of Judah to return from Babylonian Exile (1 Chron. 9:6). *3.* Leader of the tribe of Benjamin as they settled in Gibeon. He may have married a foreign woman (1 Chron. 9:35; compare 8:29). See *Maachah. 4.* Leader in David's army (1 Chron. 11:44). *5.* A Levite and porter or gatekeeper under David (1 Chron. 15:18). *6.* A Levite and harp player under David (1 Chron. 15:21). *7.* A Levite who served as worship leader at the ark of the covenant under David (1 Chron. 16:5). The Hebrew text includes two Jeiels in this verse, and interpreters since the earliest translations have changed one or the other to a slightly different spelling. *8.* Ancestor of Levite who prophesied under Jehoshaphat (2 Chron. 20:14). *9.* Royal scribe or secretary under King Uzziah (792–740 B.C.). He maintained the numbers of military personnel (2 Chron. 26:11). *10.* Levite who helped Hezekiah purify the Temple (2 Chron. 29:13). *11.* Officer among the Levites who provided them offerings to sacrifice at the Passover under Josiah about 622 B.C. (2 Chron. 35:9). *12.* Man who went with Ezra from Babylon to Judah about 458 B.C. (Ezra 8:13). *13.* Man condemned for having foreign wife and thus tempting Israel to worship foreign gods under Ezra (Ezra 10:43).

JEKABZEEL (Jė kăb′ zē ĕl) Place name meaning, "God assembled." A city in southern Judah settled by members of the tribe of Judah after the Exile (Neh. 11:25). Jekabzeel was apparently south of the boundary of the Persian province of Judah, possibly at modern khirbet Gharreh or tell Ira. It is probably the same as Kabzeel, originally assigned to the tribe of Judah (Josh. 15:21) about halfway between tell Beersheba and tell Arad. See *Kabzeel.*

JEKAMEAM (Jĕ kă′ mē ăm) Personal name meaning, "the people deliver" or "the Kinsman saves." A priest set aside to work in God's house (1 Chron. 23:19; 24:23).

JEKAMIAH (Jė kȧ mī′ ah) Personal name meaning, "Yah delivers." *1.* Member of clan of Jerahmeel in tribe of Judah (1 Chron. 2:41). *2.* Son of King Jeconiah, also called Jehoiachin, of Judah about 597 B.C. (1 Chron. 3:18).

JEKUTHIEL (Jė kū′ thĭ ĕl) Personal name meaning, "God nourishes." Member of tribe of Judah (1 Chron. 4:18).

JEMIMA (Jĕ mī′ mȧ) or **JEMIMAH** (Jĕ mī′ mah) Personal name meaning, "turtle dove." Job's first daughter after God restored his fortunes (Job 43:14).

JEMUEL (Jė mū′ ĕl) Personal name meaning, "day of God" or "sea of God." Son of Simeon, grandson of Jacob, and head of clan in Israel (Gen. 46:10; Ex. 6:15). Also called Nemuel (Num. 26:12; 1 Chron. 4:24).

JEPHTHAE (Jĕph′ thāē) KJV transliteration of Greek for Jephthah (Heb. 11:32). See *Jephthah.*

JEPHTHAH (Jĕph′ thah) Personal name meaning, "he will open." One of Israel's judges about 1100 B.C. (Judg. 11:1—12:7). A Gileadite, he was driven from his home because he was "the son of an harlot" (Judg. 11:1). He lived and raided in the land of Tob with a band of outlaws, becoming known as a "mighty warrior." When the Ammonites moved against Israel, Jephthah's people asked him to return and lead them. His victory over the Ammonites came about because of a vow he made to offer as a burnt offering the first living thing he saw upon his return from the battle. Although it was his daughter who greeted him, Jephthah did fulfill his vow. Considered as one of Yahweh's "chief" deliverers of his people (1 Sam. 12:11), Jephthah is hailed by the author of Hebrews as a hero of faith (Heb. 11:32).

See *Judges; Ammon; Human Sacrifices.*

Darlene R. Gautsch

JEPHUNNEH (Jė phŭn′ nēh) Personal name meaning, "he will be turned" or "appeased." *1.* Father of Caleb (Num. 13:6). See *Caleb. 2.* In 1 Chronicles 7:38, one of the sons of Jether in tribe of Asher.

JERAH (Jē′ rah) Personal name meaning, "moon" or "month." A descendant of Shem, son of Noah, in the Table of Nations (Gen. 10:26). The moon was the chief god in South Arabia. Since the surrounding names in the list represent Arabian tribes, this probably indicates the relationship of Semitic tribes in Arabia to the Hebrews.

JERAHMEEL (Jė răh′ mē ĕl) Personal name meaning, "God shows compassion." *1.* Son of Hezron (1 Chron. 2:9), brother of Caleb (1 Chron. 2:42), and original clan ancestor of Jerahmeelites (1 Sam. 27:10). See *Jerahmeelites. 2.* Son of Hammelech (Hebrew, "the king" and so translated by modern versions), who was one of a group whom King Jehoiakim sent to arrest Baruch and Jeremiah (Jer. 36:26); but the Lord showed He has more power than human rulers by hiding His faithful servants from the king. *3.* A Levite in time of David (1 Chron. 24:29).

JERAHMEELITE (Jĕ răh′ mē ĕl īte) Member of clan of Jerahmeel which apparently lived south of Beersheba in the Negeb. While dwelling with the Philistines, David told them he was fighting in the territory of the Jerahmeelites (1 Sam. 27:10), making Achish, the Philistine king, think he was fighting against parts of Judah, while he actually fought the other groups in the south who opposed Judah—Geshurites, Gezrites, Amalekites (1 Sam. 27:8). He divided the spoils of war with the Jerahmeelites (1 Sam. 30:29).

JERASH (Jer ash) Modern Arabic name of Gerasa. See *Gerasa.*

The excavations of Gerasa showing the Corinthian columns flanking the streets and temples of the city.

JERBOA (Jĕr′ bō à) Any of several species of leaping rodents having long hind legs and long tails of the family *Dipodidae.* The REB includes the jerboa among the unclean animals of Leviticus 11:29.

JERED (Jē′ rĕd) Alternate spelling used by English translations for Jared. See *Jared.*

JEREMAI (Jĕr′ ĕ mâi) Personal name, abbreviated form of Jeremoth or Jeremiah. Israelite condemned for foreign wife which Ezra said would lead Israel to worship foreign gods (Ezra 10:33).

JEREMIAH (Jĕr ĕ mī′ ah) Personal name meaning, "may Yahweh lift up," "throw," or "found." *1.* The head of a clan of the tribe of Manasseh in East Jordan (1 Chron. 5:24). *2.* Three soldiers of David's army at Ziklag (1 Chron. 12:4,10,13). *3.* The father-in-law of King Josiah of Judah (640–609 B.C.) and grandfather of the Kings Jehoahaz [609 B.C.] (2 Kings 23:31) and Zedekiah (597–586 B.C.) (2 Kings 24:18; Jer. 52:1). *4.* A representative of the sect of the Rechabites (Jer. 35:3). *5.* Three priests or heads of priestly families in the times of Zerubbabel about 537 B.C. (Neh. 12:1,12) and Nehemiah about 455 B.C. (Neh.

Sunset at Jerash (ancient Gerasa).

10:2; 12:34).

Other persons by the name of Jeremiah are referred to in Hebrew inscriptions from Lachish and Arad about 700 B.C. and in a number of ancient Jewish seals. The Bible has a short form of the name seventeen times and a long form 121 times. Both forms are applied to the prophet. Inscriptions use the longer form.

6. **Jeremiah, the prophet** The Bible tells us more about personal experiences of Jeremiah than of any other prophet. We read that his father's name was Hilkiah, a priest from Anathoth (Jer. 1:1). He was called to be a prophet in the thirteenth year of King Josiah (627/6 B.C.) (Jer. 1:2). He was active under the Kings Jehoahaz-Shallum (609 B.C.) (22:11), Jehoiakim (609–587 B.C.) (Jer. 1:3; 22:18; 26:1; 35:1; 36:1, 9), Jehoiachin/Jeconiah/Coniah (597 B.C.) (22:24; 24:1; 27:20; 28:3; 29:2; 37:1), and Zedekiah (597–586 B.C.) (1:3; 21:1; 27:1–12; 28:1; 32:1; 34:2; 37—38; 39:4; 52:7). When Jerusalem was destroyed by the Babylonians in 587 B.C., Jeremiah moved to Mizpah, the capital of Gedaliah, the newly appointed Jewish governor of the Babylonian province of Judah (40:5). When Gedaliah was assassinated (41:1), Jeremiah was deported to Egypt against his will by Jewish officers who had survived the catastrophes (42:1—43:7). In Egypt he continued to preach oracles against the Egyptians (43:8–13) and against his compatriots (44:1–30).

Jeremiah is depicted as living in constant friction with the authorities of his people, *religious* (priests 20:1–6; prophets 28:1; or both 26:1), *political* (kings ch. 21—22; 36—38), or *all* of them together (1:18–19; 2:26; 8:1), including Jewish leaders after the Babylonian invasion (42:1—43:13). Still his preaching emphasized a high respect for prophets whose warning words could have saved the people if they had listened (7:25; 26:4; 29:17–19; 35:13). He trusted in the promise of ideal future kings (23:5; 33:14–17). He recommended national surrender to the rule of the Babylonian Empire and called Nebuchadnezzar, Babylon's emperor and Judah's most hated enemy, the "servant of the Lord" (25:9; 27:6). He even incited his compatriots to desert to the enemy (21:8). He was accused of treason and convicted (37:11; 38:1–6), and yet the most aggressive oracles against Babylon are attributed to him (50—51). Enemies challenged his prophetic honesty and the inspiration of his message (43:1–3; 28:1; 29:24), and yet kings and nobles sought his advice (21:1; 37:3; 38:14; 42:1).

He constantly proclaimed God's judgment upon Judah and Jerusalem, and yet he was also a prophet of hope, proclaiming oracles of salvation, conditioned (3:22—4:2) or unconditioned (30—31; 32:36; 33:6; 34:4). God forbade him to intercede for his people (7:16; 11:14; 14:11; compare 15:1); yet he interceded (14:7–9,19–22). God ordered him to live without marriage and family (16:2). He had to stay away from the company of merrymakers (15:17) and from houses of feasting (16:8). He complained to and argued with God (12:1–17), complaining about the misery of his office (20:7–18). At the same time he sang hymns of praise to his God (20:13).

Jeremiah's call came in the thirteenth year of King Josiah, about 627/6 B.C. (1:2; 25:3; compare 36:2). Josiah remains however, the only Jewish king contemporary with Jeremiah to and about whom no word is spoken in the whole book. No concrete reference appears to any of the dramatic changes of national liberation and religious reformation within the last eighteen years of Josiah's reign (2 Kings 22:1—23:30). The words of the call narrative: "Before I formed you in the womb I knew you, . . . I appointed you as a prophet to the nations" (1:5 NIV), may suggest that the date of Jeremiah's call and birth is one and the same. In this case his prophetic activity must have begun many years later, but again with uncertain date. **The Book of Jeremiah** *1. Origin* This second longest book of the Bible, next to the Psalms, is the only one of the Old Testament that tells us some details of its origin. According to Jeremiah 36:1–26, Baruch had written a first version at the dictation of Jeremiah. The scroll was read first in public, and then again for the state officials and for the king. King Jehoiakim burnt it piece by piece. Jeremiah therefore dictated a second and enlarged

edition of the first book to Baruch (Jer. 36:32). Additional references to Jeremiah's own writing activity (Jer. 30:2; 51:60; compare 25:13) forbids the identification of the scroll of Jeremiah 36:32 with the present form of the biblical book.

2. Structure and Content The book may be subdivided into the following main sections:
I. Call narrative and Visions (1:1–19)
II. Prophecies and Visions (2:1—25:14)
III. Stories about Jeremiah (26:1—45:5)
IV. Oracles Against Foreign nations (25:15–38; 46:1—51:64)
V. Historical epilogue (52:1–34)
VI. Oracles on the restoration of Israel (30:1—31:40)

This structure is not based on chronology as seen above. Nor is it based on form. The so-called confessions of Jeremiah (11:18–23; 12:1–6; 15:10–21; 17:14–18; 18:19–23; 20:7–13,14–18) are scattered through chapters 11—20. Oracles of hope (chs. 30—31) interrupt the stories about Jeremiah (chs. 26—45). Words against kings (21:11—22:30) and against prophets (23:9–40) appear to be independent collections. The complex nature of the structure is further complicated by evidence from the earliest Greek translation. There the oracles against foreign nations are in a different order and appear immediately after 25:13 rather than at 46:1. This and other evidence suggests a long and complicated process of collection of the Jeremiah materials into a book. Traditional scholarly theories have tried to attribute poetic oracles to Jeremiah, stories about the prophet to Baruch, and prose sermons to a later editor who used the Book of Jeremiah to exemplify and teach the theology of the Book of Deuteronomy. Such theories are much too simplistic and must be discarded. Aside from the stories of the scroll's destruction, expansion, and recopying (ch. 36), we do not know all the processes through which God led to produce His inspired Book of Jeremiah.

3. Text of the Book The earliest Greek version of Jeremiah, dating back to pre-Christian centuries, is more than 12.5% shorter than the Hebrew text. Only a few longer sections are missing (33:14–26; 39:4–13). The Greek text rather uses less titles and epithets, and single words and verses are missing throughout the book. More than 2700 words of the Hebrew text do not have Greek equivalents. Fragments of Hebrew manuscripts from Qumran show that a longer and a shorter Hebrew text existed side-by-side in the time of Jesus. This confirms that the development of the Book of Jeremiah continued for centuries. Growing agreement among Jeremiah Bible students suggests that the shorter text represents an older stage of development.

4. The Message Theologically, the Book of Jeremiah stimulates the search for the will of God in moments when all the institutions and religious representatives normally in charge of administrat-

J

ing His will are discredited. Neither the Davidic monarchy (Jer. 21:1—22:30), nor prophets and priests (Jer. 23:9—40), nor the cultic institutions of the Temple (Jer. 7:1—34; 26:1—9) could help the people to prevent impending calamities; nor could they detect that inconspicuous apostasy that mixes up the little aims of personal egoism (Jer. 2:29—37; 7:21—26; 28:1—17) with God's commission (Jer. 4:3). God's justice and righteousness cannot be usurped by His People. He can be a stumbling block even for His prophet (Jer. 12:1—6; 20:7—12). Execution of judgment and destruction is not God's delight. God himself suffers pain because of the alienation between Himself and His people (2:1—37). Better than the prophet was able to admit, the apostate members of God's people remembered a correct notion of the nature of God. He continued to be their Father, and His anger would not last forever (3:4,12—13). Conversion is possible (3:14,22; 4:1—2), but this is no consolation for the apostate generation. Contrary to the expectations of the religious and political authorities, Judah and Jerusalem would meet the cruel catastrophe. This was not God's last word. His faithfulness prevails and creates new hope where all hope is lost (chs. 30—33).

I. God Calls His Spokesman (1:1—19).
II. God's Spokesman Warns His People (2:1—6:30).
   A. God brings a lawsuit against His unfaithful people (2:1—37).
   B. God pleads with His faithless people to return (3:1—4:4).
   C. God threatens judgment through invasion (4:5—6:30).
III. Prophetic Theology Opposes Traditional Theology (7:1—11:17).
   A. A place of worship cannot save (7:1—15).
   B. A prophet cannot fulfill his traditional role for a people who foresake God (7:16—20).
   C. Obedience, not ritual, is the most important (7:21—28).
   D. False worship will have its terrible reward (7:29—8:13).
   E. Lamentation, not praise, is the appropriate worship in face of desolation and deceitfulness (8:14—9:22).
   F. Worship of images is folly in light of God's creative power (9:23—10:16).
   G. God threatens judgment through exile (10:17—25).
   H. A covenant brings disaster on God's people (11:1—17).
IV. Struggle with God Defines the Prophetic Role (11:18—20:18).
   A. Prophesying can be life-threatening (11:18—12:6).
   B. God laments His errant people (12:7—17).

   C. God's purpose is to punish pride and promote humility (13:1—27).
   D. God can reject and prohibit prayers for forgiveness (14:1—15:9).
   E. God's spokesman makes personal sacrifices because of God's calling (15:10—16:21).
   F. Trust in humans rather than God leads to destruction (17:1—11).
   G. God's spokesman must keep listening to God and preaching (17:12—27).
   H. God's spokesman centers his message on God's freedom, not on human expectations (18:1—23).
   I. God's message leads to persecution of His spokesman (19:1—20:6).
   J. God's spokesman struggles with God over the hostility of the people (20:7—18).
V. God's Spokesman Confronts Unfaithful Leaders (21:1—29:32).
   A. God's spokesman calls for sorrow and judgment based on the king's injustice (21:1—22:30).
   B. God's spokesman bases hope on future righteous leaders (23:1—8).
   C. God's spokesman must condemn those who preach lies (23:9—40).
   D. God's word of hope is based in faithful, suffering people, not in institutions (24:1—25:38).
   E. Prophetic hope lies in repentance, not in the Temple (26:1—6).
   F. A prophetic precedent protects the endangered prophet (26:7—24).
   G. God can condemn faithless leaders to serve enemies to fulfill His purpose (27:1—22).
   H. God's true prophet overcomes false prophecy through God's divine Word (28:1—17).
   I. Hope rests in dependence on God, not on popular prophecies or political power (29:1—32).
VI. God Promises Restoration (30:1—33:26).
   A. Restoration is based on God's promises in His preserved Word (30:1—24).
   B. Restoration is based on God's faithfulness (31:1—14).
   C. Restoration is based on God's mercy (31:15—26).
   D. Restoration is based on God's promises to establish a new covenant with His people (31:27—40).
   E. God's spokesman demonstrates his trust by a purchase of land (32:1—44).
   F. Restoration is based on God's promises to restore the nation and David's dynasty (33:1—26).
VII. God Protects His Spokesman (34:1—40:6).
   A. God promises punishment upon the

privileged for their treachery to their slaves (34:1–22).

B. God commends the Rechabites for their faithfulness (35:1–19).

C. God protects His servants and His Word from a wicked ruler (36:1–32).

D. God protects His servant from a weak and foolish ruler (37:1—38:28).

E. Prophetic preaching proves true (39:1–10).

F. Even foreign leaders acknowledge prophetic authority (39:11–14).

G. God protects His servant during a national crisis (39:15—40:6).

VIII. God's Spokesman Warns Those Who Continue in Unfaithfulness (40:7—45:5).

A. Political intrigue offers no basis for hope (40:7—41:18).

B. Disobeying God's Word brings disaster, not hope, for the remnant (42:1—43:13).

C. Disobeying God's law of loyal worship brings disaster, not hope, for the remnant (44:1–14).

D. The people answer God's spokesman with continued defiance (44:15–19).

E. Jeremiah promises punishment for the people (44:20–30).

F. God promises His faithful servant his life despite desperate changes (45:1–5).

IX. God's Spokesman Warns the Nations (46:1—51:64).

A. God promises judgment upon Judah's pagan neighbors (46:1—49:39).

B. God promises perpetual desolation for the destroyer of His people (50:1—51:64).

X. Unfaithfulness Causes Destruction for God's People (52:1–34).

Hans Mallau

JEREMIAS (Jĕr ė mī′ ás) KJV transliteration of Greek for Jeremiah (Matt. 16:14). See *Jeremiah.*

JEREMOTH (Jĕr′ ė mŏth) Personal name meaning, "swellings." *1.* Member of tribe of Benjamin (1 Chron. 8:14), perhaps to be identified with Jeroham (8:27). *2.* Two Israelites with foreign wives condemned by Ezra (Ezra 10:26–27). *3.* Name written in Hebrew text of Israelite with foreign wife under Ezra (Ezra 10:29). Early Hebrew scribes and earliest translators read "and Ramoth." *4.* Descendant of Benjamin and leader in that tribe (1 Chron. 7:8). *5.* Priest in days of David and Solomon (1 Chron. 23:23; spelled Jerimoth in 24:30). *6.* Temple musician (1 Chron. 25:4, Jerimoth), possibly the same person as head of fifteenth division of priests (25:22). See *Jerimoth.*

JEREMY (Jĕr′ ě mȳ) KJV transliteration for Greek

spelling of Jeremiah, the prophet (Matt. 2:17; 27:9). See *Jeremiah.*

JERIAH (Jė rī′ ah) Personal name meaning, "Yahweh saw." Priest under David and Solomon (1 Chron. 23:19; 24:23).

JERIBAI (Jĕr ĭ′ bā ī) Personal name meaning, "he defended my case." Military leader under David (1 Chron. 11:46).

JERICHO (Jē rĭ′ chō) Place name meaning "moon." Apparently the oldest city in the world and the first city Israel conquered under Joshua. Jericho is situated in the lower Jordan Valley, which, according to Genesis 13:10, "was well watered everywhere like the garden of the Lord." The Old Testament town lies beneath tell es-Sultan near one of Palestine's strongest springs. New Testament Jericho, founded by Herod the Great, was about one and one half miles southward in the magnificent wadi Qelt. The spring, ain es-Sultan, issues some 30,000 cubit feet of water daily which falls about 160 feet in the first mile of its course down many channels to the Jordan River six miles away, irrigating about 2,500 acres.

In the foreground the tel of New Testament Jericho with the tel of Old Testament Jericho behind.

The combination of rich alluvial soil, the perennial spring, and constant sunshine made Jericho an attractive place for settlement. Only about 6.4 inches of rain fall there per year (mostly between November and February), and the average temperature for January is 59° F, while it is 88° F for August. Jericho is about 740 feet below sea level (accounting for its warm climate) but well above the Dead Sea eight miles southward which at 1,300 feet below sea level marks the earth's lowest point. Thus Jericho could be called "city of palms" (Deut. 34:3; Judg. 1:16; 3:3; 2 Chron. 28:15) and has plenty of palm trees today.

Jericho was an oasis situated in a hot plain,

Round Neolithic (New Stone Age) defense (or gate) tower at Old Testament Jericho, from ca. 7000 B.C.

Modern Arab citrus and vegetable vendors in the city of Jericho.

living in its own world with no major settlement in sight, and lying between the two focal points of Jerusalem and Amman in the mountains to the west and east. It is mentioned in the Bible usually in association with some movement from one side of the Jordan to another—the Israelite invasion, when Ehud takes tribute to the Moabite king, when David sends envoys to the king of Ammon, when Elijah and Elisha cross the Jordan, or when Zedekiah attempts to escape the Babylonians.

In New Testament times Jericho was famous for its balm (an aromatic gum known for its medicinal qualities). This along with its being the winter capital made it a wealthy city. When Jesus was

Step-trench cut into the tel of Old Testament Jericho to uncover the many levels of destruction.

hosted by Zacchaeus (Luke 19:1–10), it was probably in one of Jericho's finest houses. Its sycamore trees were quite valuable. Such a city could expect to have its share of beggars, as the Gospels tell us (Matt. 20:29–34; Mark 10:46–52; Luke 18:35–43).

The archaeology of Jericho is closely associated with the name of Kathleen Kenyon, an Oxford

Inverted Corinthian column capital as found in situ in New Testament Jericho.

University scholar who excavated there between 1952–1959. The earliest recognizable building on the site dates apparently (based on radiocarbon dating) from about 9250 B.C., a time marking the change from the Paleolithic to the Mesolithic period in Palestine. By 8,000 B.C. a walled town (the world's earliest) of about ten acres had been built. About 6000 B.C. pottery appeared in Jericho. About 4000 B.C. a period of abandonment

View from atop the tel of New Testament Jericho showing the lush greenery of the oasis.

began, but by 3300 B.C. Jericho was coming into her own again into what Kenyon calls the "Proto-Urban" age. Jericho came to have solid defense ramparts and walls. From about 2200–2000 B.C. the mound of Jericho was a campsite rather than a town, when some 346 excavated tombs show its occupants to be from various tribal units. From about 1400 to possibly slightly after 1300 B.C. Jericho was a small settlement. The town at Joshua's time was small and may have used some of its

Reconstruction of Herod the Great's Winter Palace at Jericho. Situated at the mouth of the Wadi (dry creek) Kelt along the lower slope of the western ridge of the Jordan valley, the palace had a commanding view of New Testament Jericho and the arid, fertile Jordan river valley.

Reconstruction of New Testament Jericho based on home, shop, and building architecture of the period.

earlier walls for its defenses. Thus more critical scholars underline the conflict between archaeological data and the biblical conquest narrative, while more conservative scholars have recently tried to redate the archaeological evidence or deny that tell es-Sultan is biblical Jericho without giving a satisfactory alternative. See *Archaeology; Conquest; Joshua.* *Karen Joines*

JERIEL (Jĕr' ĭ ĕl) Personal name meaning, "God sees." Member of tribe of Issachar (1 Chron. 7:2).

JERIJAH (Jĕ rī' jah) Personal name meaning, "Yah sees," a short form of Jeriah. Military hero of the Hebronite clan (1 Chron. 26:31), possibly identical with Jeriah. See *Jeriah.*

JERIMOTH (Jĕr' ĭ mŏth) Personal name possibly meaning, "fat belly." The name closely resembles Jeremoth, so that English translations are not consistent in following the Hebrew in spelling. The following represent spellings of the Hebrew text. See *Jeremoth.* *1.* Member of tribe of Benjamin (1 Chron. 7:7). *2.* Warrior of Saul's tribe Benjamin who joined David as he fled from Saul at Ziklag (1 Chron. 12:5). *3.* Levite of the house of Mushi (1 Chron. 24:30; compare 23:23). *4.* Temple musician under David and Solomon (1 Chron. 25:4; compare v. 22). *5.* Leader of tribe of Naphtali under David (1 Chron. 27:19). *6.* Son of David, whose daughter married King Rehoboam (931–913 B.C.), according to 2 Chronicles 11:18. Jerimoth does not appear in any list of David's sons. *7.* An overseer of Temple treasury under Hezekiah (2 Chron. 31:13).

JERIOTH (Jĕr' ĭ ŏth) Personal name meaning, "fearsome." Person related to Caleb, but the grammatical construction of Hebrew makes understanding of exact relationship difficult (1 Chron. 2:18): a second wife (KJV, NIV, NAS, NRSV); daughter (REB, TEV with many commentators).

JEROBOAM (Jĕr ō bō' ăm) Personal name possibly meaning, "he who contends for justice for the people" or "may the people multiply." *1.* First king of the Northern Kingdom Israel about 926–909 B.C. Jeroboam had an interesting rise to power. He managed the laborers Solomon had conscripted for his huge building projects (1 Kings 11:28). During Solomon's reign Ahijah, a prophet from Shiloh, confronted Jeroboam, tore his own coat into twelve pieces, and gave ten of them to Jeroboam (1 Kings 11:29–39). Ahijah interpreted this as God's pledge that Jeroboam would become king over ten of the twelve tribes. Upon Solomon's death, Jeroboam learned that the tribes would assemble at Shechem to make Solomon's son Rehoboam their king. Seizing upon the people's resentment toward Solomon's high-handed policies, Jeroboam led the ten tribes to revolt against the house of David. They then crowned Jeroboam king.

The inspired biblical writers did not consider Jeroboam a good king. Rather he became the example of evil kings in Israel because he built temples in Dan and Bethel with golden calves representing God's presence. What appeared to be good politics diverted people from worshiping at Jerusalem, God's chosen place. All the following northern kings suffered the biblical writers' condemnation because they walked in the ways of Jeroboam, encouraging worship at Dan and Bethel (see for example 1 Kings 15:26,34; 16:19,31). Jeroboam also instituted new worship practices at his temples (1 Kings 12:25–33), intentionally making Israelite worship different from that in Jerusalem, though claiming to worship the same God with the same worship traditions. Prophetic warnings failed to move Jeroboam (1 Kings 13:1—14:20).

2. Powerful king of Israel in the dynasty of Jehu about 793–753 B.C. (2 Kings 14:23–29). He managed to restore prosperity and territory to a weak nation but continued the religious practices of Jeroboam I and thus met condemnation from the biblical writers. Jonah, Amos, and Hosea prophesied during his reign. Jeroboam basically restored the boundaries of David's empire, reaching even into Syria. *M. Stephen Davis*

JEROHAM (Jĕ rō' hăm) Personal name meaning, "he found mercy." *1.* Father of Elkanah and grandfather of Samuel (1 Sam. 1:1; compare 1 Chron. 6:27,34). *2.* Priest after the Exile (Neh. 11:12). *3.* Member of tribe of Benjamin (1 Chron. 8:27, if proper reading is not Jeremoth as in v. 14; see *Jeremoth*). *4.* Father of one of first men to return to Jerusalem after Babylonian Exile (1 Chron. 9:8). *5.* Priest whose son was one of first to return to Jerusalem from Babylonian Exile (1 Chron. 9:12). *6.* Father of two of David's military leaders from Saul's tribe of Benjamin (1 Chron. 12:7). *7.* Father of leader of tribe of Dan under David (1 Chron. 27:22). *8.* Father of captain who helped Jehoiada, the high priest, overthrow Queen Athaliah and install Joash as king about 835 B.C. (2 Chron. 23:1).

JERUBBAAL. (Jĕr ŭb bā' ăl) Personal name meaning, "Baal judges." Another name for Gideon (Judg. 6:32). See *Gideon.*

JERUBBESHETH (Jĕ rŭb' bĕ shĕth) Personal name meaning, "may shame judge" or "shame increases." A deliberate scribal corruption of the name Jerubbaal (2 Sam. 11:21), replacing the name of the Canaanite deity Baal with a form of the Hebrew word for "shame."

JERUEL (Jĕ rū' ĕl) Place name meaning, "foundation of God." Place where Jahaziel, the prophet, predicted King Jehoshaphat and his army would find the Ammonite and Moabite army. The exact location is not known. It was on the rugged descent southeast of Tekoa going to En-Gedi.

JERUSALEM (Jė rū′ så lĕm) Place name meaning, "founded by (god) Shalem" and also known as Beth-Shalem or "House of Shalem." Chief city of Palestine, some 2500 feet above sea level and eighteen miles west of the northern end of the Dead Sea.

The name "Jerusalem" has a long and interesting history. The earliest recorded name of Jerusa-

lem is *Urushalim* and means "foundation of Shalem," a Canaanite god of twilight. The Amarna letters in Palestine refer to Beth-Shalem about 1400 B.C. It is first mentioned in the Bible as Salem (Gen. 14:18). Later the author of Hebrews (7:2) interpreted "Salem" to mean "peace" because of its similarity to *shalom*. Jerusalem is also called Zion, Jebus, Mount Moriah, and the city of David. Sometimes "city of David" refers to the whole city, and sometimes, to the part that David built.

The physical characteristics of Jerusalem include mountains, springs, and valleys. Jerusalem is built on a mountain plateau and is surrounded

The Benjamin Mazar excavations along the south end of the Temple Mount at Jerusalem.

Jerusalem in the Time of Jesus
1. The Temple (Herod's Temple)
2. Women's Court
3. The Soreg
4. The Court of the Gentiles
5. Royal Porch
6. Eastern Gate (the present-day Golden Gate)
7. Antonia Fortress
8. The Double Gate (the Western Huldah Gate)
9. The Triple Gate (the Eastern Huldah Gate)
10. Monumental Herodian Staircase (sections still remain today)
11. The City of David (established by David, the oldest part of the city)
12. Earliest defense wall (destroyed and constructed many times)
13. Herodian outer defense wall around the expanded city

14. Herodian wall separating the Upper City (or affluent district) from the Lower City (or lower economic district)
15. The Second North Wall (possible location)
16. Garden of Gethsemane (the west side of the Mount of Olives)
17. Mount of Olives
18. Kidron Valley
19. Gihon Spring
20. Pool of Siloam
21. Tyropoeon Valley (Lower City)
22. Herodian aqueduct (possible location)
23. Shops and marketplace of Jesus' day
24. Additional shops and marketplace (probably added at a later time)
25. Staircase (Robinson's Arch) leading up from the Lower City

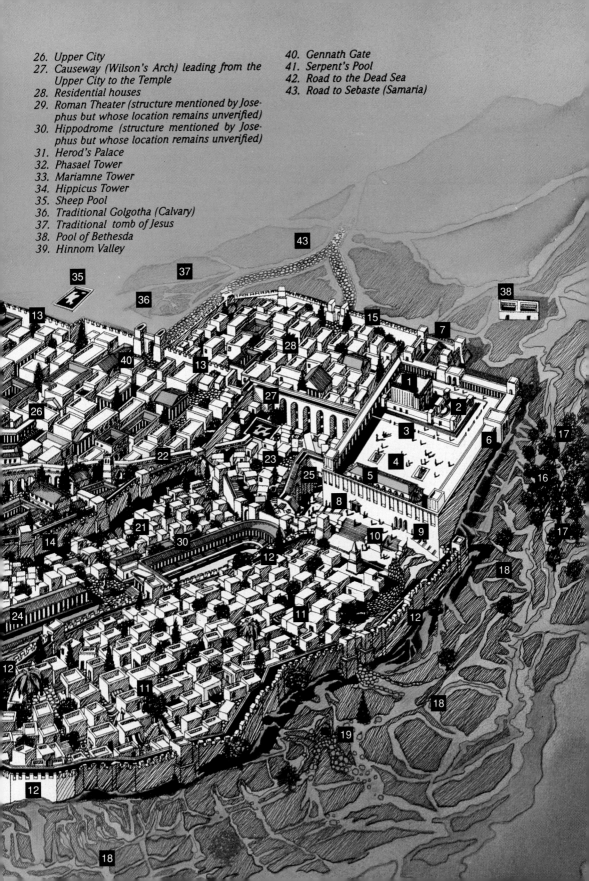

26. Upper City
27. Causeway (Wilson's Arch) leading from the Upper City to the Temple
28. Residential houses
29. Roman Theater (structure mentioned by Josephus but whose location remains unverified)
30. Hippodrome (structure mentioned by Josephus but whose location remains unverified)
31. Herod's Palace
32. Phasael Tower
33. Mariamne Tower
34. Hippicus Tower
35. Sheep Pool
36. Traditional Golgotha (Calvary)
37. Traditional tomb of Jesus
38. Pool of Bethesda
39. Hinnom Valley
40. Gennath Gate
41. Serpent's Pool
42. Road to the Dead Sea
43. Road to Sebaste (Samaria)

by mountains. Its main water source was the Gihon Spring at the foot of the hill of Zion. The plateau is related to three valleys—the Kidron on the east, the Hinnom on west and south, and the Tyropoeon which cuts into the lower part of the city dividing it into two unequal parts. The lower portion of the eastern part was the original fortress, built by prehistoric inhabitants.

All evidence indicates an early existence of the city. Jerusalem seems to have been inhabited by 3500 B.C., judging from pottery remains found on the hill of Zion. Written mention of Jerusalem may occur in the Ebla tablets (about 2500 B.C.), and certainly, in Egyptian sources (Execration Texts about 1900 B.C. and Amarna Letters). Archaeologists have discovered walls, a sanctuary, a royal palace, and a cemetery dated about 1750 B.C. About this time Abraham, returning from a victory, met Melchizedek, the king of Salem, received gifts from him, and blessed him (Gen. 14). Later Abraham was commanded to offer Isaac on one of the mountains in the land of Moriah (Gen. 22:2). Second Chronicles 3:1 understood Moriah to be where Solomon built the temple (2 Chron. 3:1) on the former threshingfloor of Araunah that David had purchased for an altar to God (2 Sam. 24:18). The Muslim mosque, the Dome of the Rock, stands in this area today.

Jerusalem became a Hebrew city under David. After the Hebrews entered Canaan under Joshua, the king of Jerusalem, Adoni-zedek fought them. He was defeated (Josh. 10), but Jerusalem was not

Model of first-century Jerusalem shows the three towers built by Herod to protect his palace.

taken. Later the men of Judah took Jerusalem and torched it (Judg. 1:8; compare 1:21). Apparently the Jebusites reclaimed it, since it had to be conquered by David almost two centuries later. The occupation of the city by the Jebusites accounts for its being referred to as Jebus (Judg. 19:10; 1 Chron. 11:4). See *Jebusites.*

Soon after being crowned king over all the tribes of Israel, David led his private forces in the capture of Jerusalem (2 Sam. 5:1–10) and made it his capital, a happy choice since it lay on the border between the northern and southern tribes. Zion, the name of the original fortress, now became synonymous with the city of David. The moving of the ark (2 Sam. 6) made Jerusalem the religious center of the nation. The city began to gather to itself those sacred associations which have made it so important. Here God made an everlasting covenant with the house of David (2 Sam. 7:16). Here Solomon built the Temple that David had wanted to build. It was understood to be a dwelling place for God (1 Kings 8:13), and the sacred ark, symbolizing His presence, was placed in the holy of holies. Other extensive building projects made Jerusalem a magnificent city.

To the Temple in Jerusalem the tribes came three times a year, so that "every one of them in Zion appeareth before God" (Ps. 84:7). The name "Zion" was often used to emphasize the religious significance of the city. One group of Psalms came to be known as "Psalms of Zion" (Pss. 46; 48; 76; 84; 87; 122; 132). The physical beauty of the city was extolled (Ps. 48), and its glorious buildings and walls were described (Ps. 87). To be a part of the festival processions there (Ps. 68:24–27) was

The Moslem Dome of the Rock mosque built on the site of Solomon's Temple.

a source of great joy (Ps. 149:3). Jerusalem, the dwelling place of both the earthly (Ps. 132) and the divine king (Ps. 5:2; 24:7), was where Israel came to appreciate and celebrate the kingship of God (Pss. 47; 93; 96—99), one of the central ideas of the entire Bible.

Jerusalem was threatened during the period of the divided kingdom. When the kingdom of Israel split at the death of Solomon, Jerusalem continued to be the capital of the Southern Kingdom. Egypt attacked it (1 Kings 14:25–26), as did Syria (2 Kings 12:17), and northern Israel (2 Kings 15:29; Isa. 7:1). Hezekiah (715–686 B.C.) had a 1750 foot tunnel dug out of solid rock to provide water from the Gihon Spring in time of seige (2 Kings 20:20). In 701 B.C. the Assyrian general Sennacherib destroyed most of the cities of Judah and shut up King Hezekiah "like a bird in a cage." The Assyrians would have destroyed Jerusalem had it not been miraculously spared (2 Kings 19:35). This deliverance, coupled with the covenant with the house of David, led some to the mistaken belief that Jerusalem could never be destroyed (Jer. 7:1–15). The true prophets of the Lord knew better. Both Micah (3:12) and Jeremiah (7:14) prophesied the destruction of Jerusalem for her unfaithfulness to God's covenant. The prophets also spoke of Jerusalem's exaltation in the "latter days" (Isa. 2:2–4). They said it would become the center to which all nations would come to learn of the true knowledge of God. This would lead them

to "beat their swords into ploughshares and their spears into pruninghooks." Isaiah 60:19 speaks of the time when the Lord will be for Jerusalem an everlasting light. The walls will be called salvation, and its gates praise. The Lord Himself will reign there (Isa. 24:23).

The Babylonians conquered Jerusalem in 598 B.C. taking 10,000 of the leading people into captivity. A further uprising led to the destruction of the city in 587 B.C. The loss was a painful blow to the exiles, but they kept memory of Zion alive deep in their hearts (Ps. 137:1–6). Actually, the Exile served to enhance the theological significance of Jerusalem. Its value was no longer dependent on its physical splendor. It became a religious symbol for the elect people of God, who centered hopes for the future upon it.

When Cyrus the Persian overran the Babylonians (539 B.C.), he encouraged the Jews to return to Jerusalem and rebuild the Temple (Ezra 1:1–4). The initial enthusiasm lagged, but Haggai and Zechariah finally motivated the people. The Temple was completed in 516 B.C. (Ezra 6:15). The city itself, however, stood unprotected until Nehemiah came to rebuild the walls. Under the influence of Ezra and Nehemiah, Jerusalem again became the living center of the Jewish faith. Worship in the restored Temple became more elaborate. Continued participation in the sacred traditions deepened the people's appreciation for Jerusalem,

The Wailing Wall, for centuries revered by Jews as the only remaining wall of the ancient Temple area.

J

the "city of our God" (Ps. 48:1).

The restoration of Jerusalem spoken of by the preexilic prophets had taken place (Jer. 29:10; 33:7—11), but only in part. The glorious vision of the exaltation of Zion (Mic. 4:1—8) and the transformation of Jerusalem (Ezek. 40—48) had not yet been fulfilled. This vision, along with the belief in the kingship of God and the coming of a Davidic messiah, continued to be cherished in the hearts of the faithful. Prophets like Zechariah painted new images concerning the future of Jerusalem (Zech. 14).

Jerusalem played an important role in apocalyptic circles of the intertestamental period. We read of a preexistent heavenly Jerusalem (Syriac Baruch 4:2) that will descend to earth at the end of the age (2 Esdras 10:27,54; 13:4—6), or, according to another conception, is the place in heaven where the righteous will eventually dwell (Slavonic Enoch 55:2). The new Jerusalem/Zion will be a place of great beauty (Tobit 13:16—17), ruled over by God Himself (Sibylline Oracles 3:787). The focus of the city is the new Temple (Tob. 13:10).

While Jewish writers pointed to future hope, Persians continued to rule Jerusalem until Alexander the Great took over in 333 B.C. The Jews finally won their freedom through the Maccabean Revolt (167—164 B.C.), but after a century of independence Jerusalem and the Jewish nation were annexed to the Roman Empire. See *In-*

A tomb, possibly dating from as early as the first century A.D., in the city of Jerusalem.

tertestamental History and Literature.

Herod the Great remodeled Jerusalem. The various conquests of Jerusalem had caused much damage. After Rome gained control, the client-king Herod the Great (37—4 B.C.) rebuilt the city extensively. This energetic ruler constructed a theater, amphitheater, hippodrome, a new palace, fortified towers, and an aqueduct to bring water from the Bethlehem area. His outstanding building project was the Temple. Doubling the Temple area, Herod constructed a magnificent building of huge white stones, richly ornamented. Here Jews from all the world came for religious festivals, and here Jesus from Nazareth came to bring His message to the leaders of the Jewish nation. See *Temple.*

This Jerusalem in which Jesus walked was de-

The modern city of Jerusalem—looking south through the Kidron Valley from Mount Scopus.

stroyed by the Roman general Titus in A.D. 70 after zealous Jews revolted against Rome. Not one stone of the Temple building remained standing on another, and widespread destruction engulfed the city. A second revolt in A.D. 135 (the Bar-Kochba Rebellion) resulted in Jews being excluded from the city. From that time until the founding of the modern state of Israel in 1948, the major role of Jerusalem in the Hebrew-Christian religion has been one of symbol, hope, and prophecy.

Jerusalem has great theological significance. All four Gospels relate that the central event of the Christian faith—the crucifixion-resurrection of Jesus—took place in Jerusalem. The most recent archaeological investigations indicate that the area now occupied by the Church of the Holy Sepulchre is almost certainly the place where these events occurred. The prophecy of the destruction of Jerusalem (Matt. 24; Mark 13; Luke 21), is mixed with prophecies concerning the coming of the Son of man at the end of the age when forsaken and desolated Jerusalem will welcome the returning Messiah (Matt. 23:39).

Several New Testament writers emphasize Jerusalem. John told us more than any other Gospel writer about Jesus' visits to Jerusalem during His public ministry, but it was Luke who emphasized Jerusalem most. Luke's opening announcement of the birth of John took place in Jerusalem. Jesus visited at age twelve. On the mount of transfiguration He spoke with Moses and Elijah of His departure (exodus) which He was to accomplish at Jerusalem. All of Luke's resurrection appearances took place in or near Jerusalem, and the disciples were instructed to stay there until the Day of Pentecost. Then the Spirit would come upon them and inaugurate the new age, beginning to undo the damage of Babel. Jerusalem is the center of the missionary activity of the church, which must extend to the end of the earth (Acts 1:8).

Paul, though sent out from Antioch, looked to Jerusalem as the center of the earthly church. He kept in contact with the Jerusalem church and brought them a significant offering towards the close of his ministry. He envisioned the "man of sin" who comes before the Day of the Lord as appearing in Jerusalem (2 Thess. 2:3–4). "Out of Zion" would come the deliverer who would enable "all Israel" to be saved after the full number of Gentiles had come in (Rom. 11:25–27). The present Jerusalem, however, still serves as the "mother" of those Jews in bondage to the law as contrasted to the "Jerusalem above" which is the mother of those persons who are set free in Christ (Gal. 4:24–31). The author of Hebrews described the heavenly Jerusalem on Mount Zion as the goal of the Christian pilgrimage (Heb. 11:10; 12:22).

Jerusalem figures in the final vision of Revelation. In Revelation the earthly Jerusalem appears for the last time after the thousand-year reign of Christ when the deceived nations, led by the temporarily loosed Satan, come against the beloved city and are destroyed by fire from heaven (Rev. 20:7–9). Finally, John saw the new Jerusalem descending from heaven to the new earth. This incomparably beautiful city is described in such a way that it is clear that the goal of the whole sweep of biblical revelation (the glory of the nations, the tree of life, a river of life, eternal vision of and communion with God) is fulfilled, and God reigns with His people forever and ever (Rev. 21–22:5). See *Revelation.*   *Joe R. Baskin*

JERUSALEM COUNCIL See *Apostolic Council.*

JERUSHA (Jė rū′ shà) Personal name meaning, "one taken in possession." Mother of Jotham, king of Judah (2 Kings 15:33). She was the daughter of Zadok, possibly of the priestly line. In 2 Chronicles 27:1 her name appears in the form Jerushah. The name of her father suggests that she may have been from a Levitical family.

JERUSHAH (Jė rü′ shàh) Form of Jerusha in 2 Chronicles 27:1, a variant spelling with different final "silent" consonant in Hebrew. See *Jerusha.*

JESAIAH (Jė saî′ ah) Shortened form of Isaiah meaning, "Yah has saved." *1.* Descendant of David in postexilic period (1 Chron. 3:21) and thus part of keeping messianic hope alive in Israel.

JESARELAH (Jĕs à rē′ lah) NIV, NRSV spelling of Jesharelah (1 Chron. 25:14), a variant spelling of Asharelah (25:2). See *Asharelah; Jesharelah.*

JESHAIAH (Jė shaî′ ah) Variant English transliteration of Hebrew name Isaiah meaning, "Yahweh delivered." *1.* Priest who used music to prophesy under David (1 Chron. 25:3). Apparently, they proclaimed God's will to the worshiping congregation. Leader of eighth course or division of priests (25:15). *2.* Member of family of Levites with responsibility for treasury of God's house under David (1 Chron. 26:25).

JESHANAH (Jė shā′ nah) Place name meaning, "old city." City that King Abijah of Judah captured from Jeroboam of Israel about 910 B.C. (2 Chron. 13:19). It was located at modern Burj el-Isane four miles south of Shiloh and eight miles northeast of Mizpah. Some interpreters follow early translations and read Jeshanah in 1 Samuel 7:12.

JESHARELAH (Jĕsh à rē′ lah) KJV, NAS, RSV transliteration of Hebrew name of leader of seventh division of Levites (1 Chron. 25:14). The Hebrew is more precisely transliterated Jesarelah and represents a variant Hebrew spelling or textual change from Asarelah (1 Chron. 25:2). Jesarelah in Hebrew is spelled like Israel with an additional final letter. See *Jesarelah; Asarelah.*

JESHEBEAB (Jĕ shĕ' bĕ ăb) Personal name meaning, "the father remains alive" or "He brings the father back." Head of fourteenth division of priests (1 Chron. 24:13).

JESHER (Jē' shēr) Personal name meaning, "he sets right, establishes justice." Son of Caleb (1 Chron. 2:18).

JESHIMON (Jĕ shī' mŏn) Place name meaning, "desert" or "wilderness." *1.* Wilderness site near where David hid from Saul. It apparently belonged to the Ziphites, who reported David's location to Saul (1 Sam. 23:19; 26:1). It lay somewhere between Hebron and the Dead Sea. *2.* Wilderness site east of the Jordan near Pisgah and Peor used to mark the places Israel passed under Moses on the way to conquer the Promised Land (Num. 21:20; 23:28). It may be another way to refer to the lower Jordan Valley. *3.* The Hebrew word also appears as a common noun meaning desert (Deut. 32:10; Ps. 68:7; 78:40; 106:14; 107:4; Isa. 43:19–20). Some interpreters take all occurrences of the word as the common noun. See also *Beth-jeshimoth; Jeshimoth.*

JESHISHAI (Jĕ shī' shâî) Personal name meaning, "advanced in years." Member of tribe of Gad (1 Chron. 5:14).

JESHOHAIAH (Jĕ shō hâî' ah) Personal name of unknown meaning. Member of tribe Simeon (1 Chron. 4:36).

JESHUA (Jĕ shū' à) Personal name spelled in Hebrew the same as Joshua and meaning, "Yahweh is salvation." *1.* Leader of the ninth course of priests under David (1 Chron. 24:11, sometimes transliterated as Jeshuah). *2.* Priest under Hezekiah (715–686 B.C.) who helped distribute food collected in tithes and offerings to the priests living in the Levitical cities outside Jerusalem (2 Chron. 31:15). *3.* High priest taken into the Exile by King Nebuchadnezzar of Babylon in 586 B.C. He returned to Jerusalem with Zerubbabel about 537 B.C. (Ezra 2:2). Descendants of his family or of *1.* above also returned (Ezra 2:36; compare 2:40). He led in rebuilding the altar and restoring sacrifice in Jerusalem (Ezra 3:2–6). They also began building the Temple but quit when strong opposition arose and appealed to King Artaxerxes (Ezra 3:8—4:24). Later correspondence led King Darius to recover Cyrus' proclamation authorizing the rebuilding of the Temple. This came after Jeshua followed the prophetic preaching of Zechariah and Haggai and renewed efforts to rebuild the Temple (Ezra 5:2—6:15; Hag. 1:1, 12—14; 2:4), finally finishing in

515 B.C. Still, some of his sons married foreign women and had to follow Ezra's teaching and divorce them (Ezra 10:18–19). Zechariah had a vision featuring Jeshua in which God announced the full cleansing of the high priest, preparing him to lead in the atonement rites for the people and pointing to the day when Messiah would come and provide complete and eternal atonement for God's people (Zech. 3). Jeshua was apparently one of the two anointed ones of Zechariah's vision (4:14; compare 6:12–13). *4.* A clan related to the Pahath-moab or governor of Moab, some of whose members returned from Exile with Zerubbabel (Ezra 2:6). *5.* Father of Exer, the Jewish governor of the district of Mizpah under Persian rule (Neh. 3:19). *6.* A Levite who signed Nehemiah's covenant to obey God's law (Neh. 10:9). *7.* A clan of Levites in the postexilic community, probably having some connection with the clan of *1.* *8.* Name for conquest hero Joshua, son of Nun (Neh. 8:17). See *Joshua.* *9.* Village in Judah where some Jews lived after returning from Exile (Neh. 11:26). It may be modern tell es-Sawi, northeast of Beersheba.

JESHUAH (Jĕ shū' ah) KJV alternative for Jeshua at 1 Chronicles 24:11. See *Jeshua; Joshua.*

JESHURUN (Jĕ shū' rŭn) Proper name meaning, "upright" or "straight." Poetic name for Israel (Deut. 32:15; 33:5,26; Isa. 44:2; compare Eccl. 37:25). It may represent a play on Jacob, the original Israel, known for deception. Jeshurun would show Israel had quit deceiving and become upright or straight in actions.

JESIAH (Jĕ sī' ah) Personal name meaning, "Yahweh forgets." Member of Saul's tribe of Benjamin who joined David at Ziklag as David fled before Saul (1 Chron. 12:6). Modern translations read, Isshiah. A shortened form in Hebrew appears at 1 Chronicles 23:20, a Levite; 7:3, leader in tribe of Issachar; 24:21, a Levite; 24:25, another Levite; Ezra 10:31, a man with a foreign wife. See *Ishiah; Isshiah; Ishijah.*

JESIMIEL (Jĕ sĭm' ĭ ĕl) Personal name meaning, "Yahweh places." Member of tribe of Simeon (1 Chron. 4:36).

JESSE (Jĕs' sĕ) Personal name meaning, "man" or "manly." Father of David the king (1 Sam. 16:1). He was a Judahite who lived in Bethlehem, the son of Obed and the grandson of Boaz and Ruth (1 Sam. 16:1; Ruth 4:17). He had eight sons, of whom David was the youngest, and two daughters. He is mentioned in the genealogies of Jesus in the Gospels of Matthew and Luke. See *David.*

JEST An act intended to provoke laughter; an utterance intended as mockery or humor. Thinking Lot was jesting about Sodom's imminent destruction, his sons-in-law remained in the city (Gen. 19:14). The jesters of Psalm 35:16 (NAS) are mockers. Isaiah 57:4 describes idolatry as making God the object of a jest (KJV sport). Ephesians 5:4 characterizes jesting or mocking speech as part of a pagan life-style.

JESUI (Jĕs' ū ī) KJV spelling of descendant of Asher (Num. 26:44), the same as Isui in Genesis 46:17. Modern translations spell both Ishvi. A son of Saul bears the same Hebrew name (1 Sam. 14:49), transliterated into English as Ishui (KJV), Ishvi (NAS, NRSV, NIV), or Ishyo (REB). See *Ishvi.*

JESUITE (Jĕs' ū īte) Member of clan founded by Jesui (Num. 26:44). See *Jesui.*

JESURUN (Jĕ sū' rŭn) KJV variant spelling of Jeshurun in Isaiah 44:2. See *Jeshurun.*

JESUS CHRIST (Jē' sŭs Chrīst) Greek form of Joshua and of title meaning, "Yahweh is salvation" and "the anointed one" or "Messiah." Proper name of the Savior of the world. The title "Christ" gathers all of the Old Testament prophetic hopes and infuses into them the meaning associated with the proper name Jesus, Man of Galilee— Man of sorrows. Jesus is the clearest picture of God the world has ever seen—that is the affirmation of believing hearts. In Jesus Christ are united the vertical of God's revelation and the horizontal of history's meaning. Christians see in this one proper name a conjunction of God and man.

The believers of the New Testament did not first "read" Jesus Christ chronologically. That is, they did not set down to construct a doctrine called Christology that would move from preexistence to *parousia* (final coming). Rather, they were caught up in the historical reality of what God was doing for them and all the world through Jesus Christ. Looking at the different episodes of the Christ event should show the New Testament understanding of Jesus, God's Christ.

Resurrection Jesus' resurrection grasped the early believers. The walk of the risen Christ with those burning hearts en route to Emmaus, the appearance of the risen Christ first to Mary Magdalene, the appearance and commissions of the risen Christ to His disciples—these things which no other experience can duplicate nor any other religious movement validate claimed the Christians' attention in an unforgetable way. People of the first century had seen people die before. None before or since had seen a person bring God's resurrection life to bear on this world's most pressing problem, death. The resurrection of Jesus Christ is the center of the Christian gospel (1 Cor. 15).

The Death of Jesus Christ He who was raised on the first day of the week was the same as the One who had died three days earlier. His was not simply a natural death. It was a ritual murder carried out by the authorities of Rome, engineered by the religious leaders of that day, but made necessary by the sins of all who ever lived. Jesus was delivered up by His own people and put to death by a cruel political regime, but the earliest New Testament communities saw in this tragedy the determinate will of God (Acts 1—12). Paul connected Jesus' death to the sacrificial ideas of the Old Testament and saw in the giving of this life a vicarious act for all humankind. Jesus' death was a major *stumbling block* for Israel. How could God's Christ be "hung on a tree" and fall under the curse of the law (Gal. 3) when He did not deserve it.

Jesus as Doer of God's Mighty Works This One who was raised, the same One who died, had performed the miracles of God's kingdom in our time and space. John testified that in the doing of God's mighty works Jesus was the prophet sent from God (John 6:14). He healed all kinds of persons, a sign of God's ultimate healing. He raised some from the dead, a sign that He would bring God's resurrection life to all who would receive it. He cast out evil spirits as a preview of God's final shutting away of the evil one (Rev. 20). He was Lord over nature, indicating that by His power God was already beginning to create a new heaven and a new earth (Rev. 21:1). The spectacular impact of His mighty works reinforced and called to mind the power of His teachings.

Jesus' Teachings "Never man spake like this man" with such authority (John 7:46; compare Matt. 7:29). His teachings were about "the Father," what He wanted, what He was like, what He would do for His creation. Jesus' teachings required absolute obedience and love for God and the kingdom of God. He dared claim that the kingdom had begun in His ministry but would not be culminated until Christ's final coming. Until that coming, Christians were to live in the world by the ethical injunctions He gave (Matt. 5—7) and in the kind of love He had shown and commanded (John 14—16). To help earthly people understand heavenly things, He spoke in parables. These parables were from realistic, real-life settings. They were about the kingdom of God— what it was like, what was required to live in it, what was the meaning of life according to its teachings, what the kingdom promised. One of the promises of the kingdom was that the King would return and rule in it.

Jesus' Ultimate Coming Just as the first coming of Jesus Christ was according to prophecy, so the final coming of Christ is to be by divine promise and prediction. The earliest Christians expected Christ's coming immediately (1 Thess. 4). This must be the expectation of the churches in every age (Rev. 1—3). It was the same Jesus who ascended who will return (Acts 1). His return heralds the end and brings an end to the struggle of good and evil, the battle between the kingdoms of this world which must become the kingdom of our God and of His Christ (Rev. 11:15). In the meanwhile His followers must work to eat (2 Thess. 3). His followers must go and tell; His followers must unite the hope of eschatology and the life of ethics in a fashion that will share the gospel with all the world (Matt. 28:19–20). The time of His final coming is not a Christian's primary concern (Acts 1:5–6). Natural calamities, man-made tragedies, and great suffering will precede His coming (Matt. 13; Matt. 24—25). All of these will find His people faithful, even as He is to His promise—found faithful even as God was to God's promises in sending this Child of promise to the world.

The Birth of Jesus Christ The Gospels began in the heart of God and in the resurrection faith of the writers, but Matthew and Luke begin with the story of Jesus' birth. His conception was virginal. His advent was announced by angels. His actual birth occurred in a place and time that seemed to be no place and time for a baby to be born. Angels announced. Shepherds heard, came, and wondered. Magi came later to bring gifts. A wrathful and jealous King (Herod) killed many innocent children hoping to find the right one. The "right One" escaped to Egypt. Upon returning, He went to Nazareth, was reared in the home of the man Joseph, was taken to Jerusalem where His knowledge of His Father's business surprised and inconvenienced them all—the doctors and the parents. At birth He seemed destined for death. At baptism He was sealed to be a suffering Messiah. Those were times in which He and the Father were working things out, so that when ministry came Jesus could "work the works of him that sent me, while it is day" (John 9:4). But Bethlehem was not the beginning of the story.

Jesus' Preexistence Eternity began the story. If this one is the Son of God, then He must be tied on to the ancient people of God. He must be in the beginning . . . with God (John 1:1). Preexistence was not the first reflection of the early church about Jesus Christ, nor was it merely an afterthought. The purpose of Jesus' preexistence is to tie Him onto God and to what God had been doing through Israel. Matthew 1 established by His genealogy that Jesus is related to David, is related to Moses, is related to Abraham—one cannot be more integrally related to Israel than that. Luke 3 established by His genealogy that Jesus is vitally related to all humans. Jesus came from Mary; but ultimately He came from God via a lineage that extends back to Adam, who was the direct child of God. Paul spoke of the fully divine Son of God who came down from God, who redeems us, and who returns to God (Eph. 3). This heavenly Christ emptied Himself and became like us for our sake (Phil. 2). God determined, before the foundation of the world, that the redemption of the world would be accomplished through Jesus, the Lord of Glory (Eph. 1). John began a new Genesis with his bold assertion that "in the beginning was the Word, and the Word was with God, and the word was God" (John 1:1). This Word (Greek, *logos*) has become flesh (John 1:14) so that qualified witnesses can see, touch, and hear the revelation of God (1 John 1:1–4). It may have been in this way from resurrection to preexistence that early Christians stitched together, under the guidance of God, the story of Jesus. But His story lay also in His names, His titles, what He was called.

The Names and Titles of Jesus Jesus' own proper name is a Greek version of the Hebrew "Joshua," salvation is from Yahweh. His very name suggests His purpose. "He shall save his people from their sins" (Matt. 1:21). This One is Immanuel, God with us (Isa. 7:14; Matt. 1:23). Mark began his brief Gospel in some manuscripts by introducing Jesus as the Son of God (Mark 1:1). Luke's shepherds knew Him as "a Saviour, which is Christ the Lord" (Luke 2:11). John pulled out all the stops in his melodic introduction of Jesus Christ: the Word who made the world (1:1–3), the Life (1:4), the Light (1:5), the Glory of God (1:14), One full of grace and truth (1:17), the Son who makes the Father known (1:18). Paul addressed Him as "the Lord"—the earliest Christian confession was that Jesus (is) Lord. The lordship of Christ is tied to the reverence for the name of God and is an assessment of Jesus' worth as well as Paul's relationship to Him. Since Christ is Lord (*kurios*), Paul is servant (*doulos*). The Gospels herald the message of the Son of Man, He who was humbled, who suffered, who will come again. Hebrews cast Jesus in the role of priest, God's great and final High Priest, who both makes the sacrifice and is the sacrifice. Thomas, known for his doubting, should also be remembered for faith's greatest application about Christ: "My Lord and my God" (John 20:28). The metaphors of John's Gospel invite us to reflect on Jesus Christ, God's great necessity. John portrays Jesus as the Water of life (4:14); the Bread of life (6:41); the Light (8:12); the Door (10:7); the Good Shepherd (10:11); the Resurrection and the Life (11:25); the Way, the Truth, the Life (14:6).

Summary Christ is the way to God. His way of being in the world was a way of obedience, faithfulness, and service. The earliest Christians saw who He was in what He did. In the great deed of the cross they saw the salvation of the world. The inspired writers offered no physical descriptions of the earthly Jesus. The functional way the New Testament portrays Him is found in the statement that He was a man "who went about doing good" (Acts 10:38). The good that He did came into dramatic conflict with the evil all mankind has done. This conflict saw Him crucified, but a Roman soldier saw in this crucified One (the) Son of God

(Mark 15:39). God did not "suffer thine Holy One to see corruption" (Acts 2:27). With the one shattering new act since creation, God raised Jesus from the dead. See *Christ; Christology.*

JESUS, LIFE AND MINISTRY OF (Jē' ṣŭs) The story of Jesus begins abruptly in the Gospel of Mark when He presented Himself at the Jordan River to the desert prophet John the Baptist as a candidate for baptism. All that is said about His origin is that He came to the river "from Nazareth" (Mark 1:9). "Jesus of Nazareth" was a designation that followed Him to the day of His death (John 19:19).

His Origins Matthew's Gospel demonstrates that although Nazareth was Jesus' home when He came to John for baptism, He was not born there. Rather, He was born (as the Jewish messiah must be) in Bethlehem, the "city of David," as a descendant of David's royal line (Matt. 1:1–17; 2:1–6). This Child born in Bethlehem ended up as an adult in Nazareth, described sarcastically by his enemies as a "Nazarene" (literally, "Nazarite" 2:23). The play on words seems intended to poke fun simultaneously at Jesus' obscure origins and at the stark contrast (in the eyes of many) between His supposed holiness (like the Nazirites of the Old Testament) and His practice of keeping company with sinners, prostitutes, and tax collectors (Mark 2:17). The Gospel of Luke supplies background information on John the Baptist, showing how the families of John and Jesus were related both by kinship and by circumstances (Luke 1:5–80). Luke added that Nazareth was the family home of Jesus' parents all along (Luke 1:26–27). Yet he confirmed Matthew's testimony that the family was of the line of David. Luke introduced the Roman census as the reason for their return to the ancestral city of Bethelehem just before Jesus' birth (Luke 2:1–7). More the biographer than either Mark or Matthew, Luke provided glimpses of Jesus as an eight-day-old infant (2:21–39), a boy of twelve years (2:40–52), and a man of 30 beginning His ministry (3:21–23). Only when this brief biographical sketch was complete did Luke append His genealogy (Luke 3:23–38), which confirms in passing Jesus' Davidic ancestry (Luke 3:31; compare 1:32–33), while emphasizing above all His solidarity with the entire human race in its descent from "Adam, which was the son of God" (Luke 3:38). The reflection on Jesus' baptism in the Gospel of John centers on John the Baptist's acknowledgement that Jesus "is preferred before me: for he was before me" (John 1:30; compare v. 15). This pronouncement allowed the Gospel writer to turn the story of Jesus' origins into a theological confession by tracing Jesus' existence back to the creation of the world and before (John 1:1–5). Despite His royal ancestry and despite His heavenly preexistence as the eternal Word and Son of God, Jesus was of humble origins humanly speaking and was viewed as such by the people of His day. When He taught in Nazareth, the townspeople asked, "Is not this the carpenter, the son of Mary, the brother of James, and Joses, and of Juda, and Simon? and are not his sisters here with us?" (Mark 6:3; compare Luke 4:22). When He taught in Capernaum, they asked, "Is not this Jesus, the son of Joseph, whose father and mother we know? how is it then that he saith, I came down from heaven?" (John 6:42). Though two Gospels, Matthew and Luke, tell of His mother Mary's miraculous conception and of Jesus' virgin birth, these matters were not public knowledge during His time on earth, for "Mary kept all these things, and pondered them in her heart" (Luke 2:19; compare v. 51).

Jesus and the God of Israel Even after the momentous events associated with Jesus' baptism in the Jordan River—the descent of God's Spirit on Him like a dove and the voice from heaven announcing "Thou art my beloved Son, in whom I am well pleased" (Mark 1:10–11)—His identity as Son of God remained hidden from those around Him. We have no evidence that anyone except Jesus, and possibly John the Baptist, either heard the voice or saw the dove. Ironically, the first intimation after the baptism that He was more than simply "Jesus of Nazareth" came not from His family or friends nor from the religious leaders of Israel, but from the devil!

Twice the devil challenged him: "If thou be the Son of God, command this stone that it be made bread" (Luke 4:3), and (on the pinnacle of the Temple in Jerusalem), "If thou be the Son of God, cast thyself down from hence" (Luke 4:9). Jesus made no attempt to defend or make use of His divine sonship but appealed instead to an authority to which any devout Jew of His day might have appealed—the holy Scriptures—and through them to the God of Israel. Citing three passages from Deuteronomy, Jesus called attention not to Himself, but to "the Lord thy God" (Luke 4:8; compare Mark 10:18; 12:29–30). Jesus apparently used this story out of His personal experience to teach His disciples that they too must "live . . . by every word that proceedeth out of the mouth of God," (Matt. 4:4), must "not tempt the Lord your God" (Luke 4:12), and must "worship the Lord thy God, and him only shalt thou serve" (Luke 4:8).

Two things about this temptation story have a special bearing on the ministry of Jesus as a whole. First, the God-centered character of His message continued in the proclamation He began in Galilee when He returned home from the desert: "The time is fulfilled, and the kingdom of God is at hand; repent ye, and believe the gospel" (Mark 1;15; compare Matt. 4:17). Mark called this proclamation "the gospel of the kingdom of God" (Mark 1:14). John's Gospel presented Jesus

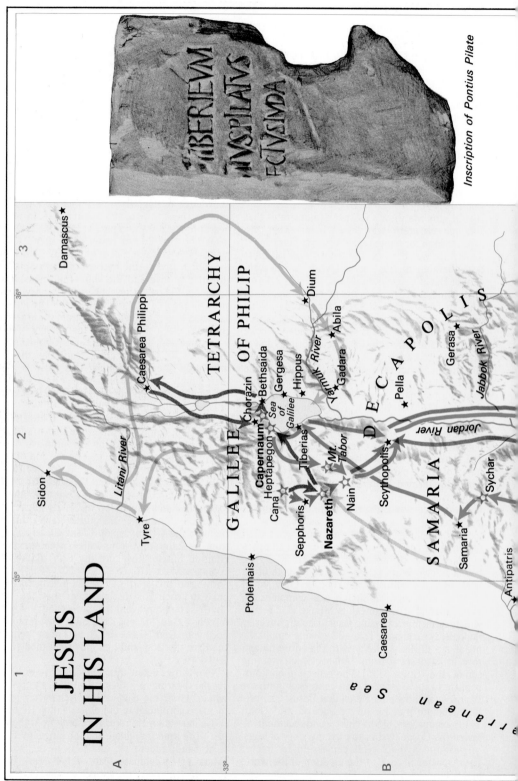

JESUS
IN HIS LAND

Inscription of Pontius Pilate

TIBERIEVM
[PON]TIVS PILATVS
[PRAEF]ECTVS IVDA[EA]E

Damascus ★

3

36°

TETRARCHY

OF PHILIP

Caesarea Philippi ★

Litani River

Sidon ★

2

Tyre ★

35°

GALILEE

Chorazin ★
Bethsaida ★
Capernaum ★
Heptapegon
Cana ★
Nazareth ★
Sepphoris ★

Sea
of
Galilee

Gergesa
Hippus ★

Tiberias ★

Mt.
Tabor ★

Nain ☆

Gadara ★

Yarmuk River

Abila ★

Dium ★

D E C A P O L I S

Pella ★

Gerasa ★

Jabbok River

Ptolemais ★

Scythopolis ★

Jordan River

S A M A R I A

Sychar ★

Samaria ★

Antipatris ★

Caesarea ★

...erranean Sea

...ea

1

A

33°

B

© carta

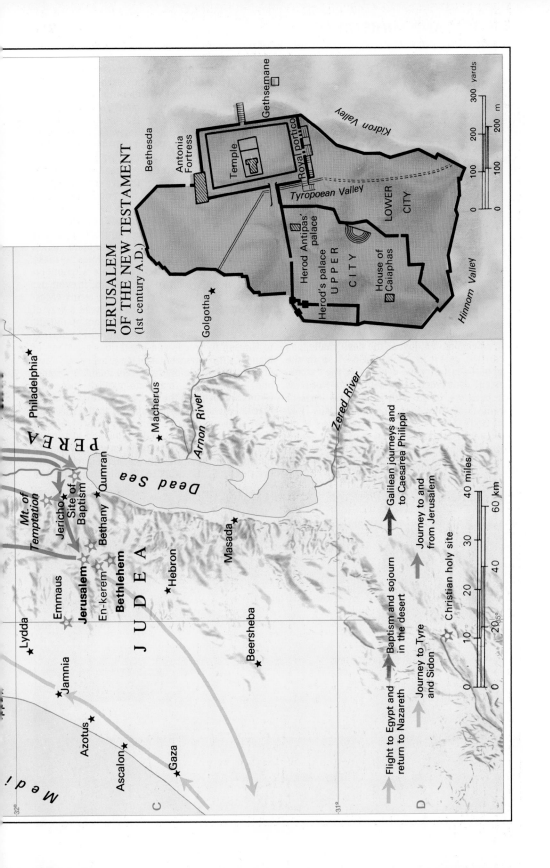

JERUSALEM OF THE NEW TESTAMENT
(1st century A.D.)

Bethesda

Antonia
Fortress

Temple

Royal portico

Gethsemane

Kidron Valley

Tyropoean Valley

Herod Antipas'
palace

Herod's palace

**U P P E R
C I T Y**

House of
Caiaphas

LOWER
CITY

Hinnom Valley

Golgotha

300   yards

200

100

0

300   m

200

100

0

Philadelphia ★

P E R E A

Mt. of
Temptation

Jericho ★

Site of
Baptism

Bethany

Qumran ★

Macherus ★

Arnon River

Zered River

Dead Sea

Masada ★

Lydda ★

Emmaus

En-kerem ★

Jerusalem ★

Bethlehem

Hebron ★

Jamnia ★

J U D E A

Beersheba ★

Azotus ★

Ascalon ★

Gaza ★

Medi

C

32°

31°

D

Flight to Egypt and
return to Nazareth

Baptism and sojourn
in the desert

Journey to Tyre
and Sidon

Galilean journeys and
to Caesarea Philippi

Journey to and
from Jerusalem

Christian holy site

0   10   20   30   40 miles

0   20   40   60 km

35°

The traditional site on the Jordan River where Jesus was baptized.

as reminding His hearers again and again that He had come not to glorify or proclaim Himself, but solely to make known "the Father," or "the One who sent me" (John 4:34; 5:19, 30; 6:38; 7:16–18,28; 8:28,42,50; 14:10,28). Second, the issue of Jesus' own identity continued to be raised first by the powers of evil. Just as the devil challenged Jesus in the desert as "Son of God," so in the course of His ministry the demons (or the demon-possessed) confronted Him with such words as "what have we to do with thee, thou Jesus of Nazareth? . . . I know thee who thou art, the Holy One of God" (Mark 1:24), or "What have I to do with thee Jesus, thou Son of the most high God?" (Mark 5:7).

15th–16th century painting in the Church of the Holy Sepulchre at Jerusalem, showing the burial of Jesus.

The mystery of Jesus' person emerged in pronouncements of this kind, but Jesus seemed not to want the question of His identity raised prematurely. He silenced the demons (Mark 1:25,34; 3:12); and when He healed the sick, He frequently told the people who were cured not to speak of it to anyone (Mark 1:43–44; 7:36a). The more He urged silence, however, the faster the word of His healing power spread (Mark 1:45; 7:36b). The crowds appear to have concluded that He must be the Messiah, the anointed King of David's line expected to come and deliver the Jews from Roman rule. If Jesus was playing out the role of Messiah, the Gospels present Him as a strangely reluctant Messiah. At one point, when the crowds tried to "take Him by force to make Him a king, "he departed again into a mountain himself alone" (John 6:15). Seldom, if ever, did He apply to Himself the customary terms "Messiah" or "Son of God." He had instead a way of using the emphatic "I" when it was not grammatically necessary and a habit sometimes of referring to Himself indirectly and mysteriously as "Son of man." In the Aramaic language Jesus spoke, "Son of man" meant simply "a certain man," or "someone." Though He made no explicit messianic claims and avoided the ready-made titles of honor that the Jews customarily applied to the Messiah, Jesus spoke and acted with the authority of God Himself. He gave sight to the blind and hearing to the deaf; He enabled the lame to walk. When He touched the unclean, He made them clean. He even raised the dead to life. In teaching the

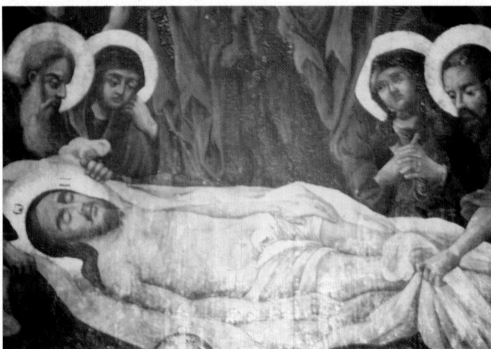

crowds that gathered around Him, He did not hesitate to say boldly, "Ye have heard that it was said . . . but I say unto you" (Matt 5:21–22, 27–28,31–32,33–34,38–39,43–44). So radical was He toward the accepted traditions that He found it necessary to state at the outset: "Think not that I am come to destroy the law, or the prophets: I am not come to destroy, but to fulfill" (Matt. 5:17).

Such speech and behavior inevitably raised questions about Jesus' identity. The crowds who heard Him "were astonished at his doctrine: for he taught them as one having authority, and not as the scribes" (Matt. 7:28–29). Despite His reluctance (or perhaps because of it), His following in the early days of His ministry was enormous. He had to get up before daylight to find time and a place for private prayer (Mark 1:35). So pressed was He by the crowds that He taught them on one occasion while standing in a boat offshore on the lake of Galilee (Mark 4:1). Once when a group of people desired healing for a paralyzed man, the huge mob around the house where Jesus was staying forced them to lower the man through a hole in the roof (Mark 2:4). Everyone needed what they knew Jesus had to give. There was no way He could meet all their needs at once.

Jesus' Mission Who were "the lost sheep" to whom Jesus was called to be the Shepherd? The apparent answer is that they were those who were not expected to benefit from the coming of the Messiah. Through their carelessness about the law, they had become the enemies of God; but God loved His enemies. Jesus' conviction was that both He and His disciples must love them, too (Matt. 5:38–48). Jesus was challenged on one occasion for enjoying table fellowship with social outcasts (known to the religious Jews as "sinners") in the house of Levi, the tax collector in Capernaum. He replied to criticism: "They that are whole have no need of the physician, but they that are sick; I came not to call the righteous, but sinners" (Mark 2:17). Another time, when the religious authorities murmured that "This man receiveth sinners, and eateth with them" (Luke 15:2), Jesus told three parables of God's inexhaustible love for those who are "lost" and of God's unbridled joy when the lost are found (the parables of the lost sheep, the lost coin, and the lost son; Luke 15:3–32). He claimed that God's joy at the recovery of all such sinners (tax collectors, prostitutes, shepherds, soldiers, and others despised by the pious in Israel) was greater than any joy "over ninety and nine just persons, which need no repentance" (Luke 15:7; compare vv. 25–32). Such an exuberant celebration of divine mercy, whether expressed in Jesus' actions or in the stories He told, must have seemed to religious leaders both in Galilee and Jerusalem a serious lowering of ancient ethical standards and a damaging compromise of the holiness of God.

We have little evidence that Jesus included non-

Jews among the "sinners" to whom He was sent. Despite the reference in Luke 4:25–27 to Elijah and Elisha and their ministry to foreigners, Jesus explicitly denied that He was sent to Gentiles or Samaritans (Matt. 15:24; see 10:5–6). Yet the principle, "not to the righteous, but to sinners," made the extension of the good news of the kingdom of God to the Gentiles after Jesus' resurrection a natural one. Even during Jesus' lifetime, He responded to the initiatives of Gentiles seeking His help (Matt. 8:5–13; Luke 7:1–10; Mark 7:24–30; Matt 15:21–28), sometimes in such a way as to put Israel to shame (Matt. 8:10). Twice He traveled through Samaria (Luke 9:51–56; John 4:4); once He stayed in a Samaritan village for two days, calling a Samaritan woman and a number of other townspeople to faith (John 4:5–42), and once He made a Samaritan the hero of one of His parables (Luke 10:29–37).

None of this was calculated to win Him friends among the priests in Jerusalem or the Pharisees throughout Israel. He described visions that many would "come from east and west, and shall sit down with Abraham, and Isaac, and Jacob, in the kingdom of heaven. But the children of the kingdom shall be cast out into outer darkness" (Matt. 8:11–12). He predicted that twelve uneducated Galileans would one day "sit upon twelve thrones, judging the twelve tribes of Israel" (Matt. 19:28; compare Luke 22:28–29). He warned the religious leaders sternly that they were in danger of "blasphemy against the Spirit" by attributing the Spirit's ministry through Him to the power of the devil (Matt. 12:31). The whole affair was complicated by the concern of Jesus' relatives over his safety and sanity (Mark 3:21) and by His consequent affirmation of His disciples as a new family based on obedience to the will of God (Mark 3:31–35).

The so-called "Beel-zebub controversy," triggered by his healing and saving activity, set a grim precedent for Jesus' relationship with the Jerusalem authorities and made His eventual arrest, trial, and execution almost inevitable (Mark 3:20–35). From that time Jesus began to speak in parables to make the truth about God's kingdom clear to His followers while hiding it from those blind to its beauty and deaf to its call (Mark 4:10–12; notice that Jesus is first said to have spoken in parables in Mark 3:23, in immediate response to the charge of demon possession). He also began to intimate, sometimes in analogy or parable (Mark 10:38; Luke 12:49–50; John 3:14; 12:24,32) and sometimes in explicit language (Mark 8:31; 9:31; 10:33–34), that He would be arrested and tried by the religious leadership in Jerusalem, die on the cross, and rise from the dead after three days. From the start He had defined His mission, at least in part, as that of the "Servant of the Lord" described in Isaiah 40—46 (see, for example the citation of Isa. 61:1–2 in Luke 4:18–19). As His

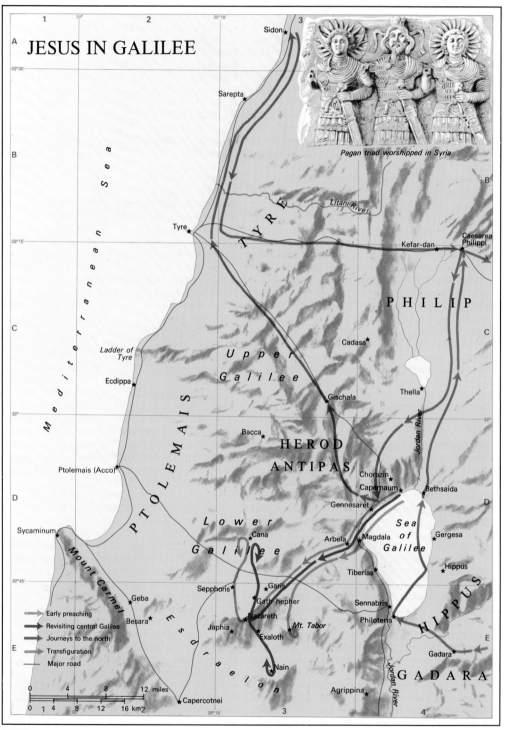

JESUS IN GALILEE

Mediterranean Sea

Sidon

Sarepta

Pagan triad worshipped in Syria

Litani River

T Y R E

Tyre

Kefar-dan

Caesarea Philippi

P H I L I P

Ladder of Tyre

Ecdippa

Upper Galilee

Cadasa

Gischala

Thella

P T O L E M A I S

Bacca

Jordan River

H E R O D

A N T I P A S

Ptolemais (Acco)

Chorazin

Capernaum

Bethsaida

Gennesaret

Lower Galilee

Cana

Arbela

Magdala

Sea of Galilee

Gergesa

Sycaminum

Hippus

Mount Carmel

Tiberias

Sepphoris

Garis

Gath-hepher

Geba

Nazareth

Sennabris

Philoteria

H I P P U S

Besara

Japhia

Mt. Tabor

Exaloth

Gadara

E s d r a e l o n

Nain

Agrippina

Jordan River

G A D A R A

Capercotnei

→ Early preaching
→ Revisiting central Galilee
→ Journeys to the north
→ Transfiguration
— Major road

0   4   8   12 miles
0 1 4 8 12 16 km

© carta

ministry moved toward its completion, the vicarious suffering of the Servant (see Isa. 52:13—53:12) came into sharper and sharper focus for Jesus (see Mark 10:45; 12:24). He also saw Himself as the stricken Shepherd of Zechariah 13:7 (Mark 14:27) and, at the very end, in the role of the righteous Sufferer of the biblical Psalms (for example Mark 15:34; Luke 23:46; John 19:28). Before His arrest He dramatized for the disciples His impending death by sharing with them in the bread and the cup of the Passover with the explanation that the bread was His body to be broken for them and that the cup of wine was His blood to be shed for their salvation. Only His death could guarantee the coming of the kingdom He had proclaimed (Matt. 26:26–29; Mark 14:22–25; Luke 22:14–20; compare 1 Cor. 11:23–26).

His Death and Resurrection The Gospel accounts of Jesus' last days in Jerusalem correspond in broad outline to the predictions attributed to Him earlier. He seems to have come to Jerusalem for the last time in the knowledge that He would die there. Though He received a royal welcome from crowds who looked to Him as the long-expected Messiah (see Matt 21:9–11; Mark 11:9–10; John 12:13), no evidence points to this as the reason for His arrest. Rather His action in driving the money changers out of the Jerusalem Temple (Matt 21:12–16; Mark 11:15–17; compare John 2:13–22), as well as certain of His pronouncements about the Temple aroused the authorities to act decisively against Him.

During His last week in Jerusalem, Jesus had predicted the Temple's destruction (Matt. 24:1–2; Mark 13:1–2; Luke 21:5–6) and claimed that "I will destroy this Temple that is made with hands, and within three days I will build another made without hands" (Mark 14:58; compare Matt. 26:61). Jesus' intention to establish a new community as a "temple," or dwelling place of God (see Matt. 16:21; John 2:19; 1 Cor. 3:16–17) was perceived as a very real threat to the old community of Judaism and to the Temple that stood as its embodiment. On this basis He was arrested and charged as a deceiver of the people.

During a hearing before the Sanhedrin, or Jewish ruling council, Jesus spoke of Himself as "Son of man sitting on the right hand of power, and coming in the clouds of heaven" (Mark 14:62; compare Matt. 26:64, Luke 22:69). Though the high priest called this blasphemy and the Sanhedrin agreed that such behavior deserved death, the results of the hearing seem to have been inconclusive. If Jesus had been formally tried and convicted by the Sanhedrin, he would have been stoned to death like Stephen in Acts 7, or like the attempted stoning of the woman caught in adultery in a story reported in some manuscripts of John 8:1–11. For whatever reason, the high priest and his cohorts apparently found no formal charges they could make stick. If Jesus were

stoned to death without a formal conviction, it would be murder, a sin the Ten Commandments forbid. (John 18:31 refers to what was forbidden to the Jews by their own law, not to what was forbidden by the Romans.) The Sanhedrin decided, therefore, to send Jesus to Pontius Pilate, the Roman governor, with charges against Him that the Romans would take seriously: "We found this fellow perverting the nation, and forbidding to give tribute to Caesar, saying that he himself is Christ a King" (Luke 23:2). Jesus' execution is therefore attributable neither to the Jewish people as a whole nor to the Sanhedrin, but rather to a small group of priests who manipulated the Romans into doing what they were not able to accomplish within the framework of their law. Though Pilate pronounced Jesus innocent three times (Luke 23:4,14,22; compare John 18:38; 19:4,6), he was maneuvered into sentencing Jesus with the thinly veiled threat, "If thou let this man go, thou art not Caesar's friend: whosoever maketh himself a king speaketh against Caesar" (John 19:12). Consequently, Jesus was crucified between two thieves, fulfilling His own prediction that "as Moses lifted up the serpent in the wilderness, even so must the Son of man be lifted up" (John 3:14). Most of His disciples fled at His arrest; only a group of women and one disciple, called the disciple whom He loved, were present at the cross when He died (John 19:25–27; compare Matt. 27:55–56; Mark 15:40; Luke 23:49).

The story did not end with the death of Jesus. His body was placed in a new tomb that belonged to a secret disciple named Joseph of Arimathea (Luke 23:50–56; John 19:38–42). The Gospels agree that two days later, the morning after the sabbath, some of the women who had remained faithful to Jesus came to the tomb. They discovered the stone over the entrance to the tomb rolled away and the body of Jesus gone. According to Mark, a young man was there (16:5; tradition calls him an angel) and told the women to send word to the rest of the disciples to go and meet Jesus in Galilee, just as He had promised them (Mark 16:7; see 14:28). The most reliable manuscripts of Mark's Gospel end the story there, leaving the rest to the reader's imagination. According to Matthew, the young man's word was confirmed to the women by the risen Jesus Himself. When they brought word to the eleven disciples (the twelve minus Judas, the betrayer), the disciples went to a mountain in Galilee, where the risen Jesus appeared to them as a group. He commanded them to make more disciples, teaching and baptizing among the Gentiles (Matt. 28:16–20). According to Luke, the risen Jesus appeared to the gathered disciples already in Jerusalem on the same day He was raised and before that to two disciples walking to the neighboring town of Emmaus. According to John, there was an appearance in Jerusalem on Easter day to one of the women,

J

Parables of Jesus

PARABLE	OCCASION	LESSON TAUGHT	REFERENCES
1. The speck and the log	When reproving the Pharisees	Do not presume to judge others	Matt. 7:1-6; Luke 6:37-43
2. The two houses	Sermon on the Mount, at the close	The strength conferred by duty	Matt. 7:24-27; Luke 6:47-49
3. Children in the marketplace	Rejection by the Pharisees of John's baptism	Evil of a fault-finding disposition	Matt. 11:16; Luke 7:32
4. The two debtors	A Pharisee's self-righteous reflections	Love to Christ proportioned to grace received	Luke 7:41
5. The unclean spirit	The Scribes demand a miracle in the heavens	Hardening power of unbelief	Matt. 12:43-45; Luke 11:24-26
6. The rich man's meditation	Dispute of two brothers	Folly of reliance upon wealth	Luke 12:16
7. The barren fig tree	Tidings of the execution of certain Galileans	Danger in the unbelief of the Jewish people	Luke 13:6-9
8. The sower	Sermon on the seashore	Effects of preaching religious truth	Matt. 13:3-8; Mark 4:3-8; Luke 8:5-8
9. The tares	The same	The severance of good and evil	Matt. 13:24-30
10. The seed	The same	Power of truth	Mark 4:20
11. The grain of mustard seed	The same	Small beginnings and growth of Christ's kingdom	Matt. 13:31,32; Mark 4:31,32; Luke 13:19
12. The leaven	The same	Dissemination of the knowledge of Christ	Matt. 13:33; Luke 13:21
13. The lamp	To the disciples alone	Effect of good example	Matt. 5:15; Mark 4:21; Luke 8:16; 11:33
14. The dragnet	The same	Mixed character of the Church	Matt. 13:47,48
15. The hidden treasure	The same	Value of religion	Matt. 13:44
16. The pearl of great value	The same	The same	Matt. 13:45,46
17. The householder	The same	Varied methods of teaching truth	Matt. 13:52
18. The marriage	To the Pharisees, who censured the disciples	Joy in Christ's companionship	Matt. 9:15; Mark 2:19,20; Luke 5:34-35
19. The patched garment	The same	The propriety of adapting actions to circumstances	Matt. 9:16; Mark 2:21; Luke 5:36
20. The wine bottles	The same	The same	Matt. 9:17; Mark 2:22; Luke 5:37
21. The harvest	Spiritual wants of the Jewish people	Need of labor and prayer	Matt. 9:37; Luke 10:2
22. The opponent	Slowness of the people to believe	Need of prompt repentance	Matt. 5:25; Luke 12:58
23. Two insolvent debtors	Peter's question	Duty of forgiveness	Matt. 18:23-35

Parables of Jesus

PARABLE	OCCASION	LESSON TAUGHT	REFERENCES
24. The good Samaritan	The lawyer's question	The golden rule for all	Luke 10:30–37
25. The three loaves	Disciples ask lesson in prayer	Effect of importunity in prayer	Luke 11:5–8
26. The good shepherd	Pharisees reject testimony of miracle	Christ the only way to God	John 10:1–16
27. The narrow gate	The question, Are there few that can be saved?	Difficulty of repentance	Matt. 7:14; Luke 13:24
28. The guests	Eagerness to take high places	Chief places not to be usurped	Luke 14:7–11
29. The marriage supper	Self-righteous remark of a guest	Rejection of unbelievers	Matt. 22:2–9; Luke 14:16–23
30. The wedding clothes	Continuation of the same discourse	Necessity of purity	Matt. 22:10–14
31. The tower	Multitudes surrounding Christ	Need of deliberation	Luke 14:28–30
32. The king going to war	The same	The same	Luke 14:31
33. The lost sheep	Pharisees objected to his receiving the wicked	Christ's love for sinners	Matt. 18:12,13; Luke 15:4–7
34. The lost coin	The same	The same	Luke 15:8, 9
35. The prodigal son	The same	The same	Luke 15:11–32
36. The unjust steward	To the disciples	Prudence in using property	Luke 16:1–9
37. The rich man and Lazarus	Derision of the Pharisees	Salvation not connected with wealth	Luke 16:19–31
38. The importunate widow	Teaching the disciples	Perseverance in prayer	Luke 18:2–5
39. The Pharisee and tax-gatherer	Teaching the self-righteous	Humility in prayer	Luke 18:10–14
40. The slave's duty	The same	Man's obedience	Luke 17:7–10
41. Laborers in the vineyard	The same	The same further illustrated	Matt. 20:1–16
42. The talents	At the house of Zaccheus	Doom-of-unfaithful-followers	Matt. 25:14–30; Luke 19:11–27
43. The two sons	The chief priests demand his authority	Obedience better than words	Matt. 21:28
44. The wicked vine-growers	The same	Rejection of the Jewish people	Matt. 21:33–43; Mark 12:1–9; Luke 20:9–15
45. The fig tree	In prophesying the destruction of Jerusalem	Duty of watching for Christ's appearance	Matt. 24:32; Mark 13:28; Luke 21:29,30
46. The watching slave	The same	The same	Matt. 24:43; Luke 12:39
47. The man on a journey	The same	The same	Mark 13:34
48. Character of two slaves	The same	Danger of unfaithfulness	Matt. 24:45–51; Luke 12:42–46
49. The ten virgins	The same	Necessity of watchfulness	Matt. 25:1–12
50. The watching slaves	The same	The same	Luke 12:36–38
51. The vine and branches	At the Last Supper	Loss and gain	John 15:1–6

Miracles of Jesus

MIRACLE	BIBLE PASSAGE			
Water Turned to Wine				John 2:1
Many Healings	Matt. 4:23	Mark 1:32		
Healing of a Leper	Matt. 8:1	Mark 1:40	Luke 5:12	
Healing of a Roman Centurion's Servant	Matt. 8:5		Luke 7:1	
Healing of Peter's Mother-in-law	Matt. 8:14	Mark 1:29	Luke 4:38	
Calming of the Storm at Sea	Matt. 8:23	Mark 4:35	Luke 8:22	
Healing of the Wild Men of Gadara	Matt. 8:28	Mark 5:1	Luke 8:26	
Healing of a Lame Man	Matt. 9:1	Mark 2:1	Luke 5:18	
Healing of a Woman with a Hemorrhage	Matt. 9:20	Mark 5:25	Luke 8:43	
Raising of Jairus' Daughter	Matt. 9:23	Mark 5:22	Luke 8:41	
Healing of Two Blind Men	Matt. 9:27			
Healing of a Demon-possessed Man	Matt. 9:32			
Healing of a Man with a Withered Hand	Matt. 12:10	Mark 3:1	Luke 6:6	
Feeding of 5,000 People	Matt. 14:15	Mark 6:35	Luke 9:12	John 6:1
Walking on the Sea	Matt. 14:22	Mark 6:47		John 6:16
Healing of the Syrophenician's Daughter	Matt. 15:21	Mark 7:24		
Feeding of 4,000 People	Matt. 15:32	Mark 8:1		
Healing of an Epileptic Boy	Matt. 17:14	Mark 9:14	Luke 9:37	
Healing of Two Blind Men at Jericho	Matt. 20:30			
Healing of a Man with an Unclean Spirit		Mark 1:23	Luke 4:33	
Healing of a Deaf, Speechless Man		Mark 7:31		
Healing of a Blind Man at Bethesda		Mark 8:22		
Healing of Blind Bartimaeus		Mark 10:46	Luke 18:35	
A Miraculous Catch of Fish			Luke 5:4	John 21:1
Raising of A Widow's Son			Luke 7:11	
Healing of a Stooped Woman			Luke 13:11	
Healing of a Man with the Dropsy			Luke 14:1	
Healing of Ten Lepers			Luke 17:11	
Healing of Malchus' Ear			Luke 22:50	
Healing of a Royal Official's Son				John 4:46
Healing of a Lame Man at Bethesda				John 5:1
Healing of a Blind Man				John 9:1
Raising of Lazarus				John 11:38

Discourses of Jesus

WHERE DELIVERED	NATURE OR STYLE	TO WHOM ADDRESSED	THE LESSON TO BE LEARNED	REFERENCES
1. Jerusalem	Conversation	Nicodemus	We must be "born of water and the Spirit" to enter the kingdom	John 3:1-21
2. At Jacob's Well	Conversation	Samaritan Woman	"God is spirit" to be worshiped in spirit and truth	John 4:1-30
3. At Jacob's Well	Conversation	The Disciples	Our food is to do His will	John 4:31-38
4. Nazareth	Sermon	Worshipers	No prophet is welcomed in his own hometown	Luke 4:16-31
5. Mountain in Galilee	Sermon	The Disciples and the People	The Beatitudes; to let our light shine before men; Christians the light of the world; how to pray; benevolence and humility; heavenly and earthly treasures contrasted; golden rule	Matt. 5-7; Luke 6:17-49
6. Bethesda—A Pool	Conversation	The Jews	To hear Him and believe on Him, is to have everlasting life	John 5:1-47
7. Near Jerusalem	Conversation	The Pharisees	Works of necessity not wrong on the Sabbath	Matt. 12:1-14; Luke 6:1-11
8. Nain	Eulogy and Denunciation	The People	Greatness of the least in heaven; judged according to the light we have	Matt. 11:2-29; Luke 7:18-35
9. Capernaum	Conversation	The Pharisees	The unforgivable sin is to sin against the Holy Spirit	Mark 3:19-30; Matt. 12:22-45
10. Capernaum	Conversation	The Disciples	The providence of God; nearness of Christ to those who serve Him	Mark 6:6-13; Matt. 10:1-42
11. Capernaum	Conversation	A Messenger	Relationship of those doing His will	Matt. 12:46-50; Mark 3:31-35
12. Capernaum	Sermon	The Multitude	Christ as the bread of life	John 6:22-71
13. Capernaum	Criticism and Reproof	The Scribes and Pharisees	Not outward conditions, but that which proceeds from the heart defiles	Matt. 15:1-20; Mark 7:1-23
14. Capernaum	Example	The Disciples	Humility the mark of greatness; be not a stumbling block	Matt. 18:1-14; Mark 9:33-50
15. Temple—Jerusalem	Instruction	The Jews	Judge not according to outward appearance	John 7:11-40
16. Temple—Jerusalem	Instruction	The Jews	To follow Christ, is to walk in the light	John 8:12-59
17. Temple—Jerusalem	Instruction	The Pharisees	Christ the door; He knows His sheep; gives His life for them	John 10:1-21
18. Capernaum	Charge	The Seventy	Need for Christian service; not to despise Christ's ministers	Luke 10:1-24
19. Bethany	Instruction	The Disciples	The efficacy of earnest prayer	Luke 11:1-13
20. Bethany	Conversation	The People	Hear and keep God's will; the state of the backslider	Luke 11:14-36
21. House of Pharisee	Reproof	The Pharisees	The meaning of inward purity	Luke 11:37-54
22. Beyond Jordan	Exhortation	The Multitude	Beware of hypocrisy; covetousness; blasphemy; be watchful	Luke 12:1-21
23. Perea	Object Lesson	The Disciples	Watchfulness; the kingdom of God is of first importance	Luke 12:22-34
24. Jerusalem	Exhortation	The People	Death for life; way of eternal life	John 12:20-50
25. Jerusalem	Denunciation	The Pharisees	Avoid hypocrisy and pretense	Matt. 23:1-39
26. Mt. of Olives	Prophecy	The Disciples	Signs of the coming of the Son of man; beware of false prophets	Matt. 24:1-51; Mark 13:1-37; Luke 21:5-36
27. Jerusalem	Exhortation	The Disciples	The lesson of humility and service	John 13:1-20
28. Jerusalem	Exhortation	The Disciples	The proof of discipleship; that He will come again	John 14-16

Mary Magdalene, another on the same day to the gathered disciples, another week later (still in Jerusalem) to the same group plus Thomas, and a fourth appearance, at an unstated time, by the lake of Galilee, in which Jesus reenacted the initial call of the disciples by providing them miraculously with an enormous catch of fish. Luke adds in the Book of Acts that the appearances of the risen Jesus went on over a period of forty days in which He continued to instruct them about the kingdom of God. Whatever the precise order of the facts, the disciples' experience of the living Jesus transformed them from a scattered and cowardly band of disillusioned visionaries into the nucleus of a coherent movement able to challenge and change forever the Roman Empire within a few short decades.

Though the physical resurrection of Jesus cannot be proven, alternate "naturalistic" explanations of the disciples' experience and of the empty tomb require without exception more credulity than the traditional confession of the Christian church that on the third day He rose from the dead. The unanimous witness of the Gospels is that the story goes on. Mark does it with the promise that Jesus will bring together His scattered flock and lead them into Galilee (Mark 16:7). Matthew does it more explicitly with Jesus' concluding words, "And, lo, I am with you alway, even unto the end of the world" (Matt. 28:20). Luke does it with the entire Book of Acts, which traces the spread of the message of the kingdom of God and the risen Jesus from Jerusalem all the way to Rome. John does it with his vivid picture of the Holy Spirit being given to the disciples directly from the mouth of Jesus Himself (John 20:21–22). Each Gospel makes the point differently, but the point is always the same. The story of Jesus is not over; He continues to fulfill His mission wherever His name is confessed and His teaching is obeyed, and the faith of Christians is that He will do so until He comes again.   *J. Ramsey Michaels*

JETHER (Jē′ thẽr) Personal name meaning, "remnant." *1.* Son of the judge Gideon who refused his father's command to kill enemy military leaders (Judg. 8:20). *2.* Father of Amasa, army leader under Judah (1 Kings 4:5,32), and descended from Ishmael (1 Chron. 2:17; compare 2 Sam. 17:25). See *Ithra. 3.* Member of clan of Jerahmeel in tribe of Judah (1 Chron. 2:32). *4.* Member of tribe of Judah (1 Chron. 4:17). *5.* Member of tribe of Asher (1 Chron. 8:38, called Ithran in 7:37). See *Ithran.*

JETHETH (Jē′ thĕth) Clan name in Edom of unknown meaning (Gen. 36:40).

JETHLAH (Jĕth′ lah) Place name meaning, "he or it hangs." Border town of tribe of Dan (Josh. 19:42). Its location is unknown. Modern transla-

tions transliterate the name Ithrah. See *Ithrah.*

JETHRO (Jĕth′ rō) Personal name meaning, "excess" or "superiority." In Exodus 3:1, a priest of Midian and the father-in-law of Moses. Some variation exists in the Bible regarding the name of Moses' father-in-law. In Exodus 2:18, his name is Reuel. In Numbers 10:29 it is Hobab. The nature of the relationship of these names to one another is uncertain. Of particular interest is that Jethro was a Midianite priest. The deity whom he served is not explicitly identified; in Exodus 18:11, however, he declared Yahweh to be greater than all gods. One school of thought has discovered the origin of Israel's Yahwism in the ancient Midianite religion represented by Jethro. Such an origin is unlikely. Yahwistic faith probably is traceable at least as far back as Abraham. See *Moses; Yahweh.*

JETUR (Jē′ tŭr) Personal name perhaps meaning, "he set in courses or layers." A son of Ishmael and thus original ancestor of Arabian tribe or clan (Gen. 25:15). The clan was a part of the Hagerites, probably descendants of Hagar (1 Chron. 5:19), who fought the East Jordan tribes. See *Hagrites.* Israel's victory illustrated the conviction that trust in God brought victory in war. See *Ituraea.*

JEUEL (Jēu′ ĕl) Personal name meaning, "God is strong" or "God heals." See *Jeiel.*

JEUSH (Jē′ ŭsh) Personal name meaning, "He helps." Hebrew is sometimes transliterated into English in different ways. See *Jehush. 1.* Son of Esau and thus head of tribe in Edom (Gen. 36:5,18). *2.* Member of tribe of Benjamin (1 Chron. 7:10; compare 8:39). *3.* Levite under David (1 Chron. 23:10–11). *4.* Son of King Rehoboam and grandson of Solomon (2 Chron. 11:19).

JEUZ (Jē′ ŭz) Personal name meaning, "He brought to safety." Member of tribe of Benjamin (1 Chron. 8:10).

JEWELS, JEWELRY Jewels are stones valued for their beauty or scarcity. Most often they are cut and polished to enhance their appearance. Jewels have been more rare in archaeological finds in Palestine than in Egyptian, Greek, or Phoenician archaeological remains. There are two reasons for this. First, the land of Israel had no natural deposits of precious stones. Jewels (sometimes in the form of jewelry) were taken as booty during war (Num. 31:50), brought as gifts to the king (2 Chron. 9:1,9); or purchased from merchants (1 Kings 10:11; compare Rev. 18:11–12). Secondly, Israel and Judah were pawns in power struggles between its neighbors. The wealth accumulated by the king and Temple was carried off by conquerors (e.g. 1 Kings 14:25–28).

Jewels functioned as a medium of exchange in the Ancient Near East before the invention of money. In Israel, jewels were used primarily in relation to worship and the monarchy.

Worship First, jewels were a fitting contribution for a special offering (Ex. 35:22). Second, the high priest was garbed in fine clothing decorated with jewels (Ex. 28; 39). The ephod worn by the high priest had an onyx stone, set in gold filigree and engraved with the names of the tribes of Israel, on each shoulder. The breastplate of the high priest (also called the "breastplate of judgment," Ex. 28:15,29) was made of the finest cloth, interwoven with gold, into which were set two precious stones, in four rows of three each. On each stone was engraved the name of one of the twelve tribes. Thus, the twelve tribes were symbolically present whenever the high priest ministered before the Lord. The Hebrew words for some of these jewels can be translated with some degree of assurance; in other cases translators must guess what stone is intended. Since the ancients had no way to cut diamonds, they were not yet precious stones. The word translated "diamond" in Exodus 28:18; 39:11 probably does refer to a very hard stone, since it is based on a root word meaning "hammer, smite." Thus it is probably not what we call a diamond (so NIV, "emerald"; REB, "jade"; NRSV, "moonstone"). The high priest would have looked quite elegant when presiding in worship.

Gold Phrygian necklace dating from 1200–650 B.C. from Gordion.

Another example of Phrygian jewelry—an armlet with facing lioness heads (1200–650 B.C.).

The Monarchy Jewels were considered a fitting gift for kings. The Queen of Sheba brought them to Solomon (1 Kings 10:2,10). Jewels were used in royal crowns (2 Sam. 12:30), and probably royal garments (Ezek. 28:13). Jewels were a form of wealth which could be accumulated and easily kept in the royal treasury. The writer of Ecclesiastes considered such accumulation of royal wealth a matter of great vanity (Eccl. 2:4–11).

Unlike precious jewels, jewelry was widely used by ordinary people in the Ancient Near East. Archaeologists have demonstrated that men and women have adorned themselves with various kinds of jewelry almost from the earliest known times. Jewelry was known in the patriarchal period. Abraham's servant, when sent to find a bride for Isaac, put a nose ring and bracelets on Rebekah (Gen. 24:47) and gave her other gold and silver jewelry. The Israelites are said to have "despoiled" the Egyptians, by begging gold and silver jewelry of their neighbors in preparation for the Exodus from Egypt (Ex. 3:22; 11:2–3). More Egyptian jewelry undoubtedly came into Israel through trade, as well as with the daughter of Pharaoh who married Solomon (1 Kings 3:1). At least 15 precious stones were mined in ancient Egypt. Egyptian metal workers were especially skilled in the art of making gold jewelry. The opulence of royal Egyptian jewelry has been dem-

Gold Roman jewelry from the first century A.D.

J

onstrated from archaeological finds, especially the tomb of Tutankhamen.

During the period of the monarchy, an ordinary man or woman might have had a few pieces of jewelry, something made of bronze or, if they could afford it, gold. Gold, which was used as a medium of exchange, was relatively plentiful, and could be made into a necklace, bracelet, or ring by a local craftsman. Royalty, of course, could wear more expensive jewelry set with precious stones.

Many kinds of jewelry are mentioned in the Old Testament. Not only women wore bracelets (Gen. 24:47); King Saul was wearing one when he died in battle (2 Sam. 1:10). Ankle bracelets might be worn (Isa. 3:16, 18). Such bracelets have been found on the leg bones of women buried in ancient Israel.

Necklaces and pendants were popular (Song of Sol. 1:10). A certain kind of gold necklace probably functioned as a symbol of authority. When Pharaoh appointed Joseph to high office, he put a gold chain around his neck (Gen. 41:42). Likewise, in the Book of Daniel, King Belshazzar proclaimed that whoever could interpret the mysterious writing on the wall should have a gold chain put around his neck and be made "the third ruler in the kingdom" (Dan. 5:7,29). The crescents mentioned in Isaiah 3:18, like those of Judges 8:21,26, which were worn by the kings of Midian, were probably moon-shaped pendants worn on chains. Gold crescent jewelry has been discovered by archaeologists. The crescent may have functioned as a royal insignia. The items referred to as chains, collars, or pendants (NRSV) (Isa. 3:19; Judg 8:26) were probably also worn around the neck, perhaps on cords.

Earrings were known in the patriarchal period. They may have had some religious significance (Gen. 35:4). Nose rings are mentioned in Genesis 24:22,30,47 (NIV) and Isaiah 3:21 (NIV). The same term, *nezem,* is used for both, so the references are often ambiguous (e.g. Num. 31:50; Prov. 25:12).

Good luck charms called "amulets" are not mentioned often in the Bible but have been widely

Gold ring inlaid with precious stone from the first century A.D.

found throughout Palestine in archaeological sites from all periods. Some represented gods and goddesses. Isaiah 3:20 may include a reference to amulets (see NRSV), though the translation is not sure. The earrings buried by Jacob under the oak near Schechem may have been amulets (Gen. 35:4). Such amulets were violations of the commandment not to make graven images (Ex. 20:4).

The most important item of jewelry mentioned in the Old Testament is the signet ring. The signet was used to make an impression on clay or wax and thus to seal and authenticate documents. Generally the signet was a finely engraved semiprecious stone. A hole could be bored through the signet and it could be hung from a cord around the neck (Gen. 38:18), or it could be used as a setting for a ring or more elaborate necklace. Pharaoh gave Joseph his signet ring as a symbol of authority (Gen. 41:42). King Ahasuerus gave his signet ring first to Haman (Esther 3:10), then to Mordecai (Esther 8:2).

Jewelry was also used to decorate animals, at least by the wealthy. The camels of the Midianite kings slain by Gideon wore crescents and decorated collars around their necks (Judg. 8:21,26). The reference in Proverbs 11:22 to a ring in a swine's snout is metaphoric; one cannot draw conclusions from it concerning the use of decorative nose rings for animals. Amulets were sometimes worn by animals to ensure good fortune on a trip.

Isaiah 3:18–23 is sometimes interpreted as an attack on women's fashions and a denunciation of the uses of jewelry. The Hebrew terms used in the passage appear to refer rather to official insignia. Thus the passage is a condemnation of the misuse of wealth and power at the expense of the poor. In Ezekiel 16:8–13, the Lord is portrayed as a Bridegroom decking His bride, Jerusalem, with fine clothing and jewlry, including a nose ring, earrings, and a crown.

The New Testament does not make much mention of jewels and jewelry. Pearls were highly valued in New Testament time and thus a fitting metaphor for the kingdom of God (Matt. 13:45–46). James warned his readers not to discriminate on the basis of wealth, as indicated by the wearing of gold rings and fine clothing (Jas. 2:1–7). In 1 Timothy 2:9–10, women are reminded that the best adornment is not braids, gold, or pearls, but good deeds.

In Revelation 21:2, which echoes the imagery of Ezekiel 16:8–31, God is pictured as a Bridegroom whose bride, the new Jerusalem, is adorned with jewels. The walls of the new Jerusalem are pictured as built of jasper, adorned with twelve kinds of jewels. Each of the twelve gates is made of a single pearl. The gems of the holy city, like those in so much jewelry, are to be put in a setting of gold. The idea of rebuilding Jerusalem with jewels as building material reflects Isaiah

54:11–12. Unlike the old Jerusalem, the new Jerusalem—associated with the completion of the kingdom of God—will not be unfaithful.

See *Minerals and Metals.*   *Wilda W. Morris*

JEWESS (Jēw′ ĕss) Female Jew. Timothy's mother was Jewish, but his father was not (Acts 16:1). Drusilla, the wife of Felix the Roman governor, was a Jewess (Acts 24:24).

JEWISH PARTIES IN THE NEW TESTAMENT
Judaism in New Testament times was diverse. We read of Pharisees, Sadducees, and Herodians. One man is called a Zealot. From other sources we learn of the Essenes.

Pharisees The Pharisees constituted the most important group. They appear in the Gospels as the opponents of Jesus. Paul claimed that he was a Pharisee before becoming a Christian (Phil. 3:5). They were the most numerous of the groups, although Josephus stated that they numbered only about six thousand. They controlled the synagogues and exercised great control over the general population.

No surviving writing gives us information about the origin of the Pharisees. The earliest reference to them is dated in the time of Jonathan (160–143 B.C.), where Josephus refers to Pharisees, Sadducees, and Essenes. Their good relations with the rulers ended in the time of John Hyrcanus (134–104 B.C.). They came to power again when Salome Alexandra became queen (76 B.C.).

The name "Pharisee" means "the separated ones." It may mean that they separated themselves from the masses of the people or that they separated themselves to the study and interpretation of the law. It is usually assumed that they were the spiritual descendants of the Hasidim, the loyal fighters for religious freedom in the time of Judas Maccabeus. They appear to be responsible for the transformation of Judaism from a religion of sacrifice to one of law. They were the developers of the oral tradition, the teachers of the twofold law: written and oral. They saw the way to God as being through obedience to the law. They were the progressives of the day, willing to adopt new ideas and adapt the law to new situations.

The Pharisees were strongly monotheistic. They accepted all the Old Testament as authoritative. They affirmed the reality of angels and demons. They had a firm belief in life beyond the grave and a resurrection of the body. They were missionary, seeking the conversion of Gentiles (Matt. 23:15). They saw God as concerned with the life of a person without denying that the individual was responsible for how he or she lived. They had little interest in politics. The Pharisees opposed Jesus because He refused to accept the teachings of the oral law.

Sadducees The Sadducees were the aristocrats of the time. They were the party of the rich and the high priestly families. They were in charge of the Temple and its services. They claimed to be descendants of Zadok, high priest in the time of Solomon. However, the true derivation of their name is unknown. In all our literature, they stand in opposition to the Pharisees. They sought to conserve the beliefs and practices of the past. They opposed the oral law, accepting the Pentateuch, the first five books of the Old Testament, as the ultimate authority. The Sadducees were materialistic in their outlook. They did not believe in life after death or any reward or punishment beyond this life. They denied the existence of angels and demons. They did not believe that God was concerned with what people did. Rather people were totally free. They were politically oriented, supporters of ruling powers, whether Seleucids or Romans. They wanted nothing to threaten their position and wealth, so they strongly opposed Jesus.

Zealots The Zealots receive only brief mention in the New Testament. Simon, one of the disciples, is called Zealot (Luke 6:15). John 18:40 uses a word for Barabbas that Josephus used for Zealot. Josephus states that the Zealots began with Judas the Galilean seeking to lead a revolt over a census for taxation purposes (A.D. 6). He did not use the name Zealot until referring to events in A.D. 66, the beginning of the Jewish revolt against Rome. The Zealots were the extreme wing of the Pharisees. In contrast with the Pharisees, they believed that only God had the right to rule over the Jews. They were willing to fight and die for that belief. For them patriotism and religion were inseparable.

Herodians The Herodians are mentioned in only three places in the New Testament (Matt. 22:16; Mark 3:6; 12:13). In the earliest reference in Mark, they joined with the Pharisees in a plot to kill Jesus. The other two passages refer to the sending of Pharisees and Herodians to ask Jesus about paying taxes to Caesar. It is assumed that they were Jews who supported Herod Antipas or sought to have a descendant of Herod the Great given authority over Palestine. At this time Judea and Samaria were under Roman governors.

Essenes We know of the Essenes through the writings of Josephus and Philo, a Jewish philosopher in Alexandria, Egypt. They are not mentioned in the New Testament. More information about the Essenes has come to light since 1947 with the discovery of the manuscripts from the caves above the Dead Sea, commonly called the Dead Sea Scrolls. It is generally believed that the people of the Scrolls were closely related to the Essenes. They may have begun at about the same time as the Pharisees and Sadducees. The Essenes were an ascetic group, many of whom lived in the desert region of Qumran, near the Dead Sea. They took vows of celibacy and perpetuated their community by adopting male children. However, some Essenes did marry. When one joined the

Jewish Parties in the New Testament

DATES OF EXISTENCE	NAME	ORIGIN	SEGMENTS OF SOCIETY	BELIEFS	SELECTED BIBLICAL REFERENCES	ACTIVITIES
PHARISEES						
Existed under Jonathan (160–143 B.C.) Declined in power under John Hyrcanus (134–104 B.C.) Began resurgence under Salome Alexandra (76 B.C.)	Pharisees = "the Separated Ones" with three possible meanings: (1) to their separating themselves *from* people (2) to their separating themselves *to* the study of the law ("dividing" or "separating" the truth) (3) to their separating themselves *from* pagan practices	Probably spiritual descendants of the Hasidim (religious freedom fighters of the time of Judas Maccabeus)	Most numerous of the Jewish parties (or sects) Probably descendants of the Hasidim—scribes and lawyers Members of the middle class—mostly businessmen (merchants and tradesmen)	Monotheistic Viewed entirety of the Old Testament (Torah, Prophets, and Writings) as authoritative Believed that the study of the law was true worship Accepted both the written and oral law More liberal in interpreting the law than were the Sadducees Quite concerned with the proper keeping of the Sabbath, tithing, and purification rituals Believed in life after death and the resurrection of the body (with divine retribution and reward) Believed in the reality of demons and angels Revered humanity and human equality Missionary-minded regarding the conversion of Gentiles Believed that individuals were responsible for how they lived	Matthew 3:7–10; 5:20; 9:14; 16:1,6–12; 22:15–22,34–46; 23:2–36 Mark 3:6; 7:3–5; 8:15; 12:13–17 Luke 6:7; 7:36–39; 11:37–44; 18:9–14 John 3:1; 9:13–16; 11:46–47; 12:19 Acts 23:6–10 Philippians 3:4b–6	Developers of oral tradition Taught that the way to God was through obedience to the law Changed Judaism from a religion of sacrifice to a religion of law Progressive thinkers regarding the adaptation of the law to new situations Opposed Jesus because He would not accept the teachings of the oral law as binding Established and controlled synagogues Exercised great control over general population Served as religious authorities for most Jews Took several ceremonies from the Temple to the home Emphasized ethical as opposed to theological action Legalistic and socially exclusive (shunned non-Pharisees as unclean) Tended to have a self-sufficient and haughty attitude
SADDUCEES						
Probably began about 200 B.C. Demise occurred in A.D. 70 (with the destruction of the Temple)	Sadducees = Three possible translations: (1) "the Righteous Ones"—based on the Hebrew consonants for the word *righteous* (2) "ones who sympathize with Zadok," or "Zadokites"—based on their possible link to Zadok the high priest (3) "syndics," "judges," or "fiscal controllers"—based on the Greek word *syndikoi*	Unknown origin Claimed to be descendants of Zadok—high priest under David (see 2 Samuel 8:17; 15:24) and Solomon (see 1 Kings 1:34–35; 1 Chronicles 12:28) Had a possible link to Aaron Were probably formed into a group about 200 B.C. as the high priest's party	Aristocracy—the rich descendants of the high-priestly line (However, not all priests were Sadducees) Possibly descendants of the Hasmonean priesthood Probably not as refined as their economic position in life would suggest	Accepted only the Torah (Genesis through Deuteronomy—the written law of Moses) as authoritative Practiced literal interpretation of the law Rigidly conservative towards the law Stressed strict observance of the law Opposed oral law as obligatory or binding Observed past beliefs and tradition Believed in the absolute freedom of human will—that people could do as they wished without attention from God Denied divine providence Denied the concept of life after death and the resurrection of the body Denied the concept of reward and punishment after death Denied the existence of angels and demons Materialistic	2 Samuel 8:17; 15:24 1 Kings 1:34 1 Chronicles 12:26–28 Ezekiel 40:45–46; 43:19; 44:15–16 Matthew 3:7–10; 16:1,6–12; 22:23–34 Mark 12:18–27 Luke 20:27–40 John 11:47 Acts 4:1–2; 5:17–18; 23:6–10	In charge of the Temple and its services Politically active Exercised great political control through the Sanhedrin of which many were members Supported the ruling power and the status quo Leaned toward Hellenism (the spreading of Greek influence)—and were thus despised by the Jewish populace Opposed both the Pharisees and Jesus because these lived by a larger canon (The Pharisees and Jesus both considered more than only Genesis through Deuteronomy as authoritative.) Opposed Jesus specifically for fear their wealth/position would be threatened if they supported Him

ZEALOTS

Origin		Location/Description	Scripture	Beliefs/Characteristics
Three possibilities for their beginning: (1) during the reign of Herod the Great (about 37 B.C.) (2) during the revolt against Rome (A.D. 6) (3) traced back to the Hassidim or the Maccabees (about 168 B.C.). Their certain demise occurred around A.D. 70–73 with Rome's conquering of Jerusalem.	Refers to their religious zeal Josephus used the term in referring to those involved in the Jewish revolt against Rome in A.D. 6—led by Judas of Galilee (According to Josephus) The Zealots began with Judas (the Galilean, son of Ezekias, who led a revolt in A.D. 6 because of a census done for tax purposes.	The extreme wing of the Pharisees	Matthew 10:4 Mark 3:18 Luke 6:15 Acts 1:13	Similar to the Pharisees with this exception: believed strongly that only God had the right to rule over the Jews. Patriotism and religion became inseparable. Believed that total obedience (supported by drastic physical measures) must be apparent before God would bring in the Messianic Age Were fanatical in their Jewish faith and in their devotion to the law—to the point of martyrdom · Extremely opposed to Roman rule over Palestine · Extremely opposed to peace with Rome · Refused to pay taxes · Demonstrated against the use of the Greek language in Palestine · Engaged in terrorism against Rome and others with whom they disagreed politically [Sicarii (or Assassins) were an extremist Zealot group who carried out acts of terrorism against Rome.]

HERODIANS

Origin		Location/Description	Scripture	Beliefs/Characteristics
Existed during the time of the Herodian dynasty (which began with Herod the Great in 37 B.C.) Uncertain demise	Based on their support of the Herodian rulers (Herod the Great or his dynasty)	Wealthy, politically-influential Jews who supported Herod Antipas (or any descendant of Herod the Great) as ruler over Palestine (Judea and Samaria were under Roman governors at this time.)	Matthew 22:5–22 Mark 3:6; 8:15; 12:13–17	Not a religious group—but a political one Membership was probably comprised of representatives of varied theological perspectives · Supported Herod and the Herodian dynasty · Accepted Hellenization · Accepted foreign rule

ESSENES

Origin		Location/Description	Scripture	Beliefs/Characteristics
Probably began during Maccabean times (about 168 B.C.)—around the same time as the Pharisees and the Sadducees began to form Uncertain demise—possibly in A.D. 68–70 with the collapse of Jerusalem	Unknown origin	Possibly developed as a reaction to the corrupt Sadducean priesthood Have been identified with various groups: Hasidim, Zealots, Greek influence, or Iranian influence	Scattered throughout the villages of Judea (possibly including the community of Qumran) (According to Philo and Josephus) About 4,000 in Palestinian Syria	None	Very strict ascetics Monastic: most took vow of celibacy (adopting male children in order to perpetuate the group), but some did marry (for the purpose of procreation) Rigidly adherent to the law (including a strict rendering of the ethical teachings) Considered other literature as authoritative (in addition to the Hebrew Scripture) Believed and lived as pacifists Rejected Temple worship and temple offerings as corrupted Believed in the immortality of the soul with no bodily resurrection Apocalyptically oriented · Devoted to the copying and studying of the manuscripts of the law · Lived in a community sense with communal property · Required a long probationary period and ritual baptisms of those wishing to join · Were highly virtuous and righteous · Were extremely self-disciplined · Were diligent manual laborers · Gave great importance to daily worship · Upheld rigid Sabbath laws · Maintained a non-Levitical priesthood · Rejected worldly pleasures as evil · Rejected matrimony—but did not forbid others to marry

Essenes, he gave all his possessions to the community. A three-year period of probation was required before full membership was granted. The Essenes devoted themselves to the study of the law. They went beyond the Pharisees in their rigid understanding of it. There is no evidence that either Jesus or John the Baptist had ever had any relation to Qumran. Jesus would have strongly opposed their understanding of the law.

The vast majority of the people were not a member of any of these parties, although they would have been most influenced by the Pharisees.

See *Intertestamental History and Literature; Dead Sea Scrolls; Synagogue; Temple.*

Clayton Harrop

JEWS IN THE NEW TESTAMENT The word *Jew* is derived ultimately from the tribe of Judah through Middle English *Iewe,* Old French *Ieu,* Latin *Iudaeus,* and Greek *Ioudaios* (compare the woman's name *Judith,* which originally meant "Jewess").

The Old Testament Era The Hebrew *yehûdim* meant originally descendants of the tribe of Judah and then those who inhabited the territories claimed by them (2 Kings 16:6; 25:25; Jer. 32:12). With the deportation and subsequent assimilation of the "Ten Lost Tribes" of the Northern Kingdom by the Assyrians after 722 B.C., the only Israelites to survive into the exilic period (with a few from the tribe of Benjamin, e.g. Mordecai, who is called a "Jew" in Esther 2:5) were those from Judah, hence the name Jews (Neh. 1:2). The corresponding Aramaic word is used in Daniel 3:8,12.

The Intertestamental Period The Greek name *Ioudaios* (plural *Ioudaioi*) was used for the Israelites in the Greek and Roman world. This is the name used in the treaty between Judas Maccabeus and the Romans, described in 1 Maccabees 8:23–32: "May all go well with the Romans and with the nation of the Jews. . . ."

Matthew, Mark, Luke The term *Ioudaios* occurs relatively rarely in the Synoptic Gospels, the first three Gospels which are closely parallel to each

From Old Testament times faithful Jews have worn phylacteries on both forehead and arm as they pray.

other. The word occurs but five times in Matthew, seven times in Mark, and five times in Luke, usually in the expression "King of the Jews" (12 of the total of 17). Of the remaining occurrences only Matthew 28:15 designates Jews as contrasted to Christian believers.

John By contrast the word *Ioudaios* occurs 70 times in the Gospel of John. Some of these references are quite positive, especially in the dialogue between Jesus and the woman of Samaria (ch. 4). In v. 9 the woman says to Jesus, "thou, being a Jew," and in v. 22 Jesus says, "salvation is of the Jews." Many of the Jews believed in Jesus (8:31; 11:45; 12:11). Other references are neutral as in John 3:1, where Nicodemus is described as a ruler of the Jews.

The description of Jesus' opponents reveals a striking difference between the Synoptic Gospels and John. Whereas the former names Jesus' enemies as scribes and Pharisees, high priests and Sadducees, the Gospel of John simply uses the general term "Jews." The term often implies Jewish authorities as in 7:13; 9:22; 19:38; 20:19.

The Jews impugned Jesus' birth and His sanity (8:48), and even alleged that He was demon possessed (8:52). The Jews questioned His statements about the Temple (2:20) and were scandalized at His claim to be the bread from heaven (6:41). They regarded His affirmations of equality with the Father as blasphemous and picked up stones to kill Him (5:18; 7:1; 10:31,33; 11:8).

The heightened use of the term "Jews" in John to serve as a general designation for those who denied that Jesus was the Christ may be explained by the fact that John's Gospel was composed at a later date than the Synoptics—after such events as the destruction of Jerusalem in A.D. 70 and the insertion of a curse upon the *minim* ("heretics," especially Christians) into the daily synagogue prayer in A.D. 80 had increased mutual hostilities between Jews and Christians.

Acts Paul was a Jew from Tarsus (Acts 21:39; 22:3). After his dramatic conversion on the road to Damascus, his fellow Jews sought to kill him (9:23). King Herod Agrippa I arrested Peter and killed the Apostle James, believing this would please the Jews (12:1–3).

Following his conviction that the gospel should be preached first to the Jews (Rom. 1:16), Paul on his missionary journeys began his preaching in the Jewish synagogues—at Salamis on Cyprus (Acts 13:5), at Iconium (14:1), at Thessalonica (17:1), at Athens (17:15–17), and at Corinth (18:1). Though he made some converts among the Jews, even converting the synagogue ruler at Corinth (18:8), and no doubt had success among the "god fearers" or proselytes who were interested in converting to Judaism (13:43; 17:4), the majority of the Jews reacted violently against Paul's message (13:50; 14:2; 17:5; 18:12). Paul therefore turned his efforts increasingly toward the Gentiles, the non-Jews.

Pauline Letters As the "apostle to the Gentiles," Paul argued against "Judaizers" that Gentile converts did not have to be circumcised, that is, become Jews first, before they became christians (Acts 15:1–5). His arguments were accepted by James and the church council at Jerusalem held about A.D. 49. Paul, who had been "an Hebrew of the Hebrews; as touching the law, a Pharisee" (Phil. 3:5) and had been more zealous in his pursuit of Judaism than his peers (Gal. 1:13,14), came to the radical conclusion that a true Jew is not one who was physically descended from Abraham (compare John 8:31–41), adhered to the Torah or Law of Moses (Rom 2:17,28) and was circumcised. For Paul a true Jew is one who believes that Jesus is the Messiah or Christ (Gal. 3:26–29), relies on God's grace and not works of the law (Eph. 2:8,9), and has been circumcised in his heart by the Holy Spirit (Gal. 2:2–9; 5:6). In spite of his grief that most of his fellow Jews did not accept his message, Paul did not teach that God had abandoned the Jews but believed that God still has a plan for them (Rom. 9–11). [Note: the word *Ioudaios* is not found in any of the non-Pauline letters of the New Testament.)

Revelation The two references in the Book of Revelation are to the church at Smyrna (2:9) and the church at Philadelphia (3:9), where there were those who claimed to be Jews but who were denounced as the "synagogue of Satan" because they opposed Christians.

See *Israel; Hebrews; Pharisees; Sadducees.*

Edwin Yamauchi

JEZANIAH (Jĕ zả nī′ ah) Personal name meaning, "Yahweh gave ear." *1.* Army captain loyal to Gedaliah, the governor Babylon appointed over Judah immediately after Babylon destroyed Jerusalem and took the Jewish leaders into Exile about 586 B.C. (Jer. 40:8). Jezaniah was one of the captains who refused to believe Jeremiah's prophecy calling the people to remain in Judah. Rather, he helped carry Jeremiah into Egypt (Jer. 42—43). In 43:2 the name is Azariah, which may be the correct reading in 4:1 rather than Jezaniah. See *Azariah.*

JEZEBEL (Jĕz′ ĕ bĕl) Personal name meaning, "Where is the prince?" perhaps derived from Phoenician name meaning, "Baal is the prince." Wife of King Ahab of Israel (874–853 B.C.), who brought the worship of Baal from Sidon, where her father Ethbaal was king (1 Kings 16:31). Jezebel tried to destroy all God's prophets in Israel (1 Kings 18:4), while installing prophets of Baal and Asherah (1 Kings 18:19, modern translations) as part of the royal household. Elijah proved these prophets to be false on Mount Carmel (1 Kings 18), bringing Jezebel's threat to kill Elijah (1 Kings 19:2). Elijah ran for his life to Beersheba.

When Ahab wanted Naboth's vineyard, Jezebel connived with the leaders of the city who falsely accused and convicted Naboth, stoning him to death. Elijah then prophesied Jezebel's death, she being the one who had "stirred up" Ahab to wickedness (1 Kings 21). She continued her evil influence as her son Joram ruled (2 Kings 9:22). Elisha anointed Jehu to replace Joram. Jehu assassinated Joram and then went to Jezreel after Jezebel. She tried to adorn herself and entice him, but her servants obeyed Jehu's call to throw her from the window to the street, where horses trod her in the ground (2 Kings 9:30–37).

Jezebel's name became so associated with wickedness that the false prophetess in the church at Thyatira was labeled, "Jezebel" (Rev. 2:20).

JEZER (Jĕ′ zēr) Personal name meaning, "He formed." Son of Naphtali (Gen. 46:24) and founding ancestor of clan in that tribe (Num. 26:49). The name Izri (1 Chron. 25:11) means member of clan of Jezer, and Zeri (1 Chron. 25:3) is probably an abbreviated form of Izri.

JEZERITE (Jē′ zēr īte) Member of clan of Jezer. See *Jezer.*

JEZIAH (Jĕ zī′ ah) Personal name meaning, "Yah sprinkled." Israelite with foreign wife condemned by Ezra (Ezra 10:25). Modern translations transliterate the Hebrew as Izziah.

JEZIEL (Jē′ zī ĕl) Personal name meaning, "God sprinkled." Military leader from tribe of Benjamin, Saul's tribe, who joined David at Ziklag as he fled from Saul (1 Chron. 12:3). The written Hebrew text has the name Jezuel, while the early Hebrew scribes noted the reading, Jeziel.

JEZLIAH (Jĕz lī′ ah) Personal name meaning, "long-lived." Member of tribe of Benjamin (1 Chron. 8:18). Modern translations transliterate the name, Izliah.

JEZOAR (Jĕ zō′ àr) Personal name perhaps meaning, "he was light-colored." Member of tribe of Judah (1 Chron. 4:7). The name in the Hebrew text is Jizhar or Izhar as read by modern translations. Early Hebrew scribes read it as "and Zohar" (NIV).

JEZRAHIAH (Jĕz rả hī′ ah) Personal name meaning, "Yah shines forth." *1.* Leader in tribe of Issachar (1 Chron. 7:3; English transliteration is usually Israhiah). *2.* Leader of Levite singers at Nehemiah's celebration of finishing the rebuilding of Jerusalem's wall (Neh. 12:42). REB transliterates Izrahiah.

JEZREEL (Jĕz′ rēēl), meaning "God sows", refers to a major valley, a northern city, a southern

J

The Valley of Jezreel (or Esdraelon, or Megiddo) as viewed from the top of the Megiddo tel.

city, and the son of Hosea. *1.* The Old Testament uses the name to refer to the entire valley of Jezreel which separates Galilee from Samaria, including the valley of Esdraelon. The valley was important militarily as a battle site for Deborah (Judg. 4—5), Gideon (Judg. 6—7), Saul (2 Sam. 4), Jehu (2 Kings 9—10), and Josiah (2 Kings 22). The geography of Palestine made Jezreel a major route for travel from north to south and from east to west. *2.* The northern city of Jezreel, which guarded the corridor to Beth-shan, was the site of the royal residence of Omri and Ahab where the incident of Naboth's vineyard occurred (1 Kings 21).

3. David's wife Ahinoam was from the southern city of Jezreel which is located in the vicinity of Ziph (1 Sam. 25:43–44). *4.* The prophet Hosea named his son Jezreel as a symbol to indicate the evil nature of the dynasty of Jehu which began with much bloodshed in Jezreel. The name also symbolized that God will sow seeds of prosperity after the destruction (Hos. 1:4,5; 1:10—2:1).

Robert Street

JEZREELITE (Jĕz' rēēl īte) A citizen of or from the home town of Jezreel. See *Jezreel.*

JIBSAM (Jĭb' săm) Personal name meaning, "he smells sweet." Early leader in tribe of Issachar (1 Chron. 7:2). Modern translations often read Ibsam.

JIDLAPH (Jĭd' lăph) Personal name meaning, "he cries or is sleepless." Son of Nahor, Abraham's brother (Gen. 22:22).

JIMNA(H) [Jĭm' nà(h)] Proper name meaning, "he allotted." *1.* Son of Asher, grandson of Jacob, and original ancestor of clan in tribe of Asher (Gen. 46:17; Num. 26:44). KJV spells the name Imnah in 1 Chronicles 7:30, as do modern translations in all occurrences. *2.* A Levite under Hezekiah (2 Chron. 31:14, spelled Imnah by English translations).

JIMNITE (Jĭm' nīte) Member of clan of Jimnah. See *Jimnah.*

JIPHTAH (Jĭph' tah) Place name meaning, "he opened or broke up." City in tribal territory of Judah (Josh. 15:43). It may have been located at modern Terqumiyeh halfway between Hebron and Beit Jibrin. Most modern translations transliterate as "Iphtah." The personal name Jephthah has the same Hebrew spelling. See *Jephthah.*

JIPHTHAH-EL (Jĭph' thah-ĕl) Place name meaning, "God opened." A valley marking the border of the tribal territories of Asher and Zebulun (Josh. 19:14,27). The modern name is wadi el-Melek. Modern translations transliterate Iphtah-el.

JOAB (Jō' ăb) Personal name meaning, "Yahweh is father." Military commander during most of David's reign. He was the oldest son of Zeruiah, the sister of David (2 Sam. 2:13; 1 Chron. 2:16). He was loyal to David and ruthless in achieving his objectives. After Saul's death, David was negotiating with Abner, Saul's military commander. Joab, whose brother had been slain in battle by Abner, deceived Abner and murdered him. David publicly lamented this assassination (2 Sam. 2—3).

Joab's exploits in the capture of Jerusalem led David to name him commander (1 Chron. 11:4—8). Joab successfully led David's armies against the Ammonites (2 Sam. 10). During this campaign David sent his infamous order to have Uriah, the husband of Bathsheba, killed (2 Sam. 11).

Joab was instrumental in the reconciliation of David and Absalom (2 Sam. 14). When Absalom led a rebellion, Joab remained loyal to David. Joab killed Absalom against the clear orders of David (2 Sam. 18:14). He also convinced David to end his obsessive grieving for Absalom (2 Sam. 19:4—8). Joab murdered Amasa, whom David had named commander (2 Sam. 20:10). He opposed David's plan for a census, but carried it out when ordered to do so (2 Sam. 24:1—9).

When David was dying, Joab supported Adonijah's claim to the throne (1 Kings 1). David named Solomon king and told him to avenge Abner and Amasa by killing Joab. Although Joab fled to the tabernacle for sanctuary, Solomon ordered Benaiah to kill Joab (1 Kings 2).   *Robert J. Dean*

JOAH (Jō′ äh) Personal name meaning, "Jah is brother." *1.* Scribe under King Hezekiah about 715–686 B.C. (2 Kings 18:18). He was one of the king's messengers to listen to the Assyrian Rab-shakeh and bring the message to the king. They did so in mourning (2 Kings 18:37). *2.* Son of royal scribe under King Josiah (640–609 B.C.). He helped repair the Temple (2 Chron. 34:8). *3.* A Levite (1 Chron. 6:21). *4.* Member of family of Levites, who were porters or gatekeepers (1 Chron. 26:4). *5.* Levite who helped cleanse the Temple under King Hezekiah about 715 B.C. (2 Chron. 29:12).

JOAHAZ (Jō′ à hăz) A short form of Jehoahaz meaning, "Yahweh grasped." *1.* See Jehoahaz (2 Kings 14:1; 2 Chron. 36:1—4). *2.* Father of a scribe under Hezekiah about 715 B.C. (2 Chron. 34:8).

JOANAN (Jō ā′ nan) Greek transliteration of Hebrew name Johanan. See *Johanan.* Ancestor of Jesus (Luke 3:27). KJV reads Joanna. Some interpreters think his father Rhesa does not represent a personal name but is a transliteration of the Aramaic word for prince, a title for Zerubbabel. Joanan would then be the Hananiah of 1 Chronicles 3:19.

JOANNA (Jō ăn′ nà) Personal name meaning,

"Yahweh's gift." *1.* In Luke 8:3, one of the women whom Jesus had healed and who ministered to Him out of their own private means. She was the wife of Herod's steward Chuza. Luke's Gospel, which gives particular prominence to women, also mentions her in 24:10. She was one of the women who came to Jesus' tomb on the Sunday following the crucifixion and reported to the eleven the message that He had risen. *2.* In Luke 3:27, the son of Rhesa mentioned in the genealogy of Jesus. See *Joanan.*

JOASH (Jō′ ăsh) Personal name meaning, "Yahweh gives." *1.* In Judges 6:11, the father of Gideon. He was a member of the tribe of Manasseh who lived at Ophrah. *2.* In 1 Chronicles 4:21–22, one of the sons of Shelah. *3.* In 1 Chronicles 7:8, one of the sons of Becher. *4.* In 1 Chronicles 12:3, one of David's warriors. He was a son of Shemaah the Gibeathite. *5.* In 1 Chronicles 27:28, one of David's officers, who was in charge of the stores of oil. *6.* In 1 Kings 22:26, a son of Ahab, the king of Israel, and one of those to whom Micaiah the prophet was handed over.

7. In 2 Kings 11:2, the infant son of King Ahaziah of Judah who survived the bloodbath carried out by Athaliah, the queen mother, following the murder of Ahaziah. Joash was hidden by Jehosheba his aunt for six years, at the end of which time he was popularly proclaimed as the legitimate ruler of Judah in a move instigated by Jehoiada. Athaliah was executed, and Joash took the throne at the age of seven. During the king's minority, Jehoiada, the priest, exercised a strong positive influence in both the civil and religious life of the nation. The death of Jehoiada, however, marked a notable decline in the quality of the rule of Joash. Finally, the king was assassinated as the result of a palace conspiracy. See *Israel; Chronology of Biblical Period; Athaliah; Jehoiada.*

8. In 2 Kings 13:10, the son and successor of Jehoahaz as king of Israel. He ruled for sixteen years during the early part of the eighth century B.C. His visit to the dying prophet Elisha is described in 2 Kings 13:14—19. During the course of that visit, the prophet promised the king three victories over Syria. Subsequently, Joash enjoyed military success not only against Syria but also against neighboring Judah. He defeated Amaziah of Judah in battle at Beth-shemesh and actually entered Jerusalem and plundered the Temple. At his death he was succeeded on the throne by his son Jeroboam II. See *Israel; Chronology of Biblical Period.*   *Gene Henderson*

JOATHAM (Jō′ à thăm) KJV transliteration of Greek for Jotham (Matt. 1:9). See *Jotham.*

JOB, THE BOOK OF (Jōb) Job apparently lived in the patriarchal or prepatriarchal days, for not only does he not mention the Law or the Exodus, but he is pictured as a wealthy nomad (Job 1:3; 42:12) who is still offering sacrifices himself (Job 1:5; 42:8). Undoubtedly, Job was a most respected man, for not only did the prophet Ezekiel refer to him as one of the greatest of Israel's ancestors (Ezek. 14:14), but even James used him as an excellent example of patient and persistent faith (Jas. 5:11).

The Book of Job presents many problems concerning the person, time, and nature of its composition. First, the text does not indicate in any way its author. The text never speaks of Job as its author, just its subject. Thus, many have concluded that Job was written by Elihu, one of the three friends, or simply some anonymous writer of that or some other age. Second, though most will agree that the character Job lived in patriarchal times, many believe that the book was written many years later. The dates of such a composition will vary from the time of Abraham to that of the Greek Empire. Third, to further complicate the issue, many believe that Job is a compilation of several different stories coming from several different ages. As one can readily see, the question of date and authorship is a very complex issue that cannot yet be settled with certainty; however, the fact that one cannot identify the human agent in no way means that the book if not inspired, for it is God's Word and is a unit as it now stands.

Job is a Perfect Illustration of True Faith.
Through the years, many purposes have been suggested for the book. Perhaps the one that has been mentioned more often than any other is that of answering the question of why the righteous suffer. Certainly this question was prominent in Job's day, for ancient society believed that human suffering was the result of one's sin or at least a god's displeasure. Even the meaning of the name Job (the persecuted one) seems to support this suggestion, but that may not be all that is involved in the book. Another popular suggestion is that the book has been preserved to illustrate for us the nature of true faith both from the point of view of people and of God. For humans, it is trusting in God as the Creator and Sustainer of life even when all is not going well and when He is not visibly present to help us. From God's point of view, the story proves His faithfulness to His creatures despite their weaknesses and inability to understand what is happening. Another, and much less frequently suggested purpose, is that of a parable concerning the nation Israel. In this case, Job becomes the nation Israel. Though this approach is possible, it seems unlikely for most parables have some type of interpretation close by which helps to explain them. Thus, perhaps it is best just to take the book as an illustration of the nature of God and His justice in dealing with humankind, a justice people often cannot recognize and never fully understand.

Job Is Unique in World Literature. Though Job shows many similarities with other Ancient Near Eastern texts, none come near to Job's beauty and message. Because the three friends have Edomite backgrounds, some have speculated that Job may have been an Edomite and that the setting for the book may have been Edom. However, there is not enough Edomite material available at this point to make any conclusions. Others have seen similarities between Job and the Egyptian poems concerning "The Protest of the Eloquent Peasant" and "A Dispute Over Suicide" or the Babylonian poems of "The Babylonian Theodicy" and "I Will Praise the Lord of Wisdom." In each of these cases, what similarities exist seem minor, indeed, and deal more with the topic than its content or form. Still others have suggested that Job is written in the form of a court room trial. No doubt, many legal terms appear in the book; yet we still know too little about ancient legal procedure to make any such conclusions. Thus, it is best to simply take the book as a unique work depicting the life of one man and his efforts to understand his God and his own situation in life.

Job's Encounter with Life Brought Him Face to Face with God. The Book of Job is most frequently pictured as a drama with a prologue (1—2) and an epilogue (42:7–17) enclosing three cycles of poetic speeches between Job and his three friends (3—27), a beautiful wisdom poem from Job (28), Job's concluding remarks (29—31), the mysterious Elihu speeches (32—37), and God's whirlwind speeches (38:1—42:6).

The prologue describes the setting for the ensuing drama. Job was a very wealthy and religious man who seemed to have life under control (1:1–5). However, unknown to him, Satan challenged his righteousness. God allowed the challenge, but limited Satan's power to Job's possessions (1:6–12). In quick succession, Satan destroyed all of Job's possessions including even his children. However, Job did not blame God nor question His integrity (1:13–22). Satan then challenged God to let him attack Job's personal health. God agreed, but warned him not to kill Job (2:1–6). Without warning, a loathsome disease fell upon Job; yet he still refused to blame God (2:7–10). Job's friends were shocked and dismayed, but nevertheless came to encourage him and offer their help (2:11–13). To this point Job displayed a traditional faith accepting suffering as inevitable and patiently enduring it.

After the traditional time of mourning had passed, Job cried out wondering why he was ever born or allowed to reach maturity (3:1–26). Job's faith turned to a challenging, seeking faith, confronting God, demanding escape and explanation. In all the bitter questioning, faith lived, for Job turned only and always to God for answers. At this point, Job's friends could remain silent no longer and thus began to speak. The first to speak was Eliphaz who told Job that he must have sinned for

God was surely punishing him. However, there was still hope if he would confess his sin and turn to God (4:1—5:27). Suffering did not have to endure always. Job was stunned and assured his friends that he was ready to meet God and work out any problem that he might have (6:1—7:21). Bildad added that if Job had not sinned it must have been his children, for obviously God was punishing him for some wrong. However, he, too, held out hope if Job would just confess (8:1—22). Job was deeply hurt and wondered aloud whether or not he could get a hearing before God (9:1—10:22). Zophar, the most brash of the friends, called upon God to meet with Job, for he was sure that when the two met, Job would see the error of his ways and repent (11:1—20). Job held to his integrity, but continued to seek an audience with God so that he could come to understand what was happening and why (12:1—14:22).

Job's friends were not satisfied, so Eliphaz spoke again and reminded him that all people (including Job) had sinned and needed to repent. Thus, if he would just repent, God would forgive him (15:1—35). Job realized that he was getting nowhere with his friends, so he called upon the rest of creation to witness to his integrity (16:1—17:16). Bildad reminded Job of the many proverbs which spoke of the fate of the wicked. In so doing, he was implying that what had happened to Job was the result of his sin (18:1—21). Job was becoming increasingly frustrated, for his friends and family seemed to have abandoned him; yet he was unwilling to give up on God. Thus, in a most beautiful way he affirmed that he would be vindicated, if not in this world, then in the world to come (19:1—29). Zophar was hurt, for he and his friends were being ignored, if not toally disagreed with. Thus, he declared that the wicked would suffer great pain and anguish and that all the forces of nature would turn against them. No doubt, Zophar included Job in this group (20:1—29). Job turned to Zophar and harshly said, "No"; for as he observed, sometimes the wicked did prosper. However, that did not mean that God was not in control or that He would not one day bring about real justice (21:1—34).

Though they listened to him patiently, Job's friends were also becoming increasingly frustrated. Thus, Eliphaz intensified his charge that Job's suffering was the result of his own sinfulness by listing the various sins of which he thought Job was guilty. Then he called upon Job to repent (22:1—30). By this time Job was in such pain that he all but ignored Elipaz's comments and cried out for relief (23:1—24:25). Bildad, not to be outdone, reminded Job again to consider the nature and character of God, for since He was not unjust, Job surely must have sinned (25:1—6). Job, in sarcastic tones, asked the friends where they got their wisdom and then pleaded with them to look to God for real understanding and faith (26:1—27:23). Apparently, at this point, the three friends, having exhausted their arguments, once again became silent.

Job then turned and reflected both upon the true nature of wisdom and his own place in existence. In one of the most beautiful descriptions of wisdom found in the entire Bible, Job concluded that real wisdom (or meaning to life) can only be found in a proper faith relationship with God ("the fear of the Lord") (28:1—28). Though Job knew this was true and though he sought to live a righteous life, he was still hurting and did not understand why. Thus, in a beautiful soliloquy he cried out unto God, reminding God of how he had lived faithfully in the past and had been respected for it (29:1—25), but now when he was suffering everyone had turned against him, and death seemed very near (30:1—31). Thus, Job issued a final plea for God to vindicate him (31:1—40). With this, Job's case was made. He paused to await an answer from God.

At this point, a young man named Elihu rose to speak. Though most of what he had to say had already been said, he gave four speeches, each of which sought to justify God's actions. First, Elihu contended that God speaks to all people, and thus, even though he was a young man, he had every right to speak and even had the understanding to do so (32:1—33:33). Second, he reiterated the view that God was just and thus what had happened to Job was well deserved (34:1—37). Third, he sought to show that God honored the righteous and condemned the prideful, just like He had Job (35:1—16). Fourth, he then pleaded with Job to accept what had happened to him as an expression of God's discipline and to humbly repent and seek His forgiveness (36:1—37:24). Finally, Elihu realized that Job really was not listening, and so he stopped speaking.

Suddenly, out of the midst of a whirlwind, God began to speak. Basically, God said two things. First, He described the marvels of creation and then asked Job if he could have done any better (38:1—40:2). Job quickly responded that he could not for he, too, was just a creature (40:3—5). Second, God described how He controlled the world and everything in it and then asked Job if he could do a better job (40:6—41:34). Job admitted that he could not and that he did not need to for now he had seen God and clearly realized that God had everything well under control (42:1—6).

God was apparently very pleased with Job and his responses. However, He rebuked the three friends and commanded that they ask Job to seek intercession for them (42:7—9). Then, God restored all Job's fortunes and even gave him more children (42:10—17). In the end Job found meaningful life, not in intellectual pursuits or even in himself, but in experiencing God and his faith relationship to Him.

Job's Message Is Still Relevant for Us Today. The

Book of Job thus wrestles with issues all people eventually face. Such issues do not admit of easy answers. The different speakers in Job address the issues from different perspectives, forcing us to admit the complexity of the issue before we accept simple answers. Two important issues are the cause and effect of suffering and the justice and care of God. Job begins by accepting suffering as a part of human life to be endured through trust in God in good and bad times. He moves to questioning, facing the theological issues head on. He illustrates human frustration with problems for which we cannot find answers. Yet, he refuses to accept his wife's perspective of giving up on God and life. Rather, he constantly confronts God with cries for help and for answers. He shows faith can be more than simple acceptance. Faith can be struggling in the dark for answers, but struggling with God not with other people. Eliphaz notes that suffering will not last forever, especially not for the innocent. Bildad notes that Job's punishment is not as bad as it could have been; after all, his children died. Being alive means Job's sin is not unforgiveable and his suffering can be endured.

Zophar emphasizes Job's sin but notes that he could suffer even more. He should give God credit for mercy in not making him endure all the pain his sin deserves. Elihu pleaded for Job to listen to God's word in the experience, for his suffering should become a means of seeing God's will and God's way in the situation. This should lead Job to confess his sin and praise God. Job's complaint is that he cannot find God. He wants to present his case to God but cannot do so, for he is unequal to God. He cannot present his claims of innocence and get his name cleared and his body healed.

God's appearance shows that God cares, that He still controls the world, even a world with unexplainable suffering, and that His creative acts and the mysterious creatures He has created only prove that humans must live under God's control. The human mind cannot control all knowledge nor understand all situations. People must be content with a God who speaks to them. They cannot demand that God give all the answers we might want. God can be trusted in the worst of circumstances as well as in the best.

See *Wisdom; Suffering; Faith.*

Outline

I. Prologue: A Righteous Man Can Endure Injustice Without Sinning (1:1—2:10).

II. First Round: Will a Just God Answer a Righteous Sufferer's Questions? (2:11—14:22).
   A. Job: Why must a person be born to a life of suffering? (2:11—3:26).
   B. Eliphaz: Do not claim to be just, but seek the disciplining God, who is just (4:1—5:27).
   C. Job: Death is the only respite for a just person persecuted by God (6:1—7:21).
   D. Bildad: A just God does not punish the innocent (8:1—22).
   E. Job: Humans cannot win an argument in court against the Creator (9:1—10:22).
   F. Zophar: Feeble, ignorant humans must confess sins (11:1—20).
   G. Job: An intelligent person demands an answer from the all-powerful, all-knowing God, not from other humans (12:1—14:22).

III. Second Round: Does the Fate of the Wicked Prove the Mercy and Justice of God? (15:1—21:34).
   A. Eliphaz: Be quiet, admit your guilt, and accept your punishment (15:1—35).
   B. Job: Oh that an innocent person might plead my case with the merciless God (16:1—17:16).
   C. Bildad: Wise up and admit you are suffering the just fate of the wicked (18:1—21).
   D. Job: In a world without justice or friends, a just person must wait for a Redeemer to win his case (19:1—29).
   E. Zophar: Your short-lived prosperity shows you are a wicked oppressor (20:1—29).
   F. Job: Lying comforters do not help my struggle against the injustice of God (21:1—34).

IV. Third Round: Can the Innocent Sufferer Ever Know God's Ways and Will? (22:1—28:28).
   A. Eliphaz: You wicked sinner, return to Almighty God and be restored (22:1–30).
   B. Job: I cannot find God, but evidence shows He pays undue attention to me but gives no attention to the wicked (23:1—24:25).
   C. Bildad: No person can be righteous before the awesome God (25:1–6).
   D. Job: Neither your meaningless counsel nor God's faint word helps the innocent sufferer (26:1—27:23).
   E. Job: Humans cannot know wisdom; only God reveals its content: Fear the Lord (28:1–28).

V. Job's Summary: Let God Restore the Good Old Days or Answer My Complaint (29:1—31:40).
   A. In the good old days I had respect and integrity (29:1–25).
   B. Now men and God are cruel to me (30:1–31).
   C. In my innocence, I cry out for a hearing before God (31:1–40).
      1. I have not looked with lust on a maiden (31:1–4).
      2. I am not guilty of lying or deceit (31:5–8).
      3. I have not committed adultery (31:9–12).
      4. I have treated my servants fairly

(31:13—15).

5. I have been generous and kind to the poor and the disadvantaged (31:16—23).
6. I have not worshiped gold nor celestial bodies (31:24—28).
7. I have not rejoiced in others' ruin (31:29—30).
8. I have not refused hospitality to anyone (31:31—32).
9. I have nothing to hide, but I wish God would give me a written statement of charges (31:33—37).
10. I have not withheld payment for the laborers on my land (31:38—40).

VI. Elihu: An Angry Young Man Defends God (32:1—37:24).
A. Elihu is angry with Job and with the friends (31:1—22).
B. Elihu speaks to Job as a man; God speaks through dreams, visions, pain, and deliverance (33:1—33).
C. God is just; Job speaks without knowledge (34:1—37).
D. Is there any advantage in serving God? Human sin is no threat to God; human righteousness is no gift to Him (35:1—16).
E. God is just, all-wise, mysterious, and sovereign over humans and nature (36:1—37:24).

VII. Dialogue: Prove Your Wisdom Is Sufficient to Contend with the Eternal Creator (38:1—42:6).
A. God: Can you control the inanimate and animate creation? (38:1—39:30).
B. Job: I am overwhelmed and powerless to answer (40:1—5).
C. God: Will you condemn God to justify yourself? (40:6—9).
D. God: Take charge of the universe. (40:10—14).
E. Two inexplicable creatures illustrate God's unfathomable ways (40:15—41:34).
F. Job: Seeing God, I confess His power and repent of sin (42:1—6).

VIII. Epilogue: Prayer Brings Reconciliation, Forgiveness, and Restoration (42:7—17).

Harry Hunt

JOBAB (Jō' băb) Personal name perhaps meaning, "wilderness" or "arm oneself for battle." *1.* Son of Joktan in Table of Nations lineage of Noah's son Shem (Gen. 10:29). He was thus the original ancestor of a Semite tribe, probably in southern Arabia. *2.* Early king of Edom centered in Bozrah (Gen. 36:33). *3.* King of city state of Madon who joined Jabin of Hazor in northern coalition against Joshua (Josh. 11:1). *4.* Two members of tribe of Benjamin (1 Chron. 8:9,18).

JOCHEBED (Jŏch' ĕ bĕd) Personal name meaning, Yahweh's glory. In Exodus 6:20, the wife of Amram and the mother of Miriam, Aaron, and Moses. She was a member of the tribe of Levi. Her name includes the divine name Yahweh, evidence that the name Yahweh was known before the time of Moses. See *Moses.*

JODA (Jō' dà) Greek transliteration of either Jehuda (thus, KJV Juda) or Joyada, a name known in Apocrypha (2 Esdras 22:10—11). An ancestor of Jesus (Luke 3:26).

JOED (Jō' ĕd) Personal name meaning, "Yah is witness." Member of tribe of Benjamin (Neh. 11:7).

JOEL (Jō' ĕl) Personal name meaning, "Yah is God." *1.* Son of Samuel who became an evil judge, leading Israel's leaders to ask Samuel to give them a king, thus introducing kingship as a form of government for Israel. Samuel argued strongly against this, but to no avail (1 Sam. 8; compare 1 Chron. 6:33). *2.* A Levite (1 Chron. 6:36). *3.* Member(s) of tribe of Reuben (1 Chron. 5:4,8). *4.* Leader among the Levites under David (1 Chron. 15:7,11,18), who brought the ark of the covenant up to Jerusalem. Compare 1 Chronicles 23:8; 26:22 for Levites named Joel. *5.* Member of tribe of Simeon (1 Chron. 4:35). *6.* Leader of tribe of Gad (1 Chron. 5:12). *7.* Leader of tribe of Issachar (1 Chron. 7:3). *8.* Military hero under David (1 Chron. 11:38; compare Igal in 2 Sam. 23:26). *9.* Leader of the western half of the tribe of Manasseh under David (1 Chron. 27:20). *10.* Levite who helped King Hezekiah cleanse the Temple about 715 B.C. (2 Chron. 29:12). *11.* Israelite Ezra condemned for having a foreign wife who might lead nation to worship other gods (Ezra 10:43). *12.* Leader of the people from tribe of Benjamin living in Jerusalem in time of Nehemiah (Neh. 11:9). *13.* Prophet whose preaching ministry produced the Book of Joel. Personal information concerning the prophet is minimal, only that he was the son of Pethuel, about whom we know nothing. That the prophet lived in Jerusalem is probable because of his avid interest in the city, his repeated references to Zion, his call to the people to assemble for worship, and his interest in the Temple rituals and sacrifices.

His use of the popular formula, "The word of the Lord came," demonstrates his devotion as God's prophet. Distinguishing himself from the priests, he respectfully urged them to lead the people in repentance. As many as twenty references to and quotations from other prophets attest to his position in the prophetic ministry.

Containing only 70 verses, the Book of Joel is one of the shortest in the Old Testament, comprising only three chapters in our English translations. The first of two natural divisions, the earlier section (1:1—2:17) describes a terrible locust plague concluding with a plea for confession of sins. The second section (2:18—3:21), written in the form of a first-person response from God, proclaims hope for the repentant people coupled with judgment upon their enemies.

An unprecedented locust plague was symbolic of the coming day of the Lord. The insects, depicted in their four stages of development, moved through the land in successive swarms, utterly destroying everything in their path. Farmers were denied a harvest. Animals desperately roamed the wasteland groaning and perishing for lack of food. Drunkards cried out for a little taste of wine. Because priests could not find enough offerings for sacrifice, altars were empty. Drought and famine followed the locust infiltration. Vegetation was stripped; the weather was hot; water was scarce. All God's creation suffered because of the sinfulness of His people.

Priests were urged to call for fasting and prayer (2:15–17). Only God's grace could avert annihilation. Then, on the basis of their repentance, God answered that He would show pity and remove their plague (2:18–27).

As a result of their return to God, His people were promised the presence of God's Spirit among them. Locusts were used to tell about a greater day of the Lord in the future. Judgment was pronounced against Phoenicia and Philistia (3:4) and eventually upon all nations as they were judged by God in the Valley of Jehoshaphat, which literally means "The Lord judges" (3:2,12). Judah faced unparalleled prosperity, but Egypt and Edom (traditional enemies) could look for terrible punishment (3:18–19). The Lord triumphed over his enemies in order that all shall "know that I am the Lord Your God" (3:17; compare 2:27).

Opinions differ regarding the date of the book. Internal evidence makes it clear that the priests were in a position of strong authority; the Temple was standing; sacrifices were considered important; and certain foreign nations stood condemned. No mention was made of the world empires of Assyria or Babylonia. No reference was made to the Northern Kingdom of Israel; neither is the name of a king mentioned.

Two approximate dates generally are given as the possible times of the authorship of the book, either before the Exile around the time of the boy-king Joash (about 836–796 B.C.) or after the return from Exile (about 500–400 B.C.). The position of the book among the early prophets in the Hebrew canon is considered as evidence for an early date. Also, the omission of a king's name would be appropriate if a young boy such as Joash had not achieved maturity.

In favor of the late date, strong arguments are given. The returning exiles, comprising a small group in Jerusalem, centered their worship in the Temple. Sacrifices were important. Emphasis on

ethical living, so characteristic of preexilic prophets such as Amos and Micah, was lacking. Idolatry and the high places were not mentioned, suggesting that they were no longer a serious problem. After the Exile, there would be no need for announcing the coming destruction of Assyria and Babylon. There would be no need to mention a king. Citation of the Grecian slave traffic (3:4–6) fits a late period. References to the scattering of the Israelites (3:2–6) would apply to an exilic period, and the use of the term "Israel" to refer to Judah (2:27; 3:2) would have been appropriate in postexilic times. In addition, the style and language reflects the period after the Exile when the prophetic emphasis was beginning to give way to the apocalyptic.

Some early theologians viewed the entire book as an allegory with the locusts representing four heathen nations that opposed God's people. Few scholars hold to such an interpretation today. Other biblical students have seen in the book primarily a prediction of future events and have related it to certain apocalyptic literature of the New Testament (Rev. 9:3–11). Most scholars, however, accept the description of the locust plague as a literal invasion which the prophet used as a point of reference to speak to the people of his own day about the coming day of the Lord, at the same time incorporating predictive elements concerning the messianic age.

Primary teachings of the Book of Joel are numerous. (1) The Creator and Redeemer God of all the universe is in complete control of nature and can use calamities to bring His people to repentance. (2) All of God's creation is interdependent. People, animals, and vegetation all suffer when people sin. (3) Whereas the Jews considered the day of the Lord as a time of punishment upon their enemies, Joel make it clear that although God controls the destinies of other nations, His people, with a responsibility to live in accordance with their relationship with Him, are not exempt from His vengeance. (4) The God of judgment also is a God of mercy who stands ready to redeem and restore when His people come before Him in repentance. (5) Of special significance is the forward look to a time when the Spirit of God would be present upon all people. All could become prophets, with no exclusions, no go-betweens, and all could know His salvation. Peter, on the day of Pentecost, proclaimed that the new day of Spirit-filled people had arrived as it had been announced earlier by the prophet Joel (Acts 2:17–21).

Outline

I. The Day of the LORD Calls for God's People to Respond (1:1—2:17).
    A. Witness to future generations (1:1–4).
    B. Mourn and grieve over the destruction (1:5–20).
    C. Sound the alarm because the day of the LORD is dreadful (2:1–11).

D. Repent inwardly because your gracious, patient God may have pity (2:12–14).

E. Assemble the congregation for mourning and repentance (2:15–17).

II. God Will Respond to His People's Mourning and Repentance (2:18–27).

A. God will have pity (2:18).

B. God will provide food needs and remove shame from His people (2:19).

C. God will defeat the enemy (2:20).

D. God will replace fear and shame with joy and praise (2:21–26).

E. God will cause His people to know and worship Him, and Him alone (2:27).

III. God Is Preparing a Great Day of Salvation (2:28—3:21).

A. God will pour out His Spirit to bring salvation to the remnant (2:28–32).

B. God will judge all nations (3:1–17).

C. God will bless His people (3:18–21).

A. O. Collins

JOELAH (Jō ē′ lah) Personal name meaning, "female mountain goat." Warrior from Saul's tribe of Benjamin who joined David at Ziklag as he fled from Saul (1 Chron. 12:7). Early manuscripts and translations give various forms of the name such as Jaalah and Azriel.

JOEZER (Jō ē′ zēr) Personal name meaning, "Yah is help." Warrior from Saul's tribe of Benjamin who joined David at Ziklag as he fled from Saul (1 Chron. 12:6).

JOGBEHAH (Jŏg′ bė hăh) Place name meaning, "height, little hill." City east of the Jordan where Gideon defeated Zeba and Zalmunna, kings of Midian (Judg. 8:11). Its location is modern khirbet el-Jubeihat twenty miles southeast of the Jordan and seven miles northwest of Amman. The tribe of Gad rebuilt it and settled it (Num. 32:35).

JOGLI (Jŏg′ lī) Personal name meaning, "He reveals." Father of Bukki, who represented tribe of Dan in distributing the Promised Land (Num. 34:22).

JOHA (Jō′ hà) Apparently a short form of the personal name Johanan meaning, "Yahweh is merciful." *1.* Member of tribe of Benjamin (1 Chron. 8:16). *2.* Military hero in David's army (1 Chron. 11:45).

JOHANAN (Jō hō′ nan) Short form of personal name Jehohanan meaning, "Yah is merciful." *1.* Military leader among Jews who remained in Judah immediately after the Exile began in 586 B.C. (2 Kings 25:23). He led the effort against Ishmael, who had assassinated Gedaliah, the governor Babylon appointed over Judah. Johanan led the people into Egypt to escape Babylonian retalia-

tion. He forced Jeremiah to go with them, refusing to follow Jeremiah's word from God (Jer. 40—43). *2.* High priest about 411 B.C. known in the Elephantine papyri as Jehohanan but in Nehemiah 12:22–23 as Johanan. He was high priest at time Nehemiah's list of priests was compiled. Some interpreters would say that Jonathan (Neh. 12:11) is a copyist's error for Johanan, but this is not likely. Others would equate this Johanan with Jehohanan of Ezra 10:6 (note the KJV equation of names despite difference in Hebrew spelling), but Ezra does not indicate Jehohanan was high priest. See *Jehohanan. 3.* A high priest whom Josephus, the early Jewish historian, says murdered his brother named Jesus, perhaps under Artaxerxes III Ochus (358–338 B.C.). *4.* Eldest son of Josiah (1 Chron. 3:15). We know nothing else of this royal son who for some reason did not become king. *5.* A descendant of David in the postexilic period about 445 B.C. (1 Chron. 3:24). *6.* High priest in the early period of Israel's monarchy (1 Chron 6:9–10). His son Azariah was high priest under Solomon (compare 1 Kings 4:2). *7.* Member of Saul's tribe of Benjamin who joined David at Ziklag when he fled from Saul (1 Chron. 12:4). *8.* Member of tribe of Gad who joined David at Ziklag, demonstrating the people east of the Jordan supported him (1 Chron. 12:12). *9.* Man who led a group going with Ezra from Babylon to Jerusalem about 458 B.C. (Ezra 8:12).

JOHANNAN (Jō hān′ nan) TEV spelling of Johanan (1 Chron. 12:12). See *Johanan.*

JOHN (Jŏhn) Greek form of Hebrew name meaning, "Yahweh has been gracious." 1. **John the Apostle,** the son of Zebedee, the brother of James. Harmonizing Matthew 27:56 with Mark 15:40 suggests that John's mother was Salome. If she was also the sister of Jesus' mother (John 19:25), then John was Jesus' first cousin. This string of associations is so conjectural, though, that we cannot be sure of it. Because James is usually mentioned first when the two brothers are identified, some have also conjectured that John was the younger of the two.

The sons of Zebedee were among the first disciples called (Matt. 4:21–22; Mark 1:19–20). They were fishermen on the Sea of Galilee and probably lived in Capernaum. Their father was sufficiently prosperous to have "hired servants" (Mark 1:20), and Luke 5:10 states that James and John were "partners with Simon" Peter.

John is always mentioned in the first four in the lists of the twelve (Matt. 10:2; Mark 3:17; Luke 6:14; Acts 1:13). John is also among the "inner three" who were with Jesus on special occasions in the Synoptic Gospels: the raising of Jairus' daughter (Mark 5:37), the transfiguration (Mark 9:2), and the Garden of Gethsemane (Mark 14:32–33). Andrew joined these three when

J

they asked Jesus about the signs of the coming destruction of Jerusalem (Mark 13:3).

The sons of Zebedee were given the surname *Boanerges,* "sons of thunder" (Mark 3:17). When a Samaritan village refused to receive Jesus, they asked, "Lord, wilt thou that we command fire to come down from heaven, and consume them?" (Luke 9:54). The only words in the Synoptic Gospels attributed specifically to John are: "Master, we saw one casting out devils in thy name . . . and we forbad him, because he followeth not us" (Mark 9:38; Luke 9:49). On another occasion the two brothers asked to sit in places of honor, on Jesus' left and right in His glory (Mark 10:35–41; compare Matt. 20:20–24). On each of these occasions Jesus challenged or rebuked John. Luke 22:8, however, identifies Peter and John as the two disciples who were sent to prepare the Passover meal for Jesus and the disciples.

The apostle John appears three times in the Book of Acts, and each time he is with Peter (1:13; 3:1–11; 4:13,20; 8:14). After Peter healed the man, they were arrested, imprisoned, and then released. They were "unlearned and ignorant men" (Acts 4:13), but they answered their accusers boldly: "we cannot but speak the things which we have seen and heard" (Acts 4:20). Later, John and Peter were sent to Samaria to confirm the conversion of Samaritans (8:14).

Paul mentioned John only once: "James, Cephas [Simon Peter], and John, who seemed to be pillars" of the church agreed that Paul and Barnabas would go to the Gentiles, while they would work among the Jews (Gal. 2:9).

The Gospel of John does not mention James or John by name, and it contains only one reference to the sons of Zebedee (21:2). An unnamed disciple who with Andrew had been one of John the Baptist's disciples is mentioned in John 1:35, and an unnamed disciple helped Peter gain access to the house of the high priest in John 18:15–16. The disciple in these verses may have been the Beloved Disciple, who reclined with Jesus during the last supper (13:23–26), stood at the cross with Jesus' mother (19:25–27), ran with Peter to the empty tomb (20:2–10), and recognized the risen Lord after the great catch of fish (21:7). The need to clarify what Jesus had said about the death of the Beloved Disciple (21:20–23) probably indicates that the Beloved Disciple had died by the time the Gospel of John was put in final form by the editor who speaks in John 21:24–25 and attributes the Gospel to this Beloved Disciple.

Five books of the New Testament have been attributed to John the Apostle: the Gospel, three Epistles, and Revelation. In each case, the traditional view that the apostle was the author of these books can be traced to writers in the second century. Neither the Gospel nor the epistles identify their author by name. The author of Revelation identifies himself as "John" (1:1, 4, 9; 22:8)

but does not claim to be the apostle. Much of the weight of the traditional view of the authorship of the Gospel rests on the testimony of Irenaeus, bishop of Lugdunum in Gaul (A.D. 130–200).

The origin of the attribution of the five writings to the apostle is difficult to trace. The strongest argument can probably be made for the traditional view of the authorship of Revelation. Its author claims to be "John," it is associated with Patmos and Ephesus, and in tone it fits the character of the apostle who was called "Boanerges." Justin Martyr, moreover, in the earliest testimony regarding the authorship of Revelation attributes it to John.

Internal evidence from the Gospel and Epistles provides many Bible students reasons to question the traditional view. The Gospel does not mention the "inner three" disciples as a group, nor does it refer to any of the events at which these three were present with Jesus: the raising of Jairus' daughter, the transfiguration, and the agony of Jesus in the Garden of Gethsemane. Clearly, the editor of the Gospel, who refers to himself in John 21:24–25, links the Gospel with the Beloved Disciple. The question is whether that disciple was John or some other apostle.

The author of the epistles identifies himself as "the elder" (2 John 1, 3 John 1), but never claims to be the apostle. Neither does the author of these epistles claim the authority to command the church to follow his instructions. Instead, he reasons with them and urges the church to abide in what it has received and what it has heard from the beginning.

In sum, a strong tradition linking the apostle John to the authorship of these five New Testament writings can be traced to the second century. Modern scholarship has raised questions about the credibility of this tradition, and discussion of these matters continues. Many would agree, however, that the strongest case can be made for the apostolic authorship of Revelation, followed in order by the Gospel and Epistles. Many Bible students continue to follow tradition and attribute all five books to the apostle.

Legends about the apostle continued to develop long after his death. According to tradition, John lived to an old age in Ephesus, where he preached love and fought heresy, especially the teachings of Cerinthus. The tomb of John was the site of a fourth-century church, over which Justinian built the splendid basilica of St. John. The ruins of this basilica are still visible in Ephesus today.

The Apocryphon of John is an early gnostic work that purports to contain a vision of the apostle John. Copies were found among the codices at Nag Hammadi. The work itself must go back at least to the second century because Irenaeus quoted from it.

The Acts of John is a third-century apocryphal writing which records miraculous events, John's journey to Rome, his exile on Patmos, accounts of several journeys, and a detailed account of John's death. In theology this work is Docetic, and it was eventually condemned by the Second Nicene Council in 787.

The apostle John also has a place in the martyrologies of the medieval church. A fifth-century writer, Philip of Side, and George the Sinner, of the ninth century, report that Papias (second century) wrote that James and John were killed by the Jews (Acts 12:2), but these reports are generally dismissed as fabrications based on interpretations of Mark 10:39.

See *John, The Gospel of; John, The Letters of; Revelation of John.*

2. **John the Baptist,** a prophet from a priestly family, who preached a message of repentance, announced the coming of the Messiah, baptized Jesus, and was beheaded by Herod Antipas.

Luke 1:5–80 records the birth of John the Baptist in terms similar to the birth of Isaac. Zechariah, John's father, was a priest from the division of Abijah. Elizabeth, his mother, was a descendant of Aaron. The angel Gabriel announced John's birth, while Zechariah was burning incense in the Temple. John would not drink wine or strong drink. He would be filled with the Holy Spirit, and as a prophet he would have the spirit and power of Elijah. His role would be to prepare the Lord's people for the coming of the Messiah.

Mark 1:3–4 records that John was in the wilderness until the time of his public ministry. There he ate locusts and wild honey. He wore the dress of a prophet, camel's hair and a leather girdle (Matt. 3:4; Mark 1:6; see 2 Kings 1:8). Because of his life in the wilderness, his priestly background, his preaching of repentance to Israel, and his practice of baptism, it is often suggested that John grew up among the Essenes at Qumran. This theory is attractive, but it cannot be confirmed. Neither can the origin of John's practice of baptizing be traced with certainty. Washings had long been part of Jewish piety, and by the time of John, Gentile converts to Judaism washed themselves as a form of ceremonial cleansing. The Essenes at Qumran practiced ritual washings and had an elaborate procedure for admission to the community. John's baptism may owe something to the Essene practices, but we cannot determine the extent of this influence.

According to Luke, John began his ministry around the Jordan River in the fifteenth year of the reign of Tiberius Caesar (Luke 3:1–3), which must have been A.D. 26 or 27. John's preaching emphasized the coming judgment, the need for repentance, and the coming of the Messiah. Luke also emphasizes the ethical teachings of John: he called the multitudes a "generation of vipers" (Luke 3:7); one who had two coats should give one to a person who had none; tax collectors were warned to collect no more than their due; and soldiers were instructed to rob no one and be content with their wages" (Luke 3:10–14).

Jesus was baptized by John, a fact that all the evangelists except Mark attempted to explain. Matthew 3:15 explains that it was "to fulfill all righteousness." Luke recorded that John was thrown in prison before he said that Jesus also was baptized (3:20–21), and John told of the baptism of Jesus but only through the testimony of John the Baptist himself. Thus, the witness of John the Baptist to Jesus is featured, deflecting any possibility that later followers of the Baptist might argue that John was superior to Jesus (Matt. 3:11–12; Mark 1:7–8; Luke 3:15–17; John 1:15, 19–36).

Various sayings give us glimpses of John's ministry. His disciples practiced fasting (Mark 2:18), and he taught them to pray (Luke 11:1). John was vigorous in his attacks on Herod. In contrast to Herod's household he lived an austere existence (Matt. 11:7–9). Some criticized John for his ascetic life-style (Matt. 11:16–19), but Jesus praised John as the greatest of the prophets (Matt. 11:11). John's popularity with the people is reflected in Matthew 21:31–32; Mark 11:27–32; Luke 7:29–30; John 10:41.

In an account that parallels the New Testament closely, Josephus stated that Herod Antipas arrested John and subsequently executed him at Machaerus because "he feared that John's so extensive influence over the people might lead to an uprising." Many believed that the defeat of Herod's armies by the Nabateans was God's judgment on Herod for the death of John the Baptist. While John was in prison, he sent two of his disciples to inquire whether Jesus was the coming One (Matt. 11:2–3; Luke 7:18–23). John's death is recorded in detail in Mark 6:14–29.

According to the Gospel of John, the ministry of Jesus overlapped with that of John (3:22–24; contrast Mark 1:14), and some of Jesus' first disciples had also been disciples of John the Baptist (John 1:35–37). Jesus even identified John with the eschatological role of Elijah (Matt. 17:12–13; Mark 9:12–13).

John's movement did not stop with his death. Indeed, some believed that Jesus was John, raised from the dead (Mark 6:14–16; 8:28). Years later, a group of John's followers were found around Ephesus, among them the eloquent Apollos (Acts 18:24–19:7); and for centuries John's influence survived among the Mandeans, who claimed to perpetuate his teachings. See *Baptism.*

3. Relative of Annas, the high priest (Acts 4:6), unless manuscripts reading Jonathan are right.

4. John Mark. See *Mark.*   R. Alan Culpepper

JOHN, THE GOSPEL OF According to tradition the fourth Gospel was written by John the apostle in Ephesus, toward the end of his life. Perhaps because it is so different from the Synoptic Gospels, Clement of Alexandria called it the "spiritual Gospel."

Since the beginning of the modern era, scholars have debated the authorship and historicity of this Gospel. The Gospel itself says only that it was written by the beloved disciple (21:20–24). Although this disciple is traditionally identified as the apostle John, the Gospel itself does not make this identification. See *John 1.*

Part of the enigma of John is its distinctiveness from the other three canonical Gospels. John does not tell of Jesus' birth in Bethlehem. Jesus tells no parables, and there is nothing like the Sermon on the Mount. Jesus heals no lepers, and demons are never mentioned. The kingdom of God, which is the primary theme of Jesus' preaching in the Synoptics, is scarcely mentioned in John. Instead of the short, pithy sayings that characterize Jesus' words in the Synoptics, one finds in John extended discourses. There is no list of the twelve disciples, and "the twelve" are mentioned only at the end of John 6 and once later (20:24). The bread and the wine are not mentioned at the last supper. Instead, Jesus washes the disciples' feet. There are also differences in chronology. In the Synoptics Jesus spends His entire ministry in and around Galilee and makes one trip to Jerusalem, just a week before His death. According to John, however, Jesus made four trips to Jerusalem (John 2:13; 5:1; 7:10; 12:12) and spent a significant part of His ministry in Judea.

The Gospel of John, therefore, gives a distinctive account of Jesus' "signs," His words, and His ministry. Parts of the Gospel are remarkably parallel to the synoptic accounts, but the distinctive elements should not be overlooked as one ponders its mystery and message.

A widely accepted theory holds that the Gospel makes use of an account of the signs Jesus performed. The first two of these are numbered (John 2:1–11; 4:46–54). At other points one can also see evidences of earlier stages in the Gospel's composition. In John 14:31 Jesus said, "Arise, let us go hence." The next three chapters, however, continue the farewell discourse. Only at 18:1 do we read the natural continuation of 14:31: "When Jesus had spoken these words, he went forth with his disciples." Many Bible students regard John 15—17 as a longer version of the discourse material contained in John 14. Similarly, the Gospel seems to reach its conclusion at the end of chapter 20. Jesus appeared to the disciples, comforted them, commissioned them, and consecrated them with the Holy Spirit. Thomas's doubt was overcome, and Thomas voiced the Gospel's climactic confession: "My Lord, and my God!" (20:28). Jesus pronounced a beatitude on all who would later believe, and the evangelist stated the purpose for which the Gospel was written (20:30–31). To many Bible students the end of John 20 appears to be the original ending of the Gospel. No ancient manuscript, however, lacks the last chapter, which these Bible students think was probably added shortly later by the final editor. Regardless of the whether material in the Gospel was added early or late in the process of composition, it all derived from the witness of the Beloved Disciple as his teachings were developed and used in the worship of the community that gathered around him. It is the inspired Word God has given us "that ye might believe that Jesus is the Christ, the Son of God; and that believing ye might have life through his name" (20:31).

The earliest period of the history of John's community took place within a Jewish synagogue. The account of Jesus' crucifixion and resurrection, which makes frequent allusions to the Hebrew Scriptures, was probably shaped during this period. Other sections of the Gospel, such as the calling of the first disciples (1:35–51) may also reflect the preaching of this group at a time when they were appealing to fellow Jews.

As a result of their confession of Jesus as the Christ, these Christian Jews were expelled from the synagogue and persecuted by the Jewish community. The Gospel reflects conflict with the Jewish authorities both during the ministry of Jesus and at the time of the writing of the Gospel. By telling about the life of Jesus in such a way that later believers saw similarities with their own struggles, the Gospel's message took on greater significance for the Christian community. The expulsion from the synagogue is referred to in John 9:22; 12:42; and 16:2, and other passages speak of "fear of the Jews" (7:13; 20:19).

The Gospel was written after the separation from the synagogue to proclaim the gospel message that gave the Christian community its identity and purpose. The Gospel of John features episodes in which individuals are caught between Jesus' call for faith and the Jewish authorities' rejection of His claims (Nicodemus, John 3; the man at the Pool of Bethesda, John 5; the crowds in Galilee, John 6; and the man born blind, John 9). The purpose of the Gospel, therefore, was twofold: (1) to call believers to reaffirm their faith and move on to a more mature faith, and (2) to call the "secret believers" (12:42; 19:38) to confess Jesus as the Christ and join the Christian community.

Eventually, a dangerous belief that either denied or diminished the significance of the incarnation began to develop. Some Johannine Christians taught that Jesus was certainly the Christ, but they denied that the Christ had come "in flesh" (see 1 John 4:2–3; 2 John 7). Finally, the community was divided. See *John, The Letters of.*

We do not know what happened to the Johannine community after the writing of the epistles, but we may conjecture that the remnant that followed the elder was assimilated into the emerging church of the second century while the elder's opponents, with their Docetic Christology, probably found their way into the developing Gnostic groups.

The roots of the Johannine tradition reach back to the ministry of Jesus, and the Gospel stands on eyewitness testimony (19:34–35; 21:24–25). The composition of the Gospel, described above, probably stretched over several decades, with the Gospel reaching its present form around A.D. 90–100. Its place in the New Testament, following the other three Gospels, may reflect the memory that it was the last of the four Gospels.

The Gospel of John draws a portrait of Jesus as the divine Logos, the Christ, the Son of God. Its message is thoroughly Christological. Jesus has a dual role as Revealer and Redeemer. He came to reveal the Father and to take away "the sin of the world" (1:18, 29). As the Logos, Jesus continued God's creative and redemptive work, turning water to wine, creating eyes for a blind man, and breathing Holy Spirit into His disciples. As the Revealer, Jesus revealed that he and the Father were one (10:30), so those who saw Him (that is, received Him in faith) saw the Father (14:9). All that Jesus does and says points beyond and above to the knowledge of God. Through Jesus' revelation of the Father, which reaches its fulfillment in His death on the cross, Jesus delivers the world from sin. Sin is understood in the Gospel of John primarily as unbelief (16:9).

John contains a profound analysis of the experience of faith. The human condition apart from God is characterized in John as "the world," which is under the power of sin. Some never believe because they love the darkness and the glory of men rather than the glory of God. All who believe are called, drawn, and chosen by the Father (6:37, 44; 10:3, 27; 17:6). Some believe only because of Jesus' signs. The Gospel accepts this response as faith but calls believers on to faith that is based on Jesus' words and on the knowledge of God revealed in Jesus.

Those who believe in His name are born "from above" (3:3 NRSV). They are the "children of God" (1:12), whose life is sustained by living water and the bread of life. They live in community as His sheep (John 10), the branches of the true Vine (John 15). Jesus' disciples are to live "just as" he lived. The twin commands of the Johannine community were to have faith and to love one another (14:1; 13:34; 1 John 3:23). Those who believe already have eternal life, here and now (John 17:3). They have already crossed from death into life (5:24), and the judgment occurs in one's response to Jesus (3:19). John emphasized the present fulfillment of future expectations. Believers, however, will also be raised "at the last day" (6:39,40,44,54).

Outline

I. The Prologue (1:1–18)

II. Jesus Before the World (1:19—12:50)
    A. Calling Disciples (1:19—2:11)

    B. The Temple and Nicodemus (2:12—3:21)
    C. An interlude in Judea (3:22–36)
    D. The Samaritan woman and the nobleman (4:1–54)
    E. The man at the pool of Bethesda (5:1–47)
    F. Feeding the multitude (6:1–71)
    G. Confrontation in Jerusalem (7:1—8:59)
    H. The blind man and the shepherd's sheep (9:1—10:42)
    I. The raising of Lazarus (11:1–54)
    J. Preparations for the Passover (11:55—12:50)

III. Jesus with His Own (13:1—20:31)
    A. The Farewell Discourse (13:1—17:26)
      1. The footwashing (13:1–30)
      2. The Farewell Discourse: Part 1 (13:31—14:31)
      3. The Farewell Discourse: Part 2 (15:1—16:4)
      4. The Farewell Discourse: Part 3 (16:5—33)
      5. The high priestly prayer (17:1–26)
    B. The trial of Jesus (18:1—19:16a)
    C. The death of Jesus (19:16b–42)
    D. The resurrection of Jesus (20:1–29)
    E. Conclusion (20:30–31)

IV. Epilogue (21:1–25)

See *John, The Letters of; John the Apostle; and Logos.*   R. Alan Culpepper

JOHN, THE LETTERS OF Three New Testament books attributed to the apostle John. Knowledge and use of 1 John is attested from an early date in the writings of Papias (according to Eusebius), Polycarp, and Justin. It was regarded as the work of the apostle John by Irenaeus, Tertullian, Clement of Alexandria, Origen, and the Muratorian Canon.

Second and Third John were accepted as Scripture more slowly. Origen reported that their authenticity was questioned, and Eusebius placed them in the list of writings that were disputed, although "well-known and acknowledged by most."

The Johannine character of the three letters is universally recognized, but debate over their authorship continues. Some scholars regard the apostle John as the author of all three letters. Others, citing stylistic and theological differences between the Gospel and the Letters, contend that they were written by an elder in the Johannine community, who was not the evangelist. It is possible that the author of the letters was the final editor of the Gospel, the "I" who speaks in John 21:25. The author never identifies himself by name. Twice he claims the title "the elder" (2 John 1; 3 John 1), but he never calls himself an apostle.

Most scholars agree that the three letters were written by the same author and that they were

J

written after the Gospel. A date of about A.D. 100 seems to be indicated, but both earlier and later dates have been proposed. Several factors support a date following the composition of the Gospel. First John 1:1–5 seems to imitate John 1:1–18. The polemic against "the Jews" that pervades much of the Gospel does not appear in the letters. Their concern was with difficulties within the Christian community. Whereas the Gospel was written "that ye might believe that Jesus is the Christ, the Son of God" (John 20:31), 1 John insists that one must confess that Jesus Christ has come in flesh (1 John 4:2). Second John 7 likewise identifies as deceivers those who do not confess "Jesus Christ come [having come or coming] in flesh." The letters are therefore concerned with correcting a false belief about Christ that was spreading in the churches.

From this emphasis on the incarnation, we may assume that the opponents held to the divinity of Christ but either denied or diminished the significance of His humanity. Their view may be an early form of Docetism, the heresy that emerged in the second century which claimed that Jesus only seemed to be human.

This false belief had already led to schism. First John 2:19 explains that those who had left the community never really belonged to it, or else they would have remained with it. First John 4:1 warns the church to test the spirits because "many false prophets are gone out into the world." These "opponents" of the elder's group are charged with not following the command to love one's fellow Christians. They apparently also claimed that they were free from sin (1 John 1:8, 10). Both groups held that believers have "passed from death unto life" (1 John 3:14), but the elder recognized the potential danger in this teaching and contended that the future coming of the Lord (1 John 3:2) requires that believers purify themselves and be righteous (1 John 3:3–7).

The Johannine letters, therefore, provide us with a window on an early Christian church, its problems, and its developing doctrine. First John seems to be a treatise written to the Johannine community. In contrast, 2 and 3 John are much briefer, about the length of a single sheet of papyrus, and they follow the conventional form of a personal letter.

First John is difficult to outline because its themes recur throughout the letter and because transitional verses may be placed either with the preceding or the following sections (2:28; 4:1–6). Outlines with varying numbers of divisions have been suggested for 1 John. The structure followed here is based on the repetition of the statement "God is" three times in the Epistle: "God is light" (1:5), "He is righteous" (2:29), and "God is love" (4:8). First John demands that these qualities must dominate the lives of believers.

As a way of refuting the false teaching that threatened the community, the elder quoted tenets of the opponents in 1 John 1:6,8,10; 2:4,6, and 9, and answered each point. He called those who remained to practice the command of love (2:3–11). The elder gave assurance to the community and warned the believers that they cannot practice love for one another and love for the world at the same time (2:15–17). "The world" here means all that is opposed to Christ. Dissension had already split the community, and the elder warned those who remained about the dangers of the false teaching (2:18–27).

One of the tests of faithfulness is righteousness (2:29). The opponents may have emphasized the present realization of the church's hope for the future, saying that the judgment was already past and Christians had already passed from death into life. The elder reasserted a more traditional eschatology (see 3:2). Hope for the future, however, carries with it the imperative of righteous, pure living. Christians cannot make sin a way of life (compare 3:6,9 with 1:8–10).

Another test of faithfulness is living by the command to love one another, which means sharing with those in need (3:11–24, especially v. 17). The false prophets, who had gone out from the community, denied the incarnation (4:1–6). The incarnation is crucial for Christian doctrine, however, because in Christ we find the love of God revealed (4:7–21). Love of God, however, requires that we love one another.

Those who have faith in Christ and love God keep His commands, and to them God gives eternal life (5:1–12). The water, the blood, and the Spirit all bear witness to Christ, His incarnation, and His death. Christians are to pray for one another, but there is sin that is "mortal" (5:16). By this the elder probably meant denying Christ, the one through whom sin is forgiven. Christ also keeps those who are "born of God." He is the only source of eternal life.

Outline

I. The Prologue: The Word of Life (1:1–4)
II. Light Among God's Children (1:5–2:27)
   A. The incompatibility of light and sin (1:5–2:2)
   B. Love as a test of knowledge (2:3–11)
   C. Conflict with the world (2:12–17)
   D. Conflict within the community (2:18–27)
III. Righteousness Among God's Children (2:28–4:6)
   A. The hope of the righteous (2:28–3:10)
   B. The love of the righteous (3:11–24)
   C. The two spirits (4:1–6)
IV. Love Among God's Children (4:7–5:12)
   A. The true nature of love (4:7–21)
   B. The true nature of faith (5:1–12)
V. The Epilogue (5:13–21)

Second John was written by the elder to a sister community to warn the church about the dangers of the false teaching that had already threatened the elder's church. The sequence of the writing of 1 and 2 John is conjectural, but they were probably written by the same author at about the same time. They share similar concerns, and in many places the same phrases appear in both letters.

The elder praised the sister church for following the truth and appealed for her to continue to show love. The elder apparently wanted to be sure that the sister church would continue in fellowship with his church. His real concern, however, was to warn "the elect lady" (v. 1) about those "who confess not that Jesus Christ is come in the flesh" (v. 7). Such deceivers and antichrists are not to be received by the church. These were apparently members of the same group referred to in 1 John 2:19 and 4:1–2.

Outline

I. The Salutation of Love for Those Who Know the Truth (1–2)

II. The Blessings of Grace, Mercy, and Peace (3)

III. Love Is the Identifying Mark for Christians (4–6).

IV. Believers Face Deceivers (7–11).

V. Personal Conclusion (12–13)

Third John is a personal letter from the elder to Gaius, who had been providing hospitality to fellow Christians and messengers from the elder's community. Diotrephes, however, refused to receive those sent by the elder. The elder charged that Diotrephes "loveth to have the preeminence among them" (v. 9), but Diotrephes' position is unclear. Some interpreters suggest that Diotrephes was an appointed leader or bishop of the church. Others conclude that Diotrephes had rejected the authority of the church's leaders, ambitiously asserting his own leadership. It may be that in an effort to prevent outsiders from spreading false teachings and dissension in the church he refused to receive any traveling prophets or teachers.

Gaius may or may not be a member of Diotrephes' church. The elder praised Gaius and commended Demetrius (who may have carried the letter) as a faithful witness. The letter closes with greetings from fellow Christians, who are called "the friends" (v. 14; see John 3:29; 11:11; 15:13–15).

See *John the Apostle; John, the Gospel of.*

Outline

I. The Address (1)

II. The Blessing of Good Health and Welfare for a Faithful Spiritual Leader (2–4)

III. Believers Should show Hospitality and Support for Visiting Believers (5–8).

IV. Pride, Gossiping, and Lack of Hospitality Bring Condemnation (9–10).

V. Imitate Good Leaders but Not Wicked Ones (11–12).

VI. Concluding Remarks (13–14).

R. Alan Culpepper

JOIADA (Joi′ à dà) Short form of personal name Jehoiada meaning, "Yah knows." *1.* Man who helped repair the old gate of Jerusalem under Nehemiah (Neh. 3:6, KJV reads, Jehoiada). *2.* High priest about 425 B.C. (Neh. 12:10–11,22). Ezra suspected one of his sons, who married Sanballat's daughter, of being a traitor (Neh. 13:28). See *Sanballat.* Such marriage of a high priest's family with a foreigner violated Jewish law (Lev. 21:14).

JOIAKIM (Joi′ à kĭm) Short form of Jehoiakim meaning, "Yah has established, set up, delivered." Son of Jeshua and high priest of Israel about 510 B.C. (Neh. 12:10,12,26).

JOIARIB (Joi à rĭb) Short form of Jehoiarib meaning, "Yah establishes justice." See *Jehoiarib. 1.* Member of group Ezra sent to get Levites to accompany him on return from Babylon to Jerusalem (Ezra 8:16). Many interpreters think Joiarib is a copyist's duplication of Jarib earlier in the verse. See *Jarib. 2.* Ancestor of member of tribe of Judah who lived in Jerusalem after the Exile (Neh. 11:5). *3.* Father of priest who lived in Jerusalem after the Exile (Neh. 11:10). *4.* Priest who returned to Jerusalem from Babylonian Exile about 537 B.C. with Zerubbabel (Neh. 12:6). *5.* Leading priestly family after return from Exile (Neh. 12:19).

JOKDEAM (Jŏk′ dĕ ăm) Place name meaning, "the people burned." City in tribal territory of Judah, possibly modern khirbet Raqqa near Ziph (Josh. 15:56).

JOKIM (Jō′ kĭm) Short form of personal name Jehoiakim meaning, "Yah has established or delivered." An early member of the tribe of Judah (1 Chron. 4:22).

JOKMEAM (Jŏk′ mĕ ăm) Place name meaning, "He establishes the people" or "the Kinsman establishes or delivers." A variant form of Jokneam. *1.* Border city of fifth district of Solomon's kingdom (1 Kings 4:12; KJV reads Jokneam). Its location was probably tell Qaimun about eighteen miles south of Haifa on the northwestern corner of the Jezreel Valley. A fortress city, it protected the pass into the Plain of Sharon. It lay on the border, perhaps outside of the tribal territory of Zebulun (Josh. 19:11, spelled Jokneam) and was assigned the Levites (Josh. 21:34, spelled Jokneam). Joshua defeated its king whose kingdom was near Mount Carmel (Josh. 12:22, spelled Jokneam). Egyptian records of Thutmose III, Egyptian Pharaoh about 1504–1450 B.C., mentioned Jokmeam.

2. City of the Levites from tribe of Ephraim (1 Chron. 6:68), either omitted in list in Joshua 21:22 or to be equated with Kibzaim there. See *Kibzaim.* It may be located at tell es-Simadi or Qusen west of Shechem.

J

JOKNEAM (Jŏk' nē ăm) Alternate spelling of Jokmeam. See *Jokmeam*.

JOKSHAN (Jŏk' shăn) Personal name meaning, "trap, snare." Son of Abraham by Keturah and ancestor of Arabian tribes in wilderness east of Jordan (Gen. 25:2–3). He links the Jews and Arabs together as belonging to a common ancestor—Abraham.

JOKTAN (Jŏk' tăn) Personal name meaning, "watchful" or "he is small." Son of Eber in line from Shem in the Table of Nations (Gen. 10:25–26). He was original ancestor of several tribes in the Arabian desert, particularly in Jemin. See *Mesha; Sephar.*

JOKTHEEL (Jŏk' thē ĕl) Place name meaning, "God nourishes" or "destroys." *1.* Town in Shephelah or valley of tribal allotment of Judah (Josh. 15:38). *2.* King Amaziah captured Selah from Edom and renamed it Joktheel (2 Kings 14:7). It may be modern es-Sela northwest of Bozrah. See *Selah.*

JONA (Jō' na) Greek transliteration of Hebrew personal name Jonah meaning, "dove." Father of Simon Peter (John 1:42; compare 21:15–17).

JONADAB (Jŏn' à dăb) Short form of personal name Jehonadab meaning, "Yah proves himself to be generous." *1.* David's nephew who counseled Ammon how to take advantage of Tamar (2 Sam. 13). Jonadab also advised the sorrowing David that of his sons only Ammon was dead (vv. 32–33). *2.* Form used at times for Jehonadab in Jeremiah 35. See *Jehonadab.*

JONAH (Jō' nah) Personal name meaning, "dove" and name of book of Bible preserving story of a part of prophet's ministry. The Book of Jonah is unique among the Minor Prophets in consisting of a short story about a prophet and in confining his message to a sentence (3:4).

The hero or rather anti-hero is mentioned in 2 Kings 14:23–29 as active in the reign of Jeroboam II (about 785–745 B.C.). His prediction of national expansion for the Northern Kingdom, evidently made early in the reign, expressed God's longing to save His people, wicked though they were. This theological background is important for the book.

A series of cumulative arguments suggest that the unknown author of the book be assigned to a comparatively late date, probably to the fifth century B.C., though many Bible students think the book came from about 750 B.C. Its Hebrew language is marked by Aramaic features, some of which can be paralleled only in Imperial Aramaic, current in the Persian period. There appear to be deliberate echoes of Jer. 18:7,8,11 (Jonah 3:8,10)

and of the postexilic Joel 2:13,14 (Jonah 3:9; 4:2). The title "king of Nineveh" (3:6) seems to imply that the city was the capital of Assyria, which it became only at the end of the eighth century. The book appears to be loosely tied to history and presents later theological reflection.

Some have regarded the book as an allegory: Jonah then stands for Israel swallowed in Exile by the Babylonian sea monster (compare Jer. 51:34, 44). Yet God used the fish not to punish Jonah but to rescue him. Rather, the book is to be regarded as a satirical parable intended to criticize and correct its readers' attitudes (compare 2 Sam. 12:1–6; 14:1–11; Isa. 5:1–7). It builds on an earlier phenomenon, as the parable in Luke 19:11–27 builds on Archelaus' visit to Rome. The book's extraordinary features—the seemingly exaggerated size of Nineveh (3:3); Jonah's survival with a song in the fish's interior, digestive juices notwithstanding; and the suddenly appearing/disappearing plant (4:6,7)—are meant to rivet the hearers' attention and to enhance the purpose of the book. The fantastic debt in Matthew 18:24 may be compared. Jonah is presented as a caricature of Elijah, who obeyed God the first time (1 Kings 17:8–10; Jonah 1:1–3; 3:1–3) and had reason for despair (1 Kings 19:4; Jonah 4:3).

The two halves of the book have a dual focus, on pagans (1:4–16; 3:3b–10) and on the Israelite prophet (1:17–2:10; 4:1–11) in their respective relations to God. The portrayal of pagans in a positive light as sensitive and submissive to God's will recognizes their worth and potential in His sight. Jonah is shown to be inconsistent: after praising God for rescuing him from threat of death, he complained when God did the same for pagans. Two credal statements represent God as universal Creator (1:9) and as Preserver of the lives of pagans in an extension of His covenant grace (4:2; compare Ex. 34:6; Ps. 145:8,9,15, 16). He so loves the world: the book has a pre-missionary role in defining a theological truth, God's relation to the world outside the sheepfold of faith. Even the Assyrians' later destruction of Israel (2 Kings 17) and their tyrannical imperialism (2 Kings 18:22–24; Nah. 3:1–4, 19), which the book appears to presuppose, could not debar them from God's loving concern for their survival.

In the Gospels, especially at Matthew 12:40, Jonah's stay in the fish (1:17) is represented as a type of Jesus' brief confinement to the grave. Exegetically the fish is the means of God's rescue of the prophet from drowning. In Jewish exposition the incident was given a negative interpretation as a threat from which Jonah had to be saved. Jesus reflected this contemporary understanding: His concern was to teach about His mission rather than to exegete the book.

Outline

I. People with Bad Reputations Can Be Pious and Know God (1:1–16).

ll. God Hears the Distress Calls of His People (1:17—2:10).
III. God in His Compassion Turns Away from Judgment When Any People Repent (3:1–10).
IV. God's People Should Mirror God's Compassion for All People (4:1–11). *Leslie C. Allen*

JONAM (Jō′ nam) Modern translation spelling of Jonan. See *Jonan.*

JONAN (Jō′ năn) Greek spelling of Hebrew personal name Jehohanan, meaning "Yahweh is gracious" (compare 1 Chron. 26:3). Ancestor of Jesus (Luke 3:30). Greek uses the "m" ending, while Hebrew has the "n." See *Jonam.*

JONAS (Jō′ nàs) KJV spelling for Jonah in New Testament. See *Jonah; Jona.*

JONATH-ELEM-RECHOKIM (Jō′ năth-ē′ lĕm-rĕ chō′ kīm) Transliteration of word in title of Psalm 56 (NAS, KJV). NIV reads, "to the tune of 'A Dove on Distant Oaks' " (compare REB, NRSV with Terebinths for oaks). This was probably the name of a tune to which the Psalm was sung.

JONATHAN (Jŏn′ à than) Personal name meaning, "Yahweh gave." *1.* A Levite who served as priest of Micah in Ephraim and later with tribe of Dan (Judg. 17—18). *2.* Eldest son of King Saul; mother: Ahinroam; brothers: Abinadab, Malchishua and Ish-baal; sisters Merab and Michal; son Mephibosheth (Meribbaal).
Jonathan possessed courage, fidelity, and friendship. He led 1,000 soldiers to defeat the Philistines at Geba (Gibeah) (1 Sam. 13:2–3). Then Jonathan took only his armor-bearer to the rocky crags at Michmash and brought panic to the Philistines by killing twenty of them (1 Sam. 14:1–16). Saul discovered that Jonathan was missing, called for the ark of God, went to battle, and defeated the Philistines. Jonathan ate honey, unaware that Saul had forbidden the people to eat that day. Saul would have had Jonathan put to death, but the people spoke in praise of Jonathan and ransomed him from death (1 Sam. 14:27–46).
The next four accounts about Jonathan focus on his friendship with David. First, Jonathan formed a close friendship with David by giving him his robe, armor, sword, bow, and girdle (18:1–5). Second, Jonathan pleaded successfully with Saul to reinstate David (19:1–7). Third, Jonathan left Saul's table angrily to inform David that the king would never receive David again (20:1–42). Fourth, Jonathan held a final meeting with David at Horesh. They made covenant with one another as Jonathan acknowledged David as the next king (23:16–18).
The end of 1 Samuel reports the end of Saul and three of his sons, Jonathan, Abinadab, and Melchishua, at Mount Gilboa (1 Sam. 31:1–13). Their

bodies were first hung on the wall of Beth-shan and later retrieved to Jabesh. Eventually, David had the bones buried in the land of Benjamin, in Zela in the tomb of Kish, Jonathan's grandfather (2 Sam. 21:12–14). See *Saul; David; Mephibosheth.*
3. Son of Abiathar the priest in service to David (2 Sam. 15:24; 17:17,20; 1 Kings 1:42–43).
4. An uncle of David who functioned as counselor and scribe in the royal court (1 Chron. 27:32).
5. Son of Shimea or Shimeah, David's brother; slew a Philistine giant (2 Sam. 21:21; 1 Chron. 20:7).
6. Son of Shammah; one of David's thirty mighty men (2 Sam. 23:32–33; 1 Chron. 11:34).
7. Son of Uzziah, a royal treasurer in reign of David; called Jehonathan in 1 Chronicle 27:25.
8. House of a scribe or secretary where Jeremiah was imprisoned (Jer. 37:15,20; 38:26).
9. Son of Kareah; "Johanan;" possibly same as *8.* (Jer. 40:8).
10. Father of Ebed, a returned exile (Ezra 8:6; 1 Esdras 8:32).
11. Priest during high priesthood of Joiakim (Neh. 12:14).
12. Priest, son of Joiada (Neh. 12:11).
13. Priest, son of Shemaiah and father of Zechariah, in a group who played musical instruments (Neh. 12:35).
14. Son of Asahel who supported foreign marriages in time of Ezra (Ezra 10:15; 1 Esdras 9:14).
15. A descendant of Jerahmeel (1 Chron. 2:32–33).   *Omer Hancock*

JOPPA (Jŏp′ pà) Place name meaning "beautiful." Situated on the Mediterranean coast, Joppa is located some thirty-five miles northwest of Jerusalem. Excavations have revealed that the city dates back at least to 1650 B.C. Originally Joppa was situated on a rocky hill just over 100 feet high, a hill that juts slightly beyond the coastline to form a small cape. To the north stretches the Plain of Sharon, to the south the Plain of Philistia.
The Old Testament name for Joppa was Japho (or Jaffe or Yafo), the name the Israeli nation has chosen as the modern designation for the city. The Phoenician form of the term comes from the name Jafe, the daughter of Aeolus, god of the winds.
Joppa is the only natural harbor on the Mediterranean between ancient Ptolemais and Egypt, and its facilities in biblical days were far less than outstanding. Reefs forming a roughly semicircular breakwater approximately 300 feet off-shore made entrance from the south impossible. Entrance from the north was shallow and treacherous, but small vessels could navigate it.
The earliest historical reference to Joppa is found in inscriptions on the walls of the Temple of Karnak at Thebes (Luxor). Thutmose III, who ruled Egypt from 1490 to 1436 B.C., boasted of

Modern produce vendors at a busy market in Tel Aviv (adjacent to ancient Joppa).

The traditional house of Simon the Tanner in Joppa where Peter received his famous vision from God.

his conquest of the cities of Palestine; Joppa is one of those named. The Amarna Letters mention Joppa twice, with observations about the beauty of her gardens and the skill of her workmen in leather, wood, and metal.

When Canaan was conquered, the tribe of Dan received Joppa; but it never came firmly into Hebrew hands. The Philistines took the city, but David recaptured it. Solomon developed it into the major port serving Jerusalem. To Joppa rafts of cedar logs were floated to be transported to Jerusalem for Solomon's splendid Temple (2 Chron. 2:16).

Phoenicia gained control of Joppa by the time of Jonah. As the prophet fled from God's call, he caught a ship at Joppa for his well-remembered voyage toward Tarshish (Jonah 1:3). In 701 B.C.

The ancient seaport of Joppa (Jaffa).

J

Sennacherib occupied the city; then, in turn, the Babylonians and the Persians. As it had been in Solomon's day, Joppa became the port that received cedar logs from Lebanon, now for the rebuilding of the Temple under the leadership of Zerubbabel.

In 164 B.C. more than 200 Jewish citizens of Joppa were treacherously drowned by angry non-Jews. In retaliation Judas Maccabeus raided the city, burned the harbor installations, torching the anchored ships as well (2 Maccabees 12:3–9). Joppa's history is linked with several notable names during the years of Roman control. Pompey conquered it in 63 B.C., joining it to the province of Syria. Antony later gave the city to Cleopatra of Egypt. Augustus Caesar added it to the kingdom of Herod the Great.

The New Testament records that Joppa was the home of Dorcas, a Christian woman known for her gracious and generous deeds. At her death the Christians of Joppa called for Simon Peter, who with the command "Tabitha, arise," restored her to life (Acts 9:36–41).

Simon Peter remained in Joppa at the home of Simon the Tanner. At noon, while Simon Peter waited for a meal to be prepared, he prayed on the flat roof of the tanner's house. In a trance Peter saw what seemed to be "a great sheet knit at the four corners" lowered before him and learned that the Gentile world was a fit audience for the gospel (Acts 10:9–16).

Joppa is now annexed to the modern city of Tel Aviv, forming a part of the southern section of the largest city of Israel. Industrial, shipping, and residential complexes have been developed on this ancient site.   *Timothy Trammell*

JORAH (Jō′ rah) Personal name meaning, "early or autumn rain." Group leader of Babylonian exiles returning to Jerusalem with Zerubbabel about 537 B.C. (Ezra 2:18). The parallel list (Neh. 7:24) has Hariph instead of Jorah (compare Neh. 10:19). Many interpreters believe Hariph to be the original reading, though it is difficult to explain the change. See *Hariph.*

JORAI (Jō′ rā ī) Personal name perhaps meaning, "Yah has seen" or a short form of Joiarim, "Yah has exalted." Member of tribe of Gad (1 Chron. 5:13).

JORAM (Jō′ ram) Personal name meaning, "Yahweh is exalted." Name of a king of Israel (849–843 B.C.) and a king of Judah (850–843 B.C.) The possibility of confusion between them is aggravated by several factors. For one thing, both are also called Jehoram. For another, they were contemporary with one another. Finally, each reigned in proximity to a person named Ahaziah: Joram of Judah was succeeded on the throne by his son, whose name was Ahaziah; Joram of Israel came to

the throne at the death of his brother, who was also named Ahaziah. The account of the reign of Joram (Jehoram) of Israel is found in 2 Kings 3. He led a coalition with Judah and Edom, advised by Elisha, to defeat Moab. The reign of Joram of Judah is treated in 2 Kings 8. He married the daughter of Ahab of Israel and brought Baal worship to Judah. Edom and Libnah gained independence from Judah in his reign. See *Israel; Chronology of Biblical Period.*

JORDAN RIVER (Jôr′ dan) Place name meaning, "the descender." River forming geographical division separating eastern and western tribes of Israel. It is the longest and most important river of Palestine. It rises from the foot of Mount Hermon and flows into the Dead Sea. The Jordan Valley proper is a strip approximately 70 miles long between the Sea of Galilee and the Dead Sea. The valley is divided by various rivers and wadis (small streams) into a number of geographically distinguishable sections. Due to the twists and turns of its course, the full length of the river is more than two hundred miles. Its headwaters lie more than a thousand feet above sea level, and its mouth nearly thirteen hundred feet below sea level. Through its descending course the river passes through a variety of climatic zones, as well as different types of terrain.

Four sources come together to form the Jordan River: Banias, el-Leddan, Hasbani, and Bareighit rivers. They all arise at the foothills of Mount Hermon. The Jordan then flows south through what can be described as three stages: (1) From the sources to Lake Huleh. The Jordan flows almost seven miles before it enters Lake Huleh. Within this distance, the river makes its way through areas of marsh consisting of reeds, bulrushes, and papyrus—the chief writing material for centuries. In this area, lions were seen in biblical times (Jer. 49:19). (2) Between Lake Huleh and the Sea of Galilee. On leaving Lake Huleh, the Jordan flows for about ten miles to the Sea of Galilee. In this short stretch, it descends to 696 feet below sea level. The river has carved a

The green waters of the Jordan River as it meanders through Israel.

J

deep and winding course for itself through the center of the valley. Much of its course is characterized by rocky gorges. (3) From the Sea of Galilee to the Dead Sea. After leaving the Sea of Galilee the river passes through an especially fertile region. The length of this stretch is around sixty-five miles, but the river curves and twists for three times this distance. The breadth of the valley is from three to fourteen miles. The river drops 590 feet during this stretch.

Several major tributaries (e.g. Yarmuk, Jabbok), flow into the Jordan emptying almost as great an amount of water as the Jordan itself. The deltas of these streams are always fertile areas which widen the extent of land that can be cultivated in the valley. Many cities of antiquity were built close to the point of juncture of the tributaries and the main river.

The Jordan River and Jordan Valley played an important role in a number of memorable events from both the Old Testament and the New Testament. The first mention of the Jordan in the Bible occurs in the story of Abram and Lot. Lot, upon his separation from Abram, chose for himself "all the plain of Jordan" (Gen. 13:11). Jacob wrestled with his adversary at the ford of the Jabbok (Gen. 32:22–26). Under the leadership of Joshua, Israel crossed the Jordan "on dry ground" (Josh. 3:15–17). During the period of the judges and the early monarchy, the possession of the fords of the Jor-

The Jordan River which flows south from Mount Hermon through Israel, finally emptying into the Dead Sea.

dan more than once meant the difference between defeat and victory. The Jordan was a strong line of defense, not to be easily forded. The Jordan River is also featured in the miracles of Elijah and Elisha.

The essential story of the Gospels begins at the Jordan River. It was there that John the Baptist came preaching the coming kingdom of heaven. The most important New Testament event relating to the Jordan is the baptism of Jesus, which was performed by John the Baptizer (Mark 1:9). The first part of Jesus' ministry was centered in and around the Sea of Galilee. The second part of His ministry followed as he pursued His course down the east side of the Jordan Valley. There He performed new miracles, and spoke to the multitudes in parables, especially those of the collection in Luke 12—18. See *Sea of Galilee; Dead Sea; Mount Hermon.*   *Philip Lee*

JORIM (Jō′ rĭm) Personal name of unknown meaning. Ancestor of Jesus (Luke 3:29).

JORKEAM (Jôr′ kė ăm) Personal name meaning, "the people is golden." Descendant of Caleb (1 Chron. 2:44). This, like other names in the list, may represent a city as well as a person. Many interpreters read Jokdeam here, equating the city with the tribal city of Judah. The location of the city is not known. See *Jokdeam; Jorkoam.*

JORKOAM (Jôr′ kō ăm) KJV spelling of Jorkeam. See *Jorkeam.*

JOSABAD (Jŏs′ à băd) KJV spelling of Jozabad (1 Chron. 12:4). See *Jozabad.*

JOSAPHAT (Jŏs′ à phăt) KJV spelling of Jehoshaphat (Matt. 1:8). See *Jehoshaphat.*

JOSE (Jō′ sè) KJV spelling of otherwise unknown ancestor of Jesus, representing Joshua in Hebrew and Jesus in Greek. Modern translations read Joshua (Luke 3:29).

JOSECH (Jō′ sĕch) Personal name of uncertain meaning. Ancestor of Jesus (Luke 3:26). KJV reads Joseph.

JOSEDECH (Jŏs′ è dĕch) Personal name meaning, "Yahweh acts in righteousness." KJV spelling of short form of Jehozadak. See *Jehozadak.*

JOSEPH (Jō′ sèph) Personal name meaning, "adding." Name of several men in the Bible, most importantly a patriarch of the nation Israel and the foster father of Jesus.
Old Testament *1.* Joseph in the Old Testament primarily refers to the patriarch, one of the sons of Israel. Joseph was the eleventh of twelve sons, the first by Jacob's favorite wife, Rachel. His name, "may he [the Lord] add," was a part of Rachel's prayer at his birth (Gen. 30:24).

As the child of Jacob's old age and Rachel's son, Joseph became the favorite and was given the famous "coat of many colors" (Gen. 37:3; "long robe with sleeves," NRSV, NEB; "richly ornamented robe" NIV) by his father. This and dreams which showed his rule over his family inspired the envy of his brothers, who sold Joseph to a caravan of Ishmaelites (Gen. 37).

Joseph was taken to Egypt where he became a trusted slave in the house of Potiphar, an official of the pharaoh. On false accusations of Potiphar's wife, Joseph was thrown in the royal prison, where he interpreted the dreams of two officials who had offended the pharaoh (Gen. 39—40). Eventually Joseph was brought to interpret some worrisome dreams for the pharaoh. Joseph predicted seven years of plenty followed by seven years of famine and recommended a program of preparation by storing grain. Pharaoh responded by making Joseph his second in command (Gen. 41:39-45).

With the famine, persons from other countries came to Egypt to buy food, including Joseph's brothers. They did not recognize him, but Joseph saw the fulfillment of his earlier dreams in which his brothers bowed down to him. After testing their character in various ways, Joseph revealed himself to them on their second visit (Gen. 42—45). Under Joseph's patronage, Jacob moved into Egypt (Gen. 46:1—47:12). Joseph died in Egypt but was embalmed and later buried in Shechem (Gen. 50:26; Ex. 13:19; Josh. 24:32).

That the influential Joseph (Gen. 47:13-26) is not known from Egyptian records would be expected if he served under a Hyksos pharaoh, as seems likely. See *Hyksos.* Later Egyptians tried to erase all evidence of that period. The pharaoh "who did not know Joseph" (Ex. 1:8, NRSV) did not "know" of him in a political or historical sense.

While in Egypt, Joseph became the father of two sons, Manasseh and Ephraim (Gen. 41:50-52), who were counted as sons of Jacob (48:5-6) and whose tribes dominated the northern nation of Israel. The name Joseph is used later in the Old Testament as a reference to the tribes of Ephraim and Manasseh (Num. 1:32; 36:1,5; 1 Kings 11:28) or as a designation for the whole Northern Kingdom (Ps. 78:67; Ezek. 37:16,19; Amos 5:6,15; 6:6; Obad. 18; Zech. 10:6).

Four other men named Joseph are mentioned in the Old Testament: *2.* the spy of the tribe of Issachar (Num. 13:7); *3.* a Levite of the sons of Asaph (1 Chron. 25:2); *4.* a contemporary of Ezra with a foreign wife (Ezra 10:42); and *5.* a priest in the days of high priest Joiakim (Neh. 12:14).
New Testament *6.* Several Josephs are mentioned in the New Testament, the most important being the husband of Mary, mother of Jesus. He was a descendant of David, a carpenter by trade (Matt. 13:55), and regarded as the legal or foster father of Jesus (Matt. 1:16,20; Luke 2:4; 3:23; 4:22; John 1:45; 6:42). Upon learning of Mary's pregnancy, Joseph, being a righteous man, sought to put her away without public disgrace. His response to God's assurances in a dream further demonstrated his piety and character (Matt. 1:18-25). Joseph took Mary to his ancestral home, Bethlehem, was with her at Jesus' birth, and shared in the naming, circumcision, and dedication of the child (Luke 2:8-33). Directed through dreams, Joseph took his family to Egypt until it was safe to return to Nazareth (Matt. 2:13-23). As dedicated father, he was anxious with Mary at the disappearance of Jesus (Luke 2:41-48). Joseph does not appear later in the Gospels, and it is likely that he died prior to Jesus' public ministry.

7. Also important in the New Testament is Joseph of Arimathea, a rich member of the Sanhedrin and a righteous man who sought the kingdom of God (Matt. 27:57; Mark 15:43; Luke 23:50). After the crucifixion, Joseph, a secret disciple of Jesus, requested the body from Pilate and laid it in his own unused tomb (Matt. 27:57-60; Mark 15:43-46; Luke 23:50-53; John 19:38-42). Arimathea is probably the same as Ramathaim-zophim (1 Sam. 1:1) northwest of Jerusalem.

Two Josephs are mentioned in the genealogy of Jesus (Luke 3:24,30). Another was a brother of Jesus, apparently named after His father (Matt. 13:55; KJV "Joses" as in Mark 6:3). It likely but uncertain that the brother of James (Matt. 27:56;

J

Joses in Mark 15:40,47) is a different person. Joseph was also another name of both Barsabbas (Acts 1:23) and Barnabas (Acts 4:36).

Daniel C. Browning Jr.

JOSEPHUS, FLAVIUS (Jō sē′ phŭs, Flā′ vĭ ŭs) Early historian of Jewish life and our most important source for the history of the Jews in the Roman period. His four surviving works are *The Jewish War* (composed about A.D. 73), *The Antiquities of the Jews* (about A.D. 93), *Life* (an autobiographical appendix to *The Antiquities*), and *Against Apion,* penned shortly after *The Antiquities.* The date of Josephus' death is unknown but was probably after A.D. 100.

Following the conflict between Rome and the Jews of Palestine (A.D. 66–73), Flavius Josephus gave an account of the struggle in his seven books of *The Jewish War,* which include a prehistory reaching back to the second century B.C. Josephus came to Rome in 73 and lived in a house provided by Vespasian, who also gave him a yearly pension. *The Antiquities, Life,* and *Against Apion* were all written in Rome. In *The Antiquities* Josephus paraphrased the Septuagint (earliest Greek translation of the Bible) to tell the story of the Hebrews through the time of Cyrus and then employed other sources to complete the account through the first century. The account of the revolt against Rome is in many respects quite different in the *The Antiquities* than it is in the earlier *War.* *Against Apion* defends the Jews against charges of the grammarian Apion as well as against other common assaults on the antiquity and moral virtue of the Jews. Josephus' *Life* focuses primarily upon the six-month period in which he was commander of Jewish forces in the Galilee and refutes the charge made by Justus of Tiberias that Josephus had organized the revolt in the Galilee.

Fred L. Horton, Jr.

JOSES (Jō′ sēs) Personal name in Mark 6:3, one of the brothers of Jesus. In Matthew 13:55 KJV follows some Greek manuscripts in reading Joses for a brother of Jesus, but modern translations follow the earliest manuscripts in reading Joseph. Some Bible students see Joses as a dialectical pronunciation or a Greek substitute for the Hebrew Joseph. Compare Matthew 27:56. Mark 15:40 mentions another Joses, the brother of James the Less, whose mother's name was Mary. This latter Joses is mentioned as if he were a disciple of Jesus. Barnabas' original name was Joseph in the Greek of Acts 4:36. KJV reads this as Joses.

JOSHAH (Jō′ shah) Personal name of uncertain meaning. Member of tribe of Simeon (1 Chron. 4:34).

JOSHAPHAT (Jŏsh′ à phăt) Short form of per-

sonal name Jehoshaphat meaning, "Yah judges." *1.* Military hero under David (1 Chron. 11:43). *2.* Priest who sounded the trumpet before the Ark of the Covenant as David brought it to Jerusalem (1 Chron. 15:24; KJV, Jehoshaphat).

JOSHAVIAH (Jŏ shȧ vī′ ah) Personal name meaning, "Yah lets inhabit," probably a short form of Joshibiah. Military hero under David (1 Chron. 11:46). See *Joshibiah.*

JOSHBEKASHAH (Jŏsh bė kā′ shah) Personal name meaning, "to live in misfortune." A Levite musician from clan of Heman, the seer, under David (1 Chron. 25:4). He headed the seventeenth course or division of Temple musicians (1 Chron. 25:24).

JOSHEB-BASSEBETH (Jō′ shĕb-Băs shē′ bĕth) Personal name meaning, "dweller of shame" (2 Sam. 23:8). See *Jashobeam.*

JOSHIBIAH (Jŏ shī bī′ ah) Personal name meaning, "Yah lets inhabit." Member of tribe of Simeon (1 Chron. 4:35).

JOSHUA (Jŏsh ū à) Personal name meaning, "Yahweh delivered." *1.* Leader of Israelites who first took control of Promised Land of Canaan. Joshua is one of the unsung heroes of the Old Testament. He, not Moses, led the people into the Promised Land. He was a person of such stature that he could succeed the incomparable Moses and compile a record of notable success (Josh. 24:31). The Hebrew variations of Joshua are Oshea (Num. 13:16); Hosea (Hos. 1:1). English versions differ in their transliteration of the Hebrew names. Its New Testament equivalent is Jesus.

Joshua was born in Egypt during the period of slavery. He was a member of Ephraim, the important tribe that later formed the heart of the Northern Kingdom of Israel. He first appeared during the battle with the Amalekites during the desert travels. He was Moses' general, who led the troops in the actual fighting while Aaron and Hur held up Moses' hands (Ex. 17:8–13).

Joshua was Moses's servant (Ex. 24:13). He was on the mountain when Moses received the Law (Ex. 32:17). He was also one of the twelve spies Moses sent to investigate Canaan (Num. 13:8). He and Caleb returned with a positive, minority report. Of all the adults alive at that time, only the two of them were allowed to live to enter the land of Canaan (Num. 14:28–30,38).

The Lord selected Joshua to be Moses' successor long before Moses' death (Num. 27:15–23; Deut. 31:14–15,23; 34:9). Joshua was a military leader, a political leader, and a spiritual leader. He was quiet and unassuming, but he was not buffaloed by his responsibilities or the task that lay before him. He was a battlefield genius, particularly in the areas of careful planning, strategy, and execution. He was a capable administrator for the nation, effective in maintaining harmony among people and groups. He was a spokesman to the people for the Lord. Though he did not receive the Law as Moses had, he communicated the Lord's will and the Lord's message much like Moses.

Joshua was at the helm of the nation during the conquest and the distribution and settlement of Canaan. He led in the covenant renewal at mount Ebal and Shechem (Josh. 8:30–35; 24:1–28). He was able to challenge his people by both word and example. His pattern is a hard one to better.

See *Joshua, The Book of; Moses.*

2. High priest of community who returned from Babylonian Exile in 538 B.C. See *Jeshua 3.*

Dan Gentry Kent

JOSHUA, THE BOOK OF The Book of Joshua is the sixth book of the English Old Testament. It is the first book of the second division of the Hebrew Old Testament, the Prophets. The book is named after its central character, Moses' successor, Joshua the son of Nun.

Authorship and Date The Former Prophets are all anonymous. That means that no author is mentioned in the book. Some Bible students think Joshua wrote the book except for the death reports (24:29–33); but the book gives no indication that Joshua had anything to do with writing the whole book, though he did write the laws on which the covenant renewal was based (Josh. 24:26).

It is also difficult to date the writing of books like this. Some Bible students suggest a time about a hundred years after Joshua's death, or at least by the time of the beginning of the monarchy. A date around 1045 B.C. would place it within the lifetime of Samuel, who was in a sense the last of the judges and the one who anointed the first two kings. Other Bible students think the Book of Joshua only reached its present form when the Former Prophets were collected together during the Exile.

The events of the book apparently took place in the last half of the thirteenth century, from about 1250 to 1200 B.C., though some would date the Exodus and the conquest earlier, in the middle of the fifteenth century.

Contents The Book of Joshua tells the story of a significant Bible event, the conquest of the land of Canaan. It tells this story in light of the theological themes of the Book of Deuteronomy, and thus the historical books of Joshua, Judges, Samuel, Kings are often spoken of as the Deuteronomic History.

The book has only two main parts, and an appendix:

I. The Conquest of the Land, 1—12.

II. The Settlement of the Land, 13—22.

III. Joshua's Farewell Addresses, 23—24.

The Book of Joshua standardizes the conquest stories to some extent. For example, the accounts are from the standpoint of the general who led the entire nation, whereas the Book of Judges is more from the standpoint of the foot soldier who did the actual fighting.

A surface reading of the Book of Joshua would give the impression that the invasion was complete and final. However, numerous passages (13:13; 15:63; 16:10; 17:12–13, 16–18) agree with the Book of Judges to show that it was up to the individual clans to root out the many pockets of Canaanite resistance still scattered throughout the land. The difference is between occupation and subjugation, the former in the Book of Joshua and the latter in the Book of Judges.

Through it all, the emphasis of the book is on the Lord's mighty acts. Joshua was rightly celebrated as an effective military leader. The people were generally obedient and courageous. However, the glory goes to God alone (3:10; 4:23–24; 6:16). He is the true hero of the book.

Nature of the Covenant in the Book of Joshua The Lord's covenant with His people was always more universalistic and inclusive than we usually realize. We see this clearly in the Book of Joshua. Rahab, the Canaanite prostitute, was accepted, along with her family, as a part of the covenant community (2:9–13; 6:22–23,25). It may well be that people related to the Hebrews who lived in the Shechem area voluntarily joined in their fellowship of faith (8:30–35). The people of Gibeon and its four-city league were accepted, and even became associated with Temple service (9:3–27). The covenant was not limited by race or nation; it was open to anyone of faith.

Holy War in the Book of Joshua The Hebrews did not divide life up into sacred and secular spheres as we do. To them all of life was holy, in the sense that it was lived under the direction of the Lord. They saw the Lord at work on behalf of His people in every area of life. Thus the soldiers were holy. They were under strict religious regulations. Religious ceremonies prepared them for battle (5:2–11).

The Lord received the credit for all victories. All of the spoils of battle belonged to Him (6:18–19). None was to be taken for personal use. This is related to the idea of *cherem* or ban. It might seem ruthless or even immoral by our modern Western standards, but it was a part of the world of that day. A certain city, for instance Jericho in chapter 6, was placed under the ban. It was devoted to destruction in the name of the Lord. Everything in it was to either be destroyed or else placed in the Lord's service in the tabernacle.

The ban was a common practice in the Semitic world and was also known among the Greeks. Some suggest that it served to control looting and that it offered an enemy encouragement to surrender without a struggle.

Moral Problems of the Book of Joshua The Book

of Joshua is filled with war, conquest, and destruction. Its teaching is that the Lord allowed his people to conquer the land of Canaan, to take possession of the area He had promised to the patriarchs.

But why would the Lord allow one nation to attack and defeat another? Several factors need to be taken into consideration in studying a book that has so little of loving your enemy or turning the other cheek.

One must begin by admitting that Joshua lived centuries before Christ appeared to reveal the Father's will fully and completely. We should not expect to find completed Christian truth in a book written so long before Christ came.

The Hebrew people saw paganism as a poison. Pagan religious views were a spiritual infection that was both highly contagious and deadly. It could be controlled only by strict quarantine and eradication. Holy war became God's method in that setting to achieve this purpose. Holy war was not set up as an eternal example (compare Deut. 20:16).

One element in the explanation for the holy wars of Joshua is judgment on sin. The iniquity of the Amorites (Canaanites) was at last full (Gen. 15:16). The catch to this arrangement is that if the other nations could be judged for their sins, the Hebrew people could, too, and later were.

See *Conquest; War; Joshua.*

Outline

I. God Brought Victory to a People of the Book (1:1—12:24).
   A. To possess the promise, God's people must be faithful to the book (1:1–18).
   B. God uses unexpected persons to fulfill His promises (2:1–24).
   C. God exalts His leaders and proves His presence so all people may know Him (3:1—4:24).
   D. God's people must worship Him to prepare for the victories He promises (5:1–15).
   E. Divine power, not human might, provides victory for God's people (6:1–27).
   F. A disobedient people cannot expect God's victories (7:1–26).
   G. A repentant people receive a strategy for victory from God (8:1–35).
   H. Human cunning and disobedience cannot overcome the purposes of God (9:1–27).
   I. God fights for His people (10:1–43).
   J. God fulfills His promises, giving victory to an obedient people (11:1—12:24).

II. God Divides the Spoils of Victory According to the Needs of His People (13:1—21:45).
   A. The complete rest is still incomplete (13:1–7).
   B. History shows God's provision for His people (13:8–33).
   C. God rewards heroes of faith (14:1–15).
   D. God fulfilled His promise of land to His people (15:1—17:13).
   E. God provided for specific needs of His people (17:14–18).
   F. God called a hesitant people to action to receive the promised gift (18:1–10).
   G. God gave the land to an obedient people (18:11—19:48).
   H. God and His people rewarded their faithful leader (19:49–51).
   I. God decreed legal protection for the accused among His people (20:1–9).
   J. God provided for the needs of His priests (21:1–42).
   K. God fulfills all His promises (21:43–45).

III. God Calls His Victorious People to Unity in Worship and Devotion (22:1—24:33).
   A. God's rest, commandments, and blessing unify His people (22:1–6).
   B. Worship unifies God's people forever despite geographical barriers (22:7–34).
   C. Israel had to be faithful to God's direction or face the loss of His gifts (23:1–16).
   D. God calls His people to remember the history of God's faithfulness and choose to serve only Him (24:1–28).
   E. Faithful leaders keep a people faithful (24:29–33).

Dan Gentry Kent

JOSIAH (Jō sī′ ah) Personal name meaning, "Yahweh heals." Judah's king from about 640–609 B.C. He succeeded his father Amon, an idolatrous king, who ruled for only two years before being murdered by his servants (2 Kings 21:19–23; 2 Chron. 33:21–24). Josiah became king at the age of eight due to wishes of "the people of the land" who put his father's assassins to death (2 Kings 21:24). Josiah's reign lasted for thirty-one years (2 Kings 22:1; 2 Chron. 34:1).

The Book of 2 Chronicles reveals much about the early years of Josiah. In his eighth year as king he began to seek the God of David (34:3). Josiah initiated a religious purge of Jerusalem, Judah, and surrounding areas during his twelfth year on the throne (34:3–7). This purge included tearing down the high places, the Asherah, and the altars to Baal. The high places were essentially Canaanite worship centers that had been taken over by Israel. The Asherah were cult objects associated with the worship of Baal, the fertility god of Canaan. See *Asherah.*

In his eighteenth year as king an unexpected event turned his energies in new directions. A "Book of the Law" was discovered while repairs were being made on the Temple. Hilkiah, the high priest, found the book and gave it to Shaphan, the scribe, who in turn read it to King Josiah. Upon hearing the message of the book, Josiah tore his clothes, a sign of repentance, and humbled himself before God. Josiah was assured that the promised destruction would not come in his time (2 Kings 22:8–20; 2 Chron. 34:15–28). The reading of this book prompted Josiah to instigate the most far-reaching religious reforms in Israel's history.

What was this "Book of the Law" and when was it written? Most scholars believe that this book included at least the core of our present Book of Deuteronomy, either chapters 5–26 or 12–26. A major thrust of the Book of Deuteronomy was to call the nation Israel to exclusive loyalty to Yahweh. Perhaps a thrust such as this inspired the Josianic revival.

The Bible is silent about the remaining years of Josiah until his death. On the international scene during those years Assyria's power was waning, and Babylon's was on the rise. Assyria had aligned itself with Egypt against Babylon. Pharoah Neco's troups were passing through territory north of Judah en route to join forces with Assyria. Josiah's army blocked the movement of Egyptian troups at Megiddo. In the battle that followed Josiah was mortally wounded (2 Kings 23:29). His body was taken to Jerusalem where he was buried. There was great mourning for him throughout the land (2 Chron. 35:24–25). Though only thirty-nine when he died, Josiah was remembered as Judah's greatest king (2 Kings 23:25):

> "Neither before nor after Josiah was there a king like him who turned to the Lord as he did—with all his heart and with all his soul and with all his strength, in accordance with the Law of Moses" (NIV).

See *Jeremiah; Deuteronomy.*

M. Stephen Davis

JOSIAS (Jō sī′ as) KJV transliteration of Greek form of Josiah (Matt. 1:10–11). See *Josiah.*

JOSIBIAH (Jŏ sī bī′ ah) KJV spelling of Joshibiah. See *Joshibiah.*

JOSIPHIAH (Jŏ sī phī′ ah) Personal name meaning, "Yah adds to," a longer form of Joseph. Leader of group of Babylonian exiles who returned to Jerusalem with Ezra (Ezra 8:10).

JOT See *Dot.*

JOTBAH (Jŏt′ bah) Place name meaning, "it is good." Home of Meshullemeth, the queen mother of King Amon of Judah about 642–640 B.C. (2 Kings 21:19). It was located at khirbet Gefat about nine miles north of Nazareth. Others would identify it with the closely related Hebrew name Jotbathah (Num. 33:34) and locate it at et-Taba twenty miles north of Akaba. See *Jotbathah; Meshullemeth.*

JOTBATHAH (Jŏt′ bȧ thah) Place name meaning, "good." Wilderness camping station the second stop before Ezion Geber for Israel in the wilderness (Num. 33:33). The context of Deuteronomy 10:7 indicates that at Jotbathah God set apart the Levites to carry the Ark of the Covenant and to do priestly service, though many interpreters would connect the address of verses 8–9 to 10:1, seeing the travel report in verses 6–7 as a historical parenthesis and not as the precise setting for verses 8ff. See *Ezion Geber; Jotbah.*

JOTHAM (Jō′ tham) Personal name meaning, "Yahweh has shown Himself to be perfect." *1.* In Judges 9:5, the youngest of Gideon's seventy sons. He survived the mass killing of Gideon's sons by Abimelech, their half brother, because he hid himself. Afterwards, when Abimelech had been hailed as king at Shechem, Jotham addressed a fable to the people of Shechem designed to mock the idea of Abimelech acting as a king. After he had told the fable and given its interpretation, Jotham fled for his life. See *Judges.*

2. In 2 Kings 15:32, the son and successor of Uzziah as king of Judah (750–732 B.C.). He was twenty-five years old when he began to reign, and he reigned for sixteen years. His mother's name was Jerusha. The sixteen-year period given for his reign may include the time that he acted as regent for his father Uzziah. Uzziah contracted leprosy during the final years of his reign and thus could not perform the functions required of royalty. Jotham evidently was an effective ruler. His reign was marked by building projects, material prosperity, and military successes. See *Chronology.*

JOY The happy state that results from knowing and serving God. A number of Greek and Hebrew words are used in the Bible to convey the ideas of joy and rejoicing. We have the same situation in English with such nearly synonymous words as joy, happiness, pleasure, delight, gladness, merriment, felicity, and enjoyment. The words *joy* and *rejoice* are the words used most often to translate the Hebrew and Greek words into English. *Joy* is found over 150 times in the Bible. If such words as "joyous" and "joyful" are included, the number comes to over 200. The verb *rejoice* appears well over 200 times.

Joy is the fruit of a right relation with God. It is not something people can create by their own efforts. The Bible distinguishes joy from pleasure. The Greek word for pleasure is the word from which we get our word *hedonism,* the philosophy of self-centered pleasure-seeking. Paul referred to false teachers as "lovers of pleasures more than lovers of God" (2 Tim. 3:4).

The Bible warns that self-indulgent pleasure-seeking does not lead to happiness and fulfillment. Ecclesiastes 2:1–11 records the sad testimony of one who sought to build his life on pleasure-seeking. The search left him empty and disillusioned. Proverbs 14:13 offers insight into this way of life, "Even in laughter the heart is sorrowful." Cares, riches, and pleasures rob people of the possibility of fruitful living (Luke 8:14). Pleasure seeking often enslaves people in a vicious cycle of addiction (Tit. 3:3). The self-indulgent person, according to 1 Timothy 5:6, is dead while seeming still to be live.

Many people think that God is the great Kill-Joy. Nothing could be a bigger lie. God Himself knows joy, and He wants His people to know joy. Psalm 104:31 speaks of God Himself rejoicing in His creative works. Isaiah 65:18 speaks of God rejoicing over His redeemed people who will be to Him "a joy."

Luke 15 is the most famous biblical reference to God's joy. The Pharisees and scribes had criticized Jesus for receiving sinners and eating with them. Then Jesus told three parables—the lost sheep, the lost coin, and the loving father. The explicit theme of each parable is joy over one sinner who repents.

The joy of God came to focus in human history in Jesus Christ. The note of joy and exultation runs through the entire biblical account of the coming of Christ (Luke 1:14,44; Matt. 2:10). The most familiar passage is the angel's announcement of "good tidings of great joy, which shall be to all people" (Luke 2:10). Jesus spoke of His own joy and of the full joy He had come to bring to others (John 15:11; 17:13). He illustrated the kingdom of heaven by telling of the joy of a man who found treasure (Matt. 13:44). Zacchaeus was in a tree when Jesus called him, but he quickly climbed down and received Jesus joyfully (Luke 19:6). He had found life's ultimate treasure in Christ.

As Jesus' death approached, He told His followers that soon they would be like a woman in labor, whose sorrow would be turned into joy (John 16:20–22). Later they understood, when the dark sorrow of the cross gave way to the joy of the resurrection (Luke 24:41). Viewed from this perspective, eventually they came to see that the cross itself was necessary for the joy to become real (Heb. 12:2). Because of His victory and the promise of His abiding presence, the disciples could rejoice even after the Lord's ascension (Luke 24:52).

The Book of Acts tells how joy continued to characterize those who followed Jesus. After Philip preached in Samaria, the people believed and "there was great joy in that city" (Acts 8:8). After the work of Paul and Barnabas in Antioch of Pisidia, "the diciples were filled with joy, and with the Holy Ghost" (Acts 13:52). Paul and Barnabas reported such conversions to other believers, "and they caused great joy unto all the brethren" (Acts 15:3). After the conversion of the Philippian jailer, he "rejoiced, believing in God with all his house" (Acts 16:34).

Joy in the Christian life is in direct proportion as believers walk with the Lord. They can rejoice because they are in the Lord (Phil. 4:4). Joy is a fruit of a Spirit-led life (Gal. 5:22). Sin in a believer's life robs the person of joy (Ps. 51:8,12).

When a person walks with the Lord, the person can continue to rejoice even when troubles come. Jesus spoke of those who could rejoice even when persecuted and killed (Matt. 5:12). Paul wrote of rejoicing in suffering because of the final fruit that would result (Rom. 5:3–5). Both Peter and James also echoed the Lord's teachings about rejoicing in troubles (1 Pet. 1:6–8; Jas. 1:2).

Joy in the Lord enables people to enjoy all that God has given. They rejoice in family (Prov. 5:18), food (1 Tim. 4:4–5), celebrations (Deut. 16:13–15), fellowship (Phil. 4:1). They share with other believers the joys and sorrows of life: "Rejoice with them that do rejoice, weep with them that weep" (Rom. 12:15). *Robert J. Dean*

JOZABAD (Jŏz′ ȧ băd) Short form of personal name Jehozabad meaning, "Yah gave." *1.* Person involved in assassination of King Joash about 782 B.C. (2 Kings 12:21, where Hebrew text says Jozabad, son of Shimeath and Jehozabad, son of Amaziah, but many Hebrew manuscripts read the first name of Jozachar). Second Chronicles 24:26 reads "Zabad son of Shimeath" and Jehozabad son of Shimrith." Copying changes have made it impossible to determine precisely the original names. Chronicles shows that because Joash killed the sons of Jehoiada the priest, his own servants paid him back. They even refused to give him royal burial in the kings' tombs. See *Jehozabad; Joash*. *2.* Man from Gederah in tribe of Benjamin who joined David as he fled from King Saul (1 Chron. 12:4). *3.* Two men of tribe of Manasseh who joined David at Ziklag as he fled from Saul (1 Chron. 12:20). *4.* Priest who promised Ezra he would divorce his foreign wife to prevent temptation of foreign worship from invading Israel (Ezra 10:22). *5.* Priest who witnessed transfer of gold Ezra's party brought from Babylon to the Temple in Jerusalem (Ezra 8:33), though a Hebrew manuscript reads Jonadab here. *6.* Levite with foreign wife Ezra condemned (Ezra 10:23). *7.* Levite who helped the people understand God's law as Ezra read it (Neh. 8:7). *8.* Levite in charge of external affairs of the Temple (Neh. 11:16). *9.* A supervisor of Temple treasures under Hezekiah about 715 B.C. (2 Chron. 31:13). He helped give Levites animals to sacrifice at Passover (2 Chron. 35:9).

JOZACAR (Jō′ zȧ cär) NAS, NRSV, TEV spelling of Jozachar (2 Kings 12:21). See *Jozachar*.

JOZACHAR (Jŏz′ ȧ chär) Personal name meaning, "Yah thought of." KJV, REB reading of conspirator who helped kill King Joash about 782 B.C. (2 Kings 12:21) based on Hebrew manuscripts differing from the base manuscript normally used for the Hebrew text. See *Jehozabad; Jozabad.*

JOZADAK (Jŏz' á dăk) Short form of personal name Jehozadak meaning, "Yah acts in righteousness." Father of high priest Joshua (Ezra 3:2 among others). See *Jehozadak.*

JUBAL (Jū' băl) Personal name meaning, "a ram," as a "ram's horn" used as a musical instrument. In Genesis 4:19–21, the son of Lamech and full brother of Jabal. He is associated with the invention of musical instruments.

JUCAL (Jū' căl) Short form of Jehucal. See *Jehucal.*

JUDA (Jū' dà) KJV spelling of Judah in New Testament. See *Judah.*

JUDAEA Alternate form of Judea used by the KJV (except in Ezra 5:8). See *Judea.*

JUDAH (Jū' dah) Personal, tribal, and territorial name meaning, "Praise Yahweh," but may have originally been related to the mountain of Jehud. *1.* In Genesis 29:35, the fourth son of Jacob and the progenitor of the tribe of Judah. His mother was Leah. Though Judah is prominent in the Genesis narratives, he seldom occupies center stage. Genesis 38 is an exception. It relates the seduction of Judah by his daughter-in-law Tamar. Their union resulted in the birth of Pharez and Zarah. Genesis 49:8–12 preserves the blessing of Judah by Jacob. Through Judah ran the genealogical line that led to Jesus.

2. The tribe of Judah occupied the strategically important territory just to the west of the Dead Sea. The city of Jerusalem was on the border between Judah and Benjamin. David was from the tribe of Judah. *3.* When the kingdom was divided following the death of Solomon, the southern kingdom took the name Judah. See *Judas; Geography; Tribes of Israel; Patriarchs; Israel.*

4. The province set up by the Persian government to rule a conquered Judean kingdom (Neh. 5:14; Hag. 1:1). Judah formed one small province alongside Samaria, Galilee, and Idumea. All these reported to the Satrap of the Persian satrapy of Abarnaharah which encompassed the land west of the Euphrates River with its center in Damascus (Ezra 5:3,6; 6:6,13). The satrap reported to a higher official over Babylon and Abarnaharah with headquarters in Babylon. When Judah's exiles returned from Babylon, Zerubbabel was governor of Judah; Tattenai, satrap of Abarnaharah or Beyond the River; and Ushtannu, satrap of Babylon and Abarnaharah.

5. Priest whose sons helped Zerubbabel and Joshua begin work on restoring the Temple after 537 B.C. (Ezra 3:9; compare Neh. 12:8). *6.* Levite whom Ezra condemned for having foreign wife who might tempt Israel to worship other gods (Ezra 10:23). *7.* Member of tribe of Benjamin who lived in Jerusalem after the return from Exile and was second in command over the city (Neh. 11:9). He may be the official who joined Nehemiah in leading the celebration of the completion of the Jerusalem wall (Neh. 12:34). *8.* Priestly musician who helped in Nehemiah's celebration (Neh. 12:36). *9.* An obscure geographical reference in the description of the tribal borders of Naphtali (Josh. 19:34). The earliest Greek translators could not understand the reference and so did not translate it. (Compare TEV, NIV). Naphtali's territory does not touch that of the tribe of Judah. Some try to define Judah here as the sixty towns of Jair east of the Jordan (Josh. 13:30). Others translate Judah as "low-lying land" (REB). Some scholars try to make another place name such as Jehuda out of the reference. It may be that a copyist confused Jordan and Judah, which resemble one another in appearance in Hebrew writing, and miscopied Jordan as Judah and then copied Jordan. No sure solution exists to explain Judah in this text. *10.* City of Judah (2 Chron. 25:28) is Jerusalem.

JUDAISM (Jū' dà ĭsm) The religion and way of life of the people of Judah, the Jews. Paul contrasted his Christian calling from his previous life in Judaism (Gal. 1:13–14). Foreigners could convert to Judaism. See *Proselytes; Jewish Parties in the New Testament.*

JUDAS (Jū' dàs) Greek transliteration of Hebrew personal name Judah meaning, "Praise Yahweh." The proper name Judas was very common in the time of Christ because it was not only the Greek form of one of the twelve patriarchs, but it was also made popular by the Jewish hero Judas Maccabaeus who led the nation in their fight for independence from Syria in 166 B.C. The New Testament mentions seven men named Judas. Most of them are only mentioned in passing. *1.* One of Jesus' ancestors (Luke 3:30). *2.* A brother of the Lord (Matt. 13:55; Mark 6:3).

Acts speaks of five others named Judas. *3.* Judas of Galilee was one of those who led a revolt against the Romans and died as a result. The exact year of this revolt is uncertain, perhaps 6 A.D. (Acts 5:37). *4.* After his experience on the road to Damascus Paul went to the house of a man named Judas who lived on Straight Street. Ananias found him there three days later. *5.* Judas, surnamed Barsabas, was one of those chosen by the Church of Jerusalem to go with Paul and Barnabas to deliver the letter from James to the church at Antioch concerning the important matter of Gentile salvation (Acts 15:22).

J

6. Jesus' twelve disciples include two named Judas. The first is always listed after James the son of Alphaeus, and is called the brother of James (Luke 6:16; Acts 1:13). He appears to have been known also by the name Lebbaeus Thaddaeus (Matt. 10:3; Mark 3:18). His only recorded words are found in John 14:22.

7. The last of these was Judas Iscariot. All of the Gospels place him at the end of the list of disciples because of his role as betrayer. Iscariot is an Aramaic word which means "man of Kerioth", a town near Hebron. He was the only disciple from Judea. He acted as treasurer for the disciples but was known as a miser and a thief (John 12:5–6). He was present at the Last Supper, during which Jesus predicted his betrayal (Luke 22:21; Matt. 26:20–21). The price of the betrayal was 30 pieces of silver, which Judas returned to Jewish leaders; then he went out and hanged himself. He died in sorrow but without repentance. The money, which could not be returned to the treasury because it was blood money, was used to buy a potter's field in Judas' name (Matt. 27:3–10; compare Acts 1:18–19). *Gerald Cowen*

JUDAS ISCARIOT (Jū' das Ĭs căr' ĭ ŏt) Personal name meaning, "Judah from Kerioth." Betrayer of Jesus. See *Judas.*

JUDE, THE BOOK OF Letter of exhortation to those who are "called" (v.1) and "beloved" (vv. 3,17,20), to "contend for the faith which was once delivered unto the saints" (v. 3). Simultaneously, it is a direct attack against the opponents of the gospel. Following his negative description of the opponents, Jude concluded the letter by urging his readers to have attitudes and life-styles different from the opponents. Then he committed them to the Lord's safekeeping in one of the most beautiful benedictions in Holy Scripture (vv. 24–25).

The authorship of this little letter has traditionally been ascribed to Jude, the half-brother of Jesus (Mark 6:3). Although the letter says nothing directly about the date, origin, or destination of the letter, it is generally thought that the book was written later than A.D. 60 and earlier than A.D. 100. This is because the content of the faith is clearly fixed (v. 3) and the congregation is comprised of second-generation Christians (v. 17). The recipients were most likely Jewish-Christians in Syria, known to have been a likely place for the kind of heresy the letter addresses.

The hard-hitting attack denounces the demoralizing faction that has slipped into the congregation (vv. 4,12). They are arrogant in theology; they boast of visions and revile angelic beings (vv. 8–10). They are self-centered (vv. 4,8,15); they create divisions (vv. 16–19) and leave disappointment behind (v. 12).

Jude, by use of a creative interpretation of Old Testament examples (some found in noncanonical sources), responds with two sets of three exhortations. His first set of examples appeal to:
(1) the murmuring Israelites
(2) the fallen angels
(3) those in Sodom and Gomorrah.
The second set appeals to:
(1) Cain
(2) Balaam (who in Rabbinic tradition is the father of the libertines)
(3) Korah (who challenged Moses' authority).
He tells the believers to:
(1) pray in the Spirit
(2) keep themselves in the love of God
(3) await the coming of the Lord Jesus Christ.
Then he concludes by exhorting them to:
(1) show mercy
(2) snatch others from the brink of disaster
(3) avoid those who have fallen under false teaching.

Jude is a helpful book, for it reminds us that God alone can safely bring believers through the hazardous environment. While false teachers may reject Christ's authority, Jesus is our Savior and Lord now and forevermore.

Outline
 I. Introduction (1–2)
 II. An Appeal to Struggle for the Faith (3–4)
   A. Authentic Christians contend for the true faith (3).
   B. Pseudo-Christians live immoral lives and deny Christ (4).
 III. The Certainty of Divine Judgment (5–7)
   A. Hebrew history shows the certainty of judgment (5).
   B. Fallen angels show the certainty of judgment (6).
   C. Immoral Sodom and Gomorrah show the certainty of judgment (7).
 IV. A Description of Heretics (8–19)
   A. They defile the body (8*a*).
   B. They flaunt authority (8*b*–11).
   C. They practice immoralities (12–16).
   D. They follow ungodly lusts (17–19).
 V. An Exhortation to the Faithful (20–23)
   A. Grow in the faith (20*a*).
   B. Pray in the Holy Spirit (20*b*).
   C. Remain in the love of God (21*a*).
   D. Anticipate the coming of Jesus (12*b*).
   E. Minister to erring Christians (22–23).
 VI. Conclusion: Praise for the Only God and Savior (24–25) *David S. Dockery*

JUDEA (Jū dē' à) Place name meaning, "Jewish." In Ezra 5:8, the Aramaic designation of a province that varied in size with changing political circumstances, but always included the city of Jerusalem and the territory immediately surrounding it. The area, formerly called Judah, was first given the name Judea following the Babylonian Exile. Dur-

The Wilderness of Judea as viewed toward the Dead Sea (left center) from atop the Herodium.

ing the Persian period, Judea occupied a very small area. Under the Maccabees, however, the territory was expanded in size and enjoyed a period of political independence. Herod the Great, appointed over roughly the same territory by Rome, had the title king of Judea. Judea, Samaria, and Galilee were generally considered, in Roman times, to be the three main geographical divisions of Palestine. See *Geography; Rome; Roman Empire.*

JUDEAN (Jū dē′ an) Resident or citizen of Judah in one of its several national and geographical meanings. See *Judah.*

JUDGE (OFFICE) (1) An official with authority to administer justice by trying cases; (2) one who usurps the perogative of a judge; (3) a military deliverer in the period between Joshua and David (for this sense, see *Judges, Book of*). Moses served as the judge of Israel, both deciding between persons and teaching Israel God's statutes (Ex. 18:16). At Jethro's suggestion, Moses himself served as the people's advocate before God and their instructor in the law (18:19–20) and appointed subordinate judges to decide minor cases (18:21–23; Num. 11:16–17; Deut. 1:12–17; 16:18–20). Elders of a community frequently served as judges at the city gate (Deut. 22:15; 25:7; Ruth 4:1–9; Job 29:7–8). Difficult cases

were referred to the priests or to the supreme judge (Deut. 17:8–13; compare Num. 5:12–31 for a case involving no witnesses). During the monarchy the king served as the supreme judge (2 Sam. 15:2–3) and appointed local judges (1 Chron. 23:4; 2 Chron. 19:5), along with an appeals process (2 Chron. 19:8–11). Following the Exile, Artaxerses gave the priest Ezra the authority to appoint judges in Judea (Ezra 7:25).

Complaints against judges are frequent in the Old Testament literature. Absalom took advantage of discontent with the legal system to instigate revolt (2 Sam. 15:4). Judges are accused of showing partiality (Prov. 24:23); of taking bribes (Isa. 61:8; Mic. 7:3; compare Ex. 23:2–9); of failing to defend the interest of the powerless (Isa. 10:2; Jer. 5:28). Zephaniah described the judges of Jerusalem as wolves on the prowl (3:3).

God is the ultimate Judge of all the earth (Gen. 18:25; Isa. 33:22; Jas. 4:12). As God's representative, Christ functions as judge as well (John 8:16; Jas. 5:9; 1 Pet. 4:5).

As is frequently the case with biblical truths, the Christian's role in exercising judgment on others is found in a tension between warnings to avoid judging others and admonitions concerning how best to judge others. Christians are forbidden to judge others when such judgment entails intolerance of another's sin coupled with blindness of one's own sin (Matt. 7:1–5; Luke 6:37; John 8:7; Rom. 2:1–4) or when human judgment impinges on God's prerogative as judge (Rom. 14:4; 1 Cor.

J

4:5; Jas. 4:11–12). Instructions on proper exercise of judgment include: the call to judge reputed prophets by their fruits (Matt. 7:5–17); encouragement for Christians to judge what is right for themselves and thus avoid pagan lawcourts (Luke 12:57–59; 1 Cor. 6:1–6); and instructions regarding church cases (Matt. 18:15–20). First Corinthians 5:3–5 illustrates the function of a church court. *Chris Church*

JUDGES, BOOK OF Second book of the group called the Former Prophets in the Hebrew Bible. In English Bible arrangement following the Greek Septuagint it is the second of the Historical Books. Judges relates important episodes in the period of Israel's settlement in Canaan between the death of Joshua and the advent of Samuel.

The Book of Judges is arranged according to its theological theme of the cyclical nature of Israel's obedience to God in the process of their gradual expansion in the land. This theme is most clearly spelled out in 2:16–19. Israel would forsake Yahweh and follow after other gods, and Yahweh would give them into the hand of an oppressor. Israel would cry out for deliverance, Yahweh would send a deliverer, and Israel would be obedient to Yahweh until the death of the deliverer, when the cycle would begin again.

The book of Judges may be outlined as follows:
I. Introduction (1:1—3:6)
   A. Judah's conquests and the land yet unconquered (1:1–36)
   B. Israel's cycles of apostasy (2:1—3:6)
II. Individual Judges (3:7—16:31)
   A. Othniel (3:7–11)
   B. Ehud delivers from Moab (3:12–30).
   C. Shamgar (3:31)
   D. Deborah (and Barak) deliver from the Canaanites (4:1—5:31).
   E. Gideon delivers from Midian (6:1—9:57).
   F. Tola and Jair (10:1–5)
   G. Jephthah delivers from Ammon (10:6—12:7).
   H. Ibzan, Elon, and Abdon (12:8–15)
   I. Samson begins the deliverance from the Philistines (13:1—16:31).
III. Illustrative Incidents (17:1—21:25)
   A. Idol worship and idol theft in Israel (17:1—18:31)
   B. The Levite's concubine and the near destruction of Benjamin (19:1—21:25).

The deliverers were called *sophetim,* "Judges." The term had a broader connotation than "judge" does today in the English-speaking world. A *shophet,* or "judge," was a military leader, civil administrator, and decider of cases at law, very likely acting as an appellate court. The Book of Judges records mostly the military exploits of five of the judges; because of this they are often called "major judges." The other judges, who receive only minimal notice, are often called "minor judges." The major judges are Ehud, Deborah (the only woman among the judges), Gideon, Jephthah, and Samson. The minor judges are Othniel, Shamgar, Tola, Jair, Ibzan, Elon, and Abdon. Abimelech, the son of Gideon, attempted to establish the dynastic principle in Israel on the strength of his father's accomplishments but was unsuccessful.

It would appear that in no case was a single judge leader over all the tribes of Israel at once. Several of the narratives make a point of noting the absence of one or more tribes from the fighting forces under a judge (5:15–17; 8:1; 12:1). Also, in working out the chronology of Israel's occupation of the land from Joshua to David, a very strong case can be made that some of the judges were contemporaries, one leading one group of tribes while another led another group of tribes.

The last five chapters (17—21) of Judges record two separate incidents unrelated to the tenure of any individual judge. The first is the setting up of an illegitimate priesthood by an individual Ephraimite named Micah, followed by the theft of Micah's priest and his "gods" by a part of the tribe of Dan who were migrating from their territory (on the west of Judah) to the northern part of the Hula Valley in the extreme north of Israel. The second episode is even more reprehensible; it concerns the rape and murder at Gibeah in Benjamin of the concubine of a nameless Levite. The eleven tribes rallied to the Levite's call for justice; Benjamin defended the town of Gibeah, and civil war followed. Benjamin was annihilated, except for six hundred warriors. Facing the destruction of one tribe of the twelve, the eleven tribes devised a dubious way around their oath not to allow any of their daughters to marry into the tribe of Benjamin. The book closes with the author's assessment of the period, which has been illustrated particularly well by these two episodes, "In those days there was no king in Israel; every man did that which was right in his own eyes," (Judg. 21:25).

The Book of Judges presents a selective and theologically oriented account of the settlement of Israel in the land of Canaan in the centuries following the initial entry under Joshua. The campaigns under Joshua meant that the Canaanite population could not deny Israel entrance into the land. The pattern of settlement, as outlined in the Book of Judges, is confirmed by archaeological survey and excavation. Archaeology has revealed a pattern of many small, brand-new settlements in large areas of the Central Hill Country of Galilee, Samaria, and Judea. Also, the southern Negev, which has been sparsely or not at all inhabited by the Canaanite population, exhibits the same pattern. Gradually, over the course of several centuries, Israel became stronger; and the Canaanite peoples became absorbed into Israel, until, under

J

David, Israel controlled all the land of Canaan and even beyond.

Some scholars have held that the Book of Judges reflects an Israelite version of the amphictyony, a group of six or twelve tribes organized around a central shrine. A comparison with Greek and Italian amphictyonies of the first millenium B.C. reveals very little similarity beyond the fact that Israel numbered twelve tribes.

The Hebrew text of Judges is among the best preserved of the Old Testament. The Song of Deborah (chapter 5) is recognized universally as one of the very earliest poems of the Bible.

Outline

I. Disobedience Causes Chaos (1:1—3:6).
  A. Partial obedience is disobedience (1:1–36).
  B. Disobedience exposes people to further temptation (2:1–5).
  C. Leaders who neglect God's covenant lead the people into punishment (2:6–15).
  D. Failure to heed God's leaders leads to defeat (2:16–23).
  E. God tests His people to see if they will obey (3:1–6).
II. Repentence Is the Only Hope of Deliverance (3:7—16:31).
  A. God listens to the agonized cries of His people (3:7–31).
  B. God uses women leaders to achieve His purpose for His people (4:1–24).
  C. A delivered people praised God for His gift of victory (5:1–31).
  D. God provided a prophet to correct His people (6:1–10).
  E. God called people even from insignificant families to deliver His people (6:11–24).
  F. God proved more powerful than Baal (6:25–32).
  G. God's Spirit gives power to God-called leaders (6:33–40).
  H. Divine power, not human numbers, provides victory for God's people (7:1–25).
  I. God is King and can rule His people without power groups, institutions, or symbols (8:1–35).
  J. God does not honor self-seeking leaders of His people (9:1–57).
  K. God's deliverance comes only to a confessing, repenting people (10:1–16).
  L. God uses leaders considered unworthy in human eyes (10:17—11:11).
  M. God honors leaders who learn the lessons of history (11:12–40).
  N. God does not honor power-seekers (12:1–15).
  O. God blesses families who honor Him (13:1–25).
  P. God can turn human trickery, treachery, and hatred to accomplish His purposes

(14:1—15:20).
  Q. Unfaithful leaders cannot follow selfish lusts and expect God's blessing (16:1–21).
  R. God delivers His people by the prayers and efforts of His leader (16:22–31).
III. Chaos Is the Moral and Social Result of Disobedience (17:1—21:25).
  A. Leaderless people use unscrupulous means even in religion (17:1—18:31).
  B. Sexual crimes can lead to civil war (19:1—20:48).
  C. Worship can become a ruse (21:1–25).

Joseph Coleson

JUDGMENT DAY Time of God's punishment and refining of the evil in the world, especially of the final, history-ending time of eternal judgment. The expression "Day of Judgment" appears several times in the Bible as a frightful day of dread (Heb. 10:27) connected with the wrath of God (Heb. 12:29) and can only be overcome through mature faith in Christ (1 John 4:17–18; compare Rom. 8:33–34; 2 Tim. 4:8). Closely connected with the second coming of Christ (2 Thess. 1:7–10), it is a part of the end-time events connected with the close of human history.

Several biblical terms are closely related to the concept of the judgment day. These refer to the wrath of God, judgment, judging, condemn, punishment, penalty, vengeance, judgment seat, destruction, and ruin.

Old Testament Background The idea of the judgment day reaches back into the Old Testament concepts of divine judgment and the day of the Lord. See *Day of the Lord.* The wrath of God is poured out in judgment upon the nation of Israel (1 Chron. 27:24; 2 Chron. 24:18; 29:8; Amos 3:2; 5:18; Hos. 13:9–11) as well as her wicked rulers (1 Sam. 15; 2 Kings 23:26–27; 1 Chron. 13:10; 2 Chron. 19:2). Other individuals became the object of God's wrath: Moses (Ex. 4:14, 24; Deut. 1:37); Aaron (Deut. 9:20), Miriam (Num. 12:9), Nadab and Abihu (Lev. 10:1–2). Surrounding nations and their rulers became objects of God's wrath (Pss. 2:5,11; 110:5; Isa. 13:3,5,9,13; Jer. 50:13,15; 51:45; Ezek. 25:14; 30:15).

His wrath is fierce (Ex. 32:12; Ezra 10:14), is kindled like a fire (Ps. 106:40), and waxes hot like molten wax (Ex. 22:24; 32:10). A day of wrath was spoken of as a specific time in which God would act in temporal judgment (Job 21:30; Prov. 11:4; Ezek. 7:12; Zeph. 1:15,18). God's wrath came to be so closely identified with divine action in judgment that its character as an emotion in the being of God receded into the background.

Also significant is the concept of God as Judge rendering judgments. The Hebrew *mishpat* brings together the ideas of judging and ruling into a single concept focused in the authority of God as Sovereign over the nation of Israel and over cre-

J

ation. Thus He instituted divine law and renders righteous verdicts based upon it as well as enforcing its requirements (Gen. 18:25; Pss. 89:27; 96:10,13; 98:9). Associated with this is the promise of a day when God will exercise His judgments with awesome power in the Day of the Lord (Isa. 24—26). The eschatological interpretation of this day is most evident in Dan. 7:22,27; 12:1–3.

Intertestamental Period This orientation became more prominent in Jewish writings in the interbiblical period (Enoch 47:3; 90:2–27; 4 Ezra 7:33; 12; Baruch 24; Testament of Benjamin 10:6–8; Judith 16:17). Judgment Day follows the resurrection of the dead and determines the eternal destiny of the righteous (either Paradise in Heaven or on a renewed earth, or life in the heavenly Jerusalem or in the heavenly Garden of Eden come down to earth) and of the wicked (Gehenna or some other place of eternal punishment) based on their obedience/disobedience to the law of God. Both Jews and Gentiles are included. Also angels will be judged as well as humans (Jubilees 5:3–16; Enoch 10:6; 16:1; 19:1; 90:20–27). God is usually pictured as the Judge although sometimes the Messiah is charged with this responsibility (Enoch 45:3; 69:27–29).

New Testament Development The New Testament builds on the foundation of the Old Testament and utilizes the language and imagery of the Jewish writings to present the full revelational picture of Judgment Day. As in the Old Testament, divine judgment is both a present and a future reality. Jesus' first coming represents a divine judgment (John 3:19; 9:39; 12:31). Sinful humanity presently stands under divine condemnation (John 3:36) and experiences in part now the wrath of God (Rom. 1:18–32). The people of God are chastised for their waywardness (Heb. 12:4–11; Prov. 3:11–12), but that final divine verdict of judgment is yet to be carried out in a future day (1 John 4:17; John 5:24–29) by the Son of Man Himself (John 12:48; 5:22). Thus human activity in this life basically determines the verdict rendered in this future judgment.

In the great white throne judgment scene (Rev. 20:11–15), the basis of judgment is first from the book of life (vv. 12a,15) and then from the books of works (vv. 12b–14). One's relationship with Christ is that determiner of eternal destiny (John 3:36), but one's faithfulness to Christ is crucial to a genuine relationship with Christ (Jas. 2:14–26; Matt. 7:21–23; 1 John 2:3–6). Very similar in emphasis is the parable of the sheep and goats (Matt. 25:31–56). Pious deeds of devotion done to those in need stands as the distinguishing criterion between the sheep and the goats and settles their eternal destiny (v. 46). Paul's discussion in Romans 2:1–16 underscores that demand for obedient commitment to Christ as well. The concept of retribution for good and bad is also applied to believers (1 Cor. 3:12–15; 2 Cor. 5:10), but the specifics of rewards and punishments are not stated. However, the New Testament is absolutely clear in declaring the certainty of Judgment Day from which no one will escape (Acts 17:30–31). Thus comes the apostolic call to repentance and faith.

See *Day of the Lord; Day of Christ; Second Coming; Last Things; Hell; Heaven.*

Lorin L. Cranford

JUDGMENT SEAT In Matthew 27:19, the raised platform or bench occupied by Pontius Pilate while he was deliberating the accusations made against Jesus and the sentence he would pronounce in connection with Jesus' case. According to Acts 18:12, Paul the apostle was brought before the judgment seat in Corinth. In these two instances the judgment seat is to be understood in its ordinary literal sense. In Romans 14:10 and 2 Corinthians 5:10, the judgment seat of Christ is a theological concept. Those verses stress that individuals are accountable to the Lord for their lives and must one day face Him in judgment. See *Cross, Crucifixion; Jesus; Jerusalem; Judgment Day.*

Place in the gate of Iron Age Dan where it is thought a judge sat to hear cases.

JUDGMENT, HALL OF (1) One of Solomon's buildings (1 Kings 7:7). See *Hall;* (2) KJV expression for the praetorium (John 18:28). See *Praetorium.*

JUDGMENT, THE LAST See *Judgment Day.*

JUDGMENTS OF GOD See *Judgment Day; Retribution, Divine; Eschatology.*

JUDITH (Jū′ dĭth) Personal name meaning, "Jewess." *1.* One of Esau's Hittite wives who caused grief for his parents because they feared the women would lead Esau away from his culture and his God (Gen. 26:33–34). *2.* Heroine of Judith in the Apocrypha. A pious widow, she beguiled Holfernes, Nebuchadnezzar's general and delivered her people from him by cutting off his head. See *Apocrypha.*

JUG A large, deep, earthenware or glass container with a narrow mouth and handle. Neither KJV nor RSV use the term. NIV uses jug in three passages: a water jug (1 Sam. 26:11,12,16; KJV, bottle; NRSV, jar); an oil jug (1 Kings 17:12,14,16; KJV, RSV, cruse; NRSV, jug); and an unspecified container (Jer. 48:12; KJV, bottle; RSV, jar). The NAS uses jug in seven passages. At 1 Samuel 1:24; 10:3; 16:20; 25:18; 2 Samuel 16:1 the translation "skins" is preferable (NIV, NRSV). At Jeremiah 13:12 the RSV translation "jar" is preferred (NIV, skin). The KJV generally rendered the underlying Hebrew terms as bottle. See *Pottery in Bible Times; Vessels and Utensils.*

JULIA (Jū′ lĭ å) Common Roman name. In Romans 16:15, a Christian woman to whom Paul the apostle extended a greeting. Her name suggests she may have had some association with the imperial household. She may have been sister or wife to Philologus and a slave of the emperor.

JULIUS (Jū′ lĭ ús) Common Roman personal name. In Acts 27:1, a centurion of the Augustan cohort assigned the responsibility of escorting Paul to Rome. Though Paul was his prisoner, Julius treated the apostle with kindness. He allowed Paul to go ashore at Sidon to visit with friends. Later, he saved the apostle's life by restraining the soldiers who wanted to kill Paul to keep him from escaping. See *Paul; Centurion.*

JULIUS CAESAR See *Rome, Roman Empire.*

JUNIA (Jū′ nĭ å) See *Junias.*

JUNIAS (Jū′ nĭ ås) Roman personal name, possibly a shortened form of Junianus. In Romans 16:7, Paul extended greeting to a certain Junia, whom he referred to as his kinsman, his fellow prisoner, and an apostle. The form of the name is feminine. Nothing is known of this individual beyond what may be inferred from this verse. Some recent commentators see the person as a woman and possibly as the wife of Andronicus. See *Andronicus; Apostle.*

JUNIPER In 1 Kings 19:4, a tree under which Elijah the prophet rested as he fled the wrath of Jezebel. The same plant is mentioned in Job 30:4 and Psalm 120:4. The Hebrew word thus translated probably refers to a kind of shrub that grows in the Arabian deserts. Modern translations read "broom." See *Broom Tree.*

JUPITER (Jū′ pī tēr) Latin name of Zeus, king of Greek gods. KJV translates Zeus as Jupiter (Acts 13:12–13). God worked through Paul to heal a crippled man at Lystra. The people responded by claiming the gods had come to earth. They named Barnabas, Zeus or Jupiter. The priest of Jupiter tried to offer sacrifices to them. Paul used the

The Temple of Jupiter at Baalbek (Helipolis).

opportunity for evangelistic preaching. KJV also inserts Jupiter in Acts 19:35, referring to the image of Artemis or Diana, the goddess for whose worship Ephesus was famous. The Greek says the image fell from heaven (NRSV, NAS, REB, NIV, TEV). See *Greece, Religion and Society of.*

JUSHAB-HESED (Jū′ shăb-hē′ sĕd) Personal name meaning, "mercy is brought back." Royal son of Zerubbabel and descendant of David, thus a part of keeping messianic hope alive (1 Chron. 3:20). See *Zerubbabel.*

JUSTICE The order God seeks to reestablish in His creation where all people receive the benefits of life with Him. As love is for the New Testament, so justice is the central ethical idea of the Old Testament. The frequency of justice is sometimes missed by the reader due to a failure to realize the wide range of the Hebrew word *mishpat,* particularly in passages that deal with the material and social necessities of life.

Nature of justice Justice has two major aspects. First, it is the standard by which penalties are assigned for breaking the obligations of the society. Second, justice is the standard by which the advantages of social life are handed out, including material goods, rights of participation, opportunities, and liberties. It is the standard for both punishment and benefits and thus can be spoken of as a plumb line. "I shall use justice as a plumbline, and righteousness as a plummet" (Isa. 28.17, REB).

Often people think of justice in the Bible only in the first sense as God's wrath on evil. This aspect of justice indeed is present, such as the judgment mentioned in John 3:19. Often more vivid words like "wrath" are used to describe punitive justice (Rom. 1:18).

Justice in the Bible very frequently also deals with benefits. Cultures differ widely in determining the basis by which the benefits are to be justly distributed. For some it is by birth and nobility. For others the basis is might or ability or merit. Or it might simply be whatever is the law or whatever has been established by contracts. The Bible takes another possibility. Benefits are distributed according to need. Justice then is very close to love and grace. God "executes justice for the orphan and the widow, and . . . loves the strangers, providing them food and clothing" (Deut. 10:18, NRSV; compare Hos. 10:12; Isa. 30:18).

Various needy groups are the recipients of justice. These groups include widows, orphans, resident aliens (also called "sojourners" or "strangers"), wage earners, the poor, and prisoners, slaves, and the sick (Job 29:12–17; Ps. 146:7–9; Mal. 3:5). Each of these groups has specific needs which keep its members from being able to participate in aspects of the life of their community. Even life itself might be threatened. Justice involves meeting those needs. The forces which deprive people of what is basic for community life are condemned as oppression (Mic. 2:2; Eccl. 4:1). To oppress is to use power for one's own advantage in depriving others of their basic rights in the community (see Mark 12:40). To do justice is to correct that abuse and to meet those needs (Isa. 1:17). Injustice is depriving others of their basic needs or failing to correct matters when those rights are not met (Jer. 5:28; Job 29:12–17). Injustice is either a sin of commission or of omission.

The content of justice, the benefits which are to be distributed as basic rights in the community, can be identified by observing what is at stake in the passages in which "justice," "righteousness," and "judgment" occur. The needs which are met include land (Ezek. 45:6–9; compare Mic. 2:2;

4:4) and the means to produce from the land, such as draft animals and millstones (Deut. 22:1–4; 24:6). These productive concerns are basic to securing other essential needs and thus avoiding dependency; thus the millstone is called the "life" of the person (Deut. 24:6). Other needs are those essential for mere physical existence and well being: food (Deut. 10:18; Ps. 146:7), clothing (Deut. 24:13), and shelter (Ps. 68:6; Job 8:6). Job 22:5–9,23; 24:1–12 decries the injustice of depriving people of each one of these needs, which are material and economic. The equal protection of each person in civil and judicial procedures is represented in the demand for due process (Deut. 16:18–20). Freedom from bondage is comparable to not being "in hunger and thirst, in nakedness and lack of everything" (Deut. 28:48 NRSV).

Justice presupposes God's intention for people to be in community. When people had become poor and weak with respect to the rest of the community, they were to be strengthened so that they could continue to be effective members of the community—living with them and beside them (Lev. 25:35–36). Thus biblical justice restores people to community. By justice those who lacked the power and resources to participate in significant aspects of the community were to be strengthened so that they could. This concern in Leviticus 25 is illustrated by the provision of the year of Jubilee, in which at the end of the fifty year period land is restored to those who had lost it through sale or foreclosure of debts (v. 28). Thus they regained economic power and were brought back into the economic community. Similarly, interest on loans was prohibited (v. 36) as a process which pulled people down, endangering their position in the community.

These legal provisions express a further characteristic of justice. Justice delivers; it does not merely relieve the immediate needs of those in dire straits (Ps. 76:9; Isa. 45:8; 58:11; 62:1–2). Helping the needy means setting them back on their feet, giving a home, leading to prosperity, restoration, ending the oppression (Ps. 68:5–10; 10:15–16; compare 107; 113:7–9). Such thorough justice can be socially disruptive. In the Jubilee year as some receive back lands, others lose recently-acquired additional land. The advantage to some is a disadvantage to others. In some cases the two aspects of justice come together. In the act of restoration, those who were victims of justice receive benefits while their exploiters are punished (1 Sam 2:7–10; compare Luke 1:51–53; 6:20–26).

The source of justice As the sovereign Creator of the universe, God is just (Ps. 99:1–4; Gen. 18:25; Deut. 32:4; Jer. 9:24), particularly as the defender of all the oppressed of the earth (Pss. 76:9; 103:6; Jer. 49:11). Justice thus is universal (Ps. 9:7–9) and applies to each covenant or dispensation. Jesus affirmed for His day the centrality of the Old Testament demand for justice (Matt. 23:23). Justice is the work of the New Testament people of God (Jas. 1:27).

God's justice is not a distant external standard. It is the source of all human justice (Prov. 29:26; 2 Chron. 19:6,9). Justice is grace received and grace shared (2 Cor. 9:8–10).

The most prominent human agent of justice is the ruler. The king receives God's justice and is a channel for it (Ps. 72:1; compare Rom. 13:1–2,4). There is not a distinction between a personal, voluntary justice and a legal, public justice. The same caring for the needy groups of the society is demanded of the ruler (Ps. 72:4; Ezek. 34:4; Jer. 22:15–16). Such justice was also required of pagan rulers (Dan. 4:27; Prov. 31:8–9).

Justice is also a central demand on all people who bear the name of God. Its claim is so basic that without it other central demands and provisions of God are not acceptable to God. Justice is required to be present with the sacrificial system (Amos 5:21–24; Mic. 6:6–8; Isa. 1:11–17; Matt. 5:23–24), fasting (Isa. 58:1–10), tithing (Matt. 23:23), obedience to the other commandments (Matt. 19:16–21), or the presence of the Temple of God (Jer. 7:1–7).

Justice in salvation Apart from describing God's condemnation of sin, Paul used the language and meaning of justice to speak of personal salvation. "The righteousness of God" represents God in grace bringing into the community of God through faith in Christ those who had been outside of the people of God (particularly in Romans but compare also Eph. 2:12–13).

See *Law; Government; Poverty; Righteousness; Welfare.*   *Stephen Charles Mott*

JUSTIFICATION Process by which an individual is brought into an unmerited, right relationship with a person, whether that relationship is established between people or with God.

Old Testament In its simplest form, the cardinal theme of Scripture could be described as God's relationship with His people. Justification is a term which explains how an individual enters into that relationship with God, contrasts the life of participants in that relationship with those outside, and outlines the obligations of that relationship. Justification is the remedy for the chief problem of sin which separates God and sinners.

God called Abraham and promised to make him into a great people (Gen. 12:1–3). Effectually, Abraham was called to counteract the sin of Adam. The only proper response to that call was faith. Although advanced in years, Abraham was promised a child Isaac, through whom innumerable descendants would emerge. Abraham's response to this promise is the crux of the whole idea of justification in the Old as well as in the New Testament. Genesis 15:6 captures this response: "Abram believed the Lord, and he cred-

ited it to him as righteousness" (NIV). Righteousness is not something Abraham possessed that prompted a reward from God. Quite to the contrary, a condition was fulfilled on the part of Abraham, and subsequently on the part of God. The Old Testament teaches that to be righteous is to fulfill the conditions of the covenant relationship. Therefore, to act righteously is to act in compliance with the covenant. The Hebrew word translated "credited" (or imputed or reckoned) originally described the important priestly task of endorsing the offerings presented to God (Lev. 7:18; 17:4; Num. 18:27). On the basis of this understanding, God accepted the response of Abraham's faith. This covenant was no mere abstraction. It was a term of relationship encompassed by the concrete, dynamic action of God. Similarly, righteousness is a term of relationship. The covenant establishes the terms of the relationship. A person who fulfills the terms of the covenant relationship is called righteous.

The search for the abstract noun "justification" in the Old Testament is fruitless. However, the verb, "to justify," is found occasionally, often in the passive "to be justified," pointing to some kind of agency involved in the action (see Job 11:2; 13:18; 25:4; Pss. 51:4; 143:2; Isa. 43:9,26; 45:25). All of these references clearly reveal the nature of justification: it is something that God does. The elemental sense in which the Old Testament employs the idea of "justifying" is best expressed in the phrase "proclaiming to be within the covenant relationship."

Ironically, God's chosen people Israel continually displayed a bent toward rebellion which can best be rendered, in covenantal language, as infidelity more than immorality. This is why the Hebrew prophets strongly decried Israel's proclivity to prostitute themselves with foreign gods. Hosea provides the best example of this infidelity because it was personified in his life. Hosea's personal experience in marriage served also as a parable of God's relationship with Israel. The names of his three children, Jezreel (God scatters), Lo-Ruhamah (not pitied), and Lo-Ammi (not my people) show the extent of the rebellion. God's perennial problem with Israel caused Him to act "justly," that is, He had to render a judgment or He would be characterized as a bad judge. This is how Hosea interpreted God's judgment upon sin and unfaithfulness to the covenant. The actions taken by God were not arbitrary; rather, they are to be seen as actions resulting directly from a major disruption in the covenantal bond. Balancing this view, the Hebrew conception of justice also included an important redemptive element. Even in the midst of Israel's rebellion, Hosea vividly portrayed God saying to them, "How can I give you up, Ephraim? How can I hand you over, Israel?" (Hos. 11:8*a* NIV). Justification always requires obedience on the part of God's

J

people, but justification also always requires judgment and restoration on the part of God. Anything less would greatly diminish the meaning of the term "justification."

New Testament The New Testament's posture, with respect to the idea of justification, is also dependent on the concrete activity of God. The major difference is that, in the New Testament, God dealt with the sin of humankind by the highest and most intimate form of revelation, His Son Jesus Christ. The earliest Christians believed that they were "made right" with God through the death and resurrection of Jesus Christ (Rom. 3:21–26; 4:18–25; 1 Cor. 1:30; 6:11; 1 Tim. 3:16; 1 Pet. 3:18). In his letter to the Romans, Paul conveyed the message that God did not consider sin lightly. Sin created a massive gulf between God and people. This gulf required a bridge to bring all of humanity into a right relationship with God. Theologians call God's bridge building "reconciliation." Reconciliation functions to bring humans "justification." The main character who effected this divine plan was Jesus Christ. Uniquely, His death on the cross made it possible for God and people to be reconciled (Rom. 5:10) and thus for humans to be justified.

Not found in the Old Testament, justification is almost as scarce in the New Testament, occurring only three times (Rom. 4:25; 5:16,18). The necessity of justification, however, is sufficiently expressed by Paul in Romans 5:12–21. Paul advanced this theme of sin and its effects no doubt with the story of Genesis 3 in mind. Paul described sin almost as a personal power controlling people, preventing them from obeying God, and leading them to death. No one is excluded from sin's domain. All people are in the deplorable state of being separated from God due to sin. All people desperately need deliverance. The redemptive activity of Christ provides the only avenue to a right relationship with God.

Justification does not encompass the whole salvation process; it does, however, mark that instantaneous point of entry or transformation which makes one "right with God." Christians are justified in the same way Abraham was, by faith (Rom. 4:16; 5:1). Human works do not achieve or earn acceptance by God. The exercise of faith alone ushers us into a right, unmerited relationship with God (Gal. 2:16; Titus 3:7). Biblically, the spiritual journey begins at the point of justification. This immediate act has far-reaching consequences. It establishes the future. God in the present moment announces the verdict He will pronounce on the day of final judgment. He declares that trusting faith in Jesus Christ puts people in the right with God, bringing eternal life now and forever.

Paul taught that faith in Jesus Christ is an obedient response which results from hearing the Gospel (Rom. 10:17). He drew a connection between the Christian's faith and the faith of Abraham. Abraham's faith in God can be seen as an exemplary foreshadowing which would find ultimate expression in every Christians' relationship to God through Jesus Christ.

Two related questions present themselves for consideration: (1) What is the relationship between faith and Old Testament law?, and (2) What is the relationship between faith and works? Paul found no room in his theology for an elitist righteousness. Special privileges were not administered by God in direct proportion to blood (nationality), brawn (strength), or brains (intellect). No justification within the law would allow anyone (Jew or not) to sidestep faith in Jesus Christ. Paul eliminated all doubt when he argued that being a Jew is neither a prerequisite (Rom. 4:1–25) nor a prerogative (9:1–33) for justification. The only stipulation, accessible to all, is faith.

Some confusion results when a comparison is made between faith and works. Paul is not the only adherent or spokesman for the doctrine of justification by faith. The apostle James, among others, taught this crucial doctrine also. However, premature appraisals of James 2:14–26 have caused some to see a contradiction in comparison with Paul's instruction. Nothing is further from the truth. The two writers merely expressed different concerns. James' idea of faith summarily eliminated all instances of imagined belief which had no observable or corresponding behavior. Paul's concept of faith emphasized a shift of focus from the world to Jesus Christ on the part of the believer. It was a reorientation which resulted in good works (see Rom. 12). By God's grace we are offered salvation, which we accept by faith. This faith results in a radical change of our natures (2 Cor. 5:17) in order that we might do good works. See *Paul; James; Reconciliation; Faith; Eternal Life.*   *Paul Jackson*

JUSTUS (Jŭs' tŭs) Common Jewish personal name. *1.* In Acts 1:23, the surname of Joseph Barsabbas, one of two men put forward to replace Judas Iscariot among the twelve. *2.* A pious man, probably a Roman citizen, whose home joined the synagogue in Corinth (Acts 18:7). Paul left the synagogue and moved into the home of Titius Justus (KJV omits Titius following some Greek manuscripts). Some scholars equate him with Titus (following some Greek manuscripts), while more identify him with Gaius of Romans 16:23. Neither identification is more than a scholarly guess based on similarity of name. *3.* Surname of a fellow minister with Paul (Col. 4:11).

JUTTAH (Jŭt' tah) Place name meaning, "spread out." Town in hill country of tribal territory of Judah (Josh. 15:55) given to the Levites (Josh. 21:16). It may be located at modern Yatta, six miles southwest of Hebron.

K

The Kidron Valley at Jerusalem.

KAB (Kăb) A measure of volume mentioned only in 2 Kings 6:25. Descriptions in ancient sources indicate a kab would be slightly larger than a quart. See *Weights and Measures.*

KABZEEL (Kăb′ zė ĕl) Place name meaning, "may God gather"; same as Jekabzeel in Nehemiah 11:25. Located in the southeast part of Judah near the border of Edom (Josh. 15:21). The home of Benaiah, an officer under David and Solomon (2 Sam. 23:20; 1 Chron. 11:22). One of the towns reoccupied by the Jews after the return from the Exile (Neh. 11:25).

KADESH (Kā′ dĕsh) See *Kadesh-Barnea.*

KADESH-BARNEA (Kā′ dĕsh-bär nē′ à) Place name meaning "consecrated." The site where the Hebrews stayed for most of thirty-eight years after leaving Mt. Sinai and before entering the Promised Land. The Old Testament locates it between the Wilderness of Paran and the Wilderness of Zin (Num. 13:3–21,26). Moses sent out the twelve spies into Canaan from Kadesh-Barnea (Num. 13:3–21,26) The Hebrews also attempted their abortive southern penetration into Canaan from there (Num. 13:26; 14:40–45). Kadesh-Barnea is mentioned as a site where Abraham fought the Amalekites (Gen. 14:7) and as the southern border of the tribe of Judah (Josh. 15:3).

The actual site of Kadesh-Barnea has been

Iron age fortress in the area of ancient Kadesh-Barnea.

much debated, but the two most frequently mentioned sites are Ein-Qedeis and Ein el-Qudeirat. Both of these sites are in the northern part of the Sinai Peninsula, and both have a spring. Most scholars today accept Ein el-Qudeirat because of its abundance of water (the largest springs and oasis in northern Sinai). Ein el-Qudeirat is located on the crossroads of two major roads of antiquity—the road from Edom to Egypt and the road from the Red Sea to the Negev and southern Canaan, later southern Judah. The location on the road from Egypt to Edom would fit well the biblical context of Kadesh-Barnea as the oasis home for the Hebrews during the wilderness wandering period. Likewise, the location of Kadesh-Barnea along the north-south road may explain the rationale for attempting the invasion of Canaan at Arad, since Arad lay north of Kadesh-Barnea on that road.

Excavations of Ein el-Qudeirat have shown major fortresses dating from the period of Solomon to the fall of the monarchy (tenth century B.C. to sixth century B.C.), but no remains from the period of the wilderness wandering have been found to date. This raises the question about the identity of the site of Kadesh-Barnea. The site has not been fully excavated, however, and as yet no better alternative site has come to light. *Joel F. Drinkard*

KADESH-MERIBAH (Kā′ dĕsh-Mĕr′ ĭ bäh) TEV transliteration of a phrase from the Hebrew text of Ezekiel 47:19. The name is translated in the KJV as "the waters of strife in Kadesh." (See Num.

20:2–13; Deut. 32:51; compare Ex. 17:1–7.) RSV has "Meribath-kadesh," and NIV has "Meribah Kadesh" at Deuteronomy 32:51; Ezekiel 47:19. NAS has "Meribah-kadesh" at Deuteronomy 32:51 and "Meribath-kadesh" at Ezekiel 47:19. TEV has "When you were at the waters of Meribah, near the town of Kadesh" at Deuteronomy 32:51. The same town as Kadesh-Barnea. See *Kadesh-Barnea.*

KADMIEL (Kăd′ mĭ ĕl) Personal name meaning, "God is of old" or "God goes before." *1.* Levite who returned from the Babylonian Exile with Zerubbabel. A representative of the line of Hodaviah (Ezra 2:40; Neh. 7:43 has Hodevah), also known as the line of Judah (Ezra 3:9). Helped rebuild the Temple. *2.* Levite who helped Ezra in the reaffirmation of the covenant after the return from the Exile (Neh. 9:4–5). *3.* Levite who signed the covenant after the Exile (Neh. 10:9). The relationship between these persons is unclear. They may all represent the same person or be father and son.

KADMONITE (Kăd′ mon īte) Name of a people meaning, "easterners." Tribe God promised (Gen. 15:19) Israel would dispossess. They probably inhabited the Syro-Arabian desert between Palestine-Syria and the Euphrates—which is to say, areas to the east of Canaan. Their names often have Arabian associations. They may be related to the "children of the east" mentioned in Judges 6:33. The sons of the concubines of Abraham were sent to live in the "east country" (Kedem) away from Isaac (Gen. 25:6). Job (Job 1:3), the camel-riding Midianite kings (Judg. 8:10–12,21,26) and the wise men whose names have Arabian associations (1 Kings 4:30–31) are all described as sons of the east.

KAIN (Kai n) A tribe and place name meaning, "smith." *1.* A clan mentioned in the fourth oracle of Balaam (Num. 24:22; KJV has Kenite). Adam and Eve's son Cain is spelled the same in Hebrew, and many scholars regard Cain as the ancestor of the Kenites. See *Kenites.* *2.* A city southeast of Hebron in southern Judah (Josh. 15:57; KJV and NEB have Cain). Identified with khirbet Yaqin. According to Arabian tradition, Abraham watched the destruction of Sodom and Gomorrah from a nearby hill. Kain was a settlement of the Kenites.

KAIWAN (Kai′ wän) Babylonian god (Amos 5:26). KJV transliterates the name as Chiun. As is often the case when foreign gods were referred to, the original vowels of the name were probably replaced with the vowels of the Hebrew word for "abomination." See *Chiun; Gods, Pagan; Sakkuth.*

KALLAI (Kăl′ lā ī) Personal name meaning, "swift" or "light." A chief priest who returned from Exile during the time of the high priest Joiakim (Neh. 12:20).

KAMON (Kā′ mŏn) City of Gilead where Jair, judge of Israel, was buried (Judg. 10:5; KJV has Camon). The precise location is unknown.

KANAH (Kā′ nah) Place name meaning, "place of reeds." *1.* The name of a brook that forms part of the boundary between Ephraim and Manasseh (Josh. 16:8; 17:9). Some of the cities of Manasseh, however, were south of the brook Kanah (Josh. 16:9). Identified by some with the modern wadi Qanah. *2.* A city on the northern border of Asher (Josh. 19:28). Identified with modern Qana, about six miles southeast of Tyre. Not to be confused with Cana of the New Testament.

KAREAH (Kȧ rē′ ah) Personal name meaning, "bald." Father of Johanan and Jonathan during the time of Jeremiah (Jer. 40:8,13,15–16; 41:11,13–14,16; 42:1,8; 43:2,4–5; spelled Careah in 2 Kings 25:23, KJV).

KARKA (Kär′ kȧ) Place name meaning, "ground" or "floor." A city on the southern border of Judah (Josh. 15:3; KJV has Karkaa). Precise location unknown.

KARKAA (Kär kā′ ȧ) KJV spelling of Karka. See *Karka.*

KARKOR (Kär′ kôr) Place name meaning "soft, level ground." A mountainous village in the eastern region of Gilead during the period of the judges. The exact site has not been located. Gideon and three hundred Israelite men conducted their second surprise attack on the Midianites at Karkor. According to Judges 8:10–11, Zebah and Zalmunna, two Midianite leaders, were encamped at Karkor with fifteen thousand troops when Gideon attacked and routed them.

KARNAIM (Kär nā′ ĭm) Place name meaning, "horns." A city in northern Transjordan. The same as Ashteroth-karnaim and Ashtaroth. Amos used the name of this city and that of Lo-Debar to make a word play (Amos 6:13). See *Ashtaroth; Lo-Debar* (for the details of the word play).

KARTAH (Kär′ tah) Place name meaning, "city." Levitical city in the territory of Zebulun (Josh. 21:34). Location unknown. See *Levitical Cities.*

KARTAN (Kär′ tăn) Place name meaning, "city." A Levitical city in the tribal territory of Naphtali (Josh. 21:32). Also called Kiriathaim (1 Chron. 6:76). It was located near the Sea of Galilee. Usually identified with modern khirbet el-Qureiyeh. See *Levitical Cities.*

KATTAH (Kăt′ tah) NAS spelling of Kattath. See *Kattath*.

KATTATH (Kăt′ tăth) Place name meaning, "small." A town in the tribal territory of Zebulun (Josh. 19:15). Probably the same as Kitron (Judg. 1:30). See *Kitron*.

KEBAR (Kē′ bär) NIV spelling of Chebar. See *Chebar*.

KEDAR (Kē′ dȧr) Personal name meaning "mighty" or "swarthy" or "black." The second son of Ishmael and a grandson of Abraham (Gen. 25:13; 1 Chron. 1:29).

The name occurs later in the Bible presumably as a reference to a tribe that took its name from Kedar. Little concrete information is known about the group, however. Apparently the descendants of Kedar occupied the area south of Palestine and east of Egypt (Gen. 25:18). They may best be described as nomadic, living in tents (Ps. 120:5; Song of Sol. 1:5) and raising sheep and goats (Isa. 60:7; Jer. 49:28–29,32), as well as camels, which they sold as far away as Tyre (Ezek. 27:21).

The Kedarites were led by princes (Ezek. 27:21) and were famous for their warriors, particularly their archers (Isa. 21:17). They evidently were of some importance during the time of Isaiah (Isa. 21:16). See *Abraham; Ishmael*.

Hugh Tobias

KEDEMAH (Kĕd′ ė mah) Personal and tribal name meaning, "eastward." The last son of Ishmael (Gen. 25:15; 1 Chron. 1:31). Probably head of an Arabian tribe of the same name. Probably considered among the Kadmonites. See *Kadmonites*.

KEDEMOTH (Kĕd′ ė mŏth) Place name meaning, "ancient places" or "eastern places." One of the Levitical cities in the tribal territory of Reuben assigned to the family of Merari (Josh. 13:18; 21:37; 1 Chron. 6:79). See *Levitical Cities*. From the wilderness nearby, Moses sent a delegation to Sihon, king of the Amorites, requesting passage through his country (Deut. 2:26). The city is associated with either Kasr ez-Za′feran or khirbet er Remeil. Both of these cities are in the same vicinity and were in existence in Abraham's day.

KEDESH (Kē′ dĕsh) Place name meaning, "sacred place" or "sanctuary." 1. A city in the southern part of Judah (Josh. 15:23). Probably the same as Kadesh-Barnea. See *Kadesh-Barnea*. 2. A Canaanite town in eastern Galilee defeated by Joshua (Josh. 12:22). The town was allotted to Naphtali (Josh. 19:32,37) and was called Kedesh in Naphtali (Judg. 4:6). It was also called Kedesh in Galilee and given to the Gershonite Levites as one of their cities (Josh. 20:7; 21:32). See *Levitical Cities*. Kedesh in Naphtali was the home

of Barak (Judg. 4:6) and the place where Deborah and Barak gathered their forces for battle (Judg. 4:1–10). Heber the Kenite pitched his tent in the vicinity where Sisera met his death at the hands of Jael, Heber's wife (Judg. 4:21; 5:24–27). Kedesh in Naphtali was captured by Tiglath-pileser III during the reign of Pekah of Israel. The inhabitants were exiled to Assyria (2 Kings 15:29). Usually identified with modern khirbet Qedish, about two miles south of Tiberias.

3. A city in Issachar allotted to the Gershomite Levites (1 Chron. 6:72). The town is also called Kishon (Josh. 21:28 KJV; Kishion in other versions). It has been suggested that "Kedesh in Issachar" may have arisen from a misreading of "Kishon" for "Kedesh." The site is uncertain. Perhaps modern tell Abu Qudeis, about two miles southeast of Megiddo. *Phil Logan*

KEDESH IN NAPHTALI (Kē′ dĕsh in Năph′ tȧ lī) See *Kedesh 2*.

KEDESH-NAPHTALI (Kē′ dĕsh-năph′ tȧ lī) See *Kedesh 2*.

KEDORLAOMER (Kĕd ôr lā′ ō mēr) NIV spelling of Chedorlaomer. See *Chedorlaomer*.

KEHELATHAH (Kē hė lā′ thah) Place name meaning, "assembly." One of the desert camps of the Israelites during the wilderness wandering (Num. 33:22–23). Location unknown.

KEILAH (Kė ī′ lah) Personal and place name perhaps meaning, "fortress." 1. A descendant of Caleb (1 Chron. 4:19). 2. A fortified city in the lowland plain (Shephelah) of the territory of Judah identified with modern khirbet Qila, about eight miles northwest of Hebron and eighteen miles southwest of Jerusalem. David rescued the city from a Philistine attack but later withdrew fearing the populace would hand him over to Saul (1 Sam. 23:1–13). The city was rebuilt by the returning exiles (Neh. 3:17–18). One of the traditional sites of the burial place of Habakkuk.

KELAIAH (Kė lâi′ ah) Personal name, perhaps meaning, "Yahweh has dishonored." One of the Levites who divorced his foreign wife during the time of Ezra. Also identified as Kelita (Ezra 10:23). See *Kelita*.

KELAL (Kē′ lăl) NIV spelling of Chelal. See *Chelal*.

KELITA (Kė lī′ tá) Personal name probably meaning, "crippled, dwarfed one," but perhaps also meaning, "adopted one." A Levite who assisted in interpreting the Law when it was read to the assembly of the people during the time of Ezra (Neh. 8:7) and who participated in the sealing of

K

the covenant (Neh. 10:10). Kelita is perhaps a nickname for Kelaiah mentioned in Ezra 10:23. There, Kelaiah (that is, the dwarf) gave up his foreign wife in accordance with the instructions of Ezra.

KELUB (Kē′ lŭb) NIV spelling of Chelub. See *Chelub.*

KELUHI (Kĕ lü′ hī) NIV and REB spelling of Chelluh. See *Chelluh.*

KEMUEL (Kĕ mū′ ĕl) Personal name of uncertain meaning; perhaps meaning, "helper of God" or "assembly of God." *1.* The father of Aram, and the son of Abraham's brother Nahor (Gen. 22:21). *2.* The son of Shiphtan and representative of Ephraim in the division of Canaan among the tribes of Israel (Num. 34:24). *3.* The father of Hashabiah, a Levite during the time of David (1 Chron. 27:17).

KENAANAH (Kĕ nā′ å nah) NIV and REB spelling of Chenaanah. See *Chenaanah.*

KENAN (Kē′ năn) Personal name of uncertain meaning. Grandson of Adam, son of Enosh, and father of Mahalaleel (Gen. 5:9–14; KJV has Cainan; 1 Chron. 1:2). Listed as Cainan among the ancestors of Jesus (Luke 3:37). See *Enosh; Cainan.*

KENANI (Kĕ nā′ nī) NIV and REB spelling of Chenani. See *Chenani.*

KENANIAH (Kĕ nå nī′ ah) NIV and REB spelling of Chenaniah. See *Chenaniah.*

KENATH (Kē′ năth) Place name of uncertain meaning. A city in eastern Gilead taken by Nobah and given his name (Num. 32:42). The city was known as Kenath at a later time when it fell into the hands of Aram and Geshur (1 Chron. 2:23). The city is usually identified with the modern Qanawat in el-Hauran. Kenath was the easternmost city of the Decapolis. See *Decapolis.*

KENAZ (Kē′ năz) Personal name of unknown meaning. *1.* Son of Eliphaz and grandson of Esau, he was a clan chieftain of the Edomites (Gen. 35:11,15). *2.* The father of Othniel, Israel's first-mentioned judge (Josh. 15:17; Judg. 1:3) and a brother to Caleb; also was the father of Seriah (1 Chron. 4:13). *3.* A grandson of Caleb and son of Elah (1 Chron. 4:15). The Kenizzites are thought to be the people of Kenaz. Their land was promised to Abraham's offspring (Gen. 15:19). They were a nomadic people from the southeast who inhabited Hebron, Debir, and parts of the Negev. They are variously associated with Judah, Edom, and the Kenites. See *Kenizzites.*

KENEZITE (Kē′ nĕz īte) KJV spelling of Kenizzite. See *Kenizzite.*

KENITES (Kĕn′ ītes) Name of a tribe meaning, "smith." Nomadic tribe, probably of blacksmiths, whose land, along with that of the Kadmonites and Kenizzites God promised to Abraham (Gen. 15:19). Their home was the southeastern hill country of Judah. Balaam pronounced doom and captivity for them (Num. 24:21–22). Moses' father-in-law, Jethro, is called a "priest of Midian" (Ex. 3:1) and is described as a Kenite (Judg. 1:16). This association suggests a close relationship between the Kenites and Midianites. Some scholars have suggested that Moses learned about the worship of Yahweh through Kenite influence, but this theory has not been accepted by all scholars.

The Kenites lived among the Amalekites during the time of Saul. The Kenites "showed kindness" to Israel during the time of the Exodus (1 Sam. 15:6). The Chronicler includes the Kenite, Hemath, the father of the Rechabites, as one of the ancestors of the tribe of Judah (1 Chron. 2:55). No mention is made of the Kenites in the late history of Israel suggesting to many scholars that they disappeared or lost their identity shortly after 1000 B.C.

The word "Kenite" is probably related to an Aramaic word that means "smith." Some scholars think the traveling blacksmiths of the Middle Ages resembled the Kenites. This would account for their relations with different peoples. In addition to their nomadic character, the biblical evidence also indicates that the Kenites were never completely absorbed by another people but maintained a separate existence throughout their history.

See *Moses; Jethro; Cain; Amalekites; Midianites.*

KENIZZITE (Kĕn′ iz zīte) Clan name of uncertain meaning. Clan God promised Abraham the Israelites would dispossess (Gen. 15:19). The Kenizzites lived in the Negev, the southern desert region of Judah, before the conquest of the land by Joshua. The tribe of Judah absorbed some of the Kenizzites while Edom absorbed others. The Kenizzites were probably related to the Kenites from whom they would have learned the craft of metalworking (1 Chron. 4:13–14). They probably derived their name from Kenaz—a descendant of Esau (Gen. 36:11,15)—who is listed among the Edomite chieftains (Gen. 36:42). Jephunneh the Kenizzite may have married a woman of the tribe of Judah. Their son was Caleb (Num. 32:12; Josh. 14:6,14; 15:13).

KENOSIS (Kĕ nō′ sĭs) The act of Christ in emptying Himself of the form of God, taking on the form of a servant, and suffering death on a cross.

The biblical passage from which the theory of kenosis is derived is Philippians 2:6–11 (a pas-

K

The Negev was home to the Kenizzites. Shown here is an area of the Negev between Arad and Beersheba.

sage considered by most modern scholars as an ancient hymn to Christ used in the early church). The kenotic theory of the incarnation takes its name from the Greek word, *kenoō,* used in verse 7 meaning "to make empty" (KJV translates the word "made himself of no reputation").

According to the kenotic theory, when the Son of God was incarnated as Jesus of Nazareth, He "emptied himself" of some of His divine attributes (for example, omnipotence, omniscience, and omnipresence) and lived for a period on earth within the limitations of human existence. Jesus retained other divine attributes according to the theory (for example, holiness, love, and righteousness). Thus, while God is omnipotent (that is, all-powerful), Jesus' power while in the flesh was limited. While God is omniscient (that is, all-knowing), Jesus' knowledge was limited. Similarly, while God is omnipresent (that is, everywhere present), Jesus was limited with respect to space and distance. This theory is, then, an attempt to understand how Jesus could be both fully human and fully divine. This theory takes all of Jesus' human limitations with full seriousness without questioning the reality of His deity.

Two major criticisms of this theory must be noted. First, as was pointed out earlier, Philippians 2:6–11 is in all likelihood a hymn. As a hymn, it utilizes poetic language, which is highly figurative in nature. For example, when Isaiah (a poetic book) is read, one would not come away believing

that mountains and hills have the ability to sing nor that the trees of the fields have the ability to clap their hands (55:12). The ancient and modern reader alike would understand that figurative language was being used and not intended to be taken literally. In like fashion, when Paul said that Christ emptied Himself in Philippians 2:5–11, he may have been saying that Jesus gave Himself sacrifically for the sake of others without intending to say anything about what attributes Christ gave up. One must decide if the language used here is literal or figurative.

Another criticism of the kenotic theory is that Paul's intention in using the hymn to Christ was for ethical rather than doctrinal purposes. That is to say, Paul was more intent on instructing the Philippians in how to live than in what to believe in this particular passage. The Philippians had exhibited selfishness and conceit in their relations with one another. Paul's exhortation to these Christians was to look not only to their own interests, but also to the interests of others (Phil. 2:3–4). The best example of selfless love and humility of which Paul was aware was the example of Jesus Christ. Therefore, Paul said to the Philippians, "Let this mind be in you, which was also in Christ Jesus" (Phil. 2:5). Paul then quoted the hymn, which shows how Jesus gave of himself to the point of enduring death on a cross for the sake of others. Paul wanted the Philippian Christians to have the same attitude toward one another. Thus, if it was Paul's intention to give ethical rather than doctrinal instruction, some would say that to use this passage to speak primar-

K

ily of doctrinal matters is a misuse of Scripture. See *Christology; Incarnation*.

James Simeon and Phil Logan

KEPHAR-AMMONI (Kē′ phär-Ăm′ mō nī) NIV and REB spelling of Chephar-Ammoni. See *Chephar-Ammoni.*

KEPHIRAH (Kė̇ phī′ rah) NIV and REB spelling of Chephirah. See *Chephirah.*

KERAN (Kē′ ran) NIV spelling of Cheran. See *Cheran.*

KERCHIEFS KJV translation of the Hebrew word translated as veils in modern translations of Ezekiel 13:18,21. Ezekiel compares the kerchiefs or veils used by women who prophesied "out of their own minds" to nets used to catch birds. According to this comparison, the kerchiefs were like nets used to catch the souls of persons. God declared through Ezekiel that he would free His people from the snares these women set for them.

KERE-KETHIB (Kė̇ rē′ -Kė̇ thîb) Transliteration of Hebrew terms meaning, "read" and "written." The terms represent notations made in the margin of the Hebrew text by early scribes called Massoretes. In such cases the text has the written consonants of the traditional text, but the scribes have placed vowel points in the text indicating how the word should be read. In the margin of the text stands the consonants of the word to be read. An example is the perpetual kere involving God's personal name, where the Hebrew text contains the consonants *yhwh* with the vowels *a, o, a* from *'adonai,* the Hebrew word for Lord in which *i* is actually a Hebrew consonant. The textual margin would read *'dni,* the consonants of *'adonai.* How such readings developed in the history of the text is not known. They may have been early attempts to correct a text known to be wrongly copied. They may have sought to make the text read in worship by the community conform to a standard written text. It may have been an attempt to record known differences between Hebrew texts at the time of the copyist. Some examples may have been theologically motivated, as the change in the divine name warned the reader not to pronounce the sacred name but to replace it with *'adonai* or Lord.

KEREN-HAPPUCH (Kĕr′ ĕn-Hăp′ pŭch) Personal name meaning "painted-horn," that is, "cosmetic box." The youngest daughter born to Job after his restoration to prosperity (Job 42:14).

KERETHITES (Kĕr′ ė̇-thītes) NIV, REB spelling for Cherethites. See *Cherethites.*

KERIOTH (Kē′ rĭ-öth) Place name meaning, "cit-

ies." A fortified city of Moab (Jer. 48:24,41; Amos 2:2, KJV has Kirioth). Kerioth may be identical to Ar, the ancient capital of Moab, since Kerioth was treated as the capital of Moab by Amos (2:2). Judas, the disciple of Jesus, may have been from Kerioth. Many scholars take the designation "Iscariot" to be derived from the Hebrew meaning, "man of Kerioth." See *Iscariot.*

KERIOTH-HEZRON (Kē′ rĭ-öth-Hĕz′ rŏn) Place name representing one or perhaps two cities. KJV takes the Hebrew to refer to two cities in Joshua 15:25—thus, Kerioth and Hezron. Some scholars still follow this. If this is a reference to two cities, Kerioth would be identified with the Kerioth of Jeremiah 48:24; Amos 2:2 See *Kerioth.* Hezron would be identified with the city of Hazor mentioned in Joshua 15:23, a city in the south of Judah near Kadesh-barnea (Josh. 15:3). See *Hazor.* Many scholars, however, take Kerioth-Hezron to refer to a village of Judah in the Negev district of Beersheba and identify it with modern khirbet el-Qaryatein, about four miles south of Maon.

KERITH (Kē′ rĭth) NIV, REB spelling of Cherith. See *Cherith.*

KEROS (Kē′ rŏs) Personal name meaning, "bent." One of the Temple servants whose descendants returned from the Exile with Zerubbabel (Ezra 2:44; Neh. 7:47).

KERUB (Kē′ rŭb) NIV, REB spelling of Cherub. See *Cherub.*

KERYGMA (Kė̇·ryg′ må) Transliteration of the Greek term which means both "the act of preaching" and "the content of the preaching." Preaching in the biblical sense is primarily the act of proclaiming the acts of God. It is more than the ability to speak in beautiful or eloquent words. This kind of preaching will not persuade anyone to become a disciple of Jesus. Preaching in the biblical sense is persuasive because it is done in the Spirit and with power (1 Cor. 2:4). God intervenes in the lives of the hearers through the act of preaching; the kingdom of God comes through the act of preaching (see Matt. 12:41; Luke 11:32). In the act of preaching the hope we have of eternal life is revealed (Titus 1:1–3).

The content of preaching in the New Testament centers on Jesus. According to Paul, some see the preaching of a crucified Savior as foolish; but for those who believe it means eternal life (1 Cor. 1:21). Of course, the preaching about Jesus concerns not only His death on a cross but also His resurrection (1 Cor. 15:12).

In modern times some scholars have attempted to determine the exact content of the preaching of the early church. One of the more prominent

K

attempts analyzed the sermons of the apostles in Acts. According to this reconstruction, the preaching of the early church included the following elements: (1) the prophecies of the coming Messiah have been fulfilled, (2) the prophecies were fulfilled by the Davidic descent, ministry, death, and resurrection of Jesus, (3) Jesus has been exalted to God's right hand as the Head of the new Israel, (4) the Holy Spirit is the sign of Christ's present power and glory, (5) Christ will return, and (6) a call for repentance. See *Gospel.*

Phil Logan

KESALON (Kĕs' á·lŏn) NIV, REB spelling of Chesalon. See *Chesalon.*

KESED (Kē' sĕd) NIV, REB spelling of Chesed. See *Chesed; Kindness.*

KESIL (Kē' sĭl) NIV, REB spelling of Chesil. See *Chesil.*

KESITAH (Kĕ sî' tăh) Transliteration of Hebrew meaning, "part, measure, piece of money." Jacob paid 100 kesitahs for land near Shechem (Gen. 33:19; compare Josh. 24:32). The earliest Greek translation translated kesitah as "lamb." (Compare REB). After God restored his fortunes, Job received a kesitah from each of his friends (Job 42:11).

KESULLOTH (Kĕ·sŭl' lŏth) NIV, REB spelling of Chesulloth. See *Chesulloth.*

KETHIB (Kĕ thîb') See *Kere-Kethib.*

KETTLE The translation of a Hebrew word for a vessel in which meat was prepared by the worshipers before being offered as a peace offering to God (1 Sam. 2:14). Hophni and Phinehas were not content with the priest's portion (1 Sam. 2:12–17; Lev. 7:14). They also reached into the worshipers' kettle with a fork to add to what was rightfully theirs. See *Hophni and Phinehas; Sacrifice and Offering.*

KETURAH (Kĕ·tū' rah) Personal name meaning "incense" or "the perfumed one." In Genesis 25:1 Keturah is called Abraham's wife, while 1 Chronicles 1:32 calls her a concubine. She was Abraham's second wife, apparently taken after Sarah's death.

Keturah bore six sons (daughters rarely are listed) to Abraham, the most notable being Midian. The list of Keturah's children substantiates the link between the Hebrews and the tribes which inhabited the areas east and southeast of Palestine. As children of a second wife, they were viewed as inferior to Isaac, Sarah's son.

KEYS The authority Christ delegated to His disci-

Kettle, or pot, hanging over coals (from the Roman time period).

ples to proclaim forgiveness and pronounce judgment.

Old Testament The holder of the keys had the power to admit or deny entrance to the house of God (1 Chron. 9:22–27; Isa. 22:22). In late Judaism, this key imagery was extended to angelic beings and to God as keepers of the keys of heaven and hell.

New Testament In the New Testament, keys are used only figuratively as a symbol of authority, particularly the authority of Christ over the final destiny of persons. The risen Christ holds the key of David and controls access to the New Jerusalem (Rev. 3:7). By overcoming death, He has the keys to the world of the dead (Rev. 1:18).

In Matthew 16:18–19, Jesus delegated the power of the keys to His disciples, combining the imagery of keys with that of binding and loosing. When Peter confessed that Jesus was the Son of God, Jesus proclaimed that the gates of death would have no power over His church. The gates would not be able to resist the keys He was giving to Peter as a representative of the church. [See also *Disciple's Study Bible,* note on Matt. 16:18–19, pp. 1198–1199.]

With the other apostles, Peter also received the power of binding and loosing (Matt. 16:19; 18:18), a phrase used to describe the work of scribes who sought God's will through a study of Scripture and declared it through teaching and judging. The scribes could also exclude persons from the community (compare Matt. 18:15–17), but Christ denounced them for misusing their key (Luke 11:52) and blocking the entrance to the kingdom (Matt. 23:13). In their place, through the gift of the Spirit, the disciples received the authority to proclaim forgiveness and judgment (John 20:23). See *Keys of the Kingdom.*

Barbara J. Bruce

KEYS OF THE KINGDOM What Jesus entrusted to Peter in Matthew 16:19, whose interpretation has been the subject of much debate between Catholics and non-Catholics. Any solution must consider: (1) the role of Peter as a leading apostle, (2) Peter's confession of Jesus as the Christ, (3) Jesus' word play regarding the "rock" (petra) upon which He would build His church, (4) the meaning of "binding" and "loosing," and (5) parallel references to both "keys" and the other abovementioned terms in biblical literature. (Compare Matt. 18:18; John 20:23; Rom. 9:32,33; Eph. 2:19–22; I Pet. 2:4–10; Rev. 1:18; 3:7–13). See *Keys.*

The phrase "keys of the kingdom" surely relates to the authority given to Peter to "bind" and "loose." This authority was delegated to Simon Peter but should not be understood as an arbitrary or even individual authority of Peter to save or condemn. Peter is a representative of the apostles, a fact observed from his frequent role as leader and spokesman. In Ephesians 2:20 it is not Peter but simply "the apostles and prophets" who are the foundation stone, with Christ Jesus the cornerstone. Moreover, in I Peter 2:4,5 (which possibly reflects Peter's own interpretation of Christ's words to him) Christians themselves are "stones" built upon Christ the "living stone."

Furthermore, the authority given to Peter/the apostles cannot be separated from the heavenly insight and confession that Jesus is the Christ, the Son of God. It is the revelation given to (and confessed by) Peter that called forth our Lord's blessing. Thus, we cannot overlook the confessional/theological component of Peter's apostolic authority. Peter's authority as an apostle was based upon his divinely given confession. Paul (like Jesus, Matt. 16:23) certainly felt free to criticize Peter when Simon's theology/behavior warranted correction (Gal. 2:6–14). Moreover, the authority to "bind" and "loose," the result of receiving "the keys of the kingdom," is a stewardship, a delegated authority from Christ (compare Matt. 16:19 with John 20:21–23 and Rev. 1:18; 3:7,8).

Finally, the related "key" passages in Scripture suggest that it is the preaching of the gospel that has been entrusted/delegated to the apostles. Though the gospel itself is certainly to be handed on (1 Tim. 6:20; 2 Tim. 2:2; 2 Pet. 1:12–16), Scripture nowhere suggests that the "power of the keys" was either a personal privilege or an ecclesi-

astical office that could be handed on by Peter or anyone else. Rather, it refers to the stewardship of the gospel (1 Cor. 3:10—4:1) entrusted to those historically unique eyewitnesses who as Christ's apostles could give authoritative testimony to the salvation that is found only in Him, a hope which could be confidently offered and promised ("on earth") as an already present gift ("in heaven") to those who confess Him. See *Apostles, Disciples; Binding and Loosing.*   *Robert B. Sloan*

KEZIA (Kė zī′ a) KJV spelling of Keziah. See *Keziah.*

KEZIAH (Kĕ·zī′ ah) Personal name meaning, "cassia" or "cinnammon." The second daughter born to Job after his property had been restored (Job 42:14).

KEZIB (Kē′ zīb) NIV, REB spelling of Chezib. See *Chezib.*

KEZIZ, VALLEY OF (Kē′ zīz) KJV translation of Emek-Keziz. See *Emek-Keziz.*

KIBROTH-HATTAAVAH (Kĭb′ rŏth·Hăt·tā′ ȧ·vah) Place name meaning, "graves of craving, lust, gluttony." The first stopping place of the Israelites after they left Sinai (Num. 33:16). The Israelites craved meat, which the Lord gave them (Num. 11:31); but because they overindulged, an epidemic broke out, and many Israelites died. The dead were buried there, giving the place its name (Num. 11:34; Deut. 9:22; Ps. 78:30–31).

KIBZAIM (Kĭb′ zā·ĭm) Place name meaning, "double gathering" or "double heap." One of the Levitical cities in the tribal territory of Ephraim also designated as a city of refuge (Josh. 21:22). In a parallel list of cities in Chronicles, the name Jokmeam appears (1 Chron. 6:68). This is not to be confused with Jokmeam (or Jokneam) of 1 Kings 4:12. The reason for the appearance of Jokmean in 1 Chronicles is unexplained. See *Levitical Cities; Cities of Refuge; Jokmeam; Jokneam.*

KID Translation of one of several Hebrew words referring to a young goat. See *Animals; Sacrifice and Offering.*

KIDON (Kī′ don) NIV, REB spelling of Chidon. See *Chidon.*

KIDNAPPING The act of capturing and holding a person using unlawful force and fraud. In modern times, a person is usually kidnapped for the purpose of extorting ransom. In biblical times the usual purpose for kidnapping was to use or sell the person into slavery (see Gen. 37:28; 40:15). NIV, NRSV translate the corresponding Greek term as "slave traders" (1 Tim. 1:10). Kidnapping free-

K

born Israelites either to treat them as slaves or to sell them into slavery was punishable by death (Ex. 21:16; Deut. 24:7).

KIDNEY One of a pair of vertebrate organs lying in a mass of fatty tissue that excrete the waste products of metabolism. In the Bible, "kidney" is used both literally and figuratively. When the word is used figuratively of humans, KJV usually translates the term as "reins" (for example, Jer. 12:2; Rev. 2:23); NRSV uses "mind" (Rev. 2:23), "heart" (Job 19:27; Pss. 7:9; 16:7, 73:21; Jer. 12:2), "vitals" (Lam. 3:13), "soul" (Prov. 23:16), or "inward parts" (Ps. 139:13; but see Job 16:13).

The kidneys are often associated with the heart as constituting the center of human personality (Pss. 7:9; 26:2; Jer. 11:20; 17:10; 20:12; Rev. 2:23). Because the areas around the kidneys are sensitive, the Hebrews believed the kidneys were the seat of the emotions (see Job 19:27; Ps. 73:21; Prov. 23:16). The kidneys were also used figuratively as the source of the knowledge and understanding of the moral life (Ps. 16:7; Jer. 12:2).

When used literally of animals (except Isa. 34:6) the kidneys are mentioned in relation to sacrifice. The kidney, along with the fat surrounding it, were reserved for God as among the choicest parts of the animal (Ex. 29:13,22). Deuteronomy 32:14 (KJV) speaks of the best wheat as the "fat of kidneys" (see NRSV).

The Kidron Valley in Jerusalem with the Greek Orthodox Church of St. Stephen in the background.

KIDRON VALLEY (Kĭd' ron) Place name meaning "turbid, dusky, gloomy." The deep ravine beside Jerusalem separating the Temple Mount and the City of David on the west from the Mount of Olives on the east. The Spring of Gihon lies on the western slope. The Garden of Gethsemane would have been above the valley on the eastern side. Cemeteries have been located in this area since the Middle Bronze Age (before 1500 B.C.). David crossed the brook when he fled Jerusalem to escape from Absalom (2 Sam. 15:23). Solomon warned Shimei not to cross it or he would die (1 Kings 2:37). Here certain kings of Judah destroyed idols and other pagan objects removed from the Temple area (1 Kings 15:13; 2 Kings 23:4,6,12; 2 Chron. 29:16; 30:14). After the Last Supper, Jesus went through the Kidron Valley on his way to the Mount of Olives (John 18:1). See *City of David; Jerusalem; Mount of Olives; Spring of Gihon; Valley of Hinnom.*

Ricky L. Johnson

KILEAB (Kĭl' ė·ab) NIV spelling of Chileab. See *Chileab.*

KILION (Kĭl' ĭ·on) NIV spelling of Chilion. See *Chilion.*

KILMAD (Kĭl' măd) NIV spelling of Chilmad. REB takes as common nouns, "all Media." See *Chilmad.*

KILN An oven, furnace, or heated enclosure used

for processing a substance by burning, firing, or drying. The Hebrew word, *tannur,* is used to refer to both the oven used in the home for baking bread and the large pottery kiln. The "paved work of a sapphire stone" in Exodus 24:10 probably refers to a glazed tile out of a potter's kiln. It is possible that the part of the wall around Jerusalem known as the "Tower of the Ovens" (Neh. 3:11 REB) got its name from a potter's kiln. The term "brickkiln" is used in Nahum 3:14, but this should probably read "brick mold" (NRSV, NAS) or "brick work" (NIV, REB), as the bricks in Palestine were usually sun-dried. See *Pottery in Bible Times.*

KIMHAM (Kĭm′ hăm) NIV, REB spelling of Chimham. See *Chimham.*

KINAH (Kī′ năh) Place name meaning, "lamentation." A city in the southeast of Judah near the boundary of Edom (Josh. 15:22). Perhaps a settlement of the Kenites. Usually identified with modern wadi el-Qeini, south of Hebron.

KINDNESS The steadfast love that maintains relationships through gracious aid in times of need.
Old Testament The principal word used to express kindness in the Old Testament (*chesed*) bears the connotation of a loyal love which manifests itself not in emotions but in actions. Originally, this loving kindness was considered an integral part of covenant relations. It was reciprocal and expected, a deed performed in return for a previous loyalty. Rahab expected kindness in return for her kindness to the spies (Josh. 2:12,14). Joseph expected kindness from the cupbearer in return for the interpretation of a dream (Gen. 40:14). In this sense, kindness was distinct from mercy or compassion which was more of an emotion and from grace which was not as closely associated with covenant keeping. In time, however, the concepts of kindness, mercy, and grace intermingled.

Kindness was shown in social relationships as the bond between host and guest (Gen. 19:19), ruler and subject (2 Sam. 16:17), or friends (1 Sam. 20:8). It was the faithfulness expected of a good person (Prov. 3:3). Primarily, kindness characterized the covenant relation between God and His people. God's faithful love accompanied the patriarchs and dwelt with those who kept His covenant (Gen. 24:27; Ex. 20:6). The Psalms developed this theme with thanksgiving for divine kindness and praise for its endurance (Pss. 86:5; 89:2,28; 100:5; 103:8,11,17; 106:1; 107:1; etc.; see especially Ps. 136). Slow to anger and abounding in love became a characteristic description of Israel's Lord, distinguishing His kindness from His wrath (Ex. 34:6; Num. 14:18; Neh. 9:17; Pss. 103:8; 145:8; Jonah 4:2; Joel 2:13).

Human response to the convenant with God,

however, was bewailed by the prophets as a youthful loyalty that vanished like the morning dew (Jer. 2:2; Hos. 6:4). In this situation God's kindness always has an aspect of freedom (Ex. 33:19) and mingles with mercy and grace. It is an everlasting love which cannot be shaken (Isa. 54:8,10).
New Testament Although both love of humankind (Acts 28:2) and brotherly love (2 Pet. 1:7) are translated as kindness in the New Testament, the Greek word bearing the richest connotation is *chrēstotēs.* This word has a basic meaning of usefulness and is translated as goodness, gentleness, and kindness. Once again, actions are emphasized, especially God's gracious actions toward sinners (Titus 3:4; Rom. 11:22). The kindness God has shown us through Christ is equivalent to His grace and embodies the fullness of salvation (Eph. 2:7). When kindness is included in lists of human virtues, it can be understood as helpfulness to others prompted by an experience of God's redemptive love (2 Cor. 6:6; Gal. 5:22; Col. 3:12). *Barbara J. Bruce*

KINE KJV plural of cow. See *Animals.*

KING, CHRIST AS The biblical teaching that Jesus of Nazareth fulfilled the Old Testament promises of a perfect King and reigns over His people and the universe. The Old Testament hope for the future included a vision of a new king like David, called the anointed one, or the Messiah in Hebrew (2 Sam. 7:16). The prophet Isaiah intensified the promises and pointed to the Messiah yet to come (see Pss. 45; 110). Daniel contains a vision of one to whom was given dominion, glory, and kingdom, one whom all peoples, nations, and languages would serve. His dominion is everlasting and shall never pass away. His kingdom shall never be destroyed (Dan. 7:13–14).

When Jesus Christ was born, His birth was announced in these categories. His earthly ministry then amplified these themes (Matt. 4:17; Luke 1:32–33). Similarly, John the Baptist proclaimed the presence of God's kingdom in the coming of Jesus (Matt. 3). The theme of Jesus as King, Ruler, or Lord dominates the New Testament from beginning to end. We find the culmination of this theme with the Lord seated on a throne, His enemies being made subject to Him and a new name given: "On his vesture and on his thigh a name written, KING OF KINGS, AND LORD OF LORDS" (Rev. 19:16).

The question arises naturally, in what sense is Christ's kingship really operating in today's world? If He is king, how is it that the world is so little changed and His kingship so little acknowledged? Some would answer that Jesus' kingship is completely future. That fails to handle Christ's own statement that the kingdom of God is "in your midst" (Luke 17:21, NAS), "among you"

K

(NRSV), or "within you" (KJV, NIV). Christ's kingship is thus both present yet still future, already here and still yet to come, spiritual and universal.

The present kingship of Christ is His royal rule over His people (Col. 1:13,18). It is a spiritual realm established in the hearts and lives of believers. He administers His kingdom by spiritual means—the Word and the Spirit. Whenever believers follow the lordship of Christ, the Savior is exercising His ruling or kingly function. From this we understand that His kingship is more concerned with Jesus' reign than with the realm over which this takes place. When we pray, "your kingdom come" as we do in the Lord's prayer (Matt. 6:10), we have in mind this present rule of Christ the King.

Christ's kingship is also present today in the natural world. Christ is the one through whom all things came into being (John 1:3) and through whom all things are held together (Col. 1:17). He is in control of the natural universe as He demonstrated during His earthly ministry (Mark 4:35–41).

The Bible recognizes Jesus' present kingship and presents the kingship as a spiritual one (John 18:36). The crowd proclaimed Jesus King during His triumphal entry on Palm Sunday (John 12:12–19). We might say the door of heaven opened a bit so that for a brief moment His true kingship appeared to people on earth. He claimed that had the people kept silent on that historic occasion, the stones would have cried out to proclaim Him King.

In addition to Christ's present rule, His kingship will become fully evident in the future. We will see and understand this clearly when Jesus returns (Matt. 19:28). The future kingdom will be essentially the same as the present rule in the sense that men and women will acknowledge Christ's rule in their hearts. It will differ, however, in that His rule will be perfect and visible (1 Cor. 15:24–28). Once manifest, the future kingdom will endure forever. Christ will rule over all things in heaven and on earth. At this time God the Father will exalt Jesus, His Son, to the highest place of authority and honor. At the name of Jesus every knee will bow, in heaven and on earth and under the earth, and every tongue will confess that Jesus is Lord to the glory of God the Father (Phil. 2:9–11).

Jesus established His kingship through His sacrificial death as each of the gospels shows clearly. Pilate recognized more than he knew when he created the sign, King of the Jews, for the charge against Jesus. Jesus' kingship finds its highest exercise as He gives the blessings He secured for His people through His atoning work (Rom. 8:32; Eph. 1:3–11,20–22). Jesus will continue to reign as the second Person of the Trinity. His God/Man personhood will not cease. Jesus Christ, the King, will reign as the God-man and will forever exercise His power for the benefit of the redeemed and for the glory of His kingdom.

David S. Dockery

KING, KINGSHIP A male monarch of a major territorial unit; especially one whose position is hereditary and who rules for life. Kingship includes the position, office, and dignity of a king. Kings were of three basic kinds in the Ancient Near East: (1) kings of great nations often identified with a god (for example, in Assyria, Babylon, and Egypt); (2) kings from a military elite who had taken control of a local population by force (for example, Canaanite city kings); and (3) kings who arose from tribal or clan-oriented groups whose election to or inheritance of the kingship was determined in part by the people's will (for example, Israel, Edom, Moab, and Ammon).

Transition from Judges to Kings Before the establishment of the monarchy in Israel, no political, administrative, or military organization encompassed all of Israel. From the time of Joshua to the time of Saul, the judges led Israel. Their leadership was temporary and local in nature, their main function being to lead those parts of Israel threatened by some outside force until the threat was gone. Israel during this period was bound together more by their covenant with God than by government.

As Israel became more settled in Canaan, the old tribal institutions of leadership began to dissolve (see, for example, 1 Sam. 8:3). This decline of tribal leadership coupled with the threat of the Philistines to all tribes of Israel threatened the existence of Israel itself. Many in Israel began to feel a need for a permanent and national leadership as a way of dealing with the threat (see 1 Sam. 8:20; 10:1).

The first national leader was Saul. Saul was anointed as the *nagid* over Israel—as a national military leader—and not king in the technical sense. The Hebrew term for king is *melek* and is never used of Saul. Saul was a charismatic leader much in the mold of the judges. Israel remained a tribal league. Saul established no central government or bureacracy, had no court or standing army, and his seat at Gibeah was a fortress and not a palace.

The significant thing about Saul's leadership is that for the first time after settlement in Canaan, Israel had a permanent national military leader. This was a very important step in the transition from the system of judges to the establishment of the monarchy.

David was also a figure much in the likeness of the judges with a charismatic personality. A prophet designated him king just as the judges and Saul had been designated before him.

David's leadership, however, represents the second stage in the transition. Unlike Saul, David was able to fuse the tribes of Israel together into a nation who owed allegiance to the crown, to establish and maintain a court, and to establish a standing army. What had been a loose union of twelve tribes became a complex empire centered around the person of David. Because of his charismatic personality, David was able to effect the union of the northern and southern tribes (something Saul was apparently unable to do). David captured Jerusalem; Jerusalem was literally the city of David. David made Jerusalem the religious and political center of Israel. The Canaanite population of Palestine was subject to the king. The foreign empire of Israel was won and held primarily by David's professional army. The subjugated lands paid tribute to David and not to the individual tribes.

During the latter days of David's reign the feeling was strong that the empire was so much David's doing and centered so much on David's person, that only a son of David could maintain what David had built. When David passed the power of the kingship along to his son, Solomon, the transition from the system of judges to that of monarchy was complete. The usual understanding of king is one whose position is hereditary and who rules for life. These conditions were met for the first time when Solomon inherited the throne from David.

Functions and Powers of the King The king functioned as military leader (1 Sam. 8:20; 15:4–5; 1 Kings 22:29–36; 2 Kings 3:6–12), supreme judge (2 Sam. 12:1–6; 14:4–8; 15:2; 1 Kings 3:16–28) and priest (1 Sam. 13:10; 14:35; 2 Sam. 6:13; 24:25; 1 Kings 3:4; 8:62–63; 9:25; 12:32; 13:1; 2 Kings 16:10–18).

Israel, unlike some nations surrounding it, placed limitations on the power of its kings. Some Israelites opposed having a king because of the excesses to which a king might go (1 Sam. 8:10–18). It was normal for the elders of the nation to make a covenant with the king (2 Sam. 5:3; 2 Kings 11:17) in which the rights and duties of the king were recorded and deposited in the sanctuary—possibly at the time of the anointment ceremony (1 Sam. 10:25). It was clearly understood that the king was not exempt from observing civil laws (see 1 Kings 21:4), nor was the king the absolute lord of life and death, a power David assumed in his murder of Uriah (2 Sam. 11; compare Ahab's murder of Naboth 1 Kings 21:14–18. See also 2 Kings 5:7; 6:26–33). The prophetic denunciation of certain kings demonstrates that they were subject to the law (2 Sam. 12:1–15; 1 Kings 21:17–24; compare Deut. 17:14–20).

The King's Court The officials at the king's court included the body guard (2 Sam. 8:18; 1 Kings 1:38; 2 Kings 11:4), captain of the host or general of the army (1 Sam. 14:50; 2 Sam. 8:16), recorder (2 Sam. 8:16; 1 Kings 4:3), secretary or scribe (2 Sam. 8:17; 2 Kings 18:18), chief administrator

over the twelve district officers (1 Kings 4:5; compare vv. 7–19), steward of the palace household (1 Kings 4:6; 18:3; 2 Kings 18:18; Isa. 22:15), overseer of forced labor (2 Sam. 20:24; 1 Kings 4:6; 5:13–17; 11:28; compare modern translations for KJV tribute), friend of the king (2 Sam. 15:37; 1 Kings 4:5; 1 Chron. 27:33), counselor (2 Sam. 15:12), keeper of the wardrobe (2 Kings 22:14), officials in charge of the royal farms (1 Chron. 27:25–31), priests (2 Sam. 8:17; 20:25; 1 Kings 4:4), and prophets (1 Sam. 22:5; 2 Sam. 7:2; 12:25; 24:10–25).

To raise the necessary revenue to support a court of this size, Solomon introduced a system of taxation. Saul's court was simple and did not require extensive financial support (1 Sam. 22:6), while David depended on spoils of war (2 Sam. 8:1–14). Solomon divided the nation into twelve districts each of which would be responsible to support the court for one month out of the year (1 Kings 4:7–19,27–28).

Other revenue for the king's court included royal property (1 Chron. 27:25–31; 2 Chron. 26:10; 32:27–29) and forced labor (2 Sam. 20:24; 1 Kings 4:6; 11:28). Solomon also received revenue from a road toll on trade routes through Israel (1 Kings 10:15), trade in horses and chariots (1 Kings 10:28–29), a merchant fleet (1 Kings 9:26–28) and, according to archaeological evidence, possibly from copper mines.

God as King Israel's faith included the confession that God was its ultimate King. Some modern scholars see the covenant between God and Israel recorded in Joshua 24 as a royal covenant made between King and people (see also Ex. 15:18; 19:6; Num. 23:21; Deut. 33:5; Judg. 8:23; 1 Sam. 8:7; 12:12). Because God was seen as King, some in Israel saw the desire for an earthly king as a turning away from God (1 Sam. 8:7; Hosea 8:4). The earthly king derived his authority from God as the Lord's anointed (1 Sam. 16:6; 2 Sam. 1:14) or the Lord's captain or prince (1 Sam. 9:16; 10:1; 13:14). Many of the Psalms speak of God as King (for example, Pss. 24; 93; 95—98). See *Kingdom of God.*   *Phil Logan*

KINGDOM OF GOD God's kingly rule or sovereignty. The Old Testament contains no references to the kingdom of God. However, in the Old Testament God is spoken of as ruling (for example, Pss. 47:2; 103:19; Dan. 4:17,25–37). The Old Testament emphasis on God's sovereign power over all kings and kingdoms sets the stage for the New Testament teaching. Jesus made the kingdom of God central in His preaching. More than a hundred references to the kingdom appear in the gospels, many in Jesus' parables. See *Parable.*

The kingdom of God was the central image in Jesus' preaching as clearly seen in Mark 1:14–15, a summary of the preaching of Jesus. The kingdom

K

of God is the heart of the summary.

In His parables Jesus spoke of the kingdom in many different ways. He said that the kingdom is like a farmer (Matt. 13:24), a seed (Matt. 13:31), a yeast (Matt. 13:33), a treasure (Matt. 13:44), a pearl merchant (Matt. 13:45), a fishnet (Matt. 13:47), an employer (Matt. 20:1), a king inviting people to a marriage feast (Matt. 22:2), and ten young women (Matt. 25:1). He spoke also of the glad tidings of the kingdom (Luke 8:1) and of the mystery of the kingdom of God (Mark 4:11).

Jesus spoke Aramaic; the gospel writers translated Jesus' sermons and parables into Greek. Mark, Luke, and John translated Jesus' words as "kingdom of God." Matthew sometimes used this phrase too, but often he preferred to translate Jesus' Aramaic words as "kingdom of heaven." The two phrases mean exactly the same thing, because they are translations of the same Aramaic words of Jesus. See *Aramaic; Greek*.

What did Jesus mean when he spoke of the kingdom of God? He meant, quite simply, the rule of God. The kingdom of God is the reign of God.

This is best understood if it is distinguished from what Jesus did not mean. He was not speaking of a geographical area such as the holy land or the Temple. He was not speaking of a political entity such as the nation of Israel or the Sanhedrin. He was not speaking of a group of people such as His disciples or the church.

Rather, the kingdom of God is God's ruling. It is the sovereign reign of God. This rule is independent of all geographical areas or political entities. It is true that the rule of God implies a people to be ruled, and Jesus called upon people to enter the kingdom. The kingdom itself should be distinguished from the people who enter it.

Jesus taught that the kingdom of God looks unimpressive, but it is going to grow into something tremendous. The kingdom is like a tiny mustard seed which grows into a bush large enough to provide shelter for God's creatures (Mark 4:30–32).

Jesus never said that people are to build the kingdom of God. On the contrary, the establishment of the kingdom is a work of God. God will reign, and people can contribute nothing to that reigning of God.

When will God establish his kingdom? In one sense, the kingdom will not come until some unspecified time in the future (see, for example, Matt. 25:1–46). There is a sense in which modern Christians may still look forward to the coming of the kingdom of God.

On the other hand, Jesus also said that there is a sense in which the kingdom of God had come in His own time. "The time is fulfilled, and the kingdom of God is at hand" (Mark 1:15). He said in an even more explicit way: "But if I with the finger of God cast out devils, no doubt the kingdom of God is come upon you" (Luke 11:20).

So the kingdom of God was the rule of God which He extended over human lives through the ministry of Jesus; and it also is His rule which will be consummated or made complete in the future. See *Eschatology; Future Hope*.

Since people cannot build the kingdom of God, what response are they to make to Jesus' message about the kingdom? First, they can make the kingdom their priority and seek it ahead of everything else (Matt. 6:33). It is a pearl of such value that they should sell everything else they have in order to be able to purchase it (Matt. 13:44–46). Second, they can repent and believe the good news of the kingdom (Mark 1:14–15), and so enter the kingdom like little children (Mark 10:14). Third, they can pray for the rule of God to come soon: "Thy kingdom come" (Matt. 6:10; compare 1 Cor. 16:22). Finally, they can be ready when the kingdom does finally come (Matt. 25:1–46).

The Lord's Prayer contains three requests, as follows: "Hallowed be thy name. Thy kingdom come. Thy will be done on earth as it is in heaven" (Matt. 6:9–10). These three phrases mean just about the same thing, and they tell us a lot about the kingdom of God. "Hallowed be thy name" means: "Let Your name be hallowed, or honored"; or, "bring all people to respect and reverence You." "Thy kingdom come" means; "extend Your rule over human lives." "Thy will be done on earth as it is in heaven" means, "Extend Your rule over human lives here and now so that they will reverence and respect You." See *Lord's Prayer*.

In His preaching Jesus regularly invited people to enter the kingdom of God, that is, to open their lives to the ruling of God. It is important to notice whom He invited.

He invited everyone. That is the great surprise. He did not restrict the invitation to the respectable people, or the religious, or the wealthy or powerful (in Jesus' day wealth and power were often thought to be signs of God's blessing). Jesus included everyone without distinction. He spoke of God sending His servants out to highways and hedges to urge people to come in to the kingdom. He even said that it is more difficult for the rich to enter the kingdom than for a camel to go through the eye of a needle (Matt. 19:24). He said that the tax-collectors and prostitutes would go into the kingdom before the moral and religious people (Matt. 21:31). In brief, God is very gracious and loving toward all people, and His kingdom is offered to everyone.

After Jesus had returned to heaven, the apostles did not continue to make the kingdom the central theme of their preaching. Instead, they began to speak of eternal life, salvation, forgiveness, and other themes. In doing this, they were not deserting Jesus' concern for the kingdom of God. They were simply expressing the same idea in their

K

way. To speak of salvation is to speak of the kingdom. We might express it as follows: God is graciously giving salvation as a free gift (extending His kingdom) to anyone who will receive it (enter the kingdom) through His Son Jesus Christ, and this salvation begins now (the kingdom is in the midst of you) and will be completed in the future (the kingdom will come like a thief in the night). As Paul put it, the kingdom of God is righteousness and peace and joy in the Holy Spirit (Rom. 14:17). See *Jesus; Christ; Salvation.*

Fisher Humphreys

KINGS, 1 AND 2 The eleventh and twelfth books of the Christian Bible interpreting God's direction of the kingdoms of Israel and Judah. Originally, 1 and 2 Kings were one book and formed a part of a larger history of Israel (see below). The first record of the division of the original work into two parts is in the Septuagint or earliest Greek translation, where 1 and 2 Kings were known as 3 and 4 Kingdoms (1 and 2 Samuel were known as 1 and 2 Kingdoms; 1 and 2 Samuel were themselves originally a single work). According to tradition, Jeremiah is the author of 1 and 2 Kings. The last recorded incident in 2 Kings is the release of Jehoiachin from prison by Evil-merodach in about 560 B.C. (2 Kings 25:27–30). While Jeremiah could have still been alive at that time and while there are certain similarities between the theology of the writer of the Books of Kings and Jeremiah, there is no way of knowing for sure who the author is. Most modern scholars do not accept Jeremiah as author. The Books of Kings do not indicate who the author was.

Part of a Larger History of Israel A common position held by many modern scholars is that 1 and 2 Kings are part of a longer history of Israel that begins with Joshua and goes through 2 Kings. Modern Bible scholars refer to this as the Deuteronomic history. The reason for this is that the reigns of the kings and many of the events in the history of Israel are evaluated according to norms set out in Deuteronomy. The Deuteronomic history was likely written shortly after the release of Jehoiachin in 560 B.C. in an attempt to explain to the Jews of the Exile why their nation had been overthrown by foreign powers even though they were the people of God. Many earlier sources were available for the final writer.

A Theological Interpretation of Israel's History This history was not written primarily for historical reasons, though the historical information contained in 1 and 2 Kings provides the basic information in reconstructing the history of the period. A reader need not look at 1 and 2 Kings long before one discovers that much of the information that could have been recorded about the events of Israel's history was not. The writer chose to tell us about some events but ignored others. The recorded events are those essential for understand-

ing what happened to Israel (as well as for understanding how we should relate to God today).

For example, when the author of 1 Kings concludes the discussion of Solomon, we find these words: the *rest* of the acts of Solomon, and *all that he did,* and his wisdom, are they not written in the book of the acts of Solomon?" (1 Kings 11:41; emphasis added). This clearly shows that the author did not give us an exhaustive history of Solomon detailing everything that went on during his reign. Only that which was important to the author's interpretation of Israel's history was included—the primary thing being the building of the Temple.

Similarly, when the reigns of other kings are described, only those things pertinent to the author's purpose are related. Many things which could have been told are not (see 1 Kings 14:19,29; 15:7,23,31; 16:5,14,20,27; 22:39,45; 2 Kings 1:18; 8:23; 10:34; 12:19; 13:8,12; 14:15,18,28; 15:6,11,15,21,26,31,36; 16:19; 20:20; 21:17,25; 23:28; 24:5).

A study of 1 and 2 Kings—as well as Joshua through 2 Samuel—indicates that the writer's intention was to evaluate Israel's history according to the principles given in the Book of Deuteronomy and in this way explain, why the nation divided after the reign of Solomon and why both nations eventually fell victim to foreign invaders. Three concerns are evident in 1 and 2 Kings as the author makes this evaluation.

The Fulfillment of the Word of God The first concern of the author is to show that God's word will be fulfilled. Deuteronomy 28 is especially important here. Deuteronomy 28:1–14 describes the blessings that will belong to Israel if they obey God's commandments. Israel would have victory over its enemies (28:1,7,10) and would prosper in all its undertakings (28:3–6,8,11–12). Israel would be established as a people holy to God (28:9) and would "always be at the top and never at the bottom" when they obeyed the command of the Lord (28:13–14 REB).

This word of God's blessing was fulfilled in Israel's history. Especially noteworthy is their success in the conquest of the land under the leadership of Joshua. They were an obedient people, and God blessed their efforts with victory. They secured for themselves a land by the hand of God (see Josh. 11:23).

Deuteronomy 28:15–68 describes in graphic detail what would happen to Israel should they turn from obeying the commandment of the Lord. They would no longer prosper (28:15–19) and would be afflicted with all kinds of plagues, pestilence, and sickness (28:20–22,58–61). Rain would be withheld from their land (28:23–24). More significantly, they would be defeated by their enemies and suffer all the consequences of defeat (28:25–33,47–57). The most serious of those consequences would be that they would no

K

longer be as numerous as the stars of the heavens (28:62–63; see Gen. 13:14–18; 15:1–6), and they would be lead into exile retracing the route of the Exodus (28:32,36–46,63–68).

God was faithful to fulfill the word of warning as well. When the people of Israel departed from God's commandment, they suffered defeat, reduction of their population, severe suffering, and exile. The Northern Kingdom of Isarel suffered defeat and exile at the hands of the Assyrians in 722 B.C. (2 Kings 17:1–41). Judah suffered a similar fate at the hands of the Babylonians between 597 and 586 B.C. (2 Kings 24:1—25:21).

God's promises came to the people not only in Deuteronomy. God's prophets continually proclaimed them to the people: Elijah (1 Kings 17—19; 21; 2 Kings 1), Elisha (2 Kings 2:1–25; 3:9–20; 4:1—8:15; 9:1–3; 13:14–21), Isaiah (2 Kings 19:1—20:19) and others. The people were without excuse. They had heard God's commandment to be faithful and His warnings of the accompanying blessings and curses.

Insistance on the Worship of the One True God in the Temple of Jerusalem The commandments found in Deuteronomy with which the author of 1 and 2 Kings was especially concerned were the commands that only God be worshiped and that God be worshiped in Jerusalem alone (Deut. 12—13). The reigns of the kings of Judah and Israel were evaluated on the basis of their adherence to these two commands.

Of the kings of Judah, only Hezekiah (2 Kings 18:3–7) and Josiah (2 Kings 22:2) were praised without reservation because they adhered to these two principles. Asa (1 Kings 15:11–14), Jehoshaphat (1 Kings 22:41–43), Jehoash (2 Kings 12:2–3), Azariah (2 Kings 15:3–4), and Jotham (2 Kings 15:34–35) were praised as having done what was right in the eyes of the Lord, but their praise is qualified with the addition that they allowed the worship of foreign gods to continue in Judah. All other kings of Judah are condemned as having done what was evil in the sight of the Lord.

Even Solomon was criticized. Although Solomon built the Temple where God was worshiped, he departed from the command of the Lord and worshiped foreign gods. This sin lead to the empire built by David being split in two at the death of Solomon (1 Kings 11:1—12:25; see 1 Kings 3:2–3).

The most notorious king of Judah was Manasseh (2 Kings 21:1–18). Manasseh negated the reforms of his father, Hezekiah, and actively promoted the worship of foreign gods. Manasseh even built altars to other gods within the Temple at Jerusalem where only God was to be worshiped. He sacrificed his own son, practiced soothsaying and augury, and dealt with mediums and wizards. Because of the sins of Manasseh and because he caused Israel to sin, the prophet delivered this word of God concerning Manasseh: "Behold, I am bringing such evil upon Jerusalem and Judah that whosoever heareth of it, both of his ears will tingle" (2 Kings 21:12). The prophet went on to speak of the defeat and exile that would eventually come because of the sin of Manasseh (2 Kings 21:13–15; see 2 Kings 23:26–27; 24:1–7; compare 2 Kings 17:19–20).

All the kings of Israel are comdemned as having done what was evil in the sight of the Lord. Most of the responsibility for the sins of Israel is placed on Jeroboam, the first king of Israel (2 Kings 17:21–23; see 1 Kings 15:30).

One of Jeroboam's faults lay in instituting the worship in a place other than Jerusalem. After the two kingdoms split, Jeroboam could not maintain the integrity of his own kingdom and allow the people of the Northern Kingdom to worship at the Temple of Jerusalem, the capital of the Southern Kingdom. As a solution to his problem, Jeroboam established places of worship at Dan and Bethel (1 Kings 12:26–29).

To complicate matters, Jeroboam made two golden calves for the people to worship (1 Kings 12:28). Thus, Jeroboam violated two of the most important principles of Deuteronomy: the worship of God only and only in the Temple of Jerusalem (Deut. 12—13). To emphasize the fact that Jeroboam was responsible for Israel's sin and ultimate downfall, many of the subsequent kings of Israel are condemned because they did not depart from the sins of Jeroboam (1 Kings 15:34; 16:2,19,26,31; 22:52; 2 Kings 3:3; 10:29,31; 13:2,6,11; 14:24; 15:9,18,24).

Hope for the Future The very fact that the Books of Kings were written indicates that the writer saw that Israel, even though suffering in the Exile, could learn from their past and begin to live in a way more pleasing to God. He could see in Israel's distress evidence of God's continual desire that Israel turn from their sins and return to God as God's people. God had shown grace and mercy when they disobeyed in the wilderness and during the lapses of the time of the judges. God would certainly show them grace and mercy now. The blessings of Deuteronomy 28:1–14 could still be theirs.

This hope is illustrated in 2 Kings 25:27–30 with the release of Jehoiachin from prison. Perhaps the writer was encouraging the exiles with the possibility that God would bless them again and raise Israel above all peoples (Deut. 28:1) just as Jehoiachin was given preference above other prisoners in captivity (2 Kings 25:28).

Outline

1 Kings

I. God Works Out His Purposes Even Through Human Revenge and Treachery (1:1—2:46).

II. God Works Through the Wisdom He Gives His Humble Leader (3:1—7:51).

A. God honors His humble leader's request and

equips him with divine wisdom (3:1–28).
B. God's leader administers his people wisely (4:1–34).
C. God's leader wisely follows divine directives to build a house of worship (5:1—7:51).
III. God Responds to the Worship and Sin of His People (8:1—11:43).
A. God fulfills His promise to His people and their leaders (8:1–21).
B. The incomparable God of heaven hears the prayers of His repentant people anywhere (8:22–53).
C. The faithful God leads His people to faithfulness and calls the nations to recognize His uniqueness (8:54–61).
D. God's people worship joyfully in His house (8:62–66).
E. God's favor is related to His people's obedience (9:1–9).
F. God blesses the efforts of His faithful leader (9:10—10:29).
G. A leader's unfaithfulness brings divine discipline on His people (11:1–43).
IV. Disobedience Brings Results (12:1—16:34).
A. A leader who refuses to be a servant loses his subjects (12:1–24).
B. False worship leads to doom for God's people and their leader (12:25—13:10).
C. God's prophets must obey God's voice (13:11–25).
D. Disobedience leads a nation to *eternal* ruin (13:26—14:20).
E. God is faithful to His promises even when a people disobey (14:21—15:8).
F. In the midst of disobedience God honors a faithful leader (15:9–24).
G. God fulfills His threats against evil leaders (15:25—16:34).
V. God Works in History Through His Prophetic Messengers (17:1—22:53).
A. God blesses and brings recognition to His faithful prophet (17:1–24).
B. Yahweh proves His claim to be the only God of Israel through His prophet (18:1–46).
C. God revives His depressed prophet and provides for His purposes to be worked out (19:1–21).
D. God uses a prophet to prove His lordship over history (20:1–30*a*).
E. God sends prophets to condemn His disobedient leaders (20:30*b*–43).
F. God uses His prophets to bring guilty leaders to repentance (21:1–29).
G. God speaks through His chosen prophet, not through those depending on human appointment and provisions (22:1–40).
H. God blesses the faithful but is angry at the disobedient (22:41–53).

2 Kings
1. Through His Prophets God Guides History and Reveals His Will (1:1—8:29).

A. God alone controls the fortunes of His people (1:1–18).
B. God provides spiritual leadership for His people (2:1–25).
C. The prophetic word from God controls history (3:1–27).
D. God's minister helps God's faithful people in their time of need (4:1–44).
E. God's mercy reaches across international lines (5:1–19*a*).
F. Greedy ministers cannot deceive God (5:19*b*–27).
G. God defeats the enemies of His people (6:1—7:20).
H. God does not forget His faithful people (8:1–6).
I. God controls the destiny of all nations (8:7–29).
II. God's Mercy Has Limits (9:1—17:41).
A. God keeps His threats against false worship but honors those who carry out His will (9:1—10:36).
B. God protects His chosen leader (11:1–21).
C. God's people support His house of worship (12:1–16).
D. God's offerings are not to be used for political purposes (12:17–21).
E. God's mercy and faithfulness protect even His disobedient people (13:1—14:29).
F. God works to punish a people who remain disobedient (15:1—16:20).
G. God brings an end to the nation that refuses to follow the prophetic word (17:1–41).
III. God Honors Righteous Rulers but Punishes a Sinful People (18:1—25:30).
A. God rewards those who trust in Him but punishes those who mock Him (18:1—19:37; compare to Isa. 36:1—37:38).
B. God hears the prayers of His faithful servant (20:1–11; compare to Isa. 38:1–22).
C. God knows the future of His people (20:12–21; compare to Isa. 39:1–8).
D. Rebellion against God brings divine rejection (21:1–26).
E. A righteous ruler can delay divine judgment (22:1–20).
F. A righteous ruler cannot avert judgment forever (23:1–30).
G. Deserved punishment comes to God's disobedient people (23:31—25:26).
H. God preserves hope for His people (25:27–30). *Phil Logan*

KING'S DALE See *Shaveh, Valley of.*

KING'S GARDEN A portion of Jerusalem containing the Pool of Shelah which was rebuilt by Shállum, ruler of the district of Mizpah (Neh. 3:15). See *Shelah, Pool of.*

KING'S HIGHWAY Major transportation route

east of the Jordan River. Literally "the way of the king," this highway has been in continuous use for over 3,000 years. It runs from Damascus to the Gulf of Aqabah and is the main caravan route for the Transjordan. It is mentioned in Numbers 20:17 and 21:22 as the route Moses and the Israelites would take through Edom and the land of Sihon. The Romans upgraded it during the reign of Trajan and renamed it Trajan's Road. The Arabic name is Tariq es-Sultani, which also means the way of the sultan or king.

KING'S POOL Probably the same as the Pool of Shelah, a reservoir in the king's garden in Jerusalem (Neh. 2:14). See *King's Garden; Shelah, Pool of.*

KING'S TREASURE HOUSE See *House of the Rolls.*

KING'S VALE See *Shaveh, Valley of.*

KING'S VALLEY See *Shaveh, Valley of.*

KINNERETH (Kĭn′ nĕ·rĕth) NIV, REB spelling of Chinnereth. See *Chinnereth.*

KINSMAN Usually refers to a blood relative based on Israel's tribal nature. The most important relationship was that of the father to the oldest son.

Certain obligations were laid on the kinsman. In the case of an untimely death of a husband without a son, the law of levirate marriage becomes operative—that is, the husband's brother was obligated to raise up a male descendant for his deceased brother and thus perpetuate the deceased's name and inheritance. The living brother was the dead brother's *goel*—his redeemer (Gen. 38:8; Deut. 25:5–10; Ruth 3:9–12). See *Levirate Law.*

The kinsman was also the blood avenger. A wrong done to a single memeber of the family was considered a crime against the entire tribe or clan. The clan had an obligation, therefore, to punish the wrongdoer. In the case of a murder committed, the kinsman should seek vengeance. According to the imagery of ancient people, the blood of the murdered man cried up from the ground for vengeance and the cry was heard loudest by that member of the clan who stood nearest to the dead in kinship; therefore, the closest of kin followed through with the blood avenger responsibility (compare Gen. 4:1–16, especially v.10). See *Vengeance.*

The kinsman was also responsible to redeem the estate which his nearest relative might have sold because of poverty (Lev. 25:25; Ruth 4:4). It was the kinsman's responsibility also to ransom a kinsman who may have sold himself (Lev. 25:47–48).

The Old Testament book of Ruth is the most

striking example of a kinsman who used his power and Jewish law to redeem. Boaz demonstrated one of the duties of the kinsman—that of marrying the widow of a deceased kinsman. A correlation is sometimes made between the redemption of Ruth by Boaz and the redemption of sinners by Christ. See *Avenger; Cities of Refuge; Redeem, Redemption, Redeemer.*   *Gary Bonner*

KIOS (Kī′ ŏs) NIV spelling of Chios. See *Chios.*

KIR (Kīr) Place name meaning "wall." *1.* A Moabite city mentioned in connection with Ar in Isaiah's prophesy against Moab (15:1). Many believe that Kir is the same as Kir-Hareseth, an ancient capital of Moab along with Ar. Located at Kerak about seventeen miles south of the Arnon and eleven miles east of the Dead Sea. See *Kir Hareseth.*

2. Kir is the Hebrew translation of the city name, Der (a word from Akkadian which also means "wall"). Kir was a Mesopotamian city east of the lower Tigris River (which is now identified with the modern Badrah) on the main road from Elam (Persia) to Babylon. During the Neo-Babylonian period (605–539 B.C.; see *Babylon*), Kir was the capital of the province of Gutium. The governor of this province joined Cyrus the Persian in the overthrow of the Babylonian empire in 539 B.C.

According to the Bible, Kir was the city from which Arameans migrated to Syria (Isa. 22:6). Their migration—like the migration of the Philistines from Caphtor—is spoken of in terms similar to that of the exodus of Israel from Egypt (Amos 9:7; see 1:5). When Tiglath-pileser III conquered the area during the reign of Ahaz (2 Kings 16:9), the descendants of the original immigrants to Syria were sent back to Kir (compare the aversion of the ancient Hebrews to being sent back to Egypt in Deut. 17:16; 28:68).   *Phil Logan*

KIR-HARESETH (Kîr-Hâr′ ĕ·sĕth) Place name meaning, "city of pottery." Known by various names in various texts and various versions of the Old Testament: Kir-Hareseth (2 Kings 3:25; Isa. 16:7), Kir-Haraseth (2 Kings 3:25 KJV), Kir-Heres ("new city"; Isa. 16:11; Jer. 48:31,36), and Kirharesh (Isa. 16:11 KJV). Perhaps also the same as Kir of Moab in Isaiah 15:1. See *Kir 1.*

During the reign of Jehoram of Israel, Mesha, king of Moab, rebelled against Israel (2 Kings 3:4–27). The kings of Judah (Jehoshaphat) and Edom joined Israel in the resulting war. The forces allied against Mesha crushed the rebellion, but they were unsuccessful in capturing Mesha. He took refuge in Kir-Hareseth—a well fortified and impregnable city. After Mesha tried unsuccessfully to break through the besiegers, he offered his son as a sacrifice upon the city walls. As a result, "there came a great wrath upon Israel"

K

(2 Kings 3:27 NRSV); and the allied forces withdrew, leaving Mesha alive in Kir-Hareseth (2 Kings 3:4–27). Apparently, the forces of Israel and Judah feared the power of the Moabite god, Chemosh, and gave up the victory that lay within their grasp. Jehoram and Jehoshaphat did not have faith that Yahweh would give them victory over the people of Chemosh.

The prophets would later correct this view. Isaiah (15:1; 16:7,11) and Jeremiah (48:31,36) prophesied that Kir-Hareseth was no match for the power of God. All human kingdoms are ultimately subject to God. Kir-Hareseth was destroyed by the Babylonians whom the prophets described as God's instrument of punishment (see Jer. 4:5–31; 6:1–8, 22–26; 25:1–14).

Kir-Hareseth is identified with modern khirbet Karnak, about 50 miles southeast of Jerusalem and 11 miles east of the Dead Sea.   *Phil Logan*

KIR-HARESH (Kĭr-Hā′ resh) The KJV spelling of Kir-Hareseth in Isaiah 16:11. See *Kir-Hareseth.*

KIR-HERES (Kĭr-Hē′ rĕs) Believed to be an alternate spelling of Kir-Hareseth found in Isaiah 16:11; Jeremiah 48:31,36. The Greek translation of the name in Isaiah 16:11 suggests that the translators of the Septuagint had a Hebrew text that read Kir-Hadesheth, a name meaning "New City," which was mistaken for Kir-Hareseth or Kir-Heres. In the context, Kir-Hares (for Kir-Hareseth) is likely the best reading (see Isaiah 16:7). The confusion between Kir-Hadesheth and Kir-Hareseth may be due to the similarity of the Hebrew "r" and "d". The name Kir-Hares may be explained by the loss of the final Hebrew letter "th" from Kir-Hareseth. See *Kir-Hareseth.*

KIR OF MOAB See *Kir 1.*

KIRIATH (Kĭr′ ĭ ath) Place name meaning, "city" in tribal territory of Benjamin (Josh. 18:28 NAS, NIV; KJV has Kirjath, an alternate spelling). The same as Kiriath-Jearim (see Josh. 18:28 NRSV, REB, TEV). See *Kiriath-Jearim.*

KIRIATHAIM (Kĭr ĭ å thā′ ĭm) Place name meaning, "double city" or "two cities." *1.* A levitical city and city of refuge in the tribal territory of Naphtali (1 Chron. 6:76, KJV has Kirjathaim). In the parallel list in Joshua 21:32, Kartan stands in the place of Kiriathaim and is probably another name for the same city. See *Levitical Cities; Cities of Refuge; Kartan. 2.* A city taken from the Emim by Chedorlaomer (Gen. 14:5, Shaveh-Kiriathaim means, "the plain of Kiriathaim"). Later the Israelites took it from the Amorites and assigned it to the tribe of Reuben (Num. 32:37; Josh. 13:19). The Moabites controlled the city during the Exile (Jer. 48:1,23; Ezek. 25:9). Perhaps to be identified with el-Qereiyat, about five miles northwest

of Dibon; however, no remains from before about 100 B.C. have been found on this site.

KIRIATH-ARBA (Kĭr′ ĭ ăth-Är′ bà) Place name meaning, "city of Arba" or "city of four." The ancient name for the city of Hebron (Josh. 15:54). It was the chief city in the hill country of Judah (Josh. 15:54) and was both a levitical city (Josh. 21:11) and a city of refuge (Josh. 20:7). Caleb captured the city for Israel (Josh. 15:13–14). Bible students dispute the origin of the name. According to some, Kiriath-Arba was originally named after Arba the Anakite hero (Josh. 14:15; see 15:13). Others point to the nearby cave of Machpelah where, according to Jewish tradition, Adam, Abraham, Isaac, and Jacob were buried—thus, "city of four." See *Levitical Cities; Cities of Refuge; Hebron.*

KIRIATH-ARIM (Kĭr ĭ ăth-Ā′ rĭm) An alternate spelling of Kiriath-Jearim in Ezra 2:25. See *Kiriath-Jearim.*

KIRIATH-BAAL (Kĭr′ ĭ ăth-Bā′ ȧl) Place name meaning, "city of Baal." Another name for Kiriath-Jearim in Joshua 15:60; 18:14. See *Kiriath-Jearim.*

KIRIATH-HUZOTH (Kĭr′ ĭ ăth-Hū′ zŏth) Place name meaning, "city of streets." A city of Moab to which Balak took Balaam to offer a sacrifice (Num. 22:39). Some suggest a location near the Arnon River (see Num. 22:36) not far from Bamoth-Baal (see Num. 22:41 NIV). The precise location is unknown.

KIRIATH-JEARIM (Kĭr′ ĭ ăth-jĕ′ ȧ-rĭm) Place name meaning, "city of forests." Kiriath-jearim was located at modern Abu Gosh nine miles north of Jerusalem. It was on the border where Dan, Benjamin, and Judah joined before Dan began their migration northward (Josh. 15:9,60; 18:14–15). Dan's army camped there in their search for new territory (Judg. 18:12). After the Philistines returned the ark of the covenant, it was kept at Kiriath-jearim for a time (1 Sam. 6:21–7:2). David attempted to move the ark to Jerusalem from there, but because he did so improperly, God struck down Uzzah (2 Sam. 6:1–8). Among Kiriath-jearim's sons was Uriah, a faithful prophet and contemporary of Jeremiah. He was executed for prophesying against the king (Jer. 26:20–24).

The Romans built a fort over the ancient ruins to guard the main route from Jerusalem to the Mediterranean Sea. A garrison from the Tenth Legion was stationed there.

Kiriath-jearim is identified with Deir al-Azhar near the modern village of Qaryet el-Inab or Abu Gosh.

KIRIATH-SANNAH (Kĭr′ ĭ·ăth-Săn′ nah) Place

K

name perhaps meaning, "city of bronze." Another name for the city of Debir, also known as Kiriath-Sepher ("city of a book") (Josh. 15:15–16,49). See *Debir 2.*

KIRIATH-SEPHER (Kĭr' ĭ-ăth-Sē' phĕr) Place name meaning, "city of book." Used in Joshua 15:15–16 as another name for Debir. Kiriath-Sannah is the same city (Josh. 15:49). See *Debir 2.*

KIRIOTH (Kĭr' ĭ-ŏth) KJV spelling of Kerioth in Amos 2:2. See *Kerioth.*

KIRJATH (Kĭr' jăth) KJV spelling of Kiriath, another name for Kiriath-Jearim. See *Kiriath-Jearim.*

KIRJATHAIM (Kĭr-jȧ-thā' ĭm) KJV spelling of Kiriathaim. See *Kiriathaim.*

KIRJATH-ARBA (Kĭr' jăth-Är' bȧ) KJV spelling of Kiriath-Arba. See *Kiriath-Arba.*

KIRJATH-ARIM (Kĭr' jăth-Ā' rĭm) KJV spelling of Kiriath-Arim. See *Kiriath-Arim.*

KIRJATH-BAAL (Kĭr' jăth-Bā' ȧl) KJV spelling of Kiriath-Baal. See *Kiriath-Baal.*

KIRJATH-HUZOTH (Kĭr' jăth-Hū' zŏth) KJV spelling of Kiriath-Huzoth. See *Kiriath-Huzoth.*

KIRJATH-JEARIM (Kĭr' jăth-Jē' ȧ-rĭm) KJV spelling of Kiriath-Jearim. See *Kiriath-Jearim.*

KIRJATH-SANNAH (Kĭr' jăth-Săn' nah) KJV spelling of Kiriath-Sannah. Kiriath-Sannah is another name for the city of Debir (Josh. 15:49) as is Kiriath-Sepher (Josh. 15:15–16). See *Debir 2.*

KIRJATH-SEPHER (Kĭr' jăth-Sē' phĕr) KJV spelling of Kiriath-Sepher. Kiriath-Sepher is another name for the city of Debir (Josh. 15:15–16) as is Kiriath-Sannah (Josh. 15:49). See *Debir 2.*

KISH (Kĭsh) Personal name of unknown meaning, perhaps "gift." *1.* Father of Saul (1 Sam. 9:2). A man of the tribe of Benjamin who lived in Gibeah. He is said to have been the son of Abiel (1 Sam. 9:1) and the son of Ner (1 Chron. 8:33). Some think he was the grandson of Abiel and son of Ner. He was apparently a man of wealth, owning both asses and servants (1 Sam. 9:3). The description of Saul as being from the humblest family of the tribe of Benjamin is probably a good example of oriental modesty (1 Sam. 9:21). He was buried in Zela of Benjamin, where Saul and Jonathan were buried (2 Sam. 21:14).
2. A Benjaminite, the third son of Jeiel of Gibeon and Maacah (1 Chron. 8:29–30; 9:35–36). *3.* The second son of Mahli who belonged to the

Merari family of Levites. Kish's sons married his brother's daughters (1 Chron. 23:21–22). Kish's son, Jerahmeel, became the head of the family of Kish (1 Chron. 24:29). *4.* Son of Abdi, also of the Merari family of Levites. He assisted in cleansing the Temple during the time of Hezekiah (2 Chron. 29:12). *5.* The Benjaminite ancestor of Mordecai (Esther 2:5).

KISHI (Kĭsh' ī) Personal name possibly meaning, "gift." A Levite of the Merari family (1 Chron. 6:44) also called Kushaiah (1 Chron. 15:17). See *Kushaiah.*

KISHION (Kĭsh' ĭ-ŏn) Place name meaning, "hard ground." A town in Issachar allotted to the Gershonite Levites (Josh. 21:28). A parallel list calls the town Kedesh (1 Chron. 6:72). It has been suggested that "Kedesh in Issachar" may have arisen from a misreading of "Kishon" for "Kedesh." The site is uncertain, perhaps modern tell Abu Qudeis, about two miles southeast of Megiddo. See *Levitical Cities; Kedesh.*

KISHON (Kī' shŏn) Place name meaning "curving, winding." A small river which flows from east to west through the Valley of Jezreel. In the spring it achieves a width of about 65 feet and a length of 23 miles.
It was at the Kishon that Deborah and Barak defeated the Canaanite Sisera when his chariots became mired in the marshes (Judg. 4:7,13; 5:21). Later, the river was the place where Elijah brought the prophets of Baal to be executed following God's display and victory on Mount Carmel (1 Kings 18:40).

KISLEV (Kĭs' lĕv) NIV, REB, TEV spelling of Chislev. See *Chislev.*

KISLON (Kĭs' lŏn) NIV, REB spelling of Chislon. See *Chislon.*

KISLOTH-TABOR (Kĭs' lŏth-Tā' bôr) NIV, REB spelling of Chisloth-Tabor. See *Chisloth-Tabor.*

KISON (Kī' sŏn) KJV spelling of Kishon in Psalm 83:9. See *Kishon.*

KISS Most often used of the touching of the lips to another person's lips, cheeks, shoulders, hands, or feet as a gesture of friendship, acceptance, respect, and reverence. The location of the kiss carried different meanings as Jesus made clear in the episode of the woman kissing his feet (Luke 7:36–50). With the exception of three occurrences (Prov. 7:13; Song of Sol. 1:2; 8:1) the term is used without any erotic overtones. Kiss translates two Hebrew words and three Greek words; the basic Hebrew term is found 32 times, and the basic Greek term is found seven times.

K

In the Old Testament close relatives kissed at greeting and departing with the connotation of acceptance most often in the foreground (Gen. 27:26–27; 29:11; 50:1; Ex. 18:7; 1 Sam. 10:1; Ruth 1:9). The term was further used of the gesture of reverence to idols (1 Kings 19:18; Hos. 13:2) as well as to the Lord (Ps. 2:12). A kiss of betrayal is also found (2 Sam. 20:9). The term "kiss" in the New Testament is used of Judas (Mark 14:44–45), of the father to the prodigal as a sign of acceptance and reconciliation (Luke 15:20), of the Ephesian elders to Paul as a sign of gratitude (Acts 20:37), of the woman who kissed the feet of Jesus (Luke 7:38), and of the "holy kiss" (1 Thess. 5:26; 1 Cor. 16:20; 2 Cor. 13:12; Rom. 16:16).

The holy kiss was widely practiced among the early Christians as a manner of greeting, a sign of acceptance, and an impartation of blessing. This custom could well have been used to express the unity of the Christian fellowship. The substitute kiss involved kissing the hand and waving it in the direction of the object to be kissed (Job 31:27). The kiss of betrayal from Judas does not belong to the category of the kiss of Joab to Amasa (2 Sam. 20:9), but was the sign of respect from pupil to master. Either the action of Judas did not accord with his inner feeling, or his action had other motivation than betrayal.

The kiss still survives in the Near Eastern culture as a sign of love, respect, and reverence.

G. Al Wright, Jr.

KITCHENS Place of meal preparation, particularly involving cooking. Ezekiel's vision of the Temple included four small courts at the corners of the Court of the Gentiles where the sacrifices that the common people were permitted to eat were boiled (Ezek. 46:24). KJV has "the place of them that boil." The sin, guilt, and cereal offerings were cooked in the kitchens within the priests' chambers to protect them from contact with persons who had not been consecrated (Ezek. 46:19–20). There is no mention in the Bible of separate rooms in homes where meals were prepared. See *Cooking and Heating.*

KITE Bird of prey, best described as a scavenger of the accipitridae family (hawk), the subfamily of milvinae of the genus milvus. Medium sized with red coloring. Found in the Bible at Leviticus 11:14; Deuteronomy 14:13; Isaiah 34:15. This bird was considered unclean and not for human consumption (Lev. 11:14). See *Birds.*

KITHLISH (Kĭth' lĭsh) KJV, REB spelling of Chitlish. See *Chitlish.*

KITLISH (Kĭt' lĭsh) NIV spelling of Chitlish. See *Chitlish.*

KITRON (Kĭt' rŏn) Place name of uncertain meaning. A city in the tribal territory of Zebulun from which the Israelites could not expel the Canaanites (Judg. 1:30). This city is probably the same as Kattath. See *Kattath.*

KITTIM (Kĭt' tĭm) Tribal name for the island of Cyprus, sometimes spelled Chittim. This name was derived from Kition, a city-state on the southeastern side of the island. Long associated with maritime lore, the island was ruled first by Greece, then the Assyrians, and finally, Rome. Genesis 10:4 traces the people's roots to Noah's son Japheth. Jeremiah and Ezekiel both mention it in their prophecies (Jer. 2:10; Ezek. 27:6; compare Isa. 23:1,12).

Kittim is used in intertestamental writings as denoting all of the land west of Cyprus. I Maccabees credits it as being the land of Alexander the Great (1:1; 8:5). The writer of Daniel understood it to be a part of the Roman Empire (11:30) used to threaten Antiochus Epipanes. The Dead Sea Scrolls contain several references to Kittim, the most notable being the defeat of her people (Romans) at the hands of God's people. See *Cyprus.*

KIYYUN (Kīy' yŭn) NAS spelling of the word spelled Chiun in Amos 5:26 (KJV). Other versions translate the word as "Kaiwan." See *Chiun; Kaiwan.*

KNEAD, KNEADING BOWL The process of making bread dough by mixing flour, water, and oil along with a piece of the previous day's dough with the hands in a kneading bowl or trough. The mixture was allowed to stand in the bowl to rise and ferment (Ex. 12:34). Kneading the dough was usually the work of the woman (Gen. 18:6; 1 Sam. 28:24) but was performed on occasion by men (Hos. 7:4). The bowls could be made of wood, earthenware, or bronze and were the objects of either God's blessing or curse (Deut. 28:5,17; see Ex. 8:3).

KNEEL The common posture when requesting a blessing from one believed able to bestow the blessing. The Hebrew word for kneel comes from the same root as the word for bless. Kneeling is also considered a sign of reverence, obedience, or respect. Kneeling was the posture of prayer (Dan. 6:10; Acts 7:60; 9:40; 20:36; Eph. 3:14; compare 1 Kings 18:42), acknowledging a superior (2 Kings 1:13; Matt. 17:14; 27:29; Mark 1:40; 10:17; Luke 5:8), or worship of God (I Kings 8:54), Jesus (Phil. 2:10), or idols (1 Kings 19:18; Isa. 66:3 where blessing an idol refers to kneeling before an idol). See *Blessing and Cursing.*

KNIFE A small instrument made of flint, copper, bronze, or iron used mainly for domestic pur-

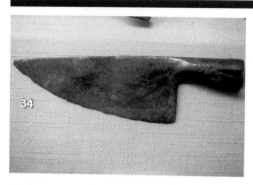

Large, wide-bladed knife from the Roman time period.

poses. Joshua was ordered to make flint knives for the circumcision of Israelite males (Josh. 5:2–3). Since flint was not the common material used to make knives in the days of Joshua, the command to make the knives of flint probably reflects a very ancient practice of circumcision (see Gen. 17:11; *Circumcision*). Knives were used most commonly for killing and skinning animals and for killing sacrificial animals (see Lev. 7:2; 8:15,20,25; 9:8–15; 1 Sam. 9:24). Some Bible students think the pruning hooks of Isaiah 18:5 were curved knives. Others believe that the lances of the priests of Baal were pointed knives with which they cut themselves to gain Baal's attention (1 Kings 18:28). According to Ezra 1:9, the furnishings for the Temple included 29 knives (KJV, NRSV), but the meaning of the Hebrew term is uncertain as seen in modern translations: NIV, "silver pans"; REB, "vessels of various kinds"; RSV, "censers"; NAS, "duplicates."

KNOB An ornamental detail on the seven-branched lampstand in the tabernacle (Ex. 25:31–36, KJV's knop; RSV's capital; NRSV's calyx; NIV's buds). Some suggest that the knob was an imitation of the almond. The word may also refer to the capital of a column (Zeph. 2:14).

KNOP *1.* KJV translation of a Hebrew word that the NRSV translates as gourd in 1 Kings 6:18; 7:24. This is a different Hebrew word from the one translated elsewhere as knob, knop, or capital. *2.* Knop is also an archaic form of the word "knob." See *Knob*.

KNOWLEDGE Translation of several Hebrew and Greek words covering a wide range of meanings: intellectual understanding, personal experience, emotion, and personal relationship (including sexual intercourse, Gen. 4:1, etc.). Knowledge is attributed both to God and to human beings.

God's knowledge is said to be omniscient. He knows all things (Job 21:22; Ps. 139:1–18); His understanding is beyond measure (Ps. 147:5). He knows the thoughts of our minds and the secrets

of our hearts (Ps. 44:21; 94:11). He knows past events (Gen. 30:22), present happenings (Job 31:4), and future events (Zech. 13:1; Luke 1:33).

The knowledge which God has of nations and human beings indicates that He has a personal interest—not merely an awareness—of people (Ps. 144:3). To be known by God may mean that a nation or individual is chosen by God to play a part in God's purposes in the world (Jer. 1:5; Amos 3:2; Gal. 4:9).

The Bible speaks often about human knowledge. Knowledge of God is the greatest knowledge (Prov. 9:10) and is the chief duty of mankind (Hos. 6:6). In the Old Testament, the Israelites know God through what He does for His people (Ex. 9:29; Lev. 23:43; Deut. 4:32–39; Ps. 9:10; 59:13; 78:16; Hos. 2:19–20). This knowledge of God is not simply theoretical or factual knowledge; it includes experiencing the reality of God in one's life (compare Phil. 3:10) and living one's life in a manner that shows a respect for the power and majesty of God (compare Jer. 22:15–16).

In the New Testament one knows God through a knowledge of Jesus Christ (John 8:19; Col. 2:2–3). The apostle Paul closely connected knowledge to faith. Knowledge gives direction, conviction, and assurance to faith (2 Cor. 4:14). Knowledge is a spiritual gift (1 Cor. 12:8) which can grow, increase, be filled, and abound (Phil. 1:9; Col. 1:9–10; 2 Cor. 8:7). It consists in having a better understanding of God's will in the ethical sense (Col. 1:9–10; Phil. 1:9), of knowing that God desires to save people (Eph. 1:8–9), and of having a deeper insight into God's will given in Christ (Eph. 1:17; 3:18–19).

But though Paul recognized the importance of knowledge, he also knew that it could be a divisive factor in churches such as at Rome and Corinth where some Christians claimed to be more spiritual because of their knowledge of spiritual matters (Rom. 14:1—15:6; 1 Cor. 8:1–13). Paul argued that knowledge puffs up but love builds up and that the knowledge exercised by the "strong" in faith could cause the "weak" in faith to go against their Christian conscience and lead to their spiritual ruin. Knowledge can be misused (1 Cor. 8). Love is more important than knowledge (1 Cor. 13), yet knowledge is still a gift, necessary for Christian teaching (1 Cor. 14:6) and for Christian growth toward a mature faith (1 Cor. 8:7; 2 Pet. 1:5–6; 3:18).

In the Gospel of John, knowledge is a key concept, although the noun "knowledge" itself never occurs in John's Gospel. John instead frequently uses the verbs "to know". Jesus and the Father have a mutual knowledge (John 10:14–15), and Jesus' knowledge of God is perfect (John 3:11; 4:22; 7:28–29, for example). Jesus brings to lost humankind the knowledge of God which is necessary for salvation (John 7:28–29; 8:19), but which mankind has distorted through sin (John

1:10). God's knowledge of Jesus consists of giving Jesus His mission and the power to perform it (John 10:18). Jesus' knowledge of the Father consists of His hearing God's word and obediently expressing it to the world.

Knowledge of God is closely related to faith, expressing the perception and understanding of faith. Full knowledge is possible only after Jesus' glorification, since the disciples sometimes failed to understand Jesus (John 4:32; 10:6; 12:16). In John, knowledge is expressed in Christian witness which may evoke belief in Jesus (John 1:7; 4:39; 12:17–18) and in love (John 17:26). Whereas Jesus' knowledge of the Father is direct, the disciples' knowledge of Jesus is indirect, qualified by believing. The Christian's knowledge of Jesus is the perception of Jesus as the revelation of God which leads to obedience to His word of love. So the Christian is caught up into God's mission of love to the world in order that the world may come to know and believe in Jesus as the revelation of the Father's love for the world.

Roger L. Omanson

KOA (Kō′ à) National name of unknown meaning. Ezekiel 23:23 lists the names of several nations God will bring against Israel. Koa, like Shoa, has not been identified to everyone's satisfaction. Some identify Koa with the Guti people of Babylon, but this is disputed.

KOHATH (Kō′ hăth) Personal name of unknown meaning. The second son of Levi (Gen. 46:11) and father of Amram, Izhar, Hebron, and Uzziel (Ex. 6:18) who became the heads of the Kohathite branch of the Levitical priesthood. Kohath went to Egypt with Levi (his father) and Jacob (his grandfather) (Gen. 46:11), had a sister named Jochebed (Ex. 6:20), and died at the age of 133 (Ex. 6:18). See *Kohathites*.

KOHATHITES (Kō′ hăth·īte) The descendants of Kohath, the son of Levi (Ex. 6:16; see *Kohath*). Since Kohath was the grandfather of Aaron, Moses, and Miriam (Ex. 6:20; Num. 26:59; see *Amram*), the Kohathites were considered the most important of the three major Levitical families (that is, Kohathites, Gershonites, and Merarites). The Kohathites were further divided into four branches according to the four sons of Kohath: Amram, Izhar, Hebron, and Uzziel (Ex. 6:18; Num. 3:19; 1 Chron. 6:1–3,16,18,33,38; 23:6,12,13,18–20; 26:23).

The Kohathites were active throughout Israel's history. The Kohathites, along with the Gershonites and Merarites, were placed around the tabernacle and were charged with caring for and moving it. The Kohathites were to camp on the south side of the tabernacle and were responsible to care for and move the ark, table, lampstand, altars, vessels of the sanctuary, and the screen (Num. 3:29–31). The Kohathites could not touch these objects and could move them only after they had been properly prepared by Aaron and his sons. The result of attempting to move these objects without their first being fit with poles for carrying was death (Num. 4:15,17–20; 7:9; compare 1 Sam. 5—6; 2 Sam. 6:6–11).

After the conquest, Kohathites descended from Aaron received thirteen cities from the tribes of Judah, Simeon, and Benjamin (Josh. 21:4,9–19; 1 Chron. 6:54–60). The remaining Kohathites received ten cities from the tribes of Dan, Ephraim, and Manasseh (Josh. 21:5,20–26; 1 Chron. 6:61,66–70). One of the latter ten was Shechem, a city of refuge. See *Levitical Cities; Cities of Refuge.*

David appointed 120 Kohathites under the leadership of Uriel to bring the ark to Jerusalem (1 Chron. 15:5). When Jehoshaphat sought deliverance from the Moabites and Ammonites, the Kohathites led the people in prayer and praise (2 Chron. 20:19). Mahath and Joel of the Kohathites helped in the purification of Israel's worship during the time of Hezekiah (2 Chron. 29:12). During Josiah's religious reforms, two Kohathite priests (Zechariah and Meshullam) helped supervise the work (2 Chron. 34:12).

When the Israelites returned from the Exile, some of the Kohathites were placed in charge of preparing the show bread every sabbath (1 Chron. 9:32). See *Levites; Gershonites; Merarites.*

Phil Logan

KOHELETH (Kō·hĕl′ ĕth) The English transliteration of the Hebrew title of Ecclesiastes (also spelled Qoheleth). Koheleth is a Hebrew word that is translated as preacher (KJV, RSV, NAS), teacher (NIV, NRSV), speaker (REB), or philosopher (TEV) in Ecclesiastes 1:1.

KOLAIAH (Kō·lâi′ ah) Personal name meaning "voice of Yah." *1.* Son of Maaseiah whose descendants lived in Jerusalem after the Exile (Neh. 11:7). *2.* The father of the false prophet, Ahab (Jer. 29:21–23).

KOPH (Kōph) Nineteenth letter of Hebrew alphabet. See *Qoph.*

KOR (kōr) Dry measure equal to a homer or to about 6.3 imperial bushels, though estimates vary greatly. Those using the metric system have estimated a kor at between 220 and 450 liters. It apparently represented the load a donkey could carry on its back. Compare 1 Kings 4:22; 5:11; 2 Chronicles 2:9; 27:5; Ezekiel 45:14. The measure in Luke 16:7 apparently represents a Greek transliteration of the Hebrew *kor*. See *Weights and Measures.*

KORAH (Kō′ rah) Personal name meaning

K

"bald." *1.* A son of Esau (Gen. 36:5,14; 1 Chron. 1:35) who became chief of a clan of Edom (Gen. 36:18).

2. A grandson of Esau, son of Eliphaz, and chief of a clan of Edom (Gen. 36:16; 1 Chron. 1:36).

3. A leader of rebellion against Moses and Aaron while Israel was camped in the wilderness of Paran (Num. 16). Korah, Dathan, and Abiram led a confederacy of 250 princes of the people against Aaron's claim to the priesthood and Moses' claim to authority in general. The rebels contended that the entire congregation was sanctified and therefore qualified to perform priestly functions. As punishment for their insubordination, God caused the earth to open and swallow the leaders and their property. A fire from the Lord consumed the 250 followers.

4. A Levite descended from Izhar, of the family of Kohath (Ex. 6:21; 1 Chron. 6:22,37), probably to be identified with *3.* above. The sons of Korah and Asaph were the two most prominent groups of Temple singers (compare 2 Chron. 20:19). Many of the Psalms with the heading "A Psalm of the Sons of Korah" may have been taken from their hymnbook (Pss. 42; 44—49; 84—85; 87—88). In a later list of Temple singers the group of Heman replaced Korah and was joined by Asaph and Ethan as the three groups of Temple singers (1 Chron. 6:33–48). The members of the group of Korah were also gatekeepers (1 Chron. 9:19; 26:1,19) and bakers of sacrificial cakes (9:31).

5. A son of Hebron in the lineage of Caleb (1 Chron. 2:43). *6.* Possibly a town in Judah near Hebron. The five Korahites who joined David at Ziklag may have been persons from this town (1 Chron. 12:6). However, since these five men are also identified as Benjamites (1 Chron. 12:2), they may have been from a town of this same name whose location has yet to be determined.

Mike Mitchell and Phil Logan

KORAHITES (Kôr' ȧ-hītes) Descendants of Korah who belonged to the Kohathite Levites. The name is also spelled Korathites (Num. 26:58) and Korhites (KJV). See *Kohathites; Korah.*

KORATHITE (Kō' răth-īte) Alternate spelling of Korahites. See *Korahites.*

KORAZIN (Kō-rā' zĭn) NIV spelling of Chorazin. See *Chorazin.*

KORHITES (Kôr' hīte) Alternate spelling of Korahites. See *Korahites.*

KORE (Kō' rė) Personal name meaning "one who proclaims." *1.* Son of Ebiasaph, a Levite of the family of Korah and father of Shallum and Meshelemiah, gatekeepers at the tabernacle (1 Chron. 9:19; 26:1). *2.* Son of Imnah, the Levite, keeper of the eastern gate, and appointed by Heze-

kiah to receive the freewill offerings and distribute them among the priests (2 Chron. 31:14). *3.* A mistake transliteration in 1 Chronicles 26:19 (KJV). The name should be Korah (see modern versions).

KOUM (Koüm) NIV and TEV spelling of *cumi.* NAS has *kum.* All three represent the Aramaic word which means "arise" in Mark 5:41.

KOZ (Kŏz) Personal name meaning "thorn." *1.* A member of the tribe of Judah (1 Chron. 4:8). He may have belonged to the priestly family of Hakkoz. *2.* The KJV transliterates the name Hakkoz in Ezra 2:61; Nehemiah 3:4,21; 7:63 with "Koz," apparently taking *Hak* to be the Hebrew article, "the." The person in these passages is probably the same as the person in 1 Chronicles 24:10. See *Hakkoz.*

KUB (Kŭb) TEV spelling of Chub. See *Chub; Libya.*

KUE (Kü' ě) Believed by many to be an ancient name for Cilicia. The name occurs in 1 Kings 10:28 and 2 Chronicles 1:16. The Masoretes (the Hebrew scholars who added the vowels to the Hebrew text which had been written only with consonants) did not seem to understand the reference and added vowels to the consonants which gave the reading now found in the KJV—"linen yarn." By adding different vowels to the consonants of the Hebrew text, modern Bible students read "from Kue." If the Masoretes and the KJV are correct, then Solomon imported horses and linen yarn from Egypt. If the NRSV, NAS, NIV, REB, and TEV are correct (which in all likelihood they are), then Solomon imported horses from Egypt and Kue—that is, Cilicia in southeast Asia Minor (see NEB which has the spelling Coa). Many think, further, that the Hebrew word translated as "Egypt" (*Mizraim*) should be translated as "Musri," a country in Asia Minor near Cilicia. From Egypt, Solomon acquired chariots (1 Kings 10:29). Thus, Solomon acted as the middle man, putting horses with chariots and exporting them to other kingdoms. This proved to be a very lucrative arrangement for Solomon. See *Cilicia; Mizraim; Musri; Solomon.*   *Phil Logan*

KUN (Kūn) TEV spelling of Cun or Chun. See *Cun.*

KUSHAIAH (Kū-shâi' ah) Personal name of unknown meaning. A Levite of the Merarite family listed as one of the sanctuary singers during the reign of David. His son Ethan was appointed as a chief assistant of Heman (1 Chron. 15:17). This same person is also listed under the name Kishi (1 Chron. 6:44).

L

Lion carving on a wall of the ruins of Baalbek (Heliopolis) in Lebanon.

LAADAH (Lā′ å dah) Personal name meaning, "throat" or "double chin." Member of tribe of Judah (1 Chron. 4:21).

LAADAN (Lā′ å dan) Personal name meaning, "throat" or "double chin." 1. Member of tribe of Ephraim (1 Chron. 7:26) and ancestor of Joshua. 2. Original ancestor of clan of Levites and son of Gershon (1 Chron. 23:7–9; 26:21), though elsewhere Gershon's son is named Libni. See *Libni*. Some suggest that Laadan originally belonged to family of Libni, but his clan became more prominent and overshadowed that of Libni in later times.

LABAN (Lā′ ban) Personal name meaning "white." 1. Rebekah's brother (Gen. 24:29) and father of Leah and Rachel (Gen. 29:16). Laban lived in the city of Nahor which was probably close to the metropolis of Haran. Laban is known primarily from Genesis 24; 29—31.

Laban was directly responsible for the betrothal of Rebekah to Isaac. After Abraham's steward related that he had come to find a wife for Isaac, Laban and his father give their permission for the marriage (Gen. 24: 50–51). Later, Jacob fled to his uncle Laban's house after stealing the blessing from Esau. Laban agreed to give his daughter, Rachel, as payment for Jacob's seven years of labor. However, Laban deceived Jacob making him marry the older daughter, Leah. After Jacob worked an additional seven years, Laban allowed him to marry Rachel (Gen. 29:15–30). See *Jacob*.

2. Town used to locate Moses' speeches in Deuteronomy (Deut. 1:1). It is sometimes identified with Libnah (Num. 33:20). See *Libnah*. Assyrian and Egyptian texts mention its location on Canaan's southern border perhaps near the brook of Egypt at Sheikh ez-Zuweid or the nearby tell Abu Seleimeh. See *Rebekah; Jacob; Leah; Rachel.*
Kenneth Craig

LABOR See *Work, Theology of.*

LACE An ornamental braid used as a trim. Blue or purple cords were used to fasten the high priest's breastpiece to the ephod (Ex. 28:28; 39:21) and the golden plate to his turban (Ex. 28:37; 39:31). The translation lace (KJV, RSV) is frequently replaced with cord (NAS, NIV, NRSV, TEV) or braid (REB). The underlying Hebrew term is used elsewhere for a belt or signet cord (Gen. 38:18), for the cords or tassels on the corners of garments (Num. 15:38), or for strands of fiber (Judg. 16:9).

LACHISH (Lā′ chĭsh) Place name meaning "obstinate." An important Old Testament city located in the Shephelah ("lowlands") southwest of Jerusalem. It has usually been identified in modern times with the archaeological site called tell ed-Duweir.

The same site has more recently come to be called tel Lachish. Lachish is also mentioned in ancient Egyptian, Assyrian and Babylonian records.

The earliest reference to Lachish is in the Amarna letters (about 1400 B.C.) It was evidently one of the important Canaanite cities of the time. The Hebrew army under Joshua's command defeated the king of Lachish, killed him and conquered his city (Josh. 10:5, 23,32–33). Later, Lachish was apportioned to the Tribe of Judah (Josh. 15:39). The next Biblical reference to Lachish comes in 2 Chronicles 11:9, from the reign of Rehoboam who "fortified the city." Lachish was also the city of refuge for Amaziah who fled there from Jerusalem to escape a conspiracy against him (2 Kings 14:19; 2 Chron. 25:27).

Lachish is perhaps most well known for the story of its siege and conquest in 701 B.C. at the hands of the Assyrian King Sennacherib (2 Kings 18; 2 Chron. 32; Isa. 36). Two later brief references appear (Jer. 34:7; Neh. 11:30).

The archaeological excavations at Lachish have been extensive and rewarding. They have shown occupation at Lachish from about 4000 B.C. to the time of its conquest by the Persian Empire (539–333 B.C.). The rich and varied finds represent almost all of the periods, but the chief interest for the student of the Bible centers on the periods beginning with the time of the Hebrew invasion of Canaan. Impressive archaeological evidence shows the city was destroyed during the period of the conquest related in the Book of Joshua, but the archaeological evidence does not indicate who the destroyers were. Some scholars date the Lachish destruction layer as late as 1150 B.C. on the basis of a cartouche of Rameses III of Egypt.

The biblical account of Sennacherib's conquest of Lachish in 701 B.C. is supported and amplified by Assyrian records of King Sennacherib's campaign (2 Kings 18; 2 Chron. 32; Isa. 36). This was graphically recorded in a large and elaborate bas relief on the walls of the royal palace in Nineveh. Presently housed in the British museum in London, these carvings show Assyrian soldiers attacking the walled city, the city inhabitants defending their city, soldiers killing some of the defenders, families with possessions being led away captive, and the king on his throne reviewing the spoils taken from the city. A replica of this relief may be found in the library of The Southern Baptist Theological Seminary in Louisville, KY.

The "Lachish Letters"—a group of messages in ancient Hebrew inscribed with ink on pottery sherds dating to around 590 B.C.—are among the most significant finds from Lachish. They provide important linguistic and historical information about this period.
Bruce C. Cresson

The definitive line of a wall at Lachish running from the south northeast up to the high place.

LADAN (Lā' dan) Modern translations' spelling of Laadan. See *Laadan.*

LADDER A series of steps used for ascent or descent. The Hebrew term may refer to steps carved out of rock or to steps constructed from wood, metal, stone, or even rope. The angels ascending and descending in Jacob's vision point to God's presence with Jacob (Gen. 28:12). Jesus' promise to Nathaniel points to Jesus as the one who incarnates God's presence (John 1:49–51).

LAEL (Lā' ĕl) Personal name meaning "belonging to God." Levite leader in clan of Gershon (Num. 3:24).

LAHAD (Lā' hăd) Personal name meaning "slow, lazybones." Member of tribe of Judah (1 Chron. 4:2).

LAHAIROI (Là hâiai' roî oi) See *Beer-Lahairoi.*

LAHMAM (Lăh' măm) Place name meaning "food" or "bread." Reading in many Hebrew manuscripts and early translations for Lahmas (Josh. 15:40). KJV, NRSV, TEV read Lahmam. Town in tribal territory of Judah near Lachish, possibly modern khirbet el-Lahm about two and a half miles south of Beth Gibrin.

LAHMAS (Lăh' màs) Place name perhaps meaning "violence." Reading of basic Hebrew manuscript (Josh. 15:40) adopted by REB, NIV, NAS. Possibly, early scribes confused final letter with similar appearing final "m" in Hebrew. See *Lahmam.*

LAHMI (Lăh' mī) Personal name meaning "my bread" or perhaps an abbreviated form of Bethlehemite. Brother of the giant Goliath. Elhanan the son of Jair killed him (1 Chron. 20:5). The parallel passage (2 Sam. 21:19) says Elhanan the Bethlehemite killed Goliath. Compare 1 Samuel 17. The Chronicler may have been using a text of Samuel which copyists had made difficult to read and have interpreted it to the best of his ability. Some interpreters think the present text of Samuel represents copyists' confusion with the Chronicler's text accurate. See *Elhanan; Goliath.*

LAISH (Lā' ĭsh) Personal and place name meaning "Strong" or "lion." The KJV form of Laishah. *1.* Father of Paltiel (Phalti in KJV) and father-in-law of Michal (King Saul's daughter) after she was given to David (1 Sam. 19:11–12; 25:44). Laish was from Gallim in Benjamin. *2.* Originally a Canaanite city in northern Palestine known for its carefree existence (Judg. 18:7). It was spied out by the Danites as a place for their dwelling after the Philistines forced them from the coastal region. After finding it suitable, the Danites invaded Laish and renamed the city and area Dan. See *Dan. 3.* Town apparently in tribal territory of Benjamin whose troubles from Assyrian invasion Isaiah mentioned (Isa. 10:30). Its location is not known. Modern translations read Laishah.

LAISHAH (Lā' ĭsh ah) Place name meaning "lioness" or "towards "Laish." City on military route from Bethel to Jerusalem which Isaiah warned of Assyrian army's approach (Isa. 10:30). It may be modern el-Esawijeh southwest of Anathoth or ras et-Tawil south of Geba. See *Laish.*

LAKE OF FIRE See *Hell; Eschatology; Fire.*

LAKE OF GENNESARET See *Gennesaret, Lake of; Galilee, Sea of.*

LAKKUM (Lăk' kŭm) Transliteration of modern translations for Lakum. See *Lakum.*

LAKUM (Lā' kŭm) Place name perhaps meaning "rising" or "fortification." Border town in tribal allotment of Naphtali (Josh. 19:33). It may be modern khirbet el-Mansurah near the southern end of the Sea of Galilee.

LAMA See *Eli, Eli, Lama Sabachthani.*

LAMB See *Animals; Sheep; Lamb of God.*

LAMB OF GOD John the Baptist identified Jesus as the Lamb of God who takes away the sin of the world (John 1:29,36). The meaning of this statement has been greatly discussed. Some regard "the Lamb of God" to be derived from an Aramaic phrase which could mean either "lamb of God" or "servant of God." John's testimony probably should be seen as a combination of both concepts. Acts 8:32–35 identifies Jesus as the servant of God whom Isaiah described as one "brought as a lamb to the slaughter" (Isa. 53:7), who "bare the sin of many" (Isa. 53:12), and who was an offering for sin (Isa. 53:10). The law for guilt offerings (Lev. 5:1—6:7) prescribed a lamb for atonement to be made before the Lord. Peter stressed this sacrificial motif when he described redemption accomplished with "the precious blood of Christ, as of a lamb without blemish and without spot" (1 Pet. 1:18). John's identification might also entail a reference to Jesus as the scapegoat sent into the wilderness on the Day of Atonement to bear the iniquities of the Israelites (Lev. 16) or to the Passover lamb (Ex. 12). Paul, in fact, referred to Christ as "our Passover" who has been sacrificed (1 Cor. 5:7). John 1:29, therefore, signifies the substitutionary, sacrificial suffering and death of Jesus, the Servant of God, by which redemption and forgiveness of sin are accomplished.

Revelation often refers to the exalted Christ as a

Lamb, but never as "the Lamb of God," nor with the same Greek word for "lamb" as used elsewhere in the New Testament. See *Atonement; Christ, Christology; Passover; Redeem, Redemption, Redeemer; Sacrifice and Offering; Servant of the Lord.*   *Barry Morgan*

LAME, LAMENESS A physical condition in which walking is difficult or impossible. In the Old Testament, lame animals were not acceptable sacrifices (Deut. 15:21; Mal. 1:8,13). The lame were prohibited from serving as priests though they were allowed to eat from the priests' provisions (Lev. 21:18). The Jebusites boasted that their stronghold of Jerusalem was so impregnable that even the blind and lame would be able to turn back David's troops (2 Sam. 5:6 NRSV, NIV). A proverb excluding the blind and lame from "the house" (that is, the Temple) is traced to the assault on Jerusalem (2 Sam. 5:8). In the New Testament, the healing of the lame forms an important part of Jesus' messianic work (Matt. 11:2–6; 15:29–31). By healing the lame in the Temple, Jesus restored these excluded ones to full participation in the worshiping community (Matt. 21:14). Acts tells of the early church continuing Jesus' healing ministry to the lame: Peter and John (Acts 3:2); Philip (8:7); Paul (14:8–10).

LAMECH (Lā′ mĕch) Personal name meaning "powerful." The son of Methuselah and father of Noah (Gen. 4:18; 5:25,29). He had two wives, Adah and Zillah, whose sons are credited with the rise of the nomadic way of life, music, and metalworking. Lamech is blamed with beginning polygamy (or bigamy) and the increase of sinful pride in the earth. The Song of Lamech (Gen. 4:23–24) is an ancient poem supporting unlimited revenge. Jesus may have had this in mind in teaching about unlimited forgiveness (Matt. 18:22).
                                        Mike Mitchell

LAMED (Là mĕd) The twelfth letter of the Hebrew alphabet used as a heading for Psalm 119:89–96. Each verse in this section of the Psalm begins with the letter *lamed.*

LAMENT See *Grief and Mourning; Lamentations; Psalms.*

LAMENTATIONS, BOOK OF (Lā mĕn tā′ tions) Twenty-fifth book of Bible preserving mourning over the fall of Jerusalem in 587 B.C. Lamentations are elegies or mournful poems which lament some great loss. The biblical Book of Lamentations is made up of such poems. The book contains five poems, each one comprising a chapter. The first four chapters are in acrostic form, where successive verses begin with successive letters of the Hebrew alphabet with slight variations.

An ancient tradition, dating back to the earliest Greek translation (about 250 B.C.), claims that Jeremiah is the author of Lamentations. However, the Hebrew text of the book does not make that claim. Factors which favor authorship by Jeremiah are the antiquity of the tradition associating him with the book, the similarity in tone between Lamentations and portions of Jeremiah's book (Jer. 8—9;14—15), and a similar perspective in Lamentations and Jeremiah as to the cause of the fall of Jerusalem (for example, Lam. 1:2–18; 2:14; 4:13–17; Jer. 2:18; 14:7; 16:10–12; 23:11–40; 37:5–10).

Factors which militate against Jeremianic authorship are differences in phraseology between the two books and differences in viewpoints on several issues. Lamentations 1:21–22 and 3:59–66 appear to be incongruent with Jeremiah's conviction that the Babylonians were functioning as God's instrument of judgment (Jer. 20:4–5). Lamentations 4:17 suggests that the author was expecting help from the Egyptians, a perspective which Jeremiah strongly opposed (Jer. 37:5–10). The view of Zedekiah, Judah's last king, in Lamentations 4:20 is also quite different from that found regarding him in Jeremiah 24:8–10. The evidence tends to favor the opinion that Lamentations was written by someone other than Jeremiah; however, Jeremianic authorship is not impossible. In either case the author was surely an eyewitness of the fall of Jerusalem.

Lamentations 1 mourns the misery resulting from the destruction of Jerusalem and explains that the desolation was God's judgment for the nation's sin. Lamentations 2 continues the lament over the ruin wrought by divine anger and calls the people to prayer. While Lamentations 3 further extends the mourning over Jerusalem's destruction, it also declares that God's steadfast love gives reason to hope that He will extend mercy in the future. In light of that hope the author calls for repentance. Lamentations 4 vividly pictures the horrors of the siege and fall of Jerusalem and places part of the blame for the judgment on the immoral prophets and priests of the city. Lamentations 5 summarizes the calamitous situation and closes with a prayer for restoration.

Lamentations served the Judeans as an expression of their grief, an explanation for the destruction, and a call for repentance and hope. The book warns modern readers that an immoral nation stands in danger of God's awesome judgment and that the only hope for survival is submission to God.

Outline

I. The Appalling Price of Sin (1:1–22)
   A. Description of punishment for sins (1:1–17)
   B. Admission of sin (1:18–20)
   C. Cry for vengeance (1:21–22)
II. God Is the One Who Punishes Sin (2:1–22)
   A. God has done as He said (2:1–17).

B. Call the people to repent (2:18–19).
C. Call on the Lord to relent (2:20–22).
III. A Personal Cry to God (3:1–66)
A. I am suffering (3:1–18).
B. I cry to God in hope (3:19–21).
C. God will hear and help (3:22–33).
D. God knows our unacceptable actions (3:34–36).
E God punishes unforgiven sin (3:37–54).
F. God will hear, respond, and require the enemy (3:55–66).
IV. A Graphic Portrayal of Suffering Caused by Sin (4:1–22)
V. A Plea to God (5:1–22)
A. Remember us, O God, (5:1–18).
B. Restore us, O God, (5:19–22).

Bob R. Ellis

LAMPS, LIGHTING, LAMPSTAND The system and articles used to illuminate homes in biblical times. Lamps are mentioned often in the Bible but seldom described. Archaeological excavations have provided numerous examples of these lighting implements used in ancient times, dating from before Abraham to after Christ. Lamps of the Old Testament period were made exclusively of pot-

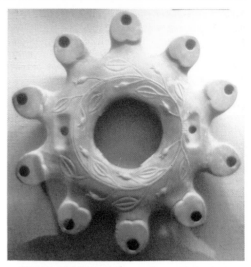

A multi-spout Roman oil lamp with ring-shaped oil chamber, made in Italy (first century A.D.).

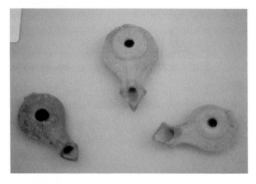

Three first-century B.C. pottery oil lamps.

tery. These lamps were of the open-bowl design with a pinched spout to support the wick. Wicks were made generally of twisted flax (Isa. 42:3). Lamps burned olive oil almost exclusively (Ex. 25:6), though in later times oil from nuts, fish, and other sources were used. Lamps from the Bronze Age to the Hellenistic times were made on the pottery wheel, after which molds were made for the enclosed forms of the Greek and Roman periods (about 500 B.C. onward). For outdoor lighting, the torch (KJV lantern) was used (Judg. 7:16; John 18:3).

A golden lampstand with three branches extending from either side of the central tier was placed in the tabernacle (Ex. 25:31–40). Each branch may have had a seven-spouted lamp (Zech. 4:2), as do some individual lamps found in Palestine. This seven-branched candelabra (menorah),

supporting seven lamps, continued in prominence through the first and second Temple periods, and later became symbolic of the nation Israel. Surrounding nations also employed multitiered and multilegged lamps and lampstands.

Lamps (lights) were used symbolically in the Old and New Testaments. Light depicted life in abundance, divine presence or life's direction versus death in darkness (compare Ps. 119:105; 1 John 1:5 with Job 18:5; Prov. 13:9). Jesus is depicted often in John as the light of the world (John 1:4–5,7–9; 3:19; 8:12; 9:5; 11:9–10; 12:35–36,46). Jesus' disciples are also described as the light of the world (Matt. 5:14–16). See *Light, Light of the World.*   *Dennis Cole*

LANCE, LANCET A weapon consisting of a long shaft with a metal head; javelin; spear (Judg. 5:8, NEB: 1 Kings 18:28, NAS, RSV; Jer. 50:42, KJV). In modern English, a lancet is a two-edged surgical instrument. The KJV used lancet for a small lance (1 Kings 18:28). See *Arms and Armor; Weapons.*

LAND OF FORGETFULNESS Description of Sheol (Ps. 88:12). See *Sheol.*

LAND, GROUND The dust of the earth and by extension the soil of territory controlled by a farmer, a tribe, a nation, or God's entire created world.

In Semitic languages, the root meaning of land or ground is "red plowed land." This implies land with a high iron content or similar coloring agent.

The land or ground as a material substance played an important role in ancient Hebrew thought. In Genesis 2 God formed the male half of humankind from dust of the ground. God breathed into the man's nostrils the breath of life, and he became a living creature (Gen. 2:7). God is pictured as using dry, loose material on the surface of the ground from which He, like a potter, formed man. There is a play on words in the Hebrew text here: 'adam (the Hebrew word for "humankind") was made from 'adamah (the Hebrew word for "ground"). Every beast and every bird was also formed from the ground (Gen. 2:19)

After sin entered the Garden of Eden, God described death in terms of the basic elements from which Adam was created: Adam would work and eat "til thou return unto the ground; for out of it wast thou taken; for dust thou art, and unto dust shalt thou return" (Gen. 3:19). The creation accounts ("You are dust or ground") thus point to the close connection of person and body.

The bold statement that humankind was made from the dust of the ground must be balanced against the statement that humankind was created in the image of God (Gen. 1:26–27). The Bible indicates that humankind as unique creatures do survive death through resurrection (John 5:28–29; Phil. 1:21–24; 2 Cor. 5:1).

In the Old Testament, an altar was important in worshiping the Lord. Exodus 20:24–25 shows altars made of two materials—ground or earth (vs. 24) and stones (vs. 25). The stone altars were not to be hewn, that is cut with a tool. The passage seems to favor altars made of ground.

The surface of the ground must be tilled to produce food. In the beginning of Genesis 2, the writer pictured the earth with nothing growing, with no rain, and with no one to till the ground (Gen. 2:5). After the fall (Gen. 3), God sent Adam and Eve away from the garden. Adam was to till the ground from which he was taken (Gen. 3:23). Cain, the firstborn son of Adam and Eve, became a tiller of the ground (Gen. 4:2–10). His offering from the fruit of the ground was not accepted by the Lord, while Abel's offering of the firstling of his flock was accepted. Cain responded by murdering his brother. The ground that formerly produced for Cain now protested the blood of Abel that fell upon it (Gen. 4:10). As a punishment, God cursed the ground where Cain was concerned so that it would no longer produce for him (Gen. 4:12).

Note how intimately ground and people are connected. God is a vital part of this connection. If His people hearken to his commands, He will bless the ground which will then produce grain, wine, and oil. This contributes to their total well-being (Deut. 7:13).

Ground or land as property During the severe famine in Egypt, the Egyptians used all their money and sold all their cattle to Joseph for food (Gen. 47:13–17). The next year, when they needed more food but had no more money or cattle, they sold themselves and their lands to Joseph. Ten times this narrative designates their individual lands or grounds as 'adhamah (ground

or land) (Gen. 47:18–23). In Genesis 47:20, the totality of their former lands that had been turned over to Pharaoh is called 'erets (meaning earth or land). In this crisis, the Egyptians lost their lands and their freedom. Note the close association between property and persons.

Ground with its produce as the sphere of living A series of blessings and curses is part of Deuteronomy 28:4,11,18,33,42,51. The people, their land, and the ground where they live will be affected by their obedience or disobedience. Faithfulness to God affects the very land where people live.

The importance of the concept of land for the ancient Hebrews is also seen in Job's final speech defending his integrity at the close of his dialogues with his three friends. He used as a witness his property and how he handled it. He said his land or ground would cry out if he did not rightly pay his workers or if, to increase his own lands, he had exploited or destroyed those who owned land around him (Job 31:38–40). The implication here is that the ground was fruitful because Job had been faithful to God and God had blessed his land (compare Deut. 28,4,11,18,33,42,51).

Qualities of Ground or Land Israel's land was a *good* land from which Israel could be removed because of disobedience (Josh. 23:13,15). Amos threatened Israel with exile to a *polluted* land (Amos 7:17). Israel's land was also called a fat or rich land when they came into it (Neh. 9:25). When Moses investigated the burning bush, he learned that the ground upon which he stood was ground of *holiness* (Ex. 3:5). The people of Judah in captivity in Babylon had difficulty singing their songs in a strange or foreign land (Ps. 137:4). These and many other qualities depend on circumstances that affect the land and the people.

Whole inhabited earth—a ground where people live This unusual universalizing of ground is found in two of the most important texts of the Old Testament. God told Abraham that all the families of the inhabited earth would be blessed in him (Gen. 12:3). This is enigmatic: God did not tell Abraham *how* they would be blessed. God said the same thing to Jacob (Gen. 28:14): Through what God did in Abraham's family, blessing would come to all families of the inhabited earth. On the other hand, God's punishment would also be over the whole inhabited earth. "In that day, that the Lord shall punish . . . and the kings of the earth (ground) upon earth (ground) (Isa. 24:21). In the New Testament, Revelation expands on this apocalyptic theme. All human families in the ground where they dwell determine their destiny in terms of what God did in Abraham's posterity—Christ.

A. Berkeley Mickelsen

LANDMARK A pillar or heap of stones serving as a boundary marker (Gen. 31:51–52). Some Babylonian and Egyptian examples are elaborately carved. Many ancient law codes (Babylonian, Egyptian, Greek, Roman) prohibited the removal of a landmark (Deut. 19:14; compare 27:17; Prov. 22:28). In Job 24:2, removal of a marker parallels theft. Proverbs 23:10 warns against removing markers to rob orphans. Hosea 5:10 condemns the ruthless rulers of Judah as like those who remove landmarks, that is, those who have no regard for justice or for the traditional law. Moving the landmark meant changing the traditional land allotments (compare Josh. 13—19) and cheating a poor landowner of what little land he owned.

LANE A narrow, constricted passageway. In English, *lane* evokes the image of a rural path between hedges or fences. The Greek Term is used for a city alley (Luke 14:21, KJV, NAS, NRSV; alley, NIV, REB, TEV). Compare Acts 9:11; 12:10 where the same Greek term is used.

LANGUAGE, CONFUSION OF See *Babel; Pentecost.*

LANGUAGES OF THE BIBLE The Old Testament was first written in Hebrew, with the exceptions of much of Ezra 4—7 and Daniel 2:4b—7:28, which appear in Aramaic. The New Testament was written in Greek, though Jesus and the early believers may have spoken Aramaic.
Characteristics of Hebrew Hebrew is a Semitic language related to Phoenician and the dialects of ancient Canaan. Semitic languages have the ability to convey abundant meaning through few words. Importance rests on the verb, which generally comes first in the sentence because action is the most significant element. Similarly, modifiers (such as adjectives) follow nouns, lending greater weight to the nouns. Typical word order for a sentence is: verb—subject—subject modifiers—object—object modifiers. Deviation from this order gives emphasis to the word which comes first.
Characteristics of Aramaic Aramaic is akin to Hebrew and shares a considerable vocabulary with it. It began as the language of Syria and was gradually adopted as the language of international communication. After about 600 B.C., it replaced Hebrew as the spoken language of Palestine. Hebrew then continued as the religious language of the Jews, but the Aramaic alphabet was borrowed for writing it.
Characteristics of Greek Greek belongs to the Indo-European language group. It spread throughout the Mediterranean world after about 335 B.C. with Alexander's conquests. The New Testament is written in a dialect called *koinē* (meaning "common") which was the dialect of the common person. New Testament Greek is heavily infused with Semitic thought modes, and many Aramaic words are found rendered with Greek letters (for example, *talitha cumi*, Mark 5:41; *ephphatha*, Mark

7:34; *Eli, Eli, lama sabachthani,* Mark 15:34; *marana-tha,* 1 Cor. 16:22). So also are such Latin words as "kenturion" (centurion) and "denarion" (denarius). Greek's accurateness of expression and widespread usage made it the ideal tongue for the early communication of the gospel. Paul no doubt knew all three biblical languages, and Latin as well. See *Alphabet; Aramaic; Daniel, Book of; Ezra, Book of; Greek; Hebrew. Larry McKinney*

LANTERN Portable container with transparent openings used to display and protect a light. The Greek term used at John 18:3 is of uncertain meaning, though some type of light is clearly intended. In John's ironic scene, the mob comes with "artificial" lights to arrest Jesus, "the light of the world" (John 8:12; 9:5; 11:9; 12:35–36,40).

LAODICEA (Lā ŏd ĭ cē′ à) A city in southwest Asia Minor on an ancient highway running from Ephesus to Syria ten miles west of Colossae and six miles south of Hierapolis. Christian communities existed in all three cities (Col. 2:1; 4:13–16), though the one in Colossae is the best known. Paul wrote a letter to the Laodiceans (Col. 4:16) which has not survived, though some scholars have attempted to identify this missing letter with either of the Books of Ephesians or Philemon.

Laodicea was well known in the ancient world for its wealth. The extent of its wealth is illustrated by the fact that Laodicea was rebuilt without the financial help of Rome after the disastrous earthquake of A.D. 60. Laodicea earned its wealth in the textile industry in the production of black wool and in the banking industry. Laodicea was also known for its medical school which concocted a spice nard for the treatment of ears and an eyesalve. The major weakness of Laodicea was its lack of a water supply. This need was met by bringing water six miles north from Denizli through a system of stone pipes (another sign of Laodicea's wealth).

Laodicea is best known today to readers of Revelation where Jesus criticized Laodicea, using imagery drawn from its daily life (Rev. 3:14–22).

Exterior view of the archways in the top tier of one of the great theaters at ancient Laodicea.

An unexcavated Roman theater, the smaller of the two theaters at ancient Laodicea.

First, Jesus said Laodicea is neither cold (like the cold, pure waters of Colossae) nor hot (like the therapeutic hot springs of Hierapolis). Laodicea is lukewarm and provides neither refreshment for the spiritually weary nor healing for the spiritually sick (Rev. 3:15–16). Despite their apparent spiritual uselessness, the Laodiceans were claiming a spiritual wealth equal to their material wealth; and further, they were claiming to have acquired both by their own efforts. In reality, however, the Laodiceans, while they may have had material wealth, were spiritually poor, blind, and naked (Rev. 3:17)—an obvious reference to the textile and banking industry and medical school of Laodicea. According to Jesus, what the Laodiceans needed more than anything else was the true gold, white (not black) garments, and eyesalve that only Christ could give (Rev. 3:18). A true spiritual foundation is laid only in Christ, not human effort.

Archaeological remains of an early church located at Laodicea in Turkey.

The letter of the risen Christ to the church at Laodicea (Rev. 3:14–22) contains numerous allusions to conditions in the city. A five-mile-long aqueduct supplied the city with tepid water that served as an image for "lukewarm" Christianity (3:15–16). The Laodicean claim to be rich and prosperous reflects the self-reliant refusal of this city to accept Roman aid for rebuilding after an earthquake of about A.D. 60 (3:17). The charge that the Laodicean Christians were naked, blind, and in need of clothing and eyesalve (3:17–18) reflects the city's well-known school of opthalmology and its fine garments of raven-black wool of local sheep.   *Phil Logan*

LAODICEAN (Lā ŏd ĭ cē′ an) Citizen of Laodicea. See *Laodicea.*

LAODICEANS, EPISTLE TO THE A short letter claiming Paul as its author. The letter was doubtless composed to fill in the gap suggested by Colossians 4:16. The date of writing is unknown. Jerome (340?–420) warned against this spurious work. Despite Jerome's protests, the letter was accepted as a genuine Pauline Epistle by Pope Gregory the Great (590–604). About one half of the Latin manuscripts of the Pauline Epistles produced between 500 and 1600 contain the Epistle to the Laodiceans. With the Reformation, the epistle quickly fell into disuse. The epistle was perhaps composed in Greek, though it survives only in Latin. Its 247 words are a patchwork of passages drawn from the authentic Pauline letters, chiefly Philippians, but also Galatians, 1 and 2 Corinthians, and 1 and 2 Timothy. There are also echoes of Matthew and 2 Peter.

LAP (Noun) (1) A loose panel or hanging flap in a garment; (2) the skirt of a robe; (3) the front part of the lower trunk and the upper part of the thighs of a seated person. Second Kings 4:39 uses lap in sense 1. This sense is also common in figurative passages concerning reward and retribution (Isa. 65:6,7; Jer. 32:18, NIV, NRSV). Sense 2 is perhaps intended at Nehemiah 5:13, though sense 1 is possible (so NIV, NRSV). KJV did not use lap in sense 3. Compare Judges 16:19 (NIV); Ruth 4:16 (NAS, NIV); 2 Kings 4:20 (NAS, NIV, RSV). The NIV frequently replaces bosom with lap (for example, Prov. 6:27; Eccl. 7:9).

LAP (Verb) To drink by licking up liquid with the tongue in the manner of a dog (Judg. 7:5–7). Gideon was to separate those who drank by cupping water in their hands and then lapping it up, still keeping watch, from those who knelt down to drink.

LAPIDOTH (Lă′ pĭ dōth) Personal name meaning "lightnings." Deborah's husband (Judg. 4:4).

LAPIS LAZULI See *Minerals and Metals.*

LAPPIDOTH (Lăp′ pĭ dōth) Transliteration in modern translations for Lapidoth. See *Lapidoth.*

LAPWING (*Vanellus vanellus*) A shore bird with a short bill and crest of feathers on its head. The

A gold staff terminal decorated with lapis lazuli lion heads.

lapwing is known for its irregular flapping flight and shrill cry. The KJV included the lapwing among the unclean birds (Lev. 11:19; Deut. 14:18). Modern translations generally identify the Hebrew term with the hoopoe.

LARGE LAND See *Broad Place.*

LARGE PLACE See *Broad Place.*

LARGE ROOM See *Broad Place.*

LASCIVIOUSNESS KJV term for an unbridled expression of sexual urges (Mark 7:22; 2 Cor. 12:21; Gal. 5:19; Eph. 4:19; 1 Pet. 4:3; Jude 4). RSV translated the underlying Greek as licentiousness; the NAS, as sensuality. Other translations used a variety of terms: debauchery; indecency; lewdness; sexual sin.

LASEA (Là sē´ à) Place name of uncertain meaning. City on south coast of Crete (Acts 27:8).

LASHA (Lā´ shà) Place name of uncertain meaning. A point on the original border of Canaan (Gen. 10:19). The traditional location is at Kallirhoe east of the Dead Sea; others identify it with Nuhashe or Laash in northern Syria near Hamath. The exact meaning of the prepositions and the direction of the borders are not clear.

LASHARON (Là shâ rōn) Place name meaning, "belonging to Sharon." Listed as one of towns whose king Joshua killed in conquering Canaan (Josh. 12:18). The early Greek translators had great difficulty with the text, some Greek manuscripts omitting the verse altogether. *L* represents the Hebrew preposition "of, to, belonging to." Sharon is the name of the plain in which the preceding town Aphek in the list is located. The original Hebrew text may have indicated Aphek in Sharon to distinguish it from other Apheks. See *Aphek.*

LAST DAY, LAST TIME See *Eschatology; Judgment Day.*

THE LAST SUPPER The last meal Jesus shared with His disciples before the crucifixion. All four Gospels link this meal with Jesus' sacrificial death. The first three Gospels picture Christ's death in the symbols of the broken bread ("This is my body which is given for you" Luke 22:19) and the outpoured wine ("This is my blood of the new testament, which is shed for many for the remission of sins" Matt. 26:28). In John, footwashing replaces the "breaking of bread" as the picture of Christ's humble acceptance of His servant role (John 13:4–20), anticipating His death on the cross which made cleansing from sin and fellowship with Him possible (John 13:8,10). See *Footwashing.*

The supper not only anticipated Christ's death but also His victory over death in the promise of His drinking wine anew in the Father's kingdom (Matt. 26:29; Mark 14:25; Luke 22:18; compare 1 Cor. 11:26). Also prominent in all four Gospels is Jesus' prediction of His betrayal by Judas (Matt. 26:21–24; Mark 14:18–21; Luke 22:21–22; John 13:21). According to the Synoptics, the Last Supper was the Passover meal (Matt. 26:17–19; Mark 14:12,16; Luke 22:7,13). In John, the last meal preceded the Passover celebration (John 13:1; John 18:28). In John, Jesus was crucified on the day of preparation at the time when lambs were slaughtered (John 19:14). The tension in the timing of Christ's death should not detract from the united New Testament witness that "Christ our passover is sacrificed for us" (1 Cor. 5:7). See *Lord's Supper; Ordinances.*

LATCHET KJV term for a leather thong or strap used to fasten sandals (Gen. 14:23; Isa. 5:27; Mark 1:7; Luke 3:16; John 1:27). According to the rabbis, untying sandals was a slave's task that could not be required of a disciple. John the Baptist thus claimed for himself a position lower than that of a slave before Jesus.

LATIN (Lă´ tĭn) Language of ancient Italy and the Roman Empire and thus one of languages in which the inscription over Christ's cross was written (John 19:20).

A stone slab inscribed with Latin found at Philippi.

LATIN See *The Bible, Texts and Versions.*

LATRINE A receptacle, generally a pit, used as a toilet (2 Kings 10:27; KJV draught house). Jehu demonstrated his utter contempt for Baal by ordering that his temple be destroyed and converted into a latrine.

The public latrine of ancient Ephesus.

LATTER DAYS See *Eschatology; Judgment Day.*

LATTICE A structure of crisscrossed strips. Lattices were used as window covering to allow some

An iron lattice over a window in ancient Pompeii dating from the first century A.D.

light to penetrate while keeping heat and rain to a minimum (Judg. 5:28; 2 Kings 1:2; Prov. 7:6, KJV casement; Song of Sol. 2:9). According to one interpretation, in Ezekiel's Temple vision the windows were latticed (Ezek. 41:16,26, NAS). Other translations describe the windows as covered. The NAS also spoke of the lattices of the doves (Isa. 60:8). Other translations use home (TEV), nests (NIV), dovecots (REB), or windows (KJV, NRSV).

LAUGH To express joy or scorn with a chuckle or explosive sound. Laughter is central to the account of the birth of Isaac. Both Abraham (Gen. 17:17) and Sarah (18:12) laughed in contempt and disbelief at God's promise that Sarah would bear a son. The name Isaac (from the Hebrew word for laughter) served as a joyful reminder that the last laugh was on those slow to believe (Gen. 21:3,6). Laughter can serve as a sign of contempt (Gen. 38:23; 2 Chron. 30:10; Job. 22:19) or of confidence (Job 5:22; 39:18,22 NAS). References to God's laughing at the wicked demonstrate God's confident contempt (Pss. 2:4; 37:13; 59:8). Laughter is frequently contrasted with signs of mourning (Job 8:21; Ps. 126:2; Luke 6:21,25). Though Hebrew wisdom recognized a time to laugh as part of God's ordering of time (Eccl. 3:4), wisdom downplayed the value of laughter, associating it with fools (Prov. 29:9; Eccl. 7:4,6), calling it madness (Eccl. 2:2), and finding sorrow preferable (Eccl. 7:3).

LAUNDERER See *Fuller; Occupations and Professions in the Bible.*

LAUREL Garlands of leaves from the laurel or bay tree (*Laurus nobilis*) were used by the Greeks to honor the winners of the Pythian games. The leaves of the tree were also used for medicine and seasoning. In Psalm 37:35, the wicked are compared to a "green bay tree" (KJV). NAS, REB, and NIV refer to a tree in its native soil. NRSV and TEV find a reference to the towering cedars of Lebanon.

LAVER A large basin or bowl used in purification rites. The Old Testament describes the lavers used in the tabernacle and in Solomon's Temple. The bronze laver of the tabernacle was constructed from metal mirrors provided by the women who ministered at the tabernacle entrance (Ex. 38:8). The priests used the laver for washing their hands and feet before priestly service (Ex. 30:18; 40:30–31). Levites also used water from this laver to purify themselves (Num. 8:7). Solomon's Temple employed a large laver, the molten sea (1 Kings 7:23–26; 2 Chron. 4:2–5), and ten smaller lavers (1 Kings 7:38–39; 2 Chron. 4:6). The priests washed in the molten sea. The ten lavers were used for washing sacrifices (1 Chron. 4:6). See *Sea, Molten; Temple.*

LAW, ADMINISTRATION OF See *Court System; Judges; Sanhedrin.*

LAW, ROMAN See *Roman Law.*

LAW, TEN COMMANDMENTS, TORAH Law refers both to the revelation of the will of God in the Old Testament and to the later elaboration on the law referred to as the "traditions of the elders" in the New Testament (for example, Mark 7:5).

Law is one of the primary concepts in the Bible. The specific translation of the term law is varied. It may be used for a commandment, a word, a decree, a judgment, a custom, or a prohibition. The first five books of the Bible (the Pentateuch) are known as books of the Law because they are based on the commandments which God revealed to Moses.

The Hebrew term most frequently translated "law" in the Old Testament is *torah,* used more than 200 times. The central idea of *torah* is that of instruction received from a superior authority on how to live. *Torah* in the Old Testament came to mean the way of life for faithful Israelites. The Torah is more than just "laws"; it includes the story of God's dealing with humankind and with Israel.

The concept of *torah* is closely linked to that of covenant in the Old Testament. The covenant agreement between God and His people at Mount Sinai provided the foundation for all of Israel's laws. God, the deliverer of the Israelites from Egypt, set forth His instructions for His people. They were to obey God's laws because of what He had done for them in saving them from Egypt (Ex. 20:2). The laws found in Exodus, Deuteronomy, Numbers, and Leviticus cover all areas of community life. The Torah is a gift of God to His people. Obeying the Torah would result in His blessing (Ex. 19:5,6). Following the Law would provide for the health and wholeness of the covenant community. The Ten Commandments are a summary of the Law (Ex. 20:2–17; Deut. 5:6–21).

Later development in Israel's history gave an expanded meaning to *torah.* By New Testament times *torah* meant not only the Old Testament Scriptures (the written Law), but also the oral law (unwritten law) of Israel as well. The religious leaders developed in applying the written Law to new life situations. This oral law is sometimes referred to as "the tradition of the elders" in the New Testament (compare Matt. 15:2; Mark 7:5; Gal. 1:14).

Two kinds of laws can be found in the Old Testament. First are broad categorical laws which set forth general principles. These laws do not specify how they are to be enforced or what penalities are to be invoked. The Ten Commandments are representative of this kind of law. They are basic policy statements for life in a covenant community with God.

Second are case laws. These laws often begin with an "if" or a "when," usually deal with very specific situations. Many times they indicate a punishment for breaking the law (e.g., Ex. 21:2,3,4; 22:1,2,4,5,25).

The Ten Commandments are prohibitions (except for Commandments 4 and 5 in Ex. 20:8–11,12). These ten laws define negatively the heart of the covenant relationship between God and Israel. The first four Commandments are related to one's relationship with God. The next six Commandments have to do with human relationships. It is important to note that right relationships with others follow being rightly related to God. Being rightly related to God compels one towards right relationships to one's neighbors. Here one can see the wonderful balance that is maintained in the Law. Duties to God and to other human beings are not separated.

The Ten Commandments were not given only for the Hebrew people but are abiding laws for all people. Some of the laws of the Bible seem to apply only to specific times, places, and persons, but the Ten Commandments have an abiding quality about them. They convey duties for everyone and reveal to us the basic morality required by God. While the Ten Commandments have universal validity, they are truly significant only when persons are committed to the God behind them. What makes the Ten Commandments unique is the character of the God who gave them. Without God, the Commandments lose their distinctiveness.

Jesus certainly knew the Law and often referred to it. It is possible to say that Jesus was both a critic of the Law and a supporter of it. He was critical of the law if one means "the tradition of the elders" or the oral laws that had grown up around the written Law. The enemies of Jesus frequently accused Him of violating the Law. It is clear that keeping the letter of the Law had become more important to some of the Jews than the purpose behind the Law.

On several occasions Jesus set His own teachings over against those of the elders (Matt. 5:21–6:48). The Pharisees accused Jesus and His disciples of not following the law with regard to "unclean" things (Matt. 15:1–20), and they accused Him of eating with tax-gatherers and sinners (Matt. 9:11). Jesus' greatest conflict came over the sabbath. He rejected their interpretation of the sabbath Law and said that the Son of man is Lord of the sabbath (Matt. 12:8); that the sabbath was made for man and not man for the sabbath (Mark 2:27); and He taught that it was permissible to do good on the sabbath (Mark 3:4).

Jesus inaugurated a new era in which the Law as understood by the Jews of His day would no longer be the guiding principle for the kingdom of God (Luke 16:16). Nevertheless, Jesus claimed not to have come to destroy the Law, but to fulfill it (Matt. 5:17–20). That is, Jesus moved the understanding of the Law from its external, legalistic meaning to its spiritual one. Moving from outward observance to inward motivation and intention is Jesus' concern (Matt. 5:21,22,27,28). He pushes the Law out to its ultimate meaning (thus filling it full). In this sense Jesus affirmed the heart and the spirit of the Law. He moved to a deeper level of meaning, to the spirit behind the Law which God had intended from the beginning.

Jesus did not give us a new law. When Jesus was asked which commandment is the greatest, He said, "Thou shalt love the Lord thy God with all thy heart, and with all thy soul and with all thy mind " (Matt. 22:36,37). Jesus said the second commandment is like the first, "Thou shalt love thy neighbor as thyself" (Matt. 22:39). Then He said, "On these two commandments hang all the Law and the Prophets" (Matt. 22:40). Incredibly, Jesus summed up the whole Law and the teaching of the prophets with these two commandments. Behind all of the Law had stood these two great principles of love for God and neighbor. It is important for us to remember that love can never be adequately portrayed in rules or in teachings. It can be seen in the life, death, and resurrection of our Lord. The commandments to love had been there all along; Jesus simply emphasized them in a way that would forever change how we should look at them.

Paul had a lifelong struggle with the Law. By the term "law," Paul meant the Law of God as contained in the Old Testament. He also spoke of a kind of natural law which existed in human beings (Rom. 7:23,25). The "law of sin" meant conduct determined by sin. Paul also used law in this sense when he referred to the "law of faith"—that is, conduct determined by faith in God (Rom. 3:27–28).

Paul's attitude toward the Mosaic Law can be summarized under several main points. First of all, he recognized that the Law had been given for a good purpose; it was holy, just and good (Rom. 7:12,14; 1 Tim. 1:8). The demands of the Law were not evil, but had the effect of pointing out the sin of human beings (Rom. 7:7). Because of man's sinfulness, the Law became a curse instead of a blessing (Gal. 3:10–13).

Second, Paul believed the Law was given for a good purpose, but it could not save (Gal. 3:11; Rom. 3:20). If persons were to become children of God, it would be by means other than keeping the Law. The third theme we find in Paul is that Christ freed us from the requirements of the Law by His death and resurrection (Rom. 8:3,4). Therefore, Christ has become the end of the Law for Christians (Rom. 10:4), and it is faith that saves and not Law (Eph. 2:8,9).

Paul, like Jesus, saw the Law fulfilled in the command to love (Rom. 13:8; Gal. 5:13). Only with the aid of the Spirit of God can we meet the requirement to love which fulfills the Law (Gal. 5:16; Rom. 8). Paul saw the Law as no longer to be viewed legalistically. Nevertheless, it is still the revelation of God, and it helps us to understand the nature of our life in Christ (Rom. 8:3; 13:8–10; Gal. 3:24).   *D. Glenn Saul*

LAWGIVER One who gives a code of law to a people (Isa. 33:22; Jas. 4:12). The KJV used lawgiver seven times. Modern translations replace lawgiver with sceptor four times (Gen. 49:10; Num. 21:18; Pss. 60:7; 108:8). At Deuteronomy 33:21 modern translations replace lawgiver with commander (NRSV), leader (NIV), ruler (NAS, REB), or an equivalent. The remaining two cases (Isa. 33:22; Jas. 4:12) identify God as lawgiver. Contrary to popular opinion, Scripture never expressly identifies Moses as "lawgiver." The earliest Greek translation twice identified God as lawgiver (Ps. 9:21; 2 Esdras 7:89) and used the verb *nomotheteō* (to give law) with God as its subject seven times (Ex. 24:12; Pss. 24:8,12; 26:11; 83:7; 118:33,102). Once the Levitical priests are the subject (Deut. 17:10; compare Heb. 7:11). The closest Scripture comes to identifying Moses as lawgiver is the question of John 7:19 ("Did not Moses give you the law?"). The New Testament more often identifies Moses as the intermediary through whom the law was given (John 1:17; Gal. 3:19). The Epistle of Aristeas is unique among Hellenistic Jewish literature in expressly identifying Moses as the lawgiver (131,148,312).

Christ is sometimes regarded as the "second Moses" or "second lawgiver," though the New Testament does not expressly identify Him as such. Rather the New Testament designates Christ as the One who fulfills the law (Matt. 5:17) or is the end of the law (Rom. 10:4; compare 7:4–6; 8:3–4). Christ does however set a new standard for judgment (Matt. 5:21) and gives a new commandment (John 13:34; 14:15,21; 15:10,12; 1 John 2:3,4,7,8).

LAWLESS, LAWLESSNESS Term used by modern translations to describe people not restrained or controlled by law, especially God's law. As rebellion against God, sin is lawlessness (1 John 3:4; compare 2 Thess. 3:4). Those responsible for Christ's death are characterized as lawless (Acts 2:23) as are Gentiles in their idolatry (1 Pet. 4:3). The leader of the eschatological (end-time) rebellion is called the man of lawlessness (2 Thess. 2:3; compare 2:8). The lawless one is already at work but is presently restrained (2:6–7). The lawless one will be revealed before the return of Christ who will slay him with His breath (2:8).

LAWYER An authoritative interpreter of the Mosaic law. Characterization of the lawyers is especially harsh in Luke's Gospel: they rejected God's purpose for themselves by refusing John's baptism

(7:30); they burdened others without offering any relief (11:45–46); they not only refused God's offer of salvation but hindered others from accepting it (11:52); they refused to answer Jesus' question concerning the legality of sabbath healing (14:3). Lawyer is used in the general sense of a jurist at Titus 3:13.

LAYING ON OF HANDS A ritual act wherein hands are placed on a person or animal in order to establish some spiritual communion.

Old Testament Laying on of hands is primarily associated in the Old Testament with the sacrifices prescribed in the Law. An Israelite making a burnt offering was to lay his hand on the animal's head that it might be an acceptable sacrifice for his atonement (Lev. 1:4; 8:18). Peace offerings (Lev. 3:2–13) and sin offerings (Lev. 4:4–33; 8:14) were made in the same way, as were the offering of the "ram of consecration" or ordination (Lev. 8:22) and the sin offering on the annual day of atonement (Lev. 16:21).

To lay hands on the sacrificial animal was a means of transferring one's iniquity to the animal (Lev. 16:22). Sins of the congregation were transferred by the elders (Lev. 4:15) or the high priest (Lev. 16:21) as the people's representatives. Later the king and princes acted on behalf of the nation (2 Chron. 29:20–24). When the Levites were presented to the Lord as a wave offering from the Israelites, the whole assembly laid hands on them (Num. 8:10). The sin of blasphemy was viewed as so severe that all who overheard one cursing the name of the Lord laid their hands on his head prior to stoning him to death (Lev. 24:14–16). While the primary texts convey little of the spiritual meaning of these rituals, later Old Testament texts emphasize the importance of "a broken spirit: a broken and a contrite heart" (Ps. 51:17).

The act of laying on of hands had other meanings in the Old Testament. Jacob ("Israel") blessed Ephraim and Manasseh by laying his hands on their heads (Gen. 48:13–20), and the psalmist celebrated the Lord's protection as a blessing bestowed by God's having "laid thine hand upon me" (Ps. 139:5). Job longed for someone who could arbitrate between himself and God by laying "his hand upon us both" (Job 9:33). Moses commissioned Joshua and transferred some of his authority to him by the laying on of hands (Num. 27:18–23; Deut. 34:9). Elisha laid his hands on King Joash's hands as a prophetic act signifying God's promise to provide Israel victory over Syria (2 Kings 13:16). In addition, the Old Testament frequently uses the image of laying hands on someone as an act of arrest, capture, or violence (Gen. 27:22; Ex. 22:11; 2 Chron. 23:15; Esther 2:21).

New Testament The most frequent usage of the expression in the New Testament relates to the arrest or capture of someone (Matt. 26:50; Mark 14:46; Luke 21:12; John 7:44; Acts 4:3; 12:1).

In contrast, miraculous healing accompanied the laying on of hands. Jesus healed a blind man (Mark 8:23–25), the sick (Mark 6:5; Luke 4:40), and a woman with "a spirit of infirmity" (Luke 13:11–13) by laying hands on them. This seems to have been a characteristic means of healing (Mark 5:23), and Jesus' disciples continued the practice (Mark 16:18; Acts 9:12–17; 28:8). Some view healing by laying on of hands as an extension of the Old Testament blessing. A more explicit example of this is Jesus' laying hands on children to bless them (Mark 10:16; Matt. 19:13–15).

Acts introduces the dynamic but fluid practice of the early church. Acts 6 relates the selection of seven men who were put in charge of the daily service to the widows of the Jerusalem congregation. These men were chosen by the congregation, brought before the apostles, and, after prayer, had hands (whether the congregation's or the apostles' is unclear) laid on them. Fasting, prayer, and the laying on of hands also accompanied the appointment of Barnabas and Saul to their missionary endeavor (Acts 13:3). Peter and John laid hands on baptized believers in Samaria so they might receive the Holy Spirit (Acts 8:14–19). Paul did the same for some disciples at Ephesus who had been baptized into John the Baptist's baptism (Acts 19:6). These disciples began speaking in tongues and prophesying as evidence of the Holy Spirit.

In 1 and 2 Timothy Paul wrote of Timothy's having been given a spiritual gift by prophecy with the laying on of the hands of the assembly of elders (1 Tim. 4:14). He also referred to a gift of God that was in Timothy through the laying on of Paul's hands (2 Tim. 1:6). Paul warned against laying hands on any one hastily (1 Tim. 5:22).

Hebrews classified laying on of hands among the elementary teachings that persons of maturity must leave behind (Heb. 6:2).   *Michael Fink*

LAZARUS (Lăz' á rŭs) Personal name meaning "One whom God helps." *1.* One of the principal characters in a parable Jesus told to warn the selfish rich that justice eventually will be done. Poor Lazarus sat outside the mansion of the nameless rich man to receive whatever food might fall from the banquet table (Luke 16:19–31). Because of his poverty, he lived in poor health, also. In death the roles of the two were reversed, with Lazarus residing comfortably in heaven and the rich man being tormented in hell. The rich man asked that Lazarus be allowed to relieve his thirst. This is refused because of the gulf fixed between heaven and hell. A second appeal came for Lazarus to go and warn the rich man's family so that they might not join him in hell. This was refused because they have had adequate warning already.

2. Lazarus (a shortened form of Eleazer) of Bethany was a personal friend of Jesus and the

The traditional site of the tomb of Lazarus in Bethany.

brother of Mary and Martha (John 11:1–3). Jesus raised Lazarus from the dead after he had been in the tomb for four days to show the glory of God. Lazarus was at the Passover celebration in Bethany six days later. He became a target for murder by the chief priests because of his celebrity. Some believe Lazarus to be the "disciple whom Jesus loved" based on John 11:3 and 21:20–22. He is not mentioned in the other Gospels, although Luke 10:38–42 names the sisters Mary and Martha. See *Beloved Disciple*.   *Mike Mitchell*

LAZINESS See *Idle*.

LEAD See *Minerals and Metals*.

LEADER See *Prince of Life*.

LEAF, LEAVES The foliage of plants or trees. Adam and Eve made their first clothes from leaves (Gen. 3:7). Leaves are frequently used to symbolize blessedness or cursedness. God's renewal of the earth following the flood was epitomized by an olive leaf (Gen. 8:11). God's providential care for the righteous is pictured by the image of a well-watered tree whose leaves do not wither (Ps. 1:3; compare Jer. 17:8). Ezekiel's vision of the new Jerusalem included trees whose leaves never wither and whose leaves have healing power (Ezek. 47:12; compare Rev. 22:2). Withered (Isa. 1:30), shaken (Isa. 33:9), fallen (Isa. 33:4), and faded (Isa. 64:4) leaves serve as images of judgment. A tree lacking fruit with withered leaves (Jer. 8:13) symbolizes a people found lacking when God judges (compare Matt. 21:19; Mark 11:13). Jesus used the appearance of fig leaves which herald the arrival of summer to illustrate the need to heed the signs of the end (Matt. 24:32; Mark 13:28).

LEAGUE KJV used league at Daniel 11:23 in the sense of an agreement (NIV), alliance (NAS, NEB, NRSV), or treaty (TEV).

LEAH (Lē′ ah) Personal name meaning "wild cow" or "gazelle." Older daughter of Laban (Gen. 29:16) and Jacob's first wife. Jacob had asked for the younger Rachel's hand but was tricked into marrying Leah. Thus was preserved the ancient Near Eastern tradition of the elder marrying first. Leah bore six sons to Jacob (Reuben, Simeon, Levi, Judah, Issachar, Zebulun) and a daughter (Dinah). Her handmaid, Zilpah, bore two sons to Jacob (Gad, Asher), which by the law of that day were officially Leah's. When Jacob returned to Palestine from Padan-aram, Leah and her children were placed in front of Rachel and Joseph, evidently to absorb any violence from Esau, Jacob's brother. This is indicative of the less-favored status of Leah to Rachel. Leah died in Palestine and was buried in the cave at Machpelah, where lay the remains of Abraham, Isaac, and their wives.

LEANNOTH (Lė ŭn′ nōth) Transliteration of

Hebrew word in title of Psalm 88 possibly meaning "to sing" or "for the poor," "for the sick." It may be part of the title of a tune to which the Psalm was sung. The meaning remains obscure and uncertain.

LEATHER Animal skins tanned and prepared for human use. Elijah the prophet was recognized by his garment of haircloth and leather belt or girdle (2 Kings 1:8). The similar dress of John the Baptist marked him as a prophet (Matt. 3:4; Mark 1:6). Leather shoes are one of the gifts that symbolize God's lavish care for His beloved bride Jerusalem (Ezek. 16:10). See *Goatskin; Skins.*

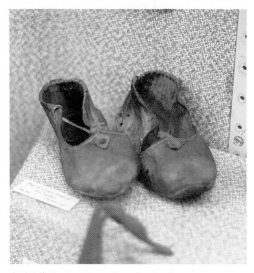

A child's leather shoes from Roman Egypt.

LEAVEN (Lēa' vĕn) A small portion of fermented dough used to ferment other dough and often symbolizing a corruptive influence. The common bread of Old Testament times was made with leaven. Such bread was acceptable as wave offerings for the priests and as loaves to accompany the peace offerings (Lev. 7:11–13; 23:17). However, bread made with leaven or honey, both associated with the process of fermentation and thus a source of corruption, was never to be used as offerings to be burned on the altar (Lev. 2:11–12). Unleavened bread was also prepared in times of haste (1 Sam. 18:24) and was required for the Feast of Unleavened Bread which was celebrated in conjunction with the Passover festival (Lev. 23:4–8). This unleavened bread, or bread of affliction, reminded the Israelites of their hasty departure from Egypt and warned them against corruptive influences (Ex. 12:14–20).

In the New Testament, leaven is a symbol of any evil influence which, if allowed to remain, can corrupt the body of believers. Jesus warned His disciples against the leaven of the Pharisees,

their teaching and hypocrisy (Matt. 16:5–12; Luke 12:1). Paul urged the Corinthians to remove wickedness from their midst and become fresh dough, unleavened loaves of sincerity and truth (1 Cor. 5:6–13). Jesus also used leaven to illustrate the pervasive growth of the kingdom of God (Matt. 13:33).   *Barbara J. Bruce*

LEBANA (Lĕ bā' nà) Personal name meaning "white" or "full moon." Original ancestor of clan of Temple servants (Ezra 2:45; Neh. 7:48). See *Nethinim.*

LEBANAH (Lĕ bā' nah) Alternate spelling of Lebana (Neh. 7:48) in most English translations despite the same names in the Hebrew text. Compare REB. See *Lebana.*

LEBANON (Lĕb' à non) Place name meaning "white" or perhaps "white mountain." A small country at the eastern end of the Mediterranean Sea and the western end of Asia. It has long been a world center of transportation and trade. The proper noun literally means the "White" (mountain), probably derived from the snow-capped Mount Hermon, also known as Sirion (Ps. 29:6). Hermon is often covered with snow, and its white crown offers a majestic and impressive view. The constant snow-coverage is contrasted with the fickleness and apostasy of Israel (Jer. 18).

Sandy beaches lie along its Mediterranean coast. Rugged mountains rise in the interior. The country itself is dominated by two mountain ridges, the Lebanon and Anti-Lebanon mountains. Both ranges run parallel to the coast. The Lebanon range extends for about 105 miles along the coast, from modern-day Tripoli in the north to Tyre in the south.

The mountain ranges are about 6,230 feet high. Some summits reach a height of more than 11,000 feet: the highest peak is el-Qurnat el-Sawda (11,024 ft.). Between the higher parts of the range lie valleys and ravines.

The Holy Valley, which collects the water from the Mountain of the Cedars, is one of the most important valleys. It was in this region that the Maronites found refuge in the beginning of their history. This Holy Valley has retained its significance throughout the ages. Ain Qadisha (Spring of the Holy Valley) is highly revered. It gushes forth in the heart of a cedar forest and mountainside near Bsherrih. Another famous valley is the Valley of Adonis, through which the River of Adonis flows; and to where the pilgrimage of Adonis took place in the spring of the year. See *Gods, Pagan.*

In the Bible, Lebanon is celebrated in various capacities. It is frequently featured in the Old Testament, in a general way, as the northern boundary of Palestine (Deut.1:24; Josh.1:4), dividing it from Phoenicia and Syria. Its imposing rage was emblematic of natural strength and solidarity, therefore a perfect poetic foil to the majesty of God revealed in a thunderstorm so powerful that it "maketh them to skip like a calf" (Ps 29:6). It was a proverbially lush land, noted for its magnificent forests (Isa. 60:13), especially the "cedars of Lebanon" (Judg. 9:15; Isa. 2:13). For the tree-poor Palestinians, Lebanon's cedars symbolized the ultimate in natural wealth and beauty. The psalmist calls these ancient and beautiful cedars the "trees of the Lord . . . which He hath planted" (Ps. 104:16). It is said that some of the cedars remaining in Lebanon are at least 2,500 years old. They share with the famous redwoods of California the distinction of being the oldest living things on earth.

Cedars, as well as other woods of Lebanon, were used in great abundance in the construction of David's palace and Solomon's Temple and palace buildings (1 Kings 5:10–18; 7:2). Cedar was obtained also for the building of the second Temple or the Temple of Zerubbabel (Ezra 3:7).

The forests of Lebanon have been victims of human greed and irresponsibility. They were exploited by Egypt and Mesopotamia long before biblical times, and they continued to supply precious timber well into the Roman Era. Under the Ottoman Empire (A.D. 1516), the forest almost entirely disappeared. Today there is not much left of the cedar woods; almost all of them are gone. The olive tree also played an important part in ancient times and is still cultivated.

Tyre to which Ezekiel 27—28 is devoted, was one of the most famous cities of the ancient world. Along with the older port of Sidon, it was one of the centers of Phoenician civilization. See *Phoenicia.*

Many foreign powers have controlled the Phoenician city-states. They include, in order of rule, the Egyptians, Hittites, Assyrians, Babylonians, and Persians. In 332 B.C. Alexander the Great conquered Lebanon. The region came under the control of the Roman Empire in 64 B.C.

Philip Lee

LEBAOTH (Lė bā′ ŏth) see *Beth-Lebaoth.*

LEBBEUS (Lĕb bē′ ŭs) Reading of some ancient Greek manuscripts for Thaddeus in Matthew 10:3 (KJV). Modern translations and interpreters follow earlier Greek manuscripts which read simply Thaddeus. See *Thaddeus; Apostles.*

LEB-KAMAI, LEB-QAMAI (Lĕb-kȧ′ mī) Transliteration of Hebrew text. A code name for Babylon (Jer. 51:1, NAS, NIV, NRSV, REB, RSV margin; Kambul, NEB). The code employed is athbash, a code which replaces each letter of a word with a letter that stands as far from the end of the alphabet as the coded letter stands from the beginning (z=a; y=b). NAS marginal reading "the heart of those who are against me" arose when the Maso-

retes added vowels to the code.

LEBO-HAMATH (Lē′ bō-hā′ măth) Place name meaning "entrance to or to come to Hamath." KJV, RSV translate; other modern translations transliterate the Hebrew name. Many modern interpreters think Lebo-hamath was an independent city in the city-state dominated by Hamath in Syria. It could be Lebwe north of Baalbek or Labau east of the Jordan. If a definite city is not meant, Lebo-hamath would represent the territory bordering the northwestern part of the Orontes River. Lebwe is close to the Litani River about 43 miles north of Damascus. Whatever its precise location, Lebo-hamath represented the northern boundary of Canaan promised to Israel (Num. 13:21; compare Ezek. 48:1), not conquered by Joshua (Josh. 13:5; Judg. 3:3), controlled by David (1 Chron. 13:5) and Solomon (1 Kings 8:65), and restored to Israel by Jeroboam II about 793–753 B.C. (2 Kings 14:25; compare 13:25). Amos predicted complete defeat for Israel starting at Lebo-hamath (6:14).

LEBONAH (Lė bō′ nah) Place name meaning "the white one." Town used to locate annual feast site by Israel's elders as they sought wives for decimated tribe of Benjamin (Judg. 21:19). It is probably modern el-Lubban three miles northwest of Shiloh and was known for its fine grapes.

LECAH (Lē′ cah) Personal name meaning "go!" Apparently the original ancestor for whom a town in Judah was named (1 Chron. 4:21). Its location is not known.

LEECH A wormlike, blood-sucking parasite of the class *Hirudinae* which serves as an symbol of an insatiable appetite (Prov. 30:15; KJV, horseleach).

LEEKS (Lēēks) Either *Allium porrum,* a bulbous vegetable, or *Tragonella foenumgraecum,* a grasslike herb. An Egyptian food eaten by the Hebrews during their captivity. After a steady diet of manna in the wilderness, they were ready to return to slavery and the foods of servitude (Num. 11:5).

LEES Solid matter that settles out of wine during the fermentation process. In ancient Palestine, wine was allowed to remain on the lees to increase its strength and flavor. Such wine "on the lees" was much preferred to the newly fermented product. At Isaiah 25:6, a banquet of wine on the well-refined lees symbolizes God's people enjoying the best God can offer. Zephaniah 1:12 pictures the inhabitants of Jerusalem who did not believe God would act as wine resting on the lees. Compare Jeremiah 48:11. Since wine was normally strained before being drunk, the prophetic images point to a temporary respite. To drink dregs or lees is to endure the bitterness of judgment or punishment (Ps. 75:8).

LEFT See *Directions* (*Geographical*).

LEFT HAND The hand located on the same side of the body as the heart; generally the weaker of the two hands. The left hand is frequently associated with the less preferable of alternatives. Joseph protested against his eldest being blest with Jacob's left hand (Gen. 48:13–19). A fool's heart inclines to the left (Eccl. 10:2). The goats' place of judgment is at the left hand (Matt. 25:33,41). Ehud, the judge, took advantage of his left-handedness to assassinate Eglon, the king of Moab (Judg. 3:15–22). To not know one's right hand from one's left hand is to be ignorant of right and wrong (Jonah 4:11).

LEG The upper leg or thigh was regarded as one of the choicest parts of a sacrifice and was reserved for the priests (Lev. 7:32–34). The first term translated leg in Isaiah 47:2 (KJV) is translated robe (NRSV) or shirt(s) (NAS, NIV, REB).

LEGION (Lē′ ġīŏn) In the New Testament a collection of demons (Mark 5:9,15; Luke 8:30) and the host of angels (Matt. 26:53). Behind this usage was the Roman military designation. The legions were the best soldiers in the army. At different times in Rome's history, the legion numbered between 4,500 and 6,000 soldiers. It was composed of differently skilled men: spearmen, commandos, skirmish specialists, calvary, and reserves. Originally, one had to be a property owner and Roman citizen to belong, but these requirements were waived depending on the need for troops. *Mike Mitchell*

LEHAB (Lē′ hăb) National name meaning, "flame." Singular of Lehabim. See *Lahabim.*

LEHABIM (Lē′ hā bĭm) See *Lehab.* "Sons" of Egypt in the Table of Nations (Gen. 10:13). Lehabim probably represents an alternative spelling of Lubim, the people of Libya. See *Lubim; Libya.*

LEHABITES (Lē′ hȧ bītes) NIV spelling of Lehabim. See *Lahabim.*

LEHEM (Lĕ′ hĕm) Place name meaning "bread" or "food." NRSV reading (1 Chron. 4:22) based on evidence from early Latin and Greek translations. The name appears in a list of members of tribe of Judah. Hebrew reads Jashubi-lehem (KJV, NAS, NIV). REB, TEV emend the text to read, "came back to" or "settled in Bethlehem." See *Jashubi-lehem.*

LEHI (Lē′ hī) Place name meaning "chin" or "jawbone." City where Samson killed 1,000 Philis-

tines with the jawbone of a donkey and where God provided water from the jawbone (Judg. 15). Many interpreters read 2 Samuel 23:11 as occurring at Lehi (TEV, NRSV, REB). The site was apparently in Judah near Beth-shemesh.

LEMUEL (Lĕm′ ū ĕl) Personal name meaning "devoted to God." A king who received words of wisdom from his mother concerning wine, women, and the legal rights of the weak and poor (Prov. 31:1–9). Exactly where his kingdom of Massa was is not known, although certain linguistic features in the text have led scholars to place it in north Arabia, possibly near Edom. This section of Proverbs apparently comes from a non-Israelite woman. See *Proverbs.*

LEND See *Banking, Interest; Loan.*

LENGTH, MEASURE OF See *Weights and Measures.*

LENT The English word *lent* (stems from an Anglo-Saxon word for "spring" and is related to the English word *lengthen*) refers to the penitential period preceding Easter. Early Christians felt that the magnitude of the Easter celebration called for special preparation. As early as the second century, many Christians observed several days of fasting as part of that preparation. Over the next few centuries, perhaps in remembrance of Jesus's fasting for forty days in the wilderness (Matt. 4:1–2), forty days became the accepted length of the Lenten season. Since, from the earliest years of Christianity, it had been considered inappropriate to fast on the day of the resurrection, Sundays were not counted in the forty days. Thus, the Wednesday 46 days before Easter came to be regarded as the beginning of Lent.

In the early centuries, the season before Easter was also the usual period of intense training for new Christians. During this period, the catechumens (those learning what it meant to be Christians) went through the final stages of preparation for baptism, which usually occurred at dawn on Easter Sunday. As the practice of infant baptism increased, the emphasis on Lent as a training period decreased. See *Church Year.*

Fred A. Grissom

LENTILS See *Plants in the Bible.*

LEOPARD See *Animals.*

LEPER See *Diseases.*

LEPROSY (Lĕp′ rō sy) A generic term applied to a variety of skin disorders from psoriasis to true leprosy. Its symptoms ranged from white patches on the skin to running sores to the loss of digits on the fingers and toes.

For the Hebrews it was a dreaded malady which rendered its victims ceremonially unclean—that is, unfit to worship God (Lev. 13:3). Anyone who came in contact with a leper was also considered unclean. Therefore, lepers were isolated from the rest of the community so that the members of the community could maintain their status as worshipers. Other physical disorders or the flow of certain bodily fluids also rendered one unclean (see Lev. 12:1—14:32; 15:1–33). Even houses and garments could have "leprosy" and, thus, be unclean (Lev. 14:33–57).

Jesus did not consider this distinction between clean and unclean valid. A person's outward condition did not make one unclean; rather that which proceeds from the heart determines one's standing before God (Mark 7:1–23; compare Acts 10:9–16). Therefore, Jesus did not hesitate about touching lepers (Mark 1:40–45) and even commanded His disciples to cleanse lepers (Matt. 10:8). Jesus even made a leper the hero of one of His parables (Luke 16:19–31). See *Diseases, Treatment of.*

LESHEM (Lē′ shĕm) Place name meaning "lion." City tribe of Dan occupied (Josh. 19:47). An alternate Hebrew spelling of Laish. See *Laish.*

LETTER A written message sent as a means of communication between persons separated by distance. Letters in the Bible consist of two categories: (1) letters mentioned and sometimes found in Bible books and (2) books of the Bible that are themselves letters.

Old Testament One of the earliest biblical references to a letter was the letter that David wrote to Joab about Uriah (2 Sam. 11:14–15). Ironically, Uriah was the bearer of the letter that contained orders for his own death. This letter was typical of many in the Old Testament in its brevity and terseness. This can be accounted for by the fact that the letter was from king to subject; thus, many standard expressions of polite address have been omitted (compare Ezra 4:17; 5:7).

Jezebel sent letters in Ahab's name ordering Naboth's death. She sealed the letters with Ahab's seal (I Kings 21:8–11). The king of Syria sent Naaman to the king of Israel with a letter instructing that Naaman be cured of his leprosy (2 Kings 5:5–6). Jehu sent letters to the guardians of the sons of Ahab, ordering that the sons of Ahab be killed (2 Kings 10:1–7). King Hezekiah of Judah sent letters by couriers ordering that the Passover be kept (2 Chron. 30:1–6). The king of Assyria sent a threatening letter to Hezekiah (2 Kings 19:8–14). The king of Babylon sent Hezekiah letters and presents (2 Kings 20:12).

Jeremiah 29 contains a different kind of letter. The prophet Jeremiah wrote a pastoral letter to Jewish exiles in Babylon. Unable to be with the exiles, Jeremiah wrote words of exhortation and encouragement. The content, purpose, and tone of this letter foreshadowed the letters that became books of the New Testament and sound very much like the letters Paul, Peter, James, and John wrote.

The period of the restoration resulted in many letters. The Persian Empire must have been a fertile period for letter writing (See *Israel, History of*). These letters are mentioned in the books of Ezra, Nehemiah, and Esther. See Ezra 4—6; Nehemiah 2; 6; Esther 3; 8; 9.

New Testament Letters are even more important in the New Testament. A number of references appear to letters within other Bible books. More than half of the books of the New Testament are letters.

The Book of Acts contains several letters and references to letters. When Saul went to Damascus to persecute believers, he went armed with letters from the high priest (Acts 9:1–2; 22:5). After the Jerusalem conference, a letter was written to inform the churches of the decision that had been reached. Men were selected to carry the letter and to explain it to the churches (Acts 15:22–23). (Compare also Acts 23:16–35; 28:21; 1 Cor. 16:3; 2 Cor. 3:1–2).

Archaeological finds have confirmed that letters were common. Many letters were written on papyrus for business and personal reasons. See *Paper; Papyrus.* These archaeological finds also show that the form of letters in the New Testament reflected the letters of that time.

The nature of Paul's work made letters an important means of communication. He traveled widely and established many churches. He spent part of his time imprisoned. He continued and expanded his ministry by writing letters. He wrote letters to places he had been and to places he hoped to visit. Paul's critics in Corinth accused Paul of being bolder in his letters than in his personal ministry. Paul denied the charge. He viewed his letters as consistent with what he would have said had he been there in person (2 Cor. 10:9–11).

Most of Paul's letters were addressed to churches. Even the letters addressed to individuals were designed to minister to churches. The so-called Pastoral Letters to Timothy and Titus were sent to men who were working with churches in given areas. Even the Letter to Philemon included the church in its greeting (Philem. 1–2).

The Roman Empire had a postal service, but it did not include personal letters. Paul's letters, therefore, were carried by messengers (see Phil. 2:25; Col. 4:7–8).

Most of Paul's letters were designed to be read to entire churches. Colossians 4:16 instructed the Colossian church to read the letter and to pass it along to the Laodicean church. The Colossians also were told to read the letter that Paul had written to the Laodiceans. Scholars disagree about the identity of the letter to the Laodiceans. Some say that it was the Letter to the Ephesians. Others feel that it was the Letter to Philemon. Or it may have been a letter that has not survived. Paul wrote other letters that have not survived. Perhaps two such letters are mentioned in 1 Corinthians 5:9 and 2 Corinthians 7:8.

Second Peter 3:15–16 mentions the difficulty some people had in understanding Paul's letters. This implies that Paul's letters were widely read. It also shows that some first-century readers had problems understanding all that Paul wrote.

The New Testament contains other letters. The two Letters of Peter and the Letter of Jude follow the familiar first-century form of letters.

The salutation is the only letter characteristic that has been postively identified in the Book of James. The content and approach of James is that of a wisdom writing. (See *James; Wisdom and Wisemen*). Hebrews on the other hand, begins like a sermon and ends like a letter. See *Hebrews.*

The three letters of John have some distinctives in style and format; only 2 and 3 John have the basic letter format. Their brevity parallels the vast majority of surviving Hellenistic letters.

Even the Book of Revelation has some characteristics of a letter. John sent it to the churches of Asia (Rev. 1:4). Chapters 2—3 contain letters to these churches from the risen Lord.

Robert J. Dean

LETTER FORM AND FUNCTION Letters may be divided into three parts: the opening, body, and close. Each part has typical conventions and its own basic function.

The basic function of the letter opening is to establish a relationship between the sender and the addresse. These parties are usually identified with the salutation formula "X to Y: Greetings" (Acts 15:23; 23:26; Jas. 1:1). In Paul's letters (and those influenced by his practice), the conventional greeting was transformed into a confession of faith: "Grace to you and peace from God our father, and the Lord Jesus Christ" (Rom. 1:7; 1 Cor. 1:3; 2 Cor. 1:2). In secular Greek letters a wish (or prayer) for the recipient's good health often follows the salutation. Third John 2 is the sole New Testament example. Pauline letters typically replace the health wish with a prayer of thanks (Rom. 1:8–15; 1 Cor. 1:4–9; 2 Cor. 1:3–11) which frequently builds relationship by mention of partnership in the gospel (2 Cor. 1:6–7; Phil. 1:5–7; 1 Thess. 1:3). In Paul's letter to the Roman Christians (a church he did not found), Paul established relationship by laying claim to a mission to *all* Gentiles, including those at Rome (Rom. 1:5–6), and by anticipating gospel partnership (Rom. 1:11–12). Hellenistic letter openings also frequently mention correspondence received (See 1 Cor. 1:11). See *Greeting.*

The basic function of the letter body is communication. The body of a Hellenistic letter fre-

quently began with a concise statement of the letter's primary theme, for example, the role of faith in salvation (Rom. 1:16–17), the problems of division in the church (1 Cor. 1:10), the impossibility of another "gospel" (Gal. 1:6). The communicative function of the body is underlined by the frequency of "disclosure" formulas: "We/I do not want you to be uninformed" (1 Cor. 10:1; 2 Cor. 1:8; 1 Thess. 4:13 NSRV); "I want you to know" (Gal. 1:11 NRSV; Phil. 1:12; Col. 2:1); "Do you not know?" (Rom. 6:3; 1 Cor. 3:16; 9:24 NRSV). Frequently, these disclosure formulas mark the beginning of a new paragraph. Another common transitional formula is "Concerning" (1 Cor. 7:1; 8:1; 12:1; 16:1; 1 Thess. 4:9,13; 2 Thess. 2:1). Letters may be distinguished according to the predominate purpose of the communication: letters of praise or blame, letters of exhortation and advice, or letters of mediation. Most New Testament letters are of a mixed type. New Testament examples of letters of censure or blame are found in Galatians (See 1:6; 3:1) and five of the letters to the churches in Asia Minor in Revelation 2—3 (excluding Smyrna and Philadelphia). Such letters are characterized by expressions of shock (Gal. 1:6), insulting address (Gal. 3:1), and the formulas "I have this against you" (Rev. 2:4,14,20 NRSV) and "I reprove and discipline" (Rev. 3:19 NRSV). The letters to the churches at Smyrna and Philadelphia serve as examples of letters of praise (Rev. 2:8–11; 3:7–13). Philemon serves as the New Testament example of a letter of mediation. (Paul interceded with Philemon on behalf of his runaway slave Onesimus). The letter of recommendation is the most common form of letter of mediation in secular letters. Recommendations are embedded in several of Paul's letters: of Phoebe (Rom. 16:1); of Timothy (1 Cor. 4:17; 16:10–11; Phil. 2:19–24); and of Epaphroditus (Phil. 2:25–30). Most New Testament letters are best characterized under the broad heading "letters of advice or exhortation." Second John serves as an excellent example of a letter offering specific advice (2 John 10–11). More often New Testament letters have broader paraenetic goals.

The letter close again highlights the relationship between the sender and addressees. Secular letters frequently concluded with an oath formula such as "I swear by the gods that I will . . ." Such formulas perhaps suggested James' concluding prohibition of oaths (5:12). A better New Testament parallel to the secular practice is Paul's calling God as witness (Rom. 1:9; Phil. 1:8). Secular letters also frequently closed with a health wish. This practice perhaps suggested James' topic of sickness (Jas. 5:13–16). Better parallels are again found in the Pauline letters in which a closing benediction (2 Cor. 13:13; Gal. 6:18; Eph. 6:23–24) expresses concern for the recipients' spiritual condition. Secular letters typically closed with the expression "farewell" (Acts 15:29). *Chris Church*

LETUSHIM (Lĕ tū' shĭm) Tribal name meaning "smiths." Descendants of Abraham and Keturah (Gen. 25:3). See *Keturah.* Nothing else is known of this tribe. They do not appear in the parallel passage (1 Chron. 1:32).

LETUSHITES (Lĕ tū' shītes) NIV spelling of Letushim. See *Letushim.*

LEUMMIM (Lĕ ŭm' mĭm) Tribal name meaning "peoples." Descendants of Abraham and Keturah. See *Keturah.* Probably an Arabian tribe of which we know nothing. They do not appear in the parallel passage (1 Chron. 1:32).

LEUMONITES (Lĕ ŭm' ō nītes) NIV spelling of Leummim. See *Leummim.*

LEVI (Lē' vī) Personal name meaning "a joining." *1.* Third son of Jacob and Leah (Gen. 29:34) and original ancestor of Israel's priests. He is characterized in Scripture as savage and merciless, avenging the rape of his sister, Dinah, by annihilating the male population of an entire city (Gen. 34:25–31). Later, Jacob spoke harshly of Levi rather than blessing him (Gen. 49:5–7). The tribe which bears his name also is characterized as instruments of wrath. After the people of Israel sinned in the wilderness by making the molten calf, Moses commanded the people of Levi to slaughter those who had participated in the debacle (Ex. 32:28). Levi's descendants became a tribe of priests. See *Levites. 2.* Name of two of Jesus' ancestors (Luke 3:24,29). *3.* A tax collector in Capernaum who became a follower of Jesus (Mark 2:14). In the parallel account in the Gospel of Matthew the man's name is given as "Matthew" instead of "Levi" (9:9). The name of Levi appears in none of the lists of apostles.

LEVIATHAN (Lĕ vī' à than) Name of an ancient sea creature subdued by God meaning "coiled one." Leviathan appears in biblical and extrabiblical literature. A serpentine form is indicated in Isaiah 27:1 ("leviathan the piercing [KJV] serpent").

The sea creature is used interchangably with other mysterious creations of the divine. Again, Isaiah 27:1 refers to leviathan as "the dragon that is in the sea." The psalmist in 74:14 presents leviathan among the supernatural enemies of God dwelling in the sea with many heads. Job 3:8; 41:1–9 present the sea creature as too formidable a foe for a person to consider arousing. Yet, leviathan was created by God and subject to Him (Ps. 104:24–30).

Apocalyptic literature depicts leviathan as throwing off his fetters at the end of the present age, only to be defeated in a final conflict with the divine. See *Apocalyptic.* Ugaritic literature of Ras Shamra during the 1300s B.C. depicts the mythi-cal Baal defeating the sea creature called *Lotan* (another linguistic form for Leviathan). The Hittites wrote of a struggle between the dragon *Illuyankas* and the mortal *Hupasiyos.* A cylinder seal found at Tel Asmar dated about 2350 B.C. shows two men fighting a seven-headed serpent.

Leviathan was seen in ancient legend as a sea monster engaged in primordial warfare with the gods. This creature represented chaos in a personified manner which any creator deity had to overcome in order to create. Leviathan was also seen as a threat to the orderliness of the universe and ultimately to be subdued at the end of time.

The ancient pagan myths concerning Leviathan were familiar to the Hebrews of the Old Testament. To what degree these myths of Leviathan influenced the Hebrews, if any, may never be known. Scripture used the name known to so many people and removed fear connected with it, showing God easily controlled Leviathan, who thus offered no threat to God's people. See *Rahab; Creation.*   *Steve Wyrick*

LEVIRATE LAW, LEVIRATE MARRIAGE The legal provision requiring a dead man's brother (levirate) to marry his childless widow and father a son who would assume the dead man's name and inherit his portion of the Promised Land (Deut. 25:5–10). The practice is an important element in the story of Ruth (Ruth 2:20; 3:2,9–13; 4:1–11). The Sadduccees appealed to levirate law in asking Jesus a question about the resurrection (Matt. 22:23–33).

LEVITES (Lē' vītes) The lowest of the three orders in Israel's priesthood. In the earliest biblical records, sacrifices were offered by the chief of a tribe, the head of a family (Gen. 12:7,8; 31:54) or possibly by a priest at a temple (Gen. 14:18). Originally, Israel's priests and Temple personnel were to be drawn from the firstborn of every family in Israel (Ex. 13:11–15). Later, God chose the tribe of Levi to carry out this responsibility for Israel (Num. 3:11–13). The tribe of Levi was appointed because it was the only tribe that stood with Moses against the people who worshiped the golden calf (Ex. 32:25–29; Deut. 10:6–9). The Levites were not given a tribal inheritance in the Promised Land (God was their inheritance) but were placed in 48 Levitical cities throughout the land (Num. 18:20; 35:1–8; Josh. 13:14,33. See *Levitical Cities.* The tithe of the rest of the nation was used to provide for the needs of the Levites (Num. 18:24–32). Since the Levites were dependent on the generosity of others, families were encouraged to invite the Levites (as well as widows, strangers, and orphans) to join them in their eating and their celebration of the joyous national feast (Deut. 12:12,18; 16:11,14). These factors point to the total dedication of the Levites to the work of the Lord rather than the earthly concerns of making a good living.

The tribe of Levi included at least three separate families: Gershon, Kohath and Merari (with the families of Moses and Aaron being treated somewhat separately from the rest of the family of Kohath). During the wilderness journey they were in charge of taking the tabernacle down, transporting it, setting it up and conducting worship at the tent where God dwelt (Num. 1:47–54; 3:14–39). In some passages (Deut. 17:9,18; 18:1; 24:8), the terms *priest* and *Levite* (or Levitical priests) seem identical, but in Exodus 28 and Levitcus 8—10 it is clear that only the family of Aaron fulfilled the priestly duties of offering sacrifices in the tabernacle. Because there appears to be a different way of handling the relationship between the priests and the Levites in these texts, interpreters differ in the way they understand the Levites. Although it is possible that the role of the Levites changed or that the distinction between the priests and Levites was not maintained in each period with equal strictness, the interpretation which maintains a general distinction between the priests and Levites seem to fit most texts.

The Levites were consecrated to God and given by God as a gift to Israel in order that they might perform the duties at the tabernacle (Ex. 29; Lev. 8). Their work made it possible for the people to come to the tabernacle and offer sacrifices for the atonement of sins. The Levites assisted the priests in their responsibilities (Num. 3:5–9; 16:9) by preparing grain offerings and the show bread, by purifying all the holy instruments used in the Temple, by singing praises to the Lord at the time of the morning and evening offerings, by assisting the priests with burnt offerings on sabbaths and feast days, and by being in charge of the Temple precinct and the chambers of the priests (1 Chron. 6:31–48; 23:1–13,24–32; 25:1–6; 2 Chron. 29:12–19). Because of their work, the holiness of the Temple was maintained; and the glory of the Lord dwelt among Israel. During David's reign, the Levites were integrated into the administration of the government, including the keeping of the gates, judges, craftsmen, muscians, and overseers of the royal treasury (1 Chron. 9:22–28; 23–26). In Jehoshaphat's time the Levites were involved with teaching the people the word of God (2 Chron. 17:7–9). This responsibility probably continued into the postexilic period of Ezra (Neh. 8:9–12). *Gary Smith*

LEVITICAL CITIES (Lĕ vĭt′ ĭ cảl) Residence and pasture lands provided the priestly tribe of Levi in lieu of a tribal inheritance. Because of their priestly duties, the tribe of Levi did not receive any part of the land of Canaan as an inheritance (Num. 18:20–24; 26:62; Deut. 10:9; 18:1,2; Josh. 18:7). To compensate them for this, they received the tithes of Israelites for their support (Num.

18:21), and 48 cities were allotted to them from the inheritance of the other tribes. On the average, four cities from each tribe were Levitical cities. The practice of setting cities aside in this manner was a common Ancient Near Eastern practice.

The Levites were not the sole possessors or occcupiers of these cities. They were simply allowed to live in them and have fields to pasture their herds. These cities did not cease to belong to the tribes within which they were located. Although six of the 48 were asylums for those guilty of manslaughter (Kedesh, Shechem, Hebron in Canaan, Bezer, Ramoth-Gilead, and Golan), Levitical cities and cities of refuge are not synonymous. See *Cities of Refuge.* The privilege of asylum was not extended to all 48 Levitical cities. The aim of having cities of refuge was to control blood revenge by making it possible for public justice to intervene between the slayer and the victim's avenger of blood. The cities of refuge were probably priestly cities containing important shrines. Cities of refuge also served as punitive dentention centers. The slayer was not permitted to leave until the death of the high priest. This was possibly interpeted as a vicarious expiation of life by life.

Levitical cities were a series of walled cities, apart from the lands surrounding them. Unwalled suburbs and fields outside the cities remained tribal property. The Levites could not sell any open plots of land.

The legal status of Levitical houses within these cities differed from ordinary property. To prevent the dispossession of Levites, it was ordained that they might at any time redeem houses in their own cities which they had been forced by need to sell. Moreover, such a house, if not redeemed, reverted to its original Levitical owner during the year of Jubilee. See *Jubilee, Year of*. Pastureland belonging to Levites could not be sold (Lev. 25:32–34).

Theological, political, and economic reasons led to establishing the cities. The cities formed bases of operation so that the Levites could better infiltrate each of the tribes to instruct them in God's covenant. Such bases would be most needed precisely where one finds them: in those areas least accessible to the central sanctuary. Obviously, there was also a political dimension. Certainly, the Levitical desire to secure Israel's loyalty to the Lord of the covenant would also imply a commitment to secure loyalty to the Lord's anointed, the king. There was a blending of covenant teaching and political involvement. The economic factor may have been the most significant. The list of cities describes the dispersion of the Levites who were not employed at the large sanctuaries, had no steady income, and who belonged, therefore, in the category of widows and orphans. The cities were established for men needing economic relief. *Gary D. Baldwin*

LEVITICUS (Lĕ vĭt ĭ cŭs) The third book of the Old Testament containing instructions for priests and worship. The title is borrowed from the Vulgate, the Latin translation of the Old Testament, and means the Levitical book. Such a title indicates that the book relates to worship, matters attended to by the Levitical priests.

The first section of Leviticus relates to the latter part of the Book of Exodus. Exodus 26—27 give the Lord's instruction for the building of the tabernacle, the place of worship during ancient Israel's sojourn in the wilderness. These instructions are carried out and the tabernacle accepted as an appropriate place of worship (Ex. 35—40). Exodus 28—29 recount the Lord's instructions for ordaining Aaron and his sons as priests. This ordination takes place in Levitcus 8—9. One of the primary tasks of the priests was to offer sacrifice at the tabernacle. Before beginning this practice, ancient Israel needed instruction on the offering of sacrifice. The Book of Leviticus begins at that point. Before listing the major types of sacrifice, we should consider its basic significance. A sacrifice is in part a gift to God, not as a way to earn God's favor but as a way to give thanks for God's gift of life. Sacrifice is also a means of facilitating communion between God and worshipers. Another important purpose of sacrifice is atonement, restoring the relationship between God and worshiper. In the offering of sacrifice, worshipers give of themselves to God. In the shedding of the blood of the sacrificial victim, the vital power of life is released (Lev. 17:11). God honors this act and gives life back to the worshiper. Thus sacrifice was important in the relationship between the ancient Israelite and God.

Leviticus lists five main types of sacrifice: (1) The whole burnt offering: a means of atonement that symbolizes the dedication of the whole life to God. The entire animal was burned on the altar (Lev. 1:3—17). (2) The cereal or grain offering; indication that everyday life is a gift from God, since grain constituted the everyday diet in ancient Israel (Lev. 2:1—16). (3) The peace, or shared, offering; the sacrifice of part of the animal and a communal meal from the remainder of the meat (Lev. 3:1—17). (4) The sin, or purification, offering; a sacrifice of repentance for sin which has broken human relations to God and has endangered the welfare of the community (Lev. 4:1—5:13). This sacrifice is for unwitting sin (Lev. 4:2,13,22,27). (5) The guilt offering: might also be called a compensation or reparation offering, for it calls for sacrifice and compensation to one who has been wronged. The guilty one repays that which has been taken plus 20 percent (Lev. 5:14—6:7).

Leviticus 6—7 provide further instruction on sacrifice for the priests, and Leviticus 8—10 describe the beginning of sacrifice at the tabernacle. Leviticus 11—15 provide instruction on that

which is clean and unclean. A person who comes into contact with an unclean object becomes unclean and is not allowed to participate in worship. Thus it is important to avoid contact with that which is unclean because worship was such a central life-giving event in the life of the community of God's people. These chapters describe various causes of uncleanness, including improper diet, childbirth, and various skin diseases. Leviticus 11 presents the famous dietary regulations, and Leviticus 12 describes uncleanness related to childbirth. Leviticus 13 gives instruction in determining uncleanness related to leprosy, and Leviticus 14 describes the way to cleanse leprosy. Leviticus 15 lists bodily discharges which cause one to be unclean.

Leviticus 16 describes the ritual of the Day of Atonement, a way of removing the impact of sin and uncleanness. First, the priest made sacrifice for himself so that he was prepared to do the same for the community. Then two goats were brought, and one chosen for sacrifice. It was offered as a purification offering, and the blood was used to cleanse the sanctuary of any sin and uncleanness. The priest then took the other goat, the scapegoat, and confessed the sin of the people with his hands over the goat, symbolically passing the sin of the people to the goat. Then the goat was taken into the wilderness, a significant symbol of the removal of the sin of the people. This central ritual assumed that ancient Israel would encounter sin and uncleanness. Since God is perfectly holy, the Lord could not dwell among sin and that which is unclean. This ritual then provided a means of removing sin and uncleanness so that God could continue to dwell among the people and be present in the sanctuary to give them life.

Leviticus 17—27 is the Holiness Code. This section gets its name from the frequent use of the phrase, "You shall be holy; for I the Lord Your God am holy." In the Old Testament, holiness means to be set apart; however, it does not indicate being set apart from the world in a separatistic way. The term is used of ancient Israel's being set apart to God. As God is holy—set apart, unique, different, distinct, "There is no other like God"—so ancient Israel as people of God was to be holy, different from other people, because they were people of God. These chapters then give instruction in how ancient Israel was to live a holy life. Leviticus 18 illustrates this. The chapter begins with a plea to live not as the Egyptians, whom ancient Israel had just left, nor as the Canaanites, whom ancient Israel would soon encounter, but as people of the Lord God. Then the chapter gives instruction in sexual conduct, particularly on forbidden sexual relations. Living according to such instruction would distinguish ancient Israel from other people in the land as people of the holy God. The conclusion of chapter 18 emphasizes this again in urging the people to be loyal to God. So holiness is not a means of removing the people from the world but of giving them a way to relate to the world as the people of God.

A number of the instructions in the Holiness Code relate to ethics and faithfulness to the Lord. Note the famous verse in Leviticus 19:18, "Thou shalt love thy neighbor as thyself." There is also instruction on keeping the sabbath as a day of rest and worship. Each seventh year was to be a sabbath year for the land, to give it renewal and also as a sign that the land is not owned by ancient Israel but a gift from God. Each fiftieth year ($7 \times 7 + 1$) was a jubilee year in which all slaves were to be freed and property revert to its original owner. This again shows that people do not own other persons or property; they are rather stewards of such gifts from God. This practice shows that life is to be structured for the good of the community rather than isolated individuals.

These chapters also contain instructions on worship. Regular worship in the tabernacle was to include the constant burning of the lamp. This symbolized both the Lord's presence with the people and light as the first of God's creations. Also of importance in the tabernacle was the bread which symbolized the relationship between God and ancient Israel and reminded the people that God gives the gift of food. The Holiness Code also gives instruction on the special feasts. In the spring came Passover and unleavened bread, reminders of the Exodus from Egypt. The summer feast (Weeks and Pentecost) related to the harvest and celebrated the giving of the law. The fall festival included the Day of Atonement and the beginning of the new year. Also here was the Feast of Tabernacles, a harvest festival remembering the time in the wilderness.

The message of Leviticus begins with the fact that God is present with the people and continues with the notion that God is perfectly holy. This is why the book gives so much instruction on holiness and includes sacrifice as a means of removing the effects of sin and uncleanness so that this perfectly holy God can continue to dwell among and give life to the people. All of this instruction is a gift from God and helps the people understand how to live as God's covenant people. The book thus provides an important part of the story of God with the people, for it gives instruction on how to maintain and, when necessary, restore that relationship. The book seeks to explore further the instruction in Exodus 19:6, "Ye shall be unto me a kingdom of priests, and an holy nation."

The New Testament uses Leviticus to speak of the atoning sacrifice of Christ.

Outline

I. Offer Yourself in Praise and Adoration to God (1:1—7:38).
   A. Offer pleasing sacrifices (1:1—6:7).
      1. Offer burnt offerings (1:1–17).
      2. Offer cereal offerings (2:1–16).
      3. Offer peace offerings (3:1–17).
      4. Offer sin offerings (4:1–35).
      5. Offer guilt offerings (5:1—6:7).
   B. Give instructions to the priests who offer pleasing sacrifices (6:8—7:38).
      1. Give priestly instructions for burnt offerings (6:8–13).
      2. Give priestly instructions for cereal offerings (6:14–23).
      3. Give priestly instructions for sin offerings (6:24–30).
      4. Give priestly instructions for guilt offerings (7:1–10).
      5. Give priestly instructions for peace offerings (7:11–38).
II. Consecrate Priests to Mediate Between God and People. (8:1—10:20).
   A. Set apart priests who mediate (8:1–36).
   B. Sacrifice for the priests who mediate (9:1–24).
   C. Warn the priests who mediate (10:1–20).
III. Purify Yourself Before God (11:1—16:34).
   A. Eat clean animals; reject unclean animals (11:1–47).
   B. Purify mother and child after childbirth (12:1–8).
   C. Test for an infectious skin disease and remove the infected one from the camp (13:1–59).
   D. Restore the cleansed inhabitant to the community (14:1–32).
   E. Remove the threat of infection from the house (14:33–57).
   F. Cleanse unhealthiness within the community (15:1–33).
   G. Make atonement for the community (16:1–34).
IV. Present Yourself in Holiness Before God (17:1—26:46).
   A. Give attention to acceptable slaughter of beasts (17:1–16).
      1. Make proper sacrifices before the Lord (17:1–9).
      2. Sanctify life by refusing to eat blood (17:10–16).
   B. Follow the commandments of the Lord (18:1—20:27).
      1. Reject abominable sexual practices (18:1–23; 20:10–21).
      2. Warn concerning the danger of abominable practices (18:24–30).
      3. Reverence God in worship (19:1–8).
      4. Show love for your neighbor by righteous living (19:9–18).
      5. Observe proper practices in agriculture, slavery, sacrifices, and the body (19:19–29).
      6. Honor God through worship (19:30–31).
      7. Honor God through life (19:32–37).

8. Worship God alone; forsake other gods (20:1–8).
9. Honor father and mother (20:9).
10. Give diligence to obeying God (20:22–27).

C. Charge mediators to follow regulations which allow presence before God (21:1—24:23).
   1. Present themselves holy before God (21:1–24).
   2. Present holy gifts to God (22:1–33).
   3. Lead worship at holy times (23:1–44).
   4. Prepare the holy place (24:1–9).
   5. Keep the congregation holy before God (24:10–23).

D. Present both land and people holy before God (25:1–55).
   1. Observe the sabbath year (25:1–7).
   2. Observe the jubilee year (25:8–22).
   3. Care for the poor brother and his land (25:23–55).

E. Remember the blessings and curses concerning the covenant people (26:1–46).

V. Offer Proper Vows Before God (27:1–34).
   A. Offer proper vows related to people (27:1–13).
   B. Offer proper vows related to a house (27:14–15).
   C. Offer proper vows related to fields (27:16–25).
   D. Offer proper vows related to firstborn animals (27:26–27).
   E. Keep your vows (27:28–34).

See *Atonement; Covenant; Holiness, Holy; Purity, Purification; Sacrifice and Offering.*

W. H. Bellinger, Jr.

LEVY To impose or collect by authority (Num. 31:28). The priests and Levites were supported in part by a levy of war gains.

LEWDNESS Lust; sexual unchastity; licentiousness. Lewdness sometimes refers to an especially heinous crime: brutal gang rape resulting in murder (Judg. 19:25–27); murder by priests (Hos. 6:9); any vicious crime (Acts 18:14). Most often lewdness is used figuratively for idolatry (Jer. 11:15; 13:27; Ezek. 16:43,58; 22:9; 23:21,27,29,35,48,49; 24:13; Hos. 2:10). Since the cults of many of Israel's neighboring peoples were fertility cults which employed sexual acts as part of worship, the application of lewdness to idolatry or unfaithfulness is easily understood. See *Fertility Cults.*

LIBATION The act of pouring liquid as a sacrifice to a god. See *Sacrifice and Offering.*

LIBERALITY NAS term for generosity or openhandedness (Rom. 12:8; 2 Cor. 8:2). The KJV used simplicity for the text of Romans 12:8 and liberal-ity for 2 Corinthians 8:2. The precise meaning of the underlying Greek is a matter of interpretation. "Simplicity" can mean wholeheartedly, generously (NIV, NRSV), or openhanded (REB). "Simplicity" can also mean purely, without mixed motives or desire for selfish gain. See *Stewardship.*

LIBERTINE (Lĭb′ ēr tîne) KJV transliteration of Greek for freedmen (Acts 6:9). See *Freedmen, Synagogue of.*

LIBERTY, LIBERATION Freedom from physical, political, and spiritual oppression. Throughout the Bible, one of God's primary purposes for His people is to free them from physical oppression and hardship and to liberate them from spiritual bondage. One of the dominant themes of the Old Testament is that Yahweh is the God who liberated the Israelites from their bondage in Egypt. In the New Testament, God is the one who liberates people from bondage to sin through Jesus Christ. Jesus showed in Luke 4:18–19 that these purposes extend to all those who are oppressed, not just those who call on His name. This liberation always comes from God, but He desires to use his people to accomplish these purposes. If they refuse, he will use other means. See *Freedom.*

Steve Arnold

LIBNAH (Lĭb′ nah) Place name meaning "white" or "storax tree." *1.* Wilderness station east of the Jordan (Num. 33:20). Its location is not known; Umm Leben 66 miles south of Haradah has been suggested. See *Haradah. 2.* Town in the Shephelah of Judah that Joshua defeated (Josh. 10:29–30). Joshua allotted it to the tribe of Judah (Josh. 15:42) and separated it as a city for the Levites (Josh. 21:13). It illustrated western border rebellion against King Joram of Judah (853–841 B.C.) just as Edom represented rebellion in the east (2 Kings 8:22). It lay on the invasion route to Jerusalem followed by Sennacherib about 701 B.C. (2 Kings 19:8). The mother of Kings Jehoahaz (609 B.C.) and Zedekiah (597–586 B.C.) came from Libnah (2 Kings 23:31; 24:18). Debate rages concerning Libnah's location: tell es-Safi at the head of the Elah Valley appears too far north; tell Bornat just west of Lachish; tell el-Judeideh, usually identified as Moresheth-gath. Tell Bornat is the most popular candidate but far from certain.

LIBNI (Lĭb′ nī) Personal name meaning "white." *1.* Original ancestor of clan of Levites (Ex. 6:17; Num. 3:21; 26:58). Compare Laadan (1 Chron. 23:7). *2.* A Levite in clan of Merari (1 Chron. 6:29).

LIBNITE (Lĭb′ nīte) Member of clan of Libni. See *Libni.*

LIBRARY A systematically arranged collection of writings. A private library is one owned by an individual; a public library is one owned corporately and open to use by many. A special library of official records is an archive. Many of the earliest libraries were archives housed in palaces or temples.

Though the Bible does not use the word *library*, it makes indirect allusions to collections of books. The Bible itself is a "library," and was called such in Latin—*bibliotheca.* It was probably not until about A.D. 300 that all 66 books were published in a single volume.

The Material and Form of Ancient Books The earliest writings, which were from Mesopotamia, were inscribed in cuneiform on clay tablets, which ranged in size from six-by-six-inches up to seven-by-thirteen inches. Longer historical texts would be placed on clay barrels or prisms. One omen series required 71 tablets for 8,000 lines. Each tablet when translated would be the equivalent of a few pages in English rather than a complete book.

Egypt provided the ancient world with its famous papyrus, made from the stalks of a reed plant. As this was imported into Greece through the Phoenician harbor of Byblos, the Greeks called a book *biblos.* The word *Bible* is derived from its plural *ta biblia,* "the books," and the Greek word for library *bibliothēkē* meant a container for such a book. Papyri sheets were normally written only on one side. They could be attached together to form long scrolls (an Egyptian royal papyrus could be over 100 feet long). Greek papyri rolls were generally shorter. The longer books of the New Testament, such as Matthew or Acts, would take a 30-foot scroll.

The Dead Sea Scrolls from Palestine were written on leather. The famous Isaiah Scroll is 23½ feet long; the newly published Temple Scroll was originally 28½ feet long. Late in 200's B.C., the city of Pergamum was supposedly forced by a shortage of papyrus to invent "parchment" (also called vellum), a specially treated animal skin which was stretched thin until it became translucent.

The Jews and pagan Greeks and Romans used both papyri and parchments in scroll form. Christians, perhaps as early as the first century, began

The re-erected marble facade of the second century A.D. Library of Celsus at Ephesus.

to use the codex form, that is, the folding of several sheets of papyrus or parchment in a "book" form. This had several advantages. Both sides of the pages could be used; it was more compact; and above all one could more readily find Scripture references. Almost all of the early Christian Scriptures preserved in Egypt's dry climate are papyri codices.

When Paul was in prison in Rome, he requested "the books but especially the parchments" (2 Tim. 4:13). The books were probably scrolls of the Old Testament. On the other hand, the parchments were probably parchment codices, possibly of his notes and letters.

Archives and Libraries in the Old Testament Era Abraham came from Mesopotamia, which had a well-developed tradition of palace and temple archives/libraries. Since 1974 over 20,000 tablets have been found in the archives of Ebla in northern Syria from pre-Abrahamic times. See *Ebla.* Many of the 25,000 tablets from Mari (1700s B.C.) and of the 4,000 tablets from Nuzi (1400s B.C.) have helped to illuminate the backgrounds of Hebrew patriarchs. See *Mari; Nuzi.* Sumerian texts from among the 20,000 tablets at Nippur (before 1500 B.C.), and Akkadian texts from among the 20,000 tablets of Ashurbanipal's (about 668–629 B.C.) famous library at Nineveh have provided literary parallels to biblical stories such as the Gilgamesh Epic. See *Sumer; Ashurbanipal; Archaeology.* Texts written in five scripts and seven languages from the libraries of Ugarit shed important light on the literary and religious background of the Canaanites. See *Ugarit, Ras Shamara.*

Joseph and Moses (Acts 7:22) had access to the royal libraries of Egypt. The excavations of Amarna have uncovered a building with shelves for storing rolls and an inscription, "Place of the Records of the Palace of the King." Ramesses II (1290–1224 B.C.) had some 20,000 rolls, which no doubt included medical works like the Ebers Papyrus, literary works like The Shipwrecked Sailor, and magical texts like The Book of the Dead.

Solomon, who was famed as a prolific author (1 Kings 4:32), must have had an extensive library. It was probably at the palace archives that such documents as the Book of the Chronicles of the Kings of Israel (1 Kings 14:19) and of the Kings of Judah (1 Kings 14:29), were housed. Sacred texts were kept in the Temple (2 Kings 23:2).

We know from the Bible that Persian kings kept careful archives (Ezra 4:15; 5:17; 6:1). Ahasuerus (Xerxes) had a servant read from his chronicle one night as a cure for his insomnia (Esther 6:1).

In 1947 the Dead Sea Scrolls were discovered in jars in caves near Qumran. These were originally from the library of the Essene monastery. They included manuscripts of all of the Old Testament books except for Esther, works from the Old Testament Apocrypha and Pseudepigrapha, and sectarian compositions such as The Manual of Discipline, The War Scroll, and The Temple Scroll. The excavators also recovered a table, a bench, and ink wells from the scriptorium, where the manuscripts were copied. See *Dead Sea Scrolls.*

Greek and Roman Libraries The tyrants of the 500s B.C., Peisistratus of Athens and Polycrates of Samos, were the first Greeks to gather libraries. Individuals such as Euripides, Plato, and Aristotle also had their own libraries. Alexander the Great took with him copies of Homer, of the Greek tragedians, and of various poets.

The first corporate Hellenistic library was conceived by Ptolemy I at Alexandria in Egypt, and then established by Demetrius of Phalerum (Athens) under Ptolemy II (285–247 B.C.). This became the greatest library in the ancient world, amassing up to 700,000 scrolls. The main building was in the palace area with a secondary collection near the Serapeum. Many of the first librarians were outstanding scholars and literary critics, such as Zenodotus of Ephesus, Apollonius of Rhodes, Callimachus the poet, and Eratosthenes the geographer. Callimachus compiled an annotated catalogue, the *Pinakes,* in 120 scrolls. It is possible that the learned Apollos (Acts 18:24) may have made use of this famous library.

The second largest Hellenistic library was established at Pergamum (Rev. 1:11) by Eumenes II (197–158 B.C.) The excavators have identified a building next to the temple of Athena as the library. Rows of holes evidently held shelves for the scrolls; stone inscriptions identified the busts of authors. Antony gave Cleopatra its 200,000 scrolls in 41 B.C.

By the first century B.C., wealthy Romans, such as Cicero and Lucullus, had well-stocked libraries in their villas. Satirists mocked those like Trimalchio, who acquired books but never read them. Some 1800 badly scorched papyri have been recovered from a wealthy man's library at Herculaneum, which was buried by volcanic mud from Vesuvius' eruption in A.D. 79.

Caesar was killed in 44 B.C. before he could erect Rome's first public library. This was built some time after 39 B.C. by Asinius Pollio. Augustus built three public libraries; Tiberius built another in the temple of Augustus. Most Roman libraries, such as Trajan's famous Biblioteca Ulpia, had both Greek and Latin collections.

The Use of Libraries The use of archives and libraries would be restricted, first of all, by literacy; and, secondly, in the case of temple or palace archives, to priests and scribes. At Alalakh (1700 B.C.) we have a record of only seven scribes out of a population of 3,000.

Though powerful individuals like the emperors could borrow books, most libraries did not permit books to circulate. An inscription from Athens reads: "No book shall be taken out, since we have sworn thus. [The library will be] open from the first hour (of daylight) until the sixth." See *Paper; Writing.*   *Edwin Yamauchi*

LIBYA (Lĭb´ ў à) A large land area between Egypt and Tunisia. Libya's northern border is the Mediterranean Sea. The people who inhabited the territory in biblical days are referred to variously as Chub (Ezek. 30:5), Put (1 Chron. 1:8; Nah. 3:9), Phut (Gen. 10:6; Ezek. 27:10), and Libyans (Ezek. 30:5; 38:5; Acts 2:10). Most of our knowledge of Libya comes from Egyptian records which mention border wars and invasions. Pharaoh Shishak I (about 950 B.C.) is thought to have been a Libyan. He began a dynasty in Egypt which reigned for over 200 years. He supported Jeroboam I in establishing the kingdom of Israel in 922 B.C. (1 Kings 11:40; 14:25–28; 2 Chron. 12:1–12).   *Mike Mitchell*

LIBYAN (Lĭb´ ў an) Person who comes from Libya. See *Libya.*

LICE See *Insects.*

LIEUTENANT KJV term for Persian officials of the rank of Satrap (Ezra 8:36; Esther 3:12; 8:9; 9:3). See *Judea; Satrap.*

LIFE A principle or force considered to underlie the distinctive quality of animate beings. What is living has movement; in death, all movement ceases. "Life" is used in the Bible to describe the animating force in both animals and humans (for example, Gen. 1:20; 2:7; 7:15). Living organisms grow and reproduce according to their kinds. Human life as bodily existence, the value of human life, and its transient nature is described (for example, Ex. 1:14; Pss. 17:14; 63:3; Jas. 4:14). This physical, bodily existence is subject to suffering, illness, toil, death, temptations, and sin (for example, Pss. 89:47; 103:14–16; 104:23; John 11:1–4,17–44; Rom. 5:12–21; 6:21–23; 8:18; 1 Cor. 7:5; 10:13; 2 Cor. 1:5–7; 11:23–29; 1 Tim. 6:9; Heb. 9:27; Jas. 5:10). "Life" as used in the Bible, however, has a much wider application than only to physical, bodily existence.

God's Unique Life Only God has life in the absolute sense. He is the living God (Deut. 5:26; Josh. 3:10; 1 Sam. 17:26; Matt. 16:16). All other life depends on God for its creation and maintenance (Gen. 2:7,19,21–22; Ps. 36:9; Acts 17:25; Rom. 4:17). God is spoken of as the God of life or as life giving (Num. 14:28; Deut. 32:40; Judg. 8:19; Ruth 3:13; 1 Sam. 14:39; 19:6; Jer. 5:2). In stark contrast to God, the idols are dead (Pss. 115:3–8; 135:15–18; Isa. 44:9–20; Jer. 10:8–10,14) as are those who depend on them for life (Pss. 115:8; 135:18).

In the same way that God is Creator by giving His breath or spirit to living creatures, so no possibility of life exists when God withholds His breath or spirit (Job 34:14–15; Ps. 104:29). Thus, God is Lord of both life and death (2 Cor. 1:9; Jas. 4:15). Life is something which only God can give (Pss. 36:9; 66:9; 139:13–14) and which only God can sustain (Job 33:4; Ps. 119:116; Isa. 38:16).

This being the case, every life is solely the possession of God. No one has a right to end a life (Ex. 20:13; Deut. 5:17; compare Gen. 4:10,19–24). Since life belongs to God, one must abstain from the consumption of blood, the vehicle of life (Gen. 9:4; Lev. 3:17; 17:10–14; Deut. 12:23–25). Thus, even animal life is valued by God as is evidenced by the fact that animal's blood was sacred to God.

Earthly existence, physical life The Bible summarizes the lives of many people. Often the biblical account includes a statement about their life-span, "These are the years of *the life* of Abraham which he *lived*—a hundred and seventy five years" (Gen. 25:7 AT. Following quotations marked AT are the author's own translation.). The Old Testament emphasizes quality of life. The person who finds wisdom is fortunate: "She [wisdom] is a tree of life to those who lay hold of her" (Prov. 3:18 NRSV). Wisdom affects how people live. Psalm 143 testifies to the dark moments of life. Then the psalmist prays for God to intervene: "For the sake of your name [person], oh Lord, revive my life; in your righteousness, bring my soul out of distress" (143:11 AT).

Jesus at His temptation quoted Deuteronomy 8:3: "A person shall not live by bread alone" (Matt. 4:4; Luke 4:4 AT). Rather each person must live "by every word that proceeds out through the mouth of God" (Matt. 4:4 AT). Earthly life involves God.

Jesus warned that "one's life does not consist in the abundance of possessions" (Luke 12:15 NRSV). Yet many people see one's belongings as the criterion of success. Jesus healed people and raised some from the dead to relieve the harshness of life (compare Mark 5:23–45). Jesus brought wholeness into human, physical life.

Life as fellowship with God The Old Testament uses bold metaphors for fellowship with God: "For with thee is the fountain of life: in thy light shall we see light" (Ps. 36:9). We come to God to receive life. We walk in fellowship with God, and in His light we see life. Otherwise, we are devoid of life and cannot see. Even when we do come to God, we may depart from Him. Another psalmist pleaded for God's hand to be upon him: "Then we will not move away or backslide from you. Revive us with fullness of life and we will call upon your name" (Ps. 80:18 AT).

The proper response to life as the gift of God is to live life in service to God (Isa. 38:10–20) by obeying the Law (Lev. 18:5), doing God's will (Matt. 6:10; 7:21), and feeding in God's Word (Deut. 6:1–9; 8:3; 32:46–47; Matt. 4:4). Only that life which lives in obedience to God deserves to be called life in the true sense of the word (Deut. 30:15–20; Ezek. 3:16–21; 18:1–32).

The New Testament deepens this emphasis. Paul points out that Christians differ in terms of food they eat and days they celebrate (Rom. 14:1–6); these things are part of custom and tradition. All Christians are to make the Lord Jesus central and live so as to show that He is their purpose for living. "Not one of us lives for himself, and not one dies for himself; for if we live, we live for the Lord, or if we die, we die for the Lord; if therefore whether we live or die, we are the Lord's. For to this end Christ died and lived again, that He might be Lord both of the dead and of the living" (Rom. 14:7–9 NAS). Such living demands fellowship with the Savior who is the purpose for living.

Paul wrote that we died with Christ and were raised together with Him (Col. 3:1–3) and that the lives of Christians (individually) have been hidden with Christ in God. When Christ (the Christians' life) comes a second time, we will be manifested with Him in glory (Col. 3:4). Our fellowship with Him now is dependent on our constantly seeking and thinking the things above (Col. 3:1,2). This is the new and transformed life.

Paul describes God's servants as an aroma for God among the people to whom they witness (2 Cor. 2:15). To those who are perishing, believers are a fragrance from death to death. To those who are being saved, they are a fragrance from life to life (2 Cor. 2:16). Those who reject the message continue on in death. Those who accept the message move from one level of life to another. The life that Christ initiates grows. Paul exclaimed: "Who is sufficient for these things?" (2 Cor. 2:16 NRSV).

Paul set forth his picture of life: *The process of living for me, Christ; the act of death, gain* (Phil. 1:21). When Christ is central, life has no boundaries.

Christ as the life, the One who imparts life. Old Testament believers identified life with God (Pss. 42:8; 27:1; 66:9). The "I am" sayings in the Gospel of John identify life with Jesus. "I am the bread of life" (John 6:35,48). "I came that they may have life (John 10:10 NRSV). "I am the resurrection and the life" (John 11:25). "I am the way, the truth, and the life" (John 14:6). John states the purpose for his Gospel: "But these things have been written that you might believe that Jesus is the Messiah, the Son of God, and because you are believing you might be having life in his name [i.e. person]" (John 20:31 AT). Since Jesus was God incarnate, He made genuine life a reality—not a distant prospect.

Life to Come, Life Beyond This Life The genuine life that comes from Jesus to those who obey God is true or eternal life. Just as physical life is the gift of God, so is eternal life (John 6:63; Rom. 6:23; 1 Cor. 15:45; Eph. 2:8–10). Eternal life, or true life, refers as much to the quality of life one has as to the quantity of life. According to the Bible, all people will have an endless duration of life either in the blessing of God's presence or in the damnation of God's absence (see, for example, Dan. 12:2; Matt. 25:31–46; John 5:28–29). The thing that distinguishes the life of these two groups of people is not its duration but its quality. Eternal life is of a quality like God's life. This kind of life is a true blessing (Luke 18:29–30; John 3:15–16; 6:40; 17:3; Rom. 2:7; I John 5:12). The quality of this life is marked by freedom from the power of sin to destroy, by holiness, and by a positive relation with God (Rom. 6:20–23). True life is not only something to be hoped for in the future; it is a present reality. Believers share in the life of God in this life (Luke 11:20; John 5:24; Rom. 6:4,11; 8:6; Col. 3:3; 1 John 3:14), but the believer does not fully experience true life until the resurrection when believers obtain the crown of life (Jas. 1:12; Rev. 2:10).

True life is offered to all, but it is received only by those who realize that the source of true life is what God has done in Jesus Christ and does not come from within the individual (John 6:63; Rom. 6:23; Eph. 2:8–10). Those who have true life as a gift are to conform themselves to the manner of life Jesus exhibited (Matt. 10:25; John 5:39–40; 1 Tim. 1:16). Christians are to lose themselves (Matt. 10:39; Rom. 6:2; 2 Cor. 5:15) and serve God in love (Matt. 25:31–46; Mark 10:17–45; Luke 10:25–37; Rom. 2:7; 14:7–8; 2 Cor. 5:15; Gal. 2:19). Just as food maintains physical life, service to God maintains true life (Matt. 4:4; John 6:27,32–58; Acts 7:38; 1 Cor. 9:14).

Eternal life is indestructible (1 Cor. 15:42–57; 1 Pet. 1:23), though threatened by the devil, the law, and death. The devil attempts to destroy this life (Matt. 10:28; Luke 12:4–5; 1 Pet. 5:8), but he is not able to harm it for God protects the believer (Rom. 8:7–39; Eph. 6:10–18). The law threatens this life by tempting people to believe that they can attain this life by their own efforts (Rom. 7:10, 13; 2 Cor. 3:4–6). Death is also an enemy of true life, but it is powerless to destroy the life that God gives (Pss. 9:13b–14; 23:4; 33:18–19; 89:48; 116:3–4,8–9; 118:18; Rom. 5:12–21; 6:9–10; 7:24—8:11, 35–39; 1 Cor. 15:51–57; Gal. 6:8; Titus 3:7).

Life beyond this life is not that of a "spirit" but that of a bodily resurrection. Paul highlighted both earthly existence and the life to come: "Godliness is profitable with respect to all things, because it has promise of life now and of the one about to be" (1 Tim. 4:8 AT). This "now" life is one of

testing. James says those who pass this test "will receive the crown, i.e. life, which God promised to those loving Him" (Jas. 1:12). This future life is one of open fellowship with God (see Col. 3:4). See *Eschatology; Eternal Life; Resurrection.*

A. Berkley Mikelson and Phil Logan

LIFE, BOOK OF A heavenly document mentioned in Psalm 139:16 and further defined in the New Testament (Luke 10:20; Rev. 13:8). In it are recorded by God the names and deeds of righteous people. The main theological teaching behind the concept is predestination. Many works of apocalyptic literature not preserved in the Bible speak of a counterpart, a book of destruction. According to this literature one's name can be removed from the book of life for certain sins against God. The Bible speaks only of the Book of Life showing God's power to know His own.

LIFE, TREE OF See *Tree of Life.*

LIFT To raise or elevate. *1.* Hands were lifted in pronouncing a blessing (Lev. 9:22). *2.* In ancient times as now, an oath required raising one's hand (Gen. 14:22; Ex. 6:8, NAS margin; Deut. 32:40). *3.* To lift a hand against someone is to attack or rebel against that one (2 Sam. 18:28; 20:21; 1 Kings 11:26–27). *4.* To lift one's heel against someone is to deal treacherously (Ps. 41:9; John 13:18).

Several uses of lift must be viewed in light of the ancient requirement of prostrating oneself before a superior (Gen. 43:26; 1 Sam. 25:23). *5.* To lift up someone's head is to accept the person (Gen. 40:13; Ps. 3:3) or even exalt the person (Ps. 27:6). *6.* To lift up one's face is to appear bold and confident of acceptance (2 Sam. 2:22; Ezra 9:6). To lift up one's face may express a rejection of another's sovereignty (Judg. 8:28). The lifting of God's face or countenance is a sign of favor (Num. 6:26; Ps. 4:6). *7.* To lift up one's eyes or heart is to be haughty or prideful (Deut. 8:14; 2 Kings 14:10; 19:22; 2 Chron. 25:19; Prov. 30:13; Isa. 37:23). *8.* Eyes, hands, heart, and soul are frequently lifted up to God in fervent prayer (Pss. 25:1; 28:2; 63:4; 134:2; 141:2; Lam. 2:19; Dan. 4:34; 1 Tim. 2:8). *9.* In John's Gospel, lifting up refers both to the lifting up of Jesus on the cross and to His exaltation (resurrection/ascension) (John 3:14; 8:28; 12:32,34).

LIGHT, LIGHT OF THE WORLD That which penetrates and dispells darkness. The concept of "light" appears numerous times in both the Old and New Testaments. God created light (Gen. 1:3). However, a careful reading of the Scriptures reveals that the physical entity that we call "light" is actually only the second form of light in the universe, since everywhere the Bible declares that God Himself is light. Psalm 27:1 says, "The

Lord is my light." In Psalm 104:2, the psalmist testified of the Lord who "covered himself" in light. In John 8:12 Jesus, the God-man, said, "I am the light of the world." Such expressions make at least two things abundantly clear. First, the origin of light rests with God. Second, in some sense God Himself is the very essence of light. Such statements do not suppose that God is light and nothing more, but they do stress that God is the ultimate source of all knowing and understanding. To this end Psalm 119:105 informs us that God's Word is a "light" to one's path. Here the emphasis lies upon perception and understanding gained when darkness is dispelled and light revealed.

This last concept becomes even clearer in John 3:19; people love darkness better than light, because their deeds are evil. Such statements reveal that the character of light is to reveal and to provide understanding and purity, while the opposite of light or darkness is designed to obscure, to deceive, and to harbor impurity.

A small problem confronts the interpreter who discovers that Jesus said to His disciples in Matthew 5:14, "Ye are the light of the world." Yet in John 8:12, Jesus said, "I am the light of the world." What appears to be a contradiction is not one at all. The moon provides light for the earth just as the sun does. Yet, the actual source of light for both the sun and the moon is the sun. The moon only reflects the light of the sun. By the same token, Jesus, the God-man, is the source of all light. His disciples become reflectors in a darkened world, transmitting through their lives the true light of the eternal Son of God. See *Lamps, Lighting, Lampstand.*   *W. A. Criswell*

LIGHTNING A flash of light resulting from a discharge of static electricity in the atmosphere. In the Old Testament, lightning is always associated with God. God is the Maker of lightning and thunder (Job 28:26; Jer. 10:13) which reveal God's power and majesty (Pss. 77:18; 97:4). Lightning and thunder frequently accompany a revelation of God (the giving of the law, Ex. 19:16; 20:18; Ezekiel's first vision, Ezek. 1:13–14). In poetic language God's voice is identified with the thunder (Job 37:3–5). Lightning also appears as God's weapon in those passages in which God is portrayed as a warrior (arrows: 2 Sam. 22:15; Pss. 18:14; 77:17; 144:6; fire: Ps. 97:3; Job 36:32). The New Testament both continues Old Testament associations and adds new uses. The Book of Revelation develops the association with power and majesty (4:5; 11:19) and with weapons/judgment (8:5; 16:18). Lightning serves as an illustration for Christ's clearly visible coming (Matt. 24:26–27) and of Satan's (sudden, catastrophic, visible?) fall (Luke 10:18).

LIGHTS, FEAST OF See *Feasts.*

LIGN ALOES KJV transliteration of the Vulgate (official Latin translation) reading at Numbers 24:6 (lignum aloes=wood of aloes). NAS, NIV, NRSV simply read aloes. The REB reflects the KJV tradition with the reading "aloe trees". See *Aloe.*

LIGURE KJV term for a gem usually identified with the jacinth which was regarded as precious in ancient times (Ex. 28:19). See *Minerals and Metals.*

LIKENESS Quality or state of being like; resemblance. Old Testament passages center around two truths: (1) that God is wholly other and cannot be properly compared to any likeness (Isa. 40:18) and (2) that humanity is created in the image and likeness of God (Gen. 1:26). The first truth forms the basis for the prohibition of making any graven images (Ex. 20:4; Deut. 4:16–18; see *Idols*) and perhaps explains Ezekiel's reluctance to speak of elements in his vision in concrete terms (Ezek. 1:5,10,16,22,26,28). The likeness of God in humanity (Gen. 1:26) has been interpreted variously. Likeness has sometimes been distinguished from image, though the terms are best regarded as synonyms. See *Image of God.* Interpreters have identified the divine likeness with the ability to think rationally, to form relationships with other humans and with God, or with the exercise of dominion over creation (cf. Ps. 8:5–8). The divine likeness is sometimes thought to have been lost in the Fall, though its passing to Seth (Gen. 5:3) argues against the popular form of this argument. Though the likeness of God was not lost with Adam's sin, neither Adam nor subsequent humanity fulfilled God's purpose. God's purpose for humanity was fulfilled in Jesus Christ who is in a unique sense the likeness of God (2 Cor. 4:4; compare John 1:14,18; 14:9; Heb. 1:3). Paul's statement that Christ came "in the likeness of sinful flesh" (Rom. 8:3) parallels "born in the likeness of men" (Phil. 2:7), testifying that the incarnate Christ was truly human. The Christian life is characterized as a new creation in the likeness of God (Eph. 4:24; compare 2 Cor. 4:4).

LIKHI (Lĭk' hī) Personal name meaning "taken." Member of tribe of Manasseh (1 Chron. 7:19).

LILY In biblical usage, any of a number of distinctive flowers ranging from the lotus of the Nile (1 Kings 7:19) to wild field flowers in Palestine (Matt. 6:28). The lily was the inspiration for the rim of the molten sea in the Temple in Jerusalem (1 Kings 7:26; compare 1 Kings 7:19,22). The Song of Solomon uses it to beautify the writer's description of love (2:1; 4:5). See *Flowers in the Bible.*

LILY BLOSSOM See *Lily Work.*

LILY OF THE COVENANT, LILY OF THE TESTIMONY Translation of the Hebrew *shushan eduth*

Mosaic of lilies at the Tabgha Church by the Sea of Galilee in Israel.

in the title of Psalm 60, taken as a reference to the hymn tune (NAS margin, NIV, NRSV, REB). KJV, RSV simply transliterate the Hebrew.

LILY WORK Decorative work capping the two free-standing columns flanking the entrance to Solomon's Temple (1 Kings 7:19,22). These columns were likely inspired by Egyptian columns with a lotus motif. The brim of the molten sea was perhaps also inspired by the shape of the lotus blossom (1 Kings 7:26). See *Temple.*

LIME A white, caustic solid consisting primarily of calcium oxide obtained by heating limestone or shells to a high temperature. Mixed with water, lime was used as a plaster (Deut. 27:2,4). Burning someone's bones to lime amounts to complete annihilation (Isa. 33:12) and was regarded as an especially heinous crime (Amos 2:1).

LINE (1) A tool used for measuring length or distance; (2) a plumb line; (3) a cord; (4) a row. Sometimes the distance to be measured is relatively short (1 Kings 7:23). Elsewhere the line serves as a surveying tool for measuring a larger distance (Ps. 16:6; Isa. 34:17; Jer. 31:39; Zech. 1:16; 2:1–2). The surveying image is applied both to contexts where judgment (Amos 7:17) and restoration (Jer. 31:39; Zech 1:16; 2:1) are in view. In contrast, references to a plumb line refer to judgment (2 Kings 21:13; Isa. 34:11; Lam. 2:8) upon those who failed to meet God's high

standards (Isa. 28:17). Line is used in the sense of a cord in story of Rahab and the spies (Josh. 2:18,21). Line can also refer to a row (of men, 2 Sam. 8:2; of writing, Isa. 28:10,13).

LINEAGE KJV and RSV term (Luke 2:4) meaning descent (compare NRSV) or family (NAS). See *Geneologies.*

LINEAR MEASURES See *Weights and Measures.*

LINEN The most common fabric used in the Ancient Near East. It was spun from the flax plant and bleached before being woven into clothing, bedding, curtains, and burial shrouds. The tabernacle curtains (Ex. 26:1) and the high priest's garments (Ex. 28:6) were of "fine linen"—cloth woven so finely that it cannot be distinguished from silk without the aid of magnification.

LINTEL A wooden crossbeam over a doorway. The lintel is most prominent in the celebration of the Passover. The people of Israel were to sprinkle the blood of the sacrificial lamb on the lintel and the doorposts as a sign to the death angel. Every household which had blood on the lintel would be spared the death of the firstborn (Ex. 12:22–23).

LINUS (Lī' nŭs) Personal name possibly meaning "linen." Paul's companion who sent greetings to Timothy (2 Tim. 4:21). Early church tradition identified him as the first bishop of the church at Rome, but it is doubtful Rome had only one bishop or pastor that early in its history.

LION See *Animals.*

Lion statue in the Faustina Baths at Miletus.

LIPS Fleshy, muscular folds surrounding the mouth. In the Old Testament, lips frequently take the character of the whole person. There are flattering and lying lips (Pss. 12:2; 31:18); joyful lips (Ps. 63:5); righteous lips (Prov. 16:13); fearful lips (Hab. 3:16). Uncircumcised lips (Ex. 6:12) most likely refer to stammering lips or lack of fluency in speech (Ex. 4:10). Mourning is expressed in part by covering the upper lip with one's hand (Lev. 13:45).

LITTER A covered and curtained couch with shafts so that it can be carried by porters (Song of Sol. 3:7 NRSV, REB; Isa. 66:20, KJV, NAS, NRSV). The term used at Isaiah 60:20 perhaps refers to covered wagons (NIV, REB). The NIV takes the term at Song of Solomon 3:7 in this sense as well (carriage).

LITTLE OWL Any species of owl other than the great owl; included in the unclean birds of Leviticus 11:17. See *Birds.*

LIVER The large organ which secretes bile. According to the NAS, the lobe of the liver was offered to God with the other choice parts of the burnt offering (Lev. 3:4,10,15). Only the covering of the liver was offered according to the NIV (also KJV). NRSV understood the offering to consist of the appendage to the liver, likely the pancreas. The ancients examined livers to discern the future. The only scriptural mention of the practice concerns the king of Babylon (Ezek. 21:21). In Lamentations 2:11, the liver is likely regarded as the seat of emotions (liver, KJV, NAS margin; heart, NAS, NIV, RSV; bile, NRSV). Several references to glory (Gen. 49:6; Pss. 16:9; 57:8) are possibly expansions of an earlier reading liver (glory, NAS; soul, RSV; spirit, REB; tongue, NIV).

LIVING BEINGS, LIVING CREATURES Characters in Ezekiel's first vision (Ezek. 1:5,13–15,19–20,22; also 3:13; 10). The creatures are later identified as cherubim (10:20). The creatures numbered four. Each had a human form but with four faces. Perhaps the best interpretation views the creatures as a pictorial representation of the total sovereignty of God. Four creatures represent the four corners of the earth. The four faces represent four classes of creation: man=humanity; lion=king of wild beasts; ox=king of domestic beasts; eagle=king of the birds. Central to this interpretation is the One seated on the throne above all the creatures (1:26–28). The Book of Revelation develops a similar image to portray God's total sovereignty (Rev. 4:7–8).

LIZARD See *Animals; Bittern.*

LOAF, LOAVES OF BREAD See *Bread.*

LO-AMMI (Lō-ăm′ mī) Symbolic personal name meaning "not my people." Son of Hosea the prophet whose name God gave to symbolize Israel's lost relationship with Him due to their sin and broken covenant (Hos. 1:9).

LOAN The grant of temporary use. Because of Israel's experience of deliverance from slavery,

her moral code gave special care to marginal folk (Ex. 22:21–24; Deut. 10:19; Ps. 82:3–4; Prov. 31:8–9). Thus, loans were to be acts of generosity, not acts for profit at the poor's expense (Lev. 25:35–37). Furthermore because the earth was God's (Lev. 25:23; Deut. 10:14) and human possessions were gifts from God (Deut. 8:1–10), lending was sharing God's gifts.

Thus Old Testament forbade charging interest to fellow Israelites (Ex. 22:25; Lev. 25:35–38; Deut 23:19), for requesting loans indicated economic hardship. One might charge interest to sojourners (Deut. 23:20), though this arrangement was not meant to be exploitative (Ex. 22:21; Lev. 19:33–34; Deut. 10:19; Ezek. 22:7). Laws for collateral focused on protecting the debtor. The pledge must not threaten the debtor's dignity (Deut. 24:10–11), livelihood (Deut. 24:6), family (Job 24:1–3,9), or physical necessities (Ex. 22:26–27; Deut. 24:12–13). Compassionate lending was one measure of a righteous person (Ps. 15; Ezek. 18:5–9).

Years of release and the jubilee year (Ex. 23:10–11; Deut. 15:1–15; Lev. 25) provided a systematic means for addressing long-term economic hardship by returning family property, freeing slaves, and canceling debts. Deuteronomy 15:7–11 warns against scheming creditors who would refuse loans because a year of release was near; lending was to be an act of generosity (v. 10). As in most human communities, greed prevailed; and the prophets railed against the exploitation of the poor (e.g., Amos 2:6–8; 8:4), including violations of charging interest and abusing pledges (Ezek. 18:12–13; 22:12; Hab. 2:6–9; see Neh. 5:6–11). See *Borrow, Borrowing; Coins; Ethics in the Bible; Jubilee, Year of; Justice; Law; Poor, Widows, Orphans, Levites; Sabbatical Year; Slavery; Stranger. David Nelson Duke*

LOBE OF THE LIVER See *Caul.*

LOCK (1) A tuft, tress, or ringlet of hair; (2) a bolt used to secure a door. As a sign of their dedication to God, Nazarites were not permitted

Mosaic of loaves and fishes at the Tabgha church commemorating Jesus' feeding of the five thousand.

to cut their locks (Num. 6:5; Judg. 16:19). Priests were likewise prohibited from shaving their heads, though they could trim their hair (Ezek. 44:20). The Hebrew term which the KJV translated locks at Song of Solomon 4:1,3; 6:7; and Isaiah 47:2 is rendered veil by modern translations. In the Old Testament period, door locks were bolts with holes into which small iron or wooden pins would drop to secure the bolt (Neh. 3:3,6,13,15; Song of Sol. 5:5; compare Judg. 3:23–24). The bolt was generally seven to nine inches long for an interior door, fourteen inches to two feet for an outside door. The key had iron pegs corresponding to the position of the pins in the bolt and worked by forcing these pins up (Judg. 3:25).

LOCUST (Lō′ cŭst) An insect species of the order *Orthoptera,* family *Acrididae.* In the Middle East the locust periodically multiplies to astronomical numbers. As the swarm moves across the land, it devours all vegetation, high and low. The Hebrew Old Testament uses different words to describe the insect at its various stages of life, from egg to larvae to adult insect. Eaten in several ways (raw, boiled, roasted), the locust is an excellent source of protein (See Lev. 11:21–22, Mark 1:6).

The locust plague is used in the Bible as a symbol for what God's judgment will be like (Joel 2:1,11; Rev. 9:3,7; compare Ex. 10:3–20; Deut. 28:38). The image of the locust plague was also used to symbolize being overwhelmed by a large and powerful army (Judg. 6:5; Isa. 33:4; Jer. 46:23; 51:27; Joel 2:20; Nah. 3:15). Similar imagery is used in other Ancient Near Eastern literature.

LOD (Lōd) Place name of unknown meaning. Town later called Lydda eleven miles southeast of Joppa. Shemed or perhaps Elpaal of tribe of Benjamin is credited with building it (1 Chron. 8:12). Returning exiles settled there about 537 B.C. (Ezra 2:33; Neh. 7:37; 11:35) at what appears as the westernmost postexilic settlement though probably outside the governing authority of Sanballat of Samaria and of Judah (Neh. 6:2). See *Lydda.*

LO-DEBAR (Lō-Dĕ bȧr) Place name variously spelled in Hebrew to mean "no word" or "to him a word" or "to speak." City which was home to Mephibosheth after his father Jonathan's death (2 Sam. 9:4,5) and to Machir who assisted David when he was fleeing Absalom (2 Sam. 17:27). The location of Lo-Debar is uncertain. The best suggestion is a city in Northern Transjordan near Mahanaim (2 Sam. 17:27), a city with well-established loyalties to the family of Saul (2 Sam. 2:8). Lo-Debar is perhaps identical with Debir in the territory of Gad (Josh 13:26). A less likely identification is Debir in the territory of Judah between Jerusalem and Jericho (Josh. 15:7).

The Hebrew text of Joshua 13:26 mentions the name of the city *Lidebir* near Mahanaim. This is usually translated "to Debir," but many see this as an alternate spelling of Lo-Debar. See *Debir.*

Lo-Debar is cryptically referred to in Amos 6:13. Prior to the delivery of this oracle, Lo-Debar and Karnaim had been recaptured by Jereboam II from the Arameans in a campaign blessed by God (2 Kings 14:25–28). Israel had taken the victory as an indication of its own strength and greatness, forgetting that God had brought them the victory. Amos took the consonants of the name Lo-Debar and added new vowels to make the name read "a thing of nought." Amos was reminding Israel that its true strength and greatness lie not in their military achievements but in God who had blessed their efforts; Amos was calling the Israelites back to faith in this God.   *Phil Logan*

LODGE In Biblical usage, a temporary resting place, for example, in a private home (Josh. 2:1; Acts 10:18), or a campground (Josh. 4:3,8; Isa. 10:29). The temporary stay might be prolonged as was the case of Paul in Rome (Acts 28:23,30). Jeremiah longed to escape to a wayfarer's desert lodge to avoid his people's sinfulness (Jer. 9:2). For the lodge in the cucumber field. See *Hut.*

LOFT KJV term for the upper room (NAS, NIV) or chamber (NRSV, compare REB) of a house (1 Kings 17:19). See *Architecture; House; Upper Room.*

LOG (1) A liquid measure (See *Weights and Measures*); (2) a section of a tree trunk. The Bible refers to splitting logs (Eccl. 10:9), to burning logs for cooking (Ezek. 24:10), and to felling logs to use in house construction (2 Kings 6:2,5). The timber which king Hiram of Tyre sent to Solomon was likely logs lashed together to form rafts (1 Kings 5:8–9). The "log" of Jesus' hyperbolic expression (Matt. 7:3–5; Luke 6:41–42) was a long, shaped piece of lumber (KJV, beam).

LOGIA (Lō gî′ ȧ) A Greek term applied to a collection of sayings. It comes from the same root as *logos,* a Greek word usually translated "word." (John 1:1,14; see *Logos*). The Church Fathers used "logia" to denote a collection of the sayings of Jesus. In his early Church history, Eusebius (about 260–about 340) quoted Papias (A.D. 100s) that Matthew compiled the "logia" in Hebrew. Apparently this is not the same as the Gospel of Matthew itself. Rather, the Hebrew logia were likely the sayings of Jesus contained in Matthew and Luke, but not in Mark.

Exactly when the "logia" might have achieved written form is a subject of debate. In addition to New Testament evidence, two modern discoveries show that "logia" existed in early Christian communities. Around 1900, remnants of an actual "logia" were unearthed near Oxyrhyncus, Egypt. Three papyrus fragments were found containing sayings ascribed to Jesus. They have been dated to the A.D. 200s, but are probably copies of an older collection. Each saying begins with "Jesus says." Some of them can be found in the Gospels, while others are known from the Church Fathers. In addition, two "logia" of a community with Gnostic tendencies were found in 1946 near Nag Hammadi, Egypt. Dating from between A.D. 300–400, they contain over 200 sayings attributed to Jesus.

The Gospels, as well as those New Testament sayings of Jesus found outside the Gospels (such as Acts 20:35), and the modern discoveries all demonstrate the early church's concern for preserving Jesus' sayings. The same concern can be seen today in our red-letter edition Bibles. See *Gnosticism; Luke; Mark; Matthew; Nag Hammadi.*

Larry McKinney

LOGOS (Lŏ′ gŏs) The Greek term ususally translated "word." In common usage it carried a variety of meanings: an account or reckoning, an argument, principle, reason, or thought. As an English suffix, it designates areas of study: theology, biology, physiology, psychology.

Among the Greek philosophers, especially the Stoics, *logos* came to mean the rational principle that gave order to the cosmos. It could therefore be equated with God. Human reason, in turn, derived from this universal *logos*. Philo of Alexandria used this concept in his efforts to interpret Jewish religion for those versed in Greek philosophy. In Philo's writings, *logos* was the mediating agency by which God created the world and by which revelation comes to God's people. The *logos* became a distinct entity, specifically the "word of God" active in creation and revelation.

In the Septuagint, the Greek translation of the Old Testament, *logos* translates the word *dabar,* which could mean "word," "thing," or "event." In Hebrew thought, the *dabar* was dynamic and filled with a power that was transmitted to those who received it. The term was often used to designate God's communication to His people, as at the beginning of many of the writings of the prophets: "The word of the Lord came." The whole of the Law, or all of Scripture, could then be referred to as God's Word.

Toward the end of the Old Testament period Wisdom was increasingly personified as the Word of God that mediated between God and the world (see Prov. 8:22–31); Wisdom of Solomon 9:1–2). Wisdom (*sophia*) was preexistent, God's first creation, His instrument and agent in all the rest of creation. God became increasingly aloof in Jewish theology and dealt with His creation only through this subordinate being and through His angels.

In the New Testament *logos* is used both with common and with technical meanings. It is used for empty words (Eph. 5:6) and evil words (3 John 10), but it could also refer to the teachings of Jesus (Matt. 24:35). Jesus preached the word (Mark 2:2) or the word of God (Luke 5:1), and judgment would be determined by one's response to Jesus' words (Mark 8:38). The gospel, the message about Jesus, could then be called "the word" (1 Thess. 1:6; Luke 1:2; Titus 1:2–3) or "the word of God" (Acts 8:14; 1 Thess. 2:13). The word carries God's power to save (1 Cor. 1:18). Those who receive the word are called to be faithful to it (Titus 1:9) and to be "doers of the word" (Jas. 1:22).

In the Johannine writings Jesus himself is called the *logos* (John 1:1,14). Paul called Jesus the "wisdom of God" (1 Cor. 1:24) and spoke of His preexistence (Phil. 2:6; Col. 1:15–16); but only in the Johannine literature do we find the full development of an understanding of Jesus as the *logos* or wisdom of God that became incarnate. As the preexistent *logos,* the Son of God was the agent of creation. In contrast to earlier wisdom speculation, John affirmed that the *logos* was with God and was God. The *logos* was not created. Elsewhere in the Gospel of John, we find *logos* used with qualifiers such as "of God" (10:35), "of Jesus" (18:32), "my word" (8:43), or "his word" (8:55). Revelation 19:13 calls Jesus the "word of God," and 1 John 1:1 speaks of Him as "the word of life" (compare Heb. 1:2), but only in the prologue of the Gospel is *logos* used of Jesus in the absolute sense. Throughout John's Gospel Jesus spoke and acted as the incarnate *logos,* continuing God's creative and redemptive work. Hence, He could change water to wine, create eyes for a man born blind, and breathe the Spirit into His disciples (20:22).

John was probably dependent upon the developments in the use of *logos* that are evident in Jewish wisdom speculation and in Philo's writings, but John's distinctive contribution was the adoption of this concept to illuminate the identity and role of Jesus more fully. The Gospel of John declares that the *logos* of whom the philosophers and sages spoke had come in human form in Jesus of Nazareth. See *Christ, Christology; Creation; Philo Judaeus; Prophets; Wisdom.*

R. Alan Culpepper

LOINS The Hebrew and Greek terms refer to the hips and lower back. Loins are used in the literal sense of the body's midsection (Ex. 28:42; 2 Kings 1:8; Isa. 11:5; Jer. 13:1; Matt. 3:4). Tying up one's long, lower garments about one's waist or loins indicated readiness for travel (Ex. 12:11; 1 Kings 18:46; 2 Kings 9:1). In the New Testament, to gird up one's loins is used in the figurative sense of preparedness (Luke 12:35; Eph. 6:14; 1 Pet. 1:13). The Old Testament sometimes uses loins as the seat of physical strength (Nah. 2:1). Thus to make someone's loins shake or loosed is to render the person helpless (Ps. 69:23; Isa. 45:1). Scripture also uses the loins as a symbol of procreative powers (Gen. 35:11; 1 Kings 8:19; Acts 2:30;

Heb. 7:5,10). Modern translations frequently hide the Hebrew expression "from his loins" behind the translation descendant.

LOIS (Lō′ ĭs) A personal name perhaps meaning "more desirable" or "better." The mother of Eunice and grandmother of Timothy (2 Tim. 1:5). Paul exalted Lois as a model of Christian faith and saw her as instrumental in nurturing her grandson in the faith. Her influence on Timothy cannot be overestimated.

LONG LOBE OF THE LIVER See *Caul.*

LONG-SUFFERING See *Patience, Patient.*

LOOKING GLASS KJV term for a (hand)mirror (Ex. 38:8). In biblical times mirrors were made of polished metal (molten mirror, Job. 37:18) which yielded a somewhat distorted image (1 Cor. 13:12). The women who ministered at the gate of the tabernacle donated their mirrors to be melted down for the bronze laver (Ex. 38:8). The KJV often refers to a mirror as a glass (Job 37:18; Isa. 3:23; 1 Cor. 13:12; Jas. 1:23). See *Glass.*

LOOM A frame used for interlacing sets of threads at right angles to form cloth. The weaving of cloth was an important industry in the ancient world. Thus it is surprising that there are so few references to the process in Scripture. In a humorous scene, Samson convinced Delilah that his strength would be sapped should someone weave his hair into a piece of cloth on a loom. While he slept, Delilah did just that but was surprised when he easily freed himself from the loom (Judg. 16:14). Here web refers to cloth on a loom. Isaiah compared his finished life with cloth which is cut off from the loom (Isa. 38:12). Job 7:6 compares the brevity of life to the speed of the weaver's shuttle, the devise used to quickly pass the woof thread between the threads of the warp. Frequent references to a spear like a weaver's beam (1 Sam. 17:7; 2 Sam. 21:19; 1 Chron. 11:23; 20:5) perhaps suggest a javelin with a cord attached so that it might be easily retrieved. In this case, the heddle rod, a rod attached to cords or wires and used to guide warp threads, is possibly in mind. Other interpreters prefer to see a reference to the great size of the spear. See *Cloth, Clothing.*

LOOPS The inner and outer coverings of the tabernacle were each made of two large curtains held together by 50 clasps which passed through curved sections of blue cord for the inner tent or of leather for the outer tent (Ex. 26:4–5,10–11; 36:11–12,17).

LORD (Lôrd) One who has power and exercises it responsibly. Lordship must include power to exercise control as well as possession of power within the boundaries of a well-defined system such as law. A despot is only a caricature of the legal term "Lord" or "ruler."

Humans as Lord The Hebrew word *adon,* "lord," is used more than 300 times in the Old Testament for a human's rule over another person. This is to be distinguished from *baal* (also "lord") in that *adon* represents a personal relationship of the subjection of one person to another, while *baal* designates the owner of things, including slaves and women. See *Baal.* At times persons would address someone of equal social status as "lord" out of respect

In the New Testament the Greek word *kurios* can designate both one who exercises rule over persons as well as the owner of goods. It is also used in respectful address to a father (Matt. 21:29–30) or to a ruler (Acts 25:26). In the era of the Roman caesars, the title *kurios* symbolized the caesar's position as absolute monarch. It did not mean that the caesar was a god. *Kurios* was not used in the cults devoted to the worship of the caesars. When the early Christians confessed Jesus as Lord, they protested against the religious claims of the state but not against the rulership of the caesar as such. On the other hand, the Jewish rebels denied the political authority of the caesar. Being exempt from the cult of the caesar, Jews could easily call the caesar, "lord." Christians had to dispute the caesar's claim to be lord when that claim was understood to mean the caesar was divine. See *Emperor Worship.*

God the Lord Nations around Israel often called their gods, "lord." We need to distinguish between the Near Eastern and Greek religions. At first the Greeks did not see themselves in a slave/lord relationship with their gods because they did not believe their gods were responsible for their creation. They could, indeed, call the gods "lord," but that was not characteristic. Instead, both they and their gods were subject to the same higher power—that is, fate. Thus the Greeks felt no personal responsibility before the gods. The divine manifested itself much more in the political governing structures. In the democracy the divine manifested itself in the law which the citizens served. In the monarchy the divine was embodied in the ruler; and, in the worship of the ruler the law (which lived in all citizens of Greece) was honored.

In the Near East the gods were lords of fate. Humans were thus responsible to the gods. Many gods were called "lord." Marduk, the national god of Babylon, was called Bel, another form of Baal (Isa. 46:1; Jer. 50:2; 51:44). From among humans, the king towered above and beyond all others. The god had transferred the administration of divine law to the king.

In the Old Testament, Lord usually describes the essence of Yahweh: His power over His people (Ex. 34:23; Isa. 1:24), over the entire earth (Josh.

3:13; Mic. 4:13), and over all gods (Deut. 10:17; Ps. 135:5). Thus *adon* could stand parallel to the personal name of God, Yahweh (Ex. 15:17): Yahweh is Lord; the Lord is Yahweh. Additional terms such as Sabbaoth (that is, Supreme Head and Commander of all the heavenly forces) underscored the absolute lordship of Yahweh (Isa. 3:1; 10:16,33). Many times *adon* or the special form *adonai* was used in direct address to God (439 times), attesting to the honor of God or His representative (2 Sam. 7:18–22,28–29; Josh. 5:14; Zech. 4:4). In time a formal designation, *adonai jahweh* ("the Lord Yahweh"), developed. This corresponded to the uniqueness of Yahweh; and, finally, Yahweh was referred to as *adonai* alone, especially in Isaiah, Psalms, and Lamentations. Israelites formed personal names with *adonai* (Adonijah, Adoniram) just as did their neighbors (Adoni-zedek, Josh. 10:1–3), since these peoples also addressed their gods as "lord."

The designation of Yahweh as *adonai* led to varied forms of conflict with Baal and his worshipers during the history of Israel: for example, prior to the conquest (Num. 25); during the time of the Judges (6:25–32); during the monarchy (1 Kings 18; 22:54; 2 Kings 3:2; 10:18–28). Even in Judah, worship of Baal proved a danger (2 Kings 11:18; 21:1–5). King Josiah's reform finally ended the conflict with Baal by destroying the worship places outside Jerusalem (2 Kings 23). The prophets Hosea, Jeremiah, Zephaniah, and Ezekiel spoke out against the hidden "Baalizing" of the religion of Yahweh. They claimed Israel went to worship Yahweh but did it in such a way they were actually worshiping Baal without naming his name. Yahweh was the supreme Lord over the world; but Baal's worshipers saw Baal as lord of at least a part of the world. He appeared and disappeared with the vegetation, being humiliated and defeated by other gods, even becoming weak, sick, and dying. See *Gods, Pagan.* These competing understandings could only mean alternatives and opposition. The revelation of God in the Old Testament, however, speaks against any such alternative or opposition, for *Yahweh* alone is Lord. He is Lord in His historical acts. Humans have no power over Him. He is Lord in His directions for life. Humans are to obey Him totally. He is the Lord who reveals Himself in His covenant, His law, and His faithfulness.

About 300 B.C. *adonai* became more frequently used than Yahweh. Thus the Books of Esther, Ecclesiastes, and Song of Solomon do not use the name Yahweh. The title "Lord" (*adonai*) was no longer an adjective modifying the divine name but was a substitute for the divine name: Yahweh. Origen reported that when Jews read the divine name Yahweh, they would pronounce it *adonai,* while non-Jews would pronounce it *kurios.*

In the Greek translation of the Old Testament (Septuagint), written before the time of Christ, "Yahweh" was written in Hebrew characters. In the Dead Sea Scrolls, the scribes out of awe for the divine name wrote it in ancient Hebrew script rather than their normal script. Later, Christian scribes replaced the Hebrew characters in the Greek Bible with *kurios.* Scribes transmitting the Hebrew Bible showed that Yahweh should not be pronounced but read as *adonai* by substituting the Hebrew vowels of *adonai* for those of Yahweh when writing the divine name. See *Kere-Kethib.* Later readers who did not know this history did not pronounce Yahweh; but neither did they pronounce *adonai,* as the scribes intended. Rather in the Middle Ages readers of the Hebrew Bible began pronouncing precisely what was written, the mixture of consonants from Yahweh and vowels from *adonai,* producing the pronunciation of Jehovah, a word that never existed for speakers of classic Hebrew.

In the majority of the books of the New Testament, also, Yahweh, or God was called Lord. That occurs above all in quotations from the Old Testament and in translating terms such as "angel," "way," "word," "day," "name," or "hand" of the Lord. In important passages *kurios* (Lord) appears in the sense of the Old Testament *adonai* as Creator of the world and Director of history (Matt. 9:38; 11:25; Acts 17:24; 1 Tim. 6:15; Book of Revelation). In this way Christians preserved and continued the Jewish understanding of God. Since the New Testament and early Christians also called Jesus "Lord," we have difficulty many times determining whether Jesus or God is meant by "Lord" (Matt. 24:42; Mark 5:19–20; Luke 1:76; Acts 10:14).

Jesus is Lord   The two words *Kurios Jesous* composed the first Christian confession of faith (1 Cor. 12:3; Rom. 10:9). The decisive reason for transferring the divine title *Lord* to Jesus was His resurrection from the dead.

Before His resurrection, Jesus was addressed with the Jewish title of honor *Rabbi* ("teacher", Mark 9:5; 11:21, for example). Luke always, and Matthew usually, translated this title into Greek as *kurios* (Lord). According to Mark only once did a non-Jew address Jesus as Lord (Mark 7:28), but even that was simply a polite and courteous way of speaking (equivalent to our "sir"). Jesus was also addressed with the Aramaic *mari* ("lord", John 13:13). The resurrection changed the respectful student/teacher relationship of the disciples with Jesus into the believers' servant/Lord relationship. The designation of Jesus as Lord in the Gospels (esp. in Luke) is an indication of this shift in relationship. Paul said that God honored Jesus with the title of Lord as His response to Jesus' obedient suffering (Phil. 2:6–11). Jesus in the form of a Servant is the humbled One with the marks of the cross, before whom the entire world will bow down. Thus the Crucified One will experience an act of homage like that due God Himself (Isa. 45:23–24). His church already gives Him such homage. He has been seated at the right hand of God, which demonstrates the elevation of Jesus to the position of Ruler next to God Himself (Ps. 110:1; see Mark 12:35–37). Still, the New Testament does not go so far as to identify Jesus with God by calling Him, "*abba*" (that is, father; see *Abba*).

Jesus as the Messiah of Israel (Acts 2:36) was installed as Head of His church and Ruler of the cosmos by His resurrection (Col. 1:17; 2:6,10; Eph. 1:20–23). As such, the church prays for His return: "Come, our Lord" (or in Aramaic, *maranatha,* 1 Cor. 16:22; 11:26; Rev. 22:20). The cosmic lordship of Jesus still remains the lordship of God. Jesus will give the judged and redeemed world back to the Father (1 Cor. 15:28). The center of this lordship is the power of administration over all things human (Rom. 14:9).

The lordship of Jesus has ethical consequences. He makes the significance of all other powers of only relative importance (1 Cor. 8:5–6; Col. 2:15). The Christian believer is foundationally freed from being servant to any thing or person in the human world (1 Cor. 7:22–23). The believer devotes self to serve others, even the ones in power, as his or her lord in voluntary service (Mark 10:42–45). Speaking the word *Lord* or calling out to Jesus with the title "Lord" is not enough for salvation. Such calling must be accompanied by actions which correspond to the teachings of the resurrected, Crucified One and to His example (Matt. 7:21–22; John 13:14–15).

Already in Acts, "Lord" had become something like a summary of the Christian message. This expresses itself in a growing, more extensive formulation of the name of Jesus: "Lord Jesus," "the Lord Jesus," "the Lord Jesus Christ." In the introductions and conclusions of Paul's Epistles—as well as at significant places of the logical argument of the Epistles—the name is expressed in especially extensive formulations (Rom. 5:1; 8:39; 15:30; 1 Cor. 15:57). The objective fact of the lordship of Christ is supplemented by the subjective element of personal bonds to Christ through the possessive pronoun: "My/our Lord Jesus Christ." The "our" in "our Lord" includes all Christians; "your Lord" does not occur in the New Testament. Jesus Christ either joins people together, or He separates them, when they deny His right to be Lord (Rom. 16:18; 1 Cor. 1:2,10–13). The personal bond or union with Jesus and with one another is especially emphasized in the formula "in the Lord" or "in Christ." Here it is evident that Lord and Christ are, in the final analysis, interchangeable (1 Cor. 7:22; 2 Cor. 4:5). The Lord is Jesus, through whom God intervened in the activities of the world in order to bring salvation.

How can humans be convinced that the cruci-fied Jesus from Nazareth is the Lord—that is, that in Him God acted in the way that the Bible says and in the way that the world needs? How can people be convinced that He is the Messiah of Israel and the Lord of all people, who comes near to all people as Friend and Brother? How does the Lord of the cosmos become our personal Lord in His church? This happens through the Holy Spirit. God has fully empowered the resurrected Jesus to send out this Spirit (Acts 2:33). Indeed, Paul could say that the Lord is the Spirit (1 Cor. 15:45; 2 Cor. 3:17). This does not signify a total identifying of Jesus with the Spirit of God (compare 2 Cor. 13:13), but it testifies to the inseparable unity of the lordship of God with the sending of Jesus and with the work of the Spirit. See *Christ; God; Holy Spirit; Messiah; Jesus; Rabbi; Resurrection.*

Christian Wolf

LORD IS MY BANNER, THE See *Jehovah-Nissi.*

LORD IS PEACE, THE See *Jehovah-shalom.*

LORD IS SHALOM, THE See *Jehovah-shalom.*

LORD IS THERE, THE See *Jehovah-shamma.*

LORD WILL PROVIDE, THE See *Jehovah-jireh.*

LORD'S DAY A designation for Sunday, the first day of the week, used only once in the New Testament (Rev. 1:10). The Greek word for "Lord's," however, is precisely the same as that used in the term for "Lord's Supper" (1 Cor. 11:20). In fact, the *Didache,* an early Christian manual for worship and instruction, links the two terms together, indicating that the Lord's Supper was observed each Lord's Day (14:1). Herein may lie the origin of the term. Because the first day of the week was the day on which the early Christians celebrated Lord's Supper, it became known as Lord's Day, the distinctively Christian day of worship.

The earliest account of a first-day worship experience is found in Acts 20:7–12. Here Paul joined the Christians of Troas on the evening of the first day of the week for the breaking of bread (probably a reference to the Lord's Supper). The actual day is somewhat uncertain. Evening of the first day could refer to Saturday evening (by Jewish reckoning) or to Sunday evening (by Roman reckoning). Since the incident involved Gentiles on Gentile soil, however, the probable reference is to Sunday night.

The importance of Sunday to first-century Christians is also intimated in 1 Corinthians 16:1–2. Giving instructions about a special relief offering he wanted to take to the Christians in Jerusalem, Paul suggested that the Corinthians should set aside their weekly contributions on the first day of the week. Paul probably mentioned this day because he knew that his readers routinely assembled on that day for worship and that would be the logical time for them to set aside their offering.

Two other second-century documents also shed light on the significance of Lord's Day for the early church. First, Ignatius in his *Epistle to the Magnesians* (about A.D. 110–117) stressed the importance of Lord's Day by contrasting the worship done on that day with that formerly observed on the Sabbath (9:1). Second, Justin Martyr (about A.D. 150) wrote the first extant Christian description of a worship service. He noted that the early Sunday morning service began with baptism, included Scripture readings, expository preaching, and prayer, and then concluded with the observance of the Lord's Supper (*Apology* 65–67).

First and second century Christian documents indicate that Sunday quickly became the standard day for Christian worship, but they do not explain how or why this change from Sabbath to Lord's Day came about. The most obvious reason, of course, was the resurrection of Jesus which took place on that *first* Lord's Day. Since the earliest collective experiences of the disciples with the risen Lord took place on Easter Sunday evening (Luke 24:36–49; John 20:19–23), one might naturally expect the disciples to gather at that *same* hour on subsequent Sundays to remember Him in the observance of the Supper. This pattern, perhaps, is reflected in the service at Troas in Acts 20.

The change in the time of worship from evening to morning, though, probably came about because of practical necessity. Writing to the emperor Trajan at the beginning of the second century, Pliny the Younger, governor of Bithynia, reported that in compliance with Trajan's edict against seditious assemblies, he had ordered that no group, including the Christians, could meet at night. Pliny then described an early morning service of the Christians. Forbidden to meet at night, they met for the observance of the Supper at the only other hour available to them on the first day of the week: early in the morning before they went to work. It is likely that the practice then spread throughout the empire wherever similar regulations against evening worship were in force.

Although some Jewish Christians probably also observed the sabbath, the early Christians saw Sunday as a day of joy and celebration, not a substitute for the sabbath. The use of the term "sabbath" to refer to Sunday did not become common until the English Puritans began to do so after A.D. 1500. Evidence from the early centuries clearly shows that Christians regarded Sunday as a day to rejoice in the new life brought by the resurrection. On other days Christians might fast and kneel when praying, but the joyous character of the Lord's day made those actions inappropriate on Sundays. Soon after Christianity became the

religion of the Roman Empire. Sunday was officially declared a day of rest. See *Didache; Lord's Supper; Sabbath; Worship.*

Fred A. Grissom and Naymond Keathley

LORD'S PRAYER, THE Words Jesus used to teach His followers to pray. Three forms of the Lord's Prayer exist in early Christian literature— two in the New Testament (Matt. 6:9–13; Luke 11:2–4) and the other in the *Didache* 8:2, a non-canonical Christian writing of the early second-century from northern Syria. See *Didache.* Their similarities and differences may be seen if the three forms are set side-by-side.

Matthew	Luke	Didache
Our *Father*	*Father:*	Our *Father*
who art		who art
in		in
heaven:		heaven:
Hallowed be	*Hallowed be*	*Hallowed be*
thy name;	*thy name;*	*thy name;*
Thy kingdom	*Thy kingdom*	*Thy kingdom*
come;	*come;*	*come;*
Thy will be		Thy will be
done		done
on earth		on earth
as it is		as it is
in		in
heaven.		heaven.
Give us this	*Give us* each	*Give us* this
day our	*day our*	*day our*
bread	*bread for*	*bread for*
for the mor-	*the morrow;*	*the morrow*
row;		
And forgive us	*And forgive us*	*And forgive us*
our debts	*our* sins	*our* debt
as *we*	for *we*	as *we*
also *have*	ourselves	also *forgive*
forgiven	*forgive* ev-	our debt-
our debtors;	ery one who	ors;
	is in-	
	debted to us;	
And cause us	*And cause us*	*And cause us*
to go not	*to go not*	*to go not*
into temp-	*into temp-*	*into temp-*
tation,	*tation.*	*tation,*
But deliver us		But deliver us
from evil.		from evil
		For thine is
		the power
		and the
		glory
		for ever.

Three conclusions derive from such comparison. First, it is the same prayer in all three cases. Second, the *Didache* likely uses the form of the prayer found in Matthew. Third, Matthew's version is longer than that of Luke at three points: at the end of the address to God, at the end of the petitions related to God, and at the end of the petitions related to humans. Also, study of the

Greek manuscripts shows that the doxology that appears at the end of the Matthean form in some translations is not original; the earliest form of the prayer with a doxology is Didache 8:2. It is likely that each Evangelist gave the prayer as it was generally used in his own church at the time.

Matthew and Luke used the Lord's Prayer in different ways in their Gospels. In Matthew the prayer appears in the Sermon on the Mount where Jesus spoke about a righteousness that exceeds that of the scribes and Pharisees (5:20). It is located in a section that warns against practicing one's piety before men in order to be seen by them (6:1–18). Almsgiving, praying, and fasting are for God's eyes and ears. When praying one should not make a public display (6:5–6) nor heap up empty phrases, thinking that one will be heard for many words (6:7). Prayer should be private and brief. The Lord's Prayer serves as an example of how to pray briefly. It is seen as a substitute for the wrong kind of prayer.

In Luke the prayer comes in the midst of Jesus' journey to Jerusalem (9:51—19:46). In His behavior Jesus is an example of one who prays. His prayer life caused one of His disciples to ask for instruction in prayer, as John the Baptist had given his disciples. What follows (11:2–13) is a teaching on prayer in which the disciples are told what to pray for (11:2–4) and why to pray (11:5–13). Here the Lord's Prayer is a model of what to pray for. To pray in this way is a distinguishing mark of Jesus' disciples.

Although all three versions of the prayer exist only in Greek the thought pattern and expressions are Jewish. In the address, God is designated "Father" or "Our Father who who art in heaven." One Jewish prayer begins: "Forgive us, Our Father" (Eighteen Benedictions, 6). Rabbi Akiba (about A.D. 130) said: "Happy are you Israelites! Before whom are you purified, and who purifies you? Your Father in heaven" (Mishnah, *Yoma,* 8:9). The *Ahaba Rabba* (Great Love) prayer, which formed part or the morning worship in the Jerusalem Temple, began: "With great love hast thou loved us, O Lord, our God, with great and exceed

Three of the many languages of the Lord's Prayer in tile at the Church of the Lord's Prayer, Jerusalem.

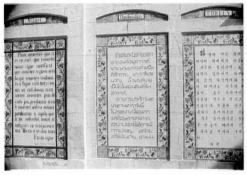

ingly great forbearance hast thou ruled over us Our Father, our King, be gracious to us."

The "Thou-petitions" are likewise Jewish in their thought and expression. The first two, "Hallowed be thy name; thy kingdom come," echo the language of the Jewish prayer, the Kaddish. It begins: "Magnified and hallowed be his great name in the world . . . And may he establish his kingdom in your lifetime and in your days . . . quickly and soon." The third, "Your will be done," is similar to a prayer of Rabbi Eliezer (about A.D. 100): "Do thy will in heaven above and give peace to those who fear thee below" (Babylonian Talmud, *Berakoth,* 29b).

The "Us-petitions" are also Jewish in their idiom. The first, "Give us our bread," is akin to the first benediction of grace at mealtime. "Blessed art thou, O Lord our God, king of the universe, who feedest the whole world with thy goodness . . . ; thou givest food to all flesh. . . . Through thy goodness food hath never failed us: O may it not fail us for ever and ever." The second, "Forgive us," echoes the Eighteen Benedictions, 6: "Forgive us, our Father, for we have sinned against thee; blot out our transgressions from before thine eyes. Blessed art thou, O Lord, who forgivest much." The accompanying phrase, "as we also have forgiven," reflects the Jewish teaching found in Sirach 28:2: "Forgive the wrong of your neighbor, and then your sins will be forgiven when you pray." The third petition, "Cause us to go not into temptation," is similar to a petition in the Jewish Morning and Evening Prayers. "Cause me to go not into the hands of sin, and not into the hands of transgression, and not into the hands of temptation, and not into the hand of dishonor."

Just as it was a practice of Jewish teachers to reduce the many commandments to one or two (compare Mark 12:28–34), so it was often the case that Jewish teachers would give synopses of the Eighteen Benedictions (Babylonian Talmud, *Berakoth,* 29a). The Lord's Prayer seems to be Jesus' synopsis of various Jewish prayers of the time.

If the language of the Lord's Prayer and that of various Jewish prayers is similar, the meaning must be determined from Jesus' overall message. Jesus and the early Christians believed in two ages, the Present Evil Age and the Coming Good Age. The Age to Come would be brought by a decisive intervention of God at the end of history. This shift of the ages would be accompanied by the resurrection from the dead and the last judgment. Before either of these events, there would be a time of great suffering or tribulation. One name given to the Age to Come was the Kingdom of God. It was a ideal state of affairs when Satan would be defeated, sin would be conquered, and death would be no more. Jesus believed that in His ministry, the activity of God that was to bring about the shift of the ages was already taking place. Within this world of thought, the Lord's Prayer must be understood.

The "Thou-petitions" are synonymous parallelism. They all mean roughly the same thing. "Hallowed be thy name," "Thy kingdom come," and "Thy will be done in earth, as it is in heaven," are all petitions for the shift of the ages to take place and for the ideal state of affairs to come about. They constitute a prayer for the final victory of God over the devil, sin, and death. It is possible that they were also understood by the early Christians to be a petition for God's rule in their lives in the here and now.

The "Us-petitions" participate in the same tension between the ultimate future and the disciples' present. "Give us our bread for the morrow" (RSV note to Matt. 6:11) may refer to the gift of manna to be renewed at the shift of the ages. As the Jewish rabbi, Joshua (about A.D. 90) said: "He who serves God up to the last day of his death, will satisfy himself with bread, namely the bread of the world to come" (*Genesis Rabbah* 82). It also refers to the bread necessary for daily life in this world as Luke 11:3 indicates: "Give us day by day." "Forgive us our debts or sins" may very well refer to the ultimate forgiveness of sins on the last day, but it also refers to the continuing forgiveness of the disciples by their Heavenly Father as they, living in this age, continually forgive those indebted to them. "And cause us to go not into temptation" may refer to protection of the disci-

Stone relief of the Lord's Supper.

ples in the final tribulation (as in Rev. 3:10), but it also speaks about being helped to avoid something evil within history where we now live. In all of the petitions, therefore, there is a tension between the present and the future. All of the petitions can be understood to refer both to the shift of the ages and to the present in which we now find ourselves. This is not surprising, considering the tension between the two in both Jesus' message and the early church's theology. The concern about the shift of the ages in the prayer sets it apart from the Jewish prayers whose language was so similar.

The Lord's Prayer in the New Testament is a community's prayer: "*Our* Father," "Give *us . . . our* bread," Forgive *us our* debts," "as *we. . .* forgive *our* debtors," "Cause *us*," "Deliver *us*." It is the prayer of the community of Jesus' disciples.

The Lord's Prayer is a prayer of petition. It is significant that the Model Prayer for Christians is not praise, thanksgiving, meditation, or contemplation, but petition. It is asking God for something.

This prayer of petition seeks two objects. First, one who prays in this way implores God to act so as to achieve His purpose in the world. Second, one who prays in this manner requests God to meet the physical and spiritual needs of the disciples. It is significant that the petitions come in the order they do: first, God's vindication; then, disciples' satisfaction.

Such a prayer of petition assumes a certain view of God. A God to whom one prays in this way is assumed to be in control; He is able to answer. He

is also assumed to be good; He wants to answer. The Father to whom Jesus taught His disciples to pray is One who is both in control and good. See *Eschatology, Kingdom of God; Mishnah; Midrash; Rabbi; Talmud and Targums.*

Charles Talbert

LORD'S SUPPER A memorial celebrated by the early church to signify Jesus' sacrificial death for humankind's sin. The form of the observance was established by the Lord at the Last Supper when He symbolically offered Himself as the paschal Lamb of atonement. His actual death the next day fulfilled the prophecy. Only Paul uses the phrase "Lord's Supper" (1 Cor. 11:20), although implication of it is made in Revelation 19:9 ("marriage supper of the Lamb"). Church fathers began to call the occasion the "Eucharist" (that is, "Thanksgiving") from the blessing pronounced over the bread and wine after about A.D. 100. Church groups celebrate the Lord's Supper regularly as a sign of the new covenant sealed by Christ's death and resurrection. See *Ordinances.*

LO-RUHAMAH (Lō-rū hǎ′ mah) Symbolic personal name meaning "without love." Name God gave Hosea for his daughter to symbolize that Israel by rebelling against God and serving foreign gods had forfeited God's love (Hos. 1:6).

LOSS See *Restitution.*

LOT (Lŏt) A personal name meaning "concealed." Lot was the son of Haran and nephew of Abraham (Gen. 11:27). Lot, whose father died in Ur (Gen. 11:28), traveled with his grandfather to Haran (Gen. 11:31). Terah had intended to travel to Canaan, but stayed in Haran instead (Gen. 11:31). When Abraham left Haran for Canaan, he was accompanied by Lot and Lot's household (Gen. 12:5).

After traveling throughout Canaan and into Egypt, Abraham and Lot finally settled between Bethel and Ai, about ten miles north of Jerusalem (Gen. 13:3). Abraham and Lot acquired herds and flocks so large that the land was unable to support both (Gen. 13:2,5). In addition, the herdsmen of Abraham and Lot did not get along (Gen. 13:7). Thus, to secure ample pasturelands for their flocks and to avoid any further trouble, Abraham suggested they separate. Abraham allowed Lot to take his choice of the land. Lot took advantage of Abraham's generosity and chose the well-watered Jordan Valley where the city of Sodom was located (13:8–12).

Some interesting details of the split between Abraham and Lot remind the reader of earlier events in Genesis. For example, the Jordan Valley is described as being well watered "like the garden of the Lord" (Gen. 13:10) reminding one of the story of Adam and Eve in the Garden of Eden.

One wonders if Lot would be more successful in this garden spot than Adam and Eve had been. The prospect of success was thrown in doubt by the way Lot's journey is described—he journeyed east, a description that recalls Adam's and Eve's journey after their expulsion from the garden (Gen. 3:24).

The Jordan Valley is also described as being fertile like Egypt (Gen. 13:10). This detail not only recalls Abraham's nearly disastrous journey to Egypt to avoid the famine in Canaan (Gen. 12:10–20) but also foreshadows the journey that Jacob and his family would later make (Gen. 42—50)—a journey that did have disastrous consequences (Ex. 1:8–14).

The mention of the cities of the Jordan Valley also carries negative connotations. One is reminded of the story of the tower of Babel where the people had gathered in one place (they had migrated from the east) to build themselves a city and make a name for themselves, so that they would not be scattered over the face of the earth and live like sojourners (Gen. 11:1–4). One is also reminded that Terah gave up his pilgrimage to Canaan to settle in the city of Haran (Gen. 11:31). To add to the negative connotations that cities have in the stories of Genesis, we are told that the people of Sodom were great sinners against the Lord (Gen. 13:13).

All in all, things did not look as good for Lot as they might at first glance appear when he chose to live in the well-watered Jordan Valley. We begin to see this unfold in Genesis 14. Not only was the Jordan Valley atttractive to herdsmen like Lot, but the riches of this valley were also attractive to foreign kings. Prominent among them was Chedorlaomer who, along with three other kings, captured and sacked Sodom, taking Lot as prisoner (Gen. 14:1–12). Abraham, upon hearing of Lot's fate, gathered an army and rescued his nephew (Gen. 14:13–16).

Lot is not mentioned again until Genesis 19 when two angels visited him. God had already told Abraham that He intended to destroy Sodom and Gomorrah (Gen. 18:20). Abraham interceded on behalf of Sodom, that if ten righteous men were found in Sodom that God would not destroy the city (Gen. 18:32). The two angels were apparently going to Sodom to inspect it. When the angels arrived, Lot received them with hospitality. When the townsmen heard that two strangers were staying with Lot, they wanted to have sexual relations with them. Lot protected his guests and offered them his daughters instead. The townsmen refused this offer and tried unsuccessfully to get the two strangers. For Lot's help, the angels revealed God's desire to destroy Sodom and urged Lot to take his family to the hills to safety. They warned Lot and his family not to look on Sodom. Lot, instead of going to the hills for safety, decided to live in another city (Zohar). In their flight from

Sodom, Lot's nameless wife looked at the destruction and turned to a pillar of salt (Gen. 19:1–29). Abraham *had rescued* Lot, again, (Gen. 19:29; compare 12:4).

As it turned out, Lot feared to live in the city of Zohar and decided to live in the surrounding caves instead. His daughters, fearing that they would never have offspring, decided to deceive their father into having intercourse with them. They got their father drunk; both conceived a son by him. The son of the eldest daughter was called Moab and became the father of the Moabites. The son of the youngest daughter was named Ben-ammi and became the father of the Ammonites (Gen. 19:30–38). Later in Israel's history, God desired to ensure the place of the Moabites and Ammonites in Palestine (Deut. 2:9). The Moabites and Ammonites betrayed their relationship, however, by joining with Assyria at a later period (Ps. 83:5–8).

In the New Testament, the day of the Son of man is compared to the destruction of Sodom and Gomorrah (Luke 17:28–29). The followers of Jesus are warned not to desire their former lives, like Lot's wife, but to be willing instead to lose their lives. Losing one's life is the only way to gain life (Luke 17:32). The story of Lot is also used to show the faithfulness of God to rescue His people (2 Pet. 2:7).   *Phil Logan*

LOTAN (Lō´ tăn) Personal and tribal name of uncertain meaning. Son of Seir the Horite and apparently the original ancestor of clan in Edom (Gen. 36:20–29). See *Seir; Edom.*

LOTS (Lŏts) Objects of unknown shape and material used to determine the divine will. Often in the Ancient Near East people, especially priests, made difficult and significant decisions by casting lots on the ground or drawing them from a receptacle. Several times Scripture mentions the practice. We do not know exactly what the lots looked like. Nor do we know how they were interpreted. We do know that people of the Old and New Testaments believed God (or gods in the case of non-Israelites or non-Christians) influenced the fall or outcome of the lots (Prov. 16:33). Thus, casting lots was a way of determining God's will.

One of the best examples of this use of lots is in Acts. Matthias was chosen to be Judas' successor by lot (Acts 1:26). The apostles' prayer immediately before shows the belief that God would express His will through this method. In the Old Testament Saul was chosen as Israel's first king through the use of lots (1 Sam. 10:20–24).

In a similar fashion God communicated knowledge unknown to human beings through lots. Saul called for the casting of lots to determine who sinned during his day-long battle with the Philistines. Specifically, he called for the use of the Urim and Thummim (1 Sam. 14:41–42; see

Urim and Thummim). When Joshua brought people near to the Lord to find the guilty party after the defeat at Ai, he may have used lots although the word is not found in the text (Josh. 7:10–15).

Lots helped God's people make a fair decision in complicated situations. God commanded that the Promised Land be divided by lot (Num. 26:52–56). Later, lots established the Temple priests' order of service (1 Chron. 24:5–19). This practice continued into Jesus' day. Zechariah, the father of John the Baptist, was burning incense in the holy place when the angel spoke to him. Zechariah was there because the lot fell to him (Luke 1:9). The awful pictue of soldiers casting lots for Jesus' garments was this kind of "fair play" use of lots (Matt. 27:35). Proverbs teaches that the use of lots is one way to put an end to a dispute when decisions are difficult (Prov. 18:18).

Lots are memorialized in the Jewish Feast of Purim. Purim, the Akkadian word for lots, celebrates the frustration of Haman's plan to destroy the Jews in Persia. Haman had used lots to find the best day for the destruction (Esther 3:7).

Finally, the word *lot* came to refer to one's portion or circumstance of life. The righteous could confess that God was their lot (Ps. 16:5). The lot of those who violated the people of God was terror and annihilation (Isa. 17:14). See *Oracles; Urim and Thummim.*   *Albert Bean*

LOTUS The lotus which serves as the habitat for behemoth (Job 40:21–22) is a thorny shrub (*Zizyphus lotus*) which flourishes in hot, damp areas of North Africa and Syria. The plant is especially abundant around the Sea of Galilee. This plant should be distinguished from the Egyptian lotus (*Nymphae lotus*) which is a water lily. The translation thorn bushes (TEV) or thorny lotus (REB) is preferable to the simple lotus (NAS, NIV, NRSV) which leaves the reader wondering what plant is in view.

LOVE Unselfish, loyal, and benevolent concern for the well-being of another. In 1 Corinthians 13, Paul described "love" as a "more excellent way" than tongues or even preaching. The New Testament maintains this estimation of love throughout. The King James Version uses the word *charity* instead of "love" to translate the Greek word Paul used (*agapē*). The word *charity* comes from the Latin *caritas* which means "dearness," "affection," or "high regard." Today, the word *charity* is normally used for acts of benevolence, and so the word *love* is to be preferred as a translation of *agapē*. Nevertheless, the reader who comes to the *agapē* of the New Testament with the idea of benevolence in mind is better off than the reader who comes with the idea of physical pleasure and satisfaction.

In the Old Testament In the Old Testament, the verb "to love" has a range of meanings as broad as the English verb. It describes physical love between the sexes, even sexual desire (Judg. 16:14; 2 Sam. 13:1–4). It describes the love within a family and among friends (Gen. 22:1–2). Love as self-giving appears in the significant commandment that Israelites love the stranger. The basis for such selfless love is God's act of redemption (Lev. 19:33–34).

Hosea used the image of married love to teach us to understand both the faithlessness of Israel and the faithfulness of God. Israel's love is "like a morning cloud, and as the early dew it goeth away" (6:4). God desires steadfast love, but Israel had been unfaithful. His own relationship with an adulterous wife allowed Hosea the insight that God had not given up Israel in spite of her faithlessness. The *Shema* (Hebrew for "hear") of Deuteronomy 6:4–6 is echoed in Paul's declaration that love is the fulfillment of the law (Rom. 13:10).

In the Teachings of Jesus In Jesus' teachings in Matthew, Mark, and Luke, the *Shema* of Deuteronomy (the command to love God) is united with Leviticus 19:8 ("Thou shalt love thy neighbor as thyself") (Matt. 22:34–40; Mark 12:28–34; Luke 10:25–28). Just before the parable of the good Samaritan, a lawyer quoted the two commands to love and then asked Jesus: "And who is my neighbor?" (Luke 10:29) Jesus gave the story of the Samaritan who took care of the man who fell among robbers to illustrate the selfless love which is to be characteristic of citizens of the Kingdom.

In Matthew 5:43–48, Jesus gave the radical command to love one's enemies and to pray for those who persecute. Loving only those who love you is, according to Jesus, no better than those who are not His disciples. The love that Jesus' disciples have for others is to be just as complete as God's love (Matt 5:48; compare Rom. 5:8).

In these teachings, of course, the selfless love is a response to God's prior activity. It is a way of living expected of those who are citizens of the Kingdom. The teachings of Jesus on love of enemy, it will be noted, are a part of the Sermon on the Mount which is directed to Christian disciples. See *Sermon on the Mount.*

In the Teachings of Paul In the poem on love in 1 Corinthians 13, Paul associated love with the all-important biblical words of faith and hope (see also 1 Thess. 5:8; Gal. 5:6) and declared love the greatest. The context for this poem on love is Paul's discussion of relationships within the church. First Corinthians 13:1–3 indicates that the gifts of the Spirit (ecstatic speech, wisdom, faith, and self-sacrifice) are good for nothing without love; only love builds up. The Spirit distributes His gifts for the common good (1 Cor. 8:1; 12:7). First Corinthians 13:4–7 characterizes love: Love is patient and kind, not jealous or boastful, not arrogant or rude. Love is not selfish, irritable, or resentful. Love does not rejoice at wrong but in the right. Love bears, believes, hopes, and endures all things.

Finally, 1 Corinthians 13:8–13 contrasts love with preaching and knowledge, on the one hand, and faith and hope, on the other. All of these (with love) are important aspects of our lives here and now. Love in contrast to these, however, is not only for the here and now; it is forever. Love, therefore, is "the greatest" of the most significant realities we experience as Christians.

Paul's understanding and discussion of love make love a central theme, and his use of the noun *agapé* makes that term almost a technical term. Prior to Paul, in fact, the Greek term *agapē* was little used. Instead of using a word for love already filled with meaning, Paul took the seldom-used term and filled it with Christian meaning. This love of which Paul wrote is somewhat different from the love we normally experience and speak about. Christian love is not simply an emotion which arises because of the character of the one loved. It is not due to the loving quality of the lover. It is a relationship of self-giving which results from God's activity in Christ. The source of Christian love is God (Rom. 5:8), and the believer's response of faith makes love a human possibility (Rom. 5:5).

Even though love does not begin in the human heart, the believer must actualize love. In Paul's admonition to Christians to love, the nature of love as self-giving is manifest (Gal. 5:13–15). The Christian walk is to be characterized by love so that Paul could even speak of "walking in love" (Rom. 14:15). The Christian is to increase and abound in love (1 Thess. 3:12).

Love is vitally connected with faith in that the believer's faithful response is one of love. Love is also connected with hope. In his prayer for love to increase and abound, Paul indicated that this increase of love has the end that the hearts of Christians might be established "unblameable in holiness" before God when Jesus returns with all his saints (1 Thess. 3:13). Paul also wrote of the hope we have of sharing the glory of God and declared that this hope does not disappoint us, because our hearts have been filled with God's love through the Holy Spirit (Rom. 5:2,5). Christian love is evidence of and a foretaste of the goal of God's purposes for His children.

In the Writings of John The Johannine writings magnify the significance of love as forcefully and fully as any other writings. John's writings account for only one tenth of the New Testament but provide one third of the references to love.

The key text in the first half of the Gospel of John is John 3:16. This passage indicates the relationship of the Father's love to the work of Christ and of both to the life of believers. These themes are repeated throughout the Gospel of John. The second half of the Gospel of John emphasizes the ethical dimension of love among Christians. The key passage is Jesus' new commandment in John 13:34–35 (see also John 14:15,21,23,24; 15:9,12,17).

This command of Jesus to love one another gives us insight into the nature of Jesus Christ for the church and the nature of Christian love. What is commanded is not an emotion; it is the disciplined will to seek the welfare of others. Jesus speaks with the authority of the Father, the only One with authority to make such demands of men and women. Jesus speaks as the incarnate Word (John 1:1,14). He has authority to give conditions for discipleship. The relationship of this commandment to Leviticus 19:18 should be noted. Both command love, but Jesus' commandment includes the clause: "as I have loved you."

When the overall importance of love in the Gospel of John is seen, the dialogue between Jesus and Peter concerning Peter's love for Jesus and Peter's tending the sheep (21:15–17) becomes more significant. Our love for Jesus Christ is closely related to our fulfillment of the pastoral task.

The Letters of John make explicit statements about the ethical implications of love. Our appreciation of these letters and the command to love is increased when we realize that John's opponents claimed that they loved God in spite of their unlovely temper and conduct. They claimed enlightenment and communion with God. (They were Gnostics or "Knowers." See *Gnosticism*). John's distress at the gap between profession and practice is seen in his repeated admonition to love. The "old commandment" which John saw as basic for Christians is belief in Jesus and love for one another (1 John 3:23). This love is be manifested in deeds (1 John 3:18). John left no doubt about the relationship of love and belief in God. Whoever hates his brother is in the darkness (1 John 2:9). Whoever does not do right and love his brother is not of God (1 John 4:20). First John 4:8 is the climax: "He that loveth not knoweth not God; for God is love."

In 2 and 3 John this command to love is repeated in direct and indirect ways. Second John 5–6 is addressed to the church, and they are explicitly reminded of the command from Jesus to love one another. Third John 5–6 speaks of the love of the "Beloved Gaius" in terms of giving service to Christian brothers. Diotrephes, however, will live in infamy, for he put himself first, refused to welcome the brethren, stopped those who wanted to welcome the brethren, and put them out of the church (3 John 9–10).

Love and Judgment The judgment account in Matthew 25:31–46 illuminates and is illuminated by the New Testament teachings on love. The account depicts not only what happens at the end. The narrative makes plain that what happens at the end is what happens here and now. Chris-

tians love because they have been loved. In such love, God's eternal purposes are being experienced and carried out by his people (Matt. 25:34–36).   *Edgar V. McKnight*

LOVE, BROTHERLY See *Brotherly Love.*

LOVE FEAST A fellowship meal the Christian community celebrated in joy in conjunction with its celebration of the Lord's Supper. See *Ordinances. Agape* (This love meal) was a significant dimension of the fellowship and worship of the early church. As a concrete manifestation of obedience to the Lord's command to love one another, it served as a practical expression of the *koinonia* or communion that characterized *the church's* life. While the only explicit New Testament reference to the agape meal is found in Jude 12, allusions to the practice may be seen in other New Testament texts. Thus, while the mention of "the breaking of bread" in Acts 2:42 is most likely a reference to a special remembrance of Jesus' last supper with His disciples, the allusion in Acts 2:46 to their taking of food "with gladness and singleness of heart" implies that a social meal was connected in some way with this celebration. Paul's discussion of the Lord's Supper in 1 Cor. 11:17–34 also suggests a combining of the ceremonial act with a common meal. Such a practice is also suggested in Acts 20:7–12. By the second century the word *agapai* had become a technical term for such a common meal which seems to have been separated from the ceremonial observance of the Lord's Supper sometime after the New Testament period.

The origin of the love feast is probably to be found in the religious fellowship meals, a common practice among first-century Jews. While the Passover meal is the most familiar of these, such meals were also celebrated to inaugurate the sabbath and festival days. On these occasions a family or a group of friends who had banded together for purposes of special devotion (know as *chaburoth* from the Hebrew word for "friends") would gather weekly before sundown for a meal in the home or another suitable place. After hors d'oeuvres were served, the company would move to the table for the meal proper. The host would pronounce a blessing (a thanksgiving to God), break the bread, and distribute it among the participants. The mealtime would be characterized by festive, joyous religious discussion. At nightfall lamps were lit and a benediction recited acknowledging God as the Creator of light. When the meal was over, hands were washed and a final benediction pronounced over the "cup of blessing" (see 1 Cor. 10:16) praising God for His provision and praying for the fulfillment of His purposes in the coming of His kingdom. The meal was concluded by the singing of a psalm. It was not uncommon for small groups of friends to gather weekly for such means.

Jesus and His disciples possibly formed just such a fellowship group. The fellowship meals of the early church appear to be a continuation of the table of fellowship which characterized the life of Jesus and His disciples. Such joyous fellowship served as a concrete manifestation of the grace of the kingdom of God which Jesus proclaimed. Jesus' last meal with His disciples may represent one specific example of such a fellowship meal causing some to trace the origins of the love feast directly to this event. See *Ordinances; Worship.*

Hulitt Gloer

LOVING KINDNESS Occasional KJV translation of the Hebrew, *chesed.* The Old Testament's highest expression for love. It is variously called God's election-, covenant-keeping, or steadfast love. It is a love which remains constant regardless of the circumstances. Although used mostly with God, it sometimes is used of love between people. See *Kindness; Love.*

LOWLAND See *Shephelah.*

LUBIM (Lū' bĭm) Racial name of uncertain meaning apparently applied to all white North Africans, especially the inhabitants of Libya (2 Chron. 12:3; 16:8; Dan. 11:43; Nah. 3:9). Many English translations read Libyans. See *Libya.*

LUCAS (Lū' căs) KJV transliteration of Greek for Luke. See *Luke.*

LUCIFER (Lū' cĭ fēr) The Latin translation (followed by the KJV) of the Hebrew word for "day star" in Isaiah 14:12, where the word was used as a title for the king of Babylon, who had exalted himself as a god. The prophet taunted the king by calling him "son of the dawn" (NIV), a play on a Hebrew term which could refer to a pagan god but normally indicated the light that appeared briefly before dawn. A later tradition associated the word with evil, although the Bible does not use it as such.

LUCIUS (Lū cī' ŭs) Personal name of uncertain meaning. *1.* Christian prophet and/or teacher from Cyrene who helped lead church at Antioch to set apart Saul and Barnabas for missionary service (Acts 13:1). Early church tradition tried, probably incorrectly, to identify him with either Luke or with 2. below. Thus an African was one of the first Christian evangelists and had an important part in the early days of the church of Antioch and in beginning the Christian world missions movement. *2.* A relative of Paul who sent greetings to the church at Rome (Rom. 16:21). He was apparently one of many Jews who adopted Greek names.

LUD (Lŭd) Racial name for person from Lydia. Plural is Ludim. *1.* Son of Egypt in the Table of Nations (Gen. 10:13) and thus, apparently, a people living near Egypt or under the political influence of Egypt. *2.* Son of Shem and grandson of Noah in Table of Nations (Gen. 10:22). Attempts to identify them with peoples mentioned in other Near Eastern sources have produced varying results: Lydians of Asia Minor called the Luddu by Assyrian records or the Lubdu living on the upper Tigris River. They were known for skill with the bow (Jer. 46:9; Ezek. 30:5 which place them under Egyptian influence and may refer to *1.* above if a distinction is to be made at all; otherwise, the reference is to mercenary soldiers from Lydia in Asia Minor serving in the Egyptians army, a practice apparently testified under Pharaoh Psammetichus before 600 B.C.). Lydian soldiers apparently served in Tyre's army (Ezek. 27:10). God promised even the isolated peoples like Lydia who had never heard of His glory would be invited to share in that glory (Isa. 66:19).

LUDIM (Lū' dīm) Hebrew plural of Lud. See *Lud.*

LUDITES (Lū' dītes) NIV spelling for Ludim. See *Lud.*

LUHITH (Lū' hĭth) Place name meaning "plateaus." It apparently identified a settlement in Moab on the road between Areopolis and Zoar, perhaps at present khirbet Medinet er-rash. Isaiah mourned for Moabite refugees who would have to climb the heights of Luhith to escape the enemy taking over their country (Isa. 15:5; compare Jer. 48:5).

LUKE Author of the Third Gospel and the Book of Acts in the New Testament, and a close friend and traveling companion of Paul. The apostle called him "beloved" (Col. 4:14). Luke referred to his journeys with Paul and his company in Acts 16:10–17; 20:5–15; 21:1–18; 27:1—28:16. Many scholars believe Luke wrote his Gospel and Acts while in Rome with Paul during the apostle's first Roman imprisonment. Apparently Luke remained nearby or with Paul also during the apostle's second Roman imprisonment. Shortly before his martyrdom, Paul wrote that "only Luke is with me" (2 Tim. 4:11).

Early church fathers Jerome (about A.D. 400) and Eusebius (about A.D. 300) identified Luke as being from Antioch. His interest in Antioch is clearly seen in his many references to that city (Acts 11:19–27; 13:1–3; 14:26; 15:22,35; 18:22). Luke adopted Philippi as his home, remaining behind there to superintend the young church while Paul went on to Corinth during the second missionary journey (Acts 16:40).

Paul identified Luke as a physician (Col. 4:14)

and distinguished Luke from those "of the circumcision" (Col. 4:11). Early sources indicate that Luke was a Gentile. Tradition holds that he was Greek. The circumstances of Luke's conversion are not revealed. An early source supplied a fitting epitaph: "He served the Lord without distraction, having neither wife nor children, and at the age of 84 he fell asleep in Boeatia, full of the Holy Spirit." See *Luke, Gospel of.*   *T. R. McNeal*

LUKE, GOSPEL OF The third and longest book in the New Testament. Luke is the first of a two-part work dedicated to the "most excellent Theophilus" (Luke 1:3; Acts 1:1). The Book of Acts forms the sequel to Luke, with the author explaining in Acts that Luke dealt with "all that Jesus began both to do and teach, until the day in which he was taken up" (Acts 1:1–2; see *Acts*).

Authorship Though the author of Luke-Acts never mentioned himself by name, he was obviously a close friend and traveling companion of Paul. In the "we-sections" of Acts (Acts 16:10–17; 20:5–15; 21:1–18; 27:1—28:16) the author of the narrative apparently joined Paul on his journeys. Through a process of elimination, the most likely choice for this person is "Luke, the beloved physician" (Col. 4:14).

Tradition for Lukan authorship is very strong, dating back to the early church. Early lists and descriptions of New Testament books dating from between A.D. 160–190 agree that Luke, the physician and companion of Paul, wrote the Gospel of Luke. Many of the early Church Fathers from as early as A.D. 185 readily accepted Luke as the author of the Third Gospel.

With the early church tradition unanimously ascribing the Third Gospel to Luke, the burden of proof is on those who argue against Lukan authorship. See *Luke.*

Date and Place of Writing The Book of Acts ends abruptly with Paul in his second year of house imprisonment in Rome. Scholars generally agree that Paul reached Rome around A.D. 60. This makes the Book of Acts written at the earliest around A.D. 61 or 62, with the Gospel written shortly before. Luke 19:41–44 and 21:20–24 records Jesus' prophecy of the destruction of Jerusalem. This cataclysmic event in ancient Judaism occurred in A.D. 70 at the hands of the Romans. It hardly seems likely that Luke would have failed to record this significant event. Assigning a date to the Gospel later than A.D. 70 would ignore this consideration. Many scholars, however, continue to favor a date about A.D. 80.

A second historical consideration pushes the dating even earlier. Many scholars feel Paul was released from the Roman imprisonment he was experiencing as Acts concludes. The apostle was later reimprisoned and martyred under the Neronian persecution which broke out in A. D. 64. Paul was enjoying considerable personal liberty and opportunities to preach the gospel (Acts 28:30,31) even though a prisoner. The optimism of the end of the Book of Acts suggests the Neronian persecution is a future event. One can hardly imagine that Paul's release would find no mention in the Acts narrative had it already occurred.

It seems best, then, to date the writing of Luke somewhere between A.D. 61 and 63. Those who argue that this does not allow Luke time to review Mark's Gospel (assuming it was written first) fail to take into account the tight web of association between those involved in Paul's ministry. See *Mark.*

As to where the Gospel was written, the most probable place is Rome. Luke reached Rome in Paul's company and was in Rome when Paul wrote Colossians (4:14) and Philemon (24) during this first Roman imprisonment. The circumstance would have allowed time for the composition of Luke-Acts. One ancient source suggested Achaia, a Greek province, as the place of writing. It seems reasonable to conclude that the Gospel, written in Rome, perhaps made its first appearance in Achaia or was finished there.

Purpose and Readership Luke himself identified the purpose of his writing the Gospel (Luke 1:1–4). He wanted to confirm for Theophilus the certainty of the things Theophilus had been taught. Luke also wanted this information available for a wider readership. Most scholars conclude that Luke's target audience were Gentile inquirers and Christians who needed strengthening in the faith.

Luke's purpose was to present a historical work "in order" (1:3). Most of his stories fall in chronological sequence. He often gave time indications (1:5,26,36,56,59; 2:42; 3:23; 9:28; 12:1,7). More than any other Gospel writer, Luke connected his story with the larger Jewish and Roman world (see 2:1; 3:1–2).

A strong argument can be presented for a second, though clearly subordinate, purpose. Some see Luke-Acts as an apology for the Christian faith, a defense of it designed to show Roman authorities that Christianity posed no political threat. Pilate declared Jesus innocent three times (Luke 23:4,14,22). Acts does not present Roman officials as unfriendly (Acts 13:4–12; 16:35–40; 18:12–17; 19:31). Agrippa remarked to Festus that Paul could have been freed if he had not appealed to Caesar (Acts 26:32). Paul is pictured as being proud of his Roman citizenship (Acts 22:28). The apostle is seen preaching and teaching in Rome openly without hindrance as Acts draws to a close. It is possible to see in all this an attempt by Luke to calm Roman authorities' fears about any supposed subversive character of Christianity.

Beyond the immediate purposes of the author, the Holy Spirit has chosen Luke's Gospel to reach all nations with the beautiful story of God's love in

Christ. Many claim the Lukan birth narrative (2:1–20) as their favorite. The canticles or songs in Luke (1:46–55; 1:67–79; 2:13–14; 2:29–32) have inspired countless melodies. Luke's Gospel has been a source for many artists, including Van Eyck, Van der Weyden, Rossetti, Plockhorst, Rubens, and Rembrandt.

Luke's sources Though Luke was not an eyewitness to the earthly life and ministry of Christ, he was in intimate contact with many who were. Luke was with Paul in Palestine in the late 50s, especially in Caesarea and Jerusalem (Acts 21:1–27:2). Members of the Jerusalem church (including James, the brother of Jesus) would have provided much oral testimony to the physician intent on writing an account of Jesus' life. Luke's association with Paul brought him into contact with leading apostolic witnesses, including James and Peter.

Most scholars believe Luke (as well as Matthew) relied on Mark's written Gospel. Mark probably was an eyewitness to some events in Jesus' life. His Gospel is generally recognized to reflect Peter's preaching about Christ. Mark was in Rome with Luke and Paul during Paul's captivity (Col. 4:10,14; Philem. 24). It would be natural to assume Luke had access to Mark's writings. Scholars have identified a source "Q" (an abbreviation for the German word *Quelle,* meaning "source"), referring to passages and sections of written material apparently available to Matthew and Luke either unavailable or unused by Mark (for example, Matt. 3:7–10/Luke 3:7–9; Matt. 24:45–51/Luke 12:42–46). This source may have been a collection of Jesus' sayings written down by His followers. See *Logia.*

John's Gospel certainly was not available for Luke (most scholars date John late in the first century). Any similarities between Luke's Gospel and John's can probably be accounted for by recognizing that a rich tradition, especially oral, provided a common source for all the Gospel writers.

Some scholars have posited an "L" source (an abbreviation for Luke) identifying some 500 verses exclusive to Luke, including the 132 verses of Luke 1 and 2. The argument that a separate document existed that only Luke had access to is not convincing. The new material introduced by Luke should be seen as the result of his own research and literary genius. One obvious example is the birth narratives of John the Baptist and Christ. The material that Luke uniquely presents give the Third Gospel much of its character.

Special emphases and characteristics As already noted, Luke took great pains to relate his narrative to contemporaneous *historical events.* Beginning with the birth narratives of John the Baptist and Jesus, he wrote with the eye for detail of a historian (see 1:5,36,56,59; 2:1,2,7,42; 3:23; 9:20,37,57; 22:1,7,66; 23:44,54; 24:1,13,29,33).

Luke stressed the *universal redemption* avail-

able to all through Christ. Samaritans enter the kingdom (9:51–6; 10:30–37; 17:11–19) as well as pagan Gentiles (2:32; 3:6,38; 4:25–27; 7:9; 10:1,47). Publicans, sinners, and outcasts (3:12; 5:27–32; 7:37–50; 19:2–10; 23:43) are welcome along with Jews (1:33;2:10) and respectable people (7:36; 11:37; 14:1). Both the poor (1:53; 2:7; 6:20; 7:22) and rich (19:2; 23:50) can have redemption.

Luke especially notes Christ's high regard for *women.* Mary and Elizabeth are central figures in chapters 1 and 2. Anna the prophetess and Joanna the disciple are mentioned only in Luke (2:36–38; 8:3; 24:10). Luke included the story of Christ's kind dealings with the widow of Nain (7:11–18) and the sinful woman who annointed Him (7:36–50). He also related Jesus' parable of the widow who persevered (18:1–8).

Outline

I. Luke's Purpose: Certainty in Christian Teaching (1:1–4).

II. Jesus Fulfilled Judaism's Expectations (1:5—2:52).
   A. John the Baptist will point Israelites to God (1:5–25).
   B. Jesus fulfilled promises to David (1:26–38).
   C. Jesus' birth fulfilled promises to patriarchs (1:39–56).
   D. John's birth a sign of God's faithfulness (1:57–80).
   E. Jesus' birth fulfilled messianic expectations (2:1–7).
   F. God verified Jesus' birth as messianic fulfillment (2:8–20).
   G. Jesus fulfilled Jewish law (2:21–24).
   H. Jesus' coming fulfilled God's promises to Israel and provided salvation for all (2:25–40).
   I. Jesus revealed divine wisdom (2:41–52).

III. Jesus Accepted Messianic Mission and Faced Rejection (3:1—4:44).
   A. John called for repentence and watchfulness (3:1–20).
   B. Jesus was baptized and acknowledged as God's Son (3:21–22).
   C. Jesus' lineage linked Him to the Davidic promise and the human race (3:23–38).
   D. Satan tempted Jesus (4:1–13).
   E. His own people rejected Jesus (4:14–30).
   F. Jesus revealed messianic power in teaching and healing (4:31–37).
   G. Jesus followed God's agenda to establish God's kingdom (4:38–44).

IV. Jesus Fulfilled His Mission in God's Way of Faith, Love, and Forgiveness (5:1—7:50).
   A. Jesus shared His mission with those of faith (5:1–16).

B. Jesus proved power to forgive (5:17–26).

C. Jesus called sinners into the joy of the messianic age (5:27–39).

D. Jesus' mission emphasized meeting human need (6:1–11).

E. Jesus called disciples to a life of loving action (6:12–49).

F. Jesus' mission was to all people (7:1–10).

G. Jesus' message was accepted by needy multitudes (7:11–17).

H. Jesus fulfilled His Spirit-given mission (7:18–23).

I. Jesus' mission inaugurated God's kingdom (7:24–30).

J. Jesus' mission emphasized forgiveness (7:31–50).

V. God's Kingdom Involves Power but Demands Faithfulness to the Point of Death (8:1—9:50).

A. Socially deprived accepted God's kingdom (8:1–3).

B. Disciples are those who learn and follow Jesus' teachings (8:4–21).

C. Jesus is Lord over threatening forces (8:22–25).

D. Jesus is Lord over demonic forces (8:26–39).

E. Jesus is Lord over incurable diseases and death (8:40–56).

F. Jesus' disciples are empowered to carry out His mission (9:1–6).

G. Jesus' power was obvious to Herod (9:7–9).

H. Jesus' power satisfies human need (9:10–17).

I. God's kingdom is revealed in self-sacrificing suffering (9:18–27).

J. God, Moses, and Elijah affirmed Jesus' sonship (9:28–36).

K. Sacrificial commitment to the kingdom's mission is the source of kingdom power (9:37–45).

L. Faith and commitment are the source of true greatness (9:46–50).

VI. The Kingdom Is Characterized by Faithful Ministry and Witness (9:51—13:21).

A. Unavoidable climax to Jesus' ministry awaited Him in Jerusalem (9:51–56).

B. Kingdom service takes top priority (9:57–62).

C. Nearing judgment calls for courageous witness (10:1–16).

D. The kingdom's mission requires joyful participation (10:17–20).

E. Prophets looked for Jesus' revelation of God (10:21–24).

F. Kingdom leaders provide loving ministry to others (10:25–37).

G. A disciple's top priority is learning the Master's teaching (10:38–42).

H. The Model Prayer characterizes kingdom members (11:1–13).

I. The kingdom's nearness is demonstrated in Jesus' power over demons (11:14–28).

J. The Son of man is the only sign of the kingdom (11:29–32).

K. The kingdom brings true light (11:33–36).

L. Kingdom members help the needy (11:37–54).

M. Kingdom members boldly witness to the Son of man (12:1–12).

N. Kingdom members seek the kingdom of God first (12:13–34).

O. Kingdom members are ready for the Master's return (12:35–48).

P. Disciples cannot avoid opposition and division (12:49–53).

Q. Now is the time for repentance (12:54—13:19).

R. The kingdom frees from human regulations and satanic domination (13:10–17).

S. The kingdom grows in a steady, surprising way (13:18–21).

VII. Entrance requirements for the kingdom (13:22—19:27)

A. Entrance not governed by human standards (13:22–30).

B. Jesus' destiny not governed by humans (13:31–35).

C. Kingdom conduct is governed by concern for people (14:1–14).

D. Kingdom membership requires only acceptance of Jesus' invitation (14:15–24).

E. Kingdom membership requires total allegiance (14:25–35).

F. Sinners are joyfully accepted into kingdom (15:1–32).

G. Earthly treasure should serve kingdom purposes and should never be one's master (16:1–13).

H. The kingdom fulfills the Old Testament (16:14–31).

I. Kingdom membership requires forgiveness and service (17:1–10).

J. Faith is the only entrance requirement for the kingdom (17:11–19).

K. Kingdom members prepare for the sudden return of Jesus (17:20–37).

L. Kingdom members are persistent in prayer (18:1–8).

M. Kingdom membership requires trusting humility (18:9–17).

N. Obedient faith qualifies one for the kingdom (18:18–30).

O. Discipleship requires allegiance to the Suffering Servant (18:31–43).

P. Recognition of lostness is necessary for

kingdom membership (19:1–10).

Q. Kingdom membership requires loyal service and patient waiting (19:11–27).

VIII. Jesus' Kingdom Power Aroused Opposition (19:28—22:6).

A. Israel rejected its promised King (19:28–44).

B. Jesus exercised authority in the Temple (19:45—20:19).

C. Jesus exercised God's authority (20:20–26).

D. Jesus' understanding was greater than that of Sadducees (20:27–40).

E. Messiah's role was greater than the political role of David (20:41–44).

F. False religious leaders face judgment (20:45–47).

G. Value of kingdom stewardship is determined by generosity (21:1–4).

H. The Son of man controls the future (21:5–36).

I. Human betrayal, not popular demand or legal justice, led to Jesus' arrest (21:37—22:6).

IX. Jesus Died as the True Passover Lamb (22:7—23:56).

A. Jesus' Passover sacrifice opens the door for kingdom service and rule (22:7–30).

B. Participation in Jesus' Passover brings satanic and human opposition (22:31–38).

C. Participation in Jesus' Passover demands prayer (22:39–46).

D. Spiritual darkness is responsible for Jesus' death (22:47–53).

E. Refusal to participate in Jesus' Passover brings sorrow (22:54–62).

F. Jesus was crucified because of religious blindness and pride (22:63–71).

G. Crowd approval, not guilt, led to Jesus' crucifixion (23:1–25).

H. Corrupt religious systems are judged by Jesus' crucifixion (23:26–31).

I. Jesus responded to opponents with forgiveness (23:32–34).

J. Jesus died to bring sinners into the kingdom (23:35–43).

K. Jesus showed faith and control in death (23:44–36).

L. Jesus died unjustly as a righteous Man (23:47–49).

M. Jesus' burial proves His death (23:50–56).

X. Jesus' Resurrection Is the Doorway to Faith and Mission (24:1–53).

A. Jesus' resurrection fulfilled prophecy, confirmed Jesus' teaching, and awakened faith (24:1–45).

B. Jesus' resurrection prepared for the church's gospel of forgiveness (24:46–48).

C. Church needed Spirit before undertaking mission (24:49).

D. Jesus' ascension leads church to worship (24:50–53).   *T. R. McNeal*

LUKEWARM Tepid; neither hot nor cold (Rev. 3:16). The city of Laodicea received its water from an aqueduct several miles long. The lukewarm water which arrived at the city served as an appropriate illustration for a tasteless, good-for-nothing Christianity.

LUNATIC KJV term for epilepsy or insanity (Matt. 4:24; 17:15). The term lunacy derives from the Latin *luna* (moon) and reflects the popular notion that the mental state of the "lunatic" fluctuated with the changing phases of the moon. The Greek terms underlying Matthew 4:24 and 17:15 are likewise related to the Greek term for moon. Lunacy was not clearly distinguished from demon possession (Matt. 17:18; compare Mark 9:17; Luke 9:39).

LUST In contemporary usage, a strong craving or desire, especially sexual desire. KJV and earlier English versions frequently used lust in the neutral sense of desire. This older English usage corresponded to the use of the underlying Hebrew and Greek terms which could be used in a positive sense: of the desire of the righteous (Prov. 10:24), of Christ's desire to eat the Passover with His disciples (Luke 22:15), or of Paul's desire to be with Christ (Phil. 1:23). Since lust has taken on the primary meaning of sexual desire, modern translations often replace the KJV's lust with a term with a different nuance. NRSV, for example, used crave/craving (Num. 11:34; Ps. 78:18); covet (Rom. 7:7); desire (Ex. 15:9; Prov. 6:25; 1 Cor. 10:6); long for (Rev. 18:14).

The unregenerate (preconversion) life is governed by deceitful lusts or desires (Eph. 4:22; 2:3; Col. 3:5; Tit. 2:12). Following conversion, such fleshly desires compete for control of the individual with spiritual desires (Gal. 5:16–17; 2 Tim. 2:22). First John 2:16–17 warns that desires of the flesh and eyes are not from God and will pass away with the sinful world. Here lust or desire includes not only sexual desire but also other vices such as materialism. James 1:14–15 warns that desire is the beginning of all sin and results in death. Jesus warned that one who lusts has already sinned (Matt. 5:28). Part of God's judgment on sin is to give persons over to their own desires (Rom. 1:24). Only the presence of the Holy Spirit in the life of the believer makes victory over sinful desires possible (Rom. 8:1–2).

LUTE A stringed instrument with a large, pear-shaped body and a neck. NRSV used lute to translate two Hebrew terms (Pss. 92:3; 150:3). NAS and NIV translated the first term as "10-stringed lute" and the second as harp. The KJV translated both terms as psaltery. See *Music, Instruments, Dancing.*

LUZ (Lŭz) Place name meaning "almond tree." *1.* Original name of Bethel (Gen. 28:19). See *Bethel.* Joshua 16:2 seems to distinguish the two places, Bethel perhaps being the worship place and Luz the city. Bethel would then be Burj Beitin and Luz, Beitin. *2.* A city in the land of the Hittites which a man founded after showing the tribe of Joseph how to conquer Bethel (Judg. 1:26). Its location is not known. See *Hittites.*

LXX The Roman numeral seventy which serves as the symbol for the Septuagint, the earliest Greek translation of the Old Testament. According to one tradition, the Septuagint was the work of seventy scholars. See *Septuagint; Bible, Texts and Versions.*

LYCAONIA (Lўc ā ō′ nĭ à) Roman province in the interior of Asia Minor including cities of Lystra, Iconium, and Derbe. See Acts 14:1–23.

LYCAONIAN (Lўc ā ō′ nĭ an) Citizen of or language of Lycaonia. See *Lycaonia.*

LYCIA (Lўc′ ĭ à) Geographical name indicating the projection on the southern coast of Asia Minor between Caria and Pamphylia. See Acts 27:5.

LYDDA (Lўd′ dà) Place name of uncertain meaning. The Old Testament Lod (1 Chron. 8:12), Lydda was a Benjaminite town near the Plain of Sharon. It was located at the intersection of the caravan routes from Egypt to Babylon and the road from Joppa to Jerusalem. According to Ezra 2:33 it was resettled after the Exile (See Neh. 7:37; 11:35). Later, it became a district captial of Samaria. The church spread to Lydda early (Acts 9:32) as the result of Peter's ministry. Christianity became a strong influence in Lydda by the second century.

LYDIA (Lўd′ ĭ à; *from king Lydus*). Both a place and personal name of uncertain meaning. *1.* The country in Asia Minor whose capital was Sardis. Habitation of the area dates from prehistory. The Hittites left their mark on the land through monuments. Lydia's most famous ruler was Croessus (560–546 BC), a name synonymous with wealth. His kingdom was captured by Cyrus, who seven years later captured Babylon and freed the exiles. Lydians were named by Ezekiel as "men of war" or mercenaries who fought to defend Tyre (27:10) and who made an alliance with Egypt (30:5) *2.* Lydia was the first European converted to Christ

under the preaching of Paul at Philippi (Acts 16:14). Her name originally might have been the designation of her home, "a woman of Lydia," since Thyatira was in the province of Lydia. Being a worshiper of God, Lydia could have been a convert to Judaism, although this cannot be stated with certainty. She did know enough about Judaism to converse with Paul about the religion. Lydia hosted Paul and his entourage in Philippi after her conversion. Her profession as a "seller of purple" meant that she probably was quite wealthy (Acts 16:12–15,50).   *Mike Mitchell*

LYDIAN (Lўd′ ĭ an) Person from Lydia. See *Lydia.*

LYE Substance used for cleansing purposes from the earliest times. Two Hebrew words are used in the Old Testament for lye. *Nethar* probably refers to sodium bicarbonate. This material occurs naturally and is referred to by ancient writers as appearing in Egypt and Armenia.

Bor likely refers to potassium carbonate and is sometimes called vegetable lye. It is a strongly alkaline solution made by burning certain plants like soapwort and leaching the lye from the ashes. This was the type of lye normally used in Palestine, for there are no known deposits of sodium bicarbonate there. The same Hebrew spelling also means, "purity" (Ps. 18:20,24) leading to confusion in English translations.

LYSANIAS (Lў sā′ nĭ as) Personal name of unknown meaning. Roman tetrarch of Abilene about A.D. 25–30 and thus at beginning of John the Baptist's ministry (Luke 3:1). See *Abilene.*

LYSIAS (Lўs′ ĭ às) Second name or birth name of Roman tribune or army captain who helped Paul escape the Jews and appear before Felix, the governor (Acts 23:26). See *Claudius.* His name also appears in some Greek manuscripts at Acts 24:7 but not in the manuscripts followed by many modern translations as the earliest. Compare 24:22.

LYSTRA (Lўs′ trà) A city in south central Asia Minor and an important Lycaonian center. According to Acts 16:1, it probably was the home of young Timothy, one of Paul's companions in the ministry. Paul's healing of a crippled man at Lystra (Acts 14:8–10) caused the inhabitants to revere him as a god. Many believed his preaching but were turned against the missionary by Judaizers from Antioch and Iconium. Paul was dragged out of Lystra, stoned, and left for dead. He revived and later went back to the city to lend strength to the new Christians.

ΒΗΘΛΕΕΜ

ΕΦΡΑΘΑ
ΡΑΜΑΦΩΝΗ
ΗΟ ΕΝΡΑΜΑ
ΗΚΥΟΘΗ

ΑΚΕΛ
ΔΑΜΑ
ΘΑΜΝΑΕΝΑΛΕΚΟΡΕΝ   ΝΙΚΟΠΟΛΙΟ
ΙΟΥΔΑΣΤΑΑΥΤΟΥΠΡΟ
ΡΑΤΑ
ΑΝΩΘΗΝΥΜ
ΒΗΘΟΑΝΝΑΒΑ ΓΕΔΟΥΡΗΚ
ΗΔΙΡΘΑ

ΑΒΛΗΚΑΧΠΟΛΙΟ

ΠΑΒΝΗΛΗΚΑ

ΕΝΕΤΑΡΑ

ΓΕΘΩΝΥΝΕΙΙ ΤΑΠΑΙΤΟ
ΟΕΛΑΝΑ Ε ΕΠΤΟΝΕΤΑΤ

ΠΡΟ ΟΔΜ

M

Detail of the famous sixth century A.D. mosaic map of Medeba (Madeba) in Jordan.

ΝΑΠΠΑΙΟΙ

M Symbol designating one of the alleged sources of Matthew's Gospel according to the four document hypothesis. The source purportedly consists of that part of Matthew not paralleled by Mark or Luke.

MAACAH (Mā′ å cah) A personal name of uncertain meaning (possibly "dull" or "stupid"). *1.* Son of Nahor, Abraham's brother (Gen. 22:24); this Maacah perhaps gave his name to the Aramean kingdom west of Basham and southwest of Mount Hermon; the residents of this kingdom, the Maachathites (Mā′ ăch å thītes), were not driven out during the Israelite conquest of Canaan (Josh. 13:13). Later, this people sided with the Ammonites against David (2 Sam. 10:6–8). This nation is perhaps personified as the wife (ally) of Machir at 1 Chronicles 7:16. *2.* Concubine of Caleb (1 Chron. 2:48). *3.* Wife of Jeiel of Gibeon (1 Chron. 8:29; 9:35). *4.* Wife of David and the mother of Absalom (2 Sam. 3:3; 1 Chron. 3:2). *5.* Father/ancestor of one of David's warriors (1 Chron. 11:43). *6.* Father/ancestor of Shephatiah who led the tribe of Simeon in David's reign (1 Chron. 27:16). *7.* Father/ancestor of Achish, king of Gath (1 Kings 2:39). *8.* Mother of King Abijam (1 Kings 15:2) and ancestress of King Asa (1 Kings 15:10,13).

MAACATH (Mā′ å căth) NRSV, NAS spelling of Maacah (Jos. 13:13).

MAACHAH (Mā å chah) KJV alternate form of Maacah.

MAACHATHITES See *Maacah 1.*

MAADAI (Mā å dā ī) An Israelite forced to give up his foreign wife as part of Ezra's reforms (Ezra 10:34).

MAADIAH (Mā å dī′ ah) Personal name of uncertain meaning (perhaps "Yah assembles," "Yahu promises," or "Yah adorns."). A priest who returned from Exile with Zerubbabel (Neh. 12:5). He is perhaps the same as Moadiah (Neh. 12:17) or Maaziah (Neh. 10:8).

MAAI (Mā ā ī) Personal name of uncertain meaning. A musician participating in Nehemiah's dedication of the rebuilt Jerusalem walls (Neh. 12:36).

MAALEH-ACRABBIM (Mā′ å lĕh ă crăb′ bĭm) KJV transliteration of a phrase meaning ascent (NAS, NRSV, REB) or pass (NIV) of Akrabbim (Josh. 15:3). See *Akrabbim.*

MAARATH (Mā å răth) Place name meaning "barren field." Name of a village in Judah's hill country (Josh. 15:59), possibly identical with Maroth (Mic. 1:12). The site is possibly modern khirbet Qufin two miles north of Beth-zur.

MAAREH-GEBA (Mā′ å rĕh-gē′ ba) Place name meaning, "clearing of Geba." Israel's army readied an ambush there for tribe of Benjamin (Judg. 20:33 NAS). Other translations translated the first part of the name or follow a Greek text in reading "west of Gibeah," a change of the final Hebrew letter. See *Gibeah.*

MAASAI (Mā′ å saî) Possibly a shortened form of Maaseiah meaning, "work of Yah. One of the priests returning from Exile (1 Chron. 9:12), Maasai is likely identical with Amashai (Neh. 11:13). KJV transliterated Maasiai.

MAASEIAH (mā å seî ah) Personal name meaning, "work of Yahweh," appearing in a longer and shorter Hebrew form. Several of the many scattered references perhaps refer to the same person, though it is no longer possible to press identifications: *1.* Levite musician during David's reign (1 Chron. 15:18,20). *2.* Participant in high priest Jehoida's revolt which put Joash on the throne (2 Chron. 23:1). *3.* One of Uzziah's military officers (2 Chron. 26:11). *4.* Son of King Ahaz of Judah (2 Chron. 28:7). *5.* Governor of Jerusalem during the reign of Josiah (2 Chron. 34:8). *6.* Father of false prophet Zedekiah (Jer. 29:21). *7.* Father of the priest Zephaniah (Jer. 21:1; 29:25; 37:3). *8.* Temple doorkeeper (Jer. 35:4). *9.* Postexilic resident of Jerusalem from tribe of Judah (Neh. 11:5), likely identical with Asaiah (1 Chron. 9:5). *10.* Benjaminite ancestor of some returned exiles (Neh. 11:7). *11.–14.* Names of three priests and one layman in Ezra's time who had taken foreign wives (Ezra 10:18,21,22,30). *15.* Father/ancestor of the Azariah participating in Nehemiah's rebuilding of the wall (Neh. 3:23). *16.* Chief of the people who signed Ezra's covenant (Neh. 10:25), possibly identical with *14* and/or *18. 17.* One of those standing beside Ezra at the reading of the law (Neh. 8:4), possibly *14* and/or *16. 18.* One of the Levites interpreting the law which Ezra read (Neh. 8:7), possibly identical with *17. 19.* Priest participating in the dedication of the rebuilt walls of Jerusalem (Neh. 12:41), perhaps identical with *11, 12,* or *13. 20.* Another priest participating in the dedication, perhaps identical with *11, 12,* or *13. 21.* KJV form for Mahseiah. See *Mahseiah.*

MAASIAI (Mā å sī′ aî) KJV form of Maasai.

MAATH (Mā′ ăth) Ancestor of Jesus (Luke 3:26).

MAAZ (Mā ăž) Personal name of uncertain meaning (possibly "angry"). See 1 Chronicles 2:27.

MAAZIAH (Mā å zī′ ah) Personal name meaning "Yahweh is a refuge." *1.* Ancestor of a division of priests serving in David's time (1 Chron. 24:18). *2.* Priest who signed Ezra's covenant (Neh. 10:8).

MACBANNAI (Măc′ băn nâi) NIV spelling of Machbanai.

MACBENAH (Măc bē′ nah) NIV spelling of Machbenah.

MACCABEES, BOOK OF See *Apocrypha*.

MACCABEES, MACCABEAN WAR Maccabees was the name given to the family of Mattathias, a faithful priest, who led in a revolt against the Hellenizing influences of the Seleucid King Antiochus Epiphanes in about 168 B.C. See *Apocrypha; Intertestamental History*.

MACE See *Weapons*.

MACEDONIA (Măç ĕ dō nĭ a) Now the northernmost province of Greece; in antiquity, the fertile plain north and west of the Thermaic Gulf from the Haliacmon river in the southwest to the Axios in the east ("Lower Macedonia") and the mountainous areas to the west and north ("Upper Macedonia," today divided between central northern Greece, southeastern Albania, and the Yugoslav province of Macedonia). Macedonia is the link between the Balkan peninsula to the north and the Greek mainland and the Mediterranean Sea to the south. The important land route from Byzantium (Istanbul) in the east to the Adriatic Sea in the west (in Roman times the "Via Egnatia") crosses it as does the north to south road from the central Balkan (the area of the Danube and Save rivers) which reached the Aegean Sea at the Thermaic Gulf and continued past Mount Olympus through the narrow valley of Tempe into Thessaly and central Greece.

History Archaeological discoveries have demonstrated that Macedonia was settled as early as the Middle Bronze Age (about 1500 B.C.) probably by Thracian and Illyrian tribes. The Macedonians, Hellenic tribes which were part of the Dorian invasion, settled first in the western mountains (the upper Haliacmon valley) before 1200 B.C. They began to conquer the central plains about 700 B.C. The Macedonian kings established their first capital in Aigai, probably not at modern Edessa but at modern Vergina south of the Haliacmon river. There a golden sarcophagus, supposedly of King Philip II (father of Alexander), was found in a vaulted tomb. Later the capital was moved to Pella (birthplace of Alexander the Great) where houses of the Macedonian nobility with beautiful pebble mosaics and the gigantic foundations of the royal palace have been excavated. Between 800 and 600 B.C. the Macedonians expelled or subjected the older populations. They extended their realm to the east where they incorporated the lands between the Axios and the Strymon. They also reached southward to the coastal lands between Mount Olympus and the Aegean Sea. For several centuries, the Macedo-

nian kings were involved in battles for the control of Upper Macedonia with its mixed Greek, Illyrian, and Thracian population. At the same time, Macedonia came increasingly under the influence of Greek culture and language (the original Macedonian language was probably a different Hellenic dialect). The famous Greek tragedian Euripides spent some time at the court of the Macedonian kings; and Aristotle, before he founded his philosophical school in Athens, served as the teacher of the Macedonian prince Alexander.

Philip II (359–336 B.C.) established firm control over the entire Macedonian area and extended it to the east beyond the Strymon into Thrace. There he founded the city of Philippi in place of the Thracian colony Crenides. It became the chief mining center for the gold and silver mines in the Pangaeon mountain. Philip II also subjected Thessaly to his rule and incorporated the Chalcidice peninsula into his realm. When he was assassinated in 336 B.C., Macedonia was the strongest military power in Greece. Its military strength and the wealth established by Philip II enabled his son Alexander to defeat the Persian Empire and to conquer the entire realm from the eastern Mediterranean to the Indus River (including today's Turkey, Egypt, Syria, Palestine, Iraq, Iran, and parts of Afghanistan and Pakistan).

In the Hellenistic period the capital was moved to Thessalonica, founded 315 B.C. at the head of the Thermaic Gulf by Cassander and named for his wife Thessalia. During the Hellenistic period, Macedonia was ruled by the Antigonids, descendants of Alexander's general Antigonus Monophthalmus. In 168 B.C. Perseus, the last Macedonian king, was defeated by the Romans. Rome first divided Macedonia into four independent "free" districts, then established it as a Roman province (148 B.C.) with Thessalonica as the capital and Beroea as the seat of the provinical assembly. During the time of Augustus, some of the Macedonian cities were refounded as Roman colonies: Dion, at the foot of Mount Olympus, became *Colonia Julia Augusta Diensis;* Philippi, where Marc Antony had defeated the assassins of Caesar—Brutus and Cassius—was settled with Roman veterans and renamed *Colonia Augusta Julia Philippensium.* While the general language of Macedonia remained Greek, the official language of the Roman colonies was Latin (until after A.D. 300 almost all inscriptions found in these cities are in Latin). At the time of the Great Persecution of the Christians (303–311), Thessalonica was one of the four capitals of the Roman Empire and served as residence of the emperor Galerius, one of the most fanatic persecutors of Christianity.

Religions Ancient Macedonian religion was dominated by two different elements. (1) The Macedonians who had conquered the country brought their own gods which are on the whole the same as the traditional gods of the Greeks. Among them, Zeus as the father of Makedon, founding hero of the Macedonians, and Herakles are the two most important deities. Also the cult of the Greek god Dionysus was widespread. Both Dionysus and Herakles appear as the patron deities of Alexander the Great. (2) At the same time, the Macedonians adopted several of the older cults and deities of the indigenous population, especially of the Thracians. A female deity of Thracian origin appears under the Greek name Artemis; numerous rock reliefs of this Artemis have been discovered on the Acropolis of Philippi where she sometimes appears with a tree of life in one hand. In Lefkopetra, a few miles west of Beroea, a temple of the "Aboriginal Mother of the Gods" has recently been discovered. Most important became the acceptance of the Thracian Cabirus. On the island of Samothrace two Cabiri were worshiped in a famous mystery cult together with a Thracian mother goddess. In the cities of Thessalonica and Philippi, one Cabirus was venerated as the founding hero of the city. As he is depicted with a hammer in one hand and a drinking horn in the other, he also seems to have been revered as the patron deity of construction workers and miners. In Thessalonica, his role was later assumed by the Christian martyr Demetrius. A widespread religious symbol was the "Macedonian rider," depicted on coins of the Macedonian kings and on many tombstones. He may have been understood as a guide to the afterlife. This originally Thracian hero became the prototype for the Christian saint George. Belief in the judgment of the dead and an afterlife is in evidence in the paintings of a Macedonian tomb found near Lefkadia.

In the Hellenistic and Roman periods, new cults were introduced to Macedonia. The cult of the Egyptian gods Sarapis, Isis, and Anubis was established in Thessalonica before 100 B.C. The Egyptian sanctuary discovered in Thessalonica included, together with many inscriptions and votive offerings, a dining club for slaves and freedmen under the tutelage of the god Anubis. An Egyptian sanctuary was also excavated on the slope of the acropolis of Philippi and in the Roman colony Dion. Worship of "God the Most High" (Zeus Hypsistos), elsewhere associated with the God of the Israelites, is also in evidence. Roman veterans who were settled in the newly founded colonies brought their gods to Macedonia; a sanctuary dedicated to the Italian god Silvanus was found on the acropolis of Philippi. Temples for the worship of the Roman emperor were established in most cities. In Thessalonica the imperial cult appears in the special form of the worship of the Roman benefactors. The evidence for ancient Judaism in Macedonia is meager. An inscription (still unpublished) recently found in Philippi mentions a synagogue. The only evidence for Israelites in Thessalonica comes from a Samaritan inscription dating after A.D. 400. A Jewish synagogue has been excavated recently in

the Macedonian city of Stobi in the valley of the Axios (Vardar) River (in Yugoslav Macedonia).

Christianity in Macedonia The Christian message came to Macedonia through the preaching of the apostle Paul. Acts 16:9–10 describes the dream vision that came to Paul in Troas: a Macedonian appeared to him and invited him to Macedonia. Paul and his associates, sailing from Troas via Samothrace, arrived in Neapolis (today Kavalla), the most important port of eastern Macedonia, and went inland to Philippi where, according to the account of Acts 16:14–15, they were received by Lydia, a God-fearer from Thyatira, and founded the first Christian community in Europe, probably in the year A.D. 50. The correspondence of Paul with this church, now preserved in the Epistle to the Philippians, gives testimony to the early development, organization, and generosity of this church. Forced to leave Philippi after an apparently brief stay (Acts 16:16–40 reports the incident of the healing of a possessed slave girl and Paul's subsequent imprisonment), Paul went to the capital Thessalonica via Amphipolis on the Via Egnatia (Acts 17:1). The church which he founded in Thessalonica (compare Acts 17:2–12) was the recipient of the oldest Christian writing, i.e., the First Letter to the Thessalonians which Paul wrote from Corinth after he had preached in Beroea and in Athens (Acts 17:13–15).

Apart from this Pauline correspondence, our information about the Macedonian churches in the first three Christian centuries is extremely slim. Shortly after A.D. 100, bishop Polycarp of Smyrna wrote to the Philippians who had asked him to forward copies of the letters of the famous martyr Ignatius of Antioch. Polycarp also wrote to advise the Philippians with respect to the case of a presbyter who had embezzled funds. Otherwise, almost no detailed information is available for the time before Constantine. *Helmut Koester*

MACEDONIANS (Mă cĕ dō′ nĭ ans) Natives or residents of Macedonia (Acts 19:29; 27:2; 2 Cor. 9:2). See *Macedonia*.

MACHAERUS (Må chē′ rŭs) Palace-fortress located about fifteen miles southeast of the mouth of the Jordan on a site rising 3,600 feet above the sea. Herod the Great rebuilt the fortress. Josephus gives the Machaerus as the site of the imprisonment and execution of John the Baptist. Mark's reference to Galilean nobles among Herod's guests has prompted some interpreters to suggest a site further north. The Gospels, however, associate John's ministry with the Judean wilderness (Mark 1:5; Matt. 3:1; John 3:22–23). That John's disciples claimed his body (Mark 6:29) suggests a site, such as the Macherus, near the center of John's ministry.

MACHBANAI (Mčh′ bå nâî) Military captain of tribe of Gad who served David (1 Chron. 12:13).

MACHBANNAI (Măch′ băn nâi) TEV spelling of Machbanai.

MACHBENA (Măch be′ nà) NAS spelling of Machbenah.

MACHBENAH (Măch bē′ nah) A descendant of Caleb or a village in Judah, possibly identical with Meconah, inhabited by descendants of Caleb (1 Chron. 2:49).

MACHI (Mā′ chī) Personal name, possibly meaning "reduced" or "bought" (Num. 13:15). Spy of tribe of Gad who explored Promised Land.

MACHIR (Mā′ chīr) Personal name meaning "sold." *1.* Oldest son of Manasseh and grandson of Joseph (Josh. 17:1). He was the father of Gilead (Josh. 17:1), Peresh, and Sheresh (1 Chron. 7:16), and a daughter whose name is not given (1 Chron. 2:21). He had a brother named Asriel (1 Chron. 7:14) and a wife named Maacah (1 Chron. 7:16). Machir was the head of the family called the Machirites (Num. 26:29). Apparently Machir along with his family had a reputation for being expert warriors (Josh. 17:1). "Because he was a man of war," Machir was allotted the territory of Bashan and Gilead, east of the Jordan (Josh. 17:1). Apparently the territory of the Machirites started at the site of Mahanaim, on the Jabbok River, extended northward, and included the region around the Yarmuk River (Josh. 13:29–31).
2. Son of Ammiel and member of the tribe of Manasseh. He came from the site of Lo-debar, perhaps a village near Mahanaim. He is recognized in the Old Testament for the assistance he provided Mephibosheth, the son of Jonathan (2 Sam. 9, especially vv. 4–5) and David during the period of Absalom's rebellion (2 Sam. 17:27–29). See *Manasseh.*　　　　*La Moine De Vries*

MACHIRITES (Mà′ chī rītes) See *Machir.*

MACHNADEBAI (Măch năd′ ē bâi) Name, possibly meaning "possession of Nebo," of one of the laymen forced to give up their foreign wives in Ezra's reform (Ezra 10:40).

MACHPELAH (Măch pē′ lah) Place name meaning, "the double cave." Burial place located near Hebron for Sarah (Gen. 23:19), Abraham (25:9), Isaac, Rebekah, Jacob, Leah, and probably other members of the family. After Sarah's death Abraham purchased the field of Machpelah and its cave as a sepulcher. The owner, Ephron the Hittite, offered it to Abraham for free, but the patriarch refused the gift and paid the fair price of 400 shekels of silver. Such conversation was typical of negotiations to purchase land in that day. Both Ephron and Abraham expected a purchase to be made. The cave became the burial place for each of the succeeding generations. Jacob requested burial there before he died in Egypt, and was returned there by his sons (Gen. 49:29; 50:13).

MACNADEBAI (Măc nă′ dē bâi) NIV spelling of Machnadebai.

MADAI (Mā′ dâi) Name of a son of Japheth (Gen. 10:2; 1 Chron. 1:5). The name means "Middle land," suggesting that Madai is to be understood as the ancester of the Medians.

MADIAN (Mā′ dī an) KJV spelling of Midian (Acts 7:29).

MADMANNAH (Măd măn′ nah) Place name meaning, "dung heap." City in the Negeb assigned to Judah (Josh. 15:31), possibly identical with Beth-marcaboth (Josh. 19:5). Suggested sites include the modern khirbet umm Demneh and khirbet Tatrit, both in the vicinity of Dharhiriyah. The reference to Shaaph as the father of Madmannah (1 Chron. 2:49) is open to various interpretations: (1) Shaaph (re)founded the city; (2) Shaaph's descendants settled in the city; or (3) Shaaph had a son named Madmannah.

MADMEN (Măd měn) A name meaning "Dung pit," applied to a city of Moab (Jer. 48:2). Dimon (Dibon), the capital city, is perhaps the intended reference. See *Dimon.* Jeremiah's dirge perhaps refers to Asshurbanipal's suppression of a Moabite revolt in 650 B.C.

MADMENAH (Măd mē nah) The place name (meaning "Dung Hill") of one of the points on the northern invasion route to Jerusalem (Isa. 10:31). The site is possibly Shu'fat. Isaiah perhaps refers to the invasion of Sennacherib in 701 B.C.

MADON (mā′ dŏn) Place name meaning, "site of justice." Town in Galilee whose king joined in an unsuccessful alliance against Israel (Josh. 11:1; 12:19). The site has been identified as the summit of Qarn Hattim, northwest of Tiberias.

MAGADAN (Măg′ a dän) A site on the Sea of Galilee (Matt. 15:39). At Mark 8:10, most translations follow other Greek manuscripts reading Dalmanutha. KJV follows the received text of its day in reading Magdala. The location of Magadan, if it is a correct reading, is not known.

MAGBISH (Măg bĭsh) Place name meaning, "pile." A town in Judah's territory, possibly identified with the modern khirbet el-Mahbiyeh three miles southwest of Adullam, to which exiles returned to reclaim their inheritance (Ezra 2:30).

MAGDALA (Măg′ dà là) Place name perhaps

The area of the village of Magdala and the plain surrounding it.

meaning, "tower." City on the western shore of the Sea of Galilee and center of a prosperous fishing operation. The town was located on a main highway coming from Tiberias. See *Magadan.* A certain Mary, who had been healed of demon possession by Jesus, was from Magdala. See *Marys of the Bible.*

MAGDALENE See *Magdala; Marys of the Bible.*

MAGDIEL (Măg dĭ' ĕl) Personal (and tribal) name meaning "choice gift of God." Edomite chieftain or the area occupied by his descendants (Gen. 36:43; 1 Chron. 1:54).

MAGGOT A soft-bodied, legless grub that is the intermediate stage of some insects (Job 25:6; Isa. 14:11). The term always occurs in parallel with worm and serves to highlight human mortality. See *Insects.*

MAGI (Mă' gī) Eastern wise men, priests, and astrologers expert in interpreting dreams and other "magic arts."

1. Men whose interpretation of the stars led them to Palestine to find and honor Jesus, the newborn King (Matt. 2). The term has a Persian background. The earliest Greek translation of Daniel 2:2,10 uses "magi" to translate the Hebrew term for astrologer (compare 4:7; 5:7). The magi who greeted Jesus' birth may have been from Babylon, Persia, or the Arabian desert. Matthew gives no number, names, or royal positions to the magi. Before A.D. 225 Tertullian called them kings. From the three gifts, the deducation was made that they were three in number. Shortly before A.D. 600 the Armenian Infancy Gospel named them: Melkon (later Melchior), Balthasar, and Gaspar. The visit of the magi affirms international recognition by leaders of other religions of Jesus' place as the expected King.

2. In Acts 8:9 the related verb describes Simon as practicing sorcery, with a bad connotation. Such negative feelings had long been associated with some uses of the term.

3. In Acts 13:6,8 Bar-Jesus or Elymas is designated a sorcerer or one of the magi as well as a false prophet. Paul blinded Simon, showing God's power over the magic arts.

MAGIC BANDS Bands or cushions placed on the wrist in magical practices (Ezek. 13:18,20). The KJV translates "pillows." Their precise nature is unknown. Apparently they represented part of a diviner's paraphanalia used to determine the destinies the gods had determined. See *Kerchiefs.*

MAGISTRATE A government official with administrative and judicial responsibilities. At Ezra 7:25 magistrate is perhaps a parallel title to judge. Possibly, judges and magistrates handled different cases, for example, cases involving traditional law and royal cases in which the state had special interest. The term for magistrate at Daniel 3:2,3 is an Old Persian term of uncertain meaning. Since magistrates follows judges, officials with judicial responsibilities may again be in view. The term for magistrate at Luke 12:11 (KJV) and 12:58 (NRSV) is *archon,* a general term for ruler. The term rendered magistrates at Acts 16:20,22,35–36,38 *stratēgoi* is a term used both for military commanders and for civil officials of a Greek city who were charged with administering the community finances, enforcing enactments of the council or citizen body, and in some cases passing sentence in legal cases. In the case of Philippi, *stratēgoi* serves as the Greek equivalent of the Latin *duumviri,* the two magistrates who served as the chief judicial officials of a Roman city or colony.

MAGNIFICAT (Mag nĭ' fĭ căt) Latin word meaning "magnify." The first word in Latin of Mary's psalm of praise (Luke 1:46–55) and thus the title of the psalm. Very similar to the psalm of Hannah (1 Sam. 2:1–10). See *Benedictus; Nunc Dimittis.*

MAGOG (Mā' gŏg) See *Gog and Magog.*

MAGOR-MISSABIB (Mā' gŏr-mĭs sā' bĭb) Name meaning "terror on every side" which Jeremiah gave to Pashur the priest after the latter had the prophet beaten and put in stocks (Jer. 20:3). The earliest Greek translation lacks the words "on every side," prompting some interpreters to conclude the words were added in imitation of the full phrase at Jeremiah 6:25; 20:10.

MAGPIASH (Măg pĭ' ăsh) Personal name, perhaps meaning "moth exterminator." Magpiash was among the chiefs of the people who signed Ezra's covenant (Neh. 10:20).

MAGUS, SIMON See *Simon Magus.*

MAHALAB (Mȧ hā' lab) A town in Asher's tribal territory (Josh. 19:29 NRSV, TEV) according to the earliest Greek translation. The existing Hebrew text lacks Mahalab as do other English translations.

MAHALAH (Mȧ hā′ lah) KJV form of Mahlah (1 Chron. 7:18). See *Mahlah.*

MAHALALEEL (Mȧ hā′ lȧ lē ĕl) KJV form of Mahalelel, a personal name meaning "God shines forth" or "praise God." *1.* Son of Kenan, father of Jared, and ancestor of Christ [Gen. 5:12–17; 1 Chron. 1:2; Luke 3:37, Greek form Malaleel (Mȧ lē lē ĕl) appears]. *2.* Ancestor of a postexilic member of the tribe of Judah (Neh. 11:4).

MAHALALEL (Mȧ hā′ lȧ lĕl) Form of Mahalaleel preferred by modern translations.

MAHALATH (Mā hȧ lăth) Personal name meaning, "dance" or "sickness" and a term used in the superscriptions of Psalms 53; 88. *1.* Granddaughter of Abraham and daughter of Ishmael who married Esau (Gen. 28:9). *2.* Granddaughter of David and wife of King Rehoboam (2 Chron. 11:18). *3.* In Psalms perhaps a choreographic instruction; the second element in the composite term mahalath-leannoth (mā′ hȧ lăth-lĕ ăn′ nŏth) perhaps refers to an antiphonal performance by two groups answering and responding to each other (Ps. 88).

MAHALATH-LEANNOTH See *Mahalath 3.*

MAHALI (Mā′ hȧ lī) KJV alternate form of *Mahli.*

MAHANAIM (Mā hȧ nā′ ĭm) Place name meaning, "two camps." City somewhere in the hill country of Gilead on the tribal borders of Gad and eastern Manasseh (Josh. 13:26,30). It was a Levitical city (Josh. 21:38). It served as a refuge twice: for Ishbosheth after Saul's death (2 Sam. 2:8–9), and for David when Absalom usurped the throne (2 Sam. 17:24–27). During Solomon's administration, the city served as a district capital (1 Kings 4:14). German archaeologists locate it at tell Heggog, half a mile south of Penuel, while Israelis point to tell edh-Dhabab el Gharbi.

MAHANEH-DAN (Mȧ′ hȧ nĕh-dăn) Hebrew term meaning "camp of Dan." During the period of the judges the tribe of Dan lacked a permanent inheritance in the Promised Land (Judg. 18:1) and continued to live according to the earlier semi-nomadic pattern. Thus it is not surprising that two places are designated "camp of Dan": *1.* a site between Zorah and Eshtaol where the Lord's Spirit first stirred Samson (Judg. 13:25). *2.* A site west of Kiriath-jearim where the Danites camped on the way to the hill country of Ephraim (Judg. 18:12).

MAHARAI (Mȧ hâ′ rā ī) Personal name mean-

ing, "hurried one." One of David's thirty elite warriors who came from the clan of the Zerahites and the town of Netophah in Judah and commanded the troups in the tenth month (2 Sam. 23:28; 1 Chron. 11:30, 27:13).

MAHATH (Mā′ hăth) Personal name meaning, "tough." *1.* Levite of the Kohathite clan (1 Chron. 6:35). *2.* Levite assisting in Hezekiah's reforms (2 Chron. 29:12; 31:13). Both Mahaths are perhaps the same individual. The second may be the Ahimoth of 1 Chronicles 6:25.

MAHAVITE (Mā′ hȧ vīte) Family name of Eliel, one of David's thirty elite warriors (1 Chron. 11:46). See *Eliel 5.*

MAHAZIOTH (Mȧ hā′ zĭ ŏth) Personal name meaning, "visions." Son of Heman who served as a Temple musician (1 Chron. 25:4,6–7,30).

MAHER-SHALAL-HASH-BAZ (Mā′ hĕr-shăl′ ăl-hăsh′ -băz) A personal name meaning "quick to the plunder, swift to the spoil" (Isa. 8:1). Symbolic name Isaiah gave his son to warn of the impending destruction of Syria and Israel as they threatened Judah and Ahaz, its king. The name appeared to show that God would deliver Judah from her enemies. The sign also called on Ahaz for faith. Without faith, Judah could become part of the spoil. The prophecy was that the two enemies of Judah would be destroyed before they could attack the Southern Kingdom. Assyria defeated Syria in 732 B.C. and Israel in 722 B.C. Judah survived until 586 B.C.

MAHLAH (Măl′ lah) Personal name, perhaps meaning, "weak one." *1.* Daughter of Zelophehad who with her sisters petitioned Moses to receive their father's inheritance in the Promised land since he had no sons (Num. 26:33; 27:1–11). God granted their request (Num. 27:6–7). The tribe of Manasseh later petitioned that daughters who inherit be required to marry within their father's tribe (Num. 36:1–12). The daughters' persistance in pressing their claim is evidenced by Joshua 17:3. *2.* A descendant of Manasseh (1 Chron. 7:18).

MAHLI (Măh′ lī) Personal name perhaps meaning, "shrewd" or "cunning." *1.* Son of Merari, a Levite who gave his name to a priestly clan (Ex. 6:19; Nu. 3:20; 1 Chron. 6:19,29; 23:21; 24:26,28; Ezra 8:18). *2.* Son of Mushi, the nephew of the above (1 Chron. 6:47; 23:23; 24:30).

MAHLITES (Măh′ lītes) Descendants of Mahli. These Levites had charge of the set up and maintenance of the tabernacle (Num. 3:33–36; 26:58).

MAHLON (Măh′ lŏn) Personal name meaning,

"sickly." One of the two sons of Elimelech and Naomi (Ruth 1:2,5), and the husband of Ruth the Moabitess (4:9–10). Mahlon died while the family was sojourning in Moab because of a famine in their homeland of Israel. The reason for Mahlon's death is not given. Boaz, a distant relative to Mahlon, married the dead man's widow, Ruth.

MAHOL (Mā′ hŏl) Personal name meaning, "place of Dancing." The name belongs to the father of three renowned wise men (1 Kings 4:31). An alternate interpretation takes the phrase "sons of the place of dancing" as a title for those who danced as part of the Temple ritual (compare Pss. 149:3; 150:4). The wisdom of the Temple dancers may be akin to the prophetic wisdom associated with musicians (1 Sam. 10:5; 2 Kings 3:15; and especially 1 Chron. 25:3).

MAHSEIAH (Mäh′ sēi ah) Personal name meaning, "Yah is a refuge." Grandfather of the scribe Baruch (Jer. 32:12; 51:59).

MAID, MAIDEN Unmarried woman, especially of the servant class. In the KJV, maid translated five Hebrew and four Greek terms. In the Old Testament *amah* and *shipchah* refer to female slaves. Alternate translations for these terms include: bondmaid; bondwoman; female slave; handmaid; and maid servant. See *Slavery* for literal uses. Both terms are used as expressions of deep humility (Ruth 3:9; 1 Sam. 25:24–31; 28:21; 2 Sam. 14:6; 1 Kings 1:13,17). A special case involves the use of these terms for the "handmaid of the Lord" (1 Sam. 1:11; Pss. 86:16; 116:16; compare *Servant of the Lord*), always with reference to prayer for the handmaid's son. KJV sometimes rendered *bethulah* as maid (Ex. 22:16; Deut. 22:17). Modern translations generally render the term *virgin*. KJV sometimes renders *almah* maid. At Exodus 2:8 *almah* means "girl." At Proverbs 30:19 a young woman of marriageable age is intended. KJV translated the term as "virgin" at Isaiah 7:14. The term *naarah* is used both for young women (2 Kings 5:2) and specifically for servants (Ruth 2:8; Esth. 2:4). In the New Testament, *korasion* refers to a child or young girl (Matt. 9:24–25). *Paidiskē* refers to a (young) female servant (Matt. 26:69; Mark 14:66; John 18:16). At Luke 8:51,54 *pais* means child. Elsewhere, the term can mean servant. Mary's reference to herself as the "handmaid [*doule*] of the Lord" (Luke 1:38,48) reflects the Old Testament use.

MAIL, COAT OF See *Weapons; Arms and Armor.*

MAIMED Mutilated, disfigured, or seriously injured, especially by loss of a limb (Matt. 18:8; Mark 9:43). In the ancient world the maimed had difficulty finding work and relied on the generos-

ity of others (Luke 14:13). A worthless shepherd (leader) does not care for the maimed (Zech. 11:16 NRSV). Christ, the Good Shepherd, cared for the maimed in His healing ministry (Matt. 15:30–31). He expected disciples to invite the maimed who could never repay (Luke 14:13). Cautioning His disciples to avoid what causes sin, Jesus taught it is preferable to enter (eternal) life maimed than to go into eternal fire with whatever causes one to sin (Matt. 18:8).

MAINSAIL The principal sail of a vessel (Acts 27:40). Modern translations render the Greek term "foresail," understanding the sail to be a smaller, auxiliary sail used in strong winds when the full force provided by the mainsail would be unnecessary or dangerous.

MAKAZ (Mā′ kăz) Place name meaning "cutting off" or "end." Center of Solomon's second administrative district (1 Kings 4:9). The site is possibly that of khirbet-el-Muskheizin south of Ekron.

MAKHELOTH (Măk hē′ lŏth) Stopping place during the wilderness wandering. Makheloth (Num. 33:25–26), like Kehelathah (Num. 33:22–23), means, "to assemble."

MAKI (Mā′ kī) NIV spelling of Machi.

MAKIR (Mā′ kīr) NIV spelling of Machir.

MAKIRITES (Mā′ kī rītes) NIV spelling of Machirites.

MAKKEDAH (Măk kē′ dah) Name meaning, "Place of shepherds," of a Canaanite city, the site of Joshua's rout of the combined forces of five Canaanite kings (Joshua 10:10). The kings sought refuge in nearby caves but were trapped there (10:16). Joshua captured the city, killing all its population (10:28). Later, Makkedah was assigned to the Shephelah (lowland) district of Judah (Josh. 15:4–1). Suggested locations include: Eusebius' suggestion of a site eight and a half miles from Eleutheropolis (Beit Jibrin); tell es-Safi south of Hulda (Libnah); el-Muqhar ("the Caves") southwest of Ekron; and a site between Lachish and Hebron.

MAKTESH (Măk′ tĕsh) KJV transliteration of the Hebrew place name meaning, "Mortar" (NAS, NRSV). District in or near Jerusalem (Zeph. 1:11). Early commentators located the site in the Kidron Valley. Recently, the site has been linked with an area of the Tyropoean Valley within the city walls (thus "lower town," REB; "market district," NIV).

MALACHI (Măl′ à chī) Personal name or common noun meaning, "my messenger," or "my angel" and name of the last book in the English

Old Testament. Some people in ancient Israel believed that an angel wrote this book because of the name. We know nothing about Malachi other than what we are told in this book. He is not mentioned anywhere else in the Old or New Testaments. The Hebrew word for "Malachi" occurs only in 1:1 and 3:1.

Date We can only estimate the date of Malachi's ministry. The dates of most Old Testament prophets are indicated in the superscription of their book by the names of the kings reigning at that time. No kings' names are listed in the superscription of Malachi. The book contains no reference to any historical incident such as an important battle, earthquake, or captivity which might give a historical context to the book. However, we do know the time was postexilic (after 536 B.C.) because of the use of the Persian word for "governor" (1:8). The Temple had been rebuilt (1:10; 3:1,10). The Edomites had suffered a crushing blow from an outisde invader, perhaps the Nabateans (1 Macc. 5:25). The Nabateans were an Arab tribe who came out of the desert and drove the Edomites out of their homeland in the fifth or sixth centuries B.C. Evidently, Malachi was a contemporary of Nehemiah. Their books show kinship. The same social and religious conditions prevail in both, and Nehemiah's reforms were probably intended to correct some of the social and religious abuses outlined by Malachi (Mal. 3:5; Neh. 5:1–13). Tithing is stressed in both (Mal. 3:7–10; Neh. 10:37–39). Divorce and mixed marriages were problems in both (Mal. 2:10–16; Neh. 10:30; 13:23–28). Nehemiah first returned to Jerusalem from Persia in 444 B.C. (Neh. 1:1; 2:1); therefore, Malachi should be dated after 450 B.C.

The people of Israel who returned to Jerusalem from Babylon and Persia in 536 B.C. came with high hopes. In Isaiah 40—55 the prophet painted a future for those repatriated people in such glowing terms that they expected the messianic age to come immediately. The prophets Haggai and Zechariah added to these hopes by assuring the people that unprecedented blessings would come when the Temple was complete. They finished the Temple in 516 B.C. (Ezra 6:14–15) and waited and waited, but no blessings came. Instead of blessings they faced drought, famine, poverty, oppression, and unfaithfulness to spouses and to God. Moral and spiritual laxity, pride, indifference, permissiveness, and skepticism were rife. Malachi tried to rekindle the fires of faith in the hearts of his discouraged people.

Book The purpose of Malachi was to assure his people that God still loved them, but He demanded honor, respect, and faithfulness from them. Malachi pointed out religious and social abuses and warned that judgment would come to purge the people of sin unless they repented. The style of the Book of Malachi is that of disputations.

This style is not unique to Malachi. Micah and Jeremiah had disputes with false prophets (Mic. 2:6–11; Jer. 27—28). Jeremiah also disputed with God (Jer. 12:1–6). Job disputed with his friends. The Book of Malachi is made up of six disputation passages and two appendices. The disputes follow a regular form: (1) the prophet stated a premise; (2) the hearers challenged the statement; and (3) God and the prophet presented the supporting evidence.

Outline

I. A dispute about God's love (1:1–5)
II. A dispute about God's honor and fear (1:6–2:9)
III. A dispute about faithfulness (2:10–16)
IV. A dispute about God's justice (2:17—3:5)
V. A dispute about repentance (3:6–12)
VI. A dispute about speaking against God (3:13—4:3)
VII. Two appendices (4:4–6)
  A. An admonition to remember the law of Moses (4:4)
  B. An announcement of the sending of Elijah (4:5–6)

Ralph L. Smith

MALACHITE (Măl′ ă chīte) A green basic carbonate of copper used as an ore and for ornamental objects; according to the NEB and REB, a component of the mosaic pavement decorating the palace of the Persian king Ahasuerus at Susa (Esth. 1:6). The Hebrew root means "glistening." Suggested meanings include: porphyry (NAS, NIV, NRSV); red marble (KJV), and white marble (TEV), in addition to malachite.

MALCAM (Măl′ căm) See *Malcham*.

MALCHAM (Măl′ chăm) KJV form for Malcam (1 Chron. 8:9) and Milcom (Zeph. 1:5). The name meaning, "their King" is applied to *1.* A Benjaminite (1 Chron. 8:9). *2.* The chief god of the Ammonites (Zeph. 1:5, KJV; Malcam, RSV and NAS margins). The Hebrew *malcam* is sometimes seen as a deliberate scribal misspelling of *Milcom* (compare Jer. 49:1,3; Zeph. 1:5), the common name for the Ammonites' god (1 Kings 11:5,33; 2 Kings 23:13). One text (1 Kings 11:7) links Milcom with Molech. At Amos 1:15 the Hebrew *malcam* is translated simply, "their king," though the word choice suggests that the Ammonites' god will go with them into Exile. See *Ammon; Milcom; Molech.*

MALCHIAH (Măl chī′ ah) Alternate form of Malchijah.

MALCHIEL (Măl′ chī ĕl) Name meaning, "My God is king," given to a descendant of Asher (Gen. 46:17; Num. 26:45; 1 Chron. 7:31).

MALCHIELITES (Măl <u>chī</u>′ ĕl ītes) Descendants of Malchiel (Num. 26:45).

MALCHIJAH (Măl <u>chī</u>′ jah) Personal name with long and short spelling meaning, "My King is Yahweh." *1.* Ancestor of the musician Asaph (1 Chron. 6:40). *2.* Priest in David's time (1 Chron. 24:9; compare 9:12; Neh. 11:12). *3.* Prince of Judah in Jeremiah's time, probably the father of Pashur (Jer. 21:1; 38:1,6); *4.–6.* Three of Ezra's contemporaries with foreign wives (Ezra 10:25,31); some modern translations replace the second Malchijah in the Hebrew text of 10:25 with Hashabiah, the early Greek reading. *7.* One standing with Ezra at the reading of the law (Neh. 8:4). *8.* Priest signing Ezra's covenant (Neh. 10:3); *9.–12.* Four contemporaries of Nehemiah involved in the rebuilding (Neh. 3:11,14,31) or dedication of the walls (Neh. 12:42). Several of the references in Ezra and Nehemiah may refer to the same person(s).

MALCHIRAM (Măl <u>chī</u>′ răm) Personal name meaning, "My king is exalted." Son of King Jeconiah of Judah (1 Chron. 3:18).

MALCHISHUA (Măl <u>chī</u> shū à) Personal name meaning, "My king is salvation." Son of King Saul and Ahinoam (1 Chron. 8:33; 9:39) killed in battle with the Philistines at Mount Gilboa (1 Sam. 14:49; 31:2; 1 Chron. 10:2).

MALCHUS (Măl′ <u>ch</u>ŭs) Personal name meaning "king," common among the Idumaeans and Palmyrenes, especially for their kings or tribal chiefs. High priest's servant whose ear Peter cut off (John 18:10). The name is unusual for slaves who commonly had names such as Onesimus ("Useful"; Philem. 10–11). Perhaps the slave was chief of the Temple guard. Only Luke recorded the healing of the ear (Luke 22:51). Possibly Luke desired to stress Jesus' compassion in the midst of His passion (compare Luke 23:28,34,43) or respect shown to the high priest and his representative (compare Acts 23:4).

MALEFACTOR used in KJV to denote the two criminals who were crucified beside Jesus. (See Luke 23:32–33,39.) The word is the Latin translation of the Greek *kakourgos,* meaning "robber" or "criminal." The Latin means "evil-doer."

MALELEEL (Mà lē lē ĕl) Greek form of Mahalaleel used by KJV (Luke 3:37).

MALICE Vicious intention; desire to hurt someone. Malice is characteristic of preconversion life in opposition to God (Rom. 1:29; Tit. 3:3). Christians are frequently called upon to rid their lives of malice (Eph. 4:31–32; Col. 3:8; 1 Pet. 2:1).

MALKIEL (Măl′ kī el) NIV spelling of Malchiel.

MALKIELITES (Măl′ kī ĕ lītes) NIV spelling of Malchielites.

MALKIJAH (Măl kī jah) NIV form of Malchiah (Malchijah).

MALKIRAM (Măl′ kī räm) NIV spelling of Malchiram.

MALLOTHI (Măl′ lō thī) Personal name meaning, "I spoke." One of David's tabernacle musicians (1 Chron. 25:4,26). Like his father Heman (25:5), he may have exercised a prophetic role (king's seer). The sons' names may have formed a prayer (see REB note).

MALLOW In Scripture mallow refers to two plants: *1. Atriplex halimus L.,* the shrubby orache, is a salt marsh plant and unpleasant food (Job 30:4; "plant of the salt marshes," NAS margin). The saltwort (REB) is another possibility for this plant associated with the marshy areas around the Dead Sea. *2.* The true mallow (genus *Malva*) is a flowering plant prominent around Jerusalem. Its fading flowers provide an image for the unrighteous according to one interpretation of Job 24:24 (NRSV, REB). Here mallow is supplied from the earliest Greek translation. Other translations follow the Hebrew text in reading "all."

MALLUCH (Măl′ lü<u>ch</u>) Personal name meaning, "being king." *1.* Ancestor of a Levitical singer in Solomon's Temple (1 Chron. 6:44); *2.* Priest who returned from Exile with Zerubbabel (Neh. 12:2, perhaps identical with the Malluchi of v. 14); *3.–6.* Four contemporaries of Ezra, two men with foreign wives (Ezra 10:29,32) and a priest (Neh. 10:4) and layperson (Neh. 10:27) who witnessed the covenant renewal. Some of the above may refer to the same person.

MALLUCHI (Mal′ lū <u>ch</u>ī) Family of priests in the time of Joiakim (Neh. 12:14). Some suggest Malluchi is a transcriptional error for Malluch (compare 12:2).

MALTA (Mal′ ta) See *Islands.*

MAMMON The Greek form of a Syriac or Aramaic word for "money," "riches," "property," "worldly goods," or "profit." In general use it was a personification of riches as an evil spirit or deity. From about 1500 it has been current in English as indicating the evil influence of wealth. The word is not used in the Old Testament. In the New Testament it is used only by Jesus (Matt. 6:24; Luke 16:9,11,13). In the Sermon on the Mount Jesus said, "Ye cannot serve God and mammon." He meant that no one can be a slave of God and worldly wealth at the same time. The undivided concentration of mind to money-getting is incompatible with wholehearted devotion to God and to His service (Col. 3:5). In the parable of the unjust steward (Luke 15:1–13), Jesus commended the steward's foresight, not his method. His object was to point out how one may best use wealth, tainted or otherwise, with a view to the future. See *Steward*.   *Ray Robbins*

MAMRE (Măm′ rē) Place name meaning, "grazing land." Main area of habitation for Abraham and his family. It apparently was named after an Amorite (Mamre) who helped Abraham defeat the evil king, Chedorlaomer (Gen. 14:1–24). Mamre was famous for its oak trees. It was just east of Mamre that Abraham purchased a cave (Machpelah) for a family burial plot. Its location was at Ramet et-Chalil, two miles north of Hebron. See *Abraham; Machpelah*.

MAN OF LAWLESSNESS See *Antichrist; Lawlessness; Man of Sin*.

MAN OF SIN KJV designation for the ultimate opponent of Christ (2 Thess. 2:3). Modern translations follow other manuscripts in reading "man of lawlessness." See *Antichrist; Lawlessness*.

MANAEN (Măn′ à ěn) Greek form of Menahem ("Comforter"); the name of a prophet and teacher in the early church at Antioch (Acts 13:1). Manaen is described as the *syntrophos* of Herod the tetrarch (Herod Antipas, reigned 4 B.C. to A.D. 37). The term literally means "one who eats with." In the Old Testament, those who shared the king's table were persons recognized as valued members of the court (2 Sam. 9:10–13; 19:28; 1 Kings 2:7; 2 Kings 25:29; Neh. 5:17). The earliest Greek translation uses *syntropoi* to refer to those generals who were reared with Alexander (1 Macc. 1:6) as well as for members of court (2 Macc. 9:29). The meanings "member of court" and "childhood companion" are both possible for Acts 13:1. A less likely alternative is the early Greek translation's use of *syntrophoi* for fellow Israelites to mean, "kin" (1 Kings 12:24).

MANAHATH (Măn′ à hăth) Place or personal name meaning "resting place" or "settlement." *1.* Ancestor of the Horite subclan of Edomites (Gen. 36:23; 1 Chron. 1:40). *2.* Site, probably outside of Palestine, to which some Benjaminites from Geba were exiled (1 Chron. 8:6). *3.* City of tribal territory of Judah according to earliest Greek text of Joshua 15:59, there called Manocho, probably el-Malcha in the hill country of Judah three miles southwest of Jerusalem. The site is perhaps the same as Nohah ("resting place") associated with Benjaminites in Judges 20:43. See 1 Chronicles 2:54.

MANAHATHITES (Măn′ à hăth ītes) Form of Manahethites preferred by NAS, NIV, NRSV.

MANAHETHITES (Măn à hěth ītes) KJV, REB spelling of residents of Manahath (1 Chron. 2:54).

MANASSEH (Mà năs′ sěh) A personal name meaning "God has caused me to forget" (trouble). *1.* One of at least two sons born to Joseph by Asenath (Gen. 41:50–51). Manasseh was adopted by Jacob as one to receive his blessing. Along with Ephraim, Manasseh became one of the twelve tribes of Israel and received a landed inheritance. In almost typical Old Testament fashion, Manasseh, the elder brother, did not receive the blessing of the firstborn (Gen. 48:13–20). Jacob crossed his hands and gave that blessing to Ephraim. When the Promised Land was apportioned, half of the tribe of Manasseh settled on the east bank of the Jordan and half on the west. See *Tribes of Israel*.
 2. King of Judah (696–642 B.C.) who was a son of Hezekiah (2 Kings 20:21). His was the longest reign of any Judean king. Manasseh's reign was known as one of unfaithfulness to Yahweh. Second Kings blames him for Judah's ultimate destruction and exile (2 Kings 21:10–16).

MANASSEH, PRAYER OF See *Apocrypha*.

MANASSITES (Mà năs′ sītes) Members of tribe of Manasseh.

MANDRAKE A small, perennial plant (*Mandragora officinarum*) native to the Middle East. Although not grown for food, its root and berries are edible. The Ancient Near East viewed it as an aphrodisiac and fertility drug. It is often called love apple or devil's apple. According to Genesis 30:14–16, a barren Rachel bargained with Reuben (Leah's oldest son) for some mandrakes which he had found. Leah, however, produced the children (Gen. 30:17–21). Only when God "remembered Rachel" did she bear Joseph (30:24). Thus Israel learned that God controlled fertility; superstition and human manipulation cannot supply what God chooses not to.

MANEH KJV alternate term for mina at Ezekiel 45:12. See *Weights and Measures*.

MANGER A feeding trough used for cattle, sheep, donkeys, or horses. Archaeologists have discovered stone mangers in the horse stables of Ahab at Megiddo. They were cut out of limestone and were approximately three feet long, eighteen inches wide, and two feet deep. Other ancient

A stone manger still in place in the archaeological excavations at ancient Megiddo.

mangers were made of masonry. Many Palestinian homes consisted of one large room which contained an elevated section and a lower section. The elevated section was the family's living quarters, while the lower section housed the family's animals. Usually a manger, in the form of a masonry box or a stone niche, was located in the lower section. Mangers were also put in cave stables or other stalls. The manger referred to in Luke 2:16 may have been in a cave stable or other shelter. There Jesus was laid to sleep after his birth. *Floyd Lewis*

MANNA (măn′ na) Grainlike substance, considered to be food from heaven, which sustained the Israelites in the wilderness and foreshadowed Christ, the true Bread from heaven.
Old Testament The small round grains or flakes, which appeared around the Israelites' camp each morning with the dew, were ground and baked into cakes or boiled (Ex. 16:13–36). Their name may have come from the question the Israelites asked when they first saw them: "What is it (*man hu*)?" Today a type of manna has been identified with the secretions left on tamarisk bushes by insects feeding on the sap. The Bible emphasizes that God caused manna to appear at the right time and place to meet His people's needs.
New Testament Jesus assured the Jews that He, and not the wilderness food, was the true Bread

from heaven which conferred eternal life on those who partook of it (John 6:30–58).
Barbara J. Bruce

MANOAH (Må̇ nō′ ah) Personal name meaning "rest." A member of the tribe of Dan and the father of Samson (Judg. 13). Manaoh petitioned God for a son when his wife could not produce an heir. God promised a son on the condition that he be reared a Nazirite. Manaoh hosted the man of God who brought the news at a meal, but was told to offer the food as a burnt offering. The man ascended in the smoke of the fire, revealing his identity as God's angel. Manaoh is buried between Zorah and Eshtaol.

MANSERVANT KJV, RSV term for a male servant or slave. See *Slavery.*

MANSION Place to dwell or abide, separate living quarters.
    Before going away, Jesus promised to make provision of a dwelling place for His disciples (John 14:2). The Greek noun means "abiding places." KJV translated this as "mansions," which meant a dwelling place but has come to represent an elaborate, expensive house in English. Thus modern translations read, "dwelling places" or "rooms." Christian theology holds that Christ's followers will abide with Him eternally in heavenly dwelling places.

MANSLAYER One guilty of involuntary manslaughter; one who accidentally causes another's death (Num. 35:9–15,22–28; Deut. 19:1–10). English translations distinguish manslayer from murderer though the underlying Hebrew term (*ratsach*) is the same. Compare Exodus 20:13.

MANSTEALING KJV term for kidnapping. See *Kidnap, Kidnapper.*

MANTLE A robe, cape, veil, or loose-fitting tunic worn as an outer garment. Many of the prophets wore them (1 Sam. 15:27; 1 Kings 19:13), as did women in Jerusalem (Isa. 3:22) and Job (Job 1:20). The transference of the mantle from Elijah to Elisha signified the passing of prophetic responsibility and God's accompanying power. These garments have been worn from at least the time of the Exodus until the present. See *Dress; Ornaments; Veil.*

MANUSCRIPT A handwritten copy of a text. Before the invention of the printing press in the fourteen hundreds, all books were handwritten. Large numbers of New Testament and some Old Testament manuscripts survive from the first few centuries B.C. until the fifteen hundreds. See *Bible, Text and Versions; Paper; Papyrus; Writing.*

MAOCH (Mā′ ŏch) Personal name meaning,

"dumb, foolish." Father of King Achish of Gath (1 Sam. 27:2). Moach is perhaps identical with Maacah (1 Kings 2:39), perhaps his ancestor.

MAON (Mā' ŏn) Name meaning "Dwelling." *1.* Descendant of Caleb who founded Beth-zur (1 Chron. 2:45). *2.* Village in the hill country of Judah (15:55). The site of Maon has been identified with tell Ma'in about eight miles south of Hebron in the vicinity of Carmel of Judah (compare 1 Sam. 25:2) and with khirbet el-Ma'in twenty-five miles northwest of Beersheba. Pottery finds at tell Ma'in demonstrate occupation from the time of David. David took refuge from Saul in the wilderness to the east of Maon (1 Sam. 23:24–25). Nabal, who foolishly refused hospitality to David, was a resident of Maon (1 Sam. 25:2).

MAONITES (Mā' ōn ītes) One of the peoples who oppressed Israel during the period of the judges (Judg. 10:12). These Maonites are perhaps the Meunites attacked by Hezekiah (1 Chron. 4:41) and Uzziah (2 Chron. 26:7), a band of marauding Arabs from south of the Dead Sea in the vicinity of Ma'an. The earliest Greek translation reads, "Midianites" (REB).

MARA (Mā' rà) Personal name meaning "bitter," chosen by Naomi to reflect God's bitter dealings with her in the death of her husband and sons (Ruth 1:20–21).

MARAH (Mā' răh) Place name meaning "bitter." Place in the Wilderness of Shur, so named because of the bitter water found there by the wandering Israelites (Ex. 15:23). The site is typical of pools in the Sinai pennisula, having undrinkable water. The people complained against Moses because of their discomfort. God answered the leader's prayer by telling him to cast a tree into the water which became sweet and drinkable. Marah cannot be located definitely.

MARALAH (Mär' à lah) Place name meaning "site on mountain ledge." Border town in Zebulun (Josh. 19:11). The site is perhaps tell Ghalta in the Jezreel Valley north of Megiddo or tell Thorah.

MARANATHA (Mär à nä' thà) An Aramaic expression Paul used (1 Cor. 16:22) in closing a letter to the church at Corinth. Having prayed that those who do not love Christ (compare 1 Cor. 13) would be *anathema* (see *anathema*), Paul used a formula probably used in celebration of the Lord's Supper to pray that Christ would come. This highlighted the urgency of showing love to Christ. One way to show such love would be to obey Paul's instructions in 1 Corinthians. Maranatha is actually two Aramaic words. Dividing it as *Marana tha* means, "Our Lord, come." *Maran atha* means, "Our Lord has come." It reveals the expectant

hope in which early Christmas lived, watching for the imminent return of Christ. The division of the phrase is disputed by scholars. Whichever division is correct, the Aramaic formula shows that very early the church applied to Jesus the word *Lord* which otherwise belonged only to God.

MARBLE See *Minerals and Metals; Alabaster.*

MARCUS (Mär' cŭs) Latin form of Mark ("large hammer") used by the KJV at Colossians 4:10; Philemon 24; and 1 Peter 5:13. See *Mark.*

MARDUK (Mär' dūk) Chief god of Babylon, sometimes called Merodach or Bel, the Babylonian equivalent of Baal meaning lord. He was credited with creation, a feat reenacted each new year and celebrated with a festival. In typical Ancient Near Eastern fashion, Marduk was proclaimed king. The reigning monarch was seen as the son of the god. As the kingdom grew, Marduk was attributed with more powers until he was acknowledged as lord of the heavens. The prophets mocked Marduk and his worshipers as products of human craftsmen who would lead Babylon to defeat and exile (Isa. 46:1; Jer. 50:2,38; 51:47). See *Babylon; Bel; Gods, Pagan.*

MARE Female horse. See *Animals; Horse.*

MAREAL (măr ė àl) RSV; TEV form of Maralah.

MARESHAH (Mår' ē shah) Personal and place name meaning, "place at the top" with two Hebrew spellings. *1.* Son of Caleb and founder of Hebron (1 Chron. 2:42). The Hebrew text apparently refers to this son as first Mesha then Meresha. *2.* Member of the tribe of Judah (1 Chron. 4:21). *3.* A Canaanite city incorporated into the Shephelah district of Judah (Josh. 15:44). The city was fortified by Rehoboam (2 Chron. 11:8). Mereshah was near the site of the battle between the forces of King Asa and the Ethiopian (Egyptian?) commander Zerah (2 Chron. 14:9–14). Mareshah was home to the prophet Eliezar (2 Chron. 20:37). Micah foretold the destruction of the city (Mic. 1:15). The site has been identified with tell Sandahannah one mile southeast of Beit Jibrin.

MARI An ancient city accidentally discovered by Arab clansmen, and later excavated by French archaeologists under the supervision of André Parrot. Today known as tell el-Hariri, the site is comprised of about 135 acres (after erosion on its northeast sector), is located adjacent to the right (west) bank of the Euphrates river, roughly fifteen miles north of the modern Syrian-Iraqi border. Some thirty archaeological campaigns have unearthed city walls and various temples and palaces that date from about 3100 B.C. to 1760, when the city was demolished by Hammurabi of Babylon, never again to rise to a stature of prominence. See *Hammurabi*.

Located about midway between the great powers of Sumeria (Kish, Ur, Akkad) and Syro-Mesopotamia (Ebla, Aleppo), Mari played a significant role in the flow of trade as early as the third millennium, though, to judge from the documents which have already been published from this era, the city experienced a dependent status to these more powerful neighbors. By about 1800, no fewer than four trading routes converged on the city; the city's geographical and commerical horizons stretched from Iran in the east to the Mediterranean and Aegean in the west, including Turkey, Lebanon, Syria, Israel, and the Arabian desert. From such an enviable position, the kingdom of Mari played a crucial role in the international trade of timber, stone, wool, resin, garments, furniture, royal horses, wine, olive and sesame oils, myrtle, copper, lapis-lazuli and perhaps most importantly, tin—an essential component in the forging or casting of bronze.

For about 25 years immediately prior to its destruction by Hammurabi, Mari experienced a "golden age" under its king Zimri-Lim. This era in Mesopotamian history has been compared by one noted historian to the age of Pericles in Greek history or of Caesar Augustus in Rome. For Mari it became a period of unsurpassed greatness in material prosperity, and its cultural remains have been matched by few sites in the neighboring areas of the Ancient Near East.

The opulent prosperity in which Mari indulged is unmistakably etched into the remains of the magnificent palace of Zimri-Lim. Encompassing a nine-acre rectangular plot and containing more than 300 rooms, this palatial estate is one of the largest and best preserved buildings in all of Mesopotamian history. The excavators uncovered interior walls as thick as thirteen feet and standing as high as sixteen feet; lintels in some doorways were still intact. Apparently a two-story edifice, the palace was constructed to include many large open courts surrounded by a constellation of rooms that were interconnected by high doorways, thereby permitting ventilation and light to penetrate throughout a ground floor in which there were no windows. Floors were usually plastered or tiled; walls were plastered and frequently adorned with ornate sculpture or painting, and wood was used decoratively to add aesthetic luster.

Exhumed from this palace was Mari's greatest legacy of all: the royal archives. Embodying more than 25,000 texts and fragments, this documentation addresses almost every aspect within a culture: internal politics, international affairs, diplomacy and treaties, domestic policy, commerce and trade, agriculture, irrigation, law and jurisprudence, political intrigue, and religion. In point of fact, Zimri-Lim's reign is presently the most heavily documented of any king in antiquity, even including personal correspondence between himself and his wife, his daughters, his local administrators, and his territorial functionaries. His archive contains hundreds of bureaucratic registers which detail in a most graphic way certain aspects of daily life in a Mesopotamian court: where and how the king worshiped and his temples were serviced; where, what, and how often the king ate or was luxuriated; how courtiers were selected for the court or enticing female dancers were selected for the royal harem; what were various forms of entertainment for the court and/or visiting dignitaries; where, how far, and how frequently did the king journey; how was royalty attired.

Mari's bearing on biblical studies is significant, if indirect. Documentation from Mari has opened the historical, geographical, and social dimension of Northern Mesopotamia, the homeland of the biblical patriarchs. Certain patriarchal behavior attested in the writings of Moses may be seen to be reflected in the literature of Mari. This includes the prominence of the firstborn within family structure, the legal procedures entailed in adoption or formalizing inheritance, the centrality and interdependence of the clan as a model for social structuring, the notion of tribal or ethnic movement of peoples and the relocation and resettlement in a new area, the importance of genealogical registers similar to those of Genesis 5 and 11 as a means of establishing personal or clan authority, the prominent role and the forms of ritual in religious practices, the procedures for census taking, and the nature of prophets and prophecy. Mari's literary sources contribute to a richly-textured reconstruction of Mesopotamian history during the early patriarchal period, just as they often provide linguistic elucidation of certain biblical concepts (compass points, tribal terms and leadership, flora and fauna, military terms).

Barry J. Beitzel

MARINER See *Ships, Sailors; Navigation.*

MARJORAM See *Hyssop; Plants in the Bible, Hyssop.*

MARK, JOHN Early missionary and church leader; author of second Gospel. He was the son of Mary in whose home the Jerusalem believers met to pray when Peter was imprisoned by Herod Agrippa I (Acts 12:12). Mark was sometimes called by his Jewish name, John, and sometimes by his Roman name, Mark.

John Mark was kin to Barnabas (Col. 4:10). After Barnabas and Saul completed a relief mission to

The south city gate (possibly Hellenistic) at Perga of Pamphylia, the port from which Mark returned home.

Jerusalem, they took Mark with them when they returned to Antioch (Acts 12:25). When Barnabas and Saul went as missionaries, they took Mark to help (Acts 13:5). They went from Antioch to Cyprus and then on to Pamphylia, where Mark left them and returned to Jerusalem (Acts 13:13). The most likely reason was because Paul had become the dominant missionary and was taking the gospel to Gentiles (Acts 13:4–12). Later, when Paul and Barnabas planned another journey, Barnabas wanted to take Mark. When Paul refused, Barnabas and Mark went together while Paul and Silas went together (Acts 15:36–40).

When Paul wrote Philemon, Mark was one of Paul's fellow workers who sent greetings (Philem. 24). Paul wrote to the Colossians to receive Mark if he came to them (Col. 4:10). When Paul wrote his final letter to Timothy, he asked Timothy to bring Mark with him because Paul considered Mark a useful helper (2 Tim. 4:11).

Peter referred to Mark as his "son," and sent greetings from him near the end of his first letter (1 Pet. 5:13).

MARK, THE GOSPEL OF The second book of the New Testament and the shortest account of the ministry of Jesus.

Author The title "according to Mark" was added to this Gospel by scribes who produced the earliest copies of the Gospel. According to early church tradition, Mark recorded and arranged the "memories" of Peter, thereby producing a Gospel based on apostolic witness. Although Mark was a common Roman name, the gospel writer is probably John Mark. Mark became an important assistant for both Paul and Peter, preaching the good news to Gentiles and preserving the gospel message for later Christians. See *Mark, John.*

Readers Mark wrote his Gospel for Gentile Christians. He explains Jewish customs in detail for the benefit of readers unfamiliar with Judaism (7:3–4; 12:18). Mark translated several Aramaic expressions for a Greek-speaking audience (5:41; 7:11,34; 15:22). Gentiles would have especially appreciated Mark's interpretation of the saying of Jesus which declared all foods clean (7:19; compare with Matt. 15:17–20). Mark's Gentile audience may explain his omission of the genealogy of Jesus. Perhaps these Gentile readers were Roman Christians. Mark's Gospel contains many terms borrowed from Latin and written in Greek, consider "taking counsel" (3:6), "Legion" (5:9), "tribute" (12:14), "scourged" (15:15).

Early Christian tradition placed Mark in Rome preserving the words of Peter for Roman Christians shortly before the apostle's death (see 1 Pet. 5:13). According to tradition, Peter was martyred in Rome during the Neronian persecution, which would place the date of Mark's Gospel about A.D. 64 to 68. Such a hostile environment motivated Mark to couch his account of the life of Jesus in terms that would comfort Christians suffering for their faith. The theme of persecution dominates the Gospel of Mark (see Mark 10:30; compare Matt. 19:29; Luke 18:29). Jesus' messianic suffering is emphasized to inspire Christians to follow the same path of servanthood (10:42–45). Roman Christians would be encouraged knowing that Jesus anticipated that "everyone shall be salted with fire" (9:49; see 13:9–13). Dying for the gospel would be equivalent to dying for Jesus (8:35; Matt. 16:25; Luke 9:24).

Style Mark has been called the "gospel of action." One of his favorite words in telling the story of Jesus is "immediately." Jesus is constantly on the move. In one day, according to Mark, Jesus instructed the multitudes by the sea, traveled across the sea of Galilee and calmed the storm, healed the Gerasene demoniac, crossed the sea again, healed the woman with a hemorrhage, and raised a little girl from the dead (4:1—6:1). Mark apparently had more interest in the work of Jesus than in the words of Jesus. Thus he omitted the Sermon on the Mount. Jesus taught as He moved from region to region, using the circumstances of His travel as valuable lessons for His disciples (8:14–21). Geographical references serve only to trace the expansive parameters of His ministry. According to Mark's "motion" picture, Jesus moved quickly—as if He were a man whose days were numbered.

Good storytellers captivate audiences by using everyday language which provokes strong imagery. Mark's language is simple, direct, and common. His sometimes rough and unrefined Greek grammar facilitates his ability to communicate the gospel message by using familiar patterns of speech. When Mark told a story, he possessed a flair for the dramatic and an eye for detail. His description of events was replete with vivid images which evoke a variety of emotions in just one story (see 5:1–20; compare Matt. 8:28–34). In the graphic account of Jesus' encounter with the demoniac boy, only Mark recorded the child's convulsion which caused him to fall on the ground, and roll "around, foaming at the mouth" (9:20, 26 NIV). Furthermore, Mark preserved Jesus' interrogation of the father as to the severity of the boy's condition and the depth of his own faith (9:21–24). Finally, only Mark recorded the actual words of Jesus' rebuke as well as the reaction of the crowd to the boy's lifeless body: "He's dead!" (9:25–26, NIV).

Mark's concern for detail, sometimes to the point of redundancy (see Mark 6:49–50 NIV, "when they *saw Him . . .* because they all *saw Him . . .* He *spoke* to them and *said*"), demonstrates his reliance upon eyewitness testimony. Mark was careful to relate not only the words of Jesus, but also His gestures, attitudes, and emotions (3:5; 6:34; 7:34; 8:12; 11:16). In the same fashion, Mark recorded the reaction of the crowds, facial expressions of conversationalists, conclusions drawn by the disciples, and private remarks made by opponents (5:40; 10:22,32,41; 11:31; 14:40). Only an observant insider would relate stories with such pertinent information. Furthermore, the prominent role of Peter in the narrative (*Peter* remembered, 11:21; see also 1:36; 14:37; 16:7) confirms early Christian tradition that Mark relied upon the recollections of the apostle when he produced "the gospel of Jesus Christ" (1:1).

Form Upon first reading, the Gospel of Mark appears to be an arbitrary collection of stories about Jesus. After the Baptist fulfilled his role as the forerunner to the Messiah (in a very brief appearance), Jesus began His public ministry in Galilee by preaching the "gospel of God" and collecting a few disciples (1:14–20). With these necessary introductions completed, Mark presented the life of Jesus by following a simple geographical scheme: from Galilee to Judea. The popular Galilean ministry of Jesus is recorded in chapters 1—9. The brief Judean ministry (10:1–31) serves primarily as a prelude to the approaching passion of Jesus. Over one-third of Mark's Gospel is devoted to describing the events of the last week in the life of Jesus (10:32—15:47). The story ends as abruptly as it began; Mark finished his Gospel account with the angelic announcement of the resurrection of Jesus the Nazarene (the earliest Greek manuscripts of the New Testament end Mark's Gospel at 16:8). Mark's chronology of Jesus leaves the reader with the impression that his only purpose in writing a Gospel was to preserve the oral tradition in written form. However, upon closer inspection, it becomes apparent to the observant reader that Mark arranged the material in a more sophisticated fashion to convey truth on a higher level.

The stories of the cleansing of the Temple and the cursing of the fig tree appear as isolated incidents in Matthew's Gospel, connected by chronological sequence (Matt. 21:12–22). In the Gospel of Mark, on the other hand, these two stories are interwoven to aid the reader in interpreting the parabolic activity of Jesus. Along the way to Jerusalem Jesus indicated to His disciples that He was hungry and approached a fig tree to harvest its fruit. The tree was full of leaves, giving every indication of life; but it possessed no fruit. Mark recorded that Jesus "answered" the tree and announced, May "no man eat fruit of thee hereafter for ever" (11:14). The disciples, who "heard him," must have been puzzled by Jesus' actions, for Mark recorded that "it was not the season for figs" (11:13, NIV). Without explanation, Jesus led His disciples into Jerusalem where he cleansed the Temple. From a distance the daily activity of the Temple gave every indication of spiritual life, but upon closer inspection Jesus found no spiritual fruit. Israel, the fig tree, was supposed to provide a "house of prayer for all the nations" (11:17, NIV). Instead, the religious leaders turned the devotion of worshipers into financial profit (11:15,17). In essence, when Jesus "answered" the fig tree, he pronounced a curse on the Jewish religious leadership and demonstrated His divine displeasure by cleansing the Temple. In word and deed, Jesus prophesied that God would no longer use Israel as the vehicle of salvation for humanity. It should have come as no surprise, then, for Peter and the disciples, during their return trip, to find the cursed fig tree dead (11:21). By purifying the Temple, Jesus marked the death of Judaism, caused His own death (11:18), and gave birth to a religion for all people. The Gentile readers of Mark's Gospel would have especially appreciated the significant arrangement of these two stories.

Mark's Gospel is not just a collection of stories about Jesus; his book tells the story of Jesus as a whole. Mark developed the unifying "plot" of the gospel story by unveiling the hidden identity of Jesus. The messianic secret is part of the mystery of the kingdom of God, understood only by insiders— "to them that are without all these things are done in parables" (4:11,33–34). Throughout Mark's Gospel, Jesus made every attempt to conceal His true identity. Jesus silenced demonic profession because they knew Him (1:34). He ordered those who witnessed miracles not to tell anyone what they saw, although silence was only a remote possibility (7:36). Even after the climactic profession of faith, when the disciples revealed that they had learned the secret ("Thou art the Christ"!), Jesus swore His followers to secrecy (8:39–30). Mark used the messianic secret to organize his story around the progressive revelation of Christ and the faith pilgrimage of His disciples. Even Gentiles demonstrated that they belonged to the community of faith when they understood Jesus' parables and recognized Him as the Christ.

The literary form of Mark's Gospel is no accident. The arrangement of the gospel material gives every indication that a skilled literary craftsman has been at work. For example, Mark found irony in pairing the story of the disciples questioning the identity of Jesus after the stilling of the storm, "What manner of man is this?" (4:41) with the account of the demons who are quick to shout, "Jesus, thou son of the most high God" (5:7). When the disciples finally offered their superlative confession of faith at Caesarea Philippi (8:27–30), they failed to understand the full implications of Jesus' messiahship (8:31–38). Mark depicted their partial spiritual vision by recording the unique miracle of Jesus healing the blind man in two stages (8:22–25). Although the disciples saw the messianic secret, their vision would not be focused until the resurrection. Beyond doubt, Mark's portrait of Jesus is a "painting" which can be appreciated both up close (style) and from a distance (form).

M

Message Jesus' favorite self-designation, especially in Mark, was "Son of Man." In Mark's Gospel, Jesus is identified with humanity in title and in kind. Mark portrayed Jesus as a Man possessing every human emotion. Moved by compassion, anger, frustration, mercy, and sorrow (1:41; 3:5; 8:17; 14:6,33), Jesus ministered among His own kind. Mark offered the full humanity of Jesus without reservation (see 3:21; 4:38; 6:3–6; 13:32); from the beginning of His earthly ministry (2:20), Jesus lived in the ominous shadow of the cross until the agony of Gethsemane almost overwhelmed Him (14:34). However, Mark penned a Gospel which was also designed to evoke faith in the deity of Jesus: the divine voice announced it from heaven, demons screamed it in agony, Peter professed it boldly, even a Roman soldier acknowledged, "Truly this man was the Son of God!" (15:39).

Outline

I. God Has Acted for His People by Sending His Son as His Agent (1:1–13).
   A. God fulfilled the words of His prophets (1:1–3).
   B. God announced His action through the herald in the wilderness (1:4–8).
   C. God's endorsement of Jesus as His beloved Son showed He is the promised Lord (1:9–11).
   D. God sustained His Son in the experience of testing in the wilderness (1:12–13).
II. The Appearance of God's Son as His Agent Signaled the Presence of the New Age (1:14–45).
   A. God's Agent announced the presence of the new age (1:14–15).
   B. The call to become fishers of men was a consequence of the presence of the new age (1:16–20).
   C. The unique authority of God's Agent demonstrated the presence of the new age (1:21–28).
   D. Healing through God's Agent revealed the saving character of the new age (1:29–34).
   E. The urgency of preaching was consistent with the presence of the new age (1:35–39).
   F. The healing of a leper was evidence of the powers of the new age (1:40–45).
III. The Old Order Failed to Recognize God's Agent or the Presence of the New Age (2:1–3:6).
   A. The old order failed to recognize that Jesus had authority to forgive sins (2:1–12).
   B. The old order resented God's Agent for forgiving outcasts and sinners (2:13–17).
   C. The old order failed to understand fasting was inappropriate when God's

Agent was present (2:18–22).
   D. The old order failed to recognize that God's Agent was the Lord of the sabbath (2:23—3:5).
   E. The old order displayed hardness of heart when it schemed to destroy God's Agent (3:6).
IV. The Presence of God's Agent Provoked a Reaction from Others (3:7—6:6).
   A. Crowds followed God's Agent to receive the blessings of the new age (3:7–10).
   B. Unclean spirits recognized the threat posed by the presence of God's Agent (3:11–12).
   C. God's Agent appointed the twelve to express His unique authority (3:13–19).
   D. God's Agent was regarded by His family as deranged (3:20–21).
   E. God's Agent was regarded by the old order as demonic (3:22–30).
   F. God's Agent identified His true family as those who do God's will in the new age (3:31–35).
   G. God's Agent used parables to clarify the character of the new age (4:1–34).
   H. When God's Agent subdued the hostile power of the sea, the reaction was awe (4:35–41).
   I. When God's Agent extended the salvation of the new age to the Gentiles, the reaction was both terror and gratitude (5:1–20).
   J. When God's Agent subdued the powers of disease and death, the reaction was fear and amazement (5:21–43).
   K. When God's Agent addressed those who knew Him well, the reaction was contempt and unbelief (6:1–6).
V. God's Agent Extended the Blessings of the New Age in Spite of Opposition (6:7–8:30).
   A. God's Agent extended the blessings of the new age through the twelve, warning them to expect opposition (6:7–13).
   B. The murder of the herald of the new age anticipated the death of God's Agent (6:14–29).
   C. God's Agent provided rest in the wilderness as a blessing of the new age (6:30–44).
   D. God's Agent provided relief to those who obey Him as a blessing of the new age (6:45–52).
   E. God's Agent provided healing for those who seek Him as a blessing of the new age (6:53–56).
   F. God's Agent challenged the old order traditions with enduring commandments (7:1–23).
   G. God's Agent extended new age blessings to believing Gentiles (7:24—8:10).
   H. God's Agent experienced the old order's

opposition in their demand for a sign (8:11–13).

I. The twelve failed to understand the significance of the blessings of the new age (8:14–21).

J. God's Agent opened blind eyes as a sign of the new age (8:22–26).

K. Jesus was recognized as God's Agent, the mediator of the blessings of the new age (8:27–30).

VI. God's Agent Exhibited the New Age Paradox: Suffering Precedes Vindication (8:31—10:52).

A. God's Agent must experience suffering prior to vindication by resurrection (8:31–33).

B. New age people participate in the paradox: the way to life is through death (8:34–38).

C. The transfiguration provides assurance: vindication will follow suffering (9:1–8).

D. Both the herald and the Agent of the new age exhibited the pattern of suffering and rejection followed by vindication (9:9–13).

E. The powers of the new age are released through faith and prayer (9:14–29).

F. The paradox of the new age that suffering precedes vindication is reaffirmed (9:30–32).

G. The paradox of the new age is that greatness is expressed through humble service (9:33–41).

H. The fact of the new age accounts for the stringent requirements of discipleship (9:42–50).

I. The creation intention of God for marriage is reaffirmed in the new age (10:1–12).

J. Entrance into the new age is through childlike faith (10:13–16).

K. Entrance into the new age requires sacrificial commitment (10:17–31).

L. The paradox of the new age is reaffirmed (10:32–45).

M. True discipleship responds immediately to the blessings of the new age (10:46–52).

VII. The Presence of God's Agent in Jerusalem Intensified the Conflict between the Old Order and the New Age (11:1—12:44).

A. The significance of the entrance of God's Agent into Jerusalem was unrecognized (11:1–11).

B. The presence of God's Agent in Jerusalem introduced judgment on the old order (11:12–25).

C. The authority of God's Agent was challenged by representatives of the old order (11:27–33).

D. God's Agent taught of His transcendent

dignity (12:1–12).

E. The wisdom of God's Agent was challenged by representatives of the old order (12:13–27).

F. God's Agent was vindicated by His teaching on the greatest commandment (12:28–34).

G. God's Agent exposed the inability of the old order to understand Scripture (12:35–37).

H. God's Agent exposed the hypocrisy of the old order (12:38–40).

I. God's Agent presented a proper response to the presence of the new age (12:41–44).

VIII. God's Agent Foresaw Impending Distress for Jerusalem and the Old Order (13:1–37).

A. God's Agent foresaw the impending destruction of the Temple (13:1–4).

B. God's Agent warned of deception through those who falsely claim to act for God (13:5–8).

C. God's Agent warned of impending persecution and called for steadfastness (13:9–13).

D. God's Agent warned of the sacrilege that causes desolation (13:14–23).

E. God's Agent looked beyond the impending distress to triumph for His people (13:24–37).

IX. The Old Order Was Unified in Its Action Against God's Agent (14:1—15:47).

A. Representatives of the old order determined to seize God's Agent (14:1–2).

B. God's Agent was anointed for His burial (14:3–9).

C. God's Agent was denied by one of the twelve who agreed to betray Him (14:10–11).

D. God's Agent announced His betrayal during the Passover meal (14:12–21).

E. God's Agent provided His own symbol of the new age (14:22–26).

F. God's Agent foresaw the failure and denial of His own followers (14:27–31).

G. God's Agent affirmed His submission to the will of God in Gethsemane (14:32–42).

H. God's Agent experienced betrayal and arrest, fulfilling Scripture (14:43–52).

I. God's Agent was condemned, mocked, and brutalized by the old order (14:53–65).

J. The prophecy of Peter's denial was fulfilled (14:66–72).

K. The old religious order joined the political order to condemn God's Agent (15:1–20).

L. God's Agent was crucified as King of the Jews (15:21–37).

M. God's Agent was acknowledged to be

M

A colonnaded street by the agora in Perga, a city significant in the life of the gospel writer Mark.

the Son of God by a Roman (15:38–39).
N. The death and burial of God's Agent was witnessed by godly women (15:40–47).
X. The Resurrection of God's Agent Validated the Presence of the New Age (16:1–8).
XI. A Later Appendix: Proof of the Vindication of God's Agent (16:9–20). *Rodney Reeves*

MARKET PLACE The narrow streets and clustered buildings of most towns and villages in ancient Paletine left little room for a public market place. Shops were built into private residences or clustered in the gate area to form bazaars (1 Kings 20:34). Merchants operated booths just inside the city gate or hawked their merchandise outside the

The shops and agora area of ancient Corinth.

gate area in an open space or square. This area also served as a marshaling place for troops (2 Chron. 32:6) and the site for public meetings (Neh. 8:1), victory celebrations (Deut. 13:16), and the display of captives (2 Sam. 21:12).

Herod rebuilt many of the cities of Palestine following the Greek pattern which included open areas for public gathering (Greek: *agora*). Amidst the shops, children played (Matt. 11:16), day laborers gathered to be hired (Matt. 20:2–3), and Pharisees and other leading citizens wandered, exchanging greetings (Matt. 23:7; Luke 11:43). Paul went to the marketplace (Greek *agora*) on his visits to Greek cities to speak to the crowd always gathered there (Acts 17:17). He and Silas were also tried by magistrates in the marketplace at Philippi after angering the local merchants (Acts 16:19). *Victor H. Matthews*

MAROTH (Mā' rŏth) Place name meaning "bitter" or "bitter fountain." Town in lowlands of Judah which would be attacked as invading armies approached Jerusalem (Mic. 1:12). The town is perhaps identical with Maarath (Josh. 15:59).

MARRIAGE The biblical standard for marriage is a monogamous relationship in which a man and a woman share a lifetime commitment to each other, second only to their commitment to God. It is an unconditional, lifetime commitment. Jesus emphasized God's intention that marriage be a lifetime commitment (Mark 10:5–9; Matt. 19:4–9). He affirmed this as the principle of marriage inherent in divine creation (Gen. 2:24). Paul cited this key principle to show the sinfullness of sexual relations outside marriage (1 Cor. 6:12–20) and to emphasize the importance of self-giving love in marriage (Eph. 5:28). Genesis 2:24 emphasizes the oneness of the marriage relationship and the priority of the relationship over all others, including the relationship of the couple to their parents. Marriage is also for companionship (Gen. 2:18–23). Paul described the kind of mutual submission that should characterize the marriage relationship (Eph. 5:21–33). Although the husband is head of the home, his role is modeled after the role of Christ as Head of the church, who "loved the church and gave Himself for it" (Eph. 5:25).

Sex is one of God's good gifts God's intention is for sexual union to be expressed exclusively within the unique monogamous relationship of marriage. Human sexuality (Gen. 1:27) and sexual union within marriage (Gen. 2:24) were part of God's good creation. Sexual union is for procreation (Gen. 1:28) and also for expressing love within the oneness of marriage (Gen. 2:24; Prov. 5:15–19; 1 Cor. 7:2–5). Although polygamy was practiced by some Old Testament personalities, monogamy was always God's ideal for humanity (Matt. 19:4–5). The New Testament clearly teaches monogamy (1 Cor. 7:2). Adultery is a violation of the commitment inherent in marriage (Ex. 20:14; 1 Thess. 4:2–3; Heb. 13:4). So is any sexual intercourse that does not express the oneness of marriage (1 Cor. 6:12–20). The biblical condemnation of adultery covers such things as communal marriage, mate swapping, and the so-called open marriage. Likewise, homosexuality violates the intended purpose of sex (Lev. 18:22; 20:13; Rom. 1:26–27). Incest also is a violation of the biblical view of sex (1 Cor. 5:1–5).

Marriage and singleness are valid options for Christians. Jesus taught that marriage demands faithfulness within a relationship based on a lifetime commitment (Matt. 19:3–9). When the disciples said that this concept made marriage too demanding, Jesus replied that singleness—whether involuntary or voluntary—has its own demand, abstinence from sexual union (Matt. 19:10–12). Paul acknowledged that marriage is best for many; but, based on his own experience, he recommended singleness to those who wanted to devote all of their energies to Christian work and could forego sexual relationships (1 Cor. 7:7–9,32–35). Neither Jesus nor Paul presented marriage or singleness as a second-class or less holy state than the other.

Christians condemn sexual immorality in all its forms. Sexual sins are serious because they undermine the foundation of family life, the oneness of the marriage relationship; however, such sins are not unforgivable. Jesus sought out and offered forgiveness to persons guilty of sexual sins (Matt. 21:31–32; Luke 7:36–50; John 4:1–42; 8:2–

11). Forgiveness does not condone such sins, but does offer a new start with God's help. David's experience shows that even when sexual sins are forgiven, the destructive consequences continue (2 Sam. 12—19). Love demands that followers of Christ seek to help persons caught in the grip of sin, being careful not to become involved in the sin themselves (Gal. 6:1). Persistent immorality is unacceptable behavior for Christians (1 Cor. 5:1–13; 6:12–20).

Christians should marry Christians, but Christians are to strive for a godly home even when this is not the case. The expectation for a Christian to marry another Christian is implicit in Paul's instructions about marrying "only in the Lord" (1 Cor. 7:39), and in his words about not being mismated with unbelievers (2 Cor. 6:14). As important as family relations are, a person's commitment to God takes precedence in those unfortunate situations when the two commitments are in conflict (Matt. 10:37; Luke 9:59–62). A Christian who is married to a non-Christian should seek to maintain the relationship, to raise any children as believers, and to win the unbelieving spouse (1 Cor. 7:12–16; 1 Pet. 3:1–12). There is no evidence that Timothy's father was a believer (Acts 16:1), but his mother passed her faith along to her son (2 Tim. 1:5; 3:14–15).

The biblical ideal is marriage that lasts a lifetime. Christians sometimes must cope with the breakup of a marriage. Because humans do not live up to the high ideals and standards of God, marriages do fail. With the strong biblical emphasis on marriage as a lifetime commitment, divorce poses a real dilemma for Christians. The dilemma of their proper attitude and response is most real for the persons directly involved and for those closest to them, but the dilemma also exists for the larger circle of friends and fellow church members. The Mosaic law allowed a man to divorce his wife but required a bill of divorce for her (Deut. 24:1). This was an advance over a time when a man simply sent his wife away. The writ of divorce was evidence of her release from the marriage and thus her freedom to be married to someone else (Deut. 24:2). Jesus explained Deuteronomy 24:1 as a concession to the hardness of human hearts; but He emphasized God's original intention as reflected in Genesis 1:27 and 2:24 (Mark 10:2–9; Matt. 19:3–9). Two verses in Matthew (5:32; 19:9) state that fornication can be grounds for divorce. Some interpreters believe that these and other relevant pasages in the Gospels (Mark 10:11–12; Luke 16:18) suggest that Jesus especially had in mind persons who divorce a spouse and marry someone else in an attempt to legitimize an adulterous relationship. The case of Herod and Herodias, who had divorced their spouses to satisfy their lust for each other, was notorious in that day. John the Baptist had been in prison for daring to rebuke Herod, and spiteful Herodias successfully plotted John's execution because of this (Mark 6:14–29; Matt. 14:1–12). Paul followed Jesus in emphasizing the permanence of marriage (1 Cor. 7:10–11), but he taught that a Christian was not bound to an unbelieving spouse if the unbeliever insisted on a separation (1 Cor. 7:12–16). Clearly, therefore, the Bible teaches permanence as the ideal; but unfortunately, human hearts are still hard; and divorce for various reasons still happens. The Gospels are filled with examples of how Jesus dealt with persons who were struggling with guilt and failure (Luke 19:1–10; John 8:2–11), including one woman who had been married five times and who was living with a man who was not her husband (John 4:1–42). Where guilt was involved, Jesus did not minimize it; but in every case He acted redemptively. That is, His goal was not to condemn people but to help them begin anew with God's grace and strength.

Marriage after the death of a spouse usually is not questioned; marriage again after a divorce is a difficult issue. Marriage after widowhood is clearly permissible in the New Testament (Rom. 7:2–3). Paul advised single persons and widows to remain unmarried if they could, but he counseled marriage for others (1 Cor. 7:8–9). For example, he advised younger widows to remarry (1 Tim. 5:10–14). Widows are free to remarry, but "only in the Lord" (1 Cor. 7:39). Those who oppose marriage again of divorced persons cite Mark 10:11–12; Luke 16:18; Romans 7:3; and 1 Corinthians 7:10–11. They interpret the statement by Jesus as teaching that divorced persons who marry again are living in adultery. They cite Paul as evidence that the apostle interpreted Jesus in this way. Based on these verses, some pastors refuse to perform a wedding involving a divorced person. Another group emphasizes Jesus' exception clause in Matthew 5:31–32 and 19:9. This clause, "Except it be for fornication," implies that when a married person commits fornication, the spouse is free to secure divorce and to marry another person. Others believe principles inherent in the gospel make marriage again a valid option for divorced persons. They cite the biblical principles of forgiveness and renewal. Those who advocate this position do not believe Jesus intended to establish a legalistic approach to marriage that would condemn every specific remarriage as an adulterous relationship.

Jesus was not a legalist. His interpretation of adultery in Matthew 5:27–28 should warn against being too heavy-handed about similar idealistic sayings. His hard sayings on divorce were intended to emphasize the biblical ideal of marriage as a lifetime commitment and to rebuke those men whose casual attitude towards divorce make a mockery of this ideal. The emphasis in Mark 10:11; Matthew 19:9; and Luke 16:18 is on the husband who divorces his wife and remarries again. This strongly implies that Jesus was talking about a man who divorces his wife to marry someone else. According to this point of view, Paul affirmed Jesus' ideal and cited Jesus as his authority (1 Cor. 7:10–11); however, he acknowledged certain exceptions in trying to apply this ideal (1 Cor. 7:12–16): "But if the unbelieving depart, let him depart, a brother or a sister is not under bondage in such cases" (1 Cor. 7:15).

Persons who hold this view believe Paul's words imply the possibility of divorce and remarriage. This approach also would leave to each divorced person the choice about marriage again. Such a decision would be based on the same biblical principles that apply to any persons considering marriage, plus the biblical principles of forgiveness and renewal. The former principles include these: companionship (Gen. 2:18), sexual fulfillment (Gen. 2:24; 1 Cor. 7:8–9), distinctive expectations of marriage or singleness (Matt. 19:3–12), parenting goals (Gen. 1:27–28; 1 Tim. 5:14), finding the right kind of person (1 Cor. 7:39).

Difference of interpretation exists about authority and submission in marriage. On the one hand are those who believe that the husband as head of the house has a delegated authority from God over his wife. In this view, the wife's response is submission. On the other side are those whose model is the modern democratic marriage in which the partners are equals in all things. In between are many Christians who advocate a mutual submission in love as the ideal (Eph. 5:21), but also believe the husband has special leadership responsibilities. The key biblical passages in this debate are Ephesians 5:21–32; Colossians 3:18–19; 1 Peter 3:1–7. Advocates of strong male authority interpret these passages in light of the various biblical passages reflecting the husband's authority (1 Cor. 14:34–35; 1 Tim. 2:11–14). Those who take a more moderate view make the following points: Jesus' actions gave women higher status than was accorded by the society of His day (Luke 8:1–3; 10:38–42; John 4:7–30). Paul's more idealistic statements (Gal. 3:28) and actual practice (Acts 16:14–15; 17:4; 18:2–3,18,26; Rom. 16:3–6) indicate that his harder teachings may have been conditioned by specific situations in some first century churches. The admonition to mutual submission in Ephesians 5:21 applies to all the relationships within the church (Eph. 5:25—6:10) and in a Christian marriage (Eph. 5:21–33). Both Paul and Peter's use of submission refers to voluntary submission in a loving relationship, not the forced subjection to authority in a military organization. The biblical references say submit yourself to one another, not *subject* the other person to yourself (Eph. 5:21–22,24; Col. 3:18; 1 Pet. 3:1). In such a relationship, the husband's role as head is modeled after the self-giving of Christ (Eph. 5:23,25,28–30 ; Phil. 2:1–11; Col. 3:19; 1 Pet. 3:7).

Differences of interpretation exist about the role of husbands and wives in marriage. The Bible presents a tension between two truths: the primacy of persons as persons whether they are male or female (Gal. 3:28) and human sexuality (maleness or femaleness) as an important aspect of human personality (Gen. 1:27). The Bible provides considerable support for traditional roles of husbands and wives; however, the Bible provides examples of a variety of masculine-feminine roles. Martha performed the traditional role of preparing a meal for guests, but Mary played the nontraditional role of learner (Luke 10:38–42). Esau was a hunter, but Jacob liked to cook (Gen. 25:27–29). In the Bible the leaders in home and in society were generally men; but there were exceptions: Deborah was a judge (Judg. 4—5); Lydia was a merchant (Acts 16:14); Priscilla and Aquila seemed to have acted as a team in teaching Apollos (Acts 18:26) and in providing a meeting place for the church (Rom. 16:3–5; 1 Cor. 16:19). Even the ideal wife of Proverbs 31 exercised considerable creativity and initiative in far-ranging projects (Prov. 31:16–20).

Douglas Anderson

MARROW The soft tissue within bone cavities. In Old Testament times, marrow was regarded as among the choicest of foods (Ps. 63:5; Isa. 25:6). Good health was characterized by bones with moist marrow (Job 21:24). To fear the Lord and

Mars Hill, where Paul preached his "unknown god" sermon, as viewed from the Acropolis of Athens.

shun evil is marrow (KJV) or refreshment (NAS, RSV) or nourishment (NIV) to the bones (Prov. 3:8). The image of the dividing of joints and marrow pictures the power of Scripture to penetrate a person's thoughts and motives (Heb. 4:12).

MARS HILL A prominent rise overlooking the city of Athens where the philosophers of the city gathered to discuss their ideas, some of which revolutionized modern thought. Paul discussed religion with the leading minds of Athens on Mars Hill. He used the altar to an "unknown god" to present Jesus to them (Acts 17:22). See *Greece*.

MARSENA (Mär′ sē nà) Aramaic or Persian personal name of uncertain meaning. One of the seven wise men or princes with access to the Persian King Ahaseurus (Esth. 1:13–14; compare Ezra 7:14).

MARSH Tract of soft, wet land (Job 8:11; 40:21). Ezekiel 47:11 refers to the salt marshes surrounding the Dead Sea.

MARSHAL Akkadian loan word for commander of troops (Jer. 51:27 NAS, NRSV; captain, KJV; commander, NIV, REB).

MARTHA (Mär′ thà) Personal name meaning "lady [of the house]" or "mistress." Sister of Mary and Lazarus of Bethany and one of Jesus' best-loved disciples. True to her name, Martha is portrayed as a person in charge: she welcomed Jesus

as a guest in *her* home (Luke 10:38); she was concerned with meeting the obligations of a hostess, whether preparing food (Luke 10:40; John 12:2) or greeting guests (John 11:20). Together with Mary, she sent for Jesus when Lazarus was ill (John 11:3). Luke 10:38–42 contrasts Martha's activist discipleship with Mary's contemplative discipleship. The church cannot minister without "Marthas" who are willing to serve alone. Jesus' gentle rebuke serves as a perpetual reminder not to major on minor matters. Jesus must not be neglected in the name of service. In John 11:21–27, Jesus led Martha from an inadequate to a lofty confession. Faced with the realities of death, Martha, however, later doubted (John 11:39). Some interpreters identify Martha as the wife (widow) or daughter of Simon the leper on the basis of harmonization with Matthew 26:6–13 and Mark 14:3–9. The three traditions which involve anointings of Jesus (*1.* Matt. 26:6–13; Mark 14:3–9; *2.* Luke 7:37–39,44–50; *3.* John 21:1–8) present a nearly insurmountable challenge to a harmonizer. A more sound approach is to appreciate each tradition within the context of the Gospel of which it is a part.

MARTYR The transliteration of a Greek word meaning "witness," in particular one who gives his life for a cause. In later usage it was applied to those who died because of their faith in Christ rather than recant. The transliteration was used for these persons and the translation "witness" came to be used for those who testified of Christ but were not put to death.

MARY (Ma′ ry) Greek personal name equivalent to Hebrew Miriam, meaning, "rebellious, bitter." See *Miriam.*

1. Mother of Jesus. Mary seems to have been related to Elizabeth, the mother of John the Baptist, and wife of the priest Zechariah. Elizabeth was also of a priestly family. If "kinswoman" in Luke 1:36 is a reference for family line and not a relationship established by marriage, then Mary's family heritage may have been priestly. Luke pre-

"Mary's House" in Ephesus where tradition says that Mary the mother of Jesus lived out her last days.

sented Mary as a person of great faith prepared to be an agent of God in the birth of the Messiah. In later church tradition, two important theological beliefs focus the significance of Mary. One has to do with what is referred to as "divine maternity," while the other is "virginal conception." Their scriptural orientation is based on Luke 1:34 that details Mary's response to the angel's announcement that she would have a son. Mary questioned how this could be since she did not have a husband. The Greek states, "I am not knowing a man." Some have interpreted the Greek text as making an eternally valid theological statement that her virginity is an on-going state that equals a "perpetual virginity." Matthew 1:24–25 (including, [Joseph] "knew her not until she had borne a son") would seem to challenge the perpetual virginity belief. The Luke text is sufficiently vague as to allow the growth of such doctrine. In contemporary Christianity, the Roman Catholic and Eastern Orthodox churches embrace these doctrines, while most Protestant churches do not. However, in all cases, Mary is a revered character in Christian tradition who is believed to represent goodness, innocence, and profound commitment to the ways of God.

Mary does not play as high a profile in the Gospels as one might expect. The Gospel writers attempted to emphasize Jesus' divine origins at the expense of deemphasizing the importance of His mother. The Gospel of John presents women in an essential place in the public ministry of Jesus, and Mary, the mother of Jesus, functions in such a role. In John 2:1–11, Mary's presence at Jesus' first public miracle of changing water to wine at the marriage at Cana underscores, in a profound manner, that Jesus' destiny challenges all norms, including that of immediate family relationships. The recurring Johannine theological theme of Jesus' "hour" being divinely directed is pointedly made by Mary's presence in the episode (compare Mark 3:31–35; Luke 11:27–28). Mary's presence at the foot of the cross (found only in John 19:25–27) highlights the mother's love. Acts 1:14 indicates that Mary was present, along with other hero figures of early Christianity, in the upper room scene in Jerusalem.

2. Mary Magdalene. Magdala was an important agricultural, fishing, and trade center of ancient Galilee. Mark 16:9 and Luke 8:2 indicate that this Mary, from Magdala, was exorcised of some seven demons. In antiquity, demon possession was an indication of physical or spiritual illness; obviously, Mary Magdalene was quite ill before her encounter with Jesus. Mary eventually became part of an inner circle of supporters of Jesus. She was a witness of His crucifixion (Mark 15:40; Matt. 27:56; John 19:25), burial (Mark 15:47; Matt. 27:61), the empty tomb (Mark 16:18; Matt. 28:1–10; Luke 24:10), and she was a witness of Jesus' resurrection (Mark 16:9; John

20:1–18). A tradition, especially prevalent in western Christianity from about A.D. 500 onward, identified Mary Magdalene with the sinful woman of Luke 7:36–50. The text gives no reason for such an association, as the introduction of Mary in Luke 8 is quite removed topically from Luke 7:36. To confuse the interpretative tradition further, the sinful woman in the anointing scene of Luke 7:36–50 is often identified incorrectly with another Mary, the sister of Martha and Lazrus. On all accounts, no evidence exists that the sinful woman of Luke 7 should be identified as Mary.

3. Mary (of Bethany), the sister of Martha and Lazarus. Mary, Martha, and Lazarus seem to have been part of an inner circle of Jesus' associates. The Gospel of John places particular emphasis on their select status. Mary from Bethany played a primary role in the episode of Lazarus' resurrection from the dead in John 11. In John 12, Mary anointed Jesus' feet with precious oil, thus serving an important confessional function of anticipating Jesus' death. Given the sequence of John's Gospel, Mary is represented as a follower of Jesus who is well acquainted with Jesus' ultimate destiny (compare Judas, the disciple in John 12:4, who is not as well informed).

4. Mary, the mother of James the younger and of Joses and Salome. This Mary would appear to be part of Jesus' following from Galilee who moved with Him during His itinerant public ministry

(compare Mark 15:40–41). She witnessed Jesus' crucifixion and was part of the group of women who encountered the empty tomb (Mark 15:47; 16:1–8; Matt. 27:55–56; 28:1–8; Luke 23:56; 24:1–10).

5. Mary, the mother of John Mark. This woman was the owner of the house in Jerusalem where the first followers of Jesus met (Acts 12:12). Her son, John Mark, eventually became a disciple of Paul and Barnabas (Acts 12:25). See *Mark, John.*

6. Mary, the wife of Clopas. She witnessed Jesus' crucifixion (John 19:25) and may be the same character as Mary, the mother of James, Joses, and Salome in the Synoptic Gospels accounts.

7. Mary, from Rome. An individual Paul greeted in Romans 16:6.   *Wayne McCready*

MASADA (Mȧ sä′ dȧ) A mesa on the western shore of the Dead Sea. It rises about 820 feet above the surrounding valleys and was used as a stronghold between 142 B.C. and A.D. 73. Jonathan Maccabeus first fortified the rock. Herod the Great made it a monument to his building activity. A band of rebellious Jews held it briefly during the first revolt against Rome (A.D. 66–73). After a long struggle to recapture the fortress, the Tenth Legion raised an enormous seige ramp and broke through the walls. They found the bodies of over 900 men, women, and children, victims of a suicide pact to keep the Romans from taking them as prisoners.

MASCHIL (Mäs′ chîl) KJV form of Maskil, a term

The natural flattop escarpment of Masada on the west shore of the Dead Sea south of En-gedi.

A view of Masada from the highest northern palace with the Roman army camp in the background.

Decorative mosaic floors decorate the Western Palace area of Masada.

From atop Masada, outlines of Roman army camps constructed during the seige of Masada can be seen.

used in the titles of thirteen Psalms (Pss. 32; 42; 44; 45; 52—55; 74; 78; 88; 89; 142). The term is translated psalm in Psalm 47:7. The origin of the term is disputed. Some see a connection with the root "to understand, ponder." Two of the maskils have clear references to instruction (Pss. 32:8–9; 78:1). Others suggest that maskil might be a musical notation or an indication that these psalms were performed at festivals (for example, Ps. 78). Though most of the maskils are laments (Pss. 42; 44; 52; 54; 55; 74; 88; 142), other form critical types are grouped as maskils as well (Ps. 32, a thanksgiving for healing; Ps. 45, a

psalm in celebration of a royal wedding; Ps. 78, a recitation of sacred history).

MASH (Măsh) A son of Aram (Gen. 10:23) in Table of Nations and thus original ancestor of Syrian tribal group, possibly from Mount Masius (Tur Abdin) in Northern Mesopotamia or the Mashu mountains of the Gilgamesh epic, probably the Lebanon and anti-Lebanon mountains. The name is copied as Meshech in 1 Chronicles 1:17.

MASHAL (Mā′ shăl) *1.* City in the tribal territory of Asher later assigned to the Levites (1 Chron. 6:74). At Joshua 19:26; 21:30 the name appears as Misheal (KJV) or Mishal (modern translations). *2.* Technical Hebrew term for proverb, parable, simile. See *Proverbs, Wisdom.*

MASKIL (Mäs kîl) See *Mischal.*

MASONS Building craftsmen using brick or stone. The professional mason in Israel first appears in the Bible in David's time, though the craft was very ancient and highly developed in Egypt by that time. The Bible suggests that no Israelites were skilled in the art of quarrying, squaring, and setting fine building stones in David's time. David relied upon the king of Tyre for craftsmen (2 Sam. 5:11–12; 1 Chron. 22:2–4,14–18). Under the reign of Solomon, Israelites may have begun to develop this craft (1 Kings 5:18). As professional craftsmen, stone masons were probably members of a guild or trade association such as other tradesmen. Such associations were primarily social organizations, though in later times they could be a political force of concern to rulers (Acts 19:23–41). It was also common for members of the same trade to live and work in one location within the larger towns and cities (2 Kings 18:17; 1 Chron. 4:14; Neh. 11:35; Jer. 37:21; Matt. 27:7; Acts 18:3).

Dressed or ashlar masonry was not ordinarily used in private dwellings. The average man built his own home of sun dried brick on a foundation of field stones. Biblical references to masons thus involve public works (2 Kings 12:11–15; 2 Kings 22:3–8; Ezra 3:7).

Limestone was a primary building stone in the hill country. It was easily cut, and it hardened when exposed to the air. To cut the stone loose from its bed, wooden wedges were driven into triangular slots cut along the line of the split. These wedges were soaked with water. As the wedges expanded, the force split the stone from the bed.

Hammers, punches, and chisels were used to batter and dress the stone followed by rubbing with fine standstone rubbing stones. Blocks could be squared and polished so finely that a blade could not be inserted between the joints.

Masons, under Herod's employ, cut massive

In Jerusalem examples of Herodian masonry are visible around the Temple Mount area.

limestone blocks as much as 46 feet long, 10 feet thick, and 10 feet high from quarries half a mile from where they were placed in the pediment of the Temple mount. Some of these stones are estimated to weigh as much as 415 tons. They can be seen today in the southwest corner of the Wailing Wall.

See *Architecture; Arts and Crafts; Building Materials; Guilds; Occupations.*   *Larry Bruce*

MASORA (Ma′ sō ra) Hebrew term meaning, "tradition," used for note added to the margins of manuscripts of the Masoretic text of the Old Testament as a safeguard to transmission of the text. See *Bible, Text and Versions.*

MASREKAH (Măs rĕ′ kah) Place name perhaps meaning, "vineyard." City in Edom whose king ruled the Edomites in the period before Israel had kings (Gen. 36:36; 1 Chron. 1:47). The site is perhaps Jebel el-Mushraq about twenty miles south-southwest of Ma'an. Eusebius (around A.D. 300) located Masrekah in Gabalene in northern Edom.

MASSA (Măs′ sà) Hebrew term meaning "burden." *1.* Seventh son of Ishmael (Gen. 25:14; 1 Chron. 1:30). *2.* Arab tribe perhaps descended from *1.* The Mas' a are listed among the peoples who paid tribute to king Tiglath-pileser III (745–727 B.C.) of Assyria. The use of Massa in the titles of collections of proverbs (Prov. 30:1; 31:1) probably refers to the nationality of the original compiler. *3.* The Hebrew term is used in the special sense of oracle, especially at the beginning of prophecies of judgment (for example, Isa. 13:1; Nah. 1:1; Hab. 1:1).

MASSAH (Măs′ sah) Place name meaning, "to test, try." Stopping place during the wilderness wandering near the base of Mount Horeb (Sinai). Moses gave the name in response to the people's desire to put God to the test by demanding water (Ex. 17:7). Massah became a reminder of Israel's disobedience or hardness of heart (Deut. 6:16;

9:22; Ps. 95:8). Massah often appears together with Meribah (meaning "to strive with, contend, find fault with"; Ex. 17:7; Deut. 33:8; Ps. 95:8). Deuteronomy 33:8 gives a poetic account of the origin of the Levitical priesthood at Massah.

MAST Long pole rising from a ship's keel which supports a sail (Prov. 23:34; Isa. 33:23; Ezek. 27:5). See *Ships, Sailors; Navigation.*

MASTER Scripture uses master in two basic senses: (1) one in authority and (2) teacher. *1.* As one in authority, master applies to slaveholders and to heads of households (which in biblical times frequently included slaves or servants). Greek terms translated master (of servants or a household) include *despotēs, kyrios, oikodespotēs* (Mark 13:35; Luke 13:25; 14:21; 16:13; Eph. 6:9). *2.* KJV regularly translated the Greek *didaskalos* (teacher) as master in the Gospels (as in Matt. 8:19; 9:11). KJV twice rendered *kathēgētsē* (guide, teacher) as master (Matt. 23:8,10). KJV sometimes also translated *rabbi* (rabbi, teacher) and *rabboni* (my rabbi, my teacher) as master (Matt. 26:25; Mark 9:5; John 4:31). Modern translations render the above terms as teacher or rabbi. Luke often uses *epistatēs* (manager, chief) where Matthew and Mark have teacher (*didaskalos*), rabbi, or Lord (for example, Luke 5:5; 8:24,45; 9:33,49; 17:13).

MATHUSALA (Mȧ thū′ sȧ là) KJV New Testament form of Methuselah, an ancestor of Christ (Luke 3:37).

MATRED (Mā trĕd) Personal name possibly meaning, "spear." The Hebrew text understands Matred to be the mother of Mehetabel (Gen. 36:39; 1 Chron. 1:50). The earliest Greek and standard Latin translations take Matred to be Mehetabel's father.

MATRI, MATRITES (Mā′ trī) The family within the tribe of Benjamin from which Saul came (1 Sam. 10:21).

MATRIX KJV term meaning womb (Ex. 13:12,15; 34:19; Num. 3:12; 18:15).

MATTAN (Măt′ tan) Personal name meaning "gift of God." *1.* Queen Athaliah's priest of Baal in Jerusalem killed in Jehoiada's purge (2 Kings 11:18). *2.* Father of Shephatiah, a contemporary of Jeremiah (Jer. 38:1).

MATTANAH (Măt′ tȧ nah) Place name meaning, "gift." Stopping place in the wilderness (Num. 21:18–19). The site is perhaps identical with khirbet el-Medeiyineh about twelve miles southeast of Madeba. Pottery shards at that site indicate occupation from before 1,200 to about 800 B.C.

MATTANIAH (Măt tȧ nī' ah) Personal name meaning "gift of Yah." *1.* Tabernacle musician-prophet in David's time (1 Chron. 25:4). *2.* Ancestor of Jahaziel (2 Chron. 20:14). *3.* Member of the Asaphite subclan of Levites who participated in Hezekiah's reforms (2 Chron. 29:13). *4.* Original name of King Zedekiah of Judah (2 Kings 24:17). *5.* Asaphite among the first to return from Exile (1 Chron. 9:15). *6.* Levitic leader of the Temple choir in Zerubbabel's time (Neh. 11:17,22). *7.* Levitic Temple gatekeeper (Neh. 12:25). *8.* Father of the Levite Shemaiah (Neh. 12:35). *9.* Grandfather of Hanan (Neh. 13:13). *10.–13.* Four of those who returned from Exile with foreign wives (Ezra 10:26,27,30,37). Some of *5—13* may be identical.

MATTATHA (Măt' tȧ thȧ) Grandson of King David and ancestor of Christ (Luke 3:31).

MATTATHIAS (Măt tȧ thī' ȧs) *1.* Two ancestors of Christ (Luke 3:25–26). *2.* Priest whose refusal to obey Antiochus' decree to offer sacrifice initiated the Maccabean revolt (1 Macc. 2). *3.* Four high priests from 5 B.C. to A.D. 65. See *Intertestamental History; High Priest.*

MATTATTAH (Măt' tȧt tah) Personal name meaning, "gift." Layman with foreign wife (Ezra 10:33).

MATTENAI (Măt' tė nâī) Personal name meaning, "my gift." *1.* Priestly contemporary of the high priest Joiakim (Neh. 12:19). *2.–3.* Two laymen with foreign wives (Ezra 10:33,37).

MATTHAN (Măt' tăn) An ancestor of Christ (Matt. 1:15).

MATTHAT (Măt' thăt) Two ancestors of Christ (Luke 3:24,29).

MATTHEW (Măt' thēw) Personal name meaning "the gift of Yahweh." A tax collector Jesus called to be an apostle (Matt. 9:9; 10:3). See *Apostle; Disciples.* Matthew's office was located on the main highway that ran from Damascus, down the Jordan Valley to Capernaum, then westward to Acre to join the coastal road to Egypt or southward to Jerusalem. His duty was to collect "toll" or "transport" taxes from both local merchants and farmers carrying their goods to market as well as distant caravans passing through Galilee. He was an employee of Herod Antipas. See *Tax Collector.* Matthew knew the value of goods of all description: wool, flax, linen, pottery, brass, silver, gold, barley, wheat, olives, figs, wheat. He

knew the value of local and foreign monetary systems. He spoke the local Aramaic language as well as Greek. Because Matthew had leased his "toll" collecting privileges by paying the annual fee in advance, he was subjected to the criticism of collecting more than enough, growing wealthy on his "profit." Thus he was hated by his fellow Jews.

Matthew is the same person as Levi, a tax collector (Mark 2:14; Luke 5:27), and thus the son of Alphaeus. James the son of Alphaeus is also listed among the Apostles (Mark 3:18; Matt. 10:3; Luke 6:15; Acts 1:13). This indicates that both Matthew and his (half) brother were in close association with Jesus. Mary, the mother of James, keeps the vigil at the foot of the cross with Mary, the mother of Jesus (Matt. 27:55–56; Mark 15:40). If the James mentioned here is the same as the son of Alphaeus, then we have a larger family closely associated with the family of Jesus.

Later legendary accounts tell of Matthew's travel to Ethiopia where he became associated with Candace, identified with the eunuch of Acts 8:27. The legends tell us of Matthew's martyrdom in that country.

Why did Jesus call Matthew? Because Matthew had the gifts to be trained as a disciple to share with others, could keep meticulous records, and was a potential recorder/author of the Gospel. From earliest times Christians affirmed that Matthew wrote the Gospel that bears his name.

See Matthew, the Gospel of. Oscar Brooks

MATTHEW'S BIBLE The Thomas Matthew Bible was a revision of Tyndale's and Coverdale's versions likely prepared by John Rogers in 1537 in Antwerp. See *Bible, Translations.*

MATTHEW, THE GOSPEL OF The opening book of the New Testament which appropriately begins with the declaration, "the book . . . of Jesus Christ." When we begin reading this book today, we should, however, have in mind its ending (28:18–20). Matthew's purpose was to show that Jesus had the power to command His disciples to spread His gospel throughout all the world.

Matthew 28:16–20 is the scene of the resurrected Jesus meeting His disciples on a hill in Galilee. Jesus immediately declared his absolute authority: "All authority in heaven and on earth has been given to me" (NIV). The disciples would be reminded of many experiences during Jesus' ministry that proved His authority. Now with this knowledge of the resurrection, it was evident to them that He had received His authority from God. Jesus then gave the disciples a Commission to "make disciples of all nations" (NIV). A disciple is (1) one who willingly becomes a learner of the Master's teaching and seeks to follow His example by implementing His teaching, and (2) who passes on to others what one has learned. Hearing Jesus' command, the disciples recalled His teaching and fellowship. Now they were called on to carry forward His mission. Jesus said they would make disciples as they went away from their meeting with Him. Their activities would include baptizing new disciples into the lordship of Jesus. This is the original commitment. The disciples would pass on to others all that Jesus taught them. In telling this story, Matthew emphasized that Jesus (1) has total authority, (2) His teachings must be transmitted, (3) and His message is for all people. If we, the modern readers, will keep these three themes in mind as we read the Gospel from the beginning, we will discover that the author shows us how Jesus demonstrated His authority, the teachings He employed, and His concern for all nations.

The Gospel is easily divided into seven sections: a beginning and an end with five teaching sections between. Because of this, Matthew has been recognized for its emphasis on the teachings of Jesus.

Matthew 1:1—4:25 opens the Gospel with the royal genealogy and builds to the proclamation of God in 3:17: "This is my beloved Son." The genealogies confirm Jesus' authoritative, kingly lineage and remind the reader of His relation to all nations by mentioning Tamar, Rahab, Ruth, and the wife of a Hittite. The wise men (Gentiles) came seeking the King of the Jews (2:2). The angel affirmed Jesus' divine nature to Joseph. The child received a messianic name (1:18—23). Joseph took the holy family to Gentile territory (Egypt) to escape the threats of Herod. When Jesus came to John for baptism, the voice from heaven proclaimed Him as God's Son. As God's Son, Jesus had the authority and power to confront Satan and overcome. Jesus then went to Galilee of the Gentiles (4:15) to begin His public ministry. This opening section makes it obvious that Jesus is designated by God to be the Messiah with authority—for all nations.

Matthew 5:1—7:29 is commonly called the Sermon on the Mount. It should be called the Teaching from the Mount since that is what the text calls it (5:2). While teaching and preaching overlap, teaching emphasizes the essential principles which must be passed on to maintain the discipline or movement at hand. Jesus gave His essential doctrine in this teaching. He stressed the importance of His commandments in 5:19; emphasized the authoritative nature of His teachings by declaring: "But *I* say unto you" (5:22,28,32,39,44); and was recognized by the crowds as a Teacher with authority (7:28—29). Matthew presented Jesus as an authoritative Teacher. When the disciples went out to teach, they knew *what* to teach. When a believer goes out to teach today, he can refer to Matthew's Gospel.

Matthew 8:1—10:42 opens with a series of ten miracles demonstrating Jesus' authority over disease, natural catastrophes, demons, and death. What He had demonstrated verbally in the teachings on the Mount, Jesus acted in displays of power. His disciples wondered "that even the winds and sea obey him!" (8:27), and the crowds stood amazed that He had the authority to forgive sins (9:8). Ministry to a Gentile centurion is in this section also. After demonstrating His power, Jesus gave authority to His disciples to go out and heal and teach as He had done (10:1), thus preparing them for their final Commission in 28:18—20. By continuing the emphasis on authority, teaching, and Gentiles, Jesus prepared His immediate disciples for their task after His death. Matthew continues to teach later generations of believers about Jesus' power and concern for all mankind.

Matthew 11:1—13:52 shows various people reacting to Jesus' authority. Various responses are noted in chapter 11, including Jesus' thanksgiving that the "babes" understand (vv. 25—30). When the leaders rejected Jesus' authority in chapter 12, Matthew implied that Jesus would go to the Gentiles by quoting Isaiah the prophet (12:18—21). Jesus continued His teaching in parables to those who were willing to listen (13:10—13). So when Jesus commissioned His disciples to go into all the world and teach, they were aware that he had already begun the movement by His example in His earthly ministry.

Matthew 13:53—18:35 opens with the story of Jesus' teaching in the synagogue in Nazareth. The people had the same response to Jesus' teaching as the crowds did at the end of the Sermon on the mount. They were astonished (compare 13:54; 7:28). Although Jesus presented His authoritative teaching, His hometown people rejected it (13:57). His disciples accepted Him (14:33), and so did the Gentile woman (15:22). Again, Jesus taught authoritatively and related to Gentiles.

Matthew 19:1—25:46 makes the transition from Galilee to Jerusalem. Jesus dramatically presented His kingly authority by His triumphal entry into Jerusalem (21:1—9) and by cleansing the Temple (21:10—17). Then, while He was teaching, the chief priests and elders challenged Him saying, "By what authority doest thou these things?" (21:23). Jesus answered with parables and other teachings (21:28—22:46). Jesus warned the people about the examples of the Pharisees and Sadducees (23:1—38). He then concentrated His teaching only on His disciples (24:1—25:46). They could recall this when He commanded them to teach what He taught. The modern believer must also hear what Jesus taught and teach it to others.

Matthew 26:1—28:20 has no teaching situations, but it tells of the conspiracy ending in Jesus'' execution. In the midst of the trial scene Jesus was asked if He was the Messiah. Jesus responded by affirming His authority: "Thou hast said" (26:64). Pilate, a Gentile, recognized, Jesus' kingly au-

M

thority, placarding over the cross: "THIS IS JESUS THE KING OF THE JEWS" (27:37). The Gentile centurion proclaimed: "Truly this was the Son of God" (27:54). As in the birth story, so in the end, the author stressed Jesus' divine, kingly authority and emphasized the inclusion of the Gentiles.

When the resurrected Lord declared His authority to His disciples in 28:18, they understood because they had seen His authority displayed as they lived with Jesus. When modern readers come to 28:18, they understand because Matthew has shown us Jesus' authority from the beginning. When Jesus commanded His disciples to make other disciples by teaching all that He taught them, they knew what to teach; and we modern believers know what Jesus intended because we know Matthew's record of His teaching. When Jesus included baptizing, they realized it was the sign of commitment to discipleship, and so do we. When Jesus assured His disciples that He would be with them even to the ends of the earth, the disciples understood because already Jesus had included all people in His ministry.

As we read through the seven sections summarized above, we should also note that Matthew presented Jesus as the "Son of God," a term that appears twenty-three times in the Gospel of Matthew. While the virgin birth story affirms Jesus' sonship, the quotation from Hosea 11:1 (Matt. 2:15) confirms it. Twice God proclaimed Jesus' sonship: at His baptism (3:17) and at the transfiguration (17:5). Peter confessed it (16:16). Jesus attested to His sonship in the Lord's prayer (6:9), His thanksgiving to God (11:25–26), and the Garden of Gethsemane (26:39). The author wanted the reader to be aware that Jesus, the Son of God, is the One crucified on the cross; so Jesus called out to "my God" from the cross (27:46), and a Gentile centurion confessed that the dying One is "truly . . . the Son of God" (27:54).

Matthew wanted the reader to be aware that forgiveness of sins comes through the death of the divine Son of God. The angel had told Joseph that Jesus would "save his people from their sins" (1:21). Jesus Himself had assured His disciples that His destiny was "to give his life a ransom for many" (20:28). Jesus left behind a continuing reminder of His role in the forgiveness of sins when He instituted the Lord's Supper. "This is my blood of the new testament, which is shed for many for the remission of sins" (26:28).

It is impossible to know the exact date when the Gospel of Matthew was written. Some contemporary writers date it as early as A.D. 60; some, as late as A.D. 95. The place of writing was probably some place along the coast of Phoenicia or Syria such as Antioch. This is because of Matthew's several references to Gentiles, a reference to Phoenicia and Syria, and the terms (in the Greek text) used for coins (17:24,27). Although the Gospel nowhere identifies the author and many modern Bible students point to a complex history of editing and collecting sources, Matthew, the tax collector, the son of Alphaeus has been identified as the author since the second century. See *Matthew.*

Outline

I. Jesus' Birth Fulfilled Prophecy (1:1—2:23).
  A. Jesus was born of the line of David (1:1–17).
  B. God directed the circumstances of Jesus' birth (1:18–25).
  C. Even Gentile foreigners worshiped the newborn Jewish king (2:1–12).
  D. God provided for His Son's survival (2:13–23).

II. The Obedient Jesus Invites People to Kingdom Service (3:1—4:25).
  A. Jesus carried out God's will by being baptized by John the Baptist (3:1–15).
  B. God approved His Son (3:16–17).
  C. Jesus obeyed God's Word and defeated Satan (4:1–11).
  D. Jesus called people to God's kingdom through repentance (4:12–22).
  E. Jesus demonstrated the power of the kingdom (4:23–25).

III. Jesus Taught God's Way to Live (5:1—7:29).
  A. Real happiness comes from a right relationship to God (5:1–12).
  B. Christians must be like salt and light (5:13–16).
  C. Love, not legalism, is the rule of the kingdom (5:17–48).
  D. The desire to be seen by others is the wrong motive for good works (6:1–4).
  E. Prayer is private seeking of forgiveness, not public search for praise (6:5–15).
  F. Fasting is of value only if the motive behind it is right (6:16–18).
  G. Only spiritual wealth really lasts (6:19–21).
  H. Each person must choose whether to give God first place (6:22–34).
  I. To judge others is wrong; to show discernment is necessary (7:1–6).
  J. The kingdom requires persistence in prayer and faith in God's goodness (7:7–11).
  K. The Golden Rule summarizes the law and the prophets (7:12).
  L. Only the narrow path of submission to God's will leads to life in His kingdom (7:13–23).
  M. Jesus and His teachings form the only lasting foundation for life (7:24–29).

IV. Jesus' Power and Call Reveal His Authority (8:1—10:42).
  A. Jesus' healing power is available to all persons of faith (8:1–17).
  B. Discipleship is first priority (8:18–22).
  C. Jesus has authority over nature, demons,

and sin (8:23—9:8).

D. Jesus calls sinners to share His authority (9:9–13).

E. Jesus' gospel requires new forms of piety (9:14–17).

F. Jesus' authority responds to faith, conquers demons, and does not come from Satan (9:18–34).

G. The compassionate Lord prays for compassionate helpers (9:35–38).

H. Jesus entrusts His disciples with His authority in word and deed (10:1–20).

I. To exercise His authority, disciples must face the dangers Jesus faced (10:21–25).

J. Jesus' authority removes cause for fear (10:26–31).

K. Disciples confess Jesus in all situations (10:32–39).

L. Those who welcome Christian messengers will receive rewards (10:40–42).

V. Jesus' Work Led to Controversy (11:1—12:50).

A. Jesus fulfilled messianic prophecy (11:1–6).

B. John marked the end of the prophetic era (11:7–15).

C. Blind religion seeks controversy rather than truth (11:16–19).

D. Repentance is the proper response to Jesus (11:20–24).

E. Discipleship requires faith in God's Son, not great human wisdom or works (11:25–30).

F. Mercy, not legalism, is the key to interpreting God's Word (12:1–14).

G. Jesus fulfilled Isaiah's servant prophecies (12:15–21).

H. Faith sees Jesus as Messiah, but blindness calls Him satanic (12:22–37).

I. Resurrection faith is the criterion for eternal judgment (12:38–45).

J. Obedient believers form God's family (12:46–50).

VI. Jesus Taught About the Kingdom (13:1–52).

A. Response to the kingdom depends on the "soil" (13:1–23).

B. God delays separating the true from the false (13:24–30).

C. God's kingdom, small at first, will finally transform the world (13:31–33).

D. Jesus' use of parables fulfills Scripture (13:34–35).

E. The Son of Man controls final judgment and will send those who reject Him to eternal punishment (13:36–43).

F. The kingdom is worth any sacrifice (13:44–46).

G. The kingdom involves both traditional and new understandings of Scripture (13:47–52).

VII. Jesus Confronts Conflict and Critical Events

(13:53—17:27).

A. Jesus faced rejection and sorrow (13:53—14:12).

B. Jesus placed compassion for others over personal needs (14:13–21).

C. Jesus' power over nature and disease shows He is God's Son (14:22–36).

D. Thoughts and motives, not ritual acts, determine spiritual purity (15:1–20).

E. Faith overcomes all obstacles that would separate us from Jesus (15:21–28).

F. Jesus' compassionate ministry leads people to raise God (15:29–39).

G. Unbelieving authorities demand a sign but cannot interpret ones they have (16:1–12).

H. Confession of Jesus as Messiah and Son of God is the church's foundation (16:13–20).

I. Willingness to suffer with Jesus is as important as proper confessions of faith (16:21–28).

J. God revealed Jesus as His Son, whom people should obey (17:1–13).

K. Faith in God overcomes obstacles (17:14–21).

L. Jesus expected His coming death and resurrection (17:22–23).

M. Concern for others may mean forfeiting one's own rights (17:24–27).

VIII. Jesus Gives Insight into Life in His Kingdom (18:1—20:34).

A. Entrance into the kingdom requires a childlike trust in God (18:1–5).

B. Christians must be careful not to lead others into sin (18:6–7).

C. Radical self-discipline prevents sin (18:8–9).

D. God takes the initiative in finding the lost (18:10–14).

E. Reconciliation must be the Christian's aim (18:15–17).

F. Jesus promises power and authority to His church (18:18–20).

G. God requires that we forgive if He is to forgive us (18:21–35).

H. Lifelong marriage is God's plan for most people, but some can accept single devotion to Him (19:1–12).

I. Children have an important place in God's kingdom (19:13–15).

J. One must give up any obstacle to discipleship, knowing reward will come (19:16–30).

K. God's rewards may be different from human expectations (20:1–16).

L. Jesus taught the necessity of His coming death and resurrection (20:17–19).

M. The truly great person serves others as Jesus did (20:20–28).

N. Those who are healed by His mercy

become His followers (20:29–34).

IX. Religious Authorities Reject Jesus as Messiah (21:1—23:36).

  A. Jesus fulfilled messianic prophecy by entering Jerusalem and cleansing the Temple (21:1–17).

  B. God punishes fruitlessness but rewards faith (21:18–22).

  C. Answerless authorities question Jesus' authority (21:23–27).

  D. Authorities must answer the call to repentance to be part of God's kingdom (21:28–46).

  E. God invites even sinners and outcasts to new life in His kingdom (22:1–4).

  F. Taxes belong to the state; we belong to God (22:15–22).

  G. Authorities do not understand Scripture and so do not believe in resurrection (22:23–33).

  H. Authorities must learn love for God and love for neighbor are the greatest commandments (22:34–40).

  I. Authorities must learn the nature of God's Messiah (22:41–46).

  J. Jesus the Authority calls for religious leaders' lives to agree with their teachings (23:1–36).

X. Jesus Has the Authoritative Word About the Future (23:37—25:46).

  A. Jerusalem faces destruction for rejecting Jesus (23:37–39).

  B. The world will hear the gospel before the end of the age (24:1–14).

  C. Jesus' disciples must flee Jerusalem when a sign appears (24:15–28).

  D. Spectacles in nature will mark Jesus' assured return (24:29–35).

  E. People must prepare for Jesus' return or face judgment (24:36—25:30).

  F. Jesus will judge us by our service to those in need (25:31–46).

XI. Jesus Prepared for Death, Obeying God and Fulfilling Scripture (26:1–56).

  A. Authorities plotted Jesus' death, as He had foretold (26:1–5).

  B. Jesus' anointing symbolized His messiahship and coming death (26:6–13).

  C. A disciple cooperated in crucifying Jesus (26:14–16).

  D. Jesus transformed Passover to His memorial supper, establishing His covenant (26:17–30).

  E. Jesus prepared His disciples for their time of falling and restoration (26:31–35).

  F. Jesus dedicated Himself to the Father's will (26:36–46).

  G. Jesus' arrest represented fulfillment of God's plan, not evidence of His weakness or God's forsaking Jesus (26:47–56).

XII. Jesus Conquered Death (26:57—28:20).

  A. The innocent Jesus was convicted on His testimony to His messiahship and to His role as Judge in the last days (26:57–68).

  B. Peter's denial showed Jesus' prophetic powers (26:69–75).

  C. Judas' guilt drove him to suicide and fulfilled Scripture (27:1–10).

  D. Government authority found no guilt in Jesus, but religious authorities accepted full responsibility for His death (27:11–26).

  E. Roman mocking pointed to the truth of Jesus' divine kingship (27:27–44).

  F. Spectacular events pointed to the saving significance of Jesus' death as God's Son (27:45–56).

  G. Jesus' dead body was entombed and could not be stolen (27:57–66).

  H. Jesus was raised from the dead (28:1–10).

  I. Religious leaders bribed people to disprove the resurrection (28:11–15).

  J. The authoritative Jesus gives His disciples a worldwide evangelistic mission (28:16–20). *Oscar Brooks*

MATTHIAS (Măt thī′ ás) Shortened form of Mattathias ("gift of Yah.") Disciple who followed Jesus from the time of John's ministry of baptism until Jesus' ascension, who was chosen by lot and prayer to succeed Judas as an apostle and official witness to the resurrection (Acts 1:20–26). This selection was regarded as necessary to fulfill Scripture concerning the band of apostles (Ps. 69:25; Acts 1:20). Scripture mentions nothing further about Matthias. See *Disciples; Acts.*

MATTITHIAH (Măt tī thī′ ah) Personal name meaning, "gift of Yah." *1.* Levite whom David appointed a Tabernacle musician with special responsibility for leading lyre music (1 Chron. 15:18,21; 25:3,21). Mattithiah also ministered before the ark (1 Chron. 16:5). *2.* Levite baker (1 Chron. 9:31). *3.* Layman with a foreign wife (Ezra 10:43). *4.* Man standing beside Ezra at the public reading of the law (Neh. 8:4).

MATTOCK See *Tools, Agricultural Tools.*

MAUL KJV term for a club (NAS, NIV, REB) or warclub (RSV) at Proverbs 25:18. See *Arms and Armor.*

MAUNDY THURSDAY *See Holy Week; Church Year.*

MAW KJV term for the fourth stomach of a cud-chewing animal. The maw was among the choice cuts of meat reserved for the priests' portion

(Deut. 18:3). Modern translations use stomach (NAS, REB, NRSV) or innerparts (NIV).

MAZZAROTH (Măz′ zȧ rŏth) Puzzling term in Job 38:22. Either a proper name for a particular constellation (so KJV, NRSV), a collective term for the twelve signs of the Zodiac (KJV margin, REB), or a general term meaning constellation or stars (NAS, NIV, TEV; compare 2 Kings 23:5).

MEADOW Tract of grassland, especially moist, low-lying pasture. The KJV used meadow at two passages. At Genesis 41:2,18, the reference is clearly to stretches of reed grass or papyrus thickets common along the Nile. The term rendered meadow in the phrase "meadows of Geba" (Judg. 20:33, KJV) is obscure. The NAS simply transliterates the phrase (Maareh-geba). In modern translations rich meadows illustrate God's blessing (Ps. 65:13, NAS, NIV, NRSV; Isa. 30:23; 44:4, NIV). Meadows are also used in pictures of God's judgment (Jer. 25:37; Hos. 4:16, NIV; Hos. 9:13, NAS; Zeph. 2:6, NRSV).

MEAH, TOWER OF (Mē′ ah) KJV transliteration of a Hebrew phrase meaning "Tower of the Hundred" (Neh. 3:1; 12:39). See *Hundred, Tower of the.*

MEAL OFFERING See *Sacrifice and Offering, Grain Offering.*

MEALS See *Banquet; Food.*

Dining area in villa in Pompeii with spaces for several persons to be seated while eating their meal.

MEARAH (Mė ā′ rah) Place name meaning, "cave." Part of the territory left unconquered following Joshua's conquest. The site is perhaps the caves called Mughar Jezzin located east of Sidon (Josh. 13:4).

MEASURING LINE A cord used to measure length (compare 1 Kings 7:15,23; 2 Chron. 4:3). References to a measuring line point to the restoration of Jerusalem (Jer. 31:39; Zech. 2:1; compare Ezek. 47:3).

MEASURING REED Ezekiel's measuring reed was a cane about 10 feet long used as a measuring tool (Ezek. 40:3,5,6,7,8; compare Rev. 21:15–16). See *Weights and Measures.*

MEAT In modern English, meat refers to animal tissue used as food, frequently in contrast to plant products. Modern translations use meat in this sense, where KJV used the term "flesh" (for example, Num. 11:4–33; Judg. 6:19–21; 1 Sam. 2:13,15). KJV used meat in two senses: (1) for food, especially solid food in contrast to drink (for example, 1 Cor. 3:2; Heb. 5:12,14); and (2) for a meal, especially the evening meal (for example, 1 Sam. 20:5; Matt. 26:7). The KJV used meat in the general sense of food about 250 times. The context frequently indicates that flesh is not in view (Gen. 1:29,30; Ezek. 47:12; Hab. 3:17). A special case of the use of meat to mean food is the frequent use of the term "meat offering" (about 130 times in the Old Testament). Here "meat offering" means food offering in contrast to a libation (drink offering). Modern translations render the expression as cereal or grain offering. Modern translations, for example NRSV, frequently replace the KJV's meat with a more specific term in light of the context: provisions (Gen. 45:23); scraps [of food] (Judg. 1:7); present (2 Sam. 11:8); meager fare (2 Sam. 12:3); solid food (1 Cor. 3:2; Heb. 5:12). KJV also used meat in the sense of a meal. Modern translations generally replace the KJV's "sit at meat" with "sit at table" which means to take a meal (1 Sam. 20:5; Matt. 9:10; 26:7; Mark 2:15). "To come to meat" (1 Sam. 20:27) is to come to supper. A "morsel of meat" (Heb. 12:16) is "a single meal" (NRSV).

MEAT OFFERING KJV term used about 130 times in the Old Testament for a food offering in contrast to a drink offering (libation). Modern translations render the term *grain* offering. See *Sacrifice and Offering.*

MEAT TO IDOLS Offerings of animal flesh sacrificed to a god. Most religions of the Ancient Near East had laws regarding offering sacrifices to the god(s). Israel's laws are in Leviticus 1–8,16–17. Part of the ritual was for the people to eat some of the sacrifice. They believed that God and the people became closer by partaking of the same animal. Since most early Christians had Jewish backgrounds, a problem arose in the church when Gentile converts ate meat that had been offered to idols. The Jerusalem council decided that Christians should abstain from eating meat offered to idols so as not to cause weak believers to stumble. Paul echoed this sentiment in 1 Corinthians 8:13.

MEAT, UNCLEAN See *Clean, Cleanness.*

MEBUNNAI (Mė bŭn′ naî) Personal name meaning, "building of Yah." One of David's thirty elite warriors (2 Sam. 23:27). The name possibly resulted from scribal confusion of the first and third letters in the Hebrew name Sibbecai which replaces Mebunnai in the parallel lists (1 Chron. 11:29; 27:11).

MECHERATHITE (Mė̇ chē' ra̅ thīte) The title of Hepher, one of David's warriors (1 Chron. 11:36). Mecherathite means inhabitant of Mecherah. The site is unknown unless it is to be identified with Maacah (2 Sam. 23:34).

MECONAH (Mė̇ cō' nah) Form of Mekonah preferred by modern translations.

MEDAD (Mē' dăd) Personal name meaning, "beloved." Israelite layman who prophesied in the wilderness camp (Num. 11:26–27). See *Eldad.*

MEDAN (Mē' dăn) Personal name meaning "judgment." Third son of Abraham and Keturah (Gen. 25:2; 1 Chron. 1:32) and ancestor of a little-known Arab tribe. The Medan should perhaps be identified with the Badan, a people conquered by Tiglath-pileser III of Assyria (732 B.C.). Others argue for textual corruption of the term Media.

MEDEBA (Mě' dĕ bà) Place name meaning "water of quiet." City in Transjordan on the main north-south road (the King's Highway) about 25 miles south of Amman. The strategic importance of Medeba is indicated by frequent references to its changing hands. Sihon King of the Amorites took Medeba from Moab only to have the area pass into Israel's control (Num. 21:24,26,30). Medeba was included in Reuben's tribal allotment (Josh. 13:9,16). According to the Moabite stone, Omri King of Israel (885–874 B.C.) recaptured Medeba. Mesha King of Moab retook the city during the reign of Omri's son. An alliance of Israel, Judah, and Edom recaptured the city but quickly withdrew (2 Kings 3:25,27). Jeroboam II again secured control of the city of Israel (2 Kings 14:25). Isaiah 15:2 reflects the city's return to Moab. The site of Medeba is that of the modern city of Madeba.

MEDES, MEDIA (Mēdes, Mē' dĭ à) The region south and southwest of the Caspian Sea in the Zagros Mountains inhabited by the Medes, an Aryan people from north and west of the Caspian Sea. It is north of Elam and west of Assyria. The traditional capital of the region was Ecbatana.

Before 1500 B.C. the region was part of the Mitanni kingdom. Later the Elamites controlled the region and its nomadic inhabitants. The people known as the Medes entered the area over a long period between 1400 and 1000 B.C.

The Medes were first reported in history by the Assyrian Shalmaneser III about 850 B.C. They were a group of nomadic tribes rather than a state or kingdom. The Assyrians controlled them or sought to for more than 200 years, though the Medes enjoyed some periods of freedom before the Scythians conquered them in 653 B.C.. Sometime before this, Deioces were united and organized the Medes. Despite the the Scythians' invasion, the Medes continued to develop as a kingdom.

The greatest Median king was Cyaxares (625–585 B.C.). He was the third ruler of the united Medes and was able to defeat the Scythians. Afterwards, Cyaxares turned his attention to the Assyrians, attacking Nineveh, the Assyrian capital. Before Nineveh fell in 612 B.C., Cyaxares conquered Asshur, the ancient center of the Assyrian Empire. Then, with the aid of the Scythians and Babylonians and others, Nineveh was taken. The end of the Assyrian Empire was near.

Babylon and Media divided the Assyrian Empire with Media taking the land east and north of the Tigris River. Nebuchadnezzar II and Cyaxares' grandaughter wed to seal the pact. The Medes turned their attention to the north and toward Asia Minor. After a five-year war with Lydia, Cyaxares concluded a peace in 584 B.C., again sealing it with a marriage. His son Astyages married the daughter of the Lydian king. Astyages became king of the Medes when Cyaxares died.

The end of the Median kingdom came with the rise of Cyrus II, founder of the Persian Empire. Cyrus was king of Anshan and a vassal to Astyages. Indeed, Cyrus' mother was Astyages' daughter. About 550 B.C., encouraged by Babylon, Cyrus rebelled against the Medes. His rebellion led to the defeat of Astyages. The kingdom of the Medes was replaced by the kingdom of the Persians. See *Persia; Cyrus.*

Though conquered by the Persians, the Medes continued to hold a place of honor in the Persian Empire. Media was the second-most important portion of the Empire after Persia itself. Biblical references frequently combine "the Medes and the Persians" (Dan. 5:28; compare Esth. 1:19; 10:2). The kings of the Persian Empire are called "the kings of Media and Persia" (Dan. 8:20). The most famous Mede in Scripture is Darius the Mede (Dan. 5:31; 9:1). See *Darius.* Media is sometimes referred to as the instrument of God, especially against Babylon (Isa. 13:17; 21:2; Jer. 51:11,28); but the Medes also had to drink the cup of God's judgment (Jer. 25:25). Their final appearance in Scripture is the presence of Jews or Jewish converts from there at Pentecost (Acts 2:9).

See Babylonia; Elam; Assyria.   *Albert F. Bean*

MEDIATOR A person midway between two parties who establishes an agreement or relationship between the parties and may act as a guarantor of that relationship.

Old Testament Only once is a specific word used for mediator in the Old Testament. Bewilderment in the midst of extreme suffering forced from Job a plea for an arbiter, one to whom he could relate, to stand between him and God in judgment (Job 9:33). The concept of someone standing between opposing persons as spokesman or reconciler is a central one in the Old Testament. In human relationships, a champion could come between armies and represent his people (1 Sam. 17:4–10), and an interpreter or spokesman helped negotiate agreements. In divine-human relations, a leader such as Abraham could negotiate with God for the sparing of a city (Gen. 18:22–32), and a father such as Job could intercede with sacrifices for his family (Job 1:5).

More often, kings, priests, and prophets took this middle position. The king embodied the people and, at times, represented God to them (Ps. 93:1). Priests were consecrated to offer sacrifices of reconciliation, with the most awesome transaction dependent upon the high priest who entered yearly into the holy of holies to make atonement for the sins of his people (Lev. 16:29–34). Israel itself was to be a kingdom of priests to channel the blessings of God to all people. Constantly, the prophets had to recall the nation to its vows of obedience and deliver God's words of judgment and hope. The Servant Songs of Isaiah told of one—whose sacrifice of Himself would bring pardon to many (Isa. 53).

One of the greatest examples of mediators is Moses. He stood between the people and God, receiving the Commandments on which the covenant was based and beseeching God's mercy when the Commandments and covenant were broken (Ex. 20:18–21; Deut. 9:25–26). Also, the wisdom, word, and Spirit of God were almost personified and used along with angels (messengers) as mediating agents (Prov. 8:22–31; Ps. 104:4).

New Testament The Greek word used for mediator in the New Testament bore several ideas. Primarily, it meant an umpire or peacemaker who came between two contestants, a negotiator who established a certain relationship, or some neutral person who could guarantee an agreement reached.

The term is used of Moses in a negative sense (Gal. 3:19–28). There Paul stressed the preeminence of the promise given directly to Abraham by grace over the law which was instituted through the mediator, Moses, when the people feared meeting God face-to-face (compare Ex. 20:18–21). In 1 Timothy 2:5, the term is used in a positive sense to designate Christ, the only necessary Mediator. This passage emphasizes not only that the legalities of the law or the ministrations of a priest are no longer necessary, but also that individuals cannot come into full communion with God by their moral or rational efforts alone.

Full communion comes through faith in the Mediator who gave Himself a ransom for others.

The only other uses of the term occur in Hebrews where Jesus is presented as the Son of God who transcends all previous agents of the divine will and who mediates a new covenant (Heb. 8:6; 9:15; 12:24). In each instance, the mediation of a new covenant is bound up with Christ's sacrificial death.

Thus, all of the mediating activities of intercession, sacrificial atonement, and covenant making and guaranteeing culminate in the New Testament with Christ. He is the great Intecessor, praying for His disciples while on earth and continuing to do so in heaven (John 17; Rom. 8:34). He is the supreme High Priest who enters once for all into the sanctuary to make a sacrifice of Himself that brings eternal redemption (Heb. 9:11–12). He is the Mediator of a better covenant which replaces the old one (Heb. 8:6; 9:15). By remaining forever, He guarantees that the covenant He establishes will forever endure since His priesthood never ends (Heb. 7:22–25). As true God and true Man, Christ stands between and with both God and humankind and is the answer to Job's plea.

Barbara J. Bruce

MEDICINE See *Diseases.*

MEDITATION The act of calling to mind some supposition, pondering upon it, and correlating it to one's own life. A wicked individual meditates upon violence (Prov. 24: 2). The meditation of a righteous person contemplates God or His great spiritual truths (Pss. 63:6; 77:12; 119:15, 23,27,48,78,97,148; 143:5). He hopes to please God by meditation (Ps. 19:14). Thus meditation by God's people is a reverent act of worship. Through it they commune with God and are thereby renewed spiritually.

Most references to meditation occur in the Old Testament, especially in the Psalms. The Hebrew words for meditation primarily were derived from two separate roots. The first (*hagah*) literally means "to utter in a low sound." The word is used to denote the growling of a lion (Isa. 31:4) or the cooing of a dove (Isa. 38:14). Therefore it has been suggested that, in ancient Hebrew meditation, Scripture frequently was recited in a low murmur. The second root word (sia*ch*) has the basic meaning of "to be occupied with," or "concerned about." Thus meditation is the repetitious going over of a matter in one's mind because it is the chief concern of life. The constant recollection of God's past deeds by the hearing of Scripture and repetition of thought produce confidence in God (Pss. 104:34; 119:15,23,48,78,97,99,148; Ps. 63:6–8; 143:5).

Meditation is only mentioned twice in the New Testament. Jesus instructed Christians to meditate beforehand on their attitude toward persecution

(Luke 21:14). Paul advised Timothy to meditate on the matters about which Paul had written Him (1 Tim. 4:15). Meditation is an important part of the Christian's relationship with Christ.

See *Prayer.*   *LeBron Matthews*

MEDITERRANEAN SEA, THE (Mĕd ĭ tēr rā′ nė an) Designated in the OT and the NT simply as "the sea" (Josh. 16:8; Acts 10:6); also referred to as the "Western Sea" (Deut. 11:24, RSV, NIV); and as the "Sea of the Philistines" (Ex. 23:31). The Mediterranean Sea is an inland ocean extending about 2,200 miles from Gibraltar to the Lebanon coast and varies in width from one hundred to six hundred miles. Most of the important nations of ancient times were either on the Mediterranean's shores or operated in its 2,200 miles of water: Israel, Syria, Greece, Rome, Egypt, Philistia, and Phoenicia. Strangely, nature has provided few natural habors for Israel (Dor, Joppa, and Acco). The shoreline is almost straight. In many places a high ridge rises up sharply from behind a narrow strip of beach.

The Hebrews were not a seafaring people. A more apt description might be that they were a sea-fearing people. The Hebrews' fear of the sea was paritally due to their desert origin; therefore, their culture developed chiefly around agriculture. The story of Jonah demonstrates the Hebrew's fear of the sea.

God exercises leadership over all creation. As part of God's creation, the sea is subservient to him. He rules over the raging sea (Ps. 89:9) and causes a storm on it (Jonah 1:4).

For the Hebrews, the Great Sea served as the western border for the land of Canaan (Num. 34:6) and the territory of Judah (Josh. 15:12). Only with the aid of the Phoenicians was Solomon able to assemble and operate a fleet of ships at Ezion Geber on the Red Sea. Timber was brought on rafts from Lebanon to Joppa (2 Chron. 2:16). Jehoshaphat's attempt at a navy ended in disaster (1 Kings 22:47–50). His ships were wrecked in the same harbor. Maritime commerce remained limited during most periods in Israel's history. Phoenicians were famous in the ancient world for their capacity as sailors and pilots.

Tyre eventually became the principal sea power in the Mediterranean. The extensive use of the Mediterranean by the Phoenicians was continued by the Romans, who called it "Our Sea." Following the conquest of Palestine by Pompey in 63 B.C., traffic on the Mediterranean increased. This development helped to make possible the missionary activity of Paul, Silas, Barnabas, and others. Paul made three missionary journeys across the Mediterranean. Under Roman arrest, Paul made his final voyage across the Mediterranean Sea and shipwrecked (Acts 27). Paul's work involved such Mediterranean cities as Caesarea, Antioch, Troas, Corinth, Tyre, Sidon, Syracuse, Rome, and Ephesus. See *Phoenicia; Tyre; Transportation and Travel.*   *Philip Lee*

Sunset over the Mediterranean Sea.

MEDIUM One possessed by (Lev. 20:22) or consulting (Deut. 18:11) a ghost or spirit of the dead, especially for information about the future. Acting as a medium was punishable by stoning (Lev. 20:27); consulting a medium, by exclusion from the congregation of Israel (Lev. 20:6). The transformation of Saul from one who expelled mediums (1 Sam. 28:3) to one who consulted a medium at En-dor (28:8–19) graphically illustrates his fall.

The Hebrew word translated medium (*ob*) may refer to the spirit of a dead person, to the medium possessed by the spirit, or to images used to conjure up spirits. Manasseh made such images (2 Kings 21:6; 2 Chron. 33:6). Josiah destroyed them as part of his reforms (2 Kings 23:24). Saul's success in quickly locating a medium (1 Sam. 28:8) points both to the popularity of the practice of consulting the dead and the difficulty of eradicating it.

Isaiah 8:19 suggests a possible connection between the consulting of mediums and ancestor worship. Those to be consulted are termed "fathers" and "gods." (Compare 1 Sam. 28:13 where Samuel is described as *elohim* or "god.") The chirping and muttering of the spirits perhaps refers to the inarticulate sounds which must be interpreted by the medium. Consulting of mediums defiled the land and was described as prostitution. God's people were to trust God in times of distress and not resort to other "gods" in an attempt to learn the future.

MEEKNESS A personality trait of gentleness and humility, the opposite of which is pride. Meekness does not refer to weakness or passivity but to controlled power. Aristotle described meekness as the middle position between excessive anger and an excessive lack of anger.

Meekness or gentleness is exemplified by God (2 Sam. 22:36, Ps. 18:35), Moses (Num. 12:1–13), and Jesus (Zech. 9:9, Matt. 11:29, 12:14–21; 21:5). In the Old Testament the meek were often the poor and the oppressed (Amos 2:7; 8:4; Job 24:4; Ps. 9:18; Pr. 3:34; 16:19). The Hebrew word translated meek (*anaw*) means, "wretched, impoverished, oppressed, in need, bowed over," but came to mean, "humble, pious."

The meek receive the special concern of God and are called blessed (Ps. 37:11; Matt. 5:5). God identifies with the poor and oppressed, hears their pleas, and helps them (Pss. 10:17; 22:26; 25:9; 147:6; 149:4). The Messiah will also have a special ministry to the meek (Isa. 11:4; 61:1; Luke 4:18).

Christians are encouraged to be meek (Eph. 4:1–2; Col. 3:12). Meekness is a fruit of the Spirit (Gal. 5:23) and should mark the Christian's attitude toward sinners (Gal. 6:1). Paul was meek with the Corinthians (1 Cor. 4:21). Pastors should be meek and teach meekness (1 Tim. 6:11; 2 Tim. 2:25; Titus 3:2). Christians should receive God's Word with meekness (Jas. 1:21). Wisdom is expressed with meekness (Jas. 3:13). Christian wives can witness to their unbelieving husbands with their meek spirit (1 Pet. 3:1–4). All Christians should be prepared to give a defense of their faith in meekness (1 Pet. 3:15).

See *Humility; Patience; Pride; Poor; Spiritual Gifts.*   *Warren McWilliams*

MEGIDDO (Mě gĭd′ dō) Place name perhaps meaning, "place of troops." One of the most strategic cities of Canaan since it guarded the main pass through the Carmel mountain range. This range was an obstacle along the international coastal highway which connected Egypt with Mesopotamia and even further destinations. Identified with current tell el-Mutesellim, Megiddo had approximately twenty-five different eras of occupation during its life from the fourth millenium to the time of the Persian Empire. The city was very active while under Egyptian authority from the time of the patriarchs through to the judges (2000–1100 B.C.), but this golden age came to an end about 1125 B.C. when it was destroyed.

The city was allotted to Manasseh (Josh. 17:11; 1 Chron. 17:29) after the partial conquest of Joshua (Josh. 12:21), but neither it nor its surrounding villages were secured by the tribe. Due to its obvious strength, it was among many cities whose overthrow was delayed until later (Judg. 1:27). Deborah and Barak fought the Canaanites and their leaders King Jabin and Sisera near the "waters of Megiddo," possibly the wadi Qina running through the surrounding hills (Judg. 5:19).

When Megiddo was finally annexed to the nation Israel is not known. Probably by the time of David the city was serving Israel's defensive and

Manger and "hitching post" stones likely from a ninth century B.C. storage area at Megiddo.

Model of ancient Megiddo.

A Solomonic gateway area at ancient Megiddo.

security purposes. Certainly by the time of Solomon the city was firmly Israelite, since he fortified the city (1 Kings 9:15), including his mighty six chambered gate which followed the pattern of his other two key fortress cities of Hazor and Gezer.

Megiddo was under the jurisdiction of Solomon's deputy, Baana (1 Kings 4:12). Buildings of current controversy have been excavated and explained variously as Solomon's or Ahab's stables, or storehouses where animals were loaded and unloaded.

During the divided monarchy, Megiddo's authority changed from Egyptian to Israelite to Assyrian. Five years into Jeroboam I's reign, (about 920 B.C.), Pharaoh Shishak burst into both Israel and

A view from Megiddo of the Valley of Jezreel with the town of Nazareth in the distance.

Judah, taking control of the coastal highway including Megiddo. However, the Egyptian grip was not long lasting. Later, the city was the place of death for the Judean king, Ahaziah, who was killed at the command of Jehu while fleeing from the scene of Jehoram's assassination (843 B.C., 2 Kings 9:27). Over a century later, the conquering Tiglath-pileser III chose Megiddo to be the seat of the *Magidu* administrative district in the Assyrian Empire (733 B.C.).

After about 650 B.C. the city was no longer strongly fortified; however, it was still strategically important. Josiah attempted to head off Pharoah Neco II as he advanced along the coastal plain on his way to Carchemish (609 B.C.), but Josiah's attack ended when Neco II's archers fatally wounded him (2 Kings 23:29–30; 2 Chron. 35:22–24).

After returning from Exile, Zechariah prophesied that the mourning for the false deities of Hadad and Rimmon (Hadad-rimmon) that took place in the plain below *Megiddon* (Megiddo) would be matched by Israel's mourning for its smitten Lord (Zech. 12:11).

Finally, in the New Testament, the Mount of Megiddo (har-Megiddon thus "Armageddon") will be where the kings of the world are gathered for that final battle in the last day of the Lord. Where Israel was initially frustrated during their conquest of Canaan is exactly where they will be victorious with Christ in the end (Rev.16:16).

Daniel C. Fredericks

MEGIDDON, VALLEY OF (Mė gĭd´ dŏn) KJV term for plain of Megiddo, the broad portion of the Jezreel Valley in the vicinity of Megiddo (Zech. 12:11). The passage perhaps alludes to the death of Josiah on this plain (2 Chron. 35:22). See *Megiddo.*

MEHETABEEL (Mė hě´ tå bē ēl) Personal name meaning "God does good." Ancestor of Shemiah, a contemporary of Nehemiah (Neh. 6:10). Modern translations use the form Mehetabel.

MEHETABEL (Mė hě´ tå běl) Personal name meaning "God does good." Wife of King Hadar of Edom (Gen. 36:39; 1 Chron. 1:50). Modern translations follow the Hebrew and also use Mehetabel for the KJV's Mehetabeel (Neh. 6:10).

MEHIDA (Mė hī´ då) Personal name meaning, "bought." Family of Temple servants (KJV, Nethinim) at Ezra 2:52; Nehemiah 7:54.

MEHIR (Mē´ hīr) Personal name meaning, "purchased." Descendant of Judah (1 Chron. 4:11).

MEHOLAH (Mė hō´ lah) TEV reading for Meholathite.

MEHOLATHITE (Mė hō lå thīte) Title meaning inhabitant of Abel-Meholah, given to Adriel, Saul's son-in-law (1 Sam. 18:19; 2 Sam. 21:8). Abel-Meholah is located in Gilead about 14 miles southeast of Beth-Shean.

MEHUJAEL (Mė hū jā´ ěl) Personal name meaning, "struck by God" or "priest of God." Son of Irad (Gen. 4:18). Some interpreters see the name as a variant form of Mahalalel (Gen. 5:12–17).

MEHUMAN (Mė hū´ măn) Personal name meaning "trusty." Eunuch serving the Persian king Ahasuerus (Esth. 1:10).

MEHUNIM (Mė hū´ nĭm) KJV form of Meunim or Meunites, an Arab tribe whose name likely derives from the city of Ma'an about twelve miles southeast of Petra. The Meunites raided Judah during the reign of Jehoshaphat (873–849 B.C.) according to 2 Chronicles 20:1 (NAS, NIV, REB, NRSV following the Greek translation; the Hebrew text reads Ammonites). Uzziah (783–742) subdued the Mehunites (2 Chron. 26:7). During the reign of Hezekiah (727–698 B.C.), Israelites dislocated the Meunites from the vicinity of Gedor in Transjordan about eighteen miles north-northwest of Heshbon (1 Chron. 4:41; KJV reads "habitations"). The Meunites are listed as Temple servants in the postexilic period (Ezra 2:50; Neh. 7:52). They were perhaps the descendants of prisoners of war.

MEJARKON (Mē jär´ kon) Name meaning, "waters of Jarkon" or "pale-green waters." Stream in the territory of Dan (Josh. 19:46), probably the Nahr el-'Auja ("winding river"), which, fed by springs at Ras el-'Ain about ten miles from the coast, flows year-round to the Mediterranean about four miles north of Joppa.

MEKERATHITE (Mė kē´ rå thīte) NIV spelling of Mecherathite.

MEKONAH (Mė kō´ nah) Place name meaning, "standing." KJV form of Meconah, town in southern Judah between Ziklag and Ain-rimmon (Neh. 11:28). The site is perhaps identical with Madmannah or Machbena (1 Chron. 2:49).

MELATIAH (Mė lå tī´ ah) Personal name meaning, "Yah has set free." Man assisting Nehemiah in building the wall (Neh. 3:7).

MELCHI (Měl´ chī) Personal name meaning, "my king." Two ancestors of Christ (Luke 3:24,28).

MELCHIAH (Měl chī´ ah) KJV alternate form of Malchijah (Jer. 21:1).

MELCHISEDEC (Měl chī´ sě děc) KJV New Testament form of Melchizedek.

MELCHISHUA (Měl chī shū´ å) KJV alternate spelling of Malchishua (1 Sam. 14:49; 31:2).

MELCHIZEDEK (Měl chĭz ě děk) Personal name meaning "Zedek is my king" or "My king is righteousness." Priest and king of Salem, a city identified with Jerusalem.

Old Testament When Abraham returned from

the Valley of Siddim where he defeated Chedorlaomer, king of Elam, and the kings aligned with Chedorlaomer, Melchizedek greeted Abraham with bread and wine. He blessed Abraham in the name of "God Most High." In return, Abraham gave Melchizedek a tenth of everything.

Melchizedek and Abraham both worshiped the one true God. Abraham also appeared to recognize the role of Melchizedek as a priest. Psalm 110:4 refers to one who would be forever a priest in the "order of Melchizedek." This messianic psalm teaches that the leader or ruler of the Hebrew nation would be able to reflect in his person the role of priest as well as the role of king.

New Testament The writer of Hebrews made several references in chapters 5—7 to Jesus' priesthood being of the "order of Melchizedek" as opposed to Levitical in nature. The author of Hebrews cited Psalm 110:4. For the writer of Hebrews, only Jesus whose life could not be destroyed by death fit the psalmist's description of a priest of the "order of Melchizedek."

Judith Wooldridge

MELEA (Mē lē′ à) Ancestor of Jesus (Luke 3:31).

MELECH (Mē lĕ<u>ch</u>) Personal name meaning, "king." Descendant of King Saul (1 Chron. 8:35; 9:41).

MELICU (Mĕ′ lĭ cū) KJV form of Malluchi (Neh. 12:14).

MELITA (Mĕ lī′ tà) KJV form of Malta (Acts 28:1). See *Islands.*

MELONS See *Plants in the Bible.*

MELZAR (Mĕl′ zär) KJV transliteration of what is likely an Assyrian loanword meaning "guard" (NIV), "overseer" (NAS), or "steward" (RSV) at Daniel 1:11,16. The KJV follows some early versions (Theodotian, Lucian, the Syriac, the Vulgate) in taking Melzar as a proper name. Modern translators point to the use of the article as evidence of a title.

MEM (Mĕm) Thirteenth letter of the Hebrew alphabet which serves as the heading for Psalm 119:97–104. Each of these verses begins with this letter.

MEMBERS *1.* Body parts. *2.* Individuals composing a group. Jesus warned of body parts which cause one to sin (Matt. 5:29). As a Christian, Paul struggled with the reality of body parts which continue to give in to sin (Rom. 6:13). The bodily members are the sphere where the law of sin (Rom. 7:23) and passions (Jas. 4:1) are at work. The image of various body parts cooperating in the life of one organism frequently serves to illus-

trate the unity of the church which is composed of different individuals exercising various, necessary functions (Rom. 12:4–5; 1 Cor. 12:12,27; compare Eph. 4:25; 5:30). See *Body; Body of Christ; Church.*

MEMORIAL Something which serves as a reminder. Scripture witnesses to God's participation in human history for the salvation of God's people. Memorials to such events reinforced faith and provided opportunities for teaching. God's covenant name (Yahweh) was to be a "memorial name" (Ex. 3:15 NAS), a reminder of God's liberation of God's people. The Passover served as a similar reminder (Ex. 12:14; 13:9). The twelve stones taken from the Jordan's bed served as a reminder of God's provision of passage across the Jordan (Josh. 4:7). In the New Testament, the Lord's Supper serves as a reminder of Christ's sacrificial death and an encouragement of His future coming (Matt. 26:13; Mark 14:9; 1 Cor. 11:25–26). All these memorials serve to "proclaim" the good news of what God has done.

MEMPHIS (Mĕm′ phĭs) Place name meaning, "the abode of the good one." An ancient capital of Egypt located just south of modern Cairo on the west bank of the Nile River. It was founded by Menes, a pharaoh of the First Dynasty (about 2800 B.C.) and became the capital of Egypt as the Third Dynasty came to power (about 2686 B.C.).

One of several small sphinxes located at Memphis on the Nile River in Egypt.

For over 300 years Memphis was the principal city of Egypt. Gradually, other cities grew in importance, and Memphis was eclipsed as the seat of power. During later dynasties Thebes and Avaris-Tanis served as the capital. Memphis regained its status as capital during the Hyksos reign (1750–1570) but was replaced when the alien occupation ended.

There remains little, architecturally, to attest to the glory and grandeur once enjoyed by the city. As the Moslems began to build Cairo, they raided the buildings of Memphis for material, even dismantling the temple of Ptah, which probably was the largest and most opulent structure in the city.

MEMUCAN (Mė mū′ căn) One of the seven princes who served as advisors to King Ahasuerus of Persia (Esth. 1:14,16,21). See *Marsena.*

MEN-PLEASERS Those who serve (only) to gain approval or win favor (Eph. 6:6; Col. 3:22).

MENAHEM (Měn′ å hěm) Personal name meaning, "consoler." King of Israel 752–742 B.C. Menahem became king by assassinating Shallum, who had killed King Zechariah only a month earlier (2 Kings 15:10–14). The period following the death of Jeroboam II in 753 B.C. was filled with turmoil. Several political factions fought for control. Shallum and Menahem each led an extremist party which sought the throne. They ruled by force. After becoming king, Menahem attacked and destroyed one of Israel's cities because it resisted his rule (2 Kings 15:16). He ruled at least ten years in Samaria. A significant event recorded about his reign is that he paid tribute to Tiglath-pileser III, the king of Assyria. This is the first mention of the Assyrian monarch in the biblical record. See *Tiglath-pileser.* It is possible that Menahem obtained the throne of Israel with Tiglath-pileser's help. In any event, Menahem was little more than a puppet of the Assyrians during his reign. He was succeeded by his son, Pekahiah.

MENAN (Mē′ năn) KJV form of Menna, the name of an ancestor of Christ (Luke 3:31).

MENE, MENE, TEKEL, UPHARSIN (Mē′ nė, mē′ nė, tē′ kěl, Ū phär′ sīn) An inscription that King Belshazzar of Babylon saw a detached hand write on his palace wall as the king was hosting a drunken party (Dan. 5:1–29). After the wise men of the kingdom could not decipher the writing, Daniel was brought in to give an interpretation.

Scholars have proposed a number of translations, the best of which probably is "mina, shekel, and halves." Daniel interpreted the inscription with a wordplay using Hebrew words which sound similar to each word of the inscription, taking it to mean, "numbered, weighed, and divided."

Daniel's interpretation was that Nebuchadnezzar and his kingdom had been weighed in the balance and found wanting. The kingdom would be divided and given to his enemies, the Medes and Persians. Daniel 5:30 records that the overthrow occurred that very night. Thus God worked through Daniel to show His wisdom was greater than that of Persia's wise counselors and magicians and that only the God of Israel controlled history and human destiny.

MENI (Mē′ nȧ) Personal name meaning, "to

count" or "to apportion." God of good luck worshiped together with the god Gad by Jewish apostates, probably in the postexilic period (Isa. 65:11 NAS margin). The god is possibly identical with Manat, a diety worshiped by the Arabs before the rise of Islam. The KJV translated the god's name as "that number." Modern translations prefer the translation "Destiny."

MENNA (Měn′ nȧ) Form of Menan preferred by modern translations.

MENORAH (Mě′ nō rah) A candelabrum used in Jewish worship, specifically the branched lampstand used in the tabernacle (Ex. 25:31–35; 37:17–20; compare Zech. 4:2,11). See *Lamps, Lighting; Lampstand.*

A large sculpture of a Jewish menorah adorns the grounds surrounding the Israeli Knesset building.

MENUHOTH (Mě nū′ hŏth) Name meaning, "resting places." Family descended from Judah (1 Chron. 2:52 NRSV) or their town (TEV). Other English translations take this family as the other half of the Manahethites (KJV, REB; Manahathites, NAS, NIV) mentioned in 1 Chronicles 2:54. Menuhoth was possibly located to the northwest of Jerusalem towards Kiriath-jearim.

MEONENIM, PLAIN OF (Mė ŏn′ ė nĭm) Meonenim is the Hebrew term for diviners or soothsayers (Deut. 18:10,14; Micah 5:12). The KJV understood Meonenim as a proper name at Judges 9:37. See *Diviner's Oak*.

MEONOTHAI (Mė ŏn′ ō thaî) Personal name meaning, "habitations of the Lord." A descendant of Judah (1 Chron. 4:14).

MEPHAATH (Mĕph ā′ ăth) Place name meaning, "height." Town in Reuben's tribal allotment (Josh. 13:18), assigned to the Levites (Josh. 21:37; 1 Chron. 6:79). In Jeremiah's time the town was in Moabite hands (Jer. 48:21). The site is perhaps that of modern Jawah about six miles south of Amman.

MEPHIBOSHETH Mĕ phĭb′ ō shĕth) Personal name meaning, "shame destroyer" or "image breaker." *1.* A son of Jonathan, who was granted special position and privilege in David's court (2 Sam. 9). Jonathan was killed in battle when Mephibosheth was five years old. Fearing that the Philistines would seek the life of the young boy, a nurse fled with him, but in her haste she dropped him and crippled him in both feet (2 Sam. 4:4). Mephibosheth may be an intentional change by copyists to avoid writing the pagan god's name "baal." The original name would be Meribaal (1 Chron. 8:34). See *Meribaal.* When David invited Mephibosheth to be a part of his court, he entrusted the family property to a steward, Ziba. During the Absalom rebellion Ziba tried unsuccessfully to turn Daivd against Mephibosheth. Upon the king's return to Jerusalem, Mephibosheth vindicated himself and was allowed to remain in the king's house (2 Sam. 16; 19). *2.* A son of Saul, who with six other members of Saul's household, was delivered by Daivd to the Gibeonites to be hanged. This was in retaliation for Saul's earlier slaughter of a band of Gibeonites (2 Sam. 21:1–9). Mephibosheth's mother guarded the bodies until the time of burial.

MERAB (Mē′ răb) Personal name from the root "to become many." Eldest daughter of King Saul (1 Sam. 14:49), who was twice promised to David in exchange for killing Goliath (1 Sam. 17:25) and for fighting the Lord's battles against the Philistines (1 Sam. 18:17–19). Saul reneged on his promise and gave Merab to Adriel. Modern translators based on context and a few ancient texts often read Merab instead of the Hebrew text's Michal in 2 Samuel 21:8.

MERAIAH (Mė râî′ ah) Personal name meaning, "Yah has promised" or "stubborn." Head of a priestly family in the time of the high priest Joiakim (Neh. 12:12).

MERAIOTH (Mė rā′ iŏth) Personal name meaning, "obstinate" or "rebellious." *1.* Ancestor of the Zadokite high priests (1 Chron. 6:6–7,52). *2.*

Ancestor of Ezra the scribe, perhaps identical with *1.* (Ezra 7:3; 1 Chron. 9:11; Neh. 11:11). *3.* Priestly family in the postexilic period (Neh. 12:15), perhaps a scribal corruption of Meremoth (Neh. 12:3).

MERARI (Mė rā′ rī) Personal name meaning, "bitterness" or "gall." Third son of Levi (Gen. 46:11; Ex. 6:16; Num. 3:17; 1 Chron. 6:1,16; 23:6). Merari was the ancestor of a division of priests, the Merarites.

MERARITES (Mė rā′ rītes) Major division of priests descended from Merari, the third son of Levi. The Merarites and Gershonites were responsible for the set up, breakdown, and transport of the tabernacle (Num. 10:17; compare 3:36–37; 4:29–33; 7:8). The Merarites received an allotment of twelve cities from the tribes of Reuben, Gad, and Zebulun, including Ramoth-Gilead, a city of refuge (Josh. 21:7,34–40; 1 Chron. 6:63,77–81). Representatives of the Merarites participated in David's move of the ark to Jerusalem (1 Chron. 15:6), served as tabernacle musicians (1 Chron. 15:17,19) and gatekeepers (1 Chron. 26:10,19), shared in Hezekiah's (2 Chron. 29:12) and Josiah's (2 Chron. 34:12) reforms, and returned from Exile to assist in the new Temple (Ezra 8:19).

MERATHAIM (Mĕr ȧ thā′ ĭm) Place name meaning, "double bitterness" or "double rebellion," possibly a play on the Akkadian phrase *mat marrati* ("Land of the Bitter River") or on *nār mārratu,* a designation for the area touching Persian gulf known from Babylonian inscriptions. Jeremiah (50:21) announced God's judgment on the land.

MERCHANT Buyer and seller of goods for profit. With the exception of the period of Solomon (1 Kings 9:26–28; 10:15,22), Israel was not known in biblical times as a nation of merchants. References to Israelites involved in trade are surprisingly few. Israelites were prohibited from selling food to fellow Israelites for profit (Lev. 25:37), but could sell even carrion to a foreigner (Deut. 14:21). Merchants purchased cloth from housewives (Prov. 31:24). Olive oil was sold (2 Kings 4:7). Abuses by mercants were often condemned: holding back grain to force up prices (Prov. 11:26); impatience for sabbath or holy days to conclude so that commerce might resume; dishonest scales (Amos 8:5); forcing fellow Israelites into slavery to buy food (Neh. 5:1–8); violation of the Sabbath (Neh. 13:15–21). Jerusalem merchants assisted in Nehemiah's reconstruction of the walls, perhaps by providing finances (Neh. 3:32).

The majority of Old Testament references to merchants concern nations other than Israel. The term translated as merchant or trader at Proverbs 31:24 and Hosea 12:7 is, in fact, the word for

Trajan's Market in Rome, a large second century A.D. "shopping center" where merchants sold their wares.

Canaanite. Men of Tyre sold fish and all kinds of merchandise in postexilic Jerusalem (Neh. 13:16). Ezekiel 27:12–25 recounts the activities of the merchants of Tyre in full. They traded in common and precious metals, slaves, livestock, precious stones, ivory, wool, cloth, clothing, agricultural produce, wine, spices, and carpets. (Compare Rev. 18:11–13.) Tyre's trading partners included twenty-two nations or peoples encompassing Asia Minor, Palestine, Syria, Arabia, and Mesopotamia. Merchants generated great wealth. The prophets railed against the pride which accompanied merchants' material successes (Isa. 23; Ezek. 27).

In the New Testament, Jesus used a merchant to illustrate the need to risk all to gain the kingdom of heaven (Matt. 13:45–46). Other references continue the prophetic attack on arrogant merchants. James 4:13 warns big businessmen who engaged in long-term foreign ventures not to dismiss God when making plans. Revelation condemns Roman merchants who grew rich on the sins of Rome (Rev. 18:3). See *Economic Life; Commerce.*   *Chris Church*

MERCURIUS (Mĕr cū′ rĭ ŭs) KJV translation of the Greek *Hermes* (Acts 14:12). The Roman god Mercury was identified with the Greek Hermes. See *Gods, Pagan; Hermes.*

MERCURY (Mĕr′ cū rē) See *Gods, Pagan; Hermes.*

MERCY SEAT A slab of pure gold measuring about 45 inches by 27 inches which sat atop the ark of the covenant which was the same size. It was the base for the golden cherubim (Ex. 25:17–19,21) and symbolized the throne from which God ruled Israel (Lev. 16:2; Num. 7:89). On the Day of Atonement the high priest sprinkled the blood of a sacrificial lamb on the mercy seat as a plea for forgiveness for the sins of the nation (Lev. 16:15). The Hebrew word means literally "to wipe out" or "cover over." This has led modern translators to render the term "cover" (REB, NRSV note), "lid" (TEV), or "atonement cover" (NIV). "Mercy seat" is based on the earliest Greek and Latin translations. The mercy seat has been replaced as the symbol and place of God's presence and atonement. Christ's cross and resurrection showed the perfect presence and accomplished atonement once for all (Heb. 9).

MERCY, MERCIFUL A personal characteristic of care for the needs of others. The biblical concept of mercy always involves help to those who are in need or distress. Such help covers a broad range, from assistance in finding a bride to God's forgiveness of sin. A wide vocabulary is employed in the original languages to express these concepts, and an even wider vocabulary is found in English translations.

Mercy in the Old Testament Three main Hebrew roots involve the idea of mercy. *1. Racham/ rachamîm* This word *family* consistently has the meaning of showing mercy, compassion, or pity.

Related to the word for womb, it may have the connotation of a mother's affection or of the bond between siblings. This sense of a mother's compassion for her child is found in 1 Kings 3:26, and a similar expression describes Joseph's feelings for his brother in Genesis 43:30. Likewise, God's mercy is often likened to family relationships: as a father to his children (Jer. 31:20; Ps. 103:13; Isa. 63:15–16), a husband to a wife (Isa. 54:6–8; Hos. 2:19), a brother to a brother (Amos 1:11), even as a mother toward a nursing child (Isa. 49:15).

God's mercy is bound up with His covenant with Israel. He is merciful to them because He chose them (Ex. 33:19; 2 Kings 13:23; Isa. 54:10; 63:7). God's mercy is never just a feeling but is expressed by His action: providing for Israel in the wilderness (Neh. 9:19; Isa. 49:10) and delivering her from enemies (Pss. 69:16–21; 79:8–11; Isa. 30:18; Jer. 42:11–12). When Israel turned from God, He showed no pity (Isa. 9:17; 27:11; Jer. 13:14; 16:5; Hos. 1:6–8; 2:4). On the other hand, He is a forgiving God and shows mercy to a penitent people (Pss. 25:4–7; 40:11–12; 51:1–4; Prov. 28:13–14; Isa. 54:7; 55:7; Lam. 3:31–33; Dan. 9:9; Mic. 7:19; Hab. 3:2). He is merciful in restoring the nation (Ps. 102:13; Isa. 14:1; 49:13; Jer. 12:15; 30:18; 33:26; Ezek. 39:25; Zech. 1:16; 10:6) and renewing His friendship with them (Hos. 2:19,23). God's mercy is the very source of His people's life (Pss. 103:4; 119:77,156).

Racham is also used to describe human mercy or lack of it. Israel's enemies were merciless (Isa. 13:18; 47:6; Jer. 6:23; 21:7; 50:42). In legal contexts, Israel was to show no mercy to criminals (Deut. 13:8; 19:13,21). On the other hand, God expected His people to be merciful to their neighbors (1 Kings 8:31–32; Prov. 3:29; 21:13). He especially expected their mercy toward the poor and needy (Zech. 7:9–10).

2. *Chesed* Chesed occurs 245 times in the Old Testament, 127 in Psalms alone. The Septuagint translators regularly rendered it with the Greek word for mercy, *eleos*. Likewise, the King James version translates it regularly as mercy or kindness. See *Kindness.* Other English versions render it as "steadfast love" (NRSV), "lovingkindness" (NAS), "loyalty" or "constant love" (REB), "love" or "unfailing love" (NIV), "faithfulness" (TEV).

Like *racham,* chesed describes a variety of human relationships: husband and wife (Gen. 20:13), next-of-kin (Gen. 24:49), father and son (Gen. 47:29), host and guest (Rahab and the spies—Josh. 2:12–14), friends like David and Jonathan (1 Sam. 20:8,14–17), king and subjects (2 Sam. 2:5). Also like *racham,* it expresses itself in action: Rahab delivered the spies; Jonathan protected David from Saul. The relationship is always reciprocal. One who experiences the *chesed* of another is to reciprocate when the opportunity presents itself. Thus, the spies promised protection for Rahab, and David pledged to protect the house of Jonathan. An element of covenantal fidelity was involved. An element of mercy was also involved. Each sought to meet the other's need. Since one can scarcely meet a need of God, this covenantal aspect of mercy was expressed in God's requirement to show mercy to others. This was often coupled with a command for justice (Mic. 6:8; compare Hos. 12:6; Zech. 7:9).

God expects His people to show *chesed* to one another because He shows *chesed* to them—to individuals such as Abraham (Gen. 24:12–14), Jacob (Gen. 32:10), David (2 Sam. 7:15), and Job (10:12). Above all, He was merciful to His chosen people Israel (Ex. 15:13; Ps. 107:8,15,21,31; Isa. 63:7; Jer. 31:2–6). The linkage of God's covenant and His *chesed* is explicit in such phrases as "keeping covenant and showing *chesed*" (1 Kings 8:23; Deut. 7:9; Neh. 1:5; 9:32; Dan. 9:4; compare Ps. 106:45; Isa. 54:10).

A final characteristic of God's *chesed* is its permanence (Pss. 23:6; 25:6; 103:17; 117:2; Isa. 54:8). This is often expressed in the set phrase, "for the Lord is good, his mercy (*chesed*) is everlasting" or "his mercy endureth forever" (Pss. 100:5; 106:1; 107:1; 118:1; 1 Chron. 16:34; 2 Chron. 5:13; 7:3; Ezra 3:11; Jer. 33:11; compare Pss. 118:2–4; 136:1–26).

3. *Chanan/chen* This is the third Hebrew word family involving mercy and pity. Job used it in appealing for pity (19:21) and with it the psalmist described one who is generous to the poor (Pss. 37:21; 112:5; compare Prov. 14:21–23; 19:17; 28:8). The latter examples show how *chanan* involves not only pity but also being gracious. It is in this sense that the word is applied to God, referring to His gracious and generous nature.

4. *Conclusion* It is difficult to draw precise distinctions between the various words used in the Old Testament for God's mercy and grace. *Racham, chesed,* and *chanan* all refer to the one gracious, forgiving, loving God who is forever faithful in reaching out to His people in their need. Nowhere is their interrelatedness more evident than in the following recurrent Old Testament liturgy which combines all three: "God is merciful (*racham*) and gracious (*chana*), slow to anger, and abounding in steadfast love (*chesed*) and faithfulness" (Ex. 34:6; Num. 14:18; Neh. 9:17; Pss. 86:15; 103:8; 145:8; Joel 2:13; Jonah 4:2).

Mercy in the New Testament Three word families express the idea of mercy in the New Testament. 1. *Splagchna* Splagchna literally refers to the upper human organs (heart, liver, lungs). This usage appears in the grim depiction of Judas' death in Acts 1:18. Much like the Hebrew *rachamîm, splagchna* developed the derived sense of strong emotional feelings, particularly of compassion and affection. The word is often used of Jesus' compassion—for the multitudes (Matt. 9:36; 14:14; 15:32), for the blind (Matt. 20:34), for a leper (Mark 1:41), for a possessed child (Mark 9:20–127), for a widow's plight (Luke 7:13). His parables use the term to describe the mercy of a master on his indebted servant (Matt. 18:27), the compassion of a father for his prodigal son (Luke 15:20), and a Samaritan's pity for a wounded Jew (Luke 10:33). With this word Paul urged the Corinthians to renew their affection for him (2 Cor. 6:12; compare 7:15), exhorted the Philippians to mutual love and concern (Phil. 2:1–2), and played on the sympathy of Philemon (Philem. 7,12,20). With it, John reminded his readers that one who closes his heart to a brother's need scarcely has God's love (1 John 3:17).

2. *Oiktirmos* This word also means "pity, mercy, compassion" and is used together with splagchna in Colossians 3:12, Philippians 2:1, and James 5:11. It can be used negatively as in Hebrews 10:28 where it describes the merciless justice of the Law. Paul pointed to the positive side of God as "the father of mercies" (2 Cor. 1:3), and he urged the Romans to sacrificial service based on God's mercy (12:1). Christian mercy is rooted in God's mercy, a principle already given by Jesus (Luke 6:36). 3. *Eleos* The most common words in the New Testament for mercy belong to the *eleos* family. In secular Greek, the word was often viewed as a sign of weakness, a sentimental inclination to be overly lenient. The New Testament does not share in this assessment, having more in common with the Old Testament perspective on God's mercy.

To be sure, the negative aspect appears. Drawing on Exodus 33:19, Paul showed how God in His sovereign purposes can withdraw His mercies (Rom. 9:15–16,18,23). The total New Testament picture is much brighter. Jesus brought the good news of a merciful, forgiving God. He embodied that good news in Himself, and everywhere He was met by cries and expectations for mercy—from two blind men (Matt. 9:27), a woman with a possessed daughter (Matt. 15:22), the father of an epileptic boy (Matt. 17:15), and by ten lepers (Luke 17:13). His healings are themselves testimony to the divine mercy (Mark 5:19). Reminiscent of *chesed,* Jesus' birth and that of John are testimonies that God is both merciful and faithful to His promises (Luke 1:58,72,78). Paul had a keen awareness of God's mercy in his own life (1 Cor. 7:25; 2 Cor. 4:1; 1 Tim. 1:13,16) and in restoring his co-worker Epaphroditus to health (Phil. 2:27).

God's mercy was shown in His readiness to forgive the penitent sinner (Luke 8:13). Especially was it transparent in the atoning work of Christ (Heb. 2:17). Through Christ, God's mercy delivers from the death of sin into life (Eph. 2:4–5) and includes the Gentiles as part of His people

(Rom. 11:30–32). In Christ the mercy of God brings new life (1 Pet. 1:3) and undergirds the hope of life to come (Jude 21). In this life the mercy of God is always available for those who approach His throne (Heb. 4:16). The Christian life is lived under this assurance of God's mercy. This is why mercy is often an element in New Testament greetings and benedictions (1 Tim. 1:2; 2 Tim. 1:2; Gal. 6:16; 2 John 3; Jude 2). See *Greetings; Benedictions.*

Those who experience God's mercy are themselves to be merciful. God does not desire the external trappings of religiosity but deeds of mercy to others (Matt. 9:13; 12:7; 23:23). One who shows no mercy to others cannot expect God's mercy (Matt. 18:33–34; Jas. 2:13). Mercy is a mark of discipleship (Matt. 5:7). Disciples show deeds of mercy to a neighbor (Luke 10:36–37) and perform them cheerfully (Rom. 12:8). God is mercy, and one who shares in God's wisdom shares His mercy (Jas. 3:17).

3. *Conclusion* As with the Old Testament, the New Testament treatment of God's mercy cannot be separated from His love, His grace, and His faithfulness. They are all part of the same fabric. The difference, of course, is that the New Testament writers had come to see the mercy of God in a much brighter light in the face of Jesus Christ. He was the ultimate manifestation of God's mercy, the assurance of that mercy for believers, and the basis of their own mercy in their relationships with others. *John Polhill*

MERED (Mē′ rĕd) Personal name meaning, "rebel." Descendant of King David who married Bithiah, a daughter of Pharaoh (1 Chron. 4:17–18), perhaps as part of a political alliance.

MEREMOTH (Mĕr ė mŏth) Personal name meaning, "heights." *1.* Priest who returned from Exile with Zerubbabel (Neh. 12:3). *2.* Priest in the time of Ezra and Nehemiah who assisted with the Temple treasury (Ezra 8:33), with the repair of the walls (Neh. 3:4,21), and witnessed the renewal of the covenant (Neh. 10:5). *3.* Layman with a foreign wife (Ezra 10:36).

MERES (Mē rĕs) One of seven princes who served as counselors to King Ahasuerus of Persia (Esther 1:14). See *Marsena.*

MERIBAH (Mĕr ĭ bäh) See *Massah.*

MERIBAH-KADESH (Mĕr′ ĭ bah-Kā′ dĕsh) See *Kadesh Meribah.*

MERIBATH-KADESH (Mĕr′ ĭ băth-kā′ dĕsh) See *Kadesh Meribah.*

MERIBBAAL (Mė rīb bả′ ȧl) Personal name of disputed meaning: "opponent of Baal," "obstinacy of Baal," "beloved or hero of Baal," or "Baal defends." Original name of Mephibosheth. See *Mephibosheth.* Apparently later copyists of text changed name with Baal to avoid use of pagan god's name (1 Chron. 8:34; 9:40, the latter with the Hebrew spelling "hero" compared to the former's spelling "opponent."

MERNEPTAH (Mĕr′ nĕ ptäh) Personal name meaning, "beloved of Ptah" (god honored in Memphis, Egypt). Ruler in the Nineteenth Dynasty of Egypt 1236–1223 B.C. or according to some recent opinions 1212–1199 B.C. and thought by many to be the pharaoh of Egypt when the Exodus occurred. A stele produced during his rule is the earliest known nonbiblical reference to the Israelites. The stele praises Merneptah's conquest of Canaan, Ashkelon, Gezer, Yanoam, and Israel, Israel being marked as a people rather than a geographical place. Merneptah claimed to have "laid waste" to Israel. The stele shows that a people Israel existed in Canaan no later than 1207 B.C. and had sufficient strength to fight Merneptah even though they lost if his account is accurate. They may have been an ally of three city-states opposing Merneptah.

MERODACH (Mĕr ō′ dăch) Hebrew form of Marduk, the chief god of Babylon, also called Bel, corresponding to the Semitic Baal or "Lord" (Jer. 50:2). Merodach is an element in the names of the Babylonian kings Merodach-baladan (2 Kings 20:12; Isa. 39:1) and Evil-Merodach (2 Kings 25:27; Jer. 52:31). With a different vocalization, Merodach yields the name Mordecai (Esther 2:5). See *Gods, Pagan.*

MERODACH-BALADAN (Mĕ rō′ dăch-băl′ å dăn) Personal name meaning, "god Marduk gave an heir." A ruler of the Bit-Yakin tribe in southern Babylonia and king of Babylon 721–711 B.C. and for a short time in 704 B.C. He was little more than a puppet of Assyria, answering to Sargon. Merodach-baladan sent envoys to King Hezekiah of Judah (Isa. 39:1; 2 Kings 20:12–13), who inventoried the palace treasures. Two years later Sennacherib laid his ill-fated siege to the Holy City. Merodach-baladan continued to rebel against the Assyrians, coming out of exile more than once to oppose the kings of Nineveh. He eventually was beaten back to his seashore tribal lands. See *Babylon; Hezekiah; Sargon; Sennacherib.*

MEROM (Mē′ rŏm) Place name meaning, "high place." Place in Galilee where Joshua led Israel to defeat a coalition of Canaanite tribes under king Jabin of Hazor in a surprise attack (Josh. 11:1–7). The location of the site has been debated, but now appears to be the modern Merion. The town is near a wadi which is fed annually by a spring during the wet season. Thutmose III and Rameses

II of Egypt claimed to have captured the area during their respective reigns.

MERONOTH (Mĕ rō nŏth′) See *Meronothite.*

MERONOTHITE (Mĕ rŏn ō thīte) A resident of Meronoth (1 Chron. 27:30; Neh. 3:7). The site is perhaps Beituniyeh northwest of Gibeon.

MEROZ (Mē′ rŏz) Place name of uncertain meaning. Town condemned in the Song of Deborah for failure to join in the Lord's battle against the oppressive forces of Sisera (Judg. 5:23). The site is unknown. Suggestions have included: khirbet Marus three miles northwest of Hazor; Madon (Josh. 12:19); and (Shimron-) Merom (Josh. 11:5; 12:20), identified with Semuniyeh north of Megiddo on the edge of the Jezreel Valley. Marus is too far removed from the battle site to have been expected to participate. Madon is closer, but still separated from the Jezreel by mountain terrain.

MESECH (Mē′ sĕch) KJV alternate form of Meshech (Ps. 120:5).

MESHA (Mē′ shà) English translation of three Hebrew names. *1.* Personal name meaning "Safety." Ruler of Moab who led a rebellion against Israel (2 Kings 3:4–27). The designation of Mesha as a sheep breeder (2 Kings 3:4 NRSV) is perhaps an honorary title for chief. The date of his revolt is uncertain. Second Kings 1:1 suggests the revolt followed immediately on Ahab's death (850 B.C.). Second Kings 3:4 sets the revolt in the reign of Jehoram (849–842 B.C.). The Moabite stone erected by Mesha to celebrate his exploits contains two apparently irreconcilable time notes: in the middle of the reign of Omri's son and forty years after the beginning of Omri's oppressive taxation of Moab. If Omri's son is taken literally, the Moabite stone places the revolt in the reign of Ahab (869–850 B.C.). "Son of Omri" was, however, used as a title for any of the kings who succeeded Omri as king in Samaria, even of Jehu who overthrew Omri's dynasty. Jehoram, Omri's grandson, might thus be the "son" of Omri of the Moabite stone. Jehoram's reign, however, ended five years before the fortieth anniversary of the earliest date of Omri's oppression of Moab. At the beginning of the revolt, Mesha succeeded in seizing Israelite border towns and in fortifying towns on his frontier. An alliance of Israel, Judah, and Edom, however, outflanked his defenses and attacked Mesha from the rear. Mesha retreated to Kir-hareseth from which he attempted, unsuccessfully, to escape to his Aramean allies. With no escape possible, Mesha sacrificed his firstborn son to his god Chemosh on the city walls. In response, the Israelites lifted their siege and returned home. The Moabite stone describes Mesha as a builder of cities and highways. Archaeological evidence, however, suggests a decline in Moabite civilization following the revolt. See *Moab*.

2. Descendant of Benjamin living in Moab (1 Chron. 8:9). *3.* Descendant of Caleb (1 Chron. 2:42; RSV follows early Greek translation in reading Mareshah). *4.* Place name meaning, "debt." City in the territory of the Joktanites (Gen. 10:30), most likely to be identified with Massa (Gen. 25:14; Prov. 31:1), located between the head of the gulf of Aqaba and the Persian Gulf. This Massa is identified with the Assyrian *Mash* and the Persian *Maciya*.   *Chris Church*

MESHACH (Mē' shăch) Personal name of unknown meaning, apparently corrupted in transmission from Babylonian to Hebrew, perhaps to avoid pronouncing or acknowledging name of Babylonian god. One of Daniel's friends exiled to Babylon after the fall of Jehoiakin in 597 B.C. (Dan. 1:6–7). His Hebrew name was Mishael ("Who is what God is") but was changed to Meshach (perhaps, "Who is what Aku is") to mock Israel's God. Declining the rich food of the king's table, he and his friends proved that the simple fare of vegetables and water was to be desired to make one wise and strong. After refusing to bow to the king's golden image, he, Shadrach, and Abednego were thrown into a furnace, but were delivered by God (Dan. 3). Thereafter, they were promoted in the king's court.

MESHECH (Mē' shĕch) Personal name meaning either, "sowing" or "possession." *1.* A people of Asia Minor (Gen. 10:2; 1 Chron. 1:5), known for trading in copper vessels (Ezek. 27:13), frequently associated with Tubal (Ezek. 32:26; 38:2–3; 39:1). This Meschech is identical to the Assyrian *Mushki* and the Greek *Moschoi*. At Psalm 120:5 the name appears in the form Mesech (KJV). *2.* An otherwise unknown Aramaean tribe (1 Chron. 1:17), perhaps identical with Mash (Gen. 10:23).

MESHEK (Mē' shĕk) TEV form of Meshech (1 Chron. 1:17).

MESHELEMIAH (Mė shĕl' ĕ mī ah) Personal name meaning, "Yahweh is recompense." Tabernacle gatekeeper in the time of David (1 Chron. 9:21; 26:1–2,9). Shelemiah is an abbreviated form of this name (1 Chron. 26:14). Other shortened forms include Shallum (1 Chron. 9:17, 19,31; Ezra 2:42) and Meshullam (Neh. 12:25). All may refer to the same Levite or various persons may be intended.

MESHEZABEEL (Mė shĕz' à bēēl) KJV form of Meshezabel, a personal name meaning, "God delivers." *1.* Ancestor of one of those working on the wall (Neh. 3:4). *2.* One of the chiefs of the people witnessing Ezra's covenant renewal (Neh. 10:21).

3. Member of the tribe of Judah (Neh. 11:24). All three are perhaps the same individual.

MESHILLEMITH (Mė shĭl' lĕ mĭth) Alternate form of Meshillemoth at 1 Chronicles 9:12.

MESHILLEMOTH (Mė shĭl' lĕ mŏth) Personal name meaning, "reconciliation." *1.* A priest (1 Chron. 9:12; Neh. 11:13); *2.* Member of the tribe of Ephraim (2 Chron. 28:12).

MESHOBAB (Mė shō' băb) Personal name from a root meaning, "return." Leader of the tribe of Simeon (1 Chron. 4:34).

MESHULLAM (Mė shūl' lăm) Personal name meaning, "allied," or "given as a replacement." *1.* Grandfather of Shaphan, King Josiah's secretary (2 Kings 22:3). See *Josiah*. *2.* A son of Zerubbabel (1 Chron. 3:19). See *Zerubbabel*. *3.* A member of the tribe of Gad who lived in Bashan (1 Chron. 5:13). *4.* A son of Elpaal (1 Chron. 8:17).

5. A son of Hodaviah, father of Sallu (1 Chron. 9:7). *6.* A son of Shephatiah (1 Chron. 9:8). *7.* A member of the priestly family, a son of Zadok, and the father of Hilkiah (1 Chron. 9:11). See *Zadok*. *8.* A son of Meshillemith of the priestly Zadokite family (1 Chron. 9:12). See *Zadok*. *9.* A descendant of Kohathite, one of the foremen during the repairs made in the Temple following the finding of the Book of Deuteronomy during Josiah's reign (2 Chron. 34:12).

10. One sent by Ezra to secure the services of a Levite for a group of returning exiles (Ezra 8:15–18). He later opposed Ezra's plan to end foreign marriages becaue he had a foreign wife himself (10:29). *11.* A son of Berechiah, he helped Nehemiah repair the walls around Jerusalem following the return from Babylon (Neh. 3:4). *12.* A son of Besodiah who helped repair the old gate (the Jeshanah Gate, NIV) when Nehemiah repaired the walls of Jerusalem (Neh. 3:6). See *Nehemiah*. *13.* He stood beside Ezra as the scribe read the Law to the people of Jerusalem (Neh. 8:2–4). *14.* One of the priests who joined Nehemiah and others setting his seal to the covenant between the people and God (Neh. 10:7). *15.* One of the leaders of the people who set his seal to the covenant between the people and God (Neh. 10:20). *16.* A son of Ezra, head of a priestly house during the time Jehoiakim was high priest (Neh. 12:13). *17.* Another head of a priestly house when Jehoiakim was high priest; son of Ginnethon (Neh. 12:16).

18. A guard of the storerooms at the gates (Neh. 12:25 NIV). *19.* A prince of Judah who participated in the procession to dedicate the rebuilt walls of Jerusalem (Neh. 12:33).

MESHULLEMETH (Mė shŭl' lĕ mĕth) Personal name meaning, "restitution." Wife of King Mannaseh and mother of Amon (2 Kings 21:19).

MESOBAITE (Mẻ sō' bả īte) KJV form of Mezobaite (NAS, NIV, NRSV), the title of one of David's 30 elite warriors (1 Chron. 11:47). The REB and TEV amended the text to give the reading "resident of Zobah."

MESOPOTAMIA (Mẻs' o po tā' mǐ à) Strictly speaking, Mesopotamia (from the Greek "between the rivers") is the designation of the area between the Tigris and Euphrates rivers. Mesopotamia applies more generally to the entire Tigris-Euphrates valley. At times in antiquity the culture of Mesopotamia dominated an even larger area, spreading east into Elam and Media, north into Asia Minor, and following the fertile crescent into Canaan and Egypt.

The Scriptures witness to a long history of contacts between the Hebrew people and the people of Mesopotamia. Mesopotamia was the homeland of the patriarchs (Gen. 11:31—12:4; 24:10; 28:6). A Mesopotamian king subdued Israel for a time during the period of the judges (Judg. 3:8). Mesopotamia supplied mercenary chariots and cavalry for the Ammonites' war with David (1 Chron. 19:6; superscription of Ps. 60). Both the Northern Kingdom of Israel (2 Kings 15:29; 1 Chron. 5:26) and the Southern Kingdom of Judah (2 Kings 24:14—16; 2 Chron. 36:20; Ezra 2:1) went into Exile in Mesopotamia.

MESSENGER One sent with a message. Messenger is often used in the literal sense (Gen. 32:3,6; Num. 20:14; 24:12; Deut. 2:26). In an extended sense, the prophets (2 Chron. 36:15—16; Isa. 44:26; Hag. 1:13) and priests (Mal. 2:7) are termed messengers in their role as bearers of God's message for humanity. The Hebrew and Greek terms for messenger are frequently rendered "angel," the heavenly messengers of God. See *Angels.* Sometimes messengers made advance travel arrangements for their master (Luke 9:52). In this sense the prophetic messenger of Malachi 3:1 prepares for the Lord's coming. The Gospel writers applied this preparatory function to John the Baptist (Matt. 11:10; Mark 1:2; Luke 7:27). See *Herald.*

MESSIAH (Mĕs sī' ah) Transliteration of Hebrew word meaning, "anointed one" that was translated into Greek as *Christos.* See *Christ, Christology.* Since apostolic times the name *Christ* has become the proper name of Jesus, the Person whom Christians recognize as the God-given Redeemer of Israel and the church's Lord. "Christ" or Messiah is therefore a name admirably suited to express both the church's link with Israel through the Old Testament and the faith that sees in Jesus Christ the worldwide scope of the salvation in Him.
The Old Testament and Early Jewish Background "Anointed" carries several senses in the Old Testament. All have to do with installing a person in an office in a way that the person will be regarded as accredited by Yahweh, Israel's God. Even a pagan king such as Cyrus was qualified as the Lord's anointed (Isa. 45:1) to execute a divinely appointed task. The usual application of the term *anointed* was to God's representatives within the covenant people. Prophets such as Elisha were set apart in this way (1 Kings 19:16). Israel probably saw a close link between the anointed persons and God's spirit though the link is specifically mentioned only occasionally (2 Kings 2:9). Israelite kings were particularly hailed as Yahweh's anointed(compare Jud. 9:8), beginning with Saul (1 Sam. 9—10 NIV) and especially referring to David (1 Sam. 16:6,13; see 2 Sam. 2:4; 5:3) and Solomon (1 Kings 1:39). The royal family of David as being the line of Israelite kings are mentioned by the title of the "anointed ones" (2 Sam. 22:51; compare 2 Kings 11:12; 23:30; Pss. 2:2; 20:6; 28:8; 84:9). The king in Israel thus became a sacred person to whom loyalty and respect were to be accorded (1 Sam. 24:6,10; 26:9,11,16,23; 2 Sam. 1:14,16). The oracle spoken by Nathan (2 Sam. 7:12—16) is important since it centers the hope of Israel on the dynasty of David for succeeding generations.

The king, especially in the Psalms, became idealized as a divine son (Ps. 2:2,7; compare 2 Sam. 7:14) and enjoyed God's protecting favor (Ps. 18:50; 20:6; 28:8). His dynasty would not fail (Ps. 132:17), and the people were encouraged to pray to God on his behalf (Ps. 72:11—15; 84:9). The fall of Jerusalem in 586 B.C. led to great confusion especially when Yahweh's anointed was taken into Exile as a prisoner (Lam. 4:20) and his authority as king rejected by the nations (Ps. 89:38,51). This humiliation of the Davidic dynasty posed a set of problems to Israel's faith, even when the people were permitted to return to the land. No revival came for the Davidic kingship; yet that restoration became the pious longing of the Jews both in Babylonian Exile (Jer. 33:14—18) and in the later centuries. One of the clearest expressions of the continuing hope was in the *Psalms of Solomon* (17—18)(70–40 B.C.), a Jewish writing of the Messiah as the son of David. There Messiah was a warrior-prince who would expel the hated Romans from Israel and bring in a kingdom in which the Jews would be promoted to world dominion.

After the Exile the Israelite priesthood came into prominence. In the absence of a king, the high priest took on a central role in the community. The rite of anointing was the outward sign of his authority to function as God's representative. This authority was traced back to Aaron and his sons (Ex. 29:7—9; 30:22—33; compare Ps. 133:2). The high priest was the anointed-priest (Lev. 4:3,5,16) and even, in one place, a "messiah" (Zech 4:14; compare 6:13; Dan. 9:25).

Messianic Prophecies of the Old Testament

PROPHECY	O.T. REFERENCES	N.T. FULFILLMENT
Seed of the woman	Gen. 3:15	Gal. 4:4; Heb. 2:14
Through Noah's sons	Gen. 9:27	Luke 6:36
Seed of Abraham	Gen. 12:3	Matt. 1:1; Gal. 3:8,16
Seed of Isaac	Gen. 17:19	Rom. 9:7; Heb. 11:18
Blessing to nations	Gen. 18:18	Gal. 3:8
Seed of Isaac	Gen. 21:12	Rom. 9:7; Heb. 11:18
Blessing to Gentiles	Gen. 22:18	Gal. 3:8,16; Heb. 6:14
Blessing to Gentiles	Gen. 26:4	Gal. 3:8,16; Heb. 6:14
Blessing through Abraham	Gen. 28:14	Gal. 3:8,16; Heb. 6:14
Of the tribe of Judah	Gen. 49:10	Rev. 5:5
No bone broken	Ex. 12:46	John 19:36
Blessing to firstborn son	Ex. 13:2	Luke 2:23
No bone broken	Num. 9:12	John 19:36
Serpent in wilderness	Num. 21:8,9	John 3:14,15
A star out of Jacob	Num. 24:17–19	Matt. 2:2; Luke 1:33,78; Rev. 22:16
As a prophet	Deut. 18:15,18,19	John 6:14; 7:40; Acts 3:22,23
Cursed on the tree	Deut. 21:23	Gal. 3:13
The throne of David established forever	2 Sam. 7:12,13,16,25,26 1 Chron. 17:11–14,23–27 2 Chron. 21:7	Matt. 19:28; 21:4; 25:31; Mark 12:37; Luke 1:32; John 7:4; Acts 2:30; 13:23; Rom. 1:3; 2 Tim. 2:8; Heb. 1:5,8; 8:1; 12:2; Rev. 22:1
A promised Redeemer	Job 19:25–27	John 5:28,29; Gal. 4:4; Eph. 1:7,11,14
Declared to be the Son of God	Ps. 2:1–12	Matt. 3:17; Mark 1:11; Acts 4:25,26; 13:33; Heb. 1:5; 5:5; Rev. 2:26,27; 19:15,16
His resurrection	Ps. 16:8–10	Acts 2:27; 13:35; 26:23
Hands and feet pierced	Ps. 22:1–31	Matt. 27:31,35,36
Mocked and insulted	Ps. 22:7–8	Matt. 27:39–43,45–49
Soldiers cast lots for coat	Ps. 22:18	Mark 15:20,24,25,34; Luke 19:24; 23:35; John 19:15–18,23,24,34; Acts 2:23,24
Accused by false witnesses	Ps. 27:12	Matt. 26:60,61
He commits His spirit	Ps. 31:5	Luke 23:46
No bone broken	Ps. 34:20	John 19:36
Accused by false witnesses	Ps. 35:11	Matt. 26:59–61; Mark 14:57,58
Hated without reason	Ps. 35:19	John 15:24,25
Friends stand afar off	Ps. 38:11	Matt. 27:55; Mark 15:40; Luke 23:49
"I come to do Thy will"	Ps. 40:6–8	Heb. 10:5–9
Betrayed by a friend	Ps. 41:9	Matt. 26:14–16,47,50; Mark 14:17–21; Luke 22:19–23; John 13:18,19
Known for righteousness	Ps. 45:2,6,7	Heb. 1:8,9
His resurrection	Ps. 49:15	Mark 16:6
Betrayed by a friend	Ps. 55:12–14	John 13:18
His ascension	Ps. 68:18	Eph. 4:8
Hated without reason	Ps. 69:4	John 15:25
Stung by reproaches	Ps. 69:9	John 2:17; Rom. 15:3
Given gall and vinegar	Ps. 69:21	Matt. 27:34,48; Mark 15:23; Luke 23:36; John 19:29
Exalted by God	Ps. 72:1–19	Matt. 2:2; Phil. 2:9–11; Heb. 1:8
He speaks in parables	Ps. 78:2	Matt. 13:34,35
Seed of David exalted	Ps. 89:3,4,19,27–29,35–37	Luke 1:32; Acts 2:30; 13:23; Rom. 1:3; 2 Tim. 2:8

Messianic Prophecies of the Old Testament

PROPHECY	O.T. REFERENCES	N.T. FULFILLMENT
Son of Man comes in glory	Ps. 102:16	Luke 21:24,27; Rev. 12:5–10
"Thou remainest"	Ps. 102:24–27	Heb. 1:10–12
Prays for His enemies	Ps. 109:4	Luke 23:34
Another to succeed Judas	Ps. 109:7,8	Acts 1:16–20
A priest like Melchizedek	Ps. 110:1–7	Matt. 22:41–45; 26:64; Mark 12:35–37; 16:19; Acts 7:56; Eph. 1:20; Col. 1:20; Heb. 1:13; 2:8; 5:6; 6:20; 7:21; 8:1; 10:11–13; 12:2
The chief corner stone	Ps. 118:22,23	Matt. 21:42; Mark 12:10,11; Luke 20:17; John 1:11; Acts 4:11; Eph. 2:20; 1 Pet. 2:4
The King comes in the name of the Lord	Ps. 118:26	Matt. 21:9; 23:39; Mark 11:9; Luke 13:35; 19:38; John 12:13
David's seed to reign	Ps. 132:11 cf. 2 Sam. 7:12,13,16,25,26,29	Matt. 1:1
Declared to be the Son of God	Prov. 30:4	Matt. 3:17; Mark 14:61,62; Luke 1:35; John 3:13; 9:35–38; 11:21; Rom. 1:2–4; 10:6–9; 2 Pet. 1:17
Repentance for the nations	Is. 2:2–4	Luke 24:47
Hearts are hardened	Is. 6:9,10	Matt. 13:14,15; John 12:39,40; Acts 28:25–27
Born of a virgin	Is. 7:14	Matt. 1:22,23
A rock of offense	Is. 8:14,15	Rom. 9:33; 1 Pet. 2:8
Light out of darkness	Is. 9:1,2	Matt. 4:14–16; Luke 2:32
God with us	Is. 9:6,7	Matt. 1:21,23; Luke 1:32,33; John 8:58; 10:30; 14:19; 2 Cor. 5:19; Col. 2:9
Full of wisdom and power	Is. 11:1–10	Matt. 3:16; John 3:34; Rom. 15:12; Heb. 1:9
Reigning in mercy	Is. 16:4,5	Luke 1:31–33
Peg in a sure place	Is. 22:21–25	Rev. 3:7
Death swallowed up in victory	Is. 25:6–12	1 Cor. 15:54
A stone in Zion	Is. 28:16	Rom. 9:33; 1 Pet. 2:6
The deaf hear, the blind see	Is. 29:18,19	Matt. 5:3; 11:5; John 9:39
King of kings, Lord of lords	Is. 32:1–4	Rev. 19:16; 20:6
Son of the Highest	Is. 33:22	Luke 1:32; 1 Tim. 1:17; 6:15
Healing for the needy	Is. 35:4–10	Matt. 9:30; 11:5; 12:22; 20:34; 21:14; 7:30; 5:9
Make ready the way of the Lord	Is. 40:3–5	Matt. 3:3; Mark 1:3; Luke 3:4,5; John 1:23
The Shepherd dies for His sheep	Is. 40:10,11	John 10:11; Heb. 13:20; 1 Pet. 2:24,25
The meek Servant	Is. 42:1–16	Matt. 12:17–21; Luke 2:32
A light to the Gentiles	Is. 49:6–12	Acts 13:47; 2 Cor. 6:2
Scourged and spat upon	Is. 50:6	Matt. 26:67; 27:26,30; Mark 14:65; 15:15,19; Luke 22:63–65; John 19:1
Rejected by His people	Is. 52:13—53:12	Matt. 8:17; 27:1,2,12–14,38
Suffered vicariously	Is. 53:4–5	Mark 15:3,4,27,28; Luke 23:1–25,32–34
Silent when accused	Is. 53:7	John 1:29; 11:49–52
Crucified with transgressors	Is. 53:12	John 12:37,38; Acts 8:28–35
Buried with the rich	Is. 53:9	Acts 10:43; 13:38,39; 1 Cor. 15:3; Eph. 1:7; 1 Pet. 2:21–25; 1 John 1:7,9

Messianic Prophecies of the Old Testament

PROPHECY	O.T. REFERENCES	N.T. FULFILLMENT
Calling of those not a people	Is. 55:4,5	John 18:37; Rom. 9:25,26; Rev. 1:5
Deliver out of Zion	Is. 59:16–20	Rom. 11:26,27
Nations walk in the light	Is. 60:1–3	Luke 2:32
Anointed to preach liberty	Is. 61:1–3	Luke 4:17–19; Acts 10:38
Called by a new name	Is. 62:1,2	Luke 2:32; Rev. 3:12
The King cometh	Is. 62:11	Matt. 21:5
A vesture dipped in blood	Is. 63:1–3	Rev. 19:13
Afflicted with the afflicted	Is. 63:8,9	Matt. 25:34–40
The elect shall inherit	Is. 65:9	Rom. 11:5,7; Heb. 7:14; Rev. 5:5
New heavens and a new earth	Is. 65:17–25	2 Pet. 3:13; Rev. 21:1
The Lord our righteousness	Jer. 23:5,6	John 2:19–21; Rom. 1:3,4; Eph. 2:20,21; 1 Pet. 2:5
Born a King	Jer. 30:9	John 18:37; Rev. 1:5
Massacre of infants	Jer. 31:15	Matt. 2:17,18
Conceived by the Holy Spirit	Jer. 31:22	Matt. 1:20; Luke 1:35
A New Covenant	Jer. 31:31–34	Matt. 26:27–29; Mark 14:22–24; Luke 22:15–20; 1 Cor. 11:25; Heb. 8:8–12; 10:15–17; 12:24; 13:20
A spiritual house	Jer. 33:15–17	John 2:19–21; Eph. 2:20,21; 1 Pet. 2:5
A tree planted by God	Ezek. 17:22–24	Matt. 13:31,32
The humble exalted	Ezek. 21:26,27	Luke 1:52
The good Shepherd	Ezek. 34:23,24	John 10:11
Stone cut without hands	Dan. 2:34,35	Acts 4:10–12
His Kingdom triumphant	Dan. 2:44,45	Luke 1:33; 1 Cor. 15:24; Rev. 11:15
An everlasting dominion	Dan. 7:13,14	Matt. 24:30; 25:31; 26:64; Mark 14:61,62; Acts 1:9–11; Rev. 1:7
Kingdom for the saints	Dan. 7:27	Luke 1:33; 1 Cor. 15:24; Rev. 11:15
Time of His birth	Dan. 9:24–27	Matt. 24:15–21; Luke 3:1
Israel restored	Hos. 3:5	John 18:37; Rom. 11:25–27
Flight into Egypt	Hos. 11:1	Matt. 2:15
Promise of the Spirit	Joel 2:28–32	Acts 2:17–21; Rom. 10:13
The sun darkened	Amos 8:9	Matt. 24:29; Acts 2:20; Rev. 6:12
Restoration of tabernacle	Amos 9:11,12	Acts 15:16–18
Israel regathered	Mic. 2:12,13	John 10:14,26
The Kingdom established	Mic. 4:1–8	Luke 1:33
Born in Bethlehem	Mic. 5:1–5	Matt. 2:1; Luke 2:4,10,11
Earth filled with knowledge of the glory of the Lord	Hab. 2:14	Rom. 11:26; Rev. 21:23–26
The Lamb on the throne	Zech. 2:10–13	Rev. 5:13; 6:9; 21:24 22:1–5
A holy priesthood	Zech. 3:8	John 2:19–21; Eph. 2:20,21; 1 Pet. 2:5
A heavenly High Priest	Zech. 6:12,13	Heb. 4:4; 8:1,2
Triumphal entry	Zech. 9:9,10	Matt. 21:4,5; Mark 11:9,10; Luke 20:38; John 12:13–15
Sold for 30 pieces of silver	Zech. 11:12,13	Matt. 26:14,15
Money buys potter's field	Zech. 11:12,13	Matt. 27:9
Piercing of His body	Zech. 12:10	John 19:34,37
Shepherd smitten—sheep scattered	Zech. 13:1,6,7	Matt. 26:31; John 16:32
Preceded by Forerunner	Mal. 3:1	Matt. 11:10; Mark 1:2; Luke 7:27
Our sins purged	Mal. 3:3	Heb. 1:3
The light of the world	Mal. 4:2,3	Luke 1:78; John 1:9; 12:46; 2 Pet. 1:19; Rev. 2:28; 19:11–16; 22:16
The coming of Elijah	Mal. 4:5,6	Matt. 11:14; 17:10–12

In the exilic and postexilic ages, the expectation of a coming Messiah came into sharper focus, commencing with Jeremiah's and Ezekiel's vision of a Messiah who would combine the traits of royalty and priestly dignity (Jer. 33:14–18; Ezek. 46:1–8; see, too, Zech. 4:1–14; 6:13). The people in the Dead Sea scrolls were evidently able to combine a dual hope of two Messiahs, one priestly and the second a royal figure. The alternation between a kingly Messiah and a priestly figure is characteristic of the two centuries of early Judaism prior to the coming of Jesus.

Messiahship in Jesus' Ministry A question posed in John 4:29; compare 7:40–43 is: "Is not this the Christ (Messiah)." It is evident that the issue of the Messiah's identity and role was one much debated among the Jews in the first century. In the Synoptic Gospels the way Jesus acted and spoke led naturally to the dialogue at Caesarea Philippi (Mark 8:29). Jesus asked His disciples, "Who do you say that I am?" a question to which Peter gave the reply, "Thou art the Christ (Messiah)" (Mark 8:29). Mark made clear that Jesus took an attitude of distinct reserve and caution to this title since it carried overtones of political power, especially in one strand of Jewish hope represented by the Psalms of Solomon. Jesus, therefore, accepted Peter's confession with great reluctance since with it went the disciple's objection that the Messiah cannot suffer (see Mark 9:32). For Peter, Messiah was a title of a glorious personage both nationalistic and victorious in battle. Jesus, on the other hand, saw His destiny in terms of a suffering Son of man and Servant of God (Mark 8:31–38; 9:31; 10:33–34). Hence He did not permit the demons to greet Him as Messiah (Luke 4:41) and downplayed all claims to privilege and overt majesty linked with the Jewish title.

The course of Jesus' ministry is one in which He sought to wean the disciples away from the traditional notion of a warrior Messiah. Instead, Jesus tried to instill in their minds the prospect that the road to His future glory was bound to run by way of the cross, with its experience of rejection, suffering, and humiliation. At the trial before His Jewish judges (Matt. 26:63–66) He once more reinterpreted the title Messiah ("Christ," KJV) and gave it a content in terms of the Son of man figure, based on Daniel 7:13–14. This confession secured His condemnation, and He went to the cross as a crucified Messiah because the Jewish leaders failed to perceive the nature of messiahship as Jesus understood it. Pilate sentenced Him as a messianic pretender who claimed (according to the false charges brought against Him) to be a rival to Caesar (Mark 15:9; Luke 23:2; John 19:14–15). It was only after the resurrection that the disciples were in a position to see how Jesus was truly a king Messiah and how Jesus then opened their minds to what true Messiahship meant (see Luke 24:45–46). The national title

Messiah then took on a broader connotation, involving a kingly role which was to embrace all peoples (Luke 24:46–47).

Messiah as a Title in the Early Church From the resurrection onward the first preachers announced that Jesus was the Messiah by divine appointment (Acts 2:36; Rom. 1:3–4). Part of the reason for this forthright declaration is to be traced to apologetic reasons. In the mission to Israel the church had to show how Jesus fulfilled the Old Testament prophecies and came into the world as the "Son of David," a title closely linked with the Messiah as a royal person. Matthew's Gospel is especially concerned to establish the identity (Matt. 1:1), but it is equally a theme common to Luke (Luke 1:32,69; 2:4,11; Acts 2:29–36; 13:22–23). Paul also saw in Jesus the fulfillment of the messianic hopes of the old covenant (1 Cor. 5:7–8). Peter, too, sought to show how the sufferings of the Messiah were foretold (1 Pet. 1:11,20; 2:21; 3:18; 4:1,13; 5:1). Luke stressed the link between Jesus as the One anointed by the Holy Spirit (Luke 4:16–22) in a way that looks back to Isaiah 61:1, and he recorded Peter's statement (in Acts 10:38 NIV) that "God anointed Jesus of Nazareth with the Holy Spirit and power" as a fulfillment of Old Testament prophecy. The letter to the Hebrews is rich in this theme. See Hebrews 1:9; 2:2–4; 9:14–15.

The final stage of development in regard to the title *Messiah* came in the way that Paul used the word more as a personal name than as an official designation (seen in Rom. 9:5, "Christ"). The reason for this shift lies in the intensely personal nature of Paul's faith which centered in Jesus Christ as the divine Lord (see Phil. 1:21; Col. 3:4). Also, Paul taught his converts who were mainly converted to Christ from paganism that Jesus was the universal Lord whose mission was wider than any Jewish hope could embrace. In Pauline thought, "Christ" is a richer term than "Messiah" could ever be, and one pointer in this direction is the fact that the early followers of the Messiah called themselves not converted Jews but "Christians," Christ's people (Acts 11:26; 1 Pet. 4:16) as a sign of their universal faith in a sovereign Lord. See *Christ; Jesus*. *Ralph P. Martin*

MESSIANIC SECRET Title Bible students use to explain Jesus' commands to His audience and His disciples not to reveal who He was after His performance of messianic wonders. Throughout the Gospel of Mark, Jesus made every attempt to conceal His true identity as the Christ. Although the messianic secret can be found in the Gospels of Matthew (8:3–4; 9:29–31; 12:15–16; 17:9) and Luke (4:41; 8:56; 9:21), Mark used the mysterious unveiling of the messiahship of Jesus as the unifying theme of his Gospel. Typically, Matthew understood the messianic secret as the fulfillment of prophecy (Matt. 12:17–21); Luke provided no explanation. Mark, however, used the messianic secret to organize his story around the progressive revelation of the person of Christ and the messianic consciousness of the disciples. Demons demonstrated that they recognized Jesus immediately: "I know who You are—the Holy One of God!" (1:24–25,34; 3:11–12; 5:6–8; 9:20 NIV); nevertheless, Jesus suppressed their confession. Jesus prohibited public profession by those who experienced miraculous healing (1:43; 5:43; 7:36; 8:26). The parables of Jesus were offered in order to keep "outsiders" from learning the secret (4:11–12). Even the disciples, once they related that they understood the "mystery of the kingdom of God" (4:11), were sworn to silence (8:30; 9:9). Why did Jesus want to keep His messiahship a secret?

Perhaps Jesus avoided the title due to the popular messianic expectations of the people—they were looking for a political deliverer. Some believe that Jesus prohibited messianic proclamation so that He could continue to move about freely in public. The only parable of Jesus which Mark recorded exclusively may provide a clue to the purpose of the messianic secret. Jesus introduced the parable of the secret growing seed (4:26–29) with the proverb: "For nothing is hidden, except to be revealed; nor has anything been secret, but that it should come to light" (4:22 NAS). Jesus intended for people of faith to learn the secret of His messiahship (4:11,34). He compared the mystery of the kingdom of God to a man who sows seed and discovers, to his amazement, that seeded ground produces plants which secretly grow at night—"he knoweth not how" (4:27). Like the seed which is covered by ground, the secret of Jesus' identity would be concealed for a season: discovering the messianic secret would take time. Jesus did not force people to accept Him as Messiah; "those who had ears to hear" must learn the secret on their own. The disciples not only needed time to recognize Jesus as Messiah (4:41; 6:52; 8:17–21), they also needed time to come to terms with His messianic agenda: messianic suffering precedes messianic glory (9:31–32). Complete human understanding of the messianic secret would only be possible after the resurrection (9:9–10). Therefore, no immediate messianic profession would possess any depth of understanding (especially demonic confession!). Jesus forced the disciples to think about the secret until they could articulate the secret.

See *Jesus; Christ; Messiah.*   *Rodney Reeves*

MESSIAS (Mĕs sī′ ăs) The Greek form of Messiah (John 1:41; 4:25; KJV).

METALSMITH, METALWORKER See *Minerals and Metals; Mines and Mining; Occupations.*

METHEG-AMMAH (Mĕth′ ĕḡ-ăm′ mah) A phrase of uncertain meaning used at 2 Samuel

8:1. KJV, NIV, NRSV take it as a place name. NAS translated the phrase as "the chief city." The parallel in 1 Chronicles 18:1 has "Gath and its villages." Other suggestions for translation include: "bridle of the water channel," reins of the forearm," "control of the mother city," "take the common land," or "wrest supremacy from."

METHUSAEL (Mĕ thū′ sā ĕl) KJV form of Methushael, a personal name of uncertain meaning. "Man of God" is possible. Canaanite patriarch (Gen. 4:18). Some scholars regard the name as a variant of Methuselah (Gen. 5:21).

METHUSELAH (Mĕ thū′ sĕ lah) Personal name meaning either, "man of the javelin" or "worshiper of Selah." A son of Enoch (who walked with God) and grandfather of Noah (Gen. 5:21,26–29). According to the biblical record, Methuselah is the oldest human ever, dying at age 969 (Gen. 5:27).

MEUNIM, MEUNITES (Mĕ′ ū nĭm; Mĕ′ ū nītes) See *Mehunim.*

MEZAHAB (Mĕz′ à hăb) Either a personal or a place name meaning, "waters of gold" (Gen. 36:39; 1 Chron. 1:50). If a person, Mezahab was the grandfather of Mehetabel, the wife of King Hadar of Edom. If a place name, Mezahab was the home of Matred which should perhaps be identified with Dizahab (Deut. 1:1).

MEZUZAH (Mĕ zū′ zăh) Hebrew term for doorpost. Ancient doors pivoted on posts set in sockets. The blood of the passover lamb was to be applied to door posts (Ex. 12:7,22–23). At the beginning of the new year blood was to be applied to the doorposts of the temple to make atonement for it (Ezek. 45:19). The command to write the words of the Shema (Deut. 6:4–9; 11:13–21) on the doorposts of one's home, like the command to write them on one's heart (Deut. 6:6), is a challenge to always remember that love of God is central to faith. At a later time, these commands were understood literally. Today Mezuzah refers to small scrolls inscribed with Deuteronomy 6:4–9; 11:13–21 placed in a container attached to the door jambs of some Jewish homes.

MIAMIN (Mī′ à mĭn) KJV form of Mijamin used at Ezra 10:25 and Nehemiah 12:5. See *Mijamin.*

MIBHAR (Mĭb′ här) Personal name meaning "best" or "chosen." One of David's 30 elite warriors (1 Chron. 11:38). The parallel at 2 Samuel 23:36, reflecting a copying error in transmission of the text, reads, "of Zobah, Bani the Godite."

MIBSAM (Mĭb′ săm) Personal name meaning, "fragrant." *1.* Arab tribe descended from a son of

Ishmael (Gen. 25:13; 1 Chron. 1:29). *2.* Descendant of Simeon (1 Chron. 4:25).

MIBZAR (Mĭb' zär) Personal name meaning, "fortification." Edomite clan chief and his tribe (Gen. 36:42; 1 Chron. 1:53). Mibzar is possibly Mabsara in northern Edom or Bozrah (Gen. 36:33; Amos 1:12).

MIC MASH (Mĭc' măsh) NIV spelling of Michmash.

MICA (Mī' ċa) See *Micha 2.* Variant spelling modern translations used for Micah reflecting Aramaic spelling in text of 2 Samuel 9:12; Nehemiah 10:11; 11:17,22; 1 Chronicles 9:15. All passages reflect Levites.

MICAH (Mī' cah) Abbreviated form of the personal name Micaiah, meaning, "Who is like Yahweh?" *1.* Ephramite whose home shrine was the source of Dan's idolotrous worship (Judg. 17—18). *2.* Descendant of Reuben (1 Chron. 5:5). *3.* Descendant of King Saul (1 Chron. 8:34–35; 9:40–44); at 2 Samuel 9:12, the KJV used the form Micha. *4.* Leader of a family of Levites in David's time (1 Chron. 23:20; 24:24–25). *5.* Father of Abdon, a contemporary of Josiah (2 Chron. 34:20); at 2 Kings 22:12, the form Micaiah is used.

MICAH, BOOK OF (Mī' cah) A prophetic book named after the eighth century B.C. prophet containing some of his messages. The prophet Micah's name means, "Who is like Yah?" People in the Ancient Near East commonly gave their children names that indicated devotion to their god, and Yahweh was the name by which the God of Israel and Judah was called. See *Micah; Micaiah; Micha.*

Micah 1:1 gives the reader three pieces of information about the prophet. He came from Maresheth (NIV) which probably should be identified with Moresheth-gath. This village was located about 25 miles southwest of Jerusalem in the tribe of Judah. Micah, however, may have lived in Jerusalem during his ministry. He worked in the reigns of Jotham (750–732 B.C.), Ahaz (735–715 B.C.), and Hezekiah (715–686 B.C.) who were kings of Judah. The identification of these kings does not mean that he was active from 750–686, but that his ministry spanned parts of each reign. Jeremiah 26:17–18 refers to Micah as prophesying during the time of Hezekiah. Determining exact dates, however, for each of the prophecies contained in the book is difficult. Micah was a contemporary of Isaiah, Hosea, and possibly Amos.

Finally, His prophecies addressed Samaria and Jerusalem. Samaria was the capital of the Northern Kingdom (Israel) and Jerusalem, of the Southern Kingdom (Judah). Even though Micah ministered in Judah, some of his messages were directed toward Israel.

Historical Background In Micah's time, many political and national crises occurred. Micah addressed those issues.

The Assyrian Empire began to dominate the Ancient Near East about 740 B.C. Judah and Israel became tribute-paying vassals of this new political power, and in 722 B.C. Israel felt the might of the Assyrian army. Shalmaneser V and Sargon II destroyed the Northern Kingdom and its capital, Samaria (2 Kings 16—17) because of an attempted rebellion. The records of Sargon II state that he "besieged and conquered Samaria, (and) led away as booty 27,290 inhabitants of it." While Judah survived, they still were vassals. Micah 1:2–7 associates the imminent destruction of Samaria as God's judgment for the people's idolatry. Hezekiah, king of Judah, instituted many reforms that caused the Assyrian king, Sennacherib, to respond with force. Many cities of Judah were destroyed, and Jerusalem was unsuccessfully besieged (2 Kings 18—19). The annals of Sennacherib boast that he laid siege to 46 cities and countless small villages. He took 200,150 people as booty along with the livestock. As for Hezekiah, Sennacherib says, "Himself I made a prisoner in Jerusalem, his royal residence, like a bird in a cage." Despite the failure to take Jerusalem, the citizens of the Southern Kingdom suffered greatly from the invasion.

The Prophet's Message The subjects of Micah's messages reveal much about the society of his day. He constantly renounced the oppression of the poor by the rich. He characterized the rich as devising ways in which to cheat the poor out of their land (2:1–5). People were evicted from their homes and had their possessions stolen. Those who committed such crimes were fellow Israelites (2:6–11). The marketplace was full of deception and injustice (6:9–16). The rulers of the country, who had the responsibility of upholding justice, did the opposite (3:1–4).

Micah also denounced the religious practices of the nation. He predicted the destruction of Judah as an act of God's judgment. Other prophets, however, led the people to believe that this could never happen because God was residing in the nation and would protect them. Micah contended that the other prophets' message was not from God. Instead, the message from God was the imminent devastation of Judah (3:5–12).

The people worshiped other gods. They did not quit believing in and worshiping the God of Judah, but they combined this worship with devotion to other details (5:10–15). The people believed all that religion required of them was to bring their sacrifices and offerings to the Temple. No relationship was acknowledged between their activity in the Temple and their activity in daily life. Micah attempted to correct this misconception by arguing that God is not just interested in the physical act of making a sacrifice but is supremely concerned with obedience that extends into daily life (6:6–8).

Micah warned of impending judgment on God's people for their disobedience. At the same time, he proclaimed messages of hope. Judgment would come, but afterwards, God would restore a remnant of the people devoted to Him (4:1–13; 7:14–20). Unlike the unjust kings that the people were accustomed to, God would bring a ruler who would allow the people to live in peace (5:1–5). Ultimately, Judah was destroyed in 586 B.C. by the Babylonians, but a remnant returned. Matthew saw in Micah's hope for a new ruler a description of Christ (Matt. 2:6). See *Ahaz; Assyria; Israel; Hezekiah; Jerusalem; Prophet; Samaria.*

Outline

I. God's Word Witnesses Against All People (1:1–2).
II. God Judges His People for Their Sins (1:3–3:12).
   A. God judges religious infidelity (1:3–16).
   B. God judges economic injustice (2:1–5).
   C. God judges false preaching (2:6–11).
   D. God's judgment looks to the remnant's restoration (2:12–13).
   E. God judges unjust leaders (3:1–4).
   F. God judges those who preach peace and prosperity for sinners (3:5–7).
   G. God judges through His Spirit-filled messenger (3:8).
   H. God judges corrupt, greedy officials (3:9–12).
III. God Promises a Day of International Peace and Worship (4:1—5:15).
   A. God plans for His people to teach His way to the nations (4:1–5).
   B. God plans to redeem and rule His weakened remnant (4:6–11).
   C. God plans to show the world His universal rule (4:12–13).
   D. God plans to raise up a Shepherd from Bethlehem to bring peace and victory to His beleagured flock (5:1–9).
   E. God plans to destroy weapons and idolatry from His people (5:10–15).
IV. God Has a Case Against His People (6:1—7:6).
   A. God has done His part, redeeming His people (6:1–5).
   B. God's expectations are clear: justice, mercy, piety (6:6–8).
   C. God's people have not met His expectations (6:9–12).
   D. God's punishment is sure for a corrupt people (6:13—7:6).
V. God in Righteousness, Love, and Faithfulness Will Forgive and Renew His People (7:7–20).
   A. God's people can trust Him for salvation (7:7).
   B. God's repentant people can expect better days ahead (7:8–14).
   C. God's enemies face shameful judgment (7:15–17).
   D. The incomparable God of patience, mercy, compassion, and faithfulness will forgive and renew His people (7:18–20).
                                        Scott Langston

M

MICAIAH (Mī caï′ ah) Personal name meaning, "Who is like Yahweh?" *1.* Son of Imlah and prophet of Yahweh who predicted the death of Ahab and the scattering of Israel's forces at Ramoth-Gilead (1 Kings 22:7–28). Having witnessed Yahweh's heavenly council, Micaiah was certain Ahab's 400 prophets were possessed by a lying spirit. When accused and imprisoned on a charge of false prophecy, Micaiah replied, "If you return in peace, the LORD has not spoken by me" (22:28 NRSV). *2.* Form of Michaiah modern translations prefer.

MICE See *Animals.*

MICHA (Mī chȧ) KJV alternate form for Micah and Mica. *1.* Descendant of King Saul (2 Sam. 9:12; See *Micah 3.*). *2.* One in a family line of Temple musicians (Neh. 11:17,22). Nehemiah 12:35 uses the longer form Micaiah.

MICHAEL (Mī′ chaėl) Personal name meaning, "Who is like God?" *1.* Father of one of the twelve Israelite spies (Num. 13:13). *2–3.*Two Gadites (1 Chron. 5:13–14). *4.* Ancestor of Asaph (1 Chron. 6:40). *5.* Leader of the tribe of Issachar (1 Chron. 7:3) perhaps identical to the father of Omri (1 Chron. 27:18). *6.* Leader of the tribe of Benjamin (1 Chron. 8:16); *7.* Manassite who defected to David's army (1 Chron. 12:20). *8.* Son of King Jehoshaphat (2 Chron. 21:2). *9.* Ancestor of one of those who returned from Exile with Ezra (Ezra 8:8). *10.* Archangel who served as the guardian of the nation of Israel (Dan. 10:13,21; 12:1). Together with Gabriel, Michael fought for Israel against the prince (angelic patron) of Persia. This angelic Michael figures in much extra-biblical literature in the intertestamental period. In Revelation 12:7 Michael commands the forces of God against the forces of the dragon in a war in heaven. Jude 9 refers to a dispute between the devil and Michael over Moses' body. According to Origin (A.D. 185? to 254?), this account formed part of the extra-biblical work, *The Assumption of Moses.* The incident is not mentioned in the surviving fragments of this work. See *Angel.*

MICHAH (Mī′ chah) Abbreviated form of the personal name Micaiah, KJV used for the leader of a family of Levites in David's time (1 Chron. 23:20; 24:24–25). Modern translations prefer the form Micah.

MICHAIAH (Mĭch âi′ ah) KJV form of Micaiah, a personal name meaning, "Who is like Yah?" *1.* Father of an officer of King Josiah (2 Kings 22:12). *2.* Wife of King Rehoboam and mother of Abijah (2 Chron. 13:1–2). *3.* Participant in Jehoshaphat's reforms (2 Chron. 17:7). *4.* Member of a leading family in Jeremiah's time (Jer. 36:11,13); *5.* Priest participating in Nehemiah's dedication of the walls (Neh. 12:41) and ancestor of a participating priest (Neh. 12:35).

MICHAL (Mĭ′ chàl) Personal name meaning, "who is like El (God)?," a variant form of Micah, "who is like Yah?" and abbreviated form of Michael. King Saul's younger daughter (1 Sam. 14:49) given to David in marriage for the price of one hundred dead Philistines (1 Sam. 18:20–29). (Saul may have thought David would be killed in the attempt). The king continued to set traps for David, but on one occasion Michal helped her husband escape (1 Sam 19:11–17). For revenge, Saul gave her to Phaltiel (1 Sam. 25:44). Following Saul's death at Gilboa, David made a treaty with Abner, Saul's general. One of the points of the pact was that Michal would be returned to David, much to Phaltiel's regret (2 Sam. 3:14–16). David's dancing before the ark of the covenant as he brought the sacred box to Jerusalem enraged Michal, who criticized the king to his face. As punishment Michal was never allowed to bear children (2 Sam. 6:16–23; compare 2 Sam. 21:8).

View of the gorge at Michmash.

MICHMASH (Mĭch′ mash) Place name meaning, "hidden place." City in Benjamin about seven miles northeast of Jerusalem, four and a half miles northeast of Gibeah, rising 1980 feet above sea level overlooking a pass going from the Jordan River to Ephraim. It is four and a half miles southeast of Bethel, which rises 2,890 feet above sea level. It is modern Mukhmas. Michmash served as a staging area, first for Saul (1 Sam. 13:2) and then for the Philistine army as they prepared to fight. It lay on the standard invasion route from the north (Isa. 10:28). The Philistines mustered 30,000 chariots and 6,000 horsemen there (1 Sam. 13:5–6). Before the battle could begin, Jonathan and his armor bearer sneaked into the Philistine camp, killed twenty sentries, and set off great confusion, resulting in the Philistines fighting each other (14:20). Exiles returning from Babylon reinhabited the city (Neh. 11:31; compare 7:31). It served as Jonathan Maccabeus' residence and seat of government (1 Macc. 9:73). See *Jonathan; Intertestamental History.*

MICHMETHAH (Mĭch′ me thah) Place name meaning, "hiding place" or "concealment." Site near Shechem (Josh. 16:6; 17:7). Michmethath has been identifed with khirbet Makhneh el-Foqa about five miles southeast of Shechem and with khirbet Juleijil east of Shechem.

MICHMETHATH (Mĭch me thăth) Spelling following Hebrew of Michmethah in NAS, NIV, NRSV, REB.

MICHRI (Mĭch′ rī) Personal name meaning, "purchase price." Member of the tribe of Benjamin (1 Chron. 9:8).

MICHTAM (Mĭch′ tăm) KJV form of Miktam. Heading for Psalms 16; 56—60. The meaning of the term is disputed. Suggestions include a musical notation or a title for psalms connected with expiation of sin. At Isaiah 38:9, Hezekiah's "writing" (Hebrew *miktab*) should perhaps be Miktam.

MICRI (Mĭc′ rī) NIV spelling of *Michri*.

MIDDAY Noon or thereabouts (Neh. 8:3; Acts 26:13).

MIDDIN (Mĭd′ dĭn) Place name meaning, "judgment." Village in the wilderness district of Judah (Josh. 15:61). The LXX identified Middin with Madon. Recently, khirbet Abu Tabaq in the Achor Valley has been suggested as a possible site.

MIDDLE GATE A city gate of Jerusalem (Jer. 39:3). Archeologists have found evidence of battle (arrowheads, charred wood) located outside the remains of a gate in the middle of the north wall of the preexilic city. It seems probable that the Babylonians attacked the city from the north and that these are, in fact, the remains of the Middle Gate. The gate is possibly identical to the Fish Gate (2 Chron. 33:14; Neh. 3:3; Zeph. 1:10).

MIDDLE WALL Term is found in Ephesians 2:14 and variously translated: "middle wall of partition" (KJV); "dividing wall of hostility" (NRSV; NIV); "barrier of the dividing wall" (NASB); "barrier of enmity which separated them" (REB). Investigation of the term has yielded several possible interpretations: (1) The wall that separated the inner and outer courts of the Temple and prevented Jews and Gentiles from worshiping together. Inscriptions in Greek and Latin warned that Gentiles who disregarded the barrier would suffer the pain of death. (2) The curtain that separated the holy of holies from the rest of the Temple. This curtain was rent at the death of Jesus (see Mark 15:38) and is representative of the separation of all humanity from God. (3) The "fence" consisting of detailed commandments and oral interpretations erected around the law by its interpreters to ensure its faithful observation. In reality, the fenced-in law generated hostility between Jews and Gentiles and further divided them, as well as furthering the enmity between God and humanity. Destruction of the law's mediators opens a new and living way to God through Christ Jesus (Eph. 2:18; 3:12; Heb. 10:20). (4) The cosmic barrier that separates God and persons, persons themselves, and other powers in the universe (Eph. 1:20–21)—angels, dominions, principalities. (5) Echoing Isaiah 59:2, the

term refers to the separation of humanity from God as a result of sin.

No one interpretation is sufficient by itself. The writer of Ephesians stressed that every conceivable barrier that exists between persons and between God and humanity has been destroyed by God's definitive work in Jesus Christ.

See *Ephesians; Gentiles; Law; Salvation; Sin; Temple.*   *William J. Ireland, Jr.*

MIDIAN, MIDIANITES (Mĭd′ ĭ an, Mĭd′ ĭ an ītes). Personal and clan name meaning, "strife"

Midian was the son of Abraham by his concubine Keturah (Gen. 25:2). Abraham sent him and his brothers away to the east, leading to the assocation of the Midianites with the "children of the east" (Judg. 6:3). Midianites took Joseph to Egypt (Gen. 37:28,36). Since the caravan in the passage is described as Ishmaelite, it is possible that these two groups descended from Abraham had become interrelated. The Old Testament mentions the Midianites in widely scattered geographical locations, but their main homeland seems to be east of the Jordan and south of Edom. Later historians locate the land of Midian in northwestern Arabia east of the Gulf of Aqabah. The people of Israel had both good and bad relationships with the Midianites. When Moses fled from Pharaoh, he went east to Midian (Ex. 2:15). Here he met Jethro (also called Reuel), the priest of Midian, and married his daughter. During the wandering in the wilderness, Reuel's father-in-law Hobab served as a guide for the Israelites (Num. 10:29–32). The Midianites are associated with the Moabites in seducing Israel into immorality and pagan worship at Baal-peor (Num. 25:1–18). For this reason God commanded Moses to execute a war of vengeance against them (Num. 31:3; compare Josh. 13:21). In the time of the judges the Midianites along with the Amalekites began to raid Israel using camels to strike swiftly over great distances. Gideon drove them out and killed their leaders (Judg. 6—8). They never again threatened Israel; but Midian did harbor Solomon's enemy Hadad (1 Kings 11:18).

See *Amalekites; Baal-peor; Gideon; Ishmaelites; Jethro; Kenites.*   *Ricky L. Johnson*

MIDNIGHT The middle of the night (Judg. 16:3; Ps. 119:62; Acts 16:25).

MIDRASH A Jewish term from the Hebrew verb *darash* meaning, "to search" and, therefore, to make exposition. Title of a body of Jewish literature that gathers together the Jewish scholars' exegesis, exposition, and homiletical interpretations of Scripture in the centuries just before and after Jesus.

Meaning to discover or develop a thought not apparent on the surface, a midrash denotes a didactic (teaching) or homiletic (preaching) exposition or an edifying religious story such as that of Tobit. Midrash also includes a religious interpretation of history, as the prophet Iddo's commentary on the acts, ways, and sayings of King Abijam (2 Chron. 13:22) and the Commentary on the Book of the Kings, in which were set forth the burdens laid upon King Joash and his rebuilding of the Temple (2 Chron. 24:27). This Jewish method of searching the Scriptures sought to discover the deeper meaning of the most minute details contained in the sacred text. The main characteristics of midrash are: (1) its starting point is an actual text or texts (often two quite different passages are combined) from the Bible itself; (2) is homiletic, essentially designed to edify and instruct; (3) it is based on a close and detailed scrutiny of the actual text, in which it seeks to establish the underlying reasons for each word, phrase, or group of words (compare rabbinical method of systematically applying the question "why"); (4) it is concerned to apply the message thus established to the present age. Midrash is divided into *halacha* (oral law), midrashic investigation of the lgeal parts of the Old Testament with the aim of establishing rules of conduct, and *haggadah,* a similar investigation of the nonlegal parts with purpose of edifying or instructing.

Ezra used Midrash in the public reading of the law (Neh. 8). Midrash became the basic work leading to the production of the *Targumin* (Aramaic paraphrases of Scripture) and of the mainline expression of Judaism (*Mishnah, Talmud*). See *Targum; Mishnah; Talmud.* Ezra also seems to have practiced the use of *midrash,* by having as his objective in life to study and apply the Torah, as well as to instruct the nation in the ordinances and statutes of the Law (Ezra 7:10). Many Bible students believe numerous examples of midrash in most, if not all, of its various forms appear in the New Testament. Thus, Matthew 2:1–12 (the first part of the infancy narrative) is held to be a midrash on Numbers 24:17. Matthew 27:3–10 (the 30 pieces of silver) is regarded as a midrash on Zechariah 11:12–13 and Jeremiah 32:6–15. Midrashic elements are also present in Paul (Gal. 3:4; Rom. 4:9–11; 2 Cor. 3) and other areas of the New Testament. It is important, therefore, for the interpretation of the New Testament to understand the characteristic methods and approach of midrash. The term *midrash* is also used of the collections of midrashic expositions; or of a manner of religious teaching that follows the midrashic method.

An important use of the Midrash is that it gives the interpreter of Scripture a greater insight into interpretation from a people closer to the original appearance of the Old Testament books, as well as an understanding of the text across history by Jewish people. Stories contained in a midrash may be totally historically accurate or simply a piece of fiction based on history, or even a work of literary fiction without any basis in history.

Midrashic material was preserved orally from its inception for a considerable period. Only after A.D. 100 were the halakic midrashim written down. The most important of these were the *Mekilta* (treatise) to Exodus and the *Sifra* (book) on Leviticus, Numbers, and Deuteronomy. The earliest written *haggadah* was the midrash on Genesis, going back to about A.D. 200 or later. This was followed by the midrashim on the rest of the Pentateuch and the Five Scrolls (Megilloth). These commentaries became known as the Midrash *Rabbah,* and with later compositions were much favored by the rabbis for homiletical purposes.

Stephenson Humphries-Brooks

MIDWIFE Woman who assists in the delivery of a child (Ex. 1:15–21). The duties of the midwife likely included cutting the umbilical cord, washing and salting the babe, and wrapping the child in cloths (Ezek. 16:4). The civil disobedience of the Hebrew midwives Siphrah and Puah confounded Pharaoh's plan to exterminate male Hebrews for a time (Ex. 1:15–21). Their faithfulness was rewarded with families of their own (Ex. 1:21), suggesting that childless women frequently served as midwives. The women of Ruth 4:14–17 and 1 Samuel 4:20 were likely serving as midwives.

MIGDAL EDER NIV transliteration of tower of Edar (Gen. 35:21). See *Edar.*

MIGDAL-EL (Mĭg' dăl-ĕl) Place name meaning, "fortress of God." Fortified town in Naphtali (Josh. 19:38). Migdal-el was located in northern Galilee in the vicinity of Iron (Yiron).

MIGDAL-GAD (Mĭg' dăl-găd) Place name meaning, "Tower of Gad." Village near Lachish in the Shephelah district of Judah (Josh. 15:37). The site is perhaps that of khirbet el-Mejdeleh five miles south of Beit Jibrin.

MIGDOL (Mĭg' dŏl) Transliteration of Hebrew word meaning, "tower, watchtower, fortress." A town or a border fortress located in the northeast corner of Egypt. The site is mentioned in reference to two events in biblical history—the Exodus and the Exile. One of the sites on or near the route of the Exodus, Migdol was located near the sites of Pi-hahiroth and Baal-Zephon, all of which were near the sea (Ex. 14:2). Jewish refugees fled to Migdol during the Exile (Jer. 44:1). The coming doom of Egypt at the hand of Nebuchadnezzar was to be proclaimed there (Jer. 46:13–14). Ezekiel prophesied that the land of Egypt would be laid waste, "from Migdol to Aswan" (Ezek. 29:10; 30:6 NIV), that is from the northern extremity of the land, Migdol, to the southern extremity of the land, Aswan.

Since *migdol* could be used as a proper name,

Migdol, or as a common noun, "tower," two questions remain unresolved. What is the exact location of the site of Migdol? Do all of the references to Migdol refer to the same site, or was there more than one site in Egypt named Migdol? More than one site may have borne the name Migdol, though the evidence we have at hand is inconclusive. The Amarna Letters from Egypt refer to an Egyptian city named Maagdali, but information about its location is not given. See *Amarna tell el.* For instance a papyrus manuscript mentions the Migdol of Pharoah Seti I. This Migdol was located near Tjeku, the location of which is still debated. Some prefer to identify Tjeku with Succoth, modern-day tell el-Maskhutah, while others identify it with tell el-Her located further north near Pelusium. For this reason we may assume with some certainty that there were at least two sites named Migdol: the Migdol referred to by Jeremiah and Ezekiel located near Pelusium, and the Migdol on the route of the Exodus located near Succoth. Both may have been part of a line of border fortresses or migdols designed to provide protection for Egypt against invasion from the Sinai. See *Watchtower, Egypt.*   *LaMoine DeVries*

MIGHTY MEN Applied to the descendants of the Nephalim, mighty men likely indicates men of great size (Gen. 6:4; perhaps Josh. 10:2). Elsewhere mighty men refers to valiant warriors, especially to the elite groups of three and thirty who served David (2 Sam. 17:8,10; 23:8–39; 1 Kings 1:10,38). Many of David's elite forces were mercenaries.

MIGRON (Mĭḡ′ rŏn) Place name meaning, "precipice." Town (or towns) in Benjamin (1 Sam. 14:2; Isa. 10:28). The town of 1 Samuel is generally located near Gibeah south of Michmash. The town of Isaiah 10 is generally located between Aiath (Ai) and Michmash, that is, to the north of Michmash. Suggested sites include Makrun, tell Miryam, and tell el 'Askar.

MIJAMIN (Mĭj′ à mĭn) Contracted form of the personal name Miniamin, meaning, "lucky" (literally, "from the right hand"). The name is attested in Neo-Babylonian and Persian business documents. *1.* Priest in David's time (1 Chron. 24:9). *2.* Priest who returned from Exile with Zerubbabel (Neh. 12:5). *3.* Priest witnessing Ezra's covenant renewal (Neh. 10:7). *4.* Layman with a foreign wife (Ezra 10:25). The KJV form of *2.* and *4.* is Miamin.

MIKLOTH (Mĭk′ lŏth) Personal name meaning, "sticks." *1.* Descendant of Jeiel and resident of Gibeon (1 Chron. 8:32; 9:37–38). *2.* Officer in David's militia (1 Chron. 27:4). REB, RSV followed the early Greek translation in omitting the name.

MIKNEIAH (Mĭk neî′ ah) Personal name meaning, "Yahweh acquires" or "Yahweh creates." Levitic musician in David's time (1 Chron. 15:18,21).

MIKTAM (Mĭk′ tăm) See *Michtam.*

MILALAI (Mĭl′ à laî) Personal name meaning, "eloquent." Musician participating in Nehemiah's dedication of the wall (Neh. 12:36). The earliest Greek translation lacks the name, prompting some to suggest a scribal corruption due to repeating the following name (Gilalai). The shorter Greek text may, however, result from omission due to the scribe skipping to a word with a similar ending.

MILCAH (Mŭl′ cah) Personal name meaning, "queen." Abraham's niece and the wife of Nahor, the patriarch's brother. She bore eight sons, one of whom was Bethuel, Rebekah's father (Gen. 11:29; 24:15). *2.* One of five daughters of Zelophehad (Num. 26:33), left without support after the death of their father. They pled their case before Moses for an inheritance as a son would receive. In a landmark ruling for Israel, God commanded Moses to give each of the daughters an inheritance from their father's estate (Num. 27:1–8; 36:11; Josh. 17:3).

MILCOM (Mĭl′ cŏm) Name of deity meaning, "king" or "their king." Apparently, a form created by Hebrew scribes to slander and avoid pronouncing the name of the national god of Ammon (1 Kings 11:5,7), who may have been identified with Chemosh, the god of Moab. See *Chemosh.* From the inscription of Mesha there appears to have been a god, Athar, whose local titles were Chemosh and Milcom. See *Moab.* This cult may have been practiced in Jerusalem before the Israelite conquest. "King" may have been the god's name or his title as King of the gods. David defeated Ammon and confiscated the crown (2 Sa. 12:30) of their king (KJV, NAS, NIV) or of the statue of the god Milcom (NRSV, REB; compare TEV). Solomon built sanctuaries to Milcom on the Mount of Olives at the request of his foreign wives, reviving the ancient cult (1 Kings 11:5,33). The sites of Solomon's sanctuaries were destroyed and defiled during Josiah's reforms in 621 B.C. (2 Kings 23:13). Jeremiah described past accomplishments attributed to Milcom, but in a play on Judges 11:24, he announced destruction and captivity for Milcom (Jer. 49:1,3 NRSV, NAS, REB; compare NIV, TEV). Worshiping Milcom was turning one's back on Yahweh (Zeph. 1:5–6). See *Molech.*

MILDEW Fungus causing a whitish growth on plants. The Hebrew term rendered mildew means, "paleness." The term may refer to the yellowing of leaves as a result of drought rather than to a fungus (Deut. 28:22–24; 1 Kings 8:37; 2 Chron. 6:28; Amos 4:9; Hag. 4:9). Mildew is one of the agricultural plagues God sent to encourage repentance.

MILE The Roman mile of Matthew 5:41 is about 4,848 feet (about 432 feet shorter than the American mile).

M

A Roman milestone.

A type of milemarker found along a Roman road.

to Miletus. The people probably were open to the gospel he preached. He chose to meet with the elders of the church at Ephesus in Miletus (Acts 20:15–17). A second visit may have been made by the apostle a few years later (2 Tim. 4:20). The harbor began to silt up by 100 A.D., bringing a gradual halt to the city's usefulness and prominence. Today the ruins are over five miles inland. See *Asia Minor; Ephesus.*   *Mike Mitchell*

MILETUM (Mī lē′ tŭm) KJV spelling of Miletus in 2 Timothy 4:20.

MILETUS (Mī lē′ tŭs) An ancient city on the west coast of Asia Minor. Miletus had four natural harbors and was a major port for the Minoan and Mycenean cultures. After 700 B.C. the Ionians developed it into an even greater center of commerce. It served as the port for Ephesus.

It featured a major school of philosophy; many artisans practiced there; and it was among the first cities to mint coins. This culture flourished until 494 B.C. when the Persians sacked the city in answer to a revolt by the Ionians. Alexander captured Miletus on his way eastward in 334 B.C., and the city saw a revival of the arts under his Hellenistic regime. In particular the architectural beauty of the city increased. Rome's influence increased the pace of economic development.

Paul encountered a robust city when he sailed

The theater of Miletus.

MILK Nourishing liquid and its by-products, the staple of the Hebrew diet. The Old Testament uses the term variously of sweet milk, soured milk, cheese, butter, and, symbolically, of blessing

A view of the walkway beneath the audience area of the theater at Miletus.

Reconstruction of the Asian city of Miletus as it appeared in the first century A.D.

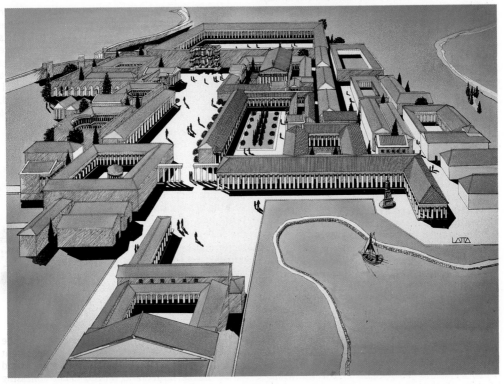

M

and abundance. The NT only has a symbolic use of what is first and basic in the Christian life. The word is used forty-three times in the OT with twenty being symbolic and only five times in the NT. Ben Sira mentions milk before wine and oil as among "the principal things for the whole use of man's life" (Ecclesiasticus 39:26). Most often milk came from sheep and goats (Prov. 27:27; Deut. 32:14); cow's milk was also known (Isa. 7:21–22), as was milk from humans (Isa. 28:9). Butter and cheese were known among the ancients (1 Sam. 17:18) as well as curdled, sour milk which still forms, after bread, the chief food of the poorer classes in Arabia and Syria. This soured milk was carried by travelers who mixed it with meat, dried it, and then dissolved it in water to make a refreshing drink such as that set by Abraham before the messengers (Gen. 18:8). After setting awhile, the drink would carry an intoxicating effect leading some to believe that the fermented variety is the drink that Jael gave to Sisera (Judg. 4:19).

The Old Testament's most extensive use of milk is in conjunction with honey to symbolize abundance and blessing (Ex. 3:17; 13:5; 33:3; Lev. 20:24, Num. 13:27; Deut. 6:3; Josh. 5:6). Milk is also used to symbolize whiteness (Lam. 4:7) and in Song of Songs as a symbol of marital bliss (5:1).

Milk as a symbol prevails in the NT where the term is used only five times (1 Cor. 3:2; 9:7; Heb. 5:12,13; 1 Pet. 2:2). In each instance it speaks concerning what is basic to the Christian life, but not all that is needed. The ancient bedouins could live on milk for days but eventually had to have meat; so must the Christian.

One of the more perplexing sayings of Scripture is the repeated rule (Ex. 23:19; 34:26; Deut. 14:21) not to boil a kid in its mother's milk. The rabbis interpreted this command to mean that milk and meat should neither be cooked or eaten together. Certain scholars have seen in the command a prohibition relating to Caananite sacrificial customs though recent archaeological investigations lend little support to this view. It remains one of the mysteries of scripture. *G. Al Wright, Jr.*

MILL Two circular stones used to grind grain. Usually, it was worked by two women facing each other. One woman fed the grain at the center, and the other guided the products into little piles. The grain to be ground is fed into the central hole in the upper stone and gradually works down between the stones. As the grain is reduced to flour, it flies out from between the stones onto a cloth or skin placed underneath the mill. To make fine flour, it is reground and sifted. The stone was made of basalt and was about a foot and a half in diameter and two to four inches thick.

It was forbidden to take millstones as a pledge because they were so important to sustaining life (Deut. 24:6). The manna which fell in the wilder-

Rotary mills at Capernaum.

ness was tough enough so that people ground it in mills before cooking it (Num. 11:7–8).

In the New Testament, our Lord prophesied that at His coming, "two women shall be grinding at the mill, one shall be taken and one other is left" (Matt. 24:41). In Revelation 18:21, the millstone was cast into the sea as a symbol of absolute destruction. See *Manna*. *Gary Bonner*

MILLENNIUM (Mĭ lĕn' nī ŭm) A term not found in Scripture but taken from Latin to express the "thousand years" mentioned six times in Revelation 20:1–7. The meaning of the thousand years and the relation of Christ's future coming to them have given rise to various millennial views.

Evangelical Christians hold three main views: amillennialism, dispensational premillennialism, and historic premillennialism. A popular view of yesteryear was postmillennialism, but it is no longer widely held, though a new form of it combined with reconstructionist theology has appeared.

The use of the prefixes *a-, pre-,* and *post-* with the term *millennial* could be misleading. Much more is involved in these viewpoints than merely positioning the return of Christ in relation to a millennium. In spite of the danger of oversimplification these terms are so widely used that they furnish the working labels for a study of end time prophecy. The names given the views suggest the general drift of each one.

Postmillennialism The growth of the church and the power of the gospel will cause the world to get better and better until the present order blends into the millennium during which the righteous will be in charge on earth. Evil will be practically nonexistent. Christ will return at the end of the millennium at a time when Satan reasserts his power. The final victory of Christ will occur at that time with final judgment and the eternal order following.

Amillennialism The term suggests "no thousand years." The idea is no literal thousand year period, but a symbolic expression related to the spiritual blessedness of present Christian experience in which Satan is a defeated enemy and believers reign in life by Christ Jesus. Therefore, this view does not look for a literal, future thousand year reign of Christ on the earth during which Satan is bound.

Premillennialism The idea is that of "before the millennium or thousand years." Such a view positions the return of Christ prior to a millennial period. There are two broad types of premillennialism.

1. Dispensational premillennialism takes the thousand years to be literal both as to fact and number. The millennium is seen to follow a seven-year tribulation period. At the beginning of the tribulation, the church will be taken out of the world. This rapture of the church is seen as the first phase of the second coming of Christ. During the millennium, Christ will reign on the earth with His saints while Satan is bound in the bottomless pit. The Jews as a nation are seen to have a major place in the events of the millennial period. This view of future events also incorporates many other aspects of biblical prophecy, such as a second phase of Christ's return following the millennium.

2. Historic premillennialism holds to a literal, future reign of Christ on earth, during which Satan is bound a thousand years and the saints reign with Christ. Many who hold this view, however, allow for symbolism in the use of the number *1,000*. While the reign of Christ will be literal, the length of the reign may or may not be exactly 1,000 years. This type of premillennialism does not divide the second coming into two phases. There is a single return between the tribulation and millennium.

See *Eschatology; Rapture; Future Hope; Seventy Weeks; Tribulation.*   *Jerry W. Batson*

MILLET (*Panicum miliacum* L.) The smallest cereal grain. Millet makes a poor quality bread and is normally mixed with other grains (Ezek. 4:9). Some identify the Hebrew term with sorghum (*Sorghum vulgare* Pers.).

MILLO (Mĭ lō) Hebrew word meaning, "filling" which describes a stone terrace system employed in ancient construction. *1.* The story of Abimelech in the Book of Judges mentions Beth Millo—"The House of the Filling." Probably a suburb of Shechem, the Beth Millo most likely was a Canaanite sanctuary. The shrine was built upon an artificial platform or fill and thus received the name "House of the Filling."

2. The extension of Jerusalem beyond the original Jebusite city David captured stretched northward to include the Hill of Moriah, the site of the future Temple. A large open space between the hill and the main city below left ample room for added construction. To provide a level platform upon which to build, a series of retaining walls

were raised along the slope of the hill. Loads of earth and rock were dumped behind the walls to form large terraces to support the royal halls and residences planned by Solomon. The area came to be called the Ophel, meaning "high" or "lofty." It is probable that additional supporting terraces were built on the southern slopes in the city proper to extend the area available for general construction. Joash's murder by his own men near the Beth Millo "on the road to Silla" may refer to terraces in this portion of the city.

MINA (Mî′ na) See *Weights and Measures.*

A Babylonian weight equaling one-third of a mina.

MIND The center of the intellectual activity, an English term translating several different Hebrew and Greek terms. The biblical languages possess no one word parallel to the English, *mind.* KJV translates at least six different Hebrew terms, *mind.* The primary word is *leb,* which means "heart." For example, Moses said, "The Lord hath sent me to do all these works; for I have not done them of mine own mind" (Num. 16:28; compare 1 Sam. 9:20; Neh. 4:6). In addition, the word *nephesh* (soul) is translated "mind" in Deuteronomy 18:6 when it refers to the desire of a man's mind (soul) and in Genesis 23:8 where it refers to mind in the sense of a decision or judgment. The word *ruach* (spirit) is rendered "mind" in Genesis 26:35. It speaks of the "grief of mind" (spirit) which Isaac and Rebekah experienced because Esau married heathen wives. Also used are the words *lebab* (heart) in Ezekiel 38:10; *yetser* (imagination) in Isaiah 26:3; and *peh* (mouth, speech) in Leviticus 24:12.

The New Testament has a similar situation because of the large number of terms which are used to describe mankind's "faculty of cognition." As in the Old Testament the term *heart* (*kardia*) is sometimes used to represent the concept *mind.*

Matthew 13:15 speaks of understanding with the "heart." Other words include *ennoia,* which means "mind" in the sense of "intent" "arm yourselves likewise with the same mind" (1 Pet. 4:1). *Gñomē* refers to mind in the sense of "purpose" (Rev. 17:13) or "opinion" (Philem. 14). *Noēma* is also used to denote the mind, especially the "thought process." Paul said that Israel's "minds were blinded" so that they could not understand the Old Testament (2 Cor. 3:14; see also 2 Cor. 4:4; 11:3). The word *phronēma* refers to what one has in the mind, the "thought": "To be carnally minded is death" (Rom. 8:6).

The more common terms for mind, however, are *nous* and *dianoia. Dianoia* occurs twelve times in the New Testament. It refers to "thinking through" or "thinking over" of something or to the "understanding" or "sentiment" which results from that process of reflection. Paul said that in times past we all lived according to the flesh, "fulfilling the desires of the flesh and of the mind" (those things we had already thought over, Eph. 2:3). *Nous* is the most prominent term for mind; it occurs twenty-four times. *Nous* represents the "seat of understanding," the place of "knowing and reasoning." It also includes feeling and deciding. Hence it sometimes includes the counsels and purposes of the mind. An example is Paul's statement: "Let every man be fully persuaded in his own mind" (Rom. 14:5). The meaning of purpose is found in Romans 11:34, which says, "Who hath known the mind of the Lord? or who hath been his counselor?"

Mind is sometimes associated with the human soul. Three times in the King James Version the word *psuchē* (soul or life) is rendered by the word *mind.* Philippians 1:27 says believers are to be of "one mind (soul)." Hebrews 12:3 urges believers not to "faint in your minds (souls)." (See Acts 14:2 also.) These passages illustrate the fact that the mind is considered to be the center of the person. However, in Scripture the heart is more often considered to be the center of the human personality. In the Old Testament, especially, this is true because of the lack of an exact equivalent for *mind.* The word *heart* fills this void, and the New Testament follows the practice of the Old Testament very closely. Why then can the mind as well as the heart be spoken of as the center of a person? Because in Hebrew thought a person is looked at as a single entity with no attempt to compartmentalize the person into separate parts which act more or less independently of one another. Therefore, the heart, mind, and soul, while in some ways different, are seen as one.

The mind is portrayed oftentimes, especially in the New Testament, as the center of a person's ethical nature. The mind can be evil. It is described as "reprobate" (Rom. 1:28), "fleshly" (Col. 2:18), vain (Eph. 4:17), corrupt (1 Tim. 6:5; 2 Tim. 3:8), and defiled (Titus 1:15). On the other hand, three Gospels command us to love God with "all" our mind (Matt. 22:37; Mark 12:30; Luke 10:27). This is possible because the mind can be revived and empowered by the Holy Spirit (Rom. 12:2) and because God's laws under the new covenant are put into our minds (Heb. 8:10; 10:16). See *Heart; Soul; Anthropology; Humanity.*

Gerald Cowen

MINERALS AND METALS Inorganic elements or compounds found naturally in nature. A number of minerals and metals are mentioned in the biblical record.

Precious Stones Stones are desirable because of rarity, hardness, and beauty, the latter expressed in terms of color, transparency, luster, and brilliance. The Bible has three main lists of precious stones: the twelve stones of Aaron's breastplate (Ex. 28:17–20; 39:10–13), the treasures of the king of Tyre (Ezek. 28:13), and the stones on the wall foundation of the New Jerusalem (Rev. 21:18–21). Other lists are found in Job 28:15–19; Isa. 54:11–12; and Ezek. 27:16. The precise identification of some of the terms is unclear, unfortunately, as can be seen by comparing these lists in various translations.

1. Adamant Appears in KJV, RSV, REB of Ezekiel 3:9 and Zechariah 7:12. The Hebrew word is sometimes translated "diamond" (Jer. 17:1 KJV, NRSV, REB, NAS). The stone was "harder than flint" (Ezek. 3:9) and may be *emery* (Ezek. 3:9 NAS) or an imaginary stone of impenetrable hardness. It is perhaps best translated "the hardest stone" (Ezek. 3:9 NIV, NRSV).

2. Agate A multicolored and banded form of chalcedony. It served on Aaron's breastplate (Ex. 28:19) and by some translations as the third stone on the New Jerusalem foundation (Rev. 21:19 NRSV).

3. Amethyst (Ex. 28:19; 39:12; Rev. 21:20) Identical with modern amethyst, a blue-violet form of quartz.

4. Beryl (beryllium aluminum silicate) Most translations show beryl to be the first stone in the fourth row of the breastplate (Ex. 28:20; 39:13;

Mineral deposits from the hot mineral springs at Hierapolis.

REB, "topaz"; NIV, "chrysolite"). The word also occurs in the list of the king of Tyre's jewels (Ezek. 28:13; RSV, NIV, "chrysolite"; NRSV, "beryl"; REB, "topaz"). The RSV translates another and the NIV a third word in the list as beryl. More certainty surrounds the use of beryl in Revelation 21:20.

5. *Carbuncle* In KJV, RSV the third stone of Aaron's breastplate (Ex. 28:17; 39:10; REB, "green feldspar;" NAS, NRSV "emerald;" TEV, "garnet"; NIV, "beryl") and material for the gates of the restored Jerusalem (Isa. 54:12; REB, "garnet"; NIV, "sparkling jewels"). RSV also appears to translate a third word as carbuncle in Ezekiel 28:13 by reversing the KJV order of emerald and carbuncle. NRSV omits carbuncle.

6. *Carnelian* (KJV and sometimes RSV, NASB, "*sardius*") A clear to brownish red variety of chalcedony. NRSV reading for one of the stones of the king of Tyre (Ezek. 28:13; NAS, TEV, NIV, "ruby"; REB, "sardin") and the sixth stone on the foundation of the new Jerusalem wall (Rev. 21:20; compare 4:3).

7. *Chalcedony* An alternate translation for agate as the third stone decorating the New Jerusalem foundation (Rev. 21:19 KJV, NAS, REB, NIV). This noncrystalline form of quartz, or silicone dioxide, has many varieties including agate, carnelian, chrysoprase, flint, jasper, and onyx.

8. *Chrysolite* (Rev. 21:20) Represents various yellowish minerals. It replaces the KJV rendering *beryl* frequently in the RSV (Ezek. 1:16; 10:9; 28:13) and throughout the NIV but not in NRSV. REB reads, "topaz."

9. *Chrysoprase* or *Chrysoprasus* (KJV) An apple-green variety of chalcedony, the tenth stone of the foundation for the New Jerusalem's wall (Rev. 21:20).

10. *Coral* (Job 28:18; Ezek. 27:16) Calcium carbonate formed by the action of marine animals. NRSV, REB, NAS translated a second word as coral (Lam. 4:7 KJV, NIV, "rubies").

11. *Crystal* Refers to quartz, the two Hebrew words so translated being related to "ice." In Job 28:18, KJV has "pearls"; the NIV, "jasper"; but NRSV, NAS, read, "crystal," while REB has "alabaster." The glassy sea (Rev. 4:6) and river of life (Rev. 22:1) are compared to crystal.

12. *Diamond* The third stone of the second row of the high priest's breastplate (Ex. 28:18; 39:11; REB, "jade"; NIV, "emerald") and one of the jewels of the king of Tyre (Ezek. 28:13; NRSV, REB, "jasper"; NIV, "emerald"). It is not clear, however, if diamonds were known in the Ancient Near East, and the translation is uncertain.

13. *Emerald* A bright green variety of beryl, readily available to the Israelites. It is the usual translation of the fourth stone of the high priest's breastplate and one of the stones of the king of Tyre (Ex. 28:18; 39:11; Ezek. 28:13; REB, "purple garnet"; NAS, NIV, NRSV, "turquoise"), with

NRSV translating another word as "emerald." The rainbow around the throne is compared to an emerald (Rev. 4:3), which also served as the fourth stone in the foundations of the New Jerusalem wall (Rev. 21:19).

14. *Jacinth* A transparent red to brown form of zirconium silicate. It appears in Aaron's breastplate (Ex. 28:19; 39:11; KJV, "ligure"; REB, TEV, "turquoise") and the New Jerusalem wall foundation (Rev. 21:20).

15. *Jasper* (Ex. 28:20; 39:13; Rev. 21:11,18–19) A red, yellow, brown, or green opaque variety of chalcedony. In the RSV for Ezekiel 28:13, *jasper* translates the word elsewhere rendered "diamond" (REB, "jade"), but NRSV reads moonstone with the sixth stone jasper as in other translations.

16. *Lapis Lazuli* Not a mineral, but a combination of minerals which yields an azure to green-blue stone popular in Egypt for jewelry. It is an alternate translation for sapphire (NAS in Ezek. 28:13; NIV marginal notes).

17. *Onyx* A flat-banded variety of chalcedony; *sardonyx* includes layers of carnelian. Onyx was used on the ephod (Ex. 25:7; 28:9; 35:27; 39:6) and in the high priest's breatplate (Ex. 28:20; 39:13). It was provided for the settings of the Temple (1 Chron. 29:2) and was one of the precious stones of the king of Tyre (Ezek. 28:13).

18. *Pearl* (Job 28:18 NAS, NRSV; KJV, NIV, "rubies"; REB, "red coral") Formed around foreign matter in some shellfish. In the New Testament, pearl serves as a simile for the kingdom of God (Matt. 13:46), a metaphor for truth (Matt. 7:6), and a symbol of immodesty (1 Tim. 2:9; Rev. 17:4; 18:16). Pearl is also material for the gates of the New Jerusalem (Rev. 21:21).

19. *Ruby* A red variety of corundum, or aluminum oxide. The first stone of Aaron's breastplate is sometimes translated "ruby" (Ex. 28:17; 39:10 NAS, NIV; KJV, RSV, REB "sardius"; NRSV "carnelian"). It also appears as a stone of the king of Tyre (Ezek. 28:13 NAS, NIV; REB, KJV, "sardius"; NRSV, "carnelian").

20. *Sapphire* (Ex. 24:10; 28:18; 39:11; Job 28:6,16; Isa. 54:11; Lam. 4:7; Ezek. 1:26; 10:1; 28:13; Rev. 21:19) The Hebrew *sappir* is a blue variety of corundum. Despite the name, it is possible that *sappir* refers to lapis lazuli (NIV marginal notes) rather than true sapphire.

21. *Topaz* Second stone of Aaron's breastplate (Ex. 28:17; 39:10); also mentioned in the wisdom list (Job 28:19) and the list of the king of Tyre's precious stones (Ezek. 28:13). True topaz is an aluminum floro silicate and quite hard, but the Old Testament topaz may refer to peridot, a magnesium olivine. The ninth decorative stone of the New Jerusalem wall foundation is topaz (Rev. 21:20). See *Beryl, Chrysolite* above.

22. *Turquoise* Sky-blue to bluish-green base phosphate of copper and aluminum was mined in the Sinai by the Egyptians and was a highly valued

stone in antiquity. Turquoise is sometimes substituted for emerald (Ex. 28:18 NAS, NIV); or jacinth (Ex. 28:19; 39:11 REB, TEV).

Common Minerals *1. Alabaster* In modern terms a fine grained gypsum, but Egyptian alabaster was crystalline calcium carbonate with a similar appearance. Alabaster may be mentioned once in the Song of Solomon (5:15 NRSV, NAS; "marble" in KJV, REB, NIV). In the New Testament (Matt. 26:7; Mark 14:3; Luke 7:37), it refers to containers for precious ointment.

2. Brimstone Refers to *sulfur* (NRSV, NIV). Burning sulfur deposits created extreme heat, molten flows, and noxious fumes, providing a graphic picture of the destruction and suffering of divine judgment (Deut. 29:23; Job 18:15; Ps. 11:6; Isa. 30:33; Ezek. 38:22; Luke 17:29).

3. Salt Sodium chloride is an abundant mineral, used as a seasoning for food (Job 6:6) and offerings (Lev. 2:13; Ezek. 43:24). As a preservative, salt was symbolic of covenants (Num. 18:19; 2 Chron. 13:5). Both meanings are present in Jesus' comparison of the disciples to salt (Matt. 5:13). Salt was also a symbol of desolation and barrenness, perhaps because of the barrenness of the Dead Sea, the biblical Salt Sea. The "saltpits" of Zephaniah 2:9 were probably located just south of the Dead Sea. Sodium chloride could leech out of the generally impure salt from this area, leaving a tasteless substance (Luke 14:34–35).

4. Soda (Prov. 25:20 NAS, NIV; Jer. 2:22 REB, NIV), or *nitre* (KJV), is probably sodium or potassium carbonate. Other translations prefer lye (Jer. 2:22 NRSV, NAS). In Proverbs 25:20 the Hebrew text refers to vinegar or lye or soda, but some modern translations follow the earliest Greek translation in reading "vinegar on a wound" (NRSV, REB; "salt in a wound," TEV).

Metals Many metals occur naturally in compound with other elements as an ore which must be smelted to obtain a usable product. Biblical lists of metals (Num. 31:22; Ezek. 22:18,20) mention gold, silver, bronze, iron, tin, and lead.

1. Brass A relatively modern alloy of copper and tin. Brass in the KJV should be rendered copper or bronze. RSV substitutes bronze, retaining brass only in a few places (Lev. 26:19, Deut. 28:23; Isa. 48:4; NRSV using brass only in Isa. 48:4). NIV does not use brass.

2. Bronze The usual translation of the Hebrew word which can indicate either copper or bronze. An alloy of copper and tin, and stronger than both, bronze was the most common metal used for utensils in the Ancient Near East. The Bible mentions armor (1 Sam. 17:5–6), shackles (2 Kings 25:7), cymbals (1 Chron. 15:19), gates (Ps. 107:16; Isa. 45:2), and idols (Rev. 9:20), as well as other bronze objects.

3. Copper Usually alloyed with tin to make bronze which possessed greater strength. The KJV uses copper only in Ezra 8:27 (NRSV, NIV

"bronze"). See *Ezion Geber.*

4. Gold Valued and used because of its rarity, beauty, and workability. It can be melted without harm and is extremely malleable. Thus it can be used for cast objects, inlays, or overlays. A number of Israel's worship objects were solid gold or gilded (Ex. 37). Gold occurs in the Bible more frequently than any other metal, being used for jewelry (Ex. 12:35; 1 Tim. 2:9), idols, scepters, worship utensils, and money (Matt. 10:9; Acts 3:6). The New Jerusalem is described as made of gold (Rev. 21:18,21).

5. Iron A more difficult metal to smelt than copper, it did not come into widespread use until about the time of Israel's conquest of Canaan. Prior to this time, metal weapons and agricultural tools were of bronze. For some time thereafter iron technology was not widespread. The Canaanites' "chariots of iron" (Josh. 17:16,18; Judg. 1:19; 4:3) represent a technological advantage over Israel, while the Philistines may have enjoyed an iron-working monopoly (1 Sam. 17:7; 13:19–21). See *Iron.* Iron was more widespread by the time of David (2 Sam. 12:31; 1 Chron. 20:3; 22:14), though it remained valuable (2 Kings 6:5–6). It was used where strength was essential and became a symbol of hardness and strength (Deut. 28:48; Ps. 2:9; Isa. 48:4; Jer. 17:1; Rev. 2:27).

6. Lead A gray metal of extremely high density (Ex. 15:10) used for weights, heavy covers (Zec. 5:7–8), and plumblines (compare Amos 7:7–8). Lead is quite pliable and useful for inlays such as lettering in rock (Job 19:24). It was also used in the refining of silver (Jer. 6:27–30).

7. Silver Used in the Near East from quite early times; though not occurring often in a natural state, silver is easily extracted from its ores. Silver was originally more valuable than gold, usually occurring before it in lists. It became a measure of wealth (Gen. 13:2; 24:35; Zeph. 1:18; Hag. 2:8). By Solomon's day it was common in Israel (1 Kings 10:27) and was the standard monetary unit, being weighed in shekels, talents, and minas (Gen. 23:15–16; 37:28; Ex. 21:32; Neh. 7:72; Isa. 7:23). See *Weights and Measures.* Silver was used for objects in Israel's worship (Ex. 26:19; 36:24; Ezra 8:26,28), idols (Ex. 20:23; Judg. 17:4; Ps. 115:4; Isa. 40:19), and jewelry (Gen. 24:53; Song of Sol. 1:11).

8. Tin (Num. 31:22; Ezek. 22:18,20) Sometimes confused with lead; articles of pure tin were rare. It was principally used in making bronze, an alloy of tin and copper. See *Mines and Mining.*

Daniel C. Browning, Jr.

MINES AND MINING The extraction of minerals from the earth.

The Earliest Mines Early mining efforts in the Fertile Crescent sought to provide people with the stones necessary to make weapons and tools.

While the earliest walled settlements in the region date back to before 6000 B.C., people had been mining stones for tools long before that. Before 10,000 B.C. people were using tools and weapons made of flint found on the surface of the ground. From exposed beds of obsidian (a black volcanic stone) and flint (chert) early people no doubt removed the stone necessary to produce the axes, knives, and scrapers used to kill and clean food. With the domestication of small animals, wheat, and barley, people found greater uses for stone tools. Sickle blades with serrated edges were chipped from flint, several pieces being fitted together in a bone or wood handle. Larger stone tools, such as the hand axe, were suitable for cutting and shaping wooden beams used in building. The greatest use of surface-mined stones was the making of weapons for hunting. Flake blades of all sizes served as knives. Finely worked arrowheads found alongside large quantities of animal bones indicated the dependence upon hunting by Neolithic man in Palestine. Flint scrapers and borers were used in the tanning and sewing of hides.

Copper The use of mined minerals to form metals began sometime around 6500 B.C. near Catal Hüyük in Asia Minor. While making pigment from crushed malachite, a greenish carbonate of copper, human beings probably stumbled upon the knowledge for smelting, ushering in the Chalcolithic Period, about 4500—3,200 B.C. (*See Minerals and Metals*). The Bible refers to Tubal-cain, a descendant of Cain, as the father of copper forging (Gen. 4:22). In the beginning, copper ore was taken from deposits above the ground. Soon, however, mine shafts and tunnels were cut into areas where surface deposits hinted at the larger ore supplies below. In the Arabah and Sinai, mining settlements were founded. Complex series of narrow shafts were bored into the mountains and hills of the Timna Valley to reach the valued copper deposits within the earth. Near the mines were constructed a series of huts, walls forming windbreaks, and areas for smelting to support the mining operations. The ruins of the mining center khirbet en-Nahas, seventeen miles south of the Dead Sea, possibly mark the location of biblical Irnahash, the "Copper City." Palestine, however, was relatively poor in copper ore. Much of what was used had to be imported from regions with greater ore concentrations. Trade relations established with settlements in Asia Minor, Armenia, and the Island of Cyprus. Copper sheets and ingots were shipped by sea and land thousands of miles to meet the growing needs for metal tools, weapons, and jewelry. In later years these ingots served as a crude style of currency. Before 3000 B.C. people discovered that copper could be mixed with arsenic to form a stronger alloy. Copper tools last longer than stone implements and could withstand greater abuse. Men continued to mine the veins of minerals which ran into the earth, often following the deposits with tunnels fifty yards long into the side of a hill. The widespread use of copper in the Ancient Near East is highlighted from the magnificent copper hoard discovered at Nahal Mishmar, near the Dead Sea. Among more than 400 copper artifacts were numerous mace heads, chisels and adzes, scepters, and small, heavy "crowns." The copper from Naham Mishmar was most likely imported from Armenia or Azerbaijan, hundreds of miles away.

Bronze Copper tools, however, were soon replaced. Around 3200 B.C., metalsmiths discovered that by combining nine parts copper with one part tin a much stronger metal—bronze—was formed. Easier to cast than copper, bronze became the most widely used metal of the period. The copper for bronze continued to be mined in the same manner it always had, although stone tools for digging out the ore were replaced with stronger bronze counterparts. Tin deposits in Mesopotamia made the growth of this new technology easier in the northern Fertile Crescent, while Palestine and Egypt, without local tin deposits and mines, were forced to import raw materials. The regions of modern-day Afghanistan exported the necessary tin throughout the Ancient Near East.

Around 2500 B.C. Phoenicians established colonies in Spain and Portugal to mine the vast local supplies of copper and tin. These and other European tin supplies were shipped throughout the Ancient Near East as late as the Roman period. Roman tin mines in Britain were worked by slave labor and had shafts cutting 350 feet deep into the ground. In Palestine, the Timna copper mines came under the control of the Egyptians during the Late Bronze period. Remains of a small open-air temple dedicated to Hathor, patron goddess of miners, have been discovered. The small enclosure has a small sacred area set with *masseboth,* standing stones dedicated to the deity. A central shrine with small niches carved into the overhanging face of a cliff was the focal point of the sanctuary, its "holy of holies." The entire shrine was covered with a woolen tent. The design of the desert temple is similar to the Israelite tabernacle or tent of meeting. Before 1100 B.C. Kenites and Midianites occupied Timna, but no remains from between 1000 and 900 have been identified. It is hard to imagine, however, that Israel during the period of the United Monarchy, especially during Solomon's reign, would not have exploited these rich deposits within its domain.

Iron The chaotic political climate after 1300 B.C. disrupted the trade routes and commercial structures of the Ancient Near East. Copper supplies dwindled, and the import of tin and copper by Egypt and Palestine was disrupted, forcing metalsmiths to develop a new method for tool manufacture. Attention was turned to iron. Although small beads discovered in Egypt give evidence of the early use of meteoric rocks for iron smelting around 4000 B.C., the much higher melting point of iron (400 degrees higher than that of copper) necessitated the development of new smelting methods. So great was the heat needed that the Bible compares the enslavement of Israel in Egypt to the iron smith's furnace (Deut. 4:20). More efficient bellows were created to produce the high temperatures needed to melt the iron ore. Since iron deposits lay close to the surface, they were much easier to mine than those of copper had been.

The Hittites were among the earliest people to use iron on a large scale. They traded iron tools and weapons to Egypt. For the most part, however, the Hittites protected iron as a monopoly. Only after the fall of the Hittite kingdom about 1200 B.C. did iron become more widely used. Still, Israel made little use of it. The Bible describes Canaan as a land "whose stones are iron and from whose hills you may mine copper" (Deut. 8:9 NRSV). Only small amounts of both ores were available. Iron mines located in the Gilead near 'Ajlun at Magharat Warda probably served as one of the earliest iron sources in Palestine, possibly providing for the iron bedstead of Og, king of Bashan.

The Bible speaks of the Philistines as controlling the ironworking skills in Palestine (1 Sam. 13:19–22), an ability that prevented Israelite domination over the Philistine settlements in the Coastal Plain and Shephelah. The domination of iron technology by these "Sea-Peoples" points to the early development and usage of iron in the Aegean region, homeland of the Philistines. At Beth-Shemesh, a Philistine stronghold in the Jordan Valley, a large industrial area with bronze and ironworking facilities was discovered. Smelting ovens and flowpipes for the fires give evidence of the metalworking that occurred. Numerous iron weapons and pieces of jewelry were also found. However, excavation in other Philistine cities such as Ashdod and tel Qasile (near modern Tel Aviv) give little evidence of the widespread use of iron. While the Philistines may have controlled the use of iron to some degree, theirs was not a monopoly. For the most part, tools in Palestine continued to be made of bronze. Common tools such as sickles were still chipped from flint even after 1000 B.C. Iron chariots, spear points, knives and swords, and common tools such as sickles and plows became more common after 900 B.C., replacing earlier bronze counterparts. During the United Monarchy, Israel gained increased control of bronze and metal exports across the Ancient Near East, bringing great wealth to the empire of David and Solomon. Solomon created a virtual trade war between Israel and the Aramaeans to the north.

Other Minerals Other minerals were also mined in the Ancient Near East but were more difficult to obtain and work. Lapis Lazuli, a deep blue stone, was quarried for its beauty and used in jewelry. Egyptian faience was an attempt to produce a synthetic lapis. Lead was mined as early as 3000 B.C., but its soft nature made it unsuitable for tools or jewelry. Lead was later incorporated into bronze and, in the Roman period, was used in glassmaking. Silver was first mined in northeast Asia Minor and taken from a lead-silver alloy. Electrum, silver mixed with small amounts of gold, was also mined. Raw gold is found in veins in quartzy granite. These veins, however, were not mined in early periods. Rather, the weathering of gold-bearing rocks put pea-sized and larger bits of the metal into streams and rivers, mixing it with alluvial gravel. Found mostly at the upper reaches of rivers in areas of Egypt, the Nubian desert, and the Caucasus, gold began to be mined rather late because of its more isolated location. Since the headwaters of rivers and streams were often in locales less accessible or desirable for pasturing flocks, gold mines only became widespread around 2500 B.C. Egyptian paintings depict the washing of river sand to extract nuggets, and authors such as Strabo and Pliny the Elder (60 B.C.) spoke in later periods of rich gold deposits in Spain. The rarity of gold made it synonymous with extravagant wealth and luxury. The apostle John's description of heaven as a city with walls and streets of gold provided the believer with a glimpse of the grandeur and glory of an eternity with God. *David C. Maltsberger*

MINGLED PEOPLE KJV term for foreigners who are perhaps of mixed race and are associated with a dominant population (Jer. 25:20,24; 50:37; Ezek. 30:5). Modern translations generally replace mingled people with foreigners or with foreign plus a noun suitable to the context (folk, tribes, troops). The underlying Hebrew consists of the same three consonants as the term for Arabia. Modern translations follow the alternate vocalization and read Arabia or Arabs at Ezekiel 30:5.

MINIAMIN (Mĭ nī´ ă mĭn) Personal name meaning, "lucky" (literally "from the right hand"). *1.* Levite in the time of Hezekiah (2 Chron. 31:15). *2.* Priestly family in the time of the high priest Joiakim (Neh. 12:17). *3.* Priest who participated in Nehemiah's dedication of the wall (Neh. 12:41).

MINNI (Mĭn´ nī) People inhabiting the mountainous area south of Lake Urmia northeast of the Tigris-Euphrates valley (Jer. 51:27). The Minni are among the tribes summoned to punish the wickedness of Babylon. The Minni are known as the Manneans in Assyrian inscriptions from 800 to 600 B.C.

MINNITH (Mĭn′ nĭth) One of twenty cities involved in Jephthah's conquest of the Ammonites (Judg. 11:29–33). The site is unknown. The city likely lay between Rabbah-ammon and Heshbon. Suggested sites include khirbet Hanizeh and khirbet umm el-Hanafish.

MINSTREL KJV term for musician (Matt. 9:23). Modern translations have flute players or musicians. These musicians were hired to assist in mourning the child's death. See *Grief.*

MINT AND CUMMIN Mint is a sweet-smelling herb used to season food. Cummin is a caraway-like herb Judaism also used in seasonings and in medicine. Jesus named cummin, dill, and mint as He criticized the Pharisees for requiring the tithe of the herbs while ignoring more important matters of the Law (Matt. 23:23).

MIPHKAD GATE (Mĭph′ kăd) KJV, TEV transliteration of the Hebrew name of a gate of Jerusalem or of the Temple (Neh. 3:31), following the earliest Greek translation in taking Miphkad as a proper name. Other translations take Miphkad as a common noun. Suggested meanings include: inspection (NAS, NIV); muster (REB, NRSV); or prison (compare Jer. 52:11). If the Miphkad Gate is a city gate, it is perhaps identical with the Benjamin Gate (Jer. 37:13; 38:7; Zech. 14:10), located at the northernmost point on the east wall (perhaps identical with the Gate of the Guard, Neh. 12:39).

MIRACLES, SIGNS, WONDERS Events which unmistakeably involve an immediate and powerful action of God designed to reveal His character or purposes. Words used in the Scriptures to describe the miraculous include sign, wonder, work, mighty work, portent, power. These point out the inspired authors' sense of God's pervasive activity in nature, history, and people.
Old Testament The two Hebrew words most frequently used for "miracle" are translated "sign" (*'ōth*) and "wonder" (*mopheth*). They are synonyms and often occur together in the same text (Ex. 7:3; Deut. 4:34; 6:22; 7:19; 13:1; 26:8; 28:46; 34:11; Neh. 9:10; Ps. 105:27; Isa. 8:18; Jer. 32:20; Dan. 6:27). "Sign" may be an object or daily activity as well as an unexpected divine action (Gen. 1:14; Ex. 12:13, RSV; Josh. 4:6; Ezek. 24:24).The basic nature of a sign is that it points people to God. "Wonders" describe God's supernatural activity, a special manifestation of His power (Ex. 7:3), but false prophets can perform actions people perceive as signs and wonders (Deut. 13:1–3). Wonders can serve as a sign of a future event. Signs seek to bring belief (Ex. 4:5; compare 10:2), but they do not compel a person to believe (Ex. 4:9). At times God invites people to ask for signs (Isa. 7:11). The signs He

has done should make all peoples on earth stand in awe (Ps. 65:8). They should join the Psalmist in confessing that the God of Israel "alone works wonders" (Ps. 72:18 NAS).
New Testament The phrase "signs and wonders" is often used in the New Testament in the same sense as it is found in the Old Testament and also in Hellenistic literature (Matt. 24:24; Mark 13:22; John 4:48; Acts 2:43; 4:30; 5:12; 6:8; 7:36; 14:3; 15:12; Rom. 15:19; 2 Cor. 12:12; 2 Thess. 2:9; Heb. 2:4).

"Sign" (*semeion*) in the New Testament is used of miracles taken as evidence of divine authority. Sometimes it is translated as "miracle" (Luke 23:8 NIV; Acts 4:16,22 NAS, NIV). John was particularly fond of using "sign" to denote miraculous activity (see 2:11,18,23; 3:2; 4:54; 6:2,14,26; 7:31; 9:16; 10:41; 11:47; 12:18; 37; 20:30; Rev. 12:1,3,; 13:13,14; 15:1; 16:14; 19:20)

"Wonders" (*teras*) translates a Greek word from which the word *terror* comes. It denotes something unusual that causes the beholder to marvel. Although it usually follows "signs," it sometimes precedes it (Acts 2:22,43; 6:8) or occurs alone (as in Acts 2:19). Whereas a sign appeals to the understanding, a wonder appeals to the imagination. "Wonders" are usually presented as God's activity (Acts 2:19; 4:30; 5:12; 6:8; 7:36; 14:3; 15:12), though sometimes they refer to the work of Satan through human instruments (Matt. 24:24; Mark 13:22; 2 Thess. 2:9; Rev. 13:11–13).

New Testament writers also used *dunamis,* power or inherent ability, to refer to activity of supernatural origin or character (Mark 6:2; Acts 8:13; 19:11; Rom. 15:19; 1 Cor. 12:10,28,29; Gal. 3:5; 2 Thess. 2:9; Heb. 2:4).

"Work" (*ergon*) is also employed in the New Testament in the sense of "miracle." John the Baptist heard of the "works" of Jesus while he was in prison (Matt. 11:2). The apostle John used the term frequently (5:20,36; 7:3; 10:38; 14:11,12; 15:24).
Worldview Considerations Contemporary philosophical and theological arguments over the possibility and definition of miracle reflect the altered worldview of the last several centuries—from a theistic to a nontheistic concept of the universe. The perceived tension between the natural and the miraculous is a by-product of a naturalism that is intent on sqeezing out the supernatural realm of reality.

The people of the Bible did not face this problem. The biblical perspective on the universe is that it is created, sustained, and providentially governed by God. The Bible makes no clear-cut distinction between the natural and supernatural. In the "natural" event the Bible views God as working providentially; whereas, in the miraculous, God works in striking ways to call attention to Himself or His purposes.

How do miracles relate to the natural order?

M

Christian thinkers have responded in different ways throughout the centuries. Some hold that miracles are not contrary to nature (Augustine and C. S. Lewis, for instance). This harmony view contends that human knowledge with limited perspective does not fully understand or comprehend the higher laws that God employs in working the miraculous. Others (like Thomas Aquinas) have maintained miracles stand outside the laws of nature. This approach is called the intervention view, based on their belief that God intervenes in the natural order to do the miraculous.

One's view of the miraculous is related to one's view of the universe. A mechanistic perspective believes the world is controlled by unalterable natural laws and cannot allow for the possibility of miracles. Christians in every century have refused to have their universe so limited. They have affirmed the continuing miraculous work of God in the universe He created, continues to care for, uses to reveal Himself, and has promised to redeem.

T. R. McNeal

MIRIAM (Mĭr' ĭ am) Personal name of uncertain meaning, perhaps "bitter," "God's gift," "beloved," or "defiant." *1.* Sister of Moses and Aaron and the daughter of Jochebed and Amram. Miriam played a key role in the rescue of Moses (Ex. 2:4–8) and in the subsequent experience of the Exodus and the wilderness community. After crossing the Red Sea, she assumed the role of prophetess and led the women in the song of victory that was steeped in faith and gratitude (Ex. 15:20–21). See *Poetry.*

At Hazeroth, Miriam sided with Aaron in an act of rebellion against Moses when he married an Ethiopian woman (Num. 12:1–15). Beneath her disapproval of Moses' choice of a wife lay a deeper problem of ambition and insubordination. Consequently, God reminded her of Moses' divinely appointed leadership and chastened her with leprosy. She was healed following Moses' intercessory prayer and a seven-day quarantine (Num. 12:15). See *Intercession; Leprosy.*

Miriam died at Kadesh (Num. 20:1). Later biblical writers remembered her as an example to Israel in cases of leprosy (Deut. 24:9) and as a leader sent by God (Mic. 6:4).

2. Member of the clan of Caleb (1 Chron. 4:17).   *R. Dean Register*

MIRMA(H) (Mĭr' mȧ) Leader of tribe of Benjamin (1 Chron. 8:10).

MIRROR A polished or smooth surface that produces images by reflection. Throughout the biblical period mirrors were made of polished metal (bronze, Ex. 38:8; molten [metal], Job 37:18). Glass mirrors became available only in the late Roman period. Paul's readers could be expected to appreciate the illustration of the unclear image

Bronze mirror with a bone handle from the Etruscan culture (ca. 350–330 B.C.).

of a metal mirror (1 Cor. 13:12). See *Glass.*

MISGAB (Mĭs' găb) KJV, REB transliteration of the Hebrew for height used as a proper place name (Jer. 48:1). Other translations treat the term as a common noun and translate as fortress or a similar term.

MISHAEL (Mĭsh' â ĕl) Personal name perhaps meaning, "who is what God is?" *1.* Cousin of Moses and Aaron (Ex. 6:22) who helped bury Nadab and Abihu (Lev. 10:4). *2.* One standing with Ezra at the public reading of the law (Neh. 8:4). *3.* One of Daniel's three friends (Dan. 1:6–7,11,19; 2:17), given the Babylonian name Meshach.

MISHAL (Mĭ' shăl) Personal name meaning, "depression." Form of Misheal in modern translations.

MISHAM (Mĭ' shăm) Benjaminite builder of Ono and Lod (1 Chron. 8:12). The name perhaps derives from the root meaning, "to inspect."

MISHEAL (Mĭ' shė̇ ȧl) Place name meaning, "place of questioning." Levitical town in the territory of Asher (Josh. 19:26). Elsewhere, the KJV used the form Mishal (Josh. 21:30) or Mashal (1 Chron. 6:74). The town appears in the list of towns conquered by Pharaoh Thut-mose III. The site is unknown.

MISHMA (Mĭsh′ mȧ) Personal name meaning, "fame." *1.* Arab tribe descended from a son of Ishmael (Gen. 25:14; 1 Chron. 1:30). *2.* Descendant of Simeon. Inclusion of the names Mibsam and Mishma in the geneologies of both Ishmael and Simeon suggest the incorporation of Arabs into that tribe as Simeon expanded southward (compare 1 Chron. 4:38–43).

MISHMANNAH (Mĭsh măn′ nah) Personal name meaning, "strength" or "tasty morsel." One of David's army officers (1 Chron. 12:10).

MISHNAH A Hebrew term that means "to repeat" and eventually, in the rabbinic period (beginning about A.D. 100), "to learn." Specifically, in rabbinic Judaism *mishnah* refers to the teaching or learning about the oral law (*halakah*) passed on by a particular teacher (rabbi). Today the Mishnah usually refers to the collected edition of rabbinic discussions of halakah compiled by Judah ha-Nasi (literally "the Prince," or Patriarch) head of the rabbinic academy at Javneh (or Jamnia) at about A.D. 220. In rabbinic tradition he is usually referred to simply as "Rabbi."

ORGANIZATION The Mishnah has six major divisions:

1. *Zeraim* (seeds) deals with agricultural produce and proper tithing;

2. *Moed* (set feasts) deals with religious festivals;

3. *Nashim* (women) deals with laws regulating women;

4. *Nazikim* (damages) deals with property rights and legal proceedings.

5. *Kodashim* (holy things) deals with the Temple;

6. *Tohoroth* (cleannesses) deals with laws of purity.

The six major divisions are each further subdivided into specific tractates. References to the Mishnah in scholarly writing are usually given according to tractate, not according to the major divisions. While these divisions appear clear and orderly, the modern reader of the Mishnah is frequently confused by the inclusion of what appears to be legal discussion unrelated to the major division in which they are found. For example, Benedictions (*Berakoth*) are treated in the first division on agricultural produce. To some extent these inconsistencies become more understandable when we look at the way in which the Mishnah was developed from earlier mishnoth of individual rabbis.

Development According to the Mishnah itself, oral tradition and its teachings goes all the way back to Moses himself who received the halakah from God on Sinai and passed it on to subsequent generations. In rabbinic tradition this understanding seems to have functioned in at least two ways. First, the teachings of previous generations is regarded as important in setting oral law. Second, this understanding did not mean that oral law was seen as the literal passing on of particular words. Halakah was to some extent a spiritual ideal only imperfectly brought to concrete realization in the teaching of specific rabbis. Therefore, halakah was a matter of exceptional religious importance and heated debate. The Mishnah frequently preserved contrary opinions, While it usually resolves the matter on one side or the other, the preservation in the tradition also allows for reconsideration by later generations.

Modern scholars see the Mishnah as a collection and editing of Jewish case law whose traditions may go back to about 150 B.C. but primarily from the period of 50 B.C. to 220 A.D. The tradition of the Mishnah appears to begin with the sect of Judaism called the Pharisees, who sought to liberalize the legal system of Judaism by applying regulations for Temple purity particularly with regard to food laws to the entirety of Judaism. This sect may be regarded as liberal since they argued that the entirety of the nation should be righteous before God in ways similar to the priesthood. The Pharisees were largely a lay movement. The major representatives of this party in the Mishnah are Hillel and Shammai who taught around A.D. 50.

After the Romans destroyed the Jerusalem Temple in A.D. 70, Yohannan ben Zakkai founded the rabbinic movement at Javneh (Jamnia) in Galilee. This movement succeeded in eventually unifying the surviving elements of Judaism into a coherent traditional system that forms the core of Judaism into the modern era. Hence, one of their primary concerns was to set the boundaries of legal interpretation or "make a fence around the Law." The Mishnah primarily represents the collections of various teachers' opinions on halakah and seeks to establish the limits of normative interpretation through an examination of case law and Scripture. Rabbi Akiba (50?–135 A.D.) is one of the towering figures who probably contributed the present system of the organization of the Mishnah. He also sought to make explicit the scriptural basis of halakah. His student Rabbi Meir appears to be the connecting link between Akiba's mishnah and the Mishnah of Rabbi.

The Mishnah of Rabbi is the basis of the Talmud which was written in Palestine about 360 A.D. and in Babylonia about 500 A.D. Those rabbis quoted in the Mishnah are referred to as the Tannaim while those in the Talmud are referred to as Amoraim. Scholars are somewhat divided on the issue to what extent Rabbi simply collected and systematized various rabbis' opinions or to what extent he functioned as an editor who left hs own stamp upon the material. It is probably safe to conclude that Rabbi was a highly respected rabbi whose opinion was considered authoritative in his day. Nevertheless, the extent to which he could creatively edit the rabbinic traditions of halakah was probably limited by the community of rabbis who would not hesitate to challenge him if he misrepresented tradition. The Mishnah may therefore be seen as a compendium of the tradition of rabbinic Judaism for the first two centuries.

Rabbinical Oral Law Several principles seem to have been used to determine the oral law that would enter the Mishnah. First, the Mishnah presumes the written Mosaic law as given in Scripture as its fundamental underpinning. Rabbi Akiba sought to give explicit scriptural precedent for decisions in the oral law, sometimes in what appear to be exceptionally strained logic. The Mishnah preserves some legal debate based upon direct scriptural commentary (referred to as *midrash*). In most of the Mishnah, however, the oral law is developed by reference to precedent and the development of case law, much on the same order that British and American jurisprudence has developed. From generation to generation certain rabbis are considered to be of particular importance in establishing the halakah. For example, almost always the halakah is according to Hillel rather than Shammai, even though Shammai's opinion is also quoted. While much of the Mishnah concerns matters of pragmatic concern to the social and religious organization (the rabbis do not distinguish between the two) of Judaism, some segments seem to preserve tradition for its own sake. For example, the Mishnah preserves an entire section dealing with the Temple organization and sacrifice, in spite of the fact that the Temple no longer existed at the time of the writing of the Mishnah. Such discussion indicates that perhaps priests were part of the academy of Yohannan ben Zakkai and also reflects the continuing hope through the first two centuries that the Temple would be rebuilt.

Mishnah and Understanding the Bible The Mishnah has proven helpful to an understanding of the Bible in two ways. First, it has helped in reconstructing specific elements in the Judaism of Palestine at the time of Jesus. Second, it has been helpful in understanding the development of Judaism during the same period that the early Christians were engaged in similar development.

1. An earlier generation of Christian scholars tended to see the Mishnah as descriptive of the practices of Judaism in Palestine during Jesus' life. More recent scholars are more cautious since they recognize the long history of development of the Mishnah and also since it has become more and more apparent that Judaism in Jesus' day was composed of many religious viewpoints and movements. See *Jewish Parties.* Particularly, the practices of the Pharisaic sect may be reflected in some of the early traditions included in the Mishnah. For example, Jesus' saying in Matthew 7:12 is quite similar to rabbinic statements in the Mishnah. Also, certain Mishnaic evidence may be helpful in better understanding social relationships depicted in the Gospels. For example, evidence from Nashim (on women) helps us to reconstruct

the social position of Palestinian Jewish women in the first century. In this context it appears that Jesus is certainly more liberal in His treatment of women than was rabbinic tradition. The evidence of the Mishnah should not be taken as representative of what all or most Jews believed in the first century. Rather, it should be taken as a clue to what some Jews believed and balanced with other historical data.

2. Since the earliest Christians were also Jews, the Mishnah may give some indication of the development of early Christianity alongside of the development of rabbinic Judaism. At the same time that Yohannan ben Zakkai was founding the academy at Javneh, Christian Jews were coping with the loss of the Temple and the development of their own religious communities. Understanding of the development of Judaism in this period alongside the development of Christianity may help in understanding the commonalities and strains between the two sibling religions.

See *Halakah; Talmud; Pharisees; Torah; Tosephta.*　　　Stephenson Humphries–Brooks

MISHRAITES (Mĭsh' rā ītes) A family from Kiriath-jearim (1 Chron. 2:53). The name designates residents of Mishra, a place of which nothing is known.

MISPAR (Mĭs' pär) Modern translation spelling of personal name meaning, "writing." Exile returning with Zerubbabel (Ezra 2:2).

MISPERETH (Mĭs' pĕ rĕth) Personal name meaning, "court recorder" or "learned." Exile who returned with Zerubbabel. Parallel list has Mizpar (Ezra 2:2).

MISREPHOTH-MAIM (Mĭs' rė phŏth mā' ĭm) Limit of pursuit of the coalition of King Jabin of Hazor (Josh. 11:8; 13:6). The most likely site is khirbet el-Mushreifeh at the north end of the plain of Acco. The meaning of the name is debated. Suggestions include: Mishrephoth on the west (REB); "eminence of the waters"; "hot springs"; "lime burning at the water."

MISSION(S) A task on which God sends a person He has called, particularly a mission to introduce another group of people to salvation in Christ. In the Christian context, the person sent is called a missionary. This person is charged with the task of spreading the gospel of Jesus Christ to people to whom he is sent. The mission of the churches is to send our missionaries to all parts of the world until everyone has had the opportunity to hear the message of Jesus and accept Him as Lord. Interestingly, the term *mission* is not found in the Scriptures, yet the concept of mission permeates the entire Bible.

Mission in the Old Testament While some scholars insist that the Old Testament has little, if anything, to say about mission, the more general understanding is that mission is an important Old Testament concept. Its foundation lies in the understanding that the transcendent God is also the God who is involved in history. He is the God who acts. The record of His involvement in history indicates that His work is both revelatory and redemptive. People know who God is by what He has done. Since the Fall (Gen. 3), God's primary activity has been redemptive, as the confessions in the Old Testament reveal (see Deut. 6:20–24; 26:5–9; Jos. 24:2–15). This redeeming activity of God is missionary because God sends His messengers to the house of Israel and His prophets as His spokesmen to all nations.

Clearly, God's mission concern is inclusive, not exclusive. As indicated in the listing of the nations in Genesis 10, God's interest has been in all people, not just in Israel. When God called Abraham and his descendants, they were chosen, not to be exclusive vessels, but rather to be a means of blessing "all families of the earth" (Gen. 12:1–3; 18:16–19; 22:9–19; 26:1–5; 28:10–14). Later, God told Israel that they had been elected as God's chosen people (Ex. 19:3–6). They are to be the recipient and guardian of God's special revelation (Heb. 1:1–3) and the channel through which the Redeemer would enter the stream of human history (Isa. 49:1–10). Still, the election was not an end in itself. God called Israel to be holy, separate, or distinct from other nations, but they were also to be priests to the other nations. To live among them and lead them to God was their purpose for being.

This truth was kept before Israel in three ways. The message of the prophets served as the first important reminder. For instance, Jeremiah was called to be a prophet to all nations (Jer. 1:3–10) and spoke out in judgment against them (Jer. 48:47; 49:6,39). He also prophesied that all nations would be gathered in Jerusalem (Jer. 3:17). In like manner, Isaiah envisioned that all nations would be redeemed by coming to Jerusalem (Isa. 25; 66:18–24). Further, he warned them of God's judgment (Isa. 12—25) and called upon Israel to be a "light to the Gentiles" (Isa. 49:6).

The second reminder of Israel's responsibility in mission came through worship. The Psalms took into account that God was the Lord of all nations (see Ps. 67:1–2; 72:8,17,19; 50; 96). The architecture of the Temple provided a place for foreigners to worship in the court of the Gentiles (1 Kings 8:41–43), and the prayer of Solomon at the Temple dedication mentioned this fact (2 Chron. 6:32–33).

Furthermore, the history of Israel reminded her of her mission responsibility through Rahab (Josh. 6:22–25) and Ruth (Ruth 1—4) becoming a part of Israel, although they were foreigners.

The Old Testament emphasized that the nations would have to come to Jerusalem to be saved. Jonah was shocked to receive a different kind of mission. God told him to go to Nineveh and call the people to repentance. He rebelled at helping the nation's oppressor escape judgment. Still, the Book of Jonah became the major Old Testament witness to God's love for and willingness to let foreigners relate to Him in worship.

Mission in the New Testament The New Testament brings to a crescendo the Bible's symphonic theme of mission. The mission begins with Jesus who was sent to earth to reveal the Father (John 1:18; 14:9), to glorify Him (John 13:31; 14:13; 17:1,6), to bring the kingdom of God on earth (Matt. 12:22–32), and to make God's love and mercy known to a lost world. He came to seek and save the lost (Luke 19:10). His mission was also inclusive. While Jesus' ministry was primarily for the Jews, He also met the needs of non-Jews. He healed the daughter of "a woman of Canaan" and praised the woman for her faith (Mat. 15:21–29). He also healed the servant of the Roman centurion (Matt. 8:5–13). On another occasion, He initiated a conversation with a Samaritan woman which led both to her conversion and to that of the entire community (John 4).

Through His teachings, Jesus made it clear that His mission was to continue after He ascended. Each of the Gospels and Acts contains an account of His mandate to His followers, telling them to go to all the world, make disciples, baptize them, and preach the gospel (Matt. 28:19–20; Mark 16:15–16; Luke 24:46–49; John 20:21–22; Acts 1:8). Jesus assumed that the church would reach out beyond itself. This commission made a dramatic change in the emphasis of mission. Instead of looking to foreigners to come to Jerusalem as did the Old Testament, the church's mission is to go into all the world and not wait for the world to come to it. Not just selected prophets like Jonah but all the believers were to go and tell what they had seen with others.

The scope of mission was inclusive. The church was to cross all barriers—to reach out to all ethnic groups, clans, tribes, social classes, and cultures. The message of salvation was to be shared with all people everywhere.

The new disciples were to be baptized and taught. The purpose of the teaching was to do more than share information. It was to provide nourishment in the faith as well.

Since the Great Commission is a mandate, the church is expected to be obedient. Even so, it does not have to do the job alone. Christ has promised that He will be with the church until "the end of the world." With this assurance, the church was obedient, for the gospel was presented first in Jerusalem (Acts 1—8), then in Samaria (Acts 8—12) and finally to all the world (Acts 13—28).

Jesus' presence would be felt through the Holy

THE GROWTH OF CHRISTIANITY

IX

VIII

VII

VIII

Eburacum

Lindum

IV

Londinium

Colonia Agrippina

Danube River

V

Vienna

Lugdunum

Arelate

Massilia

Salon

V

Rome

Corduba

Puteoli

256
Carthage

Syracuse

Medite
e

▢ Extent of Christian church, A.D. 1st cent.

▢ Extent of Christian church, A.D. 2nd cent.

⚱ Notable early church

⊕ Major church council
431 (with date)

IV Century of conversion to Christianity

COPTS Monophysite church after 431

······· Boundary of Roman Empire

||||||||| Split of Latin (western) and Greek (eastern) churches, A.D. 5th cent.

0	200	400	600 miles

0	200	400	600	800 km

© carta

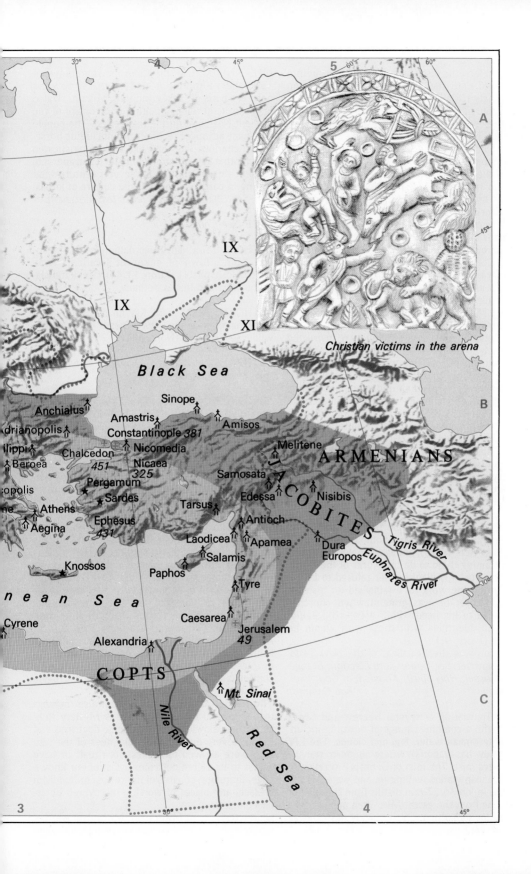

IX

IX

XI

Christian victims in the arena

Black Sea

Anchialus

Sinope

Amastris

Amisos

drianopolis

Constantinople *381*

Melitene

ilippi

Chalcedon

Nicomedia

ARMENIANS

Beroea

451

Nicaea

325

opolis

Samosata

Pergamum

Edessa

Nisibis

ne

Sardes

Tarsus

Athens

Antioch

Aegina

Ephesus

431

Laodicea

Apamea

Dura
Europos

Tigris River

Salamis

Euphrates River

Knossos

Paphos

J A C O B I T E S

Tyre

n e a n   S e a

Caesarea

Cyrene

Jerusalem
49

Alexandria

C O P T S

Mt. Sinai

Nile River

Red Sea

A

B

C

3

4

5

Spirit. In fact, the disciples were not to go out into the world until the Holy Spirit had come upon them (Acts 1:8). This is the only time in the Bible that a church is told not to be involved in mission. The reason are clear. The Holy Spirit empowers the church. He also convicts and converts sinners (Acts 5:14; 11:21,24; 18:8), performs mighty works of grace in believers (Acts 4:8–10), disciplines the church (Acts 5:13–14), sends forth workers (Acts 8:26; 13:1–3), presides over the missionary council (Acts 15), restrains and contains workers (Acts 16:6–10), and exercises supreme ecclesiastical authority (Acts 20:28).

Empowered by the Holy Spirit, the church did mission by preaching Jesus (Acts 2; 8:35; 10:36–44; 1 Cor. 2:1–2). The church's mission to the world was strengthened through its intimate fellowship and unity (Acts 2:44), and every effort was made to maintain this characteristic (Acts 6:1–7; 15; and Paul's letters to the churches in Corinth and Galatia).

The missionaries Jesus sent out were instructed to go only to the house of Israel, to preach and to meet human need. They were not to be overly concerned about their physical or material needs, nor were they to spend an undue amount of time with those who willfully rejected their message (Matt. 10:1–15). After the resurrection, missionaries were arrested (Acts 4 and 5), suffered (2 Cor. 4:7–10), and died (Acts 7).

The apostle Paul was the most outstanding of these missionaries. God had called him as a missionary to the Gentiles (Acts 26:16–18; Rom. 1:5; Eph. 3:1), and he was sent out by the church in Antioch (Acts 13:1–3). The Holy Spirit led him in his ministry (Acts 16:6–10). He preached Jesus (1 Cor. 2:1–2), met people on their own level (Acts 17), established autonomous, indigenous churches (Acts 14:23), and worked with others—often training them to do the works of the ministry (Acts 16:1–3). Paul further refused to be dependent on the work he established for his own livelihood, yet he was grateful when churches responded to his needs (Phil. 4:14–18). Significantly, he identified with those with whom he worked (1 Cor. 9:19–23).

Mission was the heartbeat of the New Testament churches. See *Confession; Election; Evangelism; Gospel; Holy Spirit; Kingdom of God; Paul; Salvation.* *Bob Compton*

MIST Translation of several Hebrew and Greek terms with a combined range of meaning including subterranean water, fog, and clouds. The KJV frequently has vapor(s) where modern translations have mist. The mist of Genesis 2:6 refers to subterranean waters welling up and watering the ground. In Job 36:27 rain distills from the mist or fog rising from the earth. Mist often appears as a symbol for something which quickly passes away (Isa. 44:22; Hos. 13:3; Jas. 4:14; 2 Pet. 2:17).

MITANNI (Mĭ tăn′ nī) Major kingdom between 1500 and 1300 B.C., located in what is now the northern parts of Turkey and Iran. Mitanni rivaled Egypt in its developed culture and control of the Ancient Near East during this period. The people had many advanced technologies, including horse-drawn chariots. They also had fairly sophisticated laws for that day. Mitanni maintained considerable influence over Palestine for several centuries, affecting in particular the Jebusite culture of Jerusalem. See *Chariots; Egypt; Jebusites; Jerusalem.*

MITE See *Coins.*

MITHAN (Mith′ an) Place name perhaps meaning, "gift." Town of unknown location; home town of Joshaphat (1 Chron. 11:43). Greek translation understood this as Bethany.

MITHCAH (Mĭth′ cah) KJV form of Mithkah, a place name meaning, "sweetness." One of the wilderness stations (Num. 33:28–29).

MITHKAH (Mĭth′ kah) Modern translations' spelling of Mithcah.

MITHNITE (Mĭth′ nīte) Title given to Joshaphat, a member of David's army (1 Chron. 11:43). See *Mithan.*

MITHRA, MITHRAISM Persian god and the mystery religion devoted to his worship.
The god Mithra Mithra was originally a Persian deity considered to be the mediator between mankind and Ahura Mazda, god of light. This god overcame evil and brought life, both animal and vegetable, to humankind. Statues of Mithra characteristically show him holding a bull by the nostrils while plunging a knife into its neck. The Romans identified Mithra with the sun god. December 25 was celebrated as his birthday. Three traditions relate the birth of Mithra: (1) he was born of an incestuous relationship between Ahura Mazda and his own mother; (2) he was born of an ordinary mortal; (3) Mithra was born from a rock. After his redemptive work on earth was finished, Mithra partook of a last supper with some of his devotees and then ascended to heaven, where he continues to assist the faithful in their struggle against demons.
The religion of Mithra Since Mithraism belongs to the general category known as Mystery Religions, our knowledge of its specific doctrines and rituals is very limited. Only devotees of the religion were allowed to witness its rituals or have access to its sacred doctrines. Most of our knowledge, therefore, consists of inferences drawn from artifacts and places of worship discovered by archaeologists.
Characteristics of Mithraism Mithraism was basically a religion of the common people, although

Mithra shrine and altar in the traditional Mithraistic cave setting.

at least one Roman emperor (Commodius, 180–192 A.D.) was initiated into its mysteries. It was the only mystery religion which excluded women from membership. It had no professional clergy. Its seven stages of initiation prepared the initiate for ascent to the god of light. These stages corresponded to the seven planetary spheres through which one must ascend to reach the abode of the blessed: the Raven, the Occult, the Soldier, the Lion, the Persian, the Runner of the Sun, and the Father. Male children were allowed to participate in the lower stages.

Rituals In its ancient rural setting the actual slaying of a bull was part of the ritual. The initiate was placed in a pit covered by an iron grate. The bull was slain on the grate, and the initiate attempted to catch its sacred blood with his tongue. By the time the religion reached the Roman Empire, this act seems to have become mere symbolism. Beyond this, we know almost nothing except that bas-reliefs depict celebrants carrying counterfeit heads of animals, Persians, etc. This suggests the wearing of costumes corresponding to the stage of initiation.

A rival to Christianity Of all the mystery religions, Mithraism became the strongest rival to Christianity. Its rivalry with Christianity may be explained by common external features. Among the more prominent are: December 25 the god's birthday, Sunday the holy day, baptism, a sacred meal, categorical ethics, belief in a final judgment with eternal life for the righteous and punishment for the wicked, and that the world would finally be destroyed by fire.

See *Mystery Religions.*   *Joe E. Lunceford*

MITHREDATH (Mĭth' rė dăth) Personal name meaning, "gift of Mithra" (a Persian diety). *1.* Cyrus' treasurer who returned the temple vessels (Ezra 1:8). *2.* Syrian officer who protested Nehemiah's rebuilding of the walls of Jerusalem (Ezra 4:7).

MITRE KJV term for a type of headdress, probably a turban (compare the related verb at Isa. 22:18). The mitre formed part of the high priest's garments (Ex. 28:4,36–39) and was required dress on the day of atonement (Lev. 16:4). Priests were prohibited from showing signs of mourning such as dishevelled hair (Ezek. 24:17; Lev. 21:10). They perhaps wore turbans whenever they went out. In Zechariah 3:5 the high priest Joshua received a clean mitre as a sign of the restoration of the priesthood.

MITYLENE (Mĭt ў lē' nė) Place name meaning, "Purity." Chief city of the Aegean island of Lesbos southeast of Asia Minor. Paul stopped at Mitylene on his return trip to Syria from Achaia as part of his third missionary journey (Acts 20:14).

MIXED MULTITUDE Term for foreigners who associate themselves with a dominant ethnic group. The term is used for those foreigners who joined with the Israelites in the Exodus from Egypt (Ex. 12:38), who became associated with the people of Judah during the Exile (Neh. 13:3), or who were associated with the Egyptians (Jer. 25:20) or Babylonians (Jer. 50:37). See *Mingled People.*

MIZAR (Mī' zår) Proper name meaning, "littleness" or an adjective meaning, "little" (Ps. 42:6). The context of the Psalm suggests a site at the headwaters of the Jordan in the territory of Dan.

MIZPAH, MIZPEH (Mĭz' päh, Mĭz' pĕh) Place name or common noun meaning, "watchtower" or "lookout." A name commonly used in Palestine to refer to places used to provide security. The name appears in two different forms, Mizpah and Mizpeh, with the same basic meaning.

The name Mizpah was used for at least two different sites in the Transjordan, one located in the territory of Gilead, the other in Moab. In Gilead, Laban and Jacob made a covenant (Gen. 31:25–55), set up a pillar, and named it Mizpah (Gen. 31:49). Mizpah was also the name of the hometown of Jephthah, the Gileadite (Judg. 11). While the location of Mizpah of Gilead is not known, it was most likely located in the northern part of Gilead, perhaps a site like Ramoth-gilead. See *Ramoth-gilead.* The location of Mizpeh in Moab has not been identified. In biblical history, this was the site to which David took his parents (1 Sam. 22:3–5) when Saul sought his life.

At least two sites and one region west of the Jordan were named Mizpah. The account of Joshua's encounter with Jabin, king of Hazor (Josh. 11), refers to "the land of Mizpah" (v. 3) and "the valley of Mizpeh" (v. 8), a region in north Palestine, the location of which is unknown. A second Mizpeh west of the Jordan was located in the tribal territory of Judah (Josh. 15:38). While the exact location is unknown, this Mizpeh may have been near Lachish.

The town of Mizpeh located in the territory of Benjamin (Josh. 18:26) seems to be the most important of the Mizpeh's in the Old Testament. In spite of the numerous references to this important Old Testament site, its location is still debated. Two major sites have been suggested as possible locations: Nebi Samwil, located about five miles north of Jerusalem, and tell en-Nasbeh, located about eight miles north of Jerusalem. While a major excavation has never been done at Nebi Samwil, the stories of Samuel seem to fit this location. On the other hand, tell en-Nasbeh has been excavated, and the archaeological data fits well the history of Mizpeh of Benjamin.

The important role Mizpah played in Old Testament history is reflected in the many events associated with the site. Mizpah was a rallying point for Israel as they gathered against the tribe of Benjamin (Judg. 20). Samuel gathered Israel to Mizpah for prayer in the light of the Philistine threat (1 Sam. 7:5–11). Mizpah was a major site at which legal decisions were made (1 Sam. 7:15–17). One of the most interesting chapters in the history of Mizpah took place after the Fall of Jerusalem. With Jerusalem in shambles following the Babylonian attack in 587 B.C., Mizpah became the administrative center of this Babylonian province. At Mizpah Gedaliah, who had been appointed governor of the province, sought to encourage those who had remained behind (Jer. 40).

See *Watchtower; Samuel; Jephthah; Gedaliah.*
LaMoine DeVries

MIZPAR (Mĭz' pår) KJV form of Mispar (Ezra 2:2).

MIZRAIM (Mĭz' rā ĭm) Hebrew word for Egypt (Gen. 12:10; 13:10; 25:18). *1.* Son of Ham (Gen. 10:6,13). *2.* The Mushri, a people of Cilicia in southeastern Asia Minor (possibly 1 Kings 10:28; 2 Kings 7:6; 2 Chron. 1:16–17 TEV; NIV note). Mushri derives from the Assyrian word for "march" and possibly designates any people living outside their borders. Some scholars revocalize the Hebrew consonantal text to read Mushri; but they have no textual evidence for this. See *Egypt.*

MIZZAH (Mĭz' zah) Personal and clan name meaning, "from this" or "light ray." Edomite clan chief (Gen. 36:13,17; 1 Chron. 1:37).

MNASON (Mnā' son) Personal name meaning, "remembering," variant of Jason. Native of Cyprus and Paul's host during his final trip to Jerusalem in about A.D. 60 (Acts 21:16).

MOAB AND THE MOABITE STONE (Mō' ăb, Mō' å bīte) Personal and national name and monument the nation left behind. The narrow strip of cultivable land directly east of the Dead Sea was known in biblical times as "Moab," and the people who lived there, as "Moabites." Moab is rolling plateau (averaging approximately 3,300 feet elevation), bounded on the west by the rugged escarpment which drops down to the Dead Sea (itself almost 1,300 feet below sea level), on the east by the desert, and running through it the steep Wady Mujib canyon (the Arnon River of biblical times). The Mujib/Arnon, which flows essentially east-west and enters the Dead Sea approximately mid-way along the latter's western shore, separates northern Moab from Moab proper.

Relatively few springs appear on the Moabite plateau, and the waters of the Mujib/Arnon are virtually inaccessible because of the steepness of the river canyon. Still, the area is well watered by winter rains brought by winds from the Mediterranean. The porous soil holds enough of the moisture for the villagers to grow cereal crops and to find good pasturage for their sheep and goats.

Moab's agricultural productivity is illustrated by the biblical passages pertaining to Ruth and King Mesha, surely the two best-known Moabites from the Bible. The Book of Ruth opens with a time of famine in Judah; thus Elimelech, Naomi, and their two sons emigrated to Moab where food was still available (Ruth 1:1–5). King Mesha, we are told, "was a sheep breeder; and he had to deliver annually to the king of Israel a hundred thousand lambs, and the wool of a hundred thousand rams" (2 Kings 3:4 RSV).

The chief cities of northern Moab were Hesbon, Medeba, and Dibon. Since this region was somewhat cut off from Moab proper by the Arnon, it was more vulnerable to international pressures and often changed hands during biblical times. In fact, the Ammonites made claim to all the territory as far south as the Arnon (Judg. 11:13), while the Book of Joshua makes the same claim for Israel (13:15–28). Other biblical passages which pertain to the region immediately north of the Arnon clearly recognize it as Moabite territory (Isa. 15; Jer. 48), as does the inscription of the Moabite Stone (see below). A crux passage for understanding the whole matter is Numbers 21:25–30, which explains that King Sihon of the Amorites took northern Moab from the Moabites and that the Israelites took it from him. Unfortunately, this passage is open to various interpretations (especially when the essentially parallel version in Jeremiah 48:45–47 is taken into account).

Moab proper was more isolated from the outside world, bounded by the Dead Sea escarpment on the west, the desert on the east, the Mujib/Arnon on the north, and a second river canyon on the south—called today Wady el-Hesa, probably, but not certainly, the River Zered of biblical times (Num. 21:12). The chief cities of Moab proper were Kir-hareseth (present-day Kerak) and a place called Ar Moab (possibly to be identified with the present-day village of Rabbah approximately nine miles northeast of Kerak). Second Kings 3 describes a military campaign undertaken by King Jehoram of Israel and supported by King Jehoshaphat of Judah which penetrated Moab proper and culminated in a siege of Kir-hareseth. The siege was lifted when King Mesha of Moab sacrificed his oldest son on the city wall.

In addition to biblical passages such as those indicated above and occasional references in Assyrian texts, our major souce of information about ancient Moab is the so-called Moabite Stone. This stone, which bears an inscription from the reign of the same King Mesha mentioned in 2 Kings 3, was discovered in 1868, near the ruins of ancient Dibon, by a German missionary. Known also as The Mesha Inscription, the monument reports the major accomplishments of King Mesha's reign. He boasts especially of having recovered Moabite independence from Israel and of having restored Moabite control over northern Moab.

Since they were neighbors, the history of the Moabites was intertwined with that of Israel. Moreover, the Israelites regarded the Moabites as close relatives, as implied by Genesis 19:30–38. We hear of peaceful interchange as well as conflicts between the Israelites and Moabites already during the time of the Judges. The story of Ruth illustrates peaceful relations, while the episode of Ehud and Eglon illustrates conflict (Judg. 3:12–30). Saul is reported to have fought against the Moabites (1 Sam. 14:47). David, a descendant of the Moabitess Ruth according to the biblical genealogies (Ruth 4:18–22), placed his parents under the protection of the king of Moab while he was on the run from Saul (1 Sam. 22:3–4). Yet he is reported to have defeated the Moabites in battle later on and to have executed two-thirds of the Moabite prisoners by arbitrary selection (2 Sam. 8:2). Moab was represented among Solomon's wives, and the worship of Chemosh, the Moabite god, accommodated in Solomon's Jerusalem (1 Kings 11:1–8).

Our most detailed information about Moabite-Israelite relations comes from the mid-ninth century B.C., the time of the Omri dynasty of Israel and King Mesha of Moab (1 Kings 16:15—2 Kings 10:18). At this point the inscription of the Moabite Stone supplements the biblical record. We learn that Omri conquered northern Moab and gained some degree of domination over Moab proper. Ahab continued Omri's policies. King Mesha ascended the throne of Moab approximately midway during Ahab's reign, however, and eventually succeeded in throwing off the Israelite yoke. Mesha apparently began the struggle for Moabite independence during the turbulent years following Ahab's death (2 Kings 1:1). Ahaziah, who succeeded Ahab to the throne of Israel, was unable to respond to Mesha's challenge because of an accident which led to his premature death (2 Kings 1). Later, when Jehoram followed Ahaziah to the throne of Israel and attempted to restore Israelite control over Mesha, he was unsuccessful (2 Kings 3).

Eventually, by 700 B.C., Moab fell under the shadow of Assyria as did Israel, Judah, Ammon, and the other petty Syro-Palestinian Kingdoms. Thus Moab and Moabite kings are mentioned in the records of Tiglath-Pileser III, Sargon II, Sennacherib, and Esarhaddon. Also, prophetic oracles such as Amos 2:1–3; Isaiah 15; and Jeremiah 48 pertain to these last, waning years of the Moabite kingdom.

See *Kir-hareseth; Arnon River; Transjordan; King Mesha; Ruth; Jehoram (of Israel); Jehoshaphat.*   Maxwell Miller

MOABITE (Mō à bīte) Resident of Moab.

MOABITESS (Mō à bīt' ess) A female resident of Moab. Prominent women from Moab include

Ruth (Ruth 1:22; 2:2,21; 4:5,10), some of Solomon's wives (1 Kings 11:1), and the mother of Jehozabad (2 Chron. 24:26).

MOADIAH (Mō à dī' ah) Personal name meaning, "Yah promises" or "Yah's ornament." Priestly clan in the time of the high priest Joiakim (Neh. 12:17), perhaps to be identified with Maadiah (Neh. 12:5).

MODERATION Self-control; calmness; temporateness (Phil. 4:5). The underlying Greek term is used in parallel with kindness (2 Macc. 9:27). Modern translations read forbearance (RSV), forbearing *spirit* (NAS), gentleness (NIV, NRSV), and "consideration of others" (REB).

MODIOS See *Weights and Measures.*

MOLADAH (Mō lā' dah) Place name meaning, "generation." City near Beersheba in southern Judah assigned both to Judah (Josh. 15:26) and to Simeon (Josh. 19:2), perhaps reflecting the political realities of different times or the dependence of Simeon on Judah. The similarity to the name Molid suggests that Moladah was a Jerahmeelite settlement (1 Sam. 27:10; 1 Chron. 2:29). The city was among those repopulated by Jews returning from Exile (Neh. 11:26). Moladah is perhaps identical to the Edomite village of Malathah which served as a retreat for Herod Agrippa I. Various sites have been proposed: khirbet Kuseifeh twelve miles east of Beersheba; tell el-Milh southeast of Beersheba; and khereibet el-Waten east of Beersheba.

MOLE See *Animals.*

MOLECH (Mō' lĕch; *king*) Transliteration of Hebrew word related to word for "king" but describing a foreign god or a practice related to foreign worship. The meaning of "Molech" is debated. Two views generally are proposed. One suggestion is that "Molech" denotes a particular type of offering—a votive sacrifice made to confirm or fulfill a vow. This viewpoint is supported by the fact that some Carthaginian-Phoenician (Punic) inscriptions from the period 400–150 B.C. imply that the word *mlk* is a general form for "sacrifice" or "offering." Such a meaning is possible in some passages (Lev. 18:21; 20:3–5; 2 Kings 23:10; Jer. 32:35).

A second suggestion is that "Molech" is the name of a pagan deity to whom human sacrifices were made. This deity often is associated with Ammon (compare 1 Kings 11:7—) "the abomination of the children of Ammon." Leviticus 20:5 condemns those who "commit whoredom with Molech" (see also Lev. 18:21; 20:3–5; 2 Kings 23:10; Jer. 32:35). Some recent archaeological evidence points to child sacrifice in ancient Ammon. Many scholars contend that all the biblical

texts referring to Molech can be understood by interpreting it as a divine name.

The etymology of the term "Molech" is interesting. Scholars suggest that it is a deliberate misvocalization of the Hebrew word for king or for the related participle (*mōlek*), "ruler." They propose that the consonants for the Hebrew word for king (*mlk*) were combined with the vowels from the word for shame (*boshet*). Thus, this title was a divine epithet expressing contempt for the pagan god.

In times of apostasy some Israelites, apparently in desperation, made their children "go through the fire to Molech" (Lev. 18:21; 20:2–5; 2 Kings 23:10; compare 2 Kings 17:31; Jer. 7:31; 19:5; 32:35). It generally is assumed that references like these are to the sacrifices of children in the Valley of Hinnom at a site known as Topheth ("Topheth" probably means "firepit" in Syriac). See *Hinnom; Topheth.* Precisely how this was done is unknown. Some contend that the children were thrown into a raging fire. Certain rabbinic writers describe a hollow bronze statute in the form of a human but with the head of an ox. According to the rabbis, children were placed in the structure which was then heated from below. Drums were pounded to drown out the cries of the children.

An alternate view contends that the expression "passed through Molech" refers not to human sacrifices but that parents gave up their children to grow up as temple prostitutes. Such a view appeals to Leviticus 18 where throughout the chapter the writer is concerned with sexual intercourse (especially vv. 19–23). Another view sees an original fire ceremony dedicating, but not harming children, that later was transformed into a burnt-offering ceremony.

The practice of offering children as human sacrifice was condemned in ancient Israel, but the implication is clear in the Old Testament that child—sacrifice was practiced by some in Israel (2 Kings 21:6; 23:10; 2 Chron. 28:3; Ps. 106:38; Jer. 7:31; 19:4–5; Ezek. 16:21; 23:37,39). The Exile seems to have put an end to this type of worship in Israel. However, it lingered on in North Africa and among the Carthaginian Phoenicians into the Christian era.

See *Gods, Pagan; Ashtoreth; Sacrifice, Child.*

Paul E. Robertson

MOLID (Mō lĭd) Personal name meaning, "begetter." Descendant of Judah (1 Chron. 2:29).

MOLOCH (Mō' lŏch) Variant form of Molech used at Acts 7:43.

MOLTEN SEA A large cast bronze basin that stood in the courtyard to the southeast of Solomon's Temple (1 Kings 7:23–26; 2 Chron. 4:2–5). The basin was cast by Hiram of Tyre who was responsible for all the bronze work in the Temple (1 Kings 7:13–14). The bronze for the molten sea was supplied by the spoils from David's campaigns (1 Chron. 18:8). The basin was over fourteen feet in diameter, over seven feet high, and over forty-three feet in circumference. It was about three inches thick. The estimated weight is about 30 tons, and the estimated volume is about 12,000 gallons (U.S.). The brim was turned outward resembling a lily, and below the brim were two rows of gourds (but compare 1 Kings 7:24; 2 Chron. 4:3). The sea rested on the backs of twelve oxen. The oxen were arranged in groups of three, each group facing toward one of the four compass directions (1 Kings 7:25; 2 Chron. 4:4). The oxen were later removed by Ahaz and replaced with a stone base (2 Kings 16:17; compare Jer. 52:20). After the fall of Jerusalem in 587 B.C., the basin was broken in pieces and taken to Babylon (2 Kings 25:13; Jer. 52:17). The basin was used for the purification of the priests (2 Chron. 4:6). Some have suggested that the molten sea was also symbolic of the great sea present when God began to create the heavens and the earth thus making the sea symbolic of God's creative activity (Gen. 1:2). *Phil Logan*

MOMENT See *Instant.*

MONEY BELT Modern rendering of the term the KJV translated as purse (Matt. 10:9; Mark 6:8). See *Purse.*

MONEY CHANGERS Persons whose profession was to sell or exchange Roman or other moneys for Jewish money acceptable in the Temple worship. In New Testament times regions and cities issued their own money. This caused Jews of the Dispersion, those who lived outside of Judea, to bring many kinds of money to Jerusalem. To help visitors change money into that acceptable in Jerusalem, money changers set up tables in the Temple court of the Gentiles. Syrian silver coins were the money of Jerusalem then, and worshipers used them to pay their Temple tax of a half shekel and to buy sacrifices for the altar.

Three words are translated "moneychangers": *kollubistōn* (Matt. 21:12; Mark 11:15; John 2:15) of Semitic origin referred to the exchange rate or commission; *kermatistas* (John 2:14) referred to a dealer in small change; and *trapetzitais* (Matt. 25:27) which Luke used in a slightly different form (*trapezan,* 19:23, or *shulhanim* in Hebrew) referred to a money agent who sat at a table.

Money changers were in the area with vendors who sold animals, birds, and other items used in Temple worship and sacrifices. Such transactions were numerous and required the service of bro-

kers who knew the value of foreign money. Some exchangers profited greatly and loaned their money along with that others invested with them. Their interest rates ranged from 20 to 300 percent per year.

In anger at this corruption of the purpose of the Temple, Jesus turned over the tables of the money changers and drove them and the sellers of animals out of the Temple court (Matt. 21:12). *Elmer L. Gray*

MONEYLENDER NIV term for one who loans money at interest (Ex. 22:25; KJV, usurer; NAS and RSV, creditor). See *Loan.*

MONITOR LIZARD See *Animals.*

MONKEY A small, long-tailed primate. TEV, REB include monkeys among the exotic animals brought as gifts to King Solomon (1 Kings 10:22; 2 Chron. 9:21). NIV, NRSV note read, "baboons." KJV, NAS, NRSV render the Hebrew term peacocks.

MONOTHEISM/POLYTHEISM The competing systems of religious belief that only one god exists or that many gods exist. Bible students often argue on the basis of biblical evidence that Israel in the first centuries of her life as a people did not have a monotheistic system of belief: indeed, that Moses' tradition does not appear in that kind of category. To support the accuracy of this statement, they examine the central text in the Old Testament for defining Israel's belief about God: the Ten Commandments. The first commandment stipulates a fundamental tenet in Israel's belief system: "Thou shalt have no other gods before me" (Ex. 20:3). That requirement for participation in Israel's community of faith does not assert that serving other gods before one serves the Lord would be foolish since no other gods exist. It assumes quite to the contrary that other gods do exist. It asserts that, even though the other gods exist, the people who follow the Mosaic Commandments shall not embrace any of those other gods as gods who compete for the loyalty of the people. The Lord who brought Israel out of the land of Egypt will allow no compromise in the loyalty of the people. That assertion assumes the existence of other false gods who could call for loyalty and commitment from the Lord's people. That kind of belief system is commonly called henotheism.

In contrast to the call for strict commitment to the Lord alone, to a kind of divine jealousy that would tolerate no commitments from the people to gods other than the Lord, even though other gods might tempt the Lord's people with offers of power, the people among whom Israel lived in the early years of occupation in Canaan believed in numerous gods whose activities influenced their lives. Principal among the gods of the Canaanite pantheon were the great father figure, El; the younger hero, Baal; the adversary against order in the created land, Yam; the consort for Baal, Anat; and the ruler of Sheol, the place of the dead, Mot. In the Canaanite story about the various events involving these gods, Baal and his consort were primarily responsible for the success or failure of the agriculture in the social structure of Canaan. The fertility of the land depended on the fertility of Baal and his consort. The cult for the Canaanite farmers sought to stimulate the fertility of the divine couple, and thus the fertility of the land, by participating in fertility rituals at central sanctuaries called high places. The sexual activities of these rituals would stimulate Baal and his consort to similar activities and thus secure the fertility of the land.

One particular phase of that cult developed its drama from a belief that in the fall of the year, the time when vegetation on the earth dies, Baal died and descended into Sheol. On hearing the news of this tragedy, Anat began a long search for Baal. She found him in Sheol and effected his resurrection from the dead by coaxing him back to activity in the world of the living. This scene of resurrection occurred in the spring when the world springs back to life. Such mythology undergirds a belief system that depended on the activities, indeed, the interrelationship, of many gods. That system can be called polytheism.

A move away from henotheism and polytheism appears first in the Old Testament among the prophets. The prophetic movement appears as early as the prophet Elijah. Competition between the people of Israel and the people of Phoenicia was highlighted by a competition for loyalty of the people between the Lord and Baal. That competition came to its sharpest focus in the story about the contest between Elijah, the prophet for the Lord, and the prophets of Baal on Mount Carmel (1 Kings 18). The issue for the contests is still competition for the loyalty of the people. That issue focused on the question of genuine claim to status as God. "If the Lord be God, follow him: but if Baal, then follow him" (v. 21). The issue of claim to genuine status as God is then focused on power. "The God that answereth by fire, let him be God" (1 Kings 18:24).

The pressure of the Exile challenged Yahweh's claim as the only God. If the Lord is really God and if that claim can be substantiated by acts of power, then how could the people of the Lord lose their independence and their land to a foreign people? Would the success of the Babylonians against Judah not undergird the claim that Marduk, the god of the Babylonians, is really God? Would it not suggest that the Lord, the God of the Judeans, had been defeated by Marduk, the god of the Babylonians? The prophets' response to this crisis was: the tragedy of the Exile was not the result of the power of Marduk against the power of the Lord, a result that would establish Marduk as God. To the contrary, the tragedy of the Exile was the result of Israel's own God using the Babylonians as an instrument of punishment against the Lord's own people since they had violated the terms of the covenant that bound them together. That theological justification for the Exile (see Amos 2:4–8) opened the door for a theological, philosophical position that asserted the existence of only one God who is Lord not only of Israel but also of all the rest of the world. That position can be called monotheism.

The beautiful poetry of Isaiah 40—66 represents the height of Israel's monotheism. For the first time in the Old Testament literature, a prophet explicitly argued that no other gods exist. The Lord alone is God. "I am the Lord, and there is none else, there is no God beside me: I girded thee, though thou hast not known me: That they may know from the rising of the sun, and from the west, that there is none beside me, I am the Lord, and there is none else (Isa. 45:5–7)." With that poetry, Israel reached a fully developed monotheism. Moreover, such monotheism asserts that the only God is Creator of the world: "I am the Lord that maketh all things; that stretcheth forth the heavens alone" (Isa. 44:24) and its Savior and Redeemer: "I, even I, am the Lord, and beside me there is no savior " (Isa. 43:11). *George W. Coats*

MONTH See *Calendars; Time.*

MOON Light in the night sky created by God and controlling the calendar (Gen. 1:14–19). Hebrew uses several words for moon, new moon, full moon, or bright, white moon. Two of Israel's greatest festivals were celebrated at the beginning of the full moon: the Passover in the spring and the Feast of Booths in the fall. Each month they celebrated the "new moon" with a little more festivity than a regular sabbath (Num. 28:11–15 NIV).

Still the Old Testament strongly teaches against worshiping the moon (Deut. 4:19; Job 31:26–28; Isa. 47:13–15) as did Israel's neighbors. The people of Israel were to remember that the moon was nothing more than an object created by Yahweh and had no power over people.

Joel said in the last days the moon would become dark (Joel 2:10; 3:15) or turn to blood (Joel 2:31). The moon will not give its light on the "Day of the Lord," the light of the sun and the moon being replaced by the everlasting light of the Lord (Isa. 13:10; 60:19–20). *James Newell*

MOON, NEW See *Calendar; Festivals; Time.*

MORASTHITE (Mō răs´ thīte) Resident of Moresheth (Jer. 26:18; Mic. 1:1).

MORDECAI (Môr′ dĕ câi) Personal name meaning, "little man." *1.* Esther's cousin and the mastermind behind her rise to power and subsequent victory over the evil Haman. Haman, a descendant of the Amalekite king Agag, sought to destroy the Jewish race. Mordecai, a descendant of King Saul's family, led Esther to thwart the attempt, Haman was hanged on the gallows he had erected for Mordecai. See *Esther.*

2. A man who returned from Babylon to Jerusalem with Zerrubbabel (Ezra 2:2; Neh. 7:7).

MOREH (Mō′ rĕh) Place name meaning, "instruction" or "archers." *1.* Place where several important events in the lives of the patriarchs and the nation Israel occurred. An oak tree at the site is mentioned several times as being the focal point. Abraham's first encampment in the land of Canaan was at Moreh. There he built an altar after God had appeared to him and entered into covenant (Gen. 12:6–7). Jacob buried there the foreign gods his family had brought from Haran (Gen. 35:4).

The hill of Moreh.

At Moreh God pronounced the blessing and curse on Israel regarding their keeping the commandments (Deut. 11:26–30). Joshua set up a memorial stone under the oak as a reminder of the covenant made between God and the people (Josh. 24:26).

2. Hill in tribal territory of Issachar where Gideon reduced his troops by testing the way they drank water (Judg. 7:1). Modern Nebi Dachi opposite Mount Gilboa.

MORESHETH, MORESHETH-GATH (Mō′ rĕ shĕth-Gặth) Place name meaning, "inheritance of Gath." Home of the prophet Micah (Mic. 1:1). The prophet pictured his home as a bride receiving a going away gift from Jerusalem, her father, a warning of exile for Jerusalem's leaders and thus separation from their neighbors (1:14). The city was apparently located near Philistine Gath and is usually identified with tell ej-Judeideh about twenty-two miles southwest of Jerusalem and nine

miles east of Gath. Recently, this identification has been questioned. This may be the Gath Rehoboam fortified (2 Chron. 11:8). It may be Muchrashti of the Amarna letters.

MORIAH (Mō rī′ ah) Place name of uncertain meaning translated in various ways, including "Amorites" by earliest translators. The rocky outcropping in Jerusalem located just north of the ancient city of David. It was on this rock that Abraham would have sacrificed Isaac as a burnt offering, but God intervened and provided a ram (Gen. 22:2,13). Later, the Jebusite city of Salem was built adjacent to the hill. After David captured the site, he purposed to build there a Temple for the ark of the covenant. However, God gave that task to his son Solomon (1 Chron. 28:3–6). It may be modern khirbet Beth-Lejj.

MORNING First part of the day by modern reckoning. Morning can refer to the time before dawn (Mark 1:35; compare Gen. 44:3), to dawn (Gen. 19:15; 29:25; Judg. 16:2), or to some time after sunrise. Morning is frequently paired with evening (Gen. 1:5,8) to indicate a complete day. The coming of morning serves as a figure for joy (Ps. 30:5) or vindication (Ps. 49:14) which comes quickly.

MORNING STAR See *Daystar.*

MORROW KJV term meaning the next day or tomorrow (Gen. 19:34; Luke 10:35; Acts 25:17).

MORTAL Subject to death in contrast to God, who is immortal or free from death (Job 4:17; Rom. 1:23). The mortal body is subject to sin (Rom. 6:12), to decay (1 Cor. 15:53,54), and to death (2 Cor. 4:11). See *Anthropology; Immortality.*

MORTAR *1.* A vessel in which substances are crushed with a pestle. Mortars were frequently fashioned from basalt or limestone. They were used to grind grain for flour, herbs for medicine, olives for oil (Ex. 27:20). By extension mortar

A stone mortar for grinding grain or other substances at Lachish.

designates a hollow place (Josh. 15:19). Mortar is used as a proper name for a district of Jerusalem in Zephaniah 1:11. *2.* A building material, usually clay (Ex. 1:14; Isa. 41:25; Nah. 3:14), though sometimes bitumen (Gen. 11:3; KJV "slime"), used to secure joints in brick or stone. Modern translations sometimes replace the mortar of the KJV with another term, for example, plaster (Lev. 14:42,45) or whitewash (Ezek. 13:10–11,14–15).

MOSERA(H), MOSEROTH (Mō sē′ rŏth) Place name meaning, "chastisements." A wilderness station (Num. 33:30–31). The singular form of the name (Mosera or Moserah) was the site of Aaron's burial (Deut. 10:6). Numbers 20:22–28 has prompted the location of Moseroth in the vicinity of Mount Hor.

MOSES (Mō′ sės) A personal name meaning, "drawn out of the water." The Old Testament depicts Moses as the leader of the Israelites in their Exodus from Egyptian slavery and oppression, their journey through the wilderness with its threats in the form of hunger, thirst, and unpredictable enemies, and finally in their audience with God at Mount Sinai/Horeb where the distinctive covenant bonding Israel and God in a special treaty became a reality. Nothing is known about Moses from sources outside the Old Testament. To be sure, the name *Moses* doubtlessly appears in Egyptian dress in compound names such as Tuthmoses III, but none of these references gives information about the Moses of Israel.

Rock traditionally considered the Rock of Rephidim that Moses struck to get water for the Israelites.

The Old Testament describes Moses as a heroic leader of the people and as a man of God who brought the people into their special relationship with God. The story about Moses in the Old Testament, found in the extensive narratives from Exodus 1 through Deuteronomy 34, can be described as a heroic saga. It is more than simply a biography of Moses, an historical document that records the events of his life. It is a special kind of ancient art form. To understand its content, the reader must appreciate its special brand of truth as beauty in the story itself.

The artistic narrative begins in Exodus 1, not with data about Moses, but with an account of events in Egypt that affected Moses' people. Since the Israelites had grown to be a large people, the Egyptian Pharaoh feared their power. To control them, he launched an official policy of oppression against them. When the oppression failed to curb the population growth of the Israelites, the Pharaoh announced a new policy for limiting that growth. "Every boy that is born to the Hebrews you shall throw into the Nile, but you shall let every girl live" (Ex. 1:22, NRSV). The very next line announces the birth of Moses. Moses' life began under the Pharaoh's judgment of death.

The mother, however, acted to protect the baby Moses from the Pharaoh's death decree. When the baby could no longer be hidden, the mother constructed an ark, a basket of bulrushes made waterproof with bitumen and pitch. She placed the child in the basket and the basket in the river. A sister stood watch over the basket to know what might happen. She witnessed an apparently terrible twist of fate, however, when the Pharaoh's own daughter came to the river. She found the ark, opened it, and recognized the child as a Hebrew. Rather than killing the child as her father had commanded, however, the woman showed compassion on the child, made the proper preparations, and, with the help of the baby's sister, established a procedure for adopting the baby as her own child. As a part of that process, the princess committed the child to a wet nurse suggested by the girl watching the ark. Of course, the wet nurse was the child's own mother.

After the baby had been weaned, the mother delivered the child to the princess. As a part of the adoption procedure, the princess named the child Moses. The young hero grew to maturity in the palace of the king who had sought to kill him. The mature Moses became concerned about the oppression of his people. The storyteller emphasized the identity between the oppressed people and Moses. "He went out to *his* people . . . , and he saw an Egyptian beating a Hebrew, *one of his kinsfolk*" (Ex. 2:11 NRSV, author's italics). Moses responded to the particular act of oppression against his people by killing the Egyptian.

In the wake of his violent act against the Egyptian taskmaster, Moses fled from Egypt and from his own people to the land of Midian. Again he intervened in the face of oppression, inviting danger and risk. Sitting at a well, the typical meeting place for the culture (see also Gen. 29:2), Moses witnessed the violent aggression of male shepherds against female shepherds who had already drawn water for their sheep. Moses saved the oppressed shepherds, whose father, the priest of Midian, invited him to live and work under the protection of the Midianite's hospitality. Eventu-

Stream in the Wilderness of Zin that local tradition says was formed when Moses and Aaron hit the rock.

ally one of the Midianite's daughters became Moses' wife. In the idyllic peace of the Midianite's hospitality, Moses took care of Jethro's sheep, fathered a child, and lived at a distance from his own people.

The event at the burning bush while Moses worked as a shepherd introduced him to the critical character of his heroic work. The burning bush caught Moses' attention. There Moses met the God of the fathers who offered Moses a distinctive name as the essential key for Moses' authority—"I am who I am." This strange formulation played on God's promise to Moses to be present with him in his special commission. God sent Moses back to the Pharaoh to secure the release of his people from their oppression. The divine speech of commission has a double character. (1) As the heroic leader of Israel, he would initiate events that would lead to Israel's Exodus from Egypt. (2) As the man of God, he would represent God in delivering the people from their Egyptian slavery. With the authority of that double commission, Moses returned to the Pharaoh to negotiate the freedom of his people.

The negotiation narratives depict Moses, the hero, in one scene of failure after the other. Moses posed his demands to the Pharaoh, announced a sign that undergirded the demand, secured some concession from the Pharaoh on the basis of the negotiations, but failed to win the release of the people. The final scene is hardly a new stage in the negotiations. To the contrary, God killed the firstborn of every Egyptian family, passing over the Israelite families. In the agony of this death scene, the Egyptians drove the Israelites out of Egypt (Ex. 12:30–36). Behind this dominant scene of violence and death lies a different interpretation of the Exodus event. The Pharaoh closed negotiations with Moses by refusing permission for the Israelites to leave in accordance with Moses' proposition (10:28). In the wake of this failure, Moses returned to the people with a plan for escaping Egypt without the knowledge of the Pharaoh. The people borrowed silver, gold, and clothing from the Egyptians in preparation for the event. When they escaped, they took the silver, gold, and clothing with them. They despoiled the Egyptians, a sign of victory over the Egyptians. Thus in leaving Egypt, Israel robbed the most powerful nation of their time of its firstborn sons and of its wealth.

Moses led the people into the wilderness, where the pursuing Egyptians trapped the Israelites at the Red Sea. God who had promised divine presence for the people defeated the enemy at the Sea. The God proved His presence with His people. He met their needs for food and water in the hostile wilderness. Even the fiery serpents and the Amalekites failed to thwart the wilderness journey of the Israelites under Moses' leadership.

Exodus 17:8–13 shows Moses to be faithful in the execution of his leadership responsibilities. Numbers 12:1–16 shows Moses to be meek, a leader of integrity who fulfilled the duties of his office despite opposition from members of his own family.

The center of the Moses traditions emerges with clarity in the events at Mount Sinai/Horeb. The law at Sinai/Horeb constitutes God's gift for Israel. The law showed Israel how to respond to God's saving act in the Exodus. The law at Sinai/Horeb showed each new generation how to follow Moses' teaching in a new setting in the life of the people. The laws carried the name of Moses as an affirmation of their authority. The law of Moses became a model for Israelite society. Indeed, Israel's historians told the entire story of Israel under the influence of the Moses model and suggested that the Davidic kings should have constructed their leadership for Israel under the influence of the Moses model (Joshua—Kings). Only the good king Josiah and, to a lesser extent, Hezekiah matched that model.

The death of Moses is marked by tragic loneliness, yet graced with God's presence. Because of Moses' sin (Num. 20), God denied Moses the privilege of entering the Promised Land. Deuteronomy 34 reports the death scene. Central to the report is the presence of God with Moses at the time of his death. Moses left his people to climb another mountain. Atop that mountain, away from the people whom he served so long, Moses died. God attended this servant at his death. Indeed, God buried him. Only God knows where the burial place is.

The Moses saga serves as a model for subsequent leaders in Israel. Jeroboam I created a new kingdom, distinct from the Davidic kingdom centered in Jerusalem. The sign of his kingship included the golden calves of Aaron. Josiah modeled a reformation in Jerusalem on the basis of the Mosaic model. As the new Moses, he almost succeeded in uniting the people of the south with the people of the north. Perhaps the most important Old Testament figure that must be interpreted as a new Moses is the servant of Isaiah 40—66, the model for understanding Jesus in the New Testament. *George W. Coats*

MOSES, BOOKS OF See *Pentateuch; Law.*

MOSES, LAW OF See *Law*

MOST HIGH The most common translation of the Hebrew word *Elyon*. It is used in conjunction with other divine names such as *El* (Gen. 14:18), and *Yahweh* (Ps. 7:17) to speak of God as the supreme being. See *Names of God.*

MOTE One translation of the Greek word *karphos* ("speck" in NRSV, NAS, NIV, TEV, REB). Jesus used the word in His Sermon on the Mount (Matt. 7:3–5) to illustrate hypocrisy, equating mote with the smallest particle of wood in contrast to a log or beam. Some older translations use "twig" or "straw."

MOTH Literally "consumer" or "waster," it is an insect whose destructive power is used to illustrate the result of sin (Ps. 39:11) and the judgment of God (Hos. 5:12). The moth's weakness is used to speak of the frailty of man (Job. 4:19). Jesus urged His followers to avoid the temptation to accumulate wealth on earth where the moth could destroy it, but to lay up immortal treasures in heaven (Matt. 6:19–20). See *Insects.*

MOTHER Female parent who carries, gives birth to, and cares for a child. Usually refers to humans but may refer to animals or even as a metaphor for deity. In the Bible a wife has two equally important roles: to love, support, and provide companionship and sexual satisfaction for her husband and to bear and rear children. So important was the latter that a stigma was attached to barrenness (Gen. 16:1–2; 18:9–15; 30:1; 1 Sam. 1:1–20; Luke 1:5–25, especially v. 25).

The Bible refers to every aspect of motherhood: conception (Gen. 4:1; Luke 1:24); pregnancy (2 Sam. 11:5; Luke 1:24); the pain of childbirth (Gen. 3:16; John 16:21); and nursing (1 Sam. 1:23; Matt. 24:19). A new mother was considered to be ritually unclean, and an offering was prescribed for her purification (Lev. 12; compare Luke 2:22–24). The Book of Proverbs (see 1:8; 31:1) indicates that even in ancient times mothers shared with fathers the responsibility for instructing and disciplining children. Mothers have the same right to obedience and respect as fathers (Ex. 20:12; Lev. 19:3), and in Old Testament times death was the fate of those who cursed or assaulted parents (Ex. 21:15; 17; Deut. 21:18–21). Jesus enforced the Fifth Commandment and protected it against scribal evasion (Matt. 15:3–6).

Motherly virtues are often extolled: compassion for children (Isa. 49:15), comfort of children (Isa. 66:13), and sorrow for children (Jer. 31:15, quoted in Matt. 2:18).

The fact that God would use a human mother to bring His Son into the world has bestowed upon motherhood its greatest honor. Jesus set an example for all to follow by the provision He made for His mother (John 19:25–27). Jesus made it plain, however, that devotion to God must take precedence to that of a mother (Matt. 12:46–50). Even the Old Testament (Gen. 2:24) indicated that a man's devotion to his wife supercedes that to his mother.

In addition to the literal sense, including that of animal mothers (see Ex. 34:26; Lev. 22:27), the word is often used metaphorically. Israel is compared to an unfaithful mother (Hos. 2:2–5; Isa. 50:1). Revelation 17:5 calls Babylon (Rome) the mother of harlots (those who are unfaithful to God). A city is the "mother" of her people (2 Sam. 20:19). Deborah was the "mother" (or deliverer) of Israel. In a more positive vein, the heavenly Jerusalem is the "mother" of Christians (Gal. 4:26). Jesus spoke of His compassion for Jerusalem as being like that of a mother hen for her chicks (Matt. 23:37). Paul compared his ministry to a mother in labor (Gal. 4:19) and a nursing mother (1 Thess. 2:7). *James A. Brooks*

MOTIONS OF SIN KJV expression for sinful desires (TEV) or passions (NAS, NIV, NRSV) at Romans 7:5.

Mount of the Beautitudes as seen from the Sea of Galilee.

MOULDY KJV spelling of moldy (Josh. 9:5,12). The underlying Hebrew term perhaps means "crumbled" (NAS, REB).

MOUNT BAAL-HERMON (Bā′ ȧl Hēr′ mon) A variant name for Mount Hermon (Judg. 3:3), perhaps indicating its use as a worship place for Baal.

MOUNT EPHRAIM See *Ephraim, Mount.*

MOUNT HERES See *Har-Heres; Heres.*

MOUNT OF ASSEMBLY See *Mount of the Congregation.*

MOUNT OF CORRUPTION Hill on the southern ridge of the Mount of Olives upon which Solomon built pagan shrines for use by his wives. These highplaces were destroyed as part of Josiah's reforms (2 Kings 23:13).

MOUNT OF THE AMALEKITES A mountainous region in the territory of Ephraim (Judg. 12:15; compare the Hebrew "in Amalek" of 5:14). Some interpreters dispute a connection with the desert tribe of the same name.

MOUNT OF THE AMORITES KJV designation for the hill country of Judah and Ephraim (Deut. 1:7,20).

MOUNT OF THE BEATITUDES The "Horns of Hattin" near Capernaum which tradition identifies as the site of the Sermon on the Mount (Matt. 5:1—7:29). The reference to Jesus' ascending the mountain is perhaps meant to recall the story of Moses at Sinai (Ex. 19:3,20).

MOUNT OF THE CONGREGATION KJV expression generally rendered Mount of Assembly by modern translations. Part of Isaiah's exposure of the pride of the King of Babylon is the charge that he desired to ascend to the distant mountain where according to Babylonian myth the gods assembled (Isa. 14:13). The desire is tantamount to a claim to divinity.

MOUNT OF THE VALLEY KJV designation for an elevation in a valley in the territory of Reuben in Transjordan (Josh. 13:19). Modern translations render the phrase hill in/of the valley.

MOUNT SINAI (Mount Sī′ nā ī) Mountain in the south central part of a peninsula in the northwestern end of Arabia. God made many significant revelations of Himself and His purposes to Israel there. The meaning of the name is unclear; but it probably means "shining" and was likely derived from the word *sin,* a Babylonian moon god. The suggestion that it means "clayey" does not in any way fit the nature of the terrain.

Looking from the top of Mt. Sinai out across the massive, rocky granite cliffs surrounding it.

The entire peninsula takes the shape of an inverted triangle whose base is 150 miles long and is bounded on the east by the north end of the Red Sea and on the west by the Gulf of Aqaba. The Gaza strip lies directly north. This peninsula contains 23,442 square miles and has a population of approximately 140,000 at time of publication. The central and southern parts are extremely mountainous, ranging from 5000 to about 9000 feet, and the land today is valued for its oil fields and manganese deposits.

The Bible uses the term *Sinai* for both the mountain and the entire wilderness area (Lev. 7:38). Sometimes Sinai is called "the mount" (Ex. 19:2); sometimes "the mountain of God" (Ex. 3:1); sometimes "the mount of the Lord" (Num. 10:33).

The term *Horeb* is often used to refer to Sinai in such a way as to make the names synonymous (Ex. 3:1). Since Horeb means "waste" or "wilderness area," it seems best to think of Horeb as the general term for the area and Sinai as the specific peak where God manifested Himself to Moses.

The modern name for the traditional site of Sinai is Jebel Musa (the mount of Moses). Jebel is the Arabic word *hill,* sometimes written Jabal or Gabel (French has Djebel).

Jebel Musa (7500 ft.) is one of three granite peaks near the southern tip of the peninsula. The highest peak, Jebel Katarin (Mount Catherine, 8,652 ft.), lies immediately on the southwest, and Ras es-Safsafeh (6,540 ft.) on the north, northeast of Jebel Musa. Many explorers think Ras es-Safsafeh is the biblical Sinai because it has a plain, *er Rahah,* on its northwest base, which is two miles long and about two thirds of a mile wide. This plain was certainly large enough to accommodate the camp of the Israelites.

Another suggested location for Mount Sinai is far north and east of Jebel Musa, near the top of the Gulf of Aqaba. The major argument for this view is that Sinai's phenomena indicate volcanic action—fire, smoke, quaking earth (Ex. 19:16–18)—and no volcano is found in the Sinaitic peninsula. The nearest volcano lies far east of the Gulf. However, the phenomena that appeared at Sinai were undoubtedly supernatural in origin, for they were accompanied by the sounds of a trumpet and the voice of God (Ex. 19:19).

Another location for Sinai is sought far north of Jebel Musa, primarily because of historical references such as the battle with the Amalekites (Ex. 17:8–16). The Amalekites lived in Canaan proper (Num. 14:42–45) and would not, it is claimed, have met the Israelites in the Sinaitic peninsula. However, the Amalekites could have followed the recently delivered Israelites to the south of their territory for the purpose of preying on the poorly organized refugees (Deut. 25:17–19).

See *Palestine; Exodus, Wilderness Journey*
J. Travis

MOUNTAIN Elevated topographical feature formed by geological faulting and erosion. The geography of Palestine featured high mountains and deep rifts. See *Palestine.* The two usual words for mountain in the Bible are *har* (Hebrew) and *oros* (Greek). The simple definition for each is mountain or hill, though they may indicate hill country or a mountainous region.

Many important events in the Bible took place on or near mountains. God called Moses to His work at Mount Horeb, sometimes called "the mountain of God." A part of God's call was the promise that the Israelite people would worship there upon their escape from Egypt (Ex. 3:1–12).

After the Exodus, God commanded Moses to gather the people at Mount Sinai (probably identical to Horeb). There God gave the Law including the Ten Commandments to Moses.

Other Old Testament mountain episodes include Aaron's death on Mount Hor (Num. 33:38), the death of Moses on Mount Nebo (Deut. 34:1–8), and Elijah's defeat of the prophets of Baal on Mount Carmel (1 Kings 18:15–40).

Much of Jesus' life and ministry also took place on mountains. One of the temptations took place on "an exceeding high mountain" (Matt. 4:8). Jesus' most famous teaching session is called the "Sermon on the Mount" (Matt. 5–7). Jesus went up to a mountain to pray (Luke 6:12) and healed the Gerasene demoniac near a mountain site (Mark 5:11).

Perhaps it is significant that the scene of the transfiguration was on a mountain (Matt. 17:1–8). Jesus was declared to be preeminent over both Moses and Elijah, the representatives of the Law and Prophets. Many of their greatest victories came on mountains. Jesus is affirmed as Lord of all at this mountain experience.

The term *mountain* also is used symbolically in the Bible. It is a natural image for stability (Ps. 30:7), obstacles (Zech. 4:7), and God's power (Ps. 121:1–2). God will remove all obstacles when His redemption is complete, "and every mountain and hill shall be made low" (Isa. 40:4).

Mountains often have been called "holy places." Jerusalem (elevation 2,670 feet) often was called Mount Zion, the hill of the Lord (Pss. 2:6; 135:21: Isa. 8:18; Joel 3:21; Mic. 4:2). God met His people there in worship. The "New Jerusalem" is also known as Mount Zion (Rev. 14:1).

Some of the more famous biblical mountains with their feet elevations are: Ebal (3,084), Gerezim (2,890), Gilboa (1,630), Hermon (9,230), Nebo (2,630), Tabor (1,930), Sinai (7,500).

See *Jerusalem,* Zion ; *Sermon on the Mount.*
Bradley S. Butler

MOUNTAIN SHEEP See *Chamois.*

MOURN, MOURNER, MOURNING See *Grief and Mourning.*

MOUSE See *Animals in the Bible.*

MOUTH Portion of head used to ingest food and to communicate. *1.* Synonymn for lips (1 Kings 19:18; 2 Kings 4:34; Job 31:27; Prov. 30:20; Song of Sol. 1:2); *2.* Organ of eating and drinking (Judg. 7:6; 1 Sam. 14:26–27), sometimes used in figurative expressions such as when wickedness (Job 20:12) or God's word (Ps. 119:10) is described as sweet to the mouth. Anthropomorphic descriptions of the earth or Sheol speak of them opening their mouths to drink blood or swallow persons (Gen. 4:11; Num. 16:30,32; Isa. 5:14). *3.* Organ of speech (Gen. 45:12; Deut. 32:1) or laughter (Job 8:21; Ps. 126:2). The phrase "the mouth of the Lord has spoken it" serves as a frequent reminder of the reliability of a prophetic message (Isa. 1:20; 40:5; Jer. 9:12; compare Deut. 8:3; Matt. 4:4). Fire (2 Sam. 22:9) or a sword (Rev. 1:16) proceeding from the mouth of God pictures the effectiveness of God's word of judgment. *4.* The Hebrew term for mouth is used for the openings of wells, caves, sacks, as well as for the edge of a sword.

MOZA (Mō′ zà) Personal name meaning, "offspring." *1.* Descendant of Judah (1 Chron. 2:46). *2.* Descendant of King Saul (1 Chron. 8:36–37; 9:42–43).

MOZAH (Mō′ zah) Place name meaning, "unleavened." City in Benjamin (Josh. 18:26), later a center for pottery production as attested by numerous vessels recovered at Jericho and tell-en-Nasbeh bearing the inscription Mozah on their handles. The site is likely that of modern Qaluniya, four miles northwest of Jerusalem on the Tel Aviv road.

MUFFLER KJV term for a scarf (NRSV) at Isaiah 3:19. The item is part of the finery of the Jerusalem socialites. Other translations render the Hebrew term as veils (NAS, NIV, TEV) or coronets (REB).

MULBERRY TREE See *Plants in the Bible; Balsam.*

MULE A hybrid animal produced by the union of a male ass and a mare. David chose a mule to symbolize royalty for Solomon's coronation (1 Kings 1:33), possibly because the Israelites did not have horses. However, this is not the donkey used in Zechariah 9:9 and Matthew 21:5 for Jesus' entry to Jerusalem. See *Animals.*

MUPPIM (Mŭp′ pĭm) Son of Benjamin (Gen. 46:21). The name perhaps derives from the root "to wave." See *Shephupham.*

MURDER Intentional taking of human life. Human life is given great value in the Bible. Persons are created in the image of God; and persons are called to obey, serve, and glorify God. Human life is viewed as a sacred trust. It is because of this that taking human life is viewed as a serious crime in the Bible.

The prohibition against murder is found in the Ten Commandments, the heart of Hebrew law (Ex. 20:13; Deut. 5:17). Murder is the unlawful killing of a human being by another. Deliberately taking the life of a human being ursurps the authority that belongs to God. The prohibition against murder is a hedge to protect human dignity.

The Old Testament (Gen. 9:6) prescribed that a murderer should be prepared to forfeit his own life. In Numbers 35:16–31, careful attention is given to determining whether a killing is to be classified as murder.

Jesus removed the concept of murder from a physical act to the intention of one's heart (Matt. 5:21–22). According to Jesus, murder really begins when one loses respect for another human being. Spitting in the face of another, looking with contempt upon another, or unleashing one's anger are signs that a murderous spirit is present. Jesus forces us to move to the spirit behind the prohibition of murder. We are compelled to do all that we can do to protect the life of our neighbor and help it flourish. The writer of 1 John pushed Jesus' teaching to its ultimate: "Whosoever hateth his brother is a murderer: and ye know that no murderer hath eternal life abiding in him (1 John 3:15).

See *Image of God; Ten Commandments.*

D. Glenn Saul

MURRAIN (Mŭ′ râin) KJV term derived from the French for to die (morir) referring to an infectious disease affecting livestock (Ex. 9:3). The earliest Greek translation used the term death. Modern translations use either disease (TEV), pestilence (NAS, NRSV), or plague (NIV, RSV).

MUSE To ponder or reflect upon something, often without coming to conclusions (Ps. 143:5; Luke 3:15).

MUSHI (Mū′ shī) Personal name meaning, "draw out." Son of Merari who gave his name to a family of priests, the Mushites (Mū′ shītes) (Ex. 6:19; Num. 3:20,33; 26:58; 1 Chron. 6:19,47; 23:21,23; 24:26,30).

MUSHITE (Mū′ shīte) Member of clan of Mushi.

MUSIC, INSTRUMENTS, DANCING The expression of the full range of human emotions vocally or instrumentally through the art of music was as much a part of the lives of biblical people as it is of modern times. Workers bringing in the harvest might sing a vintage song (Isa. 16:10; Jer.

48:33), while the working song of people digging a well (Num. 21:17) is heard as well. Indeed all of life could be touched by song. The celebrations of a community, ritual practices of worship, even the act of warfare gave rise to song.

In such a musical climate, celebration through dance found a natural place in both the religious and secular life of ancient Israel. A variety of musical instruments was available to provide instrumental accompaniment to both song and dance.

Music Music as performed in early Near Eastern times has become better known through archaeological finds of descriptive texts and the remains of actual instruments. Heptatonic and diatonic musical scales reflective of ancient Mesopotamian practice have been discerned through the research of Assyrian culture which has, over the last few decades, brought to light much pertinent information on the subject. The discovery of four Akkadian cuneiform texts describing the Mesopotamian theory of music from about 1800 to about 500 B.C. offers evidence 1400 years earlier than previously known in Greek sources for the antiquity of Western music. Giving evidence of seven different heptatonic-diatonic scales, the musical system of ancient Mesopotamia shows one similar to the major scale known today.

Textual evidence from the end of the third millennium B.C. shows ancient Sumer, the earliest center of civilization in the Fertile Crescent, to have enjoyed an expansive musical tradition. A variety of hymns offering divine praise or designed to or for kings and temples, many with musical terms, have survived and are joined by actual discoveries of instruments at the ancient site of Ur, in biblical tradition the ancestral home of Abraham (Gen. 11:31).

A cuneiform text found at ancient Ugarit in Syria dating from about 1400 B.C. is a complete piece of Hurrian cult music. As a hymn to the moon goddess Nikkal, the piece uses a notational system consisting of technical Akkadian terminology for interval names followed by numerals.

Going back to about 3000 B.C., the pictorial and written clues to Egyptian music tradition that have survived the centuries are particularly valuable in the appreciation of musical instruments, providing background information for instruments mentioned in the biblical text as well as comparative study with Mesopotamian data. Illustrations or references within the Egyptian sources include a variety of lyres, harps, and lutes. Flutes, double reed pipes, and a succession of percussion instruments (such as drums, bells, rattles, clappers) have been identified.

The secular and religious music of ancient Israel found its home against this background of Ancient Near Eastern music in which all of life could be brought under the spell of song. In reading the Old Testament, Genesis 4:21 stands as the first reference to music. As one of Lamech's sons,

Jubal "was the father of all those who play the lyre and pipe" (NAS). Jubal brought the advent of music to the portrayal of cultural advance. The name *Jubal* itself is related to the Hebrew word for "ram" (*yobel*), the horns of which served as a signaling instrument in ancient Israel.

The joy taken in music is evidenced by its prominent role in the celebrations of life. A farewell might be said "with joy and singing to the music of tambourines and harps" (Gen. 31:27 NIV); a homecoming welcomed "with timbrels and with dances" (Judg. 11:34; compare Luke 15:25). Work tasks of everyday living enjoyed the music evidenced by the songs or chants of the well diggers (Num. 21:17–18), the treaders of grapes (Jer. 48:33), and possibly the watchman (Isa. 21:12).

Under certain circumstances musical celebration brought condemnation. The account of Moses' return from the mountain to be confronted by the singing and dancing of the people around the golden calf (Ex. 32:17–19) symbolized a condition of broken covenant. The prophet Isaiah's rebuke of the idle rich who have "lyre and harp, tambourine and flute and wine" at their feasts is cast against their failure to take notice of the deeds of Yahweh (Isa. 5:12 NRSV). Both the scorn of mockers (Job 30:9) and the acclamation of heroes (1 Sam. 18:6–7) were expressed in song.

Victory in warfare provided impetus for numerous songs. The song of Miriam, one of the oldest poetic verses in the Old Testament, celebrated the defeat of Pharoah at the Sea (Ex. 15:21). Judges 5 stands as musical witness to Israel's victory over Jabin, the king of Canaan. Known as the "Song of Deborah," the verses are the musical celebration of a narrative event. Chants of victory on the lips of the victor (compare Samson following his slaying of the Philistines recorded in Judg. 15:16) or those greeting the one successful in battle (compare 1 Sam. 18:7) establish music as a medium for uncontainable joy. Celebration erupted into song. Emotions that might be limited by the restriction of prose expressed themselves through the poetry of music as seen in David's moving lament at the death of Saul and Jonathan (2 Sam. 1:19–27).

In the early days of Old Testament history a special place seems to be accorded women in musical performance. The prophetess Miriam and Deborah, a prophetess and judge, were among Israel's earliest musicians. Judges 11:34 pictures Jephthah's daughter greeting his victorious return from battle against the Ammonites "with timbrels and with dances." David's reputation for valor spread through the singing of women's voices: "Saul hath slain his thousands, and David his ten thousands" (1 Sam. 18:7). The depiction of dancing women entertaining at festive occasions found on Egyptian tomb paintings provides early Near Eastern background for the role of women in musical celebration.

The establishment of the monarchy about 1025 B.C. brought a new dimension to the musical tradition of ancient Israel with the appearance of professional musicians. Egypt and Assyria, neighboring countries to Israel, had known the tradition of professional musicians much earlier. Such musicians took their place both at court (1 Kings 1:34,39–40; 10:12; Eccl. 2:8) and in religious ritual. An Assyrian inscription, praising the victory of the Assyrian king Sennacherib over King Hezekiah of Judah, lists male and female musicians as part of the tribute carried off to Nineveh.

Although much uncertainty remains concerning the specifics of Temple worship, biblical references offer clues to the role music played in cult obervances. As a hymn proclaiming the future rule of God in all the earth, Psalm 98 calls for the employment of music in praise:

"Make a joyful noise to the Lord, all the earth; break forth into joyous song and sing praises! Sing praises to the Lord with the lyre, with the lyre and the sound of melody! With trumpets and the sound of the horn make a joyful noise before the King, the Lord!" (vv. 4–6 RSV).

Worship featured trumpet calls (compare Num. 10:10) and songs of thanksgiving, expressions of praise and petition sung after the offering of sacrifices (2 Chron. 29:20–30).

The Psalms show not only the emotional range of music from lament to praise but also provides words for some of the songs used in Temple worship. Guilds of musicians, known through reference to their founders in some psalm headings (for example, "the sons of Korah"), were evidently devoted to the discipline of liturgical music.

During the Babylonian Exile the question, "How shall we sing the Lord's song in a strange land?" (Ps. 137:4), arose. Psalm 137 further alludes to the demand of the Babylonians for the Hebrew captives to "sing us one of the songs of Zion" (v. 3). The return from Exile and reestablishment of the Temple saw the descendants of the original Levitical musicians (compare Ezra 2:40–41) reassume responsibility for liturgical music. Strabo's statement that the singing girls of Palestine were considered the most musical in the world shows that music continued in importance in Israel during Hellenistic times.

The structures of some psalms offer evidence for conjecturing the nature of vocal performance. Refrains (such as the "Lift up your heads, O ye gates; even lift them up, ye everlasting doors" of Ps. 24) and acclamations such as "Hallelujah" as well as divisions into strophes stand as performance clues. The common device of poetic parallelism, whereby a thought is balanced synonymously or antithetically with a second thought, provides further evidence for surmising the nature of musical performance, responsive and antiphonal performances being possibilities.

In light of the recognized obscurity in many of the headings, one can speak in general terms of five different types of information provided by the Psalm titles. Representatives of this classification are titles that identify psalms with persons or groups of persons (see Pss. 3; 72; 90); titles purporting to indicate historical information concerning the psalm, particularly with respect to David (see Pss. 18; 34); titles containing musical information (see Pss. 4; 5); titles with liturgical information (see Pss. 92; 100); and titles designating the "type" of psalm in question (see Ps. 120, "a song of ascents"; Ps. 145, "a song of praise").

Nearly two thirds of the psalms contain terms indicating collections, compilers, or authors in their headings: David, portrayed in biblical tradition as a composer, instrumentalist, court musician, and dancer, being most often mentioned. Others mentioned include the sons of Korah, Asaph, Solomon, Heman the Ezrahite, Ethan the Ezrahite, Moses, and Jeduthun.

Deriving from the Greek translation of the Hebrew *mizmor,* the word *psalm* is applied to some fifty-seven songs. As a technical term appearing only in the Psalter, *psalm* refers to songs with instrumental accompaniment. Other terms indicating the type of psalm include "*shiggaion*" (Ps. 7), sometimes argued to indicate a lament; "*miktam*" (Pss. 16; 56—60) connected to the Akkadian meaning "to cover"; "*maskil*" (Ps. 78) whose meaning is still unknown. Some thirty Psalms include in their heading the word *song* (Hebrew *shir*), with "song of praise," "Prayer," "a song of love," and "a song of ascent" also occurring. Headings may include as well terms which indicate the liturgical aim and usage of the particular psalm (for instance, "for the thank offering," "for the memorial offering," "for the sabbath").

Some fifty-five psalms contain the expression "to the choirmaster" in their headings. Other technical musical expressions consisting of remarks that concern types or kinds of performances include "with stringed instruments" ("*neginoth,*" see Pss. 4; 6; 54, perhaps meant to exclude percussion and wind instruments) and "for the flutes" ("*nehiloth*"), though both meanings are dubious. The terms "*higgaion*" (perhaps "musical flourish"), "*sheminith*" ("on the eighth," perhaps an octave higher), and "the *gittith*" (Pss. 8; 81; 84) remain obscure as to meaning.

The singing of psalms to other tunes popular at the time is suggested by headings such as "Hind of the Dawn" in Psalm 22 (RSV) and "to Lillies" used in Psalms 45; 69; 80 (RSV).

Although found some seventy-one times in the Psalter, the interpretation of the term "*Selah*" remains uncertain. Suggestions range from understanding the term according to its earliest Greek translation, generally thought to indicate a type of musical interlude or change in singing, to a call for repetition of the verse, louder singing, or the kneeling and bowing down of worshipers.

Musical Instruments Pictorial representations as well as remains from instruments discovered through archaeology aid in our present knowledge of ancient musical instruments. A wide scope of literary remains gives further evidence. Descriptions and comment on musical instruments are to be found in both the Old and New Testament, their early translations, rabbinic and patristic literature, and the writings of Roman and Greek authors. Caution, however, must be applied in using the data available, leaving many identifications difficult and at best hypothetical.

The most frequently named musical instrument in the Bible is the "Shophar" (ram's horn). Limited to two or three nores, the "Shophar" often translated "trumpet") served as a signaling instrument in times of peace and war (Judg. 3:27; 6:34; Neh. 4:18–20). Having as its chief function the making of noise, the Shophar announced the new moons and sabbaths, warned of approaching danger, and signaled the death of nobility. As the only ancient instrument still used in the synagogue today, the "Shophar" found a prominent place in the life of Israel, noted by its function in national celebration (1 Kings 1:34; 2 Kings 9:13).

Similar in function to the "shophar" was the trumpet, a straight metal instrument flared on the end and thought to have had a high, shrill tone. Sounded in pairs, the trumpet was known as the instrument of the priests (compare Num. 10:2–10 for a description of usages; see also 2 Chron. 5:12–13 where some twenty trumpeters are mentioned. The sound of the trumpets introduced Temple ceremony and sacrifice, the trumpet itself being counted among the sacred Temple utensils (2 Kings 12:13; Num. 31:6).

As the instrument of David and the Levites, the lyre (Hebrew, "*kinnor*"; KJV, "harp") was employed in both secular and sacred settings (compare Isa. 23:16; 2 Sam. 6:5). A popular instrument throughout the Ancient Near East, the lyre was often used to accompany singing. The number of strings on the lyre could vary; its basic shape was rectangular or trapezoidal.

The harp was a favorite instrument of the Egyptians. In Hebrew the designation *nebel,* though admittedly uncertain, may imply a type of angular harp with a vertical resonator or represent another type of lyre. Mainly a religious instrument in biblical tradition, the "*nebel*" is rarely mentioned in secular functions (compare Isa. 5:12; 14:11). Like the lyre, the harp was often associated with aristocracy, thus being often made from precious woods and metals (see 1 Kings 10:12; 2 Chron. 9:11).

Chief among "flutes" and "pipes," woodwinds generally associated with secular usages, was the "*khalil*," the most popular wind instrument in the Ancient Near East and principle among the biblical wind instuments. Perhaps better described as a primitive clarinet, the "khalil" (NAS, "flute" or KJV,"pipe") was an instrument consisting of two separate pipes made of reed, metal, or ivory; each pipe having a mouthpiece with single or double reeds. Used in the expression of joy (1 Kings 1:39–40) or mourning (Jer. 48:36; Matt. 9:23), the *khalil* was primarily a secular instrument that could be played at funerals or feasts.

Other musical instruments mentioned in the biblical texts include the timbrel or tambourine (Hebrew *toph,* often symbolic of gladness, Gen 21:27), cymbals, bells (presumably metal jingles without clappers; see Ex. 28:33–34; 39:25–26 where they are attached to the high priest's robe), and a rattle-type noisemaker translated variously as castanets, rattles, sistrums, cymbols, or clappers (2 Sam. 6:5).

Mentioned in the New Testament are pipes (RSV, "flute"), the lyre (RSV, "harp"), cymbals, and the trumpet. The "sounding brass" of 1 Corinthians 13:1 is perhaps understood through rabbinic literature in which it is seen as a characteristic instrument for weddings and joyous celebrations.

Dancing As rhythmic movement often performed to music, dancing enjoyed a prominent place in the life and worship of Israel. Various Hebrew words in the Old Testament used to express the idea of dance seem to imply different types of movement: to skip about (*raqadh,* Job 21:11), whirling about (*karar,* 2 Sam. 6:14,16), and perhaps twisting or writhing (*makhol,* Ps. 30:11). Pictured in the homecoming welcome of victorious soldiers by women, dancing could be accompanied by song and instrument music (1 Sam. 18:6).

Exodus 15:20 celebrates Israel's deliverance at the Sea of Reeds by dancing with singing and musical accompaniment. Judges 21:16–24 accords dancing a role in the celebration of the yearly feast at Shiloh, and David is pictured as dancing before the Lord as the Ark was brought to Jerusalem (2 Sam. 6:14). Psalm 150:4 calls God's people to praise Him with the dance.

As in Israel, dancing was a part of the religious practices of other peoples in the ancient Near East. Male and female dancers are known to us from Egyptian reliefs, and cultic dancers are attested in Mesopotamian texts. As an idolatrous act, dancing is mentioned in the golden-calf story (Ex. 32:19) and in the worship of Baal at Carmel (1 Kings 18:26).

In the New Testament, the return of the prodigal son was celebrated with music and dancing (Luke 15:25). The practice of dancers entertaining at royal courts in Hellenistic and Roman times is attested by the dance of Herodias' daughter, Salome, (Matt. 14:6).

See *David; Levites; Psalms, The; Shiloh.*

Kandy Queen-Sutherland

MUSTARD A large annual plant which grows quite fast. Its seeds were once thought to be the smallest in the plant world. Jesus used the mustard plant in a parable to symbolize the rapid growth of the kingdom of God (Matt 13:31–32), and its seed as a simile for faith (Matt. 17:20). See *Plants.*

MUSTER GATE NRSV, REB designation for a Jerusalem city gate where troops were mustered, that is, gathered for enlistment (Neh. 3:31). See *Miphkad Gate.*

MUTENESS The inability to speak. In the Old Testament muteness is traced to God (Ex. 4:11). God made Ezekiel mute (Ezek. 3:26) in response to Israel's failure to listen to his message. Later He restored Ezekiel's speech (24:27; 33:22) as a sign of the people's receptiveness to hear. Daniel experienced muteness in response to the appearance of a heavenly messenger (Dan. 10:15). The psalmist considered muteness an appropriate punishment for liars (Ps. 31:18). By extension, to be mute means to hold one's peace (Ps. 39:2,9; Isa. 53:7; Acts 8:32), especially in the face of injustice. In Proverbs 31:8 the mute are the symbol of all those who suffer without a voice. Isaiah 56:10 pictures Israel's leaders as mute dogs who cannot bark a warning. In Isaiah 35:6 the singing of those once mute accompanies return from the Exile. In Habakkuk 2:18–19 idols are mocked as mutes (also 1 Cor. 12:2).

In the New Testament muteness is either not explained (Mark 7:32,37) or else attributed to demons (Matt. 9:32; 12:22; Mark 9:17,25; Luke 11:14). An exception is Zechariah's muteness (Luke 1:20,22) which served as a sign of the truthfulness of Gabriel's message as well as a punishment for Zechariah's unbelief.

MUTH-LABBEN (Mŭth lăb′ bĕn) Hebrew phrase in the title of Psalm 9 which means, "death of the son." The phrase likely refers to the tune to which the psalm was performed.

MUTTER To utter words indistinctly or with a low voice. Muttering together with chirping characterized the speech of mediums (Isa. 8:19). The shades were thought to communicate through the medium in this fashion. See *Medium; Sheol.*

MUZZLE A leather or wire covering for an animal's mouth to prevent its eating or biting. Deuteronomy 25:4 is one of many laws in the Deuteronomic code concerned with humane treatment of others. Paul cited this prohibition of muzzling a treading ox to illustrate the principle that "the laborer deserves to be paid" and specifically that "those who proclaim the gospel should get their living by the gospel" (1 Cor. 9:9–14; 1 Tim. 5:17–18 NRSV).

MYRA (Mȳ′ rä) One of the six largest cities of

Lysia in southeastern Asia Minor located on the River Andracus about two and one half miles from the sea. The site of the ancient ruins is called Dembre today. Myra was a stopping point on Paul's voyage to Rome (Acts 27:5–6). Some manuscripts of the Western Text give Myra as port call after Patara in Acts 21:1.

MYRIAD (Myr î ad) Greek term literally meaning 10,000 but frequently used to mean countless or innumerable. See Jude 14; Revelation 5:11; 9:16; Luke 12:1; Acts 19:19; 21:20; Hebrews 12:22.

MYRRH An aromatic resin having many uses in the Ancient Near East. It was traded along with spices (Gen. 37:25), used as an ingredient in anointing oil (Ex. 30:23), applied as perfume (Esth. 2:12), placed in clothes to deodorize them (Ps. 45:8), given as a gift (Matt. 2:11), and used to embalm bodies (John 19:39).

MYRTLE See *Plants in the Bible.*

MYSIA (Mўs′ ĭ å) Northwest region of Asia Minor (Acts 16:7). The New Testament mentions several cities in this region: Adramyttium (Acts 27:2); Assos (Acts 20:13–14); Pergamum (Rev. 1:11; 2:12); and Troas (Acts 16:8,11; 20:5,6; 2 Cor. 2:12; 2 Tim. 4:13). Hindered from mission work in Bythinia, Paul passed through Mysia before embarking on his Macedonian mission (Acts 16:6–11). Acts 20 records Paul's seven-day stay at Troas and an overland (mission) trip to Assos. On another occasion, Paul found in Troas an open door of mission opportunity (2 Cor. 2:12).

MYSTERY/MYSTERY RELIGIONS Several different cults or societies characterized in part by elaborate initiation rituals and secret rites. Though attested in Greece before 600 B.C., the mystery religions flourished during the Hellenistic and Roman periods (after 333 B.C.) before dying out before A.D. 500. In particular, the intermingling of religious concepts made possible by Alexander the Great's far flung conquests accelerated the spread of some cults and facilitated the development of others. Knowledge of the mystery religions is fragmentary due to the strict secrecy imposed on those initiated; scattered references in ancient writers, some antagonistic to mystery religions, and archaeological data provide the most important evidence. Scholars often disagree about the interpretation of the data.

Many mystery religions emerged, but among the more important were those associated with the following deities: the Greek Demeter (the famous Eleusinian mysteries) and Dionysus, the Phyrgian Cybele (the Magna Mater) and Attis, the Syrian Adonis; the Egyptian Isis and Osiris (Sarapis); and Mithra, originally a Persian deity. Orphism and Sabazius both contributed to the mysteries of Dionysus while Samothrace was the home of the Cabiri mysteries. Many of the deities in the mystery religions were ancient and were worshiped in separate cults both before and after the development of the mystery cults.

The central feature of each mystery religion was the sacred rites, called mysteries, in which the cultic myth of the god or goddess worshiped in the cult was reenacted. Only those formally initiated into the cult could participate. The precise nature of these rites is unknown due to the vow of secrecy, but probably involved a drama based upon the cult myth and the dramatic visual presentation of certain sacred objects. Mention is made of "things said," probably sacred formulas and secret love. References exist to eating and drinking, likely a form of communion. By participating in these rites the worshiper identified with the deity and shared in the deity's fate. These powerful symbols afforded those initiated the means to overcome the suffering and difficulties of life and promised a share in the life beyond.

Many, but not all, of the deities worshiped in the mysteries were originally associated with fertility. As such, their associated myths often referred to the natural cycle as it waxes and wanes (for instance, Demeter) or to the dying and rising of a god (Attis, Adonis, Osiris). Some scholars think that the mysteries used this feature of the myth to give symbolic expression of rising to immortality with the deity. However, not all scholars agree; some deities venerated in mystery religions did not die or rise; moreover, the exact use of the myth in the mysteries is often unclear, though some concept of immortality seems to be implied.

Public festivals were given in honor of some deities worshiped in the mystery religions, but their relationship to the secret rites is not clear. The spring festival of Cybele (March 15–27) involved processions, sacrifices, music, and frenzied dancing which led to castration. The public revelry, pantomimes, theatric productions, and excesses of drink associated with the worshipers of Dionysus/Bacchus (the Bacchanalia) are well known.

Rites of initiation into the mystery religions included ritual cleansing in the sea, baptisms, and sacrifices. Mention should be made of the Taurobolium, used in the worship of Cybele, a rite in which a bull was slaughtered on a grill placed over a pit in which a priest stood; the person below eagerly covered himself with blood. Some have interpreted this as a rite of initiation, but it is more likely a purification ritual affording rebirth for a period of time, perhaps twenty years.

The mystery religions dislodged religion from the traditional foundations of state and family and made it a matter of personal choice. With a few exceptions, for instance, Mithraism which was restricted to males, the mysteries were open to all classes and sexes. Those initiated formed an association bound together by secret rites and symbols peculiar to their cult. These associations met regularly with a designated leader in houses or specially-built structures. The worshipers of Mithras met in a structure called a Mithraeum designed to imitate the cave in which Mithras killed the bull, the central act of the cult myth. Scenes of the slaying (tauroctony) appear prominently in several such structures.

The Eleusinian Caves, center of worship for the Eleusinian mystery religion.

At the meetings ritual acts or sacraments practiced by the particular cult were shared by the members. Mention is made of common meals or banquets. Members of the association were required to meet certain moral standards; some mention also is made of ascetic requirements. However, a word of caution is in order; generalizations about the mystery religions are difficult since each cult was individualistic. Exceptions to nearly all generalizations can be found.

Mystery in the New Testament The New Testament uses the word *mystery* about twenty-five times, once in the Gospels (Mark 4:11; compare Matt.13:11; Luke 8:10), twenty-one times in Paul's writings, and a few times in Revelation. The term has several facets all of which cannot be discussed here, but it is clear that the New Testament usage differs from that of the mystery religions. The mystery of the New Testament has been described as an "open secret"; matters previously kept secret in God's eternal purposes have now been or are being revealed (Eph. 3:3–5; 1 Cor. 2:7–8). In contrast to the mystery religions, the mystery of the New Testament appears in the historical activity of the person of Christ (Col. 2:2; Eph. 1:9); the indwelling Christ is the hope of glory (Col. 1:26–27). The mystery is received spiritually (Eph. 3:4–5) and manifested in the proclamation of the gospel (Eph. 6:19). Part of the mystery involves the disclosure that Gentiles share in the blessings of the gospel (Eph. 2:11–13).

Tommy Brisco

N

The Negev (Negeb) desert in southern Israel.

NAAM (Nā' ăm) Personal name meaning, "pleasantness." Descendant of Caleb (1 Chron. 4:15).

NAAMAH (Nā' ȧ mah) Name meaning, "pleasant" or "delightful." *1.* Sister of Tubal-cain (Gen. 4:22). *2.* Ammonite wife of Solomon and mother of Rehoboam (1 Kings 14:21,31; 2 Chron. 12:13). *3.* Village in the Shephelah district of Judah (Josh. 15:41), likely khirbet Farad about twenty-two miles west of Jerusalem between Timnah and Eltekeh.

NAAMAN (Nā' ȧ man) Personal name meaning, "pleasantness." Syrian general cured of leprosy under the direction of the prophet Elisha (2 Kings 5). Naaman's leprosy apparently was not contagious, nor was it seen as the result of some moral sin. Following his cleansing, he professed faith in Israel's God. See *Leprosy.*

NAAMATHITE (Nā' ȧ mȧ thīte) Title meaning, "resident of Na'ameh," given to Zophar, one of Job's three friends (Job. 2:11; 11:1; 20:1; 42:9). Na'ameh is perhaps Djebel-el-Na'ameh in northwest Arabia.

NAAMITES (Nā' ȧ mītes) Family of Benjaminites descended from Naaman (Num. 26:40).

NAARAH (Nā' ȧ răh) Name meaning, "girl" or "mill." *1.* Wife of Ashur (1 Chron. 4:5–6). *2.* Form of Naarath preferred by modern translations.

NAARAI (Nā' ȧ râi) Personal name meaning, "attendant of Yah." One of David's thirty elite warriors (1 Chron. 11:37). The parallel account gives the name Paari (2 Sam. 23:35).

NAARAN (Nā' ȧ răn) City allotted to Ephraim, likely identical with Naarah (1 Chron. 7:28; compare Josh. 16:7).

NAARATH (Nā' ȧ răth) KJV form of Naarah, a city in the tribal territory of Ephraim just north of Jericho (Josh. 16:7). Suggested sites include 'Ain Duq, khirbet el 'Nayash about five miles northeast of Jericho, and tell el-Jishr. The city is perhaps identical to Naaran (1 Chron. 7:28).

NAASHON (Nā' ăsh ŏn) KJV alternate form of Nahshon at Exodus 6:23.

NAASON (Nā ăs' on) KJV alternate form of Nahshon (Matt. 1:4; Luke 3:32).

NABAL (Nā' băl) Personal name meaning, "fool" or "rude, ill-bred." See *Abigail.*

NABATEANS (Nă ba tē' ans) Arabic people whose origins are unknown. Although not men-

The Treasury building of ancient Petra as seen from the only entranceway into the city.

tioned in the Bible, they greatly influenced Palestine during intertestamental and New Testament times. They appear to have infiltrated ancient Edom and Moab from a homeland southeast of Petra. That city later became their capital. From Petra they continued pushing northward as far as Madeba. In 85 B.C. Damascus requested a ruler of the Nabateans. The Arabs responded. Although overrun by Pompey in 63 B.C., they continued to

Part of a large stable from the Late Nabatean period at Kurnub (the ancient Nabatean town of Mampsis).

More excavations from the Nabatean time period at the ancient city of Mampsis.

influence Transjordan through a series of governors. Paul narrowly escaped being arrested by the Nabateans in Damascus (2 Cor. 11:32). Paul spent time in Arabia following his conversion, probably preaching the gospel (Gal. 1:17).

NABONIDUS (Nă bō nī′ dŭs) Personal name meaning, "Nabu is awe-inspiring." Last king of the Neo-Babylonian Empire (555–539 B.C.). See *Babylon.*

NABOPOLASSAR (Nă bō pō lăs′ săr) Personal name meaning, "Nabu, protect the son." King (626–605 B.C.) who revolted from the Assyrians and established the Neo-Babylonian Empire. He rebelled in 627 B.C. and established his capital in Babylon. His reign was one of continual warfare as he slowly captured the cities of the Assyrian realm. He made an alliance with the Median King Cyaxares in 614, and the two sacked Nineveh in 612 B.C. See *Babylon, History and Religion of.*

NABOTH (Nā′ bŏth) Personal name perhaps meaning, "sprout." Owner of a vineyard in the Jezreel Valley adjacent to the country palace of King Ahab, who desired the property for a vegetable garden. Naboth refused to sell on the grounds that the property was a family inheritance (1 Kings 21:3–4). Hebrew law only allowed farmland to be leased for the number of crops until the Jubilee year (Lev. 25:15–16). Farmland was not to be sold in perpetuity (Lev. 25:23). Jezebel, who had no regard for Israel's laws, plotted Naboth's judicial murder on the charge that he had blasphemed God and the king (1 Kings 21:8–14). Naboth's murder evoked God's judgment on Ahab and his family (1 Kings 21:17–24).

NACHON (Nā′ chŏn) KJV form of Nacon, meaning, "firm" or "prepared." Threshing floor between Baal-judah (Kiriath-jearim) and Jerusalem (2 Sam. 6:6). The designation is either a place name or the name of the owner. Chidon is given as the owner's name in the parallel account (1 Chron. 13:9).

NACHOR (Nā′ chôr) KJV alternate form of Nahor (Josh. 24:2; Luke 3:34).

NACON (Nä′ cŏn) See *Nachon.*

NADAB (Nā′ dăb) Personal name meaning, "willing" or "liberal." *1.* Aaron's eldest son (Ex. 6:23; Num. 3:2; 1 Chron. 6:3), who participated in the ratification of the covenant (Ex. 24:1,9), served as a priest (Ex. 28:1), and was consumed by fire along with his brother Abihu for offering unholy fire before the Lord (Lev. 10:1–7; Num. 26:61). Nadab died childless (Num. 3:4; 1 Chron. 24:2). *2.* Descendant of Judah and Tamar (1 Chron. 2:28,30). *3.* Descendant of Benjamin and great-uncle of Saul (1 Chron. 8:30; 9:36). *4.* Son of Rehoboam (1 Kings 14:20) and idolatrous king of Israel (901–900 B.C.). Baasha assassinated him during a siege of the Philistine city of Gibbethon (1 Kings 15:25–28). The extermination of the family of Jeroboam (15:29) was seen as fulfillment of the Ahijah's prophesy (14:10–11).

NAG HAMMADI (Năg Hăm mă′ dī) Modern Egyptian village 300 miles south of Cairo and about 60 miles north of Luxor, or ancient Thebes. Because of the close proximity of Nag Hammadi to the site of an important discovery of ancient documents relating to gnosticism, the collection of documents is usually referred to as the Nag Hammadi documents or library. Another name occasionally associated with the documents is Chenoboskion, the name of an ancient Christian community which is also near the discovery site. Although the documents were found in an abandoned cemetery near Chenoboskion, they probably had no ancient association with that community.

Unlike the Dead Sea Scroll materials, which consisted primarily of scrolls, the documents found near Nag Hammadi are codices, books containing leaves. Each codex was formed of sheets of papyrus bound in leather, and measured from about 5½ × 9½ inches to 5½ × 11½ inches. Thirteen separate codices were found containing fifty-one smaller writings. While the documents are written in the Coptic language, an ancient language of Egypt, they are probably translations of Greek originals. The date of the present documents appears to be about A.D. 350. While there is debate as to the dates of the original texts, some were probably written before A.D. 200.

The Discovery of the Nag Hammadi Documents
As in the case with many major archaeological

discoveries, the find was something quite unexpected. In 1945 an Arab peasant digging in an ancient cemetery for soft dirt to be used as fertilizer, found instead a large earthenware jar. At first he feared to open the jar due to his superstitious beliefs, but the prospect of valuable treasure inside prompted him to break open the container. He found the thirteen leather-bound books, or codices. Some of the documents may have been destroyed, but the discovery eventually came to the attention of those involved in antiquity studies.

The Contents of the Nag Hammadi Documents Practically all the materials reflect the religious outlook called gnosticism, an emerging world view that caused considerable difficulty for early Christianity. See *Gnosticism.*

Until the discovery of the Nag Hammadi Documents, our knowledge of gnosticism came primarily from early Christian writers who wrote against the movement. Christian writers such as Irenaeus, Clement of Alexandria, Origen, and Tertullian not only gave descriptions of the teachings of gnosticism, but they also quoted from gnostic writings. With the Nag Hammadi discovery, however, a small library of actual gnostic writings became available for study.

The Nag Hammadi Documents represent a rather wide diversity of content. Of special interest are several more clearly defined categories. The materials referred to as "Gospels" are especially important. In this category are such works as *The Gospel of Philip, The Gospel of Truth,* and perhaps the most important work found at Nag Hammadi, *The Gospel of Thomas,* which purports to be a collection of sayings of Jesus. See *Apocrypha, New Testament.*

Another category of documents concerns the work and circumstances of the apostles. *The Apocalypse of Paul* relates an account of the heavenly journey of Paul. *The Revelation of Peter* describes special revelations given to Peter by Jesus before Peter's imprisonment. *The Revelation of James* tells of the death of James.

An additional category of documents contains a wide variety of mythological speculations covering such topics as creation, redemption, and ultimate destiny. In this category are such works as *On the Origin of the World, Secret Book of the Great Invisible Spirit, Revelation of Adam, The Thought of our Great Power, The Paraphrase of Shem, The Second Logos of the Great Seth,* and *The Trimorphic Protennoia.*

Although the Nag Hammadi Documents represent a diversity of gnostic systems, most of the materials do reflect the gnostic orientation. A possible exception is the work called *The Acts of Peter and the Twelve Apostles* which is an apocryphal work about the twelve apostles.

Significance of the Nag Hammadi Documents

1. Provide primary source material enabling a greater understanding of Gnosticism.

2. Prove the existence of gnostic systems independent of the Christian framework. Some were primarily Jewish, and others existed as movements independent of either a Jewish or a Christian orientation.

3. Enhance the study of the New Testament, especially of the books that may have been written as reactions to Gnosticism, such as Colossians, John, and possibly 1 Corinthians.

4. Reflect the diversity of Gnosticism and point to the diversity of early Christianity and the resultant struggle for orthodoxy.

5. Reinforce an appreciation for the seriousness of the gnostic threat to early Christianity. Firsthand evidence now exists of the divergent gnostic views of creation, Christ, redemption, the doctrine of humanity, and the significance of the institutional church.

In conclusion, although not as well known as the Dead Sea Scrolls, the discovery at Nag Hammadi represents an important milestone in the understanding of the struggles and developments of the early Christian church.

Bruce Tankersley

NAGGAI (Năḡ′ ḡâi) Personal name perhaps meaning, "splendor of the sun." Ancestor of Jesus (Luke 3:25).

NAGGE (Năḡ′ ḡē) KJV form of Naggai.

NAHALAL (Nå hăl′ ål) Place name meaning, "pasture" with alternate forms: Nahallal (Josh. 19:15); Nahalol (Judg. 1:30). Town Zebulun's territory allotted to the Levites (Josh. 19:15; 21:35). The Israelites were unable to drive out the Canaanite inhabitants of the city (Judg. 1:30). The site is uncertain. Tell-en-Nahl north of the Kishon River at the southern end of the plain of Acco is possible as are modern Nahalal about six miles west of Nazareth and tell el-Beida.

NAHALIEL (Nå hā′ lĭ ĕl) Place name meaning, "palm grove of God," "torrent valley of God," or less likely, "God is my inheritance." One of Israel's stopping places in Transjordan (Num. 21:19). The stream bed is perhaps the wadi Zerqa Ma'in or the wadi Wala, a north tributary of the Arnon.

NAHALLAL (Nå hăl′ lăl) Alternate form of Nahalal (Josh. 19:15 KJV, TEV).

NAHALOL (Nå′ hå lŏl) KJV alternate form of Nahalal (Judg. 1:30).

NAHAM (Nā′ hăm) Personal name meaning, "consolation." Either the brother (KJV, REB) or brother-in-law (NAS, NIV, NRSV) of Hodiah (1 Chron. 4:19).

NAHAMANI (Nā hå mā′ nī) Personal name meaning, "comfort." Exile who returned with Zerubbabel (Neh. 7:7). The name does not appear in the parallel list (Ezra 2:2).

NAHARAI (Nā′ hå râi) Personal name meaning, "intelligent" or "snorting." One of David's thirty elite warriors who served as armor-bearer to Joab (2 Sam. 25:37; 1 Chron. 11:39). The KJV used the alternate form Nahari in 2 Samuel.

NAHARI (Nā′ hå rī) See *Naharai.*

NAHASH (Nā hăsh) Personal name meaning, "serpent" or perhaps "magnificence." *1.* Ammonite ruler whose assault of Jabesh-Gilead set the stage for Saul's consolidation of power as king (1 Sam. 11:1–11). Saul's opponent was likely the Nahash who befriended David (2 Sam. 10:1–2). His son Hanun provoked David's anger (2 Sam. 10:3–5). Another son, Shobi, served as David's ally (2 Sam. 17:27). *2.* Parent of Abigal (2 Sam. 17:25). Various harmonizations of 2 Samuel 17:25 and 1 Chronicles 2:16 have been offered. *a.* Nahash was a woman. *b.* Nahash is an alternate name for Jesse. *c.* The Amorite ruler Nahash and Jesse were at different times the husband of the same woman.

NAHATH (Nā′ hăth) Personal name meaning, "descent," "rest," "quietness," or even "pure, clear." *1.* Edomite clan chief (Gen. 36:13,17; 1 Chron. 1:37). *2.* Levite (1 Chron. 6:26), possibly identical with Toah (1 Chron. 6:34) and Tohu (1 Sam. 1:1). *3.* Overseer in Hezekiah's time (2 Chron. 31:13).

NAHBI (Năh′ bī) Personal name meaning, "hidden" or "timid." Naphtali's representative among the twelve spies sent to survey Canaan (Num. 13:14).

NAHOR (Nā′ hôr) Personal name meaning, "snore, snort." *1.* Son of Serug, father of Terah, and grandfather of Abraham (Gen. 11:22–26). *2.* Son of Terah and brother of Abraham (Gen. 11:26). He married Milcah, his niece, who bore eight sons for him (11:29; 22:20–22). Nahor's genealogy shows the link between the Hebrews and other Semitic peoples of the ancient Near East. Of special interest is his relationship to the Aramaeans who dwelled in the region of modern Syria, probably descendants of his children born to Reumah (22:24), his concubine.

3. City in Mesopotamia where Abraham's servant sought and found a wife for Isaac (Gen. 24:10); this in keeping with the ancient custom of marrying within one's family. The city probably was located southeast of Haran. It is mentioned in the Mari Texts.

NAHSHON (Năh′ shŏn) Personal name meaning, "serpent." Leader of the tribe of Judah during the wilderness years (Num. 1:7; 2:3; 7:12,17; 10:14), brother-in-law of Aaron (Ex. 6:23), and an ancestor of King David (Ruth 4:20–22) and of Jesus (Matt. 1:4; Luke 3:32).

NAHUM (Nā′ hŭm) Personal name meaning, "comfort, encourage." Hebrew prophet and the Old Testament book that contains some of his messages. Very little biographical information is known about the prophet Nahum. He is called an Elkoshite (1:1), but the location of Elkosh is unknown.

The date of the prophet's ministry can be placed between 600 and 700 B.C. by two events mentioned in his book. Nahum 3:8 refers to the destruction of the Egyptian capital, No-amon or Thebes, in 663 B.C. and indicates that the prophet was active after this time. In chapter 2, he looked forward to the destruction of Nineveh which took place in 612 B.C. Nahum, therefore, prophesied after 650 B.C., probably close to the time of the fall of Nineveh.

Historical Background Since about 730 B.C., Israel and Judah had been Assyrian vassals. Almost a century later, the Assyrian Empire began its decline. Many vassal nations revolted along with Josiah of Judah (2 Kings 22–23). A coalition of Medes, Babylonians, and Scythians attacked Assyrians and in 612 B.C. destroyed the capital, Nineveh. The Assyrians formed a coalition with the Egyptians, but in 605 B.C., they were defeated. See *Assyria.*

The Prophet's Message The Assyrian oppression created a troubling question. How could God allow such inhumanity to go unanswered? Nahum responded to Assyrian tyranny with a message marked by its vivid language. Assyria's might had been heavy upon Judah, but Nahum announced that God would destroy them.

The book opens with an affirmation of God as an avenging God. The fierceness of His wrath is pictured in terms of the destruction of nature. For over a century, the Assyrians seemed to have had an uncontrolled reign, but now God was responding. His judgment is likened to an approaching storm. Perhaps the people of Judah doubted God's justness since Assyria seemed to have no restraints. Nahum, however, sought to dispel this notion.

The second chapter graphically portrays the future fall of Assyria's capital, Nineveh. Such an event must have been hard for the people to imagine. Nineveh was a massive city with a defensive wall that measured eight miles in circumference and ranged in height from 25 to 60 feet. A moat also surrounded it. Yet, Nahum, poetically affirmed the city's fall. The enemy would rush upon the city with their chariots (2:4), and the gates would be unable to keep them out (2:5).

The great city would be plundered (2:7–10).

The Book of Nahum closes with more threats against Nineveh. Ironically, as Assyria had destroyed Thebes in 663 B.C., so the same fate would befall Nineveh (3:8–11). Preparations for a siege on the city are alluded to in 3:14. Water would be stored and fortifications strengthened by the addition of more mud bricks. Yet, these preparations would not keep away God's devastating judgment.

While the Book of Nahum is harsh and deals with the unpleasantness of war, it served to give hope to the people of Judah. They had been subjected to the cruel domination of Assyria for over a century, but now their faith in God to act on their behalf could be bolstered through God's response. God's justness was reaffirmed.

Outline

I. The Sovereign God Makes Himself Known (1:1–11).
   A. The jealous, patient Lord takes vengeance on His adversaries (1:1–3).
   B. The earth quakes at the arrival of God (1:4–5).
   C. Who can endure the heat of God's anger? (1:6).
   D. The good Lord is a refuge for His troubled, trusting people (1:7).
   E. God protects those who seek Him but will destroy the enemy (1:8–9).
   F. The enemy must drink the cup of God's wrath (1:10–11).
II. In the Enemy's Fall, God Offers Hope for His Oppressed People (1:12–15).
   A. God can defeat the enemies no matter how strong and numerous they are (1:12–13).
   B. God judges the enemy because of its false gods (1:14).
   C. God calls His delivered people to grateful worship (1:15).
III. God Will Bring Judgment Upon His Wicked Enemy (2:1—3:19).
   A. The enemy will fall, but God's people will be restored (2:1–2).
   B. Armies and wealth cannot prevent God's judgment (2:3–12).
   C. When God declares war, the enemy is helpless (2:13).
   D. God humiliates wicked peoples (3:1–19).

Scott Langston

NAIL *1.* Keratinous covering of the top ends of fingers and toes. If an Israelite desired to marry a prisoner of war, she was to cut her nails either as a sign of mourning for her parents or as part of her purification on entering the community of Israel (Deut. 21:12). *2.* Metal fasteners used in construction and for decoration (1 Chron. 22:3; 2 Chron. 3:9; Isa. 41:7; Jer. 10:4). The earliest nails were made of bronze. With the introduction of iron,

larger nails were made of iron. Smaller nails continued to be made of bronze. Nails were sometimes plaited with precious metal and nail heads decorated with gold foil when used for ornament (compare 2 Chron. 3:9). The nails used in the crucifixion of Jesus were likely iron spikes five to seven inches long (John 20:25). *3.* KJV used nail as an alternate translation for a Hebrew term modern translations consistently render peg (Ex. 35:18; Judg. 4:21–22; Zech. 10:4).

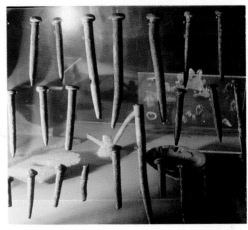

Nails from Roman times.

NAIN (Nain) Place name meaning, "pleasant." Village in southwest Galilee where Jesus raised a widow's son (Luke 7:11–15). The ancient town sat on a hillside overlooking the Plain of Esdraelon.

NAIOTH (Nai' ŏth) Place name meaning, "dwelling." The name refers either to a building or district in the city of Ramah which housed the prophetic school Samuel led (1 Sam. 19:18–24). David sought refuge from Saul at Naioth. Three groups of royal messengers and finally Saul himself fell victim to prophetic frenzy when they attempted to capture David there.

NAKED Being without clothes (Gen. 2:25; Job 1:21; Eccl. 5:15; Amos 2:16; Mic. 1:8) or else poorly clothed (Deut. 28:48; Matt. 25:36–44; Jas. 2:15). The phrase "to uncover the nakedness of" means to have sexual intercourse (Lev. 18:6–19; 20:11,17–21). Nakedness frequently occurs in conjunction with shame (Gen. 3:7; 9:21–27; Isa. 47:3; Ezek. 16:8,36–37).

NAMES OF GOD The name of God holds an important key to understanding the doctrine of God and the doctrine of revelation. The name of God is a personal disclosure and reveals His relationship with His people. His name is known only because He chooses to make it known. To the Hebrew mind, God was both hidden and revealed, transcendent and immanent. Even though he was mysterious, lofty, and unapproachable, He bridged the gap with humankind by revealing His name. See *Naming*.

The truth of God's character is focused in His name. The divine name reveals God's power, authority, and holiness. This accounts for Israel's great reverence for God's name. The Ten Commandments prohibited the violation of God's name (Ex. 20:7; Deut. 5:11). Prophets spoke with authority when they uttered God's name. Oaths taken in God's name were considered binding, and battles fought in the name of God were victorious. Other nations would fear Israel, not because it was a mighty nation, but because it rallied under the Lord's name. In the New Testament, God's name is manifested most clearly in Jesus Christ. He is called "the Word" (John 1:1), and Jesus himself makes the claim that he has revealed the name of God (John 17:6). God's name is His promise to dwell with His people.

God of the Fathers Before Moses' encounter with God in the Midianite desert, God was known generally as the God of the Fathers. Various names were used for God under this conception, most of which were associated with the primitive Semitic word *El*.

El is a generic term for God or deity. It appears in ancient languages other than Hebrew. One can see the similarities to the modern Arabic word for God, Al or Allah. The word *El* refers to an awesome power that instills within humankind a mysterious dread or reverence.

Even though *El* was a term for God in pagan or polytheistic religions, it is not a designation for an impersonal force like one would find in animism. Pagans worshipped El as a high and lofty God. He was the chief God in the Canaanite pantheon. See *Canaan*.

The word *El* in the Bible is often a reference to deity as opposed to the particular historical revelation associated with the name "Yahweh" (see below). More often than not, however, it is used interchangeably as a synonym for Yahweh, the God of Isreal, and translated God.

One of the most interesting uses of El is its alliance with other terms to reveal the character of God. Some of these combinations are:

El-Shaddai "God of the Mountains" or "The Almighty God." This term is more closely associated with the patriarchal period and can be found most frequently in the Books of Genesis and Job. Exodus 6:3 underlines El-Shaddai as the name revealed to the patriarchs. God used it to make His Covenant with Abraham (Gen. 17:1–2).

El-Elyon "The Most High God" or "The Exalted One" (Num. 24:16; 2 Sam. 22:14; Ps. 18:13). Melchizadek was a priest of El-Elyon and blessed Abraham in this name (Gen. 14:19–20), refering to El-Elyon as "Maker of heaven and earth." Canaanites at Ugarit also worshiped god as El-Elyon.

El-Elyon seems to have had close ties to Jerusalem.

El-Olam "God of Eternity" or "God the Everlasting One" (Gen. 21:33; Isa. 26:4; Ps. 90:2). God's sovereignty extends through the passing of time and beyond our ability to see or understand.

El-Berith "God of the Covenant" (Judg. 9:46) transforms the Canaanite Baal Berith (8:33) to show God alone makes and keeps covenant.

El-Roi "God who Sees me" or "God of Vision" (Gen. 16:13). God sees needs of His people and responds.

Elohim A plural form for deity. It is a frequently used term and the most comprehensive of the El combinations. The plurality of this word is not a hint of polytheism. It is a plural of majesty. It is a revelation of the infinite nature of God. In the creation narrative, we read: "Then Elohim said, 'Let us make man in our image.' " (Gen. 1:26) This name suggests that there is a mystery to the Creator-God which humankind cannot fully fathom. God is absolute, infinite Lord over creation and history. The Christian sees in this term a pointer to the trinitarian reality of creation.

Other Uses The name *El* is frequently combined with other nouns or adjectives. Some examples are: Israe-el (One who is ruled by God), Beth-el (House of God), Peni-el (Face of God). In the crucifixion narrative (Mark 15:34), Jesus employed a form of El when he cried from the cross, "Eloi, Eloi," "my God, my God," quoting Psalm 22.

The Covenant Name The covenant name for God was "Yahweh." Israel's faith was a new response to God based on His disclosure. This name was so unique and powerful that God formed a covenant with His people based upon his self-revelation. See *YHWH*.

Yahweh Titles appear in English translations as Jehovah. See *YHWH*.

Yahweh-Jireh "The Lord will Provide" (Gen. 22:14). This was the name given to the location where God provided a ram for Abraham to sacrifice in the place of Isaac. This name is a testimony to God's deliverance.

Yahweh-Nissi "The Lord is my Banner" (Ex. 17:15). Moses acribed this name to God after a victory over the Amalekites. The name of God was considered a banner under which Israel could rally for victory. The Lord's name was the battle cry.

Yahweh-Mekaddesh "The Lord Sanctifies" (Ex. 31:13). Holiness is the central revelation of God's character. God calls for a people who are set apart.

Yahweh-Shalom "The Lord is Peace" (Judg. 6:24). This was the name of the altar that Gideon built at Ophrah signifying that God brings well-being not death to His people.

Yahweh-Sabaoth "The Lord of Hosts" (1 Sam. 1:3; Jer. 11:20; compare 1 Sam. 17:45). This can also be rendered, "The Lord Almighty." It represents God's power over the nations and was closely tied to Shiloh, to the ark of the covenant, and to prophecy. The title designates God as King and ruler of Israel, its armies, its Temple, and of all the universe.

Yahweh-Rohi "The Lord is my Shepherd" (Ps. 23:1). God is the One who provides loving care for His people.

Yahweh-Tsidkenu "The Lord is Our Righteousness" (Jer. 23:5–6; 33:16). This was the name Jeremiah gave to God, the Righteous King, who would rule over Israel after the return from captivity. He would establish a new kingdom of justice.

Yahweh-Shammah "The Lord is There" (Ezk. 48:35) This is the name of God associated with the restoration of Jerusalem, God's dwelling place.

Other Names *Baal* This was the chief god of the Canaanite pantheon. In some ancient religions, Baal and El could be used interchangeably. There were tendencies within Israel to identify Baal with Yahweh, but Baal worship was incompatible with Hebrew monotheism. Prophets, such as Elijah and Hosea, called the people away from these tendencies and back to the covenant.

Adon (or *Adonai*) This is a title of authority and honor. It can be translated "Lord." It is not exclusively a title for deity because it is used in addressing a superior, such as a king or master. In this sense, it is used to ascribe the highest honor and worship to God. Adon or Adonai was often used in conjunction with Yahweh. In time, Adonai became a substitute for Yahweh. In the postexilic period, it took on the connotation of God's absolute lordship.

Symbolic Titles A prominent characteristic of Scripture is its use of figurative language. Many of the names for God are symbolic, illustrative, or figurative.

Ancient of Days (Dan. 7:9,13,22) The picture presented is of an old man who lived for many years. This, of course, is not a literal description of God, but a confession that He lives forever and His kingdom is everlasting. His rule encompasses the expanses of time. Unlike the portrait presented in other religions where the gods are bound within time, Yahweh is active in time and history. He gives history meaning and is drawing it to a conclusion. He is from "everlasting to everlasting." (Ps. 90:2)

Rock (Deut. 32:18; Ps. 19:14; Isa. 26:4) God is strong and permanent. Yahweh is sometimes identified as "The Rock of Israel."

Refuge (Ps. 9:9; Jer. 17:17) God is a haven from the enemy.

Fortress (Ps. 18:2; Nah. 1:7) God is a defense against the foe.

Shield (Gen. 15:1; Ps. 84:11) God is protection.

Sun (Ps. 84:11) God is the source of light and life.

Refiner (Mal. 3:3) God is purifier.

Political Names Many descriptions of God came from political life.

King In the Ancient East, it was common to address gods as king. Kingship was also ascribed to Yahweh. His covenant people were to obey Him as a Sovereign. This title is the key to understanding the kingdom of God, which is the most frequent title used in Scripture to describe God's rule.

Judge The Judge was the political ruler during the time of tribal confederacy. Yahweh is the Judge who arbitrates disputes, sets things right, and intervenes for Israel in its military campaigns.

Shepherd God is frequently described as a Shepherd. This was a nurturing term to describe the care given to His covenantal people. It also had political or ruling connotations. Yahweh is the Shepherd King (Ezk. 34). In the New Testament, the image of God as shepherd is continued in parables (Luke 15:4–7) and in John's protrayal of Christ as the Good Shepherd (John 10:1–18).

God the Father In the Old Testament, the word *father* is used for God to describe the close kinship that He enjoys with His worshipers. There are many figurative references to God's fatherhood. "As a father has compassion on his children, so the Lord has compassion on those who fear Him" (Ps. 103:13). God is a "father to Israel" (Jer. 31:9) and speaks of Israel as His "son" (Ex. 4:22; Hos. 11:1).

Father is the distinguishing title for God in the New Testament. Jesus taught His disciples to use the Aramaic "Abba," a term of affection that approximates our word *Daddy,* to address the heavenly Father. See *Abba.*

Father takes on a richer meaning when it is joined with other designations.

Our Father Jesus taught His disciples to address God in this manner when they prayed (Matt. 6:9):

Father of mercies (2 Cor. 1:3);
Father of lights (Jas. 1:17);
Father of glory (Eph. 1:17).

When the Father title is juxtaposed with the word *Son,* the significance of God's name in relation to Jesus Christ is understood. Christ's claim to have come in his Father's name reveals that He was God's unique representative (John 5:43). He shares the Father's essential authority and works done in his Father's name bear witness to this special relationship (John 10:25). Christ has provided a full revelation of God because He has clearly declared His name (John 12:28; 17:6).

Brad Creed

NAMING In biblical tradition the task of naming a child generally fell to the mother (Gen. 29:31—30:24; 1 Sam. 1:20) but could be performed by the father (Gen. 16:15; Ex. 2:22) and in exceptional cases by nonparental figures (Ex. 2:10; Ruth 4:17). The last son of Jacob and Rachel received a name from each parent; Jacob altering the name Rachel gave (Gen. 35:18). Naming could be attributed to God originating through a divine birth announcement (Gen. 17:19; Luke 1:13). Naming took place near birth in the Old Testament and on the eighth day accompanying circumcision in New Testament narratives (Luke 1:59; 2:21).

The biblical concept of naming was rooted in the ancient world's understanding that a name expressed essence. To know the name of a person was to know that person's total character and nature. Revealing character and destiny, personal names might express hopes for the child's future. Changing of name could occur at divine or human initiative, revealing a transformation in character or destiny (Gen. 17:5,15; 32:28; Matt. 16:17–18).

The knowing of a name implied a relationship between parties in which power to do harm or good was in force. That God knew Moses by name occasioned the granting of Moses's request for divine presence (Ex. 33:12,17). The act of naming implied the power of the namer over the named, evidenced in the naming of the animals in Genesis 2:19–20 or Pharaoh's renaming Joseph (Gen. 41:45; compare Dan. 1:6–7; 2 Kings 24:17).

Proper names consisting of one or more terms consciously chosen by the namer conveyed a readily understandable meaning within the biblical world. Reflecting circumstances of birth Rachel called the child of her death, Ben-oni, "son of my sorrow" (Gen. 35:18). Jacob was named "the supplanter" for "he took hold on Esau's heel" (Gen. 25:26). Moses, the "stranger in a strange land," named his son Gershom (Ex. 2:22). Conditions of the times proved imaginative as well: Ichabod, "The glory has departed from Israel," (NRSV) came about by the ark of the covenant falling into Philistine hands (1 Sam. 4:21–22) and the symbolic names of Isaiah's sons:Shear-jashub, "a remnant shall return," (Isa. 7:3); Maher-Shalal-hash-baz, "swift is the booty, speedy is the prey," (Isa. 8:3, NASB).

Personal characteristics, Esau means "hairy"; Careah means "bald," (Gen. 25:25; 2 Kings 25:23); and the use of animal names in early times, Deborah means "bee"; Jonah means "dove"; Rachel means "ewe," are attested. Less frequently occurring are names taken from plants: Tamar meaning "palm tree"; Susanna meaning "lily."

Simple names functioning as epithets, such as Nabal meaning "fool" and Sarah meaning "princess," gave way to compound names factual or wishful in nature, such as Mattaniah meaning "gift of Yahweh" and Ezekiel meaning "may God strengthen." Compound names in the main are theophoric, employing the divine names El and Yah (Elijah, Ishmael, Nathaniel). Titles and kinship terms (Abimelech, melech means "king"; Abigail, Ab(i) means "father") and foreign names

occur: Aramaic, Greek, and Roman (Martha, Salome, Alexandra, John Mark).

The patronymic practice whereby a child received the name of a relative, especially the grandfather (Simon Bar-Jona is "son of Jona") was common by the Christian era. Geographical identities are attested as well (Goliath of Gath and Jesus of Nazareth).

See *Family; Children; Birth; Birth Announcements.*   Kandy Queen-Sutherland

NAOMI (Nā ō′ mĭ) Personal name meaning, "*my pleasantness.*" Wife of Elimelech and mother-in-law to Orpah and Ruth (Ruth 1:2,4). Naomi suffered the deaths of her husband and two sons while in Moab. Her matchmaking betwen Ruth and Boaz was successful, and she became a forebear of David, Isreal's greatest king (Ruth 4:21–22). See *Ruth.*

NAPHATH-DOR (Nā′ phăth Dôr) Designation of the region surrounding the coastal city of Dor about fifteen miles west of Megiddo (Josh. 12:23; 1 Kings 4:11). The alternate form Naphoth-Dor is used at Joshua 11:2. KJV translated the term Naphath variously (borders, coasts, regions). NAS rendered the term "height(s)," relegating the Hebrew to the margin; REB, "districts."

NAPHISH (Nā′ phĭsh) Personal name meaning, "refreshed." A son of Ishmael and ancestor of a northwest Arabian tribe of the same name (Gen. 25:15; 1 Chron. 1:31). The tribe dwelt in Transjordan before being displaced by Reuben, Gad, and the half-tribe of Manasseh (1 Chron. 5:19).

NAPHOTH-DOR (Nā′ phŏth Dôr) RSV alternate form of Naphath-Dor (Josh. 11:2). The NIV consistently used the form Naphoth Dor (Josh. 11:2; 12:23; 1 Kings 4:11).

NAPHTALI (Năph′ tả lĭ) Personal name meaning, "*wrestler.*" Sixth son of Jacob and second son by his concubine Bilhah (Gen. 30:6–8). In blessing him, Jacob likened Naphtali to a hind let loose (49:21), probably a reference to unbridled energy. The tribe which bears his name inhabited a territory north of the Sea of Galilee that extendsalong the northwest side of Jordan beyond Lake Huleh (Josh. 19:32–39).

Naphtali is praised in the Song of Deborah for placing itself in jeopardy on behalf of Israel (Judg. 5:18). The tribe joined with Asher and Manasseh to help drive the Midianites out of the land (7:23). During Solomon's reign the territory was designated a separate economic district (1 Kings 4:7,15) and produced Hiram, the king's chief brass worker (7:13–14). The Syrians invaded Naphtali during Baasha's reign and inflicted heavy losses (15:20). The territory finally succumbed to

Tiglath-pileser III in 734 B.C. (2 Kings 15:29). See *Tribes.*

NAPHTUHIM (Năph′ tū hǐm) Residents of Naphtuh, an unidentified geographic area (Gen. 10:13; 1 Chron. 1:11; Naphtuhites, NIV and REB). The Naphtuhim were most likely residents of the Nile delta or else inhabitants of the oases to the west of the Nile Valley. The term may come from Egyptian for Ptah, pointing to Middle Egypt.

NAPKIN See *Handkerchief.*

NARCISUS (När cĭs′ sŭs) A common name among both slaves and freedmen meaning, "daffodil." The Narcissus of Romans 16:11 headed a household, perhaps including slaves and/or associated freedmen, which included some Christians. The most famous Narcissus was a freedman who served as an advisor to Emperor Claudius (A.D. 41–54). He committed suicide shortly after Nero's accession of the throne. It is possible, though not certain, that Paul had this Narcissus in mind.

NARD An expensive fragrance derived from the roots of the herb *nardostachys jatamansi.* The term appears twice in the Song of Solomon (1:12; 4:13–14) and in two of the gospel accounts of the woman anointing Jesus at Simon's house in Bethany (Mark 14:3; John 12:3; "spikenard," KJV). The disciples rebuked her for this action, stating that the ointment could have been sold for a sizeable sum and the proceeds donated to the poor.

NATHAN (Nā′ than) Personal name meaning, "gift." *1.* Prophet in royal court during reign of David and early years of Solomon. David consulted Nathan about building a Temple. Nathan responded favorably. That night the Lord spoke to Nathan with instructions for David that his successor would build the Temple. Nathan included the words of the Lord that David would have a house, a great name, and a kingdom forever. David responded with gratitude to the Lord (2 Sam. 7; 1 Chron. 17).

David committed adultery with Bathsheba and had her husband, Uriah, slain in battle. The Lord was displeased and sent Nathan to rebuke the king. The prophet told a story in which a rich man took the only little ewe lamb that belonged to a poor man and prepared a meal for one of his guests. David said the rich man should die. Nathan responded, "Thou art the man." David repented, but his first child born to Bathsheba died (2 Sam. 11—12).

Adonijah tried unsuccessfully to become king in the closing days of David's life. Nathan, along with Zadok, the priest, Benaiah the son of Jehoiada, Shimei, Rei, and David's mighty men, opposed Adonijah. Bathsheba and Nathan spoke to David about an earlier decision to appoint Solomon as the next king. David declared Solomon to be king (1 Kings 1:5–53).

Later references indicate that Nathan wrote the chronicles for David (1 Chron. 29:29) and a history of Solomon (2 Chron. 9:29). Nathan advised David in arranging the musical instruments played by the Levites (2 Chron. 29:25).

2. Son of David, born in Jerusalem (2 Sam. 5:14; 1 Chron. 14:4). His mother was Bathsheba (Bath-shua) (1 Chron. 3:5). He is in the genealogy of Jesus Christ (Luke 3:31). *3.* Nathan of Zobah, father of Igal, one of David's mighty men (2 Sam. 23:36). He may be the same as Nathan the brother of Joel (1 Chron. 11:38), within another list of David's mighty men. *4.* The two Nathans mentioned as fathers of Azariah and Zabud may be same man and identified as the prophet Nathan (1 Kings 4:5) during Solomon's reign. If Zubad (1 Chron. 2:36) is the same as Zabud, his father Nathan may be the prophet; thus, the prophet's father was Attai, a descendant of Jerahmeel (1 Chron. 2:25).

5. A returning exile whom Ezra sent on a mission to secure ministers for God's house (Ezra 8:15–17). He may be the same exile who had married a foreign wife and put her away (Ezra 10:39). *Omar Hancock*

NATHAN-MELECH (Nā′ than Mē′ lĕch) Personal name meaning, "The king has given" or perhaps "Melech [= the god Molech] has given." Nathan-Melech served as an official of King Josiah (2 Kings 23:11). See *Eunuch.*

NATHANAEL (Nȧ thăn′ ā ĕl) Personal name meaning, "*giver of God.*" An Israelite whom Jesus complimented as being guileless (John 1:47) and who, in turn confessed the Lord as being the Son of God and King of Israel (v. 49).

Nathanael was from Cana of Galilee (John 21:2) and apparently became one of the inner core of disciples who followed Jesus. Although Matthew, Mark, and Luke do not mention him by name, his two appearances in John point to his devotion to Christ. Some have equated him with Bartholomew.

Philip announced to Nathanael that Jesus was the promised Messiah (John 1:45). It was then that Nathanael made the infamous remark, "Can there any good thing come out of Nazareth?" See *Disciples.*

NATIVES Term used by several modern translations (NAS, REB, NRSV) to designate the inhabitants of Malta (Acts 28:2). Barbarous people (KJV) reflects the Greek *barbaroi* which designates the islanders as non-Greek speaking. NIV reads, "islanders."

NATIVITY OF CHRIST See *Jesus Christ; Jesus, Life and Ministry of.*

Sunset over Bethlehem with the belfry of the Church of the Nativity silhouetted in the center right.

NATURAL According to nature. *1.* Natural use (Rom. 1:26–27 KJV; natural relations, RSV) refers to heterosexual relations, thus "natural intercourse," (NRSV, REB). *2.* Natural affection refers specifically to affection for family members. Those lacking natural affection (*astorgoi*) are unloving to their families or generally inhuman or unsociable (Rom. 1:31; 2 Tim. 3:3). *3.* Natural branches refer to original or native branches as opposed to ingrafted ones (Rom. 11:21,24). *4.* The natural or unspiritual person (1 Cor. 2:14) is one not open to receiving gifts from God's Spirit or to discerning

A religious service takes place inside the Church of the Nativity in Bethlehem.

The silver star marks the traditional site of Jesus' birth in the Grotto of the Nativity in Bethlehem.

N

spiritual matters (constrast 2:15). This contrast between the spiritual and natural is also evidenced by James 3:15 (NAS) and Jude 19 (NIV). *5.* The natural face (Jas. 1:23) is literally the face of one's birth. To see one's natural face is to see oneself as one actually is.

NAUGHTINESS KJV used naughtiness to mean viciousness or wickedness (1 Sam. 17:28; Prov. 11:6; Jas. 1:21). In modern English naughtiness indicates disobedience, misbehavior, or mischievousness. Modern translations thus replace naughtiness with terms such as evil, greed, or wickedness to reflect the seriousness of the sin.

NAUM (Nā′ ŭm) KJV form of Nahum, an ancestor of Christ (Luke 3:25).

NAVE *1.* Term used by some modern translations (NAS, NRSV) for the main room of the Temple between the vestibule and the holy of holies (1 Kings 6:3,5,17; 7:50; 2 Chron. 3:4–5,13; 4:22). KJV referred to this room as the temple or house. See *Temple. 2.* KJV used nave for the center of a wheel through which an axle passes (1 Kings 7:33). Modern translations render the underlying Hebrew as rim.

NAVEL *1.* Depression in the middle of the belly marking the place where the umbilical cord was formerly attached. Ezekiel 16:4 graphically portrays Jerusalem's hopeless state before God's adoption in the image of a child whose navel string (umbilical cord) is not cut (see *Midwife*). Modern translations often replace navel with another word more appropriate to the context, for example, flesh or belly (Job 40:16; Prov. 3:8; Song of Sol. 7:2). *2.* Hebrew expression for "midst of the land" or "center of the earth" (NRSV) in Judges 9:37; Ezekiel 38:12. Israel's neighbors used the term to designate the earthly place, often a worship place or sacred city, linking heaven and earth. Some scholars use later Jewish references to Jerusalem as the cultic "navel of the earth" to interpret Gerazim and Jerusalem as places celebrated as the earth's linking point. The two biblical passages seem to have only geographical meanings, however.

The modern city of Nazareth with the Catholic Church of the Annunciation in the center of photo.

NAVY See *Fleet.*

NAZARETH, NAZARENE (Năz′ à rĕth; Năz à rēne′) Place name meaning, "branch." Nazareth did not enjoy a place of prominence until its association with Jesus. It does not appear in the Old Testament. As He became known as "Jesus of Nazareth" (Matt. 26:71; Luke 18:37; 24:19; John 1:45; Acts 2:22; 3:6; 10:38), His hometown became fixed in Christian memory.

Nazareth was located in lower Galilee about halfway between the Sea of Galilee and the Mediterranean Sea. It lay in the hill country north of the Plain of Esdraelon. The hills formed a natural basin with three sides, but open toward the south. The city was on the slopes of the basin, facing east and southeast. Cana was about five miles to the northeast. A Roman road from Capernaum westward to the coast passed near Nazareth.

It was a small village in Jesus' day, having only one spring to supply fresh water to its inhabitants. Today, the spring is referred to as "Mary's well." The modern city has about 20,000 citizens, mainly Moslems and Christians.

The angel went to Nazareth to announce to Mary and Joseph the coming birth of Jesus (Luke 1:26–28). Following Jesus' birth in Bethlehem and the sojourn in Egypt, Joseph and Mary returned with Jesus to Nazareth (Matt. 2:19–23), where Jesus grew from boyhood to manhood (Luke 2:39–40; 4:16), being stamped as a Nazarene (Matt. 2:23), apparently a midrashic play on the Hebrew term *netser,* "shoot" in Isaiah 11:1.

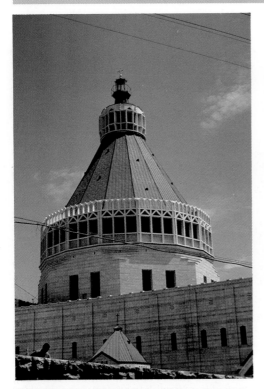

The Catholic Church of the Annunciation built over the caves where tradition says Mary and Joseph lived.

Nazareth did not possess a good reputation, as reflected in the question of Nathanael, himself a Galilean (John 1:46). The early church received similar scorn as the Nazarene sect (Acts 24:5). Such lack of respect was likely due to an unpolished dialect, a lack of culture, and quite possibly a measure of irreligion and moral laxity.

Jesus was rejected by His townspeople near the beginning of His public ministry, being cast out of the synagogue at Nazareth (Luke 4:16–30; see also Matt. 13:54–58; Mark 6:1–6).

See Galilee.   *Jerry W. Batson*

NAZIRITE (Năz′ ĭ rīte) Member of a class of individuals especially devoted to God. The Hebrew term means consecration, devotion, and separation. Two traditional forms of the Nazirite are found. One was based on a vow by the individual for a specific period; the other was a lifelong devotion following the revelatory experience of a parent which announced the impending birth of a child.

The Nazirite's outward signs—the growth of hair, abstention from wine and other alcoholic products, the avoidance of contact with the dead—are illustrative of devotion to God. Violation of these signs resulted in defilement and the need for purification so the vow could be completed. Numbers 6:1–21 regulated the practice

and lined the phenomenon to cultic law and locality. Verses 1–8 show how the Nazirite's period was begun. In case of defilement, a method of purification was given (vv. 9–12). The status was terminated (vv. 13–21) by the burning of shaven hair and the giving of various offerings. Parallels exist between the cultic purity of the high priest and the Nazirite.

The lifelong Nazirite in biblical tradition included Samson (Judg. 13), Samuel (1 Sam. 1), and John the Baptist (Luke 1:15–17). In the New Testament, Paul took the Nazirite vow for a specific period of time (Acts 18:18; 21:22–26). Amos 2:12 shows an ethical concern for protecting the status of the Nazirite.

NEAH (Nē′ ah) Place name meaning, "settlement." Border town in the tribal territory of Zebulun (Josh. 19:13). The site was perhaps that of modern Nimrin west of Kurn Hattin.

NEAPOLIS (Nė ăp′ o lĭs) Name meaning, "new city," of the seaport of Philippi (Acts 16:11). Neapolis (modern Kavala) is located about ten miles from Philippi in northeastern Macedonia. The city sits on a neck of land between two bays, each of which serve as harbors.

NEARIAH (Nē ȧ rī′ ah) Personal name perhaps meaning, "Yah's young man." *1.* Descendant of David (1 Chron. 3:22–23). *2.* Commander of Hezekiah's forces who defeated the Amalekites (1 Chron. 4:42–43).

NEBAI (Nē′ baî) Personal name meaning, "projecting" or "fruitful." One of the witnesses to Ezra's renewal of the covenant (Neh. 10:19).

NEBAIOTH (Nė baî′ ŏth) Personal name meaning, "fruitfulness." Son of Ishmael and ancestor of an Arab tribe of the same name (Gen. 25:13; 28:9; 36:3). KJV used the alternate form Nebajoth as 1 Chronicles 1:29; Isaiah 60:7.

NEBAJOTH (Nė bā′ jŏth) KJV alternate form of Nebaioth (1 Chron. 1:29; Isa. 60:7).

NEBALLAT (Nė băl′ lȧt) Place name perhaps meaning, "blessed with life." The name perhaps derives from Nabu-uballit, the personal name of an Assyrian governor of Samaria. Neballat was resettled by Benjaminites after the Exile (Neh. 11:34). The site is identical with modern Beit Nebala on the edge of the plain of Sharon about four miles east of Lod.

NEBAT (Nē′ băt) Personal name meaning, "God has regarded." Father of Jeroboam I (1 Kings 11:26; 12:2,15). Nebat was from Zeredah about ten miles west of Shiloh.

The harbor, town, and acropolis of Neapolis (modern Kavala).

NEBO (Nē' bō) Place and divine name meaning, "height." *1.* Babylonian god of speech, writing, and water. Worship of Nebo was popular during the Neo-Babylonian era (612–539 B.C.). Isaiah mocked parades featuring the idol of Nebo (Isa. 46:1).

2. Moabite city located southwest of Heshbon. The tribes Reuben and Gad requested the area around Nebo for their flocks (Num. 32:2–3). It was held by Israel until recaptured by King Mesha about 850 B.C. *3.* Town reinhabited by exiles returning from Babylon (Ezra 2:29). The site has been identified with Nob. *4.* Mountain about twelve miles east of the mouth of the Jordan River from which Moses viewed the Promised Land (Deut. 32:49). It rises over 4000 feet above the Dead Sea and gives an excellent view of the southwest, west, and as far north as Mount Hermon. Israel captured the area around Mount Nebo as they marched toward Canaan. They camped in the area of Mount Nebo opposite Jericho when the Balaam incident occurred (Num. 22—24). During the period of the judges it was the possession of Eglon of Moab. David recaptured the area (2 Sam. 8:2), and it remained a part of Israel until Mesha rebelled and took control about 850 B.C.

NEBO-SARSEKIM (Nē' bō Sär' sĕ kĭm) NIV form of the name of a Babylonian official (Jer. 39:13). The NIV and similar REB readings result from dividing the present Hebrew text differently than the majority of English translators. See *Sarsechim.*

NEBUCHADNEZZAR (Nĕb ū ch̲ăd nĕz' zàr) Personal name meaning, "Nabu protects." King of Babylon 602–562 B.C. He was the son of Nabopolassar and inherited the throne upon the death of his father. Nebuchadnezzar served as a general under his father and was a brilliant strategist. His victory over the Egyptian forces at Carchemish (605) signaled the completion of Babylon's conquest of Palestine. See *Babylon, History and Religion of.*

NEBUSHASBAN; NEBUSHAZBAN (Nĕ bū shăs' băn, Nĕ bū shăz' băn) Variant transliterations of personal name meaning, "Nabu save me." High official of Nebuchadrezzar involved in the fall of Jerusalem (Jer. 39:13).

NEBUZARADAN (Nĕb' ū zär ā' dăn) Personal name meaning, "Nebo has given offspring." An officer in the Babylonian army during King Nebuchadnezzar's reign. His title is given as "captain of the guard," a designation which is uncertain. He led his troops in a siege of Jerusalem in 587 B.C. (2 Kings 25:8–9), burned the city's buildings, tore down its walls, and carried away the people into Exile. Four years later he returned and deported still more citizens (Jer. 52:30). See *Babylon, History and Religion of.*

NECHO (Nē' ch̲ō) KJV form of Neco (2 Chron.

View of the Jordan Valley from the top of Mt. Nebo looking toward Jericho.

35:20,22; 36:4). KJV used the hyphenated form Pharaoh-Necho at Jeremiah 46:2. See *Neco.*

NECHOH (Nē' choh) KJV alternate form of Neco. This form always occurs in the hyphenated form Pharaoh-Nechoh (2 Kings 23:29,33,34–35).

NECK Portion of the body connecting the head to the torso. To put one's feet on the neck of an enemy is a sign of complete victory (Josh. 10:24). A yoke placed on the neck is a frequent emblem of servitude (Gen. 27:40; Deut. 28:48; Isa. 10:27). To fall upon someone's neck with weeping or kissing is a special sign of tenderness (Gen. 33:4; 45:14; compare Luke 15:20). To be stiff-necked

A reconstructed section of the "Procession Street" of Babylon built by Nebuchadnezzar in about 580 B.C.

or to harden one's neck is a common picture of stubborn disobedience (Ex. 32:9; 33:3,5).

NECKLACE An ornament worn around the neck (Song of Sol. 1:10; Ezek. 16:11). The gift of a gold necklace is sometimes the sign of installation to a high office (Gen. 41:42; Dan. 5:29).

NECO (Nē' cō) Second Pharaoh (609–594 B.C.) of the 26th dynasty of Egypt whose forces killed Josiah in battle (2 Kings 23:29–35; 2 Chron. 35:20–24) and who installed Jehoiakim as king of Judah in his place (2 Kings 23:34–35). The Twenty-Sixth Dynasty was established with Assyrian patronage. Neco began to reign three years after the fall of Nineveh, the Assyrian capital. The resulting power vacuum encouraged the ambitious Neco to seize Gaza as a base (Jer. 47:1) for a campaign to bring Syria under his control and to bring aid to the Assyrian remnant in their struggle with the rising force of Babylon. Josiah met Neco in battle as the latter was on route to Carchemish. There Neco was defeated by Nebuchadrezzar in 605 B.C. (Jer. 46:2). Later Nebuchadrezzar would extend his control as far as the Nile (2 Kings 24:7). See *Assyria; Egypt; Josiah.*

NECROMANCY (Nĕ crō măn' cy) Conjuring the spirits of the dead to predict or influence future events. See *Medium.*

NEDABIAH (Nĕ dā bī' ah) Personal name meaning, "Yah is generous." Son of Jeconiah, the exiled king of Judah (1 Chron. 3:18).

NEEDLE Small slender instrument used in sewing with an eye at one end through which thread is passed. The needles of New Testament times were similar in size to modern needles with the exception of our smallest needles. Needles were most often made of bronze, though bone and ivory were also used. Jesus' teaching that "it is easier for a camel to go through the eye of a needle than for a rich man to enter into the kingdom of God" (Matt. 19:24; compare Mark 10:25; Luke 18:25) illustrates the impossibility of a rich person's being saved apart from the intervention of God who does the impossible (Matt. 19:26). Some late Greek manuscripts read rope (*kamilos*) for camel (*kamēlos*). This attempt to dull the sharp edge of Jesus' saying runs counter to the context. The use of the term *needle's eye* for a gate of Jerusalem is an interpretive fiction, again designed to make Jesus' word more palatable. No such gate exists.

NEEDLEWORK Decorative work sewn upon cloth. Needlework was used in the decoration of the screens for the tabernacle door (Ex. 26:36; 36:37) and for the gate to its court (Ex. 27:16; 38:18) as well as for Aaron's girdle (Ex. 28:39; 39:29). Needlework was included in the prize spoils of war (Judg. 5:30) and in lists of luxury items for trade (Ezek. 27:16,24). Embroidered garments were the clothing of royalty (Ezek. 16:10,13,18; 26:16). The mention of material of various colors suggests that some needlework may have involved appliqué.

NEEZINGS (nēēz ings) KJV term meaning, "sneezings" or "sneezes" (Job 41:18).

NEGEB (Nĕ' gĕb) Place name meaning, "dry" referring to an arid region in southern Palestine and coming to mean "south." During biblical times it was more populated than today, indicating either more rainfall then or better conservation of the resources. It was the land of the Amalekites during Abraham's day (Gen. 14:7). There he exiled Hagar (21:14). The Israelites wandered in the Negeb after a futile attempt to enter Canaan (Num. 14:44–45). David incorporated it into his kingdom, and Solomon established fortresses in the region. Daniel used the term to refer to Egypt (Dan. 11:15,29). After Judah fell in 586 B.C. Edom took the area into its kingdom. In New Testament times it was known as Nabatea. See *Directions; Nabateans; Palestine.*

NEGEV (Nĕ' gĕv) Alternate spelling of Negeb.

NEGINAH, NEGINOTH (Nĕ ḡī' nah, Nĕḡ' ĭ nŏth) Neginoth, the plural form of Neginah, is used as a technical term in the superscriptions of several psalms (Pss. 4, 6, 54—55, 61, 67, 76) and as the subscription of Habakkuk 3:19. The term is generally understood to specify the instrumentation needed for performance, "with stringed instruments" (compare Isa. 38:20; Lam. 5:14). Other references suggest that *neginah* designates a taunt song (Job 30:9; Ps. 69:12; Lam. 3:14).

NEHELAM, NEHELAMITE (Nĕ hĕl' am, Nĕ hĕ' la mīte) Either a family name or a reference to the home of the false prophet Shemaiah (Jer. 29:24,31–32). The name is perhaps a play on the Hebrew word for dreamer (compare Jer. 23: 25,32).

NEHEMIAH (Nĕ hĕ mī' ah) Personal name meaning, "Yah comforts or encourages" and name of Old Testament book featuring work of Nehemiah. Nehemiah, the son of Hachaliah, is the main character in the book which bears his name. Two other Nehemiahs appear in the OT: one in the group who returned with Sheshbazzar (Ezra 2:2; Neh 7:7), and the other was the son of Azbuk, "the ruler of the half part of Bethzur" (Neh. 3:16), a helper with rebuilding the walls of Jerusalem.

Nehemiah and Ezra were one book in the ancient Hebrew and Greek OT, and probably were not divided until after the Interbiblical Period (see Ezra for more details). Jewish tradition says Ezra or Nehemiah was the author. Because of the close connection between Chronicles and Ezra-Nehemiah, one person might have written or compiled all three books. Those who follow this argument refer to the author as the Chronicler.

The literary style of Nehemiah is similar to that in Ezra. There are many lists (ch. 3; 10:1–27; ch. 11; 12:1–26). The author/compiler wove Ezra's and Nehemiah's stories together, Ezra being featured in Nehemiah 8.

The book has four major sections: the rebuilding of Jerusalem's walls (chs. 1—7), the Great Revival (chs. 8—10), population and census information (chs. 11—12), and the reforms of Nehemiah (ch. 13). Nehemiah made two visits from King Artaxerxes to Jerusalem (2:1–6; 13:6–7). His first, 445 B.C., was to repair the walls; they were in a state of disrepair almost a century after the first arrival from Exile in 538 B.C. The second was a problem-solving trip in the thiry-second year of Artaxerxes (13:6), 432 B.C. Nehemiah was a contemporary of Ezra and Malachi, and also Socrates in Greece (470–339 B.C.), and only a few decades later than Gautama Buddha in India (560–480 B.C.) and Confucius in China (551–479 B.C.).

Nehemiah held the distinguished position of cupbearer to the king (1:11). This was an office of trust; tasting the king's wine and food, the cupbearer stood between the king and death. That Nehemiah, a Jew and a captive, served this Gentile king in such a strategic capacity was an unusual credit and honor to this man of strong character.

Nehemiah's Memoirs include first person accounts (1:1—7:5; 12:27–47; 13:4–31), and the other material uses the third person pronoun (chs. 8—10). Thus his story is both autobiographical and biographical. Visitors to Susa informed him of the delapidation of Jerusalem's walls. He was so upset that he cried and mourned for days" (1:4). He prayed a confession (1:5–11). His grief became apparent to Artaxerxes who permitted him to go to Jerusalem.

Nehemiah's first act there was to inspect the walls at night (2:15). He then called an assembly and convinced the people of the need for a building program. He was an excellent leader who demonstrated engineering knowledge and brilliant organizing ability (ch. 3). The work began.

Trouble arose from without and from within. Sanballat and his friends tried to stop the work, but without success (ch. 4). Trouble from within was economic. Building the walls caused a labor shortage; farms were mortgaged, and high rates of interest were charged. Nehemiah said, "The thing you are doing is not good" (5:9 NRSV). He corrected the problem and even gave financial aid to those in need (ch. 5). Again Sanballat and other non-Jews made several attempts to lure Nehemiah away from the job and shut it down. They failed. Nehemiah proved to be a person of strong will and unusual boldness. "So the wall was finished . . . in fifty and two days" (6:15). The dedication of the wall is described later in 12:27–43.

The theological climax of the Book of Nehemiah and of the life of Ezra is the Great Revival (Neh 8—10). It was a grand experience. It warrants close study for revival attempts today. People assembled. They requested Ezra to read from the book of the law of Moses (8:1). The book was probably the Pentateuch (Torah) or some part of it. Ezra read, and others helped by giving "the sense, so that the people understood the reading" (8:8 NRSV). This probably included translating the Hebrew scripture into Aramaic, the commonly spoken language.

A great celebration occurred, and they observed the Feast of Tabernacles. Results were impressive: "They made confession and worshiped the Lord" (9:3 NRSV) and "separated themselves from all strangers" (9:2) that is, they divorced their foreign spouses. They prayed a long prayer of confession (9:6–37). The people responded, "Because of all this, we make a sure covenant and write it" (9:38). The signers and terms of the covenant were then recorded (ch. 10).

Nehemiah was dissatisfied with the small size of the population of Jerusalem. He made an ingenious proposal: to "cast lots to bring one out of ten to live in the holy city Jerusalem, while ninetenths remained in the other towns" (11:1 NRSV). Nehemiah's last chapter cites his reforms made during his second visit to Jerusalem in 432

B.C. He threw out a Gentile who was permitted to live in the Temple; he restored the practice of tithing to support the Levites; he corrected sabbath wrongs by those who bought and sold on the sabbath; and he dealt forthrightly with those who had married foreigners, those not in covenant relation with God.

Nehemiah was indeed an outstanding person. His theology was very practical; it affected every area of life. Note his prayers and how practical they were (1:4–11; 2:4; 4:4–5,9; 5:19; 6:9,14; 13:14,22,29,31). He boldly asked, "Remember for my good, O my God, all that I have done for this people" (5:19 NRSV; compare 13:14,31). His faith was practical: "And the king granted me what I asked, for the gracious hand of my God was upon me" (2:8 NRSV; compare 2:18 for a practical application of this concept). He believed "the God of heaven is the one who will give us success" (2:20 NRSV) and that "our God will fight for us" (4:20 NRSV). He had respect for the sabbath, the Temple and its institutions, the Levites, and tithing.

Nehemiah was an unusual person. Nehemiah was a man of action; he got things done. He knew how to use persuasion but also force. One may properly call him the father of Judaism. Because of Nehemiah, Judaism had a fortified city, a purified people, a dedicated and unified nation, renewed economic stability, and a new commitment to God's law.

Outline

I. God's Work Must Be Done (1:1—7:33).

   A. God's leaders must be informed of needs in God's work (1:1–3).

   B. God's leaders must be responsive spiritually to needs in God's work and must pray (1:4–11).

   C. God's leaders must enlist the aid of others, sometimes outside the family of God (2:1–9).

   D. God's leaders likely will encounter opposition (2:10).

   E. God's leaders must exercise caution and discretion along with careful planning (2:11–16).

   F. God's leaders must inform and challenge God's people to work (2:17–20).

   G. God's work demands hard work, good organization, plenty of cooperation, and good records to give credit where credit is due (3:1–32).

   H. God's leaders will pray in the face of ridicule and insult (4:1–9).

   I. God's leaders may expect opposition from within as well as from without (4:10–12).

   J. God's leaders must encourage weary workers with practical, prayerful faith (4:13–15).

   K. God's work gets done by hard work and

committed workers (4:16–23).
L. God's work is slowed by internal problems of unfairness (5:1–5).
M. God's leaders must confront profiteering problem causers (5:6–13).
N. God's leaders at times can be sacrificially generous to meet a pressing need (5:14–19).
O. God's leaders know opposition can be very personal and must deal with it head on (6:1–14).
P. God's help and the cooperation of many workers bring success (6:15–16).
Q. God's work can have traitors within (6:17–19).
R. God's leaders will enlist others and give them clear instructions (7:1–5).
S. God's leaders need to keep and use good records (7:6–73).
II. God's Way Must Include Revival and Reformation (8:1—13:31).
A. God's people want to hear God's Word (8:1–3).
B. God's Word must be read and then interpreted (8:4–8).
C. God's way calls for joyous celebration (8:9–12).
D. God's way prescribes formal expressions of joyous worship (8:13–18).
E. God's way elicits confession (9:1–5).
F. God's people give practical expression to prayerful repentance (9:6–37).
G. God's people are willing to commit themselves (9:38).
H. God's people will sign pledges of commitment (10:1–27).
I. God's people must give practical expressions of commitment (10:28–39).
J. God's people must be willing to make some changes (11:1–2).
K. God's work requires good records (11:3—12:26).
L. God's work should be dedicated and celebrated (12:27–47).
M. God's people must be a separated people (13:1–9).
N. God's work, including His finance program, must not be neglected (13:10–14).
O. God's day must be respected (13:15–22).
P. God's way demands purity in marriage and in ministers (13:23–31).

D. C. Martin

NEHILOTH (Nē′ hǐ lŏth) A technical musical term in the superscription of Psalm 5. The term is generally understood to specify the instrumentation for the psalm, "with flutes."

NEHUSHTA (Nė hŭsh′ tà) Personal name meaning, "serpent" or "bronze." Mother of King Jehoiachin of Judah (2 Kings 24:8). As queen mother,

she was among those deported in the first Exile (24:12,15).

NEHUSHTAN (Nė hŝh′ tăn) Name of a "brazen serpent" destroyed by King Hezekiah as part of an attempt to reform Judah's life and worship (2 Kings 18:4). The object was believed to be the one Moses fashioned to relieve a plague in the Israelite camp during the Exodus (Num. 21:8–9). The word *Nehushtan* probably is a play on words in the Hebrew, the word for bronze being very similar. Nehushtan probably was a serpentine nature god worshiped in connection with the Canaanite cults. King Jehoiachin's mother was Nehushta (2 Kings 24:8) probably in honor of this foreign deity. See *Bronze Serpent*.

NEIEL (Nė ī′ ĕl) Name meaning, "dwelling place of God." Town assigned to Asher (Josh. 19:27). The site is probably that of khirbet Ya'nin on the eastern edge of the plain of Acco about eighteen miles southeast of that city.

NEIGH The loud, prolonged cry of a horse used as a figure of approaching battle (Jer. 8:16) or of unbridled sexual desire (Jer. 5:8; 13:27; 50:11).

NEIGHBOR A person living in the same vicinity, engaging in mutual activities, and for whom one takes some responsibility. The Bible's major concern is how we treat our neighbor.
Old Testament Leviticus 19:18 stated the OT law to love your neighbor. Most of the other references shed light on how this love could be carried out, telling what *not* to do to a neighbor (see Deut. 19:11–14; 27:24; Prov. 14:21; Hab. 2:15). Refusing to respect the rights of a neighbor constituted moral disintegration and provoked punishment on the nation (Isa. 3:5; Jer. 9:4–9; Mic. 7:5–6).
Leviticus 19:18 also defined neighbor. Neighbors were "the children of thy people." That is, neighbors had to come from your kind. Anyone who believed differently from you could not be your neighbor.
Jesus By Jesus' day, the rabbis had further restricted the definition of neighbor. For them a neighbor was a Jew who strictly observed the Law. Other people were hated as enemies (Matt. 5:43). Jesus sought to broaden the definition of neighbor. Neighbors included your enemies. Love meant doing good for them (Matt. 5:44). His most comprehensive definition of neighbor came in response to a lawyer's question, "Who is my neighbor?" (Luke 10:29). Jesus replied with the story of a man who had been beaten, robbed, and left to die. First, a priest went by and did nothing. Then, a Levite went by and did nothing. Finally, a foreigner (Samaritan) came and compassionately assisted the dying man, saving his life and making provisions for his immediate future (Luke 10:30–35).

Two truths are found from the parable. First, a neighbor is any person we encounter who has any need. Since every person we encounter has a need of some kind, we can understand the term to include every person we encounter. Second, we are to *be* a neighbor. The question is not just "Who is my neighbor?" but also, "Am I being a neighbor?" Neighboring is done as we show mercy (Luke 10:37). Loving our neighbor is second in importance only to loving God (Matt. 25:35–39) and means more than all the offerings and sacrifices we could ever give (Mark 12:33). **New Testament** The remainder of New Testament thought, of course, concurs with Jesus's teachings. Both Paul (Rom. 13:9–10; Gal. 5:14) and James (2:8) regard "love your neighbor" to be of utmost importance for every Christian.   *Gil Lain*

NEKEB (Nē' kĕb) KJV transliteration of a Hebrew term meaning tunnel, shaft, or mine (Josh. 19:33). Modern translations take Nekeb as a component of the place name Adami-nekeb. If a separate site is intended, el-Bossa is possible.

NEKODA (Nè kō' dà) Personal name meaning, "speckled." *1.* Family of Temple servants returning to Jerusalem after the Exile (Ezra 2:48; Neh. 7:50). *2.* Family who returned from Exile but were unable to establish their Israelite descent (Neh. 7:62).

NEMUEL (Nĕ' mū ĕl) *1.* Ancestor of a family of Simeonites, the Nemuelites (Num. 26:12; 1 Chron. 4:24); this Nemuel is also called Jemuel (Gen. 46:10; Ex. 6:15) *2.* A Reubenite (Num. 26:9).

NEMUELITES (Nĕ' mū ĕl ītes) See *Nemuel.*

NEPHEG (Nē' phĕg) Personal name meaning, "boaster." *1.* A Levite (Ex. 6:21). *2.* Son born to David in Jerusalem (2 Sam. 5:15; 1 Chron. 3:7; 14:6).

NEPHEW *1.* The son of one's brother or sister. KJV never used nephew in this sense. NAS and NIV used nephew in this sense for Lot (Gen. 12:5; 14:12). *2.* When KJV was translated, nephew was used in the broader sense of a lineal descendant, especially a grandson (Judg. 12:14; Job 18:19; Isa. 14:22; 1 Tim. 5:4).

NEPHILIM (Nĕph' ĭ lĭm) Term probably derived from the root "to fall" and meaning either "the fallen ones" or else "ones who fall [violently] upon others." At Genesis 6:4 the term designates ancient heroes who, according to most interpreters, are the products of sexual union of heavenly beings ("sons of God"; compare Job 1:6; 2:1; 38:7; Pss. 29:1; 82:6) and human women. The account illustrates the breakdown of the God-ordained order separating heaven and earth (Gen. 1:6–10) and specifying reproduction "each according to its kind" (1:11–12,21,24–25). God intervened to reestablish limits inherent in creation (6:3; compare 3:22–23). At Numbers 13:33 Nephilim designates a race of giants descended from Anak against whom the Israelites appeared as grasshoppers. See *Sons of God; Rephaim.*

NEPHISH (Nē' phĭsh) KJV alternate form of Naphish (1 Chron. 5:19).

NEPHISHESIM (Nè phĭsh' ē sĭm) See *Nephisim.*

NEPHISIM (Nĕ phī' sĭm) Family of Temple servants who returned from Exile (Ezra 2:50), probably identical with the Nephushesim (Nephishesim, KJV) of Nehemiah 7:52.

NEPHTHALIM (Nĕph' thả lĭm) Greek form of Naphtali used by the KJV (Matt. 4:13,15; Rev. 7:6).

NEPHTOAH (Nĕph tō' ah) Name meaning, "opening," found only in the phrase "Waters of Nephtoah." Boundary marker for Judah and Benjamin (Josh. 15:9; 18:15). The site was formerly identified with Atam south of Bethlehem. The most frequent identification is now Lifta about three miles northwest of Jerusalem.

NEPHUSHESIM (Nĕ ph¨ü' shẻ sĭm) See *Nephisim.*

NER (Nēr) Personal name meaning, "light." Father of Saul's general Abner and grandfather of Saul (1 Sam. 14:51; 26:5,14; 2 Sam. 2:8; 1 Chron. 9:36).

NEREUS (Nē' reūs) Personal name borrowed from Greek mythology where Nereus is the sea god who fathers the Nereids (sea nymphs). The New Testament Nereus was a Roman Christian, possibly the son of Philogus and Julia (Rom. 16:15).

NERGAL (Nēr' g̱ăl) Name, perhaps a form of "Ne-uru-gal" (Lord of the great city), of the Mesopotamian god of the underworld whose cult was centered in the ancient city of Cuth (Cuthah, modern tell Ibrahim). Following the fall of the Northern Kingdom of Israel, the Assyrians resettled Samaria with Mesopotamian peoples who brought their gods, including Nergal, with them (2 Kings 17:30). The name is also an element in the name of the Babylonian official Nergalsharezar (Jer. 39:3,13). See *Assyria.*

NERGAL-SHAREZER (Nēr' g̱ăl-shả rē' zēr) A personal name meaning, "Nergal, protect the king." Probably a different spelling of the name

"Neriglissar." He is mentioned as being among the officers of Nebuchadnezzar's court who helped destroy Jerusalem in 586 B.C. (Jer. 39:3,13). He was a son-in-law of Nebuchadnezzar who usurped the Babylonian throne following the death of Evil-merodach. Nergal-sharezer quite possibly had something to do with the rebellion and the king's death. From the Babylonian Chronicle it is known that Nergal-sharezer mounted a military campaign across the Taurus Mountains to fight the Medes. He succeeded at first but was met with a bitter defeat later and soon died, perhaps at the hands of those who placed Nabonidus on the throne. See *Babylon, History and Religion of.*

NERI (Nē′ rī) Personal name meaning, "lamp." An ancestor of Jesus (Luke 3:27).

NERIAH (Nė rī′ ah) Personal name meaning, "Yahweh is light." Father of two men who assisted Jeremiah: Baruch the scribe (Jer. 32:12; 36:4–19) and Seraiah the quartermaster (Jer. 51:59).

NERO (Nē′ rō) Personal name meaning, "brave." Roman emperor A.D. 54–68.

Nero became emperor in A.D. 57 at the age of thirteen. He succeeded his stepfather, Claudius, who was probably murdered at the behest of Agrippina, Nero's mother.

For the first years of his reign, Nero was content to be dominated by his mother and his two mentors, Burrus and Seneca. The latter was a leading Stoic philosopher who was able, for a time, to moderate Nero's more excessive tendencies.

As he grew older, Nero threw off these moderating influences and took control. To remove opposition, he probably was involved in the death of his half brother, Britannicus, and he had his mother murdered.

Nero was a complex personality. He could be extremely cruel, and his life was marked with debauchery and excess. Yet he was also a poet, an actor, a musician, and an athlete. He attempted to turn the crowds of Rome away from the brutal gladiatorial contests to an appreciation of the Greek-style Olympic games and other forms of cultural competition.

During Nero's rule the Great Fire broke out in Rome (A.D. 64). Much of the city was destroyed including Nero's palace. The story, probably true in part, goes that Nero fiddled while Rome burned.

Nero took measures to provide relief for those affected by the fire. Still he could not dispell the rumor that he had the fire set. People knew that he planned to build a much larger palace for himself and they reasoned that he used the fire to clear off the land. Nero felt the need to divert suspicion to another group. He selected the Christians as his scapegoats. He claimed that they had set the fire. A systematic persecution of the Christians followed. Because of his life-style and the persecution, many Christians viewed him as the antichrist.

Nero neglected the army. This proved to be his downfall. He lost the loyalty of large segments of the army. Finally, several frontier armies revolted. Nero's support at home melted away. Realizing that the end was inevitable and near, he committed suicide by stabbing himself in A.D. 68. See *Rome.* *Gary Poulton*

NEST Hollow container fashioned by a bird to contain its eggs and young. Nest is often used as a simile or metaphor for a human dwelling (Num. 24:21; Job 29:18; Hab. 2:9; Prov. 27:8). The term translated "nest" (Matt. 8:20; Luke 9:58) suggests a leafy "tent" rather than a nest.

NET *1.* Loosely woven mesh of twine or cord used for catching birds, fish, or other prey. *a.* Fishing nets were of two basic types. The first was a cone-shaped net with leads around its wide mouth used for hand casting (Matt. 4:18–21; Mark 1:16–19). The second was the seine net, a large draw with floats at its head and lead sinkers at its foot. Such a net was often hauled ashore to empty (Isa. 19:8; Ezek. 26:5,14; 32:3; 47:10; Matt. 13:47). In the majority of Old Testament cases the seine net is a figure for judgment at the hands of ruthless military forces. *b.* Fowling nets frequently had hinged mouths which could clamp shut when sprung (Prov. 1:17; Hos. 7:11–12). *c.* Nets of unspecified type are frequently used as figures of the Lord's chastisement (Job 19:6; Ps. 66:11; Lam. 1:13; Ezek. 12:13) or of the plots of the wicked (Pss. 9:15; 31:4; 35:7–8). *2.* Netting or network refers to grillwork used as part of the ornament of the altar of burnt offering (Ex. 27:4–5; 38:4) and of the capitals of the Temple columns (1 Kings 7:17–20). The grillwork of the altar perhaps functioned as a vent.

NETAIM (Nė tā′ ĭm) Name meaning, "plantings." Site of a royal pottery works (1 Chron. 4:23). The site has not been identified.

NETHANEEL (Nė thăn′ ė ĕl) Personal name meaning, "given by God." *1.* Leader of the tribe Issachar and a son of Zuar (Num. 1:8). He commanded an army of 54,400 men (2:5–6).

2. The fourth son of Jesse and brother of King David (1 Chron. 2:14).

3. One of several priests to blow the trumpet before the ark of God (1 Chron. 15:24).

4. Prince of Judah whom King Jehoshaphat sent out with others to teach the law of God in the cities of Judah (2 Chron. 17:7–9).

5. A Levite and father of Shemaiah who recorded the names and order of the people who would minister in the Temple (1 Chron. 24:6).

6. The fifth son of Obed-edom who was a gate-keeper in the Temple (1 Chron. 26:4).

7. A Levite who contributed to the Passover offering when Josiah was king (2 Chron. 35:9).

8. A priest and son of Pashur who had married a foreign wife while exiled in Babylon (Ezra 10:22). He might have participated in the dedication of the wall around Jerusalem (Neh. 12:36).

9. Head of the priestly family of Jedaiah when Joiakim was high priest (Neh. 12:21).

10. A priest, one of Asaph's associates, who played a trumpet, in dedicating the rebuilding of Jerusalem's wall (Neh. 12:36). Some identify him with 8.

NETHANEL (Nĕ thăn' ĕl) Form of Nethaneel modern translations prefer.

NETHANIAH (Nĕth å nī' ah) Personal name meaning, "given of Yah." *1.* Son of Asaph who served in a company of prophets established by David. They issued their message with harps, psalteries, and cymbals (1 Chron. 25:1–2). *2.* Levite sent along with Jehoshaphat's princes to teach from the book of the law of God in all the cities of Judah (2 Chron. 17:7–9). *3.* Father of Jehudi sent to Baruch by the princes of Jehoiakim (Jer. 36:14). *4.* Father of Ishmael who killed Gedaliah (2 Kings 25:23–25; Jer. 40:8,14–16;41).

NETHINIM (Nĕth' ĭ nĭm) Name meaning, "those given (to the priests and Levites)," which Ezra and Nehemiah apply to persons of foreign extraction who performed menial tasks in the Temple. Moses assigned Midianite prisoners of war to the priests (32 servants; Num. 31:28,40) and the Levites (320 servants; Num. 31:30,47). Joshua forced the Gibeonites to serve as woodcutters and water bearers for the sanctuary (Josh. 9:27). The servants which David gave to the Levites were also likely war prisoners (Ezra 8:20). Representatives of the Nethinim returned from Exile with Zerubbabel in 538 B.C. (Ezra 2:43–54; Neh. 7:46–56). The lists of returnees contain many foreign names suggesting their origin as prisoners of war. Despite their foreign origin, the Nethinim appear to be accepted as part of the people of Israel. They were prohibited from mixed marriages with the people of the land (Neh. 10:28–30) and shared in the responsibility for repair of the Jerusalem city walls (Neh. 3:26; contrast Ezra 4:1–3). The Nethinim resided in the Ophel district of Jerusalem, likely near the water gate (Neh. 3:26), a site conducive with their task as water bearers.

NETOPHAH (Nĕ tō' phah) Name meaning, "dropping." A village and surrounding district in the hill country of Judah (2 Sam. 23:28,29; 1 Chron. 11:30; 27:13; Neh. 7:26). Netophah is frequently associated with Bethlehem, suggesting a site near that town. The inference finds added support in the inclusion of two Netophites in David's elite circle of warriors. The site is most likely khirbet Bedd Faluh about three and a half miles southeast of Bethlehem. The nearby spring, 'Ain en-Natuf, preserves the name.

NETOPHATHITES (Nĕ tŏph' å thītes) Residents of Netophah (1 Chron. 9:16; Neh. 12:27–28).

NETTLE Coarse plants with stinging hairs belonging to the family *Urtica;* generally, any prickly or stinging plant (Job 30:7; Prov. 24:31; Isa. 34:13; Hos. 9:6; Zeph. 2:9). NIV frequently replaced nettles with undergrowth, weeds, or briers. The Hebrew term used at Job 30:7 and Zephaniah 2:9 perhaps refers to wild mustard. Nettles are used as a sign of desolation and judgment.

NETWORK See *Net.*

NEW Different from one of the same which existed before; made fresh. Scripture expresses God's concern for persons and the larger creation in the broad categories of a new act and a new relationship.

God's New Act Scripture often calls to mind past acts such as the creation and Exodus which reveal God's care for God's world and people. Though rooted in God's acts in history, biblical faith does not relegate God to the distant past. Time and again, writers of Scripture called God's people to anticipate God's new intervention in their lives. Isaiah 43:14–21 promised Babylonian exiles that God was now "doing a new thing" which paralleled God's acts saving Israel from Egyptian slavery. God again acted in a new way in Jesus Christ who offered a new teaching with authority (Mark 1:27) and whose ministry could be compared to new wine bursting old expectations of God's involvement in human salvation (Mark 2:22).

New Relationships God acted in the past to establish relationships, notably with the descendants of Abraham and the people of Israel at Sinai. Jeremiah anticipated God's establishing a new covenant with God's all-too-often faithless people, a covenant in which God would make knowledge of the law a matter of the heart (Jer. 31:31–34; Heb. 8:8–13). Luke 22:20 points to Christ's sacrificial death as the basis for this new covenant. In Christ the believer experiences newness of life (Rom. 6:4; 2 Cor. 5:17). This renewed life is characterized by new relationships with God and others (Eph. 2:15–16; Col. 3:10–11). See *New Birth.*

NEW AGE A time when God acts decisively in judgment and salvation. The term *new age* does not occur in Scripture. Parallel expressions, such as the age to come, the close of the age, are common. Many biblical writers conceived of history in two periods, the present and a future time when God's salvation and judgment would be manifest. The age to come is associated with the experience of eternal life (Mark 10:30; Luke 18:30), the resurrection of the dead (Luke 20:35) and the immeasurable riches of God's gracious kindness (Eph. 2:7). The close of the age is associated with final judgment and reward (Matt. 13:39,40,49) and with the coming of Christ (Matt. 24:3). The preceding references point to a new age in God's future. Another group of New Testament texts focuses on the present reality of God's new age. According to Hebrews 9:26, Christ brought about the end of the age of sin through His sacrificial death. Paul spoke of his generation of Christians as those on whom the end of the ages has already come (1 Cor. 10:11). A biblical view of the new age must incorporate both strands. See *Eschatology*.

NEW BIRTH A term evangelicals use to describe the unique spiritual experience of beginning a changed life in Christ. The origins of the term lie in John 3:3, "Except a man be born again"; John 3:6, "That which is born of the flesh is flesh; and that which is born of the Spirit is spirit"; John 3:7, "Ye must be born again"; and 1 Peter 1:23, "Being born again, not of corruptible seed, but of incorruptible, by the word of God, which liveth and abideth forever." New birth, like the earlier physical birth, is an initiation to a new experience of life. The new birth comes from hearing the word of God (Jas. 1:21; 1 Pet. 1:23). It is not a human accomplishment but an act of God (John 1:13; Eph. 2:8; Jas. 1:18). Individuals, however, cooperate with God's saving work through their repentance (break with a life of sin, Luke 13:3) and their commitment of life to Christ (John 1:12; 3:16). New birth makes one God's child forever. Rededication and renewal may come often in one's lifetime, but the new birth never reoccurs. See *Regeneration; Salvation*.   *James L. Sullivan*

NEW COVENANT See *Covenant*.

NEW GATE A gate of the Jerusalem Temple (Jer. 26:10; 36:10), which should perhaps be identified with the Upper Gate Jothan built (2 Kings 15:35) and/or with the Upper Benjamin Gate (Jer. 20:2).

NEW JERUSALEM See *Jerusalem; Eschatology*.

NEW MOON See *Calendars in the Biblical Period; Festivals*.

NEW TESTAMENT The second major division of the Christian Bible with twenty-seven separate works (called "books") attributed to at least eight different writers. Four accounts of Jesus' life are at the core. The first three Gospels (called "Syn-

optic") are very similar in content and order. The fourth Gospel has a completely different perspective.

A history of selected events in the early church (Acts) is followed by twenty letters to churches and individuals and one apocalypse. The letters deal mainly with the interpretation of God's act of salvation in Jesus Christ. Matters of discipline, proper Christian behavior, and church polity also are included. The apocalypse is a coded message of hope to the church of the first century which has been reinterpreted by each succeeding generation of Christians for their own situations.
Mike Mitchell

NEZIAH (Nė zī′ ah) Personal name meaning, "faithful" or "illustrious." Head of a family of Temple servants (Nethinim) who returned from Exile (Ezra 2:54; Neh. 7:56).

NEZIB (Nē zĭb) Name meaning, "garrison," "idol," "pillar," or "standing place." Village in the Shephelah district of Judah (Josh. 15:43). Site is identified with Beit Nesib east of Lachish about two miles from khirbet Qila (Keilah).

NIBHAZ (Nĭb′ hăz) Deity worshiped by the residents of Avva whom the Assyrians used to resettle the area about Samaria after the fall of that city in 722 B.C. (2 Kings 17:31). The deity is otherwise unknown. The name is perhaps a deliberate corruption of the term for altar (*Mizbeah*) which had possibly become an object of worship.

NIBSAN (Nĭb′ săn) Name meaning, "prophesy." Town assigned to the tribe of Judah (Josh. 15:62). Location of the site is uncertain, though its position in the list suggests a locale on the shore of the Dead Sea.

NICANOR (Nĭ cā′ nôr) Personal name meaning, "conqueror." One of seven Hellenists "full of the Spirit and wisdom" chosen to administer food to the Greek-speaking widows of the Jerusalem church (Acts 6:5).

NICODEMUS (Nĭ co dē′ mŭs) Personal name meaning, "innocent of blood." John identifies Nicodemus as a Pharisee, "a ruler of the Jews" (John 3:1), that is, a member of the Sanhedrin, the Jewish ruling council, and as "a teacher of Israel" (John 3:10), that is, an authority on the interpretation of the Hebrew scriptures. Nicodemus' coming at night suggests his timidity and his trek from the darkness of his own sin and ignorance to the light of Jesus (John 3:2). Nicodemus greeted Jesus with a title of respect, "Rabbi" (teacher), recognizing Him as a God-sent teacher whose signs bore witness to the presence of God (John 3:2). Jesus replied that Nicodemus could never see the kingdom of God without being

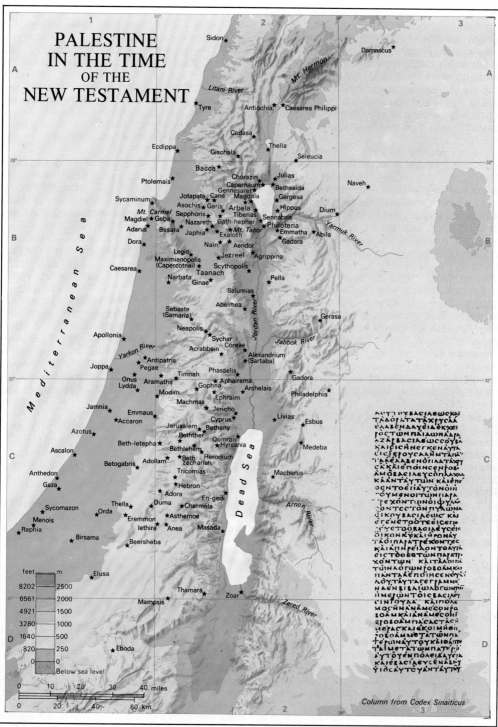

PALESTINE
IN THE TIME
OF THE
NEW TESTAMENT

Mediterranean Sea

Dead Sea

Sidon ★

Damascus ★

Mt. Hermon

Litani River

Tyre ★

Antiochia ★ ★ Caesarea Philippi

Cadasa ★

Thella ★

Ecdippa ★

Gischala ★

Seleucia ★

Bacca ★

Ptolemais ★

Chorazin ★   ★ Julias

Capernaum ★ ★ Bethsaida

Naveh ★

Gennesaret ★

Sycaminum ★

Jotapata ★ Cana ★   Magdala ★   ★ Gergesa

Asochis ★ ★ Garis   ★ Arbela   ★ Hippus

Mt. Carmel   Sepphoris ★ Tiberias ★   Dium ★

Magdiel ★ ★ Geba   Nazareth ★ Gath-hepher ★ Sennabris ★

Adarus ★ ★ Besara   Japhia ★   ★ Mt. Tabor   Philoteria ★

Dora ★   Exaloth ★   Emmatha ★ Abila ★

Nain ★ ★ Aendor   Gadara ★

Legio ★   Jezreel ★   Agrippina ★

Maximianopolis ★ (Capercotnei)   Scythopolis ★

Caesarea ★   Taanach ★

Narbata ★   Ginae ★   Pella ★

Salumias ★

Abelmea ★

Sebaste ★ (Samaria)   Gerasa ★

Neapolis ★

Apollonia ★   Sychar ★ ★ Coreae   Jabbok River

Acrabbein ★

Yarkon River   Alexandrium ★ (Sartaba)

Joppa ★ ★ Antipatris

Pegae ★   Phasaelis ★

Onus ★   Timnah ★   Aphairema ★   Gadora ★

Lydda ★ Aramatha ★   Gophna ★   Archelais ★

Modiin ★   Ephraim ★   Philadelphia ★

Jamnia ★   Machmas ★

Emmaus ★   Jericho ★   Livias ★

★ Accaron   Cyprus ★   Esbus ★

Jerusalem ★ ★ Bethany

Azotus ★   Bethther ★

Ascalon ★   Qumran ★   Medeba ★

Beth-letepha ★   Hyrcania ★

Bethlehem ★ ★ Beth   Herodium ★

Betogabris ★ Adollam ★ zechariah   Macherus ★

Anthedon ★   Tricomias ★

Gaza ★   ★ Hebron

Adora ★

Sycomazon ★   Duma ★   En-gedi ★   Arnon River

Menois ★ ★ Orda   Chermela ★

Eremmon ★ Asthemoe ★

Raphia ★   Iethira ★ ★ Anea   Masada ★

Birsama ★

Beersheba ★

feet	m
8202	2500
6561	2000
4921	1500
3280	1000
1640	500
820	250
0	0

Below sea level

Elusa ★

Thamara ★   Zoar ★

Mampsis ★   Zered River

Eboda ★

0 10 20 30 40 miles

0 20 40 60 km

Column from Codex Sinaiticus

© carta

"born again" (v. 3) or "born of water and of the Spirit" (v. 5). Nicodemus could only marvel at the impossibility of such a thing (vv. 4,9), but the text does not indicate whether Jesus was finally able to make it clear to him.

True to his name, Nicodemus defended Christ before his peers (John 7:51) who were unaware that one of their number might have believed in Him (v. 48). Their response is a twofold rebuke which may be paraphrased "Are you a Galilean peasant?" and "Are you ignorant of the Scriptures?" (v. 52).

The reference to Nicodemus' initial coming at night highlights his later public participation in Jesus' burial (John 19:39–41). Nicodemus' contribution was enough aloes and spices to prepare a king for burial, and so he did. On one level, the burial was a simple act of Pharisaic piety (compare Tobit 1:17). On a deeper level, it recognized that in His suffering and death, Christ fulfilled His role as King of the Jews.

NICOLAITANS (Nĭc ō lā′ itans) Heretical group in the early church who taught immorality and idolatry. They are condemned in Revelation 2:6,15 for their practices in Ephesus and Pergamon. Thyatira apparently had resisted the false prophecy they preached (Rev. 2:20–25). The Nicolaitans have been linked to the type of heresy taught by Balaam (Num. 25:1–2; 2 Pet. 2:15), especially the pagan feasts and orgies that they apparently propagated in the first-century church.

NICOLAS (Nĭ′ cō làs) Personal name meaning, "conqueror of people." One of seven Hellenists "full of the Spirit and wisdom" chosen to administer food to the Greek-speaking widows of the Jerusalem church (Acts 6:5). Nicolas was a proselyte, that is, a Gentile convert to Judaism, from Antioch. Some Church Fathers connect Nicolas with the heretical sect of the Nicolaitans (Rev. 2:6,15). The name, however, is common, and there is no other reason to associate this Nicolas with a sect active in Asia Minor.

NICOLAUS (Nĭ′ cō lā us) NRSV form of Nicolas (Acts 6:5), which more accurately transliterates the Greek *Nikolaus.*

NICOPOLIS (Nĭ cŏp′ ō lĭs) Place name meaning, "city of victory," shared by many cities in the ancient world. The site in which Paul most likely wintered (Titus 3:12) was Nicopolis in Epirus in northwest Greece on the north side of the Sinus Ambracicus. Octavius founded the city on the campsite from which he mounted his successful battle of Actium.

NIGER (Nī′ ḡēr) Latin nickname meaning, "black." Surname of Simeon (KJV, Symeon), one of the teacher-prophets of the early church at

Antioch. Blacks were a common sight among the populations of Egypt and north Africa in the Hellenistic period. Simeon's Latin nickname suggests that he originated from the Roman province of Africa, to the west of Cyrenica. His inclusion in Acts 13:1 demonstrates the multiracial and multinational leadership of the church at Antioch. Their concern for missions was likely rooted in their own ethnic diversity. Some have conjectured that Simeon Niger was identical to Simon of Cyrene (Mark 15:21). Acts 13:1, however, only designates Lucius as a resident of Cyrene.

NIGHT Period of darkness between sunset and dawn. Night occurs often in the simple temporal sense. Night forms part of God's ordering of time (Gen. 1:5,14; 8:22). Night is frequently a time of encounter with God, either through dreams or visions (Gen. 20:3; 31:24; 46:2; 1 Kings 3:5; Job 33:15; Dan. 2:19; 7:2,7,13; Acts 16:9; 18:9), appearances (Gen. 26:24; Num. 22:20; 1 Chron. 17:3; 2 Chron. 1:7; 7:12; Acts 23:11; 27:23), or by speech (Judg. 6:25; 7:9; 1 Sam. 15:16). Night is sometimes associated with danger (Ps. 91:5). The absence of night in the heavenly Jerusalem (Rev. 21:25; 22:5) points to the security of believers and the constant presence of God there. Night can also be associated with God's acts of deliverance (Deut. 16:1; 2 Kings 19:35; Job 34:25).

NIGHT MARCH Breaking camp and traveling at night. The term is not used in Scripture, though Exodus 13:21 records that Israel followed the pillar of fire at night (compare Num. 9:21). Advantages of night marches include cooler temperatures and avoidance of enemies. Troops were sometimes positioned at night for an ambush or attack (Josh. 8:3; 10:9; Judg. 9:32; 1 Sam. 14:36).

NIGHT MONSTER KJV translation of the Hebrew term *Lilith* (Isa. 34:14 NRSV). The term occurs only here in Scripture unless textual emendations are accepted (Job 18:15; Isa. 2:18). Interpreters divide over the natural (night creatures, NIV; nightjar, REB) or supernatural (night monster, KJV, NAS; night hag, RSV) nature of Lilith. Whatever Lilith's nature, the text stresses the great desolation which falls on God's enemies.

NIGHT WATCH An ancient division of time (Pss. 90:4; 119:148; Lam. 2:19; Matt. 14:25). According to the later Jewish system, the night was divided into three watches (evening, midnight, and morning). The Greco-Roman system added a fourth (cockcrowing) between midnight and morning (Mark 13:35). The fourth watch (Matt. 14:25; Mark 6:48) designates the time just before dawn.

NIGHTHAWK Unclean bird whose identity is uncertain (Lev. 11:16; Deut. 14:15 KJV, NRSV).

Other translations identify the bird with a type of owl (NAS, NIV, REB). See *Birds.*

NILE RIVER (Nīle) The major river considered the "life" of ancient Egypt. The Hebrew word usually used for the Nile in the Old Testament is *yʾ ʾor.* This is in fact borrowed from the Egyptian word *itrw* or *itr* by which the Egyptians referred to the Nile and the branches and canals that led from it.

The Egyptian Nile is formed by the union of the White Nile which flows out of Lake Victoria in Tanzania and the Blue Nile from Lake Tana in Ethiopia. These join at Khartum in the Sudan and are later fed by the Atbara. Thereafter the Nile flows, 1675 miles northward to the Mediterranean Sea without any further tributary. In antiquity six cataracts or falls prevented navigation at various points. The first of these, going upstream, is found at Aswan, generally recognised as the southern boundary of Egypt. From Aswan northwards, the Nile flows between two lines of cliffs which sometimes come directly down to its edge but in other places are up to nine miles away. The shore land could be cultivated as far as Nile water could be brought. This cultivated area the Egyptians called the Black Land from the color of the rich soil. Beyond lay the Red Land of the low desert stretching to the foot of the cliffs. At the cliff tops was the great inhospitable desert where few Egyptians ventured.

Below the modern capital, Cairo, and the nearby ancient capital, Memphis, the Nile forms a huge delta. The many ancient cities in this area now lie below the water table. Little archaeological excavation has been done here, though this is the area where the closest links with Palestine are likely to have been located. The eastern edge of the Delta is the site of the land of Goshen where Jacob/Israel and his descendents were settled. See *Goshen.*

The Nile is the basis of Egypt's wealth, indeed of its very life. It is the only river to flow northwards across the Sahara. Egypt was unique as an agricultural community in not being dependent on rainfall. The secret was the black silt deposited on the fields by the annual flood caused when the Blue Nile was swollen by the run-off from the winter rains in Ethiopia. This silt was remarkably fertile. Irrigation waters raised laboriously from the river, let the Egyptians produce many varieties of crops in large quantities (Num 11:5; Gen 42:1–2). If the winter rains failed, the consequent small or nonexistent inundation resulted in disastrous famine: some are recorded as lasting over a number of years (compare Gen. 41).

Even today water is brought to the individual fields by small channels leading off the arterial ditches. These channels are closed off by earth dams which can be broken down with the foot when it is a particular farmer's turn to use the water. (See Deut. 11:10.) Since life was concentrated in the valley, the river was also a natural highway. All major journeys in Egypt were under-

Sailboat on the River Nile.

taken by boat helped by the current when traveling north or by the prevailing wind when headed south. The first of the ten plagues is often linked with conditions in the river at the peak of the flood season in August when large numbers of tiny organisms turn the water red and could make it foul and undrinkable. It would also kill off the fish which would decompose and infect the frogs (the second plague) leading to successive plagues of lice, flies, and pestilences. God may have used such natural conditions with His timing to plague Egypt. See *Egypt; Plagues.*   *John Ruffle*

NIMRAH (Nĭm′ rah) Place name meaning, "clear (water)." Alternate form of Beth-Nimrah (Num. 32:36) used at Numbers 32:3.

NIMRIM (Nĭm′ rĭm) Place name meaning, "leopards" or "basins of clear waters." The name occurs in the phrase "Waters of Nimrim" (Isa. 15:6; Jer. 48:34), the stream upon which Moab's agricultural productivity depended. The stream is either the wadi en-Numeirah which flows east into the Dead Sea about eight miles north of its lower end or the wadi Nimrin which flows east into the Jordan eight miles north of its mouth.

NIMROD (Nĭm′ rŏd) Personal name meaning, "we shall rebel." Son of Cush or Ethiopia (Gen. 10:8–10; 1 Chron. 1:10). A hunter and builder of the kingdom of Babel who some Bible students

Restored gate at the site of the ancient city of Nineveh of Assyria.

have linked to Tukulti-Ninurta, an Assyrian king (about 1246–1206 B.C.). The bible does not give sufficient information to connect him with any other known figure of history. Others think that Amenophis III of Egypt (about 1411–1375 B.C.) or the heroic Gilgamesh might have been the ancient Nimrod. Regardless, extremely popular legends involve Nimrod as a ruler in both Assyrian and Egyptian lore. The prophet Micah called Assyria "the land of Nimrod" (5:6). Nimrod shows that the great Mesopotamian culture had its origin from the creative work of the God of Israel.

NIMSHI (Nĭm′ shī) Personal name meaning, "weasel." Grandfather of Jehu (2 Kings 9:2,14). Elsewhere, Jehu is called the son of Nimshi (1 Kings 19:16; 2 Kings 9:20; 2 Chron. 22:7). Either son is used loosely in the sense of descendant, or a variant tradition is involved.

NINEVE (Nĭn′ ĕ vĕ) KJV alternate form of Nineveh (Luke 11:32).

NINEVEH (Nĭn′ ĕ vĕh) The greatest of the capitals of the ancient Assyrian Empire, which flourished from about 800 to 612 B.C. It was located on the left bank of the Tigris River in northeastern Mesopotamia (Iraq today). Its remains are represented by two mounds named *Quyundjiq* "Many Sheep" and *Nebi Yunus* "The Prophet Jonah."
Biblical References Nineveh is first mentioned in the Old Testament as one of the cities established

by Nimrod (Gen. 10:9–12). It was the enemy city to which God called the reluctant prophet Jonah in the 8th century B.C. The Book of Jonah calls it "that great city" (1:2; 4:11), and "an exceeding great city" (3:3). The additional phrase "of three days' journey" (3:3) has been rendered by the NIV: "a visit required three days." The phrase could be an idiom which would refer to the first day for travel to, the second for visiting, and the third day for the return from a site. The phrase "more than a hundred and twenty thousand people who cannot tell their right hand from their left" (4:11) has sometimes been taken to refer to children, which would yield a population of 600,000. The area within the city walls, however, would not have contained more than 175,000.

The final biblical references are from Nahum, who prophesied the overthrow of the "bloody city" by the attack of the allied Medes and Chaldeans in 612 B.C. By 500 B.C. the prophet's words (Nah. 3:7) "Nineveh is laid waste" were echoed by the Greek historian Herodotus who spoke of the Tigris as "the river on which the town of Nineveh formerly stood."

Excavations A Muslim village and cemetery have occupied the site of Nebi Yunus, preventing excavations there. The tell of Quyundjiq which rises 90 feet above the plain has attracted excavators after it was first accurately sketched by C. J. Rich in 1820.

In 1842 Paul Emile Botta, the French consul at the nearby city of Mosul, became the first excavator of the Near East, when he began digging at Quyundjiq. In 1845 the Englishman, A. H. Layard, dug briefly at Quyundjiq for a month. Both moved to other sites they mistakenly believed to be Nineveh. Layard later returned in 1849 to Quyundjiq and discovered Sennacherib's palace there.

Hormuz Rassam, a native of Mosul assisted Layard and then worked at the site of Quyundjiq 1852–54 and 1878–82. He found Ashurbanipal's palace and library in 1853. George Smith, who had deciphered the Babylonian flood story in the Gilgamesh Epic in 1872, was sent to the site by *The Daily Telegraph.* In 1873 he found a tablet which contained 17 further lines of the flood story. Iraqi scholars made some soundings in 1954 at Nebi Yunus which confirmed Layard's guess that Esarhaddon's palace lay here.

Palaces Sennacherib (704–681 B.C.) built the enormous southwest palace at Quyundjiq. We observe on his reliefs captive Philistines, Tyrians, Aramaeans, and others working under the supervision of the king himself. His "palace which has no equals" covered five acres and had 71 rooms, including two large halls 180 feet long and 40 feet wide. He boasted that the materials for the palace included "fragrant cedars, cypresses, doors banded with silver and copper . . . painted brick, . . . curtain pegs of silver and copper, alabaster, breccia,

marble, ivory." The rooms were embellished with 9,880 feet of sculptured reliefs, depicting Assyrian victories over enemy cities, including the Judean city of Lachish, captured in 701 B.C. Sennacherib's city was enclosed by eight miles of walls with fifteen gates. It had gardens and parks, watered by a thirty-mile long aqueduct.

Ashurbanipal (669–28 B.C.), the last great Assyrian king, built the northern palace with its magnificent reliefs of royal lion hunts. He amassed a library of 20,000 tablets, which contained important literary epics, magical and omen collections, royal archives and letters. See *Assyria.*

Edwin Yamauchi

NINEVITES (Nĭn′ ē vītes) Residents of the Assyrian capital Nineveh (Luke 11:30,32). The Ninevites served as an example of Gentiles who repented and were accepted by God (compare Jonah 3; Luke 4:26–27; 7:9; 11:31; 17:15–18). See *Assyria.*

NIPPUR (Nĭp pŭr′) City located in Mesopotamia, approximately fifty miles southeast of the ancient city of Babylon and approximately one hundred miles south of modern Baghdad, Iraq. Although it is never mentioned in the Bible, its history is important in the larger context of the biblical world. It is believed to have been the center of one of the first true civilizations, that of Sumer.

The city was founded approximately 4000 B.C. by a primitive group called the "Ubaidians." Nippur was for more than two thousand years the undisputed cultural and religious center, although it never was used as the capital city for any kingdom.

Nippur was a flourishing center of industry and scribal education. Documents discovered in the area describe a variety of commercial enterprises. Some of the tablets, dating back to 2500 B.C. and earlier, were found, as were records of a much later time. One of the most important later discoveries appeared in the ruins of a business house. The records, known as the Murashu documents after the banking family responsible for them, give some indication of the extent of Jewish involvement in the business world after the time of the Babylonian Exile. Scribal education concerned the use of one of the earliest forms of writing called cuneiform. See *Cuneiform.* Also part of education was an emphasis on mathematics.

Nippur was most important, however, for its religion. Various gods controlled every aspect of life. The chief deity was En-lil, also occasionally called Bel ("the lord"). He was thought of as god of the terrestrial world and the father of other gods. His significance made his home, Nippur, the place where people from peasants to kings came to offer gifts.

According to tradition, kingly authority descended from heaven after the flood. The several cities in the area, except for Nippur, took turns as the seat of government and often waged war against each other for political supremacy. The undisputed source of this supremacy, however, was En-lil, the principal deity. His authority was transmitted to the human kings through the priesthood of his temple, the *Ekur* ("mountain house"), the leading shrine in the area.

Nippur's influence and prominence began to wane with the rise of Babylonian power. By the time of Hammurabi, 1792–1750 B.C., Nippur had been replaced by Babylon as the religious and cultural center. It did, however, continue to be an influential city down about 250 B.C.

See *Babylon; Cuneiform; Hammurabi; Mesopotamia; Sumer.* *Hugh Tobias*

NISAN (Nī′ săn) A foreign term used after the Exile for the first month of the Hebrew calendar (Neh. 2:1; Esth. 3:7). This month which falls within March and April was formerly called Abib. See *Calendars.*

NISROCH (Nĭs′ rŏch) God worshiped by the Assyrian king Sennacherib (2 Kings 19:37; Isa. 37:38). No god of this name is otherwise known. The name is perhaps a (deliberate?) corruption of the name Marduk, Nusku (the fire-god), or Ashur (compare early Greek readings Esdrach and Asorach).

NITER (Nī′ tēr) KJV term for lye (Prov. 25:20; Jer. 2:22).

NO, NO-AMON (Nō, Nō-ā′ mŏn) Ancient name for Egyptian city of Thebes (modern Luxor). Inherent in its name is its reputation. *No* is a word for the best of cities and Amon the name of the Egyptian god, Amun-Re. Jeremiah (46:25), Ezekiel (30:14,15,16), and Nahum (3:8) were well aware of its prominence. To attack this capital city was to strike at the heart and spirit of Egypt.

Although Thebes existed before the Middle Kingdom (about 2040–1750 B.C.), it was not particularly noteworthy. In the New Kingdom (about 1550–1070 B.C.) Thebes became the worship and cultural center of Egypt. Pharaoh after pharaoh added to the magnificent temples of Karnak and its "queen" just to the south, Luxor. These two edifices dominated the east side of the Nile while the funerary temples, and the valleys of the kings (Biban el-Moluk) and queens occupied the west side. Deir el-Bahri (Hatshepsut), the Memnon Colossi (Amenhotep III), the Ramasseum (Rameses II), and Medinet Habu (Rameses III) are just a few sites still witnessing to the past glory of Thebes. As Nahum indicated, Thebes was not invincible. In 661 B.C. Ashurbanipal (of Assyria) sacked the sacred site. Mortally wounded, the city never fully recovered. See *Egypt.* *Gary C. Huckabay*

NOADIAH (Nō å dī′ ah) Personal name meaning, "Yah has met." *1.* Levite who returned from Exile and served as a Temple treasurer (Ezra 8:33). *2.* Prophetess who discouraged Nehemiah's building of the walls of Jerusalem (Neh. 6:14).

NOAH (Nō ah) A personal name of uncertain meaning, related to "rest."

Old Testament *1.* The son of Lamech, a descendant of Adam in the line of Seth, and a survivor of the flood. A good and righteous man, Noah was the father of Shem, Ham, and Japheth who were born when he was 500 years old. God warned Noah that He was going to wipe mankind from the face of the earth. Because Noah walked with God and stood blameless among the people of that time, God gave him specific instructions for building the ark by which Noah and his family would survive the coming flood. Noah followed the building instructions down to every detail. Then a week before the flood (Gen. 7:4), Noah led his family and all of the animals into the ark just as God directed. After seven days, the rain began and lasted for 40 days. As he sought to know whether it was safe to leave the ark, he sent out first a raven and then a dove. When the dove returned with an olive leaf, Noah knew the water had receded.

Once out of the ark, Noah built an altar and sacrificed clean animals as burnt offerings on the altar. Then the Lord promised never again to destroy living creatures as He had done in the flood and established a covenant with Noah and his sons and sealed that covenant with a rainbow. See *Covenant.*

The sinful nature of humanity is one thing that remained preserved on the ark. Once on dry ground, Noah planted a vineyard, drank of its wine, became drunk, and exposed himself in his tent. Ham informed Shem and Japheth about their father's nakedness. The latter two showed respect for their father and covered him. As a result, they received rich blessings for their descendants from Noah. Ham in turn received a curse for his descendant: Canaan. Noah lived another 350 years after the flood and died at the age of 950 years.

New Testament Hebrews 11:7 affirms Noah's actions of faith in building the ark. The references to Noah in 1 Peter 3:20 and 2 Peter 2:5 speak of Noah and those of his family who were saved in the flood. See *Flood.*

2. One of Zelophehad's five daughters (Num. 26:33). Of the tribe of Manasseh, these daughters received an inheritance in the land in their father's name even though he was dead with no male offspring (27:1–11). This was most unusal in that time. *Judith Wooldridge*

NOB (Nŏb) City in Benjamin likely situated between Anathoth and Jerusalem (Neh. 11:31–32;

Isa. 10:32). Following the destruction of the Shiloh sanctuary in about 1,000 B.C. (Jer. 7:14), the priesthood relocated to Nob. Because the priest Ahimelech gave aid to the fugitive David (1 Sam. 21:1–9), Saul exterminated 85 of the priests of Nob (1 Sam. 22:9–23). Only Abiathar escaped. The site of Nob was perhaps on Mount Scopas about one mile northeast of ancient Jerusalem, on the hill Qu'meh one mile further north, or Ras el-Mesharif about one mile north of Jerusalem. See *Ahimelech.*

NOBAH (Nō′ bah) Personal name meaning, "barking" or "howling." *1.* Leader of the tribe of Manasseh who conquered Kenath in Gilead (Num. 32:42). *2.* Town in Gilead, formerly Kenath (Num. 32:42). Site is perhaps identical with Kanawat about 60 miles east of the Sea of Galilee. *3.* A town in Gilead (Judg. 8:10–11) to the east of Succoth and Penuel and west of the king's highway (KJV, "The way of them that dwell in tents"; NRSV, "caravan route").

NOD (Nŏd) Place name meaning, "wandering." After murdering his brother Abel, Cain was condemned to be "a fugitive and a wanderer on the earth" (Gen. 4:12,14; NRSV). Nod is located "away from the presence of the Lord" and "east of Eden" (Gen. 4:16). The text is not so much interested in fixing the physical location of Nod as in emphasizing the "lostness" of the wanderer Cain.

NODAB (Nō′ dab) Name meaning, "nobility." Tribe conquered by Reuben, Gad, and the half-tribe of Manasseh (1 Chron. 5:18). The name is preserved by Nudebe in Hauran. The association of Nodab with Jetur and Naphish suggests its identification with Kedemah (Gen. 25:15; 1 Chron. 1:31).

NOE (No′ e) KJV New Testament form of Noah.

NOGAH (Nō′ gäh) Personal name meaning, "brilliance" or "luster." Son born to David in Jerusalem (1 Chron. 3:7; 14:6). The omission of the name in the parallel list (2 Sam. 5:15) has suggested that the name results from dittography or copying twice of the following name, Nepheg.

NOHAH (Nō′ hăh) Personal name meaning, "quiet." Son of Benjamin (1 Chron. 8:2). The name is omitted from the parallel list (Gen. 46:21).

NON (Nŏn) KJV alternate form of the personal name Nun (1 Chron. 7:27).

NOON The middle of the day, specifically twelve o'clock noon. Noon is frequently associated with death and destruction (2 Sam. 4:5; 1 Kings

20:16; 2 Kings 4:20; Ps. 91:6; Jer. 6:4; 15:8; 20:16; Zeph. 2:4). Noon is also associated with blessings and vindication (Job 11:17; Ps. 37:6; Isa. 58:10).

NOOSE A loop of rope used as a trap (Job 18:10 NAS, NIV; Prov. 7:22 NIV). See *Fowler; Hunting.*

NOPH (Nŏph) Variant form of Moph, the Hebrew term for Memphis (Isa. 19:13; Jer. 2:16; 44:1; 46:14,19; Ezek. 30:13,16). See *Memphis.*

NOPHAH (Nō′ phah) Place name meaning, "blast." Nophah passed from Moabite to Ammonite to Israelite control (Num. 21:26,30). The REB and RSV by altering one letter of the Hebrew text read "fire spread," a reading supported by the earliest Greek translation and Samaritan Pentateuch. If Nophah was a place, it is perhaps Nobah (Num. 32:42).

NORTH See *Directions, Geographical.*

NORTH GATE Designation of two gates in Ezekiel's vision of the renewed Temple, a gate entering the outer court (Ezek. 8:14; 44:4; 46:9; 47:2) and a gate entering the inner court (Ezek. 40:35,40,44).

NORTHEASTER See *Euroclydon.*

NOSE Part of the face between the eye and mouth which bears the nostrils and covers the nasal cavity. Jewelry was worn in the nose (Gen. 24:47; Isa. 3:21; Ezek. 16:12). Prisoners of war were sometimes led captive with hooks in their noses (2 Kings 19:28; Isa. 37:29). The precise significance of placing a vine or branch to one's nose (Ezek. 8:17) is unknown. Suggestions include an act connected with idolatrous worship, a provocative gesture (compare our turning up one's nose), or, if the text is emended, to a stench from the people which reaches God's nose. Cutting off the nose of an adulteress is a penalty known from Assyrian law (Ezek. 23:25,35).

Nostrils are often associated with the breath of life (Gen. 2:7; 7:22; Job 27:3; Isa. 2:22). The Lord's nostrils pile up the waters, allowing passage through the sea (Ex. 15:8; 2 Sam 22:16) and are associated with judgment (2 Sam. 22:9; Job 41:20; Ps. 18:8; Isa. 65:5).

NOSE RINGS See *Jewels, Jewelry.*

NOSTRIL See *Nose.*

NOVICE KJV term for a recent convert (1 Tim. 3:6).

NUBIANS (Nū′ bĭ ans) Residents of an ancient kingdom along the Nile river in southern Egypt

Ivory cylinder seal showing a Nubian striking a kneeling figure.

and northern Sudan (Dan. 11:43, NIV; also NRSV margin). Cushites (REB) designates inhabitants of the same area. Other translations use Ethiopians, which formerly designated people of the same area. Modern Ethiopia lies further to the southeast. See *Ethiopia.*

NUMBER SYSTEMS AND NUMBER SYMBOL-ISM To understand properly the number systems of the biblical world, one must look to the neighbors of Israel. The Egyptians were already using relatively advanced mathematics by 3000 B.C. The construction of such structures as the pyramids required an understanding of complex mathematics. The Egyptian system was decimal. The Sumerians by that same time had developed their own number system. In fact, the Sumerians knew two systems, one based on ten (a decimal system) and one based on six or twelve (usually designated as a duodecimal system). We still make use of remnants of the Sumerian system today in our reckoning of time—12 hours for day and 12 hours for night, 60 minutes and 60 seconds as divisions of time. We also divide a circle into 360 degrees. Our calendar was originally based on the same division with the year having 12 months of 30 days for a total of 360. Even our units of the dozen (12) and gross (144) and inches to the foot may have their origin in the Sumerian mathematical system.

The Hebrews did not develop the symbols to represent numbers until the postexilic period (after 539 B.C.). In all preexilic inscriptions, small numbers are represented by individual strokes (for example, //// for four). Larger numbers

Relief of the Nubian god Mandulis.

were either represented with Egyptian symbols, or the name of the number was written out ("four" for the number 4). The Arad inscriptions regularly used Egyptian symbols for numbers, individual strokes for the units and hieratic numbers for 5, 10, and larger numbers. The Samaria ostraca more frequently wrote out the number. Letters of the Hebrew alphabet are first used to represent numbers on coins minted in the Maccabean period (after 167 B.C.).

With the coming of the Hellenistic and Roman periods to Palestine, Greek symbols for numbers and Roman numerals appeared. The Greeks used letters of their alphabet to represent numerals, while the Romans used the familiar symbols I,V,X,L,C,M, and so on.

Biblical passages show that the Hebrews were well acquainted with the four basic mathematical operations of addition (Num. 1:20–46), subtraction (Gen. 18:28–33), multiplication (Num. 7:84–86), and division (Num. 31:27). The Hebrews also used fractions such as a half (Gen 24:22), a third (Num. 15:6), and a fourth (Ex. 29:40).

In addition to their usage to designate specific numbers or quantities, many numbers in the Bible came to have a symbolic meaning. Thus seven came to symbolize completeness and perfection. God's work of creation was both complete and perfect—and it was completed in seven days. All of mankind's existence was related to God's creative activity. The seven-day week reflected God's first creative activity. The sabbath was that day of rest following the work week, reflective of God's rest (Gen. 1:1—2:4). Israelites were to remember the land also and give it a sabbath, permitting it to lie fallow in the seventh year (Lev. 25:2–7). Seven was also important in cultic matters beyond the sabbath: major festivals such as Passover and Tabernacles lasted seven days as did wedding festivals (Judg. 14:12,17). In Pharaoh's dream, the seven good years followed by seven years of famine (Gen. 41:1–36) represented a complete cycle of plenty and famine. Jacob worked a complete cycle of years for Rachel; then, when he was given Leah instead, he worked an additional cycle of seven (Gen. 29:15–30).

A major Hebrew word for making an oath or swearing, *shava'*, was closely related to the word *seven, sheva'*. The original meaning of "swear an oath" may have been "to declare seven times" or "to bind oneself by seven things."

A similar use of the number seven can be seen in the New Testament. The seven churches (Rev. 2—3) perhaps symbolized by their number all the churches. Jesus taught that forgiveness is not to be limited, even to a full number or complete number of instances. We are to forgive, not merely seven times (already a gracious number of forgivenesses), but seventy times seven (limitless forgiveness, beyond keeping count) (Matt. 18:21–22).

As the last example shows, multiples of seven frequently had symbolic meaning. The year of Jubilee came after the completion of every forty-nine years. In the year of Jubilee all Jewish bondslaves were released and land which had been sold reverted to its former owner (Lev. 25:8–55). Another multiple of seven used in the Bible is seventy. Seventy elders are mentioned (Ex. 24:1,9). Jesus sent out the seventy (Luke 10:1–17). Seventy years is specified as the length of the Exile (Jer. 25:12, 29:10; Dan. 9: 2). The messianic kingdom was to be inaugurated after a period of seventy weeks of years had passed (Dan. 9:24).

After seven, the most significant number for the Bible is undoubtedly twelve. The Sumerians used twelve as one base for their number system. Both the calendar and and the signs of the Zodiac reflect this twelve base number system. The tribes of Israel and Jesus' disciples numbered twelve. The importance of the number twelve is evident in the effort to maintain that number. When Levi ceased to be counted among the tribes, the Joseph tribes, Ephraim and Manasseh, were counted separately to keep the number twelve intact. Similarly, in the New Testament, when Judas Iscariot committed suicide, the eleven moved quickly to add another to keep their number at twelve. Twelve seems to have been especially significant in the Book of Revelation. New Jerusalem had twelve gates; its walls had twelve foundations (Rev. 21:12–14). The tree of life yielded twelve kinds of fruit (Rev. 22:2).

Multiples of twelve are also important. There were twenty-four divisions of priests (1 Chron. 24:4), and twenty-four elders around the heavenly throne (Rev. 4:4). Seventy-two elders, when one includes Eldad and Medad, were given a portion of God's spirit that rested on Moses, and they prophesied (Num. 11:24–26). An apocryphal tradition holds that seventy-two Jewish schol-

ars, six from each of the twelve tribes, translated the Old Testament into Greek, to give us the version we call today the Septuagint. The 144,000 servants of God (Rev. 7:4), were made up of 12,000 from each of the twelve tribes of Israel.

Three as a symbolic number often indicated completeness. The created cosmos had three elements: heaven, earth, and underworld. Three Persons make up the Godhead: Father, Son, and Holy Spirit. Prayer was to be lifted at least three times daily (Dan. 6:10; compare Ps. 55: 17). The sanctuary had three main parts: vestibule, nave, inner sanctuary (1 Kings 6). Three-year-old animals were mature and were, therefore, prized for special sacrifices (1 Sam. 1:24; Gen. 15:9). Jesus said He would be in the grave for three days and three nights (Matt. 12:40), the same time Jonah was in the great fish (Jonah 1:17). Paul often used triads in his writings, the most famous being "faith, hope and charity" (1 Cor. 13:13). One must also remember Paul's benediction: "The grace of the Lord Jesus Christ, and the love of God, and the communion of the Holy Ghost be with you all" (2 Cor. 13:14).

Four was often used as a sacred number. Significant biblical references to four include the four corners of the earth (Isa. 11:12), the four winds (Jer. 49:36), four rivers which flowed out of Eden to water the world (Gen. 2:10–14), and four living creatures surrounding God (Ezek. 1; Rev. 4:6–7). God sent forth the four horsemen of the Apocalypse (Rev. 6:1–8) to bring devastation to the earth.

The most significant multiple of four is forty, which often represented a large number or a long period of time. Rain flooded the earth for forty days (Gen. 7:12). For forty days Jesus withstood Satan's temptations (Mark 1:13). Forty years represented approximately a generation. Thus all the adults who had rebelled against God at Sinai died during the forty years of the Wilderness Wandering period. By age forty, a person had reached maturity (Exod. 2:11; Acts 7:23).

A special system of numerology known as *gematria* developed in later Judaism. Gematria is based on the idea that one may discover hidden meaning in the biblical text from a study of the numerial equivalence of the Hebrew letters. The first letter of the Hebrew alphabet, *aleph* represented one; *beth,* the second letter represented two, and so on. With gematria one takes the sum of the letters of a Hebrew word and seeks to find some meaning. For example, the Hebrew letters of the name Eliezer, Abraham's servant, have a numerical value of 318. When Gensis 14:14 states that Abraham took 318 trained men to pursue the kings from the east, some Jewish commentaries interpret this to mean that Abraham had but one helper, Eliezer, since Eliezer has the numerical value of 318. Likewise, the number

666 in Revelation is often taken as a reverse gematria for the emperor Nero. The name Nero Caesar, put in Hebrew characters and added up following gematria, total 666. Any interpretation based on gematria must be treated with care; such interpretation always remains speculative.

Joel F. Drinkard, Jr.

NUMBERS, BOOK OF Fourth book of Old Testament that teaches the identity of the people of God, God's provision for authority over His people, and God's plan for their fulfillment as a nation. It answers the questions: "Who are the people of God?" "Who is in charge here?" and, "What are we doing?"

Title The book title is "Numbers" in our English Bibles based upon the Vulgate (Latin translation) title, *Numeri,* and the Septuagint (Greek translation) title, *Arithmoi.* This title is based on the "numbering" of people (1:19; 1:45; 2:33; 3:42; 4:49; 26:4). The Hebrew bible uses the first word in the book, *Bemidhbar* ("in the wilderness"), as the title. This is a helpful description giving the setting for much more that happens to God's people than taking censuses. In fact, most commentators use a geographical outline to summarize the book. This outline is simply stated:

1:1—10:10 What happened at Sinai;

10:11—20:13 What happened in the wilderness; and

20:14—36:13 What happened from Kadesh to Moab.

Contents It seems most productive to consider the contents of the book in the light of the three questions asked above. The following should illuminate this.

Outline

I. Who are the People of God?
  A. Those who are ready to defend the camp through military means (chs. 1; 26);
  B. Those who dwell in a camp with provision for God's presence in their midst (ch. 2);
  C. Those who participate in a religious system under the authority of the Aaronite priesthood and ministry of the Levites (chs. 3; 4);
  D. Those who uphold the laws of ritual purity to keep the camp from becoming physically or morally contaminated or are willing to undertake appropriate rituals to restore wholeness (chs. 5; 6; 19);
  E. Those who furnish the tabernacle of God's presence with appropriate furnishings and utensils (chs. 7—8);
  F. Those who worship according to sacred rituals established by God (chs. 9; 28—30);
  G. Those who are willing to migrate according to God's instructions (ch. 10);
  H. Those who depend upon the priesthood to mediate the awesome presence of God (ch. 18);
  I. Those who recognize that secular authority is dependent on religious authority (ch. 27);
  J. Those who have an allegiance to justice beyond the idea of a family-blood feud (ch. 35).

II. Who is in charge of the People of God?
  A. Moses is prime authority under God's direction and through God's intervention in vindicating him after rebellions (chs. 11—12; 14; 16);
  B. Aaron is a prime spiritual authority due to God's active support (ch. 17);
  C. Even Moses and Aaron are inadequate without God's support (ch. 20);
  D. God Himself is final authority (ch. 21);
  E. God will guide the priesthood in directing Israel away from apostasy and toward Him (ch. 25).

III. What are the People of God to accomplish?
  A. They are to examine and investigate the land of promise (chs. 13—14);
  B. They are to be victorious over God's enemies through ritualized "holy war" (ch. 21);
  C. They are to recognize that no rival religious authority can spoil God's plan regarding the land of promise (chs. 22—24);
  D. They are to keep the land of promise within the tribes and people it was promised to (in spite of extraordinary circumstances) (ch. 27);
  E. They are to provide for "bonus" land beyond the initial promise (ch. 32);
  F. They are to provide for keeping the land of promise secure (ch. 36).

In this way, the reader is able to see that every aspect of life during the wilderness wandering was permeated with the centrality of God. Under God's instructions Israel conscripted an army; God's presence radiated both a sense of awe and well-being in the center of the camp; God's promise of a landed inheritance gave them a goal to strive for and an identity; and God was the ultimate authority and spoke both indirectly through His human representatives and directly through His miraculous power. The rebellion narratives (11:1—12:16; 14; 16; 17; 20; 21:4-9; and 25:1-18), as well as the account of Balaam the wizard (22—24), serve to show how God's plan and provision cannot be thwarted by any rival possibility or power. Israel needed to stay on God's side to find success. See *Aaron; Balaam; Eleazer; Joshua; Moses; Pentateuch; Holy War; Sacred Calendar; Tabernacle; Tribal Confederation.*

Johnny L. Wilson

NUN *1.* (Nŭn) Father of Joshua (Ex. 33:11; Num.

11:28;13:8,16); *2.* (Nūn) Fourteenth letter of the Hebrew alphabet which serves as a heading for Psalm 119:105–112 in the KJV. Each verse of this section begins with nun.

NUNC DIMITTIS Latin phrase meaning, "now lettest thou depart." The first words in Latin of Simeon's psalm of praise in Luke 2:29–32 and thus the title of the psalm. See *Benedictus; Magnificat.*

NURSE *1.* Woman who breast-feeds an infant (Gen. 21:7; Ex. 2:7; 1 Sam. 1:23). In Old Testament times children were often nursed as long as three years (1 Sam. 1:22–24). Weaning was often a time of celebration (Gen. 21:8). Generally, a mother nursed her own child; though sometimes a wet nurse was employed (Ex. 2:7). A nurse might continue as an honored family member after the child was grown (Gen. 24:59; 35:8). Paul likened the gentleness of his missionary approach to a mother nursing her children (1 Thess. 2:7). *2.* Woman who cares for a child such as a governess or nanny (Ruth 4:16; 2 Sam. 4:4). *3.* One who cares for the sick (1 Kings 1:2,4 NAS, RSV).

NURTURE KJV translation (Eph. 6:4) of the Greek *paideia* (disciple, instruction). The noun occurs elsewhere in the Pauline corpus but once (2 Tim. 3:16) which relates that all Scripture is profitable for "instruction (*paideia*) in righteousness." To rear children "in the nurture and admonition of the Lord" is to discipline and correct them as the Lord would.

NUTS See *Plants in the Bible.*

NUZI (Nū' zī) A city located in the northeast section of the fertile cresent, and then named Gasur, that flourished under Sargon shortly before 2000 B.C. Few cities that are not mentioned in the Old Testament contribute to its understanding as significantly as Nuzi (modern Yorghan Tepe). Its most relevant history, as far as the Old Testament is concerned, is its revival as part of the Hurrian kingdom, situated in the state of Mitanni, about 1500 B.C., about the time of the Israelites' bondage in Egypt. Twenty thousand Akkadian documents have been found at Nuzi that reflect primarily the legal, social, and economic situation of Mesopotamian culture about 2000–1400 B.C. The sociological importance of this discovery is estimated differently among scholars. Most scholars accept the value for general Near Eastern studies and biblical background, and some use the information to determine the date of the patriarchs and the literature about them according to biblical parallels with Nuzi customs.

Some parallels are more exact than others, but the following examples can be cited as relevant to patriarchal and later Israelite culture. *Marriage customs* of Nuzi and the patriarchs converge when we hear Rachel and Leah complain how their father Laban unfairly hoarded their dowry and left them nothing, contrary to provisions they expected under Nuzi-like marriage arrangements (Gen. 31:14–16). In spite of this injustice, Laban later relied on the honor of Jacob to conform to the custom of not marrying additional wives (Gen. 31:50). In the case of *infertility,* both Rachel and Leah offered their maids as surrogate mates that would bear sons to their husband Jacob, a convention seen also at Nuzi (Gen. 30:1–13). Jacob's grandmother, Sarah, had done the same for Abraham (Gen. 16:1–4), assuming as one would have in Nuzi, that the child would be hers (v. 2). Up to that point, Abraham had despaired that his servant Eliezer was his only legal heir, hinting that he had adopted Eliezer for this purpose, according to Nuzi custom (Gen. 15:2). Two further parallels in the area of *inheritance* are found in Jacob's verbally removing Reuben's privileges as the first born because of his sin against his father (Gen. 49:2–4), and the transfer of inheritance between the brothers Esau and Jacob (Gen. 25:27–34); both cases indicate prerogatives provided in Nuzi law. Though the exact reason why Rachel stole her father's idols is not explained in the Bible (Gen. 31:19,27–32), the importance of possessing one's father's idols appears at Nuzi as well. Nuzi parallels with Israelite law are also very interesting. The double portion granted to the firstborn on the basis of Deuteronomy 21:15–17 (compare Gen. 48:21–22), the occassional rights of daughters to be heirs (Num. 27:8), cancellation of debts after so many years (Deut. 15:1–3), are examples.

The name "Hebrew" for an alien as Joseph was in Egypt (Gen. 39:13–14), and as the Israelites were in that country (Ex. 1:15–19) or while in Philistia (1 Sam. 14:21), is very similar to the same use of the term *habiru* found in the Nuzi documents and elsewhere. This sheds light on the perpetual discussion of the source and meaning of this significant name for the Israelites. See *Archaeology; Abraham; Mesopotamia; Habiru; Patriarchs; Hurrian.*   *Dan Fredricks*

NYMPHA (Nўm' pha) Christian hostess of a house church, likely in Laodicea (Col. 4:15). Because the name occurs only in the accusative case, it is not possible to determine whether it is masculine or feminine. Modern translations follow the best Greek manuscripts in reading "her house" and using the feminine name Nympha. The KJV followed other manuscripts reading "his house" and thus used the masculine form Nymphas, an abbreviation of Nymphadorus meaning "gift of nymphs."

NYMPHAS (Nўm' phàs) See *Nympha.*

The Mount of Olives as viewed through one of the
arched eastern entryways in the Temple Mount area.

OAK See *Plants in the Bible.*

OARSMEN NIV term for those who row a galley (Ezek. 27:8,26). See *Ships, Sailors, and Navigation.*

OATHS A formal appeal to God or some sacred object as a support to fulfill a promise. Ancient societies lacked laws and documentation as a means of legal enforcement. Binding transactions depended upon the power of a person's word. Without a modern judicial system, the very security of the society demanded that people speak the truth to one another. The oath maintained the obligation to speak honestly.

Solemn oaths in the Bible were binding. Violation of an oath was serious and could not be disregarded (Ezek. 17:13,16,18–19).

The Old Testament and Oaths The making of covenants revealed the binding nature of the oath. See *Covenant.* The parties made oaths to enforce the awareness that a violator of the covenant would suffer the same fate as the sacrificed animal.

Symbolic acts often accompanied an oath. Oath takers often raised their right hands or lifted both hands to heaven (Gen. 14:22; Dan. 12:7; compare Rev. 10:5–6). Bible writers could even use human images to describe God, saying the Lord swears by His right hand (Isa. 62:8).

Invoking the name of a reigning monarch was another symbolic act joined with oath taking. Using the Lord's name in an oath directly appeals to His involvement regarding testimony and establishes Him as the supreme Enforcer and Judge. To violate the Lord's name was to violate the Lord; therefore, oaths that used God's name carelessly are condemned (Ex. 20:7; Lev. 19:12).

The oath reinforced God's promises to His people (Ex. 33:1; Deut. 6:18; Deut. 7:8; Ps. 132:11). The oath established boundaries around human speech and set guidelines for human conduct (Num. 30; Deut. 23:21). Israel ratified their treaties by oaths (Josh. 9:15,18,20), and the writer of Ecclesiastes reminded his readers that it is better not to make a vow than to make a vow and not keep it (5:4–5).

The New Testament and Oaths The New Testament raised the oath to a new level of understanding. In the Sermon on the Mount, Jesus established a different standard of speech, one based not upon oaths but upon simple integrity. A clear *yes* and *no* would be sufficient for communication (Matt. 5:33–37; compare Jas. 5:12). Jesus spurned oaths made by the Temple (Matt. 23:16–21). At His trial before Caiaphas, He was silent to the questions until a binding oath was placed upon Him (Matt. 26:63–65). Jesus did not condemn oaths, only the abuse of God's name in the taking of oaths.

Other New Testament passages reveal the gravity of oath taking. Peter's denial of Christ was first, a simple refusal to acknowledge Jesus. An oath accompanied his second denial. He issued his final denial in the form of a curse (Matt. 26:69–75). The apostle Paul frequently called upon God in the form of an oath to witness to his own sincerity (Rom. 1:9; 2 Cor. 1:23; Gal. 1:20). Hebrews establishes the superiority of Christ's priesthood over the Levitical priesthood because it was promised with an oath whereas the Levitical priesthood was not (7:20–22).

Throughout church history, some Christians have insisted that oath taking is a concession to the evil of this present age. Certain Christian groups have refused to take oaths under any conditions. Most Christians do not condemn oaths under any circumstance, but they condemn the abuse of God's name in oaths.   *Brad Creed*

OBADIAH (O bà dī' ah) Personal name meaning, "Yahweh's servant." *1.* Person in charge of Ahab's palace. He was devoted to Yahweh and saved Yahweh's prophets from Jezebel's wrath. He was the go-between for Elijah and Ahab (1 Kings 18:3–16). *2.* A descendant of David through Hananiah (1 Chron. 3:21). *3.* Son of Izrahiah of the tribe of Issachar (1 Chron. 7:3). *4.* Son of Azel of the tribe of Benjamin (1 Chron. 8:38; 9:44). *5.* A Levite who returned to Jerusalem with the first of the Babylonian exiles (1 Chron. 9:16). *6.* A Gadite who joined David, along with Ezer and Eliab. Obadiah was second in command behind Ezer (1 Chron. 12:8–9). *7.* Father of Ishmaiah, an officer from the tribe of Zebulun who served in David's army (1 Chron. 27:19). *8.* One of five officials Jehoshaphat sent throughout the cities of Judah to teach "the book of the law of the Lord" (2 Chron. 17:7–9). See *Jehoshaphat. 9.* A Levite descended from Merari appointed by Josiah to oversee the repairing of the Temple (2 Chron. 34:12). See *Josiah. 10.* A priest who returned from Babylonian Exile to Jerusalem with Ezra (Ezra 8:9). He joined other priests along with princes and Levites in putting his seal upon the covenant (Neh. 9:38) made between the people and God (Neh. 10:5). *11.* A gatekeeper and guardian of "the ward" ("the storerooms at the gates," NIV) during the leadership of Ezra and Nehemiah (Neh. 12:25).

OBADIAH (Ō bà dī' ah) The shortest book of the Minor Prophets, preserving the message of Obadiah, the prophet.

The Prophet No source outside his book mentions Obadiah. "Obadiah" is a common name in the Old Testament. Meaning "servant of Yahweh," it reflects his parents' faith and spiritual ambitions for their child. The title "The vision of Obadiah" turns attention to the divine author, "vision" being a technical term for a prophetic revelation received from God.

The Situation Historically, the book belongs to the

early postexilic period, at the end of the sixth century B.C. Its central section, verses 10—14, deals with the fall of Jerusalem to the Babylonians in 586 B.C., concentrating on the part the Edomites played in that tragic event. Edom was a state to the southeast of Judah. Despite treaty ties ("brother," v. 10) the Edomites, along with others, had failed to come to Judah's aid and had even helped Babylon by looting Jerusalem and handing over refugees. Moreover, the Edomites filled the vacuum caused by Judah's Exile by moving west and annexing the Negeb to the south of Judah and even its southern territory (compare v. 19).

Judah reacted with a strong sense of grievance. Obadiah's oracle responded to an underlying impassioned prayer of lament, like Psalms 74, 79, or 137, in which Judah appealed to God to act as providential trial Judge and Savior to set right the situation.

The Message The response begins with a prophetic messenger formula which reinforces the thrust of the title, that God is behind the message. Verses 2—9 give the divine verdict. Addressing Edom, God promised to defeat those supermen and topple the mountain capital which reflected their lofty self-conceit. Their allies would let them down, and neither their famed wisdom nor their warriors would be able to save them. This seems to look fearfully ahead to the Nabateans' infiltration from the eastern desert and their eventual takeover of Edom's traditional territory. The end of verse 1 appears to be a report from the prophet that already a coalition of neighboring groups was planning to attack Edom.

The catalog of Edom's crimes (vv. 10—14) functions as the accusation which warranted God's verdict of punishment. Repetition raises "day" to *center stage.* The underlying thought is that Judah had been the victim of "the day of the Lord" when God intervened in judgment, and had drunk the cup of God's wrath (vv. 15,16; compare Lam. 1:12; 2:21). In Old Testament theology the concept of the day of the Lord embraces not only God's people but their no-less-wicked neighbors. This wider dimension is reflected in verses 15—16 (compare Lam. 1:21). The fall of Edom was to trigger this eschatological event in which order would be restored to an unruly world. Then would come the vindication of God's people, not for their own sakes but as earthly witnesses to His glory; and so "the kingdom shall be the Lord's" (v. 21).

The Meaning Like the Book of Revelation, which proclaims the downfall of the persecuting Roman Empire, the aim of Obadiah is to sustain faith in God's moral government and hope in the eventual triumph of His just will. It brings a pastoral message to aching hearts, that God is on the throne and cares for His own.

Outline

I. God Knows and Will Judge the Sins of His People's Enemies (1—14).

  A. Pride deceives people into thinking they can escape God's judgment. (1—4).

  B. Deceitful people will be deceived by their "friends" (5—7).

  C. Human wisdom cannot avoid divine judgment (8—9).

  D. Conspiracy against "brothers" willl not go unpunished (10—14).

II. The Day of the Lord Offers Judgment for the Nations but Deliverance for God's People (15—21).

  A. Sinful peoples will receive just recompense (15—16).

  B. God will deliver His people in holiness (17—18).

  C. God's remnant will be restored (19—20)

  D. The Kingdom belongs to God alone (21)

Leslie C. Allen

OBAL (Ō' bàl) Personal name meaning, "stout." Son of Joktan and ancestor of an Arab tribe (Gen. 10:28). At 1 Chronicles 1:22 the name takes the alternate form Ebal.

OBED (Ō' bĕd) Personal name meaning, "serving." *1.* Son of Boaz and Ruth (Ruth 3:13—17), father of Jesse, and grandfather of King David. He was an ancestor of Jesus Christ (Matt. 1:5; 3:32). *2.* Son of Ephal and father of Jehu (1 Chron. 2:37—38). *3.* One of David's mighty men (1 Chron. 11:47). *4.* Gatekeeper in Solomon's Temple (1 Chron. 26:7). *5.* Father of Azariah, a commander assisting in coronation of King Josiah (2 Chron. 23). See *Athaliah.*

OBED-EDOM (Ō' bĕd-ē' dom) A Personal name meaning, "*serving Edom.*"

1. A Philistine from Gath who apparently was loyal to David and Israel. At Obed-edom's house David left the ark of the covenant following the death of Uzzah at the hand of God (2 Sam. 6:6—11). Obed-edom was unusually blessed of God (probably a reference to prosperity) during the three months the ark was at his house. *2.* A Levite who served as both gatekeeper and musician in the tabernacle in Jerusalem during David's reign (1 Chron. 15:18,24; 16:5). His duties related especially to the ark of the covenant. A guild of Levites may have adopted the name "Obed-edom" as their title as keepers of the ark. *3.* A member of the Korhites (1 Chron. 26:1,4—8) who kept the south of the Temple (v. 15). *4.* A keeper of the sacred vessels of the Temple. Joash of Israel took him with the sacred vessels to Samaria following his capture of Jerusalem and of Amaziah king of Judah (2 Chron. 25:23—24).

OBEDIENCE To hear God's Word and act accordingly. The word translated "obey" in the Old Testament means "to hear" and is often so translated.

In the New Testament, several words describe obedience. One word means "to hear or to listen in a state of submission." Another New Testament word often translated "obey" means "to trust."

The person's obedient response to God's Word is a response of trust or faith. Thus, to really hear God's Word is to obey God's Word (Ex. 19:5; Jer. 7:23).

The Bible views disobedience as a failure to hear and do God's Word (Ps. 81:11). Israel's story was one of a nation who failed to hear or to listen to God (Jer. 7:13; Hos. 9:17). Jesus warned: "He that hath ears to hear, let him hear" (Matt. 11:15).

How does obedience affect one's spiritual life? Obedience is essential to worship (1 Sam. 15:22; John 4:23–24). The obedience of faith brings about salvation (Rom. 1:5, 10:16–17). Obedience secures God's blessings (John 14:23; 1 John 2:17; Rev. 22:14). Spiritual insight is gained through obedience (John 7:17). A life of obedience to God is the fruit of faith (Jas. 2:21–26).

True obedience means imitating God in holiness, humility, and love (1 Pet. 1:15; John 13:34; Phil. 2:5–8). True disciples do the will of God (Mat. 7:21). Facing clashing claims for one's allegiance, the Christian obeys God rather than other persons (Acts 5:29).

What motivates us to obey God? Obedience springs from gratitude for grace received (Rom. 12:12). Christians obey God as an expression of their spiritual freedom (Gal. 5:13; 1 Pet. 2:16). Jesus taught that our love for God motivates us to obey Him (John 14:21, 23, 24; 15:10).

How does obedience affect our relationships with others? The Bible speaks of obedience from the wife to the husband (Eph. 5:22), from children to their parents (Eph. 6:1), from slaves to masters (Col. 3:22). Obedience with joy should be shown to church leaders (1 Thess. 5:12–13). Obedience is expected from all Christians to persons in authority (1 Pet. 2:13–14).

The New Testament places special emphasis on Jesus' obedience. Christ's obedience stands in contrast to Adam's disobedience (Rom. 5:12–21). A desire to obey the will of God motivated Jesus' actions (Luke 4:43; John 5:30). Jesus acted and spoke only as the Father directed (John 3:34). By living a life of obedience, Jesus showed Himself to be the Savior (Heb. 5:7–10). Christ's work on the cross is viewed as a sacrifice of obedience (Rom. 5:19; Heb. 10:7–10).

God has spoken in the Scriptures. Disobedience to God's Word comes from a sinful heart—a heart that will not trust God. Obedience comes from a heart that trusts God. If God's people obey Him, they find the blessings He yearns to give. If they disobey, believers receive judgment and necessary discipline. *Gary Hardin*

OBEISANCE, DO To bown down with one's face to the ground as a sign of homage and submission. KJV and RSV translate the Hebrew *shachah* as obeisance when the object of homage is a person but as worship when the object of homage is God or other gods (84 times in the RSV). Most often persons did obeisance to the king (1 Sam. 24:8; 2 Sam. 1:2; 9:6–8; 14:4) or a royal official (Gen. 43:28; Esth. 3:2,5). Moses did obeisance before his father-in-law (Ex. 18:7). Saul did obeisance before Samuel's ghost (1 Sam. 28:14).

OBELISK (Ŏb′ ĕ lĭsk) Stone pillar used in worship, especially of the Egyptian sun god Amun-Ra. Four-sided and made from one stone, obelisks tapered to the top, where a pyramid rested. They apparently symbolized the rays of the rising sun and the hope of the Pharaoh for rejuvenation and new vitality. At times, they were used in tombs to represent hope for resurrection. A four thousand-year-old obelisk still stands in modern Matariyeh, ancient On. Another has been transplanted to Central Park in New York City. Many obelisks were built from about 1550 to about 1100 B.C. Some were more than 100 feet tall. The Hebrew term translated obelisks at Jeremiah 43:13 (NAS, NRSV, RSV) means pillar or standing stone ("sacred stone," NIV, REB). The Egyptian context suggests the pillars were in fact obelisks, perhaps dedicated to the sun-god Ra. See *On.*

OBIL (Ō′ bĭl) Personal name of uncertain meaning, perhaps "camel driver," "tender," or "mourner." Overseer in charge of David's camels (1 Chron. 27:30).

OBLATION Gift offered at an altar or shrine, especially a voluntary gift not involving blood. KJV used oblation to translate four Hebrew words. Modern translations often replace oblation with either offering (Lev. 7:38; Isa. 1:13; Ezek. 44:30) or contribution (2 Chron. 31:14; Ezek. 20:40). RSV used oblation only at 1 Kings 18:29,36 where it replaced the "evening sacrifice" of the KJV, NIV, NAS. See *Sacrifice and Offerings.*

OBOTH (Ō′ bŏth) Place name meaning, "fathers" or "water skins." A wilderness station (Num. 21:10–11; 33:43–44), perhaps identical with 'Ain el-Weiba near Panon (modern Feinan).

OBSCENE OBJECT REB translation for an object the queen mother Maacah erected for the worship of Asherah, a fertility goddess (1 Kings 15:13; 2 Chron. 15:16). The precise nature of the image is unclear. The Vulgate or early Latin translation took the image to be a phallic emblem. Some recent interpreters have suggested a stylized palm tree as a symbol of fertility. Alternate translations include: idol (KJV); abominable image (NRSV); repulsive Asherah pole (NIV); and horrid image for Asherah (NAS). See *Asherah; Fertility Cults.*

Fallen Egyptian obelisk at Rameses (Tanis).

OBSCURITY KJV term for gloom or darkness (Isa. 29:11; 58:10; 59:9).

OBSERVED, SIGNS TO BE Translation of the Greek *paratērēsis* (Luke 17:20) meaning, "observation" or "observance." The Lucan context suggests that the intended meaning is that the coming of God's kingdom is not preceded by visible signs so that one could say, "Lo, here it is." Other interpreters suggest that the kingdom is not preceded by observance of a Jewish festival (such as the Passover) or brought on by adherence to ceremonial law.

OBSERVER OF TIMES KJV term for a soothsayer (Deut. 18:10,14; compare Lev. 19:26; 2 Kings 21:6; 2 Chron. 33:6). See *Divination and Magic*.

OCCUPATIONS AND PROFESSIONS IN THE BIBLE The occupations and professions of ancient civilizations were, as in modern times, related to the natural resources, commerce, and institutions of the nations. Israel was no exception. Although readers of the Bible may be

A Middle Eastern craftsman placing tiles into a mosaic inlaid box.

tempted to think of the Hebrews in general, and the Bible personalities in particular, as living lives totally absorbed by their religion, the ancients did have to make a living. In fact, few Hebrews followed a profession linked to the unique structure of their religion.

In the course of time, occupations developed from the simple task to the more complex and from unskilled to skilled labor. This evolution was spurred by Israel's shift from a nomadic existence to a settled life and from a clan-type government to that of the monarchy. The development of

A stone mason working at his craft.

O

A Middle Eastern rug weaver operating his loom.

secular occupations paralleled the settlement of the people into towns and villages, and the evolution of their government from a loose-knit tribal group to a nation involved in international politics. In earliest biblical times, the Hebrews followed their herds from pasture land to pasture land and water hole to water hole, though at times they lived for long periods near major cities (Gen. 13:18; 20:1; 26:6; 33:19). Their occupations were centered in the family enterprise.

When Israel entered into Canaan, the Hebrews moved toward a settled existence. As a settled people, agricultural pursuits became extremely important for survival. As the monarchy developed, many new occupations appear within the biblical text, mostly to maintain the royal house. Finally, as villages grew larger, and commerce between cities and nations expanded, various trades and crafts expanded with them. See *Commerce.*

A sampling of the most common occupations and professions of the Bible are briefly described and grouped around the places where they were usually practiced: the home, the palace, the market place, and the religious occupations related to the church of Christianity and Temple of Judaism. **Occupations Around the Home** The earliest occupations and professions mentioned in the Bible, as might be expected, are tasks and chores done at home. One of the principal duties around the home centered on food preparation. *1. Baker* (Gen. 40:5) is mentioned early in Scripture as a member of the Egyptian pharaoh's court. Baking bread was a frequent task performed in the Hebrew home long before it evolved into a specialized trade.

2. Butler of the pharaoh's palace was also known as a *cupbearer* (Neh. 1:11; compare Gen. 40:21), one who was responsible for providing the king with drink. He, presumably, tasted each cup of wine before it was presented to Pharaoh as a precaution against poisoning.

3. Cooks did the majority of the ancient people's food preparation (1 Sam. 9:23–24). Within the home, female family members did the cooking. As cooking became an occupation outside of

the home, men entered the trade. *4.* A related, and daily, chore of grinding grain fell to the *grinder* (Matt. 24:41) or *miller,* another trade which later entered the market place. See *Mill.*

The majority of persons in biblical times were involved in some form of food gathering or production. *5. Fishermen* (Isa. 19:8; Matt. 4:18) were one such group of food gatherers. The ancient fishermen's tools were not unlike his modern counterparts: fishing by hook and line, spears, and nets. The fisherman, and fishing, is mentioned often in Scripture, most notably as a metaphor, as in Mark 1:17 when Jesus challenged Simon and Andrew to become "fishers of men." See *Fish.*

6. Hunters (Jer. 16:16) form the second major group of food gatherers. The ancient hunter's success depended upon proficiency in the use of a bow and arrow, spear, traps and snares, and his knowledge of his prey. Nimrod (Gen. 10:9) is the first person to be designated a hunter in the Bible. See *Hunter.*

7. Shepherds (Luke 2:8) were also engaged in food production. Those persons who have rule over others are often described in terms of the shepherd's duties. They were to care for and feed the people for whom they were responsible. Psalm 23 identifies the Lord as a Shepherd and vividly describes the duties of the keeper of the sheep. Given the rugged terrain of Palestine, the constant threat from wild animals, and the ceaseless search for water and pastureland, the responsibilities and dangers of the shepherd were great. Abel is the first to be described as a "keeper of sheep" (Gen. 4:2). *8.* Closely akin to the shepherd was the *herdsman* (Gen. 4:20). Jabal is described as one "having cattle." The only distinction that might be made between a shepherd and herdsman is in their charges: the shepherd, sheep; the herdsman, cattle.

9. Abel's brother, Cain, is identified as the first *farmer* (Gen. 4:2). The Bible calls the worker of land a "tiller" or "plower" (Ps. 129:3). He is closely associated with God in Scripture, since it is God who instructs and works closely with him in producing the crops. See *Agriculture.* Farm work involved the *gleaner* (Ruth 2:3), *harvestman* (Isa. 17:5), and *reaper* (Ruth 2:3). The harvestman and reaper are, apparently, two names for the same task. It is likely, also, that the farmer served as his own harvester. The gleaner is different. See *Gleaning.* By gleaning what farmers left in the field, the poor and landless obtained food.

Nomadic existence does not require any complicated structure of government. Rule was in the hands of the leader of each tribe. Some form of government became necessary, however, when towns and villages began to form. *10.* Before the coming of the monarchy, with its more centralized system of government: *judges* (Judg. 2:16), God chose to lead His people, especially in times of crisis. Since the crises were generally wars, the judges were primarily military leaders, who rescued the Israelite tribes from destruction by their warring neighbors. These and later judges also settled disputes. (Compare Luke 18:2) See *Judge.*

Occupations Around the Palace People who worked around the home could be found doing multiple tasks on any given day. Outside the home, skills became more specialized. In Israel, with the development of the monarchy, some of the Hebrews found employment within the palace.

11. The *king* (1 Sam. 8:5) held first place. Many kings, among Israel's neighbors, were held to be gods; not so in Israel. The Israelite king was the political ruler and spiritual example and leader to his people. The king determined, by his obedience or disobedience to Israel's God, the fortunes of the nation, but he was never god. (Note, however, the poetic designation in Ps. 45:6). See *King.*

12. Joseph was a *governor* (Gen. 42:6) of Egypt. His position was second only to Pharaoh. He was, in fact, ruler (Gen. 41:43) over all the land of Egypt. *13.* Daniel was another Hebrew who enjoyed rule in a foreign nation. He was one of three *presidents* (Dan. 6:2) given rule over the Median Empire. No information is given regarding his duties.

14. In New Testament times, the Roman government used a *deputy* (Acts 13:7), also called a *proconsul,* to oversee the administrative responsibilities of its provinces. The Romans had extended their empire beyond the limits of the emperor's abilty to rule personally. Deputies were used where the Roman army was unnecessary. *15.* Where a military presence was necessary, a *governor* (Matt. 27:2), or *procurator,* was used. The New Testament names only three men employed as governors in Palestine, although there were more: Pontius Pilate, Felix, and Festus. See *Rome; Governor.*

Beyond the task of governing, the palace provided ample opportunity for military occupations to develop. *16.* The *armorbearer* (Judg. 9:54) was one of the servants provided for a warrior as he went into battle. See *Arms and Armor.*

The army was made up of men of various ranks and responsibilities. Many of the terms designating those in places of leadership are ambiguous and may refer to one and the same rank. *17.* The *commander* (Isa. 55:4) apparently referred to any leader among the people. It is possible that such ranks as *captain, lieutenant,* and *prince,* which could be included under the umbrella of "commander," were, in the first place, military ranks alone.

18. Soldiers (1 Chron. 7:4) are mentioned frequently in connection with the many wars recorded in the Bible. The geographical location of Israel put it in constant danger of invading armies. Every adult male (over the age of twenty) within the tribes of Israel, was expected to serve in the military. The Mosaic law, especially in the Book of Numbers, set forth the regulations for establishing an army.

The government included a corps of service and judicial personnel, as well. *19.* The *jailor* (Acts 16:23) is prominent in several New Testament passages. He had charge of all prisoners—political or religious. Under Roman rule, the jailor was strictly responsible for the safekeeping of the inmates. If one were to escape, or otherwise be unable to complete his sentence, the jailor was liable to fulfill the sentence of the prisoner.

In addition to providing government and a military presence, nations found it necessary to collect taxes from their citizens. *20.* The despised *publican* (Matt. 9:10) is well known from the New Testament. The principal duty was extorting as much taxes as possible. It is believed, by some, that the publican was able to keep for himself any amount of monies collected beyond that levied by the government.

21. The *scribe* (Matt. 5:20), in addition to service in a religious fashion, served in an administrative capacity in the government as well. Scribes involved in the copying and interpretation of the law of Moses are known from the time of Ezra, who is identified as a "scribe in the law of Moses" (Ezra 7:6). Within ancient governments, scribes served the royal court, keeping records of the king's reign. Each king organized his government with advisors and people responsible for different areas. The Bible lists the organization of David (2 Sam. 8:16–18; 20:23–26) and Solomon (1 Kings 4:1–19). The exact responsibility of each official is difficult to determine as a look at different translations will show.

Work Around the Marketplace The marketplace offered numerous opportunities for employment outside the home. These opportunities may be grouped around the sale of goods, many of which could be classified as arts and crafts, and dispensing of services.

22. Among early craftsmen, the *carpenter* (2 Sam. 5:11) had special meaning as the occupation of Jesus. Most of the biblical references to carpenters, however, are to foreign workers. Most notable are the workers of Hiram, King of Tyre, who labored on Solomon's Temple. Associated with these craftsmen of wood are the *feller* (Isa. 14:8) and *hewers* (Josh. 9:21), both cutters of wood.

23. In metalwork, the Bible identifies the *coppersmith* (2 Tim. 4:14), the *goldsmith* (Neh. 3:8), and the *silversmith* (Acts 19:24) as workers in their respective metals. In more general terms, metal workers are identified as *founders* (Judg. 17:4) and *smiths* (1 Sam. 13:19).

Oddly enough, *miners* are not directly mentioned in the biblical text, although craftsmen in various metals were numerous. The metals used by the craftsmen were often imported, though

Israel may have controlled some mines near the Red Sea when they controlled those regions. See *Mines and Mining.*

24. In the sphere of salesmanship, the *merchant* (Gen. 23:16) or *seller* (Isa. 24:2) held a prominent position in commerce from the earliest biblical times. Their trade developed into one of international proportions. See *Commerce.*

25. The *potter* (Jer. 18:2; Rom. 9:21) may have been one of the busiest men in the marketplace. The demands for his product would be great. Pottery was less expensive and more durable than other containers available to the Israelites, which accounts for its common use. *26.* The *mason* sold his talent of cutting stone for building purposes (2 Kings 12:12), while *27.* the *tanner* (Acts 9:43) busied himself with preparing skins for use in clothing and as containers.

28. Tentmaking (Acts 18:3) must have been a craft learned from Israel's earliest days of semi-nomadic existence in the time of the patriarchs. This trade carried over into the New Testament period. Paul, Aquila, and Priscilla are said to have made their living by making tents (Acts 18:3).

Many services were offered in biblical times. *29.* The *apothecary* (Neh. 3:8) has been characterized as the equivalent of a modern druggist. His main task involved the compounding of drugs and ointments for medical purposes. Jewish religious practices suggest that making perfume was also a part of the apothecary's craft (Ex. 30:35).

30. The *banker,* called a *lender* (Prov. 22:7), suffered a poor reputation among the Jews. Their religious law forbade the lending of money for interest. In the New Testament, these bankers were the infamous "money changers" of the Temple. See *Banking.*

31. The *fuller* (Mal. 3:2) may be best described as an ancient laundryman. He worked with soiled clothing and with the material from the loom ready for weaving. His service entailed the cleaning of any fabric.

32. A *host* (Luke 10:35), often thought of as an "innkeeper," provided minimal accommodations for travelers, in some cases, little more than provision of space for erecting a tent or a place to lie down to sleep.

33. Among the most respected persons of Scripture was the *master* (Jas. 3:1), more appropriately called an *instructor* or *teacher* (Rom. 2:20). Biblical references to this profession apply mainly to religious teaching, but the term suited anyone who offered instruction. See *Education.*

34. Prominent, throughout the Bible, are various occupations related to musical talents. Descriptive names include: *Singers* and *players* (Ps. 68:25) in the Old Testament, and *musicians, harpers, pipers,* and *trumpeters* (Rev. 18:22) in the New Testament. In both Testaments, music played a significant part in the religious life and worship of the nation.

Occupations Around the Church and Temple
While *occupation* is not a technically accurate term when referring to the early church, there were "offices" filled by Christians, normally on a voluntary basis. See *Offices in the New Testament.*

The officers of the Temple were much more authoritarian. *35.* The *priest* (Ex. 31:10) acted as an intermediary between God and the people who came to worship at the Temple. In many cases, priests sacrificed the offerings for the people and the nation, taking for themselves a share in the offering. Priests also served as advisers to the king (2 Sam. 20:25).

36. Until recently, the *prophet* (Gen. 20:7) was looked upon as the antithesis of priesthood. Many of the prophets were hostile toward the abuses of the priests and the excesses of the priesthood, but they did not condemn the priesthood, itself. In fact, some prophets were members of the Temple personnel. The prophets functioned mainly as "messengers" of their God. Where the priest was a "ritual" intermediary, the prophet was a "speaking" one. Their message, at times, had a predictive element in it; generally, however, they addressed the historical situation facing their hearers. See *Prophets; Priests; High Priest; Levite; Temple.*

Conclusion Occupations during the entire span of biblical times were many and varied, as they are today. However, they were occupations suited to a nontechnological society. The nation of Israel remained an agriculturally oriented economy throughout its existence as recorded in the biblical text. *Phillip J. Swanson*

OCHRAN (Och' răn) Form of Ocran NAS, REB, NRSV prefer.

OCRAN (Ŏc' răn) KJV, NIV form of Ochran, a personal name meaning, "troubler." Father of Pagiel, a leader of the tribe of Asher (Num. 1:13; 2:27; 7:72,77; 10:26).

ODED (Ō' dĕd) Personal name of uncertain meaning, perhaps "counter," "restorer," or "timekeeper." *1.* Father of the prophet Azariah (2 Chron. 15:1). *2.* Prophet in the time of Anaz who urged the Israelites to release the people of Judah they had taken as prisoners of war (2 Chron. 28:8–15).

ODOR Scent of fragrance, usually in the phrase "pleasing odor" (KJV, "sweet savor"). A synonym for a burnt offering (Num. 28:1–2). See *Sacrifice and Offerings.*

OFFAL NIV term for the waste remaining from the butchering of a sacrificial animal (Ex. 19:14; Lev. 4:11; 8:17; 16:27; Num. 19:5; Mal. 2:3). Other translations render the underlying Hebrew as dung.

OFFENSE Offense translates several Hebrew and Greek terms. The following two senses predominate: *1.* That which causes indignation or disgust (Gen. 31:36). Here offense approximates crime (Deut. 19:15; 22:26), guilt (Hos. 5:15), trespass (Rom. 5:15,17,18,20), or sin (2 Cor. 11:7). The application of the image of the rock of offense to Christ is a special case of this sense (Rom. 9:33; Gal. 5:11; 1 Pet. 2:8). What was especially offensive was the claim that an accursed one was the Messiah and that faith in this crucified one and not works was necessary for salvation. *2.* That which serves as a hindrance (Matt. 16:23) or obstacle (2 Cor. 6:3). This hindrance is often temptation to sin (Matt. 18:7; Luke 17:1).

OFFERINGS See *Sacrifice and Offering.*

OFFICES IN THE NEW TESTAMENT Positions of leadership in the New Testament church including *deacons, elders, pastors, apostles, bishops,* and *evangelists.* In the New Testament, the concept of "office" speaks to functions and tasks, rather than status and position. Consequently, offices are dynamic rather than static and related to charismatic gifts of the Spirit rather than to the privileges of authority. Both the general terms used for "ministry" and the specific names and requirements of offices lead to this conclusion.

Many Greek words were available to describe Christian ministry. Some of these words, such as *arche,* from which comes the prefix in "archbishop," focus on rule and headship. Others, such as *leitourgia,* the root of the word *liturgy,* were widely used in Greek culture to refer to public service, secular as well as sacred. With very few exceptions, however, the New Testament writers chose the term *diakonia,* a Greek term which denoted serving at tables and which was not used for religious service in either the Greek Old Testament or in contemporary Greek writings.

Throughout the New Testament, humble, even menial service is expected of those who lead in the name of Christ. Jesus used the analogy of a person reclining at a table and another serving, identified Himself as "one who serves," and asserted that among His followers those who lead must likewise be servants (Luke 22:26–27; see also Matt. 20:25–28; Mark 10:42–45). The clear implication is that, whatever the other qualifications for leadership may be, *diakonia* is the prerequisite.

The New Testament also clearly teaches that the call to follow Christ is a call to the responsibility of service, and the abilities for that service are gifts from God. All ministries are not the same. The most prominent image of the church's order is Paul's depiction of the church as a body (1 Cor. 12). Just as the body depends on each member fulfilling its function, so the health of the church as a whole, and the ministry of individuals, depends on each member exercising the gifts that God has given. Every Christian has an office, a ministerial function to perform. The only head of the church is Christ. The order of the church is not based on a hierarchy of position and authority but on the faithfulness of the members in exercising their gifts of ministry.

Some offices are given names or descriptive titles in the New Testament, but it gives very little discussion of the job descriptions of the various offices and no indication of a ranking of them. The nature of some of the offices, of course, makes them more prominent in the life of the church.

Perhaps the most prominent New Testament office is that of *apostle.* See *Disciples, Apostles.* Although some of the apostles apparently remained in Jerusalem, the primary task of apostles was to spread the message of Christ. To accomplish that task many apostles, such as Peter and Paul, traveled widely, ministering to many churches rather than to one church.

Other officers whose tasks apparently were not limited to one church were *prophets* and *evangelists.* The prophets, similar to those in the Old Testament, were probably those who had demonstrated a gift for inspired preaching. Although some of those termed prophets spoke in tongues, Paul valued more highly those whose message was understood by the church (1 Cor. 14:4–5). Since prophetic utterance involved a direct gift from God, prophecy carried a greater risk of abuse than most other offices. Consequently, Paul advised that prophets should be tested carefully (1 Thess. 5:19–21; 1 Cor. 14:29–33). Very few prophets are mentioned specifically; among them are the four daughters of Philip (Acts 21:8–9). Though many prophets seem to have not had a settled ministry (Acts 21:10–11), others, as evidenced by Paul's discussion in 1 Corinthians 14, apparently exercised their gift within a local church. The term *evangelist* is used only three times in the New Testament, with reference to Timothy (2 Tim. 4:5), to Philip (Acts 21:8), and to a kind of spiritual gift (Eph. 4:11). Although spreading the gospel was central to several offices, we do not have enough to know whether "evangelist" was regularly a distinct office.

Two offices which apparently appeared in almost every church, at least by the end of the New Testament period, were *elder* and *deacon.* Although the evidence is not clear and is variously interpreted, the office of bishop was probably originally equivalent to that of elder. The tasks involved in these offices are not as easy to outline as those of apostles and prophets. The qualifications for bishops (elders) indicate that the office included a wide range of pastoral and administrative functions. Elders should be mature Christians of good repute, with gifts for teaching and pastoral ministry (1 Tim. 3:1–7; Titus 1:6–9). Since the word translated "bishop" means "overseer," it is natural to assume that a principal function of the office was to oversee the spiritual and physical life of the church. In every passage in which elders and/or bishops are mentioned, they appear to be ministers settled in local churches.

The word for *deacon* is derived from *diakonia,* the basic term for Christian ministry in the New Testament. The qualifications for deacons (1 Tim. 3:8–13) imply that they performed a wide variety of important services in their churches, including visiting the sick and administering relief funds. The name of the office also leads to the conclusion that deacons assisted in serving the Lord's Supper. The account of the appointment of the seven, who are not called deacons, may indicate the origin of the office (Acts 6), although some of the functions of the seven fit other offices equally well. The New Testament apparently refers to female deacons (Rom. 16:1; 1 Tim. 3:11, Williams). Ample evidence shows that female deacons were common in the second century. Similar in function to the female deacons, perhaps identical in some cases, were the widows. Apparently referring to a distinct office, 1 Tim. 5:5–10 gives instruction for enrolling in Christian service widows who had demonstrated their maturity and faithfulness.

Apostles, commissioned by Christ Himself, and prophets, whose gifts were directly and immediately from God, did not receive any additional commissioning ceremony from the church. Although there is very little direct evidence about the procedures and ceremonies involved, those who exhibited gifts for other ministerial tasks were chosen and commissioned by the churches. In some passages, the description of one's being set apart for a particular office includes reference to prayer and laying on of hands (see Acts 6:6; 13:1–3). In these passages, the emphasis is on the presence of spiritual gifts from God and on the church's blessing the ministry of the one chosen. There is no evidence that the ceremonies conferred special rights or status.

In addition to the offices mentioned earlier, the New Testament mentions other tasks and the gifts for performing them. *Teachers* and the gift of teaching are mentioned often. Sometimes reference to a distinct office may be intended (1 Cor. 12:28), but in many cases teaching was apparently a function of the elders (1 Tim. 3:2), as well as the apostles and perhaps the prophets. *Pastors* are mentioned only once (Eph. 4:11) in a list of those with spiritual gifts. Apparently the elders (bishops) and deacons were charged with pastoral functions. Performing miracles, healing, helping, and speaking in tongues (1 Cor. 12:28) are among the other tasks mentioned for which God has supplied spiritual gifts. Though these tasks may not have involved regular distinct offices, they were important ministerial functions in the early church.

The New Testament clearly teaches that all followers of Christ share in the responsibility of service. In Christ, no one has a special status which separates an officer from the regular members. All have gifts of service, and all must serve. The whole church is a royal priesthood; the only head of the church is Christ. Every member has an "office," whether or not that office is considered "official." *Fred A. Grissom*

OFFSCOURING That which is removed by scouring; dregs; filth; refuse; scum (Lam. 3:45; 1 Cor. 4:13).

OG (Ōg̱) The Amorite king of Bashan defeated by the Israelites before they crossed the Jordan (Num. 21:33–35; Deut. 1:4; 3:1–13). Og is identified as the last member of the Rephaim or giants (Deut. 3:11). The term translated "bed" (compare Job 7:13; Amos 3:12) is perhaps better rendered "resting place" in the sense of burial place. Some interpreters suggest that this resting place was similar to black basalt sarcophagi found in Transjordan.

OHAD (Ō' hăd) Personal name meaning, "unity." Son of Simeon (Gen. 46:10; Ex. 6:15). The name is omitted in parallel lists (Num. 26:12–14; 1 Chron. 4:24).

OHEL (Ō' hĕl) Personal name meaning, "tent," "family (of God)," or "(God is) shelter." Descendant of David (1 Chron. 3:20).

OHOLAH (Ō hō' lah) Personal name meaning, "tent dweller." A woman's name Ezekiel used to portray Samaria (Ezek. 23:1–10). Oholah and her sister, Oholibah (Jerusalem), are shown as whores who consorted with various men (other nations). The obvious meaning is their spiritual adultery against God. God declared through the prophet that Samaria eventually would be delivered into the hands of her "lover," Assyria (23:9).

OHOLIAB (Ō hō' lĭ ab) Personal name meaning, "father's tent." Danite craftsman, designer, and embroiderer who assisted Bezalel in supervision of the construction of the tabernacle and its equipment (Ex. 31:6; 35:34; 36:1–2; especially 38:23).

OHOLIBAH (Ō hōl' ĭ bah) Personal name meaning, "tent worshiper." Younger sister in the allegory of Ezekiel 23 identified with Jerusalem (23:4,11–49). The sexual misconduct of these sisters represents Israel's and Judah's embrace of idolatry. See *Ohalah.*

OHOLIBAMAH (Ō' hōl ĭ bā' mah) Personal name meaning, "tent of the high place" or "tent dweller of the false cult."
1. The Hivite daughter of Anah and wife of Esau (Gen. 36:2). *2.* Edomite leader descended from Esau (Gen. 36:41).

OIL An indispensable commodity in the Ancient Near East for food, medicine, fuel, and ritual. Oil was considered a blessing given by God (Deut. 11:14), and the olive tree was a characteristic of the land which God gave to Israel (Deut. 8:8).

Preparation In biblical times, domestic oil was prepared from olives. Sometimes oil was combined with perfumes and used as a cosmetic (Esth. 2:12). The extraction of oil from olives is abundantly confirmed by archaeological findings of stone presses found at several sites in Palestine. See *Agriculture.* This oil, called "beaten oil," was lighter and considered the best oil. After the beaten oil was extracted, another grade of oil was produced by heating the pulp and pressing it again.

Domestic oil was stored in small cruses, pots, or jars (1 Kings 17:12; 2 Kings 4:2); oil used in religious ceremonies was also kept in horns (1 Sam. 16:13).

Use Oil was used in a variety of ways in biblical times; but, most often, oil was used in the preparation of food, taking the place of animal fat. Oil was used with meal in the preparation of cakes (Num. 11:8; 1 Kings 17:12–16) and with honey (Ezek. 16:13), flour (Lev. 2:1,4), and wine (Rev. 6:6).

Oil was used as fuel for lamps, both in homes (Matt. 25:3) and in the tabernacle (Ex. 25:6).

Oil was extensively used in religious ceremonies. The morning and evening sacrifices required, in addition to the lambs, a tenth of a measure of fine flour and a fourth of a hin of beaten oil. Other cereal offerings also required oil. Oil was used during the offering of purification from leprosy. In the New Testament, oil was used to anoint a body in preparation for burial (Matt. 26:12; Mark 14:8). Several persons in the Old Testament were anointed with oil: kings (1 Sam.

Ancient oil lamp decorated with two human figures.

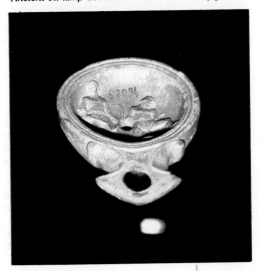

10:1; 16:13), priests (Lev. 8:30), and possibly prophets (1 Kings. 19:16; Isa. 61:1). Some objects were also anointed in dedication to God: the tabernacle and all its furniture (Ex. 40:9–11), the shields of soldiers (2 Sam. 1:21; Isa. 21:5), altars (Lev. 8:10–11), and pillars (Gen. 35:14).

As medicine, oil or ointment was used in the treatment of wounds (Isa. 1:6; Luke 10:34). James 5:14 may refer either to a symbolic use of oil or to its medicinal use.

Oil was used cosmetically as protection against the scorching sun or the dryness of the desert (Ruth 3:3; Eccl. 9:8). Since olives were found in abundance in Palestine, olive oil was also used as a commodity of trade (1 Kings 5:11; Ezek. 27:17; Hos. 12:1). See *Cosmetics; Commerce.*

Oil was regarded as a symbol of honor (Judg. 9:9), while virtue was compared to perfumed oil (Song of Sol. 1:3; Eccl. 7:1). The abundance of oil was a demonstration of blessing and prosperity (Job 29:6; Joel 2:24). However, as a symbol of affluence, oil was also associated with the arrogance of the rich (Hebrew: "valley of oil"; KJV: "fat valley," Isa. 28:1,4). Oil was a symbol of joy and gladness (Ps. 45:7), and in time of sorrow, anointing with oil was not practiced (2 Sam. 14:2). See *Anoint.*　　　*Claude F. Mariottini*

OIL TREE KJV translation of the Hebrew phrase "tree of oil" (Isa. 41:19). Other translation include olive (NAS, NIV, NRSV, TEV), oleaster (NAS margin), and wild olive (REB). The same Hebrew phrase is rendered "olivewood" at 1 Kings 6:23,31–33 and "wild olive" at Nehemiah 8:15. The latter text distinguishes the "oil tree" from the olive. Some interpreters suggest pine or cypress as the material of the carved cherubim in 1 Kings.

OINTMENT Perfumed unguents or salves of various kinds used as cosmetics, medicine, and in religious ceremonies. The use of ointments and perfumes appears to have been a common practice in the Ancient Near East, including the Hebrews.

Terminology The Old Testament uses various words to describe ointment. The most common, *shemen,* simply means oil (Gen. 28:28; Hos. 2:8). The Old Testament does not distinguish between oil and ointment. In the New Testament, *muron,* "ointment" (Matt. 26:7; Mark 14:3–4; Luke 7:37–38) was a perfumed ointment.

Manufacture The base for ointment was olive oil. Olives were very common in Palestine; however, perfumed salves were very expensive. A great demand arose for ointments as people attempted to protect themselves against the hot wind from the desert and the arid condition of the land.

The preparation of ointments was the job of skilled persons trained in the art of producing perfume. Bezaleel and Aholiab were appointed by God to prepare the sacred ointment and the incense used in worship (Ex. 31:1–11). While the blending of perfumes and ointment for secular use was probably done by women (1 Sam. 8:13), priestly families were responsible for the production of the large amount of ointments necessary for Temple use (1 Chron. 9:30). In the postexilic period a group of professional people in Jerusalem were skilled in the manufacture of perfumed ointments (Neh. 3:8). These people were called "apothecary" (KJV) or "perfumers" (RSV, NIV; Ex. 30:25,35; 37:29; Eccl. 10:1). Their function was to take the many gums, resins, roots, and barks and combine them with oil to make the various anointments used for anointing purposes. In many cases, the formula for these ointments and perfumes was a professional secret, handed down from generation to generation. Egyptian and Ugaritic sources have shown that water mixed with oil was heated in large pots (see Job 41:31). While the water was boiling, the spices were added. After the ingredients were blended, they were transferred to suitable containers. See *Containers and Vessels.* To preserve the special scents of the ointment, alabaster jars with long necks were sealed at the time the ointment was prepared and then broken just before use (Mark 14:3). Dry perfumes were kept in bags (Song of Sol. 1:13) and in perfume boxes (Isa. 3:20 NRSV; NIV: "perfume bottles"; KJV: "tablets").

Ingredients Various spices were used in the manufacturing of ointments and perfumes: aloes (Ps. 45:8; John 19:39); balsam (Ex. 30:23; 2 Chron. 9:1); galbanum (Ex. 30:34), myrrh, or more literally mastic or ladanum (Gen. 37:25; 43:11); myrrh (Esth. 2:12; Matt. 2:11), nard (Song of. Sol. 4:13–14; Mark 14:3; KJV: "spikenard"), frankincense (KJV: "incense"; Isa. 60:6; Matt. 2:11); balsam or balm (Gen. 37:25; Jer. 8:22); cassia (Ex. 30:24; Ezek. 27:19), calamus (Ex. 30:23; Song of Sol. 4:14; NRSV: "aromatic cane"), cinnamon (Ex. 30:23; Rev. 18:13), stacte (Ex. 30:34), and onycha (Ex. 30:34). Onycha, an ingredient derived from mollusks found in the Red Sea, was used in the mixture to be burned on the altar of incense. These spices were used as fragrant incense in worship. They were also mixed with oil to produce the holy anointing oil and to produce cosmetics and medicine.

Value Most of these spices were imported by the people who lived in Palestine. The great variety of spices used in the manufacture of ointments gave rise to merchants who traded in expensive spices and perfumes (Gen. 37:28; Ezek. 27:17–22). In biblical times, Arabia was one of the principal traders in aromatic spices. Spices were also imported from Africa, India, and Persia. Perfumed ointments were highly prized. Solomon received an annual payment of perfume as tribute from his subjects (1 Kings 10:25); the queen of Sheba brought many costly spices as gifts to Solomon (1 Kings 10:2); Hezekiah, king of Judah, included

valuable perfumed ointment and spices as part of his treasure (2 Kings 20:13; Isa. 39:2). When Mary anointed Jesus with a pound of costly ointment, Judas Iscariot rebuked Jesus because the ointment was worth the equivalent of one year's salary (John 12:3–8).

Use Many personal things were perfumed with spiced ointment. The breath was perfumed (Song of Sol. 7:8), probably with spiced wine (Song of Sol. 8:2). The garments of the king were perfumed with myrrh, aloes , and cassia (Ps. 45:8), or myrrh, frankincense, and "with all powders of the merchant" (Song of Sol. 3:6). The bed of the prostitute was perfumed with myrrh, aloes, and cinnamon (Prov. 7:17).

One of the most important uses of ointment in the Old Testament was in religious ceremonies. The manufacture of the anointing oil consisted of mixing olive oil with myrrh, sweet cinnamon, calamus, and cassia (Ex. 30:22–25). This ointment was considered to be holy; anyone who manufactured the sacred oil for use outside the worship place was to be cut off from the people (Ex. 30:33). See *Oil; Anoint.* Many individuals were anointed with the sacred ointment. The anointing of a person was viewed as an act of designation of that person to the service of God.

The shield of a soldier was anointed with oil (2 Sam. 1:21) as a symbol of dedication to God. Jacob anointed the pillar at Bethel, and the site where God appeared to him became a holy place (Gen. 28:18; 35:14).

Ointments were used in burial rites. See *Burial.*

Many people in the Ancient Near East believed strongly in the curative power of oil. See *Diseases; Oil.* For this reason they used ointments as medicine in the treatment of some diseases (Jer. 8:22; Mark 6:13; Jas. 5:14) and as unguents for wounds (Isa. 1:6; Luke 10:34). The law of Moses commanded the person healed of leprosy to be anointed with oil (Lev. 14:15–18,26–29).

Ointments were used as cosmetics for protection of the skin. Perfumes were used to counteract bodily odor. The whole body was usually anointed with perfume after bathing (Ruth 3:3; 2 Sam 12:20; Ezek. 16:9). Perfumes were used inside the clothes (Song of Sol. 1:13) and by women who desired to be attractive to men (Esth. 2:12).

Claude F. Mariottini

OLD GATE KJV, NAS, NRSV designation for a Jerusalem city gate repaired in Nehemiah's time (Neh. 3:6; 12:39). This rendering is doubtful on grammatical grounds (the adjective and noun do not agree). Some interpreters thus propose gate of the old (city). Others take the Hebrew *Jeshanah* as a proper name (NIV, REB, TEV). A village named Jeshanah is located near Bethel. The gate may have pointed in this direction. Still others emend the text to read "Misneh Gate" (JB). In this case the gate led from the Old City West into the New

Quarter (Mishneh). The gate is perhaps identical to the corner gate (2 Kings 14:13).

OLD TESTAMENT The first part of the Christian Bible, taken over from Israel. It tells the history of the nation Israel and God's dealings with them to the return from Exile in Babylon. For Jews it is the complete Bible, sometimes called Tanak for its three parts (Torah or Law, Nebiim or Prophets, Kethubim or Writings). Christians see its complement in the New Testament, which reveals Jesus Christ as the fulfillment of Old Testament prophecy. The Old Testament has three major divisions: Law, Prophets (Former and Latter), and Writings. The Law (Genesis—Deuteronomy) begins with the creation of the world and concludes as Israel is about to enter the Promised Land. The Prophets—Joshua, Judges, Samuel, Kings, Isaiah, Jeremiah Ezekiel, and the Twelve Minor Prophets—continue with the nation in the land of Palestine until the Exile and includes prophetic messages delivered to the nation. The Writings (all other books) contain the account of the return from Exile, collected wisdom literature from throughout the nation's history, and selected stories about God's leading in individual lives. See *Bible, Formation and Canon.*

OLD TESTAMENT QUOTATIONS IN THE NEW TESTAMENT The influence of the Old Testament is seen throughout the New Testament. The New Testament writers included approximately 250 express Old Testament quotations, and if one includes indirect or partial quotations, the number jumps to more than 1,000. It is clear that the writers of the New Testament were concerned with demonstrating the continuity between the Old Testament Scriptures and the faith they proclaimed. They were convinced that in Jesus the Old Testament promises had been fulfilled.

Types of Quotations 1. *Formula quotations* are introduced by a typical introductory quotations formula which generally employ verbs of "saying" or "writing." The most common introductory formulas are: "as the scripture hath said" (John 7:38); "What saith the Scripture" (Gal. 4:30); "it is (stands) written," emphasizing the permanent validity of the Old Testament revelation (Mark 1:2; Rom. 1:17; 3:10); "that it might be fulfilled," emphasizing the fulfillment of Old Testament prophecies (Matt. 4:14, 12:17, 21:4); "God hath said," "He saith," "the Holy Spirit says," which personify Scripture and reflect its divine dimension (Rom. 9:25; 10:21; 2 Cor. 6:16); "Moses," "David," or "Isaiah" says which emphasize the human element in Scripture (Rom. 10:16, 19,20; Heb. 4:7).

2. *Composite quotations* combine two or more Old Testament texts drawn from one or more of the sections of the Hebrew Old Testament canon (The Law, Prophets, and Writings). For example,

Romans 11:8–10 quotes from the Law (Deut. 29:4), the Prophets (Isa. 29:10) and the writings (Ps. 69:22–23). In some cases, a series of Old Testament texts may be used in a commentary-like fashion as in John 12:38–40 and Romans 9—11. Composite quotes are often organized around thematic emphases or catchwords in keeping with a practice common to Judaism and based on the notion set forth in Deuteronomy 19:15 that two or three witnesses establish the matter. The "stumbling stone" motif reflected in Romans 9:33 (Isa. 8:14; 28:16) and 1 Peter 2:6–9 (Isa. 8:14; 28:16; Ps. 118:22) is a good example of this method.

3. *Unacknowledged quotations* are often woven into the fabric of the New Testament text without acknowledgment or introduction. For example, Paul quoted Genesis 15:6 in his discussion of Abraham (Gal. 3:6) and Genesis 12:3 (Gal. 3:8) with no acknowledgment or introductory formula.

4. *Indirect quotations or allusions* form the most difficult type of Old Testament quotation to identify. The gradation from quotation to allusion may be almost imperceptible. An allusion may be little more than a clause, phrase, or even a word drawn from an Old Testament text which might easily escape the notice of the reader. For example, the reader might easily miss the fact that the words spoken from the cloud at the transfiguration of Jesus as recorded in Matthew 17:5 combine three separate Old Testament texts: "Thou art my Son" (Ps. 2:7), "in whom my soul delighteth" (Isa. 42:1), and "unto him ye shall hearken" (Deut. 18:15).

Sources of Old Testament Quotations Since the New Testament was written in Greek for predominantly Greek readers, it is not surprising that a large majority of Old Testament quotes in the New Testament are drawn from the Greek translation of the Old Testament known as the Septuagint (LXX). Of Paul's 93 quotes, 51 are in absolute or virtual agreement with the LXX, while only 4 agree with the Hebrew text. This means that 38 diverge from all known Greek or Hebrew Old Testament texts. Of Matthew's 43 quotes, 11 agree with the LXX, while the other 32 differ from all known sources. How then are these quotes to be explained? The New Testament writers may have used a version of the Old Testament which is unknown to us, or they may have been quoting from memory. It is also possible that the New Testament writers were more concerned with meaning and interpretation. It has also been suggested that the Old Testament quotations may have been drawn from "testimony books," collections of selected, combined, and interpreted Old Testament texts gathered by the early Christian community for proclamation and apologetics. The frequent use of certain Old Testament texts, such as Psalm 110, Isaiah 43, and so forth, in the preaching and writing of the early church and the

PALESTINE
IN THE TIME
OF THE
OLD TESTAMENT

Zarephath

Litani River

Ijon

Tyre
Kanah
Abel-beth-maacha
Dan
Mt. Hermon
Beth-anath
Damascus

Achziv
Abdon
Yiron
Kedesh
Merom
Hazor

Janoah
Beth-emek
Ramah

Acco
Cabul
Hukok
Chinnereth
Karnaim
Naveh

Kishon River
Aphek
Hannathon
Rimmon
Sea of Chinnereth
Karnaim

Libnath
Achshaph
Adamah
Golan
Ashtaroth
Mt. Carmel
Beth-lehem
Beth-shemesh

Geba
Shimron
Aznoth-tabor
Edrei

Joslneam
Shunem
Anaharath
En-dor
Kamon

Dor
Megiddo
Jarmuth
Jezreel
Lo-debar
Beth-arbel
Tob

Iron
Taanach
Beth-shean
Ham
Ramoth-gilead
Bezer

Hepher
Gath
Dothan
Mt. Gilboa
Pehel

Bezek
Abel-meholah
Jabesh-gilead

Socoh
Geba
Zaphon

Shiphthan
Samaria
Tirzah
Mahanaim

Shechem
Succoth
Jabbok River
Penuel

Arumah
Janoah
Zarethan

Gath-rimmon
Yarkon River
Aphek
Tappuah
Lebonah
Adam
Jogbehah

Joppa
Yehud
Zeredah
Shiloh
Geba
Betonim

Beth-dagon
Ono
Ophrah
Jazer
Rabbah

Nebellat
Beth-horon
Bethel
Ai
Gilgal
Beth-nimrah
Abel-keramim

Jabneel
Gittaim
Gezer
Ramah
Jericho
Heshbon

Eltekeh
Gibeon
Geba
Beth-jeshimoth

Gibbethon
Shaalbim
Aijalon
Gibeah
Beth-hogla

Timnah
Zorah
Kiriath-jearim
Jerusalem

Ashdod
Ekron
Chesalon
Medeba
Baal-maon

Gath
Beth-shemesh
Bethlehem

Ashkelon
Azekah
Socoh
Etam
Tekoa

Libnah
Keilah
Gedor
Zereth-shahar
Jahzah

Gaza
Mareshah
Lachish
Beth-zur
Dibon

Eglon
Beth-tappuah
Hebron
Aroer

Yurza
En-gedi
Dead Sea
Arnon River

Ziklag
Debir
Carmel

Sharuhen
Yattir
Maon
Eshtemoa
Kir-moab

Moladah
Arad

Beersheba
Kabzeel
Aroer

Zoar
Zered River

Tamar
Zalmonah
Sela
Bozrah

Punon

Rekek

Mediterranean Sea

Jordan River
Yarmuk River

feet | m
8202 | 2500
6561 | 2000
4921 | 1500
3280 | 1000
1640 | 500
820 | 250
0 | 0
Below sea level

0 10 20 30 40 miles
0 20 40 60 km

*Column from Isaiah scroll
from Dead Sea Caves*

© carta

discovery of such collections at Qumran seem to support such a possibility.

The Uses of Old Testament Quotations The New Testament writers used Old Testament quotations for at least four reasons: (1) to demonstrate that Jesus is the *fulfillment* of God's purposes and of the prophetic witness of the Old Testament Scriptures (Rom. 1:2; Matt. 4:14; 12:17–21; 21:4–5); (2) as a source for *ethical instruction* and *edification* of the church (Rom. 13:8–10; 2 Cor. 13:1); (3) to interpret contemporary events (Rom. 9—11; 15:8–12); (4) to prove a point on the assumption that the Scripture is God's Word (1 Cor. 10:26; 14:21; 15:55). The approaches employed in the use of the Old Testament are reflective of first century Judaism as represented in the Dead Sea Scrolls, Philo of Alexandra, and later rabbinic Judaism. Some Old Testament quotations are used in their *literal historical sense* and, therefore, have the same meaning in the New Testament as they had in the Old Testament. The quotation of Psalm 78:24 in John 6:31 is a good example of such usage. Some quotations reflect a typical approach to interpreting the Old Testament in first-century Judaism known as *midrash*. *Midrash* is an exposition of a text which aims at bringing out its contemporary relevance. The Old Testament text is quoted and explained so as to make it apply to or be meaningful for the current situation. The use of Genesis 15:6 in Romans 4:3–25 and the use of Psalm 78:24 in John 6:31–58 reflect such an approach.

Some Old Testament texts are interpreted *typologically*. In this approach, the New Testament writer sees a correspondence between persons, events, or things in the Old Testament and persons, events, or things in their contemporary setting. The correspondence with the past is not found in the written text, but within the historical event. Underlying typology is the conviction that certain events in the past history of Israel as recorded in earlier Scriptures revealed God's ways and purposes with persons in a typical way. Matthew's use of Hosea 11:1 (2:15) suggests that the Gospel writer saw a correspondence between Jesus' journey into Egypt and the Egyptian sojourn of the people of Israel. Jesus recapitulated or reexperienced the sacred history of Israel. The redemptive purposes of God demonstrated in the Exodus (reflected by the prophet Hosea) were being demonstrated in Jesus' life. In some cases, the understanding and application of the Old Testament quotation is dependent on an awareness of the quotation's wider context in the Old Testament. The use of the quotation is intended to call the reader's attention to the wider Old Testament context or theme and might be referred to as a "*pointer quotation*." In first-century Judaism where large portions of Scripture were known by heart, it was customary to quote only the beginning of a passage even if its continuation was to be kept in mind. A good example of this use may be seen in Romans 1—3. Paul had discussed both the faithfulness of God and the sinfulness of humanity. In Romans 3:4 Paul quoted Psalm 51:4 to support his first point. He continued his argument with a further reference to human wickedness which is, in fact, the subject of Psalm 51:5; but he did not feel the need to quote the verse, since it was already suggested to those familiar with the biblical text. Finally, there is a limited *allegorical* use of the Old Testament text in which the text is seen as a kind of code having two meanings—the literal, superficial level of meaning, and a deeper, underlying meaning such as in Galatians 4:22–31.

Despite similarities with contemporary Jewish use(s) of the Old Testament, the New Testament writers interpreted the Old Testament in a radically new way. New Testament writers did not deliberately use a different exegetical method. They wrote from a different theological perspective. The writers of the New Testament were convinced that the true meaning of the Old Testament is Jesus Christ and that He alone provides the means of understanding it. True interpretation of the Old Testament is achieved by reading Old Testament passages or incidents in light of the event of Christ. While many of the Old Testament texts quoted in the New Testament had already been accepted as messianic (for example, Ps. 110:1) or could in light of Jesus' actual life claim to be messianic (Ps. 22; Isa. 53), for the early Christians, all Scripture was to be interpreted by the fact of Christ because it is to Him that the Old Testament Scripture points (John 5:39). In summary, the New Testament writer quoted or alluded to the Old Testament in order to demonstrate how God's purposes have been fulfilled and are being fulfilled in Jesus.　　　　*Hulitt Gloer*

OLIVES See *Agriculture.*

Olive trees provide fruit for the valuable olive oil of the Middle East.

OLIVES, MOUNT OF The two and a half mile-long mountain ridge that towers over the eastern side of Jerusalem, or more precisely, the middle of the three peaks forming the ridge. Heavily cov-

An ancient olive press.

ered with olive trees, the ridge juts out in a north-south direction (like a spur) from the range of mountains running down the center of the region. Both the central Mount of Olives and Mount Scopus, the peak on its northern side, rise over two hundred feet above the Temple mount across the Kidron Valley. It provided a lookout base and signaling point for armies defending Jerusalem.

David crossed the Mount of Olives when fleeing Absalom (2 Sam. 15:30). Ezekiel saw the cherubim chariot land there (Ezek. 11:23). Zechariah described how the Mount of Olives would move to form a huge valley on the Day of the Lord (Zech. 14:3–5). Many crucial events in Jesus' life

View of the Kidron Valley to the northeast toward the Mount of Olives.

occurred on the Mount of Olives. (See, for example, Matt. 26:30; Mark 11:1–2; Luke 4:5; 22:39–46; Acts 1:9–12).   *Robert O. Byrd*

OLIVET DISCOURSE, THE (Ŏl′ ĭ vĕt) Jesus' major sermon preached on the Mount of Olives; Jesus gave instructions concerning the end of the age and the destruction of Jerusalem. The discourse (Matthew 24—25; Mark 13) is in part an apocalypse because it uses symbolic, visionary language that makes it a difficult passage to understand. Parts of it appear scattered throughout Luke 12—21.

Meaning of the Signs (Matt. 24:4–8) The opening remarks warn against misplaced belief in deceptive signs which do not in any way signal the end of the world. These signs occurred in Jesus' day and preceded the destruction of Jerusalem, the event uppermost in Jesus' mind and for which He sought to prepare His disciples. They are still operative after two thousand years, a further indication that they do not herald the end time.

A Time of Persecution (Matt. 24:9–14) These verses suggest a time of severe distress. Many would say that the reference is to a period of ultimate suffering that is to take place just before the parousia (Christ's return or second coming; see 7:14). Jesus' assertion that the gospel must be preached worldwide seems to strengthen this view. "He that shall endure unto the end" (Matt. 24:13) could refer to the period immediately prior to the parousia. It could also pertain to the end of some other event such as the destruction of Jerusalem. Oppression of Christians and family betrayal were common. That Christians were despised and subjected to great suffering is an accurate description of the situation in Judea before the Jewish War, A.D. 66–70, when Titus destroyed the city.

The Abomination that Makes Desolate (Matt. 24:15–22) Extrabiblical histories describe the desecration of the Jerusalem Temple in 167 B.C. by Antiochus Epiphanes, who built an altar there to Zeus. That event is usually seen as having fulfilled Daniel's prophecy (Dan. 11:31). However, Jesus applied the prophecy to a future overthrow of Jerusalem by Titus' armies. The horror of this siege was unprecedented. Temple and city were utterly demolished. See *Intertestamental History*.

The Second Coming of Christ (Matt. 24:26—25:46) Jesus spoke in veiled language about His coming. Unnatural occurrences in the heavens were commonly used in apocalyptic writings to describe the indescribable, but also to deliberately screen from view those things meant to remain hidden. Much of God's plans are mystery, but Jesus disclosed enough. The coming of the Son of Man will be entirely public and completely unexpected. He will come in the clouds with great power (Acts 1:9–11). The sign of His parousia is obscure in its meaning. The sermon is interrupted by the statement, "This generation shall not pass,

The western slope of the Mount of Olives on which Jesus gave His Olivet discourse.

till all these things be fulfilled" (Matt 24:34). Jesus was not confused or in error concerning these events. He referred to the destruction of Jerusalem which took place in that generation as a foretaste of the final coming. Concluding parables teach the necessity of remaining watchful. A description of final judgment ends the discourse. Its basic message is a call to be prepared when Jesus does return.   *Diane Cross*

OLYMPAS (Ō′ lўm′ pás) Perhaps a shortened form of Olympiodorus (gift of Olympus). Christian whom Paul greeted in Romans 16:15. Olympas was apparently a member of a house church including the others mentioned in 16:15.

OMAR (Ō′ már) Personal name meaning, "talkative." Son of Eliphaz and ancestor of an Edomite clan of the same name (Gen. 36:11,15; 1 Chron. 1:36).

OMEGA (Ō mē′ ḡá) Last letter in the Greek alphabet. Together with the first letter, alpha, omega designates God and Christ as the all-encompassing Reality (Rev. 1:8; 21:6; 22:13). See *Alpha.*

OMEN *1.* Sign used by diviners to predict the future. The Israelites were prohibited from interpreting omens (Deut. 18:10 NAS, NIV). Pagan prophecy employed reading of omens (Num. 24:1 NAS, RSV; Ezek. 21:21 NIV). As Lord of history, God frustrates the plans of "liars" who interpret omens (Isa. 44:25 NAS, RSV). See *Divination and Magic. 2.* Sign indicating a future event. Ahab's reference to Ben-hadad as "my brother" was understood as an omen or sign of Ahab's favor (1 Kings 20:33 NAS, NRSV). Companions of the high priest Joshua were a good omen (NRSV) or a symbol (NAS) of hope for a restored people of God (Zech. 3:8). The faithful witness of Christians in the face of opposition is likewise an omen or sign pointed to the salvation of believers and the destruction of God's enemies (Phil. 1:28).

OMER (Ō′ mēr) *1.* Unit of dry measure equal to one tenth of an ephah or a little more than two quarts (Ex. 16:13–36). See *Weights and Measurements. 2.* First sheaf (omer) of the barley harvest which was elevated as an offering (Lev. 23:9–15). See *Sacrifice and Offerings.*

OMNIPOTENCE (Ŏm nǐ′ pō tĕnce) The state of being all-powerful which theology ascribes to God. Scripture often affirms that all power belongs to God (Ps. 147:5), that all things are possible for God (Luke 1:37; 19:26), and that God's power exceeds what humans can ask or think (Eph. 3:20). For Scripture, God's omnipotence is not a matter of abstract speculation but a force to be reckoned with. God's power is revealed in God's creating and sustaining the universe (Ps. 65:6; Jer. 32:17; Heb. 1:3), in God's deliverance of Israel from Pharaoh's forces (Ex. 15:1–18), in the conquest of Canaan (Deut. 3:21–24), in the incarnation (Luke 1:35), in Christ's death on the cross (1 Cor. 1:17–18, 23–24), and in the ongoing ministry of the church (1 Cor. 2:5; Eph. 3:20).

OMNIPRESENCE See *God.*

OMNISCIENCE (Ŏm nǐ′ science) The state of being all-knowing which theology ascribes to God. Though Scripture affirms God's immeasurable understanding (Ps. 147:5), God's omniscience is not a matter of abstract speculation. Rather, God's knowing is a matter of personal experience. God knows us intimately (Ps. 139:1–6; Matt. 6:4,6,8). Such knowledge is cause for alarm for the unrighteous but for confidence for God's saints (Job 23:10; Pss. 34:15–16; 90:8; Prov. 15:3; 1 Pet. 3:12). See *God.*

OMRI (Ŏm′ rī) Personal name meaning, "pilgrim" or "life." *1.* King of Israel 885–874 B.C. and founder of the Omride dynasty, which ruled until 842. Omri came to the throne in a very odd manner. Zimri, a chariot captain in Israel's army, assassinated King Elah and took control of the palace of Tirzah (1 Kings 16:8–15). Half of the people rebelled and installed Omri ("captain of the host," v. 16) as king. When Zimri realized his situation was hopeless, he burned the palace down upon himself. Omri became king only after successfully opposing another rebellion in the person of Tibni (vv. 21–22). In his reign of eleven years, Omri's greatest accomplishment was to buy the hill of Samaria and build the capital of Israel there. He was succeeded by his son, Ahab. Assyrian sources continued to call Israel, "the land of Omri." Micah accused Jerusalem of following Omri's actions and also his son Ahab's. That was grounds for God's destroying Jerusalem (Mic. 6:16). *2.* Officer of tribe of Issachar under David (1 Chron. 27:18). *3.* Grandson of Benjamin (1 Chron. 7:8). *4.* Grandfather of member of tribe of Judah who returned to Jerusalem from Exile about 537 B.C.

ON (Ŏn) 1. Egyptian place name meaning, "city of the pillar," called in Greek Heliopolis or "city of the sun" and in Hebrew as Beth-shemesh, "city of the sun" (Jer. 43:13) and Aven. It was the cult center for the worship of the sun-god, Ra (Atum). Although not important politically, the city became a vital religious center very early in Egypt's history. Located at Matariyeh about five miles northeast of modern Cairo, the city endured as a cult center ultil very late. Joseph's Egyptian wife came from On (Gen. 41:45), her father serving as priest in the temple there. Speaking in Egypt, Jeremiah warned that God would destory On and its worship (Jer. 43:13). Ezekiel or the scribes copying his work substituted Aven, Hebrew for "trouble, deceit," for On in pronouncing judgment on it (Ezek. 30:17). 2. Personal name meaning, "powerful, rich." Member of tribe of Reuben who was one of leaders challenging authority of Moses (Num. 16:1).

ONAM (Ō' năm) Personal name meaning, "vigorous." 1. Ancestor of an Edomite subclan (Gen. 36:23; 1 Chron. 1:40). 2. Ancestor of a family of Jerahmeelites, a subclan of Judah (1 Chron. 2:26,28).

ONAN (Ō' năn) Personal name meaning, "power." A son of Judah and his Canaanite wife, Shuah (Gen. 38:2–8). Following the death of his older brother, Er, Onan was to have married the widow and produced a son who would carry on Er's name. Onan repeatedly failed to complete the responsibilities of the marriage and thus God killed him (38:8–10). (See *Levirate Law; Marriage*).

ONESIMUS (Ō nĕs' ĭ mŭs) Personal name that may mean, "profitable." The slave for whom Paul wrote his letter to Philemon. In the epistle, Paul pled with Philemon to free the servant because Onesimus had been so helpful to the apostle. Onesimus had robbed his master, escaped, met Paul, and accepted Christ. In sending him back to Philemon, Paul urged the owner to treat the slave as a Christian brother (v. 16).

Later, Onesimus accompanied Thychius in bearing Paul's letter to the church at Colossae (Col. 4:7–9). Two traditions connect Onesimus with a bishop of that name in the second-century church, and with Onesiphorus in 2 Timothy 1:16. Neither connection has been proven satisfactorily. See *Philemon*.

ONESIPHORUS (Ō nĕ sīph' ō rŭs) Personal name meaning, "profit bearing." Ephesian Christian praised for his effort to seek out the place of Paul's arrest, his disregard of the shame connected with befriending one in chains, and his past service in Ephesus (2 Tim. 1:16–18). The greeting of and prayer for the household of Onesiphorus (2 Tim. 1:16; 4:19) has suggested to some that Onesiphorus was already dead. All that can be assumed is that Onesiphorus was not at Ephesus.

ONION See *Plants in the Bible*.

ONLY BEGOTTEN KJV alternate rendering of the Greek *monogenes* (John 1:14,18; 3:16,18; Heb. 11:17; 1 John 4:9). Elsewhere the KJV rendered the term "only" (Luke 7:12; 8:42; 9:38). The phrase "only begotten" derives directly from Jerome (340?–420 A.D.) who replaced *unicus* (only), the reading of the Old Latin, with *unigenitus* (only begotten) as he translated the Latin Vulgate. Jerome's concern was to refute the Arian doctrine that claimed the Son was not begotten but made. This led Jerome to impose the terminology of the Nicene creed (325 A.D.) onto the New Testament.

Monogenes is used for an only child (Luke 7:12; 8:42; 9:38). The writer of Hebrews used *monogenes* of Isaac with full knowledge that Isaac was not Abraham's only child (Heb. 11:17–18). Here *monogenes* designates Isaac as the special child of promise through whom Abraham's descendants would be named.

KJV, NAS render *monogenes* as "only begotten" when referring to Jesus. NIV renders the term "One and Only" (Compare the NAS margin, "unique, only one of His kind.") Other translations (REB, NRSV, TEV) render *monogenes* consistently as "only." John used *monogenes* to designate the unique relationship which Jesus shares with God. John is careful to reserve the term *Son* for Jesus; believers are children (John 1:12; 1 John 3:1–2; 5:2). As unique Son of God, Jesus makes God's glory known in a unique way (John 1:14,18). As the One and Only Son, Jesus is the unique gift of God, the giving of God's own self for salvation (John 3:16; 1 John 4:9). Because Jesus is the unique representative of God, rejection of Jesus is tantamount to rejection of God. Such rejection results in swift condemnation (John 3:18). *Chris Church*

ONO (Ō' nō) Name meaning, "grief." Benjaminite town about seven miles southeast of Joppa. The town appears in a list of Pharoah Thutmose III (1490–1436 B.C.). The Mishnah regarded Ono as fortified since the time of Joshua. The city was rebuilt by Shemed, a descendant of Benjamin (2 Chron. 8:12). Ono was home to some of those who returned from Exile (Ezra 2:33; Neh. 7:37; 11:36). Ono is identified with Kefr' Ana in the wadi Musrara. This broad wadi is called the valley of craftsmen (Neh. 11:35) and the Plain of Ono (Neh. 6:2).

ONYCHA (Ŏn' ў cha) A spice probably derived from the closing flaps or the shell of a Red Sea mollusk which was used in the incense reserved for the worship of Yahweh (Ex. 30:34).

ONYX See *Minerals and Metals.*

OPHEL (Ō' phēl) Place name meaning, "swelling, fat, bulge," or "mound." It became the proper name of a portion of the hill on which the city of David was built (2 Chron. 27:3). The Ophel was just south of Mount Moriah, on which the Temple was constructed, joining the old city with the area of Solomon's palace and Temple. The hill has been inhabited since pre-Israelite times by peoples such as the Jebusites from whom David took the site. David and later kings further fortified Ophel. It served as the living quarters for those who rebuilt the ramparts following the Exile (Neh. 3:26–27). This may reflect a gradual extension of the name to an ever-larger area. Micah used the Hebrew term to name "the strong hold of the daughter of Zion" (4:8). Isaiah warned that the "forts" or "hill" (NAS) would be destroyed (32:14). The Hebrew term is used with an uncertain meaning in 2 Kings 5:24 for "tower," "hill," (NAS), "citadel" (NRSV). The term also occurs on the Moabite stone.

OPHIR (O' phīr) Place and personal name meaning, "dusty." Place famous in the Ancient Near East for its trade, especially in gold. Solomon's ships with help from Phoenician sailors brought precious goods from Ophir (1 Kings 9:28; 10:11; compare 1 Kings 22:48). Gold from Ophir was apparently highly valued, the phrase becoming a stock descriptive term in Ancient Near Eastern commercial language (Isa. 13:12; Job 22:24; 28:16; Ps. 45:10). Ophir is mentioned outside the Bible on a piece of broken pottery found at tell el-Qasileh, north of Tel Aviv on the plain of Sharon. See *Aphek.* This inscription reads, "Gold of Ophir for Beth Horon, 30 shekels."

The geographical location of Ophir is disputed among biblical scholars. Three regions have been suggested: India, Arabia, and Africa. Scholars who support an Indian location do so because of the resemblance of the Septuagint (the Greek translation of the Old Testament) form of Ophir to the Egyptian name for India. The available evidence with regard to trade practices indicates that Egyptian, Phoenician, and Greek fleets obtained eastern goods indirectly through ports in South Arabia and East Africa.

Other scholars have suggested that Ophir was located on the Arabian Peninsula. At least five areas have been identified, but the evidence for certainty with regard to any of them is lacking. The strongest argument for an Arabian location is the occurrence of the name Ophir among the names of Arabian tribes, descendants of Joktan, in the Table of Nations in Genesis 10.

Finally, one location in Africa has been suggested: the East African coast in the general vicinity of Somaliland. This location is supported because of its distance from Palestine and the products that are characteristic of Africa that are mentioned in biblical texts (1 Kings 9:28; 10:11,22).

The location of Ophir will remain a matter of uncertainty. A knowledge of ancient trade routes and practices, maritime ventures in the Ancient Near East, and economic policies in ancient Israel will be helpful in determining the cite of Ophir. See *Commerce; Economic Life.*   *James Newell*

OPHNI (Ŏph' nī) Name meaning, "high place." Town allotted to Benjamin (Josh. 18:24). Ophni was likely in the vicinity of Geba and is perhaps Jifna, three miles northwest of Bethel near the intersection of the Jerusalem-Shechem road and the road leading from the Plain of Sharon to Bethel.

OPHRAH (Ŏph' rah) Name meaning, "fawn." *1.* Descendant of Judah (1 Chron. 4:14); *2.* City in Benjamin (Josh. 18:23), likely north of Michmash (1 Sam. 13:17–18). This Ophrah is perhaps identical with Ephron (2 Chron. 13:19) and Ephraim (2 Sam. 13:23; John 11:54). Jerome located Ophrah five Roman miles east of Bethel. This site is likely et-Taiyibeh five miles north of Michmash and four miles northeast of Bethel. *3.* Town associated with the Abiezer clan of Manasseh who settled west of the Jordan (Judg. 6:11,15,24; 8:32). This Ophrah was the home of Gideon. Suggested sites include et-Taiyibeh south of modern Tulkarm, et-Taiyibeh (Afula) on the Plain of Esdraelon west of Mount Moreh, and Fer'ata west of Mount Gerazim near Shechem. The latter site is better identified with Tizrah.

ORACLES Communications from God. The term refers both to divine responses to a question asked of God and to pronouncements made by God without His being asked. In one sense, oracles were prophecies since they often referred to the future; but oracles sometimes dealt with decisions to be made in the present. Usually, in the Bible the communication was from Yahweh, the God of Israel. In times of idol worship, however, Israelites did seek a word or pronouncement from false gods (Hos. 4:12). Many of Israel's neighbors sought oracles from their gods.

Although the word *oracle* is not very frequent in the Old Testament, oracles were common in that period. This difference occurs because the Hebrew words translated "oracle" may also be translated as "burden," "saying," "word," etc. Translations are not consistent in how they render these Hebrew words. Both the NRSV and the NAS translate the same Hebrew word as "oracle" in Numbers 24:3, but it is rendered "declare" in

1 Samuel 2:30. Jeremiah 23:33–34 makes a play on a Hebrew word which may be translated either "burden" or "oracle." The NAS uses "oracle," but the NRSV and KJV use "burden." Moreover, in the KJV the English word *oracle* is used to refer to the holy of holies in the Temple.

Concordance study shows the following meaning and use of "oracle." Sometimes "oracle" refers to the whole of a prophetic book (Mal. 1:1 NRSV) or a major portion of one (Hab. 1:1 NRSV). In Isaiah, several smaller prophecies of judgment or punishment are called "oracles" (13:1 NRSV; 14:28 NRSV). The NRSV also entitles Zechariah 9 and 12 "An Oracle." Specific sayings about God's judgment on Joram (2 Kings 9:25 NRSV) and Joash (2 Chron. 24:27 NRSV) are also called oracles. Other examples, although the word *oracle* is not used, include Elijah's word to Ahab (1 Kings 21:17–19) and Elisha's word to Jehoram (2 Kings 3:13–20). On the basis of these kinds of usages, many Bible students understand oracles to be divine words of punishment or judgment. However, Balaam's oracle (Num. 24:3–9) is a blessing. Also references to Ahithophel's counsel (2 Sam. 16:23) and to oracles in Jerusalem which were pleasing but false (Lam. 2:14) show us that prophetic pronouncements were not always negative.

The New Testament does not reflect quite the same use of oracles or the word *oracle* as does the Old. The early church did have prophets like Agabus (Acts 21:10–11), who expressed God's word regarding what was to come. The word *oracles* in the New Testament most often refers to the teachings of God in the Old Testament (Acts 7:38; Rom 3:2). It may refer to Christian teachings, too (Heb 5:12).

Why Were Oracles Given? We must distinguish between oracles that were sought and those that came without any request. The first kind might be called "decision oracles." The second kind will be referred to as "pronouncement oracles." Decision oracles came when people asked God a question or sought His counsel. For example, David needed to know the right time to attack the Philistines. So he asked God. The answers he received were oracles (2 Sam. 5:19,23–24). Saul, the first king of Israel, was chosen through an oracle (1 Sam. 10:20–24). In that case, the communication from God was through the casting of lots. The falling of the lots was considered an oracle from God. Decision oracles, then, were God's response to questions and concerns in the present. They did not condemn sin or predict the future in any specific sense.

Pronouncement oracles were God's word to a situation or a person even though no word from God had been sought. (But, see comments below on Balaam's oracle.) The pronouncement oracles were sometimes brief as when Elijah foretold a drought in Israel (1 Kings 17:1). The message could be long; thus the whole Book of Malachi is a pronouncement oracle. This kind of oracle usually told what was going to happen. It also frequently condemned sin. It expressed God's view of present acts or circumstances. In that sense, many of the prophecies in the Old Testament were pronouncement oracles. Because they were God's word, these pronouncements were true, even though they could be changed as in the case of Jonah's pronouncement over Nineveh (Jonah 3:4–9).

Pronouncement oracles were given to produce an effect. People were to hear and to change their ways. With that in mind, the pronouncement oracles against foreign nations form a special group. Many of the writing prophets have pronouncements against (or concerning) nations surrounding Israel (Amos 1; Isa. 13—19; Jer. 46—51). These foreign nations had little chance to hear and heed the word of an Israelite prophet. Other nations had their own gods and their own prophets. Apparently, the pronouncements over foreign nations were intended to have an effect on the people of Israel as well as bring about the events described. At times, Israel or Judah heard their name included among foreign nations (for example, Amos 2:4–16). God cared for the other nations even though they cared little for Him. God's expression of concern by pronouncing judgment (or salvation as in Isa. 19:19–22) was intended to remind Israel of her mission to share God with others. At least, these words reminded the hearers of God's international, even universal, power and expectations.

Balaam's oracle (Num. 24) is a special case. Balak sought a pronouncement through the prophet Balaam. Balak's intention was to curse or to pronounce judgment on the Israelites. God did not allow this but gave Balaam an oracle of blessing to pronounce. Balaam's oracle, then, was positive and sought—a positive pronouncement oracle. The seeking of a pronouncement like this may have been more common than we know. Oracles came either in response to human questions or when God wished to make His views known to produce a change.

How Were Oracles Given or Received? Oracles were given through special people. Although anyone could seek a word from God and many, such as Gideon or Abraham, received an oracle directly; these divine communications usually came through either priests, prophets, or prophetesses. These two groups seemed to have their own specific ways of receiving oracles. In the earlier period, priests were more often sought out to receive a word from God. Later, the prophets were more prominent. Of course, for a long period both functioned as intermediaries. One caution about prophets and their pronouncements must be made. Often the prophets were not prophets until they received God's word (consider Amos' experience in Amos 7:14–15). The word came to some reluctantly as in the case of Jeremiah. God's giving of an oracle to a man or woman made them a prophet; for, when the divine word came, the prophet had to speak (Amos 3:8*b*).

Different methods were used by priests and prophets to receive the two forms of oracles, although we should not try to make too rigid a distinction. Decision oracles often came through the use of objects. Examples of such objects include the High Priest's Urim and Thummim and the ephod. Lots, too, were used. See *Urim and Thummim; Ephod; Lots.*

Decision oracles could also come through a person without the use of any objects. David sought the Lord's will at the point of building a temple. His answer came through Nathan, the prophet (2 Sam. 7). In 1 Kings 22, a dramatic conflict arose while the kings of Judah and Israel together sought a decision oracle. No objects were used in this case. The drama came from a true prophet receving one answer regarding the decision and a large number of false prophets giving a different answer. Prophets did sometimes use music as a means of receiving a decision oracle as did Elisha (2 Kings 3:15). However, the exact way music was used is unclear to us.

Frequently, the Old Testament gives no indication as to how God communicated His pronouncement oracles to His prophet or priest. Careful reading of the Old Testament shows a variety of methods in use. Audition—the actual hearing of a

voice—and visions undoubtedly played a part in the receiving of God's words. We cannot know how much of God's revelation came through the actual ear or eye or how much came through the mind. Balaam spoke when the Spirit came upon him (Num. 24:2). He described himself as one whose eye was opened, one who heard God's word and saw His vision. Nahum and Habakkuk wrote of a vision or of seeing their oracles (Nah. 1:1; Hab. 1:1). Through Jeremiah, God condemned those prophets who relied on dreams to receive an oracle (Jer. 23:23–32). However, Solomon earlier had received God's pronouncement in a dream (1 Kings 3:5*ff.*). Several times God used scenes which the prophet saw as a means of giving a pronouncement oracle. Some of the scenes were external (Jer. 18:1–12), and some were visionary (Ezek. 37:1–14). The frequent use of sights in pronouncements has led some to believe that the prophets had encounters with God that later they had to interpret and communicate to others.

Regardless of how the oracle came, it was to be expressed to others. This expression seems most often to have been oral. The priest or prophet told the oracle to either the individual or a group. The place may have been in a field or a king's throne room. The pronouncement oracles were often proclaimed in the city, even in a temple (Amos in Bethel and Jeremiah in Jerusalem). Many of the oracles, though, give us no indication of where or when they were spoken.

Oracles which were not simply yes or no seem

The massive structure at Cumae which was the sacred location of the famous pagan Sibylline Oracles.

most often to have been given in poetic form. This is especially true of the pronouncements of the writing prophets which have been preserved for us. Though given orally in the beginning, at some time the pronouncement oracles were written down. They may have been written by disciples of the prophet or by others who heard. They may have been written when they were first told or at a later time. Whatever the case, the oracles were given by God and preserved for us.

How Did People Respond to the Oracles? Again, a distinction should be made between the decision and the pronouncement oracles. Those who were seeking God's help or counsel in a decision-making process undoubtedly acted on what they learned. Others, who heard oracles they had neither sought nor welcomed, may not have been as quick to accept the pronouncement (consider Elijah's words to Ahab, 1 Kings 21:20–24). Most often the response of those who heard or read the oracles of God can be guessed at. Two points should be recognized. First, oracles were remembered long after their pronouncement. When Jehu killed Joram (2 Kings 9:25), he had the body taken to Naboth's vineyard in order that an oracle pronounced in Ahab's day might be fulfilled. Second, though we do not know the response of the original hearers, God's pronouncements are still being read and are producing change in people in our day. Thus, the oracles are still functioning. See *Inspiration; Priest; Prophet; Spirit.*   Albert Bean

ORATION, ORATOR An elaborate speech delivered in a formal and dignified manner and designed to persuade an audience. An orator is one distinguished for skill and persuasiveness as a public speaker. Only the RSV used the term oration and then only once (Acts 12:21); NRSV used "public address." Herod Agrippa's oration found praise for the rhetorical skill (12:22); Herod was judged for failure to give God the glory (12:23). A similar antipathy between skill in oratory and reliance on God's power is often found in Paul (1 Cor. 2:1–2,4,13; 4:19–20).

Paul, spoke of "the debater of this age" (1 Cor. 1:20 NRSV). Paul disclaimed "lofty words" and claimed to be "untrained in speech" (1 Cor. 2:1; 2 Cor. 11:6 NRSV) but elsewhere compared his preaching to a skilled builder laying a foundation (1 Cor. 3:10) and spoke of destroying arguments and obstacles to knowledge of God (2 Cor. 10:5). Acts often presents Paul as a persuasive speaker (Acts 18:4,13: 19:26; 26:28–29). Festus, in fact, recognized Paul as a man of great learning from his speech (Acts 26:24). Acts also portrays Apollos as an eloquent speaker (Acts 18:24).

The Greeks classified oratory into three modes. *1.* The judicial mode, the speech of the law court, concerns guilt and innocence. Examples of judicial rhetoric include the cases involving Paul which were brought before Gallio, Felix, and Fes-

tus (Acts 18:12–16; 24:1–21; 25:15,18–19; 26:1–29). *2.* The deliberative mode is concerned with the expediency of a course of future action. Examples include the Sanhedrin's debate over Jesus' growing following which culminated in Caiaphas' suggestion that the expedient course was to seek Jesus' death (John 11:47–50) and Demetrius' discourse on what action was necessary to save the business of the silversmiths in Ephesus (Acts 19:23–27). *3.* The epideictic mode concerns praise and blame. Examples include Paul's praise of love (1 Cor. 13) and his censure of the Galatians (Gal. 1:6–9; 3:1–5). Broadly speaking, this mode includes any exhortation to virtuous action (as in James). See *Rhetoric.*   Chris Church

ORCHARD A grove of fruit (Neh. 9:25; Eccl. 2:5) or nut trees (Song of Sol. 6:11). An enclosed orchard is sometimes called a garden (Eccl. 2:5; Song Sol. 4:13 RSV) or park (Eccl. 2:5; Song Sol. 4:13 NAS margin).

ORDINANCES Christians agree universally that baptism and the Lord's Supper were instituted by Christ and should be observed as "ordinances" or "sacraments" by His followers. Neither *ordinance* or *sacrament* is a biblical term. Some interpreters believe *sacrament* conveys the concept that God's grace is dispersed almost automatically through participation in the Lord's Supper. Others believe *ordinance* stresses obedience in doing that which Christ explicitly commanded. Extreme dangers involved in the terms range from superstition to legalism.

The "sacraments" varied in number for a thousand years in the church's early history. Peter Lombard (about A.D. 1150) defended seven, and Thomas Aquinas (about A.D. 1250) argued that all were instituted by Christ. After A.D. 1500, Martin Luther and other Protestant reformers rejected five of these, insisting that only baptism and the Lord's Supper have a biblical basis. Most Protestants agree with their assessment.

Not only the name and number but the practice and meaning of the ordinances have been matters of continuing debate. Who should receive baptism or participate in observing the Lord's Supper? What are essential elements in the observances that ensure validity? What do they accomplish in the life of the individual and the church? Definitive answers acceptable to all Christians have not been forthcoming for these or many other questions, but a survey of biblical evidence should be helpful in reaching some conclusions.

Baptism Biblical references to baptism abound in the Gospels, Acts, Pauline Epistles, and other New Testament books. John the Baptist preached and practiced a baptism of repentance (Matt. 3:11–12; Mark 1:2–8; Luke 3:2–17). His proclamation looked forward to the coming kingdom. "Repent ye: for the kingdom of heaven is at hand" (Matt.

3:2). Multitudes responded. Confessing their sins," they "were all baptized of him in the river of Jordan, (Mark 1:5). Apparently, not everyone who came received baptism, for John challenged some to "bring forth therefore fruit meet for repentance" (Matt. 3:8). John regarded his role as a transitional one to prepare the way (Matt. 3:11). The coming One would baptize with the Holy Spirit and with fire.

All the Gospel writers record that Jesus was baptized by John (Matt. 3:13–17; Mark 1:9–11; Luke 3:21–22; John 1:32–34). Matthew noted that John hesitated to baptize Jesus but finally consented "to fulfill all righteousness" (3:15). The identification of Jesus as Messiah followed as the heavens opened, the Spirit descended on Him like a dove, and a voice proclaimed Him the beloved Son. This event inaugurated His public ministry and set the stage for Christian baptism.

The coming age prophesied by John the Baptist arrived in Jesus. Jesus affirmed the ministry of John by submitting to baptism and adopted the rite for His own ministry, giving it new meaning for the new age. The Gospel of John indicates that Jesus gained and baptized more followers than John the Baptist (John 4:1–2), but notes that the actual baptizing was done by His disciples. Jesus referred to His impending death as a baptism (Luke 12:50), linking the meaning of baptism with the cross. These and other scattered references to baptism in the Gospels are evaluated and interpreted in a variety of ways by Bible students, but the total impact of evidence favors the view that Jesus practiced and commanded baptism. Central in this evidence is the Great Commission (Matt. 28:19–20).

The Acts of the Apostles reflects the practice of the earliest Christian churches regarding baptism, referring to baptism far more frequently than any other New Testament book. At Pentecost after Peter's sermon, "they that gladly received his word were baptized: and the same day there were added unto them about three thousand souls" (Acts 2:41). They had been exhorted by the apostle to "Repent, and be baptized every one of you in the name of Jesus Christ for the remission of sins, and ye shall receive the gift of the Holy Ghost" (2:38). At other times baptism was "in the name of the Lord Jesus" (8:16; 19:5). Sometimes the gift of the Spirit followed baptism; at other times, the spirit preceded baptism (10:44–48). These were apparently regarded as separate experiences.

Baptism "for" the forgiveness of sins may be translated "on the basis of." Many New Testament passages stress that forgiveness is based on repentance and trust in what Jesus had done, not on a rite—baptism or otherwise (John 3:16; Acts 16:31). The gospel is for everyone; baptism is for disciples. Salvation is provided by Christ and not through baptism. References to Jesus' blessing little children contain no indications of baptism

(Mark 10:13–16), and baptism of "households" described in Acts (16:31–33) should not be utilized to defend a later Christian practice.

If baptism is for believers only and does not convey salvation, then why do Christians universally baptize? It is highly unlikely that the early Christians would have adopted this practice without hesitation unless they were convinced strongly that Christ had intended that they do so. Further reflection upon what Christ had done enabled them to understand baptism in relation to the gospel. No New Testament writer contributed more to a fuller theological interpretation of baptism than Paul.

Paul (Saul) encountered the living Christ while on a journey to Damascus to persecute Christians. This led to a meeting in Damascus with Ananias, where Paul's sight was restored and where he was also baptized (Acts 9:17–18). What Paul had known about baptism previously must have been largely negative, but from this time baptism became a part of his missionary message and practice among both Jews and Gentiles.

Paul's basic message declared that a right relationship with God is based exclusively on faith in Jesus Christ. "For in the gospel a righteousness from God is revealed, a righteousness that is by faith from first to last, just as it is written: 'The righteous will live by faith' " (1:17 NIV). Throughout Romans Paul stressed the primacy of grace over law. Access to this grace is through faith in Jesus Christ (5:2). Where sin (breaking the law) abounds, grace much more abounds. This poses the question (6:1 NIV), "What shall we say, then? Shall we go on sinning so that grace may increase?" Paul denied emphatically that this is the case, for one dead to sin lives no longer in it. This fact is clearly illustrated in Christian baptism. "Don't you know that all of us who were baptized into Christ Jesus were baptized into his death? We were therefore buried with him through baptism into death in order that, just as Christ was raised from the dead through the glory of the Father, we too may live a new life" (vv. 3–4 NIV).

Paul assumed here the universal Christian practice of baptism and a common understanding that it symbolizes death, burial, and resurrection of the believer with Christ. The mode of immersion most clearly preserves this symbolism along with the added emphasis of death to sin and resurrection to a new life in Christ. The stress is upon what Christ has done more than what the believer does. Through faith in Him, grace is received and makes baptism meaningful.

Paul in 1 Corinthians related unity in Christ to baptism. "For by one Spirit are we all baptized into one body" (12:13). The body of Christ encompasses Jews and Greeks, slave and free, each with a diversity of gifts; but they are bound together in a unity of spirit and symbolized in baptism. Galatians 3:26–29 stresses identification with Christ and unity in Him also, using the figure of putting on clothing. "For as many of you as have been baptized into Christ have put on Christ" (3:27). But the preceding verse should be noted also. "Ye are all the children of God by faith in Christ Jesus." For those who belong to Christ, earthly distinctions disappear; and all are one in Christ, heirs according to the promise.

The subjective aspect of baptism for the believer and the objective aspect in Christ are brought together in Colossians 2:9–12. In a circumcision not by hands of men but by Christ, the sinful nature is put off. The Colossians have been buried with Christ in baptism and raised with Him through faith in the power of God, who raised Him from the dead. Consequently, they are to set their hearts on things above and put to death the earthly nature (3:1,5).

It is evident from the above and other passages that, for Paul, baptism portrayed the gospel message of the death and resurrection of Christ, affirmed the death of the believer to sin and the rising to walk in newness of life, and signified a union of the believer with Christ and a unity with other believers. The rite itself does not effect these, for they are based on what Christ has done and is doing. Baptism serves as the effective public symbol and declaration for those who trust in Christ as Savior and Lord.

The Lord's Supper The earliest written account of the institution of the Lord's Supper is in 1 Corinthians 11:23–26. The Corinthian church was divided, and many of its members were selfish and self-indulgent. In their fellowship meal, therefore, they did not eat "the Lord's Supper" (v. 20); for some overindulged, while others were left hungry and humiliated. In response to this abuse, Paul reminded them of the tradition that he had received and passed on to them regarding the Supper of the Lord with His disciples the night He was betrayed.

The Lord Jesus the same night in which he was betrayed took bread: And when he had given thanks, he brake it, and said, Take, eat: this is my body, which is broken for you: this do in remembrance of me. After the same manner also he took the cup, when he had supped, saying, This cup is the new testament in my blood: this do ye, as oft as ye drink it, in remembrance of me.

The terms *eucharist* or *thanksgiving* and *communion* or *fellowship* are often applied to the Supper, and each highlights a significant aspect of this ordinance. "The Lord's Supper" appears more satisfactory for the overall designation, reminding Christians that they share the loaf and cup at His table, not their own.

The account of the Last Supper in Mark 14:22–26 is roughly parallel to Paul's account but with some differences (see also Matt. 26:26–29 and Luke 22:17–20). Both accounts (Mark's and Paul's) record the blessing (thanksgiving) and breaking of bread. Both refer to covenant in connection with the cup as His blood, though only Paul called this a new covenant (see Jer. 31:31–34). Both contain a future emphasis, though in different forms. Mark indicated that Jesus said He would not drink again of the fruit of the vine until He drank it anew in the kingdom of God. Paul related that "whenever you eat this bread and drink this cup, you proclaim the Lord's death until he comes" (1 Cor. 11:26 NIV).

Paul stressed the memorial aspect of the Supper. "Do this in remembrance of me." Christians were to remember that the body of Christ was broken and His blood shed for them. As in baptism, sharing the Supper is a proclamation of the gospel in hope, "until he comes." As the Passover was a symbol of the old covenant, the Lord's Supper is a symbol of the new. Christians remember the sacrifice provided for their deliverance from bondage and look forward to the ultimate consummation in the land of promise, the kingdom of God.

The Supper shared in remembrance of the past and hope for the future is fulfilled in fellowship for the present. Time and again the phrase "in Christ" is repeated in the writings of Paul. Union in Christ and unity with Christians is a recurring theme. Not surprisingly, therefore, one finds these emphases related to the Lord's Supper. "Is not the cup of thanksgiving for which we give thanks a participation in the blood of Christ? And is not the bread that we break a participation in the body of Christ?" (1 Cor. 10:16 NIV). Paul was not talking about a repetition of the sacrifice of Christ, but a genuine sharing of fellowship (*koinōnia*) with the living Lord. Fellowship in Christ is basic for fellowship in his body (v. 17).

All Christians are unworthy to share the Lord's Supper, but His grace has provided for them in their unworthiness. The tragedy is that some partake in an unworthy manner, not discerning the Lord's body. Paul addressed this matter for the Corinthians and for us, urging that Christians examine themselves and respect the corporate body of Christ as they share the Supper of the Lord.

Conclusions Christ instituted both ordinances. Both portray publically and visibly the essential elements of the gospel, and both symbolize realities involving divine activity and human experience. Baptism is a once-for-all experience, but the Lord's Supper is repeated many times. Baptism follows closely one's profession of faith in Christ and actually in the New Testament was the declaration of that faith. The Lord's Supper declares one's continuing dependence upon the Christ proclaimed in the gospel, who died, was buried, and rose for our salvation.

The significance of baptism and the Lord's Supper will increase as churches and people commit themselves anew to the Christ proclaimed by the gospel. This commitment will recognize that, in observing the ordinances, they are presenting in a unique way the gospel of Christ and committing themselves fully to its demands. Calling upon Christ the Savior and Lord to provide strength and leadership for the people of God individually and collectively, believers will leave the observance of the ordinances to give faithful service in His world.   *Claude L. Howe, Jr.*

ORDINATION, ORDAIN The appointing, consecrating, or commissioning of persons for special service to the Lord and His people.

English Translations KJV uses *ordain* to translate over twenty Hebrew and Greek words. These words relate to a variety of ideas such as God's work and providence; the appointment to an office or a task; and the establishment of laws, principles, places, or observances. While all these ideas do not relate directly to ordination, they contain basic concepts of divine purpose, choice, appointment, and institution that undergird practice.

Old Testament Four primary examples provide Old Testament precedents for ordination: the consecration of Aaron and his sons as priests to God (Ex. 28—29; Lev. 8—9), the dedication of the Levites as servants of God (Num. 8:5–13), the appointment of seventy elders to assist Moses (Num. 11:16–17,24–25); and the commissioning of Joshua as Moses' successor (Num. 27:18–23). The variety in these examples helps explain the various contemporary understandings of ordination.

The ordination of the priest was based on God's choice of Aaron and his sons "that he may minister unto me in the priest's office" (Ex. 28:1). The ordination itself was a seven-day act of consecration accompanied by washing, donning vestments, anointing, sacrificing, and eating (Lev. 8). The basic Hebrew term for "ordination" literally means to "fill the hands" and may refer to filling the priest's hands with the offerings (Lev. 8:27). The ordination of the Levites also was based on God's choice of them "to do the service of the tabernacle of the congregation" (Num. 8:15). The ordination involved cleansing, presentation before the Lord, laying on of hands by the whole congregation, offering the Levites as a wave offering, and sacrifices.

The appointment of the seventy to assist Moses in bearing "the burden of the people" (Num. 11:17) was at God's initiative, but Moses selected persons who were known as elders and leaders. Their ordination involved standing with Moses and receiving from the Lord the Spirit who previously was upon Moses. When the Spirit rested on them, they prophesied (11:25). The ordination of a successor for Moses was at Moses' initiative (27:15–17), but Joshua was chosen by God because he was "a man in whom is the spirit" (v. 18). Joshua's ordination involved standing before the priest and all of the congregation and being commissioned in their sight. Moses laid his hand on Joshua, and Moses placed some of his authority on Joshua, including the role of inquiring of the judgment of the Urim.

New Testament The New Testament practice of ordination is generally associated with the laying on of hands; but other appointments, consecrations, and commissionings must be considered even if they lack formal investiture.

Jesus' appointment of the twelve "that they should be with him, and that he might send them forth to preach" (Mark 3:14) was based on prayer (Luke 6:12), His choice and call (Mark 3:13), and the apostles' responses. When He sent them out, He gave them "power and authority" (Luke 9:1) but no formal ordination. The same was true of the seventy (Luke 10:1). The Great Commission was given solely on the basis of Jesus' "power" (or authority, Matt. 28:18). The Holy Spirit was given directly without the laying on of hands (John 20:22). The disciples were chosen and appointed by Jesus for their task of bearing fruit (John 15:16).

Several other New Testament passages describe appointments without reference to ordination. Having been chosen by lot, Matthias was installed as one of the twelve (Acts 1:21–26). Barnabas and Paul appointed elders "in every church" after prayer and fasting (14:23). Titus was left in Crete to perform the same function (Titus 1:5).

Several passages describe ordination accompanied by the laying on of hands. Acts 6:1–6 tells of the appointment of seven men to the daily ministry to widows in the Jerusalem congregation. Barnabas and Paul were set apart for the work to which God had called them (Acts 13:1–3). Timothy was chosen by prophecy, recommended by Paul, and ordained to his task by the laying on of hands by Paul and the assembly of elders (1 Tim. 4:14; 2 Tim. 1:6). References to laying on of hands in 1 Timothy 5:22 and Hebrews 6:2 likely deal with other practices than ordination. See *Laying on of Hands.*

The lack of a consistent biblical pattern raises questions about ordination today. Who should be ordained? Why? By whom? On the basis of what qualifications? What is received in the act of ordination? Answers to these questions will vary with the biblical model assumed and continue to be debated in various denominations. *Michael Fink*

OREB AND ZEEB (Ō′ rĕb and Zē′ ĕb) Personal names meaning, "raven" and "wolf." Two Midianite princes captured and executed by the Ephraimites following Gideon's rout of their forces (Judg. 7:24—8:3). The Midianite nobles gave their names to the sites of their deaths, the rock of Oreb near Beth Bareh on the Jordan and the winepress of Zeeb. Israel's deliverance from Midian became proverbial for God's deliverance of His people (Ps. 83:11; Isa. 9:4; 10:26).

OREN (Ō′ rĕn) Personal name meaning, "cedar." Member of the Jerahmeelite clan of Judah (1 Chron. 2:25).

ORGAN KJV term for a musical instrument which modern translations identify as a pipe or shrill flute (Gen. 4:21; Job 21:12; 30:31; Ps. 150:4). At the time of the KJV translation organ designated any wind instrument. The modern pipe organ was not known in the biblical period, though primitive organs were used in the Jerusalem Temple after 100 B.C. and provided music for Roman games and combats. The organ came into the church use after A.D. 600.

ORION (Ō rī′ on) Constellation bearing the name of a giant Greek hunter who, according to myth, was bound and placed in the heavens. Job 38:31 perhaps alludes to this myth. God is consistently portrayed as the creator of the Orion constellation (Job 9:9; Amos 5:8). The plural of the Hebrew term for Orion is rendered constellations at Isaiah 13:10.

ORNAMENT See *Amulet; Anklet; Breastplate; Cloth, Clothing; Jewels, Jewelry; Necklace; Nose Ring.*

ORNAMENT OF THE LEGS KJV translation for armlet in Isaiah 3:20.

ORNAN (Ôr′ năn) Personal name meaning, "prince." Alternate name of Araunah (1 Chron. 21:15,18,20–25,28; 2 Chron. 3:1). See *Araunah.*

ORONTES (Ō rŏn tĕs) The principle river of Syria which originates east of the Lebanon ridge and flows 250 miles north before turning southwest into the Mediterranean south of Antioch-on-the-Orontes (Antakya). The river valley is extremely fertile and strategically significant. Cities of the Orontes valley include Antioch (Acts 11:19; 13:1), Hamath (2 Sam. 8:9; 2 Kings 17:24; 2 Chron. 8:4; Isa. 11:11), Qarqar, where King Ahab of Israel joined a coalition of Syrian kings warring against Shalmaneser III, and Riblah (2 Kings 23:33; 25:6,21). Nahr el-'Asi (rebellious river) is the modern name of the Orontes. See *Rivers and Waterways.*

ORONTES RIVER The Orontes, modern Asi (Turkish), Nahr el Assi (Arabic), rises near Heliopolis (Bealbek) in the Beka's valley of Lebanon, and flows north some 250 miles through Syria and Turkey before turning southwest through the great city of Antioch to reach the coast just south of ancient Seleucia, the seaport of Antioch. This

river is never actually mentioned in the Bible but was famous for its association with Antioch, which owed to the river the fertility of its district. See *Antioch.* *Colin J. Hemer*

ORPAH (Ôr′ pah) Personal name meaning, "neck," "girl with a full mane," or "rain cloud." Daughter-in-law of Naomi who returned to her people and gods after Naomi twice requested that she go (Ruth 1:4–15). See *Ruth.*

ORPHANS See *Fatherless.*

ORYX (Ōr′ ўx) A large, straight-horned antelope. See *Animals.*

OSEE (Ō′ sēē) Greek form of Hosea used by KJV (Rom. 9:25).

OSHEA (Ō′ shē à) KJV alternate form of Hoshea (Joshua) at Numbers 13:8,16.

OSNAPPAR (Ŏs nap′ ăr) Modern translation form of Osnapper.

OSNAPPER (Ŏs năp′ p̄er) Assyrian king who repopulated Samaria with foreigners following its capture in 722 B.C. (Ezra 4:10). Osnappar is most often identified with Ashurbanipal. KJV used the form Asnapper. See *Assyria.*

OSPRAY, OSPREY (Ŏs′ prēy) Large, flesh-eating hawk included in lists of unclean birds (Lev. 11:13; Deut. 14:12; KJV, NRSV). The identity of the bird is questionable. Other possibilities include: black vulture (NAS margin, NIV); black eagle, (KJV margin); bearded vulture (REB); and buzzard (NAS).

OSSIFRAGE (Ŏs′ sī frāge) English applies ossifrage to three birds: the bearded vulture; the osprey; and the giant petrel. The KJV included the ossifrage among the unclean birds (Lev. 11:13; Deut. 14:12). Other translations identify the bird as a black vulture (REB) or vulture (NAS, NIV, NRSV).

OSTIA (Ŏs tî à) Roman city at the mouth of the Tiber about fifteen miles from Rome which, following construction of an artificial harbor by Claudius (A.D. 41–54), served as the principle harbor for Rome. Before this construction, silt prohibited seagoing vessels from using the port. Such vessels were forced to use the port of Puteoli about 138 miles to the south of Rome (Acts 28:13).

OSTRACA (Ŏs trä că) Potsherds (pottery fragments), especially fragments used as an inexpensive writing material. See *Archaeology; Pottery; Writing.*

OSTRICH See *Birds*.

OTHNI (Ŏth' nī) Personal name perhaps meaning, "force" or "power." Levitic gatekeeper (1 Chron. 26:70).

OTHNIEL (Ŏth' nĭ ĕl) Name meaning, "God is powerful." *1.* First of Israel's judges or deliverers. Othniel received Caleb's daughter Achsah as his wife as a reward for his capture of Kiriath-sepher (Debir) (Josh. 15:15–19; Judg. 1:11–15). As the first judge, Othniel rescued Israel from the Mesopotamian king Cushan-rishathaim (Judg. 3:7–11). Othniel was the only judge to come from the southern tribes. See *Judges, Book of. 2.* Clan name associated with a resident of Netophah (1 Chron. 27:15).

OUCHES KJV term for (filagree) settings for precious stones (Ex. 28:11,13–14,25; 39:6,13,16,18). See *Jewels, Jewelry; High Priest*.

OUTCAST Scripture never employs outcast in the now common sense of one rejected by society. Outcast rather designates one banished from court (2 Sam. 14:14 RSV) or more often dispersed persons, exiles, or refugees (Deut. 30:4; Ps. 147:2; Isa. 11:12; 56:8; Jer. 30:17; Mic. 4:6–7). Outcasts often has the technical sense of diaspora. NAS employs outcast for one excommunicated from the synagogue (John 16:2).

OUTER TUNIC (Greek *chitōn*) See *Cloth, Clothing*.

OUTLANDISH KJV term meaning, "foreign" (Neh. 13:26).

OVEN A device used for baking food, especially bread (Lev. 2:4; Ex. 8:3). Ancient ovens were cylindrical structures of burnt clay two to three feet in diameter. A fire was built on pebbles in the oven bottom. Bread was baked by either placing the dough against the oven walls or upon the heated pebbles. Dried grass (Matt. 6:30; Luke 12:28), thorny shrubs, and animal dung were often used as fuels. See *Cooking and Heating*.

OVENS, TOWER OF THE See *Furnaces, Tower of the*.

OVERLIVE KJV term meaning, "outlive" (Josh. 24:31).

OVERPASS KJV term (Jer. 5:28) meaning either "surpass" previous limits or bounds (NAS, NIV, RSV, TEV) or else "passover" in the sense of overlook (NAS margin, REB).

OVERRUN KJV term meaning, "outrun" (2 Sam. 18:23).

Large domed oven.

OVERSEER A superintendent or supervisor. Various translations use overseer for a variety of secular positions (household manager, Gen. 39:4–5; prime minister, Gen. 41:34; foreman or supervisor, 2 Chron. 2:18) and ecclesiatical (Acts 20:18) offices. NAS, NIV employ overseer for the bishop of the KJV, NRSV (Phil. 1:1; 1 Tim. 3:1–2; Tit. 1:7).

OVERSHADOW To cast a shadow over; to envelope. The cloud which overshadowed the mount of transfiguration (Matt. 17:15; Mark 9:7; Luke 9:34) recalls the cloud "overshadowing" the tabernacle (Ex. 40:35 according to earliest Greek translation) when it was filled with God's glory. Luke 1:35 describes the mystery of the virginal conception in terms of Mary's being "overshadowed" by the power of God. Luke's picture does not involve sexual intercourse of a god and human woman as was common in pagan myth. The Spirit is Creator, not consort (Gen. 1:2; Ps. 33:6; and especially Job 33:40; Ps. 104:30 where the Spirit's roll is lifegiver). The Spirit which brought power and life to the church at Pentecost (Acts 1:8) and is the source of resurrection life (Ezek. 37:5–14) brought life to Mary's womb.

OWL A bird of prey belonging to the order *Strigiformes* which are generally nocturnal. Hebrew terms for various bird species cannot be indentified precisely with English terms. NRSV mentions two species of owl, the little and great owls (Deut. 14:16). KJV mentions these as well as the owl of the desert (Lev. 11:18; Deut. 14:16) and screech owl (Isa. 34:14). NIV mentions six species: the horned owl; screech owl (Lev. 11:16; Deut. 14:15); little owl (Lev. 11:17; Deut. 14:15); great owl; white owl; and desert owl (Lev. 11:18; Deut. 14:16). Owls, like other predatory birds, were classed as unclean. Owls nesting in ruins are a common image of desolation (Ps. 102:6; Isa. 34:11,15; Zeph. 2:14).

OWNERSHIP Possession of property. Two general principles guided Israelite laws of ownership: (1) All things ultimately belong to God, and (2) land possession is purely a business matter. After the division of the land among the twelve tribes, individual plots were given to family groups or clans. If the occasion demanded it, the land could be redivided at a later time. Land sales and transfers were recorded by scribes on leather or papyrus scrolls, on clay tablets, or in the presence of witnesses with the symbolic removal of a sandal (Ruth 4:7) or the stepping onto the land by the new owner. Land passed from father to son but could be given to a daughter. Private lands ultimately reverted to the king if not used for several years (2 Kings 8). The law of the kinsman-redeemer (Lev. 25:25) was developed to assure that land belonging to a particular clan did not pass out of its hands despite the death of an heirless husband. The next-of-kin was required to purchase the land and provide an heir to the name of the deceased. The impoverished widow would not be forced to sell her land to outsiders, thus diminishing the tribal area of the clan.

While it is true that the king did purchase lands from his subjects, private lands were subject to seizure by the ruler. Royal land was given as revenue-producing gifts by the ruler to members of his family or men who gained his favor. Often the land was tenant farmed for the king who continued to hold the ultimate right of its disposal. When economic times were difficult, kings exchanged their lands for other services, such as Solomon's gift of land to Hiram of Tyre for gold and laborers in the building of the Temple (1 Kings 9:11). Priestly families and local shrines also owned land, especially that surrounding the levitical cities, where the priests farmed their own fields (Josh. 21). With the consolidation of worship in the Jerusalem Temple, many of the priestly lands were sold.

Private ownership continued in much the same fashion during the New Testament era. Bills of sale and land deeds written on papyrus scrolls from this period have been discovered, attesting to the exchange of private lands. Often the sale of private land was subject to royal approval. The Romans oversaw the control of lands in Palestine, requiring heavy taxes from owners. The early Christian community existed through the generosity of those members who sold many of their possessions to help poorer believers.

David Maltsberger

OX, WILD OX See *Animals.*

Yoked oxen pulling a load.

OXGOAD See *Goad.*

OZEM (Ō′ zĕm) Personal name meaning, "irritable" or "strength." *1.* Sixth son of Jesse (1 Chron. 2:15). *2.* Fourth son of Jerahmeel (1 Chron. 2:25).

OZIAS (Ō zī′ ás) Greek form of Uzziah used by KJV (Matt. 1:8–9).

OZNI (Ŏz′ nī) Personal name meaning, "my hearing" or "attentive." Ancestor of a Gadite family, the Oznites (Ŏz′ nītes) (Num. 26:16).

OZNITES (Ŏz′ nītes) See *Ozni.*

PQ

The lush green fronds of a date palm tree in Haifa, Israel.

PADAN-ARAM KJV form of Paddan-Aram.

PADDAN-ARAM (Păd' dan-ā' răm) Place name perhaps meaning, "way of Syria," "field of Syria," or "plow of Syria." The land from where Abraham journeyed to Canaan. One of the principal cities was Haran. Later, Abraham sent his steward to Paddan-Aram to seek a wife for Isaac (Gen. 24:1–9), and Jacob fled there and married into Laban and Rebekah's branch of the patriarchal family (28:2–5). It may be modern tell Feddan near Carrhae. Hosea 12:13 calls it the field or country of Syria.

PADDLE KJV term for a digging tool (Deut. 23:13). Modern translations render the term as something to dig with (NIV), spade (NAS), stick (RSV, TEV), or trowel (NRSV, REB). The Israelites were required to respect God's presence in their camp by burying their excrement.

PADON (Pā' dŏn) Personal name meaning, "redemption." Ancestor of a family of postexilic Temple servants (Ezra 2:44; Neh. 7:47). See *Nethinim*.

PAGANS Those who worship a god or gods other than the living God to whom the Bible witnesses. NIV, REB, and RSV sometimes use pagans as the translation of the Greek *ethnoi* (1 Cor. 5:1; 10:20), which is generally translated Gentiles (so

The altar of Zeus, the highest of the pagan gods in ancient Greek religion, located at ancient Pergamum.

KJV, NAS). In English, Gentile relates to ethnic background while pagan refers to religious affiliation. See *Gentiles; Gods, Pagan*.

PAGIEL (Pā' ḡĭ ĕl) Personal name meaning, "fortune of God," "God is entreated," or "God meets." Wilderness leader of the tribe of Asher (Num. 1:13; 2:27; 7:72,77; 10:26).

PAHATH-MOAB (Pā' hăth-Mō' ăb) Title meaning, "governor of Moab." A family of returned Exiles likely descended from the Hebrew governor of Moab in the time of David (2 Sam. 8:2; Ezra 2:6; 8:4; 10:30; Neh. 7:11; 10:14).

PAI (Pā' ī) Place name meaning, "groaning." Alternate form of Pau used at 1 Chronicles 1:50 (compare Gen. 36:39). see *Pau*.

PAINT A mixture of pigment and liquid used to apply a closely adhering, colorful coat to a surface. Most scriptural references are to painting the eyes. See *Cosmetics*. The sole exception is Jeremiah 22:14 which refers to Jehoiakim's plans to paint his palace vermilion. The prohibition of making images (Ex. 20:4) perhaps curtailed development of painting in Israel. Archaeologists have uncovered numerous tomb and palace paintings in both Egypt and Mesopotamia.

PALACE The residence of a monarch or noble. KJV often used palace in passages where modern translations have substituted a term more appropriate to the context. Terms designating a strongly fortified section of the king's residence often replaced palace: citadel (1 Kings 16:18; 2 Kings 15:25); tower (Ps. 122:7 NRSV; Song of Sol. 8:9 NIV); stronghold (Isa. 34:13; Amos 1:4 NRSV); fortress (Amos 1:4 NIV); battlement (Song of Sol. 8:9 NRSV; parapet, REB). At Amos 4:3, modern translations replace palace with the proper name Harmon. The KJV used palace twice for the Greek *aulē* (Matt. 26:3; Luke 11:21). The crowd in Matthew 26 gathered in the courtyard of the high priest's residence. Modern translations rendered

An example of a wall fresco, a major art form of the Roman period which utilized types of paint.

aulē variously: palace (NIV, NRSV, TEV); court (NAS); house (REB). The strong man of Luke 11 guarded the open courtyard of his home. Modern translations are again divided on the translation of *aulē:* castle (NRSV); homestead (NAS); house (NIV, TEV); palace (REB, RSV). The KJV also used palace to translate the Latin loanword *praetorium* (Phil. 1:13). Modern translations replaced palace with praetorian guard (NAS, RSV) or an equivalent expression (imperial guard, NRSV, REB; palace guard, NIV, TEV).

Palaces served not only as royal residences but as a means of displaying the wealth of a kingdom. Esther 1:6–7 describes the palace of King Ahasuerus (Xerxes I) of Assyria which featured fine curtains, marble pillars, and ornate mosaic floors. David's palace was built by workers sent by King Hiram of Tyre and featured cedar woodwork (2 Sam. 5:11). The palace must have been large to accomodate David's growing number of wives, concubines, and children (2 Sam. 3:2–5; 5:13–16), as well as store booty, such as the golden shields which David seized (2 Sam. 8:7). Solomon's palace complex required thirteen years for completion (1 Kings 7:1). His palace complex included the "house of the forest of Lebanon" (7:2), an immense hall featuring 45 cedar pillars and Solomon's golden shields (10:16–18), the "porch of pillars" (7:6), the "Hall of Justice" (7:7 NRSV), featuring an ivory and gold throne (10:18–20), and private dwellings for both king and Pharoah's daughter (7:8). Builders used costly hewn stone and cedar throughout the palace (7:9,11). Portions of this palace complex survived the destruction of Jerusalem by the Babylonians (Neh. 3:25). King Ahab's palace in Samaria was decorated with ivory panels, some of which have been recovered by archaeologists (1 Kings 22:39).

The prophets, particularly Amos, condemned the rich for building palaces at the expense of the poor. Amos' announcements of doom refer to summer and winter residences, ivory furniture and palaces, and great houses of hewn stone (Amos 3:15; 5:11; 6:4,11). Jeremiah offered a similar critique of Jeroboam's building program in Jerusalem (22:13–15).   *Chris Church*

PALAL (Pā′ lăl) Personal name meaning, "God comes to judge." One of those assisting in Nehemiah's repair of the wall (Neh. 3:25).

PALANQUIN (Pă lăn′ quĭn) REB, RSV term for an enclosed seat or couch carried on servants' shoulders (Song of Sol. 3:9). Other translations include: carriage (NIV), chariot (KJV), and sedan chair (NAS).

PALESTINA (Păl ēs tī′ n̊a) KJV alternate name for Philistia (Ex. 15:14; Isa. 14:29,31). See *Philistines.*

PALESTINE (Păl′ ēs tīne) Geographical designation for land of Bible, particularly land west of Jordan River God allotted to Israel for an inheritance (Josh. 13—19). Various terms have been used to designate that small but significant land known in the early Old Testament era as "Canaan" (Gen. 12:5) and often referred to as the Promised Land (Deut. 9:28). The area was designated "Israel" and "Judah" at the division of the kingdoms in 931 B.C. By New Testament times the land had been divided into provincial designations, "Judea," "Samaria," "Galilee," and others. Generally, the region was considered to be a part of Syria.

Palestine is derived from the name *Pelishtim* or "Philistines." See *Philistines.* The Greeks, familiar primarily with the coastal area, applied the name Palestine to the entire southeastern Mediterranean region. Although the word *Palestine* (or *Palestina*) is found four times in the KJV (Ex. 15:14; Isaiah 14:29,31; Joel 3:4), these are references to the territory of the Philistines and so properly designate only the strip of coastland occupied by that people.

For the purposes of this article, Palestine extends to the north ten to fifteen miles beyond the ancient site of Dan and New Testament Caesarea Philippi into the gorges and mountains just south of Mount Hermon. To the east, it extends to the Arabian steppe. To the south, Palestine extends ten to fifteen miles beyond Beer-sheba. On the west is the Mediterranean Sea. It therefore includes western Palestine—between the Jordan River and the Sea, and eastern Palestine—between the Jordan and the Arabian steppe.

Palestine west of the Jordan covers approximately 6,000 square miles. East of the Jordan an area of about 4,000 square miles was included in the land of Israel.

Geographical Features Palestine is naturally divided into four narrow strips of land running north and south. *1. Coastal plain* This very fertile plain begins ten to twelve miles south of Gaza, just north of the Egyptian border, and stretches northward to the Sidon-Tyre area. Usually it is divided into three sections: (1) the Plain of Philistia, roughly from south of Gaza to Joppa (Tel Aviv); (2) the Plain of Sharon, from Joppa north to the promontory of the Carmel chain; and (3) the detached Plain of Acco, which merges with the Plain of Esdraelon, the historic gateway inland and to the regions to the north and east. The Plain of Sharon varies from a width of a few hundred yards just south of Carmel to more than twelve miles wide near Joppa. Covered with fertile alluvial soil and well watered by springs, the area was once covered with extensive forests.

Further south is the Plain of Philistia. Here were located the Philistine strongholds of Gaza, Ashkelon, Ashdod, Ekron, and Gath. Salt marshes—the Serbonian bog—located at the southern end of the

Philistine plain have been known as breeding grounds of disease.

Forming the southwestern end of the Fertile Crescent, the coastal plain has been the highway of commerce and conquest for centuries. This was the route followed by the Hittites and the Egyptians, by Cambyses, Alexander, Pompey, and Napoleon.

The coastal plain lacked an outstanding natural harbor. Joppa had roughly semicircular reefs that formed a breakwater 300 to 400 feet offshore and, consequently, was used as a port. Entrance from the south was impossible, however, and the north entrance was shallow and treacherous. Herod the Great developed Caesarea Maritima into an artificial port of considerable efficiency. See *Caesarea.*

2. Central Hill Country The second strip of land is the mountainous ridge beginning just north of Beer-sheba and extending through all of Judea and Samaria into upper Galilee. Actually, the rugged terrain running the length of the land is a continuation of the more clearly defined Lebanon Mountains to the north. The only major break in the mountain range is the Plain of Esdraelon also called the Valley of Jezreel. Three divisions are evident: Judea, Samaria, Galilee.

(1) *Judea* Rising from the parched Negeb (Negeb means "parched" or "dry land"), the Judean hills reach their highest point, 3,370 feet, near Hebron. See *Negeb.* Jerusalem is located in the Judean hills at an elevation of 2,600 feet. The eastern slopes form the barren and rugged "wilderness of Judea," then fall abruptly to the floor of the Jordan Valley. The wilderness is treeless and waterless. Deep gorges and canyons cut into the soft sedimentary formations.

The western foothills of Judea are called the "Shephelah," meaning "valley" or "lowland." The name has been inaccurately applied to the Plain of Philistia, but the towns assigned by the Old Testament to the Shephelah are all situated in the low hills rather than the plain. The Shephelah is a belt of gently rolling hills between 500 and 1,000 feet in height. Five valleys divide the region, from the Wadi el Hesy in the south to the Valley of Ajalon in northern Judea. These passes have witnessed the conflicts between Saul and the Philistines, the Maccabees and the Syrians, the Jews and the Romans, Richard I and Saladin. Here Samson grew to manhood. Here David encountered Goliath.

The Shephelah had great military importance. It formed a buffer between Judea and the enemies of the Hebrew people—Philistines, Egyptians, Syrians. Formerly heavily wooded with sycamores, the region served to impede an attack from the west.

(2) *Samaria* The hills of Samaria descend gently from the Judean mountains, averaging just over 1,000 feet in height. Several notable mountains such as Gerizim (2,890 feet), Ebal (3,083), and Gilboa (1,640 feet) dominate the area. This land

of mountains is marked by wide and fertile valleys. Here the majority of the people lived during the Old Testament era, and here significant events of Hebrew history took place. The openness of Samaria is a prominent feature of the land, making movement much easier than in Judea and thus inviting armies and chariots from the north.

The valley between Mount Ebal and Mount Gerizim was a central location, apparently providing the perfect point from which a united nation could have been governed. Roads went in all directions—to Galilee, the Jordan Valley, south to Jerusalem. Here Shechem was located, important to the patriarchs and in the day of the judges. Shechem, however, had no natural defenses and was consequently rejected by the kings of Israel as their capital.

From this region the main range of mountains sends out an arm to the northwest that reaches the coast at Mount Carmel. Carmel reaches a height of only 1,791 feet, but it seems more lofty because it rises directly from the coastline. It receives abundant rainfall, an average of 28 to 32 inches per year, and consequently is rather densely covered with vegetation, including some woodland.

The Carmel range divides the Plain of Sharon from the narrow coastal plain of Phoenicia. It forms the southern side of the Plain of Esdraelon, with the ancient fortress of Megiddo standing as one of its key cities. This natural barrier caused the passes in the Carmel chain to achieve unusual importance, lying as it does on the historic route between Egypt and Mesopotamia.

(3) *Galilee* North of the Plain of Esdraelon and south of the Leontes River lies the region called Galilee. The name comes from the Hebrew *galil,* meaning, literally "circle" or "ring." In Isaiah 9:1, the prophet refers to it as "Galilee of the Gentiles" (NIV). The tribes of Asher, Naphtali, and Zebulun were assigned to this area. There is evidence of mixed population and racial variety from early times. In the day of Jesus, many Gentiles were in Galilee.

The region is divided into Upper Galilee and Lower Galilee. Lower Galilee is a land of limestone hills and fertile valleys. Most of the region is approximately 500 feet above sea level—but with mountains like Tabor reaching a height of 1,929 feet. Grain, grass, olives, and grapes were abundant. Fish, oil, and wine were common exports. Several major international roads crossed the area, and caravan traffic from Damascus through Capernaum to the south was heavy. Josephus spoke of Galilee as "universally rich and fruitful."

Some of the most important cities of Galilee were on the shore of the Sea of Galilee. Those on the northwestern shore, such as Capernaum, were more Jewish than those to the south. Tiberias, built in A.D. 25 by Herod Antipas and named after the reigning caesar, became the capital and

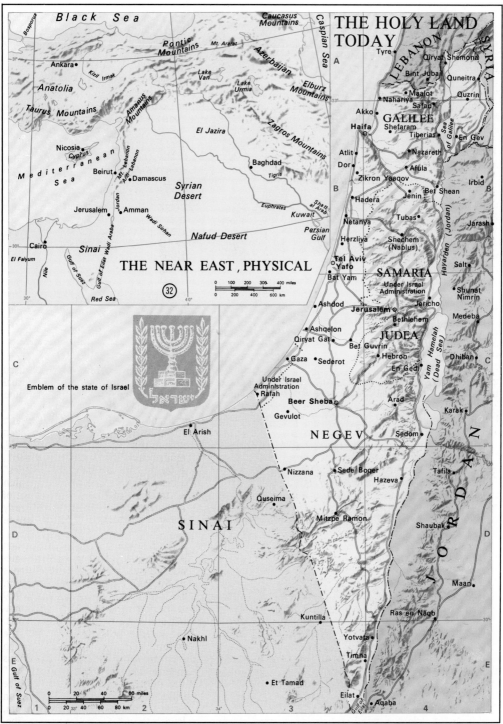

THE HOLY LAND TODAY

THE NEAR EAST, PHYSICAL

(32)

| 0 | 100 | 200 | 300 | 400 miles |

| 0 | 200 | 400 | 600 km |

Emblem of the state of Israel

| 0 | 20 | 40 | 60 miles |

| 0 | 20 | 40 | 60 | 80 km |

© carta

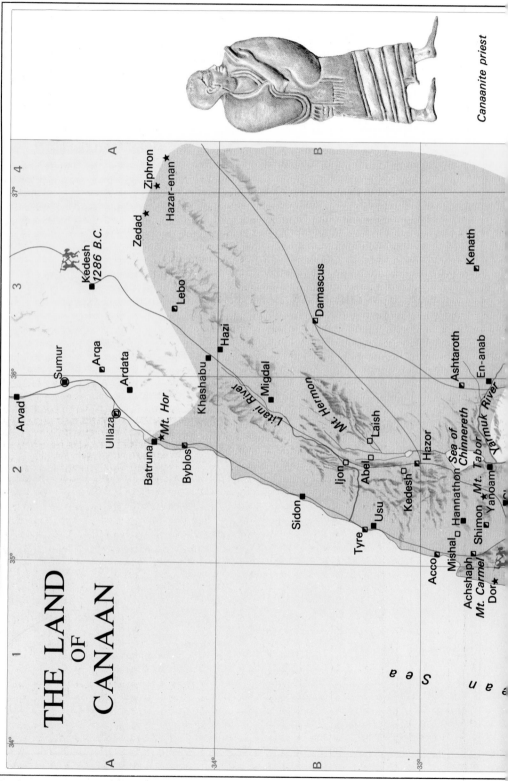

THE LAND
OF
CANAAN

Canaanite priest

Arvad ■

Sumur ◉

Arqa ■

Ardata ■

Ullaza ◉

★*Mt. Hor*

Batruna ■

Byblos ■

Khashabu ■

Hazi ■

Litani River

Migdal ■

Mt. Hermon

Sidon ■

Ijon □

Abel □

Laish □

Tyre ■

Usu ■

Kedesh □

Hazor □

Mishal □

Hannathon □

Sea of Chinnereth

Acco ■

Achshaph □

Shimon □

Mt. Tabor

Yanoam ■

Mt. Carmel

Dor ★

Kedesh
1286 B.C. ■

Zedad ★

Ziphron ★

Hazar-enan ★

Lebo ■

Damascus □

Ashtaroth ■

En-anab ■

Kenath ■

Yarmuk River

Sea

an
e
a
n

Sea

© carta

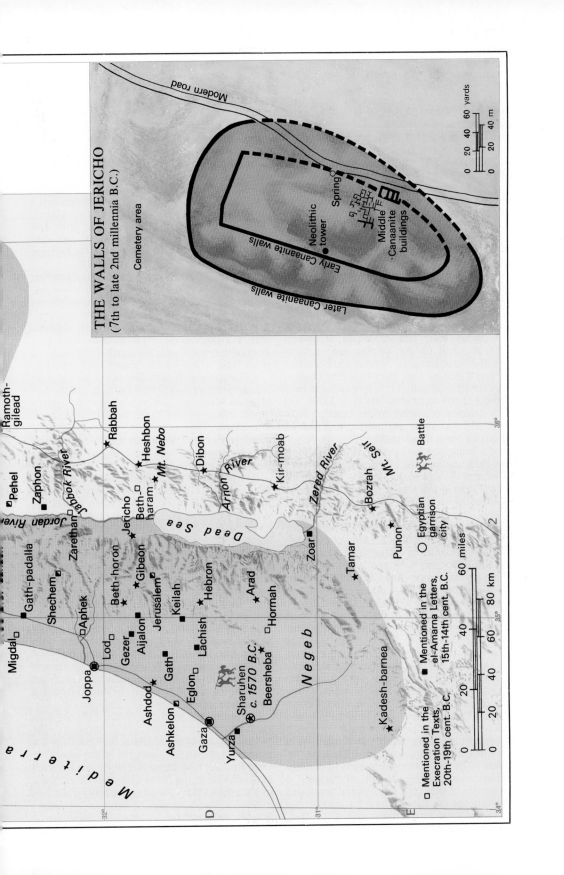

THE WALLS OF JERICHO
(7th to late 2nd millennia B.C.)

Modern road

Cemetery area

Later Canaanite walls

Early Canaanite walls

Neolithic tower

Spring

Middle Canaanite buildings

0   20   40   60 yards

0   20   40 m

Mediterranea

Migdal

Joppa

Lod

Gath-padalla

Shechem

Aphek

Gezer

Ashdod

Aijalon

Gath

Ashkelon

Jerusalem

Eglon

Gaza

Keilah

Yurza

Lachish

Beth-horon

Gibeon

Sharuhen
c. 1570 B.C.

Beersheba

Hormah

Hebron

Arad

Pehel

Zaphon

Jabbok River

Zarethan

Jordan River

Jericho

Beth-
haram

Dead Sea

Negeb

Kadesh-barnea

Ramoth-
gilead

Rabbah

Heshbon

Mt. Nebo

Dibon

Arnon River

Kir-moab

Zered River

Zoar

Tamar

Punon

Bozrah

Mt. Seir

Battle

Egyptian
garrison
city

□ Mentioned in the
  Execration Texts,
  20th-19th cent. B.C.

■ Mentioned in the
  el-Amarna Letters,
  15th-14th cent. B.C.

0   20   40   60 miles

0   20   40   60   80 km

32°

31°

34°

35°

36°

D

E

2

the most important city during the New Testament era.

The terrain of Upper Galilee is much more rugged than Lower Galilee, an area of deeply fissured and roughly eroded tableland with high peaks and many wadis. The highest peak is Mount Meron, at 3,963 feet the highest point in Palestine. The basic rock is limestone, in the eastern sections often covered with volcanic rock. In the east, Galilee drops off abruptly to the Jordan, while farther south, near the Sea of Galilee, the slopes become much more gradual and gentle.

3. Jordan Rift Valley As a result of crustal faulting, the hills of Palestine drop into the deepest split on the surface of the earth. The fault is part of a system that extends north to form the valley between the Lebanon and the Anti-Lebanon chains, also extending south to form the Dead Sea, the dry Arabah Valley, the Gulf of Aqabah, and, eventually, the chain of lakes on the African continent.

The Jordan River has its source in several springs, primarily on the western and southern slopes of Mount Hermon. Several small streams come together near Dan, then flow into shallow, reedy Lake Hula (Huleh). From its sources to Hula the Jordan drops somewhat less than 1,000 feet over a distance of twelve miles, entering Lake Hula at 230 feet above sea level (not 7 feet, as reported by some older publications). In recent years the Jordan bed has been straightened after it leaves Hula, the swamps of the valley have been drained, and the size of the lake has been greatly reduced. Most of the area is now excellent farmland. Over the eleven miles from Hula to the Sea of Galilee, the Jordan drops 926 feet, flowing in part through a narrow canyon. From Galilee to the Dead Sea there is an additional drop of 600 feet.

The Sea of Galilee is a significant part of the upper Rift Valley and is formed by a widening of it. It has several names—the Lake of Gennesaret, the Sea of Tiberias, Lake Chinnereth—but it is best known as the Sea of Galilee. Around it most of the ministry of Jesus took place. Here He could rest, escape crowds, find cool relief from the heat. Shaped much like a harp, it is thirteen miles long and seven miles wide. The hard basalt environment has given the lake an almost constant level and size. In the New Testament day, the lake was the center of a thriving fishing industry. The towns around the lake testify to this fact: Bethsaida means "fishing place," and Tarichea is from a Greek term meaning "preserved fish."

As the Jordan flows south out of the Sea of Galilee, it enters a gorge called the Ghor, or "depression." The meandering Jordan and its periodic overflows have created the Zor, or "jungle," a thick growth of entangled semitropical plants and trees. Although the distance from the lower end of the Sea of Galilee to the upper end of the Dead Sea is only 65 miles, the winding Jordan twists 200 miles to cover that distance. The Ghor is about twelve miles wide at Jericho.

Seven miles south of Jericho, the Jordan flows into the Dead Sea, one of the world's most unique bodies of water. The surface of the water is 1,296 feet below sea level, the lowest point on the surface of the earth. Forty-seven miles long and eight miles wide, the Dead Sea has no outlet. It has been calculated that an average of 6.5 million tons of water enter the sea each day. The result of centuries of evaporation is that now 25 percent of the weight of the water is mineral salts. Magnesium chloride gives the water a bitter taste, and calcium chloride gives it an oily touch. Fish cannot live in Dead Sea water. Indeed, it destroys almost all organic life in it and around it.

Thirty miles down the eastern side, a peninsula, the Lisan, or the "Tongue," juts into the sea. North of it the sea is deep, reaching a maximum depth of 1,319 feet—2,650 feet below sea level. South of the peninsula the sea is very shallow, with a maximum depth of thirteen feet. It is thought that this area is the location of "the cities of the Plain" (Gen. 13:12), Sodom and Gomorrah.

4. Transjordan Plateau East of the Jordan is an area where the tribes of Reuben, Gad, and the half tribe of Manasseh settled. In New Testament times, Decapolis and Perea were located there. The ministry of Jesus took Him to limited parts of these provinces. Transjordan is divided into sections by several rivers—the Yarmuk, the Jabbok, the Arnon, and the Zered.

(1) Across from Galilee and north of the Yarmuk River is Bashan (Hauron), an area of rich volcanic soil with rainfall in excess of sixteen inches per year. The plateau averages 1,500 feet above sea level. To the east of Bashan lies only desert that begins to slope toward the Euphrates. In the New Testament era, it was a part of the territory of Philip, the Tetrarch, son of Herod the Great. (2) South of the Yarmuk, reaching to the Jabbok River, was Gilead. During the Persian rule the boundaries were rather rigid. Both before and after Persian domination, Gilead reached as far south as Rabbah (Philadelphia, modern Amman). Formerly heavily wooded, with many springs and with gently rounded hills, Gilead is one of the most picturesque regions of Palestine. Olive groves and vineyards are found on the hillsides. Jerash and Amman, the capital of the Heshemite Kingdom of Jordan, are located here.

(3) South of Gilead lies Moab. Originally, its northern border was the Arnon River, but the Moabites pushed north, giving their name to the plains east of the spot where the Jordan enters the Dead Sea (Ammon attempted to establish herself between Gilead and Moab using Rabbath-Ammon as her stronghold. This succeeded only under the infamous Tobiah during the years of the Exile.) Moab's southern border was the Zered River, Wadi al Hasa.

(4) Still farther south is Edom, with the highest mountains of the region. The area is arid and barren. Fifty miles south of the Dead Sea lies the ancient fortress of Petra, "rose-red . . . half as old as time."

Climate Palestine lies in the semitropical belt between 30° 15′ and 33° 15′ north latitude. Temperatures are normally high in the summer and mild in the winter, but these generalizations are modified by both elevation and distance from the coast. Variety is the necessary word in describing Palestinian weather, for in spite of its relatively small size, the geographical configuration of the area produces a diversity of conditions. Because of the Mediterranean influence, the coastal plain has an average annual temperature of 57° at Joppa. Jerusalem, only 35 miles away, has an annual average of 63°. Its elevation of 2,500 feet above sea level causes the difference. Jericho is only seventeen miles further east, but it is 3,400 feet lower (900 feet below sea level), consequently having a tropical climate and very low humidity. Here bitterly cold desert nights offset rather warm desert days. Similarly, much of the area around the Sea of Galilee experiences temperate conditions, while the Dead Sea region is known for its strings of 100° plus summer days.

Palestine is a land of two seasons, a dry season and a rainy season, with intervening transitional periods. The dry season lasts from mid-May to mid-October. From June through August no rain falls except in the extreme north. Moderate, regular winds blow usually from the west or southwest. The breezes reach Jerusalem by noon, Jericho in early afternoon, and the Transjordan plateau by midafternoon. The air carries much moisture, but atmospheric conditions are such that precipitation does not occur. However, the humidity is evident from the extremely heavy dew that forms five nights out of six in July.

With late October, the "early rain" so often mentioned in Scripture begins to fall. November is punctuated with heavy thunderstorms. The months of December through February are marked by heavy showers, but it is not a time of unrelenting rain. Rainy days alternate with fair days and beautiful sunshine. The cold is not severe, with occasional frost in the higher elevations from December to February. In Jerusalem snow may fall twice during the course of the winter months.

All of Palestine experiences extremely disagreeable warm conditions occasionally. The sirocco wind (the "east wind" of Gen. 41:6 and Ezek. 19:12) blowing from the southeast during the transition months (May—June, September—October) brings dust-laden clouds across the land. It dries vegetation and has a withering effect on people and animals. On occasion the temperature may rise 30°F and the humidity fall to less than 10 percent.

Along the coastal plain, the daily temperature fluctuation is rather limited because of the Mediterranean breezes. In the mountains and in Rift Valley, daily fluctuation is much greater.

Timothy Trammel

PALLET A small, usually straw-filled, mattress light enough to be carried. All biblical references are found in accounts or summaries of the healing of invalids (Mark 2:4–12; John 5:8–12; Acts 5:15). The "bedridden" man of Acts 9:33 was one who had lain on a pallet for eight years.

PALLU (Păl′ lū) Personal name meaning, "conspicuous," "wonder," or "distinguished." Second son of Reuben (Gen. 46:9; Ex. 6:14; Num. 26:5,8; 1 Chron. 5:3). KJV used the alternate spelling Phallu in Genesis.

PALLUITES (Păl′ lū ītes) Descendants of Pallu (Nu. 26:5).

PALMERWORM The caterpillar stage of a species of locust (Joel 1:4; 2:25; Amos 4:9). See *Insects.*

PALMS The date palm (*Phoenix dactylifera*) was among the earliest cultivated trees. Five thousand-year-old inscriptions from Mesopotamia give instruction for their cultivation. Palms are characteristic of oases and watered places (Ex. 15:27; Num. 33:9). The fruit of the date palm is highly valued by desert travelers since it may be consumed fresh or else dried or made into cakes for a portable and easily storable food. Jericho was known as the city of palms (Deut. 34:3; Judg. 1:16; 3:13). The judge Deborah rendered her decisions under a palm bearing her name (Judg. 4:5). The palm was a symbol of both beauty (Song of Sol. 7:7) and prosperity (Ps. 92:12). Thus, images of palms were used in the decoration of the Temple (1 Kings 6:29,35; 7:36) and were part of Ezekiel's vision of the new Temple (Ezek. 40:16,22,26). Palms were used in the construction of the booths for the festival of booths (Lev. 23:40; Neh. 8:15). In John 12:13, the crowd used palm branches to welcome Jesus to Jerusalem. See *Dates; Plants.*

PALMS, CITY OF An alternate name for Jericho (Deut. 34:3; Judg. 1:16; 3:13; 2 Chron. 28:15).

PALSY KJV term for paralysis (Matt. 4:24; 9:2; Luke 5:18; Acts 8:7). The descriptions of the Gospel writers do not permit identifications with specific forms of paralysis. The Gospel writers were rather concerned to present Jesus as the One to whom God had entrusted the authority to forgive sins (Matt. 9:6) and whose healing ministry was a cause for glorifying God (Matt. 9:8).

Palm trees in the Wadi Feiran on the Sinai peninsula.

PALTI (Păl' tī) Personal name meaning, "my deliverance." *1.* Benjamin's representative among the twelve spies sent to survey Canaan (Num. 13:9). *2.* Second husband of Michal, King Saul's daughter who had previously been given in marriage to David (1 Sam. 25:44; KJV, Phalti). Michal was later returned to David in consequence of Abner's defection from Ishbosheth (2 Sam. 3:15–16). The fuller form *Paltiel,* meaning, "God delivers," is used in 2 Samuel (KJV, Phaltiel).

PALTIEL (Păl' tĭ ĕl) Personal name meaning, "God is (my) deliverance." *1.* Leader of Issachar whom Moses appointed to assist Joshua and Eliezer in distribution of land to the tribes west of the Jordan (Num. 34:26). *2.* Fuller form of the name of Saul's son-in-law (2 Sam. 3:15–16). See *Palti.*

PALTITE (Păl' tīte) Title meaning, "resident of Beth-Pelet," given to Helez, one of David's 30 elite warriors (2 Sam. 23:26). The parallels in 1 Chronicles read Pelonite (11:27; 27:10).

PAMPHYLIA (Păm phўl' ĭ à) One of the provinces of Asia Minor. Located in what is now southern Turkey, Pamphylia was a small district on the coast. It measured about eighty miles long and twenty miles wide. One of the chief cities was Perga, where John Mark left Paul and Barnabas during the first missionary journey (Acts 13:13). Other important cities were the ports of Side and

Attalia. The New Testament records no other significant events for the early church in Pamphylia, perhaps because of the concentration of non-Hellenized peoples in the region. This would make the spread of the gospel slower and harder to achieve.

The road north from Antalia to Isparta in the Roman province of Pamphylia (modern Turkey).

PAN A shallow, metal cooking utensil. Pans were used for baking bread for family use (2 Sam. 13:9) or as an offering (Lev. 2:5; 6:21; 1 Chron. 23:29). Deeper pans were used for boiling meat (1 Sam. 2:14). NAS used pans to refer to dishes for incense (Num. 7:14,20,26). NIV mentioned silver pans among Cyrus' gifts for rebuilding the Jerusalem Temple (Ezra 1:9). In the KJV, an iron pan (NRSV plate) serves as symbol of the coming siege of Jerusalem (Ezek. 4:3).

PANNAG Hebrew term perhaps meaning, "pastry," which the KJV took as a place name (Ezek. 27:17). NAS, NIV readings (cakes, confection) are supported by an Akkadian cognate and the Targum. RSV follows variant manuscripts in reading "early figs." REB, NRSV read "millet." TEV reads, "wheat."

A modern variety of the ancient papyrus plant from whose stalks writing material was made.

PAPER, PAPYRUS (Pȧ pȳ′ răs) Popular writing material invented by the Egyptians and used by scribes from 2500 B.C. to A.D. 700.

New Testament manuscripts produced before the fourth century were written exclusively on papyrus; after the fourth century almost all New Testament documents were preserved on parchment. See *Bible, Text and Versions; Library; Writing.*

PAPHOS (Pā′ phŏs) A town on the southwest side of Cyprus, and capital of the island during New Testament times. Paul, Barnabas, and John Mark came to the city on their first missionary journey and possibly led the proconsul, Sergius Paulus, to Christ (Acts 13:6–12). See *Cyprus.*

The ruins of ancient Paphos on the island of Cyprus.

PAPS KJV term used for a woman's breasts (Ezek. 23:21; Luke 11:27) or a man's chest (Rev. 1:13).

PARABLES Stories, especially those of Jesus, told to provide a vision of life, especially life in God's kingdom. Parable means a putting alongside for purposes of comparison and new understanding. Parables utilize pictures such as metaphors or similes and frequently extend them into a brief story to make a point or disclosure.

The difference between a parable and an allegory turns on the number of comparisons. A parable may convey other images and implications, but it has only one main point established by a basic comparison or internal juxtaposition. For example, the parable of the mustard seed (Mark 4:30–32; Matt. 13:31–32; Luke 13:18–19) compares or juxtaposes a microscopically small seed initially with a large bush eventually.

An allegory makes many comparisons through a kind of coded message. It correlates two areas of discourse, providing a series of pictures symbolizing a series of truths in another sphere. Each detail is a separate metaphor or what some call a cryptogram. If you are an insider who knows, you receive the second or intended message. Otherwise, you can follow only the surface story. Jonathan Swift's *Guilliver's Travels* is an allegory as is John Bunyan's *Pilgrim's Progress.* In the Old Testament, Ezekiel recounts an incident in nature about great eagles and vines (17:3–8) and then assigns a very allegorical application to each of the details (17:9–18).

The word *allegory* never appears in the Gospels. Parable is the basic figure Jesus used. Though no parable in the Synoptic Gospels is a pure allegory, some parables contain subordinated allegorical aspects, such as the parable of the wicked tenants (Mark 12:1–12; Matt 21:36–46; Luke 20:9–19). Even in the parable of the Mustard Seed the passing reference to the birds of heaven nesting in the branches (Mark 4:32) may be an allegorical detail, but the distinction of the parable establishing a basic, single comparison remains and aids interpretation. See *Allegory.*

Parables Prior to Jesus Though Jesus perfected the oral art of telling parables, their background can be found in the Old Testament and in secular sources. The Old Testament employs the broader category of *mashal,* which refers to all expressions that contain a comparison. A *mashal* can be a proverb (1 Sam. 10:12), a taunt (Mic. 2:4), a dark riddle (Ps. 78:2), an allegory (Ezek. 24:3–4), or a parable. The stories of Jesus are linked with the heritage of the prophetic parables in the Old Testament (Isa. 28:23–29; 5:1–7; 1 Kings 20:39–43; Eccl. 9:13–16; 2 Sam. 12:1–4).

Perhaps the most interesting antecedent of the parables of Jesus comes from Nathan's word to

David. Nathan told the unsuspecting David the seemingly harmless story of a rich man and a poor man living in the same city (2 Sam. 12:1–4). The poor man owned only a single little ewe lamb he loved as a household pet while the rich man possessed large flocks; yet when the wealthy farmer had a guest to serve, he seized the poor man's single lamb for the dinner! The teller of the story was living dangerously as he seized a teachable moment to confront the life of the most famous king of Israel. He sought to get inside David's guard and cut the iron bonds of his self-deception to strike a moral blindness from his eyes. In a sense, it was a well-laid trap since David responded with moral outrage, thus condemning himself. Nathan then applied the parable to the king's affair with Bathsheba (2 Sam. 12:5–14).

The parable was also recognized as a literary type before the time of Jesus in the writings of the Greeks concerning rhetoric. The famous writer Homer included 189 parables in *The Illiad* and 39 more in *The Odyssey.* Plato's poetic speech was rich in similitudes interwoven into his speech, but not so much independent unities like those of Jesus. Some of the illustrations of Socrates were parabolic. Aristotle recognized the place of parable in his writings.

Stormy debate rages among Bible students regarding the further question of parables from the rabbis before and during the ministry of Jesus. Scholars like C. A. Bugge and Paul Fiebig pointed to numerous rabbinic parables deriving from the beginning of the first century A.D. Others, such as Jeremias, found almost none until after the days of Jesus. We do know of parables from the rabbis soon after the time of Jesus, and we do recognize that the parables of Jesus are not only far more compelling but center in the coming kingdom of God rather than in exposition of the Law or Torah as the rabbinic parables.

Jesus' Special Use of Parables Many of the parables grew out of the conflict situations when Jesus answered His religious critics. These answering parables, usually for Pharisees and sinners simultaneously, expose and extol. Jesus exposed the self-righteousness of His critics and extolled the kingdom of God. When John the Baptizer was accosted for being too serious and Jesus for being too frivolous, Jesus came back with the parable of the playing children (Matt 11:16–19; Luke 7:31–35) to expose the inconsistency of the criticism. In His most famous parable, He extolled the forgiving love of the father and exposed the hostile criticism of the unforgiving elder brother (Luke 15:11–32).

In fact, Jesus interpreted His ministry and its place in salvation history by means of parable. He addressed different audiences such as the crowds, the disciples, and the critics with definite purposes. Indeed, the Teller as well as the tale is important. That is, the fact that Jesus was the author affects the meaning. As Jesus interpreted His ministry through parables, these sometimes have a "Christological penetration." Jesus Himself appears indirectly in the story (Mark 3:23–27). The parables are not merely clever stories but proclamation of the gospel. The hearer must respond and is invited by the story to make a decision about the kingdom and the King. The parable of the wicked tenants (Mark 12:1–12) represented a blatant confrontation.

These stories got Jesus in trouble as He made veiled claims of kingliness and exposed the hypocrisy regnant in the religious hierarchy. One of the reasons they crucified Jesus was because of His challenging parables and the claims of his Kingdom.

Jesus' Different Kinds of Parables Jesus could turn people's ears into eyes, sometimes with a still picture and then again with a moving picture. He uttered (1) parabolic sayings referring to the salt of the earth (Matt. 5:13) or throwing pearls before swine (Matt. 7:6). These parable germs or incipient parables were generally one liners with a picturesque appeal to the imagination. Remarkably, the Gospel of John has no parables as such; it does include thirteen parabolic sayings.

Jesus also spoke (2) simple parables which represent a picture elaborated into a story. These extended pictures portray a general situation growing out of a typical experience and appealing to common sense. They are often specifically concerning the kingdom of God and are introduced with a saying, "The Kingdom of God is like." Examples are the paired parables of the treasure and the pearl (Matt 13:44–46), the tower builder and the warring king (Luke 14:28–32), and the lost sheep and lost coin (Luke 15:3–10). They are extended similes.

Additionally, Jesus told his famous (3) narrative parables that represent a specific situation and often include in the first sentence reference to a certain person. While Matthew reported a great many parabolic sayings, Luke contains numerous narrative parables, such as the parable of the unjust steward (16:1–8), the compassionate Samaritan (10:30–37), and the rich fool (12:16–21). A narrative parable is a dramatic story composed of one or more scenes, drawn from daily life yet focused on an unusual, decisive circumstance.

Special Literary Considerations Narrative parables and the simple parables total more than forty examples. Certain metaphors recur in the different parables. For example, seed parables such as those of the sower, the seed growing of itself, and the mustard seed in Mark 4 focus on the nature of the coming kingdom. Master/servant parables reflect a time of critical reckoning. Kingly parables, especially in Matthew, portray the sovereignty of the divine judgment and grace. Householder parables feature an authority figure whose purpose is resisted or rejected yet whose will is finally achieved.

This latter category points to the realism of rejection of the will of God fully allowable on the one hand by the divine provision of freedom, yet on the other hand the divine insistence of the eventual triumph of His loving purpose.

Attention to parable form also brings up the prominence of the question format, the refusal parables, and the place of direct discourse. Jesus intended to involve His hearers, and so He constructed many parables that amount to one big question. The parable of the servant and his wages moves by means of two questions (Luke 17:7–10). The parable of the unjust steward (Luke 16:1–8) includes four questions. These interrogatives within parables often define a dilemma (Luke 12:20; Mark 12:9) or call for an agreeing nod in one area of life that carries over to another.

The refusal parables are those that express the intention of a character not to do what is requested: "I do not will." The elder brother refused to enter the festivities in honor of the prodigal son (Luke 15:28), and wedding guests rejected the invitation to attend the festivities of a wedding (Matt. 22:3). These and other examples of the refusal to do the will of God recognize the reality of human pride, stubbornness, hypocrisy, and rejection Jesus encountered during His proclaiming ministry.

Direct discourse is also immensely important in many of the parables because it brings the stories to life. Through the human conversation the parable often makes its point, especially in the last speech. Surely Jesus delivered these lines from each of the parabolic characters in a most animated fashion and even interpreted His parables by the tone of His voice.

Common Theme of Jesus' Parables Jesus' great thesis centers on the kingdom of God (Mark 1:15). Each parable explores and expands the theme. The kingship of God or Yahweh may be found first in the Old Testament (Ps. 24:9–10; Isa. 6:5). Daniel 4 proclaims the divine sovereignty over the secular kingdoms, and the Ten Commandments require full obedience to God.

Jesus lifted the theme to new heights and through His parables portrayed the nature of the kingdom (Mark 4:26–29), the grace of the kingdom (Luke 18:9–17), the crisis of the kingdom (Luke 12:54–56), and the conditions of the kingdom such as commitment (Luke 14:28–30), forgiveness (Matt. 18:23–35), and compassion (Luke 10:25–37).

The parables further proclaim the kingdom as ethical, experiential or existential, eschatological, and evangelistic. Several parables accentuate ethical concerns such as attitude toward one's fellows (Luke 18:9–14; 15:25–32; Matt. 18:23–35). Jesus insisted on being religious through relationships. The rousing call to repentance embodied in many parables requires a moral and spiritual reorientation of life around the kingdom.

Many parables reach the watertable of common experience and illumine existence or life. Jesus could expose a pale or petrified life. He could convey the moving experience of being lost in the far country and then to come to oneself and go home (Luke 15:17). His parables exposed the inauthentic life aggressively self-centered and greedy (Luke 12:13–21; 16:19–31).

As Jesus proclaimed through parables, God was bursting into history, the hinge of history had arrived. He announced it with urgency. He brought an otherwordly perspective to bear in the parable of the rich fool (Luke 12:13–21). He foresaw the full future coming of the kingdom (Matt. 13:8,30,32,39).

The parables are evangelistic because they sought to stimulate a decision and change a life. They invited the audience to repent and believe. The parables intended to awaken faith. The Teller's faith was contagious. The segment about the elder brother (Luke 15:25–32) is unfinished and open-ended. He could choose to swallow his pride, activate his own forgiving spirit, put on his dancing shoes, and join the party.

Unspoken Parables Like the prophets, Jesus enacted some of His intended message. His parabolic acts were boldly done. For example, He chose from His larger following a special group of twelve disciples (Mark 3:13–19), symbolizing His creation of a new Israel. Throughout His ministry, Jesus graciously received spiritual and social outcasts as the Friend of sinners, indicating the Father's loving grace. He cursed the fig tree (Mark 11:12–14,20–21), pointing to the divine judgment on Israel. He rode into Jerusalem in regal humility on the first Palm Sunday, calling forth Zechariah's expectation. He cleansed the Temple (Mark 11:15–19), enacting God's will for Israel to be a light to the nations. At the last supper as He broke the bread and poured the wine, He enacted with miniparables the loving sacrifice of Calvary.

Parables Perspective on Life Some of the stories carry a pastoral and others a prophetic relevance. They have both sugar and steel. The parable of the mustard seed speaks pastorally about ending despair, and the parable of the persistent widow (Luke 18:1–8) encourages to hang in there. The parable of the barren fig tree (Luke 13:6–9) speaks prophetically concerning national priorities; the parable of the wicked tenants accosts arrogant religious leaders; and the parable of the rich fool confronts false confidence in materialism. Through the parable of the Pharisee and the tax collector, grace peers down on two people praying in the Temple, and appearances take a pounding. Grace shines on worship, and revelation happens!

See *Kingdom of God; Jesus.*   *Peter Rhea Jones*

PARACLETE (Pâ rȧ clēte) Transliteration of the Greek word Jesus used in John's Gospel for the

Holy Spirit. Literally, "One called alongside," Paraclete is translated many ways; "advocate" (applied to Christ, 1 John 2:1) and "Comforter" (John 14:16). See *Advocate; Comforter; Counselor.*

PARADISE (Păr′ ȧ dīse) Old Persian term which means literally "enclosure" or "wooded park," used in the Old Testament to speak of King Artaxerxes' forest (Neh. 2:8), and twice of orchards (Eccl. 2:5; Song of Sol. 4:13). All three New Testament occurrences (Luke 23:43; 2 Cor. 12:4; Rev. 2:7) refer to the abode of the righteous dead (heaven). The Greek Old Testament (Septuagint) used "paradise" to translate the Hebrew words for the Garden of Eden in Genesis 2—3. Over the years, the terms became synonymous, and eventually paradise came to refer to heaven. Jewish theology then developed an opposite place for wicked persons, *gehenna,* a burning furnace. See *Future Hope; Heaven.*

PARAH (Pā′ rah) Place name meaning, "heifer" or "young cow." Village in territory of Benjamin about five miles northeast of Jerusalem, identified with modern khirbet el-Farah (Josh. 18:23). The Hebrew *parath,* often translated Euphrates (so KJV, NAS, NRSV), may refer to the spring 'Ain Farah at Jeremiah 13:4−7. (Compare NAS, NRSV margin readings, "Parah.") NIV, REB simply transliterate the term.

PARALLELISM See *Poetry.*

PARALYSIS See *Palsy; Disabilities and Deformities.*

PARAMOUR An illicit sexual partner (Ezek. 23:20 KJV, NAS, NRSV; Hos. 3:1 RSV). Other translations read: lovers (NIV); male prostitutes (REB); and oversexed men (TEV).

PARAN (Pā′ ran) *1.* Wilderness area south of Judah, west of Edom, and north of Sinai. Israel camped there after leaving Sinai during the Exodus and sent spies to scout out the Promised Land from Kadesh, a location in Paran (Num. 10:11−12; 13:3,26). Chedorlaomer turned back his military campaign at Padan (Gen. 14:5−7). Ishmael made his home there after Abraham was forced to send Hagar and him away (Gen. 21:21). King Hadad of Edom eluded Joab by going through Padan to Egypt (1 Kings 11:17−18). *2.* Mount Paran appears as a poetic parallel to Mount Sinai (Deut. 33:2; compare Hab. 3:3) as the place of revelation. If not the same place as Sinai, the location is not known.

PARBAR (Pär′ bär) Hebrew term of uncertain meaning used only at 1 Chronicles 26:18. Some translations (KJV, NAS, RSV) merely transliterate the term. Others offer plausible translations:

(western) colonnade (NRSV, REB); western pavilion (TEV); court to the west (NIV). Suggested renderings of the plural of *parbar* (or a related term) in 2 Kings 23:11 include: precincts (NAS, NRSV), court (NIV), and suburbs (KJV). It was apparently a road, an open area, or a room near the Temple.

PARCHED CORN or GRAIN A common food prepared by roasting grains in a pan or by holding heads of grain over a fire (Lev. 23:14; Josh. 5:11; Ruth 2:14; 1 Sam. 17:17; 25:18; 2 Sam. 17:28). Parched grain served as food for harvest workers, soldiers, and refugees. Mosaic law prohibited the eating of parched grain before the first fruits of the grain had been offered to God. The exact type of grain is not indicated by the Hebrew term; probably barley or wheat was meant.

PARCHED LAND See *Scorched Land.*

PARCHED PLACES Expression some translations (KJV, NIV, NRSV) use for arid land (Jer. 17:6). Other translations include: stony wastes (NAS) and among the rocks (REB).

PARCHMENT See *Writing.*

PARDON An authoritive act reversing a sentence given under a guilty verdict. Prayer for God's pardon for sin is based on the greatness of God's

The parched land and places of the Wadi Arabah area south of the Dead Sea.

covenant love and on the long history of God's acts of forgiveness (Num. 14:19; Mic. 7:18). The Old Testament believers were already aware that the condition for seeking pardon was a repentant heart rather than ritual exactness (1 Chron. 29:18). God's willingness to abundantly pardon serves as an incentive to repentance (Isa. 55:7). See *Atonement; Forgiveness; Reconciliation.*

PARE To trim or shave off. The paring of nails served as a sign of mourning for lost parents (Deut. 21:12 KJV, REB, NRSV). An Israelite desiring to marry a female prisoner of war was required to allow her to cut her hair and pare her nails first. These actions perhaps symbolized purification on entering the covenant community.

PARENTS See *Family.*

PARK See *Paradise.*

PARLOUR British variant of parlor. The KJV used parlour in three passages. In each case, modern translations replace parlor with a term more suitable to the context: (1) inner chambers (NRSV), courts (REB), or rooms (NIV) of the Temple (1 Chron. 28:11); (2) dining hall (REB) or hall (NIV, NRSV) in which Saul shared a sacred meal with Samuel (1 Sam. 9:22); (3) the upper room (NIV) or roof chamber (NRSV, REB) of a palace (Judg. 3:20,23–25).

PARMASHTA (Pär măsh´ tà) Personal name, probably of Persian origin, possibly meaning, "strong-fisted" or "the very first." One of Haman's ten sons (Esth. 9:9).

PARMENAS (Pär´ mė nàs) Personal name meaning, "faithful" or "constant." One of the seven chosen by the Jerusalem congregation to distribute food to the Greek-speaking widows of that church (Acts 6:5).

PARNACH (Pär´ nă<u>ch</u>) Persian personal name of uncertain meaning. Father of Elizaphan (Num. 34:25).

PAROSH (Pā´ rŏsh) Personal name meaning, "flea." *1.* Ancestor of a postexilic family (Ezra 2:3; 8:3; KJV, Pharosh; 10:25; Neh. 7:8). *2.* One of the witnesses to Ezra's renewal of the covenant (Neh. 10:14), possibly the father of Pedaiah (Neh. 3:25). This Parosh was likely the chief member of the family above.

PAROUSIA (Pà roū´ sĭ à) Transliteration of Greek word which means "presence" or "coming." In New Testament theology it encompasses the events surrounding the second coming of Christ. See *Day of the Lord; Eschatology; Future Hope; Kingdom of God.*

PARRI (Pā´ à râi) Personal name meaning, "revelation of Yahweh." One of David's 30 elite warriors (2 Sam. 23:35) designated an Arbite, a resident of Arbah (Josh. 15:52). The parallel list has the name Naarai (1 Chron. 11:37).

PARSHANDATHA (Pär shăn dā´ thà) Personal name, probably of Persian origin, possibly meaning, "inquisitive." One of Haman's ten sons (Esth. 9:7).

PARSIN (Pär´ sĭn) See *Mene, Mene, Tekel, Parsin.*

PARTHIANS (Pär´ thĭ ans) Tribal people who migrated from Central Asia into what is now Iran. Their homeland was an area southeast of the Caspian Sea. They spoke an Aryan dialect very close to Persian and worshiped the Persian god, Ahura Mazda. The Parthians adopted Greek culture following their fall to Alexander the Great. About 250 B.C. they revolted against the Seleucid rule and reached a height of power under King Mithradates (ruled 171–138 B.C.). In 53 B.C. the Romans invaded but were defeated on several occasions. They did not gain control of Parthia until A.D. 114. Some Parthians were among those in Jerusalem on the Day of Pentecost who heard the gospel in their own language (Acts 2:9–11).

PARTIALITY Favor shown to one person over another, particularly on the basis of external factors such as economic level or ethnic background. Old Testament law contains frequent warnings to avoid partiality in rendering legal decisions (Lev. 19:15; Deut. 1:17; 16:19). The theological grounding of this prohibition is God's character, for God shows no partiality (2 Chron. 19:7). God's impartiality served as the basis for the early church's mission to the Gentiles (Acts 10:34–35; Rom. 2:9–11). James warned that showing partiality, particularly that based on economic distinctions, is incompatible with profession of faith in Jesus as Lord (2:1) and is sin (2:9). Ephesians 6:9 warned slaveholders to be fair in treating their slaves, for God is impartial and thus not influenced by human distinctions between master and slave.

PARTIES, JEWISH See *Jewish Parties.*

PARTITION Something which divides, especially an interior dividing wall. NAS referred to the veil separating the holy place from the holy of holies as a partition (Ex. 26:33). KJV referred to the gold chains separating the same two rooms in the Temple as a partition (1 Kings 6:21; compare NIV). Christ abolished "the middle wall of partition" through His death (Eph. 2:14). Christ abolished not only the hostility between Jews and Gentiles (2:15) but also made possible full fellowship of humanity with God (2:16).

PARTRIDGE A stout-bodied, medium-size game bird with variegated plumage. David likened his life as a fugitive from Saul to a hunted partridge (1 Sam. 26:20). The translation of the proverb of the partridge (Jer. 17:11) is difficult; the Hebrew is extremely terse, and one of the verbs is of uncertain meaning (brood, gather, or lay). Various translations understand the action in the following ways: a partridge sits on eggs which will not hatch (KJV); a partridge gathers chicks it did not hatch (RSV); a partridge sits on eggs it did not lay (REB); a partridge hatches eggs it did not lay

P
Q

(NAS, NIV, NRSV TEV). The KJV interpretation is an apt picture of riches which come to nothing. In other interpretations, the partridge who steals eggs or chicks is no less fortunate than any bird whose chicks grow and leave the nest.

PARUAH (Pȧ rū′ ah) Personal name meaning, "blossoming," "joyous," or "increase." Father of Jehoshaphat (1 Kings 4:17).

PARVAIM (Pär vā′ ĭm) Source of gold for Solomon's decoration of the Temple (2 Chron. 3:6). The place is perhaps el Farwaim (Farwa) in Yemen, or else a general term for the east.

PARZITES (Pär′ zītes) KJV alternate form of Perezites (Num. 26:20).

PASACH (Pā′ săch) Personal name perhaps meaning "divider." Member of the tribe of Asher (1 Chron. 7:33).

PASCHAL Relating to the Passover. Paul used the sacrifice of the paschal lamb as a picture of the death of Christ (1 Cor. 5:7 NRSV). By dating the crucifixion on the day of preparation for the Passover, John suggested the same image of Christ as the paschal lamb who takes away the sin of the world (John 19:14; compare 1:29).

PASDAMMIN (Păs dăm′ mĭn) Place name meaning, "boundary of blood." Scene of David's victory over the Philistines (1 Chron. 11:13). The site is probably between Socoh and Azekah, the same as Ephes-dammin (1 Sam. 17:1).

PASEAH (Pȧ sē′ ah) Personal name meaning, "lame." *1.* Member of the tribe of Judah (1 Chron. 4:12). *2.* Ancestor of a family of Temple servants (Neh. 7:51; KJV Phaseah). *3.* Father of Joiada (Neh. 3:6).

PASHUR (Păsh′ ŭr) Personal name meaning, "son of (the god) Horus." *1.* Chief officer in the Jerusalem Temple in the last years before Nebuchadnezzar's victory over the city. He had Jeremiah beaten and imprisoned (Jer. 20:1–2). He or another Pashur was the father of Gedaliah (Jer. 38:1). *2.* A man in Zedekiah's court in Jerusalem (Jer. 21:1). As the Babylonian army approached, Pashhur asked Jeremiah for a word from the Lord. Jeremiah prophesied the destruction of the city (21:1–7; compare 38:1–3). *3.* Forebear of a priestly family (1 Cor. 9:12) who returned from the Exile (Ezra 2:38) and who later gave up their foreign wives (10:22; compare Neh. 10:3; 11:12).

PASSION *1.* Any bodily desire which leads to sin (Rom. 6:12; Gal. 5:24; Eph. 2:3). Passion is especially used for strong sexual desire (Rom. 1:26–

27; 1 Cor. 7:9; 1 Thess. 4:5). Unregenerate life is characterized by slavery to passions (Eph. 2:3; Titus 3:3; 1 Pet. 1:14). Those who belong to Christ have crucified fleshly passions (Gal. 5:24; compare Rom. 6:5–14). In their frequent appeals to renounce passions, New Testament letters likely echo charges to baptismal candidates (Col. 3:5; 2 Tim. 2:22; Titus 2:12). *2.* KJV twice used the phrase "like passions" (Acts 14:15; Jas. 5:17) to mean "shared human nature." *3.* KJV, RSV used passion once (Acts 1:3) to mean the suffering which Christ endured from the night of the last supper until His death. NAS, NIV, NRSV replace passion with suffering, which is the usual translation of the underlying Greek (as in Luke 17:15; 24:26). REB, TEV read, "death."

PASSOVER (Păss′ ō vĕr) The most important Hebrew feast, commemorating their deliverance from Egyptian bondage. See *Festivals.*

PASTOR *1.* KJV translation of Hebrew term for shepherd in Jeremiah (2:8; 3:15; 10:21; 12:10; 22:22; 23:1,2). Modern translations generally substituted shepherd for pastor except at Jeremiah 2:8 (leader, NIV; ruler, NAS, NRSV). *2.* Pastor translates the Greek term *poimēn* (shepherd) only at Ephesians 4:11. The background of the term lies in the biblical image of the people of God as God's flock (Jer. 23:1–4; Ezek. 34:1–16; Luke 12:32; John 10:16). Pastoral ministry is closely associated with teaching (Eph. 4:11) as God's gift to the church. Such ministry fulfills its God-ordained purpose when it trains church members to be mature in faith and equipped for ministry and unifies the church in Christian faith and knowledge (Eph. 4:12–13). Self-promotion and political divisiveness run counter to the biblical ideal for pastoral ministry. In laying down His life for His sheep (John 10:11,15), Christ set the standard for pastoral ministry that goes beyond words to deeds. His sheep recognize His voice as a trustworthy guide (John 10:3–4). Pastoral ministry is an expression of love for Christ (John 21:15–17).

PASTORALS A convenient designation for First and Second Timothy and Titus. The title, which Anton first applied to these writings in 1753, highlights their concern for proper pastoral authority in the face of heresy. Scholarly debate has centered on the related questions of authorship and setting in the history of the early church. Traditionalists have argued Pauline authorship. Such interpreters generally argue that Paul's two-year imprisonment (Acts 28:16,30) ended, not in Paul's death, but in his release, followed by further missionary work in Achaia (2 Tim. 4:20), Macedonia (1 Tim. 1:3), and Asia Minor (2 Tim. 4:13,20) and a second Roman imprisonment (compare 2 Tim. 3:16). Such critics date the Pastorals after the first imprisonment between A.D. 61 and 68. Other interpreters assign the Pastorals to a disciple of Paul writing about A.D. 100. Such critics appeal to differences in vocabulary and content—missing are Paul's emphases on the union of the believer and Christ, the Spirit as the power of the new life, and freedom from the law. The interpreter's presuppositions concerning the permissibility of pseudonymous writings in the canon and concerning the development of the early church generally determine his or her weighing of the evidence. Whether by Paul or one of his later disciples, these writings reflect a changed agenda for the church. The issue is no longer the missionary concern to incorporate Gentile believers into the church, but the institutional concern to fight heresy within established churches and to present a sober witness to a negative society. See *Timothy, First Epistle to; Timothy, Second Epistle to; Titus, Epistle to.*

PASTURE Open land surrounding towns and villages, regarded as common property to be freely used by village shepherds and herdsmen (Num. 35:2,7; Josh. 14:4; 21:11). The same Hebrew term designates open space around a city or the sanctuary (Ezek. 27:28; 45:2; 48:17).

PATARA (Păt' å rà) See *Asia Minor, Cities of.*

PATH A walkway. Two contrasting paths are a common image for rival ways of life in Hebrew wisdom literature. The path of the wicked (Prov. 4:14) who forget God (Job 8:13) is crooked (Prov. 2:15). This approach to life contrasts with the path of righteousness (Ps. 23:3; Prov. 2:13,20). This alternate path is called the path of God (compare Pss. 17:5; 25:4,10) and of light (Job 24:13). This life-path entails living by the commands or instruction of the Lord (Ps. 119:35,105; Prov. 10:17). The reward for following this path is life (Prov. 10:17; 12:28; compare Ps. 16:11; Prov. 2:19; 5:6). The wise are those who follow this way (Prov. 15:24). The paths of justice (Prov. 2:8; 8:20), peace (Prov. 3:17), and righteousness refer to the practice of these qualities.

PATHROS (Păth' rös) Hebrew transliteration of Egyptian term for Upper (southern) Egypt. Upper Egypt included the territory between modern Cairo and Aswan. The NIV translates the term; other translations transliterate (Isa. 11:11; Jer. 44:1,15; Ezek. 29:14; 30:14).

PATHRUSIM (Păth rū' sĭm) Son of Mizraim (Egypt) and ancestor of the inhabitants of Upper (southern) Egypt who bore his name (1 Chron. 1:12).

PATHRUSITES (Păth rū' sītes) NIV term for Pathrusim.

PATIENCE An active endurance of opposition, not a passive resignation. *Patience* and *patient* are used to translate several Hebrew and Greek words. Patience is endurance, steadfastness, long-suffering, and forbearance.

God is patient (Rom. 15:5). He is slow to anger in relation to the Hebrews (Ex. 34:6; Num. 14:18, Neh. 9:17; Ps. 86:15; Isa. 48:9; Hos. 11:8–9). The Hebrews were frequently rebellious, but God patiently dealt with them. Jesus' parable of the tenants depicted God's patience with His people (Mark 12:1–11). God's patience with sinners allows time for them to repent (Rom. 2:4), especially in the apparent delay of the return of Christ (2 Pet. 3:9–10).

God's people are to be patient. The psalmist learned to be patient when confronted with the prosperity of the wicked (Ps. 37:1–3,9–13,34–38). Christians should face adversity patiently (Rom. 5:3–5). Patience is a fruit of the Spirit (Gal. 5:22). Christian love is patient (1 Cor. 13:4,7). Ministers are to be patient (2 Cor. 6:6).

Christians need patient endurance in the face of persecution. Hebrews stressed endurance as the alternative to shrinking back during adversity (Heb. 6:9–15; 10:32–29). Jesus is the great example of endurance (Heb. 12:1–3). Perseverance is part of maturity (Jas. 1:2–4). Job's perseverance is another example for suffering Christians (Jas. 5:11). John frequently highlighted the patient endurance of Christians (Rev. 2:2,19; 3:10; 13:10; 14:12). Christian patience is ultimately a gift from God (Rom. 15:5–6; 2 Thess. 3:5).

Warren McWilliams

PATMOS (Păt' mos) A small island (ten miles by six miles) in the Aegean Sea located about thirty-seven miles southwest of Miletus. The Romans used such places for political exiles. John's mention of the island in Revelation 1:9 probably means that he was such a prisoner, having been sent there for preaching the gospel. Eusebius (an early church father) wrote that John was sent to Patmos by Emperor Domitian in A.D. 95 and released after 1 ½ years. See *Revelation.*

PATRIARCHS, TESTAMENT OF THE TWELVE See *Pseudepigrapha.*

PATRIARCHS, THE Israel's founding fathers—Abraham, Isaac, and Jacob and the twelve sons of Jacob (Israel). The word *patriarch* comes from a combination of the Latin word *pater,* "father," and the Greek verb *archō,* "to rule." A patriarch is thus a ruling ancestor who may have been the founding father of a family, a clan, or a nation.

The idea of a binding agreement between God and humankind antedated the patriarchs, being first expressed in the time of Noah (Gen. 6:18; 9:8–17). The growth of the Hebrew nation was promised specifically to Abraham in the patriar-

P
Q

chal covenant (Gen. 15; 17), along with the provision of a land in which Abraham's offspring would dwell. Since several generations elapsed before this situation developed, the covenant with Abraham must be regarded as promissory. The promises made to Abraham established the concept of a people descended through Abraham, Isaac, and Jacob, who would be in a special historical and spiritual relationship with God. See *Covenant.*

Abraham, or Abram as he was called in the earlier chapters of Genesis, was a ninth-generation descendant of Shem, son of Noah. Abram's father Terah was born in Ur of the Chaldees, as were his brothers Nahor and Haran (Gen. 11:26,28). See *Shem; Terah; Ur.*

At an early period, Abraham had testified that God was the Most High God (Gen. 14:22), the righteous Judge of humankind (Gen. 15:14), and the Guarantor of the covenant of promise. He experienced close communion with God (Gen. 18:33; 24:40) and worshiped Him consistently to the exclusion of all other gods. His fidelity and obedience were characteristic features of his personality and made this renowned forefather of Israel (compare Rom. 4:1–4) an example of the way in which men and women are justified before God. See *Abraham; Nuzi.*

The line of descent by which the covenant was to be perpetuated consisted solely of Abraham's son Isaac; through him the covenant promises were continued. Isaac's name is generally thought

The island of Patmos on which John was probably exiled by the Romans.

to mean "laughter," but it possibly also conveys the more subtle sense of "joker." It commemorated the occasion when both Abraham and Sarah laughed at God's promise to provide them with a son in their old age (Gen. 17:17–19; 18:9–15).

We have very little information about the maturing years of Isaac except that he was used as the supreme test of Abraham's faith in the covenant promises. Under the patriarchal system, the father had the power of life or death over every living person and thing in his household. At the very moment that Isaac's life was to be taken, his position as covenant heir was safeguarded by the provision of an alternative sacrificial offering (Gen. 22:9–13). The circumstances attending his marriage to Rebekah afforded Isaac great comfort after the death of his mother (Gen. 24:67). Isaac prayed earnestly to God for covenant heirs, and in due time Rebekah became pregnant with twins when Isaac was 60 years old. Esau grew up to be a hunter, while Jacob followed the more sedentary life-style of his father by supervising the family's flocks and herds, moving with them when it was necessary to find fresh pasture (Gen. 25:27). Isaac unfortunately provoked sibling rivalry by favoring Esau above Jacob. The former brought his father tasty venison, whereas Jacob's culinary expertise seems only to have extended to preparing lentil soup (Gen. 25:28–29). In a moment of desperate hunger, Esau traded his birthright for some of Jacob's soup, thereby transferring to his brother a double portion of Isaac's estate as well as other rights.

In old age, Isaac's sight failed; and, when it became apparent that Esau might inherit the extra birthright provision after all, Rebekah conspired with her favorite son Jacob to deceive Isaac into blessing him rather than Esau. The success of the scheme made Esau extremely angry. To escape his vengeance Jacob fled to Mesopotamia on his father's instructions. Before he arrived he received a revelation from God which confirmed his inheritance in the covenant. Jacob later encountered the family of Laban, son of Nahor, and in due course married two of Laban's daughters. After some years absence Jacob finally returned to Mamre, where his father was living, and along with Esau buried him when he died aged 180 years.

Isaac's life, though less spectacular than Abraham's, was nevertheless marked by divine favor. He was circumcised as a sign of covenant membership, and owed his life to timely divine intervention when a youth (Gen. 22:12–14). He was obedient to God's will (Gen. 22:6,9), a man of devotion and prayer (Gen. 26:25), and a follower of peace (Gen. 26:20–23). He fulfilled his role as a child of promise (Gal. 4:22–23). See *Isaac.*

The life of Jacob, the last of the three great patriarchs, was marked by migrations, as had been the case with his ancestors. Although he lived successively at Shechem (Gen. 33:18–20), Bethel 35:6–7), and Hebron (Gen. 35:27), Jacob was basically a resident alien who did not have a capital city.

Just before Isaac's death, God appeared again to Jacob (Gen. 35:9) and renewed the promise of his new name. Jacob resided in Canaan thereafter, and only left when a famine overtook the land. Jacob and his sons were invited to live in Egypt by Joseph. As his life drew to a close Jacob, like his father Isaac, became blind; but he blessed his sons by means of a spoken last will and testament, after which he died peacefully. His body was embalmed in the Egyptian manner, and he was buried subsequently in the cave of Machpelah along with his ancestors (Gen. 49:30—50:13). Despite his apparent materialism, Jacob was a person of deep spirituality who, like Abraham, was esteemed highly by his pagan neighbors. Despite his fears, he behaved honorably and correctly in dealing with his avaricious father-in-law Laban and was equally consistent in fulfilling his vow to return to Bethel. Jacob trusted the God whom he had seen at Peniel to implement the covenant promises through him; and when he died, he left behind a clearly burgeoning nation. See *Jacob.*

The date of the patriarchal period has been much discussed. A time before 2000 B.C. (Early Bronze Age) seems too early and cannot be supported easily by reference to current archaeological evidence. The Middle Bronze period (2000–1500 B.C.) seems more promising because of contemporary archaeological parallels and also be-

cause many of the Negeb irrigation systems date from that period. Some scholars have suggested the Amarna period (1500–1300 B.C.) as the one in which the patriarchs lived, but this presents problems for any dating for the Exodus. The same objection applies to a Late Bronze Age (1500–1200 B.C.) period for the patriarchs. The least likely date is in the Judges period or the time of king David. All such dates do not allow time for the patriarchal traditions to have developed and make it impossible for Abraham, Isaac, and Jacob to be fitted realistically into an already-known chronology. A date in the Middle Bronze Age seems to offer the most suitable solution to a complex problem of dating. *R. K. Harrison*

PATROBAS (Păt' rō bàs) Personal name meaning, "life of (or from) father." Member of a Roman house church whom Paul greeted (Rom. 16:14).

PAU (Pā' ū) Edomite city meaning, "they cry out." Hadar's (Hadad) capital (Gen. 36:39). The parallel in 1 Chronicles 1:50 gives the name as Pai. It may be Wadi Fai west of the southern end of the Dead Sea.

PAUL The outstanding missionary and writer of the early church. Paul the apostle and his theology are important in the New Testament not only because thirteen Epistles bear his name but also because of the extended biographical information given in the Book of Acts. From the information in these two sources, we piece together a reasonable picture of one of the major personalities of early

The traditional site of the prison of Paul and Silas at Philippi.

Christianity. The letters of Paul as listed in the New Testament include Romans through Philemon. (Dates given below are approximate.)

Early Life and Training (A.D. 1–35) Paul's Jewish name was Saul, given at birth after his father or some near kin, or even after the famous Old Testament King Saul, who like Paul was from the tribe of Benjamin. Being born in a Roman city and claiming Roman citizenship, Paul (*Paulos*) was his official Roman name. Normally, a citizen would have three names similar to our first, middle, and

Reconstruction of Caesarea Maritima where Paul was imprisoned for two years (Acts 23:31—26:32).

last names. The New Testament records only the name Paul which would have been the middle or last name, since the first name was usually indicated only by the initial. *See Rome; Roman Empire; Roman Law.*

Tarsus, the place of Paul's birth (Acts 22:3), is still a bustling city a few miles inland from the Mediteranean on Turkey's southern shore. By Paul's day it was a self-governing city, loyal to the Roman Empire. We do not know how Paul's parents or forebearers came to live in Tarsus. Many Jewish families emigrated from their homeland willingly or as a result of foreign intervention in the centuries before Christ. A nonbiblical story says that Paul's parents migrated from a village in Galilee, but this cannot be verified. *See Tarsus.*

Growing up in a Jewish family meant that Paul was well trained in the Jewish Scriptures and tradition (Acts 26:4–8; Phil. 3:5–6) beginning in the home with the celebration of the Jewish holy days: Passover, Yom Kippur, Hanukkah, and others. At an early age he entered the synagogue day school. Here he learned to read and write by copying select passages of Scripture. He learned the ancient Hebrew language from Old Testament texts. At home his parents probably spoke the current dialect—Aramaic. As Paul related to the larger community, he learned the Greek language. Every Jewish boy also learned a trade. Paul learned the art of tentmaking which he later used as a means of sustenance (Acts 18:3).

Paul eventually went to Jerusalem to study un-

der the famous rabbi, Gamaliel. He was probably 13 to 18 years old. See *Gamaliel.* Paul had been well trained by the best Jewish teacher of that day (Acts 22:3). Paul became very zealous for the traditions, that is teachings, of his people (Gal. 1:14). He was a Pharisee (Phil. 3:5).

This zealous commitment to the study of the Old Testament laws and traditions is the background of Paul's persecution of his Jewish brothers who believed Jesus was the Messiah. Luke introduced Paul in the Book of Acts at the execution of Stephen. Now Stephen was executed because he placed Jesus (1) superior to the law and (2) superior to the Temple. Furthermore he claimed (3) that the fathers of the Jewish nation had always been rebellious. Paul, from his training, vigorously disagreed with Stephen's point of view. Stephen opposed the very foundations of Judaism since the days of Moses. Stephen's sermon apparently stimulated Paul's persecution of the church (Acts 8:1–3, 9:1–2; 26:9–11; Phil. 3:6; Gal. 1:13). To be an effective persecutor, Paul would need to know as much as possible about Jesus and the church. He knew the message of Christianity: Jesus' resurrection, His messiahship, and His availability to all humankind. He simply rejected the gospel. See *Acts of the Apostles; Stephen.*

Paul's Conversion (A.D. 35) Three accounts tell of Paul's Damascus Road experience: Acts 9:3–19; 22:6–21; 26:13–23. The variations in details are accounted for by recognizing that each story is told to a different audience on a different occasion. Paul was traveling to Damascus to arrest

Jewish people who had accepted Jesus as the Messiah. This was legally possible since city governments were known to permit the Jewish sector of the city a reasonable degree of self-government. The journey would take at least a week using donkeys or mules to ride and carry provisions.

As Paul neared Damascus, a startling light forced him to the ground. The voice asked: "Why persecutest thou me," and identified the speaker as Jesus—the very one whom Stephen had seen at the right hand of God when Paul witnessed Stephen's stoning. Paul was struck blind and was led into the city. Ananias met Paul and told him that he had been chosen by God as a messenger for the Gentiles (9:17). After Paul received his sight, like other believers before him, he was baptized.

In this conversion experience, Paul accepted the claims of Jesus and the church, the very thing he was seeking to destroy. Jesus was truly the Messiah and took priority over the Temple and the law. The experience was also Paul's call to carry the gospel to the Gentile world (9:15; 22:21).

Both his conversion and call are reflected in Paul's letters. He wrote that Jesus had appeared to him (1 Cor. 15:8–10; 9:1); the gospel Paul preached had come by revelation (Gal. 1:12); he had been called by God (Gal. 1:1; Eph. 3:2–12). His conversion brought a complete change in the inner controlling power of his life. It was like dying and receiving a new life (Gal. 2:20) or being created anew (2 Cor. 5:17–20). This experience of radical change and call to the Gentiles provided the motivation to travel throughout the Roman world. See *Conversion*.

Paul's Missionary Journeys (A.D. 46–61) (1) The first missionary journey (A.D. 46–48) began at Antioch (Acts 13—14). The church at Antioch had been founded by Hellenistic Christian believers like Stephen (Acts 11:19–26). Barnabas became its prominent leader, and Paul was his associate. Acts makes it clear that the entire church was involved in the world mission project, and the church chose Paul and Barnabas to be their representatives. John Mark went along as an important assistant. Their itinerary took them from Antioch (Antakya of modern Turkey) to the seaport of Seleucia. By ship they traveled to Cyprus. They landed at Salamis and traveled the length of the island to Paphos, from whence they set sail to Perga on Turkey's southern shore. Entering the highlands, they came into the province of Galatia where they concentrated their efforts in the southern cities of Antioch, Iconium, Lystra, and Derbe. Their typical procedure was to enter a new town, seek out the synagogue, and share the gospel on the sabbath day. Usually Paul's message caused a division in the synagogue, and Paul and Barnabas would seek a Gentile audience. From Paul's earliest activities, it became evident that the gospel he preached caused tension between believers and

the synagogue. This first journey produced results. In each city many turned to the new way (Acts 13:44,52; 14:1–4,20–28); and a minimal organization was established in each locality (Acts 14:23). He later addressed an epistle to this district—Galatians. See *Asia Minor.*

(2) Paul's second journey (A.D. 49–52) departed from Antioch with Silas as his associate (Acts 15:36—18:18). They traveled overland through what is now modern Turkey to the Aegean port of Troas. A vision directed Paul to go to Philippi in the province of Macedonia. Philippi was a Roman city with no synagogue and a minimal Jewish population. Paul established a church there as further attested by his letter to the Philippians. From there he traveled to Thessalonica and Berea. His preaching in Athens met with meager results. His work in Corinth (the province of Achaia) was well received and even approved, in an oblique fashion, by the Roman governor, Gallio. From Corinth, Paul returned to Caesarea, visited Jerusalem, and then Antioch (Acts 18:22).

(3) Paul's third missionary venture (A.D. 52–57) centered in the city of Ephesus from which the gospel probably spread into the surrounding cities such as the seven churches in Revelation (Acts 18:23–20:6; Rev. 2—3). From Ephesus he carried on a correspondence with the Corinthian church and possibly other churches. While in Corinth at the end of this journey, he wrote the Epistle to the Romans. See *Romans; Corinthians.*

When Paul returned to Jerusalem for his last visit (21:17—26:32), he was soon arrested and imprisoned—first in Jerusalem and then later transferred to Caesarea (A.D. 57–59). At first the charges against him were that he had brought a Gentile into the restricted areas of the Temple. Later, he was accused of being a pestilent fellow. The real reasons for his arrest are noted: the crowd was enraged at his mentioning his call to the Gentiles (Acts 22:21–22), and he stated to the Sanhedrin that he was arrested because of his belief in the resurrection. These two reasons, or beliefs, were the controlling motivation of Paul's life from conversion to arrest. See *Resurrection; Sanhedrin.*

Paul was eventually transferred to Rome (A.D. 60–61) as a prisoner of the emperor. His story in the New Testament ends there. The tradition outside the New Testament that tells of Paul's execution in Rome is reasonable. The tradition that he traveled to Spain is problematic.

Paul and the churches (1) Paul did not hesitate to remind the churches that he possessed apostolic authority from the Lord. Galatians 1—2 is his most intensive statement of this. He blatantly stated that his appointment was from God (1:1), and that he preached the authentic gospel (1:8) because he received it by revelation (1:12).

He had been called by God to carry the gospel to the Gentiles (1:16). This call was recognized by

P
Q

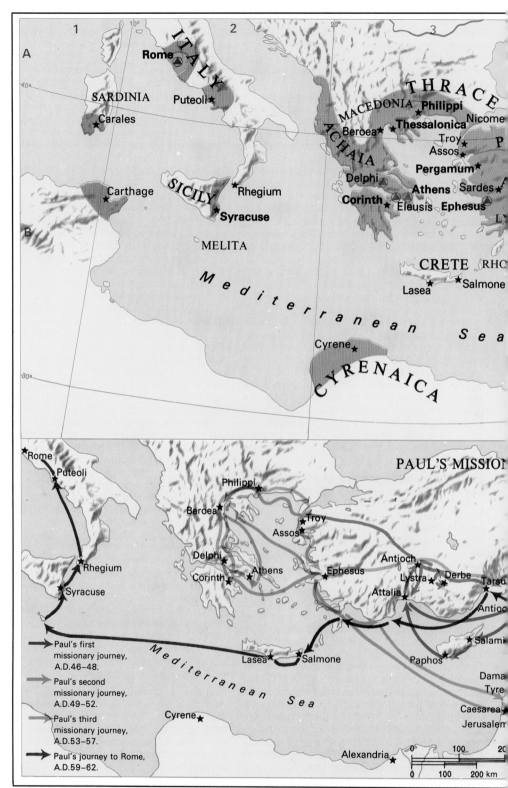

PAUL'S MISSION

Paul's first
missionary journey,
A.D. 46–48.

Paul's second
missionary journey,
A.D. 49–52.

Paul's third
missionary journey,
A.D. 53–57.

Paul's journey to Rome,
A.D. 59–62.

© carta

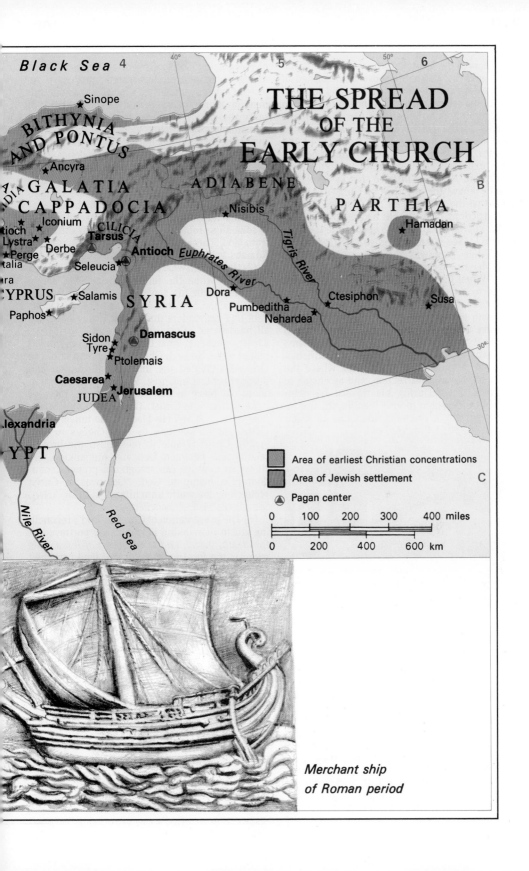

Black Sea 4

Sinope ★

BITHYNIA
AND PONTUS

Ancyra ★

GALATIA
CAPPADOCIA

★ Iconium
tioch ★ ★ CILICIA
Lystra ★ ★
★ Perge Derbe ★ Tarsus
talia
ra Seleucia ★

Antioch ★

ADIABENE

★ Nisibis

THE SPREAD
OF THE
EARLY CHURCH

B

PARTHIA

Hamadan ★

CYPRUS ★ Salamis
Paphos ★

Euphrates River

SYRIA

Dora ★
★ Pumbeditha
Nehardea ★

Tigris River

Ctesiphon ★

Susa ★

30°

Sidon ★
Tyre ★
★ Ptolemais

Damascus ◉

Caesarea ★
★ Jerusalem
JUDEA

lexandria

YPT

Nile River

Red Sea

⬛ Area of earliest Christian concentrations
⬛ Area of Jewish settlement
◉ Pagan center

C

0   100   200   300   400 miles
|___|___|___|___|___|___|___|___|
0   200   400   600 km

Merchant ship
of Roman period

the leaders of the Jerusalem church (2:7–10), the very church in which the most distinguished of the apostles resided—Peter, James, and John. In most of his letters, Paul identified himself from the beginning as an apostle of Christ Jesus. His certainty of the gospel and his relationship to Christ were the grounds of his relation to the churches. The Epistle of Paul to the Ephesians further expresses Paul's commitment to the Gentile mission. Again he insisted that by revelation (3:3) he knew the mystery of Christ which is simply that the gospel is for the Gentiles without any restrictions (3:6–9). He had been given the specific charge to carry the gospel to the Gentiles (Acts 9:15). See *Galatians, Epistle to; Gentiles.*

(2) While Paul was intensely aware of his calling, he also recognized his dependency upon others. When he was criticized for his own willingness to accept Gentiles without their being circumcised, he was willing to enter into dialogue with the Christians in Jerusalem (Acts 15) to resolve the question. Paul must have realized that he, as well as the young Gentile Christians, needed the approval and support of the Christian leaders in Jerusalem, the very place where the crucifixion, burial, resurrection, and ascension of Jesus took place. During his travels, he often returned to Jerusalem to visit the church, and he brought gifts to it on more than one occasion (Acts 11:29–30; 1 Cor. 16:1–4).

The colonnaded Arcadian Way of Ephesus, the city which became Paul's home for over two years.

(3) We must not think of Paul as an established administrator over the churches he founded. His letters give evidence that he did not command or dictate to his churches; rather he persuaded them. The lengthy correspondence with the church at Corinth was Paul's effort to persuade them to adopt the correct attitude toward specific problems as well as toward himself. He could only admonish the churches through the gospel.

Paul's Theology Paul's writings are the major source of Christian theology both because of the amount of material and because of Paul's intensively theological writing style. (1) Human beings are alienated from God. They had the opportunity of recognizing God as Creator and themselves as dependent creatures, but instead they have rejected God and established themselves as the ultimate authority. God permitted humankind to make the choice. The result of such a choice is humankind's immorality, idolatry, and the suffering that human beings impose upon one another. In short, our declaring our independence from God has given sin an opportunity. While Gentiles have made their own abilities absolute, the Jews have made the law absolute. Each group has alienated themselves from God. This is the bondage of sin. Unfortunately, humans do not have the ability to solve this problem. We are hopelessly estranged from God. These ideas are especially described in Romans 1:18–3:8. See *Sin; Anthropology.*

(2) Paul's answer to humankind's alienation was that "when the fulness of time was come, God sent forth his son" (Gal. 4:4). He further described the Son in Colossians 1:15–20. First, Paul told his readers that Christ is the model for all humankind. He is the image of God (1:15). Christ represents what God would like all human beings to be. Second, Christ is bound up with the One who created the universe. Its design and purpose centers in Christ. Whatever our question about our place in the world might be, the ultimate answer is in Christ. Third, based on Christ's relation to God and His place in the universe, He is the appropriate one to reconcile us to God (1:20). Christ is able to reestablish the broken relationship between God and humankind. He shows us how we can realign our proper dependent relationship to God. "God was in Christ reconciling the world unto himself" (2 Cor. 5:19). See *Conversion; Reconciliation.*

(3) The presentation of Christ as God's reconciling gift to humankind is graphically portrayed in the *death, burial, and resurrection of Jesus.* This event is the focal point of all that Paul preached and wrote. "For I determined not to know anything among you, save Jesus Christ, and him crucified" (1 Cor. 2:2). The *death, burial, and resurrection* of Jesus must be thought of as a unit. "If Christ be not risen, then . . . your faith is also vain" (1 Cor. 15:14). Paul could think of Christ's death as a Passover sacrifice (1 Cor. 5:7), as a representative sacrifice (2 Cor. 5:14), or as a ransom (1 Tim. 2:5–6). When Paul stressed the resurrection event, he thought in terms of the doctrine of the future which he had inherited from his Jewish background: (a) Human history has an end which will begin a new world. (b) This will begin with the coming of the Messiah. (c) An intense encounter between good and evil will take place. (d) The dead will be resurrected. Jesus' resurrection is evidence that God has already begun the messianic era. It guarantees the hope that the complete resurrection and the new world is sure to come (1 Cor. 15:20–24). Jesus' death and resurrection was God's way of verifying that Jesus

is the One who brings about reconciliation between humankind and God. See *Jesus, Life and Ministry of; Christology; Future Hope.*

(4) When Paul thought about the person who accepts God's offer of reconciliation in Christ, he described persons of faith, using Abraham as a worthy example (Rom. 4:3). Abraham had a right relation to God because of his response of faith to God's offer. Paul further described Abraham as one who was "fully convinced that God was able to do what he had promised" (Rom. 4:21 NRSV). This is applied to Christians: "It [righteousness] will be reckoned to us who believe [have faith] in him who raised Jesus our Lord from the dead" (Rom. 4:24 NRSV). Faith is simply accepting as certain the promise of salvation God has made through Christ. This response in faith is so dynamic and vital that it has transforming power and is like creating a new person (Gal. 2:20; 2 Cor. 5:17–19). The person of faith is a new creation with a new motivating, energizing force, the Holy Spirit (Rom. 8:9–11). The person of faith is truly "in Christ." See *Faith.*

(5) The believer does not come into reconciliation in isolation. It happens in a community of faith. Paul began his missionary activities out of a congregation of believers. Wherever people became believers, a community existed known by the word *church.* Paul never advised a person of faith to live alone but rather to fellowship with the church. This believing community is intimately associated with Christ, who holds a position of dignity and authority over the church—He is its Head (Eph. 1:22–23). At the same time Christ loves the church, and He gave Himself for it; the church is subject to Christ in all matters (Eph. 5:21–33). This new community performs two functions: (a) It nurtures the person of faith so that he or she may mature "unto the measure of the stature of the fulness of Christ" (Eph. 4:13). (b) It witnesses to God's power to reconcile humankind to Himself by its example of Christian fellowship within its walls and by evangelistic outreach beyond itself (Eph. 3:10). See *Church.*

(6) The reconciled person has a new life-style. Paul expressed a concern for ethics. He listed vices: Galatians 5:19–21; Colossians 3:5–11; Ephesians 4:17–19; 1 Corinthians 5; 6:9–10; 2 Corinthians 12:20–21, and others. He also listed worthy qualities: Galatians 5:22–23; Colossians 3:12–14; Philippians 4:8. He gave advice to Christian households: Colossians 3:18—4:1; Ephesians 5:21—6:9. He offered guidance in marriage matters: 1 Corinthians 7. Although Paul expected worthy Christian conduct, he was not legalistic. Legalism means keeping rules for rule's sake. Rules are essential for Christian nurture. In an extended discussion about Christian conduct (1 Cor. 8:1—11:1) he emphasized that a believer will be sensitive to the effect his conduct will have on a fellow believer (1 Cor. 8:9–12). The ultimate standard of Christian conduct is Christ Himself. After exhorting believers to be concerned about their actions toward each other, Paul gave one of his most beautiful descriptions of the example of Jesus' giving Himself for others (Phil. 2:1–11). So Christ gives Himself as God's reconciling agent to bring human beings into a right relation with God, living a life motivated by the Spirit. See *Ethics.*   *Oscar S. Brooks*

PAULUS, SERGIUS See *Sergius Paulus.*

PAVEMENT See *Gabbatha.*

PAVILION (Pă vĭl iŏ n) A large, often richly decorated tent. KJV used pavilion seven times: three times in the literal sense of tents used in military campaigns (1 Kings 20:12,16; Jer. 43:10); twice of the thick canopy of clouds surrounding God (2 Sam. 22:12; Ps. 18:11) which illustrates the mystery of God; and twice as an image of God's protection (Pss. 27:5; 31:20). NAS, NIV, and NRSV substituted various terms (booths, canopy, shelter, tabernacle, tent) in each of these passages. The NAS used pavilion in the literal sense of tent in Daniel 11:45. Elsewhere in modern translations, pavilion appears in poetic passages: a pavilion for the sun (Ps. 19:5 NIV); God's pavilion of clouds (Job 36:29 NAS, REB, NIV, NRSV); a pavilion protecting Jerusalem from heat and rain (Isa. 4:5, RSV).

Roman pavement, or paving stones, on the main street at Caesarea Maritima.

PEACE OFFERING See *Sacrifice and Offering.*

PEACE, SPIRITUAL Sense of well-being and fulfillment that comes from God and is dependent on His presence.

Old Testament The concept of spiritual peace is most often represented by the Hebrew root *slm* and its derivatives, the most familiar being the noun *shalom.* Its basic meaning is "wholeness" or "well-being." (See, for example, Gen. 28:20–22; Judg. 6:23; 18:6; 1 Kings 2:33.) The Law, the Prophets, and the Writings of the Old Testament each bear testimony that such peace is the gift of God, for God alone can give peace in all its fullness (Lev. 26:6; 1 Chron. 12:18; 22:9; 1 Kings 2:33; Isa. 26:12; 52:7; Ezek. 34:25; 37:26; Zech. 6:13; Mal. 2:5–6; Job 22:21; 25:2; Pss. 4:8; 29:11; 37:37; 85:8; 122:6–8; 147:14; Prov. 3:17). Spiritual peace may be equated with salvation (Isa. 52:7; Nah. 1:15). Its absence may be equated with judgment (Jer. 12:12; 14:19; 16:5; 25:37; Lam. 3:17; Ezek. 7:15). It is available to all who trust in God (Isa. 26:3) and love His law (Ps. 119:165—note that in vv. 166–168 this love is clearly understood to mean obedience!) This peace is clearly identified with a righteous life apart from which no one is able to find true peace (Isa. 32:17; 48:22; 57:1–2). Thus peace and righteousness are often linked in the Old Testament (Pss. 72:7; 85:10; Isa. 9:7; 32:17; 48:18; 60:17), as are peace and justice (Isa. 59:8). To be at peace is to be upright (Mal. 2:6), to be faithful (2 Sam. 20:19), to be an upholder of the truth (Esth. 9:30; Zech. 8:19), and to practice justice (Isa. 59:8; Zech. 8:16). Throughout the Old Testament spiritual peace is realized in relationship. It is realized when people are rightly related to each other and to God.

New Testament The Greek word *eirēnē* corresponds to the Hebrew *shalom* expressing the idea of peace, well-being, restoration, reconciliation with God, and salvation in the fullest sense. God is "the God of peace" (Rom. 15:33; Phil. 4:9; 1 Thess. 5:23; Heb. 13:20). The Gospel is "the good news of peace" (Eph. 6:15; Acts 10:36) because it announces the reconciliation of believers to God and to one another (Eph. 2:12–18). God has made this peace a reality in Jesus Christ, who is "our peace." We are justified through Him (Rom. 5:1), reconciled through the blood of His cross (Col. 1:20), and made one in Him (Eph. 2:14). In Him we discover that ultimate peace which only God can give (John 14:27). This peace is experienced as an inner spiritual peace by the individual believer (Phil. 4:7; Col. 3:15; Rom. 15:13). It is associated with receptiveness to God's salvation (Matt. 10:13), freedom from distress and fear (John 14:27; 16:33), security (1 Thess. 5:9–10), mercy (Gal. 6:16; 1 Tim. 1:2), joy (Rom. 14:17; 15:13), grace (Phil. 1:2; Rev. 1:4), love (2 Cor. 13:11; Jude 2), life (Rom. 8:6),

and righteousness (Rom. 14:17; Heb. 12:11; Jas. 3:18). Such peace is a fruit of the Spirit (Gal. 5:22) that forms part of the "whole armor of God" (Eph. 6:11,13), enabling the Christian to withstand the attacks of the forces of evil. Thus, the New Testament gives more attention to the understanding of spiritual peace as an inner experience of the individual believer than does the Old Testament. In both the Old and the New Testament, spiritual peace is realized in being rightly related—rightly related to God and rightly related to one another. *Hulitt Gloer*

PEACEMAKERS Those who actively work to bring about peace and reconciliation where there is hatred and enmity. God blesses peacemakers and declares them to be His children (Matt. 5:9). Those who work for peace share in Christ's ministry of bringing peace and reconciliation (2 Cor. 5:18–19; Eph. 2:14–15; Col. 1:20).

PEACOCK A male of any of several species of large pheasants, native to southeastern Asia and the East Indies, which are raised as ornamental birds. KJV translated two Hebrew words as peacock. Modern translations replaced peacock with ostrich at Job 39:13. NAS, NRSV read peacock with KJV at 1 Kings 10:22; 2 Chronicles 9:21. Other translations read monkey (REB, RSV) or baboon (NIV, NRSV margin).

PEARL See *Jewels and Jewelry; Minerals and Metals.*

PEASANTRY NAS and RSV translation of an obscure Hebrew term used only in Deborah's song of victory (Judg. 5:7,11). KJV, NIV, TEV followed the Targum (Aramaic paraphrase) and Syriac version in reading villages. REB read champion. Various commentators have suggested leading class, warriors, and strength as possible meanings.

PEDAHEL (Pĕd′ á hĕl) Personal name meaning, "God delivers." Leader of the tribe of Naphtali whom Moses appointed to assist Joshua and Eliezer in the distribution of land to the tribes living west of the Jordan (Num. 34:28).

PEDAHZUR (Pĕ dăh′ zŭr) Personal name meaning, "(the) Rock redeems." Father of Gamaliel (Num. 1:10; 2:20; 7:54,59; 10:23).

PEDAIAH (Pĕ dâi′ ah) Personal name meaning, "Yah redeems." *1.* Maternal grandfather of King Jehoiakim (2 Kings 23:36). *2.* Father (so 1 Chron. 3:18–19) or uncle (so Ezra 3:2,8; 5:2; Neh. 12:1; Haggai 1:1,12,14; 2:2,23) of Zerubbabel. First Chronicles presents Pedaiah and Shealtiel as brothers. *3.* Manassite father of Joel (1 Chron. 27:20). *4.* Son of Parosh assisting in Nehemiah's repair of the wall (Neh. 3:25). *5.* Witness to Ezra's renewal of the covenant (Neh. 8:4), perhaps identical with 4. 6. Benjaminite father of Joed (Neh. 11:7). 7. Levite whom Nehemiah appointed a Temple treasurer (Neh. 13:13).

PEDDLER One who sells goods, usually on the street or door-to-door. Paul denied being a peddler of God's word (2 Cor. 2:17). Here Paul either emphasized that he did not preach for pay (1 Cor. 9:12,15) or that he did not use tricks to gain converts (2 Cor. 4:2; 12:16).

PEDIMENT NRSV term for the stone base upon which Ahab set the bronze sea after removing it from the twelve bronze oxen (2 Kings 16:17). Other translations for pediment include: base (NIV), foundation (TEV), pavement (KJV, NAS). Ahab's changes in the Temple equipment were an attempt to gain favor with the Assyrians.

PEG A small, cylindrical or tapered piece of wood (or some other material). Pegs were used: to secure tents (Judg. 4:21–22; 5:26); to hang articles (Isa. 22:23,25; Ezek. 15:3); to weave cloth (Judg. 16:14); even to dig latrines (Deut. 23:13). Isaiah 22:23–25 used the image of a peg which gives way to picture false security in a leader. Zechariah 10:4 used the peg as one of several images for rulers. In Isaiah 33:22 secure tent pegs symbolize that God keeps Jerusalem secure. The enlarged tent and strengthened tent pegs of Isaiah 54:2 illustrate God's restoration of Jerusalem.

PEKAH (Pē' kah) A personal name meaning, "open-eyed." Officer in Israel's army who became king in a bloody coup by murdering King Pekahiah (2 Kings 15:25). His reign of twenty years (15:27) probably is the total time he held military control in Gilead and Samaria. Pekah appeared to be the leader in Gilead during Menahem's reign but surrendered control there when Tiglath-pileser III of Assyria confirmed Menahem's rule. Pekah then was given a high office in the army, and the coup followed shortly after Pekahiah succeeded Menahem. Pekah reigned in Samaria 752–732 B.C. and was in turn assassinated by Hoshea (15:30). See *Menahem.*

PEKAHIAH (Pěk' à hī' ah) A personal name meaning, "Yah has opened his eyes." King of Israel 742–740 B.C. He succeeded his father, Menahem, as a vassal of the Assyrian throne (2 Kings 15:23). The tense political situation he inherited was very hostile, as the loyalists and rebel zealots vied for control. Pekahiah's uneventful reign ended when he was assassinated by an army officer, Pekah (15:25), who was supported by Syria and opposed to the Assyrian domination. See *Pekah.*

PEKOD (Pē' kŏd) Hebrew for "punishment" or "judgment" which plays on the name Puqadu, an Aramean tribe inhabiting the area east of the mouth of the Tigris (Jer. 50:21; Ezek. 23:23). Sargon II (722–705 B.C.) incorporated Pekod into the Assyrian Empire. Pekod formed part of the Babylonian Empire in the time of Jeremiah and Ezekiel.

PELAIAH (Pē lai' ah) Personal name meaning, "Yahweh is wonderful (or performs wonders)." 1. Descendant of David (1 Chron. 3:24). 2. Levite assisting in Ezra's public reading of the law (Neh. 8:7). 3. Levite witnessing Nehemiah's covenant (Neh. 10:10), perhaps identical to 2.

PELALIAH (Pē lå lī' ah) Personal name meaning, "Yahweh intercedes." Ancestor of a priest in Ezra's time (Neh. 11:12).

PELATIAH (Pěl à tī' ah) Personal name meaning, "Yahweh delivers." 1. Descendant of David (1 Chron. 3:21). 2. One of the Simeonites destroying the remaining Amalekites at Mount Seir (1 Chron. 4:42). 2. Judean prince who offered "wicked counsel," perhaps appealing to Egypt for help in a revolt against the Babylonians (Ezek. 11:1,13; compare Jer. 27:1–3; 37:5,7,11). 4. Witness to Nehemiah's covenant (Neh. 10:22).

PELEG (Pē' lěḡ) Personal name meaning, "division" or "watercourse." Descendant of Shem (Gen. 10:25), ancestor of Abraham (Gen. 11:16–19; 1 Chron. 1:19,25) and Jesus (Luke 3:35). Peleg's name is attributed to one of the many firsts recorded in Genesis, the "division" of the earth or land. Tradition associates this division with the confusing of languages and the consequent scattering of peoples from Babel (Gen. 11:8–9). Noting that *peleg* often refers to a stream of water (Job 29:6; Pss. 1:3; 46:4; 119:136; Prov. 5:16; 21:1; Isa. 30:25; 32:2), some suggest that the "division" of the land refers to irrigation ditches crisscrossing the landscape. According to this interpretation, Peleg's name commemorates the beginnings of organized agriculture. Though Peleg's descendants are only traced through Abraham, Peleg is recognized as the ancestor of all the Semitic peoples of Mesopotamia, while his brother Joktan was ancestor of the Arabian Semites. See *Table of Nations.*

PELET (Pē' lět) Personal name derived from a root meaning, "escape." 1. Descendant of Caleb (1 Chron. 2:47). 2. Benjaminite warrior who defected from Saul to David (1 Chron. 12:3).

PELETH (Pē' lěth) Personal name meaning, "swift." 1. Father of On (Num. 16:1). The name is possibly a textual corruption of Pallu (Gen. 46:9; Num. 26:5,8), whose descendants are also associated with the Korah rebellion (Num. 26:9–10). 2. A Jerahmeelite (1 Chron. 2:33).

PELETHITES (Pē′ lĕth īte) A family name meaning, "courier." Foreign mercenaries King David employed as body guards and special forces. Their leader was Benaiah (2 Sam. 8:18). The Pelethites are mentioned in conjunction with the Cherethites. These two groups probably were sea peoples who formed a loyalty to David during his days in the Philistine country while evading Saul. They remained with him until his death, fighting for him during the rebellions against his throne. Following his death, they helped Solomon purge the kingdom of David's enemies. See *Cherethites.*

PELICAN Any member of a family of large, web-footed birds with gigantic bills having expandable pouches attached to the lower jaw. Pelicans are found in Palestine. The Hebrew term translated pelican in Leviticus 11:18; Deuteronomy 14:17, however, suggests a bird which regurgitates its food to feed its young. Other passages (Ps. 102:6; Isa. 34:11; Zeph. 2:14) associate the same Hebrew term with deserted ruins, an unlikely habitat for the pelican. Suggested identifications include the jackdaw (NAS margin), owl (NAS margin, NRSV), and vulture (RSV).

PELLA (Pĕl′ là) City just east of the Jordan River and southeast of the Sea of Galilee. It received a large part of the Jerusalem church when they fled there before the Roman destruction of the Holy City in A.D. 66. Pella became an important link in the church structure from that time. The site was inhabited as early as 1900 B.C. and is mentioned in the Egyptian Execration Texts (1850 B.C.) and the Amarna Letters (about 1400 B.C.). Pella was destroyed shortly before the Israelite conquest and not rebuilt until about 350 B.C. Alexander the Great settled the city with Macedonians. In the early years of the first century B.C. it was destroyed again but rebuilt and greatly enhanced by Pompey.

PELONITE (Pē′ lō nīte) Resident of Pelon, an unknown site. The title belongs to two of David's 30 elite warriors (1 Chron. 11:27, 36; 27:10). Pelonite is perhaps a textual corruption for Paltite, the title of Helez in the parallel in 2 Samuel 23:26.

PELUSIUM (Pĕ′ lü sĭ ŭm) Egyptian military outpost near the mouth of the easternmost branch of the Nile, about eighteen miles west of the Suez Canal, identified with modern el Farama. Some modern translations follow the Vulgate in reading Pelusium at Ezekiel 30:15–16 (NIV, NRSV, TEV; also KJV and NAS margins). Pelusium was the site of the defeat of Pharoah Psammetichus III by Cambyses of Persia in 525 B.C. KJV, NAS follow the Hebrew in reading Sin. Some Greek and Latin witnesses read Sais, the capital of the Twenty-Sixth (Saite) Dynasty (663–525 B.C.), at 30:15.

Sais was located on the westernmost branch of the Nile. The REB follows the earliest Greek translation in reading Syene (modern Aswan) at 30:16. See *Sin.*

PEN See *Writing.*

PENCIL See *Writing.*

PENDANT See *Jewels, Jewelry.*

PENIEL (Pè nī′ ĕl) Alternate form of Penuel at Genesis 32:30.

PENINNAH (Pè nĭn′ nah) Personal name perhaps meaning, "woman with rich hair," "coral," or "pearl." It may be an intentional word play meaning, "fruitful." Elkanah's second wife and rival of barren Hannah (1 Sam. 1:2,4).

PENKNIFE Another name for a scribe's knife. See *Writing.*

PENNY See *Coins.*

PENTAPOLIS A league of five Philistine city-states which banded together to oppose the Israelite occupation of Canaan. See *Philistines.*

PENTATEUCH (Pĕn′ tà teŭch) First five books of Old Testament. The word *Pentateuch* comes from two Greek words *Penta* "five" and *teuchos* meaning "box," "jar," or "scroll." Originally the word was used as an adjective meaning "a five-scrolled (book)." The common Jewish arrangement calls the first five books of the Hebrew Bible *Torah,* law or teaching. The early church fathers beginning with Tertullian (about A.D. 200) called them the Pentateuch. The fivefold division of the Pentateuch is older than the Septuagint or earliest Greek translation (about 200 B.C.). The Hebrew names of these five scrolls come mainly from the opening word(s) of each scroll. Genesis is called *bereshith,* "in beginning"; Exodus, *we'elleh shemoth,* "These are the names"; Leviticus, *wayyikra,* "and he called"; Numbers, *bemidbar,* "in the Wil-

The Samaritan Pentateuch at Nablus. Samaritans consider only the Pentateuch as canonical.

derness"; and Deuteronomy, *elleh haddebarim,* "These are the words." The names of the books in the English Bible, come through the Latin from the Greek Septuagint and are intended to be descriptive of the contents of each book. Genesis means "generation" or "origin"; Exodus means "going out"; Leviticus refers to the Levitical system; Numbers refers to the numbering of the tribes, Levites, and first born (chs. 1—4,26); and Deuteronomy means "second law" (17:18).

The dividing lines between the individual books of the Pentateuch generally mark a change in the direction of the materials. At the end of Genesis (ch. 50), the stories of the Patriarchs end, and the story of the people of Israel begins in Exodus 1. The division between Exodus and Leviticus marks the change from the building of the tabernacle in Exodus 35—40 to the inauguration of worship (Lev. 1—10). Numbers begins with preparation for leaving Sinai, and Deuteronomy stands out sharply from the end of Numbers in that Deuteronomy 1:1 begins the great speech of Moses which covers thirty chapters (Deut. 1—30). We do not know when the Pentateuch was divided into five books. The division may have taken place only when the whole material now united within it had been incorporated into one unit and this division was aimed at producing sections of approximately equal length, corresponding to the normal length of scrolls.

Contents The division of the Pentateuch into five books does not indicate adequately the richness of the contents nor the variety of the literary forms found in the whole. A division of the Pentateuch based on the contents may be outlined as: Genesis 1—11, Primeval history, from Creation to Abraham; Genesis 12—36, Patriarchal history; Genesis 37—50, Joseph stories; Exodus 1—18, The Exodus; Exodus 19—Numbers 10:10, Israel at Sinai; Numbers 10:11—21:35, Israel in the Wilderness; Numbers 22:1—Deuteronomy 34, Israel in the Plains of Moab. Within each of these larger narrative sections are a number of smaller sections dealing with various themes and subthemes couched in many literary forms.

Themes The first theme in the Pentateuch is God is Creator (Gen. 1—2). This is followed closely by a chapter on the beginning of sin (Gen. 3). Chapters 4—11 tell of the increase of world population and sin, and the judgment of God on the whole world. The themes of electon, covenant, promise, faith, and providence are introduced in the remainder of Genesis (12—50). Divine deliverance is the major theme of Exodus 1—18. Covenant and law are themes of Exodus 19—24. Worship and social ethics are the concerns of Exodus 25—Numbers 10:10. Guidance of a rebellious people through the great and terrible wilderness marks Numbers 10—21; and preparations for going over Jordan and conquering Canaan are the major topics of Numbers 22—Deuteronomy 34.

Literary forms and genres The Pentateuch includes many literary forms and genres: narratives, laws, lists, sayings, sermons, and songs. Narratives describe creation, judgment (flood), travel (wilderness wanderings), buildings (Ark, tabernacle), marriages (Isaac and Rebekah), and births (Moses).

Although the Pentateuch is often referred to as Torah or law, laws comprise only a small percentage of the text. The Ten Commandments (Ex. 20: 2–17; Deut. 5:6–21) are frequently called law, but they are not law in the technical sense because no penalties or sanctions are connected with them. Other groups of laws in the Pentateuch are: the Book of the Covenant (Ex. 20:22—23:19); the laws of sacrifice (Lev. 1—7); the laws of purity (Lev. 11—15); the Holiness Code (Lev. 17—26); and the Deuteronomy Code (Deut. 12—26). No laws appear in Genesis. Four out of forty chapters in Exodus (chs. 20—23), most of Leviticus and a small portion of Numbers contain laws. Fourteen out of thirty-four chapters of Deuteronomy consist of legal material. See *Law; Book of the Covenant; Purity; Sacrifice; Holiness.* The 65 laws in the Book of the Covenant (see Ex. 24:7) include rules about images and kinds of altars (Ex. 20:22–26); Hebrew slaves (21:1–11); offences penalized by death (21:12–17); bodily injury (21:18–24); offences against property (21:25—22:17); miscellaneous social and cultic laws (22:18—23:9); a cultic calendar (23:10–19); blessing and curse (23:20–33).

The Holiness Code (Lev. 17—26) is named from the expression, "Ye shall be holy; for I the Lord your God am holy" (Lev. 19:2; 20:7,26). The Holiness Code stresses moral and ceremonial laws rather than civil and criminal laws. Chapters 18—20; 23—26 are directed to the people; chapters 17; 21—22 are directed to the priests and the house of Aaron. This Code deals with the slaughter of animals and sacrifice (17:1–16); forbidden sexual relations (18:1–30); relationships with neighbors (19:1–37); penalties (stoning, burning); rules for personal life of the priests (20:1—22:16); the quality of sacrifices (22:17–33); a cultic calendar (23:1–44); rules for lights in the sanctuary and the shewbread (24:1–9); blasphemy (24:10–23); the sabbatic year and jubilee (25:1–55); blessings and curses (26:1–46).

The Holiness Code says very little about agriculture. Much more is said in this Code than in the Book of the Covenant about forbidden sexual relations, including homosexuality (compare Lev. 18:1–23; 20:13). All forms of witchcraft, augury, and the occult are forbidden (Lev. 17:7; 19:26,31; 20:2–6,27). Two significant passages in this group of laws are: "For the life . . . is in the blood" (17:14 RSV), and, "Thou shalt love thy neighbor as thyself" (19:18). The expression "I am the Lord your God" and similar expressions occur 46 times in Lev. 18—26.

P
Q

The Deuteronomic Code (Deut. 12—26) is part of Moses' address to the twelve tribes just before they crossed the Jordan to go into Canaan. These are "preached" laws, full of admonitions and exhortations to heed and obey so that the Lord may bless them and they may live in the land (Deut. 12:1,13,19,28; 13:18; 14; 15:10,18; 16:12; 17:20,29). Many of these 80 laws are new because they are addressed to a new generation. See *Deuteronomy.* The restriction of worship or sacrifice to one legitimate altar is limited to the Deuteronomic Code as is the expression: "the place where I will make my name to dwell." Permission for private slaughtering and eating animals is given only in Deuteronomy (Deut. 12:15). Laws for judges, prophets, priests, and kings occur only in Deuteronomy. The laws for Hebrew slaves and the calendars of worship are different in Exodus and Deuteronomy. In Deuteronomy the Passover is to be observed only at the one legitimate place and the lamb is to be boiled (Deut. 16:7), but in Exodus, Passover is a family affair and the lambs are to be roasted (Exod. 12:9). The laws for the tithes are different in Deuteronomy 14 from those in Numbers 18:21–32. Laws of holy war are given only in Deuteronomy. Idolatry and the First Commandment are major concerns of all the codes.

Many attempts have been made to classify the laws in the Old Testament according to their types. Some recent scholars have used the terms "apodictic" and "casuistic" to refer to the two main types of laws. Apodictic refers to those authoritative, unconditional laws such as the Ten Commandments which begin, "Thou shalt not," "You shall," or laws calling for the death penalty. Casuistic laws are usually case laws which begin "When a man," or, "If a man." This classification is helpful in identifying the literary form, setting, and perhaps the origin of a law. Christians often speak of Old Testament laws as moral, civil, and ceremonial, but the Old Testament does not use those categories to classify its laws. In the Pentateuch, laws of every kind are jumbled together and interspersed with narrative and descriptive sections. Rather than attempting to isolate certain moral laws, it would be better to try to detect moral and ethical principles in all types of Old Testament laws. Some recent scholars have classified the laws in the various parts of the Old Testament as: criminal law, civil laws, family laws, cultic (worship) laws, and charitable (humanitarian) laws.

Old Testament laws were given in the context of the covenant. The people had experienced deliverance (salvation) at the Exodus. God took the initiative and by grace redeemed Israel from bondage in Egypt. God acted first, then called the people to respond. Old Testament laws were given to redeemed people to tell them how to live as people of God.

The Pentateuch contains many lists: genealogical (Gen. 5; 11; Ex. 5), geographical and ethnographical (Gen. 10; 26), tribal (Gen. 49; Deut. 33); offerings (Ex. 35); census (Num. 1—4; 26), and campsites in the wilderness (Num. 33).

The Old Testament contains many "sayings" of various kinds. Some are poetic. Some are proverbial. Some are prose. These sayings may have been remembered and passed from generation to generation. Some familiar examples are:

This is now bone of my bones
    and flesh of my flesh (Gen. 2:23 NIV).
For dust you are
    and to dust you will return (Gen. 3:19 NIV).
Like Nimrod, a mighty hunter before
    the Lord (Gen. 10:9 NIV).
I . . . will be gracious to whom I will be
gracious (Ex. 33:19).

Deuteronomy is the only place in the Old Testament where long sermons are found. Even the laws in Deuteronomy are "preached" laws. The fact that many admonitions and exhortations occur throughout the book may indicate that the book was used as a covenant renewing document.

One other major literary genre is found in the Pentateuch—that of song: Israel was a singing people. They sang in times of victory (Ex. 15), at work (Num 21:17–18), in times of battle (Num. 21:14–15,27–30), and in worship (Num. 6:22–26; Deut. 32:1–43).

Date and Authorship The problem of the date and authorship of the Pentateuch is one of the major critical problems of the Old Testament. Dr. John R. Sampey wrote,

Possibly the higher criticism of the Pentateuch is the most important critical problem confronting students of the Old Testament. Fundamental and difficult it calls for patience, industry and the ability to sift evidence and estimate its value. It requires logical discipline and a well-balanced mind [John R. Sampey, *Syllabus For Old Testament Study* (Nashville: Broadman Press, 1924), p. 52].

The existence of sources for its writing is not the major issue, but its inspiration and reliability in its present form.

One reason the question of date and authorship of the Pentateuch is difficult is that the books themselves are anonymous. Most English Bibles carry the titles of the first five books as "the books of Moses." These titles are not in the Hebrew manuscripts. They came into England through Tyndale's version and were probably derived from Luther's translation which used only the numerical titles, "First Book of Moses," and so on to the fifth.

Although the books of the Pentateuch as a whole are anonymous, a number of passages refer to Moses writing at least certain things (compare 17:14; 24:4; 24:7; Num. 33:1–2; Deut. 31:9,22). Late in the Old Testament period, the tradition arose which seemingly refers to the Pentateuch as the "Book of Moses" (2 Chron. 35:12). This tradition was carried on by Jews and Christians until after A.D. 1600. Some Jews and Christians raised occasional questions about the Mosaic authorship of the Pentateuch during all that time, but the Renaissance and the Enlightenment led to the questioning of all things including the Mosaic authorship of the Pentateuch. One passage in the Pentateuch which contributed to the serious questioning of Mosaic authorship is Deuteronomy 34:5–8, describing Moses' death and the following period of mourning. Other post-Mosaic references are to Dan (Gen. 14:14; compare Josh. 19:47; Judg. 18:28b–29), and the conquest of Canaan (Deut. 2:12). The way the Hebrew text of the Pentateuch is written today is nothing like it might have appeared in Moses' day. For hundreds of years, the Hebrew text was copied by hand. In the process of copying, the shape of the letters was completely changed. Vowel points and accents were added. Words were separated word by word and divided into verses and chapters.

We do not know who wrote the completed Pentateuch. The Pentateuch makes no claim that Moses wrote all of it. Many theories and hypotheses have been advanced to explain its origin. The classical literary critical theory is associated with the name of Julius Wellhausen, a nineteenth century German scholar. He popularized and synthesized the views of many Old Testament scholars and said that the Pentateuch was a compilation of four basic literary documents identified as J, E, D, and P. J stood for Jehovah or Judah and supposedly was written in the Southern Kingdom about 850 B.C. E stood for Elohim, a favorite Hebrew name for God in this document. It was supposedly written about 750 B.C. D stands for Deuteronomy and was written according to this hypothesis about 621 B.C. P stands for the Priestly document and was written about 500 B.C. The Priestly writer might have compiled the whole Pentateuch according to this theory.

Many other theories and modifications of older theories have arisen in the twentieth century. Critical scholarship's earlier agreement on the four sources has disappeared in the 1980s. Some date P early. Some date J very late. Some see D as the dominant author. Many are more interested in the literary art of the Pentateuch than in literary sources. Scholars are thus no closer to a solution to the problem of the authorship of the Pentateuch than they were when they first asked questions about it.

Even the most conservative scholars who defend Mosaic authorship of the Pentateuch admit that Moses did not write every word of the Pentateuch. All accept the possibility of later minor alterations and additions to the work of Moses in the Pentateuch. Many discuss some development

of the material in the Pentateuch along independent lines, *after* Mosaic composition. This is especially true linguistically. There is no reason why conservatives cannot often use such symbols as P and H as a convenient shorthand to refer to certain blocks of material. Recent conservative scholars speak of sources Moses may have used.

Conclusions No agreement has been reached as to the final solution to this most difficult problem. However some things are clear: (1) We should avoid the two extreme views that Moses wrote all the Pentateuch or that he wrote none of it. We should take the claims of the Bible concerning itself seriously but keep our minds and hearts open to new and different possible interpretations. (2) We should recognize the legitimacy of certain critical methods. W. T. Conner, who taught Systematic Theology at Southwestern Seminary for almost 40 years (1910–49), said, "There are certain questions of date, authorship, historical reliability and so forth, that must be settled by historical and literary criticism. There is no other way to settle them" [W. T. Conner, *Revelation and God* (Nashville: Broadman Press, 1943), p. 99]. (3) It is not necessary that we know the date and authorship of a book in the Bible before we can read it with profit. At times we must sacrifice our need for security in certainty to God's nature as sovereign mystery.

See *Authority; Inspiration; Revelation.*

Ralph L. Smith

PENTATEUCH, SAMARITAN See *Samaritan Pentateuch; Bible, Text and Versions.*

PENTECOST (Pĕn' tĕ côst) Jewish festival at which Holy Spirit came on early church. See *Festivals; Spirit.*

PENUEL (Pė nū' ĕl) Name meaning, "face of God." *1.* Descendant of Judah and founder (father) of Gedor (1 Chron. 4:4). *2.* A Benjaminite (1 Chron. 8:25). *3.* Site on River Jabbok northeast of Succoth where Jacob wrestled with the stranger (Gen. 32:24–32; compare Hos. 12:4). The city was destroyed by Gideon because its inhabitants refused him provisions while he pursued the Midianites (Judg. 8:8–9,17). Jeroboam I built (perhaps rebuilt or fortified) the city (1 Kings 12:25). The site is identified with the easternmost of two mounds called Tulul edh-Dhahab, which commands the entrance to the Jordan Valley from the Jabbok gorge, about seven miles east of the Jordan.

PEOPLE OF GOD Group elected by God and committed to be His covenant people. Scripture repeatedly defines who is included in people of God. The history of revelation shows God electing Israel by grace.

Election and Covenant The election of Israel as people of God may be traced from Abraham (Gen.

12; compare Gal. 3:29; Rom. 9:7–8). However, the relationship between Yahweh and Israel began in the Exodus. Exodus 19 represents a special covenant form with both conditions (v. 5) and promises of the covenant (vv. 5b–6). The condition of the covenant was obedience; the promise was that "you shall be my treasured possession out of all the peoples." This promise involves a God-people and people-God relationship which is the center of the Old Testament. This promise was inherited by the church as the true Israel or the new Israel (Rom. 9:6–8; 1 Cor. 10:18–21; Gal. 6:16). Here is the unique position of the church as the people of God in the divine order (Rom. 9:25–26; 1 Cor. 6:14–17; Titus 2:14; Heb. 8:10; 1 Pet. 2:9–10; Rev. 21:3). See *Church; Covenant; Election; Israel, Spiritual.*

The faith of Israel became more concrete when the remnant idea was developed from corporate salvation out of the divine wrath and judgment. To the remnant fell the status and condition of God's long purpose for His people. The remnant as the chosen one is explained by Jesus in Matthew 22:14. Most of all, Jesus Himself is the remnant. Truly, the church carries the ideas from the Old Testament that the remnant in the figure of the Servant is the witness of universal salvation and the agent of a final revelation. The servant of Yahweh represented by Israel would be a light to the nations. The universal character of Israel's vocation is most clearly expressed here. The idea of God's people in the Old Testament culminates in the person of the Servant who is the idea of the remnant personified as an individual.

Christ claimed His servant-messiahship, for He is the Son of David, fulfilling the promise of God in the Old Testament. Jesus is the King but rejected every political interpretation of His messianic vocation. His kingdom is not of this world (John 18:36). He is the Suffering Servant, who gave His life as a ransom for many and thereby inaugurated the New Covenant.

The role of servant-messiah developed another dimension in its collectivity, that is, church. The servant idea is determinative for an understanding of the priesthood of the whole church. Christology (Christ) is related to ecclesiology (church) (2 Cor. 4:5). Christians are servants sharing that servanthood which the Servant *par excellence* creates. The call into peoplehood is a call into servanthood. The church is truly the people of God. *Samuel Tang*

PEOPLE OF THE EAST See *Kadmonites.*

PEOPLE OF THE LAND Translation of the technical Hebrew term *'am ha'arez,* used primarily in Jeremiah, Ezekiel, 2 Kings, and 2 Chronicles (see also Gen. 23:7; Ex. 5:5; Lev. 20:2; Num. 14:9; Hag. 2:4; Zech. 7:5; Dan. 9:6). In most cases, the term apparently refers to the male citizens who

lived upon their own land and who had the responsibility as citizens to participate in judicial activities, cultic festivals, and army service. Nonetheless, the references are so diverse that we cannot be sure the same people were in mind each time the term appears. Some scholars think the "people of the land" represented a particular influential element in society such as a national council, influential aristocrats, free citizens and property owners, landless poor, or non-Jerusalemites. Such theories cannot be proven.

In preexilic Judah, the "people of the land" first appear in association with the coronation of Joash (2 Kings 11:4–20). They appear slightly later in the avenging of Amon's murder and the elevation of Josiah to the kingship (2 Kings 21:24). They are depicted as being capable of liberating slaves (Jer. 34, especially vs. 18–20, where the "people of the land" both participated in the covenant making and were held responsible for breaking the same). They could also be agents of oppression (Ezek. 22:29). Second Kings 25:18–21 records that Nebuchadrezzar put to death at Riblah "sixty men of the people of the land," along with others held responsible for the revolt against Babylon resulting in the fall of Jerusalem in 587 B.C. Clearly, in these situations these are people who have social, economic, political, and religious significance.

The "people of the land" are also portrayed as "the poor of the land" who remained in Jerusalem during the Babylonian Exile (2 Kings 24:14; 25:12). It is notable that when the exiles returned they distanced themselves from those who had remained in Judah by using "people of Judah" to characterize the returning exiles (Ezra 4:4). Disapproval is expressed in Ezra and Nehemiah for the pagan half-Jew and half-Gentile, essentially non-observant Jews (see Ezra 10:2,11; Neh. 10:28–31). In Ezra 9:1–2,11 the plural, the "people of those lands," is used to designate the groupings with whom intermarriage had occurred, "the Canaanites, the Hittites, the Perizzites, the Jebusites, the Ammonites, the Moabites, the Egyptians, and the Amorites" (9:1).

There were considerable bad feelings between the "people of the land" and the Pharisees. In the Synoptic Gospels Jesus is portrayed as supporting the "people of the land" (Mark 7:1–5; Luke 6:1–5). The later postexilic use as witnessed in Ezra and Nehemiah as well as in the Synoptic Gospels (see also John 7:49) is further reflected in the rabbinical classification of the "people of the land" as those ignorant of the law and non-observant in their daily lives. Because their condition was not dependent upon birth, however, the deficiencies could be remedied by a greater awareness of and adherence to Torah.

Frank E. Eakin, Jr.

PEOR (Pē′ or) Name perhaps meaning, "opening." *1.* Mountain in Moab opposite the wilderness of Judah. Balak brought Balaam there to curse the camp of the Israelites which was visible from the site (Num. 23:28; 24:2). *2.* Abbreviated form of Baal-Peor (lord of Peor), a god whom the Israelites were led to worship (Num. 25:18; 31:16; Josh. 22:17). See *Baal-Peor. 3.* Site in Judah identified with modern khirbet Faghur southwest of Bethlehem (Josh. 15:59 REB, following the earliest Greek translation).

PERATH (Pē′ răth) See *Parah.*

PERAZIM (Pĕ′ rå zĭm) See *Baal-Perazim.*

PERDITION Describes the eternal state of death, destruction, annihilation, or ruin.
Old Testament Words of the family from which *perdition* is derived usually relate to a state of physical rather than moral or religious destruction. Perdition is held in contrast to the blessing of God. It is the penalty for disobedience (Deut. 22:24; 28:20). The Old Testament sometimes links this term to the concept of Sheol (2 Sam. 22:5; Ps. 18:4).
New Testament Perdition is the fate of all who do not come to repentance. The way that leads to this destruction is broad in contrast to the narrow road which leads to life (Matt. 7:13). Perdition, as used in the New Testament, does not convey the idea of simple extinction or annihilation. Set into the context of eternity, the Gospel writers used it to mean an everlasting state of death and judgment. Just as surely as salvation expresses the idea of eternal life, so perdition designates a hopeless eternity of destruction. The phrase "son of perdition" describes the person who has fallen victim to this destruction (compare Judas in John 17:12). The "man of sin" is doomed to perdition (2 Thess. 2:3). A form of this word is used in Revelation 9:11 to describe the ultimate enemy of God—the Destroyer. See *Death; Devil; Eternal Life; Everlasting Punishment; Hell; Sheol.*   Ken Massey

PEREA (Pĕ rē′ à) A Roman district in Transjordan which became a part of Herod the Great's king-

View from Jericho of the hills of Perea on the eastern side of the Jordan River valley.

dom. The capital was Gadara, where KJV says Jesus healed the demoniac. (Modern translations follow other manuscripts reading Gerasenes.) Other important sites in the province were the fortress of Machaerus, where John the Baptist was beheaded, and Pella, where Christians from Jerusalem fled just before the Roman destruction of the Holy City in A.D. 66. Perea was the area through which the Jews traveled to avoid going through Samaria. Although not referred to by name in the New Testament, it is mentioned as "Judea beyond the Jordan" in several texts (Matt. 19:1; Mark 10:1 RSV). See *Gadara; Machaerus; Pella; Transjordan.*

PERESH (Pē′ rĕsh) Personal name meaning, "separate." A Manassite (1 Chron. 7:16).

PEREZ (Pē rĕz) Personal name meaning, "breach." One of the twins born to the illicit affair between Judah and his daughter-in-law, Tamar (Gen. 38). After she was widowed and her brother-in-law, Onan, refused to fulfill his duties in levirate marriage (designed to carry on the name of the deceased through a son), she tricked her father-in-law, Judah, into an affair (vv. 13–30).

PEREZ-UZZA (Pē′ rĕz-Ŭz′ zà) NAS, RSV alternate form of Perez-Uzzah (1 Chron. 13:11).

PEREZ-UZZAH (Pē′ rĕz-Ŭz′ zah) Place name meaning, "breach of Uzzah." Site of the threshing floor of Nacon (or Chidon) west of Jerusalem on the Kiriath-jearim road where the anger of the Lord "broke out" against Uzzah, who touched the ark to steady it (2 Sam. 6:8; 1 Chron. 13:11). The site is perhaps that of khirbet el-Uz about two miles east of Kiriath-jearim.

PERFECT/PERFECTION Reaching an ideal state of spiritual wholeness or completeness. It is not a quality which is achieved by human effort alone, nor is it an end in itself. Christian perfection consists essentially in exercising the divine gift of love (Col. 3:14 NIV), for God, and for other people (Matt. 22:37–39). The basis of perfection lies in God Himself, whose law (Jas. 1:25), works (Deut. 32:4), and way (Ps. 18:30) are perfect. God is free from incompleteness; He can, therefore, demand from believers, and enable them to receive, completeness (Matt. 5:48).

Through a covenant relationship with His people, and by grace, God thus offers to His people the *possibility* of perfection. In the Old Testament being "perfect" is ascribed to individuals, such as Noah (Gen. 6:9) and Job (1:1), in response to their wholehearted obedience. In other contexts, corporate perfection and being "upright" belong together (Ps. 37:37; Prov. 2:21). In the New Testament, God's relationship with His people is itself fulfilled, as the old covenant is replaced, and through Christ believers can be perfected for ever (Heb. 10:14). Christians are, however, to grow from spiritual infancy to maturity so as to share the full stature of Christ, in whose image they may become renewed and perfected (Col. 3:10).

A tension exists here. Because on earth sin remains a possibility for all, believers (1 John 1:8) need to become perfect even while attaining a relative perfection (Mic. 6:6–8; Phil. 3:16,12–14). For that reason, perfection is not equated in the Bible with sinlessness (but see 1 John 3:6,9 NIV). The New Testament also stops short of deification (becoming God) as an option for believers, even if it allows for their perfect relationship with God (2 Pet. 1:4). The divine gift of perfection will be fully realized only in eternity (Phil. 3:10–14; 1 John 3:2). It is a goal to be sought (2 Cor. 7:1; Heb. 6:1) which, like the complete vision of God, cannot be found this side of heaven (Eph. 4:13; Jas. 3:2).

How, then, may even this limited perfection be achieved? The New Testament locates the means of perfection in Christ. Through His suffering and exaltation, God made Jesus perfect (Heb. 2:10) and fitted Him to win for the church and the individual believer a completeness which echoes His own (Col. 1:28; Heb. 5:9). So we and all the saints of God can be saved, and through the Spirit be given access to God and the daily help we need (Heb. 7:25; 4:14–16). See *Holy.*

Stephen S. Smalley

The south Hellenistic gate of the ancient city of Perga in Pamphylia (modern Turkey).

Carved reliefs found among the ruins of the stadium at ancient Perga.

PERFUME, PERFUMER Modern translation of a word translated as apothecary by the KJV (Ex. 30:25,35; 37:29; 2 Chron 16:14; Neh. 3:8; Eccl. 10:1). Perfumes mentioned in the Bible include: aloes, balsam (or balm), bdellium, calamus (or sweet or fragrant cane), camel's thorn, cinnamon (or cassia), frankincense, galbanum, gum, henna, myrrh, nard (or spikenard), onycha, saffron, and stacte. See *Apothecary; Cosmetics; Oil; Ointment;* and separate articles on each for further identification.

PERGA (Pĕr′ ḡȧ) An ancient city in the province of Pamphylia, about eight miles from the Mediterranean Sea. Settlement at Perga dates to prehistory. Alexander the Great passed through the town during his campaigns and used guides from

A portion of the Roman Theater located at ancient Pergamum.

there. A temple to Artemis was one of the prominent buildings. Paul, Barnabas, and John Mark came to Perga from Paphos (Acts 13:13). There young John left the team to return home.

PERGAMOS (Pĕr' g̊å mŏs) KJV form of Pergamum (Rev. 1:11; 2:12).

PERGAMUM (Pĕr' g̊å mum) Place name meaning, "citadel." A wealthy ancient city in the district of Mysia in Asia Minor. See *Asia Minor.*

PERIDA (Pė̇ rī' dà) Personal name meaning, "unique" or "separated." Head of a family of Solomon's servants, some of whom returned from Exile (Neh. 7:57; compare Peruda, Ezra 2:55).

The Temple of Athena at ancient Pergamum.

PERISHABLE Term some translations (KJV, REB, NRSV) use to describe the present, mortal body (1 Cor. 15:42,50,53–54), which is subject to death and decay. Other translations render the underlying Greek as corruptible (NAS, NIV) or mortal (TEV). Paul contrasted the perishable reward champion athletes receive with the lasting reward for which Christians compete (1 Cor. 9:25). First Peter 1:7 compares the testing of lasting faith with that of perishable gold.

PERIZZITES (Pĕr' ĭz zīte) A group name meaning, "rustic." One of the groups of people who opposed the Israelite occupation of Canaan (Josh. 9:1–2). They dwelled in the land as early as Abraham's time (Gen. 13:7). The name implies that the Perizzites probably dwelled in the open country while the Canaanites walled up their encampments.

PERJURY A false statement given voluntarily under oath. Perjury involves either false witness to past facts or the neglect of what has been previously vowed. Mosaic law prohibited false swearing (Lev. 19:12; Ex. 20:7) and giving false witness (Ex. 20:16). False witness was punishable with the sentence which would have gone to the one falsely accused of guilt (Deut. 19:16–21). Vows and oaths to perform an act were to be fulfilled (Num. 30:2). See *Oaths.*

PERSECUTION IN THE BIBLE Harassment and

suffering which people and institutions inflict upon others for being different in their faith, world'view, culture, or race. Persecution seeks to intimidate, silence, punish, or even to kill people. **Old Testament** Israel was the agent of persecution of nations (Judg. 2:11–23; Lev. 26:7–8). The Bible gives special attention to Israel's fate in Egypt (Ex. 1—3) and in the Exile (Ps. 137). On an individual level, Saul persecuted David (1 Sam. 19:9–12), and Shadrach, Meshach, and Abednego were persecuted because they refused to worship the image of the king (Dan. 3). Jezebel persecuted the prophets of the Lord, and the prophet Elijah persecuted and killed the prophets of Baal (1 Kings 18). Job felt persecuted by God himself (7:11–21). The prophets—Amos (7:10–12), Jeremiah (Jer. 1:19; 15:15; 37—38), and Urijah (Jer. 26:20–23)—suffered persecution because they fleshed out the will of God in adverse circumstances. The Psalms speak of the righteous sufferer who felt persecuted as a result of faith in God, and who prayed to God for deliverance (7; 35; 37; 79; 119:84–87).

Intertestamental period This era is important because it witnessed the concerted attempt to make the Jewish people renounce their faith in God. In this conflict, persecution took place on both sides (1 and 2 Maccabees). See *Intertestamental History.*

New Testament Jesus was persecuted and finally killed by the religious and political establishments of His day (Mark 3:6; Luke 4:29; John 5:16; Acts 3:13–15; 7:52; passion stories). He fleshed out the liberating passion of God (Luke 4:16–29) and came into conflict with the religious institutions of the cult by healing on the sabbath (Mark 3:1–6), criticizing the Temple activities (Mark 11:15–18), and the law (Matt. 5:21–48).

Jesus pronounced God's salvation upon those who are persecuted for righteousness sake (Matt. 5:10–12). In an evil world, disciples are to expect persecution (Matt. 10:16–23; Mark 4:17; 13:9; John 15:20; 16:2), just as was the case with the prophets in the Old Testament (Matt. 5:12; 23:31; Luke 11:47–51; Acts 7:52; Heb. 11:32–38). Paul (1 Cor. 4:11–13; 2 Cor. 4:8–12; 6:4–10; 11:24–27; Gal. 5:11; 1 Thess. 2:2; 3:4; Acts 17:5–10; 18:12–17; 21:30–36; 23:12–35), as well as Stephen (Acts 6:8—7:60), James (Acts 12:2), and Peter (Acts 12:3–5), together with many anonymous martyrs experienced the truth of the Johannine saying: "If they have persecuted me, they will also persecute you" (John 15:20; see Acts 4:3; 5:17–42; 8:1; 12:1; Rev. 2:26,9–10,13,19; 3:8–10; 6:9; 16:6; 17:6; 18:24; 20:4).

Whole epistles and books like 1 Peter, Hebrews, and Revelation were written to encourage Christians in a situation of persecution (1 Pet. 3:13–18; 4:12–19; 5:6–14; Heb. 10:32–39; 12:3; Rev. 2—3). Something like a theology of persecution

emerged, which emphasized patience, endurance, and steadfastness (Rom. 12:12; 1 Thess. 2:14–16; Jas. 5:7–11); prayer (Matt. 5:44; Rom. 12:14; 1 Cor. 4:12); thanksgiving (2 Thess. 1:4); testing (Mark 4:17) and the strengthening of faith (1 Thess. 3:2–3); experiencing the grace of God (Rom. 8:35; 2 Cor. 4:9, 12:10), and being blessed through suffering (Matt. 5:10–12; 1 Pet. 3:14; 4:12–14). For Paul, persecuting Christians could be a living and visible testimony to the crucified and risen Christ (2 Cor. 4:7–12).

There seems to be an element in religious fanaticism (Paul before his conversion: 1 Cor. 15:9; Gal. 1:13,23; Phil. 3:6; Acts 8:3; 9:1–2; 22:4) which breeds intolerance and can lead to persecution. Christians should repent of this element in their own history and must be radically committed to the abolition of all persecution.

See *Apostles; Maccabees; Martyr; Prophets; Prophecy; Suffering; War.*   *Thorwald Lorenzen*

PERSEVERANCE Maintaining Christian faith through the trying times of life. As a noun the term *perseverance* occurs in the New Testament only at Ephesians 6:18 (*proskarterēsei*) and Hebrews 12:1 (*hupomonēs*). The idea is inherent throughout the New Testament in the great interplay of the themes of assurance and warning.

The background setting for the idea of perseverance blossomed out of the context of persecution and temptation. The believer was expected faithfully to endure and to remain steadfast in the face of opposition, attack, and discouragement. The New Testament writers were forthright in advising believers to be consistent in prayer (Eph. 6:18; Phil. 4:6), and they employed athletic imagery to remind Christians to be effectual as they trained in the ways of God (1 Cor. 9:24–27; Rom. 12:11–12; Heb. 12:1–12). Israel's failure of faithfulness in the Exodus was also a haunting picture for Christians, and the inspired New Testament writers found it to be an important basis for warning (see 1 Cor. 10:1–14; Heb. 3:7–19). They were committed to making absolutely clear that the requirements of Christian living were recognized as an essential element of Christian believing. Authentic life and true belief are both necessary parts of being a Christian.

While the warnings are very stern, especially in Hebrews (2:3; 6:1–8; 10:26–31), the New Testament writers were firmly convinced that those who truly committed themselves to Christ should persevere to the end because they had gained a new perspective and become a people who would not treat lightly the biblical admonitions (compare Heb. 6:9–12; 10:39). They believed Christians would finish the race because Christians would focus their attention on Jesus, the lead runner and model finisher of their faith (Heb. 2:10; 12:1–2).

In the early church Christians wrestled with the problem of the renouncers during and after periods of persecution.

Christians found in the model of Peter's restoration (John 21) an important clue. Restoration for Peter was possible, but restoration still meant his death. Restoration for Christians, therefore, could be possible, but it demanded absolute seriousness for defectors. They would be expected to persevere thereafter even in the face of death. As time passed, however, baptism became regarded by some Christians as a bath which would provide cleansing from all types of sin, including renunciation. Some would thus delay baptism almost to the time of death to guarantee that all sins in life would be expunged. The need was seen by these Christians for a final rite to care for such post-baptismal, unconfessed sins. Others found such views of baptism and extreme unction to be foreign to New Testament perspectives.

But the perseverance of the saints is one of the great theological ideas that needs to be reaffirmed in this era. It is the human side of the salvation equation, and it deals with faithfulness of Christians in matters of God's will (Jas. 1:25). It encompasses the taking seriously of human weakness, without denying the mysterious nature of God's patience with His people. It permits judgment concerning the way people live in this world, but it does not exclude God's abundant graciousness.

Persevering Christians take prayer seriously as a reflection of life. They recognize the way of love and forgiveness because they understand the nature of human weakness and divine help. They know they have experienced grace beyond their human capacities. Persevering Christians recognize that the warnings of the Bible are meant for them to obey and that Christ gave His life to transform their lives. Perseverance is thus a call to faithfulness, but it is also an affirmation that somehow, in spite of our failures, God will bring His committed people through the difficulties and concerns of life to their promised destiny in Christ.

Gerald L. Borchert

PERSIA (Pĕr′ siȧ) As a nation, Persia corresponds to the modern state of Iran. As an empire, Persia was a vast collection of states and kingdoms reaching from the shores of Asia Minor in the west to the Indus River valley in the east. It reached northward to southern Russia, and in the south included Egypt and the regions bordering the Persian Gulf and the Gulf of Oman. In history, the empire defeated the Babylonians and then fell finally to Alexander the Great.

The nation was named for the southernmost region of the area, called Parsis or Persis. It was a harsh land of deserts, mountains, plateaus, and valleys. The climate was arid and showed extremes of cold and heat. Gold and silver and wheat and barley were native to the area.

The region was settled shortly after 3000 B.C. by people from the north. An Elamite culture developed which, at its peak in 1200 B.C., dominated the whole Tigris River valley. It lasted until 1050 B.C. After its destruction, other northern groups entered the area. Among these groups were tribesmen who formed a small kingdom in the region of Anshan around 700 B.C. It was ruled by Achaemenes, the great great-grandfather of Cyrus II, the Great. (Thus, the period from Achaemenes to Alexander is called the Achaemenid period.) This small kingdom was the seed of the Persian empire.

When Cyrus II came to his father's throne in 559 B.C., his kingdom was part of a larger Median kingdom. The Medes controlled the territory northeast and east of the Babylonians. In 550 B.C. Cyrus rebelled against Astyages, the Median king. His rebellion led to the capture of the king and gave Cyrus control over a kingdom stretching from Media to the Halys river in Asia Minor. Soon Cyrus challenged the king of Lydia. Victory there gave Cyrus the western portion of Asia Minor. Then, in 539 B.C., Babylon fell to Cyrus due to his skill and internal dissension in the Babylonian Empire. See *Babylon.*

Cyrus died in 530 B.C.; however, the Persian Empire continued to grow. Cambyses II, Cyrus' son, conquered Egypt in 525 B.C. Cambyses' successor Darius I expanded the empire eastward to the Indus and attempted to conquer or control the Greeks. Darius lost to the Greeks at Marathon in 490 B.C. This was the greatest extension of the empire. Later emperors did little to expand the empire. They even had difficulty holding such a far-flung empire together.

The Persian Empire is important to the history and development of civilization. It had major effects on religion, law, politics, and economics. The impact came through the Jews, the Bible, contacts with the Greeks, and through Alexander the Great's incorporation of ideas and architecture from the Persians.

Politically, the Persian Empire was the best organized the world had ever seen. By the time of Darius I, 522–486 B.C., the empire was divided into twenty satrapies (political units of varying size and population). Satrapies were subdivided into provinces. Initially, Judah was a province in the satrapy of Babylon. Later, Judah was in one named "Beyond the River." The satrapies were governed by Persians who were directly responsible to the emperor. Good administration required good communications which called for good roads. These roads did more than speed administration, though. They encouraged contacts between peoples within the empire. Ideas and goods could move hundreds of miles with little restriction. The empire became wealthy and also gave its inhabitants a sense that they were part of a larger world. A kind of "universal awareness" developed. The use of minted coins and the development of a money economy aided this identifica-

P
Q

tion with a larger world. The emperor's coins were handy reminders of the power and privileges of being part of the empire. Also, the Persians were committed to rule by law. Instead of imposing an imperial law from above, however, the emperor and his satraps gave their authority and support to local law. For the Jews this meant official support for keeping Jewish law in the land of the Jews.

The Persian Empire affected the Jews and biblical history a great deal. Babylon had conquered Jerusalem and destroyed the Temple in 586 B.C. When Cyrus conquered Babylon, he allowed the Jews to return to Judah and encouraged the rebuilding of the Temple (Ezra 1:1–4). The work was begun but not completed. Then, under Darius I, Zerubbabel and the high priest, Joshua, led the restored community with the support and encouragement of the Persians. (Ezra 3—6 tells of some of the events while Haggai's and Zechariah's prophecies were made during the days of the restoration.) Despite some local opposition, Darius supported the rebuilding of the Temple which was rededicated in his sixth year (Ezra 6:15). Also, both Ezra and Nehemiah were official representatives of the Persian government. Ezra was to teach and to appoint judges (Ezra 7). Nehemiah may have been the first governor of the province of Yehud (Judah). He undoubtedly had official support for his rebuilding of the walls of Jerusalem.

The Jews had trouble under Persian rule, too. Although Daniel was taken into Exile by the Babylonians (Dan. 1:1*ff*), his ministry continued through the fall of the Babylonians (Dan. 5) into the time of the Persians (Dan. 6*ff*). His visions projected even further. Daniel 6 shows a stable government but one in which Jews could still be at risk. His visions in a time of tranquility remind readers that human kingdoms come and go. Esther is a story of God's rescue of His people during the rule of the Persian emperor: Ahasuerus (also known as Xerxes I). The story shows an empire where law can be used and misused. Jews are already, apparently, hated by some. Malachi, too, is probably from the Persian period. His book shows an awareness of the world at large and is positive toward the Gentiles and the government.

Throughout the period, the Jews kept looking for the kind of restoration promised by prophets such as Isaiah (chapters 40—66) and Ezekiel (chapters 40—48). Prophets such as Haggai and Zechariah and Malachi helped the Jews to hope, but these men of God also reminded their hearers of the importance of present faithfulness and obedience to God.

See *Cyrus; Darius; Daniel; Esther; Ezra; Nehemiah; Temple.*   *Albert F. Bean*

PERSIS (Pĕr′ sĭs) Personal name meaning, "Persian woman." Leader in the Roman church whom

Paul greeted and commended for diligent service (Rom. 16:12).

PERSON OF CHRIST See *Christ, Christology; Jesus Christ.*

PERSONALITY See *Anthropology; Heart; Humanity; Mind.*

PERVERSE Translation of one Greek and several Hebrew terms with the literal meaning, "bent," "crooked," or "twisted," applied to persons involved in moral error. Most biblical references are in the Book of Proverbs which mention perverse: persons (Prov. 3:32; 14:14); minds (11:20; 12:8; 23:33); tongues (10:31; 17:20); words or speech (10:32; 19:1); and perverse ways (28:6). Paul urged Christians to be moral "lights" witnessing to their "crooked and perverse generation" (Phil. 2:15; compare Deut. 32:5). Jesus accused His generation of both faithlessness and perversity (Matt. 17:17; Luke 9:41; compare Deut. 32:20).

PESHITTA (Pĕ shīt′ ta) Common Syriac version of the Scriptures. The Old Testament was likely translated between A.D. 100 and 300. The New Testament translation dates from before A.D. 400. The Peshitta lacked those books rejected by the Syriac-speaking churches (2 Peter; 2 and 3 John; Jude; Revelation). See *Bible, Text and Versions.*

PESTILENCE A devastating epidemic. Old Testament writers understood pestilence to be sent by God (Ex. 9:15; Jer. 15:2; Hab. 3:5; Amos 4:10), sometimes by means of a destroying angel (2 Sam. 24:16; 1 Chron. 21:15). God sent pestilence as punishment for persistent unbelief (Num. 14:12) and failure to fulfill covenant obligations (Deut. 24:24; 28:21) as well as to encourage repentance (Amos 4:10). God withheld pestilence from Egypt to allow for survivors to witness His acts of liberation (Ex. 9:16). Earnest prayer averted pestilence (1 Kings 8:37); fasting and sacrifice without repentance did not (Jer. 14:12). Pestilence is often associated with war and siege conditions (Ex. 5:3; Lev. 26:25; Amos 4:10; Luke 21:11).

PESTLE A small, club-shaped tool used to grind in a mortar (Prov. 27:22).

PETER (Pē′ tēr) Personal name meaning, "Rock." Four names are used in the New Testament to refer to Peter: the Hebrew name *Simeon* (Acts 15:14); the Greek equivalent *Simon* (nearly fifty times in the Gospels and Acts); *Cephas*, most frequently used by Paul (1 Cor. 1:12; 3:22; 9:5; 15:5; Gal. 1:18; 2:9,11,14) and occurring only once outside his writings (John 1:42). *Cephas* and *Peter* both mean *rock. Simon* is often found in combination with *Peter,* reminding the reader that Simon was the earlier name and that Peter was a name given later by Jesus. The name *Peter* dominates the New Testament usage.

Family of Peter The Gospels preserve a surprising amount of information about Peter and his family. Simon is the son of Jona or John (Matt. 16:17; John 1:42). He and his brother, Andrew, came from Bethsaida (John 1:44) and were Galilean fishermen (Mark 1:16; Luke 5:2−3; John 21:3), in partnership with the sons of Zebedee, James and John (Luke 5:10). Peter was married (Mark 1:29−31; 1 Cor. 9:5) and maintained a residence in Capernaum (Mark 1:21,29). Before becoming disciples of Jesus, Peter and Andrew had been influenced by the teaching of John the Baptist (John 1:35−42).

Role of Peter Among the Disciples Peter is credited with being a leader of the twelve disciples, whom Jesus called. His name always occurs first in the lists of disciples (Mark 3:16; Luke 6:14; Matt. 10:2). He frequently served as the spokesman for the disciples (compare Mark 8:29) and was usually the one who raised the questions which they all seemed to be asking (Mark 10:28; 11:21; Matt 15:15; 18:21; Luke 12:41). Jesus often singled out Peter for teachings intended for the entire group of disciples (see especially Mark 8:29−33). As a member of the inner circle, Peter was present with Jesus at the raising of the synagogue ruler's daughter (Mark 5:35−41), at the Transfiguration (Mark 9:2−8), and at the arrest of Jesus in Gethsemane (Mark 14:43−50). As representative disciple, Peter frequently typified the disciple of *little faith.* His inconsistent behavior (see Matt. 14:27−31) reached a climax with his infamous denial scene (Mark 14:66−72). Peter was, however, rehabilitated in the scene where the resurrected Jesus restored Peter to his position of prominence (John 21:15−19; compare Mark 16:7).

Peter's Role in the Early Church Despite Peter's role among the disciples and the promise of his leadership in the early church (see especially Matt. 16:17−19), Peter did not emerge as the leader of either form of primitive Christianity. Though he played an influential role in establishing the Jerusalem church (see the early chapters of Acts), James, the brother of Jesus, assumed the leadership role of the Jewish community. Though Peter was active in the incipient stages of the Gentile mission (see Acts 10—11), Paul became the "apostle to the gentiles."

Peter probably sacrificed his chances to be the leader of either one of these groups because of his commitment to serve as a *bridge* in the early church, doing more than any other to hold together the diverse strands of primitive Christianity.

The Legacy of Peter Tradition holds that Peter died as a martyr in Rome in the 60s (1 Clem. 5:1—6:1). His legacy, however, lived on long after his death. Both 1 and 2 Peter in the New Testament are traditionally attributed to the apostle Peter. Significant also was the presence of a group of devotees of Peter who produced several writings in the name of the apostle—the Acts of

Church of St. Peter in Gallicantu which honors the traditional site of Peter's weeping after his denial.

P
Q

Peter, the Gospel of Peter (and some would include 2 Peter). To a great extent, subsequent generations of the church rely on the confession, witness, and ministry of Peter, the devoted, but fallible follower of Christ.   *Mikeal C. Parsons*

1 PETER (Pē' tēr) Twenty-first book of the New Testament.

Authorship The book was written from Rome (called Babylon in 5:13 for an unknown reason) by the apostle Peter. The opinion that the apostle Peter is the author is sustained by both history and careful investigation. Arguing from presuppositions about the character and background of Peter, some critics have emphatically rejected Petrine authorship. The opinion that the very fine quality of the language cannot be from a Galilean fisherman ignores the long history of Greek language in Galilee and the fact that Peter had preached for some thirty years by the time he wrote this book. Considering both style and church history, there is no compelling reason to reject Peter's authorship.

Canonicity While some modern critics have rejected it, 1 Peter was not among the disputed books by the early church. Its omission in the list of accepted books in the Muratorian Canon is due to the incomplete nature of that text, not because there was any early doubt as to 1 Peter's acceptance.

The Date During Nero's reign there was great persecution of believers, hence the most likely time period for the composition is around A.D. 62-64.

The Destination The address is to churches of the provinces in northern Asia Minor which is modern Turkey (Pontus, Galatia, Cappadocia, Asia, and Bythynia). When this area was evangelized, and what part Peter had in it is unknown unless one believes Paul worked this far north.

The Readers They were converted Jews and Gentiles. Jewishness is implied in the use of the Old Testament and factors cited in 1 Peter 1:10-12; 2:4-9,11-12. That some were Gentiles is supported in 1 Peter 1:14,18-19; 2:10. It is likely that the majority were Gentiles.

The Style The Greek is much more literary in both vocabulary and syntax than one would expect from an ignorant fisherman, but Peter was likely well educated, although not in formal schools (Acts 4:13). His preparation for this task included his background as a tradesman, requiring conversation with Greek-speaking men, training at the feet of Jesus, and the various meetings with the infant church and her leaders (Acts 1:12—2:42; 11:1-18; Gal. 1:18; 2:1-14). The place of the amanuensis in early literary work was greater than a modern secretary, and Silvanus (1 Pet. 5:12) could have been responsible for some of the stylistic sophistication.

The Purpose The persecuted believers in Asia

were encouraged to hope in God's ultimate deliverance, and hence remain steadfast in their persecutions.

Theological Contributions The vicarious atonement is stated more clearly in 1 Peter 3:18 (see also 1:18-19; 2:24) than anywhere else in Scripture. This leads to the most difficult passage in the book and one of the most difficult in the entire Scriptures.

First Peter 3:18-22 has the following problems: (1) the meaning of "preached unto the spirits in prison" 3:19; (2) the mention of Noah, 3:20; and (3) "baptism doth also now save us." Two common positions are held regarding Christ preaching to spirits in prison: (1) it is a descent of Christ into Hades to announce that He had died for sinners and victory over Satan is assured; (2) the spirit of Christ as he preached to Noah no avail to that hard-hearted generation. Peter was not teaching a second chance for salvation after death. The statement about baptism does not infer that the act of dipping in water accomplishes what Scripture affirms elsewhere is done by grace through faith (Eph. 2:8-9). It is "not a removal of dirt," but the response of a good conscience to God (1 Pet. 3:21 NRSV).

The appeals to holiness and personal Christian living are everywhere apparent (1:14—2:12; 2:24-25; 3:8-13), but it is the biblical theology of suffering which pervades the book (1:6-9; 2:18-25; 3:9-17; 4:1-6; 4:12-19). His advice to family members is typically Jewish, reflecting his background (2:18-20; 3:1-7). The doctrine of eschatology is often mentioned (1:4,7,11,13; 2:12; 4:7,13). It is the basis for the appeal to holy living and patiently suffering unjustly, knowing that God will finally establish His kingdom with justice.

See *Peter, 2 Peter, Epistle of.*

The Theme: "The Believer is to Stand in God's True Grace."

Outline

Introduction (1:1-2)
I. The coming of Grace in Salvation (1:3—2:12)
  A. The theme Presented (1:3-12)
  B. Worked into life by holiness (1:13—2:12)
    1. Positive: what to be (1:13-25)
    2. Negative: what to avoid (2:1-12)
II. The Outworking of Grace in Living (2:13—3:7)
  A. Submission to Government (2:13-17)
  B. Submission to Leaders (2:18-25)
  C. Submission to Spouses (3:1-7)
III. The Testing of Grace in Suffering (3:8—4:19)
IV. The Summary of Standing in Grace (5:1-10)
  A. Instructions to Elders (5:1-4)
  B. Instructions to the Congregation (5:5-10)
Conclusion (5:11-14)   *Duane A. Dunham*

2 PETER (Pē´ tēr) Twenty-second book of the New Testament.

Authorship The book claims to be written by the apostle Peter, but it was questioned in ancient times and is still under a cloud of uncertainty in some quarters. Usually the style and vocabulary are the critical areas of doubt. The two Petrine Letters show great differences which some explain by a change in amanuenses, or suggesting that Peter used Silas in 1 Peter while 2 Peter reflects his own unedited style. Readers can observe that in spite of differences, 2 Peter is more like 1 Peter than any other New Testament book. It was never rejected and met every test successfully, hence it rightly came into the canon.

The Date If we accept Peter's authorship, it must have been written before A.D. 68, probably shortly after 1 Peter was penned. This is the most likely date, although most modern critics place it much later. Eusebius places Peter's death in the fourteenth year of Nero that is variously dated from A.D. 64 to 68.

The Destination The address is too general to be of any help, so other data must be considered. If 2 Peter 3:1 refers to 1 Peter, then the destination must be the same as the previous letter. This is the better view, for all attempts to find another group or groups have failed. See 1 Peter.

The Readers The references to Jewishness are not as clear as 1 Peter, but still are inferred in 2 Peter 1:12; 2:1; 2:4–9; 3:5–8.

The Style If Peter wrote 2 Peter with his own hand, it explains some of the differences with 1 Peter. There are both Hellenistic and Semitic traces of vocabulary and syntax which would also fit the apostle's character. A major question is the literary affinity with Jude. First, affinity does not necessitate or even infer some dependency. It is virtually sure that Peter and Jude had some personal contact, but whether it resulted in both writing a portion of these letters in such similar style by mere conversation, or by viewing the document of the other is incapable of proof. Second, it is only one chapter of 2 Peter that is like Jude, leaving the bulk of the letter Petrine. Third, many have assumed Jude is late and that the writer of 2 Peter depended on it, hence 2 Peter is a late document and cannot be apostolic. This is incapable of proof and, furthermore, may merely show the early date of Jude! Fourth, there is no way of proving which document relied on the other. Scholars have argued convincingly on both sides of the question.

The Purpose To forestall and defeat the influence of heretics who came in the church to lead the readers into antinomianism or total freedom from the law. This temptation to a sinful life-style so affected Peter that shortly after his first letter, he followed with this one.

Theological Contributions Practical Christian living is emphasized by the motifs of growth by

addition in 1:3–8; judgment in 3:11–14; and exhortation to growth in 3:17–18. It is the Word of God that holds the forefront of this short letter: in chapter 1 by emphasizing knowledge (vv. 3,5,6,8,12,20–21) and its divine origin, in chapter 2 by showing its historicity (vv. 4–8), and in chapter 3 by indicating Paul's letters are equal with "the other Scriptures" (vv. 15–16). Peter strongly supported the influence of Scripture as the most important factor in our faith. One who could rely so much on personal experience did not and only appeals to it to further express the truth of Scripture (1:16–21).

The Theme: "Believers must continually give attention to the Word of God."

Outline

Introduction (1:1–2)

I. Recognize the Greatness of the Word (1:3–21)
    A. Its Power (1:3–11)
    B. Its Application (1:12–14)
    C. Its Truth (1:15–21)

II. Recognize the Enemies of the Word (2:1–22)
    A. Their Presence (2:1)
    B. Their Strategy (2:2–3)
    C. Their Judgment (2:4–10)
    D. Their Description (2:11–16)
    E. Their Converts (2:17–22)

III. Recognize the Prophecies of the Word (3:1–18)
    A. By What They Predict (3:1–10)
       1. False Teachers (3:1–7)
       2. Judgment (3:8–10)
    B. By What They Require: Holiness (3:11–18)   *Duane A. Dunham*

PETHAHIAH (Pĕ thà hī´ ah) Personal name meaning, "Yahweh opens." *1.* Ancestor of a postexilic priestly family (1 Chron. 24:16). *2.* Royal advisor to the Persian king, either at his court or as his representative in Jerusalem (Neh. 11:24). *3.* Levite participating in Ezra's covenant renewal (Neh. 9:5). *4.* Levite with a foreign wife (Ezra 10:23), perhaps identical with *3.*

PETHOR (Pē´ thôr) Place name meaning, "soothsayer." City in upper Mesopotamia identified with tell Ahmar, twelve miles south of Carchemish near the confluence of the Sajur and Euphrates rivers. Home of Balaam (Num. 22:5; Deut. 23:4).

PETHUEL (Pè thū´ ĕl) Personal name meaning, "vision of God" or "youth of God." Father of the prophet Joel (1:1).

PETITION See *Prayer.*

PETRA (Pĕ´ tra) Capital city of the Nabatean Arabs located about 60 miles north of the Gulf of Aqabah. Petra is sometimes identified with Sela (Judg. 1:36; 2 Kings 14:7; Isa. 16:1; 42:11),

because both names mean, "rock." Lack of archaeological evidence of Edomite settlement in the basin suggests that Sela is better identified with Um el Bayyarah on the mountain plateau overlooking Petra. The Nabatean king Aretas IV (2 Cor. 11:32–33) reigned from Petra.

PEULLETHAI (Pė ŭl′ lē thaî) Personal name meaning, "recompense." A Levitical gatekeeper (1 Chron. 26:5).

PEULTHAI (Pė ŭl thâî) KJV form of Peullethai (1 Chron. 26:5).

PHALEC (Phă′ lĕc) Greek form of Peleg which KJV used at Luke 3:35.

PHALLU (Phăl′ lū) KJV alternate form of Pallu (Gen. 46:9).

PHALTI (Phăl′ tī) KJV form of Palti (1 Sam. 25:44).

PHALTIEL (Phăl′ tī ĕl) KJV form of Paltiel (2 Sam. 3:15).

PHANUEL (Phả nū′ ĕl) Alternate form of the personal name *Penuel* meaning, "face of God." Father of the prophetess Anna (Luke 2:36).

PHARAOH A title meaning, "great house" for the ancient kings of Egypt. Every ancient pharaoh had five "great names" which he assumed on the day of his accession. Since it was not deemed

The funerary mask of King Tut (Pharaoh Tutankhamun) of Egypt.

proper to use such powerful names in direct fashion, a polite circumlocution developed; he came to be called Pharaoh.

Egyptians applied "pharaoh" to the royal palace and grounds in the fourth dynasty (about 2500 B.C.). The title *Pharaoh* came to be applied to the king from about 1500 B.C. until the Persian domi-

Valley of the Kings, containing tombs of pharaohs, across the Nile River from Luxor (at ancient Thebes).

nation, about 550 B.C.

An ancient pharaoh was an absolute monarch, supreme commander of the armies, chief justice of the royal court, and high priest of all religion. His absolute power may be seen in that justice was defined as "what Pharaoh loves"; wrongdoing as "what Pharaoh hates." An example of his divine power was that he daily conducted "the Rite of the House of the Morning," an early morning ritual in which he broke the seal to the statue of the sun god, waking him up with a prayer. This act brought the sun up and started every day for the people.

References to ten pharaohs can be clearly distinguished in the Old Testament: the Pharaoh of Abraham, Genesis 12:10–20; of Joseph, Genesis 39—50; of the Oppression, Exodus 1; of the Exodus, Exodus 2:23—15:19; of 1 Chronicles 4:18; of Solomon, 1 Kings 3—11; of Rehoboam, called Shishak, king of Egypt, 1 Kings 14:25; of Hezekiah and Isaiah, 2 Kings 18:21; Isaiah 36; of Josiah, 2 Kings 23:29; of Jeremiah 44:30 and Ezekiel 29:1–16.

See Egypt; Exodus.

PHARES (Phā′ rēṣ) KJV, NAS New Testament form of Perez (Matt. 1:3; Luke 3:33).

PHAREZ (Phā′ rĕz) KJV, NAS alternate form of Perez (Gen. 38:29; 46:12; Num. 26:20–21; Ruth 4:12,18; 1 Chron. 2:4–5; 4:1; 9:4).

PHARISEES The largest and most influential religious-political party during New Testament times. See *Jewish Parties.*

PHAROSH (Phā′ rŏsh) KJV alternate form of Parosh (Ezra 8:3).

PHARPAR (Phär′ pär) A river associated with Damascus (2 Kings 5:12). The river is perhaps the Nahr el 'A'waj which flows from Mount Hermon, passing about ten miles south of Damascus, or else the Nahr Taura.

PHARZITES (Phär′ zītes) KJV alternate form of Perezites (Num. 26:20).

PHASEAH (Phȧ sē′ ah) KJV alternate form of Paseah (Neh. 7:51).

PHEBE (Phē′ bė) KJV form of Phoebe (Rom. 16:1–2).

PHENICE, PHENICIA (Phė nī′ cė, Phė nīc′ ĭ ȧ) KJV alternate forms of Phoenicia (Phenice, Acts 11:19; 15:3; 27:12; Phenicia, Acts 21:2).

PHIBESETH (Phī bē′ sĕth) Place name derived from the Egyptian, "house of Bastet," a goddess represented as a cat (Ezek. 30:17). Bastet (Greek *Boubastos*) was located on the right shore of the old Tanite branch of the Nile about forty-five miles northeast of Cairo. Bastet served as capital of the eighteenth nome (administrative district) and, during the Twenty-Second and Twenty-Third Dynasties (940–745 B.C.), as capital of a fragmented Egyptian Empire. The site is identified with modern tell Basta.

PHICHOL (Phī′ chŏl) KJV form of Phicol.

PHICOL (Phī′ cŏl) Personal name meaning, "mighty." The chief captain of the Philistine army under King Abimelech (Gen. 21:22). He witnessed covenants between his commander and Abraham (21:32) and Isaac (26:26–28). See *Abimelech; Abraham; Covenant; Isaac.*

PHILADELPHIA (Phĭl ȧ dĕl′ phĭ ȧ) Place name meaning, "love of brother." A hellenistic city in the province of Lydia in western Asia Minor. See *Asia Minor; Revelation, Book of.*

Temple ruins at the site of the ancient city of Philadelphia in Asia Minor (modern Turkey).

PHILEMON (Phī lĕ′ mon) Personal name meaning, "affectionate" and eighteenth book of the New Testament. Philemon owed his conversion to the Christian faith to the apostle Paul (v.19). This conversion took place during Paul's extended ministry in Ephesus (Acts 19:10). There is no evidence that Paul ever visited Colosse where Philemon lived. Paul and Philemon became devoted friends. Paul referred to Philemon as a "beloved and fellow labourer" (v.1).

Paul's only epistle of a private and personal nature that is included in the New Testament was written to Philemon in A.D. 61. This epistle concerned a runaway slave. This slave, Onesimus, had robbed Philemon and escaped to Rome. There Onesimus found the apostle Paul who was imprisoned. Paul wrote to Philemon concerning Onesimus. Paul sent both the epistle and Onesimus back to Colosse. The epistle states that Onesimus was now a Christian. Paul requested that Philemon forgive and receive Onesimus not as a slave but as a brother (v.16). This request was not made from Paul's apostolic authority but tenderly as a Christian friend. Paul wrote, "Receive him as myself" (v.17).

Paul also stated that he was willing to pay any damages caused by Onesimus. Some scholars indicate that Paul may have been asking subtly that Philemon release Onesimus so that he could return and aid Paul in his evangelistic endeavors. Philemon had a judicial right to punish severely or even kill Onesimus. Paul's short epistle of some three hundred and fifty-five Greek words challenged Philemon to apply Christian love in dealing with Onesimus. Paul's approach eventually caused the end of slavery. See *Onesimus; Paul; Slavery.*

Outline

    I. Greetings of Grace and Peace (1–3)

   II. Commendation for Philemon's Love, Faith, and Example (4–7)

  III. Plea for Onesimus on Basis of Friendship (8–22)

   IV. Closing Salutation (23–25)

Kenneth Hubbard

PHILETUS (Phī lē′ tŭs) Personal name meaning, "beloved." Heretical teacher who asserted that the (general) resurrection had already occurred (2 Tim. 2:17–18), perhaps in a purely spiritual sense.

PHILIP (Phĭl′ ĭp) Personal name meaning, "fond of horses." *1.* A respected member of the church at Jerusalem who was chosen as one of the seven—first deacons (Acts 6:5). Following Stephen's martyrdom, Philip took the gospel to Samaria, where his ministry was blessed (Acts 8:5–13). Subsequently, he was led south to the Jerusalem-Gaza road where he introduced the Ethiopian eunuch to Christ and baptized him (Acts 8:26–38). He was then transported by the

Philip's Martyrium at Hierapolis built to commemorate the tradition of Philip's martyrdom here.

The agora (marketplace) in the ancient city of Philippi in Macedonia.

Spirit to Azotus (Ashdod) and from there conducted an itinerent ministry until he took up residence in Caesarea (Acts 8:39–40). Then, for nearly twenty years, we lose sight of him. He is last seen in Scripture when Paul lodged in his home on his last journey to Jerusalem (Acts 21:8). He had four unmarried daughters who were prophetesses (Acts 21:9). See *Acts; Deacon; Evangelism.*

2. One of twelve apostles (Matt. 10:3). From Bethsaida, he led his brother Nathanael to Jesus (John 1:43–51). Jesus tested Philip concerning how to feed the multitude (John 6:5–7). He and Andrew took inquiring Gentiles to Jesus (John 12:21–22). Philip asked Jesus to show them the father (John 14:8–9), opening the way for Jesus' teaching that to see Him is to see the Father. See *Disciples, Apostles.*

3. Tetrarch of Itaraea and Trachonitis (Luke 3:1). See *Herod.*   *Paul Powell*

PHILIP, HEROD See *Herods.*

PHILIPPI (Phĭl ĭp pī′) A city in the Roman province of Macedonia. Paul did missionary work in Philippi (Acts 16:12) and later wrote a letter to the church there (Phil. 1:1).
History In ancient times the site was in a gold mining area. After 400 B.C., Philip II of Macedon

seized the mines, fortified the city, and named it for himself. Philippi, along with the rest of Macedonia, came under Roman control after 200 B.C. In 42 B.C., Philippi was the site of a decisive battle that sealed the fate of Rome as a republic and set the stage for the establishment of an empire. The forces of Octavian (later to be Augustus Caesar, the first emperor) and Antony defeated the army of Brutus and Cassius. In honor of the victory, Antony settled some Roman soldiers there and made Philippi a Roman colony. After defeating Antony at the Battle of Actium in 31 B.C., the victorious Octavian dispossessed the supporters of Antony from Italy, but he allowed them to settle in places like Philippi. Octavian refounded Philippi as a Roman colony.

Paul and Philippi Paul first visited Philippi on his second missionary journey in response to his Macedonian vision (Acts 16:9). He and his companions sailed from Troas across the Aegean Sea to Neapolis, on the eastern shore of Macedonia (Acts 16:11). Then they journeyed a few miles inland to "Philippi, which is the chief city of that part of Macedonia, and a colony" (Acts 16:12).

On the sabbath, Paul went to a prayer meeting on the river bank. When Paul spoke, Lydia and others opened their hearts to the Lord (Acts 16:13–15). As a rule, Paul first went to the Jewish synagogue when he came to a new city. The fact that he did not do this in Philippi probably shows that Philippi had no synagogue.

An inscription from the Roman period at ancient Philippi.

The Roman character of the city is apparent from Paul's other experiences in Philippi. He healed a possessed slave girl whose owners charged that Jews troubled the city by teaching customs unlawful for Romans to observe (Acts 16:20–21). The city magistrates ordered Paul and Silas to be beaten and turned over to the jailer (Acts 16:20,22–23). After Paul's miraculous deliverance and the jailer's conversion, the magistrates sent the jailer word to release Paul (Acts 16:35–36). Paul informed the messengers that he was a Roman citizen. Since he had been beaten and imprisoned unlawfully, Paul insisted that the mag-

istrates themselves come and release him (Acts 16:37). The very nervous magistrates went to the jail. They pled with Paul not only to leave the jail but also to leave town (Acts 16:38–40). See *Paul; Roman Law; Philippians.* Robert J. Dean

PHILIPPIANS (Phĭ lĭp′ pĭ ans) Eleventh book of the New Testament written by Paul to the church at Philippi, the first church he established in Europe. It is one of the Prison Epistles (along with Ephesians, Colossians, and Philemon). The authenticity of the letter generally is accepted. The terminology and theology are thoroughly Pauline.

In spite of the negative circumstances from which Paul wrote, Philippians is a warm, personal, positive letter (except for chapter 3). Paul wrote to thank the church for a gift it had recently sent to Paul in prison and to inform them of his circumstances and of Timothy's and Epaphroditus' travel plans. The underlying theme which holds the letter together is a call for unity in the church.

The date of the letter depends on which imprisonment Paul was enduring. The traditional date and place of writing is A.D. 61/62 from Rome. If Philippians was written from Caesarea, we would assign a date in the late 50s; if from Ephesus, the mid-50s. See below.

Origin of Philippians Where was Paul when he wrote Philippians? The letter itself reveals only that he was in prison. Acts records Pauline imprisonments in Caesarea and in Rome. Some evidence indicates that Paul was also in prison in Ephesus (Acts 19; 2 Cor. 11:23; 1 Cor. 15:30–32).

Philippians is traditionally assigned to Rome. Reference to Caesar's household (4:22), the praetorium or palace guard (1:13 NIV), as well as the ability to receive visitors (Acts 28:16,30–31) like Epaphroditus and the possibility of execution (1:20–26) seem to mesh well with the imprisonment described in the closing verses of Acts.

An Ephesian origin for Philippians also has much in its favor. Ephesus was the capital of Asia. A provincial governor's guard occupied a "praetorium," and the governor's residence was termed "Caesar's household." An Ephesian imprisonment and origin for Philippians makes sense of Paul's stated intent to visit Philippi upon his release (Phil. 2:24; from Rome Paul intended to go to Spain, Rom. 15:23–24). In addition, Philippians 2:25–30 implies that several trips, bearing news, had been made between Paul's locale and Philippi. A trip from Rome to Philippi took several weeks; from Ephesus to Philippi required only several days. The large number of trips implied in Philippians is difficult to fit into a two-year Roman imprisonment, but is less problematic even in a much shorter Ephesian imprisonment.

A Caesarean origin for Philippians has had fewer supporters over the years. Its detractors point out Paul's intent to go to Rome (not visit

Philippi) upon his release and doubt that Paul ever feared execution in Caesarea, as Philippians implies, since he always had the option of appealing to Caesar.

Content of the Letter Philippians is structured much like a typical personal letter of that day. The introduction identifies the sender(s): Paul and Timothy, and the recipients: the saints, overseers, and deacons. This typical letter form, however, is filled with Christian content. The usual secular greeting and wish for good health is transformed into a blessing (v. 2), a thanksgiving for the Philippian church's faithful participation in the work of the gospel (1:3–8), and a prayer that they may be blessed with an ever growing, enlightened, Christian love (1:9–11). See *Letter*.

The body of the letter begins with Paul explaining his current situation (1:12–26). In vv. 12–18, Paul revealed that his primary concern (the proclamation of the gospel) was being accomplished in spite of his difficult circumstances. His captors were being evangelized (vv. 12–13). His compatriots have gained confidence through his bold example (v. 14). Even the brethren who were working with wrong motives were sharing the good news actively. (There is no hint that these were preaching a false gospel; Paul rejoiced in their work, vv. 15–18). The severity of Paul's imprisonment is reflected in 1:19–26. His death appears to be a real possibility. Death would unite him with Christ. Life would give him the joys of continued productive ministry. He found cause for genuine rejoicing in both. Paul seemed confident, however, that he would eventually be released and reunited with the Philippians.

When Paul returned to Philippi, he hoped to find a church united in Christ. Philippians 1:27—4:9 is a multifaceted call for unity in the church. The great cause of the proclamation of the gospel calls for them to be united in spirit, in task, and in confidence (1:27–30). Their common Christian experience (2:1) and purpose (2:2) should also rule out a self-centered, self-serving attitude (2:3–4). Those who follow Christ must follow him in selfless service to others (2:5–11).

Philippians 2:6–11 is known as the kenosis passage (from the Greek word translated "emptied" in 2:7 RSV). The language and structure of the passage have convinced most commentators that Paul was quoting a hymn which was already in use in the church. The purpose of the pre-Pauline hymn was probably to teach the believer about the nature and work of Christ. Preexistence, incarnation, passion, resurrection, and exaltation are all summarized in a masterful fashion. In the context of Philippians, however, the *kenosis* passage is used to highlight the humility and selfless service demonstrated by Jesus, whose example the Christian is to follow. See *Kenosis*.

Paul was concerned that the Philippians demonstrate the reality of their Christian profession in action. Neither the grumbling so characteristic of Israel in the wilderness nor the perversity of a world that does not know God should characterize the church. Paul had sacrificed himself to engender true faith in the Philippians. His desire, for them and for himself, was that he be able to rejoice that his sacrifice was not in vain (2:12–18).

Philippians 2:25–30 explained to the church why Epaphroditus was returning to Philippi. The church has sent him to take a gift to Paul (see Phil. 4:10–20) and minister to him in his imprisonment. Paul probably feared that some would criticize Epaphroditus for returning earlier than planned.

The tone of the letter changes in chapter 3. The encouragement to rejoice (3:1) unexpectedly becomes a stern warning (3:2). (The change is so marked that some scholars think chapter 3 is a later addition to the letter.) A problem was threatening the church at Philippi which had the potential of destroying the foundation of unity and the basis of joy.

The exact nature of the problem is unclear. Jewish legalism (3:2–11), Christian or gnostic perfectionism (3:12–16), and pagan libertinism (3:17–21) are all attacked. Was one heretical system blending all three together? Can one of the above be used to explain the entirety of chapter 3? Were there, in fact, three different threats to the church? Unfortunately, we do not have enough information to answer these questions with confidence. What is clear, however, is that Paul countered the heretical teachings with Christian truths: Jesus Christ is the only avenue to righteousness (3:2–11); the stature of Christ is the goal of Christian maturity (3:12–16); and the nature of Christ and His kingdom is the standard by which the Christian must live (3:17–21).

Chapter 4 returns to a more positive instruction and affirmation of the church. Two women, Euodias and Syntyche (4:2–3), were exhorted to end their conflict, for personal disagreements may be as damaging to the unity of the church as false doctrine.

General exhortations to rejoice and to remain faithful (4:4–9) led to Paul's expression of gratitude for the Philippians' faithful support of him and of the ministry (4:10–20). The letter closes in typical Pauline fashion, with an exchange of greetings and a prayer for grace.

Outline

I. Salutation (1:1–2)
II. Introduction (1:3–26)
   A. Thanksgiving prayer (1:3–11)
   B. Adverse personal circumstances may advance the gospel (1:12–26)
III. Pastoral Admonitions (1:27—2:18)
   A. Admonition to consistency (1:27)
   B. Admonition to courage (1:28–30)
   C. Admonition to unity (2:1–11)
   D. Admonition to responsibility and obedi-

ence (2:12–13)
  E. Admonition to a blameless life of rejoicing (2:14–18)
IV. Pastoral Concerns (2:19–30)
  A. Pastoral concern for the church's welfare (2:19–24)
  B. Pastoral concern for a distressed minister (2:25–30)
V. Pastoral Warning and Encouragement (3:1—4:1)
  A. Warning against legalistic zealots: Glory only in Christ (3:1–3)
  B. Warning against confidence in the flesh: Place confidence only in Christ and the resurrection hope (3:4–11)
  C. Warning against satisfaction with the past: Press onward to the heavenly prize (3:12–16)
  D. Warning against enemies of the cross: Stand firm as citizens of heaven (3:17—4:1)
VI. Final Exhortation (4:2–9)
  A. To personal reconciliation (4:2–3)
  B. To joy and gentleness (4:4–5)
  C. To peace of mind (4:6–7)
  D. To noble thoughts (4:8–9)
VII. Conclusion (4:10–23)
  A. The apostle's contentment in Christ's strength (4:10–13)
  B. The apostle's appreciation for the church's stewardship (4:14–20)
  C. The apostle's final greetings and benediction (4:21–23)   *Michael Martin*

PHILISTIA (Phĭ lĭs′ tĭ á) The coastal plain of southwestern Palestine which was under the control of the Philistines (Ex. 15:14; Pss. 60:8; 87:4; 108:9; Isa. 14:29–31). KJV sometimes referred to Philistia as Palestina (Ex. 15:14; Isa. 14:29–31). See *Philistines.*

PHILISTIM (Phĭ lĭs′ tĭm) KJV alternate form of Philistines (Gen. 10:14).

PHILISTINES, THE (Phĭl ĭs′ tînes) One of the rival groups the Israelites encountered as they settled the land of Canaan. References to the Philistines appear in the Old Testament as well as other ancient Near Eastern writings. *Philistine* refers to a group of people who occupied and gave their name to the southwest part of Palestine. Ancient Egyptian records from the time of Merneptah and Ramses III referred to them as the"prst." Ancient Assyrian records include references to the Philistines in the terms *Philisti* and *Palastu.*

The origin and background of the Philistines has not been completely clarified. Ancient Egyptian records include the "prst" as part of a larger movement of people known as the Sea Peoples, who invaded Egypt about 1188 B.C. by land and by sea, battling the forces of Ramses III, who,

according to Egyptian records, defeated them. The Sea Peoples, a massive group that originated in the Aegean area, included the Tjeker, the Skekelesh, the Denyen, the Sherden, and the Weshwesh as well as the "prst" or Pelesti, the biblical Philistines. As they moved eastward from the Aegean region, the Sea Peoples made war with people in their path including the Hittites in Anatolia and the inhabitants at sites in North Syria such as those at the site of Ugarit. According to biblical references, the homeland of the Philistines was Caphtor (Amos 9:7; Jer. 47:4). See *Caphtor.*

Philistines are first mentioned in the patriarchal stories (Gen. 21:32,34), a reference which some suggest is anachronistic and others suggest refers to the migrations of an Aegean colony in the patriarchal period. The most dramatic phase of Philistine history begins in the period of the Judges when the Philistines were the principal enemy of and the major political threat to Israel. This threat is first seen in the stories of Samson (Judg. 13—16). The threat intensified as the Philistines encroached on the territory of the tribe of Dan ultimately forcing Dan to move north (Judg. 18:11,29). The threat reached crisis proportions in the battle of Ebenezer (1 Sam. 4:1–18), when the Israelites were soundly defeated and the ark of the covenant, brought over from Shiloh (1 Sam. 4:3–4), was captured. During the time of Samuel, the Israelites defeated the Philistines at times (1 Sam. 7:5–11; 14:16–23), but, generally speaking, their advance against the Israelites continued. Saul not only failed to check their intrusion into Israelite territory but in the end lost his life fighting the Philistines at Mount Gilboa (1 Sam. 31:1–13). David finally checked the Philistine advance at Baal-perazim (2 Sam. 5:17–25).

Several features of Philistine life and culture are reflected in the Old Testament. Politically, the Philistines had a highly organized city-state system comprised of five towns in southwest Palestine: Ashdod, Gaza, Ashkelon, Gath, and Ekron (1 Sam. 6:17). Each of the city-states was ruled by a "lord" (1 Sam. 6:18), a kinglike figure. Gath was perhaps the major city of this Philistine pentapolis, and as such, served as the hub of the city-state system.

The Philistines were experts in metallurgy, the skill of processing metals (1 Sam. 13:19–23). Philistine expertise in this area put the Israelites at a decided disadvantage in their struggles with the Philistines (1 Sam. 13:22). See *Minerals and Metals.*

The Philistines had a highly trained military organization. Sea and land battles between the Egyptians and Sea Peoples are depicted on large panels at the temple of Ramses III at Medinet Habu in Thebes. The Philistines were in ships designed with a curved keel and the head of a bird on the bow. Philistine warriors wore a plumed or feathered headdress, a feature which added height to their physical appearance. On land, the Philistines were equipped with horses and chariots, numerous foot soldiers, and archers (1 Sam. 13:5; 31:3). The armor of Philistine soldiers included bronze helmets, coats of mail, leg protectors, spears, and shields (1 Sam. 17:5–7). The story of Goliath indicates that at times the Philistines used individual combat (1 Sam. 17). Most likely, the Philistine warrior went through a cursing ritual just prior to the confrontation (1 Sam. 17:43). David, who recognized the military expertise of the Philistines, selected Cherethites (Cretans) and Pelethites (Philistines) (1 Sam. 20:23) for his palace guard or mercenary army. This segment of the army provided protection for David and his family during times of revolt. See *Arms and Armor.*

While our information on Philistine religion is limited, three Philistine gods are mentioned in the Old Testament—Dagon, Ashtoreth, and Baalzebub. Dagon appears to be the chief god of the Philistines. Temples of Dagon were located at Gaza (Judg. 16:21–30) and Ashdod (1 Sam. 5:1–7). Ashtoreth, the fertility goddess of the Canaanites, was most likely adopted by the Philistines. Apparently, the Philistines had Ashtoreth temples at Beth-shan (1 Sam. 31:10 NIV) and, according to Herodotus, at Ashkelon (Herodotus I. 105). Baalzebub, the Philistine god whose name means "lord of the flies," was the god of Ekron (2 Kings 1:1–16). Most likely the Philistines worshiped Baalzebub as a god who averted pestilence or plagues.

Archaeological excavations have brought to light many features of the material culture of the Philistines. The distinctive Philistine pottery which reflects styles and designs adopted and adapted from other cultures has been found at many sites. The major types of Philistine pottery are the so-called beer jug with a spouted strainer on the side, the crater bowl, the stirrup jar, and the horn-shaped vessel. The pottery was often decorated with red and black painted designs including geometric designs often consisting of circles and cross halving and stylized birds. Clay coffins were used by the Philistines for burials. These distinctive coffins, called "anthropoid coffins" because they were made in the shape of a human body, had lids decorated with the physical features of the upper part of a human being, features such as a head, arms, and hands.

Recent excavations especially at the sites of Ashdod, tel-Qasile, tel Jemmeh, and tel Mor have added significantly to our understanding of the Philistine culture. The excavations at tel Qasile revealed a Philistine iron smeltery, a Philistine temple, offering stands, and other vessels used in religious rituals as well as many other artifacts and installations. A new series of excavations is under way at Ashkelon. The current excavations will add

yet a new dimension to our understanding of the Philistines. The political influence of the Philistines was most prominent between 1200 and 1000 B.C., but their influence continues through the use of the name Palestine, a name derived from "Philistine." See *Palestine.*

See *Gaza, Gath, Ekron, Ashdod, Ashkelon.*

LaMoine DeVries

PHILO JUDAEUS (Phī′ lō Jū dae′ ŭs) Early Jewish interpreter of Scripture known for use of allegory. Also known as Philo of Alexandria, he lived about the same time as Jesus (about 20 B.C. to A.D. 50). A member of a wealthy Jewish family in Alexandria, Egypt, he was well educated in Greek schools and used the Greek Old Testament, the Septuagint, as his Bible.

Philo's writings—particularly his commentaries on the Scriptures—influenced the early church. A literal interpretation was all right for the average scholar, but for the enlightened ones such as himself, he advocated an allegorical interpretation. See *Bible, Hermeneutics.*

James Taulman

PHILOSOPHY IN THE NEW TESTAMENT Philosophical systems abounded in the first century A.D. Among the most notable were Stoicism, Epicureanism, Platonism, Cynicism, Philonism, and Skepticism. The writers of the New Testament mention philosophy only twice. In Colossians 2:8, Paul warned his readers to beware of philosophy. Paul had in mind no particular philosophy; rather, he condemned any system of thought which denied the full divinity of Christ. The Colossian Christians were threatened by a teaching (probably Gnostic) contrary to the gospel Paul delivered. In Acts 17:18, Luke mentioned that Epicurean and Stoic philosophers engaged Paul in debate. Their motives were clearly a desire for speculation rather than an active pursuit of the truth of the gospel.

There are conceptual points of contact in the New Testament with various philosophies. The early Christians encountered the wide range of philosophies in their missionary activity. These early Christians adapted concepts familiar to their audience in their witness and writings. Paul, as a learned man, reflected a knowledge of the major philosophies in his letters. Paul quoted from Stoic works in his speech at the Areopagus (Acts 17:28). His statement in Philippians 4:11 is similar to Stoic ideas. Paul's question-and-answer style in Romans 3:1–4 and 1 Corinthians 6:2–19 are very similar to Cynic diatribe (a lively semiconversational technique). Philonic or Platonic thought is reflected in Hebrews, for example, where the writer identifies the earthly sanctuary as a copy or shadow of the perfect heavenly sanctuary (see chs. 8—10). The presence of ideas in the New Testament similar to some of the philosophical notions of the day is undeniable. It must be emphasized, however, that the theological presuppositions of a Christian writer and a first century philosopher were vastly different.   *Terence B. Ellis*

PHILOLOGUS (Phĭ lŏ' lō gŭs) Personal name meaning, "lover of words," either in the sense of "talkative" or of "lover of learning." Member, perhaps the head, of a Roman house church whom Paul greeted (Rom. 16:15). Philologus was perhaps the husband of Julia and father of Nereus and Olympas.

PHINEHAS (Phĭn' ė hȧs) Personal name meaning "dark-skinned" or "mouth of brass." *1.* Grandson of Aaron and high priest who, on several occasions, aided Moses and Joshua. See *High Priest. 2.* One of Eli the priest's worthless sons. He engaged in religious prostitution (1 Sam. 2:22) and led the people to follow. He and Hophni died in a battle with the Philistines while attempting to keep the ark from being captured (4:11). When his pregnant wife heard of his death, she immediately delivered, naming the child Ichabod ("the glory has departed").

PHLEGON (Phlē' ğŏn) Personal name meaning, "burning," perhaps in the sense of "zealous." Member of a Roman house church whom Paul greeted (Rom. 16:14).

PHOEBE (Phoē' bė) Personal name meaning, "bright." "Servant," "minister" (REB), "deaconess" (NAS, NIV note), or "deacon" (NRSV) of church at Cenchrea whom Paul recommended to church at Rome (Rom. 16:1–2). See *Deacon.*

PHOENICIA (Phoē nī' cĭ à) Place name meaning, "purple" or "crimson," translation of Hebrew "Canaan, land of purple." The narrow land between the Mediterranean Sea and the Lebanon Mountains between Tyre in the south and Arvad in the north. New Testament Phoenicia reached south to Dor. Great forest land enabled the people to build ships and become the dominant seafaring nation. The forests also provided timber for export, Phoenician cedars being the featured material of Solomon's Temple (1 Kings 5:8–10).

Culture Phoenician religion was akin to that of the Canaanites, featuring fertility rites of Baal. See *Canaan.* Later, Baal's Greek counterpart Adonis ("my lord") was worshiped in similar fashion to Tammuz. See *Fertility Cults.* The Phoenician princess Jezebel imported devotion to Baal to Israel. See *Jezebel; Elijah.* Phoenicia introduced the alphabet to the western world, but little of their literature survived.

History City-states rather than central government dominated Phoenicia. Leading cities were Tyre, Sidon, Byblos (Gebal), and Berytos (Beirut). An early Neolithic race disappeared about 3000

A relief depicting a Phoenician shepherd.

B.C., being replaced by Semitic colonizers from the east. Invading armies from north (Hittites), east (Amorites and Assyrians), and south (Egyptians) dominated history until 1000 B.C. when King Hiram of Tyre established local rule (981–947 B.C.). See *Hiram.* They were able to take advantage of their location on the sea with natural harbors and their forests to establish farflung trade. Compare Ezekiel 27. Their sailors established trading colonies to the west and south all along the Mediterranean coast. The most notable colony was Carthage on the North African coast.

Growth of Assyrian power about 750 B.C. led to Phoenicia's decline. The Persian Empire gave virtual independence to Phoenicia, using the Phoenician fleet against Egypt and Greece. Alexander the Great put an end to Phoenician political power, but the great cities retained economic power.

New Testament Jesus' ministry reached Tyre and Sidon (Matt. 15:21). Persecution beginning with Stephen's death, led the church to spread into Phoenicia (Acts 11:19; compare 15:3; 21:2–3). See *Tyre; Sidon.*   *Timothy Trammel*

PHOENIX (Phoē' nĭx) Place name perhaps meaning, "date palm." Port on the southeast coast of Crete where Paul and the ship's crew hoped to reach for winter harbor (Acts 27:12). Phoenix is often identified with Port Loutro, which, however, faces the wrong direction to offer shelter from winter storms. Phoenix is better identified with some point on Phinika Bay to the west of Loutro.

PHRYGIA (Phrỹg′ ĭa) Place name meaning, "parched." In very ancient times the area immediately west of the Hellespont. Later, the people migrated into Asia Minor. During Roman times, Phrygia was a subregion of Galatia, and her people often were slaves or servants. The area remained relatively undefined but contained Antioch of Pisidia, Laodicea, and at times, Iconium. Some of the Phrygians were present in Jerusalem on the Day of Pentecost and heard the gospel in their native language (Acts 2:10; compare 16:6; 18:23). See *Asia Minor*.

PHURAH (Phū′ rah) KJV form of Purah.

PHUT (Phŭt) KJV alternate form of Put (Gen. 10:6; Ezek. 27:10).

PHUVAH (Phū′ vah) KJV form of Puvah (Gen. 46:13).

PHYGELUS (Phỹ ġĕl′ us) Personal name meaning, "fugitive." Christian who deserted Paul (2 Tim. 1:15). The contrast with Onesiphorus, who was not ashamed of the imprisoned Paul (1:16–17), suggests that Phygelus abandoned Paul in prison.

PHYLACTERIES (Phỹ lăc′ tė rīes) See *Frontlets*.

An orthodox Jewish man wearing the traditional phylactery (frontlet) on his forehead.

A copper or bronze bucket in the form of a ram's head dating to the Phrygian period from Gordion.

PHYSICIAN See *Diseases.*

PICK See *Tools.*

PICTURE KJV term in three passages where modern translations use a term better suited to the context. *1.* Carved stone figures (Num. 33:52). *2.* Settings (NAS, NIV, NRSV) or filigree (REB) (Prov. 25:11). *3.* A sailing craft or vessel (Isa. 2:16).

PIECE OF MONEY *1.* Translation of the Hebrew *qesitah,* a coin of uncertain weight and value (Gen. 33:19; Job 42:11 KJV, NAS, NRSV). NIV reads "pieces of silver." *2.* KJV translation of the Greek term *stater* (Matt. 17:27). Modern translations read: stater (NAS); four drachma coin (NIV); shekel (RSV); coin (NRSV, REB). See *Coins.*

PIETY Translation of a Hebrew expression and several Greek terms. *1.* NIV used piety to translate the Hebrew idiom "the fear [or reverence] of the Lord" (Job 4:6; 15:4; 22:4; compare REB). *2.* NRSV used piety to translate the Greek term meaning, "righteousness" (Matt. 6:1), where the concern was with an external show of religion (Matt. 6:2–6). *3.* Piety translates two Greek terms for fear or reverence for God (Acts 3:12 NAS, NRSV; Heb. 5:7 NAS). *3.* Piety represents the religious duty of caring for the physical needs of elderly family members (1 Tim. 5:4 KJV, NAS).

PIG See *Animals.*

PIGEON See *Birds.*

PIHAHIROTH (Pī hȧ hī′ rŏth) Hebrew place name derived from the Egyptian, "house of Hathor" and interpreted in Hebrew as "mouth of canals." Pihahiroth lay in the eastern Nile delta to the east of Baal-zephon. The site is unknown. The Israelites encamped at Pihahiroth in the early days of the Exodus (Ex. 14:2,9; Num. 33:7). The alternate form Hahiroth appears at Numbers 33:8.

PILATE, PONTIUS (Pī′ lȧte, Pŏn′ tiŭs) Roman governor of Judea remembered in history as a notorious anti-Semite and in Christian creeds as the magistrate under whom Jesus Christ "suffered" (1 Tim 6:13). The New Testament refers to him as "governor," while other sources call him "procurator" or "prefect" (an inscription found in Caesarea in 1961). Pilate came to power about A.D. 26, close to the time when two of his contemporaries, Sejanus in Rome and Flaccus in Egypt, were pursuing policies apparently aimed at the destruction of the Jewish people. Pilate's policies were much the same. His procuratorship consisted of one provocation of Jewish sensibilities after another. He broke all precedent by bringing into Jerusalem military insignia bearing the image of Caesar in flagrant defiance of Jewish law. He

The only known extrabiblical mention of Pilate's name is shown here in a Latin dedicatory inscription on a stone slab found at Caesarea Maritima.

removed them only when the Jews offered to die at the hands of his soldiers rather than consent to such blasphemy. He brutally suppressed protest by planting armed soldiers, disguised as civilians, among the Jewish crowds. Against such a backdrop, it is not hard to understand the reference in Luke 13:1 to "The Galileans whose blood Pilate had mingled with their sacrifice (NIV)." Pilate was finally removed from office as the result of a similar outrage against Samaritan worshipers who had gathered on Mount Gerizim, their holy mountain, to view some sacred vessels which they believed Moses had buried there. When the Samaritans complained to Vitellius, the governor of Syria, Pilate was ordered to Rome to account for his actions to the emperor and is not mentioned again in reliable contemporary sources.

In view of his record, it is surprising that Pilate allowed himself to be pressured by a group of Jewish religious authorities into allowing Jesus to be executed. A possible explanation is that he already felt his position in the empire to be in jeopardy (note the threat implicit in John 19:12). Pilate seems to have had no personal inclination to put Jesus to death, and the New Testament writers are eager to show that he did not (Luke 23:4,14,22; John 18:38; 19:4,6; compare Matt. 17:19). The Gospel writers sought to demonstrate that Jesus was innocent from the standpoint of Roman law and that consequently Christianity in their day was not a threat to the Roman political and social order. The fact that Jesus was brought to Pilate at all probably means that He had not been formally tried and convicted by the Sanhedrin, or Jewish ruling Council (if he had, he would probably have been stoned to death like Stephen, or like James the Just in A.D. 62). Instead, a relatively small group of Jerusalem priests, including the high priest, wanted to forestall any kind of a messianic movement by the people because of the repression it would provoke from the Romans (see John 11:47–50,53). They maneuvered Pilate into doing their work for them (compare Luke 23:2). Pilate is represented in all the Gospels as questioning Jesus especially on the subject of kingship, but he remained unconvinced that Jesus was in any way a serious claimant to Jewish or Roman political power. The inscription he insisted on placing over the cross according to all the Gospels was Pilate's last grim joke at Jewish expense: "This is the King of the Jews." Anti-Jewish to the end, Pilate was telling the world, "What a sorry race this is, with such a pitiful figure for their king!" See *Cross*.   *J. Ramsey Michaels*

PILDASH (Pĭl' dăsh) Personal and clan name perhaps meaning, "powerful." Sixth son of Nahor (Gen. 22:22), probably the ancestor of an otherwise unknown north Arabian tribe.

PILEHA (Pĭ' lĕ hă) KJV form of Pilha.

PILFER To steal secretly, usually little by little (John 12:6 NAS, REB; Titus 2:10 NAS, REB, NRSV).

PILGRIMAGE A journey, especially a religious trek to a site at which God has revealed Himself in the past. KJV used pilgrimage in the nontechnical sense of journeys (Ex. 6:4). KJV, NAS, RSV used pilgrimage in a figurative sense for life journey (Gen. 47:9 KJV, only; Ps. 119:54). The only explicit mention of religious pilgrimage occurs in the NIV of Psalm 84:5 (Compare REB).

In Israel's early history, numerous local shrines were the goals of religious pilgrimage: Bethel (Gen. 28:10–22; 31:13; 35:9–15; Amos 4:4; 5:5); Gilgal (Josh. 4:19–24; Hos. 4:15; Amos 4:4; 5:5); Shiloh (Judg. 20:26–27; 1 Sam. 1:3,19); Beersheba (Amos 5:5; 8:14); Gibeon (1 Kings 3:3–5); even Horeb (1 Kings 19:8). Jerusalem was not the goal of religious pilgrims until David relocated the ark there (2 Sam. 6:12–19). Hezekiah's and Josiah's reforms attempted to destroy the pagan sites of pilgrimage and idol worship (2 Kings 18:4; 23:8) and make Jerusalem the exclusive focus of pilgrimage. Mosaic law required adult male Israelites to appear before the Lord (where the ark of the covenant rested) three times a year (Ex. 23:14–17; 34:18–23; Deut. 16:16). Crowds of pilgrims (Pss. 42:4; 55:14;

Luke 2:44) sang on the way to Jerusalem (Isa. 30:29). The Psalms of Ascent (Pss. 24; 84; 118; 120–134) were likely sung as pilgrims climbed the ascent to the Temple mount in Jerusalem. The prophets condemned the celebration of religious pilgrimages and feasts when not accompanied by genuine devotion to the Lord expressed in righteous lives (Isa. 1:12–13; Amos 4:4–5; 5:5–6,21–24).

The New Testament witnessed the continuing popularity of pilgrimage to Jerusalem (Matt. 21:8–11; Luke 2:41; John 2:13; 5:1; 7:2,10; 12:12,20; Acts 2:5–10; 20:16).   *Chris Church*

PILHA (Pĭl' hȧ) Personal name meaning, "millstone." Lay leader witnessing Ezra's covenant renewal (Neh. 10:24).

PILLAR Stone monuments (Hebrew *matstsebah*) or standing architectural structures (Hebrew *ʿamudim*). *1*. Stones set up as memorials to persons. Jacob set up a pillar on Rachel's grave as a memorial to her (Gen. 35:20). Because Absalom had no son to carry on his name, he set up a pillar and carved his name in it (2 Sam. 18:18).

2. Shrines both to the Lord and to false gods. Graven images often were pillars set up as gods. God commanded Israel to break down such "images" (Hebrew *matstseboth;* Ex. 23:24). The Canaanites erected pillars at their places of worship, and probably influenced Israelite practice. Archaeologists found pillars at Gezer. Jacob set up a pillar following his dream (Gen. 28:18) and again when God spoke to him at Bethel (35:9–15) as memorials of God's revelation. Moses set up twelve pillars to commemorate the giving of the law to the tribes of Israel (Ex. 24:4).

3. As structural supports, pillars were used extensively. The tabernacle used pillars for the veil (Ex. 26:31–32), the courts (27:9–15), and the gate (27:16). The Temple in Jerusalem used pillars for its support (1 Kings 7:2–3), and the porch had pillars (7:6). Figuratively, pillars were believed to hold up heaven (Job 26:11) and earth (1 Sam. 2:8).

4. God led Israel through the wilderness with a pillar of cloud by day and a pillar of fire by night (Ex. 13:21; compare 14:19–20). These pillars were symbols of God's presence with Israel as much as signs of where they were to go.

5. Solomon's Temple had two free-standing brass pillars (1 Kings 7:15). See *Jachin and Boaz*.
                                       Mike Mitchell

PILLAR OF CLOUD AND FIRE Visible evidence of God's presence with Israel during the Exodus and wilderness wanderings (Ex. 14:24; 33:9–10; Num. 12:5; Deut. 31:15). As a sign of God's presence, the pillar of cloud and fire was associated with divine actions: salvation (Ex. 14:19–20); revelation (Ex. 33:9–10; Ps. 99:7); judgment (Num. 12:5); commissioning (Deut. 31:15). Nehemiah used the pillar as a sign of God's faithfulness (Neh. 9:12,19). Psalm 99:7 reflects an otherwise unknown tradition that the pillar abided with Israel until the time of Samuel. Jesus' self-presentation as the incarnate Light of the world (John 8:12) recalls the guiding light of the wilderness wanderings. In Jesus' day, the celebration of the Feast of Tabernacles (John 7:2) included the lighting of great, golden lamps in the Temple court as a reminder of the pillar of fire and cloud. Jesus as the living Light challenged persons to follow Him as Israel had followed God's earlier light.

PILLOW A support for the head. KJV and REB described the rock on which Jacob rested his head as a pillow (Gen. 28:11,18). The Hebrew term translated pillow at 1 Samuel 19:13,16 (KJV, RSV, TEV) is of uncertain meaning. Possible translations include quilt (NAS), net (NRSV), and rug (REB). KJV followed the earliest Greek translation in reading pillows at Ezekiel 13:18,20. Modern translations render the underlying Hebrew as magic bands (NAS, REB, NRSV), charms (NIV), or wristbands (TEV). Jesus demonstrated His absolute trust in God by sleeping through a storm with his head on a pillow (Mark 4:38 KJV, TEV) or cushion (NAS, NIV, REB, NRSV).

PILOT A helmsman. Ancient pilots steered by positioning a side rudder which was an oversized oar pivoted in a slanting position near the vessel's stern (Jas. 3:4; KJV, governor). Most translations used pilot in Ezekiel 27:8,27–29 in parallel to terms translated mariners, rowers, or sailors. The NIV rendered the underlying Hebrew as a seaman. See *Ships.*

PILTAI (Pĭl' taî) Short form of personal name meaning, "(Yah is) my deliverance." Head of a family of postexilic priests (Neh. 12:17).

PIM See *Weights and Measures.*

PIN See *Peg.*

PINE TREE See *Plants in the Bible.*

PINNACLE (Pĭn' nă cle) The highest point of a structure. NRSV referred to the pinnacles of the Temple or the city of Jerusalem (Isa. 54:12). The underlying Hebrew suggests a structure catching the sun's rays. Other translations include battlements (NAS, NIV, REB), towers (TEV), and windows (KJV). The pinnacle (literally, "little wing") of the Temple (Matt. 4:5; Luke 4:9) is not mentioned in the Old Testament, intertestamental literature, or rabbinic sources. Possible identifications include the southeastern corner of the royal colonnade which overlooked the Kidron valley

The traditional "pinnacle of the Temple."

and a lintel or balcony above one of the Temple gates. The account of the martyrdom of James the Lord's brother by Hegesippus relates that James was thrown from the pinnacle of the Temple and then stoned and clubbed. This (likely conflated) account suggests a high structure overlooking the Temple court.

PINON (Pī' nŏn) Edomite clan chief (Gen. 36:41; 1 Chron. 1:52), whose descendants perhaps settled Punon (Num. 33:42–43).

PINT See *Weights and Measures.*

PIONEER See *Prince of Life.*

PIPE See *Music, Instruments, and Dancing.*

PIRAM (Pī' răm) Personal name perhaps meaning, "wild ass." King of Jarmuth southwest of Jerusalem and member of a coalition of five Amorite kings who battled Joshua unsuccessfully (Josh. 10:3,23).

PIRATHON, PIRATHONITE (Pī rā' thŏn, Pī rā' thŏn īte) Place name meaning, "princely" or "height, summit" and its inhabitants. The town in the hill country of Ephraim was the home of the judge Abdon (Judg. 12:13,15) and of Benaiah, one of David's elite warriors (2 Sam. 23:30; 1 Chron.

11:31). The site is identified with Far'ata about five miles southwest of Shechem.

PISGAH (Pĭs' gah) Place name perhaps meaning, "the divided one." Mountain in the Abarim range across the Jordan River from Jericho. Some Bible scholars believe it was part of Mount Nebo; others think it could have been a separate rise, either en-Neba or near modern Khirbet Tsijaga. God allowed Moses to view the Promised Land from the heights of Pisgah (Deut. 34:1) but would not let him cross into Canaan. Israel had camped near Pisgah (Num. 21:20). Balak took Balaam to its height so the prophet could see Israel and curse them (Num. 23:14). It was a limit of Sihon's kingdom (Josh. 12:23; Ashdoth-pisgah in KJV) and also for the tribe of Reuben (13:20).

PISHON (Pĭ' shŏn) Name meaning, "free-flowing," designating one of the rivers of Eden (Gen. 2:11). The identity of the river is unknown. Some suggest the "river" was a canal connecting the Tigris and Euphrates or another body of water, such as the Persian Gulf.

PISIDIA (Pĭ sĭ dĭ' à) Small area in the province of Galatia in southern Asia Minor bounded by Pamphylia, Phrygia, and Lyconia. The territory lay within the Taurus Mountain range and therefore resisted invasion by ancient peoples. Only in 25 B.C. did the Romans gain control over the region through economic diplomacy. Antioch was made the capital, although some historians contend that the city was not actually in Pisidia. Paul and Barnabas came through Antioch (Acts 13:14) after John Mark left them in Perga (v. 13). The New Testament does not record any missionary activity in Pisidia itself, probably because there were few Jews there with which to start a congregation. See *Asia Minor.*

The snow-capped mountains of the ancient Roman province of Pisidia in Asia Minor (modern Turkey).

PISPA, PISPAH (Pĭs' pà, Pĭs' pah) Personal name of unknown meaning. Member of the tribe of Asher (1 Chron. 7:38).

PISTACHIO NUTS See *Plants in the Bible.*

PIT Translation of twelve Hebrew and two Greek words in KJV for water reservoir, ditch, or place of destruction. The most common use of "pit" is to refer to a well or cistern (Gen. 37:20–29; Ex. 21:33–34; Pss. 7:15; 55:23; Prov. 26:27; 28:10). See *Cistern; Wells.*

Sometimes "pit" refers to a ditch or a marsh (Jer. 14:3; Isa. 30:14). Many times the word was used as a synonym for a place of destruction (Ps. 55:23), corruption (Ps. 16:10; 49:9; Isa. 38:17), or death (Isa. 14:15; Jonah 2:6). Three times KJV translated the word *Sheol* as "pit" (Num. 16:30,33; Job 17:16). One Greek word is translated "bottomless pit" in Revelation 9:1,2 (cf. Ps. 88:6). See *Hell; Everlasting Punishment; Sheol.*

Ralph L. Smith

PITCH *1.* Dark-colored, viscous mixture of hydrocarbons used for waterproofing sailing vessels (Gen. 6:14; compare Ex. 2:3). Mineral pitch occurs naturally and is highly flammable (Isa. 34:9). *2.* KJV used pitch as a verb meaning, "to coat or cover with pitch" (Gen. 6:14).

PITCHER A vessel with a handle and either a molded lip or a spout. For literal uses, see *Pottery.* Clay pitchers served as symbols of mortality (Eccl. 12:6) and of the commonplace (Lam. 4:2).

PITFALL A trap or snare, especially a roughly camouflaged pit. RSV used pitfall four times (Job 18:8; Ps. 119:85; Lam. 3:47; Rom. 11:9; the latter changed by NRSV to stumbling block). All uses are figurative. Pitfall in the Old Testament suggests hidden or unrecognized dangers.

PITHOM (Pĭ' thŏm) Egyptian place name Per-Atum meaning, "mansion or estate of Atum" (an Egyptian god). The only mention of this city in the Bible relates to the plight of the Israelites in Egypt (Ex. 1:11). Coupled with the city of Rameses, it becomes an important clue to the Exodus chronology. See *Exodus.*

Some recognize tell el-Retabah as Pithom, but the predominate opinion seems to see tell el-Maskhutah as Pithom, a religious name given Succoth. Papyrus Anastasi mentions Pithom in a report to Merneptah. *Gary C. Huckabay*

PITHON (Pĭ' thŏn) Personal name of unknown meaning. Descendant of Saul (1 Chron. 8:35; 9:41).

PITY Sympathetic sorrow toward one facing suffering or distress. Pity was expected of friends (Job 19:21), kin (Amos 1:11), and God (Ps. 90:13). Enemies lacked pity (Pss. 17:10; 69:20; Isa. 13:18; Jer. 21:7). Those guilty of idolatry, murder, or false witness were to be denied pity

(Deut. 7:16; 13:8; 19:13). The images of the father and shepherd illustrate God's pity (Ps. 103:13; Isa. 49:10). God pities the penitent (Judg. 2:18), the weak and needy (Ps. 72:13), Jerusalem in ruins (Ps. 102:13), those who fear God (Ps. 103:13), and the exiles (Isa. 49:10). In judgment, God withholds pity from God's people (Jer. 13:14; 20:16; Lam. 2:17; 3:43; Ezek. 5:11). Ezekiel pictured Jerusalem as an unpitied child denied the most basic postnatal care (Ezek. 16:5). Hosea illustrated the fate of Israel with *Lo-ruhamah,* a child's name meaning, "not pitied" (1:6; 2:23).

Pleas for pity are a common feature of healing narratives (Mark 9:22 NAS, NIV, NRSV; Luke 17:13 NIV). Pity moved Jesus to heal (Matt. 20:34 RSV). Jesus used a compassionate Samaritan as an unexpected example of active pity (Luke 10:33 NIV). Such active concern for those in need serves as evidence that one is a child of God (1 John 3:17 NIV).

PLACE OF THEM THAT BOIL See *Kitchen.*

PLAGUES Disease interpreted as divine judgment, translation of several Hebrew words. The ten plagues in the Book of Exodus were the mighty works of God that gained Israel's release and demonstrated God's sovereignty and were called "plagues" (Ex. 9:14; 11:1), "signs" (Ex. 7:13), and "wonders" (Ex. 7:3; 11:9). They showed the God of Moses was sovereign over the gods of Egypt, including Pharaoh who was considered a god by the Egyptians.

The primary reference to the plagues in the Bible is in Exodus 7:1—13:15 (compare Deut. 4:34; 7:19; 11:3; Jer. 32:20). Two psalms (78; 105) contain detailed accounts of the plagues, but neither includes all ten. Paul used the plagues to stress the sovereignty of God in the hardening of Pharaoh's heart (Rom. 9:17–18). The plagues of the Revelation reflect Old Testament influence (Rev. 8; 16).
Natural or Supernatural Modern distinctions between the natural and the supernatural were not allowable considerations for the Israelites. For them, whatever happened, God did it. Everything was under God's immediate control. For the inspired writer, the plagues were nothing more nor less than the Lord's judgment upon the Egyptians and His saving actions for Israel. Most interpreters point out that the plagues depict events of nature that might occur in Egypt. Clearly, the author of Exodus saw them as the product of a purposive, divine will. Since Egypt's magicians duplicated the first two events, the uniqueness of the plagues may rest in their timing, locale, intensity, and theological interpretation.
Purpose The plagues resulted in Israel's freedom. However, the central purpose was the revelation of God. Pharaoh and the Egyptians, as well as

Moses and the Israelites, would come to know the Lord through the events of the plagues (Ex. 7:17; 8:10,22; 9:14,16,29). Paul acknowledged this purpose: "that my name might be declared throughout all the earth" (Rom. 9:17). See *Exodus; Miracles.*   *Billy K. Smith*

PLAIN See *Palestine.*

PLAISTER KJV variant form of plaster (Isa. 38:21). Here plaster refers to a fig poultice (compare NIV, REB, NAS, NRSV).

PLAIT KJV term meaning, "to braid" (1 Pet. 3:3). See *Hair.*

PLANE TREE See *Plants in the Bible.*

PLANKS Long, flat pieces of timber thicker than boards, used in shipbuilding (Ezek. 27:5; Acts 27:44) and for the flooring of Solomon's Temple (1 Kings 6:15 KJV). The "thick planks upon the face of the porch" in Ezekiel's vision of the renewed Temple (Ezek. 41:25 KJV) likely refers to some type of canopy (NRSV; overhang, NIV; covering, TEV; cornice, REB) or to a threshold (NAS).

PLANTATION KJV term (Ezek. 17:7) to designate a bed (NAS, REB, NRSV) or plot (NIV) where plants are planted.

PLANTS IN THE BIBLE By plants we include all plant life such as wild and cultivated trees, shrubs, and herbs.
Lily and Rose Red lips of Song of Solomon 5:13 indicate a red-flowered "lily," such as scarlet tulip or anemone. Other references, such as Song of Solomon 2:1–2, may refer to the actual white madonna lily (*Lilium candidum*), now very rare in the area, or wild hyacinth (*Hyacinthus orientalis*) wild crocus (*Croccus* species), the rose of Isaiah 35:1–2 (see NAS). It is impossible to be sure to which "lilies" Jesus referred (Matt. 6:28; Luke 12:27): it may have been the anemone or any of the conspicuous wild flowers such as crown daisy (*Chrysanthemum coronarium*).

The biblical "rose" is similarly difficult to identify. The "rose of Sharon" (Song of Sol. 2:1) has been equated with anemone, rockrose, narcissus, tulip, and crocus.
Reeds Certain water plants may be distinguished from the several Hebrew words used. The following species are likely to be the ones referred to:

Common reed (*Phragmites communis*) forms great stands in shallow water or wet salty sand. The plumed flower head may have been given to Jesus in mockery (Matt. 27:29). Pens (3 John 13) were made from the bamboolike stems.

Papyrus sedge (*Cyperus papyrus*) also grows in shallow water in hot places such as in Lake Huleh and along the Nile, but it is now extinct in Egypt except in cultivation. Its tall, triangular, spongy stems were used for rafts (Isa. 18:1–2) and for making baskets (Ex. 2:3) and papyrus paper, on which much of the Bible may have been written.

Cattail or reed mace (*Typha domingensis*) is often associated with the above-mentioned reeds, and it seems to have been the one among which Moses was hidden (Ex. 2:3). This is often referred to as bulrush, but the tree bulrush (*Scirpus lacustris*) is a sedge with slender stems, which also occurs in lakes and pools.

Thorns Jesus' crown of thorns has led to two shrubs known as christthorn (*Ziziphus spina-christi, Paliurus spina-christi*). The former grows near the Dead Sea not far from Jerusalem (Matt. 27:29; Mark 15:17; John 19:5), while the latter does not grow nearer than Syria. However, it may have occurred on the Judean hills in biblical times. Some authors consider the common spiny burnet (*Poterium* or *Sarcopoterium spinosum*) to be the species concerned.

Even today nobody can walk far in the Holy Land without seeing prickly weeds. The ground is cursed with them (Gen. 3:18; Num. 33:55). Many different Hebrew words have been used to distinguish them, and some are identifiable. Thorns are usually woody plants, such as *Acacia, Lycium, Ononis, Prosopis, Rubus, Sarcopoterium,* while thistles are herbaceous, such as *Centaurea, Notobasis, Silybum.* The latter could have been

This large thistle plant is one of many varieties that grow in Israel.

Cactus, introduced to the Middle East from America, growing on a hill in Samaria.

the 'thorns' that suffocated the grain in Jesus' parable (Matt. 13:7).

Fragrant Plants In biblical times strong smelling plants included the following kinds:

1. Cassia and *cinnamon* are traditionally identified with the Far Eastern trees *Cinnamomum cassia* and *C. zeylanicum.* The ground bark was used in the holy anointing oil for priests (Ex. 30:24), and cinnamon was used for perfumery (Prov. 7:17; Rev. 18:13).

2. Calamus or *sweet cane* (*Acorus calamus*) was the dry rhizome of this water plant imported from temperate Asia used for perfume (Isa. 43:24 NRSV).

3. Galbanum, a very strong-smelling resin burnt as incense (Ex. 30:34), was obtained from the stem of *Ferula galbaniflua,* a relative of parsley growing on dry hills in Iran.

4. Henna (*Lawsonia inermis*) leaves were crushed and used both as a perfume (Song of Sol. 1:14 NIV) and as a yellow dye for skin, nails, and hair. It is a subtropical shrub with white flowers.

5. Hyssop used for ritual cleansing (Lev. 14:4,49) and sprinkling of blood in the tabernacle (Ex.12:22) was the white marjoram (*Origanum syriacum* or *Majorana syriacu*) which grows commonly in rocky places and is related to the mint.

6. Myrtle (*Myrtus communis*) is a shrub with fragrant leaves and white flowers frequent in bushy places. It was especially favored for temporary shelters in the fields at the Feast of Tabernacles (Lev. 23:40; Neh. 8:15).

7. Rue (*Ruta chalepensis*) grows on the hills of the Holy Land as a low straggling shrub with pungent smelling leaves. Jesus referred to it being tithed (Luke 11:42).

8. Spikenard or *nard,* an expensive perfumed oil (Song of Sol. 4:13–14; John 12:3), obtained either from the leaves of a desert grass (*Cymbopogon schoenanthus*) or, traditionally, the valerian relative *Nardostachys jatamansi* from the Himalayas.

9. Stacte, one of the spices referred to in Exodus 30:34 to be used in the incense, may be the resin of the balm-of-Gilead (*Commiphora gileadensis*) from southern Arabia.

Culinary Herbs Bitter herbs for Passover are certain wild plants with sharp-tasting leaves. The desert plant wormwood (*Artemisia*) was also bitter and depicted sorrow and suffering (Prov. 5:4 Lam. 3:15,19).

Coriander (*Coriandrum sativum*) provides both salad leaves and spicy seeds (Ex. 16:31) which were likened by the Israelites to the manna in the desert.

Cummin (*Cuminum cyminum*) and dill (*Anethum graveolens*), like coriander, are members of the parsley family with spicy seeds (Isa. 28:25–27; Matt. 23:23).

Fitches or black cummin (*Nigella sativa*) is an annual plant with black oily seeds easily damaged in harvesting (Isa. 28:25–27).

Mint (*Mentha longifolia*), a popular seasoning herb, was tithed by Jewish leaders (Luke 11:42).

Mustard (*Brassica nigra*) well known for its hot-flavored seeds is referred to by Jesus for having small seeds which grow into a tree (Matt. 13:31–32).

Saffron (*Crocus sativus*), a yellow powder prepared from the stigmas, is used as a subtle flavor (Song of Sol. 4:14) and also as a food coloring and a medicine.

Frankincense and Myrrh are resins produced by certain trees that grow in dry country in southern Arabia and northern Africa.

Frankincense is a white or colorless resin yielded by several species of *Boswellia,* chiefly *B. sacra,* which is a shrub or small tree growing on both sides of the Red Sea. The resin is obtained by cutting the branches and collecting the exuding 'tears' which are burnt as incense in religious rites or as a personal fumigant. In the Bible, frankincense was prescribed for holy incense mixture (Ex. 30:31,34; Luke 1:9). It was also brought by the wise men to the infant Jesus, together with gold and myrrh (Matt. 2:11).

Myrrh is a reddish-colored resin obtained from a spiny shrub, *Commiphora myrrha* in a similar manner to frankincense. This resin was not usually burnt but dissolved in oil and either eaten or used as a medicine and cosmetically (Ps. 45:8; Matt. 2:11).

Medicinal Plants Many medicinal herbs were gathered from the hills and valleys where the wild plants grew. Local people were well-versed in plant lore, but these common weeds are not specially mentioned in the Bible. Some special imported medicines are referred to. See *Frankincense and Myrrh* above.

Aloes of the New Testament (*Aloe vera*) were succulent plants with long swordlike leaves with serrations and erect flower heads up to three feet high imported from Yemen. The bitter pith was used as a medicine and for embalming (John 19:39). In the Old Testament, aloes refers to an expensive fragrant timber obtained from a tropical Indian eaglewood tree (*Aquilaria agallocha*).

Balm (Gen. 37:25) is a general term for medicinal ointment prepared from resin-bearing plants such as the rockrose *Cistus laurifolius,* which produces ladanum. The balm of Gilead or opobalsam is yielded by *Commiphora gileadensis,* a non-spiny shrub of dry country in Southern Arabia and said to have been cultivated by Solomon at En-Gedi near the Dead Sea (Song of Sol. 5:1, "spice"). Gum was imported with balm by the Ishmaelites (Gen. 37:25). It is extruded from cut roots of a spiny undershrub (*Astragalus tragacanth*) grown on dry Iranian hillsides.

Some plants, such as the gourd *Citrullus colocynthis,* could be medicinal purges in very small quantities but bitter poisons otherwise (2 Kings 4:39–40).

Cereal Grains for Bread Well-to-do citizens made bread primarily from wheat, but the poor man had to make do with coarse barley (2 Kings 4:42; John 6:9). No other cereals were grown, these being the Old Testament "corn." About New Testament times, however, sorghum was introduced. Rice came later still, and maize, not until America was opened up.

Wheat (emmer wheat *Triticum dicoccum;* bread wheat *T. aestivum*) is an annual crop which grows about three feet, though the primitive varieties were taller in rich soil, and with bearded ears.

Grains of wheat are hard and dry and easily kept in storehouses as Joseph did in Egypt before the time of famine (Gen. 41:49; KJV "corn"). It was important to retain seed for sowing (Gen. 47:24), but ancient tomb grain will not germinate. See *Bread.*

Barley (*Hordeum vulgare*) tolerates poorer soil than wheat, is shorter, has bearded ears, and ripens sooner (Ex. 9:31,32). It was also used for brewing beer and as horse and cattle fodder (1 Kings 4:28). Sometimes barley was eaten roasted as parched grain (Ruth 2:14).

Wheat and barley straw remaining after threshing was used for fuel (Isa. 47:14), and the fine chaff for instant heat in the oven.

Fruits *Olive* trees (*Olea europaea*) are small rounded orchard trees with narrow gray-green leaves and small cream-colored flowers in May. The stone fruits ripen toward the end of summer and are pickled in brine either unripe as green olives or ripe as black olives. However, the bulk of the crop was gathered for the sake of the olive oil. See *Oil.*

Grape vines (*Vitis vinifera*), grown either in vineyards or singly as shady bowers around houses and courtyards, have long flexible stems with tendrils and lobed leaves. Short flower heads grow among the new leaves in early summer, and the numerous tiny flowers develop into a cluster of round sweet grapes which ripen either as green or black fruits. The fruits are eaten fresh as grapes, or dried and stored as raisins (1 Sam. 30:12). Wine was prepared from the fermented juice. See *Wine.*

The common *fig* tree (*Ficus carica*) has a short stout trunk and thick branches and twigs bearing coarsely lobed rough leaves (Gen. 3:7). Rounded fruits ripen during the summer. These sweet fig fruits have numerous small seeds in their interior cavity. Fresh figs were favored as first fruits (Isa. 28:4; Jer. 24:2). Figs dry very well and were stored as cakes for future use (1 Sam. 25:18; 30:12). Jesus referred to figs and fig trees several times (Matt. 7:16; Luke 21:29–31).

Another kind of fig tree, the *sycomore* (*Ficus sycomorus*) grew in Egypt and in the warmer areas of the Holy Land. This large tree usually has low-growing branches such as would have enabled the short Zacchaeus to climb one to see Jesus passing along the streets of Jericho (Luke 19:4).

The juicy fruit of the *pomegranate* (*Punica granatum*), about the size of a tennis ball, is full of seeds and sweet pulp. It develops from beautiful scarlet flowers that cover the twiggy bush in spring. Pomegranate bushes were often grown in gardens and beside houses (Deut. 8:8; Song of Sol. 6:11). Moses was instructed to embroider pomegranate fruits on the hem of the priests' robes (Ex. 28:33), and their form ornamented the columns of Solomon's Temple in Jerusalem (1 Kings 7:18; 2 Chron. 3:16).

Only one *palm,* the date-palm (*Phoenix dactylifera*), yielded fruit in biblical times. This very tall tree with a rough unbranched trunk bearing a terminal tuft of huge feather leaves, fruits best in hot conditions of the Dead Sea oases. Hence, Jericho was known as the city of palm trees (Judg. 1:16). The wandering Israelites reached Elim where there were seventy palm trees (Ex. 15:27). The psalmist considered it to be such a fine tree that he compared the righteous flourishing to one (Ps. 92:12). Revelation 7:9 refers to the symbolic use of palm leaves (as "branches") denoting victory, as when Jesus entered Jerusalem and the people strewed the way with leaves (John 12:13).

It is doubtful whether the black *mulberry* (*Morus niger*) was present in the Holy Land until New Testament times as it originated in the Caspian Sea region. The only probable reference to it is (as "sycamine") when Jesus spoke of believers having enough faith to destroy one (Luke 17:6)—perhaps because old trees are stout, gnarled, and long-lived.

Another questionable fruit is that referred to as *"apple"* (Song of Sol. 2:3,5; 7:8), although some versions translate the word as "apricot." Either could be possible, but it is unlikely that fine varieties of apples were available so early.

Nuts Nuts are popularly considered to be hard dry fruits and seeds, as distinct from the more succu-

lent fruits described above.

The most important biblical nut was the *almond* (*Prunus dulcis*), which is a small tree with delightful whitish flowers in early spring before the leaves have sprouted. The nuts are well-known today either fresh or as marzipan; the kernel is contained in a very hard thick casing. Almond nuts were carried to Egypt by Joseph's brothers (Gen. 43:11). Aaron's walking stick budded and produced almonds overnight and proved that Aaron was God's man to assist Moses (Num. 17:8). The holy lampstand had cups like almond flowers (Ex. 25:33; 37:19).

The *walnut* tree (*Juglans regia*) originated in the Caspian region and may not have been commonly planted in the Eastern Mediterranean region until after the biblical period. However, it is possible that Solomon grew it in his garden (Song of Sol. 6:11). The tree grows to a considerable size. The leaves are compound, and the oily edible nuts look like a miniature brain—hence the ancient name Jovis glans and the scientific adaptation *Juglans.*

True *pistacio* nuts (*Pistacia vera*) also arrived late. The pistache nuts referred to in the Bible (Gen. 43:11 NIV) would be from the native terebinth trees (*Pistachia terebinthus, P. atlantica*) of the hillsides. One is a small shrubby tree, while the other is as large as an oak. Both yield small round edible fruits.

Vegetables The wandering Israelites longed for vegetables in the desert after they had left Egypt (Num. 11:5). Onions, leeks, and garlic are mentioned, as well as cucumbers and melons. Elsewhere, we read of lentils and other pulses (2 Sam. 17:28; Dan. 1:12).

Onions (*Allium cepa*) are the bulbs familiar to us nowadays. They are white or purple and grow quickly from seeds in one season. Leeks (*Allium porrum*) do not form such a distinct bulb. They are cooked, or the leaves were chopped up. Garlic (*Allium sativum*) is a strongly flavored onion that produces a bulb composed of separate scales.

The *cucumbers* of biblical Egypt were most likely the snake- or muskmelon *Cucumis melo,* which has longitudinal lines on its exterior. The *melons* were the watermelon (*Citrullus lanatus*) and not the squash or honeydew melon which are of American origin and now widely grown in the Middle East.

Several beans or pulses were grown in biblical times, especially *lentils* (*Lens culinaris*) in the more arid areas. The red pottage or soup made of lentils enabled Jacob to obtain Esau's birthright (Gen. 25:29–34). Lentil plants are small and slender with pealike flowers and small flat pods containing two seeds.

Of the other pulses the broad bean (*Vicia faba*) and the chick pea (*Cicer arietinum*) were important and may have been the vegetables Daniel and his friends ate in Babylon (Dan. 1:12).

P
Q

Trees From Genesis to Revelation trees have a special place, both factually and symbolically. We can divide them into groups according to their natural habitats.

1. Trees of dry and desert areas Rainfall is erratic and trees may be restricted to dry water courses where residual water remains.

Several species of *acacia* (KJV *shittim,* using the Hebrew word) occur in Sinai. Their timber was used for the construction of the tabernacle, the tent of meeting (Ex. 25). Acacias are usually flat-topped trees which possess strong thorns.

Tamarisk (*Tamarix species*) is a shrub or small tree with fine branchlets, scale leaves, and pink or white flowers, inhabiting salty places in the desert. Abraham planted one at Beersheba (Gen. 21:33 NIV).

2. Trees of streams, rivers and lakes Water is usually available throughout the year in these habitats.

Oleander (*Nerium oleander*) is an erect shrub with long, narrow poisonous evergreen leaves and beautiful pink flowers in summer. Although it may be found in stream beds in dry country, it is also in the marshes and streams such as those of Mount Carmel. It may be the "roses" at Jericho and the "roses" planted by the brook (Ecclesiasticus 24:14; 39:13). Even some of the references to willow trees may mean oleanders.

Plane (*Platanus orientalis*) is a large tree with flaking bark and digitate leaves. Its minute flowers are clustered in several hanging balls. The Plane tree inhabits rocky stream beds. It was one of the rods Jacob peeled (Gen. 30:37; also Ezek. 31:8, KJV, "chesnut").

Poplar (*Populus euphratica*) is another of the trees Jacob peeled (Gen. 30:37). It grows beside water, especially the rivers Euphrates and Jordan. It is a tall tree with shaking leaves and numerous suckering shoots around its base. The white poplar (*P. alba*) or the storax (*Styrax officinalis*) were more likely to be the trees upon the mountains (Hos. 4:13).

Willow (*Salix acynophylla*) Like poplars, willows root easily in wet places, but they are not as tall and usually have long narrow leaves (Job 40:22; Isa. 44:4; Ezek. 17:5).

3. Trees of hills and plains In biblical times, certainly before the Israelite conquest of Canaan, the hills of the Holy Land were well wooded, while Lebanon was famous for its dense forests. Agriculture, terracing, sheep and goat grazing, and the constant demand for fuel and timber has left little woodland at the present day. Only isolated trees remain in many places. Even the plains between the Mediterranean and the hills were covered with oaks until recent times.

Cypress (*Cupressus sempervirens*) is a dense coniferous forest tree typically with spreading branches, although often seen as a tall narrow tree planted beside cemeteries. References in the Bi-

ble to coniferous trees are confusing, but the cypress is evidently intended in Isaiah 40:20; 60:13, among others.

Cedar (*Cedrus libani*), the famous cedar of Lebanon, grew in extensive coniferous forests which are now sadly depleted. The stout flat-topped trees provide excellent timber which was used for David's house (2 Sam. 5:11) and Solomon's Temple (1 Kings 5:6–10), as well as the later one (Ezra 3:7).

Oak (*Quercus* species) trees provide excellent timber for ships (Ezek. 27:6) and other construction, although the evergreen kermes oak often grows no more than a shrub. The deciduous oak still forms woodland on some hills of Palestine, such as Carmel, Naphtali, and Bashan (Isa. 2:13). Oaks were used to mark graves (Gen. 35:8) or as landmarks (1 Sam. 10:3) or for sacrilegious ceremonies (Hos. 4:13).

Pine (*Pinus halepensis*), especially the Aleppo pine, is a tall coniferous tree with long needle-leaves and cones containing winged seeds. Its timber is workable and used for construction; probably the tree referred to in Isaiah 44:14 (KJV, ash; NRSV, cedar).

Terebinth (*Pistacia terebinthus, P. atlantica*) produced fruits used as nuts, but the timber of the large oaklike *P. atlantica* is also useful. The shade of terebinths was used for pagan sacrifices and offerings (Hos. 4:13 NIV).

4. Foreign trees Expeditions brought back rare timbers during the Old Testament period, and, in New Testament times, foreign timbers entered through normal trade routes.

Almug wood, traditionally identified as sandal wood (*Pterocarpus santalinus*), was imported from Ophir to Judah by Hiram's fleet for Solomon (1 Kings 10:10–11). Whether algum and almug are synonymous is a matter of dispute, since algum is clearly stated to be from Lebanon (2 Chron. 2:8), in which case it could have been the Cilician fir (*Abies cilicia*) or the Grecian juniper (*Juniperus excelsa*).

Ezekiel 27:15 links *ebony* with imported ivory tusks. The black-red ebony of Ancient Egypt was an African leguminous tree *Dalbergia melanoxylon,* while later the name was transferred to the tropical Asian *Diospyros ebenum* which has jet black timber.

Thyine wood is timber from the North African sanderac tree (*Tetraclinis articulata*), a coniferlike cypress, which was used by the Greeks and Romans for cabinetmaking. It is dark, hard, and fragrant (Rev. 18:12).   *F. Nigel Hepper*

PLASTER A pasty combination, usually of water, lime, and sand which hardens on drying and is isued for coating walls and ceilings. Mosaic law included regulations for treating homes in which mold or rot appeared in the plaster (Lev. 14:41–

Corner of a room in Pompeii showing the decorative way in which plaster was used in the first century.

48). Writing was easy on a surface of wet plaster (Deut. 27:2–4).

PLATE *1.* A shallow vessel from which food is eaten or served. See *Pottery.* *2.* A sheet of metal (Ex. 28:36; Num. 16:38).

PLATTER A large plate. The platter bearing the head of John the Baptist was likely of gold or silver (Matt. 14:8,11 and parallels). Ceramic platters were in common use (Luke 11:39 NAS). See *Pottery.*

PLAY See *Games.*

PLEDGE Something given as downpayment on a debt. The Old Testament regulated this practice. An outer garment given in pledge was to be returned before night since it was the only protection the poor had from the cold (Ex. 22:26; Deut. 24:12–13). One was not permitted to take as a pledge what was required for someone to earn a living (Deut. 24:6). Creditors were prohibited from entering a house to seize a pledge (Deut. 24:10). Job denounced abuses in the taking of pledges from family (22:6), from orphans and widows (24:3), as well as the practice of taking children as pledges (24:9). Ezekial warned repeatedly against failing to restore pledges. Amos rebuked those who coupled idolatry with holding garments in pledge (2:8).

PLEIADES (Plēi′ à dēs) A brilliant grouping of six or seven visible stars located in the shoulder of the constellation Taurus (Job. 9:9; 38:31; Amos 5:8). The derivation of the name has been traced to the seven daughters of Atlas and Pleione in Greek mythology, the adjective *pleos,* suggesting the "fullness" of the cluster, or to the verb *pleō* (to sail) from the cluster's usefulness in navigation.

PLOW To break up the ground to prepare it for sowing seed. For literal uses of plow, see *Agriculture.* Biblical writers often appealed to the image of a farmer plowing. Plowing served as an image

of sin (Prov. 21:4; Hos. 10:13) and of repentance (Jer. 4:3; Hos. 10:11). Plowing served as a picture of oppression (Ps. 129:3) and destruction (Jer. 26:18; Mic. 3:12) but also of expectation of reward (1 Cor. 9:10). To plow with another's heifer meant to commit adultery with his wife (Judg. 14:18). To have one's hands on the plow and look back was to have reservations about discipleship (Luke 9:62).

PLUMB LINE A cord with a weight (usually metal or stone) attached to one end. The plumb line would be dangled beside a wall during its construction to assure vertical accuracy. Prophets spoke of the measurement God would use on the nation (Isa. 28:17; Amos 7:7–8). Israel had been built straight, but, because it was out of line, it would be destroyed.

POCHERETH-HAZZEBAIM (Pŏch′ ĕ rĕth-Hăz zĕ bā′ ĭm) Personal name signifying an official office, "binder (or hunter) of Gazelles." Head of a family of Solomon's servants included in those returning from Exile (Ezra 2:57; Neh. 7:59). KJV takes "Zebaim" as a place name.

PODS Dry coverings split in the shelling of beans and similar plants. The pods of Luke 15:16 (NAS, NIV, REB, NRSV; husks, KJV; bean pods, TEV) were likely the pods of the carob tree which served as a common feed for livestock. These sweet-tasting pods may reach one foot in length.

POET One who composes poetry or verse. In ancient times, poets passed on the history and wisdom of their cultures. In witnessing to a sophisticated Greek audience at Athens, Paul appealed to poets familiar to his bearers. The line "In him we live, and move, and have our being" (Acts 17:28) is sometimes attributed to Epimenides of Crete (around 500 B.C.). The line "For we are also his offspring" is traced to the *Phaenomena of Arastus* (around 310 B.C.) or to Cleanthes' *Hymn to Zeus.*

POETRY "Poetry" calls to mind a Western pattern of balanced lines, regular stress, and rhyme. Hebrew manuscripts do not distinguish poetry from prose in such a clear-cut way. Hebrew poetry has three primary characteristics—parallelism, meter, and the grouping of lines into larger units called stanzas. Parallelism appears as two or three short lines connected in different ways. Meter may be reckoned in various ways. The most straightforward is a word count of the individual parallel lines. Stanzas may be recognized by a change of theme or the presence of a refrain. The distinction in Hebrew between poetry and prose is not so much a difference in kind as a difference in degree. Each of the three elements mentioned may be found to a lesser extent in prose.

One third of the Old Testament is cast in poetry. Poetic sections of the Old Testament are listed below in the order they appear in the Protestant canon.

Poetry in the Old Testament

Genesis 2:23; 3:14–19; 3:23–24; 8:22; 9:25–27; 14:19–20; 16:11–12; 25:23; 27:27–29,39–40; 48:15–16; 49:2–27

Exodus 15:1–18,21

Leviticus 10:3

Numbers 6:24–27; 10:35,36; 12:6–8; 21:14–15; 21:17–18,27–30; 23:7–10; 23:18–24; 24:3–9,15–24

Deuteronomy 32:1–43; 33:2–29

Joshua 10:12–13

Judges 5:2–31; 14:14,18; 15:16

Ruth 1:16–17,20–21

1 Samuel 2:1–10; 15:22–23,33; 18:7; 21:11; 29:5

2 Samuel 1:19–27; 3:33–34; 22:2–51; 23:1–7

1 Kings 8:12–13; 12:16

2 Kings 19:21–28

1 Chronicles 16:8–36

2 Chronicles 5:13; 6:41–42; 7:3; 10:16; 20:21

Ezra 3:11

Job 3:2—42:6

Psalms 1—150

Proverbs 1—31

Ecclesiastes 1:2–11,15,18; 3:2–9; 7:1–13; 8:1; 10:1–4,8–20; 11:1–4

Song of Solomon 1—8

Isaiah—largely poetry

Jeremiah—poetic selections throughout except for 32—45

Lamentations 1—5

Ezekiel 19:2–14; 23:32–34; 24:3–5; 26:17–18; 27:3–9; 27:25–36; 28:1–10; 28:12–19; 28:22–23; 29:3–5; 30:2–4; 30:6–8; 30:10–19; 31:2–9; 32:2–8; 32:12–15; 32:19

Daniel 2:20–23; 4:3; 4:34–35; 6:26–27; 7:9–10; 7:13–14; 7:23–27

Hosea—all poetry except for 1; 2:16–20; 3:1–5

Joel—all poetry except for 2:30—3:8

Amos—largely poetry

Obadiah 1

Jonah 2:2–9

Micah 1—7

Nahum 1—3

Habakkuk 1—3

Zephaniah 1—3

Zechariah 9—11:3; 11:17; 13:7–9

Parallelism The predominant feature of Hebrew poetry is parallelism. In parallelism, two or three short lines stand in one of three relationships to one another: synonymous, antithetic, or synthetic.

In synonymous parallelism, the succeeding line expresses an identical or nearly identical thought:

My mouth shall speak wisdom;
the meditation of my heart shall be understanding.

                                   Psalm 49:3 (NRSV)

The lines are not synonymous in the sense that they express exactly the same meaning. To the contrary, slight differences color the parallel lines expanding or narrowing the theme brought forward in the first line.

In antithetic parallelism, succeeding lines express opposing thoughts:

The wicked borrow, and do not pay back,
but the righteous are generous and keep giving.

                                   Psalm 37:21 (NRSV)

Line two is a positive expression of line one, but the psalmist's choice of words does more than reflect a pair of mirrored images. Each line means something more as it is linked with the other.

In synthetic parallelism, succeeding lines display little or no repetition:

How good and pleasant it is
When brothers live together in unity!

                                   Psalm 133:1 (NIV)

There is no one-to-one correspondence between the word groups. Continuity joins the parallel lines. Synthetic parallel lines may describe an order of events, list characteristics of a person or thing, or simply modify a common theme.

Meter Various methods for determining meter have been developed. Attempts to establish a classical system of meter (iambic feet, for example) have failed. Other theories use letter counts, vowel counts, stress counts, and word counts. The last mentioned is one of the most effective methods. Hebrew word units may be illustrated by the use of hyphens:

As-a-deer longs for-flowing-streams,
So-my-soul longs for-you, God.

                                   Psalm 42:1

This example shows a 3+4 meter. Particles and other words which play minor roles in the syntax of Hebrew are generally excluded from the count. Individual lines range from two to four words each, even though these "words" may be translated as two or three words in English. 3+2 and 2+3 meter is common. Parallel lines may also be 3+3. Groups of three parallel lines may express a 2+2+2 pattern or 3+3+3. Numerous metrical systems are possible. Consequently, Hebrew meter is described in terms of general patterns rather than absolute uniformity. Systems of meter, unlike parallelism, are apparent only in the Hebrew language and not in English translations.

Stanzas Sets of parallel lines are often, but not always, divided into larger units. Such stanzas may be set off by identical lines or by parallel lines expressing similar thoughts. These introductions may take the form of a refrain not unlike a musical refrain. Sections separated in this way may be dissimilar in theme, form, and vocabulary. Psalms 42—43 present a good example of clear-cut stanzas. The two chapters together form a single poem. A refrain is repeated three times: 42:5,11; 43:5. The refrain subdivides the poem into three sections.

Poetry provides imagery and tone for inspired writers to drum God's word home to His people. Awareness of poetic form alerts the reader to listen for the images and moods of a passage.

Donald K. Berry

POISON A chemical agent causing ill health or death when in contact with or ingested by an organism. Poison served as a frequent image for wickedness, especially lying speech (Deut. 32:32–33; Job 20:16; Pss. 58:4; 140:3). Poisonous weeds illustrated lawsuits springing up from broken oaths and covenants (Hos. 10:4). In Amos 6:12 poison served as an image of injustice. Poisoned water pictured God's judgment on sin (Jer. 8:14).

POKERETH-HAZZEBAIM (Pō' kě rěth-Hăz zě bā' ĭm) NIV form of Pochereth-Hazzebaim.

POLICE, POLICEMEN NAS, NRSV used police and policemen to refer to those Roman officials who attended the chief magistrates (Acts 16:35,38). See *Lictors.*

POLL *1.* KJV term for "to cut off" or "to trim" hair (2 Sam. 14:26; Ezek. 44:20; Mic. 1:16). Priests were permitted to poll their hair but not to shave their heads. Polling one's hair could be understood as a sign of mourning. *2.* KJV term for "the head," especially that part on which hair grows. To count every male "by their polls" (Num. 1:2; compare 1 Chron. 23:3,24) is to count "heads."

POLL-TAX Tax levied on a person, usually as a prerequisite for voting. NAS used poll-tax sometimes when other translations read either taxes or tribute (Matt. 17:25; 22:17; Mark 12:14). Poll-tax is perhaps misleading. The Roman Empire was not a democracy in which the Jewish people participated by voting. "Head-tax" is the meaning the NAS translators had hoped to convey. See *Poll.*

POLLUTE See *Clean, Cleanness.*

POLLUX (Pŏl' lŭx) One of the twin brothers in the constellation Gemini (Acts 28:11). See *Figurehead.*

POMEGRANATE A small tree, the fruit of which has a thick shell, many seeds, and a red pulp. See *Plants in the Bible.*

POMMELS KJV term for the bowl-shaped capitals topping the Temple pillars (2 Chron. 4:12–13).

The pomegranate is one of the many fruits found in the Middle East.

POND At Exodus 7:19; 8:5, pond renders the Hebrew *agam* meaning, "marsh" or "muddy pool." The term is usually translated pool. The Hebrew underlying "ponds for fish" (Isa. 19:10) is rendered grieved (in soul) or sick at heart by modern translations, based on a Hebrew homonym apparently occurring only in this passage.

PONTIUS PILATE See *Pilate, Pontius.*

PONTUS (Pŏn' tŭs) A province just south of the Black Sea in Asia Minor. The terrain varies from fertile plains along the shore to rugged mountains farther inland. The Greeks colonized the plains shortly after 700 B.C., but the mountains remained free of their influence. Mithradates founded the kingdom of Pontus in about 302 B.C. and it remained in his dynasty until 63 B.C. when Rome took over. Christianity spread to Pontus early. First Peter was addressed to the elect there (1:2–2). Citizens of Pontus were in Jerusalem on the Day of Pentecost (Acts 2:9). See *Asia Minor.*

POOL A collection of water, natural or artificial. Small pools were commonly seen as a place to collect rain water from the roof which was used for irrigation or drinking. These reservoirs were important sources of water supply in the arid climate of the Middle East.

The following are some of the principal pools

A pool in the Baths of Faustina from the Roman ruins of Miletus (in modern Turkey).

mentioned in Scripture: pool of Hezekiah (2 Kings 20:20), upper and lower pools of Gihon (Isa. 7:3; 22:9), old pool (Isa. 22:11), King's pool at Jerusalem (Neh. 2:14), pool of Bethesda (John 5:2,4,7), and pool of Siloam (John 9:7,11). Solomon also made pools to water his nursery (Eccl. 2:6).

Most of the pools near the cities were carved from stone, fed by rainwater channeled into them by channels cut in the rock. Pools were natural meeting places (John 9:7). Pools are also used as an illustration of God's power to transform the barren into something fruitful (Isa. 41:18), judgment (Isa. 42:15), and the beauty of a woman's eyes (Song of Sol. 7:4).

See *Cistern: Reservoir; Pond.* *C. Dale Hill*

POOR IN SPIRIT Not those who are spiritually poor, that is, lacking in faith or love, but those who have a humble spirit and thus depend on God (Matt. 5:3). Luke's parallel speaks simply of the poor (Luke 6:20). That God has "chosen those who are poor in the eyes of the world to be rich in faith and to possess the kingdom" was regarded as a well-established fact (Jas. 2:5 REB).

POOR, ORPHAN, WIDOW Three groups of people of the lower social classes in need of legal protection from the rich and powerful who sometimes abused them (Job 24:3–4). God's promise of care for the poor, the orphans, and the widows was a tremendous source of hope during times of severe difficulty.

1. Condition and Hope of the Poor The words used to describe the poor have the underlying meaning of "humble, oppressed, needy, weak, dependent." The contexts where these words are used suggest that the poor were those who had been wrongfully oppressed and impoverished (Job 24:14; 29:12; Ps. 10:9; Isa. 3:14); those who begged for food (Deut. 15:7–11; Job 31:16–21); or those who had no economic or social status (2 Sam. 12:1–4; Prov. 14:20; Eccl. 9:13–18). Ideally, there should be no poor people among the covenant people of God because of the blessings of God and the generosity of the people toward those

in need (Deut. 15:7–11). In actuality, God's blessings did not always come to His sinful people, and the rich did not always share with the poor. To provide for the poor, God allowed them to glean the remains of the fields and vineyards and harvest the corners (Lev. 19:10; 23:22). If a poor person was forced into slavery, they were to be treated like a hired servant (Lev. 25:39–43). The courts were to see that the poor received just, not favorable or unfavorable treatment (Ex. 23:3,6–7).

The hope of the poor was based on their status before God. Because they were part of the people God redeemed from the slavery of Egypt, they inherited God's blessings of freedom, protection, and a portion of the land (Lev. 25:38,42,55). The Psalms picture God as the refuge and deliverer of the poor (Pss. 12:5; 14:6; 70:5). In some passages, the poor are identified as the righteous (Ps. 14:5–6). The prophets predicted the destruction of Judah and Israel in part because of the oppression of the poor by fellow Israelites (Amos 2:6–8; 4:1–3; 5:10–13; 8:4–6). The prophets encouraged the people to defend the poor and instructed the kings to rule with equity (Prov. 29:7,14; Isa. 1:17; Jer. 22:3). God brought judgment on Sodom (Gen. 18:16—19:29) and on Judah because she did not care for the poor (Ezek. 16:46–50).

Jesus was particularly concerned with the poor. A poor man, He preached a message of good news to the poor (Matt. 11:5; Luke 4:18) and told parables that encouraged generosity toward the poor (Luke 14:13–24). The first Christians provided for the needs of poor widows (Acts 6:1–6), and Paul exerted great effort to collect funds for the poor in Jerusalem (Rom. 15:26). This positive attitude toward the poor was not present among all the early believers (Jas. 2:1–6).

2. The Condition and Hope of the Orphan and Widow Among the poor, the orphan and the widow were the most vulnerable. The orphan was a fatherless child (the mother could still be alive), while the widow was husbandless. In both cases, no mature male figure could defend against unscrupulous persons who would wish to defraud these individuals out of their inheritance. Consequently, biblical (and nonbiblical) legal codes provide for the protection of the rights of the orphan and the widow (Ex. 22:22; Deut. 10:18; 24:17–22). The prophets were particularly concerned with the injustice done to the orphan and widow (Isa. 1:17; Jer. 5:28; Mic. 2:9; Mal. 3:5). God declared that He would be a Father to the fatherless and provide justice for the widow (Deut. 10:18; Ps. 68:5).

The New Testament measured true religious character by a person's care for the orphan and the widow (Jas. 1:27). The early Christians cared for the widows (Acts 6:1–8), but Paul limited these provisions because of abuses on the part of some (1 Tim. 5:3–16). Jesus condemned the Pharisees for devouring widows' houses (Matt.

23:40). See *Ethics; Family; Fatherless; Humble; Inheritance; Oppressed.*   *Gary V. Smith*

POPLAR See *Plants in the Bible.*

PORATHA (Pō rā′ thă) Persian personal name meaning, "bounteous." One of Haman's ten sons (Esth. 9:8).

PORCH In English porch designates a covered entrance to a building, usually having a separate roof. English translations vary greatly in their use of porch for several Hebrew and Greek terms. KJV and NAS used porch freely (41 and 40 times, respectively); NIV and RSV used porch sparingly (2 and 3 times, respectively). The vast majority of Old Testament references concern the "porch" of the Jerusalem Temple as in 1 Kings 6:3,12,19. This reflects a view of a two-room Temple with an attached porch. REB and NRSV translation, "vestibule," reflects a view of a three-room Temple. The terms translated "porch" in Matthew 26:71 and Mark 14:68 can refer to a gateway or forecourt. The "porches" in John 5:2 and Acts 3:11 were likely freestanding porticoes or colonnades. See *Arch.*

PORCIUS FESTUS (Pôr′ cĭ ŭs Fĕs′ tŭs) See *Festus.*

PORPHYRY (Pôr′ phyў rў) Rock composed of feldspar crystals embedded in a dark red or purple groundmass (Esth. 1:6; KJV, "red marble").

PORPOISE Any of several species of smalltoothed whales. See *Animals, Badger.*

PORTER KJV term for a gate or doorkeeper. Such persons served at city gates (2 Sam. 18:26; 2 Kings 7:10), Temple gates (1 Chron, 9:22,24,26), the doors of private homes (Mark 13:34), and even the gate of a sheepfold (John 10:3). See *Doorkeeper.*

PORTICO See *Arch.*

PORTION Allotment, allowance, ration, share. Portion is frequently used in the literal sense of a share in food, clothing, or property as well as in a variety of figurative senses. Wisdom writings often designate one's lot in life as one's portion (Job 20:29; 27:13; Eccl. 9:9). God's chosen people are termed God's portion (Deut. 32:9; Jer. 21:10). The Levites did not receive tribal territory with the other tribes but had the Lord for their special portion (Num. 18:20). To have a portion in the Lord is to share the right of joining the community in worship of God (Josh. 22:25,27; compare Neh. 2:20). The Psalms often speak of the Lord as the portion of the faithful (Pss. 16:5; 73:26; 119:57).

POSSESSION, DEMON See *Demon Possession.*

POSTEXILIC Time in Israel's history between the return from Exile in Babylon in 538 B.C. and the Roman occupation in 63 B.C. During this period the Jews returned to Jerusalem and Palestine to rebuild what the Assyrians and Babylonians had destroyed. See *Israel; Intertestamental History.*

POT See *Pottery; Vessels and Utensils.*

POTENTATE KJV term in 1 Timothy 6:15 meaning, "ruler" (NIV) or "sovereign" (NAS, NRSV, REB), used as a title for God.

POTIPHAR (Pŏt′ ĭ phär) Personal name meaning, "belonging to the sun." Egyptian captain of the guard who purchased Joseph from the Midianite traders (Gen. 37:36; 39:1). He saw great potential in Joseph's abilities and appointed him as steward over his household. Potiphar's wife tried to seduce Joseph, but he refused her advances. Because of this rejection, she told her husband that Joseph tried to rape her. Potiphar had Joseph thrown in prison.

POTIPHERAH (Pō tĭ phēr′ ah) A priest in the Egyptian city of On (Heliopolis) where the sun god, Re, was worshiped. Joseph married his daughter, Asenath, at the pharaoh's command (Gen 41:45). Potipherah and Potiphar are the same in Egyptian, leading some to believe that one name was slightly changed in Hebrew to distinguish between the captain of the guard and the priest.

POTSHERD (Pŏt′ shērd) Fragment of a baked, clay vessel, "potsherd" (more commonly called a "sherd" by archaeologists) is used in the Old Testament with both a literal and symbolic or figurative meaning. Job used a potsherd (2:8) to scrape the sores that covered his body; the underparts of the mythological monster, Leviathan, are said to be "jagged potsherds" (41:30 NIV). The latter is a particularly arresting image for anyone familiar

Potsherds from the Sudan area south of Egypt.

with the jagged, sharp sherds always encountered in archaeological excavations where clay vessels were in use, as in the Near East.

Isaiah (30:14) used the image of a sherd as a sign of the worthlessness of ancient Judah. The psalmist (22:15) used the image of a dry potsherd as a simile for some physical illness he was experiencing.

Since the Hebrew word translated "potsherd" in the above passages can also mean "earthen vessel" in other contexts (compare Lev. 14:5,50; Num. 5:17), it is not always clear as to which meaning is to be preferred. Such is the case in Proverbs 26:23 where a comparison of the NRSV translation ("earthen vessel") with the KJV ("potsherd") highlights the problem. Elsewhere, textual confusion compounds the problem. In Isaiah 45:9, the Hebrew text literally reads: "a potsherd (or "earthen vessel") with potsherds (or "earthen vessels") of ground." In neither case is the text clear, though the symbolism of the futility of a person striving with God is obviously intended.

Finally, the obscure text in Ezekiel 23:24 assigned Judah the same fate as her sister, Samaria. She would not only drink the cup of wrath but also "gnaw its sherds" (NRSV). See *Pottery; Archaeology.*   *John C. H. Laughlin*

POTSHERD GATE See *East Gate 1.*

POTTAGE A thick soup usually made from lentils and vegetables, and spiced with various herbs.

A modern Middle Eastern potter fashioning pottery in the same manner used since biblical times.

Jacob served pottage and bread to the famished Esau in return for the birthright (Gen. 25:29–34). Elisha added meal to a tainted recipe of pottage at Gilgal (2 Kings 4:38–41).

POTTER'S FIELD Tract of land in the Hinnom Valley outside Jerusalem used as a cemetery for pilgrims to the Holy City since the interbiblical era. The field was bought with the money paid for betraying Jesus (Acts 1:18). Matthew 27:3–10 records that the priests bought the field with the money Judas returned. Their reasoning was that the money had been used to bring about bloodshed and could not be returned to the Temple treasury.

POTTERY IN BIBLE TIMES Everyday household utensils whose remains form the basis for modern dating of ancient archaeological remains. Relatively few Bible texts refer to the methods and products of the potter even though the industry formed a vital part of the economic structure of the ancient world. The few statements about the preparation of the clay, "the potter treads clay" (Isa. 41:25), and the potter's failure and success on the wheel (Jer. 18:3–4) hardly hint at the importance and abundance in antiquity of "earthen vessels" (Lev. 6:21; Num. 5:17; Jer. 32:14), the common collective term for pottery in the Bible. However, the work of the potter in shaping the worthless clay provided the imagery the biblical writers and prophets used in describ-

Storage jars from the palace complex of Knossos on the island of Crete.

ing God's creative relationship to human beings (Job 10:8,9; Isa. 45:9).

The pottery sherds (Job 2:8), those indestructible remnants of the potters' skill, are recovered in abundance at every archaeological site. They have not only clarified the pottery industries but have also shed light on the migration of peoples, their trade and commerce. They have become the key to establishing a firmer chronological framework for other cultural data, especially in those periods for which few or no written remains are available. This begins in the Neolithic period, before 5000 B.C. when pottery first appeared. See *Archaeology; Vessels.*

The Bible specifically identifies only two vessels as pottery: earthen pitchers (Lam. 4:2) and earthen bottles (Jer. 19:1), but an additional series of vessels probably came from the potter's workshop: "jar" for water (Gen. 24:14 NRSV); "pot" (Ex. 16:3); "bowl" (Num. 7:85); "bowl" (Judg. 6:38); "vial" (1 Sam. 10:1); "cruse" for oil and "jar" for flour (1 Kings 17:14 NRSV); another type of "jar" (2 Kings 4:2 NRSV); "bowl" and "cup" (Song of Sol. 7:2; Isa. 22:24); "cup" (Isa. 51:17,22); and "cup" and "pitcher" (Jer. 35:5 NRSV). Similar English words represent different Hebrew terms.

Pottery Production Two factors appear to have contributed to the late appearance of fired pottery: (1) early nomads found pottery too cumber-

some to transport and (2) a lengthy trial-and-error process in discovering and understanding the firing process.

Clay for the production of pottery may be divided into two types: pure aluminum silicate ("clean" clay) not found in Israel, and aluminum silicate mixed with iron oxides, carbon compounds, and other ingredients (sometimes referred to as "rich" clay). The potter prepared the dry clay by sifting and removing foreign matter, and letting it stand in water to achieve uniform granules. Having achieved the desired texture, the potter mixed it by treading on it or hand-kneading it. Then the potter was ready to shape the vessel.

The earliest pottery from the Neolithic period was handmade. Clay was coiled into the desired shape on a base or stand. These earliest efforts of the potter's trade were coarse and badly fired. Other vessels were hand-shaped from a clay ball. Innovations soon led to refinement of method and technique. During the Chalcolithic and Early Bronze periods (5000–2000 B.C.), turning boards or stones ("tournettes") formed the prototypes of the potter's wheel. A refinement of the wheel came with the production of two horizontal stone disks with corresponding cone and fitting socket lubricated with water or oil. While the lower stone with the socket served as a stationary base, the upper stone allowed for easy, smooth rotation to enhance the quality and productivity of the potter. Extensive use of the wheel came during the Middle Bronze age (about 1900–1550 B.C.), though a few examples have been identified belonging to the Early Bronze age.

The potter rotated the wheel and used both hands to "draw" the moist clay from base to rim into the shape of desired curvature, diameter, and height. The vessel was set aside to dry to a leatherhard consistency. At this point the vessel received its distinctive modifications such as base, handles, projecting decorations, and spout adjustment. Coloration and ornamentation followed with a variety of options such as slips and paint, burnishing, incisions, impressions, and reliefs. A

Fourteenth-century B.C. pottery found at Hazor in Israel.

second drying period further reduced water content to about three percent. Then the vessel was fired in an open or closed kiln at temperatures between 450–950 degrees Celsius.

The best wares obviously were achieved at the highest and most consistent temperatures, a result determined by the nature of the kiln. Firing may have begun by accident when people noticed the quality of clay vessels left near or in a fireplace or recovered after a building or town burned. First combustible materials were burned over the pottery in open pits. Later, the pottery appears to have been stacked above the firebox. Ultimately, the need to equalize the distribution of heat led to the closed kiln. The introduction of bellows and forced air firing provided the desirable higher temperatures.

Importance of Pottery Analysis for Historical Studies Each culture produced its own distinctive, durable pottery. That distinctiveness has enabled archaeologists to trace each culture's "fingerprints" through time. The archaeologist can describe the movement of a race from one place to another, the influence of new people in a particular region or area, and the commercial activity of the people. Archaeologists have used changes in pottery forms, shapes, decorations, and materials from one period to the next to establish a relative chronological framework for dating purposes. The type pottery in an excavated layer or strata provides the key for dating, at least in a relative way, all other cultural artifacts and architectural remains within the strata.

Developments in Pottery Production in Palestine The significance of pottery analysis may be highlighted in a general way by recognizing the major developments of pottery production in Palestine throughout biblical history period by period.

1. Neolithic Period (7000–5000 B.C.) Neolithic pottery, the earliest attempts at this important industry, were poorly handmade and badly fired, although some types including bowls and storage jars were decorated elaborately with red slip, burnished, painted (triangular and zigzag lines, herringbone design), and incised (herringbone). Jericho, Sha'ar ha-Golan and other sites in the Jordan Valley have provided the best examples of these early cultural developments.

2. Chalcolithic Period (5000–3000 B.C.) The Ghassulian (in the Jordan Valley) and Beersheba (in the Negev) cultures have provided the best assemblages for this period of pottery advancement. Rope ornamentation on this handmade pottery clearly suggests the practical strengthening of the clay vessels with various rope netting or binding. A wide variety of shapes and sizes suggests the proliferation of household and commercial uses for storage and transport of both dry and liquid products and merchandise.

3. Early Bronze Age (3000–2000 B.C.) This period has been divided into three and possibly four distinct cultural periods on the basis of the distinctive pottery. The first period (EB I) is characterized by grey burnished ware, band-slip ware, and burnished red-slip ware. The second period (EB II) is identified with "Abydos" ware (pitchers and storage jars with burnished red-slips on the lower half and brown-and-black-painted triangles and dots on the upper half), first found in Egyptian royal tombs of the First Dynasty at Abydos in Upper Egypt and most important in the chronological correlation of Egyptian and Palestinian history. The third period (EB III) includes kraters (large storage or mixing bowls), bowls, pitchers, and stands, first identified at khirbet Kerak (Beth Yerak) at the southern end of the Sea of Galilee, which has a distinctive combination of highly burnished red and black slip. This culture appears to have originated in eastern Anatolia. The fourth period (EB IV) with innovations may be a cultural continuation of the previous period.

4. Middle Bronze Age (about 2000–1500 B.C.) A transitional phase (first identified MB I, and now mostly EB–MB) resulted from nomadic or seminomadic tribes who destroyed the final phase of EB culture. They produced a distinctive pottery with gobular and cylindrical shapes. These combined hand-shaped bodies and wheel-made necks and out-flared rims. The period introduced the pinching of the rim of a small bowl to produce a four-wicked lamp. The patriarchal period usually is identified with the next period (MB IIa). The pottery reflects the arrival of a highly developed culture that results in a prosperous, urbanized, sedentary population with rich cultural ties to the upper Euphrates region from which Abraham migrated, according to the biblical text. The pottery exhibits excellent workmanship, and in many instances suggests metal prototypes. Possibly the earliest Semitic wheel-made vessels were the beautiful carinated bowls and vessels of this period. Skilled potters, with the advent of the new fast wheel were able to produce elegant new shapes with wide bodies, narrow bases, and flaring rims, all with refined details. During the MB IIb, an unusual group of juglets indicate pottery exchange with Egypt which during this period was politically joined to Syria-Palestine.

5. Late Bronze Age (about 1550–1200 B.C.) This period generally coincides with the vibrant New Kingdom period in Egypt when Palestine primarily was under Egyptian control, a rule that became more concentrated and demanding toward the end of the period. Canaan also maintained extensive trade connections with Aegean and northeastern Mediterranean powers. Cypriot pitchers called "bilbils" and shaped as poppyseed heads (upside-down), were among the most popular Palestinian imports. They may have been used to transport opium in wine or water from Cyprus to other Mediterranean sites.

Clear pottery distinctives again suggest a three

period division. The Late Bronze I (about 1550–1400) reflects a continuation of the vitality of the earlier Middle Bronze culture. The pottery of the Late Bronze IIa (about 1400–1300) shows a deterioration of forms and quality during a period of political instability associated with the el-Amarna Period. That deterioration becomes more evident during the Late Bronze IIb (about 1300–1200) as Egypt's Nineteenth Dynasty established a firmer control over the affairs of the economy and urban centers of Canaan. An abundance of Mycenaean and Cypriot pottery throughout the country would seem to suggest a growing commercial interest in the Levant for export and trade.

6. Iron Age (about 1200–587/6 B.C.) The Iron Age basically runs from the conquest of Canaan to the demise of the Judean Kingdom and usually is divided into two distinct periods. The distinguishing elements in pottery and other cultural elements for making the archaeological divisions of this period are not overly clear. Iron Age I (1200–925) pottery from the settlement to the division of the kingdom begins with a continuation of Late Bronze traditions, as Israel borrowed industrial techniques from the local Canaanite population.

The arrival of the Philistines after 1200 B.C. brought a distinctively decorated pottery with Mycenaean shapes and motifs. The deterioration of the quality and design of this pottery tends to reflect the eclectic nature of these "Sea Peoples." By 1000 B.C. the distinctive nature of the pottery in the Philistine plain had basically disappeared.

During the Iron II period (925–587/6), from the division of the United Monarchy to the fall of the Judean Kingdom to the Babylonians, the political separation produced clear distinctions in the regional pottery types, generally known as "Samaria" and "Judean" ware. During most of this period the northern pottery exhibits the higher standard of workmanship. Most prominent in imported ware up to 700 B.C. is the Cypro-Phoenician ware. From 700 to 500 B.C. imports of Assyrian origin resulted in local potters copying Assyrian prototypes.

7. Persian Period (586–330 B.C.) The deterioration of the pottery with inferior clay, firing, and general workmanship appears to reflect the general economy disruption throughout the region, a situation that seems to prevail throughout the Near East. In Palestine a growing number of Greek imports appeared, especially toward the end of the period.

8. Hellenistic Period (330–63 B.C.) While the local pottery was basically crude and uninspired, imported wares include a wide range of luxury items from molded Megarian bowls to impressed and roulette decorated black-glazed and red-glazed ware. The maritime trade connections further are evident, for example, in widespread appearance of Rhodian amorphae.

9. Roman Period (63 B.C.–A.D. 325) Only

Herodian pottery is of particular interest for an understanding of the biblical period. Local pottery basically followed earlier traditions with the dominant innovation a ribbing of many vessel surfaces. The most common imported ware is both eastern and western red-glazed terra sigillata, noted for its outstanding finish and general workmanship. The Nabataeans who controlled the trade routes of the Negev/Sinai and the Transjordan produced the finest local varieties, emulating the skills and export products of the Roman potters of the period.

George L. Kelm

POUND See *Coins; Weights and Measures.*

POVERTY See *Poor, Orphan, Widow.*

POWDERS, FRAGRANT Pulverized spices used as a fragrance (Song of Sol. 3:6). See *Spices.*

POWER The ability to act or produce an effect; the possession of authority over others. These two aspects of power are often related in Scripture. Because God has revealed His power in the act of creation, He has authority to assign dominion to whomever He wills (Jer. 10:12; 27:5). God revealed His power by miraculously delivering Israel from Egyptian slavery (Ex. 4:21; 9:16; 15:6; 32:11) and in the conquest of Canaan (Ps. 111:6). God's acts are foundational for His claim on Israel. God's power includes not only the power to judge but also the power to forgive sin (Num. 14:15–19; Jer. 32:17–18). 2 Kings 3:15 links the onrush of the power of God with prophecy. Here power approximates God's Spirit (compare Mic. 3:8; Luke 1:35).

Christ's miracles evidenced the power of God at work in His ministry (Matt. 14:2; Mark 5:30; 9:1; Luke 4:36; 5:17). Luke highlighted the role of the Holy Spirit in empowering the ministry of Jesus (Luke 4:14; Acts 10:38) and the ongoing ministry of the church (Acts 1:8; 3:12; 4:7,33; 6:8). Paul stressed the paradox that the cross—what is apparently Jesus' greatest moment of weakness—is the event in which God's power to save is realized (1 Cor. 1:17–18; compare Rom. 1:16). This scandal of God's power revealed in Christ's death continues in God's choice to work through the powerless (1 Cor. 1:26–29; 2:3–4; 2 Cor. 12:9). In some texts, powers refer to angelic powers (Rom. 8:38; Eph. 3:10; Col. 2:15; 1 Pet. 3:22).

Chris Church

PRAETORIAN GUARD (Prāē tôr′ ĭ an) Roman imperial bodyguard or troops assigned to a Roman provincial governor (Phil. 1:13 NAS, RSV). The underlying Greek (*praitōrion*) can also refer to the imperial high court. In the Gospels and Acts the term refers to the palace of a provincial governor. See *Philippians; Praetorium.*

P
Q

PRAETORIUM

PRAETORIUM (Praė tôr′ ĭ um) The barracks where Jesus was taken and mocked by the soldiers before His crucifixion (Mark 15:16). Biblical references allow the building's location next to Herod's palace or beside the Temple complex. It appears that it was the official residence of the Roman governor, which would favor the palace location.

Herod's praetorium in Caesarea (Acts 23:35 NAS, RSV) served as the residence of the Roman govenor Felix. Paul's confidence that his imprisonment had publicized the Christian cause "in the whole praetorium" (Phil. 1:13) can refer to the whole palace (KJV; NAS and RSV margins) or to the praetorian guard. See *Praetorian Guard.*

PRAISE

PRAISE One of humanity's many responses to God's revelation of Himself. The Bible recognizes that men and women may also be the objects of praise, either from other people (Prov. 27:21; 31:30) or from God Himself (Rom. 2:29), and that angels and the natural world are likewise capable of praising God (Ps. 148). Nevertheless, human praise of God is one of Scripture's major themes.

Praise comes from a Latin word meaning "value" or "price." Thus, to give praise to God is to proclaim His merit or worth. Many terms are used to express this in the Bible, including "glory," "blessing," "thanksgiving," and "hallelujah," the last named being a transliteration of the Hebrew for "Praise the Lord." The Hebrew title of

A view of the front of the praetorium at the palace of the Roman emperor Hadrian.

the book of Psalms ("Praises") comes from the same root as "hallelujah" and Psalms 113—118 have been specially designated the "Hallel" ("praise") psalms.

The modes of praise are many, including the offering of sacrifices (Lev. 7:13), physical movement (2 Sam. 6:14), silence and meditation (Ps. 77:11–12), testimony (Ps. 66:16), prayer (Phil. 4:6), and a holy life (1 Pet. 1:3–9). However, praise is almost invariably linked to music, both instrumental (Ps. 150:3–5) and, especially, vocal. Biblical songs of praise range from personal, more or less spontaneous outbursts of thanksgiving for some redemptive act of God (Ex. 15: Judg. 5; 1 Sam. 2; Luke 1:46–55,67–79) to formal psalms and hymns adapted for corporate worship in the Temple (2 Chron. 29:30) and church (Col. 3:16).

While the Bible contains frequent injunctions for people to praise God, there are also occasional warnings about the quality of this praise. Praise is to originate in the heart and not become mere outward show (Matt. 15:8). Corporate praise is to be carried on in an orderly manner (1 Cor. 14:40). Praise is also firmly linked to an individual's everyday life (Amos 5:21–24). See *Music; Psalms; Worship.*   David W. Music

PRAYER

PRAYER in the Bible involves the dialogue between God and people, especially His covenant partners.

Old Testament Israel is a nation born of prayer. Abraham heard God's call (Gen. 12:1–3), and God heard the cries of the Hebrew children (Ex.

3:7). Moses conversed with God (Ex. 3:1—4:17) and interceded for Israel (Ex. 32:11–13; Num. 11:11–15). By prayer Joshua discerned sin in the conquest community (Josh. 7:6–9), but was tricked when he did not discern God's opinion by prayer (Josh. 9). God also spoke to the Judges to deliver His people when the people called out to Him for deliverance. David's spiritual acumen is seen in his prayers of confession (2 Sam. 12:13; Ps. 51). Solomon fulfilled the promises made to David after praying for wisdom (1 Kings 3:5–9) and dedicated the Temple in prayer (1 Kings 8). God worked miracles through the prayers of Elijah and Elisha (1 Kings 17:19–22; 18:20–40). The writing prophets noted that genuine prayer calls for accompanying moral and social accountability (Hos. 7:14; Amos 4:4–5). Isaiah's call reflected the intense cleansing and commitment involved in prayer (Isa. 6). Jeremiah's dialogue and intercession frequently voiced reservation and frustration (Jer. 1; 20:7–18), teaching honesty in prayer. The Psalms teach variety and honesty in prayer are permissible; they proclaim praise, ask pardon, seek such things as communion (63), protection (57), vindication (107), and healing (6). Psalm 86 provides an excellent pattern for prayer. Daily patterned prayer becomes very important to exiles denied access to the Temple (Dan. 6:10).

New Testament Jesus' example and teaching inspire prayer. Mark emphasized that Jesus prayed in crucial moments, including the disciples' appointment (3:13), their mission (6:30–32), and the transfiguration (9:2). Jesus displayed a regular and intense prayer life (Matt. 6:5; 14:23; Mark 1:35).Luke taught that Jesus was guided by the Holy Spirit (Luke 3:22; 4:1,14,18; Luke 10:21; Acts 10:38). John reported that Jesus sometimes prayed aloud for the benefit of those present (John 11:41–42). He also reported Jesus' prayer of intercession for the first disciples and future believers (John 17). Both prayers display Jesus' unity with the Father and desire to give Him glory (John 11:4; 17:1).

The Lord's Prayer (Matt. 6:9–13; Luke 11:2–4) is taught to disciples who realize the kingdom's inbreaking, yet await its full coming. Significantly, the disciples asked Jesus to teach them to pray after watching Him pray (Luke 11:1). The prayer also provides a contrast to hypocritical prayers (Matt. 6:5). Although it is permissible to repeat this prayer, it may be well to remember Jesus was emphasizing *how* to pray, not *what* to pray. See *Lord's Prayer.*

Jesus also corrected some abuses and misunderstandings regarding prayer. (1) Prayer is not to be offered to impress others. Disciples should rather seek a storage closet or a shed and pray in private. Jesus did not reject group prayer, but his warning might apply to a believer who prays to impress a congregation (Matt. 6:5–6). (2) Jesus also prohibited long-winded attempts that try to manipulate

Jewish men praying at the Wailing Wall—a point close to the probable site of the ancient Temple.

God. While Jesus prayed for long periods of time (Luke 6:12; Mark 1:35) and repeated Himself (Mark 14:36–42), He called for people to trust their Father and not their own eloquence or fervor.

Jesus' teaching on persistence in prayer is linked to the inbreaking kingdom (Luke 11:5–28; 18:1–8). God is not like the reluctant neighbor, even though Christians may have to wait for answers (Luke 11:13; 18:6–8). The ironies of prayer are evident: God knows our needs, yet we must ask; God is ready to answer, yet we must patiently persist. Children of the kingdom will have their requests heard (Matt. 6:8; 7:7–11; 21:22; John 14:13; 15:7,16; 16:23; compare 1 John 3:22; 5:14; Jas. 1:5), particularly believers gathered in Jesus' name (Matt. 18:19).

In Hebrew thought, the name was mysteriously linked to the person's character and prerogatives. Thus prayer in Jesus' name is prayer that is seeking His will and submissive to His authority (John 14:13; 1 John 5:14).

The church remembered Jesus' teaching regarding the Spirit, prayer, and the kingdom mission. The disciples prayed awaiting the Holy Spirit's outpouring (Acts 1:14). The early church is characterized by prayer (Acts 2:42). They prayed regarding selection of leaders (Acts 1:24; 6:6; 13:3), during persecution (Acts 4:24–30; 12:5,12), and in preparing to heal (Acts 9:40; 28:8). Calling upon God's name—prayer—is the first act and

P
Q

true mark of a believer (Acts 2:21; 9:14,21; 22:16).

Paul's ministry reflected his constant prayer of intercession and thanksgiving (1 Tim. 2:1; Eph 1:16; 5:4; Acts 9:11). The Lord spoke to Paul in prayer (Acts 22:17). Prayer is crucial to continuing in the Christian life (Rom. 12:12). The indwelling Spirit enables a believer to call God "Abba" (Rom. 8:15); that is, the Spirit's work within the believer prompts him or her to address God with the confidence of a child (Rom. 8:14). The Spirit must intercede because our prayers are weak; apart from the Spirit Christians pray without discernment. He takes up our petitions with an earnest pleading beyond words (Rom. 8:26–27; Gal. 4:6).

Answered Prayers—Unanswered Petitions Not every petition is granted. Job's demand for answers from God was eclipsed by the awesome privilege of encountering Him (Job 38—41). Modern believers must also cherish communion with the Father more than their petitions.

Jesus, with His soul sorrowful to the point of death, prayed three times that His cup of suffering might pass, but He was nevertheless submissive to God's will (Matt. 26:38–39,42,45). Both the boldness of the petition to alter God's will and the submission to this "hard" path of suffering are significant.

Paul asked three times for deliverance from his "thorn in the flesh." God's answer to Paul di-

Modern orthodox Jews pray in old Jerusalem in similar manner as did the Hebrews of the Old Testament.

rected him to find comfort in God's sufficient grace. Also God declared that His power is best seen in Paul's weakness (2 Cor. 12:8–9). God gave him the problem to hinder his pride. Ironically, Paul claimed that God gave the problem, and yet he called it a messenger of Satan. Paul learned that petitions are sometimes denied in light of an eventual greater good: God's power displayed in Paul's humility.

Faith is a condition for answered petitions (Mark 11:24). Two extremes must be avoided concerning faith. (1) With Jesus' example in mind we must not think that faith will always cause our wishes to be granted. (2) Also we must not go through the motions of prayer without faith. Believers do not receive what they pray for because they pray from selfish motives (Jas. 4:2–3). Prayers are also hindered by corrupted character (Jas. 4:7) or injured relationships (Matt. 5:23–24).

Theological Insights Dialogue is what is essential to prayer. Prayer makes a difference in what happens (Jas. 4:2). Our understanding of prayer will correspond to our understanding of God. When God is seen as desiring to bless (Jas. 1:5) and sovereignly free to respond to persons (Jonah 3:9), then prayer will be seen as dialogue with God. God will respond when we faithfully pursue this dialogue. Prayer will lead to a greater communion with God and a greater understanding of His will. *Randy Hatchett*

PREACHING IN THE BIBLE Human presentation through the Holy Spirit's power of God's acts

of salvation through Jesus Christ. This proclamation of God's revelation functions as God's chosen instrument for bringing us to salvation by grace, although its message of a crucified Messiah seems to be foolishness to people of worldly wisdom and a scandalous offense to Jews (1 Cor. 1:21–23). True Christian preaching interprets the meaning of God's acts into contemporary contexts. A sermon becomes God's word to us only as God's servant reconstitutes the past realities of the biblical revelation into vital present experience.

Old Testament Traditions The great prophets of the OT heralded God's direct messages against the sins of the people, told of coming judgments, and held out future hope of the great Day of the Lord. God's revelation to families, regularly shared as private instruction (Deut. 11:19), became the foundation of the public reading of the law every seven years to all the people (Deut. 31:9–13). During periods of special revival, natural leaders traveled about sharing the revelation in great assemblies (2 Chron. 15:1–2; 17:7–9; 35:3). Nehemiah 8:7–9 records that Ezra and his associates interpreted the "sense" of what was read in such gatherings.

New Testament Practice Jesus began His ministry in the synagogue by announcing He was the Herald who fulfilled Isaiah's prophecy concerning the preaching of the kingdom and its blessings (Luke 4:16–21). By the time Peter and the other apostles preached, their emphasis focused on the person and work of Christ as the central point of history certifying the presence of God's kingdom on earth today. In the NT, this message concerned a summation of the basic facts about the life, character, death, burial, resurrection, and coming again of Christ. It continues today as the main word of revelation to the world through the church. Although the NT uses some thirty different terms to describe the preaching of John the Baptist, Jesus, and the apostles, those most commonly used can be grouped under either *proclamation* (to herald, to evangelize) or *doctrine* (to teach). Many scholars define these emphases as either *gospel preaching* (proclaiming salvation in Christ) or *pastoral teaching* (instructing, admonishing, and exhorting believers in doctrine and life-style). In practice each function melds into the other. Thus, 1 Corinthians 15:1–7 not only represents the "irreducible core" of the gospel message, but it also includes clear doctrinal teaching on the substitutionary atonement and the fulfillment of messianic prophecies. The same passage forms a foundation for the exposition of the extensive doctrine of general resurrection and its Christian dimensions taught in the following verses. Stephen's address in Acts 7:1–53 represents the best of the OT tradition, weaving narrative and historical portions of Scripture together with contemporary interpretation and application to the present situation. Peter's sermon in Acts 2 affirms

the atoning nature of Jesus' death and the reality of His resurrection together with a clear call to faith and repentance forming a balanced argument framed around the central proposition that "Jesus Christ is Lord."

Special Perspectives Paul firmly believed that proclaiming the full glory of Christ not only warns men and women of the need for salvation, but that through this preaching believers can grow towards spiritual maturity (Col. 1:28). He wrote that the ministry of God-called leaders equips believers in each local assembly for service through mutual ministries to each other and leads to the healthy upbuilding of Christ's body (Eph. 4:11–16). He defined his content as including "the whole counsel of God" and his practice as being "to Jews and Greeks," and "from house to house," as well as "publicly," and "in all seasons" (Acts 20:17–21).

Homiletics Paul underlined the need for careful attention to principles of communication in preaching. While he refused to adopt some of the cunning word craftiness of the secular rhetoricians of his day (2 Cor. 4:2; 1 Thess. 2:3,5), nevertheless, he adapted his preaching well to a variety of audiences and needs. In the synagogue Paul spoke to Jews about the special dealings God has with His people (Acts 13:16–41); but to the Greek philosophers he presented a living God as a challenge to their love for fresh ideas, quoting from their own writers as he did so (Acts 17:22–31). To Agrippa and Festus, Paul molded the gospel message in lofty and legal terms (Acts 26:2–23). When meeting a charge of apostasy from the Jewish faith, he addressed the people in their own tongue concerning his origins and his experiences in Christ (Acts 21:40—22:21). Paul also counseled young pastor Timothy to work on himself as well as on his doctrine (1 Tim. 4:16). Paul advised the need for diligent practice to improve Timothy's skills in the public reading of the Scriptures and in motivational teaching (1 Tim. 4:13–15). Paul noted that such responsibilities involved "hard labor" (1 Tim. 5:17).   *Craig Skinner*

PREDESTINATION God's work in ordaining salvation for people without their prior knowledge.
Biblical Materials The English noun, *predestination,* does not occur in the Bible. The Greek verb translated predestinate occurs only four times in two passages of the Bible (Rom. 8:29,30; Eph. 1:5,11). It is used in Acts 4:28 of human determination. The word means to determine before or ordain. On these minimal facts entire systems of doctrine have been built.

The word *predestinate* (*proorizō*) is closely related to three other more frequently used biblical words: *1. to determine; 2. to elect; 3. to foreknow.* Each of these represents several Greek and Hebrew words. Study of these words shows that for a study of predestination the key passages are

Romans 8; Ephesians 1; and 1 Peter 1. One of the appropriate things to notice in this biblical survey is that Acts refers to the purpose of God as determined (Acts 2:23; 11:29; 17:26); refers to Jesus as God's previously chosen One (2:23; 10:41–42); to the early church as those previously taken in hand by God (Acts 22:14). A wise plan is to examine the major passages keeping the verses in Acts in mind.

Romans 8 Although the word *predestinate* is used only in verses 29 and 30 of this chapter, we must explore the entire chapter to understand the use of the word. Romans 7—8 form Paul's famous battle of the flesh and of the spirit. Romans 7 speaks of the place of law in shaping life. Law makes requirements, but it has no power to help people keep them. Sin is a constant struggle and an overwhelming experience (7:23–24). Romans 8 is life in the Spirit. God's Spirit aids our spirit in the struggles of life and helps us to conquer all things through His Spirit. God purposes for His people a victorious, overcoming life. Such a life is not possible when we go it alone. God chooses and determines that it will be otherwise for His people.

The references to predestination in verses 29 and 30 come in the midst of a section of Scripture on salvation and spiritual struggle. Was Paul saying that all of his experience, before becoming a Christian and after, God decided in such a way that Paul had nothing to do with it and no decision in it? These passages could be seen that way, but they need not be. They also can be seen as the struggle of human willfulness and divine purpose and guidance. I see these passages, especially in the light of Paul's other writings, as a real struggle in which Paul realized that God's purpose for us is good and that God's determination to help us is prior to all of our struggles. In Jesus Christ, God has set the pattern. Believers are to be conformed to the image of Jesus Christ. God's determination is particularly and eternally expressed in what Christ is. He is like what we are supposed to be like. God's Spirit will help us to be like Jesus.

In a discussion of election and predestination, questions about Jacob and Esau (Rom. 9:13) arise, as do questions about God "hardening Pharaoh's heart" (Rom. 9:17–18). These verses could be interpreted to mean that God beforehand had planned things out without any regard for human response. The worst scenario would suggest that God had taken a nice young Egyptian prince and turned him into a monster. Romans 9:13 could mean that God really hated Esau and played favorites among His children. I do not believe this is the proper way to understand these passages. Paul, their human author, is looking back. Interpretations are easier after the fact. Whereas God is no respecter of persons whom He has created, He does not violate the free will He gave to humankind. God works with it. A better interpre-

tation of these passages is to say that God used what Esau and Pharoah had become. Esau, a compulsive man who sought instant gratification of his desires, would not be the kind of person who becomes a patriarch. Pharaoh, a ruthless man, God confirmed and judged as an oppressor; Pharaoh's harsh and cruel acts were punished. In that punishment God received glory to Himself, even out of Pharaoh's disobedience.

Ephesians 1 The first chapter of Ephesians is first and foremost about Jesus Christ. Christ contains, expresses, and effects God's purpose. When people hear the gospel message and believe that message (vv. 13,15), they live on earth under the leadership of Jesus Christ as Head of the body. Such believers are sealed by the Spirit (v. 13); therefore, the power of God working in us can enlarge us, open our eyes, increase our faith, and enable us to believe. Does God do this without our own willing and cooperation, or are we free participants in what God is doing through the believing community under the headship of Christ and in the power of the Spirit? It seems to me that the believers addressed are welcomed to faith and encouraged to believe and enlarge their lives in Christ's church. The specific references in verses 5 and 11 fit in this context if we do not draw them out of place and ask first what it means that *we* were predestined before the foundation of the world according to God's will. Jesus Christ is first and foremost God's chosen. He is the agent of God's redemptive plan from eternity. Jesus Christ embodies the way, the will, and the good pleasure of God. By Jesus we know the Father; in Him God's will is effected in history. We are included as we are included in Jesus. We are included, predestined, and elected as we believe in Him by the power of the Spirit. God, working His way through us, determines us. Apparently, part of God's determination is that the Ephesians and ourselves should be participants in our limited human way with God in doing God's will. God's will is that people should have a will to exercise toward God. The painful personal experience reflected in Romans 7 and the sinful corporate experiences of human divisions spoken of in the remainder of Ephesians lead us to believe that we can also exercise our wills in refusing to believe in God and in disobeying God. Predestination never eliminates human will.

1 Peter First Peter 1:2 is a part of the greeting of the author to the readers. He greets them and us in the name of the foreknowing Father, the sanctifying Spirit, and the sacrifice of the Son. The greeting is a kind of prelude under which exhortations to Christian living are given. The entire epistle presupposes both the guidance of God and the ability of people to cooperate with God in living the Christian life.

Other Passages Luke 22:22 declares that Jesus died according to the plan of God in which He freely participated. So does Acts 2:23, which adds human wickedness also entered into the betrayal of Jesus. Acts 10:41 assures us that the eyewitness apostles were especially chosen of God. The disciples determined they would provide help to the needy (Acts 11:29). God determined the basic parameters of humanity (Acts 17:26). The gist of these references is that God works according to a plan and purpose and so should we, especially as we determine to do His will.

Two special problems that arise in relation to predestination are the place of Judaism (Rom. 9—11) and of Judas (John 6:70-71) in the determination of God. Paul said that Judaism is God's preparation for the fulness of Christ, that they rejected God's fullest revelation of God in Christ, and that God confronts them with Christ inevitably and ultimately. Meanwhile, the task of the church is to confront all persons with Christ. The purpose of predestination is to be conformed to goodness and to bear witness to God in Christ. Judas was chosen by Jesus as were all of the disciples. As all disciples of Jesus, Judas had the capacity for betrayal—so did Peter. Judas exercised his will to betray. The evil one found in Judas a willing instrument (John 13:27). Jesus had to be betrayed. Judas did not have to do it, but he did.

Later Questions The above basic biblical facts were used to construct later doctrinal systems. Human logic and the desire for systematic conclusions and neat, packaged answers lead to hard solutions about freedom and destiny. Questions which lead to this development were: If God is sovereign, how can humans be free? If God knows about everything in advance, does that mean that He forces things to be the way they are? Does not God give grace to those who are to be saved and withhold it from those who are not? If God decreed that some are to be saved, does this not mean He has predestined others to be damned?

The problem with these later questions is that they go beyond Scripture in their desire to figure everything out. They ignore large portions of Scripture and Christian experience which assume human choice and the integrity of human freedom. In the last analysis, the way in which God's guidance of His creation interfaces with human freedom is unknown to us. I am convinced that God who made us with will and freedom woos us by His grace and condemns people only because of their own willfulness and unbelief. The only alternatives are to suppose that God is going to force all to be saved, whether they want to be or not; or that God, in a choosey way, is going to save some favorites but deliberately withhold salvation from others. I cannot find either of these views consistent with the full range of biblical teaching. Predestination is an assurance of God's redemptive love. There has never been a time, not even before creation, when God has not shown redemptive love for His creation. Whatever else predesti-

nation means, it assures us that God takes the initiative in relation to creation and that God pursues us with redemptive love. See *Election; Salvation.*   *Bill Hendricks*

PREEXILIC Period in Israel's history before the Exile in Babylon (586-538 B.C.). See *Israel.*

PREEXISTENCE OF SOULS Doctrine that souls exist prior to being joined to a body. Disdain for the material body as evil or disregard for the body as inferior to the soul are common corollaries of this doctrine. Scripture affirms the material body as the good creation of God. Indeed, one does not become a living "soul" apart from the material body (Gen. 2:7; 1 Cor. 15:45). Though the Greeks longed to free their souls from the prison of the body, the Hebrews feared separation from the body as the end of personal existence. Thus, Paul hoped not to be an "unclothed" soul, that is, without a body, but one clothed in a spiritual body (2 Cor. 5:41; 1 Cor. 15:44).

Jeremiah 1:5 refers not to the prophet's preexistent soul but to God's foreknowledge of a redemptive plan embracing the ministry of this prophet. The debate in John 9:2 likely concerned the possibility of sins committed in the womb (compare God's choice of Jacob over Esau while they were still in the womb Gen. 25:23; Rom. 9:11-13).

According to Josephus, the Essenes affirmed the preexistence of souls. This claim may stem from Josephus' desire to portray Jewish sects as the counterparts of Greek philosophical schools. Origen (A.D. 185?-254?) derived the doctrine of the preexistence of souls from his understanding of the nature of the soul and held the doctrine to be a necessary corollary of the immortality of souls. The consensus of the early church as evidenced by the Apostle's Creed is that the Christian hope is the resurrection of the body, not the inherent immortality of souls. See *Immortality; Resurrection; Soul.*   *Chris Church*

PREPARATION DAY Sixth day of week in which Jews prepared life's necessities to avoid work on the sabbath (compare Ex. 20:8-11; Matt. 12:1-14; John 9:14-16). Preparation of food, completing work, and spiritual purification were included. The Hebrew day began and ended at 6 p.m., so the day of preparation extended from 6 p.m. on Thursday until the beginning of the sabbath at 6 p.m. Friday.

The Feast of Passover was immediately followed by the holy convocation of the Feast of Unleavened Bread (Lev. 23:1-7). No one worked on either of these holy days, so a day of preparation was set aside to prepare for the holiday period (John 19:14). John explicitly identified the day of preparation as the day of Jesus' execution (John 19:14,31,42) and placed the Last Supper before Passover (John 13:1). The Synoptic Gospels, however, dated the Last Supper on the day of Passover (Matt. 26: 17; Mark 14:12; Luke 22:7). This apparent contradiction in dating may depend on whether the gospel writers were referring to the preparation day for the sabbath or to the preparation day for the Passover. *Steve W. Lemke*

PRESBYTER See *Elder.*

PRESENCE OF GOD God's initiative in encountering people. Biblical words for the presence of God usually relate to the "face" of God.

Old Testament Usage During the patriarchal period, God used a variety of means of revelation to communicate with the people (Gen. 15:1; 32:24–30). These are often described as theophanies, appearances of God to humanity. Moses had a close relationship with God. He encountered God in the burning bush and knew God "face to face" (Deut. 34:10). The presence of God was also closely related to the tabernacle, the place for ancient Israel to encounter God in worship. The tabernacle was the place of the Lord's name or glory, a manifestation of God's presence and activity in the world (Ex. 40:34,38). The cloud and fire symbolized the presence of God leading on the journey to Canaan.

Perhaps the primary tangible symbol of God's presence with the people was the ark of the covenant, the container for the tablet of the law and the seat of God's throne. It led the people in the journey to Canaan and into battle (Josh. 3:1–6). The ark was associated with the sanctuary and eventually came to rest in the Temple, the place of the presence of God. Here Isaiah had a powerful vision of the holy God (Isa. 6).

God also manifested Himself in other ways: in fire (1 Kings 18) and in a still small voice (1 Kings 19), both to Elijah. The Psalms speak of God's presence with the worshiping community (Ps. 139) and of the apparent absence of this present God (Ps. 13). In either case, God is still addressed. Ezekiel spoke of the Exile in terms of the glory (presence) of God leaving ancient Israel but then returning at the end of the Exile in Babylon (Ezek. 43:1–5). Much of the Old Testament discussion of the presence of God centers on the fact that God is utterly free to be where God wills but constantly chooses to be with His people to give them life.

New Testament Usage The primary New Testament manifestation of the presence of God is in Jesus Christ, Emmanuel, "God with us" (Matt. 1:23; John 1:14; Heb. 1:1–3). This presence did not end with the death of Christ. The risen Christ appeared to the disciples (John 21:1–14) and to Paul. Through the apostles, Paul and the disciples, Christ's work continued (Acts 1:8; 26:12–18). The Holy Spirit is an important manifestation of the presence of God and continues the redemp-

tive work of God. The return of Christ will bring permanence to the presence of God with His people.

The church is called to be a manifestation of God's presence. That community is fed by the presence of God found in communion between worshiper and God. *W. H. Bellinger, Jr.*

PRESSFAT KJV term for a winevat (Hag. 2:16).

PRESUMPTION See *Pride.*

PRICK See *Goads.*

PRIDE Undue confidence in and attention to one's own skills, accomplishments, state, possessions, or position. Pride is easier to recognize than to define, easier to recognize in others than in oneself. Many biblical words describe this concept, each with its own emphasis. Some of the synonyms for pride include arrogance, presumption, conceit, self-satisfaction, boasting, and high-mindedness. It is the opposite of humility, the proper attitude one should have in relation to God. Pride is rebellion against God because it attributes to self the honor and glory due to God alone. Proud persons do not think it necessary to ask forgiveness because they do not admit their sinful condition. This attitude toward God finds expression in one's attitude toward others, often causing people to have a low estimate of the ability and worth of others and therefore to treat them with either contempt or cruelty. Some have considered pride to be the root and essence of sin. Others consider it to be sin in its final form. In either case, it is a grievous sin.

"Boasting" can be committed only in the presence of other persons (1 John 2:16; Jas. 4:16). "Haughtiness" or "arrogance" measures self as above others (Mark 7:23; Luke 1:51; Rom. 1:30; 2 Tim. 3:2; Jas. 4:6; 1 Peter 5:5). This word refers primarily to the attitude of one's heart. First Timothy 3:6; 6:4; and 2 Timothy 3:4 use a word literally meaning "to wrap in smoke." It emphasizes the plight of the one who has been blinded by personal pride.

Pride may appear in many forms. Some of the more common are pride of race, spiritual pride, and pride of riches. Jesus denounced pride of race (Luke 3:8). The parable of the Pharisee and the publican was directed at those guilty of spiritual pride, the ones who "trusted in themselves that they were righteous, and despised others" (Luke 18:9). James 1:10 warns the rich against the temptation to be lifted up with pride because of their wealth. *Gerald Cowen*

PRIESTHOOD OF CHRIST That work of Christ in which He offers Himself as the supreme sacrifice for the sins of humankind and continually intercedes on their behalf. See *Atonement; Christ; Jesus; High Priest.*

PRIESTHOOD OF THE BELIEVER Christian belief that every person has direct access to God without any mediator other than Christ. All religions have developed an intricate system of priesthood, an order of religious professionals who act as mediators between the worshiper and God. The essence of the Christian gospel is that believers have direct access to God because Christ has broken down the barriers (Eph. 2:14–16). This means that the "priesthood of the believer" has become a strong Christian doctrine which developed in two directions: (1) believers can respond directly to the personal activity of God in their lives, through the Holy Spirit and through the written word of Scripture, and do not require a human priest to mediate authoritative communication with God; (2) Christians have become a "holy priesthood" (1 Pet. 2:5) and can minister to one another and to the world. No longer does a professional priesthood have an exclusive channel for holy communication. Any believer can be the channel of God's Spirit and mediate the grace of God in prayer, confession, or witness in particular situations.

The role of Christ as our only priest means that He is the only Mediator between God and the believer (1 Tim. 2:5). The priestly role of Christ is a major theme of the Epistle to the Hebrews (see 4:14–15). Further, this priesthood of Christ is said to be "after the order of Melchizedek" (Heb. 5:6), which means that God appointed Him directly and Jesus did not have to trace His priesthood through the human line of Aaron or Levi. This priestly ministry of Christ is the foundation of the doctrine, because the work of Christ is sufficient for all and His "once for all" sacrifice fulfilled the promise and purpose of the Old Testament priesthood.

Our Gospels record a dramatic event which happened at the very moment Jesus died on the cross. The great veil in the Temple which separated the holy of holies from the rest of the sanctuary was torn asunder from the top to the bottom, suggesting that God Himself opened up the direct access to the holy of holies through the death of Christ.

The priestly ministry of all believers derives directly from Christ, who calls all His followers to share in His priestly ministry. This fulfills Israel's role as a kingdom of priests and a light to the nations. First Peter compares Christian believers to living stones "built into a spiritual house, to be a holy priesthood, offering spiritual sacrifices acceptable to God through Jesus Christ" (2:5 NIV). Here the emphasis is not upon our coming directly to God without a human priest, but rather upon the priestly function of all believers as they offer "spiritual sacrifices" to God through Jesus

Christ. The question immediately arises, "What are these spiritual sacrifices?" Hebrews 13:15–16 lists praise of God in prayer and song, doing good, sharing with others. Any real sacrifice will cost us something; it should be our response in love and gratitude to the One who has given Himself for us.

Romans 12:1 emphasizes another dimension of this priestly ministry of all Christians "I appeal to you therefore, brothers and sisters, by the mercies of God, to present your bodies as a living sacrifice, holy and acceptable to God, which is your spiritual worship" (NRSV). The progression in the biblical record of sacrifice is clear. The priests of the old covenant offered the sacrifice of animals upon the altar. Christ, as High Priest, offered His own life upon the altar of the cross. Followers of Christ are called upon to offer their very bodies as a living sacrifice, a day-by-day commitment and service to God, as the truest form of worship. Biblical examples of that ministry include:

(1) We are urged to pray for one another, offering the priestly ministry of intercessory prayer.

(2) We are also urged to confess our sins to one another and to bear one another's burden. The ancient role of the priest was to receive the confession of the people and to convey it to God to receive His forgiveness. All of us have the opportunity at some time to be a special channel of blessing and help to a fellow believer on the journey.

(3) We can bring others to Christ. The ancient role of the priest was to bring people in contact with God. While Christ has come to reveal the Father, it is necessary for us to fulfill the priestly role of bringing people to Jesus in order that they may have access to the Father through Him.

Wayne Ward

PRIESTS Personnel in charge of sacrifice and offering at worship places, particularly the tabernacle and Temple.

Functions Priesthood in the Old Testament primarily involved sacrificing at the altar and worship in the shrine. Other functions were blessing the people (Num. 6:22–26), determining the will of God (Ex. 28:30), and instructing the people in the law of God (Deut. 31:9–12). This instruction included the application of the laws of cleanness (Lev. 11—15). Some of these functions, like blessing and teaching, would not be reserved for priests alone, but sacrificing and the use of the Urim and Thummim were theirs exclusively. See *Urim and Thummim.*

If the main characteristic of priesthood was sacrificing, the office is as old as Abel. Noah sacrificed; so did Abraham and the patriarchs. We may say that they were family priests. Jethro, the priest of Midian, brought sacrifices to God and worshiped with Moses, Aaron, and the elders of Israel (Ex. 18:12). God promised that Israel, if it were faithful, would be a "kingdom of priests, a holy nation" (Ex. 19:6). This may have meant that Israel was called to mediate God's word and work to the world—to be a light to the nations (Isa. 42:6).

Later, when God purposed to establish the nation, He chose Moses to organize the army, to set up a system of judges, to build a house of worship, and to ordain priests to serve therein. The formal priesthood goes with the formal worship of an organized nation of considerable size. On Mount Sinai, God gave Moses instructions to build the tabernacle. On the mount, God told Moses to appoint Aaron and his four sons to serve as priests, that is, to serve at the altar and in the sanctuary (Ex. 28:1,41). Their holy garments are prescribed in detail and their consecration ritual is given in chapters 28 and 29. As to the work of these priests, most of Leviticus and some of Numbers and Deuteronomy give details. Aaron and his descendants of the tribe of Levi served in the tabernacle and Temple as priests. Members of the tribe of Levi not related to Aaron assisted the priests but did not offer sacrifices. Priests were supported by offerings and Levites by tithes (Num. 18:20–24). See *Levites; High Priest; Aaron.*   *R. Laird Harris*

PRINCE A ruler, one of noble birth and high position; not just the limited sense of a male heir of a sovereign. (Compare Zeph. 1:8 which distinguishes princes and king's sons.) KJV used prince as a title for Israel's king (1 Sam. 13:14), a leading priest (1 Chron. 12:27), a Midianite tribal chief (Num. 25:18), the leading men of a city or province (Gen. 34:2; 1 Kings 20:15; Jer. 34:19), and for rulers in general (Matt. 20:25; 1 Cor. 2:6,8). By extension, *prince* applies to supernatural beings. "Prince of Peace" (Isa. 9:6), "Prince of life" (Acts 3:15), and "Prince and a Savior" (Acts 5:31) are messianic titles. Daniel 8:25 refers to God as "Prince of princes." Daniel 12:1 gives Michael, the angelic advocate of Israel, the title *prince.* Satan is often described as "the prince of this world" (John 12:31; 14:30; 16:11; compare Matt. 9:34; 12:24; Eph. 2:2).

PRINCE OF LIFE The word translated as "prince" (Acts 3:15; 5:31, "author" and "leader" respectively in some modern versions) is also translated as "captain" (Heb. 2:10; "pioneer" or "author" in some modern versions) and "author" (Heb. 12:2; "pioneer" in modern versions). All of these references are to Jesus as the founder of a new life which His followers now share with Him.

PRINCESS Two Hebrew constructions are translated "princess." *1.* "Daughter of a king." Solomon's 700 wives were princesses married to seal political ties with their fathers (1 Kings 11:3). Lamentations 1:1 pictures the reversal of Jerusalem's fortune in the image of a princess turned

servant. *2.* Feminine form of the common word for leader or ruler applied to a king's wife (Ps. 45:13 NIV, NRSV) and to the leading women of Judah (Jer. 43:6 NRSV). See *Prince.*

PRINCIPALITIES Supernatural spiritual powers, whether good or evil. Principalities were created by and are thus subject to Christ (Col. 1:16). Neither principalities nor any other force can separate a believer from God's love found in Christ (Rom. 8:38).

PRISCA (Prĭs′ cà) See *Priscilla.*

PRISCILLA (Prĭs cĭl′ là) See *Aquila and Priscilla.*

PRISON GATE KJV designation for a gate in Jerusalem (Neh. 12:39). Modern translations refer to the Gate of the Guard or Guardhouse Gate. The gate is perhaps identical with the Miphkad (Muster) Gate (Neh. 3:31).

PRISON, PRISONERS Any place where persons accused and/or convicted of criminal activity are confined and persons so confined or those captured in war.

Old Testament Imprisonment as a legal punishment is not a feature of ancient law codes. The Mosaic law allowed for a place of custody until the case was decided (Lev. 24:12; Num. 15:34), but beginning only in the Persian period does the Bible mention incarceration as a penalty for breaking the religious law (Ezra. 7:26).

Prisons mentioned in the Old Testament were under the control of the crown. Joseph was put in a royal prison in Egypt (Gen. 39:20), apparently attached to the house of the captain of the guard (40:3). Asa of Judah (2 Chron. 16:10) and Ahab of Israel (1 Kings 22:26–27) made use of prisons, probably associated with the palace. The experience of Jeremiah, however, provides the most interesting glimpses of prisons and prison life. The royal prisons were apparently not large, as the one in which Jeremiah was initially placed was a converted private house (Jer. 37:15). He was confined to an underground dungeon (Jer. 37:16), perhaps a converted cistern. Jeremiah later was placed under house arrest in the "court of the guard" (Jer. 37:20–21). There, he was available for consultation with the king (Jer. 38:14,28), able to conduct business (Jer. 32:2–3,6–12), and able to speak freely (Jer. 38:1–4). Because the latter enraged the princes, Jeremiah was confined for a time to a muddy cistern in the "court of the guard" (Jer. 38:4–13).

Persons were confined in royal prisons for offending the king (Gen. 40:1–3), perhaps by political intrigue. In Israel, prophets were jailed for denouncing royal policy (2 Chron. 16:10), predicting ill of the king (1 Kings 22:26–27), and suspected collaboration with the enemy (Jer. 37:11–15). Po-

Interior of the prison at Philippi where local tradition says Paul and Silas were held.

litical prisoners in Assyrian and Babylonian prisons included former kings of rebellious nations (2 Kings 17:4; 24:15; 25:27; Jer. 52:11). Samson became a prisoner in a Philistine prison (Judg. 16:21). Prisoners of war were usually either killed or enslaved.

The lot of prisoners was pitiable, sometimes consisting of meager rations (1 Kings 22:27) and hard labor (Judg. 16:21). In some cases, prisoners were restrained and tortured by the stocks or collar (2 Chron. 16:10; Jer. 29:26). Jehoiachin was clothed in special prison garments in Babylon (2 Kings 25:29). Prison life became a symbol of oppression and suffering (Ps. 79:11), and release from prison provided a picture of restoration or salvation (Pss. 102:20; 142:7; 146:7; Isa. 61:1; Zech. 9:11-12).

New Testament In New Testament times, persons could be imprisoned for nonpayment of debt (Matt. 5:25-26; Luke 12:58-59), political insurrection and criminal acts (Luke 23:19,25), as well as for certain religious practices (Luke 21:12; Acts 8:3). For some of these offenses, public prisons were also employed (Acts 5:18-19). John the Baptist was arrested for criticizing the king (Luke 3:19-20) and seems to have been held in a royal prison attached to the palace (Mark 6:17-29). Later, Peter was held under heavy security, consisting of chains, multiple guards, and iron doors (Acts 12:5-11).

Paul, who imprisoned others (Acts 8:3; 22:4; 26:10), was often in prison himself (2 Cor. 11:23). His experiences provides the most detail on prisons in the New Testament world. In Philippi, he and Silas were placed under the charge of a lone jailer, who "put them in the innermost cell and fastened their feet in the stocks" (Acts 16:23-24 NRSV). Excavations at Philippi have uncovered a crypt revered by early Christians as the prison and adorned with frescos depicting Paul and Silas in Philippi. If the identification is correct, the crypt's small size eliminates any doubt that when Paul and Silas sang hymns, "the prisoners were listening to them" (Acts 16:25 NRSV). Perhaps the crypt, originally a cistern,

served only as the "innermost cell" (Acts 16:24) for maximum security or solitary confinement. In Jerusalem, Paul was held in the barracks of the Roman cohort (Acts 23:16-18). After his transfer to Caesarea, he was confined with some freedom in the headquarters of Roman procurators and was allowed to receive visitors (Acts 23:35; 24:23). As he and other prisoners were transferred to Rome by ship, Paul was again given some freedom (Acts 27:1,3); but when shipwreck became imminent, the soldiers resolved to kill them all lest they should escape (27:42-43). While awaiting trial in Rome, Paul remained under constant guard in a kind of house arrest (28:16-17,30), met his own expenses, and was free to receive visitors and preach the gospel "openly and unhindered" (28:30). Paul considered his imprisonment as for Christ (Eph. 3:1; 4:1; Phil. 1:13-14; Philem. 1, 9).

The situation for prisoners remained dismal in New Testament times, and concern for such persons is a virtue expected by Christ of every disciple (Matt. 25:36,39,43-44). It is Satan who will be imprisoned during the millennium (Rev. 20:1-3,7).   *Daniel C. Browning, Jr.*

PRIZE A prize awarded in an athletic competition. Paul used the image to illustrate the goal of the Christian life (Phil. 3:14; compare 1 Cor. 9:24). The prize is sometimes identified as Paul's heavenly destination. More likely the "upward call" designates the total call to Christian maturity. The larger context uses multiple expressions (know Christ 2:8,10; gain Christ 2:8; know the power of Christ's resurrection; share Christ's suffering and death 2:10) to define the goal of Christian living. Though Paul used a competitive image, he was aware that the righteousness which matters was not the result of his own efforts but is God's gift through faith (3:9).

PROCHORUS (Prŏch' o rŭs) Personal name meaning, "leader of the chorus (or dance)." One of the seven selected to assist in distribution of food to the Greek-speaking widows of the Jerusalem church (Acts 6:5).

PROCLAMATION See *Kerygma; Preaching in the Bible.*

PROCONSUL An office in the Roman system of government. Proconsuls oversaw the administration of civil and military matters in a province. They are responsible to the senate in Rome. The New Testament refers to two proconsuls: Sergius Paulus in Cyprus (Acts 13:7 NRSV) and Gallio in Achaia (Acts 18:12 NRSV). Compare Acts 19:38. See *Rome.*

PROCORUS (Prŏc' o rŭs) NIV form of Prochorus.

PROCURATOR A Roman military office which developed into a powerful position by New Testament times. They had control over entire countries under the Roman system. The procurator could issue death warrants (a privilege often withheld from subject peoples) and have coins struck in his name. Three procurators are named in the New Testament: Pilate (Matt. 27:2; some question whether Pilate was a procurator), Felix (Acts 23:24), and Festus (Acts 24:27). See *Rome.*

PRODIGAL SON Popular term used to identify Jesus' parable in Luke 15:11–32. English translations do not use the term *prodigal* meaning, "reckless" or "wasteful," though they speak of the younger son's wasting or squandering his property (15:13). "The Prodigal Son" is an unfortunate designation for this parable told in defense of Jesus' practice of fellowshipping with sinners (15:1). The parable focuses not on the reckless-then-repentant younger son but on the waiting father who rushes to welcome his child home and calls all, elder brother included, to share the joy of homecoming.

PROFANE To treat that which is holy as common. Profane often approximates defile in meaning. See *Clean, Cleanness; Holy.*

PROGNOSTICATORS KJV term for those predicting the future by astrology (Isa. 47:13). See *Divination and Magic.*

PROMISE God's announcement of His plan of salvation and blessing to His people, one of the unifying themes integrating the message and the deeds of the Old and New Testaments.
Promise Embraces Both Declaration and Deed God's promise begins with a declaration by God; it covers God's future plan for not just one race, but all the nations of the earth; and it focuses on the gifts and deeds that God will bestow on a few to benefit the many. We may define God's promise this way: the divine declaration or assurance made at first to Eve, Shem, Abraham, Isaac, and Jacob and then to the whole nation of Israel that: (1) He would be their God, (2) they would be His people, and (3) He would dwell in their midst. The blessing of land and of growth as a nation as well as the call to bless the nations was part of the promise to Abraham. Added to these words of assurance were a series of divine actions in history. These words and deeds of God began to constitute the continuously unfolding divine plan by which all the peoples and nations of the earth would benefit from that day to this.

The Old Testament did not use a specific Hebrew word for promise. It used quite ordinary words to encapsulate the pivotal promise of God: speak, say, swear.

The New Testament, however, does use both the noun *promise* (51 times) and the verb (11 times).

Promise in these references can denote either the form or the content of those words. They could refer either to the words themselves as promissory notes on which to base one's confidence for the future, or they could refer to the things themselves which were promised. Since God's one promise-plan was made up of many specifications, the plural form of "promises" appears 11 times in the New Testament. Nevertheless, the singular form was greatly predominant.
Varying Formulations of the Promise in the Old Testament In Genesis 1—11, the promise of God is represented by the successive "blessings" announced both in the creative order and on the human family—even in spite of their sin. The promise of blessing therefore, was both introductory to the promise and part of the promise itself.
The Promise and the Patriarchs For the fathers of Israel (Abraham, Isaac, and Jacob) we may speak of the promise in the singular even though it announced three significant elements. Each of the three elements are incomplete without the support of each other and without being interlocked into one promise-plan.

This triple promise included: (1) the promise of a seed or offspring (an heir; Gen. 12:7; 15:4; 17:16,19; 21:12; 22:16–18; 26:3–4,24; 28:13–14; 35:11–12), (2) the promise of land (an inheritance; Gen. 12:1,7; 13:17; 15:18; 17:8; 24:7; 26:3–5; 28:13,15; 35:12; 48:4; 50:24;) (3) the promise of blessing on all the nations (a heritage of the gospel; Gen. 12:3; 18:18; 22:17–18; 26:4; 28:14).

To demonstrate the eternality and one-sidedness in the gracious offer of God, only God passed between the pieces in Genesis 15:9–21 thus obligating Himself to fulfill His promises without simultaneously and similarly obligating Abraham and the subsequent beneficiaries of the promise.
The Promise and the Law The promise was eternal, Abraham's descendants had to transmit the promise to subsequent generations until the final Seed, even Jesus the Messiah, came. They had to do more. God expected them to participate personally by faith. Where faith was present, already demands and commands were likewise present. Thus, Abraham obeyed God and left Ur (Gen. 12:1–4) and walked before God in a blameless way (Gen. 17:1). His obedience to God's "requirements," "commands," "decrees," and "laws" (Gen. 26:5 NIV) was exemplary.

The law extended these demands to the entire life of the people all the while presupposing the earlier promises as the very basis, indeed, as the lever by which such demands could be made (Ex. 2:23–25; 6:2–8; 19:3–8; 20:2). The apostle Paul will later ask whether the promises have nullified the law (Rom. 3:31). He answered, "Not at all! Rather, we uphold the law" (Rom. 3:31 NIV).

The Promises and David The monarchy, prematurely founded by the whims of a people who wished to be like the other nations, received a distinctive role through God's promise. A lad taken "from the pasture" (2 Sam. 7:8 NIV) would be given a name equal to "the greatest men of the earth" (2 Sam. 7:9 NIV); indeed, his offspring would be seated at God's "right hand" (Ps. 110:1) and inherit the nations (Ps. 2:8).

The Promise and the New Covenant The new covenant of Jeremiah 31:31-34 both repeats many of the elements and formulas already contained in the previously announced promise-plan of God and adds several new features. The new promise still contains the law of God, only now it will be internalized. It still pledges that God will be their God, and they will be His people. It still declares that He will forgive their sins and remember them no more. However, it also adds that it will no longer be necessary to teach one's neighbor or brother; for everyone, no matter what their station in life, will know the Lord.

In spite of Israel's future loss of its king, its capital, its Temple, and its former glory, God would fulfill His ancient promises by founding new promises on "the former things [foretold] long ago" (Isa. 48:3). He would send His new David, new Temple, new Elijah, new heavens and new earth—but all in continuity with what He had pledged long ago!

The New Testament Enlarges the Ancient Promises The New Testament promises may be gathered into these groups. The first, and most frequent, are the references to God's promises to Abraham about the heir he was to receive, even Jesus Christ (Rom. 4:13-16,20; 9:7-9; 15:8; Gal. 3:16-22; 4:23; Heb. 6:13-17; 7:6; 11:9, 11,17). A second major grouping may be made around David's seed and the sending of Jesus as "a Savior according to promise" (Acts 13:23,32-33; 26:6). Perhaps we should connect with this group the gift of "the promise of life that is in Christ Jesus" (2 Tim. 1:1 NIV), the "promised eternal inheritance" (Heb. 9:15 NIV), and the promise which "he has promised us, eternal life" (1 John 2:25 NRSV). This promise is "what was promised through faith in Jesus Christ" (Gal. 3:22 NRSV).

The third major group is the gift of the Holy Spirit. The promises appear after our Lord's resurrection (Luke 24:49; Acts 2:33,38-39).

There are other subjects related to God's promise: rest (Heb. 4:1); the new covenant with its prospect of an eternal inheritance (Heb. 9:15); the new heavens and new earth (2 Pet. 3:13); the resurrection (Acts 26:6); the blessing of numerous descendants (Heb. 6:14); the emergence of an unshakable kingdom (Heb. 12:28), and Gentiles as recipients of the same promise (Eph. 2:11-13).

The Promise Has Some Notable Differences from Prophecy While much of the promise doctrine is also prophetic in that it relates to the future, there are some notable differences between promise and prophecy. *1.* Promises relate to what is good, desirable, and that which blesses and enriches. Prophecy, however, also may contain notes of judgment, destruction, and calamity when people and nations fail to repent. *2.* Promises ordinarily implicate the entire human race in their provisions whereas prophecies more typically are aimed at specific nations, cultures, or peoples. *3.* Promises deliberately have a continuous fulfillment for generation after generation while prophecies invoke promise when they wish to speak to the distant future. *4.* The promise of God is unconditional while most prophecies are conditional and have a suppressed "unless" or "if" you repent attached to their predictions of judgment. Finally, *5.* The promise of God embraces many declarations of God ("very great and precious promises," 2 Pet. 1:4), whereas prophecies are usually directed to more specific events and particular individuals.

The promise-plan of God, then, is indeed His own Word and plan, both in His person and His works, to communicate a blessing to Israel and thereby to bless all the nations of the earth.

Walter C. Kaiser, Jr.

PROPERTY See *Inheritance; Ownership.*

PROPHECY, PROPHETS Reception and declaration of a word from the Lord through a direct prompting of the Holy Spirit and the human instrument thereof.

Old Testament Three key terms are used of the prophet. *Ro'eh* and *hozeh* are translated as "seer." The most important term, *nabi,* is usually translated "prophet." It probably meant "one who is called to speak."

History Moses, perhaps Israel's greatest leader, was a prophetic prototype (Acts 3:21-24). He appeared with Elijah in the transfiguration (Matt. 17:1-8). Israel looked for a prophet like Moses (Deut. 34:10).

Prophets also played a role in the conquest and settlement of the Promised Land. The prophetess Deborah predicted victory, pronounced judgment on doubting Barak, and even identified the right time to attack (Judg. 4:6-7,9,14). Samuel, who led Israel during its transition to monarchy, was a prophet, priest, and judge (1 Sam. 3:20; 7:6,15). He was able to see into the future by vision (3:11-14) and to ask God for thunder and rain (12:18). Samuel led in victory over the Philistines (1 Sam. 7), and God used him to anoint kings. Gad and Nathan served as prophets to the king. Elijah and Elisha offered critique and advice for the kings. The prophets did more than predict the future; their messages called Israel to honor God. Their prophecies were not general principles but specific words corresponding to Israel's historical context.

Similarly the classical or writing prophets were joined to history. Israel's political turmoil provided the context for the writing prophets. The Assyrian rise to power after 750 B.C. furnished the focus of the ministries of Amos, Hosea, Isaiah, and Micah. The Babylonian threat was the background and motive for much of the ministry of Jeremiah and Ezekiel. The advent of the Persian Empire in the latter part of the sixth century set the stage for prophets such as Obadiah, Haggai, Zechariah, and Malachi. Thus the prophets spoke for God throughout Israel's history.

The prophets influenced almost every institution of Israel, despite the fact that they were often viewed with contempt: they were locked up (Jer. 37), ignored (Isa. 6:9–13), and persecuted (1 Kings 19:1–2). In addition to serving judges and kings, the prophets also addressed Israel's worship. They criticized vain worship (Amos 5:23–24) and priestly failures (Amos 7:10; Mal. 2). The word of the Lord was also spoken in worship (Pss. 50:5; 60:6; 81:6–10; 91:14–16; 95:8–11). The prophets' call to covenant faithfulness revealed an awareness of the law (Isa. 58:6–9; Ezek. 18; Mic. 6:6–8; Hos. 6:6; Amos 2:4; 5:21–24).

Prophets formed guilds or schools (2 Kings 4:38; 1 Sam. 10:5; 19:20). While most references to prophetic schools belong to the period of the monarchy, there is some evidence to believe the schools continued (Jer. 23:13–14). The mere existence of the books of prophecy is probably due in part to the prophets' helpers (Jer. 36:4). Perhaps their words were recorded because they provided a moral challenge to the entire nation and not merely to a king or individual. Surely once the prophet's words were written, they were not ignored but continually studied and reapplied.

The Experience of the Prophet Prophets generally shared several key experiences and characteristics. (1) An essential mark of a prophet was a call from God. Attempting to prophesy without such a commission was false prophecy (Jer. 14:14). The prophets were at times allowed to see into the throne room or heavenly court (Isa. 6:1–7; 1 Kings 22:19–23; Jer. 23:18–22; compare Amos 3:7; Job 1:6–12; 2:1–6; 2 Cor. 12:1–4; Rev. 1:1–3; 22:18–19). (2) Prophets received a word from God through many means—direct declarations, visions, dreams, or an appearance of God. The great variety in prophetic experience prohibits any oversimplification; ecstatic experiences were not mandatory for receiving God's word. (3) Prophets spoke the word of God. They were primarily spokespersons who called His people to obedience by appealing to Israel's past and future. For example, God's past blessing and future judgment should provoke social justice and mercy for the disadvantaged. (4) Prophets relayed God's message by deed as well as by word. They worked

symbolic acts which served as dramatic, living parables. Hosea's marriage taught about God's relationship with Israel (Hos. 2:1–13; see also Isa. 20:1–3; Ezek. 4:1–3; Jer. 19:10–11). (5) The prophets also performed miracles which confirmed their message. While some prophets like Moses (Ex. 4:1–9) and Elijah (1 Kings 17) worked many miracles, virtually all prophets occasionally saw a miraculous fulfillment of God's word (Isa. 38:8). This miracle-working capacity also included healing (1 Kings 17:17–22; 2 Kings 5; Matt. 12:22–29). (6) Prophets also conveyed the word of God by writing (Isa. 8:1; Ezek. 43:11). (7) Prophets were to minister to their people. They were to test God's peoples' lives (Jer. 6:27) and be watchmen for moral compromise (Ezek. 3:17). Particularly important was the role of intercessor—sometimes even for the prophet's enemy (1 Kings 13:6; 17:17–24; 2 Kings 4:18–37; Amos 7:2; Jer. 14:17–20,21; Isa. 59:16). (8) Throughout Israel's history genuine prophets had ecstatic experiences.

False Prophets Distinguishing between false and true prophets was very difficult, though several tests of authenticity emerge in the Old Testament. The true prophet must be loyal to the biblical faith directing one to worship Yahweh alone (Deut. 13:1–3). A second test required that the words of a true prophet be fulfilled (Deut. 18:22; Jer. 42:1–6; Ezek. 33:30–33). We must remember that this is a difficult test to apply. There were often long lapses between predictions and fulfillment (Mic. 3:12; Jer. 26:16–19). Some predictions seemed very unlikely, and others were conditional—based upon the hearer's response (Jonah 3:4–5). Furthermore, prophets could behave inappropriately (Num. 12:1–2; 20:1–12; Jer. 15:19–21; 38:24–27). Prophets appeared ambivalent at times when simply delivering the word of God as it was given (2 Kings 20:1–6). Also one could predict correctly while not being loyal to Yahweh (Deut. 13:1–3). Accurate prediction was not a final test. Other tests included agreement with previous prophets' words (Jer. 28:8), good character (Mic. 3:11), and a willingness to suffer because of faithfulness (1 Kings 22:27–28; Jer. 38:3–13). Similarly, the New Testament believers had to distinguish true prophecy (1 John 4:1; 1 Cor. 14:29). See *False Prophet*.

Hints for Interpretation Prophets intended to evoke faith by proclamation, not merely to predict the future. Thus reading the prophets with a lustful curiosity is inappropriate. Our primary desire must be to know God, not just the facts of the future.

The interpreter must remember the limited perspective of the prophet. The prophets were not all-knowing but all-telling—that is they told what God had told them to tell. Prophecy has a progressive character. One must seek to read prophecy in light of its whole, deriving partial insight from different prophets. Prophecy must also be read in its historical context. Particular attention must be paid to the intention of the prophet. For example, a prophet may rebuke another country to offer assistance to Israel (Isa. 46—47), make Israel examine its own conduct (Amos 1—2), or to bring a nation to repentance (Jonah 3:4,8–9).

Caution must be exercised when reading predictive prophecy because prophecy often has more than one fulfillment. Many prophecies have an immediate application to their own situation and are also applicable to another context. Thus the prediction that Christ is born of a virgin (Matt. 1:23) also had a fulfillment in Isaiah's day (Isa. 8:3). Similarly prophecies of "the day of the Lord" had several fulfillments (partial) which also foreshadowed a final fulfillment (Obad. 15; Joel 1:15; 2:1; Zeph. 1:7,14; Ezek. 30:3; compare 2 Pet. 3:10).

Modern evangelicals understand predictive prophecies in several ways. (1) Some prophecies seem to have a direct, literal fulfillment: the Messiah was to be born in Bethlehem (Matt. 2:5–6; Mic. 5:2). (2) Not all predictions were fulfilled literally. Jesus taught that the prediction about Elijah's return was fulfilled by John the Baptist and not a literal Elijah (Matt. 11:13–15; Mal. 3:1–4). Similarly, Paul applied prophecies about literal, national Israel to the church (Rom. 9:25–26; Hos. 1:9–10, 2:23). The literal father of Israel, Abraham, was seen to be the father of the believing church (Rom. 4:11,16; Gal. 3:7). This distinctively Christian reading was thought to be legitimate because of Christ's fulfillment and interpretation of the Old Testament (Luke 4:17–21). (3) This Christian reading of the Old Testament often takes the form of typological interpretation. The New Testament authors believed Old Testament events, persons, or things foreshadowed the later Christian story. Thus, they used the images of the Old Testament to understand the New Testament realities. Christ can be compared to Adam (1 Cor. 15:22–23; see 10:11). (4) Some readers believe that Old Testament words take on a "fuller sense" or meaning. Old Testament expressions may have a divine significance, unforeseen by the Old Testament author, which comes to light only after God's later word or deed. See *Typology*.

New Testament The word *prophētēs* means "to speak before" or "to speak for." Thus it refers to one who speaks for God or Christ. Prophets were also called *pneumatics* (*pneumatikos*), "spiritual ones" (1 Cor. 14:37). The prophets played a foundational role in the early church (1 Cor. 12:28–31; Eph. 4:11; 2:20). Due to the presumed prophetic silence in the time between the Testaments, the coming of Jesus is seen as an inbreaking of the Spirit's work especially visible in prophecy. For example, in Luke the angel's visitation and prediction (1:11,26–27) provoked Mary and Zecharias to prophesy (1:46–67; 67–79). After an angelic

visitation to the shepherds, the prophet and prophetess declared Jesus to be the redemption Israel awaited (2:10–12,25,36–38). John the Baptist also predicted that Jesus would baptize in the Spirit (Matt. 3:11).

Jesus called Himself a prophet (Luke 13:33). His miracles and discernment were rightly understood as prophetic (John 4:19). He taught not by citing expert rabbis, but with His own prophetic authority (Mark 1:22; Luke 4:24).

The early believers saw the outpouring of the Spirit (Acts 2:17) as a fulfillment of Joel's prediction that all God's people, young and old, male and female, would prophesy. These gifts may intensify at the end of time as will evil. While any Christian might occasionally receive a prophecy, some seem to have a special gift of prophecy (1 Cor. 12:29; 13:2). Prophets function primarily in the worship of the church (Acts 13:2). They predict (Acts 11:28; 20:23; 27:22–26), announce judgments (Acts 13:11; 28:25–28), act symbolically (Acts 21:10–11), and receive visions (Acts 9:10–11; 2 Cor. 12:1). Prophetic insights led to missionary efforts (Acts 13:1–3; 10:10–17; 15:28,32). While teaching and prophecy are different, they also can be related (Acts 13:1–2; Rev. 2:20). Some prophets "preached" lengthy messages (Acts 15:32) and gave exposition to biblical texts (Luke 1:67–79; Eph. 3:5; Rom. 11:25–36).

The prophets used phrases such as "the Lord says" or "the Holy Spirit says" as introductory formulas for prophetic insight into the future (Acts 21:11), or for inspired adaptation of an Old Testament text (Heb. 3:7).

New Testament prophecy was limited (1 Cor. 13:9); it was to be evaluated by the congregation (1 Cor. 14:29; 1 Thess. 5:20–21). One may even respond inappropriately to prophecy (Acts 21:12). The supreme test for prophecy is loyalty to Christ (1 Cor. 12:3; Rev. 19:10). Some Christians have the gift of discernment (1 Cor. 12:10). Jesus said prophets could be known by their fruit (Matt. 7:15–20). Paul demanded orderly, Christ-honoring, upbuilding prophecy which submits to apostolic authority (1 Cor. 14:26–40). Thus prophecy is not without restraint. Circumstance may even demand that the dress of men and women prophets be stipulated (1 Cor. 11:5–7). Prophecy outside of apostolic authority can be safely ignored; thus prophecy is not a threat to Scripture's special authority (1 Cor. 14:38–39; 2 Tim. 3:16; 2 Pet. 1:20–21).　　*Randy Hatchett*

PROPHETESS 1. Female prophet; women serving as God's spokesperson. Five women are explicitly identified as prophetesses: Miriam (Ex. 15:20); Deborah (Judg. 4:4); Huldah (2 Kings 22:14); Noadiah, a "false" prophetess (Neh. 6:14); and Anna (Luke 2:36). Jezebel claimed tc be a prophetess (Rev. 2:20). The ministries of prophetesses varied greatly. Miriam called upon Israel to celebrate God's deliverance. Deborah combined the offices of prophetess and judge, even accompanying Barak into battle. Huldah spoke God's words of judgment (2 Kings 22:16–17) and forgiveness (22:18–20) to King Josiah. Anna shared the good news of Jesus' birth with the Temple crowds. The false prophetess Noadiah sought to frighten Nehemiah. Jezebel attempted to involve the church of Thyatira in idolatry.

The prophet Joel anticipated a time when all God's people, "male servants and female servants," would be filled with God's Spirit and prophesy (Joel 2:28–29). This prophetic hope was fulfilled at Pentecost (Acts 2:17–18) and in the ongoing life of the early church (Acts 21:9). Paul encouraged all believers to desire to prophesy (1 Cor. 14:1), that is, to offer speech which builds up the church (14:5). First Corinthians 11:5 presumes women were involved in prophesying and prayer in public worship. *2.* The wife of a prophet (Isa. 8:3). See *Prophet.*

PROPITIATION (Prō′ pĭ tĭ ā tĭon) See *Expiation.*

PROSELYTES Converts to a religion; non-Jews who accepted the Jewish faith and completed the rituals to become Jews. The New Testament attests to the zeal of the first century Pharisees in proselytizing Gentiles (Matt. 23:15). The success of the Jewish missionary efforts is indicated by synagogue and grave inscriptions referring to proselytes and by Roman and Jewish literary references. Tacitus (History V.5) complains, for example, that proselytes despised the gods, disdained their kindred, and abjured their fatherland.

Gentiles were impressed by three features of Judaism. First, the concept of one God who created, sustains, and rules all things was clearly superior to polytheistic views. Second, Judaism stressed a life-style of moral responsibility with its monotheism; and third, it was a religion of ancient and stable tradition in contrast to the faddish cults of the time.

Proselytes usually embraced Judaism gradually because much needed to be learned, such as the proper observance of the sabbath and the careful following of the dietary rules, before one could win acceptance into the Jewish community. Persons attracted to Judaism and keeping the sabbath and food laws were termed fearers or worshipers of God. These terms appear in the New Testament where Cornelius (Acts 10:1–2), and Lydia (Acts 16:14) are so described (see also John 12:20; Acts 17:4; 18:4).

Many God fearers went on to become proselytes or fully accepted and integrated members of the Jewish community. This involved fulfilling the Jewish demands of circumcision (males) which related one to the covenant (see Gal. 5:3), baptism (males and females) which made one ritually clean, and an offering (males and females) in the Jerusalem Temple which atoned for sin.

Harold S. Songer

PROSTITUTION The trading of sexual services for pay. It is the result of a double standard whereby men insist on the sexual purity of their wives and daughters, while desiring access to other women. This dynamic is seen clearly in Genesis 38. Judah, thinking that his daughter-in-law Tamar was a prostitute, had intercourse with her; but upon hearing that she was pregnant as the result of "playing the harlot," he demanded that she be burned. Hosea criticized the attitude which called for the punishment of prostitutes (and women committing adultery), while tolerating the men with whom these acts were committed (Hos 4:14). Because of this double standard, the prostitute or harlot, as she is also called, has had an ambiguous status in society. She was tolerated in ancient Israel—as long as she was not married—but her profession was not socially acceptable. The children of harlots suffered from social biases against them (Judg. 11:2).

Although the Old Testament records no laws prohibiting men from visiting prostitutes and making use of their services, there are strong counsels against such behavior (Prov. 23:27–28; 29:3). The apocryphal Book of Ecclesiasticus gives similar warnings (9:3–9; 19:2).

The Holiness Code prohibited Israelite fathers from turning their daughters into prostitutes (Lev. 19:29), which might have been a temptation during times when poverty was widespread. It may be that most prostitutes in Israel were foreign or Canaanite women. That would help explain why the Book of Proverbs speaks of the harlot literally as a "strange" and "foreign" woman (translated in the RSV as "loose woman," "evil woman") (Prov. 2:16; 5:3; 6:24).

Jesus told the religious leaders of His day that harlots would go into the kingdom before they would (Matt. 21:31), not because He condoned prostitution, but because harlots did not have the self-righteousness which kept the religious leaders from repentance. Paul reminded Corinthian Christians that their bodies were the temple of the Holy Spirit; therefore, they should refrain from immorality, including sexual relations with prostitutes (1 Cor. 6:15–20).

The term "cult prostitution" is frequently used to refer to certain practices in Canaanite fertility cults, including the cult of Baal. See *Fertility Cult.* This practice and the beliefs on which it was based were incompatible with monotheism and with the nature of Israel's God. The terms *kadash* (masc.) and *kedeshah* (fem.), from the word meaning "holy," are generally translated "cult prostitute" (or "sodomite"). The masculine term is probably also used in a generic sense to refer to both male and female cult prostitutes. Such prostitutes functioned in the Temple in Jerusalem at various times in Israel's history and were removed during periods of religious reform (1 Kings 14:24, 15:12, 22:46; 2 Kings 23:7). Cult prostitution is outlawed by the Deuteronomic law code (Deut. 23:17–18).

The presence of both "secular" and "cult prostitutes" provided the prophets with a powerful metaphor for the unfaithfulness of the people toward God. The covenant was imaged as a marriage between the Lord and the people; their continual interest in other gods, especially Baal, was seen as a form of harlotry. This idea is graphically presented in Ezekiel 16 (compare Ezek. 23). Because the Lord's bride has become a harlot, she will be punished as a harlot. Hosea also attacked the Israelite attraction to the fertility religion of Canaan as harlotry. He felt called of God to marry a harlot (Hos 1:2), a symbolic action (or object lesson) representing God's relationship with Israel. Hosea's love for his unfaithful and harlotrous wife was analogous to God's love for unfaithful Israel.

The Book of Revelation applies the image of harlot to Rome, which is likened to a woman in scarlet and jewels, to whom the kings of the earth go (Rev. 17:1–6).   *Wilda W. Morris*

PROVENDER (Prŏv ĕn dẽr) Grains and grasses used as animal feed (Isa. 30:24 KJV, RSV). Other translations use fodder or silage.

PROVERBS, BOOK OF The Book of Proverbs contains the essence of Israel's wisdom. It provides a godly worldview and offers insight for living. Proverbs 1:7 provides the perspective for understanding all the proverbs: "The fear of the Lord is the beginning of knowledge; fools despise wisdom and instruction." "Fear of the Lord" is biblical shorthand for an entire life in love, worship, and obedience to God.

Date and Composition Though the title of Proverbs (1:1) seems to ascribe the entire book to Solomon, closer inspection reveals that the book is composed of parts and that it was formed over a period of several hundred years. It is difficult to know precisely the role Solomon and his court may have had in starting the process which culminated in the Book of Proverbs. This process may be compared to the way psalms of Davidic authorship eventually led to the Book of Psalms. In Israel, wisdom was considered Solomonic almost by definition (see articles on *Song of Solomon,* and *Ecclesiastes,* as well as the apochryphal work, *Wisdom of Solomon*). Thus the titles in 1:1 and 10:1 are not strictly statements of authorship in the modern sense.

That Proverbs is a collection of collections which grew over time is best seen from its variety of content and from its titles. These titles introduce the book's major subcollections, and are found in 1:1; 10:1; 22:17 ("words of the wise"); 24:23; 25:1; 30:1; 31:1. For dating, 25:1 places the copying or editing of chapters 25—29 in the court of Hezekiah, thus about 700 B.C., some 250 years after Solomon. The process of compilation probably extended into the postexilic period.

Because wisdom writings have almost no historical references, they are very difficult to date. Most scholars place chapters 10—29 sometime in the period of kings. Chapters 1—9 are in a different genre (see below) from the Solomonic sayings of chapters 10:1—22:16, and their date is disputed. Some say it may be as early as Solomon. Others say it is postexilic, that chapters 1—9 were added to 10—29 to give later readers a context from which to understand the short sayings in the latter chapters. The date of chapters 30—31 is also uncertain. One scholar has argued there is a play on the Greek word for wisdom (*sophia*) in 31:27. This would date chapter 31 after the conquest of Palestine by Alexander the Great in 332 B.C.

Literary Character and Forms The Book of Proverbs uses a variety of wisdom forms or genres. The Hebrew word for proverb (*mashal*), found in the book's title, can refer to a variety of literary forms beside the proverb: prophetic "discourse" (Num. 23:7,18), "allegory" (Ezek. 17:2; 24:3), "taunt song" (Mic. 2:4). Different sections of the book specialize in characteristic forms. Long wisdom poems, which scholars call "Instructions" after their Egyptian counterpart, dominate 1:8—9:18. These usually begin with a direct address to "son/children" and contain imperatives or prohibitions, motive clauses (reasons for actions), and sometimes narrative development (7:6–23). The setting of these instructions may be a school for young aristocrats. This section also contains public speeches by personified Wisdom (1:20–33; 8:1–36; 9:1–6).

"Sayings" which express wise insights about reality are the primary forms in 10:1—22:16 and 25:1—29:27. Sayings are characterized by extreme brevity. In Hebrew they usually have two lines with only six to eight words, in contrast to their much longer English translations. These sayings may simply "tell it like it is," and let readers draw their own conclusions (11:24; 17:27–28; 18:16). They can also make clear value judgments (10:17; 14:31; 15:33; 19:17). Mostly "antithetical sayings" which contrast opposites appear in 10:1—15:33, but mixed in are a few "better—than" sayings ("Better is a dinner with herbs where love is than a fatted ox and hatred with it," 15:17; compare v. 16) which are also scattered in other sections (16:8,19; 17:1; 19:1; 21:9; 25:24; 27:5,10b; 28:6). The section 25:1—25:27 is especially rich in comparative proverbs which set two things beside one another for comparison: "Like cold water to a thirsty soul, so is good news from a far country" (25:25; compare

25:12,13,14,26,28; 26:1–3,6–11,14,20 among others). Such sayings also occur elsewhere, "Like a gold ring in a swine's snout is a beautiful woman without discretion" (11:22).

"Admonitions" characterize 22:17—24:22. Borrowing from Egyptian wisdom marks this section. These short wisdom forms contain imperatives or prohibitions, usually followed by a motive clause which gives a reason or two for doing that which is being urged: "Do not remove an ancient landmark or enter the fields of the fatherless; for their Redeemer is strong; he will plead their cause against you" (23:10–11). Admonitions are a shorter relative of the instruction.

The words of Agur (ch. 30) specializes in numerical sayings (30:15–31). The epilogue of the book (31:10–31) presents an alphabetic poem on wisdom embodied in the "valiant woman." This brief sketch of wisdom forms presents only the basic types. Even within the types here presented, a great deal of subtle variation occurs.

Themes and Worldview In spite of being a collection of collections, Proverbs displays a unified, richly complex worldview. Proverbs 1–9 introduces this worldview and lays out its main themes. The short sayings of Proverbs 10—31 are to be understood in light of the first nine chapters.

The beginning and end of wisdom is to fear God and avoid evil (1:7; 8:13; 9:10; 15:33). The world is a battleground between wisdom and folly, righteousness and wickedness, good and evil. This conflict is personified in Lady Wisdom (1:20–33; 4:5–9; 8; 9:1–6) and Harlot Folly (5:1–6; 6:24–35; 7; 9:13–18). Both "women" offer love and invite simple young men (like those in the royal school) to their homes to sample their wares. Wisdom's invitation is to life (8:34–36); the seduction of Folly leads to death (5:4–6; 7:22–27; 9:18).

Mysteriously, Lady Wisdom speaks in public places, offering wisdom to everyone who will listen (1:20–22; 8:1–5; 9:3). Wisdom does not hide, but stands there for all who seek her. Some scholars consider Wisdom to be an attribute of God, especially shown in creation (3:19–20; 8:22–31). More accurately stated, however, Wisdom is "the self-revelation of creation." That is, God has placed in creation a wise order which speaks to humankind of good and evil, urging humans toward good and away from evil. This is not just the "voice of experience," but God's general revelation which speaks to all people with authority. The world is not silent, but speaks of the Creator and His will (Pss. 19:1–2; 97:6; 145:10; 148; Job 12:7–9; Acts 14:15–17; Rom. 1:18–23; 2:14–15).

This perspective eliminates any split between faith and reason, between sacred and secular. The person who knows God also knows that every inch of life is created by God and belongs to Him. Experiences of God come only from experiences

in God's world. Experiences in the world point the person of faith to God.

Thus, the wise person "fears God" and also lives in harmony with God's order for creation. The sluggard must learn from the ant because the ant's work is in tune with the order of the seasons (Prov. 6:6–11; compare 10:5).

Thinking Proverbially The short proverbs in chapters 10—29 cover a wealth of topics from wives (11:22; 18:22; 25:24) to friends (14:20; 17:17–18; 18:17; 27:6), strong drink (23:29–35; 31:4–7), wealth and poverty, justice and injustice, table manners and social status (23:1–8; compare 25:6–7; Luke 14:7–11).

One cannot just use any proverb on any topic, for proverbs can be misused: "Like a lame man's legs, which hang useless, is a proverb in the mouth of fools" (Prov. 26:7; compare v. 9). Proverbs are designed to make one wise, but they require wisdom to be used correctly. Proverbs are true, but their truth is *realized* only when they are fitly applied in the right situation. Job's friends misapplied proverbs about the wicked to righteous Job. Many things have more than one side to them, and the wise person will know which is which. Wives can be a gift from the Lord (18:22), but sometimes singleness seems better (21:9,19). Silence can be a sign of wisdom (17:27) or a cover-up (17:28). A "friend" (Hebrew, *rea'*) can be trusted (17:17), but not always (17:18; "neighbor" = *rea'*)!

Wealth can be a sign of God's blessing (3:9–10), but some saints suffer (3:11–12). Wealth can result from wickedness (13:23; 17:23; 28:11; compare 26:12). It is better to be poor and godly: "Better is a little with righteousness than great revenues with injustice" (16:8; compare 15:16–17; 17:1; 19:1; 28:6). In the end God will judge: "He who closes his ear to the cry of the poor will himself cry out and not be heard" (21:13; compare 3:27–28; 22:16; 24:11–12; 10:2; 11:4).

The problem of fittingness is most sharply put in 26:4–5:

Answer not a fool according to his folly, lest you be like him yourself.

Answer a fool according to his folly, lest he be wise in his own eyes.

Such dilemmas force us to confront the limits of our wisdom (26:12) and to rely upon God (3:5–8).

Proverbs *generally* operate on the principle that consequences follow acts: you reap what you sow. In a fallen world, however, God's justice is sometimes delayed. The "better—than" proverbs in particular show the disorder of the present world, the "exceptions to the rule." The righteous thus works and prays, like the psalmist, for the day when God will make all things right.

Outline

   I. Proverbs Is Designed to Impart Divine Wisdom Concerning Life (1:1–6).

  II. Wisdom's Contribution to Life Is to Be

Praised (1:7—9:18).

A. The goal of all wisdom is that people "fear . . . the Lord" (1:7).

B. Wisdom identifies sin and calls sinners to repentance (1:8–33).

C. Wisdom enables the sinner to be set free and experience meaningful life (2:1–22).

D. Wisdom produces a sense of divine presence, joy, and peace in the believer (3:1–26).

E. Wisdom admonishes believers to share God's love with others (3:27–35).

F. Wisdom helps a father instruct his son how to obtain a meaningful life (4:1–27).

G. Wisdom calls for purity and honesty in all marriage relationships (5:1–23).

H. Wisdom admonishes the believer to work hard and spend wisely (6:1–19).

I. Wisdom warns against the peril of adultery (6:20—7:27).

J. Through divine wisdom, God offers Himself to humankind (8:1–36).

K. Wisdom presents us with two choices, life or death (9:1–18).

III. One's Response to Wisdom Brings About Earthly Consequences (10:1—22:16).

A. The righteous find blessings, but the wicked suffer greatly (10:1–32).

B. The deceitful pay a terrible price, but the honest find God's favor (11:1–31).

C. The righteous are open to instruction, but the wicked are not (12:1–28).

D. The righteous are obedient to God's will; however, the wicked rebel (13:1–25).

E. The foolish will be judged, but the righteous will be accepted by God (14:1–35).

F. The Lord watches over all humankind and judges each accordingly (15:1–33).

G. The Lord is the fountain of life for the faithful (16:1–33).

H. The foolish thrive on bribery, but the wise are honest yet merciful (17:1–28).

I. The foolish are haughty, but the righteous are humble (18:1–24).

J. The poor are to be pitied, but the wealthy are honored by God (19:1–29).

K. The wise work hard and treat both friend and foe with love (20:1–30).

L. God requires holy lives and not just holy rituals (21:1–31).

M. The wise discipline themselves to follow God in everything (22:1–16).

IV. Wisdom Provides Prudent Counsel for Both the Present and the Future (22:17—24).

A. Wisdom tells one when to speak and when to be silent (22:17–21).

B. The wise ones care for and protect the poor (22:22–29).

C. Wisdom warns one not to fall into the trap of another's craftiness (23:1–11).

D. Youth need instruction and correction to become what they should be (23:12–28).

E. The drunkard destroys his life and that of others (23:29–35).

F. Wisdom leads to a meaningful life, but wickedness leads to destruction (24:1–9).

G. The wise ones steadfastly trust God in both the good and bad times (24:10–22).

H. Wisdom promotes true justice (24:23–34).

V. Wisdom Constantly Reminds People of Their Past Heritage (25:1—29:27).

A. The king shares in the responsibility for promoting wisdom (25:1–14).

B. The righteous exercise self-discipline and love in all of life (25:15–28).

C. The foolish fail the test of life and face God's judgment (26:1–28).

D. Life's quest for meaning is brief and frustrating at times (27:1–22).

E. People should learn to live as responsible stewards (27:23–27).

F. God expects justice from His followers (28:1–28).

G. Discipline is an essential part of life (29:1–27).

VI. The True Source of Meaningful Existence Can Be Found Only in God (30:1—31:31).

A. Human beings cannot fully discover or understand God's wisdom (30:1–33).

B. Humans can practice righteousness and show loving-kindness (31:1–9).

C. The key to meaningful existence is found in one's faith relationship to God (31:10–31). *Raymond C. Van Leeuwen*

PROVIDENCE God's faithful and effective care and guidance of everything which He has made toward the end which He has chosen.

The opening question of the Heidelberg Catechism (1563) asks: "What is your only comfort in life and death?" Answer: "That I, with body and soul, both in life and in death, am not my own, but belong to my faithful Savior Jesus Christ who . . . so preserves me that without the will of my Father in heaven not a hair can fall from my head; yea, that all things must work together for my salvation." This statement gets at the heart of the biblical doctrine of providence. We can distinguish this understanding of providence from several distortions which have been advanced throughout the history of the church:

• fatalism: the view that all events are determined by an inviolable law of cause and effect. This was a popular doctrine among the Stoics (as in Seneca's treatise, *De Providentia*) who believed that all history and human life was subject to Fate.

- **deism:** the idea that God created the world but then withdrew from its day-to-day governance, leaving it to run by itself as a machine. Deism safeguards the transcendence of God at the expense of His immanence.
- **pantheism:** this is the opposite error of deism, for it virtually identifies God with His creation. God is a kind of World Soul or impersonal force which permeates all the universe.
- **dualism:** the view that two opposing forces in the universe are locked in struggle with each other for its control. The ancient religions of Zoroaster and Mani posited two coeternal principles, darkness and light. A modern variant of this theory is set forth by process theology which holds that God is limited by the evolving universe, caught in a struggle with forces over against His control.

In the New Testament, the Greek word for providence (*pronoia*) occurs only once, and that with reference to human rather than divine foresight (Acts 24:2). The verbal form (*pronoeō*) meaning "to know in advance" is found twice in the New Testament and eleven times in the Greek Old Testament. Yet the theme of God's provident care for the created order is present in all levels of the biblical material. The Psalms are filled with allusions to God's direction and sustenance of the creation. The heavens declare the glory of God, and the firmament proclaims His handiwork (Ps. 19:1). God directs the seasons (Ps. 104:19); the clouds are His chariot, the winds His messenger (104:3); He stills the storms and girds the mountain ranges (107:29; 65:6); everything that hath breath is exhorted to praise the Lord "for his mighty acts" (150:2,6). The so-called nature Psalms are not dedicated to the glory of nature, but to the God who created and sustains it with His fatherly care.

Providence is related to creation on the one hand and to the history of salvation on the other. Theologians speak of this second aspect as "special" providence. In Nehemiah 9:6–38, God's general and special providence are brought together in the same passage. "Thou, even thou, art Lord alone; thou hast made heaven, . . . the earth, and all things that are therein, . . . and thou preservest them all; . . . Thou art the Lord the God, who didst choose Abram, . . . And madest known unto them thy . . . precepts, . . . by the hand of Moses . . . thou art a gracious and merciful God. . . . who keepest covenant." After the destruction of Jerusalem in 587 B.C. and during the long period of Exile, confidence in God's providence sustained the children of Israel through all of their doubts and disappointments (compare Isa. 40:21–31; 42:1–6).

Two classic passages in the New Testament direct Christians to focus on God's providential care as a remedy for overanxious concerns. In the Sermon on the Mount, Jesus commanded His hearers not to worry about tomorrow, since the Heavenly Father cares much more for them than the birds of the air or the lilies of the field (Matt. 6:25–34). The point is not that following Christ will exempt one from trouble or pain. What it does provide is the assurance of God's presence in the midst of the stormy tempests of life. Armed with this assurance we can face whatever may come in the knowledge that God will care for us, as He does daily for the birds and flowers. Romans 8:28 (NIV) says: "We know that in all things God works for the good of those who love him, who have been called according to his purpose." This does not mean that everything which happens to us is good, nor necessarily the result of a "snap decision" by God. It does mean that nothing can ever happen to us apart from the knowledge, presence, and love of God, and that in the most desperate of circumstances God is always at work towards the good. We are not given to understand how this is so. We are only told that the sufferings of the present time are not worth comparing with the glory that is to be revealed to us (Rom. 8:18–25).

The doctrine of providence encompasses many other themes in the Bible as well. Scripture presents God working in various ways to accomplish His purpose. Often God works through secondary causes such as natural law or special messengers, such as the angels. Sometimes God effects His will directly through miracles or other supernatural happenings. Frequently enough, as William Cowper put it, "God moves in a mysterious way His wonders to perform." Because we are sure that God is for us, not against us, we can afford to live with this mystery which impugns neither God's sovereignty nor His goodness. In our own day, the doctrine of providence has been challenged by the enormity of evil in the world. Some theologians have attempted to devise a theodicy, a rational justification of God's providential rule, as a response to the problem of evil. Yet the Bible itself presents no systematic answer to this dilemma. It affirms only the reality of evil, its vicious, demonic power in the present age, and the certainty of Christ's ultimate victory over its every manifestation (1 Cor. 15:24–28). In the meanwhile, Christians can face the future in the confidence that nothing "in all creation, will be able to separate us from the love of God in Christ Jesus our Lord" (Rom. 8:39 NRSV). See *Election; God; Predestination.* *Timothy George*

PROVINCE A Roman political region. During New Testament times there were three types of provinces. Imperial districts were governed directly by the emperor. Senatorial provinces answered to the senate. A special type province were those composed of rugged terrain or newly conquered people. These demanded more strict control and were under the control of an imperial procurator. Judea was a special province because the Jews so fiercely hated the Roman domination.

Israel practiced a type of provincial system during Ahab's reign (1 Kings 20:14–15). Later, the Babylonians and Persians used such districts in Palestine (Esth. 4:11). The Romans refined the system dramatically and used it to maintain control over their vast empire. See *Government; Rome.*

PROVOCATION In Hebrews 3:8,15 that which aroused God's anger. Provocation corresponds to the place name Meribah meaning, "contention" (Ex. 17:1–7; Num. 20:1–13; Ps. 95:7–11 which Heb. 3:7–11 cites). See *Massah.*

PRUDENCE See *Wisdom and Wise Men.*

PRUNING HOOK See *Tools.*

PSALMIST A writer of psalms or hyms. Second Samuel 23:1 calls David the "sweet psalmist of Israel." Superscriptions ascribe about one half of the psalms to David. See *David; Psalms.*

PSALMS OF SOLOMON See *Pseudepigrapha.*

PSALMS, BOOK OF A collection of songs of praise that are theological statements and poetically represent human dialogue with God. The Psalms is the most complete collection of Hebrew poetry and worship material in the Hebrew Bible. The Psalms give clues for understanding Israelite worship on both a corporate and individual level. The psalms typify different responses to God's actions and word.

The Psalms as a collection is found in the third division of the Hebrew canon known as the Writings (Hebrew, *ketubim*). In its present canonical form, the Psalter has five divisions in the current Hebrew text. These divisions have been compared with the division of the Pentateuch into five books. Each book concludes with a doxology or closing formula. The books follow this division: (1) Psalms 1—41; (2) 42—71; (3) 73—89; (4) 90—106; and (5) 107—150. Psalm 150 closes off both book five and concludes the collection of psalms; just as Psalm 1 serves as an introduction to the psalter. Other divisions or collections appear in the Psalms. The Elohistic Psalter (Pss. 42—83) regularly uses the Hebrew *'elohim* for the divine name (compare Pss. 14; 53). The Songs of Ascent or pilgrimage psalms (Pss. 120—134) make a collection. Two different guild collections are included in the Psalms of the sons of Korah (Pss. 42—49) and the Psalms of Asaph (Pss. 73—83). Psalms has been understood as both the "hymnal" and prayerbook of the postexilic congregation of Israel with its final compilation and its inclusion within the canon.

An important key for reading and interpreting different psalms is to understand the nature of Hebrew poetry. Psalms are poetic in contrast to being narrative. See *Poetry.*

As the twentieth century began, Hermann Gunkel brought a new approach to the Psalms, seeking to discover the type or form of literary material in each Psalm and the worship situation behind each. Gunkel categorized several main types of psalms and understood that not all psalms fit neatly into one category. They might be a combination of types and thus belong to a category of mixed psalms. Following Gunkel, scholars have proposed several systems to categorize the Psalms. Most include the different types: (1) the hymn; (2) songs of thanksgiving; (3) the community laments; (4) the individual laments; (5) the individual songs of thanksgiving; (6) the royal psalms; and (7) wisdom psalms.

Clear-cut categorization is not possible for every psalm, nor does every psalm fit a particular category. Also, every cultic or original life situation is not discernible. The issue for the reader and interpreter of the psalms is to appreciate the artistry of a poet which created and crafted timeless poetic expressions which fit into many contexts of worship or an individual's life situation in different cultures and traditions.

A reader of the Psalms will find that different psalms can be grouped by similarities of form, content, and pattern. Yet, variations do occur, and each psalm is unique in both message and content. The following is descriptive of the various psalm types.

A *lament* is expressed both by the community (for example, 44; 74; 79) and by the individual (22; 38; 39; 41; 54). Both types of laments are prayers or cries to God on the occasion of distressful situations. Of the two forms, differences are related to the types of trouble and the experiences of salvation. For the community the trouble may be an enemy; with an individual it may be an illness. The basic pattern includes an invocation of God, a description of the petitioner's complaint(s), a recalling of past salvation experiences (usually community laments), petitions, a divine response (or oracle), and a concluding vow of praise.

The *thanksgiving* or psalms of narrative praise are also spoken by the community (see 106; 124; 129) and the individual (see 9; 18; 30). These psalms are related to the laments as they are responses to liberation occurring after distress. They are expressions of joy and are fuller forms of the lament's vow of praise.

The *hymn* (see 8; 19; 29) is closest in form to a song of praise as sung in modern forms of worship. These psalms are uniquely liturgical and could be sung antiphonally, some have repeating refrains (see Ps. 8). The hymn normally includes a call to praise. Then the psalm describes the reasons for praising God. The structure is not as clear-cut as other types of psalms. Creation psalms (usually reflecting a mixed form) include Psalms 8; 19; 104; and 139. These psalms are concerned with praising God and describe Him as Creator. Emphasis may be placed on God as Creator of heaven and earth, as Creator of humanity, or as the Creator of different elements of creation. The psalms affirm God who is Creator as the Lord of history.

Some psalms reflect more specific liturgical events. The *liturgical psalms* may include antiphonal responses or dialogue. There may be exhortations to listeners to prostrate themselves or to walk in a procession. These psalms include instructions for sacrifice, worship, processionals, or may invoke blessings on the worshipers. These are usually regarded as psalms of mixed type as they share similarities with the hymns. This designation includes those psalms which may have been sung by pilgrims on their way to the sanctuary (see the songs of ascents, 120—134). *Songs of Zion* (such as 46) call for God's protection of the city of God. Some psalms are considered *royal psalms* (see 2; 18; 20). These psalms are concerned with the earthly king of Israel. Again, these are usually understood as mixed psalms. They were used to celebrate the king's enthronement. They may have included an oracle for the king. In some cases (such as Ps. 72), prayers were made to intercede on behalf of the king. Another mixed type are the *enthronement psalms* which celebrate Yahweh's kingship (see Pss. 96—99). They are closely related to the hymns and to the creation psalms. However, the main difference is a celebration of Yahweh as king over all creation.

A final type of psalm (see Ps. 1) is the *wisdom psalm*. They have poetic form and style but are distinguished because of content and a tendency toward the proverbial. These psalms contemplate questions of theodicy (73), or celebrate God's Word (the Torah, Ps. 119), or deal with two different ways of living—that of the godly person or the evil person (Ps. 1). The psalms are not neatly or easily categorized, as the mixed psalms indicate. However, such identification helps the reader to know that type of psalm is being read, with a possible original context or a fitting present context in worship.

Outline The Book of Psalms is divided into five sections just as the Pentateuch has five books. Each section of the Book of Psalms concludes with a doxology. See 41:13; 72:18–19; 89:52; 106:48; 150. Psalm 1 introduces the book by dividing people into two categories and describing the fate of each. Psalm 150 closes Psalms with a symphony of praise. Otherwise, a way to describe a theological structure for the book as a whole has not been found. What devoted students of God's Word have discovered is the limited number of types of prayer represented in the Psalms. A look at the major types helps us understand how many

different functions prayer and praise can serve as we communicate with and worship God.

1. Psalms of lamentation or complaint cry out for help in a situation of distress or frustration. Psalmists protest their innocence or confess their sins. They vow to praise God and give thanks for deliverance. Such psalms show prayer as an honest communication with God in life's worst situations. The following psalms are laments: 3, 4, 6, 7, 12, 13, 17, 22, 25, 26, 28, 35, 38, 39, 40, 41, 42—43, 44, 51, 54, 55, 56, 57, 59,60, 61, 63, 64, 69, 70, 71, 74, 77, 79, 80, 83, 85, 86, 88, 90, 94, 102, 109, 123, 126, 130, 134, 137, 140, 141, 142, 143, 144.

2. Psalms of thanksgiving describe a situation of distress and how God delivered the psalmist. The psalmist promises to fulfill vows made to God during the distress and invites the congregation to join in thanksgiving and praise to God. These psalms show us our need to acknowledge God's work in our times of trouble and to witness to others of what God has done for us. Thanksgiving psalms are 9—10, 18, 30, 31, 32, 34, 66, 92, 107, 116, 118, 120, 124, 129, 138, 139.

3. Hymns lift the congregation's praise to God, describing God's greatness and majesty. In the hymn, worshipers invite one another to praise God and to provide reasons for such praise. These psalms are hymns: 8, 19, 29, 33, 65, 100, 103, 104, 105, 111; 113, 114, 117, 135, 136, 145, 146, 147, 148, 149, 150.

4. Wisdom psalms probe life's mysteries to teach the congregation about itself and God. These include psalms 1, 14, 36, 37, 49, 53, 73, 78, 112, 119, 127, 128, 133.

5. Kingship psalms detail the role of the human king in God's rule over His people. They also point ahead to the Messiah, who would inaugurate God's kingdom. From them we learn to pray for and respect the role of government officials as well as praise God's Messiah. These include psalms 2, 18, 20, 21, 28, 45, 61, 63, 72, 89, 101, 110, 132.

6. Entrance ceremonies provide questions and answers to teach the expectations God has of His worshipers. Psalms 15 and 24 are entrance ceremonies.

7. Enthronement psalms praise Yahweh as the King enthroned over His universe. They include psalms 47, 93, 96, 97, 98, 99.

8. Songs of Zion praise God indirectly by describing the Holy City where He has chosen to live among His people and be worshiped. They show God lives among His people to protect and direct their lives. These are psalms 46, 48, 76, 84, 87, 122, 132.

9. Psalms of confidence express trust in God's care for and leadership of His people. These appear in psalms 4, 11, 16, 23, 27, 62, 125, 131.

10. Prophetic psalms announce God's will to

His worshiping people. These are 50, 52, 58, 81, 82, 91, 95.

11. Liturgical psalms describe activities and responses of God's worshiping congregation. These appear in psalms 67, 68, 75, 106, 108, 115, 121.

David M. Fleming

PSALTER *1.* Alternate name for the Book of Psalms. *2.* Any collection of Psalms used in worship.

PSEUDEPIGRAPHA (Pseūd ĕ pī′ grǎ phà) Intertestamental literature not accepted into the Christian or Jewish canon of Scripture and often attributed to an ancient hero of faith. Ongoing discovery and research provide differing lists of contents. A recent publication listed 52 writings. They give much information about the development of Jewish religion and culture. *Pseudepigraphal Books*—Pseudepigrapha means, "writings falsely attributed." This is based on those books claiming to be written by Adam, Enoch, Moses, and other famous Old Testament people. Some of the writings are anonymous; thus some scholars prefer the name "outside books" for all of these writings, emphasizing that they did not become part of canon. Some ancient Christians and the Roman church have used the term "Apocrypha," since for them what Protestants call Apocrypha is part of their canon. See *Apocrypha*.

Both Palestinian and Hellenistic Jews authored books in the Pseudepigrapha. They used a variety of styles and literary types—legend, poetry, history, philosophy—but apocalypse was the dominant literary type. See *Apocalyptic*. A review of the most important and representative books will show the significance of the Pseudepigrapha in understanding the background of the New Testament.

First Enoch has been preserved in the Ethiopic language. It is a composite work of five sections, written at different times. The first section (chs. 1—36) tells how Enoch was taken up into heaven and shown its secrets. The sons of God of Genesis 6 were seen as angels. They committed sin, and the children born to them were evil giants. Emphasis is placed upon judgment and punishment. Even the realm of the dead is divided into separate places for the righteous and the wicked. The second section (chs. 37—71) is the most important for its relation to the Bible. It is the Parables or Similitudes. These chapters refer to the son of man. Opinions differ as to how such references form part of the background to the New Testament teachings about Jesus as the Son of man. There is uncertainty about the date of this section, of chapters. The rest of the book comes from between 200 and 1 B.C., but the Similitudes may have been written later, shortly before A.D. 100. Fragments of all the other sections have been found in the caves of Qumran, but no fragments of

this section have been discovered yet. The third section (chs. 78—82) deals with the heavenly bodies. The author argues for a calendar based on the movement of the sun in distinction to the standard Jewish lunar calendar. The fourth section (chs. 83–90) contains two dream visions dealing with the flood and the history of Israel from Adam to the Maccabean revolt. The final section (chs. 91—108) gives religious instruction concerning the end time. The entire book is apocalyptic.

Second Enoch is also an apocalypse preserved primarily in the Slavonic language. It was written between 100 B.C. and A.D. 100. In it Enoch was taken up into heaven and commanded to write 366 books. He was allowed to return to earth for thirty days to teach his sons, after which he returned to heaven. This writing describes the contents of the seven heavens and divides time into seven one-thousand year periods.

Second Baruch is apocalyptic and shows how some Jews responded to the destruction of Jerusalem by the Romans in A.D. 70. It was written shortly before 100 A.D. Three visions seek to console the people by showing that even though destruction has come, God has prepared something better for them. The writings teach that the Messiah will be revealed to bring in a time of great plenty. Emphasis is placed on obedience to the Law.

The *Sibylline Oracles* were very popular apocalyptic writings in the ancient world. The Jews took over the originally pagan writings and modified them by inserting ideas about monotheism, Mosaic requirements, and Jewish history. Three of the fifteen books in the collection are missing. Book 3, from between 200 and 100 B.C., is the most important and the most Jewish. It traces Jewish history from the time of Abraham to the building of the second Temple. It pronounces God's judgment upon pagan nations, but holds out hope that they may turn to God.

The *Testament of Moses* (sometimes called the *Assumption of Moses*) is also apocalyptic. The manuscripts are incomplete, and the missing portion may have contained an account of Moses' death and his being taken to heaven. Early Christian writers state that Jude 9 was to be found in the Assumption of Moses known to them. This book is a rewriting of Deuteronomy 31—34. Moses is the chosen mediator of God, prepared from the beginning of time. The book traces the history of the people from their beginning to the author's own time. Since chapters 6 and 7 seem to refer to Herod the Great, the book was probably written shortly after A.D. 1. It emphasized that God has planned all things and keeps them under His control.

The *Testaments of the Twelve Patriarchs* are patterned after Genesis 49, the closing instructions of Jacob to his sons. Each of the sons of Jacob addressed his descendants, giving a brief survey of his life, with special attention to some sin or failure. For example, Reuben stressed his adultery with Bilhah (Gen. 35:22), and Simeon told of his jealousy of Joseph. Joseph, however, emphasized the maintaining of his purity. Using the confessed sin as a background, patriarchs urged their children to live in an upright manner. Special emphasis is given to love for the neighbor and sexual purity. In most of the testaments, the children are told to give honor to Levi and Judah. The book refers to two messiahs: one from Levi, one from Judah. The earliest portions of the testaments come from after 200 B.C.

The *Book of Jubilees* is a rewriting of Genesis and the opening chapters of Exodus from after 200 B.C. It traces the history of Israel from creation to the time of Moses, dividing time into jubilee periods, forty-nine years each. The calendar is based on the sun, not the moon. The sabbath was kept by the angels in heaven who were circumcised. The writer strongly opposed the Gentile influences he found coming into Judaism urging Jews to keep separate from the Gentiles. In the Book of Jubilees, Abraham was the ideal righteous man. The book shows how a conservative, priestly Jew about 150 B.C. viewed the world.

The *Psalms of Solomon* are a collection of eighteen psalms written about 50 B.C. They reflect the situation of the people in Jerusalem following its capture by the Romans under Pompey in 63 B.C. Psalms of Solomon 17 and 18 are of special importance because of their references to the Messiah. According to these Psalms, the Messiah was to be a human figure, a descendant of David, wise and righteous, and without sin. The titles Son of David and Lord Messiah are used of Him.

Third Maccabees, written after 200 B.C., has nothing to do with the Maccabees. It tells about the attempt of Ptolemy IV to kill the Jews in Egypt. God foiled his efforts resulting in the advancement of the Jews. This book shows the vindication of the righteous.

Fourth Maccabees is based to some extent upon material found in 2 Maccabees 6—7. It is a philosophical writing, stressing that pious reason can be the master of the passions. Reason is derived from obedience to the law. In the account of the seven sons who are martyred, the author greatly expanded the account but left out all references to resurrection. The book comes from shortly after A.D. 1.

The *Life of Adam and Eve* has been preserved in both Latin and Greek. The two versions are different in length and content. Blame for the fall is placed upon Eve. Sin entered human experience through her. This writing refers to Satan being transformed into the brightness of angels (9:1; see 2 Cor. 11:14), and states that paradise is in the third heaven (compare 2 Cor. 12:2–3). The Life of Adam and Eve was written after 1 A.D.

The *Letter of Aristeas* was composed after 200

B.C., telling how the Old Testament law was translated into Greek. Actually, it is more concerned about the table conversation at banquets in Alexandria than it is about the translation of the Septuagint. It seeks to show that the Jewish law was in conformity with the highest ideals of Greek thought and life. It indicates that it is possible for Jew and Greek to live together in peace. So far as its account of the translation of the Law into Greek is concerned, its only historical validity is that it was at this time (during the reign of Ptolemy Philadelphus, 285–246 B.C.) that this translation was begun.

See *Apocalyptic; Apocrypha; Bible, Texts and Versions.*   *Clayton Harrop*

PTOLEMIES (Ptŏl' ĕ mīes) Dynastic powers which emerged in Egypt in the aftermath of the conquests of Alexander the Great.

Ptolemy I Soter (323–383 B.C.) established the dynasty which bears his name and moved the capitol of Egypt from Memphis to Alexandria, the city Alexander founded. He and his successors ruled an empire that included at times Cyrenaica, Palestine, Phoenicia, Cyprus and some parts of western Asia Minor and the Aegean. Ptolemaic policies brought great wealth to the state through taxation and trade. The Ptolemies did not force Hellenization upon native populations, but the obvious commercial, cultural, and social benefits of Ptolemaic policies led to greater acceptance of Hellenistic ideas and customs. Land was farmed

A wall relief showing Ptolemy I Soter (pictured twice) making offerings.

out under state control, and the reserves funneled to the central government. Payment of heavy yearly taxes, however, assured a measure of local autonomy. The Ptolemies introduced a ruler cult, but permitted native religions to continue unimpeded. In addition to Ptolemy I, the most energetic of these rulers were Ptolemy II Philadelphus (282–246 B.C.) and Ptolemy III Euergetes (246–221 B.C.).

The Ptolemies made Alexandria a center of learning and commerce. In particular the early Ptolemies supported a large group of scholars at the famous Museum and developed the nucleus of the great library. The Ptolemies founded or refurbished several cities in Palestine and Transjordan giving them Greek names and often endowing them with Greek features. Examples included Acco renamed Ptolemais, Bethshan now termed Scythopolis, and ancient Rabboth-Ammon refounded as Philadelphia.

Ptolemaic rule directly impacted Jews both inside and outside of Palestine. During the campaigns to secure Palestine for Egypt, Ptolemy I transported large numbers of Jews from Palestine to Alexandria for settlement. This was the beginning of a large and influential Jewish community which prospered by maintaining good relations with the Ptolemies, frequently serving as mercenaries and merchants. Soon Alexandria became a major center of world Jewry. The Alexandrian Jews imbibed Hellenism much more deeply than their counterparts in Judea as evidenced by the need to translate the Old Testament writings into Greek. This translation, known as the Septuagint, probably was begun in the reign of Ptolomy II, but was not completed until about 100 B.C.

The Ptolemies treated Judea as a Temple state given over by the king in trust to the high priest at Jerusalem. Authority in religious and most civil matters was granted the high priest in lieu of a yearly tax.

The forecourt of Ptolemy IX in the Temple of Horus, the Egyptian falcon-god, at Edfu in Upper Egypt.

During the reign of Ptolemy II, the first of five wars with the Seleucids over possession of Palestine broke out. Egypt successfully resisted the Seleucid challenge under the first three Ptolemaic rulers. However, Ptolemaic power began to wane under Ptolemy IV Philopator (221–204 B.C.), a notorious womanizer. In 200 B.C., Antiochus III defeated the Egyptian army at Banyas (later Caesarea Philippi) and seized control of Palestine. Subsequently, the Ptolemaic kingdom declined and increasingly came under the influence of Rome. Cleopatra VII was the last Ptolemaic ruler prior to

the annexation of Egypt to Rome in 30 B.C.

Tommy Brisco

PUA (Pū′ à) KJV and REB alternate form of Puvah (Num. 26:23).

PUAH (Pū′ ah) *1.* Personal name meaning, "girl." Hebrew midwife who disobeyed Pharoah's orders to kill male Hebrew infants (Ex. 1:15). *2.* Personal name meaning, "red dye." Father of the judge Tola (Judg. 10:1) and an alternate form of Puvah (1 Chron. 7:1).

PUBLICAN A political office created by the Romans to help collect taxes in the provinces. Actually, the title "tax collector" is more correct than the older term "publican" in referring to the lowest rank in the structure. Zacchaeus is called a "chief among the publicans" (Luke 19:2), probably indicating one who contracted with the government to collect taxes, and who in turn hired others to do the actual work. In New Testament times people bid for the job of chief tax collector and then exacted the tax plus a profit from the citizens. Most of the offices were filled by Romans, although some natives got the bids. Publicans were held in the lowest esteem because of their excessive profits, being placed in the same category as harlots (Matt 21:32). Jesus was accused of eating with and befriending them (Matt. 9:11).

PUBLIUS (Pŭb′ lĭ ŭs) Personal name meaning, "pertaining to the people." The highest official, either Roman or local, on Malta (Acts 28:7–8).

PUDENS (Pū′ dĕnṣ) Personal name meaning, "modest." Roman Christian who greeted Timothy (2 Tim. 4:21). This Pudens is sometimes identified with the friend of the Roman poet Martial.

PUHITES (Pū′ hītes) KJV form of Puthites.

PUITES (Pū′ ītes) NIV form of Punites.

PUL (Pŭl) *1.* Alternate name of the Assyrian king Tiglath-Pileser III (2 Kings 15:19; 1 Chron. 5:26). The name is perhaps a contraction of Pileser. See *Assyria.* *2.* The Hebrew *Pul* in Isaiah 66:19 is likely a textual corruption of Put.

PULPIT KJV, RSV term for a raised platform (NRSV, REB, NIV, TEV) on which a speaker stood (Neh. 8:4); not a lectern or high reading desk behind which a reader stands.

PULSE General term for peas, beans, and lentils (Dan. 1:12,16). Modern translations read vegetables. The Hebrew is literally "things which have been sown," a designation including grains in addition to vegetables.

PUNITES (Pū' nītes) Descendants of Puvah (Num. 26:23). Some manuscripts read Puvanites or Puvites.

PUNON (Pū' nŏn) Place name meaning, "ore pit." Edomite mining center located at the junction of the wadi el-Gheweil and wadi esh-Sheqer on the east side of the Arabah about twenty-five miles south of the Dead Sea. The site was first occupied about 2200 B.C. The second occupation began shortly before the Israelites encamped there about 1200 B.C. (Num. 33:42–43). The site was perhaps home to descendants of the clan chief Pinon (Gen. 36:41). The site is identified with modern Feinan. Two ancient smelting sites, khirbet en-Nahas and khirbet Nqeib Aseimer, lie to the north northeast.

PUR (Pŭr) See *Purim.*

PURAH (Pū' rah) Personal name meaning, "beauty" or nickname meaning, "metal container." Gideon's servant (Judg. 7:10–11). KJV used the form Phurah.

PURGE To cleanse from impurity, frequently in the figurative sense of cleansing from evil (Deut. 13:5), guilt (Deut. 19:13), idolatrous worship (2 Chron. 34:3), and sin (Ps. 51:7). See *Clean, Cleanness.*

PURIM (Pū' rĭm) See *Festivals.*

PURITY—PURIFICATION State of being or process of becoming free of inferior elements or ritual uncleanness. A basic goal of religion is to attain purity before the deity.
Old Testament Usage *1. Flawless* The primary Hebrew root word for *pure* (*thr*) often refers to pure or flawless gold (1 Kings 10:21; Job 28:19; Ps. 12:6). *Thr* and other Hebrew words for "pure" are used to describe other objects such as salt (Ex. 30:35), oil (Ex. 27:20), and incense (Ex. 37:29). Thus, a basic Old Testament meaning is that of "refined, purified, without flaw, perfect, clean." Note Lamentations 4:7.
2. Ritual Purity To be ritually pure means to be free of some flaw or uncleanness which would bar one from contact with holy objects or places, especially from contact with the holy presence of God in worship. God is the ideal of purity, and those who are to come in contact with God's presence are also to be pure. Habakkuk 1:13 indicates that God's eyes are too pure to look upon evil.
The altar for sacrifice was purified so that it would be prepared for worship (Lev. 8:15; Ezek. 43:26). The objects of gold used in the tabernacle and Temple were also pure in this sense; this

would be true of the incense in Exodus 37:29. The Levites were to purify themselves for service in the tabernacle (Num. 8:21). When that which was unclean or impure came into contact with that which was holy, danger resulted and could even lead to death. This is probably the background for the preparation made for the theophany, a manifestation of God's presence, in Exodus 19 and for the death of Uzzah when he was unprepared (not purified) to touch the ark of the covenant, a most holy object (2 Sam. 6:1–11). Malachi 1:11–12 contrasts the pure offerings of Gentiles with blemished offerings given by God's people; such a state necessitated purification (Mal. 3:3–4).
Purity qualified one to participate in worship, an activity central to the life of ancient Israel. Breaking that purity was a serious matter. Ritual impurity came as a result of bodily emissions (Lev. 15), by way of disease or menstrual flow, or discharge of semen. This chapter also shows that such impurity could be spread by contact, for anything coming into contact with the unclean person had to be purified. Leviticus 12 also discusses impurity associated with childbirth, probably because of the discharge of blood. Blood related to the mysterious power of life, and any loss of blood called for purification. Ritual impurity also came as a result of contact with a corpse since death was an enemy of God (Num. 19). Participation in war could thus cause impurity. Impurity, finally, was brought on by contact with foreign gods. This was probably the background of the need for purification when the people returned from Exile in Babylon. The priests and Levites purified themselves first and then the people and then the city gates and wall (Isa. 52:11; Ezra 6:20; Neh. 12:30). This also prepared them for worship.
3. Ethical Purity Thought and behavior befitting the people of God are pure (Pss. 24:4; 73:1; Pro. 15:26; 22:11; 30:12). Such purity of thought is to result in conduct which is appropriate for people (Ps. 119:9; Prov. 16:2; 20:9,11; 21:8). Notice also the pure prayer of Job 16:17.
Since Psalms 15 and 24 speak of qualifications for worship in terms of ethical purity, it is important not to distinguish sharply between ritual and ethical purity in the Old Testament. God expects ethical purity, and sin results in uncleanness. Thus sin and ritual uncleanness stand together in the Old Testament as unacceptable to the Lord. Their counterparts—ethical and ritual purity— also stand together.
Purification Rituals Since the Old Testament assumes that the people would encounter sin and uncleanness, it provides a way to return to cleanness.
The purification ritual usually started with a waiting period beginning when the cause of the impurity stopped. Less serious causes brought a waiting period of one day. Contact with a corpse

(Num. 19:11,14), birth of a male child (Lev. 12:2), the cure of leprosy (Lev. 14:8–9), and other discharges (Lev. 15:13,19,28), brought about a waiting period of seven days. The waiting period after the birth of a girl was fourteen days (Lev. 12:5). The same period applied to the quarantine of a suspected leper (Lev. 13:4–6).

A cleansing agent was required: water, blood, or fire (Num. 31:23). Water, the most common purifying agent, symbolized cleansing and was used in the rituals related to a waiting period. The person was to wash the clothes and bathe the body (Lev. 15:7). Blood was used to cleanse the altar and the holy place (Lev. 16:14–19). It was mixed with other ingredients for cleansing from leprosy (Lev. 14) and contact with the dead (Num. 19).

The final element of the ritual of purification is sacrifice. Purification from discharges required two pigeons or turtledoves, one for a sin offering and one for a burnt offering (Lev. 15:14–15,29–30). A lamb and pigeon or turtledove were offered after childbirth (Lev. 12:6). Sacrifice in the purification ritual for lepers was quite complicated, indicating the seriousness of leprosy as a cause of impurity (Lev. 14). The priest also touched the person's extremities with blood from the offering and with oil, cleansing and life-renewing agents. The poor were allowed to substitute less valuable animals for use in their sacrifices.

New Testament Usage Most New Testament uses of words for purity relate to cleanness of some type. Old Testament meanings are often reflected. Perfection is the meaning in Mark 14:3; this is mixed with religious purity in Hebrews 10:22; 1 John 3:3.

Ethical purity dominates in the New Testament. The person who is in right relationship with God is to live a life of purity (2 Tim. 2:21–22; Titus 1:15 and references to a pure heart—Matt. 5:8; 1 Tim. 1:5; Heb. 9:14; Jas. 4:8; 1 Peter 1:22). Purity is also listed among virtues (2 Cor. 6:6; Phil. 4:8; 1 Tim. 4:12; compare Mark 7:15).

Purification through sacrifice is also mentioned in the New Testament and applied to the death of Christ, a purification which does not need repeating and thus is on a higher level than Old Testament sacrifices (Heb. 9:13–14). The sacrifice of Christ brings purification; Christ cleansed as a part of the work of the high priest and His blood cleanses from sin (1 John 1:7).

See *Holiness; Levite; Priest; Sacrifice; Atonement; Ethics; Clean, Cleanness. W. H. Bellinger Jr.*

PURLOIN KJV term meaning, "to misappropriate" (Titus 2:10). Modern translations use pilfer or steal. See *Pilfer.*

PURPLE See *Colors.*

PURPLE GARNET REB designation of a precious stone (Ex. 28:18; 39:11) which other translations identify as an emerald or turquoise. See *Jewels.*

PURSE KJV translation of a Greek term for a belt, girdle, or waistband (Matt. 10:9; Mark 6:8). Travelers could tuck the loose ends of their garments into such a belt to allow freer movement. The folds of such waistbands were frequently used for storing money. Jesus encouraged His disciples to trust God and depend on the generosity of others as they shared the gospel. See *Girdle.*

PURSLANE (Pûrs' lāne) Fleshy-leaved, trailing plant used as a pot herb or in salads, which the RSV of Job 6:6 used as an illustration of tasteless food. Other translations follow the Targum in reading "white of an egg" (KJV, NAS, NIV) or find reference to another plant, the mallow (NRSV, REB).

PUT (Pŭt) Personal name and a geographic designation, perhaps derived from the Egyptian *pdty* meaning, "foreign bowman." *1.* Son of Ham (Gen. 10:6; 1 Chron. 1:8) in "Table of Nations" and thus ancestor of inhabitants of Put. *2.* Designation for a region of Africa bordering Egypt (Jer. 46:9; Ezek. 27:10; 30:5; 38:5; Nah. 3:9; and, by emendation, Isa. 66:19). Put is generally identified with Libya, perhaps with the city of Cyrene. All references to the men of Put involve mercenaries, that is, soldiers for hire.

PUTHITES (Pŭ' thītes) A family of Judahites (1 Chron. 2:53; KJV, Puhites).

PUTIEL (Pŭ' tĭ ĕl) Personal name meaning, "he whom God gives" or "afflicted by God." Father-in-law of the priest Eliezar (Ex. 6:25).

PUVAH (Pŭ' vah) Personal name spelled differently in Hebrew text and in various manuscripts and versions; thus rendered differently by translators. NAS (Num. 26:23) and NRSV (Gen. 46:13; Num. 26:23) form of the name of a son of Issachar. Other renderings include: Pua (KJV, REB); Puah (NIV, TEV); and Phuvah (KJV).

PUVVAH (Pŭv vah) NAS alternate form of Puvah (Gen. 46:13).

PYGARG KJV term for a white-rumped antelope (Deut. 14:5). Most modern translations identify the underlying Hebrew term with the ibex. The REB has "white-rumped deer."

PYRAMIDS (Pўr' -ĕ-mĭd) Four-sided structures have captivated visitors to Egypt for centuries. The present name apparently originated with some ancient Greek tourists who jokingly called the monuments "wheatcakes." This may describe the first "step pyramid," built by Djoser (Zoser) at Saqqara,

The step-pyramid of King Djoser (Zoser) of the Third Dynasty located at Saqqara.

but it was an injustice to those erected at Giza which represent one of the seven wonders of the world. The fourth dynasty (about 2520–2480 B.C.) reflected the zenith of pyramid construction.

The most well known of these artificial mountains rises majestically on the edge of the Nile near Cairo (at Giza). The "Great Pyramid" stands 481 feet high with a base of 755 feet. This was constructed by Cheops (Khufu) c. 2580 B.C. His son, Chephren (Khafre), and grandson, Mycerinus (Menkaure), followed in their father's footsteps literally building in his shadow. Although not as

The smallest of the three pyramids at Giza, built by Mycerinus (Menkaure).

grand, pyramids were constructed at various other places along the Nile including the distinctive "Bent Pyramid" at Dashur.

The purpose of these edifices was to intomb and immortalize the rulers. They actually act as focal points for a whole complex of buildings including a funerary temple, a causeway to a valley building near the Nile, and buried barges to carry the deceased to his eternal abode. They were not meant to be, however, astro-observatories or generators of mystical power.

See *Archaeology; Egypt.*   *Gary C. Huckabay*

The famous sphinx of Giza, built by Chephren (Khafre), measures 240 feet from front to back.

A large stone quarry in the area of Baalbek (in modern Lebanon) on the Orontes River.

PYRE Pile of material to be burned, especially that used in burning a body as part of funeral rites (Isa. 30:33 NAS, NRSV; pile, KJV; firepit, NIV, REB). God's preparation of a funeral pyre for the Assyrian king highlights the certainty of God's judgment.

PYRRHUS (Pўr rhus) Personal name meaning, "fiery red." Father of Paul's companion Sopater (Acts 20:4).

Q Abbreviation of the German *Quelle,* meaning "source," used to designate the hypothetical common source of over 200 verses found in Matthew and Luke but not in Mark. According to the two-document hypothesis, Matthew and Luke inserted sayings material stemming from Q into Mark's narrative framework of the Jesus story (compare Luke 1:1 for evidence of previous sources). Verbatim agreements in the double tradition (material shared by Matthew and Luke but not Mark), common sequence of sayings within blocks of materials, and doublets (repetition) of sayings found but once in Mark point to the common source. A common version of the Q hypothesis regards Q as written in Greek in Palestine, perhaps Caesarea, between A.D. 50–60. Luke is held to have preserved the overall order of the Q sayings better, while Matthew felt free to rearrange much of the shared material to form his five major discourses. Some scholars are so confident in their ability to decipher Q that they have written commentaries and theologies of the alleged source. Others prefer to think of Q as an "oral" source. Still others remove any need for a common source for the double tradition by arguing for the priority of Matthew. See *Harmony of the Gospels.*

QOHELETH (Qō hĕl′ ĕth) Alternate spelling of Koheleth. See *Koheleth.*

QUAIL See *Birds.*

QUARRY An area of land where stones were extracted for building various objects and buildings. Good stone lay close to the surface. In most places it was broken out of its bed by cracking the stones along lines of cleavage. Cutting these stones was obviously a dangerous business (Eccl. 10:9). KJV refers to quarries in Judges 3:19–26. The Hebrew term *pesalim* usually refers to images of gods. Thus most modern translations read: "idols" or "sculpted stones," the latter possibly referring to Joshua's stones of commemoration (Josh. 4).

Modern translations use "quarry" in 1 Kings 6:7 to make explicit the intention of the more literal KJV reading. See *Masons.*

QUARTERMASTER Officer charged with receipt and distribution of rations and supplies (Jer. 51:59 NAS, NRSV, REB). Quartermaster reflects the Hebrew "tribute-prince." The KJV reading "quiet prince" reflects a different vocalization of the Masoretic text. The NIV reading "staff-officer" likely reflects a slight change in the consonantal text to read "prince of the camp." See *Prince.*

QUARTUS (Quar'tŭs) Latin personal name meaning, "fourth." Christian, most likely from Corinth, who sent greetings to the Roman church through Paul (Rom. 16:23). Quartus and Tertius,

Famous bust of Queen Nefertiti (from about 1356 B.C.), wife of Pharaoh Akhenaton of Egypt.

whose name means "third" (Rom. 16:22), were possibly the third and fourth sons of the same family.

QUATERNION (Qua tēr' nĭ ŏn) KJV term for a squad composed of four soldiers (Acts 12:4; compare John 19:23). By translating the underlying Greek as simply squad, NAS and RSV failed to convey the size of the guard.

QUEEN The wife or widow of a monarch and the female monarch reigning in her own right. Queen mother refers to the mother of a reigning monarch. Female regents were known in the Ancient Near East (1 Kings 10:1–13, the queen of Sheba; Acts 8:27, the Ethiopian Candace). No queen ruled Israel or Judah in her own right, though Athaliah usurped power (2 Kings 11:1–3). The wives of monarchs varied in their influence. Since marriages often sealed political alliances (2 Sam. 3:3; 1 Kings 3:1; 16:31; 2 Kings 8:25–27), daughters of more powerful allies such as the Egyptian pharaoh or king of Tyre enjoyed special privileges (1 Kings 7:8) and influence (1 Kings 16:32–33; 18:19; 21:7–14). The mother of the designated heir also enjoyed special status. Nathan enlisted Bathsheba rather than Solomon in his plan to have Solomon confirmed as king (1 Kings 1:11–40). Queen mother was an official position in Israel and Judah. Great care was taken in preserving the names of the queen mothers (1 Kings 14:21; 15:2,13; 22:42; 2 Kings 8:26). Asa's removal of his mother from the office for idolatry (1 Kings 15:13) points to its official character. On her son's death, Athaliah murdered her own grandsons, the legitimate heirs, in order to retain the power she had enjoyed as queen mother (2 Kings 11:1–2). The queen mother likely served as a trusted counsel for her son (Prov. 31:1). As queen mother, Jezebel continued as a negative force after the death of Ahab (1 Kings 22:52; 2 Kings 3:2,13; 9:22).

QUEEN OF HEAVEN A goddess women in Judah worshiped to ensure fertility and material stability (Jer. 7:18; 44:17). Forms of worship included making cakes (possibly in her image as in molds found at Mari), offering drink offerings, and burning incense (Jer. 44:25). Exactly which goddess was worshiped is not certain. The words could be translated "stars of heaven" or "heavenly host." However, "queen of heaven" appears to be the best rendering. The major influence could have been Ishtar, the Mesopotamian goddess called there the queen of heaven (imported to Israel by Manassseh), or the Canaanite Ashtarte. Archaeologists have uncovered many images of nude goddesses from Israelite sites, showing why Jeremiah protested against such worship.

QUEEN OF SHEBA see *Sheba.*

QUICK, QUICKEN KJV terms meaning, "living, alive" and "make alive, revive, refresh" (Pss. 55:15; 119:25; John 5:21; Acts 10:42).

QUICKSANDS KJV translation of the Greek *syrtis* meaning, "sandbar" (Acts 27:17). Modern translations take *syrtis* as a proper name for the great sandbars off the west coast of Cyrene (modern Libya). NIV and REB paraphrase "sandbars of Syrtis" well conveys the sense.

QUILT NAS translation of a Hebrew term in 1 Samuel 19:13,16. Other possible translations include net (NRSV), pillow (KJV, RSV), and rug (REB).

QUIRINIUS Latin proper name which the KJV transliterated as Cyrenius. Modern versions prefer the Latin spelling. See *Cyrenius.*

QUIVER See *Arms and Armor.*

QUMRAN (Qŭm' răn) Archaeological site near the caves where Dead Sea Scrolls were discovered and center of Jewish Essene community.
The Location. The ruins called khirbet Qumran are located eight miles south of Jericho and three-fourths miles west of the northwestern edge of the Dead Sea. After the first discovery of the Dead Sea Scrolls in 1947, Qumran became the focus of archaeological investigation and was thoroughly excavated between 1953 and 1956. Among the areas excavated (a cemetery, extensive water system, refectory, kitchen, and prayer and study rooms), a room was discovered complete with the ruins of plaster benches and inkwells from the Roman period demonstrating that this was probably the "scriptorium" where the scrolls were copied.
The Qumran Community. The Qumran site was inhabited from about 130 B.C. to A.D. 70 by a sect so similar in nature, theology, and practice to a Jewish sect known as Essenes, that most scholars believe it was one variety of this sect. Ritual baptism, monastic life, and manual labor characterized the life of the Qumran Essenes. Although they allowed marriage, they shunned any contact with the outside world. Their main concern in life was complete and strict devotion to God. They expressed this through their scribal activity, the copying and studying of Scripture. In A.D. 70, with the Roman army posing a major threat to their existence, the Essenes of Qumran made a hasty exit, hiding their manuscripts in the surrounding caves as they left.
The Scrolls and Their Value In 1947, a young bedouin shepherd boy found an ancient scroll in a cave on the face of one of the sandstone cliffs in the Qumran area. In the following weeks and months a careful search of the area yielded 40,000 fragments of ancient manuscripts from eleven caves. Some 800 manuscripts are represented, of which 170 are fragments of Old Testament books (including manuscripts of each Old Testament book except Esther). The most impor-

The limestone cliffs of the Qumran area showing the caves in which the Dead Sea Scrolls were discovered.

A close-up view of one of the caves in which the Essenes hid their sacred scrolls from the Romans.

Ritual bath used for purification rites for the sect members at the site of the Qumran community.

tant may be a nearly complete text of Isaiah. The rest of the scrolls include commentaries on Habak-kuk and Micah, Jewish extrabiblical documents from the interbiblical and New Testament time periods, and extrabiblical writings specifically related to the community at Qumran such as the *Genesis Apocryphon, Temple Scroll,* and *Manual of Discipline.* Scrolls were found in Hebrew, Aramaic, and Greek, and the scroll material included both parchment and papyrus. (Two copper scrolls were also discovered.) While the content of many of the scrolls extends to a much earlier date, the scrolls themselves have been dated to about 200 B.C. to A.D. 70.

The value of the Dead Sea Scrolls to biblical studies is twofold. First, they provide Old Testament Hebrew manuscripts which are one thousand years older than any other extant Old Testament manuscripts. Before 1947, the earliest Hebrew Old Testament manuscripts known to exist dated to the late ninth century A.D. With the discovery of the Dead Sea Scrolls, biblical scholarship now has access to Old Testament manuscripts dating from about 200–100 B.C. The significance of this is heightened by the fact that these are copies, which presuppose originals, thus offering another verifica-

Excavations at the site of the Qumran community on the northwestern edge of the Dead Sea.

tion of an early date for the actual writing of the Old Testament. Second, the scrolls provide a glimpse into the Jewish theological and cultural milieu of the time of Christ and also provide examples of verbal expressions contemporary with the New Testament time period. See *Dead Sea Scrolls; Essenes.*   *Marsha A. Ellis Smith*

QUOTATIONS IN THE NEW TESTAMENT
See *Old Testament Quotations.*

Colossal statue of Ramses the Great at Karnak in Egypt.

R

RAAMA(H) (Rā´ à ṁa) Son of Cush (Gen. 10:7) and ancestor of Sheba and Dedan. Arab tribes occupying southwest and west-central Arabia (1 Chron. 1:9). Raamah and Sheba were trading partners of Tyre (Ezek. 27:22). Raama is likely modern Negram in Yemen, though the earliest Greek translation identified Raamah with Regmah on the Persian Gulf.

RAAMIAH (Rā à mī´ ah) Returning Exile (Neh. 7:7). Variant form of Reelaiah (Ezra 2:2).

RAAMSES (Rā ăm´ sēṣ) Alternate form of place name Rameses (Ex. 1:11).

RAB-MAG (Răb-măḡ) Title of the Babylonian official Nergal-Sharezer (Jer. 39:3,13). The name derives from the Akkadian *rab mugi*. The first element (*rab*) means, "chief." Unfortunately, the meaning of the second element is unknown. If associated with the root for magi, the Rab-mag was likely the officer in charge of divination (compare Ezek. 21:21).

RABBAH (Răb´ bah) Place name meaning, "greatness." *1.* Village near Jerusalem (Josh. 15:60) assigned to tribe of Judah but apparently in territory of Benjamin. Its location is uncertain. *2.* Capital of Ammon that Moses apparently did not conquer (Deut. 3:11; Josh. 13:25), located about twenty-three miles east of the Jordan River. Inhabited in prehistoric times and again before 1500 B.C., the city became a fortified settlement early in its history. David besieged the city (2 Sam. 11:1) and captured it (12:28–29). It remained under Israelite control throughout the period of the United Monarchy, but regained its independence shortly after the Israelite division. Rabbah was destroyed during the Babylonian sweep through the area (590–580 B.C.) and not rebuilt for several hundred years. Rabbah was renamed Philadelphia by the Hellenists and later became Amman, the modern capital of Jordan. See *Philadelphia.*

RABBATH (Răb´ bàth) KJV variant spelling of Rabbah (Deut. 3:11; Ezek. 21:20).

RABBI (Răb´ bī) Title meaning, "my master," applied to teachers and others of an exalted and revered position. During the New Testament period, the term *rabbi* came to be more narrowly applied to one learned in the law of Moses, without signifying an official office.

In the New Testament the title *rabbi* is used only in three of the gospels. In Matthew 23:7–8 scribes generally are addressed. In John 3:26 John the Baptist is thus called by his disciples. In all other occurrences "rabbi" and an alternate form "rabboni" apply to Jesus in direct address (Mark 9:5; 11:21; Mark 14:45, John 1:49; 3:2; 4:31; 6:25; 9:2; 11:8; 20:16).

Luke never used the term *rabbi,* but the word *epistata,* the equivalent of "school-master," a term more meaningful to his predominantly Greek first readers (Luke 17:13).

A unique relationship existed between Jesus and His disciples, compared to the typical rabbi and his pupils. They were forbidden to call each other "rabbi" (Matt. 23:8), and in Matthew, particularly, Jesus' disciples call Him "Lord" (*Kurie*). For Matthew, Jesus was not just a teacher to His followers; He was their Lord.   *Robert Stagg*

RABBIT (*Oractolagus cuniculus*) Small, long-eared mammal related to the hare but differing in giving birth to naked young. NAS, NIV, and TEV use rabbit for an unclean animal in Leviticus 11:6; Deuteronomy 14:7 where other English translations use hare.

RABBITH (Răb bīth) Unidentified site in territory of Issachar (Josh. 19:20). Rabbith is possibly a corruption of Daberath, a site included in other lists of Issachar's territory (Josh. 21:28; 1 Chron. 6:72) but missing in Joshua 19.

RABBONI (Rab bo´ ni) Variant spelling of *Rabbi.*

RABSARIS (Răb´ sà rīs) An Assyrian court position with strong military and diplomatic powers. The Hebrew *saris* means "eunuch," but the term here is a transliteration of Akkadian and should not be taken literally. The title literally means "he who stands by the king." The Old Testament records that the rabsaris was sent on two occasions to deal with the Israelite kings (2 Kings 18:17; Jer. 39:3). Hezekiah and Zedekiah each rebelled against the Assyrian rule and withheld tribute payment. The rabsaris was among the ambassadors who called on the kings to demand payment. See *Eunuch.*

RABSHAKEH (Răb shà´ kĕh) Assyrian title, literally, "chief cupbearer." The position probably began as a mere butler but developed into a highly influential post by the time of its mention in the Bible. The official who dealt with Hezekiah spoke for the Assyrian king much as would an ambassador. He urged the people of Jerusalem to consider turning over their king if he refused to pay the tribute demanded by the Assyrian throne (2 Kings 18:17–35).   *Mike Mitchell*

RACA (Rä´ cà) Word of reproach meaning, "empty" or "ignorant" that the Hebrew writers borrowed from the Aramaic language. Jesus used it in Matthew 5:22 as a strong term of derision, second only to "fool." He placed it in the context of anger and strongly condemned one who would use it of another person.

RACAL (Rä´ cal) Unidentified site in southern

Judah (1 Sam. 30:29). Most commentators follow the reading of the earliest Greek translation, "Carmel," and regard Racal as a textual corruption.

RACHAB (Rā′ chăb) KJV variant form of Rahab (Matt. 1:5).

RACHAL (Ra′ chȧl) KJV and REB form of Racal (1 Sam. 30:29).

RACHEL (Rā′ chĕl) Personal name meaning, "ewe." Younger daughter of Laban, the second wife and cousin of Jacob, and the mother of Joseph and Benjamin.

In flight from his brother, Esau, Jacob met her when Rachel brought the sheep to water. She immediately become the object of his attention. See *Jacob.*

Two Old Testament passages outside Genesis name Rachel. Ruth 4:11 calls her one who built up the house of Israel. Jeremiah 31:15 refers to her weeping over children being taken in Exile. Matthew (2:18) cited Jeremiah's reference of weeping in connection with Herod's order to kill male children under two.

The traditional location of Rachel's tomb in Bethlehem.

RADDAI (Răd dā ī) Personal name meaning, "Yahweh rules." Son of Jesse and brother of David (1 Chron. 2:14).

RAFT King Hiram's means of transporting timber for the Temple by lashing logs together and floating them down the coast from Tyre to Joppa (1 Kings 5:9; 2 Chron. 2:16).

RAGAU (Rā′ ḡāu) KJV alternate form of Reu (Luke 3:35).

RAGUEL (Rȧ ḡū′ ĕl) KJV alternate form of Reuel (Num. 10:29).

RAHAB (Ra′ hab) Name meaning, "arrogant, raging, turbulent, afflicter." *1.* Primeval sea monster representing the forces of chaos God overcame in creation (Job 9:13; 26:12; Ps. 89:10; Isa. 51:9;

compare Ps. 74:12–17). *2.* Symbolic name for Egypt (Ps. 87:4). Isaiah 30:7 includes a compound name *Rahab-hem-shebeth.* Translations vary: "Rahab who sits still" (NRSV); "Rahab who has been exterminated" (NAS); "Rahab the Do-Nothing" (NIV); "Rahab the Subdued" (REB). *3.* The plural appears in Psalm 40:4 for the proud, arrogant enemies.

RAHAB (Rā′ hăb) Personal name meaning, "broad." Harlot in Jericho who hid two Hebrew spies Joshua sent there to determine the strength of the city (Josh. 2:1). When the king of Jericho learned of the spies' presence, he sent men to arrest them. Rahab outsmarted the king and hid the men on her roof, sending the arresting officers on a false chase toward the Jordan River. In return for her help Joshua spared her and her clan when the Hebrews destroyed Jericho (Josh. 6:17–25). Matthew named Rahab as Boaz' mother (1:5) in his genealogy of Christ, making her one of the Lord's ancestors. Some interpreters think, however, that the Rahab in Matthew was a different woman. Hebrews 11:31 lists Rahab among the heroes of faith.

RAHAM (Rā′ hăm) Personal name meaning, "mercy, love." Descendant of Judah (1 Chron. 2:44).

RAHEL (Rā hĕl) KJV alternate form of Rachel (Jer. 31:15).

RAIL KJV term meaning, "revile," "deride," "cast contempt upon," or "scold using harsh and abusive language" (1 Sam. 25:14; 2 Chron. 32:17; Mark 15:29; Luke 23:39).

RAIMENT See *Cloth, Clothing.*

RAIN Moisture from heaven providing nourishment for plant and animal life. Palestine was a land dependent upon the yearly rains to ensure an abundant harvest and an ample food supply for the coming year. Thus, the presence or absence of rain became a symbol of God's continued blessing or displeasure with the land and its inhabitants. Rain fell in two seasons: the early rains during October and November, and the later rains in February and March. Rarely did rain of any significance fall outside these two periods. Westerly winds from the Mediterranean Sea brought wet storms during the winter, most of the rain falling along the coastal plain, in the north, and in the central hills. Lower elevations, the Jordan Valley, and the south received less rain during the year. Long droughts often were followed by flash floods that quickly filled the seasonal creeks and riverbeds. The runoff was captured in cisterns for drinking water. In the Negev, farmers plowed during the rains to allow the fine desert dust to absorb the little rain that was available. The coming of the rain was viewed as God's continued pleasure with His people. The lack of rain in spring proclaimed His judgment for sin and disobedience. The Canaanites worshiped Baal as the god of rain and thunder, and sexual orgies were enacted to provoke his presence in the land.

RAINBOW Caused by the reflection and refraction of sunlight by droplets of rain, a rainbow often appears after the passing of thunderstorms, marking its end. The bow is colored by the division of sunlight into its primary colors. The rainbow served to remind Israel and her God of His covenant with Noah to never again destroy the earth by flooding (Gen. 9:8–17). The Mesopotamian Epic of Gilgamesh, another ancient flood account, does not include the sign of the rainbow. The rainbow and its beauty became a symbol of the majesty and beauty of God. While having a vision, Ezekiel compared the brightness of the glory of God with the colors of the rainbow (1:28). Habakkuk also used the bow to describe the scene of God's final deliverance of His people (3:9). The Book of Revelation records John's vision of the throne of Christ as surrounded by the rainbow, "in sight like unto an emerald." (4:3). Later, Revelation 10:1 pictures a descending angel with the rainbow shining upon his head and having a face as the sun.

RAISIN CAKES Food prepared by pressing dried grapes together. David gave raisin cakes ("flagon," KJV) to those who accompanied the ark to Jerusalem (2 Sam. 6:19; 1 Chron. 16:3 NRSV). Hosea 3:1 (NRSV) links raisin cakes with the worship of pagan deities (compare Jer. 7:18).

RAKEM (Rā′ kĕm) Personal name meaning, "variegated, multicolored." Grandson of Manasseh (1 Chron. 7:16).

RAKKATH (Răk′ kȧth) Place name meaning, "spit," "narrow," or "swamp." Fortified town in the territory of Naphtali (Josh. 19:35), either at Tiberias or else at tell Eqlatiyeh about one and one half miles northwest of Tiberias. Artifacts spanning the Bronze Age have been recovered from the latter site.

RAKKON (Răk kon) Place name possibly meaning, "swamp" or "narrow place." Village in the vicinity of Joppa allotted to Dan (Josh. 19:46). The site is perhaps tell er-Reqqeit two miles north of the mouth of the Jarkon River (Nahr el-'Auja). The omission of the name in the earliest Greek translation suggests that Rakkon may result from a scribe having copied Me-jarkon and then started over in the middle of the word, copying the last half twice.

RAM (Răm) Personal name meaning, "high, exalted." *1.* Ancestor of David (Ruth 4:19; 1 Chron. 2:9) and Jesus (Matt. 1:3–4). *2.* Jerahmeel's eldest son (1 Chron. 2:25,27), the nephew of *1. 3.* Head of the family to which Job's friend Elihu belonged (Job 32:2).

RAM'S HORN See *Shophar.*

RAM, BATTERING See *Arms and Armor.*

RAMA (Rā′ mȧ) KJV alternate form of Ramah (Matt. 2:18).

RAMAH (Rā′ mah) Place name meaning, "high," applied to several cities located on heights, especially military strongholds. *1.* Border town in tribal territory of Asher (Josh. 19:29). The precise location of the city is unknown, although most scholars would place it in the vicinity of Tyre. *2.* Fortified city of tribal territory of Naphtali (Josh. 19:36), this town is probably to be identified with present-day er-Rameh. Ramah of Asher and Ramah of Naphtali could have been the same community since the boundaries of Asher and Naphtali join.

3. Ramah of Gilead usually called Ramoth-Gilead. Compare 2 Kings 8:28–29; 2 Chronicles 22:6. See *Ramoth-Gilead.*

4. City in the inheritance of Benjamin listed along with Gibeon, Beeroth, Jerusalem, and others (Josh. 18:25). It is to be identified with modern er-Ram five miles north of Jerusalem. In ancient times this location placed the city between the rival kingdoms of Israel and Judah, which led to dire consequences (1 Kings 15:16–22; 2 Chron. 16:1, 5,6).

The traditional site of Rachel's tomb was connected with Ramah (1 Sam. 10:2; Jer. 31:15). Deborah, the prophetess, dwelt and judged Israel from the Ramah vicinity (Judg. 4:4,5). Hosea mentioned Ramah (Hos. 5:8), and Isaiah prophesied that the approaching Assyrian army would march through Ramah (Isa. 10:29).

The Babylonians apparently used Ramah as a prisoner-of-war camp from which captives of Jerusalem were processed and sent into Babylonian Exile. There Jeremiah was released from his chains and allowed to remain in Judah (Jer. 40:1–6). People returning from captivity settled there (Ezra 2:26; Neh. 7:30). *5.* A city of the Negev, the arid desert south of Judea, in the tribal inheritance of Simeon (Josh. 19:8). David once gave presents to this town following his successful battle with the Amalekites (1 Sam 30:27). *6.* Birthplace, home, and burial place of Samuel (1 Sam. 1:19; 2:11; 7:17; 8:4; 15:34; 25:1). In 1 Samuel 1:1 the long form, Ramathaim-Zophim, is used. Samuel built an altar to the Lord at Ramah. From there he "judged" Israel and went on a yearly circuit to other cities (1 Sam. 7:15–17). Some have argued that Ramathaim-Zophim is identical with Ramah of Benjamin. It may also be the town, Arimathea, hometown of Joseph, in whose tomb Jesus was buried (Matt. 27:57–60).

J. Randall O'Brien

RAMATH (Rā′ măth) Place name meaning, "height, elevated place." An element of several names: Ramath-lehi meaning, "height of the jawbone," site of Samson's victory over the Philistines (Judg. 15:17); Ramath-Mizpeh (alternately Ramath-Mizpah) meaning, "height of lookout or watchtower" (Josh. 13:26); Ramath-Negeb meaning, "Ramath of the South," (Josh. 19:8; 1 Sam. 30:27). See *Ramah.*

RAMATH OF THE SOUTH. See *Ramah; Ramath.*

RAMATH-LEHI (Rā′ măth-Lē′ hī) See *Ramath.*

RAMATH-MIZPAH (Rā′ măth-Mĭz′ pah) See *Ramath.*

RAMATH-MIZPEH (Rā′ măth-Mĭz′ pĕh) See *Ramath.*

RAMATH-NEGEB (Rā′ măth-Ne geb) See *Ramah; Ramath.*

RAMATHAIM (Rā mȧ thā′ ĭm) NIV form of Ramathaim-Zophim.

The gateway to the city of Rameses (Tanis).

RAMATHAIM-ZOPHIM (Rā mȧ thā′ ĭm-Zō′ phĭm) Birthplace of Samuel (1 Sam. 1:1). The first element in the name means, "twin peaks." The final element distinguishes this Ramath from others. Zophim is perhaps a corruption of Zuph, the home district of Samuel (1 Sam. 9:5).

RAMATHITE (Rā′ măth īte) Resident of Ramah (1 Chron. 27:27).

RAMESES (Răm′ ĕ sēs) Egyptian capital city and royal residence during the nineteenth and twentieth dynasties (about 1320–1085 B.C.). The exact location is uncertain, although it appears to have been in the Nile delta and may be the same as Tanis or Zoan. It was near the area where the Hebrews

The head of a monumental statue of Ramses the Great, builder of the store-city of Rameses.

had settled under Joseph's administration (Gen. 47:11). After the Israelites became slaves, they were forced to help build Rameses and Pithom (Ex. 1:11) as store cities for Pharaoh Rameses II. Rameses accomodated seagoing vessels from the Mediterranean Sea and river traffic from the Nile. Surrounding the city were groves of fruit trees and vineyards. The city was quite propsperous because of the commerce which went through its port. See *Egypt; Exodus; Pithom.*

RAMIAH (Rȧ mī′ ah) Personal name meaning, "Yahweh is exalted." Israelite having a foreign wife (Ezra 10:25).

RAMOTH (Rā′ mŏth) See *Remeth.*

RAMOTH-GILEAD (Rā′ mŏth-gĭl′ ė ȧd) Place name meaning, "heights of Gilead." One of the cities of refuge Moses appointed for unintentional killers (Deut. 4:43; compare Josh. 20:8) and Levitical cities (Josh. 21:38). It probably was located in northeastern Gilead, east of the Jordan. Solomon made Ramoth-gilead a district capital (1 Kings 4:13). After the division of the kingdom about 922 B.C., the city fell to Syria (1 Kings 22:3) and remained there for almost seventy years. Ahab attempted to retake the city but was mortally wounded in the battle (1 Kings 22:29–40). Joram did recapture the city (2 Kings 9:14; compare 8:28). In Ramoth-gilead Elisha anointed Jehu as king over Israel (2 Kings 9:1–6). In 722 B.C. the region was taken by Assyria.

Mike Mitchell

RAMOTH-NEGEV (Rā′ mŏth-Nĕ ğĕb) See *Ramah; Ramath.*

RAMPART Outer ring of fortifications, usually earthworks. The underlying Hebrew term is literally, "encirclement," and can be applied to moats and walls as well as earthworks (2 Sam. 20:15; Ps. 122:7; Lam. 2:8). Because Jerusalem was ringed by steep valleys, only its north side had extensive ramparts.

RANGE KJV term for a rank or row (of soldiers) in 2 Kings 11:8,15; 2 Chronicles 23:14.

RANSOM See *Atonement; Expiation, Propitiation; Redeem, Redemption, Redeemer.*

RAPE Crime of engaging in sexual intercourse with another without consent by force and/or deception. Mosaic law required a man who had seduced a virgin to pay the bride price and offer to marry her (Ex. 22:16–17). The forcible rape of an engaged woman was a capital offense (Deut. 22:25–27). In other cases of forcible rape, the offender was required to marry his victim and was not permitted to divorce her (Deut. 22:28–29).

Lot's daughter made their father drunk and then raped him (Gen. 19:30–35). Shechem raped Dinah by force (Gen. 34:1–2). The men of Gibeah gang raped a Levite's concubine and so brutalized her that she died (Judg. 19:25). Amnon's rape of his half sister Tamar was a premeditated act involving both deception and force (2 Sam. 13:1–22). This account reveals the mind of the rapist whose uncontrolled desire quickly turned to fierce hatred for his victim (13:15). Rape was one horror associated with the fall of Jerusalem (Lam. 5:11; Zech. 14:2).

Today victims of rape are too frequently made to feel they are on trial. The Mosaic code highlighted the victim's rights, both to monetary compensation and to recovery of dignity. This quest for dignity was a driving force behind acts of retaliatory violence recorded in the narrative texts. These texts, however, suggest the ease with which the victim is forgotten in the spiral of vengeful violence. See *Sex, Biblical Teaching On.*

Chris Church

RAPHA (Rā′ phȧ) Personal name meaning, "He has healed." *1.* Fifth son of Benjamin (1 Chron. 8:2). The parallel in Genesis 46:21 gives the name Naaman. *2.* KJV form of Raphah (1 Chron. 8:37).

RAPHAH (Rā phah) Personal name from a root meaning, "heal." A descendant of Saul (1 Chron. 8:37). Raphah is identified with Rephaiah of 1 Chronicles 9:43.

RAPHU (Rā′ phû) Personal name meaning, "healed." Father of the Benjaminite representative among the twelve spies sent to survey Canaan (Num. 13:9).

RAPTURE The catching up of believers by Christ at the time of His return. The word came into use by way of the Latin *rapio* used to translate the Greek term of 1 Thessalonians 4:17, *harpagēsōmetha.* Living believers are said to be "caught up" to meet the Lord at His coming. Those of varying millennial views about end time events all hold firmly to the biblical truth of such a rapture. However, it is within the premillennial view that the teaching of a rapture finds major emphasis.

This view sees a tribulation period immediately before the second coming of Christ. Pretribulationists see the rapture occuring prior to the tribulation. This approach places the church in heaven during the time of tribulation on earth.

Mid-tribulationists place the rapture at the midpoint of a seven-year tribulation period. The church remains on earth for the first half of the tribulation, but escapes the last half which is seen to be the time of intense or great tribulation. This view, along with the previous one, sees the second coming of Christ in two phases. The first phase will be a secret coming in clouds to rapture the church. The second will be His return with the church to reign on earth.

Posttribulationists hold the church will remain on earth during the tribulation period. While that time will be one of wrath upon the world system, the church will be protected from divine wrath although experiencing tribulation. This view avoids dividing the return of Christ into two phases. See *Eschatology; Future Hope; Tribulation.*   *Jerry W. Batson*

RAS SHAMRA See *Ugarit, Ras Shamra.*

RAT See *Animals.*

RAVEN See *Birds.*

RAVEN, RAVIN KJV term for "prowl for food" or "feed greedily" (Ps. 22:13; Ezek. 22:25,27). KJV used *ravin* both as a verb meaning, "to prowl for food" (Gen. 49:27), and as a noun meaning, "something taken as prey" (Nah. 2:12).

RAZORS, SHAVING Instruments used in and process of removing facial hair. The customs of ancient nations regarding facial hair varied greatly. The availability of inscriptional and pictorial evidence as to these customs shows that nations had their own individual practices. Egyptians were known for their fastidious attention to personal cleanliness and did not shave the hair of their beard and head only in times of mourning. Their normal custom was to shave both with the motive of cleanliness. The pictures and statues of pharaohs show them with beards which we now know were fake.

The custom of shaving the face and head was less common among the Hebrews. Among them, in parallel with most Western Asiatics including the Assyrians, the beard was considered as an ornament and point of pride, and was not shaven, but only trimmed (2 Sam. 19:24; Ezek. 44:20). The beard was cherished as the badge of dignity of manhood.

Shaving was done with a sharp cutting instrument made from a variety of materials, but usually from either flint, obsidian, or iron (Isa. 7:20; Ezek. 5:1), but only in unusual circumstances. The razor could be a simple knife, probably elongated with a rounded end, or an elaborate instrument, sometimes decorated. Shaving was practiced as a sign of mourning (Job 1:20; Jer. 7:29), as a sign of subservience to a superior (Num. 8:7; Gen. 41:14), and as a treatment for a person with leprosy (Lev. 14:9).   *Jimmy Albright*

RE The chief Egyptian god, worshiped at his Temple in Thebes, credited with creating the universe and believed to have been the first pharaoh.

In images he is depicted usually as the sun disc. See *Egypt; Gods, Pagan.*

REAIA (Rė âî´ a) KJV form of Reaiah (1 Chron. 5:5).

REAIAH (Rė âî ah) Personal name meaning, "Yahweh has seen." *1.* Member of the tribe of Judah (1 Chron. 2:52). *2.* Member of the tribe of Reuben (1 Chron. 5:5). *3.* Head of a family of Temple servants (Nethanim) returning from Exile (Ezra 2:47; Neh. 7:50).

REAP To harvest grain using a sickle (Ruth 2:3–9). Reaping is used as a symbol of recompense for good (Hos. 10:12; Gal. 6:7–10) and evil (Job 4:8; Prov. 22:8; Hos. 8:7; 10:13), of evangelism (Matt. 9:37–38; Luke 10:2; John 4:35–38), and of final judgment (Matt. 13:30,39; Rev. 14:14–16).

REBA (Rē´ bà) Personal name from a root meaning, "lie down." Midianite king whom Israel defeated in the time of Moses (Num. 31:8). Joshua 13:21 connects the defeat of the Midianite kings with that of the Amorite king Sihon (Num. 21:21–35).

REBECCA (Rĕ bĕc´ cà) New Testament form of Rebekah.

REBEKAH (Rĕ bĕk´ ah) Personal name perhaps meaning, "cow." Daughter of Bethuel, Abraham's nephew (Gen. 24:15); Isaac's wife (24:67); mother of Jacob and Esau (25:25–26). Rebekah was a complex character. She is introduced as a beautiful virgin (24:16), willing servant (24:19), and as hospitable to strangers (24:25). In obedience to God's will, she left her home in Paddan-aram to be Isaac's wife (24:58). Rebekah comforted Isaac after the death of Sarah (24:67). When distressed by her problem pregnancy, she turned to God for counsel (25:22–23). Less favorable is Rebekah's favoritism towards Jacob (25:28), especially as evidenced in the plan she concocted to enable Jacob to steal Esau's blessing (27:5–17). Rebekah was forced to send her favorite to her brother's household to save Jacob from Esau's vengeance (27:42–46).

RECAB, RECHBITE (Rē´ căb) NIV form of Rechab, Rechabite.

RECAH (Rē´ cah) Unidentified site in Judah (1 Chron. 4:12). An early Greek manuscript has Rechab in place of Recah.

RECHAB (Rē´ chăb) Personal name meaning, "rider" or "charioteer." *1.* Leader, together with his brother, of a band of Benjaminite raiders. He and his brother murdered Saul's son Ish-bosheth, thinking to court David's favor. His response was their execution (2 Sam. 4:1–12). *2.* Father or ancestor of J[eh]onadab, a supporter of Jehu's purge of the family of Ahab and other worshipers of Baal (2 Kings 10:15,23). *3.* Father or ancestor of Malchijah, who assisted in Nehemiah's repair of Jerusalem's walls (Neh. 3:14), possibly identical with *2.*

RECHABITES (Rē' chă bītes) Descendants of Jehonadab ben Rechab, who supported Jehu when he overthrew the house of Ahab (2 Kings 10:15–17). About 599 B.C., the Rechabites took refuge from Nebuchadnezazar in Jerusalem (Jer. 35). At that point, the Lord commanded Jeremiah to take them to the Temple and give them wine to drink. When he did so, they refused, saying that their father Jonadab (Jehonadab) had commanded them not to drink wine, nor to live in houses, nor to engage in agriculture. These regulations may have been intended as a protest against Canaanite religion or settled life in general, but more likely they protected the Rechabites' life-style and trade secrets as itinerant metalworkers. Jeremiah contrasted their faithfulness to the commandments of their ancestor with the faithlessness of the people of Judah to the Lord. *Ricky L. Johnson*

RECHAH (Rē' chah) KJV form of Recah.

RECONCILIATION (Rĕ cŏn cĭ lĭ ā' tion) The establishment of friendly relations between parties who are at variance with each other, making peace after an engagement in war, or readmission to the presence and favor of a person after rebellion against the person. In 1525 William Tyndale, in his translation of the New Testament from the Greek text, attempted to discover an English word that would express the true meaning of the Greek *katallage* as well as the Latin reconciliation. Unable to find the word, he coined one. The word he coined was *atonement* (at-one-ment), and he used it in Romans 5:11. The *King James Version* committee followed Tyndale and used atonement. More recent versions and translations have returned to "reconciliation," largely because the word *atonement* has been encumbered with various theories of atonement.

Old Testament The idea of reconciliation between two people and between Israel and God was dominant in the Old Testament though there was no specific term to express it. The Hebrews viewed sin, whether intentional or unintentional, as a breach of the covenant between God and Israel. Sin brought about an estrangement between God and the nation or God and the individual. Provisions were made for Israel and the individual to be restored in God's favor. The Day of Atonement (*Yom Kippur*) was designated as the day when unintentional sins of the people could be forgiven (Lev. 16:1–31; 23:26–32). For these unknown sins the Hebrews were forgiven by the

sacrifices and elaborate ritual of the high priest. What about deliberate sins? These could be forgiven only by prayer and repentence. All the sacrifices in the Old Testament could never complete the act of drawing near to God and bringing a sinner into a right relationship with God (Hebrews 10:1–18). The Jewish rabbis realized this and taught that a person could be reconciled to God only by good deeds, repentance, and confession. Theirs was a self-reconciliation. A person was the subject, and God was the object. Humans took the initiative to make peace with God; God did not reconcile the person to Himself.

New Testament While the concept of reconciliation is prevalent throughout the New Testament, the term is found only in Paul's Epistles (Rom. 5:10–21; 2 Cor. 5:18–20; Eph. 2:16; Col. 1:20–21; Rom. 11:15; 1 Cor. 7:11) and in Matthew 5:23–24. However, in Matthew a different preposition is used with the Greek verb. Paul saw the need for reconciliation of humans to oneself, other people, and the environment, but his chief interest was in a person being reconciled to God.

Paul did not hint that the attitudes of God and humanity were mutually antagonistic. Hostility and estrangement had its origin in humans. Mankind through indifference, active enmity, and passive hatred had rebelled against God and stood in need of being reconciled to Him. God's creatures defied the divine purpose for life and destroyed the fellowship for which they were intended. They substituted for the true foundation of fellowship a whole series of relationships which formed a kingdom of evil and promoted estrangement from God. Thus, all mankind came under the wrath of God (the situation that pertains when a person is alienated from God).

The Sovereign of the universe, who could rightfully annihilate us, took the initiative in breaking down the estranging barrier between Himself and us. In the Old Testament humans were the subject of the action in attempting to be restored to favor with God, the object. The New Testament reverses the action. God became the subject, and a person the object. Paul said, "All things are of God, who hath reconciled us to himself by Jesus Christ" (2 Cor. 5:18). In the same context he affirmed, "God was in Christ, reconciling the world unto himself" (2 Cor. 5:19). Again he argued, "If, when we were enemies, we were reconciled to God by the death of his son, much more being reconciled, we shall be saved by his life" (Rom. 5:10). Reconciliation for Paul meant that a complete reversal of the relation between God and humans had been accomplished. Through His love manifested to us in the death of Christ on the cross even while we were in the state of being sinners, God delivered us from law, wrath, sin, and death—the tyrannies that hold humanity in check—and brought us by faith in Christ into a peaceful relationship with Himself.

The New Testament not only reveals God's act of reconciliation in Christ, but it also exhorts us to be reconciled to fellow human beings. Since God has taken the initiative in removing our hostility toward Him, it is incumbent on us to take action in overcoming the enmity that exists between us and others. In the Sermon on the Mount Jesus taught that reconciliation with one's brother was essential to genuine worship of God (Matt. 5:23–24). Paul in Ephesians 2:14–18 dramatically proclaimed that through the cross Christ reconciled both Gentile and Jew into one new humanity by terminating the hostility that existed between them. The church is commissioned to perform a ministry of reconciliation (2 Cor. 5:12–21). As the body of Christ, we have received the reconciling word, the command and power to be at peace with God and one another.

Paul used other words to express essentially the same concept. When we are reconciled to God, we have peace (Rom. 5:1; 1 Cor. 7:15; Gal. 5:22; Eph. 4:3; Phil. 4:7; Col. 3:15; 2 Thess. 3:16). No longer being alienated from God, we have freedom (Rom. 6:22; 8:2; Gal. 5:1) and sonship (Rom. 8:15; Gal. 4:5; Eph. 1:5). In Romans 5:8–10 and 2 Corinthians 5:17–21 reconciliation is used in conjunction with righteousness of God (justification). They both demonstrate an activity on the part of God in removing the barrier of sin that alienates people from God. See *Atonement; Cross; Jesus; Salvation.*   *T. C. Smith*

RECORDER Government post with unidentified responsibilities (as in 2 Sam. 8:16; 20:24). The REB identified the recorder as the secretary of state. The TEV identified the recorder as the official in charge of [court] records. The term possibly refers to a court herald. Most translations use recorder, thus leaving the function open.

RED See *Colors.* KJV used red as the translation of several Hebrew terms where modern translations substitute another meaning: "foaming" (Ps. 75:8); "pleasant" or "delight" (Isa. 27:2); and "porphyry" (Esth. 1:6).

RED HEIFER The function of the red heifer ceremony was production of ash for the water used to remove ritual impurity contracted through contact with a corpse, bones, or a grave (Num. 19). The rite involved: slaughter of a sacrificially acceptable heifer outside the camp; sprinkling blood toward the tent of meeting seven times; burning the entire heifer, including its blood and dung, together with cedarwood, hyssop, and scarlet thread (compare Lev. 14:4); and storing the ash in a clean place outside the camp. The water for removing the impurity contracted through contact with the dead was prepared by mixing running water with the ash. Impure persons and objects were sprinkled on the third and seventh days after

contamination to remove uncleanness. Hebrews 9:14 uses the image of the red heifer ceremony to picture Christ's cleansing believers of the effect of "dead works." Dead works refer either to "acts that lead to death" (NIV; "useless rituals" in view of salvation TEV) or works produced prior to being made alive in Christ (compare Heb. 6:1).

RED SEA (REED SEA) Body of water God dried up in the Exodus. Red Sea is a common translation of two Hebrew words *yam suph. Yam* means "sea," but *suph* does not normally mean "red." *Suph* often means "reeds" (Ex. 2:3,5; Isa. 19:6) or "end," "hinder part" (Joel 2:20; 2 Chron. 20:16; Eccl. 3:11). *Yam suph* could be translated "Sea of Reeds" or "Sea at the end of the world." The earliest known translation of the Hebrew Bible (the Greek Septuagint about 200 B.C.) translated *yam suph* consistently with *Erthra Thalassa* "Red Sea." Jerome continued the process in the *Latin Vulgate* (A.D. 400) by using *Mare Rubrum* "Red Sea" for *yam suph.* Most English translations have followed the Vulgate and use "Red Sea" in the text with a footnote indicating the literal translation is "Reed Sea." TEV uses various terms to translate *yam suph:* "Gulf of Suez (Ex. 10:19); "Red Sea" (see footnote on Ex. 13:18); and "Gulf of Aqaba (1 Kings 9:26).

We do not know who first suggested the translation "Reed Sea." In the eleventh century the French Jewish scholar Rashi spoke of *yam suph* in terms of a marsh overgrown with weeds. In the twelfth century Ibn Ezra, a Spanish Jew, commented that *yam suph* in Exodus 13:18 may be so named because reeds grow around it. Martin Luther translated *yam suph* as *Schilfmeer:* "Reed Sea." Although the name "Reed Sea" has been widely accepted by many scholars, there have been many recent attempts to prove the term "Sea of Reeds" is not a legitimate reading for *yam suph.*

The Old Testament uses the term *yam suph* to refer to more than one location. In Exodus 10:19 it refers to the Gulf of Suez as the place where the locusts were driven and destroyed. In 1 Kings 9:26 it refers to the Gulf of Aqaba where the ships of Solomon's navy were stationed. The same location may be indicated in Jeremiah 49:21 where the cries of Edom could be heard. The "Way of the (*yam suph*) Red Sea" is part of the name of a highway out of Egypt (Ex. 13:18; Num. 14:45; 21:4; Deut. 1:40; 2:1; Judg. 11:16). The "Red Sea" was the name of a camp along the way from Egypt (Num. 33:10,11). *Yam suph* marked the ideal southern border of Israel (Ex. 23:31), but the most significant reference of "Red Sea" in the Old Testament was to the place where God delivered Israel from Pharaoh's army (Ex. 15:4,22; Num. 21:14; Duet. 11:4; Josh. 2:10; 4:23; 24:6; Neh. 9:9; Ps. 106:7,9–11,22; 136:13–15).

No one knows the exact location of the place

A serene view of the Red Sea.

where Israel crossed the "Red Sea" on their way out of Egypt. Four primary theories have been suggested as to the place of the actual crossing of the isthmus of Suez: (1) the northern edge of the Gulf of Suez; (2) a site in the center of the isthmus near Lake Timsah; (3) a site at the northern edge of the isthmus and the southern edge of Lake Menzaleh; and (4) across a narrow stretch of sandy land which separates Lake Sirbonis from the Mediterranean Sea. Although no one knows the exact site of the crossing, the weight of the biblical evidence is on the side of suggested site number two. See *Exodus Event.*

Ralph L. Smith

REDEEM, REDEMPTION, REDEEMER To pay the required price to secure the release of a convicted criminal, the process therein involved, and the person making the payment. In early use the idea and the words related to legal and commercial activities. They provided biblical writers with one of the most basic and dynamic images for describing God's saving activity toward mankind. **Old Testament** Three Hebrew words express the legal and commercial use of the redemptive concept. *Padah* was used only in relation to the redemption of persons or other living beings. For example, if a person owned an ox which was known to be dangerous but did not keep the ox secured and the ox gored the son or daughter of a neighbor, both the ox and the owner would be stoned to death. If, however, the father of the slain person offered to accept an amount of money, the owner could pay the redemption price and live (Ex. 21:29–30; compare v. 32). Numbers 18:15–17 shows how religious practice adopted such language.

The Hebrew *ga'al* indicated a redemption price in family members involving the responsibility of a next-of-kin. See *Kinsman.* God called Jeremiah to demonstrate his confidence in God's promise by going out from Jerusalem to his ancestral village, Anathoth, and acting as next-of-kin to redeem or ransom the family land by paying the redemption price for it (Jer. 32:6–15). Such commercial practices easily passed over into religious concepts. God would redeem Israel from her iniquities.

The third Hebrew word *kipper* or "cover" came to extensive use in strictly religious concepts and practices. It is the word from which "Kippur" is derived in "Yom Kippur," Day of Atonement, or Day of Covering, perhaps the most sacred of the holy days in Judaism. The verbal form in the Old Testament is always used in a religious sense such as the covering of sin or the making of atonement for sin. See *Atonement.* The noun form, however, is sometimes used in the secular sense of a bribe (Amos 5:12) or ransom (Ex. 21:30). In Psalm 49:7–8 it is used in the sense of ransom in association with *padah* (redeem).

The doctrine of redemption in the Old Testament is not derived from abstract philosophical thought but from Hebrew concrete thinking. Religious redemption language grows out of the custom of buying back something which formerly belonged to the purchaser but for some reason had passed into the ownership of another. The original owner could regain ownership by paying a redemption price for it. In the Old Testament the terms and ideas are frequently used symbolically to emphasize dramatically the redemptive or saving activity of God. The basic Old Testament reference is the Exodus. At the sea God redeemed His people from slavery in Egypt (for example, Ex. 6:6; 15:13; Deut. 7:8; Ps. 77:15).

God similarly redeemed Israel from the Babylonian captivity by giving Egypt, Ethiopia, and Seba to King Cyrus (Isa. 43:3; compare 48:20; 51:11; 62:12). Job knew that he had a living Redeemer (Job 19:25). Psalmists prayed for redemption from distress (26:11; 49:15) and testified to God's redeeming work (31:5; 71:23; 107:2). The Old Testament witness is that God is "my strength and my redeemer" (Ps. 19:14).

New Testament The New Testament centers redemption in Jesus Christ. He purchased the church with His own blood (Acts 20:28), gave His flesh for the life of the world (John 6:51), as the Good Shepherd laid down His life for His sheep (John 10:11) and demonstrated the greatest love by laying down His life for His friends (John 15:13). The purpose of Jesus in the world was to make a deliberate sacrifice of Himself for human sin. He did something sinful people could not do for themselves. He brought hope to sinners, providing redemption from sin and fellowship with the Eternal Father. As the Suffering Servant, His was a costly sacrifice, the shameful and agonizing death of a Roman cross. New Testament redemption thus speaks of substitutionary sacrifice demonstrating divine love and righteousness. It points to a new relationship to God, the dynamic of a new life, God's leniency in the past, and the call for humility for the future.

In other ways and language the centrality of redemption through the death of Jesus Christ is expressed throughout the New Testament from the Lamb of God who lifts up and carries away the sin of the world (John 1:29) to the redeeming Lamb praised by a multitude because He was slain and by His blood redeemed unto God's people of every kindred, tongue, and nation (Rev. 5:8–14). See *Christ; Jesus; Atonement; Reconciliation.*

Ray Summers

REED PIPE See *Music, Instruments, Dancing.*

REED, VESSELS OF See *Ships, Sailors, and Navigation.*

REEDS See *Plants in the Bible.*

REELAIAH (Rē ĕl āi´ ah) Personal name meaning, "Yahweh has caused trembling." Exile who returned with Zerubbabel (Ezra 2:2); identical to Raamaiah (Neh. 7:7).

REFINE To reduce to a pure state, often used figuaratively of moral cleansing. See *Crucible; Ezion-Geber; Furnace; Minerals and Metals; Mines and Mining.*

REFINING POT See *Crucible; Fining Pot.*

REFORMATION Translation of the Greek *diorthōsis* (Heb. 9:10). The term refers either to the new order for relating to God established by Christ (NIV) or else to the process of establishing the new order (NRSV, TEV). See *Covenant.*

REFUGE, CITIES OF See *Cities of Refuge.*

REFUSE GATE See *Dung Gate.*

REGEM (Rē´ gĕm) Personal name meaning, "friend." Descendant of Caleb (1 Chron. 2:47).

REGEM-MELECH (Rē´ gĕm-Mē´ lĕch) Personal name meaning, "friend of the king." Delegate whom the people of Bethel sent to Jerusalem to inquire about continuing to fast in commemoration of the destruction of the Jerusalem Temple (Zech. 7:2). The prophet repeated the word of previous prophets: God desires moral lives rather than fasts (7:9–10).

REGENERATION (Rē´ gĕn ēr ā´ tion) The radical spiritual change in which God brings an individual from a condition of spiritual defeat and death to a renewed condition of holiness and life. The biblical doctrine of regeneration emphasizes God's role in making this spiritual change possible.

Biblical Terms The term *regeneration* (*palingenesia*) appears in Titus 3:5 as a description of the spiritual change which baptism symbolizes. The idea of regeneration is also conveyed by the use of other terms related to the idea of birth. Jesus referred to regeneration when he told Nicodemus (John 3:3) that he must be "born again" (*gennaō anōthen*). The term *born again* may also be translated as "born from above." This translation emphasizes the sovereign role of God in bringing about the experience of regeneration. In John 1:13 the term *born* (*gennaō*) refers to the act of regeneration. In 1 Peter 1:23 another Greek word (*anagennaō*) receives the translation "born again." All of these words describe the complete spiritual change which occurs when Christ enters the life of an individual.

The idea of regeneration also appears in other figures of speech which refer to concepts in addition to birth. When Paul described those in Christ as a "new creation" (2 Cor. 5:17 NIV), he was referring to the act of regeneration. In Ephesians 2:10 Paul referred to Christians as God's "workmanship" made for the purpose of good works. Sometimes the idea of receiving new life is used as a description of regeneration (compare John

5:21; 7:38; 10:10; John 10:28). In 1 Peter 2:2, the apostle described followers of Jesus as "new-born babes."

Whether the figure used involves birth, life, creation, or flowing rivers, the Bible is presenting a new experience of life which is enriching, comprehensive, and thoroughly renewed in holiness.
Need for Regeneration The great need for an experience of regeneration is apparent from the sinful condition of human beings, "dead in trespasess and sins" (Eph. 2:1). Left to themselves, human beings will corrupt God's revelation of Himself and turn to gross forms of disobedience (Rom. 1:18–32). God, however, demands holiness as a condition for having fellowship with Himself (Heb. 12:14). Human beings therefore must have a radical change in the very character of their personality. God promises such a change in the experience of regeneration.
Source of Regeneration Throughout Scripture the source of regeneration is the work of the Holy Spirit. Both Scripture (Rom. 3:10–23) and human experience indicate that people lack the power and will to reform. God works upon the human disposition by the use of truth (Jas. 1:18). This truth is the message of salvation which we find in the gospel of Jesus Christ. The role of the Holy Spirit is to take this truth and commend it to the understanding of each hearer (John 16:8–11). Regeneration occurs when the Holy Spirit takes the truth of the gospel message and allows the individual both to understand it and to commit oneself to it. There is a divine initiative through the Holy Spirit. There is a human responsibility in the response to the Spirit's urging.
Role of Baptism Some churches hold that the experience of regeneration is brought about by the act of baptism. The view which advocates this teaching is known as baptismal regeneration. The Scriptures do not present baptism as the means of regeneration but as the sign of regeneration. Peter's discussion of baptism in 1 Peter 3:21 pictures the experience of baptism as the symbol of a conscientious response to God. In other texts (Acts 2:38; Col. 2:12; Titus 3:5) we can understand the meaning of the biblical writer by distinguishing between regeneration as an inward change and baptism as the outward sign of that change. The actual change of regeneration is an instantaneous experience brought about by the Holy Spirit. Baptism becomes a means of demonstrating publicly and outwardly the nature of this change. *See Baptism.*
Result of Regeneration Ephesians 4:17–32 makes the result of regeneration apparent. Paul first discussed the nature of the spiritual change in a believer. In regeneration each believer has put off the old way of life, become clothed with a new way of life, and is in the process of having one's mind renewed in its thinking, reasoning, and willing. Because of this experience Paul urged each believer to practice truth, control anger, demonstrate kindness, and submit to the control of the Holy Spirit. The fact of regeneration formed the basis for giving an appeal to live a new life.

The experience of regeneration does not leave an individual content and passive in efforts at Christian growth. Old powers of evil have been broken. The possibility of victory in the constant struggle with sin has become certain.

Thomas D. Lea

REGIMENT NIV term for cohort, a tenth of a legion (Acts 10:1; 27:1). See *Cohort.*

REGISTER KJV term for a record of names, a genealogical registry (Ezra 2:62; Neh. 7:5,64). Modern translations use register more often in the verbal sense, to record in formal records (NAS: Num 1:18; 11:26; 2 Sam. 24:2,4; Neh. 12:22,23; Ps. 87:6). See *Census.*

REHABIAH (Rē hȧ bīʹ ah) Personal name meaning, "Yahweh has made wide." Son of Eliezer and ancestor of a group of Levites (1 Chron. 23:17; 24:21; 26:25).

REHOB (Rēʹ hŏb) Personal and place name meaning, "broad or open place." *1.* Father of a king of Zobah, an Aramaean city north of Damascus (2 Sam. 8:3,12). *2.* Witness to Nehemiah's covenant (Neh. 10:11). *3.* Town in the vicinity of Laish in upper Galilee (Num. 13:21; see *Beth-Rehob*). *4.* Town in the territory of Asher (Josh. 19:28,30). Asher was not able to drive out the Canaanite inhabitants (Judg. 1:31). Elsewhere, Rehob in Asher is assigned to the Levites (Josh. 21:31; 1 Chron. 6:75). The site is perhaps tell el-Gharbi about seven miles east-southeast of Acco.

REHOBOAM (Rē hō bōʹ am) Personal name meaning, "he enlarges the people." One of Solomon's sons and his successor to the throne of the united monarchy (1 Kings 11:43). He reigned about 931–913 B.C. While at Shechem for his crowning ceremony as king over Israel (1 Kings 12), the people asked Rehoboam if he would remove some of the tax burden and labor laws which his father had placed on them. Instead of taking the advice of the older men, he acted on the counsel of those who wanted to increase further the burden. The northern tribes revolted and made the rebel Jeroboam their king. Rehoboam was left with only the tribes of Judah and Benjamin. He continued the pagan ways which Solomon had allowed (14:21–24) and fought against Jeroboam and Shishak of Egypt. Some of his fortifications may be those at Lachish and Azekah.

REHOBOTH (Rēʹ hō bŏth) Place name meaning, "broad places." *1.* Rehoboth-Ir, "broad places of the city," likely denotes an open space within

Nineveh or its suburbs (Gen. 10:11) rather than a separate city between Nineveh and Calah. *2.* Site of a well dug and retained by Isaac's men in the valley of Gerar (Gen. 26:22). The name affirms that God had made room for them following confrontations over rights to two previous wells. *3.* Unidentified Edomite city (Gen. 36:37; 1 Chron. 1:48). KJV, NIV, and TEV distinguish this city as Rehoboth by the river. NAS, NRSV, and REB identify the river as the Euphrates. Edomite dominion reaching the Euphrates is improbable. Thus some suggest the Zered Brook, the principal stream in Edom, as the site of Rehoboth.

REHUM (Rē′ hŭm) Personal name meaning, "merciful, compassionate." *1.* One returning from Exile with Zerubbabel (Ezra 2:2); the parallel (Neh. 7:7) reads Nehum. *2.* Persian official with oversight of the Trans-Euphrates territory, including Judah. His protest of the rebuilding of the Jerusalem Temple and city walls resulted in suspension of the project (Ezra 4:8–24). *3.* Levite engaged in Nehemiah's repair of the wall (Neh. 3:17). *4.* Witness to Nehemiah's covenant (Neh. 10:25). *5.* Priest or priestly clan (Neh. 12:3), perhaps a corruption of Harim.

REI (Rē′ ī) Personal name meaning, "friendly." David's officer who sided with Solomon in his succession struggle with Adonijah (1 Kings 1:8).

REINS KJV term for kidneys, used both in a literal anatomical sense and in a figurative sense for the seat of the emotions. The substitutions made by the NRSV are illustrative of those of other modern translations: literal sense as "kidneys" (Job 16:13), "inward parts" (Ps. 139:13), and "loins" (Isa. 11:5); figurative sense as "heart" (Job 19:27; Pss. 7:9; 16:7; 26:2; 73:21; Jer. 11:20) with the exception of Proverbs 23:16 ("soul").

REKEM (Rē′ kĕm) Personal and place name meaning, "maker of multicolored cloth." *1.* One of five Midianite kings whom Israel defeated in Moses' time (Num. 31:8; Josh. 13:21). See *Reba.* Rekem was apparently the earlier name of Petra. *2.* Descendant of Caleb (1 Chron. 2:43–44). *3.* Ancestor of a family living in Gilead (1 Chron. 7:16). *4.* Unidentified site in Benjamin (Josh. 18:27).

RELEASE, YEAR OF The Hebrew expression occurs only twice (Deut. 15:9; 31:10 KJV and RSV), both times in reference to the sabbatical year as a year of release from debt. Some confusion results from modern translations using the verb release in connection with both the sabbatical year and the Year of Jubilee. See *Jubilee, Year of; Sabbatical Year.*

RELIGION A relationship of devotion or fear of God or gods. *1.* The cognate terms translated "religious" and "religion" (Acts 17:22; 25:19) can indicate positive reverence for the gods or else negative fear of the gods. The pejorative translations "superstitious" (KJV) and "superstition" (KJV, RSV) is unfortunate. Paul hardly alienated the Athenians at the outset of his speech. He rather pointed to their outward expressions of piety (Acts 17:22). Though a monotheist (believer in one God) would not use "fear of the gods" to describe Judaism, the expression is natural on pagan Roman lips (Acts 25:19). *2.* The cognate terms translated "religion" and "religious" in Acts 26:5 and James 1:26–27 point to the "fear of God" as evidenced in religious conduct, particularly ritual practice. In Acts 26:5 Paul referred to Judaism as "our" way of evidencing reverence for God. According to James 1:26–27, one who thinks himself religiously observant but who cannot control the tongue will find religious observance worthless. James continued that the religious observance God cares about is not a cultic matter but an ethical matter, care of the helpless of society. *3.* Several terms derived from *sebomai* (to fear) are translated religious or religion. The term in Acts 13:43 is rendered "religious" (KJV), "devout" (NRSV), and "God-fearing" (NAS). The term RSV translated "religion" in 1 Timothy 2:10 is literally "God-fearing," here in the sense of obedient to God's commands (compare John 9:31). The NIV translation "who profess to worship God" highlights the connection between fear and reverence. The KJV and NAS translation "godliness" accentuates the linkage of fear with an obedient life. The term RSV translated as "religion" (1 Tim. 3:16; 2 Tim. 3:5) and "religious duty" in 1 Timothy 5:4 is generally translated "godliness" or "piety." The emphasis is again on conduct. *4.* The meaning of the term the NAS translated as "self-made religion" is uncertain (Col. 2:23). The Greek roots suggest freely chosen worship (KJV, "will worship"; NIV, "self-imposed worship"; RSV, "promoting rigor of devotion"). Similar constructions with *thelō* suggest the meaning, "alleged worship." *5.* KJV translated *Ioudaïsmō* (Judaism) as the "Jews' religion" (Gal. 1:13–14). *6.* NIV frequently inserts the adjective religious into its paraphrase to clarify the nature of feasts (Amos 5:21; 8:10; Col. 2:16) or service (Heb. 10:11) when there is no corresponding term in the Greek or Hebrew text.

Chris Church

REMALIAH (Rĕm å lī′ ah) Personal name meaning, "may Yahweh be exalted" or "Yahweh adorned." Father of Pekah who murdered King Pekahiah of Israel and reigned in his stead (2 Kings 15:25; Isa. 7:1).

REMETH (Rē′ mĕth) Place name meaning, "height." Town in Issachar's territory (Josh. 19:21), likely identical with Ramoth (1 Chron.

6:73) and Jarmuth (Josh. 21:29).

REMISSION Release, forgiveness. RSV used *remission* only in the sense of refraining from exacting a tax (Esth. 2:18). Other modern translations avoided the term. KJV frequently used the expression, "remission of sins," to mean release from the guilt or penalty of sins. Modern translations generally substitute the term *forgiveness.* With the exception of Romans 3:25, the underlying Greek term is *aphesis.* Remission of sins is often linked with repentance, both in the preaching of John the Baptist (Mark 1:4; Luke 3:3) and the early church (Luke 24:47; Acts 2:38; 5:31). Remission of sins results from Christ's sacrificial death (Matt. 26:28; compare Heb. 10:17–18) and from Christ's exaltation (Acts 5:31). Remission of sins is available to all who believe in the name of Jesus (Acts 10:43; compare Luke 24:47; Acts 2:38). Because Christ's sacrifice has freed believers from the guilt and penalty of sin, no additional sacrifices are needed (Heb. 10:18). The term rendered "remission" in Romans 3:25 (*paresis*) refers to God's letting sin go unpunished in anticipation of the work of Christ.

REMMON (Rĕm´ mŏn) KJV variant of Rimmon (Josh. 19:7). RSV reads En-rimmon. Other modern translations follow the KJV in understanding two cities: Ain and Rimmon.

REMMON-METHOAR (Rĕm´ mŏn-Mĕ thō´ är) KJV took Remmon-Methoar as a proper name (Josh. 19:13). Modern translations take the second element (Methoar) to mean, "bends toward" (NRSV), "stretches to" (NAS), or a similar expression. See *Rimmon.*

REMNANT Something left over, especially the righteous people of God after divine judgment. Several Hebrew words express the remnant idea: *yether,* "that which is left over"; *she´ar,* "that which remains"; *she´rith,* "residue"; "*pelitah,* "one who escapes"; *sarid,* "a survivor"; and, *sheruth,* "one loosed from bonds." In the New Testament, remnant or left over is the equivalent of the Greek words: *kataleimma, leimma,* and *loipos.*

Several activities of everyday life are associated with these words. Objects or people may be separated from a larger group by selection, assignment, consumption (eating food), or by destruction. What is left over is the residue, or, in the case of people, those who remain after an epidemic, famine, drought, or war.

Noah and his family may be understood as survivors, or a remnant, of a divine judgment in the flood (Gen. 6:5–8; 7:1–23). The same could be said of Lot when Sodom was destroyed (Gen. 18:17–33; 19:1–29); Jacob's family in Egypt (Gen. 45:7); Elijah and the 7,000 faithful follow-ers of the Lord (1 Kings 19:17–18); and Israelites going into captivity (Ezek. 12:1–16). They were survivors because the Lord chose to show mercy to those who had believed steadfastly in Him and had been righteous in their lives.

About 750 B.C. Amos found that many people in Israel believed that God would protect all of them and their institutions. With strong language he tore down their mistaken ideas (3:12–15; 5:2–3,18–20; 6:1–7; 9:1–6). Divine judgment would be poured out on all Israel. He corrected the tenet that everyone would live happily and prosper (9:10) with the doctrine that only a few would survive and rebuild the nation (9:8b–9,11–15). This new life could be realized if one and all would repent, turn to the Lord, and be saved (5:4b–6a,14–15).

Hosea's book does not use the remnant terminology, but the concept of the Lord's mercy extended to those experiencing judgment is present in several places (2:14–23; 3:4–5; 6:1–3; 11:8–11; 13:14; 14:1–9) including calls to repentance and descriptions of what the remnant may enjoy in life.

The Book of Micah has much the same emphasis. After announcements of judgment, the Lord proclaimed that people would be assembled like sheep and led by the Lord (2:12–13) as their king (4:6–8). The Messiah would give special attention to them (5:2–5,7–9). The climax of the book is an exaltation of God as the one who pardons and removes sin from their lives after the judgment had passed (7:7–20).

The remnant doctrine was so important to Isaiah that he named one of his sons Shear-Jashub, meaning "A Remnant Shall Return" (7:3). The faithful would survive the onslaughts of the Assyrian army (4:2–6; 12:1–6) as illustrated by the remarkable deliverance of the few people in Jerusalem from the seige of the city by the Assyrians (chs. 36—38).

Many remnant passages are closely tied with the future king, the Messiah, who would be the majestic ruler of those who seek his mercies (9:1–7; 11:1–16; 32:1–8; 33:17–24). These passages have a strong eschatological thrust, expecting future generations to be the remnant. Other passages looked to the generation of Isaiah's day to provide the remnant. Numerous statements in the latter part of the book have an evident futuristic orientation. In that future, there would be a new people, a new community, a new nation, and a strong faith in one God. This remnant would be personified in the Suffering Servant (ch. 53).

Amos, Hosea, Micah, and Isaiah thus raised a chorus. Only a few would survive judgment events, basically because they repented and rested their future on the compassion of their Lord. An important segment of the remnant would be those who were afflicted (Isa. 14:32). Later, Zephaniah spoke of the humble and the lowly as the ones who would find refuge among the remnant (2:3; 3:12–13).

Jeremiah announced that Judah would be destroyed for rebelling against the Lord of the covenant. The political, religious, and social institutions of the state would be eliminated; many would lose their lives; others would be taken into Exile for seventy years. In the Exile, those who believed in the one true God would be gathered for a return to the Promised Land. God would create a new community. Statements of hope and promise for the remnant are concentrated in chapters 30—33.

Ezekiel agreed with Jeremiah that the remnant of Judah taken to Babylon would be the source of people fit for the Lord's new community. These few would participate in a new Exodus and settle in the Promised Land around a new Temple (chs. 40—48).

Zechariah spoke in glowing terms of how the remnant, the returned exiles to Jerusalem, would prosper (8:6–17; 9:9–17; 14:1–21). Ezra recognized the people who had returned to Jerusalem as members of the remnant, but in danger of re-enacting the sins of the past (9:7–15).

In the New Testament, Paul quoted (Rom 9:25–33) from Hosea and from Isaiah to demonstrate that the saving of a remnant from among the Jewish people was still part of the Lord's method of redeeming His people. There would always be a future for anyone among the covenant people who would truly turn to the Lord for salvation (9—11). *George Herbert Livingston*

REMPHAN (Rĕm' phăn) KJV form of Rephan.

RENDING OF GARMENTS Tearing or pulling garments apart, often as a sign of mourning (Gen. 37:34; Lev. 10:6; 21:10; 1 Sam. 4:12; 2 Sam. 3:31), repentance (Gen. 37:29; Josh. 7:6; 2 Chron. 34:27; Joel 2:13), or as a response to the rejection of God's plan (Num. 14:6) or (perceived) blasphemy (Matt. 26:65; Mark 14:63; Acts 14:14). See *Blasphemy; Mourning.*

REPENTANCE A feeling of regret, a changing of the mind, or a turning from sin to God. As a feeling of regret the term can apply even to God. In the days preceding the flood, God was sorry that He had created the human race (Gen. 6:6–7). He later regretted that he had made Saul the king over Israel (1 Sam. 15:11,35). God also repented in the sense of changing His mind (Ex. 32:14). Most occurrences of the term in the Bible, however, do not refer to God but to people. These also do not indicate mere regret or a change of mind; they mean a reorientation of the sinner to God. In this more common sense, then, God does not repent like humans (1 Sam. 15:29).

Old Testament In ancient Israel repentance was first expressed corporately. When national calamities such as famine, drought, defeat, or a plague of locusts arose, the people did not feel responsible individually for these catastrophes. Rather, they sensed that the incidents were caused by the guilt of the nation. All shared the responsibility and, consequently, the ritual of repentance. Fasting, the wearing of sackcloth (the traditional attire for mourning), the scattering of ashes (Is. 58:5; Neh. 9:1; Dan. 9:3), and the recitation of prayers and psalms in a penitential liturgy characterized this collective experience of worship.

With the use of such outward tokens of repentance, however, the danger of sham or pretense also arose. Ritual not accompanied by a genuine attitude of repentance was empty. Against such misleading and, therefore, futile expressions of remorse, the eighth-century prophets spoke out. Their attacks upon feigned worship and their calls for genuine contrition on the part of the individual gave flower to the characteristic biblical concept of repentance. What was needed was not ritual alone, but the active involvement of the individual in making a radical change within the heart (Ezek. 18:31) and in seeking a new direction for one's life. What was demanded was a *turning* from sin and at the same time a *turning* to God. For the prophets, such a turning or *conversion* was not just simply a change within a person; it was openly manifested in justice, kindness, and humility (Mic. 6:8; Amos 5:24; Hos. 2:19–20).

New Testament A direct connection between the prophets and the New Testament is found in John the Baptist. Appearing in the wilderness, he, like they, issued the call to his own generation for this radical kind of turning. He baptized those who by confessing their sins responded to his invitation (Mark 1:4–5). Likewise, he expected that those who had made this commitment would demonstrate by their actions the change which they had made in their hearts (Luke 3:10–14). He differed, though, from the prophets in that his message of repentance was intricately bound up with his expectation of the imminent coming of the Messiah (Luke 3:15–17; see also Acts 19:4).

The Messiah came also preaching a message of repentance (Mark 1:15). Stressing that all men needed to repent (Luke 13:1–5), Jesus summoned his followers to *turn* and become like children (Matt. 18:3). He defined His ministry in terms of calling sinners to repentance (Luke 5:32). Moreover, He illustrated His understanding of repentance in the parable of the prodigal who *returned* to the father (Luke 15:11–32). Like John, he insisted that the life that was changed was obvious by the "fruit" that it bore (Luke 6:20–45).

Jesus also differed from His predecessors in His proclamation of repentance. He related it closely to the arrival of the kingdom of God (Mark 1:14–15) and specifically associated it with one's acceptance of Him. Those who were unrepentant were those who rejected Him (Luke 10:8–15; 11:30–32); those who received Him were the truly repentant. In His name repentance and forgiveness were to be proclaimed to all nations (Luke 24:47).

Acts shows this proclamation was made. Peter (Acts 2:38; 3:19; 5:31) and Paul (Acts 17:30; 20:21) told Jews and Gentiles alike "that they should repent and turn to God, performing deeds appropriate to repentance" (Acts 26:20 NAS). The apostolic preaching virtually identified repentance with belief in Christ: both resulted in the forgiveness of sins (Acts 2:38; 10:43).

"Repentance" is infrequently found in Paul's writings and never in John. Both speak of faith which entails both a rejection of sin and a positive response to God. Other apostolic writings also note the relationship of faith and repentance (Acts 20:21; Heb. 6:1). In 1 John, moreover, *confession* of sins is tantamount to repentance from sins (1:9).

Other Usages Not all references refer to turning to God from sin. Judas repented of what he had done (Matt. 27:3). The Greek term differs from the normal word for repentance. In this context the meaning is regret or remorse; Judas' repentance was not the type that leads towards salvation.

Paul described an earlier letter he had sent to the Corinthians which caused them grief, but which eventually led them to repentance. Here Paul described a change in the Corinthians' attitude about him (2 Cor. 7:8–13). Their *repentance* resulted in their reconciliation with him.

Renewal of commitment or reaffirmation of faith seems to be the meaning of repentance in the letters to the seven churches in Revelation (2:5,16,21–22; 3:3,19). Twice the letters call for the readers to remember and thereby to return to what they had been. The call is for rededication and not initial conversion. See *Confession; Conversion; Faith; Kingdom of God; Sackcloth.*

Naymond Keathley

REPENTANCE OF GOD Old Testament description of God's reaction to human situations. The Hebrew verb (*nhm*) expresses a strong emotional content, perhaps with a reference to deep breathing of distress or relief. It should be noted that "repent" is not always the best translation for *nicham* but was the translation used by the KJV. The scope of possible translations includes "repent" (Jer. 18:8,10 RSV), "grieve" (Gen. 6:7 NIV), "pity" (Judg. 2:18 NAS), "change of mind" (Ps. 110:4 REB), and "relent" (Ps. 106:45 NAS). Therefore, the concept of the repentance of God would also include God's grieving, pitying, changing His mind, and relenting.

The concept of God's repentance is not limited to one section of the Old Testament, but can be found throughout the Law, Prophets, and Writings. The repentance of God became Israel's creed

alongside other attributes of God like "gracious," "merciful," "slow to anger," and "great in covenant-love" (Joel 2:13; Jonah 4:2).

The repentance of God was usually in response to His creation, such as human disobedience (Gen. 6:6–7), intercessory prayer (Amos 7:1–6), or repentance (Jonah 3:6–10). In many instances God is said to "change his mind" about some evil that he had planned to do (Ex. 32:12,14; Jonah 3:10). In one instance God is said to "change his mind" (Jer. 18:10) about His good intentions.

God's repentance plays an important role in our understanding about the role of prayer and about certain attributes of God, such as immutability, timelessness, and impassibility. The God who repents is free to answer prayer and to interact with people. This freedom is part of His being the same forever.   *M. Stephen Davis*

REPHAEL (Rĕph′ ā ĕl) Personal name meaning, "God heals." Temple gatekeeper (1 Chron. 26:7).

REPHAH (Rē′ phah) Personal name meaning, "overflow." An Ephraimite (1 Chron. 7:25).

REPHAIAH (Rĕ phāi′ ah) Personal name meaning, "God healed." *1.* Descendant of David (1 Chron. 3:21). *2.* Simeonite living at Mount Seir (1 Chron. 4:42). *3.* Warrior from the tribe of Issachar (1 Chron. 7:2). *4.* Descendant of Saul (1 Chron. 9:43). *5.* One helping with Nehemiah's repair of the wall who had oversight of one half of the administrative district embracing Jerusalem (Neh. 3:9).

REPHAIM (Rĕph′ ā ĭm) *1.* Residents of Sheol, often translated, "shades" or the "dead" (Job 26:5 NRSV; Ps. 88:10; Prov. 9:18; 21:16; Isa. 14:9; 26:14,19). See *Sheol. 2.* Ethnic designation of the pre-Israelite inhabitants of Palestine, equivalent to the Anakim, the Moabite term *Emim* (Deut. 2:10–11), and the Ammonite term *Zanzummim* (2:20–21). Despite their reputation for might and height, the Rephaim were defeated by a coalition of eastern kings (Gen. 14:5) and were later displaced by the Israelites (Deut. 3:11,13; compare Gen. 15:20) and their distant kin, the Moabites (Deut. 2:10–11) and the Ammonites (2:20–21). KJV regularly translated Rephaim as "giants" (except Gen. 14:5; 15:20 and some references to the valley or land of the Rephaim). NAS and RSV used the translation "giants" only in reference to individual giants in 2 Samuel and 1 Chronicles. NIV avoided the translation "giant" completely, using "Rephaim" when referring to the valley or land, "Rephaites" when referring to the pre-Israelite inhabitants, and "descendant of Rapha" for individuals in 2 Samuel and 1 Chronicles. The artificial distinction between Rephaites and descendant of Rapha apparently attempts to ease the tension between the designation of King Og of

Bashan as the last of the Rephaim (Deut. 3:11; Josh. 12:4) and the mention of later descendants in 2 Samuel 21:16,18,20,22; 1 Chronicles 20:6,8.

REPHAITES (Rĕph′ ā ītes) NIV alternate translation for the Hebrew *Rephaim* when applied to the pre-Israelite inhabitants of Canaan. See *Rephaim.*

REPHAN (Rē′ phăn) Term for a foreign, astral diety (Acts 7:43; NAS, Rompha). Acts 7 follows the earliest Greek Old Testament translation reading at Amos 5:26. The Hebrew Masoretic text reads Kaiwan, the Babylonian name for Saturn.

REPHIDIM (Rĕph′ ĭ dĭm) Site in the wilderness where the Hebrews stopped on their way to Canaan just prior to reaching Sinai (Ex. 17:1; 19:2). There the people complained of thirst, and God commanded Moses to strike the rock out of which would come water. While the Hebrews were encamped at Rephidim, the Amalekites came against them and were defeated by Israel under Joshua's leadership. Moses' father-in-law, Jethro, came to Rephidim and helped the leader delegate his authority over the people (18:13–26). The exact location is unknown.

REPROACH KJV term with five related senses: *1.* A source of blame, discredit, or disgrace due to barrenness (Gen. 30:23; Luke 1:25); rape by the uncircumcised (Gen. 34:2–5); uncircumcision (Josh. 5:9); forced mutilation (1 Sam. 11:2); Jerusalem in ruins (Neh. 2:17; Ps. 89:41); illness (Ps. 31:11); fasting (Ps. 69:10); military defeat (Ps. 79:4); sin (Prov. 14:34); mistreatment of parents (Prov. 19:26); singleness (Isa. 4:1); widowhood (Isa. 54:4); famine (Ezek. 36:30). *2.* A state of shame, disgrace, or humiliation (Neh. 1:3; Job 19:5; 27:6; Ps. 15:3). *3.* An object of scorn (Jer. 6:10; 29:18; 42:18; 44:8). *4.* An expression of rebuke or disapproval; a taunt (1 Sam. 17:26; 2 Kings 19:4,16; Neh. 4:4; 5:9). *5.* To express disappointment or disapproval (Ruth 2:15; Neh. 6:13). Of special interest theologically is reproach suffered for the sake of God (Pss. 69:7,9; 89:51) or Christ (Luke 6:22; 2 Cor. 12:10; Heb. 10:33; 11:26; 1 Pet. 4:14) and the reproach Christ suffered (Rom. 15:3; Heb. 13:13). See *Shame and Honor.*

REPROBATE KJV term used in two senses: *1.* That which fails to meet a test and is thus rejected as unworthy or unacceptable, as impure silver (Jer. 6:30); or persons (2 Cor. 13:5–7; Titus 1:16). *2.* That which is depraved or without morals (Rom. 1:28; 2 Tim. 3:8). NAS and RSV used reprobate to mean one rejected by God (Ps. 15:4; compare REB, TEV).

REPTILES See *Animals; Creeping Things.*

REPUTATION KJV term for high public esteem or regard applied to: Gamaliel (Acts 5:34); Jerusalem apostles (Gal. 2:2); Epaphroditus (Phil. 2:29). The KJV translation, "But made himself of no reputation" (Phil. 2:7) is an interpretation of *heauton ekenōsen* meaning, he "emptied himself" (NAS, NRSV).

RESEN (Rē′ sėn) Place name meaning, "fountain head." City Nimrod founded between Nineveh and Calah (Gen. 10:12). Probably modern Salemijeh two and a half miles northwest of Nimrud.

RESERVOIR Place for catching and storing water for later use, either agricultural (2 Chron. 26:10; Eccl. 2:6) or as an urban supply in anticipation of a siege (2 Kings 20:20; Isa. 22:8b–11). Reservoirs were a necessity in most of Palestine where seasonal rains were the major water source.

Large cistern (water reservoir) with column in center at ancient Pergamum.

RESH (Rēsh) Twentieth letter in the Hebrew alphabet, which the KJV used as heading for the eight verses of Psalms 119:153–160 which each begin with the letter.

RESHEPH (Rē′ shĕph) Personal name meaning, "flame." An Ephraimite (1 Chron. 7:25).

RESIN NIV translation of *bdellium* (Gen. 2:12; compare Num. 11:7). See *Bdellium.*

RESPECT OF PERSONS Honor and partiality. Respect or honor is to be shown to older men (Lev. 19:32; compare Lam. 5:12), to public officials (Rom. 13:7), to parents (1 Tim. 3:4), masters (1 Pet. 2:18), and Christian leaders (1 Thess. 5:12). Christians are to live in such a way that they command the respect of neighbors and thus serve as effective witnesses (1 Thess. 4:12). Scripture repeatedly affirms that God is no respecter of persons, that is, that God does not show partiality; thus God's people are to refrain from prejudice. See *Partiality.*

RESTITUTION (Rĕs tĭ tū′ tion) The act of returning what has wrongfully been taken or replacing what has been lost or damaged and the Divine restoration of all things to their original order.

Human Restitution The Law required "trespass offerings" to be made for sins against a neighbor (theft, deception, dishonesty, extortion, keeping lost property, or damaging property). Such crimes involved "unfaithfulness" towards God and disrupted fellowship and peace among the people. They were to be atoned for by a guilt offering to God, and "restitution" to the wronged neighbor. Atonement and forgiveness of the sin were received after restitution had been made to the victim. The sin offering to God always followed the act of restitution. Old Testament law established a principle of "punishment to fit the crime" (life for life, eye for eye, tooth for tooth, wound for wound). Restitution was consistent with this concept of equity. The stolen property was to be returned, or "full" compensation was to be made. The guidelines for making complete restitution also included a provision for punitive damages (up to five times what had been lost), justice that moved beyond "an eye for an eye." Provisions were made for complications in this process (Ex. 22:3). The act of making restitution to a victim was so closely identified with the atoning sacrifice made to God, that the two expressions could be seen as elements of the same command. Neither could stand alone. Specific examples of this law in operation are not found, but the principle in action is found (1 Kings 20:34; 2 Kings 8:6; Neh. 5:10–12). There is no legal or ritual application of this command in the New Testament; however, the principle of restitution is clearly pictured in the story of Zacchaeus (Luke 19:1–10). Jesus implicitly validated the practice when he admonished followers to "be reconciled" to a brother before offering a gift to God (Matt. 5:23–24).

Divine Restitution The New Testament word is found only once (Acts 3:21) and can be translated "restoration." It describes the future work of God that will reestablish all "things" to their pristine order and purpose. The implication here is not the restoration of persons, but of the created order, that is, the universal renewal of the earth. This divine restoration will accompany the return and triumph of Christ (1 Cor. 15:25–28). *Ken Massey*

RESURRECTION The doctrine, event, and act of persons being brought from death to unending life at the close of the age.

Old Testament The preexilic portions of the Old Testament contain no statements which point certainly to a hope of resurrection from the dead even though some of Israel's neighbors had such a belief. Death is the end of human existence, the destruction of life (Gen. 3:19; Job 30:23). In isolated instances revivification occurs (being brought back to life from death but only as a temporary escape from final death; 1 Kings 17:17–22; 2 Kings 4:18–37; 13:21). In addition,

God took from the earth two Old Testament figures before their deaths: Enoch (Gen. 5:24) and Elijah (2 Kings 2:9–11). The scarcity of these statements and the lack of reflection on their meanings, however, point to the absence of any consistent doctrinal conception of resurrection from the dead.

Similarly, the Psalms are bereft of clear thought on resurrection. Many of the songs, however, express a hope that communion with God, begun on earth, will have no end (as in Pss. 16:11; 49:15; 73:24). The Song of Moses (Deut. 32) and the Song of Hannah (1 Sam. 2) assert that Yahweh kills and makes alive. These expressions of hope in God may not suggest a doctrine of resurrection from the dead. They at least confess a conviction that the living God is able to intervene in life's darkest hours. They grope for a firm hope in justice and help beyond the grave. They may reflect the beginnings of a doctrine of resurrection.

The prophets proclaimed hope for the future in terms of national renewal (see Hos. 6:1–3; Ezek. 37). So pointed is the prophetic expression of national hope that the New Testament writers sometimes used the language of the prophets to expound the doctrine of resurrection (compare Hos. 13:14; 1 Cor. 15:55). The prophetic statements, however, do not necessarily attest to hope of individual resurrection from the dead but profess the sovereignty of God over all His subjects, even death.

On the other hand, Isaiah 26:19 and Daniel 12:2 decidedly teach a belief in resurrection. The Old Testament emphasis on the sovereignty of God in all matters easily led to the prophetic statements.

The Old Testament statements about resurrection are scant and do not reveal clear theological reflection. The emphasis upon Yahweh as the God of present life tended to make Judaism a this-worldly religion. The future was generally interpreted as a national future under the sovereign rule of Yahweh. In New Testament times the Saduccees still did not believe in resurrection. The belief, however, in God as sovereign Lord over all, even death, eventually flowered in the brief but salient assertions of the Books of Isaiah and Daniel and possibly in the Psalms. See *Eschatology; Future Hope; Sheol.*

New Testament Jesus' preaching presupposed a doctrine of resurrection. Opposition by the Saducees, who denied the resurrection, gave Jesus opportunity to assert His own thought on the matter (Mark 12:18–27; Matt. 22:23–33; Luke 20:27–38; compare Deut. 25:5–10).

John's Gospel presents Jesus as the mediator of resurrection who gives to believers the life given Him by His Father (John 6:53–58). Jesus is the resurrection and the life (11:24–26). Jesus pointed to a resurrection of the righteous to eternal life and of the wicked to eternal punishment (Matt. 8:11–

12; 25:31–34,41–46; John 5:28–29). In His postresurrection appearances Jesus had a body that was both spiritual (John 20:19,26) and physical (John 20:20,27; 21:13,15) in nature.

The greatest biblical exponent of resurrection was Paul. For him, resurrection was the final event which would usher Christians out of the bodily struggle of the present age into the bodily glory which will accompany Jesus' second coming (Phil. 3:20–21). In resurrection, God's new creation will reach completion (2 Cor. 5:17–21). The bedrock of hope for Christian resurrection is the resurrection of Christ, the foundation of gospel preaching (1 Cor. 15:12–20). Those who follow Christ are organically related to Christ in His resurrection from the dead; Christ is the first fruits of an upcoming harvest (1 Cor. 15:20–23). Destruction awaits those who do not follow Christ (Phil. 3:19).

Paul's discourses on the nature of the resurrected body broadens the Old Testament idea of a restored Israel to include the redemption of persons complete with bodies. Paul viewed the human person as a psychosomatic unity. He recognizes no truth in the Greek idea of a separation of body and soul. See *Humanity.* Persons live beyond time not because of any inherent immortality but because God gives them life (2 Cor. 5:1–10). Those united to Christ in faith become not only one with Him in spirit but also one with Him in body (1 Cor. 6:15). The resurrected body will be a spiritual body, different from the present physical body (1 Cor. 15:35–50); but it will have continuity with the present body because Christ redeems the whole person (Rom. 8:23).

The New Testament unquestionably affirms a doctrine of resurrection of all persons from the dead. Humanity has a corporate destiny to encounter just and divine response to faithfulness and unfaithfulness (Acts 24:15). A resurrection body and life in the consummated kingdom of God will characterize the resurrection of those who follow Christ. *William L. Hendricks*

RESURRECTION OF JESUS CHRIST The bodily, living appearance of Jesus of Nazareth after He died and was buried, providing certain hope for resurrection of believers. The Greek term for resurrection, *anastasis,* literally means, "to stand again." In the pagan world it was associated with the cycle of nature and the nature gods, or the survival of a "spiritual part" of a person after death. Because of Jesus Christ and His standing up again from the dead, resurrection has come to mean the restoration of the whole self by God who gave life and creates it anew in the heavenly kingdom. New Testament accounts of the resurrection fall into three categories: the empty tomb, appearances of Jesus before His ascension, and appearances of Jesus after His ascension.

The earliest written account of the resurrection

of Jesus is 1 Corinthians 15:3–8. Paul emphasized the appearances of the resurrected Christ to His followers. Paul mentioned an appearance to Cephas (compare Luke 24:34). Then Jesus appeared to the twelve (compare Luke 24:36–43). The appearance to the five hundred, some of whom had died by the time Paul wrote 1 Corinthians, is supposed by some to refer to the ascension (Acts 1:9–11). The appearance of James is nowhere else recorded. Tradition asserts that this was James the brother of Jesus, the author of the Book of James (see Acts 15:13). The second appearance to the disciples may be equated with Jesus' presentation of Himself to Thomas a week after the first appearance to the apostles (John 20:24–29). Paul mentioned last the appearance of the ascended Christ to Paul himself, an obvious reference to Saul's conversion experience (Acts 9:1–9).

Matthew reported that two Marys, Magdalene and the mother of James and Joses (Matt. 28:1–2; see 27:56,61) came to the tomb and witnessed a violent earthquake. The angel who rolled away the stone covering the tomb entrance told the women that Jesus was risen. They were invited to view the empty tomb, then to go and tell the disciples that Jesus was risen and was going to Galilee. Immediately, the resurrected Christ greeted them, urged them not to be afraid, to go and tell the "brothers" that He would meet them in Galilee. The soldiers posted at the tomb reported to their employers, the chief priests, "everything that happened"; and the entire guard was bribed to keep silent. It is not clear whether the soldiers actually saw the resurrected Christ Himself. It is assumed because of the other New Testament accounts that the resurrected Christ appeared only to believers. Matthew's final report of Jesus' resurrection is on a mountain in Galilee to His eleven disciples where He gave them the Great Commission (Matt. 28:16–20).

Mark's account of the resurrection (ch. 16) reports that three women came to the tomb wondering how they would have access to the body in order to use the spices applied to the dead. They discovered the stone rolled away and a young man in white in the tomb. He calmed their fears, told them that Jesus was risen, and that Jesus would meet the disciples in Galilee. The women left bewildered and frightened. The most ancient and reliable manuscripts of Mark end with 16:8. The long ending of Mark records several other appearances of Jesus: to Mary Magdalene (see John 20:11–18); to two walking in the country (see Luke 24:13–32); to the eleven as they were eating (see Luke 24:36–43).

Luke 24 records the visit of three women to the tomb where two angels said that He was risen. The angels reminded the women of Jesus' teachings about His death and resurrection. The women told the unbelieving disciples about the empty tomb, and Peter investigated the empty tomb. Jesus appeared to Cleopas and another disciple on the way to Emmaus and gave them a prophetic overview concerning the Messiah. At supper He was revealed as the risen Christ and disappeared. The two returned to Jerusalem to tell the disciples and heard that Simon had seen the risen Lord. After the report of the two, Jesus appeared to the apostles and assured them He was not a ghost. He showed His hands and feet, and in the most physical act of the resurrection He ate a piece of fish (v. 43). He then reminded them of prophecies of the Messiah and commissioned them on the mission task. Luke's closing paragraph is the account of the ascension. The Lukan narrative is taken up in Acts (1:6–11). Jesus taught for forty days. He told the disciples to await the Spirit in Jerusalem. When the disciples asked questions about the kingdom, He said it was a question beyond their comprehension, repeated His missionary commission, and ascended as they watched and were assured by angels of His return.

John's Gospel adds remarkable details to the other three. In the fourth Gospel another disciple (John?) accompanied Peter to the tomb. Jesus appeared to Mary Magdalene and told her not to detain him—a better translation than "do not touch me." Jesus appeared twice to the disciples in the upper room, the second time a week after the first for the sake of the unbelieving Thomas. His classic confession "my Lord and my God" (John 20:28) became the appropriate response of all believing hearts. In John 21 Jesus appeared to seven disciples in Galilee and prepared their breakfast. The occasion was the commissioning of Peter to his special ministry after Peter's three-time confession of his love for Christ, paralleling his earlier three-time denial of Christ.

The risen Christ appeared to Stephen (Acts 7:55–56), to Saul/Paul (Acts 9:1–6), and to John the Seer (Rev. 1). All of these accounts are not easy to correlate, but a composite picture reveals the following facts. The tomb was empty. Jesus appeared to many believing disciples, women and men, on numerous occasions. Jesus instructed the earliest believers about the prophetic and theological meaning of His death and resurrection. The resurrection of Jesus involved His physical body; but His resurrected life was a new kind of life called into being by God, the Effector of the resurrection (Acts 2:24). Paul, who gave the first account of the resurrection of Christ (1 Cor. 15:3–8), provided the full meaning and importance of the resurrection of Christ. Because of the resurrection of Christ, we have assurance of the resurrection of all persons—some to salvation; some to perdition—vouchsafed in the resurrection of Christ. That is God's ultimate answer to the problem of death (1 Cor. 15:12–58). See *Ascension; Christ; Jesus; Resurrection. William L. Hendricks*

RETINUE NAS, REB, NRSV, REB term for the attendants of the queen of Sheba (1 Kings 10:2; KJV, train; NIV, caravan).

RETURN OF CHRIST See *Eschatology; Future Hope; Millennium; Parousia; Second Coming.*

REU (Rē′ ū) Personal name meaning, "friend, companion." Descendant of Shem (Gen. 11:18–21; 1 Chron. 1:25), possibly the ancestor of a Semitic tribe associated with Ra'ilu, an island in the Euphrates below Anat.

REUBEN(ITES) (Reu′ běn ītes) Eldest son of Jacob, born to Leah (Gen. 29:32) while the couple was living with her father, Laban, in Paddan-aram, and the clan or tribe descended from him. Among his acts recorded in the Bible, Reuben found mandrakes (out of which a love potion probably was made for his mother to use with Jacob 30:14,16–17), and had sexual relations with one of his father's concubines (35:22), for which he later was chastised (49:4). Reuben felt compassion for young Joseph when his brothers wanted to kill the brash dreamer (37:21–22), and was willing to be responsible to his father for Benjamin's welfare when the unknown Joseph commanded that the youngest brother be brought to Egypt (42:37).

The tribe which was named for Reuben held a place of honor among the other tribes. The territory the tribe inherited was just east of the Dead Sea and was the first parcel of land to be bestowed (Num. 32).

REUEL (Reu′ ĕl) Personal name meaning, "friend of God." *1.* Son of Esau and ancestor of several Edomite clans (Gen. 36:4,10,13,17; 1 Chron. 1:35,37). *2.* Exodus 2:18 identifies Reuel as the "father" of Zipporah, Moses' wife. Numbers 10:29 presents Reuel as the father of Hobab, Moses' father-in-law. Elsewhere Moses' father-in-law is called Jethro. The tradition is also divided regarding the background of Moses' father-in-law, either Midianite (Ex. 2:16; 3:1) or Kenite (Judg. 1:16; 4:11). See *Jethro. 3.* A Gadite (Num. 2:14). *4.* A Benjaminite (1 Chron. 9:8).

REUMAH (Reu′ mah) Personal name meaning, "coral." Nahor's concubine, an ancestress of several Aramaean tribes living northwest of Damascus (Gen. 22:24).

REVELATION OF GOD The content and process of God's making Himself known to people. All knowledge of God comes by way of revelation. Human knowledge of God is revealed knowledge since God, and He alone, gives it. He bridges the gap between Himself and His creatures, disclosing Himself and His will to them. By God alone can God be known.

Modern thought often questions the possibility and/or reality of revelation. Biblical faith affirms revelation is real because the personal Creator God has chosen to let His human creatures know Him. The question remains, "How can a person know God." The Bible appears to distinguish two ways of knowing God, general and special revelation.

Biblical emphasis points to Jesus Christ as God's final revelation. God has provided ongoing generations of believers a source of knowledge about Himself and His Son. That source is the Bible.

Definition The word *revelation* means an uncovering, a removal of the veil, a disclosure of what was previously unknown. Revelation of God is God's manifestation of Himself to humankind in such a way that men and women can know and fellowship with Him. Jesus explained to Peter: "Blessed are you, Simon son of Jonah, for this was not revealed to you by man, but by my Father in heaven" (Matt. 16:17 NIV). The knowledge of Jesus' sonship was not attained by human discovery, nor could it have been; it came from God alone.

All Christians recognize that God has acted and spoken in history, revealing Himself to His creatures. Yet, a variety of opinions seek to define what constitutes revelation.

General Revelation The physical world—nature—is not a part of God as my hand is a part of me. Yet, God might reveal Himself through His actions in that world. Besides saying or writing things, persons may reveal facts about themselves in other ways, such as physical gestures or facial expressions. Sometimes persons' actions communicate whether they are selfish or generous, clumsy or skillful. A grimace, a smile, or a frown can often be telling. Transferring these things to a theological context is not simple, because God is not visible. He does not have facial features or bodily parts with which to gesture. To say God reveals Himself through nature means that through the events of the physical world God communicates to us things about Himself that we would otherwise not know.

What sort of things might God tell us in this manner? Paul explained "What can be known about God is plain to them, for God Himself made it plain. Ever since God created the world, his invisible qualities both his eternal power and his divine nature, have been clearly seen; they are perceived in the things that God has made. So those people have no excuse at all" (Rom. 1:20 TEV). The psalmist (Ps. 19:1) saw the glory of God through the spectacles of special revelation. What the psalmist saw was objectively and genuinely there. We can rephrase these observations to say that all that can be known about God in a *natural* sense has been revealed in nature. This is what we call natural or general revelation. General revelation is universal in the sense that it is *God's self-disclosure of Himself in a general way to all people at all times in all places.* General revelation occurs through (1) nature, (2) in our experience

and in our conscience, and (3) in history.

In the wonders of the heavens and in the beauty of the earth God manifests Himself. Jesus taught that God "causes His sun to rise on the evil and the good, and sends rain on the righteous and the unrighteous" (Matt. 5:45 NAS), thus revealing His goodness to all. "The living God, who made the heaven and the earth and the sea and all that is in them . . . has not left himself without a witness in doing good—giving you rains from heaven and fruitful seasons, and filling you with food and your hearts with joy" (Acts 14:15–17 NRSV). God makes Himself known in the continuing care and provision for humankind. The universe as a whole serves the Creator's purposes as a vehicle of God's self-manifestation.

God also reveals himself in men and women. They are made in the "image" and "likeness" of God (Gen. 1:26–27). Humans, as a direct creation of God, are a mirror or reflection of God. People are God's unique workmanship evidenced by their place of dominion over the rest of creation; in their capacity to reason, feel, and imagine; in their freedom to act and respond; and in their sense of right and wrong (Gen. 1:28; Rom. 2:14,15). Especially through this moral sense God reveals Himself in the consciences of men and women. The fact that religious belief and practice is universal confirms the apostle's statements in Romans 2. Yet, the creatures who worship, pray, build temples, idols and shrines, and seek after God in diverse ways do not glorify God as God nor give Him thanks (Rom. 1:21–23). Nevertheless, because each person has been given the capacity for receiving God's general revelation, they are responsible for their actions.

God manifests Himself in the workings of history. All of history, rightly understood, bears the imprint of God's activity and thus has a theological character. Primarily, God is revealed in history through the rise and fall of peoples and nations (compare Acts 17:22–31).

God's general revelation is plain, whether in nature, in human conscience, or in history. Even though it is plain, it is often misinterpreted because sinful and finite humans are trying to understand a perfect and infinite God. What we have seen so far is compatible with the following:

(1) Religious belief is a nearly universal human phenomenon.

(2) Such religious belief is implanted by God.

(3) All people ought to acknowledge God on the basis of what they learned from the world around them.

(4) All people believe in God and show their belief even though they do not admit it.

(5) No one, no matter how seemingly insignificant or weak-minded can be excused for missing God's revelation.

The light of nature is not sufficient to give the knowledge of God necessary for salvation. For

God's power (Rom. 1:20), goodness (Matt. 5:45), and righteousness (Rom. 2:14–15) have been revealed, but not His salvific grace. That is revealed only through special revelation. Special revelation is necessary to instruct people how to worship God rightly. God in His general revelation reveals Himself, but because of our sinfulness, humans pervert the reception of His general revelation, a revelation so plain it leaves all without excuse. It is as if a lawyer were offered the information necessary to solve a case, yet chose perversely to ignore it.

In sum, humans lack the willingness to come to a pure and clear knowledge of God. Men and women suppress God's truth because they do not like the truth about God. They do not like the God to which the truth leads them so they invent substitute gods and religions instead. The universality of religion on earth is evidence of truths discussed above. According to Paul, the act of suppressing the awareness of God and His demands warps our reason and conscience. Because of this rejection of God, He righteously reveals His wrath against humankind. God's general revelation does not bring one into a saving relationship with God; it does reveal God to His creatures and they are, therefore, responsible for their response. This view of general revelation can only be accepted through special revelation.

Special Revelation God has revealed Himself in nature, human experience, and history, but sin's entrance into the world has changed the revelation as well as the interpretation of it. What is needed to understand God's self-disclosure fully is His special revelation. Divine truth exists outside of special revelation, but it is consistent with and supplemental to, not a substitute for special revelation.

In contrast to God's general revelation which is available to all people, *God's special revelation is available to specific people at specific times in specific places, it is available now only by consultation of sacred Scripture.* Special revelation is first of all particular. God reveals Himself with His people. These people of God are the children of Abraham, whether by natural (Gen. 12:1–3) or spiritual descent (Gal. 3:16,29). Does this mean that God confines knowledge of Himself to a particular people? Not necessarily, because God's general revelation has been given to all, though perverted and rejected by the universal wickedness of humankind. He now chooses to whom and through whom He will make Himself known. As with Abraham, God said: "In thee shall all families of the earth be blessed" (Gen. 12:3). God manifests Himself in a particular manner to His people so they will be a channel of blessing to all others.

Special revelation is also *progressive.* Biblical history witnesses to a developing disclosure of God, His will, and His truth in the Old and New Testaments. The development is not contradictory in any fashion. It is complementary and supplementary to what had been previously revealed. We should not think of the progress from untruth to truth, but from a lesser to a fuller revelation (Heb. 1:1–3). The revelation of the law in the Old Testament is not superseded by the gospel, but is fulfilled in it.

Special revelation is primarily *redemptive* and *personal.* In recognition of the human predicament God chose at the very beginning to disclose Himself in a more direct way. Within time and space God has acted and spoken to redeem the human race from its own self-imposed evil. Through calling people, miracles, the Exodus, covenant making, and ultimately through Jesus Christ, God has revealed Himself in history.

The ultimate point of God's personal revelation is in Jesus Christ. In Him, the Word became flesh (John. 1:1,14;14:9). The Old Testament promise of salvation as a divine gift to people who cannot save themselves has been fulfilled in the gift of His Son. The redemptive revelation of God is that Jesus Christ has borne the sins of fallen humanity, has died in their place, and has been raised to assure justification. This is the *fixed center* of special revelation.

Special revelation is also *propositional.* It includes *not only those personal, redemptive acts* in history, but *also the prophetic-apostolic interpretation of those events.* God's self-disclosure is propositional in that it made known truths *about* Him to His people. Knowledge about someone precedes intimate knowledge of someone. The primary purpose of revelation is not necessarily to enlarge the scope of one's knowledge. Yet, propositional knowledge about is for the purpose of personal knowledge of.

We can thus affirm that special revelation has three stages: (1) redemption in history, ultimately centering in the work of the Lord Jesus Christ; (2) the Bible, written revelation interpreting what He has done for the redemption of men and women; (3) the work of the Holy Spirit in the lives of individuals and the corporate life of the church, applying God's revelation to the minds and hearts of His people. As a result, men and women receive Jesus Christ as Lord and Savior and are enabled to follow Him faithfully in a believing, covenant community until life's end.

The content of special revelation is primarily God Himself. Mystery remains even in God's self-revelation. God does not fully reveal Himself to any person. God, does, however, reveal himself to persons to the degree they can receive it. Special revelation is the declaration of truth about God, His character, and His action and relationship with His creation to bring all creation under Christ, the one head (Eph. 1:9–10).

The proper setting of special revelation is Christian faith. God makes Himself known to those who receive His revelation in faith (Heb. 11:1,6). Faith is the glad recognition of truth, the reception of God's revelation without reservation or hesitation (Rom. 10:17).

For today, the Bible is of crucial importance. Through the Bible the Spirit witnesses to individuals of God's grace and the need of faith response. In the Bible we learn of God's redemption of sinners in Christ Jesus. Our faith response to God's Word and acts, recorded and interpreted by the prophets and apostles, calls for us to embrace with humble teachableness, without finding fault, whatever is taught in Holy Scripture.

In sum we can say that God has initiated the revelation of Himself to men and women. This revelation is understandable to humankind and makes it possible to know God and grow in relationship with Him. God's self-manifestation provides information about Himself for the purpose of leading men and women into God's presence. For believers today, the Bible is the source of God's revelation. In the written word we can identify God, know and understand something about Him, His will, and His work, and point others to Him. Special revelation is not generally speculative. The Bible primarily speaks on matters of cosmology and history where these issues touch the nature of faith. God has manifested Himself incarnationally through human language, human thought, and human action as ultimately demonstrated in the incarnation of Jesus Christ.

David S. Dockery

REVELATION, THE BOOK OF The last book of the Bible, an apocalyptic work pointing to future hope and calling for present faithfulness. Revelation is a work of intensity, forged in the flames of the author's personal tribulation. It employs the language of biblical allusion and apocalyptic symbolism to express the heights and depths of the author's visionary experience.

To encourage Christian faithfulness, the Revelation points to the glorious world to come (a world of "no more death or mourning or crying or pain," 21:4 NIV; compare 7:16) at the reappearing of the crucified and risen Jesus. This now enthroned Lord will return to conclude world history (and the tribulations of the readers) with the destruction of God's enemies, the final salvation of His own people, and the creation of a new heaven and a new earth. The intensity of the prophet's experience is matched only by the richness of the apocalyptic symbolism he employed to warn his readers of the impending disasters and temptations which would require their steadfast allegiance to the risen Lord. To be sure, the Lord will come in power and majesty, but not before His enemies have exercised a terrible (albeit limited by the divine mercy) attack upon those who "hold to the testimony of Jesus."

Author According to early Christian traditions, the Gospel of John, the three Epistles of John, and the Revelation were all written by the apostle John. The Revelation is the only one of these books that claims to be written by someone named John. Though the author does not claim to be the *apostle* John, it seems unlikely that any other first-century Christian leader was associated closely enough with the churches of Asia Minor to have referred to himself simply as John. There are certainly some differences in style and language between the fourth Gospel and the Revelation, but, regardless of the problems related to the authorship of the fourth Gospel, it is not implausible to assume that the John of the Revelation was in fact John the apostle, son of Zebedee. See *John.*

Setting The author's situation was one of suffering. He was a "fellow partaker in the tribulation" which is "in Jesus," who, because of his testimony to Jesus, was exiled to the island of Patmos (1:9 NAS). The situation of the recipients seemed not yet so dire. To be sure, a faithful Christian in Pergamum had suffered death (2:13), and the church in Smyrna was warned of a time of impending persecution (2:10); but the persecutions described in the Revelation were still largely anticipated at the time of John's writing.

Date Scholars have traditionally suggested two dates for the writing of the Revelation based upon the repeated references to persecution (1:9; 2:2–3,10,13; 3:9–10; 6:10–11; 7:14–17; 11:7; 12:13—13:17; 14:12–20; 19:2; 21:4). From about A.D. 150, Christian authors usually referred to Domitian's reign (A.D. 81–96) as the time of John's writing, but there is no historical consensus supporting a persecution of Christians under Domitian while hard evidence does exist for a persecution under Nero (A.D. 54–68). In this century, most New Testament scholars have opted for the later date under Domitian (about A.D. 95), though there has been a resurgence of opinion (including this author's) arguing for a setting just following the reign of Nero (about A.D. 68). Whichever date is chosen, however, the setting must be closely related to a time of persecution for the author and an anticipated expansion of persecution for the original audience.

Type of Literature The Revelation has traditionally been called an apocalypse. Although the genre itself was not literarily acknowledged in the first century, what we now call "apocalyptic literature" certainly existed. In any case, John called his work a "prophecy" (1:3; 22:10,19), but also gave it some features of an epistle (1:4–7; 22:21).

Outline

   I. Introduction (1:1–8)

   II. John's Vision on the Island of Patmos (1:9–20)

   III. Letters to the Seven Churches (2:1—3:22)

   IV. The Sovereignty of the Creator God Committed to the Crucified and Now Enthroned Lamb (4:1—5:14)

   V. The Enthroned Lamb's Judgments Via

Millennial Perspectives On Revelation

	Amillennial	Historical Premillennial	Dispensational Premillennial
	Viewpoint that the present age of Christ's rule in the church is the millennium; Holds to one resurrection and judgment marking the end of history as we know it and the beginning of life eternal	Viewpoint that Christ will reign on earth for 1000 years following His Second Coming; Saints will be resurrected at the beginning of the millennium, non-believers at the end, followed by judgment	Viewpoint that after the battle of Armageddon, Christ will rule through the Jews for a literal 1000 years accompanied by two resurrections and at least three judgments
Book of Revelation	Current history written in code to confound enemies and encourage Asian Christians; message applies to all Christians	Immediate application to Asian Christians throughout the ages; applies to all Christians, but the visions also apply to a great future event	"Unveiling" of theme of Christ among churches in present dispensation, also as Judge and King in dispensations to come
Seven candlesticks (1:13)	Churches		Churches, plus end-time application
Seven stars (1:16,20)	Pastors	Symbolizes heavenly or supernatural character of the church (some believe refers to pastors)	Pastors or saints
Churches addressed (chaps. 2-3)	Specific historical situations throughout churches throughout history represent periods of church history	Specific historical situations, truths apply to churches throughout the ages; do not represent periods of church history	Specific historical situations and to all churches throughout the ages; shows progress of churches' spiritual state until end of church age
Twenty-four elders (4:4,10; 5:8,14)	Twelve patriarchs and twelve apostles; together symbolize all the redeemed	Company of angels who help execute God's rule (or elders represent twenty-four priestly and Levitical orders)	The rewarded church; also represents twelve patriarchs and twelve apostles

	Amillennial	Historical Premillennial	Dispensational Premillennial
Sealed book (5:1-9)	Scroll of history; shows God carrying out His redemptive purpose in history	Contains prophecy of end events of chapters 7-22	Title deed to the world
144,000 (7:4-8)	Redeemed on earth who will be protected against God's wrath	Church on threshold of great tribulation	Jewish converts of tribulation period who witness to Gentiles (same as 14:1)
Great Multitude (7:9-10)	Uncountable multitude in heaven praising God for their salvation	Church, having gone through great tribulation, seen in heaven	Gentiles redeemed during tribulation period through witness of 144,000
Great tribulation (first reference in 7:14)	Persecution faced by Asian Christians of John's time; symbolic of tribulation that occurs throughout history	Period at end-time of unexplained trouble, before Christ's return; church will go through it; begins with seventh seal (18:1) which includes trumpets 1-6 (8:2 to 14:20)	Period at end-time of unexplained trouble referred to in 7:14 and described in chapters 11-18; lasts three-and-one-half years, the latter half of seven-year period between rapture and millennium
"Star" (9:4)	Personified evil	Represents an angelic figure divinely commissioned to carry out God's purpose	The leader of apostasy during the great tribulation
Forty-two months (11:2); 1,260 days (11:3)	Indefinite duration of pagan desolation	A symbolic number representing period of evil with reference to last days of age	Half of seven-year tribulation period
Two witnesses (11:3-10)	Spread of gospel in first century	Two actual historical persons at end of time who witness to Israel	A witnessing remnant of Jews in Jerusalem testifying to the coming kingdom and calling Israel to repent

*Postmillennialism—Viewpoint that Christ's reign on earth is spiritual not physical. Christ returns after the millennium that is established by gospel preaching.

Millennial Perspectives On Revelation

	Amillennial	Historical Premillennial	Dispensational Premillennial
Sodom and Egypt (11:8)	Rome as seat of Empire	Earthly Jerusalem	Earthly Jerusalem
Woman (12:1-6)	True people of God under Old Covenants (true Israel)	True people of God under Old and New	Indicates Israel, not church; key is comparison with Genesis 37:9
Great red dragon (12:3)	All views identify as Satan		
Manchild (12:4-5)	Christ at His birth, life events, and crucifixion, whom Satan sought to kill	Christ, whose work Satan seeks to destroy	Christ but also the church (head and body); caught up on throne indicates rapture of church
1,260 days (12:6)	Indefinite time	Symbolic number representing period of evil with special reference to last days of age	First half of great tribulation after church is raptured
Sea beast (13:1)	Emperor Domitian, personification of Roman Empire (same as in chap. 17)	Antichrist, here shown as embodiment of the four beasts in Daniel 7	A new Rome, satanic federation of nations that come out of old Roman Empire
Seven heads (13:1)	Roman emperors	Great power, shows kinship with dragon	Seven stages of Roman Empire; sixth was imperial Rome (John's day); last will be federation of nations
Ten horns (13:1)	Symbolize power	Kings, represent limited crowns (ten) against Christ's many	Ten powers that will combine to make the federation of nations of new Rome
Earth beast (13:11)	*Concilia*, Roman body in cities responsible for emperor worship	Organized religion as servant of first beast during great tribulation period; headed by a false prophet	Antichrist, who will head apostate religion, a Jewish leader described in Daniel 11:36-45 (some identify as assistant to the Antichrist)
666 (13:18)	Imperfection, evil; personified as Domitian	Symbolic of evil, short of 777; if a personage meant, he is unknown but will be known at the proper time	Not known, but will be known when time comes
144,000 on Mount Zion (14:1)	Total body of redeemed	Redeemed in heaven	Redeemed Jews gathered in earthly Jerusalem during millennial kingdom
River of blood (14:20)	Symbol of infinite punishment for the wicked	Means God's radical judgment crushes evil thoroughly	Scene of wrath and carnage that will occur in Palestine
Babylon (woman—17:5)	Historical Rome	Capital city of future Antichrist	Apostate church of the future
Beast	Domitian	Antichrist	Head of satanic federation of nations of revived Roman Empire; linked with apostate church (seventh head)
Seven mountains (17:9)	Pagan Rome, which was built on seven hills	Indicate power, so here means a succession of empires, last of which is end-time Babylon	Rome, revived at end-time
Seven heads (17:7) and seven kings (17:10)	Roman emperors from Augustus to Titus, excluding three brief rules	Five past godless kingdoms; sixth was Rome; seventh would arise in end-time	Five distinct forms of Roman government prior to John; sixth was imperial Rome; seventh will be revived Roman Empire
Ten horns (17:7) and ten kings (17:12)	Vassal kings who ruled with Rome's permission	Symbolic of earthly powers that will be subservient to Antichrist	Ten kingdoms arising in future out of revived Roman Empire

Millennial Perspectives On Revelation

	Amillennial	Historical Premillennial	Dispensational Premillennial
Waters (17:15)	People ruled by Roman Empire	Indicates complex civilization	People dominated by apostate church
Bride, wife (19:7)	Total of all the redeemed		The church; does not include Old Testament saints or tribulation saints
Marriage supper (19:9)	Climax of the age; symbolizes complete union of Christ with His people	Union of Christ with His people at His Coming	Union of Christ with His church accompanied by Old Testament saints and tribulation saints
One on white horse (19:11-16)	Vision of Christ's victory over pagan Rome; return of Christ occurs in connection with events of 20:7-10	Second coming of Christ	
Battle of Armageddon (19:19-21; see 16:16)	Not literally at end of time but symbolizes power of God's word overcoming evil; principle applies to all ages	Literal event of some kind at end-time but not literal battle with military weapons; occurs at Christ's return at beginning of millennium	Literal bloody battle at Armageddon (valley of Megiddo) at end of great tribulation between kings of the East and federation of nations of new Rome; they are all defeated by blast from Christ's mouth and then millennium begins
Great supper (19:17)	Stands in contrast to marriage supper		Concludes series of judgments and opens way for kingdom to be established
Binding of Satan (20:2)	Symbolic of Christ's resurrection victory over Satan	Curbing of Satan's power during the millennium	
Millennium (20:2-6)	Symbolic reference to period from Christ's first coming to His second	A historical event, though length of one thousand years may be symbolic, after Armageddon during which Christ rules with His people	A literal one thousand year period after the church age during which Christ rules with His people but especially through the Jews
Those on thrones (20:4)	Martyrs in heaven, their presence with God is a judgment on those who killed them	Saints and martyrs who rule with Christ in the millennium	The redeemed ruling with Christ, appearing and disappearing on earth at will to oversee life on earth
First resurrection (20:5-6)	The spiritual presence with Christ of the redeemed that occurs after physical death	Resurrection of saints at beginning of millennium when Christ returns	Includes three groups: (1) those raptured with church (4:1); (2) Jewish tribulation saints during tribulation (11:11); (3) other Jewish believers at beginning of millennium (20:5-6)
Second death (20:6)	Spiritual death, eternal separation from God		
Second resurrection (implied)	All persons, lost and redeemed, rise when Christ returns in only resurrection that takes place	Nonbelievers, resurrected at end of millennium	
New heavens and earth (21:1)	A new order; redeemed earth		
New Jerusalem (21:2-5)	God dwelling with His saints (the church) in the new age after all other end-time events		
New Jerusalem (21:10-22:5)	Same as 21:2-5		Millennial Jerusalem from which the world will be ruled; the bride as well as the home of the saints.

Series in Revelation

	Amillennial	Historical Premillennial	Dispensational Premillennial
Seal 1 (6:1-2)	Earthly conqueror	Proclamation of gospel; others believe is earthly conqueror	Man's last effort to bring order to earth while rejecting Christ
Seals 2-4 (6:3-8)	Also with seal 1, suffering that must be endured throughout history	Constant problems of war, scarcity, and death	Sequence of disasters brought about by evil rule
Seal 5 (6:9-11)	Assurance for faithful (all ages) that God will judge evil		Jewish martyrs of tribulation period
Seal 6 (6:12-17)	End of time; God's final judgment	Real cosmic catastrophe at end of age	Symbolic description of breakup of society as a result of evil
Seal 7 (8:1)	The seven trumpets to follow		
Trumpets 1-4 (chap. 8)	Fall of Roman Empire through natural calamities	God's wrath falls on a civilization that gives allegiance to Antichrist when choice is very clear; first four trumpets involve natural catastrophes	(1) Judgment on people who refuse gospel; (2) judgment on great world-church; (3) judgment on an apostate church leader of great influence; (4) judgment on people who reject Christ and follow cults
Locusts, fifth trumpet (9:3-4)	Internal decay bringing fall of Roman Empire	Symbolic of actual demonic forces released during great tribulation, inflict torture	Predicts disastrous results that will come through demonically-led people following apostate religious leader during great tribulation
Army from East, sixth trumpet (9:13-19)	External attack bringing fall of Roman Empire	Symbolic of actual divine judgment on corrupt civilization, inflicts death	Literal invasion of West by army from East
Seventh trumpet (11:15)	God will one day claim His victory	Announces victorious outcome	Announces arrival of millennial kingdom

	Amillennial	Historical Premillennial	Dispensational Premillennial
First vial (16:2)	Judgment on adherents of false religion, including Domitian worshipers	Inflicted specifically on followers of Antichrist	Spiritual plague as great an annoyance as physical suffering
Second vial (16:3)	Destruction of sources of physical sustenance	Death of everything in sea	Death and desolation, whether literal or symbolic
Third vial (16:4-7)	Those who shed blood of saints will receive a curse of blood	Affects fresh water	Destroys the sources of life
Fourth vial (16:8-9)	Even when people recognize that source of all life fights against them for God, they blaspheme and refuse to repent	God overrules processes of nature to bring judgment, but people still refuse to repent	The primary source of humanity's comfort becomes a curse instead
Fifth vial (16:10-11)	God's judgment on seat of beast's authority; darkness indicates confused and evil plotting	Directed against the demonic civilization of end-time	Great federation of nations of new Rome is attacked at its center; darkness brought about by demonical delusions; symbolic
Sixth vial (16:12-16)	Forces against God will ultimately be destroyed; here refers specifically to Parthians	Serves as preparation for great battle of end-time; a coalition of demonically-inspired rulers	Refers to great world conflict of many nations at Armageddon in Palestine
Seventh vial (16:17-21)	Poured in the air all must breathe; strikes note of final judgment on Roman Empire	Describes fall of end-time Babylon (dealt with more fully later)	Utter destruction of every spiritual and religious institution built without God; the overthrow of civilization

the Seven Seals (6:1—8:5)
  VI. The Enthroned Lamb's Judgments Via the Seven Trumpets (8:6—11:19)
 VII. The Dragon's Persecution of the Righteous (12:1—13:18)
VIII. A Summary of Triumph, Warning, and Judgment (14:1—20)
  IX. The Enthroned Lamb's Judgments Via the Seven Cups (15:1—16:21)
   X. The Fall and Ruin of the Immoral City of the Beast (17:1—18:24)
  XI. The Rejoicing of Heaven and the Revelation of the Lamb, Bringing Judgment and the Advent of the Bride, the Holy City (19:1—22:5)
 XII. Conclusion (22:6–21)

Introduction (1:1–8) Written to "the seven churches" of the Roman province of Asia, John's work is a "revelation" of "the things which must shortly take place." The theme of John's work is clear: the Lord God Himself has guaranteed the final vindication of the crucified Jesus before all the earth (1:7–8).

John's Vision on the Island of Patmos (1:9–20) While in exile on Patmos, John saw the risen Lord (1:9–20). Appearing in the dress of power and majesty (1:9–20), the Living One revealed Himself as Lord of the churches, to whom He instructed John to send not only the seven letters, but also an account of the things which he both had seen and would see, that is, a revelation of "the things which shall be hereafter" (1:19).

Letters to the Seven Churches (2:1—3:22) The letters to the churches of Ephesus, Smyrna, Pergamum, Thyatira, Sardis, Philadelphia, and Laodicea have a fairly consistent format. First, after designating the recipients, the risen Lord as Sender describes Himself using a portion of the visionary description of Him in 1:9–20. There follows an "I know" section of either commendation or criticism. Next appears typically some form of exhortation: to those who received criticism, the usual exhortation is to repent; however, to the churches of Smyrna and Philadelphia, for whom the Lord had only praise, the exhortation is one of assurance (compare 2:10; 3:10–13). Each letter concludes, though the order may vary, with both an exhortation to "hear what the Spirit says to the churches" (NAS) and a promise of reward to the "overcomer," that is, the one who conquers by persevering in the cause of Christ.

The church at Ephesus (2:1–7) is told to return to her first love; the church at Smyrna (2:8–11), to be faithful unto death; the churches of Pergamum (2:12–17) and Thyatira (2:18–29) must beware of false teaching and the immoral deeds that so often accompany erroneous theology. The church at Sardis (3:1–6) is told to wake up and complete her works of obedience. The church at Philadelphia (3:7–13) is promised, in the face of persecution by the local synagogue, that faith in Jesus will assure access into the eternal kingdom; and the church at Laodicea (3:14–22) is told to turn from her self-deception and repent of her lukewarmness.

The Sovereignty of the Creator God Committed to the Crucified and Now Enthroned Lamb (4:1—5:14) Chapters 4 and 5 represent the pivot point of the book, tying the risen Lord's opening exhortations to the churches (chs. 2—3) to the judgments and final triumph of the Lamb (chs. 6—22). These chapters also provide the historical and theological basis of the risen Lord's authority over both the church and the world by depicting His enthronement and empowering to carry out the judging and saving purposes of God. Chapter 4 asserts the sovereign authority of the Creator God. Chapter 5 depicts the delegation of the divine authority to the risen Lord by introducing a sequence of events reminiscent of Daniel 7. In Daniel 7, the people of God were oppressed by four terrible beasts, symbolic of evil empires and kings; similarly, the Revelation is written to people who either are, or soon will be, experiencing persecution from powers of evil. Similar to Daniel 7, in Revelation 5, we see both a book of judgment—and a glorious, redemptive agent of God. Instead of an unidentified human figure, we learn that the exalted agent of God is none other than the crucified Jesus, the Lamb and Lion of God, now enthroned and therefore worthy to take the book and break the seals.

The events portrayed here are highly symbolic, but are not ahistorical myth. The scene readily suggests an otherwise well-known and important historical and theological moment within biblical history, namely, the ascension of Jesus. His redemptive death, that is, His obedience to the will of God (see also Phil. 2:8–9; Heb. 2:9–10; 5:8–9; 10:9–10), qualified Him for the role of Lord. He has "overcome" (5:5), a word which for John refers to Jesus's triumphal suffering and subsequent enthronement (see 3:21), and may therefore now as the heavenly Lord assume the role of divine agent.

The Enthroned Lamb's Judgments Via the Seven Seals (6:1—8:5) The breaking of the first four seals brings forth four differently colored horsemen (6:1–8). These riders, paralleling the chaos predicted in Mark 13, represent God's judgments through the upheavals of war and its devastating social consequences (violence, famine, pestilence, and death). The fifth seal (6:9–11) is the plea of martyred saints for divine justice upon their oppressors. For now, they must wait.

A careful look at the sixth seal is important for understanding the literary structure and episodic sequence of the Revelation. When broken, it brings forth the typical signs of the end: a great earthquake, the blackening of the sun, the ensanguining of the moon, and the falling of the stars of heaven (compare Matt. 24:29). Though the Revelation is but a few chapters old, we are brought to the end of world history. The mighty as well as the lowly of the earth realize that the great day of God's (and the Lamb's) wrath has come, and nothing can save them (6:14–17). The description of the judgments initiated by the first six seals would no doubt tend to overwhelm John's audience, so he interrupted the sequence leading to the seventh seal to remind us that the people of God need not despair, for, as the "bond-servants of God" (7:3 NAS), they have the promise of heaven.

Chapter 7 is actually two visions (7:1–8,9–17), with the second both interpreting and concluding the first. The sealing of the 144,000 (7:1–8) employs Jewish symbols to describe those who know God through Jesus Christ. Clearly, John is referring to Christians as the 144,000 for 7:3 refers to the "bond-servants" of God, a term consistently used throughout the Revelation (1:1; 2:20; 10:7; 11:18; 19:2,5; 22:3,6) to refer either to Christians in general or to the Christian prophet, but *never* to the non-Christian Jew (or Gentile). Language employed in the Old Testament to refer to the Jews is characteristically used in the New Testament to refer to those who know God through Jesus Christ (see 2 Cor. 6:16–18; Gal. 3:29; 1 Peter 2:9–10; and Rev. 1:6). The number 144,000 is an intensification ($12 \times 12 \times 10 \times 10 \times 10$) of the original number twelve (itself an obvious allusion to the twelve tribes, the Old Testament people of God), which indicates that the 144,000 comprise the full number of God's people, God's people now being all (Jew or Gentile) who are followers of Jesus.

In the second vision (7:9–17), the 144,000 have become "a great multitude, which no one could count" (NAS). Who are they? Using his favorite descriptions of heaven (see 21:3–4,23; 22:1–5), John tells us that they are those who have "come out of the great tribulation" (NAS), now to experience the joys of heaven and relief from the tribulations they have endured (compare 7:14–17 with 21:1–6; 22:1–5). To "come out of the great tribulation" (7:14) does *not* mean that they have exited the earth *before* the hour of tribulation. To the contrary, they have indeed experienced the tribulations of this evil age, but now in heaven they enjoy the presence of God (7:15; 21:3). As the true Israel of God, Christians ("the bond-servants of our God," 7:3, NAS) have the seal of *God*. Refusing the mark of the beast (13:16–17; 14:11), they hold to the testimony of Jesus (14:12) in spite of persecution (12:17; 13:7) and therefore have the promise of final deliverance in heaven from this evil age of great tribulation (7:14).

Revelation 8:1–5 gives us the seventh seal and again the traditional signs of the very end of human history and the coming of the Lord, but the prophet is not yet ready to describe the Lord's return. He still has too much to say about the nature of judgment, the mission of the church,

and the persecutions of the beast to bring his prophecy to an end. Therefore, before describing fully the end, John must start over. Now, using the symbolic vehicle of the seven trumpets, he declared that the judgments of God also have a redemptive purpose.

The Enthroned Lamb's Judgments Via the Seven Trumpets (8:6—11:19) The first four trumpets describe partial judgments ("one-third") upon the earth's vegetation, the oceans, fresh waters, and the heavenly lights (8:6–13). The last three trumpets are grouped together and also described as three "woes" upon the earth, emphasizing God's judgment upon mankind. All these judgments have no redemptive effect, for the "rest of mankind" who are not killed by these plagues do not repent of their immoralities (9:20–21 NAS).

Just as the interlude between the sixth and seventh seals reminded us that the people of God are safe from the eternally destructive effects of God's wrath, so also between the sixth and seventh trumpets we are reminded of God's protective hand on His people (10:1–11:14). In the trumpet interlude we also learn that God's protection during these days of tribulation does not mean isolation, for the people of God must bear a prophetic witness to the world.

In 10:1–8, John's call (after the pattern of Ezek. 2:1—3:11) is reaffirmed. The note of protection and witness is again struck in 11:1–13 where the measuring of the temple of God (11:1–2) alludes to God's protective hand upon His people during the hour of turmoil (11:2). Persecutions will last for "forty-two months," but His people cannot be destroyed, for the "two witnesses" (11:3–13) must bear witness to the mercy and judgment of God. The "two witnesses" ("two" suggests a confirmed, legal testimony) are also called "two lampstands" (11:4), terminology already interpreted in 1:20 to mean the church. Though engaged in great spiritual warfare, the church, like Moses and Elijah of old, must maintain a faithfully prophetic witness to the world, a witness even unto death. Though the earth rejoices that the testimony of the church is in the end apparently snuffed out, the temporary triumph of evil ("three-and-a-half days," 11:9,11) will turn to heavenly vindication as the two witnesses (the people of God) are raised from the dead (11:11–12).

With the seventh trumpet (and third woe) the end of history has come, the time "for the dead to be judged" and the saints to be rewarded (11:18 NAS). The coming of the reign of God (and Christ), as well as the day of judgment, are past events (11:17–18). John is not yet ready to describe the actual coming of the King of kings and Lord of lords. Sadly, he has more to relate regarding "the beast that comes up out of the abyss" to "make war" with the people of God (11:7, NAS). It is that "42 months," the period of persecution (and protection/witness), that John now unfolds.

The Dragon's Persecution of the Righteous (12:1—13:18) Chapter 12 is crucial for understanding John's view of the sequence of history. The number "three-and-a-half" was associated by Christians and Jews with times of evil and judgment. John variously referred to the three-and-a-half years as either "forty-two months," or "1,260 days," or "a time, times, and half a time." For John, it was the period of time when the powers of evil will do their works. During this time, God will protect His people (12:6,14) while they both bear witness to their faith (11:3) and simultaneously suffer at the hands of these evil powers (11:2,7; 12:13–17; 13:5–7). Commentators agree that this terrible period of tribulation will be brought to an end with the coming of the Lord. The critical question, however, is when the three-and-a-half year period of persecution and witness *begins.* Though some scholars have relegated the "three-and-a-half years" to some as-yet-unbegun moment in the future, chapter 12 unmistakably pinpoints its beginning with the ascension and enthronement of Christ (12:5). When the woman's (Israel's) offspring is "caught up to God *and to His throne*" (12:5, NAS, author's italics), there is war in heaven, and the dragon is cast down to the earth.

Heaven rejoices because it has been rescued from Satan, but the earth must now mourn, because the devil has been cast down to earth, and his anger is great. He knows that he has been defeated by the enthronement of Christ and that he has but a short time (12:12). The woman, who (as Israel) brought forth the Christ (12:1–2) and also "other offspring," those who "hold to the testimony of Jesus," now received the brunt of the frustrated dragon's wrath (12:17). As the enraged dragon now seeks to vent his wrath upon the woman, she is nonetheless nourished and protected for "1,260 days" (12:6), for a "time, times, and half a time" (12:14).

The dragon then brings forth two henchmen (ch. 13) to help him in his pursuit of those who believe in Jesus. Satan is thus embodied in a political ruler, the beast from the sea (13:1), who will speak blasphemies for "forty-two months" (13:5). He will "make war with the saints" (13:7 NAS), while the second beast (or false prophet, 19:20), who comes up from the earth (13:11), seeks to deceive the earth so that its inhabitants worship the first beast.

Thus, in chapters 12 and 13, each of the various ways of referring to the three-and-a-half years is a referrence to a single period of time that began with the enthronement of Christ and will conclude with His return. The time period is not a literal three-and-a-half years, but the entire time between the ascension and return of Christ which will be permitted the dragon to execute his evil work upon the earth (compare Gal. 1:4; Eph. 2:2). Almost two thousand years have elapsed since our Lord ascended to the right hand of God, but the "three-and-a-half years" still continues. Satan still rages; but his time is short, and his evil will cease at the return of Christ.

A Summary of Triumph, Warning, and Judgment (14:1—20) After the depressing news of the ongoing persecutions of the unholy trinity, John's readers need another word of encouragement and warning. Chapter 14 therefore employs seven "voices" to relate again the hopes and warnings of heaven. First is another vision of the 144,000, the full number of the people of God (14:4). Faithful in their worship of the one true God through Jesus Christ and not seduced by the satanic deceptions of the first beast and his ally, the false prophet, they will be rescued and taken to heaven's throne (14:1–5).

An angel announces the eternal gospel and warns the earth of coming judgment (14:6–7). The remaining "voices" (or oracles) follow in rapid succession. The fall of "Babylon the Great," an Old Testament symbol for a nation opposed to the people of God, is announced (14:8). The people of God are warned not to follow the beast or else those who follow him suffer separation from God (14:9–12). Finally, two voices call for harvest (14:14–20).

The Enthroned Lamb's Judgments Via the Seven Cups (15:1—16:21) Another dimension of His judgment must be revealed. The seven cups of wrath are similar to the seven trumpets and the seven seals, but also different. The wrath of God is no longer partial or temporary, but complete and everlasting, final and irrevocable. The partial judgments ("one-third") of the trumpets suggest that God uses the sufferings and evils of this life to draw mankind toward repentance and faith; but such tribulations also foreshadow the final hour of judgment when God's wrath is finished.

The seven cups have no break between the sixth and seventh outpourings of judgment. Only wrath is left with no more delay. Babylon the Great, the symbol for all who have vaunted themselves against the most high God, will fall. The end has come (16:18).

The Fall and Ruin of the Immoral City of the Beast (17:1—18:24) Chapter 17 retells the sixth cup, the fall of Babylon the Great, and chapter 18 gives a moving lament for the great city.

The Rejoicing of Heaven and the Revelation of the Lamb Bringing Judgment and the Advent of the Bride, the Holy City (19:1—22:25) Although John has withheld a description of the coming of the Lord on at least three earlier occasions (8:5; 11:15–19; 16:17–21; compare also 14:14–16), John is now prepared to describe the glories of the Lord's appearance. All of heaven rejoices over the righteous judgment of God upon evil (19:1–6). The Lamb's bride, the people of God, has made herself ready by her faithfulness to her Lord through the hour of suffering (see 19:7–8).

Heaven is opened, and the One whose coming has been faithfully petitioned from ages past appears to battle the enemies of God, a conflict whose outcome is not in doubt (19:11–16). The first beast and the second beast are thrown into the lake of fire from which there is no return (19:20). The dragon—Satan—is cast into a hellish abyss which is shut and sealed for a thousand years (20:1–3). Since the powers of evil reigned for "three-and-a-half years" (the period of time between the ascension and return of our Lord), Christ will reign for a "thousand years." The dead in Christ are raised to govern with Him (20:4–6), and God's rightful rule over the earth is vindicated.

At the end of Christ's reign, the final disposition of Satan will occur (20:7–10). Though John predicted that Satan will have one last hurrah of deception, his final insurrection will be short-lived. In one final battle, Satan and his followers are overcome, and the devil joins the beast and the false prophet in the lake of fire where "they will be tormented day and night forever and ever" (20:10 NAS). Then the final judment takes place, at which all not included in "the book of life" are thrown into the lake of fire (20:11–15 NAS).

Chapter 21 is often thought to refer to the period following the 1,000-year reign, but it is more probably a retelling of the return of Christ from the viewpoint of the bride. Just as chapter 17 was a recapitulation of the seventh cup and the fall of the harlot, Babylon the Great (compare the language of 17:1–3, which clearly introduces a "retelling," with the language of 21:9–10), so chapter 21 recapitulates the glorification of the bride of the Lamb (21:1—22:5). To be the bride is to be the holy city, the New Jerusalem, to live in the presence of God and the Lamb, and to experience protection, joy, and the everlasting, life-giving light of God (21:9–27). The throne of God and of the Lamb is there, and there His bond servants shall serve Him and reign with Him forever and ever (21:1–5).

Conclusion (22:6–21) John concluded his prophecy by declaring the utter faithfulness of his words. Those who heed his prophecy will receive the blessings of God. Those who ignore the warnings will be left outside the gates of God's presence (22:6–15). Solemnly and hopefully praying for the Lord to come, John closed his book (22:17,20). The churches must have ears to hear what the Spirit has said (22:16). The people of God must, by His grace (22:21), persevere in the hour of tribulation, knowing that their enthroned Lord will return in triumph.   *Robert B. Sloan*

REVELRY Noisy partying or merrymaking. English translations vary greatly in use of revel and its cognates (revelers, reveling, revelry). KJV used "revellings" but twice, as a work of the flesh (Gal. 5:21) and as behavior associated with Gentiles (1 Pet. 4:3). RSV used revelry once, as a character-

ization of the behavior of the rich of Samaria (Amos 6:7). NAS and NIV used cognates of revel more often (four and eleven times, respectively). In their use *revel* often means little more than rejoice or exult. Of special interest is the association of revelry and idolatry (Ex. 32:6; 1 Cor. 10:7).

REVENGE, REVENGER See *Avenger.*

REVERENCE Respect or honor paid to a worthy object. In Scripture, reverence is paid: to father and mother (Lev. 19:3; Heb. 12:9); to God (1 Kings 18:3,12; Heb. 12:28); to God's sanctuary (Lev. 19:30; 26:2); and to God's commandments (Ps. 119:48). The failure to revere God (Deut. 32:51) and the act of revering other gods (Judg. 6:10) have dire consequences. Reverence for Christ is expressed in mutual submission within the Christian community (Eph. 5:21). Christian persecution takes on new meaning as suffering becomes an opportunity for revering Christ (1 Pet. 3:14–15).

REWARD See *Restitution.*

REZEPH (Rē′ zĕph) Place name meaning, "glowing coal." Town the Assyrians conquered, most likely under Shalmaneser III (about 838 B.C.), and which the Assyrians used as a warning to king Hezekiah of Judah in 701 B.C. against relying on God to deliver him from them (2 Kings 19:12; Isa. 37:12). The site is possibly Rezzafeh about 100 miles southeast of Aleppo.

REZIA (Rē zī′ à) KJV form of Rizia.

REZIN (Rĕ′ zīn) King of Syria about 735 B.C. during the reigns of Pekah in Israel and Ahaz in Judah. When Ahaz refused to join Rezin and Pekah in fighting against Assyria, Rezin pursuaded Pekah to ally with him against the Judean king (2 Kings 15:37; 16:5). Ahaz appealed for help to Tiglath-pileser of Assyria, who came against Rezin and Pekah and destroyed their kingdoms. Rezin died in 732 B.C. when Damascus fell to the Assyrians.

REZON (Rē′ zŏn) Personal name meaning, "prince." An Aramaean leader who led a successful revolt against Solomon and established an independent state with its capital at Damascus (1 Kings 11:23–25). See *Damascus.*

RHEGIUM (Rhē′ ġĭ um) Place name either derived from the Greek *rhēgnym* (rent, torn) or from the Latin *regium* (royal). Port located at the southwestern tip of the Italian boot about seven miles across the strait of Messina from Sicily. Paul stopped there en route to Rome (Acts 28:13). Rhegium was settled by Greek colonists and retained Greek language and institutions into the first century.

RHESA (Rhē' sȧ) Ancestor of Jesus (Luke 3:27).

RHETORIC The use of language for effective communication, especially the biblical literary techniques used to communicate God's Word. The Bible was written to convince people to respond positively to God's offer of life abundant and eternal. Studying the Bible from a rhetorical perspective helps us better to understand what the Bible actually says and to become better equipped to convince others of its validity through our own rhetoric.

Rhetorical study includes the examination of *tropes* (literary devices to make langauge more colorful) and consideration of *schemes* (structural devices which aid memory and persuasion). Tropes include: metaphor, simile, personification, irony, hyperbole, assonance, and paronomasia. Schemes include: acrostic, antithesis, parallelism, rhetorical question, and syllogism.

Metaphor is a word picture which forces a comparison. Jesus' statement that He is the Good Shepherd (John 10:11) is a metaphor because believers are not really sheep. *Simile* is a word picture using *like* or *as* to explain something difficult to understand ("The kingdom of heaven is like a mustard seed" Matt. 13:31). *Personification* allows inanimate objects to take on human qualities (Judg. 9:7–15). *Irony* is overturning expectations to underscore a tension which needs to be resolved in action or belief. See *Irony*. *Hyperbole* exaggerates in order to make a point. God said He would not accept Israel's offerings or hear their worship. In other words God will not acknowledge worship He is certainly aware of (Amos 5:22–23). *Metonymy* is when one word substitutes for another which it represents. When *Zion* is used in Psalms to represent the Temple, God's throne, Jerusalem and/or all of Israel, that is a metonymy.

Assonance is the use of sounds to underscore the meaning of a phrase or verse (alliteration is assonance where the initial sounds of words make the emphasis). Such artistry with sound is difficult or impossible to reproduce in translation. REB catches part of the word play in Isaiah 7:9: "Have firm faith or you will fail to stand firm." Repetition of sound catches the reader's attention and underlines the focus on faith. *Paronomasia* is a more exact assonance, a meaningful pun. In Isaiah 5:7, God looks for righteousness (*mishpat*) but finds riots (*mishpach*) instead and for legality (*tsedhaqa*) but here is lamentation (*tse'aqa*). These techniques create interest and enhance meaning.

Other techniques involve the way sentences, phrases, and/or verses are structured. *Acrostics* begin each line of a chapter or poem with a consecutive letter of the Hebrew alphabet (Pss. 111, 112, 119, and others) as both a mnemonic (memory aid) and full expression of one's feeling. *Antithesis* is the presentation of opposites to express a truth (see Prov. 14 for extensive use of antithesis).

Parallelism is the basic building block of Hebrew poetry. One phrase is balanced by another phrase which says the same thing in slightly different words. See *Poetry*.

The Bible is full of *rhetorical questions,* those which do not need to be answered because the hearer/reader already knows the answer. In the Bible, these answers are usually negative. "Who is like unto the Lord our God?" (Ps. 113:5). No one! "Shall we continue in sin that grace may abound?" (Rom. 6:1). Not at all! "Hath God cast away his people?" (Rom. 11:1). Of course not!

Syllogism is the logical advance from one statement to another until a conclusion is derived from the premise. One of the brilliant syllogisms in the Bible is 1 Corinthians 15:12–28 in which Paul argued that the only logical conclusion to the fact of Christ's resurrection is the resurrection of all the dead.

Recognizing these techniques and studying Hebrew poetry will enhance one's ability to study the Bible. *Johnny L. Wilson*

RHODA (Rhō' dȧ) Personal name meaning, "rose." Rhoda's relationship to the household of Mary, the mother of John Mark, is not clear. She was most likely a servant, though it is possible that she was a family member or a guest at the prayer service. In her great joy at finding Peter at the door, Rhoda failed to let him in. Her joy in rushing to tell the disciples and their response accusing her of madness recall details of Luke's resurrection narrative (Acts 12:13; compare Luke 24:9–11).

RHODES (Rhōdes) Island off the southwest coast of Asia Minor in the Mediterranean Sea associated with the Dodanim (Gen. 10:4; Ezek. 27:15). See *Dodanim.* Rhodes was founded as a Minoan trading colony about 1500 B.C. and came under the control of a single government around 407 B.C. A wealthy shipping center, Rhodes developed navies

The streets of Rhodes have remained basically unchanged for centuries.

The city and harbor area of the island of Rhodes.

that controlled the eastern Mediterranean. Standing with one foot on either side of the harbor entrance was the 105-foot-tall brass Colossus, one of the Seven Wonders of the World. Set up in 288 B.C., it fell during an earthquake about 64 years

Temple ruins in the area of Lindos on the island of Rhodes.

later. Disloyalty to Roman rule met with stiff economic sanctions against the city and threw it into decline. While enjoying some popularity as the center of the cult of Helios, the sun god, Rhodes could not rise above Roman economic pressure. When the apostle Paul stopped over on his voyage from Troas to Caesarea (Acts 21:1), Rhodes was only a minor provincial city.

RIBAI (Rī' bā ī) Personal name meaning, "Yahweh contends." Father of Ittai, one of David's thirty elite warriors (2 Sam. 23:29; 1 Chron. 11:31).

RIBBAND KJV form of ribbon (Num. 15:38). Modern translations read "cord" (NAS, NIV, NRSV) or "thread" (REB).

RIBLAH (Rĭb' lăh) *1.* Syrian town located near Kadesh on the Orontes near the border with Babylonia. There Pharaoh Neco imprisoned King Jehoahaz of Judah after the young monarch had reigned only three months (2 Kings 23:31–33). Later, when Zedekiah rebelled against Nebuchadnezzar of Babylon, he was taken to Riblah as a prisoner and viewed the execution of his sons before having his eyes put out (25:4–7). See *Diblah.* *2.* Otherwise unknown town on eastern border of Canaan (Num. 34:11). Earliest translations read *Arbelah.*

RICHES See *Wealth and Materialism.*

RIDDLE An enigmatic or puzzling statement, often based on the clever use of the ambiguities of language. The classic biblical example of a riddle is that posed by Samson to the Philistines. The riddle is in poetic form (Judg. 14:12–14), and the question, "What is it?," is implied. The Philistines reply is in the form of another riddle (v. 18*a*) whose original answer was probably "love." Samson's retort may reflect yet another commonly known, and rather risque, riddle (v. 18*b*).

The Hebrew word for riddle also appears elsewhere in the Old Testament. The Lord spoke with Moses directly, not in "riddles" (Num. 12:8 NIV, REB, NRSV) or "dark speech" (KJV, NAS). The Queen of Sheba tested Solomon with "hard questions" or riddles (1 Kings 10:1–13). Riddles were a form of poetic expression (Ps. 49:4); a mark of wisdom was the ability to solve them (Prov. 1:6). Daniel had such wisdom (Dan. 5:12).

Daniel C. Browning, Jr.

RIGHT MIND Sound mind, mentally healthy (Mark 5:15; Luke 8:35). Elsewhere, the underlying Greek term is rendered "sober judgment" (Rom. 12:3 NRSV) or "self-controlled" (Titus 2:6 NRSV).

RIGHTEOUSNESS The actions and positive results of a sound relationship within a local community or between God and a person or His people. Translators have employed "righteousness" in rendering several biblical words into English: *sĕdāqāh, sedeq,* in Hebrew; and *dikaiosunē* and *euthutēs* in Greek. "Righteousness" in the original languages denotes far more than in English usage; indeed, biblical righteousness is generally at odds with current English usage. We understand righteousness to mean "uprightness" in the sense of "adherence or conformity to an established norm." In biblical usage righteousness is rooted in covenants and relationships. For biblical authors, righteousness is the fulfillment of the terms of a covenant between God and humanity or between humans in the full range of human relationships.

Old Testament The starting point is the Hebrew notion of God's "righteousness." The Hebrew mind did not understand righteousness to be an attribute of the divine, that is a characteristic of God's nature. Rather, God's righteousness is what God *does* in fulfillment of the terms of the covenant that God established with the chosen people, Israel (2 Chron. 12:6; Ps. 7:9; Jer. 9:24; Dan. 9:14). God's righteousness was not a metaphysical property but that dimension of the divine experienced by those within the covenantal community.

Most especially, God's righteousness was understood in relation to the image of God as the Judge of created order (Ps. 96:13). God's judgments are consistently redemptive in nature, God's judgments protected, delivered, and restored Israel (Isa. 11:4–5). At times God's righteousness was experienced in God's delivering Israel from enemies and oppressors (Ps. 71); at other times, in God's delivering Israel from the nation's own sinfulness (Ps. 51:19). Such deliverance involved God's righteousness of wrath against the persecutor and the wicked (Ps. 106). Salvation and condemnation exist together as the two sides of God's righteousness; the leading side is always deliverance: God condemns only because He also saves (Ps. 97).

Righteousness is a religious concept applied to humans because Israel had entered into a covenantal relationship to God. Because God had chosen Israel, the nation had the covenantal responsibility of fulfilling the terms of the covenant. Precisely here, serious misunderstanding frequently flaws thought about Israel's desire for righteousness. The Old Testament did not call on the people of Israel to attempt to earn God's favor or to strive to merit God's graces (Ps. 18). Indeed, the Old Testament teaches that God's gracious favor had been poured out on the nation in God's choosing of Abraham and his descendants. God acted to establish the covenant and in so doing bestowed salvation on Israel (Ex. 19). The law was given as an act of divine mercy to provide Israel with guidelines for keeping the nation's own portion of the covenant (Lev. 16; Ps. 40). Rather than being a ladder that Israel climbed to get to God, the law was understood to be a divine program for the *maintenance* of a healthy relationship between Israel and God (Lev. 16). God expected Israel to keep the law not to earn merit but to maintain the status God had already given the nation. As Israel kept the covenant law, the nation was righteous. Thus human righteousness in relation to God was understood as faithful adherence to the law (Lev. 19). Even so, God did not leave humans with the hopelessly impossible task of performing the law perfectly: the law God gave contained provision for atonement through repentance and appropriate acts of contrition (Lev. 19).

The concept of righteousness as faithful fulfillment of the provisions of a covenant was also meaningful in strictly human terms. The person who met the demands of a variety of social relations was thought to be righteous, to have done righteousness, though the requirements of righteousness varied with the covenantal/relational context. Some of the prominent areas were those of family (Gen. 38), friendship (1 Sam. 24), nation (Prov. 14:34), and even in relation to servants and certain foreigners (Job 31).

New Testament Greek philosophy understood righteousness to be one of the cardinal virtues, but New Testament authors show that they understood the word in terms of Old Testament thinking about covenantal relations. Human righteousness in the New Testament is absolute faith in and commitment to God (Matt. 3:15; Rom. 4:5; 1 Pet. 2:24). The one who in faith gives oneself to the doing of God's will is righteous, doing righteousness, and reckoned righteous by God (Jas. 2:23). The focus of faith in God is the saving activity of God in Jesus Christ (Rom. 3:21–26). The human-to-human dimension of righteousness observed in the Old Testament is present in New Testament thought (Phil. 1:3–11), but it seems less prominent, perhaps because of the importance of the New Testament concept of love.

At the heart of New Testament thinking about righteousness is the notion of God's righteousness (Matt. 6:33; Acts 17:31; Rom. 1:17; Eph. 4:24; Jas. 1:20). Interpreters debate whether the phrase "righteousness of God" is a *subjective genitive,* meaning "God is righteous," or an *objective genitive,* meaning "God gives righteousness."

This grammatical distinction is more than a point about subtle linguistic nuance. In the New Testament, especially in Paul's letters, "*the righteousness of God" is the key to understanding the salvation of humanity.*

Interpreters who take "the righteousness of God" to mean "God gives righteousness" see salvation as a God-created human possibility. Righteousness is that which God requires of humanity and which God gives as a gift to the person of faith. In this line of thought, faith is the condition for the reception of the gift of righteousness from God. God acts in Christ, and, in turn, humans react by having faith. Then God gives them righteousness or reckons them, on the basis of their faith, as if they were righteous.

On the other hand, interpreters who understand "the righteousness of God" to mean "God is righteous" contend that salvation is purely the work of God, God's saving activity in keeping the divine side of the covenant of creation. God acts in Christ, and part of that action is the creation of faith on the part of human beings who otherwise have no faith. Thus "the righteousness of God" is the *power of God* at work saving humanity (and the whole of creation), through the creation of faith in sinful persons.

The line between the camps of scholars holding these different interpretations of "the righteousness of God" is sharply drawn, and the debate over the validity of these interpretive options continues with intensity. See *Ethics; Grace; Law; Mercy; Salvation.*   *Marion Soards*

RIMMON (Rĭm′ mŏn) Place and divine name meaning, "pomegranate." *1.* Chief god of Syria, also called Hadad. Naaman worshiped Rimmon in Damascus (2 Kings 5:18). *2.* Town allotted to tribe of Judah (Josh. 15:32) but then given to Simeon (19:7; compare 1 Chron. 4:32). Early translations and many modern interpreters read En-rimmon in all occurrences. It is modern Khirbet er-Ramamin two miles south of Lahav. Zechariah 14:10 described it as the southern boundary of God's new exalted kingdom. See En-rimmon. *3.* A Levitical city in Zebulun (Josh. 19:13; 1 Chron. 6:77), probably the original reading for present Dimnah (Josh. 21:35). See *Dimnah.* It is present Rummaneh, six miles northeast of Nazareth. *4.* A rock near Gibeah to where the people of Benjamin fled from vengeful Israelites (Judg. 20:45–47), modern Rammun four miles east of Bethel. *5.* Father of Rechab and Baanah, who killed Saul's son Ish-Bosheth (2 Sam. 4:2,9).

RIMMON-PAREZ (Rĭm mon-Pā′ rēz) KJV form of Rimmon-Perez.

RIMMON-PEREZ (Rĭm mon-Pē′ rĕz) Place name meaning, "pomegranate of the pass." Campsite during Israel's wilderness wanderings (Num. 33: 19–20).

RIMMONO (Rĭm′ mŏn ō) Place name meaning, "his Rimmon." NIV, NAS, NRSV reading of Rimmon in 1 Chronicles 6:77. Compare Joshua 19:13; 21:25.

RING See *Jewelry, Jewels, and Precious Stones; Nose Ring.*

RINNAH (Rĭn′ nah) Personal name meaning,

"ringing cry." Descendant of Judah (1 Chron. 4:20).

RIPHATH (Rī phăth) Personal name of foreign origin. Son of Gomer, likely the ancestor of an Anatolian tribe (Gen. 10:3). The name is likely a scribal corruption of Diphath (1 Chron. 1:6).

RISHATHAIM See *Chushan-Rishathaim.* Chushan may relate to Guzana or tell Halaf.

RISSAH (Rĭs' sah) Place name possibly meaning, "dewdrop," "rain," or "ruins." Campsite during Israel's wilderness wanderings (Num. 33:21–22), modern Sharma, east of Gulf of Aqaba.

RITHMAH (Rĭth' mah) Place name meaning, "broom plant." Campsite during Israel's wilderness wanderings (Num. 33:18–19), possibly valley called er-Retame east of Gulf of Aqaba.

RITUAL See *Sacrifice and Offerings; Worship.*

RIVER OF EGYPT See *Brook of Egypt.*

RIVERS AND WATERWAYS IN THE BIBLE From the earliest efforts at permanent settlement in the Ancient Near East, people were attracted to the rivers and streams that ultimately would dictate population distribution between the mountains, deserts, and the seas. The flood plains of many of these rivers originally were inhospitable with thick, tangled jungles, wild beasts, and unpredictable flooding and disease. However, within the areas of plain and lowland that provided a more constant food supply and ease of movement, the need for a permanent water source attracted settlers to the river banks. Thus the early river civilizations of the Nile, the Tigris, and Euphrates starting about 3000 B.C., and the Indus civilization slightly later, resulted in response to the challenges and benefits these important waterways presented. Flood control, social and economic organization, and invention of writing as a means of communication developed. Trade was facilitated by means of navigable waterways. Since roads followed the lines of least resistance, the pattern of early trade routes conformed closely, especially in more rugged terrain, to channels and courses of the rivers and streams, and along the shoreline where the earliest fishing villages developed.

Rivers and Streams Each of the biblical rivers was developed to meet distinct human needs. A study of rivers helps understand the culture near the river. *1. Nile River* The name *Nile* is not explicitly mentioned in KJV, but modern translations most often translated the Hebrew *yeor* as the Nile. The Nile plays a prominent role in the early events in the life of Moses in Exodus (Moses, Ex. 2:3; the ten plagues, Ex. 7:15,20). The Nile is alluded to in many other passages as "the river" (Gen. 41:1),

the "river of Egypt" (Gen. 15:18), the "flood of Egypt" (Amos 8:8), Shihor (Josh. 13:3), river of Cush among other names. The "brook of Egypt" mostly is a reference to Wadi el-Arish, the drainage system of the central Sinai. The prophets Amos (8:8; 9:5) and Jeremiah (46:8) used the Nile as the symbol of Egypt, a concept that is readily understood in terms of the river's historical importance to the survival and well-being of the country.

For the Egyptians the predictable annual flooding of the Nile with the depositing of the fertile black alluvial soil meant the enrichment of the flood plain and the difference between food and famine. From the central highlands of East Africa, the Nile with a watershed of over one million square miles is formed by the union of the White and Blue Niles and flows a distance of nearly 3,500 miles. From its low ebb at the end of May, the flow of the river gradually rises to its maximum flood stage at the beginning of September. Historically, approximately 95 percent of Egypt's population depended upon the productivity of the 5 percent of the country's land area within the flood plain of the Nile. In the Delta at least three major branches facilitated irrigation in the extensive fan north of Memphis, the ancient capital of lower Egypt. See *Egypt; Nile.*

2. Euphrates First mentioned in Genesis 2:14 as one of the four branches of the river that watered the Garden of Eden, the Euphrates flows 1,700 miles to become the longest river in Western Asia. From the mountainous region of northeastern Turkey (Armenia), it flows southward into northern Syria and turns southeasterly to join the Tigris and flows into the Persian Gulf. On the Middle Euphrates, Carchemish, originally the center of a small city-state, became the important provincial capital of the Mitanni kingdom, later of the Hittite and Assyrian Empires. At Carchemish in 605 B.C. Nebuchadnezzar II defeated Pharaoh Necho as he began his successful drive to claim the former Assyrian Empire for Babylon (2 Kings 24:7; Jer. 46). Two important tributaries, the Belikh and Khabur, flow into the Euphrates from the north before it continues on to the ancient trade center at Mari. The Lower Euphrates generally formed the western limits of the city-states that made up the early Sumerian civilization. From the river plain to the delta, both the Tigris and Euphrates rivers regularly have formed new branches and changed their courses. About 90 percent of their flow mysteriously is lost to irrigation, evaporation, pools and lakes, and the swamps and never reaches the Persian Gulf. Lost as well in this region are the vast amounts of sediment that the Tigris and Euphrates bring from the mountainous regions. Sediment deposits along the lower courses of these rivers average 16 to 23 feet with 36-foot deposits in some regions. It has been calculated that the Tigris alone removes as much as 3 million tons of eroded highland materials in a single day. In the extreme south the two rivers join in a combined stream that today is known as the Shatt el-Arab.

The flooding of the Mesopotamian rivers in March and April differs from the Nile schedule which during that season is at its low ebb. The melting snows and rains at their sources create sudden, disastrous torrents that, along the Tigris especially, must be controlled by dams during such periods before they can supply a beneficial irrigation system. See *Euphrates and Tigris Rivers.*

The course of the Upper Euphrates was described as the northern border of the Promised Land (Gen. 15:18; Deut. 1:7; 11:24; Josh. 1:4). David, in fact, extended his military influence to its banks during the height of his power (2 Sam. 8:3; 10:16–18; 1 Kings 4:24). The terms "the river," "the flood," "the great river," and "beyond the river" (Josh. 24:2–3; Ezra 4:10–13; Neh. 2:7–9) refer to the Euphrates, historically a significant political and geographical boundary.

3. Tigris From its source in a small lake (Hazar Golu), about 100 miles west of Lake Van, in Armenia, the Tigris flows in a southeasterly direction for about 1,150 miles before joining the Euphrates and emptying into the Persian Gulf. It achieves flood stage during March and April from the melting mountain snows and subsides after mid-May. While its upper flow is swift within narrow gorges, from Mosul and Nineveh southward its course was navigable and was extensively used in antiquity for transport. A series of tributaries from the slopes of the Zagros emptied into the Tigris from the east, including the Greater and Lesser Zab and the Diyala. The Diyala flows into the Tigris near Baghdad. In antiquity its banks were inhabited by a dense population maintained and made prosperous by an excellent irrigation system. The Euphrates, flowing at a level nine meters higher than the Tigris, permitted the construction of a sequence of irrigation canals between the two rivers that resulted in unusual productivity. South of Baghdad where their courses again separated, a more complicated system of canals and diversions were necessary.

The banks of the Tigris were dotted by some of the most important cities of antiquity: Nineveh, the capital of Assyria during the Assyrian Empire; Asshur, the original capital of Assyria; Opis (in the vicinity of Baghdad), the important commercial center of Neo-Babylonian and later times; Ctesiphon, the capital of the Parthians and Sassanians; and Seleucia, capital of the Seleucid rulers of Mesopotamia.

Rivers of Anatolia Several rivers water this part of modern Turkey. See *Asia Minor.*

1. Halys River From its sources in the Armenian mountains, the Halys begins its 714-mile flow to the southwest only to be diverted by a secondary ridge into a broad loop until its direction is completely reversed into a northeasterly direction through the mountainous regions bordering the southern shore of the Black Sea. As the longest river in Anatolia, the Halys, like the other principal rivers in Turkey, is the result of heavy rainfall in the Pontic zone. Because of their winding courses within the coastal mountain chains, none of these rivers is navigable. Within this loop of the Halys in the northern Anatolian plateau the Hittites established their capital Boghazkoy. The course of the Halys generally formed the borders of the district of Pontus.

2. Rivers of the Aegean Coast The broken Aegean coastline boasted a series of sheltered havens and inlets that prompted Greek colonization and the establishment the great harbor cities of the later Greek and Roman periods. The mouths of the Aegean rivers deemed ideal for maritime centers during colonization ultimately proved disastrous. The lower courses of these rivers, relatively short and following a meandering course over their respective plains, are very shallow and sluggish during the summer months. Their upper courses however, of recent formation, carry enormous quantities of alluvium from the highlands that tended to fill the estuaries and gulfs. Constant dredging was required to maintain the harbor's access to the sea and to avoid the formation of malaria-infested swamps. Thus the Hermus (155 miles) was diverted to prevent the destruction of the harbor of Smyrna (Izmir). To the south at Ephesus, the original town site on the disease-ridden marshlands was abandoned about A.D. 400 for the construction of a new harbor on the Cayster River. During the days of Ephesus' prosperity, the constant dredging was adequately maintained. However, with the decline of the Roman Empire after A.D. 200, the silting of the harbor brought the rapid decline of the city. Miletus, on the alluvial plain of the Maeander River (236 miles), was originally established on a deep gulf well sheltered from the prevailing winds. The great Ionian city had possessed four harbors, but the silting of the harbors by the alluvial deposits of the Maeander ultimately brought about the decline and abandonment of the city. Though these Aegean rivers were not navigable, the alluvial plains that bordered them provided convenient and vital access and communications to the interior.

Rivers of Syro-Palestine In Syria and Palestine rivers often separated peoples rather than providing economic power.

1. Orontes and Litani High within the Beqa valley that forms the rift between the Lebanon and Anti-Lebanon mountain ranges, a watershed (about 3,770 feet above sea level) forms the headwaters of the Orontes and Litani Rivers. The rains and snow on the mountain summits at heights of over 11,000 feet course down into the 6—10 mile-wide Beqa which is a part of the great Rift

("Valley of Lebanon," Josh. 11:17). From the watershed, the Orontes flows northward and bends westward to empty into the Mediterranean near Antioch. The Litani flows southward and ultimately escapes to the sea north of Tyre. Unfortunately, its lower course has formed such a deep, narrow gorge that it is useless for communication. See *Palestine.*

2. Jordan River A series of springs and tributaries, resulting from the rains and snows on the heights of Mount Hermon (up to 9,100 feet above sea level) at the southern end of the Anti-Lebanon mountains east of the Rift Valley, converge in Lake Huleh to form the headwaters of the Jordan River. Along the eastern edge of the Huleh Valley, it flows southward into Lake Kinnereth (the Sea of Galilee). Only about eight miles wide and fourteen miles long, the fresh waters of the Galilee and its fishing industry sustained a dense population during most historical periods. At the Galilee's southern end, the Jordan exits and flows 65 miles on to the Dead Sea (about 1,300 feet below sea level). The Jordan flows 127 miles with a drainage area of about 6,380 square miles. The Yarmuk River joins the Jordan five miles south of the Sea of Galilee. The Jabbok River reaches the Jordan from the east twenty-five miles north of the Dead Sea.

At the Jordan's end, the Dead Sea extends another 45 miles between high, rugged cliffs of Nubian sandstone and limestone between the arid wilderness bordering the Judean watershed on the west and the Transjordanian plateau on the east. The sea and the inhospitable terrain along its shoreline discouraged regular travel and transport within the area.

The Jordan appears never to have served as a waterway for travel or transport, but rather as a natural barrier and a political boundary, that because of its steep banks and the densely wooded fringe that lined its devious route ("thickets of the Jordan," Jer. 49:19, NIV; compare 2 Kings 6:4) could be crossed without difficulty only at its fords (Josh. 3). Control of the fords during military confrontations in biblical times constituted a critical advantage (Judg. 3:28; 12:5–6). The Jordan's role as a political boundary appears to have been established already shortly after 2000 B.C. when the eastern frontier of the Egyptian province of Canaan followed the Jordan. Even though Israelite tribes were given special permission to settle in the Transjordan, it was always clear that, beyond the Jordan, they actually were residing outside the Promised Land (Josh. 22). Even in postbiblical times, the eastern boundary of the Persian and Hellenistic province of Judea followed the Jordan. Apart from the fertile oases that dotted the Jordan Valley, agricultural prosperity was assured during the Hellenistic and Roman times when irrigation was developed along the gradual slopes on either

side of the Jordan within the Rift Valley. See *Jordan.*

3. Kishon River The Kishon River forms the drainage system of the Jezreel Plain and the southern portion of the Accho Plain. While a number of its small tributaries have their sources in springs at the base of Mount Tabor, in the southern Galilee, and in the extension of the Carmel in the vicinity of Taanach and Megiddo, the Kishon is rarely more than a brook within relatively shallow and narrow banks except during the heavy rains of the winter months. During those times its course becomes a marshy bog and impassable. From the Jezreel, it passes along the base of Mount Carmel through the narrow pass formed by a spur of the Galilean hills and into the Accho Plain, where some additional tributaries join before it empties into the Mediterranean. Its total length from the springs to the sea is only twenty-three miles. In biblical history it is best known for its role in the Barak-Deborah victory over the Canaanite forces of Sisera (Judg. 4—5) and Elijah's contest with the prophets of Baal on Mount Carmel (1 Kings 18:40).

4. Yarkon River The Yarkon is formed by the seasonal runoff from the western slopes of the Samaritan and Judean hills that flows into the Brook Kanah, its major tributary, and the rich springs at the base of Aphek about eight miles inland from the Mediterranean shoreline. Though anchorages and small harbors, such as tel Qasile, a Philistine town, were established along its course and the cedar timbers from Lebanon were floated inland to Aphek for transport to Jerusalem for the construction of Solomon's palace and Temple, the Yarkon historically formed a major barrier to north-south traffic because of the extensive swamps that formed along its course. The profuse vegetation that bordered its banks probably suggested its name that was derived from the Hebrew *yarok,* meaning "green." The Yarkon, in biblical times, formed the border between the tribes of Dan and Ephraim to the north. Farther inland, the Brook Kanah formed the boundary between Ephraim and Manasseh (Josh. 16:8; 17:9).

Major Bodies of Water Two major seas heavily influenced Israel's political, economic, and cultural history.

1. Mediterranean Sea The Mediterranean Sea had a width of 100—600 miles and stretched over 2,000 miles from the Straits of Gibraltar to the Palestinian coast.

Formed by the movement of the European and North African continental plates, the greater Mediterranean consists of a series of basins and extended shoreline that historically contributed to the vitality of maritime commerce and trade. The unusually straight coast along the south portion of its eastern shoreline and the lack of natural coves and harbor facilities limited Israelite opportunities for direct involvement in Mediterranean maritime commerce. While limited port facilities existed at coastal towns such as Joppa, Dor, and Accho, they were hardly adequate to facilitate more than a local fishing fleet and an occasional refuge during a storm for the larger merchant ships that frequented the great harbors established farther to the north along the Phoenician coast. As a result, the treaties established between the Israelite kings and the Phoenicians provided for an exchange of agricultural and horticultural produce in exchange for lumber and imports (2 Chron. 2:16), and a mutually beneficial cooperation in maintaining a monopoly on both land and sea routes of commerce and trade (1 Kings 9:26,27). The Mediterranean became the "Roman" sea when the peaceful conditions of Roman control of land masses along most of the Mediterranean shoreline fostered a dramatic movement of products, merchandise and people to satisfy the diverse needs of the provinces and Roman policy in them. See *Mediterranean.*

2. *Red Sea* The Red Sea (Heb. *yam suf,* lit. "Sea of Reeds") is a long narrow body of water separating the Arabian Peninsula from the northeastern coast of Africa (Egypt, Sudan, and Ethiopia). At its southern end its narrow straits (twenty-one miles wide) open to the Indian Ocean. With a length of about 1,240 miles and a width that varies from 124 to 223 miles, the total surface area is just over 176,000 square miles. While its average depth is about 1,640 feet, as a part of the great rift or fault that runs northward from Lake Victoria to the base of the Caucasus Mountains in southern Russia, the Red Sea plunges to 7,741 feet near Port Sudan. It is the warmest and most saline of all the open seas. Though the shores of the Red Sea historically have been sparsely settled and its ports have been few, its waterway provided access to the distant ports of the Indian Ocean and the eastern shoreline of Africa where the Phoenician merchant fleets under lease to Solomon bartered for the luxury goods that graced the royal courts of the Levant (1 Kings 9:26).

In the north the Gulf of Suez and the Gulf of Elath (Aqaba) form the western and eastern arms making up the shorelines of the Sinai Peninsula. The Egyptian pharaohs used the Gulf of Suez as the shortest route to the Mediterranean. It was linked with the Bitter Lakes and the Nile by a canal that existed before 600 B.C. and was maintained by the Persians, the Ptolemies, and the Romans.

With the expansion of David's empire, the Gulf of Elath (Aqaba) provided the vital maritime trade outlet that the kings of Israel and Judah and the Phoenician allies exploited to fill the coffers of Jerusalem. After the demise of the Judean kingdom, the Nabataeans established a similar monopoly over the same marine commerce and the overland caravan routes through Petra to Damascus and Gaza for transshipment on the Mediterra-

nean. Again in Hellenistic times, the Indian trade routes were reestablished and maintained throughout Roman times. See *Red Sea.*

Apart from the significant roles played by the Nile in Egypt and the Tigris and Euphrates in Mesopotamia, the rivers of the biblical world were small and mostly unnavigable. As a result, apart from the alluvial plains that bordered their banks, these rivers played a more meaningful role as barriers and boundaries than as waterways for travel and transport. In terms of early biblical history, the Mediterranean and the Red Seas played the more dominant roles in intercultural and commercial exchange. As the Greek and Roman Empires developed, the western seas—the Aegean, Ionian, Adriatic, and Tyrrhenian—grew in importance. In the north and east, the Black Sea, the Caspian Sea, and the Persian Gulf with the mountain ranges that linked them basically formed the limits of the biblical world.

George L. Kelm

RIZIA (Rĭ′ zĭ à) Personal name meaning, "delight." Head of a family within the tribe of Asher who was a renowned warrior (1 Chron. 7:39–40).

RIZPAH (Rĭz′ pah) Personal name meaning, "glowing coals" or "bread heated over coals or ashes." Saul's concubine whom Abner took as wife in what amounted to a claim to the throne (2 Sam. 3:7; compare 1 Kings 2:22). Rizpah is best known for her faithful vigil over the bodies of her executed sons (2 Sam. 20:10–14) until David commanded their burial.

ROAD KJV term for raid (1 Sam. 27:10). For the common sense of road, see *Transportation and Travel; King's Highway.*

ROASTED GRAIN See *Parched Grain.*

ROBBERY Taking another person's property without the person's consent. The basic biblical law concerning robbery is the prohibition of the Ten Commandments, "Thou shall not steal" (Ex. 20:15; Deut. 5:19). Such an absolute statement makes it irrelevant whether the robber acquires property by force, duplicity or oppression (see Gen. 31:31; Lev. 19:13; Deut. 24:14–15; Mal. 3:5; John 10:1). Remarkably little concerning robbery is written in the law of Moses. Unlike Assyrian and Babylonian law, no specific penalty is prescribed. Instead, the emphasis is upon restoration of the stolen property to its lawful owner (Ex. 22:1,4,7,9; Lev. 6:1–7; Num. 5:5–8). If a thief could not return or replace it, the thief could be sold into slavery until restitution was made (Ex. 22:3).

During the New Testament period, robbery was the jurisdiction of Roman law. Captured robbers, on occasion, were crucified (Matt. 27:38; Mark

15:27). Robbery could be political. Palestine contained various groups called Zealots, famous for zeal in Judaism and opposition to Rome. The more militant groups, such as the Sicarii, resorted to murder and robbery.

First-century robbers frequently operated together in bands, attacking travelers (Luke 10:30). The surprise of such an attack is analogous to the suddenness of Christ's return (Rev. 3:3). Robbery threatens material possessions; therefore, Jesus commanded faith in spiritual things (Matt. 6:19–20). *LeBron Matthews*

ROBE See *Cloth, Clothing.*

ROBOAM (Rō bō′ am) KJV alternate form of Rehoboam (Matt. 1:7).

ROCK The use of rocky sites as places of refuge (Num. 24:21; Judg. 15:8; 20:47) led to the frequent image of God as a rock, that is, a source of protection. Titles of God include: the "Stone of Israel" (Gen. 49:24 NAS); the Rock (Deut. 32:4); the Rock of salvation (32:15); the Rock which begat Israel (32:18); "the rock that is higher than I" (Ps. 61:2). Isaiah 8:13–14 pictures the Lord of hosts as a "stone of stumbling" to the unholy people of Israel and Judah. Paul identified Christ as the spiritual Rock which nourished Israel in the wilderness (1 Cor. 10:4). Other texts apply to Christ the Isaiah image of a rock which causes persons to fall (Rom. 9:33; 1 Pet. 2:8). Jesus' teaching is the rock-solid foundation for life (Matt. 7:24–25). The identity of the rock upon which Christ promised to build the church (Matt. 16:18) is disputed. Possible identifications include: Peter, whose name means "rock", the larger group of disciples, Christ Himself, and Peter's confession of faith. The different Greek terms employed (*Petros* and *petra*) argue against a quick identification of Peter as the foundation. Both Christ (1 Cor. 3:11) and the larger circle of apostles (Eph. 2:20; Rev. 21:14) are pictured as the foundation of the church elsewhere. It seems unlikely that Matthew presents Christ as both Builder and foundation of the church. Application of the foundation image to evangelistic work (Rom. 15:20; 1 Cor. 3:10) suggests that Peter's God-revealed confession of faith in Jesus as the Christ, the Son of the living God (Matt. 16:16), is the foundation of the church which lays seige to the gates of Hades. See *Keys of the Kingdom; Peter.* *Chris Church*

ROCK BADGER See *Animals; Coney.*

ROD, STAFF Rod designates a straight, slender stick growing on (Jer. 1:11) or cut from (Gen. 30:37–41) a tree. Rod is sometimes used interchangeably with staff (Isa. 10:5; Rev. 11:1). Elsewhere, rod designates a shorter, clublike stick (Ps. 23:4). Rods and staffs were used as walking sticks

(Gen. 32:10), for defense (Ps. 23:4), for punishment (Ex. 21:20; Num. 22:27; Prov. 13:24; 1 Cor. 4:21), and for measurement (Rev. 11:1). Rods and staffs were also used as symbols of prophetic (Ex. 4:2–4; 7:8–24; Judg. 6:21), priestly (Num. 17:1–10), and royal (Gen. 49:10 NRSV; Judg. 5:14 NRSV; Jer. 48:17; Rev. 2:27) office.

RODANIM (Rŏd ȧ nĭm) Inhabitants of Rhodes (1 Chron. 1:7 NRSV). The parallel in Genesis 10:4 (KJV) reads "Dodanim" which should be preferred as the more difficult reading. Rhodians, however, fits well in the general geographic context.

ROE, ROEBUCK (*Capreolus capreolus*) One of the smallest species of deer, measuring about 26 inches at the shoulder. See *Animals.*

ROGELIM (Rō′ gĕ lĭm) Place name meaning, "[place of] the fullers." City on the Jabbok River in Gilead (2 Sam. 17:27–29; 19:31). The site is perhaps Zaharet's Soq′ah. Tell Barsina lacks evidence of occupation in David's time.

ROHGAH (Rōh′ ḡah) Personal name perhaps meaning, "cry out." Leader of the tribe of Asher (1 Chron. 7:34).

ROLL See *Scroll.*

ROLLER KJV term for something wrapped around the arm (Ezek. 30:21) as a bandage (NAS, REB, NRSV) or splint (NIV).

ROMAMTI-EZER (Rō măm tĭ-ē′ zēr) Personal name meaning, "I have exalted help." Temple musician (1 Chron. 25:4,31). Some scholars recognize a prayer of praise behind the names of the Temple musicians Hananiah through Mahazioth (25:4).

ROMAN LAW The broad category of Roman law stands behind an adequate understanding of the New Testament and its world. The might of the Roman Empire dominated the Ancient Near East, including Palestine and the Mediterranean world in which Christianity was born. Roman law developed over a period of one thousand years, from the publication of the XII Tables in 451–50 B.C. to Emperor Justinian's codification in A.D. 529–34. The points of major relevance of Roman law for interpreting the New Testament cluster around several categories, particularly Roman citizenship, the influence of Roman law upon family life and roles, and Roman criminal jurisprudence. **Roman Citizenship** The Book of Acts depicts Paul as a Roman citizen from birth (22:28) whose citizenship proved advantageous during his missionary travels. Roman citizenship could be obtained by one of several means, the most preferred of which was by inheriting it at birth from parents who were citizens. The New Testament is silent as to how Paul's family had acquired citizenship. The state could grant citizenship for one of several types of service to the empire, either civil or military, particularly the latter. Citizenship could be obtained by purchase (Acts 22:28).

The evidence is unclear as to how citizens were able to document their citizenship. Presumably they carried the ancient equivalent of the modern-day passport, a certificate made either of metal or wood. False claims to citizenship were punishable by death. In Acts 22:27, Paul's merely claiming citizenship seems to have sufficed without having to produce official papers.

Citizenship bestowed certain rights. These included the right to vote for magistrates, the right to be elected as a magistrate, the right to contract a legal marriage, the right to hold property in the Roman community, and the right to appeal to the people, and in later times to the emperor, against the sentences passed by magistrates or other officials of rank.

Paul's citizenship surfaced in several details of his missionary activity in Acts. Acts 16:39 records the consternation of either the lictors or magistrates in Philippi upon discovering that Paul was a Roman citizen. They realized that they had punished him without trial. By law, citizens could not be bound or scourged (compare Acts 22:24–29). Most important of all is the right of "appeal to Caesar" and trial at Rome (Acts 25:10–12).

Roman Law and Family Life The New Testament "House Codes" (Eph. 5:21—6:9; Col. 3:18—4:1; and 1 Pet. 2:18—3:7) should be interpreted against the background of the status of the family and the power of the head of the household in Roman society. If Greek society looked to belonging in one's city as the chief unit of society, Roman society, both legally and culturally, looked to the family as the primary unit of society. In early Roman law, and to a significant though diminishing extent throughout the Roman period, the paterfamilias (head of the household) was the only fully legal person in the family. The "family" included what today would be termed the "extended" family, crossing generational lines and including the wife, all unmarried sons and daughters, married sons and their families, those persons adopted into the family, and slaves. All of these persons lived under the *patria potestas,* or "absolute power," of the patriarchal head of the household. The *patria potestas* of the *paterfamilias* extended even to matters of life and death, limited only by the constraints of the habit of consulting a family council or by the restraints of certain laws. The father, for example, was the person who decided whether or not to allow a newborn infant to die. That such power flourished in the New Testament era is born out by the fact that one father had his son executed for his part in

the Catiline Conspiracy of 62 B.C. In early Roman times fathers could sell their children just as they could any other property. This absolute power of the Roman father included not only the persons directly descended from him but also their personal property. Persons living under another's *patria potestas* in actuality owned nothing. Upon their marriage, daughters passed into the power of another family's *patria potestas.* Upon the death of the *paterfamilias,* as many new families were created as there had been sons living under his power (or grandsons, in the event their fathers had died).

Against such a background, Paul's command to be subject to one another (Eph. 5:21) was a revolutionary word spoken to a society in which all were subject to the *paterfamilias.*

Roman Jurisprudence While Roman civil law relates to the New Testament only in incidental ways, Roman criminal law casts much light upon the trial of Jesus. The representative and executor of Roman law in the Gospels is, of course, Pontius Pilate, who served as the Roman *procurator,* or governor, of Judea during the years A.D. 26–36. Procurators, while lacking the full status and prestige of a Roman proconsul or imperial legate, were Roman "knights" of nonsenatorial rank and were invested with the same powers of higher officials. In modern-day terminology, Pilate was a "military governor" overseeing a province known as a seedbed of rebellion.

As the chief Roman administrator in the province, Pilate held the *imperium,* the supreme, administrative life-or-death power over the subjects in a province. The *imperium* extended particularly over the *peregrini,* or non-Roman citizens such as Jesus living in an occupied state. While Roman citizens possessed the right of appeal to Caesar, provincial subjects had little to protect them against abuses of the life and death power wielded by proconsuls and lesser governors such as Pilate. Pilate would have held the total power of Roman administration, jurisdiction, defense, and maintenance of law and order in the province of Judea. In the eyes of his superiors, Pilate's first priority was public order, not the execution of justice. They would not have categorized his conduct of the trial of Jesus as irresponsible. If an innocent Galilean peasant was the focal point of a civil disturbance, the quelling of the disturbance, and not justice for the *peregrinus* involved, was the uppermost concern for Roman officials fearful of revolts in occupied provinces.

Roman governors normally looked to a number of detailed statutes to define major offenses or felonies against persons, society, and government. The entire system, known as the *ordo iudiciorum publicoum,* perhaps is best translated as "the list of national courts." This *ordo* contained a list of crimes and punishments with the maximum and minimum penalties that could be exacted against

Roman citizens. A Roman citizen who felt that the *ordo* was misapplied could appeal to Caesar. Common offenses, and rare ones such as arson, were dealt with by magistrates *extra ordinem* ("outside the list"). In any case involving a *peregrinus,* a Roman governor such as Pilate would have been free to proceed based upon his *imperium* and his own good judgment. He functioned as prosecuting attorney, judge, and jury. He would have been free to adopt the rules and guidelines of the *ordo* if appropriate, but he would also have been free to be as harsh and arbitrary as he preferred. A good first century *procurator* would, however, have tended more and more to judge a *peregrinus* by the *ordo.*

Roman trial proceedings were public, before the tribune (compare Matt. 27:19). Interested parties brought formal charges, which had to be specific (compare Matt. 27:12). In the Gospels, Jesus was charged before Pilate with a political crime. The Romans would never execute someone simply on religious grounds. Roman criminal trials included the *cognitio,* or the questioning of the accused. After A.D. 50 enlightened officials gave accused persons three opportunities to respond to charges made against them. Interestingly enough, Pilate does this very thing in the trial account as we find it in John (compare John 18:33,35,37), following the most enlightened possible juridical rules of the day. Failure to respond to the charges resulted in conviction by default. When Jesus remained silent and made no defense, under the Roman system, Pilate had no other option but to convict. Following the *cognitio,* the governor would then render his verdict in the form of a sentence to a particular punishment.

The trial of Jesus in the Gospels conforms in many of its particulars to the fine points of Roman criminal procedure. For example, it was not unknown to transfer jurisdiction to the accused's place of origin (compare Pilate's sending Jesus to Herod in Luke 23:6–7). Similarly, according to John 18:28, the trial of Jesus took place early in the day, an odd hour to modern minds, but precisely at the time when ancient Roman officials were the busiest, ordinarily arising early to work even before breakfast. To modern thought, it might also seem strange that Pilate consulted with his wife (Matt. 27:19) concerning Jesus. Far from some unseemly intrusion by her into official affairs of state, Roman women normally shared the responsibilities of husbands serving as career diplomats. They often were the husband's best advisor.

The Roman system of criminal justice distinguished between public and private penalties. The private penalty consisted of a sum of money paid to the person wronged as a substitute for private retaliation. Public penalties ranged from light beatings to the infliction of the death penalty, which could take various forms, with decapitation, gallows or crucifixion, burning, and drowning in a sack being the most common. Imprisonment as a penalty for a crime was unknown in Roman times. In the later empire, banishment to hard labor in mines or public works projects appeared as a penalty for wrongdoing.

The appearances of Paul before governmental officials and his trials in Acts also accord with what we know elsewhere of Roman trial procedure and custom. Perhaps most notable is the fact that in Acts 24:18–19 Jews make the original charges against Paul, but later disappear from the case. Before Felix (Acts 24:19), Paul objected that his accusers ought to be present. Roman law was strongly inclined against persons who made accusations and then abandoned them. Acts closes (28:30) by giving the tantalizing detail that Paul remained under "house arrest" in Rome for two years awaiting trial. This perplexing delay could be explained by a congested court list, the failure of his accusers to appear to lodge their charges, or the upheaval that characterized Nero's reign. Also noteworthy is the fact that Acts twice links Paul with Roman proconsuls (Sergius Paulus on Cyprus in 13:6–12 and Annius Gallio at Corinth in 18:12–17). See *Trial of Jesus; Citizen, Citizenship; Marriage and Family;* and *Pilate, Pontius.*

Mike Fuhrman

ROMANS, BOOK OF The most significant theological letter ever written. Augustine of Hippo (354–430), the most influential of the church fathers, was converted upon reading Romans 13:13–14. Martin Luther, the father of the Protestant Reformation, was studying Romans when he concluded that faith alone justifies a person before God. John Wesley, the founder of Methodism, was converted on May 24, 1738, upon reading Luther's introduction to Romans.

Where was Paul when he wrote Romans? Paul discussed his situation at the time he wrote Romans in the book itself (15:25–29), indicating that he was about to leave for Jerusalem. He stated that his purpose was to deliver the monies given by the churches in Macedonia and Achaia (the name of the Roman province embracing most of Greece, south of Macedonia) for the "poor among the saints in Jerusalem" (15:26 NIV). This information from the Roman letter corresponds precisely with what Luke reported in the Acts of the Apostles about Paul's deciding to leave Ephesus, travel through Macedonia and Achaia, go to Jerusalem, and then visit Rome (Acts 19:21). Paul spent three months in Achaia (Acts 20:2–3). Scholars generally agree that Paul's close relationship with the Corinthian church would have resulted in his staying there, and this is confirmed by Paul's mentioning that he was staying with Gaius (Rom. 16:23) who was a convert in Corinth (see 1 Cor. 1:14).

That Paul wrote Romans while in Greece and before leaving for Jerusalem establishes the limits

The famous Colosseum at Rome was built in the latter part of the first century A.D.

for the dating of the letter. The fixed point for dating Paul's stay in Corinth is his appearance (on an earlier visit to Corinth) before Gallio, the proconsul of Achaia (Acts 18:12–17), who was in office between A.D. 50–54 and most likely in A.D. 51. Estimating the time from Paul's appearance before Gallio until his return to Corinth is difficult because of Luke's general statements of time—"Paul stayed many days longer" (Acts 18:18 RSV)—but most scholars would date Romans between A.D. 54 to 59, with a date of 55–56 being preferred.

Why did Paul write Romans? Paul mentioned his reasons for writing to the Roman church twice, once at the beginning and again near the end of the letter. He had for a long time had the desire to visit the Christians in Rome that "we may be mutually encouraged by each other's faith" and clearly implied that now at long last he was coming (Rom. 1:8–13). Paul thus wrote the Romans to announce his impending visit. His practice had been to preach in unevangelized areas (15:20), and he had run out of room in the eastern empire (15:23), having preached from Jerusalem to Illyricum (15:19), at the westernmost point of the eastern empire. Paul now planned to continue his ministry to the western limit of the empire and go to Spain (15:24). He shared his plans to stop and visit the Romans on his way and expressed the hope that they would provide support for his journey on to Spain (15:24). He probably looked for support in prayer, some financial assistance, and perhaps the designating of a Roman Christian

who knew the western area to travel with Paul.

Finally, Paul urged the church to pray for him as he went to Jerusalem (15:30–31). Paul's concern was twofold. He was concerned about the Jerusalem Christians' reaction to an offering from Gentile churches and hoped that the offering would draw the Jewish and Gentile Christians together (see Gal. 2:11–21; Acts 15:1–35). Paul was also aware of the threat posed by the "unbelievers in Judea" (15:31) or the Jews, loyal to their ancient traditions, who were upset by Paul's proclamation of Jesus as Messiah.

Paul's description of his purpose led earlier students of the Bible to see Romans as an outline of Paul's theology, composed at greater leisure, to acquaint the Romans with his views so they would fully support him in his mission to Spain. Scholars soon realized, however, that this perception of Romans as a summary of Paul's theology was inadequate for three reasons. First, Romans does not contain any discussion or emphasis on some things Paul clearly believed strongly as we know from his other letters—such as the Lord's Supper (1 Cor. 11:17–34) and the second coming of Christ (1 Thess. 4:13—5:11). Second, Paul stressed matters in Romans he does not give much attention to in his other letters, such as the wrath of God (Rom. 1:18–32) and the Jewish rejection of Jesus as Messiah (Rom. 9—11). Third, Romans includes materials that do not fit into the category of a summary of Paul's theology. The exhorta-

things right through the life, death, and resurrection of Jesus. See *Righteousness.*

The pivotal importance of understanding "the righteousness of God" as God in action in Christ will only clearly be seen when it is grasped that the same Greek word root occurs in the terms translated into English as righteousness, just, justification, and justify. Understanding what Paul meant by righteousness is therefore crucial for one's interpretation of Romans because it sets one's perception of justification as well.

Scholars have debated for centuries as to whether justification (God's action in making persons righteous) refers primarily to one's new status in Christ—justification would thus mean the bestowal of a righteous status before God—or to one's new moral character in Christ—justification would then mean God's action in one's life to enable a person to achieve high ethical standards. Protestant, and particularly Lutheran scholars, have argued that justification should be understood in the first sense and indicates God's acquitting or pronouncing the sinner righteous without any reference to moral change. Roman Catholic scholars have argued the opposite, holding that justification means God's making a person righteous or moral regeneration. In the heated debates over this issue, it has become clear that an undue stress on either alternative leads to a distorted view of Christianity. To stress justification as God's declaring the sinner righteous without regard to any subsequent change in the sinner's moral character is as wrong as to stress justification as moral achievement to the point that living by works overshadows living by faith. The best understanding of justification is one which includes both the new status of a person before God and the new life that this status demands. See *Justification.*

When the "righteousness of God" is understood as God's working in Christ to set things right, then it becomes clear that God declares the sinner righteous (acquits). Persons who experience this declaration at the same time repudiate sin as a way of life, enter into an intense struggle with sin, and look forward to Christ's complete victory over evil. Salvation is thus at one time, according to Paul, God's gift of a righteous status before Him in Christ (6:23) and God's demand to live the new life which Christ makes possible. Scholars refer to this reality as the indicative and imperative aspects in Paul's thought. Paul indicated what God has done in Christ (indicative) and then exhorted his readers to achieve it (imperative). Paul, for example affirmed the gift—"you have been freed from sin" (6:22 NRSV); but in the same context he exhorted his readers to live up to the demand—"Present your members as slaves to righteousness" (6:19 NRSV). Such frequent indicative and imperative statements at first glance seem contradictory. They, however, represent the way Paul understood Christianity—what God has

The interior of the Colosseum at Rome showing the area beneath the arena.

tions in 12:1—15:14 are clearly outside this category. Some of them, such as how they should relate to government (Rom. 13:1–7) or those "weak in faith" (Rom. 14:1—15:6) seem to reflect specific problems in the Roman Christian community. Taking these facts seriously, scholars now feel that Paul knew much more about the Roman Christians than earlier scholars realized and wrote to the church with several purposes in mind: (1) to request their prayers as he faced the threatening situation in Jerusalem, (2) to alert them to his intended visit, (3) to acquaint them with some of his understanding of what God had done in Christ, (4) to instruct them in areas where the church faced specific problems, and (5) to enlist their support in his planned missionary venture to Spain.

What is the key concept in Romans? The theme of Romans is generally agreed to be the "righteousness of God" (see 1:16–17), but the meaning of this phrase is disputed. Some interpret it to mean the righteousness which God bestows on persons on the basis of Christ's work, understanding "of God" to mean "from God." Other interpreters hold that "the righteousness of God" is the activity of God, understanding the term primarily from its use in the Greek translation of the Old Testament where it refers to God's acting in His saving power. This seems the better alternative—the righteousness of God is God in action, setting

done for us in Christ summons us to what we ought to do for God. See *Ethics; Salvation.*

The salvation that the power of God brings (1:16) is, therefore, not freedom from struggle. Paul understood the center of the Christian life to be intense struggle with the power of sin in one's life. The new status before God (justification) opens one's eyes to understand reality in a new way. The one who trusts Christ experiences a revelation in understanding. In the experience of faith it is "revealed" (1:17) that God came in Christ to set people free from the enslaving power of sin by enabling guilty sinners to be declared righteous and then to achieve it.

From Paul's perspective, the Christian understands the power of sin and God's action to triumph over it in a way the unbeliever does not. Paul described this new understanding and the arena of conflict it thrusts the Christian into in terms that relate to his Jewish heritage. Paul used the figures of Adam and Christ as representing the only two possibilities for human existence. Adam, the original transgressor (5:12), was the one through whom sin entered; but sin did not come alone—death is inseparably linked to sin in Paul's thought (5:12–14). These two realities—sin and death—have such great force that Paul said sin or death "reigned" (5:14,21). The third reality in his unholy trilogy of powers is the law which Paul felt is in itself holy (7:12). Sin's power demonstrated itself in using the law for its own purposes (7:8–11). This complex of powers, opposed to God and His purpose in creation, stands in unwavering hostility and opposition to another triad of powers (see 5:18–21) in the realm of Christ: righteousness (against sin), grace (against law), and life (against death). Paul's conception is that both of these power fields exist in our present world with unbelievers totally controlled by the evil forces and with believers constantly needing to struggle to free themselves from the hold sin has and tries to gain over them.

Paul also used other vehicles of expression to articulate his view of Christian life as focused in struggle with sin. Many persons in the first century world felt that an unalterable hostility existed between matter and spirit (thought or consciousness) with matter being the source of evil and spirit being the fountain of good. Paul made use of this kind of language but not with the dualism of Greek thought which opposed flesh (matter) to spirit. Flesh, as substance or material, is in itself neutral and has neither evil or good nature; but a person under sin's control is "in the flesh" (8:9), a contrast to to life "in the Spirit" (8:9–11). In this life (in the flesh) believers must rise to the demand of God's gift to us through Christ and walk "according to the Spirit" (8:4–8).

Paul alone in the New Testament explained the transition from the realm of Adam to the realm of Christ as a dying and rising with Christ (6:5–11).

This bas-relief of Rome's symbol of power, the Roman imperial eagle, was found at Jerusalem.

Our death with Christ causes us to be "united with him" (6:5) in death. This union with Christ reveals sin in all its ugliness. Believers follow God as Jesus did, repudiate sin's rule, and realize sin's end is death. Our resurrection with Christ is our rising from death with Him spiritually to live to God. This dying and rising with Christ sets us free from sin in the sense that sin's power is no longer enslaving. The Christian has the resources of God to fight sin victoriously; but intense struggle is necessary (6:11).

Dying and rising with Christ results in a person's being "in Christ." This phrase, used more than one hundred times in Paul's letters and infrequently outside Paul's writings, is Paul's favorite way of describing salvation. To be "in Christ" is to be in the power field of grace, life, and righteousness; it is to live in the strength of our having been raised with Christ; and it is a life of trust in God which struggles with the power of sin in one's life on the basis of God's powerful presence (Holy Spirit). Paul can thus speak of the power that enables Christians to overcome as "the Spirit," "the Spirit of God," "the Spirit of Christ," "Christ . . . in you," and "in Christ" (8:1–11).

What is the structure of Romans? Paul's letter to the Romans moves with logical precision as the theme of "the righteousness of God" is developed in its relevance for the Christians in Rome. The expertise of the inspired writer emerges clearly as

Paul, although dealing with the problems of a specific group of Christians in Rome, unwaveringly elevated the discussion to a level that also addresses the needs of Christians in all places and at all times.

Paul's introduction to the letter (1:1–15) sets out the apostolic calling which qualifies him (vv. 1–7) and explains his reason for writing the Romans (vv. 8–15). After the introduction, Paul crisply stated the theme of his letter—the righteousness of God, revealed in the gospel and bringing salvation (1:16–17). Paul then supported his theme in the first major section of the letter by demonstrating that all persons need salvation (1:18—3:20), showing first that the power of sin rules the Gentiles (1:18–32) and, second, that the power of sin rules the Jews as well (2:1—3:8). Paul concluded this section with a summary statement that all humanity stands under the power of sin (3:19–20).

The second major section deals with God's provision of righteousness through Jesus Christ on the basis of faith (3:21—4:25). Paul affirmed that God has manifested His righteousness apart from the law in the expiating blood of Jesus Christ and that God justified (declares righteous) persons on the basis of trust (3:21–26). Justification by faith excludes boasting or exulting in one's goodness achieved by works according to the law. The way God justified Abraham by faith demonstrates that trust as a way of relating to God preceded seeking to relate to Him by the works of the law, meeting the Jewish objection that God requires works for justification (3:27—4:25).

After establishing the reality of justification by faith, Paul discussed, in the third section of Romans, the impact and implication of what God does for us in Christ and focuses on how salvation results in a victorious new life (5:1—8:39). The immediate result of justification is a realization of peace with God based on the assurance coming from God's love for us and results in one's ability to rejoice in the face of difficulties because Christ has reversed the results of Adam's disobedience (5:1–21). The very heart of salvation is found in the Christian's continuing, but victorious, struggle with sin (6:1—7:25). This victorious struggle is possible because of the power of the risen Christ, experienced as Holy Spirit, who assists us to do what is right (8:1–39).

The salvation Christ brought raised profound questions among Jewish Christians about the destiny of the Jews who still felt themselves to be God's people even though they had rejected Christ. Paul dealt with this issue in the fourth section (chs. 9—11). He stressed that the righteousness of God is demonstrated in His faithfulness to all His promises—even those to Israel in the Old Testament. Paul confessed his personal grief over Israel's rejection of Christ (9:1–15) and affirmed that God has, as always, displayed His sovereignty in dealing with Israel (9:6–29). Israel's God-given freedom to choose explains the rejection of Jesus as the Christ (9:30—10:21). Paul reminded his readers that God's righteousness is displayed in His mercy on which all—both Jews and Gentiles—are dependent (11:1–36).

The final section is a summons to practical obedience to God (12:1—15:13). Christians should live transformed lives (12:1–2) and demonstrate this in a good stewardship of their spiritual gifts (12:3–21), in fulfilling their obligations to the state (13:1–7), in making love supreme (13:8–14), and in seeking to nurture others in the fellowship of the church, being particularly careful to bear with and edify the weak (14:1—15:13).

In the conclusion to the letter (15:14—16:27), Paul summarized his ministry and his plans for the future, requesting their prayers (15:14–33); then he commended Phoebe (16:1–2), sent greetings to individual Christians (16:3–24), and ended his letter with praise for God—"to the only wise God through Jesus Christ be glory for endless ages! Amen" (16:27 REB).

Outline

I. Introduction: Qualifications and Reason for Writing (1:1–15).
  A. Apostolic calling qualifies the author (1:1–7).
  B. Grateful, prayerful concern for the readers motivates the writing (1:8–15).

II. Theme: The Power for Salvation and the Righteousness of God Are Revealed (1:16–17).

III. All People Need Salvation from the Power of Sin (1:18—3:20).
  A. The power of sin rules among the Gentiles (1:18–32).
    1. The Gentiles reject the knowledge of God (1:18–23).
    2. The Gentiles experience the results of rebellion against God (1:24–32).
  B. The power of sin rules among the Jews (2:1—3:8).
    1. The Jews demonstrate their disobedience (2:1–16).
    2. The Jews confuse privilege and responsibility (2:17—3:8).
  C. All humanity—Jews and Gentiles—stand under the power of sin (3:9–20).

IV. God Provides Righteousness through Jesus Christ on the Basis of Faith (3:21—4:25).
  A. God manifests His righteousness (3:21–26).
    1. God's righteousness is through faith (3:21–23).
    2. God's righteousness is through the blood of Christ (3:24–25a).
    3. God's righteousness is shown in His passing over former sins (3:25b–26).
  B. Justification is by faith for all persons (3:27—4:25).

1. Justifying faith excludes all boasting (3:27–31).
2. The example of Abraham confirms justification by faith (4:1–25).

V. Salvation in Christ Results in Victorious New Life (5:1—8:39).
A. Justification results in peace and righteousness (5:1–21).
1. Peace with God results in rejoicing in all circumstances (5:1–11).
2. Christ reverses the results of Adam's sin (5:12–21).
B. Christian life is a victorious struggle with sin (6:1—7:25).
1. Faith unites believers in dying and rising with Christ (6:1–11).
2. Believers are not slaves of sin, but of righteousness (6:12–23).
3. Dying with Christ sets us free from law (7:1–6).
4. Struggle with sin is defeat without Christ (7:7–25).
C. The Spirit of Christ is the power of the Christian's life (8:1–39).
1. The Spirit is the power for freedom from sin (8:1–4).
2. Life in the Spirit is the opposite of life in the flesh (8:5–11).
3. The Spirit creates and witnesses to our status as God's children (8:12–17).
4. The Spirit confers victorious life (8:18–39).

VI. God Is Faithful in All His Promises (9:1—11:36).
A. Paul grieves over Israel's rejection of Christ (9:1–5).
B. God's sovereignty is displayed in His dealings with Israel (9:6–29).
1. God's sovereignty is illustrated in His elective choices (9:6–13).
2. God's sovereignty is seen in His mercy (9:14–18).
3. God has chosen both Jews and Gentiles (9:19–29).
C. Israel's freedom to choose explains her rejection of Christ (9:30—10:21).
1. Israel chose works rather than faith (9:30–33).
2. Israel rejected righteousness based on faith (10:1–15).
3. Israel refuses to hear and obey (10:16–21).
D. God's righteousness is displayed in His mercy (11:1–36).
1. The saved remnant of Jews shows God's mercy (11:1–6).
2. The salvation extended to the Gentiles shows God's mercy (11:7–24).
3. All persons—Jews and Gentiles—are dependent on God's mercy (11:25–32).

4. God deserves praise for His judgments (11:33–36).

VII. The Saving Mercy of God in Christ Summons Christians to Obedience (12:1—15:13).
A. Theme of the exhortations: Christians need to be transformed (12:1–2).
B. Christians must be responsible members of the body of Christ (12:3–21).
1. Christians need to view themselves and others appropriately (12:3–5).
2. Christians must express their different gifts in faith (12:6–13).
3. Christian life demands love in action (12:14–21).
C. Christians must fulfill their appropriate obligations to the state (13:1–7).
D. Christians must remember the supremacy of love and the urgency of the times (13:8–14).
1. Love fulfills the law (13:8–10).
2. The critical nature of the times calls for radical commitment to Christ (13:11–14).
E. Christians must seek to edify one another in the fellowship of the church (14:1—15:13).
1. The strong and the weak in the church must realize that Christ is the Lord of both groups (14:1–12).
2. Christians should live by their own convictions, pursue harmony, and avoid making others stumble (14:13–23).
3. Strong Christians are obligated to bear with and live in harmony with the weak (15:1–6).
4. All Christians are to receive one another as Christ has received them (15:7–13).

VIII. Conclusion (15:14—16:27)

Harold S. Songer

ROME AND THE ROMAN EMPIRE International rule the government in Rome, Italy, exercised after 27 B.C. when the Republic of Rome died and the Roman Empire was born. The reasons for the fall of the republic are not anymore clearly demonstrable than those surrounding the later fall of the empire. They were the product of a complicated interaction of numerous components that included: changes in the values, wealth, and education of the upper classes; innovations in finances, agriculture, and commerce; expansion of the senate; enormous increases in citizenship; unrest among the classes; problems in maintaining order in the districts in and around Rome, and difficulty in recruiting sufficient personnel for the army. The major factor in its demise seems to have been political. The senate lost political control of the state, and into that vacuum Julius

The Egnatian Way, shown here near Neapolis, was part of the extensive Roman road system.

Caesar stepped with ambitions of control that the senate found intolerable. His declaration of himself in early 44 B.C. as perpetual dictator provoked his assassination on the Ides of March by a group of senatorial assassins led by Brutus and Cassius. Caesar's generals, Antony and Lepidus along with Caesar's heir Octavian, formed a temporary ruling triumvirate. They defeated Caesar's assassins in the battle at Philippi in 42 B.C. This finally resulted in the exclusion of Lepidus and the division of the empire into the West, controlled by Octavian, and the East, controlled by Antony. Antony's military failure against the Parthians led to his excessive reliance on Egyptian resources and created a correspondingly inordinate influence of Egypt's Queen Cleopatra on the Roman ruler. Octavian was able to use Antony's reliance on Egypt against him, persuading the senate that Antony wanted to make Alexandria the capital of the empire. The two led their armies against each other in 31 B.C. at Actium in Greece, resulting in the defeat of Antony and the eventual suicide of both Antony and Cleopatra. Octavian became sole ruler and in 27 B.C. took the name: Augustus Caesar. The republic became the empire, and Octavian became what Julius had only dreamed of becoming—the first emperor of Rome.

Augustus was extremely efficient as an administrator and corrected many of the problems that plagued the old republic. He, unlike Julius, treated the senate with respect and gained theirs in return. He, as the adopted son of the previous ruler, inherited the affection of his army. The relationship proved so popular that, after Augustus, every emperor had to be either the real son or the adopted son of the previous emperor to command the allegiance of the army and of the people of the empire. Augustus reduced the senate gradually from 1,000 to 600 and made membership in it hereditary, although he reserved the privilege of nominating new senators.

A major achievement involved sharing power over the empire's provinces. Senatorial provinces were created, over which the senate had jurisdiction and to which they appointed governors or proconsuls. These were peaceful provinces requiring no unusual military presence. Gallio, the brother of Seneca, was made proconsul over the southern Grecian province of Achaia in A.D. 51 during the time Paul was in Corinth (Acts 18:12). Imperial provinces were controlled by the emperor. He appointed procurators over these potentially volatile areas, where the Roman legions or armies were stationed. Pontius Pilate was such a procurator or governor over Judea (Luke 3:1).

Augustus inaugurated an extensive program of social, religious, and moral reform. Special benefits were given to those couples who agreed to have children. Adultery, which previously was widely condoned, was made a public crime entailing severe penalties. Traditional religion was stressed, and 82 pagan temples were renovated. Many ancient cults were revived, further accentuating the time-honored view that the peace and prosperity of the republic was dependent upon the proper observance of religious duty. Augustus became *pontifex maximus* in 12 B.C., establishing him as both political and religious head of state.

An extensive building program was undertaken. Augustus added another forum to the already existing Roman Forum and Forum of (Julius) Caesar. The forum served as a judicial, religious, and commercial center for the city, containing basilicas, temples, and porticoes. Later, other fora were built by Vespasian, Nerva, and Trajan, all of them just north of the old Roman Forum. The great variety of other new structures included theaters, libraries, temples, baths, basilicas, arches, and warehouses. For entertainment purposes, the first permanent amphitheater in Rome's history was built. Extensive water systems were constructed that included artificial lakes, canals, aqueducts, and flood control. The sewage system was renovated. A police force of 3,000 men was created along with a fire-fighting force that numbered 7,000.

The first several emperors ruled at the time of the beginning of the Christian movement in the Roman Empire. Jesus was born during the reign of Augustus (27 B.C.–A.D. 14) and conducted His ministry during the reign of Augustus's successor, Tiberius (A.D. 14–37; compare Luke 3:1). The latter's image was stamped on a silver denarius that Jesus referred to in a discussion about taxation (Luke 20:20–26). In about A.D. 18, Herod Antipas, the son of Herod the Great, built his capital on the western shore of the Sea of Galilee and named it Tiberias after the emperor. Tiberius was an extremely able military commander and a good administrator, leaving a large surplus in the treasury when he died. He followed Augustus's example of not expanding the borders of the empire and thus avoiding war. The *pax Romana* (peace of Rome) which Augustus had inaugurated was preserved, providing easy, safe travel throughout the empire. Paul undoubtedly referred to this in Galatians 4:4 when he wrote: "In the *fullness of time* God sent forth his Son" (author's italics). Tiberius was never popular with the senate and chose to leave Rome at the first opportunity, choosing after A.D. 26, to rule the empire from his self-imposed seclusion on the Isle of Capri. In this year Pontius Pilate was appointed governor of Judea, a post he held until A.D. 36, just prior to the death of Tiberius in A.D. 37.

Tiberius was succeeded by his mentally unbalanced grandnephew, Gaius (Caligula), who proved to be a disaster. During his reign (A.D. 37–41) and that of his successor, his aging uncle Claudius (A.D. 41–54), most of the ministry of the apostle Paul took place. Claudius is reported to have expelled Jews from Rome who were creating disturbances at the instigation of Christ (compare Acts 18:2). Initially, his contemporaries viewed Claudius as inept, but he proved to have considerable hidden talents of administration and turned out to be one of Rome's more proficient emperors. He was responsible for the conquest of southern Britain in A.D. 43–47, although it took another 30 years to subjugate northern Britain and Wales. His fourth wife, Agrippina, is mentioned on a recently discovered sarcophagus in the Goliath family cemetery on the western edge of Jericho. She poisoned Claudius in A.D. 54 to speed up the succession of Nero, her son by a previous marriage.

Nero (A.D. 54–68) was in some respects worse than Caligula. He was a man without moral scruples or interest in the Roman populace except for exploitation of them. Both Paul and Peter seem to have been martyred during Nero's reign, perhaps in connection with the burning of Rome by Nero in A.D. 64, an event that he blamed on Christians. The Roman historian Tacitus wrote that when the fire subsided, only four of Rome's fourteen districts remained intact. Yet Paul wrote, "All the saints greet you, especially those of the emperor's household" (Phil. 4:22 NRSV). Nero's hedonism and utter irresponsibility led inevitably to his death. The revolt of Galba, one of his generals, led to Nero's suicide.

Galba, Otho, and Vitellius, three successive emperor-generals, died within the year of civil war (A.D. 68–69) that followed Nero's death. Vitellius's successor was Vespasian, one of the commanders who had taken Britain for Claudius and who was in Judea squelching the first Jewish revolt. He was declared emperor by the Syrian and Danube legions and returned to Rome to assume the post, leaving his son Titus to finish the destruction of Jerusalem with its holy Temple in the next year (A.D. 70). This event was prophesied by Jesus toward the end of His life when He said: "When you see Jerusalem surrounded by armies, then know that its desolation has come near" (Luke 21:20 NRSV).

The aristocratic Julio-Claudian dynasties that had reigned until the death of Nero were happily

A Roman milestone with Latin inscription at Caesarea Maritima.

replaced by the Flavian dynasty, which issued from the rural middle class of Italy and reflected a more modest and responsible approach to the use of power. Vespasian's reign (A.D. 69–79) was succeeded by the brief tenure of his son Titus (A.D. 79–81), who at his death gave way to the rule of his brother Domitian (A.D. 81–96). The fourth century historian Eusebius reported that the apostle John was exiled to Patmos (compare Rev. 1:9) in the reign of Domitian. Eusebius also claimed that in Nerva's reign the senate took away Domitian's honors and freed exiles to return home, thus letting John return to Ephesus.

Nerva's reign was brief, lasting little more than a year (A.D. 96–98). He was succeeded by Trajan (A.D. 98–117), who bathed the empire red in the blood of Christians. His persecution was more severe than that instituted by Domitian. Irenaeus wrote in the second century that John died in Ephesus in the reign of Trajan. The persecution of the church, depicted in the *Revelation of John,* probably reflects the ones initiated by Trajan and Domitian. Trajan, the adopted son of Nerva, was the first emperor of provincial origin. His family roots were in the area of Seville, Spain. Marcus Aurelius, a later emperor of Spanish descent (A.D. 161–180), also persecuted the church.

Trajan adopted Hadrian, his nephew by marriage, who succeeded him (A.D. 117–138) and quickly abandoned his predecessor's only partially

North Sea

HIBERNIA

BRITANNIA
★ Eburacum
★ Lindum
★ Aquae Sulis
★ Londinium

Atlantic Ocean

GERMANIA

Rhine River

★ Lutetia

GALLIA

★ Regina Castra
★ Vindob

★ Mediolanum
★ Lugdunum
★ Burdigala
★ Vienna

RAETIA **NORICUM**
★ Aquileia
PAN

★ Genua
ILLYR

HISPANIA
★ Nemausus
★ Narbo
★ Massilia

ITALIA
★ Ancona

★ Toletum
★ Tarraco
★ Rome

★ Corduba
★ Valentia

★ Gades

★ Neapolis
★ Brundisiu

MAURETANIA
★ Hippo Regius
AFRICA ★ Carthage
★ Syracuse

Medite

★ Leptis Magna

ROME (1st-3rd centuries A.D.)

Circus of Hadrian
Tomb of Augustus
PINCIAN HILL
Castra Praetoria

Mausoleum of Hadrian
QUIRINAL HILL
Baths of Diocletian

Circus of Nero
VATICAN HILL
Theater of Pompey
Pantheon
VIMINAL HILL

CAPITOLINE HILL
Imperial Fora
ESQUILINE HILL
Baths of Trajan

Capitol
Roman Forum
Colosseum

PALATINE HILL

Circus Maximus
T. Divi Claudii
CAELIAN HILL

AVENTINE HILL
Baths of Caracalla

✝ Earliest Christian sites

0   500   1000   1500   yards

0   500   1000   m

© carta

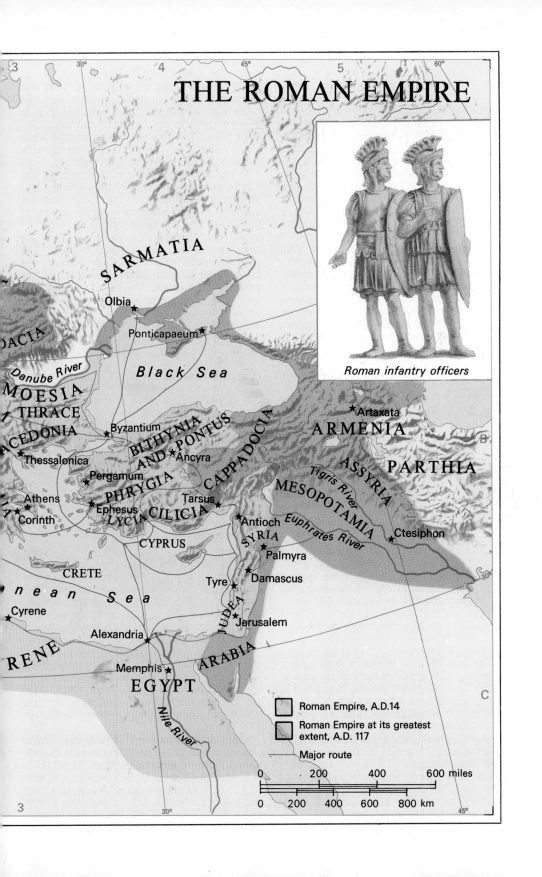

THE ROMAN EMPIRE

Roman infantry officers

SARMATIA

Olbia ★

Ponticapaeum ★

Black Sea

Danube River

DACIA

MOESIA

THRACE

MACEDONIA

Thessalonica ★

Byzantium ★

BITHYNIA AND PONTUS

★ Ancyra

PHRYGIA

Pergamum ★

Athens ★

Corinth ★

Ephesus ★

LYCIA

CILICIA

Tarsus ★

CYPRUS

CRETE

nean Sea

Cyrene ★

Alexandria ★

Memphis ★

EGYPT

Nile River

RENE

ARABIA

JUDEA

Jerusalem ★

Tyre ★

Damascus ★

Palmyra ★

SYRIA

Antioch ★

CAPPADOCIA

★ Artaxata

ARMENIA

ASSYRIA

PARTHIA

MESOPOTAMIA

Tigris River

Euphrates River

Ctesiphon ★

Roman Empire, A.D.14

Roman Empire at its greatest extent, A.D. 117

Major route

0   200   400   600 miles

0   200   400   600   800 km

successful attempts to conquer the East. More than half of Hadrian's reign was spent in traveling throughout the empire and involving himself deeply in the administration of the provinces, an activity for which he was especially talented. He left evidence of his propensity for building all over the Mediterranean world including the arch at the entrance to the precincts of the Athenian temple of Jupiter, the Ecce Homo Arch in Jerusalem, his villa near Rome, and the magnificent Pantheon in Rome, whose perfectly preserved construction continually awes the visitor. Hadrian will be best remembered by those of the Judaeo-Christian tradition, however, because of his attempt to hellenize Jerusalem by changing the name of the city to Aelia Capitolina, by erecting a temple to himself and Zeus on the site of the previous Temple of Solomon, and by prohibiting circumcision. The brutal way in which he put down the unavoidable revolt from A.D. 132–135 was consistent with Hadrian's declaration of himself as another Antiochus Ephiphanes (the second century B.C. hellenizer who, while king of Syria, also desecrated the Jewish Temple and precipitated the Maccabean Revolt). See *Intertestamental History.*

The success of the Roman Empire depended upon the ability of the legions to keep peace throughout the world. *Pax Romana* was the key to prosperity and success. Greek and Latin were universal languages; nevertheless, most of the conquered countries retained their own languages as well, including Celtic, Germanic, Semitic, Hamitic, and Berber. Not since that time has the world been able to so effectively communicate in common languages. If the Mediterranean Sea is included, the Roman Empire was roughly the size of the continental United States, reaching from Britain to Arabia and from Germany to Morocco. One could go from one end of the Mediterranean to the other by boat in three weeks. Less effectively, one could travel 90 miles a day on the fine network of roads that interlaced the empire, including the Appian Way and the Egnatian Way.

The quality of the Greco-Roman culture disseminated by Rome was strongest in the areas bordering the Mediterranean and weakest in those farthest removed from major routes of communication. The most effective resistance to the culture was, as might be expected, among the eastern countries such as Egypt, Syrian, Mesopotamia, and the Levant (Syria-Palestine) which had the longest history of civilization. Western Europe, with a comparatively recent and uncivilized history, was no opposition and was soon thoroughly and permanently immersed in the phenomenon of western civilization.

Education in the empire was the prerogative of the wealthy. The poor had neither the time, the money, nor the need for an education that was designed to prepare the upper classes for positions of public service. The goal of education was to master the spoken word. Successful civic life was tied to proficiency in the language. Oratory was indispensable. Grammar and rhetoric were the primary subjects of study with emphasis on style over content. Among Latin authors, Virgil, Terence, Sallust, and Cicero were studied most while Homer, Thucydides, Demosthenes, and the Attic tragedians were the favorite Greek writers.

In the beginning of the empire, religion was diverse and almost chaotic. Both politicians and philosophers attempted to bring the same order to religion that they achieved in other aspects of Roman life. The Roman emperor was the head of the state religion, which included worship of the emperor and the traditional gods of Rome. The emperor functioned as semidivine while alive and as a god after his death. John may refer to emperor worship in Pergamum, where the first Asian temple to a Roman emperor was erected, in his references to the place "where Satan's throne is" (perhaps meaning the altar of Zeus; Rev. 2:13 NRSV). Mystery religions such as Mithraism, and the worship of Cybele and Isis were abundant. Philosophical systems, such as Epicureanism and Stoicism, functioned virtually as religions for agnostic intellectuals. Judaism, with its monotheistic emphasis, and Christianity, with its Judaistic origin and equally high code of ethics and morals, were anomalies. The inevitable clash between Judeo-Christians and the Romans was a clash between monotheism and polytheism, between morality and immorality.   *John McRay*

ROOF See *Architecture; House.*

ROOF CHAMBER See *Architecture; Chamber.*

ROOSTER See *Birds.*

ROOT The part of a plant buried in and gaining nourishment through the ground. In Scripture root generally appears in a figurative sense. Root indicates source as when the unrighteous are pictured as a root bearing bitter and poisonous fruit (Deut. 29:18; Heb. 12:15) or when the love of money is described as the root of all kinds of evil (1 Tim. 6:10). Deep-sinking roots picture stability (Ps. 80:9; Prov. 12:3) and prosperity (Prov. 12:12; compare Ps. 1:3). Exile is termed being uprooted (1 Kings 14:15; Jer. 24:6), while taking root again pictures return from Exile and the renewal of God's blessing (2 Kings 19:30; Isa. 27:6; 37:31).

Seed that fails to take root pictures those whose commitment to Christ is not firm enough to withstand trouble or persecution (Matt. 13:6,21). To be rooted in Christ is to be established in faith (Col. 2:6). Root of Jesse (Isa. 11:10; Rom. 15:12) and root of David (Rev. 5:5; 22:16) serve as titles of the Messiah. In Paul's allegory of the grape vine Israel is the root of the plant, the church the branches (Rom. 11:16–18).

ROSE See *Plants in the Bible.*

ROSETTA STONE Stone monument engraved with a trilingual text (Egyptian hieroglyphic, Demotic, and Greek), honoring Ptolemy V Epiphanes (196 B.C.), which provided the necessary clues for deciphering the two dead languages (Egyptian hieroglyphic and Demotic). The name stems from the site of the stone's discovery in the Nile delta in 1799. See *Archaeology; Egypt.*

ROSH (Rōsh) Personal name meaning, "head" or "chief." Seventh son of Benjamin (Gen. 46:21). The earliest Greek translation regards Rosh as a son of Bela, hence Benjamin's grandson. The name is absent in parallel lists of Benjamin's sons (Num. 26:38–39; 1 Chron. 8:1–5).

ROUND TIRES KJV translation of a Hebrew term which modern translations render as crescent necklaces or ornaments (Isa. 3:18). The KJV rendered the same Hebrew term as ornaments at Judges 8:21,26. See *Jewelry, Jewels, Precious Stones.*

ROWERS, ROW See *Ships, Sailors, and Navigation.*

ROYAL CITY City having a monarchical government. Gibeon (Josh. 10:2) was compared in size and strength to cities with kings, such as Ai and Jericho. Gath (1 Sam. 27:5) was one of five Philistine cities ruled by kings or lords. Rabbah (2 Sam. 12:26) served as capital of the Ammonite kingdom.

RUBY See *Jewelry, Jewels, and Precious Stones; Minerals and Metals.*

RUDDER See *Ships, Sailors, and Navigation.*

RUDDY Having a healthy, reddish color (1 Sam. 16:12; 17:42; Song of Sol. 5:10; Lam. 4:7; compare Gen. 25:25).

RUDE IN SPEECH KJV expression (2 Cor. 11:6) to mean one ignorant or unskilled in speech. Paul perhaps meant that his speech did not meet the standards of Greek oratory.

RUDIMENTS See *Elements, Elementary Spirits.*

RUE (*Ruta graveolens*) Strong-smelling shrub used as a condiment, in medicines, and in charms (Luke 11:42). Dill appears in the Matthean parallel (Matt. 23:23).

RUFUS (Rū′ fŭs) Personal name meaning, "red haired." *1.* Son of Simon of Cyrene and brother of Alexander (Mark 15:21). *2.* Recipient of Paul's greetings in Romans 16:13. If Mark was written from Rome, both references likely refer to the same person.

RUHAMAH (Rū hä′ mah) Personal name meaning, "pitied." Name Hosea used to symbolize the change in Israel's status before God following God's judgment (2:1; compare 1:6). First Peter 2:10 applies Hosea's image to Christians who have experienced God's mercy in Christ.

RULER OF THE SYNAGOGUE See *Synagogue.*

RUMAH (Rū′ mah) Place name meaning, "elevated place." Home of Jehoiakim's mother (2 Kings 23:36), possibly identified with khirbet Rumeh near Rimmon in Galilee or with Arumah.

RUN, RUNNING Running serves as common metaphor for the struggle to live out the Christian life (1 Cor. 9:24–26; Gal. 5:7; Heb. 12:1). At Galatians 2:2 running applies specifically to Paul's struggle to evangelize.

RUNNERS Runners performed two basic functions, as messengers (2 Chron. 30:6,10; Esth. 3:13; Jer. 51:31) and royal body guards (1 Sam. 8:11; 22:17; 2 Sam. 15:1; 1 Kings 1:5; 2 Kings 10:25; 11:4).

RUNNING SORES Running sores disqualified a man from service as a priest (Lev. 21:20 NIV) and animals from serving as sacrifices (Lev. 22:22 NAS, NIV). The curse placed on Joab's descendants included affliction with running sores (2 Sam. 3:29 NIV).

RUSH, RUSHES English terms used to translate several types of reedlike plants. See *Plants in the Bible.*

RUST Coating produced by the corrosive effects of air and water on a metal, especially iron. Rust on a copper cooking pot symbolized Jerusalem's persistant wickedness in Ezekiel 24:6,12–13. Jesus highlighted the folly of relying on earthly treasures subject to rust (Matt. 6:19–20). In the style of an Old Testament prophet, James outlined God's future judgment on the wealth-reliant rich as if it were already accomplished (Jas. 5:1–6). James' mention of riches, moths, and rust (vv. 2–3) suggests that he was applying Jesus' saying. The scientific observation that gold and silver do not rust should not obscure James' primary emphasis: one is a fool to rely on riches which will not survive God's coming judgment. Ill-gotten riches will serve as evidence and witness for God's prosecution. The very riches relied on for security will provide the corrosive rust effecting God's judgment.

R

RUTH (Rūth) The woman, an ancestor of David and Jesus, and the biblical book which tells the story of the reversal of fortunes for Ruth and her mother-in-law, Naomi.

Ruth is a self-contained story and is not dependent on other Old Testament narratives for continuity. The story's time is set in the period of Israel's judges. Story place is given as the agrarian world of Moab and the environs of Bethlehem. It can be divided into a series of scenes or episodes with different narrator's comments. The story begins (1:1-5) by telling why Naomi is in Moab and her plight following the deaths of her husband and sons. Episode A (1:6-22) narrates her return to and reception in Bethlehem, and how Ruth came to be with her. Episode B (2:1-16) finds Ruth and Boaz meeting while she gleans grain during harvest. Episode C (2:17-23) shows Naomi and Ruth discussing Ruth's day in the field and identifies Boaz as a kinsman with a certain role to fulfill. Episode D (3:1-5) finds Naomi pressing Boaz's role as kinsman. Episode E (3:6-13) follows a transition in which Ruth and Boaz encounter each other, and Boaz is confronted with his responsibility as kinsman. Episode F (3:14-18) delays the plot's resolution while Naomi assures Ruth that the matter will be settled. Episode G (4:1-6) tells of Boaz at the gate settling the matters of Elimelech's property and Ruth, with another kinsman. A narrative aside (4:7-8) explains the custom of the sandal. Boaz's actions are witnessed, and he is blessed by the people and the elders for his role as kinsman in Episode H (4:9-12). Episode I (4:13-17a) reverses the fortunes of Naomi and Ruth with Obed's birth, who is declared a child of Naomi. This declaration ensures a name and a future for Naomi's family. A coda (4:18-22) ties up the story with a family genealogy.

Ruth is one of the five Megilloth (scrolls read for Jewish festivals), and is read at the Feast of Weeks. See *Festivals.* Ruth has been understood as a finely crafted historical short story. The literary artistry of Ruth speaks to multiple contexts and is multipurposed. In a social context, Ruth speaks against postexilic particularism by accepting Ruth (a native of Moab) into Israel's genealogical mainstream and the book into the Hebrew canon. See *Moab.* Ruth is concerned with Israelite family and marriage patterns and obligations. Ruth's plot shows levirate marriage (Deut. 25:5-10) as a family obligation at work. See *Levirate Law.* Religiously, the book tells the story of the faith of Naomi and Ruth and shows the ways of God in one unique family situation. A framework of devotion is deployed in the story and is variously applied to Ruth, Naomi, Boaz, and Yahweh. The text's final form speaks to political concerns by a genealogy (4:17b-22) which details David's family background and serves to legitimate him as king on Saul's throne.

Outline

I. Trial and Tragedy Seemed to Offer Little Hope for God's Redeeming Grace (1:1-22).
   A. The trial of famine gave way to the tragedy of death for Naomi (1:1-5).
   B. The hint of blessing was seen in the tearful parting of Naomi from Orpah and the determined love of Ruth for her mother-in-law (1:6-14).
   C. In spite of Naomi's urging, Ruth resisted the injunction of her mother-in-law to remain in Moab and accompanied Naomi as she returned to Judah (1:15-18).
   D. The "emptiness" of Naomi's return to Judah provided the transition to God's grace by means of Ruth (1:19-22).

II. In the Ordinary Actions of a Foreigner, God Began to Prepare the Way of Blessing (2:1-23).
   A. Ruth's initiative provided not only food for the present, but a foundation for the future welfare of her family (2:1-7).
   B. Ruth demonstrated that inclusion into the people of God is not predicated on birth alone (2:8-13).
   C. The encounter of Boaz and Ruth opened the way for God to bless in an unexpected manner (2:14-23).

III. In More Ways Than One, God Took a Potential Scandal and Made It the Way of Grace (3:1-18).
   A. Naomi proposed a daring strategy in her matchmaking effort (3:1-5).
   B. The character of both Boaz and Ruth was demonstrated in the encounter at the threshing floor (3:6-13).
   C. The blessing of God began to be given to Ruth and Naomi through Boaz (3:14-18).

IV. Through Boaz, the "Kinsman Redeemer," God "Filled" the "Emptiness" of Naomi and Demonstrated His Presence Through the Blessing of His People (4:1-22).
   A. Boaz became "kinsman redeemer" (4:1-6).
   B. Before the assembled witnesses, Boaz fulfilled the custom of levirate marriage and received the blessing of witnesses (4:7-12).
   C. God "filled" the "emptiness" of Naomi through a son born to Ruth and Boaz, a son who was none other than the grandfather of the great King David (4:13-22).

RYE (*Secale cereale*) Hardy grass grown as a cereal (Ex. 9:32 KJV) and cover crop (Isa. 28:25 KJV, NAS). Other translations render the underlying Hebrew as spelt. See *Agriculture; Grain; Plants in the Bible.*

S

A young Jewish boy at his Bar Mitzvah with the Torah scroll reverently opened before him.

SABACHTHANI (Sä bäch' thȧ nī) Transliteration of Aramaic meaning, "he has forsaken me." Word Jesus used in quoting Psalm 22:1, where Hebrew is *azabtani*. See *Eli, Eli, Lama Sabachthani*.

SABAOTH (Sä Bä' ōth) Transliteration of Hebrew meaning, "hosts, armies, heavenly bodies." Part of a divine title, "Lord of Hosts" variously interpreted as Lord of Israel's armies (compare 1 Sam. 17:45); the deposed Canaanite nature gods whose title Yahweh assumed; the stars; members of Yahweh's heavenly court or council; a comprehensive title for all beings, heavenly and earthly; an intensive title describing God as all powerful. Interestingly, the title does not appear in Genesis through Judges. The earliest Greek translation at times translated *Sabaoth* as a proper name, sometimes as Almighty, and sometimes not at all. The title was apparently closely tied to Shiloh and the ark of the covenant (1 Sam. 1:3,11; 4:4; 6:2). When David brought the ark to Jerusalem, he also introduced the title Yahweh of Hosts to Jerusalem worship (2 Sam. 6:2). Yahweh Sabaoth seems to have emphasized God's place as divine king enthroned on the cherubim with the ark as His footstool ruling over the nation, the earth, and the heavens (Ps. 24:10). He is the God without equal (Ps. 89:8) who is present with His people (Ps. 46:7,11; compare 2 Sam. 5:10).

SABBATH The day of rest, considered holy to God by His rest on the seventh day after creation and viewed as a sign of the covenant relation between God and His people and of the eternal rest He has promised them.

Old Testament The word *sabbath* comes from the Hebrew *shabbat,* meaning "to cease" or "desist." The primary meaning is that of cessation from all work. Some persons have traced the origin of the concept to the Babylonian calendar which contained certain days, corresponding to phases of the moon, in which kings and priests could not perform their official functions. Such days bore an evil connotation, and work performed on them would have harmful effects. The fifteenth of the month, the time of the full moon in their lunar calendar, was *shapattu*, the "day of pacifying the heart" (of the god) by certain ceremonies.

Although one can show similarities to the Babylonian concept, the Hebrew sabbath did not follow a lunar cycle. It was celebrated every seven days and became basic to the recognition and worship of the God of creation and redemption. Regulations concerning the sabbath are a main feature of the Mosaic laws. Both reports of the Ten Commandments stated that the sabbath belonged to the Lord. On six days the Israelites should work, but on the seventh, they as well as all slaves, foreigners, and beasts must rest. Two reasons are given. The first is that God rested on the seventh day after creation, thereby making the day holy (Ex. 29:8–11). The second was a reminder of their redemption from slavery in Egypt (Deut. 5:12–15).

The day became a time for sacred assembly and worship (Lev. 23:1–3), a token of their covenant with God (Ex. 31:12–17; Ezek. 20:12–20). Death was the penalty for desecration (Ex. 35:1–3). The true observance of not following one's own pursuits on that day would lift a person to God's holy mountain and bring spiritual nourishment (Isa. 56:1–7; 58:13), but failure to keep the sabbath would bring destruction to their earthly kingdom (Neh. 13:15–22; Jer. 17:21–27).

Interbiblical The sabbath became the heart of the law, and the prohibitions were expanded. Thirty-nine tasks were banned, such as tying or untying a knot. These in turn were extended until ingenious evasions were devised that lost the spirit but satisfied the legal requirement.

New Testament The habit of Jesus was to observe the sabbath as a day of worship in the synagogues (Luke 4:16), but His failure to comply with the minute restrictions brought conflict (Mark 2:23–28; 3:1–6; Luke 13:10–17; John 5:1–18). At first, Christians also met on the sabbath with the Jews in the synagogues to proclaim Christ (Acts 13:14). Their holy day, the day that belonged especially to the Lord, was the first day of the week, the day of resurrection (Matt. 28:1; Acts 20:7; Rev. 1:10). They viewed the sabbath and other matters of the law as a shadow of the reality which had now been revealed (Col. 2:16–23), and the sabbath became a symbol of the heavenly rest to come (Heb. 4:1–11).   *Barbara J. Bruce*

SABBATH DAY'S JOURNEY Distance a Jew in Jesus' day considered ritually legal to walk on the seventh day. This phrase appears only once in the Bible (Acts 1:12), describing the distance from the Mount of Olives to Jerusalem. Scholars have surmised that the expression came from God's instruction to the children of Israel as they prepared to cross the Jordan into Canaan (Josh. 3:4). As they followed the priests bearing the ark of the covenant, they must maintain a distance of 2,000 cubits from it. Earlier, while in the wilderness, they had been told not to leave home on the sabbath (Ex. 16:29). Rabbis eventually interpreted these commands as limiting sabbath travel to 2,000 cubits. That was the farthest that a loyal Jew should be from his center of worship on the sabbath. The length of the cubit depended on who was counting. Greeks said it was 1 foot, 6 inches; but Romans claimed it was 1 foot, 9 inches. Thus, 2,000 cubits could be from 3,000 to 3,600 feet, somewhat more than a half mile. Anyone who wanted to "bend" the rule could carry a lunch sometime before the sabbath to a place about half mile from his home. Then, by eating it on the sabbath, he could claim that place as a "legal" home and go another sabbath day's journey. See *Sabbath.* *W. J. Fallis*

SABBATICAL YEAR Every seventh year when farmers rested their land from bearing crops to renew the land and people of Israel. Mosaic law directed that every seventh year the land would not be planted in crops; food would come from what grew wild (Ex. 23:10-11; Lev. 25:1-7). Just as the the Law reserved the seventh day as holy unto God, so too, was the seventh year set aside as a time of rest and renewal. This not only assured the continued fertility of the land by allowing it to lay fallow, but also protected the rights of the poor. Peasants were allowed to eat from the natural abundance of the untended fields. It may be that only a portion of the land was allowed to rest each sabbath year, the remainder farmed as usual. Hebrews sold into slavery were to be released in that year (Ex. 21:2). Loans and debts to Israelites were also to be forgiven (Deut. 15:1-3). It is doubtful that the sabbath year was celebrated in early Israel. Jeremiah reminded the people that their fathers had ignored the observance of the law (Jer. 34:13-14; compare Lev. 26:35). Although Israel renewed her dedication to practice the sabbath year during Nehemiah's time, it is unclear whether it was carried out (Neh. 10:31). During the intertestamental period an attempt was made by Israel to observe the sabbath year despite the political turmoil of the times (1 Macc. 6:49). The sabbath year laws consistently pointed to helping the poor. *David Maltsberger*

SABEAN (Så bē′ an) Transliteration of two Hebrew national names. *1.* Descendants of Seba, son of Cush (Gen. 10:7*a*) expected to bring gifts signifying loyalty to Jerusalem (Ps. 72:10; Isa. 45:14; compare Ezek. 23:42). God could use the Sabeans to "pay for" Israel's ransom from captivity (Isa. 43:3). These are often identified with people of Meroe in Upper Egypt between the white and blue Nile, thus the capital of Ethiopia. Other scholars locate it much further south, the territory east and southeast of Cush bordering on the Red Sea. Other scholars would identify at least some references here as identical with *2.* below.

2. Descendants of Sheba, the son of Raamah (Gen. 10:7*b*) or Joktan (Gen. 10:28; compare 25:3). The rich queen of Sheba visited Solomon (1 Kings 10). Sabeans destroyed Job's flocks and herds and servants (Job 1:15). They were known as "travelling merchants" (Job 6:19 REB; compare Ps. 72:10,15; Isa. 60:6; Jer. 6:20; Ezek. 27:22; 38:13; Joel 3:8). This is usually equated with the city in southern Arabia, modern Marib in Yemen. Some scholars think this is too far south and seek biblical Sheba in northern Arabia near Medina on the wadi esh-Shaba. Sabeans could have become a general term for foreign or nomadic merchants. Sheba in southern Arabia gained riches through

trade with nearby Africa and with India, whose goods they transported and sold to the empires to the north. Sheba produced and traded incense.

SABTA(H) (Săb′ tà) Son of Cush and apparently the ancestor of citizens of Sabota, capital of Hadramaut about 270 miles north of Aden. Others identify it with an Ethiopian ruler about 700 B.C. Josephus identified it with Astaboras, modern Abare.

SABTECA(H) (Săb′ tē cà) Place name of uncertain meaning. Sometimes equated with Ethiopian ruler Sabataka (700-689 B.C.) but more probably with an Arabian city state such as Ashshabbak near Medina or Sembrachate in northern Yemen.

SABTECHA(H) (Săb′ tē <u>ch</u>à) KJV, REB spellings of Sabteca.

SACAR (Sā′ cär) Personal name meaning, "salary." *1.* Man from Harar and father of one of David's heroes (1 Chron. 11:35), called Sharar in 2 Samuel 23:33. *2.* Temple gatekeeper (1 Chron. 26:4).

SACHAR (Sā′ chär) NRSV, TEV spelling of Sacar.

SACHIA(H) (Sà <u>chī</u>′ à) NAS, NRSV, (REB) spellings of Shachia.

SACK See *Bag 5.*

SACKBUT (Săck′ bŭt) KJV term for musical instrument (Dan. 3:5), identified in modern translations as zither (TEV), lyre (NIV), trigon (NAS, NRSV), or triangle (REB). It is apparently an instrument of Asian origin, a triangular harp with four or more strings. The related Hebrew and Aramaic term refers to lattice work. Along with the other instruments in the list, it apparently was not used in worship but only in more popular settings, possibly representing a rebuke from the biblical writer for a pagan musical setting for worship.

SACKCLOTH A garment of coarse material fashioned from goat or camel hair worn as a sign of mourning or anguish, also marked by fasting and sitting on an ash heap (Isa. 58:5). Jonah 3:8 notes even animals mourned in sackcloth. The shape of the garment could have been either a loose-fitting sack placed over the shoulders or a loin cloth. The word *sack* is a transliteration of the Hebrew word rather than a translation.

SACRAMENT (Săc′ rà mĕnt) an outward and visible sign of an inward and spiritual grace. It usually refers to a religious ritual which is believed to carry a special healing or saving power. Baptism and the Lord's Supper are the two sacraments almost universally recognized in Christendom,

S

though many evangelical Christians shy away from the word *sacrament* in favor of "ordinances."

The word comes from the Latin *sacramentum,* vow, and it especially refers to the vow taken by a Roman soldier upon his induction into the army. This made it particularly appropriate for early Christians to designate their baptism, a confession and induction into the army of Christ. Later, Christians extended the use of the term to preaching, the Lord's Supper, foot washing, blessing, marriage, ordination, and any other rite seen as a channel of divine grace into the heart and life of the believer. The theological issue which most divided Christians was whether the divine grace was conveyed simply by a correct performance of the rite or whether the recipient must have an active faith and make a personal response to the power of God's spirit.

The Latin Bible translated the Greek word *mysterion* (mystery) in such passages as 1 Corinthians 2:7, Ephesians 3:3, and Colossians 1:26 with the Latin word *sacramentum.* Although none of these passages uses "mystery" to refer to baptism, Lord's Supper, or any other religious rite, the later church began to make that identification and gave that special meaning to the word.

There is strong biblical support for the theological idea of an outward sign carrying an inward spiritual power. When Paul wrote of being "buried with Christ" in baptism, he certainly meant that this visible rite demonstrates our spiritual union with Christ in His death and resurrection. It is not, however, an automatic or mechanical transmission of divine grace. It depends upon the inward faith and spiritual response of the believer. Since God became flesh in Jesus Christ, it follows that God can use anything He chooses in His created order to convey His truth and saving power to the one who believes in Him. See *Ordinances.*

Wayne Ward

SACRIFICE AND OFFERING The physical elements the worshiper brings to the Deity to express devotion, thanksgiving, or the need for forgiveness.

Iron Age sacrificial altar located at the site of ancient Arad.

Sacrifice in the Ancient Near East Israel was not unique among the nations of the Ancient Near East in their use of sacrifices and offerings as a means of religious expression. Some type of sacrificial system characterized the many religious methodologies that the nations employed in their attempts to honor their gods. The presence of sacrifices and offerings in Israel, therefore, was a reflection of the larger culture of which this nation was a part.

Many references to the offering of sacrifices exist in extrabiblical literature. The primary approach to the gods was through the sacrificial system. In Babylon, part of the ritual of purifying the temple of Bel for the new year's festival involved the slaughter of a ram. The animal was decapitated and the priest, in turn, used the body in the purification ceremony. The ram's body then was thrown into the river. The ritual accompanying the replacing of the head of the kettledrum that was used in the temple required that a black bull be selected for sacrifice. After an elaborate ceremony that culminated in the sacrifice of the bull, its hide was dipped in and rubbed with two separate mixtures and then used to cover the kettledrum.

While the above sacrifices were performed on special occasions, a variety of rams, bulls, and birds were offered as meals to the idols on a daily basis. Barley beer, mixed beer, milk, and wine also were placed before the deities, as well as loaves of bread.

The sacrifices and offerings were designed to serve the gods by meeting any physical need that they may have had. The sacrifices were the food and drink of the gods. Faithfulness to the preparation and presentation of them was an act of devotion.

The Sacrificial System in the Old Testament From the earliest times of the Old Testament, sacrifice was practiced. Cain and Abel brought offerings to the Lord from the produce of the land and from the first born of the flock (Gen. 4). Upon embarking from the ark after the great flood, Noah immediately built an altar and offered burnt sacrifices. These were a soothing aroma to the Lord (Gen. 8). Other Ancient Near Eastern flood stories have parallels to this act by Noah. The patriarchal stories in Genesis 12—50 are filled with instances of sacrifice to God. The most famous is that of Abraham and Isaac (Gen. 22).

An organized system of sacrifice does not appear in the Old Testament until after the Exodus of Israel from Egypt. In the instructions given for the building of the tabernacle and the establishment of a priestly organization, sacrifices were to be used in the consecration or ordination of the priests (Ex. 29). A bull was slaughtered as a sin offering. Other sacrifices provided Aaron and his sons a holy meal. These sacrifices were repeated each day for a week as a part of the "ordination" of the priests. The altar itself was consecrated through the offering of two lambs and a grain offering and a libation of wine. This sacrifice also was carried out each day for a week.

The sacrifices that constituted much of the worship of Israel at this time were burned on an altar that was made from accacia wood and overlaid with copper (Ex. 27). In addition to the sacrifices offered on this altar, incense was burned on a smaller altar (Ex. 30). While the sacrificial altar was placed in the courtyard, just before the door of the tabernacle, the incense altar was positioned inside the tabernacle, just before the ark of the covenant. See *Altar.*

Leviticus 1—7 gives the most detailed description of Israel's sacrificial system, including five types of sacrifices. The sacrifices and offerings that were brought by the people were to be the physical expression of their inward devotion.

1. Burnt offering (ʿolah). The burnt offering was offered both in the morning and in the evening, as well as on special days such as the sabbath, the new moon, and the yearly feasts (Num. 28—29; 2 Kings 16:15; 2 Chron. 2:4; 31:3; Ezra 3:3—6). Rituals performed after childbirth (Lev. 12:6—8), for an unclean discharge (Lev. 15:14—15) or hemorrhage (Lev. 15:29—30), or after a person who was keeping a Nazirite vow was defiled (Num. 6:10—11) required a burnt offering, as well as a sin offering.

The animal for this sacrifice could be a young bull, lamb, goat, turtledove, or young pigeon; but it had to be a perfect and complete specimen. The type of animal chosen for this sacrifice seems to be dependent on the offerer's financial ability. The one bringing the offering was to lay a hand upon the animal so as to identify that the animal was taking the person's place and then to kill it. The priest then collected the blood and sprinkled it around the altar and the sanctuary, and the worshiper cut up and skinned the animal. If a bird was brought, the priest killed it. After the priest arranged the various parts on the altar, the entire animal was burned as a sacrifice. The only portion that remained was the hide, and the priest received it (Lev. 7:8). The one who made this sacrifice did so to restore the relationship with God and to atone for some sin. When Araunah offered to David his threshing floor, oxen, and wood without cost so that David could sacrifice, David refused. His explanation was that he could not offer burnt offerings that cost him nothing (2 Sam. 24:18—25).

2. Grain offering (minchah; "meat offering" in KJV). An offering from the harvest of the land is the only type that required no bloodshed. It was composed of fine flour mixed with oil and frankincense. Sometimes, this offering was cooked into cakes prior to taking it to the priest. These cakes, however, had to be made without leaven. Every grain offering had to have salt in it (Lev. 2:13), perhaps as a symbol of the covenant. Only a portion of this offering was burned on the altar, with the remainder going to the priests. While no reason is given for the grain offering, it may have symbolized the recognition of God's blessing in the harvest by a society based to a large degree on agriculture. The bringing of a representative portion of the grain harvest was another outward expression of devotion.

3. Peace offering (zebach shelamin; well-being in NRSV; "shared" in REB; "fellowship" in NIV). This consisted of the sacrifice of a bull, cow, lamb, or goat that had no defect. As with the burnt offering, the individual laid a hand on the animal and killed it. The priests, in turn, sprinkled the blood around the altar. Only certain parts of the internal organs were burned. The priest received the breast and the right thigh (Lev. 7:28—36), but the offerer was given much of the meat to have a meal of celebration (Lev. 7:11—21). As part of the meal, various kinds of bread were offered (and ultimately kept by the priest). The idea of thanksgiving was associated with the peace offering. It often accompanied other sacrifices in celebration of events such as the dedication of the Temple (1 Kings 8:63) or spiritual renewal (2 Chron. 29:31—36).

4. Sin offering (chaṭṭaʾt; "purification" in REB). This was designed to deal with sin that was committed unintentionally. The sacrifice varied according to who committed the sin. If the priest or the congregation of Israel sinned, then a bull was required. A leader of the people had to bring a male goat, while anyone else sacrificed a female goat or a lamb. The poor were allowed to bring two turtledoves or two young pigeons. The one bringing the offering placed a hand on the animal and then slaughtered it. When the priest or the congregation sinned, the blood was sprinkled seven times before the veil in the sanctuary, and some of it was placed on the horns of the incense altar. The rest of the blood was poured out at the base of the sacrificial altar. For others who sinned, the sprinkling of the blood before the veil was omitted. The same internal organs that were designated for burning in the peace offering were likewise designated in this sacrifice. The rest of the animal was taken outside of the camp to the place where the ashes of the sacrifices were disposed, and there it was burned. These disposal procedures were not followed when the sin offering was made on behalf of a nonpriestly person (Lev. 6:24—30). In this case, the priest was allowed to eat some of the meat.

5. Guilt offering (ʾasham, trespass in KJV; reparation in REB). This is hard to distinguish from the sin offering (Lev. 4—5). In Leviticus 5:6—7, the guilt offering is called the sin offering. Both offerings also were made for similar types of sin. The guilt offering was concerned supremely with restitution. Someone who took something illegally was expected to repay it in full plus 20 percent of the value and then bring a ram for the guilt offering. Other instances in which the guilt offering was prescribed included the cleansing of a leper (Lev. 14), having sexual relations with the female slave of another person (Lev. 19:20–22), and for the renewing of a Nazirite vow that had been broken (Num. 6:11–12).

The burnt, grain, peace, sin, and guilt offering composed the basic sacrificial system of Israel. These sacrifices were commonly used in conjunction with each other and were carried out on both an individual and a corporate basis. The sacrificial system taught the necessity of dealing with sin and, at the same time, demonstrated that God had provided a way for dealing with sin.

The Prophets' Attitude Toward the Sacrificial System The prophets spoke harshly about the people's concept of sacrifice. They tended to ignore faith, confession, and devotion, thinking the mere act of sacrifice ensured forgiveness. Isaiah contended that the sacrifices were worthless when they were not accompanied by repentance and an obedient life (Isa. 1:10–17). Micah reflected the same sentiments when he proclaimed that God was not interested in the physical act of sacrifice by itself but in the life and heart of the one making the sacrifice (Mic. 6:4–6). Jeremiah condemned the belief that as long as the Temple was in Jerusalem and the people were faithful to perform the sacrifices, then God would protect them. The symbol of the sacrifice must be reflected in the individual's life (Jer. 7:1–26). Malachi chastised the people for offering the lame and sick animals to God instead of the best, as the Levitical law required. In doing this, the people were defiling the altar and despising God (Mal. 1:7–14).

The prophets did not want to abolish the sacrificial system. They, instead, denounced the people's misuse of it. God wanted more than the physical performance of meaningless sacrifices. He desired the offerings to exemplify the heart of the worshiper.

Sacrifice in the New Testament During the time of the New Testament, the people sacrificed according to the guidelines in the Old Testament. In keeping with the Levitical law (Lev. 12), Mary brought the baby Jesus to the Temple and offered a sacrifice for her purification. She sacrificed turtledoves or pigeons, indicating the family's low financial status. When Jesus healed the leper (Luke 5:12–14), He told him to go to the priest and make a sacrifice (compare Lev. 14). The cleansing of the Temple (John 2) came about because people were selling animals and birds for the various sacrifices within the Temple precincts. These people had allowed the "business" of sacrifice to overwhelm the spiritual nature of the offerings. Jesus chided the Pharisees neglecting family responsibilities by claiming that something was "corban," or offered to God, and thus unavailable for the care of their parents (Mark 7). *Corban* is the Hebrew word for offering (Lev. 1:2). See *Corban.*

The New Testament consistently describes Christ's death in sacrificial terms. Hebrews portrays Christ as the sinless high priest who offered himself up as a sacrifice for sinners (7:27). The superiority of Christ's sacrifice over the Levitical sacrificial system is seen in that His sacrifice had to be offered only once. The book ends with an encouragement to offer sacrifices of praise to God through Christ. This thought is reflected in 1 Peter 2 where believers are called a holy and royal priesthood who offer up spiritual sacrifices.

Paul used the terminology of the Old Testament sacrifices in teaching about the death of Jesus. His death was an offering and sacrifice to God and, as such, a fragrant aroma (Eph. 5:2). He associated Jesus with the Passover sacrifice (1 Cor. 5:7). Paul also spoke of himself as a libation poured out (Phil. 2:18). He called the Philippians' gift a fragrant aroma and an acceptable sacrifice to God (Phil. 4:18).

The first-century church lived in a culture that sacrificed to their gods. Paul and Barnabas at Lystra were thought to be the gods Zeus and Hermes. The priest of Zeus sought to offer sacrifices to them (Acts 14). The church at Corinth was embroiled in a controversy over whether or not it was permissible for Christians to eat meat offered to idols (1 Cor. 8—10). Paul's preaching of the gospel at Ephesus disrupted the business and worship of the goddess Artemis (Acts 19).

When the Temple in Jerusalem was destroyed in 70 A.D., the Jews' sacrificial system ceased. By this time, however, the church had begun to distance itself from Judaism. The biblical view of sacrifice changed as well. In the Old Testament and in the beginning years of the New Testament, sacrifice was the accepted mode of worship. With the death of Christ, however, physical sacrifice became unnecessary. As the temple and priest of God, the believer now has the responsibility for offering acceptable spiritual sacrifices.

Scott Langston

SADDUCEES (Săd′ dū cēes) A religious group which formed during the period between the Testaments when the Maccabees ruled Judah. They took their name from one of David's copriests, Zadok, and claimed descent from him. Their name meant "righteous ones." See *Jewish Parties.*

Mike Mitchell

SADOC (Sā′ dŏc) KJV spelling of Zadok (Matt. 1:14) following Greek.

SAFFRON (Săf′ frŏn) See *Spices.*

SAILOR See *Ships, Sailors, and Navigation.*

SAINTS Holy people, a title for all God's people but applied in some contexts to a small group seen as the most dedicated ones.

Old Testament Two words are used for saints: *qaddish* and *chasid*. *Qaddish* comes from the *qadosh* and means holy. To be holy is to separate oneself from evil and dedicate oneself to God. This separation and union is seen both with things and people. All the items of worship are separated for the Lord's use: altar (Ex. 29:37), oil (Ex. 30:25), garments (Ex. 31:10), and even the people are to be holy (Ex. 22:31). This separation reflects God's very character, for He is holy (Lev. 19:2). See *Holy; God.* Holiness is clearly portrayed as an encounter with the living God, which results in a holiness of life-style (Isa. 6). So holiness is more than a one-time separating and uniting activity. It is a way of life. "Ye shall be holy: for I . . . am holy" (Lev. 19:2). Saints are people who try to live holy lives (Dan. 7:18−28).

Chasid means "to be kind or merciful." These are qualities of God. Thus, *chasid* people are godly people because they reflect His character. Saints praise the Lord for His lifelong favor (Ps. 30:4), rejoice in goodness (2 Chron. 6:41), and know that God keeps their paths (1 Sam. 2:9). God's encounter with His people through the covenant enables them to walk as His saints.

New Testament One word, *hagios,* is used for saints in the New Testament. This word, like *qadosh,* means holy. Consequently, saints are the holy ones. There is only one reference to saints in the Gospels (Matt. 27:52). In this verse, dead saints are resurrected at the Lord's crucifixion. The death of the Holy One provides life for those who believe in God. In Acts, three of the four references occur in chapter 9 (vv. 13,32,41). First Ananias and then Peter talks of the saints as simply believers in Christ. Paul continues this use in his Epistles to the Romans, Corinthians, Ephesians, Philippians, Colossians, Thessalonians, and Philemon. In each case, saints seem simply to be people who name Jesus as Lord. In the Book of Revelation, however, where the word *saints* occurs more times than in any other single book (13 times), the meaning is further defined. Saints not only name Jesus as Lord, but they are faithful and true witnesses for Jesus.

Little wonder then that the early church considered witnesses who were martyred for their testimonies to be saints. In fact, soon these saints were accorded special honor and then even worship. Unfortunately, the term saints came to be applied only to such special people.

Biblically, though, the term *saint* is correctly applied to anyone who believes Jesus Christ is Lord. To believe in Jesus demands obedience and conformity to His will. A saint bears true and faithful witness to Christ in speech and life-style. To be a saint is a present reality when a believer seeks to let the Spirit form Christ within (Rom. 8:29; Gal. 4:19; Eph. 4:13). See *Spirit; Witness.*
William Vermillion

SAKIA (Så kī′ å) NIV spelling of Shachia.

SAKKUTH (Såk′ küth) NRSV transliteration of Assyrian divine name applied to god Ninurta (or Ninib), apparently an Assyrian name for Saturn or another astral deity. Some translators take the name as a common noun meaning, "shrine" (REB, NIV), "tabernacle" (KJV), since the Hebrew term resembles the word for "tent." Amos condemned Israel for such false worship (Amos 5:26). See *Succoth-benoth.*

SALA(H) (Sā′ là) Personal name meaning, "sprout." Father of Eber (Gen. 10:24; 11:12−15; 1 Chron. 1:18,24).

SALAMIS (Săl′ å mĭs) Most important city of Cyprus, located on its east coast and containing more than one Jewish synagogue (Acts 13:5). See *Cyprus.*

SALATHIEL (Så lā′ thĭ ĕl) Variant spelling of Shealtiel.

SALCAH (Săl′ cah) Territory and/or city on extreme eastern border of Bashan, possibly modern Salkhad, the defensive center of the Jebel el-Druze, 63 miles east of the Jordan (Deut. 3:10; Josh. 12:5). See *Bashan.*

SALCHAH (Săl′ chah) Alternate spelling of Salcah.

SALECAH (Săl′ ė cah) NAS, NRSV, NIV, TEV spelling of Salcah.

SALEM (Sā′ lĕm) Abbreviated form of Jerusalem (Gen. 14:18; Ps. 76:2; Heb. 7:1,2). See *Jerusalem; Melchizedek.*

SALIM (Sā′ lĭm) Place name meaning, "peace." Town near which John the Baptist baptized (John 3:23). Its site is disputed: northeast of Dead Sea near Bethabara; west bank of northern Jordan valley eight miles south of Scythopolis; in Samaria four miles south southeast of Shechem. The third site would identify John as well as Jesus with Samaritan ministry. See *Samaria.* The second and third sites would have John leaving for the north, allowing Jesus to minister near Jerusalem. See *Aenon; John 2.*

SALLAI (Săl′ lā ī) Personal name perhaps meaning, "the restored one." *1.* Benjaminite who lived in Jerusalem after Exile (Neh. 11:8). Commentators often emend the Hebrew text to read, "and his brothers, men of valor." Others read, "Sallu." *2.* Priestly family after the Exile (Neh. 12:20), apparently the same as Sallu (v. 7).

SALLU (Săl′ lū) Personal name perhaps meaning,

"the restored one." *1.* A Benjaminite (1 Chron. 9:7; Neh. 11:7). *2.* A leading priest after the Exile (Neh. 12:7). See *Sallai.*

SALMA (Săl′ mà) Personal name meaning, "coat." *1.* Father of Boaz and ancestor of David (1 Chron. 2:11). *2.* Descendant of Caleb and father of Bethlehem (1 Chron. 2:51).

SALMON (Săl′ mŏn) Personal and place name meaning, "coat." *1.* Father of Boaz (Ruth 4:21; Matt. 1:5; Luke 3:32). See *Salma.* *2.* KJV spelling of Zalmon (Ps. 68:14). See *Zalmon.*

SALMONE (Săl mō′ nè) Promontory on northeast coast of Crete; modern Cape Sidero. Temple to Athena Salmonia stood there. Paul sailed by there on way to Rome (Acts 27:7).

SALOME (Så lō′ mè) Personal name meaning, "pacific." Wife of Zebedee and mother of James and John (if one combines Mark 16:1; Matt. 27:56; compare John 19:25). She became a disciple of Jesus and was among the women at the crucifixion who helped prepare the Lord's body for burial. Some believe that she is mentioned in John 19:25 as Mary's sister, thus she would have been Jesus' aunt with James and John His cousins. See *Mary.*

SALT Common crystaline compound used in seasoning food and in sacrifices. See *Minerals and Metals.*

SALT SEA See *Dead Sea.*

SALT, CITY OF See *City of Salt.*

SALT, COVENANT OF See *Covenant; Covenant of Salt.*

SALT, VALLEY OF Geographical passageway south and east of the Dead Sea, often identified with wadi el-Milch south of Beersheba, but this location is not accepted by modern commentators. David killed 18,000 Edomites there (2 Sam. 8:13; compare 1 Chron. 18:12; Ps. 60). King Amaziah (796–767 B.C.) killed 10,000 Edomites (2 Kings 14:7).

SALTWORT (Sălt′ wŏrt) REB translation of "mallows" (Job 30:4). See *Mallow.*

SALU (Să′ lū) Personal name meaning, "the restored one." Father of Zimri (Num. 25:14) and tribal leader in Simeon.

SALUTATION (Săl ū tā′ tion) Act of greeting, addressing, blessing, or welcoming by gestures or words; a specific form of words serving as a greeting, especially in the opening and closing of letters.

In the Ancient Near East, a salutation covered a wide range of social practices: exchanging a greeting ("Hail"), asking politely about another's welfare, expressing personal regard, and the speaking of a parting blessing ("Go in Peace"). Physical actions, such as kneeling, kissing, and embracing, were also involved. The salutation functioned to maintain close, personal contact and to foster good relations. Though the practice continued into the first century, Jesus and early Christians transformed the act of saluting. Jesus critiqued the Pharisees for practicing long, protracted deferential salutations (Mark 12:37b–40; Luke 20:45–47; compare Matt. 23:1–36) and forbade His disciples from practicing such public displays (Luke 10:4). Instead, Jesus endorsed a salutation when it signified the long-awaited presence of messianic "peace" (Hebrew, *shalom*), that is the "peace" of the kingdom of God (Luke 10:5–13; 19:42; John 14:27; 20:21; Mark 15:18; compare Luke 2:14,29). Paul, as do other New Testament authors, also transformed the salutation to speak of newness brought on by the cross and resurrection. The typical greeting in Greek letters was the infinitive "to rejoice" (*charein*). Paul never opened his letters with this greeting; instead, the apostle fused the Greek word for the typical Hebrew blessing, "Peace" (*einrēnē*), with the noun form of the Greek blessing, "Grace" (*charis*), to yield the distinctly Christian salutation: "Grace and Peace" (*charis kai eirēnē*). By such a subtle change in the form of Greek letter writing, Paul was able to invoke the range of apostolic blessings found in Jesus: mercy from God ("grace") and eternal well-being from God's presence ("peace"). See *Letter.*   *Carey C. Newman*

SALVATION The acutely dynamic act of snatching others by force from serious peril. In its most basic sense, salvation is the saving of a life from death or harm. Scripture, particularly the New Testament, extends salvation to include deliverance from the penalty and power of sin.

Old Testament For Israelite faith, salvation never carried a purely secular sense of deliverance from death or harm. Because God and no other is the source of salvation, any saving act—even when the focus is preservation of life or release from national oppression—is a spiritual event. The primary saving event in the Old Testament is the Exodus (Ex. 14:13) which demonstrated both God's power to save and God's concern for His oppressed people (Ex. 34:6–7). Israel recounted God's deliverance from Egyptian slavery in the Passover ritual (Ex. 12:1–13), in sermon (Neh. 9:9–11), and in psalms (for example, Pss. 74:12–13; 78:13,42–54; 105:26–38). The retelling of the Exodus event and of God's provision during the wilderness years (Neh. 9:12–21; Pss. 78:14–29; 105:39–41; 114:8) provided a precedent for sharing other stories of national and even personal deliverance (Pss. 40:10; 71:15).

Some argue that the Old Testament does not link salvation with the forgiveness of sins. The recurring cycle of national sin, foreign oppression, national repentence, and salvation by a God-sent "judge," however, witnesses the linkage (Judg. 3:7–9,12,15; 4:1–4; 6:1,7,12; also Neh. 9:27; Ps. 106:34–46). God's sending of a deliverer is in effect God's act of forgiveness of the penitent (compare Pss. 79:9; 85:4). Psalms 51:12 perhaps provides the best Old Testament case for personal salvation from sin.

In the Old Testament, salvation primarily concerns God's saving acts within human history. The early prophets anticipated God's salvation to be realized in the earth's renewed fruitfulness and the rebuilding of the ruined cities of Israel (Amos 9:13–15). Salvation would extend to all nations who would stream to Zion for instruction in God's ways (Isa. 2:2–4; Mic. 4:1–4; Zech. 8:20–23). The prophets also hinted of a salvation that lies outside history (for example, Isa. 51:6). The larger context of Isaiah 25:9 reveals that God's salvation embraces abundant life (25:6) and the end of death (25:7), tears, and disgrace (25:8).

Throughout most of the Old Testament, salvation is a corporate or community experience. The Psalms, however, are especially concerned with the salvation of the individual from the threat of enemies (Pss. 13:5; 18:2,35; 24:5). Though the focus is negative—salvation involves foiling the enemies' wrongdoing—there are hints of a positive content of salvation that embraces prosperity (as in Ps. 18:35). The Psalms are especially interested in God's salvation of the "upright in heart" (Ps. 36:10) or righteous (Ps. 37:19–40) who rely on God for deliverance. Psalm 51:12 more than any other Old Testament text associates personal salvation with a conversion experience; renewed joy of salvation accompanies God's creation of a new heart and right spirit and assurance of God's abiding presence.

New Testament For convenience, salvation can be viewed from the two perspectives of Christ's saving work and the believer's experience of salvation.

Christ's saving work involves already completed, on-going, and future saving activity. Jesus' earthly ministry made salvation a present reality for His generation. Jesus' healing ministry effected salvation from disease (Mark 5:34; 10:52; Luke 17:19). Jesus offered God's forgiveness to hurting people (Mark 2:5; Luke 7:50). He assured a repentant Zacchaeus that "Today salvation has come to this house" (Luke 19:9). Through such encounters Jesus fulfilled the goal of His ministry: "to seek and to save that which was lost" (Luke 19:10).

The apex of Christ's completed work is His sacrificial death: Christ came to "give his life a ransom for many" (Mark 10:45); Christ "entered once for all into the Holy Place, . . . with his own blood,

thus obtaining eternal redemption" (Heb. 9:12 NRSV); "in Christ God was reconciling the world to himself, not counting their trespasses against them" (2 Cor. 5:19 NRSV). Here ransom, redemption, and reconciliation are synonyms for salvation. With reference to Christ's atoning work, the believer can confess, "I was saved when Jesus died for me."

Christ's present saving work primarily concerns Christ's role as mediator (Rom. 8:34; Heb. 7:25; 1 John 2:1). Christ's future saving work chiefly concerns Christ's coming again "to bring salvation to those who eagerly await him" (Heb. 9:28 REB) and salvation from the wrath of God's final judgment (Rom. 5:9–10).

Though Christ's sacrificial death is central, Christ's saving activity extends to the whole of His life, including His birth (Gal. 4:4–5), resurrection (Rom. 4:25; 1 Cor. 15:17), and ascension (Rom. 8:34).

The believer's experience also offers a perspective for viewing salvation. The experience again embraces the past, present, and future. God's initial work in the believer's life breaks down into various scenes: conviction of sin (John 16:8); repentance (turning) from sin to God (Luke 15:7,10; 2 Cor. 7:10); faith which involves commitment of one's whole life to Christ (John 3:16,36); confession of Christ as Lord (Acts 2:21; Rom. 10:9–10). Scripture uses a wealth of images to describe this act: new birth (John 3:3; Titus 3:5); new creation (2 Cor. 5:17); adoption (Rom. 8:15; Gal. 4:4–5; Eph. 1:5); empowerment to be God's children (John 1:12); the status of "saints" (1 Cor. 1:2; 2 Cor. 1:1). This initial work in the believer's life is often termed justification. Justification, however, also embraces God's final judgment (Rom. 2:13; 3:20,30).

God's ongoing work in the believer's life concerns the process of maturing in Christ (Heb. 2:3; 1 Pet. 2:2; 2 Pet. 3:18), growing in Christ's service (1 Cor. 7:20–22), and experiencing victory over sin through the power of the Holy Spirit (Rom. 7—8). Here sin remains a reality in the believer's life (Rom. 7; 1 John 1:8—2:1). The believer is caught in between what God has begun and what God is yet to complete (Phil. 1:6; 2:12).

God's yet to be finished work in the lives of all believers is sometimes called glorification (Rom. 8:17; Heb. 2:10). Scripture, however, uses a wealth of terms for this future saving work: adoption (Rom. 8:23); redemption (Luke 21:28; Rom. 8:23; Eph. 4:30); salvation (Rom. 13:11; Heb. 1:14; 9:28; 1 Pet. 1:5; 2:2); and sanctification (1 Thess. 5:23). God's future work involves more than the individual; God's future work extends to the renewal of heaven and earth.

Some Contested Issues (1) The relationship between faith and works: Scripture repeatedly affirms that salvation is the free gift of God appropri-

S

ated through faith (Eph. 2:8–9; Rom. 3:28). No individual merits salvation by fulfillment of God's law (Rom. 3:20). Saving faith is, however, obedient faith (Rom. 1:5; 16:26; 1 Pet. 1:2). We are saved for good works (Eph. 2:10). Faith that does not result in acts of Christian love is not salvific but demonic (Jas. 2:14–26, especially v. 19).

(2) The perseverance of the saints: Assurance of salvation is grounded in confidence that God is able to finish the good work begun in us (Phil. 1:6), that God who sacrificed His Son for sinners (Rom. 5:8–9) will not hold back anything necessary to save one of his children (Rom. 8:32), and that nothing can separate us from God's love in Christ (Rom. 8:35–39). Confidence in God's ability to keep those who have entrusted their lives to Christ is not, however, an excuse for any believer's inactivity or moral failure (Rom. 6:12–13; Eph. 2:10).

See *Atonement; Conversion; Election; Eschatology; Forgiveness; Future Hope; Grace; Justification; New Birth; Predestination; Reconciliation, Redeem, Redemption, Redeemer; Repentance; Sanctification; Security of the Believer.*

Chris Church

SAMARIA, SAMARITANS (Så mā′ rĭ å, Så mâr′ ĭ tan) Place name of mountain, city, and region meaning, "mountain of watching," and the residents thereof. Forty-two miles north of Jerusalem and nine miles northwest of Nablus, a hill protrudes from the broad valley which cuts across the central highlands of Israel. There lie ruins of ancient Samaria near a small village called Sebastiya. Samaria was the capital, residence, and burial place of the kings of Israel (1 Kings 16:23–28; 22:37; 2 Kings 6:24–30). Following the Northern Kingdom's fall to Assyria (721 B.C.), exiles from many nations settled Samaria (Ezra 4:9–10). Later, the Greeks conquered the region (331 B.C.) and hellenized the area with Greek inhabitants and culture. Then the Hasmoneans, under John Hyrcanus, destroyed the city (119 B.C.). After a long period without inhabitants, Samaria lived again under Pompey and the Romans (63 B.C.).

Long colonnaded street built by the emperor Severus at N.T. Sebaste (which was the O.T. city of Samaria).

Finally, Herod the Great obtained control of Samaria in 30 B.C. and made it one of the chief cities of his territory. Again, the city was resettled with people from distant places, this time mercenaries from Europe. Herod renamed the city Sebaste, using the Greek word for Augustus, the emperor. When the Jews revolted in 66 A.D., the Romans reconquered the city and destroyed it. The Romans later rebuilt Samaria, but the city never regained the prestige it once had.

Samaria is the only major city founded by Israel, the Northern Kingdom. Omri, the sixth king of Israel (885–874 B.C.), purchased the hill of Samaria for his royal residence. Shechem had been the capital of the Northern Kingdom until Jeroboam relocated it at Tirzah.

When Ahab, Omri's son, became king of Israel, he built an ivory palace at Samaria. Amos denounced him for doing this (Amos 6:1,4; 1 Kings 22:39). Jezebel influenced Ahab, her husband, to make the city the center for Baal worship (1 Kings 16:29–33). Jezebel also had many prophets of Yahweh killed in Samaria (1 Kings 18:2–4).

On two occasions, Benhadad, the king of Syria, besieged the city of Samaria; but both times he was unsuccessful (1 Kings 20; 2 Kings 6). Naaman, a Syrian leper, had come to Samaria to be healed by Elisha a short time prior to Ben hadad's attack (2 Kings 5).

Here Elijah destroyed the messengers of King Ahaziah, who were seeking the consultation of Baalzebub. He, likewise, prophesied of King Ahaziah's death (2 Kings 1). Later, Jehu killed Ahab's seventy sons in Samaria (2 Kings 10). Finally, Samaria fell to Assyria in 721 B.C. after a three years' siege (2 Kings 17:5, 18:9–12). See *Assyria.* This destruction came after many prophecies concerning its sins and many warnings about its doom (Isa. 8:4; 9:8–14; 10:9; 28:1–13; 36:19; Jer. 23:13; Ezek. 23:1–4; Hos. 7; 13:16; Amos 3:12; Mic. 1:6).

While the term *Samaria* was first identified with the city founded by Omri, it soon became associated with the entire region surrounding the city, the tribal territory of Manasseh and Ephraim. Finally, the name *Samaria* became synonymous with the entire Northern Kingdom (1 Kings 13:32; Jer. 31:5). After the Assyrian conquest, Samaria began to shrink in size. By New Testament times, it became identified with the central region of Palestine, with Galilee to the north and Judea to the south.

The name *Samaritans* originally was identified with the Israelites of the Northern Kingdom (2 Kings 17:29). When the Assyrians conquered Israel and exiled 27,290 Israelites, a "remnant of Israel" remained in the land. Assyrian captives from distant places also settled there (2 Kings 17:24). This led to the intermarriage of some, though not all, Jews with Gentiles and to widespread worship of foreign gods. By the time the

Byzantine church at Sebaste (Samaria) built over the traditional site of John the Baptist's burial place.

Jews returned to Jerusalem to rebuild the Temple and the walls of Jerusalem, Ezra and Nehemiah refused to let the Samaritans share in the experience (Ezra 4:1–3; Neh. 4:7). The old antagonism between Israel to the north and Judah to the south intensified the quarrel.

The Jewish inhabitants of Samaria identified Mount Gerizim as the chosen place of God and the only center of worship, calling it the "navel of the earth" because of a tradition that Adam sacrificed there. Their scriptures were limited to the Pentateuch, the first five books of the Bible. Moses was regarded as the only prophet and intercessor in the final judgment. They also believed that 6,000 years after creation, a Restorer would arise and would live on earth for 110 years. On the Judgment Day, the righteous would be resur-

rected in paradise and the wicked roasted in eternal fire.

In the days of Christ, the relationship between the Jews and the Samaritans was greatly strained (Luke 9:52–54; 10:25–37; 17:11–19; John 8:48). The animosity was so great that the Jews bypassed Samaria as they traveled between Galilee and Judea. They went an extra distance through the barren land of Perea on the eastern side of the Jordan to avoid going through Samaria. Yet Jesus rebuked His disciples for their hostility to the Samaritans (Luke 9:55–56), healed a Samaritan leper (Luke 17:16), honored a Samaritan for his neighborliness (Luke 10:30–37), praised a Samaritan for his gratitude (Luke 17:11–18), asked a drink of a Samaritan woman (John 4:7), and preached to the Samaritans (John 4:40–42). Then in Acts 1:8, Jesus challenged His disciples to witness in Samaria. Philip, a deacon, opened a mission in Samaria (Acts 8:5).

A small Samaritan community continues to this day to follow the traditional worship near Shechem. See *Israel; Samballat.*　　　*Donald R. Potts*

SAMARITAN PENTATEUCH The canon or "Bible" of the Samaritans, who revere the Torah as God's revelation to Moses on Mount Sinai and do not regard the rest of the Hebrew Bible as canon. The Samaritans regarded themselves as the true heirs (as versus Judahites) to the Mosaic tradition. Their scripture includes Genesis through Deuter-

Samaritans of the twentieth century celebrating their Passover at Mount Gerizim.

Samaritan priests with their sacred ancient copy of their canon—the Samaritan Pentateuch.

onomy with many variant readings from the Masoretic Text or Hebrew text currently used by scholars. See *Bible, Texts and Versions; Samaria.*

SAMGAR-NEBO (Săm′ gär-nē′ bō) Personal name of Babylonian official who accompanied Nebuchadrezzar of Babylon in capturing Jerusalem in 587 B.C. according to Hebrew text (Jer. 39:3). Many modern scholars seek to reconstruct the original Akkadian name. Such reconstructions relate the name to a city—Simmagir—known from other Babylonian records. This would mean the previous person in the list—Nergal-sharezer—was from the city (REB, compare NIV). Other scholars see Samgar-Nebo as a title describing the position Nergal-sharezer held.

SAMGAR-NEBU (Săm′ gär-nē′ bū) NAS transliteration of Hebrew for Samgar-nebo.

SAMLAH (Săm′ lah) Personal name perhaps meaning, "coat." Ruler of Edom (Gen. 36:36).

SAMOS (Sā′ mŏs) Place name meaning, "height." Small island (only 27 miles long) located in the Aegean Sea about a mile off the coast of Asia Minor near the peninsula of Trogyllium. In the strait between Samos and the mainland, the Greeks defeated the Persian fleet about 479 B.C. and turned

View of Roman period additions to the Heraion (great sanctuary of Hera of Samos) on the island of Samos.

the tide of power in the Ancient Near East. Traveling from Jerusalem to Rome, Paul's ship either put in at Samos or anchored just offshore (Acts 20:15).

SAMOTHRACE (Săm ō thrāce′) Place name perhaps meaning, "height of Thrace." Mountainous island in northern Aegean Sea thirty-eight miles south of coast of Thrace with peaks rising 5,000 feet above sea level. Paul spent a night there on his second missionary journey as he headed to Philippi (Acts 16:11). A famous mystery cult was practiced there.

SAMOTHRACIA (Săm ō thrā′ cĭ á) KJV, TEV spelling of Samothrace.

SAMSON (Săm′ son) Personal name meaning, "Of the sun." Last of the major judges over Israel about 1100 B.C. (Judg. 13:1—16:31). The son of Manoah of the tribe of Dan, Samson was a legendary hero who frequently did battle against the Philistines who, at that time, "had dominion over Israel" (14:4).

Before his conception, Samson was dedicated by his parents to be a lifelong Nazirite (13:3–7), a person especially devoted or consecrated. Part of the vow included letting the hair grow and abstaining from wine and strong drink. Samson's legendary strength did not come from his long hair. Rather, it came through the "Spirit of the Lord" who would "come upon" him to enable him to perform amazing feats of physical strength (14:6,19; 15:14; compare 16:28–29). Although a Nazirite, Samson did not live a devoted life. More frequently, he was careless in his vow. He secretly disobeyed the prohibition of approaching a dead body (14:8–9), had immoral relations with a Gaza harlot (16:1), and with Delilah (16:4–20).

Samson is portrayed as a headstrong young man with little or no self-control. None of his exploits show him as a religious enthusiast. In fact, every major crisis in his life resulting in clashes against the Philistines were brought on by his relationships with Philistine women. Samson's fascination with Delilah finally wrought his downfall. The lords of the Philistines offered her eleven hundred pieces of silver from each of them to find out the source of Samson's strength. In her first three attempts, Samson gave her false answers. However, he did not seem to equate the Philistines binding him each time with betrayal by Delilah. Finally, she coaxed the truth from him, and Samson was captured.

Ultimately, Samson proved little more than a thorn in the flesh to the Philistines. He never really freed Israel from the dominion of the Philistines. In his death, he killed more Philistines than the total he had killed during his life (16:30). He is listed with the heroes of faith in Hebrews 11:32, because his strength came from God and because in his dying act, he demonstrated his

faith. See *Nazirite; Judge; Judges, Book of; Spirit.*
                                    Darlene R. Gautsch

SAMUEL (Sā′ mū ĕl) Personal name in the Ancient Near East meaning, "Sumu is God" but understood in Israel as "The name is God," "God is exalted," or "son of God." The last judge, first king-maker, priest, and prophet who linked the period of the judges with the monachy (about 1066–1000 B.C.). Born in answer to barren Hannah's tearful prayer (1 Sam. 1:10), Samuel was dedicated to the Lord before his birth (1:11) as a "loan" for all his life (1:28; 2:20). Eli raised Samuel at the Shiloh sanctuary (1 Sam. 2:11). As a child, Samuel grew "both in stature and in favor with the Lord and with men" (1 Sam. 2:26 NAS; compare Luke 2:52). Samuel met God and received his first prophetic mission as a young lad (1 Sam. 3:1,11–14). God's initial word to Samuel concerned God's rejection of Eli's family from service as priests as punishment for the sins of Eli's sons.

Samuel was responsible for a revival of the Shiloh sanctuary (1 Sam. 3:21). Psalm 99:6–7 relates that God spoke with Samuel from out of the pillar of cloud as God had previously with Moses and Aaron. God "was with him and let none of his words fall to the ground" (1 Sam. 3:19; also 9:6). Jeremiah regarded Samuel and Moses as the two great intercessors of Israel (Jer. 15:1).

Following the death of Eli and his sons, Israel experienced twenty years (1 Sam. 7:2) of national sin and Philistine oppression. Samuel reemerged in the role of judge, calling Israel to repentance and delivering them from foreign domination. Samuel also exercised the judicial role of judge, administering justice at Bethel, Gilgal, Mizpah, and Ramah (1 Sam. 7:15–17).

Samuel served as the prototype for future prophets in tension with the kings of Israel and Judah. The sins of Samuel's sons and the Philistine threat led the elders of Israel to appeal to Samuel for a king "like all the nations" (1 Sam. 8:3,5,20). Samuel rightly understood this call for a king as rejection of

Tel Rama (Ramah)—birthplace of Samuel the prophet.

God's rule (1 Sam. 8:7; 10:19). Samuel warned Israel of the dangers of a monarchy—forced labor, seizure of property, taxation (1 Sam. 8:10–18)—before anointing Saul as Israel's first king (1 Sam. 10:1). Samuel's recording of the rights and duties of kingship (1 Sam. 10:25) set the stage for later prophets to call their monarchs to task for disobedience to God's commands and for overstepping God's limits for kingship in Israel. Samuel foreshadowed Elijah in his call for rain during the wheat harvest, the usual dry season, as vindication of his word of judgment concerning Israel's demand for a king (1 Sam. 12:17–18).

Samuel's relations with Saul highlight the conditional nature of kingship in Israel. Israel's king was designated by God and served at God's pleasure. Saul's presumption in offering burnt sacrifice before battle with the Philistines (1 Sam. 13:8–15) and his disregard of God's command to leave no survivors among the Amalekites or their flocks (1 Sam. 15) occasioned Samuel's declaration of God's rejection of Saul's kingship. Obeying God's call to anoint another king amounted to treason in Saul's eyes, and Samuel had concerns for his life. Samuel was, however, obedient in anointing David as king over Israel (1 Sam. 16:13). Later when Saul sought David's life, David took refuge with Samuel and his band of prophets at Ramah (1 Sam. 19:18–24). Finally, Samuel's death brought national mourning (1 Sam. 25:1; 28:3). It also left Saul without access to God's word. In desperation he acknowledged Samuel's power and influence by seeking to commune with Samuel's spirit (1 Sam. 28). Thus in life and death Samuel cast a long shadow over Israel's history of worship, rule, prophecy, and justice.   *Chris Church*

SAMUEL, BOOKS OF Ninth and tenth books of English Bible following the order of the earliest Greek translation but combined as the eighth book of the Hebrew canon named for the major figure of its opening section. Along with Joshua, Judges, and Kings, the Books of Samuel form the "former prophets" in the Hebrew Bible. Many modern scholars refer to these four books as the Deuteronomistic History, since they show how the teaching of Deuteronomy worked itself out in the history of God's people.

The Bible does not say who wrote these books. Many Bible students think Samuel along with Nathan and Gad had major input, pointing to 1 Chronicles 29:29 as evidence. See *Chronicles, Books of.* Others think the books had a long history of composition with various narratives or narrative sources being composed from the time of the events until the time of the Exile, when the "former prophets" were gathered into one collection. Such individual narratives would include Shiloh (1 Sam. 1—3), the Ark (1 Sam. 4:1—7:1), the Rise of Kingship (1 Sam. 9:1—11:15), Battles of Saul (1 Sam. 13—15), the History of David's

S

Rise to Power (1 Sam. 16:14—2 Sam. 5:25), and the Succession to the Throne of David (2 Sam. 9—20; 1 Kings 1—2).

The Books of Samuel arose as a reflection upon the nature of human kingship in light of Israel's tradition that Yahweh was their king. See *King, Kingship; Kingdom of God.* They answered a first generation's burning questions. Had God rejected David as He had rejected Saul? Why was the young Solomon named king rather than his older brothers? Could the violent measures Solomon undertook when he assumed the throne be justified? To answer the questions, the Books tell the narrative of three major figures: Samuel, Saul, and David. See *David; Samuel; Saul.* The story of each combines tragedy, despair, and direction toward future hope. The dangers of kingship (1 Sam. 8) and the hope for kingship (2 Sam. 7) form the narrative tension for the Books. The final chapter (2 Sam. 24) does not solve the tension. It points further ahead to the building of the Temple, where God's presence and Israel's worship can be at the center of life leading the king to be God's humble, forgiven servant.

The Books of Samuel thus point to several theological themes that can guide God's people through the generations.

Leadership is the guiding theme. Can God's people continue with a loosely knit organization as in the days of the judges, or must they have "a king to judge us like all the nations" (1 Sam. 8:5)? Samuel does not explicitly answer the question. God does not wholeheartedly accept kingship as the only alternative. Kingship means the people have rejected God (1 Sam. 8:7; 10:19). Still, kingship can flourish if the people and the king follow God (1 Sam. 12:14–15, 20–25). Saul showed God's threats could be soon realized (1 Sam. 13:13–14). A new family from a new tribe would rule. This did not mean eternal war among tribes and families. A covenant could bind the two families together (1 Sam. 20; 23:16–18). Anger on one side does not require anger from the other as David's reactions to Saul continually show, summarized in 1 Samuel 24:17: "Thou art more righteous than I: for thou has rewarded me good, whereas I have rewarded thee evil." David neither planned the demise of Saul and his family nor rewarded those who did (2 Sam. 4:9–12). David established his kingdom and sought to establish a house for God (2 Sam. 7:2). The king, however, gave in to God's plan to establish David's house and let his son build the house for God (2 Sam. 7:13). The king's response shows the nature of true leadership. He expresses praise for God not pride in personal achievement (2 Sam. 7:18–29).

Working through His promise to David, God then worked to establish His own kingdom among His people. He could work through an imperfect king who committed the outlandish sin with Bathsheba (2 Sam. 11) because the king was willing to confess his sin (2 Sam. 12:13). The rule of God's king does not promise perfect peace. Even David's own household revolted against him. Human pride and ego did not determine history. God's promise to David could not be overthrown.

Other themes are subordinate to that of leadership for Israel. The call for covenant commitment and obedience, the forgiveness and mercy of God, the sovereignty of God in human history, the significance of prayer and praise, the faithfulness of God to fulfill prophecy, the need for faithfulness to human leaders, the holy presence of God among His people, the nature of human friendship, and the importance of family relationships all echo forth from these books.

1 Samuel
Outline

I. God Gives His People an Example of Dedicated Leadership (1:1—7:17).
   A. A dedicated leader is the answer to parental prayers (1:1–28).
   B. A dedicated leader comes from grateful, sacrificial parents who worship the incomparable God (2:1–10).
   C. A dedicated leader is a priest who faithfully serves God rather than seeking selfish interests (2:11–36).
   D. A dedicated leader is a prophet who is called by the Word of God and who faithfully delivers the Word of God (3:1—4:15).
   E. Superstitious use of religious relics is not a substitute for dedicated leadership (4:16–22).
   F. Only a dedicated priest, not foreign gods nor disobedient persons, can stand before God (5:1—7:2).
   G. A dedicated political leader is a man of prayer (7:3–17).

II. Human Kingship Represents a Compromise with God by a People Who Have Rejected the Kingship of God (8:1—15:35).
   A. Hereditary kingship is a rejection of God which hurts His people and separates them from God (8:1–22; compare Judg. 8:22—9:57).
   B. A dedicated king is a humble person from a humble family who knows he owes his position to God's choice (9:1—10:27).
   C. The dedicated king is a Spirit-filled deliverer (11:1–15).
   D. The dedicated leader is morally pure and uses the history of God's people to call them to obedience (12:1–25).
   E. Kingship depends on obedience to God, not human wisdom (13:1–23).
   F. A dedicated leader is used by God to unify and deliver His people (14:1–23).
   G. God delivers His dedicated leader from inadvertent sins (14:24–46).

H. The king is responsible to defeat the enemies of the people of God (14:47–52).

I. A disobedient king is rejected by God (15:1–35).

III. God Raises Up New Leadership for His People (16:1—31:13).

  A. God gives His Spirit to the chosen person meeting His leadership qualifications (16:1–13).

  B. God provides unexpected opportunities of service for His chosen king (16:14–23).

  C. God uses the skills and faith of His leader to defeat those who would defy God (17:1–58).

  D. God provides His presence and the loyalty of friends to protect His chosen one from the jealous plots of an evil leader (18:1—20:42).

  E. God's priests affirm the special position of God's chosen leader (21:1–9).

  F. God protects His benevolent and faithful leader from the vengeance of evil enemies (21:10—22:23).

  G. God heeds the prayer of His chosen and delivers him from treacherous enemies (23:1–29).

  H. God honors the righteousness of His chosen leader (24:1–22).

  I. God avenges His chosen against the insults of foolish enemies (25:1–39a).

  J. God provides family for His chosen (25:39b–44).

  K. God rewards the righteousness and faithfulness of His chosen leader (26:1–25).

  L. The chosen leader cunningly begins building his kingdom even under adverse circumstances (27:1–12).

  M. God fulfills His prophecy and destroys disobedient leaders (28:1–25).

  N. God protects His chosen leader from compromising situations (29:1–11).

  O. God restores the property taken from His chosen leader (30:1–20).

  P. God's chosen leader shares His goods with the needy and with colleagues (30:21–31).

  Q. God destroys disobedient leaders (31:1–7).

  R. God honors people who express loyalty to their chosen leaders (31:8–13).

2 Samuel

Outline

I. To Achieve His Purposes, God Honors Obedience Not Treachery (1:1—6:23).

  A. Those who dishonor God's chosen leaders are punished (1:1–16).

  B. God's leader honors the memory of his predecessors (1:17–27).

  C. God leads people to honor His obedient leader (2:1–4a).

  D. God honors loyal, obedient people (2:4b–7).

  E. God blesses efforts for peace (2:8–28).

  F. God strengthens His obedient leader (2:29—3:19).

  G. God's leader refuses to honor treachery and revenge (3:20—4:12).

  H. God fulfills His promises to His patient servant (5:1–16).

  I. God provides victory for His people (5:17–25).

  J. God's people must honor His holy presence (6:1–23).

II. God Establishes His Purposes Through His Faithful Yet Fallible Servant (7:1—12:31).

  A. God promises to bless the house of David forever (7:1–17).

  B. God's servant praises the incomparable God (7:18–29).

  C. God gives victory to His faithful servant (8:1–18).

  D. God's servant shows kindness in memory of his departed friends (9:1–13).

  E. Enemy coalitions cannot prevent God from taking vengeance (10:1–19).

  F. Disobedience from God's leader displeases the Lord and brings judgment but also mercy (11:1—12:14a).

  G. God brings honor to His penitent servant (12:14b–31).

III. Lack of Attention to Family Relations Leads to National Problems for God's Leader (13:1—20:26).

  A. The inattention of a godly father can lead to family feuds, shame, and vengeance (13:1–39).

  B. Reconciliation, not anger and judgments, should mark the family life of God's servants (14:1–33).

  C. Unhealed family wounds lead to revolt (15:1–37).

  D. Leaders need advisors whom God can use to accomplish His purposes (16:1—17:29).

  E. The time of sorrow is too late to set family relationships right (18:1–33).

  F. God's victorious servant deals kindly with those who helped and those who opposed him (19:1–40).

  G. Victory cannot remove rivalries among God's people (19:41—20:26).

IV. God's People Learn from the Experience and Example of God's Leader (21:1—24:25).

  A. God blesses the leader who is faithful to the tradition of His people (21:1–22).

  B. God's leader praises God for His deliverance (22:1–51; compare Ps. 18).

  C. God's leader teaches what he has learned—his experiences with God (23:1–7).

D. God's leader depends on brave, faithful associates (23:8–39).

E. The leader's foolish decisions bring punishment even on a repentant leader (24:1–17).

F. Proper worship brings God's mercy for His people (24:18–25).

SANBALLAT (Săn băl' làt) Akkadian personal name meaning, "Sin (the god) has healed." According to the Elephantine Papyri from the reign of Darius I, Sanballat was governor of Samaria around 407 BC. He had sons whose names included the term *Yahweh,* for the God of Israel. Although addressed by his Babylonian name (probably acquired during the Exile), Sanballat was a practicing Jew. His daughter was married to the grandson of Jerusalem's high priest (Neh. 13:28), indicating harmonious relations between Judah and Samaria at that time. Nehemiah referred to Sanballat as the "Horonite," suggesting a connection with Upper or Lower Beth-horon. (Neh. 2:10). These cities contolled the major highway between Jerusalem and the Mediterrean Sea. If Sanballat had influence with these towns, he could greatly affect Jerusalem's economy. Sanballat, in league with Tobiah and Shemiah, opposed Nehemiah's rebuilding of Jerusalem. If the Holy City regained prominence, it would erode the powers of the surrounding cities. The struggle appears to have been more political than racial or religious. Papyri from Wadi Daliyeh appear to indicate two later Sanballats also served as governors of Samaria.

SANCTIFICATION The process of being made holy resulting in a changed life-style for the believer. The English word *sanctification* comes from the Latin *santificatio,* meaning the act/process of making holy. In the Greek New Testament, the root *hag-* is the basis of *hagiasmos,* "holiness," "consecration," "sanctification"; *hagiosyne,* "holiness"; *hagiotes,* "holiness"; *hagiazo* "to sanctify," "consecrate," "treat as holy," "purify"; and *hagios,* "holy," "saint." The root idea of the Greek stem is to stand in awe of something or someone. The New Testament usage is greatly dependent upon the Greek translation of the Old Testament, the Septuagint, for meaning. The *hag-* words in the Septuagint mostly translated the Hebrew *qadosh,* "separate, contrasting with the profane." Thus, God is separate; things and people dedicated to Him and to His use are separate. The moral implications of this word came into focus with the prophets and became a major emphasis in the New Testament. See *Holy.*
Old Testament In Old Testament thought the focus of holiness (*qadosh*) is upon God. He is holy (Ps. 99:9); His name is holy (Pss. 99:3; 111:9) and may not be profaned (Lev. 20:3). Since God exists in the realm of the holy rather than the

profane, all that pertains to Him must come into that same realm of holiness. This involves time, space, objects, and people.

Certain times are sanctified in that they are set apart especially to the Lord: the sabbath (Gen. 2:3), the various festivals (Lev. 23:4–44), the year of Jubilee (Lev. 25:12). By strictly observing the regulations governing each, Israel sanctified (or treated as holy) these special times of the year. Also the land of Canaan (Ex. 15:13), as well as Jerusalem (Isa. 11:9), was holy to the Lord and was not to be polluted by sinful conduct (Lev. 18:27–28). The tabernacle/Temple and all the objects related to it were holy (Ex. 25—Num. 10; Ezek. 40—48). The various gifts brought in worship were sanctified. These fall into three groupings: those whose sanctity was inherent (for example, firstborn males of female animals and human beings, Ex. 13:2,11–13; Lev. 27:26); objects whose sanctification was required (for example, tithes of crops and pure animals, Lev. 27:30–33; Deut. 26:13); and gifts whose sanctification was voluntary (see partial list in Lev. 27). The dedication of these objects mostly occurred not at some ritual in the sanctuary but at a prior declaration of dedication (Judg. 17:3; Lev. 27:30–33;).

Of course, the priests and Levites who functioned in the sanctuary, beginning with Aaron, were sanctified to the Lord by the anointing of oil (Ex. 30:30–32; 40:12–15). Additionally, the Nazirite was consecrated (Num. 6:8), although only for a specified period of time. Finally, the nation of Israel was sanctified to the Lord as a holy people (Ex. 19:6; Deut. 7;6; 14:2,21; 26:19). This holiness was closely identified with obedience to the Law of Holiness in Lev. 17—26, which includes both ritual and ethical commands. In the prophets especially, the ethical responsibility of being holy in conduct came to the forefront (Isa. 5; Jer. 5—7; Amos 4—5; Hos. 11).
Sanctification in the New Testament The same range of meanings reflected by the Septuagint usage is preserved in the New Testament but with extension of meaning in certain cases. Objects may be made holy (Matt. 23:17,19; 1 Tim. 4:5) or treated as holy (Matt. 6:9; Luke 11:2), but, mostly, the word group stresses the personal dimension of holiness. Here, the two streams of Old Testament meaning are significant: the cultic and the ethical. Sanctification is vitally linked to the salvation experience and is concerned with the moral/spiritual obligations assumed in that experience. We were set apart to God in conversion, and we are living out that dedication to God in holiness.

The link of New Testament thought to Old Testament antecedents in the cultic aspect of sanctification is most clearly seen in Hebrews. Christ's crucifixion makes possible the moving of the sinner from the profane to the holy (that is, sanctifies, makes holy) so that the believer can become a part of the temple where God dwells and is worshiped (Heb. 13:11–16; 2:9–11; 10:10,14,29). Paul (Rom. 15:16; 1 Cor. 1:2; 6:11; Eph. 5:26–27; 2 Thess. 2:13) and Peter (1 Pet. 1:2) both affirmed the work of the Holy Spirit in conversion as a sanctification, a making the believer holy so as to come before God in acceptance. Especially in Paul, justification and sanctification are closely related concepts. See *Justification.*

Hebrews also emphasizes the ethical aspect of sanctification. Sanctification/holiness is to be pursued as an essential aspect of the believer's life (Heb. 12:14); the blood of sanctification must not be defiled by sinful conduct (10:26–31). Paul stressed both the individual's commitment to holy living (Rom. 6:19–22; 1 Thess. 4:3–8; 2 Cor. 7:1) and the enabling power of God for it (1 Thess. 3:13; 4:8). The summation of the ethical imperative is seen in Peter's use (1 Pet. 1:15–16) of Leviticus 11:44; 19:2; 20:7: "Be ye holy; for I am holy."

See *Ethics; Hebrews; Salvation.*

Lorin L. Cranford

SANCTUARY (Sănc′ tū âr ȳ) Place set aside as sacred and holy, especially a place of worship. On sites where the patriarchs had erected altars, the people of Israel later built shrines and temples to commemorate the encounters with God. Specifically, the tabernacle and the Temple in Jerusalem were revered as sanctuaries.

SANDALS, SHOES Items worn to protect the feet. Ancient shoes are well known from paintings, sculptures, and carved reliefs. The shoe was considered the humblest article of clothing and could be bought cheaply. Two types of shoes existed: slippers of soft leather and the more popular sandals with a hard leather sole. Thongs secured the sandal across the insole and between the toes. Although shoes could be bought at a low price, they were often repaired by the poor. Shoes were removed at the doorway of the tent or house, or during a period of mourning. Shoes were also removed as evidence of humility in the presence

Close-up of the sandaled foot of a Roman statue.

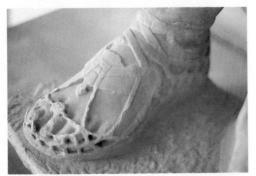

Leather thong sandals from the Roman period.

of kings. The removal of the guest's sandals was the job of the lowliest servant who was also required to wash the dusty and soiled feet of the visitor. See *Foot Washing.* In early Israel, legal contracts and oaths were often sealed with the removal and giving of a shoe by one party (Ruth 4:7). Going barefoot was a sign of poverty and reproach. Isaiah walked barefooted to symbolize the impending poverty of Israel before the judgment of God (Isa. 20:2). During New Testament times, Jewish practice forbade the wearing of sandals with multilayered leather soles nailed together, as this was the shoe worn by Roman soldiers.

David Maltsberger

SANHEDRIN (Săn hē′ drĭn) The highest Jewish council in the first century. The council had 71 members and was presided over by the high priest. The Sanhedrin included both of the main Jewish parties among its membership. Since the high priest presided, the Sadducean priestly party seems to have predominated; but some leading Pharisees also were members (Acts 5:34; 23:1–9).

The word *Sanhedrin* is usually translated "council" in the English translations of the Bible. Because of the predominance of the chief priests in the Sanhedrin, at times the words *chief priests* seem to refer to the action of the Sanhedrin, even though the name itself is not used.

According to Jewish tradition, the Sanhedrin began with the 70 elders appointed by Moses in Numbers 11:16 and was reorganized by Ezra after the Exile. However, the Old Testament provides no evidence of a council that functioned like the Sanhedrin of later times. Thus, the Sanhedrin had its origin sometime during the centuries between the Testaments. See *Intertestamental History; Jewish Parties.*

During the first century, the Sanhedrin exerted authority under the watchful eye of the Romans. Generally, the Roman governor allowed the Sanhedrin considerable autonomy and authority. The trial of Jesus, however, shows that the Sanhedrin did not have the authority to condemn people to death (John 18:31). Later, Stephen was stoned to death after a hearing before the Sanhedrin, but this may have been more a mob action than a legal execution authorized by the Sanhedrin (Acts 6:12–15; 7:54–60).

The Gospels describe the role of the Sanhedrin in the arrest, trials, and condemnation of Jesus. The Sanhedrin, under the leadership of Caiaphas the high priest, plotted to have Jesus killed (John 11:47–53). The chief priests conspired with Judas to betray Jesus (Matt. 26:14–16). After His arrest they brought Jesus into the council (Luke 22:66). They used false witnesses to condemn Jesus (Matt. 26:59–60; Mark 14:55–56). They sent Him to Pilate and pressured Pilate into pronouncing the death sentence (Mark 15:1–15).

The Book of Acts describes how the Sanhedrin harassed and threatened the apostles. The healing of the man at the Temple and Peter's sermon attracted the attention of the chief priests. Peter and John were called before the council and warned not to preach anymore in the name of Jesus (Acts 4:5–21). When the apostles continued to preach, the council had them arrested (Acts 5:21,27). The wise counsel of Gamaliel caused the council to release the apostles with a beating and a warning (Acts 5:34–42). Stephen had to appear before the Sanhedrin on charges that sounded like the false charges against Jesus (Acts 6:12–15).

After Paul was arrested in Jerusalem, the Roman commander asked the council to examine Paul to decide what was Paul's crime (Acts 22:30; 23:28). Paul identified himself as a Pharisee who was on trial for his hope of resurrection. This involved the council in a debate of the divisive issue of the resurrection (Acts 23:1–9). The chief priests and elders were part of a plot to have Paul assassinated as he was led to another hearing before the council (Acts 23:13–15,20).

Robert J. Dean

SANSANNAH (Săn săn' nah) Place name perhaps meaning, "branch of the date palm." Town in tribal territory of Judah (Josh. 15:31). Modern khirbet esh-Shamshaniyat nine miles northwest of Beersheba. Apparently the same as Hazar-susah (Josh. 19:5) and Hazar-susim (1 Chron. 4:31), thus assigned to tribe of Simeon.

SAPH (Săph) Personal name perhaps meaning, "threshold." A giant the men of David killed (2 Sam. 21:18). See *Giants; Rapha; Rephaim; Sibbechai.*

SAPHIR (Sā' phĭr) Place name meaning, "beautiful town." Town Micah lamented over (Mic. 1:11). Location is unknown; suggestions include khirbet el-Kom or tell Eitun. It must be near Lachish.

SAPPHIRA (Săp phī' rà) Personal name meaning, "beautiful" or "sapphire." See *Ananias 1.*

SAPPHIRE See *Minerals and Metals.*

SARA(H) (Sā' rà) Variant Hebrew form of name Sarai. See *Sarai.*

SARAI (Sā rah) Personal name meaning, "princess." Wife and half sister of Abraham (Gen. 11:29—25:10). Sarah, first called Sarai, had the same father as Abraham. Marriages with half brothers were not uncommon in her time. Sarah traveled with Abraham from Ur to Haran. Then at the age of 65 she accompanied him to Canaan as Abraham followed God's leadership in moving to

The building of the Cheops Pyramid at Giza, Egypt, predates Abraham's and Sarai's Egyptian sojourn.

the land God had promised. During a famine in Canaan, Abraham and Sarah fled to Egypt. This was Abraham's first attempt to pass off Sarah as his sister rather than wife because he feared that he would be killed when the Egyptians saw Sarah's beauty. Consequently, the Pharaoh thought Sarah was Abraham's sister, took Sarah into court, and treated Abraham well. When the Lord sent serious disease on Pharaoh's household, he saw the deception and sent them away. The second trick about Abraham's relationship with Sarah was in the court of Abimelech, king of Gerar, who also took in Sarah. God intervened in Abimelech's dream and protected Sarah. He sent them away with the right to live there and with a gift for Sarah.

In her grief over her barrenness, Sarah gave her maid Hagar to Abraham in the hope of an heir; but she expressed resentment when Hagar conceived. When Sarah was almost 90 years old, God changed her name and promised her a son. A year later, she bore Isaac.

At the age of 127, Sarah died at Hebron, where she was buried in the cave in the field of Machpelah near Mamre.

In the New Testament, Romans 4:19 refers to Sarah's barrenness as evidence of Abraham's faith; Romans 9:9 cites her conception of Isaac as an example of God's power in fulfilling a promise. Galatians 4:21–31 contrasts her with Hagar without naming her, Hebrews 11:11 lauds her faith,

Ruins of the Roman gymnasium at the ancient city of Sardis in Asia Minor (modern Turkey).

and 1 Peter 3:6 describes her relationship with Abraham.   *Judith Wooldridge*

SARAPH (Sā′ răph) Personal name meaning, "burning." Member of tribe of Judah who exercised power in Moab (1 Chron. 4:22).

SARDIS (Sär′ dĭs) City of one of the seven churches addressed in the Revelation (3:1–6). The church was condemned as being "dead," perhaps a reference to its ineffectiveness in the world. However, some of its members were commended (v. 4). The city of the same name was the capital of the province of Lydia and was located in the Hermus River valley northeast of Ephesus. An impressive acropolis overlooks the site. One of the major features there in New Testament times was a temple to Artemis, the goddess of love and fertility. See *Asia Minor.*

SARDITE (Sär′ dīte) Descendant of or member of clan of Sered (Num. 26:26).

SARDIUS (Sär′ dī ŭs) Precious stone sometimes used to translate Hebrew *'odem,* "red," and Greek *sardion.* Other translators use "carnelian" or "ruby." See "ruby" under *Minerals and Metals.*

SARDONYX (Sär′ dō nўx) Precious stone (Rev. 21:20), a form of agate. See "Onyx" under *Minerals and Metals.*

SAREPTA (Să rĕp′ tà) Greek transliteration of Hebrew Zarephath (Luke 4:26). See *Zarephath.*

S

Columns of the Temple of Artemis at Sardis in the modern country of Turkey.

SARGON (Sär′ gŏn) Akkadian royal name meaning, "the king is legitimate." An ancient throne name first taken by the king of Akkad about 2100 B.C. In 722 B.C., Sargon II of Assyria succeeded his brother, Shalmaneser V. His father was the famous king, Tiglath-pileser III. Sargon finished the destruction of Samaria begun by his brother. See Isaiah 20:1. He deported the people of Israel to Media and other parts of the Middle East. Sargon then launched military campaigns against King Midas of Muski in southeast Asia Minor and against the kingdom of Urartu. He conquered both. Sargon was succeeded by his son, Senneracherib. See *Assyria; Israel.*

SARID (Sā′ rĭd) Place name meaning, "survivor." Border town of tribe of Zebulun (Josh. 19:10). Spelled Sedud by some early versions, Sarid is probably modern tell Shadud at the northern edge of the Jezreel Valley about six miles northeast of Megiddo and five miles southeast of Nazareth.

SARON (Sā′ rŏn) Greek transliteration of Sharon (Acts 9:35). See *Sharon.*

SARSECHIM (Sär′ sė chĭm) Babylonian personal name or title possibly meaning, "overseer of black slaves" or "overseer of the mercenary troops." Often seen as copyist's change from Nebushasban (Jer. 39:13). A Babylonian leader during capture of Jerusalem in 587 B.C. (Jer. 39:3). Compare translations. See *Rab-saris.*

SARSEKIM (Sär′ sē kĭm) NAS spelling of Sarsechim.

SARUCH (Sā′ rŭch) Greek transliteration of Serug (Luke 3:35).

SATAN (Sā′ tan) Transliteration of Hebrew word meaning, "adversary." The Hebrew term appears in Numbers 22:22,32; 1 Samuel 29:4; 2 Samuel 19:22; 1 Kings 5:4; 11:14,23,25; Psalm 109:6, normally translated in English as adversary or accuser. In Job 1—2; Zechariah 3:2; and 1 Chronicles 21:1 the same term is translated as a proper name. See *Devil, Satan, Evil, Demonic.*

SATAN, SYNAGOGUE OF Term used in Revelation (2:9; 3:9) to describe Jewish worshipers who persecuted the church.

SATISFACTION Theory explaining Christ's atonement as satisfying demands of God's holy law and thus satisfying demands of God's wrath. See *Atonement; Expiation, Propitiation.*

SATRAP(Y) (Sā′ trăp ȳ) A political office in the Persian Empire comparable to governor. A satrap's territory was called a satrapy. KJV translated the office, "lieutenants" (Ezra 8:36). These officials aided the people of Israel in rebuilding Jerusalem and the Temple. At the height of the Persian rule, there were at least twenty satrapies. See *Persia.*

SATYR (Sā′ tȳr) A hairy, demonic figure with the appearance of a goat, translating a Hebrew term otherwise translated, "hairy" or "male goat." Bible students differ in interpreting passages as to whether a demonic figure or a normal animal is meant. Israelites apparently sacrificed to such desert-dwelling demons, since they had to have a law forbidding such sacrifice (Lev. 17:7). Some have even interpreted the scapegoat rites (Lev. 16:20–22) as sending Israel's sins back to their author, a desert demon with a different name from that translated, "satyr." Jeroboam I (926–909 B.C.) appointed priests to serve these demons (2 Chron. 11:15). Here idols in the forms of goats may be intended as parallel to the famous calves Jeroboam built. Isaiah promised that Babylon would become so desolate the desert-dwelling demons would live in the ruins (Isa. 13:21; compare 34:14). Some commentators read 2 Kings 23:8 to refer to worship places for these demons at a gate in Jerusalem (compare REB). A similar reality is expressed by a different Hebrew word in Deuteronomy 32:17; Psalm 106:37. Compare Matthew 12:43; Mark 5:13; Luke 11:24; Revelation 18:2. Lilith (Isa. 34:14 NRSV) may also be a name for the desert demons.

Sunset over the site of ancient Azekah near the location of the battle between Saul and the Philistines.

SAUL Saul) Personal name meaning, "asked for." First king of Israel and the Hebrew name of Paul, the apostle. See *Paul*.

Old Testament The Hebrew name *Sha' ul* is used of four persons in the Old Testament. It is usually rendered Shaul for a king of Edom (Gen. 36:37–38), the last son of Simeon (Gen. 46:10), and a Levite of the Kohathites (1 Chron. 6:24). Saul, however, primarily refers to the first king of a united Israel, a tall and handsome son of Kish from the tribe of Benjamin (1 Sam. 9:1–2,21). Chosen by God (1 Sam. 9:15–17) and secretly annointed by Samuel (10:1), Saul was later selected publicly by lot (10:17–24). Despite some people's skepticism (10:27), he proved himself an able leader by delivering the city of Jabesh-gilead and was acclaimed king at Gilgal (11:1–15).

The numbers in 1 Samuel 13:1 are incomplete in the Hebrew text, but Saul's reign is generally dated about 1020–1000 B.C. He made his capital at "Gibeah of Saul" ("Saul's hill," 1 Sam. 11:4), probably tell el-Ful, three miles north of Jerusalem where excavations have uncovered contemporary foundations of a modest fortresslike palace. From Gibeah, Saul drove the Philistines from the hill country (13:19—14:23) and fought other enemies of Israel (14:47–48).

A tragic figure, Saul's heart was initially changed; he had even prophesied (1 Sam. 10:9–13). See *Prophets*. His presumptuous offering

(13:8–14), however, and violation of a holy war ban led to his break with Samuel and rejection by God (15:7–23). The spirit of the Lord left Saul and was replaced by an evil spirit which tormented him. David is introduced as a musician who soothed him by playing the lyre (16:14–23). After the Goliath episode, Saul became jealous and fearful of David (18:7,12), eventually making several spontaneous and indirect attempts on David's life (18:10–11,25; 19:1,9–11). Saul's fits of rage, his obsession with David, and the slaughter of the priests at Nob (22:17–19), make it appear as though he suffered from some sort of psychotic state. His final wretched condition is betrayed by his consultation of the witch at En-dor (28:7–8). The following day, Saul and three sons were killed at the hands of the Philistines on Mount Gilboa (1 Sam. 31). Saul's body was beheaded and hung on the walls of Beth-shan, from whence it was rescued and buried by the grateful inhabitants of Jabesh-gilead (31:8–13).

The enigma of Saul was sensed by David who refused to lift his hand against "the Lord's annointed" (1 Sam. 26:9–11,23) and at his death provided a fitting elegy (2 Sam. 1:17–27).

New Testament Though the king Saul is mentioned in passing, most occurrances of the name in the New Testament refer to the Hebrew name of the apostle Paul.   *Daniel C. Browning, Jr.*

SAVIOR One who saves, used with various shades of meaning, ranging from deliverer to healer and benefactor. In the Old Testament God Himself and no other is savior (Isa. 43:11; 45:21; Hos. 13:4), though individuals such as Moses and the judges may serve as agents of God's deliverance. God reveals His role as savior primarily through the Exodus from Egypt and provision for Israel during the wilderness years (Hos. 13:4–6). In the New Testament, savior continues as a title of God; indeed, God is the savior in a full third of the New Testament cases (Luke 1:47; 1 Tim. 1:1; 2:3; 4:10; Titus 1:3; 2:10; 3:4; Jude 25). The New Testament, however, reveals God as savior primarily in the Christ event. Savior also appears as a title of Christ. The title appears only twice in the Gospels. There Christ is a savior for the outcasts of Israel (Luke 2:11) and the savior of the world (John 4:42; also 1 John 4:14). In Acts Jesus is twice described as the savior of Israel (Acts 5:31; 13:23). Here Jesus' saving role involves giving "repentance . . . and forgiveness of sins" (Acts 5:31; compare Matt. 1:21). Paul anticipated Christ's coming again as savior (Phil. 3:20). Ephesians 5:23 presents Christ as savior of the church. Over one half of the references to Christ as savior occur in the Pastorals and 2 Peter. The increased usage of savior as a Christological title in the later New Testament writings and especially in the postapostolic church perhaps results from the needs of apologetics and evangelism. In a pagan world offering numerous "saviors" such as the pagan gods Zeus and Asclepius, the Roman emperor, and various philosophers, the church witnessed to Christ as the savior who could rescue humanity from the penalty and power of sin. See *Salvation.* *Chris Church*

SAW Tool for cutting wood or stone. See *Tools.*

SCALE A skin disease involving flaking of the scalp. See *Itch; Scall.*

SCALES Instrument for weighing materials. See *Balances; Weights and Measures.*

SCALL KJV term for a skin disease (Lev. 13:30–37; 14:54). The basic Hebrew term means, "to tear away, pull loose." The disease produced head sores, itching, hair thinning, and hair turning yellow. Modern translations refer to a scale or itch. Some scholars think favus is the disease described; others speak of ringworm or eczema. See *Itch.*

SCAPEGOAT Animal that carried away the sins of the people into the wilderness on the Day of Atonement (Lev. 16:8,10,26). On the Day of Atonement, when the high priest went once a year into the holy of holies to offer sacrifices for the sins of his family and for all the people, two goats were brought before him. By lot, one was chosen to be "for the Lord." This goat was slain as a sin offering, and its blood was sprinkled on the cultic objects to help cleanse the altar, the sanctuary, and the tent of meeting from defilements of the past year.

The second goat was said to be "for Azazel." The word *Azazel* is usually interpreted to mean "the goat of removal," or scapegoat. However, the term may also refer to a rocky place in the desert or to a demon of the desert. By laying his hands on the goat's head, the priest transferred the sins of the people to it and then had the goat led away into the desert, picturing the removal of the sins.

In the Book of Enoch, Azazel is identified as the leader of the fallen angels who lies bound beneath rocks in the desert awaiting judgment. The goat is led to that area and thrown to its death from a cliff. See *Intertestamental History; Pseudepigrapha.*

Although the scapegoat is not mentioned by name in the New Testament, Hebrews 10:3–17 contrasts sanctification through the sacrifice of Christ with the blood of bulls and goats which can never take away sins. See *Sanctification.*

SCARLET Color used especially in clothing, often designating royal honor (Dan. 5:7,16,29). See *Cloth, Clothing; Colors; Crimson; Dyeing.*

SCEPTER (Scĕp′ tẽr) The official staff or baton of a king, symbolic of his authority. It probably was descended from the ancient club carried by the prehistoric rulers. Ancient Middle Eastern scepters were depicted in Scripture as the striking power of the king (Num. 24:17). As part of the royal regalia, the scepter was extended to a visitor or dignitary (Esth. 5:2) to signal approval of the visit and allow the person to approach the throne. Scepters were decorated elaborately with gold and precious stones. The shapes varied from wide short maces to long slender poles, usually with ornate heads. The type of scepter usually differed from one kingdom to the next.

SCEVA (Scē′ và) Jewish "high priest" in Ephesus with seven sons who tried unsuccessfully to exorcise demons in Jesus' name as Paul had done (Acts 19:14). The evil spirit jumped on them instead. No such Jewish high priest is known from other sources, particularly not one living in Ephesus. The title may be the result of a copyist or a title Sceva took upon himself to impress leaders of other religions in Ephesus.

SCHOOL Place and agency for education, particularly of children. The word *school* is not mentioned in the Old Testament and only once in the New where the reference is to a Greek school (Acts 19:9). Until the Exile in Babylon (586 B.C.), the education of children was like that of all ancient peoples: it was centered in the home. The main concern of the Jewish people was for religious education in the home.

A new stage in Jewish education came about due to the catastrophe of the Babylonian Exile when the upper classes of Judea were transported to Babylon. The Exiles assembled on the sabbath for prayer and worship. As time went by, buildings were erected in which the people could meet. These little gatherings were the origin of the synagogue, which ultimately became the center of Jewish religious life after the Exile. In the synagogue the scribes taught the Law to the people. Children were not taught in the synagogue until much later times. The father was responsible for transmitting what he had learned to his children.

The attempt of Antiochus Epiphanes to eradicate Judaism by force brought about the fierce nationalistic revolt of the Maccabees (Jewish patriots) in 168 B.C. See *Intertestamental History.* The Jews who had remained faithful learned a lesson. They saw that they needed schools for the young as well as adult classes for their fathers. Simon ben Shetah, the leader of the Pharisees, founded schools for boys of sixteen and seventeen to promote the study of the Scriptures. A century later, as an inevitable consequence, private schools for younger children appeared. After the destruction of Herod's Temple by Titus in A.D. 70 and the disappearance of the Jewish state after the revolt of Bar-Kochba in A.D. 135, public instruction was instituted for all children.

The elementary school, significantly called

Beth-hasepher, the "house of the book," was originally housed in some easily available room; but by A.D. 200, it had become firmly established in the synagogue. Boys entered at the age of six or seven and continued until thirteen. Here, study was wholly devoted to the written Law. This involved the learning of Hebrew, since Aramaic had long before replaced Hebrew as the everyday language of the people. Knowledge of the written word, in school as in the home, had the religious goal of bringing about obedience to the Law.

The school was not only a place of learning but a house of prayer; its aims were not cultural but religious. A strong sense of community responsibility, evidenced by an education tax on all parents, had by A.D. 200 opened all schools to the children of the poor. However, the Jewish school, like the Greek school, remained an independent fee-paying institution. See *Education; Scribes; Synagogue; Torah.*   *Jeff Cranford*

SCHOOLMASTER Law's role until coming of Christ (Gal. 3:24–25 KJV). Other translations use "disciplinarian" (NRSV), "supervision" (NIV), "tutor" (NAS), "charge" (REB; TEV; compare NIV); "custodian" (RSV). See *Custodian.*

SCIENCE KJV term (Dan. 1:4; 1 Tim. 6:20) for knowledge. Scripture describes Daniel's knowledge with admiration and approval but warns against meaningless debate of issues for the sake of human pride not leading to useful knowledge. See *Gnosticism.*

SCOFFER People who show contempt for others. Habakkuk predicted the Babylonians would be scoffers as they conquered the Near East (Hab. 1:10). 2 Peter 3:3 warns that the last days will see scoffers laughing at the idea of Christ's return (compare Jude 18). The wisdom writers repeatedly warned their students not to become scoffers (Job 11:3; Prov. 9:7–12; 13:1; 14:6; 15:12; 19:25; 21:24; 22:10; 24:9; compare Ps. 1:1; Isa. 28:14,22). Still, God is a scoffer, jeering at the feeble efforts of those who oppose Him (Ps. 2:4; Prov. 3:34). Jesus endured scoffing (Luke 16:14; compare Acts 13:41).

SCORN, SCORNFUL Dislike which turns to contempt and derision. Scorn often appears in some Bible translations where scoff appears in others. See *Scoffer.* Scorn is often expressed by laughter (2 Kings 19:21; 2 Chron. 30:10). In deep trouble psalmists often felt themselves scorned (Pss. 22:6; 31:11; 39:8; 44:13; 80:6; 89:41; 119:22; 123:4). God scorns the wicked (Prov. 3:34), who, in turn, scorn Him (2 Sam. 12:14). When His people refuse to be faithful, God can scorn them and their worship, expressed in destruction (Lam. 2:7).

SCORPION (Scôr′ pī ŏn) Small invertebrate ani-

mal (*buthus*) known for the venom and sting in its narrow segmented tail. In the wilderness God protected Israel from scorpions (Deut. 8:15) and could protect His prophet from them (Ezek. 2:6). Scorpions gave their names to an insidious instrument of punishment with lashes and spikes. Rehoboam chose to use these to enforce his harsh policies (1 Kings 12:11,14).

SCORPION PASS See *Akrabbim.*

SCOURGE (Scoûrge) A severe form of corporal punishment involving whipping and beating, usually was done with the victim tied to a post or bench and administered by a servant of the synagogue (if for religious reasons), or by a slave or soldier. John 19:1 uses this word for the beating given Jesus before His crucifixion. Matthew and Mark use a word meaning "flog" (a lesser punishment), while Luke says that Pilate offered to have Jesus "chastise[d]" (23:16), which was a still lighter punishment. The number of blows was set in Deuteronomy 25:3 at forty, but later reduced to thirty-nine. There were to be thirteen stokes on the chest and twenty-six on the back. Often the victim died from the beating.

SCREECH OWL English translation used for different Hebrew terms by different translations. KJV used for *lilith* (Isa. 34:14). See *Satyr.* NIV used it for Hebrew *qippod* (Isa. 34:11; Zeph. 2:14) but simply "owls" at Isaiah 14:23. NRSV used "screech owl" at Zephaniah 2:14. NIV also used "screech owl" for Hebrew *tachmas* (Lev. 11:16; Deut. 14:15). REB used "screech owl" for Hebrew *yanshuph* (Lev. 11:17; Deut. 14:16; Isa. 34:11). *Qippod* may be *Syrnium aluco* or *Scops giu.* Others suggest the Arabian desert fowl (*Ammoperdrix heyi*). *Tachmas* cannot be identified with any certainty. *Yanshoph* may be the eared owl (*Asiootus*) or the *Merops apiaster.* See *Owl.*

SCRIBE Person trained in writing skills and used to record events and decisions (Jer. 36:26; 1 Chron. 24:6; Esth. 3:12). During the Exile in Babylon educated scribes apparently became the experts in God's written word, copying, preserving, and teaching it. Ezra was a scribe in this sense of expert in teaching God's word (Ezra 7:6). A professional group of such scribes developed by New Testament times, most being Pharisees (Mark 2:16). They interpreted the law, taught it to disciples, and were experts in cases where people were accused of breaking the law of Moses. They led in plans to kill Jesus (Luke 19:47) and heard His stern rebuke (Matt. 23). See *Government; Sanhedrin; Jewish Parties; Secretary.*

SCRIP See *Bag 4.*

SCRIPTURE (Scrĭp′ tūre) Historic Judaeo-Christian name for the specific literature that the church receives as divine instruction. Scripture means "a writing" rendering the Latin *scriptura* and the Greek *graphe.* The term is used some fifty times in the New Testament for some or all of the Old Testament.

In the history of the church, the divine character of Scripture has been the great presupposition for the whole of Christian preaching and theology. This is apparent in the way the New Testament speaks about the Old Testament. New Testament writers often used formulas like "God says" and "the Holy Spirit says" to introduce Old Testament passages. For the New Testament authors, Scripture was the record of God speaking and revealing Himself to His people. Thus Scripture and God are so closely joined together that these writers could speak of Scripture doing what it records God as doing (Gal. 3:8; Rom. 9:17).

Because of their belief in the Scriptures' divine origin and content, the New Testament writers described it as "sure" (2 Pet. 1:19), trustworthy "of all acceptation" (1 Tim. 1:15), and "confirmed" (Heb. 2:3). Its word "endureth forever" (1 Pet. 1:24,25). Those who build their lives on Scripture "will not be disappointed" (Rom. 9:33 NAS). The Bible was written for "instruction" and "encouragement" (Rom. 15:4 NAS), to lead to saving faith (2 Tim. 3:15), to guide people toward godliness (2 Tim. 3:16b), and to equip believers for good works (2 Tim. 3:17).

The purpose of Scripture is to place men and women in a right standing before God and to enable believers to seek God's glory in all of life's activities and efforts. It is above all a book of redemptive history.

Scripture is not only a divine Book, but a divine-human Book. It is important to recognize that the biblical writers employed the linguistic resources available to them as they wrote to specific people with particular needs at particular times. The human authors were not lifted out of their culture or removed from their contexts. They functioned as members of believing communities, aware of God's leadership in their lives.

Scripture, comprised of 66 books, written by over 40 authors spanning almost 1,500 years, reveals to God's people the unifying history of His redeeming words and acts. The ultimate focus of Scripture is the incarnation and redemptive work of Jesus Christ. Jesus Christ is the center to which everything in Scripture is united and bound together—beginning and end, creation and redemption, humanity, the world, the fall, history, and future. See *Bible, Formation and Canon; Inspiration.*   *David S. Dockery*

SCROLL Sheets of papyrus glued together and rolled at each end to collect a long literature work in a form for public reading or private study. See *Paper, Papyrus; Writing.*

A Torah (Genesis–Deuteronomy) scroll being held in its wooden case at a celebration in Jerusalem.

SCURVY A disease of the gums resulting in loosening of and/or loss of teeth. KJV translation of Hebrew term for festering eruption (Lev. 21:20; 22:22), but in Deuteronomy 28:27 KJV used, "scab," while only there did RSV use "scurvy." NIV used, "festering sores." NAS used, "eczema."

SCYTHIANS (Scỹth′ ĭ ans) Nomadic, Indo-European people, speaking an Iranian dialect, who migrated from central Asia into southern Russia between 800 and 600 B.C. They were skilled horsemen who excelled in barbaric attack and plunder. Archaeologists have discovered abundant evidence of Scythian artistry in metalwork. Their forces, in pursuit of the Cimmerians, drove south through or around the Caucasus Mountains to the borders of Assyria. A Scytho-Assyrian alliance was formed about 680–670 B.C.

According to the Greek historian Herodotus, a Scythian attack forced the Medes to withdraw from an assault against Nineveh (apparently 626–620 B.C.). Later, the Scynthians advanced southward along the Palestinian coast to the Egyptian border (611 B.C.), where they were bought off by the Egyptian Pharaoh. They were eventually driven back northward into southern Russia by the Medes.

Scythian power was dominant in the area northwest of the Black Sea until about 350 B.C. Eventually, new invaders, the Sarmatians, having confined them to the Crimean area, destroyed the remaining Scythian remnants after A.D. 100.

The Old Testament refers to Scythians as Ashchenaz (Gen. 10:3; Jer. 51:27). See *Ashchenaz*. Earlier scholars identified the Scythians as Jeremiah's foe from the north and Zephaniah's threatened invader of Judah, but such theories rest on weak evidence. Colossians 3:11 uses Scythians to represent the most repugnant barbarian and slave, saying they, too, are accepted in Christ, all social and cultural barriers being abolished in His church.   *Charles Graham*

SEA COW NIV translation, explained in text note as dugong (Ex. 25:5; 26:14; Num. 4). See *Badger Skins*.

SEA GULL See *Cuckow*.

SEA MONSTER KJV translation in Lamentations 4:3. See *Dragon*.

SEA OF GALILEE See *Galilee, Sea of; Palestine*.

SEA OF GLASS See *Glass*.

SEA OF JAZER Body of water connected with town of Jazer (Jer. 48:32) but unknown to modern Bible students. Some commentators use manuscript and Isaiah 16:8 evidence to eliminate "sea of" from the text (NRSV, REB). See *Jazer*.

The Sea of Galilee as viewed from Mount Arbel.

SEA OF THE PLAIN See *Dead Sea*.

SEA, MOLTEN See *Molten Sea*.

A calm Sea of Galilee at dusk with snow-capped Mount Hermon in the distance.

S

North Syrian and Hittite stamp-type seals.

SEAL A signet containing a distinctive mark which stood for the individual who owned it. The earliest seals found so far date to before 3000 B.C. Seals varied in shapes and sizes. Some were round and were worn around the neck. Others were rings worn on the finger. The mark was made by stamping the seal into soft clay. Many cylinder seals have been found which contain scenes that communicate a message. These were rolled in the

Clay cylinder seals from ancient Uruk, biblical Erech, (in modern Iraq) dating from about 3000 B.C.

clay to form the impression. Tamar asked for Judah's signet as collateral on a pledge he made (Gen. 38:18). Joseph was given pharaoh's ring when he was placed in command of the country (Gen. 41:42), symbolizing Joseph's right to act with the ruler's authority. Jezebel used Ahab's seal to sign letters asking that Naboth be tried and stoned to death (1 Kings 21:8).

SEASON KJV translation of several Hebrew and Greek terms with different meanings. *1.* An indefinite but somewhat extended period of time (Gen. 40:4; Josh. 24:7; Luke 4:13). *2.* A regularly scheduled, recurring time (Ex. 13:10; Num. 9:2; John 5:4). *3.* To add ingredients to food to improve the flavor (Lev. 2:13; Mark 9:50). See *Salt; Spices. 4.* A particular part of a year (Gen. 1:14; 2 Kings 4:16). *5.* An indefinite part of a day (Job 30:17; Ps. 22:2). *6.* Time appointed by God (Ps. 104:27;

Matt. 24:45). *7.* The proper time for an action (Isa. 50:4). See *Time.*

SEBA, SABEANS (Sē' bȧ, Sȧ bē' ăns) A group of people thought to be akin to the Israelites through either Ham (Gen. 10:6-7) or Shem (Gen. 10:28). They settled southwest Arabia (modern Yemen) and became prosperous traders. One of the major caravan routes was in their control. They dealt mainly in rich spices, gold, and precious stones. The Sabeans also were agrarian, developing elaborate irrigation devices to make their region more fertile.

The queen of Saba (Sheba) traveled to Jerusalem (about 1,500 miles) during Solomon's reign to strike trade agreements with the thriving Israelites (1 Kings 10:1-10). The Sabeans are credited with domesticating the camel so that such journeys could be made. Matthew 12:42 promises the "Queen of the South" will condemn the people of Jesus' day in final judgment, indicating she had more faith than they. Some have tried to identify her homeland as Ethiopia. See *Sabean.*

SEBAM (Sē' băm) Place name probably meaning, "high" or "cold." Town east of the Jordan the tribes of Reuben and Gad wanted to settle after God conquered it for them (Num. 32:3). Early versions agree with verse 38 in reading, "Sibmah," which the tribes rebuilt. Its location is not certain.

SEBAT (Sē' băt) Eleventh month in Babylonian calendar used to date Zechariah's vision (1:7). This would be February–March. See *Calendars.*

SECACAH (Sė cā' cah) Place name meaning, "covered." Town in tribal territory of Judah in the Judean wilderness (Josh. 15:61). It is modern khirbet es-Samrah in the central Buqeia. Some would equate it with the site of Qumran.

SECHU (Sē' chū) Place name perhaps meaning, "lookout." Otherwise unknown site where Saul searched for David (1 Sam. 19:22). Many commentators follow the earliest Greek translation and change the Hebrew text to read "on the bare height" (NRSV note).

SECOND COMING, THE biblical teaching on the return of Jesus to earth at the end of earthly history. In the latter portion of His ministry, Jesus told His followers that He would be leaving them but would return again to the earth. This message of the second coming is referred to as the Blessed Hope (Titus 2:13). Jesus warned His followers that they should be prepared to welcome Him back (Matt. 24—25; compare Mark 13). In the upper room with His disciples, Jesus told them He was going away but promised that He would come again one day (John 14:3). At His ascension, the two angels declared that He would return (Acts 1:11).

Jesus' Form in His Coming Many who agree about the fact of Jesus's second coming are not sure about the form it will take. Some say He was referring to the coming of the Holy Spirit at Pentecost, others that He was referring to His resurrection, others to the fact that He was going to be spiritually present with us (Matt. 28:20), others to an individual's conversion experience (see Rev. 3:20).

All of these are incomplete at best. Jesus warned of misrepresentations (Matt. 24:4-5,11,23-26) and said His appearance would be bodily and unmistakable (Matt. 24:27,30; compare Acts 1:11).

Effects of Christ's Second Coming The second coming is to effect believers in a number of different ways:

Believers are to be watchful. There being no certainty as to the time of Jesus's return, it is important that we be on the alert as to the possibility that it may come at anytime (Matt. 24:42). However, they are not to believe that Christ must return in a given space of time, on a specific date. In His parable of the foolish virgins (Matt. 25:1-13) Jesus told of them sleeping and not being ready when the Bridegroom came (compare Jas. 5:7-8). Peter warned against unbelief that could blunt the expectant spirit and cause people to say, "Where is the promise of his coming? for since the fathers fell asleep, all things continue as they were from the beginning of the creation" (2 Pet. 3:3-4).

The believers are to use the hope of Christ's second return as a motivation to work. In His parable of the talents (Matt. 25:14-30), Jesus reserved His condemnation for the man who did nothing, simply taking his talent and hiding it. Convinced that their Lord will return at any moment the believers will give all their energies to serving Him. Because Jesus may return at anytime a believer strives to live a pure and blameless life: "Every man that hath this hope purifieth himself" (1 John 3:3; compare 1 Thess. 3:13; Col. 3:1-17; 1 John 2:28).

The Time of His Return One of the most difficult aspects of the second coming is the time when Jesus will come. There has been much speculation across the years. One sect even claims that Jesus returned in 1914. The emphasis on the exact time and date is mistaken. As one man says it, "I am not on the time and place, but on the welcoming committee." Jesus Himself said, "But of that day and hour knoweth no man, no, not the angels of heaven, but my Father only." (Matt. 24:36; compare 2 Thess. 2; 2 Pet. 3:4-11). This blessed hope is to mark the climax of experience for believers when they shall see Christ (1 John 3:2-3), shall be transformed (Phil. 3:20-21), receive the crown of righteousness (2 Tim. 4:8; 1 Pet. 5:4), and be made like Him (1 John 3:3).

The Meaning of the Second Coming The coming brings believers joy in Christ's presence, particularly as they see people to whom they have ministered (1 Thess. 2:19). The coming is for both those already dead in Christ and for those still alive (1 Thess. 4:15-17; compare 1 Cor. 15:23; Col. 3:4).

"Even so, come Lord Jesus" (Rev. 22:20). See *Future Hope; Eschatology; Christology; Jesus Christ; Rapture.*   *John W. Drakeford*

SECOND DEATH See *Death, Second.*

SECOND QUARTER The northern part of Jerusalem whose boundaries were extended during the monarchy. This part of the city was most open to enemy attack. See *College.*

SECOND SABBATH Chronological notation in some manuscripts of Luke 6:1 believed by many commentators to be a later addition to the text (NRSV, NIV, NAS, REB).

SECRETARY Royal official in charge of state records (2 Sam. 8:17 in modern translations; REB, "adjutant-general"). See *Government; Scribe.*

SECT A group having established their own identity and teachings over against the larger group to which they belong, especially the different parties making up Judaism in New Testament times. See *Jewish Parties.*

SECU (Sē' cū) Modern translations' transliteration of Sechu.

SECUNDUS (Sė cŭn' dŭs) Latin personal name meaning, "second." Representative of church of Thessalonica who accompanied Paul on his journey as he took the churches' contributions to the Jerusalem church (Acts 20:4).

SECURITY OF THE BELIEVER Biblical teaching that God protects believers for the completion of their salvation. Contemporary Christianity needs to deal forthrightly with the universal human problem of insecurity. The natural gulf between the invisible, infinite God and finite, fallible humanity makes the quest for assurance and security a very significant theological issue. Slogans such as "once saved, always saved," and "eternal security" often easily gain a reverential status normally reserved only for biblical texts and become symbols of "evangelical orthodoxy." Indeed, it comes as a shock to some when they discover that their symbols are not actually biblical terms.

The Bible does teach that salvation does not depend merely upon human effort. God is the author of salvation (2 Cor. 5:18-19; John 3:16). God justifies or treats as acceptable sinners who receive Christ in faith (Rom. 3:21-26). The great message of the Reformation says, No one can earn assurance or security with God. Assurance of salvation is God's gift! Security does not come by absolutions, church attendance, good works, reciting Scripture, or performances of penance. God who has begun the work of salvation in Christians also provides the necessary assurance to bring His work to its completion in the day of Christ (Phil. 1:6). God in Christ protects and keeps Christians (John 10:27–29; 2 Thess. 3:3) just as Jesus took seriously the task of preserving the disciples while He was on earth (John 17:12–15). We do not possess the strength to secure ourselves.

The biblical view of security, however, is probably best epitomized in the Christian doctrine of perseverance (Eph. 6:18; Heb. 12:1; Jas. 1:25). See *Perseverance*. Christians must realize that their security does not lie in a fairy-tale approach to life where once a person becomes a Christian everything is a happy bed of roses forever and ever. Such a view fails to take seriously the traumas of human life.

The biblical view of assurance or security is rooted in the conviction that when Jesus departed from the disciples, the Lord did not orphan them or leave them without support. He promised Christians that he would come to them and would provide them with a companion Spirit (the Comforter or Paraclete) who would not only be at their side but would be within them, as much a part of them as their very breath (John 14:16–18). The Spirit would be their sense of peace and security, their witness concerning Jesus, their attorney with the world, and their guide or teacher into all truth (John 14:25–30; 15:26–27; 16:8–15). See *Advocate; Comforter; Helper*.

Along with great promises of assurance, the Bible contains strong warnings that call Christians to consistent living, even as they have yielded to temptations and sin and capitulated to the hostile forces of evil (for example, 1 Cor. 10:1–12; Heb. 2:1–3; 3:12–19; 6:1–8; 10:26–31; Jas. 5:19–20). These and many other warnings in the Bible are not merely phantom warnings unrelated to Christian life. They are meant to be taken with great seriousness. They are no more a game with God than was the death of Christ.

These warnings appear in the New Testament within clear statements reminding believers that temptation is accompanied by God's presence. Christians are expected to resist temptations and flee ungodly activity (for example, 1 Cor. 10:13–14). Evil patterns of life are inconsistent with Christian transformation. The writers of the New Testament were convinced that Christians would heed these warnings and resist the devil (Jas. 4:7; 1 Pet. 5:8–9). It is virtually unthinkable for a Christian to do otherwise. The Christian is anchored to the person of God. Evil has to be dealt with. The Christian can find in God an enduring security for the soul. Such is the meaning of He-

brews 6:17–20. God's consistency is the basis for a Christian's security in the midst of the world's traumas.

The security of the believer is not merely focused upon this life on earth. It has a dynamic focus on the life-to-come. The New Testament writers are convinced that a Christian will take very seriously the warnings in this life because this life is related to the life with Christ in heaven. The Christian, therefore, is expected to persevere to the end (1 Pet. 1:5; 1 John 5:18; Rev. 3:10).

The confidence or secure sense of the believer with respect to the life hereafter is rooted in the united witness of the New Testament writers that the resurrection of Jesus Christ is the hinge point of the Christian faith. In raising His Son Jesus, God provided Christians with the sign of the destinies and the basis for their security. Without the resurrection, the Christian proclamation would be empty (1 Cor. 15:14). Moreover, in the coming of the Holy Spirit, God provided the guarantee of our marvelous relationship with God (2 Cor. 1:22). In our identity with Adam, humanity experienced lostness and death; but as we identify with the ultimate power of Christ in the resurrection, we, too, shall experience the effective meaning of the security of the believer in the triumph of God (1 Cor. 15:20–28).   *Gerald L. Borchert*

SEDITION Rebellion against lawful authority. Government officials in Persia's province headquartered in Samaria accused the Jews in Jerusalem of a history of rebellion as evidence against allowing Jerusalem and its Temple to be rebuilt (Ezra 4:15). Barabbas had been imprisoned for sedition (Luke 23:19). See *Barabbas*. Jewish leaders tried to convince Felix, the governor, that Paul had incited sedition (Acts 24:5). KJV used "seditions" in Galatians 5:20 for one of the works of the flesh, but modern translations are more accurate in using "dissensions." Relationships among believers rather than to governments is the apparent meaning.

SEGUB (Sē' gŭb) Personal name meaning, "He has revealed Himself as exalted" or "He has protected." *1.* Second son of Hiel, whose death during rebuilding of Jericho showed power of God's prophecy through the centuries (1 Kings 16:34). *2.* Son of Judahite father and Machirite or Manassehite mother (1 Chron. 2:21–22).

SEIR (Sē' ĭr) Place name meaning, "hairy" and thus "thicket" or "small forested region." A mountain range which runs the length of biblical Edom, leading at times to an equation of Edom and Seir. Parts of the range are almost impassable. The highest peak is about 5,600 feet about sea level. The region was home to Esau and his descendants (Gen. 32:3; Josh. 24:4). Some documents found in Egypt seem to make Seir and Edom two different tribal habitats, and it is possible that at times in its history the area was ruled over simultaneously by several local clans. The "sons of Seir" represented an early Horite clan from the region. See *Edom.*

SEIRAH (Sē′ ĭ rah) Place name meaning, "toward Seir." Modern translations' reading for KJV Seirath (Judg. 3:26). The name would seem to point to Mount Seir in Edom, but the context seems to make that location impossible. Otherwise, the location is not known. It must be a forested place in the tribal territory of Benjamin.

SEIRATH (Sē′ ĭ răth) KJV transliteration of place name in Judges 3:26. See *Seirah.*

SELA (Sē′ là) Place name meaning, "rock." Major fortified city in Edom. The biblical references lend themselves to varying interpretations, since Sela may also be read as a common noun referring to rocky country or wilderness. Judges 1:36 refers to a border of the Amorites, though some commentators change this to Edomites (REB). Amaziah of Judah (796–767 B.C.) captured Sela and renamed it Joktheel (2 Kings 14:7). Compare 2 Chronicles 25:12 in NRSV. Isaiah's oracle against Moab calls for action from Sela, which many commentators take to be the rocky wilderness bordering Moab rather than the more distant town of Sela (Isa. 16:1). Traditionally from the earliest Greek translation on, Sela has been identified with Petra, the capital of Edom, or the nearby umm-Bayyara in the wadi Musa. More recent study has placed it at es-Sela, two and a half miles northwest of Bozrah and five miles southwest of Tafileh. Modern translations include Sela in Isaiah 42:11, God's call to joy at the coming salvation.

SELAH (Sē′ lah) Term of unknown meaning appearing in psalms, outside Psalms only in Habakkuk 3. Scholars have advanced various unprovable theories: a pause either for silence or musical interlude, a signal for the congregation to sing, recite, or fall prostrate on the ground, a cue for the cymbals to crash, a word to be shouted by the congregation, a sign to the choir to sing a higher pitch or louder. The earliest Jewish traditions thought it meant "for ever."   *Mike Mitchell*

SELAH-HAMMAHLEKOTH (Sē′ là-hăm măh′ lĕ kŏth) Place name meaning, "rock of hiding, haunt, refuge." David's hiding place in the wilderness of Maon while Saul pursued him (1 Sam. 23:28). Modern translations often translate the name rather than transliterate it: "Dividing Rock" (REB), "Rock of Escape" (NRSV, NAS).

SELED (Sē′ lĕd) Personal name meaning, "jumping." Member of tribe of Judah (1 Chron. 2:30).

SELEUCIA (Sė leu′ cĭ à) Syrian city on Mediterranean coast five miles north of the Orontes River and fifteen miles from Antioch. Paul stopped there on his first missionary journey (Acts 13:4). It was founded by Seleucus Nicator, the first Seleucid king, in 301 B.C. See *Seleucids.*

SELEUCIDS (Sĕ leu′ cĭds) Descendants of Seleucus, one of the generals of Alexander the Great. Following the death of Alexander, 323 B.C., his kingdom was divided among five of his leading commanders. Seleucus chose for himself the eastern part of the empire around the city of Babylon. During the next several years, much confusion prevailed. Seleucus was forced to leave Babylon for a time and take refuge with his friend Ptolemy, ruler of Egypt. With the help of Ptolemy, he later was able to control Babylon again. The important date is 312 B.C. The Syrian calendar has its beginning at this time.

The overall situation remained unchanged until the battle of Ipsus, 301 B.C. In that battle four of the generals, including Seleucus, fought against Antigonus who had become the most powerful of the generals and claimed to be king over much of Asia Minor and northern Syria. Antigonus was slain in the battle, and his territory was given to Seleucus along with title to the land of Palestine. However, Ptolemy took control of Palestine, and his successors retained it for over a hundred years. This was a serious point of contention between the two empires throughout this period of time.

Seleucus was assassinated in 281 B.C. Antiochus I, his son, became ruler and made peace with the Egyptians. He sought throughout his reign to consolidate his rule, but the years were for the most part a time of intense struggle and warfare. At his death in 262 or early 261 B.C., his son Antiochus II became king (261–246 B.C.). During the early years of Antiochus II, conflict continued with Egypt. When peace between the two nations was reached in 253 B.C., Ptolemy offered his daughter to Antiochus as wife with the understanding that he would desert his first wife. The goal was that a son born to this marriage would become the ruler of the Seleucid Empire and cement relations between the two. However, it did not work out in this way, and Antiochus died in 246 B.C., perhaps murdered by his first wife.

The eldest son of Antiochus, Seleucus II, was named king. He ruled until his death in 226 B.C.; however, some Syrians, along with Egypt, supported the infant son of the second wife of Antiochus. The Egyptian army could not reach the area quickly enough to defend the child, and Seleucus was able to regain control of the territory ruled by his father, some of which had been lost at the time of his father's death. In 241 B.C., peace was again reached between the Seleucids and Egypt. When

Seleucus died as the result of falling from his horse, his son Alexander became king as Seleucus III. He was assassinated in 223 B.C. and was succeeded by his son Antiochus III, known as Antiochus the Great (223–187 B.C.). See *Intertestamental History* for Antiochus III, Seleucus IV, and Antiochus IV.

With the death of Antiochus Epiphanes, the situation of the Seleucids fell into disarray. From this time on it seems that more than one strong individual was contending for the crown at all times. Lysias had been left with responsibility for the care of the young son of Epiphanes. He assumed that upon the death of the king the son would become king. But before his death the king had evidently appointed Philip, a close friend with him in the East, to be king. Philip returned to Antioch, the capital in Syria, and this forced Lysias to cut off his efforts to quell the Jewish revolt. In his effort to bring peace, he granted religious freedom to the Jews. Lysias was able to thwart the effort of Philip, and the son, Antiochus V, reigned as king for a brief time (164–162 B.C.).

Demetrius, the young son of Seleucus IV, was a hostage in Rome. His desire to return home at the death of his father was denied. When Antiochus IV died, he managed to escape from Rome and fled to Syria, 162 B.C. He had himself proclaimed as king and had Lysias and Antiochus V put to death. He remained as king until 150 B.C. These years were involved in attempts to put down the Jewish revolt and to consolidate and expand his position in the East.

A strong rival appeared—Alexander Balas. He claimed to be the illegitimate son of Antiochus Epiphanes. In 153 B.C., the Roman senate acknowledged him as king of Syria although the senate was probably aware that his claim was false. The two rivals both made extensive offers to the Jews for their support. Jonathan, the Jewish leader, supported Alexander, who, in 150 B.C., gained victory over Demetrius, who was killed in battle. Alexander reigned until 145 B.C., supported at first by the ruler of Egypt, who gave Alexander his daughter in marriage. When Ptolemy learned that Alexander was plotting to kill him, he turned against Alexander, brought his daughter back, and offered her in marriage to the young son of Demetrius. Defeated in battle by Ptolemy, Alexander fled to Arabia, where he was killed. The young son of Demetrius, Demetrius II, was made king (145–139, 129–125 B.C.).

Needing their support, Demetrius granted political freedom to the Jews during the early years of his reign. One of his generals, Tryphon, supported Alexander Balas' young son, who claimed the throne as Antiochus VI (145–142 B.C.). Tryphon had Antiochus murdered and had himself proclaimed as king (142–139 B.C.). Demetrius II was taken prisoner in a campaign against the Parthians, and his brother Antiochus VII (139–128

B.C.) became king. He defeated Tryphon, who then committed suicide. Antiochus made one last effort to interfere in the life of the Jews. In 133 B.C., he invaded Judea and began a siege of Jerusalem that lasted for almost a year. Finally, peace was made between him and John Hyrcanus, guaranteeing the independence of the Jews from Syrian intervention. Antiochus made a campaign against the Parthians where he died.

With the death of Antiochus VII, the Seleucids ceased to be a major factor in the political life of the eastern Mediterranean world. Although Demetrius was released by the Parthians and resumed his role as king, neither he nor any other person was able to gain firm control of the empire. The following years were filled with internal conflict that drained the resources of the empire and saw at least ten persons claim rule in less than fifty years. In 83 B.C., the king of Armenia took possession of Syria, and the rule of the Seleucids came to an end. *Clayton Harrop*

SELF-CONTROL Modern translations' term for several Greek words indicating a sober, temperate, calm, and dispassionate approach to life, having mastered personal desires and passions. Biblical admonitions expect God's people to exercise self-control (Prov. 25:28; 1 Cor. 7:5; 1 Thess. 5:6; 1 Tim. 3:2; 2 Tim. 3:3; Gal. 5:23; 2 Tim. 1:7; Titus 1:8; 2 Pet. 1:6). Freedom in Christ does not give believers liberty to cast off all moral restraint as some members in Galatia and other churches apparently believed. Nor does it call for a withdrawal from life and its temptations. It calls for a self-disciplined life following Christ's example of being in the world but not of the world. See *Ethics; Freedom.*

SELF-WILLED To do something arbitrarily without divine permission; to act on one's own decision rather than considering the needs of others and the purpose of God. Jacob rebuked Simeon and Levi for wanton, undisciplined actions (Gen. 49:6). Titus 1:7 teaches that a bishop cannot be self-willed, that is stubborn and arrogant. Such activity is presumptuous and marks the fleshly person (2 Pet. 2:10).

SELVEDGE (Sĕl' vĕdge) KJV translation of Hebrew term for the end, edge, border, or corner (Ex. 26:4; 36:11), apparently referring to the outermost curtain of the tabernacle.

SEM (Sĕm) KJV spelling of Shem, following the Greek (Luke 3:36).

SEMACHIAH (Sĕm á chī' ah) Personal name meaning, "Yahweh supports." Levitical gatekeeper (1 Chron. 26:7), described as a valiant man or warrior, possibly a title of honor for public service.

SEMAKIAH (Sĕm à kī' ah) NIV spelling of Semachiah.

SEMEI (Sĕ' mè ī) Greek form of Hebrew personal name, Shimi, among Jesus' ancestors (Luke 3:26).

SEMEIN (Sĕ' mē ĭn) Modern translations' spelling of Semei.

SEMEN See *Discharge.*

SEMITE (Sĕm' īte) A person who claims descent from Noah's son Shem (Gen. 5:32; 10:21–31) or, more precisely as a linguistic term, those peoples speaking one of the Semitic languages. The racial list of Genesis and the list of linguists do not always include the same peoples.

Genesis 10:21–31 lists five sons and twenty-one descendants/peoples derived from Shem. These people spread geographically from Lydia to Syria, to Assyria, to Persia. Armenia formed the northern boundary while the Red Sea and Persian Gulf formed the southern boundary. The Elamites, Assyrians, Lydians, Arameans, and numerous Arab tribes are said to have been descendants of Shem.

The place of origin for the Semites is difficult to determine. The Fertile Crescent contains evidence of Semitic influence at the dawn of civilization. One unproven theory is that they migrated from northern Arabia in waves of nomadic movements into the Fertile Crescent.

Three major divisions exist in the Semitic family of languages. East Semitic would include Akkadian used in ancient Babylon and Assyria. Northwest Semitic involves Hebrew, Aramaic, Syria, Phoenician, Samaritan, Palmyrene, Nabatean, Canaanite, Moabite. South Semitic includes Arabic, Sabean, Minean, and Ethiopic. Approximately 70 distinct forms of Semitic languages are known. Some have large libraries of literature while others remain entirely unwritten or only small collections of literature exist. See *Languages of the Bible; Assyria; Babylon; Canaan.*   *Steve Wyrick*

SENAAH (Sè nā' ah) Personal name of uncertain meaning, perhaps, "thorny" or "hatred." Clan head or home town of people who returned with Zerubbabel from Babylonian Exile about 537 B.C. (Ezra 2:35).

SENATE KJV, NAS term for the Sanhedrin (Acts 5:21). See *Sanhedrin.*

SENEH (Sĕ' nĕh) Place name meaning, "shiny" or "slippery." A "cliff" (NIV) or "sharp column of rock" (REB) between Michmash and Geba (1 Sam. 14:4). See *Bozez.*

SENIR (Sĕ' nĭr) Mountain name meaning, "pointed." Amorite name for Mount Hermon (Deut. 3:9).

See *Hermon.* Song of Solomon 4:8 may indicate that Senir was a different peak than Hermon in the Antilebanon range or that it indicated the entire range (compare 1 Chron. 5:23).

SENNACHERIB (Sĕn nă<u>ch</u>' ĕr ĭb) Assyrian royal name meaning, "Sin (the god) has replaced my brother." King of Assyria (704–681 BC). See *Assyria; Israel.*

The site of Sennacherib's palace at ancient Nineveh (near modern Mosul, Iraq).

SENSUAL Activities or appearances characterized by or motivated by physical lust or luxury. God condemned Babylon for their sensual desires for pleasure and luxury (Isa. 47:8). It is part of the evil of the human heart (Mark 7:22; compare Rom. 13:13), calling for repentance (2 Cor. 12:21). See *Lasciviousness; Sex, Biblical Teaching On; Wantonness.*

SENTRY Government official with responsibility for guarding a prison (Acts 5:23; 12:6) or possibly a captain over such a guard (Jer. 37:13).

SEORIM (Sē ō' rĭm) Personal name perhaps meaning, "the shaggy-haired." Head of fourth division of priests appointed under David (1 Chron. 24:8).

SEPARATION Term used for period when a person is ritually unclean during menstruation (Lev. 12:2,5; 15:20,25–26) or for time of refraining from certain activities because of a vow (Num. 6). KJV term for water used to make one ritually pure or clean (Num. 19).

SEPHAR (Sē' phăr) Place name perhaps meaning, "numbering, census." Eastern border of sons of Joktan (Gen. 10:30). The site is apparently in southern Arabia, perhaps the coastal town of Tsaphar in Oman or Itsphar south of Hadramaut.

SEPHARAD (Sè phā' răd) Place name of uncertain meaning. Place where Jerusalem's Exiles lived. Obadiah promised them new possessions in the Negeb (v. 20). The location is disputed: possibly a country south of Lake Urmia and north and west of

S

Media, beyond the Babylonian Empire, but more likely the capital city of the Persian satrapy of Sepharad or Sardis in Lydia near the Aegean Sea. Early Syriac (Peshitta) and Aramaic (Targum) evidence points to Spain, but this is improbable.

SEPHARVAIM (Sē phär vā′ ĭm) Racial name of foreign origin. Peoples the Assyrians conquered and resettled in Israel to replace the Israelites they deported in 722 B.C. (2 Kings 17:24). The name may represent the two Sippars on the Euphrates River or Shabarain in Syria. It may be the same as Sibraim in Syria (Ezek. 47:16), a border in Ezekiel's promised restoration of Israel. Despite Assyria's claims, Sepharvaim's gods could not compare with Yahweh, the God of Israel (2 Kings 19:12–13; compare 17:31).

SEPHARVITES (Sē phär′ vītes) Citizens of Sepharvaim (2 Kings 17:31).

SEPPHORIS (Sēp phō′ rĭs) Town in Galilee that served as the capital of that region during most of Jesus' lifetime. It was near Nazareth and sat on a high ridge. The town was fortified, but suffered a violent history. Although Sepphoris is not mentioned in the Bible, Jesus probably knew it well and walked its streets.

SEPTUAGINT (Sĕp tū′ ȧ gĭnt) Title meaning, "the 70." Oldest Greek translation of the Hebrew Old Testament. It also contains several apocryphal books. Most New Testament quotations of the Old Testament are from the Septuagint. See *Apocrypha; Bible, Texts and Versions.*

SEPULCHRE (Sĕ pŭl′ chre) Tomb or grave (Gen. 23:6). It translates a Hebrew word which refers to a niche hewn out of a rock in which bodies were placed. In ancient Palestine, sepulchres usually were carved out of the walls in existing caves. Families were buried together on the carved slabs of stone. After a body had decayed to the bones, the remains were placed in a hole farther back in the cave so that the next body could be placed in

A worshiper kneels at the Stone of Unction inside the Church of the Holy Sepulchre in Jerusalem.

Inside the Church of the Holy Sepulchre, traditional site of Jesus' burial (tomb of Joseph of Arimathea).

the sepulchre. Jesus was buried in such a cave (Mark 15:46). See *Burial.*

SERAH (Sē′ rah) Personal name meaning, "progress, develop, overflow" or "splendor, pride." Daughter of Asher (Gen. 46:17; Num. 26:46, where KJV reads Sarah).

SERAIAH (Sĕ rāi′ ah) Personal name meaning, "Yah has proved Himself ruler." *1.* David's royal "scribe" and thus probably functioning as a modern secretary of state (2 Sam. 8:17). The Hebrew tradition has various spellings of the name: Sheva, Sheya (2 Sam. 20:25); Shisha (1 Kings 4:3) if this is not a Hebraic spelling of the Egyptian word for *scribe;* Shavsha (1 Chron. 18:16).
2. Chief priest taken into Babylonian Exile in 587 B.C. (2 Kings 25:18; 1 Chron. 16:14; Jer. 52:24). *3.* "Quiet prince" (KJV), "quartermaster" (REB, NAS, NRSV) Zedekiah (597–586 B.C.) sent to Babylon with instructions from himself and from Jeremiah (Jer. 51:59–64). *4.* Priest and father of Ezra (Ezra 7:1). *5.* Army officer who reported to Gedaliah when he was named governor immediately after the fall of Jerusalem in 586 B.C. (2 Kings 25:23; compare Jer. 40:8). He may have been involved in rebellion Ishmael led. *6.* Leader in tribe of Judah (1 Chron. 4:13). *7.* Member of tribe of Simeon (1 Chron. 4:35). *8.* Leader of returning Exiles under Zerubbabel (Ezra 2:2); apparently the

same as Azariah (Neh. 7:7). *9.* Priestly family (Neh. 10:2; 12:12).

SERAPHIM (Sĕr′ å phĭm) Literally, "the burning ones," seraphim (a plural word) were winged serpents whose images decorated many of the thrones of the Egyptian pharaohs. In some cases, they wore the crowns of the Egyptian kingdoms and were thought to act as guardians over the king. Israel adopted the symbolism for God's throne. Isaiah envisioned the seraphim as agents of God who prepared him to proclaim the Lord's message to Judah (Isa. 6:2). See *Angels.*

SERAPIS (Sĕ rā′ pĭs) Also known as Sarapis, this Egyptian-Greek sun deity was worshiped first at Memphis along with the bull-god, Apis. Serapis was introduced to Egypt by the Greeks and was worshiped originally as a god of the underworld. The temple to him at Alexandria was the largest and best known among several. Serapis came to be revered also as a god of healing and fertility, and his worship spread throughout the Roman Empire via the trade routes.

SERED (Sē′ rĕd) Personal name meaning, "baggage master." Clan leader in tribe of Zebulun (Gen. 46:14; Num. 26:26).

SEREDITE (Sē′ rê dīte) Member of clan of Sered in modern translations (Num. 26:26).

This bronze bust of the Egyptian-Greek god Serapis dates from the first century A.D.

SERGIUS PAULUS (Sēr′ ġĭ us Pāu′ lŭs) Personal name of proconsul of Cyprus when Paul visited the capital of Paphos on his first missionary journey (Acts 13:6–12). Sergius Paulus was under the influence of a sorcerer named Bar-jesus when Paul and Barnabas arrived. Sergius Paulus asked to hear the gospel that the two missionaries were preaching, but the sorcerer tried to keep him from the appointment. Paul temporarily blinded the sorcerer, and Sergius Paulus was converted to Christ.

SERJEANT KJV term for Roman *lictor,* a constable or policeman (Acts 16:35).

SERMON ON THE MOUNT The name given to the material found in Matthew 5—7. The Sermon on the Mount represents Jesus' expectations for those who have followed Him as disciples, both ancient and modern. The sermon begins with the beatitudes, explains the place of the law and certain religious practices in the lives of Christians, and gives various other instructions. The theme of the sermon is found in Matthew 5:20, "For I say unto you, That except your righteousness shall exceed the righteousness of the scribes and Pharisees, ye shall in no case enter into the kingdom of heaven." The Sermon on the Mount is thus a call for Jesus' disciples to observe a greater righteousness.

Approaches to Interpretation Before looking at the contents of the sermon itself, it is helpful to briefly consider the ways in which the Sermon on the Mount has been interpreted. The Sermon on the Mount confronts the reader with uncompromising demands and a lofty ethic. Many throughout the history of the church have sensed a great gap between Jesus' expectations of His disciples and their abilities to live up to those expectations. Indeed, it shocks many to read that Jesus expects us to be perfect as God is perfect (Matt. 5:48). The goal of many interpretations is to alleviate the tension between Jesus' expectations and our abilities.

Some hold that the sermon should be interpreted literally. This is, by and large, the best approach (with some exceptions). Of course, a literal approach to the sermon emphasizes the gap between Jesus' expectations and our abilities more than any other approach.

One obvious question that arises for those holding to a literal interpretation is: What do you do about a passage like 5:29–30 which talks about plucking out the eye and cutting off the hand that is offensive? Some in the history of the church have interpreted this literally. Was Jesus teaching us that we should mutilate ourselves in this fashion? That hardly seems likely. Other figurative or poetic elements as well do not lend themselves to a literal interpretation (for example 5:13–16; 6:20; 7:6,13–27). What about Matthew 5:48?

Did Jesus literally mean that His disciples must be perfect as God is perfect?

The approach that attempts to interpret the entire sermon literally, then, is insufficient by itself. This conclusion raises two other questions. First, if a strictly literal interpretation is insufficient, what other methods are acceptable? Second, which passages should be interpreted literally and which should not? Attention will be focused here on the answers given to the first question.

Some interpreters of the Sermon on the Mount have emphasized the poetic and metaphoric nature of Jesus' language (for example, calling His disciples salt and light, 5:13—16) and His use of hyperbole or consciously exaggerated speech designed to make His point vivid and memorable (for example, plucking out the eye and cutting off the hand that offends, 5:29—30). These interpreters claim that Jesus never meant His sermon to be taken literally. Jesus, according to these interpreters, was stating general principles and using exaggerated illustrations to drive home His point.

Bible interpreters have also used a variety of other approaches. Some interpreters of the sermon attempt to temper Jesus' strict ethical demands by quoting other verses from other parts of Scripture that seem to them to be more capable of human fulfillment. During the Roman Catholic church's history in the Middle Ages, only those living within the monastery were held responsible for keeping the ethics of the sermon; everyone else was bound only to keep the Ten Commandments. Martin Luther proposed the doctrine of the two kingdoms: Christians in their private lives were bound to keep the ethical standards of the sermon, but in their public and professional lives were bound only to keep the standards of the Ten Commandments. C. I. Scofield held that the ethics of the sermon were fully valid only for the new dispensation after the return of Christ.

Some interpreters feel it is impossible for us to fulfill the standards of the Sermon on the Mount (especially 5:48). For them, the sermon shows how short of perfection we really are and shows us our need of repentance. In a similar manner, some interpreters believe Jesus fulfilled the demands of the sermon for humanity since humanity was incapable of living up to standards of the sermon.

There may be some truth in all these approaches to the Sermon on the Mount, but it appears that the best approach is to take the sermon at face value (with some obvious exceptions such as 5:29—30) and to do our best to live the life Jesus outlined for us. When we fail while trying our best, we need not despair; God is a God of grace and forgiveness for all who confess and repent of their sins.

God's willingness to forgive us removes the fear and anxiety caused by failure. This will in turn give us more confidence and assurance that we can live lives that today are more godly than they were yesterday.

We must realize also, however, that we cannot live up to the standards of the sermon (being perfect as God is perfect) by our own powers and abilities. Our lives can conform to the standards of the sermon only if we allow God through the power of the Holy Spirit to work in us. Viewed in this way, the sermon becomes a picture of what God desires to make of us if we will offer ourselves to Him as living sacrifices (Rom. 12:1—2). **Contents of the Sermon on the Mount** The Sermon on the Mount opens with the beatitudes (5:3—12) and moves on to describe the function of Jesus' disciples (5:13—16). From there Jesus explained His interpretation of the law (5:17—48) and certain acts of righteousness (6:1—18), described the attitudes required of His disciples (6:19—7:12), and invited the listeners to become and continue as His disciples (7:13—27).

Jesus spoke these words directly to His disciples (5:1—2) within the hearing of the crowds who were amazed at both Jesus' teaching and the authority with which Jesus taught (7:28—29). Jesus did not teach by quoting the traditions passed down from generation to generation as other rabbis did. Jesus spoke to His disciples as "the Christ, the Son of the living God" (Matt. 16:16). Jesus showed His disciples what it meant to be a light that shines before people. The people "saw" Jesus' good works and gave glory to God (see Matt. 5:16). See *Beatitudes; Ethics; Jesus, Life and Ministry. Phil Logan*

SERPENT English translation of several biblical words for snakes. See *Animals.* A symbol for evil and Satan. See *Devil, Evil, Satan, Demonic.* God gave Moses a sign showing His control of the feared serpents (Ex. 4:3; 7:9—10; compare Job 26:13). Jesus accused the Pharisees of being as evil and deadly as serpents (Matt. 23:33). He gave the seventy power over serpents (Luke 10:19).

SERPENT CHARMERS See *Charm.*

SERPENT OF BRASS See *Bronze Serpent.*

SERPENT, BRONZE See *Bronze Serpent.*

SERUG (Sē' rŭg) Personal and place name perhaps meaning, "offshoot, descendant." Ancestor of Abraham (Gen. 11:20) and thus of Jesus (Luke 3:35) and city twenty miles northwest of Harran mentioned in Assyrian texts.

SERVANT OF THE LORD, THE Title Jesus took up from the Old Testament, especially Isaiah 40—55. The term *the servant of the Lord* (or "My servant" or "His servant" where the pronouns refer to God) is applied to many leaders of God's people: to Moses over 30 times, to David over 70 times, and to Israel as a nation a number of times.

It assumes a special significance in Isaiah 40—55.

The idea is introduced almost incidentally. Chapter 41 pictures a great crisis, as a powerful army moves westward from Persia, conquering many nations and filling all with terror. In contrast, God told Israel not to fear. "But thou, Israel, art my servant, Jacob, whom I have chosen, the seed of Abraham my friend. . . . Thou art my servant; I have chosen thee, and not cast thee away" (Isa. 41:8,9b). Israel had to be preserved, because it was God's instrument to perform a task of worldwide importance.

Isaiah 42 gives a remarkable picture of the ideal Servant of the Lord and the great work that God intends Him to accomplish. He is to "bring forth judgment to the Gentiles" (v. 1). He must "set judgment in the earth," and the distant "isles shall wait for his law" (v. 4). The tasks He is destined to accomplish are almost beyond belief. He is to bring God's justice to all the nations (vv. 1,4).

Almost more remarkable than the immensity of the task that the Servant must perform is the description of the way He is to do it. He will move forward with absolute confidence, but nothing indicates strenuous effort will be needed. He will have such an understanding of His overwhelming power that He can be absolutely gentle as He does His work (vv. 2–4) even toward those whose efforts have failed. This first part of chapter 42 pictures the ideal Servant—the goal for which Israel was to be preserved.

As an Israelite read this prediction, he would think: "How can Israel even think of performing this great task that God's Servant must do?" Soon the Lord Himself called attention to the inability of the natural Israelite to fulfill the picture of the ideal Servant. In verse 19 He says, "Who is blind, but my servant? or deaf, as my messenger that I sent?" Israel had a responsibility to fulfill this ideal, but to do so was far beyond its power. Still, the Lord says: "Ye are my witnesses, . . . and my servant whom I have chosen" (43:10; compare 44:1–2,21).

Israel had responsibility to do the work of the Servant. Yet not all Israel could be meant, for some were blasphemers and idolaters. Could part of Israel be the real Servant? Or might it really point to One who must come out of Israel—One who could represent Israel in accomplishing the task? Matthew 12:17–21 quotes Isaiah 42:1–4 as fulfilled in Jesus Christ.

Chapter 49 presents the work of the Servant in more detail. The Servant tells the "isles" and the "people, from far;" that God called Him before His birth, even mentioning His name: Israel (Isa. 49:3). Verse 4 describes the godly in Israel who know what God wants but feel their own inadequacy and provides assurance that the work belongs to God, and He will bring it to pass. Verses 5 and 6 distinguish between the One who will fulfill the work of the Servant and the nation of Israel, to which this One belongs and which He represents. Not only is He to bring judgment to all the world—He is "to bring Jacob again to him" (v. 5) and "to restore the preserved of Israel" (v. 6). He is to be "a light to the Gentiles" and "my salvation unto the end of the earth" (v. 6). In 50:4–10, we hear of the sufferings to which He will voluntarily submit.

All this leads up to the triumphal picture in Isaiah 52:13—53:12, showing the sufferings of the Servant (52:14; 53:2–5,7–8,10), their vicarious and redemptive nature (52:15; 53:4–6,8,10–12; compare 1 Pet. 1:1–2). Chapter 54 shows the outreach of the Servant's work, and chapter 55 gives the glorious call to receive the salvation won by the Servant's redemptive work, "without money and without price" (v. 1).

After chapter 53, Isaiah never again used "servant" in the singular; rather he spoke of the blessings that the followers of the Servant will receive, calling them "the servants of the Lord" (54:17); "his servants" (56:6; 65:15; 66:14); and "my servants" (65:8,9,13,14).

The New Testament pictures Jesus as the Suffering Servant fulfilling the glorious descriptions of Isaiah. In refusing to let disciples reveal His true identity, Jesus was the pleasing Servant who did not strive or cry out (Matt. 12:14–21). In the resurrection and ascension, God glorified Jesus the Servant (Acts 3;13; compare verse 26 where the same Greek word for servant appears though KJV translates "Son."). Gentile and Jewish leaders conspired to make Jesus, "your holy servant" suffer as God "had decided beforehand" (Acts 4:27–28 NIV). This led the early church to pray that as God's servants they would speak with boldness and perform miracles through the name of "your holy servant Jesus" (Acts 4:29–30 NIV). Jesus saw His mission as that of the Servant (Luke 4:18–19; compare 22:37) and symbolized it for His disciples, calling on them to serve one another and the world (John 13:4–17). See *Christology; Isaiah; Jesus Christ; Slavery; Son of God.*

Allan A. MacRae

SERVICE Work done for other people or for God and the worship of God. Jacob worked for Laban seven years for each of his wives (Gen. 29:15–30). Service could be slave labor (Ex. 5:11; Lev. 25:39; 1 Kings 12:4; Isa. 14:3; compare Lam. 1:3), farm work (1 Chron. 27:26), or daily labor on the job (Ps. 104:23). It could be service of earthly kingdoms (2 Chron 12:8; compare 1 Chron. 26:30), of God's place of worship (Ex. 30:16; compare Num. 4:47; 1 Chron 23:24), of God's ministers (Ezra 8:20), and of God (Josh. 22:27). Not only people do service; God also does service (Isa. 28:21). Even righteousness has a service (Isa. 32:17).

Service at its best is worship. This involves the service of Temple vessels (1 Chron. 9:28), of worship actions (2 Chron. 35:10; compare Ex.

S

12:25–26), of bringing offerings (Josh. 22:27), of priestly work (Num. 8:11). Interestingly, the Old Testament never ascribes service to other gods.

The New Testament similarly speaks of forced service (Matt. 27:32), sacrificial living (Rom. 12:1; Phil. 2:17 with a play on words also indicating an offering), slave labor done for Christ's sake (Eph. 6:7; Col. 3:22; compare Phil. 2:30), worship (Rom. 9:4; Heb. 12:28), offerings (Rom. 15:31; 2 Cor. 9:12), and personal ministry (Rom. 12:7; 1 Tim. 1:12; 2 Tim. 4:11). Hebrews 1:14 talks of the ministry of angels. Being in an army is also service (2 Tim. 2:4), and those who persecute Christ's followers think they do service for God (John 16:2).

SERVITUDE Hard labor done by servants or conscripted workers (Gen. 47:21; 2 Chron. 10:4; Neh. 5:18; Jer. 28:14; Lam. 1:3). The same Hebrew term is also translated, "service."

SETH (Sĕth) Personal name meaning, "He set or appointed" or "replacement." Third son of Adam and Eve born after Cain murdered Abel (Gen. 4:25; 5:3). He was an ancestor of Jesus (Luke 3:38).

SETHUR (Sē' thŭr) Personal name meaning, "hidden." Spy representing tribe of Asher in scouting out the Promised Land (Num. 13:13).

SEVEN CHURCHES OF ASIA Original recipients of Book of Revelation (Rev. 1:4). See *Asia Minor.*

SEVEN WORDS FROM THE CROSS Jesus' statements from the cross as He was crucified for our sin. The seven words from the cross were not a prepared speech but the record of Jesus responding to the events around Him during the six agonizing hours of his crucifixion. Although no single gospel records all seven sayings in order, the order that follows is the most commonly accepted.

The First Three Words Jesus' first three statements from the cross relate primarily to others, and Jesus spoke them between 9:00 a.m. and noon (Mark 15:25). First He asked forgiveness for those who were crucifying Him (Luke 23:34). Then He promised to be with the penitent thief in paradise (Luke 23:43). Jesus' provision for the care of His mother by John comprised His third remarks from the cross (John 19:26–27).

The Last Four Words Jesus' last four statements refer to Himself and were spoken between noon and 3:00 p.m. (Matt. 27:45; Mark 15:33; Luke 23:44). He uttered the cry of desolation, quoting Psalm 22:1 in the Aramaic language (Matt. 27:46; Mark 15:34), expressed His thirst, (John 19:28) and issued the cry of victory, "It is finished" (John 19:30). In His final words, Jesus quoted Psalm 31:5 as He committed His spirit to God (Luke 23:46). See *Crucifixion.*

Steve W. Lemke

SEVEN, SEVENTH The number of completeness. See *Number Systems and Number Symbolism.*

The Church of St. John in Pergamum, a city where one of the seven churches of Asia was located.

SEVENTY WEEKS The time spoken of in Daniel 9:24–27, usually understood as seventy weeks of years or 490 years. The passage groups the weeks in three parts: seven weeks (49 years), sixty-two weeks (434 years), and one week (7 years). The 49 years are associated with rebuilding Jerusalem in "times of trouble" (v. 25 NIV). The 434 years relate to the intervening time before a cutting off of the Anointed One (v. 26). The 7 years are connected with the period of a covenant between a ruler and Jerusalem, which is violated in the middle of the 7 years (v. 27).

The significance of the seventy weeks is variously understood. A historical approach relates these years to the period of history between the fall of Jerusalem and the restoration of the Temple in 164 B.C. following the atrocities of Antiochus Epiphanes. See *Intertestamental History.*

A prophetic approach sees the reference to reach to the birth of Christ, His subsequent crucifixion (the cutting off of the Anointed One), and the destruction of Jerusalem by the Romans in A.D. 70. At that time, sacrifices under the Old Covenant ceased. The same dating without reference to Jesus has been the usual Jewish understanding since Josephus. They focus on the destruction of the Temple.

The dispensational approach makes the 70 weeks a prophetic framework for end time events, rather than a prophecy of what took place in the work of Christ at His first coming. The 69th week is seen as completed at Christ's death, while the 70th week is yet to be fulfilled at a future Great Tribulation period. The interval between the two is seen as a parenthesis in the prophetic pattern which contains the present church age, a period said not to be revealed in Old Testament prophecy.

See *Dispensation; Eschatology; Millennium, Tribulation.*　　　　　　　　　　　　*Jerry W. Batson*

SEVENTY YEARS Prophetic and apocalyptic figure pointing to time of Israel's Exile in Babylon and to the end of tribulation in Daniel's vision. Seventy years represented an even number of the normal human life span (Ps. 90:10). Isaiah 23:15 and the Babylonian Black Stone of Esarhaddon may indicate that seventy years was an expected time of punishment and desolation for a defeated city. Jeremiah predicted that Judah would serve Babylon 70 years (Jer. 25:11; compare 29:10). Second Chronicles 36:21 saw the completion of the 70 years in the coming of Cyrus (538 B.C.). This apparently sees the years as from the first deporting of Judeans into Babylon (about 605 B.C.) until Cyrus came. Zechariah seems to have seen the 70 years ending in his own day with the rebuilding of the Temple (Zech. 1:12). This would span the period from the destruction of the Temple (586 B.C.) to the dedication in 516 B.C. Some interpreters see in the Chronicler's references to sabbaths an indication of a second meaning for seventy years, that is seventy sabbatical years (Lev. 25:1–7; 26:34–35) or 490 years. By this reckoning Israel had not kept the sabbatical year commandment since the period of the Judges, so God gave the land 70 consecutive sabbatical years during the Exile. See *Sabbatical Year.*

Daniel meditated on Jeremiah's prophecy (Dan. 9:2) and learned that 70 weeks of years were intended (v. 24). See *Seventy Weeks.*

SEX, BIBLICAL TEACHING ON God created humans as sexual beings, somehow reflective of His own image (Gen. 1:27), and declared that this reality was "very good" (Gen. 1:31). One will look in vain, however, in the Bible for a single word for sex. The nearest biblical terms are "male" and "female." The biblical language for sexuality is rich with variety as it describes God's will and human behavior regarding this aspect of God's creative power: the power to bring new life into being within the family and the pleasure of companions within marriage.

Attitudes toward sex The biblical writers were somewhat ambivalent about sex. Some passages truly value sex and celebrate it joyously (Gen. 18:12; 26:8; Song of Sol. 4:1–16); others call for times of abstaining from sexual activity (Ex. 19:15; 1 Sam. 21:4–5); still others raise the life without sex above the normal marital relationship (1 Cor. 7:1–9,37–38; Rev. 14:4). Positively, God blesses sex for both companionship and procreation (Gen. 1:28; 2:18–25). Fertility of women was a blessing while barrenness was a curse (Gen. 29:30—30:24; 1 Sam. 1:5–20). Basically, the Bible sees sex as good because God created it.

The interpreter should not ignore negative feelings the Bible expresses toward sex. The sinful nature of man appears to have corrupted God's good gift. Outside the first garden, a negative attitude toward nudity appears (Gen. 3:7,21; Luke 8:27,35). "Uncovering one's nakedness" refers to a shameful, incestual, or otherwise forbidden sex act (Lev. 18:6–19). Sex can be wasteful of one's strength (Prov. 31:3). Euphemisms and circumlocutions are used in referring to the body's private parts (Deut. 28:57, "feet"; Gen. 24:2, "loins" or "thigh"). Similarly, the verb "to know" is sometimes used to refer to having sex relations (Gen. 4:1; Matt. 1:25). Sin has produced a hesitancy and reservation about sex among the biblical characters and writers as compared with the lack of shame in the Garden of Eden (Gen. 2:25).

Male/Female relationships As sex is both good and bad in the Bible, so also there is a contrast of equality and dominance/submission patterns for male/female relationships in the biblical teachings. This overlording by males is a result of sin distorting God's original plan for humans. A double standard in relationships may be described throughout the Scriptures; yet before the Fall and after the coming of Christ, man and woman are set forth as equals before God.

In the garden, Adam and Eve were created equal (Gen. 1:27–28; 2:18–23). The New Testament teaches that in Christ this Edenic complementariness is restored (2 Cor. 5:17; Gal. 3:28; Eph. 5:21–33). Mates are equal in possessing one another (1 Cor. 7:4) and are interdependent (1 Cor. 11:11–12). The new creation in Christ makes this possible.

Yet the Fall ruptured God's plan for male/female equality. Sin produced male dominance and female submissiveness (Gen. 3:16). Many scholars believe that this is descriptive rather than prescriptive for all time. Much of the remainder of Scripture, therefore, describes a double standard of male superiority and female inferiority, a kind of "chain of command" of the husband ruling his wife and children. Various passages set forth women being subordinated to men (Num. 30:3–15; 1 Tim 2:11–15). Different standards of fidelity in marriage are found (Num. 5:11–31; Deut. 22:22–29) where unfaithful wives are more severely dealt with than husbands. The New Testament response to this was that of mutual equality and servanthood toward each other with the servanthood of Jesus as the basic criterion (Eph. 5:21–33). Some passages deal with specific problems that appear to be limited to the time and culture of the first-century place (1 Cor. 14:34–35; 1 Tim. 2:11–15; 1 Pet. 3:1–7), though some Bible students see such passages as establishing social orders for all times.

Sexual Deviations Several deviations of sexual behavior are condemned in the biblical teachings: homosexuality (Lev. 18:22; Rom. 1:26–27; 1 Cor. 6:9–10); bestiality (Ex. 22:19; Lev. 18:23); incest (Lev. 18:6–18; 1 Cor. 5); rape (Ex. 22:16–17; Deut. 22:23–29); adultery (Ex. 20:14; Deut. 22:22); prostitution (Prov. 7:1–27; 29:3;); fornication (1 Cor. 6:9–10; compare Matt. 19:9). These are all declared to be outside of the will of God for man and woman who are called to live together in monogamous fidelity within the covenant of marriage. The only other option is the giftedness of celibacy (Matt. 19:12b; 1 Cor. 7:7). Incidentally, the Bible is silent on the subject of masturbation (compare Lev. 15:16). It is silent on physical techniques of sexual intercourse, referring only to marital rights or enjoyment (Ex. 21:10), erotic caresses (Song of Sol. 2:6; 7:1–9), fondling (Gen. 26:8), and pleasure in conceiving (Gen. 18:12). Yet these are set forth in the context of the behavior of married couples. Intimate sexual behavior outside of marriage is considered sexual immorality in the biblical perspective.

Theology of sex The Bible reveals an ethical God who gives humans the gift of sexuality whereby they image God when they join together to complement each other as "one flesh" (Gen. 2:24). All nonmarital sex is outside the boundaries of the will of this ethical God (see Amos 2:6–8 where

Israel was to reject sex at the pagan shrines). God's people are expected to exercise self-control, not by asceticism (Col. 2:23; 1 Tim. 4:1–5), but by the power of the Holy Spirit overcoming sexual impulses (Gal. 5:16–25). For the noncelibate, marriage is the only approved outlet for sexual expression (1 Cor. 7:9; Titus 2:5–6). This view equates human wholeness with holiness of life (1 Thess. 4:3–5). One's sexuality is a vital part of Christian holiness and not a necessary evil to be rejected. Within the limits of marriage, sex is for procreation of children, the enhancement of the one-flesh relationship, and the pleasure of the married couple whose love can be nourished thereby. Outside of the limits established by God, sex becomes an evil and destructive force in human life, calling for God's redemptive power to deliver humans trapped therein. Marital sexual love is both a gift and a responsibility from God to be consecrated by the Word and prayer.

Guy Greenfield

SHAALABIN (Shā à lăb′ bīn) Place name meaning, "place of foxes." Town in tribal territory of Dan (Josh. 19:42); apparently the same as Shaalbim.

SHAALBIM (Shā ăl′ bīm) Place name meaning, "place of foxes." Spelled and interpreted differently in different texts and early Greek versions. See *Shaalabin*. Amorite stronghold eventually controlled by Manasseh and Ephraim (Judg. 1:35). Part of Solomon's second district for supplying provisions for the royal household (1 Kings 4:9). Its location is probably modern Selbit seven miles southeast of Lydda and three miles northwest of Ajalon. David's military hero Eliahba came from Shaalbim (2 Sam. 23:32).

SHAALBON (Shā ăl′ bon) RSV, NRSV, TEV, REB rendering of Shaalbonite, representing an alternative Hebrew spelling of Shaalbim.

SHAALBONITE (Shā ăl′ bō nīte) See *Shaalbon.*

SHAALIM (Shā′ à lĭm) Place name perhaps meaning, "caves, cavities." Place where Saul sought his father's lost donkeys (1 Sam. 9:4). The place is sometimes equated with Shaalbim or the land of Shual.

SHAAPH (Shā′ ăph) Clan name meaning, "balsam." Apparently two persons in Caleb's line, though some interpreters identify the two (1 Chron. 2:47,49).

SHAARAIM (Shā à rā′ ĭm) Place name meaning, "double doors." *1.* City in tribal territory of Judah (Josh. 15:36). Place where David's soldiers pursued Philistine army (1 Sam. 17:52). Some would locate it at khirbet esh-Sharia a mile northeast of Azekah. *2.* Town where tribe of Simeon lived

(1 Chron. 4:31), but the parallel texts read Shilhim (Josh. 15:32) and Sharuhen (Josh. 19:6). Many scholars think Sharuhen is meant in Chronicles.

SHAASHGAZ (Shā ăsh' gāz) Hebrew transliteration of Persian name of uncertain meaning. Eunuch in charge of Xerxes' harem of which Esther became a member before she was chosen queen (Esth. 2:14).

SHABBETHAI (Shăb' bĕ thâi) Personal name meaning, "belonging to the sabbath." Levite who explained the law to the people as Ezra read it (Neh. 8:7). He or a namesake opposed Ezra's plan of divorce for foreign wives (Ezra 10:15). He was in charge of "external business of the house of God" (Neh. 11:16 REB): either maintaining outward appearance of the Temple or collecting the tithes.

SHACHIA (Shă chī' ă) Personal name meaning, "Yahweh fenced in or protected." Clan leader in tribe of Benjamin (1 Chron. 8:10), following different manuscripts than modern translations which read Sachia. Many manuscripts and early versions read, "Shabia."

SHACKLES See *Bond; Fetter.*

SHADDAI (Shă' dâi) Transliteration of Hebrew name for God, often translated, "Almighty" following the earliest Greek translation. See *Almighty; God of the Fathers; Names of God.*

SHADOW A dark image of an object created when the object interrupts rays of light. The Bible uses the term in both literal and figurative senses. **Old Testament** The Hebrew *tsel* speaks of shadow as protection and as transitory, short-lived, and changing. The intensive heat, particularly in the summer, made shade and shadows important in Palestine. Travelers sought rest under a tree (Gen. 18:4; compare Job 40:22) or in a house (Gen. 19:8). Especially at midday when shade virtually vanished, people looked for a shadow (Isa. 16:3; compare Gen. 21:15; Jonah 4; Job 7:2). In the afternoon shadows lengthen (Jer. 6:4; compare Neh. 13:19 NIV). In the evening cool, shadows disappear (Song of Sol. 2:17). In the desert wilderness the traveler found little hope for shade but looked for shade or shadow from hills (Judges 9:36), large rocks (Isa. 32:2), a cave (Ex. 33:22; 1 Kings 19:9), or a cloud (Isa. 25:5).

Powerful people offer the shadow of protection and security (Song of Sol. 2:3). So does a king (Lam. 4:20; Ezek. 31:6). Still, Israel knew the false claims of kings to provide such protection (Judg. 9:15; compare Isa. 30:2; Ezek. 31). Biblical writers looked to the Messiah for needed shade or shadow (Isa. 32:2; Ezek. 17:23). God was the ultimate shadow of protection for His

people (Pss. 36:7; 91:1; 121:5; Isa. 25:4; 49:2; 51:16).

Human life itself is only a brief shadow (Job 8:9; 14:2; Pss. 102:11; 144:4; Eccl. 6:12; 8:13). **New Testament** The Greek *skia* can refer to a literal shadow (Mark 4:32; Acts 5:15). More often it refers to death or to an indication of something to come, a foreshadowing. References to death come from Old Testament prophecy—Matthew 4:16 and Luke 1:79 picking up Isaiah 9:2. Dietary laws and religious festivals were only a shadow preparing Israel for the reality made known in Christ (Col. 2:17; Heb. 8:5; 10:1). James used a related Greek word to say that God is not a fleeting, changing shadow (1:17).

Trent C. Butler

SHADRACH (Shăd' răch) Babylonian name meaning, "circuit of the sun." One of Daniel's three friends taken to Babylon during the Exile (Dan. 1:6–7). His Hebrew name was Hananiah. The three were cast into a fiery furnace for refusing to worship a graven image set up by King Nebuchadnezzar. The Lord miraculously delivered them, and they were given places of honor in the kingdom (Dan. 3:30). See *Daniel.*

SHAGE(E) (Shā gē) Father of one of David's military heroes (1 Chron. 11:34). The parallel text in 2 Samuel 23 has two similar names: verse 11, Shammah the son of Agee; verse 33, Shammah the Hararite. Shage may represent a combination of the two Hebrew words Shammah and Agee.

SHAHAR (Shā' här) Transliteration of Hebrew word meaning, "dawn." Part of title of Psalm 22, translated by most modern translations. NAS transliterates, "Hashshahar," including the Hebrew definite article. See *Aijeleth Shahar.*

SHAHARAIM (Shā hă rā' ĭm) Personal name meaning, "double dawns." Benjaminite who divorced his wives and lived in Moab (1 Chron. 8:8).

SHAHAZIMAH (Shā hă zī' mah) Place name meaning, "double peak." Town or mountain marking tribal boundary of Issachar (Josh. 19:22). Its location is not known. Some have suggested it is a combination of two town names: Shahaz and Yammah.

SHAHAZUMAH (Shā hă zū' mah) Modern translation spelling of Shahazimah following the written Hebrew text rather than the notes of the earliest Hebrew scribes.

SHALEM (Shā' lēm) Place name meaning, "peace, safety," according to KJV translation (Gen. 33:18; compare NIV text note). Modern translations read, "safely."

SHALIM (Shā' lǐm) KJV spelling of Shaalim.

SHALISHA(H) (Shă lī' shä) Place name meaning, "the third." Territory where Saul sought his father's lost donkeys (1 Sam. 9:4); probably the same as Baal Shalishah. Its location has recently been questioned. See *Baal Shalishah.*

SHALLECHETH (Shăl' lė chěth) Place name of uncertain meaning, sometimes thought on basis of earliest translations to have resulted from scribe's transposition of first two letters and thus to have read originally, "chamber." Jerusalem gate mentioned only in 1 Chronicles 26:16.

SHALLEKETH (Shăl' lė kěth) NIV spelling of Shallecheth.

SHALLUM (Shăl' lŭm) Personal name meaning, "replacer" or "the replaced." *1.* King of Israel (752 B.C.). He assassinated Zechariah and was, in turn, assassinated by Menahem a month later (2 Kings 15:10–15). *2.* See *3. Jehoahaz. 3.* Husband of Huldah (2 Kings 22:14). *4.* A gatekeeper (1 Chron. 9:17,19,31; compare Ezra 2:42; Neh. 7:45). This may be the same as Shelemiah (1 Chron. 26:14) and Meshelemiah (1 Chron. 9:21; 26:1–14), since these names are closely related in Hebrew. *5.* A chief priest (1 Chron. 6:13; Ezra 7:2). *6.* Descendant of Judah (1 Chron.

The monolith inscription of Shalmaneser III which records in cuneiform the Battle of Qarqar.

2:40). *7.* Jeremiah's uncle (Jer. 32:7). *8.* Temple doorkeeper (Jer. 35:4). *9.* Descendant of Simeon (1 Chron. 4:25). *10.* Descendant of Naphtali (1 Chron. 7:13). *11.* Father of Jehizkiah (2 Chron. 28:12). *12.* Porter who agreed to divorce his foreign wife (Ezra 10:24). *13.* Israelite with a foreign wife (Ezra 10:42). *14.* Supervisor of half of Jerusalem who helped Nehemiah rebuild the walls (Neh. 3:12).

SHALLUN (Shăl' lŭn) Personal name perhaps meaning, "peaceful, carefree." Man who helped Nehemiah by repairing the Fountain Gate (Neh. 3:15). NRSV, NAS, TEV follow some early version evidence and read, "Shallum."

SHALMAI (Shăl' māī) Personal name meaning, "coat." Manuscripts have several variant spellings. Servant (Nethanim) in Temple (Ezra 2:46; Neh. 7:48).

SHALMAN (Shăl' măn) Personal name meaning, "complete, peace." Mysterious figure in Hosea 10:14, sometimes identified by scholars as an abbreviation of Shalmanezer V of Assyria and sometimes as a ruler of Moab listed by Tiglath-Pileser III among kings paying him tribute. His name became synonymous with violence and ruthlessness.

SHALMANESER (Shăl man ē' sēr) Personal name meaning, "Shalmanu (the god) is the highest ranking one." *1.* An Assyrian king who ruled

1274–1245 B.C. The records of his military exploits set a precedent which succeeding kings followed. *2.* Shalmaneser III ruled Assyria 858–824 B.C. He fought a group of small kingdoms, including Israel, in the battle of Qarqar in 853 B.C. Despite claiming victory, Shalmaneser proceeded no farther.

3. Shalmaneser V ruled Assyria 726–722 B.C. He completed the attack on Samaria begun by his predecessor, Tiglath-pileser III. In 722 Israel fell to Shalmaneser (2 Kings 17:6), thus ending the Northern Kingdom forever. See *Assyria; Israel.*

SHAMA (Shā′ mȧ) Personal name meaning, "he has heard." Military hero under David (1 Chron. 11:44).

SHAMARIAH (Shă mȧ rī′ ah) KJV spelling of Shermariah (2 Chron. 11:19).

SHAME AND HONOR Sociological studies have increased appreciation for shame and honor as two pivotal values in ancient societies. As a noun, honor approximates our ideas of esteem, respect, (high) regard, or (good) reputation. Shame, the opposite of honor, approximates humiliation or loss of standing. Shame is also used as a euphemism for nakedness (Jer. 13:26; Nah. 3:5; Hab. 2:15). In a similar way, to give honor to private parts is to clothe them (1 Cor. 12:23–24). English preserves this connection between shame and nakedness when we speak of someone's guilt being exposed. In Jeremiah 2:26, for example, a thief once caught suffers shame, that is, the loss of esteem in the public eye.

To honor is to recognize the value of someone or thing and to act accordingly. Honoring parents (Ex. 20:12), for example, involves providing for their material needs (Matt. 15:4–5) so that their poverty would not be a source of shame. To honor can mean to reward with tangible signs of respect (2 Chron. 16:14; Esth. 6:8–11). To shame someone is to challenge that one's reputation or to disregard his or her worth. The ancients viewed every human action and interaction as an occasion for either gaining honor, that is, increasing one's value in the public eye, or for being shamed, that is, having one's estimation degraded. The desire to maintain one's honor and to avoid shame or dishonor was a powerful incentive for right action (Job 11:3; Ps. 70:3; Ezek. 43:10). Honor was thought of as a limited good, that is, the amount of available honor was limited. If one lost honor, another had to gain honor (Prov. 5:9).

Those who demonstrate a lack of concern for matters of honor and shame are termed shameless. Having rejected the framework for values, such will do anything (Job 19:3; Jer. 6:15). Others fail to recognize what is a source of honor and what a source of shame. Those who are ashamed of Christ and His words (Mark 8:32) are shamed by what should give them honor.

The reference to the man and woman in Gen. 2:25 being naked and unashamed likely does not highlight that they were not bashful. Rather, their honor or respect was intact in contrast to the loss of respect they suffered when God made their guilt public (Gen. 3:8–10).   *Chris Church*

SHAMED (Shā′ mĕd) Personal name meaning, "destroyed, ruin." KJV, REB reading following Hebrew of Benjaminite's name (1 Chron. 8:12). Other modern translations read, "Shemed." Many commentators follow early manuscripts and versions in reading, "Shemer."

SHAMER (Shā′ mēr) Variant spelling of Shomer or Shemer (1 Chron. 6:46; 7:34).

SHAMGAR (Shăm′ gär) Hurrian name meaning, "Shimig (the god) has given." A mysterious warrior who slew 600 Philistines with an oxgoad, a long metal-tipped pole (Judg. 3:31). His name is Hurrian, but whether that was his lineage is uncertain. In the song of Deborah (Judg. 5), Shamgar (the "son of Anath") is praised for clearing the highways of robbers, making travel once again possible. See *Anath; Judges.*

SHAMHUTH (Shăm′ hŭth) Head of fifth division of David's army, serving during the fifth month (1 Chron. 27:8). Many commentators consider the name a scribal combination of Shamman (2 Sam. 23:25) and Shammoth (1 Chron. 11:27).

SHAMIR (Shā′ mīr) Personal and place name meaning, "thorn" or "diamond." *1.* A Levite (1 Chron. 24:24), written Shamur in some manuscripts. *2.* Town in hill country of Judah assigned to tribe of Judah (Josh. 15:48). Located either at modern el-Bireh near khirbet Somera northeast of en-Rimmon or khirbet es-Sumara about twelve miles west-southwest of Hebron. *3.* Home of Tola, the judge from the tribe of Issachar, in mount Ephraim (Judg. 10:1). Located possibly at khirbet es-Sumara about seven miles south of Shechem. Some commentators would equate it with Samaria.

SHAMLAI (Shăm′ lâi) Written form of personal name in Hebrew text of Ezra 2:46. Scribal note has Shalmai and is followed by many translations. See *Shalmai.*

SHAMMA (Shăm′ mȧ) Personal name of uncertain meaning. *1.* Leader of clan of Asher (1 Chron. 7:37). *2.* Spelling of name of a military hero under David (2 Sam. 23:11; compare vv. 25,33 where Hebrew spelling is "Shammah").

SHAMMAH (Shăm′ mah) Personal name of uncertain meaning, perhaps, "frightful" or "astonishing" or "he heard." *1.* Edomite tribe descended from Esau (Gen. 36:13). *2.* Older brother of David (1 Sam. 16:9; 17:13) and father of Jonadab (2 Sam. 13:3,32) and Jonathan (2 Sam. 21:21) if the similar Hebrew spellings in 2 Samuel point to the same person mentioned in 1 Samuel. See *Shimeah.* *3.* David's military heo (2 Sam. 23:25; spelled Shammoth in 1 Chron. 11:27). *4.* Another of David's military heroes (2 Sam. 23:33) or, with a slight change of the Hebrew text suggested by many commentators, the father of Jonathan, the military hero (REB, NRSV, NIV). *5.* See *Shamma 2.* *6.* See *Shamhuth.*

SHAMMAI (Shăm' mā ī) Abbreviated form of personal name, perhaps meaning, "He heard." *1.* Member of tribe of Judah and clan of Jerahmeel (1 Chron. 2:28,32). *2.* Descendant of Caleb (1 Chron. 2:44). *3.* Another descendant of Caleb (1 Chron. 4:17).

SHAMMOTH (Shăm' mŏth) Variant spelling (1 Chron. 11:27) for Shammah (2 Sam. 23:25).

SHAMMUA(H) (Shăm mū à) Personal name meaning, "one who was heard." *1.* Spy representing tribe of Reuben (Num. 13:4). *2.* Son of David (2 Sam. 5:14; spelled "Shimea" in 1 Chron. 3:5). *3.* Father of a Levite (Neh. 11:17; spelled Shemaiah in 1 Chron. 9:16). *4.* Priest in days of Joiakim about 600 B.C. (Neh. 12:18).

SHAMSHERAI (Shăm' shē râi) Personal name of uncertain meaning; some commentators regard it as a combination of Shimshai and Shimri. Benjaminite living in Jerusalem (1 Chron. 8:26).

SHAPHAM (Shā' phăm) Personal name of unknown meaning. Leader of tribe of Gad (1 Chron. 5:12).

SHAPHAN (Shā' phăn) Personal name meaning, "coney." Prominent court official during King Josiah's reign in Judah (2 Kings 22). Shaphan served as scribe and treasurer. During Josiah's religious reforms and refurbishment of the Temple, Shaphan delivered the newfound book of the law (probably Deuteronomy) from Hilkiah the priest to the king's palace. He also was sent to Huldah the prophetess to confer concerning the book (22:14). Shaphan and his sons befriended Jeremiah on several occasions. See *Ahikam; Elasah; Gedeliah; Jaazaniah.*

SHAPHAT (Shā' phăt) Personal name meaning, "He has established justice." *1.* Spy from tribe of Simeon (Num. 13:5). *2.* Father of Elisha (2 Kings 6:31). *3.* Descendant of David and Zerubbabel (1 Chron. 3:22). *4.* Supervisor of David's cattle herds (1 Chron. 27:29). *5.* Member of tribe of Gad (1 Chron. 5:12).

SHAPHER (Shā' phēr) KJV spelling of Mount Shepher. Place name perhaps meaning, "lovely." Stop on Israel's wilderness journey (Num. 33:23), somewhere on east of the Gulf of Aqaba.

SHAPHIR (Shā' phīr) Modern translations' spelling of Saphir.

SHARAI (Shā' râi) Personal name perhaps meaning, "He loosed or redeemed." Man with a foreign wife (Ezra 10:40).

SHARAIM KJV spelling of Shaaraim in Joshua 15:36.

SHARAR (Shā' rȧr) Personal name perhaps meaning, "he is healthy." See *Sacar.*

SHARD Pottery fragment found in archaeological excavations and used for dating. See *Archaeology; Chronology; Pottery; Writing.*

SHAREZER (Shȧ rē' zēr) Abbreviated form of Akkadian name meaning, "may (god's name) protect the king." Son of Sennacherib who helped murder his father (2 Kings 19:37). Assyrian records report the death as occurring in 681 B.C. See *Assyria.* *2.* Name open to several interpretations in Zechariah 7:2. The full name may be Bethel-sharezer, meaning, "may the god Bethel protect the king" (see REB). Sharezer may be a man sent to the house of God (*beth-el* in Hebrew) to pray (KJV). The town of Bethel may have sent Sharezer to pray (NAS, NIV, NRSV, TEV). The name probably indicates the person was born in Babylonian Exile. He may have come with his questions from Babylon and have come as a representative of the people of Bethel.

SHARON, PLAIN OF (Shăr' on) Geographical name meaning, "flat land" or "wetlands." *1.* A coastal plain which runs from near modern Tel Aviv to just south of Mount Carmel (about 50 miles). The area had abundant marshes, forests, and sand dunes, but few settlements during bibli-

View of the Plain of Sharon and the Yarkon River from the excavation area at the site of Aphek.

cal days. Because of its fertility and low risk of flooding, the plain was used more by migrant herdsmen than settled farmers. Isaiah 35:2 parallels Sharon with Lebanon, which was known for its trees. Isaiah 65:10 speaks of the area as an excellent pasture for flocks, symbolic of the peace that God would one day grant to His people. See *Palestine.*

2. Area of uncertain location east of the Jordan inhabited by the tribe of Gad (1 Chron. 5:16) and mentioned by King Mesha of Moab. See *Mesha.*

SHARONITE (Shā′ rō nīte) Person who lived in Plain of Sharon.

SHARUHEN (Shå rū′ hĕn) Place name perhaps meaning, "free pasture land." Town assigned to tribe of Simeon (Josh. 19:6) located in the territory of Judah (Josh. 15:32, where spelling is Shilhim; in 1 Chron. 4:31 spelling is Shaaraim; Egyptian spelling is apparently Shurahuna). The Hyksos withdrew there after the Egyptians defeated them about 1540 B.C. See *Hyksos.* The traditional location is tell el-Farah, but recent study has favored tell el-Ajjul about four miles south of Gaza, though this has often been identified as Beth Eglayim. Excavations have shown this to have been a large, well-fortified, wealthy city.

SHASHAI (Shā′ shâi) Personal name of uncertain meaning. Man married to a foreign wife (Ezra 10:40).

SHASHAK (Shā′ shăk) Personal name of uncertain meaning, perhaps of Egyptian origin. Leader of tribe of Benjamin living in Jerusalem (1 Chron. 8:14,25).

SHAUL (Shā′ ŭl) Personal name meaning, "asked of." *1.* Transliteration of Hebrew name of King Saul. *2.* Grandson of Jacob and son of Simeon with a Canaanite mother (Gen. 46:10). *3.* Early king of Edom from Rehoboth (Gen. 36:37; 1 Chron. 1:48). *4.* Levite (1 Chron. 6:24).

SHAULITE (Shā′ ŭl īte) Member of clan of tribe of Simeon descended from Shaul (Num. 26:13).

SHAVEH (Shā′ vĕh) Place name meaning, "valley, plain" or "ruler." Place where the king of Sodom met Abraham on the latter's return from defeating the coalition of kings (Gen. 14:17). It is also called the king's valley or dale. There Absalom raised a momument to himself (2 Sam. 18:18). The Genesis Apocryphon locates it in Beth-Hakkerem, which is two and a half miles south of Jerusalem where the Kidron and Hinnom valleys join. It has also been located north, east, and west of Jerusalem.

SHAVEH-KIRIATHAIM (Shā′ vĕh-kīr ĭ å thā′ ĭm)

Place name meaning, "waste land of Kiriathaim." This valley is the high plain above the Arnon River. There Chedorlaomer and his coalition of kings defeated the Emim (Gen. 14:5). See *Chedorlaomer; Emim; Kiriathaim.*

SHAVING See *Razors.*

An ancient shaving razor with a goat's leg handle.

SHAVSHA (Shăv′ shå) spelling of Shisha (1 Kings 4:3) in 1 Chronicles 18:16. See *Shisha.*

SHEAF Harvested grain bound together into a bundle. English translation of three Hebrew terms. Joseph's dream featured sheaves still in the field (Gen. 37:7). Laws of sacrifice called for the first harvested sheaves to be sacrificed (Lev. 23:10–15). Some sheaves were for gleaners (Deut. 24:19; Ruth 2:7). The prophets used sheaves as figures of judgment (Jer. 9:22; Amos 2:13; Mic. 4:12; Zech. 12:6). See *Agriculture; Gleaning; Grain; Harvest; Sacrifice.*

SHEAL (Shē′ ăl) Personal name meaning, "ask." Many commentators change the Hebrew text slightly to read, "Yishal" or "Jishal," meaning, "he asks." Israelite who married a foreign wife (Ezra 10:29).

SHEALTIEL (Shė ăl′ tĭ ĕl) Personal name meaning, "I have asked of God." Father of Zerubbabel, the governor of Jerusalem under the Persian regime following the Exile (Ezra 3:2, Neh. 12:1; Hag. 1:1). First Chronicles 3:17 makes him Zerubbabel's uncle. This could involve the practice of Levirate marriage (Deut. 25:5–10). He was included in the genealogy of Christ (Matt. 1:12; Luke 3:27).

SHEARIAH (Shē å rī′ ah) Personal name perhaps meaning, "Yah has honored" or "Yah knows." Descendant of Saul (1 Chron. 8:38).

SHEARING HOUSE KJV translation (2 Kings 10:12,14) of what many modern translators take as place name. See *Beth-Eked.* REB reads, "shepherds' shelter."

SHEARJASHUB (Shē′ är jā′ shŭb) Symbolic personal name meaning, "a remnant shall return." First son of the prophet Isaiah, born probably around 737 B.C., near the beginning of his father's ministry in Jerusalem. Isaiah apparently named him (and his brother, Mahershalalhashbaz) as an embodiment of prophecy, that Judah would fall, but a remnant would survive. On one occasion, Shearjashub accompanied his father on a trip to assure King Ahaz that the alliance of Syria and Israel would not be allowed to harm Judah (Isa. 7:3–7). See *Isaiah.*

SHEATH Protective holder for sword attached to a belt. See *Arms and Armor; Sword.*

SHEBA (Shē′ bà) *1.* See *Sabeans. 2.* Personal name meaning, "fullness, completeness." Name of a Benjaminite who led a revolt against David (2 Sam. 20) and of a member of the tribe of Gad (1 Chron. 5:13). *3.* Personal name spelled in Hebrew like the nation of *1.* above. The name of a son of Joktan (Gen. 10:28) and of Jokshan (Gen. 25:3).

SHEBAH (Shē′ băh) Place name meaning, "overflow" or "oath." Name Isaac gave Beer-sheba (Gen. 26:33). See *Beer-Sheba.*

SHEBAM (Shē′ băm) KJV spelling for *Sebam.*

SHEBANIAH (Shĕ bà nī′ ah) Personal name appearing in short and long form in Hebrew meaning, "Yahweh came near." A clan of Levites in which the name was used for several individuals (1 Chron. 15:24; Neh. 9:4–5; 10:4,10,12; 12:14).

SHEBARIM (Shĕ′ bà rĭm) Place name meaning, "The Breaking Points." Place with symbolic name and uncertain location near Ai (Josh. 7:5), translated as "stone quarries" (NIV; compare REB). Commentators have suggested, "Breaks" or "Ravines."

SHEBAT (Shē′ băt) Modern translations' spelling for Sebat.

SHEBER (Shē′ bēr) Personal name perhaps meaning, "foolish one," "lion," or "fracture." Son of Caleb (1 Chron. 2:48).

SHEBNA(H) (Shĕb′ nah) Personal name meaning, "He came near." Royal scribe (2 Kings 18:18,37; 19:2; Isa. 36:3,22; 37:2) and "comptroller of the household" (Isa. 22:15 REB) under King Hezekiah about 715 B.C. See *Scribe.*

SHEBUEL (Shē′ bū ĕl) Personal name meaning, "Return, O God." *1.* Grandson of Moses and head of a clan of Levites (1 Chron. 23:16; 26:24; sometimes equated with Shubael of 1 Chron.

24:20). *2.* Levite, son of Heman (1 Chron. 25:4); apparently the same as Shubael (1 Chron. 25:20).

SHECANIAH (Shĕ cà nī′ ah) Personal name meaning, "Yahweh has taken up dwelling." Both long and short forms appear in the Hebrew text. *1.* Clan leader (Ezra 8:3). *2.* Leader of another clan (Ezra 8:5). *3.* Israelite with a foreign wife (Ezra 10:2). *4.* Father of man who helped Nehemiah repair Jerusalem wall and keeper of the east gate (Neh. 3:29). *5.* Father-in-law of Nehemiah's enemy, Tobiah (Neh. 6:18). *6.* Priest who returned to Jerusalem with Zerubbabel about 537 B.C. (Neh. 12:3). *7.* Descendant of David and Zerubbabel (1 Chron. 3:21). *8.* Leader of priestly division under David (1 Chron. 24:11; may be equated with founder of priestly clan of Neh. 10:4; 12:14 where spelling is Shebaniah). *9.* Priest in time of Hezekiah (2 Chron. 31:15).

SHECHANIAH (Shĕch à nī′ ah) Abbreviated Hebrew form of personal name, Shecaniah.

SHECHEM (Shĕ′ chēm) Personal and place name meaning, "shoulder, back." *1.* District and city in the hill country of Ephraim in north central Palestine. The first capital of the northern kingdom of Israel, the city was built mainly on the slope, or shoulder, of Mount Ebal. Situated where main highways and ancient trade routes converged, Shechem was an important city long before the Israelites occupied Canaan.

The city makes its earliest appearance in biblical history in connection with Abram's arrival in the land (Gen. 12:6–7). When Jacob returned from Paddan Aram, he settled down at Shechem and purchased land from the sons of Hamor (33:18–19). In Genesis 33—34, Shechem was the name of the city and also of the prince of the city. While Jacob was at Shechem, the unfortunate incident of Dinah occurred. Simeon and Levi, her full brothers, destroyed the city (Gen. 34). Later, the brothers of Joseph were herding Jacob's flock at Shechem when Joseph was sent to check on their welfare. Joseph was buried in the plot of

A view of the ruins at the site of ancient Shechem.

ground that his father Jacob had purchased here (Josh. 24:32).

As the Israelites conquered Canaan, they turned unexpectedly to Shechem. Joshua built an altar on Mount Ebal and led the people in its building, renewing their commitment to the law of Moses (Josh. 8:30–35; compare Deut. 27:12–13). Shechem lay in the tribal territory of Ephraim near their border with Manasseh (Josh. 17:7). It was a city of refuge (Josh. 20:7) and a Levitical city (21:21). See *Cities of Refuge; Levitical Cities.* Joshua led Israel to renew its covenant with God there (Josh. 24:1–17). Gideon's son Abimelech fought the leaders of Shechem (Judg. 8:31—9:49).

Rehoboam, successor to King Solomon, went to Shechem to be crowned king over all Israel (1 Kings 12:1). Later, when the nation divided into two kingdoms, Shechem became the first capital of the Northern Kingdom of Israel (1 Kings 12:25). Samaria eventually became the permanent political capital of the Northern Kingdom, but Shechem retained its religious importance. It apparently was a sanctuary for worship of God in Hosea's time about 750 B.C. (6:9).

The name Shechem occurs in historical records and other sources outside Palestine. It is mentioned as a city captured by Senusert III of Egypt (before 1800 B.C.) and appears in the Egyptian cursing texts of about the same time. "The mountain of Shechem" is referred to in a satirical letter of the Nineteenth Dynasty of Egypt. Shechem also figures in the Amarna Letters; its ruler, Lab'ayu, and his sons were accused of acting against Egypt, though the ruler protested that he was absolutely loyal to the pharaoh.

At Shechem (sometimes identified with Sychar), Jesus visited with the Samaritan woman at Jacob's Well (John 4). The Samaritans had built their temple on Mount Gerizim, where they practiced their form of religion. *Rich Murrell*

SHECHEMITE (Shĕ′ chêm īte) Resident of or native of Shechem.

SHEDEUR (Shĕ′ dė ŭr) Dialectical spelling (pronunciation) of a personal name meaning, "Shaddai is light." Father of a leader of the tribe of Reuben (Num. 1:5; 2:10; 7:30,35; 10:18).

SHEEP Animals important to the economy of ancient Israel and her neighbors. Translation of seven different Hebrew words and expressions. *Ts'on* is a collective term for small domesticated animals, particularly sheep and goats. *Seh* is an individual member of the collective *ts'on,* one sheep or goat. *Kebes* is a young ram, as is the apparently related word *keseb. Kibsah* and *kisbah* are young lambs. *Tsoneh* is either a variant spelling of or the feminine of *Ts'on. Rachel* is the mother sheep. The male sheep or ram is *'ayil,* which served as a symbol of authority and rule

Asian sheep grazing on the site of what was once a part of the ancient city of Laodicea.

(Ex. 15:15; Ezek. 17:13; 31:11). Sheep symbolized people without leadership and unity, scattered like sheep without a shepherd (1 Kings 22:17), innocent people not deserving of punishment (1 Chron. 21:17), as helpless facing slaughter (Ps. 44:11,22) and death (Ps. 49:14). God's people are His sheep enjoying His protection and listening to His voice (Pss. 78:52; 95:7; 100:3; compare Ps. 23). Sheep represent economic prosperity (Ps. 144:13) or poverty (Isa. 7:21). Straying sheep illustrate human sin (Isa. 53:6), but the silent lamb at the slaughter prepares the way for Christ's sacrifice (Isa. 53:7). Ezekiel 34 uses the life of sheep and shepherds to picture God's relationship with His people and their rulers. Human value is contrasted to that of sheep (Matt. 12:12). The shepherd's separating his *ts'on* into sheep and goats illustrates the final judgment (Matt. 25). The search for one lost sheep depicts God's love for His people (Luke 15). Jesus contrasted His care for His flock with other religious leaders, especially the Pharisees who behaved as thieves and robbers (John 10). His commission to Peter was to take care of the sheep (John 21). See *Agriculture; Cattle; Economic Life.* *Trent C. Butler*

SHEEP BREEDER See *Herdsman.*

SHEEP GATE Entrance in northeastern corner of Jerusalem's city wall (Neh. 3:1,32; 12:39). Apparently, sheep for Temple sacrifice entered the city through it. It was close to the Pool of Bethesda (John 5:2).

SHEEP MARKET KJV translation of Greek term meaning, "pertaining to sheep" and referring to the Sheep Gate (John 5:2). See *Sheep Gate.*

SHEEPCOTE KJV translation of Hebrew term meaning, "home." Modern translations usually use "pasture" as the sheep's home (2 Sam. 7:8; 1 Chron. 17:7). In 1 Samuel 24:3 the Hebrew term refers to an enclosure and is usually translated "sheepfolds" or "sheep pens."

SHEEPFOLD English translation of several Hebrew and one Greek term referring to a place where sheep were kept. The basic meanings range from stone wall, to place of confinement, and home. Related words appearing in Genesis 49:14; Judges 5:16; Ezekiel 40:43; and Psalm 68:13 are variously interpreted from the context and translated: "saddlebags," "double-pronged hooks," and "campfires" (NIV), "sheepfolds" and "pegs" (NRSV), "sheepfolds" and "double hooks" (NAS), "cattle pens," "sheepfolds," and "rims" (REB), "burdens," "sheepfolds," "pots," and "hooks" (KJV), "saddlebags," "sheep," "sheep pens," and "ledges" (TEV). The latest Hebrew dictionary completed in 1990 but published in parts over two decades gives differing meanings for the two related terms: "saddlebags" and "sheepfolds," separating the Ezekiel passage out as a meaning unto itself.

SHEEPSHEARERS Persons who cut wool from the sheep. Evidently, these are not professionals but the owners of the sheep (Gen. 31:19) or persons working for the owner (Gen. 38:12). The Hebrew does not distinguish between "sheepshearers" and "sheepshearing," so that both translations are possible in several passages. The time of shearing sheep was a festive time of parties and inviting friends (1 Sam. 25; 2 Sam. 13). The word for shearing sheep was also used for cutting human hair (Jer. 7:29; Mic. 1:16).

SHEERAH (Shē' ē rah) Personal name perhaps meaning, "blood kin." Female member of tribe of Ephraim who established the two cities of Beth-horon as well as Uzzen-sherah (1 Chron. 7:24).

SHEET English translation of Greek word meaning, "a linen cloth" and usually used for ships' sails. Such a cloth held all the clean and unclean animals in the vision that taught Peter that God loved and offered salvation to people who were not Jews (Acts 10:11; 11:5).

SHEHARIAH (Shē hȧ rī' ah) Personal name meaning, "Yah is the dawn." Leader of tribe of Benjamin who lived in Jerusalem (1 Chron. 8:26).

SHEKEL (Shě' kěl) Hebrew weight of about four tenths of an ounce. This became the name of a silver coin with that weight. See *Coins; Weights and Measures.*

SHEKINAH (Shě kī' năh) Transliteration of Hebrew word not found in the Bible but used in many of the Jewish writings to speak of God's presence. The term means "that which dwells," and is implied through out the Bible whenever it refers to God's nearness either in a person, object, or His glory. It is often used in combination with glory to speak of the presence of God's shekinah glory. See *Glory.*

SHELAH (Shē' lah) Personal name meaning, "please" or "be still, rest." Son of Judah and original ancestor of clan in tribe of Judah (Gen. 46:12; Num. 26:20; 1 Chron. 2:3; 4:21). At times Shelah is the transliteration for the Hebrew name otherwise transliterated Salah. See *Salah.*

SHELANITE (Shě' lȧ nīte) Member of clan of Shelah.

SHELEMIAH (Shě lě mī' ah) Personal name appearing in longer and shorter Hebrew forms meaning, "Yahweh restored, replaced, repaid." *1.* Father of a messenger of King Zedekiah about 590 B.C. (Jer. 37:3). *2.* Father of the captain of the guard who arrested Jeremiah (Jer. 37:13). *3.* Ancestor of an official of King Jehoiakim (Jer. 36:14). *4.* Court official whom King Jehoiakim (609–597 B.C.) ordered to arrest Jeremiah and from whom God hid Jeremiah (Jer. 36:26). *5.* Temple gatekeeper (1 Chron. 26:14) and apparently called Meshelemiah in 1 Chronicles 26:1,9. *6.* and *7.* Two Jews who married foreign women (Ezra 10:39,41). *8.* Father of man who helped Nehemiah rebuild Jerusalem's wall (Neh. 3:30). *9.* Priest whom Nehemiah made treasurer (Neh. 13:13).

SHELEPH (Shē' lěph) Tribal name perhaps meaning, "remove, take out of." Son of Joktan and original ancestor of Yemenite tribes living near Aden (Gen. 10:26).

SHELESH (Shē' lěsh) Personal name perhaps meaning, "triplet." Leader of a clan in the tribe of Asher (1 Chron. 7:35).

SHELOMI (Shě lō' mī) Personal name meaning, "my peace." Father of a leader of tribe of Asher (Num. 34:27).

SHELOMITH (Shě lō' mǐth) Feminine form of Shelomoth. *1.* Head of a family which returned from Babylonian Exile with Ezra about 458 B.C. (Ezra 8:10). *2.* Son of King Rehoboam (2 Chron. 11:20). *3.* Cousin of Moses and head of a Levitical group (1 Chron. 23:18); apparently the same as Shelomoth (1 Chron. 24:22). *4.* Priest over the cultic treasury under David (1 Chron. 26:25–28, where Hebrew scribes have interchanged Shelomith and Shelomoth). *5.* Woman of tribe of Dan whose son cursed the divine name, thus being guilty of blasphemy. The Israelites followed God's orders and stoned him to death (Lev. 24:10–23). *6.* Daughter of Zerubbabel (1 Chron. 3:19).

SHELOMOTH (Shě lō' mǒth) Personal name meaning, "peaces." See *Shelomith.* Levitical leader under David (1 Chron. 23:9; Hebrew scribal note has Shelomith).

SHELUMIEL (Shě lū′ mĭ ĕl) Personal name meaning, "God is my wholeness or health." Leader in tribe of Simeon (Num. 1:6; 2:12; 7:36,41; 10:19).

SHEM (Shĕm) Personal name meaning, "name." Noah's oldest son and original ancestor of Semitic peoples including Israel (Gen. 5:32; 6:10; 7:13; 9:18–27; 10:1,21–22,31; 11:10–11). He carried God's blessing (9:26–27). Through his line came Abraham and the covenant of blessing.

SHEMA (Shē′ mä) Transliteration of Hebrew imperative meaning, "Hear," (Deut 6:4) and applied to 6:4–9, as the basic statement of the Jewish law. The Shema became for the people of God a confession of faith by which they acknowledged the one true God and His commandments for them. Later worship practice combined Deuteronomy 6:4–9; 11:13–21; Numbers 15:37–41 into the larger Shema as the summary of Jewish confession. When Jesus was asked about the "greatest commandment," He answered by quoting the Shema (Mark 12:29).

SHEMA (Shē′ mä) Personal name meaning, "a hearing" and place name perhaps meaning, "hyena." *1.* Son of Hebron and grandson of Caleb (1 Chron. 2:43). *2.* Member and clan ancestor of tribe of Reuben(1 Chron. 5:8); possibly the same as Shemaiah (1 Chron. 5:4). *3.* Benjaminite clan leader in Aijalon (1 Chron. 8:13); apparently the same as Shimhi (1 Chron. 8:21). *4.* Man who helped Ezra teach the law (Neh. 8:4). *5.* Town in tribal territory of Judah (Josh. 15:26) and apparently occupied by Simeon (Josh. 19:2; Sheba may be a scribe's repetition of previous word instead of similar sounding Shema). It may be the same as Jeshua (Neh. 11:26). See *Jeshua 9.*

SHEMAAH (Shě mā′ ah) Personal name perhaps meaning, "a hearing." Father of Benjaminite military leaders who deserted Saul to join David at Ziklag (1 Chron. 12:3).

SHEMAIAH (Shě māī′ ah) Personal name meaning, "Yahweh heard," with both long and short forms in Hebrew. *1.* A prophet in the days of Rehoboam whose message from God prevented war between Israel and Judah about 930 B.C. (1 Kings 12:22). His preaching humbled Rehoboam and the leaders of Judah, leading God not to permit Shishak of Egypt to destroy Jerusalem (2 Chron. 12). *2.* False prophet among Babylonian Exiles who opposed Jeremiah's word (Jer. 29:24–32). *3.* Descendant of David and Zerubbabel (1 Chron. 3:22). *4.* Member of tribe of Simeon (1 Chron. 4:37). *5.* Member of tribe of Reuben (1 Chron. 5:4); perhaps identical with *Shema 2.* (1 Chron. 5:8). *6.* A Levite (Neh. 11:15; compare 1 Chron. 9:14). *7.* A Levite (1 Chron. 9:16) probably identical with *Shammua 3.* (Neh. 11:17). *8.* Head of one of the six Levitical

families under David (1 Chron. 15:8,11). *9.* Levitical scribe who recorded the priestly divisions under David (1 Chron. 24:6). *10.* Head of an important family of gatekeepers (1 Chron. 24:4–8). *11.* Levite in time of Hezekiah about 715 B.C. (2 Chron. 29:14); possibly identical with the Levite of 2 Chronicles 31:15. *12.* Head of a family that returned with Ezra from Babylonian Exile about 458 B.C. (Ezra 8:13). He may be the same man Ezra sent to get more ministers for the Temple (Ezra 8:16). *13.* Priest married to a foreign woman (Ezra 10:21). *14.* Man married to a foreign woman (Ezra 10:31). *15.* Keeper of east gate who helped Nehemiah repair Jerusalem's wall about 445 B.C. (Neh. 3:29). *16.* Prophet Tobiah and Sanballat hired against Nehemiah (Neh. 6:10–12). *17.* Original ancestor of a priestly family (Neh. 10:8; 12:6,18). *18.* Leader of Judah who participated with Nehemiah in dedicating the rebuilt walls of Jerusalem (Neh. 12:34). *19.* Priest who helped Nehemiah dedicate the walls (Neh. 12:42). *20.* Priest whose grandson helped Nehemiah dedicate the walls (Neh. 12:35). *21.* Levitical musician who helped Nehemiah dedicate the walls (Neh. 12:36). *22.* Father of the prophet Urijah (Jer. 26:20). *23.* Father of an official at Jehoikim's court about 600 B.C. (Jer. 36:12). *24.* Levite in days of Jehoshaphat (873–848 B.C.) who taught God's law to the people (2 Chron. 17:8). *25.* Levite in days of Josiah about 621 B.C. (2 Chron. 35:9).

SHEMARIAH (Shě mȧ rī′ ah) Personal name in longer and shorter Hebrew forms meaning, "Yahweh protected." *1.* Benjaminite who deserted Saul to join David's army at Ziklag (1 Chron. 12:5). *2.* Son of King Rehoboam (2 Chron. 11:19). *3.* and *4.* Men with foreign wives under Ezra (Ezra 10:32,41).

SHEMEBER (Shě mē′ ber) Royal name meaning, "powerful name." King of Zeboiim who rebelled against Chedorlaomer, leading to Abraham's rescue mission of Lot (Gen. 14:2). The Genesis Apocryphon and Samaritan Pentateuch read his name as Shemiabad, "the name is lost." See *Zeboiim.*

SHEMED (Shē′ mĕd) Personal name meaning, "destruction." Benjaminite credited with building or rebuilding Ono and Lod (1 Chron. 8:12).

SHEMER (Shē′ mĕr) Personal name meaning, "protection, preservation." *1.* Modern translations' spelling of Shamer, the father of a Temple musician under David (1 Chron. 6:46). *2.* Head of clan of tribe of Asher (1 Chron. 7:34) with variant spelling Shomer (v. 32). *3.* Original owner of the mount of Samaria for whom Samaria was named (1 Kings 16:24). See *Samaria.*

S

SHEMIDA(H) (Shḗ mī′ da) Personal name meaning, "The Name has known" or "The Name troubles Himself for." Clan head among the Gileadites in tribe of Manasseh (Num. 26:32; compare Josh. 17:2; 1 Chron. 7:19). The Samaritan Ostraca lists Shemida as a territorial name in territory of Manasseh.

SHEMIDAITE (Shḗ mī′ dà īte) Member of clan of Shemida.

SHEMINITH (Shĕ′ mī nĭth) Musical direction meaning, "the eighth" used in titles of Psalms 6; 12 and in 1 Chronicles 15:21. It may mean on an eight-stringed instrument; on the eighth string of an instrument; on a deeper octave than the Alamoth (1 Chron. 15:20); for the eighth and concluding rite of the fall new year festival; or refer to the tuning of the instrument or the scale of the melody.

SHEMIRAMOTH (Shḗ mīr′ à mŏth) Personal name of uncertain meaning. *1.* Temple Levitical musician in David's time (1 Chron. 15:18,20; 16:5). *2.* Levite under King Jehoshaphat (873–848 B.C.), who taught the law (2 Chron. 17:8).

SHEMUEL (Shḗ mū′ ĕl) Personal name meaning, "Sumu is god," "The Name is God," "God is exalted," or "Son of God." *1.* Precise transliteration of Hebrew for Samuel. See *Samuel.* *2.* Leader of tribe of Simeon (Num. 34:20). *3.* Clan chief in tribe of Issachar (1 Chron. 7:2).

SHEN (Shĕn) Place name meaning, "the tooth." Locality used to locate Eben-ezer (1 Sam. 7:12), translated and interpreted variously since the earliest translations. It may refer to a prominent hill or mountain shaped like a tooth. Early translations read it as "Jeshanah" (REB, NRSV), but that appears to be too far east for the context. Some early translators read, "Beth-shan." The exact location is debated and uncertain.

SHENA(Z)ZAR (Shḗ nā′ zär) Babylonian personal name meaning, "Sin (a god) protects" or "may Sin protect." Son of King Jehoiachin (1 Chron. 3:18). He is often identified with Sheshbazzar as an alternate transliteration of a Babylonian name, but this has been denied recently.

SHENIR (Shē′ nīr) KJV alternate spelling of Senir (Deut. 3:9; Song of Sol. 4:8).

SHEOL The abode of the dead in Hebrew thought. Sheol was thought to be deep within the earth (Ps. 88:6; Ezek. 26:20; 31:14–15; Amos 9:2) and was entered by crossing a river (Job 33:18). Sheol is pictured as a city with gates (Isa. 38:10), a place of ruins (Ezek. 26:20), or a trap (2 Sam. 22:6; Ps. 18:5). Sheol is sometimes personified as a hungry beast (Pr. 27:20; Isa. 5:14; Hab. 2:5) with an open mouth and an insatiable appetite. Sheol is described as a place of dust (Ps. 30:9; Job 17:16) and of gloom and darkness (Job. 10:21).

The Hebrews conceived of the individual as a unity of body and spirit. Thus it was impossible for the dead whose bodies had decayed (Ps. 49:14) to experience more than a marginal existence. Various terms are used by English translators to describe the residents of Sheol (Job 26:5; Isa. 14:9), including shades (NRSV, REB), spirits of the dead (TEV), or simply, the dead (KJV). The dead experience no remembrance (Pss. 6:5; 88:12), no thought (Eccl. 9:10), no speech (Pss. 31:17; 94:17), especially no words of praise (Pss. 6:5; 30:9), and no work (Eccl. 9:10). Such existence is fittingly described as sleep (Isa. 14:9). For the dead Sheol is a place of pain and distress (Ps. 116:3), weakness (Isa. 14:10), helplessness (Ps. 88:4); hopelessness (Isa. 38:10), and destruction (Isa. 38:17).

Sheol was regarded as the abode of all the dead, both righteous and wicked (Job 30:23). It was, in fact, regarded as a consolation that none escaped death (Ps. 49:10–12; Ezek. 31:16). Only once does the Old Testament speak of Sheol specifically as the abode of the wicked (Ps. 9:17). Some earthly distinctions were regarded as continuing in Sheol. Thus kings have thrones (Isa. 14:9); and warriors possess weapons and shields (Ezek. 32:27). Here the biblical writers possibly mocked the views of their neighbors. Ezekiel 32:18–30 pictures the dead as grouped by nation with the crucial distinction between the circumcised and uncircumcised continuing in the grave.

To go to Sheol alive was regarded as a punishment for exceptional wickedness (Ps. 55:15; Num. 16:30,33 where the earth swallowed Korah and his band alive). Job 24:19 speaks of Sheol snatching sinners. The righteous, wise, and well-disciplined could avoid a premature move to Sheol (Pr. 15:24; 23:14).

Though the overall picture of Sheol is grim, the Old Testament nevertheless affirms that God is there (Ps. 139:8; Prov. 15:11) or that it is impossible to hide from God in Sheol (Job 26:6; Amos 9:2). The Old Testament also affirms that God has power over Sheol and is capable of ransoming souls from its depths (Pss. 16:10; 30:3; 49:15; 86:13; Job 33:18,28–30). In the majority of these passages a restoration to physical life is clearly intended, though several (for example Ps. 49:15 with its image of God's receiving the one ransomed from Sheol) point the way toward the Christian understanding of afterlife with God. See *Death; Eschatology; Future Hope; Hell.*

Chris Church

SHEPHAM (Shē′ phăm) Place name of uncertain meaning and location in northeastern Transjordan forming the northeastern border of the Promised Land (Num. 34:10).

SHEPHATIAH (Shĕ phȧ tī′ ah) Personal name in longer and shorter Hebrew forms meaning, "Yahweh has created justice." *1.* David's fifth son (2 Sam. 3:4). *2.* King Zedekiah's (597–586 B.C.) official (Jer. 38:1). *3.* A Benjaminite (1 Chron. 9:8). *4.* Head of a family of Exiles who returned with Ezra about 458 B.C. (Ezra 2:4; 8:8; Neh. 7:9). *5.* Ancestor of family included among "Solomon's servants," that is royal officials, perhaps with Temple responsibilities (Ezra 2:57; Neh. 7:59). *6.* Member of tribe of Judah (Neh. 11:4). *7.* Benjaminite who deserted Saul to join David's army at Ziklag (1 Chron. 12:5). *8.* Leader of tribe of Simeon under David (1 Chron. 27:16). *9.* Son of King Jehoshaphat (2 Chron. 21:2).

SHEPHELAH (Shĕ′ phȧ läh) Transliteration of Hebrew geographical term meaning, "lowland." Region of low foothills between the Philistine coastal plain and the highlands of Judah farther inland. It served as a battleground for Israel and Philistia during the period of the judges and early monarchy. Joshua 15:33–41 lists about thirty villages and towns located in the region. See *Palestine.*

SHEPHER, MOUNT (Shĕ′ phēr) Place name perhaps meaning, "beauty." Stop on Israel's wilderness journey whose location is not known (Num. 33:23).

SHEPHERD A keeper of sheep. The first keeper of sheep in the Bible was Adam's son Abel (Gen. 4:2). Shepherding was the chief occupation of the Israelites in the early days of the patriarchs: Abraham (Gen. 12:16); Rachel (Gen. 29:9); Jacob (Gen. 30:31–40); Moses (Ex. 3:1).

As cultivation of crops increased, shepherding fell from favor and was assigned to younger sons, hirelings, and slaves (compare David in 1 Sam. 16:11–13). Farmers such as in Egypt even hated shepherds (Gen. 46:34).

The Bible mentions shepherds and shepherding over 200 times. However, the Hebrew word for shepherding is often translated, "feeding." Shepherds led sheep to pasture and water (Ps. 23) and protected them from wild animals (1 Sam. 17:34–35). Shepherds guarded their flocks at night whether in the open (Luke 2:8) or in sheepfolds (Zeph. 2:6) where they counted the sheep as they entered (Jer. 33:13). They took care of the sheep and even carried weak lambs in their arms (Isa. 40:11).

Shepherd came to designate not only persons who herded sheep but also kings (2 Sam. 5:2) and God Himself (Ps. 23; Isa. 40:11). Later prophets referred to Israel's leaders as shepherds (Jer. 23; Ezek. 34).

In Bible times the sheep cared for by shepherds represented wealth. They provided food (1 Sam. 14:32), milk to drink (Isa. 7:21–22), wool for clothing (Job 31:20), hides for rough clothing (Matt. 7:15), and leather for tents (Ex. 26:14). Furthermore, sheep were major offerings in the sacrificial system (Ex. 20:24). They were offered as burnt offerings (Lev. 1:10), sin offerings (Lev. 4:32), guilt offerings (Lev. 5:15), and peace offerings (Lev. 22:21).

The New Testament mentions shepherds 16 times. They were among the first to visit Jesus at His birth (Luke 2:8–20). Some New Testament references used a shepherd and the sheep to illustrate Christ's relationship to His followers who referred to Him as "our Lord Jesus, that great shepherd of the sheep" (Heb. 13:20). Jesus spoke of Himself as "the good shepherd" who knew His sheep and would lay down His life for them (John 10:7–18). Jesus commissioned Peter to feed His sheep (John 21). Paul likened the church and its leaders to a flock with shepherds (Acts 20:28). The Latin word transliterated "pastor" means shepherd.   *Elmer Gray*

SHEPHERD'S BAG See *Bag 4.*

SHEPHI (Shē′ phī) Variant spelling of Shepho (1 Chron. 1:40).

SHEPHO (Shē′ phō) Tribal name perhaps meaning, "male sheep, ram." Edomite tribe or clan (Gen. 36:23).

SHEPHUPHAM (Shĕ phū′ phăm) Personal name of uncertain meaning. Leader of Benjaminite clan according to Hebrew text (Num. 26:39) but probably a scribe repeated a letter in Shupham (KJV, REB, NIV).

SHEPHUPHAN (Shĕ phū′ phăn) Personal name of uncertain meaning. Member of tribe of Benjamin (1 Chron. 8:5). Some commentators read, "Shupham" on basis of early translations.

SHERAH (Shē′ rah) REB, KJV spelling of Sheerah.

SHERD Alternate spelling for shard often used by archaeologists. See *Shard.*

SHEREBIAH (Shĕ rē bī′ ah) Personal name of uncertain meaning: "Yah gave a new generation," "Yah understands," or "Yah made it hot." Ancestor of a family of Levites (Ezra 8:18,24; Neh. 8:7; 9:4,5; 10:12; 12:8,24). He had responsibility for the Temple gold Ezra took back to Jerusalem from Exile and helped Ezra teach the people the law.

SHERESH (Shē′ rĕsh) Personal name meaning, "sprout" or "sly, clever." Descendant of Manasseh (1 Chron. 7:16) as well as the name of a city in the kingdom of Ugarit.

SHEREZER (Shĕ rē′ zēr) KJV alternate spelling of Sharezer (Zech. 7:2).

SHESHACH (Shē' shăch) Code word Jeremiah used to indicate Babylon (25:26; 51:41). The code uses the first word of the alphabet for the last, the second for the next to last, and so on. In English *a* would stand for *z*, *b* for *y*, and so on.

SHESHAI (Shē' shâi) Probably a Hurrian name of uncertain meaning. A man or clan living near Hebron descended from the Anakim (Num. 13:22) and driven out by Caleb (Josh. 15:14) and the tribe of Judah (Judg. 1:10). See *Anak, Anakim.* They may have entered Palestine with the Sea Peoples to whom the Philistines are related.

SHESHAK (Shē' shăk) NAS spelling of Sheshach (Jer. 51:41).

SHESHAN (Shē' shăn) Personal name of uncertain meaning. Member of clan of Jerahmeel from tribe of Judah (1 Chron. 2:31–35).

SHESHBAZZAR (Shĕsh' băz' zàr) Babylonian name probably meaning, "may Shamash (sun god) protect the father." Jewish leader who accompanied the first group of Exiles from Babylon to Jerusalem in 538 BC (Ezra 1:8). King Cyrus of Persia apparently appointed Sheshbazzar governor of restored Judah and supplied his company of people with provisions and many of the treasures which the Babylonians had taken from Jerusalem. He attempted to rebuild the Temple (Ezra 5:16), but got no farther than the foundation when he was replaced by Zerubbabel. His genealogy is not clear, but some believe the Shenazar of 1 Chronicles 3:17 may be Sheshbazzar. If so, he was a son of Jehoiachin and uncle of Zerubbabel.

SHETH (Shĕth) Personal and tribal name of uncertain meaning. Moabite clan whose destruction Balaam prophesied (Num. 24:17). The Hebrew spelling is the same as Seth (Gen. 4:25). Egyptian and Babylonian texts point to a people called Sutu, semi-nomads in the Syrian and Arabian desert. Rather than a proper name, some commentators think the translation should be, "sons of tumult."

SHETHAR (Shē' thär) Persian name of uncertain meaning. Advisor of King Ahasuerus of Persia, an expert in the "law and custom" of Persia and possibly in astrology (Esth. 1:13–14 NRSV).

SHETHAR-BOZENAI (Shē' thär-Bŏz' ĕ nâi) Persian name perhaps meaning, "Mithra is deliverer." Persian provincial official who questioned Zerubbabel's right to begin rebuilding the Temple (Ezra 5:3,6) but responded to King Darius' answer by helping the Jews build (Ezra 6:13). The name appears in the Elephantine papyri.

Shepherd in Israel tending his flock of sheep.

SHETHAR-BOZNAI KJV spelling of Shethar-Bozenai.

SHETHITES (Shĕth' ītes) NRSV reading of "sons of Sheth" (Num. 24:17). See *Sheth.*

SHEVA (Shē' và) Personal name meaning, "similarity." *1.* Scribe for David (2 Sam. 20:25), perhaps the transliteration of an Egyptian title meaning, "writer of letters." The name is Seraiah in 2 Samuel 8:17; Shavsha in 1 Chronicles 18:16. See *Scribe. 2.* Descendant of Caleb and original ancestor of a clan (1 Chron. 2:49).

SHEWBREAD A sacred loaf made probably of barley or wheat which was set before the Lord as a continual sacrifice (Ex. 25:30). The old bread was then eaten by the priests (Lev. 24:5–9). David requested the bread for his hungry men as they fled from King Saul (1 Sam. 21:4–6). Jesus used this account to illustrate His teaching on the sabbath, that the day was made to benefit people (Mark 2:23–28). See *Bread of the Presence.*

SHIBAH (Shĭ' bah) Modern translation spelling of Sheba (Gen. 26:33).

SHIBBOLETH (Shĭb' bō lĕth) Transliteration of Hebrew password meaning, "ears, twigs" or "brook." People of Gilead east of the Jordan used it to detect people of Ephraim from west of the Jordan since the Ephraimite dialect evidently did not include the *sh* sound, so Ephraimites always said, "sibboleth," a word not used elsewhere in Hebrew (Judg. 12:6).

SHIBMAH (Shĭb' mah) KJV alternate spelling of Sibmah (Num. 32:38).

SHICRON (Shĭc' rŏn) Place name meaning, "henbane" (a type of nightshade plant). Border town of tribe of Judah (Josh. 15:11). It may be located at tell el-Ful north of the Soreq River and three and a half miles northwest of Ekron.

SHIELD Protective devise used in battle. See *Arms and Armor.*

SHIGGAION (Shĭg ḡai' ŏn) Transliteration of a Hebrew technical term used in psalm titles (Ps. 7; Hab. 3). Suggested translations include, "frenzied" or "emotional." Some think the basic meaning is "to wander" in reference to a wandering style of thought or melody or to the unconnected expressions of a lament.

SHIGIONOTH Hebrew plural of Shiggaion. See *Shiggaion.*

SHIHON (Shĭ' hŏn) Place name of uncertain meaning, perhaps "worthless." Some would locate it at modern Sirim, about thirteen miles southeast of Mount Tabor. It was a border town of Issachar (Josh. 19:19).

SHIHOR (Shī′ hôr) Egyptian place name meaning, "pool of Horus (a god)." It formed the border of the Promised Land (Josh. 13:3), marking the widest extent of Israel's territorial claims (1 Chron. 13:5). In Isaiah 23:3; Jeremiah 2:18, the term apparently refers to one of the branches of the Nile River inside Egypt, but the border point places it outside Egypt, identical with the Brook of Egypt or extending Israel's claim to the Nile. See *Brook of Egypt; Palestine.* The earliest translators did not understand the term in Joshua 13.

SHIHOR-LIBNATH (Shī′ hôr-lĭb′ năth) Place name perhaps meaning, "swamp of Libnath." Border of tribal territory of Asher (Josh. 19:26), variously identified as the Nahr ez-Zerqa on the southern border of Asher; the swampy territory between the rivers Nahr ed-Difleh and Nahr ez-Zerqa, and tell Abu Hawam at the mouth of the Kishon.

SHIKKERON (Shĭk′ kē rŏn) Modern translations' spelling of Shicron (Josh. 15:11).

SHILHI (Shĭl′ hī) Personal name meaning, "He sent me," "Salach (underworld god or river) has me," or "my offshoot." A similar formation has

Ruins of an ancient synagogue at the site of the city of Shiloh.

been found at tell Arad. Maternal grandfather of King Jehoshaphat (1 Kings 22:42).

SHILHIM (Shĭl′ hĭm) Alternative Hebrew spelling of Sharuhen. See *Sharuhen.*

SHILLEM (Shĭl′ lĕm) Personal name meaning, "he has replaced or repaid." Son of Naphtali and original ancestor of clan in that tribe (Gen. 46:24). First Chronicles 7:13 has "Shallum."

SHILLEMITE (Shĭl′ lĕm īte) Member of clan of Shillem (Num. 26:49).

SHILOAH, WATERS OF (Shī lō′ ah) Place name meaning, "being sent." Waters supplying Jerusalem diverted from the Gihon spring and representing God's supply making reliance on foreign kings unnecessary (Isa. 8:6). It differs from the Shiloah Tunnel Hezekiah built (2 Kings 20:20). The background may be anointing of kings at the Gihon (1 Kings 1:33–40), thus implying rejection of God's kingship represented through His anointed king.

SHILOH (Shī′ lōh) Place name perhaps meaning, "tranquil, secure." About thirty miles north of Jerusalem sat the city which would be Israel's religious center for over a century after the conquest, being the home of Israel's tabernacle (Josh. 18:1). See *Tabernacle.*

Judges 21:19 described Shiloh's location as "on the north side of Bethel, on the east side of the highway that goeth up from Bethel to Shechem,

and on the south of Lebonah." Twelve miles south of Shechem, Shiloh was in a fertile plain at 2,000 feet elevation. This is apparently modern Seilun, where archaeologists have unearthed evidence of Canaanite settlement by 1700 B.C. Perhaps when Israel chose a spot for the tabernacle, Shiloh was available for Joshua to use as the place to allot land to the tribes (Josh. 18).

Tribal annual pilgrimages to the tabernacle set the scene for another incident in Shiloh. The tribe of Benjamin had a dilemma in that no other tribe would give them their daughters for wives (Judg. 21). Because of this, the men of Benjamin waited in the vineyards (v. 20) until the dancing women went out of Shiloh where they were then captured and taken as wives.

Samuel's early years provided another connection with Shiloh (1 Sam. 1—4). At the tabernacle, Hannah vowed to the Lord that if He would give her a son she would give him back to God (1 Sam. 1). After the birth of Samuel, Hannah brought him to Shiloh in gratitude to God (1 Sam. 1:24–28). Thus, Shiloh became home for Samuel as he lived under the care of Eli, the high priest, and his two wicked sons, Hophni and Phinehas. Later, Samuel received the Lord's message that the priesthood would be taken from Eli's family (1 Sam. 3). Years later, following a defeat at Aphek, the Israelite army sent for the ark of the covenant from Shiloh. Mistakenly thinking that the ark would bring victory, the Israelites lost the second battle of Aphek to the Philistines. Results included losing the ark; the deaths of Hophni, Phinehas, and Eli; and the apparent conquering of Shiloh (1 Sam. 4).

No explicit biblical reference was made to Shiloh's final fate. According to archaeological evidence, Shiloh apparently was destroyed about 1050 B.C. by the Philistines. Supporting this was the fact that when the Philistines finally returned the ark of the covenant, it was housed at Kiriath-jearim rather than Shiloh (1 Sam. 7:1). Also, Jeremiah warned Jerusalem that it might suffer the same destructive fate as Shiloh (7:12).

Centuries later, Jeremiah used Shiloh and the tabernacle as illustrations to warn Jerusalem that it was not safe merely because it housed the Temple (7:12–14). Hearing the same message again, the people sought to kill Jeremiah (26:6–9). Jeremiah mentioned some men from Shiloh as late as 585 B.C. (41:5), indicating some occupation at that time. See *Joshua; Eli; Samuel.*

Larry McGraw

SHILONI (Shĭ lō´ nĭ) Transliteration of Hebrew for Shilonite, taken by KJV as personal name (Neh. 11:5).

SHILONITE (Shĭ´ lō nīte) Resident of or native of Shiloh.

SHILSHAH (Shĭl´ shäh) Personal name perhaps

meaning, "little triplet." Original ancestor of clan in tribe of Asher (1 Chron. 7:37).

SHIMEA (Shĭ mě´ ȧ) Personal name meaning, "hearing." *1.* Son of David (1 Chron. 3:5; spelled Shammuah in 2 Sam. 5:14). *2.* A Levite (1 Chron. 6:30). *3.* A Levite, ancestor of Asaph (1 Chron. 6:39). *4.* Older brother of David (1 Chron. 2:13; 20:7; spelled Shammah in 1 Sam. 16:9; 17:13). See *Shammah 2. 5.* See *Shimeam.*

SHIMEAH (Shĭ mě´ ah) Alternate Hebrew spelling of Shammah. See *Shammah 2.; Shimea 4.*

SHIMEAM (Shĭ mě´ ăm) Personal name perhaps meaning, "their hearing." Benjaminite who lived in Jerusalem (1 Chron. 9:38; spelled with an abbreviated form of Shimea at 1 Chron. 8:32).

SHIMEATH (Shĭ mě´ ăth) Personal name meaning, "hearing." Parent of court official who murdered King Joash about 796 B.C. (2 Kings 12:21). Second Chronicles 24:26 takes the apparently feminine form of the Hebrew name and identifies the parent as an Ammonite woman.

SHIMEATHITE (Shĭ mě´ ȧ thīte) Either a descendant of a person named Shimeath or, more likely, a native of the town of Shema (Josh. 15:26), perhaps settled by the clan of Shema (1 Chron. 2:43). See *Shema 1.* and *5.*

SHIMEI (Shĭ mě´ ī) Personal name meaning, "my being heard." *1.* Grandson of Levi and head of Levitical family (Ex. 6:17; Num. 3:18; compare 1 Chron. 6:42). *2.* A Levite (1 Chron. 23:9 if the text does not represent duplication in copying as some commentators suggest; compare v. 10). *3.* Relative of King Saul who cursed and opposed David as he fled from Absalom (2 Sam. 16). When David returned after Absalom's death, Shimei met him and pleaded for forgiveness and mercy, which David granted because of the festive occasion (2 Sam. 19). Solomon followed David's advice and had Shimei slain (1 Kings 2).

4. Court personality who refused to support Adonijah against Solomon (1 Kings 1:8). *5.* District supervisor in territory of Benjamin responsible for supplying Solomon's court one month each year (1 Kings 4:18); he could be identical with *4.* above. *6.* Ancestor of Mordecai, the cousin of Esther (Esth. 2:5). *7.* Brother of Zerubbabel (1 Chron. 3:19). *8.* Member of tribe of Simeon (1 Chron. 4:26). *9.* Member of tribe of Reuben (1 Chron. 5:4). *10.* A Levite (1 Chron. 6:29). *11.* A Benjaminite (1 Chron. 8:21; apparently identical with Shema in v. 13). *12.* Temple musician under David (1 Chron. 25:17; perhaps also in v. 3 with a Hebrew manuscript and some Greek manuscripts as in NRSV, REB, NAS, NIV, TEV . *13.* Supervisor of David's vineyards (1 Chron. 27:27).

14. and *15.* Two Levites under Hezekiah (2 Chron. 29:14; 31:12–13). *16.* Levite married to a foreign woman under Ezra (Ezra 10:23). *17.* and *18.* Two Jews married to foreign women under Ezra (Ezra 10:33,38).

SHIMEITES (Shĭ' mē ītes) Members of the clan descending from Shimei (Num. 3:21; Zech. 12:13).

SHIMEON (Shĭ' me̓ ōn) Alternate English transliteration of Hebrew Simeon. Israelite with foreign wife (Ezra 10:31).

SHIMHI (Shĭm' hī) Alternate English transliteration of Shimei (1 Chron. 8:21). See *Shimei 11.*

SHIMI (Shĭ' mī) KJV spelling of Shimei (Ex. 6:17). See *Shimei 1.*

SHIMITE (Shĭ' mīte) KJV spelling of Shimeites (Num. 3:21).

SHIMMA (Shĭm' ma) KJV spelling of Shimea (1 Chron. 2:13). See *Shimea 4.*

SHIMON (Shĭ' mŏn) Personal name of uncertain meaning. Original ancestor of clain in tribe of Judah (1 Chron. 4:20).

SHIMRATH (Shĭm' răth) Personal name meaning, "protection." Member of tribe of Benjamin (1 Chron. 8:21).

SHIMRI (Shĭm' rī) Personal name meaning, "my protection." *1.* Member of tribe of Simeon (1 Chron. 4:37). *2.* Father of one of David's military heroes (1 Chron. 11:45). *3.* Levitical gatekeeper (1 Chron. 26:10). *4.* Levite in time of Hezekiah (2 Chron. 29:13).

SHIMRITH (Shĭm' rĭth) Personal name meaning, "protection." Moabite mother whose son murdered King Joash in 796 B.C. (2 Chron. 24:26). In the parallel passage Shomer is the parent and appears to be the father (2 Kings 12:21).

SHIMROM (Shĭm' rŏm) KJV spelling of Shimron (1 Chron. 7:1).

SHIMRON (Shĭm' rŏn) Personal and place name probably meaning, "protection." *1.* Son of Issachar and original ancestor of clan in that tribe (Gen. 46:13). *2.* Canaanite city-state which joined Hazor's northern coalition against Joshua and met defeat (Josh. 11:1). Some commentators think the original name was Shimon and identify it with modern khirbet Sammuniyeh five miles west of Nazareth in the Esdraelon Valley. Others have suggested Marun er-Ras ten miles northwest of modern Safed above the Sea of Chinnereth, that is the Sea of Galilee. It was allotted to the tribe of Zebulun (Josh. 19:15).

SHIMRON-MERON (Shĭm' rŏn-mē' rŏn) Town in list of cities Joshua defeated (Josh. 12:20). Apparently a longer name of Shimron (11:1), though the earliest Greek translation and some commentators see two separate cities here.

SHIMRONITE (Shĭm' rŏn īte) Member of clan of Shimron (Num. 26:24).

SHIMSHAI (Shĭm' shâi) Personal name meaning, "little sunshine." Scribe who penned letter of Samaritan officials opposing rebuilding of Jerusalem and the Temple about 537 B.C. (Ezra 4).

SHIN (Shîn) Next to last letter of Hebrew alphabet used as title for Psalm 119:161–168 since each verse of the section begins with that letter.

SHINAB (Shī' năb) Akkadian name meaning, "Sin (a god) is father." King of Admah who joined coalition against Chedorlaomer (Gen. 14:2) leading eventually to Abraham's rescue of Lot.

SHINAR, PLAIN OF (Shī' när) Place name of uncertain meaning used in various Ancient Near Eastern documents apparently with somewhat different localities in mind. Some evidence points to a Syrian district cited as Sanhara in the Amarna letters. Some scholars equate Shinar in Assyrian texts with modern Sinjar west of Mosul in Iraq. Others think a Kassite tribe was meant originally. Whatever its meaning outside the Bible, biblical texts use Shinar as a designation for Mesopotamia (Gen. 10:10). See *Mesopotamia.*

The tower of Babel was built in Shinar (Gen. 11:2–9). The King of Shinar opposed Abraham (Gen. 14:1). Isaiah prophesied that God would bring out a remnant of His people from Shinar (11:11). Daniel 1:1–2 and probably Zechariah 5:11 equate Babylon and Shinar, thus limiting Shinar to its major city in the writers' day.

SHION (Shī' ŏn) Modern translations' spelling of Shihon.

SHIPBUILDER See *Ships, Sailors, and Navigation.*

SHIPHI (Shī' phī) Personal name meaning, "my overflow." Member of tribe of Simeon (1 Chron. 4:37).

SHIPHMITE (Shĭph' mīte) Noun indicating either the home town, native land, or clan from which Zabdi came. Some have suggested town of Shepham (Num. 34:10), but this is far from certain.

SHIPHRAH (Shĭph' rah) Personal name meaning, "beauty." Midwife for Israel in Egypt who disobeyed Pharaoh because they feared God (Ex. 1:15–21).

SHIPHTAN (Shĭp′ tan) Personal name meaning, "process of justice." Father of a leader from tribe of Ephraim (Num. 34:24).

SHIPMASTER Captain in charge of a ship (Jon. 1:6; Rev. 18:17).

SHIPS, SAILORS, AND NAVIGATION Travel by sea in biblical times. People first went down to the sea in anything that would keep them afloat. The early development of the two major centers of civilization along the major river systems of the Near Eastern world, the Tigris/Euphrates and the Nile, surely was not coincidental. Even though the first boats were punted or towed along the shore, such water-borne transportation and movement of goods facilitated the exchange of local products in more distant markets, first along the river banks and then beyond the open seas. From very basic, crude beginnings before 3000 B.C., ship technology and seamanship persistently developed as people strove to overcome the barriers that rivers and seas imposed. Thus Assyrian reliefs depict fishermen afloat on inflated bladders and soldiers lying on them to paddle across the water. In wooded areas, the single log or bundle of reeds to support one person soon developed into the raft of bound logs that could support additional personnel and produce. Along the marshy stretches of the Nile, Tigris, and Euphrates, rafts of reed bundles were refined into the reed canoe. The special requirements of rapids and swift waters of the Upper Tigris and Euphrates prompted the development of the bouyed raft, a wooden platform supported on inflated skins that continued in use until very recent times. At the destination downstream, the wooden parts could be disassembled and sold; the deflated skins, easily transported upstream for reuse.

True boats, in their earliest forms, probably consisted of sewn leather stretched and sewn over light frames of branches for ease of transport when necessary. Such boats, essential for river travel, are depicted in detail in Assyrian reliefs between 1000 and 600 B.C. In water free from rocks, such as the Nile delta where adequate materials for branch frames were lacking, clay tublike boats made their appearance. Where wood was available, the bark canoe (a troughlike strip of bark with clay ends) was followed by the dugout which required a cutting tool or controlled use of fire in its production. Wherever forests supplied the logs from Europe to India, the dugout has been familiar to waterways from the Stone Age into the Late Roman period. Modified dugouts with heightened sides and interior reinforcements were the prototypes of the planked boats

A second or third-century A.D. drawing of a ship inscribed with Latin found in Jerusalem excavations.

with keel, ribs, and strakes.

Inland Waterways Civilization arose along the two waterways that connected territories in major political units and provided internal transportation.

1. Boats on Egypt's Nile The Nile provided 750 miles of unobstructed waterway with a current that carried boats from Aswan and the First Cataract to its mouth and prevailing north winds that brought those boats under sail again. Such ideal conditions that obviously contributed to the development of water travel and transport unfortunately were offset by a lack of lumber. Thus, the Egyptians turned to the abundant reeds along the Nile to create simple rafts. Before 3000 B.C., those Nile rafts had become long slender and pointed vessels outfitted with paddles and steering oars. Modifications included cabins and a growing number of oarsmen. The shape was bowed, or sickle-shaped, with squarish prow and stern rising almost vertically from the water. A square sail was set well forward above the reed platform that served its passengers and cargo. The light weight and shallow draft made such craft most useful in the canals and marshes of the Nile River system.

Shortly after 3000 B.C., these fragile reed boats, reinforced with planks, ferried the massive granite and stone blocks used for the impressive stone architecture that began to grace the Nile's banks. These planked reed boats provided the forms for Egypt's first true boats—flat-bottomed and square-ended. Soon, however, relieved of the bulky reed bundles, Egyptian boats were outfitted with rounded bottoms, pointed prow, and rounded stern. Pictorial representations in paintings, reliefs, and models indicate that Nile rivercraft primarily constructed of Asia Minor and Lebanon cedar grew dramatically in size and diversity. Cargo boats 150 feet in length requiring 40 to 50 rowers, and, later, massive 200-by-70-foot barges towed by a fleet of oar-powered tugs, shuttled up and down the Nile to the massive building operations between Aswan and the Delta. Smaller vessels were poled, paddled, or rowed, with some

S

also equipped with a sail.

For international maritime trade, Egypt enjoyed a distinct advantage as the only nation with direct access to both the Mediterranean and the Red Seas. As a result, two long-distance maritime routes to Syria and Punt (East Africa) already were established during the Old Kingdom period. The earliest route to Byblos soon was extended to Cyprus, Crete, and possibly other Aegean sites. The earliest seagoing vessel depicted in a relief dated about 2450 B.C. had a spoon-shaped hull with a long, slender overhanging bow and stern and a rope truss that could be tightened by twisting to compensate for any sagging of bow or stern. The ships of Queen Hatshepsut's fleet trading with the East African coast reflect considerable refinement of the general lines. A two-legged forward mast with a tall, narrow rectangular sail had been replaced by a low, wide sail on a pole mast amidships. A single, massive steering oar had replaced smaller steering oars on each quarter. Fifteen rowers a side (requiring a space of not less than 45 feet) would suggest a vessel about 90 feet in length. By the end of the New Kingdom period, the ships used by Rameses III against the invading Sea Peoples (about 1170 B.C.), as depicted in his reliefs, indicate radical changes in construction. See *Egypt*.

2. Mesopotamian Shipping Mesopotamian kings and merchants also operated long-distance maritime routes in the Red Sea and Indian Ocean from several inland cities that were accessible along the Tigris and Euphrates Rivers. By 3000 B.C., overseas trade was a thriving aspect of regional economy. Maritime ventures included royal and private efforts at supplying metals, timber, and luxury items the Mesopotamian economy lacked.

A clay model of a bowllike boat, with slight evidence of prow and stern, possibly made of skins and dated about 3400 B.C., is our earliest evidence of Mesopotamian vessels. The existence of a mast and use of sails was possible, though firm evidence of sailing boats comes much later. Earliest representations on seals suggest the use of squarish reed crafts similar to Egyptian types. A

A felucca (Egyptian boat) on the Nile River near the city of Cairo, Egypt.

prevailing north wind and rapids in the Upper Tigris and Euphrates Rivers diminished the development of commercial shipping and the need for larger vessels. As a result, early light craft propelled by paddles or oars gradually evolved into wooden craft with sail as well as oars. The largest vessels appear to carry less than eleven tons with most half that size, usually constructed of edge-joined planks with framing inserted for stability. Square-ended, these boats carried a single sail of cloth or reed matting with the largest powered by eleven oarsmen.

Between 3000 and 2000 B.C. overseas trade with East Africa and India flowed through the Persian Gulf on relatively small seagoing vessels, the largest known with a capacity of only about twenty-eight tons.

International Travel and Trade Sea routes opened opportunities for evolving nations to gain wealth and explore the mysteries of far-off lands.

1. The Eastern Mediterranean: 3000–1000 B.C. Major developments of maritime travel between (2000 and 1500 B.C.) must be attributed to the island world of the Aegean and the coastlines of the eastern Mediterranean. There the Minoans of Crete especially developed an impressive naval fleet and a merchant marine that linked their island world. Ultimately, however, the Mycenaeans—Greeks from the mainland—overpowered Crete, forming an Aegean confederacy. From 1500 to 1200 B.C. they claimed control over the waters of the Eastern Mediterranean.

Cretan ships with their rounded hulls, portrayed on seals about 1500 B.C., were quite distinct from the Aegean straight-lined angular-ended vessels. Though the engravings obviously are stylized, the slender rounded hull, in some cases almost crescent-shaped, supported a pole mast with stays fore and aft and a high square sail. These Cretan vessels with ten or fifteen oars to the side were about 50 and 75 feet in length, respectively. Passenger vessels were outfitted with a cabin or shelter on deck.

An Egyptian wall painting in a 1400 B.C. tomb depicts a Syrian fleet of merchant ships with spoon-shaped hulls, with straight stempost, deck beams through the sides, and a broad square sail very much like Egyptian vessels of the period. (The Egyptian vessels were braced with a rope truss.) The representation of the sailors (their beards, profile, and clothing) clearly suggests their Syrian origin. (It is unlikely, though the evidence comes from Egypt, that these are Egyptian vessels manned by Syrians.) The rounded hulls are best related to Crete from about 1600 B.C. onwards. These merchantmen with their deck and roomy hold grew in size. By about 1200 B.C., an Ugaritic tablet suggests their size in referring to a single shipment of grain of 450 tons.

The war fleets of the Levant in 1200 B.C. were impressive in number and design. The fighting craft lost their spoon-shaped hull which was elongated and rounded. They were undecked with the oarsmen protected behind a high bulwark. The mast with an adjustable sail was crowned with a lookout. The naval battle (depicted on the Medinet Habu temple walls) between Aegean ("Sea Peoples") and Egyptian ships indicates the clear similarity of construction and design apart from ornamental or cultic aspects. The only offensive weapon appears to be the grappling irons for boarding enemy vessels. Aside from the tactical maneuvering of the vessels, sea battles were fought with bow, sword, and pike as on land. The modification of the bow for ramming appears to have been a later development.

2. The Eastern Mediterranean: 1000–500 B.C. During this period the Phoenicians gained a reputation as the ablest of seamen and maritime traders. Their primary challenge came from the Greek world where merchantmen and war vessels controlled the northern Mediterranean shoreline and the Black Sea. The low sleek "hollow" hull, with only a scant deck forward for the outlook and a slightly larger one aft for the captain and passengers, was constructed low and long primarily for speed. Several standard-sized galleys included the 20-oared dispatch and local transport, the 30-oared "triaconter" galley, the 50-oared "penteconter" for troop transport, and the 100-oared large transport. They were constructed of oak, poplar, pine, and fir, with the oars and masts of fir. A single, large-bladed steering car was replaced after 800 B.C. by double steering oars that became standard thereafter. A single square sail on a mast amidships could be raised and lowered. Sails of sewn patches of woven linen were controlled with lines of twisted papyrus and leather. Other equipment included stern mooring lines, stone anchors, punting poles, long pikes for fighting, and bags and jars for holding provisions. Screen along the sides could be closed during heavy weather.

The introduction of the ram was a dramatic innovation that revolutionized ship construction. The pointed cutwater for puncturing the hull of the enemy vessel required construction with heavier materials to withstand contact, especially in the bow area. The open or latticed bow area gave way to a cumbersome superstructure for sustaining the ram. This represented the first period of specialization in the construction and class of vessel: the open galley with a lighter hull for carrying dispatches and personnel and the galley with superstructure, including relatively high platforms as fighting stations at bow and stern, for combat. The invention of the two-banked galley soon followed to increase the number of rowers and the speed of the vessel without increasing the length and reducing the seaworthiness of its hull. The Phoenician shipwrights should be credited with many of these important innovations.

The rigging for most war galleys during this period was standard: a single square sail amidships with a retractable mast. After 600 B.C., single-banked and double-banked galleys appear in all sizes up to 100 oars.

The first Mediterranean merchant ships probably were oar driven. Plagued by calm waters during the summer months when maritime activity probably was at its peak, only oared ships could have provided the reliability and speed required for prompt delivery of merchandise. Later, as the volume of cargo grew, larger seaworthy sailing ships came into use. The merchantman was only slightly modified from the warship design to include a roomier and stronger hull and a sturdier mast for a bigger sail. Ultimately, however, the sailing ship with a rounded hull and a single square sail became the primary cargo ship from Phoenicia to Italy.

3. The Age of the Trireme: 500–323 B.C. The galley rowed by three more or less superimposed banks of oarsmen came into vogue after 500 B.C. and maintained its prominence into the later Roman Empire. The additional power and speed required by the ram seemed to outweigh the relatively unseaworthy hull of this oar arrangement. As a result, sea battles were carefully scheduled near land during the mild summer months to avoid adverse weather conditions. While the first two lines of rowers worked their oars through ports in the hull and on a second line on or just below the gunwale, the third line worked from an outrigger projecting laterally above and beyond the gunwale. Corinth appears to have been the first to launch such a fleet sometime after 700 B.C.; and a century later, it appears to have been accepted generally. Athenian naval records suggest that such ships were built with great care, and, despite their fragile construction, remained in service for an average of twenty years. The Phoenician shipwrights increased the height of their vessels to accommodate three-level rowing.

4. Warships of the Hellenistic Period: 323–31 B.C. In both Phoenician and Greek navies of the period, the primary innovation was the construction of larger and larger vessels, though the exact nature of oaring is not clearly understood. Generally, the greater power and speed was achieved with longer oars and a double banking of the rowers, while the oversized ships relied on a variety of oaring arrangements. Ramming remained a standard naval tactic, though gradually subordinated to the firing of missiles, the heaving of grapnels, and boarding. Darts and grapnels were fired from catapults at longer range, while short-range battles included archers and the slinging of javelins and stones. Shortly after 200 B.C., the Rhodians introduced the fire pot, slung from long poles (extending over the bow) onto the enemy vessel.

To complement these larger ships, light vessels

such as skiffs with speed and maneuverability made their appearance for express transport and the carrying of dispatches. Some were equipped with rams, while others were intended to disrupt the tactics and break the oars of the larger vessels. Later, the Roman imperial navy would not only add to the variety of vessels, but their architects would introduce significant defensive innovations.

5. Greek and Roman Shipbuilding The Greco-Roman shipwrights, aware of the ancient Egyptian method of edge-joining planks in the construction of the hull, created their own form of ship carpentry in which they locked the shell of planks together with mortises and then reinforced that hull with interior framing. This method was consistently used in the construction of all vessels from the smallest lake skiff to the largest seaworthy freighters. In larger vessels, massive cables for undergirding the ship during emergencies were kept on board. It was usual to smear seams and sometimes the whole hull with pitch or pitch and wax as a protective coating. Though fir, cedar, and pine appear to have been preferred for planking and frames, local availability of lumbers finally determined the choice.

The ancient Mediterranean sailor knew only the side rudder, an oversized oar pivoted in a slanting position near the stern. The pushing or pulling of a tiller bar socketed into the upper part of the loom adjusted the blade of the oar at an angle to the hull and thus maneuvered the ship. A series of ropes with individual functions fitted the mast and sail. Navigational aids were limited and simple. Handbooks with brief notes on distances, landmarks, harbors, and anchorages were available. There are no historical references to the use of charts. Soundings were taken. Flags and lights were used for signaling. Anchors were large and numerous.

The ideal sailing season in the Mediterranean was from May 27 to September 14 with an extension to outside limits from March 10 to November 10. As a result, sailing during the late fall and winter was reduced to bare essentials such as the carrying of vital dispatches, the transport of essential supplies, and urgent military movement. The severity of winter storms and the poor visibility due to fog and cloudiness made navigation before the compass most difficult.

Mediterranean currents generally are too weak seriously to affect sea travel. However, prevailing wind direction produced a definite pattern with ships traveling in most southerly directions, from Italy or Greece to Asia Minor, Syria, Egypt, and Africa, anticipating a quick and easy voyage with the aid of northerly winds. The return, on the other hand, was difficult against the prevailing winds, and thus a course near the coastline at times provided quieter waters and periodic shelter. The ancient square-riggers were designed for traveling with the wind astern or on the quarters.

Roman ships appear to have logged four and a half to six knots with the wind. Tacking, or using the familiar zigzag course, at best was difficult and slow. When rowing was unavoidable, the oarsmen were divided into squads for rotation or given regular short rest periods.

Organizational structure and rank on the earlier, smaller vessels of the Greek and Roman navy was limited to the commanding officer who manned the helm, the rowing officer who maintained the oarsmen's beat, and the bow officer ("lookout") who was responsible for the course and well-being of the ship. Around 400 B.C., when the Athenian trireme had a crew of two hundred, the officers numbered five: the executive officer or captain; the commanding officer; the rowing officer, responsible for the training and morale of the oarsmen; subordinate officer, with important administrative duties such as paymaster, purchasing, and recruiting officer; and officer of the bow. Other personnel included the ship's carpenter, flutist (to time the rowers' stroke) or time beater, side chiefs (to set the stroke), deckhands, oar tenders, and ship's doctor, among others. The number of fighting personnel (marines) varied according to strategy: the Athenian ships that relied primarily on the ram had as few as ten; others intent on boarding tactics had as many as forty. A few archers (four to six) usually were on board, together with some catapult operators.

A seagoing merchantman was controlled by its owner or charter, usually with a hired professional captain with total authority over the vessel and its crew. Under way the "sailing master" was usually in command. Two officers were in charge of operations (first mate) and administration (maintenance). The large merchantmen also had quartermasters, carpenters, guards, rowers to man the ship's boats, and others. The sailors generally wore limited or no clothing when aboard ship and wore a tunic but no sandals when ashore.

A wide variety of smaller craft, usually driven by oars and a small auxiliary sail, were prevalent in every harbor to provide various services. River and coastal craft provided towing services and transfer of cargo and merchandise to harbor warehouses and points inaccessible to the larger ships. Man-made harbors with artificial sea walls to create protected anchorage appear before 700 B.C. Gradually, quays, warehouses, and defensive towers were added to create a secure commercial port. By 400 B.C., the Piraeus harbor was surrounded by an extensive covered emporium to facilitate the handling of import and export merchandise. By Roman times, both sea and river were well endowed with harbors, with smaller ports benefitting from coastal shipping by becoming distribution centers for inland areas removed from major land routes. Unfortunately, the decline of the late Roman Empire and political weakness with a recurrence of piracy on the high seas led to a marked decline of commercial shipping in the Mediterranean. With the ultimate fragmentation of the Roman Empire, barbarian invasions in the east, and the shift of the economic center to the west, the Mediterranean, devoid of large ships, slowly was reduced to small local craft with minimal economic impact beyond the patron port.

George L. Kelm

SHIRT Modern translation of coat in some passages, reflecting Greek *chiton,* garment both sexes wore next to the skin. See *Cloth, Clothing.*

SHISHA (Shĭ′ shà) Personal name or, more likely, an official title borrowed from Egyptian: royal scribe who writes letters. Apparently, "sons of Shisha" (1 Kings 4:3) refers to members of a scribal guild. Sheva (2 Sam. 20:25) and Shavsha (1 Chron. 18:16) may represent other ways to transliterate the Egyptian title into Hebrew.

SHISHAK (Shĭ′ shăk) Egyptian royal name of unknown meaning. A pharaoh of Egypt known also as Sheshonk I. He ruled about 945–924 B.C. and founded the Twenty-Second Dynasty. Just after Rehoboam began to reign in Judah, Shishak invaded Jerusalem and carted off the Temple treasures (1 Kings 14:25–26). According to inscriptions on the walls of a temple to the god Amon in Karnak, Shishak captured over 150 towns in Palestine including Megiddo, Taanash, and Gibeon. Some equate him with the pharaoh whose daughter married Solomon (3:1) and who later burned Gezer and gave it to his daughter (9:16). See *Egypt.*

SHITRAI (Shĭt rā′ ī) Personal name perhaps meaning, "minor official." Official in charge of David's grazing animals in Sharon (1 Chron. 27:29). Early Hebrew scribes noted the spelling as Shirtai.

SHITTAH TREE KJV spelling of Shittim tree (Isa. 41:19).

SHITTIM (Shĭt′ tĭm) Transliteration of Hebrew word for accacia trees and name of *1.* a large area in Moab directly across the Jordan from Jericho and northeast of the Dead Sea. Israel camped there for a long period before crossing into the Promised Land. While at Shittim, they were blessed by Balaam (whom Balak had hired to curse Israel; Num. 22—24; compare Mic. 6:5), committed sin with the Moabite and Midianite women (Num. 25), and Joshua was announced as Moses' successor (Deut. 34:9). Joshua sent spies out from Shittim (Josh. 2:1; compare 3:1). It is modern tell el-Hammam es Samri about eight miles east of the Jordan.

2. In Joel 3:18 the symbolic meaning of acacias (note NAS) comes to the fore in the messianic

The yellow blooms of a modern variety of the acacia (shittim) tree in Israel.

picture of fertility for the Kidron Valley with a stream flowing from the Temple.

SHITTIM TREE, WOOD See *Plants.*

SHIZA (Shĭ′ zà) Abbreviated personal name of uncertain meaning. Member of tribe of Reuben in time of David (1 Chron. 11:42).

SHOA (Shō′ à) National name meaning, "help!" Nation God used to punish His people (Ezek. 23:23). They are usually identified with the Sutu, a nomadic people from the Syrian and Arabian desert known from documents from Mari, Amarna, and Assyria. Some commentators see them mentioned in Isaiah 22:5, where most translate, "crying."

SHOBAB (Shō′ băb) Personal name meaning, "one brought back" or "fallen away, rebel." *1.* Son of David (2 Sam. 5:14). *2.* Son of Caleb and ancestor of clan in tribe of Judah (1 Chron. 2:18).

SHOBACH (Shō′ băch) Personal name of uncertain meaning. Commander of Syrian army under Hadad-ezer killed by David's troops in battle (2 Sam. 10:16,18). The name appears as Shophak in 1 Chronicles 19:16,18.

SHOBAI (Shō′ bāī) Personal name of uncertain meaning. Head of family of gatekeepers (Ezra 2:42).

SHOBAL (Shō′ băl) Personal name probably meaning, "lion." *1.* Son of Seir and ruler in Edom (Gen. 36:20,23,29). *2.* Son of Caleb and founder of Kirjath-jearim (1 Chron. 2:50), listed under sons of Judah (1 Chron. 4:1), possibly an indication of "son of" denoting belonging to a tribe.

SHOBEK (Shō′ běk) Personal name meaning, "victor." Jewish leader who signed Nehemiah's covenant (Neh. 10:24).

SHOBI (Shō′ bī) Personal name of uncertain meaning. Ammonite who helped David as he fled across Jordan from Absalom (2 Sam. 17:27).

SHOCHO(H) Alternate spelling of Soco(h).

SHOHAM (Shō' hăm) Personal name meaning, "gem." Levite in time of David (1 Chron. 24:27).

SHOMER (Shō' mēr) Personal name meaning, "protector." *1.* Father of one of the murderers of King Joash (2 Kings 12:21). See *Shimrith. 2.* See *Shemer 2.*

SHOPHACH (Shō' phăch) See *Shobach.*

SHOPHAN (Shō' phăn) KJV interpretation of separate town. Modern translations have compound name. See *Atroth-shophan.*

SHOPHAR (Shō' phår) Hebrew word for the ceremonial ram's horn used to call the people of Israel together (Ex. 19:16). See *Music.* The shophar was to be blown on the Day of Atonement in the jubilee year to signal the release of slaves and debt. It also was used as a trumpet of war as the Israelites were campaigning against their enemies. *Mike Mitchell*

SHOSHANNIM (Shō shăn' nīm) Transliteration of Hebrew word meaning, "lotuses." Technical term used in titles of Psalms 45; 60; 69; 80. It may be the title of a melody, a flower used in a ceremony seeking a word from God, designation of a love song later expanded in meaning, or indication of a six-stringed instrument.

SHOSHANNIM-EDUTH (Shō' shăn' nīm-ē' dūth) See *Shoshannim.* Term in tiles of Psalms 60; 80. Eduth means, "witness" or "laws." Its implication in the Psalm titles is not clear.

SHOULDERPIECE Translation of Hebrew word meaning, "shoulder, upper arm, side." The straps going over the shoulder so the high priest could wear the ephod (Ex. 28:7).

SHOVEL Instrument used to remove ashes from the altar (Ex. 27:3).

SHRINE A small building devoted to the worship of a particular deity, usually with an image of that god. Sometimes shrines were located in larger temples, set apart by a partition or niche in a wall. An Ephraimite, Micah, had a shrine in Israel during the days of the judges (Judg. 17:5). He hired a Levite to administer worship at the site. Later, shrines were seen as pagan (2 Kings 17:29). King Josiah had them demolished during his reign (2 Kings 23:19). The apostle Paul confronted the silversmith Demitrius with his sin of selling shrines of the goddess Artemis (Acts 19:21–27). See *Artemis; High Place.*

SHRINE OF HIS OWN IDOL NIV translation in Ezekiel 8:12. See *Chambers of Imagery.*

SHROUD A linen burial cloth. Shrouds usually were very long pieces of cloth which were wound around the body. As the winding was done, spices were placed within the folds of the shroud. After His crucifixion, Jesus' body was so buried by Joseph of Arimathea and the women disciples (Matt. 27:59–61). In one recorded instance, a shroud was worn as a garment (Mark 14:51–52).

SHUA (Shū' à) Personal name meaning, "help!" *1.* Father-in-law of Judah (Gen. 38:2; 1 Chron. 2:3). *2.* Woman descended from Asher (1 Chron. 7:32), with slightly different Hebrew spelling.

SHUAH (Shū' ah) Personal name perhaps meaning, "sunken." *1.* Son of Abraham (Gen. 25:2) and possibly thought of as original ancestor the Suhu mentioned in Assyrian sources as living on the Euphrates River below the mouth of the Chabur. *2.* Home of Job's friend Bildad (Job 2:11), possibly to be identified with people mentioned in *1.* or with an otherwise unknown tribe in the Syrian and Arabian desert, perhaps an offshoot of *1.*

SHUAL (Shū' ăl) Personal and place name meaning, "jackal." *1.* Descendant of Asher (1 Chron. 7:36). *2.* Territory biblical writer used to describe path a group of Philistines took against Saul (1 Sam. 13:17). Some would identify it with the land of Shaalim (1 Sam. 9:4). The location is uncertain.

SHUBAEL (Shū' bā ĕl) See *Shebuel.*

SHUHAH (Shū' hăh) Personal name of uncertain meaning. Brother, or according to some manuscript evidence the son, of Caleb (1 Chron. 4:11). Some commentators connect the name to Suchati known from Egyptian sources and think of a forefather of a nomadic clan who lived in the Negeb.

SHUHAM (Shū' hăm) Personal name of uncertain meaning. Son of Dan (Num. 26:42). See *Hushim.*

SHUHAMITE (Shū' hăm īte) Member of clan of Shuham (Num. 26:42).

SHUHITE (Shū' hīte) Person from Shuah.

SHULAM(M)ITE (Shū' lăm īte) Description of woman in Song of Solomon 6:13 either as from Shunem through a copying change; from Shulam, an otherwise unknown town; Solomonite, referring to a relationship to Solomon; or a common noun meaning, "the replaced one."

SHUMATHITE (Shū' măth īte) Clan name of uncertain meaning descended from Caleb (1 Chron. 2:53).

SHUNAMMITE (Shū′ năm mīte) Resident of or native from Shunem.

SHUNEM, SHUNAMMITES (Shū′ něm, Shū′ năm mīte) Place name of uncertain meaning. Town in tribe of Issachar located southeast of Mount Carmel. The site was captured by the Egyptian pharaoh Thutmose III about 1450 B.C., again by Labayu of Shechem about 1350 B.C., and rebuilt by Biridya of Megiddo. The Israelites controlled it under Joshua (Josh. 19:18). The Philistines camped at Shunem while fighting with Saul (1 Sam. 28:4). About 920 B.C., the Egyptian pharaoh Shishak captured the town. See *Shishak*. As David lay dying, Abishag the Shunammite was hired to minister to the king (1 Kings 1:3; compare 2:17). The prophet Elisha stayed often at the home of a Shunammite couple, prophesied that a son would be born to them, and raised the boy from the dead after an accident in the field (2 Kings 4). It is modern Solem, about eight miles north of Jenin and three miles east of Affulah.

SHUNI (Shū′ nī) Personal name of uncertain meaning. Son of Gad and head of a clan in that tribe (Gen. 46:16).

SHUNITE (Shū′ nīte) Member of clan of Shuni (Num. 26:15).

SHUPHAM (Shū′ phăm) Personal name of uncertain meaning reconstructed by scholars as son of Benjamin on basis of the clan name Shuphamite (Num. 26:39). The personal name in Hebrew is Muppim in Genesis and Shephupham in Numbers. In 1 Chronicles 7:6 the name is absent, but in 7:12,15 Shupim occurs.

SHUPHAMITE (Shū′ phăm īte) Member of Benjaminite clan of Shupham or Shephupham. See *Shupham; Shephupham*.

SHUPPIM (Shŭp′ pīm) Personal name of uncertain meaning and plural form in Hebrew. Apparently a son of Benjamin (1 Chron. 7:12) but related to Machir in verse 15. The Chronicles texts apparently have experienced loss of words through copying. REB emends the text so that Shuppim is not included. See *Shupham*.

SHUR, WILDERNESS OF (Shūr) Place name meaning, "wall." Region on Egypt's northeastern border, perhaps named after wall Egyptians built to protect their border, where Moses made first stop after crossing the Red Sea (Ex. 15:22). Earlier, Sarah's handmaid, Hagar, had come toward Shur after her expulsion from the clan of Abraham (Gen. 16:7). Abraham lived near Shur (Gen. 20:1). Saul smote the Amalekites in that area (1 Sam. 15:7). David and his men made forays as far as Shur while eluding King Saul (1 Sam. 27:8). Shur may be modern tell el-Fara.

The Wilderness of Shur.

SHUSHAN (Shū′ shăn) Persian place name transcribed in Hebrew with word borrowed from Egyptian meaning, "lily" or "lotus." City in southwestern Iran which served as the ancient capital of the nation Elam. The site was inhabited as early as 3000 BC. It was located on the caravan routes between Arabia and points north and west, and therefore it became a very rich city. Archaeological evidence indicates that Shushan traded heavily with nations in Mesopotamia. In Esther 1:2, the city is identified as the throne city of Ahasuerus and called Susa by modern translations. The Achaemenean Dynasty between 500 and 300 B.C. took Shushan to its height politically and economically. It served as the king's winter residence; they moved to Ecbatana in summer. During periods of Seleucid and Parthian rule, it declined and finally was destroyed in the fourth century A.D. See *Elam; Persia*.

SHUSHAN-EDUTH (Shū′ shăn-ē′ dŭth) See *Shoshannim; Shoshannim-eduth*.

SHUTHALHITE (Shū thăl′ hīte) Member of clan of Shuthelah (Num. 26:35).

SHUTHELA(H)ITE (Shū thē′ lă hīte) Modern translations' spelling of Shuthalhite.

SHUTHELAH (Shū′ thē lăh) Personal name of uncertain meaning. Original ancestor of clan in tribe of Ephraim (Num. 26:35).

SHUTTLE See *Loom*.

SIA (Sī′ a) Personal name meaning, "helper." Family of Temple servants or nethanim (Neh. 7:47).

SIAHA (Sī′ ă hă) Personal name meaning, "helpers of God." Temple servants (Ezra 2:44). This is apparently a variant spelling of Sia.

SIBBEC(H)AI (Sib′ bĕ caî) Personal name of uncertain meaning. Member of David's army who killed a giant or, more literally, a descendant of the

Rephaim (2 Sam. 21:18 REB). First Chronicles 11:29 lists him among David's military heroes, leading many commentators to see Sibbecai as the original reading for Mebunnai in 2 Samuel 23:27 resulting from a confusion of Hebrew letters by early scribes. Sibbecai commanded David's forces for the eighth month (1 Chron. 27:11).

SIBBOLETH (Sĭb′ bō lĕth) See *Shibboleth*.

SIBMAH (Sĭb′ mah) Place name meaning, "cold" or "high." City tribe of Reuben rebuilt in Transjordan (Num. 32:38). It became part of their tribal inheritance (Josh. 13:19). Isaiah mentioned it in his lament over Moab (16:8–9; compare Jer. 48:32). Sebam (Num. 32:3) is often seen as a copyist's change from Sibmah. It may be located at khirbet al-qibsh about three miles east northeast of Mount Nebo and three miles southwest of Hesban.

SIBRAIM (Sĭb′ rā ĭm) Place name of uncertain meaning. Apparently the northern border between Damascus and Hamath. Some would identify it with Sepharvaim (2 Kings 17:24). The precise location is not known.

SIBYLLINE ORACLES See *Pseudepigrapha*.

SICARII (Sĭ că′ rĭĭ) See *Assassins*.

SICHEM (Sĭ′ chĕm) KJV variant spelling of Shechem (Gen. 12:6).

SICK See *Diseases*.

Inside the main tunnel at the Cumae Shrine of the Sibyl, the primary Sibylline sanctuary.

View of the harbor area of Sidon in the modern country of Lebanon.

SICKLE A curved blade of flint or metal used to cut stalks of grain. Sickles varied in size and handle length, but usually had a short wooden handle which required the user to bend near the ground to harvest the crop. They are among the oldest tools known by humans, dating to 8,500 B.C. Biblical texts often used the sickle symbolically to speak of coming judgment. Revelation 14 uses the analogy of Christ reaping the harvest of humankind at the great judgment. See *Agriculture.*

SIDDIM (Sĭd' dĭm) Place name perhaps meaning, "flats" or "fields." A variant name for the Dead Sea where the coalition faced Chedorlaomer and his allies, leading to Abraham's rescue of Lot (Gen. 14). The reference is apparently to the land bordering the Dead Sea. Some think the Hebrew should be read Shadim and interpreted as a reference to the Valley of Demons.

SIDON AND TYRE (Sī' dŏn, Tȳre) Phoenician cities located on the coastal plain between the mountains of Lebanon and the Mediterranean Sea (Gen. 10:15). Sidon and Tyre were ancient cities, having been founded long before the Israelites entered the land of Canaan. Extrabiblical sources first mention Sidon before 2000 B.C. and Tyre just after 2000 B.C. While Sidon seems to have been the most dominant of the two cities during the early part of their histories, Tyre assumed this role in the latter times. Both cities were known for their maritime exploits and as centers of trade. One of Tyre's most coveted exports was purple dye. Joshua could not conquer the territory (Josh. 13:3–4).

Israel had relations with the two cities, but especially with Tyre. David employed Tyrian stonemasons and carpenters and used cedars from that area in building a palace. (2 Sam. 5:11). The construction of the Temple in Jerusalem during Solomon's reign depended heavily on the materials and craftsmen from Tyre. About 870 B.C., Ahab married Jezebel, the daughter of the Phoenician king, bringing Baal worship to Israel's court. Ezekiel 28 characterizes the king of Tyre as the ultimate example of pride. Under Roman rule, the two cities were important ports of trade, but they did not enjoy the dominance they previously held. Jesus spent time in Tyre and Sidon and in contrast to the prophets' attitude toward the cities, He contrasted them with the Jews as examples of faith (Matt. 11:20–22). Paul spent seven days in Tyre after his third missionary journey (Acts 21:3–4). See *Phoenicia.* *Scott Langston*

SIEGE Battle tactic in which an army surrounds a city and cuts off all supplies so that the enemy army is forced to surrender for lack of food and water. Deuteronomy 28:53–57 described the horrible actions to which siege leads (compare Jer. 19:9). Ezekiel 4 describes the prophet's symbolic act of building a miniature city of Jerusalem under siege. Preparing for siege, a city stored water inside the city walls and repaired the walls (Nah. 3:14). One response was to "gather up your goods and flee the country" (Jer. 10:17 REB). To remain under siege was to "give yourselves over to die by hunger and by thirst" (2 Chron. 32:11 NAS). This was the major tactic used in Near Eastern wars. Judah suffered siege from Sennacherib (2 Kings 18—19) and from Nebuchadrezzar (2 Kings 24—25).

SIEGEWORKS Platforms or towers an army built around and above the city walls of a city under siege. This allowed the besieging army to shoot arrows and throw missiles of war down into the city. Israel's law did not allow fruit trees to be cut down to build such platforms (Deut. 20:19–20). Ramps built up to the city walls allowed soldiers to attack the walls and to shoot fire arrows and other weapons into the city. Scaling ladders lifted armies over the walls into the city. Battering rams destroyed city gates. Fires at the base of the walls weakened the sandstone bricks. Tunnels dug under the walls further weakened them. Thus the population's emotions were drained; its supplies were exhausted; and its defenses destroyed.

SIEVE Instrument used to remove unwanted materials from sand or grain. Pebbles or straw remain in the sieve, while the sand or grain passes through. God warned Israel He would place them in a sieve of judgment and none would fall through, for none of them were good grain (Amos 9:9). Another Hebrew word traditionally translated "sieve" in Isaiah 30:28 refers to a swinging action. Precisely what is swung is not clear, the noun coming from the same root as the verb. In some manner Isaiah proclaimed God's judgment would swing over His people.

SIGN That which points to something else; an object, occurrence, or person through which one recognizes, remembers, or validates something.
Old Testament *'Oth,* the usual Hebrew term for sign, appears in a nontheological sense for a military signal in the fourth Lachish letter and Joshua 2:12, and for a military standard in Numbers 2:2 and Psalms 74:4. The other 75 instances of sign carry a theological sense. Three settings predominate: the created order (Gen. 1:14; 9:12–17; Isa. 37:30; 55:13); human history (Ex. 7:3; Deut. 4:34; 6:22); and religious ritual (Gen. 17:11; Ex. 12:13; 13:9,16; 31:13). With signs, the nature of the object or event, whether commonplace, odd, or miraculous, is not the prime focus. Emphasis falls rather on the function of the sign. Old Testament signs may be classed according to seven somewhat overlapping functions: *1.* to impart knowledge; *2.* to protect; *3.* to motivate faith; *4.* to recall significant events; *5.* to witness to the covenant; *6.* to confirm; and *7.* to illustrate by means of prophetic action.

1. Signs which impart knowledge typically characterize God as Lord of history and champion of oppressed Israel. The goal of the Exodus signs is the knowledge that "I am the LORD (in the midst of the earth)" (Ex. 7:5; 8:22; 10:2) and that "the LORD is God; there is no other besides him" (Deut. 4:34–35 NRSV). The punishment to befall Pharaoh Hophra was to serve as a sign promoting the knowledge that God's word of judgment would surely stand up against the Judean refugees in Egypt (Jer. 44:29). The knowledge imparted by these signs encouraged acknowledgment of Yahweh as the only God, obedience to God's covenant, and trust in God's word. *2.* The mark of Cain (Gen. 4:15) and the blood upon the doorposts at Passover (Ex. 12:13) protected those under the sign. *3.* In addition to revealing God, a second goal of the Exodus signs was to motivate faith and worship. Israel's unbelief in spite of signs is often condemned (Num. 14:11,22; Deut. 1:29–33). The signs fulfill their goal when they inspire obedience (Deut. 11:3,8), worship (Deut. 26:8,10), and loyalty to the Lord (Josh. 24:16–17). The signs of pagan prophets similarly serve as a challenge to trust in Yahweh (Deut. 13:1–4). The reality of wonder-working false prophets underscores the truth that signs themselves are ambivalent; the function of the sign, either to evoke or challenge faith in Yahweh, is the deciding factor. *4.* Signs serve as reminders of significant events. The eating of unleavened bread at Passover (Ex. 13:9) and the redemption of the first-born (Ex. 13:16) are reminders of God's liberation of Israel. The stones at Gilgal (Josh. 4:6–7) bore similar witness to God's continuing saving presence as Israel embarked on the Conquest. The covering of the altar served as a reminder of the danger of ursurping the role of God's priests (Num. 17:10). *5.* Other signs serve as reminders of a covenant or established relationship. The rainbow witnesses God's covenant with Noah, insuring an orderly creation not threatened by flood (Gen. 9:12–17). Circumcision served as a reminder of God's covenant with Abraham (Gen. 17:11). The Sabbath, likewise, served as a reminder of God's covenant with Moses (Ex. 31:13,17; Ezek. 20:12). *6.* Still other signs serve as confirmation. Such signs often authenticated God's special call (of Moses, Ex. 3:12; 4:8; of Gideon, Judg. 6:17; of Saul, 1 Sam. 10:2–9). Elsewhere a sign confirms God's word of judgment (1 Sam. 2:34; Jer. 44:29–30) or promise of healing (2 Kings 20:8). *7.* Other signs take the form of prophetic acts. The names of Isaiah ("Yahweh is salvation") and his sons Shear-jashub ("A remnant shall return") and Maher-shalal-hash-baz ("The spoil speeds, the prey hastens") illustrate Israel's fate (Isa. 7:3; 8:3). Isaiah's walking naked and barefoot for three years illustrated the coming humiliation of Egypt and Ethiopia (Isa. 20:3). Ezekiel, likewise, illustrated the coming siege of Jerusalem using a brick, earth, and a plate (Ezek. 4:1–3).

New Testament The New Testament employs sign in the full range of Old Testament functions. *1.* Signs function simply to identify. Judas' kiss clearly designated Jesus as the One the mob was seeking (Matt. 26:48). The sign of Jesus' coming and the end of the age which the disciples requested is, likewise, an identifying mark (Matt. 24:3; Mark 13:4; Luke 21:7); it is not a matter of evoking faith in Christ's coming but of identifying that event when it occurs. The difficult "sign of the Son of Man" is probably an identifying sign as well (Matt. 24:30). The above uses approximate the nontheological use of sign by the Old Testament. Other uses of sign are distinctly theological. *2.* John's signs generally impart knowledge about Jesus and His relation to the Father. Jesus' first sign, the changing of water into wine at Cana, points to Jesus as the source of the abundant, joyful life which characterizes the anticipated Messianic Age (John 2:1–11). The three-fold repetition of the phrase "your son lives" in the healing of the official's son (John 4:46–54) points to Jesus as the life-giver. The healing of the sick man at the Sheep Gate Pool (John 5:2–9) points to Jesus as the One through whom God is still working (John 5:17). Though the just-fed crowd saw Jesus' feeding of the five thousand (John 6:2–13) as a sign that Jesus was a prophet (6:14), the sign points to Jesus as the life-giving bread which alone can satisfy (6:35). The sign of the healing of the man born blind (John 9:1–7) illustrates the ambiguity of signs: some took the sign to mean that Jesus was not from God; others, that God was with Him (9:16). John's conclusion (9:35–41) points to Jesus as both giver of spiritual insight and judge of spiritual blindness. Finally, the raising of Lazarus (John 11) points to Jesus as the resurrection and the life (11:25). *3.* Though the term sign is not used, the seal of God upon the foreheads of the redeemed (Rev. 9:4) is a sign of protection. *4.* Some signs serve to motivate faith. The signs in the Fourth Gospel were recounted so "that you may believe that Jesus is the Christ, the Son of the God, and that believing you may have life in His name" (John 20:31). John previously noted signs leading to faith (John 2:11; 4:53; 9:38). The sign of the healing of a lame man led to the praise of God in Acts 4:16,21. Philip's signs, likewise, evoked the Samaritans' faith (Acts 8:6). *5.* Other signs serve to recall God's past saving acts. The paired expression "signs and wonders" (Acts 2:19,22; 4:30; 7:36–37; 14:3) recalls the foundational saving events of the Exodus. The "signs and wonders" which Jesus and the apostles performed designate the inauguration of God's new saving event. *6.* Paul spoke of circumcision as a witness to the covenant (Rom. 4:11). *7.* Signs often serve as confirmation or authentication. The humble circumstances of the Christ-child in the manger confirmed the angel's announcement of a Savior to outcast shepherds (Luke 2:12). Jesus offered the difficult "sign of Jonah" as His authentication (Matt. 12:39–43; Luke 11:29–32). God was at work in Jesus' preaching of repentance as God had worked in Jonah. The New Testament often rebukes the demand for a sign to confirm God's work (Matt. 16:1; John 2:18; 4:48; 1 Cor. 1:22). A sign may evoke faith in a receptive heart, but no sign will convince the hard-hearted. *8.* Though the term sign is not used, Agabus' action in binding Paul with his belt (Acts 21:11) parallels the acts of the Old Testament prophets. *Chris Church*

SIGNET A seal, usually a ring with a seal carefully crafted upon it, which an important or rich person used to authenticate a document. It was used much like a signature on a document today. The ring of kings would carry the highest authority in a land and empowered subordinates to act for the king. Examples of such rings in the Bible are: Pharaoh's ring given to Joseph (Gen. 41:42), Ahasuerus' ring given to Haman and then to Mordecai after Haman was hanged (Esth. 3:10,12; 8:2), King Darius' sealing the den of lions after Daniel was thrown into it (Dan. 6:17). The signet could be worn on a chain around the neck (Song of Sol. 8:6). In an unusual use of the word, Zerubbabel is said to be "a signet" because the Lord had chosen him (Hag. 2:23). Zerubbabel was granted Yahweh's authority, and thus completion of the Temple was guaranteed. Another unusual use of the word was the special engraving of the stones on the ephod of the high priest "like the engravings of a signet" (Ex. 28:11). See *Seal*.

SIHON (Sī' hŏn) Amorite personal name of unknown meaning. Amorite king whose capital was Heshbon (Deut. 2:26). He opposed Israel's passage through his country as they journeyed toward the Promised Land (Num. 21:23). Although he allied with Og, king of Bashan, neither could withstand the Hebrew migration. The tribes of Reuben and Gad settled in the area formerly held by Sihon, just east of the Jordan River.

SIHOR (Sī' hōr) KJV spelling of Shihor. See *Shihor*.

SIKKUTH (Sĭk' kūth) NAS spelling of Sakkuth. See *Kaiwan; Rephan; Sakkuth*.

SILAS, SILVANUS (Sī' làs, Sĭl vā' nŭs) Apparently, the Greek and Latin form of same name, possibly derived from Aramaic or Hebrew name *Saul*. Leader in the early Jerusalem church. He accompanied both Peter and Paul on separate missionary journeys. One of his first missions was to carry news of the Jerusalem conference to the believers at Antioch (Acts 15:22). He and Paul left Antioch together on a mission to Asia Minor (15:40–41) and later to Macedonia. In Philippi the two were imprisoned (16:19–24), but they later won the jailer and his family to the Lord after

God delivered them from prison. Later in his ministry Silas teamed with Peter on missions in Pontus and Cappadocia. He also served as Peter's scribe, writing 1 Peter and perhaps other letters. Many believe that he composed and arranged most of the letter since Peter probably had little education. See *Paul; 1 Peter*.

SILENCE The absence of sound. The Bible uses silence in several ways: as reverence to God (Hab. 2:20), as a symbol of death (Ps. 94:17), as a symbol of Sheol (Ps. 115:17), and as an expression of despair (Lam. 2:10). It is a way to shut up the opposition (Matt. 22:34). It is also used as a dramatic pause following the opening of the seventh seal in Revelation 8:1.

SILK Cloth made from thread that came from the Chinese silk worm. Very early China and India traded. India also traded with Mesopotamia. Some think that Solomon may have gotten silk from India. Some feel that the Hebrew word translated "silk" should rather be "fine linen" or "expensive material" (see Ezek. 16:10; Prov. 31:22), the Hebrew indicating something glistening white. Revelation 18:12 indicates that the rich in Babylon bought silk from merchants.

SILLA (Sĭl' la) The house of Millo in which King Joash was murdered by his servants was said to be "on the way that goes down to Silla" (2 Kings 12:20 NRSV). Silla is an unknown place, perhaps near Jerusalem. See *Millo*.

SILOAM (Sī lō' am) Greek place name possibly derived from Hebrew, "Shiloah," meaning, "sending." Place easily confused with the waters of Shiloah mentioned in Isaiah 8:6, through similarity of spelling. Siloam was the pool created by Hezekiah's tunnel which diverted the waters of Shiloah from the Siloam Spring to a point less vulnerable to the Assyrian enemy. It was located on the southern end of the old Jebusite city of Jerusalem. See *Jerusalem*. Thus, Siloam is to be distinguished from the King's Pool mentioned in Nehemiah 3:15. See *King's Pool*. Hezekiah's inscription preserved on the tunnel wall describes the meeting of tunnel builders boring through rock from each end of the tunnel.

John 9:7,11 uses the etymological significance of the term Siloam for a play on words to press the point that the blind man was *sent* to Siloah by one who was Himself the One who was *sent*. To gain his sight, the blind man went to and obeyed the One who was sent. Luke 13:4 is a reference more to an unknown tower at Siloam than to Siloam. The tower may have been an aborted effort to protect the water supply. The theological issue of Luke 13 does not hinge on the geographical issue of Siloam.

S

The Pool of Siloam in Jerusalem.

The pool, created by Hezekiah and known by Jesus is still a source of water today.

John R. Drayer

SILVANUS (Sĭl vā′ nŭs) See *Silas, Silvanus.*

SILVER A comparatively scarce precious metal with a brilliant white color and remarkably resistant to oxidation. It melts at 960.8°C (1,861°F). Biblical references often refer to the process for refining silver (1 Chron. 29:4; Ps. 12:6; Prov. 17:3; Ezek. 22:20–22). It is so malleable that it is beaten into sheets as thin as 0.00025 mm. Until about 500 B.C., silver was the most valuable metal in the Near East. Thus, in most of the Old Testament it is given a priority over gold. Only in Chronicles and Daniel is gold considered to have more worth. Hence the analogy that in Jerusalem silver was as common as stone (1 Kings 10:27; 2 Chron. 9:27) is reflective of the lavish wealth of Solomon's empire. Coins were first minted after 700 B.C., but weight continued to be the most common standard of determining value. In the New Testament period, the drachma, a silver coin, was required for the Temple tax. Figuratively, refining silver is used in the Bible for testing human hearts (Ps. 66:10; Isa. 48:10; compare 1 Cor. 3:10–15) and the purity of God's word (Ps. 12:6). Wisdom is declared to be of more value

than silver (Job 28:10–15; Prov. 3:13–14; 8:10,19; 16:16). See *Coins; Gold; Money.*

LeBron Matthews

SILVERSMITH A person who works with silver. It could be in refining the silver from the ore or the making of the refined silver into the finished product. Silver was used for money and religious images (Judg. 17:4). Silver was used in making many of the utensils used in the tabernacle and Temple (Num. 7:13). The only mention of silversmiths in the NT was a dispute with Paul where his preaching was threatening their livelihood (Acts 19:23–41). See *Occupations and Professions in the Bible.*

SIMEON (Sĭm′ ė on) Personal name meaning, "hearing" or possibly, "little hyena beast." *1.* One of Jacob's twelve sons, the second by Leah (Gen. 29:33). He joined Levi in avenging Dinah's rape by Shechem (Gen. 34:25–31). Joseph kept Simeon bound in Egypt to ensure that he would see Benjamin (Gen. 42:24). See *Jacob; Tribes of Israel.*
2. A devout Jew who lived in Jerusalem during the time of Jesus' birth. He was seeking the fulfillment of messianic prophecy when Israel would be restored (Luke 2:25). God promised Simeon that he would not die before seeing the Christ. When Joseph and Mary brought Jesus to the Temple for

The solid silver case of a Torah (Genesis–Deuteronomy) scroll.

The traditional area of the home of Simon the tanner in ancient Joppa (modern Jaffa near Tel Aviv).

the purification rites, Simeon announced to them God's plan for the boy (2:34).

3. Ancestor of Jesus (Luke 3:30). *4.* Prophet and teacher in church at Antioch (Acts 13:1). *5.* Alternate form in Greek for Simon, original Greek name of Peter. See *Peter; Simon.*

SIMEONITES (Sĭm′ ē ō nītes) People of the tribe of Simeon, the second son of Jacob and Leah (Gen. 29:33).

SIMILITUDE "Likeness" or "similarity." *1.* The Old Testament used it of things being like God. Three words are translated "similitude" in the Old Testament: *demuth* (2 Chron. 4:3; Dan. 10:16), *tabnith* (Pss. 106:20; 144:12), and *temunah* (Num. 12:8; Deut. 4:12). *2.* In the New Testament it is used to translate *homoios* or its derivative three times (Rom. 5:14; Heb. 7:15; Jas. 3:9, "likeness" NAS).

SIMON (Sī mon) Greek personal name meaning, "flat-nosed." Used in New Testament as Greek alternative for Hebrew, "Simeon." *1.* The father of Judas Iscariot (John 6:71). *2.* One of Jesus' disciples; a son of Jonah (Matt. 16:17) and brother of Andrew. After he confessed Jesus as the Christ, the Lord changed his name to Peter (v. 18). See *Peter; Simeon.*

3. A Pharisee who hosted Jesus at a dinner (Luke 7:36–40). Simon learned valuable lessons about love, courtesy, and forgiveness after a sinful woman anointed Jesus at this event. *4.* A native of Cyrene who was forced to carry Jesus' cross to Golgotha (Mark 15:21). See *Cyrene.* *5.* A tanner of animal skins who lived in the seaport of Joppa. Peter stayed at his house (Acts 9:43) and there received a visionary message from God declaring all foods to be fit for consumption (10:9–16).

6. Jesus' disciple also called "the Canaanite" (Matt. 10:4) or the Zealot (Luke 6:15). *7.* Brother of Jesus (Matt. 13:55). *8.* A leper who hosted Jesus and saw a woman anoint Jesus with costly ointment (Matt. 26:6–13; compare *3.* above).

9. A magician from Samaria who believed Phil-

ip's preaching, was baptized, and then tried to buy the power of laying on hands and giving the Holy Spirit to people (Acts 8:9–24).

SIMPLICITY, SIMPLE Very similar to sincerity. A simple person is one who is open, honest, and direct, without hypocrisy. Sometimes there is the idea of uneducated, inexperienced, or unsophisticated. Simplicity is associated with ideas like integrity (2 Sam. 15:11), without evil (Rom. 16:18), generosity (Rom. 12:8), a life of devotion to God (2 Cor. 1:12), and simply believing the gospel truth (2 Cor. 11:3). God is said to "preserve" the simple (Ps. 116:6). Proverbs is filled with sayings about the simple, both good and bad (1:22; 14:15,18; 21:11). See *Sincerity.*

SIMRI (Sĭm′ rî) Another spelling of Shimri. See *Shimri.*

SIN (Sĭn) Actions by which humans rebel against God, miss His purpose for their life, and surrender to the power of evil rather than to God.

Sin as Rebellion One of the central affirmations throughout the Bible is humanity's estrangement from God. The cause for this estrangement is sin, the root cause of all the problems of humanity. The Bible, however, gives no formal definition for sin. It describes sin as an attitude that personifies sin as rebellion against God. Rebellion was at the root of the problem for Adam and Eve (Gen. 3) and has been at the root of humanity's plight ever since.

Sin's Origin in Humanity's Rebellious Nature Human sin is universal—we all sin. All persons without exception are under sin's dominion (Rom. 3:9–23). How did this come about? The Bible has no philosophical argument as such concerning sin's origin. God is in no way responsible for sin. Satan introduced sin when he beguiled Eve, but the Bible does not teach that sin had its origin with him either. Sin's origin is to be found in humanity's rebellious nature. Since Adam and Eve rebelled against the clear command of God, sin has infected humanity like a dread malignancy.

The Bible sets forth no systematic rationale as to how the human race was and is infected by this dread malady. Some passages such as Psalm 51:5; Ephesians 2:3 could be interpreted to mean that this sinful nature is inherited. Other passages seem to affirm that sin is due to human choice (see Ezek. 18:4,19–20; Rom. 1:18–20; 5:12.)

What then is the answer to the dilemma? A possible answer is the fact that the Jewish mind had no problem in admitting two mutually exclusive ideas into the same system of thought. Any idea that humanity inherits a sinful nature must be coupled with the corollary that every person is indeed responsible for his/her choice of sin.

Another possibility for understanding how sin has infected all of humanity may be found in the biblical understanding of the corporateness and solidarity of the human race. This understanding of the human situation would say that when Adam rebelled against God, he incorporated all of his descendants in his action (see Heb. 7:9–10 for a similar analogy). This view certainly does not eliminate the necessity for each individual to accept full responsibility for sinful acts.

Adam and Eve introduced sin into human history by their rebellious actions. The Bible affirms that every person who has lived since has followed their example. Whatever else one may say about sin's origin, this much is surely affirmed throughout the Bible.

The Bible Views Sin from Various Perspectives
One concept of sin in the Old Testament is that of transgression of the law. God established the law as a standard of righteousness; any violation of this standard is defined as sin. Deuteronomy 6:24–25 is a statement of this principle from the perspective that a person who keeps the law is righteous. The implication is that the person who does not keep the law is not righteous, that is, sinful.

Another concept of sin in the Old Testament is as breach of the covenant. God made a covenant with the nation Israel; they were bound by this covenant as a people (Ex. 19; 24; Josh. 24). Each year on the Day of Atonement, the nation went through a covenant renewal. When the high priest consecrated the people by sprinkling them with the blood of the atoning sacrifice, they renewed their vows to the Lord to be a covenant-keeping people. Any breach of this covenant was viewed as sin (Deut. 29:19–21.)

The Old Testament also pictures sin as a violation of the righteous nature of God. As the righteous and holy God, He sets forth as a criterion for His people a righteousness like His own. (Lev. 11:45.) Any deviation from God's own righteousness is viewed as sin.

The Old Testament has a rich vocabulary for sin.

Chata means "to miss the mark," as does the Greek *hamartia.* The word could be used to describe a person shooting a bow and arrow and missing the target with the arrow. When it is used to describe sin, it means that the person has missed the mark that God has established for the person's life.

Aven describes the crooked or perverse spirit associated with sin. Sinful persons have perverted their spirits and become crooked rather than straight. *Ra* describes the violence associated with sin. It also has the connotation of the breaking out of evil. Sin is the opposite of righteousness or moral straightness in the Old Testament.

The New Testament Perspective of Sin The New Testament picture is much like that of the Old Testament. Several of the words used for sin in the New Testament have almost the same mean-

ing as some of the Hebrew words used in the Old Testament. The most notable advancement in the New Testament view of sin is the fact that sin is defined against the backdrop of Jesus as the standard for righteousness. His life exemplifies perfection. The exalted purity of His life creates the norm for judging what is sinful.

In the New Testament, sin also is viewed as a lack of fellowship with God. The ideal life is one of fellowship with God. Anything which disturbs or distorts this fellowship is sin.

The New Testament view of sin is somewhat more subjective than objective. Jesus taught quite forcefully that sin is a condition of the heart. He traced sin directly to inner motives stating that the sinful thought leading to the overt act is the real sin. The outward deed is actually the fruit of sin. Anger in the heart is the same as murder (Matt. 5:21–22). The impure look is tantamount to adultery (Matt. 5:27–28). The real defilement in a person stems from the inner person (heart) which is sinful (Matt. 15:18–20). Sin, therefore, is understood as involving the essential being of a person, that is, the essential essence of human nature.

The New Testament interprets sin as unbelief. However, unbelief is not just the rejection of a dogma or a creed. Rather, it is the rejection of that spiritual light which has been revealed in Jesus Christ. Or, from another perspective, unbelief is the rejection of the supreme revelation as it is found in the person of Jesus Christ. Unbelief is resistance to the truth of God revealed by the Spirit of God and produces moral and spiritual blindness. The outcome of such rejection is judgment. The only criterion for judgment is whether or not one has accepted or rejected the revelation of God as found in Jesus Christ (John 3:18–19; 16:8–16).

The New Testament further pictures sin as being revealed by the law of Moses. The law was preparatory, and its function was to point to Christ. The law revealed sin in its true character, but this only aroused in humanity a desire to experience the forbidden fruit of sin. The law as such is not bad, but humanity simply does not have the ability to keep the law. Therefore, the law offers no means of salvation; rather, it leaves humanity with a deep sense of sin and guilt (Rom. 7). The law, therefore, serves to bring sin into bold relief, so that it is clearly perceptible.

The most common New Testament word for sin is *hamartia.* See above. *Parabasis,* "trespass" or "transgression," literally, means to step across the line. One who steps over a property line has trespassed on another person's land; the person who steps across God's standard of righteousness has committed a trespass or transgression.

Anomia means "lawlessness" or "iniquity" and is a rather general description of sinful acts, referring to almost any action in opposition to God's standard of righteousness. *Poneria,* "evil" or "wickedness," is even a more general term than *anomia. Adikia,* "unrighteousness," is just the opposite of righteous. In forensic contexts outside the New Testament, it described one who was on the wrong side of the law.

Akatharsia, "uncleanness" or "impurity," was a cultic word used to describe anything which could cause cultic impurity. It was used quite often to describe vicious acts or sexual sins. *Apistia,* "unbelief," literally refers to a lack of faith. To refuse to accept the truth of God by faith is to sin. Hence any action which can be construed as unfaithful or any disposition which is marked by a lack of faith is sinful.

Epithumia, often translated "lust," is actually a neutral word. Only the context can determine if the desire is good or evil. Jesus said, "I have eagerly desired to eat this Passover with you before I suffer" (Luke 22:15 NIV). Paul used this word with a modifier meaning, "evil," in Colossians 3:5, where it is translated "evil concupiscence" or "evil desires." When used in this way, the word could refer to almost any evil desire but was most often used to describe sexual sins (Matt. 5:28).

Sin's Consequences The Bible looks upon sin in any form as the most serious of humanity's problems. Though sinful acts may be directed against another person, ultimately every sin is against God, the Creator of all things. Perfect in righteousness, God cannot tolerate that which violates His righteous character. Therefore, sin creates a barrier between God and persons.

Sin also necessitates God's intervention in human affairs. Since humanity could not extricate itself from the entanglements of sin, it was necessary for God to intervene if humanity was ever to be freed from these entanglements. See *Salvation.*

The consequences of sin both personally and in society are far reaching. That person who constantly and consistently follows a sinful course will become so enmeshed in sin that for all practical purposes he or she is enslaved to sin (Rom. 6, for example).

Another of the awful consequences of sin is spiritual depravity in society in general as well as in the lives of individuals. Some will argue that depravity is the cause of sin, and this surely is a valid consideration. However, there can be no escaping the fact that a continuance in sin adds to this personal depravity, a moral crookedness or corruption eventually making it impossible to reject sin.

Sin also produces spiritual blindness. Spiritual truths simply are not visible to that person who has been blinded by sin.

Moral ineptitude is another devastating consequence of sin. The more people practice sin, the more inept they become as far as moral and spiritual values are concerned. Eventually, sin blurs the distinction between right and wrong.

Guilt is certainly a consequence of sin. No person can blame another person for a sin problem. Each person must accept responsibility for sin and face the guilt associated with it (Rom. 1—3).

In the Bible sin and death are corrolaries. One of the terrible byproducts of sin is death. Continual, consistent sin will bring spiritual death to that person who has not come under the lordship of Christ through repentance and faith (Rom. 6:23; Rev. 20:14.) For those who have trusted Christ Jesus for salvation, death no longer holds this dread. Christ has negated the power of Satan in making death horrible and has freed the person from slavery to this awful fear (Heb. 2:14–15.) See *Death.*

Another serious consequence of sin is that it brings separation from God, estrangement, and a lack of fellowship with God. This need not be permanent, but if a person dies not having corrected this problem by trusting Christ, then the separation does become permanent (Rom. 6:23). See *Hell.*

Sin produces estrangement from other persons just as surely as it produces an estrangement from God. All interpersonal problems have sin as their root cause (Jas. 4:1–3). The only hope for peace to be achieved on either the personal or national level is through the Prince of peace.

Billy E. Simmons

SIN, WILDERNESS OF (Sĭn) Barren region somewhere west of the Sinai plateau on the Sinai peninsula. The Hebrew people stopped here on their journey from Egypt to the Promised Land (Ex. 16:1). It was here that God first provided manna and quail for them to eat. The place sometimes has been confused with the Wilderness of Zin, which is located on the northwestern side of Sinai. See *Zin.*

SINAI See *Mount Sinai.*

SINCERITY The personal quality of living life from a pure motive without deceit. Associated with words or ideas like "truth" (1 Cor. 5:8), "genuineness" (2 Cor. 8:8), "godliness" (2 Cor.

The desolate country of the Wilderness of Zin .

1:12), and preaching sincerely the gospel (2 Cor. 2:17). It is also contrasted with words like hypocrisy, deceit, and wickedness. See *Holiness, Holy; Truth.*

SINEW The tendons and connective tissue that connect muscles to bone in the body. The literal use is seen in Scripture (Job 10:11; 30:17; Ezek. 37:6,8). Isaiah 48:4 uses it in a figurative way to show rebellion against God. Because of Jacob's wrestling with the angel that resulted in the angel's striking the sinew of his thigh, the Jews cut away this sinew and did not eat it (Gen. 32:24–32). See *Body.*

SINGING, SINGERS *See Hymns; Levites; Music.*

SINIM (Sī′ nĭm) Land from which God promised to gather the Babylonian Exiles (Isa. 49:12). Traditionally translated as China and treated variously by early translators as Persia or the south, the term received clarification from an Isaiah manuscript among the Dead Sea Scrolls, which reads, "Syenites," a reference to modern Aswan (compare NIV, REB, NRSV). See *Syene.*

SINITE (Sī′ nīte) People from a city–state controlled by Ugarit, the Hittites, and the Assyrians whose inhabitants descended from Canaan (Gen. 10:17). It is in northern Phoenicia near Arqa, either Siyanu two and a half miles east of Gebala or Shen south southeast of Halba.

View from Jebel Musa (the probable location of Mount Sinai) of the surrounding rugged landscape.

Jebel Musa (traditionally accepted as Mount Sinai) in the southern Sinai peninsula.

SINNER A person who has missed God's mark for life, rebelling against Him. The Bible considers every person a sinner (Rom. 3:23). In the Old Testament people who do not live by the law were considered sinners (Ps. 1). The New Testament uses *anomia* in a similar way (1 Tim 1:9). Jews regarded Gentiles as sinners (Gal. 2:15) as also people who did not keep the tradition of the Pharisees, including Jesus (Matt. 11:19; see Luke 15). Paul spoke of sinners as those separated from God (Rom. 5:8). See *Law; Salvation; Sin.*

SION (Sī' ŏn) *1.* KJV spelling of Sirion (Deut. 4:48). *2.* KJV spelling of Zion (Ps. 65:1; Matt. 21:5; Rom. 11:26; Rev. 14:1). See *Zion.*

SIPHMOTH (Siph' mōth) Town in southern Judah that received booty of war from David for befriending him (1 Sam. 30:26,28). The location of Siphmoth is unknown. A man named Zabdi may have been a resident of the town (1 Chron. 27:27). See *Shiphmite.*

SIPPAI (Sĭp' pā ī) Alternate rendering (1 Chron. 20:4) of the name "Saph" (2 Sam. 21:18), a son of a giant killed by Sibbechai the Hushathite. See *Saph.*

SIRAH (Sī' rah) Place name meaning, "thorn." A well ("cistern of Sirah" NRSV) where Joab and Abishai murdered Abner for killing their brother Asahel (2 Sam. 3:26–30). This well is probably the well named 'Ain Sarah, a little over a mile northwest of Hebron. See *Wells.*

SIRION (Sĭr' î ŏn) Sidonian name for Mount Hermon (Deut. 3:9). See *Hermon, Mount.*

SISAMAI (Sĭs' à mâi) KJV spelling of Sismai. See *Sismai.*

SISERA (Sĭs' ēr à) Personal name meaning, "mediation." *1.* Military leader of Jabin, king of Canaan (Judg. 4:2) who was killed by Heber's wife, Jael (v. 21). *2.* A man in a list of Nethinim descendants who returned to Palestine with Zerubbabel (Ezra 2:53; Neh. 7:55). See *Jabin; Judges.*

SISMAI (Sĭs' mâi) Personal name of uncertain meaning. Son of Eleasah and father of Shallum (1 Chron. 2:40; "Sisamai" KJV).

SISTER Female sibling counterpart to brother (Gen. 29:13; 30:1,8). In patriarchal times it was permissible to marry a sister (Gen. 20:12). Sister was also used of people held in special esteem as a counterpart to brotherly affection (Song of Sol. 4:9; 8:8). Christian women who proved helpful and assisted the church to live like family were called "sister" (Rom. 16:1–2). Martha and Mary, sisters of Lazarus, were well known as friends and supporters of Jesus. Jesus said, "For whosoever shall do the will of God, the same is my brother, and my sister, and mother" (Mark 3:35). See *Family; Women.*

SITHRI (Sĭth' rî) Personal name probably meaning, "He is my protection." A son of Uzziel in the genealogy of Levi (Ex. 6:22; "Zithri" KJV).

SITNAH (Sĭt' nah) A well Isaac's servants dug in the area of Gerar (Gen. 26:21). The well was seized by the servants of Abimelech. Therefore, the name of the well meaning "hatred" or "opponent." See *Wells.*

SIVAN (Sī' văn) Third month (May–June) of the Hebrew calendar, time of wheat harvest and Pentecost. See *Calendars.*

SKIN The outer part of the human body and of the body of animals. *1.* The mention of human skin is often in relation to disease (see Lev. 13). Human skin is also mentioned in relationship to hairiness (Gen. 27:11–12,16,22–23); to sickness (Job 7:5; Lam. 5:10); and to the color (Jer. 13:23). *2.* Genesis 3:21 is the first mention of animal skins in the Bible. Animal skins were used to make containers for various kinds of liquids: water, milk, wine (Judg. 4:19 NIV; Matt. 9:17 NIV). The most used hides probably came from the animals most in use: sheep, goats, oxen, and donkeys, although other animal's skins certainly were used when available. *3.* The sacrifice of animals sometimes called for the destruction of the entire animal (Lev. 4:11–12). At other times the skins were the property of the priests for their use (Lev. 7:8). *4.* The skin was also used in several proverbial sayings: "Skin for skin" (Job 2:4), "the skin of my teeth" (Job 19:20), and "Can the Ethiopian change his skin or the leopard his spots?" (Jer. 13:23). See *Diseases; Leprosy; Vessels and Utensils.*

SKIRT An article of clothing. Three Hebrew words are translated "skirt." *1. Kanaph* refers to the four loose corners of a garment. David cut off one of these corners of Saul's robe to show he meant Saul no harm (1 Sam. 24:4,11). "To reveal a skirt" (literal reading of Deut. 22:30; 27:20) is a euphemism for sexual relationships, since placing the skirt over a woman of marriageable age was the same as claiming her for marriage (Ruth 3:7–14). *2. Peh,* meaning "mouth," is translated "skirts" in Psalm 130:2 ("collar" NIV, NRSV; "edge" NAS). *3. Shul* refers to the part of a garment that hangs the closest to the ground. In some passages it refers to the loose garment of a woman. Several references to Jerusalem use this word figuratively to show her sin (Jer. 13:22,26; Lam. 1:9; Nah. 3:5). The lifting of the skirt brought shame because the nakedness of a person was seen (Isa. 47:1–3; Nah. 3:5). See *Cloth, Clothing.*

SKULL See *Calvary.*

SKY See *Heaven.*

SLANDER To speak critically of another person with the intent to hurt (Lev. 19:16). In a court of law it means to falsely accuse another (Ex. 20:16; Deut. 5:20). Jesus said, "Every idle word that men shall speak, they shall give account thereof in the day of judgment" (Matt. 12:36). This should cause each person to be very careful what they say about others (see Eph. 4:31; 1 Pet. 2:1). The Bible shows that slander is a mark of the unregenerate world (Jas. 4:11–12; 1 Pet. 2:12; 3:16). Jesus spoke of Satan as one who "does not stand in the truth, because there is no truth in him. When he lies, he speaks according to his own nature, for he is a liar and the father of lies" (John 8:44 NRSV). *Diabolos* can mean "slanderous" or "the slanderer" (the devil). See *Devil, Satan, Evil, Demonic; Ethics.*

SLAVE/SERVANT Person totally responsible to and dependant upon another person.

Slavery was prevalent and widely accepted in the ancient world. The economy of Egypt, Greece, and Rome was based on slave labor. In the first Christian century, one out of three persons in Italy and one out of five elsewhere was a slave. Huge gangs toiled in the fields and mines and on building projects. Many were domestic and civil servants. Some were temple slaves and others craftsmen. Some were forced to become gladiators. Some were highly intelligent and held responsible positions. Legally, a slave had no rights; but, except for the gangs, most were treated humanely and were better off than many free persons. Domestics were considered part of the family, and some were greatly loved by their masters. Canaan, Aram, Assyria, Babylonia, and Persia had fewer slaves because it proved less expensive to hire free persons. Still, the institution of slavery was unquestioned. The Stoics insisted that slaves were humans and should be treated accordingly; Israel's law protected slaves in various ways; Christian preachers called upon masters to be kind, but only the Essenes opposed slavery. See *Essenes; Jewish Parties.*

A person could become a slave as a result of capture in war, default on a debt, inability to support and "voluntarily" selling oneself, being sold as a child by destitute parents, birth to slave parents, conviction of a crime, or kidnapping and piracy. Slavery cut across races and nationalities.

Manumission or freeing of slaves was possible and common in Roman times. Masters in their wills often freed their slaves, and sometimes they did so during their lifetimes. Industrious slaves could make and save money and purchase their own freedom. By the first Christian century, a large class of freedmen had developed. There was even a synagogue of the Freedmen in Jerusalem (Acts 6:9).

Slavery in the Old Testament Slavery laws appear in Exodus 21:1–11; Leviticus 25:39–55; and Deuteronomy 15:12–18. Most of these concern humane treatment and manumission. A Hebrew sold to another Hebrew or a resident alien because of insolvency was to be released after six years of service and given provisions to start over. If he had come with a wife, she and any children were also released. If the master had given him a wife, she and the children were to remain. If, however, the slave wanted to stay with his wife and children rather than be free, he could enroll himself as a slave for life. A Hebrew who sold himself to another Hebrew or resident alien was to be released during the Jubilee Year. See *Jubilee.* A slave could be redeemed at any time by a relative. A Hebrew girl sold by her father to another Hebrew to become his wife was to be released if that man or his son did not marry her. A slave permanently maimed by his or her master was to be freed (Ex. 21:26–27). A fugitive slave—presumably one who had escaped from a foreign owner—was not to be extradited (Deut. 23:15–16). Foreigners could be enslaved permanently, but they had the right to circumcision (Ex. 12:44–48), sabbath rest (Ex. 20:10), and holidays (Deut. 16:11,14). One was to be punished for beating a slave to death (Ex. 21:20–21).

Slavery in the New Testament Paul and Peter insisted that Christian slaves be obedient to their masters (Eph. 6:5–8; Col. 3:22–25; 1 Tim. 6:1–2; 1 Pet. 2:18–21) and not seek freedom just because of conversion (1 Cor. 7:20–22). Masters were urged to be kind (Eph. 6:9; Col. 4:1). Slave trading was condemned (1 Tim. 1:10). Paul claimed that in Christ human status was unimportant (Gal. 3:28). But neither Jesus nor the apostles condemned slavery. Why? Because slavery was so much a part of their society that to call for abolition would have resulted in violence and bloodshed. That is not the Christian way! Rather, Jesus and the apostles set forth principles of human dignity and equality which eventually led to abolition.

Metaphorical Uses of Slavery In most ancient societies, few things were more despicable than to be a slave. In Israel, however, the idea emerged that it was a great privilege to be a servant or slave of God (the various Hebrew and Greek words could be translated either). Many of the heroes of the Old Testament are so called (Ex. 32:13; Deut. 34:5; 2 Sam. 7:5; 2 Kings 21:10). Very significant are the Servant Songs of Isaiah 42:1–4; 49:1–6; 50:4–9; and 52:13—53:12, which originally referred to Israel but were reinterpreted by the early church to refer to Jesus. See *Servant of the Lord.*

Jesus adopted a servant's role (John 13:4–5; Mark 10:45; compare Phil. 2:7) and indicated that His disciples should also (Matt. 6:24; 10:24; 24:45–46; Luke 17:10; John 13:12–16). Paul referred to himself as a slave or servant of Jesus Christ (Rom. 1:1; Gal. 1:10; Phil. 1:1), as did James (1:1), Peter (2 Pet. 1:1), and Jude (1).

There are three other metaphorical uses of slavery in the New Testament. A life of sin is spoken of as slavery (John 8:34; Rom. 6:6,16–20; Heb. 2:15). Legalism is a kind of slavery (Gal. 4:24–25; 5:1). Paradoxically, however, there is also a blessed slavery to righteousness (Rom. 6:16–22).

James A. Brooks

SLEEP The natural state of rest for human beings and animals (Ps. 4:8). God causes state called "deep sleep," sometimes for revelation (Gen. 2:21; 15:12; Job 4:13), and sometimes to prevent prophetic vision (Isa. 29:10; compare 1 Sam. 26:12). It is also used as a sign of laziness (Prov. 19:15). Sleep is a figure of physical death (John 11:11–14; 1 Cor. 15:51). See *Death; Eternal Life.*

SLIME See *Bitumen.*

SLING, SLINGERS, SLINGSTONES Weapon of two long straps with a piece between them at the end to hold the stone. Shepherds and professional soldiers used slings. See *Arms and Armor.*

SLOTHFUL A loose, undisciplined person. The Hebrew term can refer to a bow not strung or equipped with an arrow for action (Ps. 78:57; Hos. 7:16). A same or related Hebrew root describes a loose tongue or mind as deceitful (Job 13:7; 27:4; Pss. 32:2; 52:4; Mic. 6:12). The slothful person cannot lead but becomes subjected to another's rule (Prov. 12:24; compare 10:4; 19:15). God's work must not be done in such a spirit (Jer. 48:10). See *Ethics.* A second Hebrew term refers to that which is difficult, heavy, hindered and indicates foolish laziness or sluggishness. The tribe of Dan was encouraged to take the new territory and not be slothful or reluctant (Judg. 18:9). The wise, hardworking ant illustrates the opposite of sloth (Prov. 6:6), while the slothful wants only to sleep (Prov. 6:9; compare 10:26; 13:4; 15:19; 19:24; 20:4; 21:25; 22:13; 24:30; 26:16). The virtuous woman is the opposite of slothful, not having to live with the results of idle sloth (Prov. 31:27). Ecclesiastes apparently coined a word for slothfulness twice over and the resulting decay of present gain (10:18). Jesus condemned a wicked, slothful servant (Matt. 25:26) but praised and rewarded the "good and faithful servant" (Matt. 25:23).

SMYRNA (Smỹr′ nȧ) A major city on the West coast of Asia Minor, the modern city of Izmir, Turkey. It had good harbor facilities, was at the end of a major road, and was surrounded by rich farmland. It is the second of the seven churches addressed in Revelation (2:8–11), one of two churches of which the Lord spoke no negative

Ruins of the forum at the site of the ancient city of Smyrna in Asia Minor (modern Turkey).

word. (Philadelphia was the other.) Smyrna gave its loyalty to the Romans at an early stage (about 195 B.C.) and never wavered. The Romans often rewarded Smyrna for its loyalty. The city was headquarters for the imperial cult of emperor worship in that area of the empire. Christians were persecuted by Jews and Romans. Polycarp was a famous Christian martyr who was burned at the stake in Smyrna about A.D. 156. See *Asia Minor.*

Statues found in the ruins of Smyrna (modern Izmir, Turkey).

SNAIL Animal whose name apparently means, "moist one." It illustrates the quick end to life (Ps. 58:8). Attempts to translate "miscarriage" instead of "snail" do not seem to be based on good linguistic evidence. KJV translated the unclean reptile of Leviticus 11:30 as "snail." Other suggestions include "sand reptile" (NAS), "skink" (NIV), "sand lizard" (NRS), and "great lizard" (REB).

SNARE Trap to catch birds and animals. There were basically two kinds of snares. One used rope or cord. Either the animal stepped in the trap and was snared by the feet, or the rope fell from above and caught the animal by the neck. The most common was a trap with a net. The animal would be attracted by the bait. When the baited trigger was released, the net covered the animal and captured it. Also the opening of a pit would be camouflaged with cover. The animal would fall into the pit and be captured. Figuratively, snares spoke of peril or death and the destruction of persons (Job 22:10; Ps. 18:5; compare 1 Sam. 28:9). See *Fowler; Hunt/Hunter.*

SNOW Being basically in a hot climate, Palestine has snow only rarely. Yet Mount Hermon has a snow cap that can be seen throughout much of Palestine. Snow is used in the Bible figuratively: whiteness (Isa. 1:18), cleanness (Job 9:30), refreshing coolness (Prov. 25:13). See *Weather.*

SNUFFERS Two different instruments used to tend the lamps in the tabernacle and the Temple. One instrument seems to be a cutting tool used for trimming the wicks of the lamps. The other word is often translated "tongs" (Isa. 6:6), meaning that it consisted in two parts working together. Exodus 25:38 speaks of "tongs" and "snuffdishes." Evidently these instruments were used to trim the wicks of the lamps and dispose of the waste.

SOAP A cleaner made by mixing olive oil and alkali from burning certain salt-producing plants. It was used of washing the body (Jer. 2:22) and of washing clothes (Mal. 3:2). Perhaps the scant references to soap is due to the fact that people in the Near East use oil for cleansing the body and pound clothes on rocks while wet to cleanse them. See *Fuller.*

SOBER Characterized by self-control, seriousness, and sound moral judgment (1 Thess. 5:6,8; 1 Tim. 3:2,11; Tit. 1:8; 2:2,6; 1 Pet. 1:13; 5:8). The KJV employed sober to mean in one's right mind at 2 Corinthians 5:13.

SOCOH, SOCO, SHOCHO (Sō′ cōh) Place name meaning, "thorns." *1.* Town in southern Judah hill country used as a fortification against people approaching from the south (Josh. 15:35). It is modern Khirbet Abbad. Philistines gathered to battle Saul there (1 Sam. 17:1). Rehoboam fortified it (2 Chron. 11:7). *2.* A town in the southern hill country of Judah about ten miles southwest of Hebron (Josh. 15:48) at khirbet Shuweikeh. *3.* A town belonging to Ben-hesed (1 Kings 4:10 NRSV), one of the twelve officials who provided food for Solomon and his household. It is aš-Shuweikeh west of Nablus and two miles north of Tulkarm. *4.* A native of Judah, the son of Heber (1 Chron. 4:18). Some interpreters feel that this is a place name rather than personal name. May be the same as *2.*

SODI (Sō′ dî) Personal name meaning, "my counsel." Father of Gaddiel of Zebulun, one of the spies Moses sent to spy out Canaan (Num. 13:10).

SODOM AND GOMORRAH (Sŏ′ dŏm, Gŏ mōr′ räh) Place names of uncertain meaning. Two cities in Palestine at the time of Abraham. Sodom and Gomorrah were among the five "cities of the valley" (Gen. 13:12; 19:29; KJV, "plain") of Abraham's time. Exact locations are unknown, but they were probably situated in the Valley of Siddim (Gen. 14:3,8,10–11) near the Dead Sea, perhaps the area now covered by the Sea's shallow southern end. Lot moved to this area, eventually settling in Sodom (Gen. 13:10–12; 14:12; 19:1).

Sodom and Gomorrah were renowned for their wickedness (Gen. 18:20). Despite Abraham's successful plea (18:22–32) not even ten righteous men could be found in Sodom, and the cities were judged by the Lord, then destroyed by "brimstone and fire" (19:24; NIV, "burning sulfur").

The unnatural lusts of the men of Sodom (Gen. 19:4–8; Jude 7) have given us the modern term sodomy, but the city was guilty of a full spectrum of sins including pride, oppression of the poor, haughtiness, and "abominable things" (Ezek. 16:49–50). Together, Sodom and Gomorrah provided a point of comparison for the sinfulness of Israel and other nations (Deut. 32:32; Isa. 1:10; Jer. 23:14). The memory of their destruction provided a picture of God's judgment (Isa. 13:19; Jer. 49:18; Matt. 10:14–15; 11:23–24) and made them an example to be avoided (Deut. 29:23–25; 2 Pet. 2:6). *Daniel C. Browning, Jr.*

SODOMITE Originally a citizen of the town of Sodom, one of the cities of the plain near the Dead Sea (Gen 13:12). The term came to mean a male who has sexual relations with another male. The wickedness of Sodom became proverbial (see Gen. 19:1–11). See *Homosexuality; Sex.*

SOLDIER A person trained to fight, usually on active military duty. In early Israelite history every male was called on to fight when the tribes were threatened. David was the first to put together a national army made up of professional soldiers. Kings often had a personal group of soldiers to guard them. The New Testament soldier was usually the Roman soldier. John the Baptist indicated that the average Roman soldier extorted money from civilians by threatening them (Luke 3:14). On the other hand, the centurion (leader of 100 men) is held in esteem in the New Testament (see Acts 10). See *Army; Centurion.*

SOLEMN ASSEMBLY See *Festivals.*

SOLOMON (Sŏl′ ō mŏn) Personal name whose meaning is variously interpreted as "his peace," "(God) is peace," "Salem (a god)," "intact," or "his replacement." Tenth son of David and the second son of Bathsheba, Solomon became the third king of Israel and reigned forty years about 1000 B.C.

Cut-away view of Solomon's Temple at Jerusalem, showing the porch, the holy place, and the holy of holies—where giant protecting cherubim and the sacred ark of the covenant were placed.

Old Testament Solomon was born to David and Bathsheba after the death of their first son (2 Sam. 12:24). Although not the oldest living son of David, he was crowned king after his mother and Nathan the prophet intervened with David and secured David's decision to have Solomon succeed him (1 Kings 1—2). Solomon is remembered most for his wisdom, his building program, and his wealth generated through trade and administrative reorganization.

Solomon was remembered as having three thousand proverbs and a thousand and five songs in his repertoire (1 Kings 4:32). Thus, it is not surprising that Proverbs and Song of Solomon in the Bible are attributed to Solomon (Prov. 1:1; Song of Sol. 1:1) as are several apocryphal and pseudepigraphal books. See *Apocrypha; Pseudepigrapha.* His wisdom is also illustrated in the Bible by the accounts of the two harlots who claimed the single surviving child (1 Kings 3:16) and by the visit of the queen of Sheba (1 Kings 10).

While Solomon's Temple was the most famous of his building projects (1 Kings 5—8), it was by no means the only one. Solomon fortified a number of cities that helped provide protection to Jerusalem, built "store-cities" for stockpiling the materials required in his kingdom, and established military bases for contingents of charioteers (1 Kings 9:15–19). The Temple complex in Jerusalem was composed of several buildings including Solomon's palace, the "house of the forest of Lebanon," the "hall or porch of pillars," the "hall or porch of the throne," and a palace for one of his wives, the daughter of the pharaoh of Egypt

(1 Kings 7). See *Archaeology; Gezer; Hazor; Megiddo; Temple.*

Solomon divided the country into administrative districts that did not correspond to the old tribal boundaries (1 Kings 4:7–19) and had the districts provide provisions for the central government. This system, combined with control of vital north/south trade routes between the Red Sea and what was later known as Asia Minor, made it possible for Solomon to accumulate vast wealth. This wealth was supplemented both from trading in horses and chariots and from trade carried on by a fleet of ships (1 Kings 9:26–28; 10:26–29). See *Eloth; Ezion-geber.*

The Bible clearly notes that Solomon had faults as well as elements of greatness. The "seven hundred wives, princesses, and three hundred concubines" came from many of the kingdoms with which Solomon had treaties (1 Kings 11:1). He apparently allowed his wives to worship their native gods and even had altars to these gods constructed in Jerusalem (1 Kings 11:7–8). This kind of compromise indicated to the historian a weakness in Solomon not found in David. Rebellions led by the king of Edom, Rezon of Damascus, and Jeroboam, one of Solomon's own officers,

Reconstruction of Solomon's Temple (957–587 B.C.) at Jerusalem and its courts. Shown are the ten lavers (five on each side of the Temple), the Molten Sea (lower, center), and the Altar of Burnt Offerings (center). Solomon's palace (left) stood immediately west of the Temple court, overlooking the Temple.

indicates that Solomon's long reign was not without its turmoil.

New Testament Solomon was an ancestor of Jesus (Matt. 1:6–7) and is mentioned in Jesus' teaching about anxiety (Matt. 6:29; Luke 12:27). Jesus noted that the queen of Sheba came a long way to see Solomon and that "something greater than Solomon is here" (Matt. 12:42; Luke 11:31). Jesus walked in "Solomon's porch," a part of the Temple area (John 10:23; compare Acts 3:11; 5:12). Stephen noted that though David sought to find a place for God, it was Solomon who "built a house for him" (Acts 7:47).

Joe O. Lewis

SOLOMON'S PORCH The raised outermost part of Herod's Temple with columns that went all the way around the outer court (John 10:23; Acts 3:11). It is called "the portico of Solomon" (NAS, NRSV, REB) and "Solomon's Colonnade" (NIV), since Solomon's workers constructed at least the oldest portico on the east side. In Jesus' day this part of the Temple had been built by Herod's laborers. See *Temple.*

SON OF GOD Term used to express the deity of Jesus of Nazareth as the one, unique Son of God. In the Old Testament, certain men and angels (Gen. 6:1–4; Pss. 29:1; 82:6; 89:6) are called "sons of God" (note text notes in modern translations). The people of Israel were corporately considered the son of God (Ex. 4:22; Jer. 31:20; Hos. 11:1). The concept also is employed in the Old

S

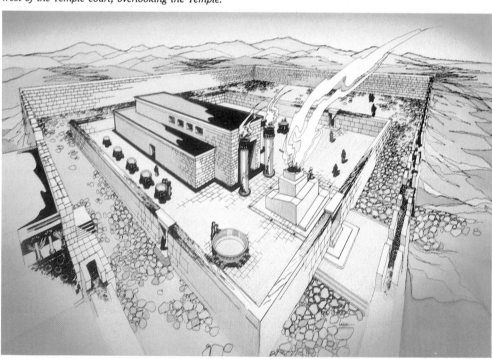

Reconstruction of Solomon's Porch in the model of first-century Jerusalem (Holyland Hotel, Jerusalem).

Testament with reference to the king as God's son (Ps. 2:7). The promises found in the Davidic covenant (2 Sam. 7:14) are the source for this special filial relationship. The title can be found occasionally in intertestamental implications (Wisd. of Sol. 2:16,18; 4 Ezra 7:28–29; 13:32,37,52; 14:9; Book of Enoch 105:2).

Jesus' own assertions and intimations indicate that references to Him as Son of God can be traced to Jesus Himself. At the center of Jesus' identity in the Fourth Gospel is His divine sonship (John 10:36). Jesus conceived of His divine sonship as unique as indicated by such assertions as "I and the Father are one" (John 10:30 NIV) and the "Father is in me and I am in the Father" (John 10:38 NRSV). Elsewhere, He frequently referred to God as "my Father" (John 5:17; 6:32; 8:54; 10:18; 15:15; Matt. 7:21; 10:32–33; 20:23; 26:29,53; Mark 8:38; Luke 2:49; 10:21–22).

At Jesus' baptism and transfiguration, God the Father identified Jesus as His son, in passages reflecting Psalm 2:7. He was identified as Son of God by an angel prior to His birth (Luke 1:32,35); by Satan at His temptation (Matt. 4:3,6); by John the Baptist (John 1:34); by the centurion at the crucifixion (Matt. 27:54). Several of His followers ascribed to Him this title in various contexts (Matt. 14:33; 16:16; John 1:49; 11:27).

The term Son of God reveals Jesus' divine sonship and is closely associated with His royal position as Messiah. Gabriel told Mary that her Son would not only be called the Son of God, but would also reign on the messianic (David's) throne (Luke 1:32–33). The connection of Son of God with Jesus' royal office is also found in John (1:49; 11:27; 20:30), in Paul (Rom. 1:3–4; 1 Cor. 15:28; Col. 1:13), and in Luke (Acts 9:20–22).

Primarily, the title Son of God affirms Jesus' deity evidenced by His person and His work. John emphasized Jesus' personal relationship to the Father. Paul stressed the salvation that Jesus provided (Rom. 1:4; 1 Thess. 1:10), and the author of Hebrews focused on Jesus' priesthood (5:5). All of

these are vitally related to His position as Son of God.   *David S. Dockery*

SON OF MAN New Testament designation for Jesus as God incarnate in flesh and agent of divine judgment. It occurs some 84 times in the Gospels, all but one being Jesus' self-description.

The Old Testament With the exception of Ezekiel and Daniel, the term *Son of man* appears in the Old Testament as a synonym for "man," "humankind" (Isa. 56:2; Jer. 50:40; Pss. 8:4; 80:17; 146:3; Job 25:6). In the Aramaic language spoken in Palestine in Jesus' day, the expression *Son of man* was similarly used to mean "the man," "a man," or simply "someone." The term appears in the rabbinic writings with the meaning, "a certain person."

1. Ezekiel In Ezekiel, God uses the term 90 times to address the prophet. The exact nuance of this usage is widely debated. Is the emphasis on the humanity and frailty of the prophet? It is used, perhaps, as a title to distinguish him from other men. Or, it may reveal the prophet's sense of identity with his people. In any event, the emphasis seems to be on the *humanity* of the prophet, a meaning which Christians also came to attach to the term when applied to Jesus.

2. Daniel The most distinctive Old Testament use of "Son of man" is in Daniel 7:13. In one of his night visions, the prophet saw "one like a son of man" (NAS) come on the clouds of heaven to appear before the throne of God. He was given dominion over all peoples and an everlasting kingdom. Scholars are divided over whether the Son of man of Daniel's vision should be seen as an angel, as the Messiah, or as all of Israel. (The latter conclusion is drawn from the fact that in Dan. 7:27 the "saints of the most High" were granted dominion over an everlasting kingdom.) Later, Jewish interpretation of Daniel 7:13, however, is at one in seeing the reference as messianic. This is true of the later apocalyptic writings such as Enoch and 2 Esdras as well as the rabbinic writings.

The New Testament The "Son of man" sayings of Jesus fall into three distinct types.

1. Apocalyptic Sayings The largest number of Son of man sayings deal with the final times when the Son of man will descend to earth to gather the elect and to judge. The picture of the Son of man in these passages is strongly reminiscent of Daniel 7:13 (quoted in Matt. 24:30; 26:64; Mark 13:26; 14:62; Luke 21:27; 22:69). The Son of man will come in glory with His angels and take His seat on His throne (Matt. 25:31). His coming will be sudden and unexpected (Matt. 10:23; 16:28; 24:27, 38–39; 24:44; Luke 17:22–27). He will come as judge to condemn the unrighteous (Matt. 13:41; 16:27; John 5:27) and to take as His own those who have faith and confess Him (Luke 12:8; 18:8; 21:36). Faithful disciples are to join the Son of man in this judgment (Matt. 19:28), which perhaps reflects the dual role of the Son of man and saints of the Most High found in Daniel 7:13,27. These sayings could be taken as referring to another than Jesus, but the Gospel writers unquestionably saw Jesus as referring to Himself and connected these events with His second coming.

2. Passion Sayings The second largest group of Son of man sayings are connected with the suffering, death, and resurrection of Jesus. Three times Jesus predicted that the Son of man would be rejected and killed by the priests and scribes but would rise on the third day (Mark 8:31; 9:31; 10:33–34; Luke 24:7). Just like John the Baptist, the Son of man would be treated with contempt (Mark 9:12–13; Matt. 17:12–13). He will be betrayed (Matt. 26:24,45; Luke 22:48). Death would be followed by victory, the resurrection from the dead (Matt. 17:9).

In his own way, John highlighted this dual emphasis on the humiliation of the cross and the glory of the resurrection. The Son of man is to be "lifted up" on the cross, but this "lifting up" is in reality His exaltation, leading to His ascension to the Father (John 3:14; 8:28; 12:34). As with a seed, death must first come for there to be new life, and thus Jesus' death became His hour of greatest glory (John 12:23–4; 13:31).

Nothing in Jewish messianic expectation connected the Son of man with suffering and death. In the Old Testament, one finds that only with the Servant of Isaiah 53. That connection is clearly made in this group of Son of man sayings, and it is explicitly made in Mark 10:45 (Matt. 20:28). The Son of man, the messianic Judge of the final time, is also the Suffering Servant of God. That connection is unique to the teaching and ministry of Jesus.

3. Sayings Connected with Jesus' Ministry The third group of Son of man sayings is the most heterogeneous, but all refer to some aspect of Jesus' earthly ministry. Many could be understood in the sense of the Hebrew idiom—"a man, this man." Yet, all have a deeper implication than any human *I,* for all point to some unique quality about Jesus' ministry. Even in these sayings, "Son of man" should be seen as a title pointing to Jesus' special role. He is the One who has authority to forgive sins (Matt. 9:6; Mark 2:10; Luke 5:24) and to interpret the meaning of the sabbath (Matt. 12:8; Mark 2:28; Luke 6:5). In His preaching, He sowed the seed of God's kingdom (Matt. 13:37), for He came to seek and to save the lost (Luke 19:10). Blessed is the disciple who suffers for His sake (Luke 6:22).

Some of these sayings reflect an incarnational emphasis. The Son of man in His earthly humiliation had no place to lay His head (Matt. 8:20; Luke 9:58). He was misunderstood and rejected (Matt. 11:19; Luke 7:34), but such personal rejection is forgivable—it is only the rejection of the work of the Spirit that is beyond forgiveness

(Matt. 12:32; Luke 12:10). John's Gospel especially highlights this incarnational emphasis. The Son of man is true flesh and blood. One must accept that humanity to find true life (John 6:53). The Son of man is also Son of God, the One who came from above, the Ladder which links all humanity with God (John 1:51).

4. The Rest of the New Testament "Son of man" occurs only four times in the New Testament outside the Gospels. All four reflect understandings of the title already found in the Gospels. In Acts 7:56, Stephen beheld the ascended Son of man standing beside the throne of God to receive him. In Revelation 1:13; 14:14–16, the Son of man appears as Judge. In Hebrews 2:6, the reference to Son of man in Psalm 8:4 which originally applied to humanity in general is specifically applied to Jesus as the unique Son of man and representative of humanity. In the context of Hebrews 2, all the Gospel emphases on Son of man coalesce—a strong incarnational emphasis on His real flesh and blood, a vivid depiction of His representative suffering, and the note that by that suffering He acquires His glory and honor and leads many to glory.

Conclusion Why are there so few references to Son of man outside the Gospels? Perhaps it was not a familiar term in the Gentile churches to which most of the New Testament writings were addressed. In any event, the significance of the term was not lost, for the New Testament writers all attest to the profound teachings which this term embodies—the true humanity of the Word made flesh, the necessity of His suffering and death for salvation, the glory of His reign over an everlasting kingdom, and His final coming to judge the just and the unjust. *John Polhill*

SONG OF SOLOMON Collection of romantic poetry comprising the twenty-second book of the English Old Testament. The Hebrew title, "Solomon's Song of Songs," means that this is the best of songs and that it in some way concerns Solomon. **Author and Date** While the title appears to name Solomon as the author, the Hebrew phrase can also mean for or about Solomon. Solomon or "king" is mentioned in the book several times (1:1,4,5,12; 3:7,9,11; 7:5; 8:11,12), but scholars remain uncertain about its author. An ancient rabbinic tradition (*Baba Bathra* 15a) attributes the Song to Hezekiah and his scribes (compare Prov. 25:1).

Similarly, it is hard to establish the date of the book from internal evidence. Some scholars argue on linguistic grounds for authorship much later than Solomon. Such grounds include the use of expressions akin to Aramaic and the presence of certain foreign loanwords (Persian: *pardes* = "orchard," 4:13; *'appiryon* from Greek *phoreion* = "carriage" or [by way of Aramaic] "canopied bed," 3:9). Others argue that such linguistic usages and borrowings can go back to the time of Solomon or merely reflect the date of the book's final editing.

Canon and Interpretation Because of its erotic language and the difficulty of its interpretation, the rabbis questioned the place of the Song of Solomon in the canon. The positive resolution of that debate is reflected in the famous declaration of Rabbi Akiva, "The whole world is not worth the day on which the Song of Songs was given to Israel; all the Writings are holy, but the Song of Songs is the holy of holies."

The problems of the book's place in the canon and its interpretation are closely related. Under the influence of Greek views, which denigrated the body, and with the loss of a biblical view of the created goodness of the body and human love, many interpreters felt compelled to find in the Song an allegory of sacred love between God and Israel, Christ and the church, or Christ and the soul. With few exceptions, allegorical readings of the Song have prevailed for most of church history.

In the modern period, most scholars have returned to a literal reading of the Song. Conflict remains even about the literal sense of the text. Some compare Egyptian and Mesopotamian poems and see the Song as a mere *collection* of secular love ditties. Another view tries to see it as an adaptation of pagan fertility rituals. (This view is in reality a modern allegorical reading.) Others see the Song as a *drama* in which the pure love of the Shulammite maid and her shepherd prevails over Solomon's callous attempt to bring the girl into his harem. This view tries to do justice to the alteration of speakers in the Song in its various dialogues. (These shifts are indicated in Hebrew by shifts in grammatical person and number.)

A recent, promising approach is aware of parallels to Egyptian love poetry but shows that the Song itself gives expression to a uniquely biblical perspective on sexual love. While containing a number of smaller love poems, the Song is unified by patterns of dialogue, repetition, the use of catch words, and above all, a consistent vision of love. Like Genesis 2:23–25, the Song celebrates God's gift of bodily love between man and woman. Here the Creator's wisdom and bounty are displayed. Thus, the Song is best taken as an example of Israel's wisdom poetry (compare Prov. 5:15–20; 6:24–29; 7:6–27; 30:18–20). Like many Psalms which praise God and also teach, the Song's *main* purpose is to celebrate rather than to instruct. Like music, it tends to joy rather than learning. Yet one can overhear in it biblical wisdom on love. "Love is as strong as death. . . . Many waters cannot quench love. . . . If one were to give all the wealth of his house for love, it would be utterly scorned" (8:6–7 NIV). Moreover, there is a right time and place for love: "Daughters of Jerusalem, I charge you. . . Do not arouse or awaken love until it so desires" (3:5 NIV). In these poems love is portrayed in its power and splendor, its freshness and devotion to the beloved. Love in all its variety parades before us: moments of union and separation, ecstacy and anguish, longing and fulfillment.

Finally, a certain validity remains in the long history of interpretation, which saw in the pure love of the Song a reflection of divine-human love (compare Eph. 5:21–32; Song of Sol. 3:6–11; and the messianic typology of Psalm 45.) Nonetheless, this parallel should not be pushed to the point of allegorizing details of the poem.

See also *Allegory, Wisdom.*

Outline

I. Longing Is a Part of Love (1:1–8).
II. Love Will Not Be Silent (1:9—2:7).
III. Spring and Love Go Together (2:8–17).
IV. Love Is Exclusive (3:1–5).
V. Love Is Enhanced by Friendship (3:6–11).
VI. Love Sees Only the Beautiful (4:1–7).
VII. Love Involves Giving and Receiving (4:8—5:1).
VIII. Love Means Risking the Possibility of Pain (5:2—6:3).
IX. Words Fail for Expressing Love (6:4—7:9).
X. Love Must Be Given Freely (7:10–13).
XI. True Love Is Priceless (8:1–14).

Raymond C. Van Leeuwen

SONS OF GOD Divine beings associated with God in the heavens in what can be called the "divine council" (Ps. 82:1 NRSV) or the "council of the holy ones" (Ps. 89:7 NAS). In Job, the earliest Greek translation translated "sons of God" as "angels of God" (Job 1:6; 2:1) and "my angels" (Job 38:7). The phrase "sons of the living God" in Hosea 1:10, however, refers to Israel.

The expression *sons of God* employs a Hebrew idiom in which "son(s)" refers to participants in a class or in a state of being, and the second word describes the class or state of being. Thus, in Genesis 5:32, Noah is said to be a "son of five hundred years," meaning he was 500 years old. In English an adjective often best translates the second term, so that "divine beings" rather than "sons of God" would be a better rendition of the Hebrew. This accords with the NRSV's translation "heavenly beings" for "sons of gods" in Psalms 29:1; 89:6.

In the New Testament, "sons of God" always refers to human beings who do God's will (Matt. 5:9; Rom. 8:14,19). Similar expressions with the same meaning are to be found in Matthew 5:45; John 1:12; Romans 9:26 (= Hos. 1:10), and 2 Corinthians 6:18. The usual designation of the heavenly beings in the New Testament is "angels."

See *Angels; Divine Council; God; Son of God.*
Fred L. Horton, Jr.

SONS OF THE PROPHETS Members of a band or guild of prophets. "Sons of" refers to membership in a group or class and does not imply a family relationship. "Sons of the prophets" suggests a community or guild of prophets. The most extensive use of the expression occurs in the Elisha stories where the prophet is portrayed as the leader of the prophetic guild. In that capacity, Elisha cared for the needs of a prophet's widow (2 Kings 4:1–7), agreed to the building of a common dwelling (2 Kings 6:1–7), and presided at a common meal (2 kings 4:38–44). The sons of the prophets functioned either as witnesses (2 Kings 2:3,5,7,15) or as agents of Elisha's ministry (2 Kings 9:1–3).

The single reference outside the Elisha cycle to the sons of the prophets is to someone identified as "a certain man of the sons of the prophets" who condemned Ahab's release of Ben-Hadad (1 Kings 20:35–42). The "company of prophets" (1 Sam. 10:5,10; 19:20) are groups of prophets whose charismatic spirit involved Saul in prophecy (1 Sam. 10:10) and, later, both Saul and his messengers (1 Sam. 19:20).

Amos' famous declaration, "I am not a prophet, nor am I the son of a prophet" (7:14 NAS) is probably a declaration of independence from the prophetic guilds of his day. Similarly, Jeremiah's claim that God made him a prophet even before conception (Jer. 1:5) may obliquely represent a rejection of association with the prophetic schools of Judah. See *Prophet*.   *Fred L. Horton, Jr.*

SOP KJV translation of *psōmion* meaning a small piece of bread that could be dipped in a dish or wine. It appears only in John 13:26–30 (compare Ruth 2:14). Most translators today use "morsel" (NAS) or "piece of bread" (NIV, NRSV). Today in Bible lands a host honors a guest by dipping a piece of bread into the sauce of the main dish and handing it to the guest. Most interpreters feel that Jesus was making his last appeal to Judas to change his mind. Then Jesus would accept him. Although Judas accepted the bread signifying friendship, John said, "Satan entered into him" (v. 27). At that moment Judas gave himself over to the will of Satan and left to betray Jesus. See *Judas.*

SOPATER (Sŏp′ ȧ tēr) A personal name meaning "sound parentage." This man accompanied Paul on his final trip to Jerusalem (Acts 20:4). Some feel he is the same as "Sosipater" in Romans 16:21.

SOPHERETH (Sōph′ ĕ reth) Personal name meaning "learning." One of Solomon's servants whose descendants returned to Jerusalem with Zerubbabel (Ezra 2:55; Neh. 7:57). Modern translations translate it "Hassophereth" in Ezra 2:55 and "Sophereth" in Nehemiah 7:57 (NAS, NIV, NRSV).

SORCERER A person who practices sorcery or divination. See *Divination and Magic.*

SORE Translation of six Hebrew words and a Greek word in RSV and of at least ten Hebrew and ten Greek words in KJV. *1.* An adverb meaning, "very, extremely" as in "sore afraid" (Gen. 20:8). *2.* An adverb meaning, "severely, insistently, with urgent pressure" as in "they pressed sore" (Gen. 19:9). *3.* To experience pain (Gen. 34:25). *4.* "Strong, severe" as in "the famine was sore" (Gen. 43:1). *5.* A wounded or diseased spot or a plague (Lev. 13:42). *6.* Something evil or bad (Deut. 6:22; 28:35). *7.* A great amount as in "wept sore" (Judg. 21:2). *8.* With vexation or anger (1 Sam. 1:6). *9.* Cruel, tough, obstinate (1 Sam. 5:7). *10.* Fully, greatly (Neh. 2:2). *11.* Hand (Ps. 77:2). *12.* Weakness or sickness (Eccl. 5:13). *13.* Horrible, terrible (Ezek. 27:35). *14.* Large, exceeding (Dan. 6:14). *15.* Pressing, irritating (Mic. 2:10). *16.* An ulcer (Rev. 16:2). *17.* Blisters or boils (Ex. 9:9). See *Boils. 18.* An inflamed spot sometimes interpreted as smallpox or a skin disease akin to leprosy (Ex. 9:9–11; Lev. 13:18–20; 2 Kings 20:7; Isa. 38:21). *19.* A wound (Gen. 4:23; Isa. 53:5).

SOREK (Sō′ rĕk) Place name meaning, "red grape." A valley on the western side of Palestine. It runs from near Jerusalem toward the Mediterranean Sea. Beth-shemesh guarded the eastern end, while the Philistines controlled the western portion during the era of the judges. Delilah, Samson's mistress, lived in the valley of Sorek (Judg. 16:4). See *Palestine.*

SORROW Emotional, mental, or physical pain or stress. Hebrew does not have a general word for sorrow. Rather it uses about fifteen different words to express the different dimensions of sorrow. Some speak to emotional pain (Ps. 13:2). Trouble and sorrow were not meant to be part of the human experience. Humanity's sin brought sorrow to them (Gen 3:16–19). Sometimes God was seen as chastising His people for their sin (Amos 4:6–12). To remove sorrow, the prophets urged repentance that led to obedience (Joel 2:12–13; Hos. 6:6).

The Greek word for sorrow is usually *lupē*. It means "grief, sorrow, pain of mind or spirit, affliction." Paul distinguished between godly and worldly sorrow (2 Cor. 7:8–11). Sorrow can lead a person to a deeper faith in God; or it can cause a person to live with regret, centered on the experience that caused the sorrow. Jesus gave believers words of hope to overcome trouble, distress, and sorrow: "I have told you these things, so that in me you may have peace. In this world you will have trouble. But take heart! I have overcome the world" (John 16:33 NIV).

SOSIPATER (Sō sīp′ ȧ tēr) Personal name meaning, "to save one's father." He is said to be a kinsman (a Jew) of Paul who sent greetings to Rome (Rom. 16:21). "Sopater of Berea" (Acts 20:4) may be the same.

SOSTHENES (Sŏs' thė nēṣ) Personal name meaning, "of safe strength." A ruler of a synagogue in Corinth (Acts 18:17). He apparently assumed the post after Crispus, the former chief ruler, became a Christian under Paul's preaching (18:8). When an attempt to prosecute Paul legally failed, the citizens of the city took revenge and beat Sosthenes. Tradition holds that Sosthenes later was converted and became one of Paul's helpers (1 Cor. 1:1). Whether the two are one person cannot be determined from existing evidence.

SOTAI (Sō' tai) One of Solomon's servants whose descendants returned to Jerusalem with Zerubbabel (Ezra 2:55; Neh. 7:57).

SOUL The vital existence of a human being. The Hebrew word *nephesh* is a key Old Testament term (755 times) referring to human beings. In the New Testament, the term *psyche* retreats behind the ideas of body, flesh, spirit to characterize human existence. In the Bible, a person is a unity. Body and soul or spirit are not opposite terms, but rather terms which supplement one another to describe aspects of the inseparable whole person. See *Anthropology; Humanity.*

Such a holistic image of a person is maintained also in the New Testament even over against the Greek culture which, since Plato, sharply separated body and soul with an analytic exactness and which saw the soul as the valuable, immortal, undying part of human beings. In the Old Testament, the use and variety of the word is much greater while in the New Testament its theological meaning appears much stronger.

The soul designates the physical life. Vitality in all of its breadth and width of meaning is meant by the soul. The basic meaning of *nephesh* is throat. Thus, the Bible refers to the hungry, thirsty, satisfied, soul (Ps. 107:5,9; Prov. 27:7; Jer. 31:12,25). The soul means the entire human being in its physical life needing food and clothing (Matt. 6:25). The breathing organs and the breath blown out from them also express individual life in animals as well as human beings (Job 11:20; 41:21; Acts 20:10). At times, then, soul can be interchanged with life (Prov. 7:23; 8:35−36) and can be identical with blood (Deut. 12:23). A person does not have a soul. A person is a living soul (Gen. 2:7). That means a living being that owes life itself to the Creator just as does the animal (Gen. 2:19). For this life or soul, one gives all one has (Job 2:4). Satan is permitted by God to take health, that is flesh and blood, but Satan cannot take the bare life of a person (Job 2:5−6).

Soul designates the feelings, the wishes, and the will of humans. The work of the throat, its hunger and appetite, stands for the desire and the longing of the human being after power and sex, after satisfaction, and after even the evil (Prov. 21:10), but also after God (Ps. 42:2−3). The soul can be incited, embittered, confirmed, unsettled, or kept in suspense (Acts 14:2,22; 15:24; John 10:24). The word mirrors the entire scale of feelings under the influence of the human being, even the psychological. The bitter soul of the childless, the sick, or the threatened (1 Sam. 1:10; 2 Kings 4:27; 2 Sam. 17:8) reminds us of the *nephesh* as the organ of taste that also stands for the entire embittered person.

The soul also knows positive emotions. The soul rejoices, praises, hopes, and is patient. Never in these cases is only one part of the human being meant. It is always the powerful soul as an expression of the entire personality (Ps. 33:20). In the command to love (Deut. 6:5; Mark 12:30), the soul stands next to other expressions for the human being to emphasize the emotional energy and willpower of the human being all rolled into one.

The soul designates the human person. Soul is not only a synoymn with life. One can also speak of the life of the soul (Prov. 3:22). Every human soul (Acts 2:43; Rom. 2:9) means each individual person. The popular expression used today "to save our souls" goes back to this biblical way of thinking (1 Pet. 3:20). It means to save the entire person. In legal texts, the soul is the individual person with juristic responsibilities (Lev. 17:10, a blood-eating soul). Connected with a figure showing statistics or numbers of people, soul becomes an idea in the arena of the statistician (Gen. 46:26−27; Acts 2:41). At times, soul simply replaces a pronoun such as the expression "let my soul live," which means "let me live" (1 Kings 20:32). It is even possible for all the nuances of meaning to sound forth together in the same expression. For instance, in Psalm 103:1, we read, "Bless, Yahweh, O my soul." This includes the throat as the organ of life, the soul as the totality of capabilities; my own personal life which experiences the saving actions of Yahweh our God; my person; my own "I"; and the vital, emotional self.

Soul designates the essential life. Physical life is given and maintained by God (Matt. 6:25−34). Meaningful and fulfilled life comes only when it is free to give itself to God as a disciple of Jesus Christ. Life is the highest good when it is lived according to God's intentions and not used up in search for material and cultural goods (Mark 8:34−37). This life is stronger than death and cannot be destroyed by human beings (Matt. 10:28). The soul does not, however, represent a divine, immortal, undying part of the human being after death as the Greeks often thought. Paul, thus, avoids the word soul in connection with eternal life. There is a continuity between the earthly and the resurrected life that does not lie in the capabilities or nature of mortal humans. It lies alone in the power of the Spirit of God (1 Cor. 15:44). According to the Bible, a human being exists as a whole unit and remains also as a whole person in the hand of God after death. A person is not at any time viewed as a bodyless soul.

Christian Wolf

SOUTH See *Directions, Geographical; Negeb.*

SOVEREIGNTY OF GOD The biblical teaching that God is the source of all creation and that all things come from and depend upon God (Ps. 24:1). Sovereignty means that God is in all and over all.

Creative Sovereignty God is the Lord of creation, the source of all things, who brought the world into being and who guides His creation toward a meaningful end. God's creativity is not the result of chance or randomness. It holds promise and purpose which God intends.

Moral Sovereignty God's sovereignty, His authority over creation, is grounded in God's essential nature which is moral. God is to be obeyed not simply because He is mighty but because He is righteous (Ps. 50:6). God judges His creation on the basis of His profound moral character. He is both the source of all creation and the source of all goodness.

Transcendent Sovereignty God's sovereignty is transcendent, beyond our complete comprehension (Isa. 6:1). God is separate from His creation and works in ways that human beings do not always understand. Transcendence is closely related to God's holiness, His surpassing moral purity and essential otherness. See *Holy.*

Purposeful Sovereignty God's sovereignty moves toward a particular end, a specific purpose (Phil. 2:13). God's purpose is to bring His creation—His whole creation—to fulness and completion, to fellowship with Him: "God was in Christ, reconciling the world unto himself" (2 Cor. 5:19). The kingdom of God is the end toward which God moves His creation.

Sovereignty and Freedom Divine sovereignty does not mean that everything which occurs in the world is God's will. God has created a world in which freedom is a real possibility. His permissive will provides for human freedom and the laws of nature. This freedom means that sovereignty must always be distinguished from "fate" or "destiny," the belief that everything which occurs in the world has been predetermined, scheduled in advance, by God. That view, carried to extremes, makes human beings pawns or puppets of a mechanical universe in which all choices are made in advance and where freedom is not possible. Yet the gospel suggests that human beings find genuine freedom, not in doing everything they wish, but in submitting themselves to the sovereign will of God, the rule and reign of God in their individual and collective lives. The sovereignty of God involves God's self-limitation in order that His creation might also choose freedom in Him.

Sovereignty and Providence God guides, sustains, loves, and longs to have fellowship with His creation. He reveals himself as a parent in love and in relationship with humanity. He "has borne our griefs, and carried our sorrows" (Isa. 53:4). God has chosen to participate in human history to care for human beings in their strengths and their weaknesses. "We know that in all things God works for the good of those who love him, who have been called according to his purpose" (Rom. 8:28 NIV). Those who belong to God will not be immune from suffering; they will not be spared the brokenness which life brings to all persons. The people of God may, however, find spiritual resources and strength to persevere in time of trouble. The sovereign God of the universe chose to identify with His creation in the cross of Christ. There is no greater example of his care for His creation. See *God; Providence.* *William Leonard*

SOW *1. To* scatter seeds on the ground (field). *2.* The female counterpart of the boar. The mature female swine. See *Animals; Swine.*

SOWER A person who held a vessel filled with seed in the left hand and scattered the seed with a practiced motion with the right hand. The seed was usually scattered on untilled ground. Then with a plow or harrow, the ground would be scratched or turned to cover the seed. It seems that any seed to be sowed had to be ceremonially clean (Lev. 11:37). Mixed seed could not be sowed together (Lev. 19:19). Purity reached into the far corners of Hebrew life. Jesus used the sower for a parable about life and illustrated the everyday hardships farmers faced (Matt. 13:3–9; Mark 4:3–9; Luke 8:4–8). See *Agriculture; Plow.*

An Arab farmer near Bethlehem sowing seeds on his land.

SPAIN The country still known by that name in the southwest corner of Europe. It was opened to the Romans just before 200 B.C. Paul wanted to go to Spain (Rom. 15:24,28). According to Clement (about A.D. 95–96) and the Muratorian Fragment (about A.D. 195–196), he did just that. See *Tarshish.*

SPAN Half a cubit. A cubit is the length of the forearm, about 18 inches. The span is measured from the thumb to the little finger both extended, about 8 or 9 inches. See *Cubit; Weights and Measures.*

SPARK A literal flame of fire (Job 18:5) used in a figurative sense of a person's dying. Also used figuratively to show that humanity lives a troubled life (Job 5:7). Leviathan is pictured with a flaming mouth (Job 41:19–21). It is used of sparks from a fire (or "torches" NIV) in Isaiah 50:11. See *Fire.*

SPARROW Often translated "bird" (Ps. 8:8; Ezek. 17:23 NAS, NIV, NRSV) as representative of all birds. It was ceremonially clean as sometimes eaten as food by the poor. Jesus used the sparrows (Matt. 10:31; Luke 12:7) to show their lack of worth as contrasted with human beings. See *Birds.*

SPECK Modern translation of KJV, "mote." See *Mote.*

SPECTACLE Theatre or play. Paul felt that he was on display before the world. The world did not appreciate the commitment of Paul to Christ but saw Paul as a spectacle, one to watch and perhaps laugh at (1 Cor. 4:9).

SPELT Wheat of an inferior quality (*Triticum satiuum*). Egyptians made bread from it. It had not sprouted when the plagues struck Egypt (Ex. 9:32). Spelt illustrates the farmer's planning, placing it on the outer edge of the field to retard the intrusion of weeds (Isa. 28:25). Compare Ezekiel 4:9. See *Agriculture.*

SPICES Aromatic, pungent substances used in the preparation of foods, sacred oils for anointings, incense, perfumes, and ointments used for personal hygiene and for burial of the dead.

Spices were very expensive and highly prized in antiquity. They were brought into Palestine from India, Arabia, Persia, Mesopotamia, and Egypt. Solomon had an extensive commercial venture with Hiram, king of Tyre, dealing in spices and other commodities. His fleet of ships brought much needed revenue into the Israelite economy (1 Kings 10:15). Solomon also taxed the caravan groups that passed through his lands. The land of Sheba, present day Yemen, had an extensive commerce in spices. The queen of Sheba made a long journey of 1,200 miles because she was afraid that her caravan spice business would be hurt by Solomon's merchant fleet. In her visit she gave to Solomon "a very great quantity of spices" (2 Chron. 9:9).

Spices were widely used in the worship service of the Temple and in the lives of the people. See *Ointment.* Several spices, which the Talmud called "food improvers," were used in the prepara-

tion of foods. These included cummin, dill, cinnamon, and mint. Frankincense, stacte, galbanum, and onycha were used in the preparation of the incense to be used in the worship of Israel (Ex. 30:34–35). Balsam, myrrh, cinnamon, cassia, and calamus were used in the preparation of the holy anointing oil (Ex. 30:23–25). Cassia, aloes, and spikenard were some of the spices used in the preparation of cosmetics (Song of Sol. 4:14; Mark 14:3; John 12:3). Myrrh and aloes were used in ointments for burial (Luke 23:56; John 19:39).

Some of the most important spices were:

1. Aloe (*Aloexyllon agallochum* and *Aquilaria agallocha*) A spice used to perfume garments and beds (Prov. 7:17; Ps. 45:8;). The aloe mentioned in John 19:39 was a different plant. The extract from its leaves was mixed with water and other spices to make ointment for the anointing of the dead.

2. Balsam (*Pistacia lentiscus*) This product of Gilead was exported to Egypt and to Tyre. The resin from this desert plant was used for medicinal and cosmetic purposes (Jer. 46:11).

3. Cummin (*Cuminum cyminum*) This seed was used as a spice in bread. Its dry seed was beaten with a stick, for it was too soft to be threshed with a sledge (Isa. 28:23–28).

4. Cassia (*Flores cassiae*) Two Hebrew words are used to translate cassia (Ex. 30:24; Ps. 45:8). The dried bark or blooms were used in the preparation of the anointing oil; the pods and leaves were used as medicine.

5. Cinnamon A highly prized plant, cinnamon was used as a condiment, in the preparation of perfumes (Prov. 7:17), and in the holy oil for anointing (Ex. 30:23). The New Testament lists cinnamon as one of the commodities found in Babylon (Rev. 18:13).

6. Coriander (*Coriandrum sativum*) An aromatic seed used as a spice in food; its oil was used in the manufacture of perfume. The Israelites compared the manna to the coriander seed (Ex. 16:31; Num. 11:7).

7. Dill The seed and the leaves were used to flavor foods and as medicine to wash skin wounds (Matt. 23:23; KJV, "anise").

8. Frankincense (*Boswellia carteri* and *Frereana*) A resin of a tree which, when burned, produced a strong aromatic scent. Frankincense was used in the preparation of the sacred oil for anointing of kings and priests and for the sacrifices in the Temple. The men from the East brought frankincense to Jesus (Matt. 2:11).

9. Galbanum A fragrant resin which gave a pleasant scent when burned; it was one of the ingredients of the holy incense (Ex. 30:34).

10. Henna A plant used as a cosmetic; its leaves produced a dye women used (Song of Sol. 1:14; 4:13). KJV translates the word as "camphire," but camphire was not native to Palestine and may not have been known in biblical times.

11. Mint Mint leaves were used as a condiment (Matt. 23:23; Luke 11:42).

12. Myrrh (*Commiphora abessinica*) The resinous gum of a plant which was included in the preparation of the holy anointing oil (Ex. 30:23). It was also used for its aromatic properties (Ps. 45:8) and used for female purification (Esth. 2:12). Myrrh was given to Jesus at His birth as a gift (Matt. 2:11) and as a drink when He was on the cross (Mark 15:23).

13. Onycha Traditionally taken as the aromatic crushed shell of a mollusc but in light of Ugaritic plant lists probably a type of cress (*Lepidium sativum*). It was used in holy incense (Ex. 30:34).

14. Rue (*Ruta graveolens*) An herb used as a condiment. It was valued for its medicinal properties. Its leaves were used in the healing of insect bites (Luke 11:42).

15. Saffron (*Curcuma longa, Crocus sativus*) A substance of a plant which produced a yellow dye and was used to color foods. When mixed with oil, it was used as medicine and perfume (Song of Sol. 4:14).

16. Spices The Hebrew word should be translated "balsam" (*Balsamodendrium opolbalsamum*). A shrub with a resin that gave a pleasant odor. Balsam was used as perfume and as medicine. The balsam was one of the ingredients of the anointing oil (Ex. 30:23).

17. Spikenard (*Nardos tachys jatamansi*) A very expensive fragrant oil used in the manufacture of perfumes and ointments (Song of Sol. 1:12; 4:13; Mark 14:3; John 12:3).

18. Stacte (*Pistacia lentiscus*) A small tree which produced a resin used in the sacred incense (Ex. 30:34). *Claude F. Mariottini*

SPIDER An animal in Palestine known in the Bible for spinning a web (Job 8:14; Isa. 59:5). The spider's web is usually used as a sign of frailty. See *Animals.*

SPIKENARD A very expensive spice used in making perfume. It is also translated "perfume" (Song of Sol. 1:12 NAS, NIV) and "nard" (Song of Sol. 1:12 NRSV). Jesus was anointed by a woman with this expensive perfume (Mark 14:3; John 12:3). See *Spices.*

SPINDLE Used only in Proverbs 31:19, KJV translates "spindle" in the first line and "distaff" in the second line. Modern translations (NAS, NIV, NRSV) reverse the words in their translations. The *distaff* was a stick which held the fibers from which thread was spun. The *spindle* was a round stick with a round disk fastened closer to one end. The spun thread was wound around the spindle. See *Cloth, Clothing.*

SPINNING AND WEAVING Major elements involved in making cloth that were familiar processes in biblical times.

A Bedouin woman spinning wool into yarn.

Spinning The threads woven into cloth were produced from raw fibers by spinning (Matt. 6:28; Luke 12:27). Flax, or linen (Lev. 13:47–48; Prov. 31:13; Jer. 13:1; Ezek. 40:3; 44:17; Hos. 2:5), and wool (Lev. 13:47) were the major fibers used in the biblical world.

In spinning, raw fibers were pulled into a loose strand and twisted to form a continuous thread. A spindle (2 Sam. 3:29; Prov. 31:19 NRSV) was a slender stick which could be twirled to twist drawn out fibers caught in a hook or slot at the top. A spindle whorl acted as a flywheel for more efficient twisting. Spun thread was wound onto the stick. Sometimes, it was plyed or twined, two or three threads being twisted together (Ex. 26:1; 36:8,35). The finished product could then be used for weaving (Ex. 35:25–26).

Weaving Weaving is the interlacing of threads to form fabric. Weaving was conducted on looms, devices designed to create openings (sheds) between alternating vertical warp threads through which the horizontal weft threads were passed. After each weft thread was placed, it was beaten against the previous one with a flat stick, thus firming up the fabric.

Three main loom designs were used in the biblical world. On a horizontal ground loom, the warp threads were stretched between beams pegged to the ground. This type is apparently referred to in the Samson story (Judg. 16:13–14), as it would have enabled Delilah to weave his locks while he slept. When Samson jumped up, he pulled away the pin(s) of the loom (v. 14b) which secured the beams to the ground. In some vertical looms, the warp was stretched between two beams fixed in a rectangular frame. Work proceeded from the bottom of the loom, and the woven cloth could be rolled onto the bottom beam (Isa. 38:12). This permitted the weaver to remain seated and to produce much longer finished products. Another type of vertical loom had the warp threads attached to an upper beam and held taut in groups by a series of stone or clay weights. Weaving was done from the top to the bottom, and the weft beaten upwards. Large numbers of excavated loom weights testify to the popularity of warp weighted looms in Old Testament Israel.

Stripes or bands of color were made by using dyed threads for portions of the warp or weft threads. Warp weighted looms allowed portions of the shed to be opened at a time, so intricate patterns could be made in the weft by covering small areas with different colors. It was forbidden, however, to wear clothes made of linen and wool woven together (Deut. 22:11). Weavers apparently were professionals who specialized in particular types of work. The Old Testament differentiates between ordinary weavers, designers, and embroiderers (Ex. 35:35). *Daniel C. Browning, Jr.*

SPIRIT The empowering perspective of human life and the Holy Spirit bringing God's presence and power to bear in the world. A translation of the Hebrew word *ruach* and the Greek word *pneuma* which can be translated as "wind," "breath," or "spirit" depending upon the context.

In both Testaments, *spirit* is used of both God and human beings. *Spirit,* whether used of God or of human beings, is difficult to define. The kinship of spirit, breath, and wind is a helpful clue in beginning to understand *spirit.* In His conversation with Nicodemus (John 3), Jesus said that the Spirit is like the wind in that one cannot see it but one can see its effects. This is true of both the Spirit of God and the spirit of a human being.

Spirit of God At the beginning of creation, the Spirit of God hovered over the waters (Gen. 1:3). Elihu acknowledged to Job that the Spirit of God had made him and was the source of his life (Job 33:4). The animals were created when God sent out His "breath" (Ps. 104:30 NRSV note).

The Spirit of God is present everywhere. The psalmist sensed that no matter where he was, God's Spirit was there (Ps. 139:7). The Pharaoh saw the Spirit of God in Joseph (Gen. 41:38). Moses realized that the Spirit of God was on him, and he desired that God's Spirit be on all of His people (Num 11:29). During the period of the Judges, the Spirit of the Lord came to individuals and empowered them to accomplish specific tasks (Judg. 3:10; 6:34; 11:29; 13:25; 14:6; 14:19).

When Samuel, the last of the judges, annointed Saul, Israel's first king, he told Saul that the Spirit of the Lord would come upon him. The result was that Saul prophesied and was changed into a different person (1 Sam. 10:6). Later, the Spirit departed from Saul (1 Sam. 16:14). Likewise, the Spirit came upon David when Samuel annointed him (1 Sam. 16:13). In his last words, David said that the Spirit of the Lord had spoken through him (2 Sam. 23:2).

Isaiah spoke of one who is to come from the line of Jesse, one on whom the Spirit of the Lord would rest. This person would have the Spirit of wisdom, understanding, counsel, power, knowledge, and the fear of the Lord (Isa. 11:1–3). Ezekiel prophesied that God would put His Spirit within His people, removing from them hearts of stone and putting within them hearts of flesh that would be obedient to God's way (Ezek. 36:26–27).

New Testament Teaching Each of the four Gospels has numerous references to the Spirit of God or the Holy Spirit. The Spirit was the agent of Jesus' miraculous conception (Matt. 1:18,20), came down on Jesus at His baptism (Matt. 3:16), led Him into the wilderness where He was tempted by the devil (Matt. 4:1), and enabled Him to heal diseases and cast out demons (Matt. 12:28). Jesus promised the Spirit to His followers as He prepared to leave the world. The Spirit would serve as Comforter and Counselor, continuing to teach Jesus' followers and reminding them of what He had said to them (John 14:25–26). Not many days after Jesus' ascension, the promised Spirit came upon His followers during the Feast of Pentecost. The advent of the Spirit was accompanied by a sound that was like a mighty wind. Those who witnessed this event saw what seemed to be tongues of fire resting on the believers. Moreover, these disciples were empowered to speak in tongues other than their native language (Acts 2:1–3). Throughout Luke's account of the early church, the Holy Spirit empowered and guided the followers of Jesus in their mission to the world surrounding the Mediterranean (Acts 11:12; 13:2; 15:28; 16:6–7; 20:22; 21:11).

The Spirit is important in Paul's understanding of the believer's relationship to God. The Spirit is a gracious personal presence who lives in one who has confessed that Jesus Christ is Lord. Relationship to God through Christ by the Spirit is revolutionary. In Galatians, Paul argued that legalism and the way of faith are incompatible. God's Spirit comes to us as a gift based on our faith in Christ and His grace (Gal. 3:1–5). God's Spirit comes into a believer's life, with assurance that we are God's children (Rom. 8:16). The Spirit is God's pledge to us that we shall be fully transformed and conformed to the image of Christ. (Rom. 8:1–29; 2 Cor. 1:22). Paul identified the Spirit with the Lord (the risen Christ) and asserted that where the Spirit of the Lord is, there is freedom, a growing freedom from the law of sin and death (2 Cor. 3:18; compare Rom. 8:2).

The Spirit distributes gifts in the church which are designed to equip God's people for serving and building up the body of Christ (1 Cor. 12; Eph. 4:7–13). Evidence that the Spirit of God is at work in a person or group of persons is love, joy, patience, kindness, goodness, faithfulness, gentleness, and self-control (Gal. 5:22–23).

At the beginning of Scripture we see the Spirit at work in creation. As Scripture closes, the Spirit and the Bride, the church, issue an invitation for all who are thirsty to come and drink of the water of life (Rev. 22:17).

Human Spirits In both the Old and New Testaments, *spirit* is used of humans and of other beings. When used of humans, *spirit* is associated with a wide range of functions including thinking and understanding, emotions, attitudes, and intentions. Elihu told Job it was *spirit* in a person, the breath of God, which gave understanding (Job 32:8). When Jesus healed the paralytic, He perceived in His "spirit" that the religious leaders present were questioning His forgiving the man's sins (Mark 2:8).

Spirit is used extensively with human emotions including sorrow (Prov. 15:4,13), anguish (Ex. 6:9; John 13:21), anger (Prov. 14:29; 16:32), vexation (Eccl. 1:14), fear (2 Tim. 1:7), and joy (Luke 1:47).

A variety of attitudes and intentions are associated with spirit. Caleb had a different spirit than most of his contemporaries in that he followed the Lord wholeheartedly (Num. 14:24). Sihon, king of Heshbon, had a stubborn spirit (Deut. 2:30). First Kings 22 refers to a lying spirit. The psalmist called persons who have no deceit in their spirits, "blessed" (Ps. 32:2). A person's spirit can be contrite (Ps. 34:18), steadfast (Ps. 51:10), willing (Ps. 51:12), broken (Ps. 51:17), and haughty (Prov. 16:18). The Gospel of Mark has numerous references to Jesus healing persons with unclean or foul spirits.

Spirit is used of nonphysical beings, both good and evil. Satan is called the ruler of the kingdom of the air, the spirit who is at work in those who are disobedient (Eph. 2:2).

One of the perennial points of conflict between the Sadducees and the Pharisees was over whether there are angels and spirits. The latter believed that there were such while the former denied that such existed. When the risen Christ appeared to the disciples, they were startled and frightened, thinking they were seeing a spirit. Jesus invited them to touch Him. He then reminded them that a spirit does not have flesh and bones (Luke 24:37–39).   *Steve Bond*

SPIRITIST See *Medium*.

SPIRITS IN PRISON A much discussed phrase in 1 Peter 3:19. Christ went and preached to the spirits in prison "who in former times did not obey, when God waited patiently in the days of Noah" (1 Pet. 3:20a, NRSV). This event, unmentioned elsewhere in the Bible, is closely associated with the resurrection of Jesus Christ from the dead (vv. 18,21).

The framework for this depiction of Christ's work is the notion, attributed to Jesus Himself, that "As it was in the days of Noah, so too it will be in the days of the Son of Man" (Luke 17:26 NRSV; compare Matt. 24:37). The immediate focus of the statement in 1 Peter is not the flood as such. The flood becomes the center of attention in verses 20b–21. Verse 19 focuses on the situation that necessitated the flood (see Gen. 6:1–8). The disobedient "spirits," accordingly, are not the people who died in the flood, but the evil spirits, or demons, whose influence brought divine judgment on the world. Peter probably viewed these evil spirits as the offspring of the strange union mentioned in Genesis 6:1–4 between the "sons of God" (that is, angelic or superhuman beings of some kind) and the "daughters of men." (Compare the Jewish apocalyptic book of 1 Enoch 15.8–10: "But now the giants who are born from (the union of) spirits and the flesh shall be called evil spirits upon the earth.") It is also likely that Peter identified them with the "unclean spirits" over which Jesus had triumphed again and again during His earthly ministry. Jesus' proclamation to these "spirits" must therefore be understood not as redemptive "good news," but as judgment and defeat at the hands of God (see their anxious question in Matthew 8:29, "Have you come here to torment us before the time?" NRSV).

That the outcome of this proclamation was the subjection of the disobedient spirits is seen from 1 Peter 3:22, where Christ is glimpsed "at the right hand of God, with angels, authorities, and powers made subject to him" (NRSV). Yet if they were already "in prison," what precisely could further defeat and subjection mean? A possible answer to this question is provided by Revelation 18:2, where "Babylon the great" (or Rome) is seen under God's final judgment as "a haunt for every unclean spirit" (REB). The word translated "haunt" in the RSV is the same word translated "prison" in 1 Peter 3:19. Peter's point is not that the disobedient spirits were "imprisoned" in the sense of being inactive when Christ came to them, but that He came to them in their "haunts" or "havens" to notify them that their power over humanity was finally broken and that now they must surrender to His universal dominion.

J. Ramsey Michaels

SPIRITUAL GIFTS The skills and abilities which God gives through His Spirit to all Christians, which equip Christians to serve God in the Christian community.

In the Old Testament, the Spirit of the Lord was given to selected leaders rather than to all of God's people. When the Spirit came to an individual, He brought with Him one or more gifts which equipped the individual to serve God by serving Israel. Examples of this are: Bezaleel, who was given the gift of craftsmanship (Ex. 31:2–3); Othniel, who was equipped to be a judge (Judg. 3:9–10); Gideon, who was given military skills (Judg. 6:34); Samson, who was given physical strength (Judg. 14:6,19); Saul, who was given political skills (1 Sam. 10:6); and Micah, who was given prophetic gifts (Mic. 3:8).

These Old Testament stories are the background for the Christian understanding of spiritual gifts. The Christian view of spiritual gifts begins with Jesus. He was the unique bearer of the Spirit (Mark 1:10). The Spirit directed and empowered Him for His ministry (Luke 4:14–18). Jesus promised His disciples that they, too, would receive the Spirit one day and that the Spirit would guide them (see Mark 13:11; Luke 11:13).

These promises were fulfilled on the day of Pentecost (Acts 2:1–47). The Spirit was given to all Christians, not just to selected leaders (2:3–4,17–18). Peter made it quite clear that the Spirit would continue to be given to all who accepted the Christian gospel (v. 38).

Paul's letters reveal that this continued to be true in all the churches; every Christian was given the gift of the Spirit, so that Paul could write: "Whoever does not have the Spirit of Christ does not belong to him" (Rom. 8:9 TEV). When the Spirit came into a person's life, He brought with Him a gift, or gifts, which that person could use to serve God. "Each one, as a good manager of God's different gifts, must use for the good of others the special gift he has received from God" (1 Pet. 4:10 TEV).

Like Peter, Paul believed that every Christian had a spiritual gift (1 Cor. 12:4–7). Neither Paul nor any other New Testament writer suggested that some Christians might be without gifts; all Christians are given gifts. Paul always set his discussion of gifts in the context of the church. In our day many people tend to think individualistically; it is easy to do this with reference to spiritual gifts. This can lead us to become arrogant about our gifts ("I have the gift of evangelism"), or else to be ashamed of our gifts ("My gift is only working with children"). Paul spoke of gifts in terms of the whole church, not in terms of individuals only. The church, he said, is the body of Christ; each Christian is a member (eye, ear, leg); and each member has its appropriate ability (to see, or hear, or walk). This understanding leaves no room for arrogance or shame concerning our gifts.

In his writings Paul referred to about twenty different gifts, including such things as preaching, teaching, and leadership. Some interpreters have suggested that by putting Paul's lists of gifts together, we get a comprehensive list of spiritual gifts. This seems unlikely, as we today can recognize some gifts which Paul did not mention, such as the gifts of music, of working with youth, and of counseling.

Some Christians today tend to want to distinguish spiritual gifts from natural abilities, but this distinction seems not to have occurred to Paul, for he included both in his lists (see, for example, Rom. 12:6–8). His assumption seems to have been that whatever skills a Christian has are given to him by God and are to be used in God's service. What matters, then, is that Christians discover what their gifts are and then develop them.

Which specific gift is the most valuable one? Paul's answer to this is clear and emphatic: the one gift all Christians should have, love (1 Cor. 12:31—13:1). Love is the ultimate spiritual gift. If we have all other gifts and lack love, we have nothing; if we have love and nothing else, we have everything. Paul said that love fulfills the entire law (Rom. 13:10; compare Matt. 22:39–40). Love makes possible the fellowship of the church and guarantees that gifts will be used unselfishly. Love is the greatest gift given to us by the God who is love.

See *Holy Spirit; Tongues, Gift of.*

Fisher Humphreys

SPIT, SPITTLE Spitting at or on someone is the strongest sign of contempt. The brother who refused to perform levirate marriage (have a child by his brother's wife to carry on the name of the brother, Deut. 25:5–6) would have his face spit in by the spurned wife of the brother (Deut. 25:7–9). The soldiers that mocked Jesus before His crucifixion spat on Him (Matt. 27:30). The religious leaders who tried Jesus before taking Him to Pilate spat in His face (Matt. 26:67). Spittle was used to heal (Mark 8:23; John 9:6). Mixing spittle with clay (John 9:6) may have been to deliberately break the sabbath laws of the Jewish religious leaders.

SPOIL Anything taken by a victorious soldier. In ancient warfare a soldier could take anything he could carry that had belonged to a foe. This plunder could be precious metals, clothes, cattle, or the vanquished people themselves. Holy war laws dedicated all such booty to God (Deut. 20). The battles of Joshua illustrated this.

SPONGE The skeleton of marine animals whose structure retains water. It was especially useful in bathing. The only instances of its use in the Bible center around giving Jesus a drink while upon the cross (Matt. 27:48; Mark 15:36; John 19:29). See *Cross.*

SPOON KJV translation for the dish in which incense was burned in the tabernacle and Temple (Num. 7:14). Other translations are "gold pan" (NAS), "golden dish" (NRSV), and "gold dish" (NIV). The twelve dishes were made of ten shekels of gold (vv. 84–86). See *Incense; Vessels and Utensils.*

SPORT To laugh at, to mock, to play with, and in one place to live in luxury. The versions do not agree on how to translate this word. For instance, Isaiah 57:4 is translated, "Against whom do ye sport yourselves?" ("jest" NAS; "mocking" NIV, NRSV). Samson is said to have made sport for the Philistines (Judg. 16:25). Modern translations use "perform" and "entertain." 2 Peter 2:13 speaks of the unrighteous as "sporting themselves with their own deceivings while they feast with you." Modern translations translate "reveling."

SPOT Skin blemishes of differing kinds indicating sickness that made a person ceremonially unclean (Lev. 13:1–8). The priest declared such persons clean or unclean. Only animals "without spot" (Num. 28:3) could be used for an offering to Yahweh. Jesus Himself was spoken of by Peter as "a lamb without blemish and without spot" (1 Pet. 1:19). The faithful are urged to obey "without spot" (1 Tim. 6:14). In this sense it means to be morally pure and obedient to God's will. See *Sacrifice and Offering.*

SPRING A place where water bubbles up freely from the ground (NAS, NIV, NRSV). KJV usually translates, "fountain." See *Fountain; Water; Well.*

SQUAD Modern translation of quaternion (Acts 12:1–11). See *Quaternion.*

STABLE A place where animals are kept either by enclosing them or tying them. Animals were usually kept in numbers rather than one animal in a stable or stall, as is often the case today. It could be a simple enclosure, a cave, or a building. Solomon kept large numbers of horses in stalls (1 Kings

An area at Megiddo thought to be a stable complex (or possibly storehouses) from the time of Ahab.

4:26). Most people just kept their animals together. Some kept them in a lower part of their homes. Jesus was born in a stable possibly belonging to an inn for He was put in a manger (trough where animals were fed) after being wrapped in swaddling cloths. See *Manger; Solomon.*

STACHYS (Stā′ chȳs) A personal name meaning, "head of grain." Man Paul called, "my beloved" (Rom. 16:9).

STACTE The gum of the storax tree which was combined with onycha, galbanum, and frankincense to make the incense to be burned in the tabernacle (Ex. 30:34). It is a small tree plentiful in rocky places in most of Palestine. See *Incense.*

STAFF See *Rod.*

STAG Modern translation of hart. See *Animals, Wild, 9. Deer.*

STAIRS A series of steps whereby a person can climb easily to another level. Houses in Palestine usually had stairs on the outside going up to the roof. Many activities were on the roof of the average house. Sometimes the steepness of city streets would make stairs from one level to another necessary. Also wells and cisterns in many cities in Palestine would have stairs leading down to the water. There were stairs in two visions in the Old Testament: Jacob's ladder may have been stairs (Gen. 28:12); Ezekiel's temple had stairs (43:17). See *Architecture; House.*

STAKE An instrument used with cords to anchor a tent. It was used figuratively of Jerusalem (Isa. 33:20; 54:2).

STALL A place where animals were kept and fed. See *Stable.*

STANDARD A flag or banner usually used by the military to identify groups of soldiers or a central flag to rally all the soldiers at one time (Num. 1:52; 2:2; 10:14,18). It is also used figuratively of God (Isa. 59:19). See *Banner.*

STARGAZER See *Astrologer.*

STARS Constellations, planets, and all heavenly bodies except the sun and the moon. God is acknowledged to be the Creator of all such (Gen. 1:16) as well as the One who knows their names and numbers (Ps. 147:4). Biblical writers knew many of the constellations. The Lord asked Job, "Can you bind the chains of Pleiades, or loose the cords of Orion?" (Job 38:31 NAS).

Individual stars are mentioned (Amos 5:26; Acts 7:43). Probably the most famous and intriguing of all the stars mentioned in Scripture is the star of Bethlehem, (Matt. 2). Many theories have been posited regarding its identity. Suffice it to say that Scripture does not name the star. It is one of many miracles that attest to the power of our God and is similar to the pillar of fire used to demonstrate God's presence and might to the children of Israel as they made their way to the land of Canaan. In the final book of the Bible the Lord Jesus is called "the bright and morning star" (Rev. 22:16).　　　　　　　　　　　　　*C. Dale Hill*

STATURE Usually refers to the height of a person, sometimes used figuratively (Ezek. 17:6; 19:11). Jesus "increased in wisdom and stature" (Luke 2:52). It was used to show the weakness of humanity and the need to rely on God (Matt. 6:27; Luke 12:25). It was also used as a measure of the maturity of the Christian (Eph. 4:13).

STATUTE A law or commandment. It could be from God or an earthly ruler. Different statutes of God were given by Moses to God's people (Ex. 15:25–26). Joseph was able to create laws as a ruler in Egypt (Gen. 47:26).

STEADFASTNESS A word meaning to endure patiently. A steadfast person is one who is reliable, faithful, and true to the end. Paul said Jesus was a person of steadfastness (Rom. 15:3–4). The NAS translates steadfastness with "perseverance" (2 Thess. 1:4). James said that trials that test our faith produce steadfastness (1:3 KJV "patience"; NAS "endurance"; NIV "perseverance").

STEEL KJV translation of a word that most modern versions translate "bronze" (2 Sam. 22:35). See *Minerals and Metals.*

STEPHANAS (Stĕph′ ȧ nȧs) Personal name meaning, "crown." A believer who, along with his family, was baptized by Paul (1 Cor. 1:16). He lived in Achaia and apparently was among the first converts of Paul's ministry there. Stephanas may have delivered a letter from the Corinthian church to Paul while the apostle was in Ephesus (1 Cor. 16:17). From existing evidence it is uncertain whether these two are the same man.

STEPHEN (Stĕ′ phĕn) Personal name meaning, "crown." The first Christian martyr; foremost of those chosen to bring peace to the quarreling church (Acts 6:1–7) and so mighty in the Scriptures that his Jewish opponents in debate could not refute him (Acts 6:10) as he argued that Jesus was the Messiah. Saul of Tarsus heard Stephen's speech to the Jewish Sanhedrin accusing the Jewish leaders of rejecting God's way as their forefathers had (Acts 6:12—7:53). Saul held the clothes of those who stoned Stephen to death; he saw him die a victorious death. Stephen may well

St. Stephen's Gate (Lion's Gate) at Jerusalem.

have been the human agency that God used to conquer him who would become the great Christian missionary.

Stephen was in the forefront of those who saw Christianity as much more than a Jewish sect. They took seriously the commission of Jesus to carry the gospel to the whole world and led to the founding of the world mission movement that took the gospel to the whole Roman Empire in the first century. The believers had to flee Jerusalem after Stephen's death while the apostles alone remained there (Acts 8:1).　　　*Fred L. Fisher*

STEWARDSHIP Utilizing and managing all resources God provides for the glory of God and the betterment of His creation.
Old Testament Stewardship Stewardship permeates the pages of the Bible because how we respond to God is at the heart of the Book. Often, stewardship is thought of only in terms of finances, but the Bible teaches that stewardship is a far greater concept, involving how we respond with all of our life to Him who is the giver and sustainer of life?

When God created humans, He made them to have "dominion" over all of the earth (Gen. 1:26). Dominion was not intended to be domination or exploitation. Dominion was God's call for human beings to be good and gracious managers of God's creation. Unfortunately, the sin of humanity interrupted God's plans for His world. Humankind became selfish, seeing the world as a means to its own self-centered ends. The things of the world were now seen as possessions with humans as owners, not as God's stewards. God's intention for His world did not change. He still desired that people see God as the Lord of everything and themselves as the managers of God's creation.
New Testament Stewardship The call to absolute commitment to Christ is the central theme of the New Testament (Mark 8:34–36). Jesus asked for obedience to God's original intention for the world. Jesus was calling for a radical reversal of the world's values (profit) and a revolutionary return to God's purpose (lose life for My sake).

Jesus never seemed to be satisfied with a slice of the pie of our obedience. He did not rejoice in the tithe or a big offering as much as He did in the sacrificial, complete giving of a widow but Jesus called all disciples to absolute surrender of ourselves and our substance to Him.

The early church certainly saw all that it had as a gift from God for the good of each other. "And the multitude of them that believed were of one heart and of one soul: neither said any of them that ought of the things which he possessed was his own; but they had all things common" (Acts 4:32).

Of course, our economic system and sheer numbers of people today prevent this kind of complete sharing, but the amazing thing was the attitude of the church members to what they possessed. They saw none of it as their own. All of it came from the loving heart of God. That is why the sin of selfishness of Ananias and Sapphira was so serious (Acts 5).

The apostle Paul preached and taught a single-minded commitment to Christ. He reminded the Philippians that the source of thanksgiving was not in things but in our relationship to God in Christ (Phil. 3:13–14).

Thus, the New Testament concept of stewardship centers in our commitment to Jesus Christ. When He becomes our Lord, He becomes Lord of our time, talents, finances, and everything. We realize that we are not our own, but we are bought with a price. *Charles Bugg*

STOCKS An instrument that secured the feet (and sometimes the neck and hands) of a prisoner (Job 13:27; Jer. 29:26; Acts 16:24). They were usually made of wood with holes to secure the feet. They could also be an instrument of torture by stretching the legs apart and causing the prisoner to sit in unnatural positions. The Romans often added chains along with the stocks.

STONE Hardened mineral matter comprising much of the earth. Palestine is a stony country. Often it was necessary to clear a field of stone

Intricate stone carving on a column piece at ancient Baalbek (Heliopolis).

Roman marble column shafts in secondary use to reinforce a Crusader sea wall at Caesarea Maritima.

preparatory to its cultivation (Isa. 5:2). An enemy's fields were marred by throwing stones on them, and his wells were choked with stones (2 Kings 3:19,25). Stones were used for various purposes: city walls (Neh. 4:3), dwellings (Lev. 14:38–40), palaces (1 Kings 7:1,9), temples (1 Kings 6:7), pavement in courtyards and columns (Esth. 1:6), and in Herodian times, at least, for paving streets. The Israelites used unhewn stones for building their altars. They often heaped stones to commemorate some great spiritual event or encounter with God (Gen. 31:46; Josh. 4). They marked the grave of notorious offenders with stones (Josh. 7:26). One of the most popular uses of stone was the building of the walls of the Temple and the building of the walls of the city of Jerusalem (1 Kings 7:9–12).

Single stones were used to close the mouth of cisterns, wells, and tombs (Gen. 29:2; Matt. 27:60; John 11:38). They were also used to mark boundaries (Deut. 19:14). The Israelites sometimes consecrated a single stone as a memorial to God (Gen. 28:18–22; 1 Sam. 7:12).

The Old Testament and the New Testament refer to stones being used as lethal weapons. See *Arms and Armor.* Two popular stories about the use of stones for weapons are those about David killing Goliath (1 Sam. 17:49) and about the enemies of the Christian faith stoning Stephen (Acts 7:58).

Stones were often used for weights on scales. They were employed for writing documents. The most obvious example is the writing of the Ten Commandments on stone by the Spirit of God when Moses went up on Mount Sinai.

Symbolically, a stone denotes hardness or insensibility (1 Sam. 25:37; Ezek. 36:26). It could also mean firmness and strength. The followers of Christ were called living stones who were built up into the spiritual temple of Christ. Christ himself became the chief cornerstone (Eph. 2:20–22; 1 Pet. 2:4–8). See *Minerals and Metals.*

Gary Bonner

STONES OF FAIR COLORS See *Antimony.*

STOOL A simply made object for a person to sit on (2 Kings 4:10). Some translate "chair" (NAS, NRSV, NIV). It is also mentioned in Exodus 1:16 (birthstool NAS, NRSV; delivery stool NIV). God is said to have a footstool where the faithful worship Him (Ps. 99:5). James speaks of a footstool being in the assembly of the early church (2:3).

STOREHOUSE, STORAGE CITY Storehouses were built early in human history to protect harvested crops from vermin and extreme weather. The typical storehouse during the Israelite period was a rectangular building with a double row of columns which divided the building into three narrow aisles. Large, thick walls supported the roof, and small side rooms led off of the main hall. Storerooms at Herod's fortress of Masada had walls eleven feet high constructed of stones weighing over 400 pounds. Community storehouses could also be used as public markets. In large cities, certain sections of the town were designated as storage areas, with several storehouses lining the streets. During the Divided Kingdom period, royal storage facilities were established in regional capitals to collect tax payments made in flour, oil, grain, or wine. Specially marked jars held these royal stores which later could be distributed to the army or royal palaces. The Temple complex included special storage areas, both for the utensils of wor-

Storage rooms, or storehouse, excavated at Tel Beersheba in the Negeb.

ship and to serve as a sort of bank where valuables might be placed. The picture of a full storehouse served as an image of God's blessing and was often used by the prophets.　　　　*David Maltsberger*

STORK One of a number of large, long-legged birds that usually wade for their food. They eat fish and an assortment of animals that live around water. They are known for the care they take of their young and for returning each year to the same nesting area. The stork migrates from Africa in the winter to Europe in the spring. It stops in Palestine during its migration. It was ceremonially unclean (Lev. 11:19). It is related to the heron. See *Birds.*

STRAIGHT STREET A street in Damascus where Paul was staying after being struck blind in his experience with the risen Christ (Acts 9:10–12). This street still exists today called *Darb al-Mustaqim.* See *Damascus.*

STRANGE WOMAN See *Adventuress.*

STRANGER See *Alien.*

STRAW Usually barley or wheat stalks after they have been cut. Sometimes translated, "chaff" (KJV). It was usually used as bedding for animals,

The "Street called Straight" in Damascus in the modern country of Syria.

S

much as many farmers use it today. The Israelites were forced to use straw in the making of bricks (Ex. 5:6–13). See *Stubble.*

STREETS Pathways established and constructed for transportation via animals and vehicles. The layout of city streets often was established by the shape of the outer city walls. In some cities a wide street encircled the city, following the line of the outer wall. In other towns, streets radiated from a main plaza or thoroughfare. The doors of shops, storehouses, and private homes opened onto the street. Often, household wastes were thrown out into the street. Small, crooked lanes and alleyways led off from main streets, ending at a central courtyard serving several homes or shops. Streets were often paved with large, flat stones, although dirt paths were not uncommon. Larger towns constructed drainage canals beneath city streets, some to carry away waste water and others to trap the run off from winter rains which was channeled into cisterns. During the New Testament era, Roman engineers designed cities throughout the empire with wide, straight, and well-constructed streets, usually leading to a central plaza or temple. Sidewalks with raised curbs bordered streets set with large polyagonal paving stones. Drains below the pavement carried away sewage and rain water. The constant traffic of carts and pedestrians often wore ruts into the streets, necessitating repair.   *David Maltsberger*

The Street of Curetes looking toward the Library of Celsus in the ruins of ancient Ephesus.

STRIPES See *Scourge.*

STRONG DRINK An intoxicating drink made from grain. It may have at first been used of beer made from barley. Wine is usually included along with strong drink but is separate from it (1 Sam. 1:15; Judg. 13:4,7,14; Luke 1:15). It was usually denied to priests (Lev. 10:8–9) and those who took the Nazirite vow (Num. 6:3). Isaiah warned against drinking too much (5:11). The Bible warns against drunkenness. The New Testament says that the drunkard will have no place in the kingdom of God (1 Cor. 6:9–10). See *Drunkenness; Wine.*

STUBBLE Stalks of grain dried out in the field or left on the threshing floor. It is sometimes translated straw or chaff. Stubble burns quickly and can be blown away by the wind. Figuratively it is used of God's judgment (Joel 2:5; Isa. 5:24). Stubble was used by God's people to make bricks while they were slaves in Egypt (Ex. 5:12).

STUFF, STUFF FOR REMOVING, STUFF FOR CAPTIVITY See *Carriage.*

STUMBLING BLOCK Anything that causes a person to stumble or to fall. It is used literally (Lev. 19:14), but most often it is used as a metaphor. It is used of idols (Ezek. 7:19), of God's work with faithless people (Jer. 6:21), and of God Himself in relation to His people (Isa. 8:14). Paul warned Christians not to let their freedom result in a stumbling block to other believers (Rom. 14:13; 1 Cor. 8:9). The disobedient are warned that Jesus Himself could be a stumbling block (Rom. 9:32–33; 1 Cor. 1:23; 1 Pet. 2:8). The Greek word, *skandalon,* was the bait stick in a trap. It was also used symbolically for the trap itself. It came to mean a temptation to sin or to have false faith.

SUAH (Sū' ah) Personal name meaning, "sweepings." Son of Zophah of the tribe of Asher (1 Chron. 7:36).

SUBURBS Pastureland around cities that were used in common for the feeding of sheep, cattle, and other animals (Lev. 25:34). Other versions translate, "open land" (NRSV); "pastureland" (NIV); and "pasture fields" (NAS). See *Cities and Urban Life.*

SUCATHITE (Sū' ca thite) A people who claimed ancestry from the Kenites and the Rechabites (1 Chron. 2:55). KJV has Suchathites.

SUCCOTH (Sūc' cōth) *1.* A place name meaning, "booths." A city east of the Jordan in the tribal territory of Gad. Jacob dwelt there upon his return to Canaan (Gen. 33:17). It was an important town during the time of Gideon. Its leaders were punished by Gideon for not helping him in a campaign against the Midianites (Judg. 8:5–7,13–16). Near Succoth Hiram made vessels for Solomon's Temple (1 Kings 7:45–46). It is usually located at tell Deir Alla, but some excavation results have called this into question. 2. A place where the Israelites camped upon leaving Egypt (Ex. 12:37; 13:20; Num. 33:5–6). It was near Pithom and is usually identified with tell el-Maskhutah or tell er-Retabah.

SUCCOTH BENOTH (Sūc′ cōth-bē′ nōth) Divine name meaning, "booths of daughters." A pagan deity which people from Babylon brought with them to Israel when it was resettled by the Assyrians after the fall of Samaria in 722 B.C. (2 Kings 17:30). Interpreters disagree concerning the identification of this idol. Many feel that it is likely Sarpanitu, the consort of Marduk. See *Gods, Pagan; Sakkuth.*

SUFFERING Enduring undesirable pains and experiences. The Bible does not treat suffering systematically nor philosophically. It relates how people and nations experience suffering in various ways for a variety of reasons. Clearly an understanding of suffering introduces the problem of evil. Suffering follows the entrance of evil into the universe. The Bible does not attempt to explain the origin of evil. It accepts evil and suffering as givens in a fallen and sinful world. The various writers present multiple perspectives on the causes of suffering and how it can be endured.
Old Testament The Semitic mind dealt with concrete situations rather than abstract forms. Their perspective was not to treat the issue of suffering as an intellectual one. The Old Testament writers, accordingly, sought to identify the causes and purposes of suffering when it happened.

The Hebrews regarded suffering as punishment for sin against the divine moral order. The wicked would surely suffer for their evil ways (Pss. 7:15,16; 37:1–3; 73:12–20; 139:19), even though they might prosper for a time (Job 21:28–33). Some writers expressed consternation that God stayed His hand of judgment against the offenders of His will (Jer. 12:1–4; Hab. 1:2–4; Mal. 3:7–15). They often interpreted their own suffering as a sign of God's wrath and punishment for sin in their lives. The highly developed sense of corporate identity in Hebrew thought meant that suffering could come as a result of parents' sin (1 Kings 21:20,22,29; an idea reflected by Jesus' disciples in John 9:2, the story of the healing of the man born blind) or the wickedness of the king (2 Kings 21:10,11).

The suffering of the righteous posed a problem. It was explained variously as a way for God to gain peoples' attention (Job 33:14; 36:15), to correct sin into obedience (2 Chron. 20:9,10; Mal. 3:3), to develop or refine character (Job 23:10; Ps. 66:10). Ultimately, the writers consigned them-

selves to trust in God's sometimes hidden wisdom (Job 42:2,3; Ps. 135:6).

The prophet gained a vision of a greater purpose in suffering—carrying the sins of others (Isa. 53). As eschatological hopes matured in late Old Testament and intertestamental times, the righteous looked forward to the Day of the Lord when they would be vindicated and justice would reign (Dan. 12:1).
New Testament Into an evil world God sent His only Son. God is Himself touched by the suffering of Christ on the cross. Christian writers in the New Testament incorporated the trials of Christ into their existing Old Testament understanding of suffering. The purposefulness and necessity of suffering in the life of the Son of God (Matt. 16:21; Mark 8:31; Luke 9:22) aided them in coping with their own.

The early Christians recognized the inevitability of their suffering. As Christ suffered, so would they (John 16:33; Acts 14:22; Rom. 8:31–39; 1 Cor. 12:26; 1 Thess. 2:14; 2 Tim. 3:12; 1 Pet. 4:12,13). Continuing His mission, they would incur tribulation (Mark 13:12,13; Rev. 17:6; 20:14) because the world hates the disciples as much as it did their Lord (see John 15:18; 1 Cor. 2:8; 1 John 3:11,12). Suffering for His sake was counted a privilege (Acts 5:41; 1 Cor. 11:32; 1 Thess. 1:4–8).

New Testament writers realized there were other types of suffering than that incurred as they lived on Christian mission. These are to be endured patiently rather than rebelliously (1 Thess. 3:3; Jas. 1:2–4) because God is working His purpose out in His children's lives (Rom. 8:28–29). Satan would tempt believers to be defeated in their suffering (2 Cor. 4:8–12; Rev. 2:10). Instead, Christians can grow stronger spiritually through trials (Rom. 6:4–8; 1 Pet. 4:1; Heb. 12:11) and share Christ's ultimate triumph (Mark 13:9; John 16:33; 2 Thess. 1:5; Rev. 5:5; 20:9,14,15) even now as they experience daily victories (Rom. 8:37; 1 John 2:13–14; 1 Pet. 5:10). Therefore, sufferings give rise to hope (Rom. 12:12; 1 Thess. 1:3), for no present suffering compares with the rewards that await the faithful follower of Christ (Rom. 8:17–18).

T. R. McNeal

SUKKIIMS (Sūk′ kiîms) Mentioned only in 2 Chronicles 12:3, these people were part of Shishak's (king of Egypt) army when he fought against Rehoboam of Judah. They may have been desert-dwelling mercenaries out of Libya, known in Egyptian sources as Tjukten from 1300 to 1100 B.C.

SULFUR NRSV, NIV, REB translate Revelation 9:17–18 "sulfur" rather than the usual "brimstone." The Near East has large deposits of this mineral. See *Brimstone; Minerals and Metals.*

SUMER (Sū′ mĕr) One of the two political divisions originally comprising what came to be Babylonia. Its principal cities were Nippur, Adab, Lagash, Umma, Larsa, Erech, Ur, and Eridu, most of which were on or near the Euphrates. The area consists primarily of the fertile plain between the Tigris and Euphrates Rivers and is now the southern part of modern Iraq.

In the Old Testament, Sumer is the territory referred to as Shinar (Gen. 10:10) or Chaldea (Jer. 50:10). See *Shinar.*

Archaeologists believe the inhabitants of ancient Sumer developed humanity's first high civilization about 3000 B.C. Perhaps the most important Sumerian contribution to civilization was the invention of cuneiform writing, a wedge-shaped script formed by pressing a reed stylus into wet clay tablets, which were later dried, baked, and stored in libraries. The Babylonians and other surrounding peoples adapted the cuneiform script to their own languages so that for centuries, cuneiform was the dominant mode of writing in ancient Mesopotamia. Most Sumerian tablets contain economic and administrative records, but others include mythology, history, hymns, wisdom texts, law, and much more. Of special interest to biblical scholars are: the law code of Ur-nammu, the Sumerian king list, the flood story of Zuisudra, the paradise myth of Enki and Ninhursag, early forms of the Gilgamesh epic, and the descent of Inanna to the underworld.

Originally, Sumer consisted of a number of city-states, each with its own protective god. Political power was held by the free citizens of the city and a governor, called *ensi.* As the city-states vied with one another for power and as pressures from outside invaders increased, the institution of kingship emerged, whereby the ruler of one city-state dominated others.

About 2100 B.C., Sumer was conquered by invading tribesmen from the west and north. A mighty warrior named Sargon (later known as Sargon I, Sargon the Great, and Sargon of Akkad), conquered this area and extended his empire from the Persian Gulf to the Mediterranean Sea. He founded a new capital city, Agade, which was, for more than half a century, the richest and most powerful capital in the world.

Sumer enjoyed a brief revival at Ur (about 2050 B.C.) only to decline before the rise of the Elamites, a people to their east. Finally, in about 1720 B.C., Hammurabi of Babylon united Sumer (the southern division of ancient Babylon) into one empire. This conquest by Hammurabi marked the end of ancient Sumer, but the cultural and intellectual impact of the Sumerians continued until after the Persians became the dominant force in this part of the ancient world.   *Rich Murrell*

SUN The source of light for earth. Ancient people considered the sun as a necessary part of the cycle of the seasons. Thus, it was often viewed as a god. Ancient Egyptians worshiped the sun as the god Ra, and the Greeks as Helios. The Canaanite city of Beth-Shemesh, "House of the Sun," probably referred to a temple in the city. The Bible simply views the sun as the "greater light" God created to rule the day (Gen. 1:16). In Israel, the new day began with sunset. The Psalms compared the sun's brightness to God's glory by which it will one day be replaced (Ps. 84:11). Zacharias described Christ's coming as a new sunrise for humankind (Luke 1:78). The darkening or eclipse of the sun was often interpreted as a sign of God's displeasure with humans. See *Gods, Pagan.*

                                       David Maltsberger

SUNDAY See *Lord's Day.*

SUNDIAL A device, generally a flat disk with numbers around its edge, used to measure time by the position of a shadow cast by the sun. The root of the Hebrew word translated, "dial," (2 Kings 20:11; Isa. 38:8) means, "to go up," and usually refers to stairs. Most interpreters thus understand Ahab's dial to be a staircase on which a shadow went up as the day progressed. The sign involved the shadow's moving back down ten steps.

SUPERSCRIPTION Usually the Romans identified a person's crime by writing it on a wooden sign, carrying it before the condemned person, and finally nailing it to their cross. All four Gospels mention such a superscription (Matt. 27:37; Mark 15:26; Luke 23:38; John 19:19) being nailed over Jesus' head. However, they do not speak of the sign being carried before Jesus as He walked to the place of crucifixion. Superscription is also used for the titles of some psalms giving information concerning the writer and the context of the psalm. See *Cross, Crucifixion; Psalms; Trial of Jesus.*

SUPERSTITIOUS KJV translation of Greek word indicating fear of or reverence for the gods. The term can be used in a good sense or in a derogatory sense. Modern translations usually take the term in the sense of "very religious" (NAS, NIV) or "uncommonly scrupulous" concerning religion (REB). Paul described the men of Athens (Acts 17:22), and Festus characterized Paul as he stood before King Agrippa (Acts 25:19) with the term.

SUPH (Sūph) Place name meaning, "reed." *1.* Hebrew name for Red Sea. See *Red Sea. 2.* Place helping locate where Moses delivered the speech behind the Book of Deuteronomy (Deut. 1:1). It may be khirbet Safe just southeast of Medeba in the mountains of Moab, but this is uncertain.

SUPHAH (Suph′ ah) Apparently a place name perhaps meaning, "toward the reeds." The Hebrew text of Numbers 21:14 has no verb and has been translated and emended in many ways to achieve one. Compare translations. KJV created "Yam-Suph," or "Red Sea." Others find a compound place name, "Waheb in Suphah," indicating two locations in Moab.

SUR, GATE OF A gate in Jerusalem. Some feel that it may be the gate leading from the king's palace to the Temple spoken of in the account of the murder of Queen Athaliah (2 Kings 11). In the parallel account (2 Chron. 23) the gate is called "the gate of the foundation" (v. 5).

SURETY A person who is legally responsible for the debt of another or the money or thing of value put down to guarantee the debt. Should there be a default, the surety would have to pay the debt or even be enslaved until the debt was paid. Judah became surety for Benjamin to Joseph (Gen. 43:9; 44:32). God was asked by a faithful psalmist to be his surety (119:121–122). Proverbs warns against being surety for someone you do not know well (11:15). In a positive sense Jesus is said to be surety for the faithful under the new covenant (Heb. 7:22). *See Loan; Pledge; Slavery.*

SUSA (Sü′ sà)The winter capital of the ancient Persian Empire. The territory is now in the modern Iran. Cyrus made Susa a capital city along with Ecbatana and Babylon. When Alexander the Great captured Susa, he found a large treasure which he confiscated. Archaeologists have excavated Susa largely around four areas: the royal palace, the acropolis, the royal city, and an artisan tell. Some believe Susa to be the place where Queen Esther and King Ahasuerus ruled. *See Esther; Nehemiah; Persia.*

SUSANCHITES (Sū′ săn chītes) Citizens of the city of Susa. See *Susa.*

SUSANNA (Sū săn′ nà) A personal name meaning, "lily." One of several women who followed Jesus and supported Him financially (Luke 8:2–3).

SUSI (Sū′ sī) A personal name meaning, "my horse." The father of Gaddi, one of the spies Moses sent from the wilderness of Paran to spy out the land of Canaan (Num. 13:11).

SWADDLE BAND The cloth in which an infant was wrapped and secured by bands which were wrapped around the outside (Luke 2:7,12). See *Swaddling Clothes.*

SWADDLING CLOTHES A long piece of linen used in ancient times to wrap babies and broken limbs. The cloth was wrapped tightly around the body to prohibit movement. Mary wrapped Jesus in swaddling clothes just after His birth (Luke 2:7).

An Arab mother watches her baby who is wrapped in swaddling clothes.

SWALLOW A bird that migrates to Palestine from March until winter. It made nests in the Temple (Ps. 84:3) and was often seen with the common sparrow. It was sometimes confused with the swift. See *Birds.*

SWAN KJV rendering of the Hebrew *tinshemet* (Lev. 11:18; Deut. 14:16). Other versions translate, "the desert owl" or "pelican" (NRSV) or "the white owl" (NIV, NAS). See *Birds; Owl.*

SWEAR See *Oaths.*

SWEAT Perspiration. Sweat usually comes from physical exertion, sickness, or mental or emotional excitement (Gen. 3:19; Ezek. 44:18; Luke 22:44).

SWEET CANE See *Calamus.*

SWIFT A bird similar to a swallow but unrelated to swallows. Jeremiah mentions the swift (8:7 NAS, NIV). Other versions translate "swallow" (KJV, NRSV). Some commentators think a bulbul or wryneck is meant. Perhaps bulbul (*Pycnonotus Reichenovi*) is the best linguistic guess. See *Birds.*

SWINE Israelites were forbidden to eat swine (Lev. 11:7; Deut. 14:8). Swine were considered ceremonially unclean and were used as metaphors for uncleanness. (Prov. 11:22; Matt. 7:6; 2 Pet. 2:22). Mark 5:11–17 speaks of a large herd of swine in the Decapolis area where Jesus saw them as fit bearers of demons. Many ancient people ate swine and used swine for sacrifice to idols. See *Animals.*

SWORD Close-range weapon. The Hebrew word *chereb* and the Greek word *machaira* designate either a dagger or a sword. The Hebrew word also designates an iron tool ("axes," Ezek. 26:9) or a chisel ("tool," Ex. 20:25). In Joshua 5:2, the word designates stone knives used in the circumcision of the people of Israel.

Archaeology has shown that different kinds of

swords were used in the Ancient Near East. The sickle or curved sword was used throughout Mesopotamia, Egypt, and in Palestine. The earlier swords were straight, relatively short, and made of bronze. Ehud's sword was the two-edged short dagger; it measured about 18 inches (Judg. 3:16). The sword used by the Israelites in the conquest of Canaan probably was the long-bladed, curved sword (Josh. 6:21).

The Sea Peoples introduced to Canaan the two-edged long sword made of iron. This type of iron sword was kept out of the hands of the Israelites by the Philistines for military and economic reasons until the times of David (1 Sam. 13:19). The Old Testament gives witness that in the wars between the Israelites and the Philistines, the Israelites did not possess this new weapon (1 Sam. 13:22). The sword was kept in a sheath (1 Sam. 17:51; Matt. 26:52). It hung from a belt (1 Sam 25:13) and was generally put on the left hip (2 Sam. 20:8).

There are many symbolic uses for the word *sword* in the Bible. The word was used as a metaphor for war (Jer. 14:15; Matt. 10:34); the sword was an instrument of divine justice (Ezek. 21:3; Rev. 1:16). Rash words are compared to a sword that pierces (Prov. 12:18); the tongue is like a sharp sword (Ps. 57:4); malicious words are "drawn swords" (Ps. 55:21). The Word of God is sharper than a "two-edged sword" (Heb. 4:12); the sword of the Spirit, which is the Word of God, is part of the Christian's armament in the fight against evil (Eph. 6:17). See *Arms and Armor.*

Claude F. Mariottini

SYCAMORE (Sÿc′ à mōre) A combination "fig" and "mulberry" tree (*Ficus sycomorus*) indicating the fig tree in the Jordan valley that had leaves like our mulberry tree. Its fruit was inferior to the fig tree and had to be punctured to make the fruit edible. Amos was employed as "one who took

Sword dating from the Middle Kingdom in Egypt.

care of sycamore-fig trees" (7:14 NIV; compare Ps. 78:47). This tree has no relation to the American sycamore tree. It was used as food for the poor and bore fruit several times a year. See 1 Kings 10:27; 2 Chronicles 1:15; 9:27. It was often planted along roadways for its shade (see Luke 19:4). Poor people used its wood rather than expensive cedar (Isa. 9:10).

SYCHAR (Sÿ′ chär) Place name intended to note "falsehood," though perhaps originally derived from "Shechem." A village in Samaria where Jacob's well is located (John 4:5−6). Jesus rested by the well and there ministered to a Samaritan woman. Jacob bought the parcel of land from "the children of Hamor, Shechem's father" (Gen. 33:19). The site has been identified variously with Shechem and a village just north of there called 'Askar. Archaeological excavations have revealed that Sychar and Shechem are part of the same ancient settlement.

SYMBOL A token or sign. While the word *symbol* does not appear in the Bible, both the Old and New Testaments are rich in symbolism and symbolic language.

Symbols, whether objects, gestures, or rituals convey meaning to the rational, emotional, and intuitive dimensions of human beings. The universal and supreme symbol of Christian faith is the cross, an instrument of execution. For Christians, this hideous object comes to be a sign of God's love for human beings.

The meaning of symbols grows and even changes over time. For the apostle Paul, the meaning conveyed by the cross changed radically as did his view of Jesus of Nazareth. As a rabbi, zealous to keep the Mosaic law and to bring others to do so, Paul believed that anyone hung on a tree was cursed by God (Deut. 21:23). For this reason and others, he strongly resisted the claims that Jesus was Messiah. How could one obviously under a

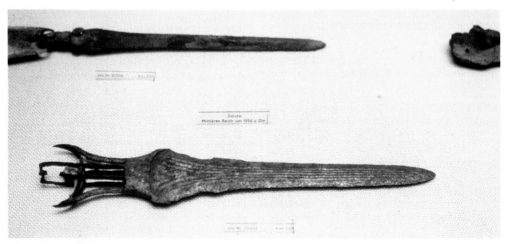

divine curse possibly be Messiah? Only when the risen Lord appeared to Saul did he realize that what appeared to be a curse had been transformed into a source of the greatest blessing. Christ's death seen through the resurrection is at the center of the two major symbolic rituals of Christian faith—baptism and the Lord's Supper or the Eucharist. See *Ordinances; Sacrament.*

Baptism is a picture of the death, burial, and resurrection of Christ. In being baptized, a person says to the world that the baptismal candidate is identifying with the saving act being pictured. That means the new believer is dying to sin and is rising to walk in new life, living now for God and with God as the center of life.

The Lord's Supper employs the ordinary elements of bread and wine to picture Christ's broken body and His blood shed for humanity's sin.

While the cross, the water, the bread, and wine are symbols at the center of Christian faith and practice, they are not the only symbols. Symbols in the Old Testament are related to symbols of the New Testament in important ways. Many of the events of the Old Testament foreshadow events of the New Testament. For example, the sacrificial lamb in the Old Testament points to the sacrificial death of Christ. The parables of Jesus are rich in symbols: grain, weeds, various kinds of soil, a lost sheep, a lost coin, and a lost son. Jesus used symbolic language in talking about Himself and His relationship to persons: Bread of life, Light of

The synagogue at the site of ancient Capernaum.

the world, Good Shepherd, Water of life, and the Door.

The apocalyptic writings of the Bible, Ezekiel, Daniel, and Revelation are rich in symbolic language. A person reading and interpreting these books is required to come to know the symbolic meaning of the terms being used in almost the same way as a person trying to break a code. See *Apocalyptic.* *Steve Bond*

SYNAGOGUE (Sĭn′ á gŏgue) The local meeting place and assembly of the Jewish people during New Testament times.

Origin Some Jewish traditions say that the synagogue was begun by Moses, but the Old Testament does not support this claim. Local worship was discouraged during most of the Old Testament because it often was associated with pagan practices. Worship centered around the Temple in Jerusalem. Psalm 74:8, written late in Old Testament times, seems to refer to local places of worship destroyed when the Temple was destroyed. Some English translations use the word *synagogues* for these local places of worship, but we know nothing else about them.

The synagogue, as we find it in the New Testament, had its roots in the time after Solomon's Temple was destroyed and many of the people were carried into Exile. Local worship and instruction became necessary. Even after many of the Jews returned to Jerusalem and rebuilt the Temple, places of local worship continued. By the time of Jesus these places and assemblies were called synagogues.

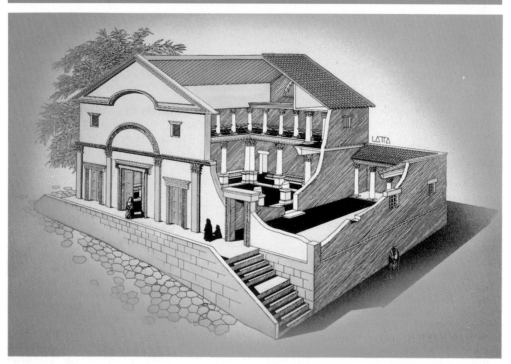

A typical synagogue of the first century A.D. showing the large inner room where the men gathered and its loft above where the women gathered. This particular drawing is patterned after the synagogue at Capernaum.

Facts about synagogues Synagogues existed not only among the many Jews who lived outside Palestine but also among those who lived in Palestine. While the Temple stood until A.D. 70, it continued to be the center for sacrificial worship. Faithful Jews continued to go to the Temple for the appointed feasts. They also participated in their local synagogues. During Jesus' time, there was even a synagogue within the Temple itself. This was probably the part of the Temple where the twelve-year-old Jesus was talking with the teachers (Luke 2:46).

Most communities of any size had at least one synagogue; some had several. Jewish sources indicate that a synagogue was to be established wherever there were as many as ten Jewish men. The principal meeting was on the sabbath. A typical service consisted of the recitation of the Shema (confession of faith in the one God), prayers, Scripture readings from the Law and the Prophets, a sermon, and a benediction. Luke 4:16–21 is the best biblical passage on what happened in a synagogue service in first-century Palestine. See *Shema.*

Local elders had general oversight of the synagogue. They often appointed a ruler of the synagogue. The ruler was a layman who cared for the building and selected those who participated in the service. The ruler was assisted by an attendant. One of his duties was to deliver the sacred scrolls to those who read and return them to the special place where they were kept (Luke 4:17,20).

Jesus and Synagogues Jesus customarily went to the synagogue in His hometown of Nazareth on the sabbath (Luke 4:16). After Jesus began His public ministry, He frequently taught and preached in synagogues throughout the land (Matt. 4:23; 9:35; Mark 1:39; Luke 4:44). Early in His ministry, Jesus healed a man in the synagogue in Capernaum (Mark 1:21–28; Luke 4:31–37).

Jesus often encountered opposition in synagogues. Luke 4:16–30 tells what happened in His home synagogue of Nazareth (see also Matt. 13:54–58; Mark 6:1–6). It shows how Jesus' preaching and teaching aroused strong negative reactions. Luke 13:10–16 tells of Jesus healing a woman in a synagogue on the sabbath. This brought an angry reaction from the ruler of the synagogue. Jesus, in turn, rebuked the man for his hypocrisy.

Jesus warned against the hypocrisy of those who paraded their righteousness in the synagogue. He warned against giving and praying in order to be seen and praised (Matt. 6:2,5). He also rebuked those who sought the chief seats (Matt. 23:6; Mark 12:39; Luke 11:43; 20:46).

As opposition to Jesus increased, He warned His disciples of a future time when they would be persecuted in the synagogues of their people (Matt. 10:17; 23:34; Mark 13:9; Luke 12:11;

The excavated remains of a third-century synagogue at the site of ancient Chorazin (Korazin), Israel.

21:12).

Synagogues in Acts The early part of the Book of Acts seems to reflect a period when some Jewish believers continued to worship in the synagogues. Saul went into the synagogues to find and persecute believers in Christ (Acts 9:2; 22:19; 26:11). This shows that Christian Jews were still in some synagogues, especially those outside Palestine. As persecution developed, the believers were forced out of the synagogues.

After Saul's conversion, he immediately preached Christ in the synagogues in Damascus (Acts 9:20). During Paul's missionary journeys, he customarily began his work in a new city by going into the synagogue (Acts 13:5,14; 14:1; 17:1,10,17; 18:4; 19:8). The exception in Philippi was probably because there were not enough Jews there to have a synagogue. Paul, therefore, went to a place where faithful Jews met to pray on the sabbath (Acts 16:13).

Generally, Paul was welcomed and given the opportunity to present his views. He found special interest among the Gentiles who attended the synagogue, but some Jews also believed (Acts 13:42–43). Others strongly opposed Paul. Usually, he was forced to leave the synagogue and go elsewhere with the band of believers (Acts 18:6–8; 19:8–10). Thus did the church and synagogue go their separate ways.

Influence of the Synagogue The synagogue was the means of preserving Jewish faith and worship. Jews all over the ancient world continued to maintain their distinctive faith. These synagogues became the seedbed for Christian faith as missionaries took the message of Christ to new places. Nearly everywhere the missionaries went, they found a Jewish synagogue. The first-century synagogue worshipers believed in the one true God, studied the Scriptures, and looked for the coming Messiah. What better place for Paul and others to go first with the message of Jesus Christ!

Robert J. Dean

SYNTYCHE (Sўn′ tў chē) Personal name meaning, "pleasant acquaintance" or "good luck."

Woman in the church at Philippi addressed by Paul concerning an argument with Euodia (Phil. 4:2).

SYRACUSE (Sўr′ a cūse) Major city on the island of Sicily. Paul stayed in the Syracuse harbor three days on his way to Rome (Acts 28:12). It was strong enough to defeat an attack from Athens in 413 B.C. but was defeated by Rome in 212 B.C. It became the residence of the governor of Sicily under Roman government. It enjoyed great prosperity during the Roman years.

SYRIA (Sўr′ ĭ a) The region or nation directly north of Palestine in the northwest corner of the Mediterranean Sea.

Name and Geography Syria is most properly a geographical term for the northwestern Mediterranean region situated between Palestine and Mesopotamia, roughly equal to the modern states of Syria and Lebanon with small portions of Turkey and Iraq. The name may come from a Greek shortening of Assyria and was only accidentally applied to the area. There is no geographical connection between Assyria and Syria.

Syria, like Palestine, has four basic geographical features as one moves from the Mediterranean eastward: (1) a narrow coastal plain; (2) a line of mountains; (3) the rift valley; and (4) fertile steppe fading into desert. The two main rivers rise near one another in the rift valley. The Orontes flows north before abruptly turning west to the sea in the plain of Antioch, while the Leontes flows south then turns west through a narrow gorge and empties into the sea. See *Palestine; Rivers.*

Old Testament Early History During the Early Bronze Age (about 3200–2200 B.C.), Syria was home to large city states similar to those found in Mesopotamia. The latter part of this period has been illuminated by the recent discovery of cuneiform tablets in the state archive at Ebla, the capital of a small empire in northern Syria. Many of these tablets are in Eblaite, an ancient language similar to Hebrew and promise to aid in biblical study. See *Ebla.*

In the Middle Bronze Age (2200–1550 B.C.), the time of the Hebrew patriarchs, north Syria was home to the kingdoms of Yamhad, with its capital at Aleppo, and Qatna. The area south of Qatna was known as Amurru (the Akkadian word for Amorite). Further south, Damascus was probably in existence (Gen. 15:2), though it is unknown from contemporary records. In the Late Bronze Age (about 1550–1200 B.C.), Syria became the frontier and sometimes battlefield between the empires of the new kingdom Egypt in the south and initially Mitanni, then the Hittites to the north. Important cities in this period included Qadesh and Ugarit. The former led a number of rebellions against Egyptian authority. Excavations at the latter yielded alphabetic cuneiform tablets in Ugaritic (a language similar to Hebrew) which have shed much light on the nature of Canaanite religion. See *Archaeology; Canaan; Ugarit.*

Aramean Kingdoms In most English versions of the Old Testament (KJV, NRSV, NAS) "Syria" and "Syrian" (NIV, NRSV "Aram" or "Aramean") translate the Hebrew word *Aram,* which refers to the nations or territories of the Arameans, a group akin to Israel (Deut. 26:5). The Arameans began to settle in Syria and northern Mesopotamia around the beginning of the Iron Age (about 1200 B.C.), establishing a number of independent states. The Old Testament mentions the Aramean kingdoms of Beth-eden in north Syria, Zobah in south-central Syria, and Damascus in the south.

By the beginning of Israel's monarchy, the kingdom of Zobah held sway in Syria and was encountered by Saul (1 Sam. 14:47). David decisively defeated Aram-Zobah (2 Sam. 10:6–19) whose king, Hadadezer, had enlisted help from his Aramean subject states (10:16,19). As a result Zobah and its vassals, apparently including Damascus, became subject to David (2 Sam. 8:3–8; 10:19). Hamath, a neo-Hittite state in north Syria which had been at war with Zobah, also established friendly relations with David (2 Sam. 8:9–10). Meanwhile, a certain Rezon broke from Hadadezer of Zobah following David's victory and became the leader of a marauding band. Late in Solomon's reign, he established himself as king in Damascus (1 Kings 11:23–25), taking southern Syria out of Israelite control. Subsequent occurrences of "Aram" or "Arameans" ("Syria" or "Syrians") in the Old Testament refer to this Aramean kingdom of Damascus.

The rise of Aram-Damascus' power was facilitated by the division of Israel following the death of Solomon. When Baasha of Israel built a fort at Ramah threatening Jerusalem, Asa of Judah enticed the king of Damascus, "Ben-hadad the son of Tabrimmon, the son of Hezion," to break his league with Israel and come to Judah's aid (1 Kings 15:18–19). Ben-hadad responded by conquering a number of cities and territory in the north of Israel (v. 20). The genealogy given in this passage has been confirmed by a stele, found near Aleppo, dedicated to the god Melqart by Ben-hadad. Rezon is not mentioned, however, and it has been suggested that he is identical to Hezion. See *Damascus.*

Syrian Culture Aramean culture was essentially borrowed from their neighbors. Typical Semitic gods were worshiped, the most important of which was the storm god, Hadad, often called by the epithet Rimmon (2 Kings 5:18; Zech. 12:11),

meaning "thunder." See *Canaan; Gods, Pagan.* The most enduring contribution of the Arameans was their language which became the language of commerce and diplomacy by the Persian period. Portions of Daniel and Ezra are written in Aramaic, which is similar to Hebrew. By New Testament times, Aramaic was the language commonly spoken in Palestine and probably used by Jesus. The Aramaic script was adopted and slightly modified for writing Hebrew. See *Aramaic.*

The Intertestamental Period In 331 B.C. Syria, with the rest of the Persian Empire, fell to the advances of Alexander the Great. At his death, the area formed the nucleus of the Hellenistic Seleucid kingdom with its capital at Antioch. It is in this period that the term *Syria* became widespread. The Seleucid kingdom oppressed Judaism, causing the Maccabean Revolt in 167 B.C. which resulted in Jewish independence. Syria continued to decline until the arrival of the Romans who made it a province in 64 B.C. See *Intertestamental History; Seleucids.*

New Testament In New Testament times, Judea was made part of a procuratorship within the larger Roman province of Syria (Matt. 4:24), the latter being ruled by a governor (Luke 2:2). Syria played an important role in the early spread of Christianity. Paul was converted on the road to Damascus (Acts 9:1–9) and subsequently evangelized in the province (Acts 15:41; Gal. 1:21). Antioch, where believers were first called "Christians" (Acts 11:26), became the base for his missionary journeys (Acts 13:1–3).

Daniel C. Browning, Jr.

SYROPHENICIAN KJV spelling of Syrophoenician.

SYROPHOENICIAN (Sȳ rō phoe̊ nĭ′ cian) A combination of Syria and Phoenicia. The word reflects the joining of the two areas into one district under Roman rule. Prior to this era, Phoenicia was the coastal area of northern Palestine, and Syria was a separate country located farther inland. Jesus encountered in the Syrophoenician district a woman whose daughter was possessed by a devil (Mark 7:26). After she prayed for her daughter's healing, the Lord granted her request.

SYRTIS (Sȳr′ tĭs) Translated "quicksands" in Acts 27:17 (KJV). Probably what is now known as the Gulf of Sidra, a place of shallow water with hidden rocks, sandbanks, and quicksands off the African coast west of Cyrene.

T

The Mount of Temptation as seen from the top of Old Testament Jericho.

TAANACH (Tā´ à nă<u>ch</u>) Place name of uncertain meaning. One of the sites along the northern slope of the Mount Carmel range protecting the accesses from the Plain of Esdraelon to the region of Samaria. Irbid, Megiddo, and Taanach each protect strategic passes through the Carmel range. Taanach thus sat along one fork of the major north-south road of antiquity that went through Palestine, usually called the Via Maris. It also sat on an east-west road that led from the Jordan Valley to the Mediterranean Sea near modern Haifa.

In the Bible, Taanach is only mentioned seven times, usually in lists such as tribal allotments (Josh. 17:11; 1 Chron. 7:29), administrative districts (1 Kings 4:12), Levitical towns (Josh. 21:25), or conquered cities (Josh. 12:21; Judg. 1:27). The most famous biblical reference to Taanach is that of the battle fought at "Taanach by the waters of Megiddo" where the Hebrew forces under Deborah and Barak defeated the Canaanites under Sisera (Judg. 5:19).

Taanach was a town of about 13 acres, about the same size as the better known Megiddo. Its history runs through the Bronze Ages and into the Iron Age, from about 2700 B.C. to about 918 B.C. when it was destroyed by the Egyptian Pharaoh Shishak. A large fortress was built on the site during the early Islamic period, and that fortress may well have continued in use during the Crusades.

While Megiddo was apparently a major Canaanite administrative center, Taanach seems to have been less heavily populated and perhaps the home for the farmers of the surrounding area and their tenants. Excavations have shown a number of cultic objects and installations at Taanach, suggesting that it was a religious center as well.

Joel F. Drinkard, Jr.

TAANATH-SHILOH (Tā´ à ñath-Shī´ lōh) Place name likely meaning, "approach to Shiloh." village located about seven miles southeast of Shechem between Michmethath and Janoah (Josh. 16:6), identified with the modern khirbet Ta'nah el Foqa.

TABBAOTH (Tăb´ bā ŏth) Personal name meaning, "signet ring." Head of a family of Temple servants (Nethinim) returning from Exile (Ezra 2:43; Neh. 7:46).

TABBATH (Tăb´ băth) Place name perhaps meaning, "sunken." Site in the mountains of Gilead east of the Jordan where Gideon ended his pursuit of the Midianites (Judg. 7:22), identified with modern Ras Abu Tabat northwest of Pakoris.

TABEEL (Tă´ beēl) Aramaic personal name meaning, "God is good." *1.* Father of a man whom king Rezin of Damascus and king Pekah of Israel hoped to install as puppet king of Judah rather than Ahaz

(Isa. 7:6). Alternately, Tabeel designates a region in northern Transjordan and home of the potential puppet. Spelling has been slightly changed in Hebrew to mean, "good for nothing." *2.* Persian official in Samaria who joined in a letter protesting the reconstruction of the Jerusalem Temple (Ezra 4:7).

TABERAH (Tăb´ ĕ rah) Place name meaning, "burning." Unidentified site in the wilderness wandering. The name commemorates God's "burning anger" which broke out in fire against the ever-complaining Israelites (Num. 11:3; Deut. 9:22). The name does not appear in the itinerary of Numbers 33.

TABERING KJV term meaning, "beating" (Nah. 2:7). See *Grief and Mourning.*

TABERNACLE (Tă bȇr´ nă cle), **TENT OF MEETING** A sacred tent, a portable and provisional sanctuary, where God met His people (Ex. 33:7–10). A tent was the dwelling place of a nomadic person. When the sacred tent was meant, it was usually used with some distinguishing epithet. Two compound phrases (*'ohel moed* and *ohel haeduth* are used in the Bible to designate this tent: "the tabernacle of the congregation" (Ex. 29:42,44), literally the "tent of meeting" (NRSV, NIV, NAS, REB) and "the tabernacle of witness" (Num. 17:7) or "tent of witness." In both cases it was the place where the God of Israel revealed Himself to and dwelled among His people. The basic Hebrew term (*mishkan*) translated as "tabernacle" (Ex. 25:9) comes from a verb which means "to dwell." In this sense it is correctly translated in some instances as "dwelling," "dwelling place," "habitation," and "abode."

The Old Testament mentions three tents or tabernacles. First, after the sin of the golden calf at Mount Sinai the "provisional" tabernacle was established outside the camp and called the "tent of meeting" (Ex. 33:7). Second, the "Sinaitic" tabernacle was built in accordance with directions given to Moses by God (Ex. 25—40). Unlike the tent of meeting, it stood at the center of the camp (Num. 2). Third, the "Davidic" tabernacle was erected in Jerusalem for the reception of the ark (2 Sam. 6:17).

The original "tent of meeting" was a provisional edifice where God met with His people (Ex. 33:7–11; 34:34–35). Apparently, only Moses actually entered the tent to meet God. Joshua, Moses' "servant" (Ex. 33:11), protected and cared for the tent. After the golden calf was made, God refused any longer to acknowledge Israel as His people and to dwell in their midst. Estrangement brought distance between God and the people because of their sin. Because of this situation and to symbolize it, Moses pitched this "tent of meeting" outside the camp (Ex. 33:7). Ultimately, God

Reconstruction of the Israelite Tabernacle and its court. The court was formed by curtains attached to erect poles. Before the tent was placed the Altar of Burnt Offerings and the Laver. The Tabernacle was always erected to face the east, so this view is from the northeast.

promised again to go into the midst of Israel (Ex. 34:9).

The exact nature of this tent is uncertain. It apparently formed the headquarters of the camp until the building of the "Sinaitic" tabernacle. Joshua guarded the tent in Moses' absence (Ex. 33:11). Since the earliest Greek translation, some would equate Moses' tent in Exodus 18:7 with the tent of meeting, but Scripture does not explicitly make this connection. The people could all go to the tent of meeting to seek the Lord (Ex. 33:7) either in looking for God's answer to a judicial case, in petition, in worship, or for a prophetic word. Apparently, Moses acted as the prophet who took the people's questions to God and received an answer, since "to seek Yahweh" usually appears in prophetic contexts. Prophetic content appears with the tent also in Numbers 11:16–29. Moses installed Joshua as his successor at the tent (Deut. 31:14–15).

Moses called it the tent of meeting because it was the place of revelation. There God met His people when the pillar of cloud descended to the door of the tent (Ex. 33:9). It may have borne its appropriate name from the first, or perhaps Moses used the name from the instructions which he received regarding the permanent tabernacle (Ex. 27:21).

Apparently, the tent did not become a national sanctuary. It did not contain an ark or those items necessary for worship, nor did it possess a priesthood. This tent was cared for by Joshua (Ex. 33:11), while Aaron was responsible for the tabernacle (Lev. 10:7). The cloud descended on this tent when Moses came to inquire of God, but the cloud stayed on the permanent tabernacle and the glory of the Lord filled it so Moses could not enter it (Ex. 40:34,35,38).

The center of attention in the wilderness narratives is the tabernacle with rich decorations, curtains, bread of the presence, ark, lights, and altar. This is the portable sanctuary Israel carefully delegates to the priests and Levites for transportation (Num. 3). The camp of Israel has this tabernacle as its center (Num. 2). This, too, is the tent of meeting (Ex. 27:21), where holy God comes to sinful people. Here the sacrifices and atonement procedures of Leviticus were carried out (Book of Leviticus). "There will I meet with the children of Israel, and the tabernacle shall be sanctified by my glory. . . . And I will dwell among the children of Israel, and will be their God" (Ex. 29:43, 45).

Jimmy Albright

TABITHA (Tăb′ ĭ thá) Aramaic personal name

TABLE

1318

meaning, "gazelle," which serves as the counterpart to the Greek name Dorcas (Acts 9:36). See *Dorcas*.

TABLE Flat surface supported by legs. *1. Dinner tables* The earliest "tables" were simply skins spread on the ground (Compare the expressions "spread a table" and "a fine spread.") Representations of tables are rare in Egyptian art before the New Kingdom (1300–1100 B.C.). The earliest scriptural mention (Judg. 1:7) falls within this same time frame. Most references concern a sovereign's table (Judg. 1:7; 2 Sam. 9:7; 1 Kings 2:7; 4:27; 10:5; 18:19; but see 1 Kings 13:20). Tables generally sat on short legs, allowing one to eat sitting or reclined on a rug (Isa. 21:5). Judges 1:7, however, reflects a table high enough for kings to rummage underneath (compare Mark 7:28). In New Testament times guests ate while reclining on couches, supporting their heads with their left hands and eating from a common bowl with their right. This practice explains a woman's standing at Jesus' feet (Luke 7:38) and the beloved disciple's position at Jesus' breast (John 13:23) during meals. See *Furniture. 2. Ritual tables* A table for the bread of the presence formed part of the furnishings for both the tabernacle (Ex. 25:23–30; 26:35; Lev. 24:5–7) and Temple (1 Kings 7:48). Other tables were used in the sacrificial cult (1 Chron. 28:14–16; 2 Chron. 4:7–8; Ezek. 40:38–43). Malachi 1:7,12 describes the altar itself as a table. To share in a god's table was an act of worship. Isaiah 65:11 and 1 Corinthians 10:21 refer to idolatrous worship. The "Lord's table" (1 Cor. 10:21) refers to the observance of the Lord's Supper. *3. Money tables* The money changers' tables were likely small trays on stands (Matt. 21:12; Mark 11:15; John 2:15). *4. Tables of law* Some translations use table in the sense of a tablet (Ex. 24:12; 31:18; Deut. 9:9). See *Tablet*.

Chris Church

TABLE OF NATIONS The Genesis 10 listing of the descendants of Noah's sons to explain the origin of the nations and peoples of the known world. The account is unique for several reasons. First, a new chapter begins in biblical history at this point; humanity has a new beginning through Noah and his three sons. Second, the account highlights the ethnic makeup of the ancient world, listing some seventy different ethnic groups that formed the basis of the known world. Third, despite our lack of knowledge about many of the groups listed in the chapter, Genesis 10 underlines the fact that the Bible is based on historical events. Fourth, Genesis 10 provides the basis for understanding Abraham, introducing his world and his relationship to that world. The account of the Table of Nations, with a few variations, also appears in 1 Chronicles 1:5–23.

The Table of Nations has three basic divisions.

The people and lands of the known world fit into one of three families, the family of Shem, Ham, or Japheth. The names which appear in each of the families are names which come from several different categories: racial descent, geographical location, language differences, or political units.

Japheth's descendants (Gen. 10:2–5) inhabited the Aegean region and Anatolia or Aisa Minor. The descendants of Ham (Gen. 10:6–20) were located especially in the regions of North Africa and the coastal regions of Canaan and Syria. The descendants of Shem (Gen. 10:21–31) are especially important because Abraham comes from the line of Shem. Thus Abraham is a Shemite or Semite. Because he is also a descendant of Eber, he is called a Hebrew (Gen. 11:14–32). The descendants of Shem were located generally in north Syria, that is, the region of the upper part of the Euphrates River, and Mesopotamia, especially the eastern part. See *Assyria; Babylon; Canaan; Habiru; Israel; Mesopotamia; Semites*.

LaMoine DeVries

TABLET KJV translation for armlet (Ex. 35:22).

TABLET Flat surface used for writing. *1. Law tablets* Scripture names the stone objects bearing the Ten Commandments the tablets (or tables) of the law (Ex. 24:12), testimony (Ex. 31:18), and covenant (Deut. 9:9). These tablets were perhaps small steles such as those other nations used to publicize their laws. *2. Writing tablets* Writing was often done on clay tablets (Ezek. 4:1) or wood tablets covered with wax (Luke 1:63). The heart is often described as a tablet upon which God writes His law (Prov. 3:3; Jer. 17:1; 2 Cor. 3:3).

TABOR (Tā′ bôr) Place name of uncertain meaning, perhaps, "height." *1.* A mountain in the valley of Jezreel. About six miles east of Nazareth, it has played an important role in Israel's history since the period of the conquest. It served as a boundary point for the tribes of Naphtali, Issachar, and Zebulun (Josh. 19:12,22), where the tribes worshiped early (Deut. 33:18–19). Barak gathered an army at Tabor to defend against Sisera (Judg. 4:6). Apparently, it was the site of false worship (Hos. 5:1). Tradition holds that Tabor was the site of Jesus' transfiguration (Mark 9:2), although no evidence exists to validate the claim.

2. Levitical city (1 Chron. 6:77), apparently replacing Nahalal in the earlier list (Josh. 21:35). It may be khirbet Dabura.

3. The "Plain of Tabor" (1 Sam. 10:3) was apparently near Gibea.

TABOR, OAK OF NAS, NRSV designation of a site between Rachel's tomb (near Bethlehem) and Gibeah of Saul (1 Sam. 10:3). Other translations read plain (KJV), great tree (NIV), or terebinth (REB) of Tabor.

Mt. Tabor, located a few miles southeast of Nazareth.

TABRET KJV term for tambourine. Scripture associates the tambourine with occasions of strong emotion: farewells (Gen. 31:27); prophetic ecstasy (1 Sam. 10:5); a victory procession (1 Sam. 18:6); the procession of the ark to Jerusalem (2 Sam. 6:5). Tambourine music often accompanied festive occasions of drinking and merrymaking (Isa. 5:12; 24:8; 30:32; Jer. 31:4). Often women were the musicians (1 Sam. 18:6; 2 Sam. 6:5; Ps. 68:25). See *Music, Instruments, Dancing.*

TABRI(M)MON (Tăb rĭm′ mon) Personal name meaning, "Rimmon is good." Father of king Ben-Hadad of Damascus (1 Kings 15:18). Rimmon was the Akkadian god of thunder. See *Hadad; Hadad-Rimmon; Rimmon.*

TACHES KJV term meaning, "hooks" or "clasps " (Ex. 26:6,11,33) used to connect the individual curtains of the tabernacle into one tent.

TACHMONITE (Tăch mo nīte) KJV, TEV form of Tahchemonite.

TACKLING KJV form of tackle, that is, gear used to handle cargo and rigging to work a ship's sails (Isa. 33:23; Acts 27:19). See *Ships, Sailors, and Navigation.*

TADMOR (Tăd′ môr) Place name of uncertain meaning. A city in northern Palestine built by Solomon (2 Chron. 8:4), probably to control a caravan route. Early Hebrew scribes read Tadmor as the city instead of Tamar of the written text in 1 Kings 9:18. The city enjoyed prosperity at various periods, but especially so during Solomon's reign and again in the third century A.D., shortly before it was destroyed. The site has been identified with Palmyra, a great Arabian city, located about 120 miles northeast of Damascus.

TAHAN (Tā′ hăn) Personal name meaning, "graciousness." *1.* Third son of Ephraim (Num. 26:35). The parallel list gives Tahath as Ephraim's third son (1 Chron. 7:20). *2.* Ephraimite ancestor of Joshua (1 Chron. 7:25).

TAHANITES (Tā′ hăn ītes) Member of the Ephraimite clan descended from Tahan (Num. 26:35).

TAHAPANES (Tȧ hă′ pȧ nĕṣ) KJV alternate form of Tahpanhes (Jer. 2:16).

TAHASH (Tā′ hăsh) Personal name meaning, "porpoise" or "dugong." Third son of Nahor and Reumah (Gen. 22:24) and ancestor of an Arab tribe, perhaps associated with Tahshi north of Damascus. The tell-el-Amarna letters and the records of Thutmose III mention Tahash.

TAHATH (Tā′ hăth) Personal and place name meaning, "beneath, low" or "substitute, compensation." *1.* A Levite (1 Chron. 6:24,37). *2.* Two descendants of Ephraim (1 Chron. 7:20). See *Ta-*

han. 3. Stopping place during the wilderness wandering (Num. 33:26–27).

TAHCHEMONITE (Täh chē′ mŏn īte) Title of one of David's thirty elite warriors (2 Sam. 23:8), likely a scribal altering of the Hebrew (ha) Hachmonite (REB), which occurs in the parallel list (1 Chron. 11:11).

TAHKEMONITE (Täh kē′ mŏn ite) NIV spelling of Tahchemonite.

TAHPANHES (Täh′ pan hēş) Hebrew transliteration of an Egyptian place name meaning, "fortress of Penhase" or "house of the Nubian." City in the Nile Delta near the eastern border of Egypt (Jer. 2:16). The site, identified with Daphnai (tell Defneh), shows little evidence of heavy occupation before the Saite dynasty (663 B.C.), which garrisoned Greek mercenaries there to hedge against Assyrian advances. In 605 B.C. then crown prince Nebuchadrezzar defeated the Egyptian forces at Carchemish on the northern Euphrates and pursued them to the border of Egypt. In 601 B.C. Nebuchadrezzar and Pharoah Neco again fought to a stalemate at the Egyptian border. Jeremiah 46:14 perhaps relates to one of these incidents. Following the destruction of Jerusalem and continuing unrest in Judah, a large group of Jews took Jeremiah with them and fled to Tahpanhes (Jer. 43:7; 44:1). Jeremiah argued against the move (Jer. 42:19), warning that Nebuchadrezzar would again reach Tahpanhes (Jer. 46:14).

TAHPENES (Täh′ pė nēş) Egyptian royal consort; title for queen of Egypt in 1 Kings 11:19–20. Her sister was given in marriage to Hadad the Edomite, an enemy of David, and later of Solomon.

TAHREA (Täh rē′ à) Alternate form of Tarea (1 Chron. 9:41).

TAHTIM-HODSHI (Täh′ tĭm-Hŏd′ shĭ) Site in northern Israel which David's census takers visited (2 Sam. 24:6). The name is not attested elsewhere, prompting various emendations: Kadesh in the land of the Hittites (REB, NRSV, TEV); and the land below Hermon.

TALENT See *Weights and Measures.*

TALITHA CUMI (Tăl′ ĭ thà-cū′ mĭ) Transliteration of Aramaic phrase meaning, "damsel, arise." Jesus' words to Jarius' daughter (Mark 5:41). The girl's relatives thought she was dead by the time the Lord arrived, but He pronounced it only as sleep (5:39). The Aramaic reflects Mark's attempt to preserve the actual words of Jesus, who probably spoke Aramaic rather than Greek in which most of the New Testament is written. See *Jairus.*

TALMAI (Tăl′ mâi) Personal name meaning, "plowman," or else derived from the Hurrian word for big. *1.* One of three Anakim (giant, pre-Israelite inhabitants of Canaan) residing in Hebron (Num. 13:22). Caleb (Josh. 15:14) and Judah (Judg. 1:10) are credited with driving the Anakim from Hebron. *2.* King of Geshur, father of David's wife Maacah and grandfather of Absalom (2 Sam. 3:3; 1 Chron. 3:2). After Absalom murdered his half brother Amnon, he took refuge with his grandfather (2 Sam. 13:37).

TALMON (Tăl′ mŏn) Personal name meaning, "brightness." *1.* Levite whom David and Samuel appointed a gatekeeper (1 Chron. 9:17), ancestor of a family of Temple gatekeepers who returned from Exile (Ezra 2:42; Neh. 7:45); *2.* Leader of the postexilic gatekeepers (Neh. 11:19; 12:25).

TALMUD Jewish commentaries. Talmud means, "study" or "learning" and refers in rabbinic Judaism to the opinions and teachings that disciples learn from their predecessors particularly with regard to the development of oral legal teachings (*halakah*). The word *Talmud* is most commonly used in Judaism to refer specifically to the digest of commentary on the *Mishnah.* The Mishnah (a codification of oral legal teachings on the written law of Moses) was probably written down at Javneh in Galilee at about 220 A.D. Between A.D. 220 and 500 the rabbinic schools in Palestine and Babylonia amplified and applied the teachings of the Mishnah for their Jewish communities. Two documents came to embody a large part of this teaching: The Jerusalem Talmud and the Babylonian Talmud.

Those scholars represented in the Mishnah are referred to as the *Tannaim.* Generally, they lived from the first through the second centuries A.D. The Talmud gives the opinions of a new generation of scholars referred to as the *Amoraim* (A.D. 200–500). Various teachers became famous and attracted students from a variety of locales in the ancient world. By this means, the decisions of rabbis resident in Babylon became normative for a broad cross section of ancient Jewish life. How strongly rabbinic decisions influenced the average Jew we cannot know. Passages from the Talmud reflect the great concern of some rabbis that their advice was not being followed by the people.

The Talmud represents a continuation of the application of the oral law (*halakah*) to every sphere of Jewish life. This process probably began with the early Jewish sect known as the *Pharisees.* Many of the discussions in the Talmud, however, seem to have no direct practical application, but are theoretical in nature.

The passing on of the tradition and the remembering of the specific decisions and reasoning of the teachers by their disciples was apparently emphasized in the rabbinic schools. There is some evidence that both Mishnah and Talmud were remembered according to chants or musical melodies.

The Babylonian Talmud became the most authoritative of the two written Talmuds due both to the political fortunes of the Jewish communities in Palestine and Babylon in the first four centuries A.D. and also to its more sophisticated style. Later generations of Jewish scholars also recognized that the Babylonian Talmud was completed later and so supposed that it absorbed or superseded the Jerusalem one.

Apart from haggadic passages that are mostly Hebrew, it was written in Eastern Aramaic, the language of Babylon at the time. The Babylonian Talmud reflects a highly developed system for settling disputed questions of *halakah* (oral law). It includes commentary on all six major divisions of the Mishnah, but deletes certain subsections. For example, discussion of the segments of Mishnah that deal with the Temple service are omitted, presumably because the Jewish community in Babylon did not anticipate the rebuilding of the Temple in the near future (interestingly, the Jerusalem Talmud does discuss these sections).

The Babylonian Talmud also contains theoretical legal discussion as well as information on the daily life of Jewish people in the first six centuries, history, medicine, astronomy, commerce, agriculture, demonology, magic, botany, zoology, and other sciences. It also incorporates a large measure of *Haggadah* (illustrative stories and poetry) in addition to legal discussion.

The Jerusalem Talmud was not compiled in Jerusalem but in the centers of Tiberias, Caesarea, and Sepphoris in Palestine, since Jerusalem ceased to be a major center of Jewish learning after the destruction of the second Temple in A.D. 70. It uses Western Aramaic, the dialect of Palestine. It is succinct and concise in its presentation of legal arguments, and does not contain the considerable body of Haggadah included in the Babylonian Talmud. The Jerusalem Talmud was completed about 400 A.D. approximately a century before the Babylonian Talmud.

The importance of the Talmud to Jewish life until the modern period can hardly be overestimated. Talmud and commentary upon it become a major focus of religious action in the medieval period. The Talmud became the central document for Jewish education during the medieval period.

New Testament scholars are especially interested in the Talmud. Some of the *halakah* embodied in the Talmud is attributed to early rabbis and may reflect Jewish practice in the time of the writers of the New Testament or of Jesus. This material must be used judiciously in historical reconstruction, however, since it was compiled five centuries after the fact. See *Haggadah and Halakah; Mishnah.*

Stephenson Humphries-Brooks

TAMAH (Tā′ mah) KJV form of Temah (Neh. 7:55).

TAMAR (Tā′ mär) Personal name meaning, "date palm." *1.* Daughter-in-law of Judah, wife of his eldest son, Er (Gen. 38:6). After her wicked husband died without fathering a child, Tamar was given to Er's brother, Onan, for the purpose of bearing a child in the name of the dead man. Onan refused to impregnate Tamar, for which God killed him. She then tricked her father-in-law into fathering her child (38:18). See *Levirate Marriage.*
2. A daughter of David raped by her half brother, Amnon (2 Sam. 13:14). The act was avenged by her full brother, Absalom, when he had Amnon murdered (13:28–29). These acts were part of Nathan's property that the sword would never depart from David's house (2 Sam. 12:10).
3. Absalom named his only daughter Tamar. She is called "a beautiful woman" (2 Sam. 14:27).
4. City built by Solomon "in the wilderness" (1 Kings 9:18). The text should perhaps read Tadmor (2 Chron. 8:4), since the Hebrew lacks the qualifying phrase "of Judah" and the Masoretic vowel points correspond to Tadmor. See *Tadmor.*
5. Fortified city at the southern end of the Dead Sea, marking the ideal limit of Israel (Ezek. 47:19; 48:28). If identical with *4,* this Tamar likely served as a supply depot for Solomon's mines in the Arabah and as a frontier post to guard the border with Edom.

TAMARISK (Tă′ mà rĭsk)A shrublike tree (*Tamarix syriaca*) common to the Sinai and southern Palestine with small white or pink flowers. Many varieties of the tree exist. Abraham planted a tamarisk at Beer-sheba (Gen. 21:33), and Saul was buried beneath one at Jabesh-gilead (1 Sam. 31:13). Saul convened his court under one (1 Sam. 22:6). KJV translated, "grave" and "tree." Some believe the resin which the tamarisk produces may have been the manna eaten by the Hebrews during the wilderness wanderings.

TAMBOURINE See *Music, Instruments, Dancing; Tabret.*

TAMMUZ (Tăm′ mŭz)A Sumerian god of vegetation. The worship of Tammuz by women in Jerusalem was revealed as one of the abominations in Ezekiel (8:14–15). According to the pagan religion, Tammuz was betrayed by his lover, Ishtar, and as a result dies each autumn. The wilting of the vegetation at that time of year is seen as a sign of his death. This caused great mourning in the ancient world, and was why the women in Jerusalem wept. See *Fertility Cults.*

TANACH (Tā′ nǎ<u>ch</u>) KJV form of Taanach (Josh. 21:25).

TANHUMETH (Tăn hū' mĕth) Personal name meaning, "comforting." Father of Seraiah, a captain of forces remaining with Gedaliah in Judah following the deportation of Babylon (2 Kings 25:23; Jer. 40:8). A Lachish stamp witnesses to the name as does an Arad inscription.

TAPHATH (Tā' phăth) Personal name meaning, "droplet." Daughter of Solomon and wife of Ben-abinadab, a Solomonic official (1 Kings 4:11).

TAPPUAH (Tăp pūáh) Personal name meaning, "apple" or "quince." *1.* A Calebite, likely a resident of a town near Hebron (1 Chron. 2:43). *2.* City in the Shephelah district of Judah (Josh. 15:34), possibly Beit Nettif about twelve miles west of Bethlehem. *3.* City of the north border of Ephraim (Josh. 16:8) whose environs were allotted to Manasseh (17:7–8), likely the Tappuah of Joshua 12:17 and 2 Kings 15:16. The site is perhaps Sheikh Abu Zarod about eight miles southwest of Shechem. Some scholars read, "Tappuah" for "Tiphsah" in 2 Kings 15:16 (REB). See *Beth-Tappuah; En-Tappuah.*

TAR See *Bitumen.*

TARAH (Tā' rah) KJV form of Terah, the wilderness campsite (Num. 33:27–28).

TARALAH (Tā' rǎ lah) Place name meaning, "strength." Unidentified site in Benjamin, likely northwest of Jerusalem (Josh. 18:27).

TAREA (Tā' rė à) Personal name of unknown derivation. Descendant of Saul (1 Chron. 8:35; Tahrea 1 Chron. 9:41).

TARES KJV term for grassy weeds resembling wheat, generally identified as darnel (genus *Lolium*). See Matthew 13:25–30,36–40.

TARGUM (Tăr' gŭm) Early translations of the Bible into Aramaic, the native language of Palestine and Babylon in the first century A.D. *Targum,* in its verbal Hebrew form, means "to explain, to translate." The most important of these translations still in existence is Targum Onkelos which was probably read weekly in synagogue services from a relatively early date. The targums are not simply translations but seem to include a large amount of biblical commentary that perhaps reflects sermons in Jewish Palestinian synagogues. Therefore, the material is of interest to New Testament scholars who attempt to understand the Judaism of which Jesus was a part. See *Aramaic.*
Stephenson Humphries-Brooks

TARPELITES (Tăr' pĕ lītes) KJV transliteration of an Aramaic title in Ezra 4:9. Most modern translations render the term, "officials" (NIV, "men of Tripolis").

TARSHISH (Tär'shĭsh) Personal and place name of uncertain derivation, either meaning, "yellow jasper," as in the Hebrew of Exodus 28:20; Ezekiel 28:13, or else derived from an Akkadian term meaning, "smelting plant." *1.* Son of Javan (Gen. 10:4; 1 Chron. 1:7) and ancestor of an Aegean people. *2.* Benjaminite warrior (1 Chron. 7:10). *3.* One of seven leading officials of King Ahasuerus of Persia (Esth. 1:14). This name possibly means "greedy one" in Old Persian. *4.* Geographic designation, most likely of Tartessus at the southern tip of Spain but possibly of Tarsus in Cilicia. Jonah sailed for Tarshish, the far limit of the western world from the Mediterranean port of Joppa in his futile attempt to escape God's call (Jonah 1:3). Tarshish traded in precious metals with Tyre, another Mediterranean port (Isa. 23:1; Jer. 10:9; Ezek. 27:12). *5.* References to Tarshish in 1 Kings and 2 Chronicles suggest a non-geographic meaning. Solomon's (1 Kings 10:22; 2 Chron. 9:21) and Jehoshaphat's (1 Kings 22:48; 2 Chron. 20:36) fleets were based at Ezion-Geber on the Red Sea. Solomon's cargo suggests east African trading partners. Thus "ships of Tarshish" may designate seagoing vessels like those of Tarshish or else ships bearing metal cargo like those of Tarshish (compare Isa. 2:16 where ships of Tarshish parallels beautiful crafts).

TARSUS (Tär' sŭs) Birthplace of Paul (Acts 9:11) and capital of Roman province of Cilicia. See *Asia Minor; Paul.*

The Cleopatra Gate at Tarsus commemorating Mark Antony's meeting of Cleopatra at this ancient city.

TARTAK (Tär' tăk) Deity worshiped by the Arvvites whom the Assyrians settled in Samaria after 722 B.C. (2 Kings 17:31). The name is otherwise unattested and is likely a deliberate corruption of Atargatis, the Syrian high goddess and wife of Hadad.

TARTAN (Tär' tăn) Title of the highest ranking Assyrian officer under the king; commander in chief; supreme commander (2 Kings 18:17; Isa. 20:1). First mention of the office occurred under Adadnirari II (911–891 B.C.).

TASKMASTER Oppressive overseers of forced labor gangs employed by monarchies for large public works projects (Egyptian: Ex. 1:11; 3:7; 5:6–14; Israelite: 2 Sam. 20:24; 1 Kings 4:6; 5:16; 12:18; 2 Chron. 10:18).

TASSEL See *Fringe.*

TATNAI (Tăt′ nâi) KJV form of Tattenai.

TATTENAI (Tăt′ tĕ nâi) Contemporary of Zerubbabel, governor of the Persian province "across the (Euphrates) River," which included Palestine (Ezra 5:3,6; 6:6,13).

TAU Twenty-second and final letter of the Hebrew alphabet which the KJV used as a heading for Psalm 119:169–176, each verse of which begins with the letter.

TAX COLLECTOR See *Publican.*

TAXES Regular payments to rulers. Early Israel only paid taxes to support the tabernacle and the priests.

Terms in the Old Testament that refer to taxes were: "assessment," "forced labor," "tribute," and "toll." Before Israel established a king, worship taxes were the only ones levied from within the nation. Tribute has to be paid, of course, to invaders such as the Philistines. During David's reign, an army was maintained by tribute paid by conquered tribes. Taxes increased under Solomon's rule. Tradesmen and merchants paid duties; subject peoples paid tribute; farmers paid taxes in kind of oil and wine; and many Israelites did forced labor on the Temple. The burden of taxation contributed to the rebellion following Solomon's death (1 Kings 12). Soon, Israel became a vassal state, paying tribute—a compulsory tax—to Assyria, and, eventually, to Rome.

In the New Testament era, Herod the Great levied a tax on the produce of the field and a tax on items bought and sold. Other duties owed to foreign powers were: a land tax, a poll tax, a kind of progressive income tax (about which the Pharisees tested Jesus, Matt. 22:17), and a tax on personal property. In Jerusalem a house tax was levied. These taxes were paid directly to Roman officials.

Export and import customs paid at seaports and city gates were farmed out to private contractors who paid a sum in advance for the right to collect taxes in a certain area. Such were Zacchaeus (Luke 19) and Matthew (Matt. 9). Rome apparently placed little restriction on how much profit the collector could take. An enrollment for the purposes of taxation under the Roman emperor brought Joseph and Mary to Bethlehem, where Jesus was born (Luke 2:1–7). In addition to the taxes owed occupying powers, the Jewish people also had to pay religious duties: A *didrachma* (half shekel) was owed to the Temple by all Jewish males throughout the world (Matt. 17:24). The second tax was a tithe, 10 percent of everything the soil produced, collected by the Levites.

The Israelites resented most deeply the duties paid to the occupying powers. Many zealous Jews considered it treason to God to pay taxes to Rome. When questioned about paying the poll tax, Jesus surprised His questioners by saying that the law should be obeyed (Mark 12:13). *Gary K. Halbrook*

TEACHING See *Education; Instruction.*

TEARS See *Mourn.*

TEBAH (Tē′ bah) Personal name meaning, "slaughter." Son of Nahor and ancestor of an Aramaean tribe (Gen. 22:24). Tebah is perhaps associated with tubihi, a site somewhere between Damascus and Kadesh.

TEBALIAH (Tĕb å lī′ ah) Personal name meaning, "Yahweh has dipped, that is, purified," or "loved by Yahweh," or "good for Yahweh." Postexilic Levitic gatekeeper (1 Chron. 26:11).

TEBETH (Tē′ bĕth) Tenth month (December–January) of the Hebrew calendar (Esth. 2:16). The name derives from an Akkadian term meaning, "sinking," and refers to the rainy month. See *Calendars.*

TEETH Hard bony structures in the jaws of persons and animals used to cut and grind food. In Old Testament thinking, the loss of a tooth was a serious matter subject to the law of retaliation (Ex. 21:23–25; Lev. 24:19–20; Deut. 19:21; compare Matt. 5:38–42). Teeth set on edge, that is made dull or insensitive, illustrates the concept of corporate or inherited guilt challenged by the prophets (Jer. 31:29–30; Ezek. 18:2–3). Gnashing of teeth displays the raging despair of those excluded from Christ's kingdom (Matt. 8:12; 13:42).

TEHAPHNEHES (tĕ hăph′ nĕhĕş) Alternate form of Tahpanhes (Ezek. 30:18).

TEHINNAH (Tĕ hĭn′ nah) Personal name meaning, "supplication" or "graciousness." Descendant of Judah responsible for founding Ir-nahash (1 Chron. 4:12).

TEIL TREE KJV term meaning, "lime" or "linden tree," used to translate a Hebrew term generally rendered oak or terebinth (Isa. 6:13). See *Plants in the Bible; Terebinth.*

TEKEL (tē′ kĕl) See *Mene, Mene, Tekel, Upharsin.*

T

Excavations at the site of ancient Tekoa, hometown of Amos the prophet.

TEKOA (Tė kō′ à) Place name meaning, "place of setting up a tent." A city in the highlands of Judah six miles south of Bethlehem and ten miles south of Jerusalem; home of the prophet Amos. God called Amos from among the shepherds of Tekoa to preach to the Northern Kingdom of Israel (Amos 1:1). The priest tried to send him back to Tekoa (7:12).

One of David's chief fighting men was Ira, the son of Ikkesh from Tekoa (2 Sam. 23:26). Sometime between 922 B.C. and 915 B.C., Rehoboam cited Tekoa as one of the cities whose fortifications were to be strengthened (2 Chron. 11:5–6). Approximately fifty years later, Jehoshaphat defeated a force of Ammonite, Meunite, and Moabite invaders in the wilderness between Tekoa and En-gedi (2 Chron. 20:20–22). After the return from Exile, Tekoa remained occupied (Neh. 3:5). See *Amos.* *Kenneth Craig*

TEKOITE (Tė ko′ īte) Resident of Tekoa (2 Sam. 23:26; Neh. 3:5).

TEL-ABIB (Tĕl-Ā′ bĭb) Place name meaning, "mound of the flood" or "mound of grain." Tel-Abib on the Chebar Canal near Nippur in Babylon was home to Ezekiel and other Exiles (Ezek. 3:15). The Babylonians may have thought it was the ruined site of the original flood.

TEL-ASSAR (Tĕl-Ăs′ sår) Place name meaning, "mound of Asshur." City in northern Mesopotamia which the Assyrians conquered (2 Kings 19:12 KJV, Thelasar; Isa. 37:12). Its location is not known.

TEL-AVIV (Tĕl-Ȧ vîv′) see *Tel-Abib.*

TEL-HARESHA (Tĕl-hȧ rē′ shȧ) KJV, NIV alternate form ot Tel-harsha (Neh. 7:61).

TEL-HARSA (Tĕl-här′ sȧ) KJV form of Tel-harsha (Ezra 2:59).

TEL-HARSHA (Tĕl-här′ shȧ) Place name meaning, "mound of the forest" or "mound of magic."

Home of Babylonian Jews unable to demonstrate their lineage (Ezra 2:59; Neh. 7:61). Tel-harsha was likely located in the flatlands near the Persian Gulf.

TEL-MELAH (Tĕl-Mē′ lah) Place name meaning, "mound of salt." Babylonian home of a group of Jews unable to demonstrate their lineage (Ezra 2:59; Neh. 7:61). Tel-Melah is perhaps Thelma of Ptolemy in the low salt tracts near the Persian Gulf.

TELAH (Tē′ lah) Personal name meaning, "breach" or "fracture." An ancestor of Joshua (1 Chron. 7:25).

TELAIM (Tė lā′ ĭm) Place name meaning, "young speckled lambs." City in southern Judah where Saul gathered forces to battle the Amalekites (1 Sam. 15:4). Suggested sites include khirbet Umm es-Salafeh southwest of Kurnub and khirbet Abu Tulul twelve miles southeast of Beer-Sheba. The earliest Greek translation of 1 Samuel 27:8 reads "from Telem" rather than "from old." See *Telem.*

TELEM (Tē′ lĕm) Personal and place name meaning, "brightness" or "lamb." *1.* Levite with a foreign wife (Ezra 10:24). *2.* City in southern Judah (Josh. 15:24), a variant form of Telaim.

TELL Semitic term meaning, "mound," applied to areas built up by successive settlement at a single site. Tell or tel is a common element in Near Eastern place names. See *Archaeology.*

TELL EL-AMARNA See *Amarna, Tell el.*

TEMA (Tē′ mȧ) Personal and place name meaning, "south country." Tema, a son of Ishmael (Gen. 25:15; 1 Chron. 1:30), is associated with Tema (modern Teima), a strategic oasis located on the Arabian penisula 250 miles southeast of Aqaba and 200 miles north-northeast of Medina. Job 6:19 alludes to Tema's importance as a caravan stop. Isaiah 21:14 likely refers to the campaign of the Assyrian king Tiglath-Pileser III (738 B.C.) when Tema escaped destruction by paying tribute. Jeremiah 25:23 perhaps refers to a campaign of Nebuchadnezzar. Having conquered and rebuilt Tema, Nabonidus, the last king of Babylon, remained there ten years, leaving his son Belshazzar as vice-regent in Babylon (Dan. 5).

TEMAH (Tē′ mah) A family of Temple servants (Nethinim) returning from Exile (Ezra 2:53; Neh. 7:55).

TEMAN (Tē′ măn) Personal and place name meaning, "right side," that is, "southern." *1.* Edomite clan descended from Esau (Gen. 36:11,

15; 1 Chron. 1:36). *2.* City of area associated with this clan (Jer. 49:7,20; Ezek. 25:13; Amos 1:12; Obad. 1:9; Hab. 3:3). Teman has often been identified with Tawilan, fifty miles south of the Dead Sea just east of Petra, though archaeological evidence does not confirm the site as the principal city of southern Edom. Others understand Teman to designate southern Edom in general. To others the linkage with Dedan (Jer. 49:7; Ezek. 25:13) suggests Tema on the Arabian peninsula. See *Tema.*

TEMANI (Tē′ măn î) KJV transliteration for Temanites (Gen. 36:34).

TEMANITES (Tē′ măn ītes) Descendants of Teman or residents of Teman, the southern area of Edom. The land of the Temanites designates (southern) Edom (Gen. 36:34; 1 Chron. 1:45). The Temanites were renowned for their wisdom (Job 2:11; compare Jer. 49:7).

TEMENI (Tē′ mĕ nĭ) Personal name perhaps meaning, "on the right hand," that is, "to the south." Descendant of Judah (1 Chron. 4:6).

TEMPERANCE See *Self-control.*

TEMPLE OF JERUSALEM A place of worship, especially the Temple of Solomon built in Jerusalem for national worship of Yahweh. Sacred or holy space is the meaning of our word *temple,* very like the two Greek words, *hieron* (temple area) and *naos* (sanctuary itself) which are translated "temple" in the New Testament. In the Old Testament, the language is usually *beth Yahweh* or *beth Elohim,* "house of the Yahweh" or "house of God" because He is said to have dwelt there. The other Hebrew expression for temple is *hekal,* "palace, great house" deriving from the Sumerian word for "great house," whether meant for God or the earthly king. So David, when he had built for himself a cedar palace, thought it only proper he should build one for Yahweh, too (2 Sam. 7:1–2). Nathan at first approved his plan, but the Lord Himself said He had been used to living in a tent since the Exodus from Egypt. He would allow David's son to build Him a house (Temple), but He would build for David a house (dynasty, 2 Sam. 7:3–16). This covenant promise became exceedingly significant to the messianic hope fulfilled in the coming of the ideal king of the line of David. See *Tabernacle, Tent of Meeting.*
Chronicles makes it clear that David planned the Temple and accumulated great wealth and gifts for it, though Solomon was the one who actually built it. Solomon's Temple may not have actually been the first temple which housed the ark of the covenant, since there was a house of Yahweh, also called a temple, at Shiloh (1 Sam. 1:7,9,24; 3:3) but in 1 Samuel 2:22 (NIV) it is

Modern orthodox Jews praying at the Wailing Wall of the Temple Mount in Jerusalem.

called "tent of meeting," whether the wilderness tabernacle or not. Jeremiah in his great Temple sermon warned all who came into the Lord's house in Jerusalem that if they trusted primarily in the Temple, instead of the Lord, He could destroy Solomon's Temple just as He had the previous one at Shiloh (Jer. 7:1–15; 26:1–6).
Israel knew other worship places with history far older than the Jerusalem Temple. Former patriarchal holy places near Shechem or Bethel (Gen. 12:6–8; 28:10–22; compare Deut. 11:29–30; 27:1–26; Josh. 8:30–35; 24:1–28; Judg. 20:26–27), these are not called temples in Scripture though local inhabitants may have called them

The southeast quadrant of the upper court of the Temple Mount in Jerusalem.

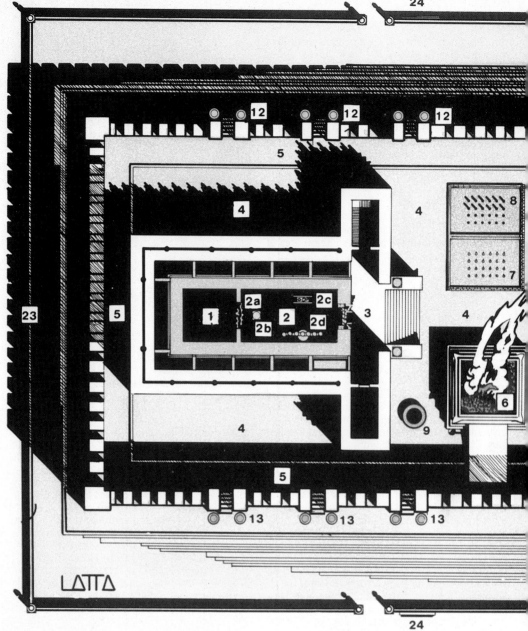

Herod's Temple (20 B.C.–A.D. 70) was begun in the eighteenth year of King Herod the Great's reign (37–4 B.C.). According to Josephus, first-century Jewish historian, Herod's Temple was constructed after removing the old foundations. The old edifice, Zerubbabel's Temple, was a modest restoration of the Temple of Solomon destroyed by the Babylonian conquest. The central building was completed in just two years—without any interruption of the Temple services. The surrounding buildings and spacious courts, considerably enlarged, were not completed until A.D. 64. The Temple was destroyed by the Romans under the command of Titus during the second Jewish revolt in A.D. 70.

1. Holy of Holies (where the ark of the covenant and the giant cherubim were once enshrined)
2. Holy Place
2a. Veil (actually two giant tapestries hung before the entrance of the holy of holies to allow the high priest entry between them without exposing the sacred shrine. It was this veil that was "wrent" upon the death of Jesus.)
2b. Altar of Incense
2c. Table of Shew Bread
2d. Seven-branched Lampstand (Great Menorah)

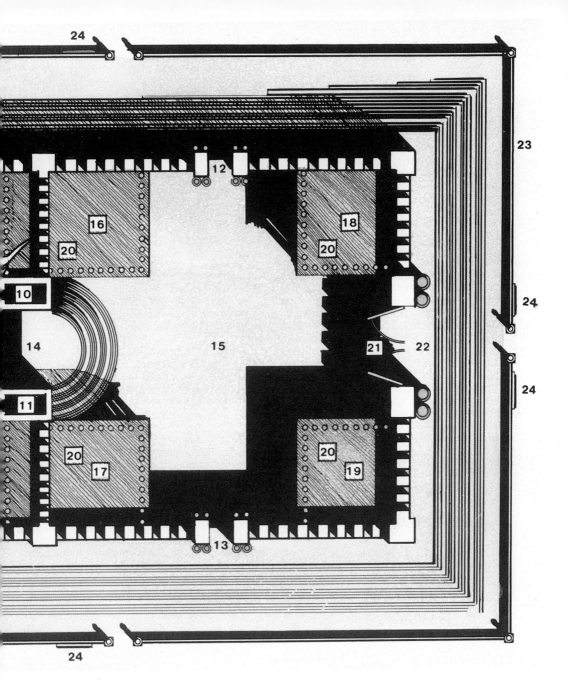

3. Temple Porch
4. Court of Priests
5. Court of Israel (Men)
6. Altar of Burnt Offerings
7. Animal Tethering Area
8. Slaughtering and Skinning Area
9. Laver
10. Chamber of Phineas (storage of vestments)
11. Chamber of the Bread Maker
12. North Gates of the Inner Courts
13. South Gates of the Inner Courts
14. East (Nicanor) Gate

15. Court of Women
16. Court of Nazirites
17. Court of Woodshed
18. Lepers' Chamber
19. Shemanyah (possibly meaning "oil of Yah")
20. Women's Balconies (for viewing Temple activities)
21. Gate Beautiful (?)
22. Terrace
23. Soreg (three-cubit high partition)
24. Warning Inscriptions to Gentiles

temples. It cannot be determined what kind of sanctuaries were at Ophrah, Gilgal, Nob, Mizpah, Ramah, or other "high places" where Yahweh was worshiped, but "the Temple" is the one at Jerusalem from Solomon's time.

Solomon's Temple There were three historical Temples in succession, those of Solomon, Zerubbabel, and Herod in the preexilic, postexilic, and New Testament periods. Herod's Temple was really a massive rebuilding of the Zerubbabel Temple, so both are called the "second Temple" by Judaism. All three were located on a prominent hill north of David's capital city, which he conquered from the Jebusites (2 Sam. 5:6–7). David had acquired the Temple hill from Araunah the Jebusite at the advice of the prophet Gad to stay a pestilence from the Lord by building an altar and offering sacrifices on the threshing floor (2 Sam. 24:18–25). Chronicles identifies this hill with Mount Moriah, where Abraham had been willing to offer Isaac (2 Chron. 3:1; Gen. 22:1–14). So the Temple mount today in Jerusalem is called Mount Moriah, and the threshing floor of Araunah is undoubtedly the large rock enshrined within the Dome of the Rock, center of the Muslim enclosure called Haram es-Sharif (the third holiest place in Islam, after Mecca and Medina). This enclosure is basically what is left of Herod's enlarged Temple platform, the masonry of which may best be seen in its Western Wall, the holiest

The Moslem Dome of the Rock on the Temple Mount in Jerusalem with the Wailing Wall in the foreground.

place within Judaism since the Roman destruction of Herod's Temple.

No stone is left that archaeologists can confidently say belonged to the Solomonic Temple. We do have the detailed literary account of its building preserved in Kings (1 Kings 5:1—9:10) and Chronicles (2 Chron. 2—7). Ezekiel's vision of the new Jerusalem Temple after the Exile (Ezek. 40—43) is idealistic and was perhaps never realized in Zerubbabel's rebuilding of the Temple, but many of its details would have reflected Solomon's Temple in which Ezekiel probably ministered as a priest before being deported to Babylon in 597 B.C. The treaty with Hiram, the king of Tyre, and the employment of the metalworker Hiram (or Huram-abi, a different person from the king) whom he provided show that considerable Phoenician influence, expertise, craftsmanship, and artistic design went into the building of the Temple.

The primary meaning of the Temple was the same as that of the ark it was constructed to enshrine: a symbol of God's presence in the midst of His people (Ex. 25:21–22). Because it was God's house, the worshipers could not enter the holy place, reserved only for priests and other worship leaders, much less the holiest place (holy of holies) to be entered by the high priest only once a year (Lev. 16). The worshipers could gather for prayer and sacrifice in the Temple courtyard(s) where they could sing psalms as they saw their offerings presented to Yahweh on His great altar. The spirit of Israel's prayer and praise is to be found in the Psalms and in the worship experiences such as that of Isaiah when he surrendered to his prophetic call experience in the forecourt of the Temple (Isa. 6:1–8).

The account of Isaiah's experience makes it clear that the earthly Temple was viewed as a microcosm of the heavenly Temple where the King of the universe really dwelt. The quaking and smoke of the Lord's presence at Sinai were now manifested in Zion (Isa. 6:4). Israel understood that it was only by God's grace that He consented to dwell with His people; and so Deu-

Notes containing prayer requests are still placed between the massive stones of the Wailing Wall.

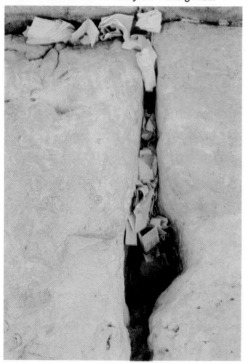

T

teronomy understood the central sanctuary as the place where Yahweh caused His name to dwell (Deut. 12:5; compare 1 Kings 8:13), and priestly thinkers viewed it as filled with His glory (compares the tabernacle, Ex. 40:34). Obviously, no one can house God: "But will God indeed dwell on the earth? Even heaven and the highest heaven cannot contain you; much less this house that I have built!" (1 Kings 8:27 NRSV).

Solomon's Temple was shaped as a "long house" of three successive rooms from east to west, a vestibule of only 15-feet depth, a nave (the holy place) of 60 feet and an inner sanctuary (the most holy place) of 30 feet (1 Kings 6:2–3; 16—17). It was approximately 30-feet wide and 45-feet high by its interior measurements for the "house" proper, not counting the porch, which was sort of an open entryway. This is similar to, though not precisely the same as, the shape of several Syrian and Canaanite temples excavated in the past few decades (at Hazor, Lachish, tell

Reconstruction of Herod's Temple (20 B.C.–A.D. 70) at Jerusalem as viewed from the southeast. The drawing reflects archaeological discoveries made since excavations began in 1967 along the south end of the Temple Mount platform. The staircase (left), leads up from the lower city to a gateway (not shown) at Robinson's Arch. The monumental Herodian staircase also leads up from the lower city to the Double and Triple (Huldah) Gates. View provides an overview of the outer and inner courts of the Temple precinct atop the Temple Mount.

Tainat). There is even one Israelite "temple" at the southeast border of Judah in the iron age fortress of Arad which some have compared with Solomon's Temple. None was so symmetrical or ornately decorated, nor even as large as the Jerusalem Temple, even though Solomon's palace complex of which the Temple was only a part (1 Kings 7:1–12) was much larger and took longer to build (tell Tainat, in northern Syria, is the closest analogy). Around the outside of the house proper was constructed three stories of side chambers for Temple storehouses, above which were recessed windows in the walls of the holy place (1 Kings 6:4–6,8–10).

The inside of the house proper was paneled with cedar, floored with cypress, and inlaid with gold throughout. It was decorated with well-known Phoenician artistic ornamentation, floral designs with cherubim, flowers, and palm trees. The most holy place, a windowless cube of about 30 feet, housed the ark of the covenant and was dominated by two guardian cherubim 15-feet tall with outstretched wings spanning fifteen feet to touch in the middle and at each side wall (1 Kings 6:15–28). One of the interesting results of archaeological research is the recovery of the form of these ancient cherubim. They are Egyptian-type sphinxes (human-headed winged lions) such as are pictured as the arms of a throne chair of a Canaanite king on one of the Megiddo ivories. The ark, the mercy-seat lid of which had its own guardian cherubim (Ex. 25:18–20), was Yahweh's "footstool." Beneath these awesome cheru-

T

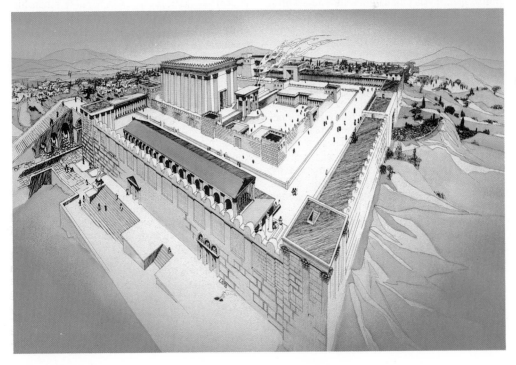

bim, God was invisibly enthroned.

The double doors of the inner sanctuary and the nave were similarly carved and inlaid of finest wood and gold (1 Kings 6:31–35). The arrangement prescribed for the wall of the inner court, "three courses of hewn stone and one course of cedar beams" was followed in Solomonic buildings excavated at Megiddo (1 Kings 6:36; 7:12). This arrangement is also known from the tell Tainat temple. This exquisite sanctuary took seven years to build (about 960 B.C.; 1 Kings 6:37–38). The marvelous furnishings of the holy place and the courtyard require another chapter to describe (1 Kings 7:9–51).

The most mysterious creations were two huge free-standing bronze pillars about thirty-five-feet tall, including their beautifully ornamented capitals of lily-work netting and rows of pomegranates (1 Kings 7:15–20). They were nearly six feet in diameter, hollow, with a thickness of bronze about three inches. The pillars were named Jachin ("He shall establish") and Boaz ("In the strength of"), perhaps to signify the visible symbolism of the Temple as a testimony to the stability of the Davidic dynasty to which it was intimately related.

The reader at this point expects an account of the bronze altar, included in Chronicles (2 Chron. 4:1), but only presumed in Kings (1 Kings 8:22,54,64; 9:25). This altar is large, thirty-feet square and fifteen-feet tall, presumably with steps.

The molten sea, which may have had some kind of cosmic symbolism, stood in the south-central quadrant of the inner courtyard opposite the bronze altar. It was round with a cup-shaped brim, fifteen feet in diameter, seven-and-a-half-feet tall, with a circumference of forty-five feet. It was cast of heavy bronze, ornately decorated, and resting on the back of twelve bronze oxen in four sets of three facing each point of the compass. Since it held about 10,000 gallons of water, it must have been for supplying water to the lavers by some sort of syphon mechanism.

The third great engineering feat was the crafting of ten ornate, rolling stands for ten lavers, five on either side of the courtyard. These were six-feet square and four-and-a-half-feet tall, each containing some 200 gallons of water, quite heavy objects to be rolled about on chariot wheels. Chronicles says they were used to wash the utensils for sacrificial worship (2 Chron. 4:6).

At the Feast of Tabernacles, Solomon conducted an elaborate dedication festival for the Temple (1 Kings 8:1—9:9). The story begins with a procession of the ark containing the two tables of the decalogue, God's glory in the shining cloud of His presence filled the sanctuary (1 Kings 8:1–11). Then the king blessed the assembly, praised God for His covenant mercies in fulfilling Nathan's promise to David, and gave a long, fervent prayer on behalf of seven different situations in which the prayers of his people should arise to the heav-

enly throne of God from His earthly temple, closing with a benediction. Solomon provided myriads of sacrifices for the seven days of the great dedication festival. God had consecrated this house of prayer, but He required covenant obedience of Solomon and each of his successors, lest He have to destroy this magnificent sanctuary because of the apostasy of His people (1 Kings 9:1–9). The consistent emphasis of Solomon's prayer and God's answer is the awareness of sin and the necessity for wholehearted repentance to keep the Temple ceremonial a meaningful symbol of worship and devotion (2 Chron. 7:13–14). The great prophets preached that, in their Temple worship, Israel was not able to avoid syncretism with pagan religious impulses or the hypocritical irrelevance of meaningless overemphasis upon ritual without righteous obedience to their sovereign Overlord (Isa. 1:10–17; Mic. 6:6–8; Jer. 7:1–26).

The history of Solomon's Temple has many ups and downs through its almost four hundred years of existence. Its treasures of gold were often plundered by foreign invaders like Shishak of Egypt (1 Kings 14:25–26). At the division of the kingdoms, Jeroboam set up rival sanctuaries at Bethel and Dan which drew worshipers away from Jerusalem for two hundred years. King Asa plundered his own Temple treasuries to buy a military ally, Ben-Hadad of Syria against Baasha, king of North Israel (1 Kings 15:18–19), though he had previously repaired the Temple altar and carried out limited worship reforms (2 Chron. 15:8–18). Temple repairs were carried out by Jehoash (Joash) of Judah after the murder of wicked Queen Athaliah, but even he had to strip the Temple treasuries to buy off Hazael, king of Syria (2 Kings 12). Jehoash (Joash), king of Israel, when foolishly challenged to battle by Amaziah, king of Judah, not only defeated him, but came to Jerusalem and plundered the Temple (1 Kings 14:12–14). King Ahaz plundered his own Temple for tribute to Assyria during the Syro-Ephraimitic war of 735 B.C., even stripping some of the bronze furnishings in the courtyard (2 Kings 16:8–9,17). Good King Hezekiah raised a hugh tribute for Sennacherib, king of Assyria, in his 701 B.C. invasion, even stripping gold off the Temple doors (2 Kings 18:13–16). During the long and disastrous reign of King Manasseh many abominable idols and pagan cult objects were placed in the Temple which good King Josiah had to remove during his reform (2 Kings 23:4–6,11–12). Both Hezekiah and Josiah were able to centralize worship in the Jerusalem Temple during their reforms and even recover some worshipers from the north for the Jerusalem sanctuary, but Josiah's successor, Jehoiakim, reversed all of Josiah's reforms and filled up the Temple with pagan abominations (Ezek. 8). Despite the warnings of Jeremiah and Ezekiel, the people refused to repent of their political and religious folly, and their Temple and holy city were first plundered by Nebuchadnezzer in 597 B.C., then burned by Nebuzaradan, his general, in 587/586 B.C.

For both groups of Judah, those in Babylon, and those still in Jerusalem, the loss of the Temple and city were a grievous blow (Ps. 137; Lam. 1—5). But Jeremiah and Ezekiel had prepared a remnant in their prophecies of hope beyond the catastrophe for a return and rebuilding.

Zerubbabel's Temple The decree of Cyrus in 538 B.C. permitted the Jews to return from the Babylonian Exile with the Temple vessels which had been taken. It charged them to rebuild the Temple of Jerusalem with Persian financial aid and free-will offerings from Jews who remained in Babylon (Ezra 1:1–4). Sheshbazzar, the governor, laid the foundation. The project was halted when the people of the land discouraged the builders (Ezra 1:8,11; 4:1–5). Then in the second year of Darius, 520 B.C., the work was renewed by the new governor Zerubbabel and Jeshua the high priest at the urging of the prophets Haggai and Zechariah (Ezra 5:1–2).

When local Persian officials tried to stop the rebuilding, Darius found a record of Cyrus' decree which included the overall dimensions (Ezra 6:1–6). The size seems to have been approximately that of Solomon's Temple. Ezekiel's temple vision had considerable influence on the new Temple (Ezek. 40—42), so that Zerubbabel's Temple perhaps was mounted on a platform and measured about 100 feet by 100 feet with the interior dimensions being virtually the same as those of Solomon's Temple. It was probably not as ornately decorated (Ezra 3:12–13; Hag. 2:3).

The differences between the two sanctuaries have to do with furniture and courtyard arrangements or gates. As Jeremiah had foreseen, the ark of the covenant was never replaced (Jer. 3:16). Jospehus said the holy of holies was empty. It was now separated from the holy place by a veil instead of a door. There was only one seven-branched lampstand, as had been true of the tabernacle, probably the one pictured by Titus in his triumphal arch at Rome as having been carried off when Herod's Temple was plundered. The importance of the new Temple was that it became a symbol of the Lord's holiness and the religious center of life for the new community. It was completed in 515 B.C. and dedicated with great joy (Ezra 6:14–16). Priesthood had replaced kingship as the authority of the postexilic community.

The Maccabean revolt changed this, and Judas Maccabeus rededicated the Temple in 167 B.C. after Antiochus had profaned it in December, 164 B.C. This joyous event is still remembered in the Jewish celebration of Hannukah. Judas' successors appointed themselves as high priests, and the Temple became more a political institution. Pompey captured the Temple in 63 B.C. but did not plunder it. See *Intertestamental History.*

Herod's Temple Herod the Great came to power in 37 B.C. and determined that he would please his Jewish subjects and show off his style of kingship to the Romans by making the Jerusalem Temple bigger and better than it had ever been. His most notable contribution was the magnificent stonework of the Temple platform which was greatly enlarged. The descriptions in Josephus and the Mishnah have been fleshed out by recent archaeological discoveries.

Herod surrounded the whole enclosure with magnificent porches, particularly the royal stoa along the southern wall. Through the Huldah gates, double and triple arches of which can still be seen, worshipers went up through enclosed passageways into the court of the Gentiles. Greek inscriptions separating this court from the court of the women and the holier inner courts of Israel (men) and the priests have been found. The steps south of the Temple, where Jesus may have taught on several occasions, have been excavated and reconstructed. An inscription: "To the place of trumpeting" was found below the southwest corner where there was a monumental staircase ascending into the Temple from the main street below. Perhaps this was the "Temple pinnacle" from which Satan tempted Jesus to throw Himself.

The Jerusalem Temple is the focus of many New Testament events. The birth of John the Baptist was announced there (Luke 1:11–20). The offering by Joseph and Mary at the circumcision of baby Jesus was brought there. Simeon and Anna greeted Jesus there (2:22–38). Jesus came there as a boy of twelve (2:42–51) and later taught there during His ministry (John 7:14). His cleansing of the Temple was instrumental in precipitating His death. He knew no earthly temple was necessary to the worship of God (4:21–24). He predicted the Temple's destruction by the Romans, and His warnings to His followers to flee when this happened actually saved many Christians' lives (Mark 13:2,14–23). Early Christians continued to worship there, and Paul was arrested there (Acts 3; 21:27–33).

After the Jewish revolt in 66 A.D., Vespasian and then his son Titus crushed all resistance. The Temple was destroyed in 70 A.D. Stephen's preaching tended to liberate Christian thinking from the necessity of a temple (Acts 7:46–50), and Paul thought of the church and Christians as the new temple (1 Cor. 3:16–17; 6:19–20). For John, the ideal which the temple represented will ultimately be realized in a "new Jerusalem."

See *Ark of the Covenant; Herods; Holy of Holies; Moriah; Shiloh; Solomon; Tabernacle, Tent of Meeting; Zerubbabel. M. Pierce Matheney*

TEMPLES, PAGAN See *Canaanite, History and Religion; Egypt; Gods, Pagan; High Place; Fertility Cult; Mystery/Mystery Religions.*

The Parthenon, a temple dedicated to Athena, dominates the Acropolis in Athens, Greece.

The Temple of Apollo at Didyma near ancient Miletus (in modern Turkey).

Ruins of the Roman Temple of Apollo at Hierapolis, Turkey.

This pylon entrance to the Luxor temple complex at ancient Thebes was built by Ramses II of Egypt.

TEMPTATION Used in KJV to refer to testing, trying, and enticing to evil. When the KJV was translated in 1611, "temptation" meant all of these, but the word has narrowed in meaning in modern times. Modern translations use "testing," "proving," "trying," and "tempting." Four distinct uses of the Hebrew (*nsh*) and Greek (*peirazō*) words for trying or tempting are:

God tests the loyalty or disloyalty of persons. "God did tempt (*nsh*) Abraham" (Gen. 22:1). God "tested" Abraham's loyalty to God when He told Abraham to sacrifice Isaac. Hebrews 11:17 says: "By faith Abraham, when he was tried, offered up Isaac." In Deuteronomy 8:2 Moses said: "God led thee these forty years in the wilderness, to humble thee, and to prove (*nsh*) thee, to know what was in thine heart, whether thou wouldest keep his commandments, or no." (Compare Ex. 20:20; Judg. 2:22.) Christ also tested the loyalty of persons. Jesus asked Philip a question "to prove (*peirazō*) him: for he himself knew what he would do (John 6:6)."

Jesus' enemies tried Him to get something to use against him. "The Pharisees also with the Sadducees came, and tempting (*peirazō*) desired him that he would show them a sign from heaven" (Matt 16:1). (Compare Matt. 19:3; 22:18,35; Mark 8:11; 10:2; 12:15; Luke 11:16; 20:23; John 8:6.)

Persons are tempted or enticed to sin. James 1:13 says, "Let no man say when he is tempted (*peirazō*), I am tempted by God: for God cannot be tempted with evil, neither tempteth he any man." Both the Old Testament and New Testament make it clear that God does not entice persons to sin, but both indicate that God allows human beings to be tempted. (Compare 1 Chron. 21:1; Matt. 4:1,3; Mark 1:13; Luke 4:2,13; 1 Cor. 7:5; 1 Thess. 3:5; Rev. 2:10.) These passages refer to the temptation as coming from the "tempter," "devil," or "Satan." In 1 Corinthians 10:13 Paul said: "There hath no temptation taken you but such as is common to man: but God is faithful, who will not suffer you to be tempted above that ye are able; but will with the temptation also make a way to escape, that ye may be able to bear it." James 1:14 says that "every man is tempted, when he drawn away of his own lust, and enticed." Persons are thus tempted from without by the tempter or from within themselves. Jesus taught His disciples to pray: "Lead us not into temptation, but deliver us from evil" (Matt 6:13). Since God does not entice to sin, this is a cry of the soul for help in the midst of temptation.

Persons are not to test God. Jesus quoted Deuteronomy 6:16 when He said: "Thou shalt not tempt the Lord thy God" (Matt. 4:7). People did put God to the test. (Compare Ex. 17:2,7; Deut. 6:16; 9:22; Num. 14:22; Acts 5:9; 15:10; 1 Cor. 10:9; Heb. 3:8–9.) When the apostles and elders from the Jerusalem church came to Antioch and questioned the admission of the Gentiles into the church, Peter said that the Holy Spirit had been given to the Gentiles: "Why tempt ye God?" (Acts 15:6–11). See *Devil, Satan, Eve, Demonic; Temptation of Jesus.*   *H. Page Lee*

TEMPTATION OF JESUS Satan's attempts at the beginning of Jesus' ministry to divert Jesus from God's way of accomplishing His mission (Matt. 4:1; Mark 1:12; Luke 4:3).

Mark (1:13–14) recorded that the Spirit drove Jesus into the wilderness where He remained 40 days, was tempted by Satan, was with the wild beasts, and was ministered to by angels. This reenforces the Old Testament ideas that the wilderness, the place of wild beasts, was the appropriate place for sin (Lev. 16) and that when one was in distress in the desert, the angels of God ministered to the afflicted.

Matthew (4:1–11) spoke of the Spirit leading Jesus into the wilderness to be tempted by the devil. The temptation was preceded by a fast of 40 days and 40 nights. Then Jesus was hungry. Before the first two temptations, the tempter mocked Jesus with the insinuating phrase "If you are the Son of God." The Greek also permits the translation, "Since you are the Son of God."

The first temptation was to turn into bread the flat stones of the desert, which looked much like the flat round loaves of Middle Eastern bread. Jesus replied in the words of Deuteronomy 8:3 that "man does not live on bread alone but on every word that comes from the mouth of the Lord" (NIV).

Matthew's setting for the second form of Jesus' temptation is the pinnacle of the Temple in Jerusalem where Jesus was challenged to jump off. The

A Christian monastery on the Mount of Temptation marks the traditional site of Jesus' temptation.

dare was accompanied by the quotation of Psalm 91:11–12 that God's angels will rescue and bear up God's anointed. The Rabbis taught that there was a specific pinnacle of the Temple where the Messiah would suddenly appear and jump off, floating down to earth sustained by angels. Jesus responded by quoting Deuteronomy 6:16 that one should not tempt "the Lord your God."

Matthew's third setting for Jesus' temptation was a high mountain from which worldly kingdoms could be seen. The taunt is missing, but Satan promised to deliver the kingdoms of this world to Jesus. Jesus concluded this temptation by quoting Deuteronomy 6:13 and by commanding Satan to leave. The devil left, and angels ministered to Jesus.

The force of the temptation experiences in Matthew is to be a bread messiah, a spectacular messiah, and a compromising messiah. Jesus was to be faced with these challenges all through His ministry and to the end of His life. When Jesus refused to continue to be a bread messiah, the crowds left Him (John 6:25–68). When Jesus came to the Temple, it was not to perform miracles but to cleanse it (Matt. 21:12–17). When the people came to make Him king, He eluded them, choosing instead to be exalted ("lifted up" in Greek) on the cross.

In Luke the second setting of the temptation is the high mountain, and the third is the Temple. This difference in arrangement may reflect Luke's Gentile/cosmopolitan interests to put the kingdoms of all people second. Luke's final phrase is that the devil left Jesus "for a time" or until an opportune time for further temptation. There is no account of the wilderness temptation in John. In the Fourth Gospel the temptation seems to be the confrontation with the religious authorities and His critics (see John 7–8) In John the devil comes to Jesus through the treachery of Judas, His friend and follower (John 6:71; 13:27). The culmination of Jesus' temptation in John's Gospel occurs where Jesus sought release from His suffering (John 17). Hebrews 4:15 says that Jesus was thoroughly and completely tempted. The evil one has nothing in which to find Him guilty (John 14:30).

The major temptation of Jesus was to do God's will the devil's way. The great purpose of Jesus was to follow the will of God. The evil one sought to have Jesus be a Messiah some other way than the way of suffering God had appointed. Jesus did not yield to this great temptation, nor did He yield to temptation at any point.

Orthodox Christology insists that Jesus was sinless. Later theologians had trouble in reconciling the reality of Jesus' divinity with the possibility of being able to sin and the reality of Jesus' humanity with His not having sinned. Was He able to sin or not able to sin. The New Testament does not answer these questions posed by the latter "two-natures-in-one-person" theory. The New Testament affirms both that He was tempted, but He did not sin; that He was divine and that He also was thoroughly human. See *Devil; Jesus, Life and Ministry.*   *William L. Hendricks*

TEN See *Numbers, Systems, Symbolism.*

TEN COMMANDMENTS See *Law, Ten Commandments, Torah.*

TENDERHEARTED KJV used tenderhearted in two senses: of timidity (2 Chron. 13:7) and of compassion (Eph. 4:32). See *Bowels; Compassion.*

TENON KJV, NAS, REB RSV translation of a Hebrew term meaning, "hands," applied to projections designed to fit into a mortice or socket to form a joint (Ex. 26:17,19; 36:22,24). Other translations employ, "projections" (NIV, TEV) or "pegs" (NRSV).

TERAH (Tē′ rah) Personal name perhaps meaning, "ibex." The father of Abraham, Nahor, and Haran (Gen. 11:26). Along with a migration of people from Ur of the Chaldees, Terah moved his family, following the Euphrates River to Haran (11:31). He intended to continue from Haran into Canaan, but died in Mesopotamia at the age of 205 (11:32). A debate has centered on Terah's religious practices, for Joshua 24:2 apparently points to his family when it claims records that the father worshiped gods other than Yahweh.

TERAPHIM (Tĕ′ rȧ phĭm) Transliteration idols used as household gods or for divination. They are idols of indeterminate size and shape (compare Gen. 31; 1 Sam. 19:13). Some scholars have understood Ancient Near Eastern rights of inheritance as being based on the possession of these images as shown in Nuzi inheritance documents. However, the evidence is ambiguous in determining the motive of Rachel's theft or their overall meaning. Jacob (Gen. 35:2) disposed of such religious artifacts before returning to Bethel. Teraphim are related to divination (Judg. 17:5; 18:14–20; 1 Sam. 15:23; 2 Kings 23:24; Hos. 3:4; Ezek. 21:21; Zech. 10:2). Prophetic literature and the Josianic reformation condemned the possession and use of teraphim. Translations used different words in different passages to translate teraphim. See *Divination.*   *David M. Fleming*

TEREBINTH (Tĕ′ rĕ bĭnth) A large, spreading tree whose species is uncertain so that translations vary in reading the Hebrew *'elah* into English (compare 2 Sam. 18:9; Isa. 1:30; 6:13). The tree had religious connections as a place under which pagan gods were worshiped (Hos. 4:13; Ezek. 6:13) which were at times taken up in Israel's religion (Gen. 35:4; Josh. 24:26; Judg. 6:11; 1 Kings 13:14).

St. Catherine's Monastery as seen from atop Mt. Sinai where Moses received the Ten Commandments.

TERESH (Tē' rĕsh) Personal name meaning, "firm, solid," or derived from an Old Persian term meaning, "desire." One of two royal eunuchs who plotted an unsuccessful assassination of the Persian king Ahasuerus. Following their exposure by Mordecai, the two were hung (Esth. 2:21–23).

TERRACE KJV translation of a Hebrew term of uncertain meaning (2 Chron. 9:11). Most modern translations follow the earliest Greek and Latin versions in reading, "steps" (NAS, NIV, RSV) or "stairs" (TEV). REB reads, "stands."

TERROR See *Fear; Fear of Isaac.*

TERTIUS (Tẽr' tĭ ŭs) Latin personal name meaning, "third [son]." Paul's amanuensis (secretary) for the writing of Romans who included his own greeting at Romans 16:22. Some suggest that Quartus, whose name means, "fourth," is perhaps Tertius' younger brother (Rom. 16:23).

TERTULLUS (Tẽr tŭl' lŭs) Diminutive of the personal name *Tertius* meaning, "third" (Acts 24:1–8). Tertullus was the prosecutor opposing Paul before Felix, the Roman governor of Judea. Tertullus accused Paul of being a political agitator and of attempting to defile the Temple. According to the longer Western text (24:7), Tertullus was a Jew. The shorter text allows for his being a Roman. Whatever his ethnic origin, he was skilled in

judicial oratory and was familiar with Roman legal conventions.

TESTAMENT See *Covenant.*

TETH Ninth letter of the Hebrew alphabet which KJV used as a heading for Psalm 119:65–72, each verse of which begins with the letter.

TETRARCH A political position in the early Roman Empire. It designated the size of the territory ruled (literally the "fourth part") and the amount of dependence on Roman authority. Luke 3:1 names one of the tetrarchs who served in the year of Jesus' birth. The position became less powerful with time, and the limits of authority narrowed. When Herod the Great died, his kingdom was

Terebinth trees are still a species found in the Middle East today.

divided among his three sons, one of whom was called "ethnarch" while the other two were named tetrarchs. See *Roman Law.*

THADDAEUS Personal name perhaps meaning, "gift of God" in Greek but derived from Hebrew or Aramaic meaning, "breast." See *Disciples, Judas 6; Lebbaeus.*

THAHASH (Thā' hǎsh) KJV form of Tahash.

THAMAH (Thā' mah) KJV alternate form of Temah (Ezra 2:53).

THAMAR (Thā' mär) KJV alternate form of Tamar (Matt. 1:3).

THANKSGIVING *1.* Gratitude directed towards God (except Luke 17:9; Acts 24:3; Rom. 16:4), generally in response to God's concrete acts in history. Thanksgiving was central to Old Testament worship. Sacrifice and offerings were to be made not grudgingly but with thanksgiving (Ps. 54:6; Jonah 2:9). The psalmist valued a song of thanksgiving more than sacrifice (Ps. 69:30–31). David employed Levites "to invoke, to thank, and to praise the Lord" (1 Chron. 16:4; also 23:30; Neh. 12:46). Pilgrimage to the Temple and Temple worship were characterized by thanksgiving (Pss. 42:4; 95:2; 100:4; 122:4). Thankfulness was expressed: for personal (Ps. 35:18) and national deliverance (Ps. 44:7–8); for God's faithfulness to the covenant (Ps. 100:5); and for forgiveness (Ps. 30:4–5; Isa. 12:1). All creation joins in offering thanks to God (Ps. 145:10). See *Psalms.*

Thanksgiving is a natural element of Christian worship (1 Cor. 14:16–17) and is to characterize all of Christian life (Col. 2:7; 4:2). Early Christians expressed thanks: for Christ's healing ministry (Luke 17:16); for Christ's deliverance of the believer from sin (Rom. 6:17–18; 7:25); for God's indescribable gift of grace in Christ (2 Cor. 9:14–15; 1 Cor. 15:57; compare Rom. 1:21); and for the faith of fellow Christians (Rom. 1:8).

2. Epistolary thanksgiving: An element in the opening of a typical Greek letter. All of the Pauline Letters with the exception of Galatians begin with a thanksgiving. See *Letters.*

THARA (Thā' rȧ) KJV alternate form of Terah (Luke 3:34).

THARSHISH (Thär' shĭsh) KJV alternate form of Tarshish (1 Kings 10:22; 22:48; 1 Chron. 7:10).

THEATER Public drama was apparently unknown in Old Testament Israel except for possible worship activities and only arrived with the Greeks after 400 B.C. As a symbol of Greco-Roman culture, the presence of theaters in Palestine was a constant reminder of Greek and Roman

The Roman Theater at the site of ancient Aspendos located in southern Turkey.

control of the Jewish state. Herod I built numerous theaters in the Greek cities during his reign in Palestine (37—4 B.C.). Their presence, especially near the Temple in Jerusalem, continually infuriated the Jews. Outside of Israel and across the Roman Empire, theaters flourished. Public performances began with a sacrifice to a pagan deity, usually the patron god of the city. Dramas and comedies included historical or political themes and were often lewd and suggestive. The semicircular seats of the theater rose step fashion either up a natural hillside or on artificial tiers. A facade of several stories (as high as the uppermost seats) was decorated with sculptures and stood behind the stage. The general public sat in the higher seats, farther back, but wealthier patrons were given seats lower and closer to the stage. A large central area was reserved for the local governor or ruler. Theaters varied in size. Those in small towns held approximately 4,000 persons, while larger theaters, such as that in Ephesus where Paul was denounced (Acts 19:29), were capable of holding 25,000 or more. See *Greece; Rome.* *David Maltsberger*

THEBES (Thēbes) The capital of Egypt's Upper Kingdom for most of its history (about 2000–661 B.C.). The city waned only during the brief Hyksos period (about 1750–1550 B.C.). Thebes

A tomb painting from the Valley of the Kings, the mortuary area across the Nile River from Thebes.

(called No in KJV) was the center of worship for the god Amon, a chief deity in Egyptian religion. Majestic temples remain as monuments to the city's dedication to Amon. See *Egypt*.

THEBEZ (Thē′ bĕz) Likely Tubas, thirteen miles northeast of Shechem where the roads from Shechem and Dothan converge to lead down to the Jordan Valley. During the seige of Thebez, a woman of the city fatally wounded Abimelech by throwing an upper millstone on his head (Judg. 9:50–53; 2 Sam. 11:21).

THEFT See *Crimes and Punishment; Ethics; Law, Ten Commandments, Torah*.

THELASAR (Thė lā′ sȧr) KJV form of Tel-assar.

THEOCRACY (Thē ŏ′ crȧ cȳ) Term not found in the Hebrew Bible, yet descriptive of a type of government in which Yahweh was king over Israel. In Israel, Yahweh was viewed as the sole Sovereign from which other authorities derived legitimacy. Passages of hope envision God's rule as one outcome in the consummation of history. See *Eschatology; Final Hope*.

Such a rule could be unmediated or mediated through a messianic ruler. Theocracy is shown in action as Yahweh is portrayed as the Heavenly King in His divine council, as He governs the affairs of humanity and His court. The divine will is expressed in decrees that are implemented by members of Yahweh's court (see 1 Kings 22; Isa.

The Hypostyle Hall of Amun-Re's Temple at Karnak in the northern part of ancient Thebes in Egypt.

Ram-headed sphinxes line the processional avenue before the Temple of Amun-Re at Thebes.

6; Job 1—2; Zech. 3). Typically, three kinds of theocracy have been outlined. *1.* A *premonarchic form* was based on the Sinaitic covenant (Ex. 19) and on the charismatic leadership of the judges and the prophets. The experience was more religious, less political. *2.* The *monarchic form* brought a compromise between anti- and pro-monarchic forces in Israel. The king was Yahweh's representative and was called Yahweh's anointed or prince. He was a king, yet he was Yahweh's subordinate. God worked or ruled through the monarchy. *3.* A *postexilic priestly form* saw both the prince and the priest as Yahweh's representative. This move reflected the rising political importance of the priest. In postexilic Israel, theocracy becomes more idealized and future looking. Throughout Israel's history theocracy was often more an ideal God's messengers proclaimed rather than a reality Israel lived out.
David M. Fleming

THEOPHANY (Thē ŏ′ phȧ nȳ) Physical appearance or personal manifestation of a god to a person. **Need for a theophany.** The basic postulate here is that to see God could be fatal. "He said, 'You cannot see My face, for no man can see Me and live!' " (Ex. 33:20 NAS; compare Gen. 16:13; Ex. 3:2–6; 19:20–21; Judg. 6:22–23; 13:20–22. Yet the record is unmistakable that people did see God, such as Moses and others at Sinai (Ex. 24:9–10); the Lord's rebuke of Aaron and Miriam (Num. 12:4–8); and the majestic vision to Isaiah (Isa. 6:1,5). Customarily, God is not revealed to ordinary sight, God at times chooses to reveal Himself in theophanies.
Kinds of theophanies. There are some five forms of theophanies.
1. In human form Without question the theophany in Exodus 24:10 involved the appearance of a human being, for the text clearly states that a pavement of sapphire appeared "under His feet." At Peniel, Jacob testified that he had seen God face-to-face (Gen. 32:30). On Mount Horeb it was the experience of Moses to speak to God "face to face, just as a man speaks to his friend" (Ex. 33:11 NAS). In the same passage when Moses begged God to show him His glory (v. 18), the Lord graciously granted Moses a vision of Himself, saying, "I will take My hand away and you shall see My back, but My face shall not be seen" (v. 23 NAS). If it is protested that the subject is enveloped in mystery, it needs to be remembered that theology without mystery is sheer nonsense. God in His wisdom does not restrict Himself to one method of self-revelation. Notice God's pronouncement in Numbers 12:6–8, which was quite unlike that of Deuteronomy 4:12–15 where only a voice was granted.
2. In vision Even self-seeking Balaam was allowed of God to see the Lord in vision (Num. 24:3–4). Isaiah, Ezekiel, and Daniel, giants among the prophets, saw God in visions (Isa. 6; Ezek. 1; Dan. 7:9). Jacob, sent off by Isaac to Paddan-aram, was granted a dream in which he saw the Lord (Gen. 28:12–13).
3. By the "Angel of the Lord" This is the most usual form of theophany, called the "Angel of the Lord" or "Angel of God." Observe it is not *an* "Angel of God," which could include any of the angelic hosts created by God. *The* "Angel of the Lord" is identified in the accounts with Yahweh Himself. He appears only occasionally in human form. The encounter of the Angel of the Lord with Hagar is of significance in this connection (Gen. 16:7–13). See *Angels.*
4. Not in human form In some instances the theophany came as at the burning bush (Ex. 3:2—4:17) and in the guidance through the wilderness (13:21; compare Acts 7:30). The glory of the Lord appears to people in numerous passages. See *Glory.* God's presence is in a cloud (Ex. 16:10; 33:9–10; Ezek. 10:4). God was also manifest in nature and history (Isa. 6:3; Ezek. 1:28; 43:2).
5. As the name of the Lord God's sacred name represented His presence (Deut. 12:5; 102:15; Isa. 30:27; 59:19).
Contrast with the incarnation The incarnate Christ was not, and indeed is not, a theophany. The phenomena of theophanies were temporary, for the occasion that required them and then disappeared. On the other hand, in the incarnate Christ His deity and humanity were joined, not for time alone, but for eternity. See *Incarnation; Jesus Christ.*
The time factor Only in the Old Testament economy did God's people need a theophany; since the incarnation, there is no such necessity. The New Testament doctrine of God is final and complete. God is always present in the risen Christ and the Holy Spirit. Still, at times, God's people are more aware of that Presence than at others.
Charles Lee Feinberg

THEOPHILUS (Thě ŏph′ ĭ lŭs) Personal name meaning, "friend of God." The person to whom the Books of Luke and Acts were written (Luke 1:3; Acts 1:1). However, his exact identity is unknown. Speculation has ranged from the generic "friend of God" intended to all Christians to a specific benefactor, perhaps in high social and/or political standing. If the latter is true, the name may be a pseudonym to protect the individual from persecution. One conjecture holds that Theophilus was unsaved and that Luke wrote the letter to persuade his belief in Christ.

1 THESSALONIANS (Thĕs să lō′ nĭ ans) Thessalonica was the largest city in first century Macedonia and the capital of the province. It was a free city. See *Macedonia.* Paul, Silas, and Timothy evangelized the city against the strong opposition of the Jews; but, though their stay was short, they were successful in establishing a church (Acts 17:4). There was not time to give much instruction to the new converts, so it is not surprising that questions arose as to the meaning of some aspects of the Christian faith and of the conduct demanded of believers.

To help the new church, Paul wrote 1 Thessalonians not long after Timothy came to him (1 Thess. 3:6). This probably means not long after Timothy's arrival at Corinth (Acts 18:5) rather than his being with Paul in Athens (1 Thess. 3:1–2), for the shorter period scarcely allows enough time for the problems with which the apostle deals in the letter to have arisen. An inscription referring to Gallio (Acts 18:12) enables us to date that proconsul's time in Corinth as the early fifties. Scholars reason from this that Paul probably wrote 1 Thessalonians early in A.D. 50 (though in view of the uncertainties this must be regarded as no more than approximate). Plainly, this is one of the earliest of Paul's letters and one of the earliest Christian documents surviving.

The authenticity of 1 Thessalonians is almost universally accepted. It is Pauline in style and is mentioned in early Christian writings such as the lists of New Testament books given by Marcion in the first half of the second century and by the Muratorian Canon a little later. Some of the problems with which it deals must have arisen quite early in the life of the church (for instance, what will happen to believers who die before Christ returns?).

Among the problems the Thessalonian church faced was persecution by pagans (2:14) and a temptation for believers to accept pagan sexual standards (4:4–8). Some of the Christians seem to have given up working and to have relied on the others to supply their needs (4:11–12). There was uncertainty about the fate of believers who had died, and some of the Thessalonians appear to have thought that Christ would come back soon and take them all to be with Him. What would happen to those who had died before the great event (4:13–18)? Paul's reply to this gives us information about Christ's return that we find nowhere else. Again, some of the believers seem to have been concerned about the time of Jesus' return (5:1–11). So Paul wrote this pastoral letter to meet the needs of inexperienced Christians and to bring them closer to Christ. See *Paul.*

Outline

I. The Church Is Founded on Past Faithfulness (1:1–10).
   A. Signature, address, and greeting (1:1).
   B. Past faith, love, and hope inspire thanksgiving (1:2–3).
   C. Election, power, conviction, and the Spirit brought the gospel (1:4–5).
   D. Model Christian living resulted from the gospel (1:6–7).

   E. Zealous witness and far-reaching Christian influence spread the gospel (1:8–9).
   F. Earnest hope in the resurrection marked the church's life (1:10).
II. Opposition and Persecution Cannot Halt the Gospel (2:1–20).
   A. Suffering and insult do not deter Christian witness (2:1–2).
   B. Sincerity of method and purpose stand behind gospel witness (2:3–6a).
   C. Love, not personal greed, motivates witness (2:6b–12).
   D. Steadfastness and endurance mark Christian converts (2:13–16).
   E. The gospel creates enduring fellowship and love (2:17–18).
   F. A new church becomes the reward for a Christian witness (2:19–20).
III. Concern for the Church Dominates the Minister's Heart (3:1—4:12).
   A. Sacrificial love leads the minister to show concern even under personal persecution (3:1–5).
   B. The church's faithfulness gives the minister encouragement and joy (3:6–10).
   C. The concerned minister prays for the church's future (3:11–13).
   D. The concerned minister teaches the church righteous living (4:1–8).
   E. The concerned minister leads the church to grow in brotherly love (4:9–12).
IV. Problems Related to the Lord's Return (4:13—5:11)
   A. Living and deceased believers have equal hope (4:13–18).
   B. The time is uncertain (5:1–3).
   C. The church needs to be alert (5:4–8).
   D. Believers have assurance (5:9–11).
V. Concluding Exhortations (5:12–28)
   A. Respect Christian leaders (5:12–13).
   B. Care for fellow Christians (5:14–15).
   C. Always be thankful (5:16–18).
   D. Test prophetic utterances to God (5:19–22).
   E. Commit yourself to God, who is faithful (5:23–24).
   F. Closing requests and benediction (5:25–28).

2 THESSALONIANS (Thĕs să lō′ nĭ ans) This letter claims to have been written by Paul (1:1), and the style, the language, and the theology fit in with this claim. Early writers like Polycarp and Ignatius seem to have known it, and it is included in the lists of New Testament books given by Marcion and the Muratorian Canon. The letter claims to have Paul's signature (3:17). Most scholars agree that this is a genuine letter of Paul written to the Thessalonian church not long after the first letter. The situation presupposed by this writing is so similar that there cannot have been a long time between the two writings, perhaps only a matter of weeks.

In recent times some have argued that this is not a genuine letter of Paul. They argue that in 1 Thessalonians the second coming of Christ is seen as very near, whereas here it is to be preceded by the appearance of the man of lawlessness and other signs. This is not a serious objection, for Christians have often held both these points of view; there is no reason why Paul should not have done so. That the teaching about the man of lawlessness is unlike anything else in Paul is of no greater force, for nowhere else does Paul face the contention that "the day of the Lord has already come" (2 Thess. 2:2 NIV).

The exact date of Paul's mission to Thessalonica is not known, and the same is true of his letters to the very young church there. Most scholars agree that 2 Thessalonians must have been written not more than a year or two after Paul and Silas left the city. The church was apparently enthusiastic, but clearly the believers had not as yet matured in their faith. Paul wrote to committed Christians who had not progressed very far in the Christian life.

The Greeks of the first century were not a stolid race. We see their enthusiasm and excitement expressed in the riots when the first Christian preachers visited them. Such a riot broke out in Thessalonica (Acts 17:5–8,13). Those who became Christians during this time did so with verve and enthusiasm. However, they had not yet had the time to come to grips with all that being a Christian meant.

The opening salutation spoke of grace and peace as coming from God the Father and the Lord Jesus Christ (1:2). Throughout the whole letter Christ is seen as in the closest relationship to the Father. This is indicated by the fact that we are sometimes uncertain whether "Lord" means the Father or the Son, as in the expression "the Lord of peace" (3:16). The greatness of Christ is seen in the description of His majestic return with the angels when He comes in judgment (1:7–10). There is not a great deal in this letter about the salvation Christ has wrought, though there are references to the gospel (1:8, 2:14), to salvation (2:13), and to the "testimony" of the preachers (1:10). It is plain enough that Paul had preached the good news of the salvation Christ had brought about by His death for sinners, and that the Thessalonians were so clear on this that Paul had no need to go over it again.

They were not allowed to study the meaning of their new faith in peace and quietness (1:4). While they exulted in what the new relationship to God meant, they apparently did not take seriously enough the demands of Christian teaching, particularly in two areas. These areas included the second coming of our Lord and that of daily living. Some of them had come to believe that "the

coming of our Lord" was at hand, or had even begun (2:2). Some of them had given up working for their living (3:6–13), perhaps because they held the view that the Lord's coming was so close that there was no point in it. Paul wrote to settle them down a little, while not restraining their enthusiasm.

The letter is not a long one and does not give us a definitive outline of the whole Christian faith. Paul wrote to meet a present need, and the arrangement of his letter focuses on local circumstances.

Perhaps we can say that there are four great teachings in this letter:
1. the greatness of God,
2. the wonder of salvation in Christ,
3. the second coming, and
4. the importance of life and work each day.

God loves people like the Thessalonians and has brought them into the church (1:4). He has elected them (2:13), called them (1:11, 2:14), and saved them. His purposes last through to the end when they will be brought to their climax with the return of Christ and judgment of all. It is interesting to see so clearly expressed in this early letter these great doctrines of election and call, which meant so much to Paul. We may see also his doctrine of justification behind the references to God counting the believers worthy (1:5,11) and, of course, in his teaching on faith (1:3; 4:11; 2:13; 3:2).

Salvation in Christ is proclaimed in the gospel and will be consummated when Christ comes again to overthrow all evil and bring rest and glory to His own. This great God loves His people and has given them comfort and hope, two important qualities for persecuted people (2:16). The apostle prayed that the hearts of his converts would be directed into "the love of God" (3:5), which may mean God's love for them or their love for God. Probably it is God's love for them that is the primary thought, but Paul also notes an answering love from the new believers. There are repeated references to revelation (1:7; 2:6,8). While the term is not used in quite the same way as in some other places, it reminds us that God has not left us to our own devices. He has revealed what is necessary and has further revelations for the last days.

The second coming is seen here in terms of the overthrow of all evil, especially the man of lawlessness. Paul made it clear that Christ's coming will be majestic, that it will mean punishment for people who refuse to know God and who reject the gospel, and that it will bring rest and glory to believers (1:7–10). In the end it is God and good that will be triumphant, not evil.

In view of God's love issuing in election and call, it is interesting to see Paul's stress on God's judgment. He spoke of God's righteous judgment (1:5) and felt that God will in due course punish those who persecute the believers and will give the believers rest (1:6–7). But others than the persecutors will suffer in the judgment. Those who refuse to know God and those who reject the gospel will receive the consequences of their actions (1:8–9). Eternal issues are involved when the gospel is preached, and Paul would not allow the Thessalonians to miss these.

But when would it all take place? From 2:2 we see that some of the converts had misunderstood either a "spirit" (i.e., a prophecy or a revelation) or a "word" (oral communication) or a letter (which may mean a genuine letter from Paul that was not understood correctly, or a letter that claimed to be from Paul and was not), with the result that they thought it would all take place very soon. In fact, they thought Christ had already returned. Of course, the glorious appearing of Christ had not taken place yet, but "the day of the Lord" was a complex event, with quite a number of features. They evidently felt "the day" had dawned, the events had begun to unfold, and all that the coming of Christ involved would very soon be accomplished.

Paul made it clear that this was not so. There were several things that must happen first; for example, "the rebellion" that occurs and the revelation of "the man of lawlessness" (2:3). He did not explain either. He was probably referring to what he had told the Thessalonians while he had been among them. Unfortunately, we do not know what he said then, so we are left to do some guessing. That a rebellion against the faith will precede the Lord's return is clearly a well-known part of Christian teaching (Matt. 24:10ff.; 1 Tim. 4:1–3; 2 Tim. 3:1–9; 4:3–4). Some manuscripts read "man of sin"(instead of "lawlessness"), but there is no real difference in meaning for "sin is lawlessness" (1 John 3:4). The Bible does not use the term *man of lawlessness* elsewhere, but clearly he is the same as the one called "antichrist" (1 John 2:18). Paul was saying that in the end time one will appear who will do the work of Satan in a special way. He will oppose the true God and claim divine honors for himself (2:4).

Paul spoke of that which remains (2:6) and He who restrains (2:7), and that which will be removed before the man of lawlessness is revealed. We do not have enough information to know precisely what is meant, and many suggestions have been made. Perhaps the best is the rule of law which may be personified in the ruler. It could be illustrated in the Roman Empire (personified in its emperor) and in other states. When this is finally removed, the time of the lawless one will come. But Paul's important point is that believers should not be rushing into premature expectations. In due course these things will take place, and God will do away with all the forces of evil (2:8–10).

Paul had a good deal to say about people he calls "disorderly" and who appear to be idle, not working at all (3:6–12). This may have been because they thought the Lord's coming was so close there was no point in it, or perhaps they were so "spiritual minded" that they concentrated on higher things and let other people provide for their needs. Paul counseled all to work for their living (3:12). No doctrinal emphasis, not even that of Christ's return, should lead Christians away from work. People able to work should earn their daily bread. Believers are to work for their living and not grow weary in doing good.

Timothy had just come to Paul from Thessalonica with fresh news (1 Thess. 3:2). Paul saw that the troubles he dealt with in the first letter were still present. So he wrote once more to rebuke the lazy (3:10) and to encourage the downhearted. There was a new error about the second coming, with some saying that the day of the Lord had already come. Paul set these people right, teaching them that evil will flourish when the man of lawlessness appears, but that they should look beyond that to the certainty that in due time Christ will return and defeat every force of evil. Christians have been heartened by such teaching from that day to this.

Outline

I. Salvation (1:1–2).

II. Church Leaders Pray for the Church (1:3–12).
   A. Growth in Christian faith, love, and perseverance inspire thanksgiving (1:3–4).
   B. God is just and will help His people who suffer injustice (1:5–7a).
   C. Christ's return will provide ultimate justice (1:7b–10).
   D. Prayer helps God's people fulfill their purposes and glorify Christ (1:11–12).

III. Christ's Return Will Defeat Satanic Forces (2:1–12).
   A. Despite deceptive reports, Christ has not returned (2:1–2).
   B. The man of lawlessness must appear before Christ returns (2:3–8).
   C. Deceived followers of lawlessness will perish (2:9–12).

IV. Election Leads to Thanksgiving (2:13–17).
   A. God chose us to share Christ's glory (2:13–14).
   B. God calls you to firm commitment to His teachings (2:15).
   C. Encouragement and hope comes from God's grace (2:16–17).

V. God Is Faithful (3:1–5).
   A. God's evangelists need our prayers (3:1–2).
   B. God is faithful to protect His people (3:3).
   C. God's people are faithful to follow His will (3:4–5).

VI. God Disciplines His People (3:6–15).
   A. God's people must not become lazy busy-

bodies (3:6–13).

    B. Disobedient people must receive brotherly discipline (3:14–15).

VII. Concluding Greetings (3:16–18).

Leon Morris

THESSALONICA (Thĕs sȧ lō nī′ cȧ) The name of modern Thessaloniki, given to the city about 315 B.C. by Cassander, a general of Alexander the Great. He founded the city in that year, naming it after his wife who was the daughter of Philip II and half sister of Alexander. Located on the Thermaic Gulf (Gulf of Salonika) with an excellent harbor—and at the termination of a major trade route from the Danube—it became, with Corinth, one of the two most important commercial centers in Greece. In the Roman period, it retained its Greek cultural orientation and functioned as the capital of Macedonia after 146 B.C. See *Macedonia*.

When the apostle Paul visited the city, it was larger than Philippi which reflected a predominantly Roman culture. Thessalonica was a free city, having no Roman garrison within its walls and maintaining the privilege of minting its own coins. Like Corinth, it had a cosmopolitan population due to the commercial prowess of the city. The recent discovery of a marble inscription, written partly in Greek and partly in a Samaritan form of Hebrew and Aramaic, testifies to the presence of Samaritans in Thessalonica. The Book of Acts testifies to the presence of a Jewish synagogue there (17:1).

Since most of the ancient city still lies under modern Thessaloniki, it has been impossible to excavate it. However, in the center of town a large open area has been excavated revealing a Roman forum (marketplace), about 70 by 110 yards, which dates to about A.D. 100 to 300. An inscription found in the general area, dating to 60 B.C., mentions an agora (Greek for the Roman "forum") and opens the possibility that a Hellenistic marketplace was located here just prior to the construction of this Roman one. In Hellenistic times there were a stadium, a gymnasium, and a temple of Serapis in the city. A third-century odeum (small theater) is preserved on the east side of the forum.

The authenticity of Acts has been questioned due to Luke's mention of Roman officials in Thessalonica by the name of *politarchs* (Acts 17:6), who are otherwise unknown in extant Greek literature. However, a Roman arch at the western end of ancient Vardar Street contained an inscription from before A.D. 100 which began, "In the time of the Politarchs." Several other inscriptions from Thessalonica, one of them dating from the reign of Augustus Caesar, mention *politarchs*. See *1 Thessalonians; 2 Thessalonians.*   *John McRay*

THEUDAS (Thēu dȧs) Personal name meaning, "gift of God." Acts 5:36 refers to a Theudas who was slain after leading an unsuccessful rebellion of

The Triumphal Arch of the Emperor Galerius, which is built over the Egnatian Way in Thessalonica.

The highway near Thessalonica (modern Salonica) going toward Athens.

T

400 men prior to the census (A.D. 6). Josephus knew a Theudas who led an unsuccessful rebellion during the consulate of Cuspius Fadus (about A.D. 44). Either two rebels are involved, or one of the historians incorporated an inaccurate source into his narrative.

THIEF See *Crimes and Punishment; Law, Ten Commandments, Torah.*

THIGH The side of the lower torso and the upper part of the leg. Sometimes the reference is simply physical (Judg. 3:16; Ps. 45:3; Song of Sol. 3:8; 7:1). More often Scripture regards the thigh as the seat of vital functions, especially procreation. English translations often obscure this connection. The Hebrew text of Genesis 46:26; Exodus 1:5; and Judges 8:30 gives the thighs (KJV loins) as the source of offspring. Marital infidelity was punishable by "the falling away of the thigh," that is, by failure of the reproductive system (Num. 5:16–21). In the Patriarchal period, oaths were taken by placing a hand "under the thigh," a veiled reference to the reproductive organs. (The English terms *testify* and *testes* witness a similar relation.) The action perhaps represents the calling of one's descendants as witnesses of the oath. When the "stranger" at Peniel did not prevail against Jacob, he touched Jacob in the hollow of his thigh, leaving him limping (Gen. 32:25–32). Jacob escaped the struggle broken but unbowed. Slapping the thigh indicated sorrow, shame, or remorse (Jer. 31:19; Ezek. 21:12). The thigh was among the portions of the sacrifice going to the priests (Lev. 7:32–34; 10:14; compare 1 Sam. 9:24 where Samuel honored Saul with this portion.)

THIMNATHAH (Thĭm' nȧ thăh) KJV alternate form of Timnah (Josh. 19:43).

THIN WORK See *Beveled Work.*

THOMAS (Thōm' ȧs) Personal name from Hebrew meaning, "a twin." One of the first twelve disciples of Jesus (Mark 3:18). The apocryphal book, *The Acts of Thomas,* uses the literal meaning of his name ("twin") in making him the twin of Jesus Himself! His personality was complex, revealing a pessimism mixed with loyalty and faith (John 11:16). Thomas sought evidence of Jesus' resurrection (John 20:25), but when convinced of the miracle made an historic confession of faith (20:28). See *Apocrypha, New Testament; Didymus; Disciples.*

THORN IN THE FLESH In 2 Corinthians 12:7 Paul referred to "a thorn in the flesh," "a messenger of Satan," given him by God to ensure his humility following a profound experience of "visions," "revelations," and "ascent into the third heaven." The nature of the "thorn in the flesh" has been the subject of many speculations. Guesses ranging from epilepsy (a popular conjec-

ture of classical liberalism, which sought to offer rational explanations for Paul's visionary experiences, especially his conversion), malaria (because of its prevalence in some of the regions of Paul's ministry), and eye disease (because of the unusual metaphorical expression in Gal. 4:15) have been suggested.

A more acceptable solution, however, relates to the context of 2 Corinthians 12:1–10 where "thorn in the flesh" parallels both "messenger of Satan" in verse 7 and the "weaknesses," "insults," "distresses," "persecutions," and "difficulties" of verse 10. The Old Testament use of the term *thorn* also offers some help. In Numbers 33:55; Ezekiel 28:24 we read of enemies who are "thorns" in Israel's side, a constant harrassment to Israel as the agent of the Lord's redemptive judgments (compare Josh. 23:13; Hos. 2:6).

Therefore, in 2 Corinthians 12:7, "thorn in the flesh" refers more to the enemy, the "messenger of Satan," than to any specific physical ailment. The "messenger of Satan" was a redemptive judgment (as Israel's enemies were also used) of God upon Paul "to keep me from exalting myself." Thus Paul's entire apostolic experience of suffering (compare 2 Cor. 1:3–11; 4:7–5:10; 6:1–10; 7:2–7; 11:16–33), abetted by Satan and operative through the evils of this world, was the "messenger of Satan," a "thorn in the flesh," which God gave and used to keep the great apostle humbly obedient. Paul could truly say that he was an earthen vessel (4:7), one who shared the sufferings of Christ (1:5), so that the life of Jesus might be manifested through his very mortality (4:11); "for when I am weak, then I am strong" (12:10 NIV). *Robert Sloan*

THREE TAVERNS Rest stop on the Appian Way thirty-three miles southeast of Rome and ten miles northwest of the Forum of Appius where Roman Christians met Paul on his trip to Rome (Acts 28:15).

THUMMIM See *Urim and Thummim.*

THUTMOSE (Thŭt' mōse) Egyptian royal name meaning, "Thoth the moon god is born." Four pharaohs of the Egyptian Eighteenth Dynasty (about 1550–1310 B.C.). Their combined efforts, especially those of Thutmose I and III, did much to expand Egyptian wealth and influence.

Thutmose I rose to power through his skills as a general and by marrying the daughter of his predecessor, Amenhotep I. His military exploits expanded Egypt to include Nubia to the south and Syria, north to the Euphrates River. The tribute from his conquests allowed Eneni, his architect, to restore and add to the temples of Thebes. Eneni was also instructed to initiate the work at Biban el-Moluk (gates of the kings) known today as the Valley of the Kings. Thutmosis I had no clear heir to the throne when he died.

Thutmose II succeeded in gaining the throne by marrying his ambitious half sister Hatshepsut. His reign lasted only a few years and was obscured by the shadow of this queen.

Thutmose III marched in the steps of his grandfather Thutmose I but only after about twenty years of "co-rule" with Hatshepsut. His hatred of her must have smoldered all those years, for he removed much of the evidence of her reign as soon as she was dead. Thutmose III conducted fourteen military campaigns in seventeen years, continuing his rule another fifteen years. The Theban temple of Karnak contains displays of his exploits. He especially enjoyed hunting and was devoted to the god Amun. Some scholars believe him to be the pharaoh of the Israelite oppression, but this is not the predominate view. Amenhotep II became coregent with his father for about three years at the conclusion of his reign.

Thutmose IV, like Thutmose II, seized his position by marriage. He seemed content to maintain the status quo and clear the sand from the Sphinx where he had dreamed of becoming Pharoah according to a stela. See *Egypt; Thebes.*

Gary C. Huckabay

THYATIRA (Thȳ å tī´ rå) A city in the Lycus River valley. Although never a magnificent city, Thyatira was the center of a number of trade guilds which used the natural resources of the area to make it a very profitable site. Thyatira had a Jewish contingent out of which grew a New Testament church. One of Paul's first converts from the European continent, Lydia, was a native of Thyatira (Acts 16:14). She probably was a member of a guild there which dealt in purple dye. The church at Thyatira was praised for its works of charity, service, and faith (Rev. 2:19), but criticized for allowing the followers of Jezebel to prosper in its midst (2:20). See *Asia Minor; Revelation, Book of.*

TIAMAT (Tī´ å mät) A Sumerian-Akkadian goddess viewed by the Babylonians as one of the major gods of their pantheon. She controlled the salt waters and was seen as a capricious goddess

The ruins of Thyatira in ancient Asia Minor (modern Turkey).

because of the destructive yet beneficial nature of the rivers and seas. In the creation epic, *Enuma Elish,* Tiamat and her consort, Apsu, gave birth to Anshar and Kishar, the universe above and below. According to the epic, the creation of the earth was the result of Tiamat's defeat by the god Marduk, who split Tiamat in two to form heaven and earth, a picture of the primordial sea being driven back and giving way to the land.

TIBERIAS (Tī bēr´ ĭ ås) Mentioned only in John 6:23 (compare 6:1; 21:1), Tiberias is a city located on the western shore of the Sea of Galilee encompassing today what was in ancient times two separate cities, Tiberias and Hammath, each surrounded by its own wall. Once a mile apart (Palestinian Talmud, *Megillah* 2.2), they were combined into a single city, apparently in the first century after Christ (Tosefta, 'Erubin 7.2,146). At this time, about A.D. 18, Herod Antipas (Luke 3:1) built the larger city on a major trade route connecting Egypt with Syria, to replace Sepphoris as the capital of Galilee (Josephus, *Antiquities* 18.36). It remained the capital until A.D. 61 when it was given to Agrippa II by Nero (*Antiquities* 20.159). It was paganized by Hadrian after the second Jewish revolt in A.D. 132–135, but became the center of Jewish learning after A.D. 200. The Mishnah, which was compiled in Sepphoris by Judah haNasi, took its final shape in Tiberias as did the Talmud and the Massoretic Text of the Hebrew Bible.

Excavations by N. Slouschz in 1921 and M. Dothan in 1961 at Hammath-Tiberias, near the warm baths, revealed several superimposed synagogues dating from about 300 to 800, some having beautiful mosaic floors. In 1973 and 1974 G. Foerster, digging just south of this area, found the southern gate of the city, having two round towers and dating to the founding of Tiberias before A.D. 100.

John McRay

T

TIBERIUS CAESAR (Tī bēr´ ĭ ŭs Çae´ sår) The person who had the unenviable task of following Augustus as Roman emperor. He ruled the empire from A.D. 14–37. Tiberius was especially ill suited to follow Augustus. A solid, taciturn man, he lacked the public relations ability of Augustus.

Tiberius was 54 when he ascended to the throne. He was a republican at heart, so he must have felt very uncomfortable with the system of government which Augustus left him. He had a deep respect for the Senate, and he took great pains to preserve the dignity of that body. Yet even Tiberius came to realize that it was too late to make the Senate an equal partner in government.

During the reign of Tiberius, Jesus began His ministry; and He was crucified. This event was probably not noted at the emperor's court. Tiberius died in A.D. 37. He was 79 years old. See *Rome.*

Gary Poulton

Modern Tiberias, built over the ancient city of Tiberias, overlooks the Sea of Galilee.

TIBHATH (Tĭb hăth) Place name meaning, "place of slaughter." City from which David took spoils (or received tribute) of bronze (1 Chron. 18:8). The site is likely in the vicinity of Zobah north of Damascus. The parallel in 2 Samuel 8:8 reads Betah.

TIBNI (Tĭb nī) Personal name meaning, "intelligent" or "straw." Likely an army officer who struggled with Omri over succession to the throne of Israel following Zimri's suicide (1 Kings 16:21–22).

TIDAL (Tī dăl) One of four kings allied against five in Genesis 14:1,9. The name is similar to Tud'alia, the name of several Hittite kings, suggesting the king's origin in eastern Asia Minor. The king is perhaps Tudhalia I (about 1700–1650 B.C.).

TIGLATH-PILESER (Tĭḡ′ lăth-Pĭ lē′ ṣĕr) Personal name meaning, "My trust is the son of Esarra (the temple of Asshur)." King of Assyria from 745 to 727 B.C. (2 Kings 16:7), also known as Tilgath-Pilneser (1 Chron. 5:6; 2 Chron. 28:20) and Pul (2 Kings 15:19; 1 Chron. 5:26). See *Assyria, History and Religion of.*

TIGRIS RIVER See *Euphrates River; Rivers.*

TIKVAH (Tĭk′ văh) Personal name meaning,

"hope, expectation." *1.* Father-in-law of Huldah, the prophetess (2 Kings 22:14; 2 Chron. 34:22). *2.* Father of Jahaziah who opposed Ezra's call for Israelites to divorce their foreign wives (Ezra 10:15).

TIKVATH (Tĭk′ văth) KJV alternate form of Tikvah (2 Chron. 34:22), perhaps representing original form of foreign name written in Hebrew as Tikvah.

TILGATH-PILNESER (Tĭl′ ḡăth-Pĭl nē′ ṣĕr) Alternate form of Tiglath-Pileser (1 Chron. 5:6; 2 Chron. 28:20).

TILON (Tī′ lŏn) Personal name of uncertain meaning. Descendant of Judah (1 Chron. 4:20).

The Tigris River flows through the country of Iraq (ancient Mesopotamia).

TIMAEUS (Tĭ maē′ ŭs) Personal name meaning, "highly prized" (Mark 10:46). Bartimaeus is Aramaic for "son of Timaeus."

TIMBREL (Tĭm brĕl) KJV term for a tambourine. See *Tabret; Music, Instruments, and Dancing.*

TIME, MEANING OF The chronological sequence of life and its significance in biblical teaching.
God and Time The biblical God is not governed by time because He is the Lord of time. God is in time in the sense that He is sovereignly present in all the events of time, confronting His people with His warnings and His promises. However, this is not the same as saying that God is caught up in time or governed by it. Humankind cannot bind Him to special sacred times; rather, He encounters humankind in each moment of their temporal existence, offering each new day as an opportunity for judgment in the event of their willful stubbornness or for redemption in the event of their repentance.

Both the Old and New Testaments speak of God as everlasting, but they do not participate in the abstract, philosophical notion that He lives in an eternity of splendid isolation. Western thinking borrowed that from the ancient Greeks. To the people of the Bible—Israelites and Jewish Christians living out of the Hebraic heritage—it would have been impossible to even think of eternity as a timelessness before and after time. The Hebrew words that are translated "eternal" and "eternity," along with the New Testament Greek equivalents, conceive only of endlessness or perpetuity, that is the absence of the temporal conditionedness marking every finite creature.

To say God is eternal from the biblical standpoint means that His existence brackets cosmic time. He was there at the beginning of all created things; He will be there when temporal reality ends; and He is present at every moment in between. This is the true meaning of eternity. Before, above, and beyond all creaturely existence, God is; yet He is intimately close in every temporal experience—not passively but actively—governing all His creatures and calling each person, to whom He has given the power of free choice, to obey and believe.

Because the Bible is no theological treatise, it never speculates about these facts. Rather, it presents them in passages whose immediate purpose is to call for true obedience and trusting faith. The poems in Isaiah 40—55 directly state God's creative presence at the beginning of all things (48:12–13; compare 41:4; 44:6). These words are addressed to a people in Exile, despairing that their God has abandoned them. The prophet assured them that the God who created in the beginning can create redemption for them.

Temporality, on the other hand, is an inescapable aspect of mankind's creaturely existence. Cre-ated of dust (Gen. 2:7), human beings must sometime die. As there is no limit to the Creator's existence, there is a necessary and inescapable limit to human existence. Genesis teaches that this is intended to keep people from seizing immortality and becoming like God (Gen. 3:22), to limit a person's lifetime in order to restrain and order the penchant for self-exaltation and violence (Gen. 6:3; 11:6). The human creature may not lay hold on the unending existence that belongs only to the Creator. Rather than attempting to seize immortality, humanity is advised to "remember your creator in the days of your youth, before the days of trouble come" (Eccl. 12: 1 NRSV; compare 11:8).

Measuring and qualifying time Like all ancient peoples, the people of the Bible were aware of the passage of time. They learned to mark seasons and measure durations. To be sure, they knew nothing of modern man's clock-watching and tight scheduling. They experienced time much more holistically. No evidence indicates that the Israelites counted seconds, minutes, or even hours (the Jews of the New Testament learned to count hours from the Romans). All their time units were based on observation and experience. Thus the day was divided up into "watches" (compare Ex. 14:24; 1 Sam. 11:11), measured by observation of the sun's position in the sky. They counted years by the cycle of the seasons, but especially by observation of the sun's return in its annual orbit. Their months were not based on an arbitrary number like our 30 days but were counted from one new moon to the next, making it necessary to add extra "intercalary" days after twelve months to make the new year (365+ days) begin on a new moon = month. (Because the Jews have continued this method, their years have a variable new beginning from September into October.) By far the most important unit of time was the day, the most basic unit of intuitive experience. Early on, the Israelites counted the day from morning till evening, or, counting the night in between, from one morning to the next. Because of the growing importance of the rising moon for festival observance, they later came to count the day from the evening, and this is the Jewish custom today. What is important for understanding the biblical view of time is the fact that days were not just counted, but were identified by their most significant event. Throughout the Scriptures we read of "day of rejoicing," "day of trouble," "day of salvation," expressions that commemorate a given day's experiential quality. As a matter of fact, the Hebrew word *yôm,* meaning "day," is the fifth most frequently used word in the Old Testament. Though used for all sorts of common experiences, it came to be used for marking special days of God's revelatory appearance, whether to individual persons or to the nation. Most notably, there was a "day" of Israel's election (Deut. 9:24; compare Ezek. 16:4–5), a "day" when God brought His people out of Egypt (Judg. 19:30; 1 Sam. 8:8; 2 Sam. 7:6; Isa. 11:16; Jer. 7:22,25), but also a "day" of restoration (Zech. 8:9–12). There was also a "day" of judgment (Lam. 1:12). A final day when God would judge the world was "the day of the Lord" (Amos 5:18–19; Isa. 13:6; Zeph. 1:7).

When the plural of *yôm* (day) is used, it may measure a significant period or sequence of days, such as the length of a king's reign (2 Sam. 2:11 NAS margin). Often the plural is synonymous with the word *'ēt,* which means "time" or "situation" and refers to an ongoing period identified by its experiential quality. There were good and evil days or times; Ecclesiastes 3:1–8 provides a list of such times while warning that mankind is unable to discern God's intent in sending them. Usually a person's "days" weigh more heavily with evil than with good (compare Gen. 47:9; Job 7:1,16; Ps. 144:4, Eccl. 2:23). Psalm 90, which measures mankind's brief life (vv. 9–10) against God's eternity (vv. 2,4), prays that God will do two things: (1) "teach us to count our days that we may gain a wise heart" (Ps. 90:12 NRSV) and (2) "make us glad as many days as you have afflicted us, and as many years as we have seen evil" (v. 15 NRSV).
Time and history The habit of the people of the Bible to identify certain days by their dominant quality is not to be compared with the ancient Babylonian notion that the quality of every day and time is set by heavenly decree, fixed so firmly that even the gods are forced to submit to it. The Babylonians observed the heavenly constellations and made them the clock that brought good or evil. If a memorable calamity had occurred under a given constellation and when the planets were in a certain convergence, the recurrence of this heavenly configuration would be the inevitable omen of evil. Thus the Babylonians saw no organic, cause and effect, interconnection between human events. Because of their fatalism, they developed no true understanding of history and saw no ultimate purpose in human striving.

Egypt, another ancient neighbor to Israel, had little of this cosmic determinism; yet the Egyptian civilization was equally unable to understand and deal with history. Time in Egyptian thought was an endless, meaningless cycle of death and rebirth, a continual return to primordial reality. Everything new was only a new incarnation of its eternal model, just as each Pharaoh was a reincarnation of the divine. Here one finds no sharp delimitation of times, as in Babylonian civilization, yet historical event remained meaningless because only the eternal order was real.

This description, little understood by Bible readers, is an illuminating preface to the biblical understanding of time and history. The Bible teaches that people are free to act—but always they are called to act in accordance with God's revealed law. Preceding all responsible human acts,

however, is God's saving act within history. The Israelites were unique in the ancient world in their belief that God had not made them with the land of Canaan, like the Egyptians with the Nile, but had brought them as strangers to settle in a land that was not theirs (Gen. 12:1–3) through a mighty act at the commencement of their existence as a people. Later, Israel became a people in the deliverance from Egypt.

God gave them His law from Sinai, and ever thereafter they strove imperfectly to be God's people and to keep His law. Because of their vacillating and backsliding, they lived constantly between the promise and the fulfillment. Their striving had historical significance because their God was present to blame their failure while urging them forward to a more perfect obedience. The people of the Bible were different because they were free in the presence of the eternal God to obey or disobey; and, in the event of their disobedience, they were free to repent and be saved (Ezek. 33:11).

Biblical humanity saw themselves standing in a present moment of critical decision making, looking back upon the records of an imperfect obedience that spoke also of God's grace and forbearance, interpreting this as a warning and a renewed promise of grace for the future. Thus the past is a mirror of the future, showing the perils and opportunities that are yet to be. This arms mankind for a commitment here and now, once and again, to decide for God.

Christ's new time After a long age of waiting and sometimes of despair, the Jewish people who were heirs of the Old Testament promises heard the announcement that God had brought history to its fulfillment in His Messiah (Mark 1:15). This Messiah eventually died a cruel death on the cross, but when He arose to everlasting life, His followers went into all the world to announce, "See, now is the acceptable time; see, now is the day of salvation" (2 Cor. 6:2 NRSV; compare 3:7–18). Just as Jesus had declined at the moment of His ascension to give His followers a clue to times and seasons (Acts 1:7), Paul refused to tell the church when the end would come, except to tell them that it would come suddenly and unexpectedly, like a thief in the night (1 Thess. 5:1–11), and that God was presently acting to overcome the mystery of "the man of lawlessness," which must first be destroyed. (2 Thess. 2:1–12)

Some are troubled that the mystery of lawlessness is still at work and has delayed the "day of the Lord" for another two thousand years. In spite of this, we must affirm with Paul and with Christ Himself that God's new age has most certainly arrived. Mankind is still lost, but only insofar as the gospel, widely proclaimed to all the world, is ignored. We too should be warned off from calculating days and seasons, for the fullness of time has already appeared. In His Son God gave mankind the most perfect revelation of Himself (John 14:5–11). For each human person, nothing counts but the present moment—the moment of decision for Christ—which brings the history of divine salvation to a climax of meaning in the life of peoples and individuals. Deciding for Christ in the present moment is the decisive act in waiting for Him.

Sacred time Israel's neighbors were very religious. They believed that their gods could be contacted at holy places (the shrines) and at holy times (the religious festivals). The biblical God, as Creator of the world and Lord of history, cannot be tied down to special places and special times. Nevertheless, His ancient people did right when they built the Temple and set aside holy seasons for His worship. This was not intended to coerce God but to hallow His holy presence for prayer and thanksgiving. Every time that Israel met for worship, it praised God for that great day at the beginning of their history, when He delivered them from Egypt; it praised Him also for every day of divine intervention. To keep His sabbaths and holy festivals and to gather in His temple, was an act of celebration and recommitment.

The Temple is long since destroyed, yet Jews and Christians gather in holy places and at holy seasons to continue their praise and renew their prayers. There is nothing sacrosanct about our church buildings or about our holy days. They are made holy by our intention. It seems a departure from biblical religion when the liturgy designs to recreate the real, bodily presence of Christ. Yet Christ must be present if worship is to be valid. It is God's greatest saving deed on our behalf, the death and resurrection of Christ, that must come to pass in our hearts anew. Then we will speak and testify in "the great congregation" (see Ps. 22:25 NRSV), recreating in our worship the reality of Christ. All time belongs to God (Gen. 1), but sacred times, especially set aside and devoutly observed, serve to show once again our participation in the great events of God's appearance. See *History*. *Simon J. DeVries*

TIMNA (Tĭm' nà) Personal name meaning, "holding in check" or "she protects." *1.* Sister of the Horite clan chief Lotan (Gen. 36:22; 1 Chron. 1:39), concubine of Esau's son Eliphaz, and mother of Amalek (Gen. 36:12). *2.* Son of Eliphaz (1 Chron. 1:36; Gen. 36:16, Teman) and Edomite clan chief (Gen. 36:40; 1 Chron. 1:51). Timna is associated with either Timna in southern Arabia or, following Genesis 36:16, Teman in southern Edom. It is the name of the capitol of Qataban. *3.* A modern name for an ancient copper-mining site fourteen miles north of Elath.

TIMNAH (Tĭm' nah) Place name meaning, "allotted portion." *1.* Town assigned to Dan (Josh. 19:43), located on the southern border with Ju-

The modern name "Timna" refers to a large copper-mining area north of the Gulf of Aqaba.

dah (Josh. 15:10). The site is likely tell el-Batashi about four miles northwest of Beth-shemesh in Judah. Philistines occupied the site at the time of Samson (Judg. 14:1–5). Uzziah likely took the site as part of his conquest of Philistine cities (2 Chron. 26:6). His grandson Ahaz lost the city to the Philistines again (2 Chron. 28:18). The city fell to the Assyrian king Sennacherib in 701 B.C. *2.* Village in the hill country of Judah (Josh. 15:57). This Timnah was the likely scene of Judah's encounter with Tamar (Gen. 38:12–14). The probable site lies south of Hebron about four miles east of Beit Nettif.

TIMNATH (Tĭm' nàth) KJV alternate form of Timnah (Gen. 38:12–14).

TIMNATH-HERES; TIMNATH-SERAH (Tĭm' nàth-Hē' rēṣ, Tĭm' nàth-Sē' rah) Place of Joshua's inheritance and burial (Judg. 2:9; Josh 19:50; 24:30). Timnath-Heres means, "portion of the sun," suggesting a site dedicated to sun worship (Judg. 2:9). Timnath-Serah means, "remaining portion," pointing to land given to Joshua following distribution of land to the tribes (Josh. 19:50; 24:30). The site is identified with khirbet Tibneh about seventeen miles southwest of Shechem.

TIMNITE (Tĭm nīte) Resident of Timnah (Judg. 15:6).

An overview of Tell Batash (site of the ancient city of Timnah).

TIMON (Tī' mŏn) Personal name meaning, "honorable." One of seven chosen to supervise distribution of food to the Greek-speaking widows of the Jerusalem church (Acts 6:5).

TIMOTHY (Tīm' ō thȳ) Personal name meaning, "honoring God." Friend and trusted coworker of Paul. When Timothy was a child, his mother Eunice and his grandmother Lois taught him the Scriptures (2 Tim. 1:5; 3:15). A native of Lystra, he may have been converted on Paul's first missionary journey (Acts 14:6–23). Paul referred to Timothy as his child in the faith (1 Cor. 4:17; 1 Tim. 1:2; 2 Tim. 1:2). This probably means that Paul was instrumental in Timothy's conversion. When Paul came to Lystra on his second journey, Timothy was a disciple who was well-respected by the believers (Acts 16:1–2). Paul asked Timothy to accompany him. Timothy's father was a Greek, and Timothy had not been circumcised. Because they would be ministering to many Jews and because Timothy's mother was Jewish, Paul had Timothy circumcised (Acts 16:3).

Timothy not only accompanied Paul but also was sent on many crucial missions by Paul (Acts 17:14–15; 18:5; 19:22; 20:4; Rom. 16:21; 1 Cor. 16:10; 2 Cor. 1:19; 1 Thess. 3:2,6). For example, when Paul was unable to go to Corinth, he sent Timothy to represent Paul and his teachings (1 Cor. 4:17). Later when Paul was in prison, he sent Timothy to Philippi (Phil. 2:19). Paul felt that no one had any more compassion and commitment than Timothy (Phil. 2:20–22).

So close were Paul and Timothy that both names are listed as the authors of six of Paul's letters (2 Cor. 1:1; Phil. 1:1; Col. 1:1; 1 Thess. 1:1; 2 Thess. 1:1; Philem. 1). In addition, Paul wrote two letters to Timothy (1 Tim. 1:2; 2 Tim. 1:2). As Paul's ministry neared the end, he challenged Timothy to remain true to his calling (1 Tim. 1:18). As Paul faced death, he asked Timothy to come to be with him (2 Tim. 4:9). At some point in his life, Timothy was imprisoned; but he was released (Heb. 13:23). See *Paul; 1 Timothy; 2 Timothy.*   *Robert J. Dean*

1 TIMOTHY First of two epistles Paul wrote to Timothy. See *Letters; Paul; Timothy.*

Date The letter was written in approximately A.D. 63, following Paul's first imprisonment in Rome. It is likely that Paul left Rome and traveled to Ephesus. There is some debate concerning the place of writing. Rome and Macedonia have been offered as possibilities. Perhaps, in light of 1 Timothy 1:3, Macedonia could be the better choice.

Recipient The letter was addressed to Timothy in Ephesus. Paul had urged Timothy to remain in Ephesus and lead this important church as its pastor (1:3).

Purpose Paul had hoped to visit Timothy in Ephesus but was fearful of a delay. If he were delayed,

he wanted Timothy to "know what is proper conduct in God's household" (3:14–15 REB). The epistle contains instructions concerning order and structure in the church and practical advice for the young pastor.

One important theme in this and the other two Pastoral Epistles (2 Tim. and Titus) is "sound doctrine." Paul urged Timothy and Titus to confront the false teaching by sound or healthy teaching. This word occurs eight times in these three letters (1 Tim. 1:10; 6:3; 2 Tim. 1:13; 4:3; Titus 1:9,13; 2:1–2).

Outline

I. Salutation (1:1–2)
II. Introductory Remarks (1:3–20)
III. The Worship of the Church (2:1–15)
IV. The Leadership of the Church (3:1–13)
V. The Mission of the Church (3:14–16)
VI. The Ministry of the Church (4:1—6:10)
VII. Concluding Remarks (6:11–21)

Overview, Chapter One: Paul wrote as an apostle of Jesus Christ. He was writing with the authority of Jesus Himself. The error described in verses 3–4 was Jewish in nature. Some were falsely teaching a mythological treatment of Old Testament genealogies. This teaching was both meaningless and controversial. Timothy was urged to teach "sound doctrine" in its place (1:10–11). Two leaders among the false teachers were Hymenaeus and Alexander, whom Paul "consigned to Satan, in the hope that through this discipline they might learn not to be taught, not to be blasphemous" (1:20 REB; compare 1 Cor. 5:5). The purpose of this and all Christian discipline was the eventual restoration of the offender.

Chapter Two: Prayer is given priority in the worship services in the church. Seven different Greek words appear in the New Testament for prayer, and four of them occur in verse 1. One of the most significant statements in the entire New Testament is found in verse 5. Paul wrote there is "one God" and "one mediator between God and men, Christ Jesus, himself man" (REB). Monotheism is clearly taught as opposed to the polytheism of the first century religious world. *Mediator* is a word that means "go-between." Jesus is humanity's "go-between" to God. He is also called our "ransom" in verse 6. A ransom was paid to a slave owner to purchase the freedom of the slave. Jesus paid for our redemption with His death on the cross.

Chapter Three: Qualifications for church leadership are discussed in this chapter. Fifteen moral and ethical requirements are mentioned in verses 2–7. See *Offices.*

Chapter Four: Paul affirmed that "everything God created is good" (4:4 NIV). Some false teachers maintained that marriage and certain foods were wrong. Paul drew from the message of Genesis in which God affirmed everything He created was good! Mankind takes God's good creation and

T

corrupts it. The apostle reminded Timothy to be a "good minister of Christ Jesus" (4:6 NIV) and to "set an example for the believers in speech, in life, in love, in faith and in purity" (4:12 NIV).

Chapter Five: Paul gave practical instructions concerning the ministry of the church to various groups that comprise its membership.

Chapter Six: The teachers of false doctrine were motivated by "financial gain" (6:5 NIV). Paul warned in light of this fact and others that "the love of money is the root of all kinds of evil" (6:10 NIV).   *Mark E. Matheson*

2 TIMOTHY The second of Paul's Epistles to Timothy, pastor of the church in Ephesus. See *Letters; Paul; Timothy.*

Authorship The letter was the last letter of which we have a record written by Paul.

Date Paul wrote this letter from his jail cell during his second imprisonment in Rome. He was awaiting trial for his faith. It is clear that he felt he would not be released (4:6). If Paul was executed by Nero and if Nero was killed in A.D. 68, then Paul had to have been executed sometime before. The letter can be dated between A.D. 63–67.

Recipient Timothy was the recipient of Paul's letter. He had been the apostle's representative in the city of Ephesus for sometime.

Purpose The letter contains Paul's stirring words of encouragement and instruction to his young disciple. Paul longed to see Timothy (1:4) and asked him to come to Rome for a visit. It is generally believed that Timothy went. Paul asked him to come before winter (4:21) and bring the winter coat Paul left in Troas (4:13). Timothy was also asked to bring the scrolls and the parchments so Paul could read and study (4:13).

Outline
I. Salutation (1:1–2)
II. Thanksgiving (1:3–7)
III. Encouragement in the Face of Hardships (1:8–14)
IV. Encouragement in the Face of Desertions (1:15—2:13)
V. Contrasts in the Church (2:14–26)
VI. Godlessness in the Last Days (3:1–9)
VII. Paul's Instructions to Timothy (3:10—4:5)
VIII. Paul's Testimony (4:6–8)
IX. Conclusion (4:9–22)

Overview, Chapter One: Paul was reminded that Timothy's faith first lived in his grandmother Lois and in his mother Eunice (1:5). Paul had in reality become Timothy's father (1:2). Timothy may have been a naturally timid person. Because of this, Paul told him to minister with "a spirit of power" (1:7 NIV). The Holy Spirit empowers believers, but we should be careful to exercise this power in a "spirit . . . of love and of self-discipline" (1:7 NIV). Two men, Phygelus and Hermogenes, deserted Paul (1:15). Onesiphorus was a refreshing friend and not ashamed of Paul's chains (1:16).

Chapter Two: Paul urged Timothy to be strong in Jesus Christ. Paul used the metaphors of a good soldier, athlete, and a hard-working farmer when describing the Christian's calling. The purpose of that calling is so all "may obtain the salvation that is in Christ Jesus" (2:10 NIV). Timothy was to be one who "correctly handles the word of truth" (2:15 NIV) in the face of those who mishandled it. Hymenaeus (1 Tim. 1:20) and Philetus were singled out. They were teaching that the resurrection had already taken place and were destroying the faith of some (2:18).

Chapter Three: "The last days" are a reference to the second coming of Jesus. The days preceding His return will be "terrible." Characteristics of these last days have appeared in many different ages, but the times before Jesus' actual return will be even more intense. Paul listed eighteen characteristics of evil men in verses 2–5. He compared them to Jannes and Jambres who opposed Moses (3:8). Although these two individuals are not mentioned in the Old Testament, Jewish tradition maintains that these men were two Egyptian magicians who opposed Moses and Aaron. The evil and false teaching is to be overcome by the Holy Scripture (3:16–17).

Chapter Four: Paul further instructed Timothy to be prepared to "preach the Word" at all times. The need is paramount, for people will not always adhere to "sound doctrine" (4:3). Paul, drawing on the imagery of Numbers 28:24, compared his life to that of a "drink offering." This was poured on a sacrifice before it was offered. He was ready to depart this life and go to be with the Lord. He anticipated the "crown of righteousness" that awaited him (4:8). The letter closes with practical instructions and pastoral remarks for Timothy.
                                                  Mark E. Matheson

TIN See *Minerals and Metals.*

TINKLING ORNAMENTS Anklets making a tinkling noise as one walked. Part of the finery of the affluent women of Jerusalem (Isa. 3:16,18).

TIPHSAH (Tǐph' sah) Place name meaning, "passage, ford." *1.* City on the west bank of the Euphrates about 75 miles south of Carchemish, representing the northeastern limit of Solomon's kingdom (1 Kings 4:24). *2.* Site near Tirzah in Samaria (2 Kings 15:16), possibly a corruption of Tappuah, the reading of the earliest Greek translation which REB, RSV, TEV follow.

TIRAS (Tī răs) Division of the descendants of Japheth who are all seagoing peoples (Gen. 10:2; 1 Chron. 1:5). Traditionally, they have been related to Turscha, part of the sea peoples Rameses III (1198–1166 B.C.) fought. Some have identified them with the Etruscans of Italy.

TIRATHITES (Tī′ răth ītes) Family of Kenite scribes (1 Chron. 2:55).

TIRE KJV term meaning, "turban" (Ezek. 24:17,23).

TIRHAKAH (Tīr hā′ kah) Egyptian pharaoh of the twenty-fifth dynasty (689–664 B.C.) who supported Hezekiah's revolt against the Assyrian king Sennacherib (2 Kings 19:8–9; Isa. 37:9).

TIRHANAH (Tīr hā′ nah) Personal name of uncertain meaning. Son of Caleb and Maacah (1 Chron. 2:48).

TIRIA (Tīr ĭ á) Personal name meaning, "fear." Descendant and family of Judah (1 Chron. 4:16).

TIRSHATHA (Tīr shắ′ tha) A title of honor designating respect for an official, sometimes translated, "your excellence" (Ezra 2:63; Neh. 7:65,70; 8:9; 10:1).

TIRZAH (Tīr′ zah) Personal and place name meaning, "she is friendly." *1.* Daughter of Zelophehad who inherited part of tribal land allotment of Manasseh since her father had no sons.
2. Originally a Canaanite city noted for its beauty (Song of Sol. 6:4) but captured in the conquest of the Promised Land (Josh. 12:24). It became one of the early capitals of Israel when Jeroboam I established his residence there (1 Kings 14:17) and continued as the capital until Omri built Samaria (1 Kings 16:23–24). Archaeological discoveries, coupled with biblical references, suggest that Tirzah is to be identified with modern tell el-Fara, a tell of extraordinary size about seven miles northeast of Shechem. The area evidently was first occupied before 3000 B.C. and flourished, off and on, as a Canaanite city until its capture by Joshua between 1550 and 1200 B.C. It remained an Israelite city until the Assyrian conquest of 722 B.C. By 600 B.C., Tirzah was completely abandoned.

Hugh Tobias

TISHBITE (Tĭsh′ bīte) Resident of an unidentified village, Tishbe, used as a title of Elijah (1 Kings 17:1; 21:17,28; 2 Kings 1:3,8; 9:36). Tishbite is possibly a corruption of Jabeshite or a class designation (compare the Hebrew *toshab* which designates a resident alien, Lev. 25:6). See *Elijah.*

TITHE A tenth part, especially as offered to God. Abraham presented a tithe of war booty to the priest-king of Jerusalem, Melchizedek (Gen. 14:18–20). Jacob pledged to offer God a tithe of all his possessions upon his safe return (Gen. 28:22). The tithe was subject to a variety of legislation. Numbers 18:20–32 provides for support of the Levites and the priests through the tithe. The Deuteronomic code stipulated that the tithe of agricultural produce be used for a family feast at the sanctuary celebrating God's provision (Deut. 14:22–27). The same code stipulated the third year's tithe for care of the Levites, orphans, widows, and foreigners (Deut. 14:28–29). Some scholars think the differences in legislation reflect different uses of the tithe at various stages of Israel's history. The rabbis of the New Testament period, however, understood the laws as referring to three separate tithes: a Levitical tithe, a tithe spent celebrating in Jerusalem, and a charity tithe. Malachi 3:8 equates neglect of the tithe with robbing God. Jesus, however, warned that strict tithing must accompany concern for the more important demands of the law, namely, for just and merciful living (Matt. 23:23; Luke 11:42). See *Stewardship.*

TITIUS JUSTUS See *Justus.*

TITTLE See *Dot.*

TITUS (Tī′ tŭs) Gentile companion of Paul (Gal. 2:3) and recipient of the New Testament letter bearing his name.
Titus may have been converted by Paul who called him "my true son in our common faith" (Titus 1:4 NIV). As one of Paul's early associates, Titus accompanied the apostle and Barnabas to Jerusalem (Gal. 2:1), probably on the famine relief visit (Acts 11:28–30).
Though Acts does not mention Titus, he was quite involved in Paul's missionary activities as shown in the Pauline letters. He was evidently known to the Galatians (Gal. 2:1,3), possibly from the first missionary journey to that region. Titus also seems to have been a very capable person, called by Paul "my partner and fellow worker" (2 Cor. 8:23 NIV). He was entrusted with the delicate task of delivering Paul's severe letter (2 Cor. 2:1–4) to Corinth and correcting problems within the church there (2 Cor. 7:13–15). Titus' genuine concern for and evenhanded dealing with the Corinthians (2 Cor. 8:16–17; 12:18) no doubt contributed to his success which he reported in person to Paul, anxiously awaiting word in Macedonia (2 Cor. 2:13; 7:5–6,13–15). Paul responded by writing 2 Corinthians which Titus probably delivered (2 Cor. 8:6,16–18,23).
Paul apparently was released after his first Roman imprisonment and made additional journeys, unrecorded in Acts. One of these took him and Titus to Crete, where Titus remained behind to oversee and administer the church (Titus 1:5). It was to Crete that Paul wrote his letter, asking Titus to join him in Nicopolis on the west coast of Greece (Titus 3:12). Following Paul's subsequent reimprisonment, Titus was sent to Dalmatia (2 Tim. 4:10). According to church tradition, Ti-

tus was the first bishop of Crete. See *Crete.*
Daniel C. Browning, Jr.

TITUS, CAESAR (Tī′ tŭs) Roman emperor A.D. 79–81, eldest son of Vespasian.

Titus, like his father, was a soldier. He served in Germany and Britain and later in the Middle East. When Vespasian left his Middle East command to become emperor in A.D. 69, he left Titus in charge of crushing the Jewish revolt. In A.D. 70, his troops captured the Temple in Jerusalem. They took the last stronghold, Masada, in A.D. 73. His victory over the Jews was vividly depicted on the Triumphal Arch erected in Rome which still stands today.

Titus was deeply admired by his soldiers; when he later became emperor, the populace loved him. He was considered an honest ruler and an efficient administrator. An adherent of Stoic philosophy, he believed that the Roman emperor was the servant of the people. He and his father before him (the so-called Flavian emperors) struggled after the excesses of Nero to reestablish stability in the empire and in the government. They managed to return the empire to sound financial footing.

Titus was constantly plagued by the activities of his younger brother, Domitian. Even though he did not believe that Domitian was worthy to be his successor, he would not dispose of him. See *Jerusalem; Rome.* *Gary Poulton*

The Arch of Titus, emperor of the Roman Empire and son of Vespasian, in the city of Rome, Italy.

TITUS, EPISTLE TO Paul's letter to Titus, who was pastor of the church on the island of Crete.

Authorship Paul, "a servant of God and an apostle of Jesus Christ," (1:1 NIV) wrote this epistle to Titus, whom he described as "my true son in our common faith" (1:4 NIV).

Date The Epistle to Titus was written after Paul's first imprisonment in Rome. The approximate date is A.D. 63. It was written after Paul left Crete, but before he reached Nicopolis (3:12). It is difficult to determine the actual place where Paul wrote, though Rome and Corinth have been mentioned by various scholars. See *Titus.*

Purpose Paul wrote to encourage and instruct Titus in the face of opposition. This letter from the apostle would strengthen Titus' ability to minister because it would be received with the authority of Paul (2:15). Titus was to admonish the people to hold "sound doctrine" and to be "sound in faith" (1:9,13; 2:1–2). This theme of sound or healthy doctrine was also prominent in 1 and 2 Timothy. See *1 Timothy.*

Outline

I. Salutation (1:1–4)

II. Instructions Concerning Elders and False Teachers (1:5–16)

III. Instructions Concerning Christian Conduct (2:1–15)

IV. Instructions Concerning Believers in the World (3:1–8)

V. Concluding Instructions (3:9–15)

Overview, Chapter One: Paul wrote that a genuine knowledge of the truth leads to godliness in the life of the believer (1:1). Titus was to "straighten out" what was left unfinished. His first duty was to appoint elders. The qualifications listed in verses 6–9 are similar to those mentioned in 1 Timothy 3:1–7. False teachers threatened the church. He mentioned the "circumcision group" (1:10 NIV), a reference to converts to the Christian faith from Judaism who apparently taught that the rite of circumcision was necessary to be a complete Christian. This group of teachers and all who sought to lead the people astray were corrupt in their minds and detestable in their actions (1:15–16).

Chapter Two: Paul urged Titus to teach "sound doctrine" to correct the false teaching. Proper teaching would lead to proper conduct in the lives of believers. Titus was to be an example to all (2:7). His teaching was to be characterized by "integrity," "seriousness," and a "soundness of speech" (2:7–8 NIV), so that the false teachers could "have nothing bad to say about us" (2:8 NIV). The basis of godly living is "the grace of God that brings salvation" (2:11 NIV). Evidence of receiving God's grace and salvation is a transformation of one's life. The anticipation of the return of Christ is called "the blessed hope" (2:13 NIV). The hope of His return should motivate us to godly living.

Chapter Three: Paul reminded the believers "to be subject to rulers and authorities" (3:1 NIV). The subjection is to be voluntary because the institution of government was created by God. The believers were to treat all persons with consideration and humility. Paul reminded them of their past and of God's kindness and love. His kindness and love were "supremely manifested in the appearance of our Savior" (3:4 NIV).

Our salvation is not because of "righteous things we had done, but because of his mercy" (3:5 NIV). Salvation is likened to the "washing of rebirth and renewal by the Holy Spirit" (3:5 NIV). The washing of rebirth is a metaphor of a divine inner act. This act is symbolized by believers' baptism. Renewal refers to the "making new" by the Holy Spirit. Rebirth takes place at salvation, and that renewal is a lifetime process. All of this results in our justification or being declared righteous and in making us heirs with Christ of eternal life.

The letter concludes with some practical instructions for Titus. Zenas, the lawyer, and Apollos probably delivered the letter to Titus (3:13). See *Apollos; Circumcision; Holy Spirit; Paul; Salvation.* *Mark E. Matheson*

TIZITE (Tī′ zīte) Title of Joha, one of David's thirty elite warriors (1 Chron. 11:45), designating his hometown or home region which is otherwise unknown.

TOAH (Tō′ ah) Personal name perhaps meaning, "humility." A Kohathite Levite (1 Chron. 6:34). The parallel lists read Nahath (1 Chron. 6:26) and Tohu (1 Sam. 1:1).

TOB (Tŏb) Place name meaning, "good." Syrian city in southern Hauran to which Jephthah fled from his brothers (Judg. 11:3–5). Tob contributed troops to an unsuccessful alliance against David (2 Sam. 10:6–13). Tob is perhaps identical with Tabeel (Isa. 7:6). The site is perhaps et-Taiyibeh about twelve miles east of Ramoth-gilead near the source of the Yarmuk River.

TOBADONIJAH (Tŏb ăd o nī′ jah) Personal name meaning, "Yah, my Lord, is good." Levite whom Jehoshaphat sent to teach the people of Judah (2 Chron. 17:8). The name is perhaps a combination of the two preceding names in the list.

TOBIAH (Tō bī′ ah) Personal name meaning, "Yah is good." *1.* One of the major adversaries to Nehemiah's rebuilding efforts at Jerusalem, Tobiah was a practicing Jew who lived in a residence chamber in the Temple. He is called an "Ammonite" (Neh. 2:10,19) probably because his family fled to that territory at the destruction of Jerusalem. He enjoyed aristocratic favor and had the title "servant" bestowed on him by the Persian ruler. He opposed the rebuilding of Jerusalem because it would weaken his political authority in the area. Tobiah allied with Sanballat and Geshem in trying to thwart Nehemiah.

2. A returned exile who apparently brought a gift of gold from Babylon for the Jerusalem community. Zechariah used him as a witness for his crowning of Joshua, the high priest, and to preserve the crowns in the Temple (Zech. 6:9–14).

3. Ancestor of clan who returned from Exile but could not show they were Israelites (Ezra 2:60).

TOBIJAH (Tō bī′ jah) Alternate form of Tobiah. Levite whom Jehoshaphat sent to teach the people (2 Chron. 17:8).

TOCHEN (Tō′ chĕn) Place name meaning, "measure." An unidentified village in Simeon (1 Chron. 4:32). The parallel lists in Joshua 15:42; 19:7 have Ether.

TOGARMAH Son of Gomer and name of a region of Asia Minor (Gen. 10:3; 1 Chron. 1:6; compare Beth-togarmah, Ezek. 38:6) inhabited by his descendants. Togarmah was famed for its horses (Ezek. 27:14). This site is likely modern Gürün 70 miles west of Malatya or an area in Armenia.

TOHU (Tō′ hū) Ancestor of Samuel (1 Sam. 1:1). Parallel lists read Nahath (1 Chron. 6:26) and Toah (6:34) in the corresponding position.

TOI (Tō′ ī) Personal name meaning, "error." King of Hammath on the Orontes who sent tribute to David following his defeat of their mutual foe, Hadadezer of Zobah (2 Sam. 8:9–11; Tou, 1 Chron. 18:9–10).

TOKEN KJV term meaning, "sign" (Gen. 9:12–17; Pss. 65:8; 135:9). See *Sign.*

TOKHATH (Tŏk′ hăth) Alternate form of Tikvah (2 Chron. 34:22).

TOLA (Tō′ là) Personal name meaning, "crimson worm." *1.* Issachar's firstborn son (Gen. 46:13; Num. 26:23; 1 Chron. 7:1–2). *2.* Judge who governed Israel for twenty-three years from Shamir, likely at or near Samaria (Judg. 10:1).

TOLAD (Tō′ lăd) Alternate form of Eltolad (1 Chron. 4:29).

TOLAITE (Tō′ là īte) Division of Issachar descended from Tola (Num. 26:23–25).

TOLL See *Publican; Taxes; Tribute.*

TOMB OF JESUS According to the New Testament accounts, the tomb of Jesus was located in a garden in the place where Jesus was crucified

(John 19:41) outside the city walls of Jerusalem (John 19:20). It was a "new tomb" which had been "hewn out in the rock" by Joseph of Arimathea (Matt. 27:60; compare Luke 23:50–56) who had apparently prepared it for his own family's use. It was not uncommon for the well-to-do to prepare such a tomb in advance because of the difficulty of digging graves in the rocky ground around Jerusalem. The tomb was large enough for someone to sit inside (Mark 16:5; compare John 20:11–12) and required that one stoop to look inside and enter (John 20:5–6,11; compare Luke 24:12). A great rolling stone sealed the entrance (Matt. 27:60; Mark 15:46; 16:3).

This description suggests a typical Jewish tomb of the Herodian period consisting of (1) an antechamber, (2) a slow doorway which could be sealed with a stone (in many cases a rolling stone fitted into a groove or track so that the tomb could be opened and closed by rolling the stone back and forth in front of the doorway), and (3) a passageway leading to a rectangular-shaped tomb chamber. Here the body (having been wrapped in a linen cloth) could be laid lengthwise in either a rectangular, horizontal, oven-shaped shaft driven back into the vertical rock face measuring 78 × 25 × 20 inches or laid on a simple rock shelf cut laterally into the rock with a vaulted arch over it. The sequence of events narrated in the Gospel accounts (especially John 20:5–6) would seem to indicate that Jesus' tomb had this vaulted arch.

The Garden Tomb is one site offered by tradition as the burial place of Jesus' body.

The traditional site of the tomb of Jesus is marked by the Church of the Holy Sepulchre which stands over the site of a first-century rock quarry which in Jesus' day was outside the city walls of Jerusalem and in which other typical first century tombs have been discovered. An alternative site known as the "the garden tomb" (adjacent to "Gordon's Calvary") and containing a tomb of the type common to the Byzantine period (A.D. 324–640) was identified in 1883.

Hulitt Gloer

TONGS Pinchers for holding coals (1 Kings 7:49; 2 Chron. 4:21; Isa. 6:6). KJV used tongs at Exodus 25:38; Numbers 4:9 where modern translations read snuffers (NAS, NRSV) or wicktrimmers (NIV).

TONGUE The organ of speech and then the language spoken (Jer. 5:15) and the people or nation speaking (Isa. 66:18). The tongue was seen to express the true nature since speech was viewed as more than just a verbal phenomenon. It was seen as the expression of a person's true nature (Pss. 64:2–3; 45:1; Prov. 10:20; 17:20). The wisdom writings of the Old Testament stressed the practical results of the use of the tongue for the individual's life (Prov. 12:18; 18:21; 21:6; 21:23; 25:23; 26:28; 28:23). Like a bit in a horse's mouth or the rudder of a ship, the tongue could control the direction of a person's life (Jas. 3:3–8). Since the tongue reveals what is in one's heart, its use had ethical conse-

quences whether for good or bad (Pss. 34:13; 37:30; 109:2; 120:2; 140:2–3; Isa. 59:3).

The tongue was seen to play a central role in the expression of a person's religious commitment. The tongue could be used to praise God (Pss. 35:28; 51:14; 71:24; Rom. 14:11; Phil. 2:11). On the other hand, the tongue could cause separation from God (Job 15:4–5; Pss. 39:1; 78:35–37). The potential for good or bad which is part of human nature is actualized through the tongue (Jas. 3:9–10).

The word *tongue* is used, of course, in the basic sense of the term to refer to the organ of eating and drinking (Judg. 7:5; Isa. 41:17). *Tongue* is, also, used figuratively to refer to objects in the material world which resemble the tongue in shape (Isa. 11:15).

See *Spiritual Gifts; Tongues, Gift of.*

Jeff Cranford

TONGUES, GIFT OF Spiritual gift involving ability to speak in foreign language(s) not previously studied or to respond to experience of the Holy Spirit by uttering sounds which those whithout the gift of interpretation could not understand. At Pentecost the church received the gift to communicate the gospel in foreign languages (Acts 2; compare 10:44–46; 19:6). God gave His Spirit to all His people to witness and prophesy. See *Pentecost.* In Corinth some members of the church uttered sounds the rest of the congregation did not understand (1 Cor. 12–14). This led to controversy and division. Paul tried to unite the church, assuring the church that there are different gifts but only one Spirit (1 Cor. 12:4–11).

TOOLS Implements or instruments used with the hands for agricultural, construction, commercial, or craft purposes.

Materials In the earliest periods, tools were made of stone, especially flint. An effective cutting surface was achieved by chipping off flakes along the edge of the shaped stone. The first metal tools were of copper, which proved to be too soft for most applications. It was soon found that much harder tools could be made from bronze, an alloy of copper and tin. Bronze, like copper, could be melted and poured into molds before final shaping by a smith. The hardest tools were made of iron (Deut. 27:5; 1 Kings 6:5–7), which required much higher temperatures to smelt. Iron only came into use in Canaan around 1200 B.C., about the time of the Israelite settlement. Handles and other parts of certain tools were made of wood, leather, bone, or ivory. See *Minerals and Metals.*

Knives One of the most common of tools is the knife. The flint knives of earlier periods continued in use even after metal became widespread. It has been suggested that the command to use flint knives for circumcision (Josh. 5:2 NIV) reflects a taboo on using new technology for ancient rites.

The winnowing fork was a tool to aid the farmer in separating chaff from the grains of wheat.

The real reason, however, is probably more practical: flint knives kept a sharp edge longer than metal blades. Nevertheless, bronze knives became the standard for general use prior to the Israelite monarchy. The blade was cast in a stone mold, and handles of wood were usually attached by a tang or rivets. Iron knives, which became popular during the Israelite monarchy, were made in a similar fashion.

The knife served various purposes and was known in different forms. The average knife in Palestine was between 6 and 10 inches, but a mold has been found to produce 16-inch blades. These would have been used for general cutting and butchering (Gen. 22:6; Judg. 19:29). A smaller version used by Jehoiakim to cut up Jeremiah's scroll (Jer. 36:23; KJV, NRSV, "penknife"; NIV, "scribe's knife") is represented by a Hebrew word elsewhere used for razors (Num. 6:5; Ezek. 5:1). The latter (Judg. 13:5; 16:17; 1 Sam. 1:11) were evidently quite sharp, as they are used as symbols of God's judgment (Isa. 7:20) and the cutting power of the tongue (Ps. 52:2).

Agricultural Tools Plows had basically the same design from the earliest models known down to those used in the present day in the Near East. The handles, crossbar, and other structural parts were of wood, while the plow point, or plowshare, needed to be of harder material to penetrate the ground. The earliest plowshares were of bronze which was only slowly replaced by iron following the Israelite settlement of Canaan. Early Iron Age levels at several archaeological sites in Palestine have produced examples of both types. Plowshares were elongated blades with a pointed end for cutting into the ground and the other end rolled like a pipe to fit on the wooden shaft. Plows were pulled by animals which were prodded with a goad, a wooden stick fitted with a metal tip (Judg. 3:31; 1 Sam. 13:21; Eccl. 12:11). On hilly or rocky terrain which was difficult to plow, the ground was broken using a hoe (Isa. 7:25 NIV; KJV, "mattock"). A similar tool, the mattock (1 Sam. 13:21), was also used for digging chores. It is probably incorrectly translated as "plowshares" in the famous prophetic passages about the tools of war and peace (Isa. 2:4; Mic. 4:3; Joel 3:10). Just prior to the monarchy, the Philistines, perhaps holding a monopoly on iron technology, forced the Israelites to come to them for sharpening of agricultural tools. The charge in silver was a pim, two-thirds of a shekel, for sharpening plowshares and mattocks and one-third of a shekel for smaller tools (1 Sam. 13:19–22). See *Weights and Measures.*

The reaping of standing grain was done with a sickle (Deut. 16:9; 23:25; Jer. 50:16), a small tool with a handle and curved blade. Sickles consisting of several serrated flint segments fitted into a shaft of bone or hollowed out wood were typical of the Canaanite culture. In Israelite and New Testament times, sickles had metal blades and short wooden handles. The sickle is used as a symbol of God's judgment (Joel 3:13) and the ingathering of the saints (Mark 4:29; Rev. 14:14–19). A tool which resembled the sickle, but with a broader and shorter blade, was the "pruning hook" (Isa. 2:4; Mic. 4:3; Joel 3:10). It was a type of knife used for pruning and harvesting grape vines (Isa. 18:5).

Building Tools The Old Testament mentions several different types of axes used in various hewing chores. The largest ax (Isa. 10:15) was used for felling trees (Deut. 19:5; 20:19) and quarrying stone (1 Kings 6:7). This type of ax was mentioned as a stone cutting tool in the Siloam Tunnel inscription in Jerusalem. See *Siloam.* A smaller ax was used for lighter jobs (Judg. 9:48; 1 Sam. 13:20–21; Ps. 74:5; Jer. 46:22). The Hebrew word used for axehead literally means "iron," indicating its material (Deut. 19:5; 2 Kings 6:5; Isa. 10:34). Trimming was done with a different tool (Jer. 10:3 REB; NIV, "chisel"), perhaps an adze with its cutting edge perpendicular to the handle. Small hand axes or hatchets were also known (Ps. 74:6 KJV; NRSV, "hammers"; REB, "pick"). A single word is used for axes in the New Testament (Matt. 3:10; Luke 3:9).

Wood and stone were also cut using saws (2 Sam. 12:31; 1 Kings 7:9; 1 Chron. 20:3; Isa. 10:15). Single and double-handled varieties are pictured in Egyptian tomb paintings. Bronze was used for the blades in the earlier periods, and iron, in the later. According to an apocryphal work (the Ascension of Isaiah), the prophet Isaiah was martyred by being sawn in two (compare Heb. 11:37).

Detail work was marked out using a "line" and "compass" (Isa. 44:13; NIV, "chisels" and "compasses"). Various types of measuring tools, lines, and chisels have been found in Egyptian tombs. Plumb lines were used quite early in Egypt and Palestine for determining verticality and levels in construction. The true levels determined by the measuring line and the plumb line are compared to the justice and righteousness God required of Israel and Judah (2 Kings 21:13; KJV, "plummet";

Isa. 28:17; Amos 7:7–8).

Hammers (Isa. 44:12; Jer. 10:4) were originally stone pounders, but in the Bronze Age holes were often bored for the insertion of a handle. Egyptian paintings show the use of broad wooden mallets not unlike those still used today in sculpture work. The "planes" used in shaping (Isa. 44:13) were probably chisels (as in the NIV). Chisels were used for rough and detail work in both wood and stone. Holes were made with awls (Ex. 21:6; Deut. 15:17) or drills.

Industrial Tools Special tools were used in the work of various industries. Early potters used wooden tools to help shape their handmade vessels. A considerable advance came with the invention of the pottery wheel (Jer. 18:3). See *Pottery.*

Weavers conducted their craft on devices called looms. A number of tools were used to assist in the weaving process. In some types of weaving, the horizontal weft threads were "beaten" in with a flat wooden stick. The weaving of patterns required picks and combs to manipulate and press up the threads. These were usually made of bone, less often of ivory or wood. See *Spinning and Weaving.*

Metalworking required unique tools as well. A bellows was needed to bring a fire to the high temperatures required for smelting ore. Hand operated bellows are shown in an Egyptian tomb painting of Semitic nomads from about the time of Abraham. These were used in small furnaces equipped with nozzles of clay to withstand the extreme heat. Molds were used to shape molten metal into tools, weapons, and other items. Metal smiths also used a variety of tongs, clamps, and hammers (Isa. 44:12), and the like.

Daniel C. Browning, Jr.

TOPAZ See *Minerals and Metals.*

TOPHEL (Tō′ phĕl) Place near the site of Moses' farewell speech to Israel (Deut. 1:1), identified with et-Tafileh about fifteen miles southeast of the Dead Sea between Kerak and Petra. It may represent the name of a territory rather than a city.

TOPHET (Tō′ phĕt) Name for a place in the Hinnom Valley outside Jerusalem derived from Aramaic or Hebrew meaning, "fireplace," but altered by Hebrew scribes to mean "shameful thing" because of the illicit worship carried on there (Jer. 7:31–32; KJV, "Tophet"). Child sacrifice was practiced at Tophet, leading the prophet to declare a slaughter of people there when God would come in vengeance (Jer. 19:6–11). See *Hinnom, Valley of.*

TOPHETH (Tō′ pheth) Modern translations' spelling of Tophet.

TORAH (Tō′ rah) Hebrew word normally translated "law" which eventually became a title for the Pentateuch, the first five books of the Old Testament.

Old Testament Though universally translated "law" in the KJV, *torah* also carries the sense of "teaching" or "instruction," as reflected in more recent translations (Job 22:22; Ps. 78:1; Prov. 1:8; 4:2; 13:14; Isa. 30:9). The meaning, *law,* is certainly present in the Old Testament. *Torah,* for example, is used in connection with terms for requirements, commands, and decrees (Gen. 26:5; Ex. 18:16). The Torah was given to Moses (Ex. 24:12) and commanded to be kept (Ex. 16:28; Deut. 17:19; Ezek. 44:24).

Within the Book of Deuteronomy, *torah* is used to represent the body of the Deuteronomic code (Deut. 4:8; 30:10; 32:46), that is, the essence of Israel's responsibilities under the covenant. Subsequent Old Testament writings continue to speak of Torah as "The Law" in this sense (Isa. 5:24; Jer. 32:23; 44:10; Dan. 9:11), often as "the book of the law," the "law of Moses," or a combination (Josh. 1:8; 8:31–32,34; 2 Kings 14:6). The "book of the law" found in the Temple which fueled Josiah's reforms (2 Kings 22:8–13) is often regarded to be roughly equivalent to the Book of Deuteronomy. By the time of Ezra and Nehemiah "the book of the law of Moses" (Neh. 8:1) included more material than the Deuteronomic code. Ezra cited the "law which the Lord had

Jewish rabbis conversing before a reverently opened and elaborately decorated scroll of the Torah.

commanded by Moses" concerning the feast of booths, which is prescribed in Leviticus (22:33–43). Eventually the name *Torah* came to be applied to the entire Pentateuch, the five books traditionally ascribed to Moses: Genesis, Exodus, Leviticus, Numbers, and Deuteronomy. In rabbinical Judaism, the scope of Torah is sometimes expanded to include all of the Scriptures or even the entirety of God's revelation.

New Testament During New Testament times the limits on the Old Testament canon were being finalized. The Jews began to think of their Scriptures as consisting of three sections: the Torah (Law), the Prophets, and the Writings (compare Luke 24:44). The books of Moses were considered "law" despite the fact that a considerable amount of their material is not legalistic in nature. The Torah was unquestionably considered the most important division of the Scriptures. The Sadducees, in fact, accepted only the Torah as inspired Scripture. The same is true of the Samaritans who considered themselves God's true chosen people.

In the New Testament period, Torah was more than merely a section of the Scriptures; it became central to Judaism. The will of God was seen as embodied in the observance of the law. Pious Jews, therefore, needed some elaboration on the commands contained in the Torah to determine more precisely their obligation, and the interpretation of various passages became the subject of much debate. The traditions of the Pharisees went far beyond the bounds of the law as spelled out in the Torah. These traditions became for them the oral Torah, considered given to Moses at Mount Sinai to accompany the written law. Jesus scathingly denounced the Pharisees' placing their tradition above the intent of the law (Mark 7:8–13). Jesus never denied the authority of the Torah, but denounced the elevation of ritual concerns above "weightier matters of the law: justice and mercy and faith" (Matt. 23:23 NRSV). Some of the precepts of the law, according to Jesus, were provided because of humanity's nature and fall short of God's perfect will (Matt. 5:33–37; 19:8–9). For true believers, Jesus demanded a commitment which went far beyond the supposed righteousness gained by keeping the law (Luke 18:18–23).

The apostle Paul preached justification by faith rather than by the keeping of the law. Thus, he had much to say about Torah. Torah, according to Paul, would lead to life if it were actually practiced (Rom. 10:5), but such practice is impossible (Rom. 3:20). The effect of the law has been to manifest a knowledge of sin and bring about its increase (Rom. 3:20; 5:20; 7:5,7–11; 1 Cor. 15:56). Mankind was thus consigned to sin and God's resulting wrath (Rom. 4:14; Gal. 3:22) which set the stage for the revelation of God's grace through Christ (Rom. 3:21–26; Gal. 3:22–25). For Paul, Torah epitomized the old covenant,

with the law written on stone (2 Cor. 3:7). In the superior new covenant, the law is in the Spirit (2 Cor. 3:6), written on the hearts of believers (compare Jer. 31:33). Believers are not subject to the Torah (Gal. 5:18), but by walking "in the Spirit" (Rom. 8:4; Gal. 5:16) they produce fruits which transcend (Gal. 5:22–25) and fulfill the essence of the law (Rom. 13:8–10; Gal. 5:14; compare Matt. 22:37–40). See *Law; Pentateuch.*
Daniel C. Browning, Jr.

TORCH Long pole with cloths dipped in oil wrapped around one end used as a light. The Greek *lampas* is generally rendered torch (John 18:3; Rev. 4:5; 8:10), unless the context suggests the translation "lamp" (Acts 20:8). The lamps of the wise and foolish virgins (Matt. 25:1–8) were perhaps torches.

TORTOISE See *Animals.*

TOSEPHTA The Hebrew term *tosafah* and its Aramaic parallel *tosephta* denote a collection of additional rabbinic opinion arranged in the order of the Mishnah of Judah ha-Nasi. It may be regarded as a collected appendix to the Mishnah. In its current form, the Tosephta was probably edited about the end of the fourth century A.D. It was compiled in Palestine at about the same time as the Jerusalem Talmud. The intent of the editor seems to have been to "update" or further supplement the Mishnah with reference to new case law developed over the two centuries that separated the two works. Its existence shows the development in the legal system of the rabbis of Palestine as they sought to adapt the law orally to new and changing social and religious conditions. See *Mishnah; Talmud.*   *Stephenson Humphries-Brooks*

TOU (Tō′ ū) Alternate form of Toi (1 Chron. 18:9–10).

TOW Short, broken fibers of flax, known to be easily broken and highly flammable, used as a figure for weakness and transience (Judg. 16:9; Isa. 1:31; 43:17).

TOWER A tall edifice erected so watchmen could guard pastures, vineyards, and cities. Towers ranged from small one-room structures to entire fortresses. Archaeological remains confirm the wide usage of towers from the earliest times. Most were made of stones, although some wooden towers have been unearthed. The word is used figuratively of God's salvation in 2 Samuel 22:51, indicating the strength of the Lord's action. For references in Jeremiah 6:27, see *Assayer.*

TOWN See *Cities and Urban Life.*

TRACHONITIS (Trăch o nī′ tĭs) Place name

Ruins of the city walls of the ancient city of Perga showing the remains of a defense tower.

meaning "heap of stones." A political and geographic district in northern Palestine on the east side of the Jordan River (Luke 3:1). Its terrain was rugged and best suited to raising sheep and goats. The area was almost totally devoid of timber. During John the Baptist's ministry Trachonitis was ruled by Philip, the brother of Herod Antipas. Known as Bashan in the Old Testament (Amos 4:1), it was just south of Damascus. See *Bashan; Herods; Philip.*

TRADE See *Commerce.*

TRADITION Little thought is generally given by the beginning Bible student to the consideration of how the written text of the Bible came to us. If any thought is given at all, it is generally assumed that God handed the text to an individual (or group of individuals), and it has thus been passed on to us. A more thorough study of the biblical text, however, has led to the conclusion that behind a great deal of the written text of the Bible stands a long stream of tradition. Jeremiah admonished his people to look for the ancient ways in order to find the way of properly living with God (Jer. 6:16). His proclamation was that their long-standing tradition should have offered a proper guide for life.

Oral tradition appears to be the foundation of many written texts. A study of the New Testament helps us to realize that it was at least ten to twenty years after the death of Jesus before any of the Gospels were written. Prior to the writing of the first Gospel, the sermons of the apostles and many of the letters of Paul had been written. Yet during that time, the early Christians clearly knew a great deal about the life and ministry of Jesus. This information was passed on by word of mouth, becoming the traditions upon which the writers of the Gospels ultimately drew. Paul frequently referred to the traditions which he had received and which he passed on to the churches (1 Cor. 11:23–25; 15:3–7). He also pointed out some things which he had not received from tradition (compare Gal. 1:11–12.)

The evidence for ancient oral traditions is even stronger in the Old Testament. The entire collection of the books of the prophets is made up of material which was originally spoken (preached). It generally appears that their sermons were passed on and remembered orally for a considerable period of time before they were ever written. Jeremiah had obviously preached for many years before his sermons were first written. At that time, he employed Baruch the scribe to record his sermons as the prophet dictated them (Jer. 36:1-4). Isaiah also appeared to have ordered his disciples to collect his messages for some future time (Isa. 8:16). This evidence can be multiplied many times.

Since the work of Herman Gunkel in the early part of the twentieth century, most Old Testament scholars have almost universally accepted the idea that many Old Testament texts had a long history of oral transmission before they were ever written. To a contemporary student, such a thought often appears to make such texts suspect. However, anyone who has tried to hurry through a favorite bedtime story with a child will recognize that audiences familiar with a story ensure its accurate transmission.

It appears that the narratives were first used around campfires or in religious rituals. Either type of use is highly structured and deeply tinged with emotions which would guard the accuracy of their use. At the same time, even as a contemporary interpreter will take an old text and apply it to a new situation, these old traditions apparently were frequently retold to apply to the new situations which the people of Israel faced. (A comparative study of 1 and 2 Kings and 1 and 2 Chronicles makes it appear that such may also have been done with written texts as well.)

Oral traditions appear to have had their origin in the life needs of the community of faith. The German term *Sitz im Leben* (life situation) is normally applied to this. The point is simply that oral traditions arose, were preserved, and were passed on because the life needs of the community were being met. This recognizes that people hold on to those things which are meaningful and meet their life needs. (God used processes which met human needs to preserve His inspired Word.) The verses of Scripture which a person memorizes and treasures are held onto for precisely the same reasons.

Such traditions, then, clearly had their origin in historical situations. The children of Abraham held onto the stories of their ancestors because they heard God speak to them through those events, guiding them in facing similar situations. They also held on to other parts of the story as the basis for their faith that God's promised blessings were ultimately going to be fulfilled for them.

On the other hand, other types of materials were preserved because they aided in the human approach to God in worship. Here again, it was the human need to worship and serve which gave the basis for preserving and passing on material which helped them meet those needs.

These ancient traditions, then, were inspired by God to meet human need in real life experiences. They were preserved and passed on precisely because they had a very specific life setting, helping people to face life as it was with the strength of God to sustain them every day. Such traditions made it easier to understand what God was doing because they could hear Him speak through what He had done in other life situations.

Furthermore, study of these ancient traditions makes it obvious that materials which were used in similar life situations were generally preserved and passed on in similar "literary" forms. The use of common forms or outlines for similar kinds of material made it even easier to maintain the accuracy of transmitting the traditions.

The traditions of Israel and of the early Christians were obviously used by the worshiping communities as a means of maintaining and transmitting their faith. In the Old Testament these were apparently collected and preserved at the various shrines where Israel worshiped. In the New Testament, this was done among the many scattered congregations.

A comparison of Psalms 14 and 53 can be seen to illustrate this process. The two psalms are almost wholly identical. Yet the name for God in Psalm 14 is Lord (Hebrew, *Yahweh*) and in Psalm 53, God (Hebrew, *Elohim;* compare NAS). It appears from other studies that Yahweh was preferred in Judah and at the Jerusalem Temple while Elohim was preferred in the Northern Kingdom of Israel, possibly at Bethel. It appears that this particular psalm was a favorite among Hebrew worshipers. However, when the kingdom divided, one nation preserved it with one divine name while the other used the tradition to meet their own particular needs with the other name for God. Each worshiping community was inspired to use the same hymn to worship God, but they used it with their own particular name for God. The same types of processes appear to be demonstrable in other instances.

Further, such worshiping communities also appear to have preserved those particular traditions which were most meaningful to them. Thus Jerusalem, the City of David, appears to have had major interests in the Davidic traditions. Bethel, on the other hand, was significantly involved in the life of Jacob. It appears that traditions concerning Jacob had a very special meaning to those who worshiped at Bethel. Paul clearly referred to conflicting traditions and allegiances at Corinth (1 Cor. 1:10-12). Such conflicts arose as the worshiping community sought to assimilate a variety of traditions into one tradition.

Obviously, in the Old Testament all the traditions of the various worship centers and worshiping communities ultimately were assimilated in Jerusalem. In the ongoing history of the nation, all other shrines ultimately passed away as the nation finally centered its entire worship experience upon the Jerusalem Temple. The New Testament experience was different in that the Christians' worship did not shrink inward to one place but spread outward to many. It was the New Testament itself which became the focal point of New Testament traditions rather than any specific worship center.

Oral traditions were recorded as written traditions at certain critical points in history. This is particularly true in the Old Testament era. It appears that the worshiping communities were generally quite content to use their traditions in predominantly oral form until a crisis arose which threatened their continuity. This contentment with things as they were was probably bolstered by the fact that reading and writing were skills limited primarily to the professional scribes in Old Testament times. Everyone could handle oral tradition, only a few could handle written traditions.

However, when historical crises arose which threatened the continued stability or existence of a worship center or of a worshiping community, then it appears that the traditions were committed to writing lest they be lost. Such situations arose when the nation divided following the reign of Solomon, when the Northern Kingdom fell before Assyria, and when Jerusalem fell under the onslaught of Babylon. At such times, there appear to have been large scale writings of traditions.

It appears that the New Testament traditions were written under the impetus of historical crises, but these were of a different nature. The Gospels were apparently written when those who had known Jesus in person began to die. There appears to have been a fear that the traditions would be lost unless they were recorded for future believers. Other New Testament materials were written to meet the crises of missions and evangelism. More people could read and write by this time. The written materials allowed people to receive the good news who had never heard a Christian preacher. As always, the handling of these materials was done under the inspiration of God's Holy Spirit.

The study of the transmission of these ancient traditions allows us to perceive the human dimension of the transmission of biblical materials as well as come to a deeper understanding of the nature of God's inspiration. The common characteristics of material preserved at specific worship centers allow us to identify many of their interests, concerns, and historical roots. On the other hand, the differences between traditions sometimes give an even greater insight into the basic human issues with which those who transmitted particular traditions were concerned. As an illus-

tration, note that Mark says of the woman who had been plagued by the issue of blood that she had spent all her money on physicians yet had steadily gotten worse (Mark 5:25–26). Luke, on the other hand, left out that bit of a sarcastic criticism of doctors (Luke 8:43). The difference in the way these two writers handled the same tradition reveals Luke's human sympathetic concern with doctors. This adds depth to our understanding of the man who was himself a physician.

This kind of study has left us with both a deeper understanding of the practices by which God has inspired, recorded, and preserved His Word and a greater awareness of the fact that God worked with human beings who had all of the feelings and concerns to which humanity is heir. The biblical traditions are rooted and grounded in the divine meeting of human need. They have their basis in real-life situations and were preserved by a living, worshiping community. This allows these same traditions better to meet present human need in the real-life situations of contemporary communities of faith. See *Bible, Formation and Canon of; Inspiration; Revelation.* Robert L. Cate

TRAIN KJV used train to refer to the part of a robe that trails behind the wearer (Isa. 6:1).

TRANCE Translation of the Greek term which literally means a change of place. The term came to mean a mental state of a person who experienced an intense emotional reaction to stimuli that were perceived as originating outside the person, the results of which were visual or auditory sensations or other impressions of the senses.

Trance is descriptive of an experience in which a person received a revelation by supernatural means (Acts 10:10; 11:5; 22:17). In these instances, the author of Acts, in reference to the experiences of Peter and Paul, seemed to be interested in showing that the trance was only a vehicle for a revelation from God. Luke illustrated that the trances that Peter and Paul experienced "happened" to them and were not self induced. The distinctions between "trance," "dream" and "vision" are not always clear. See *Ecstasy; Prophets.* James Newell

TRANSFIGURATION, THE The transformation of Jesus in His appearance with Moses and Elijah before Peter, James, and John (Matt. 17:1–13; Mark 9:1–13; Luke 9:28–36; compare 2 Peter 1:16–18).

The Accounts The event took place shortly after the confession at Caesarea Philippi, the first passion prediction, and a discourse on the cost of discipleship. Jesus took Peter, James, and John to a mountain where the event took place. Jesus' personal appearance and that of His garments were changed. Moses and Elijah appeared and talked with Jesus. Peter said it was good to be there, and they should build three booths. A cloud came over them, and God spoke from the cloud identifying Jesus as His Son (compare the voice at the baptism) and commanding the disciples to hear Him. When the cloud lifted, Jesus was alone with the disciples, who were afraid. Jesus told the disciples to tell no one.

Aside from minor differences in wording, Mark alone states that Jesus' garments became so white that no bleacher could brighten them and that Peter did not know what to say. Also Mark alone has no reference to a change in Jesus' face. Matthew alone indicates that God expressed His pleasure with Jesus, that the disciples fell on their faces, and that Jesus touched them to get them up. Instead of the six days of Matthew and Mark, Luke has about eight days. He alone indicated that Jesus and the disciples were praying, that Moses and Elijah conversed with Jesus about His coming death, that the disciples were sleepy, and that they saw Jesus' glory. Luke alone has "chosen" rather than "beloved Son." In Matthew, Jesus is addressed as Lord, in Mark as Rabbi, and in Luke as Master.

The Nature of the Event It has often been claimed that the story is a misplaced resurrection appearance; but it is Moses and Elijah, not Jesus, who appear, and there is no reference to them or a voice from heaven in any other resurrection account. Others have claimed that the transfiguration was not an objective but a visionary experience. This is possible, but there is no more of the miraculous in three different disciples actually having similar visions than in a historical event, which is certainly what the writers described.

The Place The traditional site is Mount Tabor in lower Galilee, but it is not a high mountain (only 1,850 feet) and was probably fortified and inaccessible in Jesus' day. Much more likely is Mount Hermon (9,100 feet) to the north of Caesarea Philippi. See *Hermon.*

Meaning A mountain in the Bible is often a place of revelation. Moses and Elijah represented the law and the prophets respectively, which testify to but must give way to Jesus. (The latter is the reason why Peter's suggestion was improper.) Moses and Elijah themselves were heralds of the Messiah (Deut. 18:15; Mal. 4:5–6). The three booths suggest the Feast of the Tabernacles which symbolizes a new situation, a new age. Clouds represent divine presence. The close connection of the transfiguration with the confession and passion prediction is significant. The Messiah must suffer; but glorification and enthronement, not suffering, is His ultimate fate. These involve resurrection, ascension, and return in glory. The disciples needed the reassurance of the transfiguration as they contemplated Jesus' death and their future sufferings. See *Jesus, Life and Ministry.*

James Brooks

TRANSGRESSION Image of sin as overstepping the limits of God's law. See *Evil; Forgiveness; Repentance; Salvation; Sin.*

TRANSJORDAN Area immediately east of Jordan River settled by Reuben, Gad, half of Manasseh, Edom, Moab, and Amon. The most prominent topographical feature of Palestine is the Jordan River Valley, referred to in the Old Testament as the "Arabah" and called today, in Arabic, the *Ghōr.* This valley represents a huge geographical fault line which is prominent also in Lebanon, where it creates the Beqa'a Valley, continues southward from Palestine to form the Red Sea, and extends even as far as Mozambique in east Africa. Center stage of the biblical narrative is the hill country west of the Jordan where most of the Israelite tribes were settled and where the famous cities of Samaria, Shechem, Jerusalem, and Hebron were sited. See *Jordan, Palestine.*

The highlands east of the Jordan also played a significant role, especially during Old Testament times. Transjordan included: The River Jabbok, scene of the account of Jacob's wrestling on his return from Aram (Gen. 32:22–32); the Plains of Moab, where the Israelites are said to have camped following their Exodus from Egypt and where Baalam prophesied, and Mount Nebo, from which Moses viewed the Promised Land, (Num. 22:1—24:25; Deut. 34). Three Transjordanian kingoms (Ammon, Moab, and Edom) were contemporary with the two Hebrew kingdoms (Israel and Judah) sometimes as allies, sometimes as enemies (1 Sam. 11; 14:47; 2 Sam. 8:12; 10; 2 Kings 3; Amos 1:11—2:3). The prophet Elijah was from Tishbi, a town in the Transjordanian territory of Gilead (1 Kings 17:1). Other Israelite prophets and poets often referred to the territories and peoples of the Transjordan. See, for example, the allusions in Amos 4:1 and Psalm 22:12 to the cows and bulls of Bashan.

The vast Arabian Desert stretches southeastward from the geological fault line described above. The Transjordan which figures in the biblical narratives is not the whole desert expanse, but rather the north-south strip of highlands sandwiched between the Jordan Valley and the desert. This strip of highlands receives abundant rainfall from the Mediterranean winds during the winter months, which allows farming and cattle grazing. The rainfall fades rapidly as one moves eastward, however, so that the generally rugged and cultivable land gives way to rocky desert approximately thirty to thirty-five miles east of the Jordan.

Four major rivers, along with numerous smaller and intermittently active stream beds, drain the Transjordanian highlands into the Jordan Valley. (1) The Yarmuk River, not mentioned in the Bible, drains the area known in Old Testament times as Bashan. Bashan, good cattle country as indicated above, was situated roughly east of the Sea of

Galilee. Main biblical cities in the Bashan region were Ashtoroth and Karnaim (Josh. 9:10; 12:4; Amos 6:13). (2) Nahr ex-Zerqa, the Jabbok River of Old Testament times, drains the area known then as Gilead. Gilead, situated east of that portion of the Jordan which connects the Sea of Galilee with the Dead Sea, produces grapes, olives, vegetables, cereals, and also is mentioned in the Bible as a source of balm (Gen. 37:25; Jer. 8:22). Among Gileadite cities which appear in the biblical narratives were Mizpah, Jabesh, and Ramath (Judg. 10:17; 1 Sam. 11:1; 31:12; 1 Kings 22:3, 2 Kings 8:28). (3) Wady el-Mujib, the Arnon River of ancient times, bisected the ancient land of Moab and enters the Dead Sea approximately midway along its eastern shore. (4) Wady Hesa—probably the ancient Zered but not absolutely certain—would have separated Moab from Edom and enters the Arabah at the southern end of the Dead Sea.

An important trade route passed through the Transjordan during biblical times, connecting Damascus and Bostra of Syria with the Gulf of Aqabah and western Arabia. Some scholars prefer to translate the term *derek hamelek* (Num. 20:17; 21:22) as a proper noun ("The King's Highway") and identify it with this ancient route. Others interpret the term as a common, appellative noun ("royal road") and doubt that it referred to a specific route—in the same sense that present-day terms such as "freeway" or "state road" refer to categories of roads rather than to specific highways. In either case, we know that the old trade route which traversed the Transjordan would have played an important role in the economy of ancient Palestine and was refurbished by the Romans who named it the *Via Nova Traiana.*

The Israelite tribes of Reuben and Gad along with certain Manassite clans settled in the Transjordan—primarily in Gilead, it seems, although with some spillover into Bashan and into the traditionally Moabite territory immediately north of the Arnon (see especially Num. 32). Later, after the establishment of the Hebrew monarchy, several Israelite and Judean kings attempted, some more successfully than others, to rule this portion of the Transjordan with which Israelite tribes were associated. David, Omri, Ahab, and Jeroboam II were the more successful ones. Weaker kings, such as Rehoboam and Jehoash of Judah for example, will have had little or no influence in the Transjordan. Also, of course, one reads of occasional Moabite and Edomite military campaigns which threatened even Jerusalem (2 Chron. 20).

With the rise of Assyria, especially during and following the reign of Tiglath-pileser III (744–727 B.C.), the various regions of Syria-Palestine fell under Assyrian domination. The Transjordan was no different. Several of the kings of Ammon, Moab, and Edom are mentioned in Assyrian records—usually listed among those paying tribute or providing other forms of involuntary support to the Assyrian monarch. When the Assyrian Empire collapsed and was superceded by the Babylonian Empire, presumably the Babylonians also controlled the Transjordan.

By New Testament times, a cluster of Greco-Roman-oriented cities with primarily Gentile populations (the so-called "Decapolis" cities) had emerged in the northern Transjordan (earlier Bashan, Gilead, and Ammon). The southern Transjordan (earlier Moab and Edom) was dominated, on the other hand, by the Nabateans, a people of Arab origin who established a commercial empire along the desert fringe with its capital at Petra. Eventually, the whole of the Transjordan was incorporated into the Roman Empire. Domitian annexed the northern Transjordan in A.D. 90, forming the administrative province of Arabia. Trajan added the Nabatean territory in A.D. 106 and renamed the province Arabia Petraea. See *Ammon; Arnon; Bashan; Decapolis; Edom; Gilead; Jabbok; Moab; Tribes of Israel.* *J. Maxwell Miller*

TRANSLATE *1.* KJV term meaning, "to transfer," used of the transfer of Saul's kingdom to David (2 Sam. 3:10) and the transfer of believers from the power of darkness to the sphere of Christ's control (Col. 1:14). *2.* KJV term meaning, "to take up," used of Enoch's being taken up into God's presence without experiencing death (Heb. 11:5). See *Death; Future Hope; Resurrection.*

TRANSPORTATION AND TRAVEL Means and ways of commercial and private movement among towns and nations in the biblical period. Travel in the ancient, as well as the modern world, is the result of economic, political, social, and religious factors. For the most part, transportation and travel in the biblical world was on foot (Judg. 16:3; Josh. 9:3–5; 1 Kings 18:46). At first this meant following the paths animals made through the hills and valleys of Palestine. However, as the economic and political demands of the region increased, so did the traffic. Better marked and smoother roads were needed for travelers and for the transport of larger amounts of goods from place to place. Large draft animals of various types also had to be domesticated and harnessed to this work (Ex. 23:5).

As trade began to expand beyond the local area, international highways and trade routes, like the coastal road, the Via Maris, and the Transjordanian king's highway were developed. Heavily traveled routes such as these were a factor in the founding of many cities. They also functioned as the principle link from which branched lesser roads connecting cities and towns in Palestine to the rest of the Near East (Prov. 8:2–3). These highways promoted the movement of businessmen, religious pilgrims, government officials, and armies between regions of the country and foreign nations. The resulting blend of cultures and economies created the society described in biblical and extrabiblical texts.

Geographical Factors in Travel Perhaps the greatest obstacle that travelers and road builders had to overcome was the rugged geographical character of Palestine. The desert regions of the Negev and Judean highlands in the south required the identification of wells and pasturage for the draft animals. The hilly spine of central Palestine forced the traveler to zigzag around steep ascents (such as that between Jericho and Jerusalem), or follow ridges along the hill tops (the Beth Horon route northwest of Jerusalem), or go along watersheds (Bethlehem to Mizpah). Numerous streams as well as the Jordan River had to be forded by travelers (2 Sam. 19:18), sometimes at the expense of baggage and animals.

Where valleys, such as the Jezreel, had to be traversed, roads generally followed the higher ground along the base of the hills so as to bypass marshy areas and stay away from the raging torrents which sometimes filled stream beds in the rainy season. Narrow, twisting valleys, as in the Judean desert, often provided perfect areas for ambushes by bandits. Along the coastal plain, sandy dunes required a detour further inland into the foothills of the Shephelah plateau.

The rough coastline of Palestine lacked a good,

A traveler along the Jericho road to Jerusalem riding one donkey while his other donkey leads the way.

deep-water port for shipping. As a result, an additional journey overland was required to transport agricultural and other trade goods to and from the ports of Ezion-geber (1 Kings 9:26–28) on the Red Sea and the Phoenician ports of Tyre and Sidon to the cities of Israel. Solomon kept a fleet of ships operating in the Red Sea to ply the African trade. Another group of Solomon's ocean-going vessels (Hebrew, "ships of Tarshish") joined forces with the fleets of Hiram of Tyre in the Mediterranean (1 Kings 10:22). Despite this activity, Israel's kings had a general lack of experience with the sea. This sometimes made them reluctant to rely on shipping. For instance, king Jehoshaphat of Judah rejected further attempts to obtain gold from Ophir after his first fleet of ships was sunk off Ezion-geber (1 Kings 22:48–49). See *Ships, Sailors.*

Despite these difficulties, the desire to travel and the commercial needs of nations motivated the identification of routes that were relatively safe from attack by bandits and allowed free transport of goods by pack animals and carts to every region in the land. The roads that carried this traffic varied in size from two lane thoroughfares about ten feet wide to simple tracks through fields barely wide enough for a man and donkey to pass single file. The determining factor in each case was the usage each received. Roads carrying two- and four-wheeled carts and wagons pulled by oxen required more room and a smoother road bed (Isa. 62:10) than a lane crossing a vineyard.

Kings of the ancient Near East (Shulgi of Ur III, Mesopotamia, and Mesha, king of Moab) often boasted in their official inscriptions of their road-building activities. These roadways, so important to the maintenance of political and economic control of the nation, were probably kept in shape by government-sponsored corvee workers (2 Sam. 20:24; 1 Kings 9:15) or by the army. Since bridges were unknown in the biblical period, fords were identified (Judg. 12:5–6, NIV) for general use, and, in the Roman period, were smoothed by the placement of flat stones in the river bed. Where no river crossing could be found, boats were lashed together to form temporary ferries or large transports.

Political and Military Factors in Transportation While terrain had a great deal to do with the building of roads, another important factor was the political situation in the region. In ancient Israel, roads not only linked trading and religious centers, they also protected population centers and speeded the nation's armies to war. The vast network of roads in the difficult area of the Judean hill country speaks eloquently of the importance of Jerusalem which was the hub of activities in that region. It functioned as the political center of the Davidic monarchy as well as the religious focus of the nation with many pilgrims making the ascent to Zion (Ps 122:1). An even more elaborate system of highways was built by the Roman legions to help them dominate the country and forestall organized rebellion after the revolts of A.D. 69–70, 135.

Throughout the monarchy, military campaigns required well-kept roadways to facilitate the movement of troops about the country. Protecting the valleys and highways which led to the capital at Jerusalem were a series of fortresses including Gezer, Beth Horon, Baalath, and Tadmor (1 Kings 9:17–19, NIV). Royal entourages also traveled these guarded roads in peacetime to conduct governmental business (1 Kings 12:1; 18:16).

To help with the constant flow of government travelers, way stations (every ten to fifteen miles in the Persian Empire) and administrative outposts were constructed. In a time before inns, these stations provided supplies to traveling officials and fresh mounts to couriers. The private traveler had to rely on the hospitality of towns or friends along the way (Judg. 19:10–15; 2 Kings 4:8).

The road systems and port facilities of the kings of Israel and Judah were expanded in times of prosperity and contested for in times of war (2 Kings 16:6). Megiddo, which commanded the western entrance into the Jezreel Valley, controlled the traffic along the Via Maris as it moved inland and then north to Damascus. Solomon demonstrated his awareness of its strategic importance for fortifying the site, along with Hazor and Gezer, to protect the borders of Israel (1 Kings 9:15). Foreign rulers also fought to hold the city (which was destroyed over a dozen times during its period of occupation), and king Josiah of Judah died here defending the pass against the army of Pharaoh Necho II in 609 B.C. (2 Kings 23:29).

Religious Factors in Travel One of the chief reasons given for travel in the biblical text was to visit a religious shrine and make sacrifices. Throughout much of Israel's history the people are described as making journeys to places like Shechem (Josh. 24), Shiloh (1 Sam. 1:3), Ophrah (Judg. 8:27), Dan (Judg. 18:30), and Bethel (1 Kings 12:26–33). Here they would make their devotions before a sacred image or the ark of the covenant. High places *(bamoth)* were also popular sites for religious pilgrims. In the period before Jerusalem's ascendancy as the religious focal point of the nation, prophets like Samuel regularly visited these local shrines to officiate at sacrifices (1 Sam. 9:12). Local religious rites sometimes also included an ingathering of family from across the nation as well as part of the yearly celebration (1 Sam. 20:6).

Animals Used in Travel Most of what is known about the animals used to transport people and materials in the ancient world is based on textual evidence and art. The Bible mentions several different types of draft animals: donkeys, mules, camels, and oxen. Among these, donkeys appear

to have been the most popular means of transport in the Near East. They are described in Old Assyrian texts (about 2100 B.C.) transporting copper ingots from Cappadocia in Turkey. The Beni-Hasan tomb paintings from Egypt dating to 1900 B.C. graphically portray Semitic caravaneers with their donkeys laden with baggage and trade goods.

In the biblical narrative the donkey was the chief means of private and commercial transport throughout the history of the nation of Israel. Jacob's sons carried their grain purchases from Egypt to Canaan on donkey back (Gen. 42:26); Jesse sent David and a donkey loaded with provisions to Saul's court (1 Sam. 16:20); and Nehemiah became incensed when he saw Judeans transporting grain on donkeys during the sabbath (Neh. 13:15).

Mules are less commonly mentioned. This may be due to a shortage of horses for breeding or to a custom restricting the use of mules to the upper classes (2 Sam. 13:29). For instance, David's sons Absalom (2 Sam. 18:9) and Solomon (1 Kings 1:33) are described as riding mules. One passage (Isa. 66:20) pictures the caravan of returning exiles riding on horses, mules, and dromedaries, as well as in chariots and litters. Each of these means of transport, however, fits the prophet's vision of a glorious procession on its way to Jerusalem rather than the normal groupings of travelers along the international route.

Camels appear several times in the text carrying huge loads (five times that of a donkey). One clear example of this is found in 2 Kings 8:9 (NIV). Ben-hadad, the king of Syria, sent "forty camel-loads" of goods to Elisha in an attempt to learn if he would recover from an illness. In another case Isaiah denounced the leaders of Judah for sending camel loads of gifts to Egypt to buy their aid against Assyria (30:6). Because of their broad, but tender hoofs, best fit for desert travel, the camel was of little use in the hill country. These beasts were probably used only on the major routes such as the Via Maris, along the coast, or on the smoother valley roads of the Shephelah and the Negev.

Oxen are exclusively associated with travel by wheeled vehicle and will be discussed below in that context. Israelite use of horses does not appear in the text before the 1000 B.C. when David began to incorporate them into his forces (2 Sam. 8:3–4). They are mentioned primarily in military contexts: ridden into battle (Job 39:18–25) and harnessed to chariots (1 Kings 12:18). Official messengers also rode horses (2 Kings 9:18–19), as did scouts for the army (2 Kings 7:13–15).

Wheeled Vehicles The most commonly mentioned wheeled vehicle in the biblical narrative is the chariot. It was used first by Israel's enemies during the conquest period (Judg. 1:19; 4:3). However, it could not be used effectively in the rough hill country where the tribes first settled

(Josh. 17:16). Once the monarchy was established, chariots became an integral part of the kings' battle strategy (1 Kings 10:26; 22:31–34). They were also used as a standard means of travel by kings (2 Kings 9:16) and nobles (2 Kings 5:9). Private ownership of chariots is found in Isaiah 22:18. In this passage the prophet condemns Shebna, the king's household steward for his extravagance and pride. His chariots, like his rock-cut tomb were status symbols for high-ranking members of the royal bureaucracy in Hezekiah's time (see Acts 8:26–38 for a similar case).

No physical remains of chariots have been found in Palestine, although a magnificent example of a royal Egyptian chariot was discovered in the tomb of Pharaoh Tutankhamon (about 1300 B.C.). A three-man Judean battle chariot is depicted in the Assyrian relief (about 701 B.C.) of Sennacherib's siege of Lachish. It was fitted with a yoke for four horses. Estimates of the chariot's size in this period are based on the width of ruts in the roadways in Mesopotamian and Roman cities. If these are used, the standard width of chariots was 1.23 meters between the wheels and 1.53 meters overall.

The use of large-wheeled vehicles apparently originated in Sumer where models, dating to 2500 B.C., of large covered wagons drawn by oxen have been found. These bulky vehicles, carrying heavy loads, required well-kept, broad roadways. Neglected paths could become overgrown (Prov. 15:19) or filled with stones from eroded hillsides. Thus, for traffic to be maintained, teams of workmen must have traveled the roads making necessary repairs. Gateways also had to be widened to permit the entrance of wheeled vehicles. Those excavated in Israel range in width from 2.5 to 4.5 meters. Some, like those at Gezer and Megiddo, had a cobblestone or crushed-stone roadbed within the heavily traveled gate complex.

Large two- and four-wheeled carts and wagons were also commonly used in biblical times for transporting heavy loads and people. In the patriarchal period, Joseph sent carts to Canaan to carry his father and the households of his brothers to Goshen (Gen. 45:19–27). After the completion of the wilderness tabernacle, six covered wagons, each pulled by two oxen, were donated by the tribal leaders to the Levites to transport holy items along the line of march (Num. 7:1–8).

Once the people had settled into Canaan, carts became an everyday aid to farmers who had to transport sheaves of grain to the threshing floor (Amos 2:13). A similar two-wheeled cart was used by David to carry the ark of the covenant from Kiriath-jearim (also called Baale of Judah) to his new capital in Jerusalem (2 Sam. 6:2–17). The somewhat clumsy nature of these carts can be seen in its almost over turning as it came to the threshing floor of Nacon. Several men walked beside the cart to guide the oxen and prevent the cargo from shifting.

The broader roads and heavy wheeled vehicles of Palestine were also used, in the period of the Assyrian conquest, to transport the people into Exile. Sennacherib's stone relief of his siege of Lachish includes a picture of Judeans being taken away in two-wheeled carts drawn by a team of oxen. The new exiles sit atop bundles containing their belongings while a man walks alongside the left-hand ox guiding it with a sharpened stick. Isaiah's vision of the return (66:20) must have struck a poignant note for the exiles who had seen their ancestors depicted in the Assyrian relief. See *Animals; Economic Life.*   *Victor H. Matthews*

TRAPPER See *Fowler.*

TREASURE, TREASURY What one values whether silver and gold or something intangible and the storage place of what is valuable.

In Old Testament times treasure might be stored in the king's palace (2 Kings 20:13) or in the Temple (1 Kings 7:51). In Jesus' day the term also applied to thirteen trumpet-shaped offering receptacles in the Temple court of the women where Jesus watched people make their offerings (Mark 12:41). "Treasure" and "treasury" are also used as illustrations or figures of speech. Israel was God's treasure (Ex. 19:5). This is reflected in the idea of Christians as God's own people (1 Pet. 2:9). A person's memory is a treasure (Prov. 2:1; 7:1). Fear (awe) of the Lord was Israel's treasure (Isa. 33:6).

Jesus Himself used the term frequently. He contrasted earthly treasures to those of heaven (Matt. 6:19–20). What a person treasures or values determines one's loyalty and priorities (Matt. 6:21). Paul marveled that the treasure of God's revelation of Himself in Christ had been deposited in an earthen vessel such as Paul himself (2 Cor. 4:7). See *Temple.*   *Elmer Gray*

TREATY See *Covenant.*

TREE OF KNOWLEDGE Plant in midst of Garden of Eden used to prove the first couple's loyalty to the Creator (Gen. 2—3). Reference to "the tree of the knowledge of good and evil" is in a context concerned with the fall. In Genesis 3:3 the tree is designated as "the tree which is in the midst of the garden." Eating from the tree brought the knowledge of good and evil (Gen. 3:5,22). One of many trees in the garden, this tree alone was forbidden to mankind under the penalty of death (Gen. 2:17).

The tree of knowledge was Adam and Eve's opportunity to demonstrate obedience and loyalty to God, but the serpent used it to tempt Eve to eat and to become like God "knowing good and evil" (Gen. 3:5). When Adam joined Eve in eating the forbidden fruit, the result was shame, guilt, exclusion from the garden, and separation from the tree of life and from God. The Bible's primary interest about the tree of knowledge is not what kind of knowledge it represented—moral judgment, secular knowledge, sexual knowledge, universal knowledge, or some other kind—but how it served as God's test and Satan's temptation. The result for mankind was disaster as they failed the test and fell to the temptation.

See *Adam and Eve; Eden; Tree of Life.*

Billy K. Smith

TREE OF LIFE Plant in Garden of Eden symbolizing access to eternal life and metaphor used in Proverbs. For the biblical writer the tree of life was an important consideration only after Adam and Eve disobeyed. Sin interrupted the quality of life God intended for them. They were to obey God (Gen 2:17) in a family setting (Gen. 2:18–25) and perform their assigned tasks (Gen. 2:15). The implication is that they had access to all the trees in the garden, including the tree of life, but God gave an explicit command not to eat of the tree of knowledge. Their relationship to God changed radically when they disobeyed that command. Chief among the radical changes was that they no longer had access to the tree of life (Gen. 3:22–24).

The "tree of life" appears in Proverbs four times (Prov. 3:18; 11:30; 13:12; 15:4) and in Revelation 2:7; 22:2,14. To lay hold of wisdom is to lay hold on "a tree of life" (Prov. 3:18). "The fruit of the righteous is a tree of life" (11:30 NIV). Yet another proverb has this comparison: "a longing fulfilled is a tree of life" (13:12 NIV). The author of another proverb wrote, "The tongue that brings healing is a tree of life" (15:4 NIV). None of these proverbs seems to refer to "the tree of life" mentioned in Genesis. All of the references in Revelation do. See *Adam and Eve; Eden; Tree of Knowledge.*

Billy K. Smith

TRIAL OF JESUS Two systems of justice combined to produce a sentence of death for Jesus. Jewish religious leaders accused Jesus of blasphemy, a capital offense under Jewish law (see Lev. 24:16). The Jewish leaders at Jesus' trial manipulated procedures to coerce Jesus into an admission that He was God's Son (see Luke 22:66–71). For them this constituted blasphemy.

Roman leaders allowed conquered people such as the Jews to follow their own legal system so long as they did not abuse their privileges. The Romans did not give the Jews the right of capital punishment for the accusation of blasphemy. The Jews had to convince a Roman judge that their demand for capital punishment was justified.

The Jewish Trial Jewish leaders were determined to seek Jesus' death when they put Him on trial (see Luke 22:2; Mark 14:1). They held the Jewish

trial at night hoping that Jesus' supporters would be asleep and unable to protest his arrest. The Jewish portion of the trial had three separate phases: (1) an appearance before Annas; (2) an informal investigation by Caiaphas and (3) a condemnation by the Sanhedrin. Annas was father-in-law of the high priest Caiaphas. He had been high priest himself from A.D. 7–15. He was the most influential member of the Sanhedrin. The details of the interview before Annas are meager (John 18:12–14,19–24). The high priest mentioned in John 18:19 may have been Annas. If so, he held a brief interrogation of Jesus and sent Him to his son-in-law Caiaphas (John 18:24).

The meeting with Caiaphas took place in his residence (Luke 22:54). Some members of the Sanhedrin worked frantically to locate and train witnesses against Jesus (Matt. 26:59–60). The carefully prepared witnesses could not agree in their testimony (see Mark 14:56; compare Deut. 19:15).

During this circuslike activity Caiaphas talked with Jesus and put Him under oath (Matt. 26:63–64). He charged Jesus to tell if He were God's Son. Perhaps Jesus felt that silence under this oath would be a denial of His divine origin. He affirmed that He was God's Son (Mark 14:62), knowing that this would lead to death. The Sanhedrin condemned Him but did not pronounce a sentence (Mark 14:64). After the condemnation the group broke up into wild disorder. Some began to slap and spit upon Jesus (Mark 14:65).

Shortly after dawn, the Sanhedrin convened again to bring a formal condemnation against Jesus (Luke 22:66). Jewish law stipulated that a guilty verdict in a capital crime had to be delayed until the next day. The vote for condemnation after dawn gave the semblance of following this requirement.

The procedure at this session was similar to that of the night trial. No witnesses came forward to accuse Christ. Jesus again claimed that He was God's Son (Luke 22:66–71). The Sanhedrin again approved the death sentence and took Jesus to Pilate for sentencing (Luke 23:1).

The procedures of the Jewish leaders during Jesus' trial were illegal. Jewish law required that trial for a capital crime begin during the daytime and adjourn by nightfall if incomplete. Sanhedrin members were supposed to be impartial judges. Jewish rules prohibited convicting the accused on His own testimony.

The Roman Trial The Roman trial of Jesus also had three phases: (1) first appearance before Pilate; (2) appearance before Herod Antipas; (3) second appearance before Pilate. The Jews asked Pilate to accept their verdict against Jesus without investigation (John 18:29–31). Pilate refused this, but he offered to let them carry out the maximum punishment under their law, probably beating with rods or imprisonment. They insisted that they wanted death.

The Jews knew that Pilate would laugh at their charge of blasphemy. They fabricated three additional charges against Jesus which would be of concern to a Roman governor (Luke 23:2). Pilate concerned himself only with the charge that Jesus had claimed to be a king. This charge sounded like treason. The Romans knew no greater crime than treason.

Pilate interrogated Jesus long enough to be convinced that He was no political rival to Caesar (John 18:33–37). He returned to the Jews to announce that he found Jesus no threat to Rome and hence not deserving of death (John 18:38). The Jews responded with vehement accusations against Jesus' actions in Judea and Galilee (Luke 23:5). When Pilate learned that Jesus was from Galilee, he sent Jesus to Herod Antipas of Galilee who was then in Jersusalem (Luke 23:6–12). Herod wanted Jesus to entertain him with a miracle. Jesus did not even speak a word to Herod. The king and his soldiers mocked and ridiculed Jesus, finally sending Him back to Pilate.

When Herod returned Jesus to Pilate, the Roman governor announced that he still found Jesus innocent of charges of treason. Three times Pilate tried to release Jesus. First, Pilate offered to chastise or beat Jesus and then to release him (Luke 23:16). Second, he offered to release either Jesus or Barabbas, a radical revolutionary. To Pilate's surprise the crowd chanted for Barabbas' release (Luke 23:17–19). Third, he scourged Jesus. Soldiers flailed at Jesus' bare back with a leather whip. The whip had pieces of iron or bone tied to the ends of the thongs. Pilate then presented the bleeding Jesus with a crown of thorns and a mock purple robe to the crowd as their king. He hoped that this spectacle would lead them to release Jesus out of pity. Again they chanted for crucifixion (John 19:4–6).

When Pilate seemed to waver one more time concerning crucifixion, the Jews threatened to report his conduct to Caesar (John 19:12). That threat triggered Pilate's action. After symbolically washing his hands of the entire affair (Matt. 27:24), he delivered Jesus for crucifixion (John 19:16). See *Annas; Caiaphas; Pontius Pilate; Roman Law; Sanhedrin.*   *Tommy Lea*

TRIBES OF ISRAEL, THE Social and political groups in Israel claiming descent from one of the twelve sons of Jacob.

The Tribal Unit The tribal unit played an important role in the history of the formation of the nation Israel. In ancient times a nation was referred to as "a people," an *'am;* in Israel's case it was the "people of Israel." The nation in turn was made up of "tribes." The "tribe," a *shebet* or *matteh,* was the major social unit that comprised the makeup of the nation. The tribe was comprised of "clans." The "clan," a *mishpachah,* was

a family of families or a cluster of households that had a common ancestry. The clan was comprised then of the individual households or families referred to as the "father's house" the *beth ab.* Actually, the family in ancient times might be made up of several families living together and forming one household (Num. 3:24). See *Family.*

Tribal Origins The ancestral background of "the tribes of Israel" went back to the patriarch Jacob, whose name was changed to Israel. The nation Israel was identified as "the children of Israel, or more literally "the sons of Israel." According to the biblical account, the family of Jacob, from which the tribes came, originated in north Syria during Jacob's stay at Haran with Laban his uncle. Eleven of the twelve sons were born at Haran, while the twelfth, Benjamin was born after Jacob returned to Canaan. The birth of the sons came through Jacob's wives Leah and Rachel and their maids Zilpah and Bilhah. The sons of Leah included Reuben, Simeon, Levi, Judah (Gen. 29:31–35), Issachar and Zebulun, as well as one daughter named Dinah (Gen. 30:19–21). Rachel's sons were Joseph (Gen. 30:22–24), who became the father of Ephraim and Manasseh (Gen. 41:50–52), and Benjamin (Gen. 35:16–18). Jacob's sons through Zilpah, Leah's maid, were Gad and Asher (Gen. 30:9–13), while Bilhah, the maid of Rachel, bore Dan and Naphtali (Gen. 30:1–8).

This family of families or family of tribes occupied the focal point in the history of the development of Israel as a nation. While there are details of that history that we do not clearly understand and other groups simply referred to as "a mixed multitude" (Ex. 12:38) that were perhaps incorporated into the nation, the central focus is always on the "tribes of Israel," the descendants of Jacob. For that reason lists of the twelve sons of Jacob or of the tribes appear in several places in the Old Testament, though the lists vary somewhat. Some of the major lists include that of Jacob's blessing of the twelve (Gen. 49), the review of the households as the period of oppression in Egypt is introduced (Ex. 1:1–10), Moses' blessing of the tribes (Deut. 33), and the song of Deborah (Judg. 5).

The Tribes of Israel Each tribe had its own history in its allotment of land. We know few details about the individual tribes.

1. Reuben, the firstborn son of Jacob by his wife Leah, was in line to assume a leadership role in the family, but he forfeited that right because of an illicit affair he had with his father's concubine Bilhah (Gen. 35:22). The impact of this reflected in Jacob's blessing where Reuben is addressed as "unstable as water, you shall no longer excel because you went up on to your father's bed" (Gen. 49:4 NRSV). At the time of the migration of Jacob's family to Egypt, Reuben had four sons (Gen. 46:8–9).

In some of the lists of the tribes of Israel, Reuben is mentioned first (Ex. 1:1–4; Num. 1:5), while in other lists Reuben appears further down (Num. 2:1–11). During the journey through the wilderness, the tribes of Reuben, Simeon, and Gad formed the second unit of the procession with the tribe of Reuben in the lead position (Num. 10:17–20). This cluster of tribes headed by the tribe of Reuben was next in line after the tabernacle (Num. 10:17). As the tribes approached the land of Canaan and allotments were made to each tribe, the tribe of Reuben along with Gad and the half-tribe of Manasseh occupied the Transjordan, that is the highland plateau region east of the Jordan River (Josh. 13:8–31; compare Num. 32: 1–5,33–42). The tribe of Reuben occupied the southern region extending roughly from the Arnon river to the site of Heshbon (Josh. 13:15–23). Formerly, this territory was the homeland of the kingdom of Sihon. While we know little about the tribe of Reuben during the period of the settlement, the song of Deborah suggests that the tribe was criticized by some of the other tribes for not taking a more active role in the conquest (Judg. 5:15–16). See *Transjordan.*

2. Simeon was Jacob's second son by Leah and played a key role in the encounter Dinah had with Shechem. Because Simeon and Levi were full brothers of Dinah, they sought to avenge her (Gen. 34:25–26) for Shechem's actions (Gen. 34:1–4). The radical response of the two brothers, in which they "took their swords and came against the city unawares, and killed all the males" (Gen. 34:25), is reflected in Jacob's blessing of the two: "Weapons of violence are their swords. . . . cursed be their anger, for it is fierce, and their wrath, for it is cruel! I will divide them in Jacob, and scatter them in Israel" (Gen. 49:5–7 NRSV). During the years of famine as the sons of Jacob traveled back and forth between Egypt and Canaan, Simeon was held hostage by Joseph at one point (Gen. 42:24).

In the lists of the tribes, Simeon is listed in second place, that is, next after Reuben (Ex. 1:2; 6:15; Num. 1:6,22–23; 13:5; 26:12–14). Generally, the tribe of Simeon seems to be characterized by weakness. Its status is best reflected in the final statement of Jacob's blessing of Simeon and Levi: "I will divide them in Jacob, and scatter them in Israel" (Gen. 49:7). Perhaps because of its weak status, the tribe of Simeon apparently was not given a separate inheritance in the land (Josh. 19:1–9). Rather, "its inheritance lay within the inheritance of the tribe of Judah" (Josh. 19:1), in the southern Negeb.

3. Levi was the third son of Jacob and Leah. See *Simeon* above. During the journey from Egypt to Canaan, the sons of Levi slaughtered 3,000 rebellious Hebrew males (Ex. 32:25–29). They became the landless priestly tribe. See *Levites; Levitical Cities; Priests.*

4. Judah, the fourth son of Jacob by his wife Leah (Gen. 29:35), appears as a leader and a spokesman among his brothers (Gen. 37:26; 43:3; 44:16; compare 46:28). Judah was promised preeminence over the other tribes in Jacob's blessing (Gen. 49:8–12).

In the journey from Egypt to Canaan, Judah has the lead position (Num. 2:9). As the tribes entered the land, it was Achan of the tribe of Judah who was guilty of taking some of the forbidden booty or loot from Jericho (Josh. 7). The tribe of Judah occupied the southern part of Palestine, basically the territory between the Dead Sea on the east to the Mediterranean on the west (Josh. 15). The northern boundary of Judah was marked by the territories of Benjamin and Dan. The territory of Jerusalem may have formed something of a barrier between Judah and the tribes of the north because it was not finally secured until the time of David (2 Sam. 5:6–10). The capture of Jerusalem by David paved the way for the tribes to have a kind of unity they had not previously experienced. The territory of the tribe of Judah constituted the major portion of the Southern Kingdom, thus forming the kingdom of Judah with its capital Jerusalem.

5. Issachar was the ninth son born to Jacob, but the first of a second family he had by Leah (Gen. 30:18). Beyond his birth, little else is known about his life or that of the tribe. During the journey from Mount Sinai to Canaan the tribe of Issachar followed the tribe of Judah, that is, it was a part of the first cluster of tribes located on the east side of the tabernacle (Num. 2:5). The territory occupied by the tribe of Issachar is difficult to outline precisely (Josh. 19:17–23). They were located west of the Jordan in the region just south of the Sea of Galilee stretching on down to the Valley of Jezreel. Because the blessing of Moses says that Zebulun and Issachar "call peoples to the mountain; / there they offer the right sacrifices" (Deut. 33:19 NRSV), some have speculated that the two tribes perhaps had a center of worship on Mount Tabor, a mountain located on the border between the two tribes. Because the blessing of Jacob speaks of Issachar as a beast of burden and as "a slave at forced labor" (Gen. 49:14–15 NRSV), the tribe of Issachar may have faced a variety of hardships. For instance there may have been a time during the tribal period when the people of Issachar served as slaves in the forced labor projects of their neighbors, the Canaanites.

6. Zebulun was the tenth son of Jacob and the sixth and final son by his wife Leah (Gen. 30:19–20). Little else is known about Zebulun's life. The territory allotted to the tribe of Zebulun was in the north in the region of southern Galilee bounded by Issachar on the south southeast, Naphtali on the east, and Asher on the west (Josh. 19:10–16). The blessing of Jacob speaks of Zebulun's territory including "the shore of the sea," presumably the

T

Mediterranean Sea, and "his border shall be at Sidon," (Gen. 49:13 NRSV) a city on the coast north of Mount Carmel. While this territory was traditionally occupied by the tribe of Asher, it is quite possible that at some point Zebulun occupied a part of this region and, therefore, would have had access to the sea. The blessing of Moses further states that Zebulum along with Issachar would benefit from "the affluence of the seas and the hidden treasures of the sand" (Deut. 33:19 NRSV). During the period that the tribes were settling in the land of Canaan, Zebulun apparently went beyond the call of duty in providing support. It is the only tribe in the Song of Deborah to be mentioned twice (Judg. 5:14,18).

7. *Joseph* was the first son born to Jacob by Rachel, Jacob's favorite wife (Gen. 30:22–24). Two of the tribes of Israel came from Joseph, namely, *Ephraim* and *Manasseh.*

The story of Joseph is the most eventful of the sons of Jacob. See *Joseph.* Joseph had two sons, Manasseh and Ephraim (Gen. 41:50–52), who were born in Egypt. Ephraim and Manasseh were adopted by Jacob and therefore each became the father of a tribe in Israel (Gen. 48:8–20). While Manasseh was the older of the two, Jacob gave preference to Ephraim (v. 14; compare Deut. 33:17). The Blessing of Jacob (Gen. 49:22–26) mentions only Joseph; the Blessing of Moses (Deut. 33:13–17) begins with Joseph and notes Ephriam and Manasseh, the song of Deborah (Judg. 5:14) speaks of Ephraim and Machir. See *Machir.*

a. *Ephraim* occupied a major portion of the central hill country with Manasseh during the tribal period. Ephraim's territory consisted of the region just north of Dan and Benjamin and ran from the Jordan River on the east to the Mediterranean Sea on the west. That Ephraim played a major leadership role among the tribes is reflected in the tribal history. Joshua, one of the twelve spies and a member of the tribe of Ephraim, became the successor of Moses (Num. 13:8,16; Josh. 1:1–11). Ephraim demanded leadership in the period of the judges (Judg. 3:27; 4:5; 7:24; 8:1; 10:1; 12:1–6; 17:1; 18:2,13; 19:1). Shiloh, located in the territory of the tribe of Ephraim, became the major center of worship during the tribal period (Josh. 18:1; 1 Sam. 1:1–18). Samuel, the leader of the tribes (1 Sam 7:15–17) near the end of the period of the Judges and just prior to the beginning of the kinship, came from Ephraim (1 Sam. 1:1–20).

Ephraim's influence is seen not only during the tribal period, but in Israel's later history as well. For instance, as the nation Israel divided into two kingdoms following the death of Solomon in 922 B.C., it was an Ephraimite named Jeroboam who led the northern tribes in their plea for leniency (1 Kings 12:1–5). When Rehoboam rejected their plea, the northern tribes broke their ties with the

south, formed a separate kingdom (1 Kings 12:16–19), and selected Jeroboam as their king (1 Kings 12:20). Ephraim's influence is seen also during the time of the prophets. For instance, Hosea refers to Israel some three dozen times using the name Ephraim as being synonymous with Israel.

b. *Manasseh* was the oldest son of Joseph and Asenath. The tribe of Manasseh occupied territory both east and west of the Jordan River. Manasseh's terrotory east of the Jordan included the regions of Gilead and Bashan and most likely extended from the Jabbok River to near Mount Hermon. Manasseh's territory west of the Jordan was located north of Ephraim. Apparently, the tribe of Manasseh played an important role in the conquest. For instance the sons of Machir, Manasseh's son took the land of Gilead and drove out the Amorites who occupied it (Num. 32:39; compare Judg. 5:14); while other descendants of Manasseh engaged in the activities of the conquest elsewhere (Num. 32:41–42). Perhaps Gideon is the most familiar of the descendants of Manasseh (Judg. 6:12–15). Gideon defeated the Midianites with a small band of men (Judg. 6—7).

8. *Benjamin* was Jacob's youngest son, born to him by Rachel, and the only son born after returning to Palestine from Haran (Gen. 35:16–20). He was the only full-blooded brother of Joseph. Therefore, the tribes of Benjamin, Ephraim, and Manasseh formed a special group. Benjamin's tribal territory was a small area west of the Jordan, sandwiched between Ephraim to the north and Judah to the south (Josh. 18:11–28). The Benjaminites had a reputation as men of war. The blessing of Jacob refers to them as a "ravenous wolf" (Gen. 49:27 NRSV). The Book of Judges notes their activities as warriors during the tribal period (Judg. 5:14; 20:12–16). They were referred to as those "who were left-handed" and experts with the sling (Judg. 20:16 NRSV). The story of the Levite and his concubine reflects the inhumane acts for which the Benjaminites were responsible (Judg. 19). The second judge, Ehud (Judg. 3:12–30), and the first king, Saul (1 Sam. 9:15–17; 10:1), came from the tribe of Benjamin.

9. *Dan* was the fifth son of Jacob and the first of two sons by Bilhah, Rachel's maid (Gen. 30:5–8). Therefore, Dan and Naphtali were full-blooded brothers and are often mentioned together (Gen. 46:23–24; Ex. 1:4). The tribe of Dan originally occupied the territory just west of Benjamin with Ephraim on the north and Judah and the Philistines on the south (Josh. 19:40–48). Shortly after settling in this area, the Amorites and the Philistines apparently attempted to drive them out of the region (Judg. 1:34–36). The pressure and harassment the people of Dan experienced from the Philistines is reflected in the stories of Samson, the Danite, and his encounters with them

(Judg. 13—16). The Philistine pressure resulted in the migration of the tribe to an area north of Lake Hula, to the city of Laish and its territory (Judg. 18:14–27). The people of Dan captured the city and renamed it Dan (Judg. 18:29). See *Dan.*

10. Naphtali was the sixth son of Jacob and younger full-blooded brother of Dan (Gen. 30:6–8). The name, Naphtali, which conveys the idea of "wrestling" was selected because of the personal struggles between Rachel and Leah (Gen. 30:7–8). The Bible provides little information concerning Naphtali the person or tribe. During the tribal period the tribe of Naphtali occupied the broad strip of land west of the Jordan in the area of Lake Hula and the Sea of Chinnereth (Galilee). This band of land ran from Issachar and Zebulun in the south to near Dan in the north (Josh. 19:32–39). Apparently, the tribe of Naphtali provided forces during the conquest of the land (Judg. 5:18) and during the Midianite threat (Judg. 6:35; 7:23).

11. Gad was the seventh son of Jacob and the first of two sons by Zilpah, the maid of Leah (Gen. 30:9–11). Because Leah saw this birth as a sign of "good fortune," especially in the light of the fact that she had ceased having children, she named him "Gad" which means "fortune" (Gen. 30:11 NRSV). We know very little about Gad the patriarch beyond the brief details about his birth. The tribe's territory was the east side of the Jordan River and the Dead Sea, including a part of the region called Gilead (Num. 32:34–36; Josh. 13:24–28), extending from the region of the Jabbok River in the north to the region of the Arnon River in the south. According to the blessing of Jacob the tribe of Gad perhaps experienced numerous raids (Gen. 49:19) especially from groups like the Ammonites as reflected in the story of Jephthah (Judg. 11). Perhaps such raids were prompted by the fact that Gad occupied some of the best land in the Transjordan (Deut. 33:20–21). Apparently the men of Gad achieved great expertise as warriors (1 Chron. 12:8).

12. Asher was the eighth son of Jacob, the second son by Zilpah and the younger full-blooded brother of Gad (Gen. 30:9–13). Like Gad, little information is shared about the patriarch Asher. The tribe of Asher occupied the region west of Zebulun and Naphtali, that is, the northern coastal region of Palestine. The territory extended from near Mount Carmel in the south to near Tyre in the north (Josh. 19:24–31). Asher is the only tribe not recognized as providing a judge during the tribal period. While Asher occupied choice territory (Gen. 49:20), it apparently was reproached and perhaps failed to gain the respect of some of the other tribes (Judg. 5:17b).

Conclusion While discussion and research will continue concerning the history of the tribes and the territory they occupied, the tribal period will always be recognized as an important though enig-

matic period in the development of the history of Israel. With the development of the monarchy the tribal period came to an end; however, tribal ties and traditions may have continued to be quite strong. Many scholars suggest that tribal jealousies and traditions played a major role in bringing about the division of the kingdom and the formation of two kingdoms, the Northern Kindgom and the Southern Kingdom in 922 B.C.

LaMoine DeVries

TRIBULATION Trouble or pressure of a general sort; in some passages a particular time of suffering associated with events of the end time. In this sense it is described as tribulation surpassing any trouble yet experienced in human history (Matt. 24:21).

Such a reference to "the great tribulation" as Revelation 7:14 (NIV) is seen by some (amillennialism) to refer historically to persecution faced by Christians of the latter part of the first century, but also symbolic of tribulation that occurs periodically throughout history. Others (premillennialism) take such a reference to the great tribulation to refer to an end time period. Dispensational premillennialism connects such a seven-year tribulation with the seventieth week of a prophetic framework taken from Daniel 9:24–27. A distinction is usually made between the two halves of the seven years. The last half, often called the Great Tribulation, is measured variously as three and a half years (Dan. 9:27), forty-two months (Rev. 11:2; 13:5), 1,260 days (Rev. 11:3; 12:6), or "a time, and times, and half a time" (Rev. 12:14). Distinctive to this view is the teaching the church will be raptured at the beginning of the tribulation period.

Historic premillennialism sees the period as a future time of intense trouble on earth prior to Christ's return, but holds the church will go through the tribulation. The church must endure the tribulation, but not God's wrath.

See *Dispensation; Eschatology; Future Hope; Millennium; Rapture; Revelation, Book of; Seventy Weeks.*   *Jerry W. Batson*

TRIBUTE Any payment exacted by a superior power, usually a state, from an inferior one. The weaker state, called a vassal state, normally contributed a specified amount of gold, silver, or other commodities on a yearly basis. The imposition of tribute demonstrated the subservient status of the vassal state, thus undermining political autonomy and often causing financial weakness. Powerful nations collected tribute from both hostile states and allies. Refusal to render tribute by either was regarded as rebellion and normally resulted in military reprisals.

Imposing tribute was practiced widely and can be tracked back to before 2000 B.C. The tell el Amarna Letters from Canaanite kings after 1400

B.C. clearly reveal their vassal status to Egypt. During a few periods of strength Israel took tribute from neighboring peoples. David and Solomon exacted tribute from several smaller states (2 Sam. 8:14; 1 Kings 4:21). Later, Moab payed a tribute of 100,000 lambs and the wool of 100,000 rams to Ahab of Israel (2 Kings 3:3–4).

After the division of Solomon's Kingdom in 922 B.C., the relatively weaker states of Judah and Israel more often were forced to pay tribute to the large powers which increasingly dominated the Near East. This was especially true of the Assyrian Period (850–600 B.C.) as both biblical and archaeological evidence attests. The Black Obelisk of Shalmaneser III (about 841 B.C.) shows Jehu of Israel paying tribute prostrate before the Assyrian king. Menahem of Israel (2 Kings 15:19) and Ahaz of Judah (2 Kings 16:7–9) rendered tribute to Tiglath-pileser III (Pul) for different reasons. The heavy tribute paid by Hezekiah to Sennacherib about 701 B.C. was recorded in both biblical and Assyrian texts (2 Kings 18:13–16).

The Jews later paid tribute in one form or another to Babylon, Persia, the Ptolemies and Seleucids, and Rome. The Roman *tributum* was a form of taxes. In effect the famous question posed to Jesus by the Pharisees about taxes (Matt. 22:15–22) was about tribute. See *Assyria; Babylon; Egypt; Roman Empire.* *Tommy Brisco*

TRIGON (Trī′ gŏn) Small, three-cornered harp with four strings (Dan. 3:5,7,10; KJV, sackbut).

TRINITY Theological term used to define God as an undivided unity expressed in the threefold nature of God the Father, God the Son, and God the Holy Spirit. As a distinctive Christian doctrine, the Trinity is considered as a divine mystery beyond human comprehension to be reflected upon only through scriptual revelation. The Trinity is a biblical concept that expresses the dynamic character of God, not a Greek idea pressed into Scripture from philosophical or religious speculation. While the term *trinity* does not appear in Scripture, the trinitarian structure appears throughout the New Testament to affirm that God Himself is manifested through Jesus Christ by means of the Spirit.

A proper biblical view of the Trinity balances the concepts of unity and distinctiveness. Two errors that appear in the history of the consideration of the doctrine are tritheism and unitarianism. In tritheism, error is made in emphasizing the distinctiveness of the Godhead to the point that the Trinity is seen as three separate Gods, or a Christian polytheism. On the other hand, unitarianism excludes the concept of distinctiveness while focusing solely on the aspect of God the Father. In this way, Christ and the Holy Spirit are placed in lower categories and made less than divine. Both errors compromise the effectiveness

and contribution of the activity of God in redemptive history.

The biblical concept of the Trinity developed through progressive revelation. See *Revelation.* The Old Testament consistently affirms the unity of God through such statements as, "Hear, O Israel: the Lord our God is one Lord" (Deut. 6:4). See *Shema.* God's oneness is stressed to caution the Israelites against the polytheism and practical atheism of their heathen neighbors.

The Old Testament does feature implications of the trinitarian idea. This does not mean that the Trinity was fully knowable from the Old Testament, but that a vocabulary was established through the events of God's nearness and creativity; both receive developed meaning from New Testament writers. For example, the word of God is recognized as the agent of creation (Ps. 33:6,9; compare Prov. 3:19; 8:27), revelation, and salvation (Ps. 107:20). This same vocabulary is given distinct personality in John's prologue (John 1:1–4) in the person of Jesus Christ. Other vocabulary categories include the wisdom of God (Prov. 8) and the Spirit of God (Gen. 1:2; Ps. 104:30; Zech. 4:6).

A distinguishing feature of the New Testament is the doctrine of the Trinity. It is remarkable that New Testament writers present the doctrine in such a manner that it does not violate the Old Testament concept of the oneness of God. In fact, they unanimously affirm the Hebrew monothestic faith, but they extend it to include the coming of Jesus and the outpouring of the Holy Spirit. The early Christian church experienced the God of Abraham in a new and dramatic way without abandoning the oneness of God that permeates the Old Testament. As a fresh expression of God, the concept of the Trinity—rooted in the God of the past and consistent with the God of the past—absorbs the idea of the God of the past, but goes beyond the God of the past in a more personal encounter.

The New Testament does not present a systematic presentation of the Trinity. The scattered segments from various writers that appear throughout the New Testament reflect a seemingly accepted understanding that exists without a full-length discussion. It is embedded in the framework of the Christian experience and simply assumed as true. The New Testament writers focus on statements drawn from the obvious existence of the trinitarian experience as opposed to a detailed exposition.

The New Testament evidence for the Trinity can be grouped into four types of passages. The first is the trinitarian formula of Matthew 28:19; 2 Corinthians 13:14; 1 Peter 1:2; Revelation 1:4. In each passage a trinitarian formula, repeated in summation fashion, registers a distinctive contribution of each person of the Godhead. Matthew 28:19, for example, follows the triple formula of Father, Son, and Holy Spirit that distinguishes

Christian baptism. The risen Lord commissioned the disciples to baptize converts with a trinitarian emphasis that carries the distinctiveness of each person of the Godhead while associating their inner relationship. This passage is the clearest scriptural reference to a systematic presentation of the doctrine of the Trinity.

Paul, in 2 Corinthians 13:14, finalized his thoughts to the Corinthian church with a pastoral appeal that is grounded in "the grace of the Lord Jesus Christ, and the love of God, and the fellowship of the Holy Spirit" (NIV). The formulation is designed to have the practical impact of bringing that divided church together through their personal experinece of the Trinity in their daily lives. Significantly, in the trinitarian order Christ is mentioned first. This reflects the actual process of Christian salvation, since Christ is the key to opening insight into the work of the Godhead. Paul was calling attention to the trinitarian consciousness, not in the initial work of salvation which has already been accomplished at Corinth, but in the sustaining work that enables divisive Christians to achieve unity.

In 1 Peter 1:2, the trinitarian formula is followed with reference to each person of the Godhead. The scattered Christians are reminded through reference to the Trinity that their election (foreknowledge of the Father) and redemption (the sanctifying work of the Spirit) should lead to holy living obedience to the Son.

John addressed the readers of Revelation with an expanded trinitarian formula that includes references to the persons of the Godhead (Rev. 1:4–6). The focus on the triumph of Christianity crystallizes the trinitarian greeting into a doxology that acknowledges the accomplished work and the future return of Christ. This elongated presentation serves as an encouragement to churches facing persecution.

A second type of New Testament passage is the triadic form. Two passages cast in this structure are Ephesians 4:4–6 and 1 Corinthians 12:3–6. Both passages refer to the three Persons, but not in the definitive formula of the previous passage. Each Scripture balances the unity of the church. Emphasis is placed on the administration of gifts by the Godhead.

A third category of passages mentions the three persons of the Godhead, but without a clear triadic structure. In the accounts of the baptism of Jesus (Matt. 3:3–17; Mark 1:9–11; and Luke 3:21–22), the three synoptic writers recorded the presence of the Trinity when the Son was baptized, the Spirit descended, and the Father spoke with approval. Paul, in Galatians 4:4–6, outlined the work of the Trinity in the aspect of the sending Father. Other representative passages in this category (2 Thess. 2:13–15; Titus 3:4–6; and Jude 20–21) portray each member of the Trinity in relation to a particular redemptive function.

The fourth category of trinitarian passages includes those presented in the farewell discourse of Jesus to His disciples (John 14:16; 15:26; 16:13–15). In the context of these passages, Jesus expounded the work and ministry of the third person of the Godhead as the Agent of God in the continuing ministry of the Son. The Spirit is a Teacher who facilitates understanding on the disciples' part and, in being sent from the Father and the Son, is one in nature with the other Persons of the Trinity. He makes known the Son and "at the same time makes known the Father who is revealed in the Son" (16:15). The discourse emphasizes the interrelatedness of the Trinity in equality and operational significance.

All of these passages are embryonic efforts by the early church to express its awareness of the Trinity. The New Testament is Christological in its approach, but it involves the fullness of God being made available to the individual believer through Jesus and by the Spirit. The consistent trinitarian expression is not a formulation of the doctrine, as such, but reveals an experiencing of God's persistent self-revelation.

In the postbiblical era, the Christian church tried to express its doctrine in terms that were philosophically acceptable and logically coherent. Greek categories of understanding began to appear in explanation efforts. Discussion shifted from the New Testament emphasis on the function of the Trinity in redemptive history to an analysis of the unity of essence of the Godhead.

A major question during those early centuries focused on the oneness of God. The *Sabelians* described the Godhead in terms of modes that existed only one at a time. This theory upheld the unity of God, but excluded His permanent distinctiveness. The *Docetists* understood Christ as an appearance of God in human form, while *Ebonites* described Jesus as an ordinary man indwelt with God's power at baptism. *Arius* was also an influential theologian who viewed Jesus as subordinate to God. To Arius, Jesus was a being created by God, higher than man, but less than God. This idea, as well as the others, was challenged by Athanasius at Nicea (A.D. 325), and the council decided for the position of Jesus as "of the exact same substance as the Father."

Probably the most outstanding thinker of the early centuries was Augustine of Hippo (A.D. 354–430). He began with the idea of God as one substance and sought explanation of the Godhead in psychological analogy: a person eixsts as one being with three dimensions of memory, understanding, and will; so also the Godhead exists as a unity of Father, Son, and Holy Spirit. While this explanation is helpful and contains the concept of three persons in one, it does not resolve the complex nature of God.

Perhaps four statements can summarize and clarify this study. *1. God is One.* The God of the

T

Old Testament is the same God of the New Testament. His offer of salvation in the Old Testament receives a fuller revelation in the New Testament in a way that is not different, but more complete. The doctrine of the Trinity does not abandon the monotheistic faith of Israel.

2. *God has three distinct ways of being in the redemptive event, yet He remains an undivided unity.* That God the Father imparts Himself to mankind through Son and Spirit without ceasing to be Himself is at the very heart of the Christian faith. A compromise in either the absolute sameness of the Godhead or the true diversity reduces the reality of salvation.

3. *The primary way of grasping the concept of the Trinity is through the threefold participation in salvation.* The approach of the New Testament is not to discuss the essence of the Godhead, but the particular aspects of the revelatory event that includes the definitive presence of the Father in the person of Jesus Christ through the Holy Spirit.

4. *The doctrine of the Trinity is an absolute mystery.* It is primarily known, not through speculation, but through experiencing the act of grace through personal faith. See *God; Jesus Christ; Holy Spirit.*   *Jerry M. Henry*

TRIPOLIS (Trĭ′ po lĭs) See *Tarpelites.*

TRIUMPHAL ENTRY The entry of Jesus into the city of Jerusalem on the Sunday prior to His crucifixion. Due to the fact that palm branches were placed before Him, this day is often called "Palm Sunday." The event is recorded in Matthew 21:1–9; Mark 11:1–10; Luke 19:29–38; John 12:12–15. All accounts agree in substance with each adding certain detail. Whether by prearrangement or by divine foreknowledge, the disciples found a colt in Bethphage as Jesus had described (Matthew ties the account closely to Zechariah's prophecy (9:9), mentioning the colt and its mother.) It is likely that Christ rode the donkey for the more difficult part of the journey, transferring to the colt upon actually entering Jerusalem. There a large crowd applauded Him, spreading the road with their garments and with branches. They acknowledged Him as the son of David.

The triumphal entry is of vital significance in understanding the messianic mission of Jesus. Prior to this moment, Jesus had refused to allow any public acknowledgement of His being the Messiah. By conducting His ministry outside Jerusalem, He had avoided further intensification of conflict with the Jewish religious leaders. Now, however, the time was at hand. The opponents of Jesus understood the strong messianic implications of the manner of His entry into Jerusalem. The riding upon the colt, the garments and palm branches in the road, and the shouts of the multitude—all of this pointed to Jesus as the Messiah. When He was urged to quiet the people,

Jesus replied, "If these become silent, the stones will cry out!" (Luke 19:40 NAS).

Ironically, though the triumphal entry was a public acceptance of being the Messiah and presented a direct challenge to His enemies, it must have been a disappointment to many of His followers. Christ did not enter Jerusalem upon a war horse of conquest but upon a colt representing humility. As a result, the religious leaders demanded His crucifixion, while the multitudes ultimately turned away with indifference. See *Jesus, Life and Ministry; Messiah.*   *Steve Echols*

TROAS (Trō ăs) A city in northwest Asia Minor visited by Paul during his second and third missionary journeys (Acts 16:8,11; 20:5–6; 2 Cor. 2:12; 2 Tim. 4:13). Troas was founded before 300 B.C. by Antigonus, a successor of Alexander the Great and was located about ten miles south of the city of Troy. The emperor Augustus (31 B.C.—14 A.D.) made it a Roman colony. It served as an important seaport in the Roman Empire for those traveling between Asia Minor and Macedonia. Today, ruins of the city wall (about six miles in circumference), a theater, and an aqueduct remain. See *Asia Minor; Paul.*   *Scott Langston*

TROGYLLIUM (Trō gўl′ lĭ ŭm) Promontory on the west coast of Asia Minor less than one mile across the strait from Samos, a stopping place on Paul's return to Jerusalem according to the Western text of Acts 20:15.

TROPHIMUS (Trŏph′ ĭ mŭs) Personal name meaning, "nutritious." Gentile Christian from Ephesus who accompanied Paul to Jerusalem for the presentation of the collection (Acts 20:4–5; 21:29). Paul's free association with Trophimus led to the false charge that Paul had defiled the Temple by bringing a Gentile within the Court of Israel (Acts 21:19). The Trophimus whom Paul left in Miletus (2 Tim. 4:20) is either another Trophimus or else evidence for a second Roman imprisonment. (According to Acts, Paul did not pass by Miletus on his way to Rome).

TRUMPET See *Music, Instruments, Dancing; Shophar.*

TRUTH That which is reliable and can be trusted. The Bible uses *truth* in the general "factual" sense. Truth may designate the actual fact over against appearance, pretense, or assertion. In Zechariah 8:16 (NRSV) the Lord of hosts declared: "These are the things that you shall do: Speak the truth to one another, render in your gates judgments that are true and make for peace." When Jesus asked, "Who touched my garments?" the woman who had been healed through touching Jesus' garments "fell down before him, and told him all the truth" (Mark 5:32–

A section of the ruins of the theater at Troas.

33). In 1 and 2 Timothy, truth is correct knowledge or doctrine. Certain individuals had departed from proper doctrine. Some "forbid marriage and demand abstinence from foods, which God created to be received with thanksgiving by those who believe and know the truth" (1 Tim. 4:3 NRSV.) Some have "swerved from the truth by claiming that the resurrection has already taken place (2 Tim. 2:18 NRSV.)

God and the Biblical Use of Truth The essential idea of truth in the Bible is not conformity to some external standard but faithfulness or reliability. In the case of God, of course, faithfulness or reliability is not measured by any external standard. God is the standard. God's truth (faithfulness or reliability) is the truth that is basic for all other truth, (Deut. 7:9-10). He maintains covenant and steadfast love. When God is spoken of as the true God or the God of truth (Deut. 32:4; 2 Chron. 15:3; Isa. 65:16; Jer. 10:10) the idea is that God is reliable. God "keepth truth for ever" (Ps. 146:6).

The "truth" of God's commandments grows out of the fact of God and His truth (faithfulness or reliability). The Word of God and His law are not true simply in the sense that they are in accord with science, human nature, or some abstract ethical principle. The great confession given by Ezra after the Jews returned from bondage in Babylon emphasized God's nature as truth (faithfulness) in what He did in creation, election, redemption, and the giving of the law: "You came down also upon Mount Sinai, and spoke with them from heaven and gave them right ordinances and true laws, good statutes and commandments, and you made known your holy sabbath to them and gave them commandments and statutes and a law through your servant Moses" (Neh. 9:13-14 NRSV).

The truth of God is reflected not only in His commandments; it is to be reflected in human life generally. "Only fear the Lord, and serve him in truth with all your heart: for consider how great things he hath done for you" (1 Sam. 12:24).

Important New Testament Concepts of Truth The most important uses of the word *truth* are to be found in Paul and writings of John. Paul's acceptance of the Old Testament concept of truth is seen in Romans 3:1-7. The truth of God is described in the words "faithfulness" (3:3) and "justice" (3:5). In 3:4, Paul declared, "Although everyone is a liar, let God be proved true" (NRSV).

In Paul's discussion of the relationship of Christians to truth, we find the same Old Testament emphasis: "Therefore, let us celebrate the festival, not with the old yeast, the yeast of malice and evil, but with the unleavened bread of sincerity and truth" (1 Cor. 5:8 NRSV). Truth and sincerity are associated, and both are opposed to malice and evil. Truth is not simply a matter of propositional accuracy. Paul spoke of truth as something that is to be obeyed (Rom. 2:8; Gal. 5:7). Paul spoke of the truth of God as being revealed not so much in the law as in Christ (Rom. 15:8-9). In Christ, God's kingdom has become manifested

(Rom. 1:1–6; 16:25–26; 2 Cor. 4:6). The truth and the gospel are related in the phrase "the truth of the gospel" (Gal. 2:5,14). One hears and believes the truth and is in Christ (Eph. 1:13).

The Johannine writings identify Christ with the truth: "The law indeed was given through Moses; grace and truth came through Jesus Christ. No one has ever seen God. It is God the only Son, who is close to the Father's heart, who has made him known" (John 1:17–18 NRSV). In testimony before Pilate, Jesus declared: "For this I was born, and for this I came into the world, to testify to the truth. Everyone who belongs to the truth listens to my voice" (John 18:37 NRSV). God is the truth; and since Christ shares in the truth of God, He is full of grace and truth. He is "the way, the truth, and the life" (John 14:6); He is the true Light and the true Vine (John 1:9; 15:1). In the Gospel of John, the activity of the Holy Spirit is associated with the activity of Jesus in so far as truth is concerned. When the Advocate comes, whom I will send to you from the Father, the Spirit of truth, who comes from the Father, he will testify on my behalf. You also are to testify because you have been with me from the beginning" (John 15:26–27 NRSV).

John emphasized the appropriation of the truth by disciples. In Jesus' high priestly prayer, He prayed: "Sanctify them in the truth; your word is truth. As you have sent me into the world, so I have sent them into the world. And for their sakes I sanctify myself, that they also may be sanctified in truth" (John 17:17–19 NRSV). Followers of Christ are of "the truth" (John 18:37 NRSV). This knowledge of truth is not simply "head knowledge." It is a matter of receiving Christ (John 1:11–13). This acceptance of Jesus and receiving of the truth is accompanied by walking in the truth or in the light (2 John 4; 3 John 3–4; 1 John 1:7). It is in light of this understanding of truth that John can speak of doing the truth (John 3:21; 1 John 1:6). *Edgar V. McKnight*

TRYPHAENA; TRYPHOSA (Trȳ phāē′ nà; Trȳ phō′ sà) Personal names meaning, "dainty" and "delicate." Two women whom Paul greeted as "workers in the Lord" (Rom. 16:12). The two were perhaps deacons serving the Roman church (compare Phoebe in Rom. 16:1 NRSV) or else "marketplace" evangelists like Priscilla (Acts 18:26; Rom. 16:3). The similarity of their names suggests the two were perhaps (twin) sisters.

TUBAL (Tū′ bàl) Son of Jepheth (Gen. 10:2; 1 Chron. 1:5) and ancestor of a people, known for their metalworking ability, likely of Cappadocia or Cilicia in Asia Minor (Isa. 66:19; Ezek. 27:13; 32:26; 38:2–3; 39:1).

TUBAL-CAIN (Tū′ bàl-Cain) Son of Lamech, associated with the origin of metalworking (Gen.

4:22). The two elements in his name mean, "producer" and "smith."

TUNIC Loose-fitting, knee length garment worn next to the skin (Matt. 10:10; Mark 6:9). See *Cloth, Clothing*.

Relief of two Roman men wearing tunics partially visible beneath their outer togas.

TURBAN Headdress formed by wrapping long strips of cloth around the head. A distinctive headdress formed part of the garb of the high priest (Ex. 28:4,37,39; 29:6; 39:28,31; Lev. 8:9; 16:4). Removal of one's turban was a sign of mourning or shame (Isa. 3:18–23; Ezek. 24:17,23). See *Cloth, Clothing; Headband; Headdress*.

TURNING OF THE WALL The expression used in the KJV elsewhere translated as "the corner buttress" (NAS), "the Angle" (NRSV), "the escarpment" (REB), and "the angle of the wall" (NIV). One segment of the Jerusalem ramparts probably located near the palace. It was fortified by Uzziah (2 Chron. 26:9) and rebuilt by Nehemiah (Neh. 3:19–20,24). Not to be confused with "the corner" (Neh. 3:31) nor associated with the corner gate.

See *Corner, Upper Chamber of; Corner Gate.*

TURQUOISE See *Minerals and Metals; Antimony.*

TURTLEDOVE See *Birds.*

TUTOR See *Custodian; Guardian.*

TWELVE, THE See *Apostles; Disciples, Apostles.*

TYCHICUS (Tȳch′ ĭ cŭs) Personal name meaning, "fortunate." One of Paul's fellow workers in the ministry. A native of Asia Minor (Acts 20:4), he traveled with the apostle on the third missionary journey. Tychicus and Onesimus carried the

Colossian letter from Paul (Col. 4:7–9), and were to relate to the church Paul's condition. Paul also sent Tychicus to Ephesus on one occasion (2 Tim. 4:12) and possibly to Crete on another (Titus 3:12). Tradition holds that he died a martyr.

TYPOLOGY A method of interpreting some parts of Scripture by seeing a pattern which an earlier statement sets up by which a later is explained. The Greek words that help us understand typology come under a verbal root that means "to beat, strike, or smite." In building construction, what is "beaten out" can become a pattern. This article will examine how various words in the family are used and how typology functions in interpreting the Old Testament.

Foundational Words and Meanings All of these related words show the effects of an imprint. (Translations in this article are the author's.)

1. Blow, strike, mark A literal meaning *tupos* is found in the narrative about Thomas' skepticism: "If I do not see in his hands *the mark (tupos)* of the nails and place my finger into the *mark* of the nails and place my hand into his side, I will not believe" (John 20:25). Jesus invited Thomas to examine His hands and side. Then Jesus urged: "Stop becoming an unbeliever, but rather become a believer" (John 20:27). Thomas showed he did just that when he exclaimed, "My Lord and My God" (John 20:28).

2. Technical model or pattern Both Hebrews 8:5 and Acts 7:44 use *tupos* to refer to Exodus 25:40, where the Lord commanded Moses to make the furniture and utensils of the tabernacle "by *the pattern* which you were seeing in the mountain." The Hebrew word for pattern is *tabniyth,* from a Hebrew root meaning "to build." The noun means "construction, pattern, or figure." The writer of Hebrews stressed that Christ could not be an earthly priest, for such priests served in the copy and shadow of heavenly things. Moses saw an earthly copy of the heavenly reality. Jesus became a high priest and a minister of the holy places and true tent, which the Lord pitched (Heb. 8:2). Even this earthly language shows the superiority of Christ's heavenly priesthood to that of the earthly priests.

In Acts 7:44, Stephen said that the whole tabernacle, which he called "the Tent of the Testimony" (REB), was made according to "the pattern" that Moses had seen. But did Moses see the "heavenly tabernacle" that is called the pattern? Or did God grant to Moses to see a pattern from which a rough earthly counterpart of the heavenly reality could be constructed? I think it was the latter. The word *tupos* means a *model* or pattern.

3. Image or Status In Acts 7, Stephen said that Israel took up "the tent of Moloch and the constellation of the god Rephan—*images, statues,* which you made to worship them" (Acts 7:43). Here what is "stamped or beaten out" is an idol. The imprint became an object of worship.

4. Pattern as a mold or norm While Stephen pointed out a bad pattern in the case of idolatry, Paul emphasized a good pattern in Romans 6:17. Paul thanked God that, although the Romans were once slaves of sin, they became subject to the gospel. He described the gospel as "the pattern *or norm* of teaching for the learning of which you were given over [by God]." The gospel is a norm or pattern showing how we should live (compare Rom. 1:16–17).

5. Persons as examples or patterns When people internalize the gospel, their lives begin a process of transformation. Paul spoke of himself and his fellow workers as examples or patterns. He urged the Philippians to become imitators of himself: "you have us as an example or pattern" (3:17). He said to the Thessalonians, "But we gave ourselves to you as a model or pattern that you should imitate us" (2 Thess. 3:9). Paul obtained mercy and God showed His forbearance to Paul "for a model, pattern, example for those who were about to believe in Christ" (1 Tim. 1:16).

The Thessalonians, by their faith during tribulation, became models or patterns for believers in Macedonia and Achaia. "In every place their faith had gone forth" (1 Thess. 1:7–8). Paul commanded Timothy to be a pattern or model for believers in "message, in manner of life, in love, in faith, in purity" (1 Tim. 4:12). At the same time, Timothy had his own standard to guide him: "constantly have a standard of sound words which you heard from me in the sphere of faith and love which is in Christ Jesus" (2 Tim. 1:13). Titus likewise was to be a model or pattern of good works, soundness in teaching, respectfulness, sound preaching that is beyond reproach (Titus 2:7–8). Peter urged all the elders to become *examples* or patterns for the flock rather than "lording it over" the flock (1 Pet. 5:3). Christians, and especially Christian leaders, are being watched and often imitated. The pattern or model they exhibit is crucial.

Typology as a Method of Interpreting the Old Testament Sometimes the New Testament explicitly refers to its method of interpreting the Old Testament as "type," or "typically." Usually, however, the New Testament uses typology as a method of interpreting the Old Testament without explicitly saying so. Typology involves a *correspondence,* usually in *one* particular matter between a person, event, or thing in the Old Testament with a person, event, or thing, in the New Testament. All elements except this *one* may be quite different, but the *one* element selected for comparison has a genuine similiarity in the two different historical contexts.

1. Old Testament warnings Paul used this kind of typology in 1 Corinthians 10:1–11. He rehearsed the experiences of the people of Israel in the Exodus and in their forty years years in the desert: the destruction of Pharaoh's army in the sea (Ex. 14—15); the eating of manna (Ex. 16); their conduct when thirsty—Rephidim—striking the rock (Ex. 17); Kadesh—speaking to the rock (Num. 20); sin of the gold calf (Ex. 32); fornication with the daughters of Moab at Baal of Peor (Num. 25); murmuring when going from Mount Hor around the land of Edom (Num. 21). Paul stressed *one* point of correspondence between the Old Testament events and the New Testament message: *All* the people participated in these experiences, but God was not pleased with most of them; the majority died in the desert and could not enter the Promised Land (1 Cor. 10:5). Paul pointed to this conduct of the majority who angered God as *types* or warning patterns, models, examples for Christians (1 Cor. 10:6). Christians are not to desire evil things, as in the golden calf incident, and as at Baal-Peor (1 Cor. 10:7–8). They were not to complain or murmur as the Israelites did when they were bitten by fiery serpents or in the judgment of the sons of Korah (1 Cor. 10:9–10; compare Num. 16; 21). Paul concluded, "Indeed, these things happened to them as a typological warning, but they were written for our admonition unto whom the end of the ages has arrived" (1 Cor. 10:11).

2. *Adam as a type of Christ* Paul compared Adam and Christ in Romans 5:12–21. He argued that Christ's deed is much more powerful than Adam's transgression. Paul said specifically that Adam "is a type of the one who was to come" (v. 14). Certainly, huge differences separate Adam and Christ. The one point of correspondence in the passage is *the effect of influence* upon humankind. Adam affected humankind adversely; Christ affects the same humankind for the good. Adam's trespass brought a verdict of condemnation of all people; Christ's righteous deed brought the gracious benefit to all people for the acquittal that brings life (vv. 16,18). Where sin abounded, grace was overflowing in greater abundance (v. 20). To make Christ's deed effective, people must receive the abundance of God's grace and the gift of righteousness (v. 17).

3. *Baptism as a fulfillment of the type* Peter, after discussing Christ's work in preaching in the spiritual realm to spirits in prison, mentioned Noah's ark and the flood: "Into which ark a few [eight persons] were saved through water, which water [baptism] as a fulfillment of the type now saves you through the resurrection of Jesus Christ from the dead, not through removing of dirt from the body but as a pledge of a good conscience towards God" (1 Pet. 3:20–21). Baptism is a drama of faith. Here it is called a pledge—an acted-out pledge of a good conscience. We are saved by faith expressed in water baptism. What is the one point of correspondence with the flood? The flood was a type of baptism because people of faith (and recipients of God's favor) experienced

deliverance. Noah and his family were delivered by the ark and the water; Christians expressing in baptism genuine faith are delivered from bondage to sin.

One point of correspondence between an Old Testament event and a New Testament event shows the same God at work in both covenants. Typology, a comparison stressing one point of similarity, helps us see the New Testament person, event, or institution as the fulfillment of that which was only hinted at in the Old Testament.

Berkeley Mickelson

TYRANNUS (Tӯ răn′ nŭs) Latin form of the Greek term *tyrant,* a ruler with absolute authority. After Paul withdrew from the synagogue in Ephesus, he preached for two years at the lecture hall of Tyrannus (Acts 19:9). Tyrannus was either the owner of the hall or a prominent philosopher associated with it. According to some Western texts, Paul preached from 11:00 until 4:00 p.m., the time of the afternoon break from work. If accurate, this tradition explains the availability of the hall (schools generally met in the morning) and the freedom of "all Asia" to hear Paul during their "siesta."

TYRE (Tӯre) See *Sidon and Tyre.*

TYRIAN (Tӯr′ ĭ an) Person from Tyre.

TYROPOEON VALLEY A narrow depression between Jerusalem's Ophel (Hill of David) and the western or upper hill of the city. It was much deeper in ancient times but has been filled up with debris through the centuries, especially since the destruction of the city by the Romans in A.D. 70. When David captured the city, the valley served as one of the natural defensive barriers. During Hellenistic times it was included within the city walls. During Herod's building campaign, he constructed bridges across the valley to connect the palace area with the Temple complex.

TYRUS (Tӯr′ ŭs) KJV alternate form for Tyre.

Looking at the west side of the Temple Mount from the west with the Tyropoeon valley in the foreground.

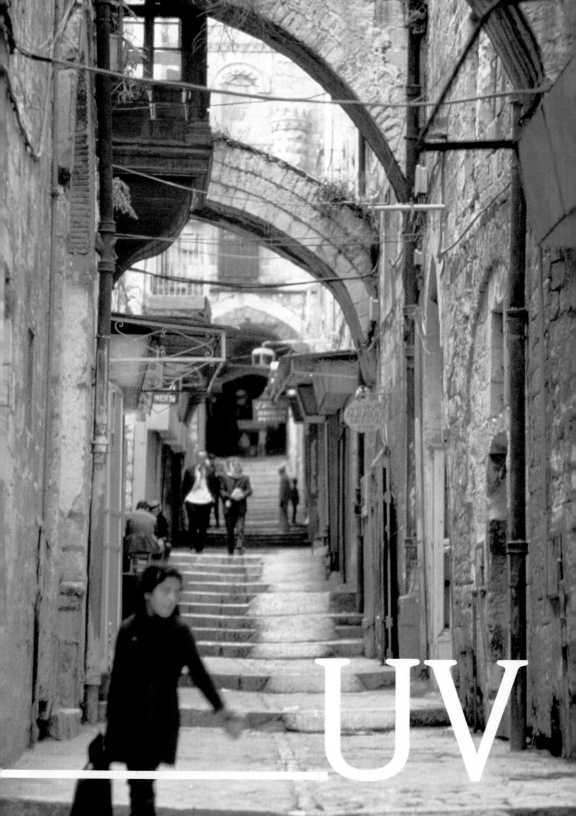

UV

The Via Dolorosa (Way of the Cross) in the old city of Jerusalem.

UCAL (Ū′ căl) Personal name meaning, "I am strong" or "I am consumed." A pupil of Agur, the wisdom teacher responsible for Proverbs 30 (Prov. 30:1). REB followed the earliest Greek translation in rendering the proper names *Ithiel* and *Ucal* as "I am weary, God, I am weary and worn out" (compare NRSV).

UEL (Ū′ ĕl) Personal name meaning, "will of God," or a contraction of Abiel, meaning, "God is father." Contemporary of Ezra with a foreign wife (Ezra 10:34; KJV, Juel).

UGARIT An important city in Syria whose excavation has provided tablets giving the closest primary evidence available for reconstructing the Canaanite religion Israel faced.

Location The ruins of the ancient city of Ugarit lie on the Mediterranean coast about nine miles north of Latakia. The contemporary name is Ras Shamra, "head [land] of fennel." Located at the juncture of major trade routes from Anatolia, northwest Mesopotamia, and Egypt and possessing a harbor (modern Minet el-Beida) which accommodated vessels from Cyprus, the Aegean, and Egypt, Ugarit was an important commercial center in most periods until the Sea People destroyed it in 1180 B.C. Its culture was cosmopolitan, so much so that it is difficult to identify those elements which were uniquely Ugaritic. Although it was the capital of a city-state, it was most often

An overview of the ruins of Ugarit, at Ras Shamra on the Syrian coast, near the Orontes River.

under the power or dominating influence of larger states.

The Excavations Although the existence of Ugarit had been known from Mesopotamian and Egyptian documents, its location was uncertain. In 1928, a farmer's discovery of what turned out to be an extensive cemetery just north of Minet el-Beida led in 1929 to excavations in the cemetery and on the tell nearby (Ras Shamra). In that first season of excavations, important texts written in a previously unknown cuneiform script were discovered, one of which mentioned that the document was written during the time of Niqmaddu, king of Ugarit. This was the first indication that the site was indeed ancient Ugarit.

Excavations were carried out annually, 1929–1939, under the direction of C. F. A. Schaeffer. After the hiatus caused by World War II, excavations were resumed and continued on a regular basis through 1976. In addition, adjacent sites have either been surveyed or excavated. The history of the city may now be traced from its earliest beginnings in the prepottery Neolithic period (about 6500 B.C.), through the Chalcolithic, Early Bronze, and Middle Bronze periods, to its complete and final destruction in the Late Bronze period soon after 1200 by the Sea Peoples. We have no evidence that the site of Ugarit was ever occupied again, although artifacts from as late as Roman times have been found.

The Late Bronze city of Ugarit, covering about seventy acres, contained the remains of palaces, temples, private dwellings, workshops, storage ar-

U
V

The excavated areas of Ugarit which have yielded much material about Canaan and Canaanite religion.

eas, and fortifications. There were found temples dedicated to Baal and to El; between these buildings was located the house of the high priest and scriptorium. On the northwestern side of the tell were located the palaces. The material culture of Late Bronze Ugarit was of the highest order, showing cultural influences from all the surrounding areas.

The most significant discoveries at Ugarit for the study of both history and religion are the discoveries of the epigraphic materials. Clay tablets and other inscriptions representing eight languages have come to light. The majority of these documents consist of economic and administrative texts, private correspondence, and liturgical-religious texts which represent major mythological themes.

From the first season of excavation there began to emerge a large number of clay tablets written in an unknown script. The new script, used to inscribe texts in the Ugaritic language, was in alphabetic cuneiform consisting of thirty-one signs, twenty-eight of which were consonants and three of which indicated the letter 'aleph as used with three different vowels. For the student of the Bible, the religious and mythological texts present a rather full picture of Canaanite religious practice and belief already known from the Bible. See *Canaan*.

The study and evaluation of all the material remains from Ugarit and contiguous sites will continue until the archaeological history can be clarified, until the fullest possible social and political history can be written, and until the full yield of information from the Ugaritic texts has been achieved.

The Religious Texts The poetic mythological texts and poetic legends have elicited the greatest interest because of the information they provide about Canaanite religion. Foremost is the Baal-Anath cycle which has survived in a number of large tablets and smaller fragments. It is difficult to determine the exact story line because there is little agreement on the order of the tablets. The central figure was Baal, the god of storm cloud and rain or the giver of life and fertility, who struggled against his foes in order to gain a dominant position in the pantheon. The head of the pantheon was El who appears in the epic as far removed, almost a god emeritus, although nothing could be accomplished without his approval. Asherah and Anath were the consorts of El and Baal, respectively. Baal's antagonists were Prince Sea (Yam) and Mot (god of the dry season and underworld). Having received permission to build a house (temple), Prince Sea struck fear into the hearts of the gods by demanding that Baal be surrendered to him. But Baal defeated Prince Sea in an episode reminiscent of Marduk's defeat of the sea monster, Tiamat, in the *enuma elish*. See *Babylon*. Then Baal was permitted to build a palace (temple) as symbol of his new status among the gods. However, Baal's mightiest foe, Mot, defeated Baal, crushing him like a kid in his gullet, and taking him down to the netherworld. The world went into mourning. El wept piteously at the news, gashing his back, chest, and arms, while Anath, having found Baal's corpse, put on sackcloth and bewailed the death of the lord of life. Mot boasted of his victory to Anath, whereupon she slew Mot, ground him up and scattered his remains over the fields. Then came the joyous cry that Baal was alive; the rains came, and the world returned to life.

The myth was closely related to the cycle of the year and described the ongoing struggles between life and death. While Baal ruled half the year, giving rain and crops, Mot held dominion over the other half: the dry season. Fertility religion consisted in part of various magical and ritual practices designed to bring Baal back to life. Hints of these practices are given in the Baal-Anath cycle. El, upon hearing that Baal was dead, gashed his body: "He harrows the roll of his arm, he plows his chest like a garden, harrows his back like a plain." Like the prophets of Baal on Mount Carmel (1 Kings 18), he was practicing imitative magic as though preparing the fields to receive the rain. For her part, Anath wept for Baal, the falling tears intended to encourage the rain to fall. In addition to these acts, in actual practice the Canaanites employed sacred prostitution and other imitative practices to restore fertility to the world. See *Fertility Cults*.

The Legend of King Keret and the Legend of Aqhat are also related in some way to the fertility cycle. King Keret, having lost his seven wives to various tragedies before they could give him an heir, bewailed his fate. In a dream, El told him to attack another kingdom to obtain another wife who could produce an heir. Keret succeeded in this, and eight sons and eight daughters were born to him. However, apparently because of an unfulfilled vow, Keret fell sick; his impending death seemed to affect the fertility of the land. El intervened, death was shattered, and Keret returned to normal life. The full significance of the Keret legend is difficult to determine, whether it

U
V

is a cultic myth or a social myth with a historical basis, but it does seem to affirm the central role of the king in the fertility of land and people.

The legend of Aqhat also treats the typical elements of the birth of a long-awaited son, the tragedy of death, and the possibility of immortality. Danel's son, Aqhat, was given a composite bow which the goddess Anath coveted. Anath promised Aqhat immortality if he would give her the bow, but Aqhat refused and was killed. The rains then failed for seven years. Aqhat's sister was sent to avenge his death, but the text broke off before the story was completed, leaving unanswered the question whether Aqhat was restored to life and the drought ended. While the connection of the legend with fertility is clear enough, there is no clear consensus on how to interpret the legend.

These myths and legends, together with others like Shachar and Shalim and Nikkal and the Kathirat, may have been used as the spoken parts of annual or periodic rituals. In any case these texts, together with other artifacts, provide a more complete picture of Canaanite religious practice which proved such a temptation to the Israelites (compare the Book of Judges) and against which the prophets protested.

Importance for Old Testament Study The Ugaritic texts and material remains offer Old Testament scholars primary resources for much of their study.

1. Lexicography. The Ugaritic texts have provided a welcome resource for clarifying the meanings and nuances of unknown and obscure words and phrases in the Old Testament. Although we must use due caution because of the chronological, geographical, and cultural factors which separate the Ugaritic texts from the Old Testament texts, no scholar today would neglect the linguistic data provided by Ugarit. New readings of biblical texts in the light of Ugaritic grammar, syntax, and lexicon open up innumerable possibilities for new or revised interpretations and translations. Translators now do not hasten so quickly to emend the Hebrew text on the basis of early translations. They look first to Ugaritic evidence.

2. Poetic studies. Poetic parallelism, the chief characteristic of Hebrew poetry, is characteristic of Ugaritic poetry as well. Indeed, the study of Ugaritic poetic texts makes one more sensitive to the sophisticated techniques of the psalmists and other poets. Clear Ugaritic cases of chiastic construction, composite divine names separated within a verse, nouns and verbs serving a double-duty function, characteristic word-pairs, and the analysis of meter by the counting of syllables are helpful in the analysis of Hebrew poetry, especially the Psalms.

3. Religion. While about 250 deity names occur in the texts from Ugarit, a much smaller number actually comprised the pantheon. Many of these names are known in the Old Testament: El, Baal, Asherah, Anath, Yarih (moon), Shahar, Shalim, Mot, Dagon, for example. The existence of the divine assembly (Ps. 82; Job 1—2) is attested at Ugarit, especially in the Baal-Anath cycle. The practice of imitative magic in order to manipulate deity and the natural order is mentioned often (compare 1 Kings 18:28; Jer. 41:5). So too was religious prostitution (compare Deut. 23:18; Hos. 4:14). All in all, the texts from Ugarit give a rather full picture of the type of fertility religion, characteristic of an agricultural people, which many Israelites adopted in most periods of Israelite history. A comparative study of Hebrew and Ugaritic texts allows one to see the common cultural and religious possessions as well as the distinctive characteristics of each. *Thomas Smothers*

ULAI (Ū′ lāi) Canal connecting the Kerkha and Abdizful rivers just north of Susa (Dan. 8:2,16).

ULAM (Ū′ lăm) Personal name meaning, "first" or "leader." *1.* Descendant of Manasseh (1 Chron. 7:16–17). *2.* Leader of a family of Benjaminite archers (1 Chron. 8:39–40).

ULLA (Ŭl′ lā) Personal name meaning, "burden" or "yoke." Descendant of Asher (1 Chron. 7:39). Scholars suggest a variety of emendations.

UMMAH (Ŭm′ mah) Place name meaning, "kin." Town in Asher (Josh. 19:30). The name is perhaps a copyist's change from Acco as may be indicated by Greek manuscript evidence.

UNCIRCUMCISED See *Circumcision.*

UNCTION KJV term meaning, "anointing" (1 John 2:20,27). See *Anoint.*

UNDEFILED Ritually clean, frequently used for moral cleanness. See *Clean, Cleanness.*

UNICORN KJV translation of several related Hebrew terms which modern translations render as wild ox (as in Num. 23:22; 24:8; Deut. 33:17).

UNITY State of being undivided; oneness.
Old Testament Central to the faith of Israel is the confession of the unity of God: "Hear, O Israel: The Lord Your God is one Lord" (Deut. 6:4). Because God is one, one set of laws was to apply to both Israelites and foreigners (Num. 15:16). Human history is a story of sin's disruption of God's ordained unity. God's ideal for marriage is for husband and wife to experience unity of life, "one flesh" (Gen. 2:24). Sin in the garden bred mistrust and accusation (3:12). Stubbornness of will ("hardness" of heart, Mark 10:5) continues to disrupt God's desired unity in marriage. God's ideal for the larger human family is again unity. The primeval unity of humanity ("one language"

Gen. 11:1) was likewise disrupted as a result of sinful pride (11:4–8). The prophetic vision of God's future anticipates the day when God will reunite the divided kingdoms of Israel and Judah, bringing back all the scattered exiles (Ezek. 37:15–23). Indeed, the prophetic hope includes the reuniting of all the peoples of the world under the sovereignty of the one Lord (Zech. 14:9).

New Testament Jesus prayed that His disciples would experience unity modeled on the unity Jesus experienced with the Father (John 17:11, 21–23). Such unity verifies Jesus' God-sent mission and the Father's love for the world. Jesus' prayer for unity was realized in the life of the earliest church. The first believers were together in one place; they shared their possessions and were of one heart and soul (Acts 2:1,43; 4:32). As in the Old Testament, sin threatened the God-ordained unity. The selfishness of Ananias and Sapphira (Acts 5:1–11), the prejudice of those who neglected the Greek-speaking widows (6:1), the rigidness of those who demanded that Gentiles become Jews before becoming disciples (15:1)—all threatened the unity of the church. In every circumstance, however, the Holy Spirit led the church in working out creative solutions that challenged the church to go beyond dissension to ministry (Acts 6:2–7; 15:6–35). Paul spoke repeatedly of believers as "one body in Christ" which transcends varieties of giftedness (Rom. 12:5–8; 1 Cor. 12:13,27–30) and human labels (Gal. 3:28; Eph. 2:14–15; 3:6). For Paul, the unity of the church reflects the unity of the Godhead: one God (1 Cor. 12:6); one Lord (Rom. 10:12; 1 Cor. 12:5; Eph. 4:5); and one Spirit (1 Cor. 12:4,11; also Acts 11:17). Christian unity has various aspects: the shared experience of Christ as Lord and confession of Christ in baptism (Eph. 4:5,13); the shared sense of mission ("one mind," Phil. 2:2); the shared concern for one another (1 Cor. 12:25; "same love," Phil. 2:2; 1 Pet. 3:8); and the shared experience of suffering for Jesus' sake (2 Cor. 1:6; Phil. 1:29–30; 1 Thess. 2:14; 1 Pet. 5:9). *Chris Church*

UNLEAVENED BREAD Bread baked without using leaven, a substance such as yeast which produces fermentation in dough. Unleavened bread was often served to guests (Gen. 19:3; Judg. 6:19; 1 Sam. 28:24). The eating of unleavened bread took on special significance through the Feast of Unleavened Bread celebrated in connection with Passover (Ex. 12:8,15,20; 13:3,6–7). See *Exodus; Festivals; Passover.*

UNNI (Ŭn′ ni) Personal name perhaps meaning, "afflicted" or "answered." *1.* Levitical harpist in David's time (1 Chron. 15:18,20). *2.* Levite returning from Exile with Zerubbabel (Neh. 12:9). The Hebrew Masoretic text reads Unno; the scribal marginal notes (Qere) read Unni.

UNNO (Ŭn′ nō) See *Unni.*

UNPARDONABLE SIN, THE Setting one's mind against the Holy Spirit and crediting Satan with what is obviously God's work. To understand the unpardonable sin referred to in Matthew 12:31–32, is to understand what it is *not.*

It is not: murder, lying, stealing, suicide, adultery, taking the Lord's name in vain, a sin committed in ignorance, a sin that a Christian can commit, or a sin that a person may feel he or she has committed.

It is: to blaspheme against the Holy Spirit. To blaspheme means to speak an insult against someone so as to defame the person's reputation and character. The unpardonable sin is a persistent and deliberate sin against light, maintained in the face of the positive work of the Holy Spirit. This can happen to people today. Jesus was not talking about a sin of His day only; it can happen anytime. It happens when a person sees a work that is without question God's work and not human work, but says it is Satan's work!

What is the Holy Spirit's work? To point one to Jesus Christ as Savior and Lord. The unpardonable sin is committed today when one sets mind and will and spirit against the Holy Spirit. This is telling the Spirit that He is trying to do something evil in the person's life by pointing one to Jesus. When do people reach that point? No one knows for sure, but each time people reject the movement of the Holy Spirit and Jesus' claim upon their lives, that sense of urgency and conviction gets weaker until, finally, it is too late.

Two points occur in a person's life when salvation may not be possible. Salvation cannot come before the Holy Spirit convicts a person; and salvation cannot come after the person no longer feels conviction, because rejection has hardened the heart. That is why the invitation to trust Jesus Christ is always *now.* See *Blasphemy; Devil; Holy Spirit; Sin.* *Jim Henry*

UPHARSIN (Ū′ phär sĭn) See *Mene, Mene, Tekel Upharsin.*

UPHAZ (Ū′ phăz) Unidentified source of fine gold (Jer. 10:9; Dan. 10:5) or else a term for fine gold. A related Hebrew term is translated "best gold" (1 Kings 10:18; Isa. 13:12). Uphaz is possibly a copyist's change for Ophir at Jeremiah 10:9 as indicated by early versions.

UPPER CHAMBER See *Chamber; Upper Room.*

UPPER ROOM An upstairs room chosen by Jesus in which to hold a final meal with His disciples before His arrest (Mark 14:14–15). Jesus commanded two of His followers to prepare the room and the meal. Tradition holds that the disciples gathered in this room following Jesus' ascension

The traditional site of the upper room, or Hall of the Coenaculum, in Jerusalem.

(Acts 1:13). More than a century after Christ's ministry on earth the room believed to be the one in which the meal was eaten was made into a shrine and still is commemorated today.

UR (Ŭr) Place name meaning, "fire oven." An ancient city in lower Mesopotamia that is mentioned in the Bible as Abraham's birthplace. Ur, Kish, and Uruk were three important population centers in Sumerian and Babylonian civilization. Abraham's family home is alluded to in Genesis 12:1 and Acts 7:2. The site associated with Ur is located in present-day Iraq, in the lower eastern portion of the Fertile Crescent. It is identified with tell el-Muqayyar some 350 km (220 mi) southeast of Baghdad. The site is an oval shape and had harbor facilities on the Euphrates River, until its course shifted twelve miles east from the city's western limit. With the river's shift, the city lost both its population and prominence. Other sites have been proposed for the biblical Ur, such as Urartu (Turkey) or Urfa (northwest of Haran). Occupation of tell el-Muqayyar began about 4000 B.C. and was important in Sumerian, Babylonian, and neo-Babylonian cultures. The third dynasty of Ur was its most prosperous and highly developed period. Important remains discovered were a ziggurat (a three stage, stepped pyramid) and royal tombs. This Sumerian site is most probably to be identified as Abraham's city of origin. Yet, as with most identifications, such can be questioned. See *Abraham; Babylon; Chaldees; Mesopotamia; Sumeria.* *David M. Fleming*

URBANE (Ŭr′ bāne) KJV spelling of Urbanus.

URBANUS (Ŭr bā′ nŭs) Personal name meaning, "of the city," that is, "elegant, refined." Roman Christian whom Paul greeted as a "helper in Christ" (Rom. 16:9).

URI (Ŭ′ rī) Personal name meaning, "fiery." *1.*

The belltower of the Church of the Dormition, adjacent to the traditional upper room, in Jerusalem.

Father of the tabernacle artisan Bezalel (Ex. 31:2; 35:30). *2.* Father of Geber, one of Solomon's officers charged with providing the royal household food for a month (1 Kings 4:19). *3.* Postexilic, Levitic singer with a foreign wife (Ezra 10:24).

URIAH (Ū rī′ ah) Personal name meaning, "fire of Yah." *1.* A Hittite mercenary, or a native, perhaps noble Israelite of Hittite ancestry, in David's army (2 Sam. 11), a member of David's elite warriors (23:39). He was the husband of Bathsheba, the woman with whom David committed adultery. The sin led to the eventual murder of Uriah after the king could cover the affair no longer. The Dead Sea Scrolls and Josephus report that Uriah was Joab's weapon-bearer. Uriah displayed more character and morality than did the king. See *Bathsheba; David.*
2. High priest in Jerusalem Temple under King Ahaz who followed the king's instructions in setting up an altar in the Temple according to a Syrian pattern (2 Kings 16:10–16). He apparently served as a witness for Isaiah (8:2).
3. Priest in time of Ezra and Nehemiah (Ezra 8:33; Neh. 3:4,21). *4.* Person who helped Ezra in informing the people of God's word (Neh. 8:4).

URIEL (Ū′ rĭ ĕl) Personal name meaning, "God is light" or "flame of God." *1.* Chief of the Levites

The outer wall of the ziggurat, or temple tower, at Ur in ancient Mesopotamia (modern Iraq).

U
V

The excavations at Ur showing the palace foundations in the foreground with the ziggurat in the distance.

assisting in David's transport of the ark to Jerusalem (1 Chron. 6:24; 15:5,11); *2.* Grandfather of King Abijah of Judah (2 Chron. 13:2).

URIJAH (Ū rī′ jah) Personal name meaning, "flame of Yahweh." Variant spelling of Uriah. *1.* Chief priest who complied with Ahab's order to build an Assyrian-style altar for the Jerusalem Temple (2 Kings 16:10–16). Ahab likely hoped the incorporation of foreign elements into Israel's worship would impress the Assyrian king Tiglath-Pileser with his loyalty. *2.* Prophet who joined Jeremiah in preaching against Jerusalem. When king Jehoiakim ordered his execution, Urijah fled to Egypt. He was, however, captured, returned to Jerusalem, and executed (Jer. 26:20–23).

URIM AND THUMMIM (Ū′ rĭm and Thŭm′ mĭm) Objects Israel, and especially the high priest, used to determine God's will. Little is known about the Urim and Thummim. They are first mentioned in Exodus as being kept by the high priest in a "breastplate of judgment" (Ex. 28:15–30). Later, Moses gave the tribe of Levi special responsibility for their care (Deut. 33:8). After Aaron's and Moses' death, Eleazar was to carry and to use the lots to inquire of the Lord (Num. 27:18–23). They apparently were two objects that served as sacred lots. See *Lots.* That is, they were used to determine God's will or to receive a divine answer to a question. Saul called for their use, for instance, in deter-

mining who had broken Saul's vow in a battle with the Philistines (1 Sam. 14:41–45). This text also hints as to how the objects were used. They were "given," perhaps drawn or shaken from a bag. One object gave one answer. The other lot gave another answer. Probably, whichever lot came out first, that was understood to be God's answer. The Urim and Thummim were not, however, automatic or mechanical. God could refuse to answer. Saul sought the spirit of Samuel through a witch because God would not answer Saul through Urim or dreams or prophets (1 Sam. 28:6–25).

The ultimate fate of the Urim and Thummim is unknown. In Nehemiah's time, expectation continued that someday a priest would arise with Urim and Thummim (Ezra 2:63; Neh. 7:65). This probably refers to the ability to receive an answer from the Lord, however, rather than a return of the lots given to Aaron. See *Oracles; Lots; High Priest.* *Albert Bean*

USURY (Ūs′ ŭ rȳ) A sum of money charged for a loan. The Old Testament laws prohibited a Jew from charging another Jew usury but permitted it when money was loaned to a Gentile (Deut. 23:19–20). Although the word has negative connotations today, it was not so in biblical days when usury simply was the interest charged for a loan. Excessive usury was condemned.

UTHAI (Ū thâî) Personal name meaning, "Yahweh is help" or "He has shown Himself supreme." *1.* Postexilic descendant of Judah

(1 Chron. 9:4). *2.* Head of a family of those returning from Exile (Ezra 8:14).

UZ (Ŭz) Personal and place name perhaps meaning, "replacement." *1.* Unspecified territory, most likely in Hauran south of Damascus (Jer. 25:20) or else between Edom and northern Arabia (Job 1:1; Lam. 4:21). *2.* Descendant of Shem's son Aram (Gen. 10:23; 1 Chron. 1:17) and progenitor of an Aramaean tribe. *3.* Descendant of Abraham's brother Nahor (Gen. 22:21). *4.* Descendant of Esau (Gen. 36:28) and member of the Horite branch of Edomites.

UZAI (Ū' zâi) Personal name meaning, "hoped for" or "He has heard." Father of one helping with Nehemiah's repair of the wall (Neh. 3:25).

UZAL (Ū' zăl) Son of Joktan and ancestor of an Arabian tribe (Gen. 10:27; 1 Chron. 1:21). Scholars have linked the tribe with Izalla in northeastern Syria and Azalla near Medina. Ezekiel 27:19 includes them among Tyre's trading partners.

UZZA (Ŭz' zà) Personal name meaning, "strength." *1.* Descendant of Benjamin (1 Chron. 8:7). *2.* Descendant of Levi (1 Chron. 6:29). *3.* Head of a family of postexilic Temple servants or nethinim (Ezra 2:49). *4.* Owner of the garden in which Manasseh and Amon were buried (2 Kings 21:18,26).

UZZA Variant English spelling of *Uzzah.*

UZZAH (Ŭz' zah) Personal name meaning, "He is strong." *1.* One of the drivers of the cart carrying the ark of the covenant when David began moving it from the house of Abinadab in Gibeah to Jerusalem (2 Sam. 6:3). When the ark started to slip from the cart, Uzzah put out his hand to steady it, and God struck him dead for touching the holy object (6:6–7). *2.* Ancestor of exiles who returned to Jerusalem from Babylon (Ezra 2:49). *3.* Name of garden in which kings Manasseh and Ammon were buried. This distinguished them from other kings who "slept with their fathers," that is, were buried in the royal tomb. Uzzah may have been a noble who owned the garden burial plot or may have been a variant spelling of the Canaanite god Attar-melek. *4.* Member of tribe of Benjamin (1 Chron. 8:7). *5.* Family of Temple servants who returned from Exile with Zerubbabel (Ezra 2:49). *6.* A Levite (1 Chron. 6:29).

UZZEN-SHEERAH (Ŭz' zĕn-Shē' ė rah) Place name meaning, "ear of Sheerah." Village which Ephraim's daughter, Sheerah, founded (1 Chron. 7:24). The site is perhaps Beit Sira three miles south of lower Beth-horon.

UZZI (Ŭz' zī) Personal name; an abbreviated form of "Yahweh is my strength." *1.* Aaronic priest (1 Chron. 6:5–6,51; Ezra 7:4). *2.* Family of the tribe of Issachar (1 Chron. 7:2–3). *3.* Descendant of Benjamin (1 Chron. 7:7; 9:8). *4.* Overseer of Jerusalem Levites after the Exile (Neh. 11:22). *5.* Postexilic priest (Neh. 12:19). *6.* Musician involved in Nehemiah's dedication of Jerusalem's walls (Neh. 12:42).

UZZIA (Ŭz zī' à) Personal name meaning, "Yahweh is strong." One of sixteen whom the Chronicler added to the list of David's "thirty" elite warriors (1 Chron. 11:44).

UZZIA(H) (Ŭz zī' ah) Personal name meaning, "Yahweh is might." *1.* Descendant of Levi (1 Chron. 6:24). *2.* Father of one of David's treasurers (1 Chron. 27:25).

3. Also known as Azariah (2 Kings 15:1,6–8,17,23,27); son and successor of King Amaziah of Judah. "All the people of Judah" declared Uzziah king when he was sixteen (2 Kings 14:21; 2 Chron. 26:1). Some conjecture that the Judeans, rather than have King Joash of Israel install a puppet king, put Uzziah forward as king following Amaziah's defeat and subsequent imprisonment by Joash (2 Chron. 25:21–24). According to this reconstruction, Uzziah began his reign about 792 B.C. and continued as joint regent after his father's release upon the death of Joash (2 Chron. 25:25).

Uzziah's reign was a time of great material prosperity for Judah. Uzziah mounted a successful campaign against the Philistines, destroying the walls of some of their chief cities, Gath, Jabneh, and Ashdod. To secure the caravan route along the Mediterranean coast (Via Maris), Uzziah built cities, perhaps military outposts, in the vicinity of Ashdod and at other sites on the Philistine plain (2 Chron. 26:6). To secure the eastern caravan route (the King's Highway), Uzziah rebuilt Elat (Eloth), the strategic port on the gulf of Aqaba (26:2) and campaigned against the Arabs of Gurbaal (possibly Gur east of Beersheba), the Meunites (a branch of Edomites), and the Ammonites (2 Chron. 26:7–8). Uzziah refortified the walls of Jerusalem with towers (2 Chron. 26:9; compare 25:23). His construction of numerous cisterns and military outposts in the wilderness (the Arad Negeb) made widespread settlement possible. Archaeological evidence confirms that construction in the Negeb flourished during Uzziah's reign. Uzziah was a lover of the soil who promoted agriculture (2 Chron. 26:10). Unlike his predecessors who relied on the troops to supply their own arms, Uzziah armed his troops with the most advanced weapons (2 Chron. 26:11–15).

Uzziah is not so much remembered as the leader who brought Judah to a golden age rivaling David's and Solomon's empires, but as the "leper king." The brief account of Uzziah's reign in

U
V

2 Kings 15:1–7 portrays the king as one who did what "was right in the sight of the Lord" (15:3). No explanation for the king's affliction is given in Kings other than "the Lord struck the king" (15:5 NRSV). The Chronicler traced Uzziah's leprosy to his prideful attempt to ursurp the priestly preroga- tive of offering incense in the Temple (2 Chron. 26:16–20; compare Num. 16:1–40; 1 Sam. 13:8–15). Thereafter, his son Jotham reigned in his stead, though Uzziah likely remained the power behind the throne (26:21). As a leper, Uzziah was denied burial in the royal tombs at Jerusalem. Rather, he was buried in a field (26:23).
4. Postexilic priest with a foreign wife (Ezra 10:21). 5. Descendant of Judah and father of a postexilic resident of Jerusalem (Neh. 11:4).

Chris Church

UZZIEL (Ŭz' zĭ ĕl) Personal name meaning, "God is strength." *1.* Descendant of Levi (Ex. 6:18; Num. 3:19; 1 Chron. 6:2,18) and ancestor of a subdivision of Levites, the Uzzielites (Num. 3:27; 1 Chron. 15:10; 26:23). *2.* One captain in the successful Simeonite attack on the Amalekites of Mount Seir (1 Chron. 4:42). *3.* Descendant of Benjamin (1 Chron. 7:7). *4.* Levitical musician (1 Chron. 25:4). *5.* Levite involved in Hezekiah's reform (2 Chron. 29:14). *6.* Goldsmith assisting in Nehemiah's repair of the Jerusalem walls (Neh. 3:8).

UZZIELITE (Ŭz zĭ e' līte) Member of Levitical clan of Uzziel.

VAIN Self-conceit, usually a translation of a num- ber of words that mean, "nothingness" or "unreli- ability." In relation to God, trying to thwart His will is vain (Ps. 2:1; see Acts 4:25). Trying to do things without God's help is vain (Ps. 127:1). We are warned not to take God's name in vain (as though it were nothing) in the Ten Command- ments (Ex. 20: 7; Deut. 5:11). Mark warned that believers are not to give God vain lip service but obedience from the heart (7:6–7; see Isa. 1:13; 29:13; Jas. 1:26).

VAIZATHA (Vai' za tha) Modern translations' spelling of Vajezatha.

VAJEZATHA (Va jez' a tha) Persian personal name perhaps meaning, "the son of the atmo- sphere." One of Haman's ten sons the Jews killed after Esther gained permission to retaliate against Haman's deadly plan (Esth. 9:9).

VALLEY Depression between mountains, a broad plain or plateau, a narrow ravine, or a low terrain. "Valleys" of varying shapes and sizes mark Pales- tine's landscape.
Five Hebrew terms are designated "valley" in

the Old Testament. *Bikeah* is a broad plain (Gen. 11:2; Isa. 41:8). *Gaye* is a deep ravine, gorge, or valley (Isa. 40:4; Zech. 14:4). *Nahal* is a wadi, that is the bed of a stream which is often dry (Num. 34:5; Ps. 124:4; Ezek. 48:28). *Emech* is a long, broad sweep between parallel ranges of hills (Num. 14:25; Josh. 8:13; Jer. 21:13). *Shephelah* is the low land, plain, or slope sweeping gently down from mountains (Deut. 10:1; Josh. 9:1; Jer. 17:26). One Greek term, *pharanx,* is used in the New Testament for each of these.
Valley is often used symbolically to refer to the difficulties of life. The classic example of this is Psalm 23:4. All people go through these trials, but God is present with His people, protecting them during these times. See *Palestine.*

Bradley S. Butler

VALLEY OF CRAFTSMEN See *Geharashim.*

VALLEY OF ZERED See *Brook of Zered.*

VANIAH (Vȧ nī' ah) Personal name possibly meaning, "worthy of love." Man who married a foreign wife (Ezra 10:36).

VASHNI (Vash' ni) Personal name perhaps mean- ing, "weak." Samuel's son according to Hebrew text of 2 Chronicles 6:28 (KJV), which reads literally, "And sons of Samuel the firstborn Vashni and Abiah." Modern translations and commenta- tors follow 1 Samuel 8:2 and manuscripts of early versions, taking Vashni as a copyist's change from the similar Hebrew word for "the second" and inserting Joel.

VASHTI (Văsh' tī) Personal name meaning, "the once desired, the beloved." Wife of King Ahasue- rus and queen of Persia and Media (Esth. 1:9). The king called for her to show off her beauty to a group he was entertaining, but she refused. Vashti was deposed as queen (1:19), and a beauty con- test was arranged to select a new queen. Esther was chosen as the new queen (2:16). No records yet have been recovered which name Vashti as the queen of any king of the Medo-Persian Em- pire, leading some to speculate whether she was a historical person. The only other queen with Ahas- uerus (also called Xerxes) was named Amestris. See *Ahasuerus; Esther; Persia; Xerxes.*

VEIL (KJV "vail") Cloth covering. *1. Womens' veils.* Rebecca veiled herself before meeting Isaac (Gen. 24:65). Her veil was perhaps the sign that she was a marriageable maiden. Tamar used her veil to conceal her identity from Judah (Gen. 38:14,19). Another Hebrew term renders veil at Isaiah 3:23. Here veils are but one of the items of finery which the elite women of Jerusalem would lose in the coming siege. The same Hebrew term is rendered, "shawl" (NAS), "cloak" (NIV, REB),

U
V

View of the western edge of the Jordan Valley from the top of Old Testament Jericho.

and "mantle" (KJV, NRSV) at Song of Solomon 5:7. There, removal of the shawl was part of a humiliating assault on the king's beloved. At Isaiah 47:2, the removal of one's veil is again a sign of shamelessness. Paul regarded the wearing of veils as necessary for women praying or preaching ("prophesying") in public (1 Cor. 11:4–16). *2. Moses' veil.* Moses spoke to God with his face unveiled and then delivered God's message to the people with his face still unveiled. Afterwards, Moses veiled his face (Ex. 34:33–35). For Paul, Moses' practice illustrated the superiority of the new covenant: Christians see the abiding splendor of the era of the Spirit and God-given righteousness; Israel saw the fading splendor of the era of death reflected in Moses' face (2 Cor. 3:7–11). Moses' veil further illustrated the mental barrier preventing Israel from recognizing Christ in the Old Testament (3:12–15). Through faith in Christ the veil is removed, and believers enjoy free access to God which transforms life (3:15–18). *3. Imagery.* The "veil which is stretched over the nations" (Isa. 25:7 NAS) is likely an image for death which is also swallowed up (25:8). The veil possibly includes reproach as well. *4. Temple veil.* This curtain separated the most holy place from the holy place (2 Chron. 3:14). Only the high priest was allowed to pass through the veil and then only on the Day of Atonement (Lev. 16:2). At Jesus' death the Temple veil was ripped from top to bottom, illustrating that in Christ God had abolished the barrier separating humanity from the presence of God (Matt. 27:51; Mark 15:38; compare Luke 23:45). Hebrews 10:20 uses the tabernacle veil, not as the image of a barrier, but of access: Access to God is gained through the flesh of the historical Jesus (compare John 10:7).

Chris Church

VEILS See *Kerchiefs* for the reference to veils in Ezekiel 13:18,20.

VENGEANCE The English word *vengeance* is a principal translation of several Hebrew words related to the stem *nqm* and of *ekdikeō* (and cognates) in the Septuagint (or earliest Greek Old Testament) and in the New Testament. Behind the Hebrew usage of *nqm* stands a sense of the solidarity and integrity of the community which, having been damaged by an offense, must be restored by some deed of retaliation or punishment. The range of meaning of the motif, however, extends beyond "vengeance" and/or "punishment" to a sense of "deliverance."

Human revenge against an enemy or enemies is demonstrated in a broad range of circumstances in the Old Testament documents (Gen. 4:23–24; Jer. 20:10). Samson's reaction to his enemies (Judg. 15:7) is so described. Vengeance might be punishment directed toward another who has committed adultery with one's wife (Prov. 6:32–34) or toward a whole ethnic group such as the Philistines (1 Sam. 18:25). On occasion, the enemies of the people of God are described as acting vengefully

(Ezek. 25:12,15,17). In the context of loving one's neighbor, human revenge toward fellow Hebrews was forbidden (Lev. 19:17–18; compare Deut. 32:35), but *nqm* may be used of legitimate punishment for a wrong (Ex. 21:20; compare Ex. 21:23–25; Lev. 24:19; Deut. 19:21).

As an activity of God on behalf of His people, *nqm* is sometimes best understood as retribution (Judg. 11:36). David was often the recipient of such favor (2 Sam. 4:48; 22:48; Ps. 18:47). The motif occurs in this sense in the prayers of Jeremiah (Jer. 11:20; 15:15; 20:12) and of the psalmist (Pss. 58:10; 79:10; 94:1). Note that *deliverance* is involved in several of these instances. The wrath of God was exhibited toward Babylon (Jer. 51:6,11,36; Isa. 47:3; Ezek. 24:7–9). In the song of Moses, such retribution is attributed to God alone (Deut. 32:35,41,43). Yet, the wrath of God might be extended toward the people of Israel because of their sin (Lev. 26:25).

Nqm has a sense of eschatological deliverance. This can be combined with an expression of God's wrath against Israel's enemies (Isa. 34:8). The parallel Isaianic phrases "day of vengeance" and "year of my redemption" have the same import (63:4; compare 61:1–3).

In the New Testament, the motif of "vengeance" (*ekdikeō* and cognates) occurs on relatively few occasions. Of the evangelists, Luke alone uses both the verb and the noun. In Jesus' parable of the unjust judge, a widow's persistent request for vendication from her enemy is grudgingly granted. Luke displayed the parable as a worst-case model of God's vendication ("deliverance") of His people (Luke 18:1–8). In another teaching of Jesus, "vengeance" has an eschatological dimension which is reflective of Isaiah 63:4 (Luke 21:22). A further Lukan example is found in Stephen's speech—this time retribution (Acts 7:24).

Paul forbade human vengeance much in the way of Deuteronomy 32:35 (compare Lev. 19:18), asserting that the Lord is the Avenger of wrong (Rom. 12:19; 1 Thess. 4:6–7). In the Corinthian correspondence, Paul used both noun and verb in the sense of "punishment." The usage seems designed to bring about repentance (2 Cor. 7:10–11; 10:5–6). On one occasion, Paul wrote of the ruler of a state as a servant of God, "a revenger to execute wrath upon him who doeth evil" (Rom. 13:4). Once, he wrote of the eschatological wrath (judgment) of God (2 Thess. 1:7–8; compare Isa. 66:15; Ps. 79:6).

The author of Hebrews also cited the Deuteronomic prohibition against human vengeance (Heb. 10:30; Deut. 32:35; compare Rom. 12:19; Lev. 19:18), and the author of 1 Peter referred to human governors as persons sent by God to punish evildoers (1 Pet. 2:14; compare Rom. 13:4).

In Hebraic fashion, the author of Revelation viewed God as the Avenger who vindicates His people against their enemies (Rev. 6:10; 19:2). Both of these usages have eschatological overtones (compare Isa. 63:1–6).

See *Avenger; Punishment; Wrath.*

Donald E. Cook

VENISON The flesh of a wild animal taken by hunting (Gen. 25:28; "game," NAS, NRSV; "wild game," NIV). The word is only used in the narrative of Jacob's stealing Esau's birthright. Isaac preferred Esau because of his love of wild game.

VENOM A poisonous secretion from an animal such as a snake, spider, or scorpion that is released into its victim by a bite or sting. Venom is a translation of *rosh* (Deut. 32:33; Job 20:16). The same Hebrew term is used for a dangerous, poisonous plant (Deut. 29:18; Hos. 10:4 among others). See *Poison.*

VESPASIAN (Vĕs pā′ sĭ ăn) Emperor of Rome A.D. 69–79. He was born into a wealthy family and became a military hero as commander of a legion under Emperor Claudius. After becoming commander of three legions, he was ordered to quell the Jewish revolt in Palestine in A.D. 66. Three years into the war, he answered the call of the army to become emperor. Vespasian left his command to his son, Titus, and went to Rome. He sought to establish a dynasty, but it lasted only through his two sons, Titus and Domitian. See *Caesar; Rome; Titus Caesar.*

VESSELS AND UTENSILS Implements or containers ordinarily used as in, for example, the Temple service or household activities. Vessels are utensils designed for holding dry or liquid products. A number of vessels and other utensils are mentioned in the Bible.

Vessel Materials Vessels in biblical times were made of a variety of materials. As early as 3000 B.C., cups and goblets of precious metals were made by silversmiths and goldsmiths throughout the Near East. These were used for religious service (Num. 7:13,19; 1 Chron. 28:17; 2 Chron. 4:8; Ezra 1:9–10; 8:27) or by persons of great wealth or authority (Gen. 44:2). Copper and bronze (Ex. 27:3; Lev. 6:28) vessels were also known.

Many containers, both large and small, were made of stone. Alabaster was easily carved and polished. It was especially prized for storage of perfumes (Matt. 26:7; Mark 14:3–4; Luke 7:37). According to rabbinical writings, stone containers were not susceptible to ritual uncleaness. Thus, a sizable industry existed in Jerusalem of New Testament times for making a variety of stone vessels. Excavations there have produced examples of all sizes and types, from large stone jars (John 2:6) turned on a lathe to cups carved by hand. By New Testament times, glass was becoming widely used for juglets and bottles. See *Glass*.

Baskets, made from reeds, were inexpensive containers which could be used for transportation and sometimes storage. Water or wine bottles were frequently made from animal skins (Josh. 9:4,13; Judg. 4:19; 1 Sam. 1:24; 10:3; 2 Sam. 16:1; Neh. 5:18; Job 32:19; Ps. 119:83; Matt. 9:17; Mark 2:22; Luke 5:37). Such leather vessels were popular among nomadic peoples for their durability.

By far the most widely used material for vessels was clay which was cheap and readily available. Indeed, pottery or "earthenware vessels" (Num. 5:17; Jer. 32:14) were among the most common objects made in antiquity. The earliest ceramics, beginning before 5000 B.C., were handmade and somewhat crude. Though making pottery by hand continued, wheel-made pottery was predominant by Israelite times. See *Pottery*.

The abundance of pottery and widespread familiarity with the process of its manufacture provided object lessons for understanding spiritual truths. Isaiah refered several time to potters and their products. He likened the fury of God's chosen instruments to a potter treading clay (Isa. 41:25). Israel is compared to a potter's vessel which, when broken, will not yield a single useful fragment (Isa. 30:14). For Isaiah, the potter's vessel demonstrated the sovereignty of the Creator (Isa. 45:9). Paul took up the same analogy to make a point about election (Rom. 9:20–21): the potter can make any sort of vessel he chooses. Jeremiah also allegorically related a potter and his work to God, who molded His people Israel (the clay) and is able to rework a spoiled produce (Jer. 18:1–6). A completed clay vessel was used by the prophet to announce the fate of Jerusalem, which like the vessel would be irreparably smashed (Jer. 19:1–2,10–11).

The fragments, or sherds, of a broken pottery vessel are extremely hard (compare Job 41:30) and thus remain forever. They are found in enormous quantities at every Near Eastern archaeological mound or tell and were quite familiar to biblical persons. Job, for example, used a handy potsherd to scrape his sores (2:8). The ubiquitous sherds served as symbols of dryness (Ps. 22:15) and useless remnants (Isa. 30:14). See *Potsherd*.

Types of Vessels The Old Testament sometimes refers to pottery by a generic term translated, "earthen(ware) vessel" (Lev. 6:28; 11:33; 14:5,50; Num. 5:17; Jer. 32:14; NIV, "clay jar"). Only two types of vessels are specifically designated as pottery, "earthen pitchers" (Lam. 4:2) and "earthen bottle" (Jer. 19:1). Nevertheless, other common vessels mentioned in the Bible were presumably made of clay as well. The terms, especially for the Old Testament, are not entirely clear and are variously rendered even within the same English translation.

One of the most common and basic pottery forms was the bowl. Large mixing and serving bowls or basins (Ex. 24:6 NRSV, "basins"; Song of Sol. 7:2 NIV, "goblet"; Isa. 22:24 NRSV, "cups"), called kraters by archaeologists, generally had handles in the Israelite period. A different Hebrew word identifies similar, perhaps smaller, serving bowls (Judg. 5:25; 6:38). Sprinkling bowls (Num. 7:84–85 NRSV, "basins") were usually of metal. A generic word for bowl designates the silver vessels used in the dedication of the altar (Num. 7:84; NAS, "dishes"; NRSV, NIV, "plates"). The main "dish" (2 Kings 21:13; Prov. 19:24 NRSV; 26:15 NRSV; Matt. 26:23) at meals was actually a medium-sized handleless bowl. It was evidently large enough to use for boiling (2 Chron. 35:13; NRSV, NIV, "pans"). Smaller versions were used for other purposes (2 Kings 2:20). Plates did not become common until New Testament times. Cups in the modern sense also were virtually unknown in Old Testament times. Three Hebrew words so translated (Gen. 40:11; Isa. 51:17,22; Jer. 35:5; Zech. 12:2) refer to small bowls. Joseph's silver "cup" (Gen. 44:2,12,16–17) was probably a goblet or chalice. New Testament cups (Luke 11:39) remained bowl-like and varied in size.

A special bowl-like trough was used for kneading dough in bread making (Ex. 8:3; 12:34; Deut. 28:5,17). Other special bowls served as fireports for holding coals (Zech. 12:6). Lamps in the Old Testament were essentially bowls for oil whose rims were pinched in to hold a wick. By New Testament times, lamps (Matt. 25:1; Mark 4:21) were molded in two parts forming a covered bowl with central opening to which a handmade spout was added. See *Lamps*.

"Pot" in the Old Testament (Ex. 16:3; Num. 11:8; 2 Kings 4:38–41; Job 41:20,31 NIV, "caldron") generally translates several Hebrew words which designate cooking pots. In pre-Israelite times, these were similar to deep bowls without handles. Israelite cooking pots of the monarchy period usually had two handles and were more closed. A more globular shape with a short neck and smaller mouth also developed. New Testament cooking pots were similar, but smaller and more delicate with thin straplike handles. Cooking pots required a clay tempered with various grit materials to withstand the expansion of extreme heating and cooling. They were produced in graduated sizes much like their modern counterparts.

Another basic vessel type in antiquity was the storejar, tall oval or pear-shaped jars usually having two or four handles. The tops were closed with an appropriately shaped potsherd or by a clay stopper. Jars were used for storage of flour or meal (1 Kings 17:14) or for transport and storage of liquid rations such as water (Mark 14:13 KJV, "pitcher"; John 4:28 KJV, "waterpot"). A smaller jar was used for storing oil (2 Kings 4:2; KJV, "pot;" NIV, "a little"). Storejars were often de-

U V

signed to hold standard measures, a common size in the Old Testament period being two baths, averaging twenty-five inches high and sixteen in diameter. Typical storejars had rounded, almost pointed, bases and were placed in stands, holes in wood planks, or pressed into soft ground. A special type was shaped like a cylinder with no handles and a ribbed rim.

Jugs or pitchers (1 Kings 14:3 KJV, "cruse"; Jer. 19:1,10 KJV, "bottle;" Jer. 35:5 KJV, "pots") were smaller than storejars and generally had a single handle attached to the neck and shoulder. There were wide and narrow-necked varieties, the former being more likely to have a pinched rim forming a slight spout. A variation on the jug was the pilgrim flask, a flattened bottle with twin handles around a thin neck which functioned like a canteen. Saul may have used one of these (1 Sam. 26:11–12 NRSV, "jar"), but the same Hebrew word (1 Kings 17:14) can refer to the smaller juglet. Juglets with round or oblong bodies, a single handle, and small necks and openings, are well known to archaeologists who work in the Holy Land. They were used for dipping liquids out of large jars and keeping oil (1 Sam. 10:1 NRSV, "vial"; NIV, "flask"; 2 Kings 9:3 NRSV, NIV, "flask"). New Testament versions (variously translated) are mentioned as containers for oil (Matt. 25:4) and, in alabaster, for perfume (Matt. 26:7).

Utensils A general word for utensils (KJV, "vessels" or "furniture") is often used in the Old Testament as a collective term for the gold and bronze articles used in the tabernacle service (Ex. 25:39; 27:3,19; 30:27–28; NIV, "accessories," "utensils," or "articles"). These included snuffers, trays, shovels, pots, basins, forks, firepans, hooks, and the like. The same word is used of utensils used in the Temple service (1 Chron. 9:28–29; 2 Chron. 24:14–19; Jer. 27:18–21; NIV, "articles" or "furnishings") and for household articles (1 Kings 10:21; 2 Chron. 9:20; NRSV, "vessels").

Common household utensils included items for cooking. In Old Testament times, grain was ground by hand (Ex. 11:5; Isa. 47:2) using grindstones usually made of basalt, a hard volcanic stone with many cavities which made natural cutting edges. See *Cooking and Heating.* In the Roman world of the New Testament, large examples of millstones were common, the heavy upper stones (Matt. 18:6; Mark 9:42; Luke 17:2; Rev. 18:21) of which required animals or two persons (Matt. 24:41) to operate. Smaller grinding and crushing chores were done with a mortar and pestle (Num. 11:8; Prov. 27:22).

Eating utensils are not usually found in excavations and were probably made of wood. Knives (Gen. 22:6; Judg. 19:29; Prov. 30:14) for various purposes were made of flint (Josh. 5:2–3), copper, bronze, or iron. See *Archaeology; Tools.*

Daniel C. Browning, Jr.

VESTIBULE See *Arch.*

VIA DOLOROSA (Vī′ ă Dō lŏ rō′ să) Literally, "the way of suffering," the Via Dolorosa was marked after A.D. 1300 as the route over which Christ was led to His crucifixion. Fourteen places along the streets of Old Jerusalem have been revered as "stations" of the cross. Nine of these spots are marked by churches and shrines. The exact route is disputed among believers, just as is the place of crucifixion.

One of the stations on the Via Dolorosa ("the Way of Suffering," or "the Way of the Cross") in Jerusalem.

VIAL Vessel that held oil, usually for annointing purposes (1 Sam. 10:1 KJV, NRSV; "flask" NAS, NIV). The same word is used a number of times in the Book of Revelation (5:8; 15:7; 16:1–4,8,10,12,17; 17:1; 21:9; "bowls," NAS, NIV, NRSV). See *Anoint; Oil; Vessels and Utensils.*

VILLAGE The Old Testament distinguishes between the city and the village. The city was usually walled and much larger. The village was characterized by no wall and usually homes consisting of one room (Lev. 25:29,31). The village had little or no organized government. Archaeology shows Israelite villages built around the circumference, house walls joining to form the only defense system, and open community space left in the middle. Many villages had twenty to thirty houses. The cattle were kept in the inner open space, where grain was stored. The main job in the villages was farming. Small craft manufacturing was practiced. Usually a common threshing floor was available. Shepherds often gathered around villages. The pastureland was seen as the possession of the village (see 1 Chron. 6:54–60). See *Agriculture; Cities and Urban Life; House.*

VINE Any plant having a flexible stem supported by creeping along a surface or by climbing a natural or artificial support. While ancient Israel grew different types of plants that produced vines, such as cucumbers and melons (Num. 11:5; Isa. 1:8), the word *vine* in the Bible almost always refers to

Grapes growing on the vine.

the grapevine or vineyard. The climate of Palestine was well suited for growing vineyards. Along with the olive and fig trees, the grapevine is used throughout the Old Testament to symbolize the fertility of the land (Deut. 6:11; Josh. 24:13; 1 Sam. 8:14; 2 Kings 5:26; Jer. 5:17; 40:10; Hos. 2:12).

The origin of viticulture lies in the antiquity of the unknown past. The Bible traces the origin of caring for vineyards to the time of Noah (Gen. 9:20–21). Such knowledge seems to have been an indigenous undertaking known in many regions of the ancient world. References to vineyards appear from the time of Gudea (a ruler in ancient Sumer before 2100 B.C.). A wall painting found in a tomb at Thebes in Egypt, dating from before 1400 B.C., depicts the entire process of wine making from the gathering and treading of the grapes to the storing of the wine in jars.

The planting and care of a vineyard required constant and intensive care. The most detailed description of the work involved is found in Isaiah 5:1–6. Hillsides are frequently mentioned as the most desirable locations for the vines, especially since they were less suitable for other forms of agriculture (compare Ps. 80:8–10; Jer. 31:5; Amos 9:13). However, vineyards were also grown in the plains and valleys; the Hebron area was particularly noted for its grapes (Num. 13:22–24).

Stone walls and/or hedges were usually built around the vineyard to protect the grapes from thirsty animals and from thieves (Song of Sol. 2:15; Jer. 49:9). Watchtowers were also built to provide further protection. The hewing out of a winepress or vat completed the vineyard installation (Isa. 5:2). During the harvesting season, the owner of the vineyard might live in a booth to stay close to his valuable crop (Isa. 1:8).

After the grapes had set on the branches, the vines were pruned (Lev. 25:4; Isa. 18:5; John 15:1–2). This process produced stronger branches and a greater fruit yield. The pruned branches were useless except to be used as fuel (Ezek. 15:2–8). The vines for the most past were allowed to run on the ground, though occasionally they might climb a nearby tree (compare Ps. 80:8–10; Ezek. 15:2; 19:11). Perhaps it was this latter occurrence that made it possible for a man to "sit under" his vine (1 Kings 4:25). Only in the Roman period were artificial trellises introduced.

The harvest of the grapes took place in August or September. How many grapes an average vineyard produced is unknown (compare Isa. 5:10), but a vineyard was considered so important that a man who had planted one was exempt from military service (Deut. 20:6). Some of the harvested grapes were eaten fresh (Jer. 31:29), and others dried into raisins (1 Sam. 25:18). Most were squeezed for their juice to make wine.

Several laws governed the use of vineyards in Old Testament times. Vineyards could not be stripped totally of their grapes; the owner was to allow gleanings for the poor and the sojourner (Lev. 19:10), and the fatherless and the widow

U
V

(Deut. 24:21). See *Gleaning.* Vineyards were to lie fallow every seventh year (Ex. 23:10–11; Lev. 25:3–5), and other plants could not be sown in them (Deut. 22:9). This latter law apparently was not followed by New Testament times (compare Luke 13:6). Vineyards were cultivated by their owners, hired laborers (Matt. 20:1–16), or rented out to others (Song of Sol. 8:11; Matt. 21:33–43).

The Bible frequently uses *vine* or *vineyard* as symbols. *Vine* is often used in speaking of Israel. Thus Israel is said to have been brought out of Egypt and planted as a vine on the land but was forsaken (Ps. 80:8–13; compare Isa. 5:1–7). Israel was planted a "choice vine" but became a "wild vine" (Jer. 2:21; compare Hos. 10:1). As the dead wood of a vine is good for nothing but fuel, so the inhabitants of Jerusalem would be consumed (Ezek. 15:1–8; 19:10–14).

On the other hand, the abundance of vines and vineyards were seen as expressions of God's favor. The fruit of the vine gladdens the heart of humankind (Ps. 104:15; Eccl. 10:19) and suppresses pain and misery (Prov. 31:6–7). Israel was "like grapes in the wilderness" when God found them (Hos. 9:10), and the remnant surviving the Exile is compared to a cluster of grapes (Isa. 65:8). Finally, an abundance of the vine symbolizes the glorious age to come when the treader of the grapes will overtake the one who sows the seed (Amos 9:13–15; compare Gen. 49:10–12).

In the New Testament, Jesus often used the vineyard as an analogy for the kingdom of God (Matt. 20:1–16). Those who hope to enter the kingdom must be like the son who at first refused to work in his father's vineyard but later repented and went (Matt. 21:28–32 and parallels). Ultimately, Jesus Himself is described as the "true vine" and His disciples (Christians) as the branches (John 15:1–11). See *Agriculture; Eschatology; Israel; Wine; Winepress.*

John C. H. Laughlin

VINEGAR Literally, "that which is soured," related to Hebrew term for "that which is leavened" and referring to a drink that has soured, either wine or beer from barley (Num. 6:3). In biblical times vinegar was most commonly produced by pouring water over the skins and stalks of grapes after the juice had been pressed out and allowing the whole to ferment. However, any fruit could be used for making wine or vinegar. Vinegar in two forms was forbidden to the Nazirite because of its association with strong drink (Num. 6:3). It irritates the teeth (Prov. 10:26) and neutralizes soda (Prov. 25:20). It was an unpleasant drink (Ps. 69:21), though some sopped bread in it (Ruth 2:14); some see this as the common Near Eastern chick-pea paste called *chimmuts.* In the New Testament it is mentioned only in connection with the crucifixion. The first instance, which Jesus refused, was a mixture used to deaden the sense of the victim and nullify the pain. Possibly the vinegar mentioned in the second instance, which Christ accepted, was the customary drink of a peasant or soldier called posca, a mixture of vinegar, water, and eggs.

Vinegar was most commonly used as a seasoning for food or as a condiment on bread (Ruth 2:14). Solomon figuratively used vinegar to describe the irritation caused by a lazy man's attitude.

See *Wine.* *C. Dale Hill*

VIOLENCE Use of force to injure or wrong. The Old Testament affirms that God hates violence (Mal. 2:16). The flood was God's response to a world filled and corrupted by violence (Gen. 6:11,13). The Exile was likewise God's response to a Jerusalem filled with violence (Ezek. 7:23). The Wisdom Literature often warns that those who live lives of violence will meet violent ends (Ps. 7:16; Prov. 1:18–19; 21:7; compare Matt. 26:52). Through the prophets God demanded an end to violence (Jer. 22:3; Ezek. 45:9). Such violence was especially evidenced in the oppression of the poor by the rich (Ps. 55:9,11; 73:6; Jer. 22:17; Mic. 6:12; Jas. 5:1–6). The servant of the Lord models a nonviolent response to violence (Isa. 53:9; compare 1 Pet. 2:23; Jas. 5:6). Isaiah anticipated the end of violence in the Messianic age (60:18).

Matthew 11:12 is one of the most difficult texts in the New Testament. Does the kingdom of heaven suffer violence (KJV, NAS, REB, NRSV), or does the kingdom come "forcefully" (NIV)? The violence which John the Baptist (Matt. 14:3–10) and believers (Matt. 5:10–11; 10:17; 23:34) suffer argues for the former. Other "violent" images of the kingdom's coming (Matt. 10:34–36; Luke 14:26–27) support the latter. Likewise, do violent men lay seige to the kingdom, or do "forceful men lay hold of it" (NIV)? Though the NIV interpretation fits well with Luke's parallel (16:16), it appears too much like an effort to tone down the real harshness of Matthew's language. Candidates for church leadership should be nonviolent persons (1 Tim. 3:3; Titus 1:7).

VIPER A poisonous snake. Several species of snakes are called vipers, and the various words used in the Bible for them probably do not designate specific types. Some scholars take the Old Testament references to refer to the *Echis Colorata.* Jesus spoke of the wicked religious leaders as vipers (Matt. 3:7) because of their venomous attacks on Him and their evil character in leading the people astray. Paul was bitten by a viper (Acts 28:3) but suffered no ill effect from it.

VIRGIN, VIRGIN BIRTH One who has not engaged in sexual intercourse and thus particular

A viper partially hidden in the surrounding grass and wildflowers.

reference to the belief that Jesus was conceived in the womb of Mary by the miraculous action of God without a human father.

In the Old Testament two words are generally translated virgin or maiden. The more common word, *bethulah,* (used about 60 times) is used in a literal way to refer to such virgins as Rebekah (Gen. 24:16), the daughter of Jephthah (Judg. 11:37–38), and Tamar (2 Sam. 13:2). Specific command was given that the high priest must marry a virgin (Lev. 21:13–14). The word was also used in a spiritual sense to refer to the nation, especially in the prophets (Isa. 23:12; 37:22; Jer. 14:17). In other places the word is often translated maid or maiden (Ps. 78:63; 148:12; Ezek. 9:6). In these instances the word means girl, although the idea of chastity may still be involved.

The other word in the Old Testament, *almah,* sometimes translated "virgin" occurs only seven times. Translators differ in their treatment of it. It is translated virgin four times in KJV (Gen. 24:43; Song of Sol. 1:3; 6:8; Isa. 7:14). Only one of these is translated virgin (Isa 7:14) in NAS, and two, in NIV (Song of Sol. 6:8; Isa. 7:14). Some versions like REB do not translate this word as *virgin* in any passage. Isaiah 7:14 is of special interest because of its use in the Gospel of Matthew. Some believe the prophet wrote of a son to be born to his wife or to some other woman of the day and only then with a further reference to the birth of the Mes-

siah. Others claim that the prophet had no reference to anyone in his day but only spoke of the coming Messiah. However, in its context in Isaiah, it seemingly was a message for King Ahaz. The word itself referred to a young woman, usually of marriageable age. God inspired Matthew to interpret Isaiah 7:14 for his day and ours in light of God's miraculous new work in Christ.

The word for virgin occurs fourteen times in the New Testament. It could refer to unmarried maidens (Matt. 25:1; Acts 21:9; 1 Cor. 7:34,36,37) or to the unmarried in general (1 Cor. 7:25). In these passages, the virginity of the unmarried is assumed. The word is also used in a spiritual sense (2 Cor. 11:2). The word is used of Mary, the mother of Jesus (Matt. 1:23; Luke 1:27). Mary was a young woman betrothed (engaged) to Joseph. From these passages the doctrine of the virgin birth is derived.

Matthew gave the account from the viewpoint of Joseph. He was betrothed to Mary. Before they were married, she was discovered to be pregnant. Joseph planned to divorce her without public scandal. Only then did God reveal to Joseph that the child was conceived through the Holy Spirit. This was seen as the fulfillment of the prophecy that a virgin would conceive and bear a son who would be named Emmanuel (Isa. 7:14). Luke gave the events from the viewpoint of Mary. An angel appeared to her while she was still a virgin betrothed to Joseph. It was revealed to her that she would bear a son who would be called "the Son of the Highest" (Luke 1:32). As in Matthew, no room is left in the account for human agency in the conception of Jesus.

Belief in the virgin birth is a central doctrine of Christian thought. Its basis lies in the two passages in Matthew 1 and Luke 1. The writers stated that Mary was a virgin when Jesus was conceived and when He was born. However, the real emphasis is upon the miraculous conception of Jesus. There was no human father. He was the Child of God. The new creative act of God is seen in His bringing His Son into the world.

One must not look upon this in a crude materialistic way. There is no thought of sexual relations between God and Mary, an idea which can be found in some pagan religions where the deities were thought of as engaging in such practices. Rather, God worked in a hidden, secret way which is beyond our ability to understand or explain.

Some believe the New Testament teaches that Mary remained a virgin, but it appears that she and Joseph had several children after the birth of Jesus: James, Joses, Judas, Simon, and sisters (Mark 6:3). Adherents of Mary's perpetual virginity believe Mark was referring to children of Joseph by a first marriage.

The virgin birth is not an explanation of the incarnation, that God became man in Jesus. The Gospels teach that it is the way that God chose to bring about the incarnation. It cannot be proved or disproved by human reason.

See *Ahaz; Christ; Divorce; Incarnation; Isaiah; Jesus; Joseph; Maid; Marys of the Bible; Messiah.*

Clayton Harrop

VISION An experience in the life of a person, whereby a special revelation from God was received. The revelation from God had two purposes. First, a vision was given for immediate direction, as with Abram in Genesis 12:1–3; Lot, Genesis 19:15; Balaam, Numbers 22:22–40; and Peter, Acts 12:7. Second, a vision was given to develop the kingdom of God by revealing the moral and spiritual deficiencies of the people of God in light of God's requirements for maintaining a proper relationship with Him. The vision of prophets such as Isaiah, Amos, Hosea, Micah, Ezekiel, Daniel, and John are representative of this aspect of revelation.

Several Greek and Hebrew terms are translated by the English word *vision.* In some references, the literal sense of perception with the physical organs of sight is the intended meaning of the word (Job 27:11–12; Prov. 22:29). In 2 Samuel 7:17; Isaiah 22:1,5; Joel 3:1; and Zechariah 13:4, the Hebrew word refers to the prophetic function of receiving and delivering the word of God by the prophet.

Vision in varying forms occurs approximately thirty times in the Book of Daniel. The term denotes the mysterious revelation of that which the prophet described as knowledge of the future. In Ezekiel, the words are used literally and metaphorically.

Among the classical prophets (Amos, Hosea, Isaiah, Micah, Obadiah, etc.) the vision was the primary means of communication between God and the prophet. By this avenue, the prophets interpreted the meaning of immediate events in the history of Israel. "Vision" and "Word of Yahweh" became synonymous in these prophetic writings (see Obad. 1:1). See *Prophecy; Revelation; Seer.*

James Newell

VOCATION See *Call, Calling.*

VOPHSI (Vŏph′ sī) Personal name of uncertain meaning. Father of Nahbi of the tribe of Naphtali (Num. 13:14). Nahbi was one of the spies Moses sent into Canaan.

VOWS Voluntary expressions of devotion usually fulfilled after some condition had been met. Vows in the Old Testament usually were conditional. A common formula for vows was the "if . . . then . . ." phrase (Gen. 28:20; Num. 21:2; Judg. 11:30). The one making the religious vow proposed that if God did something (such as give protection or victory), then he or she in return would make some act of devotion. Not all vows, however, were conditional. Some, such as the Nazirite vow (Num. 6), were made out of devotion to God with no request placed upon God. Whether conditional or not, the emphasis in the Bible is on keeping the vow. A vow unfulfilled is worse than a vow never made. While vows do not appear often in the New Testament, Paul made one that involved shaving his head (Acts 18:18).

Scott Langston

VULGATE The Latin translation by Jerome about A.D. 400 of the Bible. See *Bible, Texts and Versions.*

A mosaic in the chapel of Jerome's Room, the traditional site where he translated the Latin Vulgate, located under the Church of the Nativity, Bethlehem.

VULTURE See *Birds.*

W

Young woman carrying a can of water on her head from a village well near Jerusalem.

WADI (Wä' dĭ) Transliteration of Arabic word for a rocky watercourse that is dry except during rainy seasons. These creekbeds can become raging torrents when especially heavy rains fall. Wadis are numerous in the Middle East.

The wadi through the limestone cliffs of the Qumran area in Israel.

WAGES The terms of employment or compensation for services rendered encompass the meaning of the Hebrew and Greek words. Their usage in the text applies to commercial activities and labor service, as well as judgmental recompense for one's actions in life.

In a mixed economy of agriculture and pastoralism without coined money, wages often included little more than meals and a place of employment (Compare Job 7:2; John 10:12). Still, a skilled shepherd, like Jacob, might receive a portion of the flock and thus begin his own herd (Gen. 30:32–33; 31:8; and legal texts from both Assyria and Babylonia). No fixed wage was set for farm laborers. They may have received a portion of the harvest (John 4:36), or, as in Matthew 20:1–8 an agreed upon daily wage. By law, these landless workers were to be paid at the end of each day for their efforts (Lev. 19:13; Deut. 24:14–15). Texts mention enough instances of fraud, however, to suggest that this group was often cheated out of their wages (Jer. 22:13; Mal. 3:5; Jas. 5:4).

Kings hired mercenary troops to fight their wars (Judg. 9:4; 2 Sam. 10:6) and employed skilled laborers, along with slaves and unpaid draftees, to build and decorate their palaces and temples (1 Kings 5:6–17; Isa. 46:6; 2 Chron. 24:11–12). The services of priests (Judg 18:4; Mal. 1:10) and the advice of elders (Ezra 4:5; 1 Tim. 5:17–18) were obtained for gold or silver at fees to match their abilities. The authority of prophets could also be purchased. Balaam, for example, was paid "fees for divination" in exchange for his cursing of Israel (Num. 22:7), and Shemaiah was hired by Sanballat to trap Nehemiah with a false prophecy (Neh. 6:10–13).

Theological usage of these terms promises God's reward for the faithful (Gen. 15:1) and proper recompense for His people Israel (Isa. 40:10; 62:11). His justice also ensured that the reward of the unrighteous was equal to their crimes (Ps. 109:20; Rom. 6:23; 2 Pet. 2:15). See *Commerce; Economic Life; Slavery.*

Victor H. Matthews

WAGON A vehicle of transportation with two or four wooden wheels. The two wheeler was usually called a cart. Wagons were used to transport people and goods (Gen. 45:17–21). Sometimes, wagons were used as instruments of war (Ezek. 23:24). Wagons were usually pulled by oxen. The use of the wagon was quite different than that of the chariot. See *Transportation and Travel.*

WAIL See *Grief and Mourning; Repentance.*

WALK A slower pace contrasted with running. It is used literally in the Bible (Ex. 2:5; Matt. 4:18). It is also used figuratively to mean a person's conduct or way of life (Gen. 5:24; Rom. 8:4; 1 John 1:6–7).

WALK TO AND FRO KJV translation (Zech. 1:10–11) of a military term meaning, "patrol" (NAS, NRSV) or "go and inspect" (TEV).

WALLS The outside vertical structures of houses and the fortifications surrounding cities. In ancient times, the walls of cities and houses were constructed of bricks made of clay mixed with reed and hardened in the sun. Archaeologists estimate that the walls of Nineveh were wide enough to drive three chariots abreast and the walls of Babylon were wide enough to drive six chariots abreast on the top. See *Architecture; Fortifications.*

In scriptural language a wall is a symbol of salvation (Isa. 26:1; Isa, 60:18), of the protection of God (Zech. 2:5), of those who afford protection (1 Sam. 25:16; Isa. 2:15), and of wealth of the rich in their own conceit (Prov. 18:11). A "brazen wall" is symbolic of prophets and their testimony against the wicked (Jer. 15:20). The "wall of partition" (Eph. 2:14) represented Temple worship and Jewish practice separating Jew from Gentile.

WANDERINGS IN THE WILDERNESS Israel's movements from Egypt to the Promised Land under Moses, including the place names along the routes. A reconstruction of the Israelites' wilderness wanderings is more complex than a casual reading of the biblical account at first would seem to indicate. The "wanderings" refer to that difficult period in Israel's history between their departure from the area of Egyptian enslavement in the land of Goshen and arrival in the Jordan Valley to claim their long-standing inheritance of the Promised Land (Ex. 12:31—Num. 33:49). The sequence of that extended event is complicated by the nature of the biblical data.

W

The itinerary from the border of Egypt to the oasis of Kadesh-barnea is relatively clear. Only three established trade routes across the northern Sinai were viable options for the movement of such a large contingent of people and livestock. Decisions in Egypt during the early stages of their migration reduced those options to only one. The shortest, most northerly, route along the Mediterranean shoreline was not taken because of a possible encounter with Egyptian military guarding oasis forts or returning from regular incursions and punitive raids in Canaan (Ex. 13:17). A second relatively direct route to Kadesh-barnea appears to have been avoided by divine plan when they approached the border at Etham and then were instructed to turn back to the seeming impossible situation "by the Sea" where God miraculously delivered them from the pharaoh's forces (Ex. 13:20—14:2). This route is identified with Marah (15:23), Elim (15:27), the Wilderness of Sin (16:1), Rephidim (17:1), the Wilderness of Sinai (18:5; 19:1), Sinai (19:2), the wilderness of Paran (Num. 10:12), Taberah (11:3) or Kibrothhattaavah ("the cemetery of the lusters," 11:34), Hazeroth ("corrals," 11:35; 12:16) where the mention of enclosures for the livestock and a series of events in the biblical account suggest an extended stay, and, ultimately, Kadesh (Num. 20:1). A later reference to the distance between Mount Sinai (Horeb) and Kadesh-barnea (Deut. 1:2) seems to suggest that the early itinerary took them basically along the major trade route used by the Amalekites between modern Suez at the northern end of the Gulf of Suez and the northern end of the Gulf of Aqaba (Elath and Ezion-geber) and then northward into the extensive clustering of oases at Kadesh that would become their tribal center and the location of the tabernacle during the next 38 years.

The negative response to an immediate conquest following the spies' report resulted in the additional 38 years in the Sinai wilderness. When that generation of military died, the camp of Israel again was mobilized for the assault on Canaan. Their request to pass through Edomite territory and to proceed along the King's Highway through Moab and into the Jordan Valley opposite Jericho was blocked by a show of military force by the king of Edom. Their attempt to enter Canaan from the south was stopped by the king of Arad, and so a very difficult detour southward to the head of the Gulf of Aqaba and northeastward around Edomite and Moabite lands (Num. 20:14; Deut. 2) brought them finally to Mount Nebo overlooking the Jordan Valley north of the Dead Sea.

This itinerary is complicated by a comprehensive list of place names in Numbers 33 related to the Exodus and wanderings that includes many more locations seemingly playing a part in this extended event. Obviously, many of these places naturally may be related to the 38 years of the wanderings. More important is the fact that Numbers 33 indicates that in fact the Israelite itinerary from Egypt to the Jordan Valley did include passage through Edomite and Moabite territory along the King's Highway. This route cannot be associated with the Moses/Joshua-led Exodus because of the specific statements in Numbers 20—21. Many scholars therefore conclude that Numbers 33 is a combined compilation of place names that are related to pre-Mosaic infiltration from Egypt to Canaan by way of the King's Highway, the place along the second route around Edomite-Moabite territory followed by the Moses/Joshua-led contingent and all those places visited by the Israelites during those 38 punitive years of desert wanderings when like the nomads of every generation they sought water and pasturage for their flocks within that hostile arid environment of the Sinai. See *Exodus; Kadesh; Moses; Sinai.*

George L. Kelm

WASHING See *Ablutions; Bathing.*

WASP See *Insects.*

WATCH A division of time in which soldiers or others were on duty to guard something. They are listed as "evening," "midnight," "cockcrowing," and "morning" (Mark 13:35 NAS). Nehemiah set watches which may mean armed persons or just citizens on guard (4:9; 7:3). The Old Testament seems to have had three watches rather than four. There was the "beginning of the watches" (Lam. 2:19), the "middle watch" (Judg. 7:19), and the "morning watch" (Ex. 14:24). See *Time.*

WATCHMAN One who stands guard. Ancient cities had watchmen stationed on the walls. Their responsibility was to sound a warning if an enemy approached (2 Kings 9:17; Ezek. 33:2–3). Israel's prophets saw themselves as watchmen warning the nation of God's approaching judgment if the people did not repent. Vineyards and fields also had watchmen, especially during harvest. Their responsibility was to guard the produce from animals and thieves.

WATCHTOWER A tower on a high place or built high enough to afford a person to be able to see for some distance. The person doing the watching may be a soldier or a servant (2 Kings 9:17; Isa. 5:2; Mark 12:1). See *Tower.*

WATER The Bible speaks of water in three different ways: as a material resource, as a symbol, and as a metaphor.

A Material Necessity which God Provides Water as a material resource is necessary for life. The Bible states that God made water a part of His good creation and that He exercises sovereignty over it (Gen. 1—2; Isa. 40:12). He controls the

An ancient watchtower remains relatively unchanged in an open field in Israel.

natural processes of precipitation and evaporation, as well as the courses of bodies of water (Job 5:10; 36:27; 37:10; Pss. 33:7; 107:33; Prov. 8:29). God normally assures the provision of water for human needs (Deut. 11:14). However, water is sometimes used in punishment for sin, as with the flood of Noah's day (Gen. 6:17) or the drought proclaimed by Elijah (1 Kings 17:1). The divine control of water teaches people obedience to and dependency upon God.

Many of the great acts of God in history have involved water, such as the parting of the sea (Ex. 14:21), the provision of water for the Israelites in the wilderness (Ex. 15:25; 17:6), and the crossing of the Jordan River (Josh. 3:14–17). Water was also involved in several of Jesus' miracles (Matt. 14:25; Luke 8:24–25; John 2:1–11).

Water was a crucial element in God's gift of the Promised Land to Israel (Deut. 8:7). Palestine contains several natural sources of water: rain, springs, wells, and a few short, perennial streams. The average annual rainfall in Palestine is about 25 inches, all of which normally falls between November and April. The dry months of May to October made necessary the use of cisterns and pools for water storage. Several famous biblical cities had pools, such as Gibeon (2 Sam. 2:13), Hebron (2 Sam. 4:12), Samaria (1 Kings 22:38), and Jerusalem (2 Kings 20:20).

An Arab man drinks from the spout of a multi-spouted waterpot as he would have done in biblical times.

A Theological Symbol and Metaphor The Old Testament contains laws for the use of water in rituals as a symbol of purification. Priests, sacrificial meat, and ritual utensils were washed before involvement in rituals (Lev. 1:9; 6:28; 8:6). Unclean people and things were also washed as a symbol of ritual cleansing (Lev. 11:32–38; 14:1–9; 15:1–30; Num. 31:23). The Book of Genesis uses water as a symbol of instability before the completion of creation (1:2), and Ezekiel spoke of water as a symbol of renewal in the age to come (47:1–12).

The Bible contains dozens of metaphorical usages of water. For example, in the Old Testament water is a metaphor or simile for fear (Josh. 7:5), death (2 Sam. 14:14), sin (Job 15:16), God's presence (Ps. 72:6), marital fidelity (Prov. 5:15–16), the knowledge of God (Isa. 11:9), salvation (Isa. 12:3), the Spirit (Isa. 44:3–4), God's blessings (Isa. 58:11), God's voice (Ezek. 43:2), God's wrath (Hos. 5:10), and justice (Amos 5:24). Among the metaphorical uses of water in the New Testament are references to birth (John 3:5), the Spirit (John 4:10), spiritual training (1 Cor. 3:6), and life (Rev. 7:17). See *Creation; Famine and Drought; Flood; Rain.*   *Bob R. Ellis*

WATERPOT A vessel made for carrying water, usually made of clay although some were made of stone (John 2:6). Large pots stored water (1 Kings 18:33; John 2:6); smaller pots a woman could carry on her shoulder (John 4:28). Small pitchers were used for pouring water (Luke 22:10; see Jer. 19). Water was also carried in animal skins. See *Pottery; Skin; Vessels and Utensils.*

WAW The sixth letter in the Hebrew alphabet. Heading of Psalm 119:41–48 (KJV, Vau) in which each verse begins with the letter.

WEALTH AND MATERIALISM Physical resources God gives humans to control and the human tendency to lift those resources to replace God as the center of life.
The Bible and Wealth The Bible has two basic attitudes toward wealth. In the first place, wealth is acknowledged to be a blessing from God. This can be seen from the witness of the Old Testament. God chose Abram and promised to bless him and make his name great (Gen. 12:1–3). In the process, Abram became rich (Gen. 13:2). Further, we are told that God blessed Isaac; and he became very rich (Gen. 26:12–14). Solomon's wealth was seen as a sign of God's favor (1 Kings 3:13; 10:23). Job, too, was blessed by God, and his wealth increased greatly (Job. 42:12).

These few examples do not allow us to assume that poverty is a sign of God's disfavor. The Bible does not say that. Jesus' references to money in the New Testament consist mainly of stories or parables which show the dangers of wealth. In the parable of the seed and the sower Jesus warned that riches and the pursuit of pleasure may keep some from maturing in the faith (Luke 8:14). A harsh warning against the destructive nature of wealth is sounded in the story of the rich farmer (Luke 12:16–21). In Jesus' words, the person is a fool who labors to lay up treasures on earth rather than treasures in heaven. Of greater importance is Jesus' statement that life does not consist of one's possessions (Luke 12:15). Personal worth and success are not to be measured in terms of material wealth or possessions. This is different from the way that the world views possessions.

Jesus viewed money or wealth as a spiritual power (Matt. 6:24), identifying wealth as an object of worship, a rival to God. For this reason Jesus often asked people to turn away from it (Matt. 19:21; Luke 12:33–34). Zacchaeus offered to give half of his possessions to the poor and restore four times to any one that he had cheated (Luke 19:8). This was a sign of his desire to follow Christ. The only way to defeat the power of mammon is to give it away (Acts 20:35). See *Stewardship.*

For a while members of the Jerusalem church pooled their resources for the common good (Acts 2:44–45). To provide for the needs of those in their midst, owners of land and property sold it and gave it to the apostles (Acts 4:34–35). While this kind of sharing may not be a requirement, it provides a model for the responsibility that Christians have for one another.

Paul likewise warned against the power of money. One of the qualifications of a church officer is to be free from the love of money (1 Tim. 3:3). Deacons likewise must not be "greedy for money" (1 Tim. 3:8 NRSV). The strongest warning is found in 1 Timothy 6:10 (NRSV): "For the love of money is a root of all kinds of evil, and in their eagerness to be rich some have wandered away from the faith." Paul may be implying that people who love money will resort to all kinds of things to get it. The desire for money has a way of enslaving the person seeking it.

The answer to the wrong use of money is to use it for kingdom purposes. Money can be used to enhance our relationship to God and bless others. Paul commended the liberal giving of the Macedonian Christians (2 Cor. 8:1–4; compare 2 Cor. 9:7).

Hebrews encourages us to "Keep your lives free from the love of money, and be content with what you have (Heb. 13:5 NRSV). Jesus admonished us not to be anxious over material things, but to trust the Heavenly Father to care for our needs (Matt. 6:25–26). Christians are to recognize that God's kingdom is more important than money (Matt. 6:33). Material wealth is given to human beings as a stewardship. God is the owner of all things, and we are given a portion to use. At all times we are to keep in mind that we will one day give account to God for the use of our wealth.

The Bible and Materialism Philosophically, materialism refers to a view of life that sees physical matter as the only reality in the universe. According to this view, everything, including thought, feelings, and will can be explained according to physical laws. There is obviously no room for God in this view. Another kind of materialism tempts Christians. This is the view that values life in terms of the accumulation and consumption of goods, measuring success or worth in terms of wealth or possessions. Materialism leads us to justify spending on ourselves all that our income will bear.

Christians are to learn to possess money and not be possessed by it. Wealth is to be channeled into ministries that serve people and spread the gospel. The pursuit of wealth as an end in itself, or the desire for luxury and personal indulgence are evidences of materialism. Christians must take a stand against the persistent idolatry of materialism that focuses on the material stuff of this world and not God.   *D. Glenn Saul*

WEAPONS Since mankind's beginnings, the desire to impose one's will upon another person(s) or being has led to active conflict using many types of weapons. Human history shows marked means by which the implements were advanced technologically through the past six millennia.

Reconstruction of a Roman siege tower with battering ram of the first century A.D.

W

The implements of warfare and defense are known from three sources: excavations; pictorial representations in murals, reliefs, and models; and written documents. Tombs of Egypt contained actual weapons and models. Assyrian reliefs depicted great battles in detail. Excavations have uncovered numerous examples of stone and metal weapons; and biblical and inscriptional sources provide names of objects, strategy and tactics, and methods of construction.

Military action has been defined in terms of ability to achieve supremacy over the enemy in three fields: mobility, firepower, and security. Mobility is exemplified by the chariot and cavalry; firepower by bow, sling, spear, axe and sword; and security by shield, armor, and helmet. See *Arms and Armor; Chariots; Horse.*   *Dennis Cole*

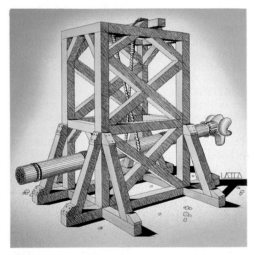

Reconstruction of a Roman battering ram of the first century A.D.

WEASEL An unclean animal (Lev. 11:29). Some translations see this animal as the "mole" (NAS) or "mole-rat" (REB). It may be a member of the mole family (*palax Sehrenberg*) found in many countries, including Palestine. See *Animals.*

WEATHER Climatic conditions in Palestine, including geographical factors and seasonal changes. The weather patterns of Palestine result from the clash between the extreme heat of the Arabian desert and the cooler Mediterranean winds from the west. The climate is subtropical with humid, cold winters and hot, dry summers. From October to April the days range from cool and sunny to overcast, cold, and rainy. The rains fill the seasonal brooks and streams, which provide the majority of water for the coming year. The elevation of the land, dropping from 3,900 feet in upper Galilee to 1,296 feet below sea level at the Dead Sea, provides natural barriers which influence the

weather. Rain generally diminishes as one travels farther south and inland. Thus, the coastal plain and Galilee receive more rain than the central hill country and Negev desert. Snow covers the higher elevations of Mount Hermon throughout most of the winter and occasionally falls on Jerusalem and the surrounding hills. The Jordan Valley, particularly in the area of the Dead Sea, remains mild in the winter, making it the traditional site of the winter palaces of kings and rulers. The Mediterranean Sea becomes windy and cold, making travel dangerous.

In April and May the climate changes dramatically. Hot desert winds blow across the land from the east in the early morning hours. The land and seasonal rivers begin to dry, and the vegetation turns brown. Near noon each day, the air turns to the west, bringing with it slightly cooler air from the sea. The difference is minimal, however, and the heat remains intense. The central hill country is cooler than the foothills and coastal areas, but the Judaean wilderness and Negev become fiercely hot. Temperatures along the Dead Sea and Arabah remain above 90 degrees Farenheit for weeks on end. Once across the Jordan Valley atop the Transjordan plateau to the east, the temperature moderates once more. Rain is uncommon in the summer months, usually falling in October, November, February, and March.

The Bible hints at the influence which the weather imposed on life in Palestine. The winds and rain were considered to be under God's personal direction. Thus, Christ's control of the elements demonstrated to the disciples His heavenly calling. The hot east wind was often viewed as the wrath of God, bringing infertility and death. Rain signified the continued blessings of God; its absence, His judgment. See *Fertility Cults; Palestine; Rain; Wind.*   *David Maltsberger*

WEAVER See *Loom.*

WEAVING See *Cloth; Loom.*

WEB *1.* A fabric usually woven on a loom (see

A Middle Eastern weaver operating his loom.

Judg. 16:13–14). See *Loom. 2.* The weaving of a spider that looks like thread. The spider's web is used figuratively to that which is impermanent and untrustworthy (Job 8:14). See *Animals, Spider.*

WEEK For the Jews, any seven consecutive days ending with the sabbath (Gen. 2:1–3). The sabbath began at sunset Friday and lasted until sunset Saturday. The Christians moved their day of worship to Sunday, the first day of the week. In this way they called attention to the resurrection of their Lord Jesus Christ (Luke 24:1–7). The week is of ancient Semitic origin. It was shared with the ancient world through the Bible and the religious practice of both Jews and Christians. See *Calendars; Time.*

WEEPING See *Grief and Mourning.*

WEIGHTS AND MEASURES Systems of measurement in the Bible. In the Ancient Near East, weights and measure varied. The prophets spoke against merchants who used deceitful weights (Mic. 6:11).

Weights Considering first the Old Testament evidence, Hebrew weights were never an exact system. An abundance of archaeological evidence demonstrates that not even inscribed weights of the same inscription weighed the same. Weights were used in a balance to weigh out silver and gold, since there was no coinage until the Persian period after 500 B.C. This medium of exchange replaced bartering early in the biblical period.

The *shekel* is the basic unit of weight in the Hebrew as well as the Babylonian and Canaanite systems, though the exact weight varied from region to region and sometimes also according to the kind of goods for sale. The Mesopotamian system was sexagesimal, based on sixes and sixties. So, for example, the Babylonian system used a *talent* of sixty minas, a *mina* of sixty shekels, and a shekel of twenty-four *gerahs.*

The Hebrew system was decimal like the Egyptian, though the weights were not the same. Variations in the weights of the shekel may be attributed to several factors other than the dishonesty condemned in the law (Deut. 25:13–16) and the prophets (Amos 8:5; Mic. 6:11). There could have been variation between official and unofficial weights, including the setting of new standards by reform administrations such as that of good King Josiah. There might have been a depreciation of standards with passage of time, or a use of different standards to weigh different goods (a heavy standard was used at Ugarit to weigh purple linen), or the influence of foreign systems. There seems to have been three kinds of shekel current in Israel: (1) a temple shekel of about ten grams (.351 ounces) which depreciated to about 9.8 grams (.345 ounces); (2) the common shekel of

about 11.7 grams (.408 ounces) which depreciated to about 11.4 grams (.401 ounces); and (3) the heavy ("royal"?) shekel of about thirteen grams (.457 ounces).

The smallest portion of the shekel was the gerah, which was ¹⁄₂₀ of a shekel (Ex. 30:13; Ezek. 45:12). The gerah has been estimated to weigh .571 grams. There were larger portions of the shekel, the most familiar of which was the *beka* or half shekel (Ex. 38:26), known also from Egypt. Inscribed examples recovered by archaeologists average over six grams and may have been half of the heavy shekel mentioned above. The *pim,* if it is ⅔ of a shekel as most scholars suppose, is also related to the heavy shekel and weighs about eight grams. It may have been a Philistine weight, since it is mentioned as the price the Philistines charged Israelite farmers to sharpen their agricultural tools when the Philistines enjoyed an iron monopoly over Israel (1 Sam. 13:19–21).

Multiples of the shekel were the *mina* and the *talent.* According to the account of the sanctuary tax (Ex. 38:25–26), three thousand shekels were in a talent, probably sixty minas of fifty shekels each. This talent may have been the same as the Assyrian weight, since both 2 Kings 18:14 and Sennacherib's inscriptions mention the tribute of King Hezekiah as thirty talents of silver and of gold. This was 28.38 to 30.27 kilograms (about seventy pounds). The mina was probably fifty shekels (as the Canaanite system), though Ezekiel 45:12 calls for a mina of sixty shekels, and the early Greek translation reads, "fifty." The mina has been estimated at 550 to 600 grams (1.213 to 1.323 lbs.). One table of Old Testament weights, estimated on a shekel of 11.424 grams is as follows:

1 talent (3000 shekels)	34.272 Kilograms	75.6 lbs.
1 mina (50 shekels)	571.2 grams	1.26 lbs.
1 shekel	11.424 grams	.403 oz.
1 pim (⅔ shekel?)	7.616 grams	.258 oz.
1 beka (½ shekel)	5.712 grams	.201 oz.
1 gerah (¹⁄₂₀ shekel)	.571 grams	.02 oz.

We should remember however, that this is misleading, for Old Testament weights were never so precise as this. The Lord's ideal was *just* weights and measures (Lev. 19:36; Prov. 16:11; Ezek. 45:10); but dishonest manipulations were all too common (Prov. 11:1; 20:23; Hos. 12:7), and archaeologists have discovered weights that have been altered by chiseling the bottom. Interesting things weighed in the Old Testament were Goliath's armor (1 Sam. 17:5–7) and Absolom's annual haircut (2 Sam. 14:26). In the New Testament, the talent and mina were large sums of money (Matt. 25:15–28; compare Luke 19:13–25), and the *pound* of precious ointment (John 12:3) is probably the Roman standard of twelve ounces.

Measures Measures of capacity, like the weights, were used from earliest times in the market place. These were also only approximate and varied

W

TABLE OF WEIGHTS AND MEASURES

WEIGHTS

Biblical Unit	Language	Biblical Measure	U.S. Equivalent	Metric Equivalent	Various Translations
Gerah	Hebrew	1/20 shekel	1/50 ounce	.6 gram	gerah; oboli
Bekah	Hebrew	1/2 shekel or 10 gerahs	1/5 ounce	5.7 grams	bekah; half a shekel; quarter ounce; fifty cents
Pim	Hebrew	2/3 shekel	1/3 ounce	7.6 grams	2/3 of a shekel; quarter
Shekel	Hebrew	2 bekahs	2/5 ounce	11.5 grams	shekel; piece; dollar; fifty dollars
Litra (Pound)	Graeco-Roman	30 shekels	12 ounces	.4 kilogram	pound; pounds
Mina	Hebrew/Greek	50 shekels	1 1/4 pounds	.6 kilogram	mina; pound
Talent	Hebrew/Greek	3000 shekels or 60 minas	75 pounds/ 88 pounds	34 kilgrams/ 40 kilograms	talents/talent; 100 pounds

LENGTH

Handbreadth	Hebrew	1/6 cubit or 1/3 span	3 inches	8 centimeters	handbreadth; three inches; four inches
Span	Hebrew	1/2 cubit or 3 handbreadths	9 inches	23 centimeters	span
Cubit/Pechys	Hebrew/Greek	2 spans	18 inches	.5 meter	cubit(s)/cubit(s); yard; half a yard; foot
Fathom	Graeco-Roman	4 cubits	2 yards	2 meters	fathom; six feet
Kalamos	Graeco-Roman	6 cubits	3 yards	3 meters	rod; reed; measuring rod
Stadion	Graeco-Roman	1/8 milion or 400 cubits	1/8 mile	185 meters	miles; furlongs; race
Milion	Graeco-Roman	8 stadia	1,620 yards	1.5 kilometer	mile

DRY MEASURE

Xestēs	Graeco-Roman	1/2 cab	.5 liter	1 1/6 pints	pots; pitchers; kettles; copper pots; copper bowls; vessels of bronze
Cab	Hebrew	1/18 epah	1 liter	1 quart	cab; kab
Choinix	Graeco-Roman	1/18 ephah	1 liter	1 quart	measure; quart
Omer	Hebrew	1/10 ephah	2 liters	2 quarts	omer; tenth of a deal; tenth of an ephah; six pints
Seah/Saton	Hebrew/Greek	1/3 ephah	7.3 liters	7 quarts	measures; pecks; large amounts
Modios	Graeco-Roman	4 omers	9 liters	1 peck or 1/4 bushel	bushel; bowl; peck-measure; corn-measure; meal-tub
Ephah [Bath]	Hebrew	10 omers	22 liters	3/5 bushel	bushel; peck; deal; part; measure; six pints, seven pints
Lethek	Hebrew	5 ephahs	110 liters	3 bushels	half homer; half sack
Cor [Homer]/Koros	Hebrew/Greek	10 ephahs	220 liters/525 liters	6 bushels or 200 quarts/14.9 bushels or 500 quarts	cor; homer; sack; measures; bushels/sacks; measures; bushels; containers

LIQUID MEASURE

Log	Hebrew	1/72 bath	.3 liter	1/3 quart	log; pint; cotulus
Xestēs	Graeco-Roman	1/8 hin	.5 liter	1 1/6 pints	pots; pitchers; kettles; copper pots; copper bowls; vessels of bronze
Hin	Hebrew	1/6 bath	4 liters	1 gallon or 4 quarts	hin; pints
Bath/Batos	Hebrew/Greek	1 ephah	22 liters	6 gallons	gallon(s); barrels; liquid measure/gallons; barrels; measures
Metretes	Graeco-Roman	10 hins	39 liters	10 gallons	firkins; gallons

Measures are approximate.

from time to time and place to place. Sometimes different names were used to designate the same unit. Some names were used to describe both liquid and dry measures as the modern liter. The basic unit of dry measure was the *ephah* which means basket. The *homer,* "ass's load," was a dry measure, the same size as the *cor,* both a dry and a liquid measure. Each contained ten ephahs or *baths,* an equivalent liquid measure (Ezek. 45:10–14). The ephah is estimated at 1.52 to 2.42 pecks, about ⅜ to ⅔ of a bushel.

The bath is estimated from two fragments of vessels so labeled from tell Beit Mirsim and Lachish to have contained 21 to 23 liters or about 5½ gallons, which would correspond roughly to an ephah of ⅜ to ⅔ of a bushel. *Lethech,* which may mean half a homer (or cor) would be five ephahs. *Seah* was a dry measure which may be a third of a ephah. *Hin,* an Egyptian liquid measure, which means "jar" was approximately a sixth of a bath. The *omer,* used only in the manna story (Ex. 16:13–36) was a daily ration and is calculated as a tenth of an ephah (also called issaron, "tenth"). A little less than half an omer is the *kab* (only 2 Kings 6:25 NRSV), which was four times the smallest unit, *log* (only Lev. 14:10–20 NRSV) which is variously estimated, according to its Greek or Latin translation as a half pint or ⅔ pint.

Although Old Testament measures of capacity varied as much as the difference between the American and English gallon, the following table at least represents the assumptions of the above discussion:

Dry Measures

kab	1.16 quarts
omer, issaron ¹⁄₁₀ ephah	2.09 quarts
seah, ⅓ ephah	⅔ peck
ephah	½ bushel
lethech, ½ homer	2.58 bushels
homer, cor	5.16 bushels

Liquid Measures

log	0.67 pint
hin	1 gallon
bath	5½ gallons
cor, homer	55 gallons

In the New Testament, measures of capacity are Greek or Roman measures. The sextarius or "pot" (Mark 7:4) was about a pint. The measure of John 2:6 (*metrētas*) is perhaps ten gallons. The bushel (*modios*) of Matthew 5:15 and parallels is a vessel large enough to cover a light, perhaps about a fourth of an American bushel. As remarked before, the amount of ointment Mary used to anoint Jesus (John 12:3) was a Roman pound of twelve ounces (a measure of both weight and capacity), and Nicodemus brought a hundred such pounds of mixed spices to anoint Jesus' body (John 19:39).

In measures of length, all over the Ancient Near East, the standard was the *cubit,* the length of the forearm from the elbow to the tip of the middle finger. Israel knew two different lengths for the cubit just as did Egypt. The common cubit, mentioned in connection with the description of the bed of Og, king of Bashan (Deut. 3:11), was about seventeen and a half inches. This may be deduced from the 1,200 cubit length mentioned in the Siloam, inscription for King Hezekiah's tunnel which has been measured to yield a cubit of this length. Ezekiel (40:5) mentions a long cubit consisting of a common cubit plus a handbreadth which would yield a "royal" cubit of about twenty and a half inches, similar to the Egyptian short and long cubits.

Even figuring with the common cubit, Goliath's height was truly gigantic at six cubits and a *span* (1 Sam. 17:4), about nine and a half feet tall. If Solomon's Temple is figured with the common cubit, it was about ninety-feet long, thirty-feet wide, and forty-five-feet high (1 Kings 6:2). The span is half a cubit (Ezek. 43:13,17), or the distance between the extended thumb and little finger. If it is half the long cubit, the span would be about ten and one-fifth inches; if half, the common cubit was about eight and three-fourths inches.

The *handbreadth* or palm is a sixth of a cubit, consisting of the breadth of the hand at the base of the four fingers. This measure is a little less than three inches. The smallest Israelite measure of length was the finger, a fourth of a handbreadth (Jer. 52:21) and was about three-fourths inch. Larger than a cubit was the *reed,* probably consisting of six common cubits. Archaeologists have noticed several monumental buildings whose size can be calculated in round numbers of such cubits or reeds. Summarizing on the basis of the common cubit, linear measurements of the Old Testament were:

Common Cubit

1 reed	6 cubits	8 ft. 9 in.
1 cubit	6 handbreadths	17.5 in.
1 handbreadth	4 fingers	2.9 in.
1 finger		.73 in.

Ezekiel's Cubit

1 reed	6 cubits	10 ft. 24 in.
1 cubit	7 handbreadths	20.4 in.

There were indefinite measures of great length, such as a day's journey or three day's journey or seven day's journey, the calculation of which would depend on the mode of transportation and the kind of terrain. Shorter indefinite distances were the bowshot (Gen. 21:16) and the furrow's length (1 Sam. 14:14 NRSV).

In the New Testament measures of length were Greek or Roman units. The cubit was probably the same as the common cubit, since the Romans reckoned it as one and a half times the Roman foot. The *fathom* (Acts 27:28) was about six feet of water in depth. The *stadion* or furlong was a Roman measure of 400 cubits or one eighth Roman mile. The Roman mile (Matt. 5:41) was 1,620 yards. Josephus calculated this as six stadia or 1,237.8 yards.

Measures of area were indefinite in the Old Testament. An "acre" was roughly what a yoke of oxen could plow in one day. Land could be measured by the amount of grain required to sow it. In New Testament times a Roman measure of land was the Latin *jugerum,* related to what a yoke of oxen could plow, figured at 28,000 square feet or five-eighths of an acre. Another was the furrow, 120 Roman feet in length.

In conclusion weights and measures in biblical times are seldom precise enough to enable one to calculate exact metric equivalents, but the Lord set forth an ideal for *just* balances, weights, and measures. Different standards in surrounding Near Eastern countries affected biblical standards. Sometimes there were two standards operating at the same time, such as short and long, light and heavy, common and royal. There is enough evidence to figure approximate metrological values for the biblical weights and measures.

M. Pierce Matheney

WELL A source of water created by digging in the earth to find available water. In the semiarid climate of ancient Israel, the availability of water was a constant concern, the Bible contains many references to the sources used for obtaining it. Several Hebrew words are used in different contexts to denote these sources, making it sometimes difficult to know which English word to use in translation. See *Cistern; Fountain; Pit; Spring; Water.*

A chaduf for raising well water near ancient Lystra in south central Asia Minor (modern Turkey).

The Hebrew word most commonly translated "well" is *beer* (Gen. 21:30–31; Num. 21:16–18). *Beer* also occurs in several place names indicating the location of important wells: Beer (Num. 21:16); Beer-elim (Isa. 15:8); Beeroth (Deut. 10:6); Beer-lahai-roi (Gen. 16:14); Beer-sheba (Gen. 21:31).

The digging of a well could be a time for celebration (Num. 21:17–18), but wells were also fought over as different people tried to control the precious resource (Gen. 21:25–26; 26:15–22; Ex. 2:16–17). Wells were located wherever a water source could be found. This included fields (Gen. 29:2), towns (2 Sam. 23:15), and the wilderness (Gen. 16:7,14).

"Well" is also used figuratively of a harlot (Prov. 23:27 NRSV) and of a wicked city (Jer. 6:7). Elsewhere it is used as a metaphor for sexual pleasure (Prov. 5:15; see Song of Sol. 4:15).

John C. H. Laughlin

WHALE KJV translation (Gen. 1:21; Job 7:12; Ezek. 32:2; and in Matt. 12:40 with reference to Jonah) for Hebrew *tan.* The Hebrew term can refer to a primeval sea monster or dragon (Isa. 27:1; 51:9 among others), to a serpent (Ex. 7:9; Ps. 91:13), or possibly a crocodile (Ezek. 29:3; 32:2). The Book of Jonah refers simply to a "great fish" (Jonah 1:17). Matthew used the Greek *ketos,* indicating a great sea monster rather than indicating a particular species. All references show that God is in sovereign control over all that humans fear might threaten life and the created order.

WHEAT The staple grain of the Ancient Near East (Num. 18:12). Wheat has been raised in this region since at least neolithic times (8300–4500 B.C.) Many species exist, and exact types cannot be determined from the biblical words. It became the major crop after the nomads began settling into agrarian societies. It is used as an analogy to speak of God's judgment (Matt. 3:12) and His care (Ps. 81:16). Wheat was used to make bread and was also parched (Lev. 23:14). KJV often translated wheat by the word *corn* (Mark 4:28). Wheat harvest was an ancient time reference (Ex. 34:22) and was celebrated by the Feast of Weeks. Wheat is said to have been harvested (1 Sam. 6:13), threshed (Judg. 6:11), and winnowed (Matt. 3:12). See *Agriculture; Bread; Harvest; Plants in the Bible.*

WHEEL A disk or circular object capable of turning on a central axis. Archaeologists and historians believe that the wheel was probably invented in Mesapotamia before 3000 B.C.

The Bible describes both a functional use and symbolic meaning for the wheel. The wheel was indispensable for transportation. It was used on wagons, carts, and chariots, and the word *wheel* could be a synonym for any of these vehicles (Ezek. 23:24; 26:10; Nah. 3:2). In Solomon's Temple, there were ten stands upon which rested ten lavers. Each of the stands were adorned with four wheels each (1 Kings 7:30–33).

Ezekiel's vision of the great wheel in the sky (1:4–28; ch. 10) was a symbol of God's presence. There were four cherubim around the throne. Beside each, there was a wheel which "sparkled like chrysolite" (1:16 NIV). Ezekiel described the rims of the wheel as "high and awesome," and "full of eyes" (v. 18 NIV). The exact meaning of

W

A burned Roman wagon wheel.

these mysterious images is unknown. Perhaps they represented the wheels of God's invisible chariot moving across the sky ("chariots of the sun," see 2 Kings 23:11) or the wheels of God's throne (Dan. 7:9).

Other symbolic uses of the wheel are a whirlwind (Ps. 77:18 NIV) and God's judgment, as a wheel is driven over the wicked (Prov. 20:26). Jeremiah described God's redemption as the reshaping of marred clay on a potter's wheel (18:13). See *Chariots.*   *Brad Creed*

WHELP A lion's cub, used figuratively in the Old Testament (see Gen. 49:9; Jer. 51:38; Nah. 2:11). See *Animals.*

WHIRLWIND English translation of four Hebrew words that designate any windstorm that is destructive. Only Psalm 77:18 uses a term indicating circular motion. True whirlwinds and tornados are rare in Palestine. They usually occur near the coast where the cool breezes of the Mediterranean Sea collide with the hot wind from the desert. Lesser whirlwinds are seen as whirling dust is thrown up into the air. The Lord used the raging wind to take Elijah to heaven (2 Kings 2:1,11) and to talk with Job (38:1; 40:6). The prophets used the stormwind as a figure for judgment (Isa. 5:28; Jer. 4:13; Hos. 8:7; Amos 1:14;

A small whirlwind in the desert of the Wadi Arabah.

Zech. 7:14). God comes to deliver His people riding the stormy winds (Zech. 9:14).

WHITE See *Colors.*

WIFE Female marriage partner. See *Family; Marriage; Woman.*

WILD ASS See *Ass.*

WILD BEASTS A designation of any wild animal in contrast to domesticated animals, translating different Hebrew words. Most often the Hebrew is *chayyah* indicating living creatures (Gen. 1:24) including wild animals (Gen. 1:25). The same Hebrew form indicates humans as "living" beings (Gen. 2:7). The context shows the precise type creature meant. See *Animals.*

WILD BEASTS OF THE ISLAND KJV phrase for a beast identified by modern translations as the hyena or jackal. See *Hyena.*

WILD DONKEY See *Animals.*

WILD GOAT See *Animals.*

WILD GOURD A poisonous plant, probably *Citrillus colocynths* (2 Kings 4:39).

WILD OX See *Animals.*

WILDERNESS Holy Land areas, particularly in the southern part, with little rainfall and few people. The words for *wilderness* in the Old Testament come close to our word *desert,* because they usually mean a rocky, dry wasteland. Desert in the lands of the Bible is usually rocks instead of sand dunes. These have been called "tame" deserts, because they have infrequent rainfall and wells or oases enough to accommodate some nomadic or seminomadic human occupancy. It was the land that neighbored inhabited land to which shepherds could drive their sheep and goats for pasture. David's older brother Eliab taunted him: "With whom have you left those few sheep in the wilderness?" (1 Sam. 17:28 NRSV). The wilderness could also have the forboding sense of uninhabitable land, as Jeremiah described it: "a land of deserts and pits . . . a land of drought and deep darkness . . . a land that no one passes through, where no one dwells" (Jer. 2:6 NRSV). It was a fearful place in which to get lost (Ps. 107:4–9).

Geographically, the wilderness lay south, east, and southwest of the inhabited land of Israel in the Negeb, Transjordan, and the Sinai. A particular wilderness, closer to home, lay on the eastern slopes of the Judean mountains in the rain shadow leading down to the Dead Sea. This particular wilderness, sometimes called Jeshimon, became a refuge for David when he fled from Saul, and was

The Wilderness of Judea (Wilderness of Judah).

the locale of the temptation of Jesus.

Historically, the wilderness was particularly connected with the wandering of the escaping Hebrews after their miraculous escape from Egypt and just prior to the conquest of Transjordan. This was remembered in their retelling of the story as "that great and terrible wilderness" (Deut. 1:19; 8:15). There was good news and bad news about this period of the nation's existence. The good news was that God had provided manna, quail, and water from the rock. He had led them in the wilderness, and revealed Himself and His covenant laws to them at Sinai/Horeb, the mountain of revelation. The bad news was they had rebelled against the Lord and murmured against Moses again and again in the wilderness. The Book of Numbers is called in the Hebrew Bible, *bᵉmidbar,* "In the desert." It tells the tragic story of Kadesh-barnea in the wilderness of Paran and the spy committee who persuaded the people not to attack the Promised Land from the south, so that a whole generation died in the desert (Num. 13—14). In the Psalms, the worshiping Israelites confessed these ancient sins (78:40; 106:26), and New Testament preachers used them as a warning to "wilderness Christians" not to make the same mistakes (1 Cor. 10:1–13; Heb. 3:16–19). There were several specific wilderness areas mentioned, such as those of Sin, Shur, Sinai, Paran, and Zin on the way of wilderness wanderings. Some specific locales were connected with David's outlaw years, such as wilderness of En-Gedi, of Judah, of Maon, of Ziph. Jeremiah once yearned for a desert lodge as a place of escape from his rebellious audience (9:2). People in biblical times mostly feared the desert as a place inhabited by beasts of prey, snakes, and scorpions (even demons) to which one might drive out the scapegoat (Lev. 16:10, 22,26; Isa. 13:21–22; 34:13–14). So it was appropriate as a place for Jesus' temptation (Matt. 4:1–11; Mark 1:12–13; Luke 4:1–13).

The prophets felt that most of Israel's religious troubles began with the settlement of Canaan and apostasy to Canaanite idolatry, but they also looked forward to a renewed pilgrimage in the wilderness (Hos. 2:14–15; 9:10, compare Deut. 32:10; Jer. 2:2–3; 31:2–3). There would be a new Exodus after the Babylonian Exile through the north Syrian desert to make the Lord their king and "prepare his way" (Ezek. 20:30–38; Isa. 40:3–5). John the Baptist appeared in the wilderness of Judea as the promised prophetic forerunner (Matt. 3:1–3; Mark 1:2–4; Luke 3:2–6; John 1:23). Not only did Jesus overcome the tempter in the wilderness, but He fed the four thousand in a desolate place east of Lake Galilee (Mark 8:1–9).

See *Desert; Paran; Shur, Wilderness of; Sin, Wilderness of; Sinai; Wanderings.*

M. Pierce Matheny

WILLOW A tree usually found where water is plentiful, particularly along the Jordan River. Often the willow and the poplar are found together. The willow can grow up to forty feet high. Willow branches were used to make the booths for the feast of tabernacles (Lev. 23:40). In Babylonian captivity the Jews hung their harps on willow trees because they did not feel like singing about Jerusalem in a foreign land (Ps. 137:1–4). NIV often translated willow as "poplar." See *Plants in the Bible.*

WIMPLE Covering women wore around their head and neck (Isa. 3:22). Other translations use "cloaks." See *Cloth, Clothing.*

WIND The natural force which represents in its extended meaning the breath of life in human beings and the creative, infilling power of God and His Spirit.

Early Concepts Two words in the Bible—the Hebrew *ruah* and the Greek *pneuma*—bear the basic meaning of wind but are often translated as spirit. Some understanding of the development of the latter word clarifies this transfer in meaning and enriches the concept.

Pneuma originally represented an elemental, vital, dynamic wind or breath. It was an effective power, but it belonged wholly to the realm of nature. This force denoted any type of wind and ranged from a soft breeze to a raging storm or fatal vapor. It was the wind in persons and animals as the breath they inhaled and exhaled. It was life, since breath was the sign of life; and it was soul, since the animating force left when breathing ceased.

Metaphorically speaking, *pneuma* could be extended to mean a kind of breath that blew from the invisible realms; thus, it could designate spirit, a sign of the influence of the gods upon persons, and the source of a relationship between humankind and the divine. In primitive mythology, this cosmic wind possessed a life-creating power, and a god could beget a son by his breath. The divine breath also inspired poets and granted ecstatic speech to prophets.

W

In all of these reflections, wind remained an impersonal, natural force. When we come to the Judeo-Christian understanding, however, the concept and terms retain their dynamic characteristics, but rise from cosmic power to personal being.

Old Testament In the Old Testament, the primary meaning of the word *ruah* is wind. There is the slight breeze (Ps. 78:39), the storm wind (Isa. 32:2), the whirlwind (2 Kings 2:11), and the scorching wind (Ps. 11:6 NRSV). Winds from the mountains and sea to the north and west brought rain and storm (1 Kings 18:43–45; see Ex. 10:19; Ezek. 1:4); those coming from the deserts of the south and east could at times be balmy but more often would sear the land and dry up the vegetation (Gen. 41:6; Job 37:1–2). Coming from different directions, wind was identified with those directions, referring to the four corners or quarters of the earth or of heaven (Jer. 49:36; Ezek. 37:9).

Theophanies, or manifestations of God, were often associated with the wind. God answered Job out of the whirlwind (Job 38:1), and the four living creatures appeared to Ezekiel in a strong wind from the north (1:4).

Wind was a symbol of transience (Ps. 78:39), fruitless striving (Eccl. 1:14 NRSV), and desperateness (Job 6:26). More importantly, it was a mighty force which only God could command (Jer. 10:13). The wind did God's bidding (Ps. 104:4 NRSV). So closely is the wind connected with God's will that it is called His breath which He blew on the sea to cover the chariots of Pharaoh (Ex. 15:10), or by which He froze rivers (Job 37:10) and withered grass (Isa. 40:7).

The wind is also breath in humans as the breath of life (Gen. 6:17). The entry of breath gives life (Ezek. 37:5–7); and, when it is taken away, the person dies (Ps. 104:29). The breath which brings death when it is withdrawn is identified as God's breath (Job 34:14–15). This same breath of the Almighty is the spirit of wisdom and understanding in a person (Job 32:8 NRSV). When *ruah* is used of the will, intellect, and emotions, or related to God, the meaning often expands from the wind to *spirit* (Isa. 40:13). Thus Psalm 51 uses *ruah* three times when referring to the steadfast, willing, and broken spirit of the psalmist and once when speaking of God's Holy Spirit (verses 10–12,17). Sometimes opinions differ whether the meaning is best served by translating the word as "wind" (breath) or "spirit" when it is specifically designated the *ruah* of God. Thus NRSV translates Genesis 1:2, "a wind from God," to meaning that a wind was moving over the primordial waters; other translations speak of God's Spirit hovering there. See *Spirit.*

New Testament God makes His angels winds (Heb. 1:7 NIV), and "with the breath of His mouth" the Lord Jesus will destroy the wicked one (2 Thess. 2:8 NIV).

The extended meaning, after the experience of Pentecost, has become dominant, and *pneuma* usually refers to a person's inner being (in distinctions from the body) with which the personal Spirit of God communicates and blends as it generates and sanctifies Christians and forms them into the body of Christ (John 3:5–8; Rom. 8:14–16; 1 Cor. 12:7–13; Gal. 5:16–23). In each of these extended meanings, we can still detect in their foundation the image of the wind (*pneuma*) which blows where it wills (John 3:8).

WINDOW English translation of several Hebrew and Greek terms indicating holes in a house. Such holes served several purposes: as a chimney for smoke to escape (Hos. 13:3); holes in places were doves live (Isa. 60:8); holes in heaven through which rain falls (Gen. 7:11; 8:2; Mal. 3:10; compare 2 Kings 7:2). The Hebrew term indicates holes in the wall for air and light (Gen. 8:6; Josh. 2:15; Judg. 5:28 among others). Recessed widows with lattice work marked elaborate public buildings such as the Temple (1 Kings 6:4) and the royal palace (2 Kings 9:30). A third Hebrew term related to enabling something to be seen (1 Kings 7:4). See *Architecture; House.*

A limestone window grill from Tel el-Amarna in Egypt dating from the Eighteenth Dynasty.

WINE Beverage made from fermented grapes. Grapes grew throughout ancient Palestine. Even in areas with limited rainfall, enough dew fell at night to support thriving vineyards. Wine was produced by pressing the juice from the grapes in large stone vats with a small drain at one end. The juice was collected in troughs, poured into large jars, and allowed to ferment while stored in cool, rock cisterns. In New Testament times, wine was kept in skin flasks and often diluted with water. It was also used as a medicine and disinfectant. Scripture condemns drunkenness and overindulgence, but pictured wine as a part of the typical ancient meal. See *Drink; Vine.* David Maltsberger

WINEPRESS The machine used for making wine from grapes. Wine making has always been a major industry in Syria-Palestine. The ancient

An ancient Pompeii wine shop where wine was served from pottery containers sunk into the bar counter.

Egyptian story of Sinuhe, dating from the time of the Middle Bronze Age (about 2200–1550 B.C.), describes this land as having "more wine than water."

In Old Testament times the presses for making wine were usually cut or hewed out of rock (Isa. 5:2) and were connected by channels to lower rock-cut vats where the juice was allowed to collect and ferment. The juice was squeezed from the grapes by treading over them with the feet (Job 24:11; Amos 9:13). Recent excavations at tel Aphek have uncovered two unusually large plastered wine presses dating from the Late Bronze Age (1550–1200 B.C.). The presses were con-

Reconstruction of a first-century wine press, showing the pressing basin with drain leading to the lower collecting basin.

nected to large collection pits which still contained the Canaanite jars for the storage of the wine.

After the juice had fermented, it was collected into jars or wineskins (Matt. 9:17, and parallels). At ancient Gibeon, archaeologists discovered a major wine-producing installation dating from about 700 B.C. In addition to the presses and fermentation tanks, 63 rock-cut cellars were found with a storage capacity of 25,000 gallons of wine. In these cellars the wine could be kept at a constant cool temperature of 65 degrees Fahrenheit. Both royal presses and cellars are mentioned in the Bible (1 Chron. 27:27; Zech. 14:10). Other activities besides the making of wine could go on at a press site (Judg. 6:11; 7:25). By the New Testament period, both beam presses and presses with mosaic pavements were in use.

The harvesting and treading of the grapes was a time of joy and celebration (Isa. 16:10; Jer. 48:33; Deut. 16:13–15); and the image of the abundance of wine is used in the Bible to speak of God's salvation and blessing (Prov. 3:10; Joel 3:18; Amos 9:13). But God's judgment is also vividly portrayed as the treading of the wine press (Isa. 63:2–3; Rev. 14:19–20). See *Agriculture; Vine; Wine.*   *John C. H. Laughlin*

WING The specialized part of the bird that allows flight (Gen. 1:21). The word is most often used figuratively: of God's help (Ruth 2:12), of God's judgment (Jer. 48:40), of strength to return from Exile (Isa. 40:31).

W

Arabs winnowing grain in the ancient way with wooden winnowing forks.

WINNOWING A step in the processing of grain whereby the grain is separated from the inedible parts. The stalks are thrown into the air, and the wind blows away the chaff and the straw, letting the heavier pure grain fall back to the ground (Isa. 30:24). John the Baptist used winnowing as an analogy of God's judgment, when the Lord would separate the sinful from the righteous (Matt. 3:12).

WINNOWING FORK, WINNOWING SHOVEL See *Fan.*

WINTER The season between fall and spring, usually short and mild in Palestine. Winter is also the rainy season for that land (Song of Sol. 2:11). See *Weather.*

WINTERHOUSE A part of a palace or a separate home of the rich that is heated and thus warmer than the rest of the house (Jer. 36:22), or built in a warmer part of the country. Amos spoke of the destruction of the winterhouse because of Israel's sin against God (3:15).

WISDOM AND WISE MEN An educated class of people responsible for preserving and transmitting the culture and learning of the society. Though wisdom and the wise men who perpetuated it have been around almost as long as have people, the study of wisdom in the Ancient Near East is a relatively new endeavor. This has been due, in part, to a lack of a clear definition of the term *wisdom,* as well as the difficult nature of the poetic language within which most of the wisdom material has been found. Sad to say, neither of these issues is completely solved today though much has been learned in recent years.

Real Wisdom Is the Fear of God Three basic definitions of wisdom summarize the status of the field of study very well. Note that the first two of these definitions are quite secular in nature while the third is religious.

First, wisdom is considered by many to be simply the art of learning how to succeed in life. Apparently, ancient persons learned very early that there was an orderliness to the world in which they lived. They also learned that success and happiness came from living in accordance with that orderliness (Prov. 22:17—24:22). Second, wisdom is considered by some to be a philosophical study of the essence of life. Certainly, much of the Books of Job and Ecclesiastes seem to deal with just such existential issues of life (see particularly Job 30:29–31). Third, though the other definitions might include this, it seems that the real essence of wisdom is spiritual, for life is more than just living by a set of rules and being rewarded in some physical manner. Undoubtedly, in this sense wisdom comes from God (Prov. 2:6). Thus, though it will involve observation and instruction, it really begins with God and one's faith in Him as Lord and Savior (Prov. 1:7; Job 28:28).

The Wise Men Preserved This Wisdom Though

at first such wisdom was probably the responsibility of the patriarch or head of the clan, it appears that every ancient culture developed a distinct class of people, the *hakam* or sages, who were responsible for the creating and preserving of their wisdom. No doubt these people were part of the more educated group of their societies who could read and write and had the economic freedom to do so.

Certainly Israel was no exception. The first clear reference to wise men in the biblical text is the one about Ahithophel and Hushai during the reign of David (2 Sam. 16:15—17:23). However, during Solomon's day, the wisdom movement took on a whole new significance, for Solomon and his court became world renowned for their wisdom (1 Kings 4:29–34; 10). Certainly his reign became known as the "golden age" of Israelite culture (Luke 12:27).

Though the movement became less visible during the early part of the divided monarchy, it was still quite active, for Hezekiah's wise men were very concerned about preserving the wisdom tradition for future generations (Prov. 25:1). Later still, Jeremiah's enemies even confronted him regarding his prophecy that the Law would perish from the priests, the prophets, and the sages (Jer. 18:18). Thus, clearly by the fall of Judah, the sage had taken his place as one of the key leaders in Israelite society.

No doubt, as the role of the prophet became less visible during the intertestamental period, the role of the sage and the priest became more prominent (see particularly Ecclesiasticus 38:24—39:11). Apparently, this development continued right on into the New Testament era where the magi (or sage) announced the birth of Christ (Matt. 2:1–12) who became the greatest of all wisdom teachers (Matt. 12:42; 13:54; Mark 6:2).

Most Wisdom Is in Poetic Form Most of the Ancient Near Eastern wisdom material has been found in some type of poetic structure. Until recent years these structures have been a mystery because they did not seem to rhyme either in meter or sound as modern languages do. However, in A.D. 1753 Bishop Robert Lowth unlocked the key to such poetic writing when he discovered that Hebrew poetry rhymed in thought. Moreover, he surmised that such thoughts were most commonly expressed in parallel patterns. Some of these patterns expressed the same thoughts (Prov. 20:1), while others expressed opposing thoughts (Prov. 10:1), or developed a given thought (Prov. 31:10–31). In time, these parallel patterns were structured into specific forms such as the proverb, riddle, allegory, hymn, disputation, autobiographical narrative, didactic narrative, and lists. No doubt, such beautiful and intricate poetic structure was clearly a mark of the sage and the wisdom schools of his day and age. See *Poetry.*

Wisdom Became the Guide for Daily Living

Though in recent years many parts of the sacred Scripture have been considered under wisdom's umbrella, no doubt the greatest contribution of Israel's sages has been the three books found in the "writings" (Job, Proverbs, and Ecclesiastes). However, certain of the other "writings" such as the Psalms, the Song of Solomon, and Lamentations contain figures of speech and stylized forms reflective of the wisdom tradition. In addition to these, the intertestamental works of Ecclesiasticus and the Wisdom of Solomon continued the tradition and laid an excellent foundation for the ultimate revelation of wisdom in Christ Jesus (Matt. 11:19; Luke 11:49–51; Col. 1:15–20; 1 Cor. 1:24,30; Rev. 5:12). See *Intertestamental History; Apocrypha; Pseudepigrapha.*

Certainly, biblical wisdom like that of other cultures emphasizes the success and well-being of the individual. This is visible not only in the topics it chooses to deal with, but also in the way it deals with them. Some of its major topics are: knowledge, the world, justice, virtue, family, and faith. The greatest of these may be faith which is constantly watching over wisdom and really all of life (Prov. 1:7). See *Ecclesiastes; Job; Proverbs.*

Harry Hunt

WITCH A female whose work was in divination and magic. See *Divination and Magic.*

WITNESS, MARTYR The testimony of a person, or something which bears testimony to a person or an event. In the Old Testament the Hebrew word *moed* is used to refer to the "meeting" place of God and His people. This meeting is testimony to a particular person or event, such as God or the giving of the covenant, and provides a place of testimony. See *Tent of Meeting.*

The second Hebrew word, *ed*, refers to the legal element of witness. One rendered testimony based on observation which was to be true and faithful. This is beautifully illustrated in Ruth 4:9–11 where Boaz called on the elders of the city to be witnesses to his act of redemption. Witnesses were also expected to be involved in the judgment. Thus, in Deuteronomy 17:7 the witness is the first to throw a stone. Joshua (24:22) called the people to awareness of their vow to serve the Lord their God by reminding them they were witnesses and thus accountable.

In this last chapter of Joshua, Joshua also set up a memorial, *edah*, to the commitment. This act of memorializing is also a witness and is commonly practiced in the Old Testament. See *Stone.* The memorial is a witness response to both present and future generations of God's activity. In Psalm 119, the law is the supreme "testimony" or monument to God. God established the law and gave it to people as a true and faithful witness for righteous living.

The legal concept of witness found in the Old

Testament is continued in the New Testament. This aspect of witness, as well as new ones, is covered by only one Greek word, *martureō,* and its many derivatives. The legal sense of witness/ testimony occurs in the synoptics during the trial of Jesus (Matt. 26:65; Mark 14:63; Luke 22:71). Paul employed this legal concept when he bore witness to the Galatians of their care for him (Gal. 4:15). In a more technical sense of witness, he reminded Timothy not to act too hastily in accusing an elder without at least two or three witnesses (1 Tim. 5:19). Nowhere is this sense of witness more developed than in John's writings. Jesus is the supreme witness to God and His love. In John 1, John the Baptist bore testimony to the truth of Jesus' witness. In John 5, Jesus argued pointedly that John the Baptist, the Father, and the Scripture all bear witness to Him. In John 8, Jesus reminded His hearers that according to the law the testimony of two people is true. Thus His hearers needed to respond to the truth of His witness. For John, Jesus's message as witness was inseparable from His very personhood. Jesus is true and faithful, and so is His message. A response is demanded.

This concept of one's person being involved in the witness informs the way witness is used to described the early believers. Believers were challenged by Christ Himself to be His witnesses throughout the world (Acts 1:8). As Jesus had indicated earlier, this witness is informed and empowered by the Holy Spirit (John 15:26−27). Throughout the New Testament, believers are instructed that their witness is to be true and faithful, reflected both in speech and life-style (Acts 4:33; 14:3; Heb. 10:15−17; 1 Thess. 2:10).

This high commitment to witness/testify exemplified by Christ resulted in His persecution and death. Likewise, with His followers there would be persecution for their witness (John 15:20). Thus, early in the Book of Acts (ch. 7), Stephen became the first martyr. That very word comes from *martureō* and really states that Stephen was first and foremost a witness, giving testimony. Ironically, the witness was put to death by witnesses to his testimony (7:58).

The death of Stephen serves as a stark reminder that true and faithful testimony to Christ requires total commitment, even one's life. As Christ is the faithful and true witness (Rev. 3:14) who clearly presented God to the world, so may believers be. See *Acts; Covenant; Evangelism; Martyr.*

William Vermillion

WIZARD See *Medium.*

WOLF The largest of wild carnivorous animals (*Canis lupus; Canis pallipes*) that include dogs, foxes, and jackals. The wolf is known for its boldness and fierceness of attack. It often killed more than it could eat because the taste of blood put it into a frenzy. Shepherds knew the wolf as the greatest enemy of sheep. The wolf was well known in biblical days (John 10:12), yet nearly every reference to wolves is in a figurative sense (Gen. 49:27; Jer. 5:6; Ezek. 22:27). Jesus used the figure of the false prophet as a wolf in sheep's clothing (Matt. 7:15). One of the signs of the messianic age is that the "wolf and the lamb shall feed together" (Isa. 65:25). See *Animals.*

WOMAN A female human. The picture of woman revealed in the Bible is far from one-dimensional. Frequently subjected to the rule of her male counterpart, often adored for her beauty and purity, and occasionally praised for her leadership in times of crisis, woman emerges from the pages of the Bible with as much complexity as man.

Woman in Bible times lived in a patriarchal society. Both the Old and New Testament worlds normally restricted the role of woman primarily to the sphere of home and family, although a few strong women emerged as leaders. In religious life she was subordinate to man. Father and then husband or other male relatives gave protection and direction to woman. Jesus raised the window for women. He paid attention to them. His manner was inclusive and acknowledged their place in the kingdom He proclaimed. By what He did and what He said He elevated the status of woman. Paul also caught Jesus' vision. Although Paul faced the need to preserve order in the early church, he exclaimed in Galatians 3:28: "There is neither Jew nor Greek, there is neither bond nor free, there is neither male nor female: for ye are all one in Christ Jesus." The final barrier preventing woman from fully participating in the kingdom of God toppled under Jesus' influence.

What the Old Testament Teaches About Woman
The Old Testament shows woman in at least two lights. The predominant view is one of woman in subjection to man. However, at times, woman is also the object of adoration and admiration. The creation narratives in Genesis foreshadow two different perspectives regarding woman. In the account in Genesis 1:26−30, man and woman are created simultaneously (Gen. 1:27). Woman, like man, is made in the image of God. Together, man and woman reflect the image of God. Woman is not in an inferior place in creation. In Genesis 2:7−25, man is created before woman. In this second account woman is viewed as being created for man as his helper. This account is often cited as supportive of the view that woman should remain subject to man since she has a subordinate position in creation, but the narrative describes woman as a "suitable partner" (v. 20 REB) for whom man leaves his family.

The subordination of woman appears more clearly in close reading the Ten Commandments. The Commandments are addressed to

An Arab village woman and small girl carrying large waterpots balanced on their heads.

men, a fact evidenced by the use of masculine pronouns. A major of evidence of women's subordination is the reference to man not coveting any of his neighbor's property. His wife is included in the list of possessions (Ex. 20:17). Marriage and divorce are areas in which woman's rights were subordinate to those of man. If a woman about to be married was suspected of not being a virgin, she was required to submit to a test. If her virginity was not established, she could be stoned to death at her father's door (Deut. 22:13–21). No such requirement was made for a man. Adultery was seen as a crime against a husband's rights. Both male and female caught in the act of adultery were stoned, but it was the husband's rights which were being vindicated (Deut. 22:22). A husband who was jealous of his wife and had some fears about her faithfulness could take her to the priest and have her submit to an intricate test to determine her innocence or guilt (Num. 5:11–31). No such avenue was open for a woman who suspected her husband of being unfaithful.

Divorce was also slanted toward the husband. He could obtain a divorce from his wife "because he finds something objectionable about her" (Deut. 24:1 NRSV). The phrase "something objectionable" was variously interpreted by the Jews and ran the gamut from adultery to burned toast!

Inequity between boy and girl babies existed from the very beginning of life. A mother who bore a girl baby was considered unclean for twice as long as a mother who bore a male child. During her "purifying" time after the birth of a baby, a mother was not to "touch any holy thing, or come into the sanctuary, until the days of her purification are completed" (Lev. 12:2–5).

Aside from specific inequities in the way men and women were treated, the Old Testament, pratically the Book of Proverbs, warned of tempting, "loose" (2:16 NRSV), "loud," "ignorant" (9:13 NRSV), and "contentious" (21:9 NRSV) women. Women were also seen as fearful (Isa. 19:16). Proverbs 31 also pictured the hardworking, praiseworthy, "virtuous" woman.

Woman's most positive image was wife and mother. Against the predominant pattern of women in subordinate roles, several positive images of women emerged from the Old Testament. Undoubtedly, woman was venerated in her role as wife and mother. The Ten Commandments cite a son's duty to honor both his father and mother (Ex. 20:12). The ideal woman, eulogized in Proverbs 31, is a wife and mother who fulfills well both roles in addition to engaging profitably in the business world.

The birth of children was a sign of God's favor bestowed upon a good woman. A particular sign of God's favor was the birth of male children (Gen. 29:31—30:24). The story of Ruth is a good example of a traditional woman who was admired for her role as a good daughter-in-law. Ruth and Naomi, whose husbands died, were women of worth whom God aided by sending Boaz as their protector (Ruth 1—4).

A thread which crosses the dominant pattern of the subjection of women is one which depicts women positively. Wisdom, which held high value for the Hebrew people, was personified as "she" (Prov. 1:20; 7:4). The prophet Isaiah used a mother's love for her child as a model for God's love for His people (Isa. 49:15: 66:13). Several women—including Miriam, Deborah, Huldah, and Esther—earned the respect and admiration of the Israelite nation by playing a significant role in times of national crisis. See *Deborah; Esther; Huldah; Miriam.*

What the New Testament Teaches About Woman Jesus was able to retain the best in the Hebrew tradition and yet cut away some of the rigid structure that restricted it. He was able to do the same for woman. Without radically changing her roles, Jesus enlarged and transformed women's possibilities for a full life. His manner and teachings elevated her status and gave her an identity and a cause. Jesus' manner in His interactions with women is at least as significant as His teachings about woman. At the risk of censure from a male-oriented society, Jesus talked to women, responded to their touch, healed them, received their emotional and financial support, and used them as main characters in His stories. Jesus saw women as persons. Martha wanted Jesus to make Mary help with the serving duties, but Jesus affirmed Mary's choice to learn as a disciple. Women of that day could not be disciples of rabbis, but Jesus recognized women's potential for intelligent thought and commitment (Luke 10:38–42).

On another occasion, Jesus welcomed a woman's anointing His head as indicative of her understanding of His real mission. Instead of rejecting her public display or chiding her for extravagance, He commended her for her act of love. He treated her as a person of insight and feeling (Mark 14:3–9). The woman at the well in Samaria is another example of Jesus seeing women as persons. Jesus would not have talked theology to her if

W

He had related to her primarily as a woman or as a Samaritan. However, He saw her as a person, so He was not restricted in His interaction by her sex or race (John 4:1–42). The woman caught in adultery was treated as a person. Her action was not condoned by Jesus, but neither did He allow her to be subjected to a double standard by her male accusers. Jesus offered her new possibilities of living with His directive: "Neither do I condemn you. Go your way, and from now on do not sin again" (John 7:53—8:11 NRSV).

Besides seeing women as persons, Jesus involved them in His earthly ministry. Luke mentioned a group of women who traveled with Jesus as He journeyed from town to town (Luke 8:1–3). Among them were Mary of Magdala, Joanna, and Susanna. These women provided financial support for Jesus and the twelve apostles. Women also proclaimed the gospel. In His encounter with the Samaritan woman, Jesus revealed Himself as the Messiah. She immediately left and began telling people, "He told me everything I have ever done" (John 4:39 NRSV). Many Samaritans believed in Jesus because of the woman's testimony.

Women were the first at the tomb after the resurrection; and, as such, they were the first to broadcast His victory over death (Luke 23:55—24:11). Matthew, Mark, and Luke all called attention to the loyal women who participated in Jesus' Galilean ministry and followed Him all the way to the cross and the grave. They shared the greatest news: "He is not here, but has risen" (Luke 24:5 NRSV).

As a master teacher, Jesus used parables to teach about the kingdom of God. He reached out to the women in His audience by telling stories about their life experiences. By capturing their attention and commitment through parables, He offered them a place in the kingdom.

God's seeking activity is the theme of two parables, the lost sheep begins, "What man of you" and the parable of the lost coin, "What woman." The woman looking for the lost coin represented God's activity in seeking the lost, just as the man represented God's seeking activity. Jesus appealed to women through their housekeeping experiences. He elevated their experiences by likening them to God's activity.

The twin parables in Luke 13:18–20 point to the way the kingdom of God grows. Again Jesus used the life experience of woman to illuminate an eternal truth. Jesus meant for women to identify with His mission. He meant to involve them in spreading the gospel. His parables taught that both women and men would be involved in the kingdom work.

Jesus spoke directly to the matter of treating a woman as a sex object. In the Sermon on the Mount, He redefined adultery to include a lustful look (Matt. 5:28). While making religion a matter of the heart instead of the law, Jesus elevated

women to the level of full personhood, from the level of sexual exploitation. Marriage and divorce were issues of great importance to women, since their lives were lived mainly in the roles of wife and mother. Their emotional, social, and financial security was dependent on their marriages. Jesus said that divorce is a testimony to the hardness of the human heart, not God's will (Matt. 19:1–9). To those who were casually divorcing their wives, Jesus stated plainly that they were committing adultery. Responsive to the plight of women, He offset the male bias toward divorce and strengthened marriage as a permanent union. (See Matt. 5:31–32; 19:1–12; Mark 10:1–12; Luke 16:18.)

Jesus' parable of the ten maidens, five foolish and five wise, hints at the way Jesus saw and dealt with woman (Matt. 25:1–13). He saw women as neither inferior nor superior, but simply as persons. He saw their potential, their sinfulness, their strengths and weaknesses, and He dealt with them directly. As a group, He elevated their status and strengthened their participation and influence in their world. But as individuals, He treated them as friends and disciples.

Paul's theological vision (Gal. 3:28) was that there was no partiality among persons with God. Yet Paul felt the tension of maintaining order in the New Testament church. He often fell back on Jewish social customs of the day to ensure that the fledgling church would not be seen unfavorably by the rest of the world. A man of his time, he still had a vision toward which he strove.

Paul moved ahead of his Jewish background when he called for mutual submission between husbands and wives (Eph. 5:21–33). The prevailing custom was for wives to be submissive. However, Paul reflected Jesus' concern that all relationships reflect the grace extended by God. Responsibilities of both husbands and wives to love each other follow the initial exhortation to submit to each other in love. In other passages Paul implied a hierarchy of submission from God, to Christ, to man, to woman, to child as the sequence. However, the tone of this hierarchy was not military, but voluntary and self-sacrificing. Here again was a concession to order and not the ideal (1 Cor. 11:2–16; 14:33–40; 1 Tim. 2:8–15).

Paul wrote in response to problems in churches. Paul was concerned that the Christians should "give no offense to Jews or to Greeks or to the church of God" (1 Cor. 10:32 NRSV). Therefore, he wrote responses to the way specific problems should be handled in different churches. Some of his remarks do not have direct relevance to our day. For example, he spoke of meat offered to idols (Rom. 14), and women wearing jewelry and braiding their hair (1 Tim. 2:8–12). In contrast to these specific problems, Paul espoused basic principles which have relevance to every age: (1) A Christian should take into account how his or her actions may influence others (1 Cor. 8:13) and (2) A Christian should do all things to to the glory of God (1 Cor. 10:31).

Of equal weight with what Paul said regarding women is how he related to them. Paul welcomed women as colaborers in the churches and commended them for their gifts and faithfulness (Rom. 16:1,3–5). Phoebe, Prisca, Lydia, and others were seen as partners in the gospel. To the Roman church Paul said, "I commend to you our sister Phoebe, a deacon of the church at Cenchreae" (Rom. 16:1 NRSV). He called Phoebe a "benefactor of many and of myself as well" (v. 2 NRSV). Evidently Paul relied on women to exercise their gifts (1 Cor. 12) as a part of the body of Christ. See *Deacon; Offices; Phoebe; Prisca.*

Summary Woman is the subject of many questions and controversies in the church today. Is she equal to man? Can she exercise the same spiritual gifts as man in the church? Should she be subject to her husband in all matters? As Christians turn to the Bible for guidance in responding to these questions, they must be careful not to focus on one verse or passage. The total impact and message of the Bible should become the guiding spirit in answering these and other questions.

The Old Testament clearly subjected woman to the will and protection of her husband. She was extolled for performing her important roles as wife and mother. On occasion she rose above those roles and led the Jewish nation in times of crisis.

The New Testament brings a different picture of woman into focus. Jesus, and later Paul, elevated the status of woman so that she could be a full participant in the kingdom of God. However, she is urged to use her responsibility as well as her freedom to find her place in the body of Christ. The spirit of freedom and love in Christ is woman's as well as man's.

See *Divorce; Family; Marriage; Sex, Teaching on.*   *Kay W. Shurden*

WOODWORKER Person who worked with wood in some sense—cutting trees in a forest (1 Kings 5:6); bringing the logs to where they were needed (v. 9); building the house and the furniture needed for it (2 Kings 22:6); and making beautiful objects of art from wood. See *Occupations and Professions in the Bible.*

WOOL The thick hair forming the coat especially of sheep and some other animals. It was made into thread and used to make clothing, blankets, and other articles. It was one of the major economic factors in Israel and the surrouding countries. Gideon used a piece of wool to determine God's will for his life (Judg. 6:35–40). Wool was also used as a symbol of whiteness and purity (Isa. 1:18). See *Cloth, Clothing; Sheep.*

WORD Utterance or saying that may refer to a single work, the entire law, the gospel message, or even Christ.

Old Testament *Dabar* is the primary Hebrew expression for word. It has various meanings. It can refer to a spoken utterance, a saying, a command, a speech, a story—linguistic communication in general. *Dabar* can also mean a thing, event, or action (Gen. 18:14). Occasionally, difficulty arises in distinguishing between these meanings (Ps. 35:20 NRSV, "deceitful words"; KJV, "deceitful matters"; REB, "intrigues"; NIV, "false accusations"). The frequent construction "the word of the Lord" or "the word of Yahweh" refers to communication made by God to people. The means of this communication are seldom related, nor must the phrase refer to a particular set of words. Three aspects of this word demand special attention.

1. A prophetic word. The prophets claimed to deliver the "word of God" (Jer. 1:9). For this purpose they were commissioned (Isa. 6:8). This word of God addressed human beings and demanded a response. Thus God's word may be visualized as a great salvation (Isa. 2:2–5) or a great judgment (Jer. 26:4–6).

2. A legal word. In the covenant law God spoke the words of the law to Moses (Ex. 20:1; 24:3–8). The heart of the law is called the ten words (Ex. 34:28; Deut. 4:13). The entire law represents the will of God and so can be called a single "word" (Deut. 4:2 KJV). This word also demands response: faithful obedience will bring God's blessing while disobedience will lead to a curse (Deut. 30:15–20).

3. Creative word. God created the world by His word (Gen. 1; Isa. 48:13; Ps. 33:9). This world reveals God's majesty (Ps. 19:1) and thus extends the sphere of His revelation beyond His work with covenant Israel to all people. The word is spoken of as if it were a person who directs the events of nature (Ps. 147:15–18; 148:8), saves (107:20), and gives life (Ezek. 37:1–4).

New Testament *Logos* and *Rhēma* are the two primary Greek words meaning "word." They are used interchangeably and variously as with the Old Testament *dabar.* The New Testament can use these words to apply to Jesus' message, the message about Jesus, and Jesus Himself.

Jesus' message of the coming kingdom can be called a "word" (Mark 2:2; 4:33; Luke 5:1) as can His individual sayings (Matt. 26:75; Luke 22:61; John 7:36). Significantly, Jesus avoided citing rabbinic authorities or using the traditional language of a prophet who would claim "that the word of the Lord came to me" or declare "thus says the Lord." Perhaps these phrases did not significantly honor His special relationship with the Father and His own authority (Matt. 11:27; compare 5:21–26; Mark 3:28–29). As in the Old Testament, so also Jesus' word demanded decision on the part of

W

the hearers (John 8:51; 12:47).

The message concerning Jesus can also be called "a word." Paul spoke of "the word of God that you heard from us" that is mediated by his human words (1 Thess. 2:13 NRSV). The content of this word is certainly the good news story concerning Jesus' death and resurrection—the heart of the gospel (1 Cor. 15:3–5). This message is the word of the cross (Gal. 3:1) and is the core content of Paul's preaching (1 Cor. 2:2). Because of His sacrifice and resurrection, the gospel message is a "word of reconciliation" (2 Cor. 5:19) and a "word of life" (Phil. 2:16). The word is witnessed and proclaimed by Jesus' followers (Luke 1:2; Acts 4:2; 6:7). The word revealed through His son (Heb. 1:1–4) brings illumination and judgment.

Jesus Himself is the Word—the living Word. The preexistent Word who was with God "in the beginning" has now become flesh (John 1:1–18). Scholars have frequently claimed that John used *logos* in a philosophical sense to refer to the world's controlling rational principle (Stoicism) or to the created intermediary between God and His world (Philo). However, John's word is not a *principle* or divine characteristic. It is a preexistent, life-giving *person.* John opposed Greek philosophy by arguing that salvation comes not by mankind's escape from this world but by God entering and redeeming creation. More probably *logos* was chosen because of its meaning in the Old Testament, its Greek translation, and contemporary Hebrew literature, where the concepts of *wisdom* and *word* were being spoken of as a distinct manifestation of God. John saw that the same agent of God who gave life in the first creation was also giving life in the new creation inaugurated by Jesus' coming. The creative Word of God became flesh; being divine He embodied divine communication. Now the Word dwells among us revealing the glory of God (John 1:14).

Power of the Word It is often assumed that in Hebrew thought words had a mysterious binding authority. For example, when Isaac discovered he had been deceived and wrongly gave his blessing to Jacob, he declared that his blessing had been given and Jacob "shall be blessed" (Gen. 27:33). Isaac's word seems magical—like an arrow once shot, it could not be recalled. Caution must be exercised here. Actually, only God's word has this type of irresistible potency (Isa. 55:11) and absolute creative power (Gen. 1:3–31; Luke 1:32–35; compare Isa. 9:8; 31:2; 45:23). Most occurrences like Isaac's may be explained in terms of their social custom. Following a prescribed social custom, a person may form a bond, or a will, by speaking a word. Even today a couple can make or create a marriage by saying "I do." We must also note that Scripture teaches that a person's word is often powerless (1 Cor. 2:4; 4:19–20) and frequently fails (Matt. 21:28–32).

Words are capable of great good and evil (Matt.

12:36; Jas. 3:5–6,8). Words can deeply injure (Prov. 12:18; 18:14), and revive (Prov. 12:18,25; 16:24). Words can have a widespread influence; words from the wicked are like a fire-spreading torch (Prov. 16:27–28); words from the good bring good fruit (Prov. 12:14; 10:11).

Randy Hatchett

WORK, THEOLOGY OF Meaning and value God places on human labor.

God's People Work Because They Are Made in His Image The Bible opens with a picture of a working God. God worked in creating a universe. He has been at the job of sustaining creation since He fashioned it. To be created in God's image means, in part, that people have the capacity to work, to fashion, to create. The notion that labor came into being as a result of humanity's fall does not reflect biblical truth. Sinless humanity was placed in the garden to cultivate it. The opportunity to labor was part of God's original commission to mankind to subdue the earth. Adam and Eve were given a situation that needed tending. Paradise had its chores.

Whereas the entrance of sin did not precipitate humanity's need to labor, it has affected the original circumstances of people's work. As He expelled them from the garden, God told Adam and Eve they would have to labor hard to carve out a living. Sin hinders the progress of men's and women's efforts and thwarts their genius. Nature does not cooperate like it would without the curse. People's physical ability has been limited by the effect of sin. A person's mental capacity has been drastically reduced by the ravages of sin.

However, the primal commission for humanity to subdue the earth remains in force. In the garden imagery, cultivation was the scope of the original pair's labor. Today the range would be broadened to include every pursuit of people—cultural, physical, social, and spiritual.

God's People Reflect Him Through Practicing Integrity in Their Work Christianity that is real shows up in the marketplace. It affects the work of employees and the attitude of employers. Christian employees are conscious of their responsibilities to their employers. Followers of Christ know they owe their employers an honest day's work. Those representing Christ should strive to be the most productive and conscientious workers in the company. Christians view their service to their employer as ultimately rendered to God, knowing He is the ultimate judge of their efforts (Eph. 6:5–8). Those in authority over others in the workplace have special responsibility. Christian supervisors or employers know they are accountable to God for how they treat those under them (Eph. 5:9). Managers' testimony for Christ is on the line in their dealings with subordinates. Fairness, reasonableness, and generosity can be maintained even when a standard of excellence is upheld.

God's People Realize His Plan for Work Also Includes a Plan for Rest After six days of creation God rested. He reflected on the worth and meaning of His work. Later He prescribed a day of rest for His people each week to do the same (Ex. 20:8–11). God knows people have physical, emotional, mental, and spiritual limits. These must be guarded by a proper balance of work and rest.

God's People See Their Primary Vocation as Serving Him For Christians, life's primary vocation is ministry. Christians view their workplace as a ministry post. Their pulpits are their desks, their cars, their classrooms, their kitchens. Seeing oneself as a mine worker, homemaker, school teacher, or professional person who happens to be a Christian is fundamentally different from seeing oneself primarily as a Christian who happens to be a secretary, salesperson, or accountant. A proper theology of work operating in the lives of believers would see many people positively influenced toward Christ in every setting where Christians are found working.   *T. R. McNeal*

WORKS Deeds leading to planned results, both by God and people. God's works are His acts and deeds in creating, saving, and sustaining (Judg. 2:7; Pss. 8:6; 103:22; 104:24; Isa. 64:8; Eph. 2:10; Phil. 1:6). Jesus Christ came to do the work of God (John 4:34; 5:17; 9:4.) The miraculous works of Christ testify to His divine nature and mission (John 5:36; 6:28–29; 10:37–38). Christ calls and enables His followers to continue His works (John 14:12; 1 Cor. 15:58; 16:10).

The works of people testify to their faith or lack of it. Those who do the works of the devil show that they are of the devil (John 8:34–44; 2 Cor. 11:14–15). Sinners are called to cast off the works of darkness (Rom. 13:12; Eph. 5:11), sometimes called wicked works (Col. 1:21) or the works of the flesh (Gal. 5:19). Because sinners cannot save themselves, they must rely on the grace of God, not on their own works (Eph. 2:8–9; Titus 3:4–7).

Paul warned against relying on the works of the law as a basis for acceptance by God (Rom. 9:32; Gal. 2:16; 3:2,5,10). Sinners are accepted as righteous before God on the basis of God's grace through faith in Christ, not on the basis of their own works (Rom. 3:27; 4:2–6). One evidence of saving faith, however, is the existence of good works in the lives of believers (Matt. 5:16; Acts 9:36; Eph. 2:10; Col. 1:10; 2 Thess. 2:17; 1 Tim. 2:10; 5:10,25; Titus. 2:7,14; Heb. 10:24; 1 Pet. 2:12).

Some people think that Paul and James contradict each other in their teachings about works. James 2:14–26 says that people are justified by faith and works, not by faith alone. However, closer examination shows that James used the word "works" to refer to what Paul meant by "good works." James and Paul were dealing with people who wanted to rely on works of the law for their salvation. James was dealing with people who professed to believe but whose lives did not show it. Paul, therefore, emphasized that sinners cannot make themselves acceptable to God by keeping the works of the law. Dealing with a different situation, James emphasized that true faith shows itself in good works, a point Paul that also made.

The Lord knows the works of His people. He commends His churches for their good works and rebukes them for the works that are not worthy of His people (Rev. 2:2,5,9,13,19,23,26; 3:1,2,8,15). God does not judge according to outward appearances but according to works (1 Pet. 1:17; Rev. 20:12–13; 22:12). Although true believers are accepted into God's eternal kingdom by grace through faith, God will condemn those whose profession is proved false by their evil works (Matt. 7:21–23). True believers are saved because their lives are built on the solid foundation of Christ Himself. They will be rewarded for good works but any unworthy works will not survive God's judgment (1 Cor. 3:10–15). See *Faith; Salvation.*   *Robert J. Dean*

WORLD, THE The created order in the totality of its space and time. The development of the biblical concept and the varieties of ways in which the term is used become evident when the Old Testament uses, Greek concept, and New Testament uses are considered in sequence.

The Old Testament The ancient Hebrews had no word for the "universe." When speaking of the totality of creation, they used descriptive phrases like "the heavens and the earth" (Gen. 1:1 NIV), "heavens and the earth, the sea, and all that is in them" (Ex. 20:11; compare Phil. 2:10 NIV), or "the heavens, even the highest heavens, and all their starry host, the earth and all that is on it, the seas and all that is in them" (Neh. 9:6 NIV). Evident in these more extended descriptions is the view that the world consisted of an expanse of land ("the earth") that was surrounded by water and set under the canopy of the heavens. More simply, they could use the inclusive "all" (Isa. 44:24; Jer. 10:16; 51:19).

Basic to Hebrew thought was the affirmation that God created everything above the earth, on the earth, and under it (Gen. 1:1—2:3; Job 38). The doctrine of creation asserted the sovereignty of God—and the superiority of the God of the Hebrews over the idols worshiped by other peoples. Four Hebrew words have been translated by "world." The word *eretz* (2,047 times) normally means "earth" or "land." It is translated as "world" four times in the KJV and twice in the RSV (Isa. 23:17; Jer. 25:26). *Olam* is translated as "world" twice in the KJV (Ps. 73:12; Eccl. 3:11).

W

Its general sense is *age,* or *long duration.* Two other rarer words appear predominantly in the poetic writings (*tebel,* which is synonymous with *eretz,* 36 times, for instance, Ps. 13:18; Job 37:12; and *cheled,* which is synonymous with *olam,* 5 times, for instance, Pss. 17:14; 49:1). The Hebrews, therefore, did not have a single concept of the world but thought of the creation in terms of its geographical and temporal extent.

Greek Thought The word *kosmos* (from which we get the English words "cosmic" and "cosmology") originally described anything that was constructed or built, then its order, or by extension its ordered beauty. The world was a perfect unity, beautiful in its order. From the time of the use of *kosmos* to describe the world, therefore, the order of the world was primary. Precisely this concept of the world as an ordered system is absent from Hebrew thought.

The order of the world was explained variously by the leading schools of philosophy. Plato held that the *kosmos* included both the visible world and all that could be known by reason. The concepts of world, heaven, and space began to merge. Heraclitus and later Aristotle rejected any notion of a beginning of the world. The world was infinite, without beginning or end. For the Stoics, the *logos* was the rational principle that gave order to the world. The idea of God as Creator and the world as God's creation was foreign to the Greeks. The world was an extension of the *logos* that gave it order. Plato considered that a demiurge formed the world in a manner consistent with perfect being. Even for Plato, however, neither was the demiurge fully God nor was the world a creation. It was an extension or emanation of the demiurge.

The use of *kosmos* in the Septuagint, the Greek translation of the Hebrew Bible, marked the beginning of a biblical concept of *world.* The merging of Hebrew and Greek thought later found its fullest expression in the works of Philo of Alexandria, who used the word more than any other writer in antiquity.

In the New Testament Three words are translated as "world" in the New Testament: *oikoumenē* (15 times, "the inhabited earth"), *aiōn* (over 30 times, similar to the Hebrew *olam* meaning "long duration," "age," or "world"), and *kosmos* (188 times). *World* can carry various nuances.

1. The whole created order Paul before the Areopagus in Athens spoke of "the God who made the world and everything in it" (Acts 17:24 NIV). The doctrine of creation was still fundamental to the New Testament writers. The early Christians in Jerusalem addressed God as "Sovereign Lord, . . . you made the heaven and the earth and the sea, and everything in them" (Acts 4:24 NIV). The biblical writers could therefore refer to "the foundation of the world" (Matt. 25:34; Luke 11:50; John 17:24; Eph. 1:4; Heb. 4:3; 9:26; 1 Pet. 1:20; Rev. 13:8; 17:8) or the creation of the world (see Rom. 1:20; compare John 17:5).

2. The earth and its inhabitants John 1:9 refers to "the true light which enlightens everyone was coming into the world" (NRSV). Similarly, in the farewell discourse in John, Jesus spoke of His departure from the world (13:1; 16:28). The authorities complained that "the world"—meaning all people—had "gone after him" (John 12:19). Satan offered Jesus "all the kingdoms of the world" (Matt. 4:8 NIV), and Paul saluted the Christians in Rome, saying, "Your faith is proclaimed throughout the world" (Rom. 1:8 NRSV). The meaning of "the world" in John 3:16 should probably be understood in this sense.

3. The arena of human activity. This especially pertains to wealth and material goods. "The cares of this world" can choke out the word (Mark 4:19). Married persons may be especially troubled over worldly affairs (1 Cor. 7:33–34). In this sense, the elder admonished the Johannine community, "Do not love the world or anything in the world" (1 John 2:15 NIV; compare 2:16–17).

"The world" can also designate all that is hostile, rebellious, and opposed to God. Paul referred to the effects of the fall on the whole cosmic order: "The creation was subjected to frustration . . . [but] the creation itself will be liberated from its bondage" (Rom 8:19–25 NIV; compare 2 Pet. 1:4). The world, therefore, is under the power of "the prince of this world" (John 12:31; 14:30; 16:11), "the prince of the power of the air" (Eph. 2:2), the "god of this world" (2 Cor. 4:4); "the whole world is under the control of the evil one" (1 John 5:19 NIV).

Paul contrasted the wisdom of this world with the wisdom of God (1 Cor. 1:20–21,26–28; 3:19). "The rulers of this age" cannot understand God's wisdom hidden in Christ (1 Cor. 2:7–8 NIV). Through the cross, Christ triumphed over all the powers of this world (Col. 2:15). Indeed, God was in Christ "reconciling the world unto himself" (2 Cor. 5:19; Col. 1:20).

The hostile sense of "the world" is especially pronounced in the Johannine writings. Nevertheless, it is important to note that the world is not inherently evil. John still affirmed the creation of the world through the *logos* (John 1:3–4). Jesus, "the lamb of God who takes away the sin of the world" (1:29 NIV), was sent to save the world (3:17; 10:36; 12:47). He is, therefore, "the light of the world" (8:12); the Samaritans acclaimed Him as "the Savior of the world" (4:42).

The coming of Jesus, however, brought judgment to the world (9:39; 12:31). The world will hate the disciples as it hated Jesus (15:18) because they are not of the world (15:19). Jesus called His disciples to show love for one another that all may recognize them through this love (13:35) The disciples are to be in the world but not "of the world" (17:14–16). Victory over the hostility of the world is assured through the cross of Jesus (16:33) and through faith (1 John 5:4–5). The world, in fact, is already passing away (1 John 2:17).

In the New Testament, therefore, *world* is influenced by both Hebrew and Greek thought and may be considered primarily in its natural order, its human order, its fallenness, or its place in God's redemptive order.

See *Creation; Earth; Heaven.*

R. Alan Culpepper

WORM A small, slender, softbodied animal without a backbone, legs, or eyes. They often improve the soil by working decaying matter into the soil while aerating it by their movements. There are many examples in the Bible where insect larvae are called worms. The earthworm is the most representative of the worms of Palestine. It is also used in the Bible as a figure of lowliness or weakness (Ps. 22:6; Job 17:14; Isa. 41:14). Both the Old Testament and the New Testament speak of the place of the ungodly and unbeliever as being that where the worm is always alive and working (Isa. 66:24: Mark 9:44,48). See *Animals.*

WORMWOOD A nonpoisonous but bitter plant common to the Middle East. Wormwood often is used in analogy to speak of bitterness and sorrow. The Old Testament prophets pictured wormwood as the opposite of justice and righteousness (Amos 5:7; Jer. 23:15). Revelation describes as wormwood one of the blazing stars which brings destruction (8:10–11).

WORSHIP Human response to the perceived presence of the divine, a presence which transcends normal human activity and is holy. Thus, Jacob, fleeing away to Haran, perceived the presence of the Lord in a dream while sleeping at "a certain place," and when he woke from his sleep, he said:

Surely the Lord is in this place—and I did not know it! . . . How awesome is this place! This is none other than the house of God, and this is the gate of heaven (Gen. 28:16–17 NRSV).

Before the dream, the place had only been a stopping place reached by sunset (18:11), but when he awoke it had become a holy place. The holy presence of God had penetrated into ordinary (profane) space in a way which had aroused acute awareness on the part of a human being. The sacred (holy) and profane are united in an experience of worship.

The consciousness of holy presence brings forth a response from those who perceived it. The response is worship and may take many forms. The response may be private and intensely personal, in the form of prayers, confessions, silence, and meditative experiences of various sorts. Jesus, leaving the disciples behind in a place called Gethsemane, went a ways from them to fall on the ground and pray alone to the Father (Mark 14:32–35). According to Matthew 26:39 (NRSV), he "threw himself on the ground and prayed"; according to Luke 22:41, he "knelt down, and prayed" (NRSV). Each of these is a physical posture considered appropriate for worship in prayer.

Jacob's response was to take the stone he had used for a pillow and to set it up as a pillar, declaring that the stone pillar would be a house of God, apparently meaning that a temple/sanctuary would be built there. This would be a place where communication could occur between the divine-heavenly realm and the human-earthly realm. The messengers of God would be continually going up and down bearing the petitions of worshipers and the responses of God. Thus Jacob proposed that his personal experience of the presence of God be made available to others.

Worship in the Bible moves back and forth between personal experience and corporate experience. Personal worship may occur in very private circumstances or may be related to public worship. This is illustrated by the shifting back and forth from plural speakers to a singular speaker in the Psalms (for instance, Ps. 44). Personal worship and corporate worship are mutually interactive. Corporate worship is empowered by personal experience, but personal experience needs affirmation and interpretation in corporate worship. Thus, early Christians were warned not to neglect meeting together in worship, "as is the habit of some," in order to encourage one another in the faith and in the spiritual life (Heb. 10:25 NRSV). Assembling together in worship is an affirmation of what the worshipers believe and an opportunity for mutual response to the gracious actions of God.

Worship in the Bible appears in varied forms and types. Times and places are among the major factors. Worship, especially of the corporate type, normally takes place according to some sort of schedule and/or calendar. There are times and seasons for worship, even though in the Bible God is present with His people at anytime. Sharpened awareness of the divine presence may result from intensive exercises of worship during special times and at special places. These occasions and places are also the contexts for religious education and the development and enjoyment of fellowship among the worshipers. Thus in ancient Israel there was the divine comand that "Three times in the year all your males shall appear before the Lord God," and "Three times in the year you shall hold a festival for me" (Ex. 23:17,14 NRSV). See *Day of Atonement; Festivals; Sabbath.*

The Psalms with expressions of lament, confession, thanksgiving, praise, teaching, and celebration show the breadth of Old Testament worship. See *Music; Psalms.*

The followers of Jesus, who became known as Christians, received a rich heritage of worship

W

from Judaism, but the new dynamics of their experience with Christ brought about major changes. The festivals of Passover and Pentecost were retained but in different forms. The Lord's Supper, the crucifixion, and the resurrection of Jesus are all closely related to the Passover celebration (1 Cor. 11:23–26; Matt. 26:17,26–28 and parallels). The Christian Easter is a form of the Passover. According to Acts 2:1–42, Pentecost was the occasion of a great filling and empowering of the disciples of Jesus by the Holy Spirit (interpreted as a fulfillment of Joel 2:28–32). Scattered references in the New Testament (1 Cor. 16:8; Acts 20:16) indicate that the early Christians converted Pentecost into a Christian observance. It has continued to be observed as a part of the Christian calendar by many churches (seventh Sunday after Easter). Tabernacles/Booths has not been continued in Christian worship except in the related forms of thanksgiving observances and harvest festivals. The Day of Atonement is used theologically to interpret Christ's sacrifice in Hebrews 8—9, but does not seem to have been a regular part of Christian worship, except in the form of penitential periods like Lent. For Christians the whole complex of Temple activities, priesthood, sacrifice, and sin-cleansing rituals either became obsolete or were reinterpreted in major ways (for instance, the church itself becomes the temple 1 Cor. 6:19; Eph. 2:21–22; 1 Pet. 2:9). See *Church Year.*

Sabbath has been a major problem for Christian worship. The early Christians are said to have met on the first day of the week (Acts 20:7; compare 1 Cor. 16:2; John 20:19,26)—though attending the Temple together on a daily basis (Acts 2:46). The early Christian meetings seem to have been joyful occasions for teaching, prophesying, singing, praying, reading apostolic letters, and the "breaking of bread" in the Lord's Supper (Acts 2:42,46; 1 Cor. 14:26; Eph. 5:19–20; Col. 3:16; 1 Thess. 5:16–18). The explanation of the emergence of the Christian Sunday from these beginnings is plagued by a lack of precise information and by doctrinal disputes. It seems clear that the first-day-of-the-week meetings of the early Christians were not sabbaths. The first-day celebration became "the Lord's day" (Rev. 1:10) with emphasis on the resurrection. In time, the Christian Sunday became the Christian sabbath for most Christians; though non-Sunday, sabbatarian groups have been very persistent in Christian history. It seems logical for Christians to observe both sabbath and Sunday, but in most cases this has been judged both impractical and unnecessary. The extent to which Sunday should be considered as sabbath is debated by Christians both in theory and in practice. One polar position is represented by a long tradition of puritanical sabbath observance on Sunday, with no works and a minimum of other activities apart from worship. The other pole gathers around it the

conviction that sabbath was annulled by the work and teaching of Jesus (compare Gal. 4:10–11; Rom. 14:5; Col. 2:16–17) and that Christians are free from any sabbath observance on Sunday. Most Christians maintain a middle position of sabbath/Sunday observance, taking Sunday as a messianic continuation of the Jewish sabbath and believing that the loss of the sabbath theology of the Old Testament would be serious and unnecessary. The sabbath theology includes the archetypal testimonies of God's saving action in creation from chaos and in Exodus from slavery. Such fundamental aspects are essential for a life of faith and merge without conflict with the celebration of the resurrection and the lordship of Christ.

The discussion above indicates that worship in the biblical context is multifaceted and complex. Some elements seem to be of vital importance. Time and places have been referred to already. The New Testament and much Christian experience move away from rigid adherence to calendars and places, but they are still important in Christian practice. The awareness of divine presence, however symbolized and realized, is absolutely essential for worship. Like Jacob, every true worshiper becomes aware that "The Lord is in this place!" As in the case of Jacob, the sense of presence may come in private and personal experience. However, the most basic pattern is found in the promise of Jesus, according to Matthew 18:20 (NRSV): "For where two or three are gathered in my name, I am there among them." The heart of Christian worship is the power of Christ's presence in a gathered community of disciples (see John 14:12–14; Acts 2:43–47; 4:9–12,32–37; 1 Cor. 5:3–4; Rev. 2:1). According to the New Testament, the presence of Christ is especially manifest in the breaking of the bread at the Lord's Supper (compare Luke 24:28–32,35). However, the Presence is not limited to the Supper and may occur wherever and whenever "two or three are gathered" in the name of Jesus Christ.

Marvin E. Tate

WRATH, WRATH OF GOD The emotional response to perceived wrong and injustice, often translated "anger," "indignation," "vexation," and "irritation." Both humans and God express wrath.

Old Testament The wrath of God appears in the Old Testament as a divine response to human sin and injustice. When the Israelites complained to God at Taberah, "the anger of the Lord blazed hotly" (Num. 11:10 RSV) Later, God reminded the people of various such experiences and warned, "Remember and do not forget how you provoked the Lord your God to wrath in the wilderness." (Deut. 9:7 NRSV) Idolatry became the occasion for divine wrath also. Psalm 78:56–66 describes Israel's idolatry: God was "full of wrath," "utterly rejected Israel," and "gave his people to the sword." The wrath of God is consistently directed towards those who do not follow His will. (Deut. 1:26–46; Josh. 7:1; Ps. 2:1–6) Historical calamity and disaster were to be expected when God was stirred to anger. God was wrathful over Saul's disobedience: "Because you did not obey the voice of the Lord, and did not carry out his fierce wrath against Amalek, . . . the Lord will also give the army of Israel into the hands of the Philistines" (1 Sam. 28:18–19 NRSV).

The Old Testament often speaks of a "day" coming in the future which will be "The great day of the Lord . . . a day of wrath" (Zeph. 1:14–15 NRSV). Isaiah spoke of "the day of the Lord" as "cruel, with wrath and fierce anger" (Isa. 13:9 NRSV) This day referred to the present day of judgment in history, as when the Assyrians conquered Israel; but it also calls to mind a future day of final judgment at the end time when all will be called to give account to God.

The wrath of God was viewed in fear and awe. Yet God provided a way to gain divine favor. Repentance turns God's wrath away from the sinner. The psalmist reminded God that He had in times past forgiven the iniquity of His people and withdrawn all of His wrath (Ps. 85:1–3). Jesus affirmed the Old Testament teaching about such a day. He predicted a day that will come at an unknown time when "the earth will pass away" (Mark 13:31; compare the entire chapter).

New Testament Jesus' teaching supports the concept of God the Father as a God of wrath who judges sin and justice. The story of the rich man and Lazarus shows the rich man in hades in torment and anguish (Luke 16:19–31). The story definitely speaks of the judgment of God and implies that there are serious consequences for the sinner. In Luke 13:3,5 (NRSV) Jesus said, "Unless you repent, you will all perish." John 15:1–11 warns that the unfruitful branches are to be "gathered, thrown into the fire, and burned" (John 15:6 NRSV; compare Matt. 3:7).

God's wrath is restrained, held back from its full and final effect. John 3:36 (NRSV) records Jesus' saying "Whoever believes in the Son has eternal life; whoever disobeys the Son will not see life, but must endure God's wrath." The grace of God, His unmerited favour, holds the full effect of wrath back at the same time that wrath "rests upon" the sinner.

In Romans 2:5 (NRSV), Paul spoke to those who do not repent of their sin, warning that "by your hard and impenitent heart you are storing up wrath for yourself on the day of wrath, when God's righteous judgment will be revealed." The image of wrath being restrained for some future release is truly awe inspiring. However, the Christian has no fear of this day, since 1 Thessalonians says that Jesus "rescues us from the wrath that is coming." (1 Thess. 1:10 NRSV). The instruments of God's

wrath may be angels (Rev. 15:1,7), nations, kings, and rulers as well as natural catastrophes.

Human wrath is always suspect. We are instructed by Paul not to take revenge (Rom. 12:19), nor to "let the sun go down on your anger" (Eph. 4:26 NRSV). Fathers should not provoke children to wrath (Eph. 6:4). We must rid ourselves of "all such things—anger, wrath, malice" (Col. 3:8 NRSV). The Old Testament psalms of lament such as Psalms 53; 137 show how humans can freely express their anger to God.

To realize this freedom from the domination of wrath, the gracious work of the Holy Spirit is needed to sanctify and cleanse the heart of the attitudes and feelings of wrath and anger. Romans 8 pictures the mind filled by the Spirit which is "life and peace" (Rom. 8:6 NRSV). Such a spirit is no longer a slave of anger and wrath but is yielded "to righteousness for sanctification" (Rom. 6:19 NRSV). There is no need to continue in the fleshly spirit of wrath for the Holy Spirit provides inner peace (Phil. 4:4–8).   *W. Stanley Johnson*

WRITING The human ability to record and communicate information through etching signs on stone or drawing them on skins or papyrus. Present knowledge shows that writing began in the Ancient Near East about 3500 B.C. The increasing complexity of commercial and civil life made some system of writing necessary. The development of writing, in turn, made possible the development of increasingly sophisticated civilizations. **Mesopotamia** About 3500 B.C. the earliest documents appeared in Mesopotamia. These were business documents used for accounting purposes. Prior to this, accounts were kept by enclosing counters or tokens of various shapes in clay or mud balls over which a cylinder seal would be rolled identifying the owner or sender. The early tablets typically were inscribed with a picture or pictures identifying the commodity, numbers, and personal names. The language used by the writers of these early tablets is not known. The Sumerians were the first to write different words having the same sound with the same picture. Soon after, the Sumerians began to use stylized pictures composed of wedges impressed in the clay tablet with a stylus. So there began to be developed the hundreds of wedge-shaped signs which comprise the cuneiform script.

The early pictographic writing, which depicted an object, developed into logographic writing in which a picture could stand for a word associated with the idea of the object. Several pictures could be combined to present a concept or a phrase. Rebus writing occurred when a picture or sign was associated with another word of the same sound. In logo-syllabic writing, a sign came to represent a sound rather than a word; this is commonly regarded as the emergence of true writing. The correct reading of signs could be indicated by the addition of phonetic complements or by prefixing determinatives which could indicate "wood," "city," "male," "mountain," and so forth. The rapid development of the cuneiform script made it suitable not only for the mundane task of keeping business accounts but also for legal documents, letters, and literary and religious documents.

The Sumerians established the scribal school in which the student spent several years learning how to write documents of all kinds. The teacher would write a text on one side of the tablet, and the student would copy the text on the other side for the teacher's evaluation. Grammars and verb charts were compiled. Trained scribes were in heavy demand for service at the temple, the court, and at trading firms.

The cuneiform script of the Sumerians was adopted by the Semitic speaking Akkadians, the Elamites, and Hurrians. Cuneiform continued to be expanded and adapted to meet the demands of the various languages. Excavations have yielded thousands of documents in Sumerian and Akkadian showing the progress of civilization, the arts, and sciences. So successful did Akkadian become that it was used as the international language of trade and diplomacy for several centuries. The modern historian is indebted most of all to king Assurbanipal of Assyria (668–626 B.C.) who founded a library at Nineveh. Assurbanipal sent his scribes all over Mesopotamia to make copies of thousands of important documents, especially literary and religious texts. The discovery of this library provided a corpus of texts coming from all periods of Mesopotamian history.

Egypt By about 3000 B.C. the Egyptians had developed a hieroglyphic system of writing, the so-called "sacred picture writing." used chiefly for inscriptions on public monuments. In a manner similar to Sumerian, hieroglyphic signs could be read as signs for words or ideas, as phonetic signs, and as determinatives. Vowels were not indicated in the script, but the debate about whether the logographic script became a syllabic script apparently continues. The decipherment of hieroglyphics was accomplished by Champollion in 1822 after several years of rigorous study.

The Egyptians developed a cursive script, called hieratic, to meet the needs of everyday life, such as record keeping, inventories of goods, and so forth. Hieratic, simplified hieroglyphics, was written with brush and ink on the smooth surfaces of stone and papyrus. About 700 B.C. hieratic was further simplified into another cursive script, demotic. By A.D. 200 Greek letters were used for the writing of the Egyptian language, then in use, called Coptic.

Asia Minor The Hittites of Anatolia, who spoke an Indo-European language, adopted the Mesopotamian cuneiform system of writing. The Hittite cuneiform texts are known mainly from the archives of Bogazkoy discovered in 1906. The pio-

neering work in the interpretation of the texts was done by F. Hrozny who recognized that the texts were characteristically written with a mixture of Sumerian logograms, Akkadian words and phrases, and phonetically written Hittite words and phrases. Variant copies of the same or similar texts often contain the phonetically written equivalents of the Sumerian and Akkadian elements. The Hittites, like the Elamites and Hurrians, also used Akkadian for documents dealing with international relations.

About 1500 B.C. a hieroglyphic system known as Hittite hieroglyphics began to appear. This system of writing was not influenced by the older Egyptian hieroglyphics. Students of the texts have determined that the language is related to but not identical with the Hittite known from the cuneiform texts. The Karatepe bilingual inscription, composed of a text in hieroglyphics and Phoenician, came to light in 1947 and confirmed not only the meanings of some words but also that the previous research, done without the aid of bilingual texts, had been on the correct course.

Syria-Palestine The first-known attempts to produce an alphabet were made in Syria-Palestine. The texts from Ugarit (Ras Shamra) date from 1500–1200 B.C. and were written in an alphabetic cuneiform. The alphabet consists of thirty-one characters, twenty-eight of which are consonants and three of which indicate the vowel accompanying the letter 'aleph.

In work carried out in 1904–1905 at Serabit el-Khadem in the Sinai, Flinders Petrie discovered inscriptions written in a script reminiscent of Egyptian hieroglyphics but consisting of only about thirty signs. Although not all the signs have been deciphered conclusively, it is possible to see the relationship of some of the characters to letters in the Phoenician alphabet from about 1000 B.C. The script of the Sinaitic inscriptions is the earliest stage in the development of the Canannite linear script.

The sources available for the study of the development of the Hebrew script are of several kinds: monumental inscriptions (incised in stone), ostraca (inscribed potshreds), inscriptions incised on seals, weights, jar handles, ossuaries, and documents written in ink on papyrus and leather. The monumental inscriptions include the Gezer Calendar (950 B.C.), the Moabite Stone (850 B.C.), the Siloam tunnel inscription and the Siloam tomb inscription (700 B.C.). The ostraca include those from Samaria (800 B.C.), Hazor (800 B.C.), Yavneh-yam (550 B.C.), and Lachish (500 B.C.). After the Exile the "square" script of Aramaic origin began to replace the cursive script, as the Elephantine papyri show. The documents from the Qumran and Wadi Murabba'at areas (200 B.C. to A.D. 150) complete the data. These source materials make it possible to trace the development of the Hebrew-Aramaic scripts for more than a thousand years and, therefore, to date with greater precision the documents which continue to come to light in the course of excavations.

Biblical References to Writing Several writing systems were in use in Syria-Palestine by the time of Moses and Joshua. Many Bible texts refer to Moses being directed to write down accounts of historical events (Ex. 17:14), laws and statutes (Ex. 34:1–9), and the words of the Lord (Ex. 24:4). Joshua wrote on stones a copy of the law of Moses (Josh. 8:32) and later wrote down statutes and ordinances in the book of the law of God (Josh. 24:26). Gideon had a young man of Succoth to write down the names of the 77 officials and elders of that town (Judg. 8:14). Samuel wrote down the rights and duties of kingship (1Sam. 10:25). David could write his own letter to his general (2 Sam. 11:14). Kings engaged in international correspondence (2 Chron. 2:11). Many references to the "chronicles of the kings of Israel" and Judah perhaps indicate court diaries or annals (1 Kings 14:19). The prophets wrote, or dictated, their oracles (Isa. 8:1,16; 30:8; Jer. 30:1–2; 36:27–28). By at least 800 B.C., court scribes were tallying the payment of taxes (compare the Samaria Ostraca). Commemorative and memorial inscriptions were in use (compare the Siloam inscription and the Siloam tomb inscription). Nehemiah as an official under Persian appointment wrote down the covenant to keep the law of God (Neh. 9:38), to which several men set their seals as witnesses (Neh. 10:1–27).

Similarly, in the New Testament period literacy was widespread. Jesus could both read (Luke 4:16–21) and write (John 8:6). The writers of the Gospels and Paul wrote in excellent Greek, with Paul regularly using an amanuensis or scribe.

The various kinds of documents and writings mentioned in the Bible were letters (personal and official), decrees (religious and civil), legal documents, deeds of sale, certificates of divorce, family registers, topographical descriptions, and books of scrolls containing laws, court records, and poetic works (see *Jashar, The Book of*).

It is difficult to determine how widespread literacy may have been in Old Testament times. Most of the persons listed as writers are those in professional capacities or in positions of leadership which required writing, such as kings, religious leaders, prophets, and governors. Even then, scribes or secretaries were most often used. One of the cabinet officials was the secretary (*sōphēr*) who handled official correspondence, including international communications (2 Sam. 8:17; 20:25). Jeremiah dictated his oracles to his scribe, Baruch (Jer. 30:2; 36:27). In addition the Hebrew inscriptions provide no firm evidence that the general populace could read or write, or even that they had much need to do so.

Writing Materials and Implements Stone was used in all periods in the Ancient Near East as a writing surface, especially for monumental and memorial inscriptions. In Egypt the wall of temples were covered with historical inscriptions chiseled into the stone. In Mesopotamia and Anatolia inscriptions were cut into the faces of mountains (compare the Behistun Rock) or into stones of various sizes for monuments on public display (compare the Code of Hammurabi and boundary markers) or for small inscriptions to be included in foundation deposits. In Syria-Palestine several monumental inscriptions were cut into stone, including the Moabite Stone, the Siloam inscription, and the inscriptions of Aramaean and Phoenician rulers from 1000 B.C. onward. In the Old Testament the law was written on stone (Ex. 24:12) and written on stones covered with plaster (Deut. 27:1–10).

Clay was the main writing medium for those cultures which used cuneiform scripts. Impressions were made on the soft clay by the use of a stylus. Often legal documents and letters would be encased in a clay envelope on which a summary of the text was written and over which cylinder seals would be rolled to identify witnesses. Although clay documents written in cuneiform scripts have been found in Palestine, there is no clear Old Testament reference to clay tablets used by Israelites.

Wooden tablets, covered by clay or wax, were used as writing surfaces in both Egypt and Mesopotamia. In the Bible there is the mention of writing on wooden staffs (Num. 17:2–3) and on wooden staves (Ezek. 37:16). The references in Isaiah 30:8 and Habakkuk 2:2 may be to writing on wooden tablets. In Luke 1:63, Zechariah wrote on a tablet of wood with a wax surface.

In several periods metal was used as a writing medium, especially bronze or copper. Inscriptions in a poorly understood syllabic script from Byblos were written on bronze sheets. Especially well known are the two copper scrolls from Qumran which contained a list of the treasures of the community.

The potsherd provided a cheap and highly useful surface for letters, economic records, and school copy texts. Inscribed potsherds (ostraca) were commonly used in Egypt in all periods and in Palestine. They were inscribed with pen (or brush) and ink. Ostraca form a major part of the corpus of Hebrew inscriptions, such as the Samaria and Lachish ostraca.

Papyrus was used very early in Egypt and continued in use through the early centuries of our era. The papyrus reed was split into thin strips which were arranged in two layers at right angles and then pressed together and polished to form a smooth surface. Sheets of papyrus could be glued together to form long scrolls. As Aramaic began to be accepted as the international language, papyrus became more widely used in Mesopotamia and Syria-Palestine. It is likely that the first edition of

Jeremiah's book was written on papyrus (Jer. 36). The documents of the Jewish community at Elephantine were written on papyrus. Several works on papyrus were among the literary remains from Qumran. Large collections of papyri from Egypt written in Koine Greek helped to elucidate the New Testament writings.

Carefully prepared leather was used for most of the biblical scrolls at Qumran. Torah scrolls are still written on leather. Sections of leather would be sewn together to form scrolls of lengths appropriate for the book or work. Horizontal lines were often pressed into the leather to act as guides for the scribe. The codex, or book, was made only from parchment.

Two words are used in the Old Testament for writing implements 'eṭ and ḥereṭ. The first term is usually rendered "pen." Psalm 45:1 (NRSV) speaks of the "pen of a ready scribe," and thus it is probably a reference to a reed pen whose end fibers were separated to form a brush. Jeremiah 17:1 and Job 19:24 refer to an iron pen designed to make inscriptions on rock. The second term, ḥereṭ, is mentioned as both a graving tool (Ex. 32:4) and as a stylus (Isa. 8:1; "pen," KJV). Since Isaiah 8:1 mentions a tablet (NRSV) as the writing surface, it is possible that the stylus was used to carve or scratch the inscription into the wood or its covering of wax.

Ink was made from carbon black and gum resin and could be washed from a writing surface such as papyrus. Papyrus could thus be used more than once. A sheet of papyrus which was used more than once, with the original writing having been rinsed away, is called a palimpsest. Paleographers have often found palimpsests to be valuable because the original writing, incompletely expunged, may be more significant than the later writing.

Ezekiel 9:2–3,11 mention the equipment of the scribe, the *qeset ha-sōphēr,* The man clothed in linen who appeared to Ezekiel had a "writing case" or "inkhorn" upon his loins (at his side). Writing cases are known in both Egyptian and Mesopotamian literature and art work. They provided containers for pens, brushes, styluses, and ink.

The last implement to be mentioned is the scribe's knife in Jeremiah 36:23. As Jeremiah's scroll was being read, the king took a scribe's knife and cut off the columns of the scroll and burned them. The knife was probably used by the scribe to size and trim papyrus, leather, or parchment. That Jeremiah's scroll was made of papyrus and not leather is indicated by the fact that the king was in his winter quarters seeking warmth from a charcoal brazier. The odor of burning leather in an enclosed space would have been obnoxious. See *Akkadian; Aramaic; Archaeology; Cuneiform; Hebrew; Pottery.*   Thomas Smothers

Hieroglyphics (Egyptian sacred picture writing) on the wall of the tomb of Seti I at ancient Thebes.

XYZ

A sycamore tree in Jericho which is like the one into which Zaccheus climbed to see Jesus.

XERXES (Xĕr′ xēș) A Persian king who reigned 486–464 B.C., known in Book of Esther as Ahasuerus. He was the son of Darius the Great and grandson of Cyrus the Great. He campaigned militarily against the Greeks, avenging the loss at Marathon in 490. However, his armada suffered a crippling defeat in the Bay of Salamis in 480, and he soon lost interest in attempting to defeat the Greeks. See *Esther; Persia.*

The intricately carved wall of the Palace of Xerxes of Persia at Persepolis (in modern Iran).

YAH Shortened form of *Yahweh,* the Hebrew name for the God of the covenant. See *God; I Am; Jehovah; Lord; YHWH.*

YEAR See *Calendar.*

The gate building of Xerxes at Persepolis which led to a mammoth terrace built by Darius the Great.

YEAR OF JUBILEE The fiftieth year after seven cycles of seven years (Lev. 25:10) in which Israel's land and people gained freedom. It was begun with a blast from a ram's horn on the Day of Atonement (Lev. 25:9). During this year of joy and liberation, the law stipulated three respects in which the land and people were to be sanctified: (1) It was to be a time of rest for the soil as well as people (Lev. 25:11). The unattended growth of the field was for the poor to glean and for the beasts of the field (Ex. 23:11). (2) All land was to revert back to the original owner (Lev. 25:10–34; 27:16–24). The original distribution of land was to remain intact. All property which the original owner had been obligated to sell (and had not yet been redeemed) was to revert (without payment) to the original owner or his lawful heirs. Some exceptions to this pattern are noted in Leviticus 25:29–30; 27:17–21. (3) Every Israelite who had sold himself—either to his fellow countryman or to a foreigner settled in the land—because of poverty and remained unredeemed was to be freed along with his children (Lev. 25:39–46).

The Year of Jubilee prevented the Israelites from oppression of one another (Lev. 25:17). It had a leveling effect of Israel's culture by giving everyone a chance for a new start. It discouraged excessive, permanent accumulations of wealth and the deprevation of an Israelite of his inheritance in the land. Families and tribes were preserved by the return of freed bondservants to their own families. Permanent slavery in Israel was rendered impossible.

X Y Z

The tomb of Xerxes located in the modern country of Iran.

This year was a constant reminder of God's interest in economic freedom (Ezek. 46:17). Purchase of property was actually tantamount to assuming a lease for a maximum of forty-nine years, and the seller always retained the right to cancel the purchase by settling with the buyer on the amount of money that was still payable, taking into account the number of years that the buyer had made use of the property. If the seller was either incapable or not desirous of making use of this right of redemption, the property nevertheless returned to his possession automatically in the next Year of Jubilee. So the sale of a house, for example, was equivalent to renting it for a specified period of time (Lev. 25:29–34). This made it difficult to accumulate vast permanent holdings of wealth (compare Isa. 5:8; Mic. 2:2). God's designed arrangement was against both large estates and pauperism. The Israelites were repeatedly given the opportunity to begin anew, and the impoverished were enabled to maintain themselves in society.

This year also reflected God's provision for the soil's conservation (Lev. 25:11–12,18–21). During the Year of Jubilee, the Israelites were once again taught that they were to live in faith that the Lord would satisfy their needs (compare Ex. 16:17–18).

YELLOW Two Hebrew words are translated "yellow." *Yeraqraq* (Ps. 68:13) refers to gold strongly alloyed with silver or the sallow color of sick skin (Lev. 13:49). *Tsahob* (Lev. 13:30,32,36) refers to the color of hair in a patch of skin that lets the priest know it is leperous. The basic meaning of *tsahob* is "shining" and represents bright red or gold. See *Colors.*

YHWH God's name in Hebrew known by the technical term "Tetragrammaton" (Greek, meaning four letters), these are the four consonants which make up the divine name (Ex. 3:15; found more than 6,000 times in the Old Testament). The written Hebrew language did not include vowels, only the consonants were used; thus readers supplied the vowels as they read (this is true even today in Hebrew newspapers). Reverence for the divine name led to the practice of avoiding its use lest one run afoul of Commandments such as Exodus 20:7 or Leviticus 24:16. In time it was thought that the divine name was too holy to pronounce at all. Thus the practice arose of using the word *Adonai:* "Lord." Many translations of the Bible followed this practice. In most English translations YHWH is recognizable where the word LORD appears in all caps. See *God; I Am; Jehovah; Lord.*

In the course of the centuries the actual pronunciation of YHWH was lost. In the Middle Ages Jewish scholars developed a system of symbols placed under and beside the consonants to indicate the vowels. YHWH appeared with the vowels from "Adonai" as a device to remind them to say "Adonai" in their reading of the text. A latinized form of this was pronounced "Jehovah," but it was

X
Y Z

actually not a real word at all. From the study of the structure of the Hebrew language most scholars today believe that YHWH was probably pronounced Yahweh (Yah ´ weh). *Mark Fountain*

YIRON (Yī' ron) NAS spelling of Iron (Josh. 19:38). See *Iron.*

YOD Tenth letter of the Hebrew alphabet used as title of Psalm 119:73–80 (KJV, Jod) in which all verses begin with the letter.

YOKE A wooden frame placed on the backs of draft animals to make them pull in tandem. The simple yokes consisted of a bar with two loops either of rope or wood which went around the animals' necks. More elaborate yokes had shafts connected to the middle with which the animals pulled plows or other implements. The word is used most often in the Bible to speak of slavery, bondage, and hardship (1 Kings 12:4, Jer. 27:8). Positive usages include the yoke of Christ (Matt. 11:29–30) and the joint nature of the church's work (Phil. 4:3).

ZAANAIM (Ză à nä' îm) KJV, TEV spelling of Zaanannim (Judg. 4:11) following written Hebrew text rather than scribal note and Joshua 19:33.

ZAANAN (Ză' à năn) Place name possibly mean-

An ox and a donkey yoked together and pulling a wooden plow.

ing, "sheep country" or "outback." Unidentified city in southernmost Judah (Mic. 1:11), probably identical with Zenan (Josh. 15:37).

ZAANANNIM (Ză' à năn nîm) Place name of uncertain meaning. Town on northeastern corner of tribal allotment of Naphtali near Kadesh (Josh. 19:33; Judg. 4:11). The "plain of Zaanaim" (Judg. 4:11 KJV) is literally translated, "great tree in Zaanannim" (NIV) or "oak in Zaanannim" (NAS; note transliterations of REB, NRSV). This probably indicates a "sacred tree" associated with a worship center. See *Elon; Terebinth.*

ZAAVAN (Ză' à văn) Personal name meaning, "tremble or quake." Son of Ezer (Gen. 36:27).

ZABAD (Ză' băd) Place name meaning, "He has given" or "gift." *1.* Member of the tribe of Judah (1 Chron. 2:36–37). *2.* An Ephramite (1 Chron. 7:21). *3.* One of David's "thirty" elite warriors (1 Chron. 11:41); the first of twenty-one names which the Chronicler appended to a list paralleling that of 2 Samuel 23:24–39. *4.* Assassin of King Joash (2 Chron. 24:26), called Jozacar in 2 Kings 12:21. *5.* Three postexilic laymen ordered to divorce their foreign wives (Ezra 10:27,33,43).

ZABBAI (Zăb' bâi) An abbreviated personal name perhaps meaning, "pure." *1.* A son of Bebai who promised Ezra he would put away his foreign wife (Ezra 10:28). *2.* The father of Baruch who

worked on the wall of Jerusalem with Nehemiah (3:20). Some say that *1.* and *2.* may be the same person. The early scribal note (*qere*) in Nehemiah writes the name, Zaccai.

ZABBUD (Zăb′ bŭd) Personal name meaning, "gift." Descendant of Bigvai who returned to Jerusalem with Ezra after the Exile (Ezra 8:14) according to written Hebrew text. Scribal note (*qere*) has Zaccur. See *Zabud.*

ZABDI (Zăb′ dī) Personal name meaning, "my gift" or short form of "Yah gives." *1.* Son of Zerah of the tribe of Judah (Josh. 7:1). *2.* Man of the tribe of Benjamin (1 Chron. 8:19). *3.* Man in charge of the wine cellars of David (1 Chron. 27:27). *4.* Son of Asaph who led in thanksgiving and prayer (Neh. 11:17).

ZABDIEL (Zăb′ dĭ ĕl) Personal name meaning, "God gives gifts" or "My gift is God." *1.* Descendant of David (1 Chron. 27:2). *2.* An overseer in Jerusalem during the time of Nehemiah (Neh. 11:14).

ZABUD (Zā′ bŭd) Personal name meaning, "endowed." Son of Nathan, a priest and Solomon's friend (1 Kings 4:5).

ZABULON (Zăb′ ū lŏn) KJV spelling of Zebulun in New Testament. See *Zebulun.*

ZACCAI (Zăc′ cā ī) Personal name meaning "pure" or "innocent." One whose descendants returned to Jerusalem with Zerubbabel (Ezra 2:9; Neh. 7:14).

ZACCHEUS (Zăc chāe′ ŭs) Greek form of Hebrew name meaning, "innocent." A corrupt tax collector in first-century Jericho (Luke 19:2–9). Out of curiosity he went to hear Jesus. Because of his short stature he had to climb a tree to catch a glimpse of the Lord. To his surprise Jesus called him by name to come down and went home with Zacchaeus. There the official believed and was converted. As a result of his newfound faith, he restored with interest the money he had taken illegally.

ZACC(H)UR (Zăc′ chŭr) Personal name meaning, "well remembered." *1.* Father of Shammua of the tribe of Reuben (Num. 13:4). *2.* Descendant of Mishma of the tribe of Simeon (1 Chron. 4:26). *3.* Descendant of Merari among the Levites (1 Chron. 24:27). *4.* Son of Asaph (1 Chron. 25:2; Neh. 12:35). *5.* Son of Imri who helped Nehemiah rebuild the walls of Jerusalem (3:2). *6.* One who sealed the covenant of reform during the time of Ezra and Nehemiah (10:12). Father of Hanan, one of the treasurers appointed by Nehemiah (13:13).

ZACHARIAH (Zăch à rī′ ah) KJV alternate spelling of Zechariah. See *Zechariah 1.*

ZACHARIAS (Zăch ăr ī′ ăs) Greek form of Hebrew personal name Zechariah, meaning, "Yah remembered." A priest in Jerusalem and the father of John the Baptist (Luke 1:5–64). As he was burning incense in the Temple as part of his duties, the angel Gabriel appeared to Zacharias and announced that he and his elderly wife, Elisabeth, would have a son. Since both were past the age of childbearing, Zacharias asked for a sign that the birth would occur. Because of his lack of faith, the angel struck him dumb. When John was born, the people assumed that he would be named after his father despite Elisabeth's objections that the boy be called "John." When Zacharias confirmed the name by writing it on a tablet, his speech returned. See *Zechariah.*

ZACHER (Zā′ chĕr) KJV alternate form of Zechariah (1 Chron. 8:31).

ZADOK (Zā′ dŏk) Personal name meaning, "righteous," a short form of Zedekiah, "the Lord is righteous." See *Zedekiah.*

1. Son of Ahitub and father of Ahimaaz, descended from Aaron through Eleazar and was a priest in the time of David (2 Sam. 8:17; 1 Chron. 6:3–8). He is named in company with Abiathar, who was descended from Aaron through Ithamar (1 Chron. 24:3). See *Abiathar.* Zadok was loyal to David when Adonijah rebelled in his father's old age (1 Kings 1). As a consequence, he continued as a priest in Solomon's day. Abiathar was soon removed in accordance with the prophecy to Eli (1 Sam. 2:31–33; 1 Kings 2:26–27). The genealogy of Zadok is given in 1 Chronicles 6:3–15 from Aaron through Eleazar on down to Jehozadak of postexilic times (compare Zech. 6:11). The genealogy mentions a second Zadok seven generations later of whom we know little, but his name emphasizes the fact that standard names do reappear in genealogical lists.

In a touching scene Zadok with Abiathar carried the ark to go with David in his flight from Absalom (2 Sam. 15:24). David sent them back to carry on their worship in Jerusalem and be spies for him. Zadok's son Ahimaaz was the go-between and was also the first to bring David news of Absalom's defeat (2 Sam 18:27). David then appealed to Zadok and Abiathar to arrange a welcome for him to come back to Jerusalem.

In later days Ezekiel declared that the priests who were sons of Zadok were the only faithful ones at the time of the Exile, and that they only would be allowed to serve in the ideal future Temple. This statement agrees with the genealogies of Chronicles which list only two families as far as the captivity—David of Judah and Zadok the descendant of Aaron through Eleazar. The return-

A tomb in Jerusalem which is said by local tradition to be Zacharias's tomb.

ing priests, including Joshua son of Jehozadak (1 Chron. 6:15) and Ezra (7:1–7), were of the line of Zadok which lasted long into the intertestamental period. The line of Ithamar after the removal of Eli's family was of less importance. The Zadokites to a degree lived up to their name as righteous priests of the Lord.

2. Grandfather of Jotham, king of Judah (2 Kings 15:33). *3.–4.* Men who helped Nehemiah rebuild the Jerusalem wall (Neh. 3:4,29). *5.* Leader who signed Nehemiah's covenant (Neh. 10:21). *6.* A faithful scribe whom Nehemiah appointed as a treasurer (Neh. 13:13).   *R. Laird Harris*

ZADOKITES (Zā′ dŏk ītes) Descendants of Zadok, a chief priest with David and Solomon. As a reward for Zadok's loyalty to Solomon and as punishment for the sins of Eli's sons, Zadok's descendants (the line of Eliezer) replaced the descendants of Ithamar as the leading priests. The developing role of Jerusalem as the exclusive center of Israel's worship furthered the position of the Zadokites. See *High Priest; Priests and Levites; Zadok.*

ZAHAM (Za′ ham) Personal name meaning, "fatness" or "loathing." Son of King Rehoboam by Abihail (2 Chron. 11:18–19).

ZAHAR (Zā′ här) Source of wool traded with Tyre (Ezek. 27:18 NIV; "Sahar," TEV; "Suhar,"

REB). KJV, NAS, and RSV translate the Hebrew as "white wool." If the Hebrew refers to a place, the association with Damascus and Helbon suggests a Syrian site, perhaps modern as-Sahra northwest of Damascus.

ZAIR (Zā′ ĭr) Place name that means, "small." Place where Joram, king of Judah (853–841 B.C.), fought with Edom (2 Kings 8:20–21). The location of Zair is still in dispute. Some place it south of the Dead Sea near Edom. Others equate it with Zoar (Gen. 13:10) or Zior (Josh. 15:54). Compare 2 Chronicles 21:9.

ZALAPH (Zā′ lăph) A personal name meaning, "caper plant." Father of Hanun, who helped Nehemiah repair the walls of Jerusalem (3:30).

ZALMON (Zăl′ mŏn) Place and personal name meaning, "little dark one" or "small image." *1.* Mountain near Shechem where Abimelech and his men cut brush with which to burn the tower of Shechem (Judg. 9:48–49). *2.* One of David's "thirty" mighty men (2 Sam. 23:28). He is also known as Ilai (1 Chron. 11:29). *3.* Psalm 68:14 mentions a "hill of Bashan" named Zalmon (KJV, "Salmon). This may refer to the Golan Heights.

ZALMONAH (Zăl mō′ nah) Place name meaning, "dark" or "shady." Israel's first stop after leaving Mount Hor (Num. 33:41–42). The place cannot be identified.

ZALMUNNA (Zăl mŭn′ nà) Personal name meaning, "Protection is withdrawn" or "Zelem (god) rules." King of Midian captured and killed by Gideon (Judg. 8:1–21; Ps. 83:11).

ZAMZUMMIM (Zăm zŭm′ mĭm) Name the Ammonites gave to the Rephaim. They lived east of the Jordan River until the Ammonites drove them out (Deut. 2:20). See *Rephaim.*

ZAMZUMMITES (Zăm zŭm′ mītes) NIV form of Zamzummin.

ZANOAH (Ză nō′ ah) Place name meaning, "broken district" or "stinking." *1.* Village in Judah identified with khirbet Zanu about three miles south southeast of Beth-Shemesh (Josh. 15:34). *2.* City in the highlands of Judah (Josh. 15:56), whose identification with khirbet Zanuta, ten miles southwest of Hebron or khirbet Beit Amra is disputed.

ZAPH(E)NATH-P(A)ANEAH (Zăph ē′ năth-păn ē′ ăh) Personal name meaning, "the god has said, he will live." Pharaoh's name for Joseph when he made Joseph second only to himself in Egypt (Gen. 41:45). See *Joseph.*

ZAPHON (Zā′ phŏn) Place name meaning, "north." *1.* City east of the Jordan River in Gad's territory (Josh. 13:27). It was probably a center of worship of the god Baal-zaphon in the days of Canaanite supremacy before the Gadites took over. It is identified with tell el-Qos, tell es-Saidiye, or tell el-Mazar. Shophan (Num. 32:35) may be another spelling of the same city. *2.* Mountain viewed as home of the gods in Canaanite thought, perhaps referred to in Psalm 48:2 (NIV), Isaiah 14:13 (NRSV), and Job 26:7 (NRSV), showing Yahweh controls what Canaan thought their gods possessed.

ZARA (Zā′ rà) KJV alternate form of Zerah (Matt. 1:3).

ZAREAH (Zā′ rė ah) KJV form of Zorah (Neh. 11:29).

ZAREATHITE (Zā′ rė ăth īte) KJV form of Zorathite in 1 Chronicles 2:53.

ZARED (Zā rĕd) KJV form of Zered in Numbers 21:12.

ZAREPHATH (Zăr′ a phăth) Place name possibly meaning, "smelting, refining." A town on the Mediterranean seacoast just south of Sidon. At the God's command Elijah fled there after prophesying a drought in Israel (1 Kings 17:2–9). While in Zarepath, he was hosted by a widow and her son. Although the drought affected the widow's in-

come, too, her supply of meal and oil were miraculously sustained (17:12–16). Elijah also restored her son to life and health (17:17–23).

ZARETAN (Zâr′ ĕ tăn) KJV form of Zarethan in Joshua 3:16.

ZARETH-SHAHAR (Zā′ rĕth-Shā här) KJV form of Zereth-Shahar.

ZARETHAN (Zăr′ ĕ thăn) Place name perhaps meaning, "cooling." The River Jordan backed up and Israel passed over into Canaan on dry ground near there (Josh. 3:16). It was near Beth-shean (1 Kings 4:12). Hiram of Tyre cast bronze Temple vessels near there (1 Kings 7:46; the parallel in 2 Chron. 4:17 reads Zeredah). Zarethan is most often identified with the two mounds of tell es-Sa′ idiyah on the east bank of the Jordan about fourteen miles north of Adam (tell ed-Damiyeh). Archaeologists have uncovered numerous bronze artifacts from the vicinity of Succoth and Zarethan, confirming activity like that attributed to Hiram. Alternate sites include tell Umm Hamad, Sleihat, and tell el-Merkbere.

ZARHITE (Zär′ hīte) KJV form of Zerahites, descendants of Zerah, one of the two twins born to Judah by Tamar (Num. 26:20; compare 1 Chron. 9:6; Neh. 11:24). See *Zerahites.*

ZARTANAH (Zăr′ tȧ nah) KJV form of Zarethan (1 Kings 4:12).

ZARTHAN (Zär′ thăn) KJV form of Zarethan (1 Kings 7:46).

ZATTHU (Zăt′ thū) KJV form of Zattu (Neh. 10:14).

ZATTU (Zăt′ tū) Head of family who returned to Jerusalem after the Exile (Ezra 2:8; Neh. 7:13). Some of the sons of Zattu put away their foreign wives (Ezra 10:27). He seems to be the same as the "Zatthu" who signed the covenant in Nehemiah's time (10:14).

ZAVAN (Zā′ văn) KJV form of Zaavah (1 Chron. 1:42).

ZAYIN Seventh letter of the Hebrew alphabet. Title of Psalm 119:49–56 where each verse begins with the letter.

ZAZA (Zā′ zà) A son of Jonathan and descendant of Jerahmeel (1 Chron. 2:33).

ZEALOT (Zăēl′ ot) A militant radical; one who acts with great zeal for a cause. The term came to designate a particular segment of the Jewish population who continually tried to overthrow foreign oppression, especially the Roman rule in Palestine. Jesus called a zealot, Simon, as one of His twelve disciples (Luke 6:15). See *Jewish Parties.*

ZEBADIAH (Zĕb a̍ dī′ ah) Personal name meaning, "Yahweh has given." *1.* Son of Beriah (1 Chron. 8:15). *2.* Son of Elpaal (1 Chron. 8:17). *3.* Son of Jehoram of Gedor (1 Chron. 12:7). *4.* A gatekeeper (1 Chron. 26:2). *5.* Fourth captain in David's army (1 Chron. 27:7). *6.* One of nine Levites sent by Jehoshaphat to teach the law in the towns of Judah (2 Chron. 17:8). *7.* Son of Ishmael who ruled civil cases in a court system Jehoshaphat set up (2 Chron. 19:11). *8.* Son of Shephatiah who returned to Jerusalem from Babylon (Ezra 8:8). *9.* Priest who put away his foreign wife in Ezra's time (10:20).

ZEBAH (Zē′ bah) Personal name meaning "slaughter" or "sacrifice." He and Zalmunna were Midianite kings that Gideon captured and killed because they had killed Gideon's brothers (Judg. 8:4–21; see Ps. 83:11; Isa. 9:4; 10:26). This account shows the act of blood revenge that often prevailed in that day and marks a turning point in Israel's struggles against Midian.

ZEBAIM (Zĕ bā′ ĭm) Home of the children of Pochereth (Ezra 2:57) who returned to Jerusalem from Babylonian capitivity (KJV). See *Pochereth-hazzebaim.*

ZEBEDEE (Zĕb′ e dēē) Greek form of Hebrew personal name meaning, "gift." See *Zabdi.* A fisherman on the Sea of Galilee and father of James and John, two of Jesus' first disciples (Mark 1:19–20). Based at Capernaum on the north shore of the sea, Zebedee ran a considerable fishing business which included several hired servants, Simon Peter, and Andrew (Luke 5:10). His wife, Mary, also followed Jesus and ministered to Him (Mark 15:40–41). The Bible does not say if Zebedee ever became a believer, but he did not stand in the way of his sons or wife becoming Jesus' disciples.

ZEBIDAH (Zĕ bī′ dah) Personal name meaning, "gift." Daughter of Pedaiah of Rumah and the mother of King Jehoiakim (2 Kings 23:36; "Zebudah," KJV).

ZEBINA (Zĕ bī′ na) Personal name meaning, "purchased." One who had a foreign wife during Ezra's time (Ezra 10:43).

ZEBOIIM (Zĕ boi ′ ĭm) Place name possibly meaning, "hyenas." One of the cities in the valley of Siddim (Gen. 14:2–3) at the southern end of the Dead Sea. The site probably is under water now. Zeboiim was ruled by King Shemeber but under the control of Chedorlaomer, king of Elam. When

Shemeber rebelled, Chedorlaomer came to suppress the rebellion. Although the text is not clear, it appears the city was delivered when Abram defeated Chedorlaomer (14:16–17). Zeboiim was destroyed when God sent fire and brimstone on Sodom and Gomorrah (Deut. 29:23; compare Hos. 11:8). Recent attempts to identify Zeboiim in the Ebla tablets have been hotly debated.

ZEBOIM (Zĕ bō′ ĭm) Place name meaning, "hyenas" or "a wild place." Not to be confused with Zeboiim. *1.* One of the towns the Benjamites occupied upon returning to Palestine from Exile (Neh. 11:34). It may be khirbet Sabije. *2.* A valley in Benjamin between Michmash and the wilderness overlooking the Jordan River (1 Sam. 13:17–18). It may be wadi el-Oelt or wadi Fara.

ZEBUDAH (Zĕ bū′ dah) KJV spelling of Zebidah.

ZEBUL (Zē′ bŭl) Personal name meaning, "prince" or "captain." Resident of Shechem who was a follower of Abimelech, son of Gideon. When Gaal plotted against Abimelech in Shechem, Zebul sent word to Abimelech who came to Shechem and defeated Gaal (Judg. 9:30–41).

ZEBULUN (Zĕb′ ū lŭn) Personal and tribal name probably meaning, "elevated dwelling." Jacob's tenth son and sixth by Leah (Gen. 30:20). The tribe named for him settled in the area between the Sea of Galilee and Mount Carmel (Josh. 19:10–16). The tribe hosted the other tribes with religious festivals at Mount Tabor (Deut. 33:18–19). Their menu included the delicacies fished from the Sea of Galilee. Militarily, the tribe distinguished itself in the struggles to possess the land, fighting faithfully in the armies of Deborah and Barak, and Gideon (Judg. 4:6; 6:35). See *Israel; Palestine; Tribes.*

ZECHARIAH (Zĕch a̍ rī′ ah) Personal name meaning, "Yah (in long form Yahweh) remembered." *1.* Son of Jeroboam II, who reigned over Israel for six months in the year 746 B.C. until he was assassinated by Shallum (2 Kings 15:8–12). See *Israel.* *2.* The prophet Zechariah, who flourished immediately after the Exile in 520–518 B.C. and urged the people of Judah to rebuild the Temple.
3. Grandfather of Hezekiah (2 Kings 18:2). *4.* Priest and prophet whom the people stoned and Joash, the king, killed (2 Chron. 24:20–22). *5.* Postexilic gatekeeper of Temple (1 Chron. 9:21). *6.* Member of family who lived in Gibeon (1 Chron. 9:37). *7.* Temple musician (1 Chron. 15:20). *8.* Community leader Jehoshaphat the king sent to teach in the cities of Judah (2 Chron. 17:7). *9.* One of Josiah's overseers in repairing the Temple (2 Chron. 34:12).
10.–11. Men who accompanied Ezra on return

X Y
Z

from Babylon (Ezra 8:3,11). *12.* Man Ezra sent to get Levites to return from Babylon (Ezra 8:16). *13.* Israelite with foreign wife (Ezra 10:26). *14.* Man who helped Ezra as he taught the law (Neh. 8:4), perhaps identical with *12.* or other one above. *15.* Ancestor of postexilic resident of Jerusalem (Neh. 11:4). *16.* Ancestor of postexilic resident of Jerusalem (Neh. 11:5). *17.* Ancestor of priest in Nehemiah's day (Neh. 11:12). *18.* Leading priest in time of Joiakim's high priesthood, possibly the same as the prophet (Neh. 12:16). *19.–20.* Priestly musicians who helped Nehemiah celebrate (Neh. 12:35,41).

21. High official Isaiah used as witness, perhaps the same as *3.* above. *22.* Son of Jehoshaphat the king whom his brother Jehoram killed upon becoming king (2 Chron. 21:2–4). *23.* Godly advisor of King Uzziah (2 Chron. 26:5). *24.* Descendant of tribe of Reuben (1 Chron. 5:7). *25.* Father of leader of eastern half of tribe of Manasseh (1 Chron. 27:21). *26.–34.* Levites (1 Chron. 15:18,24; 24:25; 26:2,14; 26:11; 2 Chron. 20:14; 29:13; 35:8).   *Paul L. Redditt*

ZECHARIAH, BOOK OF The Book of Zechariah is the eleventh of the so-called Minor Prophets.
When the book was written In 538, Cyrus the Great, emperor of the Persian Empire, issued an edict (Ezra 1:2–4; 6:3–5) allowing the Jews in Exile in Babylon to return to Jerusalem. Over the next two decades, many Exiles took advantage of Persian leniency, returned home, and began to reestablish life in Jerusalem or Judah. Apparently, an effort was made to begin rebuilding the Temple under an official named Sheshbazzar (Ezra 5:14–16) and perhaps Zerubabel (Ezra 3:1–13; Zech. 4:9), but the work stopped due to opposition from persons who had not been in Exile and local officials. Cyrus was succeeded by his son Cambysees, who died in 521 B.C. with no heir. The empire was thrown into disarray as two men, Darius I and Gautama, fought for the crown. In the midst of that turmoil, God raised two prophets, Haggai and Zechariah, to urge finishing the Temple.
What Zechariah preached The message of Zechariah may be summarized under two headings: prosperity and purification. Simply put, God promised the people of Judah and Jerusalem prosperity if they purified themselves from sin. This message is found in the first six chapters of the Book of Zechariah. Those chapters are writtin in the form of eight visions, with two messages of exhortation. The structure of the book anticipates the structure of later books called apocalypses, books like Daniel and Revelation; the Book of Zechariah itself is not, however, an apocalypse.

The opening message (1:1–6) reminds the audience that God had warned their forefathers not to sin, but they had not listened or repented. They had brought the Exile upon themselves. This mes-

sage served to validate prophecy, after which Zechariah related his visions. The first three visions predict prosperity for Judah and Jerusalem. Four horsemen ride forth in 1:7–17 to announce God's return to Zion, a new day when prosperity would come. In the second vision (1:18–21), four smiths (agents of God's deliverance) overcome four horns (symbols of the nations that ruled over Jerusalem). This reversal of fortunes would bring about the coming prosperity. In the third vision a man measures Jerusalem, only to find that it is too small to accommodate all those God would return to live there in glory. The visions conclude with a call to Exiles to return home from Babylon.

The last five visions deal with purification. In vision four (3:1–10) the high priest Joshua is symbolically cleansed for his work. The fifth vision (4:1–14) pictures God as a lampstand with two olive trees standing beside Him: Joshua and Zerubbabel. Zerubbabel is named to finish building the Temple, worship and sacrifice at which would be the means of purification. Vision six (5:1–4) involves a scroll flying through the air. The scroll and a voice condemn stealing and lying to cover up one's theft. (Was theft an especially acute problem in the poor, reduced state of Judah after the Exile?) In the seventh vision (5:5–11), Zechariah saw an ephah, in this case a container with a heavy, lead cover. Usually an ephah would hold about two-thirds of a bushel of grain. This ephah instead held a woman, who symbolizes impurity. Two women with wings came to take the iniquity back to Babylon, from which it had come. In the last vision (6:1–8), four charioteers head out in all directions to patrol the earth (and presumably to punish evil). Chapters 7 and 8 contain additional messages from Zechariah, but add no new insights.

The last six chapters of the Book of Zechariah do not seem to have been composed at the same time as the first eight chapters. For one thing, they presuppose that the Temple exists and so at least must have been written after 515, when the Temple was finished. In addition, 11:12–13 is quoted in Matthew 27:9–10 as a saying of Jeremiah. In some Old Testament manuscripts, then, the verses (and presumably their context) probably were attached to the Book of Jeremiah, while in the manuscripts preserved in our Hebrew Bibles they were attached to Zechariah. Since the chapters differ in style and contents from both Jeremiah and Zechariah, some scholars think they were prophecies from an unknown prophet either from the time of the Persian Empire (down to 332) or the Greek Empire. Others think they are the later work of Zechariah.

Whether written by Jeremiah, Zechariah, or an anonymous prophet, it is the contents of the chapters that are important. Chapters 9 through 11 depict God's deliverance of His people in terms of the victory of God and His Messiah over the neighboring peoples, including the Greeks (9:1—10:7), the return of the Exiles (10:6–12), and the punishment of the wicked leaders of Judah (11:4–17). Chapters 12—14 depict an end-time attack upon Jerusalem and the cities of Judah (12:1–3; 14:1–3), an attack in which many people would be killed as God purifies His people (13:7–9). God Himself would rescue His people (12:4–9; 14:4–5,12–15), cleanse the people from idolatry, rid the land of prophecy (which had become synonymous with false prophecy, 13:1–6), and turn Jerusalem into a paradise to which the nations of the world would come to worship. Zechariah 14 envisions the Mount of Olives splitting in two, with fresh water (representing the blessings of God) flowing east and west watering the world. Cold and night-time, representing threats to God's control, would be eliminated as He came to reign over all the world from Jerusalem.

Outline

I. God Is Just (1:1—2:13)
   A. God's anger with His sinful people is justified (1:1–2).
   B. God will return to His people if they return to Him (1:3).
   C. History shows the justice of God and the sinfulness of His people (1:4–6).
II. God Promises Prosperity to His People (1:7—2:13).
   A. Vision One: God's election mercy for His people replaces His anger (1:7–17).
   B. Vision Two: God punishes those who oppress His people (1:18–21).
   C. Vision Three: God's glorious presence will restore, protect, and expand His people (2:1–13).
III. God Calls His People to Purification (3:1—6:15).
   A. Vision Four: God wants to forgive and purify His people and their leaders (3:1–10).
   B. Vision Five: God exerciese His sovereign rule through His Spirit and His messianic leaders (4:1–14).
   C. Vision Six: God condemns stealing and lying (5:1–4).
   D. Vision Seven: God removes the wickedness of His people (5:5–11).
   E. Vision Eight: The universal God defeats the enemies of His people (6:1–8).
   F. God commissions leaders for His obedient people (6:9–15).
IV. God Seeks Righteousness, Not Ritual (7:1–14).
   A. God has always rejected selfish, insincere worship rituals (7:1–7).
   B. God seeks justice, mercy, and compassion (7:8–10).
   C. God is angry when His people reject His inspired teaching (7:11–12).
   D. God punishes His disobedient people (7:13–14).
V. God in His Jealousy Restores His Faithful Remnant (8:1–23).
   A. God's jealousy leads to hope for His people (8:1–5).
   B. The faithful God wants to renew His covenant with His people (8:6–8).
   C. God is not bound by the past (8:9–13).
   D. God has punished Judah and now will bless her (8:14–15).
   E. God commands truthfulness, justice, and peace (8:16–19).
   F. God seeks all people to worship Him (8:20–23).
VI. God Controls the Future of His People (9:1—11:17).
   A. God promises restoration (9:1–17).
   B. God punishes wicked leaders (10:1—11:3).
   C. God is not bound by past covenants from punishing His foolish people and their wicked leaders (11:4–17).
VII. God Purges and Delivers His People (12:1—14:21).
   A. The universal God exercises His control over all His world (12:1—13:6).
   B. God will make a new covenant with the remnant of His people after striking His shepherd (13:7–9).
   C. God will rule over the whole earth on the day of the Lord (14:1–21).

Paul L. Redditt

ZECHER (Zē′ chĕr) Form of Zechariah (1 Chron. 9:37) used in 1 Chronicles 8:31.

ZEDAD (Zē′ dăd) Place name meaning, "a sloping place" or "mountainous." It is Sadad, 62 miles north of Damascus. The northern border of Canaan (Num. 34:8; Ezek. 47:15).

ZEDEKIAH (Zĕd ĕ kī′ ah) Personal name meaning, "Yahweh is my righteousness" or "Yahweh is my salvation." *1.* False prophet who advised King Ahab to fight against Ramoth-gilead, assuring the king of victory (1 Kings 22). His prophecy conflicted with that of Micaiah, who predicted defeat. When Micaiah stated that God had put a lying spirit in the mouths of Zedekiah and his band of prophets, Zedekiah struck Micaiah on the cheek. Micaiah forecast that Zedekiah would feel the brunt of God's Spirit, but the text does not tell what became of the false prophet. See *Micaiah; Prophet, False.*

2. Last king of Judah (596–586 B.C.). Zedekiah was made king in Jerusalem by Nebuchadnezzar of Babylon (2 Kings 24:17). When he rebelled, the Babylonian army besieged Jerusalem and destroyed it. Zedekiah was taken to Riblah along with his family. At Riblah he witnessed the executions of his sons before his own eyes were blinded

(25:7). Then Zedekiah was taken to Babylon. He apparently died in captivity. See *Israel.*

3. Son either of Jehoiakim or Jeconiah (1 Chron. 3:16), the Hebrew text being unclear at this point. *4.* Signer of Nehemiah's covenant (10:1), spelled Zidkijah by KJV. *5.* Prophet who promised quick hope to Exiles in Babylon (Jer. 29:21). Jeremiah pronounced God's judgment on him. *6.* Royal official in Jeremiah's day (36:12).

ZEEB (Zē′ ĕb) See *Oreb and Zeeb.*

ZEKER (Zē′ kĕr) NIV form of Zecher (1 Chron. 8:31).

ZELA (Zē′ là) Form of Zelah in NRSV, REB, RSV, TEV.

ZELAH (Zē′ lah) Place name meaning, "rib, side, slope." Town allotted to Benjamin (Josh. 18:28), in which the bones of Saul and Jonathan were buried (2 Sam. 21:14). The site is probably khirbet Salah between Jerusalem and Gibeon or else another site in the hills north and west of Jerusalem.

ZELEK (Zē′ lĕk) Personal name meaning, "cleft, fissure." One of David's thirty elite warriors (2 Sam. 23:37; 1 Chron. 11:39).

ZELOPHEHAD (Zè lō′ phė hăd) Personal name meaning, "protection from terror" or the kinsman is my protector." A Hebrew who wandered in the wilderness with Moses. He had no sons to receive his property and carry on his name, so his daughters pled with Moses to receive a share of inheritance following his death (Num. 26:33; 27:1–4). Despite the inheritance customs which allowed only men to own property, God led Moses to declare the daughters eligible (27:6–7). The only stipulation was that the women had to marry within their own tribe (36:5–9).

ZELOTES (Zè lō′ tēs) KJV transliteration of name for Simon, Jesus' disciple. Modern translations translate as "Zealot." See *Simon; Zealot.*

ZELZAH (Zĕl′ zah) Unidentified site near Rachel's tomb in the territory of Benjamin, site of the first of three signs which Samuel promised Saul as confirmation of his kingship (1 Sam. 10:1–2). Many commentators use Greek manuscript evidence to emend the Hebrew text to something other than a place name.

ZEMARAIM (Zĕm à rā′ ĭm) Place name meaning, "twin peaks." *1.* Town allotted to the tribe of Benjamin (Josh. 18:22), likely Ras ex-Zeimara about five miles northeast of Bethel. *2.* Mountain in the territory of Ephraim where Abijah rebuked Jeroboam (2 Chron. 13:4). The parallel text in

1 Kings 15:7 mentions hostilities between Abijam and Jereboam but not the speech at Zemaraim. The town and mountain may be located in the same place. Some would place the town at khirbet es-Samra four miles north of Jericho.

ZEMARITES (Zĕm′ à rītes) Canaanites inhabiting the area north of Lebanon between Arvad and Tripolis (Gen. 10:18; 1 Chron. 1:16). The Zemarites possibly gave their name to the town Sumra in this region. The town figures in the tell Amarna letters and in Assyrian records. NRSV emended the text of Ezekiel 27:8 to read "men of Zemer" (KJV, "thy wise men, O Tyrus").

ZEMER (Zē′ mėr) Place name meaning, "wool." See *Zemarites.*

ZEMIRA(H) (Zè mī′ rah) Personal name meaning, "song." Descendant of Benjamin (1 Chron. 7:8).

ZENAN (Zē′ năn) Place name meaning, "flocks." Village in the Shephelah (wilderness) district of Judah (Josh. 15:37), likely identified with 'Araq el-Kharba. Zenan is perhaps identical to Zaanan (Mic. 1:11).

ZENAS (Zē′ nàs) Abbreviated form of the personal name Zenodoros meaning, "gift of Zeus." Christian lawyer whom Paul asked Titus to send, together with Apollos, on his way, lacking nothing (Titus 3:13). Paul had in mind, no doubt, material provisions for itinerant evangelistic work. Zenas and Apollos perhaps delivered Paul's letter to Titus.

ZEPHANIAH (Zĕph à nī′ ah) Personal name meaning, "Yahweh sheltered or stored up" or "Zaphon (god) is Yahweh." *1.* A prophet in the Old Testament whose preaching produced the thirty-sixth book of the Old Testament.

2. Priest whom King Zedekiah sent asking Jeremiah to pray for the nation threatened by Nebuchadrezzar of Babylon (Jer. 21:1–7; 37:3). He reported false prophecy from Babylon to Jeremiah (29:24–32). When Jerusalem fell, the priest was executed (52:24–27).

3. Father of Josiah and Hen (Zech. 6:10,14), possibly identical with *2.* above. *4.* A Levite (1 Chron. 6:36), perhaps the same as Uriel (1 Chron. 6:24).　　　　　　　*Paul L. Redditt*

ZEPHANIAH, BOOK OF The Book of Zephaniah, only three chapters in length, looks toward the punishment of all sinful nations, including Judah, followed by the restoration of Judah and the nations as well.
The Prophet Zephaniah The first verse tells all we really know about the prophet. His ancestry is traced back four generations to a man named Hezekiah. Some scholars think Hezekiah was the

king of Judah by that name who reigned in the late eighth century during the ministry of Isaiah (2 Kings 18—20). If so, Zephaniah would have belonged to the royal line. That would perhaps explain why he did not condemn the king in 1:8; 3:3–5, where he blames most of Judah's upper classes for their sins. Other scholars note that the name Hezekiah was quite common and that the ancestor is not identified as king. Further, Zephaniah's father was named Cushi, which could mean "Cushite" or "Ethiopian." They suggest that Zephaniah's ancestry was traced four generations to demonstrate that he was indeed Israelite.

The Date of Zephaniah According to 1:1 Zephaniah's ministry occurred during the reign of Josiah (640–609 B.C.). Most scholars date the book in 630 or between 630 and 621. In 621 King Josiah instituted a sweeping reformation of worship in Judah (see 2 Kings 22:3—23:25), which officially abolished the worship of Baal and the stars mentioned in Zephaniah 1:4–6. Jeremiah also condemned those practices (Jer. 2:20–28; 8:1–3). Jeremiah 26:1 shows that the practices flourished again as early as the beginning of the reign of Jehoiakim (609 B.C.); it might be the case that such worship continued secretly between 621 and 609. If that were so, Zephaniah might have prophesied during those years. In short, it is a good guess that he preached between 630 and 621, but he might have flourished anytime during the reign of Josiah.

Contents of the Book Zephaniah looked toward a future punishment. In 1:2–6 he predicted punishment upon the whole world, including Jerusalem. Verses 17–18 depict the inability of sinful humanity to escape God's punishment. The intervening verses further describe the punishment as the Day of the Lord. Verses 14–16 describe the time of God's approaching wrath. Punishment would come upon the nobles at the king's court, those who gained materially through violence, the merchants, and those who denied the power of God to reward good or punish evil.

The second chapter contains a series of threats against the Philistines (vv. 4–7), the Moabites and Ammonites (vv. 8–11), the Ethiopians (v. 12), and the Assyrians (vv. 13–15). Zephaniah called all nations to repent and become righteous and meek. Zephaniah would not presume on God's grace by promising forgiveness, but he counseled turning to righteousness and meekness as the means for possibly avoiding punishment on the Day of the Lord.

The third chapter is marked by a change in perspective between versus 7 and 8. The first seven verses pronounce a woe upon Jerusalem for oppression within her walls. Her princes preyed like lions upon their people; her prophets committed treachery, and her priests polluted the Temple. God indicted the people not only for their sins, but also for their failure to receive instruction from his dealings with other nations.

Beginning with verse 8, however, the tone is quite positive toward Israel. Many scholars think part or all of verses 8–20 was appended to the book by a later author. Whether written by Zephaniah or a later prophet, the verses complete the message of chapter 3. Verses 8 and 14 admonish the people to wait for God to act and to rejoice for what He will do, respectively. Verses 8–13 promise that God will punish the nations and convert them from idolatry. What is more, He promises to remove the haughty from Mount Zion, leaving behind a meek and humble people. Verses 14–20 predict the cessation of punishment and oppression and the return of exiles. God Himself is called the king of Israel (v. 15). His presence alleviates any reason to fear the nations. God will punish the oppressors and bring home the exiles. Thus the book ends with a message of hope, based on God's mercy.

Outline

I. Identification of the Messenger of God's Word (1:1)

II. God's Warning of Worldwide Judgment (1:2—3:8)

  A. God's day of judgment is coming (1:2—2:3).

    1. His judgment will include all mankind (1:2–3).

    2. His judgment will include His own sinful people who forsake Him (1:4–6).

    3. The day of the Lord calls for awesome silence in the face of God's judgment (1:7–11).

    4. God's skeptics will see Him in action on His day (1:12–13).

    5. God's wrath will be poured out against sin on that day (1:14–17).

    6. Wealth is good for nothing on His day (1:18).

    7. God calls His humble people to seek Him before it is too late (2:1–3).

  B. God's judgment will subject His enemies and bless the remnant of His people (2:4–15).

  C. God's righteous justice will be impartial (3:1–8).

III. God Promises to Form a New People (3:9–20).

  A. The nations will call on God (3:9–10).

  B. A purified remnant will worship Him in humility and with joy (3:11–13).

  C. God will reign as King to remove His people's fears (3:14–17).

  D. His oppressed people will be exalted (3:18–20). *Paul L. Redditt*

ZEPHATH (Zē′ phăth) Place name meaning, "watchtower." City in southwestern Judah in the vicinity of Arvad. Following their destruction of the city, the tribes of Judah and Simeon renamed the site Hormah (Judg. 1:17). The site is identified with khirbet Masas on the main road from Beer-sheba to the Arabah valley.

ZEPHATHAH (Zĕ phả' thah) Place name meaning, "watchtower." Asa met Zerah, the Ethiopian king, in battle "in the valley of Zephathah at Mareshah" (2 Chron. 14:10). The earliest Greek translation translated *Zaphon,* "north" instead of Zephathah. If Zephathah is identified with Safiyah, less than two miles northeast of Beit Jibrin, the "valley of Zephathah" is the wadi Safiyah. See *Mareshah.*

ZEPHI (Zĕ' phī) Short form of personal name meaning, "purity" or "good fortune." Descendant of Esau (1 Chron. 1:36) called Zepho in the parallel passage (Gen. 36:11,15).

ZEPHO (Zē' phō) See *Zephi.*

ZEPHON (Zē' phŏn) Personal name perhaps meaning, "north." Eldest son of Gad and ancestor of the Zephonites (Num. 26:15). The Samaritan Pentateuch and the earliest Greek translation support the identification with Ziphion (Gen. 46:16).

ZEPHONITE (Zē' phŏ nīte) Member of clan of Zephon.

ZER (Zĕr) Place name meaning, "narrow" or "enemy." Fortified town in the territory of Naphtali (Josh. 19:35), possibly identified with Madon which is conspicuously absent from this list. Commentators often take *Zer* as a copyist's modification, repeating the Hebrew for "fenced cities." See *Ziddin.*

ZERAH (Zē' rah) Personal name meaning, "sunrise." *1.* A twin born to Tamar and her father-in-law, Judah (Gen. 38:30, Zarah KJV). One of his descendants was Achan, who was executed for taking forbidden booty (Josh. 7:1,25). Zerah is included in Matthew's genealogy of Christ, although Perez was the direct ancestor (1:3). *2.* Descendant of Esau and thus clan leader of Edomites (Gen. 36:13,17). *3.* Ancestor of Edomite ruler (Gen. 36:33). *4.* Clan leader in tribe of Simeon (Num. 26:13), apparently same as Zohar (Gen. 46:10): *5.* Levite (1 Chron. 6:21,41). *6.* Cushite general God defeated in answer to Asa's prayer about 900 B.C. (2 Chron. 14:8–13). See *Cush; Ethiopia.*

ZERAHIAH (Zĕ rả hī' ah) Personal name meaning, "Yahweh has dawned." *1.* Priest descended from Phinehas (1 Chron. 6:6,51; Ezra 7:4). *2.* Descendant of Pahath-Moab ("governor of Moab") and father of Eliehoenai (Ezra 8:4). See *Izrahiah.*

ZERAHITES (Zĕr' ả hītes) Name of two families, one from the tribe of Simeon (Num. 26:13), the other from the tribe of Judah (Num. 26:20; Josh. 7:17), descended from men named Zerah. Two of David's thirty elite warriors, Sibbecai and Maharai, were Zerahites (1 Chron. 27:11,13).

ZERED (Zē' rĕd) River name perhaps meaning, "white thorn." A stream which empties into the southern end of the Dead Sea. Its entire length is only about thirty-eight miles, but it drains a large area of land. Israel crossed the Zered after wandering in the wilderness for thirty-eight years (Deut. 2:13–14). See *Palestine; Rivers.*

ZEREDA(H) (Zĕr è dah) Place name of uncertain meaning. *1.* Site in Ephraim of the home of Jeroboam (1 Kings 11:26), possibly identified as Ain Seridah iin the wadi Deir Ballut in western Samaria. *2.* City in the Jordan Valley (2 Chron. 4:17). The parallel text in 1 Kings 7:46 reads Zerethan.

ZEREDATHAH (Zĕ rĕ dả' thah) KJV spelling of Zeredah (2 Chron. 4:17).

ZERERAH (Zĕr' ĕ rah) Site on the route by which the defeated Midianites fled from Gideon (Judg. 7:22; KJV, Zereath); possibly a variant rendering of Zarethan (Josh. 3:16; 1 Kings 4:12; 7:46) or of Zeredah (2 Chron. 4:17). See *Zarethan.*

ZERERATH (Zĕr' è răth) KJV form of Zererah.

ZERESH (Zē' rĕsh) Personal name meaning, "shaggy head, disheveled." Haman's wife and counselor (Esth. 5:10,14; 6:13).

ZERETH (Zē' rĕth) Personal name perhaps meaning, "splendor." Descendant of Judah (1 Chron. 4:7).

ZERETH-SHAHAR (Zē' rĕth-Shả' här) Place name meaning, "splendor of the dawn." The city located "on the hill of the [Dead Sea] valley" was allotted to Reuben (Josh. 13:19). The site is perhaps modern Zarat near Machaerus on the eastern shore of the Dead Sea. Others suggest khirbet el-Libb seven miles south of Medeba or khirbet qurn el-Kibsh six miles northwest of Medeba.

ZERI (Zē' rī) Personal name meaning, "balsam." Levitical harpist (1 Chron. 25:3). Zeri is possibly a copying variant of Izri (25:11).

ZEROR (Zē' rôr) Personal name meaning, "bundle, pouch" or "particle of stone." Ancestor of Saul (1 Sam. 9:1).

ZERUAH (Zĕ rū' ah) Personal name meaning, "stricken" or "leprous." Mother of King Jeroboam (1 Kings 11:26).

ZERUBBABEL (Zĕ rŭb′ bå bĕl) Personal name meaning, "descendant of Babel." The grandson of King Jehoiachin (taken to Babylon in the first Exile in 597 B.C. by Nebuchadnezzar; 2 Kings 24:10–17) and the son of Shealtiel (Ezra 3:2), second son of Jehoiachin (1 Chron. 3:16–17). He is named in Ezra 2:2 among the leaders of those who returned from Exile. The list in Ezra 2:1–67 (compare Neh. 7:6–73a) probably names people who returned in 539, the first year of the reign of Cyrus the Great, ruler of the Persian Empire (Ezra 1:1), or between 539 and 529, despite the contention of many American scholars that the list belongs to an unmentioned second return led by Zerubbabel in 521/20.

According to Ezra 3, Zerubbabel and Jeshua (or Joshua, the high priest) rebuilt the altar and in their second year (538?) laid the foundation of the Temple, but their work was halted by opposition from persons who had remained in Palestine during the Exile (4:1–6,24). Darius (Persian emperor from 522—486 B.C.) granted the Jews permission to continue rebuilding the Temple (6:1–12). Under the urging of Haggai (1:1,12–15; 2:1,20) and Zechariah (4:6–10a), Zerubabel, now governor (Hag. 1:1) in place of Sheshbazzar (Ezra 5:14), resume the task (Ezra 5:1–2), completed in 515 B.C.

Zerubbabel himself, however, disappeared from view. He was a Davidic prince, so it is possible that the Jews tried to crown him king during the civil war surrounding the rise of Darius as emperor (522/21). Zechariah 6:9–14 may reflect the wish to crown Zerubbabel, but his fate remains unknown. See *Babylon; Israel; Zechariah.*

Paul L. Redditt

ZERUIAH (Zĕ rŭ ī′ ah) Personal name meaning, "perfumed with mastix" or "bleed." Mother of three of David's generals, Joab, Abishai, and Asahel (2 Sam. 2:18). According to 1 Chronicles 2:16, Zeruiah was David's (half-)sister. According to 2 Samuel 17:25, her sister, Abigail, was the (grand)daughter of Nahash rather than of Jesse, David's father. Kinship with David accounts for the positions of trust enjoyed by Zeruiah's sons.

ZETHAM (Zĕ′ thăm) Personal name meaning, "olive tree." Levite who served as a Temple treasurer (1 Chron. 23:8; 26:22).

ZETHAN (Zĕ′ thăn) Personal name meaning, "olive tree" or "olive merchant." Member of the tribe of Benjamin (1 Chron. 7:10).

ZETHAR Zĕ′ thär) Personal name perhaps meaning, "slayer," "kingdom," or "victor." One of seven eunuchs who served king Ahasuerus of Persia (Esth. 1:10).

ZEUS (Zeūs) The Greek god of the sky and chief

of the pantheon; ruler over all the gods. His devotees believed all the elements of weather were under his control. The worship of Zeus was very prevalent throughout the Roman Empire during the first century. Barnabas was mistaken for Zeus (equivalent of the Roman god, Jupiter) by the people of Lystra after Paul healed a cripple (Acts 14:8–12). See *Greece; Gods, Pagan.*

ZIA (Zī′ å) Personal name meaning, "trembling." Head of a family of the tribe of Gad (1 Chron. 5:13).

ZIBA (Zī′ bà) Personal name, perhaps Aramaic for "branch." Servant of Saul. When David desired to show kindness to surviving members of Jonathan's family, Ziba directed David to Mephibosheth (2 Sam. 9:1–8). David placed Ziba in charge of Mephibosheth's restored property (9:9–13). During Absalom's rebellion, Ziba assisted David with supplies and (falsely) accused Mephibosheth of treason (2 Sam. 16:1–4). David rewarded Ziba with Mephibosheth's property. Mephibosheth met David on his return to power in Jerusalem and accused Ziba of deception (2 Sam. 19:24–29). David, either uncertain whom to believe or else desiring to leave no strong rivals, divided Saul's property between Ziba and Mephibosheth.

ZIBEON (Zī′ bĕ on) Personal name meaning, "little hyena." Horite chieftan (Gen. 36:29) and ancestor of one of Esau's wives (Gen. 36:2). Zibeon established kinship between the Horites and Edomites (Gen. 36:20,24,29; 1 Chron. 1:38,40).

ZIBIA (Zīb′ ĭ å) Personal name meaning, "gazelle." Head of a family of Benjaminites (1 Chron. 8:9).

ZIBIAH (Zīb′ ĭ ah) Personal name meaning, "female gazelle." Mother of king Jehoash (Joash) of Judah (2 Kings 12:1; 2 Chron. 24:1).

ZICHRI (Zīch′ rī) Personal name meaning, "remembrance, mindful." *1.* Levite in Moses' time (Ex. 6:21). *2.* Heads of three families of Benjaminites (1 Chron. 8:19,23,27). *3.* Levite (1 Chron. 9:15), perhaps identical to Zaccur (1 Chron. 25:2,10; Neh. 12:35) and Zabdi (Neh. 11:17). *4.* Descendant of Moses assisting with David's treasury (1 Chron. 26:25); *5.* Reubenite (1 Chron. 27:16). *6.* Father of one of Jehosaphat's army commanders (2 Chron. 17:16). *7.* Father of one of Jehoiada's generals (2 Chron. 23:1). *8.* Ephraimite warrior assisting Pekah in the elimination of Ahab's family and advisors (2 Chron. 28:7). *9.* Father of the leading Benjaminite in postexilic Jerusalem (Neh. 11:9). *10.* Postexilic priest (Neh. 12:17).

ZICRI (Zĭc′ rī) NIV form of Zichri.

ZIDDIM (Zĭd' dĭm) Place name meaning, "sides." Fortified town in Naphtali (Josh. 19:35), perhaps identifical with Hattin el-Qadim about eight miles west northwest of Tiberias. Some commentators see it as copyist's repetition of "fenced cities." See *Zer.*

ZIDKIJAH (Zĭd kī' jah) KJV alternate form of Zedekiah (Neh. 10:1).

ZIDON, ZIDONIANS (Zī' don, Zī dō' nĭ ans) KJV alternate forms of Sidon and Sidonians.

ZIF (Zĭf) KJV form of Ziv.

ZIGGURAT (Zĭg' gŭ răt) A stepped building, usually capped by a temple. The architecture was made popular by the Babylonians. The design consisted of placing smaller levels of brick on top of larger layers. Those so far excavated reveal advanced building techniques used by ancient civilizations. Most biblical scholars believe the tower of Babel was a ziggurat (Gen. 11:3–9).

ZIHA (Zī' hà) Egyptian personal name meaning, "the face of Horus (god) has spoken." *1.* Family of

A ziggurat dating to the Babylonian period (605–550 B.C.).

The ziggurat, or temple tower, located at Ur in ancient Mesopotamia (modern Iraq).

Temple servants (nethinim) (Ezra 2:43; Neh. 7:46). *2.* Overseer of postexilic Temple servants (Neh. 11:21).

ZIKLAG (Zĭk' lăg) A village in the southern Judean plain; variously identified either as tell el-Khuweilifeh, 10 miles north northeast of Beersheba, tell esh-Shariah, 9 miles north northwest of Beersheba, or khirbet el-Mashash. City in tribal inheritance of Judah given to Simeon (Josh. 15:31; 19:5).

Ziklag appears to have belonged to the Philis-

Y X Z

tines, taken during a period of rapid expansion in the time of Israel's judges (1 Sam. 27:6). The town was given to David by Achish, king of Gath, during David's "outlaw" period. The gift may have been a means of shortening Philistia's over-extended borders. Ziklag appears never to have been a part of Philistia proper.

David made the town his headquarters as he gathered his private army and made raids against the Amalekites. On returning to his base follow-ing Philistia's refusal to allow him to fight with them against Saul, David found the town had been raided and burned by the Amalekites and his family taken hostage. A daring night raid on the base of the enemy resulted in the rescue of his people and their return to Ziklag (1 Sam. 30). Jews returning from Babylonian Exile inhabited Ziklag (Neh. 11:28).

ZILLAH (Zĭl´ lah) Personal name meaning, "shadow." Second wife of Lamech and mother of Tubal-Cain and Naamah (Gen. 4:19,22–23).

ZILLETHAI (Zĭl´ lė thâî) Personal name; an ab-breviated form of "Yahweh is a shadow," that is, a protector. *1.* Family of Benjaminites (1 Chron. 8:20). *2.* Manassite supporter of David at Ziklag (1 Chron. 12:20).

ZILPAH (Zĭl´ pah) Personal name perhaps mean-ing, "short-nosed." Leah's maid (Gen. 29:24; 46:18), given to Jacob as a concubine (30:9; 37:2); mother of Gad and Asher who were re-garded as Leah's sons (30:10,12; 35:26).

ZILTHAI (Zĭl´ thâî) KJV form of Zillethai.

ZIMMAH (Zĭm´ mah) Personal name; perhaps an abbreviation of "Yahweh has considered or resolved." A Levite (1 Chron. 6:20,42; 2 Chron. 29:12).

ZIMNAH (Zĭm´ nah) TEV alternate form of Zim-mah (2 Chron. 29:12).

ZIMRAN (Zĭm´ răn) Personal name meaning, "celebrated in song, famous" or "mountain goat." Son of Abraham and Keturah and ancestor of an Arabian tribe (Gen. 25:2; 1 Chron. 1:32), possi-bly identified with Zabram, located somewhere west of Mecca on the Red Sea, and with Zimri (Jer. 25:25).

ZIMRI (Zĭm´ rī) Short form of personal name meaning, "Yah helped," "Yah is my protection," or "Yah is my praise." *1.* Son of Zerah and grand-son of Judah (1 Chron. 2:6). *2.* A chariot captain in Israel who usurped the throne by killing Elah (1 Kings 16:9–10). His reign was the shortest of all the kings of Israel, seven days (16:15). Zimri committed suicide by burning his palace around

him after Omri besieged Tirzah. His name became a byword for king killers (2 Kings 9:31). *3.* Leader of tribe of Simeon slain by Phinehas for bringing Midianite woman into the wilderness camp (Num. 25). *4.* Descendant of Saul (1 Chron. 8:36). *5.* A difficult name of a nation God judged (Jer. 25:25), often taken as a copying change from the Hebrew for Cimmerians or a coded designa-tion for Elam clarified by the immediate mention of Elam. Nothing is known of a nation of Zimri.

ZIN (Zĭn) Rocky desert area through which Israel passed en route from Egypt to Canaan (Num. 20:1; 27:14; 33:36). The wilderness of Zin, stretching from Kadesh-barnea to the Dead Sea, formed part of the southern border of Canaan and later Judah (Num. 34:3–4; Josh. 15:1,3). "From the wilderness of Zin to Rehob" in Galilee encom-passes almost the whole Promised Land (Num. 13:21). The wilderness of Zin should be distin-guished from the wilderness of Sin which em-braces the western Sinai plateau. See *Negeb; Pal-estine; Sin, Wilderness of; Wilderness.*

ZINA (Zī´ nä) Alternate form of Zizah (1 Chron. 23:10).

ZION (Zī´ on) The transliteration of the Hebrew and Greek words that originally referred to the fortified hill of pre-Israelite Jerusalem between the Kedron and Tyropean valleys. Scholars disagree as to the root meaning of the term. Some authorities have suggested that the word was related to the Hebrew word that meant "dry place" or "parched ground." Others relate the word to an Arabic term that is interpreted as "hillcrest," or "mountainous ridge."

The name "Zion" was mentioned first in the account of David's conquest of Jerusalem (2 Sam. 5:6–10; 1 Chron. 11:4–9). The phrase "strong-hold of Zion" may have referred to only the forti-fied section of the city. Jerusalem was the name of the city state as a whole and included numerous villages and houses located outside of the fortified area of the city itself. After David captured Zion, he resided there and changed its name to the "city of David."

Zion was used by biblical writers in a variety of ways. Many of the psalmists used the term to refer to the Temple built by Solomon (2:6; 48:2; 84:7; 132:13). In Isaiah 1:27, the idea of "Zion" in-cluded the whole nation. Zion also stood for the capital of Judah (Amos 6:1). The most common usage of Zion was to refer to the city of God in the new age (Isa. 1:27; 28:16; 33:5).

Zion was understood, also, to refer to the heav-enly Jerusalem (Isa. 60:14; Heb. 12:22; Rev. 14:1), the place where the Messiah would appear at the end of time. The glorification of the messi-anic community will take place on the holy moun-tain of "Zion." See *Jerusalem.*   *James Newell*

X Y
Z Y

ZIOR (Zī' ôr) Place name meaning, "smallness." Village allotted to Judah, located in the hill country near Hebron (Josh. 15:54). Archaeological research indicates that the frequently suggested site Si'ir about five miles north northeast of Hebron was uninhabited before A.D. 400.

ZIPH (Zīph) Place and personal name perhaps meaning, "flowing." *1.* Son of Mareshah and grandson of Caleb (1 Chron. 2:42). The text perhaps means Mareshah was the founder of Ziph near Hebron. *2.* Family of the tribe of Judah (1 Chron. 4:16). *3.* Town in the Judean hill country (Josh. 15:24), likely tell Zif about three miles southeast of Hebron. Mereshah likely founded the town (1 Chron. 2:42). David hid from Saul in the surrounding wilderness (1 Sam. 23:14–15; 26:2). Ziphites, residents of Ziph, twice revealed David's hideouts to Saul (1 Sam. 23:19; 26:1). Rehoboam fortified the site (2 Chron. 11:8). *4.* Town in the Negeb (Josh. 15:24), likely khirbet ez-Zeifeh sothwest of Kurnub.

ZIPHAH (Zī' phah) Clan name perhaps meaning, "flowing." Family of the tribe of Judah (1 Chron. 4:16).

ZIPHIMS (Zīph' īms) KJV alternate form of Ziphites (superscription of Ps. 54). "Ziphims" was formed by adding *s* to the already plural Ziphim. See *Ziph.*

ZIPHION (Zīph' ĭ' ŏn) See *Zephon.*

ZIPHITES (Zīph' ītes) See *Ziph.*

ZIPHRON (Zīph' rŏn) Place name perhaps meaning, "fragrance." Site on the northern border of Canaan, near Hazar-enan (Num. 34:9). It may be modern Zapherani southeast of Restan between Hamath and Homs.

ZIPPOR (Zĭp' pôr) Personal name meaning, "(little) bird." Father of King Balak of Moab (Num. 22:2,4,10).

ZIPPORAH (Zĭp pō' rah) Personal name meaning, "small bird" or "sparrow." Moses' first wife (some believe the woman named in Numbers 12:1 may be a reference to Zipporah, too) and mother of his children, Gershom and Eliezer (Ex. 2:21–22; 18:4). She was one of the daughters of Reuel, a priest of Midian. She saved Moses' life when the Lord sought to kill him by circumcising Gershom (4:24–25). It appears that Zipporah stayed with her father until Moses had led the people out of Egypt (18:2–6).

ZITHER (Zīth' ēr) Stringed instrument composed of thirty to forty strings placed over a shallow soundboard and played with a pick and fingers (Dan. 3:5,7,10,15 NAS margin). See *Music, Instruments, Dancing.*

ZITHRI (Zīth' rī) KJV form of Sithri.

ZIV (Zīv) Second month of calendar (1 Kings 6:1). See *Calendar.*

ZIZ (Zīz) Place name meaning, "blossom." Site involved in Judah's battle plans with Ammon and Moab (2 Chron. 20:16). A pass through a steep place where the people of Ammon, Moab, and Mount Seir were going to enter Judah to attack King Jehoshaphat. It is often located at wadi Hasasa, southeast of Tekoa near the Dead Sea. The Lord won this battle for His people without their fighting (see vv. 22-30), causing surrounding nations to fear God.

ZIZA (Zī' zà) Personal name meaning, "shining" or "brightness." *1.* Son of Shiphi who was a part of the expansion of the tribe of Simeon into Gedor (1 Chron. 4:37). *2.* Son of Shimei, a Levite from Gershon, following some manuscript and early translation evidence (1 Chron. 23:10). "Zina" is the reading of KJV, NAS, REB following Hebrew text. *3.* One of Rehoboam's sons by Maachah (2 Chron. 11:20).

ZIZAH (Zī' zah) Alternate Hebrew spelling for Ziza. A Levite (1 Chron. 23:11).

ZOAN (Zōan) Hebrew name for Egyptian city of Tanis located at San el-Hagar on the Tanitic arm of the Nile. Zoan became capital of Egypt about 1070 B.C. under Smendes I and remained so until 655 B.C. Numbers 13:22 notes that Hebron was seven years older than Zoan, but the exact date when either was built is not known. The prophets used Zoan to refer to the Egyptian government and its activities (Isa. 19:11,13; 30:4; Ezek. 30:14). The psalmist praised God for Exodus miracles near there (Ps. 78:12,43).

ZOAR (Zō' àr) Place name meaning, "small." One of the cities in the valley of Siddim, also known as Bela (Gen. 14:2). It was attacked by Chedolaomer, but apparently delivered by Abraham (14:17). Lot fled to Zoar with his family just before God destroyed Sodom and Gomorrah (19:23–24). He was afraid to remain there with his two daughters, so he went up to a mountain above the city (19:30). Isaiah prophesied that the citizens of Moab would flee to Zoar when destruction would come upon their nation (Isa. 15:5; compare Jer. 48:34). It was apparently a Moabite city, perhaps Safi on the river Zered.

ZOBA(H) (Zō' bah) City-state name perhaps meaning, "battle." First Saul (1 Sam. 14:47), then David (2 Sam. 8:3) fought the kings of Zobah. Compare title of Psalm 60. Zobah seems to be roughly where Syria later became a nation, northeast of Damascus. It was the leading Syrian power before the rise of Damascus. At one time, the Ammonites hired mercenaries from Zoba (2 Sam. 10:6) to help them fight David. The Ammonites came from the South while the Zobaites came from the North causing David to fight on two fronts. David won, and the people of Zobah served him (vv. 13-19). See *David; Syria.*

ZOBEBAH (Zō bē′ bah) Personal name of uncertain meaning. Descendant of Judah (1 Chron. 4:8; NIV, "Hazzobebah").

ZOHAR (Zō′ här) Personal name perhaps meaning, "witness." *1.* Hittite (Gen. 23:8; 25:9). *2.* Son of Simeon (Gen. 46:10; Ex. 6:15), also called Zerah (Num. 26:13; 1 Chron. 4:24). *3.* Descendant of Judah according to the traditional marginal correction (Qere) at 1 Chronicles 4:24. The Hebrew text reads Izhar.

ZOHELETH (Zō′ hē lĕth) Place name meaning, "creeping one," "sliding," or "serpent stone." Stone of sacrifice where Adonijah offered sacrifices in light of his coming coronation as king (1 Kings 1:9). This place was near En-rogel, a spring or well near Jerusalem where the Kidron Valley and the Valley of Hinnom meet. Adonijah's bid for the throne was short lived. David named Solomon to follow him on the throne (vv. 29–30).

ZOHETH (Zō′ hĕth) Personal name of uncertain meaning. Son of Ishi (1 Chron. 4:20) and the head of one of the families in Judah.

ZOPHAH (Zō′ phah) Personal name perhaps meaning, "jug." Family in the tribe of Asher (1 Chron. 7:35–36).

ZOPHAI (Zō′ phâi) Personal name perhaps meaning, "honeycomb." Son of Elkanah (1 Chron. 6:26). See *Zuph.*

ZOPHAR (Zō′ phär) Personal name of uncertain meaning. One of Job's three friends who came to sit with him in his misery (2:11). Zophar probably was the youngest of the three since he is mentioned last. He was the sharpest critic of the three men and was more philosophical in his criticism of Job. His words were more coarse and his dogmatism more emphatic. Although there was a place called Naamah in Judah (Josh. 15:41), doubt remains that it was Zophar's home. The exact location is unknown.

ZOPHIM (Zō′ phĭm) Place name meaning, "watchers" or common noun meaning, "the Field of the Watchers" (REB) or lookout post. It was a high place at "the top of Pisgah," near the northeastern end of the Dead Sea. Balak took Baalim there to curse the Israelites (Num. 23:14).

ZORAH (Zō′ rah) Place name meaning, "wasps" or "hornets." City of Dan (Josh. 19:41) about thirteen miles west of Jerusalem on the border

with Judah (Josh. 15:33; "Zoreah," KJV). It was the home of Manoah, Samson's father (Judg. 13:2). Rehoboam, king of Judah, strengthened Zorah in case of war (2 Chron. 11:5–12). It is modern Sarah.

ZORATHITES (Zō′ rā thītes) Descendants of Shobal who lived in Zorah (1 Chron. 2:52–53). See *Zorah.*

ZOREAH (Zō′ rē ah) KJV alternate spelling of Zorah.

ZORITES (Zō′ rītes) People from Zorah (1 Chron. 2:54). See *Zorah.*

ZOROASTER An ancient Iranian prophet after whom a religion called Zoroastrianism was named. See *Persia.*

ZOROBABEL (Zō rŏb′ å bĕl) KJV alternate form of Zerubbabel (Matt. 1:12–13; Luke 3:27).

ZUAR (Zū′ år) Personal name meaning, "young" or "small." Member of the tribe of Issachar (Num. 1:8; 2:5; 7:18,23; 10:15).

ZUPH (Zŭph) Personal and place name meaning, "honeycomb." *1.* Levitic ancestor of Elkanah and Samuel (1 Sam. 1:1; 1 Chron. 6:16,26,35) from Ephraim. He is called a Levite in another passage (see 1 Chron. 6:16,26,35). Ephraim may be geographical rather than tribal. Others argue that late sources incorporated Samuel into the tribe of Levi because he performed priestly duties. *2.* "Land of Zuph" where Saul was looking for some donkeys (1 Sam. 9:5). Its exact location is not known.

ZUPHITE (Zū′ phīte) NIV term for a resident or descendant of Zuph (1 Sam. 1:1).

ZUR (Zŭr) Personal name meaning, "rock." *1.* Midianite tribal chief (Num. 25:15 NIV) whose daughter, Cozbi, was killed along with an Israelite man by Phinehas. Zur was later killed in a battle Moses led (Num. 31:7–8). *2.* King Saul's uncle (1 Chron. 8:30; 9:36).

ZURIEL (Zū′ rĭ ĕl) Personal name that may mean, "God is a rock." Son of Abihail and head of the Merari family of Levites (Num. 3:35).

ZURISHADDAI (Zū′ rĭ shăd′ dā ī) Personal name meaning, "shaddai is a rock." The father of Shelumiel, a leader of the tribe of Simeon, in the wilderness wanderings (Num. 1:6).

ZUZIM (Zū′ zĭm) National name of uncertain meaning. A people who lived in Ham and were defeated by Chedorlaomer (Gen. 14:5). They are apparently called the Zamzummim in Deuteronomy 2:20.

ZUZITE (Zū′ zīte) NIV term for Zuzim (Gen. 14:5).

ART CREDITS

The publishers express deep gratitude to the following persons
and institutions for the use of art materials in this book.

PHOTOGRAPHS

Museum Abbreviations

AMA = Archaeological Museum, Antakya, Turkey
AMO = Ashmolean Museum, Oxford, England
AMS = Augst Museum, Augst, Switzerland
BMB = Bergama Museum, Bergama, Turkey
BMG = Bode Museum, Berlin, Germany
BMI = Beersheba Museum, Beersheba, Israel
BML = British Museum, London, England
CMR = Capitoline (Compagdiglio) Museum, Rome, Italy
EMC = Egyptian Museum, Cairo, Egypt
GAM = Geneva Archaeological Museum, Geneva, Switzerland
GMC = Glyptothek Museum, Copenhagen, Denmark
GMM = Glyptothek Museum, Munich, Germany
HHJ = The Holyland Hotel, Jerusalem, Israel
IMJ = Israel Museum, Jerusalem, Israel

IMT = Istanbul Archaeological Museum, Istanbul, Turkey
MAO = Museum of the Ancient Orient, Istanbul, Turkey
MGV = Museum of Giulia Villa, Rome, Italy
MMM = Megiddo Museum, Megiddo, Israel
MNY = Metropolitan Museum, New York, New York
NAM = Nimes Archaeological Museum, Nimes, France
NMN = Naples Museum, Naples, Italy
RMA = Roman Museum, Augsburg, Germany
RMM = Roman Museum, Malta
SMG = Saalburg Museum, Saalburg, Germany
TAM = The Archaeological Museum, Ankara, Turkey
TLP = The Louvre, Paris, France
VMR = Vatican Museum, Rome, Italy
WMS = Windisch Museum, Windisch, Switzerland

Photographers

Arnold, Nancy, Free-lance Photographer, Nashville, Tennessee 37234: pp. 128; 217; 218, middle; 219, top; 231; 345; 347, top; 437; 478, bottom right; 579; 589; 618; 629; 683; 756, top; 855; 940; 964, top right; 989; 1037, bottom right; 1048, top; 1102; 1204; 1246, bottom; 1264; 1304, top; 1305, right; 1392; 1427.

Biblical Illustrator (David Rogers, photographer), Nashville, Tennessee, 37234: pp. 9; 10; 32; 37; 40; 46, bottom; 64; 65, top left; 65, middle; 65, bottom (AMA); 79, bottom right; 85; 99, top; 108; 122-123 (TLP); 129; 138 (TLP); 143, bottom (MAO); 156, top; 174, bottom; 208 (TAM); 215, top (TLP); 220, top; 227; 262; 263; 264, top right; 274 (TAM); 275, bottom (TAM); 290 (TAM); 291, top; 422; 425, middle; 425, bottom; 428, bottom; 513, bottom; 575, bottom; 615; 634; 638; 644, top left; 644, bottom left; 645, top; 655, bottom (MAO); 658; 659; 684 (TLP); 686 (TAM); 765; 789, top (TAM); 789, bottom left (TAM); 789, bottom right (TAM); 790 (TAM); 812, bottom left; 857; 862; 863, top; 880; 916; 919; 924, top; 968; 987, bottom; 1009, top right; 1009, bottom;

1048, bottom; 1070, bottom; 1084; 1094, bottom; 1105, top; 1111, bottom (TAM); 1115; 1117, top; 1127, bottom; 1224; 1234; 1239, top; 1259; 1266; 1269; 1273; 1281; 1306; 1322; 1325, bottom; 1332, middle left; 1359; 1407.

Biblical Illustrator (Ken Touchton, photographer), Nashville, Tennessee, 37234: pp. 12; 24; 38; 39; 52; 55; 66 (HHJ); 81; 84; 88; 105; 137; 172, top; 172, middle; 179; 201; 209; 216; 224; 236; 240; 264, bottom; 275, top; 329; 334; 341; 347, bottom; 350, bottom; 355; 356, top; 356, bottom; 357; 383; 386; 414; 419; 460; 475; 479; 485, top; 485, bottom; 511; 516; 521; 530, top; 532, top; 532, bottom; 533, bottom; 538; 566, bottom; 575, top; 596, top; 617 (IMJ); 639; 640; 649; 759; 760; 761, top left; 761, top right; 761, bottom left; 761, bottom right; 768 (HHJ); 780, bottom; 812, top; 823; 831; 840; 894; 905; 929; 999; 1000, top; 1009, top left; 1013, top; 1033; 1049; 1061; 1085; 1093; 1099; 1105, bottom; 1111, top; 1112 (IMJ); 1114; 1131; 1160, top left; 1160, top right; 1160, bottom; 1203; 1205 (IMJ); 1209; 1215; 1235; 1238; 1280, bottom; 1291 (HHJ); 1296; 1304,

bottom; 1315; 1325, top; 1328, bottom; 1333; 1342; 1343; 1358; 1364; 1379; 1384; 1385, top; 1389; 1397.

Brisco, Thomas V., Associate Professor of Biblical Backgrounds and Archaeology, Southwestern Baptist Theological Seminary, Fort Worth, Texas 76122: pp. 34, top; 59; 78; 113 (BML); 157; 159, top; 264, top left; 291, bottom; 292; 317; 502, top; 680; 827; 836; 863, bottom; 927; 930, middle; 941; 942, top left; 1010; 1103, top; 1127, top; 1218; 1232; 1233; 1246, top; 1254 (BML); 1256; 1284, top; 1298; 1302; 1303; 1305, left; 1311; 1313; 1328, top; 1332, bottom; 1337, top; 1337, bottom; 1349, bottom; 1355.

Couch, Ernie, Graphics Consultant, Nashville, Tennessee 37222-1687: pp. 1071, top; 1123.

Ellis, C. Randolph, M.D., General Practice, Surgery, and Anesthesiology, Malvern, Arkansas 72104: pp. 426-427; 428, top; 533, top; 548; 566, top; 735; 769; 770-771; 794; 813; 990; 1023; 1078; 1156, bottom; 1192.

Langston, Scott, Doctoral Candidate, Southwestern Baptist Theological Seminary, Fort Worth, Texas 76122: pp. 67; 79, top left; 79, middle right; 106, top; 106, bottom; 162, top; 162, bottom; 219, middle; 220, bottom; 225; 226; 232, top; 232, bottom; 299; 300, top; 301; 332, middle right; 333, top left; 333, top right; 425, top; 428, middle; 552; 588, top; 641, top; 642; 772, top; 814; 924, bottom; 930, top; 930, bottom; 931; 964, bottom; 965, top; 1047; 1094, top; 1095, top; 1095, bottom; 1132; 1156, top; 1157, top; 1177; 1208; 1239, bottom; 1283; 1332, top right; 1336, top; 1336, bottom; 1349, top; 1400, top; 1409.

Scofield Collection, Dargan Research Library, Nashville, Tennessee 37234: pp. 1; 11, top; 53; 82; 83; 98; 146; 167; 171; 172, bottom; 210; 241; 270; 295, top; 295, bottom; 296; 297; 326; 330; 331; 337; 338, top; 338, bottom; 339; 346, top; 377, top left; 377, top right; 381; 387; 396; 412, bottom; 432; 438, top; 445; 446; 467; 494-495; 496; 502, top; 502, bottom; 503; 512; 528; 531, left; 533, middle; 535, bottom; 543; 547; 554; 556; 568; 576, bottom; 644, top right; 645, bottom; 699; 715, top; 715, bottom; 737; 741; 780, top; 869; 910; 944; 987, top; 988; 1037, bottom left; 1038; 1079; 1103, bottom; 1104; 1125; 1126; 1153; 1157, bottom; 1165, top; 1170; 1193, top; 1193, bottom; 1225, bottom; 1226, top; 1227; 1258; 1275; 1276, bottom; 1309; 1335, bottom; 1356; 1385, bottom; 1393; 1395; 1398; 1400, bot-tom; 1402, bottom; 1412; 1415; 1426; 1428, top; 1428, bottom; 1429; 1430; 1432.

Sickelka, Susan Preshaw, Associate Minister, Evangelical United Church of Christ, Highland, Illinois 62249: p. 945.

Smith, Marsha A. Ellis, Editor/ Designer, Bibles and Academic Books, Holman Bible Publishers, Nashville, Tennessee 37234: pp. 91; 107; 150; 163 (BMI); 174, top; 212; 218, top; 219, bottom; 230; 333, bottom; 346, bottom; 350, top; 1000, bottom; 1001.

Southwestern Baptist Theological Seminary, A. Webb Roberts Library, Fort Worth, Texas 76122: pp. 3; 118; 399, bottom; 1117, bottom; 1159; 1270.

Staatliche Museen zu Berlin, Berlin, Germany: pp. 114; 121; 1013; 1240.

Stephens, Bill, Senior Curriculum Coordinator, Discipleship Training Department, Baptist Sunday School Board, Nashville, Tennessee 37234: pp. 11, bottom; 26; 33 (NMN); 46, top; 56; 60; 75, top; 75, bottom; 94; 95; 100 (BML); 102; 104 (CMR); 119; 120 (TLP); 132; 144 (BML); 156, bottom; 160; 175; 207, left (NMN); 207, right (BML); 214 (NMN); 215, bottom; 218, bottom (GMC); 234; 242; 250; 268 (RMM); 273 (NMN); 288; 298 (BML); 322, top (BML); 322, bottom (BML); 323 (MNY); 328 (BML); 353 (AMS); 412, top; 417; 421; 430; 454, bottom; 455; 478, top (NAM); 478, bottom left; 483; 497 (GMM); 499; 501 (AMS); 506, top (MGV); 506, bottom (BML); 513, top; 522; 526, top; 529, top (AMS); 529, bottom; 530, bottom; 531, right; 534 (NMN); 535, top (MNY); 576, top; 577; 578, left; 578, right (BMB); 582, top (NMN, the Farnese Collection); 588, middle; 588, bottom; 596, bottom (NMN); 623 (BML); 628; 632, top; 632, bottom (CMR); 633 (VMR); 637 (AMO); 655, top; 668 (VMR); 694 (RMM); 695 (BMI); 697 (BML); 732; 734 (NMN); 748 (GAM); 750; 796;

826; 832; 838 (WMS); 852 (BML); 860, top (BML); 860, bottom (BMB); 864 (BML); 865, top; 865, middle; 865, bottom; 870 (BML); 885, top; 885, bottom; 886; 893; 928; 937; 942, top left (MMM); 947; 964, top left (SMG); 966; 967 (BML); 974 (BML); 981; 991; 998; 1004 (MGV); 1012; 1028 (BMG); 1029 (GMM); 1037, top; 1043 (MGV); 1053; 1059; 1060; 1062, left; 1062, right (NMN); 1070, top; 1074; 1106; 1110 (IMT); 1121; 1124; 1130; 1139; 1152 (BML); 1158 (GMM); 1165, bottom; 1226, bottom; 1231, top (GMM); 1231, bottom (NMN, the Farnese Collection); 1240, top (BML); 1247 (BML); 1250; 1257 (AMS); 1276, top; 1280, top; 1310 (GMM); 1335, top; 1353; 1375; 1376 (RMA); 1378; 1396; 1408, top (SMG); 1410 (BML); 1411, top.

Tolar, William B., Vice President for Academic Affairs and Provost, Southwestern Baptist Theological Seminary, Fort Worth, Texas 76122: pp. 31, top; 31, bottom (EMC); 34; 141; 143, top; 159, bottom; 278, top; 278, bottom; 300, bottom; 325; 327; 332, top; 332, bottom; 397; 399, top (EMC and GMM); 401; 402; 403; 405; 438, bottom; 454, top; 501, top; 526, bottom; 527; 536, left; 536, right; 544; 548, bottom; 550; 553; 582, bottom; 616; 627; 630; 641, bottom; 756, bottom; 772, bottom; 812, bottom right; 942, bottom; 960; 1011; 1024; 1071, bottom; 1088; 1161; 1163; 1225, top; 1245; 1284, bottom; 1287, top; 1287, bottom; 1319; 1324; 1332, top left; 1345; 1346, top; 1346, bottom; 1380; 1381; 1386; 1408, bottom; 1441.

University of Missouri-Columbia, Museum of Art and Archaeology, Columbia, Missouri 65211: dust jacket, front cover.

ILLUSTRATIONS

Latta, Bill, Art Section Manager, Baptist Sunday School Board, Nashville, Tennessee 37234: pp. 93; 99; 126-127; 170; 342-343; 672; 673; 762-763; 766-767; 965, bottom; 1080; 1289; 1290; 1312; 1317; 1326-1327; 1329; 1401; 1402, top; 1411, bottom; 1441, bottom.

INTERNAL MAPS

Carta, The Israel Map and Publishing Company, Limited, Jerusalem, Israel: pp. 365; 390-391; 452-453; 580-581; 652-653; 656-657; 708-709; 724-725; 728-729; 778-779; 782; 978-979; 1021; 1046; 1065; 1066-1067; 1082-1083; 1210-1211.

Key to Bible Maps

Plate I   Age of the Patriarchs
               The Ancient World
Plate II   The Exodus Route
               Wilderness Wanderings & The Conquest of
               Canaan
Plate III   The Twelve Tribes in Canaan
               The Empire of David & Solomon
Plate IV   The Divided Kingdom
               Judah & Israel

Plate V   Palestine in the Time of Jesus
Plate VI   The Ministry of Jesus
               Early Galilee & Later
Plate VII   Jerusalem in New Testament Times
               David's City, The Tabernacle & Solomon's
               Temple
Plate VIII   Paul's Missionary Journeys
               The Seven Churches of Asia

Map Index

A

Abel (Abila, in Perea) V-6E; VI-9E
Abila (Abel, in Perea) V-6E, VI-9E
Abila (in the Decapolis), V-3E
Abilene V-1E
Abydos VIII-6A
Acchabare VI-1B, 3D, 5B
Acco (Ptolemais) I-5D; II-3D; III-3C;
   IV-3C; V-3C; VII-9D
Achaia VIII-4B
Achshaph III-3C; IV-3C
Acrabeta V-6D; VI-7D
Actium VIII-3B
Adam III-6E; IV-6E
Adida V-6C
Adora V-8C
Adramyttium VIII-6B
Adria, Sea of VIII-3B
Adullam III-7C; IV-7C
Aegean Sea I-2A; VIII-5B
Aenon V-5D
Africa VIII-1E
Agrigentum VIII-1C
Agrippina V-5E; VI-5D
Ai II-5E; III-6D; IV-6D
Ain II-4E; III-3E; IV-3E
Akkad I-8D
Alalakh I-5B
Aleppo (Halab) I-5B
Alexandria VIII-7E
Alexandrium V-6D; VI-7D
Altar VII-9C
Altar, Brazen VII-6B
Altar of Incense VII-7A
Alush II-8C
Amarna I-3E
Amastris VIII-8A
Amisus VIII-9A
Ammathus (of Decapolis) V-5E; VI-
   7E
Ammathus (of Galilee) V-3E; VI-2B,
   7B
Ammon II-5E; III-6E; IV-6E
Amphipolis VIII-4A
Anab III-8C; IV-8C
Ancyra VIII-8A
Anthedon V-8B
Antioch (of Pisidia) VIII-8B
Antioch (of Syria) VIII-9C
Antipatris V-5C

Antonia, Tower of VII-1C
Aphek II-4D; III-6C; IV-3E, 6C
Aphek, Tower of, V-6C
Appii Forum (Appius, Forum of)
   VIII-1A
Appius, Forum of (Appii Forum)
   VIII-1A
Apollonia V-5C; VIII-4A
Aqaba, Gulf of II-9D
Ar II-5E; III-8E; IV-8E
Arad II-6D; III-9C; IV-9C; V-9C
Aram (Syrians) IV-2E
Ararat, Mt. I-7A
Archelais V-6D; VI-8D; VIII-9B
Areopolis V-9E
Ark VII-6A
Arnon River II-5E; III-8E; IV-8E; V-
   8E
Aroer III-8E; IV-8E
Arvad I-5C; II-1E
Arzawa I-3B
Ascalon V-7B
Ashdod II-5D; III-7B; IV-7B
Asher, Allotment of III-3D
Ashkelon II-7B; IV-7B
Ashtaroth II-4E; IV-3E
Asia VIII-7B
Asphaltitis, Lake (Dead Sea, Salt
   Sea) II-5E; III-8D; IV-8D; V-8D;
   VI-9D
Asshur I-7C
Assos VIII-6B
Assuwa I-2A
Assyria I-7B
Ataroth III-7E; IV-7E
Athens I-1B; VIII-5B
Attalia VIII-7C
Azor II-5D; III-6C; IV-6C

B

Baal-meon VI-9E
Baal-zephon II-6B
Baaras V-7E
Babylon I-8D
Babylonia I-8D
Baca VI-3D
Baddan VI-7D
Bashan IV-2E
Beersheba I-5D; II-6D; III-9C; IV-
   9C; V-9C

Belzedek V-8C
Benjamin, Allotment of III-7D
Beroea VIII-4A
Beror Hayil V-8B
Berytus I-5C; II-2E; VIII-9D
Bethany V-7D; VI-9D
Bethel I-5D; II-5E; III-6D; IV-6D;
   VI-8C
Bethennabris V-6E
Bethesda, Pool of VII-1D
Beth-horon IV-6C;
Beth-jeshimoth III-7E; IV-7E
Bethlehem III-7D; IV-7D; V-7D; VI-
   9C
Bethletepha V-7C
Beth Netofa VI-1A, 6A
Beth-ramatha (Livias, Julias) V-7E;
   VI-9E
Bethsaida V-3E; VI-1C, 3E, 6C
Beth-shan II-4E
Beth-shean III-4E; IV-4E
Beth-shemesh III-7C; IV-7C
Betogabris V-7C
Bithynia VIII-8A
Bitter Lakes II-7B
Black Sea (Euxine Sea) I-5A; VIII-6A
Bronze, Sea of VII-9B
Brundisium VIII-2A
Bubastis (Pibeseth) II-6A
Buto II-5A
Buxetum VIII-1A
Byblos (Gebal) II-2E
Byzantium VIII-6A

C

Cadasa V-2E; VI-2D
Caesarea (Strato's Tower) V-4C;
   VIII-9D
Caesarea Philippi V-1E; VI-2E
Calah I-7B
Callirrhoe V-7E; VI-9E
Cana V-3D; VI-1A, 4D, 6A
Canaan II-4E
Canopus VIII-8E
Capercotnei (Kefar Otnay) V-4D
Capernaum V-3E; VI-1B, 4E, 6B
Cappadocia VIII-9A
Carchemish I-5B
Carmel, Mt. III-3C
Caspian Sea (Hyrcanian Sea) I-9A

Catania VIII-1C
Cenchreae VIII-4B
Charachmoba V-9E
Chephirah III-7C; IV-7C
Chinnereth III-3E; IV-3E
Chinnereth, Sea of III-3E; IV-3E
Chios I-2B; VIII-5B
Chorazin V-3E; VI-1B, 3E, 5B
Cilicia VIII-9B
Cilician Gates VIII-9B
Cnidus VIII-6C
Colossae VIII-7B
Corcyra VIII-3B
Coreae V-5D
Corinth VIII-4B
Cos VIII-6C
Cotiaeum VIII-7B
Crete I-2C; VIII-5D
Crocodile Lake II-8A
Crocodilopolis II-8A
Croton VIII-2B
Cuthah I-8C
Cyclades I-1B; VIII-5C
Cydonia VIII-5C
Cyprus (Elishah, Kypros) I-4C; II-1B;
    VIII-8C
Cyrenaica VIII-4E
Cyrene VIII-4E
Cyzicus VIII-6A

D

Damascus I-5C; 11-2E
Dan, Allotment of III-1E, 6B
Dan (Laish), II-3E; III-1E; IV-1E
David's City VII-8D, 4D
Dead Sea (Asphaltitis, Lake; Salt Sea)
    II-5E; III-8D; IV-8D; V-8D; VI-9D
Debir II-5D; III-8C; IV-8C
Decapolis V-4E; VI-3B, 5E, 8B
Deir el-Balah III-8A; IV-8A
Delphi VIII-4B
Derbe VIII-9B
Dibon II-5E; III-8E; IV-8E; V-8E
Dodona VIII-3B
Dophkah II-8C
Dor I-5D; II-4D; III-4C; IV-4C
Dora IV-4C
Dorylaeum VIII-7A
Dothan III-4D; IV-4D
Dyrrhachium VIII-3A

E

Eastern Desert II-9A
Ebla I-5C
Ecbatana I-9C
Ecdippa V-2C
Eder III-9E; IV-9E
Edom II-6E; III-9E; IV-9E
Edrei II-4E
Eglon II-5D; III-8B; IV-8B
Ekron IV-7B
Egypt I-3E; II-7A; VIII-7E
Egypt, River of (Wadi al' Arish, W.
    al' Arish) II-6C; III-9A; IV-9A
Ekron IV-7B
Elam I-9C
Elath II-8D

Elim II-8C
Elis VIII-4B
Elishah (Cyprus, Kypros) I-4C; II-1B;
    VIII-8C
Elusa V-9B
Emmatha VI-4E
Emmaus V-7C
Emmaus (Nicopolis, in Judea) V-7C
En Boqeq V-9D
Engedi III-8D; IV-8D; V-8D
Enkomi II-1C
Ephesus VIII-6B
Ephraim V-6D; VI-8D
Ephraim, Allotment of III-6C
Epirus VIII-3B
Erech I-8D
Escarpment VII-3C
Esdraelon VI-5D
Essene Community V-7E
Etham II-6B
Etham, Wilderness of II-7B
Etna, Mt. VIII-1C
Euphrates River I-6C
Euxine Sea (Black Sea) I-5A; VIII-6A
Ezion-geber II-8D

F

Faiyum, The II-8a
Fair Havens VIII-5D
First Wall VII-2B

G

Gabaon V-6D
Gabath Saul VI-9C
Gabbatha VII-1C
Gad, Allotment of III-5E
Gadara V-4E; VI-2C, 5E, 7C
Gadora V-6E; VI-8E
Galatia VIII-8A
Galilee V-3D; VI-2A, 4D, 7A
Galilee, Sea of V-3E; VI-1B, 4E, 6B
Gamala VI-3E
Gangra VIII-8A
Gath II-5D; III-7C; IV-7C
Gath-rimmon III-6C; IV-6C
Gaza I-4D; II-5D; III-8B; IV-8B;
    V-8B; VIII-9E
Gebal (Byblos) I-5C; II-2E
Geder II-5D
Gedor III-7C; IV-7C
Gennesaret V-3E; VI-1B, 4E, 6B
Gerar III-8B; IV-8B
Gerasa (of Samaria) V-6D
Gerasa (of the Decapolis) V-5E
Gergesa V-3E; V-1C, 4E, 6C
Geshur IV-3E
Gethsemane VII-2E
Gezer II-5D; III-7C; IV-7C
Gibeon III-6D; IV-6D
Gihon, Spring VII-3D, 7E
Gilboa, Mt. III-4D
Gilead IV-6E
Gilgal III-6D; IV-6D
Gina III-4D; IV-4D
Ginae V-4D; VI-4A, 6D, 9A
Gischala VI-3D

Golden Gate VII-2D
Gophna V-6D; VI-8C
Gordium VIII-8A
Goshen II-6A
Great Sea, The (Mediterranean Sea;
    Upper Sea) I-3C; II-5B; III-5A; IV-
    5A; V-5A; VI-1C; VIII-7D

H

Halab (Aleppo) I-5B
Halicarnassus VIII-6C
Hamath I-5C; II-1E
Hapharaim VI-3B, 8B
Haran I-6B
Hattushah I-4A
Havvoth-jair IV-4E
Hazaraddar (Hezron) II-6D
Hazeroth II-8D
Hazor I-5D; II-3E; III-2E; IV-2E
Hebron I-5D; II-5D; III-8C; IV-8C;
    V-8C
Heliopolis (On) I-3E; II-7A; VIII-8E
Hepher II-4D; III-5C; IV-5C
Heraclea VIII-7A
Heracleopolis Magna II-8A
Hermes River I-2B
Hermon, Mt. III-1E; V-1E; VI-1E
Hermopolis II-9A
Hermus River VIII-6B
Herodium V-7D; VI-9D
Herod's Palace VII-3B
Heroonpolis (Pithom) II-6A
Heshbon II-5E; III-6E; IV-6E
Hinnom Valley VII-4B
Hippus V-3E; VI-2C, 4E, 7C
Hittite Empire I-4A; II-1E
Holy of Holies VII-6A; 9A
Holy Place, VII-6A; 9A
Hor, Mt. II-6D
Hor-haggidgad II-6D
Hormah II-6D; III-9C; IV-9C
Hyrcania V-7D; VI-9D
Hyrcania Sea (Caspian Sea) I-9A

I

Iconium VIII-8B
Idumea V-9B
Ikhetaten II-9A
Illyricum VIII-2A
Imbros VIII-5A
Isin I-8D
Issachar, Allotment of III-4D
Issus VIII-9B
Italy VIII-1A

J

Jabbok River II-4E; III-5E; IV-5E;
    V-5E; VI-7E
Jabesh Gilead IV-4E
Jabneel IV-6B
Jacob's Well VI-7D
Jamnia V-7B
Jamnith V-2E; VI-3D
Japhia V-3D; VI-2A, 4D, 7A
Jazer III-6E; IV-6E
Jebus (Jerusalem) I-5D; II-5E; III-7D;

IV-7D; V-7D; VI-9D;
VII-2C, 8D; VIII-9E
Jericho I-5D; II-5E; III-6D; IV-6D;
V-6D; VI-9D
Jerusalem (Jebus) I-5D; II-5E;
III-7D; IV-7D; V-7D; VI-9D;
VII-2C, 8D; VII-9E
Jezreel IV-4D
Jogbehah III-6E; IV-6E
Jokneam III-3C
Joppa I-5D; II-5D; III-6B; IV-6B;
V-6B; VIII-9E
Jordan River II-4E; III-5E; IV-5E;
V-5E; VI-4B, 8D, 9B; VIII-9E
Judah, Allotment of III-8C
Judah, Wilderness of III-8D; VI-9D
Judaea (Judea) V-7C; VI-8D
Judea (Judaea) V-7C; VI-8D
Julias (Livias, Beth-ramatha) V-7E;
VI-9E

K

Kadesh-barnea II-6D
Kanish I-5A
Karka II-6D
Kedemoth III-7E; IV-7E
Kedesh II-3E; III-2E; IV-2E
Kefar Otnay (Capercotnei) V-4D
Kidron Valley VII-3D, 8E
Kibroth-hattaavah II-9D
Kir-hareseth IV-9E
Kish I-8D
Kition II-1C
Kizzuwatna I-4B
Knossos I-2C; VIII-5D
Kumidi II-2E
Kypros (Cyprus, Elishah) I-4C; II-1B;
VIII-8C

L

Lachish II-5D; III-8C; IV-8C
Lagash I-8D
Laish (Dan) II-3E; III-1E; IV-1E
Laodicea VIII-7B
Larissa VIII-4B
Larsa I-8D
Lasea VIII-5D
Laver VII-6B
Lebanon, Mt. II-2E; III-1E; V-1E
Lemnos VIII-5A
Leontes River III-1E; IV-1E; V-1E
Leptis Magna VIII-1E
Lesbos I-2A; VIII-6B
Letopolis II-7A
Libnah III-7C; IV-7C
Libnath II-4D; III-3C; IV-3C
Libya (Put) I-2D; VIII-4E
Livias (Julias, Beth-ramatha) V-7E;
VI-9E
Lod (Lydda) IV-6C; V-6C
Lo-debar IV-4E
Lower City VII-4C
Lower Egypt I-3D
Lower Sea (Persian Gulf) I-9E
Lycaonia VIII-8B
Lycia VIII-7C

Lydda (Lod) IV-6C; V-6C
Lystra VIII-8B

M

Macedonia VIII-3A
Machaerus V-7E; VI-9E
Madai (Media) I-9B
Maeander River I-2B; VIII-6B
Magdala V-3E; VI-1B, 6B
Malatha V-9C
Malta (Melita) VIII-1D
Manasseh, Allotment of III-4E, 5C
Mahanaim IV-5E
Marah II-8C
Mari I-6C
Markets VII-1C
Masada V-8D
Medeba III-7E; IV-7E; V-7E; VI-9E
Media (Madai) I-9B
Mediterranean Sea (Great Sea, The;
Upper Sea) I-3C; II-5B; III-5A;
IV-5A; V-5A; VI-1C; VIII-7D
Megiddo II-4E; III-4D; IV-4D
Melita (Malta) VIII-1D
Memphis (Noph) I-3E; II-7A; VIII-8E
Merom II-3E; III-2D; IV-2D
Meroth VI-2D
Messana VIII-1B
Midian, Land of II-9E
Migdal II-4C; IV-4C
Miletus VIII-6B
Minoans I-1C
Moab II-6E; III-9E; IV-9E
Moesia VIII-3A
Mycenae I-1B
Mycenaeans I-1A
Myra VIII-7C
Mysia VIII-6A
Mytilene VIII-6B

N

Nabataeans V-9E
Nain V-4D; VI-3A, 5D, 8A
Naphtali, Allotment of III-3D
Narbata V-4C
Nazareth V-3D; VI-2A, 4D, 7A
Neapolis (in Italy) VIII-1A
Neapolis (in Thrace) VIII-5A
Neara V-6D
Nebo, Mt. II-5E; III-7E; IV-7E
Nicaea VIII-7A
Nicopolis (Emmaus, in Judea) V-7C
Nicopolis (in Achaia) VIII-3B
Nile Delta I-3D; II-5A; VIII-8E
Nile River I-3E; II-9A
Nineveh I-7B
Nippur I-8D
Noph (Memphis) I-3E; II-7A; VIII-8E
Nuzi I-7C

O

Oea VIII-1E
Olives, Mount of V-7D; VII-2E
Olympia VIII-4C
Olympus, Mt. VIII-4A
On (Heliopolis) I-3E; II-7A; VIII-8E

Ophel VII-7E
Ophrah III-4D; IV-4D

P

Paestum VIII-1A
Pamphylia VIII-8C
Panormus VIII-1B
Paphlagonia VIII-8A
Paphos II-1B; VIII-8D
Paran, Wilderness of II-7C
Patara VIII-7C
Patmos VIII-5C
Patrae VIII-4B
Pehel III-4E
Pella V-4E; VI-4C, 6E, 9C; VIII-4A
Pelusium (Sin) II-6B; VIII-9E
Perea V-6E; VI-8E
Perga VIII-7C
Pergamum VIII-6B
Persian Gulf (Lower Sea) I-9E
Pessinus VIII-7A
Petra II-7E
Phasael, Tower of VII-2B
Phasaelis V-6D
Philadelphia V-6E; VIII-7B
Philippi VIII-5A
Philippopolis VIII-5A
Philistines III-7B; IV-7B
Philoteria V-3E; VI-2B, 4E, 7B
Phoenicia III-2D; IV-2D; V-1D;
VI-1D
Phrygia VIII-7B
Pibeseth (Bubastis) II-6A
Pisgah III-7E; IV-7E
Pisidia VIII-7B
Pithom (Heroonpolis) II-6A
Plain of Jezreel IV-4D
Pompeii VIII-1A
Pontus VIII-8A
Prusa VIII-6A
Ptolemais (Acco) I-5D; II-3D; III-3C;
IV-3C; V-3C; VIII-9D
Punon II-6E
Put (Libya) I-2D; VIII-4E
Puteoli VIII-1A
Pylos I-1B; VIII-4C

Q

Qumran V-7D

R

Rabbath-ammon II-5E
Ragaba V-5E; VI-7E
Rama V-6D
Ramat Rahel V-7D
Ramses (Tanis, Zoan) I-4D; II-6A
Raphia III-8A; IV-8A; V-8A
Red Sea I-4E; II-9C
Rephidim II-9C
Reuben, Allotment of III-7E
Rhegium VIII-1B
Rhinocolura II-6C
Rhodes, City of I-2B; VIII-6C
Rhodes, Province of VIII-6C
Rome VIII-1A

S

Sahara Desert I-1E; VIII-4E
Salamis II-1C; VIII-9C
Salim VI-7D
Salt Sea (Asphaltitis, Lake; Dead Sea)
  II-5E; III-8D; IV-8D; V-8D; VI-9D
Samaria, City of IV-5D; V-5D
Samaria, Province of V-5C; VI-4A,
  6D, 9A
Samos I-2B; VIII-6B
Samothrace VIII-5A
Sappho V-6C
Sardis VIII-6B
Scupi VIII-4A
Scythopolis V-4E; VI-4B, 5E, 9B
Sebennytos II-6A
Seleucia VIII-9C
Seleucia Pieria VIII-9C
Sepph V-2D; VI-3D
Sepphoris V-3D; VI-2A, 4C, 7A
Serpent's Pool VII-3A
Sharon, Plain of III-5C; IV-5C; V-5C
Sharuhen III-8A; IV-8A
Shechem I-5D; II-4E; III-5D; IV-5D;
  V-5D; VI-7D
Sheep Gate VII-1D
Shewbread, Table of VII-6A
Shiloh II-4E; III-6D
Shimron II-4E; III-3D; IV-3D
Shittim III-7E; IV-7E
Showbread, Table of VII-6A
Shur, Wilderness of II-6C
Sicily VIII-1C
Sidon I-5C; II-3E; III-1D; IV-1D;
  V-1D; VI-1D; VIII-9D
Sidonians III-1D; IV-1D
Siloam, Pool of VII-4D
Simeon, Allotment of III-9C
Sin (Pelusium) II-6B; VIII-9E
Sin, Wilderness of II-8C
Sinai, Mt. II-9C
Sinai Peninsula I-4E; II-8C; VIII-9E
Sinda II-1C
Sippar I-8C
Smyrna VIII-6B
Socoh IV-5C
Sogane V-2E; VI-1A, 3E, 4D, 6A
Soli VIII-9B
Solomon's Temple VII-9A
Sparta VIII-4C
Storerooms VII-9A

Strato's Tower (Caesarea) V-4C;
  VIII-9D
Succoth (in Canaan) III-5E; IV-5E
Succoth (Theku, in Egypt) II-6B
Suez, Gulf of II-8B
Sumer I-8D
Sumur II-1E
Susa I-9D
Sybaris VIII-2B
Sychar V-5D; VI-7D
Syracuse VIII-1C
Syria V-1D; VIII-9C
Syrtis, Greater VIII-2E

T

Taanach III-4D; IV-4D
Taberah II-9D
Tabernacle, The VII-6A
Tabor, Mt. III-3D; VI-3A, 7A
Tamar II-6E; IV-9D
Tanis (Ramses, Zoan) I-4D; II-6A
Tappuah III-6D; IV-6D
Tarbenet VI-5D
Tarentum VIII-2A
Taricheae VI-4D
Tarracina VIII-1A
Tarsus VIII-9B
Taurus Mountains I-4B
Tavium VIII-9A
Tekoa V-7D; VI-9D
Temple Mount VII-2D
Thamna V-6C
Theku (Succoth, in Egypt) II-6B
Thella V-2E; VI-3E
Thessalonica VIII-4A
Thessaly VIII-4B
Thrace VIII-5A
Three Taverns VIII-1A
Thyatira VIII-6B
Tiberias V-3E; VI-2B, 4E, 7B
Tigris River, I-7C
Timnah II-7D; III-7C; IV-7C
Tirzah III-5D; IV-5D
Tishbeh IV-5E
Tower Pool VII-2B
Tripolis VIII-9C
Troas VIII-5A
Troodos Mountains II-1B
Troy I-2A
Tyre I-5C; II-3E; III-1D; IV-1D;
  V-1D; VI-2C; VIII-9D

Tyropoeon Valley VII-3C, 8D
Tyros VI-8E
Tyrrhenian Sea VIII-1B

U

Ugarit I-5C
Upper City VII-3B
Upper Egypt I-3E
Upper Sea (Great Sea, The; Mediter-
  ranean Sea) I-3C; II-5B; III-5A;
  IV-5A; V-5A; VI-1C; VIII-7D
Ur I-8D
Urmai, Lake I-8B

V

Valley of Salt IV-9D
Van, Lake I-7A

W

Wadi al' Arish (Egypt, River of; W.
  al' Arish) II-6C; III-9A; IV-9A
W. al' Arish (Egypt, River of; Wadi
  al' Arish) II-6C; III-9A; IV-9A
Wilderness of Judah IV-8D
Wilderness of Zin IV-9C

X

Xanthus VIII-7C

Y

Yarmuk River II-4E; III-3E; IV-3E;
  V-3E; VI-3B, 4E, 8B
Yurza III-8A; IV-8A

Z

Zagros Mountains I-8C
Zalmonah II-6E
Zarephath IV-1D
Zarethan IV-5E
Zebulun, Allotment of III-4D
Zered River II-6E; III-9E; IV-9E;
  V-9E
Zia V-6E; VI-7E
Ziklag III-8B; IV-8B
Zilu II-6B
Zin, Wilderness of II-6D; III-9C
Ziph IV-8D
Zippor III-7B; IV-7B
Zoan (Ramses, Tanis) I-4D; II-6A
Zoar II-6E; III-9D; IV-9D; V-9D

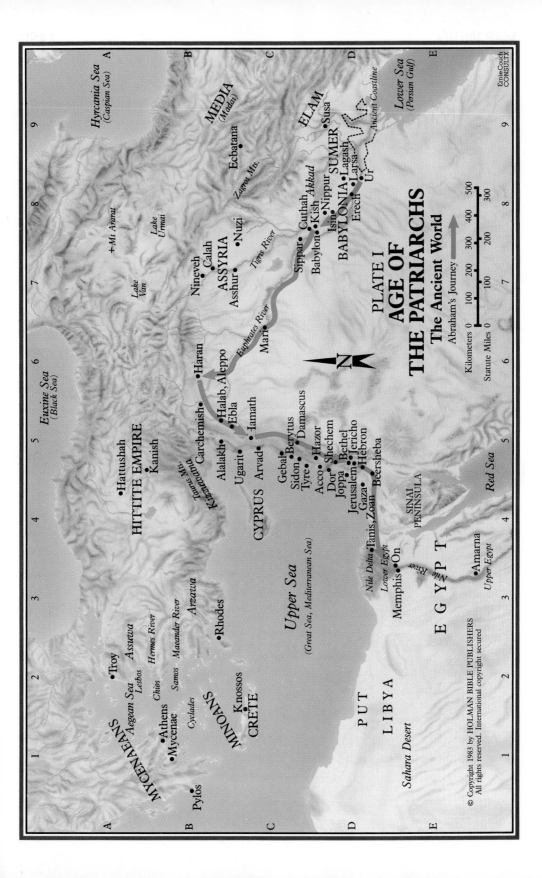

PLATE I
AGE OF THE PATRIARCHS
The Ancient World

Abraham's Journey

Kilometers 0 100 200 300 400 500
Statute Miles 0 100 200 300

ErnieCouch
CONSULTX

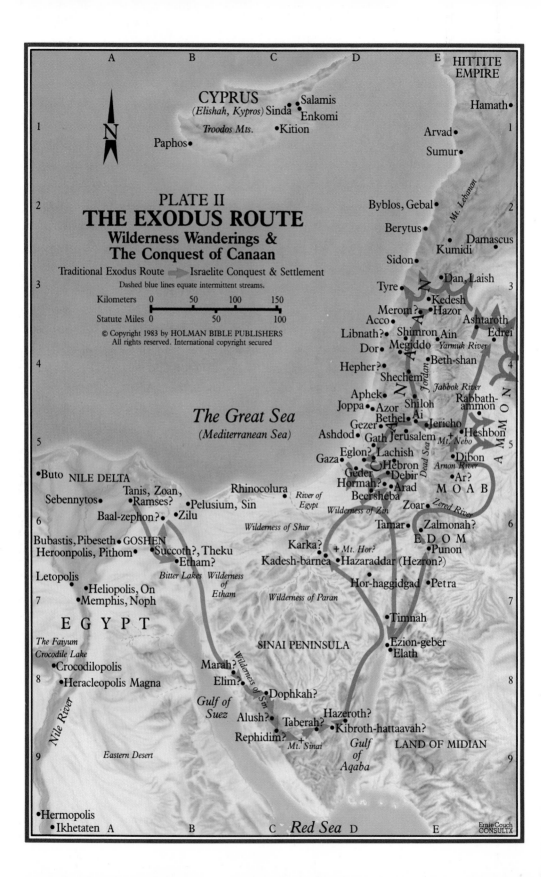

A   B   C   D   E HITTITE
EMPIRE

CYPRUS
(Elishah, Kypros) Sinda • •Salamis
•Enkomi
Troodos Mts. •Kition
Paphos•

Hamath•

Arvad•

Sumur•

1

PLATE II
THE EXODUS ROUTE
Wilderness Wanderings &
The Conquest of Canaan

Traditional Exodus Route ⟶ Israelite Conquest & Settlement
Dashed blue lines equate intermittent streams.

Kilometers 0   50   100   150
Statute Miles 0   50   100

© Copyright 1983 by HOLMAN BIBLE PUBLISHERS
All rights reserved. International copyright secured

Byblos, Gebal•
Berytus•   • Damascus
Kumidi   •
Sidon•

•Dan, Laish
Tyre•   •Kedesh
Merom?• •Hazor
Acco•   Ashtaroth
Libnath?• Shimron Ain   •Edrei
Dor• Megiddo Yarmuk River
Hepher?•   •Beth-shan
Shechem•   Jabbok River
Aphek•   •Rabbath-
Joppa•• Azor Shiloh   ammon
Gezer• Bethel• Ai Jericho
Ashdod• Gath Jerusalem   •Heshbon
Eglon?• Lachish   Mt. Nebo
Gaza• •Hebron   •Dibon
Geder• •Debir Arnon River
Hormah?• •Arad   •Ar?
Beersheba   MOAB
Zoar• Zered River

The Great Sea
(Mediterranean Sea)

•Buto NILE DELTA
Sebennytos• Tanis, Zoan, Rhinocolura   River of
•Ramses? •Pelusium, Sin Egypt
Baal-zephon?• •Zilu   Wilderness of Zin
Wilderness of Shur
Bubastis, Pibeseth• GOSHEN
Heroonpolis, Pithom• •Succoth?, Theku Karka?
•Etham?   +Mt. Hor?
Letopolis Bitter Lakes Wilderness Kadesh-barnea •Hazaraddar (Hezron?)
•Heliopolis, On of
•Memphis, Noph Etham   Wilderness of Paran   Hor-haggidgad •Petra

Tamar• •Zalmonah?
EDOM
•Punon

Timnah
•Ezion-geber
•Elath

E G Y P T

The Faiyum
Crocodile Lake
•Crocodilopolis
•Heracleopolis Magna

SINAI PENINSULA

Marah?•
Elim?•
•Dophkah?
Gulf of
Suez Alush?•
•Taberah? Hazeroth?•
Rephidim?• •Kibroth-hattaavah?
+Mt. Sinai Gulf
of
Aqaba LAND OF MIDIAN

Nile River

Eastern Desert

•Hermopolis
•Ikhetaten A   B   C *Red Sea* D   E

Dead Sea

Ernie Couch
CONSULTX

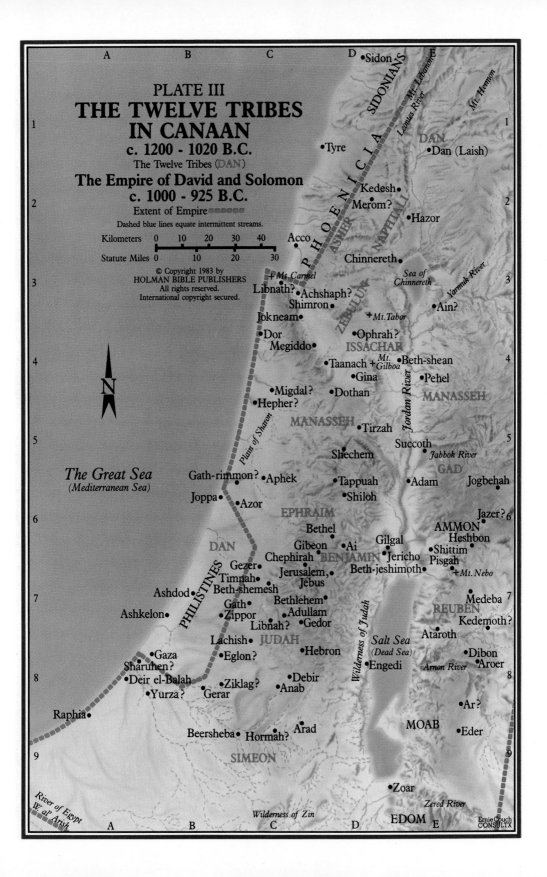

PLATE III
THE TWELVE TRIBES
IN CANAAN
c. 1200 - 1020 B.C.
The Twelve Tribes (DAN)
The Empire of David and Solomon
c. 1000 - 925 B.C.

Extent of Empire ▭▭▭▭▭

Dashed blue lines equate intermittent streams.

Kilometers 0 10 20 30 40

Statute Miles 0 10 20 30

© Copyright 1983 by
HOLMAN BIBLE PUBLISHERS
All rights reserved.
International copyright secured.

N

The Great Sea
(Mediterranean Sea)

SIDONIANS

•Sidon

•Tyre

PHOENICIA

•Kedesh
•Merom?

ASHER

NAPHTALI

•Dan (Laish)

DAN

Mt. Lebanon
Mt. Hermon
Leontas River

•Hazor

Acco•

Chinnereth•

Sea of
Chinnereth

Yarmuk River

+Mt. Carmel
Libnath?•
•Achshaph?
•Shimron

ZEBULUN

+Mt. Tabor

•Ain?

Jokneam•

•Ophrah?

•Dor
Megiddo•

ISSACHAR

•Taanach +Mt. •Beth-shean
Gilboa
•Gina

•Pehel

•Migdal?
•Hepher?

•Dothan

Plain of Sharon

MANASSEH

•Tirzah

MANASSEH

Jordan River

MANASSEH

Shechem•

Succoth•
•Jabbok River

GAD

Gath-rimmon?•
•Aphek

•Tappuah
•Shiloh

•Adam

Jogbehah

Joppa•
•Azor

EPHRAIM

Jazer?

•Bethel

Gibeon•
Chephirah•
Gezer•
Timnah•
Beth-shemesh•

•Ai
BENJAMIN
Jerusalem,•
Jebus

Gilgal
•Jericho
Beth-jeshimoth•

AMMON
Heshbon
•Shittim
Pisgah•
+Mt. Nebo

Ashdod•

PHILISTINES

Gath•
•Zippor

•Bethlehem
•Adullam
Libnah?• •Gedor

REUBEN

•Medeba

Kedemoth?

Ashkelon•

Lachish•
JUDAH

•Hebron

Ataroth•

Wilderness of Judah

Salt Sea
(Dead Sea)
•Engedi

•Dibon
Arnon River •Aroer

•Gaza
Sharuhen?•
•Deir el-Balah
•Yurza?

•Eglon?
•Ziklag?
Gerar

•Debir
•Anab

•Ar?

Raphia•

Beersheba•
Hormah?•

•Arad

MOAB

•Eder

SIMEON

•Zoar

Zered River

River of Egypt
W. al' Arish

Wilderness of Zin

EDOM

Ernie Couch
CONSULTX

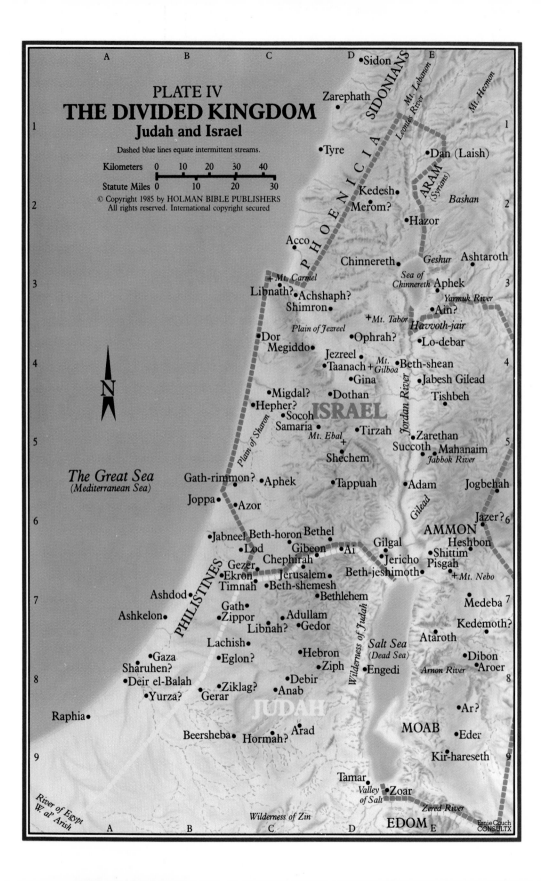

PLATE IV
THE DIVIDED KINGDOM
Judah and Israel

Dashed blue lines equate intermittent streams.

Kilometers 0 10 20 30 40

Statute Miles 0 10 20 30

© Copyright 1985 by HOLMAN BIBLE PUBLISHERS
All rights reserved. International copyright secured

A B C D E

•Sidon

SIDONIANS

Zarephath•

Mt. Lebanon

PHOENICIA

Leontes River

Mt. Hermon

•Tyre

•Dan (Laish)

ARAM (Syrians)

Kedesh•
Merom?•

Bashan

•Hazor

Acco•

Chinnereth• Geshur Ashtaroth

+ Mt. Carmel

Sea of
Chinnereth Aphek•

Libnath?•Achshaph?
Shimron•

Yarmuk River

•Ain?

+Mt. Tabor

Havvoth-jair

Plain of Jezreel

•Ophrah?   •Lo-debar

•Dor
Megiddo•

Jezreel• Mt. •Beth-shean
Taanach•+Gilboa

•Jabesh Gilead

•Gina

Tishbeh

ISRAEL

•Migdal? •Dothan

•Hepher?
•Socoh
Samaria• Mt. Ebal •Tirzah
    +

Jordan River

•Zarethan

Succoth •Mahanaim

Shechem•

Jabbok River

Gath-rimmon?• •Aphek

•Tappuah

•Adam   Jogbehah•

Plain of Sharon

Joppa•
•Azor

Gilead

Jazer?•

The Great Sea
(Mediterranean Sea)

N

Jabneel• Beth-horon Bethel•

AMMON

•Lod
Gezer•
•Ekron
Timnah•

Gibeon•
Chephirah• •Ai

•Gilgal
•Jericho

Heshbon•
•Shittim

•Jerusalem
Beth-shemesh•

Beth-jeshimoth•

Pisgah•

+Mt. Nebo

PHILISTINES

Ashdod•

Gath•
•Zippor

•Bethlehem

•Adullam
Libnah? •Gedor

•Hebron
•Ziph

Ataroth•

•Medeba

Kedemoth?•

Ashkelon•

Lachish•

Salt Sea
(Dead Sea)

•Dibon
•Aroer

Wilderness of Judah

•Gaza
Sharuhen?•
•Deir el-Balah
•Yurza?

•Eglon?

Ziklag?•
Gerar•

•Debir
•Anab

•Engedi

Arnon River

JUDAH

•Ar?

Raphia•

MOAB •Eder

Beersheba• Hormah?• •Arad

Kir-hareseth•

River of Egypt
W. el Arish

Tamar•
Valley •Zoar
of Salt

Wilderness of Zin

Zered River

EDOM

Ernie Couch
CONSULTX

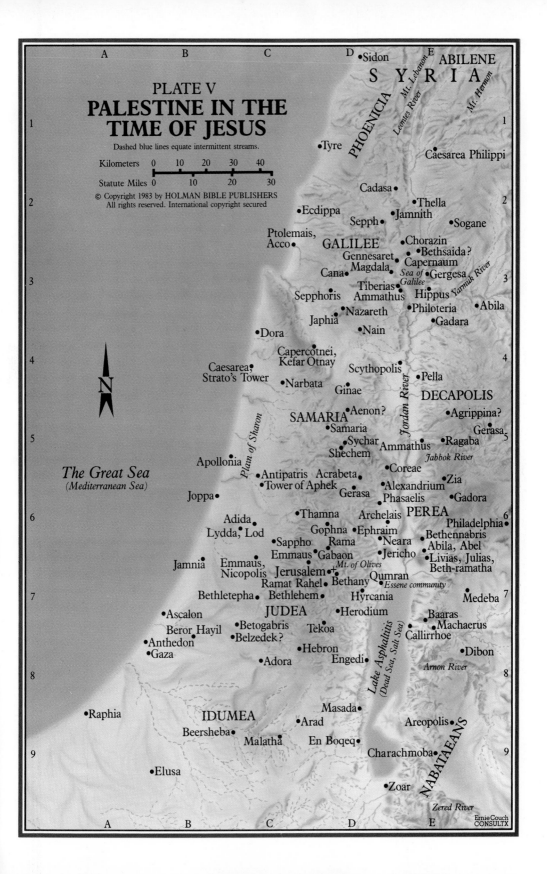

PLATE V
PALESTINE IN THE TIME OF JESUS

Dashed blue lines equate intermittent streams.

Kilometers 0   10   20   30   40

Statute Miles 0   10   20   30

© Copyright 1983 by HOLMAN BIBLE PUBLISHERS
All rights reserved. International copyright secured

A B C D E

•Sidon

E ABILENE

S Y R I A

PHOENICIA Mt. Lebanon Leontes River Mt. Hermon

•Tyre

•Caesarea Philippi

Cadasa•

•Thella
•Ecdippa   Sepph• •Jamnith   •Sogane

Ptolemais,
Acco•   GALILEE   •Chorazin
   Gennesaret   •Bethsaida?
   Magdala•   •Capernaum
Cana•   Sea of •Gergesa   Yarmuk River
   Tiberias• Galilee
Sepphoris• Ammathus •Hippus   •Abila
   Japhia• •Nazareth   •Philoteria
   •Nain   •Gadara

•Dora

Capercotnei,
Kefar Otnay
Caesarea•   Scythopolis•   •Pella
Strato's Tower •Narbata
   Ginae   DECAPOLIS

Plain of Sharon

SAMARIA •Aenon?
   •Samaria   •Agrippina?
Apollonia•   •Sychar   Gerasa•
   Shechem Ammathus •Ragaba
Joppa•   Jabbok River
   •Antipatris Acrabeta•   •Coreae
   •Tower of Aphek   •Zia
   Gerasa• •Alexandrium
      Phasaelis•   •Gadora
Adida• •Thamna Archelais• PEREA
Lydda,•Lod Gophna •Ephraim   Philadelphia•
   •Sappho Rama •Neara Bethennabris
Jamnia• Emmaus•Gabaon   •Jericho Abila, Abel
   Emmaus, Jerusalem• Mt. of Olives •Livias, Julias,
   Nicopolis   Qumran   Beth-ramatha
   Ramat Rahel• •Bethany •Essene community
Bethletepha• Bethlehem•   Hyrcania   •Medeba
   JUDEA •Herodium
•Ascalon   •Baaras
Beror Hayil •Betogabris Tekoa• •Machaerus
•Anthedon •Belzedek?   Callirrhoe
•Gaza   •Hebron   •Dibon
   •Adora Engedi•   Arnon River

The Great Sea
(Mediterranean Sea)

Jordan River

Lake Asphaltitis
(Dead Sea, Salt Sea)

Masada•
   IDUMEA •Arad   Areopolis•
•Raphia   Beersheba•   •En Boqeq   NABATAEANS
   Malatha•   Charachmoba•

•Elusa

•Zoar

Zered River

Ernie Couch
CONSULTX

1 2 3 4 5 6 7 8 9

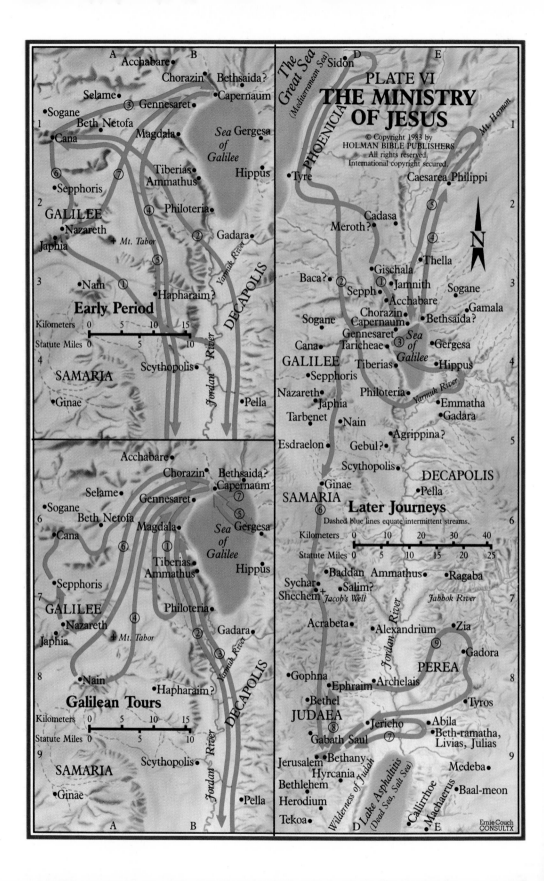

PLATE VI
THE MINISTRY OF JESUS

© Copyright 1983 by
HOLMAN BIBLE PUBLISHERS
All rights reserved,
International copyright secured.

Early Period

Kilometers 0 5 10 15
Statute Miles 0 5 10

Galilean Tours

Kilometers 0 5 10 15
Statute Miles 0 5 10

Later Journeys

Dashed blue lines equate intermittent streams.

Kilometers 0 10 20 30 40
Statute Miles 0 5 10 15 20 25

Ernie Couch
CONSULTX

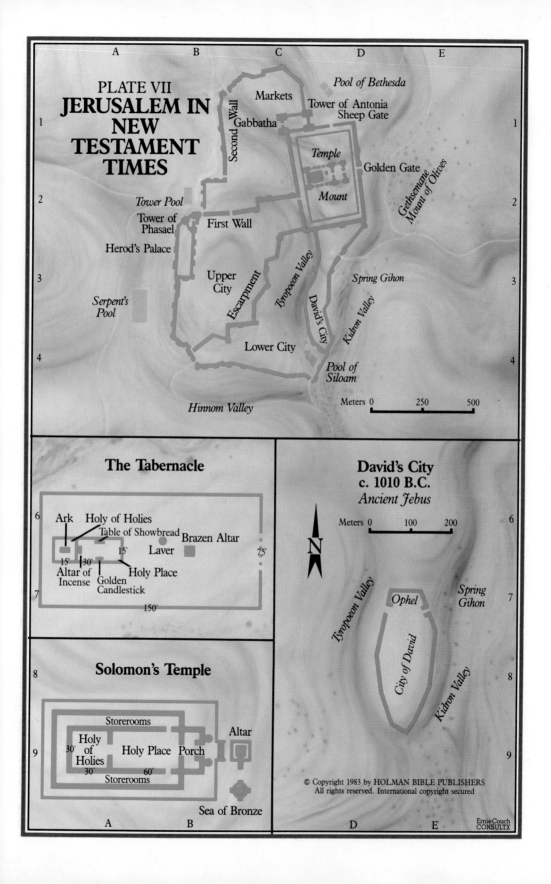

PLATE VII
JERUSALEM IN NEW TESTAMENT TIMES

Pool of Bethesda

Markets

Tower of Antonia
Sheep Gate

Second Wall

Gabbatha

Temple

Golden Gate

Mount

Gethsemane
Mount of Olives

Tower Pool

Tower of
Phasael

First Wall

Herod's Palace

Upper
City

Escarpment

Tyropoeon Valley

David's City

Spring Gihon

Kidron Valley

Serpent's
Pool

Lower City

Pool of
Siloam

Hinnom Valley

Meters 0   250   500

The Tabernacle

Ark   Holy of Holies
Table of Showbread   Brazen Altar
Laver
15'   15'   75'
15'   30'
Altar of
Incense   Golden
Candlestick   Holy Place
150'

Solomon's Temple

Storerooms
Holy
30'   of   Holy Place   Porch   Altar
Holies
30'   60'
Storerooms

Sea of Bronze

A   B

David's City
c. 1010 B.C.
Ancient Jebus

Meters 0   100   200

N

Tyropoeon Valley

Ophel

Spring
Gihon

City of David

Kidron Valley

© Copyright 1983 by HOLMAN BIBLE PUBLISHERS
All rights reserved. International copyright secured

Ernie Couch
CONSULTX

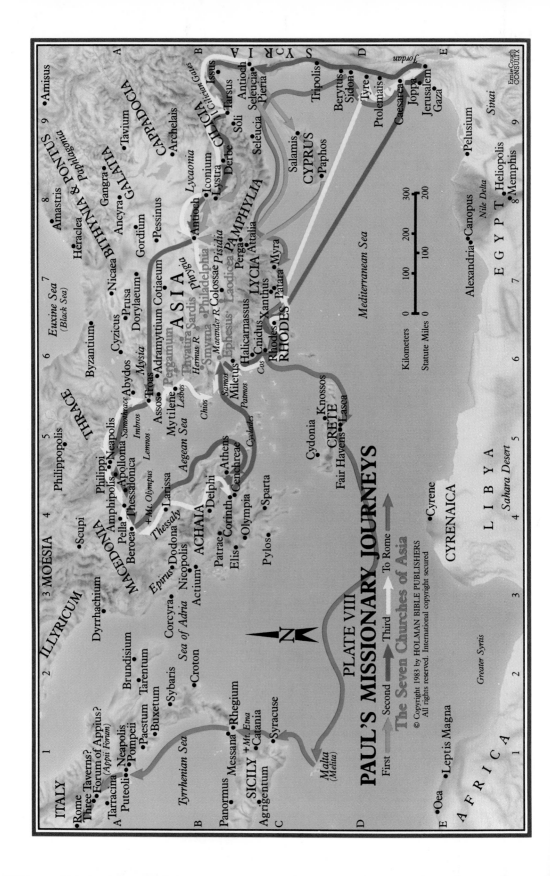

PAUL'S MISSIONARY JOURNEYS

The Seven Churches of Asia

First   Second   Third   To Rome

PLATE VIII

© Copyright 1983 by HOLMAN BIBLE PUBLISHERS
All rights reserved. International copyright secured

ErnieCouch
CONSULTX